2007 ALMANAC

BASEBALL AMERICA INC.
Durham, N.C.

Baseball america®
2007 ALMANAC

A Comprehensive Review of the 2006 Season, Featuring Statistics and Commentary

PUBLISHED BY
Baseball America Inc.

EDITOR
Will Lingo

CONTRIBUTING EDITORS
J.J. Cooper, Matt Eddy, Aaron Fitt, Chris Kline, Josh Leventhal, John Manuel, Alan Matthews, Matt Meyers

CONTRIBUTING WRITER
John Perrotto

INTERNS
Kristin Pratt, Nathan Rode, Bryan Smith

DESIGN & PRODUCTION
Phillip Daquila, Drew McDaniel, Linwood Webb

STATISTICAL CONSULTANTS
Major League Baseball
Advanced Media

Baseball america

PRESIDENT/CEO Catherine Silver
VICE PRESIDENT/PUBLISHER Lee Folger
EDITORS IN CHIEF Will Lingo, John Manuel
DESIGN & PRODUCTION DIRECTOR Phillip Daquila

COVER PHOTOS David Wright by Ed Wolfstein; Brandon Wood by Bill Mitchell; Kevin Gunderson; Andrew Miller by Sports on Film

EDITOR'S NOTE
- Major league statistics are based on final, unofficial 2006 averages.
- The organization statistics, which begin on page 55, include all players who participated in at least one game during the 2006 season. Pitchers' batting statistics are not included, nor are the pitching statistics of field players who pitched in less than two games. For players who played with more than one team in the same league, the player's cumulative statistics appear on the line immediately after the player's statistics with each team.
- Innings pitched have been rounded off to the nearest full inning.

TABLE OF
CONTENTS

LARRY GOREN

MAJOR
LEAGUES

2006 IN REVIEW
Bonds again makes steroids focal point after absence

BY JOHN PERROTTO

A total of 44 major league players hit more home runs than he did, and 90 others drove in more runs. Yet Giants left fielder Barry Bonds, perhaps the game's most compelling figure, continued to dominate the news in 2006.

Healthy again after an injury-wracked 2005 that included three knee surgeries, Bonds slugged his way to the doorstep of Hank Aaron's all-time home run record. And as always, he did it under the cloud of suspicion that his late-career surge has been fueled by banned performance-enhancing drugs.

The issue of steroid use by players surrounded the game at both the beginning and end of the regular season, much to the chagrin of Major League Baseball, which sought to re-focus attention back on the field,

"Game of Shadows" kicked things off in March. Written by San Francisco Chronicle reporters Mark Fainaru-Wada and Lance Williams, the book detailed Bonds' alleged use of steroids and his relationship with Victor Conte, the founder of the Bay Area Laboratory Co-Operative in Burlingame, Calif., the outfit around which the steroid scandal centered.

From Game of Shadows to overtaking the Babe
Barry Bonds was back in the headlines after an injury-riddled 2005

Conte, a self-proclaimed nutritionist, admitted to providing performance-enhancing drugs to professional baseball, football and track and field athletes.

Then on the next-to-last day of the regular season, the Los Angeles Times reported that former Diamondbacks righthander Jason Grimsley had implicated a handful of prominent ex-teammates as users of performance-enhancing drugs to FBI investigators.

Despite those headline-grabbing stories, Commissioner Bud Selig insisted that MLB's toughened drug-testing program was working. "I really think steroid use has been minimized," he said. "I think the numbers prove that."

Just two players on teams' 40-man rosters were suspended for failed drug tests during the season, a sharp decrease from the 12 who did so in 2005, the first year of the testing program. One of the players was Mets righthander Yusaku Iriki, who had spent the previous eight seasons pitching in his native Japan. And the other was Grimsley, who asked for and was granted his release from the Diamondbacks the day after the story surfaced that federal agents raided his home in Scottsdale, Ariz., on June 6. Investigators were searching for evidence that Grimsley was a distributor of human growth hormone (HGH) and other performance-enhancing drugs following his admission he had used HGH, steroids and amphetamines.

Federal investigators who cracked the BALCO case said Grimsley initially cooperated in a probe but withdrew his assistance in April, which prompted the search of his home nearly two months later. Authorities had tracked a package containing two kits of HGH to Grimsley's home on April 19.

Before his silence, Grimsley had identified other major leaguers who he said had used or supplied HGH. Though the names were redacted on copies of the testimony released to the media, the Times reported that Grimsley had implicated righthander Roger Clemens and lefthander Andy Pettitte, both of the Astros, along with Orioles second baseman Brian Roberts, shortstop Miguel Tejada and right fielder Jay Gibbons. All five players denied the report, and the federal prosecutor overseeing the investigation said the report contained "significant inaccuracies."

"I just think it's incredibly dangerous to just throw names out there," said Clemens, who quickly pointed out he had never failed a drug test.

Meanwhile, Bonds hit 26 home runs in 130 games to bring his career total to 734—21 shy of tying Aaron's mark—and in the process doing nothing to silence those

Santana again the Twins' sure thing

RON VESELY

MINNEAPOLIS—Santana won the American League Cy Young Award in 2004, and is the favorite to win again this season. In fact, he may be looking at a third straight Cy Young, but his 16-7 record in 2005 was the byproduct of terrible run support. As it is, he's 55-19 since 2004.

The Twins were 27-6 in games started by Santana. He swept the pitching triple crown, leading the major leagues in wins (19), strikeouts (245) and ERA (2.77) So the question is: Has Santana made a case to be the AL MVP?

PLAYER OF THE YEAR

Santana, 27, went 10-1 after the all-star break to help the Twins complete a stunning run to the AL Central title. At the same time he outclassed pitchers in both leagues with precision, smarts and dominant stuff—including a 93 mph fastball he can spot with ease, a biting 82-85 mph slider and two versions of a swing-altering changeup that comes in as slow as 78 mph.

His second-half surge helped him become the second pitcher to win Baseball America's Major League Player of the Year award. He joins Pedro Martinez, who won the award in 1999.

"Well, he deserves it," Twins general manager Terry Ryan said. "He's had a tremendous year and was tremendous last year and the one before that."

Santana's career took off three seasons ago after he learned how to adjust to hitters. If hitters swing early in the count, trying to avoid getting into conventional changeup counts, Santana will go with sliders and first-pitch changeups. If hitters try to run him out of games through high pitch counts, he'll hammer the strike zone. When one pitch isn't working, he'll win without it.

He also ignores what his body tries to tell him. Santana finished the year battling back and hip soreness, plus a blister on his left middle finger. Santana says he usually struggles to get out of bed the day after he pitches. "Throughout your career you are going to have pain—every single player is going to go through that, and it is something you have to learn to live with," he said.

He makes multiple visits to the whirlpool each week, jumping from hot to cold whirlpools to work out muscle soreness. To break up the monotony of running the day after starts, Santana will kick a soccer ball around on the field in the early afternoon. There's weightlifting and stretching.

The Astros originally signed him in 1996. In 1999, he was the No. 2 starter at low Class A Michigan, behind Roy Oswalt, and went 8-8, 4.66. He was left off the Astros' 40-man roster, making him eligible for the Rule 5 draft. Jose Marzan, the Twins' Midwest League manager at the time and now the Twins' Latin American coordinator, recommend-

ed Santana after watching him pitch a couple of times. He liked Santana's arm strength and his athleticism, though he had little other than a fastball.

The Twins were going to select Santana with the first pick in the 2000 Rule 5 draft, but the Marlins were worried the Twins were after their man, Jared Camp. So Florida agreed to select Santana with the second pick and trade him to the Twins—plus cash—if the Twins took Camp.

Santana is a hero in his native Venezuela. A national celebration erupted when he won the Cy Young in 2004, forcing president Hugo Chavez to assign body guards to protect Santana and his family. Santana hails from Tovar, located in the Andes, and lives in Golden Valley, Minn., during the season. But that doesn't mean Santana is distancing himself from his country. He's paid for chemotherapy treatments for a Venezuelan child with cancer. He's purchased new parts for police motorcycles. "I try to help people out," Santana said, "especially those in my community, my hometown."

Santana will earn $12 million next season and is signed through 2008, providing the Twins with at least two more seasons of as close to a sure thing as there is. "There's no question when he takes the mound we have a good chance to win a game," Ryan said. "I think everyone in the industry recognizes the talent."

—LA VELLE NEAL

PREVIOUS **WINNERS**
1998—Mark McGwire, 1b, Cardinals
1999—Pedro Martinez, rhp, Red Sox
2000—Alex Rodriguez, ss, Mariners
2001—Barry Bonds, of, Giants
2002—Alex Rodriguez, ss, Rangers
2003—Barry Bonds, of, Giants
2004—Barry Bonds, of, Giants
2005—Albert Pujols, 1b, Cardinals

who doubted the legitimacy of his chase. Bonds might have attained the record in 2005 had he not been limited to just 14 games and five home runs.

Bonds, who turned 42 in July and who filed for free agency following the season, indicated throughout the year he was uncertain about his future. He alternated between saying he wanted to keep playing and saying he would rather retire than continue answering questions about steroids.

"Game of Shadows," the culmination of two years of investigation by Fainaru-Wada and Williams, immediately became a best seller, creating more questions for Bonds than it answered. Bonds claimed he did not read the book and that he didn't care what it said—which was that Bonds had used steroids, HGH, insulin and other performance-enhancing drugs since 1998. The book alleged Bonds began using the substances in 2001 because he was jealous of the attention Mark McGwire received for hitting 70 home runs and breaking Roger Maris' single-season record. Bonds bested McGwire's record with 73 homers in 2001.

"All I know is that I've been tested for drugs like every other player in the major leagues and I've never failed any of the tests," Bonds said.

Alleged use of steroids wasn't Bonds' only problem: A federal grand jury investigated him for tax evasion and perjury. Bonds is alleged to have not reported income from the sale of memorabilia, resulting in the tax evasion investigation, while the perjury issue stems from his testimony to a grand jury that he had never used steroids. The grand jury expired without Bonds being charged. However, a second grand jury was convened and was continuing the investigation when the season ended.

On the heels of "Game of Shadows," Selig appointed former Senate Majority Leader George Mitchell, a member of the Red Sox board of directors, to investigate the use of performance-enhancing drugs in the major leagues. Mitchell's investigation was still ongoing when the 2006 season ended.

TOP 10 MAJOR LEAGUE STORIES OF 2006

1 **Cardinals win it all after limping into playoffs.** St. Louis wins its NL-best 10th World Series after nearly coughing up a seven-game NL Central lead down the stretch. Their 83 wins were the fewest ever by a Series winner, and six other NL teams had won the Series—including the Marlins twice—since the Cardinals last won in 1982. October made heroes out of the unassuming David Eckstein, Yadier Molina, Jeff Weaver and Jeff Suppan.

2 **Labor peace extended another five years.** The players and owners agreed on a new Collective Bargaining Agreement two months before the current one had expired. Changes to the draft and to free agent compensation were the major alterations.

3 **Twins surge from way back to win AL Central.** Though they were knocked out of the playoffs in the first round, the Twins remarkable run began May 27, when they stood 12½ games out of first, and didn't stop until they had overtaken the Tigers for first place on the last day of the season.

4 **Inaugural World Baseball Classic a rousing success.** Despite the United States' poor showing, fans turned out in droves at San Diego's Petco Park for the WBC semifinals and the Japan vs. Cuba finale. The U.S. team was eliminated in the second round, and lost once each to neighbors Canada and Mexico.

5 **Bonds passes Ruth; Griffey cracks top 10.** After missing most of the 2005 season, Bonds returned and passed Babe Ruth for second all time in home runs. He finished with 734, 21 shy of home run king Hank Aaron. Griffey tied Reggie Jackson for tenth place all time when he hit No. 563.

6 **Hoffman saves his place in history.** Padres closer Trevor Hoffman passed Lee Smith in September for the lead in career saves and finished with 482.

7 **Braves' division streak halted.** The Braves had finished first in their division in every full season since 1991. That streak came to an end in 2006 with the Mets and Phillies both finishing ahead of the Braves in the NL East.

8 **Mauer first AL catcher to win batting title.** The 23-year-old Mauer went 2-for-4 on the season's final day to win the batting title from Yankees shortstop Derek Jeter, who went 1-for-5. It was just Mauer's second full season.

9 **Marlins strike fear on $15 million budget.** Despite baseball's lowest payroll, the Marlins hung around the fringes of the NL wild card race late into the season under first-year manager Joe Girardi. They were 17-34 on June 1.

10 **Two Phillies go on extended hitting streaks.** Chase Utley hit safely in 35 straight games from June-August, and Jimmy Rollins hit in 38 straight, spanning the 2005-06 seasons. Both streaks rank among the 10 longest ever.

300-SAVES CLUB

Hoffman claimed the all-time saves lead. Rivera topped 400, and Wagner surpassed 300.

No.	Pitcher	SV
1.	Trevor Hoffman	482
2.	Lee Smith	478
3.	John Franco	424
4.	Mariano Rivera	413
5.	Dennis Eckersley	390
6.	Jeff Reardon	367
7.	Randy Myers	347
8.	Rollie Fingers	341
9.	John Wetteland	330
10.	Roberto Hernandez	326
11.	Troy Percival	324
12.	Billy Wagner	324
13.	Jose Mesa	320
14.	Rick Aguilera	318
15.	Robb Nen	314
16.	Tom Henke	311
17.	Rich Gossage	310
18.	Jeff Montgomery	304
19.	Doug Jones	303
20.	Bruce Sutter	300

Active players in bold

A tougher drug-testing policy for 2006—which for the first time included amphetamines as a banned substance—did little to ease suspicion that many players were using the undetectable HGH. Many players, though, did not agree.

"It seems to be like the testing is working pretty well," Dodgers righthander Greg Maddux said. "I know you hear things here and there around the clubhouse, and to me, guys aren't doing it anymore."

Where once the use of amphetamines, a drug legal only with a prescription, was considered routine in baseball clubhouses, not one player was suspended under the new policy.

"I think the testing changes guys' behavior, no question about it," Mets lefthander Tom Glavine said. "Guys are trying to find other ways to compensate, whether it's getting more sleep or drinking more coffee."

Braves Historic Streak Ends

The Braves went 79-83 and finished third in the National League East in 2006, snapping a streak of 14 straight division titles, the longest in American professional sports history. The streak stretched from 1991 to 2005 and did not include 1994, when no official division winner was crowned because of the players' strike.

"It does feel as bad as I thought it would," said righthander John Smoltz, the only player to be a mem-

EAST	W	L	PCT	GB	Manager	General Manager	Attendance	Average	Last Penn.
New York Yankees	97	65	.599	—	Joe Torre	Brian Cashman	4,248,067	52,445	2003
Toronto Blue Jays	87	75	.537	10	John Gibbons	J.P. Ricciardi	2,302,212	28,422	1993
Boston Red Sox	86	76	.531	11	Terry Francona	Theo Epstein	2,930,588	36,180	2004
Baltimore Orioles	70	92	.432	27	Sam Perlozzo	Mike Flanagan	2,153,139	26,582	1983
Tampa Bay Devil Rays	61	101	.377	36	Joe Maddon	Andrew Friedman	1,368,950	16,901	None
CENTRAL	W	L	PCT	GB	Manager	General Manager	Attendance	Average	Last Penn.
Minnesota Twins	96	66	.593	—	Ron Gardenhire	Terry Ryan	2,285,018	28,210	1991
Detroit Tigers*	95	67	.586	1	Jim Leyland	Dave Dombrowski	2,595,937	32,049	2006
Chicago White Sox	90	72	.556	6	Ozzie Guillen	Ken Williams	2,957,414	36,511	2005
Cleveland Indians	78	84	.481	18	Eric Wedge	Mark Shapiro	1,997,995	24,667	1997
Kansas City Royals	62	100	.383	34	Buddy Bell	A. Baird/Dayton Moore	1,372,638	16,946	1985
WEST	W	L	PCT	GB	Manager	General Manager	Attendance	Average	Last Penn.
Oakland Athletics	93	69	.574	—	Ken Macha	Billy Beane	1,976,625	24,403	1990
Los Angeles Angels	89	73	.549	4	Mike Scioscia	Bill Stoneman	3,406,790	42,059	2002
Texas Rangers	80	82	.494	13	Buck Showalter	Jon Daniels	2,388,757	29,491	None
Seattle Mariners	78	84	.481	15	Mike Hargrove	Bill Bavasi	2,481,165	30,632	None

*Won wild card.
NOTE: Team's individual batting, pitching and fielding statistics can be found on page indicated in lefthand column.

ber of the Braves in each of the 14 title years. "Not the fact that we didn't win the division but the fact that we didn't even come close to winning. It's bitter in the sense that we knew the streak was going to come to an end sooner or later. But I never thought it would be the way that we have played this year. That's been really frustrating."

Over in the American League, the Yankees continued their pursuit of the Braves' mark by winning the American League East for a ninth consecutive season. The Yankees finished at 97-65, giving them the best record in the game and a 10-game edge over the Blue Jays. The Yankees did not take this celebration for granted, though, in a season in which star outfielders Hideki Matsui and Gary Sheffield were limited to 51 and 39 games because of wrist injuries.

"The celebration lasted a little longer this year," shortstop Derek Jeter said. "You can talk about this payroll and that payroll, but it's still difficult to win. Winning year after year says a lot about our organization."

Across town, the Mets won their first NL East title since 1988 as they tied the Yankees for the best regular season record. It marked the first time both New York teams won division titles in the same season.

Red Sox righthander in select company
Curt Schilling got his 200th win and 3,000th strikeout in 2006

BILL NICHOLS

3,000 STRIKEOUTS

Pedro Martinez is poised to join the club. He has 2,998 strikeouts.

NO.	PITCHER	SO
1.	Nolan Ryan	5,714
2.	**Roger Clemens**	4,604
3.	**Randy Johnson**	4,544
4.	Steve Carlton	4,136
5.	Bert Blyleven	3,701
6.	Tom Seaver	3,640
7.	Don Sutton	3,574
8.	Gaylord Perry	3,534
9.	Walter Johnson	3,509
10.	Phil Niekro	3,342
11.	Fergie Jenkins	3,192
12.	**Greg Maddux**	3,169
13.	Bob Gibson	3,117
14.	**Curt Schilling**	3,015
Active players in bold		

"It's always a great feeling you get when you win a division title and I'm glad our organization could experience that again," said Willie Randolph, in his second season as the Mets manager after spending 11 seasons on the Yankees coaching staff. "It's that adrenaline you get when you know you've accomplished something very special. It's a very euphoric feeling."

It was certainly a euphoric season for the Twins, who stormed back from a 12½-game deficit on May 27 to overtake the Tigers on the final day of the season for the AL Central crown. The Twins went 72-38 from June onward to finish 96-66, one game better than the Tigers, who settled for the wild card after 12 consecutive losing seasons.

"People didn't even talk about us in April, May and June," Twins catcher Joe Mauer said. "We went on that run, and here we are, on top of the Central, one of the toughest divisions in baseball. So it doesn't get much better than that."

While the Twins sprinted to their division title, the Cardinals stumbled to the finish line, but persevered to become NL Central champs for the third time in four years. The Cardinals lost nine of their last twelve games and nearly squandered their seven-game lead on the Astros. Only a Houston loss on the final day of the sea-

NATIONAL LEAGUE STANDINGS

EAST	W	L	PCT	GB	Manager	General Manager	Attendance	Average	Last Penn.
New York Mets	97	65	.599	—	Willie Randolph	Omar Minaya	3,379,535	41,723	2000
Philadelphia Phillies	85	77	.525	12	Charlie Manuel	Pat Gillick	2,701,815	33,356	1993
Atlanta Braves	79	83	.488	18	Bobby Cox	John Schuerholz	2,550,524	31,488	1999
Florida Marlins	78	84	.481	19	Joe Girardi	Larry Beinfest	1,164,134	14,372	2003
Washington Nationals	71	91	.438	26	Frank Robinson	Jim Bowden	2,153,056	26,581	None
CENTRAL	**W**	**L**	**PCT**	**GB**	**Manager**	**General Manager**	**Attendance**	**Average**	**Last Penn.**
St. Louis Cardinals	83	78	.516	—	Tony LaRussa	Walt Jocketty	3,407,104	42,589	2006
Houston Astros	82	80	.506	1½	Phil Garner	Tim Purpura	3,022,763	37,318	2005
Cincinnati Reds	80	82	.494	3½	Jerry Narron	Wayne Krivsky	2,134,607	26,353	1990
Milwaukee Brewers	75	87	.463	8½	Ned Yost	Doug Melvin	2,335,643	28,835	None
Pittsburgh Pirates	67	95	.414	16½	Jim Tracy	Dave Littlefield	1,861,549	22,982	1979
Chicago Cubs	66	96	.407	17½	Dusty Baker	Jim Hendry	3,123,215	38,558	1945
WEST	**W**	**L**	**PCT**	**GB**	**Manager**	**General Manager**	**Attendance**	**Average**	**Last Penn.**
San Diego Padres	88	74	.543	—	Bruce Bochy	Kevin Towers	2,659,757	32,837	1998
Los Angeles Dodgers*	88	74	.543	—	Grady Little	Ned Colletti	3,758,545	46,402	1988
San Francisco Giants	76	85	.472	11½	Felipe Alou	Brian Sabean	3,130,313	38,646	2002
Arizona Diamondbacks	76	86	.469	12	Bob Melvin	Josh Byrnes	2,091,685	25,823	2001
Colorado Rockies	76	86	.469	12	Clint Hurdle	Dan O'Dowd	2,104,362	25,980	None

*Won wild card.
NOTE: Team's individual batting, pitching and fielding statistics can be found on page indicated in lefthand column.

son clinched the NL Central title for the Cardinals.

The Cardinals finished 83-78, which meant they narrowly missed tying the record for fewest wins by a playoff team. That distinction belongs to the 1973 Mets and 2005 Padres with 82 wins apiece. "I don't think anybody on this club wanted to be associated with mugging that lead," Cardinals manager Tony La Russa said. "That's one of those historic things that you'll never forget."

The Padres and the Dodgers finished with identical 88-74 records, but the Padres won their second consecutive NL West title because they sported the better head-to-head record. The Dodgers captured the wild card. The Athletics pulled away late to win the AL West, finishing 93-69 and four games in front of the Angels.

Closing Statements

After 14 years of playing in the shadows in San Diego, the spotlight finally shined on Padres closer Trevor Hoffman when he became baseball's all-time saves leader in September. Hoffman surpassed Lee Smith's mark of 478 at home on Sept. 24 when he pitched a 1-2-3 ninth inning to nail down a 2-1 victory over the Pirates.

Trevor Hoffman

"It's overwhelming," Hoffman said. "It becomes a very humbling experience. It's hard to put into words what it really feels like."

Hoffman finished the season with a NL-leading 46 saves, raising his career total to 482.

The save is a relatively new statistic, becoming part of baseball's official record in 1969, and has its critics. However, Padres manager Bruce Bochy said that should not detract from Hoffman's accomplishment.

"I think the perception of closers is going to change," Bochy said. "It's going to get recognized more, get more attention with Hoffman and (Yankees righthander) Mariano Rivera as they continue to accumulate saves. I think people are going to realize how important, how valuable, these guys are to the team. They're just like a position player. I mean, they're available most every day."

Rivera became just the fourth pitcher in baseball history to record 400 saves, reaching that milestone in a July 16 win over the White Sox. Rivera joined Hoffman, Smith and John Franco. Meanwhile, Mets closer Billy Wagner notched save No. 300 on July 4 against the Pirates, becoming the 20th pitcher to reach that plateau.

Closers weren't the only pitchers to reach significant milestones in 2006.

Yankees lefthander Randy Johnson joined Nolan Ryan and Roger Clemens as the only pitchers to record 4,500 strikeouts. Johnson got there Aug. 14 when he fanned the Angels' Tim Salmon. Red Sox righthander Curt Schilling joined two exclusive clubs, winning his 200th game May 27 against the Devil Rays and recording his 3,000th strikeout Aug. 30 when he whiffed Nick Swisher of the A's. Mets righthander Pedro Martinez and Tigers lefthander Kenny Rogers each reached 200 victories, Martinez against the Braves April 17 and Rogers against the Cubs June 18.

On the home run front, Padres catcher Mike Piazza and Mets first baseman Carlos Delgado each reached 400

ACTIVE WINS LEADERS

Rogers, Schilling and Martinez all reached 200 career wins. Glavine and Johnson inched closer to 300.

NO.	PITCHER	W
1.	Roger Clemens	348
2.	Greg Maddux	333
3.	Tom Glavine	290
4.	Randy Johnson	280
5.	Mike Mussina	239
6.	David Wells	230
7.	Jamie Moyer	216
8.	Kenny Rogers	207
	Curt Schilling	207
10.	Pedro Martinez	206
11.	John Smoltz	193
12.	Andy Pettitte	186

Tom Glavine

for their careers. Piazza connected off the Diamondbacks' Jose Valverde on April 26 and Delgado took the Cardinals' Jeff Weaver deep Aug. 22.

Right fielder Moises Alou and center fielder Steve Finley, both of the Giants, Pirates right fielder Jeromy Burnitz and Royals right fielder Reggie Sanders all eclipsed 300 homers. Finley and Sanders also become just the fifth and sixth members of the 300 home run-300 stolen base club, joining Barry Bonds, Willie Mays, Andre Dawson and Bobby Bonds.

With 46 homers and 41 steals, Nationals left fielder Alfonso Soriano became the fourth 40-40 player in major league history. The other three: Jose Canseco, Barry Bonds and Alex Rodriguez.

Red Sox left fielder Manny Ramirez reached a pair of significant milestones: 2,000 hits and 1,500 RBIs. Alou and Piazza also recorded their 2,000th hits, as did Yankees teammates Derek Jeter and Alex Rodriguez. Yankees outfielder Gary Sheffield and Oakland DH Frank Thomas notched their 1,500th RBIs. Astros second baseman Craig Biggio became only the 23rd player to amass 10,000 at bats, and finished the 2006 season just 70 hits shy of 3,000.

The major leagues also saw the first no-hitter since Johnson's perfect game on May 18, 2004, when Marlins rookie righthander Anibal Sanchez no-hit the Diamondbacks Sept. 6. The 6,364 games between no-hitters was the longest in history. It was also the first no-hitter by a rookie since Cardinals lefthander Bud Smith threw one in 2001. "This is the best moment of my life," said the 22-year-old Sanchez, a native of Venezuela. "You never think something like this is going to happen."

LARRY GOREN

A 2-for-4 game sealed the deal on the season's final day
Joe Mauer became the first AL catcher to win a batting title

A pair of Phillies teammates, shortstop Jimmy Rollins and second baseman Chase Utley, and Rangers right fielder Kevin Mench reeled off significant hitting streaks, but fell short of long-standing marks.

Rollins hit safely in his final 36 games of 2005 and opened the 2006 season with hits in his first two games, for a 38-game streak spanning two seasons. Utley hit safely in 35 straight from June 23 through Aug. 3. While both streaks fell well short of Joe DiMaggio's record of 56, they both ranked among the 10 longest in major league history. Obscured by the feats of Rollins and Utley, Astros center fielder Willy Taveras hit safely in 30 straight August games.

Mench homered in seven games in a row form April 21-28, falling one short of the record held by Dale Long, Don Mattingly and Ken Griffey Jr.

Batting Titlists Not Usual Suspects

Joe Mauer did something no other AL catcher had ever done before: He won the batting title. The Twins star catcher got two hits on the last day of the season to finish at .347, four points ahead of the Yankees shortstop Derek Jeter. Mauer had a razor-thin .0005 advantage going into the final day, but went 2-for-4 against the White Sox while Jeter went 1-for-5 against the Blue Jays.

The last catcher to win a batting title was Ernie Lombardi, who hit .330 for the 1942 Boston Braves to lead the National League. Lombardi also won the batting title in 1938, when he hit .342 for the Reds.

"That's something that can never be taken away from you when you're the first," Mauer said. "It's really unbelievable."

Just as unbelievable was Pirates third baseman Freddy Sanchez winning the NL batting

400-HOME RUN CLUB

Delgado and Piazza hit their 400th home runs in 2006. Griffey moved into the top 10.

STEVE MOORE

Carlos Delgado

NO.	PLAYER	HR
1.	Hank Aaron	755
2.	Barry Bonds	734
3.	Babe Ruth	714
4.	Willie Mays	660
5.	Sammy Sosa	588
6.	Frank Robinson	586
7.	Mark McGwire	583
8.	Harmon Killebrew	573
9.	Rafael Palmeiro	569
10.	Ken Griffey	563
	Reggie Jackson	563
12.	Mike Schmidt	548
13.	Mickey Mantle	536
14.	Jimmie Foxx	534
15.	Willie McCovey	521
	Ted Williams	521
17.	Ernie Banks	512
	Eddie Mathews	512
19.	Mel Ott	511
20.	Eddie Murray	504
21.	Lou Gehrig	493
	Fred McGriff	493
23.	Frank Thomas	487
24.	Stan Musial	475
	Willie Stargell	475
26.	Jim Thome	472
27.	Manny Ramirez	470
28.	Dave Winfield	465
29.	Alex Rodriguez	464
30.	Jose Canseco	462
31.	Gary Sheffield	455
32.	Carl Yastrzemski	452
33.	Jeff Bagwell	449
34.	Dave Kingman	442
35.	Andre Dawson	438
36.	Juan Gonzalez	434
37.	Cal Ripken	431
38.	Billy Williams	426
39.	Mike Piazza	419
40.	Darrell Evans	414
41.	Carlos Delgado	407
	Duke Snider	407

2006 MAJOR LEAGUE ALL-STARS

BILL MITCHELL

Durable Diamondbacks ace led NL in wins
Brandon Webb went 16-8, 3.10 in 235 innings

MORRIS FOSTOFF

Another MVP-type campaign for young Marlin
Miguel Cabrera has gotten a little better each season

Selected by Baseball America

FIRST TEAM

POS	PLAYER, TEAM	AGE	AVG	OBP	SLG	AB	R	H	2B	3B	HR	RBI	SB	CS	BB	SO
C	Joe Mauer, Twins	23	.347	.429	.507	521	86	181	36	4	13	84	8	3	79	54
1B	Albert Pujols, Cardinals	26	.331	.431	.671	535	119	177	33	1	49	137	7	2	92	50
2B	Chase Utley, Phillies	27	.309	.379	.527	658	131	203	40	4	32	102	15	4	63	132
3B	Miguel Cabrera, Marlins	23	.339	.430	.568	576	112	195	50	2	26	114	9	6	86	108
SS	Derek Jeter, Yankees	32	.343	.417	.483	623	118	214	39	3	14	97	34	5	69	102
LF	Alfonso Soriano, Nationals	30	.277	.351	.560	647	119	179	41	2	46	95	41	17	67	160
CF	Carlos Beltran, Mets	29	.275	.388	.594	510	127	140	38	1	41	116	18	3	95	99
RF	Jermaine Dye, White Sox	32	.315	.385	.622	539	103	170	27	3	44	120	7	3	59	118
DH	David Ortiz, Red Sox	30	.287	.413	.636	558	115	160	29	2	54	137	1	0	119	117

POS	PITCHER, TEAM	AGE	W	L	ERA	G	GS	CG	SV	IP	H	BB	SO	HR	G/F	AVG
SP	Chris Carpenter, Cardinals	31	15	8	3.09	32	32	5	0	222	194	43	184	21	2.04	.235
SP	Roy Oswalt, Astros	28	15	8	2.98	33	32	2	0	221	220	38	166	18	1.52	.263
SP	Johan Santana, Twins	27	19	6	2.77	34	34	1	0	234	186	47	245	24	1.06	.216
SP	Brandon Webb, Diamondbacks	27	16	8	3.10	33	33	5	0	235	216	50	178	15	4.06	.246
RP	Joe Nathan, Twins	31	7	0	1.58	64	0	0	36	68	38	16	95	3	0.87	.158

SECOND TEAM

POS	PLAYER, TEAM	AGE	AVG	OBP	SLG	AB	R	H	2B	3B	HR	RBI	SB	CS	BB	SO
C	Brian McCann, Braves	22	.333	.388	.572	442	61	147	34	0	24	93	2	0	41	54
1B	Ryan Howard, Phillies	26	.313	.425	.659	581	104	182	25	1	58	149	0	0	108	181
2B	Robinson Cano, Yankees	23	.342	.365	.525	482	62	165	41	1	15	78	5	2	18	54
3B	David Wright, Mets	23	.311	.381	.531	582	96	181	40	5	26	116	20	5	66	113
SS	Carlos Guillen, Tigers	30	.320	.400	.519	543	100	174	41	5	19	85	20	9	71	87
LF	Manny Ramirez, Red Sox	34	.321	.439	.619	449	79	144	27	1	35	102	0	1	100	102
CF	Grady Sizemore, Indians	23	.290	.375	.533	655	134	190	53	11	28	76	22	6	78	153
RF	Vladimir Guerrero, Angels	30	.329	.382	.552	607	92	200	34	1	33	116	15	5	50	68
DH	Travis Hafner, Indians	29	.308	.439	.659	454	100	140	31	1	42	117	0	0	100	111

POS	PITCHER, TEAM	AGE	W	L	ERA	G	GS	CG	SV	IP	H	BB	SO	HR	G/F	AVG
SP	Roy Halladay, Blue Jays	29	16	5	3.19	32	32	4	0	220	208	34	132	19	2.39	.251
SP	John Smoltz, Braves	39	16	9	3.49	35	35	3	0	232	221	55	211	23	1.38	.251
SP	Chien-Ming Wang, Yankees	26	19	6	3.63	34	33	2	1	218	233	52	76	12	3.06	.277
SP	Carlos Zambrano, Cubs	25	16	7	3.41	33	33	0	0	214	162	115	210	20	1.24	.208
RP	Jonathan Papelbon, Red Sox	25	4	2	0.92	59	0	0	35	68	40	13	75	3	0.78	.167

Ages as of July 1, 2006

Organization of the Year: Los Angeles Dodgers. **Executive of the Year:** Dave Dombrowski, Tigers.
Player of the Year: Johan Santana, Twins. **Rookie of the Year:** Justin Verlander, Tigers. **Manager of the Year:** Jim Leyland, Tigers.

title with a .344 average, five points higher than Marlins third baseman Miguel Cabrera. Sanchez began the season as the Pirates' utility infielder, moving into the starting lineup in May when veteran third baseman Joe Randa was injured.

"It's really something special," Sanchez said. "It's just hard to believe I could do this, especially considering I wasn't even a starter when the season began."

Phillies first baseman Ryan Howard, in his first full season, led the majors with 58 home runs and 149 RBIs.

The homer total was the highest in the major leagues since Barry Bonds hit a record 73 in 2001, but Howard's bid to hit 60 stalled in the season's final weeks as he connected just twice in his last 21 games.

Freddy Sanchez

David Ortiz, the Red Sox designated hitter, led the AL with 54 homers and 137 RBIs.

Mariners right fielder Ichiro Suzuki topped the majors with 224 hits, giving him six 200-hit campaigns in as many seasons since coming to the U.S. from Japan. The major league record is held by Wee Willie Keeler, who collected 200 hits in eight straight seasons from 1894-1901.

Both league stolen base champions repeated from 2005, as Mets shortstop Jose Reyes topped the NL with 63 (in 81 tries) and Devil Rays left fielder Carl Crawford led the AL with 58 (in 67 tries).

Not a single pitcher won 20 games, marking the first time that had happened in non-shortened season history. Twins lefthander Johan Santana captured the AL pitching triple crown with 19 wins, a 2.77 ERA and 245 strikeouts. Yankees righthander Chien-Ming Wang tied Santana for the AL victories lead, while six pitchers—all righthanders—tied for the NL lead with 16: Cincinnati's Aaron Harang, Los Angeles teammates Derek Lowe and Brad Penny, Atlanta's John Smoltz, Arizona's Brandon Webb and Chicago's Carlos Zambrano.

Harang topped the NL with 216 strikeouts, while Astros righthander Roy Oswalt was the ERA leader with a 2.98 mark. Angels righthander Francisco Rodriguez led the AL with 47 saves.

The Royals finished 62-100 to become just the 11th team in history to post three straight 100-loss seasons. The Pirates haven't been quite that bad, but did go 67-95 to notch consecutive losing season No. 14, two short of the record 16 set by hapless Phillies of 1933-48.

Tragedy Strikes Twice

The tragic deaths of two players, one active and one retired, served as bookends to the 2006 season. Hall of Fame outfielder Kirby Puckett, who collected 2,304 hits in 12 seasons with the Twins, died of a stroke March 6 at age 45. Meanwhile, Yankees righthander Cory Lidle lost his life Oct. 11 when the small plane he was piloting crashed into an apartment building on Manhattan's Upper East Side. Lidle was 34 and had been traded from the Phillies July 30 in the same trade that sent outfielder Bobby Abreu to New York. He also pitched for the Mets, Devil Rays, A's, Blue Jays and Reds in his nine-year career.

Puckett became the second-youngest player to die after being enshrined in Cooperstown. Only Lou Gehrig,

37 when he died in 1941, was younger. The short and stocky Puckett was a fan favorite, though he had put on excessive weight since his playing career ended in 1996, when glaucoma caused blindness in his right eye. He was a .318 lifetime hitter, appeared in 10 All-Star Games and won six Gold Gloves. He also led the Twins to World Series victories in 1987 and 1991.

"It's a tough thing to see a guy go through something like that and come to this extent," former teammate Kent Hrbek said. "Being forced out of the game really hurt him badly. I don't know if he ever recovered from it."

Four days after the Yankees were defeated by the Tigers in the AL Championship Series, Lidle took off in his single-engine Cirrus SR 20 to go home to Glendora, Calif., a suburb of Los Angeles. Flight instructor Tyler Stanger accompanied him.

Lidle took off from Teterboro Airport in New Jersey and decided to take a sightseeing pass over New York before heading to Nashville, Tenn., on the first leg of his trip home. Lidle circled the Statue of Liberty, flew past lower Manhattan and north above the East River. The weather conditions were hazy and windy, however, and something went terribly wrong after Lidle passed the 59th Street Bridge. The plane smashed into a luxury high-rise condominium, right between the 30th and 31st floors, sending fiery debris to the sidewalk and street below. Amazingly, no one in the building or on the ground was injured.

"This is a terrible shock," Yankees manager Joe Torre said. "I was with (coaches) Ron Guidry and Lee Mazzilli when I heard the news and we were just stunned. Cory's time with the Yankees was short, but he was a good teammate and a great competitor."

Lidle had gotten his pilot's license the previous offseason and flying had become his passion in his final months. "No matter what's going on in your life, when you get up in that plane, everything's gone," Lidle said

Fatal plane crash just four days after his season ended
Cory Lidle was just 34 when the plane he was piloting crashed

Dodgers combat injuries with prospects

LOS ANGELES—The Dodgers were supposed to nurse their celebrated stable of prospects for at least another year. Matt Kemp was supposed to spend a full season in Double-A and another in Triple-A. Russell Martin was supposed to have one more season to hone his already superior catching skills.

And then the Dodgers suffered a slew of injuries, like they had in 2005 when they were forced to bring up a slew of journeymen minor leaguers like Mike Edwards, Brian Myrow and Mike Rose. But this year, they didn't bring up journeymen. They brought up prospects, including Kemp, Martin, left fielder Andre Ethier and righthanders Jonathan Broxton and Chad Billingsley, all a year ahead of schedule. The most surprising part: All five contributed to the Dodgers winning the NL wild card.

ORGANIZATION
OF THE **YEAR**

■ Martin, 23, hit .282/.355/.436 in 121 games and finished fourth among NL catchers with 65 RBIs. He retained his starting job even after the Dodgers acquired veteran backstop Toby Hall from the Devil Rays.

■ Ethier, 24, led all rookies in hitting, on-base and slugging percentage at the all-star break and finished at .308/.365/.477. He was acquired in the offseason trade that sent outfielder Milton Bradley to the Athletics.

■ Kemp, 22, started strong, playing mostly in center field, but struggled with good breaking balls and slumped to .253/.289/.448.

■ Broxton, 22, went 4-1, 2.59, struck out 97 in 76 innings and held opposing batters to a .216 average. He pitched two innings in the NL Division Series against the Mets.

■ And the 22-year-old Billingsley, who entered the season as the Dodgers' No. 1 prospect, went 7-4, 3.80 in 90 innings, though his strikeout-walk ratio was just 59-58. Like Broxton, he pitched a couple of playoff relief innings.

Two other rookies—first baseman James Loney, 22, and lefthander Hong-Chih Kuo, 25—made the biggest impact in October when each made a playoff start.

The Dodgers emphasis on player development, which produced ready-to-contribute prospects sooner than anyone could have expected makes them Baseball America's Organization of the Year.

When general manager Ned Colletti was hired Nov. 16, 2005, after 11 seasons as the assistant GM in San Francisco, he was immediately peppered with questions about his willingness to trade from the Dodgers' stockpile of promising prospects.

And almost invariably, trade talks with other clubs quickly resulted in that club asking for one of the Dodgers' prized prospects. On Jan. 14, 2006, Colletti dealt two of them, sending lefthander Chuck Tiffany and righthander Edwin Jackson to the Devil Rays for relievers Danys Baez

LARRY GOREN

Dodgers prospect pipeline paid dividends
Russell Martin was one of five rookies to make contributions

and Lance Carter. Then on July 28 he packaged Baez and infielder Willy Aybar to the Braves for third baseman Wilson Betemit. He also sacrificed outfielders Joel Guzman and Sergio Pedroza to get shortstop Julio Lugo from the Devil Rays in a July 31 trade. Both Jackson and Guzman had previously ranked as the Dodgers' No. 1 prospect.

Billingsley, Broxton, Ethier, Martin and Kemp all were invited to major league spring training, even though none of them was expected to make the roster. Colletti asked a handful of his veteran players to make sure the youngsters felt welcome and comfortable. He saw it as an investment in the future. Both Colletti and manager Grady Little said before promoting any of these players that they wanted them to be ready to stick permanently when they did get the call.

Broxton came up May 1 after getting a taste of the big leagues in 2005, when he posted a 5.93 ERA in 14 appearances. That experience was invaluable, as the strapping righthander showed the flashes of the brilliance in 2006 that scouting director Logan White has long predicted. Billingsley's future remains bright, despite rookie stuggles.

Because of the work of White and the player development staff, the Dodgers system should continue to churn out prospects for years to come, but Colletti is glad the big league team has already started receiving dividends.

–TONY JACKSON

PREVIOUS WINNERS	
1982—Oakland Athletics	
1983—New York Mets	
1984—New York Mets	
1985—Milwaukee Brewers	
1986—Milwaukee Brewers	
1987—Milwaukee Brewers	
1988—Montreal Expos	
1989—Texas Rangers	
1990—Montreal Expos	
1991—Atlanta Braves	
1992—Cleveland Indians	
1993—Toronto Blue Jays	
1994—Kansas City Royals	
1995—New York Mets	
1996—Atlanta Braves	
1997—Detroit Tigers	
1998—New York Yankees	
1999—Oakland Athletics	
2000—Chicago White Sox	
2001—Houston Astros	
2002—Minnesota Twins	
2003—Florida Marlins	
2004—Minnesota Twins	
2005—Atlanta Braves	

Calling It Quits

Right fielder Sammy Sosa decided to stay home when the only offer he received as a free agent was a non-guaranteed one from the Nationals. He had hit just .221 with 14 home runs in an injury-plagued 2005 season with the Orioles. Sosa hit 588 homers, the fifth-highest total in history, in a 17-year career, including seasons of 66 in 1998, 63 in 1999 and 64 in 2001, all with the Cubs. He also amassed 2,194 strikeouts, trailing only Reggie Jackson for the highest total ever. Sosa, 37, was seeking a team to take a chance on him for the 2007 season.

"It wasn't about the money and it wasn't about No. 600," said Adam Katz, Sosa's agent. "It was a function of Sammy's expectation of his own performance. He didn't want to go out there and under-perform like he did last year because it was just too painful for him, and it's just something he doesn't want to go through again."

The career of first baseman Rafael Palmeiro, one of only four players with 500 home runs and 3,000 hits, came to an involuntary and unceremonious end when he received no offers as a free agent. Palmeiro was coming off a season in which he'd hit .266 with 18 home runs, but lack of contract offers had nothing to do with production. Palmeiro was suspended in August 2005 for violating MLB's drug policy.

Kevin Brown, a 19-year veteran and 211-game winner, also failed to get any offers after going 4-7, 6.50 for the Yankees in 2005. Yankees lefthander Al Leiter, Tigers righthander Troy Percival, Mets second baseman Bret Boone and Cubs outfielder Marquis Grissom all retired in spring training. Boone and Grissom were trying to catch on with new teams after signing minor-league contracts in the offseason.

Percival finished his 11-year career, spent primarily with the Angels, with 324 saves. Leiter won 162 games in his 19-year career he divided between four teams, mostly the Blue Jays and Mets. Boone hit 252 homers and drove in 1,021 runs in 14 seasons, while Grissom had 227 homers and 429 stolen bases in 17 seasons.

Rockies third baseman Vinny Castilla and Angels outfielder Tim Salmon called it quits at the end of the season. Castilla, who began the year as a regular with the Padres but was released and subsequently picked up by the Rockies, the team with which he established himself, hit 320 home runs in 16 seasons. Salmon belted 299 in 14 years, all with the Angels.

Still Going Strong

A pair of 300-game winners continued to add to their resumes in 2006.

Though he turned 44 during the season, Roger Clemens was as effective as ever, going 7-6, 2.30 in 19 starts. He didn't pitch until June 1, though, when he re-signed with the Astros as a free agent. He had pitched for the United States in the World Baseball Classic in March, but hadn't appeared in major league game since the 2005 World Series. Clemens signed a one-year contract for $22,000,000.22—his uniform number with the Astros was 22—but received only a prorated amount, which worked out to approximately $12.25 million.

Clemens had been undecided about returning to the game, but said his decision to come back was sparked by his son Koby, a third baseman with low Class A Lexington, an Astros affiliate. "Basically, he got me

---

A Baseball America survey of American League managers, conducted at midseason 2006, ranked AL players with the best tools:

BEST HITTER
1. Joe Mauer, Twins
2. Ichiro Suzuki, Mariners
3. Manny Ramirez, Red Sox

BEST POWER
1. David Ortiz, Red Sox
2. Jim Thome, White Sox
3. Manny Ramirez, Red Sox

BEST BUNTER
1. Joey Gathright, Devil Rays
2. Ichiro Suzuki, Mariners
3. Chone Figgins, Angels

BEST STRIKE-ZONE JUDGMENT
1. Travis Hafner, Indians
2. Placido Polanco, Tigers
3. Jason Giambi, Yankees

BEST HIT-AND-RUN ARTIST
1. Derek Jeter, Yankees
2. Michael Young, Rangers
3. Placido Polanco, Tigers

BEST BASERUNNER
1. Derek Jeter, Yankees
2. Ichiro Suzuki, Mariners
3. Orlando Cabrera, Angels

FASTEST BASERUNNER
1. Carl Crawford, Devil Rays
2. Joey Gathright, Royals
3. Ichiro Suzuki, Mariners

BEST PITCHER
1. Roy Halladay, Blue Jays
2. Francisco Liriano, Twins
3. Johan Santana, Twins

BEST FASTBALL
1. Joel Zumaya, Tigers
2. Justin Verlander, Tigers
3. Bobby Jenks, White Sox

BEST CURVEBALL
1. Barry Zito, Athletics
2. Josh Beckett, Red Sox
3. Mike Mussina, Yankees

BEST SLIDER
1. Francisco Liriano, Twins
2. Jeremy Bonderman, Tigers
3. Curt Schilling, Red Sox

BEST CHANGEUP
1. Johan Santana, Twins
2. Roy Halladay, Blue Jays
3. Kelvim Escobar, Angels

BEST CONTROL
1. Mike Mussina, Yankees

2. Brad Radke, Twins
3. Curt Schilling, Red Sox

BEST PICKOFF MOVE
1. Kenny Rogers, Tigers
2. Mark Buehrle, White Sox
3. Scott Kazmir, Devil Rays

BEST RELIEVER
1. Mariano Rivera, Yankees
2. B.J. Ryan, Blue Jays
3. Jonathan Papelbon, Red Sox

BEST DEFENSIVE C
1. Ivan Rodriguez, Tigers
2. Jose Molina, Angels
3. Ramon Hernandez, Orioles

BEST DEFENSIVE 1B
1. Mark Teixeira, Rangers
2. Doug Mientkiewicz, Royals
3. Travis Lee, Devil Rays

BEST DEFENSIVE 2B
1. Luis Castillo, Twins
2. Tadahito Iguchi, White Sox
3. Adam Kennedy, Angels

BEST DEFENSIVE 3B
1. Joe Crede, White Sox
2. Eric Chavez, Athletics
3. Brandon Inge, Tigers

BEST DEFENSIVE SS
1. Alex Gonzalez, Red Sox
2. Derek Jeter, Yankees
3. Yuniesky Betancourt, Mariners

BEST INFIELD ARM
1. Michael Young, Rangers
2. Adrian Beltre, Mariners
3. Eric Chavez, Athletics

BEST DEFENSIVE OF
1. Ichiro Suzuki, Mariners
2. Torii Hunter, Twins
3. Alex Rios, Blue Jays

BEST OUTFIELD ARM
1. Ichiro Suzuki, Mariners
2. Vladimir Guerrero, Angels
3. Alex Rios, Blue Jays

MOST EXCITING PLAYER
1. Ichiro Suzuki, Mariners
2. Grady Sizemore, Indians
3. Derek Jeter, Yankees

BEST MANAGER
1. Jim Leyland, Tigers
2. Joe Torre, Yankees
3. Ron Gardenhire, Twins

---

going, and that got my body moving," Clemens said.

Family ties also played a major role in what team he chose. The Red Sox, Yankees and Rangers also pursued Clemens, but Koby swung the decision to the Astros. Roger pushed his career win total to 348 in 23 seasons.

Dodgers righthander Greg Maddux, a veteran of 21 seasons, increased his win total to 333 after going 15-14, 4.20 in 34 starts. The Cubs dealt the 40-year-old Maddux to the Dodgers for shortstop Cesar Izturis at the trade deadline, after which a seemingly rejuvenated Maddux went 6-3, 3.30 for the playoff-bound Dodgers. He had gone 9-11, 4.69 in 22 starts for the Cubs.

Off The Managerial Hot Seat

All 30 managers made it through the 2006 season unscathed, though that turned out to be the calm before the storm.

Ken Macha was fired just hours after his A's lost to the Tigers in Oakland's first ALCS appearance since 1990. Both parties had briefly parted ways after the 2005 season

Verlander best in a deep rookie pool

We thought we were lucky last season. From Huston Street to Ryan Howard to Jeff Francoeur to another dozen drool-inducing rookies, there was every reason to think it would become a historic crop of baseball freshmen. And then 2006 came along.

ROOKIE
OF THE **YEAR**

It seemed as if every month—first Jonathan Papelbon, then Justin Verlander, then Francisco Liriano, then Jered Weaver—another American League phenom was blowing our eyes out. A team of rookies, the laughably underestimated Marlins, caught fire in midsummer behind shortstop Hanley Ramirez and a slew of starters and wound up staying in serious contention until the season's final two weeks. The depth was just outstanding—how else can you explain Joel Zumaya, the Tigers' flamethrowing reliever, ranking just No. 16 on our list of top rookies?

None was as impressive as Verlander, though, who led all rookies in wins and ERA and helped pitch the Tigers to the World Series. So even in the year of the rookie pitcher, Verlander rose above the other promising arms to become the Baseball America Rookie of the Year.

The No. 2 overall draft pick in 2004 out of Old Dominion, Verlander entered this spring hoping to win the No. 5 rotation spot—and wound up being the No. 1, and fast. He busted out of the gate to go 13-4, 2.69 through July as the Tigers built a huge lead. The 23-year-old Verlander tired in the later months but still finished up 17-9, 3.63 and could be considered Detroit's MVP.

He has everything you want in a frontline starter, from a high-90s fastball (he was baseball's hardest-throwing starter this year, according to Baseball Info Solutions) to a hard curveball to a plus changeup—and already has pennant-race and postseason experience. Verlander still needs to build stamina but should be the anchor of a fine rotation.

Verlander tossed 186 regular-season innings (and 22 more in the playoffs), far surpassing his previous career high. He struck out 124 batters, walked 60 and surrendered 21 home runs. He squared off with another rookie—of course—in Game 1 of World Series when he dueled Cardinals righthander Anthony Reyes. Both had entered the season as their organizations' No. 1 prospect.

Verlander's top competitor in the year of the pitcher was, oddly, not a pitcher. Marlins shortstop Ramirez, the top prospect traded by the Red Sox to acquire Josh Beckett, blossomed as much as anyone in baseball. The

A big part of Detroit's pennant winner
Justin Verlander led all rookies in wins and ERA

leadoff hitter scored 119 runs, stole 51 bases and displayed power with 17 home runs and 46 doubles. Ramirez also showed surprising plate discipline.

Twins lefthander Liriano spent the first six weeks of the season in the bullpen then exploded to go 11-2, 1.65 as starter. Subsequent elbow trouble kept him from Cy Young Award consideration, but things got worse for Liriano in November when he had Tommy John surgery.

Angels righthander Jered Weaver was demoted after four starts but eventually replaced his brother Jeff in the rotation. He started his career 9-0 and finished 11-2, 2.32 in just 18 starts.

The most dominant reliever in baseball for first five months, Red Sox righthander Papelbon saved 35 games for Red Sox with 0.92 ERA. Shoulder soreness shut him down after Sept. 1. Boston plans to make him a starter next spring, where he has the stuff to be a solid No. 2 starter.

Zumaya's electrifying 103 mph fastball made him most talked-about middle reliever of 2006. The 22-year-old Tigers righthander posted a 1.95 ERA and struck out 97 batters in 83 innings. Zumaya remained strong down the stretch, bedazzling the Yankees in the Division Series, but a sore wrist slowed him in the ALCS and World Series.

—ALAN SCHWARZ

PREVIOUS WINNERS

1989—Gregg Olson, rhp, Orioles	
1990—Sandy Alomar, c, Indians	
1991—Jeff Bagwell, 1b, Astros	
1992—Pat Listach, ss, Brewers	
1993—Mike Piazza, c, Dodgers	
1994—Raul Mondesi, of, Dodgers	
1995—Hideo Nomo, rhp, Dodgers	
1996—Derek Jeter, ss, Yankees	
1997—Nomar Garciaparra, ss, Red Sox	
1998—Kerry Wood, rhp, Cubs	
1999—Carlos Beltran, of, Royals	
2000—Rafael Furcal, ss/2b, Braves	
2001—Albert Pujols, of/3b/1b, Cardinals	
2002—Eric Hinske, 3b, Blue Jays	
2003—Brandon Webb, rhp, Diamondbacks	
2004—Khalil Greene, ss, Padres	
2005—Huston Street, rhp, Athletics	

TOP 20 ROOKIES

1.	Justin Verlander, rhp, Tigers
2.	Hanley Ramirez, ss, Marlins
3.	Francisco Liriano, lhp, Twins
4.	Jered Weaver, rhp, Angels
5.	Jonathan Papelbon, rhp, Red Sox
6.	Ryan Zimmerman, 3b, Nationals
7.	Dan Uggla, 2b, Marlins
8.	Josh Johnson, rhp, Marlins
9.	Matt Cain, rhp, Giants
10.	Russell Martin, c, Dodgers
11.	Prince Fielder, 1b, Brewers
12.	Josh Willingham, of, Marlins
13.	Nick Markakis, of, Orioles
14.	Scott Olsen, lhp, Marlins
15.	Takashi Saito, rhp, Dodgers
16.	Joel Zumaya, rhp, Tigers
17.	Andre Ethier, of, Dodgers
18.	Josh Barfield, 2b, Padres
19.	Anibal Sanchez, rhp, Marlins
20.	Ronnie Paulino, c, Pirates

but quickly reconciled and agreed on a three-year contract. Macha compiled a 368-280 record in his four seasons, but general manager Billy Beane felt communication problems between the front office and Macha, and between Macha and his players could not be resolved.

"Not to fault either side, but I felt a disconnect on a lot of levels," Beane said. "Once again, it's not to point the finger at Ken or anything like that. But that disconnect was there and it was something we needed to address as soon as possible."

Padres manager Bruce Bochy left San Diego after 12 years as manager—the longest such tenure in the majors—to take the same job with the Giants. Like Macha, Bochy was coming off a playoff appearance and had led the Padres to two straight NL West titles. Bochy, who guided the Padres to a 951-975 mark, was frustrated by the Padres' indifference to his wish for a contract extension.

"I made a commitment to myself and to my wife that if we were to make a change, it would be a place where I would have a chance to make an impact and a contribution," Bochy said. "That's the only reason I'd leave San Diego."

Four other veteran managers were also cut loose by their clubs, a list that included the Nationals' Frank Robinson, the Giants' Felipe Alou, the Cubs' Dusty Baker and the Rangers' Buck Showalter.

Robinson went 385-425 in five seasons with the Nationals franchise, which operated as Montreal Expos for his first three seasons. Alou was 342-304 in four seasons with Giants; Baker compiled a 322-326 record in four seasons with the Cubs; and Showalter had a 319-329 mark in four seasons with the Rangers.

Florida fired manager Joe Girardi after one season, though he guided the Marlins to a 78-84 record and to the fringes of the wild card race, even though Florida began the season with a payroll of $15 million, by far the lowest in the majors. One of the more bizarre moments of the season—a shouting match between Girardi and Marlins owner Jeffrey Loria—ultimately cost Girardi his job. During an Aug. 6 game against the Dodgers at Dolphin Stadium, Loria complained to umpires from his seat behind home plate, prompting Girardi to tell his boss to quiet down. Loria angrily left his seat and confronted Girardi after the game during a 90-minute clubhouse meeting, after which Loria reportedly fired Girardi then changed his mind.

"Obviously, the things I did, whether they were perfect or not, the players responded. We won," Girardi said. "I have no regrets."

The Royals' Allard Baird was the only general manager casualty during the season. He was fired May 31 and replaced with Braves assistant GM Dayton Moore, who

Bruce Bochy

took the reigns after the draft. Kansas City proceeded to go 31-44 after the all-star break, an improvement on their 31-56 first-half record.

Thirteenth Time The Charm For Sutter

Righthander Bruce Sutter became the fourth relief pitcher to be inducted into the Hall of Fame, leading a record Cooperstown class of 18 players and executives.

NATIONAL LEAGUE: BEST TOOLS

A Baseball America survey of National League managers, conducted at midseason 2006, ranked NL players with the best tools:

BEST HITTER
1. Albert Pujols, Cardinals
2. Nomar Garicaparra, Dodgers
3. David Wright, Mets

BEST POWER
1. Albert Pujols, Cardinals
2. Adam Dunn, Reds
3. Ryan Howard, Phillies

BEST BUNTER
1. Juan Pierre, Cubs
2. Jose Reyes, Mets
3. David Eckstein, Cardinals

BEST STRIKE-ZONE JUDEMENT
1. Bobby Abreu, Phillies
2. Albert Pujols, Cardinals
3. Barry Bonds, Giants

BEST HIT-AND-RUN ARTIST
1. David Eckstein, Cardinals
2. Edgar Renteria, Braves
3. Omar Vizquel, Giants

BEST BASERUNNER
1. Jose Reyes, Mets
2. Juan Pierre, Cubs
3. Bobby Abreu, Phillies

FASTEST BASERUNNER
1. Jose Reyes, Mets
2. Juan Pierre, Cubs
3. Willy Taveras, Astros

BEST PITCHER
1. Chris Carpenter, Cardinals
2. Brandon Webb, D'backs
3. Jason Schmidt, Giants

BEST FASTBALL
1. Billy Wagner, Mets
2. Derrick Turnbow, Brewers
3. Brad Penny, Dodgers

BEST CURVEBALL
1. Chris Carpenter, Cardinals
2. Tom Gordon, Phillies
3. Roy Oswalt, Astros

BEST SLIDER
1. John Smoltz, Braves
2. Brad Lidge, Astros
3. Pedro Martinez, Mets

BEST CHANGEUP
1. Trevor Hoffman, Padres
2. Pedro Martinez, Mets
3. Chris Capuano, Brewers

BEST CONTROL
1. Greg Maddux, Dodgers

2. Brandon Webb, D'backs
3. Pedro Martinez, Mets

BEST PICKOFF MOVE
1. Chris Capuano, Brewers
2. Andy Pettitte, Astros
3. Noah Lowry, Giants

BEST RELIEVER
1. Trevor Hoffman, Padres
2. Tom Gordon, Phillies
3. Jason Isringhausen, Cardinals

BEST DEFENSIVE C
1. Yadier Molina, Cardinals
2. Mike Matheny, Giants
3. Brad Ausmus, Astros

BEST DEFENSIVE 1B
1. Derrek Lee, Cubs
2. Albert Pujols, Cardinals
3. Todd Helton, Rockies

BEST DEFENSIVE 2B
1. Orlando Hudson, D'backs
2. Jose Castillo, Pirates
3. Dan Uggla, Marlins

BEST DEFENSIVE 3B
1. Scott Rolen, Cardinals
2. Ryan Zimmerman, Nationals
3. David Wright, Mets

BEST DEFENSIVE SS
1. Omar Vizquel, Giants
2. Jose Reyes, Mets
3. Adam Everett, Astros

BEST INFIELD ARM
1. Jose Reyes, Mets
2. Rafael Furcal, Dodgers
3. Scott Rolen, Cardinals

BEST DEFENSIVE OF
1. Andruw Jones, Braves
2. Jim Edmonds, Cardinals
3. Carlos Beltran, Mets

BEST OUTFIELD ARM
1. Jeff Francoeur, Braves
2. Carlos Beltran, Mets
3. Andruw Jones, Braves

MOST EXCITING PLAYER
1. Jose Reyes, Mets
2. Albert Pujols, Cardinals
3. Carlos Beltran, Mets

BEST MANAGER
1. Bobby Cox, Braves
2. Tony La Russa, Cardinals
3. Bruce Bochy, Padres

All but Sutter were selected by a special committee on African American baseball, which relied on research and statistics gleaned from old Negro Leagues box scores to narrow the ballot from 39 candidates. Included in the group was Negro Leagues owner Effa Manley, the first woman to be inducted.

Sutter recorded 300 saves with the Cubs, Cardinals and Braves in his 12-year career that stretched from 1976-88. He was on the Baseball Writers Association of America's ballot for 13 years before finally gaining the necessary 75 percent of the votes. He joins Hoyt Wilhelm, Rollie Fingers and Dennis Eckersley as the only relievers in the Hall.

"I am in awe," Sutter said. "When I got the call in January that I had been elected, it answered a question that had been ongoing for 13 years, a question, quite frankly, that I would ask myself every year at election time: `Do you belong?' The thought of having my plaque beside the greatest players who have ever played

Top executive, manager both Tigers

The Tigers improved by 24 games from 2005 to 2006 and claimed the American League pennant for the first time since 1984. Their secret was pitching—they led the majors with a 3.84 team ERA—but while they seemingly sprang from nowhere, these Tigers have been steadily building to this point.

EXECUTIVE
OF THE **YEAR**

MANAGER
OF THE **YEAR**

One can trace the Tigers' success to two figures: general manager Dave Dombrowski, the Baseball America Executive of the Year, and manager Jim Leyland, the BA Manager of the Year. The last time a GM and manager combo was honored in the same season was 2001, when GM Pat Gillick and manager Lou Piniella of the 116-win Mariners were so honored.

As the major league Tigers went mired in a run of losing seasons that stretched back to 1993—including the 119-loss debacle of 2003—the player-development system also had more than its share of notable failures. Perhaps nothing illustrated the Tigers' woes better than their run of first-round picks, beginning in '93: Matt Brunson, Cade Gaspar, Mike Drumright, Seth Greisinger, Matt Anderson, Jeff Weaver, Eric Munson, Matt Wheatland, Kenny Baugh, Scott Moore and Kyle Sleeth. Only Anderson and Weaver made any contribution in Detroit, and even they were ultimately considered disappointments.

Righthander Justin Verlander finally broke the string of failed picks in 2004, and his rise highlighted the quiet progress the Tigers have made since Dombrowski took over in April 2002. Both the arrival of Dombrowski and that of Verlander signaled a change in the organization's culture.

Verlander, righthanders Jeremy Bonderman and Joel Zumaya, as well as center fielder Curtis Granderson and third baseman Brandon Inge, were the most obvious symbols of developmental success, but infielder Omar Infante and arms such as righthander Fernando Rodney and lefthander Nate Robertson have played less-heralded, but no less valuable, roles.

And like the resourceful organization they are, the Dombrowski Tigers have found these players in all sorts of ways. Journeyman righthander Jason Grilli was signed before the 2005 season after the White Sox

LARRY GOREN

The architect of the AL's best
General manager Dave Dombrowski

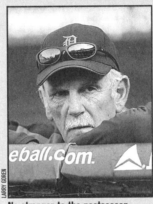

LARRY GOREN

No stranger to the postseason
Manager Jim Leyland

released him, while Robertson was part of the haul from the Marlins for Mark Redman. Left fielder Craig Monroe spent four seasons as an organization soldier before becoming a big league mainstay last year. And DH Marcus Thames had bounced between Triple-A Toledo and Detroit since signing as a minor league free agent in 2003.

Dombrowski's best acquisitions, though, were unquestionably the trades that netted Detroit its stellar middle infield—shortstop Carlos Guillen and second baseman Placido Polanco—at the cost of a few spare parts, notably Ramon Santiago, Ramon Martinez and Ugueth Urbina.

Revisionists will assign the hiring of Leyland as manager in October 2005 as the turning point in the Tiger renaissance, and many gave him credit for the whole shebang. Part of the reason for success came from Leyland. When players were sent out from big league camp in the spring, they remembered what Leyland was preaching in the major league clubhouse: Be prepared to play your best every day.

Leyland showed his deft touch all season, whether it be excoriating his troops in a television interview during an April slump or having the knack for supplying the right words of encouragement to a struggling pitcher in the heat of battle. Whatever Leyland offered, the Tigers clearly responded.

But while Leyland might be the reason the Tigers were better—he replaced a nice but clearly overmatched first-time manager in Alan Trammell—something else made them great. And Leyland himself was happy to identify it: "Talent," he said. "We have talent, and I'll always take talent."

And as the Tigers have imported talent for the big league club, they've also increased the talent level down on the farm. Detroit bottomed out at No. 29 in Baseball America's minor league talent rankings before the 2005 season, but leaped to No. 14 entering 2006. They could move up again this offseason after landing lefthander Andrew Miller with the sixth overall pick in last June's draft.

—ALAN SCHWARZ AND CHRIS KLINE

PREVIOUS WINNERS

Year	Executive, Team	Manager, Team
1998	Doug Melvin, Rangers	Larry Dierker, Astros
1999	Jim Bowden, Reds	Jimy Williams, Red Sox
2000	Walt Jocketty, Cardinals	Dusty Baker, Giants
2001	Pat Gillick, Mariners	Lou Piniella, Mariners
2002	Billy Beane, Athletics	Mike Scioscia, Angels
2003	Brian Sabean, Giants	Jack McKeon, Marlins
2004	Terry Ryan, Twins	Bobby Cox, Braves
2005	Mark Shapiro, Indians	Ozzie Guillen, White Sox

the game is truly an honor and humbling experience."

Longtime Baseball America columnist Tracy Ringolsby of the Rocky Mountain (Denver) News received the J.G. Taylor Spink Award for meritorious service to baseball writing, while longtime Astros broadcaster Gene Elston won the Ford Frick Award.

Manley was co-owner of the Newark Eagles along with her husband Abe, and used the sport to help advance civil rights causes. For example, the Eagles held an Anti-Lynching Day at the ballpark. The Eagles won the Negro Leagues World Series in 1946, one year before Jackie Robinson became the first black major league player of the 20th century.

"She did a lot for the Newark community. She was just a well-rounded, influential person," said former Giants outfielder and Hall of Famer Monte Irvin, who played for the Eagles. "She tried to organize the owners to build their own parks and have a balanced schedule and to really improve the lot of the Negro League players."

Manley was white but married a black man and passed as a black woman, said Larry Lester, a baseball author and member of the voting committee. "She campaigned to get as much money as possible for these ballplayers, and rightfully so," Lester said.

First baseman Mule Suttles and catcher Biz Mackey were the most prominent of the 12 former Negro Leagues players inducted, joining Ray Brown, Willard Brown, Andy Cooper, Cristobal Torriente and Jud Wilson. Frank Grant, Pete Hill, Jose Mendez, Louis Santop and Ben Taylor all played before the formation of the Negro Leagues. The executives enshrined were Alex Pompez, Cum Posey, J.L. Wilkinson and Sol White.

Buck O'Neil and Minnie Minoso, the only living members among the 39 candidates on the ballot, were not elected by the 12-person panel. O'Neil, who had become the preeminent historian of the Negro Leagues late in his life, was expected to be a shoo-in after a standout playing and managing career. After his playing days O'Neil

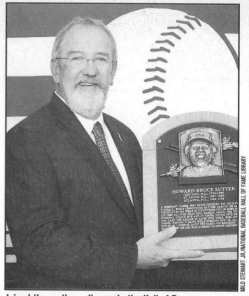

Joined three other relievers in the Hall of Fame
Bruce Sutter saved 300 games in his 12-year career

became the first black coach in major league history with the Cubs in 1962. He was a driving force in the building of the Negro Leagues Baseball Museum in Kansas City. O'Neil died on Oct. 6 at age 94 of exhaustion but professed no bitterness about his Cooperstown snub.

"Shed no tears for Buck," O'Neil said the day after he failed to gain election. "I couldn't attend Sarasota High School. That hurt. I couldn't attend the University of Florida. That hurt. But not going into the Hall of Fame, that ain't going to hurt me that much, no. Before, I wouldn't even have a chance. But this time I had that chance."

POWER AND SPEED

Alfonso Soriano is the fourth member of the 40-40 club

40-40 CLUB

Soriano joined three others who have hit 40 home runs and stolen 40 bases in the same season.

YEAR	PLAYER	TEAM	HR	SB
2006	Alfonso Soriano	Nationals	46	41
1998	Alex Rodriguez	Mariners	42	46
1996	Barry Bonds	Giants	42	40
1988	Jose Canseco	Athletics	42	40

300-300 CLUB

Finley and Sanders joined the exclusive company of four other players who have amassed more than 300 home runs and 300 stolen bases in their careers:

PLAYER	HR	SLG	SB	SB%	YEARS
Barry Bonds	734	.608	509	78%	21
Willie Mays	660	.557	338	77%	22
Andre Dawson	438	.482	314	74%	21
Bobby Bonds	332	.471	461	73%	14
Steve Finley	303	.444	320	73%	18
Reggie Sanders	303	.487	304	73%	16

Steve Finley

Reggie Sanders

Young extends AL streak with 9th inning heroics

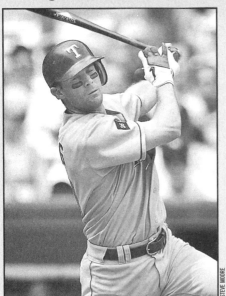

Good things came in threes
Michael Young's ninth-inning triple was the game-winner

The National League looked like a good bet to secure World Series home-field advantage for the first time since the 2003 inception of "This Time It Counts" All-Star Game.

The NL held a one-run lead going into the ninth inning of the 77th All-Star Game at PNC Park in Pittsburgh, and Padres closer Trevor Hoffman, who would lead the NL with 46 saves, was on to try to nail the game down.

While Hoffman would pass Lee Smith on the all-time saves list Sept. 24 and finish with 482 for the season, he couldn't convert this opportunity.

Rangers shortstop Michael Young's two-run triple with two outs rallied the American League to a 3-2 victory, giving the AL nine wins in the last 10 games. The 2002 game in Milwaukee ended in a tie and contributed to Commissioner Bud Selig's decision to award home-field advantage to the All-Star Game winner.

Ryan Howard

"You don't expect to get a hit off Trevor Hoffman in any situation, especially a big one like that," said Young, who won the game's MVP award. "I feel fortune to get a game-winning hit off him. It's definitely a big thrill."

Hoffman got two quick outs in the ninth, but White Sox' Paul Konerko kept the AL hopes alive with a single. The Blue Jays' Troy Glaus followed with a double,

moving pinch runner the Mariners' Jose Lopez to third.

Young then lined his triple to the gap in right-center.

"I got those two outs and it seemed like the inning was moving so quickly," Hoffman said. "But the American League kept battling and you've got to give them credit for that. That's why you compete, to be in situation like that, and unfortunately it didn't turn out well for me."

The rally made a winner of Toronto's B.J. Ryan, who pitched a scoreless eighth inning. Yankees' Mariano Rivera blanked the NL in the ninth for the save.

Angels right fielder Vladimir Guerrero hit a solo home run for the AL and Mets third baseman David Wright had a solo shot for the NL.

Phillies first baseman Ryan Howard won the home run derby, beating Wright in the finals. Howard, in his first full major league season, hit 58 home runs to lead the major leagues.

–JOHN PERROTTO

July 11 in Pittsburgh
American League 3, National League 2

AMERICAN	ab	r	h	bi	NATIONAL	ab	r	h	bi
Suzuki, rf	3	0	0	0	Soriano, lf	2	0	1	0
Dye, rf	1	0	0	0	Webb, p	0	0	0	0
Jeter, ss	3	0	0	0	Sanchez, ss-2b	2	0	0	0
Tejada, ss	1	0	0	0	Beltran, cf	4	1	2	0
Ortiz, 1b	2	0	0	0	Pujols, 1b	3	0	0	0
Konerko, 1b	2	0	2	0	Howard, 1b	1	0	0	0
J.Lopez, pr-3b	0	1	0	0	Bay, rf-lf	3	0	1	0
A.Rodriguez, 3b	2	0	0	0	D.Lee, lf	1	0	0	0
Glaus, 3b-1b	2	1	1	0	Renteria, ss	2	0	0	0
Guerrero, lf	2	1	1	1	Arroyo, p	0	0	0	0
M.Young, 2b	2	0	1	2	Fuentes, p	0	0	0	0
I.Rodriguez, c	2	0	0	0	Turnbow, p	0	0	0	0
Mauer, c	2	0	0	0	Berkman, ph	0	0	0	0
Wells, cf	2	0	1	0	M.Cabrera, 3b	0	0	0	0
Matthews, lf	1	0	1	0	Wright, 3b	3	1	1	1
Loretta, 2b	2	0	0	0	Gordon, p	0	0	0	0
Zito, p	0	0	0	0	Hoffman, p	0	0	0	0
Kazmir, p	0	0	0	0	Utley, 2b	2	0	1	0
Santana, p	0	0	0	0	McCann, c	1	0	0	0
Thome, ph	1	0	0	0	Lo Duca, c	2	0	0	0
Ryan, p	0	0	0	0	Eckstein, ss	1	0	0	0
Rivera, p	0	0	0	0	Penny, p	0	0	0	0
Rogers, p	0	0	0	0	Oswalt, p	0	0	0	0
Ordonez, ph	1	0	0	0	Holliday, ph-rf	3	0	0	0
Halladay, p	0	0	0	0					
Sizemore, cf	2	0	0	0					
Totals	**33**	**3**	**7**	**3**	**Totals**	**30**	**2**	**6**	**1**

American	0	1	0	0	0	0	0	0	2	—3
National	0	1	1	0	0	0	0	0	0	—2

LOB—American 3, National 2. **2B**—Glaus, Beltran. **3B**—M. Young. **HR**—Guerrero, Wright. **GIDP**—Glaus, Lo Duca, Renteria, Wright. **SB**—Soriano, Beltran. **E**—J. Lopez.

AMERICAN	ip	h	r	er	bb	so	NATIONAL	ip	h	r	er	bb	so
Rogers	2	3	1	1	0	1	Penny	2	1	1	1	0	3
Halladay	2	3	1	1	0	1	Oswalt	1	0	0	0	0	1
Zito	1	0	0	0	0	0	Webb	1	0	0	0	0	1
Kazmir	1	0	0	0	0	0	Arroyo	1	1	0	0	0	0
Santana	1	0	0	0	1	1	Fuentes	1	0	0	0	0	1
Ryan W	1	0	0	0	0	1	Turnbow	1	1	0	0	0	0
Rivera S	1	0	0	0	0	0	Gordon	1	1	0	0	0	1
							Hoffman BS, L 1	3	2	2	0	0	0

WP—Halladay.
Umpires: HP—Jerry Crawford. **1B**—Randy Marsh. **2B**—Fieldin Culbreth. **3B**—Jeff Nelson. **LF**—Mike Everitt. **RF**—Alfonso Marquez.
T—2:33. **A**—38,904.

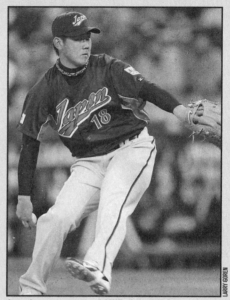
2006 WORLD BASEBALL CLASSIC

Japan bests Cuba, while USA falls in round two

Bud Selig's dream for years had been to stage a World Cup-style tournament that he felt would determine a true world champion. The commissioner's dream finally came true when Major League Baseball held the 16-team World Baseball Classic from March 3-20.

The WBC featured games at six sites in three countries and when the champion emerged, it was quite a surprise. And so was the runner-up.

Japan defeated Cuba 10-6 at San Diego's Petco Park in the final featuring two teams that entered the tournament as heavy underdogs to favorites like the United States, the Dominican Republic and Venezuela. Those three countries' rosters were loaded with major league stars, after all.

"Apart from the Olympics, I really wanted this WBC tournament to be the event that decides the true world champions, so that's why I participated," said Japan's Ichiro Suzuki, the Mariners' star outfielder. "This is probably the biggest moment of my baseball career."

That was saying quite a bit since Suzuki set the major-league record for hits in a season with 262 in 2005 and won the AL MVP award and Rookie of the Year honors in 2001 in a season Seattle won an AL-record 116 times.

While Americans seemed disinterested in the WBC at first, the idea seemed to catch on. The event drew a total of 737,112 fans, including more than 42,000 for the championship game—even though the United States did not make the final four. Furthermore, the only major leaguers on either Cuba's or Japan's roster were Suzuki and Rangers righthander Akinori Otsuka.

The championship game provided a festive event, as the fans chanted "Coo-ba! Coo-ba!" when Cuba rallied late in the game. The Japanese fans got their chance in postgame ceremonies, chanting "Nip-pon! Nip-pon!"

"The excitement wasn't the fact that they maybe just had tickets and had to go, but the excitement was already there, even if you hardly had any big leaguers," said Hall of Fame manager and WBC ambassador Tommy Lasorda. "That's the way it was the whole tournament."

Suzuki doubled, singled and drove in a run as Japan took a 4-0 lead in the first inning and never relinquished it. Righthander Daisuke Matsuzaka, who was named MVP of the tournament, went four innings, stiking out four Cuban batters and allowing a just a solo home run. Japan advanced to the final by blanking Korea, another surprise team, 4-0 in one semifinal, while Cuba defeated the Dominican Republic 3-1 in the other. Teams went through two rounds of pool play to make the final four in San Diego.

Pinch-hitter Kosuke Fukudome's two-run home run in the seventh inning of the semifinal snapped a scoreless tie and spurred Japan to victory after it had lost twice to Korea in pool play. Korea went 6-0 in pool play and was the only team to go unbeaten.

In the other semifinal, Osmani Urrutia broke a 1-1 tie with his RBI single in the seventh inning to propel

Japan's ace was named MVP of the WBC
Daisuke Matsuzaka was 3-0, 1.38 in 13 tournament innings

Cuba to victory against the Dominican Republic. Adding intrigue to the matchup was the composition of the two teams: The Dominicans featured major leaguers at several positions, many of whom make seven-figure salaries, while the Cubans play for minimal pay in their communist homeland.

The United States team was a major disappointment as it went 2-1 in both rounds of pool play, with both losses stunners against neighboring countries. They lost 8-6 to Canada in the first round at Phoenix, and 2-1 to Mexico in the second round at Anaheim. The latter game eliminated the Americans.

"This is up there with anything I've ever done," said U.S. pitcher Jake Peavy of the Padres. "It's disheartening to be eliminated. There are a lot of emotional guys in the clubhouse. It's not easy to deal with."

Instead, the Americans will have to wait for the next WBC, scheduled for 2009 and then expected to be played every four years after that.

Tweaks will be made to the second WBC, such as holding the event later in spring training when players are more game-ready and reducing the number of teams in the tournament. Major league umpires will also be employed after a series of disputed calls by minor league umps.

Lasorda, who managed the U.S. to the gold medal in 2000 Olympics in Sydney, can't wait for the next go-round, especially after the International Olympic Committee decided to eliminate baseball after the 2008 Games in Beijing.

—JOHN PERROTTO

WBC STATS

WORLD BASEBALL CLASSIC, San Diego, March 3-20, 2006

ROUND 1
POOL-PLAY STANDINGS

Tokyo POOL A	W	L	T	Phoenix POOL B	W	L	T
Korea	3	0	0	Mexico	2	1	0
Japan	2	1	0	United States	2	1	0
Taiwan	1	2	0	Canada	2	1	0
China	0	3	0	South Africa	0	3	0

San Juan, P.R. POOL C	W	L	T	Orlando POOL D	W	L	T
Puerto Rico	3	0	0	Dominican Republic	3	0	0
Cuba	2	1	0	Venezuela	2	1	0
Netherlands	1	2	0	Italy	1	2	0
Panama	0	3	0	Australia	0	3	0

ROUND 2
POOL-PLAY STANDINGS

Anaheim POOL 1	W	L	T	San Juan, P.R. POOL 2	W	L	T
Korea	3	0	0	Dominican Republic	2	1	0
Japan	1	2	0	Cuba	2	1	0
Mexico	1	2	0	Venezuela	1	2	0
United States	1	2	0	Puerto Rico	1	2	0

SEMI-FINALS: Japan 6, Korea 0; Cuba 3, Dominican Republic 1.
FINAL: Japan 10, Cuba 6.
ALL-TOURNAMENT TEAM: C—Tomoya Satozaki, Japan. **1B**—Seung Yeop Lee, Korea. **2B**—Yulieski Gourriel, Cuba. **SS**—Derek Jeter, USA. **3B**—Adrian Beltre, Dominican Republic. **OF**—Ken Griffey, USA; Ichiro Suzuki, Japan; Jong Beom Lee, Korea. **DH**—Yoandy Garlobo, Cuba. **P**—Daisuke Matsuzaka, Japan; Chan Ho Park, Korea; Yadel Marti, Cuba.
MVP: Daisuke Matsuzaka, Japan.

INDIVIDUAL BATTING LEADERS
(Minimum 2.7 plate appearances per game)

BATTER, COUNTRY	AVG	AB	R	H	2B	3B	HR	RBI	SB
Adam Stern, Canada	.667	9	3	6	1	1	1	5	1
Ken Griffey, USA	.524	21	4	11	2	0	3	10	0
Brett Willemburg, S. Africa	.500	10	2	5	1	0	0	3	0
Yoandy Garlobo, Cuba	.480	25	4	12	1	0	1	4	0
Jason Bay, Canada	.455	11	5	5	1	0	0	0	0
Sidney de Jong, Netherlands	.455	11	2	5	0	0	0	0	0
Nicholas Dempsey, S. Africa	.455	11	0	5	0	0	0	0	0
Derek Jeter, USA	.450	20	5	9	0	1	0	1	0
Nobuhiko Matsunaka, Japan	.433	30	11	13	4	0	0	2	0
Yi Feng, China	.429	7	0	3	0	0	0	0	0

INDIVIDUAL PITCHING LEADERS
(Minimum 0.8 innings pitched per game)

PITCHER, COUNTRY	W	L	ERA	SV	IP	H	BB	SO
Adzam Loewen, Canada	1	0	0.00	0	4	3	3	0
Yadel Marti, Cuba	1	0	0.00	2	13	6	4	11
Wei-Lun Pan, Taiwan	1	0	0.00	0	4	2	2	5
Jason Grilli, Italy	1	0	0.00	0	5	1	0	7
Shairon Martis, Netherlands	1	0	0.00	0	7	0	1	0
Kelvim Escobar, Venezuela	1	1	0.00	0	8	3	5	5
Carlos Silva, Venezuela	0	0	0.00	0	6	5	1	4
Po-Hsuan Keng, Taiwan	0	0	0.00	0	3	1	1	1
Erik Bedard, Canada	0	0	0.00	0	4	2	2	6
Chan Ho Park, Korea	0	0	0.00	3	10	7	0	8

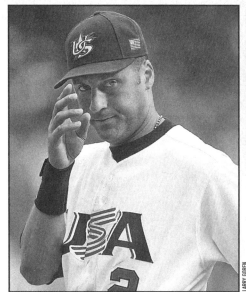

LARRY GOREN

Star shortstop and leader, regardless of uniform
Derek Jeter excelled for the Yankees and for the U.S. in the WBC

Nationals Bought By Lerner

One of the game's longest-running sagas finally ended in 2006 when real estate developer Ted Lerner purchased the Nationals for $450 million. No longer will the franchise be the ward of baseball as it had been since MLB bought the then-Montreal Expos for $120 million in 2002. MLB's purchase of the Expos precipitating a triangle of ownership changes: Jeffrey Loria vacated the Expos to buy the Marlins, while Marlins owner John Henry became part of the Red Sox ownership group. Commissioner Selig then approved the Expos move from Montreal to Washington prior to the 2005 season.

Eight groups were involved in the bidding process, which took more than a year to complete. Ultimately, Lerner's group was chosen over one headed by former Mariners owner Jeffrey Smulyan, and another by Fred Malek and Jeffrey Zients, leaders of Washington Baseball Club, which worked for seven years to bring a big league club to the nation's capital.

Lerner, 80, grew up in Washington and was a high school classmate of former Commissioner Bowie Kuhn. Lerner became the principal owner along with his son Mark and two son-in-laws, and brought in former Braves executive Stan Kasten as minority owner and club president.

In other business news, MLB sold broadcast rights to one of its League Championship Series to the cable television network Turner Broadcasting System for a reported $310 million. TBS will show the NLCS in odd-numbered years—2007, 2009, 2011 and 2013—and the ALCS in even-numbered years—2008, 2010 and 2012. The transaction was part of a new $3 billion television package in which the World Series, LCS, Division Series and All-Star Game will be aired on Fox or TBS. Fox also will continue to show Saturday regular-season games through 2013, while TBS will add 26 regular-season Sunday afternoon games in 2008. All Division Series games will move to TBS.

The ramifications of the umpires' failed 1999 mass resignation continued to be felt seven years later. MLB was ordered by a federal judge to pay umpires Gary Darling, Bill Hohn, Larry Poncino, Larry Vanover and Joe West $3.1 million in compensatory damages to cover back pay, interest and medical costs. A total of 22 umpires lost their jobs in 1999 following a failed mass resignation. An arbitrator decided in May 2001 that 11 of the umps should be rehired, and the five covered in the latest ruling were rehired in a partial settlement in February 2002.

Cardinals Take Flight In New Park

Though the Cardinals ballpark was new, it sported a familiar name. They defeated the Brewers 6-4 on April 10 in the third incarnation of Busch Stadium, this one a $365-million facility built just beyond the left-field wall of the old one. Cardinals lefthander Mark Mulder christened the new park by pitching into the ninth inning of a game in which he hit his first career home run. Mulder had also started the final game—Game 6 of the 2005 NLCS—at the 40-year-old Busch Stadium.

"Something about that old round stadium was pretty exciting," Cardinals center fielder Jim Edmonds said. "This is going to take some adjusting, but I think it's going to be a great place for everybody."

Meanwhile, the Yankees, Nationals and Mets broke ground on new ballparks. The new Yankee Stadium will be just north of the existing ballpark, which opened in 1923, and the cost is expected to be $1 billion. The Yankees plan to move into their new home in 2009.

The new Washington park is expected to cost $611 million and the Nationals are aiming for it to be ready in time to replace RFK Stadium by Opening Day 2008. The stadium is being built near the west bank of the Anacostia River, about a mile south of the Capitol.

The Mets broke ground in November on CitiField, which they expect to move into for the 2009 season. The Twins, meanwhile, finally got the green light on a downtown park, which they plan to have ready for 2010.

Last But Certainly Not Least

The most surprising news of the 2006 season bodes well for the next five seasons. Selig, representing the owners, and Donald Fehr, head of the Major League Baseball Players Association, announced prior to Game Three of the World Series that they had signed a five-year Collective Bargaining Agreement, covering the years 2007-2011. Most surprising was that the accord was struck two months before the old agreement was set to expire, ensuring continuation of 16 years of labor peace.

Baseball had seen eight work stoppages in the 23 years from 1972 to 1994, including the players' strike that led to the cancellation of the 1994 World Series and delayed start of the 1995 season by nearly a month. The last time the CBA was up for renewal in 2002, the owners and players were able to hammer out an 11th-hour agreement just before a strike deadline had been set.

"The last agreement produced stunning growth and revenue," Selig said. "I believe that five years from now people will be stunned how well we grew the sport."

The existing luxury tax and revenue-sharing rules, provisions that send money from large revenue teams to their competitors, will continue with some minor adjustments. The payroll threshold for the luxury tax increases

A change in home venue meant little to his bottom line
Albert Pujols just kept hitting in Cardinals' newest Busch Stadium

from $136.5 million in 2006 to $148 million in 2007 then increases each year until it reaches $178 million in 2011. The minimum player salary also will increase, from the present $327,000 to $380,000 in 2007.

The new CBA also instituted a signing date of Aug. 15 for all draft picks (excluding college seniors), eliminating the draft-and-follow process. Draft compensation rules were altered for 2007, as well. A team losing a Type C free agent, as defined by the Elias Sports Bureau, no longer will be awarded a draft pick, while a team losing a Type B free agent will receive one supplemental pick between the first and second round.

In addition, longstanding deadlines for teams to re-sign their own free agents were eliminated, and management agreed to take the threat of contraction off the table. Baseball's drug-testing policy will remain intact and was extended through 2011.

"There is a spirit of cooperation between management and labor in this game that is unprecedented," Selig said. "I think we all understand that we are currently in the midst of the golden age of baseball and we're all benefiting because of that."

Lance Berkman's productivity is often overlooked

HISTORIC SLUGGERS

Nine active players finished the 2006 season ranked among the top 50 batters ever for both career on-base percentage and career slugging percentage. Those nine ranked by career OPS:

PLAYER	OPS	OBP	RANK	SLG	RANK	PA
Barry Bonds	1.051	.443	6	.608	6	12,129
Albert Pujols	1.048	.419	21	.629	4	4,062
Todd Helton	1.023	.430	10	.593	9	6,073
Manny Ramirez	1.011	.411	35	.600	8	7,783
Frank Thomas	.990	.424	14	.566	16	9,162
Lance Berkman	.983	.416	24	.567	15	4,459
Jim Thome	.974	.409	39	.565	18	7,891
Jason Giambi	.954	.413	30	.541	34	6,908
Jeff Bagwell	.948	.408	44	.540	35	9,431

Players with 1,000 PA only. **Source:** Baseball-Reference.com

ARIZONA DIAMONDBACKS

Callaspo, Alberto	Aug. 6
Drew, Stephen	July 15
Gonzalez, Enrique	May 28
Montero, Miguel	Sept. 6
Pena, Tony	July 18
Quentin, Carlos	July 20
Slaten, Doug	Sept. 4
Young, Chris	Aug. 18

ATLANTA BRAVES

Barry, Kevin	July 4
Moylan, Peter	April 12
Pena, Tony	April 13
Prado, Martin	April 23
Stockman, Phil	June 15
Thorman, Scott	June 18

BALTIMORE ORIOLES

Abreu, Winston	Aug. 6
Birkins, Kurt	May 20
Britton, Chris	May 20
Burres, Brian	Sept. 8
Fahey, Brandon	April 30
Hoey, Jim	Aug. 23
Johnson, Jim	July 29
Loewen, Adam	June 18
Markakis, Nick	April 3
Rleal, Sendy	May 20

BOSTON RED SOX

Gabbard, Kason	July 22
Hansack, Devern	Sept. 23
Lester, Jon	June 16
Murphy, David	Sept. 2
Pauley, David	May 31
Pedroia, Dustin	Aug. 22

CHICAGO CUBS

Coats, Buck	Aug. 22
Guzman, Angel	April 26
Marmol, Carlos	June 4
Marshall, Sean	April 9
Mateo, Juan	Aug. 3
Moore, Scott	Sept. 4
O'Malley, Ryan	Aug. 16
Pagan, Angel	April 3
Reyes, Jose	Sept. 13
Ryu, Jae Kuk	May 14

CHICAGO WHITE SOX

Fields, Josh	Sept. 13
Haeger, Charlie	May 10
Logan, Boone	April 4
Montero, Agustin	June 18
Owens, Jerry	Sept. 11
Stewart, Chris	Sept. 6
Sweeney, Ryan	Sept. 1
Tracey, Sean	June 8

CINCINNATI REDS

Bray, Bill	June 3
Hopper, Norris	Aug. 20

CLEVELAND INDIANS

Brown, Andrew	Aug. 13
Carmona, Fausto	June 18
Inglett, Joe	June 21
Kouzmanoff, Kevin	Sept. 2
Lara, Juan	Sept. 8
Mastny, Tom	Sept. 8
Mujica, Edward	June 21
Perez, Rafael	June 18
Slocum, Brian	April 22
Sowers, Jeremy	June 25

COLORADO ROCKIES

Colina, Alvin	Sept. 18
Corpas, Manny	July 18
Hampson, Justin	Sept. 10
Iannetta, Chris	Aug. 27
Jimenez, Ubaldo	Sept. 26
Morillo, Juan	Sept. 24
Ramirez, Ramon	April 14
Salazar, Jeff	Sept. 7
Tulowitzki, Troy	Aug. 30

DETROIT TIGERS

Clevlen, Brent	July 30
Hannahan, Jack	May 25
Miller, Andrew	Aug. 30
Miner, Zach	June 20

FLORIDA MARLINS

Rabelo, Mike	Sept. 23
Tata, Jordan	April 6
Zumaya, Joel	June 16
Abercrombie, Reggie	April 4
Fulchino, Jeff	June 22
Garcia, Jose	Sept. 11
Martinez, Carlos	April 3
Nolasco, Ricky	April 5
Petit, Yusmeiro	May 14
Pinto, Renyel	May 18
Reed, Eric	April 3
Sanchez, Anibal	July 1
Tankersley, Taylor	June 3
Uggla, Dan	April 3

HOUSTON ASTROS

Albers, Matt	July 25
Barzilla, Philip	June 11
Buchholz, Taylor	April 7
Gimenez, Hector	Sept. 25
Hirsh, Jason	Aug. 12
Nieve, Fernando	April 4
Sampson, Chris	June 2

KANSAS CITY ROYALS

Andrade, Steve	May 1
Braun, Ryan	Sept. 2
Diaz, Jose	Sept. 6
Keppel, Bob	June 17
Maier, Mitch	Sept. 23
Sanchez, Angel	Sept. 23

LOS ANGELES ANGELS

Aybar, Erick	May 16
Kendrick, Howie	April 26
Morales, Kendry	May 23
Moseley, Dustin	July 17
Murphy, Tommy	May 4
Napoli, Mike	May 4
Weaver, Jered	May 27
Willits, Reggie	April 26

LOS ANGELES DODGERS

Billingsley, Chad	June 15
Ethier, Andre	May 2
Guzman, Joel	June 1
Kemp, Matt	May 28
Loney, James	April 4
Martin, Russell	May 5
Saito, Takashi	April 9
Stults, Eric	Sept. 5
Young, Delwyn	Sept. 7

MILWAUKEE BREWERS

Anderson, Drew	Sept. 11
Barnwell, Chris	June 20
Gwynn, Tony	July 15
Jackson, Zach	June 4
Mabeus, Chris	May 29
Rottino, Vinny	Sept. 1
Sarfate, Dennis	Sept. 3
Villanueva, Carlos	May 23

MINNESOTA TWINS

Bonser, Boof	May 21
Casilla, Alexi	Sept. 1
Eyre, Willie	May 20
Garza, Matt	Aug. 11
Neshek, Pat	July 7
Perkins, Glen	Sept. 21
Rabe, Josh	July 17

NEW YORK METS

Bannister, Brian	April 5
Humber, Philip	Sept. 24
Milledge, Lastings	May 30
Owens, Henry	July 7
Pelfrey, Mike	July 8
Soler, Alay	May 24

NEW YORK YANKEES

Beam, T.J.	June 17
Cannizaro, Andy	Sept. 5
Karstens, Jeff	Aug. 22
Thompson, Kevin	June 3
Veras, Jose	Aug. 5

OAKLAND ATHLETICS

Brown, Jeremy	Sept. 3
Komine, Shane	July 30
Rouse, Mike	June 9

Windsor, Jason	July 17

PHILADELPHIA PHILLIES

Bourn, Michael	July 30
Coste, Chris	May 26
Hamels, Cole	May 12
Mathieson, Scott	June 17
Roberson, Chris	May 12
Ruiz, Carlos	May 6
Sanches, Brian	June 1
Smith, Matt	June 17

PITTSBURGH PIRATES

Davis, Rajai	Aug. 14
de Caster, Yurendell	May 21
Maldonado, Carlos	Sept. 8
Perez, Juan	Sept. 7
Rogers, Brian	Sept. 1
Sharpless, Josh	Aug. 1
Youman, Shane	Sept. 10

ST. LOUIS CARDINALS

Kinney, Josh	July 3
Narveson, Chris	Sept. 8
Nelson, John	Sept. 7

SAN DIEGO PADRES

Barfield, Josh	April 3
Thompson, Mike	May 17

SAN FRANCISCO GIANTS

Alfonzo, Eliezer	June 3
Frandsen, Kevin	April 28
Ishikawa, Travis	April 18
Lewis, Fred	Sept. 1
Misch, Patrick	Sept. 21
Sadler, Billy	Sept. 15
Sanchez, Jonathan	May 28
Santos, Chad	July 16
Wilson, Brian	April 23

SEATTLE MARINERS

Bohn, T.J.	Aug. 22
Chick, Travis	Sept. 13
Feierabend, Ryan	Sept. 13
Fruto, Emiliano	June 22
Green, Sean	June 28
Huber, Jon	Aug. 30
Jimenez, Cesar	Sept. 11
Johjima, Kenji	April 3
Jones, Adam	July 14
Livingston, Bobby	April 25
Lowe, Mark	July 7
Navarro, Oswaldo	Sept. 9
O'Flaherty, Eric	Aug. 16

TAMPA BAY DEVIL RAYS

Childers, Jason	April 3
Hammel, Jason	April 11
Lugo, Ruddy	June 16
Riggans, Shawn	Sept. 5
Salas, Juan	Sept. 5
Shields, Jamie	June 16
Stokes, Brian	Sept. 3
Young, Delmon	Aug. 29
Zobrist, Ben	Aug. 1

TEXAS RANGERS

Arias, Joaquin	Sept. 13
Castro, Fabio	July 6
Kinsler, Ian	April 3
Littleton, Wes	July 4
Masset, Nick	June 27
Meyer, Drew	April 21
Rheinecker, John	June 28

TORONTO BLUE JAYS

Hattig, John	Aug. 19
Janssen, Casey	June 17
Lind, Adam	Sept. 2
Roberts, Ryan	July 30
Romero, Davis	Aug. 18
Rosario, Francisco	May 19
Taubenheim, Ty	May 20

WASHINGTON NATIONALS

Campbell, Brett	Sept. 7
Dorta, Melvin	July 21
Harper, Brandon	Aug. 9
O'Connor, Michael	April 27
Perez, Beltran	Sept. 2
Ramirez, Santiago	May 24
Rivera, Saul	May 25
Schroder, Chris	Aug. 8

2006 AMERICAN LEAGUE STATISTICS

CLUB BATTING

	AVG	G	AB	R	H	2B	3B	HR	BB	SO	SB	OBP	SLG
Minnesota	.287	162	5602	801	1608	275	34	143	490	872	101	.347	.425
N.Y. Yankees	.285	162	5651	930	1608	327	21	210	649	1053	139	.363	.461
Toronto	.284	162	5596	809	1591	348	27	199	514	906	65	.348	.463
Cleveland	.280	162	5619	870	1576	351	27	196	556	1204	55	.349	.457
Chi. White Sox	.280	162	5657	868	1586	291	20	236	502	1056	93	.342	.464
Texas	.278	162	5659	835	1571	357	23	183	505	1061	53	.338	.446
Baltimore	.277	162	5610	768	1556	288	20	164	474	878	121	.339	.424
L.A. Angels	.274	162	5609	766	1539	309	29	159	486	914	148	.334	.425
Detroit	.274	162	5642	822	1548	294	40	203	430	1133	60	.329	.449
Seattle	.272	162	5670	756	1540	266	42	172	404	974	106	.325	.424
Kansas City	.271	162	5589	757	1515	335	37	124	474	1040	65	.332	.411
Boston	.269	162	5619	820	1510	327	16	192	672	1056	51	.351	.435
Oakland	.260	162	5500	771	1429	266	22	175	650	976	61	.340	.412
Tampa Bay	.255	162	5474	689	1395	267	33	190	441	1106	134	.314	.420

CLUB PITCHING

	ERA	G	CG	SHO	SV	IP	H	R	ER	HR	BB	SO	AVG
Detroit	3.84	162	3	16	46	1448	1420	675	618	160	489	1003	.257
Minnesota	3.95	162	1	6	40	1439	1440	683	632	182	356	1164	.267
L.A. Angels	4.04	162	5	12	50	1453	1410	732	652	158	471	1164	.254
Oakland	4.21	162	5	11	54	1452	1525	727	679	162	529	1003	.272
Toronto	4.37	162	6	6	42	1428	1447	754	694	185	504	1076	.262
Cleveland	4.41	162	13	13	24	1423	1583	782	698	166	429	948	.282
N.Y. Yankees	4.41	162	5	8	43	1444	1463	768	708	170	496	1019	.262
Seattle	4.60	162	6	6	47	1447	1500	792	739	183	560	1067	.267
Texas	4.60	162	3	8	42	1431	1558	784	731	162	496	972	.278
Chi. White Sox	4.61	162	5	11	46	1449	1534	794	743	200	433	1012	.271
Boston	4.83	162	3	6	46	1441	1570	825	773	181	509	1070	.279
Tampa Bay	4.96	162	3	7	33	1420	1600	856	782	180	606	979	.286
Baltimore	5.35	162	5	9	35	1419	1579	899	843	216	613	1016	.284
Kansas City	5.65	162	3	5	35	1426	1648	971	896	213	637	904	.292

CLUB FIELDING

	PCT	PO	A	E	DP		PCT	PO	A	E	DP
Boston	.989	4324	1663	66	174	Toronto	.984	4285	1712	99	157
Oakland	.986	4355	1626	84	173	Baltimore	.983	4257	1608	102	156
Minnesota	.986	4318	1648	84	135	Detroit	.983	4344	1780	106	162
Seattle	.985	4340	1630	88	163	N.Y. Yankees	.983	4331	1593	104	145
Chi. White Sox	.985	4347	1655	90	145	Cleveland	.981	4270	1670	118	165
Kansas City	.984	4279	1658	98	189	Tampa Bay	.981	4261	1594	116	156
Texas	.984	4294	1748	98	174	L.A. Angels	.979	4358	1545	124	154

INDIVIDUAL BATTING LEADERS
(Minimum 502 Plate Appearances)

	AVG	G	AB	R	H	2B	3B	HR	RBI	BB	SO	SB
Mauer, Joe, Minnesota	.347	140	521	86	181	36	4	13	84	79	54	8
Jeter, Derek, N.Y. Yankees	.343	154	623	118	214	39	3	14	97	69	102	34
Cano, Robinson, N.Y. Yankees	.342	122	482	62	165	41	1	15	78	18	54	5
Tejada, Miguel, Baltimore	.330	162	648	99	214	37	0	24	100	46	79	6
Guerrero, Vladimir, L.A. Angels	.329	156	607	92	200	34	1	33	116	50	68	15
Suzuki, Ichiro, Seattle	.322	161	695	110	224	20	9	9	49	49	71	45
Morneau, Justin, Minnesota	.321	157	592	97	190	37	1	34	130	53	93	3
Ramirez, Manny, Boston	.321	130	449	79	144	27	1	35	102	100	102	0
Guillen, Carlos, Detroit	.320	153	543	100	174	41	5	19	85	71	87	20
Johnson, Reed, Toronto	.319	134	461	86	147	34	2	12	49	33	81	8

INDIVIDUAL PITCHING LEADERS
(Minimum 130 Innings)

	W	L	ERA	G	GS	CG	SV	IP	H	R	ER	BB	SO
Santana, Johan, Minnesota	19	6	2.77	34	34	1	0	234	186	79	72	47	245
Halladay, Roy, Toronto	16	5	3.19	32	32	4	0	220	208	82	78	34	132
Sabathia, C.C., Cleveland	12	11	3.22	28	28	6	0	193	182	83	69	44	172
Kazmir, Scott, Tampa Bay	10	8	3.24	24	24	1	0	145	132	59	52	52	163
Mussina, Mike, N.Y. Yankees	15	7	3.51	32	32	1	0	197	184	88	77	35	172
Lackey, John, L.A. Angels	13	11	3.56	33	33	3	0	218	203	98	86	72	190
Escobar, Kelvim, L.A. Angels	11	14	3.61	30	30	1	0	189	192	93	76	50	147
Verlander, Justin, Detroit	17	9	3.63	30	30	1	0	186	187	78	75	60	124
Wang, Chien-Ming, N.Y. Yankees	19	6	3.63	34	33	2	1	218	233	92	88	52	76
Bedard, Erik, Baltimore	15	11	3.76	33	33	0	0	196	196	92	82	69	171

AWARD WINNERS

Selected by Baseball Writers Association of America

MOST VALUABLE PLAYER

Player, Team	1st	2nd	3rd	Total
Justin Morneau, Minnesota	15	8	3	320
Derek Jeter, New York	12	14	0	306
David Ortiz, Boston	0	1	11	193
Frank Thomas, Oakland	0	3	4	174
Jermaine Dye, Chicago	0	1	2	156
Joe Mauer, Minnesota	0	0	3	116
Johan Santana, Minnesota	1	0	5	114
Travis Hafner, Cleveland	0	1	0	64
Vladimir Guerrero, L.A.	0	0	0	46
Carlos Guillen, Detroit	0	0	0	34
Grady Sizemore, Cleveland	0	0	0	24
Jim Thome, Chicago	0	0	0	17
Alex Rodriguez, New York	0	0	0	13
Jason Giambi, New York	0	0	0	9
Johnny Damon, New York	0	0	0	7
Justin Verlander, Detroit	0	0	0	7
Ichiro Suzuki, Seattle	0	0	0	7
Joe Nathan, Minnesota	0	0	0	6
Manny Ramirez, Boston	0	0	0	6
Miguel Tejada, Baltimore	0	0	0	5
Raul Ibanez, Seattle	0	0	0	4
Robinson Cano, New York	0	0	0	3
Paul Konerko, Chicago	0	0	0	3
Magglio Ordonez, Detroit	0	0	0	3
Vernon Wells, Toronto	0	0	0	3
Carl Crawford, Tampa Bay	0	0	0	2
Mariano Rivera, New York	0	0	0	2
Kenny Rogers, Detroit	0	0	0	2
Chien-Ming Wang, New York	0	0	0	2
Troy Glaus, Toronto	0	0	0	1
Gary Matthews Jr., Texas	0	0	0	1
A.J. Pierzynski, Chicago	0	0	0	1
Michael Young, Texas	0	0	0	1

CY YOUNG AWARD

Player, Team	1st	2nd	3rd	Total
Johan Santana, Minnesota	28	0	0	140
Chien-Ming Wang, New York	0	15	6	51
Roy Halladay, Toronto	0	12	12	48
Francisco Rodriguez, L.A.	0	1	2	5
Joe Nathan, Minnesota	0	0	3	3
Kenny Rogers, Detroit	0	0	3	3
Justin Verlander, Detroit	0	0	2	2

ROOKIE OF THE YEAR

Player, Team	1st	2nd	3rd	Total
Justin Verlander, Detroit	26	1	0	133
Jonathan Papelbon, Boston	0	20	3	63
Francisco Liriano, Minnesota	1	3	16	30
Kenji Johjima, Seattle	0	2	4	10
Jered Weaver, Los Angeles	0	2	2	8
Nick Markakis, Baltimore	1	0	2	7
Ian Kinsler, Texas	0	0	1	7

MANAGER OF THE YEAR

Manager, Team	1st	2nd	3rd	Total
Jim Leyland, Detroit	19	7	2	118
Ron Gardenhire, Minnesota	9	15	3	93
Ken Macha, Oakland	0	5	11	26
Joe Torre, New York	0	1	12	15

GOLD GLOVE AWARDS
Selected by AL managers

C—Ivan Rodriguez, Detroit. 1B—Mark Teixeira, Texas. 2B—Mark Grudzielanek, Kansas City. 3B—Eric Chavez, Oakland. SS—Derek Jeter, New York. OF—Torii Hunter, Minnesota; Ichiro Suzuki, Seattle; Vernon Wells, Toronto. P—Kenny Rogers, Detroit.

SILVER SLUGGER AWARDS
Selected by AL managers, coaches

C—Joe Mauer, Minnesota. 1B—Justin Morneau, Minnesota. 2B—Robinson Cano, New York. 3B—Joe Crede, Chicago. SS—Derek Jeter, New York. OF—Jermaine Dye, Chicago; Vladimir Guerrero, Los Angeles; Manny Ramirez, Boston. DH—David Ortiz, Boston.

︙

AMERICAN LEAGUE
DEPARTMENT LEADERS

BATTING

GAMES
Grady Sizemore, Indians 162
Mark Teixeira, Rangers 162
Miguel Tejada, Orioles.............................. 162
Michael Young, Rangers 162
Ichiro Suzuki, Mariners 161

AT-BATS
Ichiro Suzuki, Mariners 695
Michael Young, Rangers 691
Grady Sizemore, Indians 655
Miguel Tejada, Orioles.............................. 648
Mark Loretta, Red Sox 635

RUNS
Grady Sizemore, Indians 134
Derek Jeter, Yankees 118
Johnny Damon, Yankees........................... 115
David Ortiz, Red Sox 115
Alex Rodriguez, Yankees 113

HITS
Ichiro Suzuki, Mariners 224
Michael Young, Rangers 217
Derek Jeter, Yankees 214
Miguel Tejada, Orioles.............................. 214
Vladimir Guerrero, Angels 200

TOTAL BASES
David Ortiz, Red Sox 355
Grady Sizemore, Indians 349
Jermaine Dye, White Sox 335
Vladimir Guerrero, Angels 335
Justin Morneau, Twins 331
Vernon Wells, Blue Jays 331

SINGLES
Ichiro Suzuki, Mariners 186
Derek Jeter, Yankees 158
Miguel Tejada, Orioles.............................. 153
Michael Young, Rangers 148
Mark Loretta, Red Sox 143

DOUBLES
Grady Sizemore, Indians 53
Michael Young, Rangers 52
Mike Lowell, Red Sox 47
Lyle Overbay, Blue Jays 46
Orlando Cabrera, Angels 45
Mark Teixeira, Rangers 45

TRIPLES
Carl Crawford, Devil Rays 16
Grady Sizemore, Indians 11
Curtis Granderson, Tigers 9
Ichiro Suzuki, Mariners 9
Chone Figgins, Angels 8
Jose Lopez, Mariners 8

EXTRA-BASE HITS
Grady Sizemore, Indians 92
David Ortiz, Red Sox 85
Mark Teixeira, Rangers 79
Vernon Wells, Blue Jays 77
Jermaine Dye, White Sox 74
Travis Hafner, Indians 74
Richie Sexson, Mariners 74

HOME RUNS
David Ortiz, Red Sox 54
Jermaine Dye, White Sox 44
Travis Hafner, Indians 42
Jim Thome, White Sox 42
Frank Thomas, Athletics 39

HOME RUN RATIO
(At-bats per home run)
David Ortiz, Red Sox 10.3
Travis Hafner, Indians 10.8
Jim Thome, White Sox................................ 11.7

Grady Sizemore led AL in extra-base hits

Frank Thomas, Athletics 11.9
Jason Giambi, Yankees 12.1

RUNS BATTED IN
David Ortiz, Red Sox 137
Justin Morneau, Twins 130
Raul Ibanez, Mariners 123
Alex Rodriguez, Yankees 121
Jermaine Dye, White Sox 120

SACRIFICES
Jose Lopez, Mariners 12
Nick Punto, Twins 10
Vance Wilson, Tigers.................................. 10
6 tied with 9

SACRIFICE FLIES
Orlando Cabrera, Angels 11
Justin Morneau, Twins 11
Kevin Youkilis, Red Sox 11
Emil Brown, Royals 10
Alex Rios, Blue Jays 10

HIT BY PITCHES
Reed Johnson, Blue Jays 21
Jason Giambi, Yankees 16
Melvin Mora, Orioles 14
Kenji Johjima, Mariners.............................. 13
Grady Sizemore, Indians 13

WALKS
David Ortiz, Red Sox 119
Jason Giambi, Yankees 110
Jim Thome, White Sox 107
Travis Hafner, Indians 100
Manny Ramirez, Red Sox 100

INTENTIONAL WALKS
Vladimir Guerrero, Angels 25
David Ortiz, Red Sox 23
Joe Mauer, Twins 21
3 tied with 16

STOLEN BASES
Carl Crawford, Devil Rays 58
Chone Figgins, Angels 52
Corey Patterson, Orioles 45
Ichiro Suzuki, Mariners 45
Scott Podsednik, White Sox 40

CAUGHT STEALING
Scott Podsednik, White Sox 19
Chone Figgins, Angels 16
Luis Castillo, Twins 11
Johnny Damon, Yankees............................ 10
Adam Kennedy, Angels 10

STRIKEOUTS
Curtis Granderson, Tigers 174
Richie Sexson, Mariners 154
Grady Sizemore, Indians 153
Jhonny Peralta, Indians.............................. 152
Nick Swisher, Athletics 152

TOUGHEST TO STRIKE OUT
(At-bats per strikeout)
Kenji Johjima, Mariners 11.00
Jay Payton, Athletics 10.71
Orlando Cabrera, Angels 10.47
Yuniesky Betancourt, Mariners 10.33
Jason Kendall, Athletics 10.22

GROUNDED INTO DOUBLE PLAYS
Miguel Tejada, Orioles................................ 28
Victor Martinez, Indians 27
Michael Young, Rangers 27
Troy Glaus, Blue Jays 25
Paul Konerko, White Sox............................ 25

MULTIPLE-HIT GAMES
Ichiro Suzuki, Mariners 71
Michael Young, Rangers 69
Gary Matthews, Rangers 65
Derek Jeter, Yankees 63
Vladimir Guerrero, Angels 61

ON-BASE PERCENTAGE
Manny Ramirez, Red Sox........................... .439
Travis Hafner, Indians .... .439
Joe Mauer, Twins...................................... .429
Derek Jeter, Yankees .... .417
Jim Thome, White Sox................................ .416

SLUGGING PERCENTAGE
Travis Hafner, Indians .... .659
David Ortiz, Red Sox .... .636
Jermaine Dye, White Sox .... .622
Manny Ramirez, Red Sox .... .619
Jim Thome, White Sox................................ .598

PITCHING

WINS
Johan Santana, Twins 19
Chien-Ming Wang, Yankees 19
Jon Garland, White Sox.............................. 18
Freddy Garcia, White Sox 17
3 tied with 17

LOSSES
Rodrigo Lopez, Orioles 18
Carlos Silva, Twins 15
Kelvim Escobar, Angels.............................. 14
Felix Hernandez, Mariners 14
Jarrod Washburn, Mariners 14

David Ortiz was home run champ at last

WINNING PERCENTAGE

Francisco Liriano, Twins	.800
Roy Halladay, Blue Jays	.762
Johan Santana, Twins	.760
Chien-Ming Wang, Yankees	.760
Jon Garland, White Sox	.720

GAMES

Scott Proctor, Yankees	83
Shawn Camp, Devil Rays	75
Juan Rincon, Twins	75
Scot Shields, Angels	74
Kyle Farnsworth, Yankees	72
J.J. Putz, Mariners	72
George Sherrill, Mariners	72

GAMES STARTED

Jeremy Bonderman, Tigers	34
Dan Haren, Athletics	34
Kevin Millwood, Rangers	34
Johan Santana, Twins	34
Barry Zito, Athletics	34

COMPLETE GAMES

C.C. Sabathia, Indians	6
Roy Halladay, Blue Jays	4
Kris Benson, Orioles	3
John Lackey, Angels	3
Jake Westbrook, Indians	3

SHUTOUTS

John Lackey, Angels	2
C.C. Sabathia, Indians	2
Jeremy Sowers, Indians	2
Jake Westbrook, Indians	2
17 tied with	1

GAMES FINISHED

Joe Nathan, Twins	61
Mariano Rivera, Yankees	59
Bobby Jenks, White Sox	58
Francisco Rodriguez, Angels	58
2 tied with	57

SAVES

Francisco Rodriguez, Angels	47
Bobby Jenks, White Sox	41
B.J. Ryan, Blue Jays	38
Todd Jones, Tigers	37
Huston Street, Athletics	37

INNINGS PITCHED

Johan Santana, Twins	233.2
Dan Haren, Athletics	223.0
Barry Zito, Athletics	221.0
Roy Halladay, Blue Jays	220.0
Chien-Ming Wang, Yankees	218.0

HITS ALLOWED

Mark Buehrle, White Sox	247
Jon Garland, White Sox	247
Jake Westbrook, Indians	247
Carlos Silva, Twins	246
Joe Blanton, Athletics	241

Chien-Ming Wang led AL with 19 wins

RUNS ALLOWED

Carlos Silva, Twins	130
Rodrigo Lopez, Orioles	129
Randy Johnson, Yankees	125
Mark Buehrle, White Sox	124
Joel Pineiro, Mariners	123

HOME RUNS ALLOWED

Carlos Silva, Twins	38
Josh Beckett, Red Sox	36
Mark Buehrle, White Sox	36
Kris Benson, Orioles	33
Freddy Garcia, White Sox	32
Rodrigo Lopez, Orioles	32

WALKS

Daniel Cabrera, Orioles	104
Barry Zito, Athletics	99
Gil Meche, Mariners	84
Ted Lilly, Blue Jays	81
Josh Beckett, Red Sox	74

FEWEST WALKS PER NINE INNINGS

Curt Schilling, Red Sox	1.24
Roy Halladay, Blue Jays	1.39
Mike Mussina, Yankees	1.60
Carlos Silva, Twins	1.60
Jon Garland, White Sox	1.75

HIT BATSMEN

Vicente Padilla, Rangers	17
Javier Vazquez, White Sox	15
Barry Zito, Athletics	13
Casey Fossum, Devil Rays	12
Ervin Santana, Angels	11

STRIKEOUTS

Johan Santana, Twins	245
Jeremy Bonderman, Tigers	202
John Lackey, Angels	190
Javier Vazquez, White Sox	184
Curt Schilling, Red Sox	183

STRIKEOUTS PER NINE INNINGS

Johan Santana, Twins	9.44
Jeremy Bonderman, Tigers	8.50
Felix Hernandez, Mariners	8.29
Javier Vazquez, White Sox	8.17
Curt Schilling, Red Sox	8.07

STRIKEOUTS PER NINE INNINGS (RELIEVERS)

Joe Nathan, Twins	12.51
Francisco Rodriguez, Angels	12.08
J.J. Putz, Mariners	11.95
B.J. Ryan, Blue Jays	10.70
Fernando Cabrera, Indians	10.53

PICKOFFS

Mark Buehrle, White Sox	10
Justin Verlander, Tigers	7
Scott Kazmir, Devil Rays	5
Jon Lester, Red Sox	5
3 tied with	4

WILD PITCHES

Daniel Cabrera, Orioles	17
Jose Contreras, White Sox	16
John Lackey, Angels	16
Mark Redman, Royals	12
3 tied with	11

OPPONENT BATTING AVERAGE

Johan Santana, Twins	.216
Ervin Santana, Angels	.241
Mike Mussina, Yankees	.241
Josh Beckett, Red Sox	.245
John Lackey, Angels	.246

WORST ERA

Joel Pineiro, Mariners	6.36
Carlos Silva, Twins	5.94
Rodrigo Lopez, Orioles	5.90
Mark Redman, Royals	5.71
Josh Beckett, Red Sox	5.01

FIELDING

PITCHER

PCT	11 tied at	1.000
PO	Jake, Westbrook, Indians	33

Ivan Rodriguez still had best arm in AL

A	Chien-Ming Wang, Yankees	42
E	Paul Byrd, Indians	5
	Kenny Rogers, Tigers	5
TC	Jake Westbrook, Indians	74
DP	Jon Garland, White Sox	10

CATCHER

PCT	Ivan Rodriguez, Tigers	.998
PO	Jason Kendall, Athletics	924
A	Ramon Hernandez, Orioles	69
E	Ramon Hernandez, Orioles	13
TC	Jason Kendall, Athletics	983
DP	Kenji Johjima, Mariners	9
	Jason Kendall, Athletics	9
PB	Ramon Hernandez, Orioles	13
	Jorge Posada, Yankees	13
CS%	Ivan Rodriguez, Tigers	51%

FIRST BASE

PCT	Travis Lee, Devil Rays	.998
PO	Mark Teixeira, Rangers	1480
A	Justin Morneau, Twins	111
E	Ben Broussard, Mariners	9
	Lyle Overbay, Blue Jays	9
TC	Mark Teixeira, Rangers	1572
DP	Mark Teixeira, Rangers	158

SECOND BASE

PCT	Mark Ellis, Athletics	.997
PO	Jose Lopez, Mariners	282
A	Jose Lopez, Mariners	417
E	Ian Kinsler, Rangers	18
TC	Jose Lopez, Mariners	715
DP	Mark Grudzielanek, Royals	111

THIRD BASE

PCT	Eric Chavez, Athletics	.987
	Mike Lowell, Red Sox	.987
PO	Mike Lowell, Red Sox	143
A	Brandon Inge, Tigers	398
E	Alex Rodriguez, Yankees	24
TC	Brandon Inge, Tigers	555
DP	Eric Chavez, Athletics	43

SHORTSTOP

PCT	Alex Gonzalez, Red Sox	.985
PO	Orlando Cabrera, Angels	252
A	Michael Young, Rangers	492
E	Carlos Guillen, Tigers	28
TC	Michael Young, Rangers	747

OUTFIELD

PCT	Curtis Granderson, Tigers	.997
PO	Grady Sizemore, Indians	409
A	Juan Rivera, Angels	13
E	Vladimir Guerrero, Angels	11
TC	Grady Sizemore, Indians	419
DP	Joey Gathright, Royals	4
	Torii Hunter, Twins	4
	Corey Patterson, Orioles	4

CLIFF WELCH

ED WOLFSTEIN

2006 NATIONAL LEAGUE STATISTICS

CLUB BATTING

	AVG	G	AB	R	H	2B	3B	HR	BB	SO	SB	OBP	SLG
L.A. Dodgers	.276	162	5628	820	1552	307	58	153	601	959	128	.348	.432
Colorado	.270	162	5562	813	1504	325	54	157	561	1108	85	.341	.433
Atlanta	.270	162	5583	849	1510	312	26	222	526	1169	52	.337	.455
St. Louis	.269	161	5522	781	1484	292	27	184	531	922	59	.337	.431
Chi. Cubs	.268	162	5587	716	1496	271	46	166	395	928	121	.319	.422
Arizona	.267	162	5645	773	1506	331	38	160	504	965	76	.331	.424
Philadelphia	.267	162	5687	865	1518	294	41	216	626	1203	92	.347	.447
N.Y. Mets	.264	162	5558	834	1469	323	41	200	547	1071	146	.334	.445
Florida	.264	162	5502	759	1454	309	42	182	497	1249	110	.331	.435
Pittsburgh	.263	162	5558	691	1462	286	17	141	459	1200	68	.327	.397
San Diego	.263	162	5576	731	1465	298	38	161	564	1104	123	.332	.416
Washington	.262	162	5495	746	1437	322	22	164	594	1156	123	.338	.418
San Francisco	.259	161	5472	746	1418	297	52	163	494	891	58	.324	.422
Milwaukee	.258	162	5433	730	1400	301	20	180	502	1233	71	.327	.420
Cincinnati	.257	162	5515	749	1419	291	12	217	614	1192	124	.336	.432
Houston	.255	162	5521	735	1407	275	27	174	585	1076	79	.332	.409

CLUB PITCHING

	ERA	G	CG	SHO	SV	IP	H	R	ER	HR	BB	SO	AVG
San Diego	3.87	162	4	11	50	1464	1385	679	629	176	468	1097	.249
Houston	4.08	162	5	12	42	1469	1425	719	666	182	480	1160	.256
N.Y. Mets	4.14	162	5	12	43	1461	1402	731	673	180	527	1161	.253
L.A. Dodgers	4.23	162	1	10	40	1460	1524	751	686	152	492	1068	.269
Florida	4.37	162	6	6	41	1433	1465	772	696	166	622	1088	.267
Arizona	4.48	162	8	9	34	1460	1503	788	727	168	536	1115	.267
Cincinnati	4.51	162	9	10	36	1446	1576	801	725	213	464	1053	.278
Pittsburgh	4.52	162	2	10	39	1435	1545	797	720	156	620	1060	.281
St. Louis	4.54	161	6	9	38	1430	1475	762	721	193	504	970	.268
Philadelphia	4.60	162	4	6	42	1460	1561	812	747	211	512	1138	.275
Atlanta	4.60	162	6	6	38	1441	1529	805	736	183	572	1049	.273
San Francisco	4.63	161	7	9	37	1430	1422	790	735	153	584	992	.261
Colorado	4.66	162	5	8	34	1447	1549	812	749	155	553	952	.277
Chi. Cubs	4.74	162	2	7	29	1439	1396	834	758	210	687	1250	.255
Milwaukee	4.82	162	7	8	43	1426	1454	833	763	177	514	1145	.265
Washington	5.03	162	1	3	32	1436	1535	872	803	193	584	960	.274

CLUB FIELDING

	PCT	PO	A	E	DP		PCT	PO	A	E	DP
Houston	.987	4406	1753	80	164	Pittsburgh	.983	4305	1790	104	168
Colorado	.985	4342	1816	91	190	Philadelphia	.983	4381	1686	104	153
San Diego	.985	4391	1596	92	138	Chi. Cubs	.982	4317	1480	106	122
San Francisco	.985	4289	1581	91	132	L.A. Dodgers	.982	4381	1797	115	174
St. Louis	.984	4289	1780	98	170	Milwaukee	.980	4277	1583	117	126
Atlanta	.984	4324	1608	99	146	Cincinnati	.979	4337	1599	128	139
Arizona	.983	4379	1776	104	172	Florida	.979	4300	1588	126	166
N.Y. Mets	.983	4384	1638	104	131	Washington	.978	4309	1501	131	123

INDIVIDUAL BATTING LEADERS
(Minimum 502 Plate Appearances)

	AVG	G	AB	R	H	2B	3B	HR	RBI	BB	SO	SB
Sanchez, Freddy, Pittsburgh	.344	157	582	85	200	53	2	6	85	31	52	3
Cabrera, Miguel, Florida	.339	158	576	112	195	50	2	26	114	86	108	9
Pujols, Albert, St. Louis	.331	143	535	119	177	33	1	49	137	92	50	7
Atkins, Garrett, Colorado	.329	157	602	117	198	48	1	29	120	79	76	4
Holliday, Matt, Colorado	.326	155	602	119	196	45	5	34	114	47	110	10
Lo Duca, Paul, N.Y. Mets	.318	124	512	80	163	39	1	5	49	24	38	3
Berkman, Lance, Houston	.315	152	536	95	169	29	0	45	136	98	106	3
Howard, Ryan, Philadelphia	.313	159	581	104	182	25	1	58	149	108	181	0
Wright, David, N.Y. Mets	.311	154	582	96	181	40	5	26	116	66	113	20
Utley, Chase, Philadelphia	.309	160	658	131	203	40	4	32	102	63	132	15

INDIVIDUAL PITCHING LEADERS
(Minimum 130 Innings)

	W	L	ERA	G	GS	CG	SV	IP	H	R	ER	BB	SO
Oswalt, Roy, Houston	15	8	2.98	33	32	2	0	221	220	76	73	38	166
Carpenter, Chris, St. Louis	15	8	3.09	32	32	5	0	222	194	81	76	43	184
Johnson, Josh, Florida	12	7	3.10	31	24	0	0	157	136	63	54	68	133
Webb, Brandon, Arizona	16	8	3.10	33	33	5	0	235	216	91	81	50	178
Arroyo, Bronson, Cincinnati	14	11	3.29	35	35	3	0	241	222	98	88	64	184
Zambrano, Carlos, Chi. Cubs	16	7	3.41	33	33	0	0	214	162	91	81	115	210
Young, Chris, San Diego	11	5	3.46	31	31	0	0	179	134	72	69	69	164
Smoltz, John, Atlanta	16	9	3.49	35	35	3	0	232	221	93	90	55	211
Schmidt, Jason, San Francisco	11	9	3.59	32	32	3	0	213	189	94	85	80	180
Lowe, Derek, L.A. Dodgers	16	8	3.63	35	34	1	0	218	221	97	88	55	123

AWARD WINNERS

Selected by Baseball Writers Association of America.

MOST VALUABLE PLAYER

Player, Team	1st	2nd	3rd	Total
Ryan Howard, Philadelphia	20	12	0	388
Albert Pujols, St. Louis	12	19	1	347
Lance Berkman, Houston	0	0	21	230
Carlos Beltran, New York	0	1	5	211
Miguel Cabrera, Florida	0	0	2	170
Alfonso Soriano, Washington	0	1	1	106
Jose Reyes, New York	0	0	1	98
Chase Utley, Philadelphia	0	0	0	98
David Wright, New York	0	0	1	70
Trevor Hoffman, San Diego	0	0	0	46
Andruw Jones, Atlanta	0	0	0	29
Carlos Delgado, New York	0	0	0	23
Nomar Garciaparra, L.A.	0	0	0	18
Rafael Furcal, Los Angeles	0	0	0	11
Garrett Atkins, Colorado	0	0	0	10
Matt Holliday, Colorado	0	0	0	10
Aramis Ramirez, Chicago	0	0	0	5
Freddy Sanchez, Pittsburgh	0	0	0	5
Chris Carpenter, St. Louis	0	0	0	4
Chipper Jones, Atlanta	0	0	0	3
Mike Cameron, San Diego	0	0	0	2
Jimmy Rollins, Philadelphia	0	0	0	2
Bronson Arroyo, Cincinnati	0	0	0	1
Jason Bay, Pittsburgh	0	0	0	1

CY YOUNG AWARD

Player, Team	1st	2nd	3rd	Total
Brandon Webb, Arizona	15	7	7	103
Trevor Hoffman, San Diego	12	3	8	77
Chris Carpenter, St. Louis	2	16	5	63
Roy Oswalt, Houston	3	3	7	31
Carlos Zambrano, Chicago	0	1	3	6
Billy Wagner, New York	0	1	1	4
John Smoltz, Atlanta	0	1	0	3
Takashi Saito, Los Angeles	0	0	1	1

ROOKIE OF THE YEAR

Player, Team	1st	2nd	3rd	Total
Hanley Ramirez, Florida	14	11	2	105
Ryan Zimmerman, Wash.	10	16	3	101
Dan Uggla, Florida	6	3	16	55
Josh Johnson, Florida	2	0	1	11
Matt Cain, San Francisco	0	1	1	4
Andre Ethier, Los Angeles	0	1	1	4
Prince Fielder, Milwaukee	0	0	2	2
Takashi Saito, Los Angeles	0	0	2	2
Russell Martin, Los Angeles	0	0	1	1
Scott Olsen, Florida	0	0	1	1
Anibal Sanchez, Florida	0	0	1	1
Josh Willingham, Florida	0	0	1	1

MANAGER OF THE YEAR

Manager, Team	1st	2nd	3rd	Total
Joe Girardi, Florida	18	6	3	111
Willie Randolph, New York	8	11	8	81
Bruce Bochy, San Diego	5	6	7	50
Grady Little, Los Angeles	1	5	10	30
Charlie Manuel, Philadelphia	0	3	0	9
Jerry Narron, Cincinnati	0	1	3	6
Phil Garner, Houston	0	0	1	1

GOLD GLOVE AWARDS
Selected by NL managers
C—Brad Ausmus, Houston. 1B—Albert Pujols, St. Louis. 2B—Orlando Hudson, Arizona. 3B—Scott Rolen, St. Louis. SS—Omar Vizquel, San Francisco. OF—Carlos Beltran, New York; Mike Cameron, San Diego; Andruw Jones, Atlanta. P—Greg Maddux, Chicago.

SILVER SLUGGER AWARDS
Selected by NL managers, coaches
C—Brian McCann, Atlanta. 1B—Ryan Howard, Philadelphia. 2B—Chase Utley, Philadelphia. 3B—Miguel Cabrera, Florida. SS—Jose Reyes, New York. OF—Carlos Beltran, New York; Alfonso Soriano, Washington; Matt Holliday, Colorado. P—Carlos Zambrano, Chicago.

NATIONAL LEAGUE
DEPARTMENT LEADERS

BATTING

GAMES
Jeff Francoeur, Braves 162
Juan Pierre, Cubs 162
Adam Dunn, Reds 160
Pedro Feliz, Giants 160
Chase Utley, Phillies 160

AT-BATS
Juan Pierre, Cubs 699
Jimmy Rollins, Phillies 689
Chase Utley, Phillies 658
Rafael Furcal, Dodgers 654
Jeff Francoeur, Braves 651

RUNS
Chase Utley, Phillies 131
Carlos Beltran, Mets 127
Jimmy Rollins, Phillies 127
Jose Reyes, Mets 122
4 tied with 119

HITS
Juan Pierre, Cubs 204
Chase Utley, Phillies 203
Freddy Sanchez, Pirates 200
Garrett Atkins, Rockies 198
Rafael Furcal, Dodgers 196
Matt Holliday, Rockies 196

TOTAL BASES
Ryan Howard, Phillies 383
Alfonso Soriano, Nationals 362
Albert Pujols, Cardinals 359
Matt Holliday, Rockies 353
Chase Utley, Phillies 347

SINGLES
Juan Pierre, Cubs 156
Rafael Furcal, Dodgers 140
Freddy Sanchez, Pirates 139
Omar Vizquel, Giants 135
Felipe Lopez, Reds/Nationals 128
Jose Reyes, Mets 128

DOUBLES
Freddy Sanchez, Pirates 53
Luis Gonzalez, Diamondbacks 52
Miguel Cabrera, Marlins 50
Garrett Atkins, Rockies 48
Scott Rolen, Cardinals 48

TRIPLES
Jose Reyes, Mets 17
Juan Pierre, Cubs 13

Matt Holliday quietly had huge season

Carlos Beltran had a big bounceback

Dave Roberts, Padres 13
Steve Finley, Giants 12
Kenny Lofton, Dodgers 12

EXTRA-BASE HITS
Alfonso Soriano, Nationals 89
Matt Holliday, Rockies 84
Ryan Howard, Phillies 84
Albert Pujols, Cardinals 83
Carlos Beltran, Mets 80
Aramis Ramirez, Cubs 80

HOME RUNS
Ryan Howard, Phillies 58
Albert Pujols, Cardinals 49
Alfonso Soriano, Nationals 46
Lance Berkman, Astros 45
Carlos Beltran, Mets 41
Andruw Jones, Braves 41

HOME RUN RATIO
(At-bats per home run)
Ryan Howard, Phillies 10.0
Albert Pujols, Cardinals 10.9
Lance Berkman, Astros 11.9
Carlos Beltran, Mets 12.4
Andruw Jones, Braves 13.8

RUNS BATTED IN
Ryan Howard, Phillies 149
Albert Pujols, Cardinals 137
Lance Berkman, Astros 136
Andruw Jones, Braves 129
Garrett Atkins, Rockies 120

SACRIFICES
Roy Oswalt, Astros 20
Clint Barmes, Rockies 19
Cory Sullivan, Rockies 19
John Smoltz, Braves 18
2 tied with 15

SACRIFICE FLIES
Carlos Delgado, Mets 10
Jason Bay, Pirates 9
Andruw Jones, Braves 9
Freddy Sanchez, Pirates 9
6 tied with 8

HIT BY PITCHES
Rickie Weeks, Brewers 19
Aaron Rowand, Phillies 18
Jose Bautista, Pirates 16
David Eckstein, Cardinals 15
Matt Holliday, Rockies 15

WALKS
Barry Bonds, Giants 115

Adam Dunn, Reds 112
Nick Johnson, Nationals 110
Ryan Howard, Phillies 108
Brian Giles, Padres 104

INTENTIONAL WALKS
Barry Bonds, Giants 38
Ryan Howard, Phillies 37
Albert Pujols, Cardinals 28
Miguel Cabrera, Marlins 27
Lance Berkman, Astros 22

STOLEN BASES
Jose Reyes, Mets 64
Juan Pierre, Cubs 58
Hanley Ramirez, Marlins 51
Dave Roberts, Padres 49
Felipe Lopez, Reds/Nationals 44

CAUGHT STEALING
Juan Pierre, Cubs 20
Jose Reyes, Mets 17
Alfonso Soriano, Nationals 17
Hanley Ramirez, Marlins 15
Rafael Furcal, Dodgers 13

STRIKEOUTS
Adam Dunn, Reds 194
Ryan Howard, Phillies 181
Bill Hall, Brewers 162
Alfonso Soriano, Nationals 160
Jason Bay, Pirates 156

TOUGHEST TO STRIKE OUT
(At-bats per strikeout)
Juan Pierre, Cubs 18.39
Nomar Garciaparra, Dodgers 15.63
Paul Lo Duca, Mets 13.47
David Eckstein, Cardinals 12.20
Todd Walker, Cubs/Padres 11.63

GROUNDED INTO DOUBLE PLAYS
Garrett Atkins, Rockies 24
Adrian Gonzalez, Padres 24
Jose Castillo, Pirates 22
Matt Holliday, Rockies 22
Brad Ausmus, Astros 21

MULTIPLE-HIT GAMES
Juan Pierre, Cubs 64
Chase Utley, Phillies 64
Miguel Cabrera, Marlins 63
Rafael Furcal, Dodgers 62
Freddy Sanchez, Pirates 60

ON-BASE PERCENTAGE
Albert Pujols, Cardinals .... .431
Miguel Cabrera, Marlins .... .430
Nick Johnson, Nationals .... .428
Ryan Howard, Phillies .... .425
Lance Berkman, Astros .... .420

SLUGGING PERCENTAGE
Albert Pujols, Cardinals .... .671
Ryan Howard, Phillies .... .659
Lance Berkman, Astros .... .621
Carlos Beltran, Mets .... .594
Matt Holliday, Rockies .... .586

PITCHING

WINS
Aaron Harang, Reds 16
Derek Lowe, Dodgers 16
Brad Penny, Dodgers 16
John Smoltz, Braves 16
Brandon Webb, Diamondbacks 16
Carlos Zambrano, Cubs 16

LOSSES
Jason Marquis, Cardinals 16
Ramon Ortiz, Nationals 16

Aaron Cook, Rockies 15
Zach Duke, Pirates 15
Matt Morris, Giants 15

WINNING PERCENTAGE
Chuck James, Braves .... .733
Woody Williams, Padres .... .706
Carlso Zambrano, Cubs .... .696
Chris Young, Padres .... .688
Tom Glavine, Mets .... .682

GAMES
Salomon Torres, Pirates 94
Matt Capps, Pirates..................................... 85
Jon Rauch, Nationals 85
Bob Howry, Cubs 84
Mike Stanton, Nationals/Giants 82

GAMES STARTED
Bronson Arroyo, Reds.................................... 35
Aaron Harang, Reds 35
Tim Hudson, Braves 35
Andy Pettitte, Astros 35
John Smoltz, Braves 35

COMPLETE GAMES
Aaron Harang, Reds 6
Chris Carpenter, Cardinals 5
Brandon Webb, Diamondbacks 5
Dontrelle Willis, Marlins 4
7 tied with 3

SHUTOUTS
Chris Carpenter, Cardinals 3
Brandon Webb, Diamondbacks 3
Dave Bush, Brewers 2
Chris Capuano, Brewers 2
Aaron Harang, Reds 2
Jason Jennings, Rockies.............................. 2

GAMES FINISHED
Ryan Dempster, Cubs 64
Joe Borowski, Marlins................................... 60
Chad Cordero, Nationals 59
Billy Wagner, Mets 59
Brian Fuentes, Rockies 58

SAVES
Trevor Hoffman, Padres 46
Billy Wagner, Mets 40
Joe Borowski, Marlins................................... 36
Tom Gordon, Phillies 34
Jason Isringhausen, Cardinals 33

INNINGS PITCHED
Bronson Arroyo, Reds 240.2
Brandon Webb, Diamondbacks 235.0
Aaron Harang, Reds...................................... 234.1
John Smoltz, Braves 232.0
Dontrelle Willis, Marlins.......................... 223.1

HITS ALLOWED
Zach Duke, Pirates 255
Livan Hernandez, Nationals/D'backs 246
Aaron Cook, Rockies..................................... 242
Aaron Harang, Reds 242
Andy Pettitte, Astros 238

RUNS ALLOWED
Jason Marquis, Cardinals 136

Roy Oswalt led NL with a 2.98 ERA

Tim Hudson, Braves 129
Ramon Ortiz, Nationals 127
Livan Hernandez, Nationals/D'backs 125
Matt Morris, Giants 123

HOME RUNS ALLOWED
Jason Marquis, Cardinals 35
Bronson Arroyo, Reds.................................... 31
Ramon Ortiz, Nationals 31
Jorge Sosa, Braves/Cardinals 30
5 tied with 29

WALKS
Carlos Zambrano, Cubs.................................. 115
Doug Davis, Brewers...................................... 102
Matt Cain, Giants 87
Jason Jennings, Rockies................................ 85
Miguel Batista, Diamondbacks 84

FEWEST WALKS PER NINE INNINGS
Jon Lieber, Phillies 1.29
Roy Oswalt, Astros 1.55
Greg Maddux, Cubs/Dodgers 1.59
Dave Bush, Brewers 1.63
Chris Carpenter, Cardinals 1.75

HIT BATSMEN
Dontrelle Willis, Marlins 19
Dave Bush, Brewers 18
Ramon Ortiz, Nationals 18
Jason Marquis, Cardinals 16
Matt Morris, Giants 14

STRIKEOUTS
Aaron Harang, Reds 216
Jake Peavy, Padres 215
John Smoltz, Braves 211
Carlos Zambrano, Cubs.................................. 210
Brett Myers, Phillies 189

STRIKEOUTS PER NINE INNINGS
Jake Peavy, Padres 9.56
Orlando Hernandez, D'backs/Mets 9.09
Carlos Zambrano, Cubs.................................. 8.83
Brett Myers, Phillies 8.59
Matt Cain, Giants 8.45

STRIKEOUTS PER NINE INNINGS (RELIEVERS)
Brad Lidge, Astros 12.48
Takashi Saito, Dodgers 12.29
Jorge Julio, Mets/D'backs 12.00
Billy Wagner, Mets 11.70
Jonathan Broxton, Dodgers 11.44

PICKOFFS
Paul Maholm, Pirates 8
Zach Duke, Pirates 7
Joe Beimel, Dodgers 6
Chris Capuano, Brewers 6
Jamey Wright, Giants 6

WILD PITCHES
Miguel Batista, Diamondbacks 14
Ryan Madson, Phillies 12
Brad Lidge, Astros.. 11
Jason Schmidt, Giants 11
Jason Jennings, Rockies.............................. 10

OPPONENT BATTING AVERAGE
Chris Young, Padres .... .206
Carlos Zambrano, Cubs.................................. .208
Matt Cain, Giants .... .222
Chris Carpenter, Cardinals .... .235
Jason Schmidt, Giants .... .238

WORST ERA
Jason Marquis, Cardinals............................ 6.02
Ramon Ortiz, Nationals 5.57
Josh Fogg, Rockies.. 5.49
Matt Morris, Giants 4.98
Steve Trachsel, Mets 4.97

FIELDING

PITCHER
PCT	11 tied at....................................	1.000
PO	Bronson Arroyo, Reds	29
A	Zach Duke, Pirates	52
	Greg Maddux, Dodgers	52
E	Pedro Martinez, Mets........................	5
	Tomo Ohka, Brewers	5

Ryan Zimmerman great with bat, glove

	Dontrelle Willis, Marlins..................	5
TC	Derek Lowe, Dodgers......................	71
DP	Greg Maddux, Dodgers	9

CATCHER
PCT	Brad Ausmus, Astros	.998
PO	Brad Ausmus, Astros	929
A	Yadier Molina, Cardinals	79
E	Paul Lo Duca, Mets	11
	Ronny Paulino, Pirates.....................	11
TC	Brad Ausmus, Astros	994
DP	Johnny Estrada, Diamondbacks.........	11
	Miguel Olivo, Marlins	11
PB	Michael Barrett, Cubs.....................	10
	Miguel Olivo, Marlins	10
CS%	Matt Treanor, Marlins	47%

FIRST BASE
PCT	Todd Helton, Rockies	.997
PO	Ryan Howard, Phillies	1373
A	Adrian Gonzalez, Padres	116
E	Nick Johnson, Nationals	15
TC	Ryan Howard, Phillies	1478
DP	Todd Helton, Rockies	156

SECOND BASE
PCT	Jamey Carroll, Rockies...................	.995
PO	Chase Utley, Phillies.....................	357
A	Orlando Hudson, Diamondbacks ...	510
E	Rickie Weeks, Brewers.....................	22
TC	Orlando Hudson, Diamondbacks	833
DP	Orlando Hudson, Diamondbacks	116

THIRD BASE
PCT	Aramis Ramirez, Cubs	.965
	Scott Rolen, Cardinals	.965
	Ryan Zimmerman, Nationals............	.965
PO	Ryan Zimmerman, Nationals	152
A	Pedro Feliz, Giants	332
E	Edwin Encarnacion, Reds.................	25
	Chad Tracy, Diamondbacks	25
TC	Pedro Feliz, Giants	469
DP	Garrett Atkins, Rockies	36

SHORTSTOP
PCT	Omar Vizquel, Giants	.993
PO	Rafael Furcal, Dodgers....................	269
A	Rafael Furcal, Dodgers	492
E	Felipe Lopez, Nationals	28
TC	Rafael Furcal, Dodgers	788
DP	Rafael Furcal, Dodgers	117

OUTFIELD
PCT	Endy Chavez, Mets	1.000
	Juan Pierre, Cubs	1.000
	Dave Roberts, Padres	1.000
	Shane Victorino, Phillies	1.000
PO	Juan Pierre, Cubs...........................	379
A	Alfonso Soriano, Nationals..............	22
E	Adam Dunn, Reds	12
TC	Andruw Jones, Atlanta	384
	Juan Pierre, Cubs.............................	384
DP	Alfonso Soriano, Nationals............	9

POSTSEASON

Baseball crowns its seventh champ in seven seasons

BY JOHN PERROTTO

It wasn't quite as improbable as, say, a Geo Metro winning the Indianapolis 500 or a donkey capturing the Kentucky Derby. But the Cardinals' ascension to the top of the heap in 2006, capped by a five-game handling of the upstart Tigers in the World Series, was improbable, to say the least.

Consider that the Cardinals won just 83 games in the regular season and nearly blew a seven-game lead in the National League Central in the final 11 days. They clinched on the final day of the season when the second-place Astros lost. St. Louis' 83 wins were the fewest ever by a World Series winner, two fewer than the Twins had in 1987. Only the 82-win 1973 Mets had ever advanced to the Fall Classic with fewer victories.

The Cardinals entered the National League Division Series against the Padres and the National League Championship Series against the Mets as sizeable underdogs. After all, the Cardinals were a losing outfit since a 17-8 April and had lost 10 of their final 14 regular-season games. Yet the Cardinals beat the Padres in four games and the Mets in seven to advance to their second World Series in three years.

In fact, the Cardinals have been more resilient than generally given credit for since 2000. They've played in the NLCS five times in seven seasons, including each of the past three years, but somehow had not won a World Series since 1982. Even the Tigers had won it all more recently—1984—though recent years had not been so kind.

Prior to 2006, the Tigers had endured 12 consecutive losing seasons, had not appeared in the postseason since 1987 and were just three years removed from losing an AL-record 119 games. Futility was even closer than that: They lost 91 games in 2005.

The 2006 Tigers were a different story. Guided by first-year manager Jim Leyland, Detroit had been baseball's best story all season long and were heavily favored against the Cardinals. Leyland had led the Marlins to the 1997 World Series title and had spent the previous six seasons as a scout for St. Louis and was close friends with Cardinals manager Tony La Russa.

The Tigers got to the Series by upsetting the Yankees in four games in the American League Division Series then

One pitcher, one team, two celebrations
Adam Wainwright got the final out in both the NLCS (pictured) and the World Series

swept the Athletics in four games in the American League Championship Series. Detroit's early dismissal of the A's gave them a full week off before the start of the Series. The Cardinals, meanwhile, had just one day between Game Seven of the NLCS and the start of the Series.

Yet at the conclusion of Game Five, it was the Cardinals who gained their first World Series title since the early 1980s. They also supplied Major League Baseball with its seventh champion in seven years.

"I think we shocked the world," center fielder Jim Edmonds said.

"No one believed in us, but we believed in ourselves," shortstop David Eckstein said.

WORLD SERIES YEAR-BY-YEAR

Year	Winner	Manager	Loser	Manager	Result	MVP
1903	Boston (AL)	Jimmy Collins	Pittsburgh (NL)	Fred Clarke	5-3	None Selected
1904	NO SERIES					
1905	New York (NL)	John McGraw	Philadelphia (AL)	Connie Mack	4-1	None Selected
1906	Chicago (AL)	Fielder Jones	Chicago (NL)	Frank Chance	4-2	None Selected
1907	Chicago (NL)	Frank Chance	Detroit (AL)	Hugh Jennings	4-0	None Selected
1908	Chicago (NL)	Frank Chance	Detroit (AL)	Hugh Jennings	4-1	None Selected
1909	Pittsburgh (NL)	Fred Clarke	Detroit (AL)	Hugh Jennings	4-3	None Selected
1910	Philadelphia (AL)	Connie Mack	Chicago (NL)	Frank Chance	4-1	None Selected
1911	Philadelphia (AL)	Connie Mack	New York (NL)	John McGraw	4-2	None Selected
1912	Boston (AL)	Jake Stahl	New York (NL)	John McGraw	4-3-1	None Selected
1913	Philadelphia (AL)	Connie Mack	New York (NL)	John McGraw	4-1	None Selected
1914	Boston (NL)	George Stallings	Philadelphia (AL)	Connie Mack	4-0	None Selected
1915	Boston (AL)	Bill Carrigan	Philadelphia (AL)	Pat Moran	4-1	None Selected
1916	Boston (AL)	Bill Carrigan	Brooklyn (NL)	Wilbert Robinson	4-1	None Selected
1917	Chicago (AL)	Pants Rowland	New York (NL)	John McGraw	4-2	None Selected
1918	Boston (AL)	Ed Barrow	Chicago (NL)	Fred Mitchell	4-2	None Selected
1919	Cincinnati (NL)	Pat Moran	Chicago (AL)	Kid Gleason	5-3	None Selected
1920	Cleveland (AL)	Tris Speaker	Brooklyn (NL)	Wilbert Robinson	5-2	None Selected
1921	New York (NL)	John McGraw	New York (AL)	Miller Huggins	5-3	None Selected
1922	New York (NL)	John McGraw	New York (AL)	Miller Huggins	4-0	None Selected
1923	New York (AL)	Miller Huggins	New York (NL)	John McGraw	4-2	None Selected
1924	Washington (AL)	Bucky Harris	New York (NL)	John McGraw	4-3	None Selected
1925	Pittsburgh (NL)	Bill McKechnie	Washington (AL)	Bucky Harris	4-3	None Selected
1926	St. Louis (NL)	Rogers Hornsby	New York (AL)	Miller Huggins	4-3	None Selected
1927	New York (AL)	Miller Huggins	Pittsburgh (NL)	Donie Bush	4-0	None Selected
1928	New York (AL)	Miller Huggins	St. Louis (NL)	Bill McKechnie	4-0	None Selected
1929	Philadelphia (AL)	Connie Mack	Chicago (NL)	Joe McCarthy	4-1	None Selected
1930	Philadelphia (AL)	Connie Mack	St. Louis (NL)	Gabby Street	4-2	None Selected
1931	St. Louis (NL)	Gabby Street	Philadelphia (AL)	Connie Mack	4-3	None Selected
1932	New York (AL)	Joe McCarthy	Chicago (NL)	Charlie Grimm	4-0	None Selected
1933	New York (NL)	Bill Terry	Washington (AL)	Joe Cronin	4-1	None Selected
1934	St. Louis (NL)	Frankie Frisch	Detroit (AL)	Mickey Cochrane	4-3	None Selected
1935	Detroit (AL)	Mickey Cochrane	Chicago (NL)	Charlie Grimm	4-2	None Selected
1936	New York (AL)	Joe McCarthy	New York (NL)	Bill Terry	4-2	None Selected
1937	New York (AL)	Joe McCarthy	New York (NL)	Bill Terry	4-1	None Selected
1938	New York (AL)	Joe McCarthy	Chicago (NL)	Gabby Hartnett	4-0	None Selected
1939	New York (AL)	Joe McCarthy	Cincinnati (NL)	Bill McKechnie	4-0	None Selected
1940	Cincinnati (NL)	Bill McKechnie	Detroit (AL)	Del Baker	4-3	None Selected
1941	New York (AL)	Joe McCarthy	Brooklyn (NL)	Leo Durocher	4-1	None Selected
1942	St. Louis (NL)	Billy Southworth	New York (AL)	Joe McCarthy	4-1	None Selected
1943	New York (AL)	Joe McCarthy	St. Louis (NL)	Billy Southworth	4-1	None Selected
1944	St. Louis (NL)	Billy Southworth	St. Louis (AL)	Luke Sewell	4-2	None Selected
1945	Detroit (AL)	Steve O'Neill	Chicago (NL)	Charlie Grimm	4-3	None Selected
1946	St. Louis (NL)	Eddie Dyer	Boston (AL)	Joe Cronin	4-3	None Selected
1947	New York (AL)	Bucky Harris	Brooklyn (NL)	Burt Shotton	4-3	None Selected
1948	Cleveland (AL)	Lou Boudreau	Boston (NL)	Billy Southworth	4-2	None Selected
1949	New York (AL)	Casey Stengel	Brooklyn (NL)	Burt Shotton	4-1	None Selected
1950	New York (AL)	Casey Stengel	Philadelphia (NL)	Eddie Sawyer	4-0	None Selected
1951	New York (AL)	Casey Stengel	New York (NL)	Leo Durocher	4-2	None Selected
1952	New York (AL)	Casey Stengel	Brooklyn (NL)	Chuck Dressen	4-3	None Selected
1953	New York (AL)	Casey Stengel	Brooklyn (NL)	Chuck Dressen	4-2	None Selected
1954	New York (NL)	Leo Durocher	Cleveland (AL)	Al Lopez	4-0	None Selected
1955	Brooklyn (NL)	Walter Alston	New York (AL)	Casey Stengel	4-3	Johnny Podres, p, Brooklyn
1956	New York (AL)	Casey Stengel	Brooklyn (NL)	Walter Alston	4-3	Don Larsen, p, New York
1957	Milwaukee (NL)	Fred Haney	New York (AL)	Casey Stengel	4-3	Lew Burdette, p, Milwaukee
1958	New York (AL)	Casey Stengel	Milwaukee (NL)	Fred Haney	4-3	Bob Turley, p, New York
1959	Los Angeles (NL)	Walter Alston	Chicago (AL)	Al Lopez	4-2	Larry Sherry, p, Los Angeles
1960	Pittsburgh (NL)	Danny Murtaugh	New York (AL)	Casey Stengel	4-3	Bobby Richardson, 2b, New York
1961	New York (AL)	Ralph Houk	Cincinnati (NL)	Fred Hutchinson	4-1	Whitey Ford, p, New York
1962	New York (AL)	Ralph Houk	San Francisco (NL)	Alvin Dark	4-3	Ralph Terry, p, New York
1963	Los Angeles (NL)	Walter Alston	New York (AL)	Ralph Houk	4-0	Sandy Koufax, p, Los Angeles
1964	St. Louis (NL)	Johnny Keene	New York (AL)	Yogi Berra	4-3	Bob Gibson, p, St. Louis
1965	Los Angeles (NL)	Walter Alston	Minnesota (AL)	Sam Mele	4-3	Sandy Koufax, p, Los Angeles
1966	Baltimore (AL)	Hank Bauer	Los Angeles (NL)	Walter Alston	4-0	Frank Robinson, of, Baltimore
1967	St. Louis (NL)	Red Schoendienst	Boston (AL)	Dick Williams	4-3	Bob Gibson, p, St. Louis
1968	Detroit (AL)	Mayo Smith	St. Louis (NL)	Red Schoendienst	4-3	Mickey Lolich, p, Detroit
1969	New York (NL)	Gil Hodges	Baltimore (AL)	Earl Weaver	4-1	Donn Clendenon, 1b, New York
1970	Baltimore (AL)	Earl Weaver	Cincinnati (NL)	Sparky Anderson	4-1	Brooks Robinson, 3b, Baltimore
1971	Pittsburgh (NL)	Danny Murtaugh	Baltimore (AL)	Earl Weaver	4-3	Roberto Clemente, of, Pittsburgh
1972	Oakland (AL)	Dick Williams	Cincinnati (NL)	Sparky Anderson	4-3	Gene Tenace, c, Oakland
1973	Oakland (AL)	Dick Williams	New York (NL)	Yogi Berra	4-3	Reggie Jackson, of, Oakland
1974	Oakland (AL)	Alvin Dark	Los Angeles (NL)	Walter Alston	4-1	Rollie Fingers, p, Oakland
1975	Cincinnati (NL)	Sparky Anderson	Boston (AL)	Darrell Johnson	4-3	Pete Rose, 3b, Cincinnati
1976	Cincinnati (NL)	Sparky Anderson	New York (AL)	Billy Martin	4-0	Johnny Bench, c, Cincinnati
1977	New York (AL)	Billy Martin	Los Angeles (NL)	Tom Lasorda	4-2	Reggie Jackson, of, New York
1978	New York (AL)	Bob Lemon	Los Angeles (NL)	Tom Lasorda	4-2	Bucky Dent, ss, New York
1979	Pittsburgh (NL)	Chuck Tanner	Baltimore (AL)	Earl Weaver	4-3	Willie Stargell, 1b, Pittsburgh
1980	Philadelphia (NL)	Dallas Green	Kansas City (AL)	Jim Frey	4-2	Mike Schmidt, 3b, Philadelphia
1981	Los Angeles (NL)	Tom Lasorda	New York (AL)	Bob Lemon	4-2	Cey/Guerrero/Yeager, L.A.
1982	St. Louis (NL)	Whitey Herzog	Milwaukee (AL)	Harvey Kuenn	4-3	Darrell Porter, c, St. Louis
1983	Baltimore (AL)	Joe Altobelli	Philadelphia (NL)	Paul Owens	4-1	Rick Dempsey, c, Baltimore
1984	Detroit (AL)	Sparky Anderson	San Diego (NL)	Dick Williams	4-1	Alan Trammell, ss, Detroit
1985	Kansas City (AL)	Dick Howser	St. Louis (NL)	Whitey Herzog	4-3	Bret Saberhagen, p, Kansas City
1986	New York (NL)	Dave Johnson	Boston (AL)	John McNamara	4-3	Ray Knight, 3b, New York
1987	Minnesota (AL)	Tom Kelly	St. Louis (NL)	Whitey Herzog	4-3	Frank Viola, p, Minnesota
1988	Los Angeles (NL)	Tom Lasorda	Oakland (AL)	Tony La Russa	4-1	Orel Hershiser, p, Los Angeles
1989	Oakland (AL)	Tony La Russa	San Francisco (NL)	Roger Craig	4-0	Dave Stewart, p, Oakland
1990	Cincinnati (NL)	Lou Piniella	Oakland (AL)	Tony La Russa	4-0	Jose Rijo, p, Cincinnati
1991	Minnesota (AL)	Tom Kelly	Atlanta (NL)	Bobby Cox	4-3	Jack Morris, p, Minnesota
1992	Toronto (AL)	Cito Gaston	Atlanta (NL)	Bobby Cox	4-2	Pat Borders, c, Toronto
1993	Toronto (AL)	Cito Gaston	Philadelphia (NL)	Jim Fregosi	4-2	Paul Molitor, dh, Toronto
1994	NO SERIES					
1995	Atlanta (NL)	Bobby Cox	Cleveland (AL)	Mike Hargrove	4-2	Tom Glavine, p, Atlanta
1996	New York (AL)	Joe Torre	Atlanta (NL)	Bobby Cox	4-2	John Wetteland, p, New York
1997	Florida (NL)	Jim Leyland	Cleveland (AL)	Mike Hargrove	4-3	Livan Hernandez, p, Florida
1998	New York (AL)	Joe Torre	San Diego (NL)	Bruce Bochy	4-0	Scott Brosius, 3b, New York
1999	New York (AL)	Joe Torre	Atlanta (NL)	Bobby Cox	4-0	Mariano Rivera, p, New York
2000	New York (AL)	Joe Torre	New York (NL)	Bobby Valentine	4-1	Derek Jeter, ss, New York
2001	Arizona (NL)	Bob Brenly	New York (AL)	Joe Torre	4-3	Johnson, p/Schilling, p, Arizona
2002	Anaheim (AL)	Mike Scioscia	San Francisco (NL)	Dusty Baker	4-3	Troy Glaus, 3b, Anaheim
2003	Florida (NL)	Jack McKeon	New York (AL)	Joe Torre	4-2	Josh Beckett, p, Florida
2004	Boston (AL)	Terry Francona	St. Louis (NL)	Tony La Russa	4-0	Manny Ramirez, of, Boston
2005	Chicago (AL)	Ozzie Guillen	Houston (NL)	Phil Garner	4-0	Jermaine Dye, of, Chicago
2006	St. Louis (NL)	Tony La Russa	Detroit (AL)	Jim Leyland	4-1	David Eckstein, ss, St. Louis

LARRY GOREN

Shortstop for two World Series winners in five years
David Eckstein won Series MVP honors for going 8-for-22

Unlikely Heroes

The Cardinals seemed to be the only people beyond the shadow of the Gateway Arch who believed they could win, perhaps galvanized by their late-season struggles.

"It just shows you this is the best game in the world because you can't predict it," Eckstein said. "You get a bunch of guys that are on a mission, that are going out there playing as hard as they can, as smart as they can, until the game ends, anything is possible.

"Once the regular season was over, we took a deep breath, put it behind us and decided we were going to do everything we could to win the World Series."

Eckstein epitomized that attitude in the World Series as he won the Most Valuable Player award, rebounding from an 0-for-11 start to hit .364 for the Series. He drove in four runs and scored three. The 5-foot-6 Eckstein, also the shortstop on the World Series-winning 2002 Angels, did it all despite being slowed by shoulder and hamstring injuries. "He's the toughest guy I've ever seen in a uniform," La Russa said. "Whenever David is playing, there is absolutely no doubt that our club responds to how hard he plays. He is a wonderful leader."

Eckstein helped lead an offense that got little from star first baseman Albert Pujols, the first player in history to hit .300 with 30 home runs and 100 RBIs in each of his first six seasons. Pujols went just 3-for-15 (.200) with one home run and two RBIs in the World Series, but third baseman Scott Rolen, hampered by a sore shoulder in the first two rounds of the playoffs, was 8-for-19 (.421) with one homer. Catcher Yadier Molina, who supplied the go-ahead, ninth-inning home run in Game Seven of the NLCS, was 7-for-17 (.412).

Meanwhile, La Russa made history by becoming just the second manager to win a World Series in both

JOHN WILLIAMSON

Tony La Russa has managed St. Louis to the NLCS six times

Since the addition of the Division Series in 1995, teams need to clear an extra hurdle to advance to Championship Series. Here are the 11 teams to play in more than one LCS since 1995:

Bobby Cox

TEAM	LAST	TOTAL
Yankees	2004	7
Braves	2001	6
Cardinals	2006	6
Indians	1998	3
Mariners	2001	3
Mets	2006	3
Red Sox	2004	3
Angels	2005	2
Astros	2005	2
Marlins	2003	2
Orioles	1997	2

It should be no surprise that the top three teams above also have the three longest-tenured managers. Here are the six managers who will enter 2007 with five or more years with the same club:

MANAGER	W	L	PCT	YEARS
Bobby Cox, Braves	1,816	1,394	.566	17
Tony La Russa, Cardinals	977	803	.549	11
Joe Torre, Yankees	1,079	699	.607	11
Mike Scioscia, Angels	609	525	.537	7
Ron Gardenhire, Twins	455	354	.562	5
Clint Hurdle, Rockies	352	436	.447	5

leagues, joining Sparky Anderson. La Russa also led the A's to victory over the Giants in the 1989 World Series, but that Series had been interrupted by the massive Loma Prieta earthquake. The City of Oakland forewent a victory parade out of respect for the victims.

"I always wanted a championship parade and I finally got one," La Russa said. "It means so much to win another World Series. It's been a long time. And to be on the same list with Sparky, who I respect so greatly, makes it that much better." Fittingly, Anderson led the Tigers to their last World Series title and had guided the Reds to consecutive championships in 1975 and 1976.

Like the Cardinals, the Tigers stumbled down the stretch. They lost 31 of their last 50 games, blew a 10-game lead in the AL Central and settled for the wild card on the season's final day. The 2006 World Series pairing was the first between two teams with losing records after the All-Star break.

Toothless Tigers

The Tigers hit just .199 against the Cardinals, with second baseman Placido Polanco, MVP of the ALCS, a

AMERICAN LEAGUE CHAMPIONS, 1901-2006

PENNANT	PCT	PENNANT	PCT	PENNANT	PCT	PENNANT	PCT
1901 Chicago	.610	1918 Boston	.595	1935 Detroit	.616	1952 New York	.617
1902 Philadelphia	.610	1919 Chicago	.629	1936 New York	.667	1953 New York	.656
1903 Boston	.659	1920 Cleveland	.636	1937 New York	.662	1954 Cleveland	.721
1904 Boston	.617	1921 New York	.641	1938 New York	.651	1955 New York	.623
1905 Philadelphia	.622	1922 New York	.610	1939 New York	.702	1956 New York	.630
1906 Chicago	.616	1923 New York	.645	1940 Detroit	.584	1957 New York	.636
1907 Detroit	.613	1924 Washington	.597	1941 New York	.656	1958 New York	.597
1908 Detroit	.588	1925 Washington	.636	1942 New York	.669	1959 Chicago	.610
1909 Detroit	.645	1926 New York	.591	1943 New York	.636	1960 New York	.630
1910 Philadelphia	.680	1927 New York	.714	1944 St. Louis	.578	1961 New York	.673
1911 Philadelphia	.669	1928 New York	.656	1945 Detroit	.575	1962 New York	.593
1912 Boston	.691	1929 Philadelphia	.693	1946 Boston	.675	1963 New York	.646
1913 Philadelphia	.627	1930 Philadelphia	.662	1947 New York	.630	1964 New York	.611
1914 Philadelphia	.651	1931 Philadelphia	.704	1948 Cleveland	.626	1965 Minnesota	.630
1915 Boston	.669	1932 New York	.695	1949 New York	.630	1966 Baltimore	.606
1916 Boston	.591	1933 Washington	.651	1950 New York	.636	1967 Boston	.568
1917 Chicago	.649	1934 Detroit	.656	1951 New York	.636	1968 Detroit	.636

DIVISION ERA (1969-1993)

* Won pennant. ^ Won first half; defeated Milwaukee 3-2 in playoff. ^^ Won first half, defeated Kansas City 3-0.

	EAST	PCT	WEST	PCT	LCS		EAST	PCT	WEST	PCT	LCS
1969	Baltimore*	.673	Minnesota	.599	3-0	1982	Milwaukee*	.586	California	.574	3-2
1970	Baltimore*	.667	Minnesota	.605	3-0	1983	Baltimore*	.605	Chicago	.611	3-1
1971	Baltimore*	.639	Oakland	.627	3-0	1984	Detroit*	.642	Kansas City	.519	3-0
1972	Detroit	.551	Oakland*	.600	3-2	1985	Toronto	.615	Kansas City*	.562	4-3
1973	Baltimore	.599	Oakland*	.580	3-2	1986	Boston*	.590	California	.568	4-3
1974	Baltimore	.562	Oakland*	.556	3-1	1987	Detroit	.605	Minnesota*	.525	4-1
1975	Boston*	.594	Oakland	.605	3-0	1988	Boston	.549	Oakland*	.642	4-0
1976	New York*	.610	Kansas City	.556	3-2	1989	Toronto	.549	Oakland*	.611	4-1
1977	New York*	.617	Kansas City	.630	3-2	1990	Boston	.543	Oakland*	.636	4-0
1978	New York*	.613	Kansas City	.568	3-1	1991	Toronto	.562	Minnesota*	.586	4-1
1979	Baltimore*	.642	California	.543	3-1	1992	Toronto*	.593	Oakland	.593	4-2
1980	New York*	.636	Kansas City*	.599	3-0	1993	Toronto*	.586	Chicago	.580	4-2
1981	New York*^	.607	Oakland^^	.587	3-0						
	Milwaukee	.585	Kansas City	.566							

WILD CARD ERA (1994-2006)

* Won pennant. † Lost ALCS.

	EAST	PCT	CENTRAL	PCT	WEST	PCT	WILD CARD	PCT	LCS
1994	New York	.619	Chicago	.593	Texas	.456	Season incomplete	—	—
1995	Boston	.597	Cleveland*	.694	Seattle†	.545	New York (E)	.549	4-2
1996	New York*	.568	Cleveland	.615	Texas	.556	Baltimore (E)†	.543	4-1
1997	Baltimore†	.605	Cleveland*	.534	Seattle	.556	New York (E)	.593	4-2
1998	New York*	.704	Cleveland†	.549	Texas	.543	Boston (E)	.568	4-2
1999	New York*	.605	Cleveland	.599	Texas	.586	Boston (E)†	.580	4-1
2000	New York*	.540	Chicago	.586	Oakland	.565	Seattle (W)†	.562	4-2
2001	New York*	.594	Cleveland	.562	Seattle†	.716	Oakland (W)	.630	4-1
2002	New York	.640	Minnesota†	.584	Oakland	.636	Anaheim (W)*	.611	4-1
2003	New York*	.623	Minnesota	.556	Oakland	.593	Boston (E)†	.586	4-3
2004	New York†	.623	Minnesota	.568	Anaheim	.568	Boston (E)*	.605	4-3
2005	New York	.586	Chicago*	.611	Los Angeles†	.586	Boston (E)	.586	4-1
2006	New York	.599	Minnesota	.593	Oakland†	.574	Detroit (C)*	.586	4-0

key culprit. He was hitless in 17 at-bats. Right fielder Magglio Ordonez was 2-for-19 (.105), left fielder Craig Monroe 3-for-20 (.150) and catcher Ivan Rodriguez 3-for-19 (.158). Of equal consequence, the Tigers defense was atrocious. They committed eight errors in five games, including three by usually-steady third baseman Brandon Inge and an amazing five by the pitching staff, one in each game.

"In the American League you don't handle a lot of bunts and stuff," Leyland said. "We knew we were going to do that this series, so we worked on it during the time frame we were off and quite frankly we didn't execute it during the World Series. I'm responsible and I accept that responsibility. It's my job to have my team ready."

And Inge admitted maybe the Tigers weren't quite ready mentally to play in a World Series. "It's the atmosphere that can get you a little tight," Inge said. "It's the biggest stage in the world for baseball. It can make some nerves, get people a little jittery."

Nevertheless, the Tigers could still take pride in the progress they had made. "I just only hope that nobody forgets the job that we did, the players I'm talking about, to go from 71 wins to the World Series," Leyland said. "I tell you what, that's pretty impressive stuff right there."

Kenny Rogers

Cardinals rookie righthander Anthony Reyes showed some pretty impressive stuff himself in pitching the Cardinals to a 7-2 victory to open the Series in Detroit. He was opposed by righthander Justin Verlander, in the first-ever Game One featuring two rookie starters. Reyes allowed two runs and four hits in eight-plus innings and retired 17 batters in a row at one point. He went 5-8, 5.06 in 17 starts during the regular season and no Game One starter had ever won fewer games than Reyes. "I don't know if I'll ever be able to top this," Reyes said.

Verlander, the BA Rookie of the Year, went 17-9, 3.63 in the regular season, but struggled in Game One. He gave up seven runs in six innings, including home runs to Pujols and Rolen.

The Series' most controversial moment came in Game Two when Cardinals players, watching the first inning on a clubhouse TV, noticed something dark on Tigers lefthander Kenny Rogers' pitching hand. The 41-year-old Rogers had dominated in the postseason and would pitch eight two-hit, shutout innings that night to help the Tigers even the series.

Scott Rolen

La Russa talked to umpires between innings, and home plate umpire Alfonso Marquez asked Rogers to wipe the substance—which appeared to be pine tar—off his hand. Though La Russa could have argued for Rogers ejection for applying a foreign substance to the ball, he chose not to purse the matter further. "I said, 'I don't like this stuff, let's get it fixed.' If it gets fixed let's play the game. It got fixed, in my opinion," La Russa said. "If he didn't get rid of it, I would have challenged it. But I do think it's a little bit part of the game at times, and don't go crazy."

Rogers, meanwhile, proclaimed his innocence. "It was a big clump of dirt, and I wiped it off," Rogers said. "I didn't know it was there, and they told me and I took it off, and it wasn't a big deal." Rogers did not pitch again and finished the postseason with 23 scoreless innings in three starts. He became just the second pitcher in history to make three scoreless starts in the same postseason, joining Hall of Fame righthander Christy Mathewson, who threw three shutouts in the 1905 World Series for

NATIONAL LEAGUE CHAMPIONS, 1901-2006

	PENNANT	PCT		PENNANT	PCT		PENNANT	PCT		PENNANT	PCT
1901	Pittsburgh	.647	1918	Chicago	.651	1935	Chicago	.649	1952	Brooklyn	.627
1902	Pittsburgh	.741	1919	Cincinnati	.686	1936	New York	.597	1953	Brooklyn	.682
1903	Pittsburgh	.650	1920	Brooklyn	.604	1937	New York	.625	1954	New York	.630
1904	New York	.693	1921	New York	.614	1938	Chicago	.586	1955	Brooklyn	.641
1905	New York	.686	1922	New York	.604	1939	Cincinnati	.630	1956	Brooklyn	.604
1906	Chicago	.763	1923	New York	.621	1940	Cincinnati	.654	1957	Milwaukee	.617
1907	Chicago	.704	1924	New York	.608	1941	Brooklyn	.649	1958	Milwaukee	.597
1908	Chicago	.643	1925	Pittsburgh	.621	1942	St. Louis	.688	1959	Los Angeles	.564
1909	Pittsburgh	.724	1926	St. Louis	.578	1943	St. Louis	.682	1960	Pittsburgh	.617
1910	Chicago	.675	1927	Pittsburgh	.610	1944	St. Louis	.682	1961	Cincinnati	.604
1911	New York	.647	1928	St. Louis	.617	1945	Chicago	.636	1962	San Francisco	.624
1912	New York	.682	1929	Chicago	.645	1946	St. Louis	.628	1963	Los Angeles	.611
1913	New York	.664	1930	St. Louis	.597	1947	Brooklyn	.610	1964	St. Louis	.574
1914	Boston	.614	1931	St. Louis	.656	1948	Boston	.595	1965	Los Angeles	.599
1915	Philadelphia	.592	1932	Chicago	.584	1949	Brooklyn	.630	1966	Los Angeles	.586
1916	Brooklyn	.610	1933	New York	.599	1950	Philadelphia	.591	1967	St. Louis	.627
1917	New York	.636	1934	St. Louis	.621	1951	New York	.624	1968	St. Louis	.599

DIVISION ERA (1969-1993)
* Won pennant. ^ Won second half; defeated Philadelphia 3-2 in playoff. ^^ Won first half; defeated Houston 3-2 in playoff.

	EAST	PCT	WEST	PCT	LCS		EAST	PCT	WEST	PCT	LCS
1969	New York*	.617	Atlanta	.574	3-0	1982	St. Louis*	.568	Atlanta	.549	3-0
1970	Pittsburgh	.549	Cincinnati*	.630	3-0	1983	Philadelphia*	.556	Los Angeles	.562	3-1
1971	Pittsburgh*	.599	San Francisco	.556	3-1	1984	Chicago	.596	San Diego*	.568	3-2
1972	Pittsburgh	.619	Cincinnati*	.617	3-2	1985	St. Louis*	.623	Los Angeles	.586	4-2
1973	New York*	.509	Cincinnati	.611	3-2	1986	New York*	.667	Houston	.593	4-2
1974	Pittsburgh	.543	Los Angeles*	.630	3-1	1987	St. Louis*	.586	San Francisco	.556	4-3
1975	Pittsburgh	.571	Cincinnati*	.667	3-0	1988	New York	.625	Los Angeles*	.584	4-3
1976	Philadelphia	.623	Cincinnati*	.630	3-0	1989	Chicago	.571	San Francisco*	.568	4-1
1977	Philadelphia	.623	Los Angeles*	.605	3-1	1990	Pittsburgh	.586	Cincinnati*	.562	4-2
1978	Philadelphia	.556	Los Angeles*	.586	3-1	1991	Pittsburgh	.605	Atlanta*	.580	4-3
1979	Pittsburgh*	.605	Cincinnati	.559	3-0	1992	Pittsburgh	.593	Atlanta*	.605	4-3
1980	Philadelphia*	.562	Houston	.571	3-2	1993	Philadelphia*	.599	Atlanta	.642	4-2
1981	Montreal^	.566	Los Angeles*^^	.632	3-2						
	Philadelphia	.618	Houston	.623							

WILD CARD ERA (1994-2006)
* Won pennant. † Lost NLCS.

	EAST	PCT	CENTRAL	PCT	WEST	PCT	WILD CARD	PCT	LCS
1994	Montreal	.649	Cincinnati	.593	Los Angeles	.509	Season incomplete	—	—
1995	Atlanta*	.625	Cincinnati†	.590	Los Angeles	.542	Colorado (W)	.535	4-2
1996	Atlanta*	.593	St. Louis†	.543	San Diego	.562	Los Angeles (W)	.556	4-3
1997	Atlanta†	.623	Houston	.519	San Francisco	.556	Florida (E)*	.568	4-2
1998	Atlanta†	.654	Houston	.630	San Diego*	.605	Chicago (C)	.552	4-2
1999	Atlanta*	.636	Houston	.599	Arizona	.617	New York (E)†	.595	4-2
2000	Atlanta	.586	St. Louis†	.586	San Francisco	.599	New York (E)*	.580	4-1
2001	Atlanta†	.543	Houston	.574	Arizona*	.568	St. Louis (C)	.574	4-1
2002	Atlanta	.631	St. Louis†	.599	Arizona	.605	San Francisco (W)*	.590	4-1
2003	Atlanta	.623	Chicago†	.543	San Francisco	.621	Florida (E)*	.562	4-3
2004	Atlanta	.593	St. Louis*	.648	Los Angeles	.574	Houston (C)†	.568	4-3
2005	Atlanta	.556	St. Louis†	.617	San Diego	.506	Houston (C)*	.549	4-2
2006	New York†	.599	St. Louis*	.516	San Diego	.543	Los Angeles (W)	.543	4-3

the New York Giants against the Philadelphia Athletics.

With the Tigers facing elimination, Leyland could have gone back to Rogers to start Game Five in St. Louis on his normal rest. Game Four had been pushed back a day because of a rainout. However, Leyland did not want Rogers to pitch in front of a jeering Busch Stadium crowd, instead opting to pitch him in a potential Game Six that never came.

Cardinals Finish At Home

Righthander Chris Carpenter set the tone for the Cardinals once the World Series shifted to Busch Stadium for Game Three. The 2005 NL Cy Young Award winner allowed just three hits in eight shutout innings in a Cardinals 5-0 victory and 2-1 Series lead. Carpenter struck out six and walked none, needing just 82 pitches.

Cardinals righthanders shine brightest in October
Jeff Weaver (left) won the deciding Game Five, while Jeff Suppan was NLCS MVP

He was calm, cool and relaxed, despite participating in his first World Series. A nerve problem in his right biceps forced him to sit out the 2004 Series against the Red Sox. "Go one pitch at a time," Carpenter said. "All that stuff around you that's going on doesn't get in your head, so you're not even thinking about it."

By going 4-for-4 with three doubles, Eckstein helped the Cardinals notch a 5-4 win in Game Four and take a 3-1 lead in the series. Two of his doubles, including the game-winner in the bottom of the eighth, were the result of a still-soggy Busch Stadium outfield. Monroe got a late jump because of poor footing and the ball

The only Tiger with teeth
Sean Casey had six of the 15 Tigers hits in Games Four and Five

glanced off the diving left fielder's glove.

Two innings earlier, Eckstein also wound up with a double when center fielder Curtis Granderson slipped and fell while trying to catch a routine fly ball. "I went to plant my feet and they just went out from under me," Granderson said. "It was just a freak thing. If I stand up, I catch it easily. The field wasn't just wet. It was wet and soft."

The Cardinals then wrapped up their 10th World Series at home with a 4-2 victory in Game Five. They became the first team to win a World Series in their first year in a new ballpark since the 1923 Yankees beat the New York Giants in Yankee Stadium's inaugural season.

Cardinals righthander Jeff Weaver saved his best game for the clincher, in the midst of a turbulent season in which he lost his spot in the Angels rotation to his younger brother Jered. Jeff was traded to the Cardinals in July for minor league outfielder Terry Evans. In Game Five, Weaver allowed just two runs and four hits in eight innings while striking out nine. "It's all the belief in yourself, knowing that you're going to work through it," Weaver said. "Just never say die. Just keep working. Really, it's the same attitude everyone on this team had. That's why we're the World Series champions."

Rookie righthander Adam Wainright, who took over as closer in September when veteran Jason Isringhausen went down, pitched a scoreless ninth inning for the save. Wainright wound up with four saves in the postseason after having just three in the regular season.

Dramatic NLCS

Before the Tigers, the Cardinals defeated the 97-win Mets in dramatic fashion. Molina's Game Seven two-run homer off righthander Aaron Heilman snapped a 1-1 tie. "Everybody said I don't hit and I proved them wrong," said Molina, who batted just .216 with six home runs in 129 regular-season games.

Wainright escaped a bases-loaded jam in the bottom of the ninth inning of that game by freezing Mets center fielder Carlos Beltran with a sharp curveball. Cardinals righthander Jeff Suppan pitched into the eighth inning and allowed just one run. He gave up just the one run and five hits in 15 innings in two starts and was named NLCS MVP.

Veteran Mets lefthander Tom Glavine pitched seven scoreless innings in Game One and Beltran hit a two-run homer to give the Mets a 2-0 in New York. The Cardinals evened the series with a 9-6 win in Game Two and did so in improbable fashion as reserve outfielder So Taguchi's ninth-inning home run off closer Billy Wagner broke a 6-6 tie.

The series shifted to St. Louis for Game Three where the Cardinals won 5-0 behind Suppan's eight shutout innings. He also homered, matching his career total in 251 regular season at bats. Beltran homered twice and first baseman Carlos Delgado and third baseman David Wright also went deep as the Mets rolled to a 12-5 win in Game Four to even the series.

The Cardinals regained the series lead, 3-2, in Game Five when Pujols' home run off Glavine in the fourth inning to key a Cardinals' rally. They would win 4-2. Losing a Glavine start was especially harmful to the Mets, who had lost righthanders Pedro Martinez and Orlando Hernandez to injuries just a month before the playoffs. Mets rookie righthander John Maine helped ease those pitching problems when the series shifted back to New York for Game Six, which the Mets won 4-2. Maine worked 5⅓ scoreless innings

The series moved to Game Seven, which Molina won for the Cardinals, ruing a strong effort by Mets left-hander Oliver Perez, who had gone just 3-13, 6.55 during the season.

The Tigers, meanwhile, had little problem polishing off the A's in the ALCS as they won all four straight

The one batter Detroit would not let beat them
Albert Pujols hit just .200 with two RBIs in the World Series

games by at least three runs each. Despite the relatively large margins of victory, the Tigers wrapped up the series in dramatic fashion as Ordonez hit a three-run home run off A's closer Huston Street with the score tied 3-3 in the bottom of the ninth inning to give Detroit a 6-3 victory in front of delirious Comerica Park fans. "I knew it was gone as soon as I hit it," Ordonez said. "This is what I've dreamed about my whole career, my whole life. I don't even remember running around the bases."

The Tigers won the first two games of the series in Oakland by scores of 5-1 and 8-5. Inge and Rodriguez homered to power the Tigers in Game One, and seldom-used reserve outfielder Alexis Gomez, who had hit just one career home run in 158 regular-season at bats, went deep and drove in four runs to lead the way in Game Two. Rogers allowed two hits in 7⅓ scoreless innings in Game Three and the Tigers won 3-0. Polanco had three hits in Game Four and finished 9-for-17 (.529).

Carpenter won both his starts in the Cardinals' four-game NLDS win over the Padres. The Mets swept the Dodgers in the other NLDS, where Delgado went 6-for-14 (.429), in his first postseason appearance after 14 years and 1,711 regular season games.

In the ALDS, shortstop Carlos Guillen went 8-for-14 (.571) to lift the Tigers over the heavily-favored Yankees in four games, while A's reserve shortstop Marco Scutaro, subbing for the injured Bobby Crosby, drove in six runs in Oakland's three-game sweep of the Twins.

Redemption for a mediocre NLCS
Ace righthander Chris Carpenter threw eight shutout innings in his lone Series start

WORLD SERIES
BOX SCORES

GAME ONE : October 21, 2006
St. Louis Cardinals 7, Detroit Tigers 2

St. Louis	ab	r	h	bi	bb	so	Detroit	ab	r	h	bi	bb	so
Eckstein, ss	5	0	0	0	0	1	Granderson, cf	4	0	0	0	0	0
Duncan, dh	4	1	1	1	0	2	Monroe, lf	4	2	2	1	0	0
Wilson, ph-dh	1	0	0	0	0	1	Polanco, 2b	4	0	0	0	0	0
Pujols, 1b	3	2	1	2	1	1	Ordonez, rf	3	0	0	0	1	1
Edmonds, cf	4	1	2	1	0	2	Guillen, 1b	4	0	2	1	0	1
Rolen, 3b	4	2	2	1	0	1	Rodriguez, c	4	0	0	0	0	0
Encarnacion, rf	3	0	1	1	0	0	Casey, dh	3	0	0	0	0	1
Belliard, 2b	4	0	0	0	0	1	Inge, 3b	3	0	0	0	0	1
Molina, c	4	1	1	0	0	1	Santiago, ss	2	0	0	0	0	1
Taguchi, lf	4	0	1	0	0	0	Thames, ph	1	0	0	0	0	0
							Perez, ss	0	0	0	0	0	0
Totals	**36**	**7**	**8**	**6**	**2**	**10**	**Totals**	**32**	**2**	**4**	**2**	**1**	**5**

St. Louis						013 003 000—7
Detroit						100 000 001—2

LOB—Cardinals 4, Tigers 4. E— Encarnacion, Rolen, Verlander, Inge 2. 2B—Duncan (1), Rolen (1), Monroe (1). HR—Rolen (1), Pujols (1), Monroe (1).

St. Louis	ip	h	r	er	bb	so	Detroit	ip	h	r	er	bb	so
Reyes W	8	4	2	2	1	4	Verlander L	5	6	7	6	2	8
Looper	1	0	0	0	0	1	Grilli	1	0	0	0	0	0
							Rodney	1	0	0	0	0	1
							Ledezma	1	1	0	0	0	0
							Jones	⅔	1	0	0	0	0
							Walker	⅓	0	0	0	0	1

Reyes pitched to 1 batter in the 9th.
Verlander pitched to 3 batters in the 6th.
HR—Reyes 1 (1), Verlander 2 (2). WP—Walker.
Umpires: HP—Randy Marsh. 1B—Alfonso Marquez. 2B—Wally Bell. 3B—Mike Winters. LF—John Hirschbeck. RF—Tim McClelland.
T—2:54. A—42,479.

GAME TWO: October 22, 2006
Detroit Tigers 3, St. Louis Cardinals 1

St. Louis	ab	r	h	bi	bb	so	Detroit	ab	r	h	bi	bb	so
Eckstein, ss	4	0	0	0	0	0	Granderson, cf	5	0	0	0	0	2
Spiezio, dh	3	0	0	1	1	1	Monroe, lf	3	1	1	1	1	1
Pujols, 1b	3	0	0	0	1	0	Polanco, 2b	3	0	0	0	0	1
Rolen, 3b	4	1	2	0	0	1	Ordonez, rf	4	1	2	0	0	0
Encarnacion, rf	4	0	0	0	0	1	Guillen, 1b	3	1	3	1	1	0
Edmonds, cf	3	0	1	1	1	1	Rodriguez, c	4	0	0	0	0	1
Wilson, lf	3	0	0	0	0	0	Casey, dh	3	0	1	1	0	0
Molina, c	4	0	1	0	0	0	Inge, 3b	4	0	2	0	0	2

Unlikely hero hit just .216 during regular season
Yadier Molina had 19 postseason hits, including the NLCS winner

Miles, 2b | 3 | 0 | 0 | 0 | 0 | 1

Detroit (cont.)	ab	r	h	bi	bb	so		ab	r	h	bi	bb	so
Miles, 2b	3	0	0	0	0	1	Santiago, ss	3	0	1	0	0	1
Totals	**31**	**1**	**4**	**1**	**3**	**5**	**Totals**	**32**	**3**	**10**	**3**	**2**	**8**

St. Louis		000 000 001—1
Detroit		200 010 00x—3

LOB—Cardinals 7, Tigers 10. E— Pujols, Jones. 2B—Edmonds (1), Guillen (1). 3B—Guillen (1). HR—Monroe (2). SH—Santiago.

St. Louis	ip	h	r	er	bb	so	Detroit	ip	h	r	er	bb	so
Weaver L	5	9	3	3	1	5	Rogers W	8	2	0	0	3	5
Johnson	⅔	0	0	0	0	1	Jones S	1	2	1	0	0	0
Kinney	⅓	0	0	0	1	0							
Flores	1	1	0	0	0	0							
Thompson	⅔	0	0	0	0	1							
Wainwright	⅓	0	0	0	1	0							

HR—Weaver 1 (1). HBP—Casey (by Weaver), Polanco (by Kinney), Wilson (by Jones).
Umpires: HP—Alfonso Marquez. 1B—Wally Bell. 2B—Mike Winters. 3B—John Hirschbeck. LF—Tim McClelland. RF—Randy Marsh.
T—2:55. A—42,533.

GAME THREE: October 24, 2006
St. Louis Cardinals 5, Detroit Tigers 0

Detroit	ab	r	h	bi	bb	so	St. Louis	ab	r	h	bi	bb	so
Granderson, cf	4	0	0	0	0	2	Eckstein, ss	4	1	2	0	1	0
Monroe, lf	4	0	0	0	0	1	Wilson, lf	3	1	1	0	2	1
Polanco, 2b	3	0	0	0	0	0	Pujols, 1b	4	1	1	0	0	0
Ordonez, rf	3	0	0	0	0	0	Rolen, 3b	4	1	1	0	1	1
Guillen, ss	3	0	0	0	0	1	Belliard, 2b	4	0	0	0	0	1
Rodriguez, c	3	0	0	0	0	1	Edmonds, cf	2	0	1	2	2	1
Casey, 1b	3	0	2	0	0	0	Molina, c	3	0	1	0	1	0
Inge, 3b	3	0	1	0	0	1	Taguchi, lf	3	1	0	0	1	1
Rodney, p	0	0	0	0	0	0	Carpenter, p	3	0	0	0	0	0
Miner, p	0	0	0	0	0	0	Looper, p	0	0	0	0	0	0
Robertson, p	0	0	0	0	0	0							
Gomez, ph	1	0	0	0	0	0							
Ledezma, p	0	0	0	0	0	0							
Zumaya, p	0	0	0	0	0	0							
Grilli, p	0	0	0	0	0	0							
Perez, 3b	0	0	0	0	0	0							
Infante, ph	1	0	0	0	0	0							
Totals	**28**	**0**	**3**	**0**	**0**	**6**	**Totals**	**30**	**5**	**7**	**2**	**8**	**5**

Detroit		000 000 000—0
St. Louis		000 200 21x—5

LOB—Tigers 2, Cardinals 11. E—Zumaya. 2B—Pujols (1), Edmonds (2), Molina (1). SH—Robertson, Carpenter.

Detroit	ip	h	r	er	bb	so	St. Louis	ip	h	r	er	bb	so
Robertson L	5	5	2	2	3	3	Carpenter W	8	3	0	0	0	6
Ledezma	⅓	1	0	0	1	0	Looper	1	0	0	0	0	0
Zumaya	1	0	2	0	2	1							
Grilli	⅔	0	0	0	1	0							
Rodney	⅓	1	1	1	2	0							
Miner	⅔	0	0	0	0	0							

WP—Miner, Carpenter. IBB—Molina (by Robertson), Edmonds (by Grilli). HBP—Pujols (by Miner).
Umpires: HP—Wally Bell. 1B—Mike Winters. 2B—John Hirschbeck. 3B—Tim McClelland. LF—Randy Marsh. RF—Alfonso Marquez.
T—3:03. A—46,513.

GAME FOUR: October 26, 2006
St. Louis Cardinals 5, Detroit Tigers 4

Detroit	ab	r	h	bi	bb	so	St. Louis	ab	r	h	bi	bb	so
Granderson, cf	5	1	1	0	0	2	Eckstein, ss	5	1	4	2	0	0
Monroe, lf	5	0	0	0	0	1	Duncan, rf	2	0	0	0	1	0
Guillen, ss	3	1	1	0	2	1	Taguchi, ph-rf-lf	1	1	0	0	0	0
Ordonez, rf	5	0	0	0	0	2	Pujols, 1b	2	0	0	0	2	1
Casey, 1b	4	1	3	2	0	0	Edmonds, cf	4	0	0	0	0	3
Rodriguez, c	4	1	3	1	0	0	Rolen, 3b	4	1	2	0	0	1
Polanco, 2b	4	0	0	0	0	0	Wilson, lf	3	0	1	1	0	0
Inge, 3b	3	0	2	1	1	0	Wainwright, p	0	0	0	0	0	0
Bonderman, p	2	0	0	0	0	1	Molina, c	2	0	1	1	2	0
Rodney, p	0	0	0	0	0	0	Miles, 2b	3	2	1	0	1	1
Gomez, ph	1	0	0	0	0	1	Suppan, p	2	0	0	0	0	1
Zumaya, p	0	0	0	0	0	0	Rodriguez, ph	1	0	0	0	0	1
							Kinney, p	0	0	0	0	0	0
							Johnson, p	0	0	0	0	0	0
							Looper, p	0	0	0	0	0	0
							Encarnacion, rf	0	0	0	0	0	0
Totals	**36**	**4**	**10**	**4**	**3**	**8**	**Totals**	**30**	**5**	**9**	**4**	**6**	**9**

Detroit		012 000 010—4
St. Louis		001 100 21x—5

LOB—Tigers 9, Cardinals 9. E—Rodney. 2B—Granderson (1), Rodriguez (1), Inge (1), Eckstein 3 (3), Rolen 2 (3), Molina (2). HR—Casey

(1). **SB**—Guillen (1), Miles (1). **SH**—Bonderman, Wilson, Taguchi.

Detroit	ip	h	r	er	bb	so	St. Louis	ip	h	r	er	bb	so
Bonderman	5⅓	6	2	2	4	4	Suppan	6	8	3	3	2	4
Rodney BS	1⅔	2	2	0	1	4	Kinney	⅔	0	0	0	1	1
Zumaya L	1	1	1	1	1	1	Johnson	⅓	0	0	0	0	0
							Looper	⅓	1	1	1	0	0
							Wainwright BS, W1	⅔	1	0	0	0	3

HR—Suppan 1 (1). **WP**—Zumaya. **IBB**—Miles (by Bonderman), Pujols (by Rodney), Inge (by Suppan).

Umpires: HP—Mike Winters. **1B**—John Hirschbeck. **2B**—Tim McClelland. **3B**—Randy Marsh. **LF**—Alfonso Marquez. **RF**—Wally Bell.

T—3:35. **A**—46,470.

GAME FIVE: October 27, 2006
St. Louis Cardinals 4, Detroit Tigers 2

Detroit	ab	r	h	bi	bb	so	St. Louis	ab	r	h	bi	bb	so
Granderson, cf	3	0	1	0	1	1	Eckstein, ss	4	1	2	2	0	0
Monroe, lf	4	0	0	0	0	2	Duncan, rf	2	0	0	0	1	1
Zumaya, p	0	0	0	0	0	0	Wilson, lf	0	0	0	0	1	0
Guillen, ss	4	0	0	0	0	1	Pujols, 1b	3	0	1	0	1	1
Ordonez, rf	4	1	0	0	0	1	Edmonds, cf	4	0	0	0	0	1
Casey, 1b	4	1	3	2	0	1	Rolen, 3b	3	0	1	1	1	0
1-Santiago, pr	0	0	0	0	0	0	Belliard, 2b	4	0	0	0	0	1
Rodriguez, c	4	0	0	0	0	1	Molina, c	4	2	3	0	0	0
Polanco, 2b	3	0	0	0	1	0	Taguchi, lf-rf	3	1	1	0	0	1
Inge, 3b	4	0	1	0	0	2	Weaver, p	3	0	0	0	0	0
Verlander, p	2	0	0	0	0	1	Spiezio, ph	1	0	0	0	0	0
Gomez, ph	1	0	0	0	0	0	Wainwright, p	0	0	0	0	0	0
Rodney, p	0	0	0	0	0	0							
Thames, lf	0	0	0	0	0	0							
Totals	**33**	**2**	**5**	**2**	**2**	**10**	**Totals**	**31**	**4**	**8**	**3**	**4**	**5**

Detroit	**000 200 000—2**
St. Louis	**010 200 10x—4**

LOB—Tigers 6, Cardinals 8. **E**—Inge, Verlander, Duncan. **2B**—Inge (2), Casey 2 (2). **HR**—Casey (2). **CS**—Pujols (1). **SH**—Taguchi.

Detroit	ip	h	r	er	bb	so	St. Louis	ip	h	r	er	bb	so
Verlander L	6	6	3	1	3	4	Weaver W	8	4	2	1	1	9
Rodney	1	2	1	1	1	0	Wainwright S	1	1	0	0	1	1
Zumaya	1	0	0	0	0	1							

HR—Weaver 1 (2). **WP**—Verlander 2, Wainwright.

Umpires: HP—John Hirschbeck. **1B**—Tim McClelland. **2B**—Randy Marsh. **3B**—Alfonso Marquez. **LF**—Wally Bell. **RF**—Mike Winters.

T—2:56. **A**—46,638.

COMPOSITE BOX

ST. LOUIS CARDINALS

Player, Pos.	AVG	G	AB	R	H	2B	3B	HR	RBI	BB	SO	SB
Scott Rolen, 3b	.421	5	19	5	8	3	0	1	2	2	4	0
Yadier Molina, c	.412	5	17	3	7	2	0	0	1	3	1	0
David Eckstein, ss	.364	5	22	3	8	3	0	0	4	1	1	0
Jim Edmonds, of	.235	5	17	1	4	2	0	0	4	3	8	0
Albert Pujols, 1b	.200	5	15	3	3	1	0	1	2	5	3	0
Preston Wilson, of	.200	5	10	1	2	0	0	0	1	3	2	0
So Taguchi, of	.182	4	11	3	2	0	0	0	0	1	2	0
Aaron Miles, 2b	.167	2	6	2	1	0	0	0	0	1	2	1
Chris Duncan, of	.125	3	8	1	1	1	0	0	1	2	3	0
Ronnie Belliard, 2b	.000	3	12	0	0	0	0	0	0	0	3	0
Juan Encarnacion, of	.000	3	8	0	0	0	0	0	1	1	2	0
Scott Spiezio, dh	.000	2	4	0	0	0	0	0	0	1	1	0
Chris Carpenter, p	.000	1	3	0	0	0	0	0	0	0	0	0
Jeff Weaver, p	.000	1	3	0	0	0	0	0	0	0	0	0
Jeff Suppan, p	.000	1	2	0	0	0	0	0	0	0	1	0
John Rodriguez, ph	.000	1	1	0	0	0	0	0	0	0	1	0
Totals	**.228**	**5**	**158**	**22**	**36**	**12**	**0**	**2**	**16**	**23**	**34**	**1**

Pitcher	W	L	ERA	G	GS	SV	IP	H	R	ER	BB	SO
Chris Carpenter	1	0	0.00	1	1	0	8.0	3	0	0	0	6
Adam Wainwright	1	0	0.00	3	0	1	3.0	2	0	0	1	5
Randy Flores	0	0	0.00	1	0	0	1.0	1	0	0	0	0
Tyler Johnson	0	0	0.00	2	0	0	1.0	0	0	0	0	1
Josh Kinney	0	0	0.00	2	0	0	1.0	0	0	0	2	1
Brad Thompson	0	0	0.00	1	0	0	0.2	0	0	0	0	1
Anthony Reyes	1	0	2.25	1	1	0	8.0	4	2	2	1	4
Jeff Weaver	1	1	2.77	2	2	0	13.0	13	5	4	2	14
Braden Looper	0	0	3.86	3	0	0	2.1	1	1	1	0	1
Jeff Suppan	0	0	4.50	1	1	0	6.0	8	3	3	2	4
Totals	**4**	**1**	**2.05**	**5**	**5**	**1**	**44.0**	**32**	**11**	**10**	**8**	**37**

JOHN WILLIAMSON

A quiet World Series, but . . .
Magglio Ordonez hit the walk-off home run to end the ALCS

DETROIT TIGERS

Player, Pos.	AVG	G	AB	R	H	2B	3B	HR	RBI	BB	SO	SB
Sean Casey, 1b	.529	5	17	2	9	2	0	2	5	0	2	0
Carlos Guillen, ss	.353	5	17	2	6	1	1	0	2	3	4	1
Brandon Inge, 3b	.353	5	17	0	6	2	0	0	1	1	6	0
Ramon Santiago, ss	.200	3	5	0	1	0	0	0	0	0	2	0
Ivan Rodriguez, c	.158	5	19	1	3	1	0	0	1	0	3	0
Craig Monroe, of	.150	5	20	3	3	1	0	2	2	1	5	0
Magglio Ordonez, of	.105	5	19	2	2	0	0	0	0	1	4	0
Curtis Granderson, of	.095	5	21	1	2	1	0	0	0	1	7	0
Placido Polanco, 2b	.000	5	17	0	0	0	0	0	0	1	1	0
Alexis Gomez, ph	.000	3	3	0	0	0	0	0	0	0	1	0
Jeremy Bonderman, p	.000	1	2	0	0	0	0	0	0	0	1	0
Justin Verlander, p	.000	1	2	0	0	0	0	0	0	0	1	0
Omar Infante, ph	.000	1	1	0	0	0	0	0	0	0	0	0
Marcus Thames, of	.000	2	1	0	0	0	0	0	0	0	0	0
Totals	**.199**	**5**	**161**	**11**	**32**	**8**	**1**	**4**	**11**	**8**	**37**	**1**

Pitcher	W	L	ERA	G	GS	SV	IP	H	R	ER	BB	SO
Kenny Rogers	1	0	0.00	1	1	0	8.0	2	0	0	3	5
Jason Grilli	0	0	0.00	2	0	0	1.2	0	0	0	1	0
Todd Jones	0	0	0.00	2	0	1	1.2	3	1	0	0	0
Wilfredo Ledezma	0	0	0.00	2	0	0	1.1	2	0	0	0	1
Zach Miner	0	0	0.00	1	0	0	0.2	0	0	0	0	0
Jamie Walker	0	0	0.00	1	0	0	0.1	0	0	0	0	1
Joel Zumaya	0	1	3.00	3	0	0	3.0	1	3	1	3	3
Jeremy Bonderman	0	0	3.38	1	1	0	5.1	6	2	2	4	4
Nate Robertson	0	1	3.60	1	1	0	5.0	5	2	2	3	3
Fernando Rodney	0	0	4.50	4	0	0	4.0	5	4	2	4	5
Justin Verlander	0	2	5.73	2	2	0	11.0	12	10	7	5	12
Totals	**1**	**4**	**3.00**	**5**	**5**	**1**	**42.0**	**36**	**22**	**14**	**23**	**34**

SCORE BY INNING

St. Louis	**024 503 521—22**
Detroit	**312 210 011—11**

E—Encarnacion, Rolen, Verlander 2, Inge 3, Pujols, Zumaya, Rodney, Duncan. **DP**—St. Louis 3, Detroit 3. **LOB**—St. Louis 36, Detroit 31. **CS**—Pujols. **SH**—Santiago, Robertson, Carpenter, Bonderman, Wilson, Taguchi 2. **SF**—None. **HBP**—Casey (by Weaver), Polanco (by Kinney), Wilson (by Jones), Pujols (by Miner). **IBB**—Molina (by Robertson), Edmonds (by Grilli)., Miles (by Bonderman), pujols (by Rodney), Inge (by Suppan). **WP**—Walker, Miner, carpenter, Zumaya, Verlander 2, Wainwright. **PB**—None. **BK**—None.

AMERICAN LEAGUE
DIVISION SERIES

NEW YORK VS. DETROIT
COMPOSITE BOX

DETROIT

Player, Pos.	AVG	G	AB	R	H	2B	3B	HR	RBI	BB	SO	SB
Carlos Guillen, ss	.571	4	14	3	8	3	0	1	2	2	1	0
Placido Polanco, 2b	.412	4	17	3	7	1	0	0	2	1	1	0
Sean Casey, 1b	.353	4	17	1	6	3	0	0	4	0	0	0
Marcus Thames, dh	.333	4	15	2	5	2	0	0	1	1	5	0
Curtis Granderson, of	.294	4	17	3	5	0	1	2	5	0	1	1
Magglio Ordonez, of	.267	4	15	3	4	1	0	1	2	1	2	0
Ivan Rodriguez, c	.231	4	13	3	3	1	0	0	3	2	3	0
Craig Monroe, of	.188	4	16	3	3	1	0	2	3	0	3	0
Brandon Inge, 3b	.133	4	15	1	2	0	0	0	0	0	6	0
Totals	.309	4	139	22	43	12	1	6	22	7	22	1

Pitcher	W	L	ERA	G	GS	SV	IP	H	R	ER	BB	SO
Kenny Rogers	1	0	0.00	1	1	0	7.2	5	0	0	2	8
Todd Jones	0	0	0.00	2	0	1	2.0	1	0	0	0	2
Joel Zumaya	0	0	0.00	2	0	0	2.0	0	0	0	0	3
Jason Grilli	0	0	0.00	1	0	0	0.1	0	0	0	0	0
Jeremy Bonderman	1	0	2.16	1	1	0	8.1	5	2	2	1	4
Jamie Walker	0	0	4.91	3	0	0	3.2	3	2	2	1	1
Justin Verlander	0	0	5.06	1	1	0	5.1	7	3	3	4	5
Nate Robertson	0	1	11.12	1	1	0	5.2	12	7	7	0	1
Totals	3	1	3.60	4	4	1	35.0	33	14	14	8	24

NEW YORK

Player, Pos.	AVG	G	AB	R	H	2B	3B	HR	RBI	BB	SO	SB
Derek Jeter, ss	.500	4	16	4	8	4	0	1	1	1	2	0
Jorge Posada, c	.500	4	14	2	7	1	0	1	2	2	2	0
Bobby Abreu, of	.333	4	15	2	5	1	0	0	4	2	2	0
Hideki Matsui, of	.250	4	16	1	4	1	0	0	1	0	2	0
Johnny Damon, of	.235	4	17	3	4	0	0	1	3	1	2	0
Robinson Cano, 2b	.133	4	15	0	2	0	0	0	0	0	1	0
Jason Giambi, dh	.125	3	8	1	1	0	0	1	2	2	3	1
Gary Sheffield, 1b	.083	3	12	1	1	0	0	0	1	0	4	0
Alex Rodriguez, 3b	.071	4	14	0	1	0	0	0	0	0	4	0
Melky Cabrera, of	.000	2	3	0	0	0	0	0	0	0	0	0
Bernie Williams, of	.000	1	3	0	0	0	0	0	0	0	2	0
Andy Phillips, 1b	.000	1	1	0	0	0	0	0	0	0	0	0
Totals	.246	4	134	14	33	7	0	4	14	8	24	1

Pitcher	W	L	ERA	G	GS	SV	IP	H	R	ER	BB	SO
Kyle Farnsworth	0	0	0.00	2	0	0	2.0	1	0	0	1	1
Mariano Rivera	0	0	0.00	1	0	0	1.0	1	0	0	0	1
Ron Villone	0	0	0.00	1	0	0	1.0	1	0	0	1	1
Scott Proctor	0	0	2.25	3	0	0	4.0	5	1	1	1	1
Brian Bruney	0	0	3.38	3	0	0	2.2	1	1	1	0	4
Chien-Ming Wang	1	0	4.05	1	1	0	6.2	8	3	3	1	4
Mike Mussina	0	1	5.14	1	1	0	7.0	8	4	4	0	5
Randy Johnson	0	1	7.94	1	1	0	5.2	8	5	5	2	4
Jaret Wright	0	1	10.12	1	1	0	2.2	5	4	3	1	1
Cory Lidle	0	0	20.25	1	0	0	1.1	4	3	3	0	1
Mike Myers	0	0	Inf.	1	0	0	0.0	1	1	1	0	0
Totals	1	3	5.56	4	4	0	34.0	43	22	21	7	22

SCORE BY INNINGS

Detroit	071 074 300—22
New York	005 302 112—14

E—Grilli, Jeter, A.Rodriguez, Sheffield. **DP**—Detroit 3, New York 4. **LOB**—Detroit 25, New York 26. **CS**—Ordonez, Jeter, Polanco. **SH**—Inge. **SF**—Granderson, A.Rodriguez. **HBP**—Giambi 2 (by Robertson 2), A.Rodriguez (by Rogers). **IBB**—None. **WP**—Mussina. **PB**—None. **BK**—None.

OAKLAND VS. MINNESOTA
COMPOSITE BOX

MINNESOTA

Player, Pos.	AVG	G	AB	R	H	2B	3B	HR	RBI	BB	SO	SB
Justin Morneau, 1b	.417	3	12	3	5	1	0	2	2	0	0	0
Rondell White, of	.417	3	12	1	5	1	0	1	2	0	0	0
Jason Bartlett, ss	.273	3	11	0	3	1	0	0	0	0	2	0
Luis Castillo, 2b	.273	3	11	0	3	0	0	0	0	3	3	0
Torii Hunter, of	.273	3	11	1	3	1	0	1	2	0	1	0
Michael Cuddyer, of	.250	3	12	2	3	0	1	1	1	0	2	0
Joe Mauer, c	.182	3	11	0	2	0	0	0	0	1	0	0
Nick Punto, 3b	.167	3	12	0	2	0	0	0	0	0	1	0
Phil Nevin, dh	.000	1	3	0	0	0	0	0	0	0	0	0

Two home runs and five RBIs in four games
Athletics outfielder Milton Bradley had a strong ALCS

BILL MITCHELL

Player, Pos.	AVG	G	AB	R	H	2B	3B	HR	RBI	BB	SO	SB
Jason Tyner, of	.000	2	6	0	0	0	0	0	0	2	2	1
Totals	.257	3	101	7	26	4	1	5	7	6	11	1

Pitcher	W	L	ERA	G	GS	SV	IP	H	R	ER	BB	SO
Matt Guerrier	0	0	0.00	1	0	0	1.0	0	0	0	0	0
Joe Nathan	0	0	0.00	1	0	0	0.2	1	0	0	0	1
Glen Perkins	0	0	0.00	1	0	0	0.1	2	0	0	0	0
Johan Santana	0	1	2.25	1	1	0	8.0	5	2	2	1	8
Boof Bonser	0	0	3.00	1	1	0	6.0	7	2	2	1	3
Juan Rincon	0	0	3.00	2	0	0	3.0	1	1	1	0	3
Brad Radke	0	1	6.75	1	1	0	4.0	5	4	3	1	2
Jesse Crain	0	0	9.00	2	0	0	1.0	3	3	1	1	1
Pat Neshek	0	1	9.00	2	0	0	1.0	1	1	1	0	1
Dennys Reyes	0	0	9.00	2	0	0	1.0	1	3	1	2	0
Totals	0	3	3.81	3	3	0	26.0	26	16	11	6	19

OAKLAND

Player, Pos.	AVG	G	AB	R	H	2B	3B	HR	RBI	BB	SO	SB
Frank Thomas, dh	.500	3	10	3	5	1	0	2	2	2	1	0
Jay Payton, of	.333	3	12	3	4	0	0	0	0	0	1	0
Marco Scutaro, 2b	.333	3	12	1	4	4	0	0	6	0	1	0
Nick Swisher, 1b	.300	3	10	3	3	2	0	0	1	2	2	0
Mark Ellis, 2b	.286	2	7	0	2	0	0	0	0	0	2	0
Jason Kendall, c	.214	3	14	1	3	1	0	0	1	0	4	0
Eric Chavez, 3b	.200	3	10	2	2	1	0	1	1	2	4	0
Mark Kotsay, of	.143	3	14	2	2	0	0	1	2	0	2	0
Milton Bradley, of	.077	3	13	1	1	0	0	1	2	0	1	0
D'Angelo Jimenez, 2b	.000	2	4	0	0	0	0	0	0	0	0	0
Totals	.245	3	106	16	26	9	0	5	15	6	19	0

Pitcher	W	L	ERA	G	GS	SV	IP	H	R	ER	BB	SO
Kiko Calero	1	0	0.00	1	0	0	1.0	0	0	0	1	1
Barry Zito	1	0	1.12	1	1	0	8.0	4	1	1	3	1
Justin Duchscherer	0	0	2.25	2	0	0	4.0	1	1	1	0	4
Dan Haren	1	0	3.00	1	1	0	6.0	9	2	2	1	2
Huston Street	0	0	3.00	3	0	2	3.0	4	1	1	1	1
Esteban Loaiza	0	0	3.60	1	1	0	5.0	8	2	2	0	2
Totals	3	0	2.33	3	3	2	27.0	26	7	7	6	11

SCORE BY INNINGS

Minnesota	000 103 111—7
Oakland	042 020 602—16

E—Bartlett 2, Radke, Morneau, Cuddyer, Kendall. **DP**—Minnesota 2, Oakland 2. **LOB**—Minnesota 21, Oakland 18. **CS**—Castillo. **SH**—Punto, Hunter. **SF**—None. **HBP**—None. **IBB**—Thomas (by Reyes). **WP**—Nathan. **PB**—None. **BK**—None.

AMERICAN LEAGUE
CHAMPIONSHIP SERIES
OAKLAND VS. DETROIT
COMPOSITE BOX

DETROIT

Player, Pos.	AVG	G	AB	R	H	2B	3B	HR	RBI	BB	SO	SB
Placido Polanco, 2b	.529	4	17	2	9	1	0	0	2	2	1	0
Omar Infante, dh	.500	1	2	0	1	0	0	0	0	1	1	1
Alexis Gomez, dh	.444	3	9	1	4	0	0	1	4	0	2	0
Craig Monroe, of	.429	4	14	5	6	2	0	1	4	3	4	0
Sean Casey, 1b	.333	1	3	0	1	0	0	0	0	1	0	0
Brandon Inge, 3b	.333	4	12	3	4	1	0	1	3	3	3	0
Curtis Granderson, of	.333	4	15	4	5	2	0	1	2	4	2	1
Magglio Ordonez, of	.235	4	17	3	4	0	0	2	6	2	2	0
Carlos Guillen, ss	.188	4	16	1	3	1	0	0	0	1	4	0
Ivan Rodriguez, c	.125	4	16	2	2	0	0	1	1	1	4	0
Neifi Perez, ss	.000	1	4	0	0	0	0	0	0	0	1	0
Marcus Thames, dh	.000	2	5	1	0	0	0	0	0	0	1	0
Ramon Santiago, ss	.000	3	7	0	0	0	0	0	0	1	0	0
Totals	**.285**	**4**	**137**	**22**	**39**	**7**	**0**	**7**	**22**	**19**	**25**	**2**

Pitcher	W	L	ERA	G	GS	SV	IP	H	R	ER	BB	SO
Kenny Rogers	1	0	0.00	1	1	0	7.1	2	0	0	2	6
Nate Robertson	1	0	0.00	1	1	0	5.0	6	0	0	3	4
Fernando Rodney	0	0	0.00	3	0	0	3.2	1	0	0	1	4
Todd Jones	0	0	0.00	3	0	2	3.0	3	0	0	1	2
Jason Grilli	0	0	0.00	2	0	0	1.0	1	0	0	3	1
Jamie Walker	0	0	0.00	1	0	0	0.1	0	0	0	0	1
Wilfredo Ledezma	1	0	3.38	2	0	0	2.2	2	1	1	1	1
Jeremy Bonderman	0	0	4.05	1	1	0	6.2	6	3	3	2	3
Justin Verlander	1	0	6.75	1	1	0	5.1	7	4	4	1	6
Joel Zumaya	0	0	9.00	1	0	0	1.0	1	1	1	0	0
Totals	**4**	**0**	**2.25**	**4**	**4**	**2**	**36.0**	**29**	**9**	**9**	**14**	**28**

OAKLAND

Player, Pos.	AVG	G	AB	R	H	2B	3B	HR	RBI	BB	SO	SB
Milton Bradley, of	.500	4	18	4	9	2	0	2	5	0	2	0
Jason Kendall, c	.294	4	17	0	5	0	0	0	0	2	2	0
Jay Payton, of	.286	4	14	1	4	2	0	1	2	1	2	0
Mark Kotsay, of	.250	4	16	3	4	2	0	0	0	2	3	0
Eric Chavez, 3b	.231	4	13	1	3	1	0	1	2	2	4	0
D'Angelo Jimenez, 2b	.167	4	12	0	2	0	0	0	0	0	2	0
Nick Swisher, 1b	.100	4	10	0	1	0	0	0	0	5	5	0
Marco Scutaro, ss	.067	4	15	0	1	0	0	0	0	0	3	0
Adam Melhuse, ph	.000	1	1	0	0	0	0	0	0	0	1	0
Bobby Kielty, ph	.000	2	2	0	0	0	0	0	0	0	0	0
Frank Thomas, dh	.000	4	13	0	0	0	0	0	0	2	4	0
Totals	**.221**	**4**	**131**	**9**	**29**	**7**	**0**	**4**	**9**	**14**	**28**	**0**

Though hitless in 17 World Series at-bats . . .
Placido Polanco won ALCS MVP honors for hitting .529

JOHN WILLIAMSON

Pitcher	W	L	ERA	G	GS	SV	IP	H	R	ER	BB	SO
Joe Kennedy	0	0	0.00	4	0	0	3.2	2	0	0	2	2
Chad Gaudin	0	0	0.00	3	0	0	3.1	2	0	0	3	1
Joe Blanton	0	0	0.00	1	0	0	2.0	0	0	0	2	2
Kiko Calero	0	0	0.00	3	0	0	2.0	3	0	0	1	1
Rich Harden	0	1	4.76	1	1	0	5.2	5	3	3	5	4
Dan Haren	0	0	5.40	1	1	0	5.0	7	3	3	2	7
Esteban Loaiza	0	1	10.50	1	1	0	6.0	9	7	7	1	5
Huston Street	0	1	10.80	2	0	0	3.1	4	4	4	0	3
Barry Zito	0	1	12.27	1	1	0	3.2	7	5	5	3	0
Totals	**0**	**4**	**5.71**	**4**	**4**	**0**	**34.2**	**39**	**22**	**22**	**19**	**25**

SCORE BY INNINGS

Detroit	212 733 004	—22
Oakland	302 101 110	—9

E—Guillen, Jimenez 2, Chavez. **DP**—Detroit 7, Oakland 5. **LOB**—Detroit 33, Oakland 29. **CS**—None. **SH**—None. **SF**—Inge, Monroe. **HBP**—Thomas (by Rogers). **IBB**—Inge (by Kennedy), Polanco (by Gaudin). **WP**—Bonderman, Verlander, Haren 2, Kennedy. **PB**—None. **BK**—None.

NATIONAL LEAGUE DIVISION SERIES

NEW YORK VS. LOS ANGELES
COMPOSITE BOX

LOS ANGELES

Player, Pos.	AVG	G	AB	R	H	2B	3B	HR	RBI	BB	SO	SB
James Loney, 1b	.750	1	4	0	3	0	0	0	3	1	0	0
Jeff Kent, 2b	.615	3	13	2	8	1	0	1	2	0	1	0
Wilson Betemit, 3b	.500	3	8	3	4	1	0	1	1	2	1	0
Ramon Martinez, ph	.333	3	3	0	1	0	0	0	1	0	1	0
Russell Martin, c	.333	3	12	2	4	0	0	0	0	1	2	0
Marlon Anderson, of	.308	3	13	2	4	1	0	0	1	0	1	0
Julio Lugo, 3b	.250	2	4	0	1	0	0	0	0	1	1	0
Nomar Garciaparra, 1b	.222	3	9	0	2	1	0	0	2	0	1	0
Rafael Furcal, ss	.182	3	11	1	2	0	0	0	1	3	2	2
J.D. Drew, of	.154	3	13	1	2	0	0	0	0	0	3	0
Kenny Lofton, of	.077	3	13	0	1	0	0	0	0	0	4	0
Andre Ethier, of	.000	2	1	0	0	0	0	0	0	0	0	0
Derek Lowe, p	.000	1	1	0	0	0	0	0	0	0	1	0
Greg Maddux, p	.000	1	1	0	0	0	0	0	0	0	1	0
Hong-Chih Kuo, p	.000	1	2	0	0	0	0	0	0	0	1	0
Olmedo Saenz, ph	.000	2	2	0	0	0	0	0	0	0	1	0
Totals	.291	3	110	11	32	6	0	2	11	8	21	2

Pitcher	W	L	ERA	G	GS	SV	IP	H	R	ER	BB	SO
Mark Hendrickson	0	0	0.00	3	0	0	2.2	1	0	0	1	1
Takashi Saito	0	0	0.00	2	0	0	2.2	0	0	0	0	4
Chad Billingsley	0	0	0.00	2	0	0	2.0	1	0	0	0	3
Hong-Chih Kuo	0	1	4.15	1	1	0	4.1	4	2	2	2	4
Derek Lowe	0	0	6.75	1	1	0	5.1	6	4	4	2	6
Greg Maddux	0	0	9.00	1	1	0	4.0	7	4	4	2	0
Brett Tomko	0	0	9.00	2	0	0	1.0	4	4	1	2	0
Jonathan Broxton	0	1	13.50	2	0	0	2.0	5	3	3	2	3
Brad Penny	0	1	18.00	1	0	0	1.0	2	2	2	2	1
Totals	0	3	5.76	3	3	0	25.0	30	19	16	13	22

NEW YORK

Player, Pos.	AVG	G	AB	R	H	2B	3B	HR	RBI	BB	SO	SB
Chris Woodward, ph	1.000	1	1	1	1	0	0	0	0	0	0	0
Paul Lo Duca, c	.455	3	11	2	5	1	0	0	3	1	1	0
Cliff Floyd, of	.444	3	9	3	4	0	0	1	2	1	2	0
Carlos Delgado, 1b	.429	3	14	3	6	0	0	1	2	0	3	0
Endy Chavez, of	.375	3	8	1	3	0	0	0	0	0	0	0
Shawn Green, of	.333	2	9	1	3	2	0	0	2	0	2	0
David Wright, 3b	.333	3	12	1	4	2	0	0	4	1	4	0
Carlos Beltran, of	.222	3	9	2	2	0	0	0	1	5	2	1
Jose Reyes, ss	.167	3	12	2	2	0	0	0	3	2	2	1
Tom Glavine, p	.000	1	1	0	0	0	0	0	0	0	0	0
John Maine, p	.000	1	1	0	0	0	0	0	0	0	1	0
Guillermo Mota, p	.000	2	1	0	0	0	0	0	0	0	1	0
Michael Tucker, ph	.000	2	1	1	0	0	0	0	0	1	0	0
Julio Franco, ph	.000	2	2	0	0	0	0	0	1	0	1	0
Steve Trachsel, of	.000	1	2	0	0	0	0	0	0	0	0	0
Jose Valentin, 2b	.000	3	9	2	0	0	0	0	0	2	4	0
Totals	.294	3	102	19	30	6	0	2	18	13	22	2

Pitcher	W	L	ERA	G	GS	SV	IP	H	R	ER	BB	SO
Tom Glavine	1	0	0.00	1	1	0	6.0	4	0	0	2	2
Pedro Feliciano	0	0	0.00	3	0	0	1.2	0	0	0	2	2
Chad Bradford	0	0	0.00	2	0	0	0.1	1	0	0	1	0
John Maine	0	0	2.08	1	1	0	4.1	6	1	1	2	5
Aaron Heilman	0	0	3.00	3	0	0	3.0	3	1	1	0	1
Billy Wagner	0	0	3.00	3	0	2	3.0	3	1	1	0	4
Steve Trachsel	0	0	5.40	1	1	0	3.1	6	2	2	1	2
Guillermo Mota	1	0	6.75	2	0	0	4.0	6	3	3	0	5
Darren Oliver	0	0	20.25	1	0	0	1.1	3	3	3	0	0
Totals	3	0	3.67	3	3	2	27.0	32	11	11	8	21

SCORE BY INNINGS

Los Angeles	010 230 311	—11
New York	302 217 220	—19

E—Betemit, Kent, Loney, Tomko, Beltran, Valentin, Wright. DP—Los Angeles 2, New York 3. LOB—Los Angeles 27, New York 26. SB—Reyes, Beltran, Furcal 2. CS—Reyes. SH—Lowe, Glavine, Valentin. SF—Lo Duca. HBP—Valentin (by Hendrickson), Lo Duca (by Maddux). IBB—Floyd (by Lowe), Betemit (by Maine), Reyes (by Kuo), Valentin (by Maddux). WP—Kuo. PB—None. BK—Tomko.

SAN DIEGO VS. ST. LOUIS
ST. LOUIS

Player, Pos.	AVG	G	AB	R	H	2B	3B	HR	RBI	BB	SO	SB
So Taguchi, ph	1.000	2	1	1	1	0	0	1	1	0	0	0
Aaron Miles, 2b	.500	2	2	0	1	0	0	0	0	0	0	0
Jeff Weaver, p	.500	1	2	0	1	0	0	0	0	0	1	0
Ronnie Belliard, 2b	.462	4	13	2	6	1	0	0	2	1	0	1
Albert Pujols, 1b	.333	4	15	3	5	1	0	1	3	1	4	0
Jim Edmonds, of	.308	4	13	2	4	0	0	0	2	2	3	0
Yadier Molina, c	.308	4	13	0	4	1	0	0	1	0	2	0
Juan Encarnacion, of	.286	4	14	1	4	0	1	0	2	1	2	0
Preston Wilson, of	.250	2	8	2	2	1	0	0	0	1	0	0
Chris Carpenter, p	.200	2	5	0	1	0	0	0	0	0	2	0
Scott Spiezio, 3b	.200	2	5	1	1	0	0	0	1	0	1	0
Chris Duncan, of	.167	2	6	1	1	0	0	0	0	2	2	0
David Eckstein, ss	.133	4	15	1	2	0	0	0	1	0	1	0
Scott Rolen, 3b	.091	3	11	0	1	1	0	0	0	2	0	0
John Rodriguez, ph	.000	1	1	0	0	0	0	0	0	0	0	0
Jeff Suppan, p	.000	1	1	0	0	0	0	0	0	0	0	0
Totals	.272	4	125	14	34	5	1	2	13	7	21	2

Pitcher	W	L	ERA	G	GS	SV	IP	H	R	ER	BB	SO
Jeff Weaver	1	0	0.00	1	1	0	5.0	2	0	0	3	3
Adam Wainwright	0	0	0.00	3	0	1	3.2	3	0	0	0	6
Tyler Johnson	0	0	0.00	4	0	0	2.2	2	0	0	1	6
Josh Kinney	0	0	0.00	2	0	0	2.0	0	0	0	1	1
Josh Hancock	0	0	0.00	1	0	0	1.2	1	0	0	2	1
Braden Looper	0	0	0.00	1	0	0	1.2	1	0	0	0	0
Randy Flores	0	0	0.00	2	0	0	1.0	2	0	0	1	1
Brad Thompson	0	0	0.00	1	0	0	0.2	0	0	0	1	1
Chris Carpenter	2	0	2.03	2	2	0	13.1	12	3	3	4	12
Jeff Suppan	0	1	6.23	1	1	0	4.1	6	3	3	3	3
Totals	3	1	1.50	4	4	1	36.0	29	6	6	16	34

SAN DIEGO

Player, Pos.	AVG	G	AB	R	H	2B	3B	HR	RBI	BB	SO	SB
Rob Bowen, ph	1.000	1	1	0	1	0	0	0	0	0	0	0
Ryan Klesko, ph	.667	3	3	0	2	1	0	0	0	0	0	0
Dave Roberts, of	.438	4	16	1	7	0	1	0	0	1	4	1
Adrian Gonzalez, 1b	.357	4	14	2	5	0	0	0	3	3	0	0
Brian Giles, of	.286	4	14	1	4	1	0	0	1	2	3	0
Josh Barfield, 2b	.250	4	8	0	2	1	0	0	0	1	2	0
Russell Branyan, 3b	.231	4	13	1	3	1	1	0	3	1	5	0
Josh Bard, c	.143	3	7	0	1	0	0	0	0	1	2	0
Mike Cameron, of	.143	4	14	1	2	1	0	0	1	3	7	1
Geoff Blum, 3b	.125	4	8	0	1	0	0	0	1	4	1	0
Mike Piazza, c	.100	4	10	0	1	1	0	0	0	1	0	0
Mark Bellhorn, ph	.000	2	1	0	0	0	0	0	0	1	0	0
Jake Peavy, p	.000	1	1	0	0	0	0	0	0	0	1	0
David Wells, p	.000	1	1	0	0	0	0	0	0	0	0	0
Woody Williams, p	.000	1	2	0	0	0	0	0	0	0	2	0
Chris Young, p	.000	1	3	0	0	0	0	0	0	0	2	0
Khalil Greene, ss	.000	3	4	0	0	0	0	0	0	2	0	0
Todd Walker, 3b	.000	3	9	0	0	0	0	0	0	1	0	0
Totals	.225	4	129	6	29	7	2	0	6	16	34	2

Pitcher	W	L	ERA	G	GS	SV	IP	H	R	ER	BB	SO
Chris Young	1	0	0.00	1	1	0	6.2	4	0	0	2	9
Cla Meredith	0	0	0.00	2	0	0	3.2	3	2	0	0	3
Clay Hensley	0	0	0.00	2	0	0	2.2	2	0	0	1	0
Chan Park	0	0	0.00	1	0	0	2.0	1	0	0	1	0
Rudy Seanez	0	0	0.00	1	0	0	1.2	0	0	0	0	2
Trevor Hoffman	0	0	0.00	1	0	1	1.0	0	0	0	0	1
Alan Embree	0	0	0.00	1	0	0	0.1	0	0	0	0	1
David Wells	0	1	3.60	1	1	0	5.0	7	2	2	0	2
Woody Williams	0	1	6.75	1	1	0	5.1	5	4	4	2	1
Scott Linebrink	0	0	6.75	2	0	0	1.1	1	1	1	1	0
Jake Peavy	0	1	8.44	1	1	0	5.1	11	5	5	1	2
Totals	1	3	3.09	4	4	1	35.0	34	14	12	7	21

SCORE BY INNINGS

St. Louis	200 515 010	—14
San Diego	200 301 000	— 6

E—Duncan, Molina, Branyan. DP—St. Louis 4, San Diego 8. LOB—St. Louis 20, San Diego 35. CS—Encarnacion, Molina, Roberts. SH—Carpenter, Eckstein, Roberts. SF—Encarnacion, Giles, Blum. HBP—Bard (by Johnson), Rolen (by Park), Eckstein (by Wells), Edmonds (by Williams), Belliard (by Meredith). IBB—Belliard (by Peavy), Edmonds (by Young), Blum (by Suppan). WP—None. PB—None. BK—None.

NATIONAL LEAGUE CHAMPIONSHIP SERIES
NEW YORK VS. ST. LOUIS

ST. LOUIS

Player, Pos.	AVG	G	AB	R	H	2B	3B	HR	RBI	BB	SO	SB
So Taguchi, ph	1.000	5	3	1	3	1	0	1	3	0	0	0
Aaron Miles, 2b	.667	3	3	0	2	0	1	0	0	0	0	0
Yadier Molina, c	.348	7	23	2	8	1	0	2	6	3	2	0
Jeff Suppan, p	.333	2	3	1	1	0	0	1	1	0	1	0
Albert Pujols, 1b	.318	7	22	5	7	1	0	1	1	7	3	0
Jeff Weaver, p	.250	2	4	0	1	0	0	0	0	0	1	0
Ronnie Belliard, 2b	.240	7	25	0	6	0	0	0	2	2	3	1
Scott Rolen, 3b	.238	7	21	4	5	1	0	0	0	3	1	0
Scott Spiezio, of	.235	6	17	3	4	1	2	0	5	2	5	0
David Eckstein, ss	.231	7	26	3	6	1	0	1	1	4	0	3
Jim Edmonds, of	.227	7	22	5	5	0	0	2	4	5	5	0
Juan Encarnacion, of	.182	6	22	1	4	0	1	0	2	2	3	0
Preston Wilson, of	.176	6	17	2	3	1	0	0	1	1	4	0
Chris Duncan, of	.125	5	8	1	1	0	0	1	1	0	2	0
Gary Bennett, c	.000	2	1	0	0	0	0	0	0	0	1	0
Anthony Reyes, p	.000	1	1	0	0	0	0	0	0	0	1	0
Chris Carpenter, p	.000	2	4	0	0	0	0	0	0	0	1	0
John Rodriguez, ph	.000	4	4	0	0	0	0	0	0	0	1	0
Totals	.248	7	226	28	56	7	4	9	27	29	33	4

Pitcher	W	L	ERA	G	GS	SV	IP	H	R	ER	BB	SO
Randy Flores	1	0	0.00	4	0	0	3.2	2	0	0	0	3
Josh Kinney	1	0	0.00	3	0	0	3.1	3	0	0	1	4
Adam Wainwright	0	0	0.00	3	0	2	3.0	2	0	0	1	4
Jeff Suppan	1	0	0.60	2	2	0	15.0	5	1	1	6	6
Tyler Johnson	0	0	2.45	4	0	0	3.2	2	1	1	1	5
Jeff Weaver	1	1	3.09	2	2	0	11.2	10	4	4	4	2
Anthony Reyes	0	0	4.50	1	1	0	4.0	3	2	2	4	4
Chris Carpenter	0	1	5.73	2	2	0	11.0	13	7	7	4	5
Braden Looper	0	0	5.79	3	0	0	4.2	7	3	3	0	1
Brad Thompson	0	1	27.00	2	0	0	0.2	3	3	2	0	1
Josh Hancock	0	0	162.00	2	0	0	0.1	4	6	6	3	1
Totals	4	3	3.84	7	7	2	61.0	54	27	26	24	36

NEW YORK

Player, Pos.	AVG	G	AB	R	H	2B	3B	HR	RBI	BB	SO	SB
Michael Tucker, ph	.400	6	5	1	2	0	0	0	0	0	1	1
Carlos Delgado, 1b	.304	7	23	5	7	3	0	3	9	6	3	0
Shawn Green, of	.304	7	23	2	7	1	0	0	2	4	3	1
Carlos Beltran, of	.296	7	27	8	8	1	0	3	4	4	3	1
Jose Reyes, ss	.281	7	32	5	9	1	1	1	2	1	3	2
Jose Valentin, 2b	.250	7	24	0	6	2	0	0	5	2	5	0
Paul Lo Duca, c	.207	7	29	3	6	1	0	0	3	2	2	0
Endy Chavez, of	.185	7	27	1	5	2	0	0	0	0	1	0
David Wright, 3b	.160	7	25	2	4	1	0	1	2	4	4	0
Anderson Hernandez, ph	.000	2	1	0	0	0	0	0	0	0	1	0
Julio Franco, ph	.000	2	2	0	0	0	0	0	0	0	2	0
John Maine, p	.000	2	2	0	0	0	0	0	0	0	2	0
Darren Oliver, p	.000	1	2	0	0	0	0	0	0	0	2	0
Cliff Floyd, ph	.000	3	3	0	0	0	0	0	0	0	1	0
Tom Glavine, p	.000	2	4	0	0	0	0	0	0	0	0	0
Oliver Perez, p	.000	2	5	0	0	0	0	0	0	1	3	0
Totals	.231	7	234	27	54	12	1	8	27	24	36	5

Game Seven starter went 3-13, 6.55 during the season
Oliver Perez allowed just one run in six innings of NLCS finale

Pitcher	W	L	ERA	G	GS	SV	IP	H	R	ER	BB	SO
Darren Oliver	0	0	0.00	1	0	0	6.0	3	0	0	1	3
Chad Bradford	0	0	0.00	5	0	0	5.1	3	0	0	0	2
Roberto Hernandez	0	0	0.00	3	0	0	2.1	0	0	0	2	0
Tom Glavine	1	1	2.45	2	2	0	11.0	11	3	3	5	4
John Maine	1	0	2.89	2	2	0	9.1	4	4	3	9	8
Pedro Feliciano	0	0	3.00	3	0	0	3.0	2	1	1	0	1
Aaron Heilman	0	0	4.15	3	0	0	4.1	4	2	2	1	5
Guillermo Mota	0	0	4.15	5	0	0	4.1	4	2	2	2	2
Oliver Perez	1	0	4.63	2	2	0	11.2	13	6	6	3	7
Billy Wagner	0	1	16.88	3	0	1	2.2	7	5	5	1	0
Steve Trachsel	0	1	45.00	1	1	0	1.0	5	5	5	5	1
Totals	3	4	3.98	7	7	1	61.0	56	28	27	29	33

SCORE BY INNINGS

St. Louis	273	223	207—28
New York	512	349	300—27

E—Belliard 2, Rolen 2, Delgado 3, Lo Duca. **DP**—St. Louis 4, New York 10. **LOB**—St. Louis 51, New York 53. **CS**—Rolen. **SH**—Belliard, Suppan 3, Lo Duca, Maine. **SF**—None. **HBP**—Eckstein (by Bradford), Eckstein (by Perez), Encarnacion (by Maine), Green (by Johnson), Tucker (by Carpenter), Valentin (by Suppan). **IBB**—Edmonds (by R.Hernandez), Pujols (by Glavine), Pujols (by Heilman), Pujols (by Maine), Pujols (by Perez), Green (by Suppan), Wright (by Weaver). **WP**—Heilman, Oliver, Feliciano, R.Hernandez. **PB**—None. **BK**—None.

ORGANIZATION
STATISTICS

BY JACK MAGRUDER

The Diamondbacks spent 2006 in transition, bidding farewell to the final two position-player links to the 2001 World Series, Luis Gonzalez and Craig Counsell, while affirming their commitment to youth.

Brandon Webb and Chad Tracy were given long-term contracts as cornerstones of the future, manager Bob Melvin received a two-year extension, and the Diamondbacks took a first look at several pieces of their future during a disjointed season in which they were in contention for the playoffs berth before a bloody Labor Day weekend despite a 3-20 June stretch, the worst in the majors since Detroit opened 3-25 in 2003.

Gonzalez, whose 57-home run 2001 season was capped with a ninth-inning Game Seven single to win the World Series, was told in September that he would not be re-signed after eight seasons, and the final home series against San Diego became a Last Waltz celebration complete with multiple standing ovations and a final day tribute that brought some to tears and even lured former managing general partner Jerry Colangelo to the park for the first time since he left the franchise late in 2004.

New general manager Josh Byrnes also jettisoned veterans Russ Ortiz, Shawn Green and Orlando Hernandez during the 2006 season, after dealing Troy Glaus and Javier Vazquez the previous winter while acquiring Orlando Hudson, Eric Byrnes, Johnny Estrada and Miguel Batista.

All the moves created a younger, less expensive nucleus to combine with a strong next wave that the Diamondbacks believe will put them on the path to long-term competitiveness.

ORGANIZATION LEADERS

BATTING
*Minimum 250 at-bats

*AVG	Parra, Gerardo, Missoula	.328
R	Bonifacio, Emilio, Lancaster	117
H	Rahl, Chris, Lancaster	195
TB	Rahl, Chris, Lancaster	302
2B	Rahl, Chris, Lancaster	47
3B	Callaspo, Alberto, Tucson	12
HR	Reynolds, Mark, Lancaster/Tennessee	35
RBI	Reynolds, Mark, Lancaster/Tennessee	112
BB	Carter, Chris, Tucson	79
SO	Burgess, Brandon, Lancaster	132
SB	Bonifacio, Emilio, Lancaster	61
*OBP	Quentin, Carlos, Tucson	.424
*SLG	Reynolds, Mark, Lancaster/Tennessee	.635

PITCHING
#Minimum 75 innings

W	Owings, Micah, Tennessee/Tucson	16
L	Schreppel, Ryan, South Bend	13
#ERA	Dove, Shane, Yakima	2.26
G	Schultz, Mike, Tennessee/Tucson	65
CG	Ohlendorf, Ross, Tennessee/Tucson	4
SV	Elliott, Matt, Lancaster/Tennessee	25
IP	Ohlendorf, Ross, Tennessee/Tucson	183
BB	Cupps, Anthony, South Bend/Lancaster	60
SO	Nippert, Dustin, Tucson	130
	Owings, Micah, Tennessee/Tucson	130
#AVG	Norberto, Jordan, Missoula	.216

PLAYERS OF THE YEAR

MAJOR LEAGUE: Brandon Webb, rhp

BA's 2003 Major League Rookie of the Year, provided the pitching staff with a backbone the entire season—leading the club with 235 innings. He also led the Diamondbacks in nearly every other category, including wins (16), strikeouts (178), complete games (5) and shutouts (3).

MINOR LEAGUE: Micah Owings, rhp

Owings led the organization in wins with 16-2, 3.33 numbers between Double-A Tennessee and Triple-A Tucson. He didn't lose at all in Triple-A and helped the Sidewinders to their first Pacific Coast League title since 1993. Owings also tied with Dustin Nippert for tops in the system with 130 strikeouts.

BILL MITCHELL

First baseman Conor Jackson was the first rookie to test the waters, hitting .291 with 15 home runs in his first full season, while top prospects Stephen Drew, Carlos Quentin, Chris Young, Enrique Gonzalez, Miguel Montero and Alberto Callaspo saw varying degrees of playing time as Arizona finished 76-86, one victory less than in 2005.

"We bring back so much of this team into next year, I think we probably get three good moves, we can jump from a team that has a good foundation to a team that expects not just to compete but expects to win the division," Byrnes said.

Webb had a Cy Young-quality season after signing a four-year extension in January, tying for the league lead in wins and shutouts while finishing second in innings (235) and third in ERA (3.08), falling out of the league lead on the final day. Batista set a career high in innings in his return to the rotation, although the Diamondbacks suffered from inconsistent closing from Jose Valverde and Jorge Julio.

Tracy had a career-high 41 doubles as Arizona led the league with 331 doubles while finishing in the top half in runs and batting despite getting the worst production in the league from the cleanup spot. Eric Byrnes resurrected his career with 37 doubles, 26 homers and 25 stolen bases, while Hudson played Gold Glove defense and was local writers' choice as the team's MVP.

Drew hit .316 with 25 extra-base hits in 59 games, recalled when Counsell broke a rib the day after the all-star break, gave the team every reason to believe he was worth the $5.3 million deal he received after being a No. 1 pick in 2004.

The Diamondbacks farm system is loaded. Drew, Quentin, Young and Callaspo were key components as Triple-A Tucson won a minor league-high 98 games under manager Chip Hale, who was promoted to the major league staff when third base coach Carlos Tosca left for Florida. The Sidewinders also won the PCL playoffs and Triple-A championship game, and they were named Baseball America's Minor League Team of the Year.

National League

BATTING

BATTING	B-T	HT	WT	DOB	AVG	vLH	vRH	G	AB	R	H	2B	3B	HR	RBI	BB	HBP	SH	SF	SO	SB	CS	SLG	OBP
Byrnes, Eric	R-R	6-2	210	2-16-76	.267	.323	.244	143	562	82	150	37	3	26	79	34	5	2	3	88	25	3	.482	.313
Callaspo, Alberto	B-R	5-10	175	4-19-83	.238	.278	.208	23	42	2	10	1	1	0	6	4	0	0	1	6	0	1	.310	.298
Clark, Tony	B-R	6-7	245	6-15-72	.197	.125	.213	79	132	13	26	4	0	6	16	13	2	0	0	40	0	0	.364	.279
Counsell, Craig	L-R	6-0	185	8-21-70	.255	.256	.255	105	372	56	95	14	4	4	30	31	9	2	1	47	15	8	.347	.327
DaVanon, Jeff	B-R	6-0	200	12-8-73	.290	.205	.308	87	221	38	64	12	4	5	35	31	0	0	4	42	10	4	.448	.371
Drew, Stephen	L-R	6-1	185	3-16-83	.316	.350	.308	59	209	27	66	13	7	5	23	14	0	2	1	50	2	0	.517	.357
Easley, Damion	R-R	5-11	190	11-11-69	.233	.245	.217	90	189	24	44	6	1	9	28	21	5	3	2	30	1	1	.418	.323
Estrada, Johnny	B-R	5-11	215	6-27-76	.302	.296	.304	115	414	43	125	26	0	11	71	13	7	1	8	40	0	0	.444	.328
Gonzalez, Luis	L-R	6-2	200	9-3-67	.271	.259	.277	153	586	93	159	52	2	15	73	69	7	0	6	58	0	1	.444	.352
Green, Shawn	L-L	6-4	210	11-10-72	.283	.274	.287	115	417	59	118	22	3	11	51	37	6	0	2	64	4	4	.429	.348
2-team (34 New York)					.277	—	—	149	530	73	147	31	3	15	66	45	10	0	3	82	4	4	.432	.344
Green, Andy	R-R	5-9	180	7-7-77	.186	.171	.196	73	86	15	16	4	0	1	6	13	0	3	0	20	1	0	.267	.293
Hairston, Scott	R-R	6-0	200	5-25-80	.400	.375	.429	9	15	2	6	2	0	0	2	1	0	0	0	5	0	0	.533	.438
Hammock, Robby	R-R	5-10	185	5-13-77	.500	—	.500	1	2	1	1	1	0	0	0	0	0	0	0	0	0	0	1.000	.500
Hudson, Orlando	B-R	6-0	185	12-12-77	.287	.338	.270	157	579	87	166	34	9	15	67	61	2	4	4	78	9	6	.454	.354
Jackson, Conor	R-R	6-2	225	5-7-82	.291	.296	.288	140	485	75	141	26	1	15	79	54	9	1	7	73	1	0	.441	.368
Montero, Miguel	L-R	5-11	195	7-9-83	.250	.333	.231	6	16	0	4	1	0	0	3	1	0	0	0	3	0	0	.313	.294
Quentin, Carlos	R-R	6-1	225	8-28-82	.253	.171	.280	57	166	23	42	13	3	9	32	15	8	1	1	34	1	0	.530	.342
Snyder, Chris	R-R	6-3	230	2-12-81	.277	.246	.294	61	184	19	51	9	0	6	32	22	1	1	5	39	0	0	.424	.349
Tracy, Chad	L-R	6-2	200	5-22-80	.281	.231	.304	154	597	91	168	41	0	20	80	54	5	1	5	129	5	1	.451	.343
Young, Chris	R-R	6-2	180	9-5-83	.243	.360	.178	30	70	10	17	4	2	2	10	6	1	0	1	12	2	1	.386	.308

PITCHING

PITCHING	B-T	HT	WT	DOB	W	L	ERA	G	GS	CG	SV	IP	H	R	ER	HR	BB	SO	AVG	vLH	vRH	K/9	BB/9
Aquino, Greg	R-R	6-1	190	1-11-78	2	0	4.47	42	0	0	0	48	54	27	24	8	24	51	.283	.280	.286	9.50	4.47
Bajenaru, Jeff	R-R	6-1	200	3-21-78	0	1	36.00	1	0	0	0	1	4	4	4	3	0	0	.571	.667	.500	0.00	0.00
Batista, Miguel	R-R	6-1	195	2-19-71	11	8	4.58	34	33	3	0	206	231	116	105	18	84	110	.288	.321	.257	4.80	3.66
Choate, Randy	L-L	6-1	195	9-5-75	0	1	3.94	30	0	0	0	16	21	9	7	0	3	12	.304	.294	.314	6.75	1.69
Cruz, Juan	R-R	6-2	155	10-15-78	5	6	4.18	31	15	0	0	95	80	45	44	7	47	88	.230	.263	.199	8.37	4.47
Daigle, Casey	R-R	6-5	250	4-4-81	0	0	3.65	10	0	0	0	12	14	5	5	1	6	7	.311	.375	.238	5.11	4.38
Gonzalez, Edgar	R-R	6-0	225	2-23-83	3	4	4.22	11	5	0	0	43	45	20	20	7	9	28	.273	.259	.288	5.91	1.90
Gonzalez, Enrique	R-R	5-10	210	7-14-82	3	7	5.67	22	18	0	0	106	114	71	67	14	34	66	.275	.288	.265	5.59	2.88
Grimsley, Jason	R-R	6-3	205	8-7-67	1	2	4.88	19	0	0	0	28	30	15	15	4	8	10	.280	.271	.288	3.25	2.60
Hernandez, Livan	R-R	6-2	245	2-20-75	4	5	3.76	10	10	0	0	69	70	31	29	7	26	39	.266	.286	.244	5.06	3.38
2-team (24 Washington)					13	13	4.83	34	34	0	0	216	246	125	116	29	78	128	—	—	—	5.33	3.25
Hernandez, Orlando	R-R	6-2	220	10-11-69	2	4	6.11	9	9	0	0	46	52	32	31	8	20	52	.292	.376	.200	10.25	3.94
2-team (20 New York)					11	11	4.66	29	29	1	0	162	155	90	84	22	61	164	—	—	—	9.09	3.38
Jarvis, Kevin	L-R	6-2	200	8-1-69	0	1	11.91	5	1	0	0	11	18	15	15	2	5	6	.360	.333	.379	4.76	3.97
Julio, Jorge	R-R	6-1	235	3-3-79	1	2	3.83	44	0	0	15	45	31	20	19	6	25	55	.190	.161	.224	11.08	5.04
2-team (18 New York)					2	4	4.23	62	0	0	16	66	52	35	31	10	35	88	—	—	—	12.00	4.77
Koplove, Mike	R-R	5-11	175	8-30-76	0	0	3.00	2	0	0	0	3	5	1	1	0	2	1	.417	.250	.500	3.00	6.00
Lyon, Brandon	R-R	6-1	195	8-10-79	2	4	3.89	68	0	0	0	69	68	32	30	7	22	46	.258	.244	.270	5.97	2.86
Medders, Brandon	R-R	6-1	190	1-26-80	5	3	3.64	60	0	0	0	72	76	37	29	5	28	47	.270	.348	.196	5.90	3.52
Mulholland, Terry	R-L	6-3	225	3-9-63	0	0	9.00	5	0	0	0	3	7	3	3	1	1	1	.500	.250	.833	3.00	3.00
Nippert, Dustin	R-R	6-8	225	5-6-81	0	2	11.70	2	2	0	0	10	15	13	13	5	7	9	.349	.333	.375	8.10	6.30
Ortiz, Russ	R-R	6-1	220	6-5-74	0	5	7.54	6	6	0	0	23	27	21	19	3	22	21	.303	.366	.250	8.34	8.74
Pena, Tony	R-R	6-1	220	1-9-82	3	4	5.58	25	0	0	1	31	36	21	19	6	8	21	.290	.382	.179	6.16	2.35
Slaten, Doug	L-L	6-5	200	2-4-80	0	0	0.00	9	0	0	0	3	0	0	0	2	3	.167	.111	.222	4.76	3.18
Valverde, Jose	R-R	6-4	255	7-24-79	2	3	5.84	44	0	0	18	49	50	32	32	6	22	69	.256	.323	.192	12.59	4.01
Vargas, Claudio	R-R	6-3	230	6-19-78	12	10	4.83	31	30	0	0	168	185	101	90	27	52	123	.274	.275	.272	6.60	2.79
Vizcaino, Luis	R-R	5-11	185	8-6-74	4	6	3.58	70	0	0	0	65	51	26	26	8	29	72	.215	.163	.256	9.92	3.99
Webb, Brandon	R-R	6-2	230	5-9-79	16	8	3.10	33	33	5	0	235	216	91	81	15	50	178	.246	.261	.231	6.82	1.91

FIELDING

Catcher	PCT	G	PO	A	E	DP	PB
Estrada	.996	108	683	50	3	11	4
Montero	1.000	5	36	4	0	0	1
Snyder	.995	60	394	35	2	6	6

First Base	PCT	G	PO	A	E	DP
Clark	.993	53	274	21	2	27
Easley	1.000	3	6	1	0	0
S. Green	1.000	12	105	6	0	12
Hammock	1.000	1	2	0	0	0
Jackson	.990	129	1110	81	12	111
Tracy	.960	6	23	1	1	2

Second Base	PCT	G	PO	A	E	DP
Callaspo	.947	3	7	11	1	2

	PCT	G	PO	A	E	DP
Counsell	1.000	2	5	7	0	0
Easley	1.000	9	16	16	0	7
Green	1.000	6	2	8	0	2
Hudson	.984	157	310	510	13	116

Third Base	PCT	G	PO	A	E	DP
Callaspo	1.000	2	1	1	0	0
Counsell	1.000	7	2	6	0	0
Easley	.903	20	10	18	3	2
Green	1.000	7	1	8	0	0
Tracy	.935	147	101	266	25	27

Shortstop	PCT	G	PO	A	E	DP
Callaspo	.929	4	4	9	1	2
Counsell	.979	88	127	296	9	75

	PCT	G	PO	A	E	DP
Drew	.978	56	74	149	5	35
Easley	.976	27	23	58	2	9
Green	.500	2	0	1	1	0

Outfield	PCT	G	PO	A	E	DP
Byrnes	.997	137	297	5	1	1
DaVanon	.979	58	92	0	2	0
Easley	—	1	0	0	0	0
Gonzalez	.996	150	256	3	1	1
Green	1.000	7	10	0	0	0
Green	.988	100	164	1	2	1
Hairston	1.000	5	8	0	0	0
Quentin	.980	46	97	3	2	0
Young	1.000	24	50	1	0	0

General manager: Josh Byrnes. **Farm director:** A.J. Hinch. **Scouting director:** Tom Allison.

Class	Team	League	W	L	PCT	Finish*	Manager	Affiliate Since
Majors	Arizona	National	76	86	.469	11th (16)	Bob Melvin	—
Triple-A	Tucson Sidewinders	Pacific Coast	91	53	.632	+1st (16)	Chip Hale	1998
Double-A	Mobile BayBears	Southern	62	76	.449	7th (10)	Gary Jones	2005
High A	Lancaster Jethawks	California	68	72	.486	7th (10)	Brett Butler	2001
Low A	South Bend Silver Hawks	Midwest	74	62	.544	4th (14)	Mark Haley	1997
Short-season	Yakima Bears	Northwest	28	48	.368	7th (8)	Jay Gainer	1999
Rookie	Missoula Osprey	Pioneer	42	34	.553	+3rd (8)	Hector De La Cruz	1999
OVERALL 2006 MINOR LEAGUE RECORD			373	338	.525	9th (30)		

*Finish in overall standings (No. of teams in league). +League champion

ORGANIZATION STATISTICS

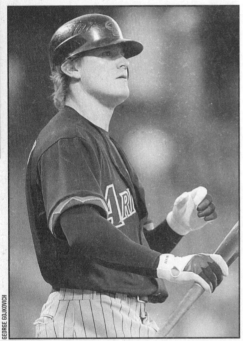

GEORGE GOJKOVICH

Eric Byrnes had 37 doubles and 26 home runs

LARRY GOREN

Mark Reynolds had a breakout season with the bat

Tucson Sidewinders
Triple-A

Pacific Coast League

BATTING	B-T	HT	WT	DOB	AVG	vLH	vRH	G	AB	R	H	2B	3B	HR	RBI	BB	HBP	SH	SF	SO	SB	CS	SLG	OBP
Barden, Brian	R-R	5-11	185	4-2-81	.298	.220	.329	128	494	80	147	35	3	16	96	44	7	2	3	92	1	3	.478	.361
Brito, Juan	R-R	5-11	220	11-7-79	.296	.310	.288	73	247	35	73	14	0	8	43	24	2	0	2	54	0	1	.449	.360
Callaspo, Alberto	B-R	5-10	175	4-19-83	.337	.292	.354	114	490	93	165	24	12	7	68	56	2	2	4	27	8	5	.478	.404
Carter, Chris	L-L	5-11	220	9-16-82	.301	.302	.300	136	509	87	153	30	3	19	97	78	1	0	0	69	10	4	.483	.395
Castillo, Wilkin	B-R	6-0	170	6-1-84	.238	.000	.278	6	21	3	5	1	0	1	4	0	1	0	0	8	1	0	.429	.273
Clark, Tony	B-R	6-7	245	6-15-72	.333	.667	.000	2	6	2	2	0	0	1	1	0	1	0	0	0	0	0	.833	.429
Counsell, Craig	L-R	6-0	185	8-21-70	.182	—	.182	2	11	2	2	0	0	0	0	1	0	0	0	1	0	0	.182	.250
DeCarlo, Mike	R-R	6-1	215	3-13-82	1.000	—	1.000	1	1	0	1	0	0	0	0	0	0	0	0	0	0	0	1.000	1.000
Drew, Stephen	L-R	6-1	185	3-16-83	.284	.376	.253	83	342	55	97	16	3	13	51	33	0	1	7	50	3	3	.462	.340
Erickson, Matt	L-R	5-11	190	7-30-75	.270	.184	.287	103	293	42	79	12	0	2	24	28	7	3	1	48	4	2	.331	.347
Gil, Jerry	R-R	6-3	195	10-14-82	.128	.133	.125	16	47	6	6	1	0	1	3	0	1	1	0	15	1	0	.213	.146
Gonzalez, Alberto	R-R	5-11	167	4-18-83	.200	.200	.200	4	15	2	3	0	0	0	1	1	0	0	1	0	0	0	.200	.294
Green, Andy	R-R	5-9	180	7-7-77	.240	.125	.294	18	75	10	18	3	0	1	6	4	1	0	0	14	0	0	.320	.288
Hairston, Scott	R-R	6-0	200	5-25-80	.323	.303	.332	98	381	83	123	22	1	26	81	52	4	0	3	78	3	0	.591	.407
Hammock, Robby	R-R	5-10	185	5-13-77	.290	.249	.297	103	369	57	107	21	1	20	65	24	7	1	4	59	2	2	.515	.342
Montero, Miguel	L-R	5-11	195	7-9-83	.321	.282	.337	36	134	21	43	5	0	7	29	14	4	0	2	21	1	1	.515	.396
Perez, Kenny	B-R	6-2	190	9-28-81	.254	.211	.273	100	284	35	72	9	2	2	29	26	1	3	1	41	6	3	.320	.317
Quentin, Carlos	R-R	6-1	225	8-28-82	.289	.253	.303	85	318	66	92	30	3	9	52	45	31	0	2	46	5	0	.487	.424
Sadler, Donnie	R-R	5-6	175	6-17-75	.279	.343	.244	76	190	36	53	13	4	1	13	26	0	5	0	40	6	2	.405	.366
Weber, Jon	L-L	5-10	190	1-20-78	.321	.255	.350	46	168	26	54	18	0	5	27	15	1	1	3	23	1	1	.518	.374
2-team (82 Las Vegas)					.283	—	—	128	428	65	121	36	1	7	58	42	4	3	4	62	10	4	.421	.349
Williams, Marland	R-R	5-9	185	6-22-81	.185	.200	.176	10	27	5	5	2	0	0	1	4	0	0	1	0	8	2	1	.259	.290
Young, Chris	R-R	6-2	180	9-5-83	.276	.209	.301	100	402	78	111	32	4	21	77	52	6	1	5	71	17	5	.532	.363

PITCHING	B-T	HT	WT	DOB	W	L	ERA	G	GS	CG	SV	IP	H	R	ER	HR	BB	SO	AVG	vLH	vRH	K/9	BB/9
Aquino, Greg	R-R	6-1	190	1-11-78	2	0	0.00	9	0	0	1	12	6	0	0	0	4	15	.154	.118	.182	11.57	3.09
Arreola, Daryl	R-R	6-0	170	11-20-82	1	0	0.00	1	0	0	0	3	1	0	0	0	1	1	.100	.000	.125	3.00	3.00
Bacsik, Mike	L-L	6-3	190	11-11-77	11	0	2.79	28	10	0	0	87	81	28	27	8	19	57	.248	.238	.253	5.90	1.97
Bajenaru, Jeff	R-R	6-1	200	3-21-78	4	3	4.50	52	3	0	7	80	79	47	40	6	40	72	.258	.277	.242	8.10	4.50
Bass, Adam	R-R	6-6	220	7-31-81	9	4	4.76	20	20	1	0	125	136	68	66	13	40	68	.278	.305	.253	4.91	2.89
Bruney, Brian	R-R	6-2	245	2-17-82	0	1	33.75	4	0	0	0	3	10	12	10	2	4	4	.556	.667	.333	13.50	13.50
Castellanos, Jonathan	R-R	6-2	214	9-17-81	0	0	4.50	1	0	0	0	2	3	1	1	0	0	1	.375	.667	.200	4.50	0.00
Choate, Randy	L-L	6-1	195	9-5-75	6	0	2.17	43	1	0	8	46	39	13	11	0	10	44	.228	.190	.250	8.67	1.97
Cruz, Juan	R-R	6-2	155	10-15-78	0	0	2.70	1	1	0	0	3	4	1	1	0	1	4	.286	.333	.250	10.80	2.70
Daigle, Casey	R-R	6-5	250	4-4-81	3	5	4.69	42	0	0	4	48	60	31	25	6	17	41	.302	.315	.291	7.69	3.19
Erickson, Matt	L-R	5-11	190	7-30-75	0	0	0.00	1	0	0	0	0	0	0	0	0	0	0	.000	.000	—	0.00	0.00
Gonzalez, Edgar	R-R	6-0	225	2-23-83	3	8	3.90	24	24	3	0	138	142	69	60	11	27	107	.268	.289	.251	6.96	1.76
Gonzalez, Enrique	R-R	5-10	210	7-14-82	4	3	2.24	10	10	0	0	60	61	22	15	2	14	35	.263	.282	.241	5.22	2.09
Jarvis, Kevin	L-R	6-2	200	8-1-69	3	6	3.44	15	13	0	0	84	76	40	32	7	22	58	.240	.287	.176	6.24	2.37
Kinsey, Chris	R-R	6-3	230	10-18-82	0	0	12.00	3	0	0	0	3	4	4	4	2	1	5	.308	.200	.375	15.00	3.00
Koplove, Mike	R-R	5-11	175	8-30-76	5	0	3.60	48	0	0	0	65	63	31	26	4	24	49	.260	.260	.261	6.78	3.32
MacLane, Evan	L-L	6-2	190	11-4-82	1	0	3.38	2	1	0	0	8	10	3	3	1	1	4	.323	.444	.273	4.50	1.13
Medders, Brandon	R-R	6-1	190	1-26-80	0	1	1.50	5	0	0	0	6	4	2	1	0	1	9	.200	.167	.250	13.50	1.50
Mulholland, Terry	R-L	6-3	225	3-9-63	1	1	3.38	3	1	0	0	11	9	4	4	0	3	5	.257	.250	.261	4.22	2.53
Murphy, Bill	L-L	5-11	215	5-9-81	5	4	5.58	37	9	0	0	81	86	53	50	5	38	72	.279	.368	.244	8.03	4.24
Musser, Neal	L-L	6-1	215	8-25-80	1	3	5.45	8	7	0	0	36	44	26	22	4	24	18	.306	.356	.283	4.46	5.94
2-team (2 Omaha)					2	3	4.70	10	9	0	0	46	51	28	24	6	27	24	—	—	—	4.70	5.28
Nippert, Dustin	R-R	6-8	225	5-6-81	13	8	4.87	25	24	1	0	140	161	85	76	11	52	130	.290	.289	.290	8.34	3.33
Ohlendorf, Ross	R-R	6-4	235	8-8-82	0	0	1.80	1	1	0	0	5	6	1	1	0	0	4	.300	.200	.333	7.20	0.00
Ortiz, Russ	R-R	6-1	220	6-5-74	1	0	2.61	4	4	0	0	21	22	7	6	1	5	10	.268	.298	.229	4.35	2.18
Owings, Micah	R-R	6-5	220	9-28-82	10	0	3.70	15	15	1	0	88	96	40	36	4	34	61	.291	.317	.266	6.26	3.49
Pena, Tony	R-R	6-1	220	1-9-82	3	1	1.71	24	0	0	7	26	17	6	5	1	2	21	.183	.200	.170	7.18	0.68
Schultz, Mike	R-R	6-7	220	11-28-79	2	4	3.52	49	0	0	4	54	58	22	21	1	19	41	.271	.337	.218	6.88	3.19
Slaten, Doug	L-L	6-5	200	2-4-80	2	1	0.45	18	0	0	2	20	10	2	1	0	7	21	.152	.069	.216	9.45	3.15
Valverde, Jose	R-R	6-4	255	7-24-79	1	0	3.06	15	0	0	3	18	13	9	6	1	10	18	.200	.229	.167	9.17	5.09

FIELDING

Catcher	PCT	G	PO	A	E	DP	PB
Brito	.998	64	423	36	1	3	5
Castillo	.962	6	46	4	2	0	1
Hammock	.992	53	341	29	3	1	6
Montero	.976	28	192	10	5	1	2

First Base	PCT	G	PO	A	E	DP
Barden	.986	10	66	3	1	9
Carter	.987	124	1042	69	15	106
Clark	1.000	1	8	2	0	1
Hammock	1.000	11	102	8	0	10
Perez	1.000	13	68	3	0	7

Second Base	PCT	G	PO	A	E	DP
Barden	.973	22	42	68	3	15
Callaspo	.982	70	113	210	6	44
Erickson	.995	45	92	124	1	41
Gil	.857	1	1	5	1	1
Green	1.000	5	10	13	0	1

	PCT	G	PO	A	E	DP
Perez	1.000	1	1	1	0	0
Sadler	.982	14	17	39	1	11
Third Base	**PCT**	**G**	**PO**	**A**	**E**	**DP**
Barden	.957	79	45	157	9	17
Callaspo	.953	23	12	49	3	6
Erickson	—	1	0	0	0	0
Gil	1.000	1	1	2	0	1
Green	1.000	3	3	6	0	1
Hammock	.500	2	1	0	1	0
Perez	.966	49	32	81	4	11
Sadler	—	1	0	0	0	0

Shortstop	PCT	G	PO	A	E	DP
Barden	.952	20	30	70	5	21
Callaspo	.955	25	31	75	5	17
Drew	.955	82	108	213	15	38
Erickson	1.000	1	1	0	0	0
Gil	1.000	1	1	4	0	2

	PCT	G	PO	A	E	DP
Gonzalez	1.000	4	10	12	0	4
Green	.957	8	9	13	1	2
Perez	1.000	4	5	15	0	4
Sadler	.850	6	4	13	3	3
Outfield	**PCT**	**G**	**PO**	**A**	**E**	**DP**
Callaspo	—	1	0	0	0	0
Erickson	.974	29	36	2	1	0
Gil	.818	10	9	0	2	0
Green	1.000	3	4	0	0	0
Hairston	.980	87	144	3	3	0
Hammock	1.000	36	58	0	0	0
Murphy	1.000	1	1	0	0	0
Perez	.957	18	21	1	1	0
Quentin	.981	81	157	2	3	0
Sadler	.986	43	65	3	1	0
Weber	.971	45	92	7	3	2
Williams	.941	9	14	2	1	1
Young	.982	100	259	8	5	3

Tennessee Smokies — Double-A

Southern League

BATTING	B-T	HT	WT	DOB	AVG	vLH	vRH	G	AB	R	H	2B	3B	HR	RBI	BB	HBP	SH	SF	SO	SB	CS	SLG	OBP
Avlas, Phil	R-R	5-11	183	12-17-82	.263	.306	.227	93	278	43	73	17	0	7	29	46	4	4	2	50	3	5	.399	.373
Ball, Jarred	B-R	6-0	185	4-18-83	.192	.300	.151	20	73	8	14	2	2	0	7	10	0	0	0	32	0	1	.274	.263
Castillo, Wilkin	B-R	6-0	170	6-1-84	.250	.259	.245	27	76	7	19	3	0	0	5	6	2	2	2	10	1	0	.289	.314
Cota, Jesus	L-R	6-3	220	11-7-81	.233	.189	.259	126	446	48	104	19	0	15	54	30	2	1	3	76	2	1	.377	.283
D'Antona, James	R-R	6-2	210	5-12-82	.310	.365	.269	126	461	72	143	29	0	17	67	54	2	0	4	88	2	1	.484	.382
Frazier, Alex	R-R	6-4	225	12-21-80	.233	.191	.256	103	313	36	73	16	0	9	43	16	6	0	5	85	1	2	.371	.279
Garrabrants, Steve	R-R	5-10	170	11-18-81	.220	.217	.222	105	241	28	53	8	0	3	26	30	7	9	0	59	4	4	.290	.324
Gil, Jerry	R-R	6-3	195	10-14-82	.269	.283	.260	112	446	71	120	27	6	26	86	18	5	8	4	111	6	6	.531	.302
Gonzalez, Alberto	R-R	5-11	167	4-18-83	.290	.273	.302	129	434	67	126	20	3	6	50	37	8	13	2	42	5	1	.392	.356
Gonzalez, Carlos	L-L	6-1	180	10-17-85	.213	.158	.238	18	61	11	13	6	0	2	5	7	0	1	0	12	1	0	.410	.294
Haley, Adam	L-R	6-0	171	9-4-80	.155	.333	.138	39	71	5	11	3	0	0	1	6	2	0	0	18	0	1	.197	.241
Montero, Miguel	L-R	5-11	195	7-9-83	.270	.248	.282	81	289	24	78	18	0	10	46	39	5	0	4	44	0	3	.436	.362
Morgan, Matthew	R-R	6-2	195	8-10-81	.364	.551	.267	6	22	4	8	2	0	0	3	2	0	1	0	5	0	0	.455	.417
Murillo, Agustin	R-R	6-2	193	5-5-82	.235	.247	.226	118	362	44	85	9	0	8	38	36	12	7	3	58	3	1	.326	.322
Reynolds, Mark	R-R	6-1	200	8-3-83	.272	.269	.274	30	114	23	31	7	0	8	21	11	2	0	0	37	0	1	.544	.346
Richar, Danny	L-R	6-0	170	6-9-83	.292	.276	.301	130	480	79	140	25	5	8	42	52	3	6	7	77	15	5	.415	.360
Zeringue, Jon	R-R	6-2	215	3-29-83	.217	.176	.237	69	203	15	44	5	1	4	19	19	2	3	1	43	1	2	.310	.289

PITCHING	B-T	HT	WT	DOB	W	L	ERA	G	GS	CG	SV	IP	H	R	ER	HR	BB	SO	AVG	vLH	vRH	K/9	BB/9
Bass, Adam	R-R	6-6	220	7-31-81	2	3	4.50	9	9	1	0	46	47	24	23	4	16	42	.266	.286	.254	8.22	3.13
Castellanos, Jonathan	R-R	6-0	214	9-17-81	3	1	4.50	24	1	0	0	36	31	21	18	5	14	23	.228	.175	.250	5.75	3.50
Chico, Matt	L-L	5-11	200	6-10-83	7	2	2.22	13	13	0	0	81	62	22	20	6	21	63	.211	.215	.210	7.00	2.33
Elliott, Matt	R-R	6-0	190	4-6-84	2	1	5.91	9	0	0	0	11	14	7	7	1	3	10	.318	.158	.440	8.44	2.53
Glant, Dustin	R-R	6-2	200	7-20-81	4	6	4.79	51	0	0	1	62	69	39	33	7	22	49	.285	.244	.306	7.11	3.19
Goocher, Clint	L-L	6-2	195	6-15-82	7	7	3.49	42	10	0	0	85	88	39	33	6	30	52	.274	.281	.271	5.51	3.18
Jackson, Steven	R-R	6-5	215	3-15-82	8	11	2.65	24	24	1	0	150	131	52	44	6	45	125	.239	.293	.204	7.52	2.71
Kinsey, Chris	R-R	6-3	230	10-18-82	2	2	3.76	45	0	0	3	55	52	25	23	6	27	39	.254	.288	.235	6.38	4.42
Mock, Garrett	R-R	6-4	215	4-25-83	4	8	4.95	23	23	0	0	131	144	81	72	14	50	117	.280	.289	.274	8.04	3.44

Name	B-T	HT	WT	DOB	W	L	ERA	G	GS	CG	SV	IP	H	R	ER	HR	BB	SO	AVG	vLH	vRH	K/9	BB/9
Murphy, Bill	L-L	5-11	215	5-9-81	0	1	5.57	5	4	0	0	21	22	13	13	2	9	26	.272	.353	.250	11.14	3.86
Ohlendorf, Ross	R-R	6-4	235	8-8-82	10	8	3.29	27	27	4	0	178	180	70	65	13	29	125	.271	.324	.236	6.33	1.47
Owings, Micah	R-R	6-5	220	9-28-82	6	2	2.91	12	12	0	0	74	66	24	24	4	17	69	.246	.286	.211	8.35	2.06
Pena, Tony	R-R	6-1	220	1-9-82	2	0	0.89	17	0	0	6	20	18	2	2	0	5	17	.231	.241	.224	7.52	2.21
Schultz, Mike	R-R	6-7	220	11-28-79	1	0	1.54	9	0	0	3	12	4	2	2	0	4	7	.108	.083	.120	5.40	3.09
Shappi, A.J.	R-R	6-2	195	10-16-82	1	3	5.59	5	5	0	0	29	40	21	18	3	9	17	.328	.429	.275	5.28	2.79
Slaten, Doug	L-L	6-5	200	2-4-80	2	3	1.88	40	0	0	8	43	31	12	9	1	15	59	.209	.208	.210	12.35	3.14
Smith, Gregory	L-L	6-2	190	12-22-83	5	4	3.90	11	11	0	0	60	65	32	26	4	23	38	.284	.231	.299	5.70	3.45
White, Bill	L-L	6-4	215	11-20-78	0	1	3.53	54	0	0	12	64	59	27	25	6	33	76	.252	.231	.263	10.74	4.66
Wilkinson, Matthew	L-R	6-3	205	10-25-77	4	6	4.19	48	0	0	2	58	68	35	27	6	25	59	.287	.300	.280	9.16	3.88

FIELDING

Catcher	PCT	G	PO	A	E	DP	PB
Avlas	.979	41	263	17	6	3	1
Castillo	.994	23	161	17	1	2	2
D'Antona	.947	7	34	2	2	0	1
Montero	.997	75	548	51	2	4	8
Morgan	.947	2	17	1	1	0	0

First Base	PCT	G	PO	A	E	DP
Avlas	.938	2	14	1	1	0
Cota	.993	73	556	50	4	53
D'Antona	.988	75	614	39	8	52
Murillo	1.000	7	35	5	0	1

Second Base	PCT	G	PO	A	E	DP
Avlas	1.000	1	1	1	0	0
Gil	.957	10	20	24	2	4
Haley	1.000	3	1	0	0	0
Reynolds	.976	8	19	21	1	2
Richar	.986	125	229	322	8	65

Third Base	PCT	G	PO	A	E	DP
Avlas	—	1	0	0	0	0
D'Antona	.927	36	14	62	6	3
Garrabrants	—	1	0	0	0	0
Gil	1.000	3	0	5	0	1
Haley	.923	6	2	10	1	0
Morgan	.600	2	1	2	2	0
Murillo	.955	103	53	178	11	14
Reynolds	.950	11	3	16	1	1

Shortstop	PCT	G	PO	A	E	DP
Gil	.924	15	24	37	5	8
A. Gonzalez	.977	128	212	391	14	82
Haley	.939	7	11	20	2	5

Outfield	PCT	G	PO	A	E	DP
Avlas	.986	50	63	5	1	3
Ball	1.000	19	34	0	0	0
Cota	.974	47	74	2	2	1
D'Antona	—	1	0	0	0	0
Frazier	.963	77	103	2	4	0
Garrabrants	.957	73	133	2	6	1
Gil	.972	90	165	11	5	2
C. Gonzalez	.969	18	28	3	1	0
Haley	1.000	11	11	0	0	0
Morgan	1.000	2	1	1	0	0
Reynolds	1.000	15	21	2	0	1
Zeringue	.975	65	111	7	3	1

Lancaster JetHawks

High Class A

California League

BATTING

Name	B-T	HT	WT	DOB	AVG	vLH	vRH	G	AB	R	H	2B	3B	HR	RBI	BB	HBP	SH	SF	SO	SB	CS	SLG	OBP
Bonifacio, Emilio	B-R	5-11	178	4-23-85	.321	.252	.347	130	546	117	175	35	7	7	50	44	6	8	4	104	61	14	.449	.375
Brito, Javier	R-R	6-3	210	3-25-83	.356	.388	.335	85	264	63	94	20	1	16	60	44	5	0	6	48	1	2	.621	.448
Bruce, Derek	R-R	6-2	190	8-3-82	.308	.291	.315	99	321	49	99	13	1	2	35	10	7	15	2	40	6	3	.374	.341
Burgess, Brandon	B-R	6-4	225	2-24-83	.265	.259	.267	123	434	74	115	15	2	26	84	39	28	0	4	132	8	8	.488	.360
Castillo, Wilkin	R-R	6-0	170	6-1-84	.285	.200	.321	56	200	25	57	10	1	3	19	13	1	2	2	24	9	2	.390	.329
Counsell, Craig	L-R	6-0	185	8-21-70	1.000	1.000	—	1	3	1	3	1	0	0	1	0	0	0	0	0	0	0	1.333	1.000
Ford, Joshua	R-R	6-2	235	1-17-83	.293	.239	.309	107	393	57	115	17	0	7	52	35	6	0	2	69	0	3	.389	.358
Gonzalez, Carlos	L-L	6-1	180	10-17-85	.300	.296	.302	104	403	82	121	35	4	21	94	30	10	0	9	104	15	8	.563	.356
Hankerd, Cyle	R-R	6-3	180	1-24-85	.369	.286	.409	18	65	15	24	4	0	8	23	8	5	0	0	9	0	0	.800	.474
Mercado, Richard	R-R	6-0	205	5-23-83	.179	.200	.171	38	117	8	21	4	2	1	15	12	0	1	3	26	1	1	.274	.256
Milons, Jereme	R-R	6-2	205	2-5-83	.301	.303	.300	100	386	56	116	11	6	11	54	30	0	1	3	95	14	5	.446	.348
Nicolas, Cesar	R-R	6-4	230	4-17-82	.302	.295	.304	120	434	78	131	34	0	14	80	60	14	2	5	81	1	2	.477	.400
Rahl, Chris	R-R	6-0	185	12-5-83	.327	.314	.333	131	568	101	186	44	8	13	83	35	5	0	5	119	19	10	.502	.369
Reynolds, Mark	R-R	6-1	200	8-3-83	.337	.282	.359	76	273	64	92	18	2	23	77	41	3	0	5	72	1	1	.670	.422
Ryal, Rusty	R-R	6-2	195	3-16-83	.277	.301	.268	97	350	53	97	17	6	11	42	23	12	1	1	78	8	3	.454	.342
Santana, Mayo	R-R	6-3	190	8-23-81	.333	.364	.313	11	27	7	9	1	0	3	7	0	0	0	0	4	0	1	.704	.333
Zeringue, Jon	R-R	6-2	215	3-29-83	.278	.400	.230	43	158	22	44	12	1	5	21	9	2	2	2	40	2	0	.462	.320

PITCHING

Name	B-T	HT	WT	DOB	W	L	ERA	G	GS	CG	SV	IP	H	R	ER	HR	BB	SO	AVG	vLH	vRH	K/9	BB/9
Baeza, Eduardo	R-R	6-1	190	10-19-84	1	4	7.57	10	6	0	0	36	57	33	30	2	21	26	.368	.364	.372	6.56	5.30
Bono, Kyle	R-R	6-3	205	6-29-83	0	0	27.00	1	0	0	0	1	4	4	4	0	4	1	.500	.333	.600	6.75	27.00
Bruce, Derek	R-R	6-2	190	8-3-82	0	0	18.00	1	0	0	0	1	3	2	2	1	1	0	.500	.400	1.000	9.00	9.00
Chico, Matt	L-L	5-11	200	6-10-83	3	4	3.75	10	10	0	0	50	48	25	21	5	11	49	.239	.341	.210	8.76	1.97
Coffin, Ryan	R-R	6-5	205	8-5-81	0	1	6.41	17	0	0	0	27	38	21	19	3	14	18	.345	.487	.268	6.08	4.73
Cupps, Anthony	R-R	6-3	198	5-31-83	3	0	5.59	5	5	0	0	29	36	18	18	2	17	16	.319	.296	.357	4.97	5.28
Doyle, Jared	R-L	6-0	200	1-30-81	3	1	5.98	46	0	0	4	65	62	49	43	3	46	40	.253	.338	.214	5.57	6.40
Elliott, Matt	R-R	6-0	190	4-6-84	2	4	4.02	43	0	0	24	47	53	27	21	6	28	66	.282	.259	.299	12.64	5.36
Evans, Cody	R-R	6-5	190	9-3-83	2	3	8.22	11	11	0	0	58	95	60	53	15	19	25	.364	.351	.372	3.88	2.95
Fowles, Matt	B-R	6-3	220	6-3-83	4	1	3.84	37	0	0	1	59	50	26	25	4	47	53	.229	.267	.197	8.13	7.21
Green, Matthew	R-R	6-5	195	1-5-82	5	12	5.14	27	27	0	0	137	182	99	78	15	51	96	.318	.324	.314	6.32	3.36
Guerrero, Hipolito	L-L	6-0	149	6-13-83	3	4	7.44	46	0	0	0	65	85	59	54	7	38	56	.315	.270	.332	7.71	5.23
Kinsey, Chris	R-R	6-3	230	10-18-82	3	0	0.00	6	0	0	0	11	8	3	0	0	9	13	.195	.286	.148	10.32	7.15
Mercado, Richard	R-R	6-0	205	5-23-83	0	0	27.00	1	0	0	0	1	4	2	2	1	0	1	.667	.750	.500	0.00	13.50
Pohlman, Daniel	R-R	6-1	215	1-1-82	3	8	6.95	55	0	0	7	66	92	59	51	5	44	58	.329	.342	.319	7.91	6.00
Raab, Kellen	L-L	6-6	225	2-16-82	9	8	6.84	30	22	0	0	122	197	104	93	13	36	79	.370	.380	.366	5.81	2.65
Rosen, Mark	L-L	5-11	210	6-30-84	2	4	5.13	38	0	0	2	60	58	44	34	5	39	52	.246	.325	.208	7.84	5.88
Shappi, A.J.	R-R	6-2	195	10-16-82	2	7	5.58	22	22	0	0	123	165	97	76	18	32	60	.322	.327	.319	4.40	2.35
Silva, Jesus	R-R	6-0	199	12-24-82	2	1	4.41	11	6	0	0	33	35	17	16	5	15	24	.285	.281	.288	6.61	4.13
Smith, Gregory	L-L	6-2	190	12-22-83	9	0	1.63	13	13	0	0	88	57	21	16	3	31	71	.190	.225	.185	7.23	3.16
Valverde, Jonatan	R-R	6-3	185	4-4-83	2	2	9.11	21	0	0	0	27	50	32	27	5	14	17	.385	.345	.413	5.74	4.73
Vasquez, Esmerling	R-R	6-1	154	11-7-83	4	9	5.89	34	18	0	0	118	129	89	77	9	51	115	.271	.301	.245	8.80	3.90

FIELDING

Catcher	PCT	G	PO	A	E	DP	PB
Castillo	.993	36	260	22	2	4	11
Ford	.987	86	541	60	8	6	19
Mercado	1.000	26	148	14	0	2	2

First Base	PCT	G	PO	A	E	DP
Brito	.986	31	205	13	3	24
Burgess	1.000	1	3	0	0	0
Mercado	1.000	2	15	1	0	2
Nicolas	.991	115	899	91	9	101
Reynolds	.967	8	26	3	1	4

Second Base	PCT	G	PO	A	E	DP
Bonifacio	.969	129	277	369	21	89
Bruce	1.000	3	4	7	0	2
Burgess	.909	1	5	5	1	0
Reynolds	.982	10	26	29	1	10
Zeringue	1.000	1	1	2	0	1

Third Base	PCT	G	PO	A	E	DP
Brito	.600	1	0	3	2	0

Outfield	PCT	G	PO	A	E	DP
Burgess	.876	51	39	74	16	6
Reynolds	.870	17	9	31	6	1
Ryal	.894	75	60	143	24	17
Santana	1.000	6	4	7	0	1

Shortstop	PCT	G	PO	A	E	DP
Bruce	.950	95	137	242	20	67
Reynolds	.963	32	48	81	5	18
Ryal	.974	23	30	46	2	7
Santana	.909	5	4	6	1	1

Outfield	PCT	G	PO	A	E	DP
Brito	1.000	27	24	2	0	0
Burgess	.952	50	76	4	4	0
Castillo	.667	1	1	1	1	0
Gonzalez	.943	101	190	10	12	4
Hankerd	1.000	17	35	2	0	0
Milons	.952	83	154	8	8	0
Rahl	.976	122	281	3	7	1
Reynolds	.933	8	13	1	1	0
Zeringue	1.000	34	61	3	0	1

South Bend Silver Hawks — Low Class A

Midwest League

BATTING	B-T	HT	WT	DOB	AVG	vLH	vRH	G	AB	R	H	2B	3B	HR	RBI	BB	HBP	SH	SF	SO	SB	CS	SLG	OBP
Batten, Joseph	R-R	5-10	175	12-14-84	.133	.000	.182	4	15	1	2	0	0	0	1	1	1	0	0	3	1	0	.133	.235
Byrne, Bryan	L-R	6-3	200	4-30-84	.286	.297	.282	120	437	68	125	24	0	10	72	70	8	0	7	88	3	2	.410	.389
Ciriaco, Pedro	R-R	6-0	150	9-27-85	.264	.268	.262	128	550	77	145	15	5	2	32	32	5	10	3	96	19	8	.320	.308
Crouch, Will	R-R	6-3	220	8-13-82	.226	.250	.217	79	283	50	64	11	1	13	34	38	10	2	2	76	0	2	.410	.336
Cruz, Ricardo	R-R	5-11	175	8-11-83	.111	.000	.133	19	54	2	6	0	0	1	5	3	0	1	1	30	1	2	.167	.155
Curreri, Frank	L-R	6-4	215	12-4-82	.285	.297	.282	64	207	35	59	15	0	6	38	37	1	3	1	56	1	2	.444	.394
Ferrer, Manuel	R-R	5-11	168	2-15-85	.246	.155	.282	78	248	20	61	5	4	1	26	23	1	5	0	58	3	5	.310	.313
Gulick, Travis	R-R	6-3	215	5-17-83	.281	.167	.350	8	32	6	9	4	0	0	3	2	0	0	0	5	0	0	.406	.324
Hendricks, Trey	B-R	6-4	200	8-8-82	.230	.226	.231	103	379	33	87	16	0	6	47	26	2	1	2	56	3	0	.319	.281
Mena, Steve	R-R	6-4	210	1-24-85	.264	.227	.276	107	349	34	92	20	0	8	47	39	9	3	1	104	1	7	.390	.352
Mercado, Orlando	R-R	5-10	215	3-13-85	.247	.271	.235	86	292	38	72	20	0	11	58	40	4	4	1	36	1	1	.428	.344
Mercado, Richard	R-R	6-0	220	5-23-83	.245	.333	.197	27	94	9	23	5	1	0	10	6	0	0	1	23	0	1	.319	.287
Septimo, Leyson	L-L	6-0	150	7-7-85	.251	.172	.275	132	529	79	133	22	5	6	51	36	9	12	0	112	10	10	.346	.310
Sosa, Ricardo	R-R	6-1	205	5-24-84	.290	.295	.289	90	334	48	97	18	2	5	36	27	8	0	2	52	5	2	.401	.356
Thomson, Gregory	L-L	6-1	205	6-4-83	.277	.250	.284	112	372	56	103	28	2	1	40	30	11	1	0	66	14	3	.395	.349
Upton, Justin	R-R	6-1	195	8-25-87	.263	.175	.290	113	438	71	115	28	1	12	66	52	5	0	6	96	15	7	.413	.343

PITCHING	B-T	HT	WT	DOB	W	L	ERA	G	GS	CG	SV	IP	H	R	ER	HR	BB	SO	AVG	vLH	vRH	K/9	BB/9
Baeza, Eduardo	R-R	6-1	190	10-19-84	3	2	2.60	10	10	0	0	55	45	18	16	1	15	53	.215	.253	.182	8.62	2.44
Baxter, Jake	R-R	6-5	210	11-9-83	3	2	4.45	19	0	0	1	30	35	15	15	2	8	17	.285	.240	.315	5.04	2.37
2-team (16 West Michigan)					3	5	3.86	35	0	0	1	58	62	30	25	7	20	39	—	—	—	6.02	3.09
Bongiovanni, Vincent	R-R	6-5	215	1-11-83	7	3	3.75	32	11	1	5	84	74	41	35	2	42	67	.229	.279	.196	7.18	4.50
Christianson, Chase	R-R	6-5	220	12-11-84	0	0	9.00	3	0	0	0	3	5	3	3	1	1	2	.385	.333	.400	6.00	3.00
Cory, Forrest	R-L	6-3	205	10-13-83	4	2	1.99	37	1	0	3	68	49	18	15	3	15	47	.199	.185	.208	6.22	1.99
Cupps, Anthony	R-R	6-3	198	5-31-83	7	4	4.72	22	22	1	0	130	159	80	68	7	43	72	.301	.284	.316	5.00	2.98
Doherty, Ryan	R-R	7-1	255	2-2-84	9	1	2.59	39	0	0	5	63	50	25	18	2	20	76	.214	.244	.196	10.91	2.87
Duran, Enmanuel	R-R	6-2	205	11-7-84	2	4	5.85	36	0	0	2	52	55	39	34	3	22	48	.268	.260	.273	8.25	3.78
Evans, Cody	R-R	6-5	190	9-3-83	5	7	3.02	16	16	3	0	104	92	40	35	7	19	70	.237	.242	.232	6.04	1.64
Howard, Adam	R-R	6-4	200	8-16-83	9	5	3.90	30	20	0	0	134	138	64	58	7	30	101	.266	.278	.258	6.78	2.01
Julio, Donald	R-R	6-1	165	8-12-83	3	1	2.66	38	1	0	3	68	58	32	20	4	15	67	.225	.223	.226	8.91	2.00
Newby, Kyler	R-R	6-4	225	2-22-85	6	1	2.05	28	0	0	11	44	22	10	10	0	19	64	.151	.241	.091	13.09	3.89
Rocha, Angel	L-L	6-3	205	11-15-84	0	0	18.00	4	0	0	0	3	6	6	6	1	1	10	.000	.167	.000	0.00	30.00
Sanchez, Ramon (Perez)	R-R	6-3	195	5-6-84	1	10	7.66	33	7	0	1	67	81	67	57	3	44	47	.303	.306	.302	6.31	5.91
Schreppel, Ryan	L-L	6-2	195	6-2-84	6	13	5.00	26	23	0	0	139	154	87	77	15	59	72	.285	.317	.276	4.67	3.83
Torra, Matthew	R-R	6-3	225	6-29-84	0	1	1.80	7	7	0	0	25	24	7	5	0	5	20	.258	.296	.242	7.20	1.80
Valverde, Jonatan	R-R	6-3	185	4-4-83	1	1	2.57	12	0	0	5	14	16	5	4	1	3	12	.314	.231	.400	7.71	1.93
Wright, Kyle	R-R	6-3	170	4-27-83	8	5	3.69	32	18	0	0	124	156	72	51	7	17	103	.305	.296	.310	7.46	1.23

FIELDING

Catcher	PCT	G	PO	A	E	DP	PB
Curreri	.990	47	345	35	4	4	4
O. Mercado	.990	78	520	52	6	4	14
R. Mercado	.981	15	91	11	2	0	1

First Base	PCT	G	PO	A	E	DP
Byrne	.990	95	815	59	9	65
Crouch	.988	29	227	11	3	19
Curreri	1.000	2	17	2	0	4
Hendricks	1.000	11	79	11	0	5
Mena	1.000	2	12	2	0	2

Second Base	PCT	G	PO	A	E	DP
Batten	.938	3	5	10	1	1

	PCT	G	PO	A	E	DP
Cruz	.971	17	27	39	2	10
Ferrer	.961	66	102	195	12	32
Hendricks	—	1	0	0	0	0
Mena	.967	58	89	149	8	28

Third Base	PCT	G	PO	A	E	DP
Cruz	1.000	2	0	4	0	0
Ferrer	—	1	0	0	0	0
Hendricks	.800	4	1	3	1	0
Mena	.929	49	37	80	9	10
Sosa	.933	85	73	150	16	9

Shortstop	PCT	G	PO	A	E	DP
Ciriaco	.927	128	200	369	45	72

	PCT	G	PO	A	E	DP
Ferrer	.838	9	11	20	6	3

Outfield	PCT	G	PO	A	E	DP
Batten	—	1	0	0	0	0
Crouch	.933	9	13	1	1	0
Gulick	1.000	8	13	1	0	0
Hendricks	.968	64	87	5	3	1
Mena	—	1	0	0	0	0
R. Mercado	—	1	0	0	0	0
Septimo	.972	131	291	21	9	5
Thomson	.978	105	212	9	5	3
Upton	.980	105	283	4	6	1

Yakima Bears — Short-Season

Northwest League

BATTING	B-T	HT	WT	DOB	AVG	vLH	vRH	G	AB	R	H	2B	3B	HR	RBI	BB	HBP	SH	SF	SO	SB	CS	SLG	OBP
Batten, Joseph	R-R	5-10	175	12-14-84	.193	.194	.193	46	145	20	28	7	1	1	11	21	6	0	1	40	3	0	.276	.318
Brashear, Justin	L-R	6-3	200	1-19-85	.213	.182	.222	40	141	22	30	7	2	6	18	18	3	1	1	46	1	1	.418	.313
Byrne, Shane	B-R	6-3	190	9-14-83	.244	.180	.270	56	213	20	52	7	2	17	15	0	1	0	44	2	1	.324	.294
Contreras, Lester	R-R	5-11	190	7-30-84	.192	.160	.208	19	73	6	14	4	0	1	8	0	0	2	22	0	0	.288	.187
Cruz, Tito	R-R	5-10	205	8-28-84	.138	.186	.091	8	29	1	4	0	0	0	1	2	0	0	7	0	0	.138	.194
DeCarlo, Mike	R-R	6-1	215	3-13-82	.253	.310	.239	43	146	22	37	8	0	5	21	21	5	0	3	35	4	0	.411	.360
Dilone, Jose	L-R	6-2	179	9-12-84	.163	.082	.195	46	172	10	28	5	0	1	11	12	3	0	1	59	1	0	.209	.229
Hankerd, Cyle	R-R	6-3	180	1-24-85	.384	.404	.377	54	216	24	83	17	0	4	38	13	4	0	3	54	0	0	.519	.424
Janes, Connor	R-R	6-4	225	8-27-83	.197	.188	.200	17	61	4	12	1	0	1	5	7	1	0	0	25	3	0	.262	.290
Lajara, Luis	L-L	6-1	180	12-12-84	.133	.200	.100	4	15	0	2	1	0	0	0	4	0	0	0	4	0	0	.200	.133
Melendez, Joel	R-R	5-11	170	9-18-84	.235	.333	.214	5	17	1	4	0	0	0	2	1	0	0	0	7	1	0	.235	.235
Miller, Brad	R-R	6-5	220	6-25-83	.251	.263	.247	61	227	28	57	14	1	11	53	18	3	0	12	45	0	1	.467	.300
Parra, Julio	R-R	6-0	200	6-12-86	.094	.056	.143	12	32	0	3	1	0	0	2	1	0	1	0	5	0	0	.125	.147
Roman, Edwin	R-R	5-10	215	4-8-86	.249	.277	.241	59	213	40	53	9	1	6	27	27	6	2	4	45	2	6	.357	.342
Sharpe, Blake	R-R	6-2	185	9-10-83	.272	.295	.266	71	268	35	73	12	0	2	27	27	6	2	4	45	2	6	.340	.348
Side, Joey	R-R	6-3	190	12-4-83	.267	.306	.256	56	217	36	58	14	2	2	20	21	6	3	2	48	2	2	.378	.343
Summers, Houston	R-R	5-8	170	11-23-83	.143	.400	.087	10	28	2	4	1	0	0	0	2	0	0	0	10	1	1	.179	.226
Tully, Travis	L-R	5-8	170	1-31-84	.267	.293	.254	51	180	20	48	12	1	0	14	24	2	0	1	40	7	4	.278	.357
Watson, Jason	R-R	5-10	160	8-28-83	.182	.185	.181	58	198	27	36	3	1	0	14	27	7	0	1	40	1	4	.207	.300

ORGANIZATION STATISTICS

PITCHING

PITCHING	B-T	HT	WT	DOB	W	L	ERA	G	GS	CG	SV	IP	H	R	ER	HR	BB	SO	AVG	vLH	vRH	K/9	BB/9
Arreola, Daryl	R-R	6-0	170	11-20-82	2	1	1.85	17	0	0	0	24	19	7	5	0	8	17	.211	.115	.250	6.29	2.96
Beck, Chad	R-R	6-4	230	1-17-85	1	5	6.25	16	2	0	0	40	47	37	28	8	18	45	.296	.261	.310	10.04	4.02
Brown, Brooks	L-R	6-3	205	6-20-85	0	2	3.42	13	1	0	0	24	23	11	9	2	12	30	.250	.371	.175	11.41	4.56
Butler, Eric	R-R	6-4	235	12-26-83	3	5	4.15	15	15	0	0	78	74	40	36	3	46	67	.253	.182	.295	7.73	5.31
Christianson, Chase	R-R	6-5	220	12-11-84	1	4	3.20	21	0	0	3	25	28	14	9	0	11	23	.272	.387	.222	8.17	3.91
Church, Lorenzo	R-R	5-11	180	8-16-86	0	1	4.85	15	0	0	0	26	29	15	14	1	13	17	.299	.324	.286	5.88	4.50
Dove, Shane	L-L	6-2	185	7-22-84	5	6	2.26	16	14	1	0	88	78	38	22	5	18	72	.232	.179	.245	7.39	1.85
Duda, Peter	R-R	6-4	215	9-10-83	0	0	18.00	10	0	0	0	9	19	18	18	1	18	5	.442	.583	.387	5.00	18.00
Familia, Roberto	R-R	5-11	178	2-20-85	0	2	4.82	20	1	0	0	37	40	24	20	7	26	42	.272	.227	.291	10.13	6.27
Mahon, Reid	R-R	6-3	215	6-1-83	2	3	4.25	22	0	0	4	36	32	20	17	4	14	25	.229	.250	.216	6.25	3.50
Perez, Jorge	R-R	5-11	163	1-16-86	0	0	0.00	4	0	0	1	7	6	0	0	0	2	6	.250	.182	.308	7.71	2.57
Pfautz, Craig	R-L	6-3	190	9-13-84	3	0	5.16	21	0	0	1	30	39	23	17	0	10	12	.315	.313	.315	3.64	3.03
Romero, Edward	L-L	5-11	180	11-7-85	2	2	3.00	12	12	0	0	39	33	13	13	0	14	34	.228	.304	.213	7.85	3.23
Souther, Scott	R-R	6-2	186	11-4-82	2	8	4.35	15	14	0	0	83	89	51	40	5	24	39	.272	.260	.279	4.25	2.61
Stout, Ross	R-R	6-0	195	2-15-84	0	1	3.18	9	0	0	0	11	9	7	4	0	8	14	.220	.000	.290	11.12	6.35
Thompson, Bryant	R-R	6-2	190	8-26-85	0	3	3.20	15	1	0	2	20	21	8	7	0	7	25	.273	.261	.278	11.44	3.20
Valdez, Cesar	R-R	6-1	175	3-17-85	7	5	3.15	16	16	2	0	97	97	43	34	5	20	81	.257	.265	.252	7.52	1.86

FIELDING

Catcher	PCT	G	PO	A	E	DP	PB
Brashear	.986	34	256	23	4	1	3
Cruz	.968	8	52	9	2	0	3
DeCarlo	.981	26	183	22	4	2	8
Parra	1.000	12	74	4	0	1	1

First Base	PCT	G	PO	A	E	DP
Brashear	1.000	1	9	0	0	0
Contreras	.986	7	66	5	1	6
DeCarlo	.975	15	146	8	4	12
Janes	1.000	1	6	0	0	0
Miller	.994	52	461	37	3	43

Second Base	PCT	G	PO	A	E	DP
Batten	.936	44	79	112	13	24
Summers	.913	5	7	14	2	2
Watson	.957	31	64	93	7	24

Third Base	PCT	G	PO	A	E	DP
Contreras	1.000	10	3	25	0	2
Dilone	.874	45	23	95	17	8
Watson	.944	23	12	55	4	2

Shortstop	PCT	G	PO	A	E	DP
Batten	.700	2	1	6	3	1
Sharpe	.958	70	92	227	14	38

Watson	.947	5	8	10	1	1

Outfield	PCT	G	PO	A	E	DP
Batten	1.000	1	1	0	0	0
Byrne	.968	53	87	5	3	1
Hankerd	.963	40	72	5	3	2
Janes	1.000	13	20	1	0	1
Lajara	1.000	3	7	0	0	0
Melendez	1.000	5	5	0	0	0
Roman	.944	34	50	1	3	0
Side	.992	43	113	4	1	0
Tully	.963	42	76	3	3	3

Missoula Osprey — Rookie

Pioneer League

BATTING	B-T	HT	WT	DOB	AVG	vLH	vRH	G	AB	R	H	2B	3B	HR	RBI	BB	HBP	SH	SF	SO	SB	CS	SLG	OBP
Beshenich, Andrew	R-R	6-2	200	2-25-88	.429	.000	.500	4	7	1	3	1	0	0	0	1	0	0	1	0	0	0	.571	.556
Brashear, Justin	L-R	6-3	200	1-19-85	.219	.250	.212	20	64	13	14	4	0	3	6	11	0	2	0	16	0	0	.422	.333
Bustamante, Gerardo	R-R	5-8	184	6-10-86	.200	.222	.190	23	60	7	12	3	0	0	8	2	0	0	0	14	0	1	.250	.226
Cruz, Ricardo	R-R	5-11	175	8-11-83	.207	.147	.220	53	184	20	38	5	0	9	26	19	2	1	2	73	5	0	.380	.285
Dijol, Jose	R-R	6-2	186	11-7-84	.226	.265	.218	53	190	25	43	5	0	6	28	18	7	0	3	46	2	2	.347	.312
Elder, Jake	R-R	6-1	205	3-21-83	.107	.000	.120	9	28	4	3	0	0	1	2	2	1	0	0	4	0	0	.214	.194
Fie, Andrew	R-R	6-3	205	10-25-87	.259	.286	.252	67	255	33	66	23	2	6	31	27	3	0	4	81	8	5	.435	.318
Hester, John	R-R	6-4	210	9-14-83	.271	.158	.299	56	192	36	52	16	4	6	41	27	5	0	3	52	6	2	.490	.370
Janes, Connor	R-R	6-2	195	4-21-84	.375	.500	.350	9	24	5	9	2	0	2	8	5	2	0	0	6	1	0	.708	.516
Jones, Tyler	L-L	6-2	195	12-29-83	.287	.438	.253	63	265	50	76	10	5	4	17	9	7	4	0	43	21	5	.408	.327
McFeely, Shea	R-R	6-2	195	4-21-84	.251	.268	.247	53	195	31	49	8	5	5	37	24	3	0	2	38	4	2	.421	.330
Oxendine, Matthew	R-R	6-1	175	10-13-83	.248	.239	.250	61	238	46	59	8	0	3	31	27	3	2	2	35	7	3	.319	.330
Parra, Gerardo	L-L	6-1	186	5-6-87	.328	.396	.312	69	271	46	89	18	4	4	43	25	3	0	4	30	23	7	.469	.386
Parra, Julio	R-R	6-0	200	6-12-86	.231	.000	.257	15	39	4	9	1	0	0	8	5	1	0	0	3	1	1	.256	.333
Perales, Daniel	L-L	5-11	165	3-18-85	.275	.188	.295	67	255	42	70	13	5	7	39	25	7	2	1	35	12	4	.447	.354
Smith, Sean	R-R	5-10	170	3-6-83	.244	.226	.250	41	135	20	33	6	0	0	17	11	7	0	2	23	5	2	.289	.329
Summers, Houston	R-R	5-10	180	8-20-87	.200	.000	.250	7	20	5	4	1	0	0	2	5	0	0	2	1	1	0	.250	.407
Walker, Derrick	R-R	6-4	215	10-10-85	.223	.216	.225	45	139	20	31	3	0	1	11	29	6	0	1	45	13	1	.266	.377

PITCHING	B-T	HT	WT	DOB	W	L	ERA	G	GS	CG	SV	IP	H	R	ER	HR	BB	SO	AVG	vLH	vRH	K/9	BB/9
Ambriz, Hector	L-R	6-1	210	5-24-84	1	3	1.91	15	4	0	3	42	29	10	9	1	11	52	.192	.240	.168	11.06	2.34
Barnette, Anthony	R-R	6-2	190	11-9-83	6	4	3.89	15	15	0	0	76	81	41	33	9	20	74	.265	.253	.269	8.72	2.36
Brewer, Matthew	R-R	6-3	225	11-11-83	1	2	8.88	15	0	0	0	24	43	30	24	2	9	9	.387	.480	.360	3.33	3.33
Caro, Luis	R-R	5-11	183	8-15-85	5	7	4.26	16	15	0	0	80	88	49	38	8	21	46	.278	.284	.275	5.15	2.35
Castillo, Osbek	R-R	6-3	195	1-29-81	6	0	1.04	12	7	0	1	52	29	8	6	2	10	71	.159	.149	.163	12.29	1.73
Cedeno, Ivan	R-R	6-3	194	4-7-85	1	0	3.86	5	1	0	0	16	14	7	7	1	8	18	.230	.318	.179	9.92	4.41
Fournier, Daniel	R-R	6-4	205	5-19-85	4	3	3.77	15	15	0	0	76	74	43	32	3	39	43	.262	.264	.262	5.07	4.60
Krohe, Matthew	L-L	6-3	200	1-9-84	3	2	2.49	22	0	0	0	43	41	18	12	3	18	32	.246	.098	.294	6.65	3.74
Neighborgall, Jason	R-R	6-5	205	12-19-83	0	2	20.77	20	1	0	0	13	11	30	30	1	46	15	.229	.154	.257	10.38	31.85
Norberto, Jordan	L-L	5-11	165	12-8-86	3	3	3.09	16	16	0	0	76	59	30	26	4	40	64	.216	.184	.221	7.61	4.76
Perez, Jorge	R-R	5-11	163	1-16-86	1	1	4.97	21	0	0	7	25	34	14	14	1	4	31	.327	.318	.329	11.01	1.42
Reynolds, Brett	R-R	6-3	195	9-28-84	3	3	4.25	20	2	0	0	42	44	22	20	2	28	45	.275	.400	.240	9.57	5.95
Sena, Giornale	R-R	6-3	186	5-28-86	1	0	6.88	19	0	0	0	17	13	14	13	3	13	19	.217	.211	.200	10.06	17.47
Stange, Daniel	R-R	6-3	185	12-22-85	5	2	4.25	27	0	0	13	36	39	19	17	2	17	48	.267	.341	.235	12.00	4.25
Zavada, Clay	L-L	6-1	195	6-28-84	2	3	3.10	22	0	0	2	49	41	29	17	3	15	51	.225	.205	.231	9.30	2.74

FIELDING

Catcher	PCT	G	PO	A	E	DP	PB
Brashear	1.000	12	96	11	0	1	2
Bustamante	1.000	8	32	6	0	0	7
Elder	.984	7	54	6	1	1	2
Hester	.997	44	368	20	1	4	7
J. Parra	1.000	12	88	7	0	1	9

First Base	PCT	G	PO	A	E	DP
Dijol	.980	47	421	22	9	40
Janes	1.000	2	17	2	0	0
McFeely	.992	29	254	10	2	24

Second Base	PCT	G	PO	A	E	DP
Cruz	.972	37	55	82	4	21
Smith	.965	41	76	91	6	21
Summers	1.000	3	3	7	0	2

Third Base	PCT	G	PO	A	E	DP
Cruz	1.000	1	0	2	0	0
Fie	.918	65	35	166	18	15
McFeely	.968	11	6	24	1	3

Shortstop	PCT	G	PO	A	E	DP
Cruz	.918	18	21	46	6	13

Oxendine	.945	61	77	197	16	33

Outfield	PCT	G	PO	A	E	DP
Janes	1.000	5	1	0	0	0
Jones	.991	62	108	2	1	0
G. Parra	.970	66	119	10	4	4
J. Parra	1.000	1	5	0	0	0
Perales	.979	61	88	6	2	0
Walker	.967	38	54	5	2	0

ATLANTA BRAVES

BY BILL BALLEW

Everyone knew the day would come when the Braves would not win their division. But they wondered when after seeing the club reach playoff competition for 14 consecutive seasons, the longest streak in professional sports history.

It finally happened in 2006. The Braves struggled through the first half, capped by a disastrous 6-21 mark in June, and failed to post a winning record for the first time since 1990 by going 79-83 to finish third in the National League East. Both the rotation and bullpen were in shambles for much of the slate. Injuries and a mediocre showing by Tim Hudson crippled the rotation, while the lack of anything resembling a closer—until the arrival of Bob Wickman from Cleveland on July 20—cost the team numerous wins.

The lineup also had its problems. Third baseman Chipper Jones missed a third of the season with a variety of ailments, though he still ended up batting .324 with 26 home runs in 411 at-bats. Second baseman Marcus Giles was miscast as a leadoff hitter, resulting in an inconsistent offensive effort.

Yet those stumbling blocks were minor compared to those in the bullpen, which suffered setbacks as early as spring training with the injuries to Blaine Boyer and John Foster. A bigger problem was the search for a reliable closer, which continued into the second half of the season, when the Braves traded for Bob Wickman. Wickman converted 18 saves in 28 appearances and had a 1.04 ERA, and the Braves extended his contract after the season.

Pitching had been the Braves' calling card throughout the previous 14 seasons, but that was not the case in 2006. The team finished tied for 10th in the NL with a team ERA of 4.60. The hitters compensated for the inef-

ORGANIZATION STATISTICS

PLAYERS OF THE YEAR

MAJOR LEAGUE: John Smoltz, rhp

Smoltz has been the Braves' best pitcher since returning to a starting role in 2005. In 2006 he led the club with a 3.49 ERA, 232 innings and 211 strikeouts, while his 16 wins tied for the NL lead. Smoltz is seven wins shy of 200 and he needs 222 strikeouts to reach 3,000.

MINOR LEAGUE: Matt Harrison, lhp

TOM PRIDDY

Harrison took the biggest step forward among Braves prospects in a year without a true standout performer. He was 11-8, 3.35 with 114-33 strikeout-walk ratio in 159 innings split between high Class A and Double-A. The 21-year-old ranked second in the system in wins, third in ERA and fifth in strikeouts.

fective arms by mashing the ball as well as any club on the senior circuit. The Braves topped the NL in home runs (222) and slugging percentage (.455), ranked second in runs (849) and total bases (2,540), and tied with the Rockies for second in batting (.270).

That the Braves were able to remain as competitive as they did was a testament to the acumen of manager Bobby Cox. The club also received impressive contributions from 22-year-old catcher Brian McCann, who earned all-star recognition in his second season and hit a team-best .333. First baseman Adam LaRoche had a breakout campaign, particularly in the power department. Shortstop Edgar Renteria also did a solid job after coming over from the Red Sox.

But the offensive leader was outfielder Andruw Jones, who also added another Gold Glove to his trophy case. Jones hit 41 home runs and had 129 RBIs, both team-leading figures.

Going home after the regular season was not the only change the Braves experienced. Bench coach Pat Corrales did not have his contract renewed, third-base coach Fredi Gonzalez was named the Marlins' new manager, and bullpen coach Bobby Dews was reassigned as a special assistant to general manager John Schuerholz.

The development-oriented Braves filled the coaching vacancies from within. Minor league field coordinator Chino Cadahia became the bench coach. Triple-A Richmond manager Brian Snitker was promoted to third-base coach, while longtime catcher Eddie Perez was selected as the new bullpen coach.

In the minors, the Braves continued to show impressive depth, particularly in young starting pitching, though the farm system does not have as much top-shelf talent after catcher Jarrod Saltalamacchia and shortstop Elvis Andrus.

Rookie-level Danville won the Appalachian League title for the first time after advancing to the championship series for the third consecutive season. Low Class A Rome was the only other club to reach postseason play, and the farm system finished with a cumulative .474 winning percentage, ranking 25th in baseball.

ORGANIZATION LEADERS

BATTING		*Minimum 250 at-bats
*AVG	Loadenthal, Carl, Mississippi/Myrtle Beach	.305
R	Blanco, Gregor, Mississippi/Richmond	99
H	Blanco, Gregor, Mississippi/Richmond	163
TB	Campbell, Eric, Rome	255
2B	Campbell, Eric, Rome	33
	Pope, Van, Myrtle Beach	33
3B	Davis, Quentin, Rome	8
HR	Kaaihue, Kala, Rome/Myrtle Beach	28
RBI	Campbell, Eric, Rome	84
	Pope, Van, Myrtle Beach	84
BB	Blanco, Gregor, Mississippi/Richmond	104
SO	Kaaihue, Kala, Rome/Myrtle Beach	123
SB	Suero, Ovandy, Rome/Myrtle Beach	53
*OBP	Fontaine, Robert, Danville	.411
*SLG	Kaaihue, Kala, Rome/Myrtle Beach	.540

PITCHING		#Minimum 75 innings
W	Reyes, Jo-Jo, Rome/Myrtle Beach	12
L	Waters, Chris, Mississippi	14
#ERA	Harrison, Matt, Myrtle Beach/Mississippi	3.35
G	Acosta, Manny, Mississippi/Richmond	55
CG	Harrison, Matt, Myrtle Beach/Mississippi	3
SV	Schreiber, Zach, Myrtle Beach/Mississippi	24
IP	Harrison, Matt, Myrtle Beach/Mississippi	159
BB	Jones, Beau, Rome	83
SO	Reyes, Jo-Jo, Rome/Myrtle Beach	142
#AVG	Reyes, Jo-Jo, Rome/Myrtle Beach	.223

Atlanta Braves · MLB

National League

BATTING	B-T	HT	WT	DOB	AVG	vLH	vRH	G	AB	R	H	2B	3B	HR	RBI	BB	HBP	SH	SF	SO	SB	CS	SLG	OBP
Aybar, Willy	B-R	5-11	200	3-9-83	.313	.408	.242	36	115	17	36	6	0	1	8	10	1	1	0	19	0	2	.391	.373
2-team (43 Los Angeles)					.280	—	—	79	243	32	68	18	0	4	30	28	4	3	0	36	1	2	.403	.364
Betemit, Wilson	B-R	6-3	200	7-28-80	.281	.222	.299	88	199	30	56	16	0	9	29	19	0	1	0	57	2	1	.497	.344
2-team (55 Los Angeles)					.263	—	—	143	373	49	98	23	0	18	53	36	0	1	2	102	3	1	.469	.326
Diaz, Matt	R-R	6-1	205	3-3-78	.327	.295	.358	124	297	37	97	15	4	7	32	11	9	1	4	49	5	5	.475	.364
Francoeur, Jeff	R-R	6-4	220	1-8-84	.260	.292	.248	162	651	83	169	24	6	29	103	23	9	0	3	132	1	6	.449	.293
Giles, Marcus	R-R	5-8	175	5-18-78	.262	.229	.273	141	550	87	144	32	2	11	60	62	6	5	3	105	10	5	.387	.341
Jones, Andruw	R-R	6-1	210	4-23-77	.262	.260	.263	156	565	107	148	29	0	41	129	82	13	0	9	127	4	1	.531	.363
Jones, Chipper	B-R	6-4	230	4-24-72	.324	.393	.332	110	411	87	133	28	3	26	86	61	1	0	4	73	6	1	.596	.409
Jordan, Brian	R-R	6-1	225	3-29-67	.231	.180	.293	48	91	11	21	2	0	3	10	7	1	0	2	23	0	0	.352	.287
Langerhans, Ryan	L-L	6-3	205	2-20-80	.241	.308	.232	131	315	46	76	16	3	7	28	50	3	0	1	91	1	2	.378	.350
LaRoche, Adam	L-L	6-3	185	11-6-79	.285	.241	.297	149	492	89	140	38	1	32	90	55	2	1	7	128	1	2	.561	.354
McCann, Brian	L-R	6-3	210	2-20-84	.333	.266	.351	130	442	61	147	34	0	24	93	41	3	0	6	54	2	0	.572	.388
Orr, Pete	L-R	6-1	185	6-8-79	.253	.182	.265	102	154	22	39	3	4	1	8	5	0	5	0	30	2	4	.344	.277
Pena, Brayan	B-R	5-11	220	1-7-82	.268	.200	.308	23	41	9	11	2	0	1	5	2	0	0	0	5	0	0	.390	.302
Pena, Tony	R-R	6-1	180	3-23-81	.227	.278	.192	40	44	12	10	2	0	1	3	2	0	0	0	10	0	0	.341	.261
Prado, Martin	R-R	6-1	170	10-27-83	.262	.310	.154	24	42	3	11	1	1	1	9	5	0	2	0	7	0	0	.405	.340
Pratt, Todd	R-R	6-3	240	2-9-67	.207	.176	.239	62	135	14	28	6	0	4	19	12	1	1	3	43	1	0	.341	.272
Renteria, Edgar	R-R	6-1	200	8-7-75	.293	.333	.281	149	598	100	175	40	2	14	70	62	3	8	2	89	17	6	.436	.361
Thorman, Scott	L-R	6-3	235	1-6-82	.234	.189	.253	55	128	13	30	11	0	5	14	5	0	0	0	21	1	0	.438	.263
Ward, Daryle	L-L	6-2	240	6-27-75	.308	.000	.381	20	26	2	8	1	0	1	7	1	0	0	0	6	0	0	.462	.333
2-team (78 Washington)					.308	—	—	98	130	17	40	10	0	7	26	15	2	0	3	27	0	1	.546	.380

PITCHING	B-T	HT	WT	DOB	W	L	ERA	G	GS	CG	SV	IP	H	R	ER	HR	BB	SO	AVG	vLH	vRH	K/9	BB/9
Baez, Danys	R-R	6-1	230	9-10-77	0	1	5.40	11	0	0	0	10	7	6	6	0	6	10	.189	.182	.192	9.00	5.40
2-team (46 Los Angeles)					5	6	4.53	57	0	0	9	59	60	35	30	3	17	39	—	—	—	5.88	2.56
Barry, Kevin	R-R	6-2	235	8-18-78	1	1	5.61	19	1	0	0	26	24	16	16	2	14	19	.253	.194	.288	6.66	4.91
Boyer, Blaine	R-R	6-3	215	7-11-81	0	0	40.50	2	0	0	0	1	4	3	3	0	1	0	.667	.750	.500	0.00	13.50
Cormier, Lance	R-R	6-1	200	8-19-80	4	5	4.89	29	9	0	0	74	90	44	40	8	39	43	.314	.271	.351	5.25	4.76
Davies, Kyle	R-R	6-2	205	9-9-83	3	7	8.38	14	14	1	0	63	90	60	59	14	33	51	.332	.333	.331	7.25	4.69
Devine, Joey	R-R	6-1	225	9-19-83	0	0	9.95	10	0	0	0	6	8	7	7	1	9	10	.308	.333	.286	14.21	12.79
Franklin, Wayne	L-L	6-2	195	3-9-74	0	0	7.04	11	0	0	0	8	8	6	6	2	6	3	.296	.308	.286	3.52	7.04
Hudson, Tim	R-R	6-1	170	7-14-75	13	12	4.86	35	35	2	0	218	235	129	118	25	79	141	.273	.281	.265	5.81	3.26
James, Chuck	L-L	6-0	190	11-9-81	11	4	3.78	25	18	0	0	119	101	54	50	20	47	91	.232	.297	.215	6.88	3.55
Lerew, Anthony	L-R	6-3	220	10-28-82	0	0	22.50	1	0	0	0	2	5	5	5	0	3	1	.455	.200	.667	4.50	13.50
McBride, Macay	L-L	5-11	210	10-24-82	4	1	3.65	71	0	0	1	57	53	28	23	2	32	46	.248	.181	.312	7.31	5.08
Moylan, Peter	R-R	6-3	220	12-2-78	0	0	4.80	15	0	0	0	15	18	8	8	1	5	14	.290	.192	.361	8.40	3.00
Paronto, Chad	R-R	6-5	250	7-28-75	2	3	3.18	65	0	0	0	57	53	23	20	5	19	41	.252	.288	.234	6.51	3.02
Ramirez, Horacio	L-L	6-1	210	11-24-79	5	5	4.48	14	14	0	0	76	85	42	38	6	31	37	.287	.286	.288	4.36	3.66
Ray, Ken	R-R	6-2	200	11-27-74	1	1	4.52	69	0	0	5	68	66	36	34	9	38	50	.259	.282	.237	6.65	5.05
Reitsma, Chris	R-R	6-5	235	12-31-77	1	2	8.68	27	0	0	8	28	46	27	27	7	8	13	.362	.422	.302	4.18	2.57
Remlinger, Mike	L-L	6-1	215	3-23-66	2	4	4.03	36	0	0	2	22	27	11	10	2	9	19	.293	.289	.298	7.66	3.63
Shiell, Jason	R-R	6-0	180	10-19-76	0	2	8.62	4	3	0	0	16	23	15	15	5	9	14	.343	.423	.293	8.04	5.17
Smith, Travis	R-R	5-10	170	11-7-72	0	1	4.15	1	1	0	0	4	5	4	2	1	1	1	.313	.364	.200	2.08	2.08
Smoltz, John	R-R	6-3	220	5-15-67	16	9	3.49	35	35	3	0	232	221	93	90	23	55	211	.251	.278	.228	8.19	2.13
Sosa, Jorge	R-R	6-2	175	4-28-77	3	10	5.46	26	13	0	3	87	105	61	53	20	32	58	.298	.327	.277	5.98	3.30
2-team (19 St. Louis)					3	11	5.42	45	13	0	4	118	138	79	71	30	40	75	—	—	—	5.72	3.05
Stockman, Phil	R-R	6-8	250	1-25-80	0	0	2.25	4	0	0	0	4	3	1	1	0	4	4	.231	.500	.182	9.00	9.00
Thomson, John	R-R	6-3	220	10-1-73	2	7	4.82	18	15	0	0	80	93	55	43	11	32	46	.295	.276	.313	5.15	3.59
Villarreal, Oscar	L-R	6-0	215	11-22-81	9	1	3.61	58	4	0	0	92	93	41	37	13	27	55	.261	.264	.259	5.36	2.63
Wickman, Bob	R-R	6-1	240	2-6-69	0	2	1.04	28	0	0	18	26	24	7	3	1	2	25	.231	.224	.236	8.65	0.69
Yates, Tyler	R-R	6-4	240	8-7-77	2	5	3.96	56	0	0	1	50	42	23	22	6	31	46	.228	.217	.235	8.28	5.58

FIELDING

Catcher	PCT	G	PO	A	E	DP	PB
McCann	.989	124	778	39	9	6	5
B. Pena	1.000	32	200	0	0	0	
Pratt	.986	54	279	11	4	2	3

First Base	PCT	G	PO	A	E	DP
Jordan	.986	25	137	9	2	13
LaRoche	.996	142	1117	97	5	109
Thorman	.992	18	112	9	1	13
Ward	1.000	4	26	2	0	2

Second Base	PCT	G	PO	A	E	DP
Betemit	1.000	10	26	20	0	7
Giles	.983	134	258	368	11	81
Orr	1.000	32	31	63	0	12
Prado	.976	11	15	26	1	4

Third Base	PCT	G	PO	A	E	DP
Aybar	.947	32	14	40	3	4
Betemit	.941	30	8	40	3	9
C. Jones	.936	105	87	177	18	22
Orr	1.000	10	5	15	0	1
B. Pena	—	1	0	0	0	0
T. Pena	1.000	1	0	1	0	0
Prado	.857	8	2	4	1	0

Shortstop	PCT	G	PO	A	E	DP
Betemit	.914	18	20	33	5	10
T. Pena	.977	22	14	28	1	7
Renteria	.978	146	185	399	13	76

Outfield	PCT	G	PO	A	E	DP
Diaz	.977	99	166	5	4	1
Francoeur	.973	162	317	13	9	4
A. Jones	.995	153	378	4	2	1
Jordan	1.000	6	6	0	0	0
Langerhans	.995	119	196	2	1	0
Thorman	1.000	21	19	1	0	0
Ward	1.000	2	1	0	0	0

Richmond Braves · Triple-A

International League

BATTING	B-T	HT	WT	DOB	AVG	vLH	vRH	G	AB	R	H	2B	3B	HR	RBI	BB	HBP	SH	SF	SO	SB	CS	SLG	OBP
Aybar, Willy	B-R	5-11	200	3-9-83	.300	.333	.286	3	10	2	3	1	0	0	1	2	0	0	0	3	0	0	.400	.417
Blanco, Gregor	L-L	5-11	170	12-24-83	.294	.244	.316	73	269	43	79	12	1	0	19	52	0	6	0	53	14	9	.346	.408
Crespo, Cesar	B-R	5-11	190	5-23-79	.239	.186	.258	116	423	52	101	15	2	5	29	55	1	5	2	85	15	6	.319	.326
Duran, Carlos	L-L	6-1	165	12-27-82	.300	.143	.348	11	30	3	9	2	0	0	2	3	0	0	0	5	0	1	.367	.364

2006 PERFORMANCE

General manager: John Schuerholz. **Farm director:** Kurt Kemp. **Scouting director:** Roy Clark.

Class	Team	League	W	L	PCT	Finish*	Manager	Affiliate Since
Majors	Atlanta	National	79	83	.488	8th (16)	Bobby Cox	—
Triple-A	Richmond Braves	International	57	86	.399	14th (14)	Brian Snitker	1966
Double-A	Mississippi Braves	Southern	58	80	.420	10th (10)	Jeff Blauser	2005
High A	Myrtle Beach Pelicans	Carolina	72	68	.514	3rd (8)	Rocket Wheeler	1999
Low A	Rome Braves	South Atlantic	71	68	.511	8th (16)	Randy Ingle	2003
Rookie	Danville Braves	Appalachian	40	27	.597	+2nd (10)	Paul Runge	1993
Rookie	GCL Braves	Gulf Coast	23	27	.460	8th (13)	Luis Ortiz	1998
OVERALL 2006 MINOR LEAGUE RECORD			321	356	.474	25th (30)		

*Finish in overall standings (No. of teams in league). +League champion

Brian McCann was one of the best-hitting catchers in the game

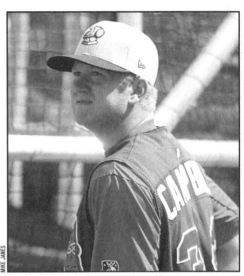

Eric Campbell led the farm system in total bases

	B-T	HT	WT	DOB	AVG	vLH	vRH	G	AB	R	H	2B	3B	HR	RBI	BB	SO	SB	CS	OBP	SLG
Hernandez, Luis	B-R	5-10	165	6-26-84	.192	.063	.228	19	73	3	14	4	0	1	5	0	0	1	0	8	0	1	.288	.192
Johnson, Kelly	L-R	6-1	205	2-22-82	.333	.350	.316	10	39	3	13	4	0	1	7	6	1	0	1	6	1	0	.513	.426
Jordan, Brian	R-R	6-1	225	3-29-67	.333	.429	.250	4	15	3	5	1	0	2	4	1	0	0	0	7	0	0	.800	.375
Jurries, J. J.	R-R	6-0	195	4-13-79	.205	.217	.200	89	307	30	63	13	0	8	27	34	5	0	0	106	2	0	.326	.295
Kelton, David	R-R	6-3	195	12-17-79	.216	.269	.188	48	153	13	33	6	1	1	10	14	1	0	1	53	2	0	.288	.284
McCarthy, Bill	R-R	6-2	205	12-2-79	.235	.200	.255	103	345	31	81	17	1	6	32	22	9	1	1	70	2	0	.342	.297
Mendez, Carlos	R-R	6-0	225	6-18-74	.290	.305	.284	98	366	28	106	13	0	5	54	5	2	2	5	35	1	2	.366	.299
Norris, Dax	R-R	5-10	190	1-14-72	.226	.200	.236	57	190	17	43	8	0	3	25	5	3	1	0	29	0	1	.316	.258
Pena, Brayan	B-R	5-11	220	1-7-82	.302	.336	.284	87	325	32	98	18	1	1	33	21	1	1	4	28	6	6	.372	.342
Pena, Tony	R-R	6-1	180	3-23-81	.282	.190	.318	81	298	38	84	12	4	1	23	12	2	5	2	56	12	3	.359	.312
Prado, Martin	R-R	6-1	170	10-27-83	.282	.301	.274	60	241	30	68	12	1	2	23	12	0	2	2	28	2	2	.365	.314
Ryan, Michael	L-R	6-0	215	7-6-77	.242	.125	.264	110	363	35	88	18	1	6	39	30	1	4	0	75	2	3	.347	.302
Schuerholz, Jonathan	R-R	5-11	190	6-25-80	.184	.190	.181	116	375	33	69	12	2	2	25	32	4	9	5	94	5	2	.243	.252
Strong, Jamal	R-R	5-10	185	8-5-78	.255	.295	.235	97	329	40	84	14	2	1	26	41	6	8	2	63	16	2	.319	.347
Thorman, Scott	L-R	6-3	235	1-6-82	.298	.293	.300	81	309	38	92	16	2	15	48	31	1	0	3	48	4	2	.508	.360
Timmons, Wes	R-R	6-0	190	7-12-79	.280	.338	.259	71	250	28	70	15	0	6	26	38	6	3	3	19	5	4	.412	.384
Trejo, Jaime	R-R	6-3	187	9-7-83	.333	—	.333	1	3	0	1	0	0	0	1	0	0	0	0	0	0	0	.333	.500

PITCHING	B-T	HT	WT	DOB	W	L	ERA	G	GS	CG	SV	IP	H	R	ER	HR	BB	SO	AVG	vLH	vRH	K/9	BB/9
Acosta, Manny	R-R	6-4	170	5-1-81	1	6	3.63	38	0	0	17	45	38	19	18	4	32	44	.238	.226	.243	8.87	6.45
Almanzar, Carlos	R-R	6-2	200	11-6-73	0	0	27.00	1	0	0	0	1	3	3	2	0	1	0	.750	.000	1.000	0.00	13.50
Baker, Brad	R-R	6-2	180	11-6-80	1	0	2.40	9	0	0	0	15	14	5	4	1	4	17	.237	.120	.324	10.20	2.40
2-team (30 Pawtucket)					3	4	5.14	39	0	0	3	61	75	38	35	7	19	49	—	—	—	7.19	2.79
Barry, Kevin	R-R	6-2	235	8-18-78	4	5	3.30	18	15	0	0	95	87	40	35	5	36	73	.241	.253	.232	6.89	3.40
Basner, Ryan	R-R	6-3	230	7-15-81	0	0	2.35	6	0	0	0	8	6	2	2	0	2	8	.194	.077	.278	9.39	2.35
Bush, Paul	R-R	6-1	175	10-5-79	0	4	3.60	17	4	0	0	40	29	17	16	3	16	36	.200	.183	.212	8.10	3.60
Cormier, Lance	R-R	6-1	200	8-19-80	4	3	3.95	9	9	1	0	55	65	26	24	4	14	27	.301	.345	.273	4.45	2.30
Curtis, Dan	R-R	6-4	215	11-3-79	3	5	4.85	13	11	0	0	72	82	41	39	5	33	51	.296	.281	.312	6.35	4.11
Davies, Kyle	R-R	6-2	205	9-9-83	2	0	0.60	2	2	0	0	15	7	1	1	0	3	8	.140	.179	.091	4.80	1.80
Devine, Joey	R-R	6-1	225	9-19-83	0	0	—	1	0	0	0	0	1	1	1	0	1	0	1.000	1.000	—	—	—
Franklin, Wayne	L-L	6-1	195	3-9-74	2	3	2.36	35	1	0	4	53	39	15	14	2	17	52	.202	.179	.214	8.78	2.87
James, Chuck	L-L	6-0	190	11-9-81	1	0	2.67	7	6	0	0	34	30	10	10	3	6	25	.236	.167	.264	6.68	1.60
Johnson, Jonathan	R-R	6-0	180	7-16-74	2	3	3.48	23	3	0	0	52	45	24	20	2	17	46	.228	.268	.206	8.01	2.96
Lerew, Anthony	L-R	6-3	220	10-28-82	3	5	7.48	16	15	1	0	71	92	63	59	12	36	69	.315	.276	.337	8.75	4.56
McBride, Macay	L-L	5-11	210	10-24-82	0	0	0.00	3	0	0	0	3	1	0	0	0	1	3	.111	—	.111	9.00	3.00
Moss, Damian	R-L	6-0	185	11-24-76	1	2	10.13	3	2	0	0	13	23	16	15	5	8	12	.383	.533	.333	8.10	5.40

LARRY GOREN

MIKE JANES

ORGANIZATION STATISTICS

Name	B-T	HT	WT	DOB	W	L	ERA	G	GS	CG	SV	IP	H	R	ER	HR	BB	SO	AVG	vLH	vRH	K/9	BB/9
Moylan, Peter	R-R	6-3	220	12-2-78	1	7	6.35	35	0	0	1	57	61	43	40	4	38	54	.272	.303	.257	8.58	6.04
Mullen, Scott	R-L	6-2	195	1-17-75	2	2	6.35	20	0	0	0	28	31	20	20	3	17	18	.274	.317	.250	5.72	5.40
Nunez, Franklin	R-R	6-0	175	1-18-77	1	6	6.09	30	0	0	2	44	55	34	30	4	26	35	.301	.356	.264	7.11	5.28
O'Connor, Brian	L-L	6-2	210	1-4-77	8	10	4.18	28	25	0	0	149	160	77	69	8	73	77	.284	.291	.283	4.66	4.42
Obermueller, Wes	R-R	6-2	210	12-22-76	0	2	2.45	2	2	0	0	11	12	4	3	1	3	5	.293	.308	.286	4.09	2.45
Paronto, Chad	R-R	6-5	250	7-28-75	1	1	1.02	12	0	0	4	18	17	3	2	1	3	15	.250	.217	.267	7.64	1.53
Ramirez, Horacio	L-L	6-1	210	11-24-79	1	1	5.68	3	3	0	0	13	18	8	8	1	1	10	.327	.467	.275	7.11	0.71
Rodriguez, Ricardo	L-R	6-3	190	5-21-78	5	9	4.62	18	18	0	0	111	130	66	57	11	34	54	.294	.324	.276	4.38	2.76
Scalamandre, Rich	R-R	5-11	195	8-20-80	1	0	3.60	11	0	0	0	15	13	6	6	2	7	10	.228	.296	.167	6.00	4.20
Schmitt, Eric	R-R	6-4	210	7-23-78	0	0	13.50	4	0	0	0	8	19	12	12	1	2	2	.452	.467	.444	0.00	2.25
Shiell, Jason	R-R	6-0	180	10-19-76	2	4	4.50	9	9	0	0	52	51	26	26	3	16	34	.263	.305	.232	5.88	2.77
Smith, Travis	R-R	5-10	170	11-7-72	3	1	2.91	8	8	0	0	46	41	15	15	2	16	44	.234	.200	.255	8.55	3.11
Startup, Will	L-L	6-0	195	8-4-84	5	2	3.43	30	0	0	0	42	45	17	16	3	11	38	.274	.288	.268	8.14	2.36
Stockman, Phil	R-R	6-8	250	1-25-80	0	0	0.81	18	0	0	2	33	13	3	3	0	10	41	.123	.156	.098	11.07	2.70
Wright, Matt	R-R	6-4	230	3-13-82	3	5	5.77	10	10	0	0	48	57	33	31	6	29	34	.298	.366	.235	6.33	5.40
Yates, Tyler	R-R	6-4	240	8-7-77	0	0	2.16	7	0	0	0	8	6	2	2	0	3	10	.214	.125	.250	10.80	3.24

FIELDING

Catcher	PCT	G	PO	A	E	DP	PB
Mendez	.991	29	202	12	2	1	1
Norris	.982	36	253	19	5	2	6
B. Pena	.993	83	515	40	4	2	15

First Base	PCT	G	PO	A	E	DP
Jurries	.994	62	508	33	3	39
Mendez	.993	39	276	23	2	32
Norris	1.000	3	16	1	0	1
Thorman	.991	52	424	24	4	34

Second Base	PCT	G	PO	A	E	DP
Aybar	1.000	1	1	2	0	1
Crespo	.976	61	110	170	7	33
Prado	.982	46	92	132	4	35

(Second Base cont.)	PCT	G	PO	A	E	DP
Schuerholz	.978	38	69	109	4	25
Timmons	1.000	2	3	5	0	1

Third Base	PCT	G	PO	A	E	DP
Aybar	1.000	2	1	3	0	1
Crespo	.938	13	6	24	2	1
Jurries	1.000	4	3	12	0	0
Mendez	.818	6	0	9	2	0
Prado	1.000	15	13	23	0	2
Schuerholz	.936	40	30	72	7	5
Timmons	.958	70	28	131	7	16
Trejo	1.000	1	0	2	0	0

Shortstop	PCT	G	PO	A	E	DP
Crespo	.955	6	11	10	1	2
Hernandez	.972	19	29	74	3	10
T. Pena	.966	81	123	244	13	44
Schuerholz	.951	40	52	103	8	23

Outfield	PCT	G	PO	A	E	DP
Blanco	.988	73	155	5	2	1
Crespo	.966	37	83	2	3	1
Duran	1.000	10	17	0	0	0
Johnson	1.000	4	7	0	0	0
Jordan	1.000	4	8	0	0	0
Kelton	.975	39	76	3	2	0
McCarthy	.990	91	193	3	2	1
Ryan	.993	71	144	3	1	0
Strong	.986	93	214	3	3	0
Thorman	.917	27	42	2	4	0

Mississippi Braves — Double-A

Southern League

BATTING	B-T	HT	WT	DOB	AVG	vLH	vRH	G	AB	R	H	2B	3B	HR	RBI	BB	HBP	SH	SF	SO	SB	CS	SLG	OBP
Arteaga, Josh	R-R	5-9	170	3-14-80	.220	.234	.212	108	328	29	72	11	0	7	27	27	2	1	4	66	2	0	.317	.280
Blanco, Gregor	L-L	5-11	170	12-24-83	.287	.205	.327	66	251	45	72	16	3	0	9	43	3	5	0	57	17	6	.375	.397
Burrus, Josh	R-R	5-11	190	8-20-83	.213	.213	.213	76	291	35	62	12	0	3	28	13	3	0	2	69	5	4	.285	.252
Canizares, Barbaro	R-R	6-3	210	11-21-79	.301	.295	.304	78	279	33	84	18	1	4	33	28	2	0	3	44	0	0	.416	.365
Darula, Bobby	L-R	5-10	190	10-29-74	.250	.429	.190	21	56	7	14	3	0	1	3	2	0	0	0	3	2	1	.357	.276
Duran, Carlos	L-L	6-1	165	12-27-82	.000	.000	.000	4	5	0	0	0	0	0	0	1	0	0	0	1	0	0	.000	.286
Escobar, Yunel	R-R	6-2	200	11-2-82	.264	.259	.266	121	428	55	113	21	4	2	45	59	8	2	4	77	7	9	.346	.361
Esquivel, Matt	R-R	6-2	225	12-17-82	.257	.272	.250	68	253	26	65	16	1	5	38	18	6	0	0	71	4	5	.387	.321
Hernandez, Luis	B-R	5-10	165	6-26-84	.268	.313	.245	104	380	39	102	12	4	1	29	20	3	7	3	46	4	4	.329	.308
James, Willie	B-R	5-8	165	4-30-81	.133	.500	.000	6	15	2	2	0	0	0	1	1	1	0	0	2	0	0	.133	.235
Jones, Brandon	L-R	6-2	195	12-10-83	.273	.323	.246	48	176	18	48	9	3	7	25	15	0	1	2	38	4	2	.477	.326
Jones, Chipper	B-R	6-4	230	4-24-72	.167	—	.167	2	6	1	1	0	0	0	0	0	0	0	0	2	0	0	.167	.167
Joseph, Onil	R-R	6-2	165	2-12-82	.266	.260	.269	92	338	33	90	10	4	3	31	13	3	0	3	90	7	7	.346	.297
Loadenthal, Carl	L-L	5-11	185	12-27-81	.167	.111	.179	19	48	7	8	2	0	1	4	6	1	0	1	5	5	0	.271	.268
Norris, Dax	R-R	5-10	190	1-14-72	.279	.286	.276	16	43	2	12	1	0	0	4	2	1	1	6	9	0	0	.302	.304
Perez, Eddie	R-R	6-1	220	5-4-68	.279	.333	.258	13	43	5	12	0	0	2	5	4	0	0	0	11	0	0	.419	.340
Prado, Martin	R-R	6-1	170	10-27-83	.278	.305	.265	43	176	17	49	6	2	1	15	14	0	0	1	35	2	2	.352	.330
Rosamond Jr., Michael	R-R	6-4	220	4-18-78	.243	.306	.213	104	338	47	82	19	3	15	47	20	5	0	3	117	5	2	.450	.292
Rozema, Mike	L-R	6-2	180	9-16-81	.232	.145	.262	80	271	26	63	9	2	0	21	16	3	2	4	54	4	3	.280	.279
Saltalamacchia, Jarrod	B-R	6-4	195	5-2-85	.230	.262	.214	92	313	30	72	18	1	9	39	55	4	0	3	71	0	1	.380	.353
Serrano, Ray	R-R	5-8	221	1-19-81	.242	.275	.228	70	227	23	55	14	0	3	22	13	1	3	0	36	1	1	.344	.255
Terrazas, Ivan	B-R	5-11	168	11-11-83	.269	.286	.267	16	52	2	14	4	0	0	3	3	0	0	0	11	1	1	.346	.309
Trejo, Jaime	B-R	6-3	187	9-7-83	.143	.500	.000	7	14	0	2	0	0	0	1	0	1	0	0	5	0	0	.143	.143
Williams, Jon	L-R	5-10	183	5-18-79	.000	.000	.000	3	3	0	0	0	0	0	0	0	0	0	0	0	0	0	.000	.000
Young, Matt	L-R	5-8	175	10-3-82	.220	.182	.231	13	50	3	11	1	0	0	6	7	0	1	1	9	1	1	.240	.310

PITCHING	B-T	HT	WT	DOB	W	L	ERA	G	GS	CG	SV	IP	H	R	ER	HR	BB	SO	AVG	vLH	vRH	K/9	BB/9
Acosta, Manny	R-R	6-4	170	5-1-81	0	0	2.35	13	0	0	4	15	7	4	4	1	15	13	.137	.148	.125	7.63	8.80
Almanzar, Carlos	R-R	6-2	200	11-6-73	0	0	2.25	3	0	0	0	4	2	1	1	1	1	3	.154	.000	.182	6.75	2.25
Ascanio, Jose	R-R	6-0	150	5-2-85	4	2	4.26	24	0	0	0	38	37	20	18	2	17	37	.253	.254	.253	8.76	4.03
Baker, Brad	R-R	6-2	180	11-6-80	0	0	0.00	2	0	0	0	2	1	0	0	0	0	1	.143	.250	.000	4.50	0.00
Basner, Ryan	R-R	6-3	230	7-15-81	4	5	4.08	35	6	0	1	75	80	40	34	8	26	64	.277	.310	.254	7.68	3.12
Bueno, Francisley	L-L	5-11	200	3-5-81	1	7	3.59	17	14	1	0	80	77	36	32	10	19	84	.252	.280	.242	9.41	2.13
Bush, Paul	R-R	6-1	175	10-5-79	5	5	4.91	20	6	0	0	59	62	36	32	8	23	60	.265	.291	.250	9.20	3.53
Coggin, David	R-R	6-4	210	10-30-76	0	3	4.95	6	3	0	0	20	25	13	11	2	9	10	.294	.310	.279	4.50	4.05
Curtis, Dan	R-R	6-4	215	11-3-79	2	5	4.22	15	13	0	0	81	78	42	38	5	33	54	.262	.277	.250	6.00	3.67
Davies, Kyle	R-R	6-2	205	9-9-83	1	1	4.50	4	4	0	0	14	11	8	7	1	5	9	.216	.095	.300	5.79	3.21
Devine, Joey	R-R	6-1	225	9-19-83	2	0	0.82	6	0	0	0	11	2	1	1	1	4	20	.065	.091	.050	16.36	3.27
Digby, Bryan	R-R	6-2	220	12-31-81	1	1	9.95	12	0	0	0	19	30	24	21	0	16	18	.349	.406	.315	8.53	7.58
Endl, Brady	R-L	6-5	230	4-14-82	0	0	0.00	1	1	0	0	4	2	0	0	0	3	4	.077	.000	.100	9.00	6.75
Harrison, Matt	L-L	6-4	221	8-16-85	3	4	3.61	13	12	1	0	77	83	36	31	6	17	55	.272	.338	.249	6.28	1.98
Lerew, Anthony	R-R	6-3	210	10-28-82	4	2	2.03	9	8	0	0	49	43	18	11	1	13	37	.234	.179	.274	6.80	2.40
McBride, Macay	L-L	5-11	210	10-24-82	0	0	9.64	4	0	0	0	5	8	5	5	1	1	6	.381	.500	.273	11.57	1.93
Roberts, Ralph	R-R	6-2	215	3-28-80	0	1	13.50	2	0	0	0	4	7	6	6	2	4	2	.368	.375	.364	4.50	9.00
Santos, Arthur	R-R	6-0	180	2-20-82	2	3	1.79	26	0	0	3	40	30	12	8	3	8	26	.207	.218	.200	5.80	1.79
Schmitt, Eric	R-R	6-4	210	7-23-78	0	4	5.98	29	0	0	1	56	67	40	37	13	14	37	.296	.371	.248	5.98	2.26
Schreiber, Zach	R-R	6-1	200	6-24-82	1	2	2.50	35	0	0	21	40	26	11	11	3	28	45	.187	.182	.190	10.21	6.35

	B-T	HT	WT	DOB	W	L	ERA	G	GS	CG	SV	IP	H	R	ER	HR	BB	SO	AVG	vLH	vRH	K/9	BB/9
Smith, Dan	L-L	6-5	250	9-9-83	3	6	3.13	28	8	0	0	60	41	26	21	3	32	86	.196	.250	.170	12.83	4.77
Sodowsky, Clint	R-R	6-4	200	7-13-72	0	0	3.60	1	1	0	0	5	6	3	2	0	1	4	.300	.286	.308	7.20	1.80
Startup, Will	L-L	6-0	195	8-4-84	3	0	0.72	16	0	0	4	25	18	2	2	0	6	29	.202	.094	.263	10.44	2.16
Stockman, Phil	R-R	6-8	250	1-25-80	0	0	0.00	3	0	0	0	7	1	0	0	0	2	12	.043	.125	.000	14.73	2.45
Thomson, John	R-R	6-3	220	10-1-73	0	0	9.00	1	1	0	0	1	2	1	1	0	1	1	.400	.333	.500	9.00	9.00
Tucker, Glenn	B-R	6-3	205	4-9-81	2	4	3.78	50	0	0	0	67	71	35	28	6	17	37	.275	.313	.253	5.00	2.30
Waters, Chris	L-L	6-0	170	8-17-80	8	14	4.82	27	27	0	0	155	152	90	83	24	79	117	.263	.252	.267	6.79	4.59
Watkins, David	R-R	6-1	210	8-18-81	0	1	6.48	4	0	0	1	8	8	6	6	0	6	7	.276	.167	.353	7.56	6.48
White, Sean	R-R	6-4	215	4-25-81	5	6	4.40	21	16	0	1	102	124	58	50	3	43	73	.300	.316	.288	6.42	3.78
Wright, Matt	R-R	6-4	230	3-13-82	7	3	2.22	15	14	0	0	89	74	26	22	3	28	84	.234	.236	.233	8.49	2.83

FIELDING

Catcher	PCT	G	PO	A	E	DP	PB
Perez	1.000	1	6	0	0	0	0
Saltalamacchia	.989	81	644	56	8	6	7
Serrano	.986	59	412	18	6	3	4
Williams	1.000	3	4	0	0	0	0

First Base	PCT	G	PO	A	E	DP
Arteaga	1.000	6	34	6	0	5
Canizares	.986	63	476	35	7	42
Darula	—	1	0	0	0	0
Norris	.970	10	62	3	2	3
Perez	.972	10	61	9	2	12
Rosamond Jr.	.984	53	344	24	6	40
Terrazas	.933	6	39	3	3	7

Second Base	PCT	G	PO	A	E	DP
Arteaga	1.000	13	38	24	0	8
Escobar	.953	24	54	69	6	17

Hernandez	.969	34	67	89	5	14	
James	1.000	6	6	5	0	0	
Prado	.961	27	58	66	5	15	
Rozema	.960	35	77	91	7	23	
Trejo	1.000	1	0	1	0	1	
Young	.889	4	7	9	2	5	

Third Base	PCT	G	PO	A	E	DP
Arteaga	.893	66	44	98	17	8
Escobar	.932	35	28	68	7	9
C. Jones	.857	2	2	4	1	0
Prado	.900	16	9	27	4	1
Rozema	.920	22	13	33	4	4
Trejo	1.000	3	3	3	0	0

Shortstop	PCT	G	PO	A	E	DP
Escobar	.953	62	102	161	13	35
Hernandez	.964	65	80	185	10	38

Rozema	.952	13	21	39	3	12	

Outfield	PCT	G	PO	A	E	DP
Arteaga	1.000	1	2	0	0	0
Blanco	.967	66	173	5	6	2
Burrus	.974	75	107	5	3	1
Canizares	.833	5	5	0	1	0
Darula	.960	12	24	0	1	0
Duran	—	1	0	0	0	0
Esquivel	.993	66	135	5	1	2
B. Jones	.991	48	105	6	1	0
Joseph	.987	88	215	5	3	0
Loadenthal	1.000	14	25	0	0	0
Rosamond Jr.	1.000	34	61	4	0	3
Terrazas	1.000	10	14	0	0	0
Young	1.000	9	31	1	0	0

Myrtle Beach Pelicans — High Class A

Carolina League

BATTING	B-T	HT	WT	DOB	AVG	vLH	vRH	G	AB	R	H	2B	3B	HR	RBI	BB	HBP	SH	SF	SO	SB	CS	SLG	OBP
Barksdale, James	R-R	5-10	215	12-7-81	.068	.050	.083	17	44	4	3	0	0	2	4	1	0	0	0	19	0	0	.205	.089
Canizares, Barbaro	R-R	6-3	210	11-21-79	.381	.667	.267	6	21	3	8	0	0	1	1	1	0	0	0	3	1	0	.524	.409
Carmona, Eliazar	R-R	6-1	170	12-12-85	.135	.056	.176	15	52	3	7	0	0	0	3	2	0	2	1	14	0	1	.135	.132
Creek, Greg	L-R	6-3	225	8-29-82	.262	.217	.283	77	256	28	67	14	1	4	33	18	4	1	3	39	4	3	.371	.317
Doetsch, Steve	R-R	6-2	195	12-2-83	.262	.250	.269	93	282	29	74	11	4	0	22	25	7	1	4	75	9	3	.330	.333
Hernandez, Diory	R-R	6-1	170	4-8-84	.238	.228	.242	76	286	37	68	10	0	6	47	19	5	0	2	51	11	1	.336	.295
Hernandez, Victor	R-R	6-1	170	1-17-85	.167	.000	.250	2	6	0	1	0	0	0	1	1	0	0	0	2	0	0	.167	.286
Holt, J.C.	L-R	5-9	175	12-8-82	.266	.277	.260	116	470	65	125	23	1	1	32	41	5	7	3	80	35	5	.326	.329
James, Willie	R-R	5-8	165	4-30-81	.217	.182	.250	11	23	3	5	0	0	0	0	6	2	0	0	4	3	1	.217	.419
Jansen, Ardley	R-R	6-2	160	2-16-83	.190	.250	.154	6	21	0	4	2	0	0	1	1	0	0	0	4	1	0	.286	.227
Jones, Brandon	L-R	6-2	195	12-10-83	.257	.241	.266	59	226	27	58	10	3	7	35	25	1	0	3	49	11	6	.420	.329
Joseph, Onil	R-R	6-5	215	2-12-82	.318	.395	.275	31	107	19	34	4	2	2	12	10	1	6	0	18	4	2	.449	.381
Jurich, Mark	L-L	5-10	195	12-29-80	.254	.240	.263	79	279	23	71	18	1	1	52	21	1	1	3	43	0	0	.401	.306
Kaaihue, Kala	R-R	6-2	230	3-29-85	.223	.230	.220	53	188	37	42	8	0	13	31	30	4	0	0	49	0	1	.473	.342
Loadenthal, Carl	L-L	5-11	185	12-27-81	.323	.308	.368	106	365	64	118	13	2	7	48	62	4	1	2	67	25	10	.427	.425
Marcial, Robert	R-R	5-10	170	4-21-84	.157	.067	.194	39	102	11	16	2	0	0	9	19	1	5	0	28	3	0	.176	.295
Parliament, Adam	R-R	6-4	220	12-16-85	.000	.000	.000	1	3	0	0	0	0	0	0	0	0	0	0	3	0	0	.000	.000
Pope, Van	R-R	6-0	200	2-26-84	.263	.323	.234	127	467	78	123	31	1	15	74	58	11	0	8	92	7	4	.430	.353
Pyzik, Steve	R-R	5-10	175	5-18-81	.224	.234	.219	57	201	14	45	6	0	0	11	9	1	1	1	16	1	0	.254	.259
Rozema, Mike	L-R	6-2	180	9-16-81	.277	.229	.299	43	155	23	43	10	1	4	11	10	1	2	1	28	4	4	.432	.323
Sammons, Clint	R-R	6-0	200	5-15-83	.258	.277	.249	103	360	36	93	21	0	8	56	32	5	4	6	65	4	4	.383	.323
Schade, Scott	R-R	6-1	220	2-22-82	.216	.273	.172	15	51	3	11	2	0	2	6	7	0	0	0	24	0	0	.373	.310
Suero, Ovandy	B-R	5-10	160	6-20-82	.250	.316	.222	19	64	10	16	1	0	0	1	3	1	0	0	19	5	2	.266	.294
Terrazas, Ivan	R-R	5-11	168	11-11-84	.250	.167	.273	10	28	1	7	3	0	0	2	2	0	0	0	4	0	0	.357	.300
Timmons, Wes	R-R	6-0	190	7-12-79	.200	—	.200	2	5	2	1	0	0	0	1	3	1	0	0	1	0	0	.200	.556
Trejo, Jaime	R-R	6-3	187	9-7-83	.213	.188	.224	34	108	14	23	4	0	1	6	9	0	2	2	32	3	1	.278	.269
Young, Matt	L-R	5-8	175	10-3-82	.281	.245	.301	118	424	65	119	13	6	4	52	71	8	9	6	55	21	10	.375	.389

PITCHING	B-T	HT	WT	DOB	W	L	ERA	G	GS	CG	SV	IP	H	R	ER	HR	BB	SO	AVG	vLH	vRH	K/9	BB/9
Anderson, Devin	L-L	6-5	220	1-24-84	1	3	6.49	20	0	0	0	35	45	27	25	1	17	27	.313	.310	.314	7.01	4.41
Ascanio, Jose	R-R	6-0	150	5-2-85	1	1	4.94	8	6	0	0	31	38	18	17	0	20	23	.314	.400	.272	6.68	5.81
Atilano, Luis	R-R	6-3	215	5-10-85	6	7	4.50	19	18	2	0	116	134	63	58	16	27	45	.298	.296	.299	3.49	2.09
Bullock, Tyler	R-R	6-3	225	1-22-84	1	2	6.18	7	4	0	1	28	31	23	19	6	13	8	.279	.314	.250	2.60	4.23
Covington, Marcus	R-R	6-0	185	5-17-85	1	0	9.00	4	0	0	0	4	3	4	4	0	9	3	.214	.273	.000	6.75	20.25
Devine, Joey	R-R	6-1	225	9-19-83	1	3	5.89	13	2	0	0	18	13	12	12	1	11	28	.203	.346	.105	13.75	5.40
Harrison, Matt	L-L	6-4	221	8-16-85	8	4	3.10	13	13	2	0	81	77	30	28	6	16	60	.252	.286	.246	6.64	1.77
Hernandez, Moises	R-R	6-1	168	3-18-84	2	4	4.76	26	4	0	10	68	75	40	36	5	23	48	.293	.381	.224	6.35	3.04
Letson, Wes	L-L	6-0	200	9-13-82	0	0	5.59	12	0	0	0	19	26	13	12	0	10	9	.325	.378	.279	4.19	4.66
Lopez, Gonzalo	R-R	6-2	175	10-6-83	0	0	2.19	4	1	0	0	12	15	4	3	0	6	6	.306	.400	.241	4.38	4.38
Morton, Charlie	R-R	6-5	218	11-12-83	6	7	5.40	30	14	0	2	100	116	70	60	14	54	75	.291	.271	.302	6.75	4.86
Nelson, Brad	R-R	6-3	200	1-5-82	1	0	0.64	10	0	0	2	28	12	2	2	0	8	21	.128	.070	.176	6.67	2.54
Nix, Michael	R-R	6-5	235	5-21-83	6	4	2.90	36	0	0	7	50	44	20	16	0	30	50	.237	.222	.248	9.06	5.44
Parr, James	R-R	6-1	185	2-27-86	7	8	4.81	24	22	2	1	135	138	76	72	14	37	90	.269	.262	.277	6.01	2.47
Payano, Nelson	L-L	6-2	180	11-13-82	0	0	6.23	2	1	0	0	4	5	3	3	1	5	5	.300	.000	.400	10.38	6.23
Reyes, Jo-Jo	L-L	6-2	230	11-20-84	4	4	4.11	14	14	0	0	66	52	36	30	0	36	58	.220	.234	.215	7.95	4.93
Roberts, Ralph	R-R	6-2	215	3-28-80	5	1	5.65	31	1	0	0	57	55	37	36	6	34	46	.257	.269	.250	7.22	5.34
Russell, Stephen	R-R	6-6	185	12-20-83	4	3	5.40	25	10	0	0	70	75	46	42	16	38	60	.278	.339	.236	7.71	4.89
Santos, Arthur	R-R	6-0	180	2-20-82	4	0	1.04	13	0	0	1	26	21	4	3	0	6	15	.236	.323	.190	5.19	2.08
Schreiber, Zach	R-R	6-1	200	6-24-82	0	0	1.10	8	0	0	0	16	13	2	2	1	8	18	.213	.111	.294	9.92	4.41
Smith, Dan	L-L	6-5	250	9-9-83	0	0	1.13	8	0	0	5	8	5	1	1	1	4	13	.172	.400	.125	14.63	4.50

	B-T	HT	WT	DOB	W	L	ERA	G	GS	CG	SV	IP	H	R	ER	HR	BB	SO	AVG	vLH	vRH	K/9	BB/9
Startup, Will	L-L	6-0	195	8-4-84	1	0	0.00	1	0	0	0	2	1	0	0	0	1	3	.143	.000	.333	13.50	4.50
Stevens, Jake	L-L	6-2	215	3-15-85	1	6	6.41	13	11	0	0	60	69	47	43	5	30	33	.303	.286	.307	4.92	4.48
Tisone, Nick	R-R	6-2	185	3-2-83	1	0	2.35	5	0	0	1	15	15	4	4	1	9	10	.250	.276	.226	5.87	5.28
Villa, Kelvin	L-L	5-10	160	12-14-85	8	6	3.83	25	19	0	1	120	121	65	51	3	47	86	.268	.253	.272	6.45	3.53
Watkins, David	R-R	6-1	210	8-18-81	2	5	4.26	29	0	0	7	38	27	23	18	3	19	32	.191	.213	.175	7.58	4.50

FIELDING

Catcher	PCT	G	PO	A	E	DP	PB
Barksdale	.982	12	51	3	1	0	0
V. Hernandez	1.000	2	7	1	0	0	2
Pyzik	.983	41	253	31	5	4	6
Sammons	.988	96	585	74	8	9	21

First Base	PCT	G	PO	A	E	DP
Creek	.993	51	396	40	3	31
Doetsch	1.000	1	1	0	0	0
Jurich	.983	21	168	8	3	20
Kaaihue	.981	51	397	16	8	38
Pyzik	1.000	8	82	7	0	6
Schade	1.000	14	122	7	0	11

Second Base	PCT	G	PO	A	E	DP
Holt	.967	107	160	281	15	51
James	1.000	3	5	4	0	0
Marcial	1.000	3	6	12	0	4

Rozema	.944	4	8	9	1	1
Trejo	.750	1	3	0	1	0
Young	.984	25	49	75	2	14

Third Base	PCT	G	PO	A	E	DP
Creek	.500	1	1	0	1	0
D. Hernandez	1.000	1	1	1	0	0
James	.833	1	4	1	1	0
Marcial	1.000	1	1	16	0	1
Pope	.962	122	113	188	12	14
Rozema	.900	3	4	5	1	1
Timmons	.800	1	1	3	1	0
Trejo	.818	6	1	8	2	1

Shortstop	PCT	G	PO	A	E	DP
D. Hernandez	.959	68	116	164	12	45
Marcial	.967	20	34	53	3	11
Rozema	.970	30	53	78	4	14

Timmons	1.000	1	2	4	0	0
Trejo	.962	27	57	69	5	15

Outfield	PCT	G	PO	A	E	DP
Canizares	1.000	6	1	1	0	0
Carmona	.977	15	41	2	1	0
Creek	.963	20	25	1	1	0
Doetsch	.969	82	148	6	5	1
James	1.000	6	8	1	0	0
Jansen	.923	6	11	1	1	0
Jones	.950	50	91	5	5	1
Joseph	.983	27	57	2	1	0
Jurich	1.000	14	29	0	0	0
Loadenthal	.971	91	198	5	6	0
Marcial	1.000	6	18	0	0	0
Suero	.960	17	23	1	1	0
Terrazas	1.000	9	12	0	0	0
Young	.996	87	223	8	1	1

South Atlantic League

BATTING

	B-T	HT	WT	DOB	AVG	vLH	vRH	G	AB	R	H	2B	3B	HR	RBI	BB	HBP	SH	SF	SO	SB	CS	SLG	OBP
Andrus, Elvis	R-R	6-0	185	8-26-88	.265	.331	.233	111	437	67	116	25	4	3	50	36	2	2	1	91	23	15	.362	.324
Arnold, Derrick	B-R	5-10	165	8-3-83	.216	.265	.189	79	231	26	50	9	2	2	14	9	4	2	3	63	4	3	.299	.255
Camarena, Jose	B-R	5-10	170	5-29-84	.191	.167	.200	37	89	9	17	4	0	4	10	11	1	5	0	21	1	1	.371	.287
Campbell, Eric	R-R	6-0	195	8-6-85	.296	.346	.275	116	449	83	133	27	3	22	77	23	5	0	3	68	18	4	.517	.335
Clark, Cody	R-R	6-2	170	9-14-81	.296	.287	.300	74	247	30	73	22	0	3	35	24	10	4	3	43	5	0	.421	.377
Davis, Quentin	L-R	5-10	170	3-7-83	.254	.307	.228	122	457	60	116	16	8	2	39	25	5	13	2	81	41	16	.337	.299
Guerra, Junior	R-R	5-11	213	1-16-85	.120	.167	.094	13	50	5	6	3	0	1	6	0	1	1	0	12	0	0	.240	.137
Hernandez, Victor	R-R	6-1	170	1-17-85	.083	.000	.111	5	12	0	1	0	0	0	0	1	0	0	0	5	0	0	.083	.154
Johnson, Kelly	L-R	6-1	205	2-22-82	.474	.500	.462	5	19	5	9	2	1	1	3	4	1	0	0	3	2	2	.842	.583
Jordan, Brian	R-R	6-1	225	3-29-67	.000	—	.000	1	1	0	0	0	0	0	0	0	0	0	0	0	0	0	.000	.750
Kaaihue, Kala	R-R	6-2	230	3-29-85	.329	.338	.325	128	228	44	75	16	2	15	49	52	3	0	1	66	3	0	.614	.458
Koko, Rubi	R-R	6-3	186	3-25-86	.040	.000	.067	12	25	1	1	0	0	0	0	2	0	1	0	15	1	0	.040	.111
Lundahl, Chad	R-R	6-2	190	8-18-84	.226	.143	.294	9	31	1	7	1	0	0	0	2	0	1	0	2	0	0	.258	.273
Marcial, Robert	R-R	5-10	170	4-21-84	.218	.200	.227	44	133	20	29	3	0	1	14	16	3	0	2	30	6	1	.263	.312
McCann, Brian	L-R	6-3	210	2-20-84	.286	—	.286	2	7	0	2	0	0	0	0	1	0	0	0	1	0	0	.286	.375
Monk, Brandon	R-R	5-11	180	2-22-87	.205	.220	.198	49	176	14	36	6	0	1	8	4	2	1	1	47	0	0	.256	.230
Morris, Joshua	R-R	6-5	230	5-11-85	.250	.232	.259	57	208	24	52	9	0	3	19	10	2	0	0	50	0	1	.337	.291
Owings, Jon	R-R	6-4	192	4-4-85	.167	.083	.250	8	24	2	4	1	0	1	2	1	0	0	0	6	0	0	.333	.200
Ramirez, Maximiliano	R-R	5-11	170	10-11-84	.285	.396	.227	80	267	50	76	17	0	9	37	54	3	0	2	72	2	0	.449	.408
2-team (37 Lake County)					.292		—	117	394	69	115	23	1	13	63	84	4	0	5	99	2	0	.454	.417
Rodriguez, Manuel	R-R	6-3	190	1-6-85	.258	.243	.263	70	264	29	68	11	1	6	23	8	2	0	1	57	0	0	.375	.284
Romak, Jamie	R-R	6-2	220	9-30-85	.247	.277	.231	108	348	55	86	26	2	16	68	59	10	0	3	102	3	1	.471	.369
Santos, Jose	R-R	6-0	165	10-7-84	.182	.231	.167	19	55	4	10	2	0	0	3	5	1	1	0	13	1	1	.218	.262
Schafer, Jordan	L-L	6-3	190	9-4-86	.240	.206	.252	114	388	49	93	15	7	8	60	28	1	0	5	95	15	9	.376	.293
Suero, Ovandy	B-R	5-10	160	6-20-82	.231	.203	.247	97	372	50	86	4	4	1	21	40	4	5	2	93	48	18	.272	.278
Trejo, Jaime	R-R	6-3	187	9-7-83	.254	.212	.271	36	118	13	30	7	0	2	16	10	1	1	2	28	2	1	.381	.313

PITCHING

	B-T	HT	WT	DOB	W	L	ERA	G	GS	CG	SV	IP	H	R	ER	HR	BB	SO	AVG	vLH	vRH	K/9	BB/9
Anderson, Devin	L-B	6-5	220	1-24-84	2	1	2.13	19	0	0	2	38	33	11	9	1	16	27	.237	.238	.237	6.39	3.79
Bullock, Tyler	R-R	6-2	225	1-22-84	7	4	4.15	23	8	0	0	80	83	44	37	5	37	58	.269	.295	.247	6.50	4.15
Cormier, Lance	R-R	6-1	200	8-19-80	0	0	0.00	1	0	0	0	1	0	0	0	0	0	2	.000	.000	.000	18.00	0.00
Covington, Marcus	R-R	6-0	185	5-17-85	0	1	0.93	6	0	0	0	10	8	3	1	0	8	8	.222	.190	.267	7.45	7.45
Cuevas, Jairo	R-R	6-2	217	1-24-84	7	12	5.55	27	23	0	0	130	123	87	80	10	65	117	.248	.231	.264	8.12	4.51
Demme, Asher	R-R	6-3	205	11-1-84	3	8	4.05	16	9	1	0	73	71	35	33	7	35	48	.265	.271	.259	5.89	4.30
Evans, Dustin	R-R	6-3	200	9-24-84	2	2	2.88	8	5	0	0	41	37	19	13	1	11	25	.242	.233	.250	5.53	2.43
Gunderson, Kevin	R-L	5-10	165	9-16-84	4	0	1.13	14	0	0	3	24	16	3	3	1	4	21	.195	.167	.207	7.88	1.50
Hernandez, Moises	R-R	6-1	168	3-18-84	2	0	1.93	11	1	0	2	33	21	8	7	1	13	34	.188	.288	.100	9.37	3.58
Hyde, Lee	R-L	6-2	185	2-14-85	0	1	3.33	13	0	0	1	27	29	14	10	2	8	19	.271	.273	.270	6.33	2.67
James, Chuck	L-L	6-0	190	11-9-81	0	0	0.00	1	0	0	0	1	0	0	0	0	0	1	.000	.000	.000	9.00	0.00
Jones, Beau	L-L	6-1	195	8-25-86	5	5	5.61	25	22	0	1	111	125	79	69	8	83	101	.286	.364	.263	8.21	6.75
Lyman, Jeffrey	R-R	6-3	215	1-14-87	6	6	4.49	22	18	0	0	100	118	57	50	3	47	80	.296	.311	.281	7.18	4.22
Nelson, Brad	R-R	6-3	200	1-5-82	1	0	0.69	10	0	0	4	13	10	1	1	0	1	10	.213	.235	.200	6.92	0.69
Nix, Michael	R-R	6-5	235	5-21-83	1	0	1.08	7	0	0	3	8	9	1	1	0	2	18	.273	.300	.261	19.44	2.16
Payano, Nelson	L-L	6-2	180	11-13-82	3	5	5.21	18	4	0	1	47	51	34	27	1	21	47	.274	.104	.333	9.06	4.05
Quinonez, Rudy	R-R	6-2	215	6-17-84	3	1	6.99	33	0	0	5	48	64	41	37	5	21	47	.309	.341	.287	8.87	3.97
Ramirez, Horacio	R-R	6-1	210	11-24-79	0	0	3.86	1	1	0	0	5	5	2	2	1	3	1	.294	—	.294	1.93	5.79
Rayo, Pedro	R-R	6-0	145	5-6-84	0	2	14.14	7	0	0	0	7	13	12	11	0	6	3	.419	.429	.412	3.86	7.71
Reyes, Jo-Jo	L-L	6-2	230	11-20-84	8	1	2.99	13	13	0	0	75	62	26	25	5	25	84	.225	.254	.217	10.04	2.99
Rivas, Carlos	R-R	6-3	160	1-3-85	0	0	2.86	5	4	0	0	22	20	9	7	1	11	15	.241	.263	.234	6.14	4.50
Russell, Stephen	R-R	6-6	185	12-20-83	3	0	2.25	9	0	0	1	20	14	5	5	1	3	21	.200	.207	.195	9.45	1.35
Santiago, Jose	R-R	6-4	180	8-1-81	1	0	4.65	17	1	0	2	31	16	16	16	2	25	40	.155	.196	.115	11.61	7.26
Stanley, Adam	L-L	6-0	201	11-20-84	3	7	3.69	27	7	0	1	76	66	37	31	8	25	56	.239	.195	.258	6.66	2.97
Stevens, Jake	L-L	6-2	215	3-15-85	2	4	4.06	18	6	1	3	62	56	35	28	4	19	48	.238	.203	.251	6.97	2.76
Stockman, Phil	R-R	6-8	250	1-25-80	0	1	0.00	3	0	0	0	5	5	0	0	0	0	5	.417	.667	.167	18.00	9.00
Thomson, John	R-R	6-3	220	10-1-73	0	1	10.80	1	1	0	0	3	6	3	2	2	0	0	.375	.000	.500	0.00	0.00

ORGANIZATION STATISTICS

	B-T	HT	WT	DOB	W	L	ERA	G	GS	CG	SV	IP	H	R	ER	HR	BB	SO	AVG	vLH	vRH	K/9	BB/9
Tisone, Nick	R-R	6-2	185	8-2-83	1	3	4.88	14	0	0	1	31	46	29	17	0	15	13	.329	.258	.392	3.73	4.31
Vines, Chris	R-R	6-5	215	2-26-85	5	2	4.39	12	12	1	0	70	80	37	34	5	20	54	.291	.263	.319	6.98	2.58
Ward, Joshua	R-R	6-3	190	4-1-86	0	0	3.18	2	0	0	0	6	5	5	2	1	1	0	.217	.091	.333	0.00	1.59
Watkins, David	R-R	6-1	210	8-18-81	2	1	5.54	4	0	0	0	13	13	8	8	3	5	12	.271	.333	.190	8.31	3.46

FIELDING

Catcher	PCT	G	PO	A	E	DP	PB
Camarena	1.000	26	106	13	0	1	2
Clark	.998	71	509	52	1	9	1
Guerra	1.000	13	131	8	0	0	6
Hernandez	1.000	3	13	2	0	1	0
Ramirez	.991	39	290	29	3	1	7
Suero	—	1	0	0	0	0	0

First Base	PCT	G	PO	A	E	DP
Camarena	1.000	2	3	2	0	0
Campbell	1.000	1	3	0	0	0
Kaaihue	.994	63	483	37	3	64
Marcial	1.000	2	2	1	0	1
Morris	.996	34	267	4	1	22
Rodriguez	.983	41	306	34	6	41
Romak	1.000	1	3	0	0	1

	PCT	G	PO	A	E	DP
Trejo	1.000	1	5	1	0	1

Second Base	PCT	G	PO	A	E	DP
Arnold	.961	42	63	111	7	26
Lundahl	.955	5	5	16	1	3
Marcial	.960	25	48	72	5	23
Monk	.941	48	73	118	12	24
Santos	.938	14	31	30	4	6
Trejo	1.000	14	31	45	0	11

Third Base	PCT	G	PO	A	E	DP
Arnold	.922	23	13	34	4	4
Campbell	.920	110	59	184	21	17
Lundahl	1.000	2	2	5	0	0
Marcial	1.000	8	5	10	0	0
Santos	.750	2	1	2	1	1
Trejo	.842	5	5	11	3	1

Shortstop	PCT	G	PO	A	E	DP
Andrus	.938	106	208	274	32	81
Arnold	.930	13	16	24	3	9
Lundahl	.800	2	1	3	1	0
Marcial	.921	7	15	20	3	6
Santos	.952	4	7	13	1	4
Trejo	.932	16	26	42	5	6

Outfield	PCT	G	PO	A	E	DP
Davis	.978	119	255	6	6	2
Johnson	1.000	4	7	0	0	0
Koko	.923	12	12	0	1	0
Owings	1.000	8	15	0	0	0
Romak	.962	98	168	9	7	0
Schafer	.993	112	259	10	2	3
Suero	.967	82	144	4	5	1

Danville Braves — Rookie

Appalachian League

BATTING	B-T	HT	WT	DOB	AVG	vLH	vRH	G	AB	R	H	2B	3B	HR	RBI	BB	HBP	SH	SF	SO	SB	CS	SLG	OBP
Bennett, Paul	R-R	5-11	180	9-6-83	.275	.231	.293	45	131	34	36	4	1	0	13	23	8	2	0	35	11	4	.321	.414
Brezeale, Danny	R-R	5-11	200	5-13-86	.270	.310	.250	51	178	18	48	11	0	5	29	7	9	3	3	49	0	3	.416	.325
Britton, Phillip	R-R	6-0	180	9-25-84	.296	.297	.295	58	223	34	66	18	0	7	35	7	2	4	2	31	1	2	.471	.321
Cabrera, Willie	R-R	5-11	185	8-3-86	.308	.300	.312	60	234	35	72	13	1	7	37	11	4	2	4	32	3	2	.462	.344
Flowers, Tyler	R-R	6-4	220	1-24-86	.279	.333	.253	34	129	24	36	9	0	5	16	16	4	0	1	30	0	0	.465	.373
Fontaine, Robert	L-R	6-2	185	10-22-85	.296	.250	.317	60	199	42	59	11	0	4	25	37	3	0	2	45	4	2	.412	.411
Mejia, Ernesto	R-R	6-6	190	12-2-85	.296	.310	.288	50	169	29	50	16	1	4	25	16	5	1	1	48	1	0	.473	.372
Miles, Cole	B-R	5-8	165	3-24-87	.250	.000	.286	5	8	2	2	0	0	0	0	2	0	0	1	0	0		.250	.400
Monk, Brandon	R-R	5-11	180	2-22-87	.162	.213	.137	46	142	21	23	4	0	0	9	12	4	5	3	32	0	2	.190	.242
Owings, Jon	R-R	6-4	192	4-4-85	.284	.309	.271	42	162	28	46	12	1	8	29	13	3	0	3	32	2	1	.519	.343
Rodriguez, Concepcion	R-R	6-2	170	9-19-86	.275	.278	.273	63	244	45	67	11	3	5	37	24	2	3	5	39	9	4	.406	.338
Santos, Jose	R-R	6-0	165	10-7-84	.250	.294	.237	25	76	14	19	3	1	1	11	7	1	2	0	16	2	2	.355	.321
Silva, Yohan	B-R	5-11	175	1-30-85	.417	.333	.444	7	12	3	5	1	0	0	4	1	0	2	0	4	0	0	.500	.462
Stevens, Jeff	R-R	6-3	215	3-28-84	.111	1.000	.000	2	9	2	1	0	0	0	1	1	0	0	0	2	0	0	.111	.200
Verastegui, Jerry	L-R	5-10	213	1-26-83	.297	.455	.270	26	74	13	22	5	2	0	12	13	0	0	1	9	0	1	.365	.398
Williams, Larry	L-R	6-2	205	4-6-85	.338	.326	.345	66	266	36	90	17	2	2	46	23	2	0	5	46	2	0	.440	.389

PITCHING	B-T	HT	WT	DOB	W	L	ERA	G	GS	CG	SV	IP	H	R	ER	HR	BB	SO	AVG	vLH	vRH	K/9	BB/9
Acosta, Jorge	L-L	5-11	185	9-18-83	3	1	3.81	17	0	0	0	26	23	11	11	0	10	36	.242	.348	.208	12.46	3.46
Broadway, Michael	R-R	6-5	190	3-30-87	4	0	3.25	9	5	0	0	36	30	15	13	1	9	18	.231	.260	.213	4.50	2.25
Chapman, Jaye	R-R	6-0	180	5-22-87	1	2	5.77	14	5	0	1	34	46	25	22	2	21	24	.338	.469	.298	6.29	5.50
Cofield, Kyle	R-R	6-5	190	1-23-87	2	3	6.21	13	8	0	0	42	50	31	29	2	22	29	.289	.343	.255	6.21	4.71
Covington, Marcus	R-R	6-0	185	5-17-85	1	1	5.94	12	1	0	0	17	21	13	11	0	17	15	.313	.290	.333	8.10	9.18
Curtis, James	R-R	6-1	205	5-6-86	3	0	4.35	12	1	0	0	21	22	13	10	3	7	16	.268	.269	.268	6.97	3.05
Evans, Dustin	R-R	6-3	200	9-24-84	1	1	1.69	2	1	0	0	11	5	2	2	0	4	10	.147	.000	.179	8.44	3.38
Guerra, Junior	R-R	6-0	185	1-16-85	0	1	9.00	2	0	0	0	2	2	2	2	0	0	1	.250	.500	.167	4.50	0.00
Gunderson, Kevin	R-L	5-10	165	9-16-84	0	0	0.00	1	0	0	0	1	0	0	0	0	0	0	.000	—	.000	0.00	0.00
Hanson, Thomas	R-R	6-6	210	8-28-86	4	1	2.09	13	8	0	0	52	42	15	12	2	9	56	.218	.263	.188	9.75	1.57
Hendricks, Donavon	L-L	6-0	175	3-9-86	1	0	6.27	16	0	0	0	19	20	14	13	1	15	21	.290	.357	.273	10.13	7.23
Hyde, Lee	R-L	6-2	185	2-14-85	1	0	0.00	3	1	0	0	5	3	0	0	0	2	6	.176	.000	.250	10.80	3.60
Johnson, Joseph	R-R	6-4	210	8-10-84	1	0	0.00	3	0	0	0	4	1	0	0	0	2	6	.100	.200	.000	14.73	4.91
Katz, Jeff	R-R	6-4	217	4-18-86	1	0	4.15	16	0	0	0	17	19	10	8	1	14	19	.271	.348	.234	9.87	7.27
Medlen, Kristopher	B-R	5-10	175	10-7-85	1	0	0.41	20	0	0	10	22	14	2	1	0	2	36	.175	.182	.170	14.73	0.82
Rayo, Pedro	R-R	6-0	145	5-6-84	1	1	4.38	11	4	0	0	25	33	18	12	2	8	23	.303	.333	.281	8.39	2.92
Richmond, Jamie	R-R	6-0	185	3-23-86	7	1	1.21	14	12	0	0	67	51	11	9	0	4	52	.210	.188	.222	6.99	0.54
Sencion, Carlos	L-L	6-6	170	11-17-84	0	4	2.56	13	9	0	1	53	41	18	15	6	17	60	.212	.241	.207	10.25	2.91
Tisone, Nick	R-R	6-2	185	8-2-83	0	3	3.00	6	0	0	0	6	6	2	2	1	3	3	.250	.300	.214	4.50	4.50
Valenzuela, Sergio	R-R	6-0	175	9-15-84	3	4	6.04	13	11	0	0	51	57	44	34	5	18	29	.286	.313	.274	5.15	3.20
Ward, Joshua	R-R	6-3	190	4-1-86	1	3	4.70	14	1	0	0	23	37	21	12	1	9	19	.363	.500	.281	7.43	3.52
Williams, David	R-R	6-4	190	5-6-85	2	1	2.52	22	0	0	4	25	20	8	7	1	11	29	.215	.235	.203	10.44	3.96
Wilson, Tyler	L-L	6-1	210	7-11-86	3	2	4.43	16	0	0	2	22	15	11	11	3	13	40	.185	.118	.203	16.12	5.24

FIELDING

Catcher	PCT	G	PO	A	E	DP	PB
Britton	.981	48	373	43	8	3	8
Flowers	1.000	8	56	5	0	0	1
Stevens	1.000	6	26	2	0	0	0
Verastegui	.990	15	89	9	1	1	1

First Base	PCT	G	PO	A	E	DP
Flowers	.995	22	180	17	1	18
Mejia	.974	33	281	19	8	25
Williams	.980	12	91	7	2	8

Second Base	PCT	G	PO	A	E	DP
Bennett	.920	11	23	23	4	4
Miles	.909	4	3	7	1	2
Monk	.961	45	68	106	7	27
Santos	.983	15	21	37	1	10

Third Base	PCT	G	PO	A	E	DP
Bennett	.938	17	12	33	3	6
Brezeale	.942	51	41	106	9	9
Santos	1.000	4	0	2	0	1

Shortstop	PCT	G	PO	A	E	DP
Bennett	.929	12	18	34	4	9

	PCT	G	PO	A	E	DP
Fontaine	.907	53	53	122	18	18
Santos	1.000	6	6	12	0	2

Outfield	PCT	G	PO	A	E	DP
Bennett	.857	5	5	1	1	0
Cabrera	.961	58	120	2	5	0
Mejia	—	1	0	0	0	0
Owings	.974	42	71	5	2	0
Rodriguez	.946	62	103	3	6	1
Silva	1.000	7	7	0	0	0
Williams	.962	33	49	1	2	0

ORGANIZATION STATISTICS

Gulf Coast League

BATTING

	B-T	HT	WT	DOB	AVG	vLH	vRH	G	AB	R	H	2B	3B	HR	RBI	BB	HBP	SH	SF	SO	SB	CS	SLG	OBP
Alexander, John	L-R	6-3	195	11-1-83	.188	.000	.214	11	16	2	3	0	0	0	2	3	1	0	0	5	0	0	.188	.350
Burrus, Josh	R-R	5-11	190	8-20-83	.154	.100	.188	8	26	4	4	1	0	0	1	2	0	0	0	7	2	1	.192	.214
Campusano, Albaro	R-R	5-11	175	12-14-86	.177	.148	.186	39	124	15	22	4	0	0	5	10	1	0	0	16	1	0	.210	.244
Carmona, Eliazar	R-R	6-1	170	12-12-85	.230	.192	.239	45	139	10	32	2	1	1	10	10	1	0	1	22	9	1	.281	.285
Casso, Jorge	R-R	6-2	180	2-4-84	.173	.150	.180	33	81	5	14	2	0	0	7	3	1	0	0	26	0	0	.198	.212
Coe, Adam	R-R	6-0	190	6-7-88	.269	.243	.277	43	156	23	42	9	1	7	32	16	2	0	1	39	0	1	.474	.343
De La Cruz, Tony	B-R	6-1	150	3-29-87	.190	.294	.152	20	63	12	12	2	0	0	3	6	3	1	0	10	5	4	.222	.292
Dominguez, Javier	B-R	6-1	150	7-14-85	.217	.211	.220	29	69	11	15	2	0	0	7	6	10	0	2	12	1	0	.246	.356
Garcia, Steven	R-R	5-11	190	9-7-86	.207	.235	.200	28	82	8	17	3	0	2	5	4	3	0	0	25	0	0	.317	.270
Griffin, Trevion	R-R	5-11	175	11-8-84	.200	.308	.173	31	65	8	13	2	0	1	9	8	2	0	0	18	2	1	.277	.307
Hamaoka, Takumi	L-R	6-1	185	9-4-86	.253	.125	.284	33	83	6	21	4	0	0	8	6	2	0	0	17	0	1	.301	.319
Hernandez, Diory	R-R	5-11	170	4-8-84	.267	.143	.304	8	30	6	8	1	0	1	2	3	2	0	0	5	0	0	.400	.371
Hernandez, Victor	R-R	6-1	170	1-17-85	.296	.286	.300	13	27	2	8	2	1	0	0	1	0	0	0	6	0	0	.444	.321
Johnson, Cody	L-R	6-4	195	8-18-88	.184	.056	.208	32	114	13	21	6	1	1	16	12	0	0	1	49	2	0	.281	.260
Koko, Rubi	R-R	6-3	185	3-25-86	.264	.320	.247	42	110	18	29	6	0	2	14	13	1	2	0	39	10	2	.373	.347
Lundahl, Chad	R-R	6-2	190	8-18-84	.444	.500	.435	11	27	5	12	3	0	0	4	4	0	0	0	2	0	0	.556	.516
Marbry, Michael	R-R	6-3	185	9-3-84	.130	.000	.143	10	23	4	3	1	0	0	0	4	0	0	0	10	0	0	.174	.259
Miles, Cole	B-R	5-8	165	3-24-87	.307	.364	.308	32	114	23	35	4	2	1	10	22	3	1	0	20	18	2	.404	.432
Owings, Jon	R-R	6-4	192	4-4-85	.368	.286	.417	13	38	5	14	4	0	0	6	6	1	0	1	6	2	0	.474	.457
Parliament, Adam	R-R	6-4	220	12-16-85	.234	.364	.201	45	167	18	39	8	1	4	21	18	5	0	1	45	3	0	.365	.325
Reyes, Cesar	R-R	5-11	205	4-7-83	.200	1.000	.000	4	5	1	1	0	0	0	0	2	0	0	0	1	0	0	.200	.429
Rivadeneira, Deivis	R-R	5-11	160	11-28-85	.277	.200	.297	16	47	5	13	2	0	0	7	5	2	0	0	4	0	0	.319	.370
Silva, Yohan	B-R	5-11	175	1-30-85	.333	—	.333	1	3	0	1	1	0	0	0	0	0	0	0	1	0	0	.667	.333
Timmons, Wes	R-R	6-0	190	7-12-79	.308	.000	.364	8	26	3	8	2	0	0	1	4	2	0	0	4	2	0	.385	.438
Weidenaar, Nate	R-R	6-2	190	12-14-86	.098	.100	.098	29	51	6	5	1	0	0	2	5	1	1	0	11	2	1	.118	.193

PITCHING

	B-T	HT	WT	DOB	W	L	ERA	G	GS	CG	SV	IP	H	R	ER	HR	BB	SO	AVG	vLH	vRH	K/9	BB/9
Beck, Casey	R-R	6-1	215	3-28-87	0	0	1.69	8	0	0	1	11	7	3	2	0	6	8	.194	.200	.192	6.75	5.06
Castro, Yeliar	R-R	6-3	180	12-8-87	1	2	5.32	8	5	0	1	24	23	18	14	1	15	19	.247	.316	.230	7.23	5.70
Evarts, Steven	L-L	6-3	180	10-13-87	2	2	2.93	11	9	0	0	43	42	19	14	0	12	33	.255	.207	.265	6.91	2.51
Feliz, Neftali	R-R	6-3	180	5-2-88	0	2	4.03	11	5	0	2	29	20	13	13	0	14	42	.192	.125	.222	13.03	4.34
Figueroa, Steven	R-R	6-0	215	5-1-88	0	0	3.00	3	1	0	0	6	8	3	2	1	1	3	.308	.000	.444	4.50	1.50
Garcia, Steven	R-R	5-11	190	9-7-86	0	0	0.00	1	0	0	0	1	0	1	0	0	1	0	.000	—	.000	9.00	9.00
Garcia, Ysidro	R-R	6-0	165	5-15-87	1	1	4.63	8	0	0	0	12	13	8	6	1	4	8	.283	.313	.267	6.17	3.09
Gonzalez, Raul	R-R	6-2	155	7-12-85	0	0	0.00	1	1	0	0	3	2	0	0	0	3	0	.182	.000	.222	0.00	9.00
Guerra, Junior	R-R	5-11	213	1-16-85	0	1	6.75	14	0	0	1	24	25	19	18	3	16	16	.266	.300	.250	6.00	6.00
Himpsl, Derick	L-L	6-4	240	6-4-86	2	1	8.68	7	0	0	0	9	11	10	9	0	5	8	.314	.500	.290	7.71	4.82
Johnson, Joseph	R-R	6-4	210	8-10-84	2	2	3.54	16	0	0	0	20	22	11	8	0	9	20	.268	.148	.327	8.85	3.98
Kent, Steve	L-L	6-0	170	5-8-89	1	4	4.00	11	6	0	0	36	32	18	16	1	16	20	.241	.286	.232	5.00	4.00
Locke, Jeffrey	L-L	6-2	180	11-20-87	4	3	4.22	10	5	0	0	32	38	18	15	4	5	38	.299	.250	.311	10.69	1.41
Lyman, Jeffrey	R-R	6-3	215	1-14-87	0	0	1.50	2	2	0	0	6	2	1	1	0	1	9	.095	.000	.154	13.50	1.50
Mehlich, Michael	R-R	6-2	180	9-5-87	1	0	3.22	13	0	0	2	22	15	8	8	1	7	25	.188	.208	.179	10.07	2.82
Ortegano, Jose	L-L	6-1	145	8-5-87	3	3	3.30	12	5	0	0	46	43	20	17	3	10	31	.247	.250	.246	6.02	1.94
Osuna, Edgar	L-L	6-1	165	11-25-87	0	1	0.92	6	2	0	2	20	15	4	2	0	1	18	.217	.100	.237	8.24	0.46
Payano, Nelson	L-L	6-2	180	11-13-82	0	0	7.20	3	0	0	0	5	5	5	4	0	4	5	.263	.667	.188	9.00	7.20
Rasmus, Cory	R-R	6-1	220	11-6-87	0	0	8.59	3	1	0	0	7	7	7	7	0	5	3	.280	.250	.308	3.68	6.14
Rivas, Carlos	L-L	6-0	160	1-3-85	0	1	0.00	3	0	0	0	6	4	3	0	0	2	5	.174	.000	.267	7.94	3.18
Rodgers, Chad	L-L	6-3	185	11-23-87	3	2	2.31	11	5	0	1	39	31	14	10	1	13	30	.217	.333	.190	6.92	3.00
Sanchez, Julio	R-R	6-1	158	7-11-85	1	0	4.50	11	0	0	2	16	14	9	8	0	4	13	.241	.250	.238	7.31	2.25
Sodowsky, Clint	L-R	6-4	200	7-13-72	0	0	0.00	1	0	0	0	1	0	0	0	0	0	2	.000	—	.000	18.00	0.00
Warren, Jesse	L-L	6-3	180	3-21-86	2	2	5.09	12	0	0	0	18	12	10	10	2	10	4	.197	.000	.240	2.04	5.09
White, Sean	R-R	6-4	215	4-25-81	0	0	0.00	3	0	0	0	7	3	0	0	0	0	6	.125	.182	.077	7.71	0.00

FIELDING

Catcher	PCT	G	PO	A	E	DP	PB
Alexander	.969	8	30	1	1	1	0
Dominguez	.943	25	132	16	9	3	3
Garcia	.963	26	148	10	6	2	4
V. Hernandez	.970	11	57	7	2	0	1
Reyes	1.000	3	8	1	0	0	0

First Base	PCT	G	PO	A	E	DP
Casso	.972	12	66	4	2	3
Hernandez	—	1	0	0	0	0
Parliament	.986	43	337	24	5	33

Second Base	PCT	G	PO	A	E	DP
Campusano	.975	21	35	42	2	7
De La Cruz	.967	5	15	14	1	4
Miles	.936	26	46	56	7	13

	PCT	G	PO	A	E	DP
Rivadeneira	.955	5	10	11	1	2
Timmons	1.000	1	2	3	0	1

Third Base	PCT	G	PO	A	E	DP
Campusano	.923	6	4	8	1	0
Coe	.906	40	28	78	11	7
Dominguez	.818	3	4	5	2	0
Lundahl	1.000	2	2	3	0	1
Timmons	1.000	6	3	9	0	2

Shortstop	PCT	G	PO	A	E	DP
Campusano	.943	13	26	40	4	7
De La Cruz	.914	11	8	24	3	4
D. Hernandez	.892	8	12	21	4	7
Lundahl	.902	8	10	27	4	5
Marbry	1.000	8	8	19	0	5

	PCT	G	PO	A	E	DP
Rivadeneira	.892	8	8	25	4	4
Timmons	1.000	1	2	0	0	0

Outfield	PCT	G	PO	A	E	DP
Burrus	1.000	4	7	0	0	0
Carmona	.975	45	107	8	3	3
Griffin	.968	25	28	2	1	0
Hamaoka	1.000	22	24	1	0	0
Johnson	.933	26	28	0	2	0
Koko	1.000	40	74	1	0	0
Miles	—	1	0	0	0	0
Owings	1.000	10	13	2	0	1
Silva	1.000	1	1	0	0	0
Weidenaar	1.000	28	29	2	0	1

ORGANIZATION STATISTICS

BALTIMORE ORIOLES

BY ROCH KUBATKO

Fourth place has become familiar to the Orioles, but it's not exactly comfortable.

For the eighth time in the last nine seasons, the Orioles finished ahead of one team, the Devil Rays, in the American League East. Their final attendance was the lowest since Camden Yards opened in 1992, and that includes the strike-shortened season. If players are frustrated, they've got nothing on the fans. By going 70-92, the Orioles posted their ninth straight losing season, the longest stretch in club history.

Sam Perlozzo's first full season as manager didn't include any players failing a steroid test. Nobody was fired, though first base coach Dave Cash was reassigned within the organization. In that regard, the year was a success, or at least gave the team some stability. But the production on the field still was lacking.

The Orioles were 34-28 against teams with a losing record, and 36-64 against teams above .500. They were the last club in the major leagues to win four games in a row.

In keeping with a recent trend, the Orioles went 16-33 against lefthanded pitchers, and their .258 average ranked last in the American League. But they were 54-59 against righthanders and ranked fourth with a .284 average.

The addition of pitching coach Leo Mazzone didn't pay immediate dividends, at least statistically. The young staff's 5.35 ERA was the second-highest in the AL and second-highest in club history. The starters ranked 13th in the league with a 5.40 ERA, and the bullpen was 19-25 with a 5.26 ERA.

ORGANIZATION LEADERS

BATTING		*Minimum 250 at-bats
*AVG	Rowell, Billy, Bluefield/Aberdeen	.328
R	Finan, Ryan, Delmarva	87
H	Keylor, Cory, Bowie	131
TB	Reimold, Nolan, Frederick	211
2B	Reed, Keith, Ottawa	35
3B	Rivas, Arturo, Delmarva/Frederick	7
HR	Fransz, Jason, Frederick	24
RBI	Fransz, Jason, Frederick	84
BB	Finan, Ryan, Delmarva	91
SO	Bass, Bryan, Frederick/Bowie	172
SB	Scott Jr., Lorenzo, Delmarva	29
*OBP	Rowell, Billy, Bluefield/Aberdeen	.415
*SLG	Rowell, Billy, Bluefield/Aberdeen	.503
XBH	Finan, Ryan, Delmarva	52

PITCHING		#Minimum 75 innings
W	Johnson, Jim, Bowie	13
L	Finch, Brian, Bowie	12
	Hamblet, Reid, Delmarva	12
#ERA	Moore, Jeffrey, Aberdeen	2.41
G	McCurdy, Nick, Ottawa/Bowie	60
CG	DuBose, Eric, Ottawa/Bowie	2
	Penn, Hayden, Bowie/Ottawa	2
SV	Hoey, Jim, Delmarva/Frederick/Bowie	33
IP	Olson, Garrett, Frederick/Bowie	166
BB	Spoone, Chorye, Delmarva	80
SO	Olson, Garrett, Frederick/Bowie	162
#AVG	Ramirez, Luis, Frederick	.226

PLAYERS OF THE YEAR

MAJOR LEAGUE: Erik Bedard, lhp

Bedard was the most consistent starter on an erratic staff, leading the club in wins (15), ERA (3.76), innings (197) and strikeouts (171). A sixth-round pick in 1999, Bedard had his best year by far in the majors, recording more victories last year than he had in his two previous big league seasons.

MINOR LEAGUE: Garrett Olson, lhp

Olson threw 200 innings between college and pro ball after the Orioles drafted him 48th overall in 2005, and he showed he could handle the workload at high Class A Frederick and Double-A Bowie in 2006, finishing with 10-9, 3.10 numbers in 166 innings. Olson also led the system in strikeouts with 162.

CARL KLINE

The Orioles also led the majors by allowing 216 home runs, the second-highest total in club history. They served up 12 grand slams—11 on the road.

On a positive note, lefthander Erik Bedard emerged as a frontline starting pitcher, going 15-11, 3.76 and winning nine more games than his previous high. And Daniel Cabrera finished with a one-hit shutout at Yankee Stadium to provide hope that he's finally turned the corner—and not hit another wall.

But the Opening Day starter, Rodrigo Lopez, was 9-18, 5.90. And Bruce Chen went from 13 wins to none while also falling out of the rotation. Relief didn't come from the bullpen, which used 19 pitchers. Only Chris Ray, in his first season as a closer, earned positive reviews.

Shortstop Miguel Tejada, the subject of trade rumors since last winter, set the single-season club record for hits with 214 and was named the team's MVP. And right fielder Nick Markakis recovered from a slow start to emerge as one of the top rookies in the majors, batting .291 with 16 home runs.

On the minor league level, the Orioles scored their most significant victory by moving their Triple-A affiliate from Ottawa to Norfolk, giving them arguably the best farm system geography in baseball. Class A Frederick reached the finals of the Carolina League playoffs before bowing out. Short-season Aberdeen missed qualifying for the New York-Penn League playoffs on the last day.

Without an abundance of position prospects in the farm system, the Orioles chose Double-A Bowie outfielder Cory Keylor as the organization's minor league player of the year. Keylor batted .294 with 20 doubles and two triples in 446 at-bats and committed just three errors.

Righthander James Hoey earned pitcher of the year honors after starting the year at low Class A Delmarva and ending it with the Orioles. Hoey went 2-1, 2.54 with 18 saves at Delmarva, walking 10 and striking out 46 in 28 innings, and holding opponents to a .175 average. He had a 0.64 ERA and 11 saves at Frederick, walking five and striking out 16 in 14 innings, and a 4.00 ERA and four saves at Bowie, walking three and striking out 11 in nine innings.

Baltimore Orioles — MLB

American League

BATTING	B-T	HT	WT	DOB	AVG	vLH	vRH	G	AB	R	H	2B	3B	HR	RBI	BB	HBP	SH	SF	SO	SB	CS	SLG	OBP
Ardoin, Danny	R-R	6-0	215	7-8-74	.077	—	.077	5	13	2	1	0	0	0	1	1	1	0	0	6	0	0	.077	.200
Chavez, Raul	R-R	5-11	180	3-18-73	.179	.000	.200	16	28	1	5	0	0	0	0	1	0	0	0	4	0	0	.179	.207
Clark, Howie	L-R	5-10	195	2-13-74	.143	.500	.000	7	7	1	1	0	0	0	0	0	2	0	1	2	0	0	.143	.333
Conine, Jeff	R-R	6-1	225	6-26-66	.265	.267	.264	114	389	43	103	20	3	9	49	35	2	1	5	53	3	2	.401	.325
Fahey, Brandon	L-R	6-2	160	1-18-81	.235	.190	.244	91	251	36	59	8	2	2	23	23	3	9	0	48	3	3	.307	.307
Fiorentino, Jeff	L-R	6-1	180	4-14-83	.256	.182	.286	19	39	8	10	2	0	0	7	7	1	2	1	3	1	0	.308	.375
Gibbons, Jay	L-L	6-0	205	3-2-77	.277	.258	.281	90	343	34	95	23	0	13	46	32	2	0	1	48	0	0	.458	.341
Gomez, Chris	R-R	6-1	190	6-16-71	.341	.333	.345	55	132	14	45	7	0	2	17	7	3	0	0	11	1	2	.439	.387
Hernandez, Ramon	R-R	6-0	225	5-20-76	.275	.291	.270	144	501	66	138	29	2	23	91	43	11	0	5	79	1	0	.479	.343
Lopez, Javy	R-R	6-3	220	11-5-70	.265	.273	.262	76	279	30	74	15	1	8	31	18	2	0	0	60	0	0	.412	.314
2-team (18 Boston)					.251	—		94	342	36	86	20	1	8	35	20	2	0	0	76	0	0	.386	.297
Markakis, Nick	L-L	6-2	195	11-17-83	.291	.286	.293	147	491	72	143	25	2	16	62	43	3	3	2	72	2	0	.448	.351
Matos, Luis	R-R	6-0	215	10-30-78	.207	.226	.191	55	121	14	25	7	1	2	5	10	2	1	0	21	7	0	.331	.278
Millar, Kevin	R-R	6-0	215	9-24-71	.272	.244	.283	132	430	64	117	26	0	15	64	59	12	0	2	74	1	1	.437	.374
Mora, Melvin	R-R	5-11	200	2-2-72	.274	.253	.282	155	624	96	171	25	0	16	83	54	14	6	7	99	11	1	.391	.342
Newhan, David	L-R	5-10	170	9-7-73	.252	.182	.266	39	131	14	33	4	0	4	18	7	2	0	3	22	4	2	.374	.294
Patterson, Corey	L-R	5-9	175	8-13-79	.276	.207	.301	135	463	75	128	19	5	16	53	21	5	8	1	94	45	9	.443	.314
Roberts, Brian	B-R	5-9	175	10-9-77	.286	.235	.308	138	563	85	161	34	3	10	55	55	0	6	5	66	36	7	.410	.347
Rogers, Ed	R-R	6-3	190	8-29-78	.200	.154	.250	17	25	1	5	0	0	0	2	0	0	0	1	3	0	0	.200	.192
Tatis, Fernando	R-R	5-10	195	1-1-75	.250	.286	.214	28	56	7	14	6	1	2	8	6	0	2	0	17	0	0	.500	.313
Tejada, Miguel	R-R	5-9	215	5-25-76	.330	.335	.329	162	648	99	214	37	0	24	100	46	9	0	6	79	6	2	.498	.379
Terrero, Luis	R-R	6-3	225	5-18-80	.200	.182	.286	27	40	4	8	1	0	1	6	1	1	0	0	7	0	3	.300	.238
Widger, Chris	R-R	6-2	220	5-21-71	.118	.200	.083	9	17	0	2	0	0	0	2	2	0	1	0	4	0	0	.118	.211
2-team (27 Chicago)					.172	—		36	93	6	16	3	0	1	9	11	0	1	2	24	0	0	.237	.255

PITCHING	B-T	HT	WT	DOB	W	L	ERA	G	GS	CG	SV	IP	H	R	ER	HR	BB	SO	AVG	vLH	vRH	K/9	BB/9
Abreu, Winston	R-R	6-2	170	4-5-77	0	0	10.13	7	0	0	0	8	10	10	9	1	6	6	.294	.286	.300	6.75	6.75
Bedard, Erik	L-L	6-1	190	3-6-79	15	11	3.76	33	33	0	0	196	196	92	82	16	69	171	.258	.200	.272	7.84	3.16
Benson, Kris	R-R	6-4	205	11-7-74	11	12	4.82	30	30	3	0	183	199	105	98	33	58	88	.287	.303	.270	4.33	2.85
Birkins, Kurt	L-L	6-2	190	8-11-80	5	2	4.94	35	0	0	0	31	25	19	17	4	16	27	.221	.212	.230	7.84	4.65
Britton, Chris	R-R	6-3	280	12-16-82	0	2	3.35	52	0	0	1	54	46	22	20	4	17	41	.228	.301	.186	6.88	2.85
Brower, Jim	R-R	6-1	215	12-29-72	0	1	13.86	12	0	0	0	12	21	19	19	1	13	9	.389	.261	.484	6.57	9.49
Burres, Brian	L-L	6-1	180	4-8-81	0	0	2.25	11	0	0	0	8	6	2	2	1	1	6	.200	.071	.313	6.75	1.13
Byrdak, Tim	L-L	5-11	195	10-31-73	1	0	12.86	16	0	0	0	7	14	10	10	2	8	2	.438	.381	.545	2.57	10.29
Cabrera, Daniel	R-R	6-7	260	5-28-81	9	10	4.74	26	26	2	0	148	130	82	78	11	104	157	.241	.231	.251	9.55	6.32
Chen, Bruce	L-L	6-1	215	6-19-77	0	7	6.93	40	12	0	0	99	137	81	76	28	35	70	.334	.328	.337	6.39	3.19
DuBose, Eric	L-L	6-3	235	5-15-76	0	0	9.64	2	0	0	0	5	10	5	5	2	3	2	.500	.400	.533	3.86	5.79
Halama, John	L-L	6-5	215	2-22-72	3	1	6.14	17	1	0	0	29	38	20	20	6	13	12	.325	.304	.338	3.68	3.99
Hawkins, LaTroy	R-R	6-5	215	12-21-72	3	2	4.48	60	0	0	0	60	73	30	30	4	15	27	.300	.323	.285	4.03	2.24
Hoey, Jim	R-R	6-6	200	12-30-82	0	1	10.24	12	0	0	0	10	14	11	11	1	5	6	.359	.375	.348	5.59	4.66
Johnson, Jim	R-R	6-5	225	6-27-83	0	1	24.00	1	1	0	0	3	9	8	8	1	3	0	.563	.375	.750	0.00	9.00
Loewen, Adam	L-L	6-5	235	4-9-84	6	6	5.37	22	19	0	0	112	111	72	67	8	62	98	.259	.277	.254	7.85	4.97
Lopez, Rodrigo	R-R	6-1	185	12-14-75	9	18	5.90	36	29	0	0	189	234	129	124	32	59	136	.302	.308	.296	6.48	2.81
Manon, Julio	R-R	6-0	200	6-10-73	0	1	5.40	22	0	0	0	20	23	13	12	5	16	22	.274	.364	.216	9.90	7.20
Ortiz, Russ	R-R	6-1	215	6-5-74	0	3	8.48	20	5	0	0	40	59	39	38	15	18	23	.349	.386	.323	5.13	4.02
Penn, Hayden	R-R	6-3	195	10-13-84	0	4	15.10	6	6	0	0	20	38	33	33	8	13	8	.392	.327	.467	3.66	5.95
Ray, Chris	R-R	6-3	225	1-12-82	4	4	2.73	61	0	0	33	66	45	22	20	10	27	51	.193	.184	.202	6.95	3.68
Rleal, Sendy	R-R	6-1	180	6-21-80	1	1	4.44	42	0	0	0	47	48	25	23	10	23	19	.274	.242	.310	3.66	4.44
Rodriguez, Eddy	R-R	6-1	215	8-8-81	1	1	7.20	9	0	0	0	15	17	14	12	5	10	11	.283	.318	.263	6.60	6.00
Williams, Todd	R-R	6-3	220	2-13-71	2	4	4.74	62	0	0	1	57	76	36	30	8	19	24	.323	.342	.314	3.79	3.00

FIELDING

Catcher	PCT	G	PO	A	E	DP	PB
Ardoin	1.000	5	35	1	0	0	1
Chavez	.985	15	60	5	1	1	0
Hernandez	.985	135	793	69	13	5	13
Lopez	1.000	21	124	9	0	1	1
Widger	1.000	6	32	3	0	1	0

First Base	PCT	G	PO	A	E	DP
Conine	.996	73	422	30	2	47
Gomez	1.000	27	116	0	0	14
Hernandez	1.000	2	5	0	0	0
Millar	.995	98	764	62	4	74
Newhan	1.000	1	3	1	0	1
Tatis	1.000	4	40	2	0	3

Second Base	PCT	G	PO	A	E	DP
Fahey	1.000	13	29	34	0	11

	PCT	G	PO	A	E	DP
Gomez	.986	15	37	33	1	10
Mora	1.000	1	0	2	0	0
Roberts	.985	137	214	375	9	98
Rogers	1.000	4	3	5	0	2
Tatis	—	1	0	0	0	0

Third Base	PCT	G	PO	A	E	DP
Clark	—	1	0	0	0	0
Conine	1.000	1	0	0	0	0
Fahey	1.000	1	1	1	0	0
Gomez	.867	5	3	10	2	1
Mora	.959	154	101	296	17	18
Rogers	.667	4	1	1	1	0
Tatis	1.000	5	1	8	0	0

Shortstop	PCT	G	PO	A	E	DP
Fahey	.935	17	11	32	3	11

	PCT	G	PO	A	E	DP
Gomez	1.000	6	5	7	0	2
Rogers	—	1	0	0	0	0
Tejada	.972	150	237	418	19	108

Outfield	PCT	G	PO	A	E	DP
Conine	.989	57	85	5	1	1
Fahey	.954	54	101	2	5	1
Fiorentino	1.000	17	28	3	0	1
Gibbons	.980	44	97	1	2	0
Markakis	.994	145	314	8	2	0
Matos	1.000	47	67	0	0	0
Newhan	.970	37	65	0	2	0
Patterson	.989	134	345	7	4	0
Rogers	.750	4	3	0	1	0
Tatis	1.000	4	7	1	0	0
Terrero	.973	23	33	3	1	1

Ottawa Lynx — Triple-A

International League

BATTING	B-T	HT	WT	DOB	AVG	vLH	vRH	G	AB	R	H	2B	3B	HR	RBI	BB	HBP	SH	SF	SO	SB	CS	SLG	OBP
Alvarez, Tony	R-R	6-1	200	5-10-79	.289	.217	.317	25	83	14	24	3	0	2	10	5	1	0	1	9	1	3	.398	.333
Badeaux, Brooks	B-R	5-10	177	10-20-76	.223	.262	.206	47	139	12	31	4	0	3	16	7	1	2	0	24	0	2	.317	.265
Bock, Brian	R-R	6-1	210	8-24-81	.000	.000	—	1	1	0	0	0	0	0	0	0	0	0	0	0	0	0	.000	.000

General manager: Mike Flanagan. **Farm director:** David Stockstill. **Scouting director:** Joe Jordan.

Class	Team	League	W	L	PCT	Finish*	Manager	Affiliate Since
Majors	Baltimore	American	70	92	.432	12th (14)	Sam Perlozzo	—
Triple-A	Ottawa Lynx	International	74	69	.517	8th (14)	Dave Trembley	2003
Double-A	Bowie Baysox	Eastern	67	74	.475	8th (12)	Don Werner	1993
High A	Frederick Keys	Carolina	61	77	.442	8th (8)	Bien Figueroa	1989
Low A	Delmarva Shorebirds	South Atlantic	64	73	.467	12th (16)	Gary Kendall	1997
Short-season	Aberdeen IronBirds	New York-Penn	41	34	.547	5th (14)	Andy Etchebarren	2002
Rookie	Bluefield Orioles	Appalachian	31	37	.456	8th (10)	Gary Allenson	1958
OVERALL 2006 MINOR LEAGUE RECORD			338	364	.481	23rd (30)		

*Finish in overall standings (No. of teams in league). +League champion

ORGANIZATION STATISTICS

	B-T	HT	WT	DOB	AVG	vLH	vRH	G	AB	R	H	2B	3B	HR	RBI	BB	HBP	SH	SF	SO	SB	CS	SLG	OBP
Bowers, Jason	R-R	5-10	183	1-27-78	.230	.167	.250	58	174	16	40	7	1	0	8	14	4	7	2	29	5	1	.282	.299
Calzado, Napoleon	R-R	6-3	200	2-9-77	.289	.317	.279	64	246	30	71	15	1	3	27	6	4	0	1	29	5	0	.394	.315
Clark, Howie	L-R	5-10	195	2-13-74	.263	.247	.270	86	308	41	81	16	1	3	27	36	2	2	2	28	2	2	.351	.342
Donovan, Todd	R-R	6-1	180	8-12-78	.216	.222	.213	45	153	17	33	3	0	2	7	14	4	1	1	26	8	6	.275	.297
Fahey, Brandon	L-R	6-2	160	1-18-81	.279	.174	.333	20	68	8	19	1	1	0	3	10	4	2	0	5	4	3	.324	.402
Freire, Alejandro	R-R	6-2	225	8-23-74	.226	.267	.205	50	177	21	40	7	0	3	13	15	5	0	1	41	0	2	.316	.303
Garabito, Eddy	B-R	5-8	200	12-2-76	.257	.298	.240	128	474	55	122	24	1	5	46	47	1	9	0	54	19	8	.344	.326
Majewski, Val	L-L	6-2	215	6-19-81	.260	.293	.249	99	323	44	84	15	6	4	39	37	5	0	1	72	7	8	.381	.344
Marsters, Brandon	R-R	5-11	225	3-14-75	.216	.271	.191	55	190	19	41	4	0	8	27	7	2	2	0	65	0	0	.363	.251
McCurdy, Joshua	R-R	6-6	220	12-28-79	.212	.174	.241	20	52	7	11	2	0	2	4	0	1	0	1	11	1	1	.365	.212
Reed, Keith	R-R	6-4	210	10-8-78	.279	.317	.263	115	426	57	119	35	2	10	66	19	6	2	0	63	14	11	.441	.319
Rogers, Ed	R-R	6-3	190	8-29-78	.298	.352	.279	86	339	40	101	18	1	5	30	13	1	4	2	52	12	7	.401	.324
Snead, Esix	B-R	5-11	185	6-7-76	.220	.200	.232	41	127	11	28	3	0	1	14	19	0	6	1	20	15	4	.268	.320
Tatis, Fernando	R-R	6-3	195	1-1-75	.298	.291	.300	90	326	44	97	15	2	7	37	36	4	0	2	56	8	2	.420	.372
Terrero, Luis	R-R	6-3	225	5-18-80	.318	.305	.323	84	302	52	96	21	2	16	44	16	8	2	1	61	18	9	.560	.367
Tracy, Andy	L-R	6-3	220	12-11-73	.237	.224	.243	132	455	64	108	29	1	20	73	69	3	0	7	107	7	6	.437	.337
Whiteside, Eli	R-R	6-2	220	10-22-79	.244	.326	.252	92	315	37	77	18	1	11	47	10	7	2	6	73	1	3	.413	.278

PITCHING	B-T	HT	WT	DOB	W	L	ERA	G	GS	CG	SV	IP	H	R	ER	HR	BB	SO	AVG	vLH	vRH	K/9	BB/9
Abreu, Winston	R-R	6-2	170	4-5-77	9	4	2.48	46	0	0	1	65	54	22	18	4	20	78	.220	.217	.222	10.74	2.76
Anderson, Craig	L-L	6-3	180	10-30-80	0	4	5.59	9	9	0	0	47	66	30	29	4	10	24	.338	.319	.345	4.63	1.93
Birkins, Kurt	L-L	6-2	190	8-11-80	1	3	3.20	5	5	0	0	25	20	10	9	2	11	19	.225	.167	.229	6.75	3.91
Bowles, Brian	R-R	6-5	220	8-18-76	10	10	3.23	30	26	1	0	156	156	66	56	12	53	78	.264	.296	.237	4.50	3.06
Burres, Brian	L-L	6-1	180	4-8-81	10	6	3.76	26	26	1	0	139	133	63	58	14	57	110	.255	.288	.246	7.12	3.69
Cabrera, Daniel	R-R	6-7	260	5-28-81	3	1	4.07	4	4	0	0	24	20	13	11	1	9	27	.220	.196	.250	9.99	3.33
DuBose, Eric	L-L	6-3	235	5-15-76	3	4	5.54	8	8	0	0	39	44	26	24	3	23	30	.293	.343	.278	6.92	5.31
Garcia, Anderson	R-R	6-2	170	3-23-81	0	0	2.70	5	1	0	0	7	4	2	2	0	3	3	.174	.300	.077	4.05	4.05
Gracesqui, Franklyn	S-L	6-5	245	8-20-79	0	2	4.75	29	0	0	0	36	35	21	19	1	20	35	.263	.345	.240	8.75	5.00
Kester, Tim	R-R	6-4	202	12-1-71	7	5	4.26	17	16	0	0	99	120	52	47	10	13	43	.303	.303	.303	3.90	1.18
Loewen, Adam	L-L	6-5	235	4-9-84	2	0	1.27	3	3	0	0	21	10	3	3	0	3	21	.143	.118	.151	8.86	1.27
Manon, Julio	R-R	6-0	200	6-10-73	0	2	2.13	47	0	0	30	51	35	13	12	4	20	61	.198	.211	.188	10.84	3.55
McCurdy, Nick	R-R	6-3	185	1-24-80	4	0	3.94	15	0	0	0	30	35	14	13	3	8	20	.302	.355	.282	6.07	2.43
Mitchell, Andy	R-R	6-3	205	9-10-79	1	1	2.27	50	1	0	0	67	72	27	17	3	27	49	.273	.326	.243	6.55	3.61
Morris, Cory	R-R	6-2	200	6-2-79	1	9	4.21	16	16	0	0	73	73	39	34	5	56	63	.266	.234	.293	7.80	6.94
Penn, Hayden	R-R	6-3	195	10-13-84	7	4	2.26	14	14	2	0	88	71	25	22	5	27	85	.221	.215	.227	8.73	2.77
Piersoll, Chris	R-R	6-4	215	9-29-77	6	2	3.90	42	2	0	0	67	65	33	29	6	27	57	.255	.264	.248	7.66	3.63
Rice, Scott	L-L	6-6	220	9-21-81	3	4	3.86	52	0	0	1	65	66	28	28	4	28	38	.262	.193	.297	5.23	3.86
Rleal, Sendy	R-R	6-1	180	6-21-80	2	2	6.65	19	0	0	0	23	29	18	17	4	5	14	.315	.282	.340	5.48	1.96
Rodriguez, Eddy	R-R	6-1	215	8-8-81	3	1	1.71	42	0	0	12	47	33	13	9	0	18	55	.191	.227	.163	10.46	3.42
Stephens, John	R-R	6-1	220	11-15-79	2	5	4.97	12	12	0	0	63	74	39	35	4	24	43	.287	.297	.280	6.11	3.41

FIELDING

Catcher	PCT	G	PO	A	E	DP	PB
Bock	1.000	1	1	0	0	0	0
Marsters	.991	52	322	25	3	3	
Whiteside	.986	92	650	58	10	2	9

First Base	PCT	G	PO	A	E	DP
Clark	1.000	10	70	9	0	8
Freire	.986	19	139	7	2	19
Majewski	.987	11	68	9	1	8
Tracy	.997	107	915	102	3	98

Second Base	PCT	G	PO	A	E	DP
Badeaux	.994	41	62	111	1	26
Clark	1.000	15	28	35	0	9
Fahey	1.000	1	2	3	0	1
Garabito	.983	79	151	199	6	56

Rogers	1.000	15	32	35	0	14

Third Base	PCT	G	PO	A	E	DP
Badeaux	—	1	0	0	0	0
Bowers	—	1	0	0	0	0
Calzado	.909	24	19	51	7	9
Clark	.940	33	21	42	4	7
Garabito	—	1	0	0	0	0
Rogers	.909	8	5	15	2	2
Tatis	.968	84	62	180	8	10

Shortstop	PCT	G	PO	A	E	DP
Badeaux	1.000	3	4	9	0	4
Bowers	.989	57	83	183	3	42
Calzado	—	1	0	0	0	0
Fahey	.946	19	34	71	6	18

Garabito	.899	23	26	63	10	7
Rogers	.963	48	85	125	8	31

Outfield	PCT	G	PO	A	E	DP
Alvarez	1.000	25	41	4	0	1
Calzado	.976	24	38	2	1	0
Clark	.963	11	25	1	1	0
Donovan	.986	42	72	0	1	0
Garabito	1.000	6	7	0	0	0
Majewski	.974	72	112	2	3	0
McCurdy	.833	18	15	0	3	0
Reed	.973	114	210	9	6	1
Rogers	1.000	20	27	2	0	0
Snead	.988	40	81	0	1	0
Terrero	.981	84	197	5	4	0

Bowie Baysox — Double-A

Eastern League

BATTING	B-T	HT	WT	DOB	AVG	vLH	vRH	G	AB	R	H	2B	3B	HR	RBI	BB	HBP	SH	SF	SO	SB	CS	SLG	OBP
Alvarez, Gerardo	R-R	5-10	185	10-31-79	.212	.138	.238	112	326	40	69	11	0	4	30	24	6	15	3	68	9	6	.282	.276
Alvarez, Tony	R-R	6-1	200	5-10-79	.255	.239	.261	68	251	27	64	11	1	5	28	16	10	0	2	56	13	8	.367	.323
Andrews, Robert	R-R	6-0	200	12-23-83	.200	1.000	.111	3	10	1	2	0	0	0	1	0	0	0	2	2	0	.200	.200
Badeaux, Brooks	B-R	5-10	177	10-20-76	.211	.139	.237	35	133	16	28	5	0	3	14	13	6	3	0	25	1	2	.316	.309
Bass, Bryan	B-R	6-1	190	4-12-82	.212	.194	.221	63	212	31	45	10	3	3	24	39	2	2	0	81	9	3	.330	.340
Bautista, Rayner	R-R	5-11	155	9-17-78	.259	.333	.230	122	424	46	110	25	1	7	38	6	1	14	1	112	4	3	.373	.271

	B-T	HT	WT	DOB	AVG	vLH	vRH	G	AB	R	H	2B	3B	HR	RBI	BB	HBP	SH	SF	SO	SB	CS	SLG	OBP
Chavez, Raul	R-R	5-11	180	3-18-73	.255	.214	.278	52	196	18	50	10	0	0	2	21	11	0	3	3	19	0	0	.337	.290
Chavez, Angel	R-R	6-1	200	7-22-81	.267	.250	.273	4	15	0	4	2	0	0	1	1	0	0	1	3	3	0	0	.400	.294
Daigle, Leo	R-R	6-4	255	9-18-79	.233	.250	.226	126	421	53	98	18	2	15	63	46	8	1	9	122	2	5	.392	.314
Delgado, Mario	L-L	6-0	220	8-5-79	.260	.163	.285	56	208	18	54	10	1	5	18	12	2	1	1	37	0	0	.389	.305
Donovan, Todd	R-R	6-1	180	8-12-78	.297	.222	.328	26	91	17	27	3	3	1	12	9	0	2	0	15	12	3	.429	.360
Duran, Carlos	L-L	6-1	165	12-27-82	.284	.417	.234	20	88	13	25	2	0	2	8	1	0	0	0	22	3	3	.375	.292
Fiorentino, Jeff	L-R	6-1	180	4-14-83	.275	.221	.295	104	385	63	106	14	0	13	62	53	3	6	3	58	9	3	.413	.365
Gibbons, Jay	L-L	6-0	205	3-2-77	.400	.000	.444	3	10	2	4	2	0	0	0	0	1	0	0	0	1	0	0	.600	.455
Gomez, Chris	R-R	6-1	200	6-16-71	.250	.429	.111	4	16	4	4	1	0	0	1	1	0	0	0	3	0	0	.313	.294
Hall, Noah	R-R	5-11	200	6-9-77	.276	.341	.249	122	431	67	119	25	6	12	58	51	15	1	1	64	18	8	.445	.371
Hubele, Ryan	R-R	5-11	195	9-9-80	.247	.237	.251	93	312	40	77	16	2	9	34	20	7	5	1	76	4	3	.397	.306
Johnson, Tripper	L-R	6-1	180	4-28-82	.198	.167	.208	36	131	10	26	4	0	2	6	7	2	2	0	24	1	1	.275	.250
Keylor, Cory	L-R	6-3	216	8-25-79	.294	.200	.323	124	446	58	131	20	2	10	68	48	4	0	3	92	6	5	.415	.365
Lopez, Javy	R-R	6-3	220	11-5-70	.286	.200	.500	2	7	1	2	1	0	0	1	1	1	0	0	1	0	0	.857	.375
Madera, Sandy	R-R	6-2	176	8-11-80	.232	.250	.222	24	69	7	16	4	0	1	6	2	1	4	0	19	0	2	.333	.264
Maestrales, Pete	B-R	5-11	190	7-4-77	.278	.333	.259	13	36	5	10	2	0	0	4	4	0	0	0	8	0	2	.333	.350
Maxey, Jason	L-R	5-11	215	3-31-83	.500	.000	.600	3	6	2	3	1	0	0	0	2	0	0	0	0	1	0	0	.667	.625
Newhan, David	L-R	5-10	170	9-7-73	.235	.167	.273	6	17	4	4	0	1	0	3	4	1	0	0	3	1	0	.353	.409
Roberts, Brian	B-R	5-9	175	10-9-77	.200	.000	.333	2	5	0	1	0	0	0	2	0	0	0	0	0	0	0	.200	.429
Shier, Peter	R-R	6-2	176	3-16-81	.286	.235	.308	69	224	25	64	17	2	0	24	12	3	6	1	39	3	8	.379	.329
Yount, Dustin	L-R	6-1	198	10-27-82	.228	.226	.228	54	167	21	38	5	0	5	20	25	1	0	5	52	0	2	.347	.323

PITCHING	B-T	HT	WT	DOB	W	L	ERA	G	GS	CG	SV	IP	H	R	ER	HR	BB	SO	AVG	vLH	vRH	K/9	BB/9
Anderson, Craig	L-L	6-3	180	10-30-80	3	0	2.28	8	6	0	0	43	32	13	11	3	5	35	.195	.220	.187	7.27	1.04
Birkins, Kurt	L-L	6-2	190	8-11-80	0	1	9.00	2	0	0	0	4	5	4	4	2	1	5	.313	.333	.308	11.25	2.25
Britton, Chris	R-R	6-3	280	12-16-82	1	0	2.81	13	0	0	2	16	14	5	5	0	6	24	.233	.286	.205	13.50	3.38
Bruback, Matt	R-R	6-5	205	1-12-79	1	4	4.81	18	5	0	0	43	53	24	23	3	9	43	.308	.314	.304	9.00	1.88
Byrdak, Tim	L-L	5-11	195	10-31-73	0	0	2.25	3	0	0	0	4	4	1	1	0	2	7	.250	.167	.300	15.75	4.50
DuBose, Eric	L-L	6-3	235	5-15-76	7	1	3.11	20	11	2	0	84	70	33	29	7	34	67	.230	.266	.217	7.18	3.64
Finch, Brian	R-R	6-4	215	9-27-81	6	12	3.65	27	26	1	0	146	146	83	59	18	69	83	.264	.246	.281	5.13	4.26
Forystek, Brian	L-L	6-1	180	10-30-78	6	3	3.57	43	1	0	2	71	53	28	28	8	32	64	.209	.197	.213	8.15	4.08
Garcia, Anderson	R-R	6-2	170	3-23-81	2	1	2.16	4	0	0	0	8	6	2	2	0	0	8	.200	.071	.313	8.64	0.00
Hale, Beau	R-R	6-2	202	12-1-78	4	6	3.22	19	12	0	0	95	85	40	34	8	20	65	.237	.287	.196	6.16	1.89
Hoey, Jim	R-R	6-6	200	12-30-82	0	0	4.00	8	0	0	0	9	9	5	4	1	3	11	.243	.273	.231	11.00	3.00
Jan, Carlos	L-L	5-11	165	11-3-79	1	2	4.43	23	0	0	0	43	35	24	21	3	30	53	.223	.326	.180	11.18	6.33
Johnson, Jim	R-R	6-5	225	6-27-83	13	6	4.44	27	26	0	0	156	165	80	77	13	57	124	.274	.275	.274	7.15	3.29
Keefer, Ryan	L-R	6-3	225	8-10-81	0	0	3.00	5	0	0	0	9	4	3	3	1	3	13	.138	.214	.067	13.00	3.00
Kester, Tim	R-R	6-4	202	12-1-71	1	0	1.17	2	2	0	0	8	6	1	1	0	3	5	.214	.235	.182	5.87	3.52
Liz, Radhames	R-R	6-2	170	6-10-83	3	1	5.36	10	10	0	0	50	55	31	30	9	31	54	.281	.247	.304	9.66	5.54
Loewen, Adam	L-L	6-5	235	4-9-84	4	2	2.72	9	8	0	0	50	46	17	15	3	26	55	.250	.164	.293	9.97	4.71
Maduro, Calvin	R-R	6-0	200	9-5-74	1	5	4.50	24	1	0	0	38	32	24	19	1	16	47	.232	.180	.273	11.13	3.79
McCurdy, Nick	R-R	6-3	185	1-24-80	1	2	2.37	37	0	0	3	49	54	14	13	2	13	40	.287	.321	.262	7.30	2.37
Morris, Cory	R-R	6-2	200	6-2-79	1	0	3.00	2	2	0	0	6	3	2	2	1	4	8	.150	.143	.154	12.00	6.00
Olson, Garrett	R-L	6-1	200	10-18-83	6	5	3.42	14	14	0	0	84	78	33	32	5	31	85	.249	.247	.250	9.07	3.31
Pearson, Jason	L-L	6-0	190	12-29-75	3	6	3.02	50	0	0	2	66	55	27	22	6	15	61	.231	.271	.209	8.36	2.06
Penn, Hayden	R-R	6-3	195	10-13-84	0	0	9.00	1	1	0	0	2	3	2	2	1	2	1	.375	.400	.333	4.50	9.00
Salas, Marino	R-R	6-0	190	2-2-81	2	6	2.92	44	0	0	19	49	39	16	16	3	16	46	.215	.226	.206	8.39	2.92
Salazar, Richard	L-L	5-11	191	10-6-81	0	0	5.06	5	0	0	0	5	4	3	3	1	4	6	.238	.600	.125	10.13	6.75
Stahl, Richard	R-L	6-7	220	4-11-81	1	10	6.50	24	14	0	0	73	85	62	53	7	53	58	.297	.260	.310	7.12	6.50
Williams, Todd	R-R	6-3	220	2-13-71	0	0	4.50	4	0	0	0	4	4	2	2	0	1	5	.250	.000	.364	11.25	2.25

FIELDING

Catcher	PCT	G	PO	A	E	DP	PB
Chavez	.987	45	340	50	5	8	5
Hubele	.993	81	631	58	5	11	14
Madera	.985	19	129	5	2	1	4

First Base	PCT	G	PO	A	E	DP
Daigle	.986	94	684	69	11	73
Delgado	.981	23	186	16	4	16
Johnson	1.000	1	2	0	0	0
Yount	.987	37	285	16	4	29

Second Base	PCT	G	PO	A	E	DP
G. Alvarez	.975	61	113	156	7	45
Badeaux	.978	35	67	111	4	21
Bautista	1.000	4	6	12	0	2
Newhan	.500	1	1	1	2	1
Roberts	1.000	1	1	0	0	0

Third Base	PCT	G	PO	A	E	DP
Shier	.972	49	94	116	6	27
G. Alvarez	.948	29	14	41	3	2
Bass	.955	60	40	107	7	8
Daigle	.929	9	4	9	1	3
Gomez	1.000	1	1	2	0	0
Johnson	.938	35	29	77	7	6
Maestrales	.750	8	1	11	4	1
Shier	.882	5	0	15	2	2

Shortstop	PCT	G	PO	A	E	DP
G. Alvarez	1.000	18	23	52	0	15
Bass	1.000	1	1	1	0	0
Bautista	.951	117	164	305	24	67
Chavez	.941	4	4	12	1	4
Gomez	1.000	2	3	9	0	3

Outfield	PCT	G	PO	A	E	DP
Shier	1.000	4	6	6	0	3
G. Alvarez	1.000	1	2	0	0	0
T. Alvarez	.977	56	82	3	2	2
Andrews	.900	3	9	0	1	0
Daigle	1.000	7	6	1	0	0
Donovan	1.000	23	54	2	0	1
Duran	.917	19	22	0	2	0
Fiorentino	.983	96	164	11	3	3
Hall	.990	107	191	1	2	0
Keylor	.984	106	182	3	3	0
Maestrales	1.000	1	1	0	0	0
Newhan	1.000	5	6	0	0	0
Shier	.966	14	27	1	1	0

Frederick Keys — High Class A

Carolina League

BATTING	B-T	HT	WT	DOB	AVG	vLH	vRH	G	AB	R	H	2B	3B	HR	RBI	BB	HBP	SH	SF	SO	SB	CS	SLG	OBP
Andrews, Robert	R-R	6-0	200	12-23-83	.200	.000	.250	2	5	1	1	0	0	0	1	0	0	0	0	2	0	0	.200	.200
Bass, Bryan	B-R	6-1	190	4-12-82	.228	.169	.254	63	197	25	45	11	1	3	20	27	5	5	2	77	5	6	.340	.333
Bock, Brian	R-R	6-1	210	8-24-81	.198	.257	.171	67	222	14	44	4	0	1	24	9	1	3	2	32	1	2	.230	.231
Brown, Travis	R-R	5-11	180	8-1-80	.235	.235	.236	112	327	44	77	11	1	1	26	49	2	8	4	59	1	8	.284	.335
Chiaravalloti, Vito	R-R	6-3	225	10-26-80	.075	.000	.091	11	40	1	3	1	0	0	1	9	0	0	0	11	0	0	.100	.245
Clendenin, Morgan	L-R	6-0	187	10-2-81	.252	.207	.266	78	242	26	61	18	1	4	33	14	8	1	3	51	0	1	.384	.311
Delgado, Mario	L-L	6-0	220	8-5-79	.286	.302	.280	62	238	30	68	15	0	11	49	12	4	0	6	43	1	2	.487	.323
Duncan, Jacob	L-L	5-11	190	11-20-81	.252	.221	.264	96	353	38	89	18	3	5	27	19	2	4	2	71	6	2	.363	.293
Duran, Carlos	L-L	6-1	165	12-27-82	.260	.250	.263	39	146	19	38	8	3	1	18	2	1	0	0	22	5	2	.377	.275
Figueroa, Paco	R-R	5-11	182	2-19-83	.284	.280	.286	90	345	62	98	17	2	4	28	30	10	9	1	46	20	13	.380	.358
Fransz, Jason	R-R	6-3	212	2-5-81	.243	.295	.222	124	444	63	108	20	1	24	84	41	13	0	7	102	1	5	.455	.321
Gibbons, Jay	L-L	6-0	205	3-2-77	.000	.000	.000	2	8	1	0	0	0	0	0	0	0	0	0	0	0	0	.000	.000
Gutierrez, Juan	R-R	6-0	195	8-1-81	.387	.667	.320	10	31	6	12	3	0	2	7	3	0	0	0	6	0	0	.677	.441
Hendricks, K. J.	B-R	5-7	165	2-20-81	.258	.125	.304	9	31	8	8	0	0	0	5	2	0	0	0	4	0	1	.258	.361

ORGANIZATION STATISTICS

Johnson, Tripper	R-R	6-1	199	4-28-82	.305	.136	.357	54	187	32	57	17	0	5	24	20	2	1	3	17	4	0	.476	.373
Madera, Sandy	R-R	6-2	176	8-11-80	.325	.314	.330	38	126	23	41	8	0	8	31	12	4	0	2	24	1	2	.579	.396
Maestrales, Pete	B-R	5-11	190	7-4-79	.285	.274	.290	103	354	68	101	24	2	7	41	68	3	2	4	55	9	2	.424	.401
Matos, Luis	R-R	6-0	215	10-30-78	.333	—	.333	2	9	1	3	0	0	1	2	0	0	0	0	1	1	0	.667	.333
McCurdy, Joshua	R-R	6-6	220	12-28-79	.172	.278	.125	16	58	7	10	2	0	0	3	2	0	0	0	12	2	1	.207	.200
Reimold, Nolan	R-R	6-4	207	10-12-83	.255	.269	.251	119	415	73	106	26	0	19	75	76	9	0	4	107	14	8	.455	.379
Rine, Jarod	L-R	6-1	190	11-14-81	.213	.216	.212	70	239	31	51	13	1	2	21	33	4	5	0	50	14	8	.301	.319
Rivas, Arturo	R-R	6-0	205	2-2-84	.275	.233	.291	35	109	14	30	9	1	3	13	21	0	1	1	35	1	2	.459	.389
Russell, Michael	R-R	6-0	197	8-14-81	.178	.108	.226	34	90	8	16	4	0	4	6	10	0	0	0	34	0	0	.356	.260
Shier, Peter	R-R	6-2	176	3-16-81	.170	.267	.132	23	53	2	9	2	0	0	2	2	1	0	0	21	0	3	.208	.214
Steinbach, Ryan	B-R	6-0	180	10-30-82	.156	.333	.111	19	45	3	7	3	0	0	2	5	0	0	1	16	0	1	.222	.235
Tucker, Jonathan	R-R	5-7	170	7-2-83	.250	.500	.222	18	60	11	15	2	0	0	3	7	2	3	1	11	5	1	.283	.343
Yount, Dustin	L-R	6-1	198	10-27-82	.271	.222	.294	67	225	33	61	12	0	7	30	43	3	0	0	41	3	0	.418	.395

PITCHING	B-T	HT	WT	DOB	W	L	ERA	G	GS	CG	SV	IP	H	R	ER	HR	BB	SO	AVG	vLH	vRH	K/9	BB/9
Anderson, Craig	L-L	6-3	180	10-30-80	5	1	4.78	11	11	0	0	58	66	36	31	8	11	37	.283	.395	.262	5.71	1.70
Basilio, Manny	R-R	6-3	218	10-20-79	4	2	2.56	22	2	0	1	39	40	22	11	2	13	36	.268	.323	.226	8.38	3.03
Baysinger, Trent	L-L	6-0	185	9-1-81	1	2	4.05	21	0	0	1	33	30	18	15	3	10	21	.227	.233	.225	5.67	2.70
Birkins, Kurt	L-L	6-2	190	8-11-80	0	0	0.00	1	0	0	0	1	0	0	0	0	1	1	.000	—	.000	9.00	9.00
Bruback, Matt	R-R	6-5	205	1-12-79	3	5	3.69	14	14	0	0	76	80	45	31	4	22	39	.273	.252	.288	4.64	2.62
Byrdak, Tim	L-L	5-11	195	10-31-73	0	0	13.50	1	0	0	0	1	4	2	2	0	1	0	.500	.667	.400	0.00	6.75
Cahill, Casey	R-R	6-3	197	3-15-82	5	2	4.75	48	0	0	4	72	72	45	38	4	33	42	.270	.266	.272	5.25	4.13
Caughey, Trevor	L-L	6-1	172	11-23-82	2	1	5.50	25	0	0	0	36	39	24	22	8	15	37	.273	.300	.262	9.25	3.75
Deza, Fredy	R-R	6-2	170	12-11-82	3	4	4.75	43	0	0	0	83	92	55	44	7	32	68	.280	.287	.277	7.34	3.46
Haehnel, David	L-L	6-4	200	7-21-82	2	11	6.22	28	27	0	0	116	121	88	80	17	61	83	.268	.238	.274	6.46	4.75
Hale, Beau	R-R	6-2	202	12-1-78	2	0	3.80	12	1	0	1	21	28	14	9	1	5	20	.304	.192	.348	8.44	2.11
Hart, Kevin	R-R	6-4	215	11-29-82	6	11	4.61	28	27	0	0	148	149	97	76	18	65	122	.258	.277	.245	7.40	3.94
Henington, Justin	R-R	6-3	210	2-24-82	0	2	5.56	10	0	0	3	11	16	9	7	1	3	8	.327	.333	.324	6.35	2.38
Hoey, Jim	R-R	6-6	200	12-30-82	0	0	0.64	14	0	0	11	14	13	3	1	0	5	16	.228	.174	.265	10.29	3.21
Jan, Carlos	L-L	5-11	165	11-3-79	2	1	3.14	8	0	0	1	14	10	6	5	1	15	15	.208	.273	.189	9.42	9.42
Lewis Jr., Rommie	L-L	6-6	200	9-2-82	5	3	2.09	31	0	0	6	52	46	16	12	3	11	36	.234	.292	.215	6.27	1.92
Liz, Radhames	R-R	6-2	170	6-10-83	6	5	2.82	16	16	0	0	83	57	32	26	8	44	95	.196	.200	.193	10.30	4.77
Montani, Jeff	R-R	5-11	174	11-22-80	1	2	7.24	18	0	0	0	27	34	24	22	7	15	26	.296	.270	.308	8.56	4.94
Neal, Tony	R-R	6-2	210	9-12-80	1	3	6.28	12	0	0	2	14	13	11	10	3	6	11	.241	.158	.286	6.91	3.77
Olson, Garrett	R-L	6-1	200	10-18-83	4	4	2.77	14	14	0	0	81	81	32	25	7	19	77	.266	.222	.274	8.52	2.10
Petrick, Russell	L-L	6-1	185	2-12-83	0	4	7.41	23	0	0	0	34	37	29	28	3	22	27	.287	.286	.287	7.15	5.82
Ramirez, Luis	R-R	6-4	202	6-9-82	8	9	4.23	23	23	0	0	126	107	68	59	15	42	122	.223	.241	.211	8.74	3.01
Salazar, Richard	L-L	5-11	191	10-6-81	1	5	3.60	36	3	0	1	65	61	29	26	5	29	48	.255	.296	.243	6.65	4.02

FIELDING

Catcher	PCT	G	PO	A	E	DP	PB
Bass	1.000	1	1	0	0	0	0
Bock	.987	66	478	46	7	2	9
Clendenin	.972	53	319	27	10	1	6
Gutierrez	1.000	6	26	3	0	0	1
Madera	.988	14	74	6	1	0	7
Russell	1.000	17	122	5	0	2	3

First Base	PCT	G	PO	A	E	DP
Chiaravalloti	.982	8	98	9	2	8
Delgado	.988	41	326	17	4	28
Fransz	.979	19	137	5	3	9
Gutierrez	1.000	1	11	0	0	2
Madera	.950	11	55	2	3	5
Russell	1.000	6	41	3	0	1
Yount	.987	62	502	27	7	50

Second Base	PCT	G	PO	A	E	DP
Figueroa	.952	89	174	222	20	49
Johnson	.982	28	47	64	2	13
Maestrales	.966	15	24	32	2	7
Shier	.960	8	10	14	1	2
Steinbach	.909	4	6	4	1	1
Tucker	1.000	6	12	16	0	3

Third Base	PCT	G	PO	A	E	DP
Bass	.908	62	33	95	13	6
Clendenin	.600	1	1	2	2	1
Johnson	.943	25	20	46	4	2
Maestrales	.905	57	27	116	15	7
Russell	1.000	5	0	1	0	0
Shier	.917	4	3	8	1	1
Steinbach	.750	2	0	3	1	0
Tucker	1.000	2	2	5	0	1

Shortstop	PCT	G	PO	A	E	DP
Brown	.942	111	155	312	29	66
Hendricks	1.000	4	5	5	0	0
Johnson	.917	7	10	12	2	0
Shier	.808	9	6	15	5	4
Steinbach	.955	12	15	27	2	2
Tucker	.915	10	13	30	4	6

Outfield	PCT	G	PO	A	E	DP
Andrews	1.000	1	2	0	0	0
Bass	1.000	1	2	0	0	0
Duncan	.989	94	169	6	2	0
Duran	.920	30	42	4	4	0
Fransz	.963	44	75	3	3	0
Hendricks	1.000	6	11	0	0	0
Maestrales	.976	26	37	3	1	1
Matos	1.000	2	6	0	0	0
McCurdy	.935	16	29	0	2	0
Reimold	.969	115	213	6	7	0
Rine	.993	68	142	1	1	0
Rivas	.972	35	103	3	3	1

Delmarva Shorebirds — Low Class A

South Atlantic League

BATTING	B-T	HT	WT	DOB	AVG	vLH	vRH	G	AB	R	H	2B	3B	HR	RBI	BB	HBP	SH	SF	SO	SB	CS	SLG	OBP
Andrews, Robert	R-R	6-0	200	12-23-83	.182	.333	.125	4	11	1	2	0	0	0	0	1	0	1	0	4	0	0	.182	.250
Aqueron, Rene	L-R	5-10	180	10-14-81	.068	.000	.075	15	44	4	3	0	0	0	1	5	0	0	0	9	2	0	.068	.163
Ascencion, Quincy	R-R	6-0	212	11-1-82	.260	.191	.286	121	400	46	104	27	2	0	36	22	12	16	2	47	14	7	.338	.317
Chiaravalloti, Vito	R-R	6-3	225	10-26-80	.262	.263	.261	28	107	21	28	7	0	8	27	17	0	0	0	22	0	0	.551	.363
Dahlberg, Kyle	R-R	6-3	211	4-9-83	.218	.212	.221	71	202	19	44	8	0	4	21	19	5	2	3	89	0	1	.317	.297
Davis, Zach	L-L	6-0	173	2-20-84	.192	.235	.184	44	104	17	20	5	0	0	9	13	0	2	0	48	2	1	.240	.282
Davis, Blake	L-R	5-11	160	12-22-83	.271	.220	.285	50	199	30	54	8	2	3	20	15	2	4	0	28	9	2	.377	.329
Dillon, Zachary	L-R	5-10	210	5-18-83	.262	.367	.239	54	172	24	45	10	0	3	21	33	0	2	2	32	1	1	.372	.377
Figueroa, Daniel	R-R	5-11	182	2-19-83	.278	.143	.364	7	18	3	5	1	0	0	1	4	0	0	0	4	2	1	.333	.409
Finan, Ryan	L-R	6-5	220	1-5-82	.262	.214	.274	131	427	80	112	31	2	17	78	85	9	1	5	100	1	1	.464	.392
Fleisher, Mark	R-R	6-4	235	9-18-83	.261	.170	.292	120	421	51	110	29	1	16	67	47	7	0	3	84	2	1	.449	.343
Gutierrez, Juan	B-R	6-0	195	8-1-81	.162	.120	.169	67	185	12	30	6	0	3	18	18	1	4	2	35	0	2	.243	.238
Marconi, Robert	R-R	6-1	200	9-14-82	.167	.200	.159	28	84	10	14	2	1	1	5	9	2	0	0	24	1	1	.250	.263
Musslewhite, Stuart	R-R	5-11	195	8-28-82	.237	.196	.249	120	409	40	97	22	1	3	53	30	7	4	3	64	7	6	.318	.298
Rine, Jarod	L-R	6-1	190	11-14-81	.155	.143	.157	37	110	13	17	3	2	1	6	17	3	1	0	31	7	1	.245	.285
Rivas, Arturo	R-R	6-0	205	2-2-84	.257	.244	.261	93	335	38	86	14	6	5	42	39	7	3	6	82	7	4	.379	.341
Rodriguez, Rafael	R-R	5-11	160	1-11-84	.193	.273	.159	61	187	14	36	9	1	3	12	7	2	3	3	51	5	4	.299	.226
Scott Jr., Lorenzo	L-L	6-3	210	3-1-82	.258	.205	.276	113	360	66	93	14	4	4	32	60	2	13	0	140	29	10	.353	.367
Shafer, Corey	L-L	6-3	221	12-17-82	.192	.333	.174	20	52	5	10	4	0	0	9	3	0	1	2	18	1	0	.269	.228
Smith, C.J.	R-R	6-3	210	2-22-82	.183	.167	.188	36	115	11	21	4	0	1	12	19	2	1	1	33	1	0	.243	.307
Snyder, Brandon	R-R	6-2	205	11-23-86	.194	.222	.182	38	144	12	28	12	0	3	20	9	0	3	3	55	0	0	.340	.237
Steinbach, Ryan	B-R	6-0	180	10-30-82	.217	.176	.233	26	60	13	13	0	1	1	4	17	1	1	0	20	0	0	.300	.397
Tucker, Jonathan	R-R	5-7	170	7-2-83	.280	.308	.268	75	261	50	73	14	4	3	30	43	2	7	1	43	9	11	.398	.384
Winterling, Paul	R-R	6-3	220	7-31-83	.125	.000	.167	6	16	1	2	1	0	0	2	2	0	0	0	5	1	0	.188	.222

PITCHING

PITCHING	B-T	HT	WT	DOB	W	L	ERA	G	GS	CG	SV	IP	H	R	ER	HR	BB	SO	AVG	vLH	vRH	K/9	BB/9
Basilio, Manny	R-R	6-3	218	10-20-79	5	3	2.34	19	9	0	2	73	59	23	19	2	17	57	.225	.196	.245	7.03	2.10
Baysinger, Trent	L-L	6-0	185	9-1-81	1	3	2.93	21	0	0	0	40	45	21	13	0	5	29	.280	.204	.313	6.53	1.13
Bergesen, Bradley	L-R	6-2	205	9-25-85	5	4	4.27	18	14	1	0	86	97	44	41	6	10	49	.280	.279	.282	5.11	1.04
Caughey, Trevor	L-L	6-1	172	11-23-82	1	1	6.75	6	0	0	0	5	8	7	4	0	7	4	.348	.444	.286	6.75	11.81
Erbe, Brandon	R-R	6-4	180	12-25-87	5	9	3.22	28	27	0	0	115	88	47	41	2	47	133	.217	.242	.203	10.44	3.69
Gallaway, Bruce	R-L	6-3	200	9-17-82	0	0	3.65	10	0	0	0	12	12	5	5	1	5	10	.240	.167	.263	7.30	3.65
Hamblet, Reid	R-R	6-1	205	9-11-83	5	12	5.08	31	24	0	1	135	151	94	76	17	55	91	.282	.314	.258	6.08	3.68
Hernandez, David	R-R	6-2	180	5-13-85	7	8	4.15	28	28	0	0	145	134	83	67	13	71	154	.244	.243	.244	9.54	4.40
Hoey, Jim	R-R	6-6	200	12-30-82	2	1	2.54	27	0	0	18	28	17	8	8	2	10	46	.175	.086	.226	14.61	3.18
Horner, Tag	L-L	6-3	220	11-12-82	0	0	0.00	3	0	0	0	3	1	0	0	0	1	5	.111	.000	.143	16.88	0.00
Lebron, Luis	R-R	6-1	172	3-15-85	1	0	27.00	2	0	0	0	1	3	4	4	1	1	1	.500	.500	.500	6.75	6.75
Lonsberry, Daniel	R-R	6-4	200	7-6-83	5	3	3.07	46	0	0	1	94	103	45	32	7	36	74	.288	.304	.278	7.11	3.46
Neal, Tony	R-R	6-2	210	9-12-80	1	3	5.48	18	0	0	0	23	21	15	14	0	9	26	.244	.275	.217	10.17	3.52
Owen, Blake	R-R	6-3	215	10-29-83	7	4	3.81	55	0	0	10	59	60	30	25	3	18	50	.259	.340	.200	7.63	2.75
Petrick, Russell	L-L	6-1	185	2-12-83	2	0	5.94	21	0	0	0	36	46	24	24	1	18	17	.322	.286	.333	4.21	4.46
Potter, Joshua	R-R	6-4	175	4-8-83	4	8	3.04	42	1	0	2	92	90	40	31	4	34	70	.256	.315	.225	6.87	3.34
Quijada, Fernando	R-R	6-3	165	10-9-84	2	1	3.08	30	0	0	0	53	49	28	18	4	24	46	.243	.270	.221	7.86	4.10
Schmidt, Kyle	R-R	6-3	220	8-25-83	4	4	4.53	10	9	1	0	50	45	29	25	8	16	51	.239	.260	.226	9.24	2.90
Soriano, Julio	R-R	6-2	160	9-24-83	0	0	1.98	7	0	0	2	14	12	4	3	0	8	12	.245	.278	.226	7.90	5.27
Spoone, Chorye	R-R	6-3	9-16-85	7	9	3.56	26	25	0	0	129	118	72	51	5	80	90	.241	.268	.221	6.28	5.58

FIELDING

Catcher	PCT	G	PO	A	E	DP	PB
Dahlberg	.990	69	474	47	5	5	16
Dillon	.967	20	131	15	5	1	9
Gutierrez	.983	39	219	18	4	2	13
Musslewhite	1.000	1	3	0	0	0	0
Snyder	.975	22	168	27	5	3	12

First Base	PCT	G	PO	A	E	DP
Chiaravalloti	.976	11	74	6	2	7
Dillon	1.000	1	3	2	0	0
Finan	1.000	15	116	7	0	8
Fleisher	.986	101	871	43	13	69
Smith	.991	15	99	7	1	10

Second Base	PCT	G	PO	A	E	DP
Aqueron	.969	15	27	35	2	8

	PCT	G	PO	A	E	DP
Marconi	.941	4	7	9	1	3
Musslewhite	.993	35	51	86	1	15
Rodriguez	.969	32	44	80	4	10
Steinbach	.864	8	4	15	3	0
Tucker	.988	56	101	150	3	42

Third Base	PCT	G	PO	A	E	DP
Dillon	—	1	0	0	0	0
Finan	.957	98	67	175	11	9
Marconi	.905	23	16	22	4	1
Musslewhite	.932	24	16	25	3	4
Rodriguez	.800	2	1	3	1	1

Shortstop	PCT	G	PO	A	E	DP
Davis	.927	50	73	143	17	24
Musslewhite	.930	61	94	172	20	32

	PCT	G	PO	A	E	DP
Rodriguez	.907	20	15	53	7	11
Steinbach	.954	16	21	41	3	10

Outfield	PCT	G	PO	A	E	DP
Andrews	.923	4	11	1	1	0
Ascension	.990	114	181	12	2	3
Davis	.984	37	59	4	1	0
Figueroa	1.000	6	12	0	0	0
Rine	.987	34	75	2	1	0
Rivas	.957	90	162	14	8	5
Rodriguez	1.000	2	3	1	0	0
Scott Jr.	.957	112	263	7	12	2
Shafer	1.000	17	26	1	0	0
Tucker	.970	16	28	4	1	0
Winterling	1.000	6	13	0	0	0

Aberdeen IronBirds — Short-Season

New York-Penn League

BATTING	B-T	HT	WT	DOB	AVG	vLH	vRH	G	AB	R	H	2B	3B	HR	RBI	BB	HBP	SH	SF	SO	SB	CS	SLG	OBP
Abreu, Miguel	R-R	6-0	190	11-14-84	.269	.241	.276	69	275	33	74	12	3	3	26	8	3	3	1	29	12	6	.367	.296
Adams, Ryan	R-R	6-0	185	4-21-87	.316	.500	.231	6	19	2	6	3	0	1	5	4	1	0	0	7	0	0	.632	.458
Andrews, Robert	R-R	6-0	200	12-23-83	.210	.238	.202	34	105	15	22	2	1	0	11	12	6	2	0	30	13	3	.248	.325
Aqueron, Rene	L-R	5-10	180	10-14-81	.250	.000	.333	1	4	1	1	0	0	0	0	0	0	0	0	0	0	0	.250	.250
Avila, Angel	R-R	6-1	170	6-26-84	.136	.000	.150	5	22	1	3	0	0	0	1	0	0	0	0	10	1	0	.136	.136
Calzado, Napoleon	R-R	6-3	200	2-9-77	.273	—	.273	5	22	4	6	3	0	0	1	1	0	0	1	3	1	0	.409	.292
Cash, David	B-R	6-3	180	11-22-85	.297	.208	.322	30	111	18	33	5	2	1	12	10	0	1	0	18	5	3	.405	.355
Castillo, Victor	B-R	5-11	222	9-12-84	.261	.242	.267	43	134	16	35	6	1	1	15	15	3	2	0	19	0	1	.343	.349
Davis, Zach	L-L	6-0	173	2-20-84	.212	.200	.215	38	113	14	24	7	1	0	11	4	3	0	1	35	5	2	.292	.256
Davison, Todd	R-R	5-10	175	10-7-83	.208	.195	.212	50	154	21	32	9	2	0	15	12	4	4	0	29	0	0	.292	.276
Figueroa, Daniel	R-R	5-11	182	2-19-83	.202	.308	.186	26	99	7	20	3	1	1	11	13	5	1	1	30	7	2	.283	.322
Florimon Jr., Pedro	B-R	6-2	165	12-10-86	.248	.238	.250	26	105	13	26	4	1	0	5	13	1	0	0	26	0	0	.305	.336
Kotch, Kevin	L-R	6-4	235	8-31-84	.000	—	.000	8	10	1	0	0	0	0	1	4	0	0	1	4	0	0	.000	.267
Marconi, Robert	R-R	6-1	200	9-14-82	.182	.167	.186	17	55	5	10	1	2	1	5	2	1	0	0	19	3	0	.327	.224
Martinez, Anthony	R-R	6-3	240	12-19-83	.263	.125	.364	5	19	3	5	0	0	1	1	0	0	0	0	6	0	0	.263	.300
Pacheco, Joel	R-R	6-2	190	3-2-82	.218	.191	.236	39	119	12	26	5	1	2	12	8	4	0	0	34	2	2	.328	.290
Pierce, Michael	R-R	6-3	185	4-19-84	.091	.000	.154	15	22	1	2	1	0	0	2	3	0	0	0	8	0	1	.136	.200
Pope, Kieron	L-R	6-1	195	10-3-86	.107	.188	.085	20	75	9	8	0	0	3	5	5	0	0	0	15	0	0	.107	.160
Pulley, Matthew	L-R	6-3	200	5-15-85	.280	.000	.286	17	50	4	14	0	0	0	6	5	0	0	0	15	0	0	.280	.345
Rowell, Billy	L-R	6-5	205	9-10-88	.326	.000	.424	11	43	8	14	4	0	1	6	4	1	0	1	12	0	0	.488	.388
Shafer, Corey	L-L	6-3	221	12-17-82	.250	.250	.248	36	128	12	32	5	1	2	14	9	1	0	0	25	3	1	.352	.304
Silveren, Pedro	R-R	6-0	160	9-2-84	.237	.091	.280	32	97	13	23	6	1	0	4	7	2	2	0	21	0	1	.320	.302
Snyder, Brandon	R-R	6-2	205	11-23-86	.234	.300	.221	34	124	14	29	8	1	1	15	5	1	0	1	43	2	1	.339	.267
Stephen, Jedidiah	R-R	6-2	190	4-30-84	.174	.143	.182	42	138	13	24	3	0	3	14	8	0	3	3	32	1	3	.261	.215
Tripp, Brandon	L-R	6-2	200	4-2-85	.221	.313	.195	43	145	20	32	8	0	2	15	16	12	0	1	49	1	2	.317	.345
Vinyard, Christopher	R-R	6-4	230	12-15-85	.284	.246	.292	73	264	40	75	26	2	8	47	28	9	0	5	62	0	0	.489	.366
Winterling, Paul	R-R	6-3	220	7-31-83	.105	.103	.106	25	76	8	8	0	0	0	2	8	1	0	1	27	1	1	.224	.198

PITCHING	B-T	HT	WT	DOB	W	L	ERA	G	GS	CG	SV	IP	H	R	ER	HR	BB	SO	AVG	vLH	vRH	K/9	BB/9
Allar, Brent	R-R	6-2	210	3-1-85	0	0	16.20	4	0	0	0	3	4	8	6	0	8	2	.286	.375	.167	5.40	21.60
Beato, Pedro	R-R	6-5	210	10-27-86	3	2	3.63	14	10	0	0	57	47	31	23	6	23	52	.222	.241	.209	8.21	3.63
Berken, Jason	R-R	6-0	175	11-27-83	1	4	2.80	9	8	0	0	45	39	20	14	4	5	46	.234	.155	.275	9.20	1.00
Birkins, Kurt	L-L	6-2	190	8-11-80	1	1	3.38	2	0	0	0	3	3	1	1	0	2	5	.375	.500	.333	6.75	0.00
Bordes, Brett	R-L	5-10	175	11-30-83	3	1	1.96	29	0	0	5	37	18	8	8	0	18	30	.146	.043	.211	7.36	4.42
Clark, Zach	R-R	6-0	195	7-11-83	1	1	7.36	3	2	0	0	11	20	10	9	0	3	5	.400	.469	.278	4.09	2.45
De Nabal, Fernando	R-R	6-3	180	6-16-84	3	4	3.97	16	5	0	0	45	36	21	20	3	35	41	.228	.203	.250	8.14	6.95
Faiola, Josh	R-R	6-3	200	10-3-83	0	0	0.00	1	0	0	0	1	0	0	0	0	2	2	.000	.333	.000	18.00	18.00
Horner, Tag	L-L	6-3	220	11-12-82	0	0	8.31	3	0	0	0	4	6	4	4	0	3	3	.333	.125	.500	6.23	6.23
Keefer, Ryan	L-R	6-3	225	8-10-81	2	0	2.20	10	0	0	0	16	14	5	4	0	11	17	.233	.045	.342	9.37	6.06
Lebron, Luis	R-R	6-1	172	3-15-85	0	2	1.17	32	0	0	20	31	17	6	4	2	15	46	.163	.146	.175	13.50	4.40
Lozado, Henry	R-R	6-3	178	1-19-84	3	1	2.82	24	0	0	0	38	34	14	12	1	16	24	.233	.157	.305	5.63	3.76
McCrory, Robert	R-R	6-1	205	5-3-82	2	2	2.33	20	1	0	2	39	34	12	10	2	16	52	.230	.231	.230	13.27	3.72

Player	B-T	HT	WT	DOB	W	L	ERA	G	GS	CG	SV	IP	H	R	ER	HR	BB	SO	AVG	vLH	vRH	K/9	BB/9
Moore, Jeffrey	R-R	6-1	195	3-26-83	6	2	2.29	15	13	0	0	79	65	26	20	2	5	60	.226	.239	.216	6.86	0.57
Morris, Cory	R-R	6-2	200	6-2-79	0	0	0.00	2	2	0	0	6	2	0	0	0	4	6	.095	.000	.222	8.53	5.68
Nery, Nathan	R-L	6-4	212	8-25-85	3	4	5.17	14	9	0	0	47	35	27	27	1	28	34	.211	.208	.211	6.51	5.36
Perez, Wilfredo	L-L	6-0	145	8-12-84	1	1	3.28	7	5	0	0	25	23	9	9	1	12	31	.256	.192	.281	11.31	4.38
Schindling, Andrew	R-R	6-2	165	8-15-86	0	0	0.00	2	1	0	0	7	4	1	0	0	2	5	.174	.100	.231	6.75	2.70
Schmidt, Kyle	R-R	6-3	220	8-25-83	1	1	3.30	5	5	0	0	30	26	12	11	2	8	37	.243	.292	.203	11.10	2.40
Soriano, Julio	R-R	6-2	160	9-24-83	0	0	2.65	15	0	0	0	17	11	5	5	0	14	21	.186	.067	.227	11.12	7.41
Stadanlick, Ryan	R-R	6-3	210	8-3-84	0	2	4.00	18	0	0	0	27	27	17	12	3	12	19	.255	.342	.206	6.33	4.00
Tamba, Josh	L-R	6-2	200	11-15-84	5	4	3.21	15	14	0	0	70	72	34	25	2	21	50	.263	.272	.252	6.43	2.70
Thall, Chad	L-L	6-4	220	8-2-85	6	2	1.83	25	0	0	1	44	36	13	9	3	14	33	.226	.217	.233	6.70	2.84

FIELDING

Catcher	PCT	G	PO	A	E	DP	PB
Castillo	.992	43	313	43	3	5	15
Kotch	1.000	7	21	4	0	0	1
Pierce	1.000	15	58	7	0	1	4
Pulley	1.000	1	1	0	0	0	0
Snyder	.973	29	223	25	7	1	8

First Base	PCT	G	PO	A	E	DP
Calzado	1.000	1	1	1	0	0
Marconi	1.000	1	5	0	0	1
Pacheco	.976	16	118	6	3	15
Vinyard	.987	62	581	21	8	48

Second Base	PCT	G	PO	A	E	DP
Abreu	.975	15	29	48	2	8
Adams	.941	6	10	22	2	4

Davison	.976	30	46	76	3	17
Silveren	.934	30	64	77	10	18
Stephen	1.000	1	2	4	0	0

Third Base	PCT	G	PO	A	E	DP
Abreu	.944	39	20	65	5	8
Calzado	.923	4	4	8	1	0
Davison	.941	8	1	15	1	0
Gomez	1.000	1	0	2	0	0
Marconi	.930	16	15	25	3	4
Rowell	.905	11	7	12	2	1
Stephen	1.000	3	1	7	0	1

Shortstop	PCT	G	PO	A	E	DP
Davison	.958	13	8	38	2	8
Florimon Jr.	.965	26	51	85	5	14
Silveren	1.000	1	1	6	0	0

Stephen	.964	38	53	106	6	23

Outfield	PCT	G	PO	A	E	DP
Abreu	.939	16	26	5	2	2
Andrews	.965	31	54	1	2	0
Avila	.938	5	14	1	1	0
Calzado	1.000	1	1	0	0	0
Cash	.896	22	42	1	5	0
Davis	.960	32	45	3	2	1
Figueroa	.979	26	46	1	1	1
Pope	.967	18	28	1	1	0
Shafer	.926	29	45	5	4	0
Silveren	.—	1	0	0	0	0
Stephen	1.000	1	1	0	0	0
Tripp	.987	42	71	3	1	1
Winterling	.966	19	27	1	1	0

Bluefield Orioles — Rookie

Appalachian League

BATTING	B-T	HT	WT	DOB	AVG	vLH	vRH	G	AB	R	H	2B	3B	HR	RBI	BB	HBP	SH	SF	SO	SB	CS	SLG	OBP
Adams, Ryan	R-R	6-0	185	4-21-87	.256	.286	.242	34	133	24	34	8	1	2	7	19	3	1	0	32	2	2	.376	.361
Bent, Brian	R-R	6-2	210	9-11-85	.283	.273	.290	16	53	9	15	2	0	0	6	4	2	2	1	11	0	0	.321	.350
Chmiel, Paul	L-R	6-5	200	5-17-87	.286	.189	.315	44	161	17	46	13	2	2	28	21	0	2	0	38	0	1	.429	.364
D Oleo, Richard	L-L	6-1	165	5-5-86	.213	.189	.224	46	169	24	36	9	1	3	21	30	0	2	2	53	6	1	.331	.328
Diaz, Andino	R-R	6-0	180	5-19-85	.179	.231	.154	13	39	1	7	1	0	0	2	1	1	0	2	12	0	0	.205	.209
Florimon Jr., Pedro	B-R	6-2	165	12-10-86	.333	.262	.372	33	120	23	40	6	1	1	8	28	0	1	1	29	7	6	.425	.456
Gonzalez, Franklin	R-R	6-0	160	4-7-86	.240	.204	.254	45	171	20	41	10	0	3	14	9	3	2	0	51	0	1	.351	.290
Henson, Bobby	R-R	6-1	190	12-15-87	.230	.356	.175	43	148	21	34	5	2	0	13	18	1	1	2	49	1	1	.291	.314
Howell, Joey	R-R	6-1	205	9-22-85	.243	.238	.246	31	111	10	27	4	3	3	16	8	1	3	1	31	1	1	.414	.309
Huches, Leonardo	R-R	5-11	195	11-9-85	.136	.174	.116	19	66	4	9	2	0	0	3	4	1	0	0	18	1	1	.167	.197
Johnson, Justin	L-R	6-1	180	11-7-82	.177	.095	.200	33	96	10	17	5	1	2	16	12	1	0	2	16	0	2	.313	.270
Lopez, Luis	R-R	6-0	180	11-24-87	.221	.217	.224	36	122	15	27	4	0	4	16	8	1	1	2	44	2	0	.352	.271
Martinez, Anthony	R-R	6-3	240	12-19-83	.304	.300	.306	47	168	20	51	13	0	1	19	18	1	0	3	24	0	0	.399	.368
Nowicki, Joseph	L-L	6-2	210	11-12-82	.228	.313	.212	29	101	12	23	3	1	0	10	10	1	0	1	21	0	1	.277	.301
Polo, Winter	B-R	6-1	160	5-10-85	.227	.250	.208	33	97	15	22	2	2	2	11	4	2	1	0	26	3	1	.351	.272
Pope, Kieron	R-R	6-1	195	10-3-86	.341	.308	.361	37	135	20	46	16	1	5	29	10	6	0	0	36	4	3	.585	.411
Rowell, Billy	L-R	6-5	205	9-10-88	.329	.298	.347	42	152	38	50	15	3	2	26	25	1	0	2	47	3	0	.507	.422
Silveren, Pedro	R-R	6-0	160	9-2-84	.231	.286	.205	17	65	7	15	2	1	0	8	5	1	2	1	8	1	1	.292	.292
Thiel, Emile	R-R	6-2	155	2-15-87	.097	.250	.074	10	31	3	3	1	0	0	2	7	0	0	0	15	0	0	.129	.263
Yeme, Leonel	L-L	6-4	198	9-25-85	.175	.143	.182	23	80	11	14	0	0	1	4	4	1	0	2	21	0	3	.213	.224

PITCHING	B-T	HT	WT	DOB	W	L	ERA	G	GS	CG	SV	IP	H	R	ER	HR	BB	SO	AVG	vLH	vRH	K/9	BB/9
Allar, Brent	R-R	6-2	210	3-1-85	0	0	1.59	14	0	0	8	17	10	5	3	0	9	21	.175	.077	.205	11.12	4.76
Basta, Samuel	L-L	6-0	165	2-21-86	1	0	8.31	3	0	0	0	4	4	5	4	0	4	4	.222	.000	.286	8.31	8.31
Britton, Zach	L-L	6-2	172	12-22-87	0	4	5.29	11	11	0	0	34	35	22	20	4	20	21	.271	.375	.257	5.56	5.29
Camacho, Gustavo	R-R	6-3	218	10-17-84	0	1	20.25	3	0	0	0	3	7	6	6	0	2	4	.438	.375	.500	13.50	6.75
Clark, Zach	R-R	6-0	195	7-11-83	5	4	2.11	13	13	0	0	64	56	26	15	1	19	58	.230	.214	.239	8.16	2.67
Escorcha, Juan	R-R	6-0	172	1-8-86	0	0	4.79	12	0	0	0	21	15	15	11	3	18	23	.197	.190	.200	10.02	7.84
Faiola, Josh	R-R	6-3	200	10-3-83	2	0	1.00	20	0	0	2	36	24	10	4	2	8	35	.180	.263	.147	8.75	2.00
Gallaway, Bruce	R-L	6-3	200	9-17-82	1	0	2.13	11	0	0	5	13	11	6	3	0	9	18	.229	.100	.263	12.79	6.39
Garcia, Adolfito	R-R	6-2	170	1-31-85	1	3	5.44	16	7	0	1	46	50	31	28	3	24	32	.281	.375	.246	6.22	4.66
Hayes, Matthew	R-L	6-3	175	3-25-83	2	0	4.94	16	0	0	0	27	38	17	15	1	10	21	.309	.526	.269	6.91	3.29
Horner, Tag	L-L	6-3	220	11-12-82	3	1	0.93	14	0	0	2	19	15	5	2	0	10	16	.211	.211	.212	7.45	4.66
Jevne, Zachary	R-R	6-7	220	8-9-82	2	3	4.27	17	2	0	2	46	56	29	22	5	5	35	.289	.259	.300	6.80	0.97
Lee, Bryan	R-R	6-5	200	1-24-85	2	0	8.57	14	0	0	0	21	19	26	20	0	28	22	.232	.308	.196	9.43	12.00
Maria, Jose	L-L	6-3	175	6-14-83	4	6	2.55	14	14	0	0	71	67	33	20	3	17	53	.245	.316	.239	6.75	2.17
Miller, Aubrey	R-R	6-4	215	9-22-83	0	4	6.59	16	5	0	0	42	50	39	31	2	19	27	.292	.269	.300	5.74	4.04
Ouellette, Ryan	R-R	5-11	185	10-4-85	2	8	6.66	13	12	0	0	53	68	52	39	3	24	26	.306	.328	.297	4.44	4.10
Schindling, Andrew	R-R	6-2	165	8-15-86	6	2	2.49	15	4	0	0	47	35	16	13	1	23	40	.200	.200	.200	7.66	4.40
Selen, Ezequiel	R-R	6-3	170	7-14-85	0	1	13.50	7	0	0	0	7	15	12	11	2	6	8	.417	.444	.407	9.82	7.36

FIELDING

Catcher	PCT	G	PO	A	E	DP	PB
Bent	.984	15	117	10	2	0	4
Diaz	1.000	5	21	3	0	0	3
Huches	.957	19	120	14	6	1	3
Johnson	1.000	33	211	27	0	7	7

First Base	PCT	G	PO	A	E	DP
Chmiel	.990	38	356	21	4	41
Martinez	.981	31	282	21	6	22

Second Base	PCT	G	PO	A	E	DP
Adams	.955	27	69	78	7	24

Gonzalez	.907	15	25	43	7	7
Henson	.957	9	20	25	2	7
Silveren	.864	17	25	45	11	13

Third Base	PCT	G	PO	A	E	DP
Gonzalez	.957	14	9	36	2	3
Henson	.818	11	10	17	6	4
Rowell	.868	36	15	90	16	9
Thiel	.800	9	1	15	4	0

Shortstop	PCT	G	PO	A	E	DP
Florimon Jr.	.891	33	46	118	20	20

Gonzalez	.935	13	14	44	4	11
Henson	.839	23	27	67	18	12

Outfield	PCT	G	PO	A	E	DP
D Oleo	.978	46	84	3	2	2
Howell	.979	31	43	4	1	1
Lopez	.979	32	44	2	1	1
Nowicki	.953	26	40	1	2	0
Polo	.900	29	33	3	4	0
Pope	.962	34	45	6	2	0
Yeme	.722	11	13	0	5	0

BOSTON RED SOX

BY JOHN TOMASE

If the 2006 season were a cross-country trip, the Red Sox would have broken down somewhere around Colorado.

The flawed squad hung around the playoff race until August, when injuries and age exposed its many holes. Not only did the Sox miss the playoffs for the first time since 2002, but they couldn't even maintain second place, finishing a game behind the Blue Jays in third.

The end came swiftly during a listless five-game August sweep to the Yankees at Fenway Park. So methodical was New York's dismantling, fans couldn't even summon the rage to label it another New York Massacre, as was the case in 1978.

That series triggered a series of blows that came in rapid succession, culminating in the awful news that top prospect Jon Lester had cancer. The diagnosis of lymphoma ended his season, though doctors were cautiously optimistic he'd make a full recovery.

MVP candidate David Ortiz was briefly hospitalized with an irregular heartbeat that turned out to be benign, and Jason Varitek, Trot Nixon, Tim Wakefield, Mike Timlin, Coco Crisp and Manny Ramirez each missed significant action.

Another player who ended the year on the sidelines was rookie closer Jonathan Papelbon, who authored a transcendent season until leaving a game with what was eventually diagnosed as a tired shoulder. While healthy, Papelbon was one of the highlights of the season. He took the closer's job from Keith Foulke just one game in and never looked back. He didn't allow his first run until May and finished with 35 saves and a 0.92 ERA.

PLAYERS OF THE YEAR

MAJOR LEAGUE: David Ortiz, dh

Manny Ramirez also was productive in 2006, but Big Papi's 54 home runs, 137 RBIs and 115 runs give him the nod. The 54 bombs rank as a career-high for Ortiz, who also drew a personal-best 119 walks to lead the club. He had 85 extra-base hits in 2006, and 23 of those free passes came intentionally.

MINOR LEAGUE: Clay Buchholz, rhp

Buchholz started his first full season with a bang, picking up back-to-back wins at low Class A Greenville, and finished even stronger. He won his final five games for the Drive, then went 2-0, 1.13 at high Class A Wilmington. Buchholz led all Red Sox farmhands with 140 strikeouts and finished with 11 wins.

TOM PRIDDY

He held together a shaky pitching staff that received little in the form of consistency beyond ace Curt Schilling. Josh Beckett, acquired from the Marlins in a ballyhooed trade for prospects Hanley Ramirez and Anibal Sanchez, among others, won 16 games and cracked 200 innings for the first time, but finished with a career worst 5.01 ERA.

The rest of the staff had to be pieced together, particularly after Wakefield cracked a rib in July and was sidelined for two months. The Red Sox used 14 different starters without finding one who could win consistently. The bullpen wasn't much better. Free-agent signees Rudy Seanez and Julian Tavarez were busts. Timlin was lights-out until going on the disabled list in May with a strained shoulder.

The uneven pitching weighed on the offense, which couldn't deliver like teams of the previous three seasons. Ortiz did his best, slamming 54 home runs to break Jimmie Foxx' 68-year-old team record. Ramirez joined him until losing interest over the final month and sitting with a knee injury that many believed to be less than serious. There weren't too many offensive highlights otherwise. Varitek took a step back behind the plate, prospective free agent Trot Nixon likely finished his 13-year Red Sox tenure with a whimper, Crisp was slowed by injuries, and veteran Mike Lowell and first-time starter Kevin Youkilis faded after strong starts.

The Red Sox played surprisingly strong defense, setting a major league record for consecutive errorless games (17) and leading baseball with a .989 fielding percentage. Shortstop Alex Gonzalez led the charge with just seven errors.

The bloom started to come off of general manager Theo Epstein, who briefly left the team during the offseason before winning a power play with CEO Larry Lucchino and returning. The Red Sox made a regrettable deal in May, reacquiring catcher Doug Mirabelli from San Diego for Josh Bard and prospect Cla Meredith. Mirabelli hit just .191 while Bard batted .338 and Meredith tossed a club-record 34 consecutive scoreless innings to finish with a 1.07 ERA.

ORGANIZATION LEADERS

BATTING
Minimum 250 at-bats

*AVG	Pedroia, Dustin, Pawtucket	.305
R	Johnson, Jay, Portland/Greenville/Wilmington	86
H	Ellsbury, Jacoby, Wilmington/Portland	149
TB	Johnson, Jay, Portland/Greenville/Wilmington	230
2B	Murphy, David, Portland/Pawtucket	40
3B	Ellsbury, Jacoby, Wilmington/Portland	10
HR	Bailey, Jeff, Pawtucket	22
RBI	Natale, Jeff, Greenville/Wilmington	87
BB	Natale, Jeff, Greenville/Wilmington	103
SO	Hall, Michael, Wilmington/Greenville	151
SB	Ellsbury, Jacoby, Wilmington/Portland	45
*OBP	Natale, Jeff, Greenville/Wilmington	.446
*SLG	Bailey, Jeff, Pawtucket	.489
XBH	Murphy, David, Portland/Pawtucket	57

PITCHING
#Minimum 75 innings

W	Jackson, Kyle, Wilmington/Portland	12
L	Galvez, Gary, Wilmington	10
	Hottovy, Thomas, Wilmington/Portland	10
#ERA	Rodriguez, Jorge, GCL Red Sox	2.35
G	Hertzler, Barry, Pawtucket/Portland	57
CG	Hottovy, Thomas, Wilmington/Portland	2
SV	James, Michael, Wilmington	25
IP	Hottovy, Thomas, Wilmington/Portland	163
BB	Vaquedano, Jose, Wilmington/Portland	73
SO	Buchholz, Clay, Greenville/Wilmington	140
#AVG	Doubront, Felix, GCL Red Sox/Lowell	.207

Boston Red Sox | MLB

American League

BATTING	B-T	HT	WT	DOB	AVG	vLH	vRH	G	AB	R	H	2B	3B	HR	RBI	BB	HBP	SH	SF	SO	SB	CS	SLG	OBP
Bard, Josh	B-R	6-3	210	3-30-78	.278	.250	.286	7	18	2	5	1	0	0	0	3	0	0	0	3	0	0	.333	.381
Cora, Alex	L-R	6-0	200	10-18-75	.238	.333	.219	96	235	31	56	7	2	1	18	19	6	4	0	29	6	2	.298	.312
Crisp, Coco	B-R	6-0	180	11-1-79	.264	.277	.259	105	413	58	109	22	2	8	36	31	1	7	0	67	22	4	.385	.317
Gonzalez, Alex	R-R	6-0	200	2-15-77	.255	.278	.244	111	388	48	99	24	2	9	50	22	5	7	7	67	1	0	.397	.299
Harris, Willie	L-R	5-9	170	6-22-78	.156	.250	.135	47	45	17	7	2	0	0	1	4	2	0	1	11	6	3	.200	.250
Hinske, Eric	L-R	6-2	235	8-5-77	.288	.273	.290	31	80	8	23	8	0	1	5	8	0	0	0	30	1	1	.425	.352
2-team (78 Toronto)..					.271	—	—	109	277	43	75	17	2	13	34	35	0	0	0	79	2	2	.487	.353
Huckaby, Ken	R-R	6-1	200	1-27-71	.200	.000	.250	8	5	0	1	0	0	0	1	0	0	0	0	0	0	0	.200	.200
Kapler, Gabe	R-R	6-2	210	7-31-75	.254	.265	.242	72	130	21	33	7	0	2	12	14	3	0	0	15	1	1	.354	.340
Lopez, Javy	R-R	6-3	220	11-5-70	.190	.250	.176	18	63	6	12	5	0	0	4	2	0	0	0	16	0	0	.270	.215
2-team (76 Baltimore)					.251	—	—	94	342	36	86	20	1	8	35	20	2	0	0	76	0	0	.386	.297
Loretta, Mark	R-R	6-0	185	8-14-71	.285	.274	.290	155	635	75	181	33	0	5	59	49	12	2	5	63	4	1	.361	.345
Lowell, Mike	R-R	6-3	210	2-24-74	.284	.241	.302	153	573	79	163	47	1	20	80	47	4	0	7	61	2	2	.475	.339
Miller, Corky	R-R	6-1	245	3-18-76	.000	.000	.000	1	4	0	0	0	0	0	0	0	0	0	0	1	0	0	.000	.000
Mirabelli, Doug	R-R	6-1	220	10-18-70	.193	.208	.186	59	161	12	31	6	0	6	25	11	4	0	0	54	0	0	.342	.261
Mohr, Dustan	R-R	6-1	210	6-19-76	.175	.250	.000	21	40	5	7	1	0	2	3	3	0	0	0	20	0	0	.350	.233
Murphy, David	L-L	6-4	190	10-18-81	.227	.000	.238	20	22	4	5	1	0	1	2	4	0	0	0	4	0	0	.409	.346
Nixon, Trot	L-L	6-2	210	4-11-74	.268	.204	.288	114	381	59	102	24	0	8	52	60	7	0	5	56	0	2	.394	.373
Ortiz, David	L-L	6-4	230	11-18-75	.287	.278	.292	151	558	115	160	29	2	54	137	119	4	0	5	117	1	0	.636	.413
Pedroia, Dustin	R-R	5-9	180	8-17-83	.191	.162	.212	31	89	5	17	4	0	2	7	7	1	1	0	7	0	1	.303	.258
Pena, Carlos	L-L	6-2	210	5-17-78	.273	.273	.273	18	33	3	9	2	0	1	3	4	0	0	0	10	0	0	.424	.351
Pena, Wily Mo	R-R	6-3	245	1-23-82	.301	.260	.326	84	276	36	83	15	2	11	42	20	3	0	5	90	0	1	.489	.349
Ramirez, Manny	R-R	6-0	200	5-30-72	.321	.326	.319	130	449	79	144	27	1	35	102	100	1	0	8	102	0	1	.619	.439
Snow, J.T.	L-L	6-2	210	2-26-68	.205	.333	.184	38	44	5	9	0	0	0	4	8	1	0	0	8	0	0	.205	.340
Stern, Adam	L-R	5-11	180	2-12-80	.150	.000	.158	10	20	3	3	1	0	0	0	4	0	1	0	4	1	0	.200	.190
Varitek, Jason	B-R	6-2	230	4-11-72	.238	.229	.244	103	365	46	87	19	2	12	55	46	2	1	2	87	1	2	.400	.325
Youkilis, Kevin	R-R	6-1	220	3-15-79	.279	.270	.283	147	569	100	159	42	2	13	72	91	9	0	11	120	5	2	.429	.381

PITCHING	B-T	HT	WT	DOB	W	L	ERA	G	GS	CG	SV	IP	H	R	ER	HR	BB	SO	AVG	vLH	vRH	K/9	BB/9
Alvarez, Abe	L-L	6-2	190	10-17-82	0	0	12.00	1	0	0	0	3	5	4	4	2	2	2	.385	1.000	.111	6.00	6.00
Beckett, Josh	R-R	6-5	220	5-15-80	16	11	5.01	33	33	0	0	205	191	120	114	36	74	158	.245	.251	.238	6.95	3.25
Breslow, Craig	L-L	6-1	180	8-8-80	0	2	3.75	13	0	0	0	12	12	5	5	0	6	12	.261	.316	.222	9.00	4.50
Burns Jr., Mike	R-R	6-1	210	7-14-78	0	0	4.70	7	0	0	0	8	10	4	4	0	1	7	.323	.231	.389	8.22	1.17
Clement, Matt	R-R	6-3	210	8-12-74	5	5	6.61	12	12	0	0	65	77	50	48	8	38	43	.291	.307	.272	5.92	5.23
Corey, Bryan	R-R	6-0	180	10-21-73	1	0	4.57	16	0	0	0	22	20	11	11	1	7	15	.250	.297	.209	6.23	2.91
2-team (16 Texas)					2	1	3.69	32	0	0	0	39	35	16	16	1	15	28	—	—	—	6.46	3.46
Delcarmen, Manny	R-R	6-2	190	2-16-82	2	0	5.06	50	0	0	0	53	68	32	30	2	17	45	.309	.319	.302	7.59	2.87
DiNardo, Lenny	L-L	6-4	190	9-19-79	1	2	7.85	13	6	0	0	39	61	35	34	6	20	17	.363	.375	.358	3.92	4.62
Foulke, Keith	R-R	6-0	210	10-19-72	3	1	4.35	44	0	0	0	50	52	24	24	9	7	36	.271	.301	.236	6.52	1.27
Gabbard, Kason	L-L	6-3	200	4-8-82	1	3	3.51	7	4	0	0	26	24	11	10	0	16	15	.255	.250	.257	5.26	5.61
Hansack, Devern	R-R	6-2	180	2-5-78	1	1	2.70	2	2	1	0	10	6	3	3	2	1	8	.171	.235	.111	7.20	0.90
Hansen, Craig	R-R	6-5	185	11-15-83	2	2	6.63	38	0	0	0	38	46	32	28	5	15	30	.305	.344	.276	7.11	3.55
Holtz, Mike	L-L	5-9	180	10-10-72	0	0	16.20	3	0	0	0	2	3	3	3	0	4	2	.429	.333	.500	10.80	21.60
Jarvis, Kevin	L-R	6-2	200	8-1-69	0	1	4.86	4	3	0	0	17	22	12	9	1	6	7	.324	.323	.324	3.78	3.24
Johnson, Jason	R-R	6-6	225	10-27-73	0	4	7.36	6	6	0	0	29	41	26	24	3	13	18	.333	.338	.327	5.52	3.99
2-team (14 Cleveland)					3	12	6.35	20	20	0	0	106	149	81	75	13	35	50	—	—	—	4.23	2.96
Lester, Jon	L-L	6-2	190	1-7-84	7	2	4.76	15	15	0	0	81	91	43	43	7	43	60	.294	.397	.271	6.64	4.76
Lopez, Javier	L-L	6-4	220	7-11-77	1	0	2.70	27	0	0	1	17	13	10	5	1	10	11	.232	.250	.208	5.94	5.40
Papelbon, Jonathan	R-R	6-4	230	11-23-80	4	2	0.92	59	0	0	35	68	40	8	7	3	13	75	.167	.203	.128	9.88	1.71
Pauley, David	R-R	6-2	185	6-17-83	0	2	7.88	3	3	0	0	16	31	14	14	1	6	10	.419	.450	.382	5.63	3.38
Riske, David	R-R	6-2	180	10-23-76	0	1	3.72	8	0	0	0	10	8	4	4	2	3	5	.222	.154	.261	4.66	2.79
2-team (33 Chicago)..					1	2	3.89	41	0	0	0	44	40	20	19	6	17	28	—	—	—	5.73	3.48
Schilling, Curt	R-R	6-5	235	11-14-66	15	7	3.97	31	31	0	0	204	220	90	90	28	28	183	.276	.277	.275	8.07	1.24
Seanez, Rudy	R-R	5-11	200	10-20-68	2	1	4.82	41	0	0	0	47	51	28	25	6	26	48	.271	.266	.275	9.26	5.01
Snyder, Kyle	B-R	6-8	215	9-9-77	4	5	6.02	16	10	0	0	58	77	42	39	11	19	55	.314	.345	.287	8.49	2.93
2-team (1 Kansas City)					4	5	6.56	17	11	0	0	60	87	51	44	12	20	57	—	—	—	8.50	2.98
Tavarez, Julian	L-R	6-2	195	5-22-73	5	4	4.47	58	6	1	1	99	110	54	49	10	44	56	.293	.248	.327	5.11	4.01
Timlin, Mike	R-R	6-4	210	3-10-66	6	6	4.36	68	0	0	9	64	78	33	31	7	16	30	.305	.306	.303	4.22	2.25
Van Buren, Jermaine	R-R	6-1	220	7-2-80	1	0	11.77	10	0	0	0	13	14	17	17	1	15	8	.292	.350	.250	5.54	10.38
Wakefield, Tim	R-R	6-2	210	8-2-66	7	11	4.63	23	23	1	0	140	135	80	72	19	51	90	.248	.222	.264	5.79	3.28
Wells, David	L-L	6-3	250	5-20-63	2	3	4.98	8	8	0	0	47	64	30	26	10	8	24	.327	.262	.344	4.60	1.53

FIELDING

Catcher	PCT	G	PO	A	E	DP	PB
Bard	1.000	7	32	7	0	2	10
Huckaby	1.000	8	11	0	0	0	0
Lopez	.990	17	98	5	1	1	2
Miller	1.000	1	6	0	0	0	0
Mirabelli	.994	57	298	18	2	3	11
Varitek	.994	99	647	28	4	3	1

First Base	PCT	G	PO	A	E	DP
Hinske	.990	12	91	5	1	9
Loretta	1.000	11	74	9	0	8
Ortiz	.971	10	62	6	2	8
C. Pena	.989	17	81	5	1	15
Snow	.990	26	86	9	1	9
Youkilis	.995	127	1035	70	5	110

Second Base	PCT	G	PO	A	E	DP
Cora	.977	18	18	24	1	6
Harris	—	1	0	0	0	0
Loretta	.994	138	246	389	4	99
Pedroia	.975	27	45	73	3	17

Third Base	PCT	G	PO	A	E	DP
Cora	1.000	3	7	0		2
Lowell	.987	153	143	314	6	39
Youkilis	.927	16	11	27	3	1

Shortstop	PCT	G	PO	A	E	DP
Cora	.975	63	66	167	6	47
Gonzalez	.985	111	163	305	7	68

Outfield	PCT	G	PO	A	E	DP
Crisp	.996	103	246	3	1	3
Harris	1.000	36	38	1	0	0
Hinske	1.000	15	15	1	0	0
Kapler	1.000	68	83	4	0	1
Mohr	1.000	20	30	0	0	0
Murphy	1.000	16	12	0	0	0
Nixon	.995	110	212	6	1	2
C. Pena	—	1	0	0	0	0
W. Pena	.981	76	146	5	3	0
Ramirez	.989	123	175	7	2	0
Stern	1.000	10	18	1	0	0
Youkilis	1.000	18	36	3	0	0

(Second Base, cont.)	PCT	G	PO	A	E	DP
Pedroia	.952	6	7	13	1	4

ORGANIZATION STATISTICS

General manager: Theo Epstein. **Farm director:** Mike Hazen. **Scouting director:** Jason McLeod.

Class	Team	League	W	L	PCT	Finish*	Manager	Affiliate Since
Majors	Boston	American	86	76	.531	8th (14)	Terry Francona	—
Triple-A	Pawtucket Red Sox	International	69	75	.479	10th (14)	Ron Johnson	1973
Double-A	Portland Sea Dogs	Eastern	72	67	.518	+4th (12)	Todd Claus	2003
High A	Wilmington Blue Rocks	Carolina	67	71	.486	4th (8)	Chad Epperson	2005
Low A	Greenville Bombers	South Atlantic	67	73	.479	11th (16)	Ivan DeJesus	2005
Short-season	Lowell Spinners	New York-Penn	39	36	.520	9th (14)	Bruce Crabbe	1996
Rookie	GCL Red Sox	Gulf Coast	35	19	.648	+1st (12)	Dave Tomlin	1993
OVERALL 2006 MINOR LEAGUE RECORD			349	341	.506	13th (30)		

*Finish in overall standings (No. of teams in league). +League champion

Pawtucket Red Sox   Triple-A

International League

BATTING	B-T	HT	WT	DOB	AVG	vLH	vRH	G	AB	R	H	2B	3B	HR	RBI	BB	HBP	SH	SF	SO	SB	CS	SLG	OBP
Allen, Luke	L-R	6-2	220	8-4-78	.241	.167	.271	52	187	16	45	12	0	4	24	19	0	0	2	42	1	1	.369	.308
Bailey, Jeff	R-R	6-2	200	11-19-78	.275	.318	.255	134	458	64	126	22	5	22	82	74	10	0	6	116	1	2	.489	.383
Buckley, Ron	R-R	6-1	223	9-14-79	.222	.200	.235	9	27	4	6	1	0	1	3	2	0	0	0	10	0	0	.370	.276
Calloway, Ron	L-L	6-1	210	9-4-76	.288	.163	.319	114	406	49	117	27	3	4	49	40	4	2	5	77	9	6	.399	.354
Choi, Hee-Seop	L-L	6-4	255	3-16-79	.207	.193	.216	66	227	35	47	9	1	8	27	47	2	0	1	56	0	0	.361	.347
Concepcion Jr., Alberto	R-R	6-1	220	4-18-81	.118	.000	.154	5	17	0	2	0	0	0	1	1	0	0	0	10	0	0	.118	.167
Crisp, Coco	B-R	6-0	180	11-1-79	.333	—	.333	1	3	0	1	0	0	0	2	1	0	0	0	0	0	0	.333	.500
De Renne, Keoni	R-R	5-7	170	4-30-79	.182	.500	.080	10	33	1	6	0	0	0	1	3	0	0	1	0	0	0	.182	.250
Durrington, Trent	R-R	5-10	190	8-27-75	.233	.261	.221	112	391	49	91	14	3	3	30	33	5	8	3	88	32	7	.307	.299
Gonzalez, Alex	R-R	6-0	200	2-15-77	.333	—	.333	1	3	0	1	0	0	0	0	0	1	0	0	1	0	0	.333	.500
Harris, Willie	L-R	5-9	170	6-22-78	.220	.238	.213	60	218	32	48	6	1	8	17	29	3	2	1	56	11	3	.367	.319
Huckaby, Ken	R-R	6-1	200	1-27-71	.219	.174	.238	88	288	18	63	10	0	2	23	9	0	4	4	72	4	0	.274	.239
Jeroloman, Chuck	R-R	6-1	190	9-14-82	.125	—	.125	7	16	1	2	0	0	1	1	0	0	0	0	7	0	0	.313	.125
Kapler, Gabe	R-R	6-2	210	7-31-75	.200	.250	.143	4	15	0	3	1	0	0	2	1	0	0	0	4	0	0	.267	.250
Kent, Mathew	L-R	6-3	190	7-2-80	.000	—	.000	4	3	0	0	0	0	0	0	1	0	0	0	1	0	0	.000	.250
Khoury, Ryan	R-R	5-10	180	3-19-84	.143	.111	.167	9	21	1	3	0	0	0	2	2	0	0	1	7	0	0	.143	.208
Machado, Alejandro	B-R	6-0	185	4-26-82	.260	.194	.285	116	373	46	97	12	4	4	32	52	5	4	3	51	21	6	.346	.356
Miller, Corky	R-R	6-1	245	3-18-76	.258	.236	.266	63	198	29	51	11	0	13	36	22	6	0	4	43	0	0	.510	.343
Minges, Tyler	R-R	6-0	180	11-15-79	.238	.277	.219	62	202	19	48	11	0	3	16	17	1	0	2	47	1	0	.337	.297
Mohr, Dustan	R-R	6-1	210	6-19-76	.169	.259	.105	22	65	10	11	2	0	1	6	21	0	0	1	23	0	0	.246	.368
2-team (54 Toledo)					.238	—	—	76	252	31	60	13	4	7	31	43	0	2	2	93	1	4	.405	.347
Murphy, David	L-L	6-4	190	10-18-81	.267	.267	.268	84	318	45	85	23	5	8	44	45	0	0	3	53	3	3	.447	.355
Nixon, Trot	L-L	6-2	210	4-11-74	.167	.000	.182	3	12	2	2	1	0	0	0	0	0	0	0	0	0	0	.250	.167
Nye, Rodney	R-R	6-4	215	12-2-76	.237	.180	.270	43	139	13	33	9	0	2	17	18	1	0	3	25	1	0	.345	.323
2-team (49 Durham)					.242	—	—	92	298	29	72	18	1	4	31	30	3	0	5	70	1	0	.349	.312
Pedroia, Dustin	R-R	5-9	180	8-17-83	.305	.273	.321	111	423	55	129	30	3	5	50	48	9	9	4	27	1	4	.426	.384
Pena, Carlos	L-L	6-2	210	5-17-78	.459	.500	.452	11	37	7	17	3	0	4	8	5	1	0	1	5	0	0	.865	.523
2-team (105 Columbus)					.278	—	—	116	418	72	116	20	0	23	74	68	10	0	10	94	4	0	.490	.383
Pena, Wily Mo	R-R	6-3	245	1-23-82	.244	.400	.194	12	41	8	10	1	0	2	7	7	3	0	1	10	0	0	.415	.385
Pressley, Josh	L-R	6-6	240	4-2-80	.050	.000	.059	7	20	0	1	0	0	0	0	3	1	0	0	5	0	0	.050	.208
Stern, Adam	L-R	5-11	180	2-12-80	.258	.231	.271	93	392	59	101	21	3	8	34	23	1	4	1	78	23	7	.388	.300
Van Der Bosch, Matt	L-L	5-8	190	4-12-82	.167	—	.167	2	6	0	1	0	0	0	1	0	0	0	0	2	0	0	.167	.167
Varitek, Jason	B-R	6-2	230	4-11-72	.429	—	.429	2	7	2	3	0	0	1	1	0	0	0	0	3	0	0	.857	.429
Wilson, Enrique	R-R	5-11	190	7-27-73	.222	.210	.227	62	203	16	45	9	2	3	18	23	1	0	1	16	3	3	.330	.303

PITCHING	B-T	HT	WT	DOB	W	L	ERA	G	GS	CG	SV	IP	H	R	ER	HR	BB	SO	AVG	vLH	vRH	K/9	BB/9
Alvarez, Abe	L-L	6-2	190	10-17-82	6	9	5.64	22	21	0	0	118	136	79	74	22	40	71	.288	.253	.295	5.42	3.05
Baker, Brad	R-R	6-2	180	11-6-80	2	4	6.02	30	0	0	3	46	61	33	31	6	15	32	.319	.314	.324	6.22	2.91
2-team (9 Richmond)					3	4	5.14	39	0	0	3	61	75	38	35	7	19	49	—	—	—	7.19	2.79
Barnes, John	R-R	6-2	210	4-24-76	0	0	6.23	1	1	0	0	4	4	3	3	1	8	3	.286	.375	.167	6.23	16.62
Bausher, Tim	R-R	6-4	200	4-23-79	4	3	4.91	37	2	0	0	70	77	41	38	4	37	40	.284	.250	.305	5.17	4.78
2-team (2 Louisville)					4	4	5.30	39	2	0	0	73	85	47	43	6	39	42	—	—	—	5.18	4.81
Breslow, Craig	L-L	6-1	180	8-8-80	7	1	2.69	39	0	0	7	67	49	21	20	3	24	77	.200	.179	.206	10.34	3.22
Bumatay, Mike	L-L	6-0	170	10-9-79	1	2	6.91	11	0	0	0	14	21	13	11	1	12	10	.368	.357	.372	6.28	7.53
Corey, Bryan	R-R	6-0	180	10-21-73	0	0	7.20	3	0	0	0	5	7	4	4	2	2	4	.333	.333	.333	7.20	3.60
Delcarmen, Manny	R-R	6-2	190	2-16-82	0	1	2.12	10	0	0	0	17	9	4	4	0	6	19	.155	.238	.108	10.06	3.18
Deschenes, Marc	R-R	6-2	175	1-6-73	8	5	4.54	29	16	0	0	117	115	62	59	8	37	73	.260	.245	.273	5.62	2.85
DiNardo, Lenny	L-L	6-4	190	9-19-79	0	0	12.00	1	0	0	0	3	6	4	4	1	1	2	.357	.500	.333	6.00	3.00
Durrington, Trent	R-R	5-10	190	8-27-75	0	0	6.00	1	0	0	0	3	1	2	2	0	3	0	.111	.167	.000	0.00	9.00
Evert, Brett	L-R	6-6	200	10-23-80	0	1	10.38	1	1	0	0	4	5	5	5	3	3	3	.278	.417	.000	6.23	6.23
Foulke, Keith	R-R	6-0	210	10-19-72	0	1	1.80	4	2	0	0	5	4	1	1	0	4	5	.235	.167	.400	9.00	7.20
Gabbard, Kason	L-L	6-3	200	4-8-82	1	7	5.23	9	8	0	0	52	51	31	30	8	26	48	.268	.313	.254	8.36	4.53
Ginter, Matt	R-R	6-1	220	12-24-77	3	9	3.64	15	15	1	0	89	88	43	36	5	18	49	.263	.288	.248	4.96	1.82
2-team (9 Indianapolis)					5	14	4.33	24	23	1	0	141	147	80	68	15	26	85	—	—	—	5.41	1.66
Guyette, Kevin	R-R	6-4	215	12-3-82	0	0	11.25	1	1	0	0	4	9	5	5	0	2	4	.450	.444	.455	9.00	4.50
Hansen, Craig	R-R	6-5	185	11-15-83	1	2	2.75	14	4	0	0	36	31	14	11	0	19	26	.238	.277	.200	6.50	4.75
Henkel, Rob	R-L	6-3	210	8-3-78	1	4	5.74	5	5	1	0	27	36	17	17	5	4	23	.324	.303	.333	7.76	1.35
Hertzler, Barry	R-R	6-2	215	2-15-81	4	2	4.87	25	0	0	2	41	48	24	22	1	27	19	.314	.403	.253	4.20	5.98
Holtz, Mike	L-L	5-9	180	10-10-72	0	0	1.93	14	0	0	3	19	10	4	4	2	7	29	.154	.077	.173	13.98	3.38
Johnson, Jason	R-R	6-6	225	10-27-73	2	0	3.32	3	3	1	0	19	15	7	7	1	6	12	.217	.250	.195	5.68	2.84
2-team (1 Louisville)					2	1	4.50	4	4	1	0	24	21	13	12	2	7	14	—	—	—	5.25	2.62
Large, Terry	R-R	6-4	185	5-28-83	0	0	5.14	3	0	0	0	7	9	5	4	1	3	2	.290	.313	.267	2.57	3.86

	B-T	HT	WT	DOB	W	L	ERA	G	GS	CG	SV	IP	H	R	ER	HR	BB	SO	AVG	vLH	vRH	K/9	BB/9
Lee, David	R-R	6-1	200	3-12-73	0	1	0.87	8	0	0	1	10	5	1	1	0	3	12	.139	.056	.222	10.45	2.61
Lester, Jon	L-L	6-2	190	1-7-84	3	4	2.70	11	11	0	0	47	43	17	14	5	25	43	.240	.129	.264	8.29	4.82
Lopez, Javier	L-L	6-4	220	7-11-77	0	0	4.86	13	0	0	4	17	20	10	9	1	8	12	.299	.300	.298	6.48	4.32
2-team (26 Charlotte)					2	1	1.99	39	0	0	16	49	48	12	11	2	14	38	—	—	—	6.89	2.54
Mathews, T.J.	R-R	6-1	225	1-19-70	0	1	14.40	1	1	0	0	5	12	8	8	2	0	3	.462	.250	.643	5.40	0.00
Meredith, Cla	R-R	6-0	180	6-4-83	0	0	5.27	8	0	0	0	14	16	9	8	1	5	14	.302	.286	.308	9.22	3.29
Nye, Rodney	R-R	6-4	215	12-2-76	0	0	0.00	1	0	0	0	2	2	0	0	0	0	2	.250	.200	.333	9.00	0.00
2-team (1 Durham)....					0	0	0.00	2	0	0	0	3	3	0	0	0	1	2	—	—	—	6.00	3.00
Pauley, David	R-R	6-2	185	6-17-83	1	3	5.54	9	9	0	0	50	60	40	31	10	18	25	.303	.432	.214	4.47	3.22
Pena, Mario	L-L	6-4	170	12-7-84	0	1	6.75	1	1	0	0	4	4	3	3	1	2	4	.267	.500	.231	9.00	4.50
Richardson, Jason	R-R	6-4	225	6-11-80	1	0	0.00	2	0	0	0	4	1	0	0	0	0	2	.083	.200	.000	4.50	0.00
Riske, David	R-R	6-2	180	10-23-76	0	1	5.40	5	2	0	0	5	5	3	3	0	5	8	.250	.200	.300	14.40	9.00
Schroyer, Ryan	R-R	6-1	215	9-28-81	0	0	6.00	4	0	0	1	9	12	7	6	0	4	7	.324	.357	.304	7.00	4.00
Seibel, Phil	L-L	6-1	195	1-28-79	2	0	1.20	9	0	0	0	15	6	2	2	1	3	22	.118	.167	.103	13.20	1.80
Serrano, Jimmy	R-R	5-10	170	5-9-76	4	5	2.50	13	11	0	0	72	72	22	20	2	26	61	.263	.236	.280	7.63	3.25
Shoemaker, Scott	R-R	6-4	210	9-21-81	2	0	5.40	2	2	0	0	10	10	6	6	1	2	10	.278	.308	.261	9.00	1.80
Smith, Chris	R-R	6-2	200	4-9-81	1	1	3.21	7	6	0	0	34	33	16	12	2	9	23	.250	.217	.286	6.15	2.41
Snyder, Kyle	B-R	6-8	215	9-9-77	1	1	3.54	3	3	0	0	20	24	8	8	1	2	7	.304	.293	.316	3.10	0.89
Van Buren, Jermaine	R-R	6-1	220	7-2-80	4	0	2.98	33	0	0	16	45	37	16	15	2	18	46	.233	.257	.213	9.13	3.57
Wells, David	L-L	6-3	250	5-20-63	1	1	8.10	2	2	0	0	10	10	9	9	2	4	4	.263	.000	.294	3.60	3.60
Zink, Charlie	R-R	6-1	190	8-26-79	9	4	4.03	23	15	0	0	109	100	54	49	7	60	58	.247	.248	.246	4.77	4.94

FIELDING

Catcher	PCT	G	PO	A	E	DP	PB
Buckley	1.000	9	62	5	0	1	3
Concepcion Jr.	.970	4	30	2	1	0	2
Durrington	1.000	2	9	0	0	1	1
Huckaby	.984	84	499	51	9	5	15
Kent	1.000	4	16	0	0	0	0
Miller	.985	54	353	36	6	6	2
Varitek	1.000	1	3	0	0	0	0

First Base	PCT	G	PO	A	E	DP
Allen	1.000	1	10	1	0	3
Bailey	.994	76	591	33	4	57
Choi	.988	49	403	21	5	37
Durrington	1.000	1	1	0	0	1
Miller	1.000	5	27	1	0	3
C. Pena	.986	10	60	11	1	3
W. Pena	1.000	3	27	1	0	4
Pressley	1.000	4	14	0	0	0

Second Base	PCT	G	PO	A	E	DP
De Renne	1.000	9	15	27	0	8
Durrington	.986	30	74	65	2	17
Harris	.934	22	42	57	7	12
Khoury	1.000	1	0	1	0	1
Machado	.989	46	93	88	2	24
Pedroia	1.000	33	63	93	0	23
Wilson	.975	11	16	23	1	5

Third Base	PCT	G	PO	A	E	DP
Allen	.800	5	1	7	2	2
Durrington	.946	56	48	91	8	4
Jeroloman	1.000	6	3	6	0	1
Nye	.960	40	27	92	5	2
Pedroia	1.000	4	5	7	0	1
Wilson	.956	43	27	81	5	9

Shortstop	PCT	G	PO	A	E	DP
De Renne	1.000	1	3	4	0	1
Durrington	1.000	1	0	2	0	0
Gonzalez	1.000	1	2	4	0	1
Khoury	1.000	6	13	14	0	4
Machado	.985	61	74	124	3	30

	PCT	G	PO	A	E	DP
Pedroia	.979	74	116	207	7	41
Wilson	1.000	4	3	14	0	3

Outfield	PCT	G	PO	A	E	DP
Allen	.918	35	60	7	6	4
Bailey	.973	18	36	0	1	0
Calloway	.978	73	163	12	4	4
Crisp	1.000	1	2	0	0	0
Durrington	.964	31	48	5	2	1
Harris	.976	37	80	2	2	0
Kapler	—	2	0	0	0	0
Machado	.968	12	30	0	1	0
Minges	.983	52	108	5	2	1
Mohr	1.000	12	29	0	0	0
Murphy	.972	83	167	8	5	3
Nixon	1.000	2	5	0	0	0
W. Pena	.833	5	10	0	2	0
Stern	.991	93	213	6	2	2
Van Der Bosch	1.000	1	2	0	0	0

Portland Sea Dogs — Double-A

Eastern League

BATTING	B-T	HT	WT	DOB	AVG	vLH	vRH	G	AB	R	H	2B	3B	HR	RBI	BB	HBP	SH	SF	SO	SB	CS	SLG	OBP
Bacani, David	R-R	5-7	170	7-30-79	.229	.254	.219	121	406	60	93	19	2	5	45	52	20	4	9	67	11	5	.323	.339
Borowiak, Zach	R-R	6-1	185	5-18-81	.216	.227	.211	107	306	36	66	13	0	3	32	14	11	5	7	59	5	3	.288	.269
Brown, Dustin	R-R	6-0	195	6-19-82	.224	.297	.186	85	295	32	66	17	0	5	40	24	3	4	5	65	2	1	.332	.284
Concepcion Jr., Alberto	R-R	6-1	220	4-18-81	.227	.182	.243	79	251	29	57	14	0	4	28	28	4	3	0	67	1	2	.331	.314
De Renne, Keoni	B-R	5-7	170	4-30-79	.224	.170	.239	74	250	33	56	6	0	1	20	22	1	2	0	27	3	1	.260	.289
Durbin, Chris	R-R	6-0	180	9-8-81	.246	.212	.260	97	341	53	84	28	1	4	34	39	7	2	3	65	3	5	.370	.333
Ellsbury, Jacoby	L-L	6-1	185	9-11-83	.308	.389	.278	50	198	39	61	10	3	3	19	24	2	0	1	25	16	8	.434	.387
Jimenez, Luis A.	L-L	6-4	205	5-7-82	.276	.258	.284	115	395	74	109	22	2	17	70	58	5	0	6	90	9	2	.471	.371
Johnson, Jay	R-R	6-2	185	12-19-82	.333	.462	.250	8	33	7	11	4	0	2	9	2	1	0	1	8	0	0	.636	.378
Kapler, Gabe	R-R	6-2	210	7-31-75	.400	—	.400	3	10	2	4	3	1	0	2	1	0	0	0	2	0	0	.900	.455
Kelly, Dustin	R-R	6-0	185	5-23-83	.185	.333	.128	21	54	2	10	3	0	0	6	3	0	0	1	11	1	0	.241	.224
Leonard, Mike	R-R	6-0	210	5-4-82	.250	.000	.400	2	8	0	2	0	1	0	2	0	0	0	0	1	0	0	.500	.250
Minges, Tyler	R-R	6-0	180	11-15-79	.308	.375	.283	58	237	40	73	21	1	3	39	14	3	1	0	41	4	2	.451	.354
Moss, Brandon	L-R	6-0	180	9-16-83	.285	.325	.266	133	508	76	145	36	3	12	83	56	3	2	4	108	8	5	.439	.357
Murphy, David	L-L	6-4	190	10-18-81	.273	.196	.310	42	172	22	47	17	1	3	25	11	0	1	1	29	4	2	.436	.315
Myrow, Brian	R-L	5-11	190	9-4-76	.270	.273	.269	20	63	3	17	5	0	0	6	3	0	0	1	17	0	0	.349	.299
Pritz, Bryan	R-R	5-10	180	5-5-82	.182	.250	.129	14	55	8	10	4	0	1	3	3	0	0	1	9	2	0	.309	.220
Spann, Chad	R-R	6-1	195	10-25-83	.294	.333	.279	99	360	53	106	28	3	10	50	29	9	0	1	85	3	3	.472	.361
Suarez, Ignacio	R-R	5-11	165	5-3-81	.130	.000	.214	8	23	4	3	0	0	1	3	0	0	0	5	0	0	.130	.231
Twomley, Jason	L-L	6-0	215	9-20-82	.095	.000	.118	10	21	2	2	2	0	0	1	7	0	0	1	10	0	0	.190	.310
Van Der Bosch, Matt	L-L	5-8	190	4-12-82	.198	.333	.159	58	162	25	32	3	1	4	17	22	0	3	0	33	13	2	.302	.293
West, Jeremy	R-R	6-0	200	11-8-81	.269	.282	.263	124	450	64	121	32	1	13	66	41	11	0	4	64	1	3	.431	.342

PITCHING	B-T	HT	WT	DOB	W	L	ERA	G	GS	CG	SV	IP	H	R	ER	HR	BB	SO	AVG	vLH	vRH	K/9	BB/9
Bacani, David	R-R	5-7	170	7-30-79	0	0	18.00	1	0	0	0	1	4	2	2	0	1	1	.600	.667	.500	0.00	9.00
Beam, Randy	L-L	6-3	205	5-21-82	3	3	4.56	35	0	0	1	51	48	32	26	10	12	41	.246	.263	.235	7.19	2.10
Brooks, Frank	L-L	6-1	190	9-6-78	2	6	3.86	17	14	0	0	82	72	45	35	16	31	75	.232	.148	.261	8.27	3.42
Bumatay, Mike	L-L	6-0	170	10-9-79	1	2	4.93	42	0	0	3	42	41	26	23	4	25	41	.256	.157	.303	8.79	5.36
DiNardo, Lenny	L-L	6-4	190	9-19-79	0	1	31.50	1	1	0	0	2	7	7	7	2	2	2	.583	—	.583	9.00	9.00
Dobies, Andrew	L-L	6-1	180	4-20-83	1	2	3.93	6	6	0	0	34	38	18	15	6	7	16	.286	.343	.265	4.19	1.83
Evert, Brett	L-R	6-6	200	10-23-80	0	0	3.27	9	0	0	0	11	10	6	4	0	8	13	.238	.091	.290	10.64	6.55
Frederick, Kevin	L-R	6-1	215	11-4-76	2	2	3.27	10	0	0	1	11	11	4	4	1	4	9	.262	.435	.053	7.36	3.27
Gabbard, Kason	L-L	6-3	200	4-8-82	9	2	2.57	13	13	1	0	74	51	26	21	4	25	68	.192	.117	.222	8.31	3.05
Goodson, Matt	R-R	6-3	195	9-26-82	1	0	3.72	2	2	0	0	10	7	4	4	2	4	8	.200	.286	.143	7.45	3.72
Hansack, Devern	R-R	6-2	180	2-5-78	8	7	3.26	31	18	0	1	132	122	55	48	14	36	124	.242	.265	.220	8.43	2.45
Hansen, Craig	R-R	6-5	185	11-15-83	1	0	0.82	5	0	0	0	11	4	1	1	0	4	12	.105	.143	.059	9.82	3.27

Hertzler, Barry	R-R	6-2	215	2-15-81	0	0	0.73	25	1	0	5	37	27	4	3	0	22	27	.208	.183	.229	6.57	5.35
Hottovy, Tom	L-L	6-1	195	7-9-81	2	4	4.17	7	7	0	0	41	28	20	19	1	15	31	.190	.273	.176	6.80	3.29
Jackson, Kyle	R-R	6-3	192	4-9-83	3	1	2.45	22	0	0	1	37	32	11	10	2	25	36	.246	.188	.280	8.84	6.14
Kelly, Dustin	R-R	6-0	185	5-23-83	0	0	0.00	1	0	0	0	1	2	0	0	0	0	0	.400	.333	.500	0.00	0.00
Martinez, Edgar	R-R	6-0	220	10-23-81	5	3	2.61	49	0	0	12	69	51	23	20	9	18	59	.205	.135	.261	7.70	2.35
Mendoza, Luis	L-R	6-3	180	10-31-83	1	5	6.38	9	9	0	0	48	73	35	34	4	14	29	.356	.388	.333	5.44	2.63
Pauley, David	R-R	6-2	185	6-17-83	2	3	2.39	10	10	0	0	60	54	20	16	6	17	47	.248	.236	.263	7.01	2.54
Ramos, Victor	L-R	6-3	220	10-4-81	3	1	5.91	29	0	0	1	35	36	26	23	7	13	30	.259	.255	.261	7.71	3.34
Rozier, Michael	L-L	6-5	210	7-4-85	0	1	1.80	1	1	0	0	5	7	4	1	1	1	8	.292	.400	.263	14.40	1.80
Searles, Jonathan	R-R	6-3	200	1-18-81	7	4	4.19	53	0	0	1	77	72	41	36	7	38	56	.249	.286	.226	6.52	4.42
Seibel, Phil	L-L	6-1	195	1-28-79	2	3	1.20	9	9	0	0	45	24	11	6	5	12	42	.153	.175	.145	8.40	2.40
Shoemaker, Scott	R-R	6-4	210	9-21-81	0	1	2.57	3	3	0	0	14	15	4	4	2	4	10	.273	.400	.200	6.43	2.57
Smith, Chris	R-R	6-2	200	4-9-81	9	6	4.05	20	20	1	0	116	114	57	52	9	29	78	.257	.281	.236	6.07	2.26
Sturge, Justin	R-L	6-4	200	5-4-81	0	0	8.31	3	0	0	0	4	7	4	4	1	2	4	.368	.556	.200	8.31	4.15
Tucker, Rusty	R-L	6-1	190	7-15-80	0	2	3.90	25	0	0	2	32	34	14	14	3	18	19	.286	.286	.286	5.29	5.01
Vaquedano, Jose	R-R	6-4	167	7-9-81	9	8	6.47	24	24	0	0	106	131	89	76	9	68	86	.308	.332	.284	7.32	5.79
Zink, Charlie	R-R	6-1	190	8-26-79	1	0	1.23	2	1	0	0	7	6	3	1	1	5	7	.214	.278	.100	8.59	6.14

FIELDING

Catcher	PCT	G	PO	A	E	DP	PB
Brown	.986	79	586	68	9	8	10
Concepcion Jr.	.989	61	400	33	5	6	6
Leonard	1.000	2	19	4	0	1	0

First Base	PCT	G	PO	A	E	DP
Concepcion Jr.	1.000	1	3	0	0	1
Jimenez	.976	84	619	40	16	63
Myrow	1.000	2	5	0	0	1
Twomley	1.000	4	27	2	0	2
West	.989	56	417	39	5	31

Second Base	PCT	G	PO	A	E	DP
Bacani	.972	109	214	244	13	65
De Renne	.957	18	43	45	4	10
Kelly	.986	19	27	42	1	9

Third Base	PCT	G	PO	A	E	DP
Borowiak	.885	6	5	18	3	4
Concepcion Jr.	.946	13	13	22	2	2
De Renne	.886	20	10	29	5	3
Myrow	.884	15	13	25	5	1
Spann	.927	97	77	165	19	13

Shortstop	PCT	G	PO	A	E	DP
Bacani	.947	13	14	22	2	4
Borowiak	.937	97	146	223	25	51
De Renne	.940	40	42	83	8	20
Suarez	.880	8	6	16	3	4

Outfield	PCT	G	PO	A	E	DP
Brown	—	1	0	0	0	0
De Renne	1.000	1	1	0	0	0
Durbin	.982	84	152	10	3	2
Ellsbury	.993	48	129	4	1	2
Johnson	1.000	8	15	0	0	0
Kapler	1.000	1	2	0	0	0
Minges	.977	56	121	9	3	2
Moss	.983	128	222	9	4	3
Murphy	.969	40	92	2	3	0
Pritz	.968	13	28	2	1	0
Twomley	1.000	2	3	0	0	0
Van Der Bosch	.986	50	71	1	1	0

Wilmington Blue Rocks — High Class A

Carolina League

BATTING	B-T	HT	WT	DOB	AVG	vLH	vRH	G	AB	R	H	2B	3B	HR	RBI	BB	HBP	SH	SF	SO	SB	CS	SLG	OBP
Arias, Claudio	R-R	6-2	218	5-9-82	.252	.228	.264	70	274	37	69	22	1	8	36	12	4	0	0	79	3	0	.427	.293
Bell, Bubba	L-R	6-0	195	10-9-82	.283	.286	.282	19	60	8	17	4	1	1	9	8	0	0	0	7	2	0	.433	.368
Bladergroen, Ian	L-L	6-5	210	2-23-83	.242	.273	.226	98	331	46	80	20	4	9	51	42	17	0	4	91	1	0	.408	.353
Corsaletti, Jeffrey	L-R	6-0	190	2-22-83	.264	.232	.283	125	447	69	118	32	1	11	60	97	6	3	3	85	11	5	.414	.400
Devries, Jonathan	R-R	6-3	235	8-22-82	.204	.167	.222	15	54	6	11	0	1	1	5	6	2	0	0	28	0	0	.296	.306
Ellsbury, Jacoby	L-L	6-1	185	9-11-83	.299	.287	.306	61	244	35	73	7	5	4	32	25	7	4	1	28	25	9	.418	.379
Farkes, Zak	R-R	5-11	190	5-30-83	.667	—	.667	2	3	0	2	0	0	0	1	1	0	0	0	0	0	0	.667	.750
Hall, Michael	L-L	6-1	195	5-20-85	.206	.181	.218	68	228	28	47	11	7	1	16	21	2	2	1	88	7	3	.329	.278
Jeroloman, Chuck	R-R	6-1	190	9-14-82	.241	.255	.233	49	137	13	33	9	0	2	19	24	0	2	2	60	2	1	.350	.350
Johnson, Jay	R-R	6-2	185	12-19-82	.262	.278	.257	37	149	21	39	7	2	5	21	12	3	2	1	26	1	1	.436	.327
Kent, Mathew	L-R	6-3	190	7-2-80	.136	.120	.140	35	125	9	17	2	0	2	9	5	1	0	0	39	0	0	.200	.176
Lowrie, Jed	B-R	6-0	180	4-17-84	.262	.248	.269	97	374	43	98	21	6	3	50	54	2	0	8	65	2	2	.374	.352
Natale, Jeff	R-R	5-9	180	8-24-82	.278	.291	.273	82	273	46	76	13	0	7	46	62	10	0	8	54	1	0	.403	.419
Otness, John	R-R	5-11	200	9-15-81	.281	.263	.292	105	402	48	113	24	2	3	45	29	9	0	6	40	1	1	.373	.339
Pinckney, Andrew	B-R	6-1	195	4-7-82	.255	.237	.264	112	431	58	110	31	5	10	47	32	6	0	4	92	6	3	.420	.313
Pritz, Bryan	R-R	5-10	180	5-5-82	.254	.250	.257	98	346	47	88	17	3	3	40	30	1	3	1	48	10	5	.347	.315
Ramos, Dominic	R-R	5-10	180	3-10-83	.163	.147	.173	31	86	10	14	6	0	0	4	9	4	2	1	19	3	2	.233	.270
Suarez, Ignacio	R-R	5-11	165	5-3-81	.265	.197	.306	94	328	50	87	17	3	4	36	28	2	4	5	70	7	6	.372	.322
Wagner, Mark	R-R	6-1	205	6-11-84	.169	.238	.136	17	65	8	11	4	0	1	5	7	0	0	2	9	0	0	.277	.243
White, Scott	R-L	6-3	196	10-18-83	.220	.221	.219	78	264	32	58	16	3	5	34	15	8	0	8	53	3	3	.360	.275

PITCHING	B-T	HT	WT	DOB	W	L	ERA	G	GS	CG	SV	IP	H	R	ER	HR	BB	SO	AVG	vLH	vRH	K/9	BB/9
Barnes, John	R-R	6-2	210	4-24-76	2	4	3.13	8	7	0	0	37	34	25	13	3	23	28	.245	.250	.242	6.75	5.54
Blackley, Adam	L-L	6-1	220	2-22-85	0	2	4.64	5	4	0	0	21	27	12	11	1	8	16	.310	.316	.309	6.75	3.38
Bowden, Michael	R-R	6-3	215	9-9-86	0	0	9.00	1	1	0	0	5	9	5	5	0	1	3	.391	.000	.474	5.40	1.80
Buchholz, Clay	L-R	6-3	190	8-14-84	2	0	1.13	3	3	0	0	16	10	4	2	0	4	23	.182	.286	.146	12.94	2.25
Cox, Timothy	R-L	5-10	165	7-8-86	0	0	0.00	1	0	0	0	3	3	0	0	0	1	1	.250	.500	.200	3.00	3.00
Cox, Bryson	R-R	6-4	205	8-10-84	2	0	0.74	13	0	0	0	24	14	4	2	0	9	25	.165	.129	.185	9.25	3.33
Dobies, Andrew	L-L	6-1	180	4-20-83	8	6	3.98	21	21	0	0	118	124	58	52	10	33	77	.270	.232	.279	5.89	2.52
Galvez, Gary	R-R	6-2	200	3-24-84	6	10	5.44	25	25	0	0	122	141	82	74	16	43	72	.296	.266	.322	5.30	3.16
Goodson, Matthew	R-R	6-3	195	9-26-82	3	7	3.92	19	19	1	0	96	84	51	42	13	42	67	.226	.237	.219	6.26	3.92
Guyette, Kevin	R-R	6-4	215	12-3-82	2	6	6.58	14	11	0	0	64	77	52	47	12	22	43	.292	.240	.323	6.02	3.08
Hottovy, Thomas	L-L	6-1	195	7-9-81	8	6	2.80	21	21	2	0	122	109	49	38	3	35	91	.237	.250	.234	6.71	2.58
Jackson, Kyle	R-R	6-3	192	4-9-83	6	0	1.59	24	0	0	1	45	24	9	8	1	24	67	.159	.155	.161	13.30	4.76
James, Michael	R-R	6-1	185	6-2-81	2	1	1.81	48	0	0	25	50	42	10	10	2	19	51	.228	.212	.237	9.24	3.44
Johnson, Jason	R-R	6-6	225	10-27-73	1	0	5.14	1	1	0	0	7	10	4	4	0	0	1	.333	.462	.235	1.29	0.00
Mann, Will	R-R	6-5	235	6-20-84	0	0	18.00	1	0	0	0	1	2	2	2	0	1	0	.500	1.000	.333	0.00	9.00
Mendoza, Luis	L-R	6-3	180	10-31-83	5	4	3.14	13	13	0	0	63	67	26	22	4	14	46	.269	.267	.271	6.57	2.00
Newsom, Randy	R-R	6-2	200	5-6-82	1	1	3.92	19	0	0	1	44	42	22	19	0	19	27	.246	.282	.215	5.56	3.92
2-team (16 Kinston)					3	3	3.50	35	0	0	2	64	65	32	25	1	26	44	—	—	—	6.16	3.64
Pena, Mario	L-L	6-4	170	12-7-84	0	0	2.33	5	2	0	0	19	18	7	5	1	9	9	.237	.345	.170	4.19	4.19
Richardson, Jason	R-R	6-4	225	6-11-80	2	7	4.92	35	0	0	0	71	83	43	39	5	29	58	.300	.387	.246	7.32	3.66
Rozier, Michael	L-L	6-5	210	7-4-85	0	0	7.71	1	1	0	0	5	6	4	4	0	3	5	.316	.333	.313	9.64	5.79
Schroyer, Ryan	R-R	6-1	215	9-28-81	1	5	4.80	31	0	0	1	51	52	28	27	2	20	49	.265	.237	.283	8.70	3.55
Shoemaker, Scott	R-R	6-4	210	9-21-81	9	2	4.05	23	8	0	0	73	65	38	33	8	20	38	.243	.247	.240	4.66	2.45
Sturge, Justin	R-L	6-4	200	5-4-81	4	5	2.92	50	0	0	4	89	82	33	29	2	30	79	.252	.197	.267	7.96	3.02
Vaquedano, Jose	R-R	6-4	167	7-9-81	0	0	6.75	1	1	0	0	4	6	3	3	0	5	1	.353	.400	.333	2.25	11.25
Vaughan, Beau	B-R	6-4	230	6-4-81	3	5	3.72	43	0	0	0	65	71	30	27	2	20	60	.273	.305	.252	8.27	2.76

FIELDING

Catcher	PCT	G	PO	A	E	DP	PB
Devries	.991	14	107	9	1	1	1
Kent	.974	29	204	20	6	5	3
Otness	.993	85	550	46	4	4	11
Wagner	.982	13	101	6	2	0	7

First Base	PCT	G	PO	A	E	DP
Bladergroen	.993	95	802	58	6	64
Kent	1.000	1	8	0	0	1
Otness	.981	6	50	3	1	4
White	.988	41	321	21	4	24

Second Base	PCT	G	PO	A	E	DP
Jeroloman	.975	24	40	76	3	16

Natale	.953	59	104	137	12	24
Ramos	.956	29	50	80	6	15
Suarez	.975	33	74	82	4	22

Third Base	PCT	G	PO	A	E	DP
Jeroloman	.925	17	12	25	3	2
Pinckney	.918	104	69	178	22	15
Suarez	.909	6	4	16	2	1
White	1.000	16	7	26	0	7

Shortstop	PCT	G	PO	A	E	DP
Jeroloman	1.000	5	6	11	0	3
Lowrie	.938	88	125	255	25	34

Suarez	.963	48	72	136	8	31

Outfield	PCT	G	PO	A	E	DP
Arias	.951	39	70	7	4	1
Bell	1.000	14	29	2	0	1
Corsaletti	.968	117	180	2	6	0
Ellsbury	.994	61	162	0	1	0
Hall	.986	67	135	6	2	1
Jeroloman	—	1	0	0	0	0
Johnson	.987	37	73	2	1	1
Pritz	.996	92	219	7	1	2

Greenville Drive — Low Class A

South Atlantic League

BATTING	B-T	HT	WT	DOB	AVG	vLH	vRH	G	AB	R	H	2B	3B	HR	RBI	BB	HBP	SH	SF	SO	SB	CS	SLG	OBP
Bates, Aaron	R-R	6-4	232	3-10-84	.270	.455	.218	43	152	13	41	7	0	4	16	17	3	0	2	26	0	0	.395	.351
Bell, Bubba	L-R	6-0	195	10-9-82	.231	.140	.259	59	208	30	48	7	1	3	28	27	3	2	1	31	5	6	.317	.326
Farkes, Zak	R-R	5-11	190	5-30-83	.256	.267	.250	13	39	7	10	2	1	1	3	4	0	0	0	11	2	0	.436	.326
Granadillo, Tony	B-R	5-10	165	8-10-84	.283	.306	.275	116	420	70	119	29	2	13	68	43	11	5	7	79	3	0	.455	.360
Hall, Michael	L-L	6-1	195	5-20-85	.236	.190	.248	51	195	22	46	8	2	2	21	30	3	0	2	63	6	4	.328	.343
Jeroloman, Chuck	R-R	6-1	190	9-14-82	.231	.091	.286	14	39	3	9	2	1	1	3	13	0	0	0	17	0	0	.410	.423
Johnson, Jay	R-R	6-2	185	12-19-82	.283	.184	.324	73	300	58	85	16	5	11	43	33	3	2	2	42	4	4	.480	.358
Kelly, Dustin	R-R	6-0	185	5-23-83	.202	.200	.202	39	129	20	26	7	1	2	8	12	1	0	0	33	0	0	.318	.275
Khoury, Ryan	R-R	5-10	180	3-19-84	.389	—	.389	6	18	3	7	1	0	0	1	1	0	0	0	2	2	0	.444	.421
Lara, Christian	B-R	5-11	150	4-11-85	.259	.263	.257	106	352	58	91	16	1	1	35	42	4	5	1	69	33	8	.318	.343
Leonard, Mike	R-R	6-0	210	5-4-82	.230	.171	.247	55	191	24	44	10	1	2	14	27	7	0	0	48	0	0	.325	.347
Mercurio, Matthew	R-R	6-2	180	11-26-82	.231	.284	.213	82	290	45	67	14	0	5	29	19	6	2	0	74	9	2	.331	.292
Mota, Willy	R-R	6-1	165	10-25-85	.091	.333	.000	4	11	0	1	1	0	0	0	2	0	0	0	5	0	0	.182	.231
Natale, Jeff	R-R	5-9	180	8-24-82	.343	.275	.371	50	175	38	60	10	0	10	41	41	11	1	3	20	2	1	.571	.487
Ramos, Dominic	R-R	5-10	180	3-10-83	.224	.237	.220	73	294	37	66	19	1	0	29	27	3	6	1	62	9	4	.296	.295
Segovia, Luis	B-R	5-10	150	7-19-86	.128	.129	.128	21	78	8	10	1	1	1	8	6	1	0	0	18	1	3	.205	.200
Sorensen, Logan	L-L	6-1	195	8-12-81	.237	.208	.250	72	257	33	61	11	4	1	29	33	0	0	1	43	10	2	.323	.323
Soto, Luis	B-R	6-1	179	12-7-85	.230	.282	.212	67	274	30	63	14	1	6	38	14	1	1	3	70	1	1	.354	.267
Stachowsky, Mitchel	R-R	6-3	230	10-2-84	.210	.300	.173	43	138	14	29	8	1	7	21	10	5	1	1	61	0	0	.435	.286
Turner, Christopher	R-R	5-11	195	12-2-83	.243	.215	.253	108	403	59	98	18	7	18	63	36	11	0	5	149	3	4	.457	.319
Vasquez, Pedro	R-R	6-0	167	6-29-86	.229	.133	.300	11	35	3	8	0	0	1	3	2	0	1	0	12	1	0	.314	.270
Wagner, Mark	R-R	6-2	205	6-11-84	.301	.295	.304	96	355	49	107	32	1	7	45	42	8	0	2	52	1	3	.456	.386
Yema, Yahmed	L-L	6-0	195	9-3-84	.289	.304	.284	112	450	51	130	22	8	8	65	23	7	4	7	70	7	4	.427	.329

PITCHING	B-T	HT	WT	DOB	W	L	ERA	G	GS	CG	SV	IP	H	R	ER	HR	BB	SO	AVG	vLH	vRH	K/9	BB/9
Barnes, John	R-R	6-2	210	4-24-76	1	4	3.23	9	5	0	0	39	27	20	14	2	28	33	.194	.121	.247	7.62	6.46
Blackey, Jason	R-R	6-4	206	4-11-83	2	2	3.32	24	0	0	8	41	34	17	15	7	8	31	.221	.127	.286	6.86	1.77
Bowden, Michael	R-R	6-3	215	9-9-86	9	6	3.51	24	24	0	0	108	91	50	42	9	31	118	.224	.216	.229	9.86	2.59
Buchholz, Clay	L-R	6-3	190	8-14-84	9	4	2.62	21	21	0	0	103	78	34	30	10	29	117	.211	.226	.200	10.22	2.53
Casillas, Ismael	R-R	6-3	215	12-8-82	3	5	3.72	31	5	0	0	87	71	42	36	7	35	88	.225	.178	.260	9.10	3.62
Colvin, Ryan	R-R	6-2	165	4-12-87	0	0	48.60	3	0	0	0	2	9	9	9	0	3	3	.692	.667	.750	16.20	16.20
Cox, Timothy	R-L	5-10	165	7-8-86	5	6	2.80	33	4	0	0	103	90	40	32	10	16	82	.231	.260	.221	7.17	1.40
Fernandes, Kyle	L-R	6-0	190	9-12-85	3	5	3.11	38	0	0	0	84	81	47	29	8	31	57	.257	.261	.256	6.11	3.32
Guyette, Kevin	R-R	6-4	215	12-3-82	5	2	3.53	13	8	0	0	51	49	24	20	1	17	51	.247	.278	.222	9.00	3.00
Hancock, Matthew	L-L	6-3	195	10-1-82	1	1	4.50	19	0	0	0	28	29	19	14	1	23	18	.266	.261	.267	5.79	7.39
Jones, Christopher	R-R	6-3	205	6-9-84	4	4	3.63	19	0	0	0	97	83	42	39	6	32	79	.229	.207	.250	7.36	2.98
Jones, Hunter	L-R	6-4	235	1-10-84	4	5	3.34	35	5	0	0	94	87	41	35	8	20	100	.246	.227	.251	9.54	1.91
Large, Terry	R-R	6-4	185	5-28-83	1	1	3.60	3	0	0	0	5	4	6	2	1	2	3	.190	.222	.167	5.40	3.60
Lawson, Ryne	L-R	6-2	180	6-21-85	0	1	12.27	1	1	0	0	4	6	5	5	1	4	1	.375	.364	.400	2.45	9.82
Mann, Will	R-R	6-5	235	6-20-84	0	0	6.00	1	0	0	0	3	5	2	2	0	1	2	.385	.200	.500	4.50	9.00
Maxwell, Blake	R-R	6-5	255	8-1-84	6	3	3.08	52	0	0	14	64	56	25	22	5	9	41	.230	.222	.234	5.74	1.26
Newsom, Randy	R-R	6-2	200	5-6-82	1	0	0.00	1	0	0	0	4	2	0	0	0	0	6	.167	.000	.250	0.00	0.00
Pena, Mario	L-L	6-4	170	12-7-84	0	2	6.89	3	3	0	0	16	28	14	12	3	4	5	.412	.412	.412	2.87	2.30
Phillips, Ryan	L-L	6-4	210	5-29-84	2	8	3.26	16	16	0	0	80	69	39	29	5	40	75	.228	.178	.237	8.44	4.50
Rhoades, Chad	R-R	5-10	175	3-10-83	1	4	3.13	17	0	0	0	37	39	19	13	2	11	24	.273	.186	.333	5.79	2.65
Rozier, Michael	L-R	6-5	210	7-4-85	5	6	3.61	25	25	0	0	130	112	70	52	8	63	88	.235	.212	.240	6.11	4.37
Seibel, Phil	L-L	6-1	195	1-28-79	2	0	1.35	4	4	0	0	20	12	3	3	2	0	19	.176	.063	.212	8.55	0.00
Timm, David	L-L	6-6	190	9-28-83	0	1	14.73	3	0	0	0	4	8	8	6	1	5	3	.421	.429	.417	7.36	2.45
Ventura, Felix	R-R	5-11	165	4-27-84	0	0	10.80	1	0	0	0	2	5	3	2	0	0	2	.500	.500	.500	10.80	0.00
Zink, J.T.	R-R	6-2	195	5-6-85	3	3	7.67	16	0	0	0	29	41	29	25	4	10	23	.331	.447	.260	7.06	3.07

FIELDING

Catcher	PCT	G	PO	A	E	DP	PB
Farkes	1.000	1	1	0	0	0	0
Leonard	.980	45	349	42	8	4	11
Stachowsky	.972	33	223	22	7	3	8
Wagner	.996	65	477	55	2	4	12

First Base	PCT	G	PO	A	E	DP
Bates	.981	43	395	28	8	30
Bell	.923	1	12	0	1	0
Farkes	1.000	4	26	1	0	1
Jeroloman	1.000	1	8	0	0	0
Leonard	1.000	4	34	2	0	3
Mercurio	.986	24	189	19	3	16
Sorensen	.997	72	615	64	2	41

Second Base	PCT	G	PO	A	E	DP
Granadillo	1.000	1	1	0	0	0

Kelly	.983	14	25	32	1	6
Mercurio	.928	27	40	63	8	15
Natale	.970	27	32	64	3	10
Ramos	.972	64	110	169	8	31
Segovia	1.000	12	20	33	0	8
Vasquez	.944	3	10	7	1	2

Third Base	PCT	G	PO	A	E	DP
Farkes	.762	8	2	14	5	1
Granadillo	.936	102	86	235	22	13
Jeroloman	.842	7	2	14	3	0
Kelly	.829	14	12	22	7	2
Mercurio	.943	15	7	43	3	3

Shortstop	PCT	G	PO	A	E	DP
Jeroloman	1.000	6	18	19	0	4
Kelly	1.000	4	4	12	0	2

Khoury	.944	5	4	13	1	3
Lara	.962	105	160	315	19	49
Ramos	.927	12	14	37	4	4
Segovia	.960	9	11	13	1	4
Vasquez	.895	8	13	21	4	4

Outfield	PCT	G	PO	A	E	DP
Bell	.962	47	74	2	3	0
Granadillo	—	1	0	0	0	0
Hall	.988	46	77	2	1	0
Johnson	.971	71	124	12	4	3
Mercurio	.833	9	5	0	1	0
Mota	1.000	4	7	0	0	0
Soto	.971	61	97	5	3	0
Turner	.923	94	125	7	11	1
Yema	.968	102	209	2	7	0

ORGANIZATION STATISTICS

New York-Penn League

BATTING

	B-T	HT	WT	DOB	AVG	vLH	vRH	G	AB	R	H	2B	3B	HR	RBI	BB	HBP	SH	SF	SO	SB	CS	SLG	OBP
Arambarris, Manuel	R-R	6-0	178	8-25-85	.282	.222	.303	29	103	16	29	6	0	2	13	13	3	0	1	9	0	0	.398	.375
Bates, Aaron	R-R	6-4	232	3-10-84	.360	.286	.400	27	100	17	36	8	0	3	14	9	6	0	2	21	2	1	.530	.436
Bell, Bubba	L-R	6-0	195	10-9-82	.429	.421	.431	23	91	22	39	9	2	2	13	13	1	1	2	13	3	3	.637	.495
Chambers, Michael	R-R	6-0	175	1-20-84	.250	.224	.261	47	164	28	41	5	0	3	20	22	5	1	4	21	0	0	.335	.349
Chiang, Chih-Hsien	L-R	6-2	170	2-21-88	.278	.000	.323	9	36	6	10	0	3	1	8	2	0	0	1	9	1	0	.528	.308
Daeges, Zachary	L-R	6-4	225	11-16-83	.288	.286	.288	55	198	24	57	10	1	4	32	35	4	0	2	40	3	1	.409	.402
Egan, Jonathan	R-R	6-4	210	10-12-86	.083	.000	.111	4	12	2	1	1	0	0	1	1	1	0	0	5	0	0	.167	.214
Engel, Reid	L-R	6-2	175	5-7-87	.251	.254	.250	56	231	20	58	8	2	4	26	10	1	0	4	48	4	2	.355	.280
Exposito, Luis	R-R	6-3	210	1-20-87	.250	.228	.258	57	208	18	52	13	0	1	23	13	3	2	2	44	1	1	.327	.301
Farkes, Zak	R-R	5-11	190	5-30-83	.297	.350	.276	41	138	18	41	9	0	2	12	13	6	1	0	33	1	1	.406	.382
Jimenez, Jorge	L-R	6-1	210	9-12-84	.257	.147	.294	41	136	19	35	3	0	0	9	18	5	0	0	17	1	1	.279	.365
Jones, Michael	L-R	6-3	220	6-14-85	.255	.071	.333	11	47	8	12	2	1	1	13	1	1	0	1	9	0	0	.404	.280
Kalish, Ryan	L-L	6-1	205	3-28-88	.200	.333	.172	11	35	8	7	0	1	0	4	2	2	0	1	14	2	0	.257	.275
Khoury, Ryan	R-R	5-10	180	3-19-84	.236	.209	.248	40	148	16	35	7	1	0	16	16	4	4	2	28	2	2	.297	.324
Moreno, Junior	R-R	6-1	185	2-27-85	.117	.167	.083	17	60	4	7	2	0	0	1	5	2	0	0	24	0	0	.150	.209
Negron, Kris	R-R	6-0	180	2-1-86	.393	.167	.455	9	28	8	11	2	1	0	5	4	1	2	0	2	5	1	.536	.485
Pena, Wily Mo	R-R	6-3	245	1-23-82	.167	.500	.000	2	6	1	1	0	0	0	0	0	0	0	0	0	0	0	.167	.167
Santa, Moises	R-R	6-0	180	12-13-85	.222	.077	.357	7	27	1	6	0	0	0	2	0	0	0	0	6	1	2	.222	.222
Segovia, Luis	B-R	5-10	150	7-19-86	.195	.250	.172	64	174	19	34	4	0	1	9	23	3	3	1	47	4	3	.236	.299
Smyth, Paul	R-R	6-2	205	4-25-83	.266	.271	.264	50	188	29	50	10	2	4	24	15	5	1	2	31	6	1	.404	.333
Still, Jonathan	R-R	6-2	210	11-16-84	.220	.222	.219	62	232	23	51	9	1	2	27	26	2	2	4	41	0	0	.293	.299
Twomley, Jason	L-L	6-0	215	9-20-82	.095	.000	.250	7	21	2	2	1	0	0	0	0	1	0	0	10	0	0	.143	.136
Vincent, Jeffrey	L-R	6-4	205	4-15-84	.254	.158	.274	38	114	12	29	2	0	1	8	13	2	0	2	41	1	1	.298	.336

PITCHING

	B-T	HT	WT	DOB	W	L	ERA	G	GS	CG	SV	IP	H	R	ER	HR	BB	SO	AVG	vLH	vRH	K/9	BB/9
Beazley, Travis	R-R	6-0	175	6-17-83	3	2	2.39	14	13	0	0	68	68	26	18	6	19	59	.257	.216	.289	7.85	2.53
Cox, Bryson	R-R	6-4	205	8-10-84	0	1	1.59	3	0	0	0	6	6	2	1	0	2	3	.261	.250	.273	4.76	3.18
Craft, Jordan	R-R	6-3	200	6-5-85	1	0	1.42	7	0	0	1	13	11	4	2	0	4	14	.229	.250	.208	9.95	2.84
Doubront, Felix	L-L	6-2	166	10-23-87	2	0	4.91	2	2	0	0	11	7	6	6	1	3	7	.179	.200	.167	5.73	2.45
Farrell, Jeffrey	R-L	6-2	180	6-16-83	2	8	6.75	13	13	0	0	53	58	43	40	4	30	28	.290	.250	.300	4.73	5.06
Foulke, Keith	R-R	6-0	210	10-19-72	0	0	0.00	1	1	0	0	1	0	0	0	0	0	1	.000	.000	.000	9.00	0.00
German, Yulkin	L-L	6-2	180	8-27-83	6	1	1.81	24	0	0	0	50	38	12	10	1	22	52	.218	.232	.212	9.42	3.99
Guillen, Jean	R-R	6-3	170	3-21-84	5	1	3.62	28	0	0	0	37	35	16	15	1	16	37	.241	.265	.229	8.92	3.86
Johnson, Kristofer	L-L	6-4	170	10-14-84	0	2	0.88	14	13	0	0	31	25	7	3	0	7	27	.229	.303	.197	7.92	2.05
Large, Terry	R-R	6-4	185	5-28-83	1	1	2.06	21	0	0	10	39	30	14	9	0	10	45	.207	.259	.172	10.30	2.29
Lawson, Ryne	L-R	6-2	180	6-21-85	2	2	5.40	13	4	0	0	57	66	38	34	3	23	34	.291	.371	.221	5.40	3.65
Masterson, Justin	R-R	6-6	250	3-22-85	3	1	0.85	14	0	0	0	32	20	4	3	0	2	33	.174	.196	.156	9.38	0.57
Papelbon, Josh	R-R	6-1	210	6-24-83	0	2	1.86	25	0	0	13	29	22	12	6	0	6	36	.195	.234	.167	11.17	1.86
Pena, Mario	L-L	6-4	170	12-7-84	4	1	2.08	7	7	0	0	39	32	9	9	0	2	18	.234	.304	.219	4.15	0.46
Richardson, Dustin	L-L	6-5	195	1-9-84	4	1	3.18	16	1	0	2	40	28	16	14	2	13	44	.199	.208	.194	9.98	2.95
Steinocher, Brian	R-R	6-1	190	8-1-84	0	2	3.64	10	6	0	0	30	28	16	12	0	11	16	.243	.254	.232	4.85	3.34
Timm, David	L-L	6-6	190	9-28-83	0	0	12.00	2	0	0	0	3	6	4	4	0	0	3	.400	.375	.429	9.00	0.00
Ventura, Felix	R-R	5-11	165	4-27-84	3	7	4.74	23	0	0	1	38	40	24	20	3	19	49	.263	.304	.240	11.61	4.50
Yeh, Ting-Jen	L-R	6-1	189	7-1-83	1	0	9.53	9	0	0	0	11	22	15	12	0	7	10	.400	.263	.472	7.94	5.56
Zink, J.T.	R-R	6-2	195	5-6-85	2	4	4.67	15	15	0	0	79	80	49	41	4	21	33	.263	.237	.285	3.76	2.39

FIELDING

Catcher	PCT	G	PO	A	E	DP	PB
Egan	1.000	2	11	2	0	0	0
Exposito	.983	40	297	45	6	2	2
Moreno	.957	9	60	7	3	1	1
Still	.990	26	181	16	2	3	0

First Base	PCT	G	PO	A	E	DP
Arambarris	.987	16	144	8	2	13
Bates	.993	26	270	17	2	16
Farkes	1.000	7	42	5	0	2
Jimenez	.975	16	143	10	4	5
Jones	1.000	10	89	4	0	9
Moreno	1.000	2	16	1	0	0
Twomley	1.000	2	17	2	0	0

Second Base	PCT	G	PO	A	E	DP
Chambers	.971	47	71	131	6	13
Chiang	.949	8	10	27	2	5
Segovia	.976	28	57	67	3	13

Third Base	PCT	G	PO	A	E	DP
Arambarris	.750	13	3	18	7	2
Daeges	.778	4	1	6	2	0
Farkes	.916	34	21	66	8	4
Jimenez	.928	20	14	50	5	2
Khoury	.895	7	8	9	2	0

Shortstop	PCT	G	PO	A	E	DP
Khoury	.942	35	59	119	11	23
Negron	.968	8	13	17	1	4
Segovia	.925	35	59	101	13	14

Outfield	PCT	G	PO	A	E	DP
Bell	.957	22	44	1	2	0
Daeges	.955	47	55	8	3	1
Engel	.990	56	100	1	1	0
Kalish	.909	11	9	1	1	0
Pena	1.000	2	1	0	0	0
Santa	.889	7	8	0	1	0
Smyth	.938	50	83	8	6	3
Twomley	1.000	4	2	0	0	0
Vincent	.987	37	75	3	1	1

Gulf Coast League

BATTING

	B-T	HT	WT	DOB	AVG	vLH	vRH	G	AB	R	H	2B	3B	HR	RBI	BB	HBP	SH	SF	SO	SB	CS	SLG	OBP
Arambarris, Manuel	R-R	6-0	178	8-25-85	.328	.263	.356	19	64	9	21	4	1	0	10	5	0	2	1	3	0	0	.422	.371
Cabreja, Rafael	L-R	5-9	170	4-14-87	.152	.333	.098	24	66	8	10	3	0	0	5	7	0	2	2	14	2	0	.197	.227
Chiang, Chih-Hsien	L-R	6-2	170	2-21-88	.287	.303	.281	33	122	12	35	8	2	1	12	4	1	1	1	11	2	0	.410	.318
De Renne, Keoni	B-R	5-7	170	4-30-79	.000	—	.000	2	4	0	0	0	0	0	0	0	0	0	0	1	0	1	.000	.333
Diaz, Argenis	R-R	5-11	155	2-12-87	.263	.270	.260	37	133	16	35	2	1	0	11	6	1	2	0	23	3	1	.293	.300
Egan, Jonathan	R-R	6-4	210	10-12-86	.339	.310	.347	37	127	22	43	10	3	4	19	13	0	0	0	36	0	0	.559	.400
Engel, Reid	L-R	6-2	175	5-7-87	.200	.300	.100	6	20	2	4	1	0	0	3	0	0	0	5	1	0	.300	.304
Fernandez-Oliva, Carlos	L-L	6-1	175	9-3-86	.297	.310	.292	43	155	33	46	12	2	3	23	20	1	3	2	26	9	5	.458	.400
Gil, Rafael	R-R	6-0	165	10-3-85	.235	.250	.231	13	17	0	4	1	0	0	2	1	0	0	2	0	0	.294	.294
Huang, Chih-Hsiang	R-R	6-1	165	11-18-87	.125	.118	.127	26	72	5	9	3	0	1	5	6	0	1	0	22	0	0	.208	.190
Jones, Michael	L-R	6-3	220	6-14-85	.311	.387	.286	34	122	24	38	9	0	9	28	9	4	0	1	28	0	0	.607	.375
Kalish, Ryan	L-L	6-1	205	3-28-88	.300	.182	.444	6	20	6	6	2	0	1	2	1	0	0	2	0	0	.550	.333
Linares, Emilio	B-R	5-11	170	5-1-86	.242	.286	.229	25	62	7	15	3	1	0	6	3	0	0	24	0	0	.323	.266
Negron, Kris	R-R	6-0	180	2-1-86	.261	.205	.282	41	142	19	37	6	2	3	16	12	5	3	0	20	10	0	.373	.340

	B-T	HT	WT	DOB																					
Place, Jason	R-R	6-3	205	5-8-88	.292	.185	.326	33	113	14	33	3	1	4	21	17	1	0	1	35	3	3	.442	.386
Sheely, Matt	R-R	5-9	160	8-30-86	.292	.276	.299	41	106	16	31	1	3	0	14	12	0	3	1	18	4	4	.358	.361
Sosa, Roberto	R-R	6-0	165	12-13-84	.213	.100	.246	28	89	8	19	6	0	2	8	11	1	0	0	26	0	0	.348	.307
Soto, Luis	B-R	6-1	179	12-7-85	.160	.091	.214	7	25	2	4	2	1	0	0	1	1	0	0	4	0	0	.320	.222
Sumoza, Luis	R-R	6-0	170	7-15-88	.205	.182	.214	38	117	13	24	5	1	1	14	10	0	0	3	38	7	2	.291	.262
Tapia, Levi	R-R	5-10	200	4-21-87	.186	.000	.250	15	43	6	8	1	0	1	3	5	0	0	1	16	0	0	.279	.265
Van Der Bosch, Matt	L-L	5-8	190	4-12-82	.263	.200	.286	5	19	3	5	0	0	2	6	3	1	0	0	3	1	1	.579	.391
Vasquez, Pedro	R-R	6-0	167	6-29-86	.257	.214	.271	33	113	19	29	4	0	2	12	15	4	1	0	23	6	4	.345	.364

PITCHING	B-T	HT	WT	DOB	W	L	ERA	G	GS	CG	SV	IP	H	R	ER	HR	BB	SO	AVG	vLH	vRH	K/9	BB/9
Barnes, John		6-2	210	4-24-76	0	0	2.57	3	0	0	0	7	6	2	2	0	3	6	.231	.222	.235	7.71	3.86
Blackley, Adam	L-L	6-1	220	2-22-85	0	0	3.86	3	2	0	0	7	3	3	3	0	1	7	.150	.000	.167	9.00	1.29
Capellan, Jose	L-L	6-2	170	7-18-86	4	1	2.79	11	6	0	0	48	42	22	15	3	9	48	.233	.167	.247	8.94	1.68
Clement, Matt	R-R	6-3	210	8-12-74	0	0	0.00	1	1	0	0	1	1	0	0	0	1	0	.250	1.000	.000	9.00	0.00
Colvin, Ryan	R-R	6-2	165	4-12-87	0	1	3.72	11	8	0	0	19	24	9	8	1	5	10	.324	.259	.357	4.66	2.33
Craft, Jordan	R-R	6-3	200	6-5-85	0	0	3.00	2	2	0	0	3	2	1	1	0	0	3	.182	.000	.286	9.00	0.00
DiNardo, Lenny	L-L	6-4	190	9-19-79	0	0	0.00	2	2	0	0	5	2	1	0	0	0	4	.118	.000	.125	7.71	0.00
Doubront, Felix	L-L	6-2	166	10-23-87	2	3	2.52	11	11	0	0	54	41	17	15	6	13	36	.212	.182	.219	6.04	2.18
Gonzalez, Carlos	R-R	6-2	175	3-10-86	4	1	2.08	7	0	0	1	17	17	6	4	0	1	12	.254	.353	.231	6.23	0.52
Guerra, Joseph	R-R	5-11	178	9-4-86	4	2	2.68	9	3	0	0	44	53	16	13	1	0	25	.305	.217	.378	5.15	0.00
Guerrero, Emilis	R-R	6-2	162	12-26-85	3	2	2.45	10	6	1	0	40	47	19	11	1	11	38	.292	.293	.291	8.48	2.45
Hancock, Matthew	L-R	6-3	195	10-1-82	0	1	14.73	2	0	0	0	4	7	6	6	0	1	4	.389	.400	.385	9.82	2.45
Lin, Wang-Yi	R-R	6-2	192	6-28-88	2	1	1.31	10	0	0	1	21	17	5	3	0	6	8	.227	.222	.229	3.48	2.61
Mann, Will	R-R	6-5	235	6-20-84	2	0	3.06	15	0	0	8	18	16	6	6	1	5	18	.239	.200	.262	9.17	2.55
Martes, Jose	L-R	6-4	165	12-23-85	1	1	8.49	9	1	0	0	12	14	15	11	0	12	12	.304	.222	.324	9.26	9.26
Mendez, Mauricio	R-R	6-6	198	9-22-85	2	1	1.50	15	1	0	2	36	30	7	6	2	5	28	.226	.184	.250	7.00	1.25
Paulino, Aregnis	R-R	6-6	205	12-12-85	1	1	4.97	6	3	0	0	13	13	7	7	0	6	9	.271	.214	.294	6.39	4.26
Rhoades, Chad	R-R	5-10	175	3-10-83	0	0	0.00	4	0	0	0	5	2	0	0	0	2	5	.133	.000	.182	9.00	3.60
Rodriguez, Jorge	R-R	6-1	160	3-11-85	4	1	2.35	9	6	0	0	46	38	20	12	1	18	34	.229	.208	.239	6.65	3.52
Salcedo, Gustavo	L-L	6-0	150	1-30-86	0	2	7.59	12	0	0	0	21	26	18	18	2	17	16	.329	.273	.317	6.75	7.17
Socolovich R., Miguel	R-R	6-1	155	7-24-86	4	0	3.20	14	2	0	2	25	20	12	9	1	11	18	.217	.167	.242	6.39	3.91
Timm, David	L-L	6-6	190	9-28-83	2	1	2.81	11	0	0	3	16	14	6	5	1	3	12	.246	.250	.245	6.75	1.69

FIELDING

Catcher	PCT	G	PO	A	E	DP	PB
Egan	.993	22	122	12	1	0	1
Gil	1.000	12	42	4	0	0	3
Sosa	.980	21	125	21	3	1	5
Tapia	.965	14	71	12	3	2	3

First Base	PCT	G	PO	A	E	DP
Arambarris	1.000	9	68	3	0	10
Huang	.929	4	25	1	2	2
Jones	.997	34	300	17	1	28
Linares	.987	12	71	3	1	4

Second Base	PCT	G	PO	A	E	DP
Chiang	.923	28	45	75	10	17

	PCT	G	PO	A	E	DP
Linares	1.000	8	8	9	0	2
Vasquez	.977	24	60	70	3	16

Third Base	PCT	G	PO	A	E	DP
Arambarris	.842	11	7	9	3	1
Diaz	1.000	1	2	1	0	0
Huang	.942	21	16	33	3	4
Linares	.636	7	2	5	4	0
Negron	.930	20	21	45	5	4

Shortstop	PCT	G	PO	A	E	DP
De Renne	.889	2	1	7	1	2
Diaz	.951	34	57	99	8	17
Negron	.927	17	31	45	6	11

	PCT	G	PO	A	E	DP
Vasquez	.969	7	12	19	1	4

Outfield	PCT	G	PO	A	E	DP
Cabreja	1.000	21	33	3	0	2
Engel	1.000	4	5	0	0	0
Fernandez-Oliva	.967	41	55	4	2	2
Huang	1.000	1	1	0	0	0
Kalish	1.000	1	3	0	0	0
Place	.973	29	71	2	2	0
Sheely	.966	39	52	4	2	0
Soto	1.000	6	8	1	0	1
Sumoza	.981	37	47	5	1	2
Van Der Bosch	1.000	2	8	1	0	1

BY JEFF VORVA

It was easy to joke that the Cubs were fielding a Triple-A type of team for a good portion of the 2006 campaign.

They used the disabled list 19 times, and that forced them to use 16 rookies—including eight starting pitchers.  While it may have been great from a developmental standpoint, not all of the players were major-league ready, and the growing pains were evident when the North Siders turned in a 66-96 season and a last-place finish in the six-team National League Central.

The season took its toll upstairs as well, when team president Andy MacPhail stepped down after the final game. The next day, manager Dusty Baker's contract was not renewed just three years removed from a deep playoff run.

John McDonough was named interim president and Lou Piniella was named manager, and McDonough proclaimed on his first day on the job: "We will win the World Series." Little evidence from the 2006 club suggests that can happen without major changes via trades and free agency.

The team was five outs away from a World Series bid in 2003 and declined to last place three seasons later. Was it a lost season? Not completely.

"Last year they had to force-feed some players because of injuries," Piniella said. "You bring in some young kids and let them learn at the big league level. Probably the problems that they went through last year will pay some dividends because they had an opportunity to pitch innings and get at-bats."

Two of the 16 rookies stood out and should have jobs

ORGANIZATION LEADERS

BATTING		*Minimum 250 at-bats
*AVG	Norwood, Ryan, Peoria	.307
R	Patterson, Eric, West Tenn/Iowa	95
H	Walker, Christopher, West Tenn	168
TB	Pie, Felix, Iowa	259
2B	Three tied at	35
3B	Patterson, Eric, West Tenn/Iowa	11
	Walker, Christopher, West Tenn	11
HR	Restovich, Michael, Iowa	27
RBI	Fox, Jacob, Daytona/West Tenn	94
BB	Chirinos, Robinson, Peoria	70
SO	Moore, Scott, West Tenn/Iowa	139
SB	Walker, Christopher, West Tenn	61
*OBP	Craig, Matt, Daytona	.384
*SLG	Restovich, Michael, Iowa	.560
XBH	Restovich, Michael, Iowa	60

PITCHING		#Minimum 75 innings
W	Atkins, Mitch, Peoria	13
	Walrond, Les, Iowa	13
L	Brownlie, Robert, Iowa/West Tenn	14
#ERA	Veal, Donald, Peoria/Daytona	2.16
G	Rapada, Clay, West Tenn/Iowa	69
CG	Mathes, J.R., West Tenn	3
SV	Campusano, Edward, Peoria/West Tenn	25
IP	Gallagher, Sean, Daytona/West Tenn	165
BB	Veal, Donald, Peoria/Daytona	82
SO	Veal, Donald, Peoria/Daytona	174
#AVG	Veal, Donald, Peoria/Daytona	.175

MAJOR LEAGUE: Carlos Zambrano, rhp

Zambrano was the dominant force on the mound for the Cubs in 2006, leading the club in nearly every pitching category. The 25-year-old tied a career-high with 16 wins and led the club with a 3.41 ERA. He also led the National League in walks with 115, but finished with 210 strikeouts and logged 183 innings.

MINOR LEAGUE: Scott Moore, 3b

Moore always had big power, but in 2006 the 23-year-old showed versatility—which could be the aspect of his game that allows him to stick in the majors. Moore batted .276/.359/.480, spending the bulk of the season at Double-A West Tenn, and logged time at first and third base and in the outfield.

with the club in 2007. Lefthander Rich Hill went 6-7, 4.17 in 17 games and should join Carlos Zambrano (16-7 with a 3.41 ERA and 210 strikeouts in 33 games) as the only locks in the rotation. Infielder Ryan Theriot hit .328/.412/.522 in 134 at-bats and may battle Ronny Cedeno for playing time at second base in 2007, unless the Cubs pick up a second baseman with power in the offseason.

Some of the other 14 rookies who played—including pitchers Sean Marshall, Juan Mateo and Carlos Marmol—showed enough potential to get consideration for major league spots when camp opens in 2007.

The Cubs suffered three huge injuries when first baseman Derrek Lee and pitchers Kerry Wood and Mark Prior spent most of the season on the disabled list. Lee was coming off a career 2005 season but played in just 50 games in '06 because of a fractured right wrist and its after-effects.

Wood made four starts and Prior made nine as both battled through shoulder problems. If the Cubs re-sign Wood, it will be as a reliever. Prior needs to show he's healthy in spring training before the Cubs count on him in the rotation.

Even in a weak division and a weak National League, the Cubs failed to contend because of a 5-23 slide from April 29-May 28 in which they scored two or fewer runs in 13 of those losses.

One of the few bright spots was Zambrano, who was a contender for the NL Cy Young Award. While Juan Pierre (204 hits) and Aramis Ramirez (38 homers, 119 RBI) had decent numbers, they both struggled in April and May when the Cubs needed a boost.

The minor league teams finished 362-328, and short-season Boise and Class A Peoria went to the playoffs in their respective leagues. First-round draft pick Tyler Colvin drove in 53 runs for Boise. Chris Walker had 50 stolen bases for Double-A West Tenn and had a team-record 150 hits and a franchise-best 11 triples. Triple-A Iowa's Felix Pie had 158 hits but also 126 strikeouts and was one of the few top prospects not brought up during the injury-filled season.

Chicago Cubs | **MLB**

National League

BATTING

BATTING	B-T	HT	WT	DOB	AVG	vLH	vRH	G	AB	R	H	2B	3B	HR	RBI	BB	HBP	SH	SF	SO	SB	CS	SLG	OBP
Barrett, Michael	R-R	6-3	210	10-22-76	.307	.313	.305	107	375	54	115	25	3	16	53	33	5	2	3	41	0	1	.517	.368
Blanco, Henry	R-R	5-11	220	8-29-71	.266	.325	.236	74	241	23	64	15	2	6	37	14	0	4	2	38	0	0	.419	.304
Bynum Jr., Freddie	L-R	6-1	185	3-15-80	.257	.130	.283	71	136	20	35	5	5	4	12	9	1	2	0	44	8	4	.456	.308
Cedeno, Ronny...............	R-R	6-0	180	2-2-83	.245	.230	.251	151	534	51	131	18	7	6	41	17	3	15	3	109	8	8	.339	.271
Coats, Buck	L-R	6-3	195	6-9-82	.167	.000	.200	18	18	2	3	1	0	1	1	0	0	0	0	6	0	0	.389	.167
Hairston Jr., Jerry	R-R	5-10	185	5-29-76	.207	.167	.239	38	82	8	17	3	0	0	4	4	1	5	0	14	3	0	.244	.253
Izturis, Cesar	S-R	5-7	190	2-10-80	.233	.167	.246	22	73	4	17	2	0	0	6	5	0	1	0	8	0	1	.260	.282
2-team (32 Los Angeles)					.245	—	—	54	192	14	47	9	1	1	18	12	2	1	1	14	1	4	.318	.295
Jones, Jacque	L-L	5-10	200	4-25-75	.285	.234	.303	149	533	73	152	31	1	27	81	35	5	2	2	116	9	1	.499	.334
Lee, Derrek	R-R	6-5	245	9-6-75	.286	.292	.283	50	175	30	50	9	0	8	30	25	0	0	4	41	8	4	.474	.368
Mabry, John	L-R	6-4	210	10-17-70	.205	.316	.194	107	210	16	43	8	1	5	25	23	1	0	3	57	0	0	.324	.283
Moore, Scott	L-R	6-2	180	11-17-83	.263	.000	.294	16	38	6	10	2	0	2	5	2	1	1	0	10	0	0	.474	.317
Murton, Matt	R-R	6-1	220	10-3-81	.297	.301	.295	144	455	70	135	22	3	13	62	45	5	1	2	62	5	2	.444	.365
Nevin, Phil	R-R	6-3	220	1-19-71	.274	.203	.318	67	179	26	49	4	0	12	33	17	0	0	1	52	0	0	.497	.335
Pagan, Angel	B-R	6-1	180	7-2-81	.247	.196	.272	77	170	28	42	6	2	5	18	15	0	1	1	28	4	2	.394	.306
Perez, Neifi	B-R	6-0	195	6-2-73	.254	.282	.241	87	236	27	60	13	1	2	24	5	0	2	3	21	0	1	.343	.266
Pierre, Juan	L-L	6-0	180	8-14-77	.292	.293	.291	162	699	87	204	32	13	3	40	32	8	10	1	38	58	20	.388	.330
Ramirez, Aramis.............	R-R	6-1	215	6-25-78	.291	.261	.301	157	594	93	173	38	4	38	119	50	9	0	7	63	2	1	.561	.352
Restovich, Michael	R-R	6-4	250	1-3-79	.167	.222	.000	10	12	0	2	1	0	0	1	1	0	0	0	5	0	0	.250	.231
Reyes, Jose	B-R	5-11	180	2-26-83	.200	.000	.333	4	5	0	1	0	0	0	2	0	0	0	0	3	0	0	.200	.200
Soto, Geovany	R-R	6-1	230	1-20-83	.200	.133	.300	11	25	1	5	1	0	0	2	0	1	0	0	5	0	0	.240	.231
Theriot, Ryan	R-R	5-11	175	12-7-79	.328	.346	.317	53	134	34	44	11	3	3	16	17	2	6	0	18	13	2	.522	.412
Walker, Todd	L-R	6-0	185	5-25-73	.277	.211	.303	94	318	38	88	16	1	6	40	38	1	1	4	27	0	1	.390	.352
2-team (44 San Diego)					.278	—	—	138	442	56	123	22	2	9	53	55	1	1	5	38	2	1	.398	.356
Womack, Tony	L-R	5-9	175	9-25-69	.280	.286	.278	19	50	6	14	1	0	1	2	4	0	3	0	4	1	1	.360	.333
2-team (9 Cincinnati)					.265	—	—	28	68	7	18	3	0	1	5	8	0	4	0	7	1	1	.353	.342

PITCHING

PITCHING	B-T	HT	WT	DOB	W	L	ERA	G	GS	CG	SV	IP	H	R	ER	HR	BB	SO	AVG	vLH	vRH	K/9	BB/9
Aardsma, David	R-R	6-4	205	12-27-81	3	0	4.08	45	0	0	0	53	41	25	24	9	28	49	.214	.190	.225	8.32	4.75
Dempster, Ryan	R-R	6-2	215	5-3-77	1	9	4.80	74	0	0	24	75	77	47	40	5	36	67	.262	.310	.226	8.04	4.32
Eyre, Scott	L-L	6-1	215	5-30-72	1	3	3.38	74	0	0	0	61	61	25	23	11	30	73	.265	.273	.261	10.71	4.40
Guzman, Angel	R-R	6-3	195	12-14-81	0	6	7.39	15	10	0	0	56	68	48	46	9	37	60	.308	.305	.309	9.64	5.95
Hill, Rich	L-L	6-5	205	3-11-80	6	7	4.17	17	16	2	0	99	83	51	46	16	39	90	.227	.262	.220	8.15	3.53
Howry, Bob	L-R	6-5	220	8-4-73	4	5	3.17	84	0	0	5	77	70	28	27	8	17	71	.245	.247	.244	8.33	2.00
Maddux, Greg	R-R	6-0	180	4-14-66	9	11	4.69	22	22	0	0	136	153	78	71	14	23	81	.284	.271	.295	5.35	1.52
2-team (12 Los Angeles)					15	14	4.20	34	34	0	0	210	219	109	98	20	37	117	—	—	—	5.01	1.59
Marmol, Carlos	R-R	6-2	180	10-14-82	5	7	6.08	19	13	0	0	77	71	54	52	14	59	59	.250	.229	.263	6.90	6.90
Marshall, Sean	L-L	6-7	205	8-30-82	6	9	5.59	24	24	0	0	126	132	85	78	20	59	77	.270	.256	.273	5.51	4.23
Mateo, Juan	R-R	6-2	180	12-17-82	1	3	5.32	11	10	0	0	46	51	31	27	6	23	35	.288	.277	.295	6.90	4.53
Miller, Wade	R-R	6-2	210	9-13-76	0	2	4.57	5	5	0	0	22	19	12	11	4	18	20	.232	.273	.184	8.31	7.48
Novoa, Roberto	R-R	6-5	200	8-15-79	2	1	4.26	66	0	0	0	76	77	47	36	15	32	53	.262	.279	.255	6.28	3.79
O'Malley, Ryan	R-L	6-1	205	4-9-80	1	1	2.13	2	2	0	0	13	10	3	3	0	7	4	.213	.000	.286	2.84	4.97
Ohman, Will	L-L	6-2	195	8-13-77	1	1	4.13	78	0	0	0	65	51	30	30	6	34	74	.208	.158	.243	10.19	4.68
Prior, Mark	R-R	6-5	230	9-7-80	1	6	7.21	9	9	0	0	44	46	39	35	9	26	38	.269	.321	.226	7.83	5.77
Rusch, Glendon	L-L	6-1	215	11-7-74	3	8	7.46	25	9	0	0	66	86	57	55	21	33	59	.320	.348	.310	8.01	4.48
Ryu, Jae Kuk	R-R	6-3	220	5-30-83	0	1	8.40	10	1	0	0	15	23	14	14	7	6	17	.348	.360	.341	10.20	3.60
Walrond, Les	L-L	6-3	205	11-7-76	0	1	6.23	10	2	0	0	17	19	13	12	2	12	21	.271	.136	.333	10.90	6.23
Williams, Jerome	R-R	6-3	240	12-4-81	0	2	7.30	5	2	0	0	12	15	12	10	2	11	5	.326	.214	.375	3.65	8.03
Williamson, Scott...........	R-R	6-0	185	2-17-76	2	3	5.08	31	0	0	0	28	27	17	16	2	16	32	.248	.167	.278	10.16	5.08
2-team (11 San Diego)					2	4	5.72	42	0	0	0	39	41	26	25	4	22	42	—	—	—	9.61	5.03
Wood, Kerry	R-R	6-5	225	6-16-77	1	2	4.12	4	4	0	0	20	19	13	9	5	8	13	.253	.206	.293	5.95	3.66
Wuertz, Michael	R-R	6-3	205	12-15-78	3	1	2.66	41	0	0	0	41	35	14	12	5	16	42	.226	.184	.245	9.30	3.54
Zambrano, Carlos...........	B-R	6-5	255	6-1-81	16	7	3.41	33	33	0	0	214	162	91	81	20	115	210	.208	.247	.174	8.83	4.84

FIELDING

Catcher	PCT	G	PO	A	E	DP	PB
Barrett......	.994	102	727	42	5	7	10
Blanco	.998	69	467	34	1	10	2
Nevin........	1.000	1	1	0	0	0	0
Reyes.........	1.000	2	7	0	0	0	0
Soto	.986	7	66	4	1	0	0

First Base	PCT	G	PO	A	E	DP
Blanco.........	1.000	6	34	3	0	3
Hairston Jr...	1.000	1	4	0	0	1
Lee	.988	47	370	26	5	34
Mabry........	.994	51	312	29	2	21
Moore	.978	6	43	2	1	1
Nevin..........	1.000	38	250	17	0	26
Walker	.990	37	274	19	3	17

Second Base	PCT	G	PO	A	E	DP
Bynum Jr..........	.930	15	34	32	5	7
Cedeno	.973	15	35	37	2	7
Hairston Jr.......	1.000	24	30	33	0	7
Perez........	.973	53	72	107	5	24
Theriot........	.984	39	62	60	2	11
Walker........	.977	46	76	93	4	24
Womack........	1.000	16	27	39	0	9

Third Base	PCT	G	PO	A	E	DP
Mabry........	1.000	2	0	1	0	0
Moore	1.000	5	3	4	0	0
Perez........	1.000	10	3	9	0	0
Ramirez........	.965	156	110	252	13	17
Theriot........	—	1	0	0	0	0

Shortstop	PCT	G	PO	A	E	DP
Cedeno........	.956	134	148	357	23	64
Izturis.................	.975	21	33	44	2	8
Perez........	.968	21	24	36	2	7
Theriot........	.875	2	3	4	1	1

Outfield	PCT	G	PO	A	E	DP
Bynum Jr........	.931	22	27	0	2	0
Coats........	1.000	4	3	0	0	0
Hairston Jr........	1.000	8	9	0	0	0
Jones	.976	143	275	4	7	2
Mabry........	1.000	11	12	0	0	0
Murton........	.988	133	240	3	3	2
Nevin........	1.000	10	9	0	0	0
Pagan........	.989	58	86	2	1	0
Pierre	1.000	162	379	5	0	0
Restovich	1.000	3	1	0	0	0

General manager: Jim Hendry. **Farm director:** Oneri Fleita. **Scouting director:** Tim Wilken

Class	Team	League	W	L	PCT	Finish*	Manager	Affiliate Since
Majors	Chicago	National	66	96	.407	16th (16)	Dusty Baker	—
Triple-A	Iowa Cubs	Pacific Coast	76	68	.528	6th (16)	Bobby Dickerson	1981
Double-A	West Tenn Diamond Jaxx	Southern	70	69	.504	5th (10)	Bill Plummer	1998
High A	Daytona Cubs	Florida State	71	66	.518	5th (12)	Don Buford	1993
Low A	Peoria Chiefs	Midwest	75	64	.540	5th (14)	Jody Davis	2005
Short-season	Boise Hawks	Northwest	44	32	.579	2nd (8)	Steve McFarland	2001
Rookie	AZL Cubs	Arizona	21	34	.382	7th (9)	Carmelo Martinez	1997
OVERALL 2006 MINOR LEAGUE RECORD			362	329	.524	10th (30)		

*Finish in overall standings (No. of teams in league). +League champion

Iowa Cubs — Triple-A

Pacific Coast League

BATTING	B-T	HT	WT	DOB	AVG	vLH	vRH	G	AB	R	H	2B	3B	HR	RBI	BB	HBP	SH	SF	SO	SB	CS	SLG	OBP
Bynum Jr., Freddie	L-R	6-1	185	3-15-80	.227	.667	.158	6	22	3	5	0	0	0	3	1	0	0	0	3	0	0	.227	.261
Coats, Buck	L-R	6-3	195	6-9-82	.282	.244	.297	124	450	60	127	21	0	7	51	38	4	4	2	87	17	4	.376	.342
Deardorff, Jeff	R-R	6-3	220	8-14-78	.238	.209	.245	98	320	41	76	21	1	11	43	32	1	0	2	85	8	1	.413	.307
Fontenot, Mike	L-R	5-8	160	6-9-80	.296	.329	.287	111	362	54	107	28	2	8	36	47	2	2	5	64	5	4	.450	.375
Greenberg, Adam	L-L	5-9	180	2-21-81	.118	.000	.167	11	17	1	2	0	0	0	0	0	0	0	0	5	0	1	.118	.118
Hoffpauir, Micah	L-L	6-3	190	3-1-80	.267	.324	.246	77	255	34	68	9	1	12	49	33	1	1	7	59	1	2	.451	.345
Hoorelbeke, Jesse	R-R	6-2	263	10-13-77	.227	.105	.320	14	44	7	10	2	0	5	9	1	0	0	17	0	0		.614	.244
Kopitzke, Casey	R-R	6-1	205	5-31-78	.239	.176	.259	30	71	7	17	1	0	0	6	8	2	1	1	13	0	0	.254	.329
Lee, Derrek	R-R	6-5	245	9-6-75	.250	—	.250	1	4	0	1	0	0	0	1	0	0	0	0	0	0	0	.250	.250
McGehee, Casey	R-R	6-1	195	10-12-82	.280	.287	.277	135	497	56	139	28	1	11	68	41	3	1	4	70	0	3	.406	.336
Montanez, Luis	R-R	6-2	185	12-15-81	.224	.261	.210	82	245	23	55	12	0	8	31	17	3	2	2	44	0	1	.371	.281
Moore, Scott	L-R	6-2	180	11-17-83	.250	—	.250	1	4	1	1	0	0	0	0	0	0	0	0	1	0	0	.500	.250
Ojeda, Augie	B-R	5-8	170	12-20-74	.248	.237	.254	115	306	40	76	11	1	3	25	46	8	13	5	38	4	1	.320	.356
Padgott, Matt	R-R	6-2	215	7-22-77	.164	.125	.178	19	61	3	10	3	0	1	4	7	0	0	1	20	0	0	.262	.246
Pagan, Angel	B-R	6-1	180	7-2-81	.267	.333	.250	4	15	2	4	1	0	0	0	1	0	0	0	4	1	0	.333	.313
Patterson, Eric	L-R	5-11	170	4-8-83	.358	.333	.375	17	67	14	24	1	1	2	12	6	0	0	3	9	8	0	.493	.395
Pie, Felix	L-L	6-2	170	2-8-85	.283	.255	.294	141	559	78	158	33	8	15	57	46	5	10	3	126	17	11	.451	.341
Restovich, Michael	R-R	6-4	250	1-3-79	.293	.311	.288	120	443	75	130	29	4	27	85	52	7	0	4	121	2	1	.560	.374
Reyes, Jose	B-R	5-11	180	2-26-83	.250	.316	.236	37	108	10	27	6	0	0	11	14	2	2	0	11	0	1	.306	.347
Sing, Brandon	R-R	6-5	215	3-13-81	.177	.174	.178	33	96	10	17	4	0	4	11	13	5	0	0	33	0	1	.344	.307
Soto, Geovany	R-R	6-1	230	1-20-83	.272	.340	.246	108	342	34	93	21	0	6	38	41	3	2	7	74	0	1	.386	.353
Sprowl, Jon-Mark	L-R	6-2	200	8-1-80	.125	.000	.167	6	8	0	1	1	0	0	1	0	0	0	1	0	0	0	.250	.125
Strong, Jamal	R-R	5-10	185	8-5-78	.071	.125	.050	14	28	3	2	0	0	0	0	1	1	0	0	7	1	0	.071	.133
Theriot, Ryan	R-R	5-11	175	12-7-79	.304	.310	.301	73	280	41	85	11	5	0	22	27	2	1	2	34	14	3	.379	.367
Womack, Tony	R-R	5-9	175	9-25-69	.467	.333	.556	5	15	2	7	1	0	0	1	3	0	2	0	3	3	1	.533	.556

PITCHING	B-T	HT	WT	DOB	W	L	ERA	G	GS	CG	SV	IP	H	R	ER	HR	BB	SO	AVG	vLH	vRH	K/9	BB/9
Aardsma, David	R-R	6-4	205	12-27-81	2	3	3.22	29	0	0	8	36	31	15	13	1	15	36	.240	.241	.240	8.92	3.72
Atlee, Thomas	R-R	5-10	200	8-6-79	0	1	4.73	10	0	0	0	13	10	7	7	2	11	7	.213	.190	.231	4.73	7.43
Baez, Federico	R-R	6-2	190	8-4-81	0	3	5.06	9	2	0	0	21	21	12	12	5	12	19	.263	.316	.214	8.02	5.06
Brownlie, Robert	R-R	6-0	205	10-5-80	0	3	10.80	8	1	0	0	12	24	15	14	4	6	14	.429	.385	.442	10.80	4.63
Castellanos, Hugo	R-R	6-1	205	6-30-80	0	0	6.75	2	0	0	0	4	4	3	3	2	3	6	.250	.444	.000	13.50	6.75
Chavez, Wilton	R-R	6-2	165	6-13-78	3	3	6.10	13	2	0	0	31	32	22	21	4	13	17	.264	.216	.300	4.94	3.77
2-team (27 Nashville)					6	4	4.54	40	5	0	0	85	83	48	43	10	39	64	—	—	—	6.75	4.11
Cherry, Rocky	R-R	6-5	215	8-19-79	1	0	10.13	2	0	0	0	3	3	3	3	0	1	2	.273	.500	.143	6.75	3.38
Emanuel, Brandon	R-R	6-3	210	4-9-76	5	2	3.57	54	1	0	1	76	79	32	30	10	26	63	.274	.272	.276	7.49	3.09
Garcia, Mike	R-R	6-2	230	5-11-68	1	0	0.00	4	0	0	0	5	0	0	0	0	4	0	.000	.000	.000	6.75	0.00
Guzman, Angel	R-R	6-3	195	12-14-81	4	4	4.04	15	15	0	0	76	72	37	34	5	24	77	.252	.276	.233	9.16	2.85
Hill, Rich	L-L	6-5	205	3-11-80	7	1	1.80	15	15	0	0	100	62	22	20	3	21	135	.179	.230	.162	12.15	1.89
Ligtenberg, Kerry	R-R	6-2	220	5-11-71	4	4	3.57	53	0	0	18	58	64	27	23	8	6	44	.272	.326	.240	6.83	0.93
Marmol, Carlos	R-R	6-2	180	10-14-82	0	0	9.00	2	0	0	0	3	4	3	3	0	1	1	.333	.000	.444	3.00	3.00
Marshall, Sean	L-L	6-7	205	8-30-82	0	2	3.32	4	4	0	0	22	17	10	8	1	14	21	.221	.167	.231	8.72	5.82
Mendez, Adalberto	R-R	6-2	160	2-22-82	0	0	7.71	2	0	0	0	2	2	2	2	0	1	3	.250	.000	.400	11.57	3.86
Miller, Wade	R-R	6-2	210	9-13-76	1	0	6.55	2	2	0	0	11	18	8	8	3	9	9	.383	.278	.448	7.36	2.45
Mueller, Jon	R-R	6-4	180	5-12-84	0	0	6.75	1	0	0	0	3	2	2	2	0	3	2	.222	.500	.000	6.75	6.75
Novoa, Roberto	R-R	6-5	205	8-15-79	1	0	2.70	4	0	0	0	7	3	2	2	0	3	3	.136	.143	.133	4.05	4.05
O'Malley, Ryan	L-L	6-1	205	4-9-80	7	7	4.08	26	19	0	0	124	135	62	56	9	30	71	.284	.279	.285	5.17	2.18
Ojeda, Augie	B-R	5-8	170	12-20-74	0	0	0.00	1	0	0	0	1	1	0	0	0	0	1	.250	.000	1.000	9.00	0.00
Pignatiello, Carmen	R-L	6-0	190	9-12-82	0	0	2.70	8	0	0	0	7	7	4	2	0	2	4	.269	.375	.222	5.40	2.70
Prior, Mark	R-R	6-5	230	9-7-80	0	0	0.00	1	1	0	0	7	4	1	0	0	1	10	.174	.118	.333	13.50	1.35
Rapada, Clay	R-L	6-5	180	3-9-81	3	2	3.04	28	0	0	0	24	27	8	8	0	15	21	.310	.243	.360	7.99	5.70
Rusch, Glendon	L-L	6-1	225	11-7-74	0	0	2.25	1	1	0	0	4	2	1	1	0	0	2	.154	.000	.200	4.50	0.00
Ryu, Jae Kuk	R-R	6-3	220	5-30-83	8	8	3.23	24	23	1	0	139	133	54	50	12	51	114	.237	.239	.235	7.36	3.29
Shipman, Andy	R-R	6-3	185	10-18-81	2	3	3.81	46	0	0	0	57	65	24	24	1	27	43	.304	.238	.343	6.83	4.29
Suzuki, Mac	R-R	6-3	205	5-31-75	1	0	4.11	11	2	0	0	15	13	7	7	2	5	7	.236	.438	.154	4.11	2.93
Valdes, Raul	L-L	5-11	190	11-27-77	1	3	7.59	7	7	0	0	32	44	27	27	5	11	20	.341	.344	.340	5.63	3.09
Walrond, Les	L-L	6-3	205	11-7-76	10	5	3.98	31	20	0	0	133	134	72	59	11	59	104	.265	.221	.282	7.02	3.98
Watson, Mark	R-L	6-2	220	1-23-74	3	1	3.38	23	0	0	1	21	20	10	8	0	13	21	.253	.297	.214	8.86	5.48
2-team (26 Sacramento)					4	3	3.14	49	0	0	2	43	42	18	15	1	22	33	—	—	—	6.91	4.60
Wells, Randy	R-R	6-5	230	8-28-82	5	5	4.96	13	12	0	0	69	87	42	38	7	23	59	.309	.297	.318	7.70	3.00

Williams, Jerome	R-R	6-3	240	12-4-81	5	7	4.76	29	16	1	0	112	145	66	59	17	35	52	.324	.329	.320	4.19	2.82
Williamson, Scott	R-R	6-0	185	2-17-76	0	0	1.80	4	0	0	1	5	4	1	1	0	2	5	.222	.125	.300	9.00	3.60
Wood, Kerry	R-R	6-5	225	6-16-77	0	1	1.80	1	1	0	0	5	5	1	1	0	2	3	.250	.200	.300	5.40	3.60
Wuertz, Michael	R-R	6-3	205	12-15-78	6	0	1.73	30	0	0	10	42	30	10	8	2	9	67	.191	.206	.180	14.47	1.94

FIELDING

Catcher	PCT	G	PO	A	E	DP	PB
Kopitzke	1.000	22	158	12	0	5	2
Reyes	.992	30	228	17	2	0	4
Soto	.990	102	712	69	8	9	3

First Base	PCT	G	PO	A	E	DP
Deardorff	.992	45	361	23	3	37
Hoffpauir	.989	63	493	27	6	41
Hoorelbeke	.988	10	69	10	1	6
Lee	1.000	1	6	0	0	0
McGehee	.960	7	20	4	1	3
Restovich	1.000	10	64	7	0	8
Reyes	1.000	1	5	0	0	0
Sing	.983	26	222	15	4	16
Sprowl	1.000	2	3	0	0	1

Second Base	PCT	G	PO	A	E	DP
Bynum Jr.	1.000	3	4	4	0	1
Coats	.926	19	23	40	5	8

	PCT	G	PO	A	E	DP	PB
Fontenot	.978	92	185	258	10	62	
McGehee	.778	3	4	3	2	0	
Patterson	.979	17	42	53	2	14	
Theriot	.969	26	39	54	3	11	
Womack	1.000	3	2	9	0	1	

Third Base	PCT	G	PO	A	E	DP
Coats	.929	5	4	9	1	1
Deardorff	.944	17	10	24	2	3
Fontenot	1.000	6	3	3	0	0
McGehee	.972	128	93	248	10	31
Reyes	—	1	0	0	0	0
Theriot	1.000	1	1	2	0	1

Shortstop	PCT	G	PO	A	E	DP
Bynum Jr.	1.000	1	2	0	0	0
Coats	.971	9	12	21	1	7
Fontenot	.750	2	0	3	1	1
McGehee	.857	2	2	4	1	2

	PCT	G	PO	A	E	DP
Moore	.714	1	3	2	2	0
Ojeda	.984	102	114	246	6	43
Theriot	.960	47	64	105	7	29
Womack	.909	2	5	5	1	0

Outfield	PCT	G	PO	A	E	DP
Bynum Jr.	1.000	2	3	0	0	0
Coats	.989	101	178	6	2	0
Deardorff	1.000	25	40	3	0	0
Greenberg	1.000	3	6	0	0	0
Hoffpauir	—	1	0	0	0	0
Montanez	.966	65	79	6	3	1
Padgett	.900	15	18	0	2	0
Pagan	.889	4	8	0	1	0
Pie	.989	139	333	18	4	8
Restovich	.979	97	139	4	3	2
Sing	—	1	0	0	0	0
Strong	1.000	7	3	0	0	0
Theriot	1.000	9	14	1	0	0

West Tenn Diamond Jaxx — Double-A

Southern League

BATTING	B-T	HT	WT	DOB	AVG	vLH	vRH	G	AB	R	H	2B	3B	HR	RBI	BB	HBP	SH	SF	SO	SB	CS	SLG	OBP
Cates Jr., Gary	R-R	5-7	155	7-3-81	.266	.256	.271	84	237	34	63	12	1	2	25	25	1	1	3	31	7	3	.350	.335
Dopirak, Brian	R-R	6-4	230	12-20-83	.257	.361	.203	52	179	16	46	12	0	1	23	16	2	0	2	41	0	0	.341	.322
Farina, Peter	R-R	6-1	205	9-7-83	.000	—	.000	3	7	0	0	0	0	0	0	0	0	0	0	2	0	0	.000	.000
Fox, Jake	R-R	6-0	210	7-20-82	.269	.313	.248	55	193	20	52	17	0	5	25	9	1	0	1	44	0	0	.435	.304
Greenberg, Adam	L-L	5-9	180	2-21-81	.179	.077	.224	32	84	9	15	2	0	1	9	1	4	0	27	3	2		.202	.266
2-team (75 Jacksonville)					.215	—	—	107	303	45	65	11	3	1	18	60	8	10	2	97	12	5	.281	.357
Hoffpauir, Micah	L-L	6-3	190	3-1-80	.268	.366	.227	40	138	28	37	11	2	10	31	20	2	0	3	29	0	0	.594	.362
Jackson, Nic	L-R	6-3	200	9-25-79	.297	.262	.309	74	256	34	76	18	5	4	39	28	2	1	2	50	16	5	.453	.368
Lewis, Richard	R-R	6-1	195	6-29-80	.252	.265	.244	115	345	42	87	18	2	2	30	29	4	5	2	64	17	5	.333	.316
Machado, Albenis	B-R	6-0	170	3-20-79	.108	.067	.136	17	37	1	4	1	0	0	4	0	0	0	0	9	0	0	.135	.195
Montanez, Luis	R-R	6-2	185	12-15-81	.369	.410	.353	38	141	24	52	11	0	2	25	15	3	2	1	26	5	3	.489	.438
Moore, Scott	L-R	6-2	180	11-17-83	.276	.259	.284	132	463	52	128	28	0	22	75	55	8	1	5	126	12	7	.479	.360
Negron, Miguel	L-L	6-1	170	8-22-82	.291	.288	.291	86	265	24	77	19	4	1	24	25	0	6	2	43	9	5	.404	.349
Patterson, Eric	L-R	5-11	170	4-8-83	.263	.234	.275	121	441	66	116	22	9	8	48	46	1	7	6	89	38	12	.408	.330
Reyes, Jose	B-R	5-11	180	2-26-83	.229	.234	.227	47	144	15	33	3	0	1	9	9	0	3	0	25	0	1	.250	.275
Richie, Anthony	R-R	6-1	215	2-9-82	.230	.225	.232	72	222	13	51	15	0	0	11	5	3	1	3	45	1	0	.297	.253
Rojas, Carlos	R-R	6-1	175	1-11-84	.204	.270	.174	114	353	27	72	8	0	0	16	28	1	12	1	54	3	0	.227	.264
Sing, Brandon	R-R	6-5	215	3-13-81	.203	.241	.184	85	241	26	49	9	0	8	39	49	2	0	3	76	1	0	.340	.339
Sprowl, Jon-Mark	L-R	6-1	200	8-1-80	.205	.167	.212	26	39	2	8	1	0	0	5	9	0	0	0	5	0	0	.231	.354
Walker, Christopher	R-R	5-8	180	7-3-80	.292	.296	.291	131	513	70	150	21	11	2	35	40	7	5	1	102	50	23	.390	.351
Weston, Aron	L-L	6-5	173	11-5-80	.270	.250	.273	32	89	8	24	6	0	3	7	4	0	1	3	31	0	1	.438	.298
Wick, Olin	B-R	6-0	180	5-6-82	.000	.000	.000	5	11	0	0	0	0	0	0	0	0	0	0	5	0	0	.000	.000

PITCHING	B-T	HT	WT	DOB	W	L	ERA	G	GS	CG	SV	IP	H	R	ER	HR	BB	SO	AVG	vLH	vRH	K/9	BB/9
Atlee, Thomas	R-R	5-10	200	8-6-79	3	5	2.71	46	0	0	6	70	57	25	21	4	28	51	.222	.242	.211	6.59	3.62
Baez, Federico	R-R	6-2	190	8-4-81	2	2	2.43	25	0	0	1	67	56	20	18	6	18	46	.230	.167	.270	6.21	2.43
Blevins, Jerry	L-L	6-6	185	9-6-83	0	0	1.42	5	0	0	1	6	5	1	1	0	1	8	.217	.300	.154	11.37	1.42
Brownlie, Robert	R-R	6-0	220	10-5-80	3	11	5.64	33	8	0	0	75	102	50	47	7	34	52	.337	.349	.330	6.24	4.08
Campusano, Edward	L-L	6-4	175	7-14-82	2	1	1.75	18	0	0	4	26	22	6	5	2	8	34	.227	.267	.209	11.92	2.81
Cash, David	R-R	6-1	180	7-25-79	1	0	0.00	1	1	0	0	5	1	0	0	0	2	6	.063	.000	.083	10.80	3.60
Castellanos, Hugo	R-R	6-1	205	6-30-80	0	1	1.88	3	2	0	0	14	9	3	3	1	10	14	.176	.333	.037	8.79	6.28
Cherry, Rocky	R-R	6-5	215	8-19-79	4	1	2.22	31	0	0	2	49	43	14	12	3	14	50	.246	.250	.243	9.25	2.59
Gallagher, Sean	R-R	6-1	210	12-30-85	7	5	2.71	15	15	0	0	86	74	30	26	4	55	91	.239	.288	.202	9.49	5.73
Holdzkom, Lincoln	R-R	6-4	240	3-23-82	2	3	1.95	18	0	0	0	32	25	7	7	0	10	27	.221	.156	.247	7.52	2.78
Jan, Carlos	L-L	5-11	165	11-3-79	0	1	2.61	8	0	0	1	10	8	5	3	2	5	7	.216	.111	.250	6.10	4.35
Lewis, Richard	R-R	6-1	195	6-29-80	0	0	0.00	1	0	0	0	1	0	0	0	0	2	0	.000	.000	.000	18.00	0.00
Marmol, Carlos	R-R	6-2	180	10-14-82	3	2	2.33	11	11	0	0	58	42	18	15	1	25	67	.207	.167	.229	10.40	3.88
Mateo, Juan	R-R	6-2	180	12-17-82	7	4	2.82	18	17	0	0	93	78	32	29	6	26	70	.229	.252	.211	6.80	2.53
Mathes, J.R.	L-L	6-3	205	11-9-81	10	8	3.27	27	27	3	0	160	165	64	58	10	31	114	.267	.243	.274	6.43	1.75
Mendez, Adalberto	R-R	6-2	160	2-22-82	0	0	0.00	8	0	0	2	10	4	0	0	0	3	11	.125	.133	.118	10.24	2.79
Miller, Wade	R-R	6-2	210	9-13-76	1	0	1.50	1	1	0	0	6	3	1	1	0	1	4	.143	.071	.286	6.00	1.50
Mueller, John	R-R	6-1	180	5-12-84	1	0	2.25	4	0	0	0	4	5	1	1	0	3	3	.313	.667	.100	4.50	6.75
Pavlik, Isaac	R-L	5-8	170	5-19-80	2	1	3.38	9	6	0	0	40	43	19	15	3	14	35	.277	.333	.255	7.88	3.15
Pignatiello, Carmen	R-L	6-0	190	9-12-82	3	1	2.69	38	1	0	0	60	52	19	18	3	19	74	.230	.222	.234	11.04	2.83
Prior, Mark	R-R	6-5	230	9-7-80	1	5	5.40	1	1	0	0	5	4	3	1	2	4	11	.211	.200	.222	7.20	3.60
Rapada, Clay	R-L	6-5	180	3-9-81	3	2	0.82	33	0	0	21	44	30	7	4	1	10	45	.192	.206	.189	9.27	2.06
Schappert, Paul	L-L	6-5	215	12-21-81	5	0	3.47	24	3	0	0	47	46	23	18	4	20	21	.269	.333	.250	4.05	3.86
Shaver, Chris	L-L	6-7	235	8-21-81	7	10	2.99	26	26	1	0	150	146	62	50	7	56	120	.256	.279	.249	7.18	3.35
Shipman, Andy	R-R	6-3	185	10-18-81	1	1	1.76	11	0	0	0	15	11	4	3	0	2	13	.193	.240	.156	7.63	1.17
Sotolongo, Roberto	R-R	6-4	200	8-18-82	0	0	15.00	2	0	0	0	3	6	5	5	1	1	4	.429	.500	.417	12.00	3.00
Vasquez, Carlos	L-L	6-2	220	12-6-82	3	5	3.55	36	0	0	3	51	41	25	20	2	32	60	.220	.176	.237	10.66	5.68
Wells, Randy	R-R	6-5	230	8-28-82	4	2	1.59	12	12	0	0	62	45	13	11	2	13	54	.199	.224	.180	7.80	1.88

FIELDING

Catcher	PCT	G	PO	A	E	DP	PB
Farina	1.000	2	15	1	0	0	0
Fox	.992	43	326	38	3	3	14
Reyes	.997	44	287	31	1	2	3
Richie	.998	61	440	36	1	6	2
Sprowl	1.000	4	13	0	0	0	0
Wick	1.000	1	7	1	0	0	0

First Base	PCT	G	PO	A	E	DP
Dopirak	.984	44	345	20	6	26
Hoffpauir	.992	39	346	18	3	25
Lewis	1.000	10	67	4	0	11
Moore	1.000	1	5	0	0	0
Sing	.990	60	454	28	5	45
Sprowl	.955	3	21	0	1	3

Second Base	PCT	G	PO	A	E	DP
Cates Jr.	.962	5	10	15	1	0

Lewis	.973	19	35	38	2	12
Machado	1.000	10	14	15	0	8
Patterson	.976	115	237	334	14	63
Rojas	1.000	1	4	3	0	1
Walker	1.000	1	1	3	0	1

Third Base	PCT	G	PO	A	E	DP
Cates Jr.	1.000	2	0	2	0	0
Lewis	.942	19	13	36	3	6
Moore	.940	123	84	216	19	18
Sprowl	—	2	0	0	0	0

Shortstop	PCT	G	PO	A	E	DP
Cates Jr.	.958	48	46	112	7	24
Lewis	1.000	3	1	5	0	0
Machado	1.000	4	2	6	0	1
Moore	1.000	1	0	2	0	0
Rojas	.975	107	151	319	12	63

Outfield	PCT	G	PO	A	E	DP
Cates Jr.	.971	25	30	4	1	2
Fox	1.000	6	4	0	0	0
Greenberg	.957	30	43	1	2	0
Hoffpauir	1.000	2	1	0	0	0
Jackson	.991	68	109	2	1	0
Lewis	.983	47	58	1	1	0
Montanez	.969	38	60	3	2	0
Moore	1.000	1	4	1	0	1
Negron	.978	78	127	8	3	1
Patterson	1.000	1	1	0	0	0
Sing	1.000	19	22	1	0	1
Walker	.990	127	281	3	3	0
Weston	1.000	22	38	1	0	0
Wick	1.000	2	2	0	0	0

Daytona Cubs — High Class A

Florida State League

BATTING	B-T	HT	WT	DOB	AVG	vLH	vRH	G	AB	R	H	2B	3B	HR	RBI	BB	HBP	SH	SF	SO	SB	CS	SLG	OBP
Ciaramella, Matthew	S-L	6-1	190	10-25-82	.219	.194	.229	64	228	20	50	9	0	2	29	14	0	4	2	47	1	2	.285	.262
Craig, Matt	B-R	6-2	200	4-16-81	.287	.275	.290	130	450	67	129	35	3	12	76	68	5	1	3	107	6	1	.458	.384
Culpepper, Jeff	L-R	6-1	190	12-30-81	.263	.208	.278	76	251	41	66	12	1	1	21	25	3	1	2	48	9	11	.331	.335
Fox, Jake	R-R	6-0	210	7-20-82	.313	.290	.321	66	249	45	78	15	1	16	61	27	6	1	8	49	4	1	.574	.383
Fuld, Sam	L-L	5-10	180	11-20-81	.300	.297	.302	89	353	63	106	19	6	4	40	40	5	6	1	54	22	3	.422	.378
Gonzalez, Daniel	B-R	6-0	185	11-20-81	.229	.220	.233	41	144	16	33	3	0	0	18	10	3	1	0	26	1	2	.250	.293
Harvey, Ryan	R-R	6-5	220	8-30-84	.248	.227	.256	122	475	64	118	25	1	20	84	25	4	0	3	125	7	0	.432	.290
Jackson, Nic	L-R	6-3	200	9-25-79	.275	.429	.236	18	69	12	19	3	3	2	7	8	3	0	0	15	6	2	.493	.375
Lane, Andrew	R-R	6-0	185	12-25-81	.178	.239	.139	44	118	14	21	2	0	0	6	20	1	2	0	23	2	0	.195	.302
Mota, Jonathan	R-R	6-0	165	6-1-87	.247	.245	.248	55	170	18	42	6	2	1	13	9	1	8	2	26	1	1	.324	.286
Muyco, Jake	R-R	6-0	190	9-16-84	.211	.216	.207	45	133	11	28	3	0	2	10	11	1	3	1	40	0	0	.278	.274
Price, Nathan	L-L	6-2	195	3-11-84	.276	.333	.260	34	98	15	27	2	1	0	5	9	1	0	1	26	4	1	.316	.343
Rick, Alan	L-R	6-3	205	9-8-83	.242	.206	.248	77	240	25	58	12	1	8	45	18	3	2	4	64	0	2	.400	.298
Robinson, Chris	R-R	6-0	200	5-12-84	.356	.400	.343	12	45	2	16	2	0	2	12	1	1	1	0	16	1	0	.533	.383
2-team (95 Lakeland)					.294	—	—	107	367	32	108	24	0	3	59	26	2	9	4	89	7	1	.384	.341
Salas, Issmael	R-R	5-10	175	7-25-82	.313	.324	.306	28	83	12	26	8	0	0	7	7	1	1	0	16	1	1	.410	.374
Simokaitis, Joseph	R-R	6-1	200	12-27-82	.259	.307	.237	110	320	47	83	10	2	1	32	37	7	11	2	65	9	7	.313	.347
Spearman, Jemel	R-R	6-0	190	12-27-80	.279	.266	.284	131	491	70	137	29	5	3	52	57	9	16	5	84	21	5	.377	.361
Spears, Nate	L-R	5-11	165	5-3-85	.246	.276	.240	97	321	45	79	15	1	1	25	31	7	7	3	53	7	4	.308	.323
Sprowl, Jon-Mark	L-R	6-1	200	8-1-80	.118	.250	.093	16	51	2	6	1	0	0	5	3	0	0	1	5	0	0	.137	.164
Weston, Aron	L-L	6-5	173	11-5-80	.241	.240	.242	48	174	33	42	4	1	2	13	13	3	0	0	36	4	0	.310	.305
Wick, Olin	B-R	6-0	180	5-6-82	.247	.250	.244	28	73	10	18	1	0	2	11	6	0	0	0	21	1	0	.342	.304
Williams, Jeremy	R-R	6-4	230	6-7-83	.200	.429	.000	7	15	2	3	0	0	2	4	0	1	0	0	8	0	0	.600	.250

PITCHING	B-T	HT	WT	DOB	W	L	ERA	G	GS	CG	SV	IP	H	R	ER	HR	BB	SO	AVG	vLH	vRH	K/9	BB/9
Berg, Justin	R-R	6-4	220	6-7-84	7	7	4.38	24	24	0	0	115	126	67	56	4	53	82	.278	.261	.287	6.42	4.15
Bicondoa, Ryan	R-R	6-3	190	1-26-79	1	3	2.23	8	7	1	0	44	37	18	11	2	12	45	.224	.274	.185	9.14	2.44
Billek, Mike	R-R	6-4	235	3-4-84	0	1	8.84	5	2	0	0	18	27	22	18	5	10	10	.333	.438	.308	4.91	4.91
Blevins, Jerry	L-L	6-6	185	9-6-83	0	1	9.00	8	0	0	1	11	18	12	11	0	4	9	.367	.500	.349	7.36	3.27
Brannon, Clint	S-L	5-11	205	12-24-82	1	0	6.14	6	0	0	0	7	12	6	5	1	6	3	.375	.500	.367	3.68	7.36
Bronder, Stephen	R-R	6-1	180	6-5-84	4	2	4.60	29	2	0	0	61	58	34	31	7	27	44	.258	.253	.261	6.53	4.01
Burrows, Angelo	L-R	6-1	195	7-2-80	2	1	10.66	8	0	0	0	13	20	15	15	5	2	9	.385	.400	.378	6.39	1.42
Gallagher, Sean	R-R	6-1	210	12-30-85	4	0	2.30	13	13	0	0	78	75	24	20	5	21	80	.260	.273	.255	9.19	2.41
Hagerty, Luke	R-L	6-7	230	4-1-81	0	2	15.00	2	2	0	0	3	4	7	5	0	9	4	.333	—	.333	12.00	27.00
Holdzkom, Lincoln	R-R	6-4	240	3-23-82	0	0	0.00	2	0	0	0	5	3	0	0	0	2	6	.167	.111	.222	10.80	3.60
Holliman, Mark	R-R	6-0	195	9-19-83	8	11	4.38	26	26	0	0	144	129	76	70	12	58	121	.241	.237	.244	7.56	3.63
Hunton, Jon	R-R	6-9	250	11-30-82	6	5	4.32	48	0	0	3	67	62	40	32	4	34	54	.244	.234	.249	7.29	4.59
Johnson, Grant	R-R	6-6	220	5-26-83	7	5	4.70	31	10	0	1	92	108	63	48	0	38	56	.294	.347	.267	5.48	3.72
Layden, Tim	L-L	6-2	180	12-22-82	7	1	2.48	45	0	0	0	54	41	23	15	3	28	46	.205	.203	.206	7.62	4.64
Mendez, Adalberto	R-R	6-2	160	2-22-82	4	2	2.14	43	0	0	14	59	48	20	14	4	17	64	.217	.205	.223	9.76	2.59
Norton, Phil	R-L	6-0	215	2-1-76	1	1	3.86	6	2	0	0	14	15	7	6	1	8	8	.288	.143	.342	5.14	5.14
Perez, Carlos	L-L	6-1	185	5-20-82	5	8	4.80	29	19	0	1	111	141	67	59	8	56	86	.322	.320	.323	6.99	4.55
Petrick, Billy	R-R	6-6	220	4-29-84	1	2	6.06	3	3	0	0	16	24	11	11	3	2	9	.343	.357	.321	4.96	1.10
Phelps, Michael	R-R	6-4	190	5-26-84	1	2	2.73	22	0	0	0	26	28	10	8	1	9	25	.269	.191	.333	8.54	3.08
Salas, Issmael	R-R	5-10	175	7-25-82	0	1	27.00	1	0	0	0	1	1	1	1	0	2	0	1.000	—	1.000	0.00	54.00
Schappert, Paul	L-L	6-5	215	12-21-81	0	1	1.76	27	0	0	20	31	20	6	6	4	9	21	.183	.077	.217	6.16	2.64
Shaver, Chris	L-L	6-7	235	8-21-81	0	0	0.00	2	0	0	0	9	4	0	0	0	0	10	.154	.333	.100	10.38	0.00
Sotolongo, Roberto	R-R	6-4	200	8-18-82	0	3	4.28	14	7	0	0	34	35	21	16	3	16	23	.267	.213	.298	6.15	4.28
Sprowl, Jon-Mark	L-R	6-1	200	8-1-80	0	0	16.20	2	0	0	0	2	4	3	3	2	4	1	.444	.500	.429	5.40	21.60
Teasley, Jeff	R-R	6-8	250	5-9-83	1	1	15.88	4	0	0	0	6	10	10	10	2	4	3	.385	.333	.400	4.76	6.35
Vasquez, Carlos	L-L	6-2	220	12-6-82	3	0	1.57	18	0	0	0	34	24	7	6	0	3	18	.198	.207	.196	8.13	2.62
Veal, Donald	L-L	6-4	215	9-18-84	6	2	1.67	14	14	0	0	81	46	18	15	3	42	88	.170	.194	.163	9.82	4.69
Weber, Matt	R-R	6-3	190	5-5-85	2	4	6.67	17	6	0	0	55	68	47	41	8	19	26	.308	.313	.303	4.23	3.09

FIELDING

Catcher	PCT	G	PO	A	E	DP	PB
Fox	.986	47	321	43	5	3	8
Muyco	.983	44	260	35	5	2	3
Rick	1.000	44	296	37	0	1	10
Robinson	.981	7	46	5	1	1	0
Wick	1.000	7	17	3	0	0	1

First Base	PCT	G	PO	A	E	DP
Craig	.992	119	976	81	8	94
Lane	1.000	10	73	6	0	9
Rick	.960	5	23	1	1	4
Salas	.975	14	73	4	2	9
Simokaitis	1.000	1	1	0	0	0
Sprowl	1.000	3	26	3	0	4

Second Base	PCT	G	PO	A	E	DP
Gonzalez	.976	18	35	45	2	17

	PCT	G	PO	A	E	DP
Lane	.962	14	20	30	2	8
Salas	.943	12	24	26	3	7
Simokaitis	.980	27	33	63	2	5
Spears	.975	88	182	203	10	50

Third Base	PCT	G	PO	A	E	DP
Craig	1.000	2	1	1	0	0
Gonzalez	—	2	0	0	0	0
Lane	.919	16	11	23	3	4
Salas	1.000	1	0	3	0	1
Spearman	.933	122	68	225	21	21

Shortstop	PCT	G	PO	A	E	DP
Gonzalez	.922	30	33	73	9	17
Lane	1.000	2	1	0	0	0
Mota	.917	54	80	152	21	30
Simokaitis	.954	73	79	231	15	45

Outfield	PCT	G	PO	A	E	DP
Ciaramella	.984	63	124	3	2	2
Culpepper	.991	62	106	1	1	0
Fuld	.991	85	219	6	2	3
Harvey	.975	118	186	9	5	5
Jackson	1.000	9	12	1	0	0
Lane	1.000	1	1	0	0	0
Price	.984	33	58	2	1	1
Salas	1.000	6	6	0	0	0
Spearman	.875	10	19	2	3	1
Sprowl	1.000	3	3	0	0	0
Weston	.938	32	59	2	4	0
Williams	1.000	5	12	1	0	1

Peoria Chiefs — Low Class A

Midwest League

BATTING	B-T	HT	WT	DOB	AVG	vLH	vRH	G	AB	R	H	2B	3B	HR	RBI	BB	HBP	SH	SF	SO	SB	CS	SLG	OBP
Carter, Yusuf	B-R	6-2	205	2-6-85	.210	.188	.217	78	276	36	58	8	1	12	54	23	1	0	4	88	3	3	.377	.270
Chirinos, Robinson	R-R	6-1	185	6-5-84	.242	.275	.233	126	433	74	105	30	2	9	47	69	14	7	6	79	19	10	.383	.360
Ciaramella, Matt	S-L	6-1	190	10-25-82	.213	.211	.214	61	164	20	35	5	1	1	10	21	2	3	1	25	2	5	.274	.309
Collins, Kevin	L-L	6-2	200	5-6-81	.246	.429	.200	18	69	12	17	5	0	4	12	4	0	0	0	20	0	0	.493	.288
Defendis, John	L-R	6-1	200	3-12-84	.172	.500	.120	9	29	1	5	2	0	0	3	0	0	0	5	1	0	.241	.250
Garcia, Alberto	R-R	6-1	180	6-5-83	.269	.295	.258	113	372	32	100	20	3	5	50	23	7	2	4	76	2	1	.379	.320
Gregg, Davy	L-R	6-1	175	5-31-83	.225	.257	.214	119	414	60	93	11	2	0	19	26	4	10	2	100	27	19	.261	.276
Heredia, Valerio	B-R	5-10	150	3-14-86	.250	.375	.208	10	32	6	8	1	0	0	5	1	1	0	5	6	3	.281	.368
Johnston, Dylan	L-R	6-0	180	3-25-87	.200	.100	.227	58	190	22	38	7	3	0	11	26	3	5	0	60	8	2	.268	.306
Lalli, Blake	R-R	6-1	210	5-12-83	.191	.091	.211	22	68	3	13	3	0	0	4	3	2	0	0	11	1	1	.235	.247
Lilly, Ryan	R-R	6-0	195	12-15-83	.319	.409	.280	22	72	14	23	4	0	3	6	4	2	0	0	14	0	2	.500	.372
Malone, Ryne	L-R	5-11	180	1-6-85	.284	.244	.297	51	183	26	52	16	2	2	29	27	3	0	0	34	6	3	.426	.385
Morgan, Justin	R-R	6-2	195	2-1-82	.273	.500	.143	6	11	0	3	1	0	0	0	0	0	0	0	5	0	0	.364	.273
Mota, Jonathan	R-R	6-0	165	6-1-87	.275	.333	.246	33	91	10	25	2	1	0	9	6	1	1	1	14	2	3	.319	.323
Muyco, Jake	R-R	6-0	190	9-16-84	.205	.114	.239	38	127	8	26	5	0	2	15	12	0	1	1	33	1	0	.291	.271
Norwood, Ryan	R-L	6-4	220	2-18-83	.307	.278	.317	134	505	62	155	28	0	15	69	27	14	0	8	106	5	0	.451	.354
Parker, Richard	R-R	6-3	200	6-19-85	.000	.000	.000	7	21	0	0	0	0	0	0	1	1	0	8	0	0	.000	.045
Price, Nathan	L-L	6-2	195	3-11-84	.229	.440	.200	16	35	6	8	0	0	0	2	7	0	3	0	9	1	2	.229	.357
Reed, Mark	L-R	5-11	175	4-13-86	.252	.304	.237	101	349	47	88	12	0	2	30	26	5	5	0	82	14	9	.304	.313
Reynolds, Kyle	L-R	6-2	190	9-1-83	.230	.194	.238	99	331	36	76	14	5	9	38	25	3	0	3	91	9	5	.384	.287
Rivera, Luis	R-R	6-1	165	1-25-84	.080	.111	.063	10	25	3	2	0	0	0	0	0	0	0	0	6	0	0	.080	.080
Taylor, Brandon	R-R	6-1	200	7-26-82	.213	.216	.212	53	188	14	40	11	1	3	18	7	5	1	2	33	2	3	.330	.257
Tirado, Francisco	B-R	6-0	175	7-30-87	.269	.000	.350	11	26	4	7	1	0	0	2	3	0	1	1	10	0	1	.308	.333
Valdez, Jesus	R-R	6-2	170	11-2-84	.302	.390	.306	130	510	63	154	25	1	5	61	22	9	3	3	73	10	6	.384	.340
Whitesides, Jake	L-R	5-11	190	6-23-81	.154	—	.154	5	13	1	2	0	0	0	1	3	0	0	0	4	0	0	.154	.313
Wick, Olin	B-R	6-0	180	5-6-82	.222	.263	.192	17	45	4	10	2	0	0	3	1	0	0	0	7	0	0	.267	.239

PITCHING	B-T	HT	WT	DOB	W	L	ERA	G	GS	CG	SV	IP	H	R	ER	HR	BB	SO	AVG	vLH	vRH	K/9	BB/9
Atkins, Mitch	R-R	6-3	230	10-1-85	13	4	2.41	25	25	0	0	138	110	47	37	10	53	127	.217	.209	.223	8.26	3.45
Avery, Matthew	R-R	6-2	230	9-7-83	4	3	2.15	48	0	0	18	67	46	17	16	4	27	76	.188	.198	.182	10.21	3.63
Billek, Mike	R-R	6-4	235	3-4-84	4	5	5.66	15	5	0	0	35	45	29	22	3	11	25	.300	.292	.306	6.43	2.83
Blackford, Todd	L-R	6-4	215	6-10-85	10	9	5.37	27	27	0	0	141	159	93	84	11	63	70	.285	.285	.285	4.48	4.03
Campusano, Edward	L-L	6-4	175	7-14-82	0	0	1.21	26	0	0	21	30	16	5	4	0	9	47	.152	.130	.159	14.26	2.73
Carrillo, Marco	R-R	—	—	2-1-87	0	0	15.00	1	1	0	0	3	7	6	5	0	1	1	.438	.500	.417	3.00	3.00
Estrada, Jesse	R-R	6-8	260	10-27-83	7	1	3.32	36	5	0	0	95	89	41	35	4	28	61	.250	.282	.231	5.78	2.65
Evenson, Roger	R-R	6-4	235	8-18-83	1	2	3.30	21	0	0	0	44	40	20	16	6	8	31	.248	.169	.302	6.39	1.65
Jimenez-Angulo, Fabian	L-L	6-2	187	8-27-86	1	3	10.13	4	4	0	0	16	30	20	18	1	6	6	.411	.389	.418	3.38	3.38
2-team (17 Fort Wayne)					6	10	5.31	21	21	0	0	103	117	69	61	6	58	60	—	—	—	5.23	5.05
Koerber, Scott	L-L	6-4	215	9-30-82	5	4	3.42	38	0	0	3	50	40	21	19	4	27	34	.220	.148	.256	6.12	4.86
Layden, Tim	L-L	6-2	180	12-22-82	0	0	2.25	7	0	0	1	12	11	3	3	0	6	15	.239	.091	.286	11.25	4.50
Miller, Wade	R-R	6-2	210	9-13-76	0	0	2.50	5	5	0	0	18	17	5	5	0	5	15	.254	.290	.222	7.50	2.50
Mueller, Jon	R-R	6-4	180	5-12-84	0	1	4.24	21	0	0	2	34	34	17	16	3	9	20	.272	.381	.217	5.29	2.38
Phelps, Michael	R-R	6-4	190	5-26-84	1	0	5.40	3	0	0	0	5	5	3	3	0	2	4	.263	.273	.250	7.20	3.60
Prior, Mark	R-R	6-5	230	9-7-80	0	2	3.86	2	2	0	0	7	7	4	3	1	0	8	.241	.333	.200	10.29	0.00
Rayborn, Justin	R-R	6-5	210	11-29-82	6	1	1.93	37	0	0	2	65	60	16	14	4	17	72	.235	.232	.238	9.92	2.34
Samardzija, Jeff	R-R	6-6	215	1-23-85	0	1	3.27	2	2	0	0	11	6	5	4	1	6	4	.167	.231	.130	3.27	4.91
Santo, Jesus	R-R	6-3	194	6-4-84	3	4	4.11	7	5	1	0	35	32	17	16	2	20	34	.248	.240	.253	6.94	5.14
2-team (20 Fort Wayne)					9	10	5.03	27	20	1	0	127	128	74	71	11	74	75	—	—	—	5.31	5.24
Sotolongo, Roberto	R-R	6-4	200	8-18-82	0	3	12.79	6	0	0	1	6	11	10	9	2	4	5	.355	.353	.357	7.11	5.68
Taylor, Scott	R-R	6-3	240	10-28-86	8	8	3.39	23	22	1	0	141	145	61	53	8	28	71	.268	.279	.258	4.54	1.79
Teasley, Jeff	R-R	6-8	250	5-9-83	2	3	4.30	29	0	0	1	46	49	25	22	6	12	38	.274	.325	.235	7.43	2.35
Veal, Donald	L-L	6-4	215	9-18-84	5	3	2.69	14	14	0	0	74	45	26	22	4	40	86	.179	.200	.173	10.51	4.89
Weber, Matt	R-R	6-3	200	5-5-85	0	1	9.95	2	2	0	0	6	14	7	7	0	4	3	.452	.364	.500	4.26	5.68
Williamson, Scott	R-R	6-0	185	2-17-76	0	0	9.00	1	0	0	0	1	1	1	1	0	0	1	.333	.000	.500	9.00	0.00
Wood, Kerry	R-R	6-5	225	6-16-77	0	0	0.00	1	1	0	0	5	1	0	0	0	1	12	.063	.000	.100	21.60	1.80
Yepez, Jesus	L-L	6-1	180	4-15-84	5	6	4.30	28	19	0	0	128	133	68	61	9	68	72	.274	.276	.274	5.08	4.79

FIELDING

Catcher	PCT	G	PO	A	E	DP	PB
Lalli	.981	17	94	9	2	0	3
Morgan	.968	6	26	4	1	0	0
Muyco	.987	38	279	20	4	2	3
Reed	.993	75	487	53	4	2	4
Wick	.977	14	80	4	2	0	1

First Base	PCT	G	PO	A	E	DP
Chirinos	1.000	1	1	0	0	0
Garcia	.985	8	62	5	1	8
Lalli	1.000	2	3	0	0	1
Norwood	.991	126	979	69	9	63
Parker	.875	2	6	1	1	1
Reed	1.000	8	63	5	0	6
Reynolds	1.000	2	2	2	0	0

Second Base	PCT	G	PO	A	E	DP
Chirinos	.981	97	184	277	9	55
Garcia	1.000	4	9	6	0	2

	PCT	G	PO	A	E	DP
Heredia	.962	8	11	14	1	0
Lilly	1.000	3	2	2	0	0
Malone	.948	16	27	46	4	5
Mota	1.000	4	5	11	0	4
Reynolds	1.000	10	16	15	0	6
Rivera	1.000	2	4	3	0	0
Tirado	1.000	4	1	2	0	0
Whitesides	.500	1	1	0	1	0

Third Base	PCT	G	PO	A	E	DP
Chirinos	1.000	1	1	0	0	0
Heredia	.667	1	0	2	1	0
Lilly	.943	15	9	24	2	2
Malone	.900	25	16	47	7	3
Parker	.889	4	3	5	1	0
Reed	1.000	2	0	4	0	0
Reynolds	.942	47	29	84	7	6
Rivera	.667	1	0	2	1	0
Taylor	.921	49	41	88	11	8

	PCT	G	PO	A	E	DP
Whitesides	1.000	1	0	1	0	0

Shortstop	PCT	G	PO	A	E	DP
Chirinos	.943	26	47	52	6	6
Johnston	.931	55	98	157	19	27
Lilly	.900	3	4	5	1	1
Mota	.941	24	35	60	6	7
Reynolds	.975	34	53	104	4	19
Rivera	.917	3	3	8	1	0
Tirado	1.000	4	8	3	0	1

Outfield	PCT	G	PO	A	E	DP
Carter	.941	74	137	7	9	2
Ciaramella	.991	60	104	3	1	1
Defendis	.889	7	13	3	2	1
Garcia	.990	52	94	3	1	0
Gregg	.989	114	269	7	3	1
Price	1.000	12	23	1	0	0
Valdez	.969	124	241	9	8	1
Whitesides	1.000	1	1	0	0	0

Boise Hawks — Short-Season

Northwest League

BATTING	B-T	HT	WT	DOB	AVG	vLH	vRH	G	AB	R	H	2B	3B	HR	RBI	BB	HBP	SH	SF	SO	SB	CS	SLG	OBP
Baez, Sammy	R-R	6-2	175	12-10-84	.310	.318	.306	19	71	8	22	3	1	0	10	1	3	1	1	9	9	4	.380	.342
Camp, Matt	L-R	6-0	175	5-29-84	.289	.272	.295	74	301	51	87	12	2	1	37	27	3	2	3	32	22	10	.352	.350
Canepa, Matthew	R-R	6-1	195	6-3-85	.223	.200	.229	45	130	14	29	4	0	1	11	19	6	3	0	21	1	2	.269	.348
Canzler, Russell	R-R	6-2	190	4-11-86	.264	.250	.270	73	280	49	74	22	4	16	61	22	3	1	5	70	7	4	.543	.319
Castillo, Welington	R-R	—	—	4-24-87	.167	—	.167	3	6	1	1	0	0	0	0	1	0	1	0	0	0	0	.167	.286
Clevenger, Steven	L-R	6-0	185	4-5-86	.286	.298	.283	63	220	35	63	8	1	2	21	26	1	1	1	28	5	2	.359	.363
Colvin, Tyler	L-L	6-3	190	9-5-85	.268	.278	.264	64	265	50	71	12	6	11	53	17	2	0	4	55	12	5	.483	.313
Episcopo, Ryan	R-R	6-2	180	7-20-85	.174	.125	.200	7	23	1	4	0	0	0	1	3	0	0	1	6	0	0	.174	.259
Gilbert, Cody	R-R	6-3	185	8-21-85	.286	—	.286	2	7	1	2	1	0	0	2	1	0	1	0	4	0	0	.429	.375
Hackstedt, Adam	B-R	6-2	215	6-1-84	.222	.000	.250	12	27	3	6	5	0	0	2	0	1	0	0	10	0	0	.407	.250
Joseph, Alfred	R-R	5-11	190	7-25-86	.306	.302	.307	67	229	35	70	14	2	3	29	17	5	2	3	35	8	4	.424	.362
Lalli, Blake	R-R	6-1	210	5-12-83	.000	.000	.000	3	7	0	0	0	0	0	0	1	0	0	1	0	0	0	.000	.125
Lansford, Joshua	R-R	6-2	220	7-3-84	.255	.203	.275	62	235	32	60	7	1	5	35	24	5	3	0	43	4	1	.357	.333
Lewis, Deryck	R-R	6-0	210	8-25-85	.257	.239	.263	52	179	26	46	17	3	5	34	15	0	0	3	41	2	1	.469	.310
Lopez, Pedro	B-R	5-10	165	10-31-86	.259	.211	.286	23	54	9	14	2	0	0	2	2	0	0	0	16	2	0	.296	.286
Matulia, Matt	B-R	6-0	185	5-24-84	.241	.230	.245	62	220	38	53	3	4	2	26	29	4	6	3	48	15	6	.318	.336
Mercedes, Mario	R-R	5-10	160	11-22-86	.315	.410	.275	37	130	19	41	8	1	0	17	4	1	0	2	10	0	2	.392	.336
Puello, Elvin	R-R	6-2	175	12-18-84	.245	.159	.270	57	196	25	48	9	0	1	21	13	8	1	4	51	2	1	.306	.312
Rosario, Lisandro	B-R	5-11	150	7-16-86	.000	—	.000	2	3	0	0	0	0	0	0	0	1	0	0	0	0	0	.000	.250

PITCHING	B-T	HT	WT	DOB	W	L	ERA	G	GS	CG	SV	IP	H	R	ER	HR	BB	SO	AVG	vLH	vRH	K/9	BB/9
Bernard, Oscar	R-R	6-2	170	6-27-83	0	0	15.00	2	0	0	0	3	8	5	5	0	3	1	.533	.500	.545	3.00	9.00
Billek, Mike	R-R	6-4	235	3-4-84	3	3	6.67	13	11	0	0	55	75	43	41	9	16	22	.326	.306	.335	3.58	2.62
Blevins, Jerry	L-L	6-6	185	9-6-83	1	2	6.04	16	0	0	0	22	27	22	15	3	8	19	.287	.320	.275	7.66	3.22
Ceda, Jose	R-R	6-4	205	1-28-87	1	0	3.27	3	3	0	0	11	5	4	4	1	2	11	.139	.188	.100	9.00	1.64
Clipp, Brad	R-R	6-2	180	8-15-84	2	0	3.23	21	0	0	1	31	22	15	11	2	9	24	.200	.114	.240	7.04	2.64
Cooper, Michael	R-R	6-6	230	11-29-84	2	0	1.23	19	0	0	9	22	15	4	3	1	11	13	.185	.235	.172	5.32	4.50
Downs, Darin	R-L	6-3	176	12-26-84	4	2	4.81	9	2	0	0	24	25	15	13	0	7	24	.260	.300	.250	8.88	2.59
Francisco, Alfredo	R-R	6-3	235	8-27-84	4	1	4.81	19	1	0	1	49	47	30	26	2	13	43	.244	.284	.222	7.95	2.40
Jackson, Brett	R-R	6-2	200	9-28-84	0	1	7.24	6	1	0	0	14	15	13	11	3	11	8	.278	.316	.257	5.27	7.24
Jimenez-Angulo, Fabian	L-L	6-2	187	8-27-86	1	0	1.56	3	3	0	0	17	8	3	3	0	6	10	.143	.143	.143	5.19	3.12
Kopach, Kitt	L-R	6-2	195	2-14-85	2	2	4.28	11	4	0	0	27	23	14	13	0	24	7	.240	.359	.158	2.30	7.90
Maestri, Alessandro	R-R	5-11	180	6-1-85	4	3	3.80	22	0	0	1	43	36	20	18	4	13	35	.232	.333	.187	7.38	2.74
Martinez, Jose	L-L	6-5	180	10-8-84	0	0	6.00	2	0	0	0	3	6	2	2	1	1	2	.462	.000	.545	3.00	3.00
Muldowney, William	R-R	6-1	185	8-9-84	1	3	2.68	11	8	0	0	44	43	15	13	2	11	42	.265	.265	.265	8.66	2.27
Papelbon, Jeremy	R-L	6-1	205	6-24-83	4	0	1.83	18	0	0	3	44	29	10	9	1	15	50	.182	.156	.193	10.15	3.05
Pawelek, Mark	L-L	6-3	190	8-18-86	3	5	2.51	15	12	0	0	61	54	24	17	1	23	52	.232	.195	.240	7.67	3.39
Petrick, Billy	R-R	6-6	220	4-29-84	5	0	2.23	7	7	0	0	36	37	10	9	0	12	28	.268	.265	.270	6.94	2.97
Pina, Jose	R-R	6-2	150	11-2-85	2	5	4.45	15	14	0	0	65	66	37	32	7	23	26	.269	.347	.235	3.62	3.20
Renshaw, Jacob	R-R	6-3	215	4-29-86	1	3	4.24	5	5	0	0	23	25	16	11	2	6	20	.266	.342	.214	7.71	2.31
Roquet, Rocky	R-R	6-2	210	11-6-82	0	0	5.49	19	0	0	3	20	21	13	12	1	5	31	.273	.188	.333	14.19	2.29
Ruhlman, Jayson	L-L	6-1	180	8-17-84	3	1	3.79	20	0	0	0	36	29	17	15	2	16	45	.216	.167	.235	11.36	4.04
Samardzija, Jeff	R-R	6-6	215	1-23-85	1	1	2.37	5	5	0	0	19	18	5	5	1	6	13	.247	.367	.163	6.16	2.84
Sotolongo, Roberto	R-R	6-4	200	8-18-82	0	0	0.00	2	0	0	0	2	0	0	0	0	1	2	.000	.000	.000	4.91	2.45

FIELDING

Catcher	PCT	G	PO	A	E	DP	PB
Canepa	.991	43	311	31	3	6	10
Castillo	1.000	3	10	2	0	0	2
Hackstedt	1.000	5	17	2	0	1	3
Lalli	1.000	3	9	2	0	0	1
Mercedes	.990	31	180	23	2	0	9

First Base	PCT	G	PO	A	E	DP
Canzler	.985	68	621	21	10	54
Puello	.988	8	79	5	1	8

Second Base	PCT	G	PO	A	E	DP
Clevenger	.966	63	133	180	11	41
Lopez	1.000	8	8	11	0	3
Matulia	.925	10	15	22	3	7
Rosario	1.000	2	4	1	0	0

Third Base	PCT	G	PO	A	E	DP
Lansford	.945	42	36	102	8	14
Matulia	.857	4	4	8	2	1
Puello	.901	34	25	66	10	9

Shortstop	PCT	G	PO	A	E	DP
Baez	.918	19	23	66	8	10
Joseph	1.000	1	1	0	0	0
Lopez	.917	13	10	34	4	5
Matulia	.960	51	67	151	9	24

Outfield	PCT	G	PO	A	E	DP
Camp	.976	74	156	6	4	1
Colvin	.983	63	109	4	2	1
Episcopo	1.000	3	7	0	0	0
Joseph	.977	66	121	6	3	1
Lewis	.912	31	46	6	5	0

Arizona League

BATTING

	B-T	HT	WT	DOB	AVG	vLH	vRH	G	AB	R	H	2B	3B	HR	RBI	BB	HBP	SH	SF	SO	SB	CS	SLG	OBP
Andersen, Clifford	L-L	6-2	185	7-24-87	.248	.250	.248	46	157	30	39	5	3	0	11	21	4	1	1	59	5	2	.318	.350
Brown, Randy	R-R	6-0	172	11-12-85	.333	.333	.333	6	12	2	4	1	0	0	1	2	0	0	0	2	0	1	.417	.429
Castillo, Welington	R-R	—	—	4-24-87	.192	.250	.182	7	26	4	5	0	0	0	0	1	1	0	0	6	0	0	.192	.250
Gilbert, Cody	R-R	6-3	185	8-21-85	.243	.242	.244	32	111	12	27	5	2	4	25	8	5	0	1	22	1	1	.432	.320
Gonzalez, Marwin	B-R	6-1	186	3-14-89	.198	.120	.230	24	86	9	17	4	1	0	11	8	0	0	0	19	0	2	.267	.266
Hackstedt, Adam	B-R	6-2	215	6-1-84	.250	.286	.233	15	44	4	11	2	0	1	8	5	1	0	1	16	0	1	.364	.333
Heredia, Valerio	B-R	5-10	150	3-14-86	.216	.286	.192	40	139	24	30	4	3	0	12	18	1	1	0	31	27	8	.288	.310
Inoa, Wilson	R-R	—	185	3-18-87	.200	.167	.211	39	120	14	24	2	0	0	11	11	5	0	1	42	7	2	.217	.292
Lilly, Ryan	R-R	6-0	195	12-15-83	.245	.333	.216	15	49	7	12	3	0	0	6	7	2	0	0	6	2	0	.306	.362
Lopez, Pedro	B-R	5-10	165	10-31-86	.225	.167	.250	15	40	9	9	1	0	0	4	10	0	1	0	6	2	2	.250	.380
Malone, Ryne	L-R	5-11	180	1-6-85	.667	—	.667	1	3	1	2	0	1	1	1	1	0	0	0	1	0	2.333	.750
Mercedes, Mario	R-R	5-10	160	11-22-86	.214	.000	.273	14	42	2	3	0	0	0	0	0	1	0	0	2	1	0	.214	.267
Murphy, Luther	R-R	6-3	225	3-15-86	.227	.188	.250	32	88	14	20	6	1	0	6	16	7	0	1	24	2	3	.318	.384
Pagan, Angel	B-R	6-1	180	7-2-81	.111	.000	.143	3	9	1	1	0	0	0	0	2	0	0	0	3	1	0	.111	.273
Parker, Richard	R-R	6-3	200	6-19-85	.262	.258	.263	39	126	17	33	13	1	2	18	20	1	1	0	27	0	1	.429	.367
Perez, Carlos	R-R	—	—	10-18-87	.215	.156	.246	30	93	7	20	5	0	1	10	3	1	0	2	18	2	1	.301	.242
Rosario, Lisandro	B-R	5-11	150	7-16-86	.314	.409	.288	32	102	17	32	4	1	0	11	11	1	1	1	25	13	3	.373	.383
Rundle, Andrew	L-L	6-4	180	11-5-87	.230	.286	.209	37	126	22	29	9	3	1	15	20	10	1	1	49	3	3	.373	.376
Samson, Nathan	R-R	6-0	170	8-19-87	.211	.333	.170	21	71	10	15	0	0	0	8	14	3	2	1	18	0	4	.211	.360
Tirado, Francisco	B-R	6-0	175	7-30-87	.286	.278	.289	16	56	6	16	2	0	0	8	3	0	0	6	1	2	.321	.322
Valentin, Cesar	R-R	5-11	155	10-19-88	.235	.368	.194	32	81	6	19	4	0	0	7	7	0	1	0	19	3	0	.284	.295
Vanderhook, Cory	B-R	6-2	190	8-19-83	.283	.292	.281	33	113	14	32	5	1	0	11	5	3	2	2	16	0	1	.345	.325
Williams, Jeremy	R-R	6-4	230	6-7-83	.233	.239	.231	39	150	26	35	9	6	1	21	14	3	0	1	50	7	3	.393	.310

PITCHING

	B-T	HT	WT	DOB	W	L	ERA	G	GS	CG	SV	IP	H	R	ER	HR	BB	SO	AVG	vLH	vRH	K/9	BB/9
Alburquerque, Alberto	R-R	6-0	150	6-10-86	0	2	5.68	8	5	0	0	13	10	8	8	1	10	15	.233	.500	.152	10.66	7.11
Astorga, Alejandro	L-L	—	—	3-14-87	1	1	4.35	5	0	0	0	10	12	7	5	0	4	8	.286	.333	.273	6.97	3.48
Bennett, Cedric	R-R	6-5	210	12-4-82	0	0	4.40	12	0	0	0	14	16	9	7	1	6	9	.291	.389	.243	5.65	3.77
Bernard, Oscar	R-R	6-2	170	6-27-83	1	4	4.03	14	2	0	0	29	36	20	13	1	13	15	.310	.375	.276	4.66	4.03
Brown, Randy	R-R	6-0	172	11-12-85	0	1	18.00	1	0	0	0	1	3	2	2	0	1	2	.500	.750	.000	18.00	9.00
Carrillo, Marco	R-R	—	—	2-1-87	4	0	1.73	13	3	0	0	42	30	10	8	3	10	34	.196	.203	.191	7.34	2.16
Castillo, Julio	R-R	6-3	212	7-10-87	2	6	8.73	15	3	0	0	33	56	39	32	1	17	13	.386	.388	.385	3.55	4.64
Ceda, Jose	R-R	6-4	205	1-28-87	0	0	0.75	5	3	0	0	12	6	2	1	0	7	21	.154	.300	.103	15.75	5.25
2-team (8 AZL Padres)					2	0	3.60	13	7	0	0	35	26	16	14	1	20	52	—	—	—	13.37	5.14
Clipp, Brad	R-R	6-2	180	8-15-84	0	0	0.00	1	0	0	0	2	1	0	0	0	2	2	.125	.000	.333	9.00	9.00
Cuevas novas, Greibal	R-R	6-9	260	8-11-83	0	0	3.18	7	1	0	0	17	14	7	6	1	8	20	.237	.375	.186	10.59	4.24
Diaz, Eli	R-R	6-3	180	11-11-86	0	0	0.00	1	1	0	0	1	0	0	0	0	0	0	.000	.000	.000	0.00	0.00
Dolis, Rafael	R-R	6-3	180	1-10-88	0	2	8.28	13	3	0	0	25	30	27	23	1	16	33	.294	.276	.301	11.88	5.76
Downs, Darin	R-L	6-3	176	12-26-84	1	1	10.80	2	1	0	0	3	5	4	4	1	1	2	.357	.333	.364	5.40	2.70
Gwaltney, Lee	R-R	6-6	210	5-6-80	0	1	5.14	3	1	0	0	7	11	4	4	0	1	5	.367	.375	.364	6.43	1.29
Hernandez, Robert	R-R	6-2	165	10-7-88	5	2	3.20	14	5	0	0	39	42	27	14	1	16	18	.266	.313	.245	4.12	3.66
Holden, Kyle	R-R	6-6	205	12-13-83	1	1	6.75	8	1	0	0	11	6	9	8	0	11	9	.167	.214	.136	7.59	9.28
Holdzkom, Lincoln	R-R	6-4	240	3-23-82	0	0	2.08	5	1	0	0	9	11	4	2	0	3	10	.324	.154	.429	10.38	3.12
Huseby, Christopher	R-R	6-7	220	1-11-88	0	2	5.19	6	6	0	0	17	21	10	10	1	6	14	.296	.400	.220	7.27	3.12
Inoa, Wilson	R-R	—	185	3-18-87	0	0	—	0	0	0	0	0	0	2	2	0	0	0	—	—	—	—	—
Kopach, Kitt	L-R	6-2	195	2-14-85	0	0	2.31	7	1	0	3	12	5	3	3	0	6	7	.135	.063	.190	5.40	4.63
Lopez, Pedro	B-R	5-10	165	10-31-86	0	0	0.00	1	0	0	0	1	0	0	0	0	0	0	.000	.000	—	0.00	0.00
Maradeo, Matthew	R-R	6-2	210	6-30-83	1	1	10.24	12	0	0	1	19	31	22	22	1	6	14	.369	.450	.344	6.52	2.79
Martinez, Jose	L-L	6-5	180	10-8-84	0	1	0.00	1	0	0	0	2	4	7	0	0	3	3	.400	1.000	.333	16.20	16.20
McCormick, Andrew	R-R	6-0	210	8-9-84	1	3	6.38	12	0	0	1	18	21	15	13	0	9	12	.288	.370	.239	5.89	4.42
Norton, Phil	R-L	6-0	215	2-1-76	0	1	5.14	3	1	0	0	7	9	4	4	1	0	8	.321	.250	.350	10.29	0.00
Parker, Taylor	L-L	5-11	150	10-2-84	2	2	2.35	14	8	0	0	54	49	16	14	0	13	39	.237	.209	.244	6.54	2.18
Perez, Leonel	R-R	6-2	175	1-3-84	0	1	9.00	6	0	0	0	7	8	8	7	0	6	3	.286	.200	.333	3.86	7.71
Phelps, Michael	R-R	6-4	190	5-26-84	0	0	0.00	1	1	0	0	2	0	0	0	0	3	2	.000	.000	.000	9.00	13.50
Platt, Charles	R-R	6-2	235	10-12-82	1	0	1.65	10	1	0	1	16	11	6	3	0	4	11	.186	.222	.171	6.06	2.20
Renshaw, Jacob	R-R	6-3	215	4-29-86	0	1	5.57	7	6	0	0	21	24	13	13	1	6	17	.296	.250	.321	7.29	2.57
Taylor, Brandon	R-R	6-1	200	7-26-82	0	1	2.57	5	1	0	1	7	6	9	2	0	2	2	.207	.182	.222	2.57	2.57
Vanderhook, Cory	B-R	6-2	190	8-19-83	0	0	0.00	1	0	0	0	1	0	0	0	0	1	1	.000	.000	.000	9.00	9.00
Walters, Donald	R-R	6-1	195	7-18-86	1	0	5.26	14	0	0	1	26	31	15	15	1	11	25	.310	.321	.306	8.77	3.86

FIELDING

Catcher	PCT	G	PO	A	E	DP	PB
Castillo	.955	3	19	2	1	0	1
Hackstedt	1.000	10	50	9	0	1	2
Mercedes	1.000	2	14	0	0	0	0
Parker	1.000	8	36	6	0	2	3
Perez	.974	28	164	25	5	1	5
Vanderhook	1.000	21	111	24	0	0	2

First Base	PCT	G	PO	A	E	DP
Castillo	.875	1	4	3	1	1
Hackstedt	.946	5	33	2	2	4
Lilly	1.000	3	12	0	0	0
Murphy	.973	29	243	11	7	15
Parker	.979	25	179	10	4	18
Vanderhook	1.000	3	21	3	0	1
Williams	1.000	1	4	1	0	0

Second Base	PCT	G	PO	A	E	DP
Heredia	.935	20	41	60	7	13
Lilly	1.000	5	13	10	0	5
Lopez	.952	7	20	20	2	8
Malone	1.000	1	1	2	0	1
Rosario	.952	18	33	47	4	7
Valentin	.933	10	16	26	3	4

Third Base	PCT	G	PO	A	E	DP
Gonzalez	.894	17	11	31	5	3
Heredia	.833	14	10	15	5	0
Lilly	.889	6	2	14	2	0
Lopez	1.000	1	0	3	0	0
Parker	.840	9	7	14	4	0
Rosario	.833	3	0	5	1	0
Tirado	.957	8	5	17	1	0
Valentin	.846	5	2	9	2	0

Shortstop	PCT	G	PO	A	E	DP
Gonzalez	.933	9	9	19	2	0
Heredia	.941	3	7	9	1	1
Lilly	.857	1	1	5	1	1
Lopez	1.000	6	5	12	0	5
Samson	.947	21	33	75	6	18
Tirado	.884	9	8	30	5	2
Valentin	.915	14	17	37	5	8

Outfield	PCT	G	PO	A	E	DP
Andersen	.921	44	67	3	6	1
Brown	.900	5	7	2	1	0
Gilbert	.957	20	20	2	1	0
Inoa	.981	29	46	5	1	1
Pagan	1.000	2	2	0	0	0
Rosario	1.000	3	7	0	0	0
Rundle	.971	35	65	3	2	0
Williams	.948	35	52	3	3	0

BY PHIL ROGERS

There was nothing wrong with the White Sox' ambition. But disappointing pitching and the emergence of the American League Central as the major leagues' deepest division caused their World Series defense to end one month ahead of schedule.

A third-place finish left the 2005 champions paying compliments to the Twins and Tigers, who made it a moot point that the Sox finished with 90-plus victories in back-to-back seasons for the first time since the late Al Lopez' teams did it in 1963-65.

With team owner Jerry Reinsdorf increasing the payroll, general manager Ken Williams was aggressive in the offseason as he tried to improve on the team that had swept the Astros in the World Series.

Williams showed a decided lack of sentimentality, dispatching clubhouse leader Aaron Rowand and postseason heroes Orlando Hernandez and Geoff Blum in a series of moves that brought Jim Thome, Javier Vazquez and Rob Mackowiak to Chicago. His biggest move might have been retaining free agent first baseman Paul Konerko, who signed a five-year, $60 million deal—the biggest in club history—after personally delivering the last-out ball from the series to Reinsdorf.

The rebuilt lineup delivered as expected, with Thome, Konerko and Jermaine Dye forming the best 3-4-5 combination in the majors. They each delivered at least 35 home runs and 109 RBIs as the White Sox scored 868 runs, the third-most in the majors.

Third baseman Joe Crede made it the first Sox team to ever feature four hitters with 30-plus homers. The majors-leading total of 236 marked the seventh consecutive season the Sox had hit at least 200 homers, extending the

PLAYERS OF THE YEAR

MAJOR LEAGUE: Jermaine Dye, of

Dye has revitalized his career in Chicago—winning World Series MVP in 2005—and he was a big reason the White Sox scored 120 more runs in 2006 than they had in 2005. Adding Jim Thome didn't hurt, but neither did Dye's .315 average, .622 slugging percentage, 44 home runs and 120 RBIs.

MINOR LEAGUE: Josh Fields, 3b

Fields homered in his first major league at-bat, which wasn't surprising considering the season he had. He has been pushed by the White Sox and has gotten a little better each year since begin drafted in 2004 out of Oklahoma State. Fields hit .305, slugged .515 and scored 85 runs at Triple-A.

ongoing club record they share with the Yankees.

Yet the White Sox went steadily downhill after a 56-29 start. They lost first place to Detroit in May and got passed by Minnesota in late August. The second half was an exercise in frustration for all involved as the Sox went 33-36, finishing the season 90-72.

Despite the presence of a five-veteran rotation that included all-stars Jose Contreras and Mark Buehrle, the staff ERA jumped from 3.61 to 4.61, which ranked 10th in the AL. While the bullpen was a question in the first part of the season, the dropoff was largely the result of erratic pitching from the starters, who showed signs of wear.

During the World Series season, Buerhle, Contreras, Jon Garland and Freddy Garcia all had ERAs of 3.87 or lower. But the best in 2006 was Contreras' 4.27.

Williams has never been shy about trading prospects for proven players, and that trend continued when he included center fielder Chris Young in the Vazquez trade with the Diamondbacks and lefthander Tyler Lumsden and righthander Daniel Cortes in a July deal with the Royals for reliever Mike MacDougal.

Young was the organization's top prospect at the time he was dealt. Lumsden had recovered from elbow surgery to become the most highly regarded pitching prospect at the time he was dealt. Dealing Young seemed more suspect after Brian Anderson, a 2003 first-round pick who had been handed the center-field job, batted .225 with eight homers as a rookie for the White Sox.

Led by third baseman Josh Fields, knuckleballer Charlie Haeger and unheralded lefthander Heath Phillips, Triple-A Charlotte advanced to the International League playoffs.

There was little cause for celebration elsewhere in the farm system. The talent in the lower levels seemed especially thin after two short-season teams and low Class A Kannapolis combined for a .333 winning percentage (92-184).

As has been the recent tendency, the White Sox used their first-round pick in the June draft on an projectable college player, Texas righthander Kyle McCullough.

ORGANIZATION LEADERS

BATTING		*Minimum 250 at-bats
*AVG	Gilbert, Archie, Great Falls	.332
R	Fields, Josh, Charlotte	86
H	Velandia, Jorge, Charlotte	153
TB	Fields, Josh, Charlotte	246
2B	Mercedes, Victor, Winston-Salem	35
3B	Orlando, Paulo, Kannapolis	10
HR	Kelly, Christopher, Winston-Salem	20
RBI	Kelly, Christopher, Winston-Salem	77
	Sweeney, Ryan, Charlotte	77
BB	Cook, David, Winston-Salem	77
SO	Fields, Josh, Charlotte	147
SB	Owens, Jerry, Charlotte	42
*OBP	Gilbert, Archie, Great Falls	.408
*SLG	Carter, Christopher, Kannapolis/Great Falls	.522
XBH	Fields, Josh, Charlotte	56

PITCHING		#Minimum 75 innings
W	Haeger, Charlie, Charlotte	14
	Redding, Tim, Charlotte	14
L	Rote, Ryan, Kannapolis/Great Falls	15
#ERA	Egbert, Jack, Winston-Salem/Birmingham	2.67
G	Wassermann, Ehren, Birmingham	68
CG	Redding, Tim, Charlotte	5
SV	Wassermann, Ehren, Birmingham	22
IP	Redding, Tim, Charlotte	207
BB	Randolph, Stephen, Charlotte	118
SO	Randolph, Stephen, Charlotte	155
	Redding, Tim, Charlotte	155
#AVG	Haeger, Charlie, Charlotte	.231

ORGANIZATION STATISTICS

Chicago White Sox — MLB

American League

BATTING	B-T	HT	WT	DOB	AVG	vLH	vRH	G	AB	R	H	2B	3B	HR	RBI	BB	HBP	SH	SF	SO	SB	CS	SLG	OBP
Alomar Jr., Sandy	R-R	6-3	235	6-18-66	.217	.235	.167	19	46	5	10	3	0	1	8	3	0	0	2	7	0	0	.348	.255
Anderson, Brian	R-R	6-2	215	3-11-82	.225	.226	.223	134	365	46	82	23	1	8	33	30	5	2	3	90	4	7	.359	.290
Cintron, Alex	B-R	6-1	205	12-17-78	.285	.274	.288	91	288	35	82	10	3	5	41	10	2	1	3	35	10	3	.392	.310
Crede, Joe	R-R	6-2	200	4-26-78	.283	.273	.288	150	544	76	154	31	0	30	94	28	7	0	7	58	0	2	.506	.323
Dye, Jermaine	R-R	6-5	235	1-28-74	.315	.337	.305	146	539	103	170	27	3	44	120	59	6	0	7	118	7	3	.622	.385
Fields, Josh	R-R	6-1	215	12-14-82	.150	.167	.143	11	20	4	3	2	0	1	2	5	0	0	0	8	0	0	.400	.320
Gload, Ross	L-L	6-1	190	4-5-76	.327	.308	.333	77	156	22	51	8	2	3	18	6	1	3	1	15	6	0	.462	.354
Iguchi, Tadahito	R-R	5-10	200	12-4-74	.281	.252	.298	138	555	97	156	24	0	18	67	59	3	8	2	110	11	5	.422	.352
Konerko, Paul	R-R	6-2	220	3-5-76	.313	.318	.310	152	566	97	177	30	0	35	113	60	8	0	9	104	1	0	.551	.381
Mackowiak, Rob	L-R	6-0	200	6-20-76	.290	.222	.308	112	255	31	74	12	1	5	23	28	3	2	2	59	5	2	.404	.365
Owens, Jerry	L-L	6-3	195	2-16-81	.333	.000	.375	12	9	4	3	1	0	0	0	0	0	0	0	2	1	0	.444	.333
Ozuna, Pablo	R-R	5-11	195	8-25-74	.328	.322	.348	79	189	25	62	12	2	2	17	7	4	3	0	16	6	6	.444	.365
Pierzynski, A.J.	L-R	6-3	235	12-30-76	.295	.270	.304	140	509	65	150	24	0	16	64	22	8	3	1	72	1	0	.436	.333
Podsednik, Scott	L-L	6-1	190	3-18-76	.261	.216	.278	139	524	86	137	27	6	3	45	54	2	8	4	96	40	19	.353	.330
Stewart, Chris	R-R	6-4	205	2-19-82	.000	.000	.000	6	8	0	0	0	0	0	0	0	0	0	0	2	0	0	.000	.000
Sweeney, Ryan	L-L	6-4	200	2-20-85	.229	.286	.214	18	35	1	8	0	0	0	5	0	0	0	0	7	0	0	.229	.229
Thome, Jim	L-R	6-4	245	8-27-70	.288	.236	.321	143	490	108	141	26	0	42	109	107	6	0	7	147	0	0	.598	.416
Uribe, Juan	R-R	6-0	220	3-22-79	.235	.224	.244	132	463	53	109	28	2	21	71	13	3	9	7	82	1	1	.441	.257
Widger, Chris	R-R	6-2	220	5-21-71	.184	.149	.241	27	76	6	14	3	0	1	7	9	0	0	2	20	0	0	.263	.264
2-team (9 Baltimore)					.172	—	—	36	93	6	16	3	0	1	9	11	0	1	2	24	0	0	.237	.255

PITCHING	B-T	HT	WT	DOB	W	L	ERA	G	GS	CG	SV	IP	H	R	ER	HR	BB	SO	AVG	vLH	vRH	K/9	BB/9
Buehrle, Mark	L-L	6-2	225	3-23-79	12	13	4.99	32	32	1	0	204	247	124	113	36	48	98	.305	.238	.322	4.32	2.12
Contreras, Jose	R-R	6-4	245	12-6-71	13	9	4.27	30	30	1	0	196	194	101	93	20	55	134	.256	.267	.248	6.15	2.53
Cotts, Neal	L-L	6-1	195	3-25-80	1	2	5.17	70	0	0	1	54	64	33	31	12	24	43	.291	.263	.314	7.17	4.00
Garcia, Freddy	R-R	6-4	250	6-10-76	17	9	4.53	33	33	1	0	216	228	116	109	32	48	135	.267	.262	.271	5.62	2.00
Garland, Jon	R-R	6-6	215	9-27-79	18	7	4.51	33	32	1	0	211	247	112	106	26	41	112	.294	.290	.297	4.77	1.75
Haeger, Charlie	R-R	6-1	200	9-19-83	1	1	3.44	7	1	0	1	18	12	10	7	0	13	19	.182	.133	.196	9.33	6.38
Hermanson, Dustin	R-R	6-2	205	12-21-72	0	0	4.05	6	0	0	0	7	6	3	3	2	1	5	.240	.167	.308	6.75	1.35
Jenks, Bobby	R-R	6-3	280	3-14-81	3	4	4.00	67	0	0	41	70	66	32	31	5	31	80	.253	.227	.268	10.33	4.00
Logan, Boone	R-L	6-5	200	8-13-84	0	0	8.31	21	0	0	1	17	21	18	16	2	15	15	.288	.357	.244	7.79	7.79
MacDougal, Mike	B-R	6-4	185	3-5-77	1	1	1.80	25	0	0	0	25	19	5	5	1	6	19	.213	.269	.190	6.84	2.16
2-team (4 Kansas City)					1	1	1.55	29	0	0	1	29	21	5	5	1	6	21	—	—	—	6.52	1.86
McCarthy, Brandon	R-R	6-7	195	7-7-83	4	7	4.68	53	2	0	0	85	77	44	44	17	33	69	.243	.197	.270	7.33	3.51
Montero, Agustin	R-R	6-3	210	8-26-77	1	0	5.14	11	0	0	0	14	15	10	8	3	2	7	.278	.368	.229	4.50	1.29
Nelson, Jeff	R-R	6-8	225	11-17-66	0	1	3.38	6	0	0	0	3	3	1	1	1	5	2	.300	.000	.429	6.75	16.88
Politte, Cliff	R-R	5-10	195	2-27-74	2	2	8.70	30	0	0	0	30	47	30	29	9	15	15	.353	.385	.340	4.50	4.50
Riske, David	R-R	6-2	180	10-23-76	1	1	3.93	33	0	0	0	34	32	16	15	4	14	23	.246	.324	.215	6.03	3.67
2-team (8 Boston)					1	2	3.89	41	0	0	0	44	40	20	19	6	17	28	—	—	—	5.73	3.48
Thornton, Matt	L-L	6-6	235	9-15-76	5	3	3.33	63	0	0	2	54	46	20	20	5	21	49	.229	.211	.240	8.17	3.50
Tracey, Sean	L-R	6-3	210	11-14-80	0	0	3.38	7	0	0	0	8	4	3	3	2	5	3	.143	.091	.176	3.38	5.63
Vazquez, Javier	R-R	6-2	215	7-25-76	11	12	4.84	33	32	1	0	203	206	116	109	23	56	184	.259	.256	.261	8.17	2.49

FIELDING

Catcher	PCT	G	PO	A	E	DP	PB
Alomar Jr.	.990	17	96	4	1	1	0
Pierzynski	.997	132	795	62	3	4	10
Stewart	1.000	5	17	2	0	0	0
Widger	.973	22	102	5	3	0	3

First Base	PCT	G	PO	A	E	DP
Gload	.986	49	266	13	4	24
Konerko	.995	140	1173	67	6	113
Thome	1.000	3	21	0	0	1

Second Base	PCT	G	PO	A	E	DP
Cintron	.990	26	43	59	1	9

	PCT	G	PO	A	E	DP
Iguchi	.988	136	270	371	8	76
Ozuna	.944	6	5	12	1	1

Third Base	PCT	G	PO	A	E	DP
Cintron	.903	11	8	20	3	1
Crede	.978	149	114	339	10	34
Fields	1.000	6	5	12	0	0
Mackowiak	1.000	6	0	4	0	0
Ozuna	1.000	17	5	11	0	0

Shortstop	PCT	G	PO	A	E	DP
Cintron	.973	41	50	94	4	19
Uribe	.977	132	217	373	14	84

Outfield	PCT	G	PO	A	E	DP
Anderson	.994	134	305	3	2	1
Dye	.981	146	305	5	6	2
Fields	—	1	0	0	0	0
Gload	1.000	19	16	0	0	0
Mackowiak	.974	96	149	2	4	0
Owens	1.000	5	6	0	0	0
Ozuna	1.000	40	45	3	0	0
Podsednik	.969	135	245	4	8	0
Sweeney	1.000	15	23	0	0	0

Charlotte Knights — Triple-A

International League

BATTING	B-T	HT	WT	DOB	AVG	vLH	vRH	G	AB	R	H	2B	3B	HR	RBI	BB	HBP	SH	SF	SO	SB	CS	SLG	OBP
Blakely, Darren	B-R	6-1	200	3-14-77	.173	.278	.122	32	110	16	19	5	1	1	6	9	2	1	2	36	3	0	.264	.244
Fields, Josh	R-R	6-1	215	12-14-82	.305	.343	.289	124	462	85	141	32	4	19	70	54	3	4	3	136	28	5	.515	.379
Gonzalez, Angel	R-R	6-2	180	12-15-81	.271	.278	.268	116	402	48	109	27	0	6	51	46	7	5	2	77	16	8	.383	.354
Hummel, Tim	R-R	6-2	205	11-18-78	.244	.226	.255	28	82	9	20	4	0	4	16	9	3	1	1	17	0	0	.451	.337
Lopez, Pedro	R-R	6-1	160	4-28-84	.274	.304	.259	59	208	32	57	12	0	5	24	11	3	6	0	28	4	0	.404	.320
Matos, Pascual	R-R	6-2	180	12-23-74	.175	.109	.198	58	177	15	31	11	0	2	16	6	2	2	36	2	0	.271	.191
Molina, Gustavo	R-R	6-2	210	2-24-82	.167	.182	.158	10	30	0	5	0	0	0	1	0	0	0	5	0	0	.167	.194
Owens, Jerry	L-L	6-3	195	2-16-81	.262	.205	.287	112	439	75	115	15	5	4	48	45	1	5	3	61	40	12	.346	.330
Quinn, Mark	R-R	6-1	190	5-21-74	.000	.000	.000	3	8	0	0	0	0	0	1	0	0	0	1	0	0	.000	.111
Rivera, Ruben	R-R	6-0	196	11-14-73	.239	.270	.220	107	331	52	79	18	2	16	42	32	10	1	3	90	4	1	.450	.322
Rogowski, Casey	L-L	6-3	230	5-1-81	.272	.282	.268	127	459	69	125	32	2	13	76	53	5	4	4	97	26	9	.436	.351
Rolls, Damian	R-R	6-2	215	9-15-77	.182	.273	.091	17	44	5	8	2	1	0	2	4	0	0	0	10	0	1	.295	.250
Rosa, Wally	R-R	6-1	182	11-28-81	.000	.000	.000	5	10	0	0	0	0	0	0	0	0	0	1	0	0	.000	.000
Smith, Bobby	R-R	6-3	210	5-10-74	.259	.367	.222	59	193	20	50	17	0	6	25	13	0	1	1	60	3	0	.440	.304

2006 PERFORMANCE

General manager: Kenny Williams. **Farm director:** David Wilder. **Scouting director:** Duane Shaffer.

Class	Team	League	W	L	PCT	Finish*	Manager(s)	Affiliate Since
Majors	Chicago	American	90	72	.556	5th (14)	Ozzie Guillen	—
Triple-A	Charlotte Knights	International	79	62	.560	2nd (14)	Razor Shines	1999
Double-A	Birmingham Barons	Southern	59	81	.421	9th (10)	Chris Cron	1986
High A	Winston-Salem Warthogs	Carolina	66	72	.478	5th (8)	Rafael Santana	1997
Low A	Kannapolis Intimidators	South Atlantic	42	94	.309	16th (16)	Omer Munoz	2001
Rookie	Great Falls White Sox	Pioneer	28	48	.368	7th (8)	Bobby Tolan	2003
Rookie	Bristol Sox	Appalachian	22	42	.344	10th (10)	Nick Leyva	1995
OVERALL 2006 MINOR LEAGUE RECORD			296	399	.426	29th (30)		

*Finish in overall standings (No. of teams in league). +League champion

Jim Thome rejuvenated his career with the White Sox

Ryan Sweeney will battle for a big league job in 2007

Name	B-T	HT	WT	DOB	AVG	vLH	vRH	G	AB	R	H	2B	3B	HR	RBI	BB	HBP	SH	SF	SO	SB	CS	SLG	OBP
Stewart, Chris	R-R	6-4	205	2-19-82	.265	.244	.274	89	272	40	72	17	3	4	28	15	5	8	1	35	3	0	.393	.314
Sweeney, Ryan	L-L	6-4	200	2-20-85	.296	.288	.300	118	449	64	133	25	3	13	70	35	3	3	2	73	7	7	.452	.350
Torcato, Tony	L-R	6-1	220	10-25-79	.249	.298	.236	78	225	22	56	11	1	2	22	17	2	1	4	35	1	1	.333	.302
Velandia, Jorge	R-R	5-9	180	1-12-75	.291	.269	.299	122	475	69	138	25	1	10	56	28	1	11	1	85	15	2	.411	.331
Young, Ernie	R-R	6-1	230	7-8-69	.300	.350	.279	105	350	52	105	26	0	13	68	55	9	0	3	85	2	2	.486	.405

PITCHING	B-T	HT	WT	DOB	W	L	ERA	G	GS	CG	SV	IP	H	R	ER	HR	BB	SO	AVG	vLH	vRH	K/9	BB/9
Bentz, Chad	R-L	6-2	210	5-5-80	4	3	4.46	23	2	0	0	34	25	17	17	10	21	21	.216	.194	.224	5.50	5.50
2-team (13 Louisville)					6	3	5.32	36	2	0	0	44	38	26	26	13	29	25	—	—		5.11	5.93
Broadway, Lance	R-R	6-2	210	8-20-83	0	0	3.00	1	1	0	0	6	5	2	2	0	1	6	.217	.091	.333	9.00	1.50
Cornejo, Nate	R-R	6-5	245	9-24-79	0	0	16.20	3	0	0	0	3	10	8	6	0	3	3	.476	.400	.500	8.10	8.10
De Los Santos, Valerio	L-L	6-2	210	10-6-72	1	1	3.02	19	8	0	0	57	47	27	19	6	24	47	.233	.308	.215	7.46	3.81
Farnsworth, Jeff	R-R	6-2	195	10-6-75	7	3	4.71	48	0	0	14	50	57	27	26	8	9	40	.286	.349	.257	7.25	1.63
Haeger, Charlie	R-R	6-1	200	9-19-83	14	6	3.07	26	25	2	0	170	143	71	58	9	78	130	.231	.249	.217	6.88	4.13
Hermanson, Dustin	R-R	6-2	205	12-21-72	0	1	3.29	14	0	0	0	14	8	5	5	1	7	16	.174	.300	.077	10.54	4.61
Logan, Boone	R-L	6-5	200	8-13-84	3	1	3.38	38	0	0	11	43	35	18	16	1	12	57	.222	.200	.229	12.02	2.53
Lopez, Javier	L-L	6-4	220	7-11-77	2	1	0.55	26	0	0	12	33	28	2	2	1	6	26	.235	.147	.271	7.09	1.64
2-team (13 Pawtucket)					2	1	1.99	39	0	0	16	49	48	12	11	2	14	38	—	—		6.89	2.54
Lorraine, Andrew	L-L	6-3	200	8-11-72	0	0	1.95	17	1	0	0	28	26	8	6	0	8	14	.248	.120	.288	4.55	2.60
Lubisich, Nik	L-L	6-2	195	4-19-79	0	2	10.38	2	2	0	0	9	13	11	10	3	3	6	.371	.286	.393	6.23	3.12
Montero, Agustin	R-R	6-3	210	8-26-77	2	3	4.85	39	0	0	1	59	54	33	32	8	20	55	.244	.247	.243	8.34	3.03
Munoz, Arnie	L-L	5-9	175	6-21-82	0	1	14.21	7	0	0	0	6	10	10	10	1	7	5	.357	.200	.391	7.11	9.95
Nelson, Jeff	R-R	6-8	225	11-17-66	1	0	0.00	4	0	0	0	5	4	1	0	0	4	7	.222	.333	.167	11.81	6.75
Nomo, Hideo	R-R	6-2	235	8-31-68	0	0	3.00	1	1	0	0	3	2	4	1	0	2	3	.167	.143	.200	9.00	6.00
Phillips, Heath	L-L	6-3	242	3-24-82	13	5	2.96	25	24	2	0	155	152	62	51	12	39	102	.263	.225	.274	5.92	2.26
Politte, Cliff	R-R	5-10	195	2-27-74	0	0	1.93	3	2	0	0	5	5	1	1	0	1	5	.263	.182	.375	9.64	1.93
Randolph, Stephen	L-L	6-3	205	5-1-74	9	9	3.67	28	27	0	0	154	130	75	63	19	114	144	.236	.216	.242	8.40	6.65
Redding, Tim	R-R	6-0	205	2-12-78	12	10	3.40	29	28	5	0	188	168	77	71	21	56	148	.238	.267	.221	7.10	2.69
Reynoso, Paulino	L-L	6-3	190	8-10-80	3	3	4.37	47	0	0	0	60	48	29	29	3	45	59	.215	.208	.218	8.90	6.79
Skrmetta, Matt	B-R	6-3	220	11-6-72	0	4	6.86	22	0	0	0	20	27	16	15	3	13	22	.325	.364	.311	10.07	5.95
Tracey, Sean	L-R	6-3	210	11-14-80	8	9	4.30	29	20	1	0	130	111	67	62	17	76	102	.238	.243	.235	7.08	5.28

FIELDING

Catcher	PCT	G	PO	A	E	DP	PB
Matos	.990	57	356	28	4	4	17
Molina	1.000	10	76	10	0	0	0
Rosa	1.000	5	20	3	0	0	7
Stewart	.994	84	600	51	4	7	17

First Base	PCT	G	PO	A	E	DP
Gonzalez	.917	1	8	3	1	1
Hummel	1.000	1	2	0	0	0
Molina	1.000	1	3	0	0	0
Rogowski	.990	127	1055	67	11	102
Smith	1.000	5	26	1	0	1
Stewart	1.000	2	14	1	0	2
Torcato	1.000	3	30	3	0	4
Young	.968	9	53	7	2	4

Second Base	PCT	G	PO	A	E	DP
Gonzalez	.970	74	143	177	10	47
Hummel	.933	5	6	8	1	2
Lopez	.988	40	70	90	2	25
Smith	.979	33	69	72	3	13

Third Base	PCT	G	PO	A	E	DP
Fields	.944	117	70	200	16	13
Gonzalez	.970	26	17	48	2	4
Hummel	.727	5	4	4	3	0
Smith	1.000	2	2	5	0	0
Stewart	—	1	0	0	0	0

Shortstop	PCT	G	PO	A	E	DP
Gonzalez	1.000	10	14	24	0	3

	PCT	G	PO	A	E	DP
Lopez	.954	19	27	56	4	12
Velandia	.979	118	139	336	10	75

Outfield	PCT	G	PO	A	E	DP
Blakely	1.000	30	49	2	0	1
Gonzalez	1.000	11	11	1	0	0
Hummel	1.000	10	15	0	0	0
Owens	.984	112	238	5	4	2
Quinn	1.000	1	1	0	0	0
Rivera	.969	94	179	7	6	0
Rolls	1.000	15	14	0	0	0
Smith	1.000	1	2	0	0	0
Sweeney	.988	116	231	10	3	3
Torcato	.981	39	48	4	1	2
Young	.941	26	45	3	3	1

Birmingham Barons — Double-A

Southern League

BATTING

	B-T	HT	WT	DOB	AVG	vLH	vRH	G	AB	R	H	2B	3B	HR	RBI	BB	HBP	SH	SF	SO	SB	CS	SLG	OBP
Aldridge, Cory	L-R	6-1	225	6-13-79	.287	.221	.310	84	293	34	84	17	4	4	30	29	2	0	4	85	7	6	.413	.351
Amador, Chris	R-R	5-10	167	12-14-82	.212	.211	.213	84	231	26	49	9	1	2	15	14	5	9	4	70	12	3	.286	.268
Armstrong, Cole	L-R	6-3	235	8-24-83	.120	.000	.125	8	25	3	3	0	0	0	0	2	0	0	2	0	0	.120	.185
Blakely, Darren	R-R	6-1	200	3-14-77	.260	.343	.217	27	104	12	27	6	1	3	12	6	3	0	0	23	2	2	.423	.319
Collaro, Thomas	R-R	6-4	216	4-4-83	.213	.168	.229	108	389	36	83	17	2	11	51	20	3	2	3	128	1	4	.352	.255
Gartrell, Maurice	R-R	6-2	220	1-14-84	.200	.000	.250	5	15	4	3	1	0	0	0	3	0	0	0	6	1	0	.267	.333
Getz, Christopher	L-R	6-0	175	8-30-83	.256	.263	.254	130	508	67	130	15	6	2	36	52	2	9	2	47	19	6	.321	.326
Hansen, Joshua	R-R	5-10	215	9-16-81	.143	.182	.129	12	42	3	6	2	0	0	2	3	1	0	0	12	0	0	.190	.217
Hollis, Eric	R-R	6-2	225	9-26-82	.188	.000	.214	5	16	1	3	0	0	0	0	2	0	0	0	4	0	0	.188	.278
Lee, Carlos	R-R	6-1	220	9-29-81	.143	.000	.167	2	7	0	1	0	0	0	0	2	1	0	0	2	0	1	.143	.250
Lopez, Pedro	R-R	6-1	160	4-28-84	.322	.303	.330	65	258	30	83	15	2	5	34	16	1	5	4	32	3	6	.453	.358
Lucy, Donny	R-R	6-3	210	8-8-82	.283	.357	.261	18	60	2	17	1	0	0	3	4	3	2	0	15	1	0	.300	.358
Molina, Gustavo	R-R	6-2	210	2-24-82	.227	.255	.215	103	344	26	78	14	0	7	34	25	4	0	1	65	5	6	.328	.286
Myers, Michael	R-R	6-1	194	12-11-79	.263	.319	.243	130	414	53	109	23	2	4	23	51	6	13	1	78	20	10	.357	.352
Nanita, Ricardo	L-L	6-1	180	6-12-81	.286	.238	.304	106	364	48	104	14	3	8	42	51	2	10	5	56	11	6	.407	.372
Quinn, Mark	R-R	6-1	190	5-21-74	.264	.241	.271	63	235	28	62	15	0	11	40	23	5	0	4	41	1	1	.468	.337
Rosa, Wally	R-R	6-1	182	11-28-81	.176	.071	.209	44	119	9	21	1	0	0	4	13	1	1	0	27	0	0	.185	.263
Sasser, Rob	R-R	6-3	205	3-9-75	.233	.290	.213	39	120	10	28	5	0	3	15	20	0	0	2	32	1	0	.350	.338
Schnurstein, Micah	R-R	6-1	207	7-18-84	.219	.180	.232	131	480	48	105	25	2	9	46	24	6	7	1	100	8	6	.335	.264
Smith, Corey	R-R	6-1	200	4-15-82	.238	.218	.246	120	425	46	101	19	2	12	52	62	4	0	5	112	5	1	.376	.337
Valido, Robert	R-R	6-2	180	5-16-85	.208	.182	.215	45	168	15	35	9	3	1	11	13	1	10	0	24	8	3	.315	.269

PITCHING

	B-T	HT	WT	DOB	W	L	ERA	G	GS	CG	SV	IP	H	R	ER	HR	BB	SO	AVG	vLH	vRH	K/9	BB/9
Bittner, Tim	L-L	6-2	210	6-9-80	1	0	5.64	18	0	0	0	22	35	16	14	3	12	8	.368	.333	.385	3.22	4.84
Broadway, Lance	R-R	6-2	210	8-20-83	8	8	2.74	25	25	2	0	154	160	59	47	10	40	111	.269	.271	.268	6.47	2.33
Cornejo, Nate	R-R	6-5	245	9-24-79	0	1	3.60	1	1	0	0	5	6	2	2	0	2	2	.300	.357	.167	3.60	3.60
Dizard, Fraser	L-L	6-0	195	8-6-81	0	1	7.54	18	0	0	2	23	27	20	19	4	9	13	.300	.400	.250	5.16	3.57
Egbert, Jack	L-R	6-3	205	5-12-83	0	2	0.86	4	4	0	0	21	17	4	2	0	8	24	.215	.239	.182	10.29	3.43
Harrell, Lucas	B-R	6-2	200	6-3-85	0	2	10.24	3	3	0	0	10	12	12	11	1	14	4	.316	.308	.320	3.72	13.03
LaMura, B.J.	R-R	6-1	200	1-1-81	5	0	1.69	34	0	0	3	53	32	12	10	2	31	67	.180	.130	.202	11.31	5.23
2-team (14 Jacksonville)					6	1	1.77	48	0	0	4	76	47	18	15	5	47	92	—			10.85	5.54
Liotta, Ray	L-L	6-3	220	4-3-83	3	8	4.93	18	18	0	0	97	109	57	53	3	46	52	.290	.278	.294	4.84	4.28
Little, Jeff	R-R	6-3	200	4-30-80	0	1	5.40	6	0	0	0	10	10	6	6	1	4	9	.278	.300	.269	8.10	3.60
Lumsden, Tyler	L-L	6-4	215	5-9-83	9	4	2.60	20	20	0	0	124	114	47	37	9	40	72	.252	.243	.256	5.24	2.91
Malone, Corwin	R-L	6-1	200	7-3-80	9	11	4.43	27	27	0	0	154	141	83	76	13	94	121	.247	.229	.253	7.06	5.48
Munoz, Arnie	L-L	5-9	175	6-21-82	2	4	3.72	26	2	0	2	46	38	20	19	4	14	48	.225	.300	.193	9.39	2.74
Myers, Michael	R-R	6-1	194	12-11-79	0	0	0.00	1	0	0	0	1	0	0	0	0	0	0	.000	.000	.000		
Perez, Oneli	R-R	6-2	163	5-26-83	0	1	0.55	7	0	0	1	16	6	1	1	1	6	20	.115	.115	.115	11.02	3.31
Pollok, Dwayne	R-R	6-3	195	11-12-80	4	5	3.16	54	0	0	3	83	88	32	29	8	20	54	.271	.301	.252	5.88	2.18
Rodriguez, Ryan	L-L	6-4	233	7-10-84	4	10	5.49	21	21	0	0	116	143	82	71	4	51	62	.310	.284	.318	4.80	3.95
Rosa, Wally	R-R	6-1	182	11-28-81	0	0	0.00	2	0	0	0	2	2	0	0	0	0	2	.250	.500	.167	9.00	0.00
Russell, Adam	R-R	6-8	250	4-14-83	3	3	4.75	10	10	0	0	55	59	33	29	5	19	47	.269	.207	.307	7.69	3.11
Sierra, Edwardo	R-R	6-4	195	4-15-82	2	1	5.65	25	2	0	0	43	44	32	27	1	30	40	.265	.258	.269	8.37	6.28
Tucker, Rusty	R-L	6-1	190	7-15-80	1	2	8.77	20	0	0	0	26	32	28	25	1	27	25	.317	.179	.370	8.77	9.47
Wassermann, Ehren	B-R	6-0	185	12-6-80	4	8	2.56	61	0	0	22	63	60	26	18	3	25	47	.253	.359	.201	6.68	3.55
West, Brian	R-R	6-4	230	8-4-80	2	6	6.00	52	0	0	4	69	75	50	46	8	28	41	.283	.293	.277	5.35	3.65
Whisler, Wesley	L-L	6-5	235	4-7-83	2	3	4.43	7	7	0	0	45	50	28	22	5	15	28	.284	.378	.259	5.64	3.02

FIELDING

Catcher	PCT	G	PO	A	E	DP	PB
Armstrong	.985	8	60	5	1	0	0
Lucy	.963	12	98	7	4	0	0
Molina	.992	95	572	78	5	2	8
Myers	—	1	0	0	0	0	0
Rosa	.985	35	174	21	3	3	6

First Base	PCT	G	PO	A	E	DP
Hansen	1.000	12	126	7	0	10
Hollis	1.000	3	18	0	0	3
Lucy	1.000	1	1	0	0	1
Molina	1.000	11	71	12	0	3
Myers	.994	30	166	9	1	18
Rosa	1.000	4	18	1	0	1
Sasser	.989	31	263	16	3	27
Smith	.984	71	629	31	11	66

Second Base	PCT	G	PO	A	E	DP
Getz	.976	129	221	349	14	75
Lopez	1.000	2	2	6	0	1
Myers	.958	15	22	24	2	8
Schnurstein	.750	1	2	1	1	0

Third Base	PCT	G	PO	A	E	DP
Myers	1.000	6	6	11	0	1
Sasser	1.000	1	1	0	0	0
Schnurstein	.929	127	97	268	28	20
Smith	.931	11	5	22	2	1

Shortstop	PCT	G	PO	A	E	DP
Getz	—	1	0	0	0	0
Lopez	.964	64	98	197	11	44
Myers	.955	37	54	116	8	26

	PCT	G	PO	A	E	DP
Smith	1.000	1	2	2	0	1
Valido	.992	44	88	147	2	36

Outfield	PCT	G	PO	A	E	DP
Aldridge	.983	68	114	3	2	1
Amador	.981	77	200	3	4	1
Blakely	.962	26	50	1	2	0
Collaro	.964	89	184	5	7	0
Gartrell	.917	5	11	0	1	0
Myers	.991	55	104	5	1	0
Nanita	.962	99	170	8	7	0
Quinn	1.000	19	20	0	0	0
Rosa	.600	3	3	0	2	0
Sasser	1.000	3	2	0	0	0
Schnurstein	1.000	3	3	0	0	0

Carolina League

BATTING

BATTING	B-T	HT	WT	DOB	AVG	vLH	vRH	G	AB	R	H	2B	3B	HR	RBI	BB	HBP	SH	SF	SO	SB	CS	SLG	OBP
Allen, Rod	R-R	6-2	210	9-21-82	.253	.312	.222	75	221	27	56	9	0	3	27	9	2	1	1	43	4	6	.335	.288
Amador, Chris	R-R	5-10	167	12-14-82	.302	.279	.313	38	139	21	42	6	4	3	21	5	8	2	0	32	7	5	.468	.362
Armstrong, Cole	L-R	6-3	235	8-24-83	.237	.222	.239	42	131	9	31	5	0	2	14	17	0	0	1	30	0	0	.321	.322
Cook, David	R-R	5-11	195	7-21-81	.233	.212	.243	130	437	76	102	24	5	16	58	77	6	3	5	108	17	4	.421	.352
De Los Santos, Jose	R-R	5-11	160	8-10-84	.297	.321	.286	99	340	34	101	17	0	1	31	18	4	6	2	43	10	4	.356	.338
Gomes, Anderson	R-R	6-1	185	3-12-85	.205	.133	.232	34	112	14	23	6	2	2	12	11	3	1	1	30	2	3	.348	.291
Guest, Garrett	R-R	5-11	170	7-3-82	.127	.167	.095	66	150	13	19	1	0	0	7	21	2	10	2	31	2	0	.133	.240
Haggerty, Cory	L-R	6-0	180	8-25-81	.225	.193	.232	102	307	42	69	18	2	6	36	32	7	10	4	67	5	2	.355	.309
Hansen, Joshua	R-R	5-10	215	9-16-81	.247	.238	.251	115	429	48	106	28	0	17	52	34	3	0	2	93	1	0	.431	.306
Kelly, Christopher	R-R	6-1	195	2-23-82	.244	.268	.232	133	496	64	121	32	2	20	77	34	5	0	8	105	1	1	.438	.295
Lucy, Donny	R-R	6-3	210	8-8-82	.262	.288	.249	97	332	48	87	17	1	7	32	33	8	6	2	67	12	3	.383	.341
Mercedes, Victor	B-R	5-11	184	4-15-79	.273	.299	.261	137	521	68	142	34	8	10	52	36	7	17	8	69	20	10	.426	.323
Ricks, Adam	B-R	5-10	195	9-24-82	.291	.381	.259	26	79	5	23	3	0	0	10	17	0	1	0	13	0	0	.329	.417
Roberts, Daron	R-R	6-0	215	2-25-83	.272	.345	.243	54	202	21	55	11	1	3	17	13	1	1	1	38	8	8	.381	.318
Smith, Sean	R-R	6-0	194	8-24-82	.258	.257	.259	131	461	69	119	31	2	9	57	47	18	13	6	76	30	14	.393	.346
Tartaglia, Evan	L-L	6-1	185	5-21-82	.188	.000	.200	5	16	1	3	0	0	0	0	2	0	1	0	5	1	1	.188	.278
Valido, Robert	R-R	6-2	180	5-16-85	.222	.200	.238	9	36	5	8	1	1	1	5	3	0	2	0	3	0	0	.389	.282
Welker, Kris	R-R	6-0	205	9-8-82	.083	.000	.167	4	12	1	1	0	0	0	0	0	0	2	0	4	0	0	.083	.083

PITCHING

PITCHING	B-T	HT	WT	DOB	W	L	ERA	G	GS	CG	SV	IP	H	R	ER	HR	BB	SO	AVG	vLH	vRH	K/9	BB/9
Bakker, Garry	R-R	6-2	208	3-28-83	1	1	4.36	45	0	0	8	54	37	26	26	4	26	46	.190	.185	.192	7.71	4.36
Banks, Demetrius	L-L	6-1	160	5-23-83	1	2	3.35	33	0	0	0	43	24	21	16	4	38	43	.161	.143	.170	9.00	7.95
Bittner, Tim	L-L	6-2	210	6-9-80	0	0	4.15	4	0	0	0	4	7	6	2	1	2	2	.318	.333	.300	4.15	4.15
Cassel, Justin	R-R	6-1	190	9-25-84	1	1	5.12	4	4	0	0	19	28	15	11	2	4	8	.333	.233	.389	3.72	1.86
Day, Dewon	R-R	6-4	210	9-29-80	1	4	3.40	40	0	0	8	48	40	23	18	3	21	63	.222	.247	.206	11.90	3.97
Egbert, Jack	L-R	6-3	205	5-12-83	9	8	2.94	25	25	0	0	141	131	57	46	2	46	120	.246	.257	.237	7.68	2.94
Harrell, Lucas	R-R	6-2	200	6-3-85	7	2	2.45	17	17	0	0	92	58	29	25	3	44	70	.182	.197	.167	6.87	4.32
Hernandez Jr., Fernando	R-R	5-11	190	7-31-84	7	5	1.93	57	0	0	13	65	50	24	14	4	32	81	.207	.243	.180	11.16	4.41
Hurd, John	R-R	5-11	185	1-29-83	1	3	8.51	16	0	0	0	24	39	24	23	0	9	12	.371	.435	.322	4.44	3.33
Liotta, Ray	L-L	6-3	220	4-3-83	1	6	8.08	10	9	0	0	42	62	49	38	5	19	30	.354	.271	.386	6.38	4.04
Marshall, Jay	L-L	6-5	185	2-25-83	5	1	1.02	58	0	0	4	62	46	11	7	2	8	44	.210	.096	.313	6.39	1.16
McCulloch, Kyle	R-R	6-3	180	3-20-85	2	5	4.08	7	7	0	0	35	37	20	16	4	17	21	.266	.309	.238	5.35	4.33
Moat, Michael	R-R	6-1	190	10-25-81	5	6	3.55	35	7	0	0	89	99	40	35	7	15	45	.280	.253	.300	4.57	1.52
Perez, Oneli	R-R	6-2	163	5-26-83	1	0	0.72	17	0	0	0	25	17	5	2	1	5	29	.181	.171	.186	10.44	1.80
Richard, Clayton	L-L	6-5	225	9-12-83	1	3	4.56	4	4	1	0	24	29	18	12	2	6	12	.315	.240	.343	4.56	2.28
Rodriguez, Ryan	L-L	6-4	233	7-10-84	1	2	5.57	6	6	0	0	32	40	23	20	5	12	14	.305	.276	.314	3.90	3.34
Rodriguez, Derek	R-R	5-11	190	5-17-83	1	1	4.91	2	2	0	0	11	15	6	6	1	3	13	.326	.190	.440	10.64	2.45
Russell, Adam	R-R	6-8	250	4-14-83	7	3	2.66	17	17	0	0	95	80	35	28	5	39	61	.235	.211	.257	5.80	3.71
Torres, Carlos	R-R	6-2	180	10-22-82	3	8	4.69	25	20	0	1	94	116	66	49	7	55	76	.304	.309	.300	7.28	5.27
Whisler, Wesley	L-L	6-5	235	4-7-83	10	7	2.97	20	20	1	0	118	112	52	39	0	44	57	.250	.246	.252	4.34	3.35
Zaleski, Matthew	R-R	6-0	205	12-2-81	1	4	3.43	42	0	0	1	63	61	27	24	5	18	40	.254	.266	.247	5.71	2.57

FIELDING

Catcher	PCT	G	PO	A	E	DP	PB
Armstrong	.990	33	182	16	2	1	4
Lucy	.980	94	633	52	14	5	11
Ricks	.986	12	65	4	1	0	4
Welker	.971	4	31	2	1	1	2

First Base	PCT	G	PO	A	E	DP
Armstrong	1.000	5	32	4	0	5
Hansen	.997	38	367	22	1	41
Kelly	.991	99	883	86	9	84

Second Base	PCT	G	PO	A	E	DP
De Los Santos	.954	67	110	223	16	43
Guest	.959	33	51	91	6	20

	PCT	G	PO	A	E	DP
Haggerty	.942	34	59	86	9	26
Mercedes	.944	9	18	33	3	10
Ricks	.889	1	4	4	1	0
Third Base	**PCT**	**G**	**PO**	**A**	**E**	**DP**
De Los Santos	.897	32	13	57	8	6
Guest	.948	27	13	60	4	3
Haggerty	.844	62	36	72	20	9
Kelly	.865	13	2	30	5	1
Ricks	.909	13	5	25	3	2
Shortstop	**PCT**	**G**	**PO**	**A**	**E**	**DP**
Guest	1.000	3	3	4	0	1
Haggerty	.750	1	0	3	1	0

	PCT	G	PO	A	E	DP
Mercedes	.948	127	190	445	35	97
Valido	.952	9	24	35	3	7
Outfield	**PCT**	**G**	**PO**	**A**	**E**	**DP**
Allen	.953	44	59	2	3	2
Amador	.985	37	61	3	1	0
Cook	.978	128	215	5	5	2
Gomes	.965	32	50	5	2	1
Roberts	.970	47	94	4	3	1
Smith	.984	130	242	11	4	1
Tartaglia	1.000	1	1	0	0	0

South Atlantic League

BATTING

BATTING	B-T	HT	WT	DOB	AVG	vLH	vRH	G	AB	R	H	2B	3B	HR	RBI	BB	HBP	SH	SF	SO	SB	CS	SLG	OBP
Acosta, Christian	R-R	5-11	178	7-14-83	.000	.000	.000	3	8	0	0	0	0	0	0	0	0	0	0	2	0	0	.000	.000
Acosta, Leonardo	R-R	6-2	165	4-29-86	.150	.206	.129	37	127	8	19	2	1	0	11	3	0	4	3	38	1	2	.181	.165
Allen, Brandon	L-R	6-2	235	2-12-86	.213	.230	.205	109	395	36	84	17	2	15	68	22	3	3	4	126	6	4	.380	.257
Blood, Randy	L-R	5-10	180	1-7-81	.160	.167	.158	6	25	1	4	1	0	1	4	2	0	0	0	8	0	0	.320	.222
Camacho, Juan	B-R	6-2	175	1-13-81	.228	.239	.223	58	224	22	51	9	0	4	27	6	3	1	0	45	0	1	.321	.258
Carter, Christopher	R-R	6-4	210	12-18-86	.130	.214	.094	13	46	4	6	1	0	1	5	5	1	0	0	17	0	0	.261	.231
Castillo, Javier	B-R	6-2	185	8-29-83	.256	.276	.249	94	344	53	88	17	5	8	42	29	4	1	0	64	8	2	.404	.321
Cunningham, Aaron	R-R	5-11	195	4-24-86	.305	.349	.285	95	341	58	104	26	3	11	41	34	13	11	3	72	19	10	.496	.386
Gomes, Anderson	R-R	6-1	185	3-12-85	.250	.284	.240	80	288	37	72	11	3	7	30	24	3	3	2	67	10	5	.382	.312
Hernandez, Francisco	B-R	5-9	160	2-4-86	.247	.196	.269	92	316	29	78	16	1	6	34	22	6	4	3	31	3	1	.361	.305
Hollis, Eric	R-R	6-2	225	9-26-82	.250	.000	.308	13	32	2	8	1	0	0	3	2	0	1	0	8	0	0	.281	.294
Johnson, Brandon	L-R	6-0	190	7-23-84	.231	.200	.240	69	221	29	51	13	3	6	20	15	5	6	2	71	8	6	.398	.292
Mesa, Eric	R-R	5-10	180	12-7-82	.221	.132	.267	41	113	11	25	2	0	3	11	12	1	0	1	33	0	1	.239	.282
Metheny, Brenton	L-R	6-0	205	10-3-80	.272	.279	.270	54	180	28	49	10	0	2	19	25	2	1	0	32	2	1	.361	.367
Moreno, Pedro	R-R	5-11	165	7-30-85	.000	.—	.000	2	6	1	0	0	0	0	0	0	0	0	0	1	0	0	.000	.000
Orlando, Paulo	R-R	6-3	165	11-1-85	.262	.246	.268	116	470	71	123	23	10	6	31	18	11	4	0	143	29	9	.391	.305
Ricks, Adam	B-R	5-10	195	9-24-82	.230	.242	.225	87	282	29	65	12	0	4	27	43	2	6	4	57	2	2	.316	.332
Roberts, Daron	R-R	6-0	215	2-25-83	.322	.348	.305	43	171	21	55	15	1	2	20	7	4	0	1	22	9	1	.456	.361

Player	B-T	HT	WT	DOB	AVG	vLH	vRH	G	AB	R	H	2B	3B	HR	RBI	BB	HBP	SH	SF	SO	SB	CS	SLG	OBP
Rodriguez, Jose	R-R	6-0	155	11-12-84	.132	.080	.157	26	76	5	10	1	0	0	5	6	1	2	1	32	1	1	.145	.202
Rodriguez, Manuel	R-R	6-2	180	5-24-83	.193	.294	.150	18	57	5	11	4	0	0	1	4	1	1	0	19	0	0	.263	.258
Sanchez, Salvador	R-R	6-6	195	9-13-85	.209	.193	.216	88	287	36	60	9	0	8	37	16	7	0	4	76	17	5	.324	.264
Tartaglia, Evan	L-L	5-11	165	5-21-82	.206	.375	.149	16	63	7	13	2	0	0	4	10	2	0	2	15	1	3	.238	.315
Valenzuela Jr., Fernando	L-L	5-10	210	9-30-82	.266	.203	.286	80	293	37	78	13	2	9	43	40	6	0	1	45	0	1	.416	.365
Welker, Kris	R-R	6-0	205	9-8-82	.200	.429	.111	17	50	4	10	2	0	0	6	10	0	0	0	11	0	1	.240	.298
Whealy, Blake	R-R	5-11	175	5-27-80	.211	.200	.218	24	90	12	19	4	0	1	6	8	0	2	1	27	0	0	.289	.273

PITCHING	B-T	HT	WT	DOB	W	L	ERA	G	GS	CG	SV	IP	H	R	ER	HR	BB	SO	AVG	vLH	vRH	K/9	BB/9
Brennan, Chris	L-L	6-0	185	12-5-82	0	0	5.59	8	0	0	0	10	5	7	6	0	15	4	.161	.182	.150	3.72	13.97
Brooks, Richard	R-R	6-3	180	7-18-84	8	11	5.17	26	26	1	0	134	161	104	77	10	46	86	.292	.301	.285	5.78	3.09
Chirino, Israel	L-L	6-1	200	11-8-83	1	1	3.43	57	0	0	1	63	47	32	24	4	39	45	.203	.205	.201	6.43	5.57
Cortes, Daniel	R-R	6-5	205	3-4-87	3	9	4.01	20	19	0	0	108	109	61	48	6	38	96	.260	.270	.252	8.02	3.18
Farfan, Alex	R-R	6-3	175	1-6-83	0	0	10.86	21	0	0	0	29	46	40	35	5	33	10	.380	.370	.387	3.10	10.24
Flores, Rafael	R-R	6-7	246	4-26-84	5	6	6.93	23	11	0	0	74	106	67	57	7	20	43	.339	.318	.354	5.23	2.43
Long, Matthew	R-R	6-5	220	2-23-84	3	5	8.02	22	0	0	1	34	51	37	30	5	13	20	.345	.355	.337	5.35	3.48
Moviel, Paul	R-R	6-6	220	9-28-82	1	5	3.13	55	0	0	2	75	66	40	26	7	29	84	.232	.245	.223	10.13	3.50
Omogrosso, Brian	R-R	6-3	230	4-26-84	1	2	3.19	22	0	0	2	37	27	14	13	2	13	23	.209	.140	.253	5.65	3.19
Perez, Oneli	R-R	6-2	163	5-26-83	3	1	0.99	30	0	0	8	36	23	5	4	1	8	42	.172	.220	.133	10.40	1.98
Rice, Jason	R-R	6-0	190	5-13-86	1	6	3.72	44	9	0	6	94	61	46	39	7	65	107	.184	.165	.198	10.21	6.20
Richard, Clayton	L-L	6-5	225	9-12-83	6	6	3.67	18	17	0	0	96	117	47	39	0	28	54	.310	.244	.330	5.08	2.63
Rodriguez, Derek	R-R	6-1	190	5-17-83	6	11	4.64	25	25	0	0	147	149	91	76	10	45	109	.258	.265	.254	6.66	2.75
Rodriguez, Noe	L-L	6-0	165	8-12-84	0	6	3.48	17	10	0	0	54	55	39	21	5	21	65	.253	.214	.263	10.77	3.48
Rote, Ryan	R-R	6-4	225	8-8-82	1	13	5.92	14	12	0	0	62	76	63	41	1	34	33	.303	.306	.301	4.76	4.91
Sabo, Tim	R-R	6-3	215	2-6-84	0	1	7.71	11	0	0	0	19	24	18	16	0	9	6	.308	.290	.319	5.30	4.34
Santeliz, Clevelan	R-R	6-0	160	9-1-86	0	2	6.85	16	0	0	0	24	30	19	18	4	15	21	.319	.306	.328	7.99	5.70
Texeira, Kanekoa	R-R	6-2	190	2-6-86	0	0	4.50	4	0	0	0	6	8	3	3	1	1	2	.333	.364	.308	3.00	1.50
Wesley, John	R-R	6-6	263	10-14-80	1	3	3.66	27	1	0	4	39	39	28	16	1	14	46	.247	.246	.247	10.53	3.20
Williamson, Logan	L-L	6-0	210	3-31-85	1	3	5.02	13	0	0	0	14	20	13	8	1	5	13	.345	.316	.359	8.16	3.14
Woodson, Alexander	L-L	6-0	190	10-10-85	0	1	7.45	3	2	0	0	10	13	8	8	1	1	10	.333	.273	.357	9.31	0.93
Zazueta, Jose	R-R	6-0	204	2-24-87	1	2	10.80	4	4	0	0	18	31	23	22	5	6	13	.369	.371	.367	6.38	2.95

FIELDING

Catcher	PCT	G	PO	A	E	DP	PB
Hernandez	.991	89	575	95	6	8	16
Hollis	.983	12	56	2	1	0	2
Metheny	.937	24	135	14	10	1	7
Ricks	1.000	9	57	3	0	0	2
Welker	.982	15	102	6	2	0	3

First Base	PCT	G	PO	A	E	DP
Allen	.982	95	804	58	16	70
Camacho	.857	1	5	1	1	1
Carter	.944	6	66	2	4	4
Ricks	.—	1	0	0	0	0
Valenzuela Jr.	.985	34	304	19	5	26

Second Base	PCT	G	PO	A	E	DP
C. Acosta	.833	2	1	4	1	0
Blood	.818	6	12	15	6	1

(2B cont.)	PCT	G	PO	A	E	DP
Johnson	.940	65	118	166	18	31
Mesa	.958	37	34	81	5	17
Moreno	.875	2	1	6	1	1
Rodriguez	.976	9	18	22	1	4
Welker	1.000	2	5	4	0	0
Whealy	.915	24	55	64	11	16

Third Base	PCT	G	PO	A	E	DP
C. Acosta	.750	1	1	2	1	0
Camacho	.882	43	21	76	13	5
Mesa	.750	4	0	3	1	0
Metheny	.500	1	2	0	2	1
Ricks	.916	79	48	138	17	8
Rodriguez	.917	8	6	16	2	0
Rodriguez	.722	8	4	9	5	1

Shortstop	PCT	G	PO	A	E	DP
L. Acosta	.918	37	59	119	16	26
Castillo	.959	94	109	269	16	45
Mesa	.875	3	2	5	1	3
Rodriguez	.889	6	6	10	2	1

Outfield	PCT	G	PO	A	E	DP
Camacho	1.000	4	11	0	0	0
Cunningham	.976	87	157	6	4	2
Gomes	.989	79	167	7	2	0
Johnson	1.000	3	4	1	0	0
Metheny	1.000	6	6	0	0	0
Orlando	.976	111	276	10	7	5
Roberts	.966	37	54	3	2	1
Rodriguez	1.000	6	9	0	0	0
Sanchez	.949	78	177	8	10	3
Tartaglia	.909	5	8	2	1	0

Great Falls White Sox — Rookie

Pioneer League

BATTING	B-T	HT	WT	DOB	AVG	vLH	vRH	G	AB	R	H	2B	3B	HR	RBI	BB	HBP	SH	SF	SO	SB	CS	SLG	OBP
Acosta, Christian	R-R	5-11	178	7-14-83	.230	.375	.208	19	61	8	14	4	0	0	3	5	1	1	1	17	0	0	.295	.294
Batista, Franklin	R-R	5-11	155	10-17-84	.197	.154	.208	29	61	10	12	3	0	0	6	7	1	1	1	24	4	0	.246	.286
Carter, Christopher	R-R	6-4	210	12-18-86	.299	.280	.303	69	251	37	75	21	1	15	59	34	8	0	1	70	4	4	.570	.398
Cruz, Lee	R-R	6-2	190	6-13-83	.301	.271	.308	69	269	38	81	17	6	5	39	9	3	3	3	37	1	2	.465	.327
Garcia, Santo	S-L	6-0	168	8-6-84	.241	.268	.227	49	116	15	28	2	0	1	14	10	1	7	0	39	3	2	.284	.307
Gilbert, Archie	R-R	5-8	180	7-8-83	.332	.378	.320	52	187	41	62	13	1	2	26	21	6	4	4	21	35	7	.444	.408
Grace, Michael	R-R	6-1	220	4-27-84	.261	.286	.255	64	234	29	61	14	0	7	32	15	2	5	3	70	0	1	.410	.307
Hunter, Joseph	R-R	6-1	190	12-2-83	.295	.455	.273	25	88	16	26	3	1	4	15	7	7	1	0	21	8	5	.489	.392
Lawrence, Tim	R-R	6-0	175	5-17-83	.264	.333	.247	45	121	23	32	8	0	0	5	14	3	4	0	27	2	2	.331	.355
Madsen, Scott	R-R	6-0	178	4-23-82	.218	.258	.207	39	142	21	31	7	2	0	8	16	6	3	0	47	6	6	.296	.323
Marrero, Christian	L-L	6-1	185	7-30-86	.252	.194	.262	72	242	24	61	17	0	3	24	30	2	5	2	37	1	0	.360	.337
Moreno, Pedro	R-R	5-11	165	7-30-83	.067	.000	.077	7	15	0	1	0	0	0	0	0	0	0	0	5	0	1	.067	.067
Reves, Tyler	R-R	5-11	208	1-15-84	.270	.319	.259	69	248	28	67	14	0	8	27	14	7	1	2	59	2	0	.423	.325
Sharp, Matt	L-R	6-0	205	8-3-82	.265	.182	.278	40	83	15	22	4	0	0	5	16	1	5	0	17	0	1	.313	.390
Shelby, John	R-R	5-10	185	8-6-85	.272	.283	.269	66	250	37	68	12	3	8	36	18	5	5	1	55	8	4	.440	.332
Tavares, Reymundo	R-R	5-10	165	2-7-83	.256	.302	.239	53	160	19	41	7	3	3	18	6	1	6	0	31	1	1	.394	.287
Welker, Kris	R-R	6-0	205	9-8-82	.224	.200	.234	27	67	8	15	3	0	2	4	3	3	3	0	16	1	0	.358	.288

PITCHING	B-T	HT	WT	DOB	W	L	ERA	G	GS	CG	SV	IP	H	R	ER	HR	BB	SO	AVG	vLH	vRH	K/9	BB/9
Brennan, Chris	L-L	6-0	185	12-5-82	0	1	13.50	11	0	0	0	6	12	14	9	0	7	4	.429	.333	.474	6.00	10.50
Cassel, Justin	R-R	6-1	190	9-25-84	3	2	2.97	13	4	0	0	39	38	17	13	1	10	37	.252	.255	.250	8.47	2.29
Corley, Tyson	R-R	6-6	200	1-26-86	0	6	6.75	21	5	0	0	47	56	38	35	2	26	32	.295	.311	.287	6.17	5.01
Day, Tim	L-R	6-4	210	9-22-82	3	3	4.24	14	14	0	0	64	90	53	30	3	7	42	.326	.440	.261	5.94	0.99
Feehan, Patrick	R-R	6-6	220	1-8-84	0	1	8.33	23	0	0	0	27	38	25	25	4	14	32	.328	.395	.295	10.67	4.67
Fields, Joshua	R-R	6-1	180	1-20-80	0	0	1.35	6	0	0	0	7	2	1	1	0	3	6	.167	.000	.222	8.10	4.05
McCulloch, Kyle	R-R	6-3	180	3-20-85	1	1	1.61	6	5	0	0	22	19	15	4	1	7	27	.213	.235	.200	10.88	2.82
Murphey, Timothy	L-L	6-3	170	3-4-85	0	0	4.09	6	2	0	0	11	12	8	5	0	13	8	.293	.235	.333	6.55	10.64
Rocco, Michael	R-R	6-2	180	8-19-85	2	3	3.82	22	1	0	6	38	31	21	16	2	12	53	.212	.256	.194	12.66	2.87
Rote, Ryan	R-R	6-4	225	8-8-82	0	2	8.90	22	0	0	0	29	43	33	29	3	23	24	.347	.375	.333	7.36	7.06
Sabo, Tim	R-R	6-3	215	2-6-84	1	1	5.09	22	0	0	0	23	21	15	13	0	12	32	.233	.346	.188	12.52	7.43
Sanchez, Ramon	R-R	5-11	175	11-3-83	6	4	5.00	15	15	0	0	72	89	57	40	10	28	56	.304	.288	.313	7.00	3.50

	B-T	HT	WT	DOB	W	L	ERA	G	GS	CG	SV	IP	H	R	ER	HR	BB	SO	AVG	vLH	vRH	K/9	BB/9
Santeliz, Clevelan	R-R	6-0	160	9-1-86	1	8	4.77	14	14	0	0	66	62	41	35	9	32	61	.248	.323	.204	8.32	4.36
Spurgeon, Steven	R-R	6-0	180	8-22-83	0	2	3.12	23	0	0	1	40	38	19	14	3	21	34	.239	.208	.255	7.59	4.69
Urena, Andrew	R-R	5-10	190	2-28-84	5	6	5.01	26	0	0	2	32	39	22	18	1	17	38	.307	.212	.340	10.58	4.73
Walters, Nick	L-L	6-2	175	9-30-85	1	1	4.55	28	0	0	1	28	29	16	14	1	16	29	.287	.191	.370	9.43	5.20
Wasylak, David	R-R	6-3	195	12-6-82	0	0	6.58	23	0	0	2	26	24	25	19	2	20	25	.226	.179	.244	8.65	6.92
Williamson, Logan	L-L	6-0	210	3-31-85	5	6	4.11	15	15	0	0	81	79	46	37	8	37	53	.261	.277	.258	5.89	4.11
Wing, Ryan	L-L	6-2	170	2-1-82	0	1	2.92	7	1	0	0	12	10	7	4	1	7	21	.217	.182	.229	15.32	5.11

FIELDING

Catcher	PCT	G	PO	A	E	DP	PB
Grace	1.000	1	5	1	0	0	2
Reves	.955	8	38	4	2	0	5
Sharp	.965	17	103	7	4	1	7
Tavares	.990	50	365	34	4	1	14
Welker	.991	22	97	16	1	3	2

First Base	PCT	G	PO	A	E	DP
Carter	.973	62	558	29	16	62
Grace	1.000	4	46	1	0	2
Moreno	—	1	0	0	0	0
Reves	1.000	4	35	0	0	2
Sharp	.989	11	87	7	1	6
Welker	.909	1	9	1	1	1

Second Base	PCT	G	PO	A	E	DP
Acosta	.889	3	2	6	1	1
Batista	.933	5	4	10	1	5
Lawrence	.956	26	39	69	5	14
Madsen	.857	1	0	6	1	0
Moreno	.882	3	9	6	2	1
Shelby	.964	43	91	123	8	36

Third Base	PCT	G	PO	A	E	DP
Acosta	.935	10	5	24	2	3
Batista	.833	4	1	9	2	0
Grace	.856	59	39	121	27	9
Lawrence	.800	5	4	12	4	0
Madsen	1.000	3	1	3	0	0

Shortstop	PCT	G	PO	A	E	DP
Acosta	.842	4	7	9	3	4

	PCT	G	PO	A	E	DP
Batista	.857	16	26	34	10	7
Lawrence	.792	5	6	13	5	0
Madsen	.916	35	47	105	14	26
Moreno	.600	1	1	2	2	1
Shelby	.945	22	28	76	6	12

Outfield	PCT	G	PO	A	E	DP
Batista	—	2	0	0	0	0
Cruz	.894	64	71	13	10	2
Garcia	.951	46	38	1	2	1
Gilbert	.955	49	85	0	4	0
Hunter	.977	19	39	4	1	1
Marrero	1.000	69	77	4	0	1
Reves	.875	6	7	0	1	0
Tavares	1.000	4	6	0	0	0

Bristol Sox — Rookie

Appalachian League

BATTING	B-T	HT	WT	DOB	AVG	vLH	vRH	G	AB	R	H	2B	3B	HR	RBI	BB	HBP	SH	SF	SO	SB	CS	SLG	OBP
Acosta, Leonardo	R-R	6-2	165	4-29-86	.184	.093	.226	43	136	8	25	2	1	0	7	13	4	4	1	41	1	0	.213	.273
Causey, Marcos	R-R	5-10	195	7-4-84	.186	.226	.154	25	70	9	13	0	0	0	2	4	0	1	1	19	0	0	.186	.227
Cody, Marquise	L-L	5-10	182	10-7-84	.111	—	.111	3	9	1	1	0	0	0	0	0	0	0	0	3	0	0	.222	.111
Enuco, Matthew	R-R	6-0	185	1-21-84	.222	.246	.210	50	185	22	41	9	1	3	18	15	6	4	1	23	5	1	.330	.300
Espinal, Jeury	R-R	6-3	196	12-4-86	.236	.246	.232	51	182	12	43	10	0	3	22	15	1	0	3	36	0	1	.341	.294
Gartrell, Maurice	R-R	6-2	220	1-14-84	.308	.305	.310	61	214	41	66	16	1	4	33	43	7	0	1	48	4	1	.449	.438
Gerst, Kent	L-R	5-10	170	2-6-88	.236	.210	.247	56	212	25	50	1	2	0	16	17	5	6	1	48	4	7	.259	.306
Hash, Rylee	B-R	6-2	205	3-31-88	.273	.111	.333	13	33	4	9	2	0	0	2	0	0	0	0	9	0	0	.333	.273
Inouye, Matthew	R-R	5-10	165	5-20-84	.258	.194	.288	57	194	23	50	9	1	4	31	20	11	1	3	32	4	3	.376	.355
Jordan, Daniel	R-R	6-0	190	5-9-86	.184	.163	.194	42	136	10	25	4	0	2	18	17	1	1	0	55	1	0	.257	.279
Madsen, Scott	R-R	6-0	190	4-23-82	.314	.194	.365	28	105	18	33	8	1	0	14	10	3	2	0	23	6	1	.410	.390
Mead, Andrew	R-R	6-1	190	4-17-84	.196	.250	.175	47	158	25	31	9	1	1	11	12	1	5	0	46	0	0	.285	.257
Morgan, Joshua	R-R	6-2	215	7-20-84	.252	.298	.235	55	214	21	53	14	3	4	31	14	2	0	1	42	0	1	.405	.304
O'Donnell, Brendon	R-R	5-11	175	10-15-84	.224	.167	.279	31	85	14	19	1	1	1	8	9	4	1	1	27	4	0	.294	.323
Rodriguez, Jose	R-R	6-0	155	11-12-84	.280	.214	.319	27	75	11	21	6	0	0	8	3	1	1	0	21	0	0	.360	.353
Valdez, Baltazar	R-R	6-1	215	1-7-83	.215	.294	.169	29	93	11	20	4	0	2	7	11	2	1	1	20	0	0	.323	.308
Wolff, John	L-R	6-0	180	11-3-83	.143	—	.143	3	7	1	1	0	0	0	0	2	0	0	0	2	0	0	.143	.333

PITCHING	B-T	HT	WT	DOB	W	L	ERA	G	GS	CG	SV	IP	H	R	ER	HR	BB	SO	AVG	vLH	vRH	K/9	BB/9
Brujan, Rafael	L-L	6-1	165	5-23-85	1	2	5.40	17	0	0	0	17	10	16	10	0	17	29	.156	.222	.130	15.66	9.18
Carter, Anthony	L-R	6-2	170	4-4-86	2	8	7.67	13	13	0	0	63	88	58	54	7	21	35	.321	.320	.322	4.97	2.98
Edwards, Justin	L-L	5-11	170	9-7-87	3	7	5.30	12	12	0	0	53	69	39	31	6	21	42	.319	.444	.302	7.18	3.59
Escolano, Enrique	R-R	6-7	185	5-4-87	0	0	5.40	6	0	0	0	8	8	5	5	0	10	4	.242	.400	.174	4.32	10.80
Evans, Raleigh	L-L	6-0	185	2-15-85	1	2	4.74	7	4	0	0	25	24	17	13	0	13	26	.247	.077	.274	9.49	4.74
Garcia, Alvin	R-R	6-0	195	3-13-87	1	1	2.60	18	1	0	1	28	20	8	8	2	23	33	.198	.231	.187	10.73	7.48
Gomez, Domingo	R-R	6-1	188	3-4-84	1	1	4.50	25	0	0	0	28	30	16	14	1	14	22	.270	.290	.263	7.07	4.50
Jean, Jacob	L-L	6-1	175	5-24-83	0	1	20.06	12	0	0	0	12	17	29	26	1	18	8	.340	.250	.382	6.17	13.89
Moreno, Juan	R-R	6-3	176	11-29-86	7	5	4.60	13	13	0	0	72	81	43	37	8	16	65	.277	.308	.261	8.09	1.99
Perez, Wander	L-L	6-3	168	1-5-85	1	0	4.22	17	1	0	0	32	32	20	15	2	20	25	.250	.143	.280	7.03	5.63
Segura, Wascar	R-R	6-3	180	7-4-85	0	0	2.25	9	0	0	0	16	7	6	4	3	7	11	.127	.143	.122	6.19	3.94
Smith, Colt	R-L	6-1	190	6-14-85	0	4	8.74	19	0	0	0	23	41	31	22	0	15	16	.366	.565	.315	6.35	5.96
Stires, Justin	R-R	6-1	190	3-3-84	0	3	4.58	14	0	0	0	39	26	24	20	0	35	27	.188	.229	.167	6.18	8.01
Texeira, Kanekoa	R-R	6-1	190	2-6-86	1	2	0.76	19	0	0	3	24	15	3	2	0	5	29	.179	.077	.224	11.03	1.90
Torres, Gaury	R-R	5-11	180	6-21-85	0	0	3.38	16	0	0	1	24	24	13	9	2	14	26	.239	.174	.261	9.75	5.25
Woodson, Alexander	L-L	6-0	190	10-10-85	2	3	4.03	16	5	0	1	45	44	24	20	2	17	54	.254	.250	.255	10.88	3.43
Zazueta, Jose	R-R	6-0	204	2-24-87	2	3	3.27	12	7	0	0	41	35	24	15	1	17	27	.215	.244	.203	5.88	3.70

FIELDING

Catcher	PCT	G	PO	A	E	DP	PB
Hash	1.000	4	26	1	0	0	2
Inouye	.982	39	285	34	6	1	8
Jordan	.981	13	87	14	2	2	6
Valdez	.961	11	68	6	3	2	5

First Base	PCT	G	PO	A	E	DP
Gartrell	.945	6	49	3	3	1
Jordan	.993	18	142	8	1	12
Morgan	.985	41	371	13	6	36
Rodriguez	1.000	1	1	0	0	0
Valdez	1.000	1	3	0	0	0
Wolff	1.000	1	7	0	0	0

Second Base	PCT	G	PO	A	E	DP
Acosta	1.000	1	0	2	0	0
Enuco	.934	48	78	121	14	22
Inouye	1.000	1	3	2	0	1
Madsen	.974	7	18	19	1	3
Rodriguez	.903	6	13	15	3	2
Wolff	1.000	2	3	7	0	1

Third Base	PCT	G	PO	A	E	DP
Espinal	.916	51	26	94	11	7
Madsen	1.000	1	0	2	0	0
Rodriguez	.778	17	9	33	12	4

Shortstop	PCT	G	PO	A	E	DP
Acosta	.919	42	61	155	19	24
Enuco	1.000	1	0	4	0	0
Madsen	.920	19	27	54	7	8
Rodriguez	.857	4	6	12	3	1

Outfield	PCT	G	PO	A	E	DP
Causey	.926	22	23	2	2	0
Cody	.667	3	2	0	1	0
Gartrell	.946	49	99	6	6	1
Gerst	.982	54	108	2	2	0
Jordan	1.000	1	2	0	0	0
Mead	.986	45	68	4	1	0
O'Donnell	.955	28	39	3	2	1

BY JOHN FAY

The Reds made significant strides on the field and in the front office in 2006, yet saw their season come to a familiar close as they missed the postseason for the 11th consecutive season.

Cincinnati got off to a great start and was in playoff contention until the last two days of the season. The team's starting pitching, long a problem, proved to be a strength as the Reds ranked seventh in ERA in the National League.

The team posted its best record since 2000 at 80-82 but couldn't escape a late-season collapse, losing 10 of 12 in late August and early September to fall back just as the NL Central looked like it would be winnable.

Overall, though, the season was eventful and productive. New ownership took over in January and team president Bob Castellini seemed to abandon his predecessor's build-for-the-future philosophy by promising "to bring championship baseball back to Cincinnati."

Castellini fired general manager Dan O'Brien three days after taking over and on Feb. 8 hired former Twins assistant GM Wayne Krivsky, who quickly made up for lost time.

Krivsky dealt outfielder Wily Mo Pena to Boston for righthander Bronson Arroyo on March 20 and brought in catcher David Ross a day later. Krivsky obtained second baseman Brandon Phillips from the Indians shortly after the season began.

The moves worked.

Arroyo went 14-11, 3.29 with a career-high 184 strikeouts. Ross played in a career-high 90 games and hit .255/.353/.579 with 21 home runs and 52 RBIs in 247 at-bats. Phillips thrived as the Reds everyday second baseman, hitting .276/.324/.427 with 17 home runs and 75

PLAYERS OF THE YEAR

MAJOR LEAGUE: Bronson Arroyo, rhp

Arroyo provided stability atop the Reds rotation, leading the club in innings (240) and ERA (3.29). The former Pirate, who helped the Red Sox to a World Series title in 2004, enjoyed his best season as a professional, setting career-highs in six categories, including strikeouts (184) and complete games (3).

MINOR LEAGUE: Joey Votto, 1b

Votto edged Homer Bailey by batting .319/.408/.547 with 22 home runs and 77 RBIs at Double-A Chattanooga. Votto's 46 doubles tied Rockies' farmhand Seth Smith for tops in the minors, and he was among the minor league's best in hits (162). He also stole 24 bases in 31 attempts and scored 85 runs.

ORGANIZATION STATISTICS

RBIs.

The Reds endured a pair of five-game losing streaks and a six-game slide but still entered the all-star break trailing the Cardinals by just two games for the NL Central lead.

Krivsky, attempting to strengthen a bullpen that converted just 36-of-60 saves for the season, made his boldest move by trading right fielder Austin Kearns and shortstop Felipe Lopez to the Nationals as part of an eight-player deal that centered around relievers Gary Majewski and lefthander Bill Bray. Krivsky also obtained closer Eddie Guardado from the Mariners and brought in lefthanders Rheal Cormier and Scott Schoeneweis and righthander Ryan Franklin.

By July 14 the Reds were back in the wild-card lead, though in the long run the moves did not give the Reds the extra push they needed.

One move Krivsky did not make was calling-up pitching prospect Homer Bailey, who went a combined 10-6, 2.47 in 139 innings at high Class A Sarasota and Double-A Chattanooga.

Despite up-and-down play, the Reds were in the postseason race until a make-or-break late-season West Coast trip. They won the first of a 10-game road trip before the bottom fell out. They lost six straight and nine of 10. The offense was suddenly silent. They averaged 2.7 runs over the next 22 games and went 6-16 as a result.

Along the way, Ken Griffey Jr. dislocated a toe and was lost for nearly all of September.

The Reds recovered during the last two weeks of the season and a late slide by the Cardinals left the Reds 2½ back with four to play. But the miracle did not happen and the Reds finished 3½ out of first at season's end, leading to reflection on games got away.

"I don't know which games they would have been," Krivsky said. "I think every team can do that . . . I don't look at that at all.

"It happened so fast. It's kind of been a blur. When we were 36-24, you really thought we had it going. We had some down times, but there were a lot of positives that went on during the year."

ORGANIZATION LEADERS

BATTING		*Minimum 250 at-bats
*AVG	Dorn, Daniel, Billings	.354
R	Strait, Cody, Sarasota/Louisville	99
H	Votto, Joey, Chattanooga	165
TB	Votto, Joey, Chattanooga	284
2B	Votto, Joey, Chattanooga	46
3B	Anderson, Drew, Sarasota/Chattanooga	12
HR	Votto, Joey, Chattanooga	23
RBI	Strait, Cody, Sarasota/Louisville	87
BB	Votto, Joey, Chattanooga	79
SO	Szymanski, Brandon, Dayton	191
SB	Strait, Cody, Sarasota/Louisville	56
*OBP	Dorn, Daniel, Billings	.457
*SLG	Dorn, Daniel, Billings	.573
XBH	Votto, Joey, Chattanooga	71

PITCHING		#Minimum 75 innings
W	Cueto, Johnny, Dayton/Sarasota	15
L	Lecure, Sam, Sarasota	12
#ERA	Bailey, Homer, Sarasota/Chattanooga	2.47
G	Chiasson, Scott, Louisville	60
CG	Cueto, Johnny, Dayton/Sarasota	3
SV	Chiasson, Scott, Louisville	29
IP	Hall, Josh, Louisville/Chattanooga	152
BB	Pelland, Tyler, Chattanooga	93
SO	Bailey, Homer, Sarasota/Chattanooga	156
#AVG	Bailey, Homer, Sarasota/Chattanooga	.198

Cincinnati Reds	MLB

National League

BATTING	B-T	HT	WT	DOB	AVG	vLH	vRH	G	AB	R	H	2B	3B	HR	RBI	BB	HBP	SH	SF	SO	SB	CS	SLG	OBP
Abad, Andy	L-L	6-0	210	8-25-72	.000	—	.000	5	3	0	0	0	0	0	0	2	0	0	0	0	0	0	.000	.400
Aurilia, Rich	R-R	6-1	190	9-2-71	.300	.347	.276	122	440	61	132	25	1	23	70	34	1	2	4	51	3	0	.518	.349
Castro, Juan	R-R	5-11	195	6-20-72	.284	.344	.254	54	95	8	27	5	1	2	14	5	0	0	0	13	0	1	.421	.320
Clayton, Royce	R-R	6-0	200	1-2-70	.235	.191	.255	50	149	13	35	8	0	2	13	11	1	2	1	32	6	3	.329	.290
2-team (87 Washington)					.258	—	—	137	454	49	117	30	1	2	40	30	5	7	6	85	14	6	.341	.307
Denorfia, Chris	R-R	6-0	195	7-15-80	.283	.317	.262	49	106	14	30	6	0	1	7	11	1	2	0	21	1	1	.368	.356
Dunn, Adam	L-R	6-6	275	11-9-79	.234	.270	.215	160	561	99	131	24	0	40	92	112	6	1	3	194	7	0	.490	.365
Encarnacion, Edwin	R-R	6-1	195	1-7-83	.276	.248	.287	117	406	60	112	33	1	15	72	41	13	0	3	78	6	3	.473	.359
Freel, Ryan	R-R	5-10	180	3-8-76	.271	.303	.261	132	454	67	123	30	2	8	27	57	9	3	0	98	37	11	.399	.363
Griffey Jr., Ken	L-L	6-3	220	11-21-69	.252	.204	.278	109	428	62	108	19	0	27	72	39	2	0	3	78	0	0	.486	.316
Harris, Brendan	R-R	6-1	200	8-26-80	.200	.500	.000	8	10	2	2	0	0	1	1	1	0	0	0	4	0	0	.500	.273
2-team (17 Washington)					.238	—	—	25	42	5	10	2	0	1	3	4	1	0	0	7	0	0	.357	.319
Hatteberg, Scott	L-R	6-1	210	12-14-69	.289	.231	.302	141	456	62	132	28	0	13	51	74	3	2	4	41	2	2	.436	.389
Hollandsworth, Todd	L-L	6-2	225	4-20-73	.265	.000	.273	34	68	6	18	6	0	1	8	6	0	0	0	19	0	1	.397	.324
Hopper, Norris	R-R	5-10	200	3-24-79	.359	.571	.111	21	39	6	14	1	0	1	5	6	0	1	1	4	2	2	.462	.435
Kearns, Austin	R-R	6-3	235	5-20-80	.274	.316	.257	87	325	53	89	21	1	16	50	35	5	0	3	85	7	1	.492	.351
2-team (63 Washington)					.264	—	—	150	537	86	142	33	2	24	86	76	10	1	5	135	9	4	.467	.363
LaRue, Jason	R-R	5-11	205	3-19-74	.194	.235	.179	72	191	22	37	5	0	8	21	27	8	3	1	51	1	0	.346	.317
Lopez, Felipe	B-R	6-1	185	5-12-80	.268	.207	.291	85	343	55	92	14	1	9	30	47	0	3	1	66	23	6	.394	.355
2-team (71 Washington)					.274	—	—	156	617	98	169	27	3	11	52	81	2	11	3	126	44	12	.381	.348
McCracken, Quinton	B-R	5-8	185	8-16-70	.208	.143	.217	45	53	5	11	1	1	1	2	4	0	3	0	9	2	0	.321	.263
Olmedo, Ray	B-R	5-11	155	5-31-81	.205	.333	.184	30	44	5	9	2	0	1	4	4	0	0	0	4	1	0	.318	.271
Phillips, Brandon	R-R	6-0	195	6-28-81	.276	.299	.268	149	536	65	148	28	1	17	75	35	6	4	6	88	25	2	.427	.324
Ross, David	R-R	6-2	205	3-19-77	.255	.316	.228	90	247	37	63	15	1	21	52	37	3	4	5	75	0	0	.579	.353
Ross, Cody	R-L	5-9	205	12-23-80	.200	.250	.000	2	5	0	1	0	0	0	0	0	0	0	0	2	0	0	.200	.200
3-team (91 Florida, 8 Los Angeles)					.227	—	—	101	269	34	61	12	2	13	46	22	4	1	2	65	1	1	.431	.293
Valentin, Javier	B-R	5-10	210	9-19-75	.269	.111	.286	92	186	24	50	6	1	8	27	13	0	0	2	29	0	0	.441	.313
Watson, Brandon	L-R	6-1	170	9-30-81	—	—	—	1	0	0	0	0	0	0	0	0	0	0	0	0	1	0	—	—
2-team (9 Washington)					.179	—	—	10	28	0	5	0	0	0	0	0	0	0	3	1	2	.179	.207
Wise, Dewayne	L-L	6-1	180	2-24-78	.184	.000	.206	31	38	3	7	2	0	1	0	0	2	0	6	0	0	.237	.184
Womack, Tony	L-R	5-9	175	9-25-69	.222	.000	.250	9	18	1	4	2	0	0	3	4	0	1	0	3	0	0	.333	.364
2-team (19 Chicago)					.265	—	—	28	68	7	18	3	0	1	5	8	0	4	0	7	1	1	.353	.342

PITCHING	B-T	HT	WT	DOB	W	L	ERA	G	GS	CG	SV	IP	H	R	ER	HR	BB	SO	AVG	vLH	vRH	K/9	BB/9
Arroyo, Bronson	R-R	6-5	190	2-24-77	14	11	3.29	35	35	3	0	241	222	98	88	31	64	184	.243	.282	.206	6.88	2.39
Belisle, Matt	R-R	6-3	195	6-6-80	2	0	3.60	30	2	0	0	40	43	18	16	5	19	26	.277	.240	.295	5.85	4.28
Bray, Bill	L-L	6-3	215	6-5-83	2	1	4.23	29	0	0	2	28	33	16	13	3	9	23	.292	.372	.243	7.48	2.93
2-team (19 Washington)					3	2	4.09	48	0	0	2	50	57	27	23	5	18	39	—	—	—	6.93	3.20
Burns Jr., Mike	R-R	6-1	210	7-14-78	0	0	8.78	11	0	0	0	13	30	13	13	2	3	9	.469	.350	.523	6.08	2.03
Claussen, Brandon	R-L	6-1	200	5-1-79	3	8	6.19	14	14	0	0	77	93	56	53	14	28	57	.301	.164	.331	6.66	3.27
Coffey, Todd	R-R	6-5	230	9-9-80	6	7	3.58	81	0	0	8	78	85	34	31	7	27	60	.274	.347	.242	6.92	3.12
Cormier, Rheal	L-L	5-10	195	4-23-67	0	1	4.50	21	0	0	0	14	21	7	7	3	4	6	.350	.345	.355	3.86	2.57
2-team (43 Philadelphia)					2	3	2.44	64	0	0	0	48	48	13	13	5	17	19	—	—	—	3.56	3.19
Franklin, Ryan	R-R	6-3	190	3-5-73	5	2	4.44	20	0	0	0	24	27	14	12	3	16	18	.297	.250	.313	6.66	5.92
2-team (46 Philadelphia)					6	7	4.54	66	0	0	0	77	86	42	39	13	33	43	—	—	—	5.00	3.84
Germano, Justin	R-R	6-3	205	8-6-82	0	1	5.40	2	1	0	0	7	8	4	4	1	3	8	.296	.000	.381	10.80	4.05
Gosling, Mike	L-L	6-2	210	9-23-80	0	0	13.50	1	0	0	0	1	1	2	2	1	1	1	.200	.000	.250	6.75	6.75
Guardado, Eddie	R-L	6-0	205	10-2-70	0	0	1.29	15	0	0	8	14	15	5	2	2	2	17	.278	.091	.326	10.93	1.29
Hammond, Chris	L-L	6-1	210	1-21-66	1	1	6.91	29	0	0	0	29	36	23	22	5	5	23	.303	.286	.314	7.22	1.57
Harang, Aaron	R-R	6-7	270	5-9-78	16	11	3.76	36	35	6	0	234	242	109	98	28	56	216	.269	.267	.270	8.30	2.15
Johnson, Jason	R-R	6-6	225	10-27-73	0	0	3.12	4	0	0	0	9	11	5	3	1	4	4	.297	.357	.261	4.15	0.00
Kim, Sun-Woo	R-R	6-1	190	9-4-77	0	1	5.40	2	1	0	0	7	7	4	4	3	0	4	.259	.333	.167	5.40	0.00
2-team (6 Colorado)					0	1	12.51	8	1	0	0	13	24	19	19	5	8	8	—	—	—	5.27	5.27
Lohse, Kyle	R-R	6-2	200	10-4-78	3	5	4.57	12	11	0	0	63	70	33	32	7	19	51	.288	.294	.284	7.29	2.71
Majewski, Gary	R-R	6-1	215	2-26-80	1	2	8.40	19	0	0	0	15	30	14	14	1	4	9	.435	.400	.455	5.40	2.40
2-team (46 Washington)					4	4	4.61	65	0	0	0	70	79	38	36	5	29	43	—	—	—	5.50	3.71
Mays, Joe	B-R	6-1	200	12-10-75	0	1	7.33	7	4	0	0	27	40	23	22	4	12	16	.342	.327	.354	5.33	4.00
Mercker, Kent	L-L	6-2	205	2-1-68	1	1	4.13	37	0	0	1	28	28	15	13	6	11	17	.259	.260	.259	5.40	3.49
Michalak, Chris	L-L	6-2	195	1-4-71	2	4	4.89	8	6	0	0	35	42	21	19	6	16	18	.304	.276	.312	2.57	4.11
Milton, Eric	L-L	6-3	205	8-4-75	8	8	5.19	26	26	0	0	153	163	94	88	29	42	90	.269	.216	.286	5.31	2.48
Ramirez, Elizardo	R-R	6-0	180	1-28-83	4	9	5.37	21	19	0	0	104	123	70	62	14	29	69	.293	.291	.294	5.97	2.51
Schoeneweis, Scott	L-L	6-0	190	10-2-73	2	0	0.63	16	0	0	3	14	9	1	1	1	8	11	.176	.133	.194	6.91	5.02
Shackelford, Brian	L-L	6-1	195	8-30-76	1	0	7.16	26	0	0	0	16	18	13	13	4	10	15	.269	.175	.407	8.27	5.51
Standridge, Jason	R-R	6-4	230	11-9-78	1	1	4.82	21	0	0	0	19	17	14	10	2	14	18	.239	.200	.261	8.68	6.75
Weathers, David	R-R	6-3	230	9-25-69	4	4	3.54	67	0	0	12	74	61	31	29	12	34	50	.226	.219	.230	6.11	4.15
White, Rick	R-R	6-4	240	12-23-68	1	0	6.26	26	0	0	1	27	34	23	19	5	5	17	.318	.333	.311	5.60	1.65
2-team (38 Philadelphia)					4	1	5.15	64	0	0	1	64	72	44	37	8	20	40	—	—	—	5.57	2.78
Williams, Dave	L-L	6-3	230	1-12-79	2	3	7.20	8	8	0	0	40	54	34	32	9	16	16	.321	.258	.336	3.60	3.60
2-team (6 New York)					5	4	6.52	14	13	0	0	69	93	52	50	14	20	32	—	—	—	4.17	2.61
Yan, Esteban	R-R	6-4	255	6-22-75	1	0	3.60	14	0	0	1	15	13	7	6	4	7	8	.245	.211	.265	4.80	4.20

FIELDING

Catcher	PCT	G	PO	A	E	DP	PB
LaRue	.995	63	374	38	2	9	3
Ross	.985	75	480	33	8	5	4

	PCT	G	PO	A	E	DP
Valentin	.974	46	244	20	7	1	2
First Base	PCT	G	PO	A	E	DP
Aurilia	.994	47	302	26	2	34

	PCT	G	PO	A	E	DP
Dunn	.941	2	15	1	1	2
Encarnacion	1.000	2	9	0	0	1
Hatteberg	.996	131	1002	69	4	86

2006 PERFORMANCE

General manager: Wayne Krivsky. **Farm director:** Johnny Almaraz. **Scouting director:** Chris Buckley.

Class	Team	League	W	L	PCT	Finish*	Manager	Affiliate Since
Majors	Cincinnati	National	80	82	.494	7th (16)	Jerry Narron	—
Triple-A	Louisville RiverBats	International	75	68	.524	6th (14)	Rick Sweet	2000
Double-A	Chattanooga Lookouts	Southern	81	59	.579	2nd (10)	Jayhawk Owens	1988
High A	Sarasota Reds	Florida State	66	73	.475	10th (12)	Donnie Scott	2005
Low A	Dayton Dragons	Midwest	67	73	.479	9th (14)	Buddy Bailey	2000
Rookie	Billings Mustangs	Pioneer	51	25	.671	1st (8)	Rick Burleson	1974
Rookie	GCL Reds	Gulf Coast	18	34	.346	13th (13)	Luis Aguayo	1999
OVERALL 2006 MINOR LEAGUE RECORD			358	332	.519	11th (30)		

*Finish in overall standings (No. of teams in league). +League champion

Second Base	PCT	G	PO	A	E	DP
Aurilia	1.000	10	13	15	0	2
Castro	1.000	1	0	2	0	0
Freel	.980	13	23	25	1	2
Harris	1.000	3	4	3	0	2
Olmedo	.900	5	5	13	2	2
Phillips	.977	142	331	334	16	83
Womack	1.000	5	11	17	0	3

Third Base	PCT	G	PO	A	E	DP
Aurilia	.953	52	24	78	5	7

Valentin 1.000 2 2 0 0 0

	PCT	G	PO	A	E	DP
Castro	1.000	20	4	16	0	2
Encarnacion	.916	111	74	197	25	17
Freel	1.000	13	7	25	0	2
Olmedo	—	3	0	0	0	0

Shortstop	PCT	G	PO	A	E	DP
Aurilia	.991	26	37	68	1	17
Castro	.985	27	23	42	1	11
Clayton	.958	43	60	100	7	15
Lopez	.959	84	98	227	14	45
Olmedo	.909	4	4	6	1	3
Phillips	.800	3	1	3	1	0

Outfield	PCT	G	PO	A	E	DP
Denorfia	1.000	37	58	2	0	1
Dunn	.960	156	279	7	12	1
Freel	.980	105	238	12	5	1
Griffey Jr.	.979	100	229	6	5	0
Hollandsworth	1.000	20	23	1	0	0
Hopper	1.000	15	27	2	0	1
Kearns	.991	85	207	5	2	1
McCracken	.955	15	21	0	1	0
Olmedo	—	1	0	0	0	0
Ross	1.000	1	1	0	0	0
Wise	.950	18	18	1	1	0

Louisville Bats

Triple-A

International League

BATTING	B-T	HT	WT	DOB	AVG	vLH	vRH	G	AB	R	H	2B	3B	HR	RBI	BB	HBP	SH	SF	SO	SB	CS	SLG	OBP
Abad, Andy	L-L	6-0	210	8-25-72	.267	.295	.259	82	266	36	71	12	0	9	32	26	6	5	1	31	0	1	.414	.344
Bannon, Jeff	R-R	6-4	185	8-21-79	.250	.281	.236	66	212	18	53	17	1	4	32	9	1	0	2	42	2	1	.396	.281
Bergolla, William	R-R	6-0	175	2-4-83	.279	.252	.288	114	416	46	116	21	2	2	33	22	2	13	2	47	14	8	.353	.317
Buchanan, Brian	R-R	6-4	230	7-21-73	.179	.115	.212	24	78	9	14	2	0	3	10	5	1	0	1	19	4	0	.321	.235
Castellano, John	R-R	5-11	180	9-8-77	.200	.000	.250	3	10	0	2	0	0	0	0	0	0	0	0	3	0	0	.200	.200
Cruz, Jacob	L-L	6-0	215	1-28-73	.250	.000	.375	3	12	1	3	1	0	1	3	0	0	0	0	2	0	0	.500	.250
2-team (55 Norfolk)					.287	—	—	58	157	19	45	16	0	1	20	22	0	0	0	33	0	0	.408	.374
Denorfia, Chris	R-R	6-0	195	7-15-80	.349	.311	.365	83	312	46	109	19	1	7	45	34	1	1	5	41	15	1	.484	.409
Encarnacion, Edwin	R-R	6-1	195	1-7-83	.306	.250	.313	10	36	6	11	3	0	1	1	2	0	0	0	11	0	0	.472	.342
Garthwaite, Jay	R-R	6-2	220	11-26-80	.000	.000	.000	2	4	0	0	0	0	0	0	0	0	0	0	1	0	0	.000	.000
Griffin, Michael	R-R	5-9	200	10-1-83	.000	.000	.000	1	3	0	0	0	0	0	0	0	0	0	0	1	0	0	.000	.000
Gutierrez, Jesse	R-R	6-2	195	6-16-78	.282	.258	.294	119	397	46	112	27	2	10	61	49	7	0	2	74	0	0	.436	.369
Hanigan, Ryan	R-R	6-0	195	8-16-80	.154	.500	.091	8	13	2	2	0	0	0	1	6	0	0	0	2	0	0	.154	.421
Harris, Brendan	R-R	6-1	200	8-26-80	.324	.378	.306	43	148	22	48	14	1	5	28	14	1	1	1	29	2	0	.534	.384
Herr, Aaron	R-R	6-1	200	3-7-81	.274	.263	.279	19	62	14	17	3	0	2	6	7	3	0	0	16	1	0	.419	.375
Holbert, Aaron	R-R	6-1	180	1-9-73	.000	.000	—	1	1	0	0	0	0	0	0	0	0	0	0	0	0	0	.000	.000
Hopper, Norris	R-R	5-10	200	3-24-79	.347	.363	.341	98	383	47	133	11	3	0	26	20	0	5	2	25	25	7	.392	.378
Jorgensen, Ryan	R-R	6-2	220	5-4-79	.213	.222	.210	74	230	25	49	9	0	8	30	31	4	2	2	57	1	0	.357	.315
Kata, Matt	B-R	6-1	195	3-14-78	.263	.278	.256	113	331	45	87	20	4	9	34	18	10	4	3	48	4	4	.429	.318
LaRue, Jason	R-R	5-11	205	3-19-74	.250	.200	.333	2	8	1	2	1	0	0	0	0	0	0	0	1	0	0	.375	.250
Long, Terrence	L-L	6-1	200	2-29-76	.229	.250	.225	15	48	2	11	3	0	0	6	2	0	0	0	10	0	0	.292	.260
2-team (69 Columbus)					.269	—	—	84	308	31	83	16	1	10	44	21	1	0	0	63	0	0	.425	.318
Menechino, Frank	R-R	5-8	200	1-7-71	.250	.000	.333	6	16	3	4	2	0	0	1	1	0	0	0	4	0	0	.375	.294
2-team (12 Columbus)					.193	—	—	18	57	9	11	3	0	3	7	4	2	0	0	9	0	0	.404	.270
Olmedo, Ray	B-R	5-11	155	5-31-81	.282	.380	.247	100	383	47	108	20	3	3	29	34	3	8	2	71	17	6	.373	.344
Patchett, Gary	R-R	6-2	180	9-25-78	.143	.000	.250	6	7	0	1	0	0	0	0	0	0	0	0	3	0	0	.143	.143
Ross, Cody	R-R	5-9	205	12-23-80	.340	.357	.333	15	50	11	17	1	0	3	6	13	1	0	0	12	2	0	.540	.484
Sanchez, Alex	L-L	5-10	180	8-26-76	.225	.194	.237	38	129	8	29	1	0	0	4	5	1	4	0	17	5	2	.233	.259
Sardinha, Dane	R-R	6-0	215	4-8-79	.175	.125	.191	71	229	19	40	7	0	2	10	15	2	2	1	64	0	0	.231	.231
Snyder, Earl	R-R	6-0	210	5-6-76	.257	.336	.227	127	463	58	119	25	2	17	77	43	3	0	9	99	1	0	.430	.319
Strait, Cody	R-R	6-1	185	5-28-83	.100	.000	.167	3	10	2	1	0	1	0	1	2	0	0	0	0	0	0	.300	.250
Stratton, Robert	R-R	6-4	250	10-7-77	.243	.300	.230	29	107	13	26	6	0	6	14	8	0	0	0	35	0	0	.467	.296
2-team (24 Columbus)					.242	—	—	53	207	23	50	9	0	13	37	15	1	0	1	75	0	1	.473	.295
Watson, Brandon	L-R	6-1	170	9-30-81	.270	.267	.271	42	137	16	37	3	0	0	8	11	0	4	0	12	6	2	.292	.324
Wise, Dewayne	L-L	6-1	180	2-24-78	.266	.146	.310	44	154	27	41	10	4	4	21	13	4	7	2	29	6	2	.461	.335

PITCHING	B-T	HT	WT	DOB	W	L	ERA	G	GS	CG	SV	IP	H	R	ER	HR	BB	SO	AVG	vLH	vRH	K/9	BB/9
Abad, Andy	L-L	6-0	210	8-25-72	0	0	0.00	1	0	0	0	1	0	0	0	0	0	1	.000	—	.000	9.00	0.00
Alvarado, Carlos	R-R	6-4	210	1-24-78	0	1	3.86	2	0	0	0	2	2	1	1	1	0	1	.250	.500	.167	3.86	0.00
Avery, James	R-R	6-1	210	6-10-84	0	0	9.00	1	1	0	0	4	5	4	4	1	2	1	.333	.200	.400	2.25	4.50
Bausher, Tim	R-R	6-4	200	4-23-79	0	1	13.50	2	0	0	0	3	8	6	5	2	2	2	.444	.286	.545	5.40	5.40
2-team (37 Pawtucket)					4	4	5.30	39	2	0	0	73	85	47	43	6	39	42	—	—	—	5.18	4.81
Belisle, Matt	R-R	6-3	195	6-6-80	1	0	0.00	8	1	0	0	9	4	0	0	0	1	9	.129	.222	.091	9.00	1.00
Bentz, Chad	R-L	6-2	210	5-5-80	2	0	8.38	13	0	0	0	10	13	9	9	3	8	4	.342	.154	.440	3.72	7.45
2-team (23 Charlotte)					6	3	5.32	36	2	0	0	44	38	26	26	13	29	25	—	—	—	5.11	5.93
Buchanan, Brian	R-R	6-4	230	7-21-73	0	0	9.00	1	0	0	0	1	1	1	1	1	1	1	.250	—	.250	9.00	9.00
Burns, Mike	R-R	6-1	210	7-14-78	6	1	1.75	40	2	0	0	57	47	11	11	5	12	56	.225	.227	.200	8.86	1.91
Chiasson, Scott	R-R	6-3	205	8-14-77	3	2	1.91	60	0	0	29	61	40	14	13	3	29	49	.195	.180	.201	7.19	4.26
Claussen, Brandon	R-L	6-1	200	5-1-79	0	2	8.34	5	5	0	0	23	31	21	21	5	8	18	.330	.250	.357	7.15	3.18

PITCHING	B-T	HT	WT	DOB	W	L	ERA	G	GS	CG	SV	IP	H	R	ER	HR	BB	SO	AVG	vLH	vRH	K/9	BB/9
Coutlangus, Jonathan	L-L	6-1	185	10-21-80	0	0	0.00	2	0	0	0	3	2	0	0	0	1	2	.222	.500	.143	6.75	3.38
Dumatrait, Phil	R-L	6-2	170	7-12-81	5	7	4.72	16	15	1	0	88	104	49	46	10	36	58	.301	.279	.306	5.95	3.70
Germano, Justin	R-R	6-3	205	8-6-82	8	6	3.69	19	18	0	0	117	124	53	48	11	22	67	.279	.283	.276	5.15	1.69
2-team (6 Scranton/WB)					10	6	3.48	25	24	0	0	155	164	66	60	13	24	92	—	—	—	5.33	1.39
Gosling, Mike	L-L	6-2	210	9-23-80	6	8	4.58	23	22	0	0	118	118	68	60	12	53	100	.263	.216	.276	7.63	4.04
Hall, Josh	R-R	6-3	195	12-16-80	1	3	4.11	7	7	0	0	35	34	20	16	3	14	22	.254	.215	.290	5.66	3.60
Johnson, Jason	R-R	6-6	225	10-27-73	0	1	9.00	1	1	0	0	5	6	6	5	1	1	2	.273	.500	.188	3.60	1.80
2-team (3 Pawtucket)					2	1	4.50	4	4	1	0	24	21	13	12	2	7	14	—	—	—	5.25	2.62
Kelly, Steven	R-R	6-1	195	9-30-79	4	7	3.16	12	10	0	0	68	68	26	24	7	29	46	.264	.223	.287	6.06	3.82
Kozlowski, Ben	L-L	6-6	230	8-16-80	0	2	12.54	7	0	0	0	9	23	13	13	1	3	3	.489	.455	.500	2.89	2.89
Majewski, Gary	R-R	6-1	215	2-26-80	0	0	0.00	4	1	0	0	4	4	2	0	0	1	3	.267	.375	.143	7.36	2.45
May, Darrell	L-L	6-2	190	6-13-72	3	3	3.86	8	8	0	0	47	41	20	20	6	13	37	.233	.224	.236	7.14	2.51
Mays, Joe	B-R	6-1	200	12-10-75	6	3	3.07	10	10	1	0	67	68	27	23	4	13	40	.267	.255	.275	5.35	1.74
Michalak, Chris	L-L	6-2	195	1-4-71	9	5	2.99	23	22	0	0	132	142	56	44	17	28	61	.278	.255	.284	4.15	1.90
Paduch, Jim	R-R	6-3	185	11-2-82	0	0	0.00	1	0	0	0	4	4	0	0	0	2	0	.286	.333	.200	0.00	4.50
Ramirez, Elizardo	L-R	6-0	180	1-28-83	0	1	4.05	4	4	0	0	20	22	9	9	2	2	19	.272	.261	.286	8.55	0.90
Robbins, Jake	R-R	6-5	220	5-23-76	2	3	3.02	51	0	0	4	54	54	24	18	4	32	52	.267	.279	.262	8.72	5.37
Salmon, Brad	L-R	6-4	220	1-3-80	5	1	2.34	39	0	0	3	58	36	18	15	3	27	72	.184	.246	.158	11.24	4.21
Shackelford, Brian	L-L	6-1	195	8-30-76	1	0	1.82	34	0	1	0	30	29	6	6	0	14	23	.259	.133	.343	6.98	4.25
Shearn, Tom	R-R	6-4	200	8-28-77	9	4	2.52	32	14	0	0	96	83	37	27	10	42	79	.234	.212	.253	7.38	3.92
Stahl, Richard	R-L	6-7	220	4-11-81	1	0	18.00	1	0	0	0	2	6	4	4	0	2	0	.545	1.000	.500	0.00	9.00
Standridge, Jason	R-R	6-4	230	11-9-78	2	2	2.93	37	0	0	0	46	40	16	15	2	15	43	.233	.230	.234	8.41	2.93
Venafro, Mike	L-L	5-10	180	8-2-73	0	0	2.45	36	0	0	2	22	19	6	6	0	8	18	.232	.171	.293	7.36	3.27
Wagner, Ryan	R-R	6-4	225	7-15-82	1	3	6.34	35	0	0	1	38	55	29	27	3	14	28	.344	.351	.340	6.57	3.29
Wilson, Paul	R-R	6-5	210	3-28-73	0	2	4.91	2	2	0	0	11	15	11	6	4	1	3	.300	.143	.361	2.45	0.82

FIELDING

Catcher	PCT	G	PO	A	E	DP	PB
Hanigan	1.000	6	35	1	0	0	0
Jorgensen	.987	72	473	48	7	5	0
LaRue	1.000	2	12	1	0	0	0
Sardinha	.992	68	430	41	4	10	3

First Base	PCT	G	PO	A	E	DP
Abad	.995	22	180	7	1	22
Castellano	1.000	1	14	1	0	1
Cruz	1.000	1	4	0	0	0
Encarnacion	1.000	2	15	1	0	2
Gutierrez	.994	104	863	78	6	87
Hanigan	1.000	1	2	0	0	0
Kata	—	1	0	0	0	0
Snyder	1.000	24	164	11	0	14

Second Base	PCT	G	PO	A	E	DP
Bergolla	.987	95	170	222	5	63
Harris	.957	11	24	21	2	7
Herr	.900	2	7	2	1	1

	PCT	G	PO	A	E	DP
Hopper	.925	11	16	21	3	2
Kata	1.000	25	49	69	0	17
Menechino	1.000	5	7	15	0	1
Olmedo	1.000	5	8	10	0	3
Patchett	1.000	1	0	2	0	0

Third Base	PCT	G	PO	A	E	DP
Bannon	.864	20	16	22	6	2
Encarnacion	.933	7	3	11	1	0
Harris	.957	23	7	37	2	2
Herr	.952	5	4	16	1	3
Kata	1.000	3	1	5	0	0
Menechino	—	1	0	0	0	0
Snyder	.943	98	57	224	17	21

Shortstop	PCT	G	PO	A	E	DP
Bannon	.899	25	28	70	11	12
Bergolla	.929	18	28	50	6	5
Harris	.963	7	7	19	1	5
Kata	.909	3	1	9	1	1

	PCT	G	PO	A	E	DP
Olmedo	.960	95	165	311	20	83
Patchett	1.000	2	0	1	0	0

Outfield	PCT	G	PO	A	E	DP
Abad	.961	36	48	1	2	0
Bannon	1.000	13	32	1	0	1
Buchanan	1.000	15	27	0	0	0
Castellano	1.000	2	2	0	0	0
Denorfia	.989	80	180	6	2	2
Garthwaite	1.000	1	3	0	0	0
Griffin	1.000	1	1	0	0	0
Hopper	1.000	86	150	6	0	2
Kata	.986	70	133	8	2	2
Long	.960	14	23	1	1	1
Ross	.968	13	27	3	1	0
Sanchez	.983	34	57	1	1	1
Strait	1.000	3	6	0	0	0
Stratton	.900	7	9	0	1	0
Watson	.975	39	76	2	2	0
Wise	.982	42	103	4	2	2

Chattanooga Lookouts — Double-A

Southern League

BATTING	B-T	HT	WT	DOB	AVG	vLH	vRH	G	AB	R	H	2B	3B	HR	RBI	BB	HBP	SH	SF	SO	SB	CS	SLG	OBP
Anderson, Drew	B-R	5-9	170	2-2-83	.277	.291	.269	43	148	19	41	9	3	2	15	14	0	5	1	25	2		.419	.337
Asadoorian, Rick	R-R	6-2	180	7-23-80	.267	.237	.285	99	300	37	80	12	4	4	29	19	1	4	2	76	5	6	.373	.311
Bannon, Jeff	R-R	6-4	185	8-21-79	.246	.210	.276	40	138	14	34	6	0	3	12	6	0	3	0	21	3	2	.355	.278
Bolivar, Luis	B-R	6-1	150	2-15-81	.274	.318	.250	109	318	44	87	13	2	4	29	22	4	4	1	52	12	4	.365	.328
Colina, Javier	R-R	6-1	190	2-15-79	.215	.168	.242	120	358	42	77	23	2	7	42	32	1	0	6	81	5	2	.349	.277
Crozier, Eric	L-L	6-4	200	8-11-78	.267	.217	.286	33	86	13	23	4	1	3	15	6	0	0	0	33	1	0	.442	.315
Dickerson, Chris	L-L	6-4	212	4-10-82	.242	.196	.260	115	389	65	94	21	7	12	48	65	5	3	3	129	21	6	.424	.355
Hanigan, Ryan	R-R	6-0	195	8-16-80	.246	.255	.241	56	126	17	31	2	0	0	14	19	2	0	3	23	0	0	.262	.347
Herr, Aaron	R-R	6-0	205	3-7-81	.287	.324	.269	84	327	41	94	24	0	11	52	23	3	0	1	86	3	5	.462	.339
Hopper, Norris	R-R	5-10	180	3-24-79	.283	.238	.320	13	46	7	13	2	1	0	10	6	0	0	3		0		.370	.365
Janish, Paul	R-R	6-2	185	10-12-82	.267	.286	.250	4	15	1	4	1	0	0	2	5	0	0		5	0		.333	.313
Machado, Anderson	L-R	5-11	160	1-25-81	.237	.181	.258	129	396	48	94	20	2	7	39	53	3	11	4	104	15	6	.351	.329
Moran, Javon	R-R	5-11	175	9-30-82	.320	.279	.341	63	250	34	80	11	3	1	12	11	3	4	1	26	16	7	.400	.355
Motooka, Rafael	R-R	6-0	200	4-18-82	.171	.167	.174	13	35	3	6	2	0	0	1	7	2	0	0	5	0	0	.314	.211
Patchett, Gary	R-R	6-2	180	9-25-78	.296	.214	.385	25	27	2	8	0	0	0	2	9	1	0	0	11	0	0	.296	.486
Perez, Miguel	R-R	6-3	190	9-25-83	.241	.261	.230	111	394	33	95	16	0	3	33	19	10	6	5	88	5	1	.305	.290
Ross, David	R-R	6-2	225	3-19-77	.333	.333	.333	2	6	0	2	0	0	0	2	0	0	0		2	0	0	.333	.500
Sanchez, Alex	L-L	5-10	180	8-26-76	.297	.235	.350	20	74	9	22	2	2	2	11	2	0	1	2	7	1	0	.459	.308
Varner, Noochie	R-R	6-0	204	12-7-80	.285	.308	.271	133	460	63	131	33	2	10	73	33	8	1	11	90	2	0	.430	.336
Votto, Joey	L-R	6-3	220	9-10-83	.319	.262	.351	136	508	85	162	46	2	22	77	78	1	0	3	109	24	7	.547	.408
Wise, Dewayne	L-L	6-1	180	2-24-78	.420	.333	.447	13	50	11	21	7	0	3	7	3	1	0	1	9	1	0	.740	.455

PITCHING	B-T	HT	WT	DOB	W	L	ERA	G	GS	CG	SV	IP	H	R	ER	HR	BB	SO	AVG	vLH	vRH	K/9	BB/9
Abbott, Jim	B-R	6-3	192	10-12-79	1	2	6.32	14	0	0	1	16	18	15	11	0	8	18	.277	.333	.250	10.34	4.60
Alvarado, Carlos	R-R	6-4	210	1-24-78	5	1	3.28	31	1	0	0	49	38	20	18	1	25	58	.209	.227	.198	10.58	4.56
Asadoorian, Rick	R-R	6-2	180	7-23-80	1	0	0.00	3	0	0	0	4	4	0	0	0	0	7	.235	.400	.167	15.75	0.00
Bailey, Homer	R-R	6-4	205	5-3-86	7	1	1.59	13	13	0	0	68	50	13	12	1	28	77	.208	.182	.224	10.19	3.71
Bannon, Jeff	R-R	6-4	185	8-21-79	0	0	0.00	1	0	0	0	1	2	2	0	0	2	0	.333	.333	.333	0.00	18.00
Belisle, Matt	R-R	6-3	195	6-6-80	0	0	0.00	2	1	0	0	4	4	0	0	0	0	4	.231	.000	.375	10.80	0.00
Bentz, Chad	R-L	6-2	210	5-5-80	0	1	5.68	3	1	0	0	6	3	4	4	1	5	6	.095	.143	.071	9.95	7.11
Bong, Jung	L-L	6-3	215	7-15-80	1	1	5.09	4	2	0	0	18	20	11	10	2	8	17	.282	.231	.311	8.66	4.08
Bruksch, Jeff	R-R	6-4	212	4-29-80	0	0	2.25	2	0	0	0	4	3	1	1	0	2	1	.214	.000	.300	2.25	4.50
Chick, Travis	R-R	6-3	215	6-10-84	4	5	4.61	16	16	0	0	84	79	45	43	12	36	77	.249	.288	.222	8.25	3.86

Player	B-T	HT	WT	DOB	W	L	ERA	G	GS	CG	SV	IP	H	R	ER	HR	BB	SO	AVG	vLH	vRH	K/9	BB/9
Coutlangus, Jon	L-L	6-1	185	10-21-80	1	3	2.86	49	0	0	9	63	40	24	20	0	32	56	.185	.179	.188	8.00	4.57
Dumatrait, Phil	R-L	6-2	170	7-12-81	3	4	3.62	10	10	0	0	50	39	24	20	4	22	45	.218	.182	.230	8.15	3.99
Granado, Jan	L-L	6-0	190	9-26-82	0	0	0.00	2	0	0	0	3	0	0	0	0	1	2	.000	.000	.000	6.00	3.00
Guevara, Carlos	R-R	6-0	175	3-18-82	2	3	3.72	49	0	0	1	77	74	35	32	6	27	89	.247	.215	.264	10.36	3.14
Hall, Josh	R-R	6-3	195	12-16-80	9	6	3.39	19	19	1	0	117	130	61	44	11	34	69	.284	.289	.281	5.32	2.62
Kelly, Steven	R-R	6-1	195	9-30-79	9	4	2.82	15	14	0	0	83	88	34	26	4	24	63	.273	.264	.282	6.83	2.60
Kozlowski, Ben	L-L	6-6	230	8-16-80	2	1	1.17	10	0	0	0	23	20	5	3	1	11	13	.241	.207	.259	5.09	4.30
2-team (23 Jacksonville)					3	3	2.39	33	7	0	1	83	75	30	22	7	35	72	—	—		7.81	3.80
Mallett, Justin	R-R	6-7	215	11-11-81	0	0	0.00	1	0	0	0	4	3	0	0	0	1	3	.214	.500	.100	6.75	2.25
Medlock, Calvin	R-R	5-10	175	11-8-82	7	2	2.97	42	0	0	2	64	54	24	21	4	28	70	.226	.262	.206	9.90	3.96
Motooka, Rafael	R-R	6-0	200	4-18-82	0	0	45.00	1	0	0	0	1	3	5	5	0	3	0	.500	.333	.667	0.00	27.00
Nannini, Mike	R-R	5-11	190	8-9-80	0	1	2.31	7	1	0	0	12	8	3	3	2	3	10	.190	.286	.143	7.71	2.31
Ondrusek, Logan	R-R	6-8	195	2-13-85	0	0	0.00	1	0	0	0	4	0	0	0	0	0	3	.000	.000	.000	15.75	6.75
Pelland, Tyler	R-L	6-0	198	10-9-83	9	5	3.99	28	28	0	0	142	144	78	63	11	89	107	.275	.225	.288	6.78	5.64
Salmon, Brad	L-R	6-4	220	1-3-80	2	1	2.70	16	0	0	2	23	18	7	7	0	16	24	.214	.200	.224	9.26	6.17
Shafer, David	R-R	6-3	185	3-7-82	1	2	2.36	44	0	0	26	50	37	14	13	2	16	52	.204	.183	.215	9.42	2.90
Shearn, Tom	R-R	6-4	200	8-28-77	0	0	7.71	1	0	0	0	2	4	2	2	0	1	4	.364	.667	.000	15.43	3.86
Stahl, Richard	R-L	6-7	220	4-11-81	1	0	3.60	3	0	0	0	5	2	2	2	0	10	3	.154	.000	.286	5.40	18.00
Till, Brock	R-R	5-10	195	7-1-80	6	1	2.17	40	0	0	6	62	50	19	15	1	30	40	.222	.160	.257	5.78	4.33
Valdez, Edward	R-R	6-2	165	2-8-80	7	10	3.89	29	23	0	0	137	134	66	59	9	38	111	.260	.260	.261	7.31	2.50
Vazquez, Camilo	L-L	6-0	180	10-3-83	3	5	4.33	11	11	0	0	60	66	39	29	6	25	56	.283	.261	.289	8.35	3.73

FIELDING

Catcher	PCT	G	PO	A	E	DP	PB
Hanigan	1.000	26	186	12	0	2	0
Motooka	.942	10	62	3	4	0	2
Perez	.985	107	864	74	14	14	13
Ross	1.000	2	11	2	0	0	0

First Base	PCT	G	PO	A	E	DP
Asadoorian	.857	1	5	1	1	1
Bannon	1.000	1	8	1	0	1
Hanigan	.935	6	24	5	2	0
Patchett	1.000	1	2	0	0	0
Votto	.988	136	1068	127	14	99

Second Base	PCT	G	PO	A	E	DP
Anderson	.987	33	66	82	2	22
Bannon	.846	3	5	6	2	4
Bolivar	.967	31	56	62	4	14

	PCT	G	PO	A	E	DP
Colina	.958	80	134	184	14	29
Hopper	.833	1	1	4	1	1
Machado	1.000	7	7	19	0	4
Patchett	1.000	2	4	5	0	3

Third Base	PCT	G	PO	A	E	DP
Bannon	.938	14	11	19	2	1
Bolivar	.913	50	27	99	12	10
Colina	1.000	5	1	5	0	0
Herr	.904	83	59	158	23	17
Patchett	1.000	1	1	0	0	0

Shortstop	PCT	G	PO	A	E	DP
Bannon	.980	17	20	29	1	4
Bolivar	.962	16	18	33	2	6
Janish	1.000	4	8	16	0	3
Machado	.962	119	158	299	18	54

	PCT	G	PO	A	E	DP
Patchett	1.000	3	4	8	0	1

Outfield	PCT	G	PO	A	E	DP
Anderson	1.000	10	9	0	0	0
Asadoorian	.980	79	136	8	3	2
Bannon	1.000	7	11	0	0	0
Bolivar	1.000	1	1	0	0	0
Crozier	.973	25	33	3	1	1
Dickerson	.989	112	250	9	3	2
Hanigan	1.000	1	1	0	0	0
Hopper	1.000	12	17	3	0	1
Moran	1.000	56	118	5	0	3
Motooka	1.000	—	1	0	0	0
Sanchez	.967	19	28	1	1	0
Varner	.989	117	167	9	2	1
Wise	.967	13	26	3	1	0

Sarasota Reds — High Class A

Florida State League

BATTING	B-T	HT	WT	DOB	AVG	vLH	vRH	G	AB	R	H	2B	3B	HR	RBI	BB	HBP	SH	SF	SO	SB	CS	SLG	OBP
Anderson, Drew	B-R	5-9	170	2-2-83	.300	.355	.287	83	327	48	98	19	9	4	31	29	2	3	0	51	7	4	.450	.360
Bolivar, Luis	B-R	5-9	150	2-15-81	.182	.333	.148	11	33	6	6	0	0	1	1	1	0	0	6	0	0		.273	.229
Garthwaite, Jay	R-R	6-2	220	11-26-80	.262	.281	.256	125	450	62	118	28	3	21	72	39	11	1	4	125	6	7	.478	.333
Gentry, Philip	L-R	5-11	195	9-2-80	.223	.250	.220	86	264	11	59	14	2	0	23	6	1	2	3	50	3	4	.292	.241
Gutierrez, Tonys	L-L	6-2	180	8-18-83	.283	.197	.307	92	325	49	92	17	4	2	34	55	6	2	0	60	4	0	.378	.396
Hernandez, Habelito	R-R	6-0	180	1-11-81	.316	.000	.353	5	19	1	6	1	0	0	1	0	0	0	4	1	0		.368	.316
Janish, Paul	R-R	6-2	185	10-12-82	.278	.333	.256	91	335	53	93	17	2	9	55	38	6	7	7	39	8	2	.421	.355
Key, Brad	R-R	6-0	185	3-14-83	.188	.200	.200	7	16	2	3	1	0	0	4	0	0	0	0	8	0	0	.250	.278
Kroski, Chris	L-R	6-1	231	5-17-82	.215	.143	.231	61	191	15	41	10	0	2	15	9	3	2	1	52	1	0	.298	.260
LaRue, Jason	R-R	5-11	205	3-19-74	.167	—	.167	3	12	1	2	0	0	0	1	1	0	0	0	3	0	0	.167	.231
Lasso, Yoni	R-R	5-11	170	11-22-84	.067	.143	.000	7	15	0	1	0	0	0	0	0	0	0	0	3	0	0	.067	.067
Lawhorn, Trevor	R-R	6-2	182	12-18-82	.224	.209	.229	91	326	32	73	10	2	4	28	16	2	2	0	66	4	7	.304	.265
McCracken, Quinton	B-R	5-8	185	8-16-70	.500	.500	.500	4	16	3	8	1	0	1	0	0	0	0	0	0	0	0	.625	.500
Moran, Javon	R-R	5-11	175	9-30-82	.372	.250	.419	10	43	5	16	2	0	0	3	2	1	0	0	5	4	4	.419	.413
Patchett, Gary	R-R	6-2	180	9-25-78	.143	.167	.132	21	56	7	8	0	0	0	2	6	2	0	0	7	0	0	.143	.250
Piepkorn, Jeremiah	R-R	6-3	215	2-18-81	.256	.237	.262	121	481	60	123	29	3	10	79	13	8	1	5	107	6	4	.391	.284
Purdom, John	R-R	6-2	230	5-28-81	.233	.240	.231	98	326	36	76	14	2	2	35	18	16	2	6	54	1	5	.307	.301
Roberts, J.D.	L-R	6-4	225	8-8-81	.155	.158	.154	34	60	7	10	15	3	0	5	0	0	0		36	0	0	.247	.226
Roberts, Brandon	L-R	6-0	185	11-9-84	.267	.340	.249	60	247	40	66	5	1	1	15	16	6	2	2	39	23	7	.352	.349
2-team (71 Fort Myers)					.293	—		131	532	80	156	17	2	4	49	36	11	4	3	82	50	14	.355	.349
Rosales, Adam	R-R	6-2	195	5-20-83	.213	.182	.225	34	122	15	26	8	2	2	14	20	2	1	2	27	3	3	.361	.329
Schramek, Mark	L-R	6-3	230	6-2-80	.185	.000	.192	8	27	1	5	1	0	0	2	4	0	0	0	7	0	0	.222	.290
Strait, Cody	R-R	6-1	185	5-28-83	.258	.267	.255	131	489	85	126	36	4	17	74	36	14	2	3	108	50	9	.452	.325
Tiburcio, Hector	B-R	6-0	185	6-11-81	.201	.283	.171	56	169	14	34	6	2	3	15	8	1	6	3	38	3	1	.314	.238
Williams, Marland	R-R	5-9	185	6-22-81	.221	.260	.204	75	235	40	52	3	6	3	18	25	3	0	2	88	35	9	.396	.312

PITCHING	B-T	HT	WT	DOB	W	L	ERA	G	GS	CG	SV	IP	H	R	ER	HR	BB	SO	AVG	vLH	vRH	K/9	BB/9
Abbott, Jim	B-R	6-3	192	10-12-79	3	0	2.25	11	0	0	3	16	10	4	4	0	3	16	.185	.267	.154	9.00	1.69
Alvarado, Carlos	R-R	6-4	210	1-24-78	1	1	1.17	9	0	0	2	15	6	2	2	1	4	20	.118	.143	.100	11.74	2.35
Avery, James	R-R	6-1	210	6-10-84	8	8	4.43	26	26	1	0	130	136	73	64	14	48	86	.264	.274	.273	5.95	3.32
Bailey, Homer	R-R	6-4	205	5-3-86	3	5	3.31	13	13	0	0	71	49	35	26	6	22	79	.189	.188	.190	10.06	2.80
Balfour, Grant	R-R	6-2	195	12-30-77	0	0	7.94	5	0	0	0	6	8	7	5	0	3	7	.320	.417	.231	11.12	4.76
Bohorquez, Carlos	R-R	5-11	165	10-6-81	3	3	2.80	41	0	0	1	64	55	24	20	3	28	51	.226	.200	.243	7.13	3.92
Bruksch, Jeff	R-R	6-4	212	4-29-80	1	1	3.98	25	0	0	2	43	37	23	19	5	31	32	.231	.258	.214	6.70	6.49
Camardese, Brandon	R-L	6-2	205	7-2-83	0	2	10.38	3	2	0	0	9	12	10	10	1	6	6	.333	.200	.385	6.23	3.12
Cueto, Johnny	R-R	5-11	194	2-15-86	7	2	3.50	12	12	1	0	62	48	25	24	6	23	61	.214	.291	.167	8.93	3.36
DeJesus, Misael	R-R	6-3	190	11-4-84	0	0	5.40	2	0	0	0	2	4	1	1	0	2	3	.500	.400	.667	16.20	10.80
Edens, Kyle	R-R	5-10	210	1-25-80	2	1	5.46	18	0	0	0	30	41	19	18	1	9	25	.333	.340	.329	7.58	2.73
Feliz, Rainer	R-R	6-5	170	3-22-83	0	1	16.88	3	0	0	0	3	6	5	5	0	4	2	.462	.500	.400	3.38	3.38
Gardner, Richie	R-R	6-3	185	2-1-82	0	3	6.97	5	5	0	0	21	26	19	16	4	9	21	.310	.324	.300	6.53	3.92

Player	B-T	HT	WT	DOB	W	L	ERA	G	GS	CG	SV	IP	H	R	ER	HR	BB	SO	AVG	vLH	vRH	K/9	BB/9
George, Jon	R-R	6-4	220	7-6-84	0	0	9.00	2	0	0	0	3	4	4	3	1	3	1	.267	.222	.333	3.00	9.00
Granado, Jan	L-L	6-0	190	9-26-82	2	4	2.22	29	0	0	11	49	33	17	12	4	13	50	.189	.189	.188	9.25	2.40
Guerrero, Daniel	R-R	6-1	190	7-21-85	0	0	0.00	1	0	0	0	1	0	0	0	0	0	1	.000	.000	.000	9.00	0.00
Haltiwanger, Russell	R-R	6-2	180	4-21-84	0	0	2.25	1	1	0	0	4	1	1	1	1	4	2	.077	.000	.125	4.50	9.00
Hendley, Blake	R-R	6-3	195	9-1-81	4	0	4.40	27	0	0	1	45	48	31	22	4	15	25	.270	.257	.278	5.00	3.00
Lecure, Sam	R-R	6-1	190	5-4-84	7	12	3.43	27	27	0	0	142	130	63	54	12	46	115	.243	.251	.237	7.31	2.92
Lundgren, Wayne	R-R	6-6	180	4-21-82	0	2	7.62	8	0	0	0	13	25	14	11	0	5	10	.379	.458	.333	6.92	3.46
Mallett, Justin	R-R	6-7	215	11-11-81	2	2	3.51	11	7	0	0	41	43	21	16	3	13	32	.267	.289	.247	7.02	2.85
Manuel, Robert	R-R	6-3	190	7-9-83	0	0	4.50	6	0	0	0	8	10	7	4	3	2	4	.313	.545	.190	4.50	2.25
Medina, Ruben	R-R	5-11	157	7-28-86	0	0	0.00	1	0	0	0	0	0	0	0	0	2	0	.000	—	.000	0.00	54.00
Nannini, Mike	R-R	5-11	190	8-9-80	0	0	3.86	3	0	0	0	5	6	2	2	0	1	2	.316	.600	.214	3.86	1.93
Paduch, Jim	R-R	6-3	185	11-2-82	6	5	4.61	21	16	0	1	105	132	67	54	14	34	55	.308	.303	.313	4.70	2.91
Patchett, Gary	R-R	6-2	180	9-25-78	0	0	0.00	1	0	0	0	1	0	0	0	0	0	1	.000	.000	.000	0.00	9.00
Ramirez, Ramon	R-R	6-0	160	9-16-82	4	5	4.29	15	11	1	0	65	66	33	31	11	21	53	.261	.215	.288	7.34	2.91
Rincon, Daniel	R-R	6-3	165	10-11-82	0	0	81.00	1	0	0	0	0	2	3	3	1	1	0	.667	1.000	.500	0.00	27.00
Schmidt, Jeremy	R-R	6-2	203	11-15-79	0	3	6.27	16	0	0	0	19	22	18	13	2	14	16	.293	.345	.261	7.71	6.75
Smiley, Wes	R-R	6-1	217	7-21-81	0	0	0.00	1	0	0	0	0	0	0	0	0	0	0	.000	.000	—	0.00	0.00
Stahl, Richard	R-L	6-7	220	4-11-81	0	0	3.00	2	0	0	0	3	2	2	1	0	4	2	.167	.000	.200	6.00	12.00
Stott, Zac	R-R	6-4	205	7-26-83	1	2	2.53	17	0	0	0	32	23	9	9	2	10	22	.200	.146	.230	6.19	2.81
2-team (7 Clearwater)					1	2	3.21	24	0	0	1	42	36	16	15	6	12	27	—	—	—	5.79	2.57
Tabor, Lee	L-L	6-2	175	12-17-84	0	1	7.11	4	3	0	0	13	15	11	10	1	5	6	.288	.154	.333	4.26	3.55
Till, Brock	R-R	5-10	195	7-1-80	2	0	5.25	9	0	0	0	12	11	7	7	0	6	10	.256	.389	.160	7.50	4.50
Vazquez, Camilo	L-L	6-0	180	10-3-83	4	5	4.00	16	15	0	0	83	84	42	37	10	32	79	.261	.254	.262	8.53	3.46
Villalon, Julio	R-R	6-2	172	5-11-78	0	0	0.00	2	0	0	0	4	2	0	0	0	1	4	.154	.250	.111	9.00	2.25
Wilson, Paul	R-R	6-5	210	3-28-73	1	0	3.00	1	1	0	0	6	9	2	2	0	1	1	.360	.600	.300	1.50	1.50
Woody, Abe	R-R	5-10	195	11-9-82	5	5	2.92	49	0	0	12	83	80	36	27	1	38	62	.256	.256	.255	6.70	4.10

FIELDING

Catcher

Catcher	PCT	G	PO	A	E	DP	PB
Kroski	.985	48	304	26	5	3	8
LaRue	1.000	2	23	1	0	1	0
Purdom	.987	97	643	49	9	7	21
Lasso	1.000	4	3	7	0	2	
Lawhorn	.959	29	70	71	6	16	
Patchett	.977	12	16	27	1	5	
Tiburcio	.954	25	45	58	5	16	
Janish	.977	84	135	251	9	51	
Patchett	.950	8	12	26	2	9	
Rosales	.944	20	32	53	5	13	
Tiburcio	.872	26	37	65	15	13	

First Base

First Base	PCT	G	PO	A	E	DP
Garthwaite	.981	26	193	14	4	19
Gutierrez	.990	90	703	59	8	73
Hernandez	.964	5	49	4	2	5
Piepkorn	.988	11	81	3	1	5
Purdom	.909	2	7	3	1	1
Roberts	1.000	8	60	3	0	13

Second Base

Second Base	PCT	G	PO	A	E	DP
Anderson	.949	67	132	167	16	37
Bolivar	.964	6	10	17	1	5

Third Base

Third Base	PCT	G	PO	A	E	DP
Anderson	1.000	1	1	1	0	0
Bolivar	1.000	2	0	1	0	0
Key	1.000	6	2	9	0	0
Lawhorn	.876	38	26	52	11	7
Piepkorn	.916	90	78	172	23	12
Schramek	.947	8	5	13	1	2

Shortstop

Shortstop	PCT	G	PO	A	E	DP
Anderson	.857	2	2	4	1	1
Bolivar	1.000	2	1	0	0	

Outfield

Outfield	PCT	G	PO	A	E	DP
Anderson	.938	10	14	1	1	0
Garthwaite	.984	68	120	6	2	1
Gentry	.975	66	114	2	3	0
McCracken	1.000	3	5	1	0	0
Moran	.962	10	25	0	1	0
Piepkorn	1.000	10	25	0	0	0
Roberts	—	1	0	0	0	0
Roberts	.984	60	121	4	2	1
Strait	.977	130	279	23	7	6
Williams	.978	74	174	5	4	0

Dayton Dragons — Low Class A

Midwest League

BATTING

Player	B-T	HT	WT	DOB	AVG	vLH	vRH	G	AB	R	H	2B	3B	HR	RBI	BB	HBP	SH	SF	SO	SB	CS	SLG	OBP
Bruce, Jay	L-L	6-3	195	4-3-87	.291	.236	.312	117	444	69	129	42	5	16	81	44	4	0	6	106	19	9	.516	.355
Cabrera, Gerardo	R-R	6-2	185	12-23-83	.232	.340	.188	103	323	35	75	15	3	4	24	36	5	7	0	74	4	2	.334	.319
Colon, Angel	R-R	6-4	210	9-27-83	.097	.111	.091	10	31	3	3	0	0	0	2	2	2	0	1	17	0	1	.097	.194
DeJesus, Michael	L-R	5-8	180	7-16-83	.246	.298	.232	112	394	52	97	12	1	3	42	59	1	6	4	60	11	4	.305	.343
Denove, Christopher	R-R	6-1	200	12-9-82	.179	.295	.136	55	162	16	29	6	0	1	17	13	2	3	2	38	0	0	.235	.246
Eymann, Eric	R-R	6-3	185	2-9-84	.238	.188	.255	119	437	51	104	29	5	4	41	35	6	2	2	95	2	4	.355	.302
Griffin, Michael	R-R	5-9	200	10-1-83	.263	.299	.251	131	548	75	144	33	6	6	52	20	13	3	2	94	10	5	.378	.304
Hernandez, Habelito	R-R	6-0	180	1-11-81	.271	.215	.289	115	436	57	118	16	5	7	53	7	2	5	2	49	3	3	.378	.284
Holden, Josh	L-L	6-2	220	12-10-80	.248	.267	.246	90	262	30	65	8	4	0	18	16	4	2	3	49	11	5	.309	.298
Janish, Paul	R-R	6-2	185	10-12-82	.398	.545	.355	26	98	19	39	6	0	5	18	7	1	0	2	10	0	0	.612	.435
Key, Brad	R-R	6-0	185	3-14-83	.224	.167	.241	35	107	9	24	7	0	1	5	11	1	0	0	25	0	0	.318	.303
Lasso, Yoni	R-S	5-11	170	11-22-84	.100		.143	5	10	3	1	1	0	0	0	2	0	0		3	0	0	.200	.357
Mosby, Bobby	R-R	6-2	240	4-9-82	.237	.333	.198	86	291	31	69	15	0	12	45	26	4	0	2	91	0	0	.412	.307
Reininger, Jarrett	R-R	5-10	190	12-3-82	.219	.207	.224	34	105	16	23	6	1	2	10	21	2	0	0	38	0	0	.333	.359
Roberts, J.D.	L-R	6-4	225	8-8-81	.154	.100	.174	8	26	2	4	1	0	1	1	1	0	0	0	11	0	0	.269	.185
Rosales, Adam	R-R	6-2	195	5-20-83	.270	.340	.249	55	222	36	60	9	3	6	29	15	5	2	2	40	5	1	.419	.328
Szymanski, Brandon	B-R	6-5	210	10-1-82	.239	.302	.216	128	482	68	115	31	3	16	59	46	4	0	2	191	22	10	.415	.309
Tatum, Craig	R-R	6-1	215	3-18-83	.277	.253	.285	98	343	41	95	21	0	8	37	32	4	0	2	70	3	1	.408	.344

PITCHING

Player	B-T	HT	WT	DOB	W	L	ERA	G	GS	CG	SV	IP	H	R	ER	HR	BB	SO	AVG	vLH	vRH	K/9	BB/9
Balfour, Grant	R-R	6-2	195	12-30-77	0	0	0.00	2	0	0	0	3	0	0	0	0	0	3	.000	.000	.000	13.50	0.00
Belisle, Matt	R-R	6-3	195	6-6-80	1	0	0.00	2	0	0	1	4	3	1	0	0	0	3	.200	.333	.167	6.75	0.00
Camardese, Brandon	R-L	6-2	205	7-2-83	0	0	14.29	6	0	0	0	6	14	9	9	0	3	6	.412	.300	.524	9.53	4.76
Cueto, Johnny	R-R	5-11	174	2-15-86	8	1	2.59	14	14	2	0	76	52	22	22	5	15	82	.191	.195	.188	9.67	1.77
Donaldson, Daniel	R-L	6-4	180	7-23-84	1	0	3.38	2	0	0	0	3	3	2	1	0	5	0	.250	.250	.250	0.00	16.88
Feliz, Rainer	R-R	6-5	170	3-22-83	1	0	5.23	17	1	0	0	31	38	20	18	3	16	27	.295	.241	.333	7.84	4.65
Fisher, Carlos	R-R	6-4	220	2-22-83	12	5	2.76	27	27	0	0	150	133	53	46	5	38	122	.237	.261	.218	7.32	2.28
George, Jon	R-R	6-4	220	7-6-84	0	1	3.29	8	0	0	0	14	19	7	5	0	2	13	.333	.350	.324	8.56	1.32
Gonzalez, Rafael	R-R	6-3	225	3-21-86	2	4	5.22	9	9	0	0	40	32	25	23	7	25	33	.221	.191	.247	7.49	5.67
Guerrero, Daniel	R-R	6-1	190	7-21-85	4	5	3.94	12	12	1	0	59	62	28	26	4	17	39	.272	.333	.220	5.92	2.58
Haltiwanger, Russell	R-R	6-2	180	4-21-84	0	4	4.15	40	5	0	1	82	72	46	38	10	45	78	.233	.236	.231	8.53	4.92
Hendley, Blake	R-R	6-3	195	9-1-81	1	3	3.34	22	0	0	15	30	33	12	11	1	3	28	.270	.333	.210	8.49	0.91
Huddy, Kyle	R-R	6-2	220	6-13-83	0	1	6.55	7	1	0	0	11	14	9	8	0	2	12	.326	.222	.400	9.82	7.36
Lanier, Thomas	R-R	6-0	160	11-20-82	3	11	3.03	49	0	0	9	74	57	27	25	3	33	58	.214	.248	.194	7.02	4.00
Lundgren, Wayne	R-R	6-6	180	4-21-82	2	1	2.60	12	0	0	1	17	19	5	5	1	3	9	.271	.240	.289	4.67	1.56
Lutz, Derrik	R-R	6-0	210	4-22-85	2	1	2.39	13	0	0	0	26	26	10	7	2	11	22	.255	.233	.271	7.52	3.76

Name	B-T	HT	WT	DOB	W	L	ERA	G	GS	CG	SV	IP	H	R	ER	HR	BB	SO	AVG	vLH	vRH	K/9	BB/9
Mallett, Justin	R-R	6-7	215	11-11-81	0	3	4.02	11	0	0	3	16	13	8	7	1	8	18	.228	.240	.219	10.34	4.60
Manuel, Robert	R-R	6-3	190	7-9-83	0	3	4.31	13	7	0	1	48	58	27	23	5	4	36	.294	.333	.265	6.75	0.75
Melendez, German	R-R	6-0	185	9-13-80	0	1	27.00	2	0	0	0	2	7	5	5	0	1	0	.583	.500	.667	0.00	5.40
Montano, Luis	R-R	6-0	180	3-20-85	0	1	6.75	2	2	0	0	8	10	7	6	2	3	9	.286	.308	.273	10.13	3.38
Ondrusek, Logan	R-R	6-8	195	2-13-85	4	5	3.42	27	0	0	0	53	48	24	20	2	19	47	.240	.321	.189	8.03	3.25
Ramirez, Elizardo	L-R	6-0	180	1-28-83	0	0	4.50	1	1	0	0	6	6	3	3	1	0	3	.250	.333	.200	4.50	0.00
Rojas, Jose A.	R-R	6-0	165	3-2-83	3	1	1.07	25	0	0	4	42	27	7	5	2	22	63	.184	.212	.168	13.50	4.71
Stevens, Jeffrey	R-R	6-1	220	9-5-83	2	4	4.43	14	6	0	0	43	42	22	21	6	16	43	.261	.240	.279	9.07	3.38
Stott, Zac	R-R	6-4	205	7-26-83	0	2	5.40	14	0	0	4	17	22	13	10	1	4	15	.310	.423	.244	8.10	2.16
Ursin, Damian	R-R	6-0	197	11-27-82	1	2	3.71	34	0	0	5	44	46	22	18	3	20	40	.266	.269	.264	8.24	4.12
Valiquette, Philippe-Alexandre	L-L	6-0	175	2-14-87	2	4	7.54	12	9	0	0	37	52	39	31	5	21	24	.327	.340	.321	5.84	5.11
Ward, Zach	R-R	6-3	235	1-14-84	7	0	2.29	20	18	0	0	114	74	35	29	2	37	95	.188	.181	.194	7.50	2.92
2-team (6 Beloit)					8	4	3.06	26	24	0	0	144	103	55	49	3	48	118	—	—	—	7.36	2.99
Watson, Sean	R-R	6-1	210	7-24-85	1	2	8.59	10	0	0	0	15	22	14	14	2	5	16	.349	.375	.333	9.82	3.07
Weimer, Andrew	R-R	6-2	180	3-20-81	0	1	9.00	2	0	0	0	3	5	7	3	0	3	3	.313	.500	.200	9.00	9.00
Wilson, Paul	R-R	6-5	210	3-28-73	0	1	5.14	1	1	0	0	7	10	6	4	1	0	4	.313	.357	.278	5.14	0.00
Wood, Travis	R-L	6-0	165	2-6-87	10	5	3.66	27	27	0	0	140	108	65	57	14	56	133	.215	.203	.220	8.55	3.60
Young, Terrell	R-R	6-3	175	8-7-85	0	1	8.10	4	0	0	0	7	6	7	6	0	6	5	.231	.385	.077	6.75	8.10

FIELDING

Catcher	PCT	G	PO	A	E	DP	PB
Denove	.986	54	377	37	6	6	7
Tatum	.986	94	699	92	11	9	12

First Base	PCT	G	PO	A	E	DP
Colon	1.000	4	29	1	0	3
Hernandez	.990	108	898	78	10	72
Mosby	.988	32	225	27	3	20
Roberts	.982	5	50	4	1	4

Second Base	PCT	G	PO	A	E	DP
DeJesus	.943	87	134	212	21	34
Eymann	1.000	1	1	0	0	0
Griffin	.962	57	103	149	10	29
Key	1.000	1	0	1	0	0

Third Base	PCT	G	PO	A	E	DP
Colon	.889	3	1	7	1	0
Eymann	.955	55	52	97	7	6
Griffin	.930	33	20	60	6	3
Hernandez	1.000	3	1	4	0	0
Key	.862	30	25	50	12	2
Lasso	.500	1	0	1	1	0
Reininger	.804	26	13	32	11	2

Shortstop	PCT	G	PO	A	E	DP
Eymann	.975	68	87	188	7	37
Griffin	.964	7	9	18	1	3
Janish	.975	26	41	74	3	19
Lasso	1.000	3	2	6	0	0
Rosales	.944	44	63	124	11	18

Outfield	PCT	G	PO	A	E	DP
Bruce	.975	94	188	5	5	5
Cabrera	.981	102	149	5	3	1
Griffin	.979	33	45	2	1	1
Holden	.955	81	124	2	6	0
Key	.667	2	2	0	1	0
Szymanski	.973	124	243	8	7	2

Billings Mustangs — Rookie

Pioneer League

BATTING	B-T	HT	WT	DOB	AVG	vLH	vRH	G	AB	R	H	2B	3B	HR	RBI	BB	HBP	SH	SF	SO	SB	CS	SLG	OBP
Brown, Ryan	L-R	6-4	235	10-17-82	.211	.160	.225	39	114	13	24	7	0	0	13	18	2	0	3	26	0	1	.272	.321
Colon, Angel	R-R	6-0	210	9-27-83	.207	.189	.214	40	121	17	25	2	0	3	16	11	6	0	1	37	1	2	.298	.302
Dorn, Daniel	L-L	6-2	190	7-20-84	.354	.182	.387	60	206	48	73	17	2	8	40	36	4	2	1	36	3	0	.573	.457
Esquer, Anthony	R-R	6-1	215	9-3-84	.331	.300	.341	36	121	16	40	5	0	0	19	8	3	4	0	13	0	0	.372	.386
Feiner, Kevyn	R-R	6-1	170	6-11-87	.353	.750	.231	8	17	6	6	0	0	0	2	2	0	0	0	4	0	0	.353	.421
Francisco, Juan	B-R	6-2	180	6-24-87	.333	.000	.414	9	36	6	12	3	0	0	2	0	0	0	0	8	2	1	.417	.333
Gonzalez, Rey	R-R	6-0	185	8-16-84	.150	.250	.125	13	20	1	3	0	0	0	2	1	0	1	0	5	0	0	.150	.190
Heisey, Chris	R-R	6-1	195	12-14-84	.286	.311	.277	70	245	46	70	10	0	6	37	28	2	9	1	33	11	5	.400	.362
Lasso, Yoni	R-R	5-11	170	11-22-84	.167	.000	.182	7	12	1	2	0	0	0	0	2	0	0	0	4	0	0	.167	.286
Long, Jacob	R-R	6-1	180	4-17-86	.158	.000	.188	8	19	5	3	0	0	0	2	0	0	0	0	4	0	0	.158	.238
Louwsma, Jason	R-R	6-2	210	9-9-83	.298	.278	.305	54	208	37	62	16	0	2	31	17	4	0	4	28	1	2	.404	.356
McKennon, Michael	L-R	6-3	210	3-31-85	.234	.160	.250	46	137	11	32	5	3	0	28	7	3	0	2	36	0	2	.380	.282
Mesa, Maikol	R-R	6-3	180	9-24-85	.214	.125	.269	19	42	6	9	1	2	0	4	4	0	1	1	8	0	0	.333	.277
Parker, Logan	L-L	6-3	220	7-18-84	.329	.313	.333	66	231	43	76	12	3	9	51	41	0	0	3	47	2	1	.524	.425
Phipps, Denis	R-R	6-2	176	7-22-85	.315	.294	.324	17	54	7	17	3	0	1	10	5	0	2	1	19	1	0	.426	.367
Rojo, Billy	R-R	5-10	144	4-23-83	.297	.271	.308	55	202	40	60	14	1	1	19	26	2	1	1	31	7	6	.391	.381
Stubbs, Drew	R-R	6-5	190	10-4-84	.252	.180	.275	56	210	39	53	7	3	6	24	32	7	2	1	64	19	4	.400	.368
Tordi, Justin	R-R	6-1	195	4-9-84	.168	.160	.171	37	101	11	17	2	0	0	9	11	3	1	1	25	0	0	.188	.267
Turner, Justin	R-R	5-11	180	11-23-84	.338	.392	.322	60	231	53	78	16	3	6	41	23	7	0	2	38	12	2	.511	.411
Valaika, Chris	R-R	6-0	190	8-14-85	.324	.310	.327	70	275	58	89	22	4	8	60	24	8	2	6	61	2	2	.520	.387
Winkler, Jason	R-R	6-2	215	5-7-84	.143	.500	.000	4	7	0	1	0	0	0	1	0	0	0	0	0	0	0	.143	.143

PITCHING	B-T	HT	WT	DOB	W	L	ERA	G	GS	CG	SV	IP	H	R	ER	HR	BB	SO	AVG	vLH	vRH	K/9	BB/9
Arneson, Jamie	L-L	6-5	195	11-5-85	2	1	3.35	17	0	0	3	43	31	20	16	3	24	46	.199	.286	.174	9.63	5.02
Burchett, Jeremy	R-R	6-3	195	11-25-83	3	2	2.16	13	0	0	1	33	25	12	8	2	11	19	.210	.129	.239	5.13	2.97
Camardese, Brandon	R-L	6-2	205	7-2-83	1	1	3.20	11	0	0	0	25	29	11	9	0	6	24	.284	.222	.318	8.53	2.13
DeJesus, Misael	R-R	6-3	190	11-4-84	2	1	5.17	16	7	0	2	54	49	33	31	9	16	48	.245	.180	.273	8.00	2.67
Donaldson, Daniel	R-L	6-4	180	7-23-84	0	0	9.64	5	0	0	0	5	11	5	5	1	5	3	.440	.667	.368	5.79	9.64
Gonzalez, Rafael	R-R	6-3	225	3-21-86	1	1	2.40	3	3	0	0	15	12	6	4	3	2	6	.222	.273	.209	3.60	1.20
Gressick, Anthony	R-R	6-3	200	1-1-84	6	2	4.50	14	14	0	0	62	72	36	31	5	21	44	.304	.273	.319	6.39	3.05
Guerrero, Daniel	R-R	6-1	190	7-21-85	2	0	0.75	2	2	0	0	12	6	1	1	0	0	5	.146	.200	.129	3.75	0.00
Gunter, Kevin	R-R	6-3	210	11-5-83	3	1	4.67	17	1	0	2	44	43	27	23	6	19	32	.256	.304	.238	6.50	3.86
Huddy, Kyle	R-R	6-2	220	6-13-83	0	0	5.50	10	1	0	0	18	16	14	11	2	20	17	.242	.235	.245	8.50	10.00
Mason, Dane	R-R	6-0	175	12-3-82	3	4	4.40	11	10	0	0	45	50	36	22	3	17	34	.281	.226	.310	6.80	3.40
Mateo, Marcos	R-R	6-1	160	4-18-84	5	1	3.20	18	0	0	1	45	43	17	16	2	20	30	.262	.326	.240	6.00	4.00
Morris, James	L-L	6-8	255	6-3-83	1	1	4.84	19	0	0	1	22	22	17	12	1	16	30	.253	.250	.254	12.09	6.45
Moya, Luis	R-R	6-0	170	1-4-84	3	2	3.52	22	0	0	0	31	26	13	12	3	14	23	.243	.100	.299	6.75	4.11
Ondrusek, Logan	R-R	6-8	195	2-13-85	0	1	27.00	1	0	0	0	1	4	3	3	0	1	3	.571	—	.571	27.00	9.00
Pointer, Adam	R-R	5-11	170	9-21-84	3	0	6.14	10	1	0	0	15	17	10	10	3	6	5	.309	.333	.300	3.07	3.68
Ravin, Josh	R-R	6-4	195	1-21-88	0	0	3.52	4	4	0	0	15	10	7	6	1	13	18	.189	.286	.154	10.57	7.63
Roenicke, Joshua	R-R	6-3	195	8-4-82	1	1	6.32	14	0	0	6	16	10	11	11	1	12	24	.179	.294	.128	13.79	6.89
Smiley, Wes	R-R	6-1	217	7-21-81	0	1	13.50	1	0	0	0	2	7	4	3	1	1	1	.700	1.000	.667	4.50	4.50
Smith, Jordan	R-R	6-4	210	2-4-86	6	3	3.01	14	14	0	0	69	58	29	23	3	20	49	.227	.229	.226	6.42	2.62
Watson, Sean	R-R	6-1	210	7-24-85	0	0	1.52	7	4	0	1	24	16	7	4	0	5	19	.190	.138	.218	7.23	1.90
Webb, Travis	L-L	6-4	200	8-2-84	5	2	3.40	13	7	0	0	40	41	21	15	5	16	32	.273	.385	.234	7.26	3.63
White, Christopher	R-R	6-2	205	10-14-82	1	0	6.08	5	1	0	0	13	16	9	9	3	6	12	.291	.214	.317	8.10	4.05
Young, Terrell	R-R	6-3	175	8-7-85	3	1	2.70	25	0	0	9	23	11	10	7	2	20	32	.145	.154	.140	12.34	7.71

FIELDING

Catcher	PCT	G	PO	A	E	DP	PB
Esquer	.978	35	238	28	6	3	9
Gonzalez	.986	13	57	15	1	0	3
Long	1.000	8	55	3	0	2	2
Tordi	.983	35	207	27	4	2	11

First Base	PCT	G	PO	A	E	DP
Brown	.983	14	108	8	2	14
Colon	.982	10	54	1	1	8
Lasso	1.000	1	4	0	0	0
Parker	.983	59	488	30	9	56
Turner	1.000	1	1	0	0	0
Winkler	.857	2	6	0	1	1

Second Base	PCT	G	PO	A	E	DP
Feiner	1.000	2	3	5	0	2
Lasso	—	1	0	0	0	0
Rojo	.968	43	95	120	7	36
Turner	.966	37	71	99	6	26

Third Base	PCT	G	PO	A	E	DP
Colon	.875	19	14	35	7	3
Francisco	.917	6	2	9	1	2
Lasso	1.000	2	0	4	0	0
Louwsma	.930	48	31	116	11	13
Turner	.929	7	4	9	1	1

Shortstop	PCT	G	PO	A	E	DP
Feiner	.900	5	3	6	1	1
Lasso	.667	2	1	3	2	2

	PCT	G	PO	A	E	DP
Tordi	1.000	2	0	1	0	0
Turner	.971	7	11	22	1	3
Valaika	.951	66	99	194	15	51

Outfield	PCT	G	PO	A	E	DP
Dorn	.988	53	74	6	1	5
Feiner	—	1	0	0	0	0
Heisey	.970	69	125	3	4	0
Louwsma	1.000	1	1	0	0	0
McKennon	1.000	30	36	0	0	0
Mesa	.900	16	17	1	2	0
Phipps	.951	17	37	2	2	0
Stubbs	.985	55	123	7	2	2
Turner	1.000	8	11	0	0	0

GCL Reds
Rookie

Gulf Coast League

BATTING	B-T	HT	WT	DOB	AVG	vLH	vRH	G	AB	R	H	2B	3B	HR	RBI	BB	HBP	SH	SF	SO	SB	CS	SLG	OBP
Bastardo, Jose	R-R	5-11	165	11-16-85	.188	.143	.222	8	16	4	3	0	0	0	0	3	0	0	0	8	0	0	.188	.316
Brown, Ryan	L-R	6-4	235	10-17-82	.348	.500	.333	7	23	3	8	2	0	0	7	1	0	0	1	3	1	0	.435	.360
Cabrera, Angel	R-R	6-0	185	10-14-85	.293	.303	.291	48	167	31	49	15	2	3	17	24	2	2	2	31	2	1	.461	.385
Cabrera, Enmanuel	R-R	5-10	170	8-9-85	.292	.323	.281	35	120	15	35	0	2	0	5	6	2	2	0	28	11	6	.325	.336
Encarnacion, Fernando	R-R	6-0	185	7-23-85	.333	.333	.333	20	45	2	15	3	1	0	5	0	1	0	1	9	0	0	.444	.340
Feiner, Kevyn	R-R	6-1	170	6-11-87	.227	.267	.219	28	88	4	20	2	0	1	6	3	0	1	0	14	0	2	.284	.253
Francisco, Juan	B-R	6-2	180	6-24-87	.280	.222	.295	45	182	24	51	14	0	3	30	6	1	0	1	35	2	0	.407	.305
Hauschild, Tyler	R-R	6-0	210	11-24-85	.209	.000	.243	23	43	0	9	0	0	0	5	2	4	0	0	9	0	0	.209	.306
Jones, Keltavious	L-L	5-9	170	9-21-85	.256	.438	.210	28	78	20	20	4	1	0	2	12	3	0	1	15	6	1	.333	.372
Jones, Michael	R-R	6-3	180	11-19-86	.176	.192	.173	43	136	11	24	6	0	0	6	10	3	4	1	24	3	3	.221	.247
Long, Jacob	R-R	6-1	180	4-17-86	.333	.263	.354	27	84	12	28	6	0	0	14	0	0	1	0	14	0	0	.405	.378
Loo, Milton	R-R	6-1	185	4-2-86	.372	.600	.303	14	43	10	16	6	0	1	7	1	2	0	0	5	0	1	.581	.413
Martinez, Juan	R-R	5-11	162	3-14-86	.321	.211	.354	30	84	12	27	3	1	0	6	2	3	0	2	18	2	3	.381	.352
Phipps, Denis	R-R	6-2	176	7-22-85	.280	.436	.232	43	164	21	46	10	1	3	22	8	3	0	1	31	6	6	.409	.324
Reed, Justin	L-R	5-11	179	11-29-87	.180	.160	.184	44	161	17	29	2	6	1	16	19	1	6	0	45	6	5	.286	.271
Rodriguez, Eddy	R-R	6-0	205	12-1-85	.235	.500	.000	7	17	1	4	2	0	1	4	1	1	0	1	5	0	0	.529	.300
Rumbos, Javier	R-R	5-10	170	7-5-85	.286	.273	.292	15	35	1	10	2	0	0	3	4	0	1	1	6	0	0	.343	.350
Sanchez, Rafael	L-R	6-1	190	8-1-86	.207	.185	.213	37	116	10	24	2	1	0	11	20	4	0	2	22	0	2	.241	.343
Scott, David	L-R	6-2	220	3-29-85	.202	.238	.192	31	99	8	20	5	0	1	9	13	1	0	3	29	1	1	.283	.293
Winkler, Jason	R-R	6-2	215	5-7-84	.174	.143	.179	18	46	3	8	2	0	1	4	5	0	0	1	10	0	0	.283	.250

PITCHING	B-T	HT	WT	DOB	W	L	ERA	G	GS	CG	SV	IP	H	R	ER	HR	BB	SO	AVG	vLH	vRH	K/9	BB/9
Alford, Brandon	R-L	6-3	225	10-31-82	2	3	5.91	11	3	0	0	35	40	26	23	2	17	26	.292	.343	.275	6.69	4.37
Balfour, Grant	R-R	6-2	195	12-30-77	0	0	13.50	2	2	0	0	1	1	2	2	0	3	0	.250	1.000	.000	13.50	20.25
Burchett, Jeremy	R-R	6-3	195	11-25-83	0	0	2.70	3	0	0	0	7	6	4	2	0	2	3	.250	.375	.188	4.05	2.70
Camardese, Brandon	R-L	6-2	205	7-2-83	0	1	9.00	2	2	0	0	7	7	7	7	0	0	4	.259	.000	.304	5.14	0.00
Caudill, William	R-R	6-4	230	9-28-82	0	2	4.57	13	0	0	1	22	16	14	11	0	14	14	.208	.167	.234	5.82	5.82
Clark, Matt	L-L	6-2	185	3-12-87	1	0	3.75	8	1	0	0	12	7	7	5	0	17	7	.194	.000	.241	5.25	12.75
Dicso, Greg	R-R	6-5	195	2-24-84	0	0	0.00	3	0	0	0	4	1	0	0	0	2	2	.077	.100	.100	4.91	4.91
Donaldson, Daniel	R-L	6-4	190	7-23-84	0	1	4.91	9	2	0	0	26	22	14	14	3	12	25	.229	.467	.185	8.77	4.21
Gardner, Richard	R-R	6-3	185	2-1-82	1	0	1.64	4	0	0	0	11	5	3	2	0	3	14	.147	.222	.120	11.45	2.45
Gonzalez, Rafael	R-R	6-3	225	3-21-86	0	1	15.00	1	0	0	0	3	6	5	5	0	2	2	.500	.600	.429	6.00	6.00
Gruler, Christopher	R-R	6-3	200	9-11-83	1	1	3.60	5	5	0	0	15	17	9	6	1	8	11	.274	.174	.333	6.60	4.80
Herrera, Andres	L-L	6-2	165	3-29-88	0	1	13.50	2	2	0	0	4	5	7	6	0	4	0	.294	.333	.286	0.00	9.00
Leach, Jarred	R-R	6-2	210	8-4-87	0	1	4.76	12	0	0	0	23	22	13	12	0	19	15	.265	.233	.283	5.96	7.54
Lutz, Derrik	R-R	6-0	210	4-22-85	1	0	1.59	2	0	0	0	6	3	1	1	0	0	5	.158	.200	.143	7.94	0.00
Medina, Ruben	R-R	5-11	157	7-28-86	1	1	0.00	10	0	0	0	12	8	1	0	0	4	4	.200	.286	.154	3.00	3.00
Montano, Luis	R-R	6-0	180	3-20-85	0	3	3.52	10	8	0	0	38	49	19	15	2	9	34	.304	.240	.333	7.98	2.11
Newman, Justin	L-R	6-0	200	4-6-84	0	6	9.70	14	0	0	1	21	31	25	23	4	14	9	.348	.267	.390	3.80	5.91
Nickols, Robert	L-L	6-5	215	3-4-86	0	0	3.00	2	0	0	0	3	2	1	1	0	4	4	.182	—	1	12.00	12.00
Pointer, Adam	R-R	5-11	170	9-21-84	2	1	2.41	11	0	0	1	19	13	6	5	0	8	15	.194	.353	.140	8.68	1.93
Ravin, Joshua	R-R	6-4	195	1-21-88	0	1	4.29	7	6	0	0	21	21	13	10	0	10	22	.266	.304	.250	9.43	4.29
Rice, Brandon	R-R	6-4	210	1-11-88	2	2	2.73	10	9	0	0	33	28	16	10	0	10	20	.222	.092	5.45	2.73
Roenicke, Josh	R-R	6-3	195	8-4-82	1	0	1.17	7	0	0	0	8	8	2	1	0	3	9	.258	.400	.190	10.57	3.52
Rojas, Jose A.	R-R	6-0	165	3-2-83	0	0	0.00	3	0	0	0	3	3	0	0	0	5	2	.273	.400	.167	16.88	0.00
Schaler, Eric	R-R	6-4	210	3-5-84	0	1	20.25	4	0	0	0	3	5	7	6	0	2	4	.385	.333	.400	6.75	6.75
Smiley, Wes	R-R	6-1	217	7-21-81	1	0	2.45	2	0	0	0	4	4	1	1	0	2	6	.091	.000	.167	7.36	4.91
Tabor, Lee	L-L	6-2	175	12-17-84	2	1	3.69	9	5	0	0	32	34	17	13	4	3	27	.268	.355	.240	7.67	0.85
Thompson, Daryl	R-R	6-1	170	11-2-85	0	0	2.57	5	4	0	0	14	10	4	4	1	6	18	.222	.278	.185	10.29	2.57
Wandless, Nicholas	R-R	6-2	220	11-15-83	2	2	2.18	16	0	0	1	33	25	8	8	0	9	40	.214	.163	.243	10.91	2.45
White, Christopher	R-R	6-2	205	10-14-82	0	1	3.45	6	3	0	0	16	19	11	6	1	6	15	.288	.150	.348	8.62	3.45
Williams, Ryan	L-L	6-0	197	9-21-82	2	4	3.00	10	0	0	0	18	17	10	6	1	4	19	.243	.267	.236	9.50	2.00
Yount, Andrew	R-R	6-2	180	2-14-77	0	0	0.00	5	0	0	0	6	2	1	0	0	5	1	.111	.000	.182	1.59	7.94

FIELDING

Catcher	PCT	G	PO	A	E	DP	PB
Encarnacion	1.000	19	81	16	0	1	6
Hauschild	.961	23	89	9	4	1	1
Long	.989	25	163	22	2	1	3
Rodriguez	.977	7	31	12	1	0	2
Rumbos	1.000	7	15	1	0	0	0

First Base	PCT	G	PO	A	E	DP
Brown	1.000	4	31	3	0	2
Sanchez	.994	16	148	5	1	8
Scott	.987	26	211	12	3	18

		PCT	G	PO	A	E	DP
Winkler		.989	12	87	3	1	5

Second Base	PCT	G	PO	A	E	DP
Cabrera	.925	26	37	49	7	12
Feiner	.933	10	22	20	3	2
Martinez	.920	22	48	56	9	9
Sanchez	—	1	0	0	0	0

Third Base	PCT	G	PO	A	E	DP
Francisco	.884	37	22	85	14	10
Sanchez	.844	15	7	20	5	1
Winkler	1.000	2	1	1	0	0

Shortstop	PCT	G	PO	A	E	DP
Cabrera	.923	48	81	160	20	18
Feiner	1.000	4	1	13	0	1
Loo	1.000	2	1	3	0	0
Martinez	.889	4	4	12	2	2

Outfield	PCT	G	PO	A	E	DP
Feiner	1.000	14	21	2	0	2
M. Jones	.980	42	46	4	1	1
K. Jones	.979	25	44	2	1	0
Phipps	.972	43	97	7	3	3
Reed	.984	44	60	2	1	0

CLEVELAND INDIANS

BY ANDY CALL

It's not as if there were no positive story lines for the Indians.

Grady Sizemore developed into an all-star. Travis Hafner was being mentioned in the MVP race until a broken bone in his right hand sidelined him in September. C.C. Sabathia experienced the best season of his career. Some of the team's rookies demonstrated considerable promise.

But when looking at the big picture, the Indians may have been the biggest disappointment in baseball in 2006. The team that had won 93 games a year earlier fell out of the division race in June, sold off many of its veteran players in July, and spent the second half of the season sending out a lineup of young players to take part in meaningless games.

"There were a lot of expectations on us this year, for the first time," manager Eric Wedge said. "That was some of the difficulty."

There were more tangible difficulties as well. Cleveland's bullpen, the best in baseball in 2005, ranked 11th in the American League with a 4.66 ERA. Nearly all of the team's offseason moves seemed to backfire.

"Our bullpen wasn't capable, it was terrible," general manager Mark Shapiro said. "That, and our infield defense, were two factors that undermined our ability to win games. Maybe we could have overcome one, but not both."

The Indians also could not overcome the loss of pitchers Kevin Millwood and Bobby Howry to free agency, the early struggles of its starting rotation, the regression of shortstop Jhonny Peralta and third baseman Aaron Boone reaching the end of the line.

ORGANIZATION LEADERS

BATTING		*Minimum 250 at-bats
*AVG	Kouzmanoff, Kevin, Akron/Buffalo	.379
R	Francisco, Ben, Buffalo	91
H	Francisco, Ben, Buffalo	161
TB	Francisco, Ben, Buffalo	264
2B	Francisco, Ben, Buffalo	35
3B	Constanza, Jose, Lake County/Kinston	9
HR	Goleski, Ryan, Kinston/Akron	27
RBI	Goleski, Ryan, Kinston/Akron	106
BB	Crowe, Trevor, Kinston/Lake County/Akron	76
SO	Snyder, Brad, Akron	158
SB	Crowe, Trevor, Kinston/Lake County/Akron	47
*OBP	Kouzmanoff, Kevin, Akron/Buffalo	.437
*SLG	Kouzmanoff, Kevin, Akron/Buffalo	.656
XBH	Francisco, Ben, Buffalo	59

PITCHING		#Minimum 75 innings
W	Lofgren, Charles, Kinston	17
L	Vargas, Albert, Lake County	14
#ERA	Lewis, Scott, Kinston	1.48
G	Collins, Kyle, Akron/Kinston	60
CG	Guthrie, Jeremy, Buffalo	2
	Sowers, Jeremy, Buffalo	2
SV	Davis, Matt, Lake County/Akron	27
IP	Smith, Sean, Kinston/Akron	169
BB	Ness, Joe, Kinston	55
SO	Miller, Adam, Buffalo/Akron	161
#AVG	Tomlin, Joshua, Mahoning Valley	.196

The Tigers led the Indians by 15 games on June 19. When the hopelessness of the situation became apparent, the team began trading away marketable veterans (Bob Wickman, Ronnie Belliard, Ben Broussard, Eduardo Perez and Todd Hollandsworth) for prospects.

Some of those who stayed forged memorable seasons. Sizemore finished with 53 doubles, 11 triples, 28 home runs and 22 stolen bases, the first player in club history to reach double digits in all four categories in two consecutive seasons. His 92 extra-base hits were the most by any leadoff batter in 50 years. The 24-year-old center fielder also led the league in runs (134).

Hafner was batting .308/.439/.659 with 42 homers and 117 RBIs when his season-ending injury occurred Sept. 1. Sabathia's 3.22 ERA ranked third in the AL, and he set career highs in innings pitched (193) and strikeouts (172) despite missing the first month of the season with a strained oblique.

Those three players, as well as catcher Victor Martinez and lefthander Cliff Lee, make up the core the Indians will attempt to build around. A few youngsters (lefthander Jeremy Sowers, first baseman Ryan Garko, outfielder Shin-Soo Choo) seized their second-half opportunity and offer Tribe fans some hope for the future.

"We took a little bit of a detour, but we're still headed in the right direction," Shapiro said.

Cleveland's traditionally strong minor league system experienced some success, but lost farm director John Farrell when he decided to become pitching coach for the Red Sox. High Class A Kinston won the Carolina League championship, Double-A Akron lost in the Eastern League finals and three of the five other affiliates finished with winning records.

Kinston lefthander Scott Lewis (3-3, 1.48) had one of the best seasons in the minors, while teammates Jordan Brown and Chuck Lofgren were named the Carolina League's MVP and pitcher of the year respectively. Akron's Adam Miller (15-6, 2.75) was named the Eastern League's top pitcher. Third baseman Kevin Kouzmanoff batted a combined .379 at Akron and Triple-A Buffalo, earning a September callup.

Cleveland Indians — MLB

American League

BATTING	B-T	HT	WT	DOB	AVG	vLH	vRH	G	AB	R	H	2B	3B	HR	RBI	BB	HBP	SH	SF	SO	SB	CS	SLG	OBP
Belliard, Ronnie	R-R	5-8	195	4-7-75	.291	.248	.313	93	350	43	102	21	0	8	44	21	4	2	2	45	2	0	.420	.337
Blake, Casey	R-R	6-2	210	8-23-73	.282	.272	.286	109	401	63	113	20	1	19	68	45	4	1	5	93	6	0	.479	.356
Boone, Aaron	R-R	6-2	200	3-9-73	.251	.280	.239	104	354	50	89	19	1	7	46	27	6	4	1	62	5	4	.370	.314
Broussard, Ben	L-L	6-2	220	9-24-76	.321	.130	.360	88	268	44	86	14	0	13	46	17	1	0	2	58	0	1	.519	.361
2-team (56 Seattle)					.289	—	—	144	432	61	125	21	0	21	63	26	3	0	4	103	2	1	.484	.331
Choo, Shin-Soo	L-L	5-11	210	7-13-82	.295	.278	.297	45	146	23	43	11	3	3	22	18	1	1	1	46	5	3	.473	.373
2-team (4 Seattle)					.280	—	—	49	157	23	44	12	3	3	22	18	2	1	1	50	5	3	.452	.360
Garko, Ryan	R-R	6-2	225	1-2-81	.292	.333	.281	50	185	28	54	12	0	7	45	14	7	0	3	37	0	0	.470	.359
Gutierrez, Franklin	R-R	6-2	180	2-21-83	.272	.262	.277	43	136	21	37	9	0	1	8	3	0	2	0	28	0	0	.360	.288
Hafner, Travis	L-R	6-3	240	6-3-77	.308	.321	.300	129	454	100	140	31	1	42	117	100	7	0	2	111	0	0	.659	.439
Hollandsworth, Todd	L-L	6-2	225	4-20-73	.237	.190	.244	56	156	21	37	12	1	6	27	4	0	0	2	33	0	1	.442	.253
Inglett, Joe	L-R	5-10	180	6-29-78	.284	.217	.292	64	201	26	57	8	3	2	21	14	1	5	1	39	5	1	.383	.332
Kouzmanoff, Kevin	R-R	6-1	210	7-25-81	.214	.167	.227	16	56	4	12	2	0	3	11	5	0	0	0	12	0	0	.411	.279
Laker, Tim	R-R	6-3	225	11-27-69	.308	.400	.250	4	13	1	4	1	0	0	2	0	0	0	0	4	0	0	.385	.308
Luna, Hector	R-R	6-1	170	2-1-80	.276	.326	.247	37	127	14	35	7	1	2	17	6	0	1	0	26	0	1	.394	.306
Marte, Andy	R-R	6-1	190	10-21-83	.226	.227	.225	50	164	20	37	15	1	5	23	13	1	0	0	38	0	0	.421	.287
Martinez, Victor	B-R	6-2	195	12-23-78	.316	.290	.332	153	572	82	181	37	0	16	93	71	3	0	6	78	0	0	.465	.391
Merloni, Lou	R-R	5-10	200	4-6-71	.211	.222	.200	9	19	1	4	1	0	0	1	2	0	2	0	5	1	0	.263	.286
Michaels, Jason	R-R	6-0	205	5-4-76	.267	.291	.252	123	494	77	132	32	1	9	55	43	3	2	6	101	9	5	.391	.326
Peralta, Jhonny	R-R	6-1	195	5-28-82	.257	.267	.252	149	569	84	146	28	3	13	68	56	1	3	3	152	0	1	.385	.323
Perez, Eduardo	R-R	6-4	240	9-11-69	.303	.330	.091	37	99	16	30	9	0	8	22	5	2	0	2	11	0	0	.636	.343
2-team (43 Seattle)					.253	—	—	80	186	22	47	10	0	9	33	18	3	0	3	33	0	1	.452	.324
Shoppach, Kelly	R-R	6-0	220	4-29-80	.245	.314	.213	41	110	7	27	6	0	3	16	8	0	2	0	45	0	0	.382	.297
Sizemore, Grady	L-L	6-2	200	8-2-82	.290	.214	.329	162	655	134	190	53	11	28	76	78	13	1	4	153	22	6	.533	.375
Vazquez, Ramon	L-R	5-11	170	8-21-76	.209	.286	.200	34	67	11	14	2	0	1	8	6	0	2	2	18	0	0	.284	.267

PITCHING	B-T	HT	WT	DOB	W	L	ERA	G	GS	CG	SV	IP	H	R	ER	HR	BB	SO	AVG	vLH	vRH	K/9	BB/9
Betancourt, Rafael	R-R	6-2	200	4-29-75	3	4	3.81	50	0	0	3	57	52	25	24	7	11	48	.241	.221	.254	7.62	1.75
Brown, Andrew	R-R	6-6	230	2-17-81	0	0	3.60	9	0	0	0	10	6	4	4	0	8	7	.171	.286	.095	6.30	7.20
Byrd, Paul	R-R	6-1	190	12-3-70	10	9	4.88	31	31	1	0	179	232	120	97	26	38	88	.308	.369	.256	4.42	1.91
Cabrera, Fernando	R-R	6-4	220	11-16-81	3	3	5.19	51	0	0	0	61	53	36	35	12	32	71	.243	.235	.248	10.53	4.75
Carmona, Fausto	R-R	6-4	220	12-7-83	1	10	5.42	38	7	0	0	75	88	46	45	9	31	58	.298	.299	.298	6.99	3.74
Davis, Jason	R-R	6-6	225	5-8-80	3	2	3.74	39	0	0	1	55	67	28	23	1	14	37	.302	.316	.294	6.02	2.28
Graves, Danny	R-R	6-0	200	8-7-73	2	1	5.79	13	0	0	0	14	18	12	9	3	5	3	.305	.348	.278	1.93	3.21
Guthrie, Jeremy	R-R	6-1	200	4-8-79	0	0	6.98	9	1	0	0	19	24	15	15	2	15	14	.316	.394	.256	6.52	6.98
Johnson, Jason	R-R	6-6	225	10-27-73	3	8	5.96	14	14	0	0	77	108	55	51	10	22	32	.341	.403	.292	3.74	2.57
2-team (6 Boston)					3	12	6.35	20	20	0	0	106	149	81	75	13	35	50	—	—	—	4.23	2.96
Lara, Juan	R-L	6-2	190	1-26-81	0	0	1.80	9	0	0	0	5	4	2	1	0	1	2	.222	.091	.429	3.60	1.80
Lee, Cliff	L-L	6-3	190	8-30-78	14	11	4.40	33	33	1	0	201	224	114	98	29	58	129	.278	.261	.282	5.79	2.60
Mastny, Tom	R-R	6-6	220	2-4-81	0	1	5.51	15	0	0	5	16	17	10	10	1	8	14	.279	.273	.282	7.71	4.41
Miller, Matt	R-R	6-3	215	11-23-71	1	0	3.45	14	0	0	0	16	11	6	6	2	9	12	.212	.250	.188	6.89	5.17
Mota, Guillermo	R-R	6-4	210	7-25-73	1	3	6.21	34	0	0	0	38	45	27	26	9	19	27	.298	.267	.329	6.45	4.54
Mujica, Edward	R-R	6-2	220	5-10-84	0	1	2.95	10	0	0	0	18	25	6	6	1	0	12	.333	.324	.341	5.89	0.00
Perez, Rafael	L-L	6-3	185	5-15-82	0	0	4.38	18	0	0	0	12	10	6	6	2	6	15	.204	.130	.269	10.95	4.38
Sabathia, C.C.	L-L	6-7	290	7-21-80	12	11	3.22	28	28	6	0	193	182	83	69	17	44	172	.247	.271	.242	8.03	2.06
Sauerbeck, Scott	R-L	6-3	200	11-9-71	0	1	6.23	24	0	0	0	13	9	9	9	2	9	11	.196	.250	.136	7.62	6.23
2-team (22 Oakland)					0	1	4.97	46	0	0	0	25	22	17	14	3	18	17	—	—	—	6.04	6.39
Sikorski, Brian	R-R	6-1	190	7-27-74	2	1	4.58	17	0	0	0	20	20	10	10	4	4	24	.267	.333	.235	10.98	1.83
Slocum, Brian	R-R	6-4	200	3-27-81	0	0	5.60	8	2	0	0	18	27	11	11	3	9	11	.360	.367	.356	5.60	4.58
Sowers, Jeremy	L-L	6-1	180	5-17-83	7	4	3.57	14	14	2	0	88	85	36	35	10	20	35	.252	.225	.259	3.57	2.04
Westbrook, Jake	R-R	6-3	200	9-29-77	15	10	4.17	32	32	3	0	211	247	106	98	15	55	109	.296	.290	.300	4.64	2.34
Wickman, Bob	R-R	6-1	240	2-6-69	1	4	4.18	29	0	0	15	28	29	15	13	1	11	17	.271	.308	.236	5.46	3.54

FIELDING

Catcher	PCT	G	PO	A	E	DP	PB
Laker	1.000	4	24	1	0	1	0
Martinez	.990	133	753	46	8	7	4
Shoppach	.991	40	208	20	2	5	3

First Base	PCT	G	PO	A	E	DP
Blake	.984	9	62	1	1	6
Broussard	.989	80	578	51	7	58
Garko	.986	45	398	30	6	50
Hafner	1.000	4	18	4	0	2
Martinez	1.000	22	149	5	0	15
Perez	.991	29	210	14	2	23

Second Base	PCT	G	PO	A	E	DP
Belliard	.981	91	169	252	8	54
Boone	1.000	1	1	1	0	0

Inglett	.984	53	112	142	4	43
Luna	.947	20	39	50	5	14
Merloni	1.000	3	3	3	0	0
Vazquez	1.000	7	8	20	0	5

Third Base	PCT	G	PO	A	E	DP
Belliard	1.000	1	1	1	0	0
Boone	.938	101	56	186	16	16
Kouzmanoff	.857	2	2	4	1	0
Luna		2	0	0	0	0
Marte	.962	50	32	118	6	14
Merloni	1.000	3	1	3	0	0
Vazquez	.960	14	4	20	1	1

Shortstop	PCT	G	PO	A	E	DP
Inglett	1.000	1	3	1	0	0

Luna	1.000	10	15	34	0	10
Merloni	1.000	3	0	4	0	1
Peralta	.977	147	235	459	16	95
Vazquez	.885	7	8	15	3	3

Outfield	PCT	G	PO	A	E	DP
Blake	.986	93	210	6	3	0
Choo	.976	39	81	2	2	1
Gutierrez	.966	42	85	1	3	0
Hollandsworth	.976	44	76	4	2	0
Inglett	1.000	9	14	0	0	0
Luna		1	0	0	0	0
Michaels	.991	118	216	6	2	2
Perez	1.000	5	4	2	0	0
Sizemore	.993	160	409	7	3	1

General manager: Mark Shapiro. **Farm director:** John Farrell. **Scouting director:** John Mirabelli.

Class	Team	League	W	L	PCT	Finish*	Manager(s)	Affiliate Since
Majors	Cleveland	American	78	84	.481	11th (14)	Eric Wedge	—
Triple-A	Buffalo Bisons	International	73	68	.518	7th (14)	Torey Lovullo	1995
Double-A	Akron Aeros	Eastern	87	55	.613	1st (12)	Tim Bogar	1997
High A	Kinston Indians	Carolina	85	54	.612	+1st (8)	Mike Sarbaugh	1987
Low A	Lake County Captains	South Atlantic	64	74	.464	13th (16)	Lee May	2003
Short-season	Mahoning Valley Indians	New York-Penn	40	36	.526	7th (14)	Rouglas Odor	1999
Rookie	Burlington Indians	Appalachian	34	33	.507	4th (10)	Kevin Higgins	1986
Rookie	GCL Indians	Gulf Coast	21	29	.420	11th (13)	Chris Tremie	2006
OVERALL 2006 MINOR LEAGUE RECORD			404	349	.537	5th (30)		

*Finish in overall standings (No. of teams in league). +League champion

Buffalo Bisons   Triple-A

International League

BATTING	B-T	HT	WT	DOB	AVG	vLH	vRH	G	AB	R	H	2B	3B	HR	RBI	BB	HBP	SH	SF	SO	SB	CS	SLG	OBP
Alfaro, Jason	R-R	5-9	210	11-29-77	.276	.222	.297	74	283	33	78	21	1	8	48	20	2	2	4	29	2	4	.442	.324
2-team (27 Indianapolis)					.257	—	—	101	374	40	96	24	1	11	56	25	2	2	5	51	2	4	.414	.303
Cabrera, Asdrubal	B-R	6-0	170	11-13-85	.263	.207	.288	52	190	26	50	11	0	1	14	8	3	4	6	39	5	4	.337	.295
Camacaro, Armando	R-R	5-11	215	4-6-79	.211	.300	.179	11	38	4	8	1	0	4	4	1	1	2	0	5	0	0	.237	.250
Chavez, Jose	B-R	5-10	170	1-2-85	.250	—	.250	1	4	2	1	0	0	0	0	1	0	0	0	0	0	0	.250	.400
Cooper, Jason	L-L	6-2	215	12-6-80	.228	.198	.240	116	412	56	94	23	4	13	61	41	5	0	4	126	5	2	.398	.303
Diaz, Einar	R-R	5-10	200	12-28-72	.218	.259	.205	64	220	22	48	13	0	3	29	14	1	6	1	23	0	1	.318	.267
Dubois, Jason	R-R	6-5	220	3-26-79	.275	.256	.281	121	455	65	125	31	1	22	87	45	5	1	6	131	4	1	.492	.342
Flores, Jose	R-R	5-11	185	6-28-73	.262	.269	.260	32	103	13	27	4	0	1	16	17	1	1	1	15	1	1	.330	.369
Francisco, Ben	R-R	6-1	190	10-23-81	.278	.297	.270	134	515	80	143	32	4	17	59	45	10	5	4	72	25	5	.454	.345
Garko, Ryan	R-R	6-2	225	1-2-81	.247	.277	.236	103	364	43	90	18	0	15	59	45	19	0	9	67	4	5	.420	.352
Gautreau, Jake	L-R	6-0	195	11-14-79	.198	.149	.218	76	248	27	49	12	0	7	29	25	0	0	0	63	1	1	.331	.271
Gutierrez, Franklin	R-R	6-2	180	2-21-83	.278	.320	.260	90	349	63	97	27	0	9	38	49	5	8	2	84	13	8	.433	.373
Inglett, Joe	L-R	5-10	180	6-29-78	.299	.304	.297	40	157	21	47	7	2	1	13	13	2	8	1	24	3	2	.389	.358
Kouzmanoff, Kevin	R-R	6-1	210	7-25-81	.353	.484	.296	27	102	22	36	9	0	7	20	10	1	0	2	12	2	1	.647	.409
Laker, Tim	R-R	6-3	225	11-27-69	.207	.200	.210	54	188	24	39	14	0	4	12	13	2	2	1	50	0	0	.282	.265
Marte, Andy	R-R	6-1	190	10-21-83	.261	.275	.256	96	357	49	93	23	0	15	46	34	0	0	3	81	1	0	.451	.322
Merloni, Lou	R-R	5-10	200	4-6-71	.285	.232	.302	91	330	33	94	22	0	7	38	29	11	3	1	49	0	2	.415	.361
Michaels, Jason	R-R	6-0	205	5-4-76	.429	.333	.500	2	7	1	3	0	0	1	1	1	0	0	0	0	0	0	.857	.429
Ochoa, Ivan	B-R	5-10	175	12-16-82	.205	.200	.207	16	39	4	8	2	1	0	2	4	3	1	0	5	4	0	.308	.326
Shoppach, Kelly	R-R	6-0	220	4-29-80	.282	.250	.300	21	78	11	22	8	0	4	9	6	3	0	0	25	0	1	.538	.356
Torres, Eider	B-R	5-9	175	1-16-83	.205	.154	.226	11	44	5	9	0	0	0	2	2	0	2	0	4	3	1	.205	.239
Van Every, Jonathan	L-L	6-1	195	11-27-79	.258	.143	.303	47	151	23	39	9	2	5	16	16	3	0	1	51	5	2	.444	.339
Vazquez, Ramon	L-R	5-11	170	8-21-76	.242	.222	.250	28	99	19	24	2	1	2	11	22	0	1	1	27	2	1	.343	.377

PITCHING	B-T	HT	WT	DOB	W	L	ERA	G	GS	CG	SV	IP	H	R	ER	HR	BB	SO	AVG	vLH	vRH	K/9	BB/9
Adams, Mike	R-R	6-5	190	7-29-78	0	0	1.93	3	0	0	0	5	4	1	1	0	0	3	.250	.000	.364	5.79	0.00
2-team (13 Norfolk)					0	0	4.19	16	0	0	0	19	17	9	9	0	7	15	—	—	—	6.98	3.26
Bay, Ronald	R-R	6-3	155	8-7-83	1	0	0.00	1	1	0	0	5	1	0	0	0	6	6	.067	.000	.111	10.80	10.80
Bell, Rob	R-R	6-5	225	1-17-77	9	10	4.25	30	21	0	1	142	145	75	67	20	35	98	.260	.284	.239	6.21	2.22
Brown, Andrew	R-R	6-6	230	2-17-81	5	4	2.60	39	0	0	5	62	52	21	18	5	36	53	.228	.191	.254	7.65	5.20
Cabrera, Fernando	R-R	6-4	220	11-16-81	1	0	1.08	4	0	0	0	8	8	1	1	1	2	13	.242	.214	.263	14.04	2.16
Carmona, Fausto	R-R	6-4	220	12-7-83	1	3	5.53	6	5	0	0	28	28	21	17	2	8	28	.264	.241	.288	9.11	2.60
Choi, Hyang-Nam	R-R	6-3	190	3-28-71	8	5	2.37	34	11	0	0	106	95	32	28	5	35	103	.237	.258	.217	8.72	2.96
Darensbourg, Vic	L-L	5-8	175	11-13-70	1	5	3.92	33	0	0	0	41	41	20	18	2	15	39	.258	.328	.214	8.49	3.27
Davis, Jason	R-R	6-6	225	5-8-80	0	2	0.54	11	0	0	4	17	8	2	1	0	3	15	.138	.174	.114	8.10	1.62
Denham, Dan	R-R	6-2	195	12-24-82	1	2	8.28	9	4	0	0	25	41	24	23	3	11	14	.369	.442	.305	5.04	3.96
Diaz, Einar	R-R	5-10	200	12-28-72	0	1	9.00	1	0	0	0	1	2	1	1	0	1	0	.500	1.000	.333	0.00	9.00
Dittler, Jake	R-R	6-4	220	11-24-82	5	12	4.70	25	24	0	0	130	152	88	68	6	50	54	.290	.325	.259	3.73	3.45
Foley, Travis	R-R	6-0	205	3-11-83	0	0	3.18	2	0	0	0	6	6	2	2	1	1	2	.286	.333	.250	3.18	1.59
Graves, Danny	R-R	6-0	200	8-7-73	1	1	4.01	33	1	0	1	52	55	26	23	5	13	27	.278	.280	.276	4.70	2.26
Guthrie, Jeremy	R-R	6-1	200	4-8-79	9	5	3.14	21	20	2	0	123	104	50	43	6	48	88	.229	.221	.236	6.42	3.50
Heredia, Felix	L-L	6-0	180	6-18-75	0	0	6.75	8	0	0	0	8	16	8	6	1	7	4	.400	.533	.320	4.50	7.88
Howard, Ben	R-R	6-2	210	1-15-79	2	1	3.98	34	0	0	11	41	38	20	18	1	14	21	.252	.255	.250	4.65	3.10
2-team (11 Syracuse)					3	2	5.37	45	0	0	11	57	59	36	34	7	21	29	—	—	—	4.58	3.32
Karsay, Steve	R-R	6-3	215	3-24-72	1	1	2.00	8	0	0	0	18	12	6	4	2	1	14	.188	.161	.212	7.00	0.50
Laker, Tim	R-R	6-3	225	11-27-69	0	0	0.00	1	0	0	0	1	0	0	0	0	1	0	.000	.000	.000	9.00	0.00
Lara, Juan	R-L	6-2	190	1-26-81	1	1	3.00	13	0	0	1	15	17	6	5	1	3	15	.279	.200	.317	9.00	1.80
Mastny, Tom	R-R	6-6	220	2-4-81	2	1	2.61	24	0	0	9	38	25	11	11	0	16	46	.184	.235	.153	10.89	3.79
Miller, Adam	R-R	6-4	175	11-26-84	0	0	5.79	1	1	0	0	5	4	3	3	0	3	4	.235	.231	.250	7.71	5.79
Miller, Matt	R-R	6-3	215	11-23-71	0	0	0.00	1	0	0	1	1	0	0	0	0	0	2	.000	.000	.000	18.00	0.00
Mujica, Edward	R-R	6-2	220	5-10-84	3	1	2.48	22	0	0	5	33	31	10	9	1	5	29	.258	.309	.215	7.99	1.38
Perez, Rafael	L-L	6-3	185	5-15-82	0	3	2.63	13	0	0	0	27	20	11	8	0	8	33	.202	.115	.233	10.87	2.63
Sabathia, C.C.	L-L	6-7	290	7-21-80	1	0	1.80	1	1	0	0	5	6	2	1	0	1	5	.300	.000	.333	9.00	1.80
Slocum, Brian	R-R	6-4	200	3-27-81	6	3	3.35	27	15	0	1	94	78	42	35	5	37	91	.227	.202	.253	8.71	3.54
Sowers, Jeremy	L-L	6-1	180	5-17-83	5	1	1.39	15	15	2	0	97	78	20	15	1	29	54	.224	.205	.230	4.99	2.68
Stanford, Jason	L-L	6-2	200	1-23-77	6	6	4.01	22	18	0	0	112	102	52	50	11	38	81	.242	.257	.236	6.49	3.04

FIELDING

Catcher

	PCT	G	PO	A	E	DP	PB
Camacaro	1.000	10	72	2	0	0	2
Diaz	.989	63	426	35	5	7	6
Garko	1.000	1	2	0	0	0	0
Laker	.983	50	333	18	6	2	7
Shoppach	.975	20	138	17	4	2	1

First Base

	PCT	G	PO	A	E	DP
Garko	.993	87	746	76	6	74
Gautreau	1.000	17	145	16	0	19
Kouzmanoff	1.000	6	49	2	0	3
Laker	1.000	2	19	2	0	0
Merloni	.993	36	276	25	2	31
Vazquez	1.000	2	14	0	0	4

Second Base

	PCT	G	PO	A	E	DP
Alfaro	.988	47	95	142	3	42
Chavez	1.000	1	4	0	0	0
Flores	1.000	3	7	7	0	1
Gautreau	.959	29	62	78	6	20
Inglett	1.000	14	33	38	0	13
Merloni	.971	29	50	83	4	14
Ochoa	.875	2	4	3	1	0
Torres	.968	11	20	40	2	4
Vazquez	.981	10	19	33	1	7

Third Base

	PCT	G	PO	A	E	DP
Alfaro	1.000	1	1	3	0	0
Flores	1.000	3	3	3	0	1
Gautreau	.956	20	11	32	2	4
Kouzmanoff	.932	20	14	54	5	7
Marte	.935	91	61	213	19	25
Merloni	.963	11	7	19	1	0
Vazquez	—	1	0	0	0	0

Shortstop

	PCT	G	PO	A	E	DP
Alfaro	.909	23	29	61	9	11
Cabrera	.942	52	80	147	14	37
Flores	.940	23	30	64	6	10
Inglett	.948	13	24	31	3	9
Merloni	.957	8	14	30	2	4
Ochoa	.946	13	16	37	3	5
Vazquez	.968	13	24	37	2	12

Outfield

	PCT	G	PO	A	E	DP
Cooper	.988	99	169	2	2	1
Dubois	.987	89	149	7	2	0
Francisco	.981	103	193	9	4	0
Gutierrez	.995	85	180	6	1	3
Inglett	.944	8	17	0	1	0
Michaels	1.000	2	6	0	0	0
Van Every	1.000	46	104	4	0	2

Akron Aeros — Double-A

Eastern League

BATTING

	B-T	HT	WT	DOB	AVG	vLH	vRH	G	AB	R	H	2B	3B	HR	RBI	BB	HBP	SH	SF	SO	SB	CS	SLG	OBP
Aubrey, Michael	L-L	6-0	195	4-15-82	.269	.400	.188	6	26	3	7	2	0	1	2	2	1	0	0	4	0	0	.462	.345
Barton, Brian	R-R	6-3	187	4-25-82	.351	.219	.387	42	151	32	53	5	0	6	26	13	5	0	2	26	15	5	.503	.415
Blake, Casey	R-R	6-2	210	8-23-73	.333	—	.333	1	3	0	1	1	0	0	1	0	0	0	0	0	0	0	.667	.333
Brock, Caleb	R-R	5-11	200	3-30-80	.667	—	.667	1	3	1	2	0	1	0	1	0	0	0	0	0	0	0	1.333	.667
Camacaro, Armando	R-R	5-11	215	4-6-79	.056	.100	.000	6	18	3	1	0	0	1	3	0	0	0	7	1	0		.056	.190
Crowe, Trevor	B-R	6-0	190	11-17-83	.234	.229	.235	39	154	20	36	7	2	1	13	20	0	0	2	24	16	6	.325	.318
Donovan, Todd	R-R	6-1	180	8-12-78	.289	.211	.346	24	90	10	26	4	0	0	3	9	0	0	1	12	17	3	.333	.350
2-team (26 Bowie)					.293	—		50	181	27	53	7	3	1	15	18	0	2	1	27	29	6	.381	.355
Goleski, Ryan	R-R	6-3	225	3-19-82	.296	.301	.295	87	324	48	96	24	0	17	63	36	5	0	5	87	4	2	.528	.370
Herrera, Javi	R-R	6-1	200	10-8-81	.207	.250	.184	44	150	15	31	7	0	3	11	8	6	6	0	33	3	0	.313	.274
Inglett, Joe	L-R	5-10	180	6-29-78	.516	.478	.537	18	64	20	33	9	3	9	11	6	2	0	4	7	3		.797	.587
Kouzmanoff, Kevin	R-R	6-1	210	7-25-81	.389	.436	.367	67	244	46	95	19	1	15	55	23	6	0	3	34	2	3	.660	.449
Larkin, Shaun	L-R	5-9	175	9-7-79	.253	.257	.252	110	391	39	99	23	0	6	47	33	2	0	2	47	1	4	.358	.313
Mulhern, Ryan	R-R	6-2	205	11-29-80	.268	.267	.268	121	452	65	121	26	3	15	69	40	7	0	2	123	1	4	.438	.335
Ochoa, Ivan	B-R	5-10	175	12-16-82	.251	.251	.251	104	335	53	84	10	2	1	28	37	8	6	3	63	20	4	.301	.337
Osborn, Pat	R-R	6-1	210	2-27-81	.250	.248	.251	114	408	47	102	14	2	1	37	33	2	0	5	63	14	10	.301	.306
Panther, Nathan	L-L	6-1	180	7-12-81	.231	.186	.242	66	221	30	51	8	4	0	23	21	2	3	3	47	3	4	.303	.300
Pinckney, Brandon	R-R	5-10	165	4-12-82	.308	.500	.245	18	65	13	20	6	2	0	13	1	1	0	1	6	0	0	.492	.324
Sandberg, Jared	R-R	6-3	225	3-2-78	.232	.250	.226	39	125	17	29	14	0	3	22	15	3	0	1	36	2	1	.416	.326
Snyder, Brad	L-L	6-3	200	5-25-82	.270	.255	.276	135	523	86	141	28	5	18	72	62	5	1	3	158	20	2	.446	.351
Toregas, Wyatt	R-R	5-11	200	12-2-82	.258	.385	.234	48	163	21	42	10	0	4	29	14	2	2	3	33	1	3	.393	.319
Torres, Eider	B-R	5-9	175	1-16-83	.273	.294	.265	104	428	49	117	12	2	2	42	32	2	11	2	54	41	12	.325	.325
Valdes, Juan	B-R	6-0	150	6-22-85	.160	.100	.182	10	25	1	4	0	0	1	3	0	0	1	0	11	0	2	.160	.250
Van Every, Jonathan	L-L	6-1	195	11-27-79	.258	.333	.224	66	236	35	61	16	5	10	40	26	5	0	5	80	5	1	.496	.338
Wallace, David	R-R	6-4	230	10-17-79	.232	.289	.209	49	155	25	36	8	0	6	22	17	3	0	1	33	3	1	.400	.318

PITCHING

	B-T	HT	WT	DOB	W	L	ERA	G	GS	CG	SV	IP	H	R	ER	HR	BB	SO	AVG	vLH	vRH	K/9	BB/9
Bay, Ronald	R-R	6-3	155	8-7-83	7	8	4.33	27	19	1	0	133	126	72	64	24	48	114	.249	.288	.218	7.71	3.25
Betancourt, Rafael	R-R	6-2	200	4-29-75	0	0	0.00	1	1	0	0	1	0	0	0	0	1	2	.000	.000		18.00	9.00
Buzachero, Edward	R-R	5-11	180	6-13-81	8	3	2.72	49	0	0	4	79	74	27	24	2	25	71	.252	.277	.232	8.05	2.84
Collins, Kyle	R-R	6-1	165	8-17-81	1	1	5.12	18	0	0	0	19	23	13	11	3	14	15	.295	.364	.244	6.98	6.52
Cooper, Chris	L-L	5-11	195	10-31-78	1	0	6.75	4	0	0	0	5	5	4	4	0	2	6	.250	.429	.154	10.13	3.38
Cowley, Thomas	L-L	6-3	190	12-30-83	1	0	2.70	2	2	0	0	10	7	3	3	2	7	11	.194	.273	.160	9.90	6.30
Davis, Matt	R-R	6-2	205	11-19-81	0	0	6.00	4	0	0	1	6	6	4	4	3	1	6	.261	.167	.294	9.00	1.50
Denham, Dan	R-R	6-2	195	12-24-82	6	2	4.88	23	10	0	0	66	66	37	36	3	39	40	.262	.339	.200	5.43	5.29
Foley, Travis	R-R	6-0	205	3-11-83	4	5	3.83	41	0	0	3	80	79	39	34	6	31	86	.252	.284	.232	9.68	3.49
Gomez, Mariano	L-L	6-6	190	9-12-82	0	0	9.82	3	1	0	0	7	14	8	8	1	1	5	.389	.444	.370	6.14	1.23
Kleine, Victor	L-L	6-4	185	9-12-79	0	0	15.88	5	0	0	0	6	12	10	10	0	3	4	.462	.556	.412	6.35	4.76
Laffey, Aaron	L-L	6-0	170	4-15-85	8	3	3.53	19	19	0	0	112	121	50	44	9	33	61	.286	.320	.272	4.89	2.64
Lara, Juan	R-L	6-2	190	1-26-81	4	2	2.70	40	0	0	7	47	32	14	14	2	21	48	.189	.188	.190	9.26	4.05
Larkin, Shaun	L-R	5-9	175	9-7-79	0	0	18.00	1	0	0	0	1	1	2	2	0	1	0	.250	.333	.000	0.00	9.00
Lewis, Jensen	R-R	6-3	195	5-16-84	1	2	3.89	7	7	0	0	39	41	21	17	4	12	44	.270	.294	.250	10.07	2.75
Mastny, Tom	R-R	6-6	220	2-4-81	1	1	1.09	12	1	0	1	25	15	5	3	0	8	30	.169	.189	.154	10.95	2.92
Miller, Matt	R-R	6-3	215	11-23-71	0	0	0.00	2	0	0	0	2	2	0	0	1	0	5	.286	.500	.000	0.00	1.50
Miller, Adam	R-R	6-4	175	11-26-84	15	6	2.75	26	24	1	0	154	129	56	47	9	43	157	.226	.198	.250	9.20	2.52
Mujica, Edward	R-R	6-2	220	5-10-84	1	0	0.00	12	0	0	8	19	11	1	0	0	9	17	.169	.267	.086	8.05	4.26
Perez, Rafael	L-L	6-3	185	5-15-82	4	5	2.81	12	1	0	0	67	53	25	21	3	22	53	.218	.145	.243	7.08	2.94
Pesco, Nick	R-R	6-2	195	9-17-83	6	8	5.81	18	18	0	0	88	100	60	57	13	40	64	.290	.318	.267	6.52	4.08
Roehl, Scott	R-R	6-1	195	8-19-81	0	0	9.82	7	0	0	0	7	12	8	8	2	7	5	.375	.375	.375	6.14	8.59
Santos, Reid	L-L	6-1	170	8-24-82	1	0	2.61	9	0	0	0	10	11	4	3	0	0	20	.262	.273	.258	17.42	0.00
Sipp, Tony	L-L	6-0	190	7-12-83	4	2	3.13	29	4	0	3	60	44	25	21	2	21	80	.201	.226	.191	11.93	3.13
Smith, Sean	R-R	6-4	195	10-13-83	10	5	3.88	25	24	1	0	144	140	66	62	10	45	94	.258	.232	.283	5.88	2.81
Wallace, David	R-R	6-4	230	10-17-79	0	0	27.00	1	0	0	0	1	3	3	3	0	2	0	.500	.000	.600	0.00	18.00
Warden, Jim Ed	R-R	6-7	195	5-7-79	5	2	2.90	55	0	0	11	59	35	25	19	3	29	47	.172	.187	.159	7.17	4.42

FIELDING

Catcher	PCT	G	PO	A	E	DP	PB
Brock	.800	1	8	0	2	0	0
Camacaro	1.000	5	49	4	0	0	1
Herrera	.979	44	353	26	8	0	1
Toregas	.995	48	381	34	2	1	6
Wallace	.986	46	308	32	5	1	7

First Base	PCT	G	PO	A	E	DP
Aubrey	1.000	5	40	3	0	4
Camacaro	1.000	1	3	0	0	0
Larkin	.981	14	94	8	2	7
Mulhern	.993	90	739	57	6	61
Osborn	.979	23	171	15	4	17
Sandberg	.994	18	143	12	1	13
Wallace	1.000	1	1	1	0	0

Second Base	PCT	G	PO	A	E	DP
Crowe	.778	7	11	10	6	1
Larkin	.971	36	72	94	5	24
Osborn	1.000	5	9	11	0	2
Pinckney	.964	7	14	13	1	4
Torres	.979	91	148	270	9	54

Third Base	PCT	G	PO	A	E	DP
Kouzmanoff	.938	56	33	117	10	9
Larkin	.857	7	2	4	1	0
Osborn	.955	71	36	154	9	13
Sandberg	.872	17	10	24	5	4

Shortstop	PCT	G	PO	A	E	DP
Inglett	.973	17	27	44	2	9
Ochoa	.963	104	172	293	18	61
Osborn	1.000	3	5	11	0	2

	PCT	G	PO	A	E	DP
Pinckney	.884	8	13	25	5	3
Sandberg	1.000	1	0	1	0	0
Torres	1.000	13	20	33	0	3

Outfield	PCT	G	PO	A	E	DP
Barton	1.000	38	81	1	0	0
Blake	1.000	1	2	0	0	0
Crowe	.965	22	54	1	2	0
Donovan	.971	18	33	0	1	0
Goleski	.979	84	130	12	3	1
Mulhern	1.000	23	26	3	0	1
Osborn	1.000	1	2	0	0	0
Panther	.989	49	83	3	1	1
Pinckney	1.000	2	3	0	0	0
Snyder	.967	126	227	11	8	4
Valdes	1.000	9	17	0	0	0
Van Every	1.000	63	143	3	0	1

Kinston Indians — High Class A

Carolina League

BATTING	B-T	HT	WT	DOB	AVG	vLH	vRH	G	AB	R	H	2B	3B	HR	RBI	BB	HBP	SH	SF	SO	SB	CS	SLG	OBP
Aubrey, Michael	L-L	6-0	195	4-15-82	.286	.400	.222	8	28	8	8	3	0	2	10	5	2	0	1	5	0	0	.607	.417
Barton, Brian	R-R	6-3	187	4-25-82	.308	.358	.290	82	295	56	91	16	3	13	57	39	16	3	6	83	26	3	.515	.410
Brock, Caleb	R-R	5-11	200	3-30-80	.168	.234	.125	43	119	12	20	1	1	0	4	6	1	1	1	25	1	0	.193	.213
Brown, Jordan	L-L	6-0	205	12-18-83	.290	.338	.269	125	473	71	137	26	7	15	87	51	4	2	3	59	4	0	.469	.362
Camacaro, Armando	R-R	5-11	215	4-6-79	.218	.095	.263	25	78	9	17	3	0	0	6	7	3	3	1	15	1	0	.256	.303
Choy Foo, Rodney	B-R	6-1	190	12-12-81	.293	.234	.324	89	314	55	92	17	2	12	60	49	0	1	6	77	14	1	.475	.382
Constanza, Jose	S-L	5-9	150	9-1-83	.327	.415	.300	76	275	55	90	15	6	1	27	42	2	1	1	50	20	4	.436	.419
Crowe, Trevor	B-R	6-0	190	11-17-83	.329	.366	.311	60	219	51	72	15	2	4	31	48	2	1	3	46	29	6	.470	.449
De La Cruz, Chris	B-R	6-0	190	5-3-82	.250	.333	.200	4	16	2	4	0	0	1	5	1	0	0	1	0	0	0	.438	.278
Drennen, John	L-L	6-0	190	8-26-86	.239	.294	.215	31	113	15	27	6	2	0	8	12	3	0	0	21	2	1	.327	.328
Finegan, Brian	R-R	6-0	190	12-15-81	.266	.329	.230	47	192	35	51	10	2	2	23	21	4	4	1	39	14	2	.370	.349
Goleski, Ryan	R-R	6-3	225	3-19-82	.331	.340	.324	38	121	28	40	7	0	10	43	25	2	1	4	30	2	2	.636	.441
Head, Stephen	L-L	6-3	220	1-13-84	.235	.273	.217	130	477	65	112	26	0	14	73	54	7	2	5	73	2	1	.377	.319
Herrera, Javi	R-R	6-0	200	10-8-81	.286	.306	.277	50	168	24	48	13	0	1	24	21	9	1	1	27	0	2	.381	.392
Panther, Nathan	L-L	6-1	180	7-12-81	.221	.208	.226	25	77	12	17	4	0	3	10	14	0	0	1	16	0	1	.390	.337
Pinckney, Brandon	R-R	5-10	165	4-12-82	.277	.321	.254	100	382	57	106	26	2	5	55	35	5	7	5	54	5	1	.395	.342
Reyes, Argenis	B-R	5-10	165	9-25-82	.266	.315	.243	130	516	71	137	16	6	2	58	48	4	10	8	73	24	6	.331	.328
Schilling, Micah	L-R	5-11	185	12-27-82	.261	.277	.256	87	284	53	74	10	6	3	33	58	5	3	3	61	10	2	.370	.391
Toregas, Wyatt	R-R	5-11	200	12-2-82	.336	.347	.330	44	146	25	49	14	0	4	23	20	2	1	2	28	0	0	.514	.418
Whitney, Matthew	R-R	6-4	200	2-13-84	.206	.256	.177	96	345	40	71	20	2	10	39	41	3	0	2	131	0	2	.362	.294

PITCHING	B-T	HT	WT	DOB	W	L	ERA	G	GS	CG	SV	IP	H	R	ER	HR	BB	SO	AVG	vLH	vRH	K/9	BB/9
Allen, Wyatt	R-R	6-4	205	4-12-80	1	1	1.17	11	0	0	0	15	8	2	2	0	11	13	.167	.200	.143	7.63	6.46
Bunkelman, Cody	R-R	6-3	225	2-6-85	3	1	6.65	13	0	0	0	23	23	18	17	3	19	23	.261	.194	.298	9.00	7.43
Burton, TJ	L-R	6-3	185	7-30-83	2	5	5.36	48	0	0	19	50	67	35	30	3	18	46	.318	.365	.292	8.23	3.22
Collins, Kyle	R-R	6-1	165	8-17-81	3	0	2.00	35	0	0	7	36	22	9	8	1	19	39	.176	.158	.184	9.75	4.75
Cowley, Thomas	L-L	6-3	190	12-30-83	1	1	5.04	5	4	0	0	25	22	14	14	2	10	14	.239	.250	.253	5.04	3.60
Dixon, Kevin	R-R	6-3	225	12-16-83	6	3	5.19	13	13	0	0	69	76	40	40	8	23	40	.283	.264	.297	5.19	2.99
Finocchi, Michael	R-R	6-0	190	4-28-85	1	2	2.72	20	0	0	1	36	35	17	11	0	25	23	.267	.342	.237	5.70	6.19
Gomez, Mariano	L-L	6-6	190	9-12-82	2	3	3.86	22	8	0	0	56	57	28	24	4	23	41	.270	.229	.291	6.59	3.70
Hicks, Christopher	L-L	5-11	165	11-28-85	5	2	5.18	11	1	0	0	33	29	22	19	5	15	21	.244	.161	.273	5.73	4.09
Knippschild, Ryan	L-L	6-1	195	9-24-82	6	4	3.88	41	0	0	0	70	59	36	30	9	19	54	.223	.195	.236	6.98	2.45
Laffey, Aaron	L-L	6-0	170	4-15-85	4	1	2.18	10	4	1	1	41	38	16	10	0	6	24	.241	.280	.203	5.23	1.31
Lewis, Jensen	R-R	6-3	195	5-16-84	7	6	3.99	21	20	0	0	108	110	59	48	11	29	94	.261	.308	.225	7.81	2.41
Lewis, Scott	S-L	6-0	185	9-26-83	3	3	1.48	27	26	0	0	116	84	24	19	3	28	123	.203	.178	.210	9.57	2.18
Lofgren, Charles	L-L	6-3	205	1-29-86	17	5	2.32	25	25	1	0	140	108	51	36	5	54	125	.217	.192	.223	8.05	3.48
Martin, J.D.	R-R	6-4	170	1-2-83	1	0	0.00	3	2	0	0	11	6	0	0	0	1	11	.154	.053	.250	8.74	0.79
Ness, Joe	R-R	6-5	230	11-4-83	9	6	3.62	26	26	0	0	139	128	64	56	9	55	120	.247	.236	.253	7.75	3.55
Newsom, Randy	R-R	6-2	200	5-6-82	2	2	2.61	16	0	0	1	21	23	10	6	1	7	17	.280	.500	.179	7.40	3.05
Niesel, Christopher	R-R	5-11	195	11-18-82	3	0	4.65	17	0	0	0	31	35	17	16	6	15	34	.285	.304	.273	9.87	4.35
Nottingham, Shawn	L-L	6-1	190	1-22-85	0	0	2.25	1	1	0	0	4	6	1	1	0	2	2	.400	—	.400	4.50	0.00
Roehl, Scott	R-R	6-1	195	8-19-81	4	6	3.84	37	3	0	4	68	70	32	29	2	21	54	.271	.340	.226	7.15	2.78
Santos, Reid	L-L	6-1	170	8-24-82	2	0	3.44	35	2	0	4	71	55	28	27	2	28	65	.223	.165	.250	8.28	3.57
Smith, Sean	R-R	6-4	195	10-13-83	1	2	3.60	4	4	0	0	25	20	10	10	2	6	23	.225	.170	.286	8.28	2.16
Soto, Jesus	R-R	5-11	170	8-26-80	1	0	4.50	16	0	0	0	16	15	10	8	1	9	16	.247	.194	.257	9.00	5.06
Sumner, Scott	R-R	6-2	185	7-21-83	1	1	2.70	2	0	0	0	3	2	1	1	0	1	5	.200	.250	.167	2.70	13.50

FIELDING

Catcher	PCT	G	PO	A	E	DP	PB
Brock	.990	34	179	15	2	3	3
Camacaro	.991	25	198	25	2	4	4
Herrera	1.000	49	330	33	0	2	3
Toregas	.992	43	332	30	3	0	1

First Base	PCT	G	PO	A	E	DP
Aubrey	1.000	6	51	2	0	6
Brown	1.000	7	41	4	0	2
Choy Foo	1.000	22	187	12	0	18
Head	.992	109	907	61	8	86

Second Base	PCT	G	PO	A	E	DP
Choy Foo	1.000	2	1	1	0	0
Pinckney	.964	8	14	13	1	2

	PCT	G	PO	A	E	DP
Reyes	.974	72	129	205	9	46
Schilling	.970	62	105	155	8	37

Third Base	PCT	G	PO	A	E	DP
Brock	1.000	1	0	1	0	0
Choy Foo	.926	17	5	20	2	1
Pinckney	.769	5	2	8	3	2
Reyes	.935	34	19	67	6	8
Schilling	.600	1	2	2	0	0
Whitney	.894	85	47	156	24	13

Shortstop	PCT	G	PO	A	E	DP
De La Cruz	.955	4	10	11	1	4
Finegan	.962	46	68	133	8	13
Pinckney	.961	81	105	217	13	53

	PCT	G	PO	A	E	DP
Reyes	.972	10	15	20	1	5

Outfield	PCT	G	PO	A	E	DP
Barton	.979	64	136	3	3	0
Brock	1.000	7	8	0	0	0
Brown	.990	113	183	10	2	2
Constanza	.981	75	152	5	3	1
Crowe	.982	59	108	3	2	1
Drennen	.982	30	53	3	1	1
Goleski	.975	38	75	4	2	1
Mortensen	—	1	0	0	0	0
Panther	.983	24	56	2	1	0
Reyes	1.000	16	32	2	0	0

Lake County Captains — Low Class A

South Atlantic League

BATTING	B-T	HT	WT	DOB	AVG	vLH	vRH	G	AB	R	H	2B	3B	HR	RBI	BB	HBP	SH	SF	SO	SB	CS	SLG	OBP
Blake, Casey	R-R	6-2	210	8-23-73	.500	—	.500	1	2	1	1	0	0	1	2	2	0	0	0	0	0	0	2.000	.750
Butia, Mike	L-R	6-2	215	11-29-82	.292	.361	.272	39	161	25	47	8	2	5	16	13	3	0	0	21	0	1	.460	.356
Casillas, Omar	R-R	6-1	200	9-17-83	.212	.244	.196	41	137	14	29	7	0	1	12	14	0	1	1	40	2	1	.285	.283
Chavez, Jose	B-R	5-10	170	1-2-85	.195	.176	.208	12	41	5	8	1	0	0	0	6	0	0	0	8	1	1	.220	.298
Conroy, Mike	L-L	6-3	215	10-3-82	.228	.246	.222	120	447	54	102	16	5	12	70	44	3	3	6	134	8	6	.367	.298
Constanza, Jose	S-L	5-9	150	9-1-83	.277	.207	.292	44	159	31	44	5	3	1	9	30	1	1	0	30	19	4	.365	.395
Crowe, Trevor	B-R	6-0	190	11-17-83	.000	.000	.000	2	5	0	0	0	0	0	0	0	0	0	0	1	0	0	.000	.000
Cumberbatch, Cirilo	B-R	6-2	185	7-11-86	.156	.333	.138	8	32	0	5	1	0	0	1	0	0	0	0	13	0	1	.188	.156
De La Cruz, Chris	B-R	6-0	165	5-3-82	.260	.202	.283	83	296	44	77	11	1	1	21	32	2	5	3	36	10	1	.314	.333
Denham, Jason	L-L	6-0	170	5-1-86	.206	.200	.211	14	34	1	7	2	0	0	0	5	0	0	0	5	3	0	.265	.308
Drennen, John	L-L	6-0	190	8-26-86	.321	.232	.348	67	240	33	77	12	3	6	30	31	5	1	0	52	6	6	.471	.409
Fornasiere, Matthew	L-R	6-1	195	11-19-83	.246	.266	.241	101	345	28	85	13	3	2	36	51	2	4	2	74	2	1	.319	.345
Gimenez, Chris	R-R	6-2	190	12-27-82	.255	.304	.240	91	329	55	84	25	1	11	40	33	26	1	5	72	6	8	.438	.364
Head, Jerad	R-R	6-1	195	11-15-82	.000	.000	.000	1	4	1	0	0	0	0	0	0	0	0	0	1	0	0	.000	.000
Hiser, P.J.	R-R	6-1	205	8-18-81	.261	.261	.261	89	326	45	85	21	5	10	50	17	3	1	6	104	12	4	.448	.298
Lytle, Andrew	R-R	6-1	165	9-15-82	.118	.000	.222	6	17	2	2	1	0	0	2	1	0	0	0	4	0	0	.176	.167
Noviskey, Joshua	L-R	6-4	230	3-15-83	.227	.164	.250	64	211	28	48	5	0	7	41	30	5	2	2	49	1	0	.351	.335
Pacheco, Fernando	L-L	6-1	205	10-1-84	.237	.246	.235	103	337	41	80	9	1	13	46	30	9	0	3	87	1	0	.386	.314
Pena, Roman	L-L	6-0	185	9-2-86	.278	.308	.268	13	54	6	15	1	0	2	3	2	1	1	0	19	1	0	.407	.316
Petrucci, Nicholas	R-R	6-1	190	7-16-85	.202	.239	.189	91	321	24	65	19	0	3	28	22	2	2	4	85	0	0	.290	.255
Ramirez, Maximiliano	R-R	5-11	170	10-11-84	.307	.138	.357	37	127	19	39	6	1	4	26	30	1	0	3	27	0	0	.465	.435
2-team (80 Rome)					.292	—	—	117	394	69	115	23	1	13	63	84	4	0	5	99	2	0	.454	.417
Roberts, Joshua	L-R	6-1	175	7-17-86	.235	.000	.286	4	17	1	4	0	0	0	1	1	0	0	0	4	1	0	.235	.278
Romero, Niuman	B-R	6-0	160	1-24-85	.228	.204	.235	114	412	45	94	11	1	2	36	55	1	9	3	83	10	8	.274	.318
Szabo, Marshall	B-R	5-11	180	2-13-83	.260	.316	.237	58	196	24	51	9	1	0	14	20	2	5	1	40	5	4	.316	.333
Valdes, Juan	B-R	6-0	150	6-22-85	.225	.247	.217	94	329	41	74	12	2	6	31	56	1	3	2	88	14	10	.328	.338

PITCHING	B-T	HT	WT	DOB	W	L	ERA	G	GS	CG	SV	IP	H	R	ER	HR	BB	SO	AVG	vLH	vRH	K/9	BB/9
Bunkelman, Cody	R-R	6-3	225	2-6-85	1	2	2.82	24	0	0	0	45	26	16	14	2	28	48	.169	.237	.147	9.67	5.64
Cevette, Dan	L-L	6-4	205	10-19-83	0	1	7.20	3	3	0	0	5	4	4	4	1	4	3	.222	.333	.200	5.40	7.20
Cowley, Thomas	L-L	6-3	190	12-30-83	4	5	1.99	15	10	0	0	72	38	20	16	7	13	65	.154	.234	.135	8.09	1.62
Davis, Matt	R-R	6-2	205	11-19-81	2	7	3.13	54	0	0	26	55	45	21	19	5	26	67	.223	.203	.231	11.03	4.28
Deters, James	R-R	6-4	180	6-4-83	12	9	3.11	28	28	1	0	168	178	77	58	10	29	106	.270	.282	.264	5.69	1.56
Dixon, Kevin	R-R	6-3	225	12-16-83	2	1	1.36	7	7	0	0	40	32	10	6	0	7	21	.230	.159	.263	4.76	1.59
Edell, Ryan	L-L	6-1	215	7-6-83	0	1	3.44	6	6	0	0	18	19	8	7	2	5	12	.279	.000	.333	5.89	2.45
Eisentrager, Dan	R-R	6-3	180	12-30-80	0	1	4.38	6	0	0	0	12	14	7	6	3	2	10	.275	.368	.219	7.30	1.46
Finocchi, Michael	R-R	6-0	190	4-28-85	4	1	3.44	19	0	0	0	37	42	15	14	1	14	24	.298	.327	.283	5.89	3.44
Herrmann, Frank	L-R	6-4	220	5-30-84	4	6	3.90	26	26	0	0	122	122	61	53	8	47	89	.261	.231	.276	6.55	3.46
Hicks, Christopher	L-L	5-11	165	11-28-85	3	2	4.66	12	0	0	0	37	40	25	19	2	15	29	.280	.316	.267	7.12	3.68
Jecmen, Mark	R-R	6-8	235	2-16-83	4	3	4.34	29	0	0	1	48	35	26	23	1	37	37	.212	.143	.241	6.99	6.99
Knippschild, Ryan	L-L	6-1	195	9-24-82	2	1	2.63	8	0	0	0	14	14	5	4	0	5	15	.264	.214	.282	9.88	3.29
Loberg, Matthew	R-R	6-3	235	8-31-82	3	4	3.94	44	0	0	3	80	89	46	35	8	27	63	.280	.356	.243	7.09	3.04
Martin, J.D.	R-R	6-4	170	1-2-83	0	1	4.20	5	5	0	0	15	13	7	7	2	3	16	.241	.174	.290	9.60	1.80
Newsom, Randy	R-R	6-2	200	5-6-82	0	0	2.25	3	0	0	0	4	6	2	1	0	0	3	.333	.429	.273	6.75	0.00
2-team (1 Greenville)					1	0	1.12	4	0	0	0	8	8	2	1	0	0	3	—	—	—	3.38	0.00
Pinto, Julio	R-R	6-0	170	10-23-84	2	4	4.60	36	1	0	1	76	66	46	39	10	26	68	.235	.237	.234	8.02	3.07
Riera, Jorge	R-R	6-0	170	6-17-83	1	1	2.50	16	3	0	0	36	36	11	10	1	14	35	.267	.250	.273	8.75	3.50
Roberts, Joshua	L-R	6-1	175	7-17-86	0	0	18.00	1	0	0	0	1	2	2	2	1	0	1	.400	—	.400	9.00	0.00
Roddy, Dustin	R-R	6-2	195	11-10-82	2	2	3.72	26	0	0	1	39	44	23	16	0	28	21	.295	.349	.274	4.89	6.52
Schutt, Jason	R-R	6-3	225	12-11-83	2	3	4.68	19	0	0	0	33	36	20	17	3	6	17	.288	.370	.241	4.68	1.65
Smith, Carlton	L-R	6-1	200	1-23-86	3	3	4.09	11	11	0	0	55	49	27	25	4	24	38	.239	.347	.205	6.22	3.93
Stevens, Jeffrey	R-R	6-1	220	9-5-83	7	3	4.42	16	15	0	0	73	65	40	36	4	23	60	.232	.218	.241	7.36	2.82
Vargas, Albert	R-R	6-0	175	10-19-84	6	13	3.83	27	23	0	0	139	152	74	59	11	28	95	.279	.234	.302	6.17	1.82

FIELDING

Catcher	PCT	G	PO	A	E	DP	PB
Casillas	.977	37	255	36	7	2	8
Gimenez	.985	62	417	32	7	5	8
Noviskey	.989	27	166	16	2	3	11
Ramirez	.972	18	130	9	4	3	3
Roberts	1.000	1	8	0	0	0	1

First Base	PCT	G	PO	A	E	DP
Gimenez	1.000	1	9	0	0	0
Hiser	.997	33	274	14	1	19
Lytle	1.000	6	54	3	0	2
Noviskey	.988	13	75	9	1	8
Pacheco	.994	101	813	64	5	88

Second Base	PCT	G	PO	A	E	DP
Chavez	1.000	9	20	31	0	9
De La Cruz	.967	6	10	19	1	1
Fornasiere	.965	80	153	207	13	44
Szabo	.972	48	87	122	6	34

Third Base	PCT	G	PO	A	E	DP
De La Cruz	.949	38	18	93	6	9
Fornasiere	1.000	1	1	2	0	0
Gimenez	1.000	3	0	1	0	0
Head	1.000	1	0	4	0	0
Petrucci	.887	89	56	203	33	14
Romero	.947	5	3	15	1	0
Szabo	.909	7	2	8	1	0

Shortstop	PCT	G	PO	A	E	DP
Chavez	.929	3	3	10	1	1
De La Cruz	.959	33	48	92	6	22
Romero	.966	103	158	291	16	60
Szabo	.857	2	2	4	1	1

Outfield	PCT	G	PO	A	E	DP
Blake	1.000	1	2	0	0	0
Butia	.971	34	64	2	2	1
Conroy	.975	107	193	4	5	2
Constanza	1.000	44	58	6	0	3
Crowe	1.000	2	3	0	0	0
Cumberbatch	.909	8	8	2	1	0
Denham	1.000	13	27	1	0	0
Drennen	.994	66	165	2	1	0
Hiser	.963	43	72	7	3	1
Pena	.970	12	30	2	1	0
Roberts	1.000	1	2	0	0	0
Valdes	1.000	93	203	10	0	3

Mahoning Valley Scrappers — Short-Season

New York-Penn League

BATTING	B-T	HT	WT	DOB	AVG	vLH	vRH	G	AB	R	H	2B	3B	HR	RBI	BB	HBP	SH	SF	SO	SB	CS	SLG	OBP
Cumberbatch, Cirilo	B-R	6-2	185	7-11-86	.214	.227	.210	55	182	23	39	4	0	3	15	20	3	0	0	42	5	2	.286	.302
Davis, Adam	B-R	5-9	185	10-15-84	.213	.190	.219	66	254	37	54	9	5	1	15	21	1	2	1	49	9	5	.299	.274
De Leon, Evandy	R-R	6-0	175	6-29-83	.231	.222	.234	55	173	25	40	7	3	5	22	12	3	4	3	45	0	7	.393	.288
Denham, Jason	L-L	6-0	170	5-1-86	.302	.371	.289	53	215	22	65	9	2	0	14	18	1	0	2	34	6	4	.363	.356

ORGANIZATION STATISTICS

	B-T	HT	WT	DOB	AVG	vLH	vRH	G	AB	R	H	2B	3B	HR	RBI	BB	HBP	SH	SF	SO	SB	CS	SLG	OBP
Douglas, Stephen	L-R	6-2	185	5-10-85	.263	.067	.298	56	198	16	52	3	2	0	23	8	0	3	1	31	8	5	.298	.290
Edmundson, Kelly	R-R	6-0	195	10-3-83	.191	.147	.206	44	141	10	27	8	0	2	13	6	8	3	0	40	1	0	.291	.265
Goedert, Jared	R-R	6-1	180	5-25-85	.269	.417	.232	63	238	31	64	14	2	3	27	19	3	2	2	28	1	0	.382	.328
Lacy, Brent	R-R	6-1	200	11-22-82	.125	.182	.111	19	56	5	7	0	0	0	2	6	2	1	0	16	2	1	.125	.234
Lytle, Andrew	R-R	6-1	165	9-15-82	.292	.280	.296	65	236	36	69	10	0	1	22	20	4	2	3	34	10	4	.347	.354
McBride, Matthew	R-R	6-2	215	5-23-85	.272	.154	.303	52	184	24	50	12	0	4	31	16	9	0	2	22	5	2	.402	.355
Montero, Lucas	B-R	5-11	180	10-18-84	.235	.250	.231	6	17	0	4	0	0	0	1	1	0	0	3	0	3		.235	.278
Realini, Dustin	R-R	6-2	200	5-14-84	.239	.262	.233	63	222	26	53	13	1	5	37	18	2	3	6	48	1	3	.374	.294
Roberts, Joshua	L-R	6-1	175	7-17-86	.209	.267	.203	46	153	11	32	6	1	2	23	13	1	2	1	33	4	2	.301	.274
Rodriguez, Joshua	R-R	6-0	175	12-18-84	.268	.214	.279	45	157	26	42	11	4	4	24	14	3	0	1	33	2	0	.465	.337
Thomas, Brent	R-R	6-0	165	2-12-83	.171	.231	.143	19	41	5	7	3	0	0	3	4	0	0		17	2	1	.244	.244

PITCHING	B-T	HT	WT	DOB	W	L	ERA	G	GS	CG	SV	IP	H	R	ER	HR	BB	SO	AVG	vLH	vRH	K/9	BB/9
Bunton, Nathan	R-R	6-1	205	6-1-84	0	0	0.00	1	0	0	0	1	2	0	0	0	1	0	.400	.500	.000	0.00	9.00
Collina, Kyle	R-R	6-2	185	1-21-84	1	0	4.50	7	1	0	0	12	11	7	6	0	5	10	.239	.250	.231	7.50	3.75
Cooper, Chris	L-L	5-11	195	10-31-78	1	1	5.17	10	0	0	0	16	18	9	9	3	3	15	.290	.182	.350	8.62	1.72
Delage, William	L-L	6-1	170	7-12-84	2	7	4.34	14	14	0	0	66	68	39	32	4	15	67	.264	.265	.263	9.09	2.04
Eisenberg, Michael	L-R	6-7	200	2-19-85	3	1	4.29	14	13	0	0	63	72	32	30	1	24	40	.287	.260	.305	5.71	3.43
Eisentrager, Dan	R-R	6-3	180	12-30-80	1	0	2.87	7	0	0	0	16	16	7	5	0	2	13	.254	.214	.286	7.47	1.15
Frega, Daniel	R-R	6-5	195	11-16-84	2	4	7.50	11	0	0	0	24	31	27	20	1	17	17	.316	.324	.311	6.38	6.38
Hering, Hart	R-R	6-3	220	12-12-83	3	3	2.20	19	0	0	2	29	27	7	7	1	9	23	.250	.250	.250	7.22	2.83
Hernandez, Mike	L-L	6-4	215	4-8-81	0	0	3.86	5	0	0	0	5	5	2	2	0	4	2	.278	.200	.308	3.86	7.71
Huff, David	L-L	6-2	190	8-22-84	0	1	5.87	4	4	0	0	8	9	5	5	0	7	8	.300	.313	.286	9.39	8.22
Loop, Derrick	R-L	6-3	220	12-11-83	1	2	2.95	22	0	0	2	37	31	19	12	1	15	25	.225	.100	.276	6.14	3.68
Martin, J.D.	R-R	6-4	170	1-2-83	0	1	1.50	6	6	0	0	18	11	3	3	1	1	13	.169	.156	.182	6.50	0.50
Meyer, Matthew	L-L	6-4	210	1-17-85	2	2	1.98	19	0	0	2	27	23	6	6	0	5	31	.230	.333	.186	10.21	4.94
Miltenberger, Daniel	R-R	6-0	180	9-15-83	2	0	6.85	15	0	0	0	24	33	18	18	1	16	11	.337	.400	.302	4.18	6.08
Pesco, Nick	R-R	6-6	195	9-17-83	1	0	0.50	4	4	0	0	18	13	2	1	0	4	13	.200	.200	.200	6.50	2.00
Riera, Jorge	R-R	6-0	170	6-17-83	2	0	1.98	13	0	0	2	27	20	7	6	1	6	23	.206	.172	.221	7.57	1.98
Schutt, Jason	R-R	6-3	225	12-11-83	0	1	1.80	4	0	0	2	5	5	1	1	0	0	6	.263	.286	.250	10.80	0.00
Stiller, Erik	R-R	6-5	200	7-10-84	3	3	3.23	9	8	0	0	47	40	17	17	3	7	22	.229	.190	.260	4.18	1.33
Tomlin, Joshua	R-R	6-1	175	10-19-84	8	2	2.09	15	15	0	0	77	56	24	18	5	15	69	.196	.204	.192	8.03	1.75
Valdez, Luis	R-R	6-4	175	3-11-84	7	5	2.62	17	11	0	0	76	60	33	22	2	18	70	.213	.274	.176	8.33	2.14
Wagner, Neil	R-R	6-0	195	1-1-84	0	1	1.39	26	0	0	17	32	16	5	5	1	9	50	.143	.170	.123	13.92	2.51
Woods, Andy	L-L	6-3	210	11-26-83	1	2	9.74	14	0	0	0	20	24	27	22	4	10	12	.279	.300	.273	5.31	4.43

FIELDING

Catcher	PCT	G	PO	A	E	DP	PB
Edmundson	.990	40	270	32	3	2	6
Lacy	.957	12	78	10	4	0	0
McBride	.990	26	184	11	2	2	5

First Base	PCT	G	PO	A	E	DP
Lytle	.996	27	213	16	1	15
Realini	.994	37	314	21	2	20
Roberts	.955	15	116	11	6	6

Second Base	PCT	G	PO	A	E	DP
Davis	.973	49	95	123	6	25

	PCT	G	PO	A	E	DP
Goedert	1.000	1	2	1	0	0
Lacy	.933	4	6	8	1	0
Lytle	.969	14	25	38	2	6
Realini	.957	5	7	15	1	1
Rodriguez	1.000	3	3	5	0	2

Third Base	PCT	G	PO	A	E	DP
Goedert	.947	62	41	139	10	8
Lytle	1.000	1	0	2	0	0
Realini	.903	15	7	21	3	1

Shortstop	PCT	G	PO	A	E	DP
Davis	.884	17	20	41	8	7

	PCT	G	PO	A	E	DP
Lytle	.927	20	23	53	6	10
Rodriguez	.931	42	50	98	11	16

Outfield	PCT	G	PO	A	E	DP
Cumberbatch	.970	50	95	1	3	0
De Leon	.964	53	104	3	4	0
Denham	.983	45	113	3	2	1
Douglas	.959	52	70	0	3	0
Montero	1.000	6	13	0	0	0
Roberts	.970	16	32	0	1	0
Thomas	.969	14	30	1	1	1

Burlington Indians — Rookie

Appalachian League

BATTING	B-T	HT	WT	DOB	AVG	vLH	vRH	G	AB	R	H	2B	3B	HR	RBI	BB	HBP	SH	SF	SO	SB	CS	SLG	OBP
Alcombrack, Robert	R-R	6-0	205	6-10-88	.286	.167	1.000	3	7	1	2	0	0	0	0	0	0	0	0	3	0	0	.286	.286
Alvarado, Ramon	R-R	6-1	185	6-3-85	.194	.226	.179	31	98	16	19	2	0	3	10	10	4	1	1	22	4	2	.306	.292
Ard, Alfred	R-R	6-0	185	8-3-82	.216	.259	.192	51	153	25	33	9	0	1	18	22	3	6	1	33	12	3	.294	.324
Armstrong, Corteze	L-R	5-11	180	6-9-84	.275	.295	.266	49	153	24	42	2	0	0	9	15	6	1	0	38	12	1	.288	.362
Butia, Mike	L-R	6-2	215	11-29-82	.337	.250	.351	25	89	13	30	5	0	2	12	10	1	0	0	14	1	2	.461	.410
Chavez, Jose	B-R	5-10	170	1-2-85	.233	.250	.225	32	120	16	28	5	0	2	17	13	0	0	3	19	3	2	.325	.301
Clark, Boodle	R-R	6-0	200	12-28-83	.191	.214	.178	32	115	19	22	5	0	0	6	20	5	1	2	34	1	1	.391	.288
Garcia, Felipe	R-R	6-3	225	5-15-83	.298	.355	.270	59	235	26	70	10	1	7	41	17	3	0	3	34	1	1	.438	.349
Head, Jerad	R-R	6-1	195	11-15-82	.246	.253	.242	59	240	44	59	12	5	10	52	16	6	0	1	41	7	2	.463	.308
Infante, Jansy	R-R	6-1	170	2-27-86	.287	.345	.263	49	188	23	54	7	0	2	21	11	0	5	1	26	9	3	.356	.325
Kinning, Brett	R-R	5-10	175	12-30-83	.245	.288	.228	56	204	37	50	8	1	1	21	32	2	2	3	31	13	4	.309	.349
Martinez, Richard	R-R	6-0	165	6-19-87	.313	.343	.304	23	64	11	20	2	0	2	10	8	1	1	1	12	0	0	.438	.392
Merrell, Cody	R-R	6-3	240	2-8-84	.163	.219	.136	36	98	12	16	2	0	1	8	7	5	0	3	24	1	2	.214	.255
Mortensen, Trevor	R-R	5-10	190	2-12-83	.282	.349	.252	55	202	39	57	15	0	2	24	29	2	3	2	29	4	2	.386	.374
Ortega, Jose	R-R	5-11	180	12-29-80	.500	.000	1.000	2	2	0	1	0	0	0	0	0	0	0	0	0	0	0	.500	.500
Rivero, Carlos	R-R	6-3	198	5-20-88	.212	.211	.213	16	66	3	14	3	0	1	7	5	0	1	1	11	0	1	.303	.264
Tavarez, Aregenis	B-R	5-11	165	2-19-84	.272	.163	.311	53	184	22	50	6	0	0	20	23	1	1	2	34	7	1	.304	.352
Vasquez, Enrique	R-R	6-0	195	3-14-84	.195	.219	.182	29	87	9	17	5	0	0	6	13	1	1	1	27	0	2	.253	.304

PITCHING	B-T	HT	WT	DOB	W	L	ERA	G	GS	CG	SV	IP	H	R	ER	HR	BB	SO	AVG	vLH	vRH	K/9	BB/9
Andrade, Brett	R-R	6-4	200	11-4-83	2	1	3.12	23	0	0	1	35	36	17	12	1	12	24	.269	.326	.242	6.23	3.12
Archer, Christopher	R-R	6-2	165	9-26-88	0	0	10.80	1	0	0	0	2	2	2	2	1	1	1	.333	1.000	.200	5.40	5.40
Brech, Alan	L-L	6-0	195	9-10-84	2	2	3.35	12	12	0	0	51	44	22	19	1	11	57	.220	.179	.227	10.06	1.94
Brettl, James	L-L	6-0	180	2-21-84	5	0	3.50	18	0	0	0	46	50	23	18	3	18	33	.282	.366	.257	6.41	3.50
Bunton, Nathan	R-R	6-1	205	6-1-84	1	0	1.71	23	0	0	11	26	21	6	5	1	7	30	.214	.130	.240	10.25	2.39
Collina, Kyle	R-R	6-2	185	1-21-84	0	1	3.46	9	3	0	0	26	28	13	10	3	8	30	.272	.265	.275	10.38	2.77
Cruz, Wilander	R-R	6-3	185	12-15-84	3	1	4.71	13	0	0	0	21	23	11	11	5	11	25	.274	.158	.308	10.71	4.71
De La Rosa, Alexis	R-R	6-3	179	5-4-85	0	1	9.82	3	1	0	0	7	11	8	8	3	2	1	.344	.200	.409	2.45	3.68
Fairchild, Richard	R-R	6-3	205	5-17-83	4	3	5.74	12	12	0	0	47	60	36	30	4	14	35	.308	.281	.319	6.70	2.68
Halverson, Brady	R-R	6-2	185	3-25-82	0	4	5.60	18	5	0	0	35	39	31	22	1	20	22	.260	.280	.250	5.60	5.09
Heredia, Felix	R-R	6-1	185	11-19-83	1	2	7.56	13	0	0	1	17	21	15	14	5	6	14	.328	.385	.289	7.56	3.24

Name	B-T	HT	WT	DOB	W	L	ERA	G	GS	CG	SV	IP	H	R	ER	HR	BB	SO	AVG	vLH	vRH	K/9	BB/9
Johnson, Zachary	L-L	6-5	210	5-9-84	0	1	5.49	13	0	0	0	20	21	12	12	1	15	13	.304	.182	.328	5.95	6.86
Montero, Joanniel	R-R	6-5	191	2-2-86	2	6	4.97	14	14	0	0	67	77	41	37	9	24	41	.288	.247	.310	5.51	3.22
Morris, Ryan	L-L	6-3	175	1-10-88	0	0	18.00	1	0	0	0	1	2	2	2	0	2	0	.500	—	.500	0.00	18.00
Perez, Osiris	R-R	6-3	175	4-19-82	5	1	3.16	18	0	0	0	43	42	27	15	3	17	40	.247	.288	.229	8.44	3.59
Sanders, Brandt	L-L	5-11	195	8-16-84	4	1	2.70	18	0	0	0	33	27	12	10	3	12	26	.218	.091	.264	7.02	3.24
Soto, Jesus	R-R	5-11	170	8-26-80	0	0	9.00	3	0	0	0	2	5	4	2	1	1	0	.385	.200	.500	0.00	4.50
Stiller, Erik	R-R	6-5	200	7-10-84	2	2	6.45	4	4	0	0	22	27	16	16	4	6	15	.307	.261	.323	6.04	2.42
Storey, Mike	S-L	6-3	189	9-4-85	3	6	4.11	14	14	0	0	61	64	36	28	5	20	37	.271	.265	.272	5.43	2.93
Sumner, Scott	R-R	6-2	185	7-21-83	0	1	2.37	15	2	0	0	38	25	13	10	1	17	47	.197	.176	.204	11.13	4.03

FIELDING

Catcher	PCT	G	PO	A	E	DP	PB
Alcombrack	1.000	2	6	0	0	0	1
Garcia	1.000	2	1	0	0	0	0
Martinez	.992	20	100	19	1	3	5
Tavarez	.989	36	248	33	3	3	13
Vasquez	1.000	21	128	14	0	1	4

First Base	PCT	G	PO	A	E	DP
Clark	.979	25	214	15	5	27
Garcia	.983	35	322	21	6	34
Merrell	1.000	2	11	0	0	1
Tavarez	.956	6	58	7	3	3
Vasquez	1.000	3	20	1	0	2

Second Base	PCT	G	PO	A	E	DP
Chavez	.945	20	36	50	5	15
Head	1.000	2	5	4	0	1
Infante	—	1	0	0	0	0
Kinning	.978	48	99	128	5	37

Third Base	PCT	G	PO	A	E	DP
Head	.914	28	19	77	9	7
Kinning	.800	3	0	8	2	0
Merrell	.842	30	14	66	15	3
Rivero	.846	9	5	17	4	1

Shortstop	PCT	G	PO	A	E	DP
Chavez	.938	14	31	45	5	14

	PCT	G	PO	A	E	DP
Head	1.000	4	6	14	0	6
Infante	.937	48	82	157	16	34
Ortega	—	2	0	0	0	0
Rivero	.895	7	12	22	4	5

Outfield	PCT	G	PO	A	E	DP
Alvarado	.943	30	48	2	3	0
Ard	.984	49	118	3	2	2
Armstrong	.958	45	65	3	3	1
Butia	.875	20	12	2	2	1
Head	.939	20	30	1	2	0
Mortensen	.987	48	75	2	1	1

GCL Indians — Rookie

Gulf Coast League

BATTING

Name	B-T	HT	WT	DOB	AVG	vLH	vRH	G	AB	R	H	2B	3B	HR	RBI	BB	HBP	SH	SF	SO	SB	CS	SLG	OBP
Alcombrack, Robert	R-R	6-0	205	6-10-88	.198	.276	.167	32	101	9	20	5	0	0	9	5	0	1	2	31	0	0	.248	.231
Arias, Janel	B-R	6-2	160	2-8-86	.250	.239	.255	39	144	13	36	8	2	1	19	6	2	0	2	26	6	0	.354	.286
Arnal, Cristo	R-R	6-0	177	9-17-85	.229	.244	.222	44	140	19	32	5	1	1	16	15	2	2	1	21	11	3	.300	.310
Castillo, Alex	R-R	6-0	168	11-29-85	.283	.267	.289	33	106	16	30	6	0	2	7	8	2	0	0	27	3	1	.396	.345
Fermin Jr., Felix	R-R	5-11	155	11-27-84	.245	.278	.229	20	53	10	13	3	0	0	6	8	1	0	1	8	2	1	.302	.349
Hargis, Charles	R-R	6-0	185	11-10-83	.247	.276	.232	27	85	9	21	1	0	0	8	7	0	0	1	20	6	1	.259	.301
Hernandez, Ramon	R-R	6-1	170	8-25-86	.256	.314	.230	47	164	22	42	4	0	0	13	10	0	2	0	39	16	4	.280	.299
King, Daryl	R-R	6-4	228	1-21-88	.192	.238	.173	23	73	10	14	1	1	0	7	7	0	0	2	10	2	0	.233	.263
Martin, Collin	L-L	6-3	203	4-29-83	.221	.172	.237	37	122	21	27	3	1	3	16	15	1	1	1	33	2	3	.336	.309
Martin, Todd	L-L	6-3	210	6-25-83	.217	.400	.167	11	23	4	5	2	0	0	2	3	0	0	0	10	0	0	.304	.308
Martinez, Richard	R-R	6-0	186	6-19-87	.300	.200	.350	11	30	5	9	3	0	0	5	1	0	1	1	4	0	0	.400	.313
Montero, Lucas	B-R	5-11	180	10-18-84	.263	.250	.268	45	171	35	45	7	2	6	26	18	5	2	1	32	23	7	.433	.349
Nilsson, Jay	R-R	6-1	185	11-1-87	.276	.375	.231	22	76	15	21	6	0	3	15	7	5	1	1	18	3	0	.474	.371
Pena, Roman	L-L	6-0	185	9-2-86	.311	.327	.303	43	151	27	47	12	1	5	23	22	4	1	2	48	6	3	.503	.408
Rincon, Luis	R-R	6-1	200	4-30-87	.258	.160	.297	25	89	8	23	1	0	1	14	2	1	0	0	13	0	0	.303	.283
Rivero, Carlos	R-R	6-3	198	5-20-88	.284	.375	.255	37	134	17	38	6	0	2	22	10	2	0	2	20	0	0	.373	.338
Weglarz, NicK	L-L	6-3	215	12-16-87	.000	.000	.000	—	1	2	0	0	0	0	0	0	0	0	0	2	0	0	.000	.000

PITCHING

Name	B-T	HT	WT	DOB	W	L	ERA	G	GS	CG	SV	IP	H	R	ER	HR	BB	SO	AVG	vLH	vRH	K/9	BB/9
Archer, Christopher	R-R	6-2	165	9-26-88	0	3	7.45	7	6	0	0	19	17	22	16	1	17	21	.224	.174	.245	9.78	7.91
Bolivar, Julio	R-R	6-3	168	2-28-87	1	1	4.67	15	1	0	0	35	26	19	18	1	22	21	.203	.268	.172	5.45	5.71
Carlin, Brett	L-L	5-11	180	4-3-85	2	1	4.94	17	0	0	0	24	21	17	13	1	11	20	.226	.167	.240	7.61	4.18
Claudio, Angel	R-R	6-3	191	12-19-86	1	1	5.96	13	0	0	0	23	23	17	15	3	12	14	.247	.235	.254	5.56	4.76
De La Cruz, Kelvin	L-L	6-5	187	1-8-88	1	2	10.98	9	4	0	0	20	32	29	24	2	13	15	.360	.786	.280	6.86	5.95
De La Rosa, Alexis	R-R	6-3	179	5-4-85	0	2	6.65	13	0	0	0	23	29	23	17	3	18	17	.296	.290	.299	6.65	7.04
Diaz, Kelvin N.	R-R	6-4	189	2-7-87	3	2	3.65	10	5	0	1	44	38	19	18	2	19	43	.236	.233	.238	8.73	3.86
Frega, Daniel	R-R	6-5	195	11-16-84	2	0	3.16	6	0	0	0	26	25	12	9	0	10	22	.260	.244	.273	7.71	3.51
Gomez, Jeanmar	R-R	6-3	168	10-2-88	4	3	2.48	11	9	0	0	54	50	24	15	2	12	34	.238	.324	.197	5.63	1.99
Heredia, Felix	R-R	6-1	185	11-19-83	0	2	0.90	8	0	0	0	10	9	4	1	0	1	7	.231	.400	.206	6.30	0.90
Hernandez, Ramon	R-R	6-5	225	11-10-84	0	0	—	0	0	0	0	0	0	0	1	0	0	0	—	—	—	—	—
Libeg, Kevin	R-R	6-5	225	1-10-84	1	0	3.86	12	0	0	0	21	21	10	9	0	11	23	.263	.360	.218	9.86	4.71
Morris, Ryan	L-L	6-3	175	1-10-88	1	5	4.61	8	8	0	0	27	27	22	14	2	12	21	.245	.304	.230	6.91	3.95
Perdomo, Luis	R-R	6-0	170	4-27-84	0	2	3.60	19	0	0	9	20	11	9	8	1	5	29	.155	.208	.128	13.05	2.25
Robinson, Matthew	R-R	6-1	190	12-20-83	3	1	3.62	17	0	0	0	32	30	16	13	1	13	28	.238	.163	.277	7.79	3.62
Rondon, Hector	R-R	6-3	165	2-26-88	3	4	5.13	11	11	0	0	53	62	34	30	6	3	32	.286	.310	.254	5.47	0.51

FIELDING

Catcher	PCT	G	PO	A	E	DP	PB
Alcombrack	.983	25	160	14	3	1	4
Castillo	.982	23	137	23	3	2	9
Martinez	.981	7	42	9	1	1	2
Rincon	.923	2	10	2	1	0	1

First Base	PCT	G	PO	A	E	DP
C. Martin	.974	36	250	16	7	21
T. Martin	1.000	1	5	0	0	0
Rincon	.988	21	154	16	2	11

Second Base	PCT	G	PO	A	E	DP
Arnal	.953	32	73	68	7	19

	PCT	G	PO	A	E	DP
Fermin Jr.	.947	18	37	34	4	6
Hargis	1.000	7	12	15	0	4
Nilsson	.917	3	4	7	1	0

Third Base	PCT	G	PO	A	E	DP
Arias	.904	33	25	78	11	4
Hargis	.889	5	2	14	2	1
Nilsson	.780	13	10	29	11	4

Shortstop	PCT	G	PO	A	E	DP
Arias	1.000	4	4	14	0	0
Arnal	.917	5	5	6	1	0
Castillo	1.000	1	0	1	0	0

	PCT	G	PO	A	E	DP
Hargis	.897	11	12	23	4	3
Rivero	.902	35	42	87	14	14

Outfield	PCT	G	PO	A	E	DP
Arnal	1.000	10	11	0	0	0
Hernandez	.938	46	103	2	7	0
King	.909	19	20	0	2	0
C. Martin	1.000	1	1	0	0	0
T. Martin	1.000	8	9	1	0	0
Montero	.975	43	70	7	2	3
Pena	.946	37	64	6	4	2

COLORADO ROCKIES

BY JACK ETKIN

The Rockies were better but by no means good in 2005. There was notable progress from several players the Rockies expect will be a vital part of the mix when they can throw their weight around in the National League West for an entire season. The team also reaped benefits from a much-improved farm system.

Still, though, the Rockies finished 76-86, a gloomy record that nonetheless was a nine-game improvement from a year earlier as well as the most victories since the Rockies crept above .500 with 82 wins in 2000, their last winning season. They entered the final day of the regular season with a chance to finish in third place but settled for a fourth-place tie with Arizona.

"We played better at times this year," general manager Dan O'Dowd said, "and there has been another level of maturity for the organization. But we are tired of losing. We have to take the next step."

The Rockies were tied for first place July 5, the latest they had been atop the NL West since 1996. But the three months of promise ended rather suddenly, as Colorado was swept by Arizona in three games leading into the all-star break. That proved to be the start of an eight-game losing streak, a stretch of 11 losses in 12 games and an unfulfilling 32-43 record after the break.

Winning on the road has been an eternal mystery for the Rockies. They thought it was finally solved in 2005 because of their improved pitching and the use of the humidor. That combination seemed to normalize Coors Field, until a run-filled September, and make it easier for the Rockies deal with conditions away from their mile-high home.

But the road problem persists. After the break, the Rockies went went 10-28 on the road—compared to 22-

PLAYERS OF THE YEAR

MAJOR LEAGUE: Matt Holliday, of

Holliday had a solid rookie season in 2005 and he built upon that success in 2006, hitting .326/.387/.586 and leading the Rockies in OPS (.973), homers (34), runs (119) and total bases (353). Holliday hit both righties (.327) and lefties (.325), and finished second to Garrett Atkins on the club in RBIs with 114.

MINOR LEAGUE: Troy Tulowitzki, ss

In his first full season, Tulowitzki was asked to hit leadoff for the first time in his career at Double-A Tulsa, and his plate discipline and pitch recognition improved as a result. An above-average defender at a premium position, he received a September callup and could be the everyday shortstop in 2007.

21 in the first half—losing 20 of their final 26 games away from Coors Field.

Where the Rockies played mattered little to Garrett Atkins and Matt Holliday. Atkins hit .329/.409/.556 with 29 homers, 120 RBIs and 198 hits. Holliday hit .326/.387/.586 with 34 homers, 114 RBIs and 196 hits. Their success allowed Todd Helton to bat fifth, where the Rockies expect him to revert to his more productive self. He returned too soon from an intestinal infection in early May that hospitalized him for four days and was climbing uphill the balance of what for him was an off year.

Jason Jennings, who pitched 212 innings, Aaron Cook (213) and Jeff Francis (199) emerged as pillars in a home-grown rotation, as the Rockies hoped.

Right fielder Brad Hawpe was a run producer at times. He could share time in 2007 with Jeff Baker, who put to rest questions about whether he could stay healthy and had a big season at Triple-A followed by an eye-opening September in Colorado.

Relievers Ramon Ramirez and Manuel Corpas gave the bullpen a lift after beginning the year in the minors. The fearless Corpas, who throws strikes with superb stuff, opened the season at Double-A Tulsa, as did shortstop Troy Tulowitzki and catcher Chris Iannetta. They reached the big leagues in late August and showed they might be able to solve the problems that existed at those positions in 2006. And Ubaldo Jimenez, who began last year at Tulsa and did well in his start for the Rockies on the last day of the regular season, could factor into their plans at some point in 2007.

Lefthander Franklin Morales, who will start 2007 at Tulsa and appears to be on a fast track, could reach Colorado next season, along with right fielder Seth Smith and third baseman Ian Stewart, who might face a move to the outfield. Righthander Greg Reynolds, the second overall pick in 2006, started off in high Class A Modesto and could move quickly.

And making his way through the system is exciting center fielder Dexter Fowler, a switch-hitter with an abundance of tools who is expected to begin next season at Modesto.

ORGANIZATION LEADERS

BATTING *Minimum 250 at-bats

*AVG	Rivera, Carlos, Colorado Springs	.325
	Wimberly, Corey, Modesto	.325
R	Garner, Cole, Asheville	105
H	Young Jr., Eric, Asheville	164
TB	Koshansky, Joseph, Tulsa	278
2B	Smith, Seth, Tulsa	46
3B	Three players tied at	9
HR	Koshansky, Joseph, Tulsa	33
RBI	Koshansky, Joseph, Tulsa	116
BB	Young Jr., Eric, Asheville	72
SO	Nelson, Justin, Modesto	156
SB	Young Jr., Eric, Asheville	97
*OBP	Wimberly, Corey, Modesto	.404
*SLG	Koshansky, Joseph, Tulsa	.510
XBH	Smith, Seth, Tulsa	65

PITCHING #Minimum 75 innings

W	Jimenez, Ubaldo, Tulsa/Colorado Springs	14
L	Esposito, Mike, Colorado Springs	13
#ERA	Hynick, Brandon, Casper/Tri-City	2.41
G	Newman, Joshua, Tulsa	68
CG	Kaiser, Marc, Tulsa	4
SV	Field, Nate, Colorado Springs	25
	Johnston, Andrew, Asheville	25
IP	Kaiser, Marc, Tulsa	165
BB	Deduno, Samuel, Modesto	92
SO	Morales, Franklin, Modesto	179
#AVG	Sullivan, Joshua, Tri-City	.188

National League

BATTING	B-T	HT	WT	DOB	AVG	vLH	vRH	G	AB	R	H	2B	3B	HR	RBI	BB	HBP	SH	SF	SO	SB	CS	SLG	OBP
Ardoin, Danny	R-R	6-0	215	7-8-74	.193	.250	.186	35	109	12	21	5	1	0	2	8	2	1	0	27	0	0	.257	.261
Atkins, Garrett	R-R	6-3	215	12-12-79	.329	.341	.327	157	602	117	198	48	1	29	120	79	7	0	7	76	4	0	.556	.409
Baker, Jeff	R-R	6-2	220	6-21-81	.368	.438	.341	18	57	13	21	7	2	5	21	1	0	0	0	14	2	0	.825	.379
Barmes, Clint	R-R	6-0	210	3-6-79	.220	.267	.209	131	478	57	105	26	4	7	56	22	9	19	7	72	5	4	.335	.264
Carroll, Jamey	R-R	5-9	170	2-18-74	.300	.359	.283	136	463	84	139	23	5	5	36	56	3	9	3	66	10	12	.404	.377
Castilla, Vinny	R-R	6-1	205	7-4-67	.190	.167	.200	15	21	2	4	0	0	1	4	0	1	0	0	3	0	0	.333	.227
2-team (72 San Diego)					.229	—	—	87	275	26	63	10	0	5	27	9	3	0	4	49	0	0	.320	.258
Closser, J.D.	B-R	5-10	200	1-15-80	.196	.083	.212	32	97	10	19	3	1	2	11	12	1	1	1	23	0	1	.309	.288
Colina, Alvin	R-R	6-3	210	12-26-81	.200	.250	.000	2	5	0	1	0	0	0	1	0	0	0	0	1	0	0	.200	.200
Freeman, Choo	R-R	6-2	200	10-20-79	.237	.276	.206	88	173	24	41	6	3	2	18	14	1	3	0	42	5	6	.341	.298
Gonzalez, Luis	R-R	5-11	205	6-26-79	.242	.219	.248	61	149	7	36	9	1	2	14	4	2	2	1	27	1	1	.356	.269
Hawpe, Brad	L-L	6-3	205	6-22-79	.293	.232	.302	150	499	67	146	33	6	22	84	74	0	0	2	123	5	5	.515	.383
Helton, Todd	L-L	6-2	210	8-20-73	.302	.326	.295	145	546	94	165	40	5	15	81	91	6	0	6	64	3	2	.476	.404
Holliday, Matt	R-R	6-4	235	1-15-80	.326	.327	.325	155	602	119	196	45	5	34	114	47	15	0	3	110	10	5	.586	.387
Iannetta, Chris	R-R	5-11	195	4-8-83	.260	.231	.266	21	77	12	20	4	0	2	10	13	1	1	1	17	0	1	.390	.370
Marrero, Eli	R-R	6-1	180	11-17-73	.217	.071	.261	30	60	7	13	3	0	4	10	11	1	0	0	16	3	0	.467	.342
2-team (25 New York)					.204	—	—	55	93	11	19	4	0	6	15	15	2	1	0	31	5	0	.441	.324
Matsui, Kazuo	B-R	5-10	185	10-23-75	.345	.125	.381	32	113	22	39	6	3	2	19	10	0	1	2	27	8	1	.504	.392
2-team (38 New York)					.267	—	—	70	243	32	65	12	3	3	26	16	0	4	2	46	10	1	.379	.310
Ojeda, Miguel	R-R	6-1	230	1-29-75	.230	.333	.215	25	74	5	17	3	0	2	11	8	0	0	0	16	0	0	.351	.305
Piedra, Jorge	L-L	6-0	200	4-17-79	.169	.000	.189	43	59	4	10	2	0	3	10	3	1	0	2	11	0	1	.356	.222
Quintanilla, Omar	L-R	5-9	190	10-24-81	.176	.250	.167	11	34	3	6	1	1	0	3	3	0	1	0	9	1	1	.265	.243
Salazar, Jeff	L-L	6-0	190	11-24-80	.283	.000	.294	19	53	13	15	4	0	1	8	11	1	1	1	16	2	0	.415	.409
Shealy, Ryan	R-R	6-5	250	8-29-79	.222	.500	.000	5	9	2	2	2	0	0	1	0	0	0	0	4	0	0	.444	.222
Smith, Jason	L-R	6-3	200	7-24-77	.263	.400	.255	49	99	9	26	1	0	5	13	7	2	0	0	29	3	0	.424	.324
Spilborghs, Ryan	R-R	6-1	190	9-5-79	.287	.323	.267	67	167	26	48	6	3	4	21	14	0	2	3	30	5	2	.431	.337
Sullivan, Cory	L-L	6-0	190	8-20-79	.267	.280	.266	126	386	47	103	26	10	2	30	32	1	19	5	100	10	6	.402	.321
Torrealba, Yorvit	R-R	5-11	200	7-19-78	.247	.246	.247	65	223	23	55	16	3	7	43	11	4	2	1	49	4	3	.439	.293
Tulowitzki, Troy	R-R	6-3	205	10-10-84	.240	.150	.263	25	96	15	23	2	0	1	6	10	1	1	0	25	3	0	.292	.318

PITCHING	B-T	HT	WT	DOB	W	L	ERA	G	GS	CG	SV	IP	H	R	ER	HR	BB	SO	AVG	vLH	vRH	K/9	BB/9
Affeldt, Jeremy	L-L	6-4	225	6-6-79	4	2	6.91	27	0	0	1	27	31	23	21	4	13	20	.277	.268	.282	6.59	4.28
Asencio, Miguel	R-R	6-2	190	9-29-80	1	0	4.70	3	1	0	0	8	9	8	4	1	4	7	.281	.133	.412	8.22	4.70
Bautista, Denny	R-R	6-5	190	8-23-80	0	1	5.40	4	1	0	0	7	9	10	4	0	4	5	.310	.286	.333	6.75	5.40
Cook, Aaron	R-R	6-3	215	2-8-79	9	15	4.23	32	32	0	0	213	242	107	100	17	55	92	.288	.314	.258	3.89	2.33
Corpas, Manny	R-R	6-3	170	12-3-82	1	2	3.62	35	0	0	0	32	36	13	13	3	8	27	.286	.281	.290	7.52	2.23
Cortes, David	R-R	5-11	225	10-15-73	3	1	4.30	30	0	0	0	29	35	14	14	3	6	14	.310	.279	.329	4.30	1.84
Day, Zach	R-R	6-4	215	6-15-78	1	2	10.80	3	3	0	0	13	22	17	16	3	10	6	.373	.400	.353	4.05	6.75
2-team (5 Washington)					2	5	6.75	8	8	0	0	40	51	32	30	5	21	19	—	—	—	4.28	4.72
DeJean, Mike	R-R	6-2	220	9-28-70	1	0	0.00	2	0	0	0	2	1	0	0	0	2	0	.167	.000	.250	0.00	10.80
Dohmann, Scott	R-R	6-1	200	2-13-78	1	1	6.20	27	0	0	1	25	26	18	17	4	15	22	.277	.290	.270	8.03	5.47
Field, Nate	R-R	6-2	205	12-11-75	1	1	4.00	14	0	0	0	9	9	4	4	2	5	14	.257	.417	.174	14.00	5.00
Fogg, Josh	R-R	6-0	205	12-13-76	11	9	5.49	31	31	1	0	172	206	115	105	24	60	93	.300	.309	.291	4.87	3.14
Francis, Jeff	L-L	6-5	205	1-8-81	13	11	4.16	32	32	1	0	199	187	101	92	18	69	117	.250	.241	.252	5.29	3.12
Fuentes, Brian	L-L	6-4	230	8-9-75	3	4	3.44	66	0	0	30	66	51	25	25	8	26	73	.209	.186	.217	10.06	3.58
Hampson, Justin	L-L	6-1	200	5-24-80	1	0	7.50	5	1	0	0	12	19	10	10	3	5	9	.352	.364	.349	6.75	3.75
Jennings, Jason	L-R	6-2	235	7-17-78	9	13	3.78	32	32	3	0	212	206	94	89	17	85	142	.258	.254	.261	6.03	3.61
Jimenez, Ubaldo	R-R	6-4	200	1-22-84	0	0	3.52	2	1	0	0	8	5	4	3	1	3	3	.185	.182	.188	3.52	3.52
Kim, Byung-Hyun	R-R	5-9	175	1-19-79	8	12	5.57	27	27	0	0	155	179	103	96	18	61	129	.295	.325	.265	7.49	3.54
Kim, Sun-Woo	R-R	6-1	190	9-4-77	0	0	19.29	1	0	0	0	7	17	15	15	2	8	4	.500	.579	.400	5.14	10.29
2-team (2 Cincinnati)					0	0	12.51	8	1	0	0	13	24	19	19	5	8	8	—	—	—	5.27	5.27
King, Ray	L-L	6-1	240	1-15-74	1	4	4.43	67	0	0	1	45	56	26	22	6	20	23	.327	.303	.347	4.63	4.03
Martin, Tom	L-L	6-1	205	5-21-70	2	0	5.07	68	0	0	0	60	62	37	34	4	25	46	.264	.268	.261	6.86	3.73
Mesa, Jose	R-R	6-3	235	5-22-66	1	5	3.86	79	0	0	1	72	73	32	31	9	36	39	.270	.270	.271	4.85	4.48
Morillo, Juan	R-R	6-3	190	11-5-83	0	0	15.75	1	1	0	0	4	8	7	7	3	3	4	.421	.625	.273	9.00	6.75
Ramirez, Ramon	R-R	5-11	190	8-31-81	4	3	3.46	61	0	0	0	68	58	28	26	5	27	61	.230	.274	.194	8.11	3.59
Venafro, Mike	L-L	5-10	180	8-2-73	1	0	2.45	7	0	0	0	4	3	1	1	0	3	2	.250	.200	.286	4.91	7.36

FIELDING

Catcher	PCT	G	PO	A	E	DP	PB
Ardoin	.986	35	204	15	3	1	1
Closser	.989	29	173	13	2	3	1
Colina	1.000	1	8	0	0	0	0
Iannetta	1.000	21	139	8	0	3	2
Marrero	1.000	5	11	1	0	1	0
Ojeda	.993	24	126	9	1	0	0
Torrealba	.987	63	337	34	5	7	4

First Base	PCT	G	PO	A	E	DP
Atkins	1.000	3	5	0	0	1
Baker	1.000	1	4	0	0	0
Castilla	1.000	7	19	0	0	3
Gonzalez	1.000	7	40	1	0	5
Helton	.997	145	1367	87	4	156
Marrero	1.000	7	58	8	0	8
Shealy	1.000	2	13	0	0	1

	PCT	G	PO	A	E	DP
Smith	1.000	6	34	3	0	1

Second Base	PCT	G	PO	A	E	DP
Barmes	1.000	4	2	9	0	1
Carroll	.995	109	186	397	3	98
Gonzalez	.984	32	51	69	2	7
Matsui	.984	21	48	73	2	26
Quintanilla	1.000	3	8	4	0	2
Smith	.975	18	32	46	2	13

Third Base	PCT	G	PO	A	E	DP
Atkins	.953	157	98	286	19	36
Carroll	.917	3	8	1	2	
Castilla	1.000	1	1	3	0	0
Gonzalez	1.000	3	2	1	0	0
Smith	1.000	3	2	4	0	0

Shortstop	PCT	G	PO	A	E	DP
Barmes	.969	125	192	371	18	89

	PCT	G	PO	A	E	DP
Carroll	.971	10	9	24	1	6
Matsui	1.000	3	4	1	0	1
Quintanilla	1.000	8	10	26	0	7
Smith	1.000	1	0	1	0	0
Tulowitzki	.983	25	47	69	2	25

Outfield	PCT	G	PO	A	E	DP
Baker	1.000	12	11	1	0	0
Freeman	.991	51	107	0	1	0
Gonzalez	1.000	7	10	0	0	0
Hawpe	.987	145	280	16	4	3
Holliday	.979	153	277	8	6	2
Marrero	.933	6	13	1	1	0
Piedra	1.000	5	7	0	0	0
Salazar	1.000	14	25	0	0	0
Spilborghs	.988	46	75	4	1	2
Sullivan	.996	114	225	4	1	0

General manager: Dan O'Dowd. **Farm director:** Marc Gustafson. **Scouting director:** Bill Schmidt.

Class	Team	League	W	L	PCT	Finish*	Manager	Affiliate Since
Majors	Colorado	National	76	86	.469	12th (16)	Clint Hurdle	—
Triple-A	Colorado Springs Sky Sox	Pacific Coast	66	77	.465	13th (16)	Tom Runnells	1993
Double-A	Tulsa Drillers	Texas	75	64	.540	4th (8)	Stu Cole	2003
High A	Modesto Nuts	California	66	74	.471	8th (10)	Chad Kreuter	2005
Low A	Asheville Tourists	South Atlantic	74	63	.540	6th (16)	Joe Mikulik	1994
Short-season	Tri-City Dust Devils	Northwest	38	38	.500	5th (8)	Fred Ocasio	2001
Rookie	Casper Rockies	Pioneer	27	49	.355	8th (8)	Paul Carey	2001
OVERALL 2006 MINOR LEAGUE RECORD			346	365	.487	21st (30)		

*Finish in overall standings (No. of teams in league). +League champion

Colorado Springs Sky Sox — Triple-A

Pacific Coast League

ORGANIZATION STATISTICS

BATTING	B-T	HT	WT	DOB	AVG	vLH	vRH	G	AB	R	H	2B	3B	HR	RBI	BB	HBP	SH	SF	SO	SB	CS	SLG	OBP
Apodaca, Luis	R-R	5-11	175	7-15-82	.000	—	.000	1	1	0	0	0	0	0	0	0	0	0	0	0	0	0	.000	.000
Ardoin, Danny	R-R	6-0	215	7-8-74	.267	.000	.333	6	15	2	4	2	0	0	2	2	1	1	0	5	0	0	.400	.389
Baker, Jeff	R-R	6-2	220	6-21-81	.305	.347	.291	128	482	71	147	30	4	20	108	46	5	1	4	110	7	1	.508	.369
Barker, Sean	R-R	6-3	220	5-26-80	.297	.278	.304	106	330	53	98	14	9	13	55	29	5	0	1	104	17	7	.512	.362
Berglund, Bret	R-R	6-4	210	12-9-82	.000	—	.000	1	4	0	0	0	0	0	0	0	0	0	0	0	0	0	.000	.000
Castilla, Vinny	R-R	6-1	205	7-4-67	.387	.333	.409	8	31	6	12	3	0	0	4	2	1	0	0	5	0	0	.484	.441
Closser, JD	B-R	5-10	200	1-15-80	.298	.310	.293	70	225	32	67	15	1	8	30	31	1	0	1	38	8	2	.480	.384
Conway, Dan	R-R	6-2	190	10-13-79	.219	.208	.225	48	128	12	28	6	0	2	10	9	0	1	0	30	0	1	.313	.268
Gonzalez, Luis	R-R	5-11	205	6-26-79	.268	.080	.333	27	97	15	26	4	2	2	10	6	0	1	0	11	1	0	.412	.345
Hart, Bo	R-R	5-11	175	9-27-76	.252	.295	.225	39	115	16	29	6	1	1	6	10	2	1	0	18	1	1	.348	.323
2-team (54 Memphis)					.215	—	—	93	261	33	56	12	2	3	14	22	5	1	2	48	4	1	.310	.286
Helton, Todd	L-L	6-2	210	8-20-73	.333	—	.333	2	6	0	2	0	0	0	0	0	1	0	0	1	0	0	.333	.429
Iannetta, Chris	R-R	5-11	195	4-8-83	.351	.410	.330	47	151	23	53	12	1	3	22	34	3	1	1	29	0	0	.503	.447
Matsui, Kazuo	R-R	5-10	185	10-23-75	.278	.323	.262	31	115	26	32	4	0	3	16	9	1	1	3	20	3	1	.391	.328
Melo, Juan	B-R	6-1	160	10-11-76	.211	.222	.209	33	109	7	23	2	1	3	11	6	0	0	0	24	0	0	.330	.252
2-team (82 Fresno)					.263	—	—	115	384	43	101	12	2	8	50	24	2	3	5	70	2	2	.367	.306
Miller, Matt	R-R	6-2	210	12-26-82	.333	.444	.267	8	24	2	8	0	0	0	3	3	0	0	1	6	0	1	.333	.393
Miller, Tony	R-R	5-9	200	8-18-80	.143	.214	.122	22	63	2	9	1	0	0	1	8	0	1	0	22	1	1	.159	.239
Nazario, Radames	R-R	6-0	166	6-14-87	.000	—	.000	1	1	0	0	0	0	0	0	0	0	0	0	0	0	0	.000	.000
Nix, Jayson	R-R	5-11	185	8-26-82	.251	.262	.247	103	358	39	90	14	1	2	26	32	3	3	1	61	15	3	.313	.317
Ojeda, Miguel	R-R	6-1	230	1-29-75	.288	.444	.256	17	52	11	15	4	1	2	4	12	0	1	1	10	1	0	.519	.415
2-team (14 Oklahoma)					.313	—	—	31	99	19	31	6	1	2	8	18	0	1	1	18	1	0	.455	.415
Piedra, Jorge	L-L	6-0	200	4-17-79	.239	.091	.267	41	138	15	33	8	0	6	18	15	1	0	2	31	0	2	.428	.314
Quintanilla, Omar	L-R	5-9	190	10-24-81	.276	.217	.298	82	308	48	85	23	2	4	29	28	4	7	2	55	4	1	.403	.342
Rivera, Carlos	L-L	5-11	230	6-10-78	.325	.290	.338	120	421	54	137	25	1	9	70	18	6	0	5	51	3	2	.454	.358
Salazar, Jeff	L-L	6-0	190	11-24-80	.265	.205	.284	85	328	62	87	14	7	9	39	46	2	3	2	64	12	5	.433	.357
Shealy, Ryan	R-R	6-5	250	8-29-79	.284	.333	.268	58	222	37	63	16	1	15	55	20	4	0	2	34	0	0	.568	.351
Slavik, Corey	L-R	6-0	190	3-24-80	.200	.429	.164	20	35	5	7	1	1	1	7	3	2	0	0	3	0	0	.371	.300
Smith, Jason	L-R	6-3	200	7-24-77	.291	.219	.312	41	141	26	41	9	5	4	23	15	0	1	2	41	3	1	.511	.354
Spilborghs, Ryan	R-R	6-1	190	9-5-79	.338	.315	.347	68	269	50	91	20	1	5	34	30	1	1	5	49	8	2	.476	.400
Torrealba, Yorvit	R-R	5-11	200	7-19-78	.167	.111	.185	10	36	0	6	2	0	0	2	4	0	0	0	9	0	0	.222	.250
Whiteman, Tommy	R-R	6-3	180	7-14-79	.163	.111	.180	60	147	11	24	3	1	2	10	7	0	4	1	53	1	1	.238	.200
Wilson, Josh	R-R	6-1	180	3-26-81	.307	.329	.300	89	335	61	103	18	4	10	45	37	4	1	7	41	15	4	.475	.376

PITCHING	B-T	HT	WT	DOB	W	L	ERA	G	GS	CG	SV	IP	H	R	ER	HR	BB	SO	AVG	vLH	vRH	K/9	BB/9
Acevedo, Jose	R-R	6-0	220	12-18-77	6	8	5.59	15	15	0	0	87	108	59	54	10	19	53	.310	.356	.271	5.48	1.97
Apodaca, Luis	R-R	5-11	175	7-15-82	0	0	6.00	1	0	0	0	3	3	2	2	0	0	0	.273	.125	.667	0.00	9.00
Asahina, Jonathan	B-R	6-1	190	12-31-80	3	7	6.12	16	15	0	0	90	107	67	61	11	24	42	.301	.284	.318	4.22	2.41
Asencio, Miguel	R-R	6-2	190	9-29-80	8	7	5.03	38	16	0	1	111	127	69	62	13	41	71	.294	.321	.269	5.76	3.32
Bautista, Denny	R-R	6-5	190	8-23-80	1	4	4.50	6	6	0	0	36	46	24	18	2	16	35	.311	.314	.308	8.75	4.00
2-team (10 Omaha) ..					3	9	6.08	16	16	0	0	80	98	62	54	5	48	63	—	—		7.09	5.40
Beckstead, Jentry	R-R	6-0	175	6-9-80	1	3	3.52	7	0	0	0	8	11	6	3	1	3	9	.333	.176	.500	10.57	3.52
Cerda, Jaime	L-L	6-0	200	10-26-78	3	3	5.72	36	0	0	1	46	48	30	29	8	26	41	.268	.167	.312	8.08	5.12
Colyer, Steve	L-L	6-4	235	2-22-79	2	2	5.71	48	0	0	0	58	54	39	37	7	48	52	.257	.207	.289	8.02	7.41
Corpas, Manny	R-R	6-3	170	12-3-82	0	0	1.04	8	0	0	0	9	5	1	1	1	2	7	.167	.222	.143	7.27	2.08
Cortes, David	R-R	5-11	225	10-15-73	1	1	4.82	18	0	0	2	19	22	10	10	2	9	16	.282	.240	.302	7.71	4.34
Dohmann, Scott	R-R	6-1	200	2-13-78	0	0	2.53	10	0	0	1	11	6	3	3	2	1	12	.158	.118	.190	10.13	0.84
Esposito, Mike	R-R	6-1	190	9-27-81	6	13	6.67	27	26	0	0	140	187	109	104	20	45	91	.318	.291	.351	5.84	2.89
Field, Nate	R-R	6-2	205	12-11-75	3	3	4.74	49	0	0	25	49	63	28	26	7	9	55	.313	.344	.288	10.03	1.64
Hampson, Justin	L-L	6-1	200	5-24-80	8	4	3.33	31	13	0	0	122	121	57	45	10	39	95	.264	.257	.268	7.03	2.88
Jimenez, Ubaldo	R-R	6-4	200	1-22-84	5	2	5.06	13	13	0	0	78	74	49	44	7	43	64	.252	.266	.236	7.35	4.94
Kim, Byung-Hyun	R-R	5-9	175	1-19-79	0	1	6.23	3	3	0	0	13	18	11	9	0	4	11	.310	.258	.370	7.62	2.77
Kim, Sun-Woo	R-R	6-1	190	9-4-77	8	6	5.05	21	21	2	0	125	149	77	70	14	36	71	.305	.317	.295	5.13	2.60
McClellan, Zach	R-R	6-5	210	11-25-78	4	3	4.18	54	0	0	3	65	77	33	30	3	29	49	.297	.294	.300	6.82	4.04
Nin, Sandy	R-R	6-0	170	8-13-80	1	3	4.55	6	6	0	0	32	32	17	16	3	8	26	.274	.333	.217	7.39	2.27
Parker, Zack	R-L	6-2	205	8-19-81	2	6	6.63	15	8	0	0	57	68	44	42	9	39	36	.297	.460	.235	5.68	6.16
Prinz, Bret	R-R	6-3	210	6-15-77	0	0	0.00	8	0	0	3	9	7	0	0	0	1	8	.219	.188	.250	8.31	1.04
Ramirez, Ramon	R-R	5-11	190	8-31-81	0	0	0.00	1	0	0	0	1	0	0	0	0	0	1	.000	.000	.000	9.00	0.00
Sierra, Edwardo	R-R	6-4	195	4-15-82	0	0	5.14	6	0	0	0	7	4	4	4	1	6	7	.280	.455	.143	9.00	7.71
Ulloa, Enmanuel	R-R	6-2	190	11-26-78	0	1	0.00	1	0	0	0	6	3	2	2	0	2	2	.150	.111	.182	3.00	3.00
Venafro, Mike	L-L	5-10	180	8-2-73	3	1	3.20	20	0	0	0	16	10	4	4	1	5	10	.175	.217	.147	5.51	2.76
Williams, Randy	L-L	6-3	195	9-18-75	1	2	6.41	47	0	0	0	59	71	45	42	6	30	46	.306	.275	.322	7.02	4.58

FIELDING

Catcher

Catcher	PCT	G	PO	A	E	DP	PB
Apodaca	1.000	1	1	0	0	0	0
Ardoin	.952	4	19	1	1	0	1
Closser	.988	57	371	31	5	7	6
Conway	.994	31	161	14	1	2	8
Iannetta	.992	37	230	23	2	1	3
Ojeda	1.000	17	106	10	0	3	1
Torrealba	1.000	8	60	4	0	1	1
Matsui	1.000	3	4	13	0	4	
Nix	.982	100	225	369	11	88	
Quintanilla	.989	32	59	114	2	24	
Smith	1.000	3	6	6	0	2	
Wilson	1.000	4	7	6	0	3	
Hart	1.000	4	7	15	0	2	
Matsui	.956	28	40	91	6	20	
Nazario	—	1	0	0	0	0	
Quintanilla	.978	49	73	146	5	37	
Smith	.842	4	8	8	3	2	
Whiteman	.929	5	4	9	1	3	
Wilson	.975	62	93	181	7	46	

First Base

First Base	PCT	G	PO	A	E	DP
Castilla	.941	1	16	0	1	2
Conway	.944	2	16	1	1	3
Helton	1.000	2	17	3	0	2
Melo	1.000	5	27	1	0	3
Rivera	.998	91	797	83	2	78
Shealy	.996	44	419	29	2	64
Slavik	1.000	1	5	1	0	0
Smith	.966	4	26	2	1	3

Second Base

Second Base	PCT	G	PO	A	E	DP
Gonzalez	1.000	2	6	8	0	3
Hart	1.000	4	7	8	0	4

Third Base

Third Base	PCT	G	PO	A	E	DP
Baker	—	1	0	0	0	0
Castilla	.833	2	2	3	1	0
Closser	—	1	0	0	0	0
Conway	—	1	0	0	0	0
Gonzalez	1.000	10	5	22	0	5
Hart	.938	21	12	33	3	6
Melo	.946	25	15	38	3	6
Nix	1.000	2	2	2	0	0
Slavik	.944	11	2	15	1	2
Smith	.989	32	23	71	1	12
Whiteman	.843	36	17	42	11	4
Wilson	.958	27	17	51	3	6

Shortstop

Shortstop	PCT	G	PO	A	E	DP
Gonzalez	.875	1	4	3	1	1

Outfield

Outfield	PCT	G	PO	A	E	DP
Baker	.985	120	192	10	3	4
Barker	.957	93	152	4	7	1
Berglund	—	1	0	0	0	0
Conway	—	1	0	0	0	0
Gonzalez	1.000	12	7	0	0	0
Hart	1.000	3	2	0	0	0
M. Miller	.909	6	10	0	1	0
T. Miller	.917	19	33	0	3	0
Piedra	.957	38	63	4	3	2
Rivera	1.000	3	3	0	0	0
Salazar	.973	84	175	6	5	1
Spilborghs	.979	66	131	9	3	2

Tulsa Drillers — Double-A

Texas League

BATTING

	B-T	HT	WT	DOB	AVG	vLH	vRH	G	AB	R	H	2B	3B	HR	RBI	BB	HBP	SH	SF	SO	SB	CS	SLG	OBP
Apodaca, Luis	R-R	5-11	175	7-15-82	.000	.000	.000	3	7	0	0	0	0	0	0	0	0	0	0	4	0	0	.000	.000
Bernier, Douglas	B-R	5-11	175	6-24-80	.280	.383	.256	87	246	44	69	16	3	1	27	30	2	9	2	46	4	1	.382	.361
Colina, Alvin	R-R	6-3	210	12-26-81	.254	.260	.252	92	323	45	82	14	1	12	46	23	6	0	2	77	3	2	.415	.314
Colonel, Christian	R-R	6-2	210	12-25-81	.271	.287	.267	115	387	47	105	24	0	10	43	35	5	2	6	64	11	5	.411	.335
Czarniecki, Jordan	R-R	6-1	175	10-4-80	.275	.341	.256	117	408	61	112	27	4	11	57	46	6	5	3	86	20	4	.441	.354
Dragicevich, Jeffrey	R-R	6-2	200	8-1-82	.250	.200	.265	16	44	6	11	2	0	1	5	7	1	1	0	13	2	0	.364	.365
Gaetti, Joe	R-R	6-2	205	10-16-81	.296	.376	.274	109	392	68	116	23	4	16	62	38	10	2	4	99	5	2	.497	.369
Iannetta, Chris	R-R	5-11	195	4-8-83	.321	.214	.344	44	156	38	50	10	2	11	26	24	3	1	1	26	1	0	.622	.418
Koshansky, Joseph	L-L	6-4	225	5-26-82	.284	.216	.305	132	500	84	142	28	0	31	109	64	6	1	2	134	3	2	.526	.371
Macri, Matt	R-R	6-2	200	5-29-82	.233	.241	.230	83	288	35	67	12	2	8	35	22	5	6	5	66	2	4	.372	.294
Miller, Matt	R-R	6-2	210	12-26-82	.229	.261	.217	27	83	14	19	1	1	1	7	11	2	0	1	13	1	1	.301	.330
Sanchez, Tino	B-R	6-0	175	2-2-79	.325	.263	.344	23	83	12	27	6	0	3	24	9	0	1	1	6	0	0	.506	.387
Smith, Seth	L-L	6-3	215	9-30-82	.294	.286	.296	130	524	79	154	46	4	15	71	51	4	3	0	74	4	4	.483	.361
Stewart, Ian	L-R	6-3	205	4-5-85	.268	.252	.273	120	462	75	124	41	7	10	71	50	11	1	4	103	3	8	.452	.351
Thigpen, Jud	R-R	6-0	180	10-3-80	.232	.222	.235	92	310	37	72	16	1	5	35	15	10	5	10	60	6	2	.339	.281
Tulowitzki, Troy	R-R	6-3	205	10-10-84	.291	.396	.262	104	423	75	123	34	2	13	61	46	10	1	5	71	6	5	.473	.370

PITCHING

	B-T	HT	WT	DOB	W	L	ERA	G	GS	CG	SV	IP	H	R	ER	HR	BB	SO	AVG	vLH	vRH	K/9	BB/9
Arias, Alberto	R-R	5-11	155	10-14-83	8	6	4.35	49	9	0	0	112	102	59	54	15	45	83	.245	.287	.217	6.69	3.63
Asahina, Jonathan	B-R	6-1	190	12-31-80	1	3	6.24	13	9	0	0	58	86	46	40	12	20	25	.351	.395	.313	3.90	3.12
Beckstead, Jentry	R-R	6-0	175	6-9-80	6	2	2.64	41	0	0	0	65	53	31	19	7	22	59	.225	.234	.217	8.21	3.06
Burch, Jason	R-R	6-5	215	10-15-82	3	4	4.95	45	0	0	0	64	62	45	35	5	28	52	.254	.262	.248	7.35	3.96
Colyer, Steve	L-R	6-4	235	2-22-79	0	1	9.00	6	0	0	1	5	7	5	5	2	3	4	.350	.000	.500	7.20	5.40
Corpas, Manny	R-R	6-3	170	12-3-82	2	1	0.98	34	0	0	19	37	22	7	4	0	4	35	.177	.096	.236	8.59	0.98
Daley, Matt	R-R	6-2	175	6-23-82	0	0	1.42	3	0	0	0	6	4	1	1	0	3	2	.200	.333	.000	2.84	4.26
Jimenez, Ubaldo	R-R	6-4	200	1-22-84	9	2	2.45	13	13	1	0	73	49	21	20	2	40	86	.194	.178	.209	10.55	4.91
Kaiser, Marc	R-R	6-2	205	5-7-82	10	10	4.15	25	25	4	0	165	174	89	76	15	40	73	.276	.268	.283	3.99	2.19
Miller, Jim	R-R	6-1	200	4-28-82	0	3	3.86	45	0	0	12	44	50	23	19	10	14	41	.275	.307	.245	8.32	2.84
Morillo, Juan	R-R	6-3	190	11-5-83	12	8	4.62	27	27	1	0	140	128	82	72	13	80	132	.248	.261	.240	8.47	5.13
Newman, Joshua	L-L	6-1	190	6-11-82	9	5	3.16	62	0	0	2	77	56	27	27	8	24	77	.204	.181	.222	9.00	2.81
Parker, Zack	R-L	6-2	205	8-19-81	2	2	10.24	10	6	0	0	29	33	37	33	3	33	28	.270	.172	.301	8.69	10.24
Register, Steven	R-R	6-1	175	10-6-82	4	10	5.57	27	27	2	0	155	189	114	96	25	53	77	.308	.314	.304	4.47	3.08
Songster, Judd	R-R	6-3	195	12-26-79	2	1	3.18	47	0	0	2	65	46	26	23	9	29	73	.197	.215	.184	10.11	4.02
Ulloa, Enmanuel	R-R	6-2	190	11-26-78	7	6	3.91	23	23	0	0	127	125	65	55	14	35	112	.254	.291	.224	7.96	2.49

FIELDING

Catcher	PCT	G	PO	A	E	DP	PB
Colina	.994	87	604	59	4	7	11
Iannetta	.990	38	272	14	3	4	3
Sanchez	.983	18	108	9	2	1	1

First Base	PCT	G	PO	A	E	DP
Bernier	1.000	1	2	0	0	1
Colonel	1.000	12	98	12	0	11
Koshansky	.991	125	1108	96	11	126
Sanchez	1.000	4	30	2	0	3

Second Base	PCT	G	PO	A	E	DP
Bernier	.983	44	71	104	3	28
Colonel	.975	21	33	44	2	12
Dragicevich	1.000	6	16	20	0	5
Macri	.972	81	148	234	11	70

Third Base	PCT	G	PO	A	E	DP
Bernier	1.000	4	3	7	0	3
Colonel	.950	23	9	48	3	7
Dragicevich	1.000	1	0	3	0	0
Stewart	.945	114	73	252	19	38

Shortstop	PCT	G	PO	A	E	DP
Bernier	.953	33	61	82	7	19
Dragicevich	1.000	7	5	15	0	1
Tulowitzki	.948	102	161	291	25	70

Outfield	PCT	G	PO	A	E	DP
Colonel	1.000	32	43	5	0	1
Czarniecki	.981	111	258	6	5	0
Gaetti	.939	86	151	4	10	2
Miller	.971	20	32	2	1	0
Smith	.976	119	192	13	5	5
Thigpen	.973	61	100	7	3	1

Modesto Nuts — High Class A

California League

BATTING

	B-T	HT	WT	DOB	AVG	vLH	vRH	G	AB	R	H	2B	3B	HR	RBI	BB	HBP	SH	SF	SO	SB	CS	SLG	OBP
Almonte, Sandy	B-R	5-11	150	11-19-82	.263	.231	.280	11	38	4	10	2	1	0	2	1	0	0	2	8	2	1	.368	.282
Apodaca, Luis	R-R	5-11	175	7-15-82	.311	.333	.306	16	45	9	14	3	0	0	3	4	1	0	0	6	2	2	.378	.380
Ardoin, Danny	R-R	6-0	215	7-8-74	.077	.111	.059	7	26	4	2	2	0	0	0	2	0	0	0	6	0	0	.154	.200
Brooks, Doc	R-R	5-10	190	1-21-80	.277	.264	.281	98	357	64	99	18	4	16	62	53	13	1	1	110	10	5	.485	.389
Davies, Michael	L-L	6-3	195	3-29-81	.217	.164	.230	80	281	32	61	17	1	4	36	33	0	2	2	93	1	4	.327	.297

	B-T	HT	WT	DOB	AVG	vLH	vRH	G	AB	R	H	2B	3B	HR	RBI	BB	HBP	SH	SF	SO	SB	CS	SLG	OBP
Dragicevich, Jeffrey	R-R	6-2	200	8-1-82	.275	.246	.285	75	244	36	67	16	1	3	33	41	4	7	1	62	1	3	.385	.386
Frey, Christopher	L-L	6-1	180	8-11-83	.281	.311	.271	125	455	69	128	26	9	2	54	48	6	17	10	81	22	13	.391	.351
Granato, Anthony	B-R	6-0	200	3-18-81	.213	.176	.222	27	89	20	19	5	0	1	9	20	2	1	1	24	9	2	.303	.366
Guarno, Rick	R-R	6-0	185	8-16-82	.250	.278	.238	20	60	10	15	5	0	1	6	7	4	2	0	22	0	2	.383	.366
Hahn, Dustin	L-R	6-1	200	10-21-82	.180	.154	.186	45	139	13	25	4	0	0	6	13	1	1	0	48	1	1	.209	.255
Herrera, Jonathan	B-R	5-9	155	11-3-84	.310	.289	.317	127	487	87	151	20	8	7	77	58	3	13	7	67	34	15	.427	.382
Miller, Matt	R-R	6-2	210	12-26-82	.323	.292	.333	92	368	52	119	20	2	12	77	31	8	0	8	37	4	9	.486	.381
Nelson, Justin	L-L	6-3	205	4-23-83	.241	.270	.231	134	489	75	118	33	8	20	86	62	8	0	8	156	7	8	.464	.332
Robledo, Nelson	R-R	6-1	180	6-13-84	.000	—	.000	1	1	0	0	0	0	0	0	0	1	0	0	0	0	0	.000	.500
Sardinha, Duke	R-R	6-0	200	12-9-80	.235	.276	.222	106	371	44	87	21	2	12	45	33	4	6	3	112	8	4	.399	.302
Sargent, Luke	R-R	5-9	190	7-14-82	.242	.207	.253	44	120	12	29	4	0	0	9	13	1	2	0	45	1	0	.275	.321
Valdez, Jose	L-R	6-1	152	9-6-83	.225	.240	.220	79	284	37	64	15	1	11	41	30	0	1	2	55	0	4	.401	.297
Wilson, Kyle	R-R	6-1	215	8-23-82	.230	.250	.220	78	261	34	60	16	0	4	28	10	9	2	1	51	0	1	.337	.281
Wilson, Neil	R-R	6-1	190	12-7-83	.290	.186	.333	62	241	30	70	13	1	2	30	19	1	0	1	39	0	1	.378	.344
Wimberly, Corey	R-R	5-8	180	10-26-83	.325	.292	.337	87	342	72	111	6	4	2	24	30	17	8	2	42	50	16	.383	.404

PITCHING	B-T	HT	WT	DOB	W	L	ERA	G	GS	CG	SV	IP	H	R	ER	HR	BB	SO	AVG	vLH	vRH	K/9	BB/9
Beerer, Scott	R-R	6-1	200	7-4-82	3	1	3.81	28	0	0	11	28	28	18	12	0	19	27	.252	.265	.242	8.58	6.04
Bright, Adam	L-L	6-0	180	8-11-84	3	6	5.18	49	0	0	0	57	56	42	33	1	34	35	.268	.182	.308	5.49	5.34
Cardenas, Humberto	R-R	6-1	210	3-25-83	8	9	4.44	28	16	0	0	130	150	73	64	16	29	80	.298	.276	.311	5.55	2.01
Clarke, Darren	R-R	6-8	235	3-19-81	1	1	1.35	25	0	0	5	27	13	5	4	1	7	37	.140	.200	.083	12.49	2.36
Daley, Matt	R-R	6-2	175	6-23-82	4	3	3.15	51	0	0	15	69	70	27	24	3	20	79	.258	.154	.323	10.35	2.62
Deduno, Samuel	R-R	6-1	156	7-2-83	5	8	4.80	27	26	0	0	146	121	88	78	3	92	167	.222	.219	.225	10.27	5.66
Dohmann, Scott	R-R	6-1	200	2-13-78	0	1	2.25	3	3	0	0	4	2	1	1	0	2	5	.154	.167	.143	11.25	4.50
Fox, Ryan	R-R	6-3	220	10-13-80	2	0	8.63	25	0	0	1	32	52	35	31	3	19	24	.369	.357	.376	6.68	5.29
Grube, Jarrett	R-R	6-4	220	11-5-81	4	2	3.69	42	1	0	0	71	72	34	29	10	17	64	.264	.307	.238	8.15	2.17
Kreidermacher, Andrew	B-R	6-2	195	1-27-83	1	1	4.32	13	0	0	0	25	21	17	12	0	13	21	.228	.268	.196	7.56	4.68
Lo, Ching Lung	R-R	6-6	190	8-20-85	10	5	5.39	27	25	0	0	155	179	108	93	14	54	128	.285	.272	.295	7.42	3.13
Mattheus, Ryan	R-R	6-3	215	11-10-83	7	12	5.19	28	28	1	0	156	198	103	90	5	65	131	.313	.331	.301	7.56	3.75
Merrell, Darric	R-R	6-4	210	1-22-82	4	7	5.09	45	0	0	1	58	70	39	33	3	23	53	.294	.327	.271	8.18	3.55
Morales, Franklin	L-L	6-0	175	1-24-86	10	9	3.68	27	26	0	0	154	126	77	63	9	89	179	.223	.193	.231	10.46	5.20
Postlewait, Jacob	S-L	6-0	195	11-3-81	0	6	5.94	26	4	0	0	50	65	37	33	3	26	34	.317	.358	.303	6.12	4.68
Reynolds, Greg	R-R	6-7	220	7-3-85	2	1	3.33	11	11	0	0	49	51	22	18	1	14	29	.271	.183	.325	5.36	2.59
Santiago, Tomas	R-R	6-4	210	10-30-81	2	2	6.04	15	0	0	1	22	30	17	15	0	7	20	.313	.300	.318	8.06	2.82

FIELDING

Catcher	PCT	G	PO	A	E	DP	PB
Apodaca	.979	14	90	4	2	0	6
Ardoin	.941	4	24	8	2	2	1
Guarno	.994	20	139	24	1	1	3
Robledo	1.000	1	6	0	0	0	0
Sargent	.985	42	300	28	5	3	6
N. Wilson	.995	50	406	26	2	2	12
K. Wilson	.970	26	153	8	5	0	15

First Base	PCT	G	PO	A	E	DP
Davies	.996	77	629	59	3	62
Dragicevich	.982	13	102	10	2	9
Frey	1.000	1	3	0	0	1
Hahn	.949	7	54	2	3	5
Sardinha	1.000	15	119	16	0	13
Valdez	1.000	1	6	1	0	0
K. Wilson	.986	33	260	25	4	23

Second Base	PCT	G	PO	A	E	DP
Almonte	.941	7	11	21	2	6
Dragicevich	.993	34	66	80	1	24
Granato	.960	14	30	42	3	7
Herrera	1.000	2	3	5	0	0
Valdez	.972	13	30	39	2	11
Wimberly	.961	78	143	202	14	48

Third Base	PCT	G	PO	A	E	DP
Almonte	1.000	1	0	1	0	0
Davies	1.000	1	0	1	0	0
Dragicevich	.833	4	0	10	2	0
Granato	.917	7	4	18	2	1
Hahn	1.000	2	0	1	0	0
Herrera	1.000	2	4	5	0	0
Sardinha	.886	69	43	135	23	11
Valdez	.919	58	21	115	12	9
Wimberly	1.000	1	1	1	0	0

Shortstop	PCT	G	PO	A	E	DP
Almonte	1.000	2	5	11	0	3
Dragicevich	.914	15	18	35	5	14
Herrera	.964	121	208	373	22	68
Valdez	1.000	3	1	8	0	2

Outfield	PCT	G	PO	A	E	DP
Brooks	.980	59	92	6	2	0
Dragicevich	.—	1	0	0	0	0
Frey	.980	121	239	8	5	2
Granato	1.000	6	7	3	0	0
Hahn	1.000	26	44	3	0	1
Miller	.978	88	173	8	4	1
Nelson	.982	122	160	7	3	0
Sardinha	1.000	1	1	0	0	0
K. Wilson	1.000	5	2	0	0	0
Wimberly	1.000	2	1	0	0	0

Asheville Tourists — Low Class A

South Atlantic League

BATTING	B-T	HT	WT	DOB	AVG	vLH	vRH	G	AB	R	H	2B	3B	HR	RBI	BB	HBP	SH	SF	SO	SB	CS	SLG	OBP
Anderson, Nate	L-R	6-2	220	10-22-83	.133	.067	.200	10	30	1	4	0	0	0	1	1	0	0	0	8	0	0	.133	.161
Becktel, Travis	R-R	6-1	201	4-3-83	.272	.244	.284	78	268	45	73	16	1	1	23	43	3	2	1	66	21	11	.351	.378
Blumenthal, Kyle	L-R	5-10	195	1-11-83	.272	.297	.259	80	261	43	71	18	3	8	49	35	2	1	3	61	7	2	.456	.359
Carte, Daniel	R-R	6-0	190	5-18-84	.258	.223	.272	117	426	73	110	26	1	14	66	42	13	2	2	107	11	11	.423	.342
Cook, Chris	R-R	6-4	222	7-3-83	.255	.260	.253	83	274	36	70	15	0	7	44	31	4	0	8	72	3	9	.387	.340
Cuadrado, Phillip	R-R	6-1	210	11-4-83	.296	.345	.275	105	378	58	112	20	2	15	86	35	14	1	4	72	3	9	.479	.374
Fowler, Dexter	B-R	6-4	173	3-22-86	.296	.296	.296	99	405	92	120	31	6	8	46	43	7	2	1	79	43	23	.462	.373
Garner, Cole	R-R	6-2	210	12-15-84	.302	.302	.301	120	464	100	140	40	2	19	88	25	15	2	6	127	35	13	.519	.353
Nazario, Radames	R-R	6-0	166	6-14-87	.286	—	.286	4	7	2	2	0	0	0	0	2	0	1	0	2	1	1	.286	.444
Nelson, Chris	R-R	5-11	176	9-3-85	.260	.282	.251	118	466	69	121	38	1	11	76	32	7	5	7	101	14	2	.416	.313
Nunez, Florentino	B-R	6-0	164	3-23-84	.198	.217	.190	30	81	7	16	3	0	1	8	5	1	4	1	23	2	2	.272	.250
Paulk, Michael	L-L	6-2	195	4-23-84	.245	.202	.258	106	376	40	92	15	0	3	48	43	4	3	2	62	7	5	.309	.326
Restrepo, John	L-L	6-1	185	7-27-82	.241	.263	.233	28	79	13	19	3	1	1	9	10	2	1	1	24	5	0	.342	.337
Robledo, Nelson	R-R	6-1	180	6-13-84	.208	.172	.221	63	212	24	44	10	0	3	35	14	5	5	1	54	3	1	.297	.272
Sargent, Luke	R-R	5-9	190	7-14-82	.286	.500	.200	2	7	1	2	0	0	0	1	0	3	0	0	0	0	0	.286	.286
Van Kooten, Jason	R-R	6-0	170	9-1-84	.283	.274	.286	98	357	59	101	22	2	2	39	27	11	5	2	80	20	15	.373	.350
Young Jr., Eric	R-R	5-10	180	5-25-85	.295	.234	.320	128	482	92	142	28	6	5	49	67	10	9	1	75	87	31	.409	.391

PITCHING	B-T	HT	WT	DOB	W	L	ERA	G	GS	CG	SV	IP	H	R	ER	HR	BB	SO	AVG	vLH	vRH	K/9	BB/9
Bailey, Chad	L-L	6-4	190	6-24-83	2	0	3.68	27	0	0	1	37	43	21	15	1	17	21	.297	.300	.295	5.15	4.17
Binda, Byron	R-R	6-0	185	6-30-83	2	2	7.43	17	0	0	0	23	31	21	19	3	8	20	.323	.389	.283	7.83	3.13
Burok, James	R-R	6-3	212	11-16-82	4	6	4.91	43	0	0	3	55	62	39	30	3	30	37	.287	.305	.276	6.05	4.91
Cedeno, Xavier	L-L	6-1	165	8-26-86	8	9	4.04	27	27	0	0	138	144	79	62	8	63	99	.270	.286	.266	6.46	4.11
Delgado, George	R-R	6-2	175	3-22-84	0	0	5.09	11	0	0	0	18	25	10	10	3	2	20	.342	.303	.375	10.19	1.53
Durden, Brandon	R-L	6-3	215	7-20-84	10	4	3.64	26	26	0	0	151	172	83	61	14	43	119	.293	.305	.290	7.18	2.56
Ferrer, Simon	B-R	5-10	175	6-24-80	0	0	0.00	3	0	0	0	10	6	0	0	0	1	8	.182	.200	.167	7.20	1.80
George, Jon	R-R	6-4	220	7-6-84	4	4	2.88	34	0	0	0	50	43	20	16	1	13	35	.225	.174	.254	6.30	2.34

Name	B-T	HT	WT	DOB	W	L	ERA	G	GS	CG	SV	IP	H	R	ER	HR	BB	SO	AVG	vLH	vRH	K/9	BB/9
Johnson, Alan	R-R	6-1	180	8-24-83	13	5	4.04	27	27	0	0	160	171	82	72	11	40	123	.274	.257	.285	6.90	2.25
Johnston, Andrew	R-R	6-5	205	4-20-84	0	3	2.84	45	0	0	25	44	43	21	14	5	5	23	.246	.246	.245	4.67	1.02
Katz, Ethan	R-R	6-5	210	7-4-83	2	0	6.05	11	0	0	0	19	29	13	13	2	7	15	.354	.258	.412	6.98	3.26
Lindsay, Shane	R-R	6-1	205	1-25-85	2	1	2.67	7	7	0	0	34	26	15	10	2	27	43	.211	.259	.174	11.50	7.22
Patton, David	R-R	6-3	175	5-18-84	7	4	1.95	52	0	0	3	74	51	18	16	1	26	79	.191	.180	.199	9.65	3.18
Postlewait, Jacob	S-L	6-0	195	11-3-81	2	3	3.29	7	7	0	0	41	36	22	15	3	17	31	.234	.200	.240	6.80	3.73
Roe, Chaz	R-R	6-5	180	10-9-86	7	4	4.06	19	19	0	0	100	105	54	45	4	47	80	.273	.288	.260	7.22	4.24
Simons, Zachary	L-R	6-3	200	5-23-85	6	9	6.29	26	21	1	0	112	134	91	78	14	49	60	.295	.305	.286	4.84	3.95
Strickland, Brett	R-R	6-0	170	2-15-83	0	5	3.68	49	0	0	9	51	55	30	21	5	23	48	.270	.298	.250	8.42	4.03
Strop, Pedro	B-R	6-0	160	6-13-85	2	1	4.73	11	0	0	0	13	10	7	7	3	5	13	.213	.227	.200	8.78	3.38
Vargas, Buzz	R-R	6-6	220	10-21-83	3	3	4.38	31	3	0	0	64	63	34	31	6	17	50	.260	.281	.248	7.07	2.40

FIELDING

Catcher	PCT	G	PO	A	E	DP	PB
Anderson	1.000	9	46	3	0	0	2
Blumenthal	.988	67	434	49	6	1	19
Robledo	.998	63	447	52	1	8	19
Sargent	.933	2	12	2	1	0	0

First Base	PCT	G	PO	A	E	DP
Cook	.985	53	480	47	8	40
Cuadrado	1.000	1	1	0	0	0
Paulk	.990	86	804	53	9	65

Second Base	PCT	G	PO	A	E	DP
Cuadrado	1.000	1	1	3	0	0

	PCT	G	PO	A	E	DP
Van Kooten	.991	20	41	65	1	12
Young Jr.	.959	118	267	369	27	72

Third Base	PCT	G	PO	A	E	DP
Cook	.909	14	10	20	3	2
Cuadrado	.914	88	60	218	26	16
Nazario	1.000	1	0	1	0	0
Van Kooten	.949	42	37	93	7	12

Shortstop	PCT	G	PO	A	E	DP
Cuadrado	1.000	3	1	5	0	0
Nazario	.900	3	3	6	1	0
Nelson	.918	109	142	316	41	62

	PCT	G	PO	A	E	DP
Van Kooten	.931	24	40	68	8	13

Outfield	PCT	G	PO	A	E	DP
Becktel	.984	74	113	9	2	0
Carte	.983	111	165	11	3	5
Fowler	.964	97	205	8	8	3
Garner	.983	87	114	2	2	1
Nunez	.886	24	30	1	4	2
Paulk	1.000	3	5	0	0	0
Restrepo	.933	23	40	2	3	1

Tri-City Dust Devils — Short-Season

Northwest League

BATTING	B-T	HT	WT	DOB	AVG	vLH	vRH	G	AB	R	H	2B	3B	HR	RBI	BB	HBP	SH	SF	SO	SB	CS	SLG	OBP
Aguilar, Brian	L-R	5-11	185	4-29-84	.311	.333	.307	23	90	11	28	5	1	0	6	5	0	0	0	15	7	0	0	.389	.347
Banda, Joshua	R-R	6-1	195	9-7-85	.235	.191	.255	44	153	17	36	6	0	4	21	10	4	1	1	41	1	3	.353	.298
Berglund, Bret	R-R	6-4	210	12-9-82	.217	.258	.203	71	253	36	55	9	4	4	28	21	11	2	2	77	11	2	.332	.303
Boggs, Steve	B-R	5-10	170	2-29-84	.204	.167	.213	32	93	6	19	2	0	0	8	11	2	4	0	17	4	2	.226	.302
Ferrante, Victor	R-R	6-3	215	12-6-84	.254	.203	.271	73	276	32	70	17	2	6	34	17	8	0	0	89	3	1	.395	.316
Gomez, Hector	R-R	6-1	157	3-5-88	.244	.250	.242	12	45	4	11	3	0	0	6	0	1	1	1	14	0	1	.311	.255
Jackson, Anthony	B-R	5-7	170	6-17-84	.246	.243	.247	62	252	32	62	4	2	1	21	18	4	1	0	55	18	5	.290	.307
Kindel, Jeff	L-L	6-3	205	9-1-83	.287	.245	.304	47	174	26	50	12	2	1	30	23	2	0	4	29	4	1	.397	.369
Mayora, Daniel	R-R	5-11	145	7-27-85	.304	.333	.294	74	276	40	84	19	2	5	30	23	9	3	1	70	8	4	.442	.375
McKenry, Michael	R-R	5-10	200	3-4-85	.216	.271	.194	66	245	28	53	16	1	4	23	22	11	6	6	49	3	3	.339	.303
Nagy, Spence	R-R	5-11	185	6-14-85	.125	.000	.143	3	8	1	1	0	0	0	0	0	0	0	0	4	0	0	.125	.125
Repec, Matthew	R-R	6-1	190	8-30-83	.229	.220	.233	63	231	20	53	14	2	4	27	22	3	1	5	59	1	0	.359	.299
Rifkin, Aaron	L-L	6-3	220	3-12-79	.220	.333	.182	15	59	10	13	2	1	3	7	7	3	0	0	18	0	1	.441	.333
Rodriguez, Ramon	R-R	5-11	200	9-3-84	.186	.276	.140	26	86	5	16	1	1	0	6	10	1	1	0	23	1	0	.221	.278
Strickland, Geoff	B-R	5-10	180	7-1-84	.204	.229	.192	64	221	25	45	10	1	1	22	43	2	4	2	64	17	7	.271	.336
Suarez, Gabriel	R-R	6-0	170	12-14-84	.165	.154	.169	28	91	8	15	5	0	0	5	7	2	0	1	35	2	2	.220	.238

PITCHING	B-T	HT	WT	DOB	W	L	ERA	G	GS	CG	SV	IP	H	R	ER	HR	BB	SO	AVG	vLH	vRH	K/9	BB/9
Bailey, Chad	L-L	6-4	190	6-24-83	1	0	0.96	9	0	0	0	9	5	1	1	0	2	12	.152	.111	.167	11.57	1.93
Baumgardner, Thomas	L-L	6-3	220	10-15-83	1	1	1.04	24	0	0	2	26	16	7	3	0	10	33	.176	.091	.224	11.42	3.46
Chivilli, Pedro	R-R	6-0	150	2-21-83	1	2	2.31	9	0	0	2	12	8	4	3	2	2	14	.195	.231	.179	10.80	1.54
Collis, Devin	L-L	6-2	180	4-27-84	1	2	3.93	18	0	0	0	18	20	10	8	1	10	10	.278	.292	.271	4.91	4.91
Dardar, Chase	R-R	6-0	190	9-26-83	0	0	4.50	4	0	0	0	4	5	3	2	1	1	3	.294	.429	.200	6.75	2.25
Delgado, George	R-R	6-2	175	3-22-84	2	3	3.38	23	0	0	7	24	23	17	9	1	5	25	.237	.306	.197	9.38	1.88
Ferrer, Simon	B-R	5-10	175	6-24-80	0	0	2.25	15	0	0	0	24	15	8	6	1	13	18	.179	.161	.189	6.75	4.88
Freeman, James	L-L	5-11	205	3-27-82	2	1	5.23	10	0	0	0	10	8	6	6	1	14	9	.235	.200	.263	7.84	12.19
Graham, Andrew	R-R	6-4	210	6-29-84	3	1	2.65	15	10	0	0	58	43	22	17	7	21	55	.213	.238	.197	8.58	3.28
Harris, William	R-R	6-4	225	8-28-84	2	3	1.16	22	0	0	6	31	20	6	4	0	9	42	.183	.343	.108	12.19	2.61
Hayes, Alvin	R-R	6-6	195	8-19-83	0	0	3.26	18	0	0	0	19	11	8	7	1	24	27	.172	.200	.159	12.57	11.17
Hynick, Brandon	R-R	6-3	205	3-7-85	0	0	2.57	2	1	0	0	7	5	2	2	0	1	9	.208	.154	.273	11.57	1.29
Jarrett, Sean	R-R	6-5	210	4-26-83	4	1	2.78	27	0	0	0	36	29	13	11	0	9	41	.215	.200	.222	10.35	2.27
Katz, Ethan	R-R	6-5	210	7-4-83	4	4	2.15	29	1	0	0	46	31	15	11	2	12	41	.193	.218	.179	8.02	2.35
Kreidermacher, Andrew	R-R	6-2	195	1-27-83	6	5	3.48	15	15	2	0	96	91	46	37	3	24	61	.248	.216	.269	5.74	2.26
Lindsay, Shane	R-R	6-1	205	1-25-85	2	2	2.79	6	5	0	0	29	18	10	9	0	17	48	.176	.158	.188	14.90	5.28
Rodriguez, Aneury	R-R	6-3	180	12-13-87	4	4	4.14	15	15	1	0	76	78	42	35	2	30	69	.261	.311	.228	8.17	3.55
Santiago, Tomas	R-R	6-4	210	10-30-81	1	3	4.30	6	5	0	0	29	28	15	14	0	10	23	.255	.227	.273	7.06	3.07
Sullivan, Joshua	R-R	6-4	205	7-5-84	3	4	2.71	13	13	0	0	70	49	30	21	2	21	74	.188	.178	.195	9.56	2.71
Weiser, Keith	R-L	6-2	190	9-21-84	1	2	3.79	12	11	0	0	57	63	25	24		8	53	.283	.292	.280	8.37	1.26

FIELDING

Catcher	PCT	G	PO	A	E	DP	PB
Aguilar	1.000	10	84	4	0	0	0
McKenry	.987	46	426	35	6	4	5
Rodriguez	.989	21	149	30	2	1	7

First Base	PCT	G	PO	A	E	DP
Aguilar	1.000	1	8	0	0	0
Banda	1.000	9	58	8	0	5
Kindel	.981	47	390	30	8	36
Repec	1.000	6	45	7	0	7
Rifkin	.909	3	26	4	3	4
Strickland	1.000	5	36	1	0	3
Suarez	1.000	7	64	5	0	7

Second Base	PCT	G	PO	A	E	DP
Jackson	.854	12	16	19	6	3
Mayora	.977	12	19	24	1	8
Strickland	.959	49	96	138	10	28
Suarez	.963	7	7	19	1	4

Third Base	PCT	G	PO	A	E	DP
Gomez	.500	1	0	1	1	0
Mayora	.800	2	1	7	2	2
Repec	.934	58	40	101	10	7
Strickland	.706	4	3	9	5	1
Suarez	.926	12	10	15	2	1

Shortstop	PCT	G	PO	A	E	DP
Gomez	.930	11	14	26	3	7
Mayora	.941	60	101	169	17	38
Nagy	.833	3	3	7	2	1
Strickland	1.000	1	2	0	0	1
Suarez	1.000	3	4	6	0	2

Outfield	PCT	G	PO	A	E	DP
Banda	1.000	18	23	0	0	0
Berglund	.992	71	121	2	1	1
Boggs	1.000	25	36	1	0	0
Ferrante	.982	73	107	4	2	0
Jackson	.982	49	106	3	2	1

Pioneer League

BATTING	B-T	HT	WT	DOB	AVG	vLH	vRH	G	AB	R	H	2B	3B	HR	RBI	BB	HBP	SH	SF	SO	SB	CS	SLG	OBP
Agustin, Jhaysson	R-R	6-0	170	3-16-85	.222	.250	.212	55	203	27	45	12	0	3	22	23	2	0	0	60	5	3	.325	.307
Brownell, Jesse	R-R	6-1	195	3-15-82	.132	.211	.088	20	53	3	7	1	0	0	1	1	1	1	0	17	0	2	.151	.164
Cabrera, Everth	B-R	5-8	160	11-17-86	.254	.189	.280	54	185	30	47	4	2	0	14	37	2	3	1	45	18	7	.297	.382
Christensen, David	R-R	6-1	195	2-11-88	.198	.216	.192	58	207	26	41	11	2	5	20	22	2	0	2	93	2	6	.343	.279
Clark, Kevin	L-L	6-0	195	12-10-85	.242	.302	.226	56	207	33	50	10	4	5	23	28	3	0	2	65	6	4	.401	.338
Cox, Jay	L-R	6-0	200	10-30-84	.242	.121	.276	44	149	25	36	8	1	2	20	31	3	0	0	49	5	1	.349	.383
Gomez, Hector	R-R	6-1	157	3-5-88	.327	.260	.349	50	202	24	66	9	4	5	35	11	3	1	4	26	5	3	.485	.364
Kinzler, Derek	L-R	6-0	176	11-27-84	.162	.143	.167	23	74	8	12	1	0	1	7	1	5	1	0	14	1	2	.216	.225
Loupadiere, Maruis	R-R	6-1	150	4-28-85	.250	.326	.205	32	116	12	29	4	0	2	12	3	0	3	1	20	2	0	.336	.267
Milliron, Michael	R-R	6-0	175	8-3-82	.243	.317	.211	40	136	25	33	8	1	2	15	16	1	0	0	44	5	3	.360	.327
Nazario, Radames	R-R	6-0	166	6-14-87	.211	.280	.181	52	166	22	35	2	0	0	10	22	4	4	0	34	8	2	.223	.318
Perez, Pedro	L-L	6-1	162	6-19-86	.223	.160	.235	43	157	21	35	8	2	1	15	5	6	0	2	53	7	5	.318	.271
Rauch, Austin	R-R	6-3	210	3-30-88	.216	.174	.228	32	102	15	22	3	0	1	10	18	0	0	0	36	1	1	.275	.333
Sandes, Jorge	B-R	6-0	170	2-25-85	.230	.350	.185	23	74	8	17	3	0	2	10	6	0	1	0	16	1	0	.351	.288
Suarez, Steven	L-R	6-0	205	2-24-82	.246	.162	.268	49	179	20	44	8	2	3	23	18	2	0	3	46	1	1	.363	.317
Velazquez, Helder	R-R	6-3	165	10-14-88	.255	.282	.246	40	157	12	40	7	1	2	19	3	1	1	1	27	3	1	.350	.272
Wiens, Logan	R-R	6-6	210	1-13-86	.234	.283	.215	48	167	23	39	8	1	7	25	17	2	0	2	49	1	1	.419	.309

PITCHING	B-T	HT	WT	DOB	W	L	ERA	G	GS	CG	SV	IP	H	R	ER	HR	BB	SO	AVG	vLH	vRH	K/9	BB/9
Arias, Agustin	R-R	5-10	165	5-28-85	0	1	7.33	26	0	0	5	27	33	24	22	9	12	28	.297	.306	.293	9.33	4.00
Arnold, David	R-R	6-1	220	3-6-86	0	1	6.51	20	0	0	0	28	27	24	20	2	21	28	.257	.235	.268	9.11	6.83
Bechtold, David	L-L	6-2	200	2-11-83	2	1	3.04	21	0	0	0	27	21	14	9	3	7	26	.214	.240	.205	8.78	2.36
Buechner, Christopher	R-R	6-3	235	8-23-83	1	1	5.19	18	0	0	1	17	18	10	10	2	6	17	.273	.308	.250	8.83	3.12
Collis, Devin	L-L	6-2	180	4-27-84	0	0	3.86	1	0	0	0	2	1	1	1	0	1	0	.125	.000	.200	0.00	3.86
De Los Santos, Riquy	R-R	6-2	162	6-17-85	3	2	3.35	21	3	0	2	48	42	22	18	3	26	50	.235	.292	.202	9.31	4.84
Espinosa, Sandy	R-R	6-1	145	12-28-84	0	1	8.24	20	0	0	0	32	42	34	29	2	23	31	.311	.260	.341	8.81	6.54
Fabian, Robinson	R-R	6-3	152	2-10-86	3	5	4.91	13	12	0	0	62	55	44	34	4	36	49	.230	.226	.232	7.07	5.20
Gibbs, Michael	R-R	6-5	195	9-18-84	0	0	9.99	22	0	0	0	24	30	30	27	3	27	29	.306	.333	.286	10.73	9.99
Guzman, Henry	L-L	6-4	170	7-25-84	1	1	5.97	23	0	0	0	35	30	25	23	2	26	25	.240	.269	.232	6.49	6.75
Hanna, Daniel	L-R	6-3	195	12-14-80	2	3	5.71	27	0	0	0	35	33	23	22	3	25	32	.248	.216	.268	8.31	6.49
Hayes, Alvin	R-R	6-6	195	8-19-83	1	0	0.00	2	0	0	0	3	0	0	0	2	3	.000	.000	.000	10.13	6.75
Hynick, Brandon	R-R	6-3	205	3-7-85	4	3	2.39	12	12	0	0	64	55	23	17	3	8	70	.227	.225	.228	9.84	1.13
Lopez, Ronny	R-R	6-2	185	8-12-86	1	10	9.46	15	15	0	0	66	104	81	69	6	26	48	.365	.323	.387	6.58	3.56
Nin, Sandy	R-R	6-0	170	8-13-80	0	3	5.84	3	3	0	0	12	17	10	8	1	3	6	.340	.400	.300	4.38	2.19
Rogers, Esmil	R-R	6-1	146	8-14-85	3	6	6.96	15	15	1	0	63	78	53	49	8	24	40	.306	.272	.325	5.68	3.41
Shetrone, Drew	R-R	6-2	185	9-18-84	1	4	5.98	19	4	0	0	41	48	29	27	2	18	40	.294	.333	.277	8.85	3.98
Silano, Yull	R-R	6-2	165	5-13-86	4	6	4.97	16	12	0	0	63	52	40	35	5	25	61	.223	.245	.209	8.67	3.55
Strop, Pedro	B-R	6-0	160	6-13-85	1	0	2.08	11	0	0	0	13	9	3	3	1	2	22	.188	.143	.195	15.23	1.38

FIELDING

Catcher	PCT	G	PO	A	E	DP	PB
Agustin	.981	51	377	35	8	3	17
Rauch	.988	20	160	9	2	1	11
Suarez	.972	9	61	9	2	0	8

First Base	PCT	G	PO	A	E	DP
Milliron	1.000	2	13	0	0	0
Suarez	.982	30	251	23	5	29
Wiens	.991	46	395	33	4	43

Second Base	PCT	G	PO	A	E	DP
Cabrera	.977	51	100	156	6	38

	PCT	G	PO	A	E	DP
Kinzler	1.000	3	8	7	0	3
Milliron	.938	3	6	9	1	2
Nazario	.942	20	50	48	6	8

Third Base	PCT	G	PO	A	E	DP
Gomez	.888	21	19	52	9	6
Kinzler	.949	16	9	28	2	2
Milliron	.916	29	17	59	7	4
Velazquez	.852	14	6	17	4	4

Shortstop	PCT	G	PO	A	E	DP
Gomez	.929	25	39	66	8	16

	PCT	G	PO	A	E	DP
Nazario	.963	32	50	104	6	21
Velazquez	.937	22	27	62	6	13

Outfield	PCT	G	PO	A	E	DP
Brownell	.800	14	11	1	3	0
Christensen	.935	54	82	5	6	0
Clark	.983	40	55	4	1	0
Cox	.974	37	32	6	1	0
Loupadiere	1.000	32	78	1	0	1
Milliron	1.000	2	3	0	0	0
Perez	.973	40	70	1	2	0
Sandes	.960	17	22	1	1	0

BY DANNY KNOBLER

The last five days of the regular season were bad. The last four days of the World Series were bad.

As for the rest of the Tigers' 2006 season, well, they made it to the World Series in a year when a .500 record would have been considered a success. What more do you need to know?

For a team coming off 12 straight losing seasons, it was an incredible turnaround. For a team that had lost 90 games each of the last five years, including an American League-record 119 just three seasons ago, it was downright historic.

At the end of the season, the Tigers couldn't win a game, and they watched the Twins pass them for the AL Central title on the season's final day. At the end of the World Series, the Tigers couldn't win a game, and they watched the Cardinals celebrate a championship.

In the World Series, the Tigers were bad at the plate, and worse in the field. They batted .199 as a team, and they became the first team in series history to have errors from pitchers in five straight games. They won only one game, and only won that one because Kenny Rogers shut out the Cardinals for eight innings.

Rogers was brilliant throughout the playoffs, pitching 23 scoreless innings in three starts against New York, Oakland and St. Louis. He was good during the season, too, winning 17 games at age 41 after the Tigers signed him as a free agent.

Yet the Tigers' season belonged more to the young pitchers, in particular outstanding rookies Justin Verlander and Joel Zumaya. When the Tigers went to spring training, Verlander and Zumaya were competing to be the fifth starter. By the end of the spring, new man-

PLAYERS OF THE YEAR

MAJOR LEAGUE: Carlos Guillen, ss

Since coming over from the Mariners in 2004, Guillen put up good numbers for Detroit, but none more meaningful than what he contributed to the American League pennant in 2006. He batted .320/.400/.519 and led the club in on-base and slugging percentage, as well as runs (100) and stolen bases (20).

MINOR LEAGUE: Cameron Maybin, of

Maybin made a splash in his first full season, batting .304/.387/.457 and helping low Class A West Michigan win the Midwest League title. Maybin is also a true center fielder with outstanding range. The 2005 first-round pick finished the season with 20 doubles, six triples and nine homers in 487 at-bats.

ager Jim Leyland decided they both belonged on the team, and he moved Zumaya to the bullpen. Verlander won 17 games and was Baseball America's Rookie of the Year. Zumaya became a key set-up man, and a fan favorite with his ability to throw a baseball up to 103 mph.

Leyland had been away from the dugout for six years, after quitting as manager of the Rockies at the end of the 1999 season. He came back to the organization he had played for as a minor leaguer, and the organization he grew up in as a minor league manager.

Leyland's Tigers played well right from the start of the season, and by early August they were 40 games over .500, at 76-36. Even after their late-season slip, they recovered to storm past the Yankees in an AL Division Series, then sweep through the AL Championship Series, reaching the World Series on Magglio Ordonez' dramatic ninth-inning home run in Game Four.

The 61-year-old Leyland showed a great ability to get along with and motivate all his players, but he proved that he meant it when he said he wasn't worried about experience. "I'll take talent," Leyland said.

He put Zumaya in a one-run game on Opening Day. He had Verlander start Game One of the World Series. He took a long look at 22-year-old outfielder Brent Clevlen in spring training, then put Clevlen in the lineup when he joined the major league team from Double-A Erie in July.

And when the Tigers brought first-round draft pick Andrew Miller to the big leagues in late August, Leyland put him right into a game at Yankee Stadium. Miller became the third straight big-money, big-talent first-rounder for the Tigers, following Verlander in 2004 and Cameron Maybin in 2005. Maybin had an outstanding debut season himself, batting .304 at Class A West Michigan.

The Whitecaps won the Midwest League title, the second in three years for manager Matt Walbeck. The Tigers' Triple-A Toledo team was also a champion, taking its second straight International League title under manager Larry Parrish.

The only real disappointment was Double-A Erie, where the SeaWolves finished 60-81 and manager Duffy Dyer and his staff were fired at the end of the season.

ORGANIZATION LEADERS

BATTING		*Minimum 250 at-bats
*AVG	Hernandez, Gorkys, GCL Tigers	.327
	Sizemore, Scott, Oneonta	.327
R	Ludwick, Ryan, Toledo	81
H	Phelps, Josh, Toledo	143
TB	Ludwick, Ryan, Toledo	257
2B	Larish, Jeffrey, Lakeland	34
	Ludwick, Ryan, Toledo	34
3B	Hollimon, Michael, West Michigan	13
HR	Ludwick, Ryan, Toledo	28
RBI	Phelps, Josh, Toledo	90
BB	Airoso, Kurt, Erie	81
	Larish, Jeffrey, Lakeland	81
SO	Kirkland, Kody, Toledo/Erie	184
SB	Thomas, Clete, Lakeland	34
*OBP	Carlson, Christopher, GCL Tigers	.402
*SLG	Carlson, Christopher, GCL Tigers	.588
XBH	Ludwick, Ryan, Toledo	64

PITCHING		#Minimum 75 innings
W	Badenhop, Burke, West Michigan	14
L	Bumstead, Nathan, Erie	14
#ERA	Martinez, Cristhian, Lakeland/GCL Tigers/Oneonta	2.56
G	Gardner, Lee, Toledo	58
CG	Trahern, Dallas, Lakeland	4
SV	Gardner, Lee, Toledo	30
IP	Durbin, Chad, Toledo	185
BB	Bumstead, Nathan, Erie	79
SO	Durbin, Chad, Toledo	149
#AVG	Sanchez, Humberto, Erie/Toledo	.220

Detroit Tigers — MLB

American League

BATTING	B-T	HT	WT	DOB	AVG	vLH	vRH	G	AB	R	H	2B	3B	HR	RBI	BB	HBP	SH	SF	SO	SB	CS	SLG	OBP
Casey, Sean	L-R	6-4	235	7-2-74	.245	.256	.241	53	184	17	45	7	0	5	30	10	1	0	1	21	0	1	.364	.286
Clevlen, Brent	R-R	6-2	190	10-27-83	.282	.333	.200	31	39	9	11	1	2	3	6	2	0	1	0	15	0	0	.641	.317
Gomez, Alexis	L-L	6-2	180	8-8-78	.272	.188	.287	62	103	17	28	5	2	1	6	6	1	1	0	21	4	0	.388	.318
Granderson, Curtis	L-R	6-1	185	3-16-81	.260	.218	.274	159	596	90	155	31	9	19	68	66	4	7	6	174	8	5	.438	.335
Guillen, Carlos	B-R	6-1	215	9-30-75	.320	.291	.332	153	543	100	174	41	5	19	85	71	4	0	4	87	20	9	.519	.400
Hannahan, Jack	L-R	6-2	205	3-4-80	.000	.000	.000	3	9	0	0	0	0	0	0	1	0	0	0	1	0	0	.000	.100
Hooper, Kevin	R-R	5-10	160	12-7-76	.000	—	.000	8	3	1	0	0	0	0	0	1	0	1	0	1	0	0	.000	.250
Infante, Omar	R-R	6-0	180	12-26-81	.277	.286	.273	78	224	35	62	11	4	4	25	14	3	2	2	45	3	2	.415	.325
Inge, Brandon	R-R	5-11	190	5-19-77	.253	.243	.256	159	542	83	137	29	2	27	83	43	7	4	5	128	7	4	.463	.313
Monroe, Craig	R-R	6-1	205	2-27-77	.255	.271	.249	147	541	89	138	35	2	28	92	37	1	0	6	126	2	2	.482	.301
Ordonez, Magglio	R-R	6-0	215	1-28-74	.298	.294	.300	155	593	82	177	32	1	24	104	45	4	0	4	87	1	4	.477	.350
Perez, Neifi	B-R	6-0	195	6-2-73	.200	.200	.200	21	65	4	13	1	0	0	5	3	0	2	0	4	1	0	.215	.235
Polanco, Placido	R-R	5-10	195	10-10-75	.295	.272	.305	110	461	58	136	18	1	4	52	17	7	8	2	27	1	2	.364	.329
Rabelo, Mike	B-R	6-1	200	1-17-80	.000	.000	—	1	1	0	0	0	0	0	0	0	0	0	0	1	0	0	.000	.000
Rodriguez, Ivan	R-R	5-9	195	11-30-71	.300	.340	.284	136	547	74	164	28	4	13	69	26	1	4	2	86	8	3	.437	.332
Santiago, Ramon	B-R	5-11	175	8-31-79	.225	.208	.232	43	80	9	18	1	1	0	3	1	4	0	14	2	0	.263	.244
Shelton, Chris	R-R	6-0	215	6-26-80	.273	.276	.273	115	373	50	102	16	4	16	47	34	4	0	1	107	1	2	.466	.340
Stairs, Matt	L-R	5-9	215	2-27-68	.244	.000	.250	14	41	5	10	3	0	2	8	3	0	0	0	12	0	0	.463	.295
3-team (77 Kansas City, 26 Texas)					.247	—	—	117	348	42	86	21	0	13	51	40	3	0	2	86	0	0	.420	.328
Thames, Marcus	R-R	6-2	220	3-6-77	.256	.238	.266	110	348	61	89	20	2	26	60	37	4	0	1	92	1	1	.549	.333
Wilson, Vance	R-R	5-11	215	3-17-73	.283	.326	.266	56	152	18	43	9	0	5	18	2	3	10	1	33	0	4	.441	.304
Young, Dmitri	B-R	6-2	220	10-11-73	.250	.136	.267	48	172	19	43	4	1	7	23	11	0	0	1	39	1	1	.407	.293

PITCHING	B-T	HT	WT	DOB	W	L	ERA	G	GS	CG	SV	IP	H	R	ER	HR	BB	SO	AVG	vLH	vRH	K/9	BB/9
Bonderman, Jeremy	R-R	6-2	220	10-28-82	14	8	4.08	34	34	0	0	214	214	104	97	18	64	202	.259	.284	.235	8.50	2.69
Colon, Roman	R-R	6-6	225	8-13-79	2	0	4.89	20	1	0	1	39	46	21	21	6	14	25	.303	.271	.323	5.82	3.26
Durbin, Chad	B-R	6-2	200	12-3-77	0	0	1.50	3	0	0	0	6	6	1	1	0	3	.250	.286	.235	4.50	0.00
Grilli, Jason	R-R	6-5	225	11-11-76	2	3	4.21	51	0	0	0	62	61	31	29	6	25	31	.261	.292	.249	4.50	3.63
Jones, Todd	L-R	6-3	230	4-24-68	2	6	3.94	62	0	0	37	64	70	31	28	4	11	28	.276	.264	.284	3.94	1.55
Ledezma, Wilfredo	L-L	6-2	210	1-21-81	3	3	3.58	24	7	0	0	60	60	28	24	5	23	39	.254	.241	.261	5.82	3.43
Lewis, Colby	R-R	6-4	230	8-2-79	0	0	3.00	2	0	0	0	3	8	1	1	1	1	5	.471	.429	.500	15.00	3.00
Maroth, Mike	L-L	6-0	190	8-17-77	5	2	4.19	13	9	0	0	54	64	26	25	11	16	24	.295	.250	.309	4.02	2.68
Miller, Andrew	R-L	6-6	210	5-21-85	0	1	6.10	8	0	0	0	10	8	9	7	0	10	6	.205	.333	.167	5.23	8.71
Miner, Zach	R-R	6-3	200	3-12-82	7	6	4.84	27	16	1	0	93	100	53	50	11	32	59	.276	.320	.245	5.71	3.10
Robertson, Nate	R-L	6-2	225	9-3-77	13	13	3.84	32	32	1	0	209	206	98	89	29	67	137	.259	.111	.284	5.91	2.89
Rodney, Fernando	R-R	5-11	220	3-18-77	7	4	3.52	63	0	0	7	72	51	36	28	6	34	65	.196	.202	.192	8.16	4.27
Rogers, Kenny	L-L	6-1	190	11-10-64	17	8	3.84	34	33	0	0	204	195	97	87	23	62	99	.253	.200	.268	4.37	2.74
Seay, Bobby	L-L	6-2	235	6-20-78	0	0	6.46	14	0	0	0	15	14	11	11	1	9	12	.246	.227	.257	7.04	5.28
Spurling, Chris	R-R	6-5	240	6-28-77	0	0	3.18	9	0	0	0	11	13	4	4	2	4	4	.289	.071	.387	3.18	3.18
Tata, Jordan	R-R	6-6	220	9-20-81	0	0	6.14	8	0	0	0	15	14	11	10	1	7	6	.250	.259	.241	3.68	4.30
Verlander, Justin	R-R	6-5	200	2-20-83	17	9	3.63	30	30	1	0	186	187	78	75	21	60	124	.266	.279	.253	6.00	2.90
Walker, Jamie	L-L	6-2	185	7-1-71	0	1	2.81	56	0	0	0	48	47	15	15	8	8	37	.251	.238	.262	6.94	1.50
Zumaya, Joel	R-R	6-3	210	11-9-84	6	3	1.94	62	0	0	1	83	56	20	18	6	42	97	.187	.183	.188	10.48	4.54

FIELDING

Catcher	PCT	G	PO	A	E	DP	PB
Rodriguez	.998	123	740	59	2	7	4
Wilson	.997	55	282	30	1	2	2

First Base	PCT	G	PO	A	E	DP
Casey	.996	51	467	14	2	40
Guillen	1.000	8	30	4	0	4
Hannahan	1.000	1	6	0	0	0
Rodriguez	.984	7	56	6	1	6
Shelton	.994	115	1004	55	6	93
Young	.889	3	19	5	3	3

Second Base	PCT	G	PO	A	E	DP
Hooper	1.000	3	0	3	0	1

	PCT	G	PO	A	E	DP
Infante	.977	37	65	108	4	30
Perez	1.000	14	34	42	0	12
Polanco	.989	108	224	325	6	81
Rodriguez	1.000	1	1	0	0	0
Santiago	1.000	12	14	19	0	4

Third Base	PCT	G	PO	A	E	DP
Hooper	1.000	2	0	2	0	0
Infante	1.000	7	3	8	0	0
Inge	.960	159	135	398	22	34
Perez	—	1	0	0	0	0
Santiago	1.000	1	0	2	0	0

Shortstop	PCT	G	PO	A	E	DP
Guillen	.956	145	178	428	28	88
Infante	.958	10	7	16	1	5
Perez	.963	7	9	17	1	7
Santiago	1.000	27	17	48	0	6

Outfield	PCT	G	PO	A	E	DP
Clevlen	1.000	29	29	3	0	1
Gomez	1.000	52	44	2	0	0
Granderson	.997	157	385	3	1	0
Infante	1.000	4	1	0	0	0
Monroe	.980	116	181	12	4	2
Ordonez	.974	148	258	9	7	1
Thames	.977	59	84	1	2	0

Toledo Mud Hens — Triple-A

International League

BATTING	B-T	HT	WT	DOB	AVG	vLH	vRH	G	AB	R	H	2B	3B	HR	RBI	BB	HBP	SH	SF	SO	SB	CS	SLG	OBP
Dlugach, Brent	R-R	6-4	200	3-3-83	.000	.000	.000	2	6	0	0	0	0	0	0	0	0	0	0	2	0	0	.000	.000
Espinosa, David	B-R	6-2	190	12-16-81	.266	.291	.251	96	293	50	78	13	7	9	27	43	3	6	4	70	12	6	.451	.362
Gomez, Alexis	L-L	6-2	180	8-8-78	.288	.305	.281	58	226	36	65	18	3	11	36	18	2	3	2	48	8	4	.540	.343
Hannahan, Jack	L-R	6-2	205	3-4-80	.282	.207	.313	119	415	59	117	27	0	9	62	61	8	3	7	114	9	6	.412	.379
Hessman, Mike	R-R	6-5	215	3-5-78	.165	.165	.165	101	345	45	57	11	0	24	49	45	4	0	129	3	1	.406	.269
Hooper, Kevin	R-R	5-10	160	12-7-76	.276	.344	.244	121	504	66	139	15	4	1	29	23	3	15	4	71	24	12	.327	.309
Kelly, Don	L-R	6-4	190	2-15-80	.228	.208	.236	66	237	23	54	14	3	0	19	24	2	4	0	32	18	7	.312	.304
Kirkland, Kody	R-R	6-4	200	6-9-83	.176	.000	.214	4	17	1	3	2	0	0	1	0	0	0	0	10	0	0	.294	.176
Logan, Nook	B-R	6-3	180	11-28-79	.185	.077	.212	19	65	9	12	2	1	0	4	2	0	0	0	18	3	2	.246	.284
Ludwick, Ryan	R-L	6-3	210	7-13-78	.266	.262	.267	134	508	81	135	34	2	28	80	48	12	1	2	167	2	6	.506	.342

General manager: Dave Dombrowski. **Farm director:** Dan Lunetta. **Scouting director:** David Chadd.

Class	Team	League	W	L	PCT	Finish*	Manager	Affiliate Since
Majors	Detroit	American	95	67	.586	+3rd (14)	Jim Leyland	—
Triple-A	Toledo Mud Hens	International	76	66	.535	5th (14)	Larry Parrish	1987
Double-A	Erie Sea Wolves	Eastern	60	81	.426	12th (12)	Duffy Dyer	2001
High A	Lakeland Tigers	Florida State	68	68	.500	6th (12)	Mike Rojas	1967
Low A	West Michigan Whitecaps	Midwest	89	48	.650	+1st (14)	Matt Walbeck	1997
Short-season	Oneonta Tigers	New York-Penn	40	34	.541	6th (14)	Tom Brookens	1999
Rookie	GCL Tigers	Gulf Coast	32	18	.640	2nd (13)	Kevin Bradshaw	1995

OVERALL 2006 MINOR LEAGUE RECORD 365 315 .537 4th (30)

*Finish in overall standings (No. of teams in league). +League champion

	B-T	HT	WT	DOB	AVG	vLH	vRH	G	AB	R	H	2B	3B	HR	RBI	BB	HBP	SH	SF	SO	SB	CS	SLG	OBP
Maples, Chris	R-R	5-10	180	10-31-79	.206	.235	.176	13	34	3	7	1	0	2	5	1	0	0	0	8	0	0	.412	.229
Melian, Jackson	R-R	6-2	205	1-7-80	.000	.000	.000	5	13	1	0	0	0	0	0	1	0	0	0	8	0	0	.000	.071
Mendez, Victor	B-R	5-11	160	6-28-80	.238	.300	.182	7	21	5	5	2	0	1	3	3	0	0	0	8	0	0	.476	.333
Mohr, Dustan	R-R	6-1	210	6-19-76	.262	.254	.267	54	187	21	49	11	4	6	25	22	0	2	1	70	1	4	.460	.338
2-team (22 Pawtucket)					.238	—	—	76	252	31	60	13	4	7	31	43	0	2	2	93	1	4	.405	.347
Peterson, Brian	R-R	6-2	225	10-22-78	.263	.364	.222	36	114	13	30	6	2	4	13	7	0	1	0	32	0	1	.456	.306
Phelps, Josh	R-R	6-3	225	5-12-78	.308	.322	.301	126	464	60	143	26	3	24	90	38	12	1	7	124	6	1	.532	.370
Rabelo, Mike	B-R	6-1	200	1-17-80	.270	.323	.255	38	137	19	37	12	0	3	22	11	3	0	2	33	1	1	.423	.333
Raburn, Ryan	R-R	6-0	185	4-17-81	.275	.283	.271	118	451	68	124	29	4	20	79	51	5	1	4	120	16	4	.490	.352
Redman, Tike	L-L	5-11	175	3-10-77	.253	.151	.286	79	300	30	76	15	2	1	13	13	1	1	0	35	12	4	.327	.277
Santiago, Ramon	B-R	5-11	175	8-31-79	.253	.273	.240	25	83	13	21	6	0	2	12	9	1	7	0	18	2	1	.398	.333
Shelton, Chris	R-R	6-0	215	6-26-80	.266	.250	.270	28	109	20	29	6	2	3	14	18	1	0	1	37	1	0	.440	.372
St. Pierre, Max	R-R	6-0	175	4-17-80	.202	.188	.210	78	247	25	50	14	1	3	31	16	3	9	5	36	0	0	.304	.255
Young, Dmitri	B-R	6-2	220	10-11-73	.452	.333	.500	8	31	4	14	3	0	1	6	4	0	0	0	4	0	0	.645	.514

PITCHING	B-T	HT	WT	DOB	W	L	ERA	G	GS	CG	SV	IP	H	R	ER	HR	BB	SO	AVG	vLH	vRH	K/9	BB/9
Boehringer, Brian	B-R	6-2	195	1-8-70	3	1	4.83	10	3	1	0	32	36	17	17	5	4	15	.300	.290	.303	4.26	1.14
Claggett, Anthony	R-R	6-2	185	7-15-84	0	0	0.00	1	0	0	0	1	1	0	0	0	1	0	.200	.000	.250	18.00	9.00
Colon, Roman	R-R	6-6	225	8-13-79	0	0	0.00	2	2	0	0	7	4	5	0	0	2	6	.160	.000	.222	8.10	2.70
Connolly, Jonathan	R-L	6-0	205	8-24-83	0	0	5.40	1	1	0	0	5	7	3	3	0	1	4	.318	—	.318	7.20	1.80
Davis, Lance	R-L	6-0	170	9-1-76	3	4	4.73	28	5	0	1	59	70	33	31	7	12	32	.297	.234	.320	4.88	1.83
De La Cruz, Eulogio	R-R	5-11	175	3-12-84	0	0	11.57	1	1	0	0	2	4	3	3	1	2	3	.333	.500	.250	11.57	7.71
Durbin, Chad	B-R	6-2	200	12-3-77	11	8	3.11	28	28	2	0	185	169	72	64	17	46	149	.242	.251	.236	7.25	2.24
Ennis, John	R-R	6-5	240	10-17-79	0	1	2.45	22	1	0	0	37	30	14	10	2	13	32	.224	.196	.239	7.85	3.19
Fiore, Tony	R-R	6-4	230	10-12-71	3	4	7.62	13	2	0	1	26	32	22	22	7	12	18	.302	.250	.329	6.23	4.15
Gardner, Lee	R-R	6-0	220	1-16-75	5	5	2.92	58	0	0	30	62	46	21	20	3	17	45	.212	.188	.227	6.57	2.48
Green, Steve	R-R	6-2	200	1-26-78	5	5	3.62	32	3	0	2	55	52	25	22	2	29	35	.260	.315	.228	5.76	4.77
Hamman, Corey	L-L	6-2	198	4-12-80	2	8	4.02	37	13	0	0	103	103	51	46	15	27	56	.260	.211	.276	4.89	2.36
Herrera, Alex	L-L	5-11	190	11-5-76	1	1	5.06	15	1	0	0	21	24	12	12	3	11	18	.276	.323	.250	7.59	4.64
Karnuth, Jason	R-R	6-2	190	5-15-76	2	0	4.08	24	0	0	2	29	31	15	13	4	5	16	.279	.433	.222	5.02	1.57
Larrison, Preston	R-R	6-4	235	11-19-80	1	0	1.74	6	0	0	0	10	12	3	2	1	5	3	.324	.231	.375	2.61	4.35
Ledezma, Wilfredo	L-L	6-4	210	1-21-81	4	3	2.52	12	12	0	0	71	60	22	20	6	23	56	.235	.176	.250	8.33	2.90
Lewis, Colby	R-R	6-4	230	8-2-79	6	7	3.96	24	24	0	0	148	154	70	65	13	36	104	.271	.233	.298	6.34	2.19
Mantei, Matt	R-R	6-1	205	7-7-73	0	0	0.00	4	0	0	1	5	1	1	0	0	5	5	.067	.000	.091	9.00	9.00
Maroth, Mike	L-L	6-0	190	8-17-77	3	0	4.50	4	4	0	0	20	18	10	10	4	4	11	.243	.200	.254	4.95	1.80
Mercado, Hector	L-L	6-3	230	4-29-74	3	2	3.94	26	0	0	1	32	36	16	14	1	18	25	.283	.366	.244	7.03	5.06
Miner, Zach	R-R	6-3	200	3-12-82	6	0	2.82	9	9	1	0	51	43	18	16	2	21	40	.232	.247	.221	7.06	3.71
Sanchez, Humberto	R-R	6-6	230	5-28-83	5	3	3.86	9	9	0	0	51	50	23	22	2	20	40	.260	.224	.298	7.54	3.51
Seay, Bobby	L-L	6-2	235	6-20-78	1	2	4.74	24	1	0	0	25	25	15	13	3	6	14	.278	.265	.286	5.11	2.19
Spurling, Chris	R-R	6-4	240	6-28-77	1	4	2.05	49	0	0	5	66	61	20	15	1	10	34	.254	.218	.272	4.64	1.36
Tata, Jordan	R-R	6-6	220	9-20-81	10	6	3.84	21	21	1	0	122	117	58	52	11	49	86	.252	.269	.240	6.34	3.61
Woodyard, Mark	R-R	6-2	195	12-19-78	1	4	7.93	28	2	0	1	36	42	33	32	7	20	31	.284	.327	.258	7.68	4.95

FIELDING

Catcher	PCT	G	PO	A	E	DP	PB
Peterson	.987	36	212	23	3	5	2
Rabelo	.996	38	221	20	1	1	0
St-Pierre	.985	77	474	57	8	5	8

First Base	PCT	G	PO	A	E	DP
Hannahan	.995	19	176	10	1	19
Hessman	1.000	1	14	1	0	0
Kelly	.985	7	54	10	1	5
Maples	1.000	2	12	1	0	1
Phelps	.992	87	813	62	7	75
Shelton	.976	23	238	9	6	25
Young	.956	5	40	3	2	4

Second Base	PCT	G	PO	A	E	DP
Hannahan	.975	53	93	141	6	32

Hooper	.985	39	75	117	3	28
Kelly	.941	7	17	15	2	3
Maples	1.000	1	1	3	0	0
Raburn	.968	34	65	88	5	22
Santiago	.972	14	27	42	2	11

Third Base	PCT	G	PO	A	E	DP
Hannahan	.934	39	32	95	9	11
Hessman	.973	98	82	210	8	23
Kirkland	1.000	4	2	13	0	1
Maples	.944	5	3	14	1	2

Shortstop	PCT	G	PO	A	E	DP
Dlugach	.917	2	3	8	1	2
Hessman	1.000	2	3	5	0	0
Hooper	.973	78	106	251	10	41

Kelly	.958	50	70	134	9	36
Maples	1.000	2	1	1	0	0
Santiago	.982	12	16	38	1	9

Outfield	PCT	G	PO	A	E	DP
Espinosa	.976	46	78	5	2	0
Gomez	.961	56	121	5	5	0
Hooper	1.000	2	4	0	0	0
Logan	1.000	19	41	1	0	0
Ludwick	.986	109	196	14	3	3
Melian	1.000	1	3	0	0	0
Mendez	1.000	7	11	0	0	0
Mohr	1.000	49	117	1	0	0
Raburn	.986	77	127	11	2	2
Redman	1.000	73	149	2	0	2

Erie SeaWolves — Double-A

Eastern League

BATTING	B-T	HT	WT	DOB	AVG	vLH	vRH	G	AB	R	H	2B	3B	HR	RBI	BB	HBP	SH	SF	SO	SB	CS	SLG	OBP
Airoso, Kurt	R-R	6-2	190	2-12-75	.237	.253	.228	126	430	64	102	18	1	16	63	81	5	0	1	123	1	2	.395	.364
Blue, Vincent	L-R	6-2	180	2-8-83	.232	.158	.263	124	409	47	95	14	1	0	21	50	1	4	3	107	24	14	.271	.315

	B-T	HT	WT	DOB	AVG	vLH	vRH	G	AB	R	H	2B	3B	HR	RBI	BB	HBP	SH	SF	SO	SB	CS	SLG	OBP
Clevlen, Brent	R-R	6-2	190	10-27-83	.230	.250	.220	109	395	47	91	17	0	11	45	47	3	1	5	138	6	2	.357	.313
Francia, Juan	B-R	5-9	145	1-4-82	.163	.167	.161	56	190	21	31	4	2	0	9	7	2	5	0	27	11	4	.205	.201
Giarratano, Tony	B-R	6-0	180	11-29-82	.283	.271	.290	67	269	35	76	19	5	0	19	22	2	1	1	45	16	4	.390	.340
Graham, Andrew	R-R	6-4	215	4-22-82	.276	.400	.211	20	58	5	16	2	0	1	5	5	1	0	0	13	0	2	.362	.344
Haley, Adam	L-R	6-0	171	9-4-80	.228	.211	.235	67	219	21	50	8	2	2	17	28	1	2	1	46	4	2	.311	.317
Hunt, Kelly	R-R	6-5	240	4-15-81	.228	.197	.248	107	382	38	87	16	1	22	52	9	1	1	3	123	0	1	.448	.246
Kelly, Don	L-R	6-4	190	2-15-80	.275	.308	.261	58	207	30	57	11	1	0	24	27	1	0	5	23	5	3	.338	.354
Kirkland, Kody	R-R	6-4	200	6-9-83	.217	.268	.190	119	428	61	93	25	5	22	65	26	19	2	3	157	9	10	.453	.290
Leon, Maxwell	B-R	5-11	190	6-28-84	.067	.000	.091	6	15	2	1	0	0	1	3	1	0	0	0	6	0	0	.267	.125
Logan, Nook	B-R	6-3	180	11-28-79	.247	.293	.194	20	77	14	19	2	1	0	2	11	0	0	0	23	9	3	.299	.341
Maples, Chris	R-R	5-10	180	10-31-79	.281	.229	.318	100	342	52	96	27	1	20	71	24	4	2	7	93	4	4	.541	.329
McIntyre, Nick	B-R	5-10	185	3-11-81	.178	.167	.182	24	73	7	13	3	0	0	4	3	0	0	1	18	3	1	.219	.208
McKinney, Garth	R-R	6-3	210	5-7-82	.200	.143	.226	27	90	9	18	2	0	3	5	7	0	2	0	45	2	0	.322	.258
Melian, Jackson	R-R	6-2	205	1-7-80	.269	.336	.232	103	364	52	98	23	4	15	60	24	7	2	4	69	4	1	.478	.323
Mendez, Victor	B-R	5-11	160	6-28-80	.225	.231	.222	21	80	12	18	2	0	2	5	7	0	1	1	18	0	0	.325	.284
Rabelo, Mike	B-R	6-1	200	1-17-80	.277	.328	.253	62	213	31	59	13	1	6	28	19	9	1	0	38	2	1	.432	.361
Sanchez, Danilo	R-R	5-11	215	10-25-80	.181	.218	.160	79	237	19	43	7	0	7	24	24	4	4	3	48	1	0	.300	.265
Tousa, Scott	L-R	5-11	180	8-3-79	.184	.182	.185	37	114	4	21	2	0	0	7	12	3	2	2	26	1	1	.202	.275
Young, Dmitri	B-R	6-2	220	10-11-73	.150	.200	.100	6	20	2	3	1	0	0	1	4	0	0	0	6	0	0	.200	.292

PITCHING	B-T	HT	WT	DOB	W	L	ERA	G	GS	CG	SV	IP	H	R	ER	HR	BB	SO	AVG	vLH	vRH	K/9	BB/9
Bonine, Eddie	R-R	6-5	220	6-6-81	0	1	9.00	1	1	0	0	6	8	6	6	3	0	2	.320	.222	.375	3.00	0.00
Bumstead, Nathan	R-R	6-2	215	5-5-82	7	14	4.90	27	27	3	0	158	171	102	86	14	79	127	.277	.264	.288	7.23	4.50
Connolly, Jonathan	R-L	6-0	205	8-24-83	3	4	6.14	10	10	1	0	59	74	44	40	6	16	34	.308	.229	.341	5.22	2.45
Davis, Lance	R-L	6-0	170	9-1-76	0	1	1.74	2	2	1	0	10	7	3	2	0	1	5	.189	.182	.192	4.35	0.87
De La Cruz, Eulogio	R-R	5-11	175	3-12-84	5	6	3.43	38	12	0	2	105	103	46	40	3	45	87	.258	.262	.255	7.46	3.86
Ennis, John	R-R	6-5	240	10-17-79	2	3	3.08	24	0	0	13	26	27	9	9	1	11	25	.273	.234	.308	8.54	3.76
Finigan, P.J.	R-R	6-0	185	9-30-82	0	2	5.00	11	3	0	1	27	27	15	15	4	7	16	.257	.286	.238	5.33	2.33
Homer, Chris	R-R	6-1	190	3-6-81	1	4	7.26	42	0	0	13	48	60	40	39	10	14	42	.308	.282	.325	7.82	2.61
Johnson, Jeremy	R-R	6-3	170	7-19-82	2	4	6.39	8	7	0	0	38	57	30	27	6	11	24	.345	.368	.326	5.68	2.61
Jones, Bobby M.	R-L	6-0	170	4-11-72	3	4	3.92	28	12	0	0	80	81	45	35	11	41	68	.260	.308	.240	7.62	4.59
Jurrjens, Jair	R-R	6-1	160	1-29-86	4	3	3.36	12	12	0	0	67	71	30	25	7	21	53	.277	.281	.273	7.12	2.82
Larrison, Preston	R-R	6-4	235	11-19-80	4	10	3.92	26	15	1	1	106	108	48	46	10	40	48	.272	.326	.221	4.09	3.41
Maples, Chris	R-R	5-10	180	10-31-79	0	0	0.00	1	0	0	0	1	0	0	0	0	0	0	.500	—	.500	0.00	0.00
Nannini, Mike	R-R	5-11	190	8-9-80	1	1	3.35	23	0	0	2	40	34	18	15	6	15	39	.222	.263	.178	8.70	3.35
Ostlund, Ian	R-L	6-1	200	10-17-78	9	5	4.43	53	0	0	0	65	67	34	32	6	24	70	.266	.263	.268	9.69	3.32
Rogers, Brian	R-R	6-4	190	7-17-82	3	2	2.39	37	0	0	1	64	49	19	17	7	14	69	.210	.213	.209	9.70	1.97
2-team (2 Altoona)					3	2	2.25	39	0	0	2	68	51	19	17	7	16	74	—		—	9.79	2.12
Sanchez, Humberto	R-R	6-6	230	5-28-83	5	3	1.76	11	11	0	0	72	47	17	14	2	27	86	.190	.218	.163	10.80	3.39
Sikaras, Pete	R-R	6-2	205	5-5-79	1	0	5.79	22	0	0	0	28	32	18	18	5	16	15	.302	.341	.277	4.82	5.14
Vasquez, Virgil	R-R	6-3	205	6-7-82	7	12	3.73	27	27	3	0	174	174	79	72	21	50	129	.265	.288	.243	6.69	2.59
Woodyard, Mark	R-R	6-2	195	12-19-78	1	2	4.50	11	2	0	0	22	29	16	11	2	15	26	.312	.340	.283	10.64	6.14
Zell, Danny	L-L	6-5	210	11-27-81	2	0	4.66	19	0	0	0	19	29	11	10	0	11	16	.349	.382	.327	7.45	5.12

FIELDING

Catcher	PCT	G	PO	A	E	DP	PB
Graham	1.000	20	124	7	0	0	3
Rabelo	.995	56	330	48	2	3	4
Sanchez	.986	76	524	40	8	5	10

First Base	PCT	G	PO	A	E	DP
Hunt	.987	105	923	63	13	107
Kelly	.926	4	23	2	2	2
Maples	.989	27	168	11	2	17
Melian	1.000	1	8	1	0	1
Rabelo	.941	2	14	2	1	3
Tousa	1.000	9	67	7	0	7
Young	.933	3	26	2	2	1

Second Base	PCT	G	PO	A	E	DP
Francia	.967	50	102	130	8	33
Haley	.973	6	12	24	1	5
Kelly	.989	35	63	111	2	31
Leon	.923	5	10	14	2	4
Maples	.943	16	32	34	4	8
McIntyre	.963	19	35	68	4	23
Tousa	.981	22	40	62	2	21

Third Base	PCT	G	PO	A	E	DP
Kelly	.909	8	4	16	2	3
Kirkland	.924	111	74	217	24	20
Maples	.935	21	8	35	3	4
McIntyre	1.000	2	1	3	0	0
Tousa	1.000	1	1	0	0	0

Shortstop	PCT	G	PO	A	E	DP
Francia	1.000	1	2	1	0	1
Giarratano	.979	66	100	184	6	40
Haley	.981	61	85	176	5	44
Kelly	.945	13	17	35	3	9
Maples	.964	4	7	20	1	7
Tousa	1.000	2	4	0	0	0

Outfield	PCT	G	PO	A	E	DP
Airoso	1.000	9	17	0	0	0
Blue	.981	120	249	5	5	2
Clevlen	.980	108	192	7	4	1
Logan	.953	19	39	2	2	0
Maples	.984	36	55	7	1	4
McKinney	.946	26	32	3	2	0
Melian	.974	96	145	7	4	3
Mendez	.970	19	28	4	1	0
Tousa	1.000	2	4	0	0	0
Young	1.000	1	1	0	0	0

Lakeland Tigers — High Class A

Florida State League

BATTING	B-T	HT	WT	DOB	AVG	vLH	vRH	G	AB	R	H	2B	3B	HR	RBI	BB	HBP	SH	SF	SO	SB	CS	SLG	OBP
Casanova, Adrian	R-R	6-1	200	5-6-83	.149	.167	.143	25	74	6	11	4	0	0	5	11	1	3	1	26	1	1	.203	.264
Dlugach, Brent	R-R	6-4	200	3-3-83	.256	.280	.247	125	465	51	119	24	6	5	52	27	2	9	1	144	13	8	.366	.299
Essian, James	B-R	6-3	215	11-8-79	.251	.317	.227	82	239	39	60	19	4	4	22	44	0	0	2	75	17	8	.414	.365
Francia, Juan	B-R	5-9	145	1-4-82	.297	.171	.340	35	138	17	41	3	0	0	9	7	2	3	1	19	15	7	.319	.338
Frazier, Jeffrey	R-R	6-3	195	8-10-82	.228	.203	.238	135	526	61	120	21	1	13	73	37	3	0	7	88	12	3	.346	.279
Graham, Andrew	R-R	6-4	215	4-22-82	.127	.091	.146	27	63	6	8	0	0	2	8	3	2	0	17	1	1	.127	.257
Larish, Jeffrey	L-R	6-2	200	10-11-82	.258	.270	.254	135	457	76	118	34	2	18	65	81	10	0	4	101	9	1	.460	.379
Linares, Miguel	R-R	6-2	180	12-16-83	.165	.115	.177	57	139	10	23	3	0	0	6	10	1	4	1	42	1	4	.187	.225
McIntyre, Nick	B-R	5-10	185	3-11-81	.283	.309	.309	94	315	36	89	11	3	7	35	26	4	5	5	68	14	4	.403	.340
McKinney, Garth	R-R	6-3	210	5-7-82	.201	.224	.193	86	283	43	57	10	0	12	38	26	4	0	0	115	11	4	.364	.278
Mejia, Gilberto	B-R	5-9	160	9-1-82	.248	.230	.255	122	455	56	113	19	7	5	48	55	5	9	4	88	25	14	.354	.334
Melian, Jackson	R-R	6-2	205	1-7-80	.226	.250	.218	9	31	3	7	1	0	1	3	0	1	0	1	6	0	0	.290	.242
Mendez, Victor	B-R	5-11	160	6-28-80	.281	.292	.276	46	171	25	48	11	3	4	24	18	0	1	0	44	8	2	.450	.347
Patino, Jorge	R-R	5-10	150	1-25-86	.000	—	.000	3	5	0	0	0	0	0	0	0	0	0	0	2	0	0	.000	.000
Ramirez, Wilkin	R-R	6-2	190	10-25-85	.225	.240	.218	66	249	31	56	10	4	8	33	10	2	0	2	69	8	2	.394	.259
Roberson, Ryan	R-R	6-5	240	8-1-83	.250	.250	.250	5	16	0	4	1	0	0	2	1	0	0	0	10	0	0	.313	.294
Robinson, Chris	R-R	6-0	200	5-12-84	.286	.375	.256	95	322	30	92	22	0	1	47	25	1	8	4	73	6	1	.363	.335
2-team (12 Daytona)..					.294	—	—	107	367	32	108	24	0	3	59	26	2	9	4	89	7	1	.384	.341

ORGANIZATION STATISTICS

BATTING	B-T	HT	WT	DOB	AVG	vLH	vRH	G	AB	R	H	2B	3B	HR	RBI	BB	HBP	SH	SF	SO	SB	CS	SLG	OBP
Sandoval, Daniel	R-R	5-11	170	5-7-85	.000	.000	.000	6	6	0	0	0	0	0	0	1	1	0	0	0	1	0	1	.000	.143
Thomas, Clete	L-R	5-11	195	11-14-83	.257	.217	.272	132	529	67	136	30	5	6	40	56	6	1	3	127	34	13	.367	.333
Wells, Casper	R-R	6-2	210	11-23-84	.152	.100	.174	11	33	4	5	1	0	1	4	4	3	1	0	9	1	0	.273	.300
Young, Dmitri	R-R	6-2	220	10-11-73	.400	—	.400	2	5	1	2	1	0	0	0	0	1	0	0	0	1	0	0	.600	.500

PITCHING	B-T	HT	WT	DOB	W	L	ERA	G	GS	CG	SV	IP	H	R	ER	HR	BB	SO	AVG	vLH	vRH	K/9	BB/9
Aponte, Eleazar	R-R	6-1	160	3-4-85	0	2	3.22	4	4	1	0	22	14	10	8	2	8	11	.184	.146	.229	4.43	3.22
Ardoin, Kevin	R-R	6-1	167	8-6-82	9	9	4.11	26	26	2	0	155	176	79	71	16	22	86	.288	.296	.282	4.98	1.27
Bonine, Eddie	R-R	6-5	220	6-6-81	4	4	3.98	41	11	0	1	106	108	62	47	9	27	83	.262	.230	.286	7.03	2.29
Caraballo, Jesse	R-R	6-1	190	7-17-86	0	0	0.00	1	0	0	0	2	0	2	0	0	3	3	.000	.000	.000	13.50	13.50
Clelland, Edward	L-L	6-0	165	6-27-82	0	1	19.29	3	0	0	0	2	8	6	5	0	2	1	.615	.667	.571	3.86	7.71
Connolly, Jonathan	R-L	6-0	205	8-24-83	3	0	1.66	3	3	0	0	22	14	5	4	0	4	5	.189	.000	.222	2.08	1.66
Davis, Lance	R-L	6-2	170	9-1-76	2	3	5.26	7	7	0	0	39	57	27	23	4	8	28	.333	.325	.336	6.41	1.83
Dolsi, Freddy	R-R	6-0	160	1-9-83	4	4	4.01	30	0	0	1	43	47	25	19	5	17	29	.278	.292	.268	6.12	3.59
Finigan, P.J.	R-R	6-0	185	9-30-82	9	2	3.16	33	2	0	0	63	55	24	22	2	21	36	.234	.244	.228	5.17	3.02
Fraser, Loren	R-R	6-6	235	8-20-82	0	1	6.23	11	0	0	0	13	21	11	9	1	4	7	.368	.379	.357	4.85	2.77
Hahn, Jeff	R-R	6-1	180	9-28-81	8	5	4.08	50	0	0	3	71	72	41	32	4	42	50	.265	.269	.261	6.37	5.35
Hammond, Paul	L-L	5-11	205	9-20-82	0	1	2.84	4	0	0	0	6	5	4	2	1	3	4	.208	.400	.158	5.68	4.26
Johnson, Jeremy	R-R	6-3	170	7-19-82	2	5	3.99	22	11	0	1	90	81	45	40	6	39	50	.238	.234	.241	4.98	3.89
Jurrjens, Jair	R-R	6-1	160	1-29-86	5	0	2.08	12	12	0	0	74	53	23	17	4	10	59	.198	.215	.184	7.21	1.22
Kauten, Joshua	R-R	6-3	200	4-5-82	0	0	5.40	7	0	0	0	12	11	10	7	1	6	8	.244	.292	.190	6.17	4.63
Kown, Andrew	L-R	6-7	210	10-7-82	6	5	3.53	18	18	2	0	105	99	53	41	9	43	67	.246	.250	.242	5.76	3.70
Martinez, Cristhian	R-R	6-1	160	3-6-82	1	1	4.98	5	5	0	0	22	27	14	12	3	5	15	.314	.300	.326	6.23	2.08
McIntyre, Nick	B-R	5-10	185	3-11-81	0	0	0.00	1	0	0	0	1	1	0	0	0	0	0	.333	1.000	.000	0.00	0.00
Miller, Andrew	R-L	6-6	210	5-21-85	0	0	0.00	3	0	0	0	5	2	0	0	0	1	9	.118	.000	.154	16.20	1.80
Peralta, Tony	L-L	6-2	187	9-13-83	1	1	2.65	27	1	0	0	37	35	15	11	4	9	35	.243	.238	.245	8.44	2.17
Rainwater, Josh	R-R	6-1	220	4-9-85	0	2	6.17	5	4	0	0	23	32	18	16	2	7	9	.327	.415	.263	3.47	2.70
Rodriguez, Jermy	R-R	5-10	160	1-10-80	0	0	16.20	1	0	0	0	3	7	6	6	2	2	4	.438	.600	.167	10.80	5.40
Sleeth, Kyle	R-R	6-5	205	12-20-81	1	4	11.90	8	7	0	0	20	23	27	26	2	21	7	.291	.267	.306	3.20	9.61
Tomey, Anthony	R-R	6-4	245	8-17-81	2	3	2.51	23	0	0	0	32	17	9	9	0	12	37	.155	.163	.149	10.30	3.34
Trahern, Dallas	R-R	6-3	190	11-29-85	6	11	3.30	25	25	4	0	145	129	66	53	9	41	86	.238	.289	.197	5.35	2.55
Whelan, Kevin	R-R	6-0	200	1-8-84	4	1	2.67	51	0	0	27	54	33	20	16	1	29	69	.178	.211	.158	11.50	4.83
Zell, Danny	L-L	6-5	210	11-27-81	1	3	4.64	34	0	0	1	33	41	19	17	3	10	25	.311	.265	.337	6.82	2.73

FIELDING

Catcher	PCT	G	PO	A	E	DP	PB
Casanova	.972	25	161	14	5	3	2
Graham	.975	27	143	12	4	4	4
Robinson	.988	93	520	52	7	4	16
Sandoval	.929	5	13	0	1	0	0

First Base	PCT	G	PO	A	E	DP
Essian	.919	6	30	4	3	2
Larish	.990	135	1245	92	13	128
Roberson	1.000	2	13	1	0	3

Second Base	PCT	G	PO	A	E	DP
Francia	.959	32	63	101	7	23
Linares	1.000	1	2	2	0	0

	PCT	G	PO	A	E	DP
McIntyre	1.000	10	18	31	0	3
Mejia	.955	94	181	291	22	66
Patino	1.000	1	2	0	0	0

Third Base	PCT	G	PO	A	E	DP
Linares	.937	38	18	56	5	4
McIntyre	.924	41	32	101	11	13
Mejia	—	1	0	0	0	0
Patino	—	1	0	0	0	0
Ramirez	.881	65	40	123	22	9
Roberson	—	1	0	0	0	0

Shortstop	PCT	G	PO	A	E	DP
Dlugach	.951	125	192	423	32	92

	PCT	G	PO	A	E	DP
Francia	1.000	3	7	3	0	1
Linares	.956	16	28	37	3	8
McIntyre	1.000	2	2	3	0	0

Outfield	PCT	G	PO	A	E	DP
Essian	.956	21	42	1	2	0
Frazier	.976	134	228	12	6	1
McKinney	.946	78	119	4	7	0
Melian	1.000	5	9	0	0	0
Mendez	.958	45	86	6	4	1
Thomas	.991	132	321	8	3	6
Wells	1.000	2	2	0	0	0

West Michigan Whitecaps — Low Class A
Midwest League

BATTING	B-T	HT	WT	DOB	AVG	vLH	vRH	G	AB	R	H	2B	3B	HR	RBI	BB	HBP	SH	SF	SO	SB	CS	SLG	OBP
Cotto, Pedro	L-L	5-11	175	5-26-82	.278	.260	.282	108	421	61	117	19	1	0	34	39	5	2	4	29	7	3	.328	.343
Haske, Mark	L-R	5-10	165	5-28-83	.239	.189	.250	100	309	35	74	5	0	1	24	43	3	2	2	46	7	6	.265	.336
Hernandez, Michael	R-R	6-0	175	12-18-83	.278	.284	.276	87	349	40	97	19	3	13	63	19	4	0	5	68	2	1	.461	.318
Hollimon, Michael	B-R	6-1	185	6-14-82	.278	.206	.300	128	449	69	125	29	13	15	54	77	4	3	4	124	19	5	.501	.386
Joyce, Matt	L-R	6-2	185	8-3-84	.258	.250	.260	122	465	75	120	30	5	11	86	56	3	1	5	70	5	4	.415	.338
Justice, Justin	L-L	6-0	185	2-19-85	.295	.238	.309	112	414	51	122	22	9	6	67	41	6	3	8	101	15	5	.435	.360
Kunkel, Jeff	B-R	5-11	200	3-11-83	.000	.000	.000	2	8	0	0	0	0	0	0	0	0	0	0	3	0	0	.000	.000
Laster, Jeramy	R-R	6-1	185	4-5-85	.233	.295	.206	75	253	31	59	11	4	9	31	21	6	0	2	107	4	4	.415	.305
Leon, Maxwell	B-R	5-11	190	6-28-84	.167	.000	.222	6	12	1	2	2	0	0	1	1	0	0	0	2	1	0	.333	.231
Maybin, Cameron	R-R	6-3	200	4-4-87	.304	.325	.298	101	385	59	117	20	6	9	69	50	5	0	5	116	27	7	.457	.387
Mendez, Rafael	R-R	6-0	190	4-24-84	.200	.177	.210	69	200	27	40	11	2	3	21	31	3	2	2	74	3	1	.320	.314
Middleton, Cory	R-R	6-1	185	10-3-85	.180	.218	.165	80	278	24	50	14	0	3	29	20	4	2	2	73	3	4	.263	.243
Rhymes, William	L-R	5-9	155	4-13-83	.261	.217	.273	126	506	80	132	19	2	3	39	53	3	12	4	53	23	6	.324	.332
Roa, Joel	R-R	6-0	175	1-2-84	.130	.098	.144	54	162	7	21	3	0	2	7	13	5	1	0	56	1	1	.185	.160
Roberson, Ryan	R-R	6-5	240	8-1-83	.233	.290	.216	34	133	11	31	5	1	0	13	8	1	0	0	42	3	1	.286	.282
Ryan, Dusty	R-R	6-4	220	9-2-84	.245	.217	.252	98	322	49	79	13	2	6	35	44	5	3	1	102	3	4	.354	.344

PITCHING	B-T	HT	WT	DOB	W	L	ERA	G	GS	CG	SV	IP	H	R	ER	HR	BB	SO	AVG	vLH	vRH	K/9	BB/9
Averill, Erik	L-L	6-2	190	2-9-84	9	8	3.73	28	28	0	0	171	171	89	71	12	48	111	.261	.281	.255	5.83	2.52
Badenhop, Burke	R-R	6-5	220	2-8-83	14	3	2.84	27	27	3	0	171	170	59	54	6	31	124	.260	.293	.237	6.53	1.63
Baxter, Jake	R-R	6-5	210	11-9-83	0	3	3.21	16	0	0	0	28	27	15	10	5	12	22	.257	.216	.279	7.07	3.86
2-team (19 South Bend)					3	5	3.86	35	0	0	1	58	62	30	25	7	20	39	—	—		6.02	3.09
Claggett, Anthony	B-R	6-2	185	7-15-84	7	2	0.91	51	0	0	14	59	35	7	6	0	20	58	.174	.209	.157	8.80	3.03
Fragoso, Jose	R-R	6-0	175	11-12-84	1	0	2.33	13	0	0	0	19	10	6	5	0	11	23	.154	.167	.146	10.71	5.12
Fraser, Loren	R-R	6-6	235	8-20-82	1	1	2.65	8	0	0	0	17	14	5	5	1	3	17	.219	.136	.262	9.00	1.59
French, Lucas	L-L	6-4	220	9-13-85	11	8	3.72	26	26	1	0	157	156	75	65	10	44	94	.258	.272	.254	5.38	2.52
Garcia, Ramon	L-L	6-2	165	10-30-84	7	2	1.92	12	12	2	0	75	51	17	16	5	11	55	.194	.167	.202	6.60	1.32
Hammond, Paul	L-L	5-11	205	9-20-82	0	0	0.00	5	0	0	2	7	3	0	0	0	1	5	.136	.125	.143	6.75	1.35
Kauten, Joshua	R-R	6-3	200	4-5-82	2	1	3.24	20	1	0	1	42	32	16	15	1	19	27	.213	.214	.213	5.83	4.10

Name	B-T	HT	WT	DOB	W	L	ERA	G	GS	CG	SV	IP	H	R	ER	HR	BB	SO	AVG	vLH	vRH	K/9	BB/9
Kown, Andrew	L-R	6-7	210	10-7-82	2	0	0.00	6	0	0	0	16	10	0	0	0	0	16	.179	.273	.118	9.00	0.00
Lewis, Lavon	R-R	6-3	205	12-17-83	0	0	2.08	8	0	0	0	13	11	4	3	2	4	8	.244	.357	.194	5.54	2.77
Napolitan, Phil	R-R	6-1	185	1-29-82	0	0	5.18	17	0	0	1	24	24	15	14	1	8	17	.253	.194	.288	6.29	2.96
O'Brien, Matt	R-R	6-3	215	8-10-82	3	1	2.25	4	4	0	0	24	24	9	6	0	5	11	.258	.207	.281	4.13	1.88
Perdomo, Orlando	R-R	6-0	160	5-3-84	0	2	4.15	48	0	0	28	43	44	23	20	2	12	48	.256	.243	.265	9.97	2.49
Rainwater, Josh	R-R	6-1	220	4-9-85	6	4	3.84	14	10	0	0	63	69	34	27	4	12	53	.278	.267	.287	7.53	1.71
Rusch, Matthew	R-R	5-11	180	5-20-83	9	3	1.79	39	3	0	1	80	63	19	16	5	10	66	.219	.231	.212	7.39	1.12
Santos, Adriano	R-R	6-2	170	9-8-84	0	0	0.00	1	0	0	0	3	1	0	0	0	0	3	.111	.000	.143	10.13	0.00
Sborz, Jay	R-R	6-4	210	1-24-85	1	0	5.40	3	0	0	0	5	8	3	3	0	4	4	.364	.286	.400	7.20	7.20
Steik, Ricky	L-R	6-4	220	1-24-84	3	4	2.63	44	0	0	2	68	59	24	20	2	15	80	.229	.152	.277	10.54	1.98
Vasquez, Sendy	B-R	6-1	160	8-10-82	13	6	2.97	26	26	0	0	142	129	64	47	7	49	112	.240	.235	.244	7.08	3.10
Wilson, Gibbs	R-R	6-2	170	6-9-85	0	0	5.68	8	0	0	0	6	4	8	4	1	6	8	.154	.091	.200	11.37	8.53

FIELDING

Catcher	PCT	G	PO	A	E	DP	PB
Kunkel	1.000	2	12	2	0	0	0
Mendez	1.000	5	14	1	0	1	1
Roa	.987	54	356	34	5	3	5
Ryan	.988	95	587	61	8	5	7

First Base	PCT	G	PO	A	E	DP
Cotto	.996	51	453	27	2	34
Haske	1.000	6	61	4	0	10
Hernandez	.952	5	38	2	2	4
Leon	1.000	1	5	0	0	2
Mendez	.989	54	438	22	5	35

	PCT	G	PO	A	E	DP
Roberson	.980	27	230	20	5	18

Second Base	PCT	G	PO	A	E	DP
Haske	1.000	12	17	38	0	4
Leon	.929	4	7	6	1	3
Mendez	.909	3	3	7	1	0
Rhymes	.969	122	220	316	17	80

Third Base	PCT	G	PO	A	E	DP
Haske	.946	59	40	101	8	9
Mendez	1.000	7	4	8	0	0
Middleton	.919	78	55	160	19	16

Shortstop	PCT	G	PO	A	E	DP
Haske	.985	16	19	47	1	5
Hollimon	.955	124	200	394	28	77
Middleton	.500	0	1	1	0	0

Outfield	PCT	G	PO	A	E	DP
Cotto	.977	37	82	3	2	0
Hernandez	.967	29	53	5	2	1
Joyce	.974	109	222	7	6	4
Justice	.984	93	185	4	3	1
Laster	.962	66	121	6	5	0
Maybin	.995	88	211	6	1	3
Roberson	—	1	0	0	0	0

Oneonta Tigers — Short-Season

New York-Penn League

BATTING	B-T	HT	WT	DOB	AVG	vLH	vRH	G	AB	R	H	2B	3B	HR	RBI	BB	HBP	SH	SF	SO	SB	CS	SLG	OBP
Boesch, Brennan	L-L	6-5	185	4-12-85	.291	.279	.298	70	292	27	85	15	6	5	54	21	3	0	1	42	3	4	.435	.344
Bourquin, Ronald	L-R	6-3	205	4-29-85	.266	.329	.237	67	252	37	67	13	1	2	24	46	6	0	0	46	3	4	.349	.391
De Leon, Santo	R-R	6-2	175	11-1-83	.253	.293	.222	41	174	24	44	11	0	3	21	2	1	0	1	43	0	2	.368	.264
Kunkel, Jeffrey	B-R	5-11	200	3-11-83	.260	.364	.211	30	104	7	27	4	0	0	10	11	0	0	0	28	0	1	.298	.330
Leon, Maxwell	B-R	5-11	190	6-28-84	.220	.167	.261	12	41	6	9	0	0	0	2	5	0	0	0	9	0	0	.220	.304
Newton, Jordan	R-R	5-10	180	8-29-85	.179	.213	.158	37	123	16	22	3	1	2	11	19	5	3	2	37	3	1	.268	.309
Ott, Louis	B-R	6-0	185	2-22-85	.241	.286	.221	50	162	29	39	3	3	0	20	28	3	6	0	23	5	3	.296	.363
Reyes, Angel	R-R	6-3	180	1-9-84	.242	.154	.300	20	66	5	16	3	0	1	7	4	0	3	1	25	0	0	.333	.282
Scram, Deik	L-R	6-2	180	2-1-84	.281	.290	.277	59	235	30	66	12	6	2	29	26	5	2	2	62	3	7	.409	.362
Sizemore, Scott	R-R	6-0	185	1-4-85	.327	.300	.340	70	294	49	96	15	4	3	37	32	2	3	2	47	7	5	.435	.394
Skelton, James	L-R	5-11	165	10-28-85	.300	.346	.288	42	130	20	39	8	1	1	22	21	2	0	1	29	1	1	.400	.403
Strieby, Ryan	R-R	6-6	220	8-9-85	.241	.225	.248	61	224	26	54	9	0	4	25	25	2	0	3	58	1	1	.335	.319
Timm, Brandon	R-R	6-2	200	12-4-84	.259	.305	.228	55	205	26	53	6	7	1	18	16	2	1	1	47	8	2	.371	.317
Tucker, Joseph	R-R	5-11	180	11-25-84	.240	.230	.248	49	179	27	43	7	1	0	16	16	4	1	3	37	5	5	.291	.312
Wells, Casper	R-R	6-2	210	11-23-84	.229	.311	.167	35	105	19	24	8	0	1	14	9	3	1	1	27	1	1	.333	.305

PITCHING	B-T	HT	WT	DOB	W	L	ERA	G	GS	CG	SV	IP	H	R	ER	HR	BB	SO	AVG	vLH	vRH	K/9	BB/9
Below, Duane	L-L	6-2	205	11-15-85	0	0	3.86	2	2	0	0	9	11	6	4	0	5	8	.282	.071	.400	7.71	4.82
Bierd, Randor	R-R	6-4	190	3-14-84	5	0	6.57	20	2	0	0	38	48	30	28	2	15	41	.298	.362	.262	9.63	3.52
Cody, Christopher	L-L	6-0	180	1-7-84	4	1	2.38	11	11	0	0	53	48	23	14	1	9	50	.238	.220	.243	8.49	1.53
Fien, Casey	R-R	6-2	195	10-21-83	1	1	2.74	20	0	0	1	43	39	17	13	1	8	37	.248	.259	.242	7.80	1.69
Fragoso, Jose	R-R	6-0	175	11-12-84	3	0	1.50	10	0	0	1	24	10	4	4	0	7	25	.133	.138	.130	9.38	2.63
Gagnier, Lauren	R-R	6-2	210	2-28-85	1	1	0.70	9	1	0	0	26	13	2	2	1	12	21	.155	.229	.102	7.36	4.21
Gerbe, Jeffrey	R-R	6-3	195	7-4-84	1	4	5.08	8	8	0	0	39	52	30	22	1	8	23	.325	.347	.306	5.31	1.85
Jensen, Brett	R-R	6-7	180	11-29-83	1	0	0.68	25	0	0	17	27	17	4	2	0	5	31	.177	.132	.207	10.46	1.69
Krawczyk, Christopher	R-R	6-1	200	7-21-83	2	2	3.47	18	0	0	0	36	39	15	14	2	11	26	.279	.313	.247	6.44	2.72
Martinez, Cristhian	R-R	6-1	160	3-6-82	1	2	2.16	7	7	0	0	42	38	15	10	4	5	30	.241	.256	.225	6.48	1.08
Napolitan, Phil	R-R	6-1	185	1-29-82	1	0	2.25	3	0	0	1	4	2	1	1	0	4	4	.182	.000	.222	9.00	9.00
Nickerson, Jonah	R-R	6-0	210	3-9-85	0	0	2.77	5	0	0	2	13	8	4	4	1	4	12	.190	.167	.208	8.31	2.77
O'Brien, Matt	R-R	6-3	215	8-10-82	8	1	2.79	11	11	1	0	68	66	22	21	1	16	42	.264	.279	.253	5.59	2.13
Piccola, Zachary	R-L	6-3	225	3-27-85	1	7	4.04	14	13	0	0	62	66	41	28	1	31	35	.282	.241	.295	5.05	4.48
Robertson, Timothy	R-R	6-2	215	12-27-82	1	3	6.26	15	0	0	1	27	39	28	19	1	8	19	.322	.366	.300	6.26	2.63
Thornton, Thomas	L-L	6-6	220	10-30-83	2	4	3.33	12	11	0	0	51	55	24	19	1	9	39	.278	.341	.261	6.84	1.58
Wise, Brendan	L-R	6-2	190	1-9-86	3	6	3.46	16	8	0	0	65	67	30	25	0	15	39	.268	.282	.259	5.40	2.08
Witt, Derek	R-R	6-1	180	12-31-83	5	2	1.16	17	0	0	0	39	28	6	5	0	10	22	.206	.154	.254	5.12	2.33

FIELDING

Catcher	PCT	G	PO	A	E	DP	PB
Kunkel	.979	21	128	13	3	1	0
Newton	.970	32	233	23	8	2	3
Skelton	1.000	26	149	21	0	1	2

First Base	PCT	G	PO	A	E	DP
De Leon	.990	10	83	17	1	11
Ott	1.000	1	11	1	0	2
Reyes	1.000	14	145	18	0	15
Strieby	.987	51	471	45	7	46

Second Base	PCT	G	PO	A	E	DP
Leon	.981	9	19	34	1	9
Ott	.975	46	102	135	6	32
Sizemore	.944	4	7	10	1	1
Strieby	1.000	1	3	5	0	2
Tucker	.978	16	40	51	2	16

Third Base	PCT	G	PO	A	E	DP
Bourquin	.926	58	37	126	13	15
De Leon	.906	16	10	38	5	4

Shortstop	PCT	G	PO	A	E	DP
De Leon	1.000	1	2	3	0	0
Ott	.882	3	7	8	2	3
Sizemore	.948	63	85	187	15	42
Tucker	.867	9	11	28	6	5

Outfield	PCT	G	PO	A	E	DP
Boesch	.950	69	113	2	6	0
Scram	.970	58	122	6	4	0
Timm	.973	52	65	6	2	1
Tucker	.974	20	35	2	1	0
Wells	.977	31	40	3	1	0

Gulf Coast League

BATTING	B-T	HT	WT	DOB	AVG	vLH	vRH	G	AB	R	H	2B	3B	HR	RBI	BB	HBP	SH	SF	SO	SB	CS	SLG	OBP
Arlet, Luis....................	R-R	5-11	174	11-8-84	.300	.220	.328	44	160	33	48	4	3	6	20	9	1	0	1	54	20	1	.475	.339
Bertram, Michael	L-R	6-2	220	2-25-84	.250	.298	.231	44	164	22	41	10	1	1	25	3	3	2	4	26	8	1	.341	.270
Bowen, Joseph...............	B-R	6-1	190	9-25-87	.262	.143	.302	35	84	13	22	2	1	0	8	15	1	0	0	27	6	1	.310	.380
Carlson, Christopher	R-R	6-4	230	1-7-84	.311	.326	.305	49	177	27	55	16	0	11	47	24	5	0	3	31	3	1	.588	.402
Casanova, Adrian	R-R	6-1	200	5-6-83	.250	.500	.167	2	8	1	2	1	0	0	2	0	0	0	0	0	0	0	.375	.250
Ciriaco, Audy	R-R	6-3	195	6-16-87	.217	.309	.175	50	175	26	38	7	1	4	19	9	1	1	1	30	9	1	.337	.258
Collet, Cody	R-R	6-0	195	1-22-85	.184	.235	.156	22	49	2	9	1	0	1	8	2	1	1	0	15	1	0	.265	.231
Flores, Angel	R-R	6-0	195	8-16-86	.234	.235	.233	21	47	2	11	1	0	1	8	7	0	2	0	5	2	0	.319	.333
Hernandez, Gorkys........	R-R	6-0	175	9-7-87	.327	.356	.315	50	205	41	67	9	2	5	23	10	0	1	1	27	20	4	.463	.356
Leon, Maxwell	B-R	5-11	190	6-28-84	.184	.286	.143	17	49	9	9	3	0	1	5	6	0	0	0	13	0	0	.306	.273
Mendez, Victor	B-R	5-11	160	6-28-80	.229	.143	.250	11	35	7	8	1	0	1	9	7	0	0	0	9	6	0	.343	.357
Parrott, Hayden	R-R	6-1	195	4-11-88	.429	.333	.478	10	35	5	15	4	1	0	3	3	1	0	1	6	2	0	.600	.475
Patino, Jorge	R-R	5-10	150	1-25-86	.270	.313	.259	27	74	12	20	2	0	0	4	5	1	0	0	7	0	3	.297	.325
Ramirez, Carlos	R-R	5-11	190	9-1-85	.197	.185	.204	25	76	9	15	3	0	1	6	1	3	1	0	32	1	0	.276	.238
Roberson, Ryan	R-R	6-5	240	8-1-83	.083	.143	.000	4	12	2	1	0	0	0	1	2	2	0	0	6	0	0	.083	.313
Rodriguez, Orlando	R-R	6-0	180	8-29-85	.200	.171	.217	35	95	14	19	2	0	3	14	5	1	0	1	18	3	0	.316	.245
Sandoval, Daniel	R-R	5-11	170	5-7-85	.091	.083	.095	14	33	0	3	2	0	0	3	4	0	0	0	5	0	1	.152	.189
Sullivan, Michael	L-R	6-2	190	12-16-83	.287	.224	.313	47	164	28	47	7	4	0	14	19	1	6	0	35	10	0	.378	.364
Trapani, Michael............	R-R	5-10	185	1-5-83	.034	.000	.050	12	29	1	1	1	0	0	0	3	1	0	0	6	0	0	.069	.152

PITCHING	B-T	HT	WT	DOB	W	L	ERA	G	GS	CG	SV	IP	H	R	ER	HR	BB	SO	AVG	vLH	vRH	K/9	BB/9
Aponte, Eleazar	R-R	6-1	160	3-4-85	4	0	1.77	8	6	1	0	46	37	10	9	2	7	33	.220	.288	.190	6.50	1.38
Arrowood, Dana	R-R	6-4	215	11-22-82	0	1	7.20	11	0	0	0	15	11	15	12	1	13	9	.212	.333	.162	5.40	7.80
Beattie, Eric	R-R	6-3	190	4-2-83	3	2	4.17	11	8	0	0	37	23	18	17	1	30	34	.183	.140	.205	8.35	7.36
Below, Duane	L-L	6-2	205	11-15-85	2	0	1.60	15	4	0	0	34	27	8	6	1	10	30	.216	.233	.211	8.02	2.67
Caraballo, Jesse	R-R	6-1	190	7-17-86	3	3	3.00	18	1	0	4	27	15	11	9	1	14	31	.163	.162	.164	10.33	4.67
Darrow, Rudy	R-R	5-10	180	2-11-84	0	0	11.25	5	0	0	1	4	3	5	5	0	4	5	.200	.000	.300	11.25	9.00
Figaro, Alfredo	R-R	6-0	173	7-7-84	3	1	0.70	14	4	0	1	38	29	7	3	0	12	31	.210	.200	.215	7.28	2.82
Franco, Santo	L-L	5-11	157	5-7-85	1	3	6.35	10	4	0	0	23	19	16	16	0	17	27	.229	.167	.239	10.72	6.75
Fuhrman, Aaron	L-L	6-0	185	4-2-88	0	0	16.20	4	0	0	0	3	6	6	6	0	3	4	.375	.000	.400	10.80	8.10
Hammond, Paul	L-L	5-11	205	9-20-82	3	0	0.44	15	0	0	4	20	11	1	1	0	3	18	.167	.091	.182	7.97	1.33
Martinez, Cristhian	R-R	6-1	160	3-6-82	3	2	1.54	7	6	0	0	35	30	11	6	1	4	27	.233	.234	.232	6.94	1.03
Moscoso, Guillermo	R-R	6-1	165	11-14-83	3	2	2.50	13	3	0	0	36	37	14	10	3	8	33	.264	.279	.258	8.25	2.00
Ramos, Jacob	L-L	5-9	170	5-18-83	1	0	5.59	7	0	0	0	10	12	6	6	0	6	9	.316	.143	.355	8.38	5.59
Righter, Matthew	R-R	6-5	190	8-7-81	4	1	2.47	10	10	0	0	47	44	19	13	5	17	27	.237	.270	.214	5.13	3.23
Santos, Adriano	R-R	6-2	170	9-8-84	1	1	2.57	18	0	0	3	28	23	8	8	1	15	27	.225	.300	.194	8.68	4.82
Shepherd, Alec..............	R-R	6-3	190	1-17-86	0	2	9.90	11	0	0	0	10	14	12	11	0	8	10	.318	.250	.344	9.00	7.20
Sleeth, Kyle	R-R	6-5	205	12-20-81	1	0	3.63	5	4	0	1	17	22	9	7	0	3	17	.319	.273	.340	8.83	1.56

FIELDING

Catcher	PCT	G	PO	A	E	DP	PB
Bowen.................	.989	31	163	10	2	1	1
Collet.................	1.000	16	80	7	0	1	3
Flores	1.000	18	90	10	0	1	2
Sandoval	.981	10	42	9	1	1	3

First Base	PCT	G	PO	A	E	DP
Bertram	1.000	10	78	7	0	7
Carlson..............	.987	40	369	19	5	36
Roberson	1.000	1	4	1	0	0

Second Base	PCT	G	PO	A	E	DP
Bertram	1.000	1	0	3	0	1
Leon.................	.950	14	24	33	3	8
Parrott..............	.957	8	10	12	1	3
Patino................	.971	24	36	64	3	19
Trapani	.957	11	15	29	2	6

Third Base	PCT	G	PO	A	E	DP
Bertram..............	.899	34	21	68	10	4
Patino.................	—	1	0	0	0	0
Ramirez..............	.912	19	11	41	5	5

Shortstop	PCT	G	PO	A	E	DP
Ciriaco.................	.936	50	78	140	15	31
Patino.................	1.000	1	0	1	0	0

Outfield	PCT	G	PO	A	E	DP
Arlet	.981	29	51	2	1	2
Hernandez...........	.979	50	90	4	2	1
Mendez.............	1.000	5	9	0	0	0
Ramirez.............	1.000	3	2	1	0	0
Rodriguez...........	1.000	29	36	2	0	1
Sullivan	.952	47	56	3	3	0

ORGANIZATION STATISTICS

FLORIDA MARLINS

BY MIKE BERARDINO

They opened the year with the youngest starting line-up in modern history, the majors' smallest payroll in seven years and a halfway decent chance of breaking the 1962 Mets' record for most losses in a season.

But the 2006 Marlins turned out to be a pleasant surprise on a number of levels.

Under rookie manager Joe Girardi—who was a manager of the year candidate but was fired at season's end due to poor communication with the front office—the Mini Marlins went 78-84 and chased a wild-card spot until the season's penultimate weekend.

How did they do it? For starters, most of those kids could really play. Of the 22 rookies the Marlins used during the season, at least a half dozen figured to receive some consideration for National League rookie of the year.

Second baseman Dan Uggla led the charge for much of the summer, becoming the first major league Rule 5 draft pick (coming over from the Diamondbacks organization) to make the all-star team the very next year. He also broke Joe Gordon's rookie record for home runs by a second baseman.

Shortstop Hanley Ramirez, acquired in a trade from the Red Sox, led off and finished the year with 119 runs and 51 stolen bases. Over the final six weeks, only Ryan Howard posted a higher combined on-base/slugging percentage in the majors.

Outfielder Josh Willingham, who finally got an extended big league opportunity, hit 26 home runs to go with a .356 on-base percentage and .496 slugging percentage.

And of course seasoned veteran Miguel Cabrera, in his

PLAYERS OF THE YEAR

MAJOR LEAGUE: Miguel Cabrera, 3b

Cabrera played 30 games at third base in 2005, but he went back to the hot corner for 2006 and put up his most productive season in the majors. Cabrera batted .339/.430/.568 with a career-high 50 doubles, and led the club in average, hits (195) RBIs (114) and total bases (327).

MINOR LEAGUE: Jose Garcia, rhp

Garcia went 12-10, 2.88 over three levels in 2006, representing the Marlins organization in the Futures Game in July. After making just four starts at low Class A Greensboro in 2005, Garcia firmly entrenched himself among the top pitching prospects in the organization.

third full big league season, batted .339/.430/.568 with 26 home runs and 114 RBIs.

On the pitching staff, rookie righthander Anibal Sanchez, the other key piece in that Red Sox deal, tossed the majors' first no-hitter in 2½ seasons on Sept. 6 against Arizona. Sanchez, who didn't even make the jump from Double-A until mid-June, also finished 10-3, giving the Marlins four rookie starters with 10 wins or more. No team had ever done that before with rookies, whether they were starters or relievers.

Fellow righty Josh Johnson kept his name among the National League ERA leaders for much of the year before a late bout with forearm woes shut him down in September. Lefty Scott Olsen tied with Dontrelle Willis for the team lead in starts with 31, while righty Ricky Nolasco was a revelation after spending the first five weeks in the bullpen.

All told those rookie starters went a combined 45-31 and became the envy of the game.

Not bad for a team that opened the year with a $15 million payroll after selling off a boatload of established stars (Carlos Delgado, Josh Beckett, Mike Lowell, Juan Pierre, Luis Castillo, Paul Lo Duca) in salary-dump trades the previous winter.

If the rookies make similar improvement in 2007, new manager Fredi Gonzalez figures to enjoy his dugout debut immensely. Gonzalez, formerly the Braves' third-base coach, was announced as Girardi's replacement two days after the season ended, returning to the organization where he spent a decade (1992-2001).

In the minors, the Marlins struggled to a combined .465 winning percentage. Just one affiliate managed a winning record: the Rookie-level Gulf Coast League team at 29-24.

This was understandable considering 13 of the organization's top 18 prospects coming into the season saw time in the majors in 2006. Even so, there was considerable hope for the Class of 2005, a handful of young starting pitchers (including first-rounders Chris Volstad and Aaron Thompson) who spent much of last season at low Class A Greensboro.

ORGANIZATION LEADERS

BATTING
*Minimum 250 at-bats

*AVG	Kinkade, Mike, Albuquerque	.328
R	Andino, Robert, Albuquerque	70
H	Gonzalez, Edgar, Jupiter/Carolina/Albuquerque	154
TB	Gonzalez, Edgar., Jupiter/Carolina/Albuquerque	234
2B	Mitchell, Lee, Carolina	37
3B	Reed, Eric, Albuquerque	9
HR	Carroll, Brett, Jupiter/Carolina	20
RBI	Wood, Jason, Albuquerque	77
BB	Sanchez, Gabriel, Greensboro/GCL Marlins/Jupiter	67
SO	Brinkley, Dante, Jupiter	139
	Mitchell, Lee, Carolina	139
SB	Campusano, Jose, Carolina	37
*OBP	Sanchez, Gabriel, Greensboro/GCL Marlins/Jupiter	424
*SLG	Sanchez, Gabriel, Greensboro/GCL Marlins/Jupiter	523
XBH	Carroll, Brett, Jupiter/Carolina	55

PITCHING
#Minimum 75 innings

W	Garcia, Jose, Jupiter/Albuquerque/Carolina	12
L	Tucker, Ryan, Greensboro	13
#ERA	Winters, Kyle, Jamestown	2.45
G	Yourkin, Matt, Carolina/Albuquerque	61
CG	Ungs, Nic, Albuquerque	3
SV	Clontz, Brad, Albuquerque	23
IP	Mildren, Paul, Carolina	167
BB	Bostick, Adam, Carolina/Albuquerque	85
SO	Garcia, Jose, Jupiter/Albuquerque/Carolina	161
#AVG	Winters, Kyle, Jamestown	.194

Florida Marlins MLB

National League

BATTING	B-T	HT	WT	DOB	AVG	vLH	vRH	G	AB	R	H	2B	3B	HR	RBI	BB	HBP	SH	SF	SO	SB	CS	SLG	OBP
Abercrombie, Reggie	R-R	6-3	220	7-15-80	.212	.220	.208	111	255	40	54	12	2	5	24	18	3	4	1	78	6	5	.333	.271
Aguila, Chris..................	R-R	5-11	180	2-23-79	.232	.195	.259	47	95	5	22	8	1	0	7	9	0	0	0	26	2	1	.337	.298
Amezaga, Alfredo	B-R	5-10	165	1-16-78	.260	.091	.294	132	334	42	87	9	3	3	19	33	3	7	1	46	20	12	.332	.332
Andino, Robert...............	R-R	6-0	170	4-25-84	.167	.111	.200	11	24	0	4	1	0	0	2	1	0	1	2	6	1	0	.208	.185
Borchard, Joe.................	R-R	6-4	230	11-25-78	.230	.155	.256	108	230	30	53	7	1	10	28	28	3	0	0	66	0	2	.400	.322
Cabrera, Miguel	R-R	6-2	210	4-18-83	.339	.321	.344	158	576	112	195	50	2	26	114	86	10	0	4	108	9	6	.568	.430
Cepicky, Matt	L-R	6-2	215	11-10-77	.111	.500	.063	9	18	0	2	0	0	0	0	1	0	0	0	4	0	0	.111	.158
Helms, Wes	R-R	6-4	230	5-12-76	.329	.336	.323	140	240	30	79	19	5	10	47	21	6	3	5	55	0	4	.575	.390
Hermida, Jeremy	L-R	6-4	200	1-30-84	.251	.236	.261	99	307	37	77	19	1	5	28	33	5	2	1	70	4	1	.368	.332
Hoover, Paul	R-R	6-1	200	4-14-76	.400	.400	—	4	5	0	2	0	0	0	1	0	0	0	0	0	0	0	.400	.400
Jacobs, Mike	L-R	6-2	200	10-30-80	.262	.182	.281	136	469	54	123	37	1	20	77	45	1	0	5	105	3	0	.473	.325
Olivo, Miguel	R-R	6-0	220	7-15-78	.263	.273	.258	127	430	52	113	22	3	16	58	9	7	3	3	103	2	3	.440	.287
Ramirez, Hanley	R-R	6-3	195	12-23-83	.292	.307	.288	158	633	119	185	46	11	17	59	56	4	5	2	128	51	15	.480	.353
Reed, Eric	L-L	5-11	170	12-2-80	.098	.000	.100	42	41	6	4	0	0	0	0	2	2	0	0	9	3	1	.098	.178
Ross, Cody	R-L	5-9	205	12-23-80	.212	.216	.210	91	250	30	53	11	1	11	37	22	4	1	2	61	0	1	.396	.284
3-team (2 Cincinnati, 8 Los Angeles)					.227	—	—	101	269	34	61	12	2	13	46	22	4	1	2	65	1	1	.431	.293
Treanor, Matt	R-R	6-0	205	3-3-76	.229	.268	.216	67	157	12	36	6	1	2	14	19	5	2	2	34	0	1	.318	.328
Uggla, Dan	R-R	5-11	200	3-11-80	.282	.307	.273	154	611	105	172	26	7	27	90	48	9	7	8	123	6	6	.480	.339
Willingham, Josh	R-R	6-2	200	2-17-79	.277	.299	.269	142	502	62	139	28	2	26	74	54	11	0	6	109	2	0	.496	.356
Wood, Jason	R-R	6-1	200	12-16-69	.462	.500	.444	12	13	3	6	2	0	0	1	0	0	0	0	2	1	0	.615	.500

PITCHING	B-T	HT	WT	DOB	W	L	ERA	G	GS	CG	SV	IP	H	R	ER	HR	BB	SO	AVG	vLH	vRH	K/9	BB/9
Borowski, Joe	R-R	6-2	225	5-4-71	3	3	3.75	72	0	0	36	70	63	31	29	7	33	64	.235	.167	.291	8.27	4.26
Fulchino, Jeff	R-R	6-5	250	11-26-79	0	0	0.00	1	0	0	0	0	0	0	0	0	0	1	.000	—	.000	0.00	27.00
Garcia, Jose	R-R	5-11	165	1-7-85	0	0	4.91	5	0	0	0	11	10	6	6	1	5	8	.233	.267	.154	6.55	4.09
German, Franklyn	R-R	6-7	260	1-20-80	0	0	3.00	12	0	0	0	12	7	4	4	1	14	6	.171	.235	.125	4.50	10.50
Herges, Matt	L-R	6-0	210	4-1-70	2	3	4.31	66	0	0	0	71	94	42	34	5	28	36	.321	.300	.340	4.56	3.55
Johnson, Josh	L-R	6-7	240	1-31-84	12	7	3.10	31	24	0	0	157	136	63	54	14	68	133	.236	.246	.227	7.62	3.90
Kensing, Logan	R-R	6-1	185	7-3-82	1	3	4.54	37	0	0	1	38	30	19	19	6	19	45	.221	.218	.222	10.75	4.54
Martinez, Carlos	R-R	6-1	170	5-26-82	0	1	1.74	12	0	0	0	10	9	2	2	0	6	11	.250	.250	.250	9.58	5.23
Messenger, Randy	R-R	6-6	245	8-13-81	2	7	5.67	59	0	0	0	60	72	42	38	8	24	45	.296	.333	.267	6.71	3.58
Mitre, Sergio	R-R	6-4	210	2-16-81	1	5	5.71	15	7	0	0	41	44	28	26	7	20	31	.275	.344	.232	6.80	4.39
Moehler, Brian	R-R	6-3	235	12-31-71	7	11	6.57	29	21	0	0	122	164	95	89	19	38	58	.325	.351	.297	4.28	2.80
Nolasco, Ricky	R-R	6-2	220	12-13-82	11	11	4.82	35	22	0	0	140	157	86	75	20	41	99	.286	.338	.240	6.36	2.64
Olsen, Scott	L-L	6-4	200	1-12-84	12	10	4.04	31	31	0	0	181	160	94	81	23	75	166	.239	.182	.255	8.27	3.74
Petit, Yusmeiro	R-R	6-0	180	11-22-84	1	1	9.57	15	1	0	0	26	46	28	28	7	9	20	.390	.381	.400	6.84	3.08
Pinto, Renyel	L-L	6-4	195	7-8-82	0	0	3.03	27	0	0	1	30	20	12	10	3	27	36	.190	.171	.200	10.92	8.19
Resop, Chris	R-R	6-3	220	11-4-82	1	2	3.38	22	0	0	0	21	26	9	8	1	16	10	.310	.279	.341	4.22	6.75
Sanchez, Anibal	R-R	6-0	180	2-27-84	10	3	2.83	18	17	2	0	114	90	39	36	9	46	72	.217	.229	.202	5.67	3.62
Tankersley, Taylor	L-L	6-1	220	3-7-83	2	1	2.85	49	0	0	3	41	33	14	13	4	26	46	.228	.236	.222	10.10	5.71
Vargas, Jason	L-L	6-0	215	2-2-83	1	2	7.33	12	5	0	0	43	50	39	35	9	30	25	.292	.262	.302	5.23	6.28
Wellemeyer, Todd	R-R	6-3	205	8-30-78	0	2	5.48	18	0	0	0	21	20	13	13	1	13	17	.256	.241	.265	7.17	5.48
Willis, Dontrelle	L-L	6-4	240	1-12-82	12	12	3.87	34	34	4	0	223	234	106	96	21	83	160	.274	.231	.281	6.45	3.34

FIELDING

Catcher	PCT	G	PO	A	E	DP	PB
Hoover	.875	3	7	0	1	0	1
Olivo....................	.991	124	732	65	7	11	10
Treanor	.993	61	374	26	3	2	2
Willingham............	1.000	2	11	1	0	0	1

First Base	PCT	G	PO	A	E	DP
Amezaga.............	1.000	2	4	0	0	0
Borchard.............	1.000	1	2	0	0	1
Helms.................	1.000	88	375	25	0	48
Jacobs...............	.993	124	931	57	7	101
Olivo..................	1.000	5	4	1	0	1
Willingham............	1.000	2	5	0	0	0

Wood	1.000	5	16	1	0	2

Second Base	PCT	G	PO	A	E	DP
Amezaga.............	.974	23	33	41	2	15
Uggla.................	.980	151	314	423	15	112
Wood.................	—	1	0	0	0	0

Third Base	PCT	G	PO	A	E	DP
Amezaga.............	1.000	4	1	0	0	0
Cabrera..............	.957	157	114	266	17	33
Helms.................	.938	24	7	23	2	0

Shortstop	PCT	G	PO	A	E	DP
Amezaga.............	1.000	11	5	21	0	5
Andino................	.964	9	7	20	1	2

	PCT	G	PO	A	E	DP
Ramirez...............	.963	154	258	411	26	111

Outfield	PCT	G	PO	A	E	DP
Abercrombie........	.973	93	176	3	5	1
Aguila................	1.000	31	39	2	0	0
Amezaga.............	.977	78	166	2	4	0
Borchard.............	.982	63	101	7	2	2
Cepicky..............	1.000	6	8	0	0	0
Helms.................	1.000	1	1	0	0	0
Hermida..............	.957	89	177	1	8	0
Reed..................	1.000	32	33	1	0	1
Ross..................	.985	79	125	3	2	0
Willingham..........	.968	132	206	5	7	0

Albuquerque Isotopes Triple-A

Pacific Coast League

BATTING	B-T	HT	WT	DOB	AVG	vLH	vRH	G	AB	R	H	2B	3B	HR	RBI	BB	HBP	SH	SF	SO	SB	CS	SLG	OBP
Aceves, Jonathan	R-R	6-2	220	3-7-78	.333	.000	.500	1	3	0	1	0	0	0	0	1	0	0	0	0	0	0	.333	.500
Aguila, Chris..................	R-R	5-11	180	2-23-79	.318	.354	.305	78	302	53	96	15	3	11	61	26	1	0	4	54	7	3	.497	.369
Andino, Robert...............	R-R	6-0	170	4-25-84	.255	.274	.248	120	498	70	127	18	4	6	46	33	4	8	6	100	13	11	.363	.303
Ashby, Chris..................	R-R	6-3	213	12-15-74	.308	.346	.295	68	198	27	61	12	0	4	38	16	2	0	3	38	1	0	.429	.361
Cepicky, Matt	L-R	6-2	215	11-10-77	.266	.293	.256	107	320	39	85	19	2	7	34	44	0	0	2	66	2	1	.403	.352
Colangelo, Mike	R-R	6-1	200	10-22-76	.318	.396	.285	65	176	32	56	17	0	5	21	21	9	0	2	35	0	2	.500	.413
Gonzalez, Edgar V.	R-R	6-0	182	6-14-78	.392	.400	.388	46	143	29	56	10	1	5	36	20	1	2	32	1	1	.580	.473
Hoover, Paul	R-R	6-1	200	4-14-76	.278	.366	.251	92	302	38	84	21	1	6	41	33	3	1	4	71	3	2	.414	.351
Kinkade, Mike	R-R	6-1	210	5-6-73	.328	.353	.319	106	381	59	125	26	3	4	50	29	22	1	3	56	6	5	.444	.405

2006 PERFORMANCE

General manager: Larry Beinfest. **Farm director:** Brian Chattin. **Scouting director:** Jim Fleming.

Class	Team	League	W	L	PCT	Finish*	Manager	Affiliate Since
Majors	Florida	National	78	84	.481	9th (16)	Joe Girardi	—
Triple-A	Albuquerque Isotopes	Pacific Coast	70	72	.493	10th (16)	Dean Treanor	2003
Double-A	Carolina Mudcats	Southern	61	79	.436	8th (10)	Luis Dorante	2003
High A	Jupiter Hammerheads	Florida State	55	80	.407	11th (12)	Tim Cossins	2002
Low A	Greensboro Grasshoppers	South Atlantic	68	69	.496	9th (16)	Brandon Hyde	2003
Short-season	Jamestown Jammers	New York-Penn	33	39	.458	11th (14)	Bo Porter	2002
Rookie	GCL Marlins	Gulf Coast	29	24	.547	5th (11)	Edwin Rodriguez	1992

OVERALL 2006 MINOR LEAGUE RECORD   316 363 .465   26th (30)

*Finish in overall standings (No. of teams in league). +League champion

	B-T	HT	WT	DOB	AVG	OBP	SLG	G	AB	R	H	2B	3B	HR	RBI	BB	SO	SB	CS	HBP	SH	SF	vLH	vRH
Little, Mark	R-R	6-0	190	7-11-72	.291	.240	.303	88	251	39	73	16	3	3	30	31	20	6	1	70	8	6	.414	.409
Niles, Drew	B-R	6-1	185	3-17-77	.237	.160	.252	63	152	8	36	5	1	1	11	17	0	3	2	38	1	2	.303	.310
Reed, Eric	L-L	5-11	170	12-2-80	.303	.260	.316	95	390	68	118	20	9	5	39	24	2	1	3	94	20	9	.438	.344
Rundgren, Rex	R-R	6-1	170	11-20-80	.192	.143	.211	8	26	1	5	1	0	0	2	1	0	0	0	4	0	0	.231	.222
Schrager, Tony	R-R	6-1	170	6-14-77	.254	.296	.222	27	63	12	16	4	1	1	8	7	2	0	0	21	0	0	.397	.347
Seabol, Scott	R-R	6-4	200	5-17-75	.314	.333	.310	71	242	39	76	18	1	17	46	29	4	0	4	55	0	3	.607	.391
Sears, Todd	L-R	6-6	205	10-23-75	.222	.000	.250	2	9	0	2	0	0	0	0	0	0	0	0	2	0	0	.222	.222
2-team (45 Tacoma)					.265			—	47		181	25	48	9	1	5	26	14	1	1	39	3	0	.409	.320
Shanks, James	R-R	6-0	190	1-26-79	.299	.262	.312	66	231	31	69	15	3	5	29	14	3	0	51	9	6	.455	.347
Stokes, Jason	R-R	6-4	225	1-23-82	.257	.316	.230	65	237	39	61	13	2	7	34	35	0	0	2	85	2	1	.418	.350
Trzesniak, Nick	R-R	6-0	210	11-19-80	.286	.294	.281	18	49	8	14	1	1	3	14	7	0	0	1	9	0	0	.531	.368
2-team (50 Oklahoma)					.262			—	68		210	28	55	10	1	4	26	22	0	3	2	38	4	2	.376	.329
Wilson, Tom	R-R	6-3	220	12-19-70	.299	.333	.288	86	278	49	83	24	0	10	46	31	2	1	3	68	1	2	.493	.369
Wood, Jason	R-R	6-1	200	12-16-69	.288	.325	.273	123	441	64	127	23	3	11	77	42	2	1	8	92	1	1	.429	.347

PITCHING	B-T	HT	WT	DOB	W	L	ERA	G	GS	CG	SV	IP	H	R	ER	HR	BB	SO	AVG	vLH	vRH	K/9	BB/9
Anderson, Jimmy	L-L	6-1	210	1-22-76	2	3	5.77	22	4	0	0	44	58	36	28	7	19	35	.326	.412	.291	7.21	3.92
Blank, Matt	L-L	6-2	190	4-5-76	2	2	4.98	14	7	0	0	47	56	28	26	7	24	28	.318	.345	.306	5.36	4.60
2-team (7 Portland)					3	3	5.64	21	10	0	0	68	80	46	43	10	32	38	—	—	—	4.98	4.19
Bostick, Adam	L-L	6-1	220	3-17-83	1	2	4.67	5	5	0	0	27	39	20	14	4	13	30	.339	.265	.370	10.00	4.33
Brower, Jim	R-R	6-3	215	12-29-72	0	1	3.93	15	0	0	0	18	20	9	8	3	3	13	.282	.351	.206	6.38	1.47
2-team (24 Portland)					5	3	4.61	39	0	0	1	52	57	30	27	8	21	41	—	—	—	7.01	3.59
Bump, Nate	R-R	6-2	195	7-24-76	0	2	6.35	6	2	0	0	11	23	9	8	2	6	6	.426	.286	.577	4.76	2.38
Carlyle, Buddy	L-R	6-3	185	12-21-77	3	1	1.93	13	2	0	0	28	17	6	6	3	7	22	.177	.171	.182	7.07	2.25
Clontz, Brad	R-R	6-1	195	4-25-71	6	5	3.57	57	0	0	23	58	58	29	23	4	14	54	.261	.259	.263	8.38	4.03
Fulchino, Jeff	R-R	6-5	250	11-26-79	6	10	4.50	25	24	0	0	140	144	82	70	12	56	109	.271	.288	.250	7.01	3.60
Gaillard, Eddie	R-R	6-1	180	8-13-70	2	1	3.91	22	0	0	1	25	27	16	11	2	12	22	.276	.231	.305	7.82	4.26
Garcia, Jose	R-R	5-11	165	1-7-85	0	1	11.25	1	1	0	0	4	5	5	5	0	4	5	.294	.429	.200	11.25	9.00
George, Chris	L-L	6-2	195	9-16-79	5	6	5.62	22	19	0	0	107	132	76	67	6	52	81	.311	.286	.323	6.79	4.36
German, Franklyn	R-R	6-7	260	1-20-80	0	1	8.53	8	0	0	0	6	11	6	6	0	2	6	.393	.462	.333	8.53	2.84
Horgan, Joe	L-L	6-1	200	6-7-77	5	6	3.98	45	0	0	3	43	36	19	19	6	17	32	.232	.194	.258	6.70	3.56
Kensing, Logan	R-R	6-1	185	7-3-82	1	1	3.00	13	0	0	2	18	11	6	6	2	5	18	.180	.273	.128	9.00	2.50
Lee, David	R-R	6-1	200	3-12-73	0	0	6.00	10	0	0	0	9	12	7	6	2	5	6	.300	.348	.235	6.00	5.00
2-team (22 Round Rock)					1	1	4.72	28	0	0	0	40	42	23	21	5	27	40	—	—	—	9.00	6.08
Messenger, Randy	R-R	6-6	245	8-13-81	0	0	9.00	4	0	0	0	3	1	3	3	0	1	3	.125	.333	.000	3.00	9.00
Miadich, J.B.	R-R	6-4	225	2-3-76	3	2	3.67	35	0	0	0	42	21	21	17	4	28	55	.147	.177	.123	11.88	6.05
Olsen, Scott	L-L	6-4	200	1-12-84	0	0	0.00	1	1	0	0	6	5	1	0	0	3	5	.227	.333	.188	7.11	4.26
Petit, Yusmeiro	R-R	6-0	180	11-22-84	4	6	4.28	17	17	0	0	97	101	53	46	14	20	68	.268	.289	.244	6.33	1.86
Pinto, Renyel	L-L	6-4	195	7-8-82	8	2	3.40	18	18	1	0	95	82	40	36	8	47	96	.232	.299	.203	9.06	4.44
Resop, Chris	R-R	6-3	220	11-4-82	4	0	3.81	40	0	0	2	50	49	21	21	4	15	43	.258	.287	.233	7.79	2.72
Rupe, Ryan	R-R	6-5	250	3-31-75	0	1	6.00	2	0	0	0	3	3	2	2	1	0	3	.273	.667	.125	9.00	0.00
Stewart, Josh	L-L	6-3	205	12-5-78	1	3	6.37	13	5	0	0	35	42	29	25	5	15	21	.309	.333	.301	5.35	3.82
Ungs, Nic	R-R	6-2	220	9-3-79	9	9	3.99	26	24	3	0	144	165	80	64	14	45	80	.289	.330	.252	4.99	2.81
Vargas, Jason	L-L	6-0	215	2-2-83	3	6	7.43	13	13	0	0	69	98	60	57	11	28	51	.348	.306	.362	6.65	3.65
Wilkerson, Wes	R-R	6-4	216	9-11-76	0	0	4.46	30	0	0	0	40	39	22	20	2	17	34	.247	.267	.222	7.59	3.79
Wolf, Ross	R-R	6-0	185	10-18-82	4	1	5.18	48	0	0	0	49	65	28	28	1	15	29	.335	.398	.277	5.36	2.77
Young, Christopher	R-R	6-4	218	4-19-81	1	0	12.00	3	0	0	0	6	12	10	8	1	5	2	.444	.417	.467	3.00	7.50
Yourkin, Matt	R-L	6-3	225	7-4-81	0	0	2.95	12	0	0	0	18	22	6	6	3	3	20	.310	.556	.226	9.82	1.47

FIELDING

Catcher	PCT	G	PO	A	E	DP	PB
Aceves	1.000	1	5	0	0	0	
Ashby	.989	25	162	12	2	1	7
Hoover	.981	86	565	59	12	8	10
Trzesniak	.983	15	112	6	2	0	1
Wilson	.962	23	164	14	7	2	0

First Base	PCT	G	PO	A	E	DP
Ashby	.991	13	104	7	1	14
Seabol	1.000	8	55	4	0	5
Sears	1.000	2	18	4	0	1
Stokes	.994	63	508	44	4	65
Wilson	.986	43	335	28	5	38
Wood	.990	20	186	10	2	23

Second Base	PCT	G	PO	A	E	DP
Andino	.955	5	8	13	1	5

	PCT	G	PO	A	E	DP
Gonzalez	.964	38	54	78	5	18
Niles	.995	47	81	108	1	37
Rundgren	1.000	4	5	4	0	0
Schrager	1.000	4	5	6	0	1
Seabol	.981	42	83	121	4	44
Wood	.992	24	56	61	1	16

Third Base	PCT	G	PO	A	E	DP
Kinkade	.922	71	55	133	16	13
Schrager	1.000	5	2	6	0	0
Seabol	.960	10	9	15	1	1
Wilson	.857	3	0	6	1	0
Wood	.947	65	49	128	10	19

Shortstop	PCT	G	PO	A	E	DP
Andino	.965	115	169	361	19	81
Niles	.905	5	2	17	2	4

	PCT	G	PO	A	E	DP
Rundgren	1.000	4	3	9	0	1
Schrager	1.000	4	0	13	0	0
Seabol	.988	15	29	51	1	14
Wood	1.000	2	4	8	0	2

Outfield	PCT	G	PO	A	E	DP
Aguila	.984	74	116	6	2	0
Ashby	1.000	16	16	1	0	0
Cepicky	.979	68	91	3	2	1
Colangelo	1.000	43	48	1	0	0
Kinkade	.957	26	43	1	2	0
Little	.964	78	130	5	5	1
Reed	.987	93	217	9	3	4
Schrager	1.000	5	10	0	0	0
Shanks	.980	59	95	5	2	0
Wood	1.000	1	3	1	0	0

Southern League

BATTING	B-T	HT	WT	DOB	AVG	vLH	vRH	G	AB	R	H	2B	3B	HR	RBI	BB	HBP	SH	SF	SO	SB	CS	SLG	OBP
Aceves, Jonathan	R-R	6-2	220	3-7-78	.238	.212	.247	81	252	37	60	22	0	6	31	21	5	2	2	63	0	1	.397	.307
Arlis, Patrick	R-R	6-0	215	12-18-80	.234	.281	.213	68	205	20	48	14	0	2	13	35	2	3	0	46	2	1	.332	.351
Athas, Jamie	L-R	6-2	190	10-14-79	.208	.186	.216	68	159	16	33	4	1	3	10	14	3	3	0	32	3	0	.302	.284
Bear, Ryan	R-R	6-2	220	1-26-81	.243	.264	.233	133	477	36	116	21	1	7	59	60	4	0	3	89	4	5	.335	.331
Brown, Greg	R-R	5-11	195	5-4-80	.000	.000	—	2	3	0	0	0	0	0	0	0	0	0	0	1	0	0	.000	.000
Campusano, Jose	B-R	5-11	165	12-19-83	.285	.243	.297	99	337	41	96	14	1	1	15	15	8	10	1	78	37	12	.341	.330
Carroll, Brett	R-R	6-0	190	10-3-82	.231	.235	.229	74	251	29	58	15	3	9	30	18	8	3	0	62	4	1	.422	.303
Cleveland, Brian	R-R	6-1	182	1-7-82	.216	.218	.215	38	134	16	29	4	1	1	7	8	1	5	0	28	1	0	.284	.266
De Aza, Alejandro	L-L	6-0	174	4-11-84	.278	.218	.297	69	230	40	64	12	2	2	16	21	4	9	2	46	27	10	.374	.346
Garbe, B.J.	R-R	6-2	195	2-3-81	.184	.172	.188	35	98	12	18	5	0	3	8	7	1	0	1	28	4	2	.327	.243
Gendron, Steve	R-R	6-3	195	11-25-81	.500	.500	—	2	2	0	1	0	0	0	1	0	0	0	0	0	0	1	.500	.500
Gonzalez, Edgar V.	R-R	6-0	182	6-14-78	.295	.277	.303	64	210	19	62	10	3	6	25	24	3	0	3	37	9	6	.457	.371
Hill, Jason	R-R	6-3	210	3-17-77	.211	.143	.256	24	71	6	15	4	0	0	11	8	2	1	2	16	0	0	.268	.301
Mitchell, Lee	R-R	6-1	198	4-21-82	.253	.234	.262	131	462	56	117	37	1	11	56	46	8	1	3	139	2	6	.409	.329
Molina, Angel	R-R	6-2	226	11-4-81	.233	.246	.227	67	189	15	44	12	0	3	21	24	3	1	1	44	3	2	.344	.327
Moore, Frank	L-R	6-2	213	7-2-78	.210	.196	.216	46	157	14	33	5	1	2	12	15	1	2	1	34	4	3	.293	.282
Muniz, JC	R-R	6-1	175	1-28-76	.248	.235	.256	66	206	28	51	15	1	9	27	21	0	2	0	56	1	1	.461	.317
Pressley, Josh	L-R	6-6	240	4-2-80	.231	.320	.175	24	65	2	15	1	1	0	7	11	0	0	1	13	1	0	.277	.338
Randel, Kevin	L-R	6-1	180	6-11-81	.280	.250	.289	123	325	54	91	26	2	12	57	47	6	5	8	87	3	3	.483	.376
Rundgren, Rex	R-R	6-1	170	11-20-80	.232	.248	.224	113	371	33	86	10	0	0	28	33	3	12	1	81	1	4	.259	.299
Schrager, Tony	R-R	6-1	170	6-14-77	.391	.375	.400	13	46	8	18	5	1	0	3	6	0	1	0	2	0	2	.543	.462
Tucker, Michael	R-R	6-3	225	11-7-79	.289	.385	.240	22	38	5	11	3	0	0	2	7	1	0	0	13	0	0	.368	.413
Willingham, Josh	R-R	6-1	200	2-17-79	.250	.000	.286	2	8	0	2	0	0	0	0	0	0	0	0	3	0	0	.250	.250

PITCHING	B-T	HT	WT	DOB	W	L	ERA	G	GS	CG	SV	IP	H	R	ER	HR	BB	SO	AVG	vLH	vRH	K/9	BB/9
Athas, Jamie	L-R	6-2	190	10-14-79	0	0	4.50	2	0	0	0	2	4	1	1	0	1	0	.500	—	.500	0.00	4.50
Barone, Daniel	R-R	6-2	185	4-24-83	1	0	1.80	3	2	0	0	20	13	4	4	1	6	13	.183	.222	.159	5.85	2.70
Blank, Matt	L-L	6-2	190	4-5-76	1	0	1.50	7	0	0	0	12	10	2	2	1	7	11	.233	.133	.286	8.25	5.25
Bostick, Adam	L-L	6-2	220	3-17-83	8	7	3.52	22	22	0	0	115	100	58	45	7	67	109	.235	.218	.241	8.53	5.24
Brandenburg, Adam	L-L	6-5	225	8-17-81	1	2	7.01	21	3	0	0	35	46	31	27	3	19	20	.319	.316	.321	5.19	4.93
Brauer, James	R-R	6-4	210	7-16-82	1	0	0.00	1	1	0	0	6	4	0	0	0	2	2	.200	.200	.200	3.00	3.00
Cave, Kevin	R-R	6-2	220	5-25-80	3	2	4.21	43	0	0	5	51	55	31	24	6	34	43	.268	.256	.279	7.54	5.96
Garcia, Jose	R-R	5-11	165	1-7-85	6	7	3.40	14	14	0	0	85	78	37	32	10	25	87	.242	.273	.221	9.25	2.66
Humen, David	R-R	6-2	210	6-11-81	0	0	0.00	1	1	0	0	5	4	0	0	0	4	6	.211	.200	.222	10.80	7.20
Hutchinson, Trevor	R-R	6-5	220	10-8-79	1	4	10.61	5	4	0	0	19	39	25	22	4	2	9	.443	.412	.463	4.34	0.96
Julianel, Ben	S-L	6-2	180	9-4-79	1	3	2.38	7	6	0	0	34	24	12	9	0	8	22	.195	.204	.188	5.82	2.12
Koehler, Kurt	R-R	6-1	190	9-5-84	0	0	4.50	2	0	0	0	2	3	1	1	0	1	1	.333	.500	.286	4.50	4.50
McNutt, Michael	R-R	6-2	190	10-18-79	0	0	11.57	6	0	0	0	7	12	9	9	1	5	5	.375	.100	.500	6.43	1.29
Mildren, Paul	R-L	6-1	160	5-3-84	10	10	4.14	28	28	2	0	167	161	88	77	19	54	150	.255	.246	.266	8.07	2.90
Mobley, Chris	R-R	5-11	171	8-16-83	1	4	3.99	52	0	0	4	59	58	27	26	5	30	51	.259	.288	.243	7.82	4.57
Nestor, Scott	R-R	6-4	225	8-20-84	2	2	7.43	12	0	0	0	13	18	15	11	1	13	13	.310	.474	.231	8.78	8.78
Olivera, Manuel	R-L	5-11	205	12-8-77	5	9	3.99	25	17	0	0	108	120	55	48	4	39	65	.286	.257	.295	5.40	3.24
Rundgren, Rex	R-R	6-1	170	11-20-80	0	0	0.00	1	0	0	0	1	0	0	0	0	1	0	.000	.000	—	0.00	9.00
Russ, James	R-R	6-4	210	10-24-80	6	10	3.80	28	27	1	0	156	154	74	66	16	63	125	.261	.248	.272	7.20	3.63
Sanchez, Anibal	R-R	6-0	180	2-27-84	3	6	3.15	15	15	2	0	86	82	41	30	7	27	92	.246	.228	.261	9.67	2.84
Tankersley, Taylor	L-L	6-1	220	3-7-83	4	1	0.95	22	0	0	6	28	11	4	3	0	14	40	.125	.147	.111	12.71	4.45
Tyler, Scott	R-R	6-5	265	8-20-82	1	2	3.67	48	0	0	3	61	56	29	25	5	44	52	.239	.253	.231	7.63	6.46
Wolf, Ross	R-R	6-0	185	10-18-82	1	2	1.00	12	0	0	0	18	12	3	2	0	2	12	.190	.226	.156	6.00	1.00
Young, Christopher	R-R	6-4	218	4-19-81	4	4	2.42	46	0	0	12	71	60	24	19	1	18	61	.233	.230	.234	7.77	2.29
Yourkin, Matt	R-L	6-3	225	7-4-81	1	4	3.91	44	0	0	3	48	45	22	21	2	25	47	.251	.292	.228	8.75	4.66

FIELDING

Catcher	PCT	G	PO	A	E	DP	PB
Aceves	.990	75	585	36	6	4	5
Arlis	.990	67	454	40	5	4	6
Brown	1.000	2	9	0	0	0	0
Hill	1.000	4	21	1	0	0	0

First Base	PCT	G	PO	A	E	DP
Aceves	—	1	0	0	0	0
Athas	.988	14	79	4	1	4
Bear	.992	103	775	62	7	55
Hill	.991	15	107	8	1	10
Moore	1.000	4	5	2	0	1
Pressley	.987	19	149	7	2	12
Randel	1.000	1	2	0	0	0
Tucker	1.000	6	32	1	0	5

Second Base	PCT	G	PO	A	E	DP
Athas	.980	18	21	27	1	6
Cleveland	1.000	30	51	92	0	12

	PCT	G	PO	A	E	DP
Gonzalez	.959	32	53	63	5	13
Moore	.800	2	3	1	1	1
Randel	.971	76	118	179	9	33
Rundgren	1.000	3	3	5	0	2
Schrager	1.000	5	5	2	0	2
Tucker	1.000	4	3	2	0	0

Third Base	PCT	G	PO	A	E	DP
Athas	1.000	7	4	7	0	1
Gonzalez	.833	11	10	15	5	1
Mitchell	.972	117	71	208	8	13
Moore	1.000	1	0	1	0	0
Randel	.932	20	11	30	3	2
Schrager	.500	2	1	0	1	0
Tucker	1.000	3	3	5	0	0

Shortstop	PCT	G	PO	A	E	DP
Athas	.975	21	28	49	2	6
Campusano	—	1	1	0	0	0

	PCT	G	PO	A	E	DP
Cleveland	.900	6	10	17	3	6
Gonzalez	.964	18	9	44	2	7
Randel	—	1	0	0	0	0
Rundgren	.949	107	143	264	22	55
Schrager	.960	7	9	15	1	1

Outfield	PCT	G	PO	A	E	DP
Athas	—	1	0	0	0	0
Bear	1.000	39	48	0	0	0
Campusano	.943	87	140	8	9	2
Carroll	.984	73	169	19	3	5
De Aza	.961	66	145	1	6	0
Garbe	1.000	31	37	4	0	1
Hill	1.000	3	2	0	0	0
Molina	.963	60	73	4	3	0
Moore	.970	42	61	3	2	1
Muniz	.952	64	99	1	5	0
Schrager	.900	4	9	0	1	0
Willingham	1.000	2	3	0	0	0

Florida State League

BATTING	B-T	HT	WT	DOB	AVG	vLH	vRH	G	AB	R	H	2B	3B	HR	RBI	BB	HBP	SH	SF	SO	SB	CS	SLG	OBP
Ambrosini, Dominick	L-L	5-10	185	2-21-81	.165	.091	.185	38	103	8	17	4	1	1	8	6	2	0	2	31	1	2	.252	.221
Brinkley, Dante	R-R	5-11	180	8-21-81	.234	.220	.239	116	406	64	95	19	4	8	48	53	20	4	5	139	34	13	.360	.347
Brown, Greg	R-R	5-11	195	5-4-80	.162	.100	.177	35	99	8	16	2	0	0	4	6	1	2	0	35	1	0	.182	.217
Carroll, Brett	R-R	6-0	190	10-3-82	.241	.235	.242	59	216	31	52	12	1	8	30	16	9	0	1	48	9	3	.417	.324

ORGANIZATION STATISTICS

Cleveland, Brian	R-R	6-1	182	1-7-82	.238	.163	.257	63	240	29	57	14	0	1	17	14	7	8	3	41	7	3	.308	.295
D'Antonio, Trent	B-R	5-9	180	8-14-85	.250	—	.250	2	4	0	1	0	0	0	0	1	0	0	0	0	1	0	.250	.400
Davis, Bradley	R-R	6-2	185	12-29-82	.262	.281	.256	106	347	43	91	21	1	4	46	34	5	7	1	62	5	5	.363	.336
De Aza, Alejandro	L-L	6-0	174	4-11-84	.143	.000	.250	2	7	1	1	0	1	0	0	0	0	1	0	2	0	1	.429	.143
Figueroa, Juan	L-L	6-0	200	12-9-81	.207	.276	.186	77	241	27	50	9	1	8	35	26	1	1	3	78	3	3	.353	.284
Gaston, Jared	R-R	6-2	195	4-15-84	.167	.000	.286	6	12	1	2	0	0	0	2	1	0	1	0	4	0	0	.167	.231
Gendron, Steve	R-R	6-3	195	11-25-81	.223	.169	.243	86	273	19	61	6	1	0	14	16	3	4	3	78	8	5	.253	.271
Gonzalez, Edgar V.	R-R	6-0	182	6-14-78	.293	.385	.274	21	75	10	22	8	0	2	10	6	0	1	1	18	1	3	.480	.341
Gonzalez, Juan	R-R	6-0	165	2-23-82	.254	.458	.206	36	126	16	32	2	1	1	11	15	1	1	2	33	7	5	.310	.333
Hermida, Jeremy	L-R	6-4	200	1-30-84	.176	.143	.200	6	17	3	3	1	0	0	2	3	0	0	0	7	0	0	.235	.300
Langley, Torre	R-R	5-9	175	10-9-87	.286	.000	.333	3	7	1	2	1	0	0	2	0	0	0	0	4	0	0	.429	.286
Lisk, Charles	R-R	6-3	206	1-3-83	.000	.000	.000	4	6	0	0	0	0	0	0	1	0	0	0	2	0	0	.000	.143
McCallum, Geoff	B-R	6-0	185	11-22-77	.185	.172	.190	32	108	13	20	1	1	0	9	11	1	3	2	16	2	1	.213	.262
McCann, Brad	R-R	6-3	190	12-9-82	.231	.270	.219	121	458	47	106	23	0	12	40	32	5	0	1	108	3	5	.360	.288
Miller, Jai	R-R	6-4	195	1-17-85	.209	.173	.219	111	344	40	72	16	2	0	24	45	5	5	2	115	24	10	.267	.308
Moore, Frank	L-R	6-2	213	7-2-78	.421	.167	.538	5	19	2	8	3	0	0	1	3	0	0	1	3	0	1	.579	.478
Muniz, JC	R-R	6-1	175	1-28-76	.239	.111	.279	35	113	10	27	3	0	4	15	11	3	1	0	23	2	4	.372	.323
Padgett, Kyle	R-R	6-1	185	1-16-83	.214	.286	.190	20	56	3	12	2	0	1	4	5	1	1	0	20	0	4	.304	.290
Piste, Carlos	B-R	6-1	179	3-8-85	.218	.222	.217	67	211	27	46	8	2	2	19	18	4	8	2	54	3	4	.303	.289
Psomas, Grant	R-R	6-3	210	9-2-82	.291	.346	.275	92	358	39	104	25	0	8	53	28	2	0	5	64	7	2	.427	.341
Restko, J.T.	R-R	6-5	190	12-15-84	.255	.189	.275	87	314	30	80	10	1	6	34	26	7	0	1	70	0	1	.350	.325
Roberson, Colin	R-R	6-5	205	7-15-83	.246	.100	.275	16	61	6	15	4	1	0	2	1	0	0	0	15	0	2	.344	.258
Rogers, Tanner	R-R	6-0	180	1-11-85	.143	.125	.154	15	21	2	3	0	0	0	0	2	0	0	0	6	4	0	.143	.217
Sanchez, Gabriel	R-R	6-2	225	9-2-83	.182	.211	.167	16	55	13	10	3	1	1	7	12	0	0	1	12	1	0	.327	.324
Varela, Edgar	L-R	6-1	213	8-9-80	.160	.125	.183	32	100	5	16	5	0	1	6	7	1	0	0	24	0	0	.240	.222
Webb, Justin	R-R	6-1	175	11-5-82	.000	.000	.000	2	2	0	0	0	0	0	0	0	0	0	0	1	0	0	.000	.000
Witt, Paul	R-R	5-11	180	12-8-82	.108	.143	.087	15	37	3	4	0	0	0	1	0	1	2	0	10	1	0	.108	.132

PITCHING	B-T	HT	WT	DOB	W	L	ERA	G	GS	CG	SV	IP	H	R	ER	HR	BB	SO	AVG	vLH	vRH	K/9	BB/9
Barone, Daniel	R-R	6-2	185	4-24-83	3	5	4.30	17	8	0	0	73	84	44	35	9	18	57	.289	.282	.293	7.00	2.21
Baxter, Allen	R-R	6-4	215	7-6-83	0	0	9.64	5	0	0	0	5	5	8	5	0	8	4	.238	.286	.214	7.71	15.43
Brandenburg, Adam	L-L	6-5	225	8-17-81	4	1	3.38	18	2	0	0	40	35	24	15	1	25	28	.241	.333	.211	6.30	5.63
Brauer, James	R-R	6-4	210	7-16-82	5	8	5.56	21	20	0	0	102	128	73	63	14	32	57	.307	.312	.302	5.03	2.82
Camilo, Juan	R-R	6-3	168	4-22-83	0	0	0.00	1	0	0	0	1	1	0	0	0	0	0	.250	.000	.500	0.00	0.00
Castor, Parrish	L-L	6-2	180	9-18-83	0	1	9.00	1	0	0	0	1	1	1	1	0	2	1	.250	.000	.333	9.00	18.00
Delgado, Jesus	R-R	6-1	200	4-19-84	2	4	2.58	28	0	0	0	38	33	19	11	0	18	40	.231	.258	.208	9.39	4.23
Doolittle, Michael	R-R	5-10	175	11-1-82	3	1	0.84	16	0	0	0	21	12	2	2	0	7	26	.160	.226	.114	10.97	2.95
Figueroa, Juan	L-L	6-0	200	12-9-81	0	0	27.00	1	0	0	0	1	4	3	3	0	1	0	.667	1.000	.600	0.00	9.00
Garcia, Harvey	R-R	6-2	170	3-16-84	0	7	2.92	55	0	0	21	65	54	27	21	5	32	83	.221	.229	.216	11.55	4.45
Garcia, Jose	R-R	5-11	165	1-7-85	6	2	1.87	12	11	1	0	77	60	31	16	3	16	69	.210	.221	.201	8.06	1.87
German, Franklyn	R-R	6-7	260	1-20-80	0	0	0.00	4	4	0	0	4	2	0	0	0	1	1	.143	.000	.250	2.25	2.25
Goyen, Matthew	R-L	6-5	220	1-19-83	2	5	4.60	16	16	0	0	86	90	48	44	6	27	56	.266	.266	.266	5.86	2.83
Hernandez, Gabriel	R-R	6-3	210	5-21-86	9	7	3.68	21	20	0	0	120	120	60	49	7	35	115	.259	.288	.233	8.63	2.63
Hutchinson, Trevor	R-R	6-5	220	10-8-79	3	3	3.27	16	11	0	0	72	82	37	26	3	19	45	.283	.261	.303	5.65	2.39
Jackson, Andy	L-L	6-1	185	8-8-83	0	0	0.00	1	0	0	0	1	1	0	0	0	0	0	.333	—	.333	0.00	0.00
Jarrett, Jason	R-R	6-5	195	5-29-82	1	2	2.82	27	0	0	0	45	44	21	14	2	21	29	.256	.299	.221	5.84	4.23
Jones, Blake	R-R	6-5	220	4-15-81	2	2	3.72	7	0	0	0	10	10	4	4	0	2	6	.294	.182	.348	5.59	1.86
Koehler, Kurt	R-R	6-1	190	9-5-84	0	0	0.00	5	0	0	1	8	5	0	0	0	1	11	.179	.125	.200	12.38	1.13
Letson, Wes	L-L	6-0	200	9-13-82	1	0	3.05	18	0	0	0	21	15	9	7	2	7	10	.192	.150	.207	4.35	3.05
Madden, Corey	R-R	6-1	195	3-30-84	0	0	7.36	2	0	0	0	4	7	3	3	0	1	2	.412	.500	.385	4.91	2.45
Mangieri, John	R-R	6-2	200	9-24-76	3	2	3.07	30	0	0	1	41	38	15	14	3	12	28	.248	.353	.165	6.15	2.63
Marceaux, Jacob	R-R	6-1	195	2-14-84	4	11	3.99	22	22	1	0	117	115	65	52	8	49	80	.254	.265	.247	6.14	3.76
Martinez, Carlos	R-R	6-1	170	5-26-82	0	0	0.00	2	1	0	0	2	0	0	0	0	1	0	.000	.000	.000	0.00	4.50
Messenger, Randy	R-R	6-6	245	8-13-81	0	0	0.00	1	0	0	0	1	1	0	0	0	0	1	.250	.000	.500	9.00	0.00
Molldrem, Craig	R-R	6-6	205	9-17-81	0	2	3.68	6	0	0	0	7	8	5	3	1	3	6	.258	.500	.200	7.36	3.68
Nestor, Scott	R-R	6-4	225	8-20-84	2	2	2.52	33	0	0	10	39	19	12	11	0	26	48	.142	.154	.130	10.98	5.95
Olivera, Manuel	R-L	5-11	205	12-8-77	1	0	5.30	10	1	0	0	19	19	13	11	1	5	20	.268	.111	.321	9.64	2.41
Padgett, Kyle	R-R	6-1	185	1-16-83	0	0	0.00	1	0	0	0	1	2	0	0	0	0	0	.400	.500	.000	0.00	0.00
Santos, Jarrett	R-R	6-4	215	8-18-81	2	6	1.84	42	0	0	0	83	78	29	17	3	14	51	.241	.226	.253	5.51	1.51
Talbott, Travis	L-L	5-11	175	5-23-82	0	1	2.31	10	0	0	0	12	17	10	3	1	3	8	.340	.316	.355	6.17	2.31
Vanden Hurk, Rick	R-R	6-5	195	5-22-85	0	0	2.70	3	3	0	0	10	5	4	3	1	6	15	.147	.133	.158	13.50	5.40
Wood, Timothy	R-R	6-1	185	11-16-82	2	7	5.83	16	16	0	0	63	65	43	41	4	25	52	.273	.305	.248	7.39	3.55
Young, Christopher	R-R	6-4	218	4-19-81	0	1	3.00	2	0	0	0	3	4	1	1	0	0	2	.333	.250	.375	6.00	0.00

FIELDING

Catcher	PCT	G	PO	A	E	DP	PB
Brown	.974	34	198	23	6	3	6
D'Antonio	1.000	2	12	0	0	0	0
Davis	.990	103	726	58	8	7	8
Langley	1.000	3	12	1	0	0	0
Lisk	1.000	2	2	1	0	0	0
Rogers	1.000	7	29	3	0	1	0
Sanchez	.800	1	3	1	1	0	1

First Base	PCT	G	PO	A	E	DP
Ambrosini	1.000	4	18	2	0	0
Davis	1.000	1	5	1	0	1
Figueroa	.988	37	296	22	4	31
Gendron	1.000	5	24	4	0	1
Lisk	.500	1	1	0	1	0
McCann	.991	91	781	62	8	64
Sanchez	1.000	7	51	3	0	6
Varela	1.000	1	3	0	0	0

Second Base	PCT	G	PO	A	E	DP
Cleveland	.968	48	92	152	8	33
Gendron	.927	32	53	86	11	16
E. Gonzalez	.974	17	27	47	2	7
Moore	.875	2	2	5	1	2
Padgett	.938	15	22	39	4	8
Piste	.978	22	42	46	2	12
Rogers	1.000	1	0	2	0	1
Webb	—	1	0	0	0	0
Witt	1.000	7	10	13	0	2

Third Base	PCT	G	PO	A	E	DP
Gendron	.939	19	11	35	3	7
Padgett	1.000	2	2	1	0	0
Psomas	.911	84	65	149	21	7
Sanchez	.929	7	2	11	1	2
Varela	.921	29	10	60	6	5
Webb	—	1	0	0	0	0
Witt	—	1	0	0	0	0

Shortstop	PCT	G	PO	A	E	DP
Cleveland	.923	13	14	34	4	9
Gendron	.947	10	13	23	2	6
E. Gonzalez	1.000	2	0	1	0	0
J. Gonzalez	.926	36	54	120	14	16
McCallum	.929	31	37	81	9	14
Padgett	1.000	2	0	1	0	0
Piste	.937	45	60	119	12	23
Witt	.966	7	14	14	1	6

Outfield	PCT	G	PO	A	E	DP
Ambrosini	1.000	33	52	3	0	2
Brinkley	.975	109	224	8	6	4
Carroll	.952	56	92	8	5	3
De Aza	.750	2	6	0	2	0
Figueroa	1.000	11	17	0	0	0
Gaston	1.000	4	3	0	0	0
Gendron	1.000	19	27	3	0	1
Hermida	1.000	4	3	0	0	0
Miller	.996	104	248	2	1	0
Moore	1.000	2	2	1	0	0
Muniz	.977	23	38	4	1	0
Restko	.953	56	76	5	4	0
Roberson	.917	10	10	1	1	0
Witt	—	1	0	0	0	0

South Atlantic League

BATTING

BATTING	B-T	HT	WT	DOB	AVG	vLH	vRH	G	AB	R	H	2B	3B	HR	RBI	BB	HBP	SH	SF	SO	SB	CS	SLG	OBP
Adduci, James	L-L	6-2	185	5-15-85	.000	—	.000	2	3	1	0	0	0	0	0	0	0	0	0	1	0	0	.000	.000
Batista, Norberto	R-R	6-1	150	8-5-83	.059	.000	.067	12	17	1	1	0	0	0	0	0	1	0	1	0	5	0	0	.059	.111
Batz, Daniel	R-R	6-2	210	3-19-82	.096	.100	.094	28	83	5	8	4	0	0	3	7	1	0	1	10	0	0	.145	.174
Burns, Gregory	L-L	6-2	185	11-7-86	.231	.109	.259	105	342	44	79	13	8	2	23	38	0	6	1	109	20	13	.333	.307
Correll, Brad	R-R	6-2	205	6-17-81	.254	.174	.273	35	122	23	31	6	1	8	24	17	7	0	1	19	3	2	.516	.374
D'Antonio, Trent	B-R	5-9	180	8-14-85	.245	.227	.247	64	204	26	50	8	1	12	34	19	3	4	2	37	6	3	.471	.316
Figueroa, Juan	L-L	6-0	200	12-9-81	.264	.333	.250	31	110	12	29	5	0	2	12	11	1	0	0	25	1	0	.364	.336
Fulton, Jonathan	R-R	6-4	200	12-1-83	.262	.211	.278	110	385	48	101	26	1	12	43	22	5	0	3	108	4	3	.429	.308
Gaston, Jared	R-R	6-2	195	4-15-84	.221	.105	.259	45	154	18	34	7	1	2	15	8	6	1	1	42	6	3	.318	.284
Guerrero, James	R-R	5-7	175	6-8-84	.226	.169	.241	108	372	61	84	18	1	5	28	65	9	4	4	54	7	11	.320	.351
Harvey, Kris	R-R	6-2	195	1-5-84	.245	.263	.241	96	367	46	90	18	2	15	60	24	1	0	3	82	9	4	.428	.291
Hayes, Brett	R-R	6-2	200	2-13-84	.245	.255	.242	82	278	39	68	13	1	9	38	29	4	1	4	61	4	3	.396	.321
Jenkins, Andrew	R-R	6-0	205	7-23-83	.288	.394	.261	128	479	52	138	26	2	5	73	41	10	0	5	89	6	4	.382	.353
Kutler, Matthew	L-L	6-0	185	2-25-82	.283	.348	.275	67	205	21	58	13	0	1	20	10	3	1	0	33	0	2	.361	.326
Roberson, Colin	R-R	6-5	205	7-15-83	.222	.152	.245	51	189	22	42	8	1	3	17	12	0	0	0	65	11	4	.323	.269
Roche, Gary	R-R	5-11	180	12-28-83	.252	.239	.255	94	322	35	81	14	1	2	25	23	8	5	1	52	2	2	.320	.316
Rogers, Tanner	R-R	6-0	180	1-11-85	.238	.333	.200	9	21	3	5	0	0	1	3	2	1	0	0	7	0	1	.381	.333
Sanchez, Gabriel	R-R	6-2	225	9-2-83	.317	.406	.299	55	189	43	60	12	0	14	40	39	7	0	2	20	6	2	.603	.447
Septimo, Agustin	L-R	5-11	170	5-27-84	.263	.188	.286	74	289	44	76	10	2	7	25	30	1	5	1	71	20	3	.384	.333
Van Houten, Jeffrey	R-R	5-10	175	11-14-82	.246	.200	.257	75	268	41	66	14	2	14	47	31	2	0	2	66	2	2	.470	.327
Walton, Jamar	L-R	6-4	195	1-5-86	.000	—	.000	2	1	0	0	0	0	0	0	0	0	0	0	1	0	0	.000	.000
Webb, Justin	R-R	6-1	175	11-5-82	.000	.000	.000	3	8	0	0	0	0	0	0	1	0	1	0	2	0	0	.000	.000
Westerfeld, Travis	R-R	6-2	200	12-17-83	.500	—	.500	1	2	0	1	0	0	0	1	0	0	0	0	1	0	0	.500	.500
Witt, Paul	R-R	5-11	180	12-8-82	.240	.370	.210	56	146	21	35	4	0	0	7	14	3	5	1	24	7	2	.267	.317

PITCHING

PITCHING	B-T	HT	WT	DOB	W	L	ERA	G	GS	CG	SV	IP	H	R	ER	HR	BB	SO	AVG	vLH	vRH	K/9	BB/9
Barone, Daniel	R-R	6-2	185	4-24-83	4	0	2.39	9	6	0	0	49	36	15	13	1	9	60	.199	.167	.213	11.02	1.65
Camilo, Juan	R-R	6-3	168	4-22-83	0	0	27.00	1	0	0	0	1	2	3	3	1	0	2	.400	.000	.500	18.00	9.00
Doolittle, Michael	R-R	5-10	175	11-1-82	4	1	1.37	30	2	0	2	59	36	11	9	1	21	79	.176	.148	.194	12.05	3.20
Fountain, Joel	R-R	6-4	175	11-10-83	1	0	0.00	2	1	0	0	6	6	0	0	0	1	1	.261	.222	.286	1.50	1.50
Galbizo, Rafael	R-R	6-1	185	2-18-85	4	7	5.22	41	5	0	0	79	72	53	46	9	39	50	.251	.260	.246	5.67	4.42
Goyen, Matthew	R-L	6-5	220	1-19-83	0	0	4.50	2	2	0	0	8	8	5	4	2	3	8	.276	.400	.250	9.00	3.38
Humen, David	R-R	6-2	210	6-11-81	2	3	4.39	30	8	0	0	70	61	40	34	7	36	62	.234	.188	.271	8.01	4.65
Iehl, Jason	R-R	6-2	185	4-23-84	3	3	2.55	33	0	0	1	53	38	23	15	3	31	49	.198	.169	.211	8.32	5.26
Jackson, Andy	L-L	6-1	185	8-8-83	0	0	13.50	1	0	0	0	2	5	3	3	0	1	2	.455	.333	.500	9.00	4.50
Jarrett, Jason	R-R	6-5	195	5-29-82	0	0	2.25	3	0	0	0	4	1	1	1	1	2	4	.083	.000	.125	9.00	4.50
Jones, Blake	R-R	6-5	220	4-15-81	6	5	4.73	45	0	0	17	51	57	27	27	3	24	66	.285	.400	.230	11.57	4.21
Lamacchia, Marc	R-R	6-1	190	3-27-82	1	2	5.88	15	4	0	0	34	40	22	22	3	8	28	.303	.250	.333	7.49	2.14
Leroux, Christopher	L-R	6-6	210	4-14-84	0	3	6.10	3	3	0	0	10	13	7	7	2	6	9	.325	.500	.281	7.84	5.23
Letson, Wes	L-L	6-0	200	9-13-82	2	0	1.23	7	0	0	1	7	8	5	1	1	4	11	.276	.100	.368	13.50	4.91
Rasowky, Avi	L-L	6-1	195	5-17-83	1	1	6.16	9	2	0	0	19	26	13	13	2	3	16	.325	.476	.271	7.58	1.42
Santos, Jarrett	R-R	6-4	215	8-18-81	0	0	1.59	6	0	0	0	11	9	3	2	1	1	5	.214	.333	.167	3.97	0.79
Sinkbeil, Brett	R-R	6-2	170	12-26-84	1	1	4.99	8	8	0	0	40	45	22	22	5	14	32	.290	.226	.333	7.26	3.18
Sosa, Alexis	S-L	6-1	160	6-25-83	0	0	8.53	7	0	0	0	6	9	6	6	2	3	4	.259	.143	.300	5.68	4.26
Stone, Bradley	R-R	6-3	190	5-20-84	1	3	2.10	20	0	0	4	34	36	13	8	2	11	17	.279	.278	.280	4.46	2.88
Talbott, Travis	L-L	5-11	175	5-23-82	1	1	1.69	31	0	0	0	43	38	11	8	1	13	36	.255	.348	.214	7.59	2.74
Thompson, Aaron	L-L	6-3	195	2-28-87	8	8	3.63	24	24	0	0	134	139	68	54	12	35	114	.270	.239	.277	7.66	2.35
Tucker, Ryan	R-R	6-2	190	12-6-86	7	13	5.00	25	25	2	0	131	123	86	73	14	67	133	.246	.249	.243	9.11	4.59
Volstad, Christopher	R-R	6-7	190	9-23-86	11	8	3.08	26	26	0	0	152	161	73	52	12	36	99	.275	.298	.259	5.86	2.13
West, Sean	L-L	6-8	200	6-15-86	8	5	3.74	21	21	0	0	120	115	55	50	13	40	102	.255	.215	.263	7.63	2.99
Witt, Paul	R-R	5-11	180	12-8-82	0	0	0.00	1	0	0	0	0	2	0	0	0	0	0	.667	.500	1.000	0.00	0.00
Zabala, Felix	R-R	5-10	150	7-1-84	0	0	0.00	1	0	0	0	0	1	0	0	0	1	0	.500	—	.500	0.00	27.00
Zarate, Mauro	R-R	6-1	180	2-8-83	3	5	3.19	53	0	0	7	79	75	33	28	7	30	80	.244	.207	.269	9.11	3.42

FIELDING

Catcher	PCT	G	PO	A	E	DP	PB
D'Antonio	.979	22	176	12	4	0	6
Hayes	.993	71	517	61	4	8	14
Jenkins	.991	39	300	26	3	1	4
Rogers	.933	3	10	4	1	0	0
Sanchez	1.000	9	54	9	0	0	3
Webb	1.000	1	14	0	0	0	1
Westerfeld	1.000	1	5	0	0	0	0

First Base	PCT	G	PO	A	E	DP
Adduci	.500	1	1	0	1	1
Batz	.989	11	82	6	1	15
Figueroa	.995	22	185	14	1	11
Hayes	—	1	0	0	0	0
Jenkins	.992	63	559	28	5	51
Roche	1.000	2	15	1	0	0
Sanchez	.990	40	364	23	4	34
Witt	.972	6	30	5	1	4

Second Base	PCT	G	PO	A	E	DP
Batista	1.000	5	0	1	0	0
Guerrero	.969	71	136	207	11	35
Roche	.982	68	108	169	5	40
Van Houten	1.000	5	7	6	0	2
Webb	1.000	1	2	2	0	0
Witt	.800	1	3	1	1	0

Third Base	PCT	G	PO	A	E	DP
Batista	.867	5	3	10	2	1
Fulton	.948	106	62	209	15	23
Guerrero	1.000	1	0	2	0	0
Jenkins	.943	14	8	25	2	2
Roche	.929	20	6	33	3	4
Webb	—	1	0	0	0	0
Witt	.714	2	1	4	2	0

Shortstop	PCT	G	PO	A	E	DP
Batista	—	1	0	0	0	0

	PCT	G	PO	A	E	DP
Fulton	1.000	2	1	3	0	1
Guerrero	.965	37	55	111	6	22
Septimo	.955	71	112	229	16	42
Witt	.925	35	54	94	12	14

Outfield	PCT	G	PO	A	E	DP
Batz	1.000	11	15	1	0	0
Burns	.991	103	210	6	2	1
Correll	.979	34	44	2	1	1
DAntonio	.000	1	0	0	2	0
Figueroa	1.000	7	6	1	0	0
Gaston	.971	42	63	3	2	0
Harvey	.921	75	121	8	11	2
Kutler	1.000	41	53	2	0	0
Roberson	.947	51	83	7	5	1
Rogers	.857	4	6	0	1	0
Van Houten	1.000	56	81	4	0	0
Witt	1.000	8	10	2	0	0

New York-Penn League

BATTING	B-T	HT	WT	DOB	AVG	vLH	vRH	G	AB	R	H	2B	3B	HR	RBI	BB	HBP	SH	SF	SO	SB	CS	SLG	OBP
Agustin, Juan	R-R	5-11	160	10-30-84	.200	.000	.308	9	20	2	4	0	1	0	1	0	0	0	0	7	0	0	.300	.200
Blackwood, Jacob	R-R	6-0	195	9-14-85	.300	.220	.322	69	267	30	80	16	1	2	32	11	2	0	2	33	5	4	.390	.330
Coghlan, Christopher	L-R	6-1	190	6-18-85	.298	.231	.309	28	94	14	28	5	1	0	12	13	0	1	3	9	5	2	.372	.373
Cousins, Scott	L-L	6-2	190	1-22-85	.211	.190	.217	21	90	11	19	1	0	1	6	4	1	2	0	17	3	1	.256	.253
Garcia, Daniel	R-R	6-0	165	12-27-87	.222	.182	.240	12	36	7	8	1	0	0	2	4	0	2	1	11	0	0	.250	.293
Hatcher, Chris	B-R	6-2	180	1-12-85	.181	.242	.160	36	127	19	23	4	2	2	17	11	5	1	0	40	3	1	.291	.273
Jacobs, Justin	R-R	6-1	180	7-31-88	.208	.333	.167	10	24	2	5	2	0	1	5	2	1	0	1	5	3	0	.417	.286
Kaats, Dustin	R-R	6-0	175	12-18-86	.222	.167	.244	22	63	12	14	2	1	2	5	7	1	1	1	26	2	2	.381	.306
Martinez, Guillermo	R-R	6-0	180	10-5-84	.193	.233	.179	38	114	6	22	2	0	0	11	4	0	1	1	26	0	0	.211	.218
McDougall, Spike	R-R	6-3	180	2-7-84	.254	.283	.246	67	236	33	60	17	5	2	31	30	3	1	0	67	6	2	.394	.346
Mense, David	L-L	5-11	185	8-30-84	.255	.216	.262	65	220	30	56	9	3	0	23	24	9	0	2	43	3	5	.323	.349
Messner, Nathan	R-R	6-3	210	11-21-85	.238	.333	.212	39	143	15	34	5	0	1	22	13	1	1	0	29	0	1	.294	.306
Morrison, Logan	L-L	6-2	215	8-25-87	.203	.154	.213	23	74	6	15	3	0	1	11	11	0	0	3	17	0	0	.284	.295
Munoz, Jose	R-R	5-10	160	7-1-85	.203	.250	.190	26	79	4	16	2	0	0	8	9	0	0	0	16	1	0	.228	.284
Ochoa, Blake	R-R	6-0	180	9-5-85	.211	.182	.216	41	133	12	28	6	1	1	13	7	5	1	1	22	1	3	.293	.274
Raynor, John	R-R	6-2	185	1-4-84	.286	.286	.287	54	199	36	57	8	4	4	21	17	5	1	1	51	21	2	.427	.356
Rogers, Tanner	R-R	6-0	180	1-11-85	.274	.238	.282	41	106	21	29	4	0	1	13	14	6	2	0	31	3	3	.340	.389
Saylor, Andrew	R-R	6-0	195	1-9-84	.148	.200	.128	46	149	13	22	2	1	1	9	15	5	2	1	21	3	2	.195	.247
Silverio, Rigoberto	B-R	6-1	156	7-2-86	.188	.000	.200	7	16	2	3	0	0	0	3	1	0	0	0	2	0	0	.188	.235
Walton, Jamar	L-R	6-4	195	1-5-86	.000	—	.000	3	6	1	0	0	0	0	0	1	0	1	0	3	0	0	.000	.143
Webb, Justin	R-R	6-0	175	11-5-82	.231	.385	.200	54	156	24	36	12	2	2	26	22	3	5	3	37	2	4	.372	.332
Westerfeld, Travis	R-R	6-2	200	12-17-83	.100	.167	.000	5	10	2	1	1	0	0	0	0	0	0	0	4	0	0	.200	.100

PITCHING	B-T	HT	WT	DOB	W	L	ERA	G	GS	CG	SV	IP	H	R	ER	HR	BB	SO	AVG	vLH	vRH	K/9	BB/9
Alexander, Stu	R-R	6-5	210	10-25-84	0	5	7.12	9	9	0	0	37	54	35	29	1	10	15	.355	.304	.398	3.68	2.45
Benitez, Gabriel	R-R	6-4	165	3-1-83	1	1	7.04	17	0	0	0	23	22	18	18	3	12	22	.244	.235	.250	8.61	4.70
Bird, Zach	R-R	6-0	205	5-17-84	0	1	3.94	11	7	0	0	32	30	16	14	1	21	28	.244	.357	.149	7.88	5.91
Buente, Jay	R-R	6-2	185	9-28-83	2	3	3.09	22	3	0	1	44	40	17	15	2	13	41	.242	.200	.274	8.45	2.68
Camilo, Juan	R-R	6-3	168	4-22-83	1	2	2.93	19	0	0	0	28	24	17	9	0	17	25	.229	.286	.200	8.13	5.53
Castor, Parrish	L-R	6-2	180	9-18-83	4	2	5.11	18	6	0	0	49	58	30	28	4	15	39	.290	.182	.331	7.11	2.74
Czyz, Don	R-R	6-2	200	9-16-83	3	1	4.91	22	0	0	6	22	20	15	12	0	11	20	.225	.200	.250	8.18	4.50
Davis, Jordan	R-R	6-0	190	11-12-82	1	2	6.21	24	0	0	2	29	35	22	20	1	11	30	.307	.420	.219	9.31	3.41
Encarnacion, Rodolfo	R-R	5-11	180	5-8-86	1	3	2.61	25	0	0	6	31	25	11	9	2	17	32	.227	.245	.213	9.29	4.94
Jackson, Andy	L-L	6-1	185	8-8-83	1	0	4.50	7	0	0	0	8	8	5	4	1	7	7	.242	.000	.320	7.88	7.88
Jarrett, Jason	R-R	6-5	195	5-29-82	0	0	2.25	1	1	0	0	4	3	3	1	0	1	2	.200	.200	.200	4.50	2.25
Leroux, Christopher	R-R	6-6	210	4-14-84	0	1	7.94	4	4	0	0	11	13	13	10	0	12	4	.283	.174	.391	3.18	9.53
Liersemann, Ross	R-R	6-4	205	8-14-83	3	1	3.16	19	2	0	0	43	38	18	15	3	6	36	.236	.194	.266	7.59	1.27
Madden, Corey	R-R	6-1	195	3-30-84	1	2	7.36	5	0	0	0	7	7	7	6	0	5	7	.233	.250	.222	8.59	6.14
Pie, Esequier	R-R	6-2	165	3-6-84	2	3	5.32	14	7	0	0	44	51	29	26	1	27	30	.302	.290	.310	6.14	5.52
Sinkbeil, Brett	R-R	6-2	170	12-26-84	2	0	1.23	5	5	0	0	22	14	4	3	1	8	22	.192	.321	.111	9.00	3.27
Sosa, Alexis	S-L	6-1	160	6-25-83	2	1	5.20	18	0	0	0	28	25	18	16	1	19	22	.245	.333	.203	7.16	6.18
Stone, Bradley	R-R	6-3	190	5-20-84	0	0	1.17	4	0	0	0	8	6	2	1	1	3	4	.250	.111	.333	4.70	3.52
Taylor, Graham	L-L	6-3	225	5-25-84	3	5	2.47	13	13	0	0	66	59	26	18	2	4	48	.243	.184	.258	6.58	0.55
Winters, Kyle	R-R	6-4	190	4-22-87	6	6	2.45	15	15	0	0	88	63	31	24	2	15	60	.194	.212	.174	6.11	1.53

FIELDING

Catcher	PCT	G	PO	A	E	DP	PB
Hatcher	.991	31	195	25	2	1	6
Ochoa	.987	38	265	32	4	2	8
Rogers	.929	2	13	0	1	1	0
Westerfeld	1.000	5	25	5	0	0	0

First Base	PCT	G	PO	A	E	DP
Blackwood	.982	15	106	4	2	10
McDougall	1.000	4	36	0	0	4
Messner	.973	35	286	35	9	32
Morrison	.978	20	170	12	4	15
Saylor	1.000	1	3	0	0	0

Second Base	PCT	G	PO	A	E	DP
Blackwood	.893	5	6	19	3	4
Coghlan	1.000	5	2	10	0	2
Jacobs	.857	1	3	3	1	1

	PCT	G	PO	A	E	DP	PB
Martinez	1.000	8	11	22	0	1	
Munoz	1.000	3	7	13	0	3	
Rogers	1.000	3	3	5	0	0	
Saylor	.954	37	61	106	8	29	
Silverio	.857	3	3	3	1	2	
Webb	.969	18	43	50	3	5	

Third Base	PCT	G	PO	A	E	DP
Blackwood	.946	39	29	58	5	4
Coghlan	.919	19	22	35	5	1
Munoz	.500	1	1	0	1	0
Rogers	1.000	2	3	2	0	0
Webb	.909	15	13	27	4	4

Shortstop	PCT	G	PO	A	E	DP
Blackwood	—	1	0	0	0	0
Garcia	.844	12	11	16	5	2

	PCT	G	PO	A	E	DP
Martinez	.923	27	44	76	10	17
Munoz	.944	22	34	67	6	15
Silverio	.667	2	1	1	1	1
Webb	.932	15	20	48	5	13

Outfield	PCT	G	PO	A	E	DP
Agustin	1.000	7	8	0	0	0
Blackwood	.900	2	8	1	1	0
Cousins	.941	18	32	0	2	0
Kaats	.949	19	33	4	2	1
Martinez	—	1	0	0	0	0
McDougall	.975	60	115	2	3	0
Mense	.962	55	72	4	3	1
Raynor	.975	46	114	4	3	2
Rogers	.926	22	22	3	2	1
Walton	1.000	2	2	0	0	0
Webb	1.000	2	3	0	0	0

ORGANIZATION STATISTICS

Gulf Coast League

BATTING	B-T	HT	WT	DOB	AVG	vLH	vRH	G	AB	R	H	2B	3B	HR	RBI	BB	HBP	SH	SF	SO	SB	CS	SLG	OBP
Adduci, James	L-L	6-2	185	5-15-85	.286	.400	.267	12	35	3	10	2	1	1	5	5	0	0	0	8	1	1	.486	.375
Agustin, Juan	R-R	5-11	160	10-30-84	.222	.222	.222	21	72	11	16	2	0	4	9	4	0	0	1	21	2	2	.417	.260
Allen, Cody	R-R	6-2	190	9-19-86	.150	.129	.157	43	133	15	20	2	0	0	4	15	3	3	1	40	4	1	.165	.250
Arias, Rene	R-R	6-0	182	6-22-87	.259	.100	.295	21	54	8	14	0	0	0	4	4	0	0	0	9	1	2	.259	.310
Coghlan, Christopher	L-R	6-1	190	6-18-85	.286	—	.286	2	7	2	2	0	0	0	3	0	0	0	0	1	0	0	.286	.286
De Aza, Alejandro	L-L	6-0	174	4-11-84	.458	.167	.556	7	24	7	11	1	0	0	4	4	0	0	0	2	3	2	.500	.536
Garcia, Daniel	R-R	6-0	165	12-27-87	.216	.286	.196	33	125	21	27	6	3	2	12	8	0	0	0	28	1	1	.360	.263
Haupt, Christopher	R-R	6-0	200	5-18-87	.077	.000	.091	19	26	3	2	0	0	0	1	6	2	1	0	9	1	0	.077	.294
Hickman, Thomas	L-L	6-1	180	4-18-88	.263	.167	.288	50	175	28	46	12	4	2	20	30	2	0	0	43	4	5	.411	.377
Howard, Adam	R-R	6-2	195	10-3-85	.205	.321	.180	49	161	7	33	5	3	0	15	13	2	1	0	40	3	1	.273	.273
Jacobs, Justin	R-R	6-1	180	7-31-88	.284	.167	.312	31	95	14	27	1	0	1	8	11	2	3	0	15	8	2	.326	.370
Kaats, Dustin	R-R	6-0	175	12-18-86	.196	.214	.192	30	92	9	18	5	0	2	15	18	3	0	2	28	0	4	.315	.339
Langley, Torre	R-R	5-9	175	10-9-87	.169	.071	.190	25	77	2	13	1	0	0	1	0	0	0	0	12	0	0	.182	.169
Martinez, Osvaldo	R-R	5-10	170	5-7-88	.263	.250	.267	49	171	21	45	4	1	1	21	19	0	3	1	21	7	4	.316	.335
Messner, Nathan	R-R	6-3	210	11-21-85	.366	.444	.344	11	41	9	15	1	0	0	7	6	1	0	0	7	2	1	.390	.458
Morrison, Logan	L-L	6-2	215	8-25-87	.270	.267	.270	26	89	10	24	4	0	1	7	10	0	0	0	12	1	0	.348	.343
Padgett, Kyle	R-R	6-1	185	1-16-83	.172	.400	.151	18	58	2	10	1	0	0	7	6	1	0	1	16	0	2	.190	.258
Ramos, Luis	L-R	6-2	180	3-10-87	.159	.188	.149	25	63	8	10	1	1	0	0	10	1	3	0	15	2	2	.206	.284
Sanchez, Gabriel	R-R	6-2	225	9-2-83	.333	1.000	.200	3	6	1	2	1	0	0	3	5	0	0	0	0	0	0	.500	.636
Septimo, Agustin	L-R	5-11	170	5-27-84	.333	.200	.385	5	18	3	6	2	0	0	1	2	1	0	0	1	0	0	.444	.429
Silverio, Rigoberto	B-R	6-1	156	7-2-86	.228	.161	.244	44	162	13	37	5	0	0	8	12	1	4	0	30	3	2	.259	.286
Stokes, Jason	R-R	6-4	225	1-23-82	1.000	—	1.000	1	3	1	3	1	0	1	2	0	0	0	0	0	0	0	2.333	1.000
Verley, Brandon	L-L	6-2	202	6-25-85	—	—	—	1	0	1	0	0	0	0	0	0	0	0	0	0	0	0	—	—
Walton, Jamar	L-R	6-4	195	1-5-86	.000	.000	—	1	1	0	0	0	0	0	0	0	0	0	0	0	0	0	.000	.000
Westerfeld, Travis	R-R	6-2	200	12-17-83	.231	.000	.300	11	13	0	3	0	0	0	3	3	0	1	1	4	0	0	.231	.353

PITCHING	B-T	HT	WT	DOB	W	L	ERA	G	GS	CG	SV	IP	H	R	ER	HR	BB	SO	AVG	vLH	vRH	K/9	BB/9
Alexander, Stu	R-R	6-5	210	10-25-84	0	2	5.73	4	4	0	0	11	15	9	7	1	1	11	.306	.364	.289	9.00	0.82
Barradas, Arturo	L-L	6-3	190	8-10-87	3	2	3.42	10	8	0	0	47	46	21	18	1	7	35	.260	.250	.261	6.65	1.33
Baxter, Allen	R-R	6-4	215	7-6-83	0	0	0.00	4	0	0	0	5	3	1	0	0	2	5	.188	.000	.250	9.64	3.86
Campusano, Joelmy	L-L	6-2	180	7-17-86	0	0	18.00	1	0	0	0	2	3	4	4	0	3	1	.333	—	.333	4.50	13.50
Correa, Hector	R-R	6-3	165	3-18-88	1	2	1.76	10	5	0	0	41	38	13	8	1	15	38	.244	.255	.238	8.34	3.29
Faria, Carlos	R R	6-1	185	10-7-84	0	0	4.05	9	0	0	0	7	4	4	3	2	5	6	.160	.125	.176	8.10	6.75
Fountain, Joel	R-R	6-4	175	11-10-83	3	2	2.30	10	6	0	1	43	31	12	11	0	9	32	.197	.189	.202	6.70	1.88
German, Franklyn	R-R	6-7	260	1-20-80	0	0	0.00	1	0	0	0	1	0	0	0	0	0	1	.000	.000	.000	9.00	0.00
Gonzalez, Jose	R-R	6-2	170	7-18-85	2	2	1.73	9	5	0	0	42	40	15	8	1	6	28	.253	.250	.255	6.05	1.30
Iehl, Jason	R-R	6-2	185	4-23-84	1	0	0.00	2	1	0	0	2	0	0	0	0	3	4	.000	.000	.000	18.00	13.50
Jackson, Andy	L-L	6-1	185	8-8-83	0	1	1.00	18	0	0	5	27	19	5	3	0	4	31	.186	.083	.200	10.33	1.33
Kelley, Kevan	L-L	6-0	200	6-4-84	0	0	54.00	4	0	0	0	1	3	8	8	0	6	0	.375	—	.375	0.00	40.50
Leroux, Christopher	L-R	6-6	210	4-14-84	0	0	4.09	4	0	0	0	11	10	9	5	0	1	9	.250	.235	.261	7.36	0.82
Madden, Corey	R-R	6-1	195	3-30-84	4	2	2.63	14	0	0	0	24	15	8	7	0	11	29	.179	.235	.164	10.88	4.13
Mitre, Sergio	R-R	6-4	210	2-16-81	0	0	0.00	1	1	0	0	1	0	0	0	0	0	1	.000	—	.000	9.00	0.00
Moehler, Brian	R-R	6-3	235	12-31-71	0	1	3.60	1	1	0	0	5	8	2	2	0	0	4	.348	.500	.294	7.20	0.00
Molldrem, Craig	R-R	6-6	205	9-17-81	0	0	6.52	7	1	0	0	10	9	7	7	0	6	7	.257	.300	.240	6.52	5.59
O'Neal, Charles	R-L	6-4	165	9-12-83	0	1	4.50	6	0	0	0	6	10	4	3	0	3	8	.370	.667	.333	12.00	4.50
Rasowky, Avi	L-L	6-1	195	5-17-83	0	0	9.00	2	0	0	0	4	5	4	4	1	2	4	.333	.500	.286	9.00	4.50
Rosario, Sandy	R-R	6-1	170	8-22-85	3	2	2.25	10	6	0	0	40	41	20	10	0	10	27	.256	.284	.237	6.08	2.25
Sanabia, Alejandro	R-R	6-1	180	9-8-88	3	1	3.24	11	0	0	0	17	10	7	6	0	7	16	.169	.188	.163	8.64	3.78
Smolarski, Freddy	R-R	6-1	180	9-24-84	0	0	6.10	7	0	0	0	10	12	8	7	1	4	9	.300	.154	.370	7.84	3.48
Stewart, Josh	L-L	6-3	205	12-5-78	0	0	3.00	4	4	0	0	9	8	3	3	1	3	6	.235	.286	.222	6.00	3.00
Suarez, Luis	R-R	6-1	195	9-21-84	0	1	4.40	16	0	0	6	14	11	12	7	1	15	14	.200	.250	.186	8.79	9.42
Vanden Hurk, Rick	R-R	6-5	195	5-22-85	0	0	1.20	5	5	0	0	15	4	2	2	0	8	26	.085	.063	.097	15.60	4.80
Vasquez, Yanery	L-L	5-11	150	10-22-86	5	2	1.26	19	1	0	1	36	23	8	5	1	12	32	.178	.071	.191	8.07	3.03
Zabala, Felix	R-R	5-10	150	7-1-84	4	3	2.43	20	0	0	5	30	23	10	8	1	7	36	.211	.281	.182	10.92	2.12

FIELDING

Catcher	PCT	G	PO	A	E	DP	PB
Arias	1.000	15	79	10	0	0	1
Haupt	1.000	16	76	7	0	0	8
Howard	1.000	13	72	3	0	0	2
Langley	.974	25	132	16	4	1	4
Smolarski	1.000	1	4	0	0	0	1
Westerfeld	1.000	11	45	2	0	0	2

First Base	PCT	G	PO	A	E	DP
Adduci	.984	9	59	3	1	5
Arias	1.000	3	10	1	0	0
Howard	1.000	14	118	7	0	6
Messner	.978	11	86	5	2	4
Morrison	.973	21	169	8	5	14
Sanchez	1.000	2	14	1	0	3

Second Base	PCT	G	PO	A	E	DP
Allen	1.000	1	0	1	0	0

	PCT	G	PO	A	E	DP
Garcia	.833	3	3	2	1	0
Jacobs	1.000	1	1	0	0	0
Martinez	.973	20	33	38	2	6
Septimo	1.000	1	2	6	0	1
Silverio	.980	32	59	90	3	20

Third Base	PCT	G	PO	A	E	DP
Allen	.333	2	1	0	2	0
Coghlan	.833	2	1	4	1	0
Howard	.813	12	6	20	6	0
Jacobs	.842	22	8	40	9	1
Martinez	.905	13	12	26	4	3
Padgett	.950	8	5	14	1	2

Shortstop	PCT	G	PO	A	E	DP
Garcia	.912	24	31	62	9	5
Jacobs	1.000	2	0	2	0	0
Martinez	.902	12	20	35	6	10

	PCT	G	PO	A	E	DP
Padgett	.963	6	7	19	1	3
Septimo	1.000	2	2	2	0	1
Silverio	.956	10	18	25	2	6

Outfield	PCT	G	PO	A	E	DP
Adduci	.500	1	1	0	1	0
Agustin	.967	15	27	2	1	1
Allen	.982	38	52	4	1	1
De Aza	1.000	7	16	0	0	0
Hickman	.979	49	88	7	2	1
Howard	1.000	2	4	0	0	0
Jacobs	.875	3	7	0	1	0
Kaats	1.000	30	65	3	0	1
Martinez	1.000	6	6	1	0	0
Ramos	.962	16	23	2	1	0

BY BRIAN McTAGGART

As poorly as the Astros played for most of the season, they nearly pulled off their most improbable playoff run yet when they won 10 of their final 12 games to get within one-half game of the National League Central Division lead in the final week of the season.

The Astros, who won 36 of their final 46 games in 2004 and overcame a 15-30 start in 2005 to make the playoffs, couldn't finish the job this time. That's because the Cardinals righted their ship in time to clinch the division on the final day of the season.

The Astros finished 82-80, marking their sixth consecutive winning season and 14th in the previous 15 seasons.

"We took it to the wire, and I'm proud of our guys," manager Phil Garner said. "There was a time it didn't look like there was any way to fight back in this thing and we did and fought back to the last day and essentially to the last inning.

"I'm proud of what we did. Even though we didn't achieve our goal and we didn't get there, we showed a lot of pride and a lot of grit."

Staying in contention until the final day of the regular season was remarkable. The Astros were 8 ½ games behind the Cardinals on Sept. 19 before winning nine games in a row behind the pitching of Roy Oswalt and a resurgent offense.

"It's one of those situations where the ending of the season is not what frustrates us, it's the fact we played below what we would have liked for the first part of the season, and had we played up to our capability we would

PLAYERS OF THE YEAR

MAJOR LEAGUE: Lance Berkman, of

Berkman had arguably his best year since 2001, hitting .315/.420/.621 with a career-high 45 home runs. He led the team in homers, on-base and slugging percentage, as well as hits (169), runs (95), total bases (333), and RBIs (136). He also stayed healthy all season, playing in 152 games.

MINOR LEAGUE: Hunter Pence, of

Pence has always hit for average and power since being a second-round pick in 2004, and he did more of the same in 2006 by hitting .283/.357/.533 with 28 homers. He has become a much-improved defensive outfielder and has speed for a big man, stealing 17 bases in 2006.

have won the division easily," slugger Lance Berkman said.

Coming off their World Series berth, the Astros started the season 19-9 before trudging through the next four months. The starting pitching was iffy, but the Astros' biggest problem was their inconsistent offense, which finished last in the NL with a .255 average and was terrible with runners in scoring position.

The lack of offense was another reason the Astros were somewhat of a surprise to be contending for a division on the final day of the season.

"Any time you lose the last game of the year—we lost the last game of the year last year and it just happened to be in the World Series—it's not any easier and doesn't make it any better," shortstop Adam Everett said. "We put a good run together toward the end. We just didn't have enough. We never quit, and that's something about this team and something we can build on."

The Astros never pressed the panic button no matter how many games back they fell in September, thanks to their previous late-season runs. But after getting swept by the Phillies at home in mid-September, some of the players appeared to accept that the Astros weren't going to win the wild card for the third year in a row.

It was then the Astros turned it on, however, taking two of three from the Reds before the dramatic sweep of the Cardinals to get within 3½ games. While the Cardinals threatened to come up with the biggest last-season collapse since the 1964 Phillies, the Astros kept winning.

They entered the final day of the season needing to win to force a playoff with the Cardinals, but their playoff nemesis—the Braves—beat the Astros 3-1 to end their season.

It was another successful season on the farm for the Astros, as a talented Double-A Corpus Christi team won the Texas League title, led by outfield prospect Hunter Pence. Triple-A Round Rock and short-season Tri-City made it to the finals of the playoffs in their leagues as well, and the farm system finished with the second-best cumulative record in baseball.

ORGANIZATION LEADERS

BATTING		*Minimum 250 at-bats
*AVG	House, J.R., Corpus Christi/Round Rock	.345
R	Pence, Hunter, Corpus Christi	107
H	Anderson, Josh, Corpus Christi	173
TB	Pence, Hunter, Corpus Christi	314
2B	Caraballo, Francisco, Salem	40
	Conrad, Brooks, Round Rock	40
	Sellers, Neil, Salem	40
3B	Conrad, Brooks, Round Rock	15
HR	Pence, Hunter, Corpus Christi	31
RBI	Pence, Hunter, Corpus Christi	106
BB	Sheldon, Ole, Lexington/Salem	74
SO	Jimerson, Charlton, Round Rock	183
SB	Anderson, Josh, Corpus Christi	43
*OBP	Zobrist, Ben, Corpus Christi/Durham	.434
*SLG	Pence, Hunter, Corpus Christi	.537
XBH	Conrad, Brooks, Round Rock	79

PITCHING		#Minimum 75 innings
W	Fairchild, Thomas, Lexington/Salem	14
L	Patton, Troy, Salem/Corpus Christi	12
#ERA	Salamida, Christopher, Tri-City	1.06
G	Estrada, Paul, Corpus Christi	56
CG	Douglass, Chance, Corpus Christi	2
	Sampson, Chris, Round Rock	2
SV	Escobar, Rodrigo, Salem	17
IP	Fairchild, Thomas, Lexington/Salem	173
BB	Barthmaier, James, Salem	67
SO	Patton, Troy, Salem/Corpus Christi	148
#AVG	Salamida, Christopher, Tri-City	.189

Houston Astros — MLB

National League

BATTING	B-T	HT	WT	DOB	AVG	vLH	vRH	G	AB	R	H	2B	3B	HR	RBI	BB	HBP	SH	SF	SO	SB	CS	SLG	OBP
Ausmus, Brad	R-R	5-11	190	4-14-69	.230	.266	.220	139	439	37	101	16	1	2	39	45	6	9	3	71	3	1	.285	.308
Berkman, Lance	B-L	6-1	220	2-10-76	.315	.266	.335	152	536	95	169	29	0	45	136	98	4	0	8	106	3	2	.621	.420
Biggio, Craig	R-R	5-11	185	12-14-65	.246	.297	.233	145	548	79	135	33	0	21	62	40	9	5	5	84	3	2	.422	.306
Bruntlett, Eric	R-R	6-0	190	3-29-78	.277	.350	.241	73	119	11	33	8	0	0	10	13	1	2	1	21	3	1	.345	.351
Burke, Chris	R-R	5-11	180	3-11-80	.276	.327	.257	123	366	58	101	23	1	9	40	27	14	4	2	77	11	1	.418	.347
Ensberg, Morgan	R-R	6-2	220	8-26-75	.235	.245	.232	127	387	67	91	17	1	23	58	101	4	0	3	96	1	4	.463	.396
Everett, Adam	R-R	6-0	170	2-5-77	.239	.250	.237	150	514	52	123	28	6	6	59	34	4	10	4	71	9	6	.352	.290
Gimenez, Hector	B-R	5-10	180	9-28-82	.000	.000	.000	2	2	0	0	0	0	0	0	0	0	0	0	1	0	0	.000	.000
House, J.R.	R-R	5-10	200	11-11-79	.000	.000	.000	4	9	0	0	0	0	0	0	0	0	0	0	2	0	0	.000	.000
Huff, Aubrey	L-R	6-4	230	12-20-76	.250	.235	.254	68	224	31	56	10	1	13	38	26	7	0	4	39	0	0	.478	.341
Jimerson, Charlton	R-R	6-3	210	9-22-79	.333	.667	.000	17	6	2	2	0	0	1	1	0	0	0	0	3	2	0	.833	.333
Lamb, Mike	L-R	6-1	190	8-9-75	.307	.211	.324	126	381	70	117	22	3	12	45	35	0	0	5	55	2	4	.475	.361
Lane, Jason	R-L	6-2	220	12-22-76	.201	.198	.203	112	288	44	58	10	0	15	45	49	2	4	2	75	1	2	.392	.318
McEwing, Joe	R-R	5-11	170	10-19-72	.000	.000	.000	7	6	0	0	0	0	0	0	0	0	0	0	2	0	0	.000	.000
Munson, Eric	L-R	6-3	220	10-3-77	.199	.318	.176	53	141	10	28	6	0	5	19	11	3	0	1	32	0	0	.348	.269
Palmeiro, Orlando	L-L	5-11	185	1-19-69	.252	.000	.259	103	119	12	30	6	1	0	17	6	1	2	0	17	0	1	.319	.294
Quintero, Humberto	R-R	5-9	215	8-2-79	.333	.571	.214	11	21	2	7	2	0	0	2	1	0	0	0	3	0	0	.429	.364
Scott, Luke	L-R	6-0	210	6-25-78	.336	.240	.366	65	214	31	72	19	6	10	37	30	4	0	1	43	2	1	.621	.426
Taveras, Willy	R-R	6-0	160	12-25-81	.278	.254	.285	149	529	83	147	19	5	1	30	34	11	11	2	88	33	9	.338	.333
Wilson, Preston	R-R	6-2	215	7-19-74	.269	.312	.259	102	390	40	105	22	2	9	55	22	2	0	3	94	6	2	.405	.309
2-team (33 St. Louis)					.263	—	135	501	58	132	25	2	17	72	29	4	0	3	121	12	2	.423	.307	

PITCHING	B-T	HT	WT	DOB	W	L	ERA	G	GS	CG	SV	IP	H	R	ER	HR	BB	SO	AVG	vLH	vRH	K/9	BB/9
Albers, Matt	L-R	6-0	205	1-20-83	0	2	6.00	4	2	0	0	15	17	10	10	1	7	11	.298	.333	.267	6.60	4.20
Astacio, Ezequiel	R-R	6-3	150	11-4-79	2	0	11.12	6	0	0	0	6	7	7	7	2	6	6	.292	.182	.385	9.53	9.53
Backe, Brandon	R-R	6-0	195	4-5-78	3	2	3.77	8	8	0	0	43	43	18	18	4	18	19	.261	.317	.205	3.98	3.77
Barzilla, Philip	L-L	6-0	180	1-25-79	0	0	0.00	1	0	0	0	1	0	0	0	0	0	1	.500	—	.500	0.00	0.00
Borkowski, Dave	R-R	6-1	230	2-7-77	3	2	4.69	40	0	0	0	71	70	38	37	8	23	52	.257	.262	.255	6.59	2.92
Buchholz, Taylor	R-R	6-4	220	10-13-81	6	10	5.89	22	19	1	0	113	107	80	74	21	34	77	.248	.249	.248	6.13	2.71
Clemens, Roger	R-R	6-4	235	8-4-62	7	6	2.30	19	19	0	0	113	89	34	29	7	29	102	.216	.254	.185	8.10	2.30
Gallo, Mike	L-L	6-0	175	4-2-77	1	2	6.06	23	0	0	0	16	28	11	11	3	7	7	.400	.360	.422	3.86	3.86
Hirsh, Jason	R-R	6-8	250	2-20-82	3	4	6.04	9	9	0	0	45	48	32	30	11	22	29	.267	.211	.303	5.84	4.43
Lidge, Brad	R-R	6-5	210	12-23-76	1	5	5.28	78	0	0	32	75	69	47	44	10	36	104	.238	.286	.201	12.48	4.32
Miller, Trever	R-L	6-3	200	5-29-73	2	3	3.02	79	0	0	0	51	42	17	17	7	13	56	.225	.224	.225	9.95	2.31
Nieve, Fernando	R-R	6-0	195	7-15-82	3	3	4.20	40	11	0	0	96	87	46	45	18	41	70	.242	.262	.224	6.54	3.83
Oswalt, Roy	R-R	6-0	185	8-29-77	15	8	2.98	33	32	2	0	221	220	76	73	18	38	166	.263	.264	.262	6.77	1.55
Pettitte, Andy	L-L	6-5	225	6-15-72	14	13	4.20	36	35	2	0	214	238	114	100	27	70	178	.284	.259	.290	7.47	2.94
Qualls, Chad	R-R	6-5	220	8-17-78	7	3	3.76	81	0	0	0	89	76	38	37	10	28	56	.242	.229	.251	5.68	2.84
Rodriguez, Wandy	B-L	5-11	160	1-18-79	9	10	5.64	30	24	0	0	136	154	96	85	17	63	98	.290	.262	.298	6.50	4.18
Sampson, Chris	R-R	6-1	190	5-23-78	2	1	2.12	12	3	0	0	34	25	10	8	3	5	15	.205	.154	.243	3.97	1.32
Springer, Russ	R-R	6-4	215	11-7-68	1	1	3.47	72	0	0	0	60	46	23	23	10	16	46	.211	.253	.187	6.94	2.41
Wheeler, Dan	R-R	6-3	220	12-10-77	3	5	2.52	75	0	0	9	71	58	22	20	5	24	68	.221	.273	.183	8.58	3.03

FIELDING

Catcher	PCT	G	PO	A	E	DP	PB
Ausmus	.998	138	929	63	2	9	1
House	1.000	3	10	1	0	0	1
Munson	.995	37	197	10	1	2	4
Quintero	1.000	10	42	6	0	3	1

First Base	PCT	G	PO	A	E	DP
Ausmus	—	1	0	0	0	0
Berkman	.994	112	964	71	6	96
House	1.000	2	8	0	0	0
Huff	1.000	3	6	3	0	1
Lamb	.990	68	475	41	5	48
Lane	1.000	1	3	0	0	0
Munson	1.000	4	29	1	0	4

Second Base	PCT	G	PO	A	E	DP
Ausmus	1.000	2	0	1	0	0
Biggio	.989	129	219	334	6	80
Bruntlett	.938	23	13	17	2	5
Burke	.974	69	68	117	5	26
Lamb	1.000	2	1	0	1	0
McEwing	1.000	2	1	2	0	0

Third Base	PCT	G	PO	A	E	DP
Bruntlett	1.000	2	1	2	0	0
Ensberg	.963	117	80	230	12	25
Huff	.972	30	23	47	2	3
Lamb	.940	36	24	70	6	8

Shortstop	PCT	G	PO	A	E	DP
Bruntlett	.951	21	20	57	4	9

	PCT	G	PO	A	E	DP
Burke	.909	8	2	8	1	1
Everett	.990	149	202	479	7	105

Outfield	PCT	G	PO	A	E	DP
Berkman	.955	44	61	3	3	2
Bruntlett	.950	18	18	1	1	0
Burke	.990	61	96	2	1	0
Huff	.953	37	40	1	2	0
Jimerson	1.000	9	6	0	0	0
Lane	1.000	98	166	1	0	0
Palmeiro	1.000	23	15	0	0	0
Scott	1.000	60	96	1	0	1
Taveras	.986	138	335	9	5	3
Wilson	1.000	100	155	2	0	0

Round Rock Express — Triple-A

Pacific Coast League

BATTING	B-T	HT	WT	DOB	AVG	vLH	vRH	G	AB	R	H	2B	3B	HR	RBI	BB	HBP	SH	SF	SO	SB	CS	SLG	OBP
Bruntlett, Eric	R-R	6-0	190	3-29-78	.219	.118	.250	22	73	11	16	3	1	1	7	17	2	1	0	13	3	2	.329	.380
Burke, Chris	R-R	5-11	180	3-11-80	.500	1.000	.429	2	8	2	4	1	0	1	2	1	0	0	1	1	0	1.000	.556
Conrad, Brooks	B-R	5-11	185	1-16-80	.267	.256	.271	138	532	100	142	40	15	24	94	54	4	1	8	135	15	6	.534	.334
Ensberg, Morgan	R-R	6-2	220	8-26-75	.500	.333	.556	3	12	2	6	2	0	2	7	3	0	0	0	1	0	1.167	.600
Garcia, Jesse	R-R	5-10	170	9-24-73	.259	.294	.246	73	255	33	66	14	1	6	26	7	2	7	2	48	5	1	.392	.282
Gimenez, Hector	B-R	5-10	180	9-28-82	.273	.164	.312	76	275	31	75	8	0	8	37	24	1	0	2	42	2	3	.389	.331
Gordon, Brian	L-R	6-0	190	8-16-78	.241	.212	.249	102	303	48	73	21	3	16	59	28	3	4	2	110	1	3	.488	.310
House, J.R.	R-R	5-10	200	11-11-79	.412	.394	.420	31	114	25	47	15	0	5	36	9	1	0	4	15	0	0	.675	.445

General manager: Tim Purpura. **Farm director:** Ricky Bennett. **Scouting director:** Paul Ricciarini.

Class	Team	League	W	L	PCT	Finish*	Manager	Affiliate Since
Majors	Houston	National	82	80	.506	6th (16)	Phil Garner	—
Triple-A	Round Rock Express	Pacific Coast	85	59	.590	2nd (16)	Jackie Moore	2005
Double-A	Corpus Christi Hooks	Texas	76	63	.547	+3rd (8)	Dave Clark	2005
High A	Salem Avalanche	Carolina	76	61	.555	2nd (8)	Jim Pankovits	2003
Low A	Lexington Legends	South Atlantic	75	63	.543	5th (16)	Jack Lind	2001
Short-season	Tri-City ValleyCats	New York-Penn	43	31	.581	9th (14)	Gregg Langbehn	2001
Rookie	Greeneville Astros	Appalachian	34	33	.507	5th (10)	Ivan DeJesus	2004

OVERALL 2006 MINOR LEAGUE RECORD 389 310 .557 2nd (30)

*Finish in overall standings (No. of teams in league). +League champion

ORGANIZATION STATISTICS

	B-T	HT	WT	DOB	AVG	OBP	SLG	G	AB	R	H	2B	3B	HR	RBI	BB	SO	SB	CS	vLH	vRH
Huffman, Royce	R-R	6-0	205	1-11-77	.299	.290	.302	98	351	62	105	25	2	10	59	50	8	0	3	73 3 2	.467 .396
Jimerson, Charlton	R-R	6-3	210	9-22-79	.247	.281	.231	123	470	56	116	27	6	18	45	23	4	3	1	183 28 8	.445 .287
Lane, Jason	R-L	6-2	220	12-22-76	.261	.125	.333	12	46	7	12	2	0	1	11	5	1	0	3	16 1 0	.370 .327
McEwing, Joe	R-R	5-11	170	10-19-72	.315	.377	.288	112	422	64	133	21	1	10	46	23	3	7	5	65 16 7	.441 .351
Munson, Eric	L-R	6-3	220	10-3-77	.250	1.000	.200	9	32	6	8	1	0	2	8	3	2	0	0	4 0 0	.469 .351
Nicholson, Derek	L-R	5-11	205	6-17-76	.231	.000	.250	9	26	5	6	1	0	3	6	5	0	0	0	5 0 0	.615 .355
Orie, Kevin	R-R	6-4	220	9-1-72	.000	—	.000	1	2	1	0	0	0	0	0	0	0	0	0	0 0 0	.000 .000
Quintero, Humberto	R-R	5-9	215	8-2-79	.298	.230	.300	82	292	39	87	21	2	4	37	19	7	1	3	48 4 0	.425 .352
Ransom, Cody	R-R	6-2	205	2-17-76	.247	.226	.255	122	380	64	94	23	1	21	62	54	4	2	2	103 2 1	.479 .345
Robinson, Wade	L-R	6-2	165	1-12-81	.329	.500	.315	27	79	5	26	1	0	0	10	5	0	2	1	15 0 2	.342 .365
Rodriguez, Mike	L-L	5-10	180	10-15-80	.276	.239	.288	113	439	70	121	16	7	6	38	51	2	7	2	55 28 6	.385 .352
Scott, Luke	L-R	6-0	210	6-25-78	.299	.324	.287	87	318	63	95	15	1	20	63	52	5	1	5	66 6 1	.541 .400
Zinter, Alan	B-R	6-2	195	5-19-68	.259	.222	.282	99	212	41	55	11	2	12	44	35	0	0	1	63 1 0	.500 .363

PITCHING	B-T	HT	WT	DOB	W	L	ERA	G	GS	CG	SV	IP	H	R	ER	HR	BB	SO	AVG	vLH	vRH	K/9	BB/9
Albers, Matt	L-R	6-0	205	1-20-83	2	1	3.96	4	4	0	0	25	24	11	11	2	10	26	.253	.286	.226	9.36	3.60
Astacio, Ezequiel	R-R	6-3	150	11-4-79	8	4	4.86	21	17	0	0	93	95	51	50	15	43	76	.262	.269	.256	7.38	4.18
Backe, Brandon	R-R	6-0	195	4-5-78	1	2	5.31	4	4	0	0	20	23	12	12	1	13	13	.311	.382	.250	5.75	5.75
Baker, Chris	R-R	6-1	195	8-24-77	9	4	2.68	26	6	0	1	84	77	33	25	5	28	40	.253	.271	.240	4.29	3.00
Barzilla, Philip	L-L	6-0	180	1-25-79	8	5	3.85	25	14	1	1	112	114	57	48	5	48	80	.262	.243	.271	6.41	3.85
Borkowski, Dave	R-R	6-1	230	2-7-77	0	1	2.57	6	0	0	3	7	6	2	2	1	2	6	.250	.273	.231	7.71	2.57
Buchholz, Taylor	R-R	6-4	220	10-13-81	1	3	4.91	7	7	0	0	44	47	27	24	2	17	37	.278	.211	.333	7.57	3.48
Clemens, Roger	R-R	6-4	235	8-4-62	1	1	4.76	1	1	0	0	6	5	3	3	0	3	5	.227	.154	.333	7.94	4.76
Driskill, Travis	R-R	6-0	215	8-1-71	4	8	3.20	52	0	0	15	65	57	29	23	8	13	58	.237	.235	.237	8.07	1.81
Gallo, Mike	L-L	6-0	175	4-2-77	2	0	5.63	33	0	0	0	40	46	25	25	4	25	25	.303	.368	.263	5.63	3.60
Giron, Roberto	R-R	6-2	195	3-24-76	2	5	4.78	47	6	0	13	87	93	48	46	11	32	66	.278	.261	.292	6.85	3.32
Gothreaux, Jared	R-R	6-0	200	1-27-80	9	9	4.34	29	27	0	0	143	164	78	69	19	40	89	.288	.324	.259	5.60	2.52
Hirsh, Jason	R-R	6-8	250	2-20-82	13	2	2.10	23	23	1	0	137	94	37	32	5	51	118	.193	.186	.197	7.73	3.34
Huisman, Justin	R-R	6-1	200	4-16-79	0	0	11.25	6	0	0	0	8	11	10	10	0	4	4	.355	.417	.316	4.50	4.50
3-team (2 Omaha, 14 Tacoma)					2	0	8.10	22	1	0	0	40	50	36	36	8	20	32	—	—	—	7.20	4.50
Kent, Steve	B-L	5-11	170	10-3-78	1	0	2.43	27	0	0	2	30	24	10	8	4	20	15	.224	.224	.224	4.55	6.07
Lee, David	R-R	6-1	200	3-12-73	1	1	4.35	22	0	0	0	31	30	16	15	3	22	34	.244	.255	.237	9.87	6.39
2-team (6 Albuquerque)					1	1	4.72	28	0	0	0	40	42	23	21	5	27	40	—	—	—	9.00	6.08
McLemore, Mark	L-L	6-2	220	10-9-80	2	3	2.81	21	9	0	0	58	48	27	18	5	38	52	.226	.241	.222	8.12	5.93
Miller, Trever	R-L	6-3	200	5-29-73	0	0	0.00	2	0	0	0	2	0	0	0	0	1	3	.000	.000	.000	13.50	4.50
Nieve, Fernando	R-R	6-0	195	7-15-82	0	0	0.00	4	0	0	2	5	2	0	0	0	0	7	.105	.077	.167	11.81	0.00
Peguero, Jailen	R-R	5-11	180	1-4-81	1	2	3.47	21	0	0	1	36	34	18	14	3	18	30	.245	.207	.272	7.43	4.46
Puffer, Brandon	R-R	6-3	190	10-5-75	5	1	4.47	37	0	0	4	52	46	27	26	6	16	37	.241	.195	.279	6.36	2.75
2-team (13 Sacramento)					5	1	4.67	50	0	0	4	69	67	37	36	10	20	51	—	—	—	6.62	2.60
Rodriguez, Wandy	B-L	5-11	160	1-18-79	2	2	6.92	5	5	0	0	26	32	21	20	2	13	13	.305	.269	.316	4.50	4.50
Sampson, Chris	R-R	6-1	190	5-23-78	12	3	2.51	27	18	2	4	126	110	48	35	12	14	68	.234	.253	.212	4.87	1.00
Valentine, Joe	R-R	6-2	210	12-24-79	1	2	4.70	20	1	0	0	31	34	19	16	2	21	17	.298	.182	.371	4.99	6.16
Williams, Aaron	R-R	6-2	180	10-7-80	0	1	4.70	5	0	0	0	8	10	4	4	0	3	5	.313	.188	.438	5.87	3.52

FIELDING

Catcher	PCT	G	PO	A	E	DP	PB
Gimenez	.988	62	384	32	5	4	8
House	.933	2	13	1	1	0	0
Munson	.955	3	19	2	1	1	2
Quintero	.993	81	534	53	4	6	4

First Base	PCT	G	PO	A	E	DP
Gimenez	1.000	12	83	5	0	6
House	.990	25	190	16	2	19
Huffman	.995	81	685	53	4	82
McEwing	1.000	8	33	4	0	1
Munson	1.000	3	22	1	0	4
Zinter	.992	27	244	17	2	23

Second Base	PCT	G	PO	A	E	DP
Bruntlett	1.000	2	3	4	0	0
Burke	.857	1	3	3	1	1
Conrad	.987	100	205	307	7	67

	PCT	G	PO	A	E	DP
House	1.000	1	0	2	0	0
Huffman	.903	7	18	10	3	2
McEwing	.981	34	57	96	3	21
Ransom	.833	1	2	3	1	1
Robinson	.906	8	8	21	3	6

Third Base	PCT	G	PO	A	E	DP
Bruntlett	1.000	1	0	2	0	1
Conrad	.948	38	25	66	5	11
Ensberg	.692	3	4	5	4	1
Huffman	.852	8	7	16	4	0
McEwing	.921	52	27	90	10	5
Orie	1.000	1	0	1	0	0
Ransom	.935	51	33	68	7	5

Shortstop	PCT	G	PO	A	E	DP
Bruntlett	1.000	5	8	18	0	3
Garcia	.981	72	111	201	6	58

		PCT	G	PO	A	E	DP
McEwing		—	2	0	0	0	0
Ransom		.964	61	97	173	10	41
Robinson		.949	15	25	49	4	7

Outfield	PCT	G	PO	A	E	DP
Bruntlett	.952	14	18	2	1	1
Burke	1.000	1	1	0	0	0
Gordon	.982	84	163	4	3	0
Huffman	1.000	3	5	0	0	0
Jimerson	.986	121	280	8	4	3
Lane	1.000	12	20	0	0	0
McEwing	1.000	16	20	0	0	1
Munson	1.000	3	4	0	0	0
Nicholson	1.000	8	14	2	0	0
Rodriguez	.988	104	236	12	3	1
Scott	.994	83	151	2	1	1

Texas League

BATTING

	B-T	HT	WT	DOB	AVG	vLH	vRH	G	AB	R	H	2B	3B	HR	RBI	BB	HBP	SH	SF	SO	SB	CS	SLG	OBP
Anderson, Josh	L-R	6-2	195	8-10-82	.308	.354	.295	130	561	83	173	26	4	3	50	27	10	8	4	73	43	13	.385	.349
Ash, Jonny	L-R	5-9	185	9-11-82	.314	.323	.311	112	392	40	123	22	5	1	28	25	11	8	2	36	5	8	.403	.357
Bonifay, Josh	R-R	6-0	185	7-30-78	.261	.275	.256	113	394	61	103	25	2	19	75	37	0	0	9	97	5	4	.480	.318
Cortes, Jorge	L-L	5-10	195	10-17-80	.293	.231	.312	126	457	58	134	31	3	8	51	50	4	4	3	63	4	7	.427	.366
Davidson, Kevin	R-R	5-7	180	7-21-80	.203	.195	.206	60	172	24	35	2	1	3	13	31	1	4	4	33	2	1	.279	.322
Fagan, John	R-R	6-5	217	8-8-79	.244	.216	.256	45	127	11	31	8	1	3	16	14	5	3	2	34	3	3	.394	.338
Fernando, Osvaldo	R-R	6-0	175	10-15-80	.217	.240	.200	74	180	17	39	6	0	0	7	8	2	11	0	28	8	5	.250	.258
House, J.R.	R-R	5-10	200	11-11-79	.325	.253	.343	97	379	58	123	23	2	10	69	32	4	0	8	44	2	2	.475	.376
Nicholson, Derek	L-R	5-11	205	6-17-76	.243	.227	.246	59	136	11	33	10	1	2	18	20	0	0	2	28	1	0	.375	.335
Pence, Hunter	R-R	6-4	220	4-13-83	.283	.289	.281	136	523	97	148	31	8	28	95	60	3	1	5	109	17	4	.533	.357
Peterson, Brian	R-R	6-2	225	10-22-78	.329	.500	.245	24	79	11	26	3	0	3	6	4	1	1	0	14	2	1	.481	.369
Redman, Tike	L-L	5-11	175	3-10-77	.311	.217	.338	27	103	17	32	3	0	1	6	16	1	1	0	6	4	2	.369	.408
Robinson, Wade	R-R	6-2	165	1-12-81	.244	.125	.256	32	90	6	22	1	1	1	4	2	0	2	1	15	0	2	.311	.258
Saccomanno, Mark	R-R	6-3	210	4-30-80	.245	.250	.243	83	298	42	73	15	3	20	63	23	2	2	2	84	2	1	.517	.302
Sandberg, Jared	R-R	6-3	225	3-2-78	.186	.258	.165	39	140	16	26	9	0	4	13	9	1	0	0	43	2	0	.336	.240
Young, Walter	L-R	6-5	315	2-18-80	.277	.288	.275	95	346	32	96	16	0	10	60	12	5	0	3	44	4	6	.410	.309
Zobrist, Ben	B-R	6-3	200	5-26-81	.327	.360	.317	83	315	57	103	25	6	3	30	55	5	5	1	46	9	5	.473	.434

PITCHING

	B-T	HT	WT	DOB	W	L	ERA	G	GS	CG	SV	IP	H	R	ER	HR	BB	SO	AVG	vLH	vRH	K/9	BB/9
Albers, Matt	L-R	6-0	205	1-20-83	10	2	2.17	19	19	0	0	116	96	40	28	4	47	95	.223	.284	.191	7.37	3.65
Allen, Blake	R-L	6-2	205	7-17-81	4	2	4.15	19	1	0	0	26	31	22	12	1	13	21	.277	.283	.273	7.27	4.50
Clemens, Roger	R-R	6-4	235	8-4-62	1	0	0.00	1	1	0	0	6	2	0	0	0	1	6	.105	.000	.143	16.50	0.00
Douglass, Chance	R-R	6-1	200	2-24-84	7	8	3.52	28	26	2	0	161	144	67	63	13	56	102	.241	.241	.241	5.70	3.13
Estrada, Paul	R-R	6-2	215	9-10-82	8	5	3.05	56	0	0	15	89	61	33	30	10	37	134	.191	.219	.173	13.60	3.76
Gutierrez, Juan	R-R	6-3	200	7-14-83	8	4	3.04	20	20	0	0	104	94	39	35	10	34	106	.237	.229	.244	9.20	2.95
Hernandez, Carlos	B-L	5-10	200	4-22-80	0	2	12.86	7	3	0	0	14	21	20	20	3	16	10	.362	.300	.395	6.43	10.29
Kent, Steve	B-L	5-11	170	10-3-78	0	0	8.74	11	0	0	0	11	21	12	11	1	12	6	.396	.524	.313	4.76	9.53
Mansfield, Monte	R-R	6-4	215	3-22-81	2	1	3.76	30	0	0	0	53	53	31	22	3	33	49	.255	.287	.231	8.37	5.64
Martinez, Ronnie	R-R	5-11	205	7-6-83	3	1	5.51	19	0	0	0	49	56	30	30	6	18	45	.280	.303	.261	8.27	3.31
Miller, Joshua	R-R	6-1	200	2-7-79	11	10	4.14	33	22	1	0	152	163	83	70	14	41	103	.278	.306	.259	6.10	2.43
Muecke, Joshua	L-L	6-3	195	1-9-82	0	7	7.40	25	9	0	0	62	92	54	51	8	27	43	.351	.397	.335	6.24	3.92
Patton, Troy	B-L	6-1	185	9-3-85	2	5	4.37	8	8	0	0	45	48	26	22	6	13	37	.271	.275	.270	7.35	2.58
Peguero, Jailen	R-R	5-11	180	1-4-81	2	0	0.70	27	0	0	14	39	18	4	3	0	16	48	.144	.173	.123	11.17	3.72
Reineke, Chad	R-R	6-6	210	4-9-82	1	3	3.05	15	4	0	0	44	33	17	15	3	26	45	.209	.231	.194	9.14	5.28
Rollandini, David	R-R	6-5	220	2-6-79	4	4	4.50	47	0	0	2	76	70	42	38	11	28	50	.242	.283	.219	5.92	3.32
Skaggs, Jon	R-R	6-5	225	3-27-78	0	0	5.93	14	0	0	1	30	30	20	20	4	21	28	.268	.333	.229	8.31	6.23
Talbot, Mitch	R-R	6-2	175	10-17-83	6	4	3.39	18	17	0	1	90	94	49	34	4	29	96	.269	.274	.265	9.56	2.89
Williams, Aaron	R-R	6-2	180	10-7-80	7	5	5.25	46	0	0	4	60	67	38	35	10	16	40	.282	.286	.279	6.00	2.40

FIELDING

Catcher	PCT	G	PO	A	E	DP	PB
Davidson	.990	58	368	35	4	1	1
House	.992	68	562	48	5	3	5
Peterson	.977	24	153	17	4	4	0

First Base	PCT	G	PO	A	E	DP
Bonifay	.972	21	155	16	5	20
Fagan	.995	26	178	23	1	20
House	.992	31	243	15	2	17
Nicholson	.989	17	83	11	1	8
Sandberg	1.000	2	14	2	0	2
Young	.983	57	431	44	8	51

Second Base	PCT	G	PO	A	E	DP
Ash	.985	112	186	273	7	60
Bonifay	.948	20	22	33	3	7
Davidson	1.000	1	3	4	0	0
Fernando	1.000	16	21	31	0	10
Robinson	.923	2	4	8	1	2

Third Base	PCT	G	PO	A	E	DP
Bonifay	.754	22	13	33	15	2
Fernando	.750	1	0	3	1	0
Saccomanno	.895	83	74	140	25	8
Sandberg	.901	35	23	68	10	6
Zobrist	.857	2	1	5	1	1

Shortstop	PCT	G	PO	A	E	DP
Fernando	.951	44	77	116	10	34
Robinson	.965	27	42	69	4	19
Zobrist	.958	79	138	203	15	41

Outfield	PCT	G	PO	A	E	DP
Anderson	.972	129	269	7	8	1
Cortes	.972	123	199	8	6	0
Fagan	1.000	20	26	1	0	0
Nicholson	1.000	7	12	0	0	0
Pence	.967	129	251	13	9	2
Redman	.959	19	45	2	2	0

Carolina League

BATTING

	B-T	HT	WT	DOB	AVG	vLH	vRH	G	AB	R	H	2B	3B	HR	RBI	BB	HBP	SH	SF	SO	SB	CS	SLG	OBP
Alcantara, Ervin	R-R	5-11	180	10-3-80	.252	.248	.254	125	452	61	114	21	4	5	39	36	3	13	3	104	20	6	.350	.310
Caraballo, Francisco	R-R	6-1	200	10-21-83	.238	.227	.245	126	449	57	107	40	4	14	65	40	4	4	6	125	2	1	.439	.303
Cunningham, Matthew	R-R	6-2	205	9-24-81	.187	.171	.198	75	187	18	35	13	0	2	19	18	11	10	0	42	2	1	.289	.296
Garza, Mario	L-R	6-0	205	5-26-82	.222	.219	.222	86	230	23	51	12	0	6	33	50	4	2	0	58	1	3	.352	.370
Hart, Billy	R-R	6-2	215	11-2-82	.221	.237	.211	91	285	42	63	19	0	5	33	36	4	5	4	67	7	6	.340	.313
Mackor, Jeffrey	R-R	6-0	210	6-17-80	.272	.292	.262	51	151	20	41	8	1	2	31	11	4	2	2	22	1	2	.377	.333
Maysonet, Edwin	R-R	6-1	180	10-17-81	.254	.229	.269	113	378	58	96	32	0	8	38	20	8	11	4	58	21	3	.402	.302
Robinson, Scott	L-L	6-1	195	10-14-83	.230	.152	.266	70	248	20	57	13	0	3	21	17	1	1	3	33	1	2	.319	.281
Robinson, Wade	L-R	6-2	165	1-12-81	.294	.250	.300	26	68	12	20	1	0	0	9	4	0	2	0	14	5	2	.309	.333
Santangelo, Louis	R-R	6-1	200	3-16-83	.241	.289	.205	98	357	48	86	19	5	18	56	36	0	0	1	112	0	4	.473	.310
Sellers, Neil	R-R	6-0	195	4-3-82	.271	.347	.240	127	451	53	122	40	2	2	61	48	10	1	5	60	10	6	.381	.350
Sheldon, Ole	R-R	6-4	210	11-25-82	.292	.310	.282	46	161	19	47	6	0	1	24	31	5	0	0	32	2	1	.348	.421
Sutil, Wladimir	R-R	5-10	135	10-31-84	.227	.243	.217	29	97	14	22	5	0	0	9	9	0	7	0	10	8	3	.278	.292
Sutton, Drew	B-R	6-3	185	6-30-83	.263	.246	.266	125	456	65	120	27	2	15	48	69	3	17	6	84	20	15	.430	.360
Thompson, Michael	R-R	6-4	210	2-9-84	.224	.324	.083	18	58	3	13	2	0	1	3	0	3	0	2	0	10	1	0	.259	.262
Torbert, Wallace	R-R	6-4	205	5-1-83	.305	.333	.290	119	455	69	139	31	1	5	52	24	6	1	7	71	24	10	.411	.343

ORGANIZATION STATISTICS

PITCHING	B-T	HT	WT	DOB	W	L	ERA	G	GS	CG	SV	IP	H	R	ER	HR	BB	SO	AVG	vLH	vRH	K/9	BB/9
Barthmaier, James	R-R	6-4	210	1-6-84	11	8	3.62	27	27	0	0	147	137	64	59	6	67	134	.252	.270	.236	8.22	4.11
Dewitt, Anthony	R-R	6-0	225	5-30-82	0	2	6.52	7	0	0	0	10	12	9	7	2	5	4	.300	.263	.333	3.72	4.66
Diaz, Raymar	R-R	6-7	190	11-13-83	3	2	3.56	8	8	0	0	43	42	18	17	2	13	29	.264	.328	.224	6.07	2.72
Englebrook, Evan	R-R	6-8	225	4-28-82	9	4	3.31	36	10	0	0	109	95	46	40	6	46	82	.235	.296	.186	6.79	3.81
Escobar, Rodrigo	R-R	5-11	170	2-11-83	3	3	5.37	49	0	0	17	64	58	39	38	8	41	64	.247	.284	.221	9.05	5.80
Fairchild, Thomas	R-R	6-2	200	12-5-83	4	4	3.78	11	11	0	0	64	63	31	27	3	19	44	.254	.238	.266	6.16	2.66
Martinez, Ronnie	R-R	5-11	205	7-6-83	3	4	1.93	10	10	0	0	56	52	17	12	2	17	44	.256	.200	.293	7.07	2.73
Melendez, German	R-R	6-0	185	9-13-80	1	1	3.15	16	0	0	6	20	16	7	7	1	8	17	.213	.258	.182	7.65	3.60
Patton, Troy	B-L	6-1	185	9-3-85	7	7	2.93	19	19	1	0	101	92	49	33	4	37	102	.240	.244	.238	9.06	3.29
Paulino Del Guidice, Felipe	R-R	6-2	180	10-5-83	9	7	4.35	27	26	0	0	126	119	67	61	13	59	91	.250	.239	.258	6.48	4.20
Pence, Howard	R-R	6-5	210	10-1-79	0	0	0.00	1	0	0	0	2	2	0	0	0	1	1	.286	.333	.250	5.40	5.40
Reineke, Chad	R-R	6-6	210	4-9-82	6	5	2.98	17	17	1	0	100	82	42	33	5	29	87	.220	.219	.222	7.86	2.62
Shortell, Rory	R-R	6-3	205	6-3-81	8	7	3.23	36	9	0	2	103	89	39	37	3	43	61	.244	.274	.219	5.33	3.76
Soto, Enyelbert	L-L	6-1	200	8-20-82	2	3	1.75	44	0	0	1	57	57	19	11	1	19	43	.264	.266	.262	6.83	3.02
Stiehl, Robert	R-R	6-3	215	12-9-80	2	2	4.55	36	0	0	3	55	55	30	28	1	27	51	.257	.340	.192	8.30	4.39
Thompson, Ryan	R-R	6-4	220	8-6-82	2	0	2.93	48	0	0	10	77	59	25	25	8	17	66	.216	.283	.174	7.75	2.00
Wigdahl, Jeffrey	L-L	6-0	190	6-4-82	6	2	2.00	46	0	0	2	67	45	16	15	1	36	58	.197	.198	.197	7.75	4.81

FIELDING

Catcher	PCT	G	PO	A	E	DP	PB
Garza	.944	4	15	2	1	1	2
Mackor	.987	44	265	28	4	3	5
Santangelo	.992	97	703	73	6	4	13

	PCT	G	PO	A	E	DP
Sellers	1.000	4	2	5	0	2
Sutil	1.000	7	19	18	0	2
Sutton	.978	121	183	361	12	65
Thompson	1.000	3	6	7	0	2

	PCT	G	PO	A	E	DP
Robinson	.853	8	13	16	5	4
Sutil	.986	20	26	46	1	10
Sutton	1.000	7	7	24	0	3

First Base	PCT	G	PO	A	E	DP
Garza	.989	23	170	12	2	19
Robinson	.983	48	418	34	8	34
Sellers	.985	31	247	18	4	28
Sheldon	.991	43	397	25	4	38

Third Base	PCT	G	PO	A	E	DP
Hart	.914	75	40	120	15	7
Mackor	—	2	0	0	0	0
Sellers	.980	54	30	70	2	7
Thompson	.974	16	12	25	1	2

Outfield	PCT	G	PO	A	E	DP
Alcantara	.993	124	268	13	2	4
Caraballo	.991	126	221	10	2	2
Cunningham	.989	66	87	1	1	0
Garza	—	2	0	0	0	0
Torbert	.981	115	194	10	4	3

Second Base	PCT	G	PO	A	E	DP
Robinson	.958	11	17	29	2	7

Shortstop	PCT	G	PO	A	E	DP
Maysonet	.975	112	176	329	13	71

Lexington Legends — Low Class A

South Atlantic League

BATTING	B-T	HT	WT	DOB	AVG	vLH	vRH	G	AB	R	H	2B	3B	HR	RBI	BB	HBP	SH	SF	SO	SB	CS	SLG	OBP
Cavers, Eric	R-R	6-1	205	11-9-82	.165	.267	.141	28	79	3	13	0	0	0	6	10	0	3	1	22	2	1	.203	.256
Clemens, Koby	R-R	5-11	193	12-4-86	.229	.265	.215	91	306	40	70	19	1	5	39	32	7	4	3	67	2	1	.346	.313
Einertson, Mitch	R-R	5-10	178	4-4-86	.211	.243	.199	122	426	51	90	25	1	12	62	31	8	1	3	77	6	2	.359	.276
Espinoza, Pedro	R-R	6-1	170	5-6-85	.237	.200	.258	58	190	15	45	10	2	0	20	10	1	6	1	12	3	0	.311	.277
Flores, Joshua	R-R	6-0	195	11-18-85	.253	.189	.276	125	475	81	120	19	2	11	35	33	9	9	0	107	28	6	.371	.313
Iorg, Eli	R-R	6-3	200	3-14-83	.256	.315	.233	125	469	68	120	32	4	15	85	33	8	2	4	119	42	6	.437	.313
Kady, David	L-R	5-11	205	7-29-80	.141	.133	.143	22	64	4	9	1	0	0	5	7	1	0	0	19	0	0	.156	.236
King, Eric	R-R	5-9	175	7-2-82	.244	.295	.226	106	397	56	97	21	3	1	44	36	4	11	7	56	15	1	.320	.309
Lopez, Jose	R-R	5-11	195	3-8-85	.188	.222	.173	38	117	10	22	5	0	1	7	6	4	2	1	30	0	1	.256	.250
Mackor, Jeffrey	R-R	6-0	210	6-17-80	.333	—	.333	1	3	1	1	0	0	0	1	0	0	1	0	0	1		.667	.500
Manzella, Thomas	R-R	6-2	190	4-16-83	.275	.222	.292	99	338	50	93	22	1	7	43	33	3	8	5	80	16	8	.408	.340
Ori, Mark	L-R	6-4	225	12-16-83	.274	.287	.271	117	412	63	113	25	3	8	60	40	11	0	3	94	4	5	.408	.352
Ramirez, Ronald	R-R	6-0	149	1-30-86	.200	.250	.167	3	10	0	2	0	0	0	0	0	0	0	0	1	0	0	.200	.200
Reed, Ryan	L-L	6-4	210	12-19-83	.219	.229	.217	86	292	30	64	12	4	7	37	21	3	1	2	103	14	6	.360	.277
Sheldon, Ole	R-R	6-4	210	11-25-82	.328	.279	.344	70	241	46	79	27	0	4	32	43	5	0	2	43	7	3	.490	.436
Sutil, Wladimir	R-R	5-10	135	10-31-84	.272	.308	.259	60	195	31	53	8	0	0	12	19	5	4	0	15	20	5	.313	.352
Thompson, Michael	R-R	6-4	210	2-9-84	.212	.262	.195	54	170	14	36	10	0	4	18	4	3	3	1	40	0	1	.341	.242
Towles, Justin	R-R	6-2	195	2-11-84	.317	.253	.341	81	284	39	90	19	2	12	55	21	10	4	2	46	13	5	.525	.382
Warrick, Nathan	R-R	6-0	170	9-10-83	.245	.261	.241	36	110	16	27	5	0	0	4	7	0	3	0	25	9	4	.291	.346

PITCHING	B-T	HT	WT	DOB	W	L	ERA	G	GS	CG	SV	IP	H	R	ER	HR	BB	SO	AVG	vLH	vRH	K/9	BB/9
Arguello, Douglas	L-L	6-3	190	11-21-84	0	3	6.42	10	0	0	0	34	32	27	24	7	19	33	.242	.261	.239	8.82	5.08
Blazek, Christopher	L-L	6-0	195	3-2-84	2	1	3.82	41	0	0	4	71	66	35	30	6	42	66	.248	.253	.246	8.41	5.35
Bogusevic, Brian	L-L	6-3	215	2-18-84	2	5	4.73	17	17	0	0	70	76	44	37	6	24	60	.274	.377	.250	7.68	3.07
Campos, Christian	L-L	6-1	210	8-28-83	1	5	4.85	25	0	0	0	43	31	29	23	3	33	43	.201	.229	.189	9.07	6.96
Cavanaugh, Nick	R-R	6-2	210	3-14-82	1	0	2.89	6	0	0	1	9	7	3	3	1	3	14	.206	.308	.143	13.50	2.89
Clemens, Roger	R-R	6-4	235	8-4-62	0	0	3.00	1	1	0	0	3	3	1	1	1	0	6	.250	.273	.000	18.00	0.00
Diaz, Raymar	R-R	6-7	190	11-13-83	8	5	2.36	23	14	0	0	99	84	35	26	8	35	107	.231	.209	.246	9.69	3.17
Espinoza, Pedro	R-R	6-1	170	5-6-85	0	0	27.00	1	0	0	0	1	4	3	3	1	1	0	.667	.333	1.000	0.00	9.00
Fairchild, Thomas	R-R	6-2	200	12-5-83	10	3	1.66	18	16	1	0	109	90	25	20	5	19	98	.227	.198	.248	8.12	1.57
Gant, James	R-R	6-2	190	9-14-82	2	4	5.58	29	0	0	1	50	47	39	31	6	29	46	.240	.227	.248	8.28	5.22
Gervacio, Samuel	R-R	5-11	160	1-10-85	7	5	2.58	47	0	0	10	84	58	28	24	8	28	89	.197	.221	.181	9.57	3.01
Hurry, Jacob	L-L	6-3	220	8-12-82	4	2	3.24	12	1	0	1	25	28	10	9	1	8	11	.298	.357	.273	3.96	2.88
James, Brad	R-R	6-2	200	6-19-84	6	2	1.36	17	14	1	0	92	75	24	14	3	28	51	.220	.217	.222	4.97	2.73
Martinez, Ronnie	R-R	5-11	205	7-6-83	0	0	4.76	2	2	0	0	6	3	3	3	0	2	7	.150	.182	.111	11.12	3.18
McKeller, Ryan	R-R	6-5	220	7-8-83	4	3	4.04	11	8	0	1	42	51	25	19	4	22	30	.302	.212	.359	6.38	4.68
Melendez, German	R-R	6-0	185	9-13-80	2	0	1.32	23	0	0	7	34	17	5	5	1	9	44	.150	.205	.116	11.65	2.38
Murdy, Garrett	R-R	6-4	215	3-15-83	6	5	3.38	32	13	0	2	114	112	57	43	11	37	75	.253	.249	.256	5.90	2.91
Owens, Ryan	R-L	6-1	185	8-9-83	1	3	2.17	16	2	0	3	37	34	15	9	1	24	30	.246	.182	.277	7.23	5.79
Perez, Sergio	R-R	6-3	230	12-5-84	3	0	2.20	11	0	0	0	16	9	6	4	0	8	21	.153	.190	.132	11.57	4.41
Romero, Levi	R-R	6-5	185	4-12-84	5	5	5.43	15	15	0	0	66	80	43	40	7	26	49	.300	.290	.308	6.65	3.53
Sarver, Scott	L-L	6-2	205	11-4-82	1	0	8.41	15	0	0	1	20	39	20	19	6	10	18	.424	.375	.441	7.97	4.43
Stricklen, Brandon	R-R	6-1	200	2-20-84	4	2	5.03	29	0	0	9	39	44	22	22	8	21	29	.289	.276	.298	6.64	4.81
Thompson, Michael	R-R	6-4	210	2-9-84	0	0	0.00	1	0	0	1	1	0	0	0	0	1	1	.250	.000	.333	9.00	0.00
Walker, Sean	R-R	6-1	175	10-31-82	6	10	4.61	25	25	1	0	139	149	87	71	14	44	113	.270	.299	.251	7.33	2.86

FIELDING

Catcher	PCT	G	PO	A	E	DP	PB
Cavers	.986	25	180	25	3	3	15
Kady	.981	20	145	6	3	2	4
Lopez	.965	38	253	24	10	3	8
Mackor	.933	1	14	0	1	0	0
Sheldon	1.000	1	4	1	0	0	0
Towles	.990	61	454	28	5	4	4

First Base	PCT	G	PO	A	E	DP
Espinoza	1.000	4	29	2	0	2
Ori	.987	91	771	65	11	77
Sheldon	.989	41	322	34	4	24
Thompson	.957	7	45	0	2	9

Second Base	PCT	G	PO	A	E	DP
Clemens	1.000	1	2	4	0	1

	PCT	G	PO	A	E	DP
Espinoza	.949	21	38	56	5	9
King	.980	102	194	284	10	69
Ramirez	1.000	1	2	2	0	0
Sutil	.988	15	37	46	1	10
Thompson	.889	4	9	7	2	3

Third Base	PCT	G	PO	A	E	DP
Clemens	.887	84	50	131	23	10
Espinoza	.882	11	6	24	4	5
Sheldon	1.000	1	0	3	0	0
Sutil	.840	15	7	14	4	2
Thompson	.904	38	17	68	9	3

Shortstop	PCT	G	PO	A	E	DP
Einertson	.900	1	3	6	1	1
Espinoza	.958	20	27	64	4	17

	PCT	G	PO	A	E	DP
King	.667	1	1	3	2	1
Manzella	.956	94	125	269	18	57
Ramirez	.875	2	1	6	1	0
Sutil	.952	29	36	63	5	19

Outfield	PCT	G	PO	A	E	DP
Einertson	.971	112	189	14	6	2
Flores	.975	115	229	4	6	1
Iorg	.961	120	216	8	9	0
Reed	.910	57	80	1	8	1
Sutil	.833	1	4	1	1	0
Towles	1.000	1	1	0	0	0
Warrick	1.000	27	46	1	0	0

Tri-City ValleyCats — Short-Season

New York-Penn League

BATTING

	B-T	HT	WT	DOB	AVG	vLH	vRH	G	AB	R	H	2B	3B	HR	RBI	BB	HBP	SH	SF	SO	SB	CS	SLG	OBP
Buchanan, Greg	B-R	5-11	180	11-16-83	.272	.323	.251	60	232	34	63	8	2	2	18	18	3	1	2	31	8	1	.349	.329
Bulkley, Aaron	R-R	6-4	195	5-6-83	.228	.314	.182	33	101	6	23	4	1	2	7	11	3	1	0	38	5	2	.347	.322
Caipen, Brandon	R-R	6-0	180	8-4-83	.167	.000	.250	2	6	1	1	0	0	0	0	2	0	0	0	2	0	0	.167	.375
Espinoza, Pedro	R-R	6-1	170	5-6-85	.250	1.000	.143	2	8	1	2	0	0	0	0	0	0	0	0	0	0	0	.250	.250
Florentino, Jhon	R-R	6-0	155	8-22-83	.221	.246	.211	62	222	21	49	12	2	4	27	15	5	1	3	53	7	1	.347	.282
Goethals, James	R-R	5-11	195	7-12-82	.000	.000	.000	4	10	0	0	0	0	0	0	1	0	0	0	6	0	0	.000	.091
Holder, Andrew	R-R	6-0	210	10-2-83	.221	.138	.247	34	122	17	27	3	1	2	10	9	0	1	0	32	0	2	.311	.275
Johnson, Christopher	R-R	6-3	220	10-1-84	.212	.250	.198	60	222	18	47	7	1	1	29	11	2	0	4	35	7	3	.266	.251
Kroeker, Andrew	L-R	6-1	205	6-1-83	.259	.040	.304	21	54	6	14	2	0	2	6	6	2	2	0	20	0	0	.407	.355
Moresi, Nicholas	R-R	6-4	180	11-22-84	.180	.236	.159	57	206	17	37	5	1	2	21	15	7	3	1	59	6	2	.243	.258
Parraz, Jordan	R-R	6-3	220	10-8-84	.336	.309	.346	70	253	46	85	18	2	6	38	33	7	1	4	44	23	3	.494	.421
Quintero, Cesar A.	R-R	5-11	165	1-7-83	.333	.263	.358	18	72	15	24	3	1	1	9	6	1	1	1	17	6	1	.444	.388
Rosales, Orlando	R-R	5-8	180	4-9-84	.250	.400	.192	10	36	6	9	0	0	1	6	5	1	0	2	9	1	0	.333	.341
Sapp, Maxwell	L-R	6-2	220	2-21-88	.229	.213	.235	50	166	20	38	9	1	0	20	22	0	0	1	37	0	0	.301	.317
Smith, Andrew	R-R	6-1	190	1-10-84	.077	.000	.083	6	13	3	1	0	0	0	1	2	0	0	0	6	0	0	.077	.200
Taylor, Eric	R-R		195	7-29-85	.315	.333	.308	68	251	42	79	18	1	2	20	27	7	4	2	40	9	3	.418	.394
Tellam, Justin	R-R	6-3	190	11-20-84	.250	.286	.233	41	128	15	32	4	1	3	25	8	2	1	2	35	0	0	.367	.300
Torres, Tim	B-R	6-2	180	11-12-83	.217	.302	.184	64	226	35	49	14	2	1	28	41	1	8	3	50	13	4	.310	.336
Van Ostrand, James	R-R	6-4	210	8-7-84	.215	.324	.183	40	149	14	32	6	0	2	13	9	3	1	1	36	2	3	.295	.272
Warrick, Nathan	L-L	6-0	170	9-10-83	.500	.500	.500	3	10	4	5	1	0	0	2	3	0	0	0	2	3	0	.600	.615

PITCHING

	B-T	HT	WT	DOB	W	L	ERA	G	GS	CG	SV	IP	H	R	ER	HR	BB	SO	AVG	vLH	vRH	K/9	BB/9
Arguello, Douglas	L-L	6-3	190	11-21-84	6	6	4.14	14	14	0	0	72	68	37	33	5	19	65	.260	.325	.232	8.16	2.39
Babilonia, Edgar	R-R	5-10	190	8-5-83	0	1	8.59	3	0	0	0	7	7	7	7	0	8	5	.259	.455	.125	6.14	9.82
Bogusevic, Brian	L-L	6-3	215	2-18-84	0	0	4.09	3	3	0	0	11	10	8	5	1	5	6	.233	.308	.200	4.91	4.09
DeYoung, Kyle	R-R	6-0	190	8-15-84	1	4	5.25	20	0	0	4	36	45	25	21	3	8	24	.302	.379	.253	6.00	2.00
Garate, Victor	L-L	6-1	160	9-25-84	4	0	0.92	21	0	0	8	39	14	6	4	2	21	59	.112	.103	.116	13.50	4.81
Hallberg, Bryan	R-R	6-0	185	4-23-85	4	3	2.44	15	12	0	1	70	63	23	19	3	21	53	.243	.248	.240	6.81	2.70
Hudspeth, Casey	R-R	6-0	165	10-1-84	3	4	3.78	15	12	0	1	64	71	34	27	6	19	50	.276	.276	.276	6.99	2.66
Hurry, Jacob	L-L	6-3	220	8-12-82	1	0	3.80	8	1	0	1	24	13	10	10	2	12	22	.160	.273	.119	8.37	4.56
Lapinski, Cory	R-L	6-0	210	3-8-84	2	1	2.41	18	0	0	2	37	17	11	10	0	29	45	.139	.171	.126	10.85	6.99
Mayora, Cesar	R-R	6-2	185	1-1-84	1	0	1.98	17	0	0	0	27	21	6	6	2	11	23	.202	.231	.185	7.57	3.62
Norris, Bud	R-R	6-0	195	3-2-85	2	0	3.79	15	3	0	2	38	28	20	16	1	13	46	.200	.235	.167	10.89	3.08
Polanco, Celson	R-R	6-5	200	8-28-84	1	1	4.89	19	0	0	2	39	47	25	21	4	18	30	.305	.265	.337	6.98	4.19
Qualben, David	L-L	6-3	200	7-29-85	5	5	2.25	14	14	0	0	72	54	26	18	5	20	43	.218	.181	.233	5.38	2.50
Salamida, Christopher	L-L	6-0	180	5-7-84	10	1	1.06	14	14	0	0	68	44	12	8	2	23	53	.189	.234	.172	7.01	3.04
Stiver, Justin	R-R	6-2	190	8-7-84	2	0	0.00	4	0	0	0	6	1	0	0	1	0	3	.056	.125	.000	4.50	1.50
Trinidad, Polin	L-L	6-2	170	11-19-84	0	0	4.50	2	1	0	0	8	14	4	4	0	3	5	.389	.375	.400	5.63	3.38
Wagler, Chad	R-R	6-1	185	9-11-83	1	5	2.87	20	0	0	0	47	43	22	15	3	13	33	.249	.269	.232	6.32	2.49

FIELDING

Catcher	PCT	G	PO	A	E	DP	PB
Goethals	1.000	4	20	0	0	0	0
Kroeker	1.000	18	110	7	0	1	2
Sapp	.972	31	191	18	6	1	11
Tellam	.993	37	251	24	2	1	7

First Base	PCT	G	PO	A	E	DP
Johnson	1.000	2	13	2	0	2
Kroeker	1.000	2	9	0	0	0
Taylor	.997	63	523	57	2	36
Van Ostrand	1.000	9	86	17	0	9

Second Base	PCT	G	PO	A	E	DP
Buchanan	.997	59	126	177	1	36

	PCT	G	PO	A	E	DP
Espinoza	1.000	2	0	7	0	0
Quintero	.945	10	28	24	3	8
Torres	.947	5	8	10	1	1

Third Base	PCT	G	PO	A	E	DP
Caipen	1.000	2	1	4	0	0
Florentino	.920	20	11	35	4	1
Johnson	.969	49	26	68	3	8
Torres	.789	6	5	10	4	2

Shortstop	PCT	G	PO	A	E	DP
Buchanan	1.000	1	2	0	0	0
Florentino	.916	31	27	71	9	12
Smith	1.000	2	3	7	0	2

	PCT	G	PO	A	E	DP
Torres	.961	43	69	126	8	21

Outfield	PCT	G	PO	A	E	DP
Bulkley	.980	26	46	3	1	1
Holder	.979	31	46	1	1	0
Moresi	.965	57	135	3	5	0
Parraz	.987	69	146	7	2	1
Quintero	1.000	8	15	1	0	1
Rosales	1.000	9	25	0	0	0
Taylor	—	1	0	0	0	0
Van Ostrand	.967	22	26	3	1	1
Warrick	1.000	3	0	1	0	0

Appalachian League

BATTING

BATTING	B-T	HT	WT	DOB	AVG	vLH	vRH	G	AB	R	H	2B	3B	HR	RBI	BB	HBP	SH	SF	SO	SB	CS	SLG	OBP
Barnes, Brandon	R-R	6-2	210	5-15-86	.220	.300	.195	52	173	19	38	11	1	2	14	16	2	0	0	47	5	3	.329	.293
Brown, Steve	R-R	6-0	180	9-3-86	.306	.346	.291	54	193	36	59	3	2	1	12	9	4	2	3	35	12	5	.358	.344
Caipen, Brandon	R-R	6-0	180	8-4-83	.265	.250	.269	66	249	39	66	11	1	3	20	37	7	1	1	28	15	9	.353	.374
Cruz, Cirilo	R-R	6-2	215	2-13-85	.220	.314	.192	64	223	32	49	13	1	7	27	29	9	1	0	78	1	0	.381	.333
Darnell, Andrew	R-R	6-1	215	7-15-86	.211	.162	.227	47	147	19	31	4	1	4	16	17	3	1	1	51	2	1	.333	.304
Goethals, James	R-R	5-11	195	7-12-82	.189	.273	.154	27	74	11	14	3	1	2	9	15	0	2	0	31	1	2	.338	.326
Henriquez, Ralph	B-R	6-1	190	4-7-87	.231	.200	.239	62	238	15	55	11	0	5	37	15	1	0	5	56	1	1	.340	.274
Johnson, Timothy	R-R	6-1	180	10-15-86	.127	.167	.119	28	71	4	9	2	0	0	5	10	3	3	0	20	2	0	.155	.262
Langdon, Allen	L-R	5-11	220	9-7-86	.232	.185	.243	46	142	18	33	8	1	1	16	17	7	0	0	51	2	1	.324	.343
Pestana, Reinaldo	R-R	6-1	180	5-24-87	.146	.308	.071	18	41	6	6	2	0	1	3	3	4	0	0	9	0	0	.268	.271
Ramirez, Reinaldo	R-R	6-1	160	9-16-85	.237	.235	.238	56	198	22	47	4	5	1	15	14	4	4	0	50	12	5	.323	.301
Ramirez, Ronald	R-R	6-0	149	1-30-86	.314	.316	.314	57	229	23	72	20	2	3	33	11	1	3	0	42	7	3	.459	.349
Rosales, Orlando	R-R	5-8	180	4-9-84	.248	.205	.258	53	202	25	50	7	3	2	24	14	4	1	4	31	5	2	.342	.304
Spath, Matthew	R-R	6-2	185	10-21-86	.222	.154	.261	15	36	6	8	0	0	1	3	4	2	1	0	12	0	1	.306	.333
Zazueta, Amadeo	B-R	5-10	160	1-31-86	.170	.333	.122	28	53	4	9	2	0	1	5	3	0	1	0	9	0	0	.264	.214

PITCHING

PITCHING	B-T	HT	WT	DOB	W	L	ERA	G	GS	CG	SV	IP	H	R	ER	HR	BB	SO	AVG	vLH	vRH	K/9	BB/9
Adams, Colt	R-R	6-5	220	5-23-85	1	1	11.77	10	0	0	0	13	25	19	17	0	7	12	.403	.450	.381	8.31	4.85
Bailey, Griffin	R-R	6-5	220	9-19-84	0	1	4.50	5	0	0	0	8	11	7	4	0	5	6	.355	.571	.292	6.75	5.63
Bass, Corey	R-R	6-3	210	2-8-85	5	2	3.75	13	13	0	0	70	76	44	29	5	17	47	.275	.354	.233	6.07	2.20
Bello, Anthony	L-L	6-2	200	10-9-85	2	2	1.94	14	8	0	0	51	53	14	11	2	14	30	.272	.393	.251	5.29	2.47
Fox, Kevin	L-L	6-1	180	8-24-85	2	2	3.26	17	0	0	1	30	26	22	11	4	14	22	.228	.304	.209	6.53	4.15
Hale, Adam	L-R	6-4	205	3-7-85	1	0	2.13	17	0	0	2	25	22	7	6	0	13	19	.234	.273	.222	6.75	4.62
Kelly, Reid	R-R	6-1	182	10-31-86	4	0	3.66	20	0	0	3	39	37	19	16	1	9	26	.250	.316	.227	5.95	2.06
Ladeuth, Carlos	R-R	5-11	180	6-13-84	1	1	1.58	21	0	0	1	40	25	9	7	1	15	43	.170	.208	.152	9.68	3.38
Luis, Santo	R-R	6-5	205	1-27-84	2	2	1.82	25	0	0	10	35	24	11	7	2	16	40	.202	.267	.180	10.38	4.15
Mayora, Cesar	R-R	6-2	185	1-1-84	1	1	0.84	4	0	0	1	11	7	2	1	0	2	13	.194	.200	.192	10.97	1.69
Mitchell, Ryan	R-R	6-5	235	8-13-87	4	4	4.40	11	11	0	0	57	59	35	28	7	11	39	.257	.310	.226	6.12	1.73
Nelson, Jack	L-L	6-0	205	6-7-84	0	4	5.67	16	0	0	0	27	42	18	17	0	7	19	.350	.333	.353	6.33	2.33
Owens, Ryan	R-L	6-1	185	8-9-83	0	1	3.00	2	0	0	0	6	3	2	2	0	4	5	.143	.000	.200	7.50	6.00
Severino, Sergio	L-L	5-11	150	9-1-84	6	3	2.90	13	13	0	0	68	50	24	22	4	27	90	.204	.107	.217	11.85	3.56
Trinidad, Polin	L-L	6-2	170	11-19-84	4	4	2.39	13	13	0	0	75	59	24	20	2	10	66	.208	.103	.225	7.88	1.19
Vessella, Thomas	R-L	6-6	205	10-12-85	1	5	4.60	13	9	0	0	43	48	25	22	2	17	30	.286	.320	.280	6.28	3.56

FIELDING

Catcher	PCT	G	PO	A	E	DP	PB
Goethals	.995	26	180	16	1	0	4
Henriquez	.990	40	281	30	3	2	11
Pestana	1.000	7	46	0	0	0	0

First Base	PCT	G	PO	A	E	DP
Cruz	.984	63	516	31	9	51
Pestana	.982	7	52	4	1	4

Second Base	PCT	G	PO	A	E	DP
Remirez	.970	51	89	136	7	31

Third Base	PCT	G	PO	A	E	DP
Remirez	1.000	13	38	35	0	11
Zazueta	.957	6	9	13	1	2
Caipen	.924	60	45	113	13	11
Zazueta	.939	22	7	24	2	2

Shortstop	PCT	G	PO	A	E	DP
Johnson	.846	27	40	70	20	11
Remirez	1.000	1	2	4	0	1
Remirez	.919	44	70	146	19	31

Outfield	PCT	G	PO	A	E	DP
Barnes	.981	50	102	3	2	1
Brown	.961	50	71	3	3	0
Caipen	1.000	3	3	0	0	0
Darnell	.986	39	64	4	1	1
Langdon	.929	7	13	0	1	0
Rosales	.977	53	122	7	3	4
Spath	.882	13	15	0	2	0

ORGANIZATION STATISTICS

KANSAS CITY ROYALS

BY ALAN ESKEW

The Royals were doomed to a dreadful season almost from the beginning of spring training, and a terrible start cost general manager Allard Baird his job.

Zack Greinke, Runelvys Hernandez and Mark Redman were three pitchers the Royals were counting on for their 2006 rotation. Greinke left camp before the first exhibition game, returning home for personal reasons and reportedly for counseling. When he returned, he spent most of the season with Double-A Wichita and made three relief appearances in the majors after a September callup.

Hernandez reported to camp overweight and out of shape and began the season in the minors. Redman needed knee surgery after his first spring training appearance and began the season on the disabled list, though he recovered to lead the team with 11 wins.

Closer Mike MacDougal also went down with a shoulder injury and missed the first three months of the season. He was traded to the White Sox in late July.

With 60 percent of their rotation and closer on the shelf to start the season, the Royals lost 43 of their first 57 games before Dayton Moore, who was an assistant to Atlanta GM John Schuerholz, took over on June 8.

Moore, who became the sixth GM in franchise history, quickly went to work reshaping the organization. He acquired speedy outfielder Joey Gathright from the Devil Rays, first baseman Ryan Shealy and reliever Scott Dohmann from the Rockies, lefthander Odalis Perez from the Dodgers, lefthander Jorge de la Rosa from the Brewers and utility player Jeff Keppinger from the Mets, as well as pitching prospects Tyler Lumsden and Daniel Cortes from the White Sox, Blake Johnson and Julio Pimentel

from the Dodgers and Jose Diaz from the Rangers.

The Royals went through a club-record 31 pitchers, including 16 starters. The staff's 5.65 ERA was the worst in the majors. With the ineffective pitching, the Royals had their third consecutive 100-loss season and their fourth in five seasons.

Scott Elarton, who was the Opening Day starter, needed shoulder surgery in July and is unlikely to return before June 2007. Most other members of the rotation to start the season were not with the team by the end of July. Jeremy Affeldt and Denny Bautista were traded to Colorado, while Joe Mays was released after compiling a 10.27 ERA in six starts.

Mark Teahen, David DeJesus and Mark Grudzielanek were among the bright spots. Teahen, who was sent to Triple-A Omaha after a slow start, led the club with 18 home runs and hit .290, but he had season-ending shoulder surgery on Sept. 8 to repair a torn right labrum and rotator cuff. DeJesus missed more than a month with a left hamstring injury, but hit .295 in 119 games. Grudzielanek led the team with a .297 average and 83 runs, while his .994 fielding percentage ranked third among big league second basemen.

DH Mike Sweeney sustained another back injury and was limited to 60 games and hit just .258 with eight home runs. Aging outfielder Reggie Sanders hit .246 and appeared in just 88 games before needing knee surgery in August.

Third baseman Alex Gordon and outfielder Billy Butler hold much of the hope for the future. Gordon, the second overall pick in the 2005 draft, was Baseball America's Minor League Player of the Year after hitting .325/.427/.588 with Double-A Wichita in his first professional season. Teammate Butler led the Texas League with a .331 average.

The Royals had the first overall pick in the draft for the first time in franchise history and chose righthander Luke Hochevar, who did not sign with the Dodgers after being selected by the Dodgers in 2005. The Royals will have the second overall pick in the 2007 draft, the third straight year they have picked first or second.

ORGANIZATION LEADERS

BATTING
*Minimum 250 at-bats

*AVG	Mertins, Kurt, Idaho Falls	.342
R	Gordon, Alex, Wichita	111
H	Maier, Mitch, Wichita	183
TB	Gordon, Alex, Wichita	286
2B	Gordon, Alex, Wichita	39
3B	Lubanski, Chris, Wichita	11
HR	Gordon, Alex, Wichita	29
RBI	Gordon, Alex, Wichita	101
BB	Johnson, Joshua, Burlington	93
SO	Senreiso, Juan, Wichita/High Desert	122
SB	Lisson, Mario, Burlington	41
*OBP	Doscher, Nicholas, AZL Royals	.462
*SLG	Gordon, Alex, Wichita	.588
XBH	Gordon, Alex, Wichita	69

PITCHING
#Minimum 75 innings

W	Plummer, Jarod, High Desert/Wichita	13
L	Cota, Luis, High Desert	11
	Middleton, Kyle, Wichita/Omaha	11
#ERA	Fisher, Brent, AZL Royals/Idaho Falls	2.12
G	DeHoyos, Gabe, High Desert/Wichita	58
CG	Bernero, Adam, Scranton/WB/Omaha	2
SV	DeHoyos, Gabe, High Desert/Wichita	20
IP	Buckner, Billy, High Desert/Wichita	166
BB	Buckner, Billy, High Desert/Wichita	86
SO	Nicoll, Christopher, Burlington/High Desert	166
#AVG	Fisher, Brent, AZL Royals/Idaho Falls	.169

Kansas City Royals · MLB

American League

BATTING

BATTING	B-T	HT	WT	DOB	AVG	vLH	vRH	G	AB	R	H	2B	3B	HR	RBI	BB	HBP	SH	SF	SO	SB	CS	SLG	OBP
Bako, Paul	L-R	6-2	215	6-20-72	.209	.200	.210	56	153	7	32	3	0	0	10	11	0	2	1	46	0	0	.229	.261
Berroa, Angel	R-R	6-0	190	1-27-78	.234	.217	.241	132	474	45	111	18	1	9	54	14	3	9	3	88	3	1	.333	.259
Blanco, Andres	B-R	5-10	185	4-11-84	.241	.500	.174	33	87	9	21	4	1	0	9	5	1	3	0	14	0	1	.310	.290
Brown, Emil	R-R	6-2	210	12-29-74	.287	.236	.308	147	527	77	151	41	2	15	81	59	5	0	10	95	6	3	.457	.358
Buck, John	R-R	6-3	220	7-7-80	.245	.246	.245	114	371	37	91	21	1	11	50	26	7	4	1	84	0	2	.396	.306
Costa, Shane	L-R	6-0	200	12-12-81	.274	.244	.281	72	237	23	65	20	1	3	23	6	5	2	2	29	2	0	.405	.304
DeJesus, David	L-L	6-0	185	12-20-79	.295	.307	.291	119	491	83	145	36	7	8	56	43	12	2	4	70	6	3	.446	.364
Gathright, Joey	L-R	5-10	170	4-27-81	.262	.256	.263	79	229	34	60	6	3	1	28	22	4	4	4	45	10	6	.328	.332
2-team (55 Tampa Bay)					.238	—		134	383	59	91	12	3	1	41	42	7	9	4	75	22	9	.292	.321
German, Esteban	R-R	5-9	165	1-26-78	.326	.347	.311	106	279	44	91	18	5	3	34	40	6	6	0	49	7	3	.459	.422
Graffanino, Tony	R-R	6-1	190	6-6-72	.268	.263	.271	69	220	34	59	16	0	5	32	25	1	4	0	31	3	4	.409	.346
Grudzielanek, Mark	R-R	6-1	190	6-30-70	.297	.277	.305	134	548	85	163	32	4	7	52	28	2	3	5	69	3	2	.409	.331
Guiel, Aaron	L-R	5-10	200	10-5-72	.220	.182	.231	19	50	9	11	3	0	3	7	7	2	0	0	11	0	0	.460	.339
2-team (44 New York)					.242	—		63	132	25	32	6	0	7	18	14	5	0	0	31	2	1	.447	.338
Huber, Justin	R-R	6-2	195	7-1-82	.200	.125	.500	5	10	1	2	1	0	0	1	1	0	0	0	4	1	0	.300	.273
Keppinger, Jeff	R-R	6-0	180	4-21-80	.267	.222	.303	22	60	11	16	2	0	2	8	5	0	2	0	6	0	0	.400	.323
Maier, Mitch	L-R	6-2	210	6-30-82	.154	.000	.250	5	13	3	2	0	0	0	0	2	0	0	0	4	0	0	.154	.267
Mientkiewicz, Doug	L-R	6-2	205	6-19-74	.283	.274	.286	91	314	37	89	24	2	4	43	35	5	1	5	50	3	0	.411	.359
Phillips, Paul	R-R	5-11	205	4-15-77	.277	.304	.262	23	65	8	18	3	0	1	5	1	0	2	1	8	0	0	.369	.284
Robinson, Kerry	L-L	6-0	175	10-3-73	.266	.182	.283	18	64	8	17	2	1	0	5	1	0	2	0	7	1	1	.328	.277
Sanchez, Angel	R-R	6-2	185	9-20-83	.222	.250	.200	8	27	2	6	0	0	0	1	0	0	1	0	4	0	0	.222	.214
Sanders, Reggie	R-R	6-1	205	12-1-67	.246	.268	.237	88	325	45	80	23	1	11	49	28	1	0	4	86	7	7	.425	.304
Shealy, Ryan	R-R	6-5	250	8-29-79	.280	.160	.322	51	193	29	54	10	1	7	36	15	2	0	0	50	1	1	.451	.338
Stairs, Matt	L-R	5-9	215	2-27-68	.261	.241	.264	77	226	31	59	14	0	8	32	31	2	0	2	52	0	0	.429	.352
3-team (14 Detroit, 26 Texas)					.247	—		117	348	42	86	21	0	13	51	40	3	0	2	86	0	0	.420	.328
Sweeney, Mike	R-R	6-3	220	7-22-73	.258	.266	.255	60	217	23	56	15	0	8	33	28	4	0	3	48	2	0	.438	.349
Teahen, Mark	L-R	6-3	220	9-6-81	.290	.274	.296	109	393	70	114	21	7	18	69	40	2	2	2	85	10	0	.517	.357

PITCHING

PITCHING	B-T	HT	WT	DOB	W	L	ERA	G	GS	CG	SV	IP	H	R	ER	HR	BB	SO	AVG	vLH	vRH	K/9	BB/9
Affeldt, Jeremy	L-L	6-4	225	6-6-79	4	6	5.91	27	9	0	0	70	71	51	46	9	42	28	.262	.181	.291	3.60	5.40
Andrade, Steve	R-R	6-1	220	2-6-78	0	0	9.64	4	0	0	0	5	5	5	5	0	4	5	.278	.286	.273	9.64	7.71
Bautista, Denny	R-R	6-5	190	8-23-80	0	2	5.66	8	7	0	0	35	38	24	22	5	17	22	.277	.269	.286	5.66	4.37
Bernero, Adam	R-R	6-4	225	11-28-76	1	0	1.38	3	2	0	0	13	15	2	2	0	0	12	.283	.188	.429	8.31	0.00
Booker, Chris	R-R	6-3	235	12-9-76	0	0	54.00	1	0	0	0	1	5	6	6	3	3	0	.625	.000	.714	0.00	27.00
Braun, Ryan	R-R	6-1	215	7-29-80	0	1	6.75	9	0	0	0	11	13	8	8	2	6	3	.317	.357	.296	5.06	2.53
Burgos, Ambiorix	R-R	6-3	235	4-19-84	4	5	5.52	68	1	0	18	73	83	49	45	16	37	72	.288	.345	.249	8.84	4.54
De La Rosa, Jorge	L-L	6-1	210	4-5-81	3	4	5.18	10	10	0	0	49	49	29	28	10	32	36	.263	.324	.250	6.66	5.92
Dessens, Elmer	R-R	5-11	200	1-13-71	5	7	4.50	43	0	0	2	54	63	31	27	4	13	36	.292	.238	.324	6.00	2.17
Diaz, Jose	R-R	6-0	240	4-13-80	0	0	10.80	4	0	0	0	7	10	8	8	2	8	3	.345	.333	.353	4.05	10.80
Dohmann, Scott	R-R	6-1	200	2-13-78	1	3	7.99	21	0	0	0	23	31	21	21	5	18	22	.347	.440	.314	8.37	6.85
Duckworth, Brandon	R-R	6-1	215	1-23-76	1	5	6.11	10	8	0	0	46	62	36	31	5	31	31	.332	.232	.390	5.32	4.73
Elarton, Scott	R-R	6-7	255	2-23-76	4	9	5.34	20	20	0	0	115	117	73	68	26	52	49	.267	.253	.278	3.85	4.08
Etherton, Seth	R-R	6-1	200	10-17-76	1	1	9.39	2	2	0	0	8	10	9	8	3	6	4	.313	.231	.368	4.70	7.04
Gobble, Jimmy	L-L	6-3	205	7-19-81	4	6	5.14	60	6	0	2	84	95	51	48	12	29	80	.282	.255	.294	8.57	3.11
Greinke, Zack	R-R	6-2	185	10-21-83	1	0	4.26	3	0	0	0	6	7	3	3	1	3	5	.280	.400	.200	7.11	4.26
Hernandez, Runelvys	R-R	6-1	250	4-27-78	6	10	6.48	21	21	1	0	110	145	87	79	22	48	50	.327	.325	.329	4.10	3.94
Hudson, Luke	R-R	6-3	195	5-2-77	7	6	5.12	26	15	0	0	102	109	62	58	7	38	64	.276	.258	.293	5.65	3.35
Keppel, Bob	R-R	6-5	205	6-11-82	0	4	5.50	8	6	0	0	34	45	21	21	6	15	20	.326	.394	.264	5.24	3.93
MacDougal, Mike	B-R	6-4	185	3-5-77	0	0	0.00	4	0	0	1	4	2	0	0	0	0	2	.154	.333	.000	4.50	0.00
2-team (25 Chicago)					1	1	1.55	29	0	0	1	29	21	5	5	1	6	21	—	—		6.52	1.86
Mays, Joe	B-R	6-1	200	12-10-75	0	4	10.27	6	6	0	0	24	38	33	27	7	14	9	.369	.262	.443	3.42	5.32
Nelson, Joe	R-R	6-1	210	10-25-74	1	1	4.43	43	0	0	0	45	37	22	22	5	24	44	.226	.180	.252	8.87	4.84
Nunez, Leo	R-R	6-1	165	8-14-83	0	0	4.73	7	0	0	0	13	15	7	7	2	5	7	.300	.211	.355	4.73	3.38
Peralta, Joel	R-R	5-11	180	3-23-76	1	3	4.40	64	0	0	1	74	74	37	36	10	17	57	.263	.338	.234	6.96	2.08
Perez, Odalis	L-L	6-0	220	6-11-77	2	4	5.64	12	12	0	0	67	80	44	42	9	18	48	.295	.311	.292	6.45	2.42
Redman, Mark	L-L	6-5	245	1-5-74	11	10	5.71	29	29	2	0	167	202	110	106	19	63	76	.307	.229	.326	4.10	3.40
Sisco, Andrew	L-L	6-10	270	1-13-83	1	3	7.10	65	0	0	1	58	66	47	46	8	40	52	.289	.318	.271	8.02	6.17
Snyder, Kyle	B-R	6-8	215	9-9-77	0	0	22.50	1	1	0	0	2	10	9	5	1	1	2	.556	.400	.750	9.00	4.50
Stemle, Steve	R-R	6-4	200	5-20-77	0	1	15.00	5	0	0	0	6	15	10	10	1	3	0	.455	.429	.474	0.00	4.50
Wellemeyer, Todd	R-R	6-3	205	8-30-78	1	2	3.63	28	0	0	0	57	48	25	23	5	37	37	.235	.198	.265	5.84	5.84
Wood, Mike	R-R	6-3	220	4-26-80	3	3	5.71	23	7	0	0	65	86	51	41	10	23	29	.314	.320	.309	4.04	3.20

FIELDING

Catcher	PCT	G	PO	A	E	DP	PB
Bako	.993	53	258	20	2	3	4
Buck	.991	112	615	37	6	7	5
Phillips	.988	13	74	9	1	2	1

First Base	PCT	G	PO	A	E	DP
Graffanino	.981	16	96	6	2	14
Keppinger	1.000	4	37	1	0	1
Mientkiewicz	.996	90	749	42	3	83
Phillips	1.000	5	34	0	0	4
Shealy	.993	51	418	27	3	59
Stairs	1.000	11	67	1	0	7

Second Base	PCT	G	PO	A	E	DP
Blanco	1.000	7	5	8	0	3
German	.987	26	36	41	1	12
Graffanino	1.000	10	19	24	0	7
Grudzielanek	.994	132	261	372	4	111
Keppinger	1.000	1	3	3	0	2
Sanchez	1.000	4	13	22	0	3

Third Base	PCT	G	PO	A	E	DP
German	.929	24	9	43	4	5
Graffanino	.975	27	15	63	2	2
Keppinger	.947	12	7	29	2	3
Teahen	.958	109	79	237	14	34

Shortstop	PCT	G	PO	A	E	DP
Berroa	.969	131	188	366	18	95
Blanco	.956	25	31	77	5	25
German	—	1	0	0	0	0
Graffanino	.963	9	10	16	1	3
Grudzielanek	1.000	4	0	1	0	0
Sanchez	1.000	4	2	9	0	2

Outfield	PCT	G	PO	A	E	DP
Brown	.990	134	273	10	3	2
Costa	.959	65	142	0	6	0
DeJesus	.990	119	287	12	3	1
Gathright	.990	76	186	3	2	2
German	.925	25	36	1	3	1
Guiel	1.000	14	30	1	0	0
Keppinger	—	1	0	0	0	0
Maier	.800	4	4	0	1	0
Robinson	1.000	16	40	1	0	0
Sanders	.989	73	170	4	2	0
Stairs	1.000	2	4	0	0	0

General manager: Dayton Moore. **Farm director:** J.J. Picollo. **Scouting director:** Deric Ladnier.

Class	Team	League	W	L	PCT	Finish*	Manager	Affiliate Since
Majors	Kansas City	American	62	100	.383	13th (14)	Buddy Bell	—
Triple-A	Omaha Royals	Pacific Coast	53	91	.368	16th (16)	Mike Jirschele	1969
Double-A	Wichita Wranglers	Texas	77	62	.554	2nd (8)	Frank White	1995
High A	High Desert Mavericks	California	73	67	.521	4th (10)	Jeff Carter	2005
Low A	Burlington Bees	Midwest	64	73	.467	11th (14)	Jim Gabella	2001
Rookie	Idaho Falls Chukars	Pioneer	40	36	.526	4th (8)	Brian Rupp	2004
Rookie	AZL Royals	Arizona	36	20	.643	2nd (9)	Lloyd Simmons	2003
OVERALL 2006 MINOR LEAGUE RECORD			343	349	.496	17th (30)		

*Finish in overall standings (No. of teams in league). +League champion

Omaha Royals · Triple-A

Pacific Coast League

BATTING	B-T	HT	WT	DOB	AVG	vLH	vRH	G	AB	R	H	2B	3B	HR	RBI	BB	HBP	SH	SF	SO	SB	CS	SLG	OBP
Allen, Chad	R-R	6-1	210	2-6-75	.314	.375	.290	105	417	39	131	26	4	14	78	32	1	0	0	60	1	4	.496	.364
Ambres, Chip	R-R	6-1	200	12-19-79	.203	.167	.214	56	187	19	38	8	1	3	15	22	0	2	2	41	2	4	.305	.284
Aviles, Mike	R-R	5-11	198	3-13-81	.264	.236	.273	129	469	52	124	21	3	8	47	28	2	0	3	48	14	5	.373	.307
Bell, Ricky	R-R	6-2	195	4-5-79	.212	.204	.214	102	364	28	77	12	2	4	32	17	2	2	4	67	2	1	.288	.248
Blanco, Andres	B-R	5-10	185	4-11-84	.237	.247	.232	88	283	30	67	9	4	2	20	21	9	5	1	41	6	4	.318	.309
Brown, Dee	L-R	6-0	225	3-27-78	.151	.100	.163	16	53	3	8	1	0	0	2	4	1	0	0	11	0	0	.170	.224
Clapinski, Chris	B-R	6-1	180	8-20-71	.179	.286	.103	19	67	6	12	4	0	1	8	8	1	2	2	14	1	0	.284	.269
Coolbaugh, Mike	R-R	6-1	190	6-5-72	.223	.292	.201	57	197	19	44	9	0	8	25	31	3	3	1	48	1	1	.391	.336
Cortez, Fernando	L-R	6-1	175	8-10-81	.244	.211	.257	67	258	29	63	6	2	0	13	12	1	3	0	30	5	6	.283	.280
Costa, Shane	L-R	6-0	200	12-12-81	.342	.355	.333	52	199	35	68	12	4	10	29	13	7	3	2	25	4	0	.593	.398
DeJesus, David	L-L	6-0	185	12-20-79	.385	—	.385	3	13	0	5	0	0	0	2	0	0	0	0	2	0	0	.385	.385
Gotay, Ruben	B-R	5-11	190	12-25-82	.264	.250	.271	87	337	45	89	16	2	9	43	26	4	5	2	67	7	1	.404	.322
Guiel, Aaron	L-R	5-10	200	10-5-72	.249	.217	.265	52	177	32	44	14	1	11	32	35	8	0	4	45	2	2	.525	.388
Huber, Justin	R-R	6-2	195	7-1-82	.278	.350	.257	100	352	47	98	22	2	15	44	40	4	1	1	94	2	2	.480	.358
Keppinger, Jeff	R-R	6-0	180	4-21-80	.354	.387	.381	32	127	21	45	6	1	2	17	12	0	2	1	9	0	0	.465	.407
Phillips, Paul	R-R	5-11	205	4-15-77	.243	.270	.234	91	345	43	84	11	1	9	39	22	1	1	6	37	0	0	.359	.286
Price, Jared	R-R	6-1	220	3-18-82	.158	.108	.176	42	139	12	22	6	0	4	12	9	0	1	1	51	1	0	.288	.208
Prieto, Alejandro	R-R	5-11	205	6-19-76	.226	.227	.226	63	221	24	50	8	0	3	18	22	0	2	2	43	2	2	.303	.294
Robinson, Kerry	L-L	6-0	175	10-3-73	.311	.289	.321	100	396	68	123	24	3	2	40	33	4	0	36	17	14		.402	.370
Sweeney, Mike	R-R	6-3	220	7-22-73	.333	.500	.273	5	15	3	5	2	0	1	4	5	0	0	1	0	0		.667	.476
Teahen, Mark	L-R	6-3	220	9-6-81	.380	.364	.382	24	79	14	30	8	4	2	14	19	0	0	0	12	0	0	.658	.500
Tupman, Matt	L-R	5-11	185	11-25-79	.247	.133	.276	21	73	9	18	0	0	4	8	8	0	0	0	6	0	0	.247	.321

PITCHING	B-T	HT	WT	DOB	W	L	ERA	G	GS	CG	SV	IP	H	R	ER	HR	BB	SO	AVG	vLH	vRH	K/9	BB/9
Andrade, Steve	R-R	6-1	220	2-6-78	0	2	4.63	12	0	0	0	23	21	13	12	3	8	22	.233	.205	.261	8.49	3.09
2-team (26 Portland)					3	3	3.19	38	0	0	0	67	54	26	24	4	30	67	—	—	—	8.91	3.99
Baerlocher, Ryan	R-R	6-5	240	8-6-77	5	4	4.05	20	9	0	1	80	78	42	36	9	30	59	.260	.224	.297	6.64	3.38
Bass, Brian	R-R	6-0	215	1-6-82	1	5	7.59	7	7	0	0	32	49	35	27	7	14	11	.348	.400	.319	3.09	3.94
Bautista, Denny	R-R	6-5	190	8-23-80	2	5	7.36	10	10	0	0	44	52	38	36	3	32	28	.304	.288	.319	5.73	6.55
2-team (6 Colorado Springs)					3	9	6.08	16	16	0	0	80	98	62	54	5	48	63	—	—	—	7.09	5.40
Bernero, Adam	R-R	6-4	225	11-28-76	5	3	2.84	16	12	1	1	79	64	27	25	5	23	47	.225	.232	.218	5.33	2.61
Boehringer, Brian	B-R	6-2	195	1-8-70	2	4	2.75	8	5	0	0	39	50	20	12	1	8	17	.311	.293	.329	3.89	1.83
Booker, Chris	R-R	6-3	235	12-9-76	0	0	7.71	4	0	0	0	5	4	4	2	3	6	.375	.222	.571	11.57	5.79
2-team (15 New Orleans)					2	2	4.79	19	0	0	0	20	20	11	11	2	16	35	—	—	—	15.24	6.97
Braun, Ryan	R-R	6-1	215	7-29-80	0	2	2.16	17	0	0	3	25	23	9	6	0	13	22	.247	.184	.291	7.92	4.68
Brooks, Frank	L-L	5-11	190	9-6-78	0	2	5.96	17	0	0	0	23	29	15	15	1	14	18	.312	.303	.317	7.15	5.56
Diaz, Jose	R-R	6-0	240	4-13-80	2	3	5.40	13	0	0	0	18	14	13	11	3	15	16	.219	.286	.186	7.85	7.36
2-team (28 Oklahoma)					2	3	4.00	41	1	0	4	54	42	27	24	5	37	62	—	—	—	10.33	6.17
Elder, Dave	R-R	6-0	190	9-23-75	1	0	2.61	20	3	0	1	38	43	18	11	1	18	28	.276	.246	.299	6.63	4.26
Etherton, Seth	R-R	6-1	200	10-17-76	1	4	6.49	10	6	0	0	35	43	25	25	11	13	29	.307	.343	.271	7.53	3.38
2-team (9 Portland) ..					3	6	5.25	19	15	0	0	84	91	50	49	19	27	78	—	—	—	8.36	2.89
Hernandez, Runelvys	R-R	6-1	250	4-27-78	5	6	4.59	12	11	1	0	65	65	35	33	6	27	43	.261	.277	.246	5.98	3.76
Howell, J.P.	L-L	6-0	175	4-25-83	3	2	4.75	8	8	0	0	36	39	19	19	3	14	33	.287	.235	.304	8.25	3.50
Hudson, Luke	R-R	6-3	195	5-2-77	2	0	2.80	13	2	0	1	35	30	14	11	0	7	21	.226	.197	.254	5.35	1.78
Huisman, Justin	R-R	6-2	200	4-16-79	1	0	5.40	2	0	0	0	3	3	2	2	1	7	.222	.333	.167	12.60	1.80
3-team (6 Round Rock, 14 Tacoma)					2	0	8.10	22	1	0	0	40	50	36	36	8	20	32	—	—	—	7.20	4.50
Keppel, Bob	R-R	6-5	205	6-11-82	6	7	5.67	25	14	0	1	98	126	73	62	12	28	43	.318	.404	.253	3.94	2.56
Loux, Shane	R-R	6-2	235	8-31-79	2	5	6.46	31	0	0	2	54	74	48	39	2	15	23	.327	.363	.298	3.81	2.48
MacDougal, Mike	R-R	6-4	185	3-5-77	0	1	4.70	8	4	0	1	8	4	4	4	0	5	6	.160	.167	.154	7.04	5.87
Mahomes, Pat	R-R	6-4	200	8-9-70	1	1	5.60	7	5	0	0	35	37	22	22	3	15	27	.274	.347	.233	6.88	3.82
Middleton, Kyle	R-R	6-2	200	12-6-80	0	8	5.33	13	13	0	0	73	95	53	43	12	24	34	.329	.301	.353	4.21	2.97
Musser, Neal	L-L	6-1	215	8-25-80	1	0	1.86	2	2	0	0	10	7	2	2	2	3	6	.200	.200	.200	5.59	2.79
2-team (8 Tucson)					2	3	4.70	10	9	0	0	46	51	28	24	6	27	24	—	—	—	4.70	5.28
Nelson, Joe	R-R	6-1	210	10-25-74	2	2	1.97	24	0	0	7	32	19	9	7	4	12	39	.181	.158	.194	10.97	3.38
Nunez, Leo	R-R	6-1	165	8-14-83	2	2	2.13	23	4	0	0	38	37	11	9	5	13	33	.255	.246	.261	7.82	3.08
Osborne, Donovan	L-R	6-2	215	6-21-69	0	6	6.66	17	4	0	0	53	66	45	39	9	14	30	.374	.406	.360	5.13	2.39
Peralta, Joel	R-R	5-11	180	3-23-76	1	0	2.35	6	0	0	2	8	2	1	1	3	8	.296	.385	.214	9.39	3.52
Price, Jared	R-R	6-1	220	3-18-82	0	0	6.00	2	0	0	0	3	4	2	2	0	0	0	.333	.333	.333	0.00	0.00
Sisco, Andrew	L-L	6-10	270	1-13-83	0	0	1.93	5	0	0	0	3	3	1	1	1	1	6	.176	.000	.300	11.57	1.93
Snyder, Kyle	B-R	6-8	215	9-9-77	0	4	3.88	10	9	0	1	60	63	36	26	4	9	43	.264	.223	.294	6.41	1.34

					W	L	ERA	G	GS	CG	SV	IP	H	R	ER	HR	BB	SO	AVG	vLH	vRH	K/9	BB/9
Tamayo, Danny	R-R	6-1	219	6-3-79	3	2	4.21	7	3	0	0	26	24	12	12	4	4	26	.245	.182	.277	9.12	1.40
Van Hekken, Andy	R-L	6-3	185	7-31-79	3	5	4.36	9	9	0	0	54	60	32	26	7	11	33	.287	.364	.260	5.53	1.84
Wood, Mike	R-R	6-3	220	4-26-80	0	2	6.32	4	4	0	0	16	22	12	11	3	3	5	.349	.273	.390	2.87	1.72
Yan, Esteban	R-R	6-4	255	6-22-75	0	1	7.32	11	0	0	0	20	24	16	16	3	9	16	.296	.286	.304	7.32	4.12
Yarnall, Ed	L-L	6-3	235	12-4-75	2	3	3.19	29	4	0	1	62	57	24	22	8	15	58	.243	.225	.250	8.42	2.18

FIELDING

Catcher	PCT	G	PO	A	E	DP	PB
Phillips	.983	87	523	57	10	4	5
Price	.988	38	217	23	3	1	10
Tupman	.978	21	124	11	3	2	2

First Base	PCT	G	PO	A	E	DP
Bell	.989	60	525	34	6	58
Coolbaugh	.992	25	234	18	2	29
Cortez	.991	12	108	5	1	16
Huber	.981	30	254	9	5	28
Keppinger	1.000	2	16	2	0	4
Phillips	1.000	3	33	2	0	3
Price	.833	1	5	0	1	2
Prieto	.969	14	115	12	4	10

Second Base	PCT	G	PO	A	E	DP
Aviles	1.000	1	2	6	0	1

	PCT	G	PO	A	E	DP
Clapinski	.917	7	13	20	3	10
Cortez	.980	36	81	114	4	29
Gotay	.969	80	117	229	11	56
Keppinger	.984	16	30	33	1	15
Prieto	1.000	5	11	14	0	5

Third Base	PCT	G	PO	A	E	DP
Aviles	.927	95	63	192	20	14
Bell	1.000	3	0	6	0	0
Clapinski	.833	6	3	7	2	2
Cortez	.875	11	7	14	3	0
Keppinger	.973	10	9	27	1	2
Teahen	.981	21	16	36	1	3

Shortstop	PCT	G	PO	A	E	DP
Aviles	.975	15	24	55	2	14
Blanco	.956	88	161	298	21	74

	PCT	G	PO	A	E	DP
Clapinski	1.000	2	3	8	0	2
Cortez	.500	1	1	0	1	0
Keppinger	1.000	2	1	11	0	1
Prieto	.965	36	54	113	6	31

Outfield	PCT	G	PO	A	E	DP
Allen	.946	64	118	4	7	3
Ambres	.976	50	113	7	3	3
Bell	.955	29	40	2	2	0
Brown	1.000	14	18	0	0	0
Cortez	1.000	5	10	0	0	0
Costa	1.000	52	95	1	0	0
DeJesus	1.000	3	5	0	0	0
Guiel	.983	50	111	4	2	0
Huber	.977	69	117	8	3	2
Keppinger	1.000	2	9	0	0	0
Robinson	.992	100	241	5	2	2

Wichita Wranglers — Double-A

Texas League

BATTING	B-T	HT	WT	DOB	AVG	vLH	vRH	G	AB	R	H	2B	3B	HR	RBI	BB	HBP	SH	SF	SO	SB	CS	SLG	OBP
Bako, Paul	L-R	6-2	215	6-20-72	.167	.000	.182	3	12	3	2	0	0	0	2	0	0	0	0	1	0	0	.167	.167
Brown, Dee	L-R	6-0	225	3-27-78	.307	.345	.297	95	384	56	118	22	0	16	78	24	4	0	10	64	2	0	.490	.346
Butler, Billy	R-R	6-2	225	4-18-86	.331	.430	.309	119	477	82	158	33	1	15	96	41	8	1	8	67	1	0	.499	.388
Costa, Shane	L-R	6-0	200	12-12-81	.375	—	.375	2	8	0	3	0	0	0	1	0	0	0	0	1	0	0	.375	.375
Donahie, Adam	R-R	6-1	215	3-3-84	.191	.174	.197	29	94	21	18	5	0	2	10	19	0	0	1	20	0	1	.309	.325
Espino, Damaso	R-R	6-1	205	5-8-83	.242	.250	.239	54	182	18	44	2	0	0	18	20	1	4	3	16	0	2	.253	.316
Gemoll, Justin	R-R	6-2	218	11-19-77	.167	.333	.000	5	18	5	3	0	0	0	2	2	0	0	0	4	0	0	.167	.250
Gordon, Alex	L-R	6-1	220	2-10-84	.325	.339	.321	130	486	111	158	39	1	29	101	72	16	0	2	113	22	3	.588	.427
Groves, Brett	B-R	5-11	180	10-1-78	.205	.214	.202	55	166	18	34	3	0	0	18	26	1	4	3	29	1	2	.223	.311
Kaaihue, Kila	L-R	6-3	233	3-29-84	.199	.302	.179	103	327	40	65	15	0	6	45	49	4	5	10	73	0	1	.300	.303
Keim, Adam	R-R	5-11	196	1-5-81	.237	.333	.207	63	228	19	54	12	2	2	30	8	1	2	2	25	2	3	.325	.264
Lubanski, Chris	L-R	6-3	206	3-24-85	.282	.225	.296	137	524	93	148	34	11	15	70	72	3	9	5	112	11	7	.475	.369
Maier, Mitch	L-R	6-2	210	6-30-82	.306	.340	.297	138	543	95	166	35	7	14	92	41	7	3	9	96	13	12	.473	.357
Murphy, Donnie	R-R	5-10	185	3-10-83	.249	.171	.267	94	366	57	91	25	1	14	45	19	8	2	0	65	6	3	.437	.300
Ruiz, Randy	R-R	6-3	235	10-19-77	.217	.333	.200	6	23	3	5	1	0	2	3	6	0	0	0	6	0	0	.522	.379
Sanchez, Angel	R-R	6-2	185	9-20-83	.282	.255	.289	133	542	105	153	24	1	4	57	44	7	11	8	63	8	9	.352	.339
Senreiso, Juan	R-R	6-0	191	8-4-81	.267	.333	.250	4	15	2	4	0	0	1	4	1	0	0	1	5	0	0	.467	.294
Sevilla, Walter	R-R	5-8	180	8-24-81	.196	.270	.175	50	163	18	32	3	4	1	14	18	0	1	1	40	2	0	.282	.275
Sweeney, Mike	R-R	6-3	220	7-22-73	.385	—	.385	4	13	3	5	1	0	2	5	2	0	0	0	2	0	0	.923	.467
Thibault, Kiel	R-R	6-1	185	3-2-84	.200	—	.200	2	5	1	1	0	0	0	0	0	0	0	0	2	0	0	.200	.200
Tupman, Matt	L-R	5-11	185	11-25-79	.305	.257	.314	73	220	35	67	8	1	1	31	48	1	7	4	27	1	1	.364	.425

PITCHING	B-T	HT	WT	DOB	W	L	ERA	G	GS	CG	SV	IP	H	R	ER	HR	BB	SO	AVG	vLH	vRH	K/9	BB/9
Armitage, Barry	R-R	6-5	275	5-11-79	1	0	6.75	5	0	0	0	8	9	6	6	2	5	6	.281	.250	.292	6.75	5.63
Atencio, Greg	R-R	6-2	191	7-15-81	0	0	18.90	2	0	0	0	3	7	7	7	1	4	3	.412	.400	.417	8.10	10.80
Bass, Brian	R-R	6-0	215	1-6-82	4	1	4.00	6	5	1	0	27	29	14	12	2	6	18	.269	.260	.276	6.00	2.00
Booker, Chris	R-R	6-3	235	12-9-76	0	0	4.15	4	0	0	0	4	6	4	2	0	0	5	.300	.273	.333	10.38	0.00
Braun, Ryan	R-R	6-1	215	7-29-80	1	6	2.21	26	0	0	10	41	30	11	10	2	16	58	.204	.154	.222	12.84	3.54
Buckner, Billy	R-R	6-2	210	8-27-83	5	3	4.64	13	13	0	0	76	78	40	39	7	39	63	.265	.309	.239	7.49	4.64
Cedeno, Juan	L-L	6-1	165	8-19-83	2	9	5.78	37	11	0	2	90	92	68	58	8	78	65	.271	.263	.273	6.48	7.77
DeHoyos, Gabe	R-R	5-11	220	4-14-80	2	1	1.64	22	0	0	7	33	20	7	6	1	19	28	.175	.152	.191	7.64	5.18
DePriest, Derrick	R-R	6-8	235	11-21-76	0	4	7.01	24	0	0	1	35	44	30	27	4	18	23	.326	.326	.326	5.97	4.67
Gragg, John	L-L	5-8	170	5-9-81	1	1	5.02	10	0	0	0	14	16	8	8	1	8	5	.286	.292	.281	3.14	5.02
Greinke, Zack	R-R	6-2	185	10-21-83	8	3	4.34	18	17	1	0	106	96	53	51	12	24	77	.240	.272	.216	8.01	2.30
Herndon, Junior	R-R	6-1	190	9-11-78	12	6	5.29	27	26	0	0	160	197	104	94	21	38	87	.308	.301	.312	4.89	2.14
Hoelscher, Nate	L-L	6-2	183	11-11-79	0	5	5.40	44	0	0	3	47	46	32	28	6	14	41	.257	.232	.286	7.91	2.70
Lowery, Devon	R-R	6-3	195	3-24-83	5	1	5.67	24	0	0	4	33	29	22	21	5	19	31	.228	.216	.237	8.37	5.13
Lumsden, Tyler	L-L	6-4	215	5-9-83	2	1	3.06	7	6	0	0	35	35	12	12	3	20	24	.276	.238	.294	6.11	5.09
MacDougal, Mike	B-R	6-4	185	3-5-77	0	0	0.00	1	1	0	0	1	0	0	0	0	0	1	.000	.000	.000	9.00	0.00
Markray, Thad	R-R	6-2	236	9-20-79	5	0	2.78	35	0	0	1	65	59	21	20	9	24	45	.245	.268	.233	6.26	3.34
Middleton, Kyle	R-R	6-4	232	6-13-80	5	3	4.17	16	15	0	0	86	108	48	40	8	29	63	.309	.307	.311	6.57	3.02
Musser, Neal	L-L	6-1	215	8-25-80	6	3	4.95	18	11	0	2	84	80	53	46	12	48	67	.255	.250	.257	7.21	5.16
Nunez, Leo	R-R	6-1	165	8-14-83	1	2	4.29	15	0	0	3	21	18	10	10	3	12	22	.228	.240	.222	9.43	5.14
Plummer, Jarod	R-R	6-5	200	1-27-84	1	0	0.00	1	0	0	0	2	1	0	0	2	0	3	.143	.000	.200	13.50	9.00
Redman, Mark	L-R	6-5	245	1-5-74	0	0	0.90	2	2	0	0	10	6	2	1	0	1	9	.162	.125	.172	8.10	0.90
Sevilla, Walter	R-R	5-8	180	8-24-81	0	1	3.86	1	0	0	0	2	3	1	1	0	2	0	.375	.000	.500	0.00	7.71
Smith, Cody	R-R	6-3	200	4-20-82	9	0	2.71	46	2	0	4	86	87	30	26	5	23	59	.264	.267	.263	6.15	2.40
Snare, Ryan	L-L	6-0	200	2-8-79	2	2	6.62	7	7	0	0	35	48	31	26	4	20	26	.327	.462	.298	6.62	5.09
Song, Seung	R-R	6-1	190	6-29-80	5	10	5.37	27	22	0	0	131	138	83	78	16	70	99	.277	.284	.273	6.82	4.82
Wood, Mike	R-R	6-3	220	4-26-80	0	0	6.75	2	2	0	0	4	5	4	3	0	0	3	.294	.333	.250	6.75	0.00

FIELDING

Catcher	PCT	G	PO	A	E	DP	PB
Bako	1.000	3	15	1	0	0	0
Donachie	.987	29	212	18	3	1	2
Espino	.981	44	285	30	6	4	2
Thibault	.938	2	12	3	1	0	0
Tupman	.988	67	437	40	6	4	2

First Base	PCT	G	PO	A	E	DP
Espino	1.000	6	43	4	0	1
Gemoll	.978	5	39	5	1	3
Gordon	1.000	4	22	2	0	2
Groves	.985	14	121	12	2	13
Kaaihue	.988	91	778	65	10	85
Keim	.996	29	245	20	1	29

	PCT	G	PO	A	E	DP
Ruiz	1.000	1	10	0	0	1

Second Base	PCT	G	PO	A	E	DP
Espino	.800	2	1	3	1	0
Groves	.976	11	12	29	1	4
Keim	.975	10	13	26	1	7
Murphy	.989	91	200	245	5	61
Sevilla	.994	34	70	98	1	24

Third Base	PCT	G	PO	A	E	DP
Gordon	.955	122	90	246	16	26
Groves	.765	6	3	10	4	0
Keim	1.000	16	8	34	0	3
Sevilla	1.000	2	1	4	0	2

Shortstop	PCT	G	PO	A	E	DP
Sanchez	.960	133	200	423	26	99
Sevilla	.939	10	10	21	2	5

Outfield	PCT	G	PO	A	E	DP
Brown	1.000	27	49	1	0	1
Butler	.967	115	197	8	7	1
Costa	1.000	1	1	0	0	0
Groves	1.000	11	22	2	0	1
Keim	1.000	1	1	0	0	0
Lubanski	.966	133	190	8	7	3
Maier	.980	133	333	10	7	2
Senreiso	1.000	2	3	0	0	0

High Desert Mavericks — High Class A

California League

BATTING	B-T	HT	WT	DOB	AVG	vLH	vRH	G	AB	R	H	2B	3B	HR	RBI	BB	HBP	SH	SF	SO	SB	CS	SLG	OBP
Brown, Rusty	R-R	6-3	210	8-19-81	.261	.381	.218	112	425	54	111	18	2	14	61	46	4	2	10	88	0	2	.412	.332
Donachie, Adam	R-R	6-1	215	3-3-84	.271	.324	.245	62	210	32	57	12	0	6	21	31	1	6	2	46	0	1	.414	.365
Duenas, Tomas	R-R	5-11	205	7-16-81	.297	.333	.286	76	273	48	81	19	0	14	54	27	5	2	2	55	1	0	.520	.368
Falu, Irving	B-R	6-0	173	6-6-83	.299	.310	.296	126	531	87	159	23	7	3	49	40	3	10	1	46	31	11	.386	.351
Gaffney, Michael	R-R	6-1	190	11-11-81	.250	.183	.268	73	288	33	72	9	1	1	37	17	4	6	4	42	1	3	.299	.297
Galloway, Michael	R-R	6-2	220	5-9-81	.271	.208	.310	40	140	16	38	10	3	0	17	20	6	0	1	34	0	1	.386	.383
Jirschele, Jeremy	R-R	5-9	195	11-14-82	.211	.143	.250	8	19	2	4	1	0	0	3	3	1	0	0	7	0	0	.263	.348
Lucas, Edward	R-R	6-4	205	5-21-82	.281	.286	.280	124	455	71	128	26	4	8	66	46	3	2	3	83	19	6	.409	.349
McFall, Brian	R-R	6-3	215	3-17-84	.239	.220	.246	115	398	58	95	25	0	21	73	30	13	3	5	120	7	5	.460	.309
Melgarejo, Ransel	R-R	6-0	199	8-28-81	.264	.115	.323	26	91	12	24	5	0	1	6	12	2	0	0	28	7	4	.352	.362
Perez, Wilver	R-R	5-11	163	8-29-83	.262	.273	.258	98	351	54	92	13	3	4	30	39	6	5	3	79	9	6	.350	.343
Senreiso, Juan	R-R	6-0	191	8-4-81	.287	.299	.284	106	407	64	117	16	6	15	60	22	3	3	1	117	19	4	.467	.328
Sevilla, Walter	R-R	5-8	180	8-24-81	.217	.500	.118	7	23	4	5	1	0	1	7	4	0	0	1	1	0	0	.391	.321
Stodolka, Mike	L-L	6-2	210	9-24-81	.284	.283	.284	115	423	81	120	33	2	11	67	78	5	0	7	103	4	3	.449	.396
Thibault, Kiel	R-R	6-0	200	3-2-84	.340	.364	.328	28	97	15	33	11	0	1	18	9	1	1	1	18	0	1	.485	.398
Tomlin, James	R-R	6-0	183	8-12-82	.301	.274	.310	76	276	41	83	24	1	3	37	14	0	6	0	30	3	3	.428	.334
Valentin, Geraldo	R-R	6-0	184	9-8-82	.283	.287	.282	107	406	57	115	13	3	6	51	32	8	3	4	60	3	6	.374	.344

PITCHING	B-T	HT	WT	DOB	W	L	ERA	G	GS	CG	SV	IP	H	R	ER	HR	BB	SO	AVG	vLH	vRH	K/9	BB/9
Atencio, Greg	R-R	6-2	191	7-15-81	2	0	3.86	13	0	0	4	16	13	7	7	0	7	16	.232	.269	.200	8.82	3.86
Barnes, Justin	R-R	6-4	200	8-21-82	5	3	4.19	38	1	0	4	82	91	42	38	8	25	80	.281	.277	.284	8.82	2.76
Buckner, Billy	R-R	6-2	210	8-27-83	7	1	3.90	16	16	0	0	90	92	44	39	6	47	85	.271	.267	.276	8.50	4.70
Christensen, Daniel	L-L	6-1	205	8-10-83	6	6	4.89	28	28	1	0	162	175	94	88	23	58	153	.285	.302	.281	8.50	3.22
Cota, Luis	R-R	6-2	200	8-19-85	5	11	7.09	27	26	0	0	132	153	113	104	19	63	126	.290	.288	.291	8.59	4.30
Crist, Kyle	R-R	6-3	194	6-27-83	5	2	4.15	15	15	1	0	80	90	38	37	6	22	56	.291	.292	.291	6.27	2.46
de la Vara, Gilbert	L-L	5-11	160	10-4-84	0	5	5.61	16	3	0	4	34	43	30	21	3	14	36	.316	.259	.330	9.62	3.74
DeHoyos, Gabe	R-R	5-11	226	4-14-80	3	1	2.51	28	0	0	13	29	13	10	8	0	14	37	.138	.167	.109	11.62	4.40
Gaffney, Michael	R-R	6-1	190	11-11-81	0	0	0.00	1	0	0	0	1	0	0	0	0	0	1	.000	.000	.000	0.00	9.00
Gragg III, John	L-R	5-8	170	5-9-81	8	9	4.29	20	20	1	0	130	142	66	62	13	36	95	.277	.203	.302	6.58	2.49
Green, Patrick	L-R	6-2	193	2-13-82	3	1	5.40	7	7	0	0	32	30	19	19	6	14	22	.261	.220	.292	6.25	3.98
Hicklen, Patrick	R-R	6-4	210	12-30-81	3	10	6.15	27	6	0	0	72	87	53	49	13	27	54	.299	.325	.281	6.78	3.39
Johnson, Blake	R-R	6-3	185	6-14-85	1	1	5.73	3	2	0	0	11	15	7	7	1	0	9	.319	.333	.313	7.36	0.00
Moore, Nate	R-R	6-2	225	6-14-83	0	2	4.01	24	0	0	4	34	32	15	15	4	11	29	.244	.328	.171	7.75	2.94
Nicoll, Christopher	R-R	6-2	190	10-30-83	2	0	4.86	3	3	0	0	17	17	11	9	3	6	26	.258	.265	.250	14.04	3.24
Pimentel, Julio Cesar	R-R	6-1	190	12-14-85	2	1	3.18	12	0	0	2	23	21	8	8	3	10	26	.244	.235	.250	10.32	3.97
Plummer, Jarod	R-R	6-5	200	1-27-84	11	5	4.05	39	6	0	10	96	92	50	43	11	20	114	.249	.264	.237	10.72	1.88
Rodriguez, Ricardo	R-R	6-0	170	4-28-81	0	0	5.40	2	0	0	0	3	4	2	2	0	3	4	.286	.333	.200	10.80	8.10
Rosa, Carlos	R-R	6-1	185	9-21-84	0	1	7.15	3	0	0	0	11	20	12	9	1	4	13	.392	.348	.429	10.32	3.18
Rowe, Nate	L-R	6-0	192	1-24-82	3	2	5.10	36	0	0	0	60	78	37	34	6	16	55	.315	.279	.333	8.25	2.40
Schambough, Kraig	R-R	6-0	185	1-21-82	0	1	13.50	2	0	0	0	4	8	6	6	3	1	1	.444	.444	.444	2.25	2.25
Vacek, Chase	R-R	6-0	210	8-12-83	0	0	13.50	2	0	0	0	2	3	3	3	0	4	0	.333	.333	.333	0.00	18.00
Weeden, Brandon	R-R	6-4	195	10-14-83	6	5	6.03	32	4	0	0	78	96	53	52	10	32	74	.307	.303	.310	8.58	3.71
Woodrow, C.J.	R-R	6-3	200	8-21-81	1	0	4.60	14	0	0	0	29	39	22	15	4	6	22	.307	.339	.282	6.75	1.84

FIELDING

Catcher	PCT	G	PO	A	E	DP	PB
Donachie	.991	62	491	54	5	11	8
Duenas	.994	60	454	48	3	4	14
Thibault	.990	25	183	15	2	0	3

First Base	PCT	G	PO	A	E	DP
Brown	.980	60	504	36	11	52
Lucas	1.000	1	5	0	0	0
Stodolka	.984	80	688	53	12	72

Second Base	PCT	G	PO	A	E	DP
Falu	.952	3	6	14	1	4
Gaffney	.994	36	67	90	1	19

	PCT	G	PO	A	E	DP
Jirschele	1.000	7	8	15	0	4
Perez	.967	94	175	260	15	65
Sevilla	1.000	3	4	4	0	0
Valentin	.917	3	8	3	1	2

Third Base	PCT	G	PO	A	E	DP
Gaffney	.889	14	7	17	3	0
Lucas	.957	120	85	268	16	27
Sevilla	1.000	2	2	6	0	2
Valentin	1.000	6	5	13	0	0

Shortstop	PCT	G	PO	A	E	DP
Falu	.971	121	190	347	16	82

	PCT	G	PO	A	E	DP
Gaffney	.975	21	28	51	2	12
Sevilla	1.000	3	1	4	0	1

Outfield	PCT	G	PO	A	E	DP
Gaffney	.—	4	0	0	0	0
Galloway	.969	30	30	1	1	0
Mc Fall	.965	106	155	10	6	1
Melgarejo	.977	25	41	1	1	0
Senreiso	.963	102	198	12	8	3
Tomlin	.973	70	104	4	3	0
Valentin	.951	96	151	5	8	1

Burlington Bees — Low Class A

Midwest League

BATTING	B-T	HT	WT	DOB	AVG	vLH	vRH	G	AB	R	H	2B	3B	HR	RBI	BB	HBP	SH	SF	SO	SB	CS	SLG	OBP
Arce, Valentino	R-R	5-11	167	6-7-85	.259	.267	.255	99	336	40	87	11	0	1	20	26	11	3	2	37	8	4	.301	.331

Name	B-T	HT	WT	DOB	AVG	vLH	vRH	G	AB	R	H	2B	3B	HR	RBI	BB	HBP	SH	SF	SO	SB	CS	SLG	OBP
Arroyo, Carlos	L-L	6-0	190	5-30-81	.271	.213	.280	104	343	38	93	8	3	2	37	29	0	5	1	33	11	6	.329	.327
Duarte, Jose	R-R	5-10	165	3-7-85	.266	.317	.247	127	466	65	124	24	5	1	38	49	2	3	0	99	31	9	.345	.338
Everett, Brady	R-R	6-0	205	7-8-83	.256	.316	.234	86	297	40	76	13	0	5	22	37	11	2	1	45	4	4	.350	.358
Howell, Jeffrey	R-R	6-0	200	4-1-83	.249	.191	.268	109	374	40	93	17	2	5	35	44	3	4	5	82	2	3	.345	.329
Jirschele, Jeremy	R-R	5-9	195	11-14-82	.194	.207	.188	84	263	27	51	8	1	0	20	34	10	4	5	58	5	3	.232	.304
Johnson, Joshua	B-R	5-11	170	1-11-86	.241	.222	.248	112	381	59	92	8	5	3	40	93	2	19	2	72	18	9	.312	.391
Lisson, Mario	R-R	6-2	193	5-31-84	.263	.295	.251	130	463	67	122	30	2	13	73	65	14	5	4	109	41	11	.421	.368
Lowen, J.P.	L-R	6-3	215	3-27-84	.230	.158	.240	47	148	19	34	8	0	2	21	12	0	1	3	35	0	0	.324	.282
McConnell, Christopher	R-R	5-11	170	12-18-85	.172	.145	.181	69	239	23	41	4	0	1	18	17	10	10	2	47	8	6	.201	.254
Nunez, Eduardo	R-R	6-2	170	9-21-85	.200	.077	.259	14	40	3	8	2	1	0	3	2	0	1	0	14	1	0	.300	.238
Pena, Omar	R-R	5-11	175	3-2-82	.250	.296	.233	29	100	11	25	4	0	3	14	6	0	1	1	25	2	1	.380	.290
Peralta, Felix	R-R	6-0	175	9-30-85	.250	.400	.000	13	40	4	10	1	1	0	3	5	2	0	1	12	1	2	.325	.354
Sabatini, Antonio	R-L	6-0	195	4-1-83	.143	.154	.137	42	112	14	16	0	2	1	9	11	3	7	3	47	0	2	.205	.233
Santana, Ethien	L-L	5-11	153	1-25-84	.244	.212	.247	107	312	34	76	5	5	1	20	30	2	3	0	82	21	12	.301	.314
Sweeney, Mike	R-R	6-3	220	7-22-73	.143	.250	.000	7	7	2	1	0	0	1	1	1	0	0	0	2	0	0	.571	.250
Thibault, Kiel	R-R	6-0	200	3-2-84	.218	.133	.255	46	147	13	32	6	0	0	19	14	6	1	1	35	3	0	.259	.310
Vega, Miguel	R-R	6-3	224	7-31-85	.248	.305	.225	113	416	40	103	17	1	13	75	13	4	4	9	121	2	2	.387	.271

PITCHING	B-T	HT	WT	DOB	W	L	ERA	G	GS	CG	SV	IP	H	R	ER	HR	BB	SO	AVG	vLH	vRH	K/9	BB/9
Cordier, Erik	R-R	6-3	214	2-25-86	3	1	2.70	7	7	0	0	37	27	17	11	3	14	23	.203	.185	.215	5.65	3.44
Cortes, Daniel	R-R	6-5	205	3-4-87	1	2	6.69	7	7	0	0	35	40	27	26	7	17	30	.284	.234	.325	7.71	4.37
D'Amico, Yovany	R-R	5-11	223	8-18-84	1	5	4.00	26	0	0	1	54	51	27	24	6	17	50	.252	.217	.282	8.33	2.83
de la Vara, Gilbert	L-L	5-11	160	10-4-84	4	4	3.38	27	1	0	9	51	35	21	19	3	12	64	.196	.138	.228	11.37	2.13
Di Pietro, Ryan	L-L	6-0	175	7-21-84	1	1	4.03	5	5	0	0	22	22	13	10	2	10	8	.253	.345	.207	3.22	4.03
Garcia, Eliezer	L-L	6-1	185	6-7-84	4	3	4.26	43	0	0	1	51	41	30	24	3	31	42	.212	.160	.246	7.46	5.51
Harkcom, Cody	R-R	6-1	180	12-15-83	3	3	3.71	40	0	0	1	68	67	34	28	6	32	42	.261	.284	.245	5.56	4.24
Hayes, Chris	R-R	6-1	195	2-5-83	3	6	2.79	45	0	0	7	68	69	24	21	0	16	47	.263	.323	.229	6.25	2.13
Henninger, David	R-R	6-7	210	8-23-83	3	7	5.40	28	16	0	0	97	105	69	58	5	43	65	.277	.280	.275	6.05	4.00
Hochevar, Luke	R-R	6-5	205	9-15-83	0	1	1.17	4	4	0	0	15	8	3	2	2	2	16	.148	.103	.200	9.39	1.17
Jirschele, Jeremy	R-R	5-9	195	11-14-82	0	0	0.00	1	0	0	0	0	0	0	0	0	0	0	.000	—	.000	0.00	0.00
Kalkhof, Adam	L-L	6-6	230	9-4-83	0	0	0.00	4	0	0	0	4	4	0	0	1	1	1	.286	.000	.400	2.45	2.45
Kniginyzky, Matthew	L-R	6-3	185	10-5-82	9	5	3.51	23	23	0	0	131	124	53	51	16	34	100	.255	.265	.246	6.89	2.34
Morales, Angelo	R-R	6-1	192	5-2-86	0	0	5.06	1	1	0	0	5	7	4	3	0	2	2	.350	.667	.294	3.38	3.38
Nicoll, Christopher	R-R	6-2	190	10-30-83	4	9	2.82	23	23	0	0	134	105	49	42	13	40	140	.210	.196	.223	9.40	2.69
Oliveros, Rayner	R-R	6-2	180	9-23-85	7	4	2.84	32	5	0	2	98	91	35	31	8	17	57	.246	.250	.243	5.22	1.56
Penn, Michael	R-R	6-4	205	4-21-82	6	2	2.62	19	13	0	0	82	79	29	24	3	20	52	.252	.222	.284	5.68	2.19
Rosa, Carlos	R-R	6-1	185	9-21-84	8	6	2.53	24	24	1	0	139	121	50	39	6	54	102	.239	.245	.235	6.62	3.50
Santiago, Mario	R-R	6-2	210	12-16-85	3	6	5.37	12	8	0	1	60	78	40	36	5	14	38	.329	.358	.310	5.67	2.09
Schambough, Kraig	R-R	6-0	185	1-21-82	4	8	3.14	40	0	0	12	63	53	26	22	2	24	61	.232	.275	.204	8.71	3.43

FIELDING

Catcher	PCT	G	PO	A	E	DP	PB
Everett	.989	26	156	19	2	0	6
Howell	.991	73	486	67	5	7	16
Lowen	.983	25	156	22	3	1	3
Thibault	1.000	25	175	23	0	4	2

First Base	PCT	G	PO	A	E	DP
Everett	.982	13	105	6	2	10
Jirschele	1.000	12	84	5	0	8
Lisson	1.000	4	11	1	0	1
Lowen	.979	14	90	3	2	7
Nunez	1.000	3	27	3	0	1
Vega	.980	104	822	54	18	71

Second Base	PCT	G	PO	A	E	DP
Arce	.965	32	63	102	6	18
Jirschele	.939	8	20	11	2	3
Johnson	.982	99	198	300	9	55
Nunez	1.000	1	4	4	0	2

Third Base	PCT	G	PO	A	E	DP
Arce	1.000	2	1	2	0	0
Jirschele	.942	16	18	31	3	0
Lisson	.926	124	111	203	25	17
Nunez	1.000	2	3	1	0	1

Shortstop	PCT	G	PO	A	E	DP
Arce	.935	30	41	74	8	17
Jirschele	—	1	1	0	0	0

	PCT	G	PO	A	E	DP
Johnson	.973	10	17	19	1	5
McConnell	.932	67	86	162	18	37
Nunez	.952	8	9	11	1	2
Pena	.965	28	40	70	4	13

Outfield	PCT	G	PO	A	E	DP
Arce	.961	20	45	4	2	0
Arroyo	.978	96	174	7	4	2
Duarte	.985	126	300	22	5	7
Everett	.857	2	5	1	1	0
Jirschele	1.000	44	64	4	0	3
Lowen	—	1	0	0	0	0
Peralta	.952	10	20	0	1	0
Sabatini	.963	42	75	2	3	0
Santana	.982	102	157	6	3	0

Idaho Falls Chukars — Rookie

Pioneer League

BATTING	B-T	HT	WT	DOB	AVG	vLH	vRH	G	AB	R	H	2B	3B	HR	RBI	BB	HBP	SH	SF	SO	SB	CS	SLG	OBP
Balduf, Todd	B-R	6-2	200	7-6-84	.224	.316	.188	24	67	7	15	1	0	0	7	6	1	0	0	14	1	0	.239	.297
Bigler, Brett	L-L	6-1	185	10-16-84	.276	.196	.299	66	210	42	58	5	0	0	24	39	1	5	0	27	20	2	.300	.392
Boudreaux, Ross	R-R	5-11	197	4-30-82	.171	.100	.181	32	82	9	14	2	0	0	9	5	3	3	1	24	1	0	.195	.242
Castillo, Luis	R-R	6-3	175	1-18-84	.383	.400	.381	27	94	18	36	6	0	3	23	18	1	1	1	13	2	0	.543	.482
Dickerson, Joseph	L-L	6-1	190	10-3-86	.281	.185	.309	63	242	36	68	14	3	7	38	19	5	0	6	34	9	8	.450	.338
Gil, Gilbert	R-R	5-10	180	12-12-84	.223	.143	.244	37	103	22	23	3	0	2	15	7	0	3	0	21	5	0	.311	.273
Gonzalez, O.D.	R-R	6-0	180	9-12-84	.282	.311	.275	67	238	46	67	10	2	5	20	38	1	5	1	65	25	7	.403	.381
Hayes, Shawn	L-R	6-4	220	11-5-84	.263	.286	.256	15	57	9	15	3	1	0	13	4	2	2	1	26	1	0	.351	.328
Herrera, Brenan	R-R	6-1	180	6-16-82	.236	.277	.225	65	220	22	52	16	2	2	27	34	5	3	2	54	5	2	.355	.349
Lance, Brandon	R-R	6-0	215	10-3-83	.190	.125	.206	30	84	8	16	2	0	0	6	14	1	0	1	15	2	0	.214	.310
Maddox, Marc	R-R	5-11	185	9-16-83	.336	.154	.389	62	232	46	78	22	4	4	40	33	5	1	1	31	7	0	.504	.428
McConnell, Christopher	R-R	5-11	170	12-18-85	.262	.237	.269	47	183	25	48	8	4	4	35	15	2	1	3	35	8	4	.415	.320
Mertins, Kurt	R-R	6-0	175	4-22-86	.342	.233	.368	61	225	46	77	11	3	1	26	18	3	1	3	39	26	4	.431	.397
Morel, Alvi	L-L	6-0	153	8-28-84	.301	.333	.293	45	176	34	53	6	3	1	24	18	2	4	1	38	19	3	.386	.371
Morizio, Matthew	L-R	6-2	198	12-14-83	.264	.185	.300	30	87	12	23	5	0	0	7	25	0	0	0	16	1	1	.322	.429
Nunez, Eduardo	R-R	6-2	170	9-21-85	.182	.000	.200	23	66	9	12	3	2	0	9	10	2	1	1	16	0	0	.288	.304
Turner, Jase	L-R	6-3	215	2-22-83	.229	.263	.223	66	231	30	53	18	1	8	41	38	1	2	4	85	1	2	.420	.341
Van Stratten, Nick	R-R	6-1	185	5-22-85	.294	.000	.385	7	17	2	5	1	0	0	2	2	1	0	0	5	2	0	.353	.400

PITCHING	B-T	HT	WT	DOB	W	L	ERA	G	GS	CG	SV	IP	H	R	ER	HR	BB	SO	AVG	vLH	vRH	K/9	BB/9
Abreu, Juan	R-R	6-0	167	4-8-85	4	2	5.76	20	0	0	2	50	39	34	32	4	35	57	.223	.150	.244	10.26	6.30
Baldwin, Burke	R-L	6-5	215	5-28-85	1	2	4.15	15	0	0	2	30	25	17	14	3	15	39	.225	.318	.202	11.57	4.45
Best, Daniel	R-R	6-3	170	3-30-84	5	3	2.92	21	0	0	2	37	42	16	12	3	8	15	.280	.204	.317	3.65	1.95
Casey, Bryan	R-R	6-0	200	6-5-86	0	6	6.04	24	0	0	5	25	32	21	17	2	13	17	.302	.243	.333	6.04	4.62
Chambliss, Tyler	R-R	5-11	175	12-4-84	4	3	4.20	12	6	0	0	49	45	26	23	3	19	42	.237	.258	.227	7.66	3.47

	B-T	HT	WT	DOB	W	L	ERA	G	GS	CG	SV	IP	H	R	ER	HR	BB	SO	AVG	vLH	vRH	K/9	BB/9
Cordier, Erik	R-R	6-3	214	2-25-86	1	0	3.38	3	3	0	0	16	11	6	6	0	3	19	.186	.257	.083	10.69	1.69
Cribb, Josh	R-R	5-10	190	2-24-83	2	6	5.19	13	6	0	0	52	73	35	30	5	11	39	.351	.443	.304	6.75	1.90
Eckley, Jacob	L-L	6-2	220	6-27-83	1	1	5.92	22	0	0	2	24	27	16	16	1	2	27	.281	.235	.291	9.99	0.74
Fisher, Brent	L-L	6-2	190	8-6-87	0	0	2.25	1	0	0	1	4	2	1	1	0	1	9	.143	.143	.143	20.25	0.00
Godin, Jason	R-R	6-5	170	9-23-84	0	1	2.49	6	4	0	0	22	23	6	6	2	8	18	.288	.400	.250	7.48	3.32
Gutierrez, Daniel	R-R	6-1	180	3-8-87	0	4	6.57	14	9	0	0	49	74	42	36	6	21	36	.359	.394	.341	6.57	3.83
Hardy, Rowdy	L-L	6-4	170	10-26-82	5	3	2.80	15	15	0	0	80	79	29	25	4	5	52	.262	.200	.268	5.83	0.56
Hartsock, Aaron	R-R	6-3	200	1-17-84	6	2	2.91	18	0	0	2	46	33	17	15	2	13	43	.202	.156	.220	8.35	2.53
Mozingo, Harold	R-R	6-1	175	3-29-85	3	1	6.17	15	9	0	2	54	64	40	37	6	21	46	.299	.359	.273	7.67	3.50
Teaford, Everett	L-L	6-0	155	5-15-84	5	1	3.71	15	12	0	0	63	54	29	26	3	20	51	.228	.364	.214	7.29	2.86
Vacek, Chase	R-R	6-0	210	8-12-83	0	0	13.85	9	0	0	0	13	30	22	20	3	6	13	.448	.563	.412	9.00	4.15
Wood, Blake	R-R	6-4	225	8-8-85	3	1	4.50	12	12	0	0	52	50	28	26	1	15	46	.258	.263	.255	7.96	2.60

FIELDING

Catcher	PCT	G	PO	A	E	DP	PB
Balduf	.994	17	132	24	1	4	3
Boudreaux	.984	22	165	21	3	2	4
Lance	.982	23	138	24	3	4	3
Morizio	.993	19	123	18	1	3	2

First Base	PCT	G	PO	A	E	DP
Boudreaux	1.000	6	7	0	0	0
Castillo	1.000	19	165	7	0	13
Herrera	1.000	1	2	0	0	0
Lance	1.000	1	6	1	0	1
Maddox	.962	8	71	4	3	7
Turner	.992	51	454	29	4	49

Second Base	PCT	G	PO	A	E	DP
Gil	.968	11	12	18	1	5
Maddox	.986	29	62	82	2	18
Mertins	.952	42	73	107	9	26
Nunez	.833	1	0	5	1	1

Third Base	PCT	G	PO	A	E	DP
Castillo	.933	4	2	12	1	1
Gil	1.000	2	0	3	0	0
Hayes	.952	7	6	14	1	2
Herrera	.920	58	45	127	15	13
Maddox	.923	4	3	9	1	2
Morizio	.667	1	0	2	1	0

	Nunez	.900	3	2	7	1	1

Shortstop	PCT	G	PO	A	E	DP
Gil	.926	19	20	55	6	8
McConnell	.917	47	70	130	18	34
Nunez	.974	18	22	53	2	7

Outfield	PCT	G	PO	A	E	DP
Bigler	.955	62	81	3	4	0
Dickerson	.959	62	116	0	5	0
Gonzalez	.960	65	115	4	5	2
Morel	.985	41	62	2	1	0
Van Stratten	1.000	5	12	0	0	0

AZL Royals — Rookie

Arizona League

BATTING	B-T	HT	WT	DOB	AVG	vLH	vRH	G	AB	R	H	2B	3B	HR	RBI	BB	HBP	SH	SF	SO	SB	CS	SLG	OBP
Avila, Carlos	R-R	5-9	146	5-8-85	.262	.182	.290	21	42	10	11	1	0	1	6	5	0	0	0	10	1	1	.357	.340
Bianchi, Jeffrey	R-R	6-0	175	10-5-86	.429	.556	.394	12	42	13	18	4	0	2	6	9	2	0	1	3	1	1	.667	.537
Coolbaugh, Mike	R-R	6-1	190	6-5-72	.333	.500	.294	6	21	6	7	1	0	0	6	2	0	0	4	2	0		.381	.517
Dickson, Eric	R-R	—		2-3-83	.138	.125	.143	30	29	2	4	0	0	0	10	5	1	1	0	5	2	0	.138	.286
Doscher, Nicholas	R-R	6-2	205	5-20-87	.258	.314	.236	46	124	26	32	5	0	0	13	41	6	1	0	41	4	3	.298	.462
Dyson, Jarrod	L-R	5-10	160	8-15-84	.273	.286	.269	51	161	40	44	4	6	0	19	18	5	2	3	30	19	4	.373	.358
Francis, Nicholas	R-R	6-3	195	3-5-86	.303	.333	.293	46	155	30	47	8	4	1	27	15	1	0	1	41	3	2	.426	.366
Juan, Manuel	R-R	5-11	168	2-5-86	.271	.239	.282	49	170	24	46	10	1	3	27	8	3	2	0	32	6	3	.394	.315
Lucas, Scott	L-L	6-2	195	6-23-82	.279	.149	.318	55	204	41	57	11	9	1	51	20	15	0	5	38	11	5	.436	.377
Marrero, Oscar	B-R	6-0	177	1-26-87	.136	.333	.105	25	22	3	3	1	0	0	1	4	0	0	0	3	0	1	.182	.269
Mojica, Jose	R-R	6-0	177	12-26-88	.100	.000	.111	7	10	2	1	0	0	0	3	5	0	0	0	3	0	0	.100	.400
Peralta, Felix	R-R	6-0	175	9-30-85	.272	.200	.289	33	103	18	28	4	1	3	19	10	3	0	2	19	5	1	.417	.347
Perez, Alwin	L-R	6-0	150	4-4-87	.281	.174	.318	49	178	32	50	9	3	0	30	22	1	3	0	35	19	5	.365	.363
Robinson, Derrick	B-L	5-11	170	9-28-87	.233	.357	.194	54	176	25	41	6	3	1	24	24	3	5	0	55	20	14	.318	.335
Saldana, Pedro	R-R	6-1	198	2-10-84	.154	.000	.182	16	39	1	6	0	0	0	3	7	1	1	0	9	1	1	.154	.298
Taylor, Jason	R-R	6-0	210	1-14-88	.258	.293	.245	46	151	27	39	8	1	0	22	26	3	0	2	30	7	2	.325	.374
Van Stratten, Nick	R-R	6-1	185	5-22-85	.292	.271	.298	54	209	46	61	8	7	3	35	25	9	1	3	17	14	1	.440	.386
Wilson, Tyrone	L-R	5-9	180	10-8-87	.233	.250	.228	30	73	19	17	0	1	0	8	22	1	0	0	21	14	2	.260	.417

PITCHING	B-T	HT	WT	DOB	W	L	ERA	G	GS	CG	SV	IP	H	R	ER	HR	BB	SO	AVG	vLH	vRH	K/9	BB/9
Arias, Henry	R-R	6-3	201	1-6-85	4	5	3.59	14	10	0	1	58	53	31	23	1	27	47	.251	.314	.208	7.34	4.21
Barrera, Henry	R-R	6-0	205	11-25-85	0	1	5.48	16	0	0	2	23	20	18	14	0	17	30	.225	.192	.238	11.74	6.65
Bass, Brian	R-R	6-0	215	1-6-82	1	1	4.50	3	3	0	0	12	15	7	6	0	0	9	.294	.421	.219	6.75	0.00
Chavez, Chris	L-R	6-3	195	9-11-84	1	0	4.12	12	1	0	1	20	20	10	9	1	8	17	.260	.458	.170	7.78	3.63
Cummings, Tyler	R-R	6-3	220	3-25-84	1	0	1.69	15	0	0	4	21	20	8	4	1	4	13	.244	.321	.204	5.48	1.69
D'Amico, Yovany	R-R	5-11	223	8-18-84	3	1	3.96	5	5	0	0	25	27	12	11	1	6	25	.281	.152	.349	9.00	2.16
Fisher, Brent	L-L	6-2	190	8-6-87	3	1	2.11	14	14	0	0	68	41	18	16	2	19	98	.171	.233	.157	12.91	2.50
Hauff, Michael	R-R	6-1	230	3-7-84	1	1	1.35	12	0	0	3	20	10	3	3	1	5	21	.145	.125	.151	9.45	2.25
Lopez, Yensi	R-R	6-0	160	3-13-86	4	0	4.99	16	0	0	0	31	27	20	17	4	16	17	.245	.231	.254	4.99	4.70
Martinez, Angel	R-R	—	—	4-18-85	1	2	5.18	16	1	0	2	33	47	23	19	5	6	21	.338	.313	.333	5.73	1.64
McLintock, Jake	R-R	6-1	200	1-26-83	4	1	2.97	19	0	0	4	30	30	16	10	1	9	24	.261	.238	.274	7.12	2.67
Morales, Miguel	L-L	6-1	180	12-5-85	3	1	3.86	17	0	0	0	28	33	16	12	1	12	20	.300	.227	.318	6.43	3.86
Morales, Angelo	R-R	6-1	192	5-2-86	6	6	4.50	14	14	1	0	76	98	45	38	6	16	47	.311	.362	.286	5.57	1.89
Raglione, Paul	R-R	6-5	195	11-5-87	3	0	3.11	10	7	0	2	46	53	27	16	1	10	48	.273	.212	.296	9.32	1.94
Santiago, Mario	R-R	6-2	210	12-16-85	0	0	0.00	1	0	0	0	4	4	0	0	0	4	4	.267	.286	.250	9.00	0.00
Vacek, Chase	R-R	6-0	210	8-12-83	1	0	0.00	3	0	0	1	4	1	0	0	0	4	4	.077	.000	.111	9.82	0.00

FIELDING

Catcher	PCT	G	PO	A	E	DP	PB
Doscher	.986	46	329	32	5	1	6
Marrero	.909	10	18	2	2	0	3
Saldana	.983	16	107	6	2	0	2

First Base	PCT	G	PO	A	E	DP
Lucas	.986	55	463	21	7	41
Marrero	.968	11	30	0	1	3

Second Base	PCT	G	PO	A	E	DP
Avila	.917	13	7	15	2	2
Perez	.948	37	62	84	8	26

	Wilson	.881	27	31	43	10	7

Third Base	PCT	G	PO	A	E	DP
Avila	—	1	0	0	0	0
Coolbaugh	1.000	6	2	16	0	1
Juan	1.000	2	1	2	0	0
Perez	.806	12	5	20	6	4
Taylor	.917	42	32	78	10	6

Shortstop	PCT	G	PO	A	E	DP
Avila	1.000	7	4	11	0	1
Bianchi	.975	10	11	28	1	5

	Juan	.923	46	70	110	15	23
	Perez	.938	6	2	13	1	3

Outfield	PCT	G	PO	A	E	DP
Dickson	.947	26	18	0	1	0
Dyson	.968	39	49	11	2	2
Francis	.955	27	40	2	2	0
Mojica	1.000	7	5	1	0	0
Peralta	.944	13	16	1	1	0
Robinson	.969	53	92	1	3	0
Van Stratten	.989	50	87	4	1	1

BY BILL SHAIKIN

If the Angels had billed 2006 as a rebuilding year, they could have hailed the season a success.

Instead, they sold themselves as a championship contender and won 89 games, more than all but one  National League club. But they finished second in the American League West and missed the playoffs for the first time in three years.

So they branded the season a disappointment.

As the season approached its end, owner Arte Moreno pledged the Angels would add a big bat or two for the 2007 season—not from the minor leagues, but via trades or free agency.

"I'll guarantee we're going to do something major," Moreno said.

They did nothing major going into the 2006 season, a nod to the talent they believed was coming from their touted farm system. They abandoned catcher Bengie Molina and starter Jarrod Washburn to free agency, clearing space for catcher Jeff Mathis and starter Ervin Santana. They moved Darin Erstad to center field to allow Casey Kotchman to play first base. When Erstad got hurt, they moved Chone Figgins to center field, making way for Dallas McPherson at third base.

Santana led the team in victories at 16-8, 4.28. The other youngsters did not fare as well.

Mathis struggled defensively and was demoted after hitting .103 in 12 games. Kotchman lasted 29 games, hitting .152 before the Angels revealed he had contracted mononucleosis in spring training.

For the second consecutive season, McPherson showed flashes of power interrupted by injuries. He hit .261/.298/.478 with seven home runs in 40 games, but

ORGANIZATION STATISTICS

PLAYERS OF THE YEAR

MAJOR LEAGUE: Vladimir Guerrero, of

One of the best hitters in the game, Guerrero went .329/.382/.552 and topped the 200-hit plateau for the fourth time in his career. The 30-year-old was by far the Angels' best hitter, leading the club in on-base plus slugging percentage (.934), hits (200), total bases (335), home runs (33) and RBIs (116).

MINOR LEAGUE: Brandon Wood, ss

Wood struck out 149 times in 453 at-bats, but he's one of the best power hitters in the minors. He could have won his second straight extra-base hits title had he not committed to play for Team USA in an Olympic qualifier in Cuba. Still, Wood hit .276/.355/.552 with 25 homers and 42 doubles.

his injuries taxed the patience of management.

Other youngsters did well, and in the case of Jered Weaver, so well that he forced the Angels to make room for him by cutting his older brother Jeff. Jered Weaver won his first nine major league decisions and went 11-2, 2.56. Mike Napoli, a Double-A catcher in 2005, replaced Mathis and hit .228 with 16 home runs, fourth on the team.

Howie Kendrick showed again he was one of the best batting prospects in the minors, batting .369 at Triple-A Salt Lake before joining the Angels in July. In lieu of trading for a big bat, the Angels put Kendrick in the lineup—out of position at first base—and he hit .285/.314/.416. After the season, the Angels bid farewell to Adam Kennedy so Kendrick can play his natural position of second base in 2007.

All-star outfielder Vladimir Guerrero hit a team-high .329/.382/.552 with 33 home runs and 116 RBIs. Francisco Rodriguez, in his second season as closer, led the league and set a franchise record with 47 saves.

Juan Rivera, bidding to establish himself as an everyday player, hit .310/.362/.525 with 23 homers and 85 RBIs in 448 at-bats and led the league in outfield assists. John Lackey (13-11, 3.56) and Kelvim Escobar (11-14, 3.61) ranked among league leaders in ERA.

Outfielder Tim Salmon retired after playing his entire career with the Angels. Salmon won the Angels' only rookie of the year award in 1993 and ended his career as the club's all-time home run leader.

In the minor leagues, shortstop Brandon Wood (.276/.355/.552 at Double-A Arkansas) and righthander Nick Adenhart (15-4, 2.61 between low Class A Cedar Rapids and high A Rancho Cucamonga) represented the Angels on the U.S. Olympic qualifying team that won a spot in the 2008 Beijing Games.

The two also solidified themselves as the top hitting and pitching prospects in the organization, though the Angels selected shortstop Sean Rodriguez (.307/.387/.557 with 29 home runs and 86 RBIs between Rancho Cucamonga and Arkansas) as the organizational player of the year.

ORGANIZATION LEADERS

BATTING

		*Minimum 250 at-bats
*AVG	Pettit, Christopher, Orem	.336
R	Rodriguez, Sean, Rancho Cuca./Arkansas/Salt Lake	94
H	Eylward, Mike, Arkansas/Salt Lake	166
TB	Rodriguez, Sean, Rancho Cuca./Arkansas/Salt Lake	291
2B	Brown, Matthew, Arkansas	44
3B	Reilly, Patrick, Cedar Rapids/Rancho Cucamonga	11
HR	Rodriguez, Sean, Rancho Cuca./Arkansas/Salt Lake	29
RBI	Eylward, Mike, Arkansas/Salt Lake	88
BB	Willits, Reggie, Salt Lake	77
SO	Renz, Jordan, Cedar Rapids	178
SB	Coon, Bradley, Cedar Rapids	57
*OBP	Willits, Reggie, Salt Lake	.448
*SLG	Pettit, Christopher, Orem	.566
XBH	Wood, Brandon, Arkansas	71

PITCHING

		#Minimum 75 innings
W	Adenhart, Nick, Cedar Rapids/Rancho Cucamonga	15
L	Hunter, Christopher, Arkansas	14
#ERA	Veras, Nicolas, AZL Angels	1.35
G	Wilhite, Matt, Salt Lake	61
CG	Mosebach, Robert, Cedar Rapids/Rancho Cucamonga	3
	Moseley, Dustin, Salt Lake	3
SV	Aldridge, Richard, Cedar Rapids/Rancho Cucamonga	25
IP	Mosebach, Robert, Cedar Rapids/Rancho Cucamonga	182
BB	Torres, Joe, Rancho Cucamonga	75
SO	Arredondo, Jose, Rancho Cucamonga/Arkansas	163
#AVG	Veras, Nicolas, AZL Angels	.210

Los Angeles Angels | MLB

American League

BATTING	B-T	HT	WT	DOB	AVG	vLH	vRH	G	AB	R	H	2B	3B	HR	RBI	BB	HBP	SH	SF	SO	SB	CS	SLG	OBP
Alfonzo, Edgardo	R-R	5-11	210	11-8-73	.100	.080	.120	18	50	1	5	1	0	0	1	2	0	0	0	3	0	0	.120	.135
2-team (12 Toronto) ..					.126	—	—	30	87	5	11	2	0	0	5	7	1	0	0	4	0	0	.149	.200
Anderson, Garret	L-L	6-3	225	6-30-72	.280	.248	.294	141	543	63	152	28	2	17	85	38	0	0	7	95	1	0	.433	.323
Aybar, Erick	B-R	5-10	170	1-14-84	.250	.250	.250	34	40	5	10	1	0	0	2	0	0	0	0	8	1	0	.325	.250
Cabrera, Orlando	R-R	5-9	180	11-2-74	.282	.243	.297	153	607	95	171	45	1	9	72	51	3	3	11	58	27	3	.404	.335
Erstad, Darin	L-L	6-2	215	6-4-74	.221	.192	.232	40	95	8	21	8	1	0	5	6	2	1	1	18	1	1	.326	.279
Figgins, Chone	B-R	5-7	180	1-22-78	.267	.233	.280	155	604	93	161	23	8	9	62	65	2	5	7	100	52	16	.376	.336
Guerrero, Vladimir	R-R	6-3	235	2-9-76	.329	.401	.307	156	607	92	200	34	1	33	116	50	4	0	4	68	15	5	.552	.382
Izturis, Maicer	B-R	5-8	160	9-12-80	.293	.247	.307	104	352	64	103	21	3	5	44	38	3	5	1	35	14	6	.412	.365
Kendrick, Howie	R-R	5-10	195	7-12-83	.285	.264	.295	72	267	25	76	21	1	4	30	9	4	0	3	44	6	0	.416	.314
Kennedy, Adam	L-R	6-0	185	1-10-76	.273	.193	.291	139	451	50	123	26	6	4	55	39	5	3	5	72	16	10	.384	.334
Kotchman, Casey	L-L	6-3	215	2-22-83	.152	.214	.138	29	79	6	12	2	0	1	6	7	0	2	0	13	0	1	.215	.221
Mathis, Jeff	R-R	6-0	185	3-31-83	.145	.133	.150	23	55	9	8	2	0	2	6	7	0	1	0	14	0	0	.291	.238
McPherson, Dallas	L-R	6-4	230	7-23-80	.261	.231	.265	40	115	16	30	4	0	7	13	6	0	0	0	40	1	0	.478	.298
Molina, Jose	R-R	6-2	220	6-3-75	.240	.218	.254	78	225	18	54	17	0	4	22	9	2	7	2	49	1	0	.369	.273
Morales, Kendry	B-R	6-1	220	6-20-83	.234	.229	.235	57	197	21	46	10	1	5	22	17	0	0	1	28	1	1	.371	.293
Murphy, Tommy	B-R	6-0	185	8-27-79	.229	.318	.188	48	70	12	16	4	1	1	6	5	0	1	1	21	4	1	.357	.276
Napoli, Mike	R-R	6-0	205	10-31-81	.228	.185	.241	99	268	47	61	13	0	16	42	51	5	0	1	90	2	3	.455	.360
Pride, Curtis	L-R	6-0	210	12-17-68	.222	.000	.240	22	27	6	6	2	0	1	2	6	0	0	0	6	0	0	.407	.364
Quinlan, Robb	R-R	6-1	200	3-17-77	.321	.326	.313	86	234	28	75	11	1	9	32	7	2	0	1	28	2	1	.491	.344
Rivera, Juan	R-R	6-2	205	7-3-78	.310	.351	.293	124	448	65	139	27	0	23	85	33	7	0	6	59	0	4	.525	.362
Salmon, Tim	R-R	6-3	235	8-24-68	.265	.298	.234	76	211	30	56	8	2	9	27	29	3	0	1	44	0	2	.450	.361
Willits, Reggie	B-R	5-11	185	5-30-81	.267	.083	.333	28	45	12	12	1	0	0	2	11	0	2	0	10	4	3	.289	.411

PITCHING	B-T	HT	WT	DOB	W	L	ERA	G	GS	CG	SV	IP	H	R	ER	HR	BB	SO	AVG	vLH	vRH	K/9	BB/9
Bootcheck, Chris	R-R	6-5	200	10-24-78	0	1	10.45	7	0	0	0	10	16	12	12	3	9	7	.364	.250	.458	6.10	7.84
Bulger, Jason	R-R	6-4	215	12-6-78	0	0	16.20	2	0	0	0	2	1	3	3	0	3	1	.167	.333	.000	5.40	16.20
Carrasco, Hector	R-R	6-2	220	10-22-69	7	3	3.41	56	3	0	1	100	93	42	38	10	27	72	.244	.249	.240	6.46	2.42
Colon, Bartolo	R-R	5-11	250	5-24-73	1	5	5.11	10	10	1	0	56	71	39	32	11	11	31	.306	.354	.261	4.95	1.76
Donnelly, Brendan	R-R	6-3	240	7-4-71	6	0	3.94	62	0	0	0	64	58	32	28	8	28	53	.240	.290	.204	7.45	3.94
Escobar, Kelvim	R-R	6-1	230	4-11-76	11	14	3.61	30	30	1	0	189	192	93	76	17	50	147	.264	.258	.270	6.99	2.38
Gregg, Kevin	B-R	6-6	235	6-20-78	3	4	4.14	32	3	0	0	78	88	41	36	10	21	71	.280	.298	.268	8.16	2.41
Jones, Greg	R-R	6-2	195	11-15-76	0	0	6.00	5	0	0	0	6	8	5	4	1	2	1	.348	.000	.444	1.50	3.00
Lackey, John	R-R	6-6	235	10-23-78	13	11	3.56	33	33	3	0	218	203	98	86	14	72	190	.246	.263	.231	7.86	2.98
Moseley, Dustin	R-R	6-4	190	12-26-81	1	0	9.00	3	2	0	0	11	22	11	11	3	2	3	.440	.500	.375	2.45	1.64
Rodriguez, Francisco	R-R	6-0	180	1-7-82	2	3	1.73	69	0	0	47	73	52	16	14	6	28	98	.197	.215	.179	12.08	3.45
Romero, J.C.	B-L	5-11	205	6-4-76	1	2	6.70	65	0	0	0	48	57	40	36	3	28	31	.298	.202	.382	5.77	5.21
Santana, Ervin	R-R	6-2	160	12-12-82	16	8	4.28	33	33	0	0	204	181	106	97	21	70	141	.241	.254	.229	6.22	3.09
Saunders, Joe	L-L	6-3	210	6-16-81	7	3	4.71	13	13	0	0	71	71	42	37	6	29	51	.264	.220	.274	6.50	3.69
Shields, Scot	R-R	6-1	170	7-22-75	7	7	2.87	74	0	0	2	88	70	30	28	8	24	84	.217	.207	.227	8.62	2.46
Weaver, Jeff	R-R	6-5	200	8-22-76	3	10	6.29	16	16	0	0	89	114	68	62	18	21	62	.309	.326	.290	6.29	2.13
Weaver, Jered	R-R	6-7	205	10-4-82	11	2	2.56	19	19	0	0	123	94	36	35	15	33	105	.209	.250	.174	7.68	2.41
Yan, Esteban	R-R	6-4	255	6-22-75	0	0	6.85	13	0	0	0	22	19	18	17	4	13	16	.232	.344	.160	6.45	5.24

FIELDING

Catcher	PCT	G	PO	A	E	DP	PB
Mathis	.970	20	92	6	3	1	1
Molina	.986	76	502	50	8	4	5
Napoli	.987	94	575	48	8	2	2

First Base	PCT	G	PO	A	E	DP
Alfonzo	1.000	2	0	1	0	0
Erstad	1.000	13	31	1	0	1
Kendrick	.994	44	330	29	2	43
Kotchman	1.000	26	180	15	0	12
McPherson	1.000	6	32	0	0	5
Molina	1.000	3	4	0	0	2
Morales	.989	56	424	37	5	40
Quinlan	.992	54	353	24	3	40

Second Base	PCT	G	PO	A	E	DP
Aybar	1.000	3	1	3	0	0
Figgins	.967	9	9	20	1	6
Izturis	1.000	4	3	8	0	2
Kendrick	1.000	28	48	67	0	25
Kennedy	.984	133	205	361	9	76

Third Base	PCT	G	PO	A	E	DP
Alfonzo	1.000	15	5	20	0	1
Figgins	.878	34	22	50	10	5
Izturis	.936	87	45	145	13	12
Kendrick	—	1	0	0	0	0
McPherson	.954	31	13	49	3	4
Quinlan	.972	18	11	24	1	1

Shortstop	PCT	G	PO	A	E	DP
Aybar	.897	19	13	22	4	6

	PCT	G	PO	A	E	DP
Cabrera	.975	152	252	377	16	100
Figgins	1.000	2	0	1	0	0
Izturis	.957	10	9	13	1	7

Outfield	PCT	G	PO	A	E	DP
Anderson	1.000	94	192	1	0	0
Erstad	1.000	27	71	1	0	0
Figgins	.982	112	265	8	5	3
Guerrero	.959	126	251	7	11	2
Murphy	1.000	42	64	2	0	2
Pride	1.000	11	12	0	0	0
Quinlan	1.000	16	13	0	0	0
Rivera	.974	103	210	13	6	1
Salmon	1.000	4	3	0	0	0
Willits	.974	20	36	1	1	0

Salt Lake Bees | Triple-A

Pacific Coast League

BATTING	B-T	HT	WT	DOB	AVG	vLH	vRH	G	AB	R	H	2B	3B	HR	RBI	BB	HBP	SH	SF	SO	SB	CS	SLG	OBP
Aspito, Jason	L-R	6-0	210	1-3-79	.238	.263	.235	57	172	21	41	4	2	6	27	13	5	1	3	45	1	2	.390	.306
Aybar, Erick	B-R	5-10	170	1-14-84	.283	.247	.297	81	339	63	96	20	3	6	45	21	3	1	4	36	32	18	.413	.327
Blakely, Darren	B-R	6-1	230	3-14-77	.207	.226	.196	31	87	11	18	3	0	3	9	2	4	1	3	26	1	0	.345	.250
Budde, Ryan	R-R	5-11	205	8-15-79	.233	.208	.246	72	215	32	50	15	0	8	33	22	7	0	0	55	1	1	.414	.324
Erstad, Darin	L-L	6-2	215	6-4-74	.100	.143	.087	7	30	0	3	0	0	0	3	1	0	0	0	2	1	0	.100	.129
Eylward, Mike	R-R	6-2	215	9-28-79	.314	.330	.309	109	405	57	127	22	0	8	63	43	9	1	3	60	1	6	.427	.389
Gorneault, Nick	R-R	6-3	220	4-19-79	.283	.337	.265	107	407	66	115	25	9	15	78	38	2	0	5	106	6	4	.499	.343
Haynes, Nathan	L-L	5-9	190	9-7-79	.228	.273	.217	16	57	7	13	1	2	1	11	4	1	2	1	15	3	2	.368	.286

General manager: Bill Stoneman. **Farm director:** Tony Reagins. **Scouting director:** Eddie Bane.

Class	Team	League	W	L	PCT	Finish*	Manager	Affiliate Since
Majors	Los Angeles	American	89	73	.549	6th (14)	Mike Scioscia	—
Triple-A	Salt Lake Bees	Pacific Coast	81	63	.563	3rd (16)	Brian Harper	2001
Double-A	Arkansas Travelers	Texas	51	87	.370	8th (8)	Tyrone Boykin	2001
High A	Rancho Cucamonga Quakes	California	63	77	.450	9th (10)	Bobby Mitchell	2001
Low A	Cedar Rapids Kernels	Midwest	65	74	.468	10th (14)	Bobby Magallanes	1993
Rookie	Orem Owlz	Pioneer	45	31	.592	2nd (8)	Tom Kotchman	2001
Rookie	AZL Angels	Arizona	34	21	.618	3rd (9)	Brian Harper	2001
OVERALL 2006 MINOR LEAGUE RECORD			339	353	.490	20th (30)		

*Finish in overall standings (No. of teams in league). +League champion

	B-T	HT	WT	DOB			AVG	OBP	SLG	G	AB	R	H	2B	3B	HR	RBI	BB	SO	SB	CS	vLH	vRH	OBP	SLG
Infante, Larry	B-R	5-10	160	4-4-85			.000	—	.000	2	2	0	0	0	0	0	0	0	0	0	1	0	0	.000	.000
Izturis, Maicer	B-R	5-8	160	9-12-80			.306	.143	.345	9	36	5	11	5	1	0	5	5	0	0	2	5	1	0	.500	.372
Kendrick, Howie	R-R	5-10	195	7-12-83			.369	.431	.351	69	290	57	107	25	6	13	62	12	8	1	1	48	11	3	.631	.408
Kotchman, Casey	L-L	6-3	215	2-22-83			.000	.000	.000	3	7	0	0	0	0	0	0	1	1	0	0	1	0	0	.000	.125
Mathis, Jeff	R-R	6-0	185	3-31-83			.289	.325	.279	99	384	62	111	33	3	5	45	26	2	0	5	75	3	1	.430	.333
McPherson, Dallas	L-R	6-4	230	7-23-80			.250	.291	.235	56	208	35	52	11	5	17	45	15	4	0	4	88	3	1	.596	.307
Morales, Kendry	B-R	6-1	220	6-20-83			.320	.269	.339	66	256	41	82	13	1	12	52	14	2	0	1	40	0	3	.520	.359
Murphy, Tommy	B-R	6-0	185	8-27-79			.302	.288	.307	73	285	43	86	16	3	7	36	19	3	2	1	62	6	13	.453	.351
Myers, Corey	R-R	6-1	225	6-5-80			.263	.263	.263	52	156	23	41	5	0	2	12	19	1	0	1	29	1	1	.333	.345
Napoli, Mike	R-R	6-0	205	10-31-81			.244	.333	.217	21	78	12	19	6	0	3	10	8	4	0	0	29	1	1	.436	.344
Nieves, Abel	R-R	5-11	175	8-14-85			.111	1.000	.000	3	9	1	1	0	0	0	1	0	0	0	0	2	0	1	.111	.200
Pavkovich, Adam	R-R	6-2	190	12-31-81			.246	.305	.221	104	317	40	78	16	2	11	46	35	3	3	8	66	7	6	.413	.320
Pride, Curtis	L-R	6-0	210	12-17-68			.311	.292	.316	87	273	54	85	18	0	8	44	54	1	1	2	75	21	6	.465	.424
Remole, Clifton	L-L	6-1	205	10-24-82			.214	.000	.231	4	14	2	3	0	0	0	1	0	0	0	0	3	0	0	.214	.214
Rivera, Juan	R-R	6-2	205	7-3-78			.556	.667	.500	2	9	3	5	3	0	1	6	1	0	0	0	0	0	0	1.222	.600
Rodriguez, Sean	R-R	6-1	198	4-26-85			.000	—	.000	1	2	0	0	0	0	0	0	0	0	0	0	2	0	0	.000	.000
Rosario, Anderson	R-R	6-0	170	3-2-85			.118	.111	.125	18	17	0	2	0	0	0	0	0	0	0	0	11	0	1	.118	.118
Smith, Casey	R-R	6-2	200	3-18-79			.280	.309	.270	110	397	62	111	27	4	4	55	21	4	8	4	57	4	8	.398	.319
Specht, Brian	B-R	5-11	185	10-19-80			.269	.273	.268	28	93	16	25	3	1	3	13	11	0	1	0	22	7	1	.419	.346
Willits, Reggie	B-R	5-11	185	5-30-81			.327	.295	.339	97	352	85	115	18	4	3	39	77	2	4	2	50	31	15	.426	.448

PITCHING	B-T	HT	WT	DOB	W	L	ERA	G	GS	CG	SV	IP	H	R	ER	HR	BB	SO	AVG	vLH	vRH	K/9	BB/9
Aspito, Jason	L-R	6-0	210	1-3-79	0	0	18.00	1	0	0	1	5	2	0	0	1	1	0	.625	.667	.600	0.00	0.00
Bland, Nate	L-L	6-5	210	12-27-74	7	6	5.57	33	15	0	0	108	134	83	67	14	27	81	.306	.231	.338	6.73	2.24
Bootcheck, Chris	R-R	6-5	200	10-24-78	4	3	6.72	40	5	0	1	66	84	56	49	10	34	43	.318	.314	.322	5.89	4.66
Bulger, Jason	R-R	6-4	215	12-6-78	2	2	4.72	27	0	0	4	34	30	19	18	0	15	44	.233	.288	.161	11.53	3.93
Colon, Bartolo	R-R	5-11	250	5-24-73	0	1	6.17	2	2	0	0	12	14	8	8	4	2	3	.311	.290	.357	2.31	1.54
Cruz Chavez, Rafael	R-R	6-2	175	8-20-85	0	0	11.81	5	0	0	0	5	8	7	7	3	1	4	.348	.462	.200	6.75	1.69
Davidson, Daniel	L-L	6-4	225	1-8-81	1	2	5.79	4	4	1	0	23	32	16	15	3	6	17	.323	.297	.339	6.56	2.31
Gelinas, Karl	L-L	6-4	202	8-6-83	0	0	3.60	1	1	0	0	5	5	2	2	1	0	1	.278	.250	.333	1.80	0.00
Gregg, Kevin	B-R	6-6	235	6-20-78	1	0	0.00	3	2	0	0	10	5	0	0	0	4	8	.152	.182	.091	7.20	3.60
Gwyn, Marcus	R-R	6-3	219	11-4-77	3	1	3.65	50	0	0	6	67	66	33	27	6	30	56	.257	.259	.255	7.56	4.05
Heaverlo, Jeff	R-R	6-1	205	1-13-78	2	4	7.14	20	6	0	0	52	62	51	41	9	36	34	.304	.349	.253	5.92	6.27
Hensley, Matt	R-R	6-2	220	8-18-78	2	1	5.40	20	0	0	2	33	41	24	20	3	11	27	.308	.288	.321	7.29	2.97
Jones, Greg	R-R	6-2	195	11-15-76	5	6	4.25	47	0	0	17	55	52	28	26	7	19	45	.252	.212	.290	7.36	3.11
Moseley, Dustin	R-R	6-4	190	12-26-81	13	8	4.69	26	26	3	0	150	164	89	78	18	51	114	.283	.303	.262	6.86	3.07
Olenberger, Kasey	R-R	6-4	235	3-18-78	7	5	5.10	25	22	0	0	122	131	79	69	16	48	72	.274	.268	.280	5.33	3.55
Rouwenhorst, Jonathon	L-L	6-1	180	9-25-79	6	7	4.32	50	7	0	1	90	96	47	43	12	38	65	.274	.202	.312	6.52	3.81
Saunders, Joe	L-L	6-3	210	6-16-81	10	4	2.67	21	20	1	0	135	117	44	40	12	38	97	.234	.269	.221	6.47	2.53
Shell, Steven	R-R	6-5	190	1-1-83	5	9	6.16	24	22	0	0	123	156	91	84	16	32	82	.318	.302	.335	6.02	2.35
Smith, Jesse	R-R	6-2	214	7-11-80	0	0	0.00	1	1	0	0	7	4	1	0	0	0	5	.167	.143	.176	6.43	0.00
Thompson, Richard	R-R	6-0	180	7-1-84	0	1	12.46	4	0	0	1	4	9	6	6	1	4	3	.500	.429	.545	6.23	8.31
Weaver, Jered	R-R	6-7	205	10-4-82	6	1	2.10	12	11	2	0	77	63	19	18	7	10	93	.223	.247	.199	10.87	1.17
Wilhite, Matt	R-R	6-1	185	7-3-81	7	2	3.49	54	0	0	1	80	79	34	31	7	21	36	.266	.255	.275	4.05	2.36

FIELDING

Catcher	PCT	G	PO	A	E	DP	PB
Budde	.992	38	242	18	2	0	3
Mathis	.990	83	547	61	6	9	6
Myers	1.000	8	41	4	0	1	1
Napoli	.993	18	126	12	1	1	0
Pavkovich	1.000	1	1	0	0	0	0

First Base	PCT	G	PO	A	E	DP
Budde	.951	12	72	5	4	10
Eylward	.990	51	442	40	5	57
Kotchman	.857	2	6	0	1	0
McPherson	.962	17	123	5	5	10
Morales	.998	51	439	28	1	49
Myers	1.000	18	114	10	0	18
Napoli	1.000	3	21	2	0	4
Pavkovich	1.000	1	1	0	0	0
Pride	.—	1	0	0	0	0
Remole	.974	4	32	6	1	5

Second Base	PCT	G	PO	A	E	DP
Infante	1.000	1	1	3	0	2

	PCT	G	PO	A	E	DP
Izturis	1.000	1	0	5	0	0
Kendrick	.982	59	95	185	5	50
Myers	1.000	3	0	4	0	0
Pavkovich	.959	23	44	50	4	20
Smith	.979	49	83	154	5	50
Specht	.981	15	15	38	1	8

Third Base	PCT	G	PO	A	E	DP
Eylward	.942	40	31	67	6	7
Izturis	1.000	2	0	3	0	0
Kendrick	1.000	7	4	15	0	4
McPherson	.963	25	13	39	2	1
Myers	.895	20	9	25	4	3
Pavkovich	.938	51	33	88	8	14
Smith	.893	11	7	18	3	0
Specht	.952	5	5	15	1	3

Shortstop	PCT	G	PO	A	E	DP
Aybar	.946	81	142	241	22	63
Izturis	.917	6	8	14	2	6
Nieves	.818	3	4	5	2	2

	PCT	G	PO	A	E	DP
Pavkovich	.875	3	5	9	2	2
Rodriguez	1.000	1	0	1	0	1
Smith	.969	53	86	133	7	40
Specht	.963	5	10	16	1	3

Outfield	PCT	G	PO	A	E	DP
Aspito	.959	50	68	3	3	0
Blakely	.984	28	60	0	1	0
Erstad	1.000	5	14	0	0	0
Gorneault	.971	92	160	10	5	3
Haynes	1.000	15	29	2	0	0
Murphy	.986	71	139	6	2	1
Pavkovich	.981	28	49	4	1	0
Pride	.975	62	112	3	3	0
Rivera	.600	1	3	0	2	0
Rosario	1.000	16	8	0	0	0
Specht	1.000	4	7	0	0	0
Willits	.983	96	230	8	4	2

(sidebar, vertical text:) ORGANIZATION STATISTICS

Texas League

BATTING	B-T	HT	WT	DOB	AVG	vLH	vRH	G	AB	R	H	2B	3B	HR	RBI	BB	HBP	SH	SF	SO	SB	CS	SLG	OBP
Aspito, Jason	L-R	6-0	210	1-3-79	.266	.341	.247	60	214	33	57	10	0	11	30	18	12	1	2	37	3	5	.467	.354
Bacon, Dwaine	B-R	5-11	190	4-11-79	.215	.227	.212	93	339	42	73	15	4	5	28	37	3	8	2	81	35	11	.327	.297
Blakely, Darren	B-R	6-1	200	3-14-77	.150	.200	.133	7	20	0	3	0	0	0	1	1	0	0	1	4	0	0	.150	.200
Brown, Matthew	R-R	6-0	200	8-8-82	.293	.339	.280	134	515	77	151	41	3	19	79	47	10	2	2	108	7	6	.495	.362
Day, Devin	R-R	6-2	200	9-3-80	.168	.208	.150	52	173	21	29	8	0	2	14	10	6	1	1	52	2	3	.249	.237
Del Chiaro, Brent	R-R	6-3	240	6-26-79	.161	.057	.186	54	180	16	29	3	0	5	18	11	3	5	0	75	1	0	.261	.222
Duff, Tim	R-R	6-2	210	6-26-81	.111	.167	.095	8	27	1	3	1	0	0	1	1	0	0	0	9	0	0	.148	.143
Evans, Terry	R-R	6-3	200	1-19-82	.309	.279	.317	52	188	48	58	9	2	11	22	18	6	0	1	56	11	6	.553	.385
2-team (21 Springfield)					.308	—	—	73	263	61	81	13	2	18	42	21	11	0	2	77	16	7	.578	.380
Eylward, Mike	R-R	6-2	215	9-28-79	.365	.367	.365	26	104	16	38	12	1	5	25	7	1	2	1	13	2	2	.644	.407
Gates, David	R-R	6-1	185	9-23-80	.207	.258	.189	35	121	16	25	6	2	5	15	14	8	1	0	46	2	0	.413	.329
Haynes, Nathan	L-L	5-9	190	9-7-79	.280	.259	.289	52	207	38	58	14	3	2	19	22	1	3	1	49	18	10	.406	.351
Pali, Matt	L-L	6-1	220	12-10-80	.232	.221	.235	96	345	39	80	13	0	9	45	20	2	2	1	70	7	3	.348	.277
Peel, Marlon	R-R	6-0	195	2-8-83	.285	.229	.298	123	495	67	141	37	4	16	66	28	18	4	3	105	13	11	.473	.344
Porter, Gregory	L-R	6-5	240	8-15-80	.298	.267	.306	118	440	73	131	28	0	20	71	26	6	0	4	103	4	3	.498	.342
Rodland, Eric	L-R	6-1	180	2-23-80	.300	.265	.309	118	397	64	119	22	2	8	51	58	6	3	5	54	2	5	.426	.394
Rodriguez, Sean	R-R	6-1	198	4-26-85	.354	.600	.359	18	65	16	23	5	0	5	9	11	2	1	0	18	0	3	.662	.462
Smith, Casey	R-R	6-2	200	3-18-79	.179	.222	.158	9	28	3	5	1	0	1	3	3	0	1	0	2	2	0	.321	.258
Wilson, Bobby	R-R	6-0	205	4-8-83	.286	.329	.274	103	374	45	107	26	0	9	53	33	5	4	2	47	1	6	.428	.350
Wood, Brandon	R-R	6-3	185	3-2-85	.276	.278	.275	118	453	74	125	42	4	25	83	54	6	1	8	149	19	3	.552	.355

PITCHING	B-T	HT	WT	DOB	W	L	ERA	G	GS	CG	SV	IP	H	R	ER	HR	BB	SO	AVG	vLH	vRH	K/9	BB/9
Arredondo, Jose	R-R	6-0	170	3-30-84	2	3	6.53	11	11	1	0	61	80	47	44	8	22	48	.317	.301	.329	7.12	3.26
Aspito, Jason	L-R	6-0	210	1-3-79	0	0	0.00	1	0	0	0	1	0	0	0	0	0	0	.000	.000	.000	0.00	0.00
Bittner, Tim	L-L	6-2	210	6-9-80	2	2	6.97	17	0	0	0	21	27	18	16	1	19	17	.342	.341	.342	7.40	8.27
Buckley, Allen	R-R	6-6	240	9-18-79	1	2	4.84	10	0	0	0	22	25	12	12	5	13	16	.287	.278	.294	7.66	5.24
Davidson, Daniel	L-L	6-4	225	1-8-81	2	8	5.64	29	16	0	0	113	146	81	71	13	43	62	.319	.361	.300	4.92	3.41
Day, Devin	R-R	6-2	200	9-3-80	0	0	0.00	1	0	0	0	1	1	0	0	0	0	0	.250	.333	.000	0.00	0.00
Edens, Kyle	R-R	5-10	210	1-25-80	3	3	6.46	25	1	0	1	47	69	40	34	6	30	32	.345	.370	.328	6.08	5.70
Edwards, Bill	R-R	6-3	185	3-26-81	8	7	5.71	52	0	0	4	80	94	59	51	5	39	45	.302	.336	.280	5.04	4.37
Gonzalez, Miguel	R-R	6-1	165	5-27-84	0	2	3.88	31	0	0	4	53	41	23	23	8	17	38	.214	.221	.209	6.41	2.87
Green, Nick	R-R	6-4	180	8-20-84	8	5	4.41	17	17	0	0	112	115	64	55	23	21	77	.268	.263	.272	6.17	1.68
Gwyn, Marcus	R-R	6-3	219	11-4-77	0	0	0.00	1	0	0	0	1	1	0	0	0	0	0	.250	.000	.333	9.00	0.00
Heaverlo, Jeff	R-R	6-1	205	1-13-78	0	1	1.04	5	0	0	0	9	8	3	1	0	2	6	.250	.273	.238	6.23	2.08
Holcomb, James	R-R	6-4	205	11-28-80	0	7	5.46	13	13	0	0	63	75	51	38	6	20	42	.301	.315	.291	6.03	2.87
Hunter, Christopher	R-R	6-4	200	12-12-80	4	14	7.45	25	25	0	0	126	168	113	104	21	69	49	.326	.324	.327	3.51	4.94
Pali, Matt	L-L	6-1	220	12-10-80	0	0	13.50	2	0	0	0	1	2	2	2	1	2	2	.333	.500	.000	13.50	13.50
Pullin, Aaron	R-R	6-3	200	2-17-81	2	4	4.70	28	0	0	1	46	46	25	24	5	27	28	.263	.385	.191	5.48	5.28
Rodriguez, Rafael	R-R	6-1	175	9-24-84	5	10	6.63	24	24	0	0	133	175	111	98	28	55	83	.321	.328	.316	5.62	3.72
Shell, Steven	R-R	6-5	190	1-1-83	1	2	4.00	3	3	0	0	18	20	12	8	1	4	10	.286	.414	.195	5.00	2.00
Simard, Michel	R-R	6-4	200	9-4-81	0	1	6.42	16	2	0	0	34	46	27	24	5	17	24	.317	.328	.309	6.42	4.54
Smith, Jesse	R-R	6-2	214	7-11-80	8	13	5.22	28	27	2	0	160	199	113	93	24	64	94	.309	.296	.318	5.28	3.59
Thompson, Richard	R-R	6-1	180	7-1-84	3	4	5.13	40	0	0	10	67	52	39	38	13	27	60	.218	.223	.213	8.10	3.65
Zimmermann, Bob	R-R	6-5	245	11-17-81	2	3	6.11	34	0	0	5	46	44	32	31	5	35	26	.260	.227	.282	5.12	6.90

FIELDING

Catcher	PCT	G	PO	A	E	DP	PB
Del Chiaro	.994	54	300	27	2	3	6
Duff	.980	7	43	5	1	1	1
Wilson	.982	81	431	63	9	3	8

First Base	PCT	G	PO	A	E	DP
Eylward	1.000	10	92	7	0	6
Pali	.990	58	462	39	5	65
Porter	.986	74	619	34	9	85

Second Base	PCT	G	PO	A	E	DP
Day	.970	19	46	52	3	17

	PCT	G	PO	A	E	DP
Rodland	.977	116	238	359	14	111
Smith	.955	5	9	12	1	0

Third Base	PCT	G	PO	A	E	DP
Brown	.922	129	96	225	27	31
Day	.871	10	6	21	4	4
Smith	1.000	1	0	1	0	1

Shortstop	PCT	G	PO	A	E	DP
Day	.950	5	6	13	1	3
Rodriguez	.938	18	36	54	6	19
Smith	1.000	1	2	2	0	1

	PCT	G	PO	A	E	DP
Wood	.956	115	219	362	27	99

Outfield	PCT	G	PO	A	E	DP
Aspito	.957	40	86	3	4	0
Bacon	.965	91	237	8	9	3
Blakely	1.000	6	11	1	0	0
Day	.953	16	39	2	2	1
Evans	.993	48	131	4	1	2
Gates	1.000	21	43	2	0	0
Haynes	.973	51	142	3	4	2
Pali	.986	34	69	4	1	0
Peel	.986	119	204	6	3	1

California League

BATTING	B-T	HT	WT	DOB	AVG	vLH	vRH	G	AB	R	H	2B	3B	HR	RBI	BB	HBP	SH	SF	SO	SB	CS	SLG	OBP
Collins, Michael	R-R	6-3	215	7-18-84	.291	.264	.303	125	477	61	139	29	1	7	82	29	33	1	3	74	9	9	.400	.371
Day, Devin	R-R	6-2	200	9-3-80	.273	.231	.300	10	33	4	9	4	0	0	7	5	0	0	0	9	0	1	.394	.368
Duff, Tim	R-R	6-2	210	6-26-81	.267	.200	.303	36	116	12	31	5	0	1	10	11	4	1	1	31	0	2	.336	.348
Erstad, Darin	L-L	6-2	215	6-4-74	.214	.000	.231	7	14	4	3	0	0	0	4	0	0	0	0	2	0	0	.214	.389
Fuller, Cody	R-R	6-0	190	9-19-82	.284	.295	.277	109	352	65	100	23	5	5	36	31	23	8	1	91	9	10	.420	.378
Johnson, Ben	R-R	6-1	196	10-17-81	.252	.311	.221	99	353	57	89	20	2	19	60	34	8	0	2	83	5	0	.482	.330
Leahy, Ryan	R-R	5-10	180	7-8-81	.260	.303	.228	78	281	32	73	13	0	1	41	35	6	7	3	46	3	6	.317	.351
Leblanc, Josh	L-R	6-1	190	9-15-81	.242	.212	.253	105	372	59	90	19	6	4	45	44	6	4	2	109	22	7	.358	.330
Lopez, Baltazar	L-L	6-1	185	11-22-83	.300	.227	.321	58	200	26	60	9	1	3	25	20	2	0	2	54	1	2	.400	.366
Nieves, Abel	R-R	5-11	175	8-14-85	.000	.000	—	4	6	0	0	0	0	0	0	0	0	0	0	0	0	0	.000	.000
Pali, Matt	L-L	6-1	220	12-10-80	.242	.250	.238	24	91	12	22	1	0	3	16	6	2	0	2	17	0	1	.352	.297
Reilly, Patrick	L-L	6-1	205	12-2-81	.271	.260	.275	100	373	63	101	21	7	14	64	23	10	2	3	101	5	3	.477	.328
Remole, Clifton	L-L	6-1	205	10-24-82	.267	.240	.276	105	397	50	106	13	2	4	41	21	4	5	1	44	0	5	.340	.310
Rodriguez, Sean	R-R	6-1	198	4-26-85	.301	.338	.286	116	455	78	137	29	5	24	77	47	12	3	6	124	15	3	.545	.377
Sandoval, Freddy	B-R	6-2	205	8-16-82	.258	.252	.261	113	434	60	112	28	2	5	54	59	1	7	8	98	30	8	.366	.343

ORGANIZATION STATISTICS

	B-T	HT	WT	DOB	AVG	vLH	vRH	G	AB	R	H	2B	3B	HR	RBI	BB	HBP	SH	SF	SO	SB	CS	SLG	OBP
Statia, Hainley	B-R	5-11	160	1-19-86	.300	.217	.351	18	60	8	18	2	1	0	8	8	1	0	1	7	1	1	.367	.386
Sutton, Nate	L-R	6-0	190	9-1-82	.278	.308	.269	118	442	75	123	16	8	12	46	46	4	5	1	77	27	7	.432	.351
Toussaint, Drew	R-R	6-2	175	10-24-82	.242	.224	.252	108	372	47	90	25	1	12	42	35	11	1	0	119	2	2	.411	.325

PITCHING	B-T	HT	WT	DOB	W	L	ERA	G	GS	CG	SV	IP	H	R	ER	HR	BB	SO	AVG	vLH	vRH	K/9	BB/9
Adenhart, Nick	R-R	6-3	185	8-24-86	5	2	3.78	9	9	0	0	52	51	23	22	1	16	46	.258	.238	.272	7.91	2.75
Aldridge, Richard	R-R	6-2	210	9-10-83	0	0	9.00	5	0	0	1	4	5	4	4	0	6	6	.333	.400	.300	13.50	13.50
Arredondo, Jose	R-R	6-0	170	3-30-84	5	6	2.30	15	15	0	0	90	62	28	23	4	35	115	.198	.252	.161	11.50	3.50
Beck, Bradley	L-L	5-11	185	1-10-85	1	2	2.10	26	0	0	1	30	20	7	7	1	8	18	.196	.152	.217	5.40	2.40
Colon, Bartolo	R-R	5-11	250	5-24-73	0	0	0.00	1	1	0	0	4	2	0	0	0	1	3	.154	.200	.125	6.75	2.25
Cruz Chavez, Rafael	R-R	6-2	175	8-20-85	2	1	7.25	24	0	0	0	36	54	31	29	2	4	10	.353	.490	.288	2.50	1.00
DeLoizaga-Carney, Frederic..	R-R	6-3	220	8-21-82	1	3	4.06	23	0	0	3	38	38	19	17	2	23	32	.259	.217	.277	7.65	5.50
Diaz, Amalio	R-R	6-2	170	9-10-86	3	0	1.52	4	4	0	0	24	24	4	4	1	5	10	.264	.135	.352	3.80	1.90
Gelinas, Karl	R-R	6-4	202	8-6-83	3	8	5.68	16	15	1	0	90	115	63	57	12	17	52	.309	.304	.312	5.18	1.69
Gonzalez, Miguel	R-R	6-1	165	5-27-84	1	0	1.71	14	0	0	1	26	17	5	5	2	2	24	.173	.098	.228	8.20	0.68
Green, Nick	R-R	6-4	180	8-20-84	5	3	4.15	11	11	1	0	65	77	31	30	9	19	57	.291	.337	.266	7.89	2.63
Hawkins, Daniel	R-R	6-3	200	8-11-82	1	1	8.38	19	0	0	0	29	45	31	27	3	17	10	.366	.279	.413	3.10	5.28
Herrera, Pedro	R-R	6-0	155	2-14-86	0	1	2.84	6	0	0	0	6	6	4	2	0	5	5	.231	.500	.150	7.11	7.11
Jepsen, Kevin	R-R	6-3	215	7-26-84	4	4	3.58	47	0	0	16	50	51	26	20	2	34	46	.270	.294	.256	8.23	6.08
Leahy, Ryan	R-R	5-10	180	7-8-81	0	0	0.00	2	0	0	0	2	0	0	0	0	2	0	.000	.000	.000	0.00	9.00
Lynch, Kevin	R-R	6-2	200	1-2-83	2	3	2.40	45	0	0	0	56	41	18	15	3	25	53	.206	.277	.184	8.47	3.99
Marek, Stephen	R-R	6-2	200	9-3-83	2	3	3.94	6	6	0	0	32	26	14	14	4	13	33	.230	.298	.182	9.28	3.66
Mosebach, Robert	R-R	6-4	195	9-14-84	1	1	6.35	4	4	0	0	23	23	17	16	1	8	15	.258	.333	.214	5.96	3.18
Ortega, Anthony	R-R	6-0	170	8-24-85	0	1	2.08	5	1	0	1	9	9	6	2	0	5	5	.281	.286	.278	5.19	5.19
Pali, Matt	L-L	6-1	220	12-10-80	0	0	0.00	1	0	0	0	0	0	0	0	0	0	1	.000	—	.000	27.00	0.00
Pete, Mike	L-L	6-0	170	1-29-83	2	1	5.80	26	0	0	0	36	43	27	23	3	24	17	.293	.313	.287	4.29	6.06
Posey, Micah	L-L	6-5	220	10-18-82	4	10	5.65	32	19	0	0	121	154	95	76	15	70	61	.317	.313	.318	4.54	5.21
Pullin, Aaron	R-R	6-3	200	2-17-81	0	1	3.90	22	0	0	1	28	27	16	12	6	11	18	.250	.303	.227	5.86	3.58
Rodriguez, Fernando	R-R	6-3	210	6-18-84	11	8	4.57	28	27	1	0	163	188	92	83	15	49	112	.293	.276	.304	6.17	2.70
Rodriguez, Francisco	R-R	6-2	200	2-26-83	5	13	5.47	26	25	1	0	133	158	95	81	11	68	83	.300	.335	.277	5.60	4.59
Rodriguez, Rafael	R-R	6-1	175	9-24-84	3	0	0.53	3	3	0	0	17	15	1	1	0	2	20	.234	.250	.225	10.59	1.06
Simard, Michel	R-R	6-4	200	9-4-81	0	1	4.93	23	0	0	0	38	40	28	21	2	10	23	.261	.185	.303	5.40	2.35
Torres, Joseph	L-L	6-2	193	9-3-82	2	4	8.14	43	0	0	0	42	38	46	38	0	75	45	.245	.186	.268	9.64	16.07

FIELDING

Catcher	PCT	G	PO	A	E	DP	PB
Collins	.983	72	478	44	9	4	15
Duff	.996	36	244	32	1	4	9
Johnson	.977	35	231	21	6	1	7

First Base	PCT	G	PO	A	E	DP
Collins	.977	24	201	11	5	28
Erstad	1.000	6	27	2	0	2
Johnson	.982	11	103	7	2	17
Lopez	.993	35	272	24	2	29
Pali	.957	3	22	0	1	3
Reilly	1.000	4	39	2	0	2
Remole	.987	69	558	37	8	55

Second Base	PCT	G	PO	A	E	DP
Day	.973	6	16	20	1	5
Leahy	.981	41	88	114	4	34
Nieves	1.000	2	3	1	0	0
Sandoval	1.000	1	0	1	0	0
Sutton	.963	103	235	262	19	64

Third Base	PCT	G	PO	A	E	DP
Leahy	.931	31	22	72	7	6
Nieves	1.000	1	0	1	0	0
Sandoval	.934	110	78	247	23	26

Shortstop	PCT	G	PO	A	E	DP
Day	.950	4	5	14	1	2

	PCT	G	PO	A	E	DP
Leahy	.974	8	16	21	1	8
Nieves	1.000	1	0	1	0	0
Rodriguez	.950	113	188	360	29	80
Statia	.972	16	23	47	2	6

Outfield	PCT	G	PO	A	E	DP
Fuller	.964	107	212	5	8	1
Johnson	.931	12	25	2	2	1
Leblanc	.961	104	221	3	9	1
Pali	1.000	15	27	3	0	0
Reilly	.991	72	111	4	1	0
Remole	.981	29	49	2	1	0
Rodriguez	1.000	1	2	0	0	0
Toussaint	.951	105	171	5	9	0

Cedar Rapids Kernels — Low Class A

Midwest League

BATTING	B-T	HT	WT	DOB	AVG	vLH	vRH	G	AB	R	H	2B	3B	HR	RBI	BB	HBP	SH	SF	SO	SB	CS	SLG	OBP
Albano, Marco	R-R	5-11	215	8-26-83	.217	.282	.183	77	254	29	55	10	1	2	32	14	8	3	1	77	15	6	.287	.278
Coon, Bradley	L-L	6-0	175	12-11-82	.278	.277	.278	124	457	79	127	18	8	0	29	75	6	11	6	82	55	21	.352	.382
Davies, Josh	R-R	6-4	200	9-12-85	.242	.176	.261	41	153	23	37	5	5	3	22	10	0	1	0	45	4	3	.399	.288
Edwards, Madison	L-R	5-11	175	9-1-83	.216	.231	.214	70	199	24	43	3	4	2	11	28	3	2	0	56	10	6	.302	.322
Infante, Larry	B-R	5-10	160	4-4-85	.254	.069	.261	85	291	42	74	19	4	3	34	23	5	9	5	58	7	6	.378	.315
Johnson, Tyler	R-R	6-2	220	11-2-85	.128	.000	.156	11	39	1	5	2	0	0	1	5	0	1	0	19	0	1	.179	.227
Leahy, Ryan	R-R	5-10	180	7-8-81	.263	.300	.222	12	38	6	10	1	0	0	1	3	0	4	0	7	1	1	.289	.317
Madrigal, Warner	R-R	6-0	200	3-21-84	.235	.268	.216	30	115	11	27	1	0	4	13	5	1	1	0	28	2	3	.348	.273
Martinez, Brett	R-R	6-0	200	10-14-83	.226	.264	.213	100	354	33	80	9	1	4	35	36	3	2	5	87	6	8	.291	.299
Morris, Dallas	R-R	6-2	210	7-13-82	.260	.280	.254	122	453	48	118	23	4	7	60	25	6	1	7	66	24	10	.375	.303
Reilly, Patrick	L-L	6-1	205	12-2-81	.315	.353	.291	23	89	16	28	6	4	1	17	8	3	0	0	26	6	5	.506	.390
Renz, Jordan	R-R	6-3	225	7-21-83	.222	.298	.199	118	450	56	100	22	9	24	86	35	9	0	5	178	6	4	.440	.289
Rosario, Anderson	R-R	6-0	170	3-2-85	.273	.323	.259	39	143	19	39	13	2	3	11	3	2	1	1	48	9	3	.455	.295
Schlichting, Travis	R-R	6-4	190	10-19-84	.242	.303	.212	31	99	18	24	5	1	3	9	12	6	1	1	23	6	4	.404	.356
Smith, Stantrel	R-R	6-4	211	10-21-83	.210	.288	.181	76	243	31	51	3	5	2	21	7	2	2	1	56	11	5	.288	.237
Statia, Hainley	B-R	5-11	160	1-19-86	.297	.274	.306	111	417	68	124	31	1	1	38	52	3	8	0	54	23	15	.384	.379
Trumbo, Mark	R-R	6-4	220	1-16-86	.220	.168	.235	118	428	43	94	19	0	13	59	44	3	0	7	99	5	5	.355	.293
Wipke, Flint	R-R	6-2	195	1-22-83	.236	.291	.217	108	403	45	95	18	8	6	34	33	7	0	2	110	11	12	.365	.303

PITCHING	B-T	HT	WT	DOB	W	L	ERA	G	GS	CG	SV	IP	H	R	ER	HR	BB	SO	AVG	vLH	vRH	K/9	BB/9
Adenhart, Nick	R-R	6-3	185	8-24-86	10	2	1.95	16	16	1	0	106	84	33	23	2	26	99	.215	.214	.216	8.41	2.21
Aldridge, Richard	R-R	6-2	210	9-10-83	2	3	2.37	50	0	0	24	57	34	17	15	4	21	81	.169	.194	.148	12.79	3.32
Beck, Bradley	L-L	5-11	185	1-10-85	0	0	4.05	11	0	0	0	7	8	3	3	0	4	7	.286	.400	.154	9.45	0.00
Butcher, Brok	R-R	6-1	180	10-13-83	4	3	3.94	19	7	1	0	59	64	29	26	4	12	32	.278	.271	.285	4.85	1.82
Cruz Chavez, Rafael	R-R	6-2	175	8-20-85	0	0	1.69	12	0	0	0	21	22	6	4	2	5	22	.272	.212	.313	2.11	0.84
Diaz, Amalio	R-R	6-2	170	9-10-86	2	1	5.18	7	6	0	0	33	51	20	19	5	8	26	.357	.345	.365	7.09	2.18
Didjurgis, Timothy	R-R	6-5	230	12-16-82	0	7	4.25	42	1	0	0	66	58	36	31	3	35	51	.244	.224	.257	6.99	4.80
Hawkins, Daniel	R-R	6-3	200	8-11-82	0	4	3.97	20	1	0	0	34	29	16	15	1	26	20	.244	.265	.229	5.29	6.88
Hill, Andrew	R-R	6-3	195	10-31-84	4	10	4.27	18	17	1	0	105	115	59	50	9	34	52	.267	.252	.286	4.61	1.71
Howell, Chris	R-R	6-0	210	5-11-83	2	6	4.39	41	0	0	2	70	71	46	34	10	22	51	.283	.314	.249	6.59	2.84

	B-T	HT	WT	DOB	W	L	ERA	G	GS	CG	SV	IP	H	R	ER	HR	BB	SO	AVG	vLH	vRH	K/9	BB/9
Lynch, Kevin	R-R	6-2	200	1-2-83	0	0	0.00	2	0	0	0	3	2	0	0	0	0	4	.182	.333	.125	10.80	0.00
Marek, Stephen	R-R	6-2	200	9-3-83	10	2	1.96	19	19	1	0	119	95	27	26	8	24	100	.216	.267	.177	7.54	1.81
Mattison, Tim	R-R	6-1	225	6-22-82	3	5	4.83	37	0	0	4	54	67	34	29	6	10	36	.312	.400	.259	6.00	1.67
Mendoza, Thomas	R-R	6-2	195	8-18-87	11	6	4.17	27	27	1	0	171	169	83	79	15	32	134	.261	.250	.269	7.07	1.69
Mosebach, Robert	R-R	6-4	195	9-14-84	6	3	3.04	24	24	3	0	160	166	67	54	5	29	97	.273	.304	.247	5.47	1.63
O'Day, Darren	R-R	6-4	220	10-22-82	3	1	2.70	17	0	0	1	23	20	8	7	1	2	14	.235	.219	.245	5.40	0.77
Ortega, Anthony	R-R	6-0	170	8-24-85	1	6	4.21	12	12	0	0	66	71	36	31	5	27	55	.280	.289	.271	7.46	3.66
Pete, Mike	L-L	6-0	170	1-29-83	1	2	5.89	22	0	0	0	18	14	13	12	0	15	18	.219	.206	.233	8.84	7.36
Romero, Robert	R-R	5-10	190	3-28-85	0	3	3.16	23	0	0	0	26	15	9	9	0	16	20	.179	.235	.140	7.01	5.61
Shearer, Kelly	L-L	6-3	200	4-8-85	1	5	5.02	9	9	0	0	43	51	31	24	1	26	31	.293	.311	.287	6.49	5.44
West, James	R-R	6-2	175	12-21-84	0	2	9.00	4	0	0	0	4	4	4	4	1	3	4	.267	.286	.250	9.00	6.75
Wilson, Brendan	R-R	6-1	183	10-7-85	1	0	1.50	2	0	0	0	6	7	1	1	0	3	3	.304	.400	.231	4.50	4.50

FIELDING

Catcher	PCT	G	PO	A	E	DP	PB
Edwards	.957	6	21	1	1	0	0
Martinez	.985	86	570	92	10	9	15
Wipke	.995	50	348	37	2	7	11

First Base	PCT	G	PO	A	E	DP
Davies	1.000	11	78	6	0	13
Morris	.960	3	21	3	1	1
Reilly	1.000	2	17	2	0	0
Schlichting	1.000	5	33	1	0	3
Trumbo	.984	111	1033	75	18	80
Wipke	.983	13	112	5	2	17

Second Base	PCT	G	PO	A	E	DP
Albano	.961	59	93	155	10	32
Davies	.941	12	26	38	4	14

	PCT	G	PO	A	E	DP
Infante	.985	58	107	150	4	34
Leahy	1.000	11	15	24	0	3
Morris	.977	10	13	29	1	3
Statia	1.000	1	3	1	0	0

Third Base	PCT	G	PO	A	E	DP
Davies	.917	8	4	18	2	1
Infante	1.000	3	2	8	0	0
Leahy	.750	1	2	1	1	0
Morris	.943	109	94	235	20	28
Schlichting	.860	23	9	40	8	4

Shortstop	PCT	G	PO	A	E	DP
Albano	.973	6	15	21	1	7
Davies	1.000	1	2	1	0	0
Infante	.972	28	47	94	4	16

	PCT	G	PO	A	E	DP
Statia	.972	109	209	341	16	76

Outfield	PCT	G	PO	A	E	DP
Albano	.947	9	17	1	1	0
Coon	.986	121	270	11	4	6
Davies	.958	12	23	0	1	0
Edwards	.980	60	92	5	2	1
Johnson	.957	9	21	1	1	0
Madrigal	.958	27	42	4	2	2
Reilly	.973	21	35	1	1	0
Renz	.975	71	105	11	3	0
Rosario	.974	38	71	3	2	0
Smith	.957	65	103	8	5	2
Wipke	.667	5	4	0	2	0

Orem Owlz — Rookie

Pioneer League

BATTING	B-T	HT	WT	DOB	AVG	vLH	vRH	G	AB	R	H	2B	3B	HR	RBI	BB	HBP	SH	SF	SO	SB	CS	SLG	OBP
Bambino, Richard	R-R	6-4	210	4-16-83	.151	.154	.150	19	53	6	8	1	1	0	4	4	3	2	0	13	0	0	.208	.250
Bourjos, Peter	R-R	6-1	175	3-31-87	.292	.239	.304	65	250	42	73	16	7	5	28	22	2	5	0	67	13	5	.472	.354
Brewer, Tadd	R-R	6-1	190	5-4-84	.285	.162	.314	56	193	17	55	9	3	1	27	22	10	7	2	26	9	6	.378	.383
Colmenares, Carlos	B-R	6-0	175	2-11-86	.205	.167	.212	12	39	6	8	1	0	0	1	1	0	2	0	5	0	0	.231	.225
Fuller, Clayton	R-R	6-2	180	6-17-87	.000	—	.000	1	2	0	0	0	0	0	0	0	1	0	0	2	1	0	.000	.333
Gronkowski, Grodon	R-R	6-6	250	6-26-83	.282	.400	.265	13	39	5	11	2	0	0	3	8	0	0	0	10	0	0	.333	.404
Hodach, Jonathan	R-R	5-11	205	4-18-84	.105	.000	.118	8	19	1	2	0	0	0	1	0	1	0	7	0	0		.105	.150
Johnson, Tyler	R-R	6-2	220	11-2-85	.257	.238	.262	59	206	43	53	7	1	8	36	26	11	1	2	76	10	3	.417	.367
Knazek, Scott	R-R	6-1	215	11-4-84	.243	.265	.238	64	230	24	56	7	3	2	33	21	4	0	1	48	1	0	.326	.316
Mount, Ryan	L-R	6-1	180	8-17-86	.285	.173	.311	69	277	54	79	14	2	9	38	36	2	3	1	67	10	3	.448	.370
Nieves, Abel	R-R	5-11	175	8-14-85	.259	.261	.259	62	220	36	57	10	2	1	29	28	2	6	4	35	3	2	.336	.343
Perez, Julio	R-R	6-2	160	9-28-85	.368	.000	.389	5	19	7	7	3	0	2	7	3	1	0	0	6	1	0	.842	.478
Pettit, Christopher	R-R	6-0	193	8-15-84	.336	.349	.333	68	226	41	76	25	3	7	54	31	14	0	1	48	5	1	.566	.445
Phillips, P.J.	R-R	6-3	170	9-23-86	.240	.232	.242	69	263	36	63	12	1	6	27	20	2	2	0	75	11	8	.361	.298
Reinhardt, Douglas	R-R	6-3	210	10-22-85	.188	.143	.200	23	64	5	12	3	0	0	5	6	0	2	2	18	2	0	.234	.250
Rivera, Luis	R-R	6-1	190	10-12-86	.256	.269	.253	64	242	34	62	11	2	5	26	24	3	2	2	65	4	3	.380	.328
Sales, Darrell	R-R	6-1	210	9-12-85	.224	.207	.228	46	156	27	35	8	2	0	19	15	3	2	1	44	1	2	.301	.303
Shankle, Brooks	R-R	6-4	217	2-4-83	.144	.111	.157	30	97	14	14	3	0	2	7	16	1	1	1	32	0	0	.237	.270
Sweeney, Matt	L-R	6-3	210	4-4-88	.167	—	.167	2	6	0	1	0	0	0	0	1	0	0	0	2	0	0	.167	.286
Villaescusa, Ivan	B-R	6-1	210	10-13-86	.077	.000	.083	8	13	0	1	1	0	0	0	0	0	0	0	6	0	0	.154	.077

PITCHING	B-T	HT	WT	DOB	W	L	ERA	G	GS	CG	SV	IP	H	R	ER	HR	BB	SO	AVG	vLH	vRH	K/9	BB/9
Arredondo, Felipe	R-R	6-4	225	10-4-86	5	2	2.20	24	0	0	11	41	22	12	10	4	13	56	.162	.227	.130	12.29	2.85
Bell, Trevor	L-R	6-1	180	10-12-86	4	2	3.50	16	16	0	0	82	82	35	32	8	15	53	.261	.264	.259	5.79	1.64
Browning, Barret	L-L	6-1	170	12-28-84	3	2	3.05	23	0	0	1	41	33	17	14	3	13	40	.220	.220	.220	8.71	2.83
Butcher, Brok	R-R	6-1	180	10-13-83	0	0	9.00	1	0	0	0	5	6	5	5	1	3	0	.300	.600	.200	0.00	5.40
Calderon, Leonardo	L-L	5-11	170	7-31-86	2	2	8.39	13	3	0	0	25	27	25	23	5	20	16	.281	.321	.265	5.84	7.30
Cassevah, Robert	R-R	6-3	195	9-11-85	5	6	6.80	16	10	0	0	41	57	40	31	1	38	32	.337	.271	.364	7.02	8.34
Connelly, Patrick	L-R	6-1	195	6-27-83	4	2	2.95	19	0	0	0	37	35	20	12	1	13	33	.240	.292	.214	8.10	3.19
Cook, Aaron	R-R	6-5	175	10-20-83	3	2	4.50	23	0	0	2	30	36	17	15	2	15	23	.303	.256	.329	6.90	4.50
Cowles, Joshua	R-R	6-2	210	6-7-84	0	0	5.23	10	0	0	0	10	12	10	6	1	8	10	.267	.300	.240	8.71	6.97
Diaz, Amalio	R-R	6-2	170	9-10-86	0	2	3.38	3	3	0	0	16	17	8	6	2	2	11	.262	.182	.302	6.19	1.13
Dixon, Jacob	R-R	6-5	190	4-26-83	0	0	22.85	4	0	0	0	4	11	11	11	3	4	3	.440	.500	.385	6.23	8.31
Haynes, Jeremy	R-R	6-2	180	5-28-86	3	1	2.76	16	14	0	0	59	46	21	18	5	41	68	.217	.179	.239	10.43	6.29
Herndon, Kenneth	R-R	6-5	200	9-4-85	5	2	2.21	14	14	0	0	69	65	25	17	6	10	36	.242	.274	.218	4.67	1.30
Herrera, Pedro	R-R	6-1	155	2-14-86	2	0	1.69	5	0	0	0	11	3	4	2	1	4	9	.083	.083	.083	7.59	3.38
Holler, Blake	L-L	6-4	165	1-22-85	2	2	4.99	21	0	0	1	31	28	27	17	3	20	33	.231	.286	.203	9.68	5.87
Incinelli, Jared	R-R	6-4	200	4-12-83	2	2	3.77	21	0	0	1	31	26	13	13	4	11	36	.230	.214	.239	10.45	3.19
O'Day, Darren	R-R	6-4	220	10-22-82	0	1	2.51	14	0	0	7	14	11	5	4	1	5	15	.208	.261	.167	9.42	3.14
O'Sullivan, Sean	R-R	6-1	220	9-1-87	4	0	2.14	14	14	0	0	71	65	23	17	2	7	55	.242	.234	.242	6.94	0.88
Ortega, Anthony	R-R	6-0	170	8-24-85	1	1	0.79	3	3	0	0	23	18	5	2	0	2	22	.162	.211	.111	8.74	1.59
Pellegrine, Dave	L-R	6-4	215	11-4-85	1	0	4.50	12	0	0	0	12	9	7	6	0	12	16	.209	.059	.308	8.25	9.00
Schoeninger, Tim	R-R	6-2	220	9-7-84	0	0	0.00	1	0	0	0	2	0	0	0	1	1	0	.286	.500	.200	4.50	0.00
Sullivan, John	R-R	5-11	185	7-2-84	2	1	3.97	20	0	0	0	34	33	16	15	2	15	35	.248	.265	.238	9.26	3.97

FIELDING

Catcher	PCT	G	PO	A	E	DP	PB
Bambino	.956	19	121	10	6	0	2
Hodach	1.000	6	23	4	0	0	0
Knazek	.988	59	438	41	6	2	12
Villaescusa	1.000	1	4	0	0	0	0

First Base	PCT	G	PO	A	E	DP
Gronkowski	.984	12	109	11	2	11
Nieves	.988	33	243	13	3	22
Reinhardt	1.000	12	112	3	0	5
Shankle	.982	27	252	18	5	19

Second Base	PCT	G	PO	A	E	DP
Brewer	.962	52	86	164	10	35

	PCT	G	PO	A	E	DP
Colmenares	.941	5	10	6	1	2
Mount	1.000	4	7	9	0	4
Nieves	.932	17	30	52	6	9
Phillips	.667	1	0	2	1	0

Third Base	PCT	G	PO	A	E	DP
Brewer	.917	5	4	7	1	2
Nieves	.875	15	6	43	7	2
Phillips	.869	56	37	102	21	10
Reinhardt	.833	9	4	11	3	0
Sweeney	1.000	2	1	4	0	0

Shortstop	PCT	G	PO	A	E	DP
Colmenares	.931	7	11	16	2	3

	PCT	G	PO	A	E	DP
Mount	.961	58	87	162	10	34
Phillips	.952	16	21	38	3	9

Outfield	PCT	G	PO	A	E	DP
Bourjos	.979	64	138	2	3	0
Fuller	1.000	1	2	0	0	0
Hodach	—	1	0	0	0	0
Johnson	.976	25	38	3	1	0
Perez	.857	5	11	1	2	0
Pettit	.980	60	90	6	2	1
Rivera	.967	62	80	7	3	1
Sales	.944	26	33	1	2	0

Arizona League

BATTING	B-T	HT	WT	DOB	AVG	vLH	vRH	G	AB	R	H	2B	3B	HR	RBI	BB	HBP	SH	SF	SO	SB	CS	SLG	OBP
Castillo, Angel	R-R	6-3	190	6-7-89	.255	.233	.262	36	137	22	35	7	2	2	15	15	3	1	1	45	5	3	.380	.340
Colmenares, Carlos	B-R	6-0	175	2-11-86	.243	.263	.234	33	115	21	28	8	1	1	11	17	1	5	0	19	3	6	.357	.346
Conger, Hank	B-R	6-0	205	1-29-88	.319	.217	.370	19	69	11	22	3	4	1	11	7	0	0	0	11	1	0	.522	.382
De Los Santos, Anel	R-R	6-0	180	6-19-88	.250	.130	.284	29	104	12	26	4	3	1	11	6	1	0	1	28	2	2	.375	.295
Fonseca, Alex	R-R	5-10	170	9-13-83	.316	.360	.306	36	136	21	43	13	1	1	18	26	3	3	0	23	10	3	.449	.436
Fuller, Clayton	B-R	6-2	180	6-17-87	.268	.250	.274	45	157	28	42	3	5	0	10	25	5	1	1	47	14	4	.350	.383
Hodach, Jonathan	R-R	5-11	205	4-18-84	.667	—	.667	3	3	0	2	0	0	0	0	0	1	1	0	0	0	0	.667	.800
Lewis, Christopher	R-R	6-1	190	1-25-84	.295	.436	.248	42	156	24	46	10	5	2	23	18	1	1	1	26	9	6	.462	.369
Loman, Seth	B-R	6-3	190	12-16-85	.206	.042	.239	42	141	24	29	11	1	4	24	23	5	0	2	49	0	0	.383	.333
Maldonado, Martin	R-R	6-1	190	8-16-86	.222	.188	.234	21	63	9	14	1	1	0	6	7	3	3	0	12	0	2	.270	.329
Moore, Jeremy	L-R	6-1	190	6-29-87	.254	.219	.264	41	142	25	36	7	2	3	19	18	3	1	1	37	4	8	.394	.348
Ortiz, Norberto	R-R	6-1	170	1-19-85	.281	.297	.276	45	171	28	48	10	4	5	31	6	4	1	3	45	10	5	.474	.315
Ortiz, Wilberto	R-R	5-10	180	11-30-85	.299	.333	.294	36	137	28	41	8	1	0	10	13	5	3	1	18	3	1	.372	.378
Pressley, Ryan	B-R	6-6	255	9-29-86	.040	.125	.000	10	25	2	1	0	0	1	1	1	0	0	0	13	1	0	.040	.077
Ryan, Matt	L-L	6-4	205	4-4-86	.250	.217	.258	33	112	18	28	4	1	1	22	16	2	1	2	28	1	0	.330	.348
Sweeney, Matt	L-R	6-3	210	4-4-88	.341	.250	.369	44	170	38	58	11	7	5	39	23	6	0	3	27	4	1	.576	.431
Villaescusa, Ivan	B-R	6-1	210	10-13-86	.250	.500	.125	4	12	1	3	1	0	0	3	0	0	0	0	4	1	0	.333	.250

PITCHING	B-T	HT	WT	DOB	W	L	ERA	G	GS	CG	SV	IP	H	R	ER	HR	BB	SO	AVG	vLH	vRH	K/9	BB/9
Armstrong, Christopher	L-L	5-10	195	2-10-88	1	1	0.90	7	0	0	0	10	6	3	1	1	2	8	.182	.071	.263	7.20	1.80
Brandt, Douglas	L-L	6-0	205	10-23-84	1	1	4.79	14	0	0	1	21	20	12	11	0	10	29	.253	.176	.274	12.63	4.35
Butcher, Brok	R-R	6-1	180	10-13-83	1	0	1.56	4	4	0	0	17	11	3	3	0	4	16	.183	.125	.250	8.31	2.08
Carmona, Ismael	R-R	6-0	165	2-12-85	0	0	13.09	10	1	0	0	11	19	22	16	1	16	10	.373	.231	.421	8.18	13.09
Chile, Eduardo	R-R	6-0	195	2-6-84	0	1	6.28	11	0	0	0	14	16	11	10	1	10	10	.286	.294	.282	6.28	6.28
Diaz, Amalio	R-R	6-2	170	9-10-86	0	1	6.00	1	1	0	0	6	7	5	4	1	0	2	.280	.375	.235	3.00	0.00
Fish, Robert	L-L	6-2	215	1-19-88	1	0	3.21	10	1	0	0	14	13	5	5	0	12	16	.245	.417	.195	10.29	7.71
Hensley, Matt	R-R	6-2	220	5-18-84	1	0	0.00	2	0	0	0	2	0	0	0	0	0	3	.000	.000	.000	13.50	0.00
Herrera, Pedro	R-R	6-0	155	2-14-86	0	0	0.00	6	0	0	0	11	7	0	0	0	2	13	.189	.167	.200	10.32	1.59
Jimenez, Esmerlin	R-R	6-2	170	8-1-84	5	3	3.57	14	13	0	0	63	60	29	25	4	17	60	.253	.244	.258	8.57	2.43
Leon, Sammy	R-R	6-0	160	5-19-85	2	1	3.38	16	0	0	0	27	27	11	10	2	15	18	.270	.310	.254	6.08	5.06
Madrigal, Warner	R-R	6-0	200	3-21-84	2	1	3.75	12	0	0	5	12	11	5	5	0	3	13	.250	.071	.333	9.75	2.25
Miller, Dustin	R-R	6-4	200	3-9-83	1	0	1.10	6	1	0	0	16	13	5	2	1	2	25	.206	.167	.231	13.78	1.10
Peacock, Dylan	R-R	6-3	190	4-29-86	0	1	6.43	10	0	0	0	14	19	15	10	3	4	10	.292	.333	.268	6.43	2.57
Reilly, Matthew	R-R	6-0	194	1-24-84	2	1	5.52	10	0	0	1	15	16	11	9	1	8	9	.271	.214	.289	5.52	4.91
Sauls, Mark	R-R	6-5	215	8-8-84	0	1	5.73	11	0	0	0	11	12	9	7	0	6	9	.286	.375	.265	7.36	4.91
Schlichting, Travis	R-R	6-4	190	10-19-84	0	0	0.00	5	0	0	0	8	4	0	0	0	2	13	.148	.167	.143	15.26	2.35
Schoeninger, Tim	R-R	6-2	220	9-7-84	6	2	1.79	14	13	0	0	75	64	22	15	2	4	64	.223	.226	.222	7.65	0.48
Sempey, Edward	R-R	6-2	215	3-31-83	1	0	10.61	9	0	0	0	9	16	15	11	1	7	8	.356	.250	.414	7.71	6.75
Torres, Alexander	L-L	5-10	160	12-28-87	2	5	4.29	14	9	0	1	50	42	28	24	1	36	47	.235	.292	.226	8.40	6.44
Veras, Nicolas	R-R	6-0	150	1-9-86	8	2	1.35	12	12	0	0	60	46	15	9	0	13	58	.210	.179	.221	8.70	1.95
Wilson, Brendan	R-R	6-1	183	10-7-85	0	0	3.72	12	0	0	0	19	20	8	8	0	4	14	.270	.300	.259	6.52	1.86

FIELDING

Catcher	PCT	G	PO	A	E	DP	PB
Conger	.969	9	57	5	2	1	0
De Los Santos	.974	26	196	25	6	5	6
Hodach	.900	1	6	3	1	0	0
Maldonado	.968	20	158	25	6	1	3
Villaescusa	1.000	4	41	4	0	1	3

First Base	PCT	G	PO	A	E	DP
Loman	.970	21	188	8	6	13
Pressley	.971	5	33	1	1	1
Ryan	.982	32	260	19	5	18

Second Base	PCT	G	PO	A	E	DP
Colmenares	1.000	2	8	5	0	1
Fonseca	.951	30	41	96	7	9
Lewis	.942	23	48	50	6	16
Ortiz	1.000	1	2	3	0	0

Third Base	PCT	G	PO	A	E	DP
Colmenares	.844	12	8	19	5	2
Lewis	.714	4	1	9	4	1
Sweeney	.823	40	21	72	20	4

Shortstop	PCT	G	PO	A	E	DP
Colmenares	.913	17	32	52	8	10
Fonseca	.938	6	13	17	2	6
W. Ortiz	.917	33	47	96	13	12

Outfield	PCT	G	PO	A	E	DP
Castillo	1.000	30	57	4	0	1
Fuller	.917	45	77	0	7	0
Lewis	1.000	9	17	1	0	0
Moore	.965	39	55	0	2	0
N. Ortiz	.973	43	62	9	2	4

ORGANIZATION STATISTICS

BY TONY JACKSON

In their first season under new general manager Ned Colletti and manager Grady Little, the Dodgers took a giant step forward. Colletti's personnel moves and Little's calm demeanor transformed the club from laughingstock to contender, and the Dodgers should compete for playoff berths for years to come.

The Dodgers won the National League wild card, and with their combination of young talent in the big leagues and prospects still in the farm system, they were the choice as Baseball America's Organization of the Year.

The catalyst for the 2006 team was shortstop Rafael Furcal, whom Colletti lured to Los Angeles with a three-year, $39 million contract just as Furcal seemed ready to sign a five-year deal with the Cubs. Furcal became the leadoff man the Dodgers had lacked for so many years, batting .300 with 32 doubles, 15 homers, 63 RBIs and a .369 on-base percentage.

The team also benefited from the resurgence of Nomar Garciaparra, who signed as a free agent and accepted a move to first base, a position he never had played before. He played it like a natural. More important, he produced at the plate, hitting .303 and coming up with several clutch hits, most notably a pair of walkoff homers on the Dodgers' final homestand that helped the club win the wild card.

And then there were the moves Colletti made at the trading deadline. Wilson Betemit, long a hot prospect without a place to play in Atlanta, sizzled when he was acquired to play third base. Julio Lugo didn't hit especially well, but was a valuable presence because he could play

PLAYERS OF THE YEAR

MAJOR LEAGUE: Derek Lowe, rhp

Lowe provided stability to the rotation by pitching 218 innings—eclipsing the 200-inning plateau for the fourth time in his career. The 33-year-old tied with Brad Penny to lead the club with 16 wins and led the team in ERA (3.29). He also made 34 starts, marking the fourth straight season he made 30 or more.

MINOR LEAGUE: James Loney, 1b

Loney won the minor league batting title with a .380 average at Triple-A Las Vegas, then made the big league postseason roster, starting in place of an injured Nomar Garciaparra in Game Three of the Division Series against the Mets. He also hit a career-high 33 doubles and added eight homers in Triple-A.

three positions. But the biggest pickup was Greg Maddux, who captured his vintage form after coming over from the Cubs, going 6-3, 3.30 in 12 starts.

Just half an hour before the Aug. 31 deadline for newly acquired players to be eligible for the playoffs, Colletti got utilityman Marlon Anderson from the Nationals. Anderson played so well that he eventually wrested the left-field job from Andre Ethier, who had been in contention for the rookie of the year award before slumping down the stretch.

And then there was Takashi Saito, the veteran reliever whom the scouting staff talked Colletti into signing to a minor league deal before spring training. After Eric Gagne had gone down for the season with another injury and Danys Baez had failed, Saito became the dependable closer the Dodgers desperately needed. He finished with 24 saves, a franchise rookie record.

The Dodgers dealt with more than their share of injuries, losing Gagne, third baseman Bill Mueller and reliever Yhency Brazoban for the season early on. While that forced them to bring up several of their vaunted prospects far ahead of schedule, most of those rookies seemed more than up to the challenge.

Russell Martin quickly became the everyday catcher. Ethier, whom the Dodgers had acquired from Oakland while ridding themselves of Milton Bradley, batted .308 with 11 homers and 55 RBIs. Meanwhile, top pitching prospect Chad Billingsley, top outfield prospect Matt Kemp and top first-base prospect James Loney all got major league experience as well, and all will come to camp next spring ready to compete for jobs, which should help the Dodgers make a seamless transition into 2007 after getting swept by the Mets in a Division Series.

Down on the farm, Loney won the minor league batting title, hitting a cool .380 for Triple-A Las Vegas. Double-A Jacksonville, depleted after the slew of prospects that helped the Suns run away with the Southern League in 2005 moved up to Las Vegas, made the playoffs again. Farm director Terry Collins left the organization after the season to become manager of the Orix Buffaloes of the Japanese Pacific League.

ORGANIZATION LEADERS

BATTING
*Minimum 250 at-bats

*AVG	Loney, James, Las Vegas	.380
R	Valdez, Wilson, Las Vegas	94
H	Valdez, Wilson, Las Vegas	157
TB	Young, Delwyn, Las Vegas	243
2B	Young, Delwyn, Las Vegas	42
3B	May, Lucas, Columbus	9
HR	Pedroza, Sergio, Columbus/Vero Beach/Visalia	24
RBI	Young, Delwyn, Las Vegas	98
BB	Dunlap, Cory, Vero Beach/Las Vegas	97
SO	Paul, Xavier, Vero Beach	133
SB	Godwin, Adam, Columbus	30
	Rogowski, Ryan, Ogden	30
*OBP	Dunlap, Cory, Vero Beach/Las Vegas	.433
*SLG	Pedroza, Sergio, Columbus/Vero Beach/Visalia	.548
XBH	Mitchell, Russell, Columbus/Vero Beach	61
	Young, Delwyn, Las Vegas	61

PITCHING
#Minimum 75 innings

W	Lundberg, Spike, Las Vegas/Jacksonville	17
L	Houlton, D.J., Las Vegas	11
	Stults, Eric, Las Vegas	11
#ERA	Nunez, Jhonny, GCL Dodgers	1.58
G	Hoorelbeke, Casey, Jacksonville	59
CG	McDonald, James, Columbus	2
	Nall, T.J., Las Vegas/Jacksonville	2
SV	Alexander, Mark, Las Vegas/Jacksonville	27
IP	Lundberg, Spike, Las Vegas	187
BB	Elbert, Scott, Vero Beach/Jacksonville	85
SO	Elbert, Scott, Vero Beach/Jacksonville	173
#AVG	Nunez, Jhonny, GCL Dodgers	.177

Los Angeles Dodgers

National League

BATTING	B-T	HT	WT	DOB	AVG	vLH	vRH	G	AB	R	H	2B	3B	HR	RBI	BB	HBP	SH	SF	SO	SB	CS	SLG	OBP
Alomar, Sandy	R-R	6-3	235	6-18-66	.323	.500	.250	27	62	3	20	5	0	0	9	0	0	0	0	7	0	0	.403	.323
Anderson, Marlon	L-R	5-11	200	1-6-74	.375	.250	.404	25	64	12	24	3	2	7	15	7	0	1	1	8	2	2	.813	.431
2-team (109 Washington)					.297	—	—	134	279	43	83	16	4	12	38	25	1	4	3	49	4	6	.513	.354
Aybar, Willy	B-R	5-11	200	3-9-83	.250	.067	.274	43	128	15	32	12	0	3	22	18	3	2	0	17	1	0	.414	.356
2-team (36 Atlanta)....					.280	—	—	79	243	32	68	18	0	4	30	28	4	3	0	36	1	2	.403	.364
Betemit, Wilson	B-R	6-3	200	7-28-80	.241	.138	.262	55	174	19	42	7	0	9	24	17	0	0	2	45	1	0	.437	.306
2-team (88 Atlanta)....					.263	—	—	143	373	49	98	23	0	18	53	36	0	1	2	102	3	1	.469	.326
Cruz, Jose	B-R	6-0	210	4-19-74	.233	.313	.199	86	223	34	52	16	1	5	17	43	0	4	3	54	5	1	.381	.353
Diaz, Einar	R-R	5-10	200	12-28-72	.667	.000	1.000	3	3	0	2	0	0	0	0	0	0	0	0	0	0	0	.667	.667
Drew, J.D.	L-R	6-1	200	11-20-75	.283	.244	.296	146	494	84	140	34	6	20	100	89	4	1	6	106	2	3	.498	.393
Ethier, Andre	L-L	6-1	210	4-10-82	.308	.351	.298	126	396	50	122	20	4	11	55	34	5	0	6	77	5	5	.477	.365
Furcal, Rafael	B-R	5-8	195	10-24-77	.300	.324	.293	159	654	113	196	32	9	15	63	73	1	5	3	98	37	13	.445	.369
Garciaparra, Nomar	R-R	6-0	190	7-23-73	.303	.341	.294	122	469	82	142	31	2	20	93	42	8	0	4	30	3	0	.505	.367
Guzman, Joel	R-R	6-6	250	11-24-84	.211	.143	.250	8	19	2	4	0	0	0	3	3	1	0	0	2	0	0	.211	.348
Hall, Toby	R-R	6-3	240	10-21-75	.368	.438	.341	21	57	2	21	4	0	0	8	2	0	0	1	5	0	0	.439	.383
Izturis, Cesar	B-R	5-7	190	2-10-80	.252	.227	.258	32	119	10	30	7	1	1	12	7	2	0	1	6	1	3	.353	.302
2-team (22 Chicago)..					.245	—	—	54	192	14	47	9	1	1	18	12	2	1	1	14	1	4	.318	.295
Kemp, Matt	R-R	6-2	230	9-23-84	.253	.229	.264	52	154	30	39	7	1	7	23	9	0	0	3	53	6	0	.448	.289
Kent, Jeff	R-R	6-1	210	3-7-68	.292	.347	.275	115	407	61	119	27	3	14	68	55	8	0	3	69	1	2	.477	.385
Ledee, Ricky	L-L	6-1	225	11-22-73	.245	.500	.235	43	53	4	13	5	0	1	8	2	0	0	0	10	1	0	.396	.273
2-team (27 New York)					.188	—	—	70	85	8	16	6	0	2	9	6	0	0	0	16	1	0	.329	.242
Lofton, Kenny	L-L	5-11	190	5-31-67	.301	.214	.319	129	469	79	141	15	12	3	41	45	0	6	2	42	32	5	.403	.360
Loney, James	L-L	6-2	220	5-7-84	.284	.350	.268	48	102	20	29	6	5	4	18	8	1	0	0	10	1	0	.559	.342
Lugo, Julio	R-R	6-1	175	11-16-75	.219	.196	.233	49	146	16	32	5	1	0	10	12	1	2	3	29	6	5	.267	.278
Martin, Russell	R-R	5-10	210	2-15-83	.282	.366	.265	121	415	65	117	26	4	10	65	45	4	1	3	57	10	5	.436	.355
Martinez, Ramon	R-R	6-1	190	10-10-72	.278	.289	.275	82	176	20	49	7	1	2	24	15	1	2	0	20	0	0	.364	.339
Mueller, Bill	B-R	5-10	180	3-17-71	.252	.280	.244	32	107	12	27	7	0	3	15	17	1	0	1	9	1	1	.402	.357
Navarro, Dioner	B-R	5-9	215	2-9-84	.280	.333	.267	25	75	5	21	2	0	2	8	11	0	0	0	18	1	0	.387	.372
Repko, Jason	R-R	5-10	190	12-27-80	.254	.239	.262	69	130	21	33	5	1	3	16	15	3	2	0	24	10	4	.377	.345
Robles, Oscar	L-R	5-10	185	4-9-76	.152	.000	.172	29	33	6	5	0	1	0	0	5	0	1	0	5	0	0	.212	.263
Ross, Cody	R-L	5-9	205	12-23-80	.500	.500	.500	8	14	4	7	1	1	2	9	0	0	0	2	1	0	1.143	.500
3-team (2 Cincinnati, 91 Florida)					.227	—	—	101	269	34	61	12	2	13	46	22	4	1	2	65	1	1	.431	.293
Saenz, Olmedo	R-R	5-11	220	10-8-70	.296	.397	.248	103	179	30	53	15	0	11	48	14	7	0	4	47	0	0	.564	.363
Young, Delwyn	B-R	5-8	210	6-30-82	.000	—	.000	8	5	0	0	0	0	0	0	0	0	0	0	1	0	0	.000	.000

PITCHING	B-T	HT	WT	DOB	W	L	ERA	G	GS	CG	SV	IP	H	R	ER	HR	BB	SO	AVG	vLH	vRH	K/9	BB/9
Baez, Danys	R-R	6-1	230	9-10-77	5	5	4.35	46	0	0	9	50	53	29	24	3	11	29	.283	.309	.258	5.26	1.99
2-team (11 Atlanta)....					5	6	4.53	57	0	0	9	59	60	35	30	3	17	39	—	—	—	5.88	2.56
Beimel, Joe	L-L	6-2	215	4-19-77	2	1	2.96	62	0	0	2	70	70	26	23	7	21	30	.262	.234	.277	3.86	2.70
Billingsley, Chad	R-R	6-0	245	7-29-84	7	4	3.80	18	16	0	0	90	92	43	38	7	58	59	.272	.328	.213	5.90	5.80
Brazoban, Yhency	R-R	6-0	240	6-11-80	0	0	5.40	5	0	0	0	5	7	3	3	0	2	4	.350	.333	.364	7.20	3.60
Broxton, Jonathan	R-R	6-3	290	6-16-84	4	1	2.59	68	0	0	3	76	61	25	22	7	33	97	.216	.244	.196	11.44	3.89
Carrara, Giovanni	R-R	6-2	230	3-4-68	0	1	4.55	25	0	0	1	28	27	14	14	5	7	25	.250	.157	.333	8.13	2.28
Carter, Lance	R-R	6-1	190	12-18-74	0	1	8.49	10	0	0	0	12	17	11	11	1	8	5	.347	.429	.286	3.86	6.17
Dessens, Elmer	R-R	5-11	200	1-13-71	0	1	4.70	19	0	0	0	23	23	12	12	4	9	16	.258	.325	.204	6.26	3.52
Gagne, Eric	R-R	6-0	245	1-7-76	0	0	0.00	2	0	0	1	2	0	0	0	0	1	3	.000	.000	.000	13.50	4.50
Hamulack, Tim	R-L	6-2	220	11-14-76	0	3	6.35	33	0	0	0	34	36	28	24	7	22	34	.265	.302	.247	9.00	5.82
Hendrickson, Mark	L-L	6-9	230	6-23-74	2	7	4.68	18	12	0	0	75	92	45	39	7	28	48	.299	.258	.309	5.76	3.36
Kuo, Hong-Chih	L-L	6-0	235	7-23-81	1	5	4.22	28	5	0	0	60	54	30	28	3	33	71	.244	.241	.246	10.71	4.98
Lowe, Derek	R-R	6-6	230	6-1-73	16	8	3.63	35	34	1	0	218	221	97	88	14	55	123	.262	.270	.255	5.08	2.27
Maddux, Greg	R-R	6-0	180	4-14-66	6	3	3.30	12	12	0	0	74	66	31	27	6	14	36	.244	.218	.265	4.40	1.71
2-team (22 Chicago)..					15	14	4.20	34	34	0	0	210	219	109	98	20	37	117	—	—	—	5.01	1.59
Osoria, Franquelis	R-R	5-11	200	9-12-81	0	2	7.13	12	0	0	0	18	27	14	14	4	9	13	.360	.520	.280	6.62	4.58
Penny, Brad	R-R	6-4	260	5-24-78	16	9	4.33	34	33	0	0	189	206	94	91	19	54	148	.279	.275	.283	7.05	2.57
Perez, Odalis	L-L	6-0	220	6-11-77	4	4	6.83	20	8	0	0	59	89	49	45	13	13	33	.346	.353	.344	5.01	1.97
Saito, Takashi	L-R	6-2	200	2-14-70	6	2	2.07	72	0	0	24	78	48	19	18	3	23	107	.177	.229	.129	12.29	2.64
Sele, Aaron	R-R	6-3	220	6-25-70	8	6	4.53	28	15	0	0	103	120	57	52	11	30	57	.290	.280	.298	4.96	2.61
Seo, Jae	R-R	6-0	230	5-24-77	2	4	5.78	19	10	0	0	67	75	45	43	14	25	40	.284	.252	.309	6.58	3.36
Stults, Eric	L-L	6-0	215	12-9-79	1	0	5.60	6	2	0	0	18	17	12	11	4	7	5	.266	.467	.204	2.55	3.57
Tomko, Brett	R-R	6-2	225	4-7-73	8	7	4.73	44	15	0	0	112	123	67	59	17	29	76	.276	.300	.258	6.09	2.32

FIELDING

Catcher	PCT	G	PO	A	E	DP	PB
Alomar	.988	18	80	2	1	1	1
Diaz	—	1	0	0	0	0	0
Hall	.989	21	84	9	1	1	0
Martin	.993	117	788	62	6	8	5
Navarro	.993	24	149	3	1	1	1

First Base	PCT	G	PO	A	E	DP
Garciaparra	.996	118	1059	61	4	113
Kent	1.000	5	32	0	0	6
Loney	.996	39	212	15	1	17
Martinez	1.000	1	5	0	0	2
Saenz	.989	30	173	7	2	27

Second Base	PCT	G	PO	A	E	DP
Anderson	1.000	1	0	1	0	0
Aybar	.985	15	25	42	1	11
Izturis	1.000	1	4	8	0	2

	PCT	G	PO	A	E	DP
Kent	.985	108	217	314	8	73
Lugo	.980	29	37	63	2	11
Martinez	1.000	39	55	79	0	13
Robles	1.000	13	9	10	0	4

Third Base	PCT	G	PO	A	E	DP
Aybar	.922	29	9	50	5	2
Betemit	.964	49	24	83	4	9
Guzman	1.000	6	0	7	0	1
Izturis	.955	28	12	73	4	3
Lugo	.975	16	10	29	1	4
Martinez	.933	20	8	20	2	4
Mueller	.905	30	15	61	8	7
Robles	.857	6	0	6	1	0
Saenz	.938	16	6	24	2	0

Shortstop	PCT	G	PO	A	E	DP
Furcal	.966	156	269	492	27	111

	PCT	G	PO	A	E	DP
Izturis	1.000	2	1	5	0	2
Lugo	.875	8	3	11	2	0
Martinez	1.000	12	6	17	0	5

Outfield	PCT	G	PO	A	E	DP
Anderson	.955	15	21	0	1	0
Cruz	1.000	71	129	0	0	0
Drew	.983	135	284	3	5	0
Ethier	.968	109	172	8	6	1
Kemp	.929	46	63	2	5	1
Ledee	1.000	9	4	0	0	0
Lofton	.988	120	241	4	3	0
Lugo	1.000	3	1	0	0	0
Martinez	1.000	1	1	0	0	0
Repko	.977	62	82	4	2	2
Ross	1.000	3	4	0	0	0
Young	—	2	0	0	0	0

General manager: Ned Colletti. **Farm director:** DeJon Watson. **Scouting director:** Logan White.

Class	Team	League	W	L	PCT	Finish*	Manager	Affiliate Since
Majors	Los Angeles	National	88	74	.543	2nd (16)	Grady Little	—
Triple-A	Las Vegas 51s	Pacific Coast	67	77	.465	12th (16)	Jerry Royster	2001
Double-A	Jacksonville Suns	Southern	86	54	.614	1st (10)	John Shoemaker	2002
High A	Vero Beach Dodgers	Florida State	51	80	.389	12th (12)	Luis Salazar	1980
Low A	Columbus Catfish	South Atlantic	72	68	.514	7th (16)	Travis Barbary	2002
Rookie	Ogden Raptors	Pioneer	37	39	.487	5th (8)	Lance Parrish	2003
Rookie	GCL Dodgers	Gulf Coast	32	22	.593	4th (13)	Juan Bustabad	2001
OVERALL 2006 MINOR LEAGUE RECORD			345	340	.504	14th (30)		

*Finish in overall standings (No. of teams in league). +League champion

ORGANIZATION STATISTICS

Las Vegas 51s — Triple-A

Pacific Coast League

BATTING	B-T	HT	WT	DOB	AVG	vLH	vRH	G	AB	R	H	2B	3B	HR	RBI	BB	HBP	SH	SF	SO	SB	CS	SLG	OBP
Alvarez, Nick	R-R	6-3	207	2-8-77	.293	.333	.275	54	157	27	46	7	1	3	14	13	2	1	0	28	5	1	.408	.355
Aybar, Willy	B-R	5-11	200	3-9-83	.315	.288	.324	50	197	30	62	12	1	10	41	22	1	0	2	24	1	3	.538	.383
Bellorin, Edwin	R-R	5-9	225	2-21-82	.234	.183	.248	96	321	32	75	13	1	7	49	14	2	8	5	59	1	2	.346	.266
Borders, Pat	R-R	6-2	200	5-14-63	.053	.000	.077	6	19	0	1	0	0	0	0	0	0	0	0	2	0	0	.053	.053
Brown, Jeremy	R-R	6-1	195	4-2-84	.000	.000	.000	3	4	1	0	0	0	0	0	0	1	0	0	1	0	0	.000	.200
Diaz, Einar	R-R	5-10	200	12-28-72	.429	.000	.600	2	7	0	3	2	0	0	2	0	0	0	0	1	0	0	.714	.429
Duncan, Jeff	L-L	6-2	190	12-9-78	.299	.279	.305	89	278	53	83	10	2	6	26	32	8	1	2	55	21	7	.414	.384
Dunlap, Cory	L-L	6-1	205	4-13-84	.250	—	.250	3	4	0	1	0	0	0	0	2	1	0	0	1	2	0	.250	.333
Ethier, Andre	L-L	6-1	210	4-10-82	.349	.316	.358	25	86	15	30	4	3	1	12	14	2	0	1	16	2	1	.500	.447
Garcia, Sergio	R-R	5-10	170	3-29-80	.328	.263	.347	71	247	54	81	15	0	8	37	28	7	8	5	29	7	0	.486	.404
Garciaparra, Nomar	R-R	6-0	190	7-23-73	.500	—	.500	2	8	3	4	2	0	0	1	0	0	0	0	0	0	0	.750	.500
Guzman, Joel	R-R	6-6	250	11-24-84	.297	.315	.289	85	317	44	94	16	2	11	55	26	4	1	4	72	9	5	.464	.353
Hoffmann, Jamie	R-R	6-3	205	8-20-84	.300	.250	.333	4	10	0	3	0	0	0	0	1	1	0	3	1	0	.300	.417
Izturis, Cesar	B-R	5-7	190	2-10-80	.271	.250	.279	15	59	9	16	3	0	0	3	10	0	0	1	3	0	0	.322	.371
Kemp, Matt	R-R	6-2	230	9-23-84	.368	.452	.343	44	182	37	67	14	6	3	36	17	2	1	0	26	14	3	.560	.428
Langill, Eric	R-R	5-9	190	4-4-79	.181	.095	.210	35	83	12	15	3	0	0	5	7	3	3	0	17	0	0	.217	.269
LaRoche, Andy	R-R	6-1	215	9-13-83	.322	.347	.314	55	202	35	65	14	1	10	35	25	2	0	1	32	3	2	.550	.400
Loney, James	L-L	6-2	210	5-7-84	.380	.337	.392	98	366	64	139	33	4	8	67	32	2	0	6	34	9	5	.546	.426
Martin, Russell	R-R	5-10	210	2-15-83	.297	.444	.250	23	74	14	22	9	0	0	9	13	0	1	3	11	0	2	.419	.389
Mathias, Ryder	R-R	6-1	190	9-28-81	.333	—	.333	2	3	0	1	0	0	0	1	0	0	0	0	0	0	0	.333	.333
Meadows, Tydus	R-R	6-1	245	9-5-77	.278	.200	.308	9	18	2	5	0	0	0	2	1	1	0	0	7	0	0	.278	.350
Navarro, Dioner	B-R	5-9	215	2-9-84	.175	.200	.167	11	40	3	7	2	0	0	2	3	0	0	0	7	1	0	.225	.233
Repko, Jason	R-R	5-10	190	12-27-80	.276	.500	.217	9	29	3	8	2	0	0	2	3	2	0	0	6	1	0	.345	.382
Riggs, Eric	B-R	6-2	190	8-19-76	.300	.273	.308	90	303	33	91	14	2	9	45	29	2	5	6	59	3	0	.449	.359
Robles, Oscar	L-R	5-10	185	4-9-76	.287	.239	.303	86	275	29	79	10	0	0	28	36	0	2	3	20	0	1	.324	.366
Ruan, Wilkin	R-R	6-0	180	9-18-78	.325	.250	.344	10	40	6	13	4	1	0	3	2	0	1	0	4	3	0	.475	.357
Soto, Jesus	R-R	5-11	178	9-7-86	.000	—	.000	2	2	0	0	0	0	0	0	0	0	0	0	1	0	0	.000	.000
Truby, Chris	R-R	6-2	220	12-9-73	.215	.300	.178	42	130	12	28	7	0	2	19	11	1	0	2	38	0	1	.315	.278
Valdez, Wilson	R-R	5-11	160	5-20-78	.297	.315	.292	137	528	74	157	24	1	6	53	56	1	14	10	52	26	17	.381	.366
Weber, Jon	L-L	5-10	190	1-20-78	.258	.241	.262	82	260	39	67	18	1	2	31	27	3	2	1	39	9	3	.358	.333
2-team (46 Tucson)					.283	—	—	128	428	65	121	36	1	7	58	42	4	3	4	62	10	4	.421	.349
Young, Delwyn	B-R	5-8	210	6-30-82	.273	.198	.296	140	532	76	145	42	1	18	98	42	3	1	5	104	3	4	.457	.326

PITCHING	B-T	HT	WT	DOB	W	L	ERA	G	GS	CG	SV	IP	H	R	ER	HR	BB	SO	AVG	vLH	vRH	K/9	BB/9
Alexander, Mark	R-R	5-10	190	12-6-80	2	1	3.14	12	0	0	1	14	11	6	5	0	10	13	.216	.318	.138	8.16	6.28
Beimel, Joe	L-L	6-2	215	4-19-77	3	0	1.38	10	0	0	0	13	9	2	2	0	4	9	.209	.167	.240	6.23	2.77
Billingsley, Chad	R-R	6-0	245	7-29-84	6	3	3.95	13	13	0	0	71	57	32	31	7	32	78	.221	.263	.174	9.93	4.08
Broxton, Jonathan	R-R	6-3	290	6-16-84	1	0	0.00	11	0	0	5	11	6	0	0	0	3	18	.154	.150	.158	14.29	2.38
Carrara, Giovanni	R-R	6-2	230	3-4-68	2	1	4.62	21	0	0	4	25	23	13	13	3	12	19	.240	.275	.214	6.75	4.26
Carter, Lance	R-R	6-1	190	12-18-74	2	4	3.92	45	0	0	13	57	58	25	25	7	16	51	.267	.253	.278	8.01	2.51
Dessens, Elmer	R-R	5-11	200	1-13-71	0	1	13.50	1	0	0	0	1	2	2	1	1	0	0	.400	.667	.000	0.00	13.50
Eckert, Harold	R-R	6-3	218	7-18-77	5	10	7.49	29	19	0	1	119	162	113	99	25	67	88	.329	.358	.301	6.66	5.07
Gagne, Eric	R-R	6-0	245	1-7-76	0	0	0.00	2	0	0	2	2	1	0	0	0	1	3	.143	.000	.200	13.50	4.50
Gonzalez, Luis	L-L	6-0	205	2-27-83	2	4	5.52	35	0	0	1	44	47	28	27	4	40	39	.281	.347	.228	7.98	8.18
Hammes, Zach	R-R	6-6	225	5-15-84	0	0	5.63	2	1	0	0	8	7	5	5	0	4	8	.241	.250	.231	9.00	5.63
Hamulack, Tim	R-L	6-2	220	11-14-76	0	1	1.42	28	0	0	3	38	30	9	6	1	26	44	.222	.167	.253	10.42	6.16
Hanrahan, Joel	R-R	6-3	215	10-6-81	4	3	4.48	14	14	0	0	74	70	47	37	7	39	46	.249	.231	.263	5.57	4.72
Houlton, D.J.	R-R	6-3	220	8-12-79	9	11	5.60	29	29	1	0	162	180	115	101	25	60	132	.285	.275	.294	7.32	3.33
Hull, Eric	R-R	5-11	190	12-3-79	2	4	4.19	44	2	0	2	73	54	39	34	6	43	78	.207	.182	.225	9.62	5.30
Juarez, William	R-R	6-2	203	4-22-81	4	5	4.08	11	11	1	0	57	50	34	26	7	38	28	.229	.221	.237	4.40	5.97
Ketchner, Ryan	L-L	6-1	190	4-19-82	0	0	9.00	1	0	0	0	4	4	2	2	0	1	2	.400	.400	.400	9.00	4.50
Kozlowski, Ben	L-L	6-6	230	8-16-80	1	0	10.80	1	1	0	0	5	7	7	6	2	2	3	.304	.273	.333	5.40	3.60
Kuo, Hong-Chih	L-L	6-0	235	7-23-81	4	3	3.06	23	9	0	1	53	52	24	18	5	22	63	.260	.303	.239	10.70	3.74
Lundberg, Spike	R-R	6-1	185	5-4-77	0	4	7.17	4	4	0	0	21	28	19	17	3	5	14	.380	.405	.362	5.91	2.11
Miller, Greg	L-L	6-5	220	11-3-84	3	0	4.38	33	0	0	0	37	33	19	18	1	33	32	.243	.227	.250	7.78	8.03
Nall, T.J.	L-L	6-1	207	11-4-80	0	0	9.00	2	0	0	0	3	3	3	3	0	1	1	.533	.556	.500	3.00	3.00
Osoria, Franquelis	R-R	5-11	200	9-12-81	2	2	4.35	44	0	0	2	52	61	31	25	2	21	28	.362	.398	.331	4.88	3.66
Reid, Justin	R-R	6-5	225	6-30-77	2	3	4.53	43	9	0	3	108	117	78	65	15	47	88	.279	.304	.258	7.36	3.93
Sele, Aaron	R-R	6-3	220	6-25-70	3	0	2.43	5	5	0	0	30	33	9	8	1	5	28	.227	.270	.170	8.49	1.52
Simmons, Justin	L-L	6-3	225	10-5-81	0	0	6.00	14	0	0	0	21	26	21	14	6	14	14	.302	.281	.315	6.00	6.00
Stults, Eric	L-L	6-0	215	12-9-79	10	11	4.23	26	26	1	0	153	153	85	72	10	68	128	.268	.265	.269	7.51	3.99
Thomas, Adam	R-R	6-4	190	5-22-79	0	0	0.00	1	1	0	0	5	4	1	0	0	1	3	.250	.333	.143	5.40	1.80
Tomko, Brett	R-R	6-2	225	4-7-73	0	0	0.00	1	1	0	0	2	3	0	0	0	1	3	.375	.500	.250	13.50	4.50
Wunsch, Kelly	L-L	6-4	215	7-12-72	1	1	8.31	11	0	0	0	9	14	8	8	0	4	10	.364	.385	.350	10.38	4.15

ED WOLFSTEIN

MIKE JANES

Derek Lowe was a workhorse for the Dodgers

James Loney was the minors' leading hitter

FIELDING

Catcher	PCT	G	PO	A	E	DP	PB
Bellorin	.985	85	620	41	10	6	9
Borders	.970	5	29	3	1	0	1
Diaz	1.000	2	6	1	0	0	0
Langill	.994	26	159	13	1	4	2
Martin	.991	22	208	14	2	3	3
Mathias	—	1	0	0	0	0	0
Navarro	1.000	11	79	7	0	2	0

First Base	PCT	G	PO	A	E	DP
Alvarez	.991	18	96	11	1	9
Dunlap	1.000	1	11	0	0	1
Garciaparra	1.000	2	11	0	0	0
Guzman	.990	27	185	19	2	29
Loney	.986	85	640	68	10	68
Riggs	.974	28	172	13	5	29
Truby	1.000	3	15	0	0	0

Second Base	PCT	G	PO	A	E	DP
Aybar	.982	21	44	66	2	15
Garcia	.961	49	81	116	8	27
Izturis	1.000	3	3	5	0	2
Riggs	1.000	24	29	66	0	18
Robles	.992	54	104	159	2	42
Valdez	.963	7	13	13	1	5
Young	1.000	1	2	1	0	1

Third Base	PCT	G	PO	A	E	DP
Aybar	1.000	27	15	50	0	8
Bellorin	1.000	2	1	1	0	0
Garcia	1.000	5	4	10	0	1
Guzman	.833	9	4	11	3	0
LaRoche	.964	54	38	94	5	20
Riggs	.909	27	19	41	6	5
Robles	1.000	7	0	12	0	0
Truby	.879	28	14	37	7	1

Shortstop	PCT	G	PO	A	E	DP
Garcia	.941	12	18	30	3	6
Izturis	.978	10	16	29	1	9
Riggs	1.000	3	2	9	0	0
Robles	1.000	11	16	25	0	6
Valdez	.980	117	215	314	11	83

Outfield	PCT	G	PO	A	E	DP
Alvarez	.982	29	53	2	1	1
Brown	1.000	3	3	0	0	0
Duncan	.979	79	180	3	4	1
Ethier	.977	25	40	3	1	0
Garcia	.600	3	2	1	2	0
Guzman	.986	42	69	2	1	0
Hoffmann	1.000	4	6	0	0	0
Kemp	.990	44	100	3	1	1
Loney	.909	13	17	3	2	0
Meadows	1.000	3	4	0	0	0
Repko	.944	7	17	0	1	0
Ruan	1.000	10	19	0	0	0
Valdez	.857	9	21	3	4	2
Weber	.986	74	139	5	2	1
Young	.957	127	188	14	9	3

Jacksonville Suns — Double-A

Southern League

BATTING	B-T	HT	WT	DOB	AVG	vLH	vRH	G	AB	R	H	2B	3B	HR	RBI	BB	HBP	SH	SF	SO	SB	CS	SLG	OBP
Abreu, Tony	R-R	5-9	185	11-13-84	.287	.272	.294	118	457	66	131	24	3	6	55	33	9	4	6	69	8	4	.392	.343
Alvarez, Nick	R-R	6-3	207	2-8-77	.178	.217	.136	16	45	6	8	1	0	0	4	0	1	0	0	8	0	1	.200	.196
Brazell, Craig	L-R	6-3	210	5-10-80	.247	.258	.242	117	421	56	104	26	1	21	91	19	4	0	4	94	1	0	.463	.283
Bruce, Cole	R-R	6-3	200	1-20-82	.167	.174	.163	27	72	4	12	3	0	1	4	7	0	0	0	31	0	1	.250	.241
Cresse, Brad	R-R	6-2	230	7-31-78	.259	.261	.258	47	162	19	42	8	0	7	28	23	1	0	2	47	0	0	.438	.351
Dewitt, Blake	L-R	5-11	175	8-20-85	.183	.194	.176	26	104	6	19	1	0	1	6	8	0	0	0	21	0	1	.221	.241
Ellis, A.J.	R-R	6-3	240	4-9-81	.250	.304	.230	81	252	34	63	9	1	0	21	53	3	3	3	53	2	0	.294	.383
Garcia, Sergio	R-R	5-10	170	3-29-80	.217	.317	.175	45	138	18	30	10	0	0	15	15	0	1	3	20	0	2	.290	.288
Greenberg, Adam	L-L	5-9	180	2-21-81	.228	.455	.152	75	219	36	50	9	3	1	18	51	7	6	2	70	9	3	.311	.387
2-team (32 West Tenn)					.215	—	—	107	303	45	65	11	3	1	18	60	8	10	2	97	12	5	.281	.357
Gutierrez, Gabriel	R-R	5-11	175	11-24-83	.268	.375	.200	13	41	3	11	0	0	0	6	4	0	0	1	9	0	0	.268	.326
Hu, Chin Lung	R-R	5-9	150	2-2-84	.254	.205	.280	125	488	71	124	20	2	5	34	49	4	13	2	63	11	5	.334	.326
Kemp, Matt	R-R	6-2	230	9-23-84	.327	.329	.325	48	199	38	65	15	2	7	34	20	5	0	0	38	11	2	.528	.402
Langill, Eric	R-R	5-9	190	4-4-79	.200	.500	.091	4	15	2	3	3	0	0	2	0	0	0	0	6	0	0	.400	.200
LaRoche, Andy	R-R	6-1	215	9-13-83	.309	.333	.294	62	230	42	71	13	0	9	46	41	4	0	2	32	6	3	.483	.419
Ledee, Ricky	L-L	6-1	225	11-22-73	.100	.200	.000	3	10	0	1	0	0	0	1	2	0	0		5	0	0	.100	.250
Meadows, Tydus	R-R	6-1	245	9-5-77	.299	.327	.290	72	231	41	69	10	1	11	42	64	3	0	2	56	1	2	.494	.453
Raglani, Anthony	L-L	6-2	215	4-6-83	.244	.263	.237	105	336	49	82	25	0	9	40	44	4	2	0	88	6	2	.399	.339
Rohan, Jimmy	R-R	6-1	190	5-13-84	.247	.276	.234	66	182	14	45	9	0	0	20	21	0	4	1	21	0	3	.297	.324
Ruan, Wilkin	R-R	6-0	180	9-18-78	.260	.272	.254	101	300	39	78	15	1	1	18	13	2	4	1	29	11	4	.327	.294

	B-T	HT	WT	DOB	AVG	vLH	vRH	G	AB	R	H	2B	3B	HR	RBI	BB	HBP	SH	SF	SO	SB	CS	SLG	OBP
Ruggiano, Justin	R-R	6-2	205	4-12-82	.260	.248	.267	89	292	51	76	18	3	9	45	46	5	0	3	74	10	5	.435	.367
2-team (31 Montgomery)					.280	—	—	120	400	76	112	32	6	13	72	65	7	1	3	103	14	9	.488	.387
Sprout, Brian	R-R	6-0	205	6-28-80	.211	.100	.333	8	19	3	4	1	0	0	1	5	2	0	0	4	2	0	.263	.423
Zapp, A.J.	L-R	6-3	190	4-24-78	.223	.259	.207	91	269	29	60	16	0	8	33	41	4	0	2	99	0	1	.372	.332

PITCHING	B-T	HT	WT	DOB	W	L	ERA	G	GS	CG	SV	IP	H	R	ER	HR	BB	SO	AVG	vLH	vRH	K/9	BB/9
Akin, Brian	R-R	6-3	185	10-13-81	2	1	2.95	20	0	0	6	37	25	12	12	2	22	46	.198	.317	.141	11.29	5.40
Alexander, Mark	R-R	5-10	190	12-6-80	3	2	0.96	40	0	0	26	47	26	8	5	2	13	72	.158	.119	.179	13.79	2.49
Alvarez, Carlos	L-L	5-9	160	3-31-85	4	1	2.93	33	0	0	1	55	49	22	18	7	14	55	.236	.194	.257	8.95	2.28
Diaz, Jose	R-R	6-4	300	2-27-84	0	1	3.46	8	0	0	0	13	13	5	5	0	5	4	.283	.500	.188	2.77	3.46
Elbert, Scott	L-L	6-2	190	8-13-85	6	4	3.61	11	11	0	0	62	40	26	25	11	44	76	.187	.111	.202	10.97	6.35
Ellis, A.J.	R-R	6-3	240	4-9-81	1	1	4.15	2	0	0	0	4	7	2	2	0	3	2	.412	.500	.364	4.15	6.23
Hanrahan, Joel	R-R	6-3	215	10-6-81	7	2	2.58	12	12	0	0	66	49	19	19	4	38	67	.216	.242	.199	9.09	5.16
Hoorelbeke, Casey	R-R	6-8	245	4-4-80	2	2	2.63	52	0	0	7	72	42	24	21	4	30	60	.174	.207	.156	7.50	3.75
Johnson, Steven	R-R	6-1	185	8-31-87	0	0	0.00	2	0	0	0	5	2	0	0	0	2	3	.133	.000	.182	5.79	3.86
Kozlowski, Ben	L-L	6-6	230	8-16-80	1	2	2.85	23	7	0	1	60	55	25	19	6	24	59	.247	.180	.272	8.85	3.60
2-team (10 Chattanooga)					3	3	2.39	33	7	0	1	83	75	30	22	7	35	72	—	—		7.81	3.80
LaMura, B.J.	R-R	6-1	200	1-1-81	1	1	1.96	14	0	0	1	23	15	6	5	3	16	25	.192	.192	.192	9.78	6.26
2-team (34 Birmingham)					6	1	1.77	48	0	0	4	76	47	18	15	5	47	92	—	—		10.85	5.54
Lundberg, Spike	R-R	6-1	185	5-4-77	15	2	2.27	24	24	1	0	151	124	42	38	3	42	110	.225	.241	.215	6.57	2.51
Meloan, Jonathan	R-R	6-3	225	7-11-84	1	0	1.69	5	0	0	0	11	3	2	2	1	5	23	.086	.000	.143	19.41	4.22
Miller, Greg	L-L	6-5	220	11-3-84	1	0	0.79	11	0	0	1	23	12	8	2	0	13	24	.154	.150	.155	9.53	5.16
Muegge, Danny	L-R	6-5	180	3-6-81	9	9	3.88	25	25	1	0	142	144	73	61	19	37	84	.264	.293	.242	5.34	2.35
Nall, T.J.	R-R	6-1	207	11-4-80	10	7	2.82	29	19	2	2	141	116	51	44	10	30	155	.224	.258	.197	9.92	1.92
Ojeda, Alvis	R-R	6-0	170	9-23-83	7	3	2.95	30	7	0	1	85	82	31	28	5	36	63	.259	.304	.230	6.64	3.83
Orenduff, Justin	R-R	6-2	205	5-27-83	4	2	3.40	10	10	0	0	50	40	24	19	4	19	54	.217	.297	.164	9.66	3.40
Simmons, Justin	L-L	6-2	205	10-5-81	1	3	3.94	17	0	0	1	32	21	16	14	4	18	20	.186	.094	.222	5.63	5.06
Thomas, Adam	R-R	6-4	190	5-22-79	2	5	6.23	11	4	0	1	30	36	25	21	0	20	24	.310	.400	.230	7.12	5.93
Totten, Heath	R-R	6-2	235	9-30-78	8	5	3.29	21	21	1	0	126	123	52	46	8	27	81	.258	.233	.278	5.79	1.93
Wright, Wesley	R-L	5-11	160	1-28-85	1	1	4.64	15	0	0	1	21	14	13	11	2	11	28	.189	.167	.196	11.81	4.64

FIELDING

Catcher	PCT	G	PO	A	E	DP	PB
Cresse	.998	47	371	37	1	6	3
Ellis	.993	79	672	62	5	6	14
Gutierrez	.990	13	87	14	1	2	0
Langill	1.000	4	23	2	0	0	1

First Base	PCT	G	PO	A	E	DP
Alvarez	1.000	9	51	5	0	3
Brazell	.991	77	616	51	6	63
Bruce	1.000	5	23	2	0	3
Rohan	1.000	4	6	1	0	0
Zapp	.987	61	482	44	7	50

Second Base	PCT	G	PO	A	E	DP
Abreu	.970	117	202	322	16	82
Bruce	.905	5	6	13	2	0
Dewitt	1.000	3	4	7	0	3
Garcia	.929	4	3	10	1	2

	PCT	G	PO	A	E	DP
Rohan	.968	20	28	32	2	6
Sprout	1.000	4	4	10	0	1

Third Base	PCT	G	PO	A	E	DP
Alvarez	.000	2	0	0	1	0
Brazell	.923	6	3	9	1	0
Bruce	.800	5	3	5	2	0
Dewitt	.897	23	16	45	7	3
Garcia	.918	37	20	70	8	3
LaRoche	.937	61	40	109	10	13
Rohan	.964	22	6	21	1	3
Sprout	.833	1	0	5	1	0

Shortstop	PCT	G	PO	A	E	DP
Abreu	.900	3	4	5	1	1
Bruce	1.000	2	4	2	0	0
Garcia	1.000	1	0	3	0	1
Hu	.981	125	192	333	10	71

	PCT	G	PO	A	E	DP
Rohan	.930	19	30	36	5	14

Outfield	PCT	G	PO	A	E	DP
Alvarez	—	2	0	0	0	0
Brazell	1.000	5	11	0	0	0
Bruce	1.000	7	5	0	0	0
Garcia	.875	8	7	0	1	0
Greenberg	.993	68	147	3	1	1
Kemp	.981	48	101	5	2	1
Ledee	.833	3	4	1	1	0
Meadows	1.000	66	96	3	0	0
Raglani	.986	98	143	2	2	0
Rohan	—	2	0	0	0	0
Ruan	1.000	75	125	9	0	5
Ruggiano	.978	82	132	4	3	0
Zapp	1.000	3	3	0	0	0

Vero Beach Dodgers — High Class A

Florida State League

BATTING	B-T	HT	WT	DOB	AVG	vLH	vRH	G	AB	R	H	2B	3B	HR	RBI	BB	HBP	SH	SF	SO	SB	CS	SLG	OBP
Apodaca, Juan	R-R	5-11	188	7-15-86	.257	.273	.253	34	109	17	28	5	0	4	14	13	1	1	0	23	3	1	.413	.341
Borders, Pat	R-R	6-2	200	5-14-63	.181	.300	.161	20	72	6	13	3	0	1	7	5	0	0	0	13	0	0	.264	.234
Bruce, Cole	R-R	6-2	200	1-20-82	.284	.358	.259	85	313	43	89	23	0	10	34	23	2	1	2	77	0	1	.454	.335
Carter, Ryan	R-R	6-2	190	1-4-83	.205	.154	.217	37	132	18	27	7	6	3	16	7	1	1	2	54	0	0	.417	.246
Denker, Travis	R-R	5-9	170	8-5-85	.220	.267	.205	54	191	24	42	6	0	5	25	24	2	0	3	36	0	2	.330	.309
Dewitt, Blake	L-R	5-11	175	8-20-85	.268	.227	.280	106	425	61	114	18	1	18	61	45	3	0	5	79	8	5	.442	.339
Dunlap, Cory	L-L	6-1	205	4-13-84	.261	.145	.303	89	284	43	74	15	0	14	47	88	3	1	4	69	0	1	.461	.435
Gonzalez, Adolfo	B-R	5-11	160	6-13-85	.248	.173	.273	59	202	29	50	12	0	6	19	9	2	2	2	49	3	1	.396	.284
Gutierrez, Eloy	B-R	6-1	178	11-25-84	.217	.000	.250	26	69	11	15	2	1	0	5	9	1	0	0	24	5	0	.275	.316
Gutierrez, Gabriel	R-R	5-11	175	11-24-83	.198	.154	.205	39	96	7	19	1	0	0	14	8	2	5	2	18	0	1	.208	.269
Hoffmann, Jamie	R-R	6-3	205	8-20-84	.252	.267	.247	121	433	50	109	16	0	5	29	35	2	7	2	94	15	11	.323	.309
Jackson, D.J.	R-R	6-1	190	6-13-84	.211	.125	.273	10	19	3	4	0	0	1	1	1	1	0	0	10	0	0	.368	.286
Justis, Shane	R-R	5-10	175	3-11-83	.278	.267	.281	24	79	10	22	3	1	3	12	10	0	2	0	10	0	1	.456	.360
Lizarraga, Francisco	B-R	6-1	170	10-1-85	.000	.000	.000	3	5	0	0	0	0	0	0	0	0	0	0	2	0	0	.000	.000
Locke, Andrew	R-R	6-1	205	2-28-83	.286	.113	.337	61	231	33	66	16	0	7	39	20	4	0	1	37	5	3	.446	.352
Mathews, Brian	R-R	6-0	210	8-26-87	.167	.333	.000	2	6	2	1	1	0	0	3	0	0	0	0	1	0	0	.333	.286
Mathias, Ryder	R-R	6-1	190	9-28-81	.190	.095	.222	29	84	9	16	4	0	1	10	8	2	1	0	13	2	0	.274	.277
Mitchell, Russell	R-R	6-1	182	2-15-85	.277	.176	.303	22	83	12	23	8	0	4	16	4	1	2	1	14	1	1	.518	.315
Mooneyham, Jason	L-L	5-11	210	4-19-82	.279	.000	.288	22	68	5	19	3	0	0	5	2	0	1		9	0	3	.324	.355
Nicholson, David	B-R	6-0	175	10-22-82	.285	.244	.298	106	361	54	103	16	5	1	28	39	3	7	2	81	23	11	.366	.358
Paul, Xavier	L-R	6-1	205	2-25-85	.285	.259	.291	120	470	62	134	23	3	13	49	38	4	7	1	114	22	15	.430	.343
Pedroza, Sergio	L-R	6-1	180	2-23-84	.154	.000	.214	13	39	7	6	2	0	3	7	10	1	0	1	18	0	0	.436	.292
Raglani, Anthony	L-L	6-2	215	4-6-83	.317	.176	.370	17	63	10	20	4	1	1	7	10	1	0	0	10	0	1	.460	.419
Robinson, Trayvon	R-R	5-10	175	9-1-87	.400	.500	.000	3	5	1	2	0	0	0	0	1	0	0	0	2	1	0	.400	.400
Rohan, Jimmy	R-R	6-1	190	5-13-84	.271	.214	.286	21	70	3	19	1	0	0	4	6	1	0	1	11	0	0	.371	.320
Russ, Ryan	B-R	6-2	193	3-7-81	.223	.179	.240	33	103	13	23	2	0	0	9	11	2	0	2	30	3	0	.243	.286
Santana, Carlos	B-R	5-11	170	4-8-86	.268	.270	.267	54	198	36	53	10	2	3	18	31	0	1	0	43	0	3	.384	.345
Todd, Jeremy	L-R	6-2	210	1-30-78	.167	.000	.178	20	48	4	8	1	0	0	4	5	0	0	0	15	0	0	.333	.298
Westervelt, Chris	R-R	5-11	210	11-20-81	.225	.222	.226	41	129	18	29	3	0	0	16	10	0	4	4	41	2	1	.388	.302

PITCHING	B-T	HT	WT	DOB	W	L	ERA	G	GS	CG	SV	IP	H	R	ER	HR	BB	SO	AVG	vLH	vRH	K/9	BB/9
Akin, Brian	R-R	6-3	185	10-13-81	3	3	1.80	22	0	0	7	35	23	13	7	2	16	48	.178	.204	.160	12.34	4.11
Arias, Marlon	L-L	6-3	155	9-1-84	0	1	2.63	5	4	0	0	24	19	7	7	4	14	32	.216	.308	.177	12.00	5.25
Bastardo, Alberto	L-L	6-0	160	4-6-84	5	5	4.53	20	19	0	0	93	97	55	47	12	47	105	.264	.236	.272	10.13	4.53
Castillo, Albenis	R-R	6-4	178	12-24-83	3	5	6.37	35	0	0	0	65	83	52	46	12	27	55	.306	.333	.293	7.62	3.74
Diaz, Jose	R-R	6-4	300	2-27-84	0	1	5.27	9	0	0	2	14	12	9	8	2	4	11	.226	.333	.171	7.24	2.63
Elbert, Scott	L-L	6-2	190	8-13-85	5	5	2.37	17	15	0	0	84	57	27	22	4	41	97	.193	.185	.194	10.43	4.41
Figueroa, Jonathan	L-L	6-5	205	9-15-83	1	7	7.29	17	11	0	1	54	67	50	44	7	40	49	.302	.231	.324	8.12	6.63
Hammes, Zachary	R-R	6-6	225	5-15-84	6	3	4.32	41	3	0	1	92	95	48	44	9	46	90	.269	.292	.255	8.84	4.52
Johnson, Blake	R-R	6-3	185	6-14-85	4	5	4.92	20	18	0	0	106	121	70	58	11	19	73	.285	.322	.260	6.20	1.61
Ketchner, Ryan	L-L	6-1	190	4-19-82	2	1	1.45	9	0	0	0	19	10	3	3	2	5	19	.159	.235	.130	9.16	2.41
Leach, Brent	L-L	6-5	205	11-18-82	3	4	4.56	30	0	0	1	49	48	34	25	1	32	57	.265	.259	.268	10.40	5.84
Malone, Christopher	R-R	6-4	230	6-28-83	2	6	6.02	17	16	0	0	84	112	64	56	10	28	77	.323	.238	.371	8.28	3.01
Megrew, Mike	L-L	6-6	210	1-29-84	2	3	3.52	18	8	0	0	54	44	23	21	5	44	62	.224	.167	.238	10.40	7.38
Meloan, Jonathan	R-R	6-3	225	7-11-84	1	0	2.50	4	3	0	0	18	15	6	5	2	4	27	.221	.120	.279	13.50	2.00
Merricks, Matt	L-L	5-11	180	8-6-82	0	3	4.11	9	7	0	0	35	29	22	16	4	17	48	.225	.333	.200	12.34	4.37
Pimentel, Julio	R-R	6-1	190	12-14-85	3	8	5.69	30	9	0	2	74	85	56	47	4	45	77	.290	.296	.287	9.32	5.45
Quintana, Eduardo	R-R	6-2	175	6-30-85	0	0	18.00	1	0	0	0	1	2	2	2	0	1	0	.400	.333	.500	0.00	9.00
Ramirez, Miguel	R-R	5-11	180	7-15-83	0	0	0.00	1	0	0	0	2	0	0	0	0	0	3	.000	.000	.000	11.57	0.00
Thomas, Adam	R-R	6-4	190	5-22-79	3	4	2.30	19	7	0	2	63	57	23	16	6	16	59	.241	.215	.262	8.47	2.30
Troncoso, Ramon	R-R	6-7	187	2-16-83	1	3	6.75	18	0	0	0	29	43	27	22	1	14	31	.347	.372	.333	9.51	4.30
Wade, Cory	R-R	6-2	180	5-28-83	2	4	8.24	7	7	0	0	39	52	40	36	9	13	32	.317	.243	.372	7.32	2.97
Wilson, Kyle	R-R	6-2	200	4-21-83	2	6	3.62	35	4	0	9	60	49	28	24	3	29	67	.228	.188	.247	10.11	4.37
Wright, Wesley	R-L	5-11	160	1-28-85	3	3	1.49	26	0	0	0	42	29	11	7	0	23	51	.197	.289	.165	10.84	4.89

FIELDING

Catcher	PCT	G	PO	A	E	DP	PB
Apodaca	.993	31	270	17	2	2	3
Borders	1.000	18	155	18	0	1	0
Gutierrez	.984	39	276	41	5	3	4
Mathias	.982	27	203	13	4	1	5
Todd	1.000	8	65	0	0	0	4
Westervelt	.996	22	214	16	1	0	8

First Base	PCT	G	PO	A	E	DP
Bruce	.986	26	196	12	3	18
Dunlap	.980	74	540	38	12	40
Gonzalez	.966	12	27	1	1	2
Mitchell	1.000	3	16	2	0	2
Mooneyham	1.000	21	168	9	0	21
Rohan	.972	6	34	1	1	3
Todd	1.000	2	18	0	0	2
Westervelt	1.000	1	3	0	0	1

Second Base	PCT	G	PO	A	E	DP
Denker	.967	8	15	14	1	2

Dewitt	.951	90	169	217	20	49	
Gonzalez	.965	22	46	37	3	13	
Justis	.962	13	27	24	2	5	
Nicholson	1.000	1	3	2	0	0	
Rohan	.875	1	2	5	1	3	

Third Base	PCT	G	PO	A	E	DP
Bruce	.967	16	12	17	1	1
Denker	.878	40	19	53	10	9
Dewitt	.973	16	9	27	1	4
Gonzalez	1.000	4	0	10	0	1
Hoffmann	.000	1	0	0	1	0
Justis	.909	4	4	6	1	1
Mitchell	.971	20	11	22	1	2
Rohan	.875	3	3	4	1	1
Santana	.846	32	18	48	12	6

Shortstop	PCT	G	PO	A	E	DP
Bruce	.667	3	3	3	3	1
Gonzalez	.921	21	26	56	7	11

Justis	.929	3	5	8	1	0
Lizarraga	1.000	3	0	5	0	0
Nicholson	.953	101	108	257	18	41
Rohan	.892	7	14	19	4	3

Outfield	PCT	G	PO	A	E	DP
Carter	.919	29	32	2	3	0
Gutierrez	.933	12	13	1	1	0
Hoffmann	.982	119	262	7	5	2
Jackson	1.000	7	12	0	0	0
Locke	.959	46	70	0	3	0
Paul	.979	114	178	12	4	1
Pedroza	1.000	9	14	0	0	0
Raglani	1.000	13	16	1	0	0
Robinson	1.000	2	3	0	0	0
Rohan	1.000	3	8	1	0	0
Russ	.958	29	46	0	2	0
Santana	.935	21	28	1	2	0

Columbus Catfish — Low Class A

South Atlantic League

BATTING	B-T	HT	WT	DOB	AVG	vLH	vRH	G	AB	R	H	2B	3B	HR	RBI	BB	HBP	SH	SF	SO	SB	CS	SLG	OBP
Apodaca, Juan	R-R	5-11	188	7-15-86	.249	.297	.204	55	189	23	47	8	0	1	22	25	1	0	2	35	1	0	.307	.336
Carter, Brandon	L-R	5-7	170	11-12-82	.194	.176	.200	17	62	9	12	5	1	1	7	9	1	0	0	11	0	0	.355	.306
De Jesus, Ivan	R-R	5-11	182	5-1-87	.277	.272	.280	126	483	65	134	17	2	1	44	63	4	6	7	85	16	5	.327	.361
Denker, Travis	R-R	5-9	170	8-5-85	.268	.329	.241	75	250	47	67	11	1	11	45	65	2	1	2	37	2	1	.452	.420
Godwin, Adam	R-R	5-11	170	12-13-82	.269	.246	.280	109	383	58	103	12	6	2	36	28	9	16	2	53	30	15	.347	.332
Harper, Anthony	L-R	6-0	200	10-15-84	.287	.214	.305	78	279	30	80	12	0	6	32	22	2	0	0	69	0	0	.394	.343
Hunt, Bridger	R-R	6-0	185	7-24-85	.314	.324	.310	67	236	45	74	12	1	1	24	23	2	1	2	32	12	9	.386	.376
Jensen, Christopher	L-R	6-2	190	5-23-83	.141	.231	.096	25	78	3	11	1	0	0	7	8	2	0	2	23	2	1	.154	.233
Justis, Shane	R-R	5-10	175	3-11-83	.289	.326	.269	39	121	17	35	3	0	4	21	18	6	3	2	20	2	1	.413	.401
Laurin, Dominique	R-R	6-0	185	10-7-82	.000	.000	.000	2	7	0	0	0	0	0	0	0	0	0	0	3	0	0	.000	.000
Locke, Andrew	R-R	6-1	205	2-28-83	.325	.307	.335	62	243	49	79	16	4	8	50	21	7	1	0	42	5	1	.523	.395
May, Lucas	R-R	6-0	190	10-24-84	.273	.266	.277	119	450	76	123	27	9	18	82	35	7	0	5	130	14	2	.493	.332
McGeehan, Conor	R-R	6-2	205	6-24-83	.237	.316	.200	23	59	10	14	5	0	1	4	18	0	0	0	12	0	1	.373	.416
Mitchell, Russell	R-R	6-1	182	2-15-85	.239	.267	.225	105	435	71	104	32	2	15	75	29	3	1	5	83	3	0	.425	.288
Mooneyham, Jason	L-L	5-11	210	4-19-82	.247	.220	.260	77	255	41	63	10	0	1	27	62	24	2	2	40	4	1	.298	.434
Pedroza, Sergio	L-R	6-1	190	2-23-84	.281	.254	.296	89	317	61	89	21	1	21	75	73	17	0	3	91	2	6	.562	.437
Perez, Eduardo	B-R	6-1	175	8-30-84	.249	.217	.264	51	185	24	46	13	1	4	28	21	4	0	3	38	3	1	.395	.333
Rivera, Juan	B-R	6-0	148	2-19-87	.256	.191	.293	40	129	13	33	4	0	2	15	6	1	2	1	24	1	2	.333	.292
Soto, Jesus	R-R	5-11	178	9-7-86	.213	.276	.183	22	89	11	19	5	0	1	5	3	0	1	0	23	2	0	.303	.239
Sutherland, David	L-L	6-6	175	5-2-85	.268	.240	.280	119	447	58	120	20	0	6	42	40	5	1	7	57	1	0	.353	.331

PITCHING	B-T	HT	WT	DOB	W	L	ERA	G	GS	CG	SV	IP	H	R	ER	HR	BB	SO	AVG	vLH	vRH	K/9	BB/9
Alvarez, Mario	R-R	6-0	150	3-26-84	7	10	5.89	27	25	0	0	128	155	101	84	8	56	102	.303	.310	.296	7.15	3.93
Arias, Marlon	L-L	6-3	155	9-1-84	7	6	5.27	23	18	1	0	108	107	73	63	17	38	109	.255	.179	.272	9.13	3.18
Bastardo, Alberto	L-L	6-0	160	4-6-84	3	1	1.39	6	0	0	0	32	22	8	5	2	14	33	.193	.158	.200	9.19	3.90
Brooks, Douglas	R-R	6-4	210	8-12-82	1	0	5.40	7	0	0	1	10	11	8	6	0	2	7	.289	.444	.241	6.30	1.80
Castillo, Arismendy	R-R	6-3	190	12-10-84	8	5	4.59	33	9	0	2	98	100	58	50	4	54	66	.270	.256	.279	6.06	4.96
Felix, Francisco	R-R	5-11	191	7-28-83	1	2	5.46	21	0	0	5	30	35	19	18	1	19	27	.297	.313	.286	8.19	5.76
Garrison, Kale	L-L	6-1	175	3-1-82	1	1	3.24	21	0	0	1	33	25	14	12	0	32	30	.204	.208	.202	8.10	8.64
Gomez de Segura, Matt	R-R	6-5	230	5-9-84	3	4	4.94	36	0	0	6	51	45	35	28	5	40	53	.237	.301	.187	9.35	7.06
Hochgesang, Nathan	R-R	6-4	220	12-18-81	1	0	9.75	7	0	0	0	12	21	13	13	0	5	11	.389	.444	.333	8.25	3.75
Horlacher, David	R-R	6-4	175	6-22-82	2	4	4.61	19	14	0	2	80	87	47	41	13	26	75	.275	.320	.245	8.44	2.93
Jones, Joseph	R-R	6-5	210	11-16-82	1	2	2.68	9	6	0	0	40	29	16	12	4	18	22	.200	.308	.140	4.91	4.02
Leach, Brent	L-L	6-5	205	11-18-82	4	2	3.27	14	0	0	0	52	41	22	19	2	31	67	.230	.167	.243	11.52	5.33

	B-T	HT	WT	DOB	W	L	ERA	G	GS	CG	SV	IP	H	R	ER	HR	BB	SO	AVG	vLH	vRH	K/9	BB/9
McDonald, James	L-R	6-5	195	10-19-84	5	10	3.98	30	22	2	0	142	119	72	63	15	65	146	.229	.206	.245	9.23	4.11
Meloan, Jonathan	R-R	6-3	225	7-11-84	1	1	1.54	12	0	0	1	23	9	5	4	2	7	41	.118	.097	.133	15.81	2.70
Norrito, Giuseppe	R-R	5-10	180	8-4-82	2	3	3.55	13	1	0	0	25	22	13	10	2	7	12	.232	.091	.306	4.26	2.49
Pfeiffer, David	L-L	6-3	190	8-17-85	2	5	5.73	30	10	0	2	82	105	69	52	2	45	59	.309	.310	.309	6.50	4.96
Pratt, Jordan	R-R	6-3	195	5-17-85	8	4	4.85	34	1	0	0	78	76	46	42	1	58	83	.254	.248	.259	9.58	6.69
Preziosi, Dave	L-L	6-1	190	2-17-83	1	0	11.25	8	0	0	0	4	6	5	5	0	2	5	.316	.167	.385	4.50	11.25
Rodriguez, Jesus	R-R	5-10	187	9-13-85	2	1	6.27	12	4	0	0	33	47	26	23	5	8	25	.324	.265	.377	6.82	2.18
Sanfler, Miguel	L-L	5-11	165	10-5-84	1	4	9.14	15	0	0	1	22	25	26	22	1	21	16	.294	.313	.290	6.65	8.72
Troncoso, Ramon	R-R	6-7	187	2-16-83	4	0	2.41	23	0	0	15	34	28	11	9	1	7	22	.241	.286	.200	5.88	1.87
Wade, Cory	R-R	6-2	180	5-28-83	6	5	4.96	23	14	1	2	94	101	56	52	9	11	94	.269	.275	.263	8.97	1.05

FIELDING

Catcher	PCT	G	PO	A	E	DP	PB
Apodaca	.989	54	439	26	5	2	8
Harper	.987	74	530	55	8	6	12
McGeehan	.993	23	129	21	1	4	2

First Base	PCT	G	PO	A	E	DP
Mitchell	.990	11	101	3	1	4
Mooneyham	.990	47	370	30	4	42
Sutherland	.990	82	716	45	8	98

Second Base	PCT	G	PO	A	E	DP
Carter	.941	16	28	52	5	13
De Jesus	.889	7	11	21	4	5
Denker	.966	67	126	189	11	52

	PCT	G	PO	A	E	DP
Justis	.974	25	46	67	3	16
Laurin	1.000	1	0	7	0	0
Rivera	.906	7	12	17	3	6
Soto	.946	19	30	57	5	14

Third Base	PCT	G	PO	A	E	DP
De Jesus	1.000	1	0	1	0	0
Justis	1.000	6	2	9	0	2
Laurin	—	1	0	0	0	0
Mitchell	.938	90	63	162	15	27
Perez	.921	36	35	70	9	6
Rivera	.957	9	2	20	1	1

Shortstop	PCT	G	PO	A	E	DP
De Jesus	.957	117	208	323	24	86

	PCT	G	PO	A	E	DP
Justis	.963	6	13	13	1	6
Rivera	.908	22	24	55	8	12

Outfield	PCT	G	PO	A	E	DP
Carter	1.000	1	1	0	0	0
Godwin	.960	102	180	10	8	1
Hunt	.976	58	123	1	3	2
Jensen	1.000	19	34	0	0	0
Locke	.948	50	52	3	3	0
May	.956	108	185	10	9	3
Pedroza	.933	87	120	5	9	2
Rivera	1.000	1	1	0	0	0

Ogden Raptors — Rookie

Pioneer League

BATTING	B-T	HT	WT	DOB	AVG	vLH	vRH	G	AB	R	H	2B	3B	HR	RBI	BB	HBP	SH	SF	SO	SB	CS	SLG	OBP
Bell, Joshua	B-R	6-3	205	11-13-86	.308	.250	.322	64	250	45	77	17	3	12	53	23	1	1	5	72	4	0	.544	.367
Berezay, Matthew	L-R	5-11	175	11-15-83	.296	.226	.312	48	169	38	50	14	1	8	30	35	1	2	2	37	4	2	.533	.415
Brooks, Parker	R-R	5-10	175	8-1-81	.261	.333	.241	24	69	10	18	3	0	0	10	5	2	6	1	10	1	0	.304	.325
Brown, Jeremy	R-R	6-1	195	4-2-84	.244	.079	.312	45	131	28	32	7	1	3	19	17	4	0	3	43	6	3	.382	.342
Fuller, Justin	L-R	6-1	175	7-10-83	.230	.133	.243	39	122	24	28	4	2	0	13	21	0	7	1	24	4	2	.295	.340
Giles, Thomas	L-L	6-0	190	8-28-83	.291	.091	.313	33	110	14	32	6	1	5	23	4	2	1	5	22	3	2	.500	.314
Jackson, D.J.	R-R	6-1	190	6-13-84	.143	.100	.167	24	56	7	8	2	1	1	6	7	2	0	0	24	2	1	.268	.262
Jensen, Christopher	L-R	6-2	190	5-23-83	.281	.375	.265	15	57	10	16	2	0	1	7	6	1	1	0	10	1	1	.368	.359
Martin, John	R-R	6-3	205	12-13-83	.256	.286	.248	42	129	19	33	9	1	1	18	21	3	5	2	45	0	0	.364	.368
Medero-Stullz, Carlos	R-R	5-8	190	5-30-86	.197	.313	.179	40	122	18	24	4	0	1	14	9	11	1	2	35	0	1	.254	.306
Perez, Eduardo	B-R	6-1	175	8-30-84	.255	.125	.293	30	106	13	27	4	0	0	13	21	4	2	1	21	0	0	.292	.394
Rivera, Michael	R-R	6-0	186	5-13-85	.253	.262	.250	51	174	28	44	6	0	1	9	11	9	1	0	37	10	8	.305	.330
Rivera, Juan	B-R	6-0	148	2-19-87	.238	.346	.185	20	80	4	19	0	1	1	7	4	2	3	0		2	2	.300	.291
Rogowski, Ryan	L-L	6-2	195	1-26-84	.312	.348	.304	70	263	64	82	14	8	4	36	52	4	5	3	40	30	5	.471	.429
Santana, Carlos	B-R	5-11	170	4-8-86	.303	.500	.255	37	132	31	40	5	1	7	27	30	1	0	5	19	4	0	.515	.423
Soto, Jesus	R-R	5-11	178	9-7-86	.309	.261	.322	56	223	32	69	11	1	7	38	15	1	2	1	44	6	2	.462	.343
Taloa, Rick	R-R	6-4	250	12-14-84	.271	.204	.288	65	247	35	67	13	0	11	48	12	8	1	4	42	0	0	.457	.321
Van Slyke, Scott	R-R	6-5	195	7-24-86	.256	.275	.250	45	156	18	40	5	2	2	17	14	1	0	1	41	5	3	.353	.320

PITCHING	B-T	HT	WT	DOB	W	L	ERA	G	GS	CG	SV	IP	H	R	ER	HR	BB	SO	AVG	vLH	vRH	K/9	BB/9
Acheatel, Greg	R-R	6-4	205	9-29-83	2	0	2.70	11	0	0	0	13	8	4	4	3	4	12	.170	.286	.121	8.10	2.70
Brooks, Douglas	R-R	6-4	210	8-12-82	0	1	1.64	12	1	0	0	22	18	8	4	1	6	14	.225	.308	.185	5.73	2.45
Castillo, Jesus	R-R	6-1	190	5-31-84	2	5	2.88	14	14	0	0	72	65	29	23	3	25	55	.241	.228	.247	6.88	3.13
Coleman, Paul	L-L	6-4	195	5-11-84	1	1	2.70	13	2	0	0	40	38	17	12	1	20	38	.248	.063	.298	8.55	4.50
Dasni, Chales	R-R	6-3	170	7-21-85	4	3	5.63	13	8	0	0	48	54	36	30	7	26	64	.267	.250	.274	12.00	4.88
Gardner, Michael	R-R	5-11	175	11-2-83	0	1	8.10	3	0	0	0	7	12	8	6	0	6	6	.353	.364	.348	8.10	8.10
Gearhart, Kalen	R-R	6-2	210	8-12-85	0	1	7.89	18	0	0	0	22	32	22	19	5	6	18	.323	.360	.311	7.48	2.49
Guerra, Javy	R-R	6-1	185	10-31-85	1	3	4.82	7	7	0	0	28	37	18	15	1	20	22	.330	.391	.315	7.07	6.43
Hochgesang, Nathan	R-R	6-4	220	12-18-81	2	0	5.79	6	0	0	0	9	11	8	6	0	5	11	.275	.273	.276	10.61	4.82
Johnson, Steven	R-R	6-1	185	8-31-87	5	5	3.89	14	14	0	0	79	79	37	34	4	25	86	.267	.242	.278	9.84	2.86
Jones, Joseph	R-R	6-3	210	11-16-82	1	0	6.60	10	0	0	0	15	22	11	11	0	1	12	.338	.333	.347	7.20	0.60
Morris, Bryan	L-R	6-3	200	3-28-87	4	5	5.13	14	14	0	0	60	64	44	34	3	40	79	.267	.272	.264	11.92	6.03
Norrito, Giuseppe	R-R	5-10	180	8-4-82	0	0	1.17	5	0	0	0	8	11	3	1	0	2	3	.344	.417	.300	3.52	2.35
Ramirez, Miguel	R-R	5-11	180	7-15-83	2	3	3.82	21	0	0	0	35	26	16	15	4	9	46	.202	.226	.194	11.72	2.29
Renfrow, Wayne	R-R	6-2	220	4-18-84	0	0	54.00	1	0	0	0	0	2	2	2	0	1	1	.667	—	.667	27.00	27.00
Rodriguez, Jesus	R-R	5-10	187	9-13-85	3	0	5.40	16	0	0	0	45	71	32	27	2	5	44	.353	.382	.342	8.80	1.00
Sanfler, Miguel	L-L	5-11	165	10-5-84	2	1	2.18	23	0	0	0	33	32	18	8	0	17	31	.246	.121	.289	8.45	4.64
Wall, Joshua	R-R	6-6	190	1-21-87	3	5	5.86	14	14	0	0	66	80	56	43	5	33	41	.305	.294	.311	5.59	4.50
White, Cody	L-L	6-3	185	2-27-85	4	2	2.68	25	0	0	0	44	30	17	13	2	23	44	.190	.103	.218	9.07	4.74
White, Garrett	L-L	6-5	235	5-22-84	1	3	7.62	28	0	0	0	28	32	25	24	2	14	40	.286	.300	.280	12.71	4.45

FIELDING

Catcher	PCT	G	PO	A	E	DP	PB
Brooks	1.000	3	3	0	0	0	1
Martin	.987	42	357	23	5	3	12
Medero-Stullz	.997	40	318	32	1	3	6

First Base	PCT	G	PO	A	E	DP
Bell	1.000	1	12	0	0	0
Perez	.983	20	161	11	3	16
Taloa	.986	56	432	45	7	35
Van Slyke	1.000	3	13	0	0	1

Second Base	PCT	G	PO	A	E	DP
Brooks	1.000	13	21	31	0	5

	PCT	G	PO	A	E	DP
Rivera	.950	23	44	51	5	12
Rivera	.950	8	17	21	2	4
Soto	.927	39	64	89	12	16

Third Base	PCT	G	PO	A	E	DP
Bell	.879	52	33	90	17	5
Brooks	1.000	1	0	1	0	0
Perez	.800	6	0	12	3	0
Santana	1.000	6	2	6	0	0
Soto	.917	14	10	23	3	3

Shortstop	PCT	G	PO	A	E	DP
Brooks	.967	7	12	17	1	2

	PCT	G	PO	A	E	DP
Fuller	.945	36	51	105	9	16
Rivera	.945	27	43	61	6	13
Rivera	.909	13	13	37	5	10

Outfield	PCT	G	PO	A	E	DP
Brown	.960	41	70	2	3	0
Giles	.889	28	52	4	7	1
Jackson	.885	19	23	0	3	0
Jensen	1.000	15	25	0	0	0
Rogowski	.989	69	81	7	1	1
Santana	.970	31	57	7	2	2
Van Slyke	.983	42	58	1	1	0

Gulf Coast League

BATTING	B-T	HT	WT	DOB	AVG	vLH	vRH	G	AB	R	H	2B	3B	HR	RBI	BB	HBP	SH	SF	SO	SB	CS	SLG	OBP
Alvarez, Nick	R-R	6-3	207	2-8-77	.385	.500	.364	5	13	4	5	1	0	0	1	2	0	0	0	3	1	0	.462	.467
Anthony, Jason	R-R	6-0	210	5-26-84	.286	.000	.294	10	35	4	10	2	0	1	3	2	1	0	0	3	1	0	.429	.342
Carter, Ryan	R-R	6-2	200	1-4-83	.348	.000	.421	7	23	8	8	4	0	1	5	3	0	0	0	5	2	0	.652	.423
Cresse, Brad	R-R	6-2	230	7-31-78	.176	.000	.200	4	17	2	3	0	0	0	3	3	0	0	0	8	0	0	.176	.300
Garcia, Yosanddy	R-R	6-0	170	10-20-87	.243	.250	.241	33	111	17	27	7	1	3	19	8	1	1	0	36	3	1	.405	.300
Gutierrez, Eloy	B-R	6-1	178	11-25-84	.262	.143	.294	19	65	13	17	4	0	1	6	11	0	1	0	17	7	0	.369	.368
Herrera, Elian	B-R	5-11	169	2-1-85	.327	.400	.311	36	110	19	36	4	0	1	17	19	1	5	2	17	2	3	.391	.424
Hunt, Bridger	R-R	6-0	185	7-24-85	.125	.000	.143	2	8	0	1	0	0	0	1	0	0	0	1	1	0	0	.125	.111
Jansen, Kenley	B-R	6-2	178	9-30-87	.248	.114	.305	35	117	14	29	2	1	1	10	19	2	0	0	32	1	0	.308	.362
Lizarraga, Francisco	B-R	6-1	170	10-1-85	.273	.279	.271	47	172	25	47	9	0	1	20	12	0	11	4	19	5	3	.343	.314
Lopez, Esteban	R-R	6-1	210	6-20-84	.279	.571	.222	13	43	4	12	1	0	0	5	4	3	1	0	5	0	0	.302	.380
Mathews, Brian	R-R	6-0	210	8-26-87	.250	.250	.250	44	156	26	39	11	1	3	26	21	1	1	0	30	2	1	.391	.343
Mattingly, Preston	R-R	6-3	205	8-28-87	.290	.114	.331	47	186	22	54	12	3	1	29	9	1	0	3	39	12	3	.403	.322
McGeehan, Conor	R-R	6-2	205	6-24-83	.571	1.000	.500	2	7	2	4	0	0	0	3	1	0	0	0	0	0	0	.571	.625
Mora, Jesus	R-R	6-2	185	12-25-83	.313	.231	.343	15	48	8	15	2	1	1	7	3	0	2	0	8	0	0	.458	.353
Ortiz, Jaime	L-L	6-3	200	7-14-88	.232	.270	.222	50	181	21	42	5	1	2	22	18	3	1	1	45	1	2	.304	.310
Poole, Lyndon	R-R	6-0	185	8-30-86	.238	.200	.243	17	42	7	10	1	3	0	6	5	1	0	1	16	1	0	.405	.327
Robinson, Trayvon	R-R	5-10	175	9-1-87	.254	.267	.250	39	134	24	34	7	2	2	20	16	2	2	1	48	5	1	.381	.340
Rosario, Jovanny	B-R	5-9	160	4-12-85	.283	.261	.291	46	180	34	51	9	2	1	15	15	2	4	0	28	7	2	.372	.345
Schwab, Jason	L-R	5-9	170	3-18-84	.237	.292	.219	30	97	14	23	4	1	0	9	9	1	1	1	11	5	6	.299	.306
Vetters, Travis	R-R	6-2	195	9-11-83	.146	.000	.162	14	41	2	6	0	0	1	2	2	1	0	3	12	2	2	.146	.222
Zapp, A.J.	L-R	6-3	190	4-24-78	.467	.500	.462	5	15	2	7	2	0	1	2	3	2	0	0	4	0	0	.800	.600

PITCHING	B-T	HT	WT	DOB	W	L	ERA	G	GS	CG	SV	IP	H	R	ER	HR	BB	SO	AVG	vLH	vRH	K/9	BB/9
Diaz, Jose	R-R	6-4	300	2-27-84	0	0	4.50	1	1	0	0	2	2	1	1	1	0	0	.250	.000	.286	0.00	0.00
Diaz, Wilfredo	L-L	5-11	180	1-22-87	3	2	1.78	12	0	0	3	30	26	8	6	0	11	28	.220	.333	.187	8.31	3.26
Dutton, Johnathan	L-L	6-1	155	9-30-87	3	4	3.77	12	3	0	0	31	23	15	13	0	22	28	.207	.200	.209	8.13	6.39
Gardner, Michael	R-R	5-11	175	11-2-83	4	1	2.08	9	5	0	2	35	25	8	8	1	3	29	.205	.267	.185	7.53	0.78
Gilbert, James	R-R	6-2	195	4-2-85	0	0	13.50	1	1	0	0	1	2	1	1	0	2	2	.500	—	.500	27.00	27.00
Gracia, Mario	R-R	5-11	185	8-11-83	3	2	2.62	13	1	0	2	45	32	14	13	2	13	28	.201	.244	.186	5.64	2.62
Guerra, Luis	R-R	6-1	180	7-18-79	0	1	4.15	4	4	0	0	9	10	4	4	0	4	11	.278	.111	.333	11.42	4.15
Haldis, Jon	R-R	6-1	170	3-9-87	2	4	3.09	11	7	1	0	55	55	32	19	4	16	29	.248	.232	.255	4.72	2.60
Kershaw, Clayton	L-L	6-3	210	3-19-88	2	0	1.95	10	8	0	1	37	28	10	8	0	5	54	.201	.217	.198	13.14	1.22
Ketchner, Ryan	L-L	6-1	190	4-19-82	0	0	0.00	3	2	0	0	6	3	0	0	0	1	8	.150	.333	.118	12.00	1.50
Melgarejo, Thomas	L-L	6-1	216	1-10-87	3	1	3.60	9	7	0	0	40	35	21	16	2	19	36	.227	.300	.216	8.10	4.28
Nunez, Jhonny	R-R	6-3	185	11-26-85	6	0	1.58	10	7	0	0	57	35	12	10	0	19	56	.177	.188	.173	8.84	3.00
Paris, Gary	L-L	6-1	160	11-6-86	2	0	5.11	13	2	0	0	25	15	17	14	0	27	27	.170	.364	.143	9.85	9.85
Preziosi, Dave	L-L	6-1	190	2-17-83	0	0	3.24	7	0	0	2	17	18	6	6	0	3	13	.277	.100	.309	7.02	1.62
Pujols, Kengshill	R-R	6-0	187	3-3-85	0	0	3.43	9	0	0	1	21	18	14	8	4	10	20	.228	.308	.189	8.57	4.29
Quintana, Eduardo	R-R	6-2	175	6-30-85	2	2	4.67	16	0	0	4	27	29	14	14	0	11	31	.276	.286	.273	10.33	3.67
Renfrow, Wayne	R-R	6-2	220	4-18-84	1	1	0.60	3	3	0	0	15	9	3	1	0	5	16	.167	.143	.182	9.60	3.00
Smit, Kyle	R-R	6-3	165	10-14-87	0	2	4.09	6	3	0	1	11	15	5	5	1	2	9	.319	.214	.364	7.36	1.64
Tripp, Skyler	L-L	6-2	170	10-10-86	1	0	18.47	7	0	0	0	6	2	13	13	0	20	3	.118	.000	.133	4.26	28.42

FIELDING

Catcher	PCT	G	PO	A	E	DP	PB
Anthony	1.000	5	35	2	0	1	2
Cresse	1.000	2	20	1	0	0	2
Jansen	.977	34	262	31	7	4	5
Lopez	1.000	13	93	7	0	1	2
McGeehan	1.000	2	15	2	0	0	0

First Base	PCT	G	PO	A	E	DP
Alvarez	1.000	2	19	1	0	0
Anthony	1.000	1	3	0	0	0
Garcia	1.000	2	14	2	0	0
Ortiz	.986	47	397	15	6	27
Zapp	1.000	4	28	5	0	2

Second Base	PCT	G	PO	A	E	DP
Garcia	.974	17	33	42	2	7
Herrera	.953	35	66	75	7	14
Lizarraga	.943	8	12	21	2	2
Mathews	.750	1	2	1	1	0

Third Base	PCT	G	PO	A	E	DP
Garcia	.643	4	3	6	5	1
Lizarraga	.971	12	6	28	1	3
Mathews	.898	40	26	71	11	6
Robinson	—	1	0	0	0	0

Shortstop	PCT	G	PO	A	E	DP
Lizarraga	.963	26	31	74	4	8

Mattingly	.898	30	26	62	10	5

Outfield	PCT	G	PO	A	E	DP
Alvarez	1.000	2	2	0	0	0
Gutierrez	.968	19	28	2	1	0
Herrera	1.000	1	1	0	0	0
Hunt	1.000	2	3	0	0	0
Mora	.958	13	20	3	1	0
Poole	1.000	14	28	0	0	0
Robinson	.986	39	65	4	1	0
Rosario	.977	46	80	5	2	4
Schwab	.978	25	43	1	1	0
Vetters	1.000	14	20	0	0	0

BY TOM HAUDRICOURT

At the outset of the 2006 season, when most of the talk centered on the Brewers' up-and-coming younger players, general manager Doug Melvin had something else on his mind.

"I wasn't as concerned about the young players as I was the veterans," Melvin said. "Young players take time to develop. But when your veterans make mistakes and your veterans don't perform, that's an issue."

It became an issue that plagued the Brewers throughout the season. Veterans such as Geoff Jenkins, Brady Clark and Damian Miller had down seasons, and others such as Ben Sheets, Tomo Ohka and Corey Koskie spent too much time on the disabled list.

The Brewers didn't perform well in any area, finishing 14th in the National League in hitting (.258), 15th in pitching (4.82 ERA) and 13th in defense (.980). Under those circumstances, and taking into consideration the spate of injuries that tore apart their roster, it's no mystery why they produced six fewer victories (75-87) than the previous season.

What made the team's play even more disappointing was that the NL Central was there to be had. Surviving a late-season collapse, St. Louis finished first with a mere 83 victories.

"We were on target when we said the Astros, Cardinals and Cubs were not as good as the year before," Melvin said. "The division wasn't as strong. I really did think we had a chance."

But only if the team avoided injuries and received solid

MAJOR LEAGUE: Bill Hall, ss/3b

Not even guaranteed a regular role entering the season, Hall did more than fill in when injuries struck every Milwaukee infielder. Hall, 26, led the Brewers in slugging percentage (.553), runs (101), doubles (39), home runs (35), RBIs (85), walks (63), strikeouts (162) and extra-base hits (78).

MINOR LEAGUE: Yovani Gallardo, rhp

Gallardo established himself as one of the best pitching prospects in baseball. The 20-year-old dominated two levels and led all minor leaguers with 188 strikeouts. He finished among the leaders in strikeouts per nine innings, ERA and opponent average, and led Brewers farmhands with 11 wins and a 1.86 ERA.

performances from their veterans. Neither of those things happened, leaving the Brewers and their long-suffering fans unfulfilled.

Things started going awry in early May when Sheets and Ohka were shelved with long-term injuries. A series of pitchers summoned from the minors flopped badly, and the Brewers went 6-17 in those spots until Sheets and Ohka returned.

Then, one by one, the Brewers began losing infielders. Shortstop J.J. Hardy went down with an ankle injury in mid-May, had surgery and never returned. Koskie, the veteran third baseman, didn't play a game in the second half with post-concussion syndrome.

In perhaps the most damaging loss of all, second baseman Rickie Weeks sustained a wrist injury in late July that also required surgery. At the time, Weeks had recovered nicely from early-season fielding yips and was on pace to score 100 runs out of the leadoff spot.

One positive aspect of the injuries was the emergence of Bill Hall, who took over at shortstop. Hall broke through with 35 homers and 85 RBIs, both club highs, assuring himself a regular spot in the lineup in 2007.

For the first time since 1983, the Brewers put three players in the All-Star Game—lefthander Chris Capuano, closer Derrick Turnbow and left fielder Carlos Lee. Before the end of July, however, Lee had been traded to Texas and Turnbow melted down, losing the closer job en route to a 13.75 ERA in the second half. And after going 10-4 before the break, Capuano went 1-8 afterward, finishing with a losing record.

The Brewers also were a schizophrenic team, home and away. They were stout at Miller Park with a 48-33 record, yet meek as kittens on the road with a 27-54 mark.

On the minor league front, righthander Yovani Gallardo and third baseman Ryan Braun cemented their status as the top prospects in the organization, earning berths in the Futures Game and finishing strong at Double-A Huntsville after promotions from Class A Brevard County. Both could be in Milwaukee before the 2007 season is done.

ORGANIZATION LEADERS

BATTING *Minimum 250 at-bats

*AVG	Lefave, Andrew, AZL Brewers	.353
R	Ford, Darren, West Virginia	103
H	Cain, Lorenzo, West Virginia	176
TB	Braun, Ryan, Brevard County/Huntsville	275
2B	Cain, Lorenzo, West Virginia	37
3B	Chapman, Stephen, West Virginia/Helena	8
	Ezi, Travis, Brevard County/Huntsville	8
HR	Braun, Ryan, Brevard County/Huntsville	27
RBI	Braun, Ryan, Brevard County/Huntsville	99
BB	Nelson, Brad, Nashville/Huntsville	81
SO	Ford, Darren, West Virginia	156
SB	Ford, Darren, West Virginia	76
*OBP	Gillespie, Cole, Helena	.464
*SLG	Gillespie, Cole, Helena	.548
XBH	Braun, Ryan, Brevard County/Huntsville	67

PITCHING #Minimum 75 innings

W	Gallardo, Yovani, Brevard County/Huntsville	11
	Hammond, Steven, Brevard County/Huntsville	11
	Sarfate, Dennis, Nashville	11
	Villanueva, Carlos, Huntsville/Nashville	11
L	Hammond, Steven, Brevard County/Huntsville	11
	Thurman, Corey, Nashville/Huntsville	11
#ERA	Gallardo, Yovani, Brevard County/Huntsville	1.86
G	Zumwalt, Alec, Huntsville/Nashville	58
CG	Fernandez, Jared, Nashville	4
SV	Zumwalt, Alec, Huntsville/Nashville	20
IP	Thurman, Corey, Nashville/Huntsville	168
BB	Sarfate, Dennis, Nashville	80
SO	Gallardo, Yovani, Brevard County/Huntsville	188
#AVG	Gallardo, Yovani, Brevard County/Huntsville	.192

Milwaukee Brewers — MLB

National League

BATTING	B-T	HT	WT	DOB	AVG	vLH	vRH	G	AB	R	H	2B	3B	HR	RBI	BB	HBP	SH	SF	SO	SB	CS	SLG	OBP
Anderson, Drew	L-R	6-2	195	6-9-81	.111	.000	.125	9	9	3	1	0	0	0	0	1	0	0	0	4	0	0	.111	.200
Barnwell, Chris	R-R	5-10	180	3-1-79	.067	.100	.050	13	30	2	2	0	0	0	1	1	0	0	0	6	1	0	.067	.097
Bell, David	R-R	5-10	195	9-14-72	.256	.302	.241	53	180	21	46	10	2	4	29	18	1	0	2	30	2	1	.400	.323
2-team (92 Philadelphia)					.270	—	—	145	504	60	136	27	4	10	63	50	4	3	5	68	3	1	.399	.337
Cirillo, Jeff	R-R	6-1	200	9-23-69	.319	.413	.282	112	263	33	84	16	0	3	23	21	1	3	2	33	1	1	.414	.369
Clark, Brady	R-R	6-2	205	4-18-73	.263	.273	.258	138	415	51	109	14	2	4	29	43	14	5	5	60	3	4	.335	.348
Fielder, Prince	L-R	6-0	260	5-9-84	.271	.247	.280	157	569	82	154	35	1	28	81	59	12	0	8	125	7	2	.483	.347
Graffanino, Tony	R-R	6-1	190	6-6-72	.280	.290	.276	60	236	34	66	17	3	2	27	20	4	0	1	37	2	0	.403	.345
Gross, Gabe	L-R	6-3	210	10-21-79	.274	.095	.294	117	208	42	57	15	0	9	38	36	2	3	3	60	1	0	.476	.382
Gwynn, Tony	L-R	6-0	185	10-4-82	.260	.167	.268	32	77	5	20	2	1	0	4	2	0	0	1	15	3	1	.312	.275
Hall, Bill	R-R	6-0	210	12-28-79	.270	.300	.261	148	537	101	145	39	4	35	85	63	1	3	4	162	8	9	.553	.345
Hardy, J.J.	R-R	6-2	190	8-19-82	.242	.294	.223	35	128	13	31	5	0	5	14	10	0	0	1	23	1	1	.398	.295
Hart, Corey	R-R	6-6	215	3-24-82	.283	.304	.272	87	237	32	67	13	2	9	33	17	0	0	2	58	5	8	.468	.328
Jenkins, Geoff	L-R	6-1	210	7-21-74	.271	.133	.306	147	484	62	131	26	1	17	70	56	11	0	4	129	4	1	.434	.357
Koskie, Corey	L-R	6-3	220	6-28-73	.261	.263	.260	76	257	29	67	23	0	12	33	29	3	0	0	58	1	2	.490	.343
Lee, Carlos	R-R	6-2	240	6-20-76	.286	.295	.283	102	388	60	111	18	0	28	81	38	2	0	7	39	12	2	.549	.347
Mench, Kevin	R-R	6-0	225	1-7-78	.230	.244	.224	40	126	9	29	6	1	1	18	4	0	0	3	17	0	0	.317	.248
Miller, Damian	R-R	6-3	220	10-13-69	.251	.280	.241	101	331	34	83	28	0	6	38	33	4	3	5	86	0	0	.390	.322
Moeller, Chad	R-R	6-3	215	2-18-75	.184	.211	.177	29	98	9	18	3	0	2	5	4	2	0	0	26	0	0	.276	.231
Nix, Laynce	L-L	6-0	200	10-30-80	.229	.000	.258	10	35	2	8	1	0	1	6	0	1	0	0	11	0	0	.343	.250
Rivera, Mike	R-R	6-0	210	9-8-76	.268	.226	.279	46	142	16	38	9	0	6	24	10	3	1	2	21	0	0	.458	.325
Rottino, Vinny	R-R	6-0	195	4-7-80	.214	.143	.286	9	14	1	3	1	0	0	1	1	0	0	0	2	1	0	.286	.267
Weeks, Rickie	R-R	6-0	205	9-13-82	.279	.271	.280	95	359	73	100	15	3	8	34	30	19	2	3	92	19	5	.404	.363

PITCHING	B-T	HT	WT	DOB	W	L	ERA	G	GS	CG	SV	IP	H	R	ER	HR	BB	SO	AVG	vLH	vRH	K/9	BB/9
Adams, Mike	R-R	6-5	190	7-29-78	0	0	11.57	2	0	0	0	2	4	3	3	1	2	1	.364	.000	.571	3.86	7.71
Bush, Dave	R-R	6-2	210	11-9-79	12	11	4.41	34	32	3	0	210	201	111	103	26	38	166	.252	.258	.246	7.11	1.63
Capellan, Jose	R-R	6-4	235	1-13-81	4	2	4.40	61	0	0	0	72	65	37	35	11	31	58	.244	.248	.242	7.28	3.89
Capuano, Chris	L-L	6-2	220	8-19-78	11	12	4.03	34	34	3	0	221	229	108	99	29	47	174	.265	.273	.264	7.08	1.91
Cordero, Francisco	R-R	6-2	235	5-11-75	3	1	1.69	28	0	0	16	27	20	5	5	2	16	30	.213	.297	.158	10.13	5.40
Davis, Doug	R-L	6-4	210	9-21-75	11	11	4.91	34	34	1	0	203	206	118	111	19	102	159	.266	.307	.253	7.04	4.51
De La Rosa, Jorge	L-L	6-1	210	4-5-81	2	2	8.60	18	3	0	0	30	32	30	29	4	22	31	.269	.154	.301	9.20	6.53
Demaria, Chris	R-R	6-3	210	9-28-80	0	1	5.93	10	0	0	0	14	10	11	9	4	9	11	.200	.263	.161	7.24	5.93
Eveland, Dana	L-L	6-1	250	10-29-83	0	3	8.13	9	5	0	0	28	39	25	25	4	16	32	.331	.421	.288	10.41	5.20
Fernandez, Jared	R-R	6-1	235	2-2-72	0	0	9.95	4	0	0	0	6	11	7	7	2	1	1	.367	.429	.313	1.42	1.42
Gonzalez, Geremi	R-R	6-0	220	1-8-75	4	2	5.14	21	1	0	0	42	50	31	24	6	17	36	.298	.464	.214	7.71	3.64
2-team (3 New York)					4	2	5.79	24	4	0	0	56	71	43	36	10	23	44	—	—	—	7.07	3.70
Helling, Rick	R-R	6-3	255	12-15-70	0	2	4.11	20	2	0	0	35	25	17	16	6	15	32	.202	.250	.171	8.23	3.86
Hendrickson, Ben	R-R	6-4	190	2-4-81	0	2	12.00	4	3	0	0	12	21	17	16	0	9	8	.382	.571	.265	6.00	6.75
Jackson, Zach	L-L	6-5	220	5-13-83	2	2	5.40	8	7	0	0	38	48	26	23	6	14	22	.304	.333	.294	5.17	3.29
Kolb, Dan	R-R	6-4	210	3-29-75	2	2	4.84	53	0	0	1	48	53	28	26	4	20	26	.282	.323	.260	4.84	3.72
Lehr, Justin	R-R	6-2	215	8-3-77	2	1	8.62	16	0	0	0	16	24	16	15	2	7	12	.369	.323	.412	6.89	4.02
Mabeus, Chris	R-R	6-3	235	2-11-79	0	0	21.60	1	0	0	0	2	4	4	4	1	3	2	.444	.000	.500	10.80	16.20
Ohka, Tomo	B-R	6-1	200	3-18-76	4	5	4.82	18	18	0	0	97	98	58	52	12	35	50	.266	.265	.266	4.64	3.25
Sarfate, Dennis	R-R	6-4	210	4-9-81	0	0	4.32	8	0	0	0	8	9	4	4	0	4	11	.265	.267	.263	11.88	4.32
Sheets, Ben	R-R	6-1	220	7-18-78	6	7	3.82	17	17	0	0	106	105	47	45	9	11	116	.259	.248	.266	9.85	0.93
Shouse, Brian	L-L	5-11	190	9-26-68	1	3	3.97	59	0	0	2	34	34	16	15	3	17	20	.264	.214	.322	5.29	4.50
Simpson, Allan	R-R	6-4	200	8-26-77	0	0	3.38	2	0	0	0	3	1	2	1	0	4	5	.111	.167	.000	16.88	13.50
Spurling, Chris	R-R	6-5	240	6-28-77	0	0	7.20	7	0	0	0	10	12	8	8	3	4	3	.286	.375	.167	2.70	3.60
Turnbow, Derrick	R-R	6-3	210	1-25-78	4	9	6.87	64	0	0	24	56	56	51	43	8	39	69	.255	.245	.263	11.02	6.23
Villanueva, Carlos	R-R	6-2	190	11-28-83	2	2	3.69	10	6	0	0	54	43	22	22	8	11	39	.216	.226	.204	6.54	1.84
Winkelsas, Joe	R-R	6-3	188	9-14-73	0	1	7.71	7	0	0	0	7	9	7	6	1	6	4	.310	.300	.316	5.14	7.71
Wise, Matt	R-R	6-4	200	11-18-75	5	6	3.86	40	0	0	0	44	45	24	19	6	14	27	.268	.206	.310	5.48	2.84

FIELDING

Catcher	PCT	G	PO	A	E	DP	PB
Miller	.997	98	648	44	2	4	3
Moeller	.995	29	192	15	1	0	0
Rivera	.988	44	299	31	4	2	0
Rottino	1.000	1	3	0	0	0	0

First Base	PCT	G	PO	A	E	DP
Cirillo	1.000	14	110	6	0	3
Fielder	.992	152	1259	88	11	113
Hart	.889	2	8	0	1	1

Second Base	PCT	G	PO	A	E	DP
Barnwell	.875	3	3	4	1	1
Cirillo	1.000	12	20	30	0	9
Graffanino	.987	57	111	119	3	20

	PCT	G	PO	A	E	DP	PB
Hall	1.000	4	6	9	0	1	
Weeks	.952	92	177	261	22	68	

Third Base	PCT	G	PO	A	E	DP
Barnwell	1.000	3	2	3	0	0
Bell	.965	53	28	110	5	4
Cirillo	.978	42	27	64	2	9
Hall	.909	11	5	15	2	2
Koskie	.967	70	54	151	7	11
Rottino	1.000	3	2	3	0	0

Shortstop	PCT	G	PO	A	E	DP
Barnwell	.960	5	13	11	1	3
Cirillo	1.000	3	4	3	0	2
Graffanino	1.000	4	4	13	0	3

	PCT	G	PO	A	E	DP
Hall	.967	127	173	321	17	56
Hardy	.986	32	51	91	2	25

Outfield	PCT	G	PO	A	E	DP
Anderson	1.000	2	1	0	0	0
Clark	.985	119	257	2	4	0
Gross	.984	59	121	6	2	1
Gwynn	1.000	19	42	1	0	0
Hall	1.000	7	11	1	0	0
Hart	.991	61	103	3	1	0
Jenkins	.977	133	247	6	6	2
Lee	.974	98	145	4	4	0
Mench	.985	38	64	1	1	0
Nix	1.000	9	20	0	0	0
Rottino	1.000	2	3	0	0	0

General manager: Doug Melvin. **Farm director:** Reid Nichols. **Scouting director:** Jack Zduriencik.

Class	Team	League	W	L	PCT	Finish*	Manager	Affiliate Since
Majors	Milwaukee	National	75	87	.463	13th (16)	Ned Yost	—
Triple-A	Nashville Sounds	Pacific Coast	76	68	.528	5th (16)	Frank Kremblas	2005
Double-A	Huntsville Stars	Southern	67	71	.486	6th (10)	Don Money	1999
High A	Brevard County Manatees	Florida State	64	65	.496	7th (12)	Ramon Aviles	2005
Low A	West Virginia Power	South Atlantic	74	62	.544	4th (16)	Mike Guerrero	2005
Rookie	Helena Brewers	Pioneer	34	42	.447	6th (8)	Eddie Sedar	2003
Rookie	AZL Brewers	Arizona	21	35	.375	8th (9)	Charlie Greene	2001
OVERALL 2006 MINOR LEAGUE RECORD			336	343	.495	18th (30)		

*Finish in overall standings (No. of teams in league). +League champion

Nashville Sounds — Triple-A

Pacific Coast League

BATTING	B-T	HT	WT	DOB	AVG	vLH	vRH	G	AB	R	H	2B	3B	HR	RBI	BB	HBP	SH	SF	SO	SB	CS	SLG	OBP
Abernathy, Brent	R-R	6-0	185	9-23-77	.287	.279	.290	123	439	63	126	16	0	5	42	40	1	4	58	18	10	.358	.345
Anderson, Drew	L-R	6-2	195	6-9-81	.333	.438	.298	16	63	15	21	5	1	1	9	2	0	3	1	12	3	1	.492	.348
Barnwell, Chris	R-R	5-10	180	3-1-79	.300	.314	.294	106	383	46	115	18	2	4	37	38	10	5	4	60	16	6	.389	.375
Beattie, Andrew	B-R	5-8	175	2-28-78	.259	.250	.262	33	116	13	30	3	1	3	18	16	0	0	0	28	3	1	.379	.348
2-team (44 Sacramento)					.264	—	—	77	276	42	73	12	2	9	48	39	0	1	5	58	6	3	.420	.350
Bibbs, Kennard	L-L	5-9	143	3-5-80	.218	.100	.246	67	156	19	34	5	0	1	13	17	3	3	0	29	9	2	.269	.307
Boscan, J.C.	R-R	6-2	215	12-26-79	.250	.000	.286	2	8	0	2	1	0	0	1	0	0	0	0	3	0	0	.375	.250
Chavez, Ozzie	B-R	6-1	159	7-31-83	.231	.278	.217	24	78	6	18	1	2	1	6	1	1	1	0	11	1	1	.333	.250
Clark, Jermaine	L-R	5-10	170	9-29-76	.235	.238	.234	121	375	57	88	13	2	5	37	48	1	0	5	72	33	6	.320	.319
Cruz, Enrique	R-R	6-1	205	11-21-81	.261	.286	.244	25	69	6	18	5	0	1	10	6	0	1	0	23	2	2	.377	.320
Cruz, Nelson	R-R	6-3	225	7-1-80	.302	.350	.284	104	371	68	112	22	1	20	73	42	6	0	4	100	17	6	.528	.378
Gwynn, Tony	L-R	6-0	185	10-4-82	.300	.321	.290	112	447	73	134	21	5	4	42	42	2	0	3	84	30	11	.396	.360
Hart, Corey	R-R	6-6	215	3-24-82	.320	.276	.338	26	100	19	32	10	1	4	21	12	1	0	2	25	11	2	.560	.391
Jaramillo, Milko	B-R	5-10	182	1-21-80	.176	.125	.222	8	17	1	3	0	0	0	3	2	0	0	0	5	3	0	.176	.263
Johnson, Mark	L-R	6-0	180	9-12-75	.203	.167	.212	48	143	14	29	7	0	2	10	14	2	2	1	31	1	0	.294	.281
Koonce, Graham	L-L	6-4	230	5-15-75	.256	.266	.252	88	297	44	76	16	1	19	52	51	3	0	3	79	2	1	.508	.367
Krynzel, Dave	L-L	6-1	180	11-7-81	.231	.227	.233	116	359	49	83	17	4	7	40	42	2	11	2	107	23	4	.359	.314
Moeller, Chad	R-R	6-3	215	2-18-75	.220	.216	.221	41	132	10	29	6	0	2	18	15	3	1	3	28	0	2	.311	.307
Nelson, Brad	L-R	6-2	220	12-23-82	.215	.188	.224	40	130	24	28	10	0	3	17	18	2	0	2	36	4	3	.362	.316
Nix, Laynce	L-L	6-0	200	10-30-80	.412	.700	.292	18	68	16	28	5	1	7	13	4	1	0	0	18	0	0	.824	.452
2-team (77 Oklahoma)					.297	—	—	95	354	55	105	19	2	17	68	22	7	1	3	95	4	1	.506	.347
Rivera, Mike	R-R	6-0	210	9-8-76	.296	.364	.257	60	213	30	63	11	0	10	46	13	4	0	6	40	3	3	.488	.339
Rottino, Vinny	R-R	6-0	195	4-7-80	.314	.377	.286	117	398	55	125	25	2	7	42	40	5	4	5	74	12	7	.440	.379
Sorensen, Zach	B-R	6-0	190	1-3-77	.262	.309	.231	75	202	21	53	7	1	2	22	26	1	13	3	44	5	4	.337	.345

PITCHING	B-T	HT	WT	DOB	W	L	ERA	G	GS	CG	SV	IP	H	R	ER	HR	BB	SO	AVG	vLH	vRH	K/9	BB/9
Adams, Mike	R-R	6-5	190	7-29-78	1	1	3.31	15	0	0	2	16	17	8	6	2	8	18	.274	.190	.317	9.92	4.41
2-team (17 Portland)					1	3	3.82	32	0	0	2	40	46	24	17	3	15	33	—	—	—	7.42	3.38
Barnwell, Chris	R-R	5-10	180	3-1-79	0	0	0.00	2	0	0	0	1	1	0	0	0	0	1	.500	1.000	.000	13.50	0.00
Bray, Steve	R-R	6-1	193	12-22-80	2	0	1.25	21	0	0	0	22	11	3	3	3	4	18	.149	.154	.146	7.48	1.66
Chavez, Wilton	R-R	6-2	165	6-13-78	3	1	3.64	27	3	0	0	54	51	26	22	6	26	47	.244	.198	.280	7.79	4.31
2-team (13 Iowa)					6	4	4.54	40	5	0	0	85	83	48	43	10	39	64	—	—	—	6.75	4.11
Clark, Jermaine	L-R	5-10	170	9-29-76	0	0	0.00	1	0	0	0	2	0	0	0	0	0	0	.000	.000	.000	0.00	0.00
Demaria, Chris	R-R	6-3	210	9-28-80	4	0	2.96	38	0	0	1	52	48	20	17	4	17	50	.242	.209	.268	8.71	2.96
Eveland, Dana	L-L	6-1	250	10-29-83	6	5	2.74	20	19	0	0	105	71	40	32	4	41	110	.191	.131	.208	9.43	3.51
Evert, Brett	R-R	6-6	200	10-23-81	1	1	6.55	13	1	0	0	22	25	17	16	5	12	19	.287	.367	.246	7.77	4.91
Fernandez, Jared	R-R	6-1	235	2-2-72	6	4	3.27	24	15	4	3	129	141	64	47	9	23	76	.274	.244	.296	5.29	1.60
Hackman, Luther	R-R	6-4	195	10-6-74	0	0	0.00	1	0	0	1	2	0	0	0	0	1	0	.000	.000	.000	0.00	4.50
Helling, Rick	R-R	6-3	255	12-15-70	1	0	3.75	2	2	0	0	12	9	5	5	0	2	6	.205	.318	.091	4.50	1.50
Hendrickson, Ben	R-R	6-4	190	2-4-81	9	8	3.36	23	23	1	0	139	121	60	52	9	46	97	.241	.231	.249	6.27	2.97
Jackson, Zach	L-L	6-5	220	5-13-83	4	6	4.12	18	18	1	0	107	106	55	49	11	44	58	.262	.247	.267	4.88	3.70
Kershner, Jason	L-L	6-2	190	12-19-76	3	2	3.48	23	0	0	2	34	41	13	13	1	9	25	.306	.395	.271	6.68	2.41
Lehr, Justin	R-R	6-2	215	8-3-77	4	7	3.94	19	17	0	0	112	120	53	49	15	31	90	.278	.254	.301	7.23	2.49
Mabeus, Chris	R-R	6-3	235	2-11-79	1	0	5.68	6	0	0	0	6	7	4	4	1	5	6	.280	.364	.214	8.53	7.11
2-team (12 Sacramento)					1	1	4.85	18	0	0	0	26	23	19	14	2	15	26	—	—	—	9.00	5.19
Meyers, Mike	R-R	6-2	210	10-18-77	4	5	3.43	28	3	0	0	66	53	26	25	5	24	66	.223	.226	.221	9.05	3.29
Sarfate, Dennis	R-R	6-4	210	4-9-81	10	7	3.67	34	21	0	0	125	125	63	51	7	78	117	.265	.312	.230	8.42	5.62
Sheets, Ben	R-R	6-1	220	7-18-78	2	1	2.40	3	3	0	0	15	9	4	4	1	5	15	.173	.167	.179	9.00	3.00
Simpson, Allan	R-R	6-4	200	8-26-77	2	4	3.34	42	0	0	10	57	45	26	21	7	27	53	.223	.267	.197	8.42	4.29
Stetter, Mitch	L-L	6-4	195	1-16-81	2	5	4.46	51	0	0	0	38	38	20	19	3	16	36	.271	.230	.318	8.45	3.76
Thompson, Justin	L-L	6-4	210	3-8-73	2	3	6.11	8	8	1	0	35	44	27	24	7	7	23	.291	.211	.319	5.86	1.78
Thurman, Corey	R-R	6-1	235	11-5-78	1	1	13.50	2	0	0	0	8	15	12	12	2	3	7	.429	.529	.333	7.88	3.38
Villanueva, Carlos	R-R	6-2	190	11-28-83	7	1	2.71	11	9	1	0	66	42	20	20	6	26	61	.182	.235	.140	8.28	3.53
Winkelsas, Joe	R-R	6-3	188	9-14-73	1	3	5.06	6	0	0	1	11	11	6	6	0	2	7	.268	.222	.304	5.91	1.69
Zumwalt, Alec	R-R	6-2	205	1-20-81	0	3	3.69	40	0	0	15	39	37	18	16	6	15	45	.247	.232	.255	10.38	3.46

FIELDING

Catcher	PCT	G	PO	A	E	DP	PB
Boscan	1.000	2	14	2	0	0	1
Johnson	.997	45	311	16	1	0	11
Moeller	.986	38	248	34	4	3	5
Rivera	.985	51	351	42	6	2	7

	PCT	G	PO	A	E	DP	
Rottino	.970	18	117	13	4	4	2

First Base	PCT	G	PO	A	E	DP
Abernathy	1.000	30	229	15	0	17
Hart	1.000	5	35	2	0	4

	PCT	G	PO	A	E	DP
Koonce	.994	78	674	46	4	60
Krynzel	1.000	1	6	0	0	0
Nelson	1.000	34	283	22	0	30
Rivera	1.000	6	35	5	0	2
Rottino	1.000	2	23	2	0	0

Sorensen..........1.000 3 7 0 0 1

Second Base	PCT	G	PO	A	E	DP
Abernathy	.983	39	62	116	3	22
Beattie	.977	18	34	52	2	9
Clark	.988	55	89	164	3	37
Cruz	1.000	3	6	3	0	1
Jaramillo	1.000	3	5	5	0	1
Sorensen	1.000	38	58	98	0	19

Third Base	PCT	G	PO	A	E	DP
Beattie	.962	13	4	21	1	1
Clark	.977	36	17	67	2	8
Cruz	.900	15	8	19	3	1

Jaramillo 1.000 2 1 4 0 0
Rivera............... — 1 0 0 0 0
Rottino .945 85 56 167 13 15
Sorensen .905 8 4 15 2 1

Shortstop	PCT	G	PO	A	E	DP
Barnwell	.979	106	178	323	11	74
Chavez	1.000	22	29	59	0	12
Clark	.975	13	14	25	1	2
Cruz	.850	5	9	8	3	2
Sorensen	1.000	6	10	9	0	3

Outfield	PCT	G	PO	A	E	DP
Abernathy	.950	29	34	4	2	0

Anderson..........1.000 14 27 0 0 0
Beattie 1.000 2 4 1 0 0
Bibbs 1.000 46 61 4 0 0
Clark 1.000 6 5 1 0 0
Cruz .960 95 187 4 8 2
Gwynn .981 107 247 5 5 0
Hart .964 22 27 0 1 0
Johnson 1.000 1 2 0 0 0
Krynzel .971 102 163 6 5 1
Meyers — 1 0 0 0 0
Nix 1.000 15 27 0 0 0
Rottino 1.000 14 19 1 0 0
Sorensen 1.000 10 17 0 0 0

Huntsville Stars — Double-A
Southern League

BATTING	B-T	HT	WT	DOB	AVG	vLH	vRH	G	AB	R	H	2B	3B	HR	RBI	BB	HBP	SH	SF	SO	SB	CS	SLG	OBP
Acuna, Ron	R-R	6-0	215	6-30-79	.268	.274	.263	113	400	47	107	18	3	1	51	27	5	2	5	79	3	6	.335	.318
Anderson, Drew	L-R	6-2	195	6-9-81	.291	.319	.277	108	402	60	117	24	4	6	43	39	5	4	2	80	17	8	.415	.359
Bibbs, Kennard	L-L	5-9	143	3-5-80	.245	.222	.250	33	98	9	24	4	1	0	7	14	0	0	1	13	8	3	.306	.336
Boscan, J.C.	R-R	6-2	215	12-26-79	.194	.238	.171	43	124	7	24	7	0	0	14	11	1	1	3	38	0	1	.250	.259
Braun, Ryan	R-R	6-2	200	11-17-83	.303	.341	.279	59	231	42	70	19	1	15	40	21	3	1	1	46	12	0	.589	.367
Chavez, Ozzie	B-R	6-1	159	7-31-83	.259	.277	.249	96	320	32	83	15	3	1	33	35	2	8	3	53	6	4	.334	.333
Corporan, Carlos	B-R	6-3	210	1-7-84	.333	.500	.063	3	9	2	3	0	0	0	1	0	0	0	0	3	0	0	.333	.333
Crabbe, Callix	B-R	5-7	171	2-14-83	.267	.240	.283	129	472	59	126	18	2	5	46	71	7	16	5	62	32	13	.345	.368
Eure, Jeffrey	R-R	6-1	215	8-17-80	.253	.198	.289	107	332	44	84	18	1	12	54	21	5	2	1	87	4	4	.422	.306
Ezi, Travis	B-L	6-0	175	9-5-81	.226	.236	.221	72	168	27	38	4	3	2	18	19	3	2	1	56	8	4	.321	.314
Heether, Adam	R-R	6-0	190	1-14-82	.213	.226	.206	70	244	21	52	6	0	1	18	26	1	1	1	51	1	1	.250	.290
Jaramillo, Milko	B-R	5-10	182	1-21-80	.154	.136	.167	20	52	3	8	0	1	0	1	2	1	0	0	11	0	0	.192	.200
Katin, Brendan	R-R	6-1	235	1-28-83	.224	.296	.161	15	58	11	13	2	0	4	8	1	1	0	0	11	0	0	.466	.333
Lee, Carlos	R-R	6-1	220	9-29-81	.242	.143	.269	21	33	4	8	0	1	1	7	1	1	0	1	8	1	0	.333	.278
2-team (2 Birmingham)					.225	—		23	40	4	9	0	1	1	9	2	1	0	1	10	1	1	.300	.273
Moss, Steve	R-R	6-2	185	1-24-84	.242	.272	.222	131	484	68	117	27	1	7	43	71	3	4	2	136	7	12	.345	.341
Nelson, Brad	L-R	6-2	220	12-23-82	.264	.297	.247	80	265	47	70	14	1	6	39	63	0	4		62	6	3	.392	.401
Palmisano, Lou	R-R	6-1	185	9-16-82	.241	.254	.234	99	332	39	80	17	1	4	37	48	2	8	3	65	2	0	.334	.338
Rodriguez, Guilder	B-R	6-0	151	7-24-83	.219	.210	.224	69	160	21	35	3	1	0	7	22	3	5	0	31	2	1	.250	.324
Sain, Greg	R-R	6-2	218	12-26-79	.171	.195	.159	41	129	17	22	3	0	8	25	15	1	0	0	49	3	0	.380	.262

PITCHING	B-T	HT	WT	DOB	W	L	ERA	G	GS	CG	SV	IP	H	R	ER	HR	BB	SO	AVG	vLH	vRH	K/9	BB/9
Acuna, Ron	R-R	6-0	215	6-30-79	0	0	4.50	1	0	0	0	2	2	1	1	0	0	1	.286	—	.286	4.50	0.00
Ballouli, Khalid	R-R	6-2	188	3-20-80	2	4	4.15	23	7	0	1	56	59	37	26	4	20	52	.271	.314	.242	8.31	3.20
Bray, Steve	R-R	6-1	193	12-22-80	5	4	2.70	29	2	0	1	63	57	19	19	4	7	57	.241	.293	.207	8.10	0.99
Capellan, Jose	R-R	6-4	235	1-13-81	0	0	0.00	1	1	0	0	1	0	0	0	0	0	2	.000	.000	.000	18.00	0.00
De La Rosa, Jorge	L-L	6-1	210	4-5-81	3	1	2.40	6	6	0	0	30	31	12	8	1	3	23	.277	.355	.247	6.90	0.90
Dillard, Tim	B-R	6-4	228	7-19-83	10	7	3.15	29	25	1	0	163	167	76	57	10	36	108	.261	.269	.255	5.96	1.99
Eure, Jeffrey	R-R	6-1	215	8-17-80	0	0	0.00	1	0	0	1	1	1	0	0	0	0	2	.250	—	.250	18.00	0.00
Evert, Brett	L-R	6-6	200	10-23-80	0	4	2.65	14	0	0	0	17	14	5	5	3	7	13	.237	.333	.184	6.88	3.71
Gallardo, Yovani	R-R	6-3	215	2-27-86	5	2	1.63	13	13	0	0	77	50	19	14	2	28	85	.187	.194	.183	9.89	3.26
Hackman, Luther	R-R	6-4	195	10-6-74	3	0	0.66	8	0	0	0	14	9	1	1	1	0	15	.188	.176	.194	9.88	0.00
Hammond, Steven	R-L	6-2	205	4-30-82	5	6	2.93	13	13	1	0	74	63	29	24	7	25	58	.229	.234	.227	7.09	3.05
Housman, Jeff	L-L	6-3	180	8-4-81	3	3	3.67	12	11	0	0	56	56	23	23	1	19	44	.271	.260	.274	7.03	3.04
Jones, Mike	R-R	6-4	200	4-23-83	0	0	0.00	1	1	0	0	4	1	0	0	0	3	3	.083	.091	.091	6.75	6.75
Mabeus, Chris	R-R	6-3	235	2-11-79	1	2	6.04	18	1	0	0	22	21	15	15	1	20	15	.256	.250	.259	6.04	8.06
Meyers, Mike	R-R	6-2	210	10-18-77	1	1	6.75	4	0	0	0	7	10	6	5	0	6	5	.345	.500	.304	6.75	4.05
Parra, Manuel	L-L	6-3	200	10-30-82	2	7	2.87	6	6	0	0	31	26	13	10	4	8	23	.232	.179	.250	8.33	2.30
Phelps, Travis	R-R	6-2	170	7-25-77	5	8	3.54	31	9	0	5	86	75	43	34	7	40	79	.234	.304	.202	8.24	4.17
Pratt, Andy	L-L	6-0	180	8-27-79	1	2	5.64	16	0	0	0	22	26	19	14	3	11	17	.295	.233	.328	6.85	4.43
Rohlicek, Russ	R-L	6-6	230	12-26-79	0	2	4.50	14	0	0	0	34	32	20	17	3	16	33	.252	.260	.247	8.74	4.24
Sheets, Ben	R-R	6-1	220	7-18-78	0	0	3.38	1	1	0	0	3	4	2	1	0	0	5	.308	.200	.375	16.88	0.00
Simpson, Gerrit	R-R	6-3	200	12-18-79	3	3	2.61	51	1	0	0	76	62	27	22	7	24	59	.224	.215	.228	6.99	2.84
Smith, Matt	R-R	6-5	240	3-18-83	0	4	6.84	13	2	0	1	25	36	24	19	3	11	14	.346	.432	.299	5.04	3.96
Thatcher, Joe	L-L	6-2	203	4-10-81	1	0	1.69	4	0	0	0	5	2	1	1	0	2	6	.111	.333	.000	10.13	3.38
Thurman, Corey	R-R	6-1	235	11-5-78	5	9	2.96	24	24	0	0	140	129	56	46	8	42	124	.249	.258	.243	7.97	2.70
Valentine, Joe	R-R	6-2	210	10-24-79	2	2	2.97	22	0	0	13	30	26	11	10	3	8	23	.234	.231	.236	6.82	2.37
Villanueva, Carlos	R-R	6-2	190	11-28-83	4	5	3.75	11	10	1	0	62	60	31	26	6	14	59	.247	.194	.286	8.52	2.02
Winkelsas, Joe	R-R	6-3	188	9-14-73	1	1	1.72	13	0	0	4	16	15	3	3	1	2	15	.242	.308	.194	8.62	1.15
Yeatman, Matt	R-R	6-4	230	8-2-82	5	2	4.63	40	5	0	1	70	87	39	36	9	37	57	.314	.308	.317	7.33	4.76
Zumwalt, Alec	R-R	6-2	205	1-20-81	1	0	2.93	10	0	0	5	15	14	5	5	2	5	14	.241	.217	.257	8.22	2.93

FIELDING

Catcher	PCT	G	PO	A	E	DP	PB
Boscan	.987	40	284	24	4	5	3
Corporan	.958	3	21	2	1	1	0
Eure	1.000	5	25	1	0	0	2
Lee	1.000	2	14	2	0	1	0
Palmisano	.993	96	708	50	5	6	6

First Base	PCT	G	PO	A	E	DP
Acuna	1.000	1	3	0	0	0
Chavez	1.000	1	1	0	0	0
Corporan	1.000	1	1	0	0	0
Crabbe	1.000	1	1	0	0	0
Eure	.990	50	387	25	4	33
Nelson	.995	67	518	49	3	47

Sain .977 26 195 17 5 22

Second Base	PCT	G	PO	A	E	DP
Crabbe	.978	128	237	352	13	85
Eure	—	1	0	0	0	0
Jaramillo	1.000	2	1	5	0	1
Rodriguez	1.000	14	18	18	0	2

Third Base	PCT	G	PO	A	E	DP
Braun	.869	57	30	76	16	7
Eure	.867	19	4	22	4	1
Heether	.948	67	43	122	9	9
Rodriguez	1.000	1	2	1	0	0

Shortstop	PCT	G	PO	A	E	DP
Chavez	.962	95	137	272	16	51

Eure 1.000 2 2 5 0 1
Jaramillo .872 12 12 29 6 6
Rodriguez .978 44 52 127 4 28

Outfield	PCT	G	PO	A	E	DP
Acuna	1.000	104	179	19	0	5
Anderson	.987	105	214	7	3	1
Bibbs	1.000	26	44	6	0	1
Eure	.900	7	9	0	1	0
Ezi	.979	47	89	3	2	1
Katin	.867	13	12	1	2	0
Moss	.990	125	283	6	3	2
Nelson	1.000	4	7	0	0	0

Florida State League

BATTING	B-T	HT	WT	DOB	AVG	vLH	vRH	G	AB	R	H	2B	3B	HR	RBI	BB	HBP	SH	SF	SO	SB	CS	SLG	OBP
Braun, Ryan	R-R	6-2	200	11-17-83	.274	.302	.268	59	226	34	62	12	2	7	37	23	4	3	4	54	14	4	.438	.346
Corporan, Carlos	B-R	6-3	210	1-7-84	.270	.269	.270	86	282	29	76	14	0	3	38	13	10	5	3	45	0	2	.351	.321
Corredor, Nestor	R-R	6-1	180	5-25-84	.183	.231	.172	22	71	5	13	2	0	0	6	4	0	1	0	14	0	0	.211	.227
Crew, Ryan	R-R	6-0	175	8-31-83	.296	.277	.304	61	223	33	66	11	2	1	14	27	1	0	2	34	5	1	.377	.372
De La Cruz, Carlos	R-R	6-3	175	3-1-82	.167	.250	.115	17	42	6	7	3	0	1	4	4	0	2	0	11	0	0	.310	.239
Escobar, Alcides	R-R	6-1	155	12-16-86	.257	.253	.259	87	350	47	90	9	1	2	33	19	3	7	7	56	28	8	.306	.296
Ezi, Travis	B-L	6-0	175	9-5-81	.300	.478	.262	33	130	27	39	7	5	2	14	9	4	1	0	29	13	3	.477	.364
Fermaint, Charlie	R-R	5-9	180	10-11-85	.276	.283	.273	110	424	67	117	20	4	7	33	42	8	1	4	119	27	14	.392	.349
Heether, Adam	R-R	6-0	190	1-14-82	.217	.178	.231	49	166	20	36	10	0	3	16	25	4	0	2	37	0	0	.331	.330
Hopf, J.R.	L-R	6-1	205	11-4-82	.333	.000	.500	1	3	0	1	1	0	0	1	0	0	0	0	1	0	0	.667	.333
Iribarren, Hernan	L-R	6-1	160	6-29-84	.319	.310	.322	108	398	50	127	12	4	2	50	39	1	11	6	57	19	15	.384	.376
Jaramillo, Milko	B-R	5-10	182	1-21-80	.256	.250	.261	12	39	3	10	1	0	1	3	2	1	1	0	4	0	0	.359	.310
Katin, Brendan	R-R	6-1	235	1-28-83	.289	.330	.278	116	450	64	130	34	3	13	75	34	9	0	3	112	4	6	.464	.349
McKnight, Scott	L-R	6-1	155	12-22-84	.198	.231	.191	26	81	9	16	1	0	0	3	6	1	6	0	31	1	2	.210	.261
Medlin, C.J.	R-R	6-2	210	3-3-82	.220	.236	.212	49	159	12	35	6	0	2	19	25	3	0	1	58	1	0	.296	.335
Murray, Josh	R-R	6-1	193	8-12-84	.211	.296	.176	29	95	13	20	2	0	2	6	12	3	1	1	32	0	0	.295	.315
Parejo, Freddy	R-R	6-2	175	10-16-84	.236	.258	.228	107	347	42	82	18	3	6	48	21	2	9	6	57	14	6	.349	.279
Phillips, Kyle	L-R	6-3	235	4-3-84	.236	.313	.214	58	216	13	51	4	0	3	35	21	1	2	2	40	1	1	.296	.304
Rasheed, Hasan	L-L	5-8	170	1-26-84	.238	.222	.239	51	160	18	38	1	1	0	12	22	0	3	0	53	4	3	.256	.330
Rodriguez, Guilder	B-R	6-0	151	7-24-83	.143	.500	.000	5	7	1	1	0	0	0	0	1	0	0	0	1	0	0	.143	.250
Sollmann, Steven	R-R	5-11	195	4-1-82	.284	.256	.293	97	345	51	98	16	0	1	38	45	19	6	2	37	13	4	.339	.394
Yost IV, Ned	R-R	6-2	195	7-8-82	.139	.045	.175	24	79	11	11	3	0	1	6	8	1	0	1	23	0	1	.215	.225

PITCHING	B-T	HT	WT	DOB	W	L	ERA	G	GS	CG	SV	IP	H	R	ER	HR	BB	SO	AVG	vLH	vRH	K/9	BB/9
Alliston, Josh	R-R	6-5	232	2-29-80	5	3	2.28	38	0	0	9	43	36	13	11	0	11	40	.220	.211	.226	8.31	2.28
Gallardo, Yovani	R-R	6-3	215	2-27-86	6	3	2.09	13	13	0	0	78	54	24	18	4	23	103	.196	.185	.207	11.94	2.67
Hall, Bo	R-R	6-0	187	9-5-80	5	5	5.77	36	3	0	1	83	86	58	53	15	28	102	.260	.244	.270	11.10	3.05
Hammond, Steven	R-L	6-2	205	4-30-82	6	5	2.53	14	14	0	0	85	68	32	24	7	23	70	.215	.213	.216	7.38	2.43
Harmsen, Brandon	R-R	6-3	205	12-13-81	1	0	5.51	10	0	0	1	16	13	10	10	1	11	19	.210	.250	.176	10.47	6.06
Hinton, Robert	R-R	6-2	190	8-13-84	5	4	3.31	36	6	0	2	90	88	40	33	6	26	95	.255	.246	.261	9.54	2.61
Johnson, Dave	R-R	6-5	205	8-25-82	7	6	4.16	41	0	0	1	89	92	51	41	8	32	77	.268	.254	.277	7.82	3.25
Jones, Mike	R-R	6-4	200	4-23-83	0	2	2.80	19	13	0	0	55	45	19	17	1	27	30	.226	.222	.228	4.94	4.45
Lewis, Jeremy	R-L	6-4	180	9-12-80	2	6	3.65	43	1	0	6	69	71	32	28	3	25	64	.273	.192	.305	8.35	3.26
Miller, Derek	L-L	6-0	195	11-8-81	1	3	3.91	9	7	0	0	46	39	23	20	2	19	43	.234	.200	.242	8.41	3.72
Narron, Sam	L-L	6-7	200	7-12-81	2	4	3.25	18	9	0	1	55	48	21	20	5	15	46	.235	.211	.241	7.48	2.44
Ohka, Tomo	B-R	6-3	200	3-18-76	1	0	0.00	2	2	0	0	11	12	2	0	0	1	10	.273	.136	.409	8.44	0.84
Parra, Manuel	L-L	6-3	200	10-30-82	1	3	2.96	15	14	0	0	55	47	29	18	4	32	61	.235	.226	.237	10.04	5.27
Pena, Luis	R-R	6-5	190	1-10-83	4	6	4.41	23	11	0	1	65	68	34	32	6	33	59	.274	.245	.295	8.13	4.55
Rogers, Mark	R-R	6-2	205	1-30-86	1	2	5.07	16	16	0	0	71	68	46	40	6	53	96	.253	.267	.244	12.17	6.72
Stanczyk, Ben	R-R	6-2	210	9-26-82	8	4	4.54	39	0	0	1	81	91	45	41	5	22	82	.286	.279	.290	9.07	2.43
Thatcher, Joe	L-L	6-2	203	4-10-81	3	1	0.29	16	0	0	2	31	12	6	1	1	9	32	.119	.125	.117	9.39	2.64
Wahpepah, Joshua	R-R	6-4	185	7-17-84	6	8	4.49	24	20	0	1	100	104	55	50	9	58	64	.266	.265	.267	5.74	5.20

FIELDING

Catcher	PCT	G	PO	A	E	DP	PB
Corporan	.987	53	429	39	6	4	7
Corredor	.991	21	189	23	2	4	4
Hopf	.889	1	8	0	1	0	0
Medlin	.988	39	305	23	4	3	4
Phillips	1.000	20	165	9	0	1	3

First Base	PCT	G	PO	A	E	DP
Corporan	.993	15	120	15	1	9
De La Cruz	1.000	3	22	4	0	2
Murray	.984	16	121	4	2	8
Sollmann	.998	75	580	35	1	47
Yost IV	1.000	23	177	16	0	17

Second Base	PCT	G	PO	A	E	DP
Crew	1.000	5	7	10	0	0

	PCT	G	PO	A	E	DP
De La Cruz	1.000	1	1	0	0	0
Iribarren	.971	105	215	253	14	52
Jaramillo	.979	8	13	34	1	8
Rodriguez	1.000	3	6	8	0	3
Sollmann	.959	11	19	28	2	5

Third Base	PCT	G	PO	A	E	DP
Braun	.907	58	38	108	15	7
Crew	.867	11	7	19	4	2
De La Cruz	.750	1	3	0	1	0
Heether	.967	49	24	92	4	11
Murray	.789	8	5	10	4	1
Sollmann	.700	5	0	7	3	0

Shortstop	PCT	G	PO	A	E	DP
Crew	1.000	5	8	13	0	1

	PCT	G	PO	A	E	DP
De La Cruz	.939	8	6	25	2	5
Escobar	.941	80	138	199	21	44
Jaramillo	.950	4	10	9	1	3
McKnight	.924	26	28	57	7	6
Murray	1.000	3	3	5	0	0
Sollmann	.893	6	10	15	3	4

Outfield	PCT	G	PO	A	E	DP
Crew	.946	34	48	5	3	0
Ezi	.930	26	40	0	3	0
Fermaint	.983	110	223	6	4	2
Katin	.959	87	132	7	6	2
Parejo	.977	103	163	9	4	1
Rasheed	1.000	33	46	0	0	0

South Atlantic League

BATTING	B-T	HT	WT	DOB	AVG	vLH	vRH	G	AB	R	H	2B	3B	HR	RBI	BB	HBP	SH	SF	SO	SB	CS	SLG	OBP
Barba, Ryan	R-R	6-0	190	12-6-84	.191	.240	.176	32	110	13	21	3	1	0	13	5	3	3	1	23	1	0	.236	.244
Bell, Mike	R-R	6-0	185	3-30-85	.277	.350	.248	116	430	77	119	32	5	12	68	42	6	5	4	72	9	6	.458	.346
Bernal, Hector	L-R	5-11	175	6-14-86	.206	.375	.154	13	34	4	7	1	0	0	3	0	0	0	4	0	0	.235	.270
Brantley, Michael	L-L	6-2	180	5-15-87	.300	.340	.285	108	360	47	108	10	2	0	42	61	4	5	5	51	24	7	.339	.402
Cain, Lorenzo	R-R	6-2	165	4-13-86	.307	.294	.313	132	527	91	162	36	4	6	60	58	11	2	5	104	34	11	.425	.384
Chapman, Stephen	L-L	6-0	180	10-12-85	.176	.000	.231	7	17	3	3	0	0	0	1	1	0	0	0	6	0	1	.176	.222
Corredor, Nestor	R-R	6-1	180	5-25-84	.269	.333	.245	40	130	17	35	6	0	2	9	4	3	1	1	27	3	0	.362	.304
Crew, Ryan	R-R	6-0	175	8-31-83	.280	.302	.275	62	232	29	65	15	1	2	23	22	0	1	2	37	8	4	.379	.340
Festa, John	L-R	6-2	200	12-1-80	.290	.279	.294	110	372	55	108	19	2	6	60	42	12	3	3	56	4	6	.401	.378
Ford, Darren	R-R	6-1	195	10-1-85	.283	.273	.286	125	491	93	139	24	3	7	54	56	4	14	1	133	69	15	.387	.361
Gamel, Mat	L-R	6-0	205	7-26-85	.288	.325	.276	129	493	65	142	28	5	17	88	52	5	0	5	81	9	2	.469	.359
Holmberg, Kenneth	R-R	5-9	175	2-21-83	.235	.190	.253	72	221	34	52	15	0	7	36	41	4	2	7	49	3	3	.398	.362
McKnight, Scott	L-R	6-1	155	12-22-84	.294	.143	.318	18	51	11	15	2	1	0	8	4	1	1	0	17	0	1	.373	.357
Salome, Angel	R-R	5-7	190	6-8-86	.292	.287	.293	105	418	63	122	31	2	10	85	39	2	0	8	63	7	3	.447	.349
Willcutt, Bradley	R-R	6-1	220	2-18-82	.229	.231	.228	44	118	15	27	8	0	1	12	20	3	1	2	29	1	1	.322	.350

ORGANIZATION STATISTICS

	B-T	HT	WT	DOB	AVG	vLH	vRH	G	AB	R	H	2B	3B	HR	RBI	BB	HBP	SH	SF	SO	SB	CS	SLG	OBP
Yoho, Nathan	L-R	5-11	190	12-21-82	.188	.194	.187	80	239	26	45	5	2	3	21	17	2	6	1	43	5	2	.264	.247
Yost IV, Ned	R-R	6-2	195	7-8-82	.287	.352	.263	93	331	48	95	21	6	6	46	33	5	3	6	87	7	3	.441	.355

PITCHING	B-T	HT	WT	DOB	W	L	ERA	G	GS	CG	SV	IP	H	R	ER	HR	BB	SO	AVG	vLH	vRH	K/9	BB/9
Cordero, Julian	L-L	6-0	165	9-28-84	1	0	7.82	5	1	0	0	13	20	11	11	2	5	12	.385	.500	.364	8.53	3.55
Ferguson, Shawn	R-R	6-2	205	1-12-83	2	3	6.69	9	9	0	0	36	34	27	27	3	27	31	.254	.178	.292	7.68	6.69
Festa, Tony	L-R	6-2	200	12-1-80	0	0	0.00	1	0	0	0	1	0	0	0	1	0	0	.000	.000	.000	9.00	0.00
Garrison, Steve	B-L	6-1	185	9-12-86	7	6	3.45	17	16	0	0	89	86	38	34	10	22	77	.253	.260	.251	7.82	2.23
Inman, Will	R-R	6-0	200	2-6-87	10	2	1.71	23	20	0	0	111	75	22	21	3	24	134	.190	.185	.194	10.90	1.95
Kretzschmar, Matt	R-R	6-3	215	8-2-86	4	4	5.90	23	13	0	0	76	90	60	50	6	49	56	.296	.262	.320	6.60	5.78
Laureano, Wilfrido	R-R	6-6	165	3-4-84	3	2	4.10	29	0	0	1	64	54	32	29	8	36	62	.223	.258	.201	8.76	5.09
2-team (7 Lakewood)					6	3	4.10	36	2	0	1	85	75	42	39	9	40	75	—	—	—	7.88	4.20
Llueres, Rafael	L-L	6-4	155	9-21-84	4	7	3.72	28	16	0	0	114	106	61	47	11	59	62	.251	.304	.234	4.91	4.67
Louis, Joshua	R-R	6-2	220	3-9-85	1	1	4.88	13	0	0	0	24	22	15	13	1	14	15	.253	.250	.255	5.63	5.25
Malave, Ronny	R-R	6-1	181	1-1-86	3	1	3.74	11	3	0	2	34	44	22	14	3	6	15	.301	.313	.296	4.01	1.60
Marion, Ryan	R-R	6-1	215	9-23-84	1	1	8.58	24	2	0	1	43	56	45	41	4	37	42	.318	.284	.343	8.79	7.74
Miller, Derek	L-L	6-0	195	11-8-81	8	2	3.57	18	18	1	0	93	93	41	37	6	34	105	.257	.250	.259	10.13	3.28
Palazzolo, Steve	R-R	6-10	260	3-31-82	1	0	8.25	10	0	0	0	12	18	11	11	4	1	9	.360	.267	.400	6.75	0.75
Parillo, Brandon	L-L	5-10	185	9-22-85	3	1	6.31	11	3	0	0	26	30	22	18	0	17	23	.286	.304	.280	6.06	5.96
Pawelczyk, Kyle	R-R	6-5	200	11-18-81	0	0	2.70	3	0	0	0	3	5	2	1	0	1	4	.333	.400	.300	10.80	2.70
Renkert, Dane	R-R	6-1	210	10-17-81	5	8	3.40	48	0	0	6	77	74	44	29	3	23	62	.254	.170	.307	7.28	2.70
Roberts, Kevin	R-R	6-0	190	5-15-84	6	10	4.51	39	13	0	8	104	92	61	52	8	51	102	.237	.219	.248	8.86	4.43
Ryan, Patrick	R-R	6-0	200	5-31-83	5	2	1.87	45	0	0	2	92	77	26	19	4	27	73	.230	.169	.271	7.17	2.65
Thatcher, Joe	L-L	6-2	203	4-10-81	1	3	2.43	26	0	0	10	30	28	13	8	2	6	42	.243	.120	.278	12.74	1.82
Welch, David	R-L	6-4	215	6-2-83	8	6	2.41	25	16	1	1	101	75	32	27	8	23	85	.207	.156	.224	7.60	2.06
Willcutt, Bradley	R-R	6-1	220	2-18-82	0	0	0.00	1	0	0	0	1	0	0	0	0	0	0	.000	.000	.000	0.00	0.00
Wooley, Robert	R-R	6-1	190	12-7-84	1	3	4.86	13	6	0	0	37	45	30	20	3	21	14	.304	.327	.292	3.41	5.11

FIELDING

Catcher	PCT	G	PO	A	E	DP	PB
Corredor	.981	40	284	29	6	3	3
Salome	.975	76	541	55	15	3	17
Willcutt	.982	29	201	15	4	1	2

	PCT	G	PO	A	E	DP	PB
Crew	.964	40	71	116	7	31	
Festa	1.000	1	2	1	0	1	
Holmberg	.951	51	71	103	9	27	
McKnight	1.000	2	4	3	0	1	

	PCT	G	PO	A	E	DP	PB
Crew	.931	23	31	64	7	17	
Holmberg	1.000	2	4	4	0	0	
McKnight	.982	15	18	37	1	9	

First Base	PCT	G	PO	A	E	DP
Festa	.991	66	495	48	5	56
Willcutt	1.000	3	7	0	0	0
Yost IV	.993	68	573	21	4	64

Second Base	PCT	G	PO	A	E	DP
Bell	.964	44	79	108	7	27
Bernal	1.000	10	16	18	0	6

Third Base	PCT	G	PO	A	E	DP
Festa	.942	28	20	61	5	7
Gamel	.890	109	63	212	34	20

Shortstop	PCT	G	PO	A	E	DP
Barba	.928	32	49	80	10	18
Bell	.898	70	118	181	34	48
Bernal	.714	2	3	2	2	0

Outfield	PCT	G	PO	A	E	DP
Bell	—	1	0	0	0	0
Brantley	.989	108	172	3	2	1
Cain	.960	129	276	15	12	6
Chapman	1.000	5	6	0	0	0
Crew	1.000	2	4	0	0	0
Ford	.974	119	289	6	8	2
Yoho	.963	50	76	2	3	0
Yost IV	1.000	5	5	0	0	0

Helena Brewers — Rookie

Pioneer League

BATTING	B-T	HT	WT	DOB	AVG	vLH	vRH	G	AB	R	H	2B	3B	HR	RBI	BB	HBP	SH	SF	SO	SB	CS	SLG	OBP
Bouchie, Andy	R-R	6-1	205	8-6-85	.265	.188	.286	61	223	42	59	11	1	7	46	42	2	0	1	53	2	3	.417	.384
Caufield, Charles	R-R	6-1	180	7-6-83	.262	.218	.275	58	248	37	65	11	4	4	19	14	12	4	0	34	16	4	.387	.332
Chapman, Stephen	L-L	6-0	180	10-12-85	.308	.279	.316	70	276	50	85	18	8	6	40	29	8	3	2	63	20	6	.496	.387
Clem, Zach	R-R	6-2	210	9-20-83	.231	.167	.264	38	108	14	25	5	0	3	18	15	7	0	1	26	2	0	.361	.359
De La Cruz, Carlos	R-R	6-3	175	3-1-82	.278	.258	.284	38	133	20	37	5	0	1	7	11	2	2	0	25	4	1	.338	.342
De La Cruz, Fredy	R-R	6-0	180	10-17-85	.268	.190	.287	63	213	31	57	9	1	7	36	26	2	1	4	46	4	1	.418	.351
Errecart, Chris	R-L	6-1	210	2-11-85	.316	.379	.296	70	272	49	86	16	0	13	61	25	16	0	0	56	5	3	.518	.406
Gillespie, Cole	R-R	6-1	205	6-20-84	.344	.370	.336	51	186	49	64	12	1	8	31	40	4	0	3	34	18	4	.548	.464
Green, Taylor	L-R	5-10	180	11-2-86	.231	.188	.238	62	221	36	51	12	1	1	23	29	4	2	2	35	0	1	.308	.328
Hopf, J.R.	L-R	6-1	205	11-4-82	.188	.222	.183	27	80	4	15	3	0	0	2	12	0	1	0	27	0	0	.225	.293
Miller, Brad	R-R	6-0	185	12-11-85	.200	.143	.221	52	185	25	37	7	0	2	14	23	3	3	2	33	9	3	.270	.296
Newton, Eric	R-R	6-0		6-17-84	.143	.000	.200	6	21	4	3	0	0	1	3	5	0	0	0	5	0	0	.286	.308
Neyens, D.J.	R-R	5-11	200	9-19-83	.227	.214	.231	20	66	4	15	1	0	0	4	6	0	0	1	18	0	1	.242	.288
Parker, David	R-R	6-0	180	12-5-82	.160	.146	.167	42	125	15	20	3	0	0	5	18	0	3	0	22	2	1	.184	.266
Rowe, Bill	L-L	6-3	230	8-24-83	.279	.091	.297	44	129	22	36	6	1	2	23	18	4	0	1	29	1	0	.388	.382
Savas, Garry	R-R	6-0	200	2-24-83	.115	.000	.143	11	26	2	3	0	0	0	1	5	1	1	0	4	1	1	.115	.281
Swaydan, Jordan	R-R	6-2	185	2-1-84	.224	.300	.191	32	98	5	22	2	0	0	7	9	0	0	1	20	0	0	.245	.287

PITCHING	B-T	HT	WT	DOB	W	L	ERA	G	GS	CG	SV	IP	H	R	ER	HR	BB	SO	AVG	vLH	vRH	K/9	BB/9
Beltre, Jose	R-R	6-3	170	11-27-84	1	3	5.36	17	7	0	0	47	54	35	28	4	32	32	.290	.323	.273	6.13	6.13
Braddock, Zach	L-L	6-4	230	8-23-87	2	2	5.49	14	8	0	0	39	32	26	24	3	31	30	.227	.182	.235	6.86	7.09
Ferguson, Shawn	R-R	6-2	205	1-12-83	0	2	3.86	5	3	0	0	16	15	9	7	0	9	15	.254	.333	.172	8.27	4.96
Jean, Chris	R-R	6-4	175	10-31-82	4	5	5.47	17	12	1	1	72	91	45	44	6	17	43	.313	.370	.286	5.35	2.12
King, J.T.	R-R	6-2	210	1-25-85	0	1	6.75	2	0	0	0	3	2	3	2	0	0	2	.200	.000	.222	9.00	0.00
Kjeldgaard, Brock	R-R	6-5	215	1-22-86	1	2	5.29	16	8	0	1	49	56	33	29	4	21	25	.287	.278	.291	4.56	3.83
Logan, Brian	L-L	5-11	185	4-26-86	1	0	5.14	14	0	0	0	21	22	14	12	1	19	19	.289	.211	.316	8.14	8.14
McClendon, Mike	R-R	6-5	215	4-3-85	3	2	4.23	18	4	0	0	45	54	23	21	4	8	34	.297	.360	.273	6.85	1.61
Mercedes, Roque	R-R	6-3	186	10-16-86	5	5	4.92	15	9	0	0	60	57	42	33	7	21	29	.243	.181	.276	4.33	3.13
Palazzolo, Steve	R-R	6-10	260	3-31-82	1	1	1.82	17	0	0	6	30	23	7	6	3	11	30	.217	.238	.200	9.10	3.34
Parillo, Brandon	L-L	5-10	185	9-22-85	3	3	3.77	12	8	0	0	45	39	29	19	3	20	36	.223	.300	.213	7.15	3.97
Ramirez, Luis	L-R	6-3	170	5-3-88	2	1	3.79	5	4	0	0	19	18	9	8	1	12	14	.247	.278	.226	6.63	5.68
Ramlow, Mike	L-L	6-6	185	3-2-86	0	2	5.63	3	1	0	0	8	11	5	5	0	3	3	.355	.250	.370	3.38	3.38
Rivas, Amaury	R-R	6-2	185	12-20-85	5	4	3.02	10	10	0	0	54	48	28	18	6	18	36	.236	.215	.246	6.04	2.68
Romero, Jose	L-L	6-0	170	6-2-86	2	1	4.61	18	0	0	1	27	32	18	14	0	13	23	.296	.323	.286	7.57	3.95
Sutherland, Stuart	R-R	6-1	180	1-28-84	2	3	6.55	18	1	0	0	33	45	30	25	6	18	21	.317	.350	.304	5.50	4.72
Toneguzzi, Chris	B-R	6-4	260	2-6-83	2	2	4.54	19	0	0	3	34	42	20	17	2	16	22	.307	.463	.240	5.88	4.01
Wendte, Travis	R-R	6-2	195	11-17-82	0	1	3.05	17	0	0	3	41	46	16	14	5	4	31	.297	.372	.268	6.75	0.87
Wright, Brae	L-L	6-4	205	11-1-83	0	2	5.93	16	1	0	2	27	34	21	18	4	12	15	.315	.300	.321	3.95	4.61

FIELDING

Catcher	PCT	G	PO	A	E	DP	PB
Bouchie	.978	37	237	27	6	2	7
Hopf	1.000	5	27	2	0	1	3
Neyens	.988	12	76	8	1	0	3
Savas	.979	10	43	3	1	1	6
Swaydan	1.000	19	104	17	0	2	3

First Base	PCT	G	PO	A	E	DP
C. De La Cruz	.979	10	86	8	2	6
Errecart	.979	26	213	16	5	18
Hopf	1.000	10	89	2	0	11
Rowe	.987	40	370	15	5	27

	PCT	G	PO	A	E	DP
Swaydan	—	1	0	0	0	0
Second Base						
C. De La Cruz	1.000	1	1	4	0	0
Green	.968	60	125	179	10	45
Parker	.967	23	37	51	3	8

Third Base	PCT	G	PO	A	E	DP
C. De La Cruz	.902	23	16	58	8	8
F. De La Cruz	.933	54	43	124	12	14
Swaydan	.750	4	1	5	2	0

Shortstop	PCT	G	PO	A	E	DP
F. De La Cruz	.953	9	11	30	2	3

	PCT	G	PO	A	E	DP
Miller	.958	52	71	159	10	30
Parker	.970	18	32	66	3	10
Outfield						
Caufield	.974	56	104	7	3	1
Chapman	.986	68	135	7	2	1
Clem	.962	22	25	0	1	0
C. De La Cruz	.714	6	4	1	2	0
Errecart	1.000	39	50	6	0	1
Gillespie	.988	44	79	3	1	0
Neyens	.500	5	0	1	1	1
Parker	—	1	0	0	0	0
Swaydan	.800	5	4	0	1	0

AZL Brewers — Arizona League — Rookie

BATTING

	B-T	HT	WT	DOB	AVG	vLH	vRH	G	AB	R	H	2B	3B	HR	RBI	BB	HBP	SH	SF	SO	SB	CS	SLG	OBP
Alonso, John	R-R	6-0	215	2-19-86	.301	.414	.281	47	176	27	53	17	2	6	35	10	3	0	0	31	0	2	.523	.349
Barba, Ryan	R-R	6-0	190	12-6-84	.231	.333	.217	7	26	4	6	1	2	0	7	0	2	0	0	4	0	0	.423	.286
Bernal, Hector	L-R	5-11	175	6-14-86	.385	.375	.389	5	26	2	10	2	0	0	5	0	0	0	0	2	0	0	.462	.385
Brewer, Brent	R-R	6-2	190	12-19-87	.264	.086	.308	45	182	25	48	3	6	3	22	16	2	0	1	53	10	0	.396	.328
Caufield, Charles	R-R	6-1	180	7-6-83	.481	.571	.450	7	27	5	13	3	2	0	3	1	0	0	1	2	1		.741	.500
D'Amico, Jesse	L-R	6-2	210	1-26-88	.219	.000	.275	22	64	9	14	5	1	1	8	5	0	1	1	19	0	1	.375	.271
Delarosa, Anderson	R-R	6-0	166	8-13-84	.292	.143	.353	10	24	6	7	1	1	0	6	1	1	0	0	4	2	0	.417	.346
Dennis III, Bernie	R-R	6-0	200	7-5-83	.000	—	.000	1	1	0	0	0	0	0	0	0	0	0	0	0	0	0	.000	.000
Felix, Jovanny	B-R	5-11	160	11-6-86	.260	.306	.248	49	181	18	47	5	0	0	25	17	1	3	1	52	4	8	.287	.325
Goetz, Mike	L-R	5-10	180	7-22-84	.289	.233	.295	50	180	40	52	3	2	1	14	29	3	5	2	17	31	9	.344	.393
Iacono, Charles	L-L	5-8	170	4-21-84	.228	.364	.213	35	92	17	21	1	0	0	7	15	2	0	0	16	16	2	.239	.349
Leclercq, Lenny	R-R	6-2	180	9-7-85	.270	.300	.266	25	74	12	20	3	1	0	7	12	0	0	0	26	7	2	.338	.386
Lee, Carlos	R-R	6-1	220	9-29-81	.444	.500	.438	5	18	5	8	2	0	0	6	3	1	0	1	0	0	0	.556	.522
Lefave, Andrew	L-L	5-10	205	4-26-84	.353	.370	.352	35	136	27	48	8	4	1	22	17	2	0	2	17	3	0	.493	.427
McAngus, Zach	R-R	6-1	210	5-10-84	.260	.192	.273	41	154	30	40	11	2	2	21	18	5	0	3	39	2	2	.396	.350
Metcalf, Ryan	R-R	5-10	165	3-13-84	.257	.200	.267	34	105	13	27	3	0	0	16	14	2	4	0	16	6	6	.286	.355
Newton, Eric	R-R	6-1	200	6-17-84	.240	.125	.294	7	25	4	6	2	0	2	2	9	3	0	0	10	1	0	.560	.321
Palencia, Isaac	R-R	6-4	202	8-14-85	.247	.214	.254	28	81	17	20	3	2	0	12	6	4	0	1	15	0	0	.333	.326
Snijders, Ulrich	R-R	6-1	210	7-8-86	.260	.273	.258	28	77	14	20	3	1	1	11	11	3	0	0	27	3	0	.364	.374
Whiteside, Brett	R-R	6-2	200	3-29-88	.242	.211	.248	38	120	17	29	8	3	1	20	10	2	0	0	44	1	1	.383	.311
Wycklendt, Anthony	R-R	6-2	220	4-4-84	.240	.103	.268	48	179	29	43	12	1	4	24	17	5	0	1	59	3	2	.385	.322

PITCHING

	B-T	HT	WT	DOB	W	L	ERA	G	GS	CG	SV	IP	H	R	ER	HR	BB	SO	AVG	vLH	vRH	K/9	BB/9
Aguilar, Omar	R-R	6-0	220	3-31-85	0	1	6.00	6	6	0	0	9	5	6	6	0	9	10	.167	.308	.059	10.00	9.00
Anundsen, Evan	R-R	6-3	210	5-17-88	2	3	4.50	12	4	0	0	32	36	22	16	0	7	22	.273	.275	.272	6.19	1.97
Chaya, Yonny	R-R	6-5	193	4-22-89	1	0	8.35	13	0	0	0	18	19	23	17	2	13	15	.250	.355	.178	7.36	6.38
De La Cruz, Joel	B-R	6-1	190	6-9-89	0	0	0.00	2	0	0	0	3	1	1	0	0	4	4	.100	.000	.167	12.00	12.00
De Leon, Noel	R-R	6-5	176	7-6-88	0	1	8.46	11	1	0	0	22	37	23	21	3	11	10	.370	.405	.349	4.03	4.43
Garcia, Jose	R-R	6-4	175	5-25-88	0	3	5.31	9	3	0	0	20	23	15	12	0	8	22	.288	.250	.308	9.74	3.54
Harper, Jesse	R-R	6-4	210	11-11-80	0	0	0.00	4	0	0	0	5	3	0	0	0	5	5	.200	.222	.273	9.00	9.00
Hill, Charles	R-R	6-4	185	7-5-88	0	1	7.58	10	3	0	0	19	24	21	16	0	18	14	.300	.276	.314	6.63	8.53
James, Mark	R-R	6-1	185	7-24-87	2	2	6.91	15	1	0	0	27	31	23	21	1	23	17	.292	.286	.297	5.60	7.57
Jeffress, Jeremy	R-R	6-0	175	9-21-87	2	5	5.88	13	4	0	0	34	30	26	22	0	25	37	.237	.294	.185	9.89	6.68
Jimenez, Luis	R-R	5-7	207	9-18-88	0	0	15.70	11	0	0	0	14	15	26	25	0	30	16	.268	.333	.207	10.05	18.84
King, J.T.	R-R	6-2	210	1-25-85	0	1	18.00	1	1	0	0	1	3	3	2	0	1	1	.375	.000	.600	9.00	9.00
Langille, Craig	R-R	6-2	190	11-12-85	1	0	3.18	16	0	0	0	34	40	19	12	2	20	14	.301	.259	.333	3.71	5.29
Logan, Brian	L-L	5-11	185	4-26-86	0	0	9.00	2	0	0	0	3	5	3	3	0	3	1	.385	.000	.417	3.00	9.00
Manzanillo, Santo	R-R	6-0	175	12-20-88	0	0	13.22	14	0	0	0	16	14	29	24	1	47	13	.230	.304	.184	7.16	25.90
Mejia, Harold	R-R	6-1	155	8-28-87	1	4	5.79	17	0	0	0	19	18	15	12	0	11	20	.237	.250	.229	9.64	5.30
Ohka, Tomo	B-R	6-1	200	3-18-76	0	1	6.00	1	1	0	0	3	7	4	2	0	0	6	.438	1.000	.400	0.00	0.00
Pascual, Rolando	B-R	6-6	218	2-8-89	3	7	9.94	14	7	0	0	42	44	51	46	1	37	22	.277	.282	.273	4.75	7.99
Peralta, Wily	R-R	6-2	191	5-8-89	2	5	6.63	14	0	0	0	38	51	37	28	5	20	28	.319	.246	.364	6.63	4.74
Periard, Alexandre	L-R	6-1	180	6-15-87	3	1	4.64	13	4	0	0	43	45	31	22	1	18	25	.266	.250	.277	5.27	3.80
Ramirez, Luis	L-L	6-3	170	5-3-88	2	0	2.43	11	0	0	0	33	27	13	9	0	6	30	.216	.125	.238	8.10	1.62
Ramlow, Mike	L-L	6-6	185	3-24-86	0	0	0.00	2	0	0	0	4	2	0	0	0	0	1	.143	.000	.154	2.25	0.00
Rivas, Amaury	R-R	6-2	185	12-20-85	1	0	6.43	4	0	0	0	14	17	12	10	1	3	12	.293	.300	.289	7.71	1.93
Rogers, Mark	R-R	6-2	205	1-30-86	0	0	2.25	3	3	0	0	4	2	1	1	0	2	5	.294	.333	.273	11.25	4.50
Romero, Jose	L-L	6-0	170	6-2-86	0	0	0.00	3	2	0	0	4	2	1	0	0	2	1	.143	—	1.43	6.75	0.00
Salinas, Guillermo	R-R	6-1	180	10-28-88	1	0	4.15	14	0	0	0	22	17	12	10	0	24	24	.213	.185	.226	9.97	5.40
Sheets, Ben	R-R	6-1	220	7-18-78	0	0	10.38	1	1	0	0	4	5	5	5	0	2	8	.294	.273	.333	16.62	4.15

FIELDING

Catcher	PCT	G	PO	A	E	DP	PB
D'Amico	.978	16	80	7	2	1	3
Delarosa	.979	8	41	6	1	0	3
Dennis III	1.000	1	1	0	0	0	0
Lee	.933	2	11	3	1	0	1
Snijders	.979	25	125	14	3	3	9
Whiteside	.972	28	129	12	4	0	24

First Base	PCT	G	PO	A	E	DP
Alonso	.976	42	371	29	10	26
Leclercq	—	1	0	0	0	0
Lefave	.934	8	51	6	4	6
McAngus	.800	2	3	1	1	1
Palencia	.991	18	105	5	1	5

Second Base	PCT	G	PO	A	E	DP
Barba	1.000	3	4	7	0	1
Bernal	1.000	3	8	7	0	1
Felix	.915	29	41	99	13	12
Leclercq	.936	9	15	29	3	6
Metcalf	.984	14	27	33	1	8

Third Base	PCT	G	PO	A	E	DP
Leclercq	.765	12	7	18	1	1
McAngus	.866	34	19	65	13	3
Metcalf	.879	13	6	23	4	3

Shortstop	PCT	G	PO	A	E	DP
Barba	.909	3	2	13	1	1
Bernal	1.000	2	3	10	0	0
Brewer	.874	33	50	116	24	17

	PCT	G	PO	A	E	DP
Felix	.866	15	13	45	9	6
Metcalf	.917	5	8	14	2	2
Outfield						
Caufield	.900	7	16	2	2	0
Delarosa	1.000	2	4	0	0	0
Goetz	.984	49	117	3	2	2
Iacono	.979	32	45	1	1	0
Leclercq	.800	2	4	0	1	0
Lefave	.953	21	36	5	2	1
McAngus	1.000	7	7	0	0	0
Metcalf	1.000	2	1	0	0	0
Palencia	.917	10	10	1	1	0
Whiteside	.900	4	8	1	1	1
Wycklendt	.971	47	63	3	2	0

ORGANIZATION STATISTICS

BY JOHN MILLEA

There were questions up and down the Twins' lineup as the 2006 season began, and the early returns didn't provide many answers.

But the tune changed in June, and the Twins won a

division title for the fourth time in five years. Despite a three-game sweep at the hands of Oakland in the Division Series, it was a memorable year in Minnesota.

The club began slowly and was floundering with a 25-33 record when manager Ron Gardenhire made some changes. Nick Punto became the regular third baseman and Jason Bartlett took over at shortstop, and the manager had a heart-to-heart talk with struggling young first baseman Justin Morneau.

And then everything changed. The Twins became the hottest team in baseball, beginning with a 15-1 record in interleague play and finishing with a 71-33 surge. They finished with 96 wins and jumped past Detroit on the final day of the regular season to win the American League Central.

There were setbacks along the way, too. The biggest hurdles were injuries to starting pitchers. Veteran Brad Radke was sidelined with a shoulder injury and rookie star Francisco Liriano, who had a sterling debut, was shut down because of elbow problems. Radke may retire and Liriano had Tommy John surgery after the season, but the Twins do know a lot more about what they have for the future than in past years.

For one thing, they have legitimate middle-of-the-order hitters. Joe Mauer became the first catcher in AL history to win a batting title, as he batted .347 with a .429 on-base percentage. Michael Cuddyer drove in 109 runs and solidified his grip on a spot in the Minnesota

ORGANIZATION STATISTICS

PLAYERS OF THE YEAR

MAJOR LEAGUE: Johan Santana, lhp

It's tough to ignore first baseman Justin Morneau or catcher Joe Mauer, but Santana, BA's Major League Player of the Year, has become the best pitcher in the game. He went 19-6, 2.77 with 245 strikeouts and tied a career high with 34 starts. His 234 innings led the American League, and he held opponents to a .216 average.

MINOR LEAGUE: Matt Garza, rhp

Garza pitched at three different levels before heading to Minnesota for the stretch run, where he went 3-6, 5.76. But he was dominant in the minors. Garza, a 2005 first-rounder in his first full season, went 14-4, 1.99 in 136 innings between high Class A Fort Myers, Double-A New Britain and Triple-A Rochester.

KEVIN PATAKY

outfield. And Morneau had one of the best seasons in Twins history with a .321 average, 34 homers and 130 RBIs. That trio, with an average age of 25, combined to hit .316 with 71 homers and 323 RBIs.

The heart of the pitching staff is solid with ace Johan Santana, Baseball America's Major League Player of the Year, and closer Joe Nathan. Santana has established himself as the best pitcher in the game, and Nathan had 36 saves and a 1.58 ERA. And even when Radke and Liriano went down, rookies Boof Bonser and Matt Garza stepped in and performed admirably.

Even without Liriano, the rotation should be solid with the likes of Santana, Bonser, Garza and Glen Perkins. The infield looks all but set with Morneau at first base, Luis Castillo at second, Bartlett at shortstop and Punto at third. Cuddyer is set in right field, but there are questions after that. The Twins picked up the $12 million option on Torii Hunter's contract, which means he will play at least one more season in center field.

Left field is the main question mark. The Twins are likely to let Shannon Stewart and Rondell White exit as free agents. Jason Kubel was given a chance to win the job but didn't pan out in 2006. He has dealt with injuries and trips between the minor leagues and the big club. The front office maintains confidence in Kubel, however, and he'll get another chance to win the job come spring training.

Liriano went on the disabled list in early August and was sidelined for a month. His return was brief, but his numbers for the season were outstanding: 12-3 with a 2.16 ERA in 28 games (16 starts).

Gardenhire has quietly built a sterling record in five years after taking over for the retired Tom Kelly. Gardenhire has a career record of 455-354; the only active managers with more victories are Joe Torre, Tony LaRussa and Bobby Cox.

Twins farm teams posted the sixth-best winning percentage in baseball in 2006, and both high Class A Fort Myers and Rookie-level Elizabethton finished with the best records in their leagues. Garza was one of the best pitchers in the minors before getting called to Minnesota.

ORGANIZATION LEADERS

BATTING		*Minimum 250 at-bats
*AVG	Lis, Erik, Beloit	.326
R	Span, Denard, New Britain	92
H	Span, Denard, New Britain	170
TB	Jones, Garrett, Rochester	251
2B	Lis, Erik, Beloit	37
3B	Oeltjen, Trent, New Britain	10
	Pickrel, Jeremy, Fort Myers	10
HR	Jones, Garrett, Rochester	24
RBI	Jones, Garrett, Rochester	105
BB	Deeds, Doug, New Britain	70
SO	Jones, Garrett, Rochester	132
SB	Casilla, Alexi, Fort Myers/New Britain	50
*OBP	Lis, Erik, Beloit	.402
*SLG	Lis, Erik, Beloit	.547
XBH	Jones, Garrett, Rochester	61

PITCHING		#Minimum 75 innings
W	Pino, Yohan, Beloit	15
L	Simonitsch, Errol, New Britain	15
#ERA	Slowey, Kevin, Fort Myers/New Britain	1.90
G	Shinskie, David, Beloit/New Britain	59
CG	Nine tied at	2
SV	Hernandez, Danny, Elizabethton	18
IP	Sosa, Oswaldo, Beloit/Fort Myers	163
BB	Harben, Adam, New Britain	67
SO	Slowey, Kevin, Fort Myers/New Britain	158
#AVG	Garza, Matt, Fort Myers/New Britain/Rochester	.179

Minnesota Twins — MLB

American League

BATTING	B-T	HT	WT	DOB	AVG	vLH	vRH	G	AB	R	H	2B	3B	HR	RBI	BB	HBP	SH	SF	SO	SB	CS	SLG	OBP
Bartlett, Jason	R-R	6-0	180	10-30-79	.309	.314	.307	99	333	44	103	18	2	2	32	22	11	1	5	46	10	5	.393	.367
Batista, Tony	R-R	6-0	225	12-9-73	.236	.204	.240	50	178	24	42	12	0	5	21	15	2	0	0	27	0	1	.388	.303
Casilla, Alexi	B-R	5-9	160	7-20-84	.250	.000	.333	9	4	1	1	0	0	0	0	2	0	0	0	1	0	0	.250	.500
Castillo, Luis	B-R	5-11	190	9-12-75	.296	.246	.317	142	584	84	173	22	6	0	49	56	1	9	2	58	25	11	.370	.358
Castro, Juan	R-R	5-11	195	6-20-72	.231	.167	.233	50	156	10	36	5	2	1	14	6	0	1	1	23	1	1	.308	.258
Cuddyer, Michael	R-R	6-2	220	3-27-79	.284	.292	.276	150	557	102	158	41	5	24	109	62	10	0	6	130	6	0	.504	.362
Ford, Lew	R-R	6-0	200	8-12-76	.226	.214	.237	104	234	40	53	6	1	4	18	16	4	1	0	43	9	1	.312	.287
Heintz, Chris	R-R	6-1	210	8-6-74	.000	—	.000	2	1	0	0	0	0	0	0	0	0	0	0	0	0	0	.000	.000
Hunter, Torii	R-R	6-2	215	7-18-75	.278	.316	.263	147	557	86	155	21	2	31	98	45	5	0	4	108	12	6	.490	.336
Kubel, Jason	L-R	5-11	200	5-25-82	.241	.243	.240	73	220	23	53	8	0	8	26	12	0	2	1	45	2	0	.386	.279
Mauer, Joe	L-R	6-4	220	4-19-83	.347	.328	.356	140	521	86	181	36	4	13	84	79	1	0	7	54	8	3	.507	.429
Morneau, Justin	L-R	6-4	225	5-15-81	.321	.319	.325	157	592	97	190	37	1	34	130	53	5	0	11	93	3	3	.559	.375
Nevin, Phil	R-R	6-3	220	1-19-71	.190	.211	.174	16	42	2	8	1	0	1	4	10	0	1	1	15	0	0	.286	.340
2-team (46 Texas)					.211	—		62	218	28	46	9	0	10	35	31	2	1	1	54	0	0	.390	.313
Punto, Nick	B-R	5-9	185	11-8-77	.290	.331	.267	135	459	73	133	21	7	1	45	47	1	10	7	68	17	5	.373	.352
Rabe, Josh	R-R	6-3	215	10-15-78	.286	.375	.200	24	49	8	14	1	0	3	7	2	0	0	0	11	0	1	.490	.314
Redmond, Mike	R-R	5-11	200	5-5-71	.341	.443	.275	47	179	20	61	13	0	0	23	4	4	1	2	18	0	1	.413	.365
Rodriguez, Luis	B-R	5-9	190	6-27-80	.235	.250	.231	59	115	11	27	4	0	2	6	14	0	2	1	16	0	0	.322	.315
Sierra, Ruben	B-R	6-1	220	10-6-65	.179	.250	.150	14	28	3	5	1	0	0	4	4	0	0	1	7	0	0	.214	.273
Stewart, Shannon	R-R	5-11	210	2-25-74	.293	.288	.295	44	174	21	51	5	1	2	21	14	1	0	1	19	3	1	.368	.347
Tiffee, Terry	B-R	6-3	215	4-21-79	.244	.200	.267	20	45	4	11	1	0	2	6	4	0	0	0	8	0	1	.400	.306
Tyner, Jason	L-L	6-1	175	4-23-77	.312	.269	.325	62	218	29	68	5	2	0	18	11	1	0	2	18	4	2	.353	.345
White, Rondell	R-R	6-1	225	2-23-72	.246	.279	.236	99	337	32	83	17	1	7	38	11	4	0	3	54	1	1	.365	.276

PITCHING	B-T	HT	WT	DOB	W	L	ERA	G	GS	CG	SV	IP	H	R	ER	HR	BB	SO	AVG	vLH	vRH	K/9	BB/9
Baker, Scott	R-R	6-4	210	9-19-81	5	8	6.37	16	16	0	0	83	114	63	59	17	16	62	.324	.349	.299	6.70	1.73
Bonser, Boof	R-R	6-4	260	10-14-81	7	6	4.22	18	18	0	0	100	104	50	47	18	24	84	.267	.251	.280	7.53	2.15
Crain, Jesse	R-R	6-1	205	7-5-81	4	5	3.52	68	0	0	1	77	79	31	30	6	18	60	.262	.259	.263	7.04	2.11
Eyre, Willie	R-R	6-2	205	7-21-78	1	0	5.31	42	0	0	0	59	75	36	35	8	22	26	.309	.379	.257	3.94	3.34
Garza, Matt	R-R	6-4	185	11-26-83	3	6	5.76	10	9	0	0	50	62	33	32	6	23	38	.301	.245	.356	6.84	4.14
Guerrier, Matt	R-R	6-3	194	8-2-78	1	0	3.36	39	1	0	1	70	78	29	26	9	21	37	.287	.333	.256	4.78	2.71
Liriano, Francisco	L-L	6-2	200	10-26-83	12	3	2.16	28	16	0	1	121	89	31	29	9	32	144	.205	.202	.206	10.71	2.38
Lohse, Kyle	R-R	6-2	200	10-4-78	2	5	7.07	22	8	0	0	64	80	50	50	8	25	46	.308	.283	.325	6.50	3.53
Nathan, Joe	R-R	6-4	220	11-22-74	7	0	1.58	64	0	0	36	68	38	12	12	3	16	95	.158	.193	.130	12.51	2.11
Neshek, Pat	R-R	6-3	205	9-4-80	4	2	2.19	32	0	0	0	37	23	9	9	6	6	53	.176	.244	.140	12.89	1.46
Perkins, Glen	L-L	5-11	200	3-2-83	0	0	1.59	4	0	0	0	6	3	1	1	0	0	6	.150	.250	.083	9.53	0.00
Radke, Brad	R-R	6-2	185	10-27-72	12	9	4.32	28	28	0	0	162	197	87	78	24	32	83	.307	.303	.311	4.60	1.77
Reyes, Dennys	R-L	6-3	245	4-19-77	5	0	0.89	66	0	0	0	51	35	8	5	3	15	49	.197	.148	.244	8.70	2.66
Rincon, Juan	R-R	5-11	205	1-23-79	3	1	2.91	75	0	0	1	74	76	30	24	2	24	65	.270	.222	.303	7.87	2.91
Santana, Johan	L-L	6-0	210	3-13-79	19	6	2.77	34	34	1	0	234	186	79	72	24	47	245	.216	.254	.206	9.44	1.81
Silva, Carlos	R-R	6-4	245	4-23-79	11	15	5.94	36	31	0	0	180	246	130	119	38	32	70	.324	.329	.320	3.49	1.60
Smith, Mike	R-R	5-11	205	9-19-77	0	0	12.00	1	1	0	0	3	5	4	4	1	3	1	.357	.375	.333	3.00	9.00

FIELDING

Catcher	PCT	G	PO	A	E	DP	PB
Heintz	—	2	0	0	0	0	0
Mauer	.996	120	866	44	4	7	5
Redmond	1.000	43	317	21	0	2	0

First Base	PCT	G	PO	A	E	DP
Cuddyer	1.000	6	48	3	0	4
Morneau	.994	153	1297	111	8	113
Nevin	1.000	5	29	1	0	6
Rodriguez	1.000	1	1	0	0	0
Tiffee	.889	3	8	0	1	0

Second Base	PCT	G	PO	A	E	DP
Casilla	1.000	4	5	8	0	4

Third Base	PCT	G	PO	A	E	DP
Batista	.954	50	27	98	6	6
Punto	.962	89	53	175	9	18
Rodriguez	1.000	29	18	41	0	9
Tiffee	.941	6	3	13	1	2

Shortstop	PCT	G	PO	A	E	DP
Bartlett	.971	99	131	298	13	46
Casilla	1.000	2	1	2	0	2
Castro	.968	50	67	147	7	28

	PCT	G	PO	A	E	DP
Castillo	.991	142	267	378	6	78
Punto	.973	17	21	50	2	9
Rodriguez	.974	14	11	26	1	6

	PCT	G	PO	A	E	DP
Punto	.970	26	14	50	2	7
Rodriguez	.500	2	0	1	1	0

Outfield	PCT	G	PO	A	E	DP
Cuddyer	.981	143	244	11	5	2
Ford	.986	92	132	4	2	2
Hunter	.989	143	343	8	4	4
Kubel	.953	37	40	1	2	0
Punto	1.000	3	6	0	0	0
Rabe	.917	11	22	0	2	0
Stewart	.984	34	58	3	1	1
Tyner	.993	50	129	4	1	1
White	1.000	38	57	0	0	0

Rochester Red Wings — Triple-A

International League

BATTING	B-T	HT	WT	DOB	AVG	vLH	vRH	G	AB	R	H	2B	3B	HR	RBI	BB	HBP	SH	SF	SO	SB	CS	SLG	OBP
Bartlett, Jason	R-R	6-0	180	10-30-79	.306	.233	.340	58	235	42	72	23	3	1	20	10	2	0	3	28	6	3	.443	.336
Durazo, Erubiel	L-L	6-3	240	1-23-75	.264	.125	.289	17	53	7	14	6	0	1	12	0	0	0	14	0	0	.434	.400
2-team (19 Columbus)					.278	—		36	115	13	32	8	0	3	13	23	1	0	1	26	0	0	.426	.400
Ford, Lew	R-R	6-0	200	8-12-76	.276	.091	.389	8	29	5	8	2	0	0	2	6	3	0	0	5	0	1	.345	.447
Hart, Jason	R-R	6-4	235	9-5-77	.225	.235	.217	30	80	12	18	4	0	4	8	5	0	0	1	27	0	1	.425	.267
Heintz, Chris	R-R	6-1	210	8-6-74	.286	.222	.309	100	374	46	107	22	0	3	39	23	0	4	5	63	0	4	.369	.323
Jones, Garrett	L-L	6-4	245	6-21-81	.238	.255	.231	140	525	72	125	32	3	21	92	49	2	0	6	121	3	4	.430	.302
Kubel, Jason	L-R	5-11	200	5-25-82	.283	.306	.274	30	120	18	34	7	2	4	22	12	0	0	2	23	2	0	.475	.343
Lomasney, Steve	R-R	6-0	205	8-29-77	.200	.200	.200	3	10	2	2	0	0	1	3	0	0	0	2	0	0	.500	.200
Maza, Luis	R-R	5-9	180	6-22-80	.207	.225	.197	95	305	29	63	10	6	3	35	15	6	10	3	57	2	2	.308	.255
McCracken, Quinton	B-R	5-8	185	8-16-70	.284	.200	.310	31	109	10	31	4	0	1	11	9	0	1	0	17	2	1	.349	.339
Mendez, Donaldo	R-R	6-1	190	6-7-78	.276	.444	.200	19	29	8	8	1	0	3	4	1	0	1	0	10	1	0	.621	.300

General manager: Terry Ryan. **Farm director:** Jim Rantz. **Scouting director:** Mike Radcliff.

Class	Team	League	W	L	PCT	Finish*	Manager(s)	Affiliate Since
Majors	Minnesota	American	96	66	.593	2nd (14)	Ron Gardenhire	—
Triple-A	Rochester Red Wings	International	79	64	.552	3rd (14)	Stan Cliburn	2003
Double-A	New Britain Rock Cats	Eastern	64	78	.451	11th (12)	Riccardo Ingram	1995
High A	Fort Myers Miracle	Florida State	80	60	.571	1st (12)	Kevin Boles	1993
Low A	Beloit Snappers	Midwest	74	62	.536	6th (14)	Jeff Smith	2005
Rookie	Elizabethton Twins	Appalachian	42	26	.618	1st (10)	Ray Smith	1974
Rookie	GCL Twins	Gulf Coast	26	27	.491	7th (12)	Nelson Prada	1989

OVERALL 2006 MINOR LEAGUE RECORD   365   319   .534   6th (30)

*Finish in overall standings (No. of teams in league). +League champion

ORGANIZATION STATISTICS

	B-T	HT	WT	DOB	AVG	vLH	vRH	G	AB	R	H	2B	3B	HR	RBI	BB	HBP	SH	SF	SO	SB	CS	SLG	OBP
Morales, Jose	B-R	6-0	195	2-20-83	.143	.250	.000	2	7	0	1	0	0	0	0	0	0	0	0	0	0	0	.143	.143
Rabe, Josh	R-R	6-3	215	10-15-78	.299	.294	.300	93	355	51	106	20	1	6	47	35	3	0	5	37	7	4	.411	.362
Romero, Alex	L-R	6-0	190	9-9-83	.250	.259	.247	71	236	20	59	8	2	0	26	15	3	5	3	22	6	2	.301	.300
Sierra, Ruben	B-R	6-1	220	10-6-65	.333	.333	.333	2	6	1	2	0	0	0	2	2	0	0	0	2	0	0	.333	.500
Stewart, Shannon	R-R	5-11	210	2-25-74	.278	.667	.200	5	18	2	5	1	0	0	1	2	0	0	1	4	1	0	.333	.333
Tiffee, Terry	B-R	6-3	215	4-21-79	.273	.268	.274	79	308	37	84	20	0	4	38	20	0	0	3	50	1	0	.377	.314
Torres, Andres	B-R	5-10	190	1-26-78	.236	.216	.243	116	348	46	82	17	9	2	30	49	3	12	2	87	19	7	.353	.333
Tyner, Jason	L-L	6-1	175	4-23-77	.329	.307	.338	80	316	52	104	14	5	0	22	25	3	4	4	39	8	2	.405	.379
Velazquez, Gil	R-R	6-2	170	10-17-79	.250	.304	.222	56	164	26	41	4	1	1	17	11	2	3	2	33	2	2	.305	.302
Watkins, Tommy	R-R	5-10	200	6-18-80	.276	.224	.296	60	174	25	48	10	0	4	23	18	1	5	1	25	7	2	.402	.345
West, Kevin	R-R	6-2	225	1-1-80	.246	.232	.253	76	256	34	63	9	1	11	41	20	9	0	4	69	0	2	.418	.318
White, Rondell	R-R	6-1	225	2-23-72	.235	.077	.289	13	51	8	12	0	0	1	5	1	0	0	1	6	0	0	.294	.245
Williams, Glenn	B-R	6-2	195	7-18-77	.257	.260	.256	113	370	37	95	20	4	7	36	36	3	3	2	84	3	1	.389	.326
Wooten, Shawn	R-R	5-10	230	7-24-72	.253	.270	.247	104	352	24	89	20	0	6	41	23	3	0	5	77	1	0	.361	.300

PITCHING	B-T	HT	WT	DOB	W	L	ERA	G	GS	CG	SV	IP	H	R	ER	HR	BB	SO	AVG	vLH	vRH	K/9	BB/9
Baker, Scott	R-R	6-4	210	9-19-81	5	4	2.67	12	12	1	0	84	77	26	25	4	25	68	.246	.235	.254	7.26	2.67
Barrett, Ricky	L-L	6-0	200	3-9-81	5	1	3.42	27	0	0	1	47	31	21	18	0	26	49	.191	.125	.213	9.32	4.94
Bonilla, Henry	R-R	6-0	195	8-16-78	3	7	4.26	35	8	1	1	95	89	46	45	6	32	63	.251	.248	.252	5.97	3.03
Bonser, Boof	R-R	6-4	260	10-14-81	6	4	2.81	14	14	0	0	86	68	31	27	4	35	83	.211	.191	.227	8.65	3.65
Cameron, Kevin	R-R	6-1	192	12-15-79	6	4	2.98	40	0	0	9	66	53	25	22	2	26	65	.216	.196	.230	8.82	3.53
Durbin, J.D.	R-R	6-0	210	2-24-82	4	3	2.33	16	16	0	0	89	67	27	23	3	50	81	.209	.237	.189	8.19	5.06
Ford, Matt	B-L	6-1	190	4-8-81	1	2	4.50	33	6	0	0	58	61	31	29	7	25	33	.266	.281	.261	5.12	3.88
Garza, Matt	R-R	6-4	185	11-26-83	3	1	1.85	5	5	2	0	34	20	7	7	1	7	33	.174	.261	.116	8.74	1.85
Gassner, Dave	R-L	6-2	190	12-14-78	2	0	4.73	6	5	0	0	27	29	15	14	2	9	14	.293	.294	.292	4.73	3.04
Glynn, Ryan	R-R	6-3	200	11-1-74	0	1	3.86	1	1	0	0	5	4	2	2	1	4	2	.222	.300	.125	7.71	3.86
Kemp, Beau	R-R	6-0	195	10-31-80	7	4	2.32	49	0	0	3	89	92	28	23	2	26	35	.274	.262	.283	3.53	2.62
Korecky, Bobby	R-R	5-11	180	9-16-79	5	3	3.33	34	0	0	8	51	52	25	19	4	16	28	.260	.296	.235	4.91	2.81
Lohse, Kyle	R-R	6-2	200	10-4-78	2	1	1.50	4	4	2	0	24	15	6	4	1	6	12	.176	.231	.130	4.50	2.25
Miller, Jason	L-L	6-1	200	7-20-82	3	8	3.81	32	15	1	1	99	101	48	42	10	36	87	.264	.271	.262	7.88	3.26
Munro, Pete	R-R	6-3	210	6-14-75	8	12	4.32	30	29	1	0	162	188	95	78	14	47	97	.291	.285	.296	5.38	2.61
Neshek, Pat	B-R	6-3	205	9-4-80	6	2	1.95	33	0	0	14	60	41	13	13	7	14	87	.189	.238	.161	13.05	2.11
Perkins, Glen	L-L	5-11	200	3-2-83	0	1	2.08	1	1	0	0	4	6	1	1	0	5	3	.333	.400	.250	6.23	10.38
Reyes, Dennys	R-L	6-3	245	4-19-77	1	0	0.50	4	3	0	0	18	11	1	1	0	3	13	.183	.167	.190	6.50	1.50
Smith, Mike	R-R	5-11	205	9-19-77	11	5	3.88	28	24	2	0	151	152	76	65	12	57	110	.261	.297	.234	6.57	3.40
Speigner, Levale	R-R	5-11	170	9-24-80	1	1	4.97	9	0	0	1	13	16	7	7	1	5	8	.296	.346	.250	5.68	3.55

FIELDING

Catcher	PCT	G	PO	A	E	DP	PB
Heintz	.982	48	316	13	6	3	4
Lomasney	1.000	3	17	0	0	0	2
Morales	1.000	2	12	1	0	0	0
Wooten	.993	99	655	50	5	2	6

First Base	PCT	G	PO	A	E	DP
Hart	1.000	13	68	4	0	8
Jones	.993	121	990	124	8	91
Tiffee	1.000	9	56	5	0	5
Williams	.978	9	85	5	2	4

Second Base	PCT	G	PO	A	E	DP
Maza	.982	89	145	231	7	46
Velazquez	.984	11	30	33	1	8

	PCT			E	DP
Watkins	1.000	12	10	26	0	7
Williams	.959	45	65	99	7	22

Third Base	PCT	G	PO	A	E	DP
Heintz	.946	36	24	63	5	5
Maza	1.000	1	0	1	0	0
Tiffee	.909	60	35	95	13	3
Velazquez	.905	9	3	16	2	2
Watkins	1.000	2	1	1	0	0
Williams	.937	48	29	75	7	8

Shortstop	PCT	G	PO	A	E	DP
Bartlett	.968	58	84	160	8	32
Mendez	.968	13	7	23	1	6
Velazquez	.977	30	52	75	3	13

	PCT			E	DP
Watkins	.957	48	70	128	9	32
Williams	.907	10	12	27	4	4

Outfield	PCT	G	PO	A	E	DP
Ford	1.000	7	18	0	0	0
Jones	.970	23	31	1	1	0
Kubel	1.000	22	30	2	0	0
McCracken	1.000	27	48	2	0	1
Rabe	.983	92	169	4	3	1
Romero	.961	68	142	4	6	2
Stewart	1.000	3	5	0	0	0
Torres	.972	97	239	4	7	0
Tyner	.989	77	170	4	2	0
West	1.000	31	44	3	0	0
White	.000	1	0	0	1	0

Eastern League

BATTING	B-T	HT	WT	DOB	AVG	vLH	vRH	G	AB	R	H	2B	3B	HR	RBI	BB	HBP	SH	SF	SO	SB	CS	SLG	OBP
Casilla, Alexi	B-R	5-9	160	7-20-84	.294	.302	.291	45	170	28	50	10	1	1	13	18	4	7	0	20	19	4	.382	.375
Christy, Jeffrey	R-R	6-0	210	4-13-84	.000	.000	.000	2	6	1	0	0	0	0	1	0	0	0	1	0	0	0	.000	.000
Deeds, Doug	L-L	6-2	195	6-2-81	.282	.227	.302	132	440	71	124	35	3	14	72	70	5	2	4	107	4	3	.470	.383
Geiger, Kyle	R-R	6-3	215	5-8-82	.137	.108	.154	30	102	5	14	1	0	2	5	7	1	2	0	33	1	0	.206	.200
Grove, Jason	L-L	6-2	200	8-15-78	.235	.000	.250	11	34	4	8	1	0	0	1	6	0	0	0	2	1	0	.265	.350
Guzman, Garrett	L-L	5-10	180	2-7-83	.275	.288	.270	64	222	34	61	15	1	7	26	18	2	5	1	27	4	3	.446	.333
Leger, Jose	R-R	5-10	175	5-19-82	.143	.000	.250	3	7	0	1	0	0	0	1	1	0	0	1	3	0	0	.143	.222

Name	B-T	HT	WT	DOB	AVG	vLH	vRH	G	AB	R	H	2B	3B	HR	RBI	BB	HBP	SH	SF	SO	SB	CS	SLG	OBP
Lomasney, Steve	R-R	6-0	205	8-29-77	.199	.159	.216	45	141	7	28	5	0	2	13	7	1	1	2	49	0	3	.277	.238
Matienzo, Daniel	R-R	5-11	200	9-3-80	.252	.259	.248	125	472	58	119	24	1	17	76	25	6	1	5	117	2	2	.415	.295
Molina, Felix	B-R	5-9	175	5-5-83	.270	.198	.293	116	385	39	104	16	4	9	50	28	1	16	3	65	9	9	.403	.319
Morales, Jose	B-R	6-0	195	2-20-83	.211	.187	.222	80	251	23	53	14	1	3	26	19	5	3	4	56	2	1	.311	.276
Moses, Matt	L-R	6-0	210	2-20-85	.249	.237	.255	125	474	47	118	16	2	15	72	35	3	1	3	113	2	2	.386	.303
Oeltjen, Trent	L-L	6-1	190	2-28-83	.299	.233	.322	113	401	61	120	16	10	3	44	36	16	9	2	58	23	11	.411	.378
Romero, Alex	L-R	6-0	190	9-9-83	.281	.204	.314	48	167	29	47	11	2	5	16	26	3	2	2	19	15	7	.461	.384
Span, Denard	L-L	6-0	190	2-27-84	.285	.275	.289	134	536	80	153	16	6	2	45	40	5	15	1	78	24	11	.349	.340
Taylor, JR	B-R	5-8	170	11-6-82	.207	.271	.181	71	203	20	42	10	0	1	13	35	5	8	1	37	5	4	.271	.336
Tolbert, Matt	B-R	6-0	180	5-4-82	.258	.305	.235	72	248	33	64	15	1	3	35	30	4	5	5	43	5	1	.363	.341
Velazquez, Gil	R-R	6-2	170	10-17-79	.375	.333	.400	6	16	1	6	2	0	0	3	3	0	2	0	2	0	0	.500	.474
Watkins, Tommy	R-R	5-10	200	6-18-80	.218	.244	.196	32	101	9	22	2	1	0	8	10	1	2	0	26	3	1	.257	.295
Whitrock, Scott	R-R	6-2	190	12-18-80	.207	.224	.189	72	222	31	46	12	2	3	16	18	5	6	0	79	15	1	.320	.282

PITCHING	B-T	HT	WT	DOB	W	L	ERA	G	GS	CG	SV	IP	H	R	ER	HR	BB	SO	AVG	vLH	vRH	K/9	BB/9
Blackburn, Nick	R-R	6-4	230	2-24-82	7	8	4.42	30	19	2	0	132	141	72	65	11	37	81	.275	.278	.273	5.51	2.52
Crawford, Tristan	R-R	6-2	200	7-22-82	6	5	3.66	46	2	0	2	98	89	48	40	8	33	97	.238	.233	.242	8.88	3.02
DePaula, Julio	R-R	6-0	180	12-31-82	2	2	2.57	43	0	0	7	67	58	25	19	1	27	43	.230	.223	.235	5.81	3.65
Duensing, Brian	L-L	5-11	195	2-22-83	1	2	3.65	10	9	0	0	49	51	29	20	6	18	30	.277	.313	.265	5.47	3.28
Garza, Matt	R-R	6-4	185	11-26-83	6	2	2.51	10	10	0	0	57	40	22	16	2	14	68	.190	.216	.176	10.67	2.20
Guerrier, Matt	R-R	6-3	194	8-2-78	2	0	1.04	4	0	0	0	9	3	1	1	0	3	10	.111	.222	.056	10.38	3.12
Harben, Adam	R-R	6-5	210	8-19-83	4	9	3.96	29	22	1	1	123	118	64	54	5	67	74	.254	.321	.197	5.43	4.92
Jones, Justin	L-L	6-3	215	9-25-84	2	2	3.25	6	6	0	0	28	30	14	10	0	15	29	.280	.242	.297	9.43	4.88
Korecky, Bobby	R-R	5-11	180	9-16-79	1	2	3.24	16	0	0	5	25	30	15	9	1	13	14	.297	.342	.270	5.04	4.68
Miller, Colby	R-R	6-2	190	3-19-82	1	1	2.55	5	2	1	0	18	8	5	5	1	10	8	.140	.100	.185	4.08	5.09
Olson, Justin	R-R	6-3	215	4-5-80	7	7	5.09	32	9	0	1	88	96	55	50	10	40	102	.279	.305	.258	10.39	4.08
Perkins, Glen	L-L	5-11	200	3-2-83	4	11	3.91	23	23	2	0	117	109	60	51	11	45	131	.243	.250	.241	10.05	3.45
Sawatski, Jay	L-L	6-2	195	5-7-82	4	2	2.87	44	2	0	0	75	69	29	24	3	22	69	.241	.200	.262	8.24	2.63
Schutt, Chris	R-R	6-1	200	2-8-82	1	0	10.13	7	0	0	0	11	9	12	12	0	10	7	.220	.214	.222	5.91	8.44
Shinskie, David	R-R	6-4	205	5-4-84	0	4	8.44	11	0	0	0	16	20	20	15	1	8	11	.303	.333	.267	6.19	4.50
Simonitsch, Errol	L-R	6-4	230	8-24-82	8	14	4.48	27	26	2	0	149	186	89	74	19	39	89	.308	.303	.310	5.39	2.36
Slowey, Kevin	R-R	6-3	190	5-4-84	4	3	3.19	9	9	1	0	59	50	23	21	6	13	52	.223	.226	.221	7.89	1.97
Speigner, Levale	R-R	5-11	170	9-24-80	3	2	3.26	40	0	0	13	58	61	27	21	5	14	37	.266	.280	.257	5.74	2.17
Thomas, John	L-L	6-2	207	7-24-81	1	2	6.25	14	3	0	0	36	46	29	25	3	20	30	.322	.310	.327	7.50	5.00

FIELDING

Catcher	PCT	G	PO	A	E	DP	PB
Christy	1.000	2	9	3	0	1	0
Geiger	.982	29	213	8	4	1	4
Leger	1.000	1	1	0	0	0	0
Lomasney	.982	42	253	18	5	4	8
Matienzo	1.000	1	4	1	0	0	1
Morales	.977	76	520	39	13	8	13

First Base	PCT	G	PO	A	E	DP
Deeds	.994	74	634	40	4	63
Matienzo	.988	69	527	44	7	50

Second Base	PCT	G	PO	A	E	DP
Molina	.958	101	185	249	19	71

	PCT	G	PO	A	E	DP
Taylor	.957	11	12	33	2	9
Tolbert	.963	26	49	55	4	17
Watkins	.962	5	14	11	1	3

Third Base	PCT	G	PO	A	E	DP
Leger	1.000	1	1	0	0	0
Morales	—	1	0	0	0	0
Moses	.921	102	55	214	23	17
Tolbert	.939	26	11	51	4	5
Velazquez	1.000	1	3	5	0	1
Watkins	.951	16	12	27	2	2

Shortstop	PCT	G	PO	A	E	DP
Casilla	.977	45	74	134	5	37

	PCT	G	PO	A	E	DP
Molina	.949	8	10	27	2	5
Taylor	.948	58	82	154	13	34
Tolbert	.944	18	29	56	5	9
Velazquez	.923	5	4	20	2	2
Watkins	.917	10	13	20	3	6

Outfield	PCT	G	PO	A	E	DP
Deeds	.960	25	47	1	2	0
Grove	1.000	4	7	1	0	0
Guzman	.964	56	78	3	3	1
Oeltjen	.986	103	205	5	3	3
Romero	.988	45	80	4	1	0
Span	.987	130	306	9	4	5
Whitrock	.978	69	130	6	3	1

Fort Myers Miracle — High Class A

Florida State League

BATTING	B-T	HT	WT	DOB	AVG	vLH	vRH	G	AB	R	H	2B	3B	HR	RBI	BB	HBP	SH	SF	SO	SB	CS	SLG	OBP
Andrus, Erold	B-L	6-2	170	7-16-84	.207	.125	.233	56	198	26	41	7	3	5	30	16	2	1	1	39	1	6	.348	.272
Arneson, Justin	B-R	5-11	175	12-17-81	.232	.186	.250	70	203	26	47	6	2	3	24	19	3	5	2	52	8	2	.325	.304
Burns, Deacon	L-L	5-8	185	10-28-82	.228	.261	.218	114	404	53	92	17	3	5	33	29	6	1	1	62	19	4	.322	.289
Casilla, Alexi	B-R	5-9	160	7-20-84	.331	.333	.331	78	323	56	107	12	6	0	33	30	2	3	1	36	31	6	.406	.390
Christy, Jeffrey	R-R	6-0	210	4-13-84	.063	.000	.091	6	16	0	1	0	0	0	1	1	0	0	0	4	0	0	.063	.118
Cowgill, Thomas	R-R	5-9	185	7-21-83	.000	.000	.000	2	7	1	0	0	0	0	0	2	0	0	0	2	1	0	.000	.222
Delgado, Juan	B-R	6-3	170	7-18-86	.333	.333	.333	2	9	1	3	0	0	1	2	0	0	0	0	3	1	0	.667	.333
Feiner, Korey	R-R	5-11	220	9-25-81	.219	.271	.206	81	237	33	52	7	0	1	21	41	6	2	3	49	0	0	.262	.345
Geiger, Kyle	B-R	6-3	225	5-8-82	.248	.315	.227	61	226	27	56	10	0	1	21	14	3	1	1	40	0	0	.305	.299
Guzman, Garrett	L-L	5-10	180	2-7-83	.274	.281	.272	65	259	35	71	9	1	8	51	15	1	0	6	31	1	1	.409	.310
Hughes, Luke	R-R	6-0	190	8-2-84	.231	.232	.231	95	333	31	77	15	0	4	37	23	5	2	5	72	6	2	.312	.289
Leger, Jose	R-R	5-10	175	5-19-82	.239	.111	.270	17	46	6	11	2	0	0	3	9	5	0	0	3	0	0	.283	.417
Moore, Caleb	R-R	5-11	205	5-17-83	.220	.190	.230	27	82	8	18	5	0	1	7	5	3	0	2	20	0	0	.317	.289
Peterson, Brock	R-R	6-3	215	11-20-83	.291	.299	.289	121	447	65	130	21	4	21	75	40	8	0	5	93	6	6	.497	.356
Pickrel, Jeremy	L-R	6-4	225	4-3-83	.231	.143	.250	93	316	44	73	11	10	4	36	35	2	0	3	119	12	4	.367	.309
Plouffe, Trevor	R-R	6-1	175	6-15-86	.246	.276	.238	125	455	60	112	26	4	4	45	58	4	2	5	93	8	5	.347	.333
Roberts, Brandon	L-R	6-0	185	11-9-84	.316	.288	.325	71	285	40	90	12	1	3	34	20	5	2	1	43	27	7	.396	.370
2-team (60 Sarasota)					.293	—	—	131	532	80	156	17	2	4	49	36	11	4	3	82	50	14	.355	.349
Sierra, Ruben	B-R	6-1	220	10-6-85	.250	.167	.333	3	12	2	3	1	0	0	1	1	0	0	0	3	0	0	.333	.308
Taylor, JR	B-R	5-8	170	11-6-82	.222	.200	.229	37	126	17	28	5	0	0	11	20	1	0	2	18	7	2	.262	.329
Tolbert, Matt	B-R	6-0	180	5-4-82	.303	.303	.303	40	155	20	47	6	3	4	24	14	1	1	2	17	7	2	.458	.360
Tolleson, Steven	R-R	5-10	180	11-1-83	.268	.325	.248	49	157	23	42	8	1	4	23	22	1	2	4	24	3	1	.408	.353
West, Kevin	R-R	6-2	225	1-1-80	.222	.333	.167	6	18	2	4	1	0	1	8	6	1	0	0	4	2	0	.444	.400
Winfree, David	R-R	6-3	215	8-5-85	.276	.293	.271	67	261	43	72	13	2	13	48	19	3	0	4	59	2	0	.490	.328
Woodard, Johnny	L-R	6-4	208	9-15-84	.181	.154	.186	23	72	11	13	2	0	2	8	6	2	0	2	27	0	0	.292	.256

PITCHING

PITCHING	B-T	HT	WT	DOB	W	L	ERA	G	GS	CG	SV	IP	H	R	ER	HR	BB	SO	AVG	vLH	vRH	K/9	BB/9
Aselton, Kyle	R-L	6-5	215	2-28-83	9	5	3.79	22	22	0	0	97	89	45	41	4	54	90	.243	.214	.251	8.32	4.99
Callahan, Ryan	L-L	6-0	165	11-19-80	3	5	3.79	38	1	0	1	74	81	41	31	3	27	57	.284	.384	.250	6.96	3.30
Delaney, Robert	L-R	6-3	225	9-8-84	0	0	5.40	3	0	0	0	5	7	3	3	1	0	3	.333	.400	.313	5.40	0.00
DePaula, Julio	R-R	6-0	180	12-31-82	1	1	0.00	8	0	0	3	15	8	4	0	1	6	10	.145	.190	.118	5.87	3.52
Duensing, Brian	L-L	5-11	195	2-22-83	2	5	4.24	7	7	0	0	40	47	25	19	4	8	33	.296	.171	.331	7.36	1.79
Farfan, Alexander	R-R	6-3	175	1-6-83	0	1	14.81	7	0	0	0	10	15	19	17	5	14	4	.326	.423	.200	3.48	12.19
Feiner, Korey	R-R	5-11	200	9-25-81	0	0	27.00	2	0	0	0	2	3	5	5	1	3	0	.429	1.000	.333	0.00	16.20
Garcia, Angel	R-R	6-7	220	10-28-83	2	1	2.93	8	0	0	0	15	11	5	5	0	9	13	.204	.111	.250	7.63	5.28
Garza, Matt	R-R	6-4	185	11-26-83	5	1	1.42	8	8	0	0	44	27	13	7	3	11	53	.169	.138	.200	10.76	2.23
Gassner, Dave	R-L	6-2	190	12-14-78	0	1	3.75	3	3	0	0	12	11	5	5	1	2	2	.239	.214	.250	1.50	1.50
Hill, Joshua	R-R	6-3	225	3-27-83	6	6	4.88	33	13	1	0	107	104	72	58	9	42	80	.254	.250	.257	6.73	3.53
Jones, Justin	L-L	6-3	215	9-25-84	1	3	5.20	12	10	0	0	54	72	40	31	3	22	32	.324	.277	.337	5.37	3.69
Lahey, Timothy	R-R	6-4	235	2-7-82	7	1	4.33	45	0	0	9	73	74	36	35	1	27	57	.264	.330	.222	7.06	3.34
Leger, Jose	R-R	5-10	175	5-19-82	0	0	0.00	1	0	0	0	1	0	0	0	0	0	0	.000	.000	.000	0.00	0.00
Manship, Jeff	R-R	6-0	165	1-16-85	0	0	2.08	4	3	0	0	9	7	3	2	0	2	12	.212	.214	.211	12.46	2.08
Martinez, J.P.	R-R	6-2	205	6-8-82	4	4	2.91	48	0	0	12	77	67	30	25	3	44	88	.237	.271	.216	10.24	5.12
Mijares, Jose	L-L	6-0	230	10-29-84	3	5	3.57	27	5	0	0	63	52	30	25	10	27	77	.226	.233	.224	11.00	3.86
Miller, Colby	R-R	6-2	190	3-19-82	3	4	5.22	20	5	0	0	50	49	33	29	6	25	30	.262	.310	.233	5.40	4.50
Powers, Daniel	R-R	6-1	195	7-24-82	6	2	3.10	30	2	0	10	58	44	22	20	4	18	61	.214	.312	.155	9.47	2.79
Sawatski, Jake	L-L	6-2	195	5-7-82	1	0	2.25	2	2	0	0	8	10	3	2	0	2	5	.278	.167	.300	5.63	2.25
Schutt, Chris	R-R	6-1	200	2-8-82	4	2	2.76	37	0	0	8	62	52	23	19	4	30	64	.227	.239	.219	9.29	4.35
Slowey, Kevin	R-R	6-3	190	5-4-84	4	2	1.01	14	14	0	0	89	52	19	10	2	9	99	.164	.119	.204	9.97	0.91
Sosa, Oswaldo	R-R	6-2	187	9-19-85	4	1	2.08	6	6	0	0	35	23	12	8	1	18	27	.189	.205	.179	7.01	4.67
Swarzak, Anthony	R-L	6-3	195	9-10-85	11	7	3.27	27	27	2	0	146	131	56	53	8	60	131	.242	.240	.243	8.09	3.71
Thomas, John	L-L	6-2	207	7-24-81	1	1	4.01	5	5	0	0	25	27	12	11	1	3	24	.273	.059	.317	8.76	1.09
Waldrop, Kyle	R-R	6-4	190	10-27-85	3	2	3.57	8	7	1	0	45	48	27	18	4	17	25	.265	.289	.248	4.96	3.38

FIELDING

Catcher	PCT	G	PO	A	E	DP	PB
Christy	1.000	6	48	5	0	0	1
Feiner	.995	81	599	53	3	4	4
Geiger	.986	29	199	18	3	2	7
Leger	.983	9	47	10	1	0	2
Moore	.991	27	196	15	2	2	5

First Base	PCT	G	PO	A	E	DP
Geiger	.956	18	122	7	6	8
Hughes	1.000	1	1	0	0	0
Peterson	.991	91	745	48	7	76
Pickrel	1.000	2	7	0	0	1
Winfree	.983	17	162	8	3	15
Woodard	.980	19	136	10	3	9

Second Base	PCT	G	PO	A	E	DP
Arneson	.933	6	16	12	2	2
Casilla	.958	42	88	119	9	31

Cowgill	1.000	2	3	6	0	0
Hughes	.951	9	16	23	2	5
Peterson	.000	1	0	0	1	0
Taylor	.968	29	41	79	4	16
Tolbert	.980	25	39	60	2	10
Tolleson	.978	29	49	87	3	21

Third Base	PCT	G	PO	A	E	DP
Geiger	.600	1	1	2	2	0
Hughes	.931	82	56	173	17	14
Leger	.750	6	0	6	2	1
Peterson	—	1	0	0	0	0
Plouffe	.921	25	15	43	5	1
Tolbert	1.000	1	0	1	0	0
Winfree	.889	29	21	43	8	4

Shortstop	PCT	G	PO	A	E	DP
Casilla	.958	37	56	102	7	13

Delgado	1.000	2	5	5	0	0
Hughes	1.000	1	2	2	0	1
Plouffe	.947	94	153	276	24	62
Taylor	1.000	6	10	24	0	4
Tolbert	.800	2	1	3	1	0

Outfield	PCT	G	PO	A	E	DP
Andrus	1.000	41	55	5	0	0
Arneson	.983	59	111	8	2	4
Burns	.990	108	190	4	2	1
Guzman	.968	50	60	1	2	0
Martinez	—	1	0	0	0	0
Pickrel	.984	91	175	7	3	2
Roberts	.979	69	137	2	3	0
Sierra	1.000	2	1	0	0	0
Tolbert	1.000	9	18	0	0	0
West	1.000	2	1	0	0	0

Beloit Snappers — Low Class A

Midwest League

BATTING	B-T	HT	WT	DOB	AVG	vLH	vRH	G	AB	R	H	2B	3B	HR	RBI	BB	HBP	SH	SF	SO	SB	CS	SLG	OBP
Benson, Joe	R-R	6-1	205	3-5-88	.263	.750	.133	8	19	2	5	0	0	0	0	0	0	0	0	6	1	0	.263	.263
Berg, Daniel	R-R	6-0	190	11-21-84	.192	.667	.130	9	26	4	5	1	1	0	4	4	1	1	1	8	0	1	.308	.313
Betsill, Matthew	B-R	6-5	190	8-16-84	.280	.286	.278	28	100	10	28	4	0	0	7	12	1	0	0	19	0	1	.320	.363
de San Miguel, Allan	R-R	5-9	180	2-1-88	.208	.070	.245	71	202	20	42	10	0	0	21	17	12	7	1	61	2	0	.257	.306
Gardenhire, Toby	R-R	6-0	170	9-11-82	.198	.257	.176	87	258	22	51	4	2	0	18	15	3	9	1	51	1	7	.229	.249
Kelly, Paul	R-R	6-3	185	10-19-86	.280	.264	.287	95	378	58	106	22	4	3	48	32	11	0	2	60	4	5	.384	.352
Land, Josh	L-L	6-2	187	2-6-85	.207	.333	.200	18	58	6	12	4	0	0	7	5	0	1	1	6	3	0	.276	.266
Leger, Jose	R-R	5-10	175	5-19-82	.248	.235	.253	45	121	13	30	5	2	0	16	13	1	3	4	21	1	1	.322	.317
Lis, Erik	L-L	6-1	220	3-8-84	.326	.284	.339	105	411	69	134	37	3	16	70	51	2	0	1	83	4	3	.547	.402
Luque, William	R-R	5-9	165	4-24-84	.247	.280	.234	30	89	13	22	2	4	0	9	14	0	8	0	20	1	4	.360	.350
Moore, Caleb	R-R	5-11	205	5-17-83	.286	.320	.271	68	245	25	70	12	5	2	27	17	3	1	3	33	3	4	.400	.336
Ortiz, Yancarlos	B-R	5-9	145	9-15-84	.200	.077	.231	21	65	6	13	3	0	0	4	7	1	2	1	15	2	2	.246	.284
Ovalle, Edward	R-R	5-11	178	6-15-85	.261	.312	.243	128	471	65	123	24	2	9	55	26	20	7	5	121	15	7	.378	.324
Parmelee, Chris	L-L	6-1	200	2-24-88	.227	.000	.250	11	22	2	5	1	0	0	2	5	0	0	0	9	0	2	.273	.370
Patterson, Tarrence	R-R	5-7	168	6-12-84	.257	.188	.280	99	382	62	98	12	2	1	19	28	6	11	1	75	35	16	.306	.317
Portes, Juan	R-R	5-11	170	11-26-85	.231	.200	.242	75	268	23	62	9	3	2	33	15	3	1	2	55	8	6	.310	.278
Robbins, Whitney	L-R	6-0	205	9-25-84	.304	.353	.282	32	112	12	34	9	1	3	26	22	3	0	3	17	1	0	.482	.421
Robinson, Mark	B-R	6-1	188	4-7-86	.178	.268	.138	42	135	14	24	5	0	0	7	14	4	1	1	25	3	4	.215	.273
Sanchez, Henry	R-R	6-3	235	11-29-86	.202	.189	.209	48	168	18	34	12	1	0	18	13	3	0	0	69	1	0	.345	.272
Thompson, Andrew	L-R	6-1	160	11-7-86	.261	.260	.265	74	283	40	74	11	7	3	23	22	3	3	0	59	8	6	.382	.321
Tintor, Eli	R-R	6-2	190	12-24-84	.285	.345	.263	116	410	52	117	19	2	12	54	19	3	1	3	96	7	5	.429	.320
Tolleson, Steven	R-R	5-10	180	11-1-83	.287	.294	.283	47	171	23	49	8	2	2	16	27	2	4	0	34	7	9	.392	.390
White, Dwayne	L-L	6-1	195	4-7-83	.258	.208	.266	97	322	43	83	17	2	8	43	21	2	1	5	47	6	4	.398	.303

PITCHING	B-T	HT	WT	DOB	W	L	ERA	G	GS	CG	SV	IP	H	R	ER	HR	BB	SO	AVG	vLH	vRH	K/9	BB/9
Cline, Jon-Michael	L-L	6-2	180	10-31-81	0	2	8.53	5	0	0	1	6	9	6	6	0	4	8	.259	.400	.176	11.37	5.68
Cordero, Jose	R-R	6-2	230	8-7-83	3	2	4.24	23	5	1	1	51	47	28	24	5	24	50	.244	.244	.243	8.82	4.24
Duensing, Brian	L-L	5-11	195	2-22-83	2	3	2.94	11	11	0	0	70	68	26	23	3	14	55	.257	.264	.254	7.04	1.79
Gabino, Armando	R-R	6-3	200	8-31-83	2	3	4.15	16	0	0	1	30	29	15	14	4	5	20	.261	.262	.261	5.93	1.48
Hawes, Adam	L-R	6-4	190	4-25-83	4	4	4.02	24	14	0	1	87	92	41	39	6	37	65	.267	.247	.288	6.70	3.81

Name	B-T	HT	WT	DOB	W	L	ERA	G	GS	CG	SV	IP	H	R	ER	HR	BB	SO	AVG	vLH	vRH	K/9	BB/9
Leatherman, Dan	R-R	6-2	210	7-12-85	0	1	2.45	13	0	0	4	22	17	6	6	1	8	25	.213	.281	.167	10.23	3.27
Lugo, Jose	L-L	6-1	159	4-10-84	1	4	4.45	22	0	0	2	28	30	16	14	1	13	32	.273	.267	.277	10.16	4.13
Mata, Frank	R-R	6-0	168	3-11-84	5	3	4.22	41	0	0	5	53	58	30	25	4	18	30	.282	.338	.250	5.06	3.04
Morlan, Eduardo	R-R	6-2	178	3-1-86	5	5	2.29	28	18	1	2	106	78	31	27	6	38	125	.202	.192	.209	10.58	3.22
Mullins, Ryan	L-L	6-6	180	11-13-83	5	8	3.86	27	26	1	0	156	157	85	67	14	53	139	.257	.257	.256	8.00	3.05
Pino, Yohan	R-R	6-3	158	12-26-83	14	2	1.91	42	7	0	3	94	69	25	20	4	20	99	.198	.191	.203	9.48	1.91
Powers, Daniel	R-R	6-1	195	7-24-82	1	0	0.43	9	0	0	2	21	16	2	1	0	4	20	.213	.269	.184	8.57	1.71
Shinskie, David	R-R	6-4	205	5-4-84	6	7	2.13	48	0	0	11	76	76	25	18	3	15	61	.260	.300	.233	7.22	1.78
Smit, Alexander	L-L	6-4	205	10-2-85	7	2	2.99	34	13	0	0	108	77	48	36	6	53	141	.199	.267	.170	11.71	4.40
Sosa, Oswaldo	R-R	6-2	187	9-19-85	9	7	2.75	20	20	1	0	118	102	44	36	1	36	95	.233	.188	.271	7.27	2.75
Vais, Danny	R-R	6-1	210	11-21-84	3	4	2.12	47	0	0	2	81	80	27	19	2	26	78	.260	.219	.281	8.70	2.90
Waldrop, Kyle	R-R	6-4	190	10-27-85	6	3	3.85	18	18	1	0	110	110	54	47	8	17	62	.259	.274	.246	5.07	1.39
Ward, Zachary	R-R	6-3	235	1-14-84	1	4	5.93	6	6	0	0	30	29	20	20	1	11	23	.250	.250	.250	6.82	3.26
2-team (20 Dayton) ..					8	4	3.06	26	24	0	0	144	103	55	49	3	48	118	—	—	—	7.36	2.99

FIELDING

Catcher	PCT	G	PO	A	E	DP	PB
de San Miguel	.990	71	541	36	6	7	11
Leger	.984	37	289	22	5	2	10
Moore	.988	45	314	27	4	4	4
Tintor	—	1	0	0	0	0	0

First Base	PCT	G	PO	A	E	DP
Betsill	1.000	19	149	7	0	14
Gardenhire	.929	2	11	2	1	0
Lis	.973	80	642	43	19	56
Moore	1.000	2	8	0	0	1
Parmelee	1.000	8	38	1	0	1
Robbins	1.000	7	72	4	0	6
Sanchez	.982	34	306	20	6	23

Second Base	PCT	G	PO	A	E	DP
Gardenhire	.965	21	27	56	3	14
Luque	1.000	5	6	7	0	2

	PCT	G	PO	A	E	DP
Portes	.949	44	72	95	9	16
Thompson	.959	65	106	198	13	44
Tolleson	.911	19	25	47	7	6

Third Base	PCT	G	PO	A	E	DP
Berg	.938	9	5	10	1	1
Betsill	.880	12	11	11	3	2
Gardenhire	.961	35	22	52	3	6
Kelly	.968	12	4	26	1	3
Leger	.833	6	2	8	2	1
Luque	.900	20	9	36	5	2
Moore	.667	1	0	2	1	0
Ortiz	.933	4	2	12	1	1
Portes	.796	21	10	29	10	2
Robbins	.923	19	13	23	3	4
Tolleson	.927	22	13	38	4	5

Shortstop	PCT	G	PO	A	E	DP
Gardenhire	.918	31	35	66	9	12

	PCT	G	PO	A	E	DP
Kelly	.975	81	118	238	9	46
Luque	.917	6	6	5	1	2
Ortiz	.881	16	16	36	7	4
Thompson	.886	8	9	30	5	5
Tolleson	.889	6	11	13	3	3

Outfield	PCT	G	PO	A	E	DP
Benson	1.000	2	6	0	0	0
Gardenhire	—	1	0	0	0	0
Land	1.000	11	17	0	0	0
Lis	1.000	13	15	0	0	0
Ovalle	.976	115	236	8	6	3
Patterson	.944	87	147	4	9	2
Portes	.947	7	17	1	1	0
Robinson	1.000	29	50	2	0	0
Tintor	.946	99	166	9	10	1
White	.977	71	123	3	3	0

Elizabethton Twins — Rookie

Appalachian League

BATTING	B-T	HT	WT	DOB	AVG	vLH	vRH	G	AB	R	H	2B	3B	HR	RBI	BB	HBP	SH	SF	SO	SB	CS	SLG	OBP
Berg, Daniel	R-R	6-0	190	11-21-84	.253	.232	.267	51	174	35	44	13	3	6	27	23	4	0	0	48	0	0	.466	.353
Betsill, Matthew	B-R	6-5	190	8-16-84	.250	.000	.273	3	12	3	3	0	0	2	8	1	0	0	0	1	0	0	.750	.368
Christy, Jeffrey	R-R	6-0	210	4-13-84	.259	.296	.241	24	81	10	21	4	0	1	11	14	1	0	0	13	0	0	.346	.375
Connor, Wesley	B-R	6-2	195	4-11-85	.188	.212	.176	32	101	17	19	3	0	0	9	3	5	0	0	23	4	1	.218	.248
Dean, Joshua	L-R	6-1	205	12-24-86	.231	.071	.260	30	91	12	21	3	0	2	15	12	1	1	1	25	0	0	.330	.324
Dinkelman, Brian	L-R	5-11	195	11-10-83	.298	.333	.287	46	188	24	56	11	0	4	32	10	2	2	1	29	2	1	.420	.338
Land, Josh	L-L	6-2	187	2-6-85	.211	.143	.224	36	128	18	27	4	1	2	15	10	1	0	0	23	3	0	.305	.273
Luque, William	B-R	5-9	165	4-24-84	.243	.188	.259	21	74	10	18	4	1	0	6	8	1	0	0	13	1	1	.324	.325
Lysaght, Michael	R-R	5-11	175	9-30-85	.163	.108	.209	28	80	14	13	5	0	0	4	11	2	1	1	36	2	2	.225	.277
Olson, Garrett	R-R	6-2	200	3-10-85	.313	.419	.254	49	176	31	55	8	2	0	20	19	6	0	1	30	2	3	.381	.396
Ortiz, Yancarlos	B-R	5-9	145	9-15-84	.275	.341	.224	34	102	21	28	3	1	1	11	13	2	1	1	11	3	2	.353	.364
Sanchez, Henry	R-R	6-3	235	11-29-86	.220	.300	.194	12	41	2	9	4	0	1	8	0	1	0	1	13	0	0	.390	.233
Santiesteban, Danny	R-R	6-2	170	2-17-85	.250	.266	.242	64	244	32	61	14	2	6	30	23	6	0	1	63	8	1	.398	.328
Singleton, Steven	B-R	6-0	180	9-12-85	.340	.344	.330	41	144	26	49	9	5	4	24	5	3	1	3	19	1	3	.556	.368
Sojo, Richard	R-R	6-2	194	9-24-84	.228	.180	.266	34	114	20	26	5	2	0	11	12	3	1	0	31	3	1	.307	.318
Valencia, Daniel	R-R	6-2	190	9-19-84	.311	.345	.296	48	190	30	59	13	0	8	29	15	3	0	3	34	0	2	.505	.365
Wilson, J.W.	R-R	6-2	195	8-19-86	.228	.196	.243	48	171	28	39	4	0	6	23	18	1	2	1	44	2	4	.357	.304
Yersich, Gregory	R-R	6-0	205	10-7-86	.244	.207	.259	50	197	28	48	12	1	4	21	8	3	0	2	44	1	0	.376	.281

PITCHING	B-T	HT	WT	DOB	W	L	ERA	G	GS	CG	SV	IP	H	R	ER	HR	BB	SO	AVG	vLH	vRH	K/9	BB/9
Bryant, Patrick	R-R	6-4	190	10-26-85	0	1	6.61	14	3	0	0	33	40	25	24	2	18	36	.301	.282	.309	9.92	4.96
Burnett, Alex	R-R	6-0	190	7-26-87	4	3	4.04	13	13	1	0	71	66	41	32	6	13	71	.242	.236	.245	8.96	1.64
Castillo, Jose	R-R	6-1	175	12-23-84	4	3	3.17	13	12	0	0	71	64	28	25	6	23	56	.247	.256	.243	7.10	2.92
Craig, Aaron	R-R	6-1	205	3-22-86	2	1	5.11	20	0	0	0	25	26	16	14	1	15	17	.274	.375	.239	6.20	5.47
Fox, Matthew	R-R	6-3	192	12-4-82	4	0	3.79	20	1	0	2	40	32	18	17	1	13	46	.216	.211	.218	10.26	2.90
Gabino, Armando	R-R	6-3	200	8-31-83	1	0	0.87	5	1	0	0	10	5	1	1	0	2	8	.139	.077	.174	6.97	1.74
Hernandez, Danny	R-R	6-1	158	11-19-85	1	1	3.81	28	0	0	18	28	20	13	12	2	9	40	.190	.111	.218	12.71	2.86
Kirwan, Brian	R-R	6-4	205	6-9-87	5	5	5.63	13	13	0	0	64	67	41	40	9	23	58	.270	.263	.273	8.16	3.23
Land, Sean	L-L	6-5	230	9-27-84	3	5	4.45	13	11	0	0	61	58	32	30	7	27	57	.262	.222	.268	8.46	4.01
Leatherman, Dan	R-R	6-2	210	7-12-85	3	0	0.64	5	0	0	0	14	7	1	1	1	1	14	.146	.158	.138	9.00	0.64
Lugo, Jose	L-L	6-1	159	4-10-84	8	4	3.56	13	13	0	0	73	71	33	29	3	21	70	.253	.212	.268	8.59	2.58
McConnell, Brandon	R-R	6-4	205	2-8-85	1	1	7.30	10	1	0	0	37	47	33	30	3	12	33	.301	.298	.303	8.03	2.92
Patton, Walter	R-R	6-1	190	3-13-85	0	0	135.00	3	0	0	0	1	7	10	10	0	8	2	.778	1.000	.600	27.00	108.00
Staatz, Justin	R-R	6-7	235	10-30-83	2	0	4.15	16	0	0	1	22	18	11	10	1	10	17	.228	.286	.207	7.06	4.15
Williams, Matthew	R-R	6-1	170	2-18-87	4	2	3.89	24	0	0	1	39	47	17	17	2	10	41	.301	.351	.286	9.38	2.29

FIELDING

Catcher	PCT	G	PO	A	E	DP	PB
Berg	.974	9	69	6	2	2	6
Christy	.989	21	163	16	2	1	5
Yersich	.984	40	334	34	6	1	3

First Base	PCT	G	PO	A	E	DP
Berg	1.000	24	169	7	0	14
Dean	1.000	26	203	11	0	24
Sanchez	1.000	7	52	3	0	10
Valencia	1.000	18	154	8	0	17

Second Base	PCT	G	PO	A	E	DP
Dinkelman	.979	36	63	80	3	25

	PCT	G	PO	A	E	DP
Luque	1.000	10	20	21	0	12
Lysaught	.955	25	42	42	4	12

Third Base	PCT	G	PO	A	E	DP
Berg	1.000	1	1	2	0	0
Betsill	.818	2	2	7	2	3
Luque	.842	9	6	10	3	0
Lysaught	.750	1	1	2	1	0
Olson	.903	40	18	84	11	6
Valencia	1.000	17	15	35	0	3

Shortstop	PCT	G	PO	A	E	DP
Lysaught	1.000	1	1	1	0	0

	PCT	G	PO	A	E	DP
Olson	1.000	1	2	3	0	1
Ortiz	.964	28	32	102	5	22
Singleton	.940	39	59	129	12	26

Outfield	PCT	G	PO	A	E	DP
Connor	.953	29	39	2	2	0
Dinkelman	—	1	0	0	0	0
Land	1.000	1	1	0	0	0
Land	.946	34	52	1	3	1
Santiesteban	.983	64	110	3	2	0
Sojo	.962	33	49	2	2	0
Wilson	.952	48	76	3	4	0

GCL Twins   Rookie

Gulf Coast League

BATTING

	B-T	HT	WT	DOB	AVG	vLH	vRH	G	AB	R	H	2B	3B	HR	RBI	BB	HBP	SH	SF	SO	SB	CS	SLG	OBP
Arratia, Jilmer	R-R	5-11	170	6-28-84	.333	.000	1.000	1	3	1	1	0	0	0	1	0	1	0	0	0	0	0	.333	.500
Barrientos, Miguel	L-R	5-10	185	9-26-86	.143	—	.143	8	28	1	4	0	0	0	2	2	0	1	0	8	0	0	.143	.200
Benson, Joe	R-R	6-1	205	3-5-88	.260	.293	.246	52	196	30	51	11	5	5	28	21	2	0	2	41	9	10	.444	.335
Betsill, Matthew	B-R	6-5	190	8-16-84	.118	.214	.050	10	34	1	4	0	0	0	2	1	0	1	1	10	0	1	.118	.139
Buenrostro, Gilbert	R-R	5-11	185	12-30-85	.281	.222	.304	13	32	5	9	3	0	0	3	4	0	0	9	1	1		.375	.410
Connor, Wesley	B-R	6-2	195	4-11-85	.444	.000	.500	2	9	1	4	1	0	0	3	0	0	0	0	3	1	0	.556	.444
Cowgill, Thomas	R-R	5-9	185	7-21-83	.185	.167	.195	35	119	20	22	6	2	2	13	19	2	0	4	37	0	3	.319	.299
De Los Santos, Starling	B-R	5-10	155	1-20-87	.195	.200	.192	24	82	12	16	1	2	0	8	3	1	0	18	2	1		.256	.290
Dean, Joshua	L-R	6-1	205	12-24-86	.222	.000	.250	2	9	3	2	1	0	0	0	1	0	1	0	1	0	0	.333	.300
Delgado, Juan	B-R	6-3	170	7-18-86	.228	.279	.204	40	136	17	31	4	3	1	15	9	2	0	0	40	5	4	.324	.286
Dolenc, Mark	R-R	6-3	215	11-8-84	.212	.155	.237	51	189	28	40	4	2	1	26	16	1	3	3	43	10	4	.270	.273
Harrington, Kevin	L-R	6-6	185	4-8-88	.136	.103	.155	36	110	13	15	2	0	0	6	16	3	0	2	31	4	2	.155	.264
Lawman, Matthew	R-S	6-1	170	6-26-87	.256	.296	.237	28	86	9	22	2	0	0	4	8	1	3	0	20	2	3	.279	.326
Palacios, Rodolfo	R-R	5-10	176	6-26-85	.279	.308	.264	37	111	14	31	5	0	0	16	16	0	0	0	13	0	1	.324	.370
Parmelee, Chris	L-L	6-1	200	2-24-88	.279	.326	.259	45	154	29	43	7	4	8	32	23	0	2	47	3	3		.532	.369
Ramos, Wilson	R-R	6-0	178	8-10-87	.286	.217	.315	46	154	18	44	12	1	3	26	12	2	1	3	14	4	2	.435	.339
Romero, Deibinson	R-R	6-1	170	9-24-86	.313	.345	.297	50	176	37	55	10	2	4	38	13	4	0	4	37	6	3	.460	.365
Santiago, Eric	R-R	6-0	185	7-10-87	.250	.100	.323	35	92	15	23	2	0	0	8	12	14	2	1	21	8	6	.272	.412
Tolleson, Steven	R-R	5-10	180	11-1-83	.250	—	.250	2	8	1	2	0	0	0	1	0	0	1	0	0	0	0	.250	.222
Winfree, David	R-R	6-3	215	8-5-85	.200	.500	.091	4	15	2	3	1	0	0	1	1	0	0	0	4	0	0	.267	.250

PITCHING

	B-T	HT	WT	DOB	W	L	ERA	G	GS	CG	SV	IP	H	R	ER	HR	BB	SO	AVG	vLH	vRH	K/9	BB/9
Acosta, Jose	R-R	6-2	186	11-11-86	0	1	1.50	4	0	0	0	6	3	1	1	1	1	3	.136	.167	.125	4.50	1.50
Alcala, Omar	L-L	5-11	145	12-24-86	3	1	4.02	11	0	0	0	54	46	26	24	5	26	41	.236	.193	.254	6.88	4.36
Allen, Michael	R-R	6-3	220	5-27-87	0	2	4.91	6	6	0	0	22	29	14	12	2	8	22	.309	.324	.300	9.00	3.27
Bromberg, David	L-R	6-5	230	9-14-87	3	3	2.66	10	10	2	0	51	42	21	15	2	18	31	.230	.259	.217	5.51	3.20
Carreras, Luis	R-R	6-3	210	9-1-83	1	1	3.34	14	0	0	1	30	28	12	11	1	5	23	.259	.270	.254	6.98	1.52
Crawford, Nathan	R-R	6-6	200	11-5-86	0	0	18.00	2	0	0	0	2	7	4	4	0	1	2	.583	.500	.625	9.00	4.50
Delaney, Robert	L-R	6-3	225	9-8-84	1	3	4.64	17	0	0	2	33	37	23	17	4	1	27	.278	.319	.256	7.36	0.27
Garcia, Carlos	L-L	6-1	160	3-27-87	3	0	3.68	15	0	0	1	22	17	9	9	0	15	16	.210	.214	.209	6.55	6.14
Gassner, Dave	R-L	6-2	190	12-14-78	0	0	3.60	2	2	0	0	5	4	3	2	0	0	4	.235	.250	.231	7.20	0.00
Leatherman, Dan	R-R	6-2	210	7-12-85	1	0	0.00	3	0	0	1	9	5	1	0	0	3	8	.167	.143	.174	8.00	3.00
Leavitt, Curtis	R-R	6-4	195	1-10-87	0	2	7.59	9	6	0	0	32	45	33	27	3	16	33	.317	.277	.337	9.28	4.50
Manship, Jeff	R-R	6-0	165	1-16-85	0	0	0.00	2	0	0	0	6	3	0	0	0	1	10	.150	.167	.143	15.88	1.59
Ortiz, Joan	R-R	6-4	220	11-1-88	1	0	3.86	1	0	0	0	2	3	1	1	0	1	0	.300	.167	.500	0.00	3.86
Patton, Walter	R-R	6-1	190	3-13-85	0	0	9.00	2	0	0	0	2	2	2	2	0	4	1	.250	.000	.400	4.50	18.00
Revelette, Adam	L-L	6-2	195	5-25-84	2	1	4.78	8	1	0	0	26	33	20	14	2	3	18	.311	.281	.326	6.15	1.03
Robertson, Tyler	L-L	6-5	220	12-23-87	4	2	4.25	11	10	0	0	49	54	23	23	2	15	54	.280	.326	.265	9.99	2.77
Sanchez, Bruno	R-R	6-6	170	11-8-86	1	3	8.31	11	1	0	0	17	31	18	16	2	9	7	.397	.444	.373	3.63	4.67
Schoenbachler, Jeffrey	L-L	6-1	185	9-13-85	0	0	0.00	1	0	0	0	1	1	0	0	0	0	0	.333	—	.333	0.00	0.00
Staatz, Justin	R-R	6-7	235	10-30-83	2	0	3.09	6	0	0	0	12	8	5	4	1	3	20	.186	.111	.240	15.43	2.31
Tippett, Bradley	R-R	6-2	176	2-11-88	3	5	2.53	19	0	0	10	21	27	8	6	1	5	18	.303	.294	.309	7.59	2.11
Toufar, Jakub	R-R	—	—	3-20-87	0	0	4.70	10	0	0	0	15	15	8	8	3	6	5	.268	.200	.293	2.93	3.52
Van Mil, Ludovicus	R-R	7-1	225	9-15-84	1	2	3.30	11	0	8	0	44	51	31	16	3	17	24	.290	.296	.286	4.95	3.50
Wright, Thomas	B-R	6-3	185	1-28-88	0	1	11.74	9	0	0	0	8	15	14	10	0	9	3	.429	.357	.476	3.52	10.57

FIELDING

Catcher	PCT	G	PO	A	E	DP	PB
Barrientos	1.000	1	8	1	0	0	0
Betsill	1.000	1	2	0	0	0	0
Buenrostro	.983	8	54	5	1	0	1
Palacios	1.000	17	84	17	0	0	3
Ramos	.970	34	227	36	8	2	8

First Base	PCT	G	PO	A	E	DP
Betsill	.929	1	10	3	1	1
Dean	1.000	2	15	3	0	1
Delgado	1.000	3	13	2	0	3
Palacios	.983	14	108	6	2	4
Parmelee	1.000	11	84	4	0	7
Ramos	.990	12	93	5	1	6
Romero	.990	13	91	8	1	9
Santiago	.964	5	27	0	1	1

	PCT	G	PO	A	E	DP
Winfree	1.000	1	12	0	0	4

Second Base	PCT	G	PO	A	E	DP
Cowgill	.953	28	39	84	6	13
De Los Santos	.913	6	9	12	2	1
Lawman	.914	22	44	62	10	15
Tolleson	1.000	1	1	1	0	0

Third Base	PCT	G	PO	A	E	DP
Betsill	.810	6	8	9	4	1
Cowgill	—	1	0	0	0	0
Delgado	.926	8	7	18	2	1
Lawman	.000	1	0	0	1	0
Romero	.885	34	24	68	12	5
Santiago	1.000	6	6	9	0	2
Tolleson	.667	1	0	4	2	3

	PCT	G	PO	A	E	DP
Winfree	.900	3	1	8	1	0

Shortstop	PCT	G	PO	A	E	DP
De Los Santos	.878	15	24	41	9	7
Delgado	.889	25	50	54	13	11
Santiago	.984	18	33	30	1	11

Outfield	PCT	G	PO	A	E	DP
Arratia	1.000	1	1	0	0	0
Benson	.960	47	116	4	5	0
Connor	.857	2	6	0	1	0
De Los Santos	1.000	2	2	0	0	0
Dolenc	.968	50	85	5	3	0
Harrington	.980	34	46	2	1	0
Lawman	—	1	0	0	0	0
Parmelee	.926	33	52	11	5	1

NEW YORK METS

BY ADAM RUBIN

The Mets won their first NL East title since 1998 and ended the Braves' 14-year run atop the division in general manager Omar Minaya's second full year in Flushing.

The Mets also tied the crosstown rival Yankees for baseball's best record at 97-65 and were within one inning of reaching the World Series. Cardinals catcher Yadier Molina helped eliminate New York with a ninth-inning home run en route to a 3-1 win in Game Seven of the NL Championship Series at Shea Stadium.

The Mets' accomplishments came despite a rash of injuries to starting pitchers. Pedro Martinez, who had a career-high 4.48 ERA while the Mets went 11-12 in his starts, spent two monthlong stints on the disabled list–once for right-hip inflammation, the other for a right-calf tear. Martinez was diagnosed with a torn rotator cuff in October that required surgery and likely will sideline him for at least the first half of 2007. Orlando Hernandez suffered a leg injury while working out prior to Game One of the Division Series and missed the postseason. The Mets used 13 different starting pitchers during the regular season. Victor Zambrano was lost in May to Tommy John surgery.

The injuries to Martinez and Hernandez propelled younger pitchers into the spotlight. Rookie John Maine (1-0, 2.63 in three postseason starts) and Oliver Perez performed well during the postseason–Maine won Game One of the Division Series and helped the Mets to a three-game sweep of the Dodgers. Maine's biggest moment came in Game Six of the NLCS. With the Mets

ORGANIZATION STATISTICS

PLAYERS OF THE YEAR

MAJOR LEAGUE: Carlos Beltran, of

Beltran played like an MVP candidate, until a September slump. While he is no longer a prolific basestealer, Beltran showed he's still a five-tool player for the National League East champions. He played a stellar center field and hit .275/.388/.594 with 41 home runs, 116 RBIs, 127 runs and 80 extra-base hits.

MINOR LEAGUE: Mike Pelfrey, rhp

Pelfrey went from being the ninth overall pick in 2005 to the Mets rotation in a little over a year. Pelfrey made four major league starts and missed time with a back injury, but he did go 4-2, 2.71 for Double-A Binghamton in 12 starts. He also struck out 109 batters in 96 minor league innings.

facing elimination, he held St. Louis scoreless for five innings.

Perez went a combined 3-13 during the regular season with the Pirates and Mets but held St. Louis to one run in six innings in Game Seven of the NLCS. Perez was acquired at the July 31 non-waiver trade deadline from Pittsburgh with Roberto Hernandez when Minaya scrambled to retool his bullpen after Duaner Sanchez was lost for the rest of the season after separating his shoulder in a car accident.

Tom Glavine lifted his career win total to 290 and contributed 13 scoreless innings in his first two postseason starts.

Carlos Beltran, who struggled in 2005 after signing a seven-year, $119 million contract, thrived during his second year as a Met. Beltran, one of six Mets all-star selections, hit .275/.388/.594 with 41 homers and 116 RBIs and matched Todd Hundley's 1996 franchise record for homers.

Delgado's arrival from the Marlins in November 2005 for Mike Jacobs, Yusmeiro Petit and Grant Psomas helped Beltran on and off the field. Delgado, who hit .265/.361/.548 with 38 home runs and 114 RBIs, provided Beltran protection batting cleanup and also a comrade for the player who felt alone socially during his inaugural season.

Reyes and Wright, both 23, signed long-term contracts–Wright's six-year, $55 million deal coming a year before he was eligible for arbitration. The speedy Reyes (four years, $23 million) hit .300/.354/.487 and led the majors with 64 steals and 17 triples. Wright went .311/.381/.531 and ended the season on a 12-game hitting streak. He matched Beltran's team-high 116 RBIs, though only six of his 26 homers came after the all-star break, where he finished runner-up to Ryan Howard in the Home Run Derby.

Outfield prospect Lastings Milledge and fellow first-round picks Mike Pelfrey and Philip Humber made their major league debuts but were not included on the postseason roster. Pelfrey (forearm) and Humber (shoulder) were sent home from the Arizona Fall League with what the team labeled minor injuries.

ORGANIZATION LEADERS

BATTING
*Minimum 250 at-bats

*AVG	Coles, Corey, St. Lucie	.341
R	Carp, Mike, St. Lucie	77
H	Coles, Corey, St. Lucie	156
TB	Abreu, Michel, St. Lucie/Binghamton	245
2B	Evans, Nick, Hagerstown	33
3B	Gomez, Carlos, Binghamton	8
HR	Flores, Jesus, St. Lucie	21
RBI	Carp, Mike, St. Lucie	98
BB	Caligiuri, Jay, Binghamton	59
SO	Ragsdale, Corey, Binghamton	182
SB	Gomez, Carlos, Binghamton	41
*OBP	Coles, Corey, St. Lucie	.407
*SLG	Abreu, Michel, St. Lucie/Binghamton	.546
XBH	Abreu, Michel, St. Lucie/Binghamton	54

PITCHING
#Minimum 75 innings

W	Devaney, Michael, St. Lucie/Binghamton	12
	MacLane, Evan, Binghamton/Norfolk/Tucson	12
L	Landing, Jeffrey, Hagerstown	11
	Niese, Jonathan, Hagerstown/St. Lucie	11
	Parnell, Robert, Hagerstown/St. Lucie	11
	Scobie, Jason, Norfolk/New Hampshire/Syracuse	11
#ERA	Devaney, Michael, St. Lucie/Binghamton	2.13
G	Camacho, Eddie, Binghamton	53
CG	Devaney, Michael, St. Lucie/Binghamton	4
SV	Muniz, Carlos, St. Lucie	31
IP	Pinango, Miguel, Binghamton	160
BB	Devaney, Michael, St. Lucie/Binghamton	70
SO	Niese, Jonathan, Hagerstown/St. Lucie	142
#AVG	Devaney, Michael, St. Lucie/Binghamton	.196

New York Mets | MLB

National League

BATTING	B-T	HT	WT	DOB	AVG	vLH	vRH	G	AB	R	H	2B	3B	HR	RBI	BB	HBP	SH	SF	SO	SB	CS	SLG	OBP
Beltran, Carlos	B-R	6-1	200	4-24-77	.275	.247	.288	140	510	127	140	38	1	41	116	95	4	1	7	99	18	3	.594	.388
Castro, Ramon	R-R	6-3	235	3-1-76	.238	.269	.230	40	126	13	30	7	0	4	12	15	1	1	1	40	0	0	.389	.322
Chavez, Endy	L-L	6-0	165	2-7-78	.306	.333	.298	133	353	48	108	22	5	4	42	24	0	11	2	44	12	3	.431	.348
Delgado, Carlos	L-R	6-3	240	6-25-72	.265	.226	.282	144	524	89	139	30	2	38	114	74	10	0	10	120	0	1	.548	.361
Diaz, Victor	R-R	6-0	200	12-10-81	.182	.143	.250	6	11	0	2	1	0	0	2	0	0	0	0	5	0	0	.273	.182
DiFelice, Mike	R-R	6-2	200	5-28-69	.080	.143	.056	15	25	3	2	1	0	0	1	5	0	0	0	10	0	0	.120	.233
Floyd, Cliff	L-R	6-4	230	12-5-72	.244	.179	.266	97	332	45	81	19	1	11	44	29	12	0	3	58	6	0	.407	.324
Franco, Julio	R-R	6-1	210	8-23-58	.273	.227	.303	95	165	14	45	10	0	2	26	13	1	0	0	49	6	1	.370	.330
Green, Shawn	L-L	6-4	210	11-10-72	.257	.244	.264	34	113	14	29	9	1	4	15	8	4	0	1	18	0	0	.442	.325
2-team (115 Arizona)					.277	—	—	149	530	73	147	31	3	15	66	45	10	0	3	82	4	4	.432	.344
Hernandez, Anderson	B-R	5-9	170	10-30-82	.152	.211	.128	25	66	4	10	1	1	1	3	1	0	0	0	12	0	0	.242	.164
Ledee, Ricky	L-L	6-1	225	11-22-73	.094	.000	.120	27	32	4	3	1	0	1	1	4	0	0	0	6	0	0	.219	.194
2-team (43 Los Angeles)					.188	—	—	70	85	8	16	6	0	2	9	6	0	0	0	16	1	0	.329	.242
Lo Duca, Paul	R-R	5-10	185	4-12-72	.318	.336	.311	124	512	80	163	39	1	5	49	24	6	7	2	38	3	0	.428	.355
Marrero, Eli	R-R	6-1	180	11-17-73	.182	.200	.167	25	33	4	6	1	0	2	5	4	1	2	1	15	2	0	.394	.282
2-team (30 Colorado)					.204	—	—	55	93	11	19	4	0	6	15	15	2	2	1	31	5	0	.441	.304
Matsui, Kazuo	B-R	5-10	185	10-23-75	.200	.115	.221	38	130	10	26	6	0	1	7	6	0	3	0	19	2	0	.269	.235
2-team (32 Colorado)					.267	—	—	70	243	32	65	12	3	3	26	16	0	4	2	46	10	1	.379	.310
Milledge, Lastings	R-R	6-1	185	4-5-85	.241	.241	.241	56	166	14	40	7	2	4	22	12	5	1	1	39	1	2	.380	.310
Nady, Xavier	R-R	6-2	205	11-14-78	.264	.304	.250	75	265	37	70	15	1	14	40	19	6	1	1	51	2	1	.487	.326
2-team (55 Pittsburgh)					.280	—	—	130	468	57	131	28	1	17	63	30	11	2	1	85	3	3	.453	.337
Reyes, Jose	B-R	6-0	175	6-11-83	.300	.330	.288	153	647	122	194	30	17	19	81	53	1	2	0	81	64	17	.487	.354
Stinnett, Kelly	R-R	5-11	235	2-4-70	.083	.000	.125	7	12	0	1	0	0	0	0	0	0	0	0	4	0	0	.083	.083
Tucker, Michael	L-R	6-2	210	6-25-71	.196	.294	.154	35	56	3	11	4	0	1	6	16	1	0	1	14	2	0	.321	.378
Valentin, Jose	B-R	5-10	190	10-12-69	.271	.219	.288	137	384	56	104	24	3	18	62	37	0	5	6	71	6	2	.490	.330
Woodward, Chris	R-R	6-0	190	6-27-76	.216	.226	.209	83	222	25	48	10	1	3	25	23	1	4	3	55	1	1	.311	.289
Wright, David	R-R	6-0	200	12-20-82	.311	.285	.321	154	582	96	181	40	5	26	116	66	5	0	8	113	20	5	.531	.381

PITCHING	B-T	HT	WT	DOB	W	L	ERA	G	GS	CG	SV	IP	H	R	ER	HR	BB	SO	AVG	vLH	vRH	K/9	BB/9
Bannister, Brian	R-R	6-2	200	2-28-81	2	1	4.26	8	6	0	0	38	34	18	18	4	22	19	.239	.286	.185	4.50	5.21
Bell, Heath	R-R	6-3	225	9-29-77	0	0	5.11	22	0	0	0	37	51	25	21	6	11	35	.331	.308	.348	8.51	2.68
Bradford, Chad	R-R	6-5	205	9-14-74	4	2	2.90	70	0	0	2	62	59	22	20	1	13	45	.254	.250	.256	6.53	1.89
Feliciano, Pedro	L-L	5-10	185	8-25-76	7	2	2.09	64	0	0	0	60	56	15	14	4	20	54	.248	.231	.266	8.06	2.98
Fortunato, Bartolome	R-R	6-1	195	8-24-74	1	0	27.00	2	0	0	0	3	7	9	9	2	2	0	.467	.667	.333	0.00	6.00
Glavine, Tom	L-L	6-0	185	3-25-66	15	7	3.82	32	32	0	0	198	202	94	84	22	62	131	.267	.200	.287	5.95	2.82
Gonzalez, Geremi	R-R	6-0	220	1-8-75	0	0	7.71	3	3	0	0	14	21	12	12	4	6	8	.362	.400	.321	5.14	3.86
2-team (21 Milwaukee)					4	2	5.79	24	4	0	0	56	71	43	36	10	23	44	—	—	—	7.07	3.70
Heilman, Aaron	R-R	6-5	220	11-12-78	4	5	3.62	74	0	0	0	87	73	37	35	5	28	73	.231	.231	.231	7.55	2.90
Hernandez, Roberto	R-R	6-4	245	11-11-64	0	0	3.48	22	0	0	0	21	15	8	8	2	8	15	.208	.179	.227	6.53	3.48
2-team (46 Pittsburgh)					0	3	3.11	68	0	0	2	63	61	32	22	5	32	48	—	—	—	6.79	4.52
Hernandez, Orlando	R-R	6-2	220	10-11-69	9	7	4.09	20	20	1	0	117	103	58	53	14	41	112	.236	.269	.198	8.64	3.16
2-team (9 Arizona)					11	11	4.66	29	29	1	0	162	155	90	84	22	61	164	—	—	—	9.09	3.38
Humber, Philip	R-R	6-4	210	12-21-82	0	0	0.00	2	0	0	0	2	0	0	0	0	1	2	.000	.000	.000	9.00	4.50
Julio, Jorge	R-R	6-1	235	3-3-79	1	2	5.06	18	0	0	1	21	21	15	12	4	10	33	.247	.243	.250	13.92	4.22
2-team (44 Arizona)					2	4	4.23	62	0	0	16	66	52	35	31	10	35	88	—	—	—	12.00	4.77
Lima, Jose	R-R	6-2	210	9-30-72	0	4	9.87	4	4	0	0	17	25	22	19	3	10	12	.329	.412	.262	6.23	5.19
Maine, John	R-R	6-4	205	5-8-81	6	5	3.60	16	15	1	0	90	69	40	36	15	31	71	.212	.231	.191	7.10	3.30
Martinez, Pedro	R-R	5-11	180	10-25-71	9	8	4.48	23	23	0	0	133	108	72	66	19	39	137	.220	.231	.211	9.29	2.65
Mota, Guillermo	R-R	6-4	210	7-25-73	3	0	1.00	18	0	0	0	18	10	2	2	2	5	19	.159	.214	.114	9.50	2.50
Oliver, Darren	R-L	6-2	220	10-6-70	4	1	3.44	45	0	0	0	81	70	33	31	13	21	60	.231	.208	.244	6.67	2.33
Owens, Henry	R-R	6-3	230	4-23-79	0	0	9.00	3	0	0	0	4	4	4	4	0	4	2	.286	.167	.375	4.50	9.00
Pelfrey, Mike	R-R	6-7	210	1-14-84	2	1	5.48	4	4	0	0	21	24	13	13	1	12	13	.305	.278	.326	5.48	5.06
Perez, Oliver	L-L	6-3	210	8-15-81	1	3	6.38	7	7	1	0	37	41	26	26	7	17	41	.287	.310	.281	10.06	4.17
2-team (15 Pittsburgh)					3	13	6.55	22	22	1	0	112	129	90	82	20	68	102	—	—	—	8.15	5.43
Ring, Royce	L-L	6-0	220	12-21-80	0	0	2.13	11	0	0	0	13	7	3	3	2	3	8	.156	.150	.160	5.68	2.13
Sanchez, Duaner	R-R	6-2	210	10-14-79	5	1	2.60	49	0	0	0	55	43	19	16	3	24	44	.223	.276	.179	7.16	3.90
Soler, Alay	R-R	6-1	240	10-9-79	2	3	6.00	8	8	1	0	45	50	33	30	7	21	23	.275	.252	.307	4.60	4.20
Trachsel, Steve	R-R	6-4	205	10-31-70	15	8	4.97	30	30	1	0	165	185	94	91	23	78	79	.288	.267	.306	4.32	4.26
Wagner, Billy	L-L	5-11	205	7-25-71	3	2	2.24	70	0	0	40	72	59	22	18	7	21	94	.219	.161	.234	11.70	2.61
Williams, Dave	L-L	6-3	230	3-12-79	3	1	5.59	6	5	0	0	29	39	18	18	5	4	16	.333	.333	.333	4.97	1.24
2-team (8 Cincinnati)					5	4	6.52	14	13	0	0	69	93	52	50	14	20	32	—	—	—	4.17	2.61
Zambrano, Victor	B-R	6-0	205	8-6-75	1	2	6.75	5	5	0	0	21	25	16	16	5	11	15	.291	.344	.259	6.33	4.64

FIELDING

Catcher	PCT	G	PO	A	E	DP	PB
Castro	.996	37	267	16	1	3	1
DiFelice	.974	15	71	3	2	0	0
Lo Duca	.987	118	802	59	11	4	9
Marrero	1.000	2	1	0	0	0	0
Stinnett	.976	7	35	5	1	1	0

First Base	PCT	G	PO	A	E	DP
Delgado	.994	141	1199	70	8	95
Franco	.995	27	197	5	1	22
Green	1.000	1	2	0	0	0
Marrero	1.000	1	1	0	0	0

	PCT	G	PO	A	E	DP
Nady	1.000	1	3	0	0	1
Tucker	1.000	1	8	0	0	0
Valentin	1.000	1	3	0	0	0
Woodward	1.000	1	2	0	0	0

Second Base	PCT	G	PO	A	E	DP
Hernandez	1.000	13	26	27	0	3
Matsui	.994	31	72	85	1	23
Valentin	.988	94	194	286	6	52
Woodward	.976	39	72	93	4	20

Third Base	PCT	G	PO	A	E	DP
Franco	1.000	3	0	6	0	0

	PCT	G	PO	A	E	DP
Marrero	1.000	1	0	2	0	0
Valentin	1.000	1	1	1	0	0
Woodward	1.000	11	3	17	0	2
Wright	.954	153	107	288	19	31

Shortstop	PCT	G	PO	A	E	DP
Hernandez	1.000	10	3	7	0	0
Reyes	.971	149	176	390	17	72
Woodward	.979	13	13	33	1	10

Outfield	PCT	G	PO	A	E	DP
Beltran	.995	136	357	13	2	6
Chavez	1.000	120	209	9	0	3

General manager: Omar Minaya. **Farm director:** Adam Wogan. **Scouting director:** Rudy Terrasas.

Class	Team	League	W	L	PCT	Finish*	Manager	Affiliate Since
Majors	New York	National	97	65	.599	1st (16)	Willie Randolph	—
Triple-A	Norfolk Tides	International	57	84	.404	13th (14)	Ken Oberkfell	1969
Double-A	Binghamton Mets	Eastern	70	70	.500	6th (12)	Juan Samuel	1992
High A	St. Lucie Mets	Florida State	77	62	.554	+3rd (12)	Gary Carter	1988
Low A	Hagerstown Suns	South Atlantic	58	82	.414	14th (16)	Frank Cacciatore	2005
Short-season	Brooklyn Cyclones	New York-Penn	41	33	.554	4th (14)	George Greer	2001
Rookie	Kingsport Mets	Appalachian	34	33	.507	6th (10)	Donovan Mitchell	1980
Rookie	GCL Mets	Gulf Coast	23	30	.434	9th (13)	Bobby Floyd	2004
OVERALL 2006 MINOR LEAGUE RECORD			360	394	.477	24th (30)		

*Finish in overall standings (No. of teams in league). +League champion

Diaz	.800	4	4	0	1	0	Marrero	.909	7	10	0	1	0	Valentin	1.000	7	13	2	0	0
Floyd	.987	92	148	3	2	0	Milledge	.977	50	80	4	2	0	Woodward	1.000	9	12	0	0	0
Green	.949	31	56	0	3	0	Nady	.973	71	137	5	4	0							
Ledee	1.000	4	5	0	0	0	Tucker	1.000	18	27	2	0	0							

Norfolk Tides — Triple-A

International League

BATTING	B-T	HT	WT	DOB	AVG	vLH	vRH	G	AB	R	H	2B	3B	HR	RBI	BB	HBP	SH	SF	SO	SB	CS	SLG	OBP
Aldridge, Cory	L-R	6-1	225	6-13-79	.157	.100	.175	26	83	2	13	2	0	0	6	2	0	1	2	31	3	0	.181	.172
Alfonzo, Edgardo	R-R	5-11	210	11-8-73	.241	.205	.255	42	141	10	34	6	0	3	19	16	2	0	2	15	0	1	.348	.323
Basak, Chris	R-R	6-2	190	12-6-78	.267	.220	.286	119	371	53	99	22	3	8	36	39	5	2	0	76	17	3	.407	.345
Bozied, Tagg	R-R	6-3	210	7-24-79	.256	.261	.253	60	160	18	41	12	0	8	23	21	5	1	1	44	0	1	.481	.358
Cruz, Jacob	L-L	6-0	215	1-28-73	.290	.269	.294	55	145	18	42	16	0	0	17	22	0	0	0	31	0	0	.400	.383
2-team (3 Louisville)..					.287	—		58	157	19	45	16	0	1	20	22	0	0	0	33	0	0	.408	.374
Diaz, Victor	R-R	6-0	200	12-10-81	.224	.221	.226	103	379	30	85	16	0	8	38	25	3	2	2	99	5	5	.330	.276
DiFelice, Mike	R-R	6-2	200	5-28-69	.000	—	.000	1	2	1	0	0	0	0	0	1	0	0	0	0	0	0	.000	.333
Eldridge, Rashad	B-R	6-1	185	10-16-81	.222	.355	.153	30	90	4	20	5	1	1	10	7	0	0	0	21	0	2	.333	.278
Garcia, Yunir	R-R	6-0	170	8-3-82	.250	.222	.273	9	20	2	5	2	0	1	3	4	2	0	0	7	0	0	.500	.423
Gotay, Ruben	B-R	5-11	190	12-25-82	.266	.200	.294	42	154	19	41	12	1	3	21	10	2	2	1	29	4	5	.416	.317
Hernandez, Anderson	R-R	5-9	170	10-30-82	.249	.293	.232	102	414	44	103	11	4	0	23	21	0	9	0	70	15	5	.295	.285
Hietpas, Joe	R-R	6-3	220	5-1-79	.185	.177	.191	62	168	15	31	6	0	2	10	9	4	5	0	42	0	1	.256	.243
Keppinger, Jeff	R-R	6-0	180	4-21-80	.300	.357	.280	87	323	36	97	13	0	2	26	28	0	12	3	21	0	4	.359	.353
Lambin, Chase	B-R	6-2	195	7-7-79	.222	.184	.237	83	270	28	60	9	3	2	31	36	4	3	3	56	3	3	.300	.319
Ledee, Ricky	L-L	6-1	225	11-22-73	.083	.000	.143	4	12	1	1	0	0	0	1	0	0	0	0	2	0	0	.083	.083
Malek, Bobby	L-R	6-1	205	7-6-81	.179	.000	.213	18	56	5	10	2	0	0	3	2	1	3	0	11	1	0	.214	.220
Martinez, Sandy	L-R	6-2	215	10-8-70	.224	.226	.224	85	272	31	61	10	0	11	39	28	0	2	2	65	1	0	.382	.295
Matsui, Kazuo	B-R	5-10	185	10-23-75	.333	.200	.429	4	12	2	4	2	0	0	1	0	1	0	2	0	0	0	.500	.333
Milledge, Lastings	R-R	6-1	185	4-5-85	.277	.277	.277	84	307	52	85	21	4	7	36	43	14	1	2	67	13	10	.440	.388
Nady, Xavier	R-R	6-2	205	11-14-78	.364	.667	.250	3	11	2	4	1	0	0	3	1	0	0	0	3	0	0	.455	.417
Navarrete, Ray	R-R	6-0	202	5-20-78	.184	.000	.243	19	49	7	9	2	0	1	2	1	0	0	0	10	0	0	.286	.200
Offerman, Jose	B-R	6-1	200	11-8-68	.238	.216	.249	97	344	42	82	12	1	8	43	54	0	0	5	60	9	0	.349	.337
Ramirez, Julio	R-R	5-11	195	8-10-77	.188	.109	.222	50	154	15	29	5	0	2	9	15	9	0	1	54	4	3	.260	.232
Self, Todd	L-R	6-5	215	11-9-78	.108	.000	.114	14	37	2	4	0	0	0	3	6	0	0	0	18	0	0	.108	.298
Stinnett, Kelly	R-R	5-11	235	2-4-70	.375	.429	.333	5	16	2	6	1	0	1	1	2	0	0	2	0	0	0	.625	.444
Tejeda, Juan	R-R	6-2	195	1-26-82	.217	.205	.221	42	152	10	33	3	1	2	16	10	2	0	2	35	0	1	.289	.271
Tucker, Michael	L-R	6-2	195	6-25-71	.265	.288	.256	83	275	44	73	18	2	6	33	49	5	0	4	45	10	3	.411	.381

PITCHING	B-T	HT	WT	DOB	W	L	ERA	G	GS	CG	SV	IP	H	R	ER	HR	BB	SO	AVG	vLH	vRH	K/9	BB/9
Adams, Mike	R-R	6-5	190	7-29-78	0	0	4.91	13	0	0	0	15	13	8	8	0	7	12	.245	.308	.225	7.36	4.30
2-team (3 Buffalo)					0	0	4.19	16	0	0	0	19	17	9	9	0	7	15	—	—	—	6.98	3.26
Bannister, Brian	R-R	6-2	200	2-28-81	3	3	3.86	6	6	1	0	30	34	15	13	4	5	24	.279	.226	.297	7.12	1.48
Bell, Heath	R-R	6-3	225	9-29-77	3	3	1.29	30	0	0	12	35	27	7	5	1	8	56	.208	.196	.216	14.40	2.06
Clements, Zachary	R-R	6-0	215	4-17-80	0	0	0.00	1	0	0	0	1	0	0	0	0	0	0	.000	.000	.000	0.00	0.00
Collazo, Willie	L-L	5-9	175	11-7-79	3	3	4.79	7	5	0	0	41	45	24	22	4	13	26	.280	.406	.248	5.66	2.83
Cullen, Ryan	L-L	6-2	204	1-20-80	0	0	5.87	4	0	0	0	8	8	5	5	1	2	6	.250	.308	.211	7.04	2.35
Feliciano, Pedro	L-L	5-10	185	8-25-76	0	0	6.23	4	0	0	0	4	3	3	3	1	1	5	.250	.167	.300	10.38	2.08
Fortunato, Bartolome	R-R	6-1	195	8-24-74	1	0	2.70	11	0	0	0	17	12	6	5	0	4	21	.197	.154	.229	11.34	2.16
Garcia, Anderson	R-R	6-2	170	3-23-81	1	4	6.32	20	0	0	0	31	35	25	22	4	14	18	.287	.224	.329	5.17	4.02
2-team (5 Ottawa)					1	4	5.68	25	1	0	0	38	39	27	24	4	17	21	—	—	—	4.97	4.03
Gonzalez, Geremi	R-R	6-0	220	1-8-75	1	2	3.03	6	6	0	0	36	31	14	12	1	9	30	.230	.215	.243	7.57	2.27
Hietpas, Joe	R-R	6-3	220	5-1-79	0	0	0.00	1	0	0	0	1	2	0	0	0	0	1	.400	.667	.000	9.00	0.00
Iriki, Yusaku	R-R	5-10	180	8-13-72	4	8	4.70	19	16	0	0	77	92	42	40	8	32	62	.306	.283	.320	7.28	3.76
Lavigne, Tim	R-R	5-10	210	7-4-78	3	2	2.62	45	4	0	4	82	73	29	24	7	25	49	.241	.252	.234	5.36	2.73
Lima, Jose	R-R	6-2	210	9-30-72	7	8	3.92	25	22	0	0	140	140	64	61	15	20	88	.264	.225	.286	5.66	1.29
MacLane, Evan	L-L	6-2	190	11-4-82	9	8	3.86	20	20	1	0	121	136	61	52	11	35	67	.285	.160	.314	4.97	2.60
Maine, John	R-R	6-4	205	5-8-81	3	5	3.49	10	10	0	0	57	55	25	22	2	10	48	.253	.240	.264	7.62	3.18
McGinley, Blake	R-L	6-1	175	8-2-78	2	2	2.95	22	8	0	1	58	59	20	19	6	14	36	.266	.259	.268	5.59	2.17
McNab, Tim	R-R	6-0	175	6-4-80	0	0	6.43	3	0	0	0	7	9	5	5	1	0	7	.310	.625	.190	9.00	0.00
Navarrete, Ray	R-R	6-0	202	5-20-78	0	0	4.50	1	0	0	0	2	4	1	1	1	0	1	.400	.400	.400	4.50	0.00
Paulk, Robert	R-R	5-11	175	3-14-81	1	0	0.00	2	0	0	0	5	4	0	0	0	1	3	.211	.444	.000	5.40	1.80
Pelfrey, Mike	R-R	6-7	210	1-14-84	1	0	2.25	2	2	0	0	8	4	2	2	0	5	6	.148	.143	.150	6.75	5.63
Perez, Oliver	L-L	6-3	210	8-15-81	1	2	6.05	4	4	0	0	19	18	13	13	4	12	26	.250	.133	.281	12.10	5.59
2-team (6 Indianapolis)					2	5	5.79	10	10	0	0	51	46	34	33	10	23	60	—	—	—	10.52	4.03

ORGANIZATION STATISTICS

	B-T	HT	WT	DOB	W	L	ERA	G	GS	CG	SV	IP	H	R	ER	HR	BB	SO	AVG	vLH	vRH	K/9	BB/9
Perez, Juan	R-L	6-0	170	9-3-78	0	1	2.86	43	0	0	0	63	65	24	20	4	34	55	.266	.225	.287	7.86	4.86
2-team (4 Indianapolis)					0	1	2.57	47	0	0	0	70	68	24	20	4	37	61	—	—	—	7.84	4.76
Perez, Miguel	R-R	6-1	192	2-19-76	0	2	3.86	5	5	0	0	28	33	14	12	1	13	18	.308	.333	.290	5.79	4.18
Ring, Royce	L-L	6-0	220	12-21-80	2	2	2.97	36	0	0	11	39	30	14	13	2	15	40	.210	.140	.247	9.15	3.43
Robertson, Jeriome	L-L	6-2	215	3-30-77	1	6	7.68	11	7	0	0	39	58	34	33	6	18	21	.354	.487	.312	4.89	4.19
Roman, Orlando	R-R	6-1	210	11-28-78	0	1	4.05	8	1	0	1	13	15	7	6	0	7	10	.283	.294	.278	6.75	4.73
Schmoll, Steve	R-R	6-3	220	2-4-80	5	4	4.69	42	0	0	0	56	56	31	29	4	19	42	.271	.352	.228	6.79	3.07
Scobie, Jason	R-R	6-1	195	9-1-79	1	11	7.91	16	15	0	0	77	117	70	68	9	31	47	.355	.320	.383	5.47	3.61
2-team (12 Syracuse)					3	18	6.53	28	23	1	1	133	177	101	97	19	47	83	—	—	—	5.59	3.16
Smith, Chuck	R-R	6-3	205	12-13-81	0	0	108.00	1	0	0	0	0	4	4	4	1	1	0	.800	1.000	.750	0.00	27.00
Soler, Alay	R-R	6-1	240	10-9-79	1	1	6.30	2	2	0	0	10	13	7	7	0	4	12	.317	.357	.296	10.80	3.60
Vazquez, William	R-R	6-1	160	12-26-79	0	0	10.13	2	0	0	0	3	8	4	3	0	0	1	.571	.429	.714	3.38	0.00
Williams, Dave	L-L	6-3	230	3-12-79	2	2	3.68	7	6	0	0	37	33	20	15	3	10	17	.236	.286	.219	4.17	2.45
Wylie, Mitch	R-R	6-3	220	1-14-77	2	4	2.96	27	2	0	1	49	47	21	16	0	11	53	.251	.175	.285	9.80	2.03

FIELDING

Catcher	PCT	G	PO	A	E	DP	PB
Clements	1.000	2	14	1	0	2	0
DiFelice	1.000	1	3	2	0	0	0
Garcia	1.000	8	58	0	0	1	1
Hietpas	.982	57	301	19	6	4	2
Martinez	.983	81	529	35	10	9	3
Stinnett	1.000	5	40	2	0	0	0

First Base	PCT	G	PO	A	E	DP
Bozied	1.000	3	16	1	0	1
Cruz	1.000	11	75	4	0	9
Hietpas	1.000	4	21	0	0	5
Navarrete	1.000	4	24	3	0	2
Offerman	.993	88	767	43	6	78
Self	.960	8	67	5	3	5
Tejeda	.973	29	232	21	7	26

Second Base	PCT	G	PO	A	E	DP
Alfonzo	1.000	5	12	22	0	4

	PCT	G	PO	A	E	DP
Basak	1.000	10	19	14	0	5
Gotay	.988	37	79	88	2	19
Hernandez	.994	31	73	97	1	23
Keppinger	.979	56	120	160	6	46
Matsui	1.000	4	3	11	0	2
Navarrete	1.000	5	10	11	0	2

Third Base	PCT	G	PO	A	E	DP
Alfonzo	1.000	35	22	73	0	8
Basak	1.000	26	10	59	0	4
Bozied	1.000	1	0	1	0	0
Gotay	1.000	2	0	6	0	1
Keppinger	1.000	9	7	16	0	3
Lambin	.929	71	39	145	14	12
Navarrete	1.000	2	0	2	0	0

Shortstop	PCT	G	PO	A	E	DP
Basak	.953	67	101	200	15	47
Gotay	1.000	2	3	6	0	1
Hernandez	.963	72	108	226	13	44
Lambin	.889	3	4	12	2	4

Outfield	PCT	G	PO	A	E	DP
Aldridge	1.000	21	29	1	0	0
Basak	1.000	11	15	0	0	0
Bozied	.963	37	49	3	2	0
Cruz	1.000	18	24	1	0	0
Diaz	.963	86	148	7	6	4
Eldridge	1.000	28	58	0	0	0
Keppinger	.966	14	27	1	1	0
Lambin	—	1	0	0	0	0
Ledee	1.000	4	9	0	0	0
Malek	1.000	18	35	1	0	1
Milledge	.990	84	185	6	2	1
Nady	1.000	3	4	0	0	0
Navarrete	1.000	1	1	0	0	0
Ramirez	.979	44	88	6	2	2
Self	1.000	3	1	0	0	0
Tucker	.985	71	131	2	2	0

Binghamton Mets — Double-A

Eastern League

BATTING	B-T	HT	WT	DOB	AVG	vLH	vRH	G	AB	R	H	2B	3B	HR	RBI	BB	HBP	SH	SF	SO	SB	CS	SLG	OBP
Abreu, Michel	R-R	6-0	220	1-2-79	.332	.316	.337	111	398	62	132	26	1	17	70	45	5	0	2	87	0	0	.530	.404
Batista, Wilson	B-R	6-0	170	2-7-81	.241	.240	.242	119	468	63	113	19	2	11	41	42	4	8	1	84	6	8	.361	.309
Caligiuri, Jay	R-R	6-0	190	3-29-80	.232	.279	.214	126	410	51	95	16	1	18	64	59	15	2	5	90	1	1	.407	.346
Concepcion, Ambiorix	R-R	6-2	180	3-19-82	.261	.295	.248	63	218	24	57	11	1	3	29	7	3	5	2	57	11	2	.362	.291
Cruz, Enrique	R-R	5-10	185	7-13-81	.200	.385	.091	16	35	2	7	3	0	0	3	8	0	1	0	10	1	1	.286	.341
DiFelice, Mike	R-R	6-2	200	5-28-69	.277	.318	.267	39	112	9	31	7	0	1	19	15	4	0	3	24	0	0	.366	.373
Eldridge, Rashad	B-R	6-1	185	10-16-81	.284	.250	.300	31	116	17	33	6	2	1	10	9	0	0	0	35	1	2	.397	.336
Garcia, Yunir	R-R	6-0	170	8-3-82	.110	.182	.087	47	136	15	15	3	0	0	3	21	1	3	0	66	0	0	.132	.234
Gomez, Carlos	R-R	6-2	175	12-4-85	.281	.233	.299	120	430	53	121	24	8	7	48	27	20	6	3	97	41	9	.423	.350
Harper, Brett	L-R	6-4	185	7-31-81	.338	.471	.292	19	65	8	22	7	0	0	8	7	3	0	0	19	1	0	.446	.427
Hietpas, Joe	R-R	6-3	220	5-1-79	.130	.227	.085	21	69	2	9	0	0	1	7	4	1	1	0	22	0	0	.174	.189
Lambin, Chase	B-R	6-2	195	7-7-79	.271	.250	.275	39	133	29	36	13	0	7	20	20	4	3	1	35	2	1	.526	.380
Malek, Bobby	L-R	6-1	205	7-6-81	.240	.276	.227	63	221	28	53	9	5	5	27	19	1	6	1	42	2	3	.376	.302
Navarrete, Ray	R-R	6-0	202	5-20-78	.207	.194	.213	33	116	15	24	5	0	4	12	8	0	0	1	14	1	1	.353	.256
Nickeas, Mike	R-R	6-0	205	2-13-83	.167	—	.167	4	12	1	2	0	0	0	3	1	1	0	1	4	0	0	.167	.267
Padilla, Jorge	R-R	6-2	205	8-11-79	.295	.300	.293	129	482	66	142	26	1	10	54	42	6	3	1	87	8	5	.415	.358
Ragsdale, Corey	R-R	6-4	175	11-10-82	.204	.200	.205	129	437	47	89	19	3	10	37	40	3	5	2	182	12	9	.330	.274
Rios, Kevin	R-R	6-2	180	7-21-81	.223	.196	.239	53	139	11	31	7	0	1	20	5	2	0	0	36	1	0	.295	.260
Slack, Jonathan	L-L	5-11	180	12-4-81	.172	.054	.200	48	157	14	27	4	1	0	9	12	1	2	2	41	5	3	.210	.233
Turay, Alhaji	R-R	6-0	205	9-22-82	.256	.238	.278	12	39	4	10	1	0	2	1	1	0	0	0	15	0	1	.282	.293
Wilson, Andy	R-R	6-1	210	11-20-80	.226	.242	.219	95	319	31	72	17	0	8	28	31	5	1	2	87	0	2	.335	.303

PITCHING	B-T	HT	WT	DOB	W	L	ERA	G	GS	CG	SV	IP	H	R	ER	HR	BB	SO	AVG	vLH	vRH	K/9	BB/9
Camacho, Eddie	L-L	6-1	180	9-17-82	3	4	3.63	53	0	0	1	79	71	36	32	6	25	61	.235	.246	.227	6.92	2.84
Collazo, Willie	L-L	5-9	175	11-7-79	7	6	3.11	18	18	1	0	119	104	44	41	7	16	79	.239	.238	.239	5.99	1.21
Cordova, Vincent	R-R	6-3	210	4-16-82	0	1	4.66	5	0	0	0	10	12	5	5	0	1	9	.316	.316	.318	8.38	0.93
Cullen, Ryan	L-L	6-2	204	1-20-80	5	4	2.98	35	0	0	1	60	47	23	20	4	16	52	.212	.221	.205	7.76	2.39
Devaney, Michael	R-R	6-4	220	7-31-82	4	2	3.06	11	10	2	0	53	39	19	18	5	35	43	.211	.186	.232	7.30	5.94
Eager, Blake	R-R	6-3	205	5-19-82	0	0	2.70	1	1	0	0	7	3	2	2	2	0	5	.125	.000	.167	6.75	0.00
Edwards, Bryan	R-R	6-5	195	8-21-79	4	8	4.72	21	18	0	0	88	85	55	46	7	36	54	.253	.249	.257	5.54	3.70
Garcia, Anderson	R-R	6-2	170	3-23-81	1	1	1.29	11	0	0	1	21	21	5	3	0	6	17	.266	.361	.186	7.29	2.57
2-team (4 Bowie)					3	2	1.53	15	0	0	1	29	27	7	5	0	6	25	—	—	—	7.67	1.84
Humber, Philip	R-R	6-4	210	12-21-82	2	2	2.88	6	6	0	0	34	25	12	11	4	10	36	.195	.210	.182	9.44	2.62
Lindstrom, Matt	R-R	6-4	210	2-11-80	2	4	3.76	35	0	0	11	41	42	19	17	2	14	54	.266	.296	.241	11.95	3.10
MacLane, Evan	L-L	6-2	190	11-4-82	3	1	4.64	6	6	0	0	33	34	17	17	4	2	25	.266	.297	.253	6.82	0.55
Maldonado, Ivan	R-R	6-3	210	6-7-80	2	3	2.51	48	0	0	3	61	62	19	17	6	27	57	.263	.224	.290	8.41	3.98
McNab, Tim	R-R	6-0	175	6-4-80	3	3	3.34	13	3	0	0	35	43	17	13	2	2	19	.312	.319	.303	4.89	0.51
Mulvey, Kevin	R-R	6-1	175	5-26-85	0	1	1.35	3	3	1	0	13	10	4	2	1	5	10	.217	.241	.176	6.75	3.38
Nall, Brandon	R-R	6-4	190	3-18-82	0	0	0.00	2	0	0	0	4	1	0	0	1	1	4	.083	.000	.143	9.00	2.25
Owens, Henry	R-R	6-3	230	4-23-79	2	2	1.58	37	0	0	20	40	19	9	7	1	10	74	.137	.111	.158	16.65	2.25
Paulk, Robert	R-R	5-11	175	3-14-81	5	2	2.82	26	2	0	0	51	48	17	16	1	16	29	.242	.250	.236	5.12	2.82
Pelfrey, Mike	R-R	6-7	210	1-14-84	3	2	2.71	12	12	0	0	66	60	23	20	2	20	64	.244	.220	.268	10.45	3.53
Perez, Miguel	R-R	6-1	192	2-19-76	6	7	4.94	19	19	0	0	102	111	60	56	10	40	71	.278	.323	.237	6.26	3.53
Pinango, Miguel	R-R	6-1	160	1-20-83	10	7	4.44	28	27	2	0	152	159	86	75	20	41	80	.270	.260	.279	4.74	2.43
Portobanco, Luz	R-R	6-3	205	9-15-79	0	0	3.00	2	0	0	0	3	2	1	1	0	3	2	.000	.000	.000	6.00	9.00

Name	B-T	HT	WT	DOB	W	L	ERA	G	GS	CG	SV	IP	H	R	ER	HR	BB	SO	AVG	vLH	vRH	K/9	BB/9
Rios, Kevin	R-R	6-2	180	7-21-81	0	1	9.00	1	0	0	0	1	2	1	1	0	1	1	.400	.500	.333	9.00	9.00
Roman, Orlando	R-R	6-1	210	11-28-78	4	2	3.79	31	2	0	1	55	50	28	23	4	27	44	.244	.275	.219	7.24	4.45
Rundles, Rich	L-L	6-5	180	6-3-81	1	3	4.57	12	7	0	0	43	53	32	22	4	23	23	.305	.300	.307	4.78	4.78
Smith, Chuck	R-R	6-3	205	12-13-81	1	0	2.84	4	1	0	0	13	8	4	4	1	3	11	.186	.136	.238	7.82	2.13
Smith, Joseph	R-R	6-2	205	3-22-84	0	2	5.68	10	0	0	0	13	12	8	8	1	11	12	.267	.500	.080	8.53	7.82
Soler, Alay	R-R	6-1	240	10-9-79	1	0	2.75	3	3	0	0	20	16	6	6	0	3	22	.222	.250	.194	10.07	1.37
Urdaneta, Lino	R-R	6-1	170	11-20-79	0	1	2.25	5	0	0	0	4	3	1	1	0	1	2	.214	.333	.125	4.50	2.25
Vazquez, William	R-R	6-1	160	12-26-79	0	2	9.82	2	2	0	0	7	15	8	8	1	3	4	.405	.500	.267	4.91	3.68

FIELDING

Catcher	PCT	G	PO	A	E	DP	PB
Clements	1.000	6	34	3	0	1	1
DiFelice	.989	38	256	19	3	6	3
Garcia	.994	45	331	16	2	1	1
Hietpas	.980	21	138	10	3	1	4
Nickeas	.958	4	23	0	1	0	1
Wilson	.992	36	225	15	2	5	5

First Base	PCT	G	PO	A	E	DP
Abreu	.993	96	812	64	6	84
Caligiuri	.993	17	130	11	1	9
Harper	1.000	17	136	15	0	11
Malek	—	1	0	0	0	0
Navarrete	1.000	1	4	1	0	1
Wilson	.992	15	118	7	1	9

Second Base	PCT	G	PO	A	E	DP
Batista	.964	113	198	334	20	69
Cruz	.938	6	5	10	1	0
Navarrete	.966	7	7	21	1	1
Rios	1.000	18	30	42	0	8

Third Base	PCT	G	PO	A	E	DP
Caligiuri	.926	92	57	168	18	10
Cruz	—	1	0	0	0	0
Lambin	.878	33	23	78	14	8
Navarrete	.909	5	3	7	1	0
Rios	.895	9	4	13	2	1
Wilson	.929	7	0	13	1	1

Shortstop	PCT	G	PO	A	E	DP
Batista	1.000	2	1	3	0	0

	PCT	G	PO	A	E	DP
Ragsdale	.963	128	221	357	22	81
Rios	.955	17	26	37	3	7

Outfield	PCT	G	PO	A	E	DP
Concepcion	.975	61	113	5	3	1
Eldridge	1.000	23	34	0	0	0
Gomez	.977	118	300	3	7	0
Lambin	—	1	0	0	0	0
Malek	.955	54	99	7	5	2
Navarrete	1.000	18	21	1	0	0
Padilla	.984	113	183	4	3	2
Rios	1.000	2	2	0	0	0
Slack	1.000	41	70	2	0	0
Turay	1.000	3	6	0	0	0

St. Lucie Mets — High Class A

Florida State League

BATTING	B-T	HT	WT	DOB	AVG	vLH	vRH	G	AB	R	H	2B	3B	HR	RBI	BB	HBP	SH	SF	SO	SB	CS	SLG	OBP
Abreu, Michel	R-R	6-0	220	1-2-79	.333	.000	.500	2	9	2	3	1	0	0	0	0	0	0	0	2	0	0	.444	.333
Blaquiere, Jean Luc	R-R	6-0	196	2-27-86	.250	1.000	.000	2	4	1	1	0	0	0	0	0	1	0	1	2	0	0	.250	.400
Bowman, Shawn	R-R	6-2	205	12-9-84	.252	.320	.234	32	119	17	30	5	1	3	19	8	3	0	2	39	0	0	.387	.311
Bucce, Yasmil	R-R	6-1	180	8-29-84	.364	.333	.375	4	11	1	4	1	0	0	3	1	0	0	1	3	0	0	.455	.385
Carp, Mike	L-R	6-2	205	6-30-86	.287	.238	.309	137	491	69	141	27	1	17	88	51	25	0	6	107	2	1	.450	.379
Coles, Corey	L-L	6-1	170	1-30-82	.341	.248	.372	124	458	65	156	26	4	1	45	48	5	9	2	59	21	9	.421	.407
Concepcion, Ambiorix	R-R	6-2	180	3-19-82	.287	.260	.297	71	282	38	81	21	2	1	33	25	1	4	4	67	18	9	.387	.343
Coronado, Jose	B-R	6-1	175	4-13-86	.226	.208	.233	138	544	61	123	20	4	0	37	41	3	31	2	119	14	7	.278	.283
Coultas, Ryan	R-R	6-3	180	4-24-82	.146	.200	.128	50	144	10	21	3	0	0	8	7	0	3	2	31	3	0	.167	.183
Cruz, Enrique	R-R	5-10	185	7-13-81	.278	.384	.233	98	335	37	93	22	3	5	42	39	5	5	2	69	6	0	.406	.360
Cummins, Daniel	R-R	5-9	190	12-11-82	.204	.364	.158	18	49	5	10	2	0	2	13	6	0	0	0	9	0	1	.367	.291
Flores, Jesus	R-R	6-1	180	10-26-84	.266	.263	.267	120	429	66	114	32	0	21	70	28	18	2	3	127	2	0	.487	.335
Floyd, Cliff	L-R	6-4	230	12-5-72	.400	.250	.500	3	10	2	4	0	0	2	4	1	0	0	0	0	1	0	1.000	.455
Gaerlan, Armand	R-R	5-10	180	8-22-82	.000	.000	.000	6	14	2	0	0	0	0	0	0	0	3	0	2	0	1	.000	.125
Garcia, Yunir	R-R	6-0	170	8-3-82	.219	.333	.174	13	32	7	7	3	0	0	2	8	2	0	0	9	0	0	.313	.405
Hernandez, Anderson	B-R	5-9	170	10-30-82	.111	—	.111	2	9	0	1	0	0	0	0	0	0	0	0	1	0	0	.111	.111
Hill, Jamar	R-R	6-3	200	9-20-82	.235	.262	.226	78	251	32	59	13	3	6	28	19	4	3	1	77	7	1	.382	.298
Malek, Bobby	L-R	6-1	205	7-6-81	.318	.500	.278	6	22	3	7	3	0	0	1	2	0	0	0	3	1	0	.455	.375
Malo, Jonathan	R-R	6-1	175	9-29-83	.239	.244	.237	91	284	42	68	13	4	1	33	34	7	3	2	53	3	3	.366	.333
Martinez, Fernando	L-R	6-0	185	10-10-88	.193	.204	.186	30	119	18	23	4	2	5	11	6	4	0	1	24	1	1	.387	.254
Matsui, Kazuo	B-R	5-10	185	10-23-75	.286	.000	.400	2	7	1	2	0	0	0	0	0	1	0	0	0	0	0	.286	.375
Naccarata, Ivan	L-R	6-0	190	2-26-82	.273	.400	.256	13	44	7	12	3	0	1	4	2	0	1	1	10	1	0	.409	.298
Petersen, Joshua	R-R	6-3	215	4-15-83	.234	.274	.220	91	320	34	75	14	0	6	30	14	4	2	1	71	2	1	.334	.274
Piazza, Tony	R-R	6-2	215	6-22-80	.239	.182	.257	16	46	4	11	1	0	2	4	8	1	0	1	17	0	0	.391	.352
Stewart, Caleb	R-R	6-2	230	6-11-82	.259	.299	.241	74	243	38	63	17	2	14	42	24	8	2	2	52	1	1	.519	.343
Turay, Alhaji	R-R	6-0	205	9-22-82	.244	.153	.271	77	266	46	65	12	1	9	37	14	5	2	3	81	12	2	.398	.292

PITCHING	B-T	HT	WT	DOB	W	L	ERA	G	GS	CG	SV	IP	H	R	ER	HR	BB	SO	AVG	vLH	vRH	K/9	BB/9
Aguilar, Salvador	R-R	6-0	190	1-9-82	7	5	3.25	20	19	0	0	114	124	48	41	5	32	65	.277	.278	.277	5.15	2.53
Alfonzo, Edgar	L-L	5-10	170	12-14-84	5	7	3.95	39	0	0	6	73	75	36	32	4	29	45	.270	.262	.273	5.55	3.58
Bannister, Brian	R-R	6-2	200	2-28-81	1	0	1.50	2	2	0	0	12	10	4	2	0	4	9	.233	.238	.227	6.75	3.00
Cova, Rafael	R-R	6-1	170	3-5-82	3	2	6.21	24	0	0	3	38	47	29	26	3	22	42	.296	.254	.323	10.04	5.26
Devaney, Michael	R-R	6-4	220	7-31-82	8	3	1.62	16	16	2	0	95	63	26	17	4	35	86	.188	.208	.173	8.18	3.33
Eager, Blake	R-R	6-3	205	5-19-82	5	3	3.78	15	15	1	0	86	84	38	36	8	20	59	.257	.246	.263	6.20	2.10
Guerra, Deolis	R-R	6-5	200	4-17-89	1	1	6.14	2	2	0	0	7	9	6	5	1	5	6	.290	.400	.238	6.14	7.36
Hope, Travis	R-R	6-3	200	1-29-81	3	1	3.69	25	1	0	2	63	72	30	26	6	17	26	.294	.286	.300	3.69	2.42
Humber, Philip	R-R	6-4	210	12-21-82	3	1	2.37	7	7	0	0	38	24	12	10	4	9	36	.178	.136	.198	8.53	2.13
Iriki, Yusaku	R-R	5-10	180	8-13-72	0	0	0.00	1	0	0	0	3	2	0	0	1	0	2	.222	1.000	.125	0.00	3.00
Lindstrom, Matt	R-R	6-4	210	2-11-80	1	0	2.50	11	0	0	2	18	14	7	5	2	7	16	.212	.185	.231	8.00	3.50
Maine, John	R-R	6-4	205	5-8-81	1	0	0.00	1	1	0	0	5	3	0	0	0	2	7	.167	.200	.125	12.60	3.60
McNab, Tim	R-R	6-0	175	6-4-80	1	1	5.19	4	0	0	0	5	5	5	3	1	0	5	.286	.167	.348	5.19	0.00
Muniz, Carlos	R-R	6-1	180	3-12-81	4	3	3.08	48	0	0	31	50	39	21	17	5	18	45	.213	.227	.205	8.15	3.26
Niese, Jonathan	L-L	6-3	190	10-27-86	0	2	4.50	2	2	0	0	10	8	8	5	0	5	10	.216	.250	.212	9.00	4.50
Parnell, Robert	R-R	6-3	190	9-8-84	0	1	9.26	3	3	0	0	12	16	13	12	3	9	13	.333	.095	.519	10.03	6.94
Paulk, Robert	R-R	5-11	175	3-14-81	2	0	4.08	12	3	1	0	29	35	19	13	2	11	12	.302	.244	.333	3.77	3.45
Pelfrey, Mike	R-R	6-7	210	1-14-84	2	1	1.64	4	4	0	0	22	17	5	4	1	2	26	.224	.278	.175	10.64	0.82
Perez, Marcelo	R-R	6-1	166	10-10-80	4	3	3.07	28	0	0	1	44	39	19	15	4	25	52	.235	.241	.231	10.64	5.11
Quintero, Mayque	R-R	6-2	225	4-19-78	1	3	8.51	7	5	0	0	24	33	26	23	3	8	22	.320	.250	.373	8.14	2.96
Ruckle, Jacob	R-R	6-1	180	5-27-86	4	3	1.60	9	6	0	0	51	47	12	9	3	7	25	.244	.237	.250	4.44	1.24
Rundles, Rich	L-L	6-5	180	6-3-81	1	2	1.83	3	0	0	0	20	27	8	4	2	4	12	.329	.176	.369	4.12	2.75
Sanchez, Jose	R-R	6-0	170	5-12-84	11	9	3.87	26	26	1	0	156	148	77	67	12	43	83	.254	.257	.253	4.79	2.48
Santana, Yury	R-R	5-11	160	8-15-82	0	0	0.00	1	0	0	0	1	1	0	0	0	1	1	.333	.500	.000	9.00	9.00
Serfass, Joseph	R-R	6-3	215	5-6-81	1	2	2.32	24	0	0	0	43	35	11	11	6	9	37	.266	.281	.173	7.80	1.90
Smith, Chuck	R-R	6-3	205	12-13-81	4	5	4.24	26	9	0	0	87	83	57	41	11	48	60	.256	.239	.266	6.21	4.97

Player	B-T	HT	WT	DOB	W	L	ERA	G	GS	CG	SV	IP	H	R	ER	HR	BB	SO	AVG	vLH	vRH	K/9	BB/9
Soler, Alay	R-R	6-1	240	10-9-79	2	0	0.60	6	6	0	0	30	13	2	2	0	9	33	.129	.103	.145	9.90	2.70
Swindell, Mike	R-R	6-1	190	9-26-81	2	4	4.46	8	8	0	0	34	42	23	17	3	10	23	.304	.407	.238	6.03	2.62
Tomasiewicz, Kevin	L-L	6-2	225	9-17-83	0	0	9.00	1	0	0	1	2	2	2	2	1	1	4	.250	—	.250	18.00	4.50
Vazquez, William	R-R	6-1	160	12-26-79	0	0	1.08	8	0	0	0	17	11	2	2	0	4	15	.193	.208	.182	8.10	2.16

FIELDING

Catcher	PCT	G	PO	A	E	DP	PB
Bucce	1.000	3	21	4	0	0	1
Cummins	1.000	13	59	4	0	0	2
Flores	.995	101	670	85	4	7	12
Garcia	.988	12	70	9	1	1	0
Piazza	.971	15	62	5	2	0	2

First Base	PCT	G	PO	A	E	DP
Abreu	1.000	1	9	0	0	2
Carp	.989	136	1130	84	14	105
Cruz	1.000	2	8	1	0	1
Petersen	1.000	5	27	1	0	1

Second Base	PCT	G	PO	A	E	DP
Coultas	.933	41	65	89	11	14

	PCT	G	PO	A	E	DP
Cruz	.974	77	146	187	9	44
Gaerlan	1.000	5	6	5	0	1
Hernandez	.923	2	4	8	1	2
Malo	.973	22	45	63	3	18
Matsui	.909	2	3	7	1	2

Third Base	PCT	G	PO	A	E	DP
Bowman	.905	32	19	57	8	7
Cruz	.700	2	1	6	3	0
Malo	.915	68	49	146	18	9
Naccarata	.935	13	8	35	3	3
Petersen	.896	28	20	40	7	2

Shortstop	PCT	G	PO	A	E	DP
Coronado	.952	138	233	408	32	90

	PCT	G	PO	A	E	DP
Malo	1.000	1	4	2	0	1

Outfield	PCT	G	PO	A	E	DP
Coles	.984	119	245	7	4	2
Concepcion	.983	71	165	5	3	0
Floyd	.750	2	3	0	1	0
Hill	.978	64	130	6	3	1
Malek	1.000	6	11	1	0	0
Martinez	.986	30	67	2	1	0
Petersen	.975	28	39	0	1	0
Stewart	.961	65	118	6	5	1
Turay	.944	44	66	1	4	0

Hagerstown Suns   Low Class A

South Atlantic League

BATTING

Player	B-T	HT	WT	DOB	AVG	vLH	vRH	G	AB	R	H	2B	3B	HR	RBI	BB	HBP	SH	SF	SO	SB	CS	SLG	OBP
Anderson, Matthew	L-R	6-2	205	12-9-82	.207	.171	.214	77	222	30	46	7	0	1	19	37	1	3	3	51	1	2	.252	.319
Arroyo, Rafael	R-R	5-9	170	10-26-82	.209	.152	.234	53	153	22	32	11	0	1	18	22	9	3	2	52	3	1	.301	.339
Austin, Parris	R-R	6-2	185	12-13-85	.281	.143	.320	12	32	4	9	0	0	1	5	5	0	1	0	8	2	3	.281	.378
Butera, Andrew	R-R	6-1	190	8-9-83	.186	.183	.188	95	295	24	55	13	0	5	38	42	7	5	6	72	1	0	.281	.297
Castro, Jose	B-R	5-8	160	11-5-86	.219	.263	.206	118	434	38	95	12	1	0	38	21	20	21	0	52	6	4	.284	.286
Coultas, Ryan	R-R	5-9	180	4-24-82	.232	.214	.239	26	95	10	22	5	0	1	5	14	5	1	1	22	4	0	.284	.277
Cruz, Elvis	R-R	6-2	195	11-23-83	.260	.342	.226	40	131	8	34	5	1	3	14	5	1	3	2	29	3	2	.382	.288
Evans, Nick	R-R	6-2	180	1-30-86	.254	.256	.254	137	511	55	130	33	3	15	67	45	6	0	3	99	2	0	.419	.320
Gaerlan, Armand	R-R	5-10	180	8-22-82	.197	.130	.226	24	76	14	15	7	1	3	7	4	1	1	1	15	1	1	.434	.244
Gamero, Jesus	R-R	6-1	170	1-24-84	.310	.235	.343	44	132	22	44	7	1	3	17	8	4	0	2	17	2	2	.437	.359
Henry, Sean	R-R	5-10	154	8-18-85	.254	.364	.204	21	71	7	18	5	0	3	14	3	0	1	1	16	7	4	.451	.280
Holden, Joe	L-R	5-11	175	4-10-84	.300	.314	.295	38	140	24	42	5	0	6	25	15	1	2	3	31	12	2	.464	.367
Lietz, Todd	R-R	6-0	175	12-21-82	.143	.000	.167	2	7	0	1	0	0	0	0	0	0	0	0	2	0	0	.143	.143
Manuel, Anthony	R-R	6-0	175	8-17-82	.000	.000	.000	8	10	1	0	0	0	0	0	1	1	0	0	13	0	0	.000	.091
Martinez, Joan	B-R	5-11	175	5-7-84	.030	.091	.000	13	33	2	1	1	0	1	3	0	0	0	0	13	0	0	.061	.111
Martinez, Fernando	L-R	6-0	185	10-10-88	.333	.284	.360	45	192	24	64	14	2	5	28	15	3	0	1	36	7	4	.505	.389
Pacheco, Jonel	R-R	5-9	170	10-3-82	.264	.233	.275	127	462	61	122	25	2	10	47	37	4	4	5	75	21	15	.392	.321
Pellot, Hector	R-R	5-11	184	2-8-87	.189	.242	.170	100	359	30	68	17	1	2	16	41	11	9	0	95	5	5	.259	.292
Piazza, Tony	R-R	6-2	215	6-22-80	.247	.364	.196	23	73	9	18	9	0	2	6	9	2	0	0	24	1	0	.452	.345
Rivera, Luis	R-R	6-1	165	1-25-84	.222	.333	.167	4	9	0	2	0	0	0	0	0	0	0	0	0	1	0	.222	.222
Sanchez, Jonathan	L-L	6-2	175	9-3-85	.238	.275	.227	85	324	39	77	9	1	9	27	19	1	2	1	58	12	6	.355	.281
Schemmel, Jon	R-R	5-11	190	1-27-82	.297	.222	.315	30	91	8	27	5	0	1	7	18	2	0	1	14	1	4	.352	.387
Ventura, Leivi	R-R	6-1	185	7-19-83	.231	.175	.251	132	471	63	109	21	2	11	48	48	14	2	2	134	2	9	.362	.320
Vogl, Will	R-R	5-9	175	12-10-83	.250	.167	.279	55	188	24	47	7	1	4	21	18	5	2	0	64	4	0	.362	.332
Voyles, Jeffery	R-R	5-10	185	11-29-83	.238	.600	.125										1	0	0		2	0	.238	.304

PITCHING

Player	B-T	HT	WT	DOB	W	L	ERA	G	GS	CG	SV	IP	H	R	ER	HR	BB	SO	AVG	vLH	vRH	K/9	BB/9
Abel, Nick	R-R	6-4	200	2-18-83	1	1	1.35	15	0	0	0	20	18	5	3	0	5	17	.243	.294	.200	7.65	2.25
Aguilar, Salvador	R-R	6-0	190	1-9-82	0	0	2.54	5	5	0	0	28	28	11	8	3	2	19	.259	.310	.200	6.04	0.64
Appell, Josh	L-L	6-1	195	6-23-83	0	4	8.76	18	0	0	0	25	27	28	24	2	24	32	.281	.333	.264	11.68	8.76
Brown, Eric	R-R	6-6	225	2-23-84	3	2	5.29	20	6	1	0	63	74	42	37	5	24	51	.288	.296	.284	7.29	3.43
Cheney, Steven	R-R	6-5	200	7-3-86	0	1	0.00	2	0	0	1	3	3	1	0	0	1	2	.273	.333	.200	6.00	3.00
Clements, Zachary	R-R	6-0	215	4-17-80	0	4	6.32	7	7	0	0	31	29	25	22	2	28	18	.242	.241	.242	5.17	8.04
Domangue, Eric	L-L	6-5	200	8-16-84	2	0	2.11	13	0	0	0	21	19	6	5	0	4	18	.247	.250	.246	7.59	4.64
Durkin, Matt	R-R	6-4	220	2-22-83	0	0	0.00	1	1	0	0	3	2	0	0	0	3	4	.182	.167	.200	12.00	9.00
Guerra, Deolis	R-R	6-5	200	4-17-89	6	7	2.20	17	17	0	0	82	59	22	20	3	37	64	.208	.196	.216	7.05	4.08
Hinchman, Grady	R-R	5-9	170	9-10-81	1	2	4.50	14	0	0	1	30	19	15	15	4	15	29	.181	.087	.207	8.70	4.50
Landing, Jeffrey	R-R	6-3	190	7-31-83	6	11	4.70	21	16	0	0	98	104	61	51	9	45	60	.278	.243	.308	5.53	4.15
Marte, German	R-R	6-1	180	4-29-85	3	0	2.58	32	0	0	4	59	49	19	17	6	20	62	.223	.209	.231	9.40	3.03
Mateo, Waner	R-R	6-5	175	2-5-85	0	5	3.94	21	8	0	0	64	73	35	28	5	16	34	.294	.270	.314	4.78	2.25
Meyers, Ryan	L-R	6-5	195	7-17-85	3	10	4.89	31	13	0	2	105	105	65	57	8	57	67	.263	.241	.278	5.74	4.89
Nall, Brandon	R-R	6-4	190	3-18-82	5	5	2.91	38	0	0	0	87	69	32	28	3	35	88	.220	.288	.179	9.14	3.63
Neguilis, Jacobo	R-R	6-3	180	4-25-84	0	1	5.68	4	0	0	0	13	12	10	8	2	9	9	.245	.308	.174	6.39	6.39
Niese, Jon	L-L	6-3	190	10-27-86	11	9	3.93	25	25	1	0	124	121	67	54	7	62	132	.256	.231	.261	9.61	4.51
Parnell, Robert	R-R	6-3	180	9-8-84	5	10	4.04	18	18	1	0	94	84	50	42	7	40	84	.239	.240	.238	8.07	3.84
Perez, Marcelo	R-R	6-1	166	10-10-80	2	0	0.92	15	0	0	4	20	13	2	2	0	10	29	.194	.240	.167	13.27	4.58
Piazza, Tony	R-R	6-2	215	6-22-80	0	0	0.00	1	0	0	0	1	2	0	0	0	0	1	.400	.500	.333	9.00	0.00
Portillo, Nelson	R-R	6-0	180	9-8-85	0	0	5.19	2	2	0	0	9	10	5	5	3	2	8	.238	.083	.300	7.27	5.19
Reyes, Jorge	R-R	6-4	170	5-15-84	0	0	2.45	2	2	0	0	11	10	3	3	2	2	8	.238	.160	.300	6.55	1.64
Serfass, Joey	R-R	6-3	215	5-6-81	0	1	3.05	14	0	0	1	21	15	9	7	3	3	13	.197	.269	.160	5.66	1.31
Simmons, Jeramy	R-R	6-0	200	9-30-82	3	4	4.13	10	10	1	0	57	50	31	26	4	23	44	.237	.238	.236	6.99	3.65
Stinson, Joshua	R-R	6-4	195	3-14-88	0	1	1.35	3	3	0	0	13	11	2	2	0	4	5	.239	.231	.250	3.38	2.70
Tomasiewicz, Kevin	L-L	6-2	225	9-17-83	6	2	2.60	47	0	0	19	66	64	26	19	2	13	51	.257	.198	.286	6.99	1.78
Wilson, Brandon	R-R	6-4	195	9-1-82	1	1	3.00	3	3	0	0	12	14	4	4	0	0	7	.292	.240	.348	5.25	0.00
Wladyka, Jim	R-R	6-1	190	5-15-83	0	1	3.99	35	0	0	0	50	51	28	22	7	23	39	.270	.292	.256	7.07	4.17

FIELDING

Catcher	PCT	G	PO	A	E	DP	PB
Arroyo	.989	34	233	36	3	3	4
Butera	.988	95	669	79	9	14	21
J. Martinez	.929	4	12	1	1	1	1
Piazza	.979	13	82	10	2	2	1
Schemmel	.911	9	23	18	4		8
Voyles	.962	8	23	28	2		6
Rivera	.900	3	4	5	1		2
Schemmel	.926	15	15	48	5		3

First Base	PCT	G	PO	A	E	DP
Anderson	1.000	15	102	8	0	10
Evans	.988	127	1124	81	15	109

Second Base	PCT	G	PO	A	E	DP
Coultas	.955	16	21	43	3	11
Gaerlan	.985	16	23	42	1	10
Henry	1.000	1	0	0	0	0
Manuel	.—	1	0	0	0	0
Pellot	.939	96	186	242	28	56

Third Base	PCT	G	PO	A	E	DP
Anderson	.956	20	15	28	2	4
Coultas	1.000	2	1	5	0	1
Gaerlan	1.000	2	2	2	0	2
Lietz	1.000	2	0	5	0	0
Schemmel	1.000	2	1	3	0	0
Ventura	.900	115	79	246	36	31

Shortstop	PCT	G	PO	A	E	DP
Castro	.948	116	177	350	29	78
Coultas	.867	4	3	10	2	0
Gaerlan	.909	5	7	13	2	2
Manuel	1.000	3	1	9	0	1

Outfield	PCT	G	PO	A	E	DP
Anderson	1.000	1	1	0	0	0
Austin	1.000	10	14	1	0	1
Coultas	1.000	1	1	0	0	0
Cruz	.981	31	48	4	1	1
Gamero	.934	36	54	3	4	0
Henry	.970	18	29	3	1	1
Holden	.947	36	69	2	4	0
F. Martinez	.988	42	84	1	1	1
Pacheco	.978	115	215	11	5	5
Sanchez	.941	83	120	8	8	0
Vogl	.980	55	94	5	2	5

Brooklyn Cyclones — Short-Season

New York-Penn League

BATTING	B-T	HT	WT	DOB	AVG	vLH	vRH	G	AB	R	H	2B	3B	HR	RBI	BB	HBP	SH	SF	SO	SB	CS	SLG	OBP
Bashelor, Will	R-R	6-0	180	4-23-85	.231	.667	.100	6	13	1	3	1	0	0	0	2	0	0	0	7	1	0	.308	.333
Contreras, Junior	R-R	6-5	220	1-12-86	.250	.000	.333	7	24	1	6	0	0	0	0	5	0	0	0	6	0	0	.250	.379
Cruz, Elvis	R-R	6-2	195	11-23-83	.173	.160	.179	32	81	13	14	4	0	2	4	11	0	0	1	26	0	1	.296	.269
Cummins, Daniel	R-R	5-9	190	12-11-82	.192	.211	.188	33	99	5	19	6	0	0	11	10	3	3	1	22	2	0	.253	.283
Dziuba, Teddy	L-R	5-10	185	10-26-84	.000	.000	.000	12	19	0	0	0	0	0	0	3	0	1	0	4	0	0	.000	.136
Eigsti, Jacob	R-R	6-0	185	6-13-84	.194	.222	.185	25	72	8	14	4	0	0	5	4	1	2	0	17	1	0	.250	.247
Floyd, Cliff	L-R	6-4	230	12-5-72	.000	.—	.000	1	2	0	0	0	0	0	0	1	0	0	0	1	0	0	.000	.333
Gaerlan, Armand	R-R	5-10	180	8-22-82	.190	.200	.188	6	21	2	4	2	0	0	3	3	0	1	1	3	0	0	.286	.280
Gamero, Jesus	R-R	6-1	170	1-24-84	.207	.308	.167	26	92	10	19	2	0	1	13	5	1	3	2	11	1	1	.261	.250
Garcia, Emmanuel	L-R	6-2	180	3-4-86	.240	.111	.313	13	50	7	12	0	0	0	3	5	1	2	1	13	3	0	.240	.316
Grogan, Timothy	L-R	6-0	195	3-30-84	.230	.095	.247	65	183	14	42	10	0	1	23	23	2	1	3	41	0	2	.301	.318
Hambrice, Jeremy	R-R	6-2	195	3-14-86	.222	.211	.231	45	90	9	20	4	0	1	7	6	4	0	0	24	4	4	.300	.300
Holden, Joe	L-R	5-11	175	4-10-84	.225	.148	.245	65	258	31	58	11	1	6	24	13	1	4	1	57	4	5	.345	.264
Jacobs, Jason	R-R	6-0	210	12-9-83	.217	.114	.252	45	138	12	30	7	0	2	14	30	2	2	1	27	2	2	.312	.363
Malek, Bobby	R-R	6-1	205	7-6-81	.000	.000	.000	3	11	0	0	0	0	0	0	1	0	0	3	0	0		.000	.083
Malo, Jonathan	R-R	6-1	175	9-29-83	.179	.308	.148	20	67	7	12	3	0	0	5	12	1	2	1	16	0	4	.224	.309
Martin, Dustin	L-L	6-2	210	4-4-84	.315	.306	.317	72	251	22	79	15	7	2	35	28	9	2	3	50	7	5	.454	.399
Martinez, Joan	B-R	5-11	175	5-7-84	.000	.000	.—	1	2	0	0	0	0	0	0	1	0	0	1	0	0		.000	.333
McCraw, Sean	L-R	6-0	185	3-11-86	.167	.—	.167	9	6	1	1	0	0	0	0	2	1	0	3	0	0		.167	.444
Murphy, Daniel	L-R	6-1	210	1-4-85	.241	.417	.118	8	29	2	7	1	0	0	3	4	0	1	3	0	0		.276	.324
Naccarata, Ivan	L-R	6-0	190	2-26-82	.263	.190	.276	42	137	17	36	6	4	2	12	12	2	0	27	1	1		.409	.331
Price, Ritchie	B-R	6-2	175	7-13-84	.000	.000	.000	5	12	1	0	0	0	0	0	0	1	0	4	0	0		.000	.000
Puhl, Stephen	B-R	6-1	195	7-6-84	.200	.—	.200	6	15	2	3	2	0	0	2	0	0	1	2	0	0		.333	.200
Rivera, Luis	R-R	6-1	165	1-25-84	.272	.264	.275	69	224	29	61	7	0	0	14	9	6	8	3	21	7	1	.304	.314
Rodriguez, Joaquin	R-R	6-4	180	10-29-84	.000	.000	.—	2	2	0	0	0	0	0	0	0	0	0	1	0	0	.000	.000
Sanchez, Jonathan	L-L	6-2	175	9-3-85	.195	.133	.209	45	169	21	33	5	3	1	12	16	0	2	1	48	5	4	.278	.263
Schemmel, Jon	R-R	5-11	190	1-27-83	.263	.326	.247	57	217	26	57	8	2	0	18	18	7	9	3	25	5	0	.318	.335
Sharpe, Michael	L-R	6-0	190	3-10-83	.000	.—	.000	2	2	0	0	0	0	0	0	1	0	0	1	0	0	.000	.000
Vogl, Will	R-R	5-9	175	12-10-83	.000	.—	.000	2	3	0	0	0	0	0	0	1	0	0	2	0	0	.000	.250
Wabick, David	L-R	6-2	185	5-30-84	.240	.273	.231	19	50	1	12	5	0	0	3	3	1	0	11	1	0	.340	.296
Wright, Mark	R-R	6-1	195	9-12-83	.222	.214	.226	31	90	9	20	2	0	1	7	4	2	0	1	31	0	0	.278	.268

PITCHING	B-T	HT	WT	DOB	W	L	ERA	G	GS	CG	SV	IP	H	R	ER	HR	BB	SO	AVG	vLH	vRH	K/9	BB/9
Abel, Nick	R-R	6-4	200	2-18-83	0	2	3.07	7	0	0	0	15	10	5	5	0	6	9	.185	.176	.189	5.52	3.68
Appell, Josh	R-R	6-1	195	6-23-83	0	1	5.40	9	0	0	0	13	13	8	8	1	5	12	.260	.158	.323	8.10	3.38
Brown, Eric	R-R	6-6	225	2-23-84	7	1	1.16	10	10	1	0	70	53	16	9	2	4	55	.204	.219	.192	7.07	0.51
Castillo, Jonathan	R-R	5-11	195	12-27-83	3	2	4.09	15	1	0	1	33	36	22	15	3	16	28	.271	.340	.225	7.64	4.36
Cullen, Ryan	L-L	6-2	204	1-20-80	0	0	2.70	2	0	0	0	3	3	1	1	0	0	4	.231	.000	.300	10.80	0.00
De La Torre, Jose	R-R	5-11	165	10-17-85	2	2	2.84	17	0	0	5	25	18	9	8	1	12	29	.189	.229	.167	10.30	4.26
Domangue, Eric	L-L	6-5	200	8-16-84	0	0	15.43	1	0	0	0	2	5	4	4	0	2	1	.417	.429	.400	3.86	7.71
Haines, Timothy	B-R	6-1	175	5-19-85	2	0	3.09	10	0	0	3	12	7	5	4	0	6	7	.167	.214	.143	5.40	4.63
Hinchman, Grady	L-L	5-9	170	9-10-81	4	1	3.34	22	0	0	1	35	30	19	13	0	23	47	.236	.273	.208	12.09	5.91
Koons, David	R-R	6-1	180	3-13-84	0	0	6.75	6	0	0	0	7	13	8	5	0	1	6	.371	.529	.222	8.10	1.35
Marte, German	R-R	6-1	180	4-09-84	2	0	0.00	9	0	0	4	9	7	0	0	0	6	8	.219	.263	.154	6.00	6.00
Mizell, Jeremy	R-R	6-6	177	6-18-83	2	0	1.34	18	0	0	1	34	29	11	5	0	12	25	.238	.233	.241	6.68	3.21
Mullens, Greg	R-R	6-6	245	1-30-85	0	1	2.61	2	2	0	0	10	7	5	3	1	4	5	.184	.333	.050	4.35	3.48
Portillo, Nelson	R-R	6-0	180	9-8-85	3	5	3.68	14	13	0	0	71	77	34	29	8	16	35	.282	.273	.290	4.44	2.03
Privett, Todd	L-L	6-0	185	4-22-86	1	2	2.11	8	8	0	0	47	44	14	11	4	8	38	.246	.259	.240	7.28	1.53
Rainey, Matthew	R-R	6-0	195	4-21-84	0	0	54.00	1	0	0	0	0	1	2	2	0	1	0	.500	.000	1.000	0.00	27.00
Reyes, Jorge	R-R	6-4	170	5-15-84	1	4	5.63	7	7	0	0	32	42	22	20	3	12	26	.323	.322	.324	7.31	3.38
Ruckle, Jacob	R-R	6-1	180	5-27-86	5	3	3.38	14	14	0	0	80	88	41	30	2	8	51	.274	.273	.275	5.74	0.90
Simmons, Jeramy	R-R	6-0	200	9-30-82	2	2	3.43	4	4	0	0	21	25	10	8	0	4	19	.298	.333	.275	8.14	1.71
Smith, Joseph	R-R	6-2	205	3-22-84	0	1	0.45	17	0	0	9	20	10	3	1	0	3	28	.141	.172	.119	12.60	1.35
Soler, Alay	R-R	6-1	240	10-9-79	0	1	6.23	1	0	0	0	4	6	3	3	1	2	6	.333	.000	.143	18.69	4.15
Sparks, Richard	R-R	6-5	205	10-10-84	0	0	6.75	3	0	0	0	4	3	3	3	0	4	3	.214	.250	.200	6.75	9.00
Stoner, Tobi	B-R	6-2	192	12-3-84	6	2	2.15	14	14	1	0	84	66	25	20	1	17	62	.219	.192	.234	6.67	1.83
Waechter, Nicholas	R-R	6-3	200	11-30-84	0	0	0.00	1	0	0	0	2	0	0	0	0	1	2	.250	.167	.500	9.00	4.50
Warren, Rip	L-L	6-2	180	5-5-84	1	2	2.96	13	0	0	0	27	24	9	9	0	9	34	.238	.250	.232	11.20	2.96
Wright, Mark	R-R	6-1	195	9-12-83	0	1	13.50	1	0	0	0	2	4	5	3	0	2	0	.400	.400	.400	0.00	9.00

FIELDING

Catcher	PCT	G	PO	A	E	DP	PB
Cummins	.986	27	180	24	3	0	3
Dziuba	1.000	12	42	10	0	0	2
Jacobs	.990	39	257	35	3	2	7
Martinez	.750	1	3	0	1	0	0
McCraw	1.000	8	21	4	0	1	0
Puhl	1.000	6	27	2	0	0	1

First Base	PCT	G	PO	A	E	DP
Contreras	.969	7	60	3	2	9
Grogan	.974	40	338	30	10	22
Hambrice	.973	25	162	16	5	16
Wabick	.977	15	116	10	3	17

Second Base	PCT	G	PO	A	E	DP
Gaerlan	1.000	6	12	18	0	4

	PCT	G	PO	A	E	DP
Malo	1.000	2	8	4	0	2
Rivera	.936	13	34	39	5	10
Schemmel	.964	55	94	171	10	31

Third Base	PCT	G	PO	A	E	DP
Eigsti	.960	19	15	33	2	2
Grogan	.909	23	14	26	4	3
Malo	.966	14	16	41	2	4
Naccarata	.861	32	13	49	10	7
Rodriguez	—	1	0	0	0	0

Shortstop	PCT	G	PO	A	E	DP
Eigsti	.885	6	6	17	3	1
Garcia	.885	10	9	37	6	6
Malo	1.000	3	6	2	0	0
Price	1.000	4	4	10	0	2

	PCT	G	PO	A	E	DP
Rivera	.953	55	92	172	13	33

Outfield	PCT	G	PO	A	E	DP
Bashelor	1.000	5	9	2	0	1
Cruz	.960	22	23	1	1	0
Floyd	1.000	1	2	0	0	0
Gamero	1.000	26	35	4	0	2
Hambrice	.667	4	2	0	1	0
Holden	.992	64	112	7	1	3
Malek	—	1	0	0	0	0
Martin	.965	68	130	9	5	1
Sanchez	.953	45	94	7	5	0
Sharpe	—	1	0	0	0	0
Vogl	—	2	0	0	0	0
Wright	—	1	0	0	0	0

Kingsport Mets   Rookie

Appalachian League

BATTING	B-T	HT	WT	DOB	AVG	vLH	vRH	G	AB	R	H	2B	3B	HR	RBI	BB	HBP	SH	SF	SO	SB	CS	SLG	OBP
Austin, Parris	R-R	6-2	185	12-13-85	.167	.000	.214	5	18	2	3	0	1	0	1	0	0	0	0	6	0	0	.278	.167
Bashelor, Will	R-R	6-0	180	4-23-85	.250	.250	.250	44	144	21	36	5	2	2	11	14	3	4	0	27	8	2	.354	.329
Contreras, Junior	R-R	6-5	220	1-12-86	.288	.271	.297	47	177	16	51	8	0	3	25	17	3	0	1	41	0	0	.384	.359
Garcia, Emmanuel	L-R	6-2	180	3-4-86	.291	.207	.324	51	206	35	60	5	2	3	25	27	0	5	0	41	19	6	.379	.373
Green, Donald	R-R	6-1	200	7-29-85	.216	.250	.197	38	102	13	22	3	0	0	7	8	1	2	0	41	2	0	.245	.279
Henry, Sean	R-R	5-10	154	8-18-85	.275	.234	.294	41	149	28	41	12	2	4	27	21	0	1	0	29	23	3	.463	.365
Hubbert, Bradley	R-R	6-4	210	8-24-85	.250	.225	.273	25	84	14	21	6	0	3	6	7	2	0	0	31	1	2	.429	.323
Lietz, Todd	R-R	6-0	175	12-21-82	.250	.214	.265	30	96	11	24	2	0	0	9	6	3	0	0	27	4	2	.271	.314
Maldonado, Brahiam	R-R	6-0	185	9-18-85	.281	.246	.298	56	185	29	52	17	4	7	35	23	2	2	2	49	5	2	.530	.363
Manuel, Anthony	R-R	6-0	175	8-17-82	.237	.194	.258	34	93	13	22	5	0	0	17	16	4	3	2	11	4	5	.290	.365
Martinez, Joan	B-R	5-11	175	5-7-84	.375	.500	.250	4	8	1	3	0	0	1	2	0	0	0	0	2	0	1	.750	.375
Mateo, Jose	R-R	6-1	175	12-18-85	.227	.143	.243	26	44	11	10	3	1	2	7	9	3	3	2	16	0	1	.477	.379
McCraw, Sean	L-R	6-0	185	3-11-86	.266	.273	.264	40	139	23	37	7	1	5	25	23	3	1	2	36	3	1	.439	.377
Murphy, Daniel	L-R	6-1	210	1-4-85	.273	.150	.462	9	33	2	9	0	0	2	7	4	0	0	0	1	0	0	.455	.351
Naccarata, Ivan	L-R	6-0	190	2-26-82	.563	.333	.615	5	16	7	9	0	1	2	6	4	0	0	1	3	0	1.063	.650
Price, Ritchie	B-R	6-2	175	7-13-84	.252	.205	.275	40	119	17	30	3	0	0	19	23	4	5	1	27	0	5	.277	.388
Puhl, Stephen	B-R	6-0	195	7-6-84	.079	.133	.043	15	38	3	3	0	0	0	2	1	0	2	1	6	1	0	.079	.100
Reyes, Raul	L-L	6-0	183	12-30-86	.273	.214	.290	37	121	34	33	10	2	1	18	20	4	3	0	34	3	2	.413	.393
Thole, Joshua	L-R	6-1	190	10-28-86	.235	.167	.257	36	98	13	23	4	1	0	12	7	3	0	2	25	1	1	.306	.300
Wabick, David	L-R	6-2	185	5-30-84	.327	.294	.336	45	156	29	51	14	0	2	28	25	0	0	2	25	0	1	.455	.415
Zuaznabar, Alejandro	R-R	6-0	180	6-24-84	.244	.203	.263	51	201	35	49	11	0	2	16	23	0	5	1	19	2	0	.328	.320

PITCHING	B-T	HT	WT	DOB	W	L	ERA	G	GS	CG	SV	IP	H	R	ER	HR	BB	SO	AVG	vLH	vRH	K/9	BB/9
Arizmendi, Daniel	L-L	5-11	200	6-13-84	1	1	3.42	20	0	0	4	24	24	15	9	4	15	29	.267	.300	.257	11.03	5.70
Battista, Michael	R-R	6-2	210	1-16-83	1	0	1.02	11	0	0	3	18	20	2	2	0	5	17	.290	.333	.278	8.66	2.55
Baxter, James	L-L	6-0	195	8-8-83	0	3	5.54	11	0	0	1	13	9	9	8	0	14	16	.196	.222	.189	11.08	9.69
Carr, Nicholas	R-R	6-1	195	4-19-87	3	3	4.88	12	11	0	0	48	49	29	26	5	23	44	.265	.286	.259	8.25	4.31
Cheney, Steven	R-R	6-5	200	7-3-86	4	1	2.73	17	0	0	2	30	30	10	9	4	6	19	.265	.321	.247	5.76	1.82
Childress, Dustin	L-L	6-0	182	5-19-83	3	1	2.61	20	1	0	2	38	39	12	11	1	9	28	.262	.182	.257	6.63	2.13
De La Torre, Jose	R-R	5-11	165	10-17-85	0	1	0.00	7	0	0	3	12	11	5	0	0	2	17	.239	.182	.257	12.75	1.50
Durkin, Matt	R-R	6-4	220	2-22-83	0	0	0.00	2	0	0	0	5	1	0	0	0	3	4	.067	.250	.000	7.71	5.79
Figueroa, Jorge	R-R	6-1	194	2-24-85	0	2	1.62	13	0	0	1	17	13	6	3	0	8	12	.228	.333	.200	6.48	4.32
Frias, Jusef	R-R	6-2	180	12-31-84	1	1	4.61	14	3	0	0	41	41	22	21	5	19	22	.261	.326	.237	4.83	4.17
Gonzalez, Jose	R-R	6-2	170	8-17-84	2	3	5.32	16	0	0	0	24	27	17	14	1	14	22	.239	.318	.212	8.37	5.32
Holquin, Steven	R-R	6-3	215	6-30-85	0	1	5.27	6	6	0	0	27	26	19	16	1	18	18	.252	.222	.263	5.93	5.93
Mullens, Greg	R-R	6-6	245	1-30-85	7	2	3.06	12	12	0	0	62	73	32	21	5	17	38	.287	.333	.270	5.55	2.48
Polanco, Julio	L-L	6-0	163	11-29-86	1	3	4.53	12	12	0	0	54	57	33	27	4	21	44	.274	.313	.271	7.38	3.52
Privett, Todd	L-L	6-0	185	4-22-86	1	2	4.03	5	5	0	0	22	24	12	10	1	4	22	.264	.375	.240	8.87	1.61
Rainey, Matthew	R-R	6-0	195	4-21-84	0	0	0.00	4	0	0	0	5	2	0	0	0	3	4	.100	.000	.118	6.75	5.06
Ramirez, Edgar	R-R	6-4	215	11-30-83	2	3	3.53	17	1	0	1	36	32	15	14	0	19	33	.241	.303	.220	8.33	4.79
Santana, Yury	R-R	5-11	160	8-15-82	1	0	7.36	3	0	0	0	4	5	3	3	2	4	3	.357	.000	.385	9.82	4.91
Sparks, Richard	R-R	6-5	205	10-10-84	1	1	1.59	7	0	0	0	11	8	5	2	1	4	5	.195	.167	.207	3.97	3.18
Stronach, Timothy	L-R	6-5	185	12-20-85	4	2	3.76	13	13	0	0	65	65	35	27	6	20	40	.256	.284	.241	5.57	2.78
Wilson, Brandon	R-R	6-4	195	9-1-82	2	3	5.84	8	3	0	0	25	30	18	16	5	4	10	.300	.205	.361	3.65	1.46

FIELDING

Catcher	PCT	G	PO	A	E	DP	PB
Cummins	.986	27	180	24	3	0	3

FIELDING

Catcher	PCT	G	PO	A	E	DP	PB
Hubbert	.980	14	86	10	2	1	6
Martinez	1.000	3	9	1	0	0	1
McCraw	.977	36	220	36	6	2	5
Puhl	.967	14	79	8	3	0	3
Thole	.981	8	44	7	1	0	5

First Base	PCT	G	PO	A	E	DP
Contreras	.983	33	269	19	5	20
Thole	.978	18	130	1	3	12
Wabick	.992	26	221	13	2	22

Second Base	PCT	G	PO	A	E	DP
Bashelor	1.000	1	4	3	0	2
Garcia	1.000	1	1	1	0	0
Lietz	1.000	15	26	31	0	8
Manuel	.933	34	71	68	10	16
Naccarata	.950	4	11	8	1	1
Price	.959	20	41	53	4	16

Third Base	PCT	G	PO	A	E	DP
Lietz	.884	13	12	26	5	2
Naccarata	1.000	1	1	4	0	0
Price	.917	3	1	10	1	3
Zuaznabar	.931	51	29	146	13	13

Shortstop	PCT	G	PO	A	E	DP
Garcia	.953	50	76	167	12	32
Lietz	1.000	1	1	2	0	0
Price	.935	18	21	51	5	3

Outfield	PCT	G	PO	A	E	DP
Austin	1.000	5	10	0	0	0
Bashelor	.972	39	68	1	2	0
Green	1.000	33	48	3	0	1
Henry	.984	34	60	0	1	0
Maldonado	.957	51	88	1	4	0
Mateo	.960	20	22	2	1	0
Price	1.000	1	1	0	0	0
Reyes	.952	37	58	1	3	0

ORGANIZATION STATISTICS

Gulf Coast League

BATTING	B-T	HT	WT	DOB	AVG	vLH	vRH	G	AB	R	H	2B	3B	HR	RBI	BB	HBP	SH	SF	SO	SB	CS	SLG	OBP
Billingslea, Courtney	R-R	6-6	200	2-16-86	.125	.154	.114	27	96	8	12	3	0	3	6	6	2	0	0	47	3	1	.250	.192
Blaquiere, Jean Luc	R-R	6-0	196	2-27-86	.257	.238	.264	27	74	7	19	3	0	1	8	5	2	1	0	13	0	1	.338	.321
Cain, Gregory	R-R	6-1	205	5-1-87	.186	.179	.190	28	86	13	16	2	2	0	12	16	3	1	2	29	3	2	.256	.327
Castro, Ramon	R-R	6-3	235	3-1-76	.667	—	.667	1	3	0	2	0	0	0	2	0	0	0	0	0	0	0	.667	.667
Cherry, John	R-R	6-2	210	8-26-82	.241	.000	.280	12	29	3	7	1	0	0	5	4	0	0	0	13	1	0	.276	.333
Del Campo, Rogelio	L-R	5-10	195	7-25-86	.192	.222	.176	12	26	4	5	1	0	1	4	4	0	0	0	5	0	0	.346	.300
Floyd, Cliff	L-R	6-4	230	12-5-72	.500	.500	—	2	6	2	3	0	0	1	4	1	0	0	0	0	0	0	1.000	.571
Garcia, Aaron	R-R	5-11	195	1-5-84	.237	.091	.296	16	38	6	9	1	0	0	4	7	0	2	1	8	1	1	.263	.348
Giarraputo, Nicholas	R-R	6-3	200	5-29-88	.215	.180	.233	47	181	16	39	7	0	0	11	13	1	1	1	40	1	1	.254	.270
Malek, Bobby	L-R	6-1	205	7-6-81	.300	.250	.333	2	10	1	3	1	0	0	2	0	0	0	0	1	0	0	.400	.300
Malvagna, Stephen	R-R	5-11	195	11-28-85	.200	.333	.158	11	25	2	5	0	0	0	2	2	1	0	0	7	0	0	.200	.286
Martinez, Fernando	L-R	6-0	185	10-10-88	.250	.000	.333	1	4	1	1	0	0	0	0	0	0	0	0	1	0	0	.250	.250
Montero, Juan	R-R	6-2	165	10-5-85	.254	.193	.281	45	185	22	47	4	6	2	20	2	3	0	2	36	6	2	.373	.271
Murphy, Daniel	L-R	6-1	210	1-4-85	.056	.143	.000	8	18	2	1	0	0	0	0	4	0	0	0	3	0	0	.056	.227
Newman, James	R-R	5-10	180	10-23-83	.262	.313	.231	12	42	4	11	0	0	0	6	6	2	0	7	0	1	.262	.354
Pena, Richard	R-R	6-2	175	8-15-87	.248	.281	.239	39	141	21	35	10	1	2	13	19	2	1	2	38	8	1	.376	.341
Ramos, Valentin	R-R	6-3	185	7-21-88	.053	.000	.083	5	19	0	1	0	0	0	0	1	0	0	0	7	0	0	.053	.100
Rodriguez, Joaquin	R-R	6-4	180	10-29-84	.292	.286	.296	30	106	19	31	4	3	1	14	16	1	0	2	17	1	3	.415	.384
Santos, Jonathan	B-R	5-11	165	11-26-85	.260	.154	.316	41	150	24	39	5	1	0	8	23	3	3	0	19	10	2	.307	.369
Saylor, Ben	L-R	6-4	215	2-14-82	.268	.277	.263	39	142	17	38	10	0	2	20	22	3	0	0	37	0	0	.380	.377
Spath, Matthew	R-R	6-2	185	10-21-86	.229	.231	.229	27	96	10	22	3	2	0	13	11	1	1	0	28	0	1	.302	.315
Stegall, Daniel	L-R	6-3	180	9-24-87	.214	.196	.222	40	145	18	31	5	1	0	18	23	1	1	1	42	5	2	.262	.324
Voyles, Jeffery	R-R	5-10	185	11-29-83	.250	.354	.205	45	160	27	40	6	0	0	19	22	1	8	1	31	2	1	.288	.342

PITCHING	B-T	HT	WT	DOB	W	L	ERA	G	GS	CG	SV	IP	H	R	ER	HR	BB	SO	AVG	vLH	vRH	K/9	BB/9
Baxter, James	L-L	6-0	195	8-8-83	0	0	7.71	2	0	0	0	2	4	2	2	0	3	4	.400	1.000	.333	15.43	11.57
Beard, Hayden	R-R	6-1	175	1-22-85	5	2	5.34	15	0	0	2	30	25	21	18	2	17	19	.221	.277	.182	5.64	5.04
Beras, Alexis	R-R	6-5	215	9-24-83	1	2	6.14	17	0	0	2	22	22	18	15	0	22	19	.268	.240	.281	7.77	9.00
Calero, Angel	L-L	6-3	170	9-25-86	2	2	6.83	9	3	0	0	28	28	27	21	2	23	27	.267	.222	.271	8.78	7.48
Clements, Zachary	R-R	6-0	215	4-17-80	1	1	3.66	7	3	0	0	32	24	17	13	0	29	27	.218	.238	.206	7.59	8.16
Deaton, Kevin	R-R	6-4	265	8-7-81	0	0	2.31	3	3	0	0	12	11	3	3	1	2	10	.244	.318	.174	7.71	1.54
Durkin, Matt	R-R	6-4	220	2-22-83	0	1	8.59	6	5	0	0	15	20	16	14	2	12	13	.328	.353	.318	7.98	7.36
Eager, Blake	R-R	6-3	205	5-19-82	1	1	4.00	3	2	0	0	9	12	5	4	1	1	8	.316	.385	.280	8.00	1.00
Garcia, Anderson	R-R	6-2	170	3-23-81	0	0	3.00	2	0	0	0	3	0	1	1	0	2	3	.000	.000	.000	9.00	6.00
Hedrick, Nathan	R-R	6-10	220	9-13-86	3	4	5.16	11	5	0	0	30	34	24	17	2	19	20	.286	.378	.244	6.07	5.76
Holdzkom, John	R-R	6-7	225	10-19-87	2	5	7.71	16	2	0	0	23	28	28	20	0	20	23	.289	.269	.296	8.87	7.71
Holquin, Steven	R-R	6-3	215	6-30-85	0	2	3.81	6	3	0	0	28	25	13	12	2	7	29	.231	.262	.212	9.21	2.22
Humber, Philip	R-R	6-4	210	12-21-82	0	0	6.75	1	1	0	0	4	7	3	3	0	1	7	.389	.250	.429	15.75	2.25
Johnson, Kyle	R-R	6-3	225	1-21-85	0	1	21.94	4	1	0	0	5	12	15	13	1	9	1	.480	.364	.571	1.69	15.19
Jostock, Will	R-R	6-6	190	9-10-86	0	1	6.85	13	0	0	1	22	24	22	17	2	15	18	.267	.276	.262	7.25	6.04
Koller, Jonathan	R-R	6-5	235	7-2-83	1	0	4.43	8	2	0	0	20	25	11	10	0	6	21	.305	.385	.268	9.30	2.66
Koons, David	R-R	6-1	180	3-13-84	1	0	0.00	3	0	0	0	4	2	0	0	0	0	4	.154	.200	.125	9.00	0.00
Leaper, Joseph	R-R	6-1	160	3-12-87	2	2	4.18	9	6	0	0	28	35	13	13	1	10	20	.321	.371	.297	6.43	3.21
Mulvey, Kevin	R-R	6-1	175	5-26-85	0	0	0.00	1	1	0	0	2	1	0	0	0	1	1	.143	.000	.200	4.50	0.00
Pujols, Stanly	R-R	6-2	185	5-13-85	2	1	4.46	13	2	0	1	36	41	20	18	2	12	18	.295	.182	.347	4.46	2.97
Rainey, Matthew	R-R	6-0	195	4-21-84	0	0	1.13	10	1	0	1	16	10	2	2	0	8	15	.172	.240	.121	8.44	4.50
Santana, Yury	R-R	5-11	160	8-15-82	0	0	0.00	10	0	0	1	15	3	1	0	0	5	19	.064	.000	.094	11.66	3.07
Schafer, Scott	R-R	6-1	180	9-25-87	0	0	0.00	1	1	0	0	2	1	0	0	0	1	3	.143	.000	.250	13.50	9.00
Simeoli, Luis	R-R	6-3	194	6-28-88	0	2	6.26	9	4	0	0	23	22	20	16	4	21	12	.244	.200	.267	4.70	8.22
Stinson, Joshua	R-R	6-4	195	3-14-88	1	2	2.00	9	4	0	0	27	27	10	6	0	5	14	.273	.250	.286	4.67	1.67
Swindell, Mike	R-R	6-1	190	9-26-81	0	1	4.05	2	2	0	0	7	6	3	3	0	2	7	.240	.429	.167	9.45	2.70
Urdaneta, Lino	R-R	6-1	170	11-20-79	0	0	1.29	6	0	0	0	7	8	3	1	0	0	6	.296	.417	.200	7.71	0.00
Williams, Dave	L-L	6-3	230	3-12-79	1	0	0.00	2	2	0	0	8	2	0	0	0	0	10	.080	.000	.091	11.25	0.00

FIELDING

Catcher	PCT	G	PO	A	E	DP	PB
Blaquiere	.982	25	146	19	3	1	5
Castro	1.000	1	2	0	0	0	1
Cherry	.986	12	64	7	1	0	5
Del Campo	1.000	12	54	5	0	2	5
Garcia	.978	15	73	16	2	0	3
Malvagna	.952	6	37	3	2	0	3

First Base	PCT	G	PO	A	E	DP
Garcia	—	1	0	0	0	0
Ramos	.974	5	37	1	1	3
Saylor	.986	39	329	13	5	26
Spath	.977	10	81	4	2	8
Voyles	1.000	1	3	0	0	0

Second Base	PCT	G	PO	A	E	DP
Newman	.965	12	22	33	2	5
Santos	1.000	1	5	4	0	2
Voyles	.980	42	95	106	4	25

Third Base	PCT	G	PO	A	E	DP
Giarraputo	.931	44	47	87	10	10
Rodriguez	.853	9	6	23	5	1

Shortstop	PCT	G	PO	A	E	DP
Rodriguez	.929	16	29	50	6	1
Santos	.938	38	49	116	11	18
Voyles	1.000	1	0	2	0	0

Outfield	PCT	G	PO	A	E	DP
Billingslea	.972	23	33	2	1	0
Cain	1.000	18	21	1	0	0
Floyd	—	1	0	0	0	0
Malek	1.000	1	2	0	0	0
Martinez	1.000	1	2	1	0	0
Montero	.977	41	81	5	2	1
Pena	.929	37	62	3	5	1
Spath	1.000	11	15	4	0	0
Stegall	1.000	33	66	1	0	0

BY GEORGE KING

How different is it around the Yankees?

The team won its ninth straight American League East title despite losing its corner outfielders for four months and second baseman for six weeks. The reigning AL MVP

batted .290 with 35 homers and 121 RBIs and was booed after every out. Then after a disastrous AL Division Series, the consensus is the Yankees would be better off without Alex Rodriguez.

Hours after the Yankees were eliminated by the Tigers in four games, George Steinbrenner contemplated firing Joe Torre, who may have turned in the finest job of his 11-year tenure as Steinbrenner's manager.

Eventually, Steinbrenner was talked out of firing Torre by general manager Brian Cashman, with the following orders from The Boss: "You are back for (2007). I expect a great deal from you and the entire team. I have high expectations and I want to see enthusiasm, a fighting spirit and a team that works together."

Such is the nature of working for Steinbrenner and in New York. Even though the Yankees were ousted by the Angels in a Division Series in 2005, Steinbrenner didn't think about boxing Torre. And the media didn't write that the eventual Hall of Fame manager should go.

This time it was different. Steinbrenner was livid about the Tigers, who stumbled into the postseason, beating his $209 million Yankees. This time the columnists said it was time for the Torre Era to end.

Torre wasn't pleased with being left to dangle for three days and felt like he had to re-apply for his job. Still, as always, he said the right things.

"It's something you understand goes with the territory," Torre said. "We go to spring training to win the World Series. You know going in what the requirements

PLAYERS OF THE YEAR

MAJOR LEAGUE: Derek Jeter, ss

Jeter had his best offensive season since 1999, hitting .343/.417/.483, and won another Gold Glove. He led the club in average, on-base percentage, runs (118), total bases (301) and steals (34). His .343 average and 118 runs both ranked second in the American League, and his .417 OBP ranked fourth.

MINOR LEAGUE: Philip Hughes, rhp

Hughes emerged as one of the top pitching prospects in the minors in 2006. He was dominant in the high Class A Florida State League, where he carried a 30-2 strikeout-walk ratio, and was even better in Double-A. Hughes went 10-3, 2.25 for Trenton, then had two strong starts in the Eastern League playoffs.

STEVE MOORE

are. He expects a lot. You can't pick and choose what parts you like about working with George Steinbrenner. You have to understand the whole package and the whole package is pretty damn good."

For six months the Yankees' package was very good. The Red Sox faded in the final two months and the Yankees pulled away. The last two weeks were spent seeing if Gary Sheffield's left wrist had healed enough to be on the postseason roster. It was deemed well enough, but Sheffield didn't look right against the Tigers, going 1-for-12 (.083). Hideki Matsui returned from left wrist surgery and looked better than Sheffield.

While Matsui and Sheffield missed significant time, A-Rod continued to be the target of Yankee Stadium boo birds. And when he batted .071 (1-for-14) against the Tigers, the pressure to trade A-Rod reached its zenith.

"I want to be part of the solution," said Rodriguez, who insists he would invoke his no-trade clause unless the Yankees came to him and said there was no way they wanted to keep him. Cashman spent October saying he wasn't going to move Rodriguez.

In a disappointing season, there were pluses. In his first full year in the big leagues Chien-Ming Wang won 19 games and took over the role of staff ace from Randy Johnson, a 17-game winner who had back surgery in late October. Second baseman Robinson Cano's first full season resulted in him batting .342. Derek Jeter finished second in the AL batting race with a .343 average. Jorge Posada had his best all-around season and had a $12 million option kick in for next season. Scott Proctor turned into a very good set-up man in the bullpen.

Of course, the Yankees made a high-profile trade at the deadline when they acquired right fielder Bob Abreu from the Phillies. Unlike other years, though, they didn't give up high-end prospects. In the past Philip Hughes would have been sacrificed for Abreu.

Now, Hughes figures to be in the major league rotation by the 2007 all-star break, or possibly at the beginning of the season, after dazzling at two minor league stops in 2006 and establishing himself as one of the best pitching prospects in the game.

ORGANIZATION LEADERS

BATTING		*Minimum 250 at-bats
*AVG	Pino, Wilmer, Staten Island	.326
R	Gardner, Brett, Tampa/Trenton	106
H	Gardner, Brett, Tampa/Trenton	152
TB	Ruiz, Randy, Wichita/Trenton	249
2B	Ehlers, Cody, Tampa	38
3B	Gardner, Brett, Tampa/Trenton	10
HR	Ruiz, Randy, Wichita/Trenton	26
RBI	Ehlers, Cody, Tampa	106
BB	Gardner, Brett, Tampa/Trenton	88
SO	Jackson, Austin, Charleston	151
SB	Christian, Justin, Trenton	76
*OBP	Gardner, Brett, Tampa/Trenton	.407
*SLG	Ruiz, Randy, Wichita/Trenton	.532
XBH	Ruiz, Randy, Wichita/Trenton	62

PITCHING		#Minimum 75 innings
W	Jones, Jason, Tampa/Trenton	13
L	De Paula, Jorge, Trenton/Columbus	15
#ERA	Reyes, Angel, GCL Yankees/Staten Island	1.40
G	Casadiego, Gerardo, Tampa/Trenton	58
CG	White, Steven, Trenton/Columbus	2
	Wilson, Kris, Trenton/Columbus	2
SV	Pope, Justin, Columbus/Trenton	23
IP	White, Steven, Trenton/Columbus	175
BB	DeSalvo, Matt, Columbus/Trenton	93
SO	Clippard, Tyler, Trenton	175
#AVG	Reyes, Angel, GCL Yankees/Staten Island	.171

American League

BATTING	B-T	HT	WT	DOB	AVG	vLH	vRH	G	AB	R	H	2B	3B	HR	RBI	BB	HBP	SH	SF	SO	SB	CS	SLG	OBP
Abreu, Bobby	L-R	6-0	210	3-11-74	.330	.281	.349	58	209	37	69	16	0	7	42	33	1	2	3	52	10	2	.507	.419
Cabrera, Melky	B-L	5-11	170	8-11-84	.280	.286	.278	130	460	75	129	26	2	7	50	56	2	5	1	59	12	5	.391	.360
Cairo, Miguel	R-R	6-1	210	5-4-74	.239	.279	.221	81	222	28	53	12	3	0	30	13	1	5	3	31	13	1	.320	.280
Cannizaro, Andy	R-R	5-10	170	12-19-78	.250	1.000	.000	13	8	5	2	0	0	1	1	1	0	0	0	1	0	0	.625	.333
Cano, Robinson	L-R	6-0	190	10-22-82	.342	.287	.363	122	482	62	165	41	1	15	78	18	2	1	5	54	5	2	.525	.365
Crosby, Bubba	L-L	5-11	190	8-11-76	.207	.300	.195	65	87	9	18	3	1	1	6	4	2	3	0	21	3	1	.299	.258
Damon, Johnny	L-L	6-2	205	11-5-73	.285	.297	.280	149	593	115	169	35	5	24	80	67	4	2	5	85	25	10	.482	.359
Fasano, Sal	R-R	6-2	245	8-10-71	.143	.190	.107	28	49	3	7	4	0	1	5	2	3	0	0	14	0	0	.286	.222
Giambi, Jason	L-R	6-3	230	1-8-71	.253	.213	.270	139	446	92	113	25	0	37	113	110	16	0	7	106	2	0	.558	.413
Green, Nick	R-R	6-0	175	9-10-78	.240	.227	.245	46	75	8	18	5	0	2	4	5	1	1	0	29	1	1	.387	.296
2-team (17 Tampa Bay)					.184	—		63	114	12	21	5	0	2	4	11	1	1	0	40	1	4	.281	.262
Guiel, Aaron	L-R	5-10	200	10-5-72	.256	.167	.271	44	82	16	21	3	0	4	11	7	3	0	0	20	2	1	.439	.337
2-team (19 Kansas City)					.242	—		63	132	25	32	6	0	7	18	14	5	0	0	31	2	1	.447	.338
Jeter, Derek	R-R	6-3	195	6-26-74	.343	.390	.328	154	623	118	214	39	3	14	97	69	12	7	4	102	34	5	.483	.417
Long, Terrence	L-L	6-1	200	2-29-76	.167	.143	.172	12	36	6	6	1	0	0	2	4	0	0	0	8	0	0	.194	.250
Matsui, Hideki	L-R	6-2	230	6-12-74	.302	.226	.336	51	172	32	52	9	0	8	29	27	0	0	2	23	1	0	.494	.393
Nieves, Wil	R-R	5-11	190	9-25-77	.000	.000	.000	6	6	0	0	0	0	0	0	0	0	0	0	1	0	0	.000	.000
Phillips, Andy	R-R	6-0	205	4-6-77	.240	.195	.262	110	246	30	59	11	3	7	29	15	0	0	2	56	3	2	.394	.281
Posada, Jorge	B-R	6-2	205	8-17-71	.277	.263	.284	143	465	65	129	27	2	23	93	64	11	0	5	97	3	0	.492	.374
Reese, Kevin	L-L	5-11	195	3-11-78	.417	—	.417	10	12	2	5	0	0	0	1	1	0	0	0	1	0	0	.417	.500
Rodriguez, Alex	R-R	6-3	225	7-27-75	.290	.294	.289	154	572	113	166	26	1	35	121	90	8	0	4	139	15	4	.523	.392
Sheffield, Gary	R-R	6-0	215	11-18-68	.298	.344	.286	39	151	22	45	5	0	6	25	13	1	0	1	16	5	1	.450	.355
Stinnett, Kelly	R-R	5-11	235	2-4-70	.228	.231	.226	34	79	6	18	3	0	1	9	5	1	2	0	29	0	0	.304	.282
Thompson, Kevin	R-R	5-10	185	9-18-79	.300	.182	.368	19	30	5	9	3	0	1	6	6	1	0	9	2	0		.500	.417
Williams, Bernie	B-R	6-2	205	9-13-68	.281	.323	.261	131	420	65	118	29	0	12	61	33	2	1	6	53	2	0	.436	.332
Wilson, Craig	R-R	6-2	220	11-30-76	.212	.222	.203	40	104	15	22	4	0	4	8	4	1	0	0	34	0	0	.365	.248

PITCHING	B-T	HT	WT	DOB	W	L	ERA	G	GS	CG	SV	IP	H	R	ER	HR	BB	SO	AVG	vLH	vRH	K/9	BB/9
Beam, T.J.	R-R	6-7	215	8-28-80	2	0	8.50	20	0	0	0	18	26	17	17	5	6	12	.338	.357	.327	6.00	3.00
Bean, Colter	L-R	6-6	255	1-16-77	0	0	9.00	2	0	0	0	2	2	2	2	0	2	1	.333	.333	.333	4.50	9.00
Bruney, Brian	R-R	6-2	245	2-17-82	1	1	0.87	19	0	0	0	21	14	2	2	1	15	25	.189	.115	.229	10.89	6.53
Chacon, Shawn	R-R	6-3	220	12-23-77	5	3	7.00	17	11	0	0	63	77	55	49	11	36	35	.300	.305	.295	5.00	5.14
Dotel, Octavio	R-R	6-0	210	11-25-73	0	0	10.80	14	0	0	0	10	18	13	12	2	11	7	.383	.333	.414	6.30	9.90
Erickson, Scott	R-R	6-4	230	2-2-68	0	0	7.94	9	0	0	0	11	13	12	10	2	7	2	.283	.333	.240	1.59	5.56
Farnsworth, Kyle	R-R	6-4	240	4-14-76	3	6	4.36	72	0	0	6	66	62	34	32	8	28	75	.243	.215	.264	10.23	3.82
Henn, Sean	R-L	6-5	200	4-23-81	0	1	4.82	4	1	0	0	9	11	5	5	2	5	6	.297	.357	.261	6.75	4.82
Johnson, Randy	R-L	6-10	230	9-10-63	17	11	5.00	33	33	2	0	205	194	125	114	28	60	172	.250	.194	.259	7.55	2.63
Karstens, Jeff	R-R	6-3	175	9-24-82	2	1	3.80	8	6	0	0	43	40	20	18	6	11	16	.242	.253	.233	3.38	2.32
Lidle, Cory	R-R	5-11	190	3-22-72	4	3	5.16	10	9	0	0	45	49	26	26	11	19	32	.272	.256	.287	6.35	3.77
Mussina, Mike	L-R	6-2	190	12-8-68	15	7	3.51	32	32	1	0	197	184	88	77	22	35	172	.241	.223	.258	7.84	1.60
Myers, Mike	L-L	6-3	220	6-26-69	1	2	3.23	62	0	0	0	31	29	14	11	3	10	22	.244	.257	.224	6.46	2.93
Ponson, Sidney	R-R	6-1	255	11-2-76	0	1	10.47	5	3	0	0	16	26	20	19	3	7	15	.351	.333	.362	8.27	3.86
Proctor, Scott	R-R	6-1	200	1-2-77	6	4	3.52	83	0	0	1	102	89	41	40	12	33	89	.232	.204	.250	7.83	2.90
Rasner, Darrell	R-R	6-3	210	1-13-81	3	1	4.43	6	4	0	0	20	18	10	10	5	5	11	.237	.189	.282	4.87	2.21
Rivera, Mariano	R-R	6-2	195	11-29-69	5	5	1.80	63	0	0	34	75	61	16	15	3	11	55	.223	.192	.250	6.60	1.32
Small, Aaron	R-R	6-5	235	11-23-71	0	3	8.46	11	3	0	0	28	42	29	26	9	12	12	.341	.358	.329	3.90	3.90
Smith, Matt	L-L	6-5	225	6-15-79	0	0	0.00	12	0	0	0	12	4	0	0	0	8	9	.105	.200	.071	6.75	6.00
Sturtze, Tanyon	R-R	6-5	230	10-12-70	0	0	7.59	18	0	0	0	11	17	10	9	3	6	6	.354	.333	.361	5.06	5.06
Veras, Jose	R-R	6-5	230	10-20-80	0	0	4.09	12	0	0	1	11	8	5	5	2	5	6	.211	.188	.227	4.91	4.09
Villone, Ron	L-L	6-3	245	1-16-70	3	3	5.04	70	0	0	0	80	75	48	45	9	51	72	.250	.179	.289	8.07	5.71
Wang, Chien-Ming	R-R	6-3	200	3-31-80	19	6	3.63	34	33	2	1	218	233	92	88	12	52	76	.277	.275	.279	3.14	2.15
Wilson, Kris	R-R	6-4	220	8-6-76	0	0	8.64	5	1	0	0	8	14	8	8	4	4	6	.368	.200	.478	6.48	4.32
Wright, Jaret	R-R	6-2	230	12-29-75	11	7	4.49	30	27	0	0	140	157	76	70	10	57	84	.283	.314	.255	5.39	3.66

FIELDING

Catcher	PCT	G	PO	A	E	DP	PB
Fasano	.991	27	104	9	1	0	2
Nieves	1.000	6	15	1	0	0	1
Posada	.990	134	787	68	9	7	13
Stinnett	.989	34	169	10	2	3	1

First Base	PCT	G	PO	A	E	DP
Cairo	1.000	16	60	5	0	5
Damon	1.000	1	3	0	0	0
Giambi	.985	68	459	11	7	43
Green	1.000	1	1	1	0	0
Guiel	1.000	15	69	1	0	2
Phillips	.988	94	536	27	7	56
Posada	1.000	1	2	0	0	2
Sheffield	.983	9	56	3	1	4
Wilson	.992	35	226	9	2	22

Second Base	PCT	G	PO	A	E	DP
Cairo	.990	45	79	116	2	28
Cannizaro	—	2	0	0	0	0
Cano	.984	118	230	333	9	73
Green	.985	19	37	29	1	6
Phillips	1.000	1	0	1	0	0

Third Base	PCT	G	PO	A	E	DP
Cairo	1.000	8	3	8	0	0
Cannizaro	—	2	0	0	0	0
Green	.926	17	7	18	2	4
Phillips	1.000	1	1	0	0	0
Rodriguez	.937	151	96	262	24	24

Shortstop	PCT	G	PO	A	E	DP
Cairo	.979	14	18	28	1	8
Cannizaro	.909	10	5	5	1	0

	PCT	G	PO	A	E	DP
Green	.913	10	10	11	2	4
Jeter	.975	150	214	381	15	81

Outfield	PCT	G	PO	A	E	DP
Abreu	.984	57	114	6	2	0
Cabrera	.992	127	245	12	2	1
Cairo	1.000	1	3	0	0	0
Crosby	1.000	62	64	1	0	0
Damon	.990	131	306	3	3	1
Guiel	1.000	27	32	1	0	0
Long	.958	10	22	1	1	0
Matsui	.988	36	82	1	1	1
Reese	.667	4	2	0	1	0
Sheffield	.976	21	39	1	1	0
Thompson	1.000	15	22	0	0	0
Williams	.994	89	154	1	1	0
Wilson	1.000	2	2	0	0	0

General Manager: Brian Cashman. **Farm director:** Mark Newman. **Scouting director:** Damon Oppenheimer.

Class	Team	League	W	L	PCT	Finish*	Manager(s)	Affiliate Since
Majors	New York	American	97	65	.599	1st (14)	Joe Torre	—
Triple-A	Columbus Clippers	International	69	73	.486	9th (14)	Dave Miley	1979
Double-A	Trenton Thunder	Eastern	80	62	.547	2nd (12)	Bill Masse	2003
High A	Tampa Yankees	Florida State	75	62	.547	4th (12)	Luis Sojo	1994
Low A	Charleston Riverdogs	South Atlantic	78	62	.557	3rd (16)	Bill Mosiello	2005
Short-season	Staten Island Yankees	New York-Penn	45	29	.608	+1st (14)	Gaylen Pitts	1999
Rookie	GCL Yankees	Gulf Coast	33	20	.608	3rd (13)	Oscar Acosta	1980
OVERALL 2006 MINOR LEAGUE RECORD			378	308	.551	3rd (30)		

*Finish in overall standings (No. of teams in league). +League champion

Columbus Clippers — Triple-A

International League

BATTING	B-T	HT	WT	DOB	AVG	vLH	vRH	G	AB	R	H	2B	3B	HR	RBI	BB	HBP	SH	SF	SO	SB	CS	SLG	OBP
Brown, Jason	R-R	6-2	200	5-22-74	.200	.250	.167	5	10	0	2	1	0	0	0	2	0	0	0	4	0	0	.300	.333
Cabrera, Melky	B-L	5-11	170	8-11-84	.385	.444	.351	31	122	19	47	6	2	4	24	10	1	0	2	9	3	1	.566	.430
Cannizaro, Andy	R-R	5-10	170	12-19-78	.276	.361	.241	116	416	69	115	32	1	3	32	51	10	7	3	59	6	5	.380	.367
Conti, Jason	L-R	5-11	180	1-27-75	.259	.263	.258	23	85	12	22	5	0	2	9	2	2	0	19	1	1	.388	.344
Cosme, Caonabo	R-R	6-2	160	3-18-79	.209	.214	.207	61	172	24	36	8	0	5	18	12	1	0	2	47	0	1	.343	.262
Crosby, Bubba	L-L	5-11	190	8-11-76	.238	.111	.273	22	84	13	20	5	1	2	10	11	3	0	16	7	0	.393	.347
Davis, Ben	B-R	6-4	215	3-10-77	.222	.300	.197	48	162	10	36	6	0	4	20	7	0	1	0	37	1	1	.333	.254
Duncan, Eric	L-R	6-3	195	12-7-84	.209	.323	.165	31	110	7	23	3	1	0	6	9	2	0	1	24	0	1	.255	.279
Duncan, Shelley	R-R	6-5	215	9-29-79	.186	.222	.160	12	43	1	8	1	0	1	4	5	0	0	10	0	0	.279	.271
Durazo, Erubiel	L-L	6-3	240	1-23-75	.290	.364	.275	19	62	6	18	2	0	2	10	11	1	0	12	0	0	.419	.400
2-team (17 Rochester)					.278	—	—	36	115	13	32	8	0	3	13	23	1	0	26	0	0	.426	.400
Escalona, Felix	R-R	6-0	190	3-12-79	.186	.333	.135	20	70	6	13	4	0	1	9	1	1	1	12	0	0	.286	.205
Garcia, Danny	R-R	6-1	175	4-12-80	.242	.296	.220	123	392	46	95	25	2	3	39	35	16	4	4	66	21	7	.339	.327
Green, Nick	R-R	6-0	175	9-10-78	.208	.214	.206	14	48	3	10	4	0	0	4	7	1	1	1	13	1	0	.292	.316
2-team (10 Durham)					.222	—	—	24	90	5	20	4	0	1	6	7	2	2	1	27	1	0	.300	.290
Guiel, Aaron	L-R	5-10	200	10-5-72	.260	.278	.250	16	50	10	13	2	1	2	8	8	3	0	1	10	0	0	.460	.387
Hill, Koyie	B-R	6-0	190	3-9-79	.143	.263	.098	20	70	4	10	2	0	1	5	5	0	0	1	17	0	0	.214	.197
Johnson, Russ	R-R	5-10	185	2-22-73	.275	.330	.251	106	375	58	103	18	2	14	40	65	2	2	5	53	2	3	.445	.380
Jones, Mitch	R-R	6-2	215	10-15-77	.234	.272	.214	121	441	56	103	27	2	21	78	51	6	0	5	145	4	3	.447	.318
Long, Terrence	L-L	6-1	200	2-29-76	.277	.272	.279	69	260	29	72	13	1	10	38	19	1	0	53	0	0	.450	.329
2-team (15 Louisville)					.269	—	—	84	308	31	83	16	1	10	44	21	1	0	63	0	0	.425	.318
McDonald, Keith	R-R	6-2	235	2-8-73	.257	.250	.261	11	35	2	9	4	0	0	6	2	1	0	1	14	0	0	.371	.308
Menechino, Frank	R-R	5-8	200	1-7-71	.171	.125	.182	12	41	6	7	1	0	3	6	3	2	0	5	0	0	.415	.261
2-team (6 Louisville)					.193	—	—	18	57	9	11	3	0	3	7	4	2	0	9	0	0	.404	.270
Nelson, Kevin	R-R	6-3	215	4-8-81	.000	.000	.000	3	4	0	0	0	0	0	0	0	0	0	0	2	0	0	.000	.000
Nieves, Wil	R-R	5-11	190	9-25-77	.259	.262	.257	88	321	29	83	13	0	5	34	18	1	6	2	29	2	1	.346	.298
Parrish, David	R-R	6-3	220	6-13-79	.417	.800	.143	4	12	2	5	1	0	0	2	2	0	0	3	0	0	.500	.500
Pena, Carlos	L-L	6-2	210	5-17-78	.260	.255	.262	105	381	65	99	17	0	19	66	63	9	0	9	89	4	0	.454	.370
2-team (11 Pawtucket)					.278	—	—	116	418	72	116	20	0	23	74	68	10	0	10	94	4	0	.490	.383
Reese, Kevin	L-L	5-11	195	3-11-78	.283	.328	.265	53	212	30	60	8	2	5	21	15	10	0	3	37	4	6	.410	.354
Rolls, Damian	R-R	6-2	215	9-15-77	.048	.111	.000	7	21	1	1	1	0	0	1	2	1	0	6	1	0	.095	.167
2-team (17 Charlotte)					.138	—	—	24	65	6	9	3	0	1	2	5	2	1	0	16	0	1	.231	.222
Sardinha, Bronson	L-R	6-1	195	4-6-83	.286	.185	.342	52	185	27	53	10	5	6	27	23	1	0	2	36	3	2	.492	.365
Stotts, JT	R-R	5-11	190	1-21-80	.241	.208	.265	22	58	6	14	0	0	0	4	9	0	3	1	11	2	0	.241	.338
Stratton, Robert	R-R	6-4	250	10-7-77	.240	.182	.269	24	100	10	24	3	0	7	23	7	1	0	1	40	0	1	.480	.294
2-team (29 Louisville)					.242	—	—	53	207	23	50	9	0	13	37	15	1	0	1	75	0	1	.473	.295
Thompson, Kevin	R-R	5-10	185	9-18-79	.265	.286	.256	91	362	69	96	22	5	9	44	44	2	4	4	63	17	7	.428	.345

PITCHING	B-T	HT	WT	DOB	W	L	ERA	G	GS	CG	SV	IP	H	R	ER	HR	BB	SO	AVG	vLH	vRH	K/9	BB/9
Beam, T.J.	R-R	6-7	215	8-28-80	2	0	1.71	19	0	0	1	32	16	6	6	1	13	37	.151	.159	.145	10.52	3.69
Bean, Colter	L-R	6-6	255	1-16-77	9	2	2.65	47	6	0	0	88	61	26	26	2	53	116	.198	.198	.198	11.82	5.40
Bergman, Dusty	L-L	6-5	200	2-1-78	0	4	3.79	35	0	0	1	36	45	18	15	2	11	23	.308	.250	.333	5.80	2.78
Bruney, Brian	R-R	6-2	245	2-17-82	1	1	3.14	11	0	0	0	3	14	10	6	5	2	8	22	.196	.333	.121	13.81	5.02
Butto, Francisco	R-R	6-1	200	5-11-80	0	0	4.50	4	0	0	0	6	9	3	3	1	1	6	.333	.231	.429	9.00	1.50
Childers, Matt	R-R	6-5	190	12-3-78	1	4	5.68	26	6	0	0	57	71	37	36	8	15	38	.303	.291	.311	6.00	2.37
Colome, Jesus	R-R	6-2	205	12-23-77	1	1	3.78	25	0	0	0	33	35	17	14	3	15	25	.265	.340	.224	6.75	4.05
Corey, Mark	R-R	6-3	220	11-16-74	7	4	4.44	53	1	0	8	81	79	44	40	4	28	68	.254	.223	.271	7.56	3.11
Cosme, Caonabo	R-R	6-2	160	3-18-79	0	0	36.00	1	0	0	0	1	4	4	4	1	0	0	.571	.667	.500	0.00	0.00
De Paula, Jorge	R-R	6-1	210	11-10-78	4	10	4.63	19	18	1	0	105	122	63	54	14	23	61	.291	.287	.294	5.23	1.97
DeSalvo, Matt	R-R	6-0	170	9-11-80	1	6	7.68	11	8	0	0	39	47	39	33	4	34	30	.303	.393	.245	6.98	7.91
Dotel, Octavio	R-R	6-0	210	11-25-73	0	0	3.38	5	0	0	0	5	6	2	2	1	0	8	.286	.333	.250	13.50	0.00
Erickson, Scott	R-R	6-4	230	2-2-68	1	2	4.24	12	0	0	0	17	11	10	8	1	11	11	.180	.083	.243	5.82	5.82
Henn, Sean	R-L	6-5	200	4-23-81	3	1	4.01	18	6	0	0	43	44	19	19	1	20	33	.275	.269	.279	6.96	4.22
Karstens, Jeff	R-R	6-3	175	9-24-82	5	5	4.28	14	14	1	0	74	80	42	35	9	30	48	.275	.288	.267	5.86	3.67
Manning, Charlie	L-L	6-2	180	3-31-79	0	0	0.00	1	0	0	0	1	3	3	0	0	0	1	.429	1.000	.333	9.00	0.00
Mendoza, Ramiro	R-R	6-2	195	6-15-72	2	5	6.96	24	9	0	0	63	89	55	49	11	14	37	.328	.320	.333	5.26	1.99
Pavano, Carl	R-R	6-5	240	1-8-76	1	0	3.00	1	1	0	0	6	8	2	2	0	1	5	.381	.000	.471	7.50	1.50
Phelps, Tommy	L-L	6-2	205	3-4-74	7	4	4.45	17	17	0	0	95	111	57	47	10	29	59	.294	.260	.302	5.59	2.75
Pope, Justin	B-R	6-0	190	11-8-79	0	1	7.30	8	0	0	0	12	18	10	10	3	6	6	.346	.273	.400	4.38	4.38
Rasner, Darrell	R-R	6-3	210	1-13-81	4	0	2.76	10	10	0	0	59	60	22	18	4	11	47	.263	.262	.264	7.21	1.69
Small, Aaron	R-R	6-5	235	11-23-71	2	4	5.62	11	8	0	0	42	64	29	26	4	12	17	.350	.345	.352	3.67	2.59
Smith, Matt	L-L	6-5	225	6-15-79	0	1	2.08	24	0	0	0	26	27	9	6	3	8	22	.267	.250	.277	7.62	2.77

					0	1	2.06	33	0	0	4	35	32	11	8	4	14	28	—	—	—	7.20	3.60
2-team (9 Scranton/WB)																							
Stotts, J.T.	R-R	5-11	190	1-21-80	0	0	27.00	1	0	0	0	1	3	3	3	0	2	0	.500	.667	.333	0.00	18.00
Swindle, Robert	L-L	6-3	190	7-7-83	0	0	0.00	1	0	0	1	2	1	0	0	0	0	1	.167	.000	.200	0.00	0.00
Veras, Jose	R-R	6-5	230	10-20-80	5	3	2.41	50	0	0	21	60	49	17	16	3	19	68	.224	.169	.257	10.26	2.87
White, Steven	R-R	6-5	205	6-15-81	4	9	4.71	17	17	1	0	107	100	58	56	8	42	88	.256	.307	.227	7.40	3.53
Wilson, Kris	R-R	6-4	220	8-6-76	9	6	3.40	21	21	2	0	132	120	54	50	7	24	103	.240	.244	.238	7.01	1.63
Wordekemper, Eric	R-R	6-1	200	8-8-83	0	0	0.00	1	0	0	0	2	0	0	0	0	0	2	.000	.000	.000	9.00	0.00

FIELDING

Catcher	PCT	G	PO	A	E	DP	PB
Brown	.964	5	26	1	1	0	0
Davis	.989	32	247	17	3	6	5
Hill	1.000	14	91	6	0	0	2
McDonald	.988	11	76	4	1	2	1
Nelson	1.000	3	14	2	0	0	0
Nieves	.979	80	537	56	13	10	4
Parrish	1.000	4	33	4	0	1	0

First Base	PCT	G	PO	A	E	DP
Cosme	1.000	7	38	1	0	5
Davis	1.000	1	1	0	0	0
Duncan	.989	19	178	7	2	15
Durazo	1.000	2	21	0	0	3
Guiel	1.000	2	21	1	0	1
Johnson	1.000	2	14	2	0	4
Jones	.990	25	173	18	2	21
Pena	.989	86	727	69	9	56

Second Base	PCT	G	PO	A	E	DP
Cannizaro	.930	11	18	22	3	5

Cosme	.920	5	5	18	2	1
Escalona	.875	2	4	3	1	1
Garcia	.971	114	232	306	16	61
Johnson	1.000	4	8	12	0	2
Menechino	1.000	4	2	4	0	0
Rolls	.857	1	2	4	1	0
Stotts	.976	8	23	17	1	8

Third Base	PCT	G	PO	A	E	DP
Cannizaro	.909	4	5	1	1	
Cosme	.909	37	12	58	7	6
Duncan	1.000	6	0	4	0	0
Garcia	1.000	2	2	1	0	0
Johnson	.969	86	54	164	7	19
Jones	—	1	0	0	0	0
Menechino	1.000	7	6	10	0	6
Rolls	1.000	3	5	8	0	0
Stotts	.970	15	13	19	1	0

Shortstop	PCT	G	PO	A	E	DP
Cannizaro	.966	100	128	332	16	54

Cosme	.912	9	13	18	3	2
Escalona	.985	18	26	40	1	10
Green	.907	14	19	30	5	4
Johnson	1.000	1	0	1	0	0
Menechino	1.000	1	1	1	0	1

Outfield	PCT	G	PO	A	E	DP
Cabrera	.967	28	57	2	2	1
Conti	1.000	22	55	4	0	2
Crosby	1.000	20	49	0	0	0
Duncan	.963	11	24	2	1	0
Garcia	—	1	0	0	0	0
Guiel	1.000	11	19	1	0	0
Johnson	1.000	11	21	0	0	0
Jones	.986	87	128	9	2	2
Long	.984	32	57	4	1	2
Reese	.972	50	98	7	3	0
Sardinha	.981	51	104	2	2	0
Stratton	1.000	20	40	1	0	1
Thompson	.971	87	192	6	6	0

Trenton Thunder
Double-A

Eastern League

BATTING	B-T	HT	WT	DOB	AVG	vLH	vRH	G	AB	R	H	2B	3B	HR	RBI	BB	HBP	SH	SF	SO	SB	CS	SLG	OBP
Brown, Jason	R-R	6-2	200	5-22-74	.196	.200	.194	31	97	13	19	6	0	4	18	9	0	1	1	31	0	1	.381	.262
Cano, Robinson	L-R	6-0	190	10-22-82	.500	.667	.429	3	10	1	5	2	0	0	2	3	0	0	1	0	0	0	.700	.615
Carson, Matt	R-R	6-2	195	7-1-81	.256	.179	.293	29	86	10	22	8	1	2	9	4	2	5	0	25	0	0	.442	.304
Christian, Justin	R-R	6-1	188	4-3-80	.276	.283	.272	129	467	76	129	19	6	6	43	43	3	3	0	73	68	13	.394	.341
Cosme, Caonabo	R-R	6-2	160	3-18-79	.256	.235	.273	12	39	5	10	2	0	1	3	6	0	0	1	12	1	1	.385	.348
Duncan, Eric	L-R	6-3	195	12-7-84	.248	.333	.204	57	206	32	51	15	2	10	29	32	3	0	1	38	0	0	.485	.355
Duncan, Shelley	R-R	6-5	215	9-29-79	.256	.290	.236	92	351	47	90	24	0	19	61	34	5	0	4	77	3	1	.487	.327
Escalona, Felix	R-R	6-0	190	3-12-79	.254	.269	.247	76	287	37	73	19	0	10	45	19	11	3	2	54	1	0	.425	.323
Faison, Vince	L-R	6-0	180	1-22-81	.260	.295	.242	120	408	69	106	22	8	14	66	50	3	6	3	91	5	4	.456	.342
Gardner, Brett	L-L	5-10	180	8-24-83	.272	.266	.275	55	217	41	59	4	3	0	13	27	2	1	4	39	28	5	.318	.352
Guillen, Rodolfo	R-R	6-3	186	11-23-83	.173	.154	.194	21	75	4	13	4	0	1	6	2	0	0	0	27	1	0	.267	.195
Howard, Kevin	L-R	6-2	190	6-25-81	.255	.269	.248	102	376	44	96	19	4	8	62	26	3	2	6	67	1	6	.391	.309
Lopez, Gabe	R-R	5-8	170	3-11-80	.263	.295	.244	127	479	67	126	24	3	4	47	72	3	8	4	60	2	1	.351	.360
Pena, Ramiro	B-R	5-11	165	7-18-85	.198	.147	.231	26	86	6	17	2	0	0	6	5	1	5	1	19	0	1	.221	.247
Plumley, Grant	R-R	6-0	185	12-21-81	.267	.343	.229	31	105	12	28	8	0	2	15	7	2	2	2	19	0	0	.400	.319
Rojas, Tom	R-R	6-2	185	3-31-82	.182	.222	.169	27	77	9	14	4	0	0	11	7	2	1	0	20	1	1	.234	.264
Ruiz, Randy	R-R	6-3	235	10-19-77	.286	.285	.287	119	468	72	134	35	1	26	87	41	15	0	2	132	2	0	.532	.361
Santos, Omir	R-R	6-0	200	4-29-81	.269	.212	.301	101	324	31	87	18	0	4	38	19	6	3	4	65	1	0	.361	.317
Sardinha, Bronson	L-R	6-1	195	4-6-83	.254	.262	.250	86	334	47	85	10	1	10	40	34	2	0	3	78	0	4	.380	.324
Self, Todd	L-R	6-5	215	11-9-78	.133	.000	.174	9	30	2	4	2	0	0	1	0	0	0	0	11	0	0	.200	.161
Sheffield, Gary	R-R	6-0	215	11-18-68	.333	—	.333	1	3	0	1	0	0	0	1	0	0	0	0	1	0	0	.333	.250
Stotts, J.T.	R-R	5-11	190	1-21-80	.228	.222	.231	86	263	34	60	6	0	0	21	34	2	9	1	48	8	3	.251	.320

PITCHING	B-T	HT	WT	DOB	W	L	ERA	G	GS	CG	SV	IP	H	R	ER	HR	BB	SO	AVG	vLH	vRH	K/9	BB/9
Beam, T.J.	R-R	6-7	215	8-28-80	4	0	0.86	18	0	0	3	42	26	5	4	1	12	34	.182	.179	.184	7.29	2.57
Borrell, Danny	L-L	6-3	200	1-24-79	3	5	4.54	15	14	0	0	81	76	46	41	10	25	70	.251	.253	.250	7.75	2.77
Brunet, Michael	R-R	6-2	195	3-5-77	0	2	6.75	7	0	0	0	11	15	9	8	3	6	2	.349	.333	.368	1.69	5.06
Butto, Francisco	R-R	6-1	200	5-11-80	3	2	2.99	28	6	0	0	72	65	25	24	3	29	57	.237	.253	.229	7.09	3.61
Casadiego, Gerardo	R-R	6-0	185	12-19-80	2	3	2.12	22	0	0	1	34	25	9	8	1	14	33	.219	.194	.231	8.74	3.71
Chacon, Shawn	R-R	6-3	220	12-23-77	0	0	5.40	1	1	0	0	5	4	3	3	0	2	3	.211	.250	.182	5.40	3.60
Childers, Matt	R-R	6-5	190	12-3-78	3	3	3.81	10	9	1	0	54	47	27	23	6	15	41	.228	.250	.213	6.79	2.48
Clippard, Tyler	R-R	6-4	170	2-14-85	12	10	3.35	28	28	1	0	166	118	72	62	14	55	175	.200	.172	.226	9.47	2.98
Colome, Jesus	R-R	6-2	205	12-23-77	2	0	1.93	9	0	0	3	3	1	1	3	2	1	2	.125	.143	.111	3.86	5.79
Cox, J.B.	L-R	6-3	205	5-13-84	6	2	1.75	41	0	0	8	77	54	21	15	2	24	60	.196	.150	.226	7.01	2.81
De Paula, Jorge	R-R	6-1	210	11-10-78	0	4	4.00	5	0	0	0	27	35	13	12	3	9	18	.313	.262	.373	6.00	3.00
DeSalvo, Matt	R-R	6-0	170	9-11-80	5	4	5.77	16	16	0	0	78	80	60	50	7	59	52	.268	.311	.235	6.00	6.81
Dotel, Octavio	R-R	6-0	210	11-25-73	0	0	0.00	2	0	0	0	2	1	0	0	0	0	3	.167	—	.167	13.50	0.00
Hughes, Philip	R-R	6-5	220	6-24-86	10	3	2.25	21	21	0	0	116	73	30	29	5	32	138	.179	.161	.192	10.71	2.48
Jones, Jason	R-R	6-5	225	11-20-82	4	3	4.83	14	9	0	0	50	65	32	27	11	18	28	.323	.315	.330	5.01	3.22
Karstens, Jeff	R-R	6-3	175	9-24-82	6	0	2.31	11	11	0	0	74	54	20	19	4	14	67	.198	.143	.232	8.15	1.70
Kennard, Jeff	R-R	6-2	195	7-26-81	3	6	3.29	27	0	0	1	55	51	25	20	5	21	58	.243	.241	.244	9.55	3.46
King, Jeremy	R-R	6-2	210	11-12-81	2	3	6.56	10	5	0	0	23	30	22	17	2	11	16	.343	.309	.383	6.17	4.24
Manning, Charlie	L-L	6-2	180	3-31-79	8	3	2.71	48	1	0	1	83	60	30	25	5	28	81	.197	.163	.221	8.78	3.04
Patterson, Scott	R-R	6-7	227	6-20-79	10	2	2.33	26	0	0	1	39	26	11	10	6	8	44	.186	.154	.198	10.24	1.86
Pavano, Carl	R-R	6-5	240	1-8-76	1	0	1.64	3	3	0	0	11	6	2	2	0	2	12	.150	.158	.143	9.82	0.00
Pope, Justin	B-R	6-0	190	11-8-79	2	2	2.47	38	0	0	23	51	42	14	14	2	21	49	.228	.203	.245	8.65	3.71
Stotts, J.T.	R-R	5-11	190	1-21-80	0	1	27.00	1	0	0	0	1	1	3	3	0	2	0	.500	1.000	.000	0.00	54.00
Thorp, Paul	R-R	6-1	200	9-23-80	0	2	2.89	12	0	0	0	19	18	8	6	2	13	17	.261	.212	.306	8.20	6.27
White, Steven	R-R	6-5	205	6-15-81	4	1	2.11	11	11	1	0	68	54	16	16	0	28	45	.217	.218	.216	5.93	3.69
Wilson, Kris	R-R	6-4	220	8-6-76	0	2	9.35	2	0	0	0	9	13	10	9	4	2	2	.342	.333	.350	2.08	2.08

FIELDING

Catcher	PCT	G	PO	A	E	DP	PB
Brown	.996	30	228	13	1	2	3
Rojas	.994	25	154	5	1	1	2
Santos	.996	100	755	47	3	6	6

First Base	PCT	G	PO	A	E	DP
Cosme	1.000	1	10	0	0	0
E. Duncan	.984	44	344	17	6	28
S. Duncan	.990	56	469	28	5	38
Rojas	1.000	2	2	0	0	0
Ruiz	.984	42	361	17	6	35

Second Base	PCT	G	PO	A	E	DP
Cano	1.000	3	7	4	0	0
Christian	—	1	0	0	0	0
Escalona	1.000	1	0	1	0	0

Howard	1.000	1	3	1	0	0
Lopez	.980	122	248	326	12	65
Plumley	1.000	4	4	12	0	3
Stotts	.968	15	33	57	3	14

Third Base	PCT	G	PO	A	E	DP
Cosme	1.000	2	3	5	0	0
E. Duncan	.857	6	3	9	2	1
Howard	.939	94	80	165	16	15
Plumley	.957	17	5	40	2	2
Stotts	.906	26	12	46	6	6

Shortstop	PCT	G	PO	A	E	DP
Cosme	1.000	3	2	6	0	1
Escalona	.959	73	83	195	12	40
Lopez	1.000	1	0	1	0	0

Pena	.981	23	39	64	2	15
Plumley	.949	10	12	25	2	4
Stotts	.911	39	35	88	12	14

Outfield	PCT	G	PO	A	E	DP
Carson	1.000	27	40	1	0	0
Christian	.993	124	259	6	2	1
DeSalvo	—	1	0	0	0	0
S. Duncan	.971	20	33	0	1	0
Faison	.981	105	196	8	4	2
Gardner	1.000	52	127	0	0	0
Guillen	.956	19	38	5	2	0
Sardinha	.969	83	119	6	4	1
Self	1.000	6	5	0	0	0
Stotts	1.000	1	1	0	0	0

Tampa Yankees · High Class A

Florida State League

BATTING	B-T	HT	WT	DOB	AVG	vLH	vRH	G	AB	R	H	2B	3B	HR	RBI	BB	HBP	SH	SF	SO	SB	CS	SLG	OBP
Battle, Tim	R-R	6-2	185	9-10-85	.133	.200	.120	36	128	12	17	2	1	1	8	7	1	0	0	47	6	5	.188	.184
Beachum, Jeff	R-R	6-0	185	11-5-83	.235	.200	.286	9	17	3	4	0	0	0	4	0	0	1	0	1	0	0	.235	.235
Brown, Jason	R-R	6-2	200	5-22-74	.188	—	.188	5	16	1	3	0	0	0	2	3	0	0	0	4	0	0	.188	.316
Burke, Joseph	L-R	6-0	195	12-16-83	.293	.000	.329	29	82	13	24	5	0	0	9	10	0	2	1	8	2	1	.354	.366
Carroll, Mark	R-R	6-1	200	10-14-81	.245	.197	.264	88	249	31	61	13	2	3	24	17	5	2	0	50	8	1	.349	.306
Carson, Matt	R-R	6-2	195	7-1-81	.243	.185	.257	40	136	15	33	4	1	8	21	21	2	3	3	31	5	3	.463	.346
Corona, Reegie	R-R	5-11	160	11-7-86	.297	.250	.310	9	37	5	11	1	0	1	7	1	0	0	1	5	2	0	.405	.308
Crosby, Bubba	L-L	5-11	190	8-11-76	.125	.000	.333	3	8	0	1	0	0	0	0	1	1	0	0	2	0	0	.125	.300
Davis, Ben	B-R	6-4	215	3-10-77	.188	.000	.200	4	16	2	3	1	0	1	2	1	0	0	0	4	0	0	.438	.235
Ehlers, Cody	L-L	5-11	190	4-16-82	.298	.316	.292	134	497	68	148	38	1	18	106	64	3	0	9	88	5	3	.487	.375
Gardner, Brett	L-L	5-10	180	8-24-83	.323	.429	.295	63	232	46	75	12	5	0	22	43	2	1	0	51	30	7	.418	.433
Gonzalez, Edwar	R-R	5-10	200	1-1-83	.260	.291	.252	99	384	58	100	19	4	10	43	23	5	0	2	81	18	6	.409	.309
Greenwood, Jared	L-R	5-10	210	2-28-83	.256	.135	.285	61	195	29	50	7	0	13	31	26	0	0	3	53	3	3	.492	.339
Guillen, Rodolfo	R-R	6-3	186	11-23-83	.267	.274	.265	85	326	43	87	12	1	10	46	16	6	0	3	65	14	3	.402	.311
Hall, Victor	L-L	5-10	160	9-16-80	.320	.259	.337	63	247	48	79	11	5	4	19	29	8	6	2	46	35	8	.453	.406
Himes, Ben	L-R	6-4	205	3-9-81	.227	.200	.232	92	299	35	68	10	4	5	26	23	2	3	3	91	3	7	.338	.284
Holmann, Mario	B-R	6-0	165	5-21-84	.254	.167	.271	28	71	10	18	2	1	0	3	16	0	1	0	13	3	6	.310	.391
Jones, Ben	R-R	6-3	196	7-3-81	.125	.000	.179	13	40	3	5	1	0	1	4	6	1	0	0	17	0	1	.225	.255
Made, Hector	R-R	6-1	155	12-18-84	.286	.250	.295	86	315	37	90	22	2	3	28	13	0	4	2	42	6	8	.397	.312
2-team (28 Clearwater)					.267	—	—	114	419	42	112	24	2	4	32	15	0	5	2	64	6	8	.363	.291
Malec, Christopher	B-R	5-11	195	8-28-82	.205	.077	.227	63	176	25	36	6	1	0	19	32	7	2	2	19	2	1	.250	.346
Mendoza, Carlos	B-R	6-0	191	11-27-79	.270	.308	.258	31	115	19	31	4	0	4	16	11	0	3	2	18	3	4	.409	.328
Nelson, Kevin	R-R	6-3	215	4-8-81	.000	.000	—	1	1	0	0	0	0	0	0	0	0	0	0	1	0	0	.000	.000
Nunez, Eduardo	B-R	6-0	155	6-15-87	.184	.240	.172	37	147	17	27	5	3	4	26	8	0	4	2	28	6	1	.340	.223
Nunez, Luis	R-R	5-11	160	11-21-86	.279	.200	.321	16	43	7	12	2	0	1	1	4	0	3	0	5	3	2	.395	.340
Pena, Ramiro	B-R	5-11	165	7-18-85	.280	.240	.292	54	218	31	61	4	2	0	23	16	4	4	4	24	8	7	.317	.335
Pilittere, P.J.	R-R	6-0	215	11-23-81	.302	.302	.302	87	291	39	88	14	2	5	38	20	5	5	2	24	3	2	.416	.355
Plumley, Grant	R-R	6-0	185	12-21-81	.284	.267	.288	19	67	9	19	1	0	0	6	8	0	1	0	14	3	3	.299	.360
Rojas, Irwil	L-R	6-1	175	8-11-84	.244	.333	.237	13	41	2	10	1	0	0	2	3	0	1	0	7	0	1	.268	.295
Sain, Greg	R-R	6-2	218	12-26-79	.154	.185	.132	20	65	10	10	5	0	2	7	7	2	1	0	19	0	0	.323	.257
Vechionacci, Marcos	B-R	6-2	170	8-7-86	.178	.074	.204	36	135	15	24	3	1	1	15	11	1	0	2	29	1	2	.237	.242

PITCHING	B-T	HT	WT	DOB	W	L	ERA	G	GS	CG	SV	IP	H	R	ER	HR	BB	SO	AVG	vLH	vRH	K/9	BB/9
Beltran, Saydel	L-L	5-11	175	1-23-83	0	0	10.50	4	0	0	0	6	7	7	7	3	4	4	.304	.143	.375	10.50	6.00
Casadiego, Gerardo	R-R	6-0	185	12-19-80	1	1	3.51	28	0	0	13	33	36	16	13	2	13	27	.281	.333	.247	7.29	3.51
Coke, Phil	L-L	6-1	210	7-19-82	5	7	3.60	22	18	1	0	110	101	52	44	6	35	88	.239	.236	.240	7.20	2.86
Dotel, Octavio	R-R	6-0	210	11-25-73	0	0	0.00	2	1	0	0	2	1	0	0	0	0	1	.143	.250	.000	9.00	0.00
Gardner, Michael	R-R	6-0	190	5-23-81	3	2	3.11	33	0	0	1	46	46	22	16	2	22	45	.258	.254	.262	8.74	4.27
Horne, William	R-R	6-4	195	1-5-83	6	9	4.84	28	26	0	0	123	105	72	66	10	61	122	.230	.227	.233	8.95	4.48
Hughes, Philip	R-R	6-5	220	6-24-86	2	3	1.80	5	5	0	0	30	19	7	6	0	3	30	.178	.207	.143	9.00	0.60
Jones, Jason	R-R	6-5	225	11-20-82	9	2	2.55	19	11	0	0	88	88	30	25	4	17	52	.262	.246	.273	5.30	1.73
Kennard, Jeff	R-R	6-2	205	1-20-81	3	0	1.33	14	0	0	2	27	17	4	4	0	9	19	.183	.186	.180	6.33	3.00
King, Jeremy	R-R	6-2	210	11-12-81	0	2	4.75	9	5	0	0	36	43	21	19	1	13	29	.295	.369	.235	7.25	3.25
2-team (6 Dunedin)					3	3	5.58	15	6	0	0	50	60	33	31	3	19	35	—	—	—	6.30	3.42
Kroenke, Zach	R-L	6-3	210	4-21-84	0	8	8.36	4	4	0	0	14	23	19	13	0	8	8	.354	.538	.308	5.14	5.14
Márquez, Jeff	R-R	6-2	175	8-10-84	7	5	3.61	18	17	0	0	92	102	56	37	4	29	82	.279	.265	.290	7.99	2.83
Martinez, Mike	R-R	6-2	190	4-12-81	1	3	2.74	36	0	0	1	66	58	21	20	6	17	53	.241	.243	.239	7.26	2.33
Medina, Gabriel	R-R	6-5	235	2-17-84	0	1	13.50	2	0	0	0	2	3	3	3	1	0	1	.375	.000	.429	4.50	0.00
Mendez, Jesus	R-R	6-2	163	2-14-86	0	0	27.00	3	0	0	0	2	8	11	7	0	2	2	.471	.500	.444	7.71	7.71
Pavano, Carl	R-R	6-5	240	1-8-76	0	2	2.31	3	3	0	0	12	10	6	3	2	3	10	.238	.267	.222	7.71	2.31
Quezada, Elvys	R-R	6-1	210	12-15-81	3	2	2.97	25	4	0	0	67	56	26	22	1	26	75	.225	.232	.220	10.13	3.51
Ramirez, Edwar	R-R	6-3	155	3-28-81	4	1	1.17	19	0	0	3	31	14	4	4	0	6	47	.133	.162	.118	13.79	1.76
Rasner, Darrell	R-R	6-3	210	1-13-81	0	0	2.57	2	2	0	0	7	12	3	2	0	3	6	.387	.500	.316	7.71	3.86
Rawson, Anthony	L-R	5-10	180	7-31-80	0	0	1.80	8	0	0	0	10	5	2	2	0	6	10	.147	.143	.150	9.00	5.40
Rueger, Bryan	L-L	6-3	185	2-22-83	1	2	4.71	14	1	0	0	21	26	14	11	3	8	14	.302	.371	.255	6.00	3.43
Schmidt, Joshua	R-R	6-4	175	11-14-82	4	4	4.24	39	0	0	1	68	56	37	32	4	31	66	.223	.276	.190	8.74	4.10
Schroer, Steve	R-R	6-2	195	12-28-82	0	0	0.00	2	0	0	0	2	0	0	0	0	1	3	.095	.000	.167	10.29	2.57
Smith, Brett	R-R	6-5	220	8-12-83	8	9	3.81	28	26	0	0	158	166	82	67	14	56	119	.272	.256	.284	6.76	3.18
Thorp, Paul	R-R	6-1	200	9-23-80	4	1	0.96	27	0	0	8	38	22	6	4	1	9	29	.168	.185	.156	6.93	2.15
Wright, Chase	L-L	6-2	190	2-8-83	12	3	1.88	37	14	1	0	120	95	32	25	1	43	100	.218	.228	.216	7.52	3.23

FIELDING

Catcher	PCT	G	PO	A	E	DP	PB
Brown	1.000	5	48	5	0	0	0
Burke	.967	4	26	3	1	1	0
Davis	1.000	3	20	2	0	0	0
Greenwood	.994	45	313	28	2	4	9
Nelson	1.000	1	1	0	0	0	0
Pilittere	.998	78	545	41	1	3	8
Rojas	.991	13	95	14	1	0	4

First Base	PCT	G	PO	A	E	DP
Carroll	.973	8	36	0	1	4
Ehlers	.994	127	1083	86	7	98
Gonzalez	1.000	2	7	1	0	0
Greenwood	1.000	1	11	2	0	0
Himes	—	1	0	0	0	0
Jones	1.000	5	40	3	0	5
Pilittere	1.000	1	6	1	0	2
Sain	1.000	4	16	1	0	1

Second Base	PCT	G	PO	A	E	DP
Beachum	1.000	1	1	6	0	2

	PCT	G	PO	A	E	DP
Carroll	.966	15	17	39	2	8
Corona	1.000	1	2	1	0	0
Holmann	.992	26	43	85	1	16
Made	.976	80	142	222	9	44
Malec	.974	9	14	23	1	7
Mendoza	.917	4	3	8	1	2
Nunez	.966	6	14	14	1	3
Plumley	1.000	2	8	6	0	4

Third Base	PCT	G	PO	A	E	DP
Carroll	.821	43	24	63	19	5
Gonzalez	—	1	0	0	0	0
Malec	.908	43	16	73	9	7
Mendoza	1.000	5	0	9	0	0
Nunez	1.000	3	0	5	0	0
Plumley	.933	12	6	22	2	0
Sain	.875	13	7	14	3	1
Vechionacci	.869	34	10	63	11	7

Shortstop	PCT	G	PO	A	E	DP
Beachum	1.000	8	3	6	0	1

	PCT	G	PO	A	E	DP
Carroll	.909	10	11	19	3	2
Corona	.912	8	11	20	3	7
Mendoza	.952	23	31	69	5	18
Nunez	.910	36	47	95	14	21
Nunez	.944	4	6	11	1	6
Pena	.959	54	81	197	12	31
Plumley	.926	5	9	16	2	2

Outfield	PCT	G	PO	A	E	DP
Battle	1.000	35	87	4	0	2
Burke	1.000	12	22	0	0	0
Carroll	1.000	10	11	0	0	0
Carson	1.000	26	53	1	0	0
Crosby	1.000	2	4	0	0	0
Gardner	1.000	60	130	3	0	0
Gonzalez	.994	86	148	8	1	1
Guillen	.985	76	130	2	2	0
Hall	.986	63	143	1	2	1
Himes	.956	53	83	4	4	1
Mendoza	—	1	0	0	0	0
Nunez	1.000	2	1	0	0	0

Charleston RiverDogs — Low Class A

South Atlantic League

BATTING	B-T	HT	WT	DOB	AVG	vLH	vRH	G	AB	R	H	2B	3B	HR	RBI	BB	HBP	SH	SF	SO	SB	CS	SLG	OBP
Battle, Tim	R-R	6-2	185	9-10-85	.265	.257	.269	94	362	56	96	14	5	5	38	25	8	4	2	95	24	8	.373	.325
Beachum, Jeff	R-R	6-0	185	11-5-83	.156	.286	.120	11	32	4	5	0	1	0	4	1	0	1	0	5	1	0	.219	.182
Calzado, Josue	R-R	6-1	160	11-6-85	.375	.556	.323	12	40	4	15	3	0	0	6	2	1	0	0	8	2	0	.450	.419
Cooper, James	L-R	5-10	190	2-18-84	.211	.182	.221	35	90	8	19	3	0	1	8	6	5	1	1	17	0	0	.278	.294
Corona, Reegie	B-R	5-11	160	11-7-86	.292	.248	.315	96	359	52	105	13	2	3	40	30	5	3	5	45	26	7	.365	.351
De La Rosa, Wilkins	L-L	6-0	156	2-21-85	.220	.231	.217	28	59	13	13	1	0	0	5	10	2	2	1	24	2	1	.237	.347
Dunn, Michael	L-L	6-1	185	5-23-85	.086	.143	.071	14	35	7	3	2	0	0	2	8	0	0	0	13	1	1	.143	.256
Gil, Jose	B-R	6-0	170	9-4-86	.189	.167	.200	22	74	5	14	1	0	0	6	4	1	0	1	15	0	0	.203	.238
Harris, Estee	L-R	5-11	170	1-8-85	.177	.200	.173	74	158	20	28	4	1	1	14	20	0	2	2	64	7	4	.234	.267
Henry, C.J.	R-R	6-3	205	5-31-86	.240	.231	.246	77	275	35	66	19	3	2	33	32	6	1	2	86	14	4	.353	.330
2-team (25 Lakewood)					.243	—	—	102	366	48	89	22	7	3	49	39	7	1	2	111	15	4	.366	.326
Holmann, Mario	B-R	6-0	165	5-21-84	.213	.236	.204	71	197	27	42	5	0	0	19	35	2	3	2	46	24	4	.239	.335
Jackson, Austin	R-R	6-1	185	2-1-87	.260	.306	.238	134	535	90	139	24	5	4	47	61	6	5	4	151	37	12	.346	.340
Jones, Ben	R-R	6-3	196	7-3-81	.298	.309	.293	110	383	63	114	18	4	21	88	59	13	0	9	85	0	2	.530	.409
Lafountain, J.T.	B-R	6-0	190	10-26-81	.255	.310	.232	41	98	10	25	2	0	1	10	16	3	0	1	25	1	2	.306	.373
Larsen, Kyle	L-L	6-5	240	6-30-83	.179	.118	.194	23	84	7	15	3	0	1	13	5	1	0	1	18	2	0	.250	.231
Malec, Chris	B-R	5-11	185	8-28-82	.262	.216	.280	36	130	15	34	4	0	1	14	6	1	1	2	14	0	1	.315	.295
Muich, Joseph	R-R	6-1	205	8-18-82	.276	.232	.299	61	196	15	54	12	0	4	24	18	1	1	2	38	1	0	.398	.336
Nelson, Kevin	R-R	6-3	215	4-8-81	.283	.300	.273	40	106	12	30	7	2	1	17	18	4	2	0	24	1	1	.415	.406
Nunez, Eduardo	R-R	6-0	155	6-15-87	.227	.229	.226	90	344	36	78	11	3	2	40	23	2	0	2	48	16	5	.294	.278
Poterson, Jonathan	R-R	6-1	215	2-10-86	.167	.097	.213	24	78	7	13	3	0	1	5	3	2	0	0	30	1	0	.244	.217
Rojas, Irwil	L-R	6-1	175	8-11-84	.281	.263	.286	53	171	18	48	7	0	0	17	21	1	1	2	12	1	1	.322	.359
Roth, Tony	R-R	6-0	175	10-20-82	.195	.143	.232	47	118	22	23	3	0	1	9	25	2	3	1	23	5	2	.246	.342
Tabata, Jose	R-R	5-11	160	8-12-88	.298	.326	.286	86	319	50	95	22	1	5	51	30	12	0	2	66	15	5	.420	.377
Vechionacci, Marcos	B-R	6-2	170	8-7-86	.255	.261	.253	98	368	56	94	15	6	7	44	55	4	0	2	52	7	4	.386	.357

PITCHING	B-T	HT	WT	DOB	W	L	ERA	G	GS	CG	SV	IP	H	R	ER	HR	BB	SO	AVG	vLH	vRH	K/9	BB/9
Abreu, Erick	R-R	6-1	175	8-9-83	6	2	1.88	16	13	0	1	86	65	21	18	8	31	79	.208	.165	.239	8.27	3.24
Arias, Wilkins	L-L	6-1	150	11-4-80	9	6	3.01	31	22	1	2	141	118	50	47	9	53	114	.231	.222	.234	7.29	3.39
Coke, Phil	L-L	6-1	210	7-19-82	0	1	0.53	5	2	0	1	17	10	1	1	0	4	19	.169	.143	.173	10.06	2.12
Conroy, James	R-R	6-4	195	11-4-82	4	4	4.56	24	9	0	0	73	81	43	37	8	26	58	.285	.225	.342	7.15	3.21
Everitt, Keaton	R-R	6-7	220	2-4-83	2	0	1.93	14	0	0	0	23	21	7	5	0	6	20	.241	.158	.306	7.71	2.31
Garcia, Christian	R-R	6-4	195	8-24-85	2	3	3.46	7	7	0	0	42	37	19	16	2	12	45	.243	.266	.219	9.72	2.59
Gomez, Abel	L-L	6-0	170	11-29-84	2	3	3.25	29	10	0	2	72	59	38	26	3	59	69	.222	.231	.219	8.63	7.38
Japa, Rolando	R-R	6-1	165	1-24-85	2	7	5.01	13	7	0	1	47	56	47	26	3	21	50	.283	.242	.320	9.64	4.05
Jones, Ben	R-R	6-3	196	7-3-81	1	0	0.00	1	0	0	0	2	2	0	0	0	1	1	.250	.200	.333	4.50	0.00
Kroenke, Zach	R-L	6-3	210	4-21-84	8	6	3.58	25	20	0	0	113	124	65	45	9	41	86	.277	.274	.278	6.85	3.27
McCutchen, Daniel	R-R	6-2	195	9-26-82	1	0	2.14	7	0	0	1	21	13	5	5	2	5	18	.186	.143	.204	7.71	2.14
Medina, Gabriel	R-R	6-5	235	2-17-84	0	0	2.70	4	0	0	0	10	13	4	3	1	0	12	.310	.316	.304	10.80	0.90
Patterson, Paul	R-R	6-7	200	5-8-84	0	0	5.06	2	0	0	1	5	1	3	3	0	2	6	.063	.125	.000	10.13	3.38
Patterson, Garrett	L-L	6-2	220	5-11-82	2	5	4.50	14	12	0	0	50	47	40	25	3	37	39	.251	.278	.245	7.02	6.66
Quezada, Elvys	R-R	6-1	210	12-15-81	2	0	0.00	9	0	0	3	9	3	0	0	0	2	11	.103	.154	.063	10.61	1.93
Roth, Tony	R-R	6-0	175	10-20-82	1	0	0.00	2	0	0	0	3	1	0	0	0	1	1	.111	.000	.143	3.00	3.00
Rueger, Bryan	L-L	6-3	185	2-22-83	2	0	1.78	26	0	0	0	30	26	8	6	1	5	18	.234	.152	.269	5.34	1.48
Schroer, Steve	R-R	6-2	195	12-28-82	1	2	4.94	21	0	0	1	27	29	16	15	4	14	24	.276	.277	.276	7.90	4.61
Seccombe, David	R-R	6-1	200	1-9-82	5	4	5.33	33	0	0	1	49	52	32	29	4	23	41	.275	.217	.330	7.53	4.22
Soto, Edgar	L-L	5-11	175	12-28-84	1	2	4.95	11	6	0	2	36	35	27	20	2	22	25	.257	.314	.238	6.19	5.45
Stephens, Jason	R-R	6-4	190	10-10-84	4	1	1.80	8	6	0	0	35	31	10	7	1	5	34	.228	.208	.254	8.74	1.29
Stuart, Cory	R-R	6-3	190	3-15-82	6	1	3.06	38	0	0	9	50	45	21	17	1	20	48	.238	.244	.234	8.64	3.60
Swindle, Robert	L-L	6-3	190	7-7-83	4	2	0.61	21	0	0	2	44	35	5	3	0	5	46	.210	.218	.205	9.34	1.02
Valdez, Jose	R-R	6-4	186	1-22-83	0	1	1.08	5	0	0	0	8	8	1	1	0	2	6	.267	.385	.176	6.48	2.16
Velazquez, Juan	R-R	6-4	190	10-11-83	0	0	4.32	6	0	0	0	8	11	5	4	1	6	6	.324	.273	.348	6.48	6.48
Villalona, Bryan	R-R	6-2	170	9-15-82	9	10	3.98	27	22	1	0	138	147	70	61	16	25	81	.271	.303	.242	5.28	1.63
Wordekemper, Eric	R-R	6-1	200	8-8-83	4	3	1.81	39	4	0	7	80	62	24	16	3	21	69	.212	.210	.214	7.79	2.37

FIELDING

Catcher	PCT	G	PO	A	E	DP	PB
Gil	.972	18	120	17	4	2	1
Lafountain	1.000	13	68	0	0	0	4
Muich	.988	51	384	34	5	3	10
Nelson	.991	36	215	13	2	4	4
Rojas	.989	42	249	22	3	0	6

First Base	PCT	G	PO	A	E	DP
Corona	1.000	1	6	2	0	1
Dunn	1.000	4	21	2	0	1
Gil	1.000	1	10	1	0	1
Jones	.983	90	742	70	14	80
Lafountain	1.000	8	36	1	0	6
Larsen	.990	22	179	19	2	11
Poterson	1.000	3	26	2	0	1
Roth	.995	27	182	10	1	22
Vechionacci	1.000	1	2	0	0	0

Second Base	PCT	G	PO	A	E	DP
Beachum	.978	10	13	31	1	9
Corona	.966	51	96	156	9	37
Holmann	.972	62	117	200	9	41
Lafountain	.972	6	7	28	1	4
Nunez	.973	14	21	52	2	12
Roth	1.000	8	9	20	0	7

Third Base	PCT	G	PO	A	E	DP
Corona	.889	10	2	22	3	0
Lafountain	.900	6	2	7	1	0
Malec	.942	29	14	51	4	5
Nunez	.933	6	3	11	1	6
Roth	1.000	2	0	2	0	0
Vechionacci	.945	93	47	160	12	14

Shortstop	PCT	G	PO	A	E	DP
Beachum	1.000	1	1	3	0	1

	PCT	G	PO	A	E	DP
Corona	.912	25	34	49	8	9
Henry	.914	58	95	172	25	43
Nunez	.913	59	89	153	23	37

Outfield	PCT	G	PO	A	E	DP
Battle	.950	93	216	13	12	1
Calzado	1.000	12	17	0	0	0
Cooper	.976	32	38	3	1	0
Corona	1.000	6	12	0	0	0
De La Rosa	.963	27	25	1	1	0
Dunn	.909	9	10	0	1	0
Harris	.952	41	59	1	3	0
Jackson	.988	131	248	5	3	1
Lafountain	1.000	8	9	0	0	0
Poterson	1.000	14	14	1	0	0
Roth	.909	5	10	0	1	0
Tabata	.992	74	125	6	1	0

Staten Island Yankees — Short-Season

New York-Penn League

BATTING	B-T	HT	WT	DOB	AVG	vLH	vRH	G	AB	R	H	2B	3B	HR	RBI	BB	HBP	SH	SF	SO	SB	CS	SLG	OBP
Aragon, Brian	L-L	6-1	190	1-12-84	.237	.167	.262	41	131	18	31	8	0	2	16	6	1	2	3	36	4	0	.344	.270
Baisley, Brian	R-R	6-3	223	12-19-82	.290	.111	.364	9	31	2	9	0	1	1	4	0	0	0	0	8	0	0	.452	.290
Beachum, Jeff	R-R	6-0	185	11-5-83	.300	—	.300	3	10	1	3	1	0	0	1	0	1	0	0	0	0	0	.400	.364
Cervelli, Francisco	B-R	6-1	175	3-6-86	.309	.282	.323	42	136	21	42	10	0	2	16	13	7	1	0	30	0	0	.426	.397
Cooper, James	L-R	5-10	190	2-18-84	.260	.188	.279	22	77	10	20	5	1	0	10	6	5	1	1	8	3	1	.351	.348
Curtis, Colin	L-L	6-0	190	2-1-85	.302	.292	.308	44	159	25	48	9	2	1	18	12	4	0	2	19	4	5	.403	.362
De La Rosa, Wilkins	L-L	6-0	156	2-21-85	.201	.205	.200	66	204	34	41	4	0	0	15	35	5	4	0	62	11	7	.221	.332
Fortenberry, Seth	L-L	6-2	175	9-1-83	.268	.333	.240	67	254	34	68	11	5	4	25	24	7	2	2	65	12	5	.398	.345
Gil, Jose	B-R	6-0	170	9-4-86	.257	.250	.259	34	105	10	27	4	0	2	15	17	0	1	1	16	0	0	.352	.358
Hilligoss, Mitch	R-R	6-1	195	6-17-85	.292	.397	.251	67	267	40	78	8	1	2	36	24	4	0	2	47	12	2	.352	.357
Kunda, Christopher	R-R	6-1	175	11-1-84	.225	.222	.231	46	142	18	32	6	1	2	15	25	0	1	2	31	0	1	.324	.337
Larsen, Kyle	L-R	6-5	240	6-30-83	.235	.188	.241	68	264	35	62	7	0	8	47	23	6	0	1	42	2	0	.352	.310
Lasala, James	R-R	6-1	205	5-12-84	.000	—	.000	1	3	0	0	0	0	0	0	0	0	0	0	0	0	0	.000	.000
O'Brien, Timothy	R-R	6-2	210	12-22-83	.268	.370	.227	47	157	19	42	8	0	1	17	15	3	1	1	36	1	0	.338	.341
Pino, Wilmer	R-R	5-11	165	1-23-86	.326	.391	.302	61	227	43	74	15	2	0	31	7	8	1	3	35	18	2	.410	.363
Poterson, Jonathan	B-R	6-1	215	2-10-86	.163	.067	.172	24	80	10	13	5	0	1	5	7	0	2	1	27	0	0	.263	.227
Raley, Russell	R-R	5-10	185	12-30-83	.338	.471	.298	18	74	12	25	5	0	0	11	6	0	0	1	10	0	1	.405	.383
Roth, Tony	R-R	6-1	175	10-20-82	.500	.750	.429	5	18	5	9	1	1	1	5	3	0	0	0	5	2	1	.833	.571
Smith, Kevin	L-R	6-1	215	1-15-84	.277	.235	.291	43	155	28	43	12	1	2	21	5	3	0	3	30	1	0	.406	.307

PITCHING	B-T	HT	WT	DOB	W	L	ERA	G	GS	CG	SV	IP	H	R	ER	HR	BB	SO	AVG	vLH	vRH	K/9	BB/9
Addison, Tyler	R-R	6-1	215	7-26-84	1	1	5.79	17	0	0	0	23	26	16	15	0	6	13	.292	.364	.250	5.01	2.31
Castillo, Francisco	R-R	6-2	195	10-3-86	3	2	4.03	13	9	0	0	51	52	27	23	4	25	53	.264	.222	.267	9.29	4.38
Conroy, James	R-R	6-4	195	11-4-82	0	2	4.44	7	4	0	0	24	26	13	12	2	6	22	.283	.333	.240	8.14	2.22
Dotel, Octavio	R-R	6-0	210	11-25-73	0	0	0.00	1	0	0	0	1	2	0	0	0	0	1	.500	.333	1.000	9.00	0.00
Duff, Grant	R-R	6-6	210	12-19-82	0	3	5.25	3	3	0	0	12	10	9	7	0	11	8	.222	.150	.280	6.00	8.25
Dunn, Michael	L-L	6-1	185	5-23-85	0	0	5.68	3	0	0	0	6	3	6	4	0	7	7	.125	.000	.136	9.95	9.95
Everitt, Keaton	R-R	6-7	220	2-4-83	3	0	1.02	8	1	0	0	18	12	4	2	0	4	17	.190	.182	.195	8.66	2.04
Hovis, Jonathan	R-R	5-11	185	12-27-83	5	1	1.73	25	0	0	0	36	25	10	7	0	13	30	.200	.220	.187	7.43	3.22
Japa, Rolando	R-R	6-1	165	1-24-85	3	1	4.98	8	8	0	0	34	31	22	19	1	19	19	.244	.289	.220	4.98	4.98
Keadle, Justin	R-R	6-2	211	12-6-82	3	2	1.99	27	0	0	1	41	32	10	9	1	8	38	.215	.276	.176	8.41	1.77
Kennedy, Ian	R-R	6-0	190	12-19-84	0	0	0.00	1	1	0	0	3	2	0	0	0	2	2	.250	.250	.167	6.75	6.75
Kontos, George	R-R	6-3	215	6-12-85	7	3	2.64	14	14	0	0	78	64	25	23	3	19	82	.227	.245	.215	9.42	2.18
Lara, Toni	L-L	6-0	155	1-31-84	1	0	6.00	4	0	0	0	6	8	4	4	1	5	6	.308	.333	.304	9.00	7.50
McCutchen, Daniel	R-R	6-2	195	9-26-82	1	0	1.13	2	2	0	0	8	4	1	1	1	1	11	.148	.000	.154	12.38	1.13
Melancon, Mark	R-R	6-1	175	3-28-85	0	1	3.52	7	0	0	0	8	9	7	3	0	2	8	.281	.313	.250	9.39	2.35
Norton, Tim	R-R	6-5	230	5-23-83	3	3	2.60	15	15	0	0	73	60	29	21	1	14	83	.222	.205	.235	10.28	1.73
O'Brien, Timothy	R-R	6-2	210	12-22-83	0	0	0.00	1	0	0	0	1	0	0	0	0	1	0	.000	.000	.000	0.00	9.00
Omana, Edgar	L-L	6-3	175	9-12-83	1	1	7.85	14	0	0	0	18	20	19	16	0	21	15	.286	.250	.304	7.36	10.31
Patterson, Paul	R-R	6-7	200	5-8-84	3	0	3.48	15	2	0	1	31	30	12	12	3	9	16	.254	.149	.324	4.65	2.61
Peterson, Nicholas	R-R	6-3	210	10-3-84	5	3	1.93	30	0	0	14	37	20	8	8	1	29	53	.157	.205	.133	12.78	6.99
Reyes, Angel	L-L	5-11	170	1-8-87	1	1	1.53	3	3	0	0	18	12	4	3	0	6	16	.211	.182	.217	8.15	3.06
Smith, Kevin	L-R	6-1	215	1-15-84	0	0	36.00	1	0	0	0	1	3	4	4	0	2	1	.600	.500	.667	9.00	18.00
Soto, Edgar	L-L	5-11	175	12-28-84	2	3	4.31	12	12	0	0	54	51	29	26	2	23	49	.243	.211	.250	8.12	3.81
Trubee, Luke	R-R	6-3	195	11-20-83	2	2	2.28	31	0	0	6	51	41	14	13	2	13	27	.224	.145	.259	4.73	2.28
Velazquez, Juan	R-R	6-4	190	10-11-83	1	0	3.18	8	0	0	0	11	11	4	4	0	5	9	.244	.105	.346	7.15	3.97

FIELDING

Catcher	PCT	G	PO	A	E	DP	PB
Baisley	1.000	8	49	9	0	0	1
Cervelli	.979	39	279	46	7	3	7
Gil	.983	32	254	27	5	2	4
Lasala	1.000	1	5	0	0	0	1

First Base	PCT	G	PO	A	E	DP
Larsen	.992	38	343	29	3	24
O'Brien	—	1	0	0	0	0
Smith	1.000	36	303	18	0	19

Second Base	PCT	G	PO	A	E	DP
Kunda	1.000	5	16	14	0	3
Pino	.960	54	88	126	9	20
Raley	.986	16	26	45	1	7

Third Base	PCT	G	PO	A	E	DP
Hilligoss	.971	36	18	81	3	3
O'Brien	.952	37	21	59	4	6
Roth	1.000	5	3	10	0	1

Shortstop	PCT	G	PO	A	E	DP
Beachum	1.000	3	3	6	0	2

	PCT	G	PO	A	E	DP
Hilligoss	.964	32	45	89	5	14
Kunda	.951	41	72	103	9	17
Raley	1.000	1	0	4	0	1

Outfield	PCT	G	PO	A	E	DP
Aragon	.891	29	39	2	5	0
Cooper	1.000	20	27	0	0	0
Curtis	.988	42	76	4	1	0
De La Rosa	.973	64	103	6	3	0
Fortenberry	.944	67	95	7	6	0
Poterson	1.000	13	29	1	0	0
Smith	—	1	0	0	0	0

Gulf Coast League

BATTING

BATTING	B-T	HT	WT	DOB	AVG	vLH	vRH	G	AB	R	H	2B	3B	HR	RBI	BB	HBP	SH	SF	SO	SB	CS	SLG	OBP
Baez, Wangel	R-R	6-0	165	8-30-87	.250	.118	.314	15	52	8	13	4	0	0	4	6	1	2	0	13	3	0	.327	.339
Baisley, Brian	R-R	6-3	223	12-19-82	.345	.167	.432	14	55	10	19	3	0	1	8	4	0	1	0	8	0	1	.455	.390
Beachum, Jeff	R-R	6-0	185	11-5-83	.196	.050	.308	15	46	8	9	1	0	1	2	10	0	0	4	2	0	.283	.339
Calzado, Josue	R-R	6-1	160	11-6-85	.250	.233	.256	47	172	31	43	7	3	3	26	21	0	0	4	26	10	4	.378	.325
Cano, Robinson	L-R	6-0	190	10-22-82	.400	—	.400	1	5	0	2	0	0	0	1	0	0	0	0	0	0	0	.400	.400
Curtis, Colin	L-L	6-0	190	2-1-85	.500	.667	.400	3	8	3	4	2	0	1	4	1	1	0	0	0	1	0	1.125	.600
Diyorio, Nicholas	L-L	5-10	175	11-28-83	.286	.324	.273	36	133	22	38	7	1	0	12	16	0	1	2	17	7	2	.353	.358
Felix, Jose	R-R	6-1	172	11-22-85	.173	.143	.184	23	52	5	9	2	0	1	9	9	0	0	2	25	3	1	.269	.286
Fermin, Angel	R-R	6-2	190	10-30-85	.222	.238	.217	25	81	9	18	4	1	1	9	8	5	2	0	23	1	0	.333	.330
Hollingsworth, Donald	L-L	5-9	175	5-28-85	.216	.233	.207	31	88	24	19	2	0	0	8	30	9	1	2	16	11	8	.239	.450
Ibarra, Walter	B-R	5-11	150	11-1-87	.264	.500	.207	24	72	4	19	2	0	0	7	12	1	1	0	8	3	2	.292	.376
Ketron, Brandon	R-R	6-0	205	8-22-83	.500	—	.500	3	2	1	1	1	0	0	2	0	0	0	0	1	0	0	1.000	.500
Lafountain, J.T.	B-R	6-0	190	10-26-81	.172	.071	.267	11	29	5	5	1	0	0	2	10	2	0	0	4	2	2	.276	.415
Lasala, James	R-R	6-1	205	5-12-84	.063	.000	.091	11	16	0	1	0	0	0	2	4	0	0	0	7	0	0	.063	.250
Mesa, Melquisedec	R-R	6-1	165	1-31-87	.207	.250	.193	40	145	20	30	7	2	3	22	11	1	1	1	45	3	3	.345	.266
Odenreider, Chase	R-R	6-1	209	8-19-83	.254	.231	.259	21	67	8	17	2	0	0	4	2	4	0	0	11	2	0	.284	.315
Perez, Yang Carlos	B-R	6-2	160	6-23-85	.191	.217	.184	38	110	18	21	2	0	2	12	12	3	2	1	28	0	2	.264	.286
Plumley, Grant	R-R	6-0	185	12-21-81	.276	.143	.318	9	29	4	8	0	1	0	3	2	0	0	1	2	0	0	.345	.313
Rodriguez, Gerardo	R-R	6-1	194	10-25-87	.285	.259	.291	38	137	18	39	13	0	3	28	11	2	0	2	34	2	1	.445	.342
Rodriguez, Reynaldo	R-R	6-0	165	2-7-86	.200	—	.200	1	5	1	1	0	0	0	0	1	0	0	0	1	0	0	.200	.333
Rufino, Wady	R-R	6-2	195	4-8-85	.183	.208	.170	19	71	9	13	6	0	1	9	4	0	0	1	12	0	0	.310	.224
Russo, Kevin	R-R	5-11	190	7-8-84	.273	.244	.284	45	150	23	41	10	0	3	23	20	8	1	2	18	6	2	.400	.383
Sanchez, Jesus	R-R	—		9-24-87	.269	.292	.261	24	93	10	25	5	0	0	10	9	2	0	0	19	3	0	.323	.346
2-team (8 GCL Phillies)					.252	—	—	32	119	11	30	7	0	0	11	10	3	0	1	27	4	0	.311	.323
Ungricht, Brock	R-R	5-10	190	12-31-84	.185	.286	.150	14	27	0	5	1	0	0	2	7	0	0	0	6	0	0	.222	.353

PITCHING

PITCHING	B-T	HT	WT	DOB	W	L	ERA	G	GS	CG	SV	IP	H	R	ER	HR	BB	SO	AVG	vLH	vRH	K/9	BB/9
Amador, Anderson	R-R	6-2	180	11-4-84	1	1	3.78	4	2	0	0	17	15	7	7	2	4	13	.242	.250	.239	7.02	2.16
Betances, Dellin	R-R	6-7	185	3-23-88	0	1	1.16	7	7	0	0	23	14	5	3	1	7	27	.173	.143	.189	10.41	2.70
Bruney, Brian	R-R	6-2	245	2-17-82	0	0	4.91	3	0	0	0	4	1	2	2	0	3	6	.091	.000	.111	12.27	7.36
Cabrera, Domingo	L-L	6-1	150	2-23-86	2	2	6.35	8	3	0	0	23	26	24	16	3	15	22	.268	.200	.280	8.74	5.96
Dotel, Octavio	R-R	6-0	210	11-25-73	0	0	0.00	3	2	0	0	3	0	0	0	0	1	6	.000	.000	.000	18.00	3.00
Duff, Grant	R-R	6-6	210	12-19-82	5	1	1.14	11	8	0	0	47	26	12	6	2	17	59	.155	.172	.145	11.22	3.23
Dunn, Michael	L-L	6-1	185	5-23-85	3	0	0.73	11	0	0	4	25	13	2	2	0	9	26	.155	.125	.162	9.49	3.28
Erickson, Casey	R-R	6-3	187	8-28-85	3	2	4.91	10	0	0	1	29	26	18	16	2	6	26	.232	.308	.192	7.98	1.84
Garcia, Christian	R-R	6-4	175	8-24-85	0	1	9.53	5	3	0	0	11	15	13	12	1	4	15	.313	.333	.303	11.91	3.18
Keadle, Justin	R-R	6-2	211	12-6-82	0	0	3.00	2	0	0	1	3	3	1	1	0	0	3	.273	.400	.167	9.00	0.00
Marquez, Jeffrey	R-R	6-2	175	8-10-84	0	1	3.18	2	2	0	0	6	7	2	2	1	1	8	.304	.429	.250	12.71	1.59
Martinez, Brady	R-R	5-10	185	12-21-82	0	1	3.00	11	0	0	0	12	17	5	4	0	2	10	.340	.500	.265	7.50	1.50
McAllister, Zachary	R-R	6-5	230	12-8-87	5	2	3.09	11	1	0	0	35	35	14	12	1	12	28	.259	.241	.272	7.20	3.09
Medina, Gabriel	R-R	6-5	235	2-17-84	1	0	1.96	6	1	0	1	18	11	4	4	1	6	23	.172	.238	.140	11.29	2.95
Mendez, Jesus	R-R	6-2	163	2-14-86	1	1	5.19	6	0	0	0	9	9	5	5	1	0	9	.257	.214	.286	9.35	0.00
Monasterios, Carlos	R-R	6-2	175	3-21-86	1	2	2.97	7	3	0	0	30	23	12	10	2	3	24	.207	.189	.216	7.12	0.89
2-team (4 GCL Phillies)					1	4	3.20	11	6	0	0	45	41	19	16	3	6	35	—	—	—	7.00	1.20
Noesi, Hector	R-R	6-2	174	1-26-87	0	0	1.29	5	0	0	1	7	5	1	1	0	1	11	.192	.143	.250	14.14	1.29
Nova, Ivan	R-R	—		1-12-87	3	0	2.72	10	5	0	1	43	36	13	13	5	7	36	.229	.193	.250	7.53	1.47
Omana, Edgar	L-L	6-3	175	9-23-84	1	0	0.00	2	1	0	0	3	1	0	0	1	1	1	.111	1.000	.000	3.00	3.00
Rasner, Darrell	R-R	6-3	210	1-13-81	0	0	4.50	2	2	0	0	6	5	3	3	0	1	6	.227	.125	.286	9.00	1.50
Reyes, Angel	L-L	5-11	170	1-8-87	3	2	1.35	11	5	0	3	47	25	10	7	1	14	45	.156	.143	.159	8.68	2.70
Salter, Brady	R-R	6-5	220	12-26-82	0	0	4.22	8	0	0	1	11	11	5	5	0	4	9	.275	.286	.269	7.59	3.38
Selenes, Josue	R-R	6-0	180	10-8-85	1	1	3.68	9	1	0	1	15	15	7	6	1	2	16	.268	.300	.250	9.82	1.23
Tejeda, Ferdin	R-R	6-0	185	9-15-82	0	1	4.50	7	5	0	0	8	10	4	4	1	2	7	.323	.231	.389	7.88	2.25
Valdez, Jose	R-R	6-4	186	1-22-83	1	1	2.61	9	0	0	1	10	12	7	3	2	1	7	.293	.455	.233	6.10	0.87

FIELDING

Catcher	PCT	G	PO	A	E	DP	PB
Baisley	1.000	14	142	11	0	3	2
Ketron	1.000	3	7	1	0	0	1
Lafountain	.750	1	3	0	1	0	0
Lasala	1.000	7	31	0	0	0	2
Rodriguez	1.000	10	77	9	0	1	6
Sanchez	.980	24	174	23	4	2	1
Ungricht	1.000	2	3	0	0	0	0

First Base	PCT	G	PO	A	E	DP
Fermin	.977	17	161	6	4	10
Lasala	1.000	1	3	1	0	0
Odenreider	.944	4	34	0	2	4
Perez	1.000	1	4	0	0	1
Rodriguez	1.000	9	65	3	0	5
Rufino	.986	19	133	7	2	9

Second Base	PCT	G	PO	A	E	DP
Baez	1.000	6	8	14	0	0
Beachum	1.000	8	8	23	0	3
Ibarra	.917	5	6	5	1	0
Russo	.986	36	58	82	2	17
Ungricht	1.000	1	3	1	0	0

Third Base	PCT	G	PO	A	E	DP
Fermin	.950	8	4	15	1	0
Lafountain	.938	6	6	9	1	1
Odenreider	.917	6	4	7	1	0
Perez	.939	20	11	35	3	1
Plumley	1.000	6	3	14	0	3
Russo	.943	11	11	22	2	3

Shortstop	PCT	G	PO	A	E	DP
Baez	.972	9	15	20	1	3
Beachum	.968	7	7	23	1	6
Ibarra	.957	19	18	71	4	9
Perez	.863	17	19	44	10	6

Outfield	PCT	G	PO	A	E	DP
Calzado	.989	47	87	7	1	1
Curtis	1.000	3	3	0	0	0
Diyorio	1.000	35	40	3	0	0
Felix	.968	21	28	2	1	0
Hollingsworth	.938	15	14	1	1	0
Mesa	.971	39	62	5	2	1
Odenreider	.900	3	9	0	1	

Ungricht	1.000	8	41	7	0	1
Ungricht	.667	1	0	2	1	0

OAKLAND ATHLETICS

BY CASEY TEFERTILLER

As the numbers piled up, they grew as haunting as they were daunting. Nine consecutive times the Athletics had played postseason games where a win would advance them to the American League Championship Series. Nine consecutive times they lost. Beginning in 2000, the A's had lost in the Division Series to the Yankees twice, then Minnesota and Boston.

That streak ended with a flourish when the A's swept the Twins in the 2006 ALDS, capping a stunning season when the A's outlasted the Angels to win the American League West. Oakland's playoff life would last just four more games, though, as the Tigers muscled past the A's in a four-game sweep of the ALCS.

Before the players even had time to clear their lockers, general manager Billy Beane made an announcement that surprised the public far more than the players: He fired manager Ken Macha. Beane said only a "disconnect" existed between Macha and others in the organization. Center fielder Mark Kotsay and catcher Jason Kendall, two of the team's veterans, came forward to endorse the firing.

Beane had surprised baseball after the 2004 season by trading away top pitchers Tim Hudson and Mark Mulder for younger talent. Even when he made the moves, Beane said he was not thinking as much about '05 as he was about building a contender for '06 and beyond. With new owner Lew Wolff loosening the budget, Beane signed free-agent pitcher Esteban Loaiza, then found a bargain in Frank Thomas, who had missed most of two seasons with injuries. Thomas would

become a force, hitting .270 with 39 homers and 114 RBIs. Loaiza was 11-6, 4.42 after returning from the DL on June 8.

Beane and the A's believed they were loaded for contention in '06. What they didn't expect was a round of injuries that had the team playing at limited strength through much of the schedule. Shortstop Bobby Crosby, the 2004 AL rookie of the year, played only 96 games and missed the last month. Third baseman Eric Chavez fought injuries most of the season and finished at .241 with 22 homers, well below his usual marks.

Several players emerged in their absences, notably Nick Swisher, who hit 35 homers and drove in 95, and utility infielder Marco Scutaro, who filled in capably for Crosby. Second baseman Mark Ellis made two errors all season and set a major league record for fielding percentage at his position with a .997 mark.

Despite the injuries and the hidden internal turbulence, the A's finished 93-69 to win the West by four games over the Angels. They advanced to the ALCS for the first time since 1992.

In the minors, the results were mixed. Oakland's farm teams posted a 367-320 record overall, with Double-A Midland and Class A affiliates Stockton and Kane County all reaching the playoffs. Kane County won the first two rounds before losing to West Michigan in the Midwest League championship series.

However, many of the brightest prospects in the organization were plagued by injuries. Shortstop Cliff Pennington had leg problems and hit .203 in 42 games for Stockton. Outfielders Richie Robnett, Travis Buck, Javier Herrera and Danny Putnam, plus first baseman Daric Barton, all went down with injuries that limited their development.

The breakout players were both pitchers: starter Jason Windsor and reliever Marcus McBeth. Windsor put together a 17-2 record in the minors, enough to earn a pair of shots in the major leagues. McBeth, a converted outfielder, emerged as a closer and collected 25 saves in 31 opportunities for Midland. Third baseman Jeff Baisley was the Midwest League player of the year.

ORGANIZATION LEADERS

BATTING		*Minimum 250 at-bats
*AVG	Perez, Luis, Stockton	.333
R	Clark, Doug, Sacramento	108
H	Clark, Doug, Sacramento	155
TB	McClain, Scott, Sacramento	255
2B	Buck, Travis, Stockton/Midland	41
3B	Three players tied with	8
HR	McClain, Scott, Sacramento	28
RBI	Baisley, Jeff, Kane County	110
BB	Stavisky, Brian, Sacramento/Midland	80
SO	Pineda, Jose, Kane County	132
SB	Clark, Doug, Sacramento	25
*OBP	Stavisky, Brian, Sacramento/Midland	.406
*SLG	Baisley, Jeff, Kane County	.519
XBH	McClain, Scott, Sacramento	61

PITCHING		#Minimum 75 innings
W	Windsor, Jason, Midland/Sacramento	17
L	Ford, Ryan, Stockton	12
#ERA	Piekarz, Joe, Kane County	3.26
G	McBeth, Marcus, Stockton/Sacramento/Midland	65
CG	Lansford, Jared, Kane County/Stockton	2
	Olsen, Kevin, Midland	2
	Ray, Jason, Kane County/Stockton	2
SV	McBeth, Marcus, Stockton/Sacramento/Midland	34
IP	Fritz, Ben, Midland/Sacramento	168
BB	Ray, Jason, Kane County/Stockton	68
SO	Windsor, Jason, Midland/Sacramento	158
#AVG	Ray, Jason, Kane County/Stockton	.232

ORGANIZATION STATISTICS

Oakland Athletics

American League

BATTING	B-T	HT	WT	DOB	AVG	vLH	vRH	G	AB	R	H	2B	3B	HR	RBI	BB	HBP	SH	SF	SO	SB	CS	SLG	OBP
Bocachica, Hiram	R-R	5-11	195	3-4-76	.231	.500	.182	8	13	3	3	0	0	0	0	3	0	0	0	4	1	0	.231	.375
Bradley, Milton	B-R	6-0	190	4-15-78	.276	.293	.270	96	351	53	97	14	2	14	52	51	2	0	1	65	10	2	.447	.370
Brown, Jeremy	R-R	5-10	225	10-25-79	.300	.500	.250	5	10	1	3	2	0	0	0	1	0	0	0	1	0	0	.500	.364
Chavez, Eric	L-R	6-1	210	12-7-77	.241	.197	.257	137	485	74	117	24	2	22	72	84	1	0	6	100	3	0	.435	.351
Clark, Doug	L-R	6-2	205	3-5-76	.167	—	.167	6	6	0	1	0	0	0	0	0	0	0	0	3	1	0	.167	.167
Crosby, Bobby	R-R	6-3	215	1-12-80	.229	.185	.242	96	358	42	82	12	0	9	40	36	0	2	2	76	8	1	.338	.298
Ellis, Mark	R-R	5-11	195	6-6-77	.249	.278	.242	124	441	64	110	25	1	11	52	40	8	4	7	76	4	0	.385	.319
Jimenez, D'Angelo	B-R	6-0	215	12-21-77	.071	.000	.077	8	14	1	1	0	0	0	0	0	0	0	7	0	0	0	.071	.350
2-team (20 Texas)					.183	—		28	71	8	13	3	0	1	8	16	0	1	0	13	0	0	.268	.333
Johnson, Dan	L-R	6-2	225	8-10-79	.234	.217	.238	91	286	30	67	13	1	9	37	40	0	5	4	5	45	0	0	.381	.323
Kendall, Jason	R-R	6-0	205	6-26-74	.295	.331	.285	143	552	76	163	23	0	1	50	53	12	4	5	54	11	5	.342	.367
Kielty, Bobby	B-R	6-1	220	8-5-76	.270	.325	.229	81	270	35	73	20	1	8	36	22	2	2	1	49	2	0	.441	.329
Kotsay, Mark	L-L	6-0	205	12-2-75	.275	.265	.278	129	502	57	138	29	3	7	59	44	2	4	6	55	6	3	.386	.332
Melhuse, Adam	B-R	6-2	210	3-27-72	.219	.222	.218	49	128	10	28	8	0	4	18	9	1	0	1	34	0	1	.375	.273
Payton, Jay	R-R	5-10	185	11-22-72	.296	.296	.296	142	557	78	165	32	3	10	59	22	4	0	5	52	8	4	.418	.325
Perez, Antonio	R-R	5-11	175	1-26-80	.102	.129	.090	57	98	10	10	5	1	1	8	10	0	1	0	44	0	1	.204	.185
Rouse, Mike	L-R	5-11	200	4-25-80	.292	.200	.316	8	24	2	7	3	0	0	2	1	1	0	0	4	1	0	.417	.346
Scutaro, Marco	R-R	5-10	190	10-30-75	.266	.218	.279	117	365	52	97	21	6	5	41	50	0	3	5	66	5	1	.397	.350
Swisher, Nick	B-L	6-0	215	11-25-80	.254	.291	.241	157	556	106	141	24	2	35	95	97	11	2	6	152	1	2	.493	.372
Thomas, Frank	R-R	6-5	275	5-27-68	.270	.245	.278	137	466	77	126	11	0	39	114	81	6	0	6	81	0	0	.545	.381

PITCHING	B-T	HT	WT	DOB	W	L	ERA	G	GS	CG	SV	IP	H	R	ER	HR	BB	SO	AVG	vLH	vRH	K/9	BB/9
Blanton, Joe	R-R	6-3	240	12-11-80	16	12	4.82	32	31	1	0	194	241	111	104	17	58	107	.309	.314	.304	4.96	2.69
Calero, Kiko	R-R	6-1	200	1-9-75	3	2	3.41	70	0	0	2	58	50	22	22	4	24	67	.231	.278	.208	10.40	3.72
Casilla, Santiago	R-R	6-0	200	6-25-80	0	0	11.57	2	0	0	0	2	2	3	3	0	2	2	.250	.400	.000	7.71	7.71
Duchscherer, Justin	R-R	6-3	200	11-19-77	2	1	2.91	53	0	0	9	56	52	18	18	4	9	51	.244	.248	.241	8.25	1.46
Flores, Ron	L-L	5-11	200	8-9-79	1	2	3.34	25	0	0	1	30	28	11	11	3	10	20	.255	.323	.228	6.07	3.03
Gaudin, Chad	R-R	5-11	165	3-24-83	4	2	3.09	55	0	0	2	64	51	24	22	3	42	36	.222	.253	.201	5.06	5.91
Halsey, Brad	L-L	6-1	185	2-14-81	5	4	4.67	52	7	0	0	94	108	53	49	11	46	53	.288	.317	.277	5.06	4.39
Harden, Rich	L-R	6-1	195	11-30-81	4	0	4.24	9	9	0	0	47	31	22	22	5	26	49	.191	.176	.211	9.45	5.01
Haren, Dan	R-R	6-5	220	9-17-80	14	13	4.12	34	34	2	0	223	224	109	102	31	45	176	.258	.246	.268	7.10	1.82
Karsay, Steve	R-R	6-3	215	3-24-72	1	0	5.79	9	0	0	0	9	13	6	6	4	3	5	.351	.444	.263	4.82	2.89
Keisler, Randy	L-L	6-3	190	2-24-76	0	0	4.50	11	0	0	0	10	14	5	5	3	2	5	.350	.353	.348	4.50	1.80
Kennedy, Joe	R-L	6-4	245	5-24-79	4	1	2.31	39	0	0	1	35	34	10	9	1	13	29	.254	.326	.220	7.46	3.34
Komine, Shane	R-R	5-9	175	10-18-80	0	0	5.00	2	2	0	0	9	10	5	5	3	4	8	.270	.250	.280	1.00	8.00
Loaiza, Esteban	R-R	6-3	235	12-31-71	11	9	4.89	26	26	2	0	155	179	92	84	17	40	97	.288	.319	.265	5.64	2.33
Roney, Matt	R-R	6-3	245	1-10-80	0	1	4.50	3	0	0	0	4	5	2	2	0	1	0	.333	.250	.364	0.00	2.25
Saarloos, Kirk	R-R	6-0	185	5-23-79	7	7	4.75	35	16	0	2	121	149	70	64	19	53	52	.308	.319	.298	3.86	3.93
Sauerbeck, Scott	R-L	6-3	200	11-9-71	0	0	3.65	22	0	0	0	12	13	8	5	1	9	6	.271	.217	.320	4.38	6.57
2-team (24 Cleveland)					0	1	4.97	46	0	0	0	25	22	17	14	3	18	17	—	—	—	6.04	6.39
Street, Huston	R-R	6-0	190	8-2-83	4	4	3.31	69	0	0	37	71	64	28	26	4	13	67	.238	.274	.211	8.53	1.66
Windsor, Jason	R-R	6-2	235	7-16-82	0	1	6.59	4	3	0	0	14	21	12	10	2	5	6	.375	.381	.371	3.95	3.29
Witasick, Jay	R-R	6-4	240	8-28-72	1	0	6.75	20	0	0	0	23	25	17	17	3	21	23	.281	.138	.350	9.13	8.34
Zito, Barry	L-L	6-4	210	5-13-78	16	10	3.83	34	34	0	0	221	211	99	94	27	99	151	.257	.260	.257	6.15	4.03

FIELDING

Catcher	PCT	G	PO	A	E	DP	PB
Brown	1.000	1	2	0	0	0	0
Kendall	.995	141	924	54	5	9	7
Melhuse	1.000	24	129	14	0	3	3

First Base	PCT	G	PO	A	E	DP
Ellis	1.000	1	1	0	0	0
Johnson	.995	85	689	64	4	96
Kotsay	.933	4	28	0	2	6
Melhuse	1.000	2	9	0	0	1
Swisher	.993	90	666	42	5	56

Second Base	PCT	G	PO	A	E	DP
Ellis	.997	123	273	357	2	91

	PCT	G	PO	A	E	DP
Jimenez	1.000	2	2	1	0	0
Perez	1.000	2	1	1	0	1
Rouse	1.000	7	9	16	0	4
Scutaro	.994	37	72	93	1	32

Third Base	PCT	G	PO	A	E	DP
Chavez	.987	134	105	281	5	43
Jimenez	.667	3	1	1	1	0
Melhuse	1.000	3	0	2	0	0
Perez	.944	27	20	47	4	4
Scutaro	.893	12	4	21	3	1

Shortstop	PCT	G	PO	A	E	DP
Crosby	.972	95	145	268	12	59

	PCT	G	PO	A	E	DP
Jimenez	1.000	3	3	7	0	0
Perez	1.000	4	6	8	0	3
Scutaro	.966	69	86	168	9	38

Outfield	PCT	G	PO	A	E	DP
Bocachica	1.000	8	5	0	0	0
Bradley	.980	94	191	4	4	0
Clark	—	1	0	0	0	0
Kielty	.993	73	136	3	1	1
Kotsay	.993	127	281	6	2	2
Payton	.978	137	311	5	7	0
Scutaro	1.000	2	1	0	0	0
Swisher	.984	80	174	5	3	3

Sacramento River Cats

Pacific Coast League

BATTING	B-T	HT	WT	DOB	AVG	vLH	vRH	G	AB	R	H	2B	3B	HR	RBI	BB	HBP	SH	SF	SO	SB	CS	SLG	OBP
Baker, John	L-R	6-1	210	1-20-81	.273	.184	.291	83	293	49	80	19	1	4	38	40	2	2	3	77	6	0	.386	.361
Barton, Daric	L-R	6-0	225	8-16-85	.259	.361	.225	43	147	25	38	6	1	2	22	32	0	1	1	26	1	0	.395	.389
Beattie, Andrew	B-R	5-8	175	2-28-78	.269	.234	.283	44	160	29	43	9	1	6	30	23	0	1	5	30	3	2	.450	.351
2-team (33 Nashville)					.264	—		77	276	42	73	12	2	9	48	39	0	1	5	58	6	3	.420	.350
Bocachica, Hiram	R-R	5-11	195	3-4-76	.326	.364	.316	77	291	61	95	15	3	19	60	43	7	0	3	55	18	3	.595	.422
Bradley, Milton	B-R	6-0	190	4-15-78	.208	.143	.235	6	24	3	5	0	0	2	6	2	1	0	0	10	1	0	.458	.296
Brown, Jeremy	R-R	5-10	225	10-25-79	.255	.256	.254	77	275	41	70	14	0	13	40	23	4	0	4	60	0	0	.447	.317
Brummett, John	R-R	6-1	205	12-7-83	.000	.000	.000	2	5	0	0	0	0	0	0	0	0	0	0	1	0	0	.000	.000
Casanova, Raul	B-R	6-0	230	8-23-72	.250	.250	.250	4	16	0	4	0	0	0	3	1	0	0	0	3	0	0	.250	.250
Castillo, David	R-R	5-9	185	9-15-81	.000	—	.000	1	1	0	0	0	0	0	0	0	0	0	0	0	0	0	.000	.000
Clark, Doug	L-R	6-2	205	3-5-76	.287	.258	.298	122	494	93	142	22	2	15	67	57	8	8	7	104	25	8	.431	.366
Cobb, Larry	R-R	5-9	175	7-10-85	.000	.000	.000	2	4	0	0	0	0	0	0	0	0	0	1	0	0	0	.000	.000

190 • BASEBALL AMERICA 2007 ALMANAC

General manager: Billy Beane. **Farm director:** Keith Lieppman. **Scouting director:** Eric Kubota.

Class	Team	League	W	L	PCT	Finish*	Manager	Affiliate Since
Majors	Oakland	American	93	69	.574	4th (14)	Ken Macha	—
Triple-A	Sacramento River Cats	Pacific Coast	78	66	.542	4th (16)	Tony DeFrancesco	2000
Double-A	Midland RockHounds	Texas	78	61	.561	1st (8)	Von Hayes	1999
High A	Stockton Ports	California	69	71	.493	6th (10)	Todd Steverson	2005
Low A	Kane County Cougars	Midwest	79	60	.568	2nd (14)	Aaron Nieckula	2003
Short-season	Vancouver Canadians	Northwest	39	37	.513	4th (8)	Richard Magnante	1979
Rookie	AZL Athletics	Arizona	24	31	.436	6th (9)	Ruben Escalera	1988
OVERALL 2006 MINOR LEAGUE RECORD			367	326	.530	7th (30)		

*Finish in overall standings (No. of teams in league). +League champion

ORGANIZATION STATISTICS

	B-T	HT	WT	DOB	AVG	OBP	SLG	AB	R	H	2B	3B	HR	RBI	BB	SO	SB	CS	vLH	vRH
Ellis, Mark	R-R	5-11	195	6-6-77	.167	.000	.200	4	12	1	2	0	0	2	4	0	0	2	0	0	.167	.375
Espy, Nate	R-R	6-3	215	4-24-78	.275	.297	.266	99	357	44	98	25	0	10	48	51	6	1	4	81	2	0	.429	.371
Ginter, Keith	R-R	5-10	195	5-5-76	.268	.330	.249	114	422	71	113	29	0	13	68	58	15	4	7	74	3	0	.429	.371
Jimenez, D'Angelo	B-R	6-0	215	12-21-77	.304	.414	.271	35	125	30	38	8	1	4	23	24	0	1	1	14	2	4	.480	.413
Johnson, Dan	L-R	6-2	225	8-10-79	.314	.346	.300	46	172	34	54	13	1	7	44	32	3	0	2	27	0	1	.523	.426
Kielty, Bobby	B-R	6-1	220	8-5-76	.222	.222	.222	10	36	5	8	0	0	1	4	7	0	0	0	12	0	0	.306	.349
Kiger, Mark	R-R	5-10	180	5-30-80	.233	.196	.248	61	176	34	41	8	0	3	14	30	2	6	2	47	4	1	.330	.348
McClain, Scott	R-R	6-4	220	5-19-72	.252	.228	.260	140	547	84	138	33	0	28	107	48	3	1	6	117	7	4	.466	.313
Perez, Wilber	B-R	6-1	183	5-15-84	.000	.000	—	1	1	0	0	0	0	0	0	0	0	0	0	0	0	.000	.000
Perry, Jason	L-R	6-0	200	8-18-80	.252	.235	.257	90	318	36	80	15	2	8	47	23	4	2	3	84	3	2	.387	.307
Pratt, Haas	R-R	6-3	215	9-17-81	1.000	—	1.000	1	1	0	1	0	0	0	1	0	0	0	0	0	0	2.000	1.000
Robnett, Richie	L-L	5-10	200	9-17-83	.091	.000	.167	5	11	0	1	1	0	0	0	0	0	0	3	0	0	.182	.091
Rouse, Mike	L-R	5-11	200	4-25-80	.258	.218	.271	99	345	59	89	21	1	6	47	42	6	7	2	67	4	1	.377	.342
Stavisky, Brian	L-R	6-2	210	7-6-80	.239	.069	.300	33	109	16	26	6	0	2	8	16	0	0	1	23	0	0	.349	.333
Thomas, Charles	L-L	6-0	205	12-26-78	.274	.243	.287	114	383	58	105	8	2	9	43	38	7	6	0	77	8	9	.376	.350
Watson, Matt	L-R	5-11	210	9-5-78	.317	.357	.306	32	126	21	40	8	1	5	28	19	1	0	0	15	0	1	.516	.411

PITCHING	B-T	HT	WT	DOB	W	L	ERA	G	GS	CG	SV	IP	H	R	ER	HR	BB	SO	AVG	vLH	vRH	K/9	BB/9
Birtwell, John	R-R	6-2	225	9-4-79	0	0	3.38	24	0	0	0	29	31	13	11	1	16	26	.272	.245	.292	7.98	4.91
Casilla, Santiago	R-R	6-2	190	6-25-80	2	0	3.27	25	0	0	4	33	25	13	12	2	10	32	.207	.152	.273	8.73	2.73
Crowell, Kyle	R-R	5-11	190	6-16-79	0	0	18.00	2	0	0	0	2	2	4	4	0	3	0	.286	.333	.250	0.00	13.50
Dominguez, Juan	R-R	6-1	225	5-18-80	5	10	5.85	17	16	0	0	88	104	64	57	10	39	48	.301	.314	.287	4.93	4.00
Duchscherer, Justin	R-R	6-3	200	11-19-77	0	0	0.00	2	1	0	0	2	2	0	0	0	0	1	.286	.000	.667	4.50	0.00
Flores, Ron	L-L	5-11	200	8-9-79	5	5	6.48	26	0	0	2	25	25	20	18	0	14	27	.260	.238	.278	9.72	5.04
Fritz, Benjamin	R-R	6-4	238	3-29-81	6	6	5.83	17	17	0	0	97	111	65	63	15	44	58	.289	.282	.294	5.36	4.07
Gaudin, Chad	R-R	5-11	165	3-24-83	3	0	0.37	4	4	0	0	24	14	6	1	0	8	26	.173	.205	.143	9.62	2.96
Guzman, Jose	R-R	6-1	185	11-5-87	0	0	13.50	1	0	0	0	1	3	1	1	0	0	0	.600	1.000	.500	0.00	0.00
Halsey, Brad	L-L	6-1	185	2-14-81	1	0	0.96	2	2	0	0	9	4	1	1	0	1	3	.129	.111	.136	2.89	0.96
Harden, Rich	L-R	6-1	195	11-30-81	0	0	0.00	1	1	0	0	2	1	0	0	0	0	3	.125	.167	.000	13.50	0.00
Johnson, Adam	R-R	6-2	210	7-12-79	1	2	12.54	9	3	0	0	19	29	27	26	6	15	10	.349	.356	.342	4.82	7.23
Karnuth, Jason	R-R	6-2	190	5-15-76	0	7	4.43	38	0	0	15	43	39	24	21	2	20	25	.244	.197	.281	5.27	4.22
Keisler, Randy	L-L	6-3	190	2-24-76	9	5	3.83	25	16	0	0	103	107	53	44	2	47	82	.268	.215	.288	7.14	4.09
Kennedy, Joe	R-L	6-4	245	5-24-79	0	0	0.00	3	1	0	0	4	2	0	0	0	1	2	.154	.000	.200	4.50	2.25
Kohn, Shawn	R-R	6-2	208	1-28-80	2	2	3.40	40	0	0	2	53	42	23	20	5	15	48	.213	.293	.157	8.15	2.55
Komine, Shane	R-R	5-9	175	10-18-80	11	8	4.05	24	22	1	0	140	145	67	63	13	38	116	.267	.257	.276	7.46	2.44
Loaiza, Esteban	R-R	6-3	215	12-31-71	1	1	5.87	2	1	0	0	8	11	5	5	0	2	4	.344	.333	.364	4.70	2.35
Mabeus, Chris	R-R	6-3	235	2-11-79	0	1	4.58	12	0	0	0	20	16	11	10	1	10	20	.219	.266	.156	9.15	4.58
McBeth, Marcus	R-R	6-2	183	8-23-80	0	1	11.05	6	0	0	0	7	7	9	9	3	6	7	.241	.214	.267	8.59	7.36
Meyer, Dan	R-L	6-3	220	7-3-81	3	3	5.07	10	10	0	0	50	63	32	28	10	20	29	.315	.411	.278	5.26	3.62
Mitchell, Michael	R-R	6-3	180	10-27-81	0	0	4.50	5	0	0	0	6	5	3	3	1	1	3	.227	.167	.250	4.50	1.50
Moreno, Victor	R-R	6-0	212	6-10-79	5	4	5.38	34	14	0	4	100	117	63	60	7	41	68	.299	.289	.308	6.10	3.68
Peterson, Trent	R-L	6-1	180	11-16-81	0	0	13.50	1	0	0	0	2	5	3	3	0	0	0	.455	.667	.375	0.00	0.00
Pettyjohn, Adam	L-R	6-1	190	6-11-77	3	2	4.57	11	9	0	1	63	74	34	32	6	21	43	.292	.221	.324	6.14	3.00
Puffer, Brandon	R-R	6-3	190	10-5-75	0	0	5.29	13	0	0	0	17	21	10	10	4	4	14	.309	.393	.250	7.41	2.12
2-team (37 Round Rock)					5	1	4.67	50	0	0	4	69	67	37	36	10	20	51	—	—	—	6.62	2.60
Rall, Tim	R-L	6-0	200	9-30-79	0	0	4.15	3	0	0	0	4	3	2	2	1	2	5	.188	.125	.250	10.38	4.15
Roney, Matt	R-R	6-3	245	1-10-80	4	3	2.95	47	0	0	6	58	58	26	19	4	19	65	.260	.283	.242	10.09	2.95
Santos, Alex	R-R	6-1	230	8-9-77	0	0	3.45	10	0	0	0	16	18	7	6	2	4	7	.300	.333	.278	4.02	2.30
Sauerbeck, Scott	L-L	6-3	200	11-9-71	0	0	0.00	1	0	0	0	2	2	0	0	1	0	1	.286	.500	.200	9.00	4.50
Tadano, Kazuhito	R-R	6-0	180	4-25-80	2	4	5.08	34	3	0	3	57	68	36	32	9	19	60	.292	.277	.303	9.53	3.02
Watson, Mark	L-R	6-3	220	1-23-74	1	2	2.91	26	0	0	1	22	22	8	7	1	9	12	.262	.222	.292	4.98	3.74
2-team (23 Iowa)					4	3	3.14	49	0	0	2	43	42	18	15	1	22	33	—	—	—	6.91	4.60
Windsor, Jason	R-R	6-2	235	7-16-82	13	1	3.81	20	20	1	0	118	128	53	50	7	32	123	.272	.258	.289	9.38	2.44
Witasick, Jay	R-R	6-4	240	8-28-72	1	0	3.86	12	0	0	1	14	10	7	6	2	4	6	.196	.263	.156	3.86	2.57
Ziegler, Brad	R-R	6-4	190	10-10-79	0	1	6.00	4	0	0	0	21	32	17	14	3	5	11	.360	.351	.365	4.71	2.14

FIELDING

Catcher	PCT	G	PO	A	E	DP	PB
Baker	.986	76	541	35	8	5	7
Brown	.998	66	436	43	1	4	9
Brummett	1.000	1	3	0	0	0	0
Casanova	1.000	3	29	0	0	0	0
Castillo	1.000	3	13	0	0	0	0

First Base	PCT	G	PO	A	E	DP
Barton	.978	37	282	28	7	22
Espy	.989	67	506	52	6	40
Johnson	.992	38	315	40	3	28
McClain	1.000	5	41	1	0	2

Second Base	PCT	G	PO	A	E	DP
Beattie	.957	15	28	38	3	9
Bocachica	—	1	0	0	0	0
Ellis	1.000	3	5	7	0	1
Ginter	.971	90	168	238	12	42
Jimenez	.979	23	44	51	2	13
Kiger	.986	18	28	42	1	4

Third Base	PCT	G	PO	A	E	DP
Beattie	1.000	2	2	3	0	0
Bocachica	.688	5	2	9	5	0
Brown	1.000	2	2	3	0	1

	PCT	G	PO	A	E	DP
Ginter	.700	5	3	4	3	0
Johnson	.667	1	0	2	1	0
Kiger	1.000	7	2	9	0	1
McClain	.977	129	102	199	7	14

Shortstop	PCT	G	PO	A	E	DP
Beattie	.923	7	9	27	3	6
Jimenez	.905	9	15	23	4	5
Kiger	.973	30	39	71	3	14
McClain	1.000	3	2	6	0	0
Rouse	.980	98	136	260	8	41

Outfield	PCT	G	PO	A	E	DP
Beattie	1.000	13	22	3	0	1
Bocachica	.976	55	116	4	3	1
Bradley	1.000	1	1	0	0	0
Clark	.992	113	246	11	2	2
Cobb	—	1	0	0	0	0
Kielty	.960	7	23	1	1	1
Kiger	1.000	2	2	0	0	1
McClain	1.000	1	1	0	0	0
Perry	.961	88	162	11	7	4
Robnett	1.000	4	7	0	0	0
Stavisky	1.000	24	49	1	0	0
Thomas	.986	111	274	5	4	1
Watson	.976	28	41	0	1	0

Midland RockHounds — Double-A

Texas League

BATTING	B-T	HT	WT	DOB	AVG	vLH	vRH	G	AB	R	H	2B	3B	HR	RBI	BB	HBP	SH	SF	SO	SB	CS	SLG	OBP
Allegra, Matt	R-R	6-3	214	7-10-81	.265	.253	.268	96	355	52	94	27	1	15	62	38	5	3	7	117	4	3	.473	.338
Buck, Travis	L-R	6-2	205	11-18-83	.302	.405	.276	50	212	32	64	22	1	4	22	22	3	1	0	39	9	1	.472	.376
Casanova, Raul	B-R	6-0	230	8-23-72	.182	—	.182	2	11	1	2	1	0	0	2	0	0	0	0	0	0	0	.273	.182
Castillo, David	R-R	5-9	185	9-15-81	.208	.071	.241	24	72	7	15	2	0	0	10	6	0	0	2	11	0	0	.236	.263
Colamarino, Brant	L-L	6-2	221	12-4-80	.285	.235	.301	126	495	69	141	35	8	17	91	60	6	0	7	109	2	2	.491	.364
Cornejo, Eduardo	L-R	5-10	175	11-19-81	.210	.235	.203	47	157	17	33	6	0	0	8	16	2	4	2	14	0	0	.248	.288
Coughlan, Cameron	B-R	5-11	178	8-12-81	.258	.214	.294	21	31	7	8	1	0	1	7	6	2	2	0	5	0	1	.387	.410
Kiger, Mark	R-R	5-10	180	5-30-80	.307	.452	.259	58	251	43	77	12	3	6	20	30	0	1	1	58	7	2	.450	.379
Melillo, Kevin	L-R	5-11	185	5-14-82	.280	.292	.276	136	500	73	140	31	3	12	73	68	4	6	98	14	7	.426	.367
Merrill, Ronnie	B-R	6-1	185	11-13-78	.244	.252	.242	118	446	47	109	30	2	5	45	40	7	5	4	95	9	12	.354	.314
Morris, Jed	L-R	5-11	200	3-4-80	.306	.350	.300	45	170	27	52	6	0	6	17	22	3	3	0	25	1	1	.447	.395
Myers, Casey	R-R	5-10	209	10-23-78	.310	.286	.315	24	87	12	27	4	0	1	14	19	1	1	3	9	0	0	.391	.427
Perry, Jason	L-R	6-0	200	8-18-80	.402	.394	.405	28	107	28	43	8	2	4	17	12	4	0	1	23	2	1	.626	.476
Powell, Landon	B-R	6-3	240	3-19-82	.268	.167	.286	12	41	4	11	0	0	1	4	3	1	0	0	12	0	0	.341	.333
Putnam, Danny	L-L	5-10	200	9-17-82	.244	.232	.249	60	225	33	55	13	2	8	37	23	2	2	2	37	2	1	.427	.317
Robnett, Richie	L-L	5-10	200	9-17-83	.357	.000	.455	5	14	5	5	1	0	1	2	4	0	0	1	4	0	0	.643	.474
Snyder, Brian	R-R	6-0	195	3-17-82	.205	.219	.202	48	151	24	31	6	2	5	25	39	1	3	1	45	1	1	.371	.370
Spanos, Vasili	R-R	6-1	225	2-25-81	.308	.384	.285	120	439	70	135	29	1	9	67	52	25	3	8	73	0	1	.440	.405
Stanley, Steve	L-L	5-8	161	12-23-79	.133	.000	.200	7	30	3	4	1	0	0	4	2	0	0	0	3	1	0	.167	.188
Stavisky, Brian	L-R	6-2	210	7-6-80	.316	.363	.301	85	329	60	104	22	2	6	49	64	2	3	1	53	3	1	.450	.429
Suzuki, Kurt	R-R	6-0	205	10-4-83	.285	.382	.254	99	376	64	107	26	1	7	55	58	9	0	1	50	5	3	.415	.392
Turner, Lloyd	R-R	6-1	175	4-11-80	.208	.258	.188	100	318	37	66	5	6	8	42	30	5	8	3	70	12	5	.336	.284

PITCHING	B-T	HT	WT	DOB	W	L	ERA	G	GS	CG	SV	IP	H	R	ER	HR	BB	SO	AVG	vLH	vRH	K/9	BB/9
Aguilar, Ray	B-L	5-11	210	1-18-80	12	7	4.54	28	28	0	0	159	190	88	80	13	42	100	.303	.285	.310	5.67	2.38
Braden, Dallas	L-L	6-1	180	8-13-83	0	0	16.20	1	1	0	0	3	9	6	6	1	0	2	.500	.667	.467	5.40	1.00
Bradley, David	R-R	6-1	175	8-28-77	6	11	5.41	31	24	0	0	131	156	92	79	11	58	81	.302	.351	.271	5.55	3.97
Burton, Jared	R-R	6-5	224	6-2-81	6	5	4.14	53	0	0	1	74	71	36	34	7	27	66	.255	.260	.253	8.03	3.28
Coleman, Jeffrey	R-R	5-11	193	10-6-80	4	0	4.44	16	0	0	0	24	22	13	12	2	14	29	.239	.211	.259	10.73	5.18
Crowder, Justin	L-L	6-0	208	9-24-79	1	2	4.79	41	0	0	2	47	50	27	25	7	19	43	.276	.343	.237	8.23	3.64
Fritz, Benjamin	R-R	6-4	238	3-29-81	1	4	3.30	12	12	0	0	71	63	31	26	4	22	51	.241	.288	.207	6.46	2.79
Knox, Brad	R-R	6-2	230	5-27-82	12	5	3.67	27	25	1	0	162	154	74	66	10	62	100	.255	.282	.236	5.57	3.45
Kohn, Shawn	R-R	6-2	208	1-28-80	1	2	3.52	12	0	0	2	15	10	7	6	1	2	20	.182	.125	.205	11.74	1.17
Lynch, Matt	L-L	6-1	195	1-14-81	0	1	13.50	2	0	0	0	3	8	4	4	0	1	3	.533	.500	.545	10.13	3.38
Madsen, Michael	R-R	6-0	160	11-29-82	0	0	18.41	2	2	0	0	7	19	15	15	0	3	5	.487	.636	.429	6.14	3.68
McBeth, Marcus	R-R	6-2	183	8-23-80	3	2	2.48	45	0	0	25	54	43	16	15	4	20	65	.213	.276	.175	10.77	3.31
Mitchell, Michael	R-R	6-2	185	10-27-81	2	1	3.60	14	0	0	0	20	24	11	8	1	11	15	.316	.308	.320	6.75	4.95
Muessig, Jeff	R-R	6-2	208	2-27-82	0	1	1.96	11	0	0	1	18	12	5	4	3	4	22	.182	.240	.146	10.80	1.96
Olsen, Kevin	R-R	6-2	195	7-26-76	6	1	3.61	13	13	2	0	85	77	37	34	7	20	49	.239	.221	.251	5.21	2.13
Rall, Tim	R-L	6-0	200	9-30-79	1	0	1.26	10	0	0	2	14	11	2	2	0	5	11	.220	.167	.267	6.91	3.14
Rawson, Anthony	L-L	5-10	180	7-31-80	1	2	5.86	31	0	0	0	35	46	26	23	2	26	33	.319	.338	.303	8.41	6.62
Robertson, Connor	R-R	6-2	215	9-10-81	7	2	2.80	55	0	0	6	84	73	28	26	1	22	97	.246	.267	.234	10.43	2.37
Rogers, Michael	R-R	6-1	205	10-24-82	0	2	9.53	6	6	0	0	28	40	31	30	4	13	20	.336	.350	.329	6.35	4.13
Santos, Alex	R-R	6-1	230	8-9-77	1	2	5.51	15	0	0	4	16	20	10	10	2	8	15	.313	.269	.342	8.27	4.41
Walton, Sam	L-L	6-5	225	12-1-78	1	4	3.12	17	0	0	0	26	15	9	9	0	18	22	.179	.162	.191	7.62	6.23
2-team (3 Springfield)					1	4	3.07	20	0	0	0	29	17	10	10	0	22	27	—	—	—	8.28	6.75
Windsor, Jason	R-R	6-2	235	7-16-82	4	1	2.97	6	6	0	0	33	27	12	11	2	10	35	.227	.222	.231	9.45	2.70
Ziegler, Brad	R-R	6-4	190	10-10-79	9	6	3.37	23	22	1	0	142	151	60	53	17	37	88	.279	.282	.277	5.59	2.35

FIELDING

Catcher	PCT	G	PO	A	E	DP	PB
Casanova	1.000	2	20	3	0	0	1
Castillo	.966	19	101	13	4	2	1
Morris	.989	25	175	10	2	2	2
Powell	.977	12	80	5	2	0	0
Suzuki	.997	91	623	38	2	6	6

First Base	PCT	G	PO	A	E	DP
Castillo	1.000	1	9	2	0	0
Colamarino	.991	104	900	87	9	89
Kiger	1.000	1	6	1	0	2
Myers	1.000	8	77	2	0	4
Snyder	1.000	1	3	0	0	0
Spanos	.984	29	233	9	4	28
Suzuki	1.000	1	6	1	0	3

Second Base	PCT	G	PO	A	E	DP
Cornejo	.857	2	4	8	2	0
Kiger	.947	5	9	9	1	4
Melillo	.990	134	249	363	6	88
Turner	1.000	3	9	14	0	3

Third Base	PCT	G	PO	A	E	DP
Cornejo	.958	11	5	18	1	2
Kiger	.937	47	30	89	8	8
Morris	—	1	0	0	0	0
Snyder	.980	45	23	75	2	6
Spanos	.916	37	19	79	9	6
Turner	.960	10	5	19	1	2

Shortstop	PCT	G	PO	A	E	DP
Cornejo	.947	19	27	44	4	8
Kiger	1.000	6	11	19	0	4
Merrill	.974	117	188	344	14	79

	PCT	G	PO	A	E	DP
Turner	1.000	3	4	8	0	4

Outfield	PCT	G	PO	A	E	DP
Allegra	.969	95	241	11	8	3
Buck	1.000	49	100	4	0	1
Cornejo	1.000	4	2	1	0	0
Coughlan	1.000	9	7	0	0	0
Kiger	1.000	4	11	0	0	0
Melillo	—	1	0	0	0	0
Morris	1.000	21	41	4	0	1
Perry	1.000	25	56	3	0	2
Putnam	1.000	60	98	5	0	1
Robnett	.857	4	6	0	1	0
Stanley	1.000	7	11	0	0	0
Stavisky	1.000	75	149	5	0	0
Turner	.987	80	150	4	2	1

Stockton Ports — High Class A

California League

BATTING	B-T	HT	WT	DOB	AVG	vLH	vRH	G	AB	R	H	2B	3B	HR	RBI	BB	HBP	SH	SF	SO	SB	CS	SLG	OBP
Allegra, Matt	R-R	6-3	214	7-10-81	.042	.000	.045	8	24	2	1	0	0	1	3	3	1	0	1	11	1	0	.167	.172
Appert, Luke	L-R	6-0	185	7-14-80	.289	.375	.275	55	173	35	50	11	0	5	27	43	4	1	1	20	4	1	.439	.439
Blasi, Nick	R-R	5-10	200	9-23-81	.309	.270	.326	59	249	43	77	19	3	5	27	21	7	1	1	50	2	5	.470	.378
Bocachica, Hiram	R-R	5-11	195	3-4-76	.286	.250	.300	4	14	3	4	2	0	0	2	0	0	4	0	1	.429	.375

	B-T	HT	WT	DOB	AVG	vLH	vRH	G	AB	R	H	2B	3B	HR	RBI	BB	HBP	SH	SF	SO	SB	CS	SLG	OBP
Bradley, Milton	B-R	6-0	190	4-15-78	.143	.000	.200	2	7	1	1	0	0	0	0	1	0	0	0	1	0	0	.143	.250
Buck, Travis	L-R	6-2	205	11-18-83	.349	.316	.364	34	126	24	44	17	3	3	26	14	0	0	5	18	2	1	.603	.400
Casanova, Raul	B-R	6-0	230	8-23-72	.429	—	.429	2	7	0	3	0	0	0	2	1	0	0	0	1	0	0	.429	.500
Castillo, David	R-R	5-9	185	9-15-81	.222	.185	.238	28	90	8	20	6	0	0	10	11	3	4	0	16	0	2	.289	.327
Cornejo, Eduardo	L-R	5-10	175	11-19-81	.361	.348	.366	62	252	45	91	19	1	3	27	38	5	1	2	26	2	3	.480	.451
Coughlan, Cameron	B-R	5-11	178	8-12-81	.289	.319	.277	69	228	42	66	11	3	2	25	34	6	6	1	53	20	8	.390	.394
Espy, Nate	R-R	6-3	215	4-24-78	.382	.200	.414	10	34	10	13	4	0	1	3	7	0	0	0	9	0	0	.588	.488
Everidge, Tommy	R-R	6-1	215	4-20-83	.252	.258	.250	133	504	89	127	32	2	20	83	44	13	0	9	116	5	5	.442	.323
Leslie, Myron	B-R	6-3	220	5-2-82	.273	.230	.290	136	513	81	140	25	0	17	100	71	6	0	5	98	6	3	.421	.365
McCurdy, John	R-R	6-1	200	4-17-81	.271	.336	.241	101	361	54	98	21	0	12	55	17	6	0	6	79	2	3	.429	.310
Pennington, Cliff	R-R	5-11	185	6-15-84	.203	.157	.222	46	177	36	36	7	0	2	21	24	1	0	0	35	7	1	.277	.302
Perez, Luis	R-R	5-10	193	8-17-83	.334	.339	.332	101	359	51	120	21	4	7	58	20	6	0	5	50	2	2	.474	.374
Petit, Gregorio	R-R	5-10	160	12-10-84	.256	.291	.244	137	519	71	133	25	7	8	63	38	5	9	5	96	22	13	.378	.310
Powell, Landon	B-R	6-3	240	3-19-82	.264	.200	.290	90	326	44	86	12	0	15	47	43	2	1	3	77	0	0	.439	.350
Pratt, Haas	R-R	6-3	215	9-17-81	.239	.265	.229	35	117	17	28	7	1	2	16	8	2	1	1	26	0	0	.368	.297
Putnam, Danny	L-L	5-10	200	9-17-82	.375	.429	.346	10	40	7	15	2	0	1	9	6	0	0	0	8	0	0	.500	.457
Rivera, Julio	R-R	5-11	178	7-20-87	.167	.000	.182	3	12	1	2	0	0	1	1	0	0	0	0	7	0	0	.417	.167
Robnett, Richie	L-L	5-10	200	9-17-83	.266	.324	.245	69	267	46	71	8	2	11	38	35	4	0	1	73	4	3	.434	.358
Singleton, Matthew	R-R	6-3	185	1-25-83	.183	.115	.209	26	93	12	17	1	0	2	14	9	0	3	0	32	1	0	.258	.255
Snyder, Brian	R-R	6-0	195	3-17-82	.279	.344	.253	63	226	42	63	11	0	4	28	35	1	0	0	59	0	0	.381	.378
Turner, Lloyd	R-R	6-1	175	4-11-80	.203	.063	.250	18	64	14	13	4	0	5	15	11	2	2	2	17	1	2	.500	.329
Wayment, Kory	R-R	6-1	173	2-18-81	.200	—	.200	2	5	1	1	1	0	0	2	1	0	0	1	0	0	0	.400	.333

PITCHING	B-T	HT	WT	DOB	W	L	ERA	G	GS	CG	SV	IP	H	R	ER	HR	BB	SO	AVG	vLH	vRH	K/9	BB/9
Avendano, Elvis	R-R	6-1	196	2-8-83	0	1	22.50	3	0	0	0	2	7	5	5	0	3	1	.636	.667	.600	4.50	13.50
Birtwell, John	R-R	6-2	225	9-4-79	0	0	0.00	1	0	0	0	1	1	0	0	0	2	2	.200	.500	.000	13.50	13.50
Braden, Dallas	L-L	6-1	180	8-13-83	2	0	6.23	3	3	0	0	13	12	9	9	3	5	17	.240	.231	.243	11.77	3.46
Castle, Heath	L-L	6-0	200	1-6-82	0	1	5.55	27	6	0	0	47	67	31	29	5	25	39	.342	.324	.352	7.47	4.79
Coleman, Jeffrey	R-R	5-11	193	10-6-80	3	1	3.90	21	0	0	1	30	30	15	13	5	6	31	.259	.294	.231	9.30	1.80
Corchado, Jose	R-R	6-0	196	4-5-84	0	0	0.00	1	0	0	0	3	0	0	0	0	0	2	.000	.000	.000	6.75	0.00
Crowell, Kyle	R-R	5-11	190	6-16-79	0	0	3.18	4	0	0	0	6	7	2	2	0	2	2	.318	.417	.200	3.18	3.18
Davis, Bradley	R-L	6-1	185	12-20-82	5	1	3.99	33	0	0	0	68	72	35	30	9	25	59	.270	.280	.264	7.85	3.33
Drucker, Scot	R-R	6-2	192	5-30-82	9	6	4.78	37	11	0	2	113	135	66	60	10	29	73	.297	.314	.285	5.81	2.31
Durost, Kenneth	R-R	6-3	191	10-10-81	3	1	4.09	7	6	0	0	33	37	18	15	4	13	28	.282	.286	.280	7.64	3.55
Ford, Ryan	L-L	6-3	180	7-10-82	7	12	5.87	30	21	1	0	127	157	92	83	12	40	88	.312	.238	.337	6.22	2.83
Gray, Jeffrey	R-R	6-3	205	11-19-81	1	1	3.41	19	0	0	1	32	32	15	12	0	6	26	.269	.302	.250	7.39	1.71
Johnson, Adam	R-R	6-2	210	7-12-79	1	1	4.91	3	2	0	1	15	14	8	8	2	2	14	.246	.333	.182	8.59	1.23
Landeros, Leonard	L-L	6-3	177	12-12-80	1	1	3.31	15	0	0	0	16	13	8	6	1	11	15	.220	.182	.243	8.27	6.06
Lansford, Jared	R-R	6-2	190	10-22-86	0	1	12.71	3	3	0	0	11	23	19	16	4	5	9	.397	.400	.393	7.15	3.97
Madsen, Michael	R-R	6-0	160	11-29-82	6	11	6.68	24	24	1	0	121	149	94	90	12	44	102	.302	.338	.272	7.57	3.26
McBeth, Marcus	R-R	6-2	183	8-23-80	0	0	0.00	0	0	0	7	9	1	0	0	0	2	14	.037	.000	.067	14.54	2.08
Mitchell, Michael	R-R	6-2	185	10-27-81	1	1	2.85	33	0	0	18	41	37	14	13	0	14	41	.240	.254	.232	9.00	3.07
Muessig, Jeff	R-R	6-2	208	2-27-82	1	1	3.86	13	0	0	0	19	15	9	8	2	8	25	.221	.250	.200	12.05	3.86
Obenchain, Stephen	R-R	6-5	220	7-29-81	1	1	2.08	6	0	0	0	13	13	5	3	0	2	16	.271	.235	.290	11.08	1.38
Peterson, Trent	R-L	6-1	180	11-16-81	3	6	3.17	41	5	0	0	88	91	38	31	6	28	68	.269	.290	.261	6.95	2.86
Posey, Joel	R-R	6-1	205	2-19-81	0	2	4.79	10	3	0	0	21	23	16	11	1	10	18	.291	.341	.237	7.84	4.35
Rapp, Randy	R-R	6-1	185	9-9-81	0	0	3.78	11	0	0	0	17	17	10	7	1	8	13	.258	.318	.227	7.02	4.32
Ray, Jason	R-R	5-11	195	7-14-84	5	5	4.95	18	7	0	0	60	59	36	33	9	33	48	.266	.296	.242	7.20	4.95
Rogers, Michael	R-R	6-1	205	10-24-82	11	6	4.67	22	20	0	0	116	124	73	60	20	39	108	.274	.268	.280	8.40	3.03
Sauerbeck, Scott	R-L	6-3	200	11-9-71	0	0	0.00	1	0	0	0	1	2	0	0	0	1	0	.667	1.000	.000	9.00	9.00
Scott, Joseph	R-R	6-0	185	7-30-80	1	0	7.20	5	1	0	0	10	17	8	8	3	4	5	.395	.500	.286	4.50	3.60
Sharpe, Steven	R-R	6-1	195	7-20-81	0	1	2.00	21	0	0	7	27	30	7	6	0	6	26	.286	.262	.302	8.67	2.00
Sheridan, Eric	R-R	6-1	175	9-22-83	0	0	0.00	1	1	0	0	1	1	0	0	0	0	1	.333	.000	.500	9.00	0.00
Shull, Jimmy	R-R	6-2	185	8-21-83	0	1	2.38	2	2	0	0	11	9	3	3	0	2	16	.280	.280	.125	12.71	1.59
Sullivan, Brad	R-R	6-0	195	9-12-81	0	0	12.12	21	0	0	0	26	38	40	35	3	30	14	.345	.356	.338	4.85	10.38
Tadano, Kazuhito	R-R	6-0	180	4-25-80	0	0	3.00	1	0	0	0	3	3	1	1	0	1	2	.273	.000	.375	6.00	3.00
Webb, Ryan	R-R	6-6	195	2-5-86	8	9	5.28	23	23	0	0	118	160	75	69	9	37	96	.332	.309	.353	7.34	2.83
Witasick, Jay	R-R	6-4	240	8-28-72	0	0	3.60	3	3	0	0	5	4	2	2	0	1	6	.222	.167	.250	10.80	1.80

FIELDING

Catcher	PCT	G	PO	A	E	DP	PB
Casanova	1.000	2	12	3	0	0	0
Castillo	.981	28	184	20	4	2	2
Powell	.994	82	611	69	4	8	11
Rivera	1.000	3	25	4	0	0	2
Singleton	1.000	26	202	17	0	1	1

First Base	PCT	G	PO	A	E	DP
Espy	1.000	3	22	1	0	1
Everidge	.985	128	982	95	16	108
Pratt	.986	10	67	4	1	6

Second Base	PCT	G	PO	A	E	DP
Appert	.800	5	8	8	4	0
Cornejo	.983	58	125	159	5	44
Petit	.981	77	189	217	8	49

	PCT	G	PO	A	E	DP
Turner	1.000	1	3	3	0	0

Third Base	PCT	G	PO	A	E	DP
Appert	1.000	1	0	3	0	0
Bocabica	1.000	2	0	2	0	0
Leslie	.916	64	49	147	18	9
McCurdy	.986	25	18	53	1	4
Snyder	.922	53	29	78	9	9

Shortstop	PCT	G	PO	A	E	DP
Cornejo	.947	4	9	9	1	4
McCurdy	.908	35	61	68	13	22
Pennington	.947	46	67	112	10	26
Petit	.940	60	120	160	18	40
Wayment	1.000	1	2	4	0	1

Outfield	PCT	G	PO	A	E	DP
Allegra	1.000	8	14	0	0	0
Appert	.949	26	35	2	2	0
Blasi	.972	59	133	4	4	2
Bocabica	1.000	2	8	2	0	1
Bradley	1.000	1	2	0	0	0
Buck	.985	34	67	0	1	0
Coughlan	.992	67	121	4	1	0
Everidge	.667	2	2	0	1	0
Leslie	.923	46	78	6	7	0
Perez	.971	90	152	15	5	3
Pratt	1.000	5	4	0	0	0
Putnam	.950	9	18	1	1	0
Robnett	.980	66	138	8	3	1
Turner	.951	16	39	0	2	0

Kane County Cougars — Low Class A

Midwest League

BATTING	B-T	HT	WT	DOB	AVG	vLH	vRH	G	AB	R	H	2B	3B	HR	RBI	BB	HBP	SH	SF	SO	SB	CS	SLG	OBP
Baisley, Jeff	R-R	6-3	210	12-19-82	.298	.359	.281	124	466	86	139	35	1	22	110	62	7	0	10	86	6	1	.519	.382
Bieker, Jeff	R-R	6-4	190	6-3-83	.247	.160	.279	28	93	11	23	3	0	0	13	6	4	1	0	14	0	1	.280	.320
Blasi, Nick	R-R	5-10	200	9-23-81	.253	.316	.223	75	288	44	73	12	5	0	25	33	3	8	5	69	17	1	.330	.331
Boyd, Chad	R-R	6-1	185	3-21-85	.346	.348	.346	64	257	43	89	27	0	2	37	24	2	0	4	27	3	4	.475	.401
Johnson, Toddric	L-L	6-1	165	12-17-84	.286	.286	.286	28	105	21	30	2	1	0	12	5	0	1	0	15	3	3	.324	.318
Kleen, Steve	R-R	6-4	200	5-21-83	.281	.243	.293	126	466	79	131	24	4	5	59	48	13	1	4	87	5	3	.382	.362

Long, Wes	R-R	5-11	195	6-12-82	.198	.229	.186	84	247	31	49	9	0	1	14	39	1	3	2	40	8	3	.247	.308
Martinez, Frank	B-R	6-0	164	7-19-85	.261	.210	.277	117	414	72	108	25	2	7	58	44	10	5	3	81	11	3	.382	.344
Massaro, Michael	L-L	5-11	160	4-15-84	.254	.213	.272	50	197	34	50	7	0	1	19	29	0	4	1	31	5	10	.305	.348
Omura, Isaac	L-R	5-10	175	1-21-84	.296	.240	.311	93	348	48	103	19	1	5	47	32	3	5	7	49	1	1	.399	.354
Padron, Raul	L-R	6-0	195	9-17-84	.242	.306	.227	99	339	36	82	16	1	2	52	30	0	4	6	83	3	2	.313	.299
Perez, Wilber	B-R	6-1	183	5-15-84	.111	.000	.120	8	27	4	3	1	0	0	0	2	0	0	0	9	0	0	.148	.172
Pineda, Jose	R-R	6-2	175	2-25-82	.254	.262	.252	130	468	72	119	15	6	15	74	65	10	0	4	132	21	8	.408	.355
Piper-Jordan, Andre	R-R	6-0	195	12-5-83	.167	.000	.200	4	6	0	1	0	0	0	0	0	1	0	0	3	0	1	.167	.286
Recker, Anthony	R-R	6-2	225	8-29-83	.287	.363	.262	109	407	52	117	24	3	14	57	42	3	0	1	115	5	5	.464	.358
Sellers, Justin	R-R	5-10	160	2-1-86	.241	.217	.248	119	411	75	99	21	2	5	46	58	11	10	5	65	17	5	.338	.346
Sulentic, Matthew	L-R	5-10	170	10-6-87	.235	.250	.233	30	98	12	23	4	1	1	13	12	2	0	1	19	1	2	.327	.327

PITCHING	B-T	HT	WT	DOB	W	L	ERA	G	GS	CG	SV	IP	H	R	ER	HR	BB	SO	AVG	vLH	vRH	K/9	BB/9
Davis, Bradley	R-L	6-1	185	12-20-82	2	0	0.00	9	0	0	0	18	6	0	0	0	1	16	.100	.000	.150	8.00	0.50
Dewing, Branden	L-L	6-0	165	1-1-84	0	3	5.21	15	0	0	0	19	26	11	11	1	8	14	.351	.280	.388	6.63	3.79
Durost, Kenneth	R-R	6-3	191	10-10-81	1	1	4.61	5	5	0	0	27	26	14	14	2	9	26	.257	.283	.236	8.56	2.96
Franco, T.J.	R-R	6-2	190	6-28-83	3	2	5.84	20	7	0	3	49	66	38	32	6	12	37	.317	.338	.305	6.75	2.19
Fyvie, Dan	R-R	6-0	207	8-12-82	1	1	3.76	19	0	0	4	26	22	12	11	1	18	32	.220	.206	.227	10.94	6.15
Gray, Jeffrey	R-R	6-3	205	11-19-81	5	5	4.71	22	11	0	0	78	77	47	41	2	19	62	.263	.259	.266	7.12	2.18
Herrera, John	R-R	6-6	195	3-8-83	3	1	3.90	39	1	0	3	60	56	30	26	1	32	51	.252	.303	.226	7.65	4.80
Italiano, Craig	R-R	6-3	190	7-22-86	0	1	3.50	4	4	0	0	18	18	12	7	1	9	23	.261	.289	.226	11.50	4.50
Jukich, Ben	L-L	6-4	190	10-17-82	3	2	2.38	13	4	0	0	42	41	15	11	1	25	40	.261	.303	.250	8.64	5.40
Kilby, Brad	L-L	6-2	225	2-19-83	5	1	1.63	49	0	0	9	61	38	13	11	0	23	73	.179	.183	.177	10.83	3.41
Lansford, Jared	R-R	6-2	190	10-22-86	11	6	2.86	18	18	2	0	104	87	40	33	1	42	50	.236	.261	.218	4.33	3.63
Madej, Ronald	L-L	6-1	200	5-23-83	2	7	4.46	31	8	0	0	69	59	38	34	3	56	58	.243	.232	.247	7.60	7.34
Mazzaro, Vincent	R-R	6-2	190	9-27-86	9	9	5.05	24	24	0	0	119	146	81	67	7	42	81	.310	.346	.287	6.11	3.17
Moore, Scott	R-R	6-2	245	12-4-83	0	0	0.00	2	0	0	0	2	1	0	0	0	0	3	.125	.000	.143	11.57	0.00
Newby, Joey	R-R	6-2	205	3-8-82	5	0	3.22	32	0	0	2	50	43	22	18	1	22	53	.231	.250	.223	9.48	3.93
Piekarz, Joe	R-L	6-2	175	1-1-82	8	7	3.26	35	16	1	0	127	137	60	46	7	34	94	.275	.254	.281	6.66	2.41
Posey, Joel	R-R	6-1	205	2-19-81	1	0	6.85	18	0	0	1	24	32	19	18	1	15	26	.323	.333	.317	9.89	5.70
Rapp, Randy	R-R	6-1	185	9-9-81	2	0	4.02	18	0	0	2	31	20	15	14	4	15	39	.179	.273	.139	11.20	4.31
Ray, Jason	R-R	5-11	195	7-14-84	6	1	3.02	13	13	2	0	66	48	29	22	1	35	68	.201	.224	.179	9.32	4.80
Semerano, Rob	R-R	6-1	185	7-18-81	1	3	4.20	26	0	0	4	30	28	15	14	1	18	23	.246	.279	.225	6.90	5.40
Sharpe, Steven	R-R	6-1	195	7-20-81	1	1	2.64	25	0	0	12	31	13	10	9	1	10	36	.127	.171	.104	10.57	2.93
Shields, Trey	R-R	6-6	225	5-27-84	10	9	4.90	28	28	1	0	156	190	95	85	19	49	94	.304	.333	.280	5.42	2.83

FIELDING

Catcher	PCT	G	PO	A	E	DP	PB
Padron	.979	49	340	34	8	3	7
Recker	.984	95	669	82	12	8	14

First Base	PCT	G	PO	A	E	DP
Boyd	—	1	0	0	0	0
Kleen	.989	111	985	83	12	96
Padron	.985	28	249	17	4	25

Second Base	PCT	G	PO	A	E	DP
Long	1.000	11	11	19	0	2
Martinez	.961	57	91	153	10	30
Omura	.974	73	124	176	8	45
Perez	.750	2	0	6	2	1

Third Base	PCT	G	PO	A	E	DP
Baisley	.963	112	94	243	13	26
Long	.980	15	17	32	1	4
Martinez	.879	13	11	18	4	3
Perez	1.000	1	0	1	0	0

Shortstop	PCT	G	PO	A	E	DP
Martinez	.917	27	34	66	9	11
Sellers	.954	117	217	367	28	81

Outfield	PCT	G	PO	A	E	DP
Bieker	1.000	21	19	2	0	0
Blasi	.976	73	121	3	3	1
Boyd	.983	62	111	2	2	1
Johnson	.980	27	49	1	1	1
Long	.966	39	51	6	2	0
Massaro	.989	49	83	4	1	2
Padron	1.000	2	1	0	0	0
Pineda	.974	123	213	11	6	5
Piper-Jordan	1.000	4	1	0	0	0
Sulentic	.953	29	40	1	2	0

Vancouver Canadians — Short-Season

Northwest League

BATTING	B-T	HT	WT	DOB	AVG	vLH	vRH	G	AB	R	H	2B	3B	HR	RBI	BB	HBP	SH	SF	SO	SB	CS	SLG	OBP
Affronti, Michael	R-R	6-2	195	2-13-84	.212	.208	.214	72	273	43	58	10	1	4	31	21	5	9	5	47	8	3	.300	.276
Boyd, Chad	L-L	5-10	190	3-21-85	.389	.400	.385	5	18	4	7	0	0	0	4	3	0	0	1	2	2	1	.389	.455
Cobb, Larry	R-R	5-9	175	7-10-85	.292	.268	.302	63	253	42	74	14	2	1	14	27	1	5	4	49	9	6	.375	.358
Dowling, Greg	L-L	6-3	240	11-15-83	.268	.225	.284	72	261	20	70	17	0	1	28	26	3	1	5	50	2	1	.345	.336
Hernandez, Samuel	R-R	5-10	162	9-9-84	.212	.275	.190	47	156	24	33	7	0	1	16	23	3	3	1	39	9	4	.276	.322
Johnson, Toddric	L-L	6-1	165	12-17-84	.333	.400	.323	10	36	9	12	3	1	0	3	5	1	1	0	7	3	0	.472	.429
Klug, Michael	R-R	5-9	190	10-7-82	.183	.176	.185	45	115	21	21	6	0	2	9	13	5	7	1	45	3	1	.287	.291
Macias, Lorenzo	R-R	6-2	188	8-17-85	.165	.154	.170	35	133	15	22	4	1	2	9	6	2	0	2	24	2	0	.256	.210
Mendez, Ramiro	R-R	6-2	175	4-14-85	.196	.071	.243	28	102	15	20	3	0	6	17	10	0	1	2	33	1	1	.402	.263
Mitchell, Jermaine	L-L	6-0	200	11-2-84	.362	.381	.354	37	138	23	50	7	2	3	23	22	3	0	0	27	14	6	.507	.460
Myers, Casey	R-R	5-10	209	10-23-78	.229	.286	.206	17	48	2	11	4	0	0	6	6	1	1	1	3	0	0	.313	.321
Perez, Wilber	B-R	6-1	183	5-15-84	.209	.195	.216	40	129	18	27	5	1	0	11	9	2	1	2	21	1	2	.264	.268
Piper-Jordan, Andre	R-R	6-0	195	12-5-83	.255	.143	.305	45	137	19	35	8	1	3	14	11	3	0	0	40	4	4	.394	.325
Rosendo, Gustavo	R-R	6-2	205	3-1-86	.155	.182	.148	32	103	6	16	2	1	0	9	4	1	3	0	13	0	1	.194	.194
Smith, Jacob	R-R	6-2	217	6-5-83	.215	.283	.185	51	172	16	37	15	1	2	32	21	2	0	4	20	2	2	.349	.302
Sulentic, Matthew	L-R	5-10	170	10-6-87	.354	.354	.354	38	144	24	51	10	1	2	22	14	0	3	1	30	3	4	.479	.409
Sutton III, Don	R-R	6-1	220	11-21-83	.154	.143	.158	19	52	8	8	2	0	3	8	13	0	0	2	14	0	0	.365	.313
Valdez, Alexander	R-R	6-1	160	9-2-84	.273	.222	.294	67	249	30	68	16	4	3	31	15	4	4	4	63	3	2	.406	.320
Vitters, Christian	L-R	6-2	205	6-26-85	.244	.200	.267	12	45	3	11	4	1	0	7	4	0	0	1	9	1	0	.378	.300

PITCHING	B-T	HT	WT	DOB	W	L	ERA	G	GS	CG	SV	IP	H	R	ER	HR	BB	SO	AVG	vLH	vRH	K/9	BB/9
Bailey, Andrew	R-R	6-3	220	5-31-84	2	5	2.02	13	10	0	0	58	39	20	13	2	20	53	.187	.225	.158	8.22	3.10
Bunch, Kevin	R-R	6-5	215	11-4-86	0	1	11.57	10	1	0	1	16	31	21	21	3	9	7	.403	.455	.364	3.86	4.96
Currin, Patrick	R-R	6-0	190	5-12-84	2	5	3.66	19	0	0	2	32	32	16	13	2	8	38	.254	.317	.224	10.69	2.25
Deal, Scott	R-R	6-4	180	12-11-86	8	4	3.91	15	15	0	0	76	73	37	33	3	17	35	.259	.282	.244	4.14	2.01
Deaza, Inoel	R-R	6-2	180	5-10-86	5	5	4.18	16	16	0	0	84	80	43	39	7	21	45	.256	.282	.240	4.82	2.25
Dewing, Branden	L-L	6-0	165	1-1-84	0	0	0.90	5	0	0	1	10	5	1	1	0	3	10	.143	.333	.125	9.00	2.70
Eusebio, Keith	B-R	5-10	173	1-31-83	3	0	3.31	20	0	0	0	35	25	14	13	1	22	16	.208	.200	.213	4.08	5.60
Fernandez, Jason	R-R	6-2	175	1-8-85	1	2	3.24	12	3	0	1	33	37	17	12	1	13	23	.285	.314	.266	6.21	3.51
Franco, T.J.	R-R	6-2	190	6-28-83	1	0	2.76	10	4	0	2	29	22	10	9	1	6	18	.210	.231	.203	5.52	1.84
Gordon, Derrick	L-L	5-9	185	10-16-83	1	2	4.97	18	0	0	0	25	25	21	14	3	21	22	.250	.400	.186	7.82	7.46
Heuser, James	L-L	6-5	200	3-30-84	5	4	4.13	14	12	0	0	65	58	33	30	5	26	55	.237	.250	.233	7.58	3.58
Jukich, Ben	L-L	6-4	190	10-17-82	0	0	3.24	3	1	0	2	8	9	3	3	0	5	10	.273	.000	.290	10.80	5.40
Lee, Chad	R-R	6-4	200	12-20-85	3	2	4.29	12	10	0	0	50	50	28	24	5	15	31	.254	.230	.268	5.54	2.68

	B-T	HT	WT	DOB	W	L	ERA	G	GS	CG	SV	IP	H	R	ER	HR	BB	SO	AVG	vLH	vRH	K/9	BB/9
Manship, Matt	R-R	6-4	205	11-25-83	1	1	2.94	17	0	0	0	34	33	12	11	2	13	32	.252	.302	.218	8.55	3.48
Manzueta, Pascual	R-R	6-5	190	12-25-84	1	0	1.80	2	2	0	0	10	8	2	2	0	3	8	.242	.333	.208	7.20	2.70
Moore, Scott	R-R	6-2	245	12-4-83	1	1	1.45	16	0	0	9	19	14	5	3	1	5	27	.197	.179	.209	13.02	2.41
Oakes, Earl	R-R	6-3	225	9-3-85	2	4	4.55	18	0	0	1	30	33	18	15	5	14	29	.273	.220	.300	8.80	4.25
Pena, Francisco	R-R	6-1	188	1-22-85	0	0	0.00	2	2	0	0	10	6	1	0	0	7	2	.188	.400	.091	1.86	6.52
Presutti, Shane	R-R	6-3	187	11-29-84	1	1	6.86	14	0	0	0	20	33	20	15	2	12	11	.384	.480	.344	5.03	5.49
Rea, Anthony	R-R	5-11	180	8-3-82	2	1	1.82	23	0	0	1	35	27	9	7	4	7	31	.206	.087	.271	8.05	1.82
Sheridan, Eric	R-R	6-1	175	9-22-83	0	0	0.00	1	0	0	0	2	1	1	0	0	3	1	.167	.000	.333	5.40	16.20

FIELDING

Catcher	PCT	G	PO	A	E	DP	PB
Rosendo	.996	31	205	17	1	1	10
Smith	.994	49	297	36	2	5	8
Sutton III	1.000	3	15	4	0	0	0

First Base	PCT	G	PO	A	E	DP
Affronti	1.000	1	2	0	0	0
Boyd	1.000	1	11	1	0	0
Dowling	.979	67	558	35	13	56
Sutton III	1.000	10	71	7	0	4

Second Base	PCT	G	PO	A	E	DP
Affronti	.971	7	17	16	1	6

	PCT	G	PO	A	E	DP
Hernandez	.958	28	69	68	6	21
Klug	.978	29	64	67	3	15
Perez	.940	19	33	45	5	8

Third Base	PCT	G	PO	A	E	DP
Hernandez	1.000	1	2	1	0	1
Klug	.750	3	2	4	2	0
Perez	.930	16	5	35	3	6
Valdez	.928	58	44	123	13	14

Shortstop	PCT	G	PO	A	E	DP
Affronti	.941	66	93	193	18	27
Hernandez	.769	5	3	7	3	0

	PCT	G	PO	A	E	DP
Vitters	.889	8	15	17	4	3

Outfield	PCT	G	PO	A	E	DP
Boyd	1.000	3	7	0	0	0
Cobb	.993	54	144	3	1	0
Johnson	1.000	10	18	0	0	0
Klug	1.000	7	6	1	0	0
Macias	.944	34	60	7	4	2
Mendez	.933	22	40	2	3	0
Mitchell	.977	35	85	1	2	0
Piper-Jordan	.974	33	70	6	2	2
Rea	1.000	1	2	0	0	0
Sulentic	.944	38	66	1	4	0

AZL Athletics — Rookie

Arizona League

BATTING	B-T	HT	WT	DOB	AVG	vLH	vRH	G	AB	R	H	2B	3B	HR	RBI	BB	HBP	SH	SF	SO	SB	CS	SLG	OBP
Arrieche, Carlos	R-R	6-1	177	3-30-85	.251	.276	.246	46	167	27	42	8	1	0	22	21	7	2	2	33	11	2	.311	.355
Barton, Daric	L-R	6-0	225	8-16-85	.200	—	.200	2	5	1	1	1	0	0	2	3	0	0	0	0	0	0	.400	.200
Brummett, John	R-R	6-1	205	12-7-83	.191	.000	.225	14	47	8	9	3	1	0	4	6	5	1	0	20	0	0	.298	.345
Corporan, Angel	R-R	6-1	170	11-15-85	.269	.118	.310	44	160	19	43	6	1	1	21	15	3	5	2	39	2	6	.338	.339
Correa, Walter	R-R	6-1	180	7-17-86	.200	.235	.189	42	145	18	29	6	2	0	14	16	4	3	0	32	7	2	.269	.297
Gutierrez, Carlos	R-R	6-1	185	8-2-82	.185	.167	.190	47	151	26	28	3	2	0	11	40	0	8	2	48	6	2	.232	.378
James, Javier	R-R	6-0	172	3-1-85	.188	.000	.207	19	64	8	12	3	0	0	3	13	4	0	0	25	0	4	.234	.358
Luis, Marcos	R-R	5-11	180	11-27-85	.281	.159	.297	45	178	18	50	9	0	1	15	10	1	1	0	31	2	2	.348	.323
Macias, Lorenzo	R-R	6-2	188	8-17-85	.293	.370	.264	24	99	14	29	6	3	0	17	7	1	1	1	15	7	1	.414	.343
Medina, Fernando	R-R	6-2	183	12-18-84	.183	.222	.170	22	71	5	13	6	0	0	7	6	0	0	1	31	1	0	.268	.247
Mendez, Ramiro	R-R	6-2	175	4-14-85	.227	.200	.234	33	132	23	30	5	2	3	18	16	0	1	0	33	8	2	.364	.309
Morales, Carlos	R-R	6-3	170	7-20-85	.232	.171	.247	55	211	30	49	11	2	4	27	21	9	4	1	56	1	2	.360	.326
Ortiz, Gabriel	R-R	6-1	215	11-7-85	.268	.333	.245	20	71	11	19	2	1	3	15	3	0	1	0	17	2	0	.451	.297
Pennington, Cliff	B-R	5-11	185	6-15-84	.464	.333	.500	9	28	3	13	3	1	0	6	4	0	0	0	2	0	0	.643	.531
Perez, Wilber	B-R	6-1	183	5-15-84	.289	.364	.259	10	38	6	11	4	0	1	6	3	1	0	0	5	2	3	.474	.357
Putnam, Danny	L-L	5-10	200	9-17-82	.278	.500	.250	6	18	2	5	1	0	0	2	6	0	0	2	0	0	0	.333	.458
Rivera, Julio	R-R	5-11	178	7-20-87	.195	.118	.214	25	87	15	17	8	1	1	7	6	2	4	0	30	1	1	.345	.263
Sierra, Angel	B-R	6-0	172	8-2-88	.199	.129	.215	48	161	14	32	5	2	0	15	24	3	4	0	59	15	4	.255	.314
Singleton, Matthew	R-R	6-1	185	1-25-83	.455	.500	.400	3	11	4	5	1	0	0	1	1	1	0	0	3	0	0	.545	.571

PITCHING	B-T	HT	WT	DOB	W	L	ERA	G	GS	CG	SV	IP	H	R	ER	HR	BB	SO	AVG	vLH	vRH	K/9	BB/9
Acosta, Fernando	R-R	6-3	185	12-20-85	0	0	0.00	2	0	0	0	4	1	0	0	0	2	7	.077	.000	.091	15.75	4.50
Bondurant, Steven	L-L	6-1	185	3-3-80	0	1	3.95	5	4	0	0	14	14	6	6	1	5	14	.259	.250	.263	9.22	3.29
Braden, Dallas	L-L	6-1	180	8-13-83	2	0	0.86	6	6	0	0	21	12	2	2	0	3	36	.174	.071	.200	15.43	1.29
Bunch, Kevin	R-R	6-5	215	11-4-86	0	1	4.38	4	4	0	0	12	12	11	6	0	10	14	.245	.208	.280	10.22	7.30
Cahill, Trevor	R-R	6-3	195	3-1-88	0	0	3.00	4	4	0	0	9	2	4	3	0	7	11	.071	.125	.000	11.00	7.00
Christensen, Kyle	R-R	6-3	225	9-18-88	0	1	10.03	7	2	0	0	12	14	15	13	1	14	9	.326	.250	.355	6.94	10.80
Corchado, Jose	R-R	6-0	196	4-5-84	2	2	4.96	15	0	0	2	16	12	11	9	1	12	29	.211	.154	.258	15.98	6.61
Epstein, Seth	L-L	6-1	205	1-30-82	0	1	31.91	6	1	0	0	4	9	14	13	1	13	8	.450	.400	.467	19.64	31.91
Espinal, Leonardo	R-R	6-3	203	2-6-84	1	3	2.41	14	2	0	1	37	36	14	10	3	16	27	.247	.244	.248	6.51	3.86
Figueroa, Pedro	L-L	6-1	164	11-23-85	1	6	6.07	13	8	0	0	43	59	39	29	4	11	27	.321	.333	.315	5.65	2.30
Granados, Ivan	L-L	6-2	185	9-30-85	0	0	0.00	2	0	0	0	2	0	0	0	0	0	2	.000	.000	.000	9.00	0.00
Guzman, Jose	R-R	5-11	185	11-5-87	2	0	3.03	13	3	0	0	36	31	18	12	2	7	27	.225	.219	.230	6.81	1.77
Landeros, Leonard	L-L	6-3	177	12-12-80	0	0	0.00	4	0	0	1	4	2	0	0	0	0	3	.154	.000	.182	6.75	0.00
Manzueta, Pascual	R-R	6-5	190	12-25-84	1	1	7.20	11	3	0	0	30	42	24	24	1	17	23	.321	.233	.364	6.90	5.10
Marrero, Miguel	R-R	6-1	174	2-4-86	1	1	4.15	16	0	0	0	17	21	9	8	0	5	15	.288	.267	.302	7.79	2.60
Martinez, Leonardo	L-L	6-0	185	12-5-86	2	5	4.10	14	5	0	0	53	48	28	24	4	19	56	.238	.171	.251	9.57	3.25
O'Hagan, David	R-R	6-1	200	6-5-82	0	0	21.60	2	0	0	0	2	4	4	4	0	3	1	.286	.000	.333	5.40	16.20
Obenchain, Stephen	R-R	6-5	220	7-29-81	0	0	1.08	4	0	0	0	8	10	4	1	0	1	9	.286	.438	.158	9.72	1.08
Pena, Francisco	R-R	6-1	188	1-22-85	1	1	4.82	10	1	0	0	28	27	16	15	1	13	16	.245	.265	.237	5.14	4.18
Reyes, Carmelo	R-R	6-2	165	9-9-85	2	0	6.00	12	0	0	1	24	28	24	16	1	18	13	.295	.346	.275	4.88	6.75
Rodriguez, Henry	R-R	6-1	175	2-25-87	5	2	7.42	15	4	0	1	44	46	39	36	1	50	59	.284	.350	.245	12.16	10.31
Sheridan, Eric	R-R	6-1	175	9-22-83	0	0	9.22	12	0	0	3	14	17	15	14	0	10	22	.293	.391	.229	14.49	6.59
Sullivan, Brad	R-R	6-0	195	9-12-81	1	1	3.52	8	0	0	0	8	9	5	3	0	7	3	.321	.286	.333	3.52	8.22
Tejeda, Edgar	R-R	6-0	160	3-4-87	3	4	7.23	14	5	0	0	42	52	40	34	1	21	44	.302	.317	.294	9.35	4.46

FIELDING

Catcher	PCT	G	PO	A	E	DP	PB
Brummett	.992	13	108	10	1	0	4
Ortiz	.967	17	159	19	6	0	6
Rivera	.956	25	192	26	10	2	11
Singleton	1.000	2	13	2	0	1	0

First Base	PCT	G	PO	A	E	DP
Barton	1.000	2	3	1	0	0
Correa	.987	10	66	8	1	5
Morales	.985	45	363	24	6	29
Perez	1.000	1	10	1	0	0

Second Base	PCT	G	PO	A	E	DP
Arrieche	1.000	3	6	7	0	2

	PCT	G	PO	A	E	DP
Corporan	.933	11	20	22	3	3
Correa	.667	1	1	1	1	0
Luis	.919	35	50	86	12	15
Perez	.974	8	23	15	1	7

Third Base	PCT	G	PO	A	E	DP
Arrieche	.891	39	17	65	10	2
Corporan	1.000	3	3	0	0	0
Correa	.839	10	10	16	5	3
Luis	.901	6	3	12	3	1

Shortstop	PCT	G	PO	A	E	DP
Corporan	.928	31	56	86	11	15
Correa	.901	25	30	52	9	9

	PCT	G	PO	A	E	DP
Luis	—	1	0	0	0	0
Pennington	.913	8	5	16	2	3

Outfield	PCT	G	PO	A	E	DP
Correa	1.000	1	1	0	0	0
Gutierrez	.872	31	34	0	5	0
James	.933	19	25	3	2	1
Macias	.971	19	32	1	1	1
Medina	1.000	12	19	3	0	1
Mendez	.958	29	63	5	3	1
Morales	1.000	4	2	0	0	0
Perez	1.000	1	2	0	0	0
Putnam	.750	6	3	0	1	0
Sierra	.972	47	100	3	3	1

BY JIM SALISBURY

An impressive second-half turnaround and a series of brilliant individual efforts, highlighted by Ryan Howard's 58 homers, made for an exciting season in Philadelphia.

But ultimately, 2006 was a flop as the Phillies' playoff drought swelled to 13 years.

For the second straight year, the Phils finished one game shy of the National League wild card winner. This failure was particularly galling because the Phils entered the final seven games of the season leading the wild-card race by a half-game only to blow the lead with three losses over a four-game span.

"It stinks because of how well we played the past couple of months," said catcher Mike Lieberthal, who ended a 13-year run with the club.

The Phillies went 1-6 to start the season and were 9-18 in June. They went 5-13 in interleague play and were seven games under .500 at the all-star break.

After the break, they won 45 games, more than any other NL team. Most of those wins came after general manager Pat Gillick began breaking up the disappointing team by trading veteran third baseman David Bell to Milwaukee on July 28. The Phils were in 10th place in the wild-card race when Gillick made that trade. Two days later, he dumped the salaries of Bobby Abreu and Cory Lidle on the Yankees.

Gillick didn't just wave the white flag on the 2006 season. In announcing the Abreu trade, he said it would be a stretch to think the Phils would contend before 2008.

An impressive August surge had Gillick happily eating his words. In less than a month, he went from selling off talent to acquiring it for the stretch drive. Veterans Jamie Moyer and Jeff Conine came on board and helped the

PLAYERS OF THE YEAR

MAJOR LEAGUE: Ryan Howard, 1b

Howard has given Philadelphia its best homegrown slugger since Mike Schmidt. He topped Schmidt's single-season home run mark by hitting 58 homers—tops in the big leagues—in his first full season. He also had .313/.425/.659 numbers and led the majors with 149 RBIs.

MINOR LEAGUE: Carlos Carrasco, rhp

Carrasco came into his own in 2006, going 12-6, 2.26 in 159 innings at low Class A Lakewood. He finished fifth in the organization with 159 strikeouts while throwing three quality pitches for strikes. He held opponents to a .182 average and tossed two complete games.

DAVID SCHOFIELD

team stay in contention until the final day.

Starting pitching fueled the late-season surge, with the quintet of Moyer, Brett Myers, Jon Lieber, Cole Hamels and Randy Wolf going 26-10, 3.91 over the final two months.

Hamels, a 22-year-old rookie and former first-round draft pick, finally put together a healthy season. He zoomed through Triple-A and arrived in the majors in May. The lefthanded changeup artist was dazzling over his final 11 starts, going 6-3, 2.60 while striking out 76 in 69⅓ innings.

The Phils led the NL in runs (865) and were second in on-base percentage (.347).

The season began with leadoff man Jimmy Rollins extending his hitting streak to 38 games, en route to 191 hits. Later, all-star second baseman Chase Utley produced a 35-game hitting streak, the longest in the majors in 2006. Utley had 203 hits, second-most in the NL.

The individual highlight was authored by Howard, who a year after winning the NL Rookie of the Year award shattered Mike Schmidt's 26-year-old team record (48) for home runs. In addition to leading the majors in homers, Howard was also first with 149 RBIs. After the all-star break, he hit .355 after with 30 homers, 70 RBIs, a .509 on-base percentage and a .751 slugging percentage. He won the Hank Aaron Award as the top offensive player in the NL.

"I think the season I had opened some eyes," Howard said. "It was a fun ride."

Howard's bid for 60 homers fell short when he hit just two in the final 21 games. The Phils struggled to find a consistent No. 5 hitter to bat behind Howard and the slugging cleanup man saw fewer and fewer hittable pitches down the stretch. Pat Burrell, often given the responsibility of hitting behind Howard, hit just .222 with runners in scoring position and frequently found himself on the bench in the second half.

On the minor league front, speedy outfielder Michael Bourn continued to make strides toward regular duty in Philadelphia, while an outstanding rotation led Lakewood to its first low Class A South Atlantic League title.

ORGANIZATION LEADERS

BATTING		*Minimum 250 at-bats
*AVG	Florence, Branden, Clearwater/Reading	.324
R	Burgamy, Brian, Clearwater/Reading	112
H	Florence, Branden, Clearwater/Reading	162
TB	Florence, Branden, Clearwater/Reading	217
2B	Slayden, Jeremy, Lakewood	44
3B	Bourn, Michael, Reading/Scranton/WB	13
HR	Burnham, Gary, Reading/Scranton/WB	17
RBI	Florence, Branden, Clearwater/Reading	86
BB	Burgamy, Brian, Clearwater/Reading	95
SO	Golson, Greg, Lakewood/Clearwater	160
SB	Bourn, Michael, Reading/Scranton/WB	45
*OBP	Leon, Carlos, Reading/Scranton/WB	.394
*SLG	Slayden, Jeremy, Lakewood	.510
XBH	Slayden, Jeremy, Lakewood	57

PITCHING		#Minimum 75 innings
W	Segovia, Zach, Clearwater/Reading	17
L	Gonzalez, Gio, Reading	12
#ERA	Maloney, Matt, Lakewood	2.03
G	Bisenius, Joseph, Clearwater/Reading	52
CG	Segovia, Zach, Clearwater/Reading	3
SV	Key, Chris, Clearwater/Reading	21
IP	Kendrick, Kyle, Lakewood/Clearwater	182
BB	Gonzalez, Gio, Reading	84
SO	Maloney, Matt, Lakewood	180
#AVG	Carrasco, Carlos, Lakewood	.182

Philadelphia Phillies · MLB

National League

BATTING	B-T	HT	WT	DOB	AVG	vLH	vRH	G	AB	R	H	2B	3B	HR	RBI	BB	HBP	SH	SF	SO	SB	CS	SLG	OBP
Abreu, Bobby	L-R	6-0	210	3-11-74	.277	.300	.266	98	339	61	94	25	2	8	65	91	2	0	6	86	20	4	.434	.427
Bell, David	R-R	5-10	195	9-14-72	.278	.269	.280	92	324	39	90	17	2	6	34	32	3	3	3	38	1	0	.398	.345
2-team (53 Milwaukee)					.270	—	145	504	60	136	27	4	10	63	50	4	3	5	68	3	1		.399	.337
Bourn, Michael	L-R	5-11	180	12-27-82	.125	.000	.143	17	8	2	1	0	0	0	0	1	0	2	0	3	1	2	.125	.222
Burrell, Pat	R-R	6-4	235	10-10-76	.258	.290	.244	144	462	80	119	24	1	29	95	98	3	0	4	131	0	0	.502	.388
Conine, Jeff	R-R	6-1	225	6-26-66	.280	.235	.303	28	100	11	28	6	1	1	17	5	2	0	0	12	0	0	.390	.327
Coste, Chris	R-R	6-1	200	2-4-73	.328	.288	.345	65	198	25	65	14	0	7	32	10	5	0	0	31	0	0	.505	.376
Dellucci, David	L-L	5-11	195	10-31-73	.292	.200	.299	132	264	41	77	14	5	13	39	28	6	0	3	62	1	3	.530	.369
Fasano, Sal	R-R	6-2	245	8-10-71	.243	.273	.234	50	140	9	34	8	0	4	10	5	3	1	0	47	0	1	.386	.284
Gonzalez, Alex	R-R	6-0	200	4-8-73	.111	.130	.077	20	36	4	4	0	0	0	1	2	0	0	0	10	0	0	.111	.158
Hernandez, Jose	R-R	6-1	190	7-14-69	.250	.143	.333	18	32	4	8	2	0	1	7	1	0	1	0	11	0	0	.406	.273
2-team (67 Pittsburgh)					.263	—	85	152	12	40	4	1	3	19	12	0	2	0	40	0	0		.362	.317
Howard, Ryan	L-L	6-4	250	11-19-79	.313	.279	.331	159	581	104	182	25	1	58	149	108	9	0	6	181	0	0	.659	.425
Lieberthal, Mike	R-R	6-0	190	1-18-72	.273	.286	.269	67	209	22	57	14	0	9	36	8	6	5	2	19	0	0	.469	.316
Nunez, Abraham	B-R	5-11	190	3-16-76	.211	.171	.225	123	322	42	68	10	2	2	32	41	2	3	1	58	1	0	.273	.303
Roberson, Chris	B-R	6-2	180	8-23-79	.195	.111	.261	57	41	9	8	0	1	0	1	0	1	1	0	9	3	0	.244	.214
Rollins, Jimmy	B-B	5-8	170	11-27-78	.277	.277	.277	158	689	127	191	45	9	25	83	57	5	0	7	80	36	4	.478	.334
Rowand, Aaron	R-R	6-0	200	8-29-77	.262	.222	.275	109	405	59	106	24	3	12	47	18	18	2	2	76	10	4	.425	.321
Ruiz, Carlos	R-R	5-10	200	1-22-79	.261	.263	.260	27	69	5	18	1	1	3	10	5	1	2	1	8	0	0	.435	.316
Sandoval, Danny	B-R	5-11	200	4-7-79	.211	.286	.167	28	38	1	8	1	0	0	4	4	0	0	1	3	0	0	.237	.279
Simon, Randall	L-L	6-0	240	5-25-75	.238	—	.238	23	21	0	5	0	0	0	2	2	0	0	0	6	0	0	.238	.304
Thurston, Joe	L-R	5-11	190	9-29-79	.222	—	.222	18	18	3	4	1	0	0	0	1	0	0	0	2	0	0	.278	.300
Utley, Chase	L-R	6-1	185	12-17-78	.309	.301	.312	160	658	131	203	40	4	32	102	63	14	0	4	132	15	4	.527	.379
Victorino, Shane	B-R	5-9	180	11-30-80	.287	.273	.293	153	415	70	119	19	8	6	46	24	14	8	1	54	4	3	.414	.346

PITCHING	B-T	HT	WT	DOB	W	L	ERA	G	GS	CG	SV	IP	H	R	ER	HR	BB	SO	AVG	vLH	vRH	K/9	BB/9
Bernero, Adam	R-R	6-4	225	11-28-76	0	1	36.00	1	1	0	0	2	7	8	8	3	2	0	.538	.600	.500	9.00	9.00
Brito, Eude	L-L	5-11	160	8-19-78	1	2	7.36	5	2	0	0	18	21	15	15	2	12	9	.296	.238	.320	4.42	5.89
Castro, Fabio	L-L	5-7	175	1-20-85	0	1	1.54	16	0	0	1	23	12	4	4	1	6	13	.158	.043	.208	5.01	2.31
Condrey, Clay	R-R	6-3	195	11-19-75	2	2	3.14	21	0	0	0	29	35	11	10	3	9	16	.318	.383	.270	5.02	2.83
Cormier, Rheal	L-L	5-10	195	4-23-67	2	2	1.59	43	0	0	0	34	27	6	6	2	13	13	.225	.259	.197	3.44	3.44
2-team (21 Cincinnati)					2	3	2.44	64	0	0	0	48	48	13	13	5	17	19	—	—	—	3.56	3.19
Floyd, Gavin	R-R	6-4	220	1-27-83	4	3	7.29	11	11	1	0	54	70	48	44	14	32	34	.315	.306	.323	5.63	5.30
Franklin, Ryan	R-R	6-3	190	3-5-73	1	5	4.58	46	0	0	0	53	59	28	27	10	17	25	.280	.270	.285	4.25	2.89
2-team (20 Cincinnati)					6	7	4.54	66	0	0	0	77	86	42	39	13	33	43	—	—	—	5.00	3.84
Fultz, Aaron	L-L	6-0	210	9-4-73	3	1	4.54	66	1	0	0	71	80	39	36	7	28	62	.288	.277	.293	7.82	3.53
Geary, Geoff	R-R	6-0	175	8-26-76	7	1	2.96	81	0	0	1	91	103	34	30	6	20	60	.287	.348	.249	5.91	1.97
Gordon, Tom	R-R	5-10	195	11-18-67	3	4	3.34	59	0	0	34	59	53	23	22	9	22	68	.233	.185	.277	10.31	3.34
Hamels, Cole	L-L	6-4	195	12-27-83	9	8	4.08	23	23	0	0	132	117	66	60	19	48	145	.237	.207	.244	9.86	3.26
Lidle, Cory	R-R	5-11	190	3-22-72	8	7	4.74	21	21	0	0	125	132	74	66	19	39	98	.271	.303	.244	7.04	2.80
Lieber, Jon	L-R	6-2	235	4-2-70	9	11	4.93	27	27	2	0	168	196	100	92	27	24	100	.291	.304	.278	5.36	1.29
Madson, Ryan	L-R	6-6	195	8-28-80	11	9	5.69	50	17	0	2	134	176	92	85	20	50	99	.321	.307	.335	6.63	3.35
Mathieson, Scott	R-R	6-3	190	2-27-84	1	4	7.47	9	8	0	0	37	48	36	31	8	16	28	.312	.279	.337	6.75	3.86
Moyer, Jamie	L-L	6-0	180	11-18-62	5	2	4.03	8	8	0	0	51	49	25	23	8	7	26	.251	.219	.258	4.56	1.23
Myers, Brett	R-R	6-4	240	8-17-80	12	7	3.91	31	31	1	0	198	194	93	86	29	63	189	.257	.259	.254	8.59	2.86
Rhodes, Arthur	L-L	6-2	210	10-24-69	0	5	5.32	55	0	0	4	46	47	27	27	2	30	48	.261	.290	.246	9.46	5.91
Sanches, Brian	R-R	6-0	190	8-8-78	0	0	5.91	18	0	0	0	21	23	14	14	5	13	22	.271	.282	.261	9.28	5.48
Santana, Julio	R-R	6-0	210	1-20-74	0	0	7.56	7	0	0	0	8	8	9	7	1	9	4	.258	.143	.353	4.32	9.72
Smith, Matt	L-L	6-5	225	6-15-79	0	1	2.08	14	0	0	0	9	3	2	2	0	4	12	.111	.125	.105	12.46	4.15
White, Rick	R-R	6-4	240	12-23-68	3	1	4.34	38	0	0	0	37	38	21	18	3	15	23	.273	.267	.277	5.54	3.62
2-team (26 Cincinnati)					4	1	5.15	64	0	0	1	64	72	44	37	8	20	40	—	—	—	5.57	2.78
Wolf, Randy	L-L	6-0	205	8-22-76	4	0	5.56	12	12	0	0	57	63	37	35	13	33	44	.285	.086	.323	6.99	5.24

FIELDING

Catcher	PCT	G	PO	A	E	DP	PB
Coste	.988	54	328	12	4	0	4
Fasano	.990	50	265	26	3	2	2
Lieberthal	.991	60	428	33	4	2	4
Ruiz	.981	24	147	11	3	1	1

First Base	PCT	G	PO	A	E	DP
Coste	1.000	2	3	0	0	1
Gonzalez	1.000	3	17	4	0	2
Hernandez	1.000	1	2	0	0	0
Howard	.991	159	1373	91	14	139
Utley	1.000	2	15	0	0	0

Second Base	PCT	G	PO	A	E	DP
Nunez	1.000	6	7	13	0	2

	PCT	G	PO	A	E	DP
Sandoval	1.000	8	7	7	0	1
Thurston	1.000	4	6	2	0	1
Utley	.978	156	357	425	18	115

Third Base	PCT	G	PO	A	E	DP
Bell	.945	90	55	186	14	23
Gonzalez	.500	2	1	0	1	0
Hernandez	1.000	7	2	11	0	3
Nunez	.959	74	36	151	8	10

Shortstop	PCT	G	PO	A	E	DP
Gonzalez	1.000	3	2	4	0	0
Hernandez	1.000	2	1	4	0	1
Nunez	1.000	3	0	4	0	1
Rollins	.984	157	213	446	11	96

		PCT	G	PO	A	E	DP
Sandoval		.933	6	5	9	1	4
Outfield	PCT	G	PO	A	E	DP
Abreu	.995	97	178	4	1	0
Bourn	1.000	15	8	0	0	0
Burrell	.986	126	204	8	3	1
Conine	.973	26	36	1	1	0
Dellucci	.990	67	95	1	1	0
Gonzalez	.—	1	0	0	0	0
Hernandez	1.000	2	2	0	0	0
Roberson	1.000	45	19	0	0	0
Rowand	.981	107	251	6	5	2
Thurston	1.000	3	5	1	0	0
Victorino	1.000	122	221	11	0	3

Scranton/Wilkes-Barre Red Barons · Triple-A

International League

BATTING	B-T	HT	WT	DOB	AVG	vLH	vRH	G	AB	R	H	2B	3B	HR	RBI	BB	HBP	SH	SF	SO	SB	CS	SLG	OBP
Bergeron, Peter	L-R	6-0	190	11-9-77	.202	.188	.208	34	104	12	21	7	0	2	9	10	0	2	0	21	1	0	.327	.272
Bourn, Michael	L-R	5-11	180	12-27-82	.283	.273	.287	38	152	34	43	5	7	1	15	20	1	0	1	33	15	1	.428	.368
Burnham, Gary	L-L	5-11	219	10-13-74	.391	.667	.294	10	46	9	18	5	0	1	8	3	0	0	0	7	0	0	.565	.429
Chavez, Angel	R-R	6-1	200	7-22-81	.276	.370	.244	60	210	27	58	22	1	6	28	13	0	7	1	41	6	0	.419	.317

General manager: Pat Gillick. **Farm director:** Steve Noworyta. **Scouting director:** Marti Wolever.

Class	Team	League	W	L	PCT	Finish*	Manager	Affiliate Since
Majors	Philadelphia	National	85	77	.525	4th (16)	Charlie Manuel	—
Triple-A	Scranton/W-B Red Barons	International	84	58	.592	1st (14)	John Russell	1989
Double-A	Reading Phillies	Eastern	71	69	.507	5th (12)	P.J. Forbes	1967
High A	Clearwater Threshers	Florida State	67	72	.482	9th (12)	Greg Legg	1985
Low A	Lakewood BlueClaws	South Atlantic	84	55	.604	+2nd (16)	Dave Huppert	2001
Short-season	Batavia Muckdogs	New York-Penn	35	38	.479	10th (14)	Steve Roadcap	1988
Rookie	GCL Phillies	Gulf Coast	18	31	.367	12th (13)	Jim Morrison	1999
OVERALL 2006 MINOR LEAGUE RECORD			359	323	.526	8th (30)		

*Finish in overall standings (No. of teams in league). +League champion

LARRY GOREH

Chase Utley has become one of the NL's best second basemen

MIKE JANES

Carlos Carrasco held hitters to a .182 average

Coste, Chris	R-R	6-1	200	2-4-73	.177	.179	.176	39	147	12	26	8	0	2	14	9	3	0	2	28	1	1	.272	.236			
Fleming, Ryan	L-L	5-9	177	2-11-76	.233	.172	.241	85	232	27	54	11	3	1	20	20	1	5	2	37	4	5	.319	.294			
Garrett, Shawn	B-R	6-3	220	11-2-78	.220	.214	.222	69	245	21	54	12	5	3	26	16	1	1	3	66	1	1	.347	.268			
Gradoville, Tim	R-R	6-3	195	1-30-80	.000	.000	.000	1	4	0	0	0	0	0	0	0	0	0	0	3	0	0	.000	.000			
Guevara, Orlando	B-R	6-1	175	9-13-83	.143	.250	.000	3	7	0	1	0	0	0	0	1	0	0	0	4	0	0	.143	.250			
Jaramillo, Jason	B-R	6-0	200	10-9-82	.167	.000	.333	2	6	0	1	0	0	0	1	0	0	0	1	1	0	0	.167	.143			
King, Brennan	R-R	6-3	218	1-20-81	.261	.250	.265	97	364	40	95	25	2	12	48	20	3	1	4	69	5	0	.440	.302			
Kroeger, Josh	L-L	6-3	220	8-31-82	.231	.210	.238	119	441	41	102	26	4	9	41	23	1	2	2	104	6	3	.370	.270			
Leon, Carlos	B-R	5-10	181	8-31-79	.277	.318	.264	28	94	11	26	2	0	0	14	10	5	1	1	12	2	0	.298	.373			
Lieberthal, Mike	R-R	6-0	190	1-18-72	.667	—	.667	2	6	3	4	1	0	0	2	0	1	0	0	0	0	0	.833	.714			
Ramos, Peeter	R-R	5-11	180	3-18-82	.000	—	.000	1	2	0	0	0	0	0	0	0	0	0	0	2	0	0	.000	.000			
Roberson, Chris	B-R	6-2	180	8-23-79	.292	.280	.297	74	284	44	83	14	2	1	17	23	3	4	2	57	25	9	.366	.349			
Ruiz, Carlos	R-R	5-10	200	1-22-79	.307	.315	.305	100	368	56	113	25	0	16	69	42	9	1	3	56	4	3	.505	.389			
Rushford, Jim	L-L	6-1	220	3-24-74	.272	.257	.277	76	276	30	75	13	0	4	33	25	5	3	4	28	4	0	.362	.339			
Sandoval, Danny	B-R	5-11	200	4-7-79	.255	.212	.274	91	345	31	88	17	1	2	39	14	3	4	2	50	1	1	.328	.288			
Scales, Bobby	B-R	6-0	170	10-4-77	.291	.301	.287	105	357	46	104	22	7	7	44	44	3	6	5	100	3	3	.451	.369			
Sosa, Juan	R-R	6-1	175	8-19-75	.195	.231	.164	48	113	11	22	3	0	0	5	9	0	6	0	23	1	1	.221	.254			
Swann, Pedro	L-R	6-0	205	10-27-70	.282	.214	.303	28	117	17	33	8	1	2	14	9	1	0	1	26	6	0	.419	.336			
Thurston, Joe	L-R	5-11	190	9-29-79	.282	.246	.296	127	479	74	135	29	9	9	55	43	7	14	1	65	20	10	.436	.349			
Tugwell, Marc	R-R	6-0	190	4-16-81	.000	.000	.000	1	3	0	0	0	0	0	0	0	0	0	0	0	0	0	.000	.000			
Wathan, Dusty	R-R	6-4	215	8-22-73	.239	.250	.234	80	238	25	57	10	0	5	27	21	8	4	2	47	1	0	.345	.320			

PITCHING	B-T	HT	WT	DOB	W	L	ERA	G	GS	CG	SV	IP	H	R	ER	HR	BB	SO	AVG	vLH	vRH	K/9	BB/9
Bernero, Adam	R-R	6-4	225	11-28-76	1	1	1.80	5	5	1	0	25	11	5	5	2	4	17	.131	.206	.080	6.12	1.44
Booker, Chris	R-R	6-3	235	12-9-76	0	0	1.29	6	0	0	0	7	4	1	1	1	3	7	.174	.143	.188	9.00	3.86
Brito, Fude	L-L	5-11	160	8-19-78	10	8	3.17	26	23	2	1	148	116	60	52	11	55	103	.214	.214	.214	6.28	3.35
Cameron, Ryan	R-R	6-1	175	9-13-77	6	2	3.19	45	1	0	7	59	48	21	21	4	31	45	.226	.259	.206	6.83	4.70
Condrey, Clay	R-R	6-3	195	11-19-75	4	2	1.93	39	0	0	6	51	41	12	11	1	15	28	.229	.225	.231	4.91	2.63

Name	B-T	HT	WT	DOB	W	L	ERA	G	GS	CG	SV	IP	H	R	ER	HR	BB	SO	AVG	vLH	vRH	K/9	BB/9
Crowell, Jim	R-L	6-4	225	5-14-74	2	3	3.67	40	7	0	2	74	82	31	30	5	22	43	.285	.239	.300	5.25	2.69
Cummings, Jeremy	R-R	6-2	215	11-7-76	8	6	3.97	25	25	1	0	138	119	64	61	18	49	102	.236	.227	.243	6.64	3.19
Davis, Allen	L-L	6-4	220	10-1-75	3	2	8.59	5	4	0	0	22	32	21	21	4	7	15	.344	.400	.329	6.14	2.86
Floyd, Gavin	R-R	6-4	220	1-27-83	7	4	4.23	17	17	2	0	115	117	57	54	9	38	85	.267	.280	.257	6.65	2.97
Germano, Justin	R-R	6-3	205	8-6-82	2	0	2.82	6	6	0	0	38	40	13	12	2	2	25	.265	.277	.256	5.87	0.47
Giese, Dan	R-R	6-3	200	5-19-77	2	2	3.03	25	0	0	0	36	46	17	12	3	4	33	.317	.340	.305	8.33	1.01
Haines, Talley	R-R	6-5	205	11-16-76	0	1	2.95	9	0	0	0	18	15	8	6	1	4	5	.211	.261	.188	2.45	1.96
Hamels, Cole	L-L	6-4	195	12-27-83	2	0	0.39	3	3	1	0	23	10	1	1	0	1	36	.130	.182	.121	14.09	0.39
Happ, J.A.	L-L	6-5	205	10-19-82	1	0	1.50	1	1	0	0	6	3	1	1	1	1	4	.136	.250	.111	6.00	1.50
Hernandez, Yoel	R-R	6-2	210	4-15-80	1	0	1.74	9	0	0	6	10	11	3	2	0	4	8	.275	.333	.240	6.97	3.48
Lee, Seung Hak	R-R	6-4	225	6-2-79	8	9	4.35	31	12	0	2	93	89	47	45	10	33	62	.259	.286	.244	6.00	3.19
Mathieson, Scott	R-R	6-3	190	2-27-84	3	1	3.93	5	5	0	0	34	26	16	15	2	10	36	.208	.340	.128	9.44	2.62
Mattioni, Nick	R-R	6-3	195	3-14-79	0	0	3.60	3	0	0	0	5	3	4	2	0	3	2	.158	.333	.077	3.60	5.40
Mazone, Brian	L-L	6-4	205	7-26-76	13	3	2.03	20	20	0	0	128	108	40	29	6	36	85	.230	.204	.238	5.96	2.52
Minix, Travis	R-R	6-1	190	8-8-77	1	3	2.40	40	0	0	3	49	44	18	13	4	12	27	.237	.246	.231	4.99	2.22
Sanches, Brian	R-R	6-0	190	8-8-78	3	2	1.85	36	0	0	19	44	24	9	9	2	13	52	.164	.164	.165	10.72	2.68
Shaffar, Ben	B-R	6-3	195	9-28-77	0	0	10.13	3	0	0	0	5	6	6	6	0	4	2	.316	.200	.357	3.58	6.75
Smith, Matt	L-L	6-5	225	6-15-79	0	0	2.00	9	0	0	4	9	5	2	2	1	6	6	.161	.077	.222	6.00	6.00
White, Matt	R-L	6-1	180	8-19-77	7	9	3.58	38	13	0	1	111	111	46	44	8	36	69	.267	.245	.274	5.61	2.93

FIELDING

Catcher	PCT	G	PO	A	E	DP	PB
Coste	1.000	12	77	5	0	1	0
Gradoville	1.000	1	10	0	0	0	0
Guevara	.941	3	12	4	1	1	0
Jaramillo	1.000	2	10	0	0	0	0
Lieberthal	1.000	2	12	1	0	0	0
Ruiz	.995	79	526	38	3	6	6
Wathan	.991	51	305	23	3	3	3

First Base	PCT	G	PO	A	E	DP
Chavez	1.000	2	23	1	0	1
Coste	1.000	26	240	11	0	23
Garrett	.989	22	172	15	2	13
Rushford	.995	68	528	43	3	50
Scales	1.000	4	32	3	0	1
Sosa	1.000	1	6	0	0	0
Tugwell	1.000	1	14	2	0	1

Second Base	PCT	G	PO	A	E	DP
Wathan	.994	22	144	12	1	19
Chavez	1.000	7	16	19	0	3
Leon	.977	8	24	18	1	4
Ramos	1.000	1	0	1	0	0
Scales	.962	9	12	13	1	3
Thurston	.979	121	292	325	13	75

Third Base	PCT	G	PO	A	E	DP
King	.946	94	50	215	15	19
Leon	.964	15	13	41	2	5
Sandoval	1.000	1	0	2	0	0
Scales	.927	17	12	26	3	3
Sosa	.979	20	19	28	1	0

Shortstop	PCT	G	PO	A	E	DP
Chavez	.982	45	61	102	3	23
Leon	.900	5	8	10	2	2
Sandoval	.958	77	97	225	14	39
Sosa	.937	19	22	37	4	5
Thurston	.909	2	2	8	1	1

Outfield	PCT	G	PO	A	E	DP
Bergeron	1.000	32	66	2	0	1
Bourn	.989	36	91	3	1	1
Burnham	1.000	2	4	0	0	0
Fleming	.993	66	139	5	1	1
Garrett	.978	27	42	2	1	0
Kroeger	.989	118	264	10	3	2
Roberson	.957	74	177	3	8	2
Rushford	1.000	2	3	0	0	0
Scales	.991	54	99	6	1	1
Swann	.978	22	43	1	1	1
Thurston	1.000	6	11	2	0	1

Reading Phillies — Double-A

Eastern League

BATTING	B-T	HT	WT	DOB	AVG	vLH	vRH	G	AB	R	H	2B	3B	HR	RBI	BB	HBP	SH	SF	SO	SB	CS	SLG	OBP
Bergeron, Peter	L-R	6-0	190	11-9-77	.266	.255	.270	90	342	51	91	16	3	7	34	44	1	4	0	64	10	11	.392	.351
Bourn, Michael	L-R	5-11	180	12-27-82	.274	.263	.278	80	318	62	87	5	6	4	26	36	2	4	1	67	30	4	.365	.350
Burgamy, Brian	B-R	5-10	190	6-27-81	.194	.375	.130	10	31	2	6	0	1	0	3	7	0	0	1	6	0	0	.258	.333
Burnham, Gary	L-L	5-11	219	10-13-74	.341	.397	.321	80	290	51	99	20	0	16	60	30	6	0	2	31	2	1	.576	.412
Castellano, John	R-R	5-11	180	9-8-77	.309	.279	.319	47	178	16	55	8	0	4	27	7	5	0	4	21	0	0	.421	.345
Chavez, Angel	R-R	6-1	200	7-22-81	.255	.228	.269	63	239	35	61	9	1	5	32	16	1	1	4	46	6	3	.364	.300
2-team (4 Bowie)					.256	—	—	67	254	35	65	11	1	5	33	17	1	1	5	49	9	3	.366	.300
Diaz, Dennis	R-R	5-9	185	2-7-83	.143	.000	.167	3	7	0	1	0	0	0	0	0	0	0	0	5	0	0	.143	.143
Fasano, Sal	R-R	6-2	245	8-10-71	.000	—	.000	1	3	0	0	0	0	0	0	0	0	0	0	0	0	0	.000	.000
Florence, Branden	R-R	6-0	195	4-3-78	.000	—	.000	1	4	0	0	0	0	0	0	0	0	0	0	0	0	0	.000	.000
Gemoll, Brandon	L-L	6-1	212	9-15-80	.237	.172	.256	92	283	21	67	22	2	3	27	20	1	4	1	61	1	2	.360	.289
Gradoville, Tim	R-R	6-3	195	1-30-80	.261	.316	.234	35	115	12	30	7	0	1	13	7	2	3	1	34	0	0	.348	.312
Guevara, Orlando	B-R	6-1	175	9-13-83	.000	.000	—	1	1	0	0	0	0	0	0	1	0	0	0	0	0	0	.000	.667
Hammond, Joey	R-R	6-1	186	10-27-77	.267	.252	.272	129	469	57	125	15	3	8	55	57	3	5	5	71	3	4	.362	.346
Hansen, Bryan	L-L	6-2	200	5-8-83	.146	.188	.136	24	82	3	12	3	0	0	6	4	0	0	0	16	0	0	.183	.186
Harris, Gary	L-R	5-10	185	9-9-79	.297	.200	.327	19	64	7	19	6	0	0	11	6	0	0	1	15	0	0	.391	.352
Jaramillo, Jason	B-R	6-0	200	10-9-82	.248	.266	.241	93	322	35	80	25	1	6	39	32	4	1	5	55	0	1	.388	.320
Johnson, J.J.	R-R	6-2	195	11-3-81	.100	.000	.143	9	20	2	2	0	0	1	1	3	0	0	0	6	0	0	.250	.217
Johnston, Trey	R-R	5-11	190	7-4-85	.000	.000	.000	1	2	0	0	0	0	0	0	0	0	0	0	1	0	0	.000	.000
Leon, Carlos	B-R	5-10	181	8-31-79	.299	.291	.302	81	278	53	83	13	2	3	28	37	12	8	0	34	6	6	.392	.404
Lieberthal, Mike	R-R	6-0	190	1-18-72	.167	—	.167	2	6	0	1	0	0	0	0	0	0	0	0	2	0	0	.167	.167
Merchan, Jesus	R-R	6-0	184	3-26-81	.274	.288	.268	100	317	43	87	15	1	1	38	13	5	2	1	16	7	4	.363	.313
Moss, Timothy	R-R	5-9	150	1-26-82	.180	.107	.207	58	206	23	37	5	6	7	23	16	2	3	3	82	6	2	.364	.242
Padgett, Matt	L-R	6-2	215	7-22-77	.304	.297	.306	39	135	22	41	9	2	4	22	18	3	0	1	34	0	0	.489	.395
Ramos, Peeter	R-R	5-11	180	3-18-82	.271	.294	.262	65	236	38	64	9	2	4	27	19	1	3	3	34	4	6	.377	.324
Rushford, Jim	L-L	6-1	220	3-24-74	.262	.245	.269	48	168	17	44	10	0	1	20	22	3	0	4	15	0	1	.339	.350
Sandoval, Danny	B-R	5-11	200	4-7-79	.290	.167	.320	8	31	1	9	1	0	0	2	1	0	0	0	4	2	0	.323	.313
Sellier, Brian	L-R	6-0	180	1-12-78	.280	.190	.298	42	125	17	35	8	1	6	15	14	1	2	0	14	0	0	.504	.357
Sosa, Juan	R-R	6-1	175	8-19-75	.194	.300	.154	10	36	2	7	2	0	0	4	2	0	2	1	6	0	0	.250	.231
Swann, Pedro	L-R	6-0	205	10-27-70	.365	.353	.371	25	96	22	35	8	0	4	25	12	2	0	3	20	4	1	.573	.434
Tugwell, Marc	R-R	6-0	190	4-16-81	.179	.278	.095	28	78	6	14	1	0	0	6	4	2	0	2	18	0	0	.192	.233
Winchester, Jeff	R-R	6-0	205	1-21-80	.120	.071	.145	27	83	6	10	1	0	0	1	5	5	1	3	1	24	0	.157	.178

PITCHING	B-T	HT	WT	DOB	W	L	ERA	G	GS	CG	SV	IP	H	R	ER	HR	BB	SO	AVG	vLH	vRH	K/9	BB/9
Bisenius, Joseph	R-R	6-4	205	9-18-82	4	2	3.09	16	0	0	5	23	14	9	8	2	8	33	.182	.140	.235	12.73	3.09
Davis, Allen	L-L	6-4	220	10-1-75	5	6	3.95	21	19	1	0	118	122	59	52	20	34	71	.264	.260	.266	5.40	2.59
Evangelista, Nicholas	R-R	6-4	215	3-17-82	3	0	2.93	22	0	0	1	43	34	19	14	3	10	23	.215	.280	.157	4.81	2.09
Fahrner, Evan	R-R	6-2	200	3-4-78	1	4	3.38	33	0	0	3	45	38	22	17	3	24	50	.224	.240	.211	9.93	4.76
Giese, Dan	R-R	6-3	200	5-19-77	1	2	2.48	23	0	0	1	36	27	11	10	5	14	27	.213	.213	.213	6.69	3.47
Gonzalez, Gio	R-L	5-11	185	9-19-85	7	12	4.66	27	27	0	0	155	140	88	80	24	81	166	.239	.246	.236	9.66	4.71
Haigwood, Daniel	R-L	6-2	200	11-19-83	2	5	3.54	15	15	0	0	84	72	36	33	7	42	85	.231	.283	.209	9.11	4.50

Name	B-T	HT	WT	DOB	W	L	ERA	G	GS	CG	SV	IP	H	R	ER	HR	BB	SO	AVG	vLH	vRH	K/9	BB/9
Haines, Talley	R-R	6-5	205	11-16-76	5	2	3.67	29	0	0	0	49	46	20	20	4	14	43	.249	.265	.235	7.90	2.57
Happ, J.A.	L-L	6-5	205	10-19-82	6	2	2.65	12	12	0	0	75	58	27	22	2	29	81	.214	.212	.215	9.76	3.50
Johnson, Nathan	R-R	6-1	210	1-13-82	0	0	0.00	1	0	0	0	1	0	0	0	0	0	0	.000	.000	.000	0.00	0.00
Key, Chris	R-L	6-3	210	10-30-77	3	2	2.55	37	0	0	20	49	60	21	14	2	13	20	.311	.269	.326	3.65	2.37
Langone, Steve	R-R	6-2	193	1-12-78	0	0	0.00	7	0	0	0	11	7	0	0	0	2	6	.189	.188	.190	4.91	1.64
Lockwood, Luke	L-L	6-3	197	7-21-81	3	2	5.00	20	1	0	1	27	29	15	15	5	8	17	.269	.121	.333	5.67	2.67
Mathieson, Scott	R-R	6-3	190	2-27-84	7	2	3.21	14	14	0	0	93	73	35	33	8	29	99	.221	.252	.196	9.62	2.82
Mattioni, Nick	R-R	6-3	195	3-14-79	5	5	3.39	37	3	0	5	66	63	26	25	10	14	52	.252	.262	.242	7.06	1.90
Mazone, Brian	L-L	6-4	205	7-26-76	1	3	2.39	6	6	1	0	38	32	10	10	3	7	26	.230	.261	.215	6.21	1.67
McClaskey, Tim	B-R	6-1	175	1-11-76	4	8	4.97	32	18	1	0	129	139	76	71	12	21	81	.279	.295	.261	5.67	1.47
Reed, Brian	R-R	6-1	210	3-6-81	1	1	7.61	16	0	0	2	24	31	21	20	2	7	15	.301	.296	.306	5.70	2.66
Santana, Julio	R-R	6-0	210	1-20-74	0	0	0.00	2	0	0	0	2	1	1	0	0	0	3	.111	.000	.167	13.50	0.00
Segovia, Zach	R-R	6-2	245	4-11-83	11	5	3.11	17	16	3	0	107	90	45	37	8	24	75	.226	.239	.215	6.31	2.02
Shafer, Adam	L-R	6-5	250	2-1-79	1	2	8.10	11	0	0	3	10	15	10	9	3	6	11	.357	.450	.273	9.90	5.40
Stephens, John	R-R	6-1	220	11-15-79	0	2	6.26	8	6	0	0	23	23	17	16	3	11	16	.277	.238	.317	6.26	4.30
Sweeney, Matt	R-R	6-2	195	2-25-83	0	1	8.64	13	0	0	1	17	25	17	16	2	9	12	.342	.333	.350	6.48	4.86
Wolf, Randy	L-L	6-0	205	8-22-76	1	1	6.75	3	3	0	0	12	15	10	9	0	7	11	.306	.313	.303	8.25	5.25

FIELDING

Catcher	PCT	G	PO	A	E	DP	PB
Castellano	.750	1	3	0	1	0	0
Fasano	1.000	1	4	1	0	0	0
Gradoville	.992	35	238	24	2	2	4
Guevara	1.000	1	8	0	0	0	0
Jaramillo	.985	85	612	62	10	7	8
Johnston	1.000	1	4	1	0	0	0
Lieberthal	1.000	2	15	0	0	0	0
Winchester	.994	25	156	10	1	1	3

First Base	PCT	G	PO	A	E	DP
Burnham	.993	18	135	12	1	15
Castellano	.990	11	91	7	1	9
Gemoll	.986	72	520	53	8	48
Hammond	1.000	4	31	2	0	5
Hansen	1.000	21	144	6	0	10
Padgett	1.000	4	13	3	0	3
Rushford	.988	11	76	8	1	9
Tugwell	1.000	7	57	8	0	5

Second Base	PCT	G	PO	A	E	DP
Hammond	.500	1	1	0	1	0
Leon	.967	12	24	35	2	5
Merchan	.917	11	23	21	4	4
Moss	.964	58	95	144	9	31
Ramos	.966	64	144	193	12	46
Sosa	1.000	1	1	3	0	1

Third Base	PCT	G	PO	A	E	DP
Chavez	1.000	1	0	2	0	0
Hammond	.941	76	51	125	11	9
Leon	.889	20	15	25	5	2
Merchan	.941	45	25	55	5	7
Padgett	1.000	1	0	1	0	0
Sosa	1.000	2	0	5	0	0
Tugwell	.950	9	5	14	1	1

Shortstop	PCT	G	PO	A	E	DP
Chavez	.951	61	111	163	14	38
Leon	.981	38	70	81	3	20
Merchan	.966	30	61	81	5	13

Outfield	PCT	G	PO	A	E	DP
Sandoval	.969	8	10	21	1	3
Sosa	.882	7	9	21	4	6
Bergeron	.981	89	203	8	4	2
Bourn	.981	80	202	6	4	2
Burgamy	.833	10	15	0	3	0
Burnham	1.000	33	35	3	0	0
Castellano	.974	19	36	1	1	0
Diaz	1.000	1	1	0	0	0
Florence	1.000	1	1	0	0	0
Gemoll	1.000	2	1	1	0	0
Hammond	.990	56	97	6	1	1
Harris	.974	18	35	2	1	1
Johnson	1.000	7	20	0	0	0
Leon	1.000	11	12	1	0	0
Padgett	1.000	33	48	2	0	0
Rushford	.976	24	41	0	1	0
Sellier	1.000	39	85	1	0	0
Swann	.980	20	46	2	1	0

Clearwater Threshers — High Class A

Florida State League

BATTING	B-T	HT	WT	DOB	AVG	vLH	vRH	G	AB	R	H	2B	3B	HR	RBI	BB	HBP	SH	SF	SO	SB	CS	SLG	OBP
Antoniato, P.J.	R-R	5-9	185	7-2-83	.244	.167	.256	16	45	5	11	3	0	1	5	0	2	1	0	2	0	0	.378	.277
Asprilla, Avelino	R-R	5-11	190	1-1-82	.293	.429	.265	14	41	5	12	5	0	0	5	2	1	1	0	10	0	1	.415	.341
Burgamy, Brian	B-R	5-10	190	6-27-81	.274	.320	.262	118	441	110	121	21	5	13	51	88	2	3	1	96	24	8	.433	.397
Cambero, Alberto	B-R	5-9	152	4-23-86	—	—	—	2	0	1	0	0	0	0	0	0	0	0	0	0	0	0	—	—
Costanzo, Michael	L-R	6-3	215	9-9-83	.258	.186	.279	135	504	72	130	33	1	14	81	74	11	2	2	133	3	2	.411	.364
Cuevas, Phillip	R-R	5-11	168	6-30-85	.200	.000	.250	6	15	2	3	0	0	1	5	1	1	0	0	1	1	0	.400	.294
Diaz, Dennis	R-R	5-9	185	2-7-83	.000	.000	.000	5	3	1	0	0	0	0	0	0	0	0	0	0	0	0	.000	.000
Dzurilla, Michael	R-R	6-0	192	5-4-78	.217	.227	.214	30	120	13	26	5	1	0	6	9	1	0	2	11	1	1	.275	.273
Fasano, Sal	R-R	6-2	245	8-10-71	.083	.000	.111	4	12	0	1	0	0	0	1	0	1	0	0	1	0	0	.083	.083
Florence, Branden	R-R	6-0	195	4-3-78	.327	.311	.332	130	496	46	162	30	2	7	86	31	11	0	10	62	6	3	.438	.372
Golson, Greg	R-R	6-0	190	9-17-85	.264	.290	.258	40	159	31	42	11	2	6	17	11	3	1	0	53	7	3	.472	.324
Gosewisch, Tuffy	R-R	5-11	190	8-17-83	.252	.239	.256	95	305	32	77	14	0	9	39	24	6	1	2	55	1	0	.387	.318
Guevara, Orlando	B-R	6-1	175	9-13-83	.000	.000	.000	8	13	0	0	0	0	0	0	2	0	0	0	7	0	0	.000	.133
Hansen, Bryan	L-L	6-2	200	5-8-83	.270	.216	.284	102	352	37	95	17	0	4	55	47	4	6	7	53	0	2	.352	.356
Harman, Brad	R-R	6-1	175	11-19-85	.241	.280	.230	119	423	59	102	19	1	2	25	48	3	7	1	102	6	2	.305	.322
Harris, Gary	L-R	5-10	185	9-9-79	.385	.400	.417	3	13	3	5	0	0	0	0	0	0	0	0	4	0	0	.385	.385
Johnson, J.J.	R-R	6-2	195	11-3-81	.261	.290	.251	103	364	42	95	22	2	12	59	34	2	1	1	85	7	7	.431	.327
Made, Hector	R-R	6-1	155	12-18-84	.212	.269	.192	28	104	5	22	2	0	1	4	2	0	1	0	22	0	0	.260	.226
2-team (86 Tampa)					.267	—	—	114	419	42	112	24	2	4	32	15	0	5	2	64	6	8	.363	.291
Merchan, Jesus	R-R	6-0	184	3-26-81	.333	.000	.364	4	12	4	4	1	0	0	1	3	0	0	0	3	1	0	.417	.467
Morales, Douglas	L-L	6-0	180	6-22-86	.250	.286	.241	13	36	5	9	1	0	0	5	1	2	0	0	6	0	1	.278	.308
Moss, Timothy	R-R	5-9	150	1-26-82	.284	.316	.275	70	264	43	75	12	6	6	38	20	9	5	2	66	20	4	.443	.353
Norman, Zachary	R-R	6-0	210	1-20-82	.200	.111	.226	14	40	6	8	2	0	1	8	0	2	0	1	16	0	0	.325	.233
Paterson, Tom	L-L	6-2	195	9-18-82	.125	—	.125	5	8	0	1	0	0	0	1	1	0	0	1	2	0	1	.125	.111
Ramos, Peeter	R-R	5-11	180	3-18-82	.288	.375	.261	60	236	32	68	7	2	1	20	24	4	1	2	38	8	5	.347	.361
Sellier, Brian	L-R	6-0	200	1-12-78	.245	.163	.262	70	249	31	61	9	4	6	24	26	1	3	2	31	7	1	.386	.317
Thayer, Matt	R-L	5-10	173	2-21-82	.235	.236	.234	76	247	28	58	11	4	2	18	30	1	6	3	54	14	7	.312	.317
Tugwell, Marc	R-R	6-0	190	4-16-81	.135	.074	.170	26	74	7	10	1	0	1	6	8	0	2	1	13	0	0	.189	.217
Winchester, Jeff	R-R	6-0	205	1-21-80	.160	.100	.176	35	94	11	15	4	0	2	8	11	7	1	0	23	0	1	.266	.295

PITCHING	B-T	HT	WT	DOB	W	L	ERA	G	GS	CG	SV	IP	H	R	ER	HR	BB	SO	AVG	vLH	vRH	K/9	BB/9
Baldwin, Andrew	R-R	6-5	215	10-20-82	8	8	4.04	27	20	1	0	147	164	78	66	11	22	100	.285	.282	.288	6.12	1.35
Barrack, Jacob	R-R	5-11	165	5-19-82	2	1	5.40	25	0	0	0	30	28	18	18	4	20	31	.259	.209	.292	9.30	6.00
Bisenius, Joseph	R-R	5-11	190	9-18-82	4	1	1.93	35	0	0	2	61	48	17	13	4	22	62	.216	.223	.210	9.20	3.26
Booker, Chris	R-R	6-3	235	12-9-76	0	0	5.40	6	0	0	0	10	7	6	6	2	2	20	.194	.267	.143	18.00	1.80
Cline, Zachary	L-L	6-3	215	7-17-83	0	1	5.93	3	3	1	0	14	12	9	9	3	5	15	.231	.286	.211	9.88	3.29
De La Cruz, Julio	R-R	6-1	161	10-7-80	6	11	4.56	27	25	1	0	140	125	84	71	11	62	100	.239	.261	.223	6.94	3.99
Dueitt, Cory	R-R	6-0	212	8-16-82	0	2	5.24	27	0	0	0	46	49	32	27	2	20	31	.277	.216	.320	6.02	3.88
Evangelista, Nicholas	R-R	6-4	215	3-17-82	2	0	0.00	4	0	0	0	5	5	0	0	0	2	9	.263	.200	.286	16.20	3.60
Gordon, Tom	R-R	5-10	195	11-18-67	0	0	0.00	2	2	0	0	4	1	0	0	1	0	5	.083	.000	.143	11.25	2.25

Name	B-T	HT	WT	DOB	W	L	ERA	G	GS	CG	SV	IP	H	R	ER	HR	BB	SO	AVG	vLH	vRH	K/9	BB/9
Griffith, Derek	L-L	6-6	205	10-28-82	9	11	4.52	27	27	0	0	151	162	85	76	12	57	95	.273	.221	.291	5.65	3.39
Hamels, Cole	L-L	6-4	195	12-27-83	1	1	1.77	4	4	0	0	20	16	8	4	0	9	29	.205	.429	.156	12.84	3.98
Happ, J.A.	L-L	6-5	205	10-19-82	3	7	2.81	13	13	0	0	80	63	35	25	9	19	77	.216	.246	.209	8.66	2.14
Hill, Ronald	R-R	6-3	225	11-29-82	0	1	7.88	9	2	0	0	16	26	17	14	3	4	12	.371	.346	.386	6.75	2.25
Honsa, Chris	R-R	6-3	185	8-13-83	0	0	19.80	5	0	0	0	5	11	13	11	2	3	4	.423	.500	.357	7.20	5.40
Johnson, Nathan	R-R	6-1	210	1-13-82	8	3	2.57	45	0	0	6	67	59	25	19	3	10	55	.238	.245	.232	7.43	1.35
Kelly, Mark	R-R	6-4	210	4-18-84	0	0	0.00	1	0	0	0	1	0	0	0	0	0	1	.000	.000	—	9.00	0.00
Kendrick, Kyle	R-R	6-3	185	8-26-84	9	7	3.53	21	20	2	0	130	117	59	51	15	37	79	.241	.269	.221	5.47	2.56
Key, Chris	R-L	6-3	210	10-30-77	0	1	2.70	3	0	0	1	3	3	1	1	0	1	4	.250	.000	.375	10.80	2.70
Lieber, Jon	L-R	6-2	235	4-2-70	0	2	7.15	2	2	0	0	11	19	10	9	1	0	6	.380	.419	.316	4.76	0.00
Lockwood, Luke	L-L	6-3	170	7-21-81	2	3	4.24	18	11	0	0	64	68	36	30	8	19	39	.266	.236	.274	5.51	2.69
Overholt, Patrick	R-R	6-0	190	2-8-84	5	3	4.10	15	0	0	0	26	20	17	12	5	10	41	.196	.184	.203	14.01	3.42
Parris, Matthew	R-R	6-3	190	10-4-82	1	0	6.94	9	0	0	0	12	14	9	9	1	13	8	.298	.318	.280	6.17	10.03
Reed, Brian	R-R	6-1	210	3-6-81	0	3	3.89	29	0	0	9	39	38	19	17	0	12	19	.259	.224	.288	4.35	2.75
Segovia, Zach	R-R	6-2	245	4-11-83	5	1	2.19	7	7	0	0	49	39	14	12	2	12	41	.222	.258	.184	7.48	2.19
Shafer, Adam	L-R	6-5	250	2-1-79	2	1	5.08	29	0	0	15	34	30	19	19	3	12	30	.246	.255	.240	8.02	3.21
Smith, Matt	L-L	6-5	225	6-15-79	0	0	0.00	2	0	0	0	2	0	0	0	0	0	6	.000	.000	.000	27.00	0.00
Stott, Zac	R-R	6-4	205	7-26-83	0	0	5.40	7	0	0	0	10	13	7	6	4	2	5	.302	.500	.207	4.50	1.80
2-team (17 Sarasota)					1	2	3.21	24	0	0	1	42	36	16	15	6	12	27	—	—	—	5.79	2.57
Sweeney, Matt	R-R	6-2	195	2-25-83	0	4	4.66	22	1	0	0	37	37	20	19	8	21	23	.274	.313	.239	5.65	5.15
Wolf, Randy	L-L	6-0	205	8-22-76	0	0	0.00	2	2	0	0	6	6	1	0	0	4	4	.300	.250	.313	6.35	6.35

FIELDING

Catcher	PCT	G	PO	A	E	DP	PB
Fasano	1.000	2	1	2	0	0	0
Gosewisch	.991	90	623	76	6	7	6
Guevara	1.000	8	25	3	0	0	0
Norman	1.000	8	58	6	0	2	3
Tugwell	.988	12	76	3	1	0	4
Winchester	.987	35	205	17	3	0	5

First Base	PCT	G	PO	A	E	DP
Costanzo	1.000	1	8	1	0	2
Dzurilla	.993	30	273	21	2	26
Hansen	.989	102	826	67	10	75
Morales	1.000	1	1	0	0	0
Norman	1.000	3	24	0	0	2
Tugwell	1.000	5	41	7	0	5

Second Base	PCT	G	PO	A	E	DP
Antoniato	.964	6	12	15	1	5

(2B cont.)	PCT	G	PO	A	E	DP
Asprilla	.944	5	3	14	1	0
Cambero	1.000	1	0	2	0	0
Cuevas	—	1	0	0	0	0
Harman	1.000	3	4	5	0	0
Made	.929	3	8	5	1	2
Moss	.977	68	119	179	7	44
Ramos	.961	60	111	159	11	34

Third Base	PCT	G	PO	A	E	DP
Antoniato	1.000	2	1	4	0	0
Asprilla	1.000	2	0	1	0	0
Costanzo	.928	133	79	242	25	21
Cuevas	.800	2	1	3	1	0
Harman	.000	1	0	0	1	0
Tugwell	1.000	5	2	6	0	1

Shortstop	PCT	G	PO	A	E	DP
Antoniato	.963	7	9	17	1	4
Asprilla	.909	2	4	6	1	1

(SS cont.)	PCT	G	PO	A	E	DP
Harman	.935	112	202	316	36	72
Made	.934	20	27	58	6	12
Merchan	1.000	3	4	6	0	1

Outfield	PCT	G	PO	A	E	DP
Asprilla	1.000	1	1	0	0	0
Burgamy	.981	111	251	13	5	4
Cuevas	1.000	3	4	1	0	0
Diaz	—	1	0	0	0	0
Florence	1.000	39	64	1	0	0
Golson	.990	40	93	5	1	0
Harris	1.000	3	8	0	0	0
Johnson	.980	100	185	14	4	1
Morales	.952	12	19	1	1	0
Norman	1.000	1	0	0	0	0
Paterson	1.000	4	4	0	0	0
Sellier	.988	49	79	2	1	0
Thayer	.969	72	123	1	4	0

Lakewood BlueClaws — Low Class A

South Atlantic League

BATTING	B-T	HT	WT	DOB	AVG	vLH	vRH	G	AB	R	H	2B	3B	HR	RBI	BB	HBP	SH	SF	SO	SB	CS	SLG	OBP
Asprilla, Avelino	R-R	5-11	190	1-1-82	.242	.241	.242	99	388	54	94	23	1	7	48	24	8	6	2	76	12	4	.361	.299
Baez, Welinson	R-R	6-3	190	7-7-84	.232	.264	.225	122	427	48	99	34	3	6	51	41	5	3	2	158	5	5	.368	.305
Castellano, John	R-R	5-11	180	9-8-77	.465	.400	.474	11	43	7	20	8	0	3	7	7	2	0	0	7	0	2	.860	.558
Cheesman, Aaron	R-R	5-10	195	9-25-81	.250	.240	.253	31	100	14	25	5	0	1	15	13	2	0	1	10	1	0	.330	.345
Diaz, Dennis	R-R	5-9	185	2-7-83	.190	.304	.114	25	58	5	11	2	0	0	3	4	0	3	0	21	7	1	.224	.242
Frith, Ryan	R-R	6-2	185	8-17-82	.200	.167	.205	13	45	4	9	4	0	0	4	6	1	1	1	20	1	2	.289	.302
Gamble, Sean	L-L	6-0	195	6-23-83	.264	.267	.264	31	121	14	32	2	0	3	13	6	1	1	1	22	2	1	.355	.302
Golson, Gregory	R-R	6-0	190	9-17-85	.220	.143	.233	93	387	56	85	15	4	7	31	19	2	8	3	107	23	7	.333	.258
Guevara, Orlando	B-R	6-1	175	9-13-83	.188	.286	.160	10	32	0	6	1	0	0	2	2	1	2	0	8	0	0	.219	.257
Hardy, John	R-R	6-1	180	9-28-82	.077	.250	.032	11	39	1	3	1	0	0	1	2	0	0	0	12	0	0	.103	.122
Harris, Clay	R-R	6-4	220	8-25-82	.255	.217	.263	132	471	68	120	32	1	13	81	75	10	0	11	109	0	1	.410	.362
Henry, C.J.	R-R	6-3	205	5-31-86	.253	.204	.243	25	91	13	23	3	4	1	16	7	1	0	0	25	1	0	.407	.313
2-team (77 Charleston)					.243	—		102	366	48	89	22	7	3	49	39	7	1	2	111	15	4	.366	.326
Hernandez, Fidel	R-R	5-11	160	1-18-86	.250	.296	.242	99	356	36	89	11	0	1	31	11	1	5	3	52	9	5	.289	.272
Johnston, Trey	R-R	5-11	190	7-4-85	.000	—		1	3	0	0	0	0	0	0	0	0	0	0	2	0	0	.000	.000
Kennelly, Timothy	R-R	6-0	180	12-5-86	.200	.000	.263	8	25	1	5	2	0	1	2	0	0	2	0	9	0	0	.400	.200
Marson, Lou	R-R	6-1	195	6-26-86	.243	.226	.246	104	350	44	85	16	5	4	39	49	5	5	1	82	4	0	.351	.343
Morales, Douglas	L-L	6-0	180	6-22-86	.182	.000	.200	7	22	2	4	0	0	0	2	3	0	0	1	4	0	0	.182	.269
Osteen, Cooper	B-R	5-10	170	11-10-82	.232	.294	.219	55	194	21	45	4	0	0	17	22	2	7	1	25	6	2	.253	.315
Slayden, Jeremy	L-R	6-0	185	7-28-82	.310	.236	.322	107	400	65	124	44	3	10	81	41	8	0	5	89	5	0	.510	.381
Spidale, Mike	L-L	5-9	180	3-12-82	.345	.292	.355	80	313	58	108	19	3	1	37	37	5	2	4	33	29	4	.435	.418
Thayer, Matt	R-L	5-10	173	2-21-82	.262	.379	.218	25	107	15	28	4	2	1	9	7	2	1	1	13	3	0	.364	.316
Urick, John	L-L	6-2	210	2-22-82	.265	.241	.269	100	359	52	95	27	2	6	53	53	9	2	6	100	1	2	.401	.368
Williams, Julian	R-R	5-11	175	7-27-83	.251	.269	.246	97	347	59	87	22	1	1	23	57	18	5	2	73	9	3	.329	.382

PITCHING	B-T	HT	WT	DOB	W	L	ERA	G	GS	CG	SV	IP	H	R	ER	HR	BB	SO	AVG	vLH	vRH	K/9	BB/9
Barb, Andrew	R-R	6-3	190	10-6-84	6	2	2.23	38	0	0	18	61	35	16	15	0	28	71	.166	.185	.154	10.53	4.15
Blaine, Justin	L-L	6-4	188	3-12-84	2	2	3.83	18	6	0	0	56	58	34	24	0	34	37	.261	.275	.257	5.91	5.43
Brauer, Daniel	L-L	6-0	210	10-14-83	0	1	4.50	3	2	0	0	8	10	4	4	1	5	10	.303	.583	.143	11.25	5.63
Carrasco, Carlos	R-R	6-3	180	3-21-87	12	6	2.26	26	26	2	0	159	103	50	40	6	65	159	.182	.178	.186	8.98	3.67
Cline, Zachary	L-L	6-3	215	7-17-83	7	3	5.08	15	14	0	0	73	77	44	41	7	22	47	.283	.350	.264	5.82	2.72
De La Cruz, Maximino	R-R	6-1	160	3-24-85	5	2	4.90	22	11	0	0	90	98	60	49	9	35	58	.275	.322	.243	5.80	3.50
Hamels, Cole	L-L	6-4	195	12-27-83	0	0	1.59	1	1	0	0	6	3	1	1	1	2	3	.176	.000	.200	4.76	3.18
Harker, Brett	R-R	6-3	185	7-9-84	1	4	2.92	46	0	0	17	65	53	23	21	4	19	55	.224	.140	.278	7.65	2.64
Hill, Ronald	R-R	6-3	225	11-29-82	2	3	3.20	28	0	0	2	55	52	19	14	6	15	56	.249	.343	.199	9.22	2.47
Kendrick, Kyle	R-R	6-3	185	8-26-84	3	2	2.15	7	7	0	0	46	34	14	11	0	5	54	.199	.162	.227	10.57	2.93
Kirk, Bill	R-R	6-4	195	7-7-83	1	0	4.63	6	0	0	0	12	14	8	6	1	6	6	.292	.250	.300	4.63	3.86
Laureano, Wilfrido	R-R	6-6	165	3-4-84	3	1	4.09	7	2	0	0	22	21	10	10	1	4	13	.256	.308	.209	5.32	1.64

				6	3	4.10	36	2	0	1	85	75	42	39	9	40	75	—	—	—	7.88	4.20
2-team (29 West Virginia)																						
Maloney, Matthew	L-L	6-4	220	1-16-84	16	9	2.03	27	27	2	0	169	120	54	38	5	73	180	.194	.227	.184	9.60	3.90
Mitchinson, Scott	R-R	6-3	185	12-28-84	3	3	3.96	15	10	0	0	61	53	27	27	4	18	64	.238	.214	.258	9.39	2.64
Outman, Joshua	L-L	6-1	180	9-14-84	14	6	2.95	27	27	1	0	155	119	61	51	5	75	161	.213	.203	.217	9.33	4.35
Overholt, Patrick	R-R	6-0	190	2-8-84	3	3	3.15	29	0	0	2	46	37	17	16	4	26	52	.223	.097	.298	10.25	5.12
Pfinsgraff, Ben	R-R	6-0	180	11-13-83	1	2	2.28	4	4	0	0	24	17	9	6	0	8	25	.205	.233	.175	9.51	3.04
Raulinaitis, Christopher	R-R	6-3	235	11-25-83	1	1	4.56	13	0	0	0	26	22	14	13	3	10	13	.237	.231	.241	4.56	3.51
Rawl, Aaron	R-R	6-0	190	7-21-83	0	0	5.40	2	0	0	1	3	5	2	2	0	1	2	.385	.000	.500	5.40	2.70
Savage, William	R-R	6-4	210	8-25-84	0	1	3.45	15	0	0	3	31	31	14	12	0	5	28	.261	.276	.246	8.04	1.44
Wolf, Randy	L-L	6-0	205	8-22-76	0	0	1.13	2	2	0	0	8	2	1	1	0	3	7	.087	.200	.056	7.88	3.38
Zagurski, Michael	L-L	6-0	225	1-27-83	4	4	3.51	42	0	0	1	56	46	22	22	0	22	75	.224	.268	.208	11.98	3.51

FIELDING

Catcher	PCT	G	PO	A	E	DP	PB
Cheesman	.981	30	241	18	5	1	4
Guevara	.988	10	69	11	1	2	1
Johnston	1.000	1	4	0	0	0	1
Marson	.988	102	868	71	11	8	9

First Base	PCT	G	PO	A	E	DP
Harris	.988	81	631	44	8	62
Kennelly	.947	3	17	1	1	1
Urick	.994	55	466	38	3	50

Second Base	PCT	G	PO	A	E	DP
Asprilla	.980	95	170	229	8	74
Diaz	.846	4	4	7	2	2
Hardy	.933	3	6	8	1	1

	PCT	G	PO	A	E	DP
Hernandez	1.000	5	4	17	0	3
Osteen	.954	38	65	81	7	16

Third Base	PCT	G	PO	A	E	DP
Asprilla	1.000	1	1	0	0	0
Baez	.912	120	82	248	32	21
Castellano	1.000	1	0	2	0	0
Harris	.974	12	9	28	1	0
Kennelly	1.000	3	1	7	0	0
Osteen	1.000	4	4	8	0	2

Shortstop	PCT	G	PO	A	E	DP
Asprilla	1.000	1	0	2	0	0
Hardy	.875	8	8	20	4	3
Henry	.867	25	31	54	13	20

	PCT	G	PO	A	E	DP
Hernandez	.937	94	117	254	25	47
Osteen	.895	13	15	36	6	8

Outfield	PCT	G	PO	A	E	DP
Castellano	1.000	2	4	0	0	0
Diaz	.955	16	20	1	1	0
Frith	1.000	11	24	0	0	0
Gamble	.939	25	29	2	2	0
Golson	.985	93	186	12	3	4
Morales	1.000	7	15	1	0	0
Slayden	.964	77	130	5	5	2
Spidale	.994	77	174	1	1	0
Thayer	.900	24	47	2	1	0
Williams	.984	96	177	9	3	2

Batavia Muckdogs — Short-Season

New York-Penn League

BATTING	B-T	HT	WT	DOB	AVG	vLH	vRH	G	AB	R	H	2B	3B	HR	RBI	BB	HBP	SH	SF	SO	SB	CS	SLG	OBP
Antoniato, P.J.	R-R	5-9	185	7-2-83	.300	.342	.280	32	120	19	36	4	0	0	11	6	3	0	2	8	6	1	.333	.344
Berry, Quintin	L-L	6-1	165	11-21-84	.219	.231	.215	62	210	34	46	2	2	0	13	25	5	5	2	51	19	4	.248	.314
Capps, Brian	B-R	5-10	170	9-3-82	.256	.211	.300	34	78	13	20	5	0	1	10	3	1	3	0	10	4	4	.359	.293
Cuevas, Phillip	R-R	5-11	168	6-30-85	.176	.273	.086	26	68	6	12	3	1	0	3	2	0	1	0	21	2	0	.250	.200
Dempsey, Jacob	L-R	6-1	225	9-24-83	.262	.346	.234	58	210	32	55	17	0	7	36	14	3	0	3	65	4	0	.443	.313
Donald, Jason	R-R	6-1	190	9-4-84	.263	.159	.313	63	213	33	56	14	2	1	24	23	5	1	1	42	12	1	.362	.347
Kennelly, Timothy	R-R	6-0	180	12-5-86	.224	.191	.241	42	134	10	30	6	1	0	12	11	3	2	2	26	2	1	.284	.293
McGill, Shawn	R-R	6-4	195	2-29-84	.200	.190	.205	21	60	6	12	1	0	0	3	7	0	0		17	2	0	.217	.284
Miller, Jay	R-R	5-10	180	8-11-83	.258	.243	.265	65	225	34	58	11	2	2	27	14	7	3	4	39	5	2	.351	.316
Milner, Gus	R-R	6-5	240	4-21-84	.261	.308	.239	70	241	28	63	10	6	3	39	20	7	1	1	55	4	3	.390	.335
Montgomery, Cody	R-R	6-3	185	10-28-83	.156	.186	.143	46	141	10	22	4	0	0	5	7	1	4	2	31	3	4	.184	.199
Morales, Douglas	L-L	6-0	180	6-22-86	.239	.188	.250	48	88	9	21	1	0	0	6	11	1	1	2	15	3	1	.250	.324
Naughton, Joel	L-R	6-1	180	8-27-86	.206	.172	.215	45	136	13	28	5	0	1	8	12	0	1	1	20	0	1	.265	.268
Penprase, Zachary	R-R	6-2	180	2-16-85	.211	.176	.223	59	190	26	40	3	2	0	19	19	1	3	3	40	19	6	.247	.282
Yarbrough, Charlie	R-R	6-6	250	11-7-84	.211	.186	.224	60	204	16	43	15	1	4	27	15	3	0	2	58	0	0	.353	.272

PITCHING	B-T	HT	WT	DOB	W	L	ERA	G	GS	CG	SV	IP	H	R	ER	HR	BB	SO	AVG	vLH	vRH	K/9	BB/9
Antoniato, P.J.	R-R	5-9	185	7-2-83	0	0	9.00	1	0	0	0	2	3	2	2	0	1	0	.333	.250	.400	0.00	4.50
Brauer, Daniel	L-L	6-0	210	10-14-83	3	4	1.96	11	10	0	0	55	39	14	12	1	18	65	.206	.191	.211	10.64	2.95
Brownell, John	R-R	6-3	175	6-28-83	1	3	3.89	19	1	0	0	37	32	20	16	2	19	37	.230	.213	.244	9.00	4.62
Byrd, Darren	R-R	6-3	170	10-24-86	2	0	2.30	4	2	0	0	16	10	5	4	0	11	14	.189	.241	.125	8.04	6.32
Carpenter, Andrew	R-R	6-3	230	5-18-85	0	0	0.77	3	3	0	0	12	10	1	1	0	5	12	.250	.200	.300	9.26	3.86
Concepcion, Alexander	R-R	6-1	180	9-27-84	6	6	3.76	14	13	1	0	84	73	38	35	8	17	72	.232	.230	.235	7.75	1.83
Cruse, Andrew	R-R	6-0	200	5-31-84	4	4	2.57	13	13	0	0	67	60	29	19	2	19	48	.244	.217	.270	6.48	2.57
Cruz, Reymond	R-R	6-2	170	10-23-83	0	1	1.25	23	0	0	6	36	19	8	5	1	9	42	.150	.157	.145	10.50	2.25
Dubee, Michael	R-R	6-2	177	1-12-86	1	2	4.82	10	9	0	0	37	49	24	20	2	15	27	.327	.282	.367	6.51	3.62
Garcia, Edgar	R-R	6-2	190	9-20-87	3	5	2.98	12	12	1	0	66	62	28	22	5	10	46	.243	.243	.243	6.24	1.36
Gazo, Lenin	R-R	6-1	145	7-25-84	3	0	2.83	16	0	0	1	29	29	10	9	0	7	23	.257	.354	.185	7.22	2.20
Hill, Garet	R-R	6-5	217	5-24-84	4	3	2.49	17	4	0	2	47	39	18	13	1	7	35	.220	.293	.158	6.70	1.34
Kelly, Mark	R-R	6-4	210	4-18-84	0	1	4.50	11	0	0	1	14	13	11	7	0	10	12	.245	.214	.280	7.71	6.43
Kirk, Bill	R-R	6-4	195	7-7-83	0	0	9.00	8	0	0	1	13	21	13	13	3	6	8	.362	.333	.393	5.54	4.15
Morales, Douglas	L-L	6-0	180	6-22-86	0	0	0.00	1	0	0	0	2	1	1	0	0	2	1	.125	.200	.000	4.50	9.00
Pfinsgraff, Ben	R-R	6-0	180	11-13-83	4	4	1.12	13	4	1	1	40	25	9	5	0	10	44	.176	.132	.216	9.82	2.23
Raulinaitis, Christopher	R-R	6-3	235	11-25-83	1	0	1.04	7	0	0	2	9	7	1	1	0	4	16	.219	.188	.250	10.38	4.15
Salmon, Kevin	R-R	6-2	220	11-9-83	1	3	2.84	14	0	0	1	19	18	9	6	1	11	21	.237	.216	.256	9.95	5.21
Savage, William	R-R	6-4	210	8-25-84	1	0	0.00	7	0	0	0	8	4	0	0	0	1	8	.176	.250	.136	8.00	1.00
Walls, Samuel	R-R	5-11	195	10-31-83	1	2	2.67	19	2	0	4	30	32	13	9	1	6	26	.274	.268	.279	7.71	1.78

FIELDING

Catcher	PCT	G	PO	A	E	DP	PB
Kennelly	.987	16	137	12	2	2	3
McGill	.980	19	134	14	3	0	2
Morales	1.000	1	0	0	0	0	0
Naughton	.982	45	289	36	6	0	4

First Base	PCT	G	PO	A	E	DP
Kennelly	.954	12	55	7	3	2
Montgomery	1.000	1	1	0	0	1
Morales	.992	32	114	9	1	6
Yarbrough	.989	56	420	30	5	23

Second Base	PCT	G	PO	A	E	DP
Antoniato	.983	16	28	31	1	7
Capps	.957	5	8	14	1	3
Cuevas	.947	17	26	46	4	8
Penprase	.968	45	69	110	6	14

Third Base	PCT	G	PO	A	E	DP
Antoniato	.946	18	9	26	2	3
Cuevas	1.000	5	1	5	0	0
Dempsey	1.000	1	0	3	0	0
Kennelly	.848	13	9	19	5	1
Montgomery	.898	42	32	65	11	9

Shortstop	PCT	G	PO	A	E	DP
Antoniato	.800	3	1	3	1	0
Donald	.959	62	65	144	9	19
Penprase	.934	16	19	38	4	6

Outfield	PCT	G	PO	A	E	DP
Berry	.984	61	124	2	2	1
Capps	.944	10	17	0	1	0
Dempsey	—	2	0	0	0	0
Kennelly	1.000	3	3	0	0	0
Miller	.990	65	98	3	1	1
Milner	.960	68	139	5	6	2
Morales	.920	17	23	0	2	0

ORGANIZATION STATISTICS

Gulf Coast League

BATTING	B-T	HT	WT	DOB	AVG	vLH	vRH	G	AB	R	H	2B	3B	HR	RBI	BB	HBP	SH	SF	SO	SB	CS	SLG	OBP
Arzeno, Luis Ramon	R-R	5-11	190	8-9-84	.169	.125	.186	18	59	3	10	1	0	0	3	3	0	0	0	18	2	0	.186	.210
Brown, Dominic	L-L	6-5	204	9-3-87	.214	.048	.250	34	117	13	25	3	0	1	7	12	1	1	0	30	13	3	.265	.292
Cambero, Alberto	B-R	5-9	152	4-23-86	.204	.261	.187	27	98	18	20	6	0	1	8	12	3	1	1	22	12	1	.296	.307
Cardenas, Adrian	L-R	6-0	185	10-10-87	.318	.167	.364	41	154	22	49	5	4	2	21	17	2	0	4	28	13	3	.442	.384
Dalton, Brett	R-R	5-10	180	11-26-82	.196	.100	.217	17	56	11	11	1	0	1	3	7	1	0	0	10	2	2	.268	.297
Demmink, Herman	L-R	5-11	190	9-21-83	.281	.313	.271	18	64	16	18	2	1	0	8	4	0	3	0	6	9	0	.344	.324
Deveaux, Mike	R-R	6-3	210	5-9-84	.269	.304	.255	21	78	5	21	4	0	1	12	8	0	3	2	18	0	1	.359	.330
Durant, Michael	R-R	6-5	230	1-2-87	.226	.111	.273	11	31	3	7	2	0	0	2	3	2	0	0	14	2	1	.290	.333
Fuentes, Michael	L-R	6-1	210	12-15-83	.163	.091	.188	14	43	4	7	4	0	0	4	3	1	0	1	12	1	0	.256	.229
McDonald, Darin	R-R	6-3	195	11-3-87	.266	.229	.280	37	128	13	34	7	0	0	15	7	6	0	1	31	5	3	.320	.331
Miaso, Curt	R-R	6-3	205	9-28-85	.200	.091	.245	27	75	5	15	2	1	1	11	14	2	0	1	13	0	3	.293	.337
Mitchell, Derrick	R-R	6-2	170	1-5-87	.213	.154	.232	32	108	12	23	6	0	2	12	8	3	1	0	21	6	4	.324	.286
Montanez, Agustin	B-R	6-3	170	12-28-86	.176	.000	.200	13	34	2	6	0	0	0	2	3	0	0	1	11	1	1	.176	.237
Moron, Robert	L-L	6-0	172	9-14-85	.200	.286	.184	13	45	3	9	0	1	0	5	4	0	0	0	9	4	2	.244	.265
Myers, D'Arby	R-R	6-3	175	12-9-88	.313	.385	.294	31	128	20	40	7	1	2	13	7	1	0	0	32	11	4	.430	.353
Reed, Matthew	R-R	6-2	225	8-24-82	.216	.136	.250	25	74	8	16	5	1	2	10	7	1	0	0	22	3	1	.392	.293
Robbins, Alan	L-R	6-0	205	7-7-83	.178	.167	.179	17	45	3	8	4	0	0	4	3	2	0	1	10	1	1	.267	.255
Sanchez, Jesus	R-R	—	—	9-24-87	.192	.125	.222	8	26	1	5	2	0	0	1	1	1	0	1	8	1	0	.269	.241
2-team (24 GCL Yankees)					.252	—	—	32	119	11	30	7	0	0	11	10	3	0	1	27	4	0	.311	.323
Warren, T.J.	R-R	6-4	190	8-17-88	.206	.212	.204	39	136	13	28	6	0	1	16	11	0	3	3	50	5	1	.272	.260
Williams, Jermaine	R-R	6-3	210	3-25-87	.079	.074	.082	23	76	4	6	1	0	0	1	2	1	0	0	21	2	0	.092	.114

PITCHING	B-T	HT	WT	DOB	W	L	ERA	G	GS	CG	SV	IP	H	R	ER	HR	BB	SO	AVG	vLH	vRH	K/9	BB/9
Bastardo, Antonio	L-L	5-11	—	9-21-85	1	2	3.91	9	2	0	0	23	20	16	10	1	14	27	.220	.214	.221	10.57	5.48
Byrd, Darren	R-R	6-3	170	10-24-86	2	1	3.22	9	5	0	0	36	33	22	13	1	15	27	.246	.333	.221	6.69	3.72
Carpenter, Andrew	R-R	6-3	230	5-18-85	0	0	0.00	2	1	0	0	3	2	0	0	0	0	4	.200	.000	.222	12.00	0.00
Correa, Heitor	R-R	6-3	200	8-25-89	0	3	7.83	8	4	0	0	23	35	21	20	1	7	14	.365	.375	.361	5.48	2.74
Drabek, Kyle	R-R	6-0	185	12-8-87	1	3	7.71	6	6	0	0	23	33	24	20	2	11	14	.333	.351	.323	5.40	4.24
Dubee, Michael	R-R	6-2	177	11-26-86	0	1	1.29	2	1	0	0	7	9	1	1	0	0	1	.333	.143	.400	1.29	0.00
Freeman, Jarrod	R-R	6-3	195	11-20-87	1	2	3.38	11	6	1	0	45	47	23	17	3	5	37	.267	.224	.288	7.35	0.99
Hall, Nick	R-R	6-5	225	1-10-84	2	1	6.91	12	0	0	0	14	17	12	11	0	12	10	.298	.250	.324	6.28	7.53
Kelly, Mark	R-R	6-4	210	4-18-84	0	0	0.00	1	1	0	0	1	0	0	0	0	2	1	.000	.000	—	13.50	27.00
Lieber, Jon	L-R	6-2	235	4-2-70	0	0	3.00	1	1	0	0	3	4	1	1	0	0	1	.308	.000	.364	3.00	0.00
Lin, Yen-Feng	R-R	6-1	205	5-22-85	3	0	3.92	12	0	0	2	21	20	11	9	0	6	17	.250	.227	.259	7.40	2.61
McEnaney, Alex	R-R	6-4	175	1-8-86	0	0	3.31	11	0	0	4	16	15	9	6	2	5	10	.238	.182	.268	5.51	2.76
Mitchinson, Scott	R-R	6-3	185	12-28-84	0	1	0.00	1	0	0	0	2	4	2	0	0	0	4	.364	.250	.429	18.00	0.00
Monasterios, Carlos	R-R	6-2	175	3-21-86	0	2	3.68	4	3	0	0	15	18	7	6	1	3	11	.295	.321	.273	6.75	1.84
2-team (7 GCL Yankees)					1	4	3.20	11	6	0	0	45	41	19	16	3	6	35	—	—	—	7.00	1.20
Naylor, Drew	R-R	6-4	210	5-31-86	2	3	4.66	12	2	0	1	37	43	26	19	2	9	22	.297	.304	.293	5.40	2.21
Olson, Matthew	R-R	6-4	200	11-27-86	2	4	3.48	9	6	1	0	41	36	19	16	2	9	21	.234	.200	.248	4.57	1.96
Pena, Carlos	R-R	6-4	165	5-11-85	1	2	2.96	15	0	0	2	27	34	10	9	3	1	22	.315	.355	.299	7.24	0.33
Pereira, Gilmar	R-R	6-2	210	6-17-88	0	1	9.88	5	2	0	0	14	24	17	15	3	11	11	.375	.381	.372	7.24	7.24
Roth, Robert	R-R	6-1	195	8-5-88	1	3	5.67	12	4	0	1	33	33	27	21	2	31	24	.252	.333	.217	6.48	8.37
Tejeda, Walter	L-L	6-3	187	9-28-85	2	2	4.91	9	5	0	0	37	39	27	20	4	18	33	.255	.120	.281	8.10	4.42

FIELDING

Catcher	PCT	G	PO	A	E	DP	PB
Arzeno	.963	18	133	22	6	0	2
Fuentes	.986	13	68	5	1	2	5
Reed	1.000	1	1	0	0	0	1
Robbins	.978	17	77	12	2	2	6
Sanchez	.980	8	44	6	1	0	0
Williams	1.000	1	0	1	0	0	0

First Base	PCT	G	PO	A	E	DP
Dalton	.994	15	151	5	1	10
Durant	1.000	6	33	2	0	3
Moron	.972	13	103	3	3	9
Reed	.995	22	192	7	1	16

Second Base	PCT	G	PO	A	E	DP
Cambero	.962	27	55	73	5	19
Dalton	.875	1	3	4	1	1
Demmink	.930	9	22	18	3	3
Deveaux	.980	8	15	33	1	4
Montanez	.939	6	10	21	2	4

Third Base	PCT	G	PO	A	E	DP
Dalton	1.000	1	1	3	0	1
Demmink	.909	9	3	17	2	4
Deveaux	.958	11	12	34	2	0
Mitchell	.875	27	25	66	13	7
Montanez	1.000	2	2	1	0	0

Shortstop	PCT	G	PO	A	E	DP
Cardenas	.923	41	59	122	15	24
Mitchell	.893	5	5	20	3	3
Montanez	.813	5	5	8	3	1

Outfield	PCT	G	PO	A	E	DP
Brown	.956	30	41	2	2	1
McDonald	.903	31	50	6	6	2
Miaso	1.000	16	22	1	0	0
Myers	.922	29	45	2	4	0
Warren	.925	32	58	4	5	0
Williams	.929	12	12	1	1	0

ORGANIZATION STATISTICS

BY JOHN PERROTTO

The Pirates' 2006 season boiled down to this: 30-60 and 37-35.

The Pirates went 30-60 in the first half leading up to hosting the All-Star Game at PNC Park. They then had a

37-35 record in the second half, the first time they have finished above .500 after the all-star break since 1992.

While the second-half record was more palatable, it didn't disguise the fact that the Pirates finished 67-95 under first-year manager Jim Tracy. That was the same record they had in 2005, a mark that got Lloyd McClendon fired as manager.

The poor start also doomed the Pirates to their 14th consecutive losing seasons and the second-worst record in the National League. The Pirates are two sub-.500 seasons away from breaking the major league record of 16 straight, set by the Phillies from 1933-48.

The Pirates' turnaround coincided with becoming younger in the second half, as general manager Dave Littlefield's offseason strategy of loading up on veteran hitters failed miserably. The Pirates traded with Cincinnati for first baseman Sean Casey and signed third baseman Joe Randa and right fielder Jeromy Burnitz as free agents. They combined to hit 23 home runs and 106 RBIs, and the Pirates finished last in the NL in home runs and slugging percentage.

Casey was traded to the Tigers at midseason, while Randa suffered a stress fracture in his right foot in early May and lost his job to eventual batting champion Freddy Sanchez. Burnitz was reduced to a bench player after the all-star break.

Sanchez, who began the season as a utility infielder despite ending 2005 on a 17-game hitting streak, was a

ORGANIZATION **LEADERS**

BATTING		*Minimum 250 at-bats
*AVG	Keel, Jared, GCL Pirates/Williamsport	.313
R	Lillibridge, Brent, Hickory/Lynchburg	106
H	Bixler, Brian, Lynchburg/Altoona	164
TB	Pearce, Steven, Hickory/Lynchburg	255
2B	Pearce, Steven, Hickory/Lynchburg	40
3B	Buttler, Vic, Altoona/Indianapolis	15
HR	Pearce, Steven, Hickory/Lynchburg	26
RBI	Corley, Brad, Hickory	100
BB	Lillibridge, Brent, Hickory/Lynchburg	87
SO	Lerud, Steven, Hickory	160
SB	Morgan, Nyjer, Lynchburg/Altoona	72
*OBP	Lillibridge, Brent, Hickory/Lynchburg	.419
*SLG	Pearce, Steven, Hickory/Lynchburg	.523
XBH	Pearce, Steven, Hickory/Lynchburg	68

PITCHING		#Minimum 75 innings
W	Jacobsen, Landon, Indianapolis/Altoona	14
L	Four players tied at	11
#ERA	Bresnahan, Pat, Williamsport	2.25
G	Knight, Brandon, Altoona	58
	Nitkowski, C.J., Indianapolis	58
CG	Starling, Wardell, Lynchburg/Altoona	2
	Valdez, Luis, Lynchburg/Hickory	2
SV	Knight, Brandon, Altoona	32
IP	Starling, Wardell, Lynchburg/Altoona	179
BB	Connolly, Michael, Indianapolis/Altoona	62
SO	Redmond, Todd, Hickory	148
#AVG	Bresnahan, Pat, Williamsport	.201

MAJOR LEAGUE: Freddy Sanchez, 3b

Sanchez broke out in 2006, hitting .344/.378/.473 en route to the National League batting title. He also led the NL with 53 doubles, while hitting .442 against lefthanded pitching. The 28-year-old became the eighth Pirate in team history to win a batting title, and the first since Bill Madlock in 1983.

MINOR LEAGUE: Andrew McCutchen, of

McCutchen raked his way to Double-A Altoona in his first full season, skipping high Class A Lynchburg altogether. He batted .294/.359/.450 with 17 homers and 23 steals. Playing the whole season as a 19-year-old, McCutchen ranked among the organization's top 10 in batting, home runs and RBIs.

revelation. He batted .344/.378/.473 to become the Pirates' first batting champion since Bill Madlock in 1983, while also finishing with 200 hits and a league-leading 53 doubles.

Sanchez was selected to the All-Star Game along with left fielder Jason Bay, who became the first Pirates' player elected to the NL starting lineup since 1993. Bay had another outstanding season, hitting .286/.396/.532 with 35 homers and 109 RBIs.

Center fielder Chris Duffy provided a spark from the leadoff spot after being recalled from Triple-A Indianapolis on Aug. 1, hitting .282/.345/.366 with 16 steals in 53 games. He began the season as the starter but lost his job when he batted .194 in the first six weeks of the season, and then he spent a month away from the game while contemplating retirement.

Rookie catcher Ronny Paulino was a pleasant surprise after beginning the season at Indianapolis, batting .310/.360/.394 in the big leagues.

The bullpen was the strength of a young pitching staff that finished ninth in the 16-team NL in ERA. Lefthander Mike Gonzalez was a perfect 24-for-24 in save conversions in his first season as the closer before being sidelined for the season with elbow tendinitis on Aug. 25.

Veteran Salomon Torres converted 12 of 13 saves after Gonzalez was injured and pitched in a major league-high 94 games. Torres became just the fourth pitcher in major league history to appear in at least 90 games in a season. Matt Capps also proved to be a workhorse as he made 85 appearances, a Pirates' rookie record.

Lefties Zach Duke, Tom Gorzelanny and Paul Maholm, and righthander Ian Snell combined to go 34-41, but all were 24 or younger and showed enough improvement in the second half to give the Pirates reason to believe they had the nucleus of a good rotation moving forward.

Reliever Josh Sharpless, then with Indianapolis, provided the highlight of the season when he retired all four batters he faced in the Futures Game at PNC Park. Sharpless, a native of nearby Freedom, Pa., was a 24th-round draft pick in 2003 from Division III Allegheny (Pa.) and had a 1.50 ERA in his first shot at the major leagues.

Pittsburgh Pirates | MLB

National League

BATTING	B-T	HT	WT	DOB	AVG	vLH	vRH	G	AB	R	H	2B	3B	HR	RBI	BB	HBP	SH	SF	SO	SB	CS	SLG	OBP
Bautista, Jose	R-R	6-0	190	10-19-80	.235	.283	.216	117	400	58	94	20	3	16	51	46	16	3	4	110	2	4	.420	.335
Bay, Jason	R-R	6-2	205	9-20-78	.286	.304	.280	159	570	101	163	29	3	35	109	102	8	0	9	156	11	2	.532	.396
Burnitz, Jeromy	L-R	6-0	210	4-15-69	.230	.224	.231	111	313	35	72	12	0	16	49	22	5	0	2	74	1	1	.422	.289
Casey, Sean	L-R	6-4	235	7-2-74	.296	.304	.292	59	213	30	63	15	0	3	29	23	6	0	2	22	0	0	.408	.377
Castillo, Jose	R-R	6-0	210	3-19-81	.253	.259	.251	148	518	54	131	25	0	14	65	32	5	1	6	98	6	4	.382	.299
Cota, Humberto	R-R	5-11	215	2-7-79	.190	.125	.211	38	100	5	19	1	0	0	5	8	0	1	1	26	0	0	.200	.248
Davis, Rajai	R-R	5-11	195	10-19-80	.143	.000	.167	20	14	1	2	1	0	0	0	2	0	1	0	3	1	3	.214	.250
de Caster, Yurendell	R-R	6-1	205	9-26-79	.000	—	.000	3	2	0	0	0	0	0	0	0	0	0	0	2	0	0	.000	.000
Doumit, Ryan	B-R	6-1	215	4-3-81	.208	.208	.208	61	149	15	31	9	0	6	17	15	11	1	2	42	0	0	.389	.322
Duffy, Chris	L-L	5-9	190	4-20-80	.255	.229	.264	84	314	46	80	14	3	2	18	19	10	4	1	71	26	1	.338	.317
Edwards, Mike	R-R	6-1	200	11-24-76	.188	.000	.214	14	16	1	3	0	0	0	1	0	1	0	0	5	0	0	.188	.235
Hernandez, Jose	R-R	6-1	190	7-14-69	.267	.333	.222	67	120	8	32	2	1	2	12	11	0	1	0	29	0	0	.350	.328
2-team (18 Philadelphia)					.263	—		85	152	12	40	4	1	3	19	12	0	2	0	40	0	0	.362	.317
Maldonado, Carlos	R-R	6-1	245	1-3-79	.105	—	.105	8	19	0	2	0	0	0	0	1	0	0	0	10	1	0	.105	.150
McLouth, Nate	L-R	5-11	185	10-28-81	.233	.260	.227	106	270	50	63	16	2	7	16	18	5	3	1	59	10	1	.385	.293
Nady, Xavier	R-R	6-2	205	11-14-78	.300	.395	.279	55	203	20	61	13	0	3	23	11	5	1	0	34	1	2	.409	.352
2-team (75 New York)					.280	—		130	468	57	131	28	1	17	63	30	11	2	1	85	3	3	.453	.337
Paulino, Ronny	R-R	6-2	240	4-21-81	.310	.339	.300	129	442	37	137	19	0	6	55	34	2	1	2	79	0	0	.394	.360
Randa, Joe	R-R	5-11	190	12-18-69	.267	.275	.263	89	206	23	55	13	0	4	28	16	0	2	3	26	0	0	.388	.316
Sanchez, Freddy	R-R	5-10	185	12-21-77	.344	.442	.316	157	582	85	200	53	2	6	85	31	7	3	9	52	3	2	.473	.378
Wilson, Jack	R-R	6-0	185	12-29-77	.273	.301	.262	142	543	70	148	27	1	8	35	33	4	9	5	65	4	3	.370	.316
Wilson, Craig	R-R	6-2	220	11-30-76	.267	.307	.246	85	255	38	68	11	2	13	41	24	5	0	2	88	1	0	.478	.339

PITCHING	B-T	HT	WT	DOB	W	L	ERA	G	GS	CG	SV	IP	H	R	ER	HR	BB	SO	AVG	vLH	vRH	K/9	BB/9
Bayliss, Jonah	R-R	6-2	200	8-13-80	1	1	4.30	11	0	0	0	15	13	7	7	1	11	15	.241	.176	.270	9.20	6.75
Capps, Matt	R-R	6-2	240	9-3-83	9	1	3.79	85	0	0	1	81	81	37	34	12	12	56	.266	.250	.275	6.25	1.34
Chacon, Shawn	R-R	6-3	220	12-23-77	2	3	5.48	9	9	0	0	46	47	32	28	12	27	27	.272	.305	.242	5.28	5.28
Duke, Zach	L-L	6-2	220	4-19-83	10	15	4.47	34	34	2	0	215	255	116	107	17	68	117	.302	.264	.310	4.89	2.84
Gonzalez, Mike	R-L	6-2	220	5-23-78	3	4	2.17	54	0	0	24	54	42	13	13	1	31	64	.213	.163	.227	10.67	5.17
Gorzelanny, Tom	L-L	6-2	210	7-12-82	2	5	3.79	11	11	0	0	62	50	29	26	3	31	40	.226	.239	.223	5.84	4.52
Grabow, John	L-L	6-2	210	11-4-78	4	2	4.13	72	0	0	0	70	68	34	32	7	30	66	.260	.275	.251	8.53	3.88
Hernandez, Roberto	R-R	6-4	245	11-11-64	0	3	2.93	46	0	0	2	43	46	24	14	3	24	33	.264	.333	.216	6.91	5.02
2-team (22 New York)					0	3	3.11	68	0	0	2	63	61	32	22	5	32	48	—	—		6.79	4.52
Maholm, Paul	L-L	6-2	230	6-25-82	8	10	4.76	30	30	0	0	176	202	98	93	19	81	117	.295	.233	.313	5.98	4.14
Marte, Damaso	L-L	6-2	210	2-14-75	1	7	3.70	75	0	0	0	58	51	30	24	5	31	63	.244	.225	.258	9.72	4.78
McLeary, Marty	R-R	6-3	225	10-26-74	2	0	2.04	5	2	0	0	18	17	5	4	1	6	8	.258	.167	.333	4.08	3.06
Perez, Oliver	L-L	6-3	210	8-15-81	2	10	6.63	15	15	0	0	76	88	64	56	13	51	61	.296	.229	.309	7.22	6.04
2-team (7 New York)					3	13	6.55	22	22	1	0	112	129	90	82	20	68	102	—	—		8.15	5.43
Perez, Juan	R-L	6-0	170	9-3-78	0	1	8.10	7	0	0	0	3	5	3	3	1	1	3	.385	.240	.500	8.10	2.70
Reames, Britt	R-R	5-11	180	8-19-73	0	0	9.82	6	0	0	0	7	11	8	8	2	5	6	.355	.444	.318	7.36	6.14
Rogers, Brian	R-R	6-4	190	7-17-82	0	0	8.31	10	0	0	0	9	11	8	8	2	7	7	.324	.444	.280	7.27	2.08
Santos, Victor	R-R	6-2	205	10-2-76	5	9	5.70	25	19	0	0	115	150	80	73	16	42	81	.321	.264	.361	6.32	3.28
Sharpless, Josh	R-R	6-5	235	1-26-81	0	0	1.50	14	0	0	0	12	7	2	2	0	11	7	.175	.000	.219	5.25	8.25
Snell, Ian	R-R	5-11	190	10-30-81	14	11	4.74	32	32	0	0	186	198	104	98	29	74	169	.277	.305	.251	8.18	3.58
Torres, Salomon	R-R	5-11	210	3-11-72	3	6	3.28	94	0	0	12	93	98	42	34	6	38	72	.274	.281	.269	6.94	3.66
Vogelsong, Ryan	R-R	6-3	215	7-22-77	0	0	6.39	20	0	0	0	38	44	27	27	2	16	27	.301	.239	.330	6.39	3.79
Wells, Kip	R-R	6-3	205	4-21-77	1	5	6.69	7	7	0	0	36	46	27	27	3	18	16	.319	.373	.273	3.96	4.46
Youman, Shane	L-L	6-4	220	10-11-79	0	2	2.91	5	3	0	0	22	15	7	7	1	10	5	.200	.250	.186	2.08	4.15

FIELDING

Catcher	PCT	G	PO	A	E	DP	PB
Cota	1.000	33	179	16	0	1	5
Doumit	.987	11	66	12	1	0	2
Maldonado	.968	8	26	4	1	0	0
Paulino	.988	124	799	72	11	3	9

First Base	PCT	G	PO	A	E	DP
Casey	1.000	55	471	20	0	44
Doumit	.987	28	213	12	3	22
Hernandez	.991	18	97	11	1	15
Nady	.993	34	247	32	2	29
Randa	.986	15	69	4	1	5
Wilson	.997	43	346	19	1	42

Second Base	PCT	G	PO	A	E	DP
Bautista	1.000	3	9	9	0	3
Castillo	.975	145	344	350	18	106
Hernandez	1.000	3	1	6	0	1
Sanchez	1.000	23	39	41	0	15

Third Base	PCT	G	PO	A	E	DP
Bautista	.927	33	22	54	6	5
Edwards	1.000	3	2	3	0	0
Hernandez	1.000	4	0	7	0	0
Randa	.962	42	31	70	4	8
Sanchez	.981	99	59	243	6	24

Shortstop	PCT	G	PO	A	E	DP
Hernandez	1.000	9	12	25	0	6
Sanchez	.971	28	47	88	4	24
Wilson	.972	131	198	426	18	88

Outfield	PCT	G	PO	A	E	DP
Bautista	.988	85	154	8	2	1
Bay	.991	157	316	10	3	1
Burnitz	.984	84	120	1	2	0
Davis	.—	1	0	0	0	0
Duffy	.983	77	166	4	3	2
Hernandez	1.000	10	0	0	0	0
McLouth	.982	75	109	1	2	1
Nady	1.000	28	50	1	0	0
Wilson	1.000	30	37	2	0	0

Indianapolis Indians | Triple-A

International League

BATTING	B-T	HT	WT	DOB	AVG	vLH	vRH	G	AB	R	H	2B	3B	HR	RBI	BB	HBP	SH	SF	SO	SB	CS	SLG	OBP
Alfaro, Jason	R-R	5-9	210	11-29-77	.198	.216	.185	27	91	7	18	3	0	3	8	5	0	0	1	22	0	0	.330	.237
2-team (74 Buffalo)					.257	—		101	374	40	96	24	1	11	56	25	2	2	5	51	2	4	.414	.303
Bautista, Jose	R-R	6-0	190	10-19-80	.277	.333	.250	29	101	12	28	9	0	2	9	14	2	0	2	19	2	1	.426	.370
Boeve, Adam	R-R	6-2	216	6-20-80	.269	.308	.253	91	316	32	85	20	0	6	37	28	6	1	1	81	24	5	.389	.339
Buttler, Vic	L-L	6-4	178	8-12-80	.316	.474	.267	20	79	13	25	3	1	0	8	11	0	0	1	9	4	1	.380	.386
Chiaffredo, Paul	R-R	6-2	210	5-30-76	.124	.167	.103	51	129	8	16	6	0	1	8	6	1	4	0	45	1	1	.194	.169
Davis, Rajai	R-R	5-11	195	10-19-80	.283	.256	.296	100	385	53	109	17	1	2	21	27	3	2	0	59	45	13	.348	.335
Dawkins, Gookie	R-R	6-1	180	5-12-79	.266	.320	.234	67	203	22	54	13	1	4	26	13	1	1	1	55	3	6	.419	.312
de Caster, Yurendell	R-R	6-1	205	9-26-79	.273	.293	.265	119	421	47	115	22	3	11	51	35	2	1	3	100	7	7	.418	.330

General manager: David Littlefield. **Farm director:** Brian Graham. **Scouting director:** Ed Creech.

Class	Team	League	W	L	PCT	Finish*	Manager	Affiliate Since
Majors	Pittsburgh	National	67	95	.414	15 (16)	Jim Tracy	—
Triple-A	Indianapolis Indians	International	76	66	.535	4th (14)	Trent Jewett	2005
Double-A	Altoona Curve	Eastern	75	64	.540	3rd (12)	Tim Leiper	1999
High A	Lynchburg Hillcats	Carolina	63	75	.457	7th (8)	Gary Green	1995
Low A	Hickory Crawdads	South Atlantic	67	70	.489	10th (16)	Jeff Branson	1999
Short-season	Williamsport Crosscutters	New York-Penn	28	47	.373	13th (14)	Tom Prince	1999
Rookie	GCL Pirates	Gulf Coast	27	26	.509	6th (13)	Turner Ward	1967
OVERALL 2006 MINOR LEAGUE RECORD			336	348	.491	19th (30)		

*Finish in overall standings (No. of teams in league). +League champion

	B-T	HT	WT	DOB	AVG	vLH	vRH	G	AB	R	H	2B	3B	HR	RBI	BB	HBP	SH	SF	SO	SB	CS	SLG	OBP
Doumit, Ryan	B-R	6-1	215	4-3-81	.318	.750	.222	6	22	3	7	1	1	0	7	2	0	0	0	4	0	0	.455	.375
Duffy, Chris	L-L	5-9	190	4-20-80	.349	.281	.378	26	106	18	37	7	2	2	19	10	2	0	0	13	13	3	.509	.415
Edwards, Mike	R-R	6-1	200	11-24-76	.258	.277	.250	92	325	40	84	21	3	3	29	27	4	0	3	48	5	4	.369	.320
Eldred, Brad	R-R	6-5	275	7-12-80	.226	.087	.308	18	62	10	14	7	0	3	10	8	0	0	1	18	1	1	.484	.310
Elliott, Justin	R-R	5-11	195	4-27-82	.333	.000	.500	3	3	0	1	0	0	0	0	0	0	0	0	1	0	0	.333	.333
Furmaniak, J.J.	R-R	5-11	185	7-31-79	.213	.229	.206	114	371	43	79	12	3	6	27	25	2	4	1	85	15	5	.310	.266
Gonzalez, Raul	R-R	5-9	190	12-27-73	.263	.321	.232	112	399	49	105	23	2	7	56	54	2	0	3	59	4	5	.383	.352
Lee, Taber	B-R	6-1	185	10-18-80	.218	.243	.207	44	124	16	27	6	0	2	11	5	4	1	0	23	5	1	.315	.271
Maldonado, Carlos	R-R	6-1	245	1-3-79	.283	.330	.264	103	336	37	95	18	0	6	47	36	3	5	4	67	2	0	.390	.354
Paulino, Ronny	R-R	6-2	240	4-21-81	.241	.231	.250	8	29	2	7	3	0	0	3	0	0	0	8	1	0		.345	.313
Richard, Chris	L-L	6-2	210	6-7-74	.243	.227	.247	106	337	53	82	16	4	17	67	58	5	0	4	81	6	5	.466	.359
Sadler, Ray	R-R	6-1	200	9-19-80	.186	.275	.141	36	118	12	22	4	0	2	6	13	0	0	1	39	5	3	.271	.265
Stansberry, Craig	R-R	5-11	185	3-8-82	.223	.167	.242	60	197	30	44	10	2	3	25	35	2	3	1	35	10	3	.340	.345
Thompson, Rich	L-R	6-1	185	4-23-79	.280	.143	.324	80	232	43	65	12	6	2	22	31	12	11	1	39	16	8	.409	.391
Truby, Chris	R-R	6-2	220	12-9-73	.222	.242	.212	60	203	21	45	12	1	5	25	20	2	2	2	48	8	1	.365	.295

PITCHING	B-T	HT	WT	DOB	W	L	ERA	G	GS	CG	SV	IP	H	R	ER	HR	BB	SO	AVG	vLH	vRH	K/9	BB/9
Adams, Terry	R-R	6-2	235	3-6-73	5	3	4.26	48	0	0	1	63	66	33	30	7	22	43	.263	.296	.242	6.11	3.13
Bayliss, Jonah	R-R	6-2	200	8-13-80	3	3	2.17	46	0	0	23	58	37	15	14	4	28	67	.181	.160	.194	10.40	4.34
Burnett, Sean	L-L	6-1	190	9-17-82	8	11	5.16	25	24	0	0	120	136	74	69	13	46	46	.291	.196	.315	3.44	3.44
Carrara, Giovanni	R-R	6-2	230	3-4-68	1	1	3.00	9	1	0	0	15	8	5	5	1	5	14	.170	.211	.143	8.40	3.00
Chavez, Jesse	R-R	6-1	160	8-21-83	2	1	4.24	12	0	0	0	17	18	9	8	0	9	15	.273	.286	.267	7.94	4.76
Chiavacci, Ron	R-R	6-0	240	9-5-77	4	4	4.71	17	6	1	0	50	57	28	26	5	17	34	.297	.346	.261	6.16	3.08
Connolly, Michael	L-L	6-0	197	6-2-82	1	2	6.32	4	4	0	0	26	20	12	11	1	6	11	.303	.474	.234	6.32	3.45
Duckworth, Brandon	R-R	6-1	215	1-23-76	8	3	2.42	12	12	0	0	74	67	23	20	8	23	57	.242	.209	.265	6.90	2.78
Ginter, Matt	R-R	6-1	220	12-24-77	2	5	5.50	9	8	0	1	52	59	37	32	10	8	36	.281	.317	.258	6.19	1.38
Gorzelanny, Tom	L-L	6-2	210	7-12-82	6	5	2.35	16	16	0	0	100	67	28	26	4	27	94	.194	.232	.182	8.49	2.44
Jacobsen, Landon	R-R	6-3	220	5-4-79	0	1	10.80	2	2	0	0	10	16	12	12	1	4	3	.364	.357	.367	2.70	3.60
Johnston, Mike	L-L	6-3	220	3-30-79	1	3	5.74	28	0	0	0	42	49	27	27	6	20	36	.306	.180	.364	7.65	4.25
McLeary, Marty	R-R	6-3	225	10-26-74	3	4	2.68	35	13	0	2	104	96	32	31	6	33	115	.242	.252	.238	9.95	2.86
Nitkowski, C.J.	L-L	6-3	210	3-9-73	5	1	2.97	58	1	0	4	61	57	20	20	6	28	57	.256	.327	.232	8.46	4.15
Perez, Oliver	L-L	6-3	210	8-15-81	1	3	5.63	6	6	0	0	32	28	21	20	6	11	34	.233	.133	.248	9.56	3.09
Perez, Juan	R-L	6-0	170	9-3-78	0	0	0.00	4	0	0	0	3	0	0	0	0	3	6	.136	.000	.200	7.71	3.86
Reames, Britt	R-R	5-11	180	8-19-73	4	2	2.80	14	11	0	0	64	62	22	20	3	14	43	.261	.222	.292	6.02	1.96
Roach, Jason	R-R	6-4	205	4-20-76	2	2	3.54	10	9	0	0	56	58	33	22	6	12	22	.261	.255	.266	3.54	1.93
Rodriguez, Nerio	R-R	6-1	220	3-4-71	1	2	4.72	9	8	0	0	48	44	25	25	7	11	38	.243	.234	.250	7.17	2.08
Rogers, Brian	R-R	6-4	190	7-17-82	1	1	1.08	7	0	0	1	8	2	1	1	1	1	8	.077	.000	.118	8.64	1.08
Santos, Victor	R-R	6-2	205	10-2-76	1	0	0.00	1	1	0	0	5	1	0	0	0	0	4	.067	.000	.083	0.00	0.00
Sharpless, Josh	R-R	6-5	235	1-26-81	1	1	2.45	23	0	0	1	33	32	11	9	1	15	30	.250	.255	.247	8.18	4.09
Strickland, Scott	R-R	5-10	215	4-26-76	5	2	2.09	53	0	0	5	73	63	17	17	4	15	70	.233	.224	.238	8.59	1.84
Van Benschoten, John	R-R	6-4	215	4-14-80	1	1	5.40	3	3	0	0	12	10	7	7	2	7	13	.233	.313	.185	10.03	5.40
Vogelsong, Ryan	R-R	6-3	215	7-22-77	4	5	2.66	11	10	1	0	68	54	23	20	5	12	43	.217	.200	.231	5.72	1.60
Whiteside, Matt	R-R	6-0	200	8-8-67	2	0	1.69	20	0	0	10	27	18	6	5	2	6	20	.186	.086	.242	6.75	2.03
Youman, Shane	L-L	6-4	220	10-11-79	4	0	4.04	8	7	0	0	42	42	20	19	2	10	19	.259	.200	.268	4.04	2.13

FIELDING

Catcher	PCT	G	PO	A	E	DP	PB
Chiaffredo	1.000	47	230	27	0	4	3
Doumit	1.000	5	27	2	0	0	1
Maldonado	.996	100	675	51	3	8	3
Paulino	1.000	7	64	3	0	0	0

First Base	PCT	G	PO	A	E	DP
de Caster	.994	37	304	16	2	29
Edwards	1.000	9	56	3	0	4
Eldred	.990	14	99	4	1	13
Richard	.994	95	798	49	5	71
Truby	.929	3	12	1	1	2

Second Base	PCT	G	PO	A	E	DP
Alfaro	.962	12	23	28	2	12
Bautista	1.000	1	1	0	0	0
Dawkins	.984	32	52	75	2	18

	PCT	G	PO	A	E	DP
de Caster	.949	18	33	42	4	8
Furmaniak	1.000	2	0	3	0	0
Lee	1.000	23	38	72	0	23
Stansberry	.978	57	90	137	5	32
Truby	1.000	7	15	24	0	5

Third Base	PCT	G	PO	A	E	DP
Alfaro	.962	12	7	18	1	0
Bautista	.983	23	16	41	1	5
de Caster	.897	55	26	104	15	11
Edwards	.969	26	14	48	2	4
Furmaniak	1.000	1	1	0	0	0
Randa	.889	2	0	8	1	0
Truby	.963	40	18	59	3	10

Shortstop	PCT	G	PO	A	E	DP
Dawkins	.971	21	22	46	2	11

	PCT	G	PO	A	E	DP
Furmaniak	.967	109	170	326	17	69
Lee	.927	14	17	21	3	6
Truby	.933	13	16	26	3	3

Outfield	PCT	G	PO	A	E	DP
Bautista	1.000	5	2	0	0	0
Boeve	.981	82	150	4	3	1
Buttler	1.000	20	46	0	0	0
Davis	.991	98	216	3	2	1
de Caster	1.000	12	11	0	0	0
Duffy	.970	24	64	0	2	0
Edwards	1.000	48	76	2	0	0
Gonzalez	.993	72	137	8	1	1
Sadler	1.000	33	58	0	0	0
Thompson	.993	70	131	4	1	0

Altoona Curve — Double-A

Eastern League

BATTING	B-T	HT	WT	DOB	AVG	vLH	vRH	G	AB	R	H	2B	3B	HR	RBI	BB	HBP	SH	SF	SO	SB	CS	SLG	OBP
Alvarez, Rafael	L-L	6-0	198	1-22-77	.250	.254	.249	78	244	31	61	6	4	4	26	23	1	0	3	71	0	0	.357	.314
Bixler, Brian	R-R	6-1	190	10-22-82	.301	.314	.295	60	226	36	68	13	1	3	19	16	7	2	2	57	6	2	.407	.363

Boeve, Adam	R-R	6-2	216	6-20-80	.333	.281	.349	38	138	26	46	7	2	3	24	18	2	0	4	35	3	2	.478	.407
Buttler, Vic	L-L	6-0	174	8-12-80	.292	.295	.290	109	411	52	120	20	14	5	51	33	3	2	5	53	21	3	.445	.345
Casey, Sean	L-R	6-4	235	7-2-74	.273	.000	.375	3	11	1	3	0	0	1	2	1	0	0	0	0	0	0	.545	.333
Chapman, Travis	R-R	6-2	180	6-5-78	.275	.111	.323	11	40	4	11	3	0	1	7	4	0	0	1	6	0	0	.425	.333
Chaves, Brandon	B-R	6-3	181	8-5-79	.228	.291	.202	120	377	41	86	15	3	5	52	50	11	7	7	76	9	1	.324	.330
Doumit, Ryan	B-R	6-1	215	4-3-81	.333	.200	.400	4	15	4	5	3	0	0	4	0	2	0	0	1	0	0	.533	.412
Guzman, Javier	B-R	6-0	170	5-4-82	.268	.344	.234	129	485	57	130	23	5	7	40	25	4	6	4	64	12	8	.379	.307
Lee, Taber	B-R	6-1	185	10-18-80	.216	.271	.167	46	102	9	22	3	2	1	5	5	1	1	1	29	3	0	.314	.257
Lytle, Chaz	L-L	6-1	190	10-27-80	.111	.000	.125	5	9	1	1	0	0	0	0	0	0	0	0	1	0	0	.111	.111
Maldonado, Carlos	R-R	6-1	245	1-3-79	.278	.167	.333	5	18	1	5	2	0	0	0	0	0	0	0	6	0	0	.389	.278
Martinez, Octavio	R-R	6-0	190	7-30-79	.259	.308	.236	24	81	9	21	2	0	0	8	3	4	0	1	11	1	1	.284	.315
McCutchen, Andrew	R-R	5-11	170	10-10-86	.308	.304	.309	20	78	12	24	4	0	3	12	8	1	0	0	20	1	1	.474	.379
Morgan, Nyjer	L-L	6-0	170	7-2-80	.306	.338	.291	56	219	39	67	6	5	1	10	15	3	7	0	28	21	11	.393	.359
Parrish, David	R-R	6-3	220	6-13-79	.292	.295	.290	72	240	28	70	15	1	4	32	29	1	0	5	38	0	0	.413	.364
Pond, Simon	L-R	6-1	190	10-27-76	.249	.247	.251	128	461	64	115	32	3	13	78	59	2	0	4	121	3	3	.416	.335
Reyes, Milver	R-R	5-11	200	9-3-82	.193	.205	.189	49	166	9	32	4	0	0	11	6	1	0	0	19	0	0	.217	.225
Roneberg, Brett	L-L	6-2	205	2-5-79	.303	.264	.321	109	400	63	121	19	1	10	74	51	1	0	5	58	9	1	.430	.379
Sadler, Ray	R-R	6-1	200	9-19-80	.234	.287	.207	86	282	38	66	9	5	15	46	34	3	0	5	88	5	3	.461	.318
Stansberry, Craig	R-R	5-11	185	3-8-82	.258	.231	.269	72	260	46	67	18	3	10	30	31	4	1	1	62	8	3	.465	.345
Thompson, Rich	L-R	6-1	185	4-23-79	.340	.467	.286	14	50	11	17	3	0	0	5	8	1	0	0	11	1	3	.400	.441
Ust, Brant	R-R	6-2	200	7-17-78	.199	.231	.184	55	166	14	33	3	0	4	17	13	2	0	2	38	0	1	.289	.262
Walker, Neil	B-R	6-2	215	9-10-85	.161	.500	.111	10	31	5	5	0	0	2	3	1	0	0	0	4	0	0	.355	.188

PITCHING	B-T	HT	WT	DOB	W	L	ERA	G	GS	CG	SV	IP	H	R	ER	HR	BB	SO	AVG	vLH	vRH	K/9	BB/9
Albaladejo, Jonathan	R-R	6-5	260	10-30-82	1	2	4.00	18	1	0	1	36	41	18	16	4	5	27	.295	.283	.304	6.75	1.25
Blackwell, Chad	R-R	6-1	145	1-7-83	0	0	7.50	4	0	0	0	6	8	5	5	0	2	6	.320	.571	.222	9.00	3.00
Borner, Brady	L-L	5-10	182	4-12-79	2	0	7.11	13	0	0	0	19	28	15	15	3	6	13	.337	.357	.327	6.16	2.84
Chiavacci, Ron	R-R	6-0	240	9-5-77	1	3	3.06	10	7	0	0	50	40	26	17	6	13	49	.213	.148	.262	8.82	2.34
Connolly, Michael	L-L	6-0	197	6-2-82	7	8	4.98	25	24	0	0	121	117	75	67	18	53	87	.253	.274	.246	6.47	3.94
Davidson, David	L-L	6-1	187	4-23-84	1	1	2.31	10	1	0	0	12	8	4	3	0	10	13	.186	.231	.167	10.03	7.71
Hernandez, Chris	R-R	6-0	204	8-3-80	5	3	3.65	42	0	0	2	67	58	31	27	3	21	71	.239	.216	.258	9.59	2.84
Jacobsen, Landon	R-R	6-3	220	5-4-79	14	9	3.21	26	25	1	0	154	144	64	55	8	55	80	.252	.259	.246	4.68	3.21
Johnson, James	B-L	6-0	175	8-7-76	0	0	6.62	11	0	0	0	18	20	13	13	3	12	15	.290	.167	.333	7.64	6.11
Knight, Brandon	L-R	6-0	195	10-1-75	2	7	2.25	51	0	0	27	64	51	19	16	6	20	86	.212	.214	.210	12.09	2.81
Lorenzo, Matt	L-R	6-3	205	6-21-82	0	1	15.00	1	1	0	0	3	4	5	5	0	4	1	.333	.200	.429	3.00	12.00
Moeves, Derrik	R-R	6-3	190	8-5-83	0	1	5.40	5	0	0	0	7	6	4	4	1	5	6	.231	.231	.231	8.10	6.75
Neal, Blaine	L-R	6-5	230	4-6-78	2	0	1.99	29	0	0	2	41	34	13	9	2	10	46	.218	.270	.171	10.18	2.21
Perez, Franklin	R-R	6-2	230	6-10-78	2	1	2.57	16	0	0	2	28	18	9	8	3	8	21	.182	.178	.185	6.75	2.57
Peterson, Matt	R-R	6-4	220	2-11-82	6	6	5.03	31	17	0	0	113	115	65	63	10	47	83	.271	.246	.293	6.63	3.75
Roach, Jason	R-R	6-4	205	4-20-76	6	7	3.65	17	17	0	0	94	99	47	38	11	27	50	.278	.236	.329	4.80	2.59
Rodriguez, Nerio	R-R	6-1	220	3-4-71	0	2	7.07	3	3	0	0	14	15	11	11	2	6	16	.273	.300	.240	10.29	3.86
Rogers, Brian	R-R	6-4	190	7-17-82	0	0	0.00	2	0	0	1	4	2	0	0	0	2	5	.167	.000	.250	11.25	4.50
2-team (37 Erie)					3	2	2.25	39	0	0	2	68	51	19	17	7	16	74	—	—	—	9.79	2.12
Rojas, Chris	R-R	6-2	180	3-30-77	0	1	4.91	3	3	0	0	11	13	8	6	0	6	10	.295	.294	.296	8.18	4.91
Sanchez, Romulo	R-R	6-6	208	4-28-84	0	0	5.00	8	0	0	0	9	8	5	5	1	8	5	.242	.222	.267	5.00	8.00
Sharpless, Josh	R-R	6-5	235	1-26-81	2	0	0.86	14	0	0	8	21	8	2	2	0	9	30	.114	.207	.049	12.86	3.86
Shortslef, Josh	R-L	6-4	230	2-1-82	6	2	4.45	12	12	0	0	61	62	33	30	4	13	50	.262	.188	.280	7.42	1.93
Starling, Wardell	R-R	6-4	205	3-14-83	6	5	2.80	15	15	1	0	87	81	36	27	6	27	42	.249	.228	.269	4.36	2.80
Van Benschoten, John	R-R	6-4	215	4-14-80	1	0	3.60	1	1	0	0	5	3	2	2	0	3	3	.176	.222	.125	5.40	5.40
Vasquez, Jorge	R-R	6-1	175	7-16-78	3	3	2.22	47	0	0	5	65	45	21	16	2	28	87	.196	.271	.130	12.05	3.88
Wells, Kip	R-R	6-3	205	4-21-77	1	0	3.68	1	1	0	0	7	6	3	3	1	1	4	.231	.182	.267	4.91	1.23
Youman, Shane	L-L	6-4	220	10-11-79	7	2	1.51	23	11	0	1	95	70	27	16	4	20	64	.201	.181	.208	6.04	1.89

FIELDING

Catcher	PCT	G	PO	A	E	DP	PB
Doumit	1.000	2	9	1	0	0	0
Maldonado	1.000	5	46	6	0	0	0
Martinez	.983	23	158	20	3	0	1
Parrish	.985	60	409	48	7	4	3
Reyes	.980	48	318	29	7	3	2
Walker	1.000	5	25	5	0	0	1

First Base	PCT	G	PO	A	E	DP
Casey	1.000	2	9	0	0	1
Chapman	1.000	1	8	2	0	1
Doumit	1.000	1	5	0	0	0
Lee	1.000	2	15	1	0	2
Pond	.995	107	879	87	5	82
Roneberg	1.000	30	223	13	0	18
Ust	1.000	3	26	3	0	5

Second Base	PCT	G	PO	A	E	DP
Chaves	1.000	3	6	10	0	2
Guzman	.944	56	88	146	14	32
Lee	.968	15	31	29	2	7
Stansberry	.978	70	143	206	8	45

Third Base	PCT	G	PO	A	E	DP
Chapman	.933	10	4	24	2	2
Chaves	.926	90	44	168	17	15
Lee	1.000	2	0	1	0	1
Pond	.870	10	3	17	3	1
Ust	.930	39	15	78	7	6

Shortstop	PCT	G	PO	A	E	DP
Bixler	.949	58	90	152	13	31
Chaves	.968	11	9	21	1	3
Guzman	.939	70	115	175	19	35
Lee	.962	7	7	18	1	5

Outfield	PCT	G	PO	A	E	DP
Alvarez	.952	49	76	3	4	0
Boeve	.973	37	70	1	2	0
Buttler	.992	109	251	6	2	2
Chaves	1.000	16	34	2	0	0
Lee	1.000	1	1	0	0	0
Lytle	1.000	3	10	0	0	0
McCutchen	1.000	19	39	1	0	1
Morgan	.967	54	116	2	4	0
Pond	1.000	7	7	0	0	0
Roneberg	.988	41	79	1	1	0
Sadler	.987	84	144	11	2	1
Thompson	1.000	14	34	0	0	0
Ust	1.000	2	1	0	0	0

Lynchburg Hillcats — High Class A

Carolina League

BATTING	B-T	HT	WT	DOB	AVG	vLH	vRH	G	AB	R	H	2B	3B	HR	RBI	BB	HBP	SH	SF	SO	SB	CS	SLG	OBP
Bixler, Brian	R-R	6-1	190	10-22-82	.303	.307	.302	73	267	46	81	16	2	5	33	35	9	6	0	58	18	7	.434	.402
Carlin, Michael	R-R	6-0	205	7-6-81	.274	.341	.244	116	423	70	116	23	6	13	74	51	9	2	10	78	11	4	.449	.357
Correll, Brad	R-R	6-2	205	6-17-81	.254	.266	.248	86	315	42	80	21	2	6	38	24	0	0	2	45	2	3	.390	.305
Harris, Justin	R-R	6-0	169	5-25-81	.242	.299	.217	87	285	32	69	10	1	2	22	11	4	4	0	30	6	1	.305	.280
Jones, Christopher	R-R	6-0	205	2-27-83	.237	.308	.200	13	38	5	9	4	0	0	0	2	1	2	0	10	0	0	.342	.293
Lillibridge, Brent	R-R	5-11	180	9-18-83	.313	.327	.308	54	201	47	63	10	3	2	28	36	5	8	2	43	24	5	.423	.426
Lytle, Chaz	L-L	6-1	190	10-27-80	.167	.077	.217	14	36	2	6	0	0	0	2	1	0	0	0	4	2	1	.167	.189
Martinez, Octavio	R-R	6-0	190	7-30-79	.383	.385	.382	12	47	5	18	4	0	0	8	1	2	0	1	3	0	1	.468	.412
Meath, Matt	B-R	6-0	175	10-6-79	.232	.333	.196	41	69	14	16	3	1	0	9	14	0	1	0	22	3	2	.304	.361
Morgan, Nyjer	L-L	6-0	170	7-2-80	.303	.286	.314	61	228	43	69	7	3	0	22	20	15	7	4	40	38	11	.360	.390
Munoz, David	B-R	6-2	177	12-28-84	.000	.000	.000	1	3	0	0	0	0	0	1	1	0	0	0	0	0	0	.000	.250
Nino, Denny	R-R	6-1	211	6-4-83	.273	.333	.263	6	22	4	6	3	0	0	3	0	0	0	1	8	0	0	.409	.261

BASEBALL AMERICA 2007 ALMANAC • 207

	B-T	HT	WT	DOB	AVG	vLH	vRH	G	AB	R	H	2B	3B	HR	RBI	BB	HBP	SH	SF	SO	SB	CS	SLG	OBP
Pearce, Steven	R-R	5-11	200	4-13-83	.265	.266	.265	90	328	48	87	27	1	14	60	34	10	1	4	65	7	5	.482	.348
Powell, Pedro	B-R	5-7	143	5-20-84	.263	.301	.245	131	434	64	114	4	2	0	36	43	2	17	2	87	63	16	.281	.331
Rea, Brad	R-R	6-4	220	7-29-79	.254	.219	.271	54	193	22	49	15	0	2	27	26	0	0	0	46	1	0	.363	.342
Reyes, Milver	R-R	5-11	200	9-3-82	.273	.200	.333	4	11	0	3	0	0	0	1	0	0	0	0	0	0	0	.273	.273
Rooi, Vince	R-R	6-1	190	12-13-81	.247	.236	.252	111	381	43	94	15	1	8	46	52	5	4	2	83	4	8	.354	.343
Schwartzbauer, Daniel	R-R	5-11	175	11-2-81	.259	.256	.260	105	359	44	93	20	1	2	55	30	4	13	6	66	8	4	.337	.318
Sucre, Antonio	R-R	6-2	180	8-13-83	.223	.185	.241	58	202	30	45	18	1	6	25	12	2	0	1	71	2	1	.411	.272
Suomi, John	L-R	5-11	199	10-5-80	.260	.289	.247	81	246	30	64	19	1	3	34	25	5	2	4	43	0	1	.382	.336
Tejeda, Juan	R-R	6-2	195	1-26-82	.270	.276	.268	53	185	28	50	11	1	6	28	28	2	0	2	29	2	2	.438	.369
Ust, Brant	R-R	6-2	200	7-17-78	.167	.250	.143	7	18	1	3	1	0	0	1	4	2	1	0	9	0	0	.222	.375
Walker, Neil	B-R	6-2	215	9-10-85	.284	.220	.313	72	264	32	75	22	1	3	35	19	6	4	1	41	3	5	.409	.345

PITCHING	B-T	HT	WT	DOB	W	L	ERA	G	GS	CG	SV	IP	H	R	ER	HR	BB	SO	AVG	vLH	vRH	K/9	BB/9
Antelo, Derek	R-R	6-1	205	11-30-82	0	0	4.91	1	0	0	0	4	3	2	2	1	2	2	.273	.429	.000	4.91	4.91
Bishop, Matthew	R-R	6-2	215	6-5-82	0	0	6.89	21	0	0	1	33	39	29	25	3	17	25	.291	.263	.312	6.89	4.68
Blackwell, Chad	R-R	6-1	145	1-7-83	2	7	5.35	19	0	0	1	35	43	25	21	1	18	27	.307	.377	.253	6.88	4.58
Bloom, Kyle	R-L	6-3	185	2-21-83	7	8	4.30	25	25	0	0	128	122	63	61	15	61	108	.261	.241	.267	7.61	4.30
Craig, Dustin	R-R	6-4	240	4-9-82	2	4	3.69	20	9	0	0	61	52	34	25	6	37	52	.232	.290	.179	7.67	5.46
Davidson, David	L-L	6-1	187	4-23-84	0	0	2.16	5	0	0	0	8	6	2	2	0	2	11	.194	.214	.176	11.88	2.16
Drage, Derek	R-R	6-3	215	12-10-81	3	2	5.52	17	1	0	1	31	35	20	19	2	9	22	.292	.346	.250	6.39	2.61
Duguay, Steven	R-R	6-1	200	10-29-82	8	3	3.38	44	0	0	15	59	45	22	22	4	19	55	.208	.253	.171	8.44	2.91
Garcia, Felipe	R-R	5-11	165	9-20-82	2	1	3.52	15	0	0	1	38	28	17	15	0	17	31	.203	.204	.202	7.28	3.99
Guillory, Matt	R-R	6-4	175	3-13-83	5	5	6.83	20	8	0	0	59	82	53	45	17	19	38	.333	.410	.277	5.76	2.88
Hamilton, Clayton	R-R	6-5	200	6-15-82	4	5	4.34	14	14	0	0	66	57	33	32	5	19	41	.228	.244	.214	5.56	2.58
Hankins, Derek	R-R	6-4	190	7-1-83	5	11	4.73	26	26	1	0	143	157	82	75	13	36	70	.284	.306	.269	4.42	2.27
Heisel, Ian	R-R	6-3	225	10-19-81	1	0	2.84	11	0	0	1	19	15	6	6	0	9	15	.224	.200	.243	7.11	4.26
Holliday, Brian	L-L	6-2	202	6-1-84	1	5	8.38	8	7	0	0	29	43	34	27	3	27	6	.374	.375	.374	1.86	8.38
Linares, Ramon	R-R	6-1	215	4-28-79	3	3	4.61	36	0	0	3	66	61	39	34	8	31	57	.248	.269	.232	7.73	4.21
Lorenzo, Matt	L-R	6-3	205	6-21-82	2	4	4.39	14	14	0	0	68	70	42	33	5	28	45	.276	.306	.256	5.99	3.72
Martin, Greg	L-L	6-1	190	4-10-80	0	2	4.96	27	1	0	0	45	49	27	25	2	23	44	.280	.196	.319	8.74	4.57
Moeves, Derrik	R-R	6-3	190	8-5-83	1	0	3.16	17	0	0	3	26	22	11	9	2	15	7	.232	.306	.186	2.45	5.26
Munoz, Luis	R-R	6-2	150	1-10-82	4	3	3.82	11	11	1	0	66	66	32	28	4	29	36	.261	.297	.230	4.91	3.95
Rodriguez, Nerio	R-R	6-1	220	3-4-71	2	2	5.09	4	4	0	0	23	31	14	13	2	6	14	.316	.293	.333	5.48	2.35
Sanchez, Romulo	R-R	6-6	208	4-28-84	0	0	1.04	8	0	0	1	9	7	1	1	0	4	6	.212	.214	.211	6.23	4.15
Starling, Wardell	R-R	6-4	205	3-14-83	4	4	3.18	13	13	1	0	74	53	35	26	3	17	45	.202	.202	.203	5.50	2.08
Torrealba, Yoann	R-R	5-11	187	6-24-82	6	6	4.01	43	3	0	3	101	102	49	45	5	35	56	.264	.253	.272	4.99	3.12
Valdez, Luis	R-R	6-2	180	5-5-84	0	0	14.73	1	1	0	0	4	7	6	6	0	5	1	.412	.444	.375	2.45	12.27
Wells, Kip	R-R	6-3	205	4-21-77	1	0	0.00	1	1	0	0	6	3	0	0	0	2	5	.158	.167	.154	7.50	3.00

FIELDING

Catcher	PCT	G	PO	A	E	DP	PB
Jones	1.000	13	70	13	0	0	1
Martinez	1.000	12	79	5	0	0	0
Nino	.970	6	27	5	1	0	1
Reyes	1.000	4	14	3	0	0	1
Suomi	.992	56	329	45	3	5	13
Walker	.991	54	303	40	3	4	4

First Base	PCT	G	PO	A	E	DP
Carlin	.991	47	410	26	4	29
Pearce	.987	87	708	57	10	76
Rea	.955	2	18	3	1	1
Tejeda	.966	5	26	2	1	2

Second Base	PCT	G	PO	A	E	DP
Harris	.974	53	90	132	6	26
Schwartzbauer	.980	90	200	251	9	60

Third Base	PCT	G	PO	A	E	DP
Carlin	.885	8	4	19	3	1
Harris	.929	20	14	25	3	3
Rooi	.950	108	73	215	15	20
Ust	1.000	6	3	8	0	1

Shortstop	PCT	G	PO	A	E	DP
Bixler	.962	72	110	216	13	33
Lillibridge	.957	54	90	155	11	38
Munoz	1.000	1	0	3	0	0
Schwartzbauer	.983	14	20	38	1	7

Outfield	PCT	G	PO	A	E	DP
Carlin	.987	59	145	3	2	2
Correll	.977	83	163	7	4	1
Harris	1.000	9	16	2	0	0
Lytle	1.000	14	19	1	0	0
Meath	.917	25	30	3	3	1
Morgan	.988	61	153	8	2	0
Powell	.984	130	296	16	5	3
Sucre	.991	55	105	6	1	2

Hickory Crawdads — Low Class A

South Atlantic League

BATTING	B-T	HT	WT	DOB	AVG	vLH	vRH	G	AB	R	H	2B	3B	HR	RBI	BB	HBP	SH	SF	SO	SB	CS	SLG	OBP
Blair, Cameron	R-R	5-11	175	10-27-82	.248	.216	.262	98	363	62	90	12	1	5	42	41	9	7	3	53	12	12	.328	.337
Boone, James	B-R	6-2	175	3-16-83	.192	.121	.227	28	99	11	19	3	0	0	3	13	3	0	1	30	3	0	.222	.302
Carlin, Michael	R-R	6-0	205	7-6-81	.359	.350	.364	16	64	12	23	8	1	2	10	3	1	0	1	15	0	1	.609	.391
Corley, Brad	R-R	6-2	198	12-28-83	.281	.221	.304	134	534	87	150	32	2	16	100	18	18	0	5	109	9	3	.438	.323
Delaney, Jason	R-R	6-3	215	11-9-82	.300	.312	.296	128	456	64	137	27	3	9	75	56	2	3	1	79	5	5	.432	.379
Ford, Shelby	B-R	6-3	190	12-15-84	.265	.317	.245	55	223	43	59	16	3	6	27	14	8	3	1	51	4	3	.444	.329
Hofius, Mike	L-L	6-2	210	5-3-82	.200	1.000	.000	3	5	0	1	0	0	0	0	1	0	0	0	2	0	0	.200	.333
Igsema, Victor	R-R	6-2	172	11-16-85	.250	—	.250	2	4	1	1	1	0	0	0	0	0	0	0	2	0	0	.500	.250
Jones, Christopher	R-R	6-0	205	2-27-83	.203	.129	.250	30	79	11	16	4	0	0	7	11	3	0	0	15	1	1	.253	.323
Lerud, Steven	L-R	6-1	210	10-13-84	.239	.275	.227	117	393	45	94	28	0	12	57	40	13	0	0	146	4	3	.402	.330
Lillibridge, Brent	R-R	5-11	180	9-18-83	.299	.392	.265	74	274	59	82	18	5	11	43	51	4	2	2	61	29	8	.522	.414
Macia, Wanell	L-L	5-11	180	7-20-82	.284	.161	.315	47	155	18	44	4	1	0	15	3	0	2	3	24	3	2	.323	.292
Mansolino, Anthony	R-R	6-0	190	9-28-82	.234	.252	.226	106	376	43	88	11	1	7	46	29	2	3	3	72	1	4	.324	.290
McCuistion, Mike	L-R	6-2	213	5-14-82	.259	.302	.240	74	278	45	72	7	1	8	46	37	6	0	2	50	8	2	.378	.356
McCutchen, Andrew	R-R	5-11	170	10-10-86	.291	.344	.271	114	453	77	132	20	4	14	62	42	5	0	3	91	22	7	.446	.356
Pearce, Steven	R-R	5-11	200	4-13-83	.288	.214	.314	41	160	35	46	13	1	12	38	15	4	0	0	32	1	3	.606	.363
Poni, Francis	R-R	6-0	223	8-1-83	.000	.000	.000	3	6	0	0	0	0	0	0	0	0	0	0	3	0	0	.000	.000
Prasch, Edward	L-R	6-0	180	1-25-86	.241	.192	.254	108	369	46	89	18	2	5	36	29	6	1	5	103	7	5	.341	.303
Reddinger, Brandon	R-R	6-2	210	8-16-82	.143	.214	.095	11	35	2	5	0	0	0	1	1	1	1	0	14	0	0	.143	.189
Santiago, John	R-R	6-1	157	12-26-84	.264	.313	.238	58	193	29	51	9	0	3	20	9	4	0	1	32	6	0	.358	.309
Solano, Euvi	R-R	6-0	167	4-28-82	.236	.231	.240	37	127	11	30	5	1	1	10	6	0	9	0	33	0	4	.315	.271
Stillwagon, Nicholas	R-R	6-0	190	11-21-82	.500	—	.500	1	2	1	1	1	0	0	1	0	0	0	0	1	0	0	1.000	.500

PITCHING	B-T	HT	WT	DOB	W	L	ERA	G	GS	CG	SV	IP	H	R	ER	HR	BB	SO	AVG	vLH	vRH	K/9	BB/9
Antelo, Derek	R-R	6-1	205	11-30-82	2	4	6.00	31	5	1	0	75	89	59	50	10	29	61	.299	.339	.273	7.32	3.48
Bauserman, Joseph	R-R	6-2	220	10-4-85	6	8	4.01	21	21	0	0	110	117	66	49	11	38	63	.267	.238	.285	5.15	3.11
Bishop, Matthew	R-R	6-2	215	6-5-82	0	0	0.00	1	0	0	0	2	0	0	0	0	1	2	.000	.000	.000	9.00	4.50
Craig, Dustin	R-R	6-4	240	4-9-82	1	2	4.19	11	5	0	1	39	39	21	18	3	14	26	.260	.259	.261	6.05	3.26
Crotta, Michael	R-R	6-6	210	9-24-84	1	2	10.38	4	4	0	0	17	36	20	20	1	2	7	.424	.357	.456	3.63	1.04
Cuffman, Jacob	R-R	6-4	200	3-3-85	0	3	6.75	29	0	0	0	44	52	46	33	5	26	35	.283	.310	.260	7.16	5.32

Davidson, David	L-L	6-1	187	4-23-84	2	1	1.93	27	0	0	0	56	39	18	12	2	21	72	.195	.127	.221	11.57	3.38
Drage, Derek	R-R	6-3	215	12-10-81	0	0	0.72	16	0	0	0	25	12	3	2	1	5	20	.145	.120	.155	7.20	1.80
Garavito, Jean	R-R	5-11	186	1-11-85	8	6	3.44	41	0	0	2	84	71	38	32	5	32	61	.226	.226	.226	6.56	3.44
Holliday, Brian	L-L	6-2	202	6-1-84	0	3	6.62	14	2	0	0	34	49	34	25	6	13	11	.325	.273	.346	2.91	3.44
Hughes, Jared	R-R	6-7	220	7-4-85	5	4	5.77	10	10	0	0	48	46	38	31	6	31	25	.250	.278	.232	4.66	5.77
Johnson, Blair	R-R	6-4	218	3-25-84	3	4	4.95	9	9	0	0	44	49	32	24	5	11	28	.278	.261	.295	5.77	2.27
Lincoln, Brad	L-R	5-11	180	5-25-85	1	2	6.75	4	4	0	0	16	25	15	12	2	6	10	.368	.423	.333	5.63	3.38
Lopez, Luis	R-R	6-1	145	7-22-85	0	0	6.75	1	1	0	0	4	5	3	3	0	2	1	.313	.167	.400	2.25	4.50
Moeves, Derrik	R-R	6-3	190	8-5-83	1	2	1.47	13	0	0	0	18	11	4	3	1	6	22	.175	.304	.100	10.80	2.95
Munoz, Luis	R-R	6-2	150	1-10-82	6	2	3.28	16	14	0	0	85	82	39	31	5	20	55	.255	.310	.219	5.82	2.12
Pearson, Kyle	R-R	6-1	200	10-8-84	3	4	5.46	17	9	0	0	63	71	41	38	7	25	31	.286	.318	.262	4.45	3.59
Redmond, Todd	R-R	6-3	185	5-17-85	13	6	2.75	27	27	0	0	160	137	64	49	13	33	148	.227	.237	.220	8.31	1.85
Sanchez, Romulo	R-R	6-6	208	4-28-84	0	3	7.08	21	3	0	4	41	51	36	32	4	18	28	.302	.311	.296	6.20	3.98
Silva, Sergio	R-R	6-4	210	12-22-81	0	0	11.57	2	0	0	0	2	3	3	3	0	3	3	.300	.333	.250	11.57	11.57
Suero, Nicolas	R-R	6-2	160	12-10-84	0	0	14.40	2	1	0	0	5	9	8	8	2	3	2	.391	.500	.333	3.60	5.40
Swanson, Matt	R-R	6-8	240	10-17-82	4	4	4.61	48	0	0	11	53	57	33	27	4	27	43	.285	.321	.261	7.35	4.61
Vaclavik, Justin	R-R	6-1	185	5-27-84	4	2	3.16	47	0	0	18	51	44	22	18	6	21	59	.229	.289	.183	10.34	3.68
Valdez, Luis	R-R	6-2	180	5-5-84	7	8	4.28	22	22	2	0	122	131	73	58	20	26	71	.273	.274	.273	5.24	1.92

FIELDING

Catcher	PCT	G	PO	A	E	DP	PB
Jones	.985	29	181	17	3	0	7
Lerud	.982	97	566	81	12	8	35
McCuistion	.988	11	76	8	1	1	1
Poni	1.000	3	18	3	0	1	0
Reddinger	.927	8	44	7	4	1	2
Stillwagon	1.000	1	1	0	0	0	1

First Base	PCT	G	PO	A	E	DP
Carlin	.993	16	139	12	1	10
Hofius	1.000	1	1	1	0	0
Mansolino	.993	58	547	42	4	34
McCuistion	.961	24	204	17	9	14
Pearce	.986	39	397	35	6	34
Santiago	.778	1	7	0	2	1

Second Base	PCT	G	PO	A	E	DP
Blair	.956	50	98	163	12	32
Ford	.965	55	120	186	11	28
Lillibridge	1.000	1	0	3	0	0
Mansolino	.931	8	10	17	2	4
Santiago	.938	16	24	37	4	7
Solano	.913	16	30	43	7	10

Third Base	PCT	G	PO	A	E	DP
Mansolino	.854	20	11	30	7	3
Prasch	.892	105	56	199	31	8
Santiago	.957	16	9	36	2	1
Solano	1.000	1	1	0	0	0

Shortstop	PCT	G	PO	A	E	DP
Blair	.946	48	87	157	14	24
Lillibridge	.942	73	116	259	23	44
Santiago	.913	20	22	51	7	7

Outfield	PCT	G	PO	A	E	DP
Corley	.957	133	237	7	11	0
Delaney	.966	121	165	3	6	0
Igsema	1.000	1	2	0	0	0
Macia	.966	43	80	4	3	0
Mansolino	1.000	3	2	0	0	0
McCutchen	.977	114	246	6	6	2
Solano	1.000	6	11	2	0	0

Williamsport Crosscutters — Short-Season

New York-Penn League

BATTING	B-T	HT	WT	DOB	AVG	vLH	vRH	G	AB	R	H	2B	3B	HR	RBI	BB	HBP	SH	SF	SO	SB	CS	SLG	OBP
Barksdale, James	L-L	5-10	175	5-7-85	.209	.147	.226	50	158	18	33	2	0	0	9	6	0	1	2	32	8	5	.222	.235
Byler, Justin	R-R	6-1	190	8-12-85	.184	.000	.259	12	38	5	7	1	0	0	7	6	1	0	0	10	1	0	.211	.311
Clarkson, Matthew	L-R	6-3	200	2-24-84	.107	.071	.119	17	56	4	6	1	0	0	5	5	0	0	1	20	1	0	.125	.177
De Los Santos, Jose	R-R	5-11	160	2-17-85	.000	.000	.000	3	3	0	0	0	0	0	0	0	0	0	0	2	0	1	.000	.000
Durham, Miles	R-R	6-4	205	3-21-83	.201	.172	.214	58	189	8	38	7	3	2	15	7	3	2	2	49	4	4	.302	.239
Ford, Shelby	B-R	6-3	190	12-15-84	.400	.444	.375	7	25	3	10	3	0	0	2	3	1	0	0	3	1	0	.520	.483
Gonzalez, Angel	B-R	5-11	165	12-28-85	.274	.338	.253	65	259	31	71	12	1	0	11	14	1	5	1	43	15	10	.328	.313
Hicks, Joseph	R-R	5-11	187	4-22-84	.184	.286	.125	13	38	2	7	1	0	0	2	3	0	0	0	13	3	2	.211	.244
Johnson, A.J.	R-R	6-1	190	9-26-83	.162	.308	.083	11	37	4	6	0	0	0	2	4	0	0	0	9	0	1	.162	.244
Keel, Jared	R-R	6-1	190	8-3-84	.250	.241	.252	39	140	19	35	10	1	3	11	15	1	0	3	30	2	3	.400	.321
Laboy, Albert	R-R	6-0	175	12-1-86	.249	.240	.252	47	173	19	43	1	2	0	13	13	0	2	4	25	10	3	.277	.295
Munoz, David	B-R	6-2	177	12-28-84	.167	.250	.143	8	18	2	3	1	0	0	2	2	0	0	0	5	0	1	.222	.250
Negrych, Jim	L-R	5-10	180	3-2-85	.267	.289	.257	42	146	12	39	7	2	2	17	13	2	1	4	19	1	1	.384	.327
Peabody, John	R-R	6-4	215	8-24-85	.190	.200	.188	9	21	3	4	1	0	0	1	3	0	0	0	7	1	0	.238	.292
Peralta, Alexander	R-R	5-11	170	12-27-84	.238	.279	.217	50	181	19	43	7	3	1	19	13	1	0	5	32	2	0	.326	.285
Perez, Smelin	B-R	5-10	150	8-26-85	.133	.000	.182	10	30	3	4	1	0	0	1	4	1	1	0	6	1	1	.167	.257
Picart, Greg	B-R	5-11	175	9-25-85	.228	.208	.232	35	123	12	28	7	1	0	8	3	1	2	2	24	1	6	.301	.248
Poni, Francis	R-R	6-0	223	8-1-83	.275	.259	.281	31	91	11	25	6	0	2	7	9	4	1	1	28	2	1	.407	.362
Presley, Alexander	L-L	5-9	180	7-25-85	.260	.146	.291	61	223	26	58	7	8	3	23	17	1	1	2	55	3	3	.404	.313
Rios, Daniel	L-L	6-1	200	7-10-85	.231	.294	.222	41	143	14	33	5	1	1	13	11	1	0	3	34	0	1	.301	.285
Sakamoto, Kent	R-R	6-0	215	11-3-83	.228	.137	.270	47	162	15	37	12	1	3	23	10	3	0	3	48	0	1	.370	.281
Searage, Ryan	R-R	5-11	200	11-23-82	.111	.125	.100	17	54	2	6	1	0	0	3	1	0	0	0	22	0	1	.130	.127
Smith, Gregory	L-L	6-0	205	2-20-84	.121	.143	.115	12	33	4	4	1	0	0	1	3	1	0	0	7	1	0	.152	.216
Watts, Kris	L-R	6-1	200	7-15-84	.200	.103	.231	39	120	7	24	3	0	0	11	12	2	1	1	26	0	1	.225	.281

PITCHING	B-T	HT	WT	DOB	W	L	ERA	G	GS	CG	SV	IP	H	R	ER	HR	BB	SO	AVG	vLH	vRH	K/9	BB/9
Alvarez, Basilio	R-R	6-3	160	1-2-84	2	1	3.98	21	0	0	2	32	39	18	14	3	8	26	.305	.327	.291	7.39	2.27
Astacio, Olivo	R-R	6-5	190	7-28-84	2	3	3.49	22	0	0	9	28	16	12	11	0	15	39	.162	.167	.159	12.39	4.76
Benoit, Charles	L-L	6-2	210	9-24-84	1	3	4.97	14	5	0	1	38	35	24	21	2	21	33	.250	.237	.255	7.82	4.97
Bresnahan, Pat	R-R	6-1	195	4-23-85	4	5	2.25	15	10	0	0	68	50	21	17	3	17	59	.201	.202	.200	7.81	2.25
Cabrera, Henry	R-R	6-4	190	12-17-83	6	3	3.99	15	8	0	1	59	50	29	26	6	17	59	.230	.183	.259	9.05	2.61
Clapp, Bradley	R-R	6-4	215	5-19-86	1	3	5.33	6	6	0	0	27	31	18	16	2	12	20	.290	.244	.318	6.67	4.00
Crotta, Michael	R-R	6-6	210	9-24-84	1	3	2.68	11	7	0	0	44	43	14	13	1	4	28	.262	.262	.263	5.77	0.82
Cuffman, Jacob	R-R	6-4	200	3-3-85	0	1	2.92	6	0	0	0	12	11	5	4	1	4	14	.234	.133	.281	10.22	2.92
Felix, Mike	L-L	5-11	190	8-13-85	1	6	3.56	13	13	0	0	48	41	24	19	3	33	49	.236	.379	.207	9.19	6.19
Heisel, Ian	R-R	6-3	225	10-19-81	1	1	0.47	13	0	0	2	19	10	1	1	0	3	30	.149	.250	.106	13.97	1.40
Herman, Jason	R-R	6-3	210	12-9-81	0	2	2.00	15	0	0	0	27	20	11	6	1	5	24	.204	.171	.222	8.00	1.67
Hughes, Jared	R-R	6-7	220	7-4-85	1	2	2.74	5	5	0	0	23	14	7	7	2	7	11	.179	.120	.208	4.30	2.74
Krebs, Eric	R-R	6-3	185	5-16-85	0	1	3.49	7	7	0	0	28	25	11	11	0	14	31	.234	.283	.197	9.85	4.45
MacFarland, Steven	R-R	6-2	185	11-17-85	1	2	3.04	13	1	0	0	24	16	9	8	0	19	23	.190	.156	.212	8.75	7.23
Martinez, Yoffri	R-R	6-3	170	12-3-85	0	0	0.00	2	0	0	0	2	0	0	0	0	3	2	.000	.000	.000	9.00	13.50
Molleken, Dustin	L-R	6-4	228	8-21-84	1	2	2.51	13	0	0	0	32	30	11	9	1	8	22	.248	.214	.266	6.12	2.23
Pearson, Kyle	R-R	6-1	200	10-8-84	3	4	3.92	11	11	1	0	57	61	29	25	2	24	39	.282	.322	.256	6.12	3.77
Pluta III, Anthony	R-R	6-2	225	10-28-82	0	0	21.60	3	0	0	0	2	0	5	4	0	6	5	.000	.000	.000	27.00	32.40
Rodriguez, Dionis	R-R	6-2	181	2-8-86	0	1	5.19	2	1	0	0	9	13	6	5	1	2	5	.351	.353	.350	5.19	2.08
Silva, Sergio	R-R	6-4	210	12-22-81	1	0	0.00	9	0	0	3	12	2	0	0	0	3	19	.051	.059	.045	13.86	2.19
Suero, Nicolas	R-R	6-2	160	12-10-84	2	4	2.61	13	1	0	0	48	45	19	14	0	2	30	.249	.231	.259	5.59	0.37
Williams, Brandon	R-R	6-6	230	9-6-84	0	0	2.92	3	0	0	0	12	13	5	4	1	1	7	.265	.167	.360	5.11	0.73

FIELDING

Catcher	PCT	G	PO	A	E	DP	PB
Clarkson	.993	17	138	14	1	2	3
Johnson	.978	10	73	14	2	0	4
Poni	1.000	16	100	13	0	2	5
Watts	.993	37	258	40	2	4	6

First Base	PCT	G	PO	A	E	DP
Peabody	.971	9	62	5	2	3
Poni	1.000	2	28	3	0	3
Rios	.985	31	236	26	4	21
Sakamoto	.978	37	333	30	8	38

Second Base	PCT	G	PO	A	E	DP
Ford	1.000	5	8	11	0	4

Munoz	1.000	1	3	0	0	1
Negrych	.975	33	70	85	4	22
Peralta	.987	16	33	44	1	10
Perez	.920	7	10	13	2	1
Picart	.984	15	21	39	1	9

Third Base	PCT	G	PO	A	E	DP
Gonzalez	1.000	1	2	0	0	0
Keel	.899	35	35	54	10	5
Munoz	.800	1	1	3	1	0
Peralta	.916	30	23	75	9	8
Picart	.885	9	5	18	3	3

Shortstop	PCT	G	PO	A	E	DP
De Los Santos	1.000	2	0	4	0	0

Gonzalez	.921	63	95	196	25	30
Perez	1.000	3	2	6	0	2
Picart	.947	10	10	26	2	7

Outfield	PCT	G	PO	A	E	DP
Barksdale	1.000	43	69	2	0	2
Byler	.750	2	3	0	1	0
Durham	1.000	55	69	5	0	0
Hicks	.950	9	19	0	1	0
Laboy	1.000	46	74	7	0	2
Presley	.988	56	78	6	1	0
Searage	.964	16	26	1	1	0
Smith	1.000	9	10	0	0	0

GCL Pirates — Rookie

Gulf Coast League

BATTING

	B-T	HT	WT	DOB	AVG	vLH	vRH	G	AB	R	H	2B	3B	HR	RBI	BB	HBP	SH	SF	SO	SB	CS	SLG	OBP
Alvarez, Victor	B-R	5-11	185	6-17-83	.167	.111	.194	17	54	12	9	2	0	0	6	7	0	0	0	6	0	1	.204	.262
Byler, Justin	R-R	6-1	190	8-12-85	.306	.283	.317	34	147	22	45	13	1	5	28	9	5	0	3	24	5	0	.510	.360
Canal, Yonelvy	R-R	6-2	175	12-9-84	.200	.371	.133	39	125	14	25	6	1	2	12	10	1	3	1	47	2	2	.312	.263
Chapman, Travis	R-R	6-2	180	6-5-78	.143	.000	.214	7	21	1	3	1	0	0	5	3	1	0	0	2	0	0	.190	.280
Clarkson, Matthew	L-R	6-3	200	2-24-84	.358	.263	.387	25	81	6	29	4	0	1	13	5	4	0	1	10	0	1	.444	.418
De Los Santos, Jose	R-R	5-11	160	2-17-85	.277	.244	.289	44	159	29	44	6	0	0	11	13	3	5	1	22	18	5	.314	.341
Doumit, Ryan	B-R	6-1	215	4-3-81	.000	.000	.000	5	14	1	0	0	0	0	0	1	1	0	0	4	0	0	.000	.125
Gonzalez, Issael	R-R	5-11	175	8-16-86	.226	.176	.250	21	53	4	12	2	1	0	3	5	2	0	0	12	2	1	.302	.317
Hagan, Thomas	L-R	6-2	195	9-22-83	.268	.297	.253	38	112	18	30	3	1	1	7	17	6	1	0	18	6	2	.339	.393
Igsema, Victor	R-R	6-2	172	11-16-85	.286	.412	.242	39	133	17	38	7	1	5	26	13	4	1	1	34	5	2	.466	.364
Johnson, A.J.	R-R	6-1	190	9-26-83	.342	.364	.333	12	38	5	13	1	1	1	6	6	0	0	0	5	0	0	.500	.432
Keel, Jared	R-R	6-1	190	8-3-84	.432	.400	.441	21	74	15	32	6	1	2	13	7	1	0	2	10	5	1	.622	.476
Laboy, Albert	R-R	6-0	175	12-1-86	.267	.125	.305	19	75	10	20	3	2	1	9	6	0	1	1	14	4	4	.400	.317
McClune, Austin	R-R	6-2	175	11-15-87	.291	.333	.268	42	148	17	43	7	0	0	10	5	2	1	1	32	2	3	.338	.321
Mesa, Juan	R-R	6-1	190	4-8-85	.263	.350	.216	20	57	6	15	2	1	0	7	3	3	0	0	16	0	1	.333	.333
Munoz, David	B-R	6-2	177	12-28-84	.188	.000	.231	6	16	2	3	1	0	0	0	5	0	1	0	2	0	1	.250	.381
Perez, Smelin	B-R	5-10	150	8-26-85	.295	.304	.289	47	190	27	56	8	3	1	13	12	1	2	1	23	13	5	.384	.338
Rius, Daniel	L-L	6-1	200	7-10-85	.226	.133	.263	17	53	10	12	3	0	0	8	6	0	1	0	10	0	1	.283	.323
Roman, Willman	R-R	6-1	160	9-7-84	.167	.182	.158	20	60	4	10	3	0	0	2	2	0	0	1	14	0	1	.217	.215
Smith, Gregory	L-L	6-0	205	2-20-84	.226	.100	.286	11	31	2	7	2	0	0	2	4	0	1	1	5	1	0	.290	.306
Solano, Euvi	R-R	6-0	167	4-28-82	.244	.250	.240	13	45	2	11	1	0	1	8	1	0	0	0	7	0	0	.333	.261
Stillwagon, Nicholas	R-R	6-0	190	11-21-82	.265	.200	.310	16	49	7	13	1	0	2	6	5	0	1	0	10	0	0	.408	.333
Walk, John	R-R	6-2	220	9-12-82	.053	.000	.091	10	19	2	1	1	0	0	0	3	1	0	0	9	0	0	.105	.217
Wulf, Kent	B-R	5-11	175	4-26-85	.000	.000	.000	1	2	0	0	0	0	0	0	0	0	0	0	1	0	0	.000	.000

PITCHING

	B-T	HT	WT	DOB	W	L	ERA	G	GS	CG	SV	IP	H	R	ER	HR	BB	SO	AVG	vLH	vRH	K/9	BB/9
Albaladejo, Jonathan	R-R	6-5	260	10-30-82	1	0	2.92	3	2	0	0	12	12	4	4	1	3	16	.267	.083	.333	11.68	2.19
Alvarez, Eric	R-R	6-4	205	6-22-83	0	0	10.50	6	0	0	0	6	9	8	7	1	5	3	.333	.417	.267	4.50	7.50
Charry, Jorge	R-R	6-1	185	12-10-86	2	1	2.77	11	2	0	1	26	19	10	8	2	9	20	.204	.269	.226	6.92	3.12
Delossantos, Rafael	R-R	6-3	160	12-10-85	0	3	4.04	9	8	0	0	36	42	20	16	3	15	24	.307	.333	.308	6.06	3.79
Herbort, Ryan	R-R	6-2	200	3-13-86	0	2	3.80	14	0	0	0	21	20	14	9	0	8	16	.250	.172	.294	6.75	3.38
Holliday, Brian	L-L	6-2	202	6-1-84	0	0	0.00	2	2	0	0	6	3	0	0	0	2	5	.158	.250	.133	7.50	3.00
Johnson, Blair	R-R	6-4	218	3-25-84	0	1	1.17	2	2	0	0	8	5	2	1	0	1	8	.179	.111	.211	9.39	1.17
Krebs, Eric	R-R	6-3	185	5-16-85	0	1	5.27	4	4	0	0	14	18	8	8	0	3	15	.327	.500	.268	9.88	1.98
Lincoln, Brad	L-R	5-11	180	5-25-85	0	0	0.00	2	2	0	0	8	6	1	0	0	1	9	.222	.273	.188	10.57	1.17
Lopez, Luis	R-R	6-1	145	7-22-85	3	1	3.14	4	1	0	0	14	9	5	5	0	4	8	.173	.133	.189	5.02	2.51
Marte, Enmanuel	L-L	6-2	165	8-15-85	2	2	5.10	9	0	0	0	30	34	21	17	2	15	18	.291	.333	.283	5.40	4.50
Martinez, Yoffri	R-R	6-3	170	12-3-85	2	1	1.32	17	0	0	3	27	15	6	4	2	10	29	.156	.167	.150	9.55	3.29
Massey, Scott	R-R	6-2	185	8-16-83	0	0	2.70	2	0	0	0	7	8	2	2	0	2	3	.296	.375	.263	4.05	2.70
McCullen, Matthew	R-R	6-1	205	1-22-83	2	2	2.05	14	0	0	0	22	17	5	5	0	5	16	.210	.200	.214	6.55	2.05
McSwain, Matt	R-R	6-2	185	8-15-85	1	0	0.00	4	0	0	0	4	0	0	0	0	1	4	.000	.000	.000	9.00	2.25
Ortiz, Francisco	R-R	6-3	213	3-9-87	2	1	2.92	9	3	0	0	25	19	12	8	1	11	17	.211	.200	.218	6.20	4.01
Ridener, Eric	R-R	6-5	230	9-11-85	3	1	2.67	14	0	0	1	27	19	9	8	1	5	34	.196	.226	.190	11.33	1.67
Rodriguez, Dionis	R-R	6-2	181	2-8-86	3	3	2.36	11	9	0	0	46	43	18	12	0	12	41	.244	.183	.286	8.08	2.36
Shortslef, Josh	R-L	6-4	230	2-1-82	1	1	3.78	3	2	0	0	17	15	9	7	1	3	12	.246	.250	.244	6.48	1.62
Silva, Sergio	R-R	6-4	210	12-22-81	1	0	2.08	10	0	0	4	13	13	4	3	0	2	12	.271	.286	.265	8.31	1.38
Simon, Adam	R-R	5-10	170	1-26-84	0	0	4.50	15	0	0	4	18	25	11	9	1	4	18	.321	.258	.362	9.00	2.00
Van Benschoten, John	R-R	6-4	215	4-14-80	0	1	4.50	1	1	0	0	6	1	3	3	1	2	4	.053	.000	.077	6.00	3.00
Vasquez, Malvin	R-R	6-3	165	5-10-86	1	4	4.45	10	6	0	0	30	33	22	15	2	14	20	.268	.275	.265	5.93	4.15
Williams, Brandon	R-R	6-6	230	9-6-84	3	0	3.24	11	2	0	1	33	31	13	12	2	8	20	.252	.231	.262	5.40	2.16

FIELDING

Catcher	PCT	G	PO	A	E	DP	PB
Clarkson	.983	25	148	21	3	1	5
Doumit	.960	3	22	2	1	1	0
Johnson	.800	1	4	0	1	0	2
Roman	.977	10	74	11	2	1	4
Stillwagon	.990	16	86	11	1	0	6
Walk	.976	10	38	2	1	0	4

First Base	PCT	G	PO	A	E	DP
Byler	.947	3	17	1	1	2
Chapman	1.000	1	7	0	0	0
Doumit	1.000	1	9	0	0	1
Hagan	1.000	33	275	19	0	34
Rios	.969	16	111	13	4	4
Roman	1.000	3	14	1	0	0

Smith	1.000	4	18	1	0	3

Second Base	PCT	G	PO	A	E	DP
Alvarez	.938	3	9	6	1	2
Gonzalez	.981	11	21	30	1	3
McClune	—	1	0	0	0	0
Perez	.977	41	105	107	5	29

Third Base	PCT	G	PO	A	E	DP
Alvarez	.867	6	6	7	2	1
Chapman	.933	4	3	11	1	2
Gonzalez	.900	10	5	13	2	0
Keel	.943	20	17	33	3	5
Munoz	.923	6	2	10	1	0
Solano	.923	13	9	27	3	6

Shortstop	PCT	G	PO	A	E	DP
Alvarez	.929	7	6	20	2	4
De Los Santos	.931	42	55	135	14	24
Keel	.857	1	2	4	1	1
Perez	1.000	6	6	23	0	1

Outfield	PCT	G	PO	A	E	DP
Byler	.944	17	14	3	1	0
Canal	.961	34	49	0	2	0
Hagan	—	1	0	0	0	0
Igsema	.985	37	57	7	1	1
Laboy	1.000	18	35	1	0	0
McClune	.977	42	78	8	2	2
Mesa	.923	20	23	1	2	1
Smith	1.000	1	3	0	0	0
Wulf	1.000	1	3	0	0	0

ST. LOUIS CARDINALS

BY DERRICK GOOLD

The Cardinals had many descriptions pinned to them all summer as their fan base groped for ways to articulate an unfamiliar sense of angst. Team executives called the Cardinals "underachieving." They averted a late-September "nightmare finish," according to manager Tony La Russa. They were scuffling and splintered, bruised, bumbling and often mind-boggling.

But by the end of the season only one word stuck to the 2006 Cardinals: champions.

Led by a ragtag group of newcomers and rookie relievers and a title-hungry nucleus, the 83-win Cardinals did what their 105- and 100-win predecessors could not: deliver the franchise's 10th World Series championship.

Jeff Weaver, jettisoned from the Angels in July, aced the World Series-clinching Game Five with nine strikeouts against the Tigers. Scott Rolen, hitless and frustrated in the 2004 World Series, mashed a tone-setting home run and batted .421 in the 2006 Series. A .216 hitter in the regular season, Yadier Molina had more postseason hits than any player. And sparkplug shortstop David Eckstein seized the MVP award. He started the World Series 0-for-11 with an aching shoulder and finished with eight hits in his final 11 at-bats.

"It's been a unique season because we've had so many ups and downs," general manager Walt Jocketty said. "But this team continued to be resilient, bounce back and play well . . . It is very gratifying, based on the problems we had, the injures we had, everything that went into this season."

The Cardinals became the first team since the 1923 Yankees to christen a new ballpark with a title. The club's $365 million downtown stadium, also named Busch

ORGANIZATION **LEADERS**

BATTING		*Minimum 250 at-bats
*AVG	Garcia, Isaias, Johnson City	.339
R	Greene, Tyler, Palm Beach/Quad Cities	80
H	Roth, Randy, Quad Cities/Palm Beach	149
TB	Roth, Randy, Quad Cities/Palm Beach	248
2B	Roth, Randy, Quad Cities/Palm Beach	35
3B	Rasmus, Colby, Quad Cities/Palm Beach	8
HR	Evans, Terry, Palm Beach/Springfield/Arkansas	22
RBI	Rasmus, Colby, Quad Cities/Palm Beach	85
BB	Washington, Rico, Springfield/Memphis	77
SO	Greene, Tyler, Palm Beach/Quad Cities	155
SB	Greene, Tyler, Palm Beach/Quad Cities	33
*OBP	Garcia, Isaias, Johnson City	.395
*SLG	Garcia, Isaias, Johnson City	.510
	Shorey, Mark, Johnson City	.510
XBH	Roth, Randy, Quad Cities/Palm Beach	57

PITCHING		#Minimum 75 innings
W	Meacham, Cory, Quad Cities/Palm Beach	13
L	Tankersley, Dennis, Memphis	15
#ERA	Hearne, Trey, Quad Cities	2.25
G	Cavazos, Andy, Springfield/Memphis	67
CG	Herron, Tyler, Johnson City/State College	2
SV	Sillman, Mike, Palm Beach	35
IP	Webb, John, Memphis	200
BB	Parisi, Mike, Springfield	68
SO	Garcia, Jaime, Quad Cities/Palm Beach	131
#AVG	King, Blake, Johnson City	.167

PLAYERS OF THE YEAR

MAJOR LEAGUE: Albert Pujols, 1b

Chris Carpenter may have been one of the National League's top pitchers, but he still can't unseat Pujols as Cardinals player of the year. Sure, he led the Cardinals in nearly every offensive category, but amazingly, he also set personal bests with 49 home runs, 137 RBIs and a .671 slugging percentage.

MINOR LEAGUE: Colby Rasmus, of

PAUL GIERHART

The multi-dimensional Rasmus began in low Class A Quad Cities and hit his way to high Class A Palm Beach in July. The 20-year-old Rasmus led all Cardinals minor leaguers with 85 RBIs and was third with 28 stolen bases. He capped his year by ranking among the Top 10 Prospects in two minor leagues.

Stadium, debuted with a record April. The team won a franchise-best 17 games and Albert Pujols hit a record 14 home runs in April.

Then the Cardinals hit the skids. Starter Mark Mulder was essentially lost in June to a shoulder injury that required surgery. Closer Jason Isringhausen attempted to pitch through a degenerative hip condition, but surrendered to surgery in September. Jocketty, spackling his roster together, signed or traded for four players designated for assignment.

A seven-game losing streak at the end of the season had them chancing the biggest division-lead collapse in history. The Cardinals managed to win their sixth division title in seven years despite having only the 13th-best regular season record in the majors.

Rookie Adam Wainwright, cast as closer in Isringhausen's absence, was the postseason's breakout star. Starters Chris Carpenter, Jeff Suppan and Weaver were a combined 7-4, 2.58 in the playoffs. Suppan pitched the Cardinals to a National League Championship Series Game Seven win for the second time in three seasons.

Pitching also put luster on the Cardinals' minor league seasons. Righthander Blake Hawksworth reasserted his place as a premium prospect by going a combined 11-4, 2.92. Lefthander Jaime Garcia shined in his first professional season, going 10-8, 3.37 at two Class A stops. Reliever Josh Kinney surfaced from Triple-A Memphis' dismal summer with a 1.52 ERA in 71 innings and was a pivotal piece of the Cardinals' postseason bullpen.

Jeff Luhnow, who engineered the 2004 and '05 drafts, was given the reins of player development as well. His task is to shepherd a system that has lacked top prospects but did produce integral pieces of a title winner: Pujols, Molina, outfielder Chris Duncan (22 home runs), Anthony Reyes, Tyler Johnson and Kinney.

Kinney packed his car and was ready to drive away from baseball five years ago. The Cardinals persuaded him to keep climbing. He fit right in with the team's crew of castoffs, superstars, fallen stars, overachievers and rookies.

ORGANIZATION STATISTICS

St. Louis Cardinals — MLB

National League

BATTING	B-T	HT	WT	DOB	AVG	vLH	vRH	G	AB	R	H	2B	3B	HR	RBI	BB	HBP	SH	SF	SO	SB	CS	SLG	OBP
Belliard, Ronnie	R-R	5-8	195	4-7-75	.237	.157	.266	54	194	20	46	9	1	5	23	15	1	1	0	36	0	3	.371	.295
Bennett, Gary	R-R	6-0	210	4-17-72	.223	.400	.172	60	157	13	35	5	0	4	22	11	0	2	0	30	0	0	.331	.274
Bigbie, Larry	L-R	6-4	215	11-4-77	.240	.333	.227	17	25	2	6	1	0	0	1	3	0	0	0	9	0	0	.280	.321
Duncan, Chris	L-R	6-5	210	5-5-81	.293	.170	.318	90	280	60	82	11	3	22	43	30	2	0	2	69	0	0	.589	.363
Eckstein, David	R-R	5-7	165	1-20-75	.292	.280	.298	123	500	68	146	18	1	2	23	31	15	3	3	41	7	6	.344	.350
Edmonds, Jim	L-L	6-1	210	6-27-70	.257	.156	.295	110	350	52	90	18	0	19	70	53	0	0	5	101	4	0	.471	.350
Encarnacion, Juan	R-R	6-3	215	3-8-76	.278	.316	.261	153	557	74	155	25	5	19	79	30	4	1	6	86	6	5	.443	.317
Gall, John	R-R	6-0	195	4-2-78	.250	.333	.167	8	12	1	3	0	0	0	1	0	0	0	0	5	0	0	.250	.250
Luna, Hector	R-R	6-1	170	2-1-80	.291	.310	.271	76	223	27	65	14	1	4	21	21	1	0	0	34	5	3	.417	.355
Miles, Aaron	B-R	5-8	175	12-15-76	.263	.291	.256	135	426	48	112	20	5	2	30	38	2	2	3	42	2	1	.347	.324
Molina, Yadier	R-R	5-11	225	7-13-82	.216	.213	.217	129	417	29	90	26	0	6	49	26	8	2	8	41	1	2	.321	.274
Nelson, John	R-R	6-1	190	3-3-79	.000	—	.000	8	5	2	0	0	0	0	0	0	0	0	0	4	0	0	.000	.000
Perez, Timo	L-L	5-9	180	4-8-75	.194	.400	.154	23	31	3	6	1	0	1	3	3	1	0	0	4	0	0	.323	.286
Pujols, Albert	R-R	6-3	225	1-16-80	.331	.336	.329	143	535	119	177	33	1	49	137	92	4	0	3	50	7	2	.671	.431
Rodriguez, John	L-L	6-0	205	1-20-78	.301	.308	.300	102	183	31	55	12	3	2	19	21	3	1	4	45	0	0	.432	.374
Rolen, Scott	R-R	6-4	240	4-4-75	.296	.259	.310	142	521	94	154	48	1	22	95	56	9	0	8	69	7	4	.518	.369
Rose, Mike	B-R	6-1	215	8-25-76	.222	—	.286	10	9	2	2	0	0	0	0	1	0	0	0	2	0	0	.222	.222
Schumaker, Skip	L-R	5-10	175	2-3-80	.185	.000	.222	28	54	3	10	1	0	1	2	5	0	1	0	6	2	1	.259	.254
Spiezio, Scott	B-R	6-2	220	9-21-72	.272	.318	.251	119	276	44	75	15	4	13	52	37	5	1	2	66	1	0	.496	.366
Taguchi, So	R-R	5-10	165	7-2-69	.266	.280	.252	134	316	46	84	19	1	2	31	32	2	9	2	48	11	3	.351	.335
Vizcaino, Jose	B-R	6-1	190	3-26-68	.348	.000	.400	16	23	3	8	3	0	1	3	1	0	1	0	4	0	0	.609	.375
2-team (64 San Francisco)					.232	—		80	142	19	33	6	0	2	8	17	0	2	0	14	0	2	.317	.314
Wilson, Preston	R-R	6-2	215	7-19-74	.243	.250	.240	33	111	18	27	3	0	8	17	7	2	0	0	27	6	0	.486	.300
2-team (102 Houston)					.263	—	—	135	501	58	132	25	2	17	72	29	4	0	3	121	12	2	.423	.307

PITCHING	B-T	HT	WT	DOB	W	L	ERA	G	GS	CG	SV	IP	H	R	ER	HR	BB	SO	AVG	vLH	vRH	K/9	BB/9
Carpenter, Chris	R-R	6-6	230	4-27-75	15	8	3.09	32	32	5	0	222	194	81	76	21	43	184	.235	.266	.210	7.47	1.75
Falkenborg, Brian	R-R	6-6	225	1-18-78	0	1	2.84	5	0	0	0	6	5	2	2	0	0	5	.217	.250	.200	7.11	0.00
Flores, Randy	L-L	6-0	180	7-31-75	1	1	5.62	65	0	0	0	42	49	29	26	5	22	40	.290	.258	.329	8.64	4.75
Hancock, Josh	R-R	6-3	205	4-11-78	3	3	4.09	62	0	0	1	77	70	37	35	9	23	50	.241	.239	.241	5.84	2.69
Isringhausen, Jason	R-R	6-3	230	9-7-72	4	8	3.55	59	0	0	33	58	47	25	23	10	38	52	.222	.270	.187	8.02	5.86
Johnson, Tyler	B-L	6-2	180	6-7-81	2	4	4.95	56	0	0	0	36	33	21	20	5	23	37	.244	.221	.276	9.17	5.70
Kinney, Josh	R-R	6-1	195	3-31-79	0	0	3.24	21	0	0	0	25	17	9	9	3	8	22	.189	.162	.208	7.92	2.88
Looper, Braden	R-R	6-3	220	10-28-74	9	3	3.56	69	0	0	0	73	76	30	29	3	20	41	.277	.287	.272	5.03	2.45
Marquis, Jason	L-R	6-1	210	8-21-78	14	16	6.02	33	33	0	0	194	221	136	130	35	75	96	.289	.288	.291	4.45	3.47
Mulder, Mark	L-L	6-6	215	8-5-77	6	7	7.14	17	17	0	0	93	124	77	74	19	35	50	.327	.241	.351	4.82	3.38
Narveson, Chris	L-L	6-3	205	12-20-81	0	0	4.82	5	1	0	0	9	6	5	5	1	5	12	.176	.000	.214	11.57	4.82
Ponson, Sidney	R-R	6-1	250	11-2-76	4	4	5.24	14	13	0	0	69	82	42	40	7	29	33	.308	.298	.317	4.33	3.80
Reyes, Anthony	R-R	6-2	215	10-16-81	5	8	5.06	17	17	1	0	85	84	48	48	17	34	72	.262	.278	.249	7.59	3.59
Rincon, Ricardo	L-L	5-9	190	4-13-70	0	0	10.80	5	0	0	0	3	6	4	4	1	4	6	.375	.111	.714	16.20	10.80
Sosa, Jorge	R-R	6-2	175	4-28-77	0	1	5.28	19	0	0	1	31	33	18	18	10	8	17	.275	.325	.250	4.99	2.35
2-team (26 Atlanta)					3	11	5.42	45	13	0	4	118	138	79	71	30	40	75	—	—	—	5.72	3.05
Suppan, Jeff	R-R	6-2	220	1-2-75	12	7	4.12	32	32	0	0	190	207	100	87	21	69	104	.277	.302	.257	4.93	3.27
Thompson, Brad	R-R	6-1	190	1-31-82	1	2	3.34	43	1	0	0	57	58	23	21	4	20	32	.267	.284	.256	5.08	3.18
Wainwright, Adam	R-R	6-7	205	8-30-81	2	1	3.12	61	0	0	3	75	64	26	26	6	22	72	.230	.301	.182	8.64	2.64
Weaver, Jeff	R-R	6-5	200	8-22-76	5	4	5.18	15	15	0	0	83	99	49	48	16	26	53	.297	.357	.244	4.86	2.81

FIELDING

Catcher	PCT	G	PO	A	E	DP	PB
Bennett	.988	56	243	14	3	1	1
Molina	.995	127	734	78	4	6	7
Rose	1.000	4	10	0	0	0	0

First Base	PCT	G	PO	A	E	DP
Bennett	—	1	0	0	0	0
Duncan	1.000	11	54	3	0	6
Edmonds	1.000	6	43	2	0	5
Gall	—	1	0	0	0	0
Luna	1.000	6	25	1	0	3
Molina	.833	4	5	0	1	1
Nelson	1.000	1	1	0	0	0
Pujols	.996	143	1348	110	6	145
Spiezio	1.000	13	57	3	0	3
Vizcaino	1.000	1	1	0	0	0

Second Base	PCT	G	PO	A	E	DP
Belliard	.988	54	98	152	3	43
Luna	.976	41	69	94	4	22
Miles	.975	88	165	232	10	58
Spiezio	1.000	8	7	13	0	4
Taguchi	1.000	1	1	1	0	0
Vizcaino	1.000	2	0	1	0	0

Third Base	PCT	G	PO	A	E	DP
Luna	1.000	2	1	4	0	0
Miles	—	1	0	0	0	0
Rolen	.965	142	93	319	15	32
Spiezio	.932	38	10	45	4	4

Shortstop	PCT	G	PO	A	E	DP
Eckstein	.989	120	178	363	6	87
Luna	1.000	14	9	17	0	4

	PCT	G	PO	A	E	DP
Miles	.959	39	54	108	7	26
Nelson	1.000	1	1	1	0	0
Vizcaino	.905	7	9	10	2	3

Outfield	PCT	G	PO	A	E	DP
Bigbie	1.000	12	9	0	0	0
Duncan	.948	70	107	2	6	0
Edmonds	.987	99	223	4	3	0
Encarnacion	.978	148	265	4	6	0
Gall	1.000	2	2	0	0	0
Luna	.960	18	24	0	1	0
Perez	1.000	7	6	0	0	0
Rodriguez	.986	51	68	1	1	0
Schumaker	1.000	25	27	0	0	0
Spiezio	.972	35	34	1	1	0
Taguchi	.969	123	182	3	6	0
Wilson	.960	28	48	0	2	0

Memphis Redbirds — Triple-A

Pacific Coast League

BATTING	B-T	HT	WT	DOB	AVG	vLH	vRH	G	AB	R	H	2B	3B	HR	RBI	BB	HBP	SH	SF	SO	SB	CS	SLG	OBP
Bigbie, Larry	L-R	6-4	215	11-4-77	.143	.143	.143	11	35	4	5	0	0	0	2	7	0	0	0	14	0	1	.143	.286
Boyd, Shaun	R-R	5-11	188	8-15-81	.188	.250	.163	49	112	11	21	3	0	1	12	14	1	0	0	18	4	0	.241	.283
Conti, Jason	L-R	5-11	180	1-27-75	.267	.125	.282	38	86	10	23	3	0	1	7	7	0	1	1	19	1	0	.337	.319
Daubach, Brian	L-R	6-1	230	2-11-72	.279	.263	.284	67	226	29	63	12	0	11	38	36	6	1	3	48	0	1	.478	.387
Diaz, Juan	R-R	6-2	270	2-19-74	.229	.333	.194	13	48	5	11	3	0	3	13	6	0	0	0	11	0	0	.479	.302
Duncan, Chris	L-R	6-5	210	5-5-81	.271	.229	.286	52	181	23	49	11	0	7	31	25	0	0	0	53	1	2	.448	.359
Esposito, Brian	R-R	6-1	190	2-24-79	.234	.245	.230	55	175	13	41	9	0	4	20	10	4	0	1	32	0	1	.320	.264
Estrada, Kevin	B-R	6-2	185	10-1-80	.217	.200	.221	48	115	16	25	1	0	0	6	14	1	1	2	23	0	0	.226	.308
Gall, John	R-R	6-0	195	4-2-78	.287	.375	.258	82	289	31	83	13	2	6	34	28	6	0	1	36	3	4	.408	.361

2006 PERFORMANCE

General manager: Walt Jocketty. **Farm director:** Bruce Manno. **Scouting director:** Jeff Luhnow.

Class	Team	League	W	L	PCT	Finish*	Manager	Affiliate Since
Majors	St. Louis	National	83	78	.516	5th (16)	Tony La Russa	XX
Triple-A	Memphis Redbirds	Pacific Coast	58	86	.403	15th (16)	Danny Sheaffer	1998
Double-A	Springfield Cardinals	Texas	66	72	.478	6th (8)	Chris Maloney	2005
High A	Palm Beach Cardinals	Florida State	75	60	.556	2nd (12)	Ron Warner	2003
Low A	Swing of the Quad Cities	Midwest	76	61	.555	3rd (14)	Keith Mitchell	2005
Short-season	State College Spikes	New York-Penn	39	36	.420	8th (14)	Mark DeJohn	2006
Rookie	Johnson City Cardinals	Appalachian	34	34	.500	7th (10)	Dan Radison	1974
OVERALL 2006 MINOR LEAGUE RECORD			348	349	.499	15th (30)		

*Finish in overall standings (No. of teams in league). +League champion

ORGANIZATION STATISTICS

	B-T	HT	WT	DOB	AVG	OBP	SLG	G	AB	R	H	2B	3B	HR	RBI	BB	SO	SB	CS	vLH	vRH
Garrett, Shawn	B-R	6-3	220	11-2-78	.221	.129	.248	45	140	19	31	8	2	3	24	4	20	2	0	2 27	1 0	.371 .250
Gorecki, Reid	R-R	6-1	180	12-22-80	.162	.042	.220	21	74	7	12	4	0	1	9	9	1	1	2	21	3 3	.257 .256
Hanson, Travis	L-R	6-2	195	1-24-81	.220	.128	.244	67	223	21	49	11	1	1	18	20	0	2	2	43	1 1	.291 .282
Hart, Bo	R-R	5-11	175	9-27-76	.185	.104	.224	54	146	17	27	6	1	2	8	12	3	0	2	30	3 0	.281 .258
Hernandez, Michel	R-R	6-0	211	8-12-78	.274	.325	.255	90	285	24	78	10	1	2	28	27	2	3	4	29	3 1	.337 .336
Johnson, Gabe	R-R	6-1	195	9-21-79	.059	.125	.000	8	17	1	1	1	0	0	1	0	1	0	0	9	0 0	.118 .111
Martin, Brian	R-R	6-2	224	6-14-80	.232	.267	.209	56	151	11	35	6	0	3	21	7	4	1	0	57	0 1	.331 .284
Nelson, John	R-R	6-1	190	3-3-79	.215	.206	.219	125	423	55	91	16	2	21	48	42	5	1	4	153	12 2	.411 .291
Perez, Timo	L-L	5-9	180	4-8-75	.295	.262	.304	75	268	42	79	16	2	13	41	21	2	4	1	27	4 2	.515 .349
Redman, Prentice	R-R	6-3	185	8-23-79	.268	.381	.200	24	56	6	15	3	0	1	8	4	0	0	0	15	1 0	.375 .317
Relaford, Desi	R-R	5-9	185	9-16-73	.121	.143	.115	11	33	0	4	0	0	0	3	3	0	0	2	7	0 0	.121 .184
Rodriguez, John	L-L	6-0	205	1-20-78	.266	.217	.293	20	64	10	17	4	1	3	7	11	0	1	0	18	0 0	.500 .373
Rose, Mike	B-R	6-1	225	8-25-76	.262	.260	.263	82	271	38	71	19	0	15	36	40	2	3	0	83	2 1	.498 .361
Ryan, Brendan	R-R	6-2	195	3-26-82	.154	.000	.200	7	26	4	4	0	0	1	6	1	0	0	0	3	1 0	.269 .185
Schumaker, Skip	L-R	5-10	175	2-3-80	.306	.333	.297	95	369	47	113	13	3	3	27	23	3	4	4	48	11 4	.382 .348
Spivey, Junior	R-R	6-0	200	1-28-75	.200	.203	.199	89	285	37	57	12	2	9	29	58	7	2	2	65	13 5	.351 .347
Toca, Jorge	R-R	6-3	220	1-7-75	.329	.241	.386	22	73	7	24	10	0	2	10	3	1	0	2	14	0 0	.548 .354
Washington, Rico	L-R	5-9	195	5-30-78	.242	.259	.236	68	219	28	53	10	1	5	20	28	2	2	0	38	4 2	.365 .333
Wathan, Derek	B-R	6-3	190	12-13-76	.272	.325	.249	68	250	26	68	16	7	5	19	10	0	2	0	41	8 3	.452 .300

PITCHING	B-T	HT	WT	DOB	W	L	ERA	G	GS	CG	SV	IP	H	R	ER	HR	BB	SO	AVG	vLH	vRH	K/9	BB/9
Benes, Alan	R-R	6-5	215	1-21-72	5	6	4.75	30	4	0	0	66	67	41	35	15	23	45	.262	.287	.243	6.11	3.12
Cali, Carmen	L-L	5-10	185	11-4-78	1	4	5.60	27	0	0	0	27	32	22	17	5	19	19	.288	.175	.352	6.26	6.26
Cavazos, Andy	R-R	6-3	225	1-5-81	1	5	3.51	44	0	0	4	56	47	23	22	2	16	55	.228	.236	.224	8.79	2.56
Cunnane, Will	R-R	6-1	200	4-24-74	0	1	6.92	6	5	0	0	26	37	22	20	0	13	9	.343	.432	.281	3.12	4.50
Doyne, Cory	R-R	6-0	210	8-13-81	0	0	0.00	2	0	0	0	5	3	0	0	0	3	3	.188	.333	.154	5.40	5.40
Falkenborg, Brian	R-R	6-6	225	1-18-78	4	5	4.18	47	0	0	16	52	51	29	24	6	15	53	.259	.280	.243	9.23	2.61
Johnson, Tyler	B-L	6-2	180	6-7-81	0	0	8.64	8	0	0	0	8	12	8	8	1	4	8	.316	.438	.227	8.64	4.32
Kinney, Josh	R-R	6-1	195	3-31-79	2	2	1.52	51	0	0	3	71	46	16	12	2	29	76	.186	.258	.140	9.63	3.68
Lambert, Chris	R-R	6-1	205	3-8-83	0	1	6.75	1	1	0	0	4	5	3	3	0	0	2	.357	.250	.500	4.50	0.00
Leek, Randy	L-L	6-0	175	4-18-77	3	7	4.60	17	16	1	0	102	126	56	52	18	23	51	.310	.239	.324	4.51	2.04
Moreno, Orber	R-R	6-3	225	4-27-77	0	0	5.03	14	0	0	0	20	21	11	11	1	11	13	.280	.355	.227	5.95	5.03
Mulder, Mark	L-L	6-6	215	8-5-77	0	1	9.00	2	2	0	0	8	11	9	8	2	5	5	.324	.222	.360	5.63	10.13
Narveson, Chris	L-L	6-3	205	12-20-81	8	5	2.81	15	15	0	0	80	70	26	25	9	33	58	.238	.290	.222	6.53	3.71
Perez, Franklin	R-R	6-2	230	6-10-78	0	4	5.82	17	0	0	1	22	26	15	14	3	11	16	.295	.243	.333	6.65	4.57
Perisho, Matt	L-L	6-0	200	6-8-75	2	4	5.28	47	0	0	1	46	53	31	27	4	22	48	.299	.274	.317	9.39	4.30
Reyes, Anthony	R-R	6-2	215	10-16-81	6	1	2.57	13	13	0	0	84	70	27	24	9	11	82	.221	.242	.202	8.79	1.18
Riedling, John	R-R	5-11	180	8-29-75	1	2	6.27	16	0	0	1	19	26	14	13	1	9	13	.325	.241	.373	6.27	4.34
Rodriguez, Ricardo	L-R	6-3	190	5-21-78	3	3	6.88	9	7	1	0	51	63	42	39	13	16	29	.306	.299	.310	5.12	2.82
Scalamandre, Rich	R-R	5-11	195	8-20-80	3	0	4.26	15	0	0	0	19	19	9	9	2	8	18	.264	.200	.310	8.53	3.79
Smith, Travis	R-R	5-10	170	11-7-72	5	6	5.66	15	15	1	0	89	109	60	56	9	26	49	.306	.279	.332	4.96	2.63
Smith, Matt	R-R	6-5	240	8-14-78	1	3	7.71	7	2	0	0	19	27	20	16	2	7	8	.351	.419	.304	3.86	3.38
Tankersley, Dennis	R-R	6-2	215	2-24-79	4	15	4.35	29	28	1	0	168	173	93	81	20	60	123	.271	.311	.239	6.60	3.22
Thompson, Brad	R-R	6-1	190	1-31-82	2	0	2.11	14	5	0	0	43	36	12	10	3	6	33	.235	.274	.200	6.96	1.27
Voyles, Brad	R-R	6-1	190	12-30-76	1	0	1.50	3	3	0	0	18	17	3	3	1	5	13	.258	.333	.194	6.50	2.50
Webb, John	R-R	6-3	220	5-23-79	6	11	4.18	29	28	1	0	177	201	92	82	13	55	112	.289	.282	.295	5.71	2.80

FIELDING

Catcher	PCT	G	PO	A	E	DP	PB
Esposito	.980	48	269	26	6	0	4
Hernandez	.994	68	425	42	3	8	5
Rose	.987	39	268	25	4	3	1

First Base	PCT	G	PO	A	E	DP
Daubach	.995	63	527	50	3	63
Diaz	.970	6	61	4	2	3
Esposito	.966	4	26	2	1	1
Gall	.988	30	234	7	3	24
Garrett	.979	22	172	15	4	22
Hernandez	1.000	1	6	1	0	0
Johnson	.958	4	23	0	1	1
Rose	1.000	1	5	1	0	0
Toca	.994	19	148	12	1	11
Washington	—	1	0	0	0	0
Wathan	.991	14	99	6	1	7

Second Base	PCT	G	PO	A	E	DP
Estrada	1.000	15	34	31	0	7
Hanson	1.000	2	2	1	0	1

Third Base	PCT	G	PO	A	E	DP
Hart	.990	23	32	64	1	12
Relaford	1.000	6	17	17	0	5
Spivey	.969	82	185	216	13	56
Wathan	.989	32	74	99	2	28

Third Base	PCT	G	PO	A	E	DP
Estrada	1.000	8	3	7	0	1
Gall	.833	6	3	7	2	1
Hanson	.935	67	36	136	12	9
Hart	.912	16	11	20	3	6
Johnson	1.000	4	1	2	0	0
Washington	.963	64	52	131	7	15
Wathan	1.000	6	3	8	0	1

Shortstop	PCT	G	PO	A	E	DP
Estrada	.948	18	18	55	4	12
Hart	1.000	12	8	19	0	3
Nelson	.958	119	148	333	21	71
Relaford	.800	3	1	7	2	2
Ryan	.964	7	8	19	1	5
Wathan	1.000	8	5	10	0	2

Outfield	PCT	G	PO	A	E	DP
Bigbie	1.000	10	14	1	0	0
Boyd	.975	39	75	3	2	3
Conti	.972	27	33	2	1	0
Duncan	.935	45	58	0	4	0
Esposito	1.000	1	1	0	0	0
Gall	.963	53	76	3	3	1
Garrett	.850	18	15	2	3	0
Gorecki	.983	21	57	1	1	0
Martin	.966	44	82	3	3	1
Nelson	1.000	3	4	0	0	0
Perez	.975	64	109	6	3	1
Redman	1.000	16	14	0	0	0
Rodriguez	1.000	19	42	1	0	0
Rose	.976	31	34	6	1	0
Schumaker	.991	94	215	9	2	2
Smith	—	1	0	0	0	0
Wathan	.938	9	14	1	1	0

Texas League

BATTING	B-T	HT	WT	DOB	AVG	vLH	vRH	G	AB	R	H	2B	3B	HR	RBI	BB	HBP	SH	SF	SO	SB	CS	SLG	OBP
Bigbie, Larry	L-R	6-4	215	11-4-77	.286	.000	.308	6	14	3	4	0	0	1	2	5	0	1	5	0	0		.500	.450
Boyd, Shaun	R-R	5-11	188	8-15-81	.279	.289	.276	59	208	38	58	12	2	2	16	22	4	0	2	32	8	4	.385	.356
Cazana-Marti, Amaury	R-R	6-1	212	9-2-74	.227	.111	.246	40	132	17	30	4	0	6	13	13	4	0	0	41	1	1	.394	.315
Dryer, Matt	R-R	6-2	195	11-12-79	.217	.154	.234	20	60	11	13	3	0	2	7	8	2	1	0	20	0	0	.367	.329
Estrada, Kevin	B-R	6-2	185	10-1-80	.236	.333	.220	47	127	19	30	6	2	2	10	16	2	3	0	26	12	3	.362	.331
Evans, Terry	R-R	6-3	200	1-19-82	.307	.389	.281	21	75	13	23	4	0	7	20	3	5	0	1	21	5	1	.640	.369
2-team (52 Arkansas)					.308	—	—	73	263	61	81	13	2	18	42	21	11	0	2	77	16	7	.578	.380
Franco, Iker	R-R	6-1	210	5-5-81	.232	.200	.242	96	340	47	79	16	1	10	46	24	1	1	1	79	0	1	.374	.284
Gorecki, Reid	R-R	6-1	180	12-22-80	.251	.218	.257	85	327	56	82	21	2	16	51	42	3	7	2	80	17	9	.474	.340
Haerther, Cody	L-R	6-1	198	7-14-83	.277	.186	.292	120	412	56	114	27	3	11	52	37	1	0	2	59	3	4	.437	.336
Hanson, Travis	L-R	6-2	195	1-24-81	.226	.211	.229	65	252	21	57	12	0	2	20	16	1	1	0	52	0	0	.298	.275
Hoffpauir, Jarrett	R-R	5-9	165	6-18-83	.249	.216	.254	119	393	55	98	20	1	7	46	54	5	5	3	41	8	6	.359	.345
Johnson, Gabe	R-R	6-1	195	9-21-79	.200	.265	.178	63	195	28	39	9	1	9	34	23	1	0	0	60	0	1	.395	.288
Laya, Rayner	R-R	5-10	150	9-30-80	.286	.367	.234	32	77	10	22	1	0	0	4	3	0	0	0	7	1	2	.299	.313
Martin, Brian	R-R	6-2	224	6-14-80	.293	.302	.289	42	133	21	39	11	0	4	18	19	5	0	0	25	0	0	.466	.401
McCoy, Mike	R-R	5-9	171	4-2-81	.249	.213	.257	129	474	64	118	14	2	3	37	62	7	16	0	98	30	9	.306	.344
Moylan, Dan	L-R	6-0	190	4-24-79	.310	.330	.306	23	58	5	18	2	0	1	4	11	0	0	0	7	0	1	.397	.420
Parker, Tyler	R-R	6-2	205	5-13-81	.159	.263	.080	17	44	3	7	0	0	1	3	2	0	0	0	15	0	0	.227	.196
Pressley, Josh	L-R	6-6	240	4-2-80	.250	.286	.247	33	92	12	23	5	0	2	14	20	0	0	0	17	0	0	.370	.384
Richardson, Juan	R-R	6-1	215	1-27-79	.311	.321	.121	121	444	71	138	31	1	17	78	46	7	1	3	114	0	7	.500	.382
Ryan, Brendan	R-R	6-2	195	3-26-82	.302	.375	.286	10	43	6	13	1	0	0	3	3	0	1	0	6	1	1	.326	.348
Stavinoha, Nick	R-R	6-2	225	5-3-82	.297	.244	.310	111	417	55	124	26	3	12	73	28	2	0	6	81	2	1	.460	.340
Washington, Rico	L-R	5-9	195	5-30-78	.323	.259	.345	66	232	49	75	23	3	13	56	49	3	0	2	48	4	1	.616	.444

PITCHING	B-T	HT	WT	DOB	W	L	ERA	G	GS	CG	SV	IP	H	R	ER	HR	BB	SO	AVG	vLH	vRH	K/9	BB/9
Cali, Carmen	L-L	5-10	185	11-4-78	0	2	3.00	23	3	0	1	39	47	19	13	0	15	35	.296	.281	.305	8.08	3.46
Cate, Troy	L-L	6-1	200	10-21-80	1	1	0.57	10	0	0	1	16	5	2	1	0	6	20	.096	.067	.108	11.49	3.45
Cavazos, Andy	R-R	6-3	225	1-5-81	2	2	0.45	16	0	0	0	20	6	2	1	0	12	19	.094	.077	.105	8.55	5.40
Dove, Dennis	R-R	6-4	205	8-31-81	0	3	8.79	13	0	0	0	14	18	16	14	6	8	15	.295	.321	.273	9.42	5.02
Doyne, Cory	R-R	6-0	210	8-13-81	1	7	3.39	54	0	0	6	66	48	29	25	1	42	78	.204	.252	.167	10.58	5.70
Estrada, Kevin	B-R	6-2	185	10-1-80	0	0	3.86	2	0	0	0	2	3	3	1	0	1	2	.333	.200	.500	7.71	3.86
Garcia, Jose	R-R	6-1	160	6-2-81	0	1	1.35	3	0	0	0	7	7	1	1	0	4	5	.269	.308	.231	6.75	5.40
Garza, Justin	R-R	6-1	190	7-13-82	2	3	2.97	25	0	0	0	39	36	14	13	1	25	27	.243	.186	.295	6.18	5.72
Haberer, Eric	L-L	6-2	205	9-14-82	3	3	5.43	11	11	0	0	61	65	41	37	10	34	37	.278	.277	.278	5.43	4.99
Hawksworth, Blake	R-R	6-3	199	3-1-83	4	2	3.39	13	13	0	0	80	72	34	30	8	31	66	.248	.269	.231	7.46	3.50
Lambert, Chris	R-R	6-1	205	3-8-83	10	9	5.30	23	23	0	0	121	126	84	71	20	63	113	.268	.275	.262	8.43	4.70
Ool, Kevin	L-L	5-11	185	1-4-81	3	3	4.10	45	2	0	0	83	84	43	38	10	20	43	.264	.284	.252	4.64	2.16
Pals, Jordan	R-R	6-8	205	10-18-80	8	7	4.94	27	27	0	0	160	201	96	88	24	40	89	.312	.313	.310	5.00	2.25
Parisi, Mike	R-R	5-11	185	4-18-83	9	8	4.60	27	27	0	0	151	168	92	77	13	63	107	.281	.308	.257	6.39	3.76
Pomeranz, Stuart	R-R	6-7	220	12-17-84	7	4	4.39	18	18	0	0	98	107	50	48	13	30	63	.282	.297	.269	5.86	2.75
Rundles, Rich	L-L	6-5	180	6-3-81	5	6	4.60	15	14	1	0	86	100	52	44	9	28	47	.292	.255	.310	4.92	2.93
Russ, Chris	R-R	5-11	175	3-27-79	4	4	4.17	55	0	0	0	73	77	38	34	3	25	50	.271	.303	.247	6.14	3.07
Scalamandre, Rich	R-R	5-11	195	8-20-80	4	0	4.55	29	0	0	2	30	28	17	15	1	10	30	.246	.234	.254	9.10	3.03
Walton, Sam	L-L	6-5	225	12-1-78	0	0	2.70	3	0	0	0	3	2	1	1	0	4	5	.167	.200	.143	13.50	10.80
2-team (17 Midland)					1	4	3.07	20	0	0	0	29	17	10	10	0	22	27	—	—	—	8.28	6.75
Worrell, Mark	R-R	6-1	190	3-8-83	3	7	4.52	57	0	0	27	62	52	34	31	10	20	75	.226	.263	.198	10.95	2.92

FIELDING

Catcher	PCT	G	PO	A	E	DP	PB
Franco	.988	90	618	61	8	10	9
Johnson	.969	43	248	35	9	3	10
Motte	1.000	1	2	0	0	0	
Moylan	.977	15	79	6	2	0	0

First Base	PCT	G	PO	A	E	DP
Dryer	.994	20	159	12	1	17
Estrada	1.000	10	88	5	0	5
Johnson	.986	16	131	9	2	16
Richardson	.993	102	849	62	6	78
Washington	1.000	1	5	0	0	0

Second Base	PCT	G	PO	A	E	DP
Estrada	1.000	7	11	20	0	3
Hoffpauir	.963	118	239	353	23	73

Laya	1.000	13	26	31	0	9
McCoy	.931	4	10	17	2	4

Third Base	PCT	G	PO	A	E	DP
Estrada	.667	2	0	4	2	0
Hanson	.944	62	46	138	11	15
McCoy	.750	4	0	3	1	0
Richardson	.971	12	3	30	1	1
Washington	.936	66	38	138	12	13

Shortstop	PCT	G	PO	A	E	DP
Estrada	.957	5	8	14	1	3
Laya	.970	10	9	23	1	1
McCoy	.952	117	208	324	27	66
Ryan	.960	10	18	30	2	10
Washington	—	1	0	0	0	0

Outfield	PCT	G	PO	A	E	DP
Bigbie	1.000	2	3	0	0	0
Boyd	.982	55	107	2	2	0
Cazana-Marti	1.000	19	18	5	0	1
Estrada	1.000	16	24	1	0	0
Evans	1.000	21	45	2	0	0
Gorecki	.977	84	207	8	5	3
Haerther	.975	96	148	5	4	1
Martin	.982	32	53	2	1	1
McCoy	1.000	5	8	0	0	0
Moylan	.500	1	1	0	1	0
Parker	1.000	7	9	1	0	0
Stavinoha	.970	100	150	11	5	1

Florida State League

BATTING	B-T	HT	WT	DOB	AVG	vLH	vRH	G	AB	R	H	2B	3B	HR	RBI	BB	HBP	SH	SF	SO	SB	CS	SLG	OBP
Barthelemy, Ryan	L-R	6-3	225	5-19-80	.270	.247	.275	121	463	64	125	29	7	14	68	50	6	0	0	87	1	3	.454	.349
Cazana-Marti, Amaury	R-R	6-1	212	9-2-74	.282	.333	.274	20	85	17	24	6	0	4	16	9	0	0	0	26	3	1	.494	.351
Collins, Kevin	L-L	6-2	200	5-6-81	.143	.067	.176	14	49	3	7	2	0	2	7	4	0	1	0	14	0	0	.306	.222
Cotto, Luis	R-R	6-0	175	7-9-81	.185	.125	.220	20	65	10	12	3	0	0	4	6	1	0	0	19	0	1	.231	.264
Danielson, Sean	B-R	5-8	165	8-8-82	.249	.250	.248	114	402	65	100	12	5	0	32	60	5	15	2	77	22	14	.303	.352
Dryer, Matt	R-R	6-2	195	11-12-79	.272	.279	.271	80	301	51	82	17	0	14	54	22	5	0	3	92	1	1	.468	.329
Evans, Terry	R-R	6-3	200	1-19-82	.311	.325	.308	60	238	43	74	10	1	15	45	20	4	0	1	50	21	1	.550	.373
Ferris, Mike	L-L	6-2	220	12-31-82	.205	.233	.199	99	341	48	70	18	1	8	38	47	3	2	2	105	0	2	.334	.305
Greene, Tyler	R-R	6-2	185	8-17-83	.224	.128	.244	71	268	38	60	10	1	5	19	29	4	1	1	90	22	3	.325	.308
Laya, Rayner	R-R	5-10	150	9-30-80	.259	.208	.277	55	189	24	49	2	0	0	21	10	0	7	2	16	12	3	.270	.294
Lucena, Juan	R-R	5-10	155	1-20-84	.288	.320	.280	120	490	58	141	24	3	1	32	34	3	16	2	34	1	2	.347	.320
Mather, Joe	R-R	6-5	210	7-23-82	.269	.326	.253	124	443	64	119	33	1	16	74	36	8	3	4	91	9	0	.456	.332
Moylan, Dan	L-R	6-0	190	4-24-79	.267	.000	.286	6	15	1	4	0	0	0	4	6	0	0	0	3	0	0	.267	.476

	B-T	HT	WT	DOB	AVG	vLH	vRH	G	AB	R	H	2B	3B	HR	RBI	BB	HBP	SH	SF	SO	SB	CS	SLG	OBP
Pagnozzi, Matt	R-R	6-2	195	11-10-82	.216	.253	.202	77	268	25	58	15	3	3	27	20	5	2	0	67	0	1	.328	.283
Parker, Tyler	R-R	6-2	200	5-13-81	.191	.400	.175	20	68	9	13	4	0	2	6	9	0	0	1	23	0	1	.338	.282
Patrick, Christopher	R-R	5-9	180	2-20-82	.303	.364	.273	12	33	3	10	5	0	0	5	6	1	1	0	11	0	0	.455	.425
Rasmus, Colby	L-L	6-1	175	8-11-86	.254	.308	.234	53	193	22	49	4	5	5	35	27	3	0	2	35	11	3	.404	.351
Roth, Randy	R-R	6-1	205	3-5-82	.295	.250	.315	30	105	17	31	10	0	2	13	8	4	0	0	12	0	0	.448	.368
Ryan, Brendan	R-R	6-2	195	3-26-82	.429	.000	.500	3	14	2	6	1	0	0	1	0	0	0	0	2	1	0	.500	.429
Shepherd, Matt	B-R	5-10	175	5-5-83	.211	.226	.208	50	161	20	34	6	1	0	12	18	0	5	2	33	3	1	.261	.287
Swackhamer, Wes	L-L	6-2	210	1-21-83	.210	.143	.218	22	62	6	13	1	1	0	9	9	0	1	1	15	4	2	.258	.306
Toops, Brady	R-R	6-2	200	7-31-81	.194	.400	.161	12	36	1	7	1	0	0	2	5	0	0	1	12	0	0	.222	.286
Williams, Simon	R-L	6-2	220	6-30-82	.154	.200	.140	26	65	10	10	1	0	5	8	12	1	1	0	35	1	0	.400	.295
Yarbrough, Brandon	L-R	6-2	180	11-9-84	.222	.091	.246	43	144	18	32	5	1	1	13	19	0	1	1	37	0	0	.292	.311

PITCHING	B-T	HT	WT	DOB	W	L	ERA	G	GS	CG	SV	IP	H	R	ER	HR	BB	SO	AVG	vLH	vRH	K/9	BB/9
Adamczyk, Tyler	R-R	6-6	202	11-9-82	0	4	4.21	33	2	0	0	66	62	40	31	4	33	29	.245	.211	.266	3.93	4.48
Boggs, Mitchell	R-R	6-3	195	2-15-84	10	6	3.41	27	27	1	0	145	153	69	55	7	51	126	.271	.262	.277	7.82	3.17
Cate, Troy	L-L	6-1	200	10-21-80	2	2	1.54	34	0	0	1	41	19	8	7	3	13	58	.139	.174	.121	12.73	2.85
Dove, Dennis	R-R	6-4	205	8-31-81	3	3	2.81	41	0	0	4	51	38	20	16	3	13	56	.212	.176	.238	9.82	2.28
Garcia, Jaime	L-L	6-1	175	7-8-86	5	4	3.84	12	12	0	0	77	84	33	33	3	16	51	.282	.203	.303	5.94	1.86
Garcia, Jose	R-R	6-1	160	6-2-81	5	2	5.02	28	7	0	0	72	81	43	40	4	22	60	.288	.325	.262	7.53	2.76
Garza, Justin	R-R	6-1	190	7-13-82	3	1	3.30	23	0	0	1	30	34	14	11	3	10	26	.281	.378	.224	7.80	3.00
Haberer, Eric	L-L	6-2	205	9-14-82	4	7	3.83	17	16	0	0	99	95	49	42	7	28	64	.255	.178	.273	5.84	2.55
Hawksworth, Blake	R-R	6-3	199	3-1-83	7	2	2.47	14	14	0	0	84	75	23	23	0	19	55	.247	.258	.239	5.92	2.04
McCormick, Mark	R-R	6-5	195	10-15-83	0	0	11.25	2	2	0	0	4	5	5	5	0	3	5	.294	.333	.273	11.25	6.75
Meacham, Cory	R-R	6-1	185	7-31-84	3	3	3.45	8	8	0	0	47	45	23	18	2	13	30	.259	.264	.253	5.74	2.49
Michael, Mark	R-R	6-4	215	8-25-82	2	7	5.64	18	17	1	0	97	114	71	61	11	29	63	.296	.323	.282	5.83	2.68
Narveson, Chris	L-L	6-2	205	12-20-81	0	0	2.12	3	3	0	0	17	9	4	4	2	1	13	.150	.200	.140	6.88	0.53
Parrott, Rhett	R-R	6-2	190	11-12-79	0	1	135.00	1	1	0	0	2	6	8	5	0	1	0	.857	.667	1.000	0.00	27.00
Scherer, Matthew	R-R	6-5	230	1-20-83	9	5	3.25	53	0	0	0	80	71	34	29	9	20	106	.234	.250	.225	11.88	2.24
Sillman, Mike	R-R	6-1	190	12-3-81	4	3	1.10	57	0	0	35	57	34	10	7	2	20	86	.167	.211	.142	13.50	3.14
Stitt, Brian	R-R	5-11	201	8-26-82	4	2	3.60	16	0	0	0	25	17	11	10	3	9	20	.200	.175	.222	7.20	3.24
Webber, Nick	R-R	6-7	210	5-9-84	6	6	4.21	27	26	1	0	135	153	78	63	7	63	65	.289	.316	.268	4.34	4.21
Zuercher, Zach	L-L	6-2	215	4-10-84	6	2	4.12	43	0	0	0	59	68	30	27	5	14	47	.294	.254	.310	7.17	2.14

FIELDING

Catcher	PCT	G	PO	A	E	DP	PB
Motte	.986	9	63	9	1	3	1
Moylan	1.000	2	4	0	0	0	0
Pagnozzi	.995	76	521	72	3	2	8
Toops	1.000	10	69	11	0	0	0
Yarbrough	.974	42	281	18	8	0	6

First Base	PCT	G	PO	A	E	DP
Barthelemy	1.000	21	174	21	0	22
Dryer	1.000	6	66	2	0	6
Ferris	.986	91	858	64	13	79
Mather	1.000	4	11	0	0	1
Roth	.994	18	158	9	1	14

Second Base	PCT	G	PO	A	E	DP
Cotto	.923	3	3	9	1	1
Laya	1.000	1	1	3	0	2

	PCT	G	PO	A	E	DP
Lucena	.975	111	230	312	14	76
Shepherd	.991	27	41	71	1	13

Third Base	PCT	G	PO	A	E	DP
Barthelemy	.949	74	37	131	9	9
Cotto	.927	18	8	30	3	2
Dryer	.873	20	17	45	9	2
Lucena	1.000	1	0	1	0	0
Patrick	.912	8	5	26	3	0
Shepherd	.938	21	10	35	3	4

Shortstop	PCT	G	PO	A	E	DP
Cotto	—	1	0	0	0	0
Greene	.936	71	106	228	23	52
Laya	.969	54	84	199	9	33
Lucena	.913	12	16	26	4	6
Ryan	1.000	2	4	12	0	3

Outfield	PCT	G	PO	A	E	DP
Barthelemy	1.000	8	12	1	0	0
Cazana-Marti	1.000	16	30	2	0	0
Collins	.833	4	5	0	1	0
Danielson	.941	109	182	10	12	1
Evans	.993	59	128	5	1	0
Mather	.971	118	192	10	6	2
Moylan	1.000	1	1	0	0	0
Parker	1.000	11	15	1	0	0
Patrick	—	1	0	0	0	0
Rasmus	.971	53	101	1	3	0
Roth	1.000	7	11	0	0	0
Swackhamer	.952	18	20	1	1	0
Williams	.958	15	22	1	1	0

Swing of the Quad Cities — Low Class A

Midwest League

BATTING	B-T	HT	WT	DOB	AVG	vLH	vRH	G	AB	R	H	2B	3B	HR	RBI	BB	HBP	SH	SF	SO	SB	CS	SLG	OBP
Anderson, Bryan	L-R	6-1	200	12-16-86	.302	.271	.309	109	381	50	115	29	3	3	51	42	5	1	2	66	2	6	.417	.377
Bigbie, Larry	L-R	6-4	215	11-4-77	.357	.500	.250	4	14	2	5	0	0	0	1	2	0	0	0	4	0	0	.357	.438
Carter, Charles	R-R	6-2	215	9-27-82	.115	.111	.118	9	26	1	3	1	0	0	2	4	0	0	1	5	1	1	.154	.226
Cotto, Luis	R-R	6-0	175	7-9-81	.265	.162	.303	45	136	24	36	5	2	0	14	18	5	4	1	34	6	4	.331	.369
Gabriel, Chad	R-R	6-2	195	5-19-84	.272	.244	.284	81	287	40	78	10	1	7	32	12	6	2	0	48	4	5	.387	.315
Giannotti, Richard	B-R	6-3	210	8-9-83	.125	.000	.200	7	16	2	2	0	0	0	2	5	0	0	0	4	0	0	.125	.333
Greene, Tyler	R-R	6-2	185	8-17-83	.287	.407	.244	59	223	42	64	8	3	15	47	20	12	0	1	65	11	0	.552	.375
Guerrero, Henry	R-R	6-0	189	4-4-82	.250	.147	.315	31	88	14	22	6	0	1	14	11	1	3	0	22	0	0	.352	.340
Hamilton, Mark	L-L	6-3	220	7-29-84	.254	.188	.273	38	142	16	36	8	0	3	25	10	1	0	0	32	0	0	.373	.307
Hayes, Calvin	R-R	5-9	187	3-21-84	.137	.222	.091	17	51	6	7	1	0	0	4	5	0	1	1	8	1	1	.157	.211
Jay, Jonathan	L-L	6-0	200	3-15-85	.342	.305	.354	60	234	42	80	13	3	3	45	28	3	1	2	27	9	4	.462	.416
Jones, Daryl	L-L	5-11	180	6-25-87	.235	.333	.227	26	81	15	19	5	1	1	7	6	3	1	1	23	2	2	.358	.308
Martinez, Jose	R-R	5-11	175	1-24-86	.270	.306	.257	91	326	47	88	20	2	8	36	18	6	4	4	26	7	6	.417	.320
Nelson, Dan	B-R	5-11	180	2-12-84	.253	.278	.244	129	486	76	123	25	3	7	48	63	6	9	4	87	27	13	.360	.343
Rasmus, Colby	L-L	6-1	175	8-11-86	.310	.261	.330	78	303	49	94	22	3	11	50	29	3	3	3	55	17	5	.512	.373
Robinson, Shane	R-R	5-9	160	10-30-84	.282	.295	.277	63	252	41	71	9	2	0	21	20	6	1	2	20	13	3	.333	.346
Rodgers, Adam	R-R	6-1	200	12-1-82	.244	.265	.236	49	176	26	43	9	1	2	20	16	2	2	2	31	2	0	.341	.311
Roth, Randy	R-R	6-1	205	3-5-82	.307	.314	.304	74	127	25	23	6	2	18	67	20	10	0	4	49	9	6	.523	.354
Rowlett, Casey	R-R	5-8	175	2-8-83	.269	.258	.274	118	442	74	119	30	1	5	58	41	6	5	7	68	20	8	.376	.335
Salazar, Jose	R-R	5-10	170	12-30-83	.250	.500	.200	8	24	2	6	0	0	0	3	0	0	0	0	7	0	0	.250	.333
Sivira, Yonathan	R-R	6-1	165	1-25-84	.200	.286	.000	4	10	2	2	0	0	0	1	0	0	0	0	2	1	0	.200	.273
Smith, C.J.	R-R	6-3	210	2-22-82	.237	.286	.218	25	76	10	18	5	1	0	2	15	10	1	0	18	0	1	.395	.333
Swackhamer, Wes	L-L	6-2	210	1-21-83	.292	.462	.250	63	65	19	19	1	0	0	20	18	0	0	4	34	4	2	.270	.278
Van Slyke, A.J.	L-R	6-2	210	11-19-83	.223	.298	.196	63	251	28	56	12	2	6	30	30	4	3	3	28	6	2	.382	.320
Wilkerson, Matthew	R-R	6-4	215	12-18-82	.230	.333	.189	23	74	8	17	1	0	2	10	10	0	0	2	17	3	1	.324	.337
Williams, Simon	R-L	6-2	220	6-30-82	.123	.130	.119	24	65	9	8	1	0	0	7	10	7	1	0	30	3	1	.246	.219
Yarbrough, Brandon	L-R	6-2	180	11-9-84	.303	.367	.278	74	142	18	43	6	2	3	24	19	0	3	1	37	0	0	.423	.339

PITCHING	B-T	HT	WT	DOB	W	L	ERA	G	GS	CG	SV	IP	H	R	ER	HR	BB	SO	AVG	vLH	vRH	K/9	BB/9
Andersen, Phillip	R-R	6-3	175	10-28-83	0	2	7.11	4	4	0	0	19	22	18	15	1	6	14	.282	.222	.333	6.63	2.84
Borne, Danny	L-L	6-3	185	5-5-83	1	2	3.38	44	0	0	1	45	40	23	17	2	22	50	.238	.267	.215	9.93	4.37

Name	B-T	HT	WT	DOB	W	L	ERA	G	GS	CG	SV	IP	H	R	ER	HR	BB	SO	AVG	vLH	vRH	K/9	BB/9
Cairns, Jason	R-R	6-4	205	11-13-82	6	5	3.21	43	0	0	0	62	64	34	22	1	23	43	.267	.291	.255	6.28	3.36
Daniels, Adam	L-L	6-2	190	8-16-82	7	11	3.07	24	24	1	0	138	139	67	47	3	44	128	.268	.199	.292	8.37	2.88
Garcia, Jaime	L-L	6-1	200	7-8-86	5	4	2.90	13	13	1	0	78	67	28	25	1	18	80	.229	.246	.225	9.27	2.09
Hearne, Trey	R-R	6-1	190	8-19-83	12	3	2.25	31	17	0	0	128	102	42	32	10	34	106	.216	.234	.204	7.45	2.39
Hooks, Ashley	R-R	6-3	190	5-18-83	3	2	5.63	20	0	0	0	38	48	28	24	4	13	21	.302	.313	.295	4.93	3.05
McCormick, Mark	R-R	6-2	195	10-15-83	2	4	3.78	11	11	0	0	52	38	25	22	3	38	63	.207	.181	.228	10.83	6.54
Meacham, Cory	R-R	6-1	185	7-31-84	8	5	3.16	17	17	1	0	100	87	47	35	5	29	51	.238	.249	.229	4.61	2.62
Mikrut, Jon	R-R	6-4	195	11-22-82	3	1	3.45	50	0	0	0	60	45	27	23	4	20	56	.206	.291	.158	8.40	3.00
Moreno, Victor	R-R	6-0	168	12-22-82	1	2	3.96	16	6	0	0	39	41	22	17	1	10	33	.275	.321	.250	7.68	2.33
Motte, Jason	R-R	6-0	200	6-22-82	1	1	4.97	8	0	0	0	13	16	8	7	1	3	13	.296	.174	.387	9.24	2.13
Mulder, Mark	L-L	6-6	215	8-5-77	0	0	1.80	1	1	0	0	5	2	2	1	1	2	1	.125	.000	.182	1.80	3.60
Norrick, Tyler	L-L	6-3	190	9-27-83	2	2	3.72	13	12	0	1	65	60	28	27	3	35	60	.252	.321	.232	8.27	4.82
Ottavino, Adam	R-R	6-5	215	11-22-85	2	3	3.44	8	8	0	0	37	28	21	14	3	19	38	.211	.368	.092	9.33	4.66
Perez, Chris	R-R	6-4	225	7-1-85	2	0	1.84	25	0	0	12	29	20	9	6	0	19	32	.198	.263	.159	9.82	5.83
Sadlowski, Kyle	R-R	6-3	190	6-19-84	4	3	4.86	18	13	1	0	74	77	43	40	5	24	42	.267	.284	.253	5.11	2.92
Smith, Donnie	R-R	6-2	210	1-14-83	4	2	3.57	8	8	0	0	40	40	18	16	2	13	30	.260	.290	.239	6.69	2.90
Stitt, Brian	R-R	5-11	201	8-26-82	0	2	2.57	20	0	0	9	21	17	7	6	0	2	20	.210	.233	.196	8.57	0.86
Trent, Matthew	R-R	6-2	220	8-7-82	4	3	2.61	50	0	0	0	69	54	25	20	0	34	79	.218	.253	.200	10.30	4.43
Vander Weg, Scott	R-R	6-3	210	12-14-82	8	2	3.43	51	0	0	7	66	55	27	25	4	26	55	.224	.207	.233	7.54	3.56
Wilson, Joshua	R-R	5-11	180	9-6-86	0	2	9.00	3	3	0	0	13	21	15	13	4	5	10	.368	.385	.355	6.92	3.46
Zick, Jeremy	R-R	6-1	210	8-25-82	1	0	4.86	12	0	0	0	17	16	13	9	0	7	9	.250	.250	.250	4.86	3.78

FIELDING

Catcher	PCT	G	PO	A	E	DP	PB
Anderson	.992	92	653	75	6	7	17
Guerrero	.984	31	218	25	4	3	10
Yarbrough	.976	20	149	17	4	2	4

First Base	PCT	G	PO	A	E	DP
Hamilton	.997	35	289	15	1	25
Rodgers	.989	38	330	30	4	15
Roth	.987	53	481	31	7	54
Smith	.984	10	58	2	1	6
Van Slyke	.940	12	103	6	7	8

Second Base	PCT	G	PO	A	E	DP
Cotto	1.000	1	2	2	0	0
Hayes	.932	16	29	53	6	11
Martinez	.980	61	115	175	6	49
Nelson	.972	23	31	74	3	9

	PCT	G	PO	A	E	DP
Rowlett	.957	36	59	96	7	16
Salazar	1.000	8	11	22	0	2

Third Base	PCT	G	PO	A	E	DP
Cotto	.889	3	1	7	1	1
Martinez	—	1	0	0	0	0
Nelson	.894	91	55	173	27	16
Roth	.846	28	14	41	10	3
Rowlett	.944	21	9	42	3	3

Shortstop	PCT	G	PO	A	E	DP
Cotto	.940	38	55	103	10	18
Greene	.958	56	78	151	10	36
Martinez	.939	27	50	73	8	14
Nelson	.902	17	26	48	8	9
Rowlett	1.000	3	6	4	0	1

Outfield	PCT	G	PO	A	E	DP
Carter	1.000	9	14	0	0	0
Gabriel	.946	60	82	6	5	0
Giannotti	1.000	4	6	1	0	0
Jay	1.000	58	77	2	0	0
Jones	.957	10	21	1	1	1
Rasmus	.954	74	142	4	7	1
Robinson	.993	61	140	5	1	1
Roth	1.000	2	4	0	0	0
Rowlett	.938	60	101	5	7	0
Sivira	1.000	3	1	1	0	0
Smith	1.000	8	15	0	0	0
Swackhamer	.923	15	24	0	2	0
Van Slyke	1.000	28	40	0	0	0
Wilkerson	.960	22	44	4	2	2
Williams	1.000	22	33	1	0	0

State College Spikes — Short-Season

New York-Penn League

BATTING	B-T	HT	WT	DOB	AVG	vLH	vRH	G	AB	R	H	2B	3B	HR	RBI	BB	HBP	SH	SF	SO	SB	CS	SLG	OBP
Carpenter, David	R-R	6-2	200	7-15-85	.189	.125	.207	37	111	6	21	4	0	0	9	11	3	1	1	38	1	1	.225	.278
Carter, Charles	R-R	6-2	215	9-27-82	.209	.000	.265	12	43	4	9	1	1	1	5	2	0	0	1	8	1	0	.349	.239
Craig, Allen	R-R	6-2	190	7-18-84	.257	.281	.252	48	175	21	45	13	0	4	29	13	7	1	5	28	0	0	.400	.325
Gonzalez, Steve	R-R	5-10	190	5-31-87	.207	.192	.211	38	116	11	24	2	0	1	8	11	4	2	1	25	0	1	.250	.295
Gorsett, Luke	R-R	6-1	195	5-28-85	.211	.125	.233	24	76	7	16	2	0	2	5	9	4	2	0	23	1	1	.316	.326
Hamilton, Mark	L-L	6-3	220	7-29-84	.264	.100	.302	30	106	18	28	3	1	8	24	13	1	0	1	24	1	1	.538	.347
Morris, Adam	R-R	6-2	190	12-1-82	.178	.429	.132	13	45	7	8	5	0	2	3	2	0	0	0	17	0	0	.422	.213
Rapoport, James	L-L	5-11	160	6-25-85	.216	.278	.205	66	241	42	52	8	3	1	21	30	2	1	1	76	24	4	.286	.307
Reyes, Christian	R-R	6-0	190	4-24-86	.000	—	.000	1	1	0	0	0	0	0	0	0	0	0	0	0	0	0	.000	.000
Ryan, Brendan	R-R	6-2	195	3-26-82	.235	.667	.143	8	34	5	8	0	0	0	3	3	0	1	2	4	1	0	.235	.282
Salazar, Jose	R-R	5-10	170	12-30-83	.283	.313	.279	42	145	14	41	4	1	1	20	13	5	5	1	22	1	1	.345	.360
Sandoval, Willian	B-R	5-10	170	12-27-85	.208	.214	.207	57	149	15	31	5	3	0	11	11	8	11	2	30	21	9	.282	.294
Schweitzer, Jared	R-R	6-1	185	10-13-83	.252	.342	.223	49	159	20	40	7	0	0	15	17	1	2	1	27	0	3	.296	.326
Sivira, Yonathan	R-R	6-1	165	1-25-84	.214	.161	.227	55	159	24	34	7	1	1	16	9	1	3	0	22	4	1	.289	.260
Solano, Donovan	R-R	5-10	165	12-17-87	.282	.250	.292	44	149	22	42	2	0	0	13	12	2	3	1	17	2	1	.295	.341
Southard, Nathan	R-R	6-1	185	10-27-83	.306	.500	.253	66	242	43	74	21	4	5	44	27	5	0	2	42	16	2	.488	.384
Thomas, Scott	L-R	5-11	202	3-21-85	.190	.056	.213	39	126	5	24	3	2	0	6	7	3	1	3	26	2	1	.246	.245
Van Slyke, A.J.	L-R	6-2	210	11-19-83	.282	.259	.287	46	170	15	48	14	1	0	18	11	2	0	1	25	2	0	.376	.354
Wilkerson, Matthew	R-R	6-4	215	12-18-82	.228	.235	.226	53	180	20	41	12	2	7	29	14	2	0	3	48	0	0	.433	.286

PITCHING	B-T	HT	WT	DOB	W	L	ERA	G	GS	CG	SV	IP	H	R	ER	HR	BB	SO	AVG	vLH	vRH	K/9	BB/9
Daley, Gary	R-R	6-3	200	11-1-85	5	6	3.28	15	14	0	0	74	76	37	27	0	32	64	.267	.264	.269	7.78	3.89
Degerman, Eddie	R-R	6-4	205	9-14-83	2	1	2.76	9	9	0	0	42	37	18	13	1	20	53	.227	.247	.209	11.27	4.25
Furnish, Brad	B-L	6-1	185	1-19-85	3	6	3.94	15	15	0	0	75	65	36	33	5	19	68	.234	.203	.242	8.12	2.27
Gonzalez, Marco	R-R	6-2	205	5-28-84	0	0	4.63	11	0	0	0	12	8	6	6	0	6	9	.186	.313	.111	6.94	4.63
Gregerson, Luke	L-R	6-3	200	5-14-84	6	1	1.72	12	0	0	4	16	9	5	3	0	9	22	.164	.174	.156	12.64	5.17
Herron, Tyler	R-R	6-3	190	8-5-86	0	1	3.00	1	1	1	0	6	7	2	2	1	1	3	.318	.273	.364	4.50	1.50
Hodinka, Ryan	L-L	6-1	175	2-25-84	1	2	4.73	19	1	0	1	27	29	17	14	0	16	17	.290	.242	.313	5.74	5.40
Hooks, Ashley	R-R	6-3	190	5-18-83	1	1	6.48	5	1	0	0	8	16	9	6	1	1	4	.410	.400	.421	4.32	1.08
Lane, Matthew	R-R	6-8	225	8-17-84	3	3	3.29	14	8	1	0	66	51	28	24	4	13	45	.209	.195	.224	6.17	1.78
Maiques, Kenneth	R-R	6-1	185	6-25-85	0	0	6.75	1	1	0	0	4	3	3	3	0	3	6	.231	.500	.111	9.00	6.75
Marcum, Lance	R-R	6-2	190	7-5-83	1	3	5.94	19	2	0	1	36	43	24	24	2	15	18	.301	.318	.286	4.46	3.72
Motte, Jason	R-R	6-0	200	6-22-82	1	2	3.08	21	0	0	8	26	30	12	9	1	4	25	.280	.256	.294	8.54	1.37
Mura, Kyle	R-R	6-4	215	11-24-84	3	0	5.97	20	0	0	0	29	34	22	19	1	18	28	.298	.347	.262	5.65	2.20
Norrick, Tyler	L-L	6-3	190	9-27-83	1	0	2.25	1	0	0	0	4	4	1	1	0	0	9	.250	.000	.333	20.25	0.00
Ottavino, Adam	R-R	6-5	215	11-22-85	2	2	3.14	4	4	0	0	29	23	12	10	1	10	26	.211	.238	.194	8.16	4.08
Parrott, Rhett	R-R	6-2	190	11-12-79	1	2	2.40	4	4	0	0	15	11	5	4	1	6	10	.200	.200	.200	5.40	3.60
Repole, Michael	R-R	6-5	225	7-12-83	0	0	5.84	1	0	0	0	12	14	10	8	1	4	13	.292	.278	.300	9.49	2.92
Sadlowski, Kyle	R-R	6-3	190	6-19-84	3	2	2.56	14	7	0	0	56	50	20	16	5	15	29	.233	.281	.193	4.63	2.40
Sandoval, Willian	B-R	5-10	170	12-27-85	0	0	0.00	1	0	0	0	1	0	0	0	0	1	0	.000	.000	.000	9.00	9.00
Sauceda, Matt	L-L	6-2	190	12-26-83	1	0	5.30	14	0	0	0	19	18	11	11	0	19	9	.269	.294	.260	4.34	9.16

	B-T	HT	WT	DOB	W	L	ERA	G	GS	CG	SV	IP	H	R	ER	HR	BB	SO	AVG	vLH	vRH	K/9	BB/9
Schroeder, Brian	L-L	6-1	205	11-19-84	2	2	3.56	25	0	0	0	30	31	14	12	1	9	25	.258	.227	.276	7.42	2.67
Smith, Donnie	R-R	6-2	210	1-14-83	1	1	3.23	6	6	0	0	31	31	12	11	2	5	13	.265	.321	.213	3.82	1.47
Walters, P.J.	R-R	6-4	200	3-12-85	2	1	3.56	26	0	0	8	30	29	15	12	1	9	31	.242	.245	.239	9.20	2.67

FIELDING

Catcher	PCT	G	PO	A	E	DP	PB
Carpenter	.989	27	161	19	2	0	9
Gonzalez	.969	35	228	25	8	0	8
Thomas	.992	19	107	12	1	1	1

First Base	PCT	G	PO	A	E	DP
Hamilton	.985	30	258	13	4	21
Morris	1.000	1	7	0	0	0
Thomas	1.000	3	19	1	0	2
Van Slyke	.972	27	259	17	8	21
Wilkerson	.964	20	155	6	6	13

Second Base	PCT	G	PO	A	E	DP
Craig	1.000	1	1	2	0	0
Morris	1.000	1	2	2	0	0
Salazar	1.000	9	15	25	0	6

	PCT	G	PO	A	E	DP
Sandoval	.951	21	39	78	6	18
Schweitzer	.964	38	52	108	6	16
Solano	.959	11	15	32	2	6

Third Base	PCT	G	PO	A	E	DP
Craig	.906	35	30	47	8	3
Morris	.909	11	7	23	3	4
Sandoval	1.000	1	0	3	0	1
Schweitzer	.750	5	3	6	3	0
Solano	.961	29	18	55	3	6
Thomas	—	1	0	0	0	0

Shortstop	PCT	G	PO	A	E	DP
Craig	.857	3	2	4	1	0
Ryan	.958	8	20	26	2	6
Salazar	.966	36	49	94	5	15

	PCT	G	PO	A	E	DP
Sandoval	.954	28	47	77	6	9
Schweitzer	1.000	1	1	3	0	2
Solano	.967	5	10	19	1	4

Outfield	PCT	G	PO	A	E	DP
Carter	.947	11	18	0	1	0
Gorsett	.976	19	39	1	1	0
Rapoport	1.000	64	145	2	0	1
Sandoval	—	2	0	0	0	0
Sivira	.965	49	80	3	3	1
Southard	.959	66	92	2	4	0
Thomas	1.000	1	1	0	0	0
Van Slyke	—	1	0	0	0	0
Wilkerson	.977	25	40	2	1	0

Johnson City Cardinals — Rookie

Appalachian League

BATTING	B-T	HT	WT	DOB	AVG	vLH	vRH	G	AB	R	H	2B	3B	HR	RBI	BB	HBP	SH	SF	SO	SB	CS	SLG	OBP
Buckman, Brandon	L-L	6-6	205	2-14-84	.300	.317	.291	62	230	33	69	17	0	8	34	24	1	0	1	31	0	2	.478	.367
Bussiere, Garrett	R-R	6-2	180	8-28-85	.156	.190	.140	22	64	8	10	1	0	3	5	8	0	0	0	22	0	1	.313	.270
Caldera, Ciro	R-R	5-10	175	6-16-86	.250	.323	.204	28	80	7	20	3	0	0	9	4	1	1	0	12	1	0	.288	.294
Edwards, Jonathan	R-R	6-5	230	1-8-88	.266	.283	.257	48	154	23	41	16	1	4	27	20	3	0	1	33	0	0	.461	.360
Garcia, Isaias	R-R	5-10	180	8-20-84	.339	.449	.276	57	192	35	65	17	2	4	25	15	3	0	0	13	4	1	.510	.395
Jones, Daryl	L-L	5-11	180	6-25-87	.265	.118	.314	20	68	15	18	3	1	3	13	8	3	0	0	8	3	0	.471	.367
Lopez, Christian	R-R	6-0	160	1-23-87	.244	.188	.266	53	172	21	42	5	5	3	18	12	2	1	1	56	5	7	.384	.299
Lugo, Nelson	R-R	6-0	175	4-24-85	.240	.209	.256	43	125	18	30	4	1	1	10	14	2	0	2	36	12	3	.312	.322
Mitchell, Travis	R-R	6-3	185	9-27-87	.207	.231	.197	58	179	20	37	5	0	0	14	13	2	3	0	40	12	3	.235	.268
Mulligan, Casey	R-R	6-2	190	10-5-87	.201	.143	.221	60	189	17	38	7	1	0	9	16	3	1	1	34	0	1	.249	.273
Naylor, Keith	R-R	5-11	190	1-12-83	.157	.158	.156	30	51	7	8	3	0	0	2	3	2	0	1	21	2	0	.216	.228
Owens, Malcolm	R-R	6-3	210	3-23-84	.000	.000	.000	3	8	1	0	0	0	0	0	1	0	0	0	4	0	1	.000	.111
Pham, Thomas	R-R	6-1	175	3-8-88	.231	.125	.288	54	182	26	42	8	3	1	19	26	5	1	2	42	12	3	.324	.340
Puello, Melvin	R-R	6-1	180	11-27-85	.235	.277	.213	45	136	19	32	7	1	0	5	2	2	2	0	41	5	2	.301	.257
Pujols, Wilfrido	R-R	6-1	185	9-11-87	.202	.167	.230	40	109	11	22	3	0	0	7	5	3	1	1	37	1	2	.229	.254
Ramirez, Jose	R-R	5-11	175	3-12-85	.000	.000	.000	6	18	1	0	0	0	0	0	1	0	0	0	4	0	0	.000	.053
Reyes, Christian	R-R	6-0	190	4-24-86	.264	.286	.253	37	121	17	32	5	1	8	20	10	2	0	1	31	0	1	.521	.328
Sandoval, Willian	B-R	5-10	170	12-27-85	.200	—	.200	1	5	1	1	0	0	0	0	0	0	0	0	1	0	0	.200	.200
Schoendienst, Jesse	R-R	6-1	160	7-10-82	.000	.000	.000	9	12	2	0	0	0	0	0	2	2	1	0	6	0	0	.000	.250
Shorey, Mark	L-L	6-0	230	8-13-84	.265	.236	.276	58	200	32	53	8	1	13	47	16	4	0	1	53	0	0	.510	.330

PITCHING	B-T	HT	WT	DOB	W	L	ERA	G	GS	CG	SV	IP	H	R	ER	HR	BB	SO	AVG	vLH	vRH	K/9	BB/9
Adams, Jason	R-R	6-2	185	4-27-85	2	1	2.51	12	0	0	1	14	14	7	4	1	3	19	.250	.267	.244	11.93	1.88
Bakey, Kris	R-R	6-3	225	9-15-84	2	5	3.38	25	0	0	4	35	40	19	13	0	13	30	.288	.368	.257	7.79	3.38
Carrasco, Armando	R-R	6-1	205	7-1-85	1	1	2.63	22	0	0	4	27	18	15	8	2	19	31	.186	.154	.207	10.21	6.26
Collier, Logan	R-R	6-7	185	4-5-85	1	2	5.36	14	9	0	0	42	40	27	25	4	25	37	.252	.224	.264	7.93	5.36
Dickson, Brandon	R-R	6-5	190	11-3-84	1	0	6.35	9	0	0	1	11	16	11	8	1	6	15	.320	.333	.314	11.91	4.76
Garner, Brandon	R-R	6-0	165	8-27-86	1	0	4.71	20	2	0	0	36	46	26	19	3	17	18	.307	.286	.317	4.46	4.21
Gonzalez, Marco	R-R	6-2	205	5-28-84	3	0	0.73	7	0	0	0	12	3	1	1	0	3	14	.073	.188	.000	10.22	2.19
Gregerson, Luke	L-R	6-3	200	5-14-84	0	1	3.86	15	0	0	5	16	14	10	7	0	6	24	.222	.167	.235	13.22	3.31
Hernandez, Elvis	R-R	6-3	180	4-27-85	3	3	3.48	13	13	0	0	67	55	32	26	5	27	54	.217	.241	.206	7.22	3.61
Herron, Tyler	R-R	6-3	190	8-5-86	5	6	4.13	13	13	1	0	70	69	41	32	6	22	54	.259	.271	.254	6.98	2.84
King, Blake	R-R	6-1	195	4-11-87	4	3	3.02	13	13	0	0	63	37	25	21	3	29	74	.167	.224	.137	10.63	4.16
Lara, Oscar	R-R	5-11	185	4-10-84	3	0	3.91	20	0	0	1	25	24	12	11	1	15	13	.255	.222	.269	4.62	5.33
Lugo, Henderson	R-R	6-4	205	9-15-84	1	4	3.50	21	3	0	0	44	46	22	17	1	11	37	.271	.200	.300	7.63	2.27
Marquez, Fabian	R-R	6-1	170	11-12-86	0	1	10.89	15	1	0	0	21	25	30	25	1	26	15	.291	.346	.267	6.53	11.32
McClellan, Kyle	R-R	6-4	205	6-12-84	0	1	9.45	3	3	0	0	7	7	7	7	0	3	4	.259	.286	.250	5.40	4.05
Michael, Matt	L-L	5-11	190	11-13-83	0	0	3.72	19	0	0	0	19	15	10	8	0	12	20	.217	.174	.239	9.31	5.59
Montano, A.J.	R-R	6-1	205	1-30-84	3	0	2.57	9	0	0	0	14	8	4	4	1	6	8	.170	.091	.194	5.14	3.86
North, Matthew	R-R	6-5	170	5-23-88	2	5	6.41	11	9	0	0	39	51	34	28	1	27	20	.319	.333	.311	4.58	6.18
Oliveros, Frank	L-L	6-0	165	8-9-86	0	0	9.00	14	0	0	0	14	19	14	14	2	10	17	.328	.313	.333	10.93	6.43
Peralta, Senger	L-L	6-1	160	8-14-87	1	1	5.00	3	2	0	0	9	6	6	5	2	3	7	.182	.143	.192	7.00	3.00
Pol, Frank	R-R	6-6	245	2-23-88	0	0	4.91	3	0	0	0	4	2	2	2	0	2	3	.154	.500	.091	7.36	4.91
Valera, Yeury	R-R	6-4	210	3-1-86	1	0	7.88	7	0	0	0	8	10	9	7	0	10	8	.323	.400	.286	9.00	11.25

FIELDING

Catcher	PCT	G	PO	A	E	DP	PB
Bussiere	.993	21	129	17	1	1	1
Caldera	.984	28	162	21	3	0	13
Mulligan	.992	16	115	8	1	3	8
Reyes	.956	19	114	15	6	1	5

First Base	PCT	G	PO	A	E	DP
Buckman	.989	61	493	37	6	51
Lugo	.984	7	58	2	1	4
Reyes	1.000	2	25	1	0	1
Shorey	1.000	7	29	4	0	3

Second Base	PCT	G	PO	A	E	DP
Garcia	.978	42	80	99	4	24
Lopez	.989	26	35	53	1	9

	PCT	G	PO	A	E	DP
Lugo	1.000	1	1	1	0	1
Puello	.941	8	15	17	2	9
Sandoval	.667	1	0	2	1	0
Schoendienst	1.000	3	3	5	0	1

Third Base	PCT	G	PO	A	E	DP
Garcia	.900	5	1	8	1	1
Lopez	.864	21	9	48	9	7
Lugo	—	1	0	0	0	0
Mulligan	.932	47	23	101	9	4
Puello	.941	6	5	11	1	0
Schoendienst	1.000	3	2	4	0	0

Shortstop	PCT	G	PO	A	E	DP
Lopez	.960	8	10	14	1	4

	PCT	G	PO	A	E	DP
Pham	.849	37	51	73	22	19
Puello	.888	29	44	75	15	12
Schoendienst	.333	1	1	0	2	0

Outfield	PCT	G	PO	A	E	DP
Edwards	.949	47	70	4	4	1
Jones	1.000	16	27	0	0	0
Lopez	1.000	1	1	0	0	0
Lugo	.957	30	41	3	2	1
Mitchell	.960	57	115	4	5	0
Naylor	1.000	20	13	4	0	0
Owens	1.000	2	4	0	0	0
Pujols	.892	35	31	2	4	0
Ramirez	1.000	6	4	1	0	0
Shorey	1.000	32	45	5	0	4

BY JOHN MAFFEI

A lot went right for the Padres before 2006 ended with a quick exit in the postseason.

They won 88 games and captured the NL West title for the second consecutive season—a first for the 37-year-old franchise. Several young players established themselves as front-line major leaguers, including first baseman Adrian Gonzalez, rookie second baseman Josh Barfield and catcher Josh Bard.

Pitchers Chris Young, Clay Hensley and Cla Meredith helped the Padres post an NL-best 3.87 ERA.

Gonzalez led the team with 24 home runs and played solid defense. Barfield hit .280/.318/.423 though he was traded to the Indians after the season. Bard, acquired in a trade with Boston for disgruntled Doug Mirabelli, hit .338/.406/.537 in 93 games and was a rock behind the plate.

Young, acquired from Texas with Gonzalez for Adam Eaton and Akinori Otsuka, was 11-5, 3.46. Hensley joined the rotation early in the season and finished 11-12, 3.71 in 29 starts. Meredith, also acquired from Boston, set a franchise record by throwing 33⅔ consecutive scoreless innings. He appeared in 45 games with San Diego and finished 5-1, 1.07 using a baffling sidearm delivery.

Closer Trevor Hoffman converted 46 of 51 save opportunities and passed Lee Smith as baseball's all-time saves leader. Catcher Mike Piazza platooned with Bard and Rob Bowen and hit .283/.342/.501 with 22 home runs while handling the pitching staff like a veteran.

Leadoff left fielder Dave Roberts hit .293/.360/.393 and set career-highs in steals (49) and games played (129). Veteran Mike Cameron, acquired for Xavier Nady in a

PLAYERS OF THE YEAR

MAJOR LEAGUE: Adrian Gonzalez, 1b

Gonzalez surprised everyone with his breakout season, leading the team with a .304 average, .500 slugging percentage, 24 home runs and 38 doubles. The No. 1 overall pick by the Marlins in 2000—and acquired by the Padres in a deal with the Rangers—had never hit more than 18 home runs in a season.

MINOR LEAGUE: Will Venable, of

While older than his Midwest League competition, Venable was unquestionably one of the league's top hitters. He finished second with a .314 average and 91 RBIs, first with 86 runs and fourth with 34 doubles. Venable, 23, was all-Ivy League in baseball and basketball at Princeton and stole 18 bases in 2006.

PAUL GIERHART

deal with the Mets, hit .268/.355/.482 and won a Gold Glove in center field.

Veteran righthander Woody Williams was the backbone of the staff, finishing 12-5, 3.65.

The season ended in disappointment when the underdog Cardinals won the first two games of the Division Series in San Diego and put the Padres away in Game Four in St. Louis.

"It was a tough ending to a very good season," General manager Kevin Towers said. "We really had some young guys take positive steps. Cameron gave us everything we could have asked for in center and Piazza was the veteran leader we needed. And with Young, Hensley and Jake Peavy, we have three young, quality arms in the rotation."

The Padres will look to improve an uninspiring rotation at third base that included Vinny Castilla, Todd Walker, Geoff Blum, Mark Bellhorn, Manny Alexander and Russell Branyan. Shortstop Khalil Greene played in just 117 games and right fielder Brian Giles was inconsistent despite hitting .263/.374/.397.

Towers will need to look outside of the organization for help and should have some financial flexibility with the contracts of Chan Ho Park, Ryan Klesko and Phil Nevin expiring. Towers will find little immediate help in the farm system.

Outfielders Jack Cust and Jon Knott had huge years at Triple-A Portland but may not be in the Padres' plans. Paul McAnulty, a versatile lefthanded hitter who played first, third and the outfield, could get an opportunity as a pinch-hitter.

The Padres have some prospects at Double-A Mobile: catcher Colt Morton, outfielders Kennard Jones, Vince Sinisi and Drew Macias. Righthanders Cesar Carrillo, the 2005 first-round pick, and John Hudgins have been slowed by elbow problems.

The Padres are deep in talent at the lower-levels of the organization. A long list of prospects at least two years away from the big league is highlighted by third baseman Chris Headley (.291/.389/.434) and outfielder Will Venable (.314/.389/.477).

ORGANIZATION LEADERS

BATTING		*Minimum 250 at-bats
*AVG	Durango, Luis, AZL Padres	.378
R	Kazmar, Sean, Lake Elsinore	98
H	Venable, William, Fort Wayne	160
TB	Knott, Jon, Portland	274
2B	Cruz, Luis, Mobile	39
	Venable, William, Fort Wayne	39
3B	Baxter, Michael, Fort Wayne	7
HR	Knott, Jon, Portland	32
RBI	Knott, Jon, Portland	113
BB	Cust, Jack, Portland	143
SO	Adams, Skip, Lake Elsinore	137
SB	Ramirez, Yordany, Lake Elsinore	23
*OBP	Durango, Luis, AZL Padres	.470
*SLG	Sledge, Terrmel, Portland	.583
XBH	Knott, Jon, Portland	70

PITCHING		#Minimum 75 innings
W	Geer, Joshua, Fort Wayne/Lake Elsinore	13
L	Hayhurst, Dirk, Lake Elsinore/Mobile/Portland	14
#ERA	Dunn, Brooks, Eugene	2.41
G	Jamison, Neil, Fort Wayne/Lake Elsinore	74
CG	Ekstrom, Michael, Lake Elsinore/Mobile	4
SV	Jamison, Neil, Fort Wayne/Lake Elsinore	37
IP	Ekstrom, Michael, Lake Elsinore/Mobile	167
BB	Oyervidez, Jose, Mobile	75
SO	Thompson, Sean, Mobile	134
#AVG	Dunn, Brooks, Eugene	.232

San Diego Padres

National League

BATTING	B-T	HT	WT	DOB	AVG	vLH	vRH	G	AB	R	H	2B	3B	HR	RBI	BB	HBP	SH	SF	SO	SB	CS	SLG	OBP
Alexander, Manny	R-R	5-10	180	3-20-71	.176	.182	.167	22	34	2	6	1	1	0	4	2	0	2	1	5	0	1	.265	.216
Bard, Josh	B-R	6-3	210	3-30-78	.338	.339	.337	93	231	28	78	19	0	9	40	27	1	2	2	39	1	0	.537	.406
Barfield, Josh	R-R	6-0	190	12-17-82	.280	.331	.266	150	539	72	151	32	3	13	58	30	2	2	5	81	21	5	.423	.318
Bellhorn, Mark	B-R	6-1	205	8-23-74	.190	.224	.175	115	253	26	48	11	2	8	27	32	2	0	1	90	0	0	.344	.285
Blum, Geoff	B-R	6-3	205	4-26-73	.254	.167	.267	109	276	27	70	17	1	4	34	17	0	2	4	51	0	1	.366	.293
Bowen, Rob	B-R	6-3	225	2-24-81	.245	.167	.263	94	94	22	23	5	0	3	13	13	1	1	1	26	0	1	.394	.339
Branyan, Russell	L-R	6-3	195	12-19-75	.292	.286	.293	27	72	14	21	1	0	6	9	15	1	0	1	27	0	0	.556	.416
Cameron, Mike	R-R	6-2	200	1-8-73	.268	.252	.273	141	552	88	148	34	9	22	83	71	6	0	5	142	25	9	.482	.355
Castilla, Vinny	R-R	6-1	205	7-4-67	.232	.206	.242	72	254	24	59	10	0	4	23	9	2	0	4	46	0	0	.319	.260
2-team (15 Colorado)					.229	—	—	87	275	26	63	10	0	5	27	9	3	0	4	49	0	0	.320	.258
Cust, Jack	L-R	6-1	230	1-16-79	.333	—	.333	4	3	1	1	0	0	0	0	0	0	0	0	1	0	0	.333	.333
Giles, Brian	L-L	5-10	205	1-20-71	.263	.217	.282	158	604	87	159	37	1	14	83	104	5	0	4	60	9	4	.397	.374
Gonzalez, Adrian	L-L	6-2	220	5-8-82	.304	.312	.301	156	570	83	173	38	1	24	82	52	3	1	5	113	0	1	.500	.362
Greene, Khalil	R-R	5-11	195	10-21-79	.245	.271	.237	121	412	56	101	26	2	15	55	39	7	0	2	87	5	1	.427	.320
Johnson, Ben	R-R	6-1	220	6-18-81	.250	.275	.232	58	120	19	30	5	2	4	12	14	1	0	0	36	3	0	.425	.333
Klesko, Ryan	L-L	6-3	220	6-12-71	.750	1.000	.667	6	4	0	3	1	0	0	2	2	0	0	0	0	1	0	1.000	.833
Knott, Jon	R-R	6-3	220	8-4-78	.000	.000	—	3	3	0	0	0	0	0	0	0	0	0	0	1	0	0	.000	.000
Leone, Justin	R-R	6-1	210	3-9-77	.000	—	.000	1	1	0	0	0	0	0	0	0	0	0	0	0	0	0	.000	.000
McAnulty, Paul	L-R	5-10	220	2-24-81	.231	.000	.250	16	13	3	3	1	0	1	3	2	0	0	0	4	0	0	.538	.333
Mirabelli, Doug	R-R	6-1	220	10-18-70	.182	.143	.200	14	22	1	4	1	0	0	0	4	0	0	0	5	0	0	.227	.308
Piazza, Mike	R-R	6-3	215	9-4-68	.283	.359	.257	126	399	39	113	19	1	22	68	34	3	0	3	66	0	0	.501	.342
Roberts, Dave	L-L	5-10	180	5-31-72	.293	.292	.293	129	499	80	146	18	13	2	44	51	4	7	5	61	49	6	.393	.360
Sledge, Terrmel	L-L	6-0	185	3-18-77	.229	.400	.215	38	70	7	16	3	0	2	7	8	0	0	0	17	0	0	.357	.308
Walker, Todd	L-R	6-0	185	5-25-73	.282	.167	.302	44	124	18	35	6	1	3	13	17	0	0	1	11	2	0	.419	.366
2-team (94 Chicago)					.278	—	—	138	442	56	123	22	2	9	53	55	1	1	5	38	2	1	.398	.356
Young, Eric	R-R	5-9	185	5-11-67	.203	.258	.145	56	128	19	26	5	0	3	13	13	2	1	3	16	8	2	.313	.281

PITCHING	B-T	HT	WT	DOB	W	L	ERA	G	GS	CG	SV	IP	H	R	ER	HR	BB	SO	AVG	vLH	vRH	K/9	BB/9
Adkins, Jon	L-R	6-0	200	8-30-77	2	1	3.98	55	0	0	0	54	55	26	24	3	20	30	.271	.287	.259	4.97	3.31
Brazelton, Dewon	R-R	6-4	215	6-16-80	0	2	12.00	9	2	0	0	18	28	25	24	6	9	9	.354	.361	.349	4.50	4.50
Brocail, Doug	L-R	6-5	250	5-16-67	2	2	4.76	25	0	0	0	28	27	16	15	1	8	19	.252	.280	.228	6.04	2.54
Brower, Jim	R-R	6-3	215	12-29-72	0	0	9.39	6	0	0	0	8	11	8	8	1	1	5	.344	.467	.235	5.87	1.17
Cassidy, Scott	R-R	6-2	180	10-3-75	6	4	2.53	42	0	0	0	43	39	18	12	8	19	49	.248	.237	.255	10.34	4.01
Embree, Alan	L-L	6-2	190	1-23-70	4	3	3.27	73	0	0	0	52	50	21	19	4	15	53	.249	.240	.258	9.11	2.58
Estes, Shawn	R-L	6-2	200	2-18-73	0	1	4.50	1	1	0	0	6	5	3	3	0	3	4	.217	.000	.227	6.00	4.50
Hensley, Clay	R-R	5-11	190	8-31-79	11	12	3.71	37	29	1	0	187	174	82	77	15	76	122	.250	.263	.239	5.87	3.66
Hoffman, Trevor	R-R	6-0	215	10-13-67	0	2	2.14	65	0	0	46	63	48	16	15	6	13	50	.205	.194	.214	7.14	1.86
Linebrink, Scott	R-R	6-2	200	8-4-76	7	4	3.57	73	0	0	2	76	70	31	30	9	22	68	.243	.204	.294	8.09	2.62
Meredith, Cla	R-R	6-0	180	6-4-83	5	1	1.07	45	0	0	0	51	30	6	6	3	6	37	.170	.281	.107	6.57	1.07
Park, Chan Ho	R-R	6-2	210	6-30-73	7	7	4.81	24	21	1	0	137	146	81	73	20	44	96	.271	.266	.278	6.32	2.90
Peavy, Jake	R-R	6-1	180	5-31-81	11	14	4.09	32	32	2	0	202	187	93	92	23	62	215	.242	.242	.243	9.56	2.76
Seanez, Rudy	R-R	5-11	200	10-20-68	1	2	5.68	8	0	0	0	6	7	4	4	2	6	6	.259	.267	.250	8.53	8.53
Sikorski, Brian	R-R	6-1	190	7-27-74	1	1	5.65	13	0	0	0	14	16	9	9	4	3	14	.281	.357	.207	8.79	1.88
Stauffer, Tim	R-R	6-1	205	6-2-82	1	0	1.50	1	1	0	0	6	3	2	1	0	1	2	.150	.091	.222	3.00	1.50
Sweeney, Brian	R-R	6-2	200	6-13-74	2	0	3.20	37	0	0	2	56	53	22	20	6	16	23	.249	.263	.237	3.67	2.56
Thompson, Mike	R-R	6-4	200	11-6-80	4	5	4.99	19	16	0	0	92	103	56	51	13	30	35	.285	.283	.288	3.42	2.93
Wells, David	L-L	6-3	250	5-20-63	1	2	3.49	5	5	0	0	28	33	11	11	1	4	14	.292	.375	.270	4.45	1.27
Williams, Woody	R-R	6-0	200	8-19-66	12	5	3.65	25	24	0	0	145	152	68	59	21	35	72	.267	.245	.287	4.46	2.17
Williamson, Scott	R-R	6-0	185	2-17-76	0	1	7.36	11	0	0	0	11	14	9	9	2	6	10	.333	.250	.409	8.18	4.91
2-team (31 Chicago)					2	4	5.72	42	0	0	0	39	41	26	25	4	22	42	—	—	—	9.61	5.03
Young, Chris	R-R	6-10	260	5-25-79	11	5	3.46	31	31	0	0	179	134	72	69	28	69	164	.206	.175	.234	8.23	3.46

FIELDING

Catcher	PCT	G	PO	A	E	DP	PB
Bard	.993	71	385	30	3	5	0
Bowen	.994	65	144	14	1	1	3
Mirabelli	1.000	9	37	2	0	0	1
Piazza	.987	99	553	34	8	3	7

First Base	PCT	G	PO	A	E	DP
Bellhorn	.980	18	90	6	2	9
Blum	1.000	2	4	0	0	2
Bowen	1.000	1	1	0	0	0
Gonzalez	.995	155	1242	116	7	117
Walker	1.000	3	26	1	0	0

Second Base	PCT	G	PO	A	E	DP
Barfield	.987	147	294	381	9	84

	PCT	G	PO	A	E	DP
Bellhorn	1.000	11	22	33	0	5
Blum	1.000	1	3	6	0	1
Walker	.981	14	21	32	1	8
Young	—	1	0	0	0	0

Third Base	PCT	G	PO	A	E	DP
Alexander	.900	13	2	7	1	1
Bellhorn	.959	50	28	66	4	8
Blum	1.000	34	18	36	0	1
Branyan	.933	26	14	28	3	3
Castilla	.971	69	54	112	5	8
Walker	.896	23	12	31	5	2

Shortstop	PCT	G	PO	A	E	DP
Alexander	.975	9	12	27	1	8

	PCT	G	PO	A	E	DP
Blum	.971	49	72	129	6	28
Greene	.980	113	138	309	9	60

Outfield	PCT	G	PO	A	E	DP
Bellhorn	—	1	0	0	0	0
Blum	1.000	1	1	0	0	0
Cameron	.984	141	367	6	6	2
Cust	—	1	0	0	0	0
Giles	.978	158	299	7	7	2
Johnson	1.000	43	88	1	0	0
McAnulty	—	1	0	0	0	0
Roberts	1.000	127	273	1	0	0
Sledge	.971	22	32	1	1	0
Young	.980	39	50	0	1	0

General manager: Kevin Towers. **Farm director:** Grady Fuson. **Scouting director:** Bill Gayton.

Class	Team	League	W	L	PCT	Finish*	Manager	Affiliate Since
Majors	San Diego	National	88	74	.543	3rd (16)	Bruce Bochy	—
Triple-A	Portland Beavers	Pacific Coast	68	76	.472	11th (16)	Craig Colbert	2001
Double-A	Mobile BayBears	Southern	62	76	.449	7th (10)	Gary Jones	1997
High A	Lake Elsinore Storm	California	74	66	.529	3rd (10)	Rick Renteria	2001
Low A	Fort Wayne Wizards	Midwest	71	66	.518	8th (14)	Randy Ready	1999
Short-season	Eugene Emeralds	Northwest	43	33	.566	3rd (8)	Doug Dascenzo	2001
Rookie	AZL Padres	Arizona	36	19	.655	+1st (9)	Carlos Lezcano	2004
OVERALL 2006 MINOR LEAGUE RECORD			354	336	.513	12th (30)		

*Finish in overall standings (No. of teams in league). +League champion

Portland Beavers — Triple-A
Pacific Coast League

BATTING	B-T	HT	WT	DOB	AVG	vLH	vRH	G	AB	R	H	2B	3B	HR	RBI	BB	HBP	SH	SF	SO	SB	CS	SLG	OBP
Alexander, Manny	R-R	5-10	180	3-20-71	.265	.271	.263	102	430	78	114	21	0	7	37	35	3	1	3	58	14	4	.363	.323
Allen, Luke	L-R	6-2	220	8-4-78	.305	.378	.272	34	118	17	36	4	1	5	25	10	0	4	0	23	0	0	.483	.348
Carlin, Luke	B-R	5-11	185	12-20-80	.266	.348	.234	73	244	27	65	14	1	4	29	49	2	1	1	54	0	0	.381	.392
Chang, Ray	R-R	6-1	195	8-24-83	.222	.333	.200	12	18	2	4	1	1	1	2	1	0	0	0	7	0	0	.556	.263
Cust, Jack	L-R	6-1	230	1-16-79	.293	.279	.298	138	441	97	129	23	0	30	77	143	4	0	3	124	0	3	.549	.467
Davidiuk, A.J.	R-R	6-1	185	12-12-83	.000	.000	.000	2	5	0	0	0	0	0	0	0	0	0	0	0	0	0	.000	.000
Delucchi, Dustin	L-L	6-0	190	12-23-77	.216	.143	.233	14	37	1	8	2	0	0	4	4	1	0	0	8	0	0	.270	.310
Dowdy, Brett	R-R	6-0	190	2-22-82	.167	—	.167	4	12	1	2	0	0	0	0	1	0	0	2	0	0	0	.167	.231
Gutierrez, Ricky	R-R	6-1	195	5-23-70	.200	.143	.214	11	35	2	7	2	0	0	3	2	0	0	0	7	0	0	.257	.243
Guzman, Freddy	B-R	5-10	165	1-20-81	.274	.296	.268	30	124	15	34	7	2	2	14	14	0	1	0	19	11	3	.411	.348
2-team (69 Oklahoma)					.279	—	—	99	376	60	105	16	4	3	28	50	2	3	1	55	42	12	.367	.366
Hernandez, Brian	R-R	6-1	180	11-4-83	.333	.000	.500	1	3	0	1	1	0	0	1	0	0	0	0	0	0	0	.667	.333
Hill, Bobby	B-R	5-10	175	4-3-78	.282	.211	.303	96	309	55	87	23	0	4	33	48	12	2	2	67	0	1	.395	.396
Hill, Jason	R-R	6-3	210	3-17-77	.241	.293	.225	45	170	13	41	7	0	3	22	14	1	0	1	23	0	0	.335	.301
Johnson, Ben	R-R	6-1	220	6-18-81	.263	.316	.241	51	198	35	52	11	1	7	22	23	3	0	3	55	7	1	.434	.344
Jones, Kennard	L-L	5-11	185	9-8-81	.186	.170	.193	68	161	14	30	2	1	0	10	20	0	0	2	41	6	2	.211	.273
Knott, Jon	R-R	6-2	230	8-4-78	.280	.331	.261	136	479	80	134	32	6	32	113	52	6	0	7	103	3	3	.572	.353
Kottaras, George	L-R	6-0	185	5-16-83	.210	.111	.253	33	119	14	25	10	1	2	17	12	1	0	1	30	0	0	.361	.286
Leone, Justin	R-R	6-1	210	3-9-77	.260	.227	.271	124	453	66	118	20	0	20	73	61	6	0	4	106	4	4	.437	.353
Matos, Julius	R-R	5-11	170	12-12-74	.304	.400	.231	16	46	4	14	1	0	0	5	1	0	1	1	11	0	0	.326	.313
Matranga, Dave	R-R	6-0	185	1-8-77	.219	.190	.229	92	302	39	66	11	0	11	31	22	10	5	0	80	4	1	.364	.293
McAnulty, Paul	L-R	5-10	220	2-24-81	.310	.252	.331	125	478	76	148	34	5	19	79	62	4	0	8	79	1	2	.521	.388
Risinger, Ben	R-R	6-1	170	11-25-77	.000	—	.000	1	3	0	0	0	0	0	0	0	0	0	0	0	0	0	.000	.000
Sledge, Terrmel	L-L	6-0	185	3-18-77	.311	.382	.288	101	367	69	114	18	5	24	73	59	1	1	6	75	5	3	.583	.402
Valent, Eric	L-L	5-11	195	4-4-77	.209	.333	.169	30	86	10	18	4	0	0	4	9	0	0	0	23	0	0	.256	.284
Young, Walter	L-R	6-5	315	2-18-80	.200	.000	.233	13	35	4	7	1	0	3	6	3	1	0	3	5	0	0	.486	.262

PITCHING	B-T	HT	WT	DOB	W	L	ERA	G	GS	CG	SV	IP	H	R	ER	HR	BB	SO	AVG	vLH	vRH	K/9	BB/9
Adams, Mike	R-R	6-5	190	7-29-78	0	2	4.18	17	0	0	0	24	29	16	11	1	7	15	.299	.214	.364	5.70	2.66
2-team (15 Nashville)					1	3	3.82	32	0	0	2	40	46	24	17	3	15	33	—	—	—	7.42	3.38
Adkins, Jon	L-R	6-0	200	8-30-77	1	0	1.38	13	0	0	7	13	12	2	2	0	3	11	.235	.172	.318	7.62	2.08
Anderson, Jason	L-R	6-0	190	6-9-79	5	2	3.29	60	0	0	4	79	74	33	29	8	29	62	.247	.250	.245	7.03	3.29
Andrade, Steve	R-R	6-1	220	2-6-78	3	0	2.44	26	0	0	0	44	33	13	12	1	22	45	.209	.152	.250	9.14	4.47
2-team (12 Omaha)					3	2	3.19	38	0	0	0	67	54	26	24	4	30	67	—	—	—	8.91	3.99
Ayala, Manny	R-R	6-3	225	11-6-84	0	0	0.00	1	0	0	0	2	2	0	0	0	0	1	.286	.000	.667	4.50	0.00
Blank, Matt	L-L	6-2	190	4-5-76	1	1	7.06	7	3	0	0	22	24	18	17	3	8	10	.286	.286	.286	4.15	3.32
2-team (14 Albuquerque)					3	3	5.64	21	10	0	0	68	80	46	43	10	32	38	—	—	—	4.98	4.19
Brazelton, Dewon	R-R	6-4	215	6-16-80	5	7	4.53	17	16	1	0	91	100	50	46	15	25	53	.281	.276	.285	5.22	2.46
Brower, Jim	R-R	6-3	215	12-29-72	5	2	4.98	24	0	0	1	34	37	21	19	5	18	28	.276	.333	.221	7.34	4.72
2-team (15 Albuquerque)					5	3	4.61	39	0	0	1	52	57	30	27	8	21	41	—	—	—	7.01	3.59
Burke, Erick	L-L	6-4	230	8-14-77	3	3	4.15	49	1	0	0	80	78	45	37	10	45	79	.261	.263	.260	8.85	5.04
Carrillo, Cesar	R-R	6-3	175	4-29-84	0	0	6.75	1	1	0	0	3	2	2	2	0	3	1	.222	.200	.250	3.38	10.13
Cassel, Jack	R-R	6-2	180	8-8-80	3	5	6.48	18	11	0	0	76	96	60	55	12	28	44	.306	.348	.263	5.19	3.30
Cassidy, Scott	R-R	6-2	180	10-3-75	3	1	2.70	17	0	0	9	20	21	6	6	0	6	23	.269	.400	.200	10.35	2.70
Deago, Roger	R-L	5-10	180	6-21-77	4	5	5.28	11	11	0	0	60	67	37	35	10	32	40	.286	.255	.296	6.03	4.83
Etherton, Seth	R-R	6-1	200	10-17-76	2	2	4.38	9	9	0	0	49	48	25	24	8	14	49	.253	.262	.241	8.94	2.55
2-team (10 Omaha)					3	6	5.25	19	15	0	0	84	91	50	49	19	27	78	—	—	—	8.36	2.89
Hayhurst, Dirk	L-R	6-3	200	3-24-81	1	2	6.75	4	4	0	0	20	29	15	15	4	9	12	.345	.419	.302	5.40	4.05
Hudgins, John	R-R	6-2	195	8-31-81	1	1	2.70	2	2	0	0	7	11	8	2	1	1	7	.355	.385	.333	9.45	1.35
2-team (7 Oklahoma)					2	2	5.40	9	4	0	0	25	29	25	15	4	8	23	—	—	—	8.28	2.88
Junge, Eric	R-R	6-5	215	1-5-77	4	5	5.15	21	13	0	0	72	86	45	41	7	26	61	.305	.298	.311	7.66	3.27
Lopez, Aquilino	R-R	6-3	185	4-21-75	3	4	5.52	41	0	0	2	62	66	41	38	16	24	52	.264	.248	.279	10.45	3.48
Matranga, Dave	R-R	6-0	185	1-8-77	0	0	0.00	1	0	0	0	1	0	0	0	0	0	0	.000	.000	.000	0.00	0.00
Meaux, Ryan	R-L	5-11	170	10-5-78	2	3	6.11	40	0	0	0	74	99	55	50	9	29	59	.335	.330	.322	7.1	3.54
Meredith, Cla	R-R	6-0	180	6-4-83	3	0	1.39	24	0	0	2	32	26	5	5	2	4	24	.222	.186	.259	6.68	1.11
Pena, Eduardo	R-R	6-4	205	6-18-83	0	0	5.68	5	0	0	0	6	5	4	4	0	2	2	.227	.200	.235	2.84	7.11
Ramos, Mario	L-L	5-11	180	10-19-77	0	3	7.92	11	6	0	0	31	42	30	27	6	15	23	.333	.306	.344	6.5	4.26
Sikorski, Brian	R-R	6-1	190	7-27-74	2	3	3.14	22	0	0	7	29	25	12	10	3	7	44	.225	.228	.222	13.81	2.20
Stauffer, Tim	R-R	6-1	205	6-2-82	7	12	5.53	28	26	0	0	153	199	108	94	20	52	89	.320	.329	.310	5.24	3.06
Sterry, Vern	R-R	6-2	210	2-7-82	0	0	0.00	4	0	0	0	4	0	0	0	0	3	3	.150	.250	.083	4.76	4.76
Sweeney, Brian	R-R	6-2	200	6-13-74	2	1	4.70	7	5	0	0	31	33	17	16	3	7	22	.280	.233	.307	6.46	2.05
Thayer, Dale	R-R	6-0	190	12-17-80	0	0	3.00	2	0	0	0	3	2	1	1	1	4	.200	.500	.000	12.00	3.00

	B-T	HT	WT	DOB	W	L	ERA	G	GS	CG	SV	IP	H	R	ER	HR	BB	SO	AVG	vLH	vRH	K/9	BB/9
Thompson, Mike	R-R	6-4	200	11-6-80	6	1	3.76	13	13	0	0	69	69	30	29	4	20	41	.263	.271	.256	5.32	2.60
Valdez, Rolando	R-R	6-1	191	1-8-86	0	1	6.75	1	1	0	0	4	2	3	3	0	3	2	.143	.167	.125	4.50	6.75
Wells, Jared	R-R	6-4	200	10-31-81	2	9	7.27	15	15	0	0	73	87	66	59	8	46	55	.296	.328	.269	6.78	5.67
Williams, Woody	R-R	6-0	200	8-19-66	0	1	20.25	1	1	0	0	3	8	6	6	1	2	2	.500	.714	.333	6.75	6.75

FIELDING

Catcher	PCT	G	PO	A	E	DP	PB
Carlin	.991	71	505	40	5	2	5
Hernandez	1.000	1	3	0	0	0	0
Hill	.989	44	327	23	4	4	7
Kottaras	.990	28	180	11	2	2	4
Risinger	1.000	1	8	0	0	0	0

First Base	PCT	G	PO	A	E	DP
Allen	1.000	3	21	5	0	0
Knott	.989	73	607	44	7	65
McAnulty	.987	70	559	32	8	63
Young	1.000	5	44	4	0	5

Second Base	PCT	G	PO	A	E	DP
Carlin	1.000	1	2	3	0	2
Chang	1.000	2	1	3	0	0
Davidiuk	1.000	2	4	2	0	1

	PCT	G	PO	A	E	DP
Dowdy	1.000	2	1	7	0	1
Hill	.981	86	163	245	8	64
Leone	.958	17	28	40	3	6
Matos	.982	13	27	29	1	2
Matranga	.977	38	54	73	3	14

Third Base	PCT	G	PO	A	E	DP
Leone	.950	87	92	175	14	14
Matos	1.000	1	1	1	0	1
Matranga	.943	12	8	25	2	1
McAnulty	.909	50	39	81	12	5

Shortstop	PCT	G	PO	A	E	DP
Alexander	.977	99	164	299	11	73
Chang	.750	3	2	4	2	0
Gutierrez	.941	9	14	18	2	4
Leone	.927	6	15	23	3	5

	PCT	G	PO	A	E	DP
Matranga	.975	31	48	107	4	17

Outfield	PCT	G	PO	A	E	DP
Allen	.964	24	49	4	2	2
Cust	.974	119	175	10	5	0
Delucchi	1.000	10	11	0	0	0
Dowdy	1.000	2	3	0	0	0
Guzman	.977	29	82	2	2	1
Johnson	.983	50	114	2	2	0
Jones	.981	47	98	4	2	2
Knott	.974	50	73	2	2	0
Leone	1.000	7	12	0	0	0
Matranga	.—	1	0	0	0	0
McAnulty	.800	6	4	0	1	0
Sledge	.975	90	152	3	4	1
Valent	1.000	24	58	1	0	0

Mobile BayBears — Double-A

Southern League

BATTING	B-T	HT	WT	DOB	AVG	vLH	vRH	G	AB	R	H	2B	3B	HR	RBI	BB	HBP	SH	SF	SO	SB	CS	SLG	OBP
Baker, Steve	R-R	6-3	200	4-20-80	.234	.174	.268	38	128	14	30	5	1	1	11	15	0	1	1	41	1	0	.313	.313
Bonvechio, Brett	L-R	6-1	200	11-13-82	.236	.258	.224	81	263	30	62	14	3	1	33	41	1	0	1	87	0	1	.392	.340
Bourassa, Adam	L-L	5-8	165	3-31-81	.203	.188	.208	30	64	8	13	0	0	0	3	9	2	2	0	14	0	0	.203	.320
Carlin, Luke	B-R	5-11	185	12-20-80	.000	.000	.000	2	5	0	0	0	0	0	0	0	0	0	0	1	0	0	.000	.000
Chang, Ray	R-R	6-1	195	8-24-83	.233	.211	.250	14	43	4	10	3	0	0	2	0	0	2	1	8	0	0	.302	.227
Ciofrone, Peter	L-R	5-10	201	9-28-83	.231	.000	.300	15	26	2	6	0	0	0	2	5	4	0	0	6	0	1	.231	.429
Ciriaco, Juan	R-R	6-0	159	8-15-83	.222	.245	.211	122	442	46	98	20	3	3	33	32	3	7	3	97	9	3	.301	.277
Cleveland, Jeremy	R-R	6-2	185	9-10-81	.278	.354	.190	37	90	9	25	7	0	1	10	6	2	1	2	18	1	2	.389	.330
Cruz, Luis	R-R	6-1	180	2-10-84	.261	.281	.250	130	499	65	130	35	3	12	65	29	2	5	4	62	8	4	.415	.301
Delucchi, Dustin	L-L	6-0	190	12-23-77	.244	.227	.250	53	160	19	39	5	0	0	9	25	2	2	0	28	3	2	.275	.353
Dowdy, Brett	R-R	6-2	190	2-22-82	.260	.211	.282	70	250	36	65	10	2	1	38	30	3	6	0	45	10	5	.328	.346
Gomes, Joey	R-R	6-2	210	11-2-79	.279	.417	.226	25	86	11	24	4	0	2	11	3	3	0	0	16	0	1	.395	.326
Hagen, Matt	R-R	6-4	230	1-3-80	.000	.000	.000	4	11	0	0	0	0	0	0	0	0	0	0	7	0	0	.000	.000
Hatcher, Justin	R-R	5-10	200	5-12-80	.167	.000	.250	4	12	1	2	0	0	0	2	2	0	0	1	2	0	0	.167	.267
Howard, Joshua	L-L	5-11	180	4-6-83	.000	.000	.000	4	7	0	0	0	0	0	0	0	0	0	1	0	0	.000	.000
Johnson, Michael	L-L	6-3	225	6-25-80	.235	.242	.222	61	183	22	43	8	0	10	38	30	4	0	3	49	0	0	.443	.350
Jones, Kennard	L-L	5-11	185	9-8-81	.263	.246	.272	49	171	27	45	6	1	0	13	35	1	1	2	42	2	4	.310	.388
Kottaras, George	L-R	6-0	185	5-16-83	.276	.263	.282	78	257	40	71	19	1	8	33	50	1	0	2	68	0	1	.451	.394
Lauderdale, Matt	R-R	5-10	200	4-14-81	.233	.250	.224	44	116	12	27	7	1	3	15	19	1	1	0	26	0	0	.388	.346
Macias, Drew	L-L	6-3	175	3-7-83	.256	.270	.249	134	430	43	110	20	3	7	46	44	8	1	3	94	4	12	.365	.334
Matos, Julius	R-R	5-11	170	12-12-74	.259	.105	.333	21	58	6	15	0	0	0	1	9	0	1	0	13	0	0	.259	.358
Morton, Colt	R-R	6-5	230	4-10-82	.266	.362	.217	41	139	15	37	10	0	6	21	11	2	0	4	44	0	0	.468	.329
O'Riordan, Chris	R-R	5-8	175	1-29-80	.168	.162	.171	47	113	9	19	4	0	1	10	17	3	0	0	24	0	1	.230	.293
Rivera, Jodam	B-R	5-10	180	2-4-86	.250	.333	.200	4	8	1	2	1	0	0	0	0	2	0	4	0	1	.375	.250
Sanchez, Luany	R-R	6-1	180	6-18-85	.269	.250	.167	7	10	1	2	0	0	0	0	2	0	0	4	0	0	.200	.333
Sinisi, Vince	L-L	6-0	195	11-7-81	.269	.315	.246	120	379	52	102	33	1	7	48	50	0	3	7	71	7	2	.417	.349
Smitherman, Stephen	R-R	6-4	235	9-1-78	.237	.287	.212	85	287	37	68	18	0	19	58	33	6	0	5	97	0	0	.498	.323
Valenzuela Jr., Fernando	L-L	5-10	210	9-30-82	.169	.111	.189	28	71	5	12	2	0	0	5	6	2	0	2	27	0	1	.197	.228

PITCHING	B-T	HT	WT	DOB	W	L	ERA	G	GS	CG	SV	IP	H	R	ER	HR	BB	SO	AVG	vLH	vRH	K/9	BB/9
Abraham, Paul	R-R	6-2	220	1-10-80	3	4	3.18	43	0	0	1	65	60	26	23	5	32	55	.248	.289	.221	7.62	4.43
Basham, Bobby	R-R	6-3	205	3-7-80	0	1	5.00	2	2	0	0	9	14	6	5	1	3	5	.368	.400	.348	5.00	3.00
Bullard, Jim	L-L	6-7	225	12-29-79	1	0	2.63	10	0	0	0	14	15	4	4	2	5	15	.273	.391	.188	9.88	3.29
Carrillo, Cesar	R-R	6-3	175	4-29-84	1	3	3.02	9	9	0	0	51	45	23	17	5	15	43	.239	.269	.223	7.64	2.66
Cassel, Jack	R-R	6-2	215	8-8-80	6	3	2.29	12	12	1	0	79	66	30	20	3	18	75	.224	.211	.234	8.58	2.06
Deago, Roger	R-L	5-10	180	6-21-77	6	3	3.76	17	10	0	0	65	53	31	27	5	21	44	.221	.180	.232	6.12	2.92
Ekstrom, Michael	R-R	6-0	185	8-30-83	3	7	3.84	14	14	3	0	84	87	46	36	2	19	49	.261	.273	.253	5.23	2.03
Ellis, Jonathan	R-R	6-0	190	10-3-82	0	1	2.30	12	2	0	0	16	20	5	4	1	6	17	.317	.280	.342	9.77	3.45
Hayhurst, Dirk	L-R	6-3	200	3-24-81	3	5	4.82	12	10	0	0	52	58	35	28	6	18	49	.280	.280	.280	8.43	3.10
Hudgins, John	R-R	6-2	195	8-31-81	4	3	2.79	9	9	0	0	52	41	16	16	2	16	55	.217	.193	.236	9.58	2.79
Jones, Geoffrey	L-L	6-5	230	8-10-79	1	1	4.26	53	0	0	1	61	65	34	29	3	24	60	.270	.214	.308	8.80	3.52
Klatt, Ryan	R-R	6-0	185	9-30-81	0	0	6.97	5	0	0	0	10	13	9	8	2	2	9	.317	.368	.273	7.84	1.74
Lopez, Arturo	L-L	5-10	165	2-23-83	0	0	5.09	14	0	0	0	18	20	12	10	0	5	15	.274	.238	.288	7.64	2.55
Matos, Julius	R-R	5-11	170	12-12-74	0	0	54.00	1	0	0	0	1	6	6	6	2	0	0	.750	1.000	.333	0.00	0.00
Meaux, James	R-L	5-11	170	10-5-78	1	1	0.73	8	0	0	1	12	7	3	1	0	5	9	.171	.143	.185	6.57	3.65
Nelson, Bubba	R-R	6-1	195	8-26-81	5	7	3.80	52	3	0	2	83	67	41	35	7	44	82	.220	.196	.234	8.89	4.77
Oyervidez, Jose	R-R	5-11	195	2-18-82	6	12	3.92	28	28	0	0	149	146	79	65	11	75	131	.257	.258	.256	7.90	4.52
Pena, Eduardo	R-R	6-5	205	6-18-83	0	0	0.00	2	0	0	0	4	2	0	0	0	4	2	.182	.333	.125	4.91	9.82
Ramos, Mario	L-L	5-11	180	10-19-77	0	0	1.80	4	0	0	0	5	4	1	1	0	1	3	.250	.333	.231	5.40	1.80
Rosales, Leonel	R-R	6-1	185	5-28-81	5	6	3.21	53	0	0	6	62	53	35	22	6	18	54	.223	.186	.248	7.88	2.63
Thayer, Dale	R-R	5-11	190	12-17-80	7	4	2.48	57	0	0	27	65	59	18	18	3	22	57	.243	.227	.253	7.83	3.03
Thompson, Sean	L-L	5-11	170	10-13-82	6	10	3.86	27	27	2	0	154	148	79	66	18	46	134	.255	.231	.263	7.83	2.69
Trytten, Ryan	R-R	6-3	216	5-10-81	0	1	5.83	17	0	0	0	29	32	19	19	5	9	20	.278	.279	.278	6.14	2.76
Wells, Jared	R-R	6-4	200	10-31-81	4	3	2.64	12	12	1	0	61	53	20	18	4	27	49	.235	.234	.235	7.19	3.96

FIELDING

Catcher	PCT	G	PO	A	E	DP	PB
Carlin	1.000	1	9	2	0	0	0
Hatcher	.957	4	39	5	2	0	0
Kottaras	.990	69	471	47	5	3	8
Lauderdale	.991	31	197	22	2	3	4
Morton	.994	38	307	25	2	0	3
Sanchez	.929	2	13	0	1	0	0

First Base	PCT	G	PO	A	E	DP
Bonvechio	.972	28	232	10	7	14
Hagen	1.000	3	16	3	0	3
Johnson	.990	56	461	22	5	38
Sinisi	.988	31	236	20	3	16
Smitherman	.961	14	140	8	6	6
Valenzuela Jr.	.984	19	172	9	3	17

Second Base	PCT	G	PO	A	E	DP
Chang	.951	9	15	24	2	6

Second Base (cont.)	PCT	G	PO	A	E	DP
Ciriaco	.979	18	35	58	2	8
Cruz	.974	86	194	263	12	46
Dowdy	1.000	8	20	21	0	7
Matos	1.000	3	6	2	0	0
O'Riordan	.975	20	21	57	2	9
Rivera	1.000	3	2	8	0	1

Third Base	PCT	G	PO	A	E	DP
Bonvechio	.894	49	27	66	11	5
Chang	1.000	2	1	3	0	0
Ciofrone	.870	9	6	14	3	1
Cruz	.824	11	8	20	6	2
Dowdy	.917	46	27	84	10	6
Matos	.974	15	6	31	1	1
O'Riordan	.943	21	7	26	2	1

Shortstop	PCT	G	PO	A	E	DP
Chang	1.000	1	2	4	0	1

Shortstop (cont.)	PCT	G	PO	A	E	DP
Ciriaco	.948	104	133	321	25	55
Cruz	.935	36	53	104	11	20

Outfield	PCT	G	PO	A	E	DP
Baker	.984	34	61	1	1	0
Bourassa	1.000	16	21	0	0	0
Ciofrone	1.000	1	1	0	0	0
Cleveland	.960	25	22	2	1	1
Delucchi	.944	47	50	1	3	0
Dowdy	1.000	14	21	0	0	0
Gomes	1.000	20	24	2	0	0
Howard	1.000	2	2	0	0	0
Jones	.949	45	72	2	4	0
Macias	.988	130	245	6	3	1
Sinisi	.982	76	101	6	2	2
Smitherman	.983	43	55	2	1	0

Lake Elsinore Storm — High Class A

California League

BATTING	B-T	HT	WT	DOB	AVG	vLH	vRH	G	AB	R	H	2B	3B	HR	RBI	BB	HBP	SH	SF	SO	SB	CS	SLG	OBP
Adams, Skip	R-R	6-0	200	10-18-79	.228	.215	.233	130	461	57	105	17	4	10	58	44	10	6	5	137	12	6	.347	.306
Bourassa, Adam	L-L	6-3	195	3-31-81	.317	.000	.325	13	41	13	13	3	0	0	5	13	0	0	3	3	3	1	.390	.481
Bowen, Rob	B-R	6-3	225	2-24-81	.143	.143	—	2	7	0	1	0	0	0	0	0	0	0	0	2	0	0	.143	.143
Brown, Tim	L-L	6-3	228	2-21-83	.299	.260	.312	130	428	74	128	37	1	10	75	79	20	1	4	90	4	1	.460	.427
Cameron, Mike	R-R	6-2	200	1-8-73	.333	—	.333	2	6	1	2	1	0	0	1	1	0	0	0	2	0	0	.500	.429
Ciofrone, Peter	L-R	5-10	201	9-28-83	.292	.317	.283	86	319	44	93	17	1	8	74	47	14	1	9	64	4	2	.426	.396
Cleveland, Jeremy	R-R	6-2	185	9-10-81	.275	.267	.279	80	305	30	84	18	2	1	37	25	3	0	4	62	1	6	.357	.332
Crosta, Nick	R-R	6-2	215	11-17-82	.267	.282	.260	71	281	42	75	22	4	6	44	29	5	0	4	71	4	0	.438	.342
Davidson, Drew	R-R	6-0	190	5-7-82	.209	.281	.167	28	86	7	18	5	1	1	13	9	2	0	2	26	0	0	.326	.293
Diaz, Javis	L-L	5-10	165	6-25-84	.262	.158	.286	31	103	13	27	0	2	0	4	14	1	0	1	20	1	2	.301	.353
Dowdy, Brett	R-R	6-0	190	2-22-82	.350	.350	.350	12	40	6	14	0	0	0	2	3	0	0	4	0	0	0	.350	.395
Hagen, Matt	R-R	6-4	230	1-3-80	.176	.257	.134	74	216	25	38	5	3	6	25	31	1	1	3	63	3	2	.310	.279
Headley, Chase	B-R	6-2	195	5-9-84	.291	.237	.322	129	484	79	141	33	0	12	73	74	5	5	3	96	4	5	.434	.389
Howard, Joshua	L-L	5-11	180	4-6-83	.294	.121	.323	66	228	50	67	10	3	2	12	45	2	3	2	47	22	9	.390	.412
Hundley, Nicholas	R-R	6-1	210	9-8-83	.278	.277	.279	47	176	18	49	13	0	3	23	20	2	1	1	44	1	1	.403	.357
Kazmar, Sean	R-R	5-9	160	8-5-84	.250	.248	.251	133	540	86	135	19	5	13	72	63	2	5	6	80	10	1	.376	.327
Klesko, Ryan	L-L	6-3	220	6-12-71	.273	.333	.263	8	22	2	6	2	0	0	1	5	0	0	0	5	0	0	.364	.407
Lauderdale, Matt	R-R	5-10	180	4-14-81	.222	.167	.333	4	9	2	2	1	0	0	2	2	0	1	0	3	0	0	.333	.364
Lobaton, Jose	B-R	6-0	175	10-21-84	.213	.250	.198	42	122	12	26	7	0	4	15	20	1	1	1	42	0	2	.369	.326
Morton, Colt	R-R	6-5	230	4-10-82	.227	.254	.214	53	176	30	40	15	0	5	22	36	7	0	3	44	0	1	.398	.374
O'Riordan, Chris	R-R	5-8	175	1-29-80	.219	.143	.250	24	73	11	16	2	0	0	10	11	1	1	1	11	2	0	.247	.326
Ramirez, Yordany	R-R	6-2	180	7-31-84	.252	.210	.269	78	278	36	70	16	5	3	38	12	1	3	0	50	23	4	.378	.285
Rivera, Jodam	R-R	6-2	180	2-4-86	.200	.333	.163	19	55	10	11	1	0	0	2	5	0	2	0	8	0	0	.218	.267
Roberts, Dave	L-L	5-10	180	5-31-72	.333	.333	—	1	3	0	1	0	0	0	0	0	0	0	0	2	0	0	.333	.333
Sansoe, Mike	R-R	6-0	185	11-6-82	.280	.222	.313	7	25	4	7	0	1	0	4	3	0	0	0	6	0	0	.360	.357
Stocco, Mark	R-R	6-1	210	8-16-83	.211	.143	.250	7	19	2	4	2	0	0	3	0	1	0	0	8	0	1	.316	.250
Susdorf, William	R-R	6-1	210	5-7-83	.267	.250	.278	15	60	8	16	5	1	0	3	3	1	0	0	7	0	1	.383	.313
Turner, Tim	R-L	6-2	190	6-12-82	.233	.272	.210	79	219	27	51	6	0	3	19	14	3	1	1	92	13	3	.301	.287

PITCHING	B-T	HT	WT	DOB	W	L	ERA	G	GS	CG	SV	IP	H	R	ER	HR	BB	SO	AVG	vLH	vRH	K/9	BB/9
Ayala, Manny	R-R	6-3	220	11-6-84	5	4	4.05	23	12	0	0	91	90	42	41	8	12	71	.262	.258	.264	7.02	1.19
Brocail, Doug	L-R	6-5	250	5-16-67	0	0	0.00	6	2	0	0	6	3	1	0	0	2	12	.130	.000	.231	17.05	2.84
Burke, Greg	R-R	6-4	180	9-21-82	2	1	5.79	12	0	0	0	19	24	14	12	1	5	9	.324	.357	.304	4.34	2.41
Buschmann, Matt	R-R	6-3	195	2-13-84	1	0	3.55	2	2	0	0	13	9	5	5	0	4	5	.205	.212	.182	3.55	2.84
Carter, Brenton	R-L	6-3	200	10-10-82	5	2	3.62	15	13	1	0	80	83	37	32	5	11	49	.271	.377	.236	5.54	1.24
Daigle, Richie	R-R	6-0	185	9-9-82	6	1	3.42	53	0	0	0	68	68	28	26	1	26	36	.267	.277	.260	4.74	3.42
Ekstrom, Michael	R-R	6-0	185	8-30-83	7	4	2.30	14	14	1	0	82	76	32	21	2	21	68	.251	.231	.266	7.43	2.30
Ellis, Jonathan	R-R	6-0	190	10-3-82	1	2	2.57	24	0	0	1	28	25	9	8	0	9	37	.238	.171	.281	11.89	2.89
Frieri, Ernesto	R-R	6-2	168	7-19-85	0	0	6.00	2	0	0	0	6	8	4	4	0	3	4	.348	.200	.389	6.00	4.50
Geer, Joshua	R-R	6-3	190	6-2-83	7	4	4.96	15	15	0	0	89	116	60	49	7	16	56	.316	.301	.330	5.66	1.62
Hayhurst, Dirk	L-R	6-3	200	3-24-81	2	7	3.97	12	11	0	0	59	61	34	26	3	20	51	.265	.279	.257	7.78	3.05
Jaile, Chris	R-R	6-2	210	2-20-81	6	6	5.41	35	18	0	0	125	141	86	75	16	43	98	.286	.278	.292	7.07	3.10
Jamison, Neil	R-R	6-3	185	8-4-83	5	6	3.31	61	0	0	31	65	63	30	24	10	15	62	.248	.303	.207	8.54	2.07
Klatt, Ryan	R-R	6-0	185	9-30-81	6	6	3.02	55	0	0	3	57	56	24	19	6	13	51	.249	.216	.281	8.10	2.06
Lopez, Arturo	L-L	5-10	165	2-23-83	0	1	6.28	5	3	0	0	14	18	10	10	2	3	9	.321	.111	.362	5.65	1.88
Meek, Evan	R-R	6-1	190	5-12-83	6	6	4.98	26	25	0	0	119	136	80	66	5	62	113	.288	.284	.292	8.52	4.68
2-team (2 Visalia)					6	7	5.14	28	25	0	0	124	142	85	71	5	66	120	—	—		8.69	4.78
Ramos, Cesar	L-L	6-2	190	6-22-84	7	8	3.70	26	24	0	0	141	161	72	58	9	44	70	.292	.294	.291	4.47	2.81
Roberts, Mark	R-R	5-11	190	6-24-82	1	1	5.01	27	0	0	1	32	30	18	18	4	11	27	.250	.237	.262	7.52	3.06
Rosales, Leonel	R-R	6-1	185	5-28-81	1	0	0.00	5	0	0	0	6	1	0	0	0	2	7	.050	.000	.077	9.95	2.84
Sterry, Vern	R-R	6-2	210	2-7-82	0	0	4.50	1	0	0	0	2	3	1	1	0	1	1	.375	.333	.400	4.50	0.00
Stutes, Kyle	L-L	5-10	195	1-22-82	4	2	3.07	40	0	0	0	56	44	20	19	4	8	51	.213	.300	.185	8.25	1.29
Thomas, John	L-L	6-2	207	7-24-81	0	0	2.73	15	0	0	0	26	20	8	8	1	13	25	.217	.292	.191	8.54	4.44
Trytten, Ryan	R-R	6-3	216	5-10-81	0	0	0.00	3	0	0	0	3	1	0	0	0	0	4	.100	.167	.000	12.00	0.00
Turner, Tim	R-L	6-2	190	6-12-82	0	0	16.20	2	0	0	0	2	3	3	3	0	1	1	.333	.500	.286	5.40	5.40
Valdez, Rolando	R-R	6-1	191	1-8-86	0	0	13.50	4	0	0	0	4	4	6	6	0	5	2	.286	.364	.000	4.50	11.25
Varner, Matt	R-R	5-11	200	1-16-82	1	5	2.28	43	0	0	0	43	53	24	11	4	12	36	.312	.366	.261	7.48	2.49
Williams, Woody	R-R	6-0	200	8-19-66	0	0	0.00	1	1	0	0	3	0	0	0	0	1	5	.000	.000	.000	15.00	3.00

FIELDING

Catcher	PCT	G	PO	A	E	DP	PB
Bowen	1.000	2	14	1	0	0	0
Hagen	1.000	16	71	12	0	1	10
Hundley	.972	42	291	27	9	3	9
Lauderdale	.857	3	16	2	3	1	0
Lobaton	.962	36	236	18	10	4	5
Morton	.983	48	314	43	6	7	2
Stocco	.976	6	37	3	1	0	2

First Base	PCT	G	PO	A	E	DP
Brown	.989	127	1064	75	13	95
Hagen	.994	29	154	16	1	18
Klesko	1.000	5	26	4	0	3

Second Base	PCT	G	PO	A	E	DP
Dowdy	.857	2	3	3	1	1
Hagen	1.000	3	7	7	0	3

	PCT	G	PO	A	E	DP
Kazmar	.966	125	256	375	22	91
O'Riordan	1.000	7	8	19	0	3
Rivera	1.000	8	10	24	0	4

Third Base	PCT	G	PO	A	E	DP
Ciofrone	1.000	2	0	4	0	1
Dowdy	1.000	3	0	6	0	1
Hagen	1.000	3	0	1	0	0
Headley	.945	127	82	229	18	18
O'Riordan	.909	8	7	13	2	1
Ramirez	—	1	0	0	0	0
Rivera	.867	3	4	9	2	1

Shortstop	PCT	G	PO	A	E	DP
Adams	.955	129	206	413	29	86
Dowdy	1.000	2	5	10	0	2
Kazmar	1.000	6	8	13	0	6
Rivera	.950	6	5	14	1	4

Outfield	PCT	G	PO	A	E	DP
Bourassa	1.000	11	23	0	0	0
Cameron	1.000	2	3	0	0	0
Ciofrone	.988	54	82	3	1	1
Cleveland	.950	57	90	5	5	0
Crosta	.946	67	116	6	7	0
Davidson	.968	22	28	2	1	2
Diaz	.900	16	24	3	3	0
Dowdy	1.000	3	5	0	0	0
Hagen	.944	12	16	1	1	0
Howard	.978	53	85	4	2	1
Ramirez	.953	73	175	8	9	3
Roberts	—	1	0	0	0	0
Sansoe	.952	7	19	1	1	0
Susdorf	1.000	6	11	0	0	0
Turner	.957	66	129	4	6	1

Fort Wayne Wizards — Low Class A

Midwest League

BATTING	B-T	HT	WT	DOB	AVG	vLH	vRH	G	AB	R	H	2B	3B	HR	RBI	BB	HBP	SH	SF	SO	SB	CS	SLG	OBP
Aguilar, Abraham	R-R	6-2	155	9-18-84	.203	.167	.214	46	133	18	27	4	0	0	7	19	3	2	1	36	3	3	.233	.314
Alley, Joshua	L-L	5-9	180	9-6-83	.205	.167	.215	67	234	27	48	11	0	2	23	52	0	2	1	33	11	6	.278	.348
Antonelli, Matt	R-R	6-1	190	4-8-85	.125	.333	.077	5	16	3	2	1	1	0	0	2	0	0	0	6	0	0	.313	.222
Baxter, Michael	L-R	6-0	190	12-7-84	.256	.257	.256	117	476	67	122	28	7	3	40	31	4	1	5	66	13	5	.363	.304
Blanks, Kyle	R-R	6-6	270	9-11-86	.292	.272	.300	86	308	41	90	20	0	10	52	36	11	0	4	79	2	0	.455	.382
Bush, Matt	R-R	5-11	170	2-8-86	.268	.188	.291	21	71	8	19	3	0	0	7	6	1	0	0	13	2	1	.310	.333
Campbell, Michael	L-L	6-1	165	11-14-83	.280	.300	.275	12	50	7	14	4	0	0	3	0	1	0	1	9	0	0	.360	.288
Chang, Ray	R-R	6-1	195	8-24-83	.286	.367	.246	27	91	19	26	4	0	3	8	16	3	0	0	19	0	1	.429	.390
Contreras, Rayner	R-R	6-0	150	9-21-86	.105	.091	.111	12	38	2	4	0	0	0	1	2	0	0	0	9	0	0	.105	.150
Cooper, Craig	R-L	6-3	185	10-27-84	.333	.333	.333	6	21	6	7	1	1	0	5	3	1	0	1	3	0	0	.476	.423
Crosta, Nick	R-R	6-2	215	11-17-82	.382	.375	.385	37	123	26	47	12	1	7	30	26	2	0	2	35	2	2	.667	.490
Davidiuk, A.J.	R-R	6-1	185	12-12-83	.205	.200	.207	27	88	7	18	1	0	0	7	7	3	0	0	14	1	1	.216	.286
Davidson, Drew	R-R	6-0	190	5-7-82	.247	.292	.200	28	93	18	23	7	4	0	12	11	3	0	3	27	1	0	.409	.336
Diaz, Javis	L-L	5-10	165	6-25-84	.306	.091	.330	29	111	20	34	3	1	0	7	14	0	1	0	34	8	1	.351	.384
Freese, David	R-R	6-2	220	4-28-83	.299	.368	.272	53	204	27	61	13	3	8	44	21	4	0	1	44	1	1	.510	.374
Gottier, Brandon	R-R	5-11	195	1-5-82	.213	.193	.220	62	207	16	44	13	0	1	16	17	3	1	1	52	1	3	.290	.281
Guerrero, Santiago	R-R	6-0	176	11-28-83	.182	.200	.176	6	22	2	4	1	0	0	3	2	0	0	0	8	1	0	.227	.250
Huffman, Chad	R-R	6-1	205	4-29-85	.214	.000	.250	5	14	3	3	1	0	0	2	0	0	0		2	0	1	.357	.313
Hundley, Nicholas	R-R	6-1	210	9-8-83	.274	.157	.311	57	215	29	59	19	0	8	44	25	4	0	4	45	1	1	.474	.355
Johnston, Seth	R-R	6-3	200	3-12-83	.275	.231	.289	112	458	72	126	33	0	10	58	32	5	0	1	80	3	1	.413	.329
Jones, Daryl	R-R	6-3	200	9-1-86	.242	.291	.225	121	442	50	107	22	1	12	58	46	11	1	6	114	1	3	.378	.325
Lobaton, Jose	B-R	6-0	175	10-21-84	.279	.375	.264	20	61	15	17	3	1	1	11	12	2	1	1	12	0	0	.410	.408
Lopez, Jesus	R-R	5-11	165	9-12-87	.207	.250	.197	55	179	23	37	6	0	3	19	19	1	4	1	32	0	0	.291	.285
Rivera, Jodam	B-R	5-10	180	2-4-86	.217	.182	.226	31	106	11	23	1	0	0	8	6	1	1	2	22	1	1	.226	.261
Sanchez, Luany	R-R	6-1	180	6-18-85	.400	—	.400	3	10	4	0	0	0	0	2	0	0	0	1	0	0		.400	.400
Sansoe, Mike	R-R	6-0	185	11-6-82	.293	.330	.271	74	276	60	81	12	4	1	32	37	4	6	3	54	21	7	.377	.381
Steiner, Chad	R-R	6-2	190	12-25-83	.215	.167	.231	38	144	10	31	5	1	1	20	7	2	1	1	24	0	0	.285	.260
Venable, Will	L-L	6-2	205	10-29-82	.314	.314	.313	124	472	86	148	34	5	11	91	55	7	1	6	81	18	5	.477	.389

PITCHING	B-T	HT	WT	DOB	W	L	ERA	G	GS	CG	SV	IP	H	R	ER	HR	BB	SO	AVG	vLH	vRH	K/9	BB/9
Ayala, Manny	R-R	6-3	225	11-6-84	0	0	7.56	3	1	0	0	8	13	7	7	1	2	9	.351	.381	.313	9.72	2.16
Burke, Greg	R-R	6-4	180	9-21-82	6	5	3.58	24	17	0	0	121	130	58	48	8	14	87	.275	.322	.242	6.49	1.04
Culp, Nate	L-L	6-2	180	10-9-84	4	2	4.09	7	7	0	0	33	36	20	15	2	13	16	.281	.333	.261	4.36	3.55
Delabar, Steve	R-R	6-5	220	7-17-83	8	9	3.41	27	27	1	0	145	129	66	55	8	65	118	.242	.213	.262	7.32	4.03
Fernandez, Alfredo	R-R	6-4	224	9-15-84	5	2	2.89	52	0	0	0	65	61	28	21	3	13	45	.243	.255	.235	6.20	1.79
Frieri, Ernesto	R-R	6-2	168	7-19-85	0	0	9.00	1	0	0	0	1	1	4	1	0	5	1	.333	.500	.000	9.00	45.00
Gardner, Jarrett	R-R	6-1	175	3-26-81	5	4	4.50	13	13	0	0	68	86	43	34	6	5	37	.315	.367	.275	4.90	0.66
Geer, Josh	R-R	6-3	190	6-2-83	6	2	3.10	12	11	1	0	73	72	27	25	3	13	46	.263	.293	.234	5.70	1.61
Higelin, Brandon	L-L	6-0	195	4-8-83	3	4	2.28	53	0	0	0	67	60	21	17	4	21	62	.241	.185	.274	8.33	2.82
Jamison, Neil	R-R	6-3	185	8-4-83	0	0	0.00	4	0	0	3	4	1	0	0	0	3	9	.077	.167	.000	20.25	6.75
Jimenez, Fabian	L-L	6-2	187	8-27-86	5	7	4.43	17	17	0	0	87	87	49	43	5	52	54	.271	.188	.301	5.56	5.36
2-team (4 Peoria)					6	10	5.31	21	21	0	0	103	117	69	61	6	58	60	—	—	—	5.23	5.05
Kirby, Jonathan	R-R	5-11	198	12-5-83	0	0	2.45	3	0	0	0	4	3	1	1	0	6	5	.200	.167	.222	12.27	14.73
Krosschell, Ben	R-R	6-1	165	10-2-85	1	3	8.47	4	4	0	0	17	22	19	16	2	8	10	.314	.424	.216	5.29	4.24
Leblanc, Wade	L-L	6-3	190	8-7-84	4	1	2.20	7	7	0	0	33	31	8	8	1	10	27	.250	.270	.241	7.44	2.76
Link, Jon	R-R	6-1	175	3-23-84	5	5	4.91	53	0	0	0	62	72	45	34	9	24	57	.283	.333	.256	8.23	3.47
Madden, Chris	R-R	6-4	225	12-13-82	2	3	2.12	49	0	0	20	51	39	18	12	1	19	48	.202	.275	.150	8.47	3.35
Pawelczyk, Kyle	L-L	6-5	200	11-18-81	1	0	5.56	7	0	0	0	11	11	9	7	4	8	6	.250	.231	.258	4.76	6.35
Pena, Eduardo	R-R	6-4	205	6-18-83	0	2	3.99	27	0	0	0	47	51	33	21	5	9	38	.259	.243	.268	7.23	1.71
Roberts, Mark	R-R	5-11	190	6-24-82	0	1	1.80	15	0	0	0	20	16	4	4	1	8	26	.225	.231	.222	11.70	3.60
Santo, Joel	R-R	6-3	194	6-4-84	6	6	5.38	20	15	0	0	92	96	57	55	9	54	48	.281	.300	.269	4.70	5.28
2-team (7 Peoria)					9	10	5.03	27	20	1	0	127	128	74	71	11	74	75	—	—	—	5.31	5.24
Soria, Joakim	R-R	6-2	170	5-18-84	1	0	2.31	7	0	0	0	12	5	3	3	1	2	11	.132	.150	.111	8.49	1.54
Staggs, Nathan	R-R	6-4	210	3-4-82	5	1	3.16	28	1	0	0	63	57	23	22	6	22	59	.247	.270	.232	8.47	3.16
Sterry, Vern	R-R	6-2	210	2-7-82	0	0	0.00	1	0	0	0	3	0	0	0	0	0	2	.333	.333	.333	9.00	0.00
Varnell, Grant	R-R	6-2	215	9-27-82	4	10	4.09	27	17	1	1	112	143	69	51	9	19	63	.304	.317	.294	5.05	1.52

FIELDING

Catcher	PCT	G	PO	A	E	DP	PB
Gottier	.981	61	384	38	8	7	5
Hundley	.988	57	362	51	5	2	9
Lobaton	.987	19	135	16	2	1	3

	PCT	G	PO	A	E	DP	PB
Sanchez	1.000	3	17	2	0	0	1

First Base	PCT	G	PO	A	E	DP
Baxter	.982	7	53	3	1	5
Blanks	.990	51	477	32	5	55

	PCT	G	PO	A	E	DP
Cooper	1.000	3	29	2	0	7
Jones	.987	79	730	42	10	59

Second Base	PCT	G	PO	A	E	DP
Aguilar	.969	13	27	36	2	7

	PCT	G	PO	A	E	DP
Antonelli	.929	2	3	10	1	5
Baxter	1.000	1	1	0	0	0
Chang	.979	8	15	32	1	8
Contreras	.951	12	25	33	3	5
Johnston	.965	78	169	241	15	64
Lopez	.964	13	23	30	2	9
Rivera	.969	18	33	60	3	7

Third Base	PCT	G	PO	A	E	DP
Aguilar	.949	13	12	25	2	2
Antonelli	1.000	3	1	5	0	0
Davidiuk	1.000	1	0	2	0	0
Freese	.963	53	32	99	5	10

	PCT	G	PO	A	E	DP
Johnston	.909	34	15	65	8	9
Steiner	.911	38	20	72	9	7

Shortstop	PCT	G	PO	A	E	DP
Aguilar	.899	21	24	56	9	12
Bush	.932	21	29	80	8	10
Chang	.900	19	37	53	10	15
Davidiuk	.948	26	40	70	6	17
Lopez	.968	45	65	149	7	34
Rivera	.963	14	26	52	3	12

Outfield	PCT	G	PO	A	E	DP
Alley	.984	63	122	2	2	0

	PCT	G	PO	A	E	DP
Baxter	.970	99	153	9	5	3
Campbell	1.000	2	8	0	0	0
Crosta	.971	25	30	4	1	3
Davidson	.903	17	27	1	3	0
Diaz	1.000	22	46	4	0	1
Gardner	.—	1	0	0	0	0
Guerrero	1.000	6	12	0	0	0
Huffman	1.000	4	6	0	0	0
Sansoe	.981	71	153	5	3	2
Venable	.980	115	190	8	4	2

Eugene Emeralds · Short-Season

Northwest League

BATTING	B-T	HT	WT	DOB	AVG	vLH	vRH	G	AB	R	H	2B	3B	HR	RBI	BB	HBP	SH	SF	SO	SB	CS	SLG	OBP
Aguilar, Abraham	R-R	6-2	155	9-18-84	.219	.250	.204	25	73	6	16	1	0	1	9	4	1	0	1	15	0	1	.274	.266
Antonelli, Matt	R-R	6-1	190	4-8-85	.286	.229	.305	55	189	38	54	12	1	0	22	46	4	1	5	31	9	1	.360	.426
Campbell, Michael	L-L	6-1	165	11-14-83	.253	.161	.294	28	99	11	25	4	0	5	19	10	1	0	2	10	0	1	.444	.321
Cannon, Luke	L-L	6-1	195	8-19-84	.213	.261	.204	44	136	19	29	3	1	5	14	17	2	0	1	52	0	0	.360	.308
Carter, Sam	R-R	6-4	210	6-5-83	.250	.250	.250	4	12	0	3	2	0	0	0	1	1	0	0	4	0	0	.417	.357
Cooper, Craig	R-L	6-3	185	10-27-84	.320	.315	.322	60	231	45	74	18	1	6	46	32	8	0	2	44	5	1	.485	.418
Crafort, Willy	R-R	6-3	165	2-9-85	.194	.208	.189	47	170	11	33	9	2	2	22	9	1	0	2	50	0	0	.306	.236
Epping, Michael	L-L	5-11	190	8-28-83	.265	.225	.279	68	268	53	71	16	0	3	19	34	4	4	3	66	17	5	.358	.353
Freese, David	R-R	6-2	220	4-28-83	.379	.556	.300	18	58	19	22	8	0	5	26	7	4	0	2	12	0	0	.776	.465
Guerrero, Santiago	R-R	6-0	176	11-28-83	.294	.333	.286	4	17	1	5	2	0	0	2	1	0	0	0	2	0	1	.412	.333
Huffman, Chad	R-R	6-1	205	4-29-85	.343	.383	.331	54	198	41	68	17	1	9	40	25	14	0	7	34	2	3	.576	.439
Hunt, Jeremy	R-R	6-2	210	12-22-83	.176	.286	.100	6	17	5	3	0	0	2	3	3	0	0	1	0	0	0	.529	.300
Hunter, Cedric	L-L	6-0	185	3-10-88	.267	.125	.429	5	15	0	4	0	0	0	0	1	0	0	0	3	0	1	.267	.313
King, Tom	R-R	5-11	180	8-3-84	.231	.286	.210	69	277	38	64	19	0	3	22	29	3	1	0	39	3	0	.332	.311
Kliebert, Nicholas	R-R	5-11	180	11-16-83	.256	.400	.212	13	43	12	11	3	0	0	11	0	0	1	0	11	0	0	.326	.360
Lauderdale, Brian	R-R	5-10	170	6-29-83	.237	.176	.250	28	93	12	22	4	0	1	5	2	3	1	0	31	3	2	.312	.276
Lopez, Jesus	R-R	5-11	165	9-12-87	.246	.258	.243	40	134	18	33	8	2	0	14	15	1	1	1	27	2	1	.336	.325
Rivera, Jodam	B-R	5-10	180	2-4-86	.361	.267	.429	10	36	8	13	2	0	0	3	5	1	2	0	5	1	0	.417	.452
Sanchez, Luany	R-R	6-1	180	6-18-85	.255	.318	.238	26	106	10	27	8	0	2	16	3	0	0	0	18	0	0	.387	.275
Smith, Casey	R-R	6-4	230	2-24-84	.216	.152	.250	29	97	7	21	3	0	1	7	12	0	0	1	40	0	0	.278	.300
Stocco, Matt	R-R	6-2	210	8-16-83	.200	.167	.222	22	75	7	15	5	0	0	3	13	3	2	0	30	0	0	.387	.250
Stokes, Raymond	R-R	5-10	160	10-30-85	.186	.167	.200	11	43	5	8	1	0	0	1	3	0	0	1	7	0	0	.209	.239
Valverde, Kody	R-R	6-0	205	3-14-83	.217	.231	.212	40	138	13	30	8	0	2	24	24	3	1	6	25	0	0	.319	.333
Wetzel, Garner	R-R	6-2	210	4-26-84	.208	.194	.215	27	96	12	20	3	0	1	9	7	3	0	0	19	1	2	.271	.283

PITCHING	B-T	HT	WT	DOB	W	L	ERA	G	GS	CG	SV	IP	H	R	ER	HR	BB	SO	AVG	vLH	vRH	K/9	BB/9
Breit, Aaron	R-R	6-3	180	4-19-86	2	3	3.08	18	12	0	0	64	60	31	22	2	22	69	.250	.214	.277	9.65	3.08
Buschmann, Matt	R-R	6-3	195	2-13-84	3	4	3.12	15	10	0	0	61	54	26	21	5	11	63	.242	.213	.261	9.35	1.63
Clayton, Patrick	R-R	6-5	220	8-13-84	0	0	10.80	7	0	0	0	7	7	8	8	3	8	10	.280	.143	.333	13.50	10.80
Culp, Nathanial	L-L	6-2	180	10-9-84	0	1	1.50	9	3	0	0	18	19	6	3	0	4	8	.271	.200	.291	4.00	2.00
Dunn, Brooks	L-L	6-2	205	5-6-84	5	6	2.41	19	12	0	1	78	68	34	21	0	19	45	.232	.220	.237	5.17	2.18
Faris, Stephen	R-R	6-1	190	6-30-84	2	1	4.65	11	7	0	0	41	49	25	21	3	10	23	.295	.333	.275	5.09	2.21
Farrington, Matt	L-L	5-11	180	9-9-83	0	2	9.82	6	0	0	0	4	7	4	4	1	3	2	.389	1.000	.313	4.91	7.36
Frieri, Ernesto	R-R	6-2	168	7-19-85	3	3	3.82	27	1	0	2	38	31	18	16	3	15	38	.231	.151	.284	9.08	3.58
Handley, Matt	L-L	6-2	200	6-7-83	0	0	2.70	2	0	0	0	3	4	2	1	1	2	4	.286	.500	.200	10.80	5.40
Huff, Matthew	R-R	6-2	185	2-18-84	0	0	0.00	1	0	0	0	2	1	0	0	0	0	1	.143	.200	.000	0.00	0.00
Kirby, Jonathan	R-R	5-11	198	12-5-83	2	2	3.31	21	0	0	0	33	32	13	12	1	12	18	.254	.191	.291	4.96	3.31
Krosschell, Ben	R-R	6-1	165	10-2-85	2	0	6.85	22	0	0	0	24	26	22	18	2	16	12	.283	.194	.328	4.56	6.08
Lara, Orlando	L-L	5-10	185	5-20-85	2	1	3.23	16	10	0	0	47	37	17	17	4	14	59	.216	.195	.223	11.22	2.66
Leblanc, Wade	L-L	6-3	190	8-7-84	1	0	4.29	7	3	0	0	21	19	10	10	0	6	20	.250	.400	.213	8.57	2.57
Mattison, Justin	L-L	6-0	190	6-24-81	3	1	3.29	26	0	0	5	27	22	12	10	1	26	22	.227	.212	.234	7.24	8.56
Menchaca, Pablo	R-R	6-4	225	11-28-87	0	0	3.00	1	0	0	0	3	3	1	1	0	1	2	.273	.250	.333	6.00	3.00
Miller, Andrew	R-R	6-4	190	2-24-86	2	1	3.62	9	8	0	0	37	39	24	15	0	20	23	.267	.262	.272	5.54	4.82
Paewai, Riki	R-R	6-2	180	3-28-86	1	0	1.50	4	0	0	0	6	4	2	1	0	6	4	.200	.125	.250	6.00	9.00
Quezada, Jackson	R-R	6-4	170	8-9-86	2	2	4.19	18	4	0	0	34	30	18	16	1	13	34	.236	.286	.212	8.91	3.41
Rodriguez, R.J.	R-R	6-0	175	7-5-84	2	3	1.78	26	0	0	14	30	23	9	6	1	5	27	.207	.256	.176	8.01	1.48
Tucci, Nicholas	R-R	6-3	205	3-23-83	3	0	4.45	28	0	0	0	32	45	17	16	5	17	23	.338	.341	.337	4.73	1.95
Underwood, Andrew	R-R	6-4	185	5-20-85	0	2	3.74	7	3	0	0	22	22	11	9	2	3	11	.253	.167	.298	4.57	1.25
Valdez, Rolando	R-R	6-1	191	1-8-86	7	1	2.70	27	2	0	0	43	34	16	13	2	13	39	.218	.259	.194	8.10	3.95
Vandel, Geoff	L-L	6-1	190	6-9-87	1	0	9.82	4	1	0	0	11	19	13	12	1	10	11	.388	.375	.394	9.00	8.18

FIELDING

Catcher	PCT	G	PO	A	E	DP	PB
Sanchez	.986	23	192	21	3	3	7
Stocco	.971	22	153	13	5	2	5
Valverde	.974	34	235	26	7	3	3

First Base	PCT	G	PO	A	E	DP
Cooper	.987	54	478	35	7	40
Hunt	.980	6	47	1	1	5
Smith	.954	19	158	8	8	11

Second Base	PCT	G	PO	A	E	DP
Aguilar	1.000	4	3	11	0	2
King	.969	35	66	89	5	14
Kliebert	.930	10	16	24	3	5
Lauderdale	.930	13	29	37	5	8
Rivera	.977	9	15	28	1	7
Stokes	.940	11	24	39	4	6

Third Base	PCT	G	PO	A	E	DP
Aguilar	.979	20	17	30	1	0
Antonelli	.943	45	35	80	7	6
Freese	.905	9	5	14	2	2
Lauderdale	.870	12	5	15	3	0

Shortstop	PCT	G	PO	A	E	DP
Aguilar	.—	1	0	0	0	0
King	.962	35	42	109	6	20
Kliebert	.941	3	4	12	1	1
Lopez	.951	40	72	124	10	28
Rivera	1.000	2	6	4	0	2

Outfield	PCT	G	PO	A	E	DP
Campbell	.984	28	61	2	1	0
Cannon	.917	28	30	3	3	1
Carter	1.000	4	7	1	0	0
Crafort	.878	31	40	3	6	1
Epping	.986	66	142	3	2	1
Guerrero	1.000	4	7	1	0	0
Huffman	.979	50	82	10	2	1
Hunter	.929	4	13	0	1	0
Wetzel	.953	24	39	2	2	2

Arizona League

BATTING	B-T	HT	WT	DOB	AVG	vLH	vRH	G	AB	R	H	2B	3B	HR	RBI	BB	HBP	SH	SF	SO	SB	CS	SLG	OBP
Alley, Joshua	L-L	5-9	180	9-6-83	.323	.273	.350	7	31	6	10	2	2	0	6	3	1	0	0	8	0	1	.516	.400
Angulo, Yancarlo	R-R	6-0	160	1-6-87	.205	.000	.243	16	44	8	9	2	0	2	3	8	0	0	0	19	1	0	.386	.327
Bonvechio, Brett	L-R	6-1	200	11-13-82	.300	.000	.429	4	10	3	3	1	0	0	2	3	0	0	1	5	0	0	.400	.429
Bourassa, Adam	L-L	5-8	165	3-31-81	.412	—	.412	6	17	6	7	2	0	0	7	8	0	0	0	1	1	1	.529	.600
Burke, Kyler	L-L	6-3	205	4-20-88	.209	.200	.211	45	163	24	34	3	4	1	15	26	0	0	3	56	1	3	.294	.313
Bush, Matt	R-R	5-11	170	2-8-86	.000	—	.000	1	1	1	0	0	0	0	0	1	3	0	0	0	0	0	.000	.750
Campbell, Michael	L-L	6-1	165	11-14-83	.407	.571	.350	8	27	6	11	0	0	1	6	5	1	0	0	2	1	0	.519	.515
Carrasco, Felix	B-R	6-2	220	2-14-87	.273	.233	.287	46	172	32	47	12	1	4	37	17	4	0	3	48	2	0	.424	.347
Carter, Sam	R-R	6-4	210	6-5-83	.278	.200	.300	34	115	22	32	9	1	3	24	24	5	1	2	36	0	4	.452	.418
Carvajal, Yefri	R-R	5-11	190	1-22-89	.253	.286	.241	19	75	14	19	3	0	2	9	3	1	0	1	16	2	0	.373	.288
Contreras, Rayner	R-R	6-0	150	9-21-86	.316	.342	.308	44	171	36	54	9	3	2	52	20	1	2	1	34	4	2	.439	.389
Davidiuk, A.J.	R-R	6-1	185	12-12-83	.300	.304	.298	20	80	12	24	4	1	1	14	4	7	1	0	12	1	1	.413	.385
Diaz, Javis	L-L	5-10	165	6-25-84	.667	—	.667	1	3	2	2	1	1	0	0	0	0	0	0	0	0	1	1.667	.667
Durango, Luis	B-R	5-10	145	4-23-86	.378	.344	.387	39	143	35	54	2	4	0	14	23	2	2	0	16	17	6	.448	.470
Gonzalez, Jarol	R-R	6-0	171	12-28-84	.250	.333	.217	9	32	4	8	1	1	0	1	1	1	2	1	7	0	1	.344	.286
Hernandez, Brian	R-R	6-1	180	11-4-83	.258	.292	.246	30	93	11	24	4	0	0	15	9	1	1	2	10	1	1	.301	.324
Hopley, Murray	R-R	5-10	165	12-27-87	.077	.500	.000	10	13	3	1	0	0	0	1	7	0	2	0	6	0	0	.077	.400
Hunt, Jeremy	R-R	6-2	210	12-22-83	.323	.457	.287	45	164	32	53	8	3	5	32	28	2	0	2	37	0	1	.500	.423
Hunter, Cedric	L-L	6-0	185	3-10-88	.371	.339	.382	52	213	46	79	13	4	1	44	40	3	1	5	22	17	5	.484	.467
Johnston, Seth	R-R	6-3	200	3-12-83	.100	.000	.111	3	10	1	1	0	0	0	0	0	0	0	0	4	0	0	.100	.100
Laforest, Pete	L-R	6-2	210	1-27-78	.067	.000	.091	5	15	1	1	0	0	0	0	3	0	0	0	7	0	0	.067	.222
Lauderdale, Brian	R-R	5-10	170	6-29-83	.417	.200	.571	3	12	2	5	1	0	0	2	0	0	0	0	2	0	0	.500	.417
Naylor, Clinton	L-R	6-0	176	8-3-88	.167	.286	.143	20	42	11	7	0	0	0	3	23	1	0	0	10	0	1	.167	.462
Pickett, Justin	R-R	6-1	205	6-16-85	.260	.250	.264	23	77	11	20	3	0	1	14	5	0	1	0	27	0	0	.338	.305
Rivera, Jodam	B-R	5-10	180	2-4-86	.409	.429	.400	11	44	16	18	1	0	0	7	6	0	1	0	7	0	0	.432	.480
Rodriguez, Jorge	R-R	6-0	192	7-29-82	.242	.300	.231	22	62	17	15	2	1	0	7	15	1	0	2	20	4	2	.306	.388
Solis, Ali	R-R	6-0	176	9-29-87	.250	.231	.256	17	56	7	14	5	0	0	6	7	0	0	0	10	0	0	.339	.333
Stokes, Raymond	R-R	5-10	160	10-30-85	.254	.267	.250	21	59	13	15	2	0	0	5	9	12	4	3	2	6	3	2	.288	.403
Wetzel, Garner	R-R	6-2	210	4-26-84	.133	.250	.091	7	15	2	2	0	0	0	1	2	0	0	0	4	0	0	.133	.235

PITCHING	B-T	HT	WT	DOB	W	L	ERA	G	GS	CG	SV	IP	H	R	ER	HR	BB	SO	AVG	vLH	vRH	K/9	BB/9
Brazelton, Dewon	R-R	6-4	215	6-16-80	0	0	0.00	1	1	0	0	2	1	2	0	0	2	2	.125	.500	.000	9.00	9.00
Ceda, Jose	R-R	6-4	205	1-28-87	2	0	5.09	8	4	0	0	23	20	14	13	1	13	31	.235	.294	.196	12.13	5.09
2-team (5 AZL Cubs)					2	0	3.60	13	7	0	0	35	26	16	14	1	20	52	—	—	—	13.37	5.14
Ellis, Jonathan	R-R	6-0	190	10-3-82	0	1	9.00	1	1	0	0	1	0	1	1	0	1	0	.000	.000	.000	0.00	9.00
Farrington, Matt	L-L	5-11	180	9-9-83	2	0	4.07	17	0	0	1	24	24	13	11	0	9	22	.255	.143	.288	8.14	3.33
Garramone, Robert	R-R	6-2	175	8-22-87	3	3	4.01	14	4	0	0	43	43	25	19	2	14	31	.269	.368	.214	6.54	2.95
Handley, Matt	L-L	6-2	200	6-7-83	2	0	2.36	20	0	0	3	27	15	7	7	2	6	32	.163	.167	.162	10.80	2.03
Huff, Matthew	R-R	6-2	185	2-18-84	4	1	3.15	23	0	0	1	34	33	14	12	3	7	38	.256	.282	.244	9.96	1.83
Hussey, John	R-R	6-3	172	11-22-86	3	1	2.44	13	7	0	0	44	39	16	12	1	16	32	.253	.231	.265	6.50	3.25
Juan, Pascual	L-L	6-2	163	2-14-85	2	1	7.78	14	1	0	0	20	21	17	17	3	18	21	.276	.200	.288	9.43	8.24
Lopez, Arturo	L-L	5-10	165	2-23-83	0	0	9.00	1	0	0	0	1	3	1	1	0	0	2	.429	1.000	.333	18.00	0.00
Mead, Tyler	L-R	6-1	180	8-15-87	2	2	6.35	13	6	0	0	34	48	31	24	2	24	28	.327	.378	.304	7.41	6.35
Medina, Vantroit	R-R	6-3	175	1-30-87	3	5	5.91	14	6	0	0	46	61	40	30	2	13	38	.313	.408	.258	7.49	2.56
Menchaca, Pablo	R-R	6-4	225	11-28-87	3	1	3.35	13	7	0	0	51	52	23	19	0	9	39	.265	.262	.267	6.88	1.59
Miller, Andrew	R-R	6-4	180	2-24-86	3	0	3.47	7	4	0	0	23	19	15	9	1	10	14	.218	.146	.283	5.40	3.86
Paewai, Riki	R-R	6-2	180	3-28-86	0	0	9.00	10	0	0	0	6	12	7	6	2	6	6	.400	.273	.474	9.00	9.00
Ramos, Mario	L-L	5-11	180	10-19-77	0	0	2.25	9	3	0	1	12	7	3	3	0	5	10	.163	.357	.069	7.50	3.75
Rodriguez, R.J.	R-R	6-0	175	7-5-84	0	0	0.00	4	0	0	1	5	1	2	0	0	5	7	.059	.125	.000	13.50	9.64
Salazar, Yesid	R-R	6-1	175	11-2-86	4	3	4.25	14	8	1	0	55	68	31	26	1	9	28	.315	.333	.306	4.58	1.47
Sterry, Vern	R-R	6-2	210	2-7-82	1	1	5.59	7	0	0	0	10	11	6	6	0	5	14	.282	.417	.222	13.03	4.66
Tucci, Nicholas	R-R	6-3	205	3-23-83	0	0	0.00	2	0	0	0	2	1	0	0	0	1	0	.143	.000	.167	0.00	3.86
Vandel, Geoff	L-L	6-1	190	6-9-87	2	0	3.48	13	3	0	0	31	30	17	12	1	10	33	.244	.250	.242	9.58	2.90

FIELDING

Catcher	PCT	G	PO	A	E	DP	PB
Hernandez	.983	30	208	24	4	2	5
Laforest	1.000	2	11	2	0	1	0
Naylor	.961	20	111	12	5	1	6
Solis	.957	17	106	29	6	1	2

First Base	PCT	G	PO	A	E	DP
Hunt	.992	42	332	21	3	28
Pickett	.965	19	128	11	5	10

Second Base	PCT	G	PO	A	E	DP
Contreras	.959	25	51	66	5	12
Davidiuk	1.000	1	1	4	0	0
Hopley	.950	6	6	13	1	1
Johnston	1.000	3	3	4	0	2
Lauderdale	.923	3	6	6	1	1

	PCT	G	PO	A	E	DP
Rivera	.964	5	14	13	1	3
Stokes	.989	18	42	45	1	14

Third Base	PCT	G	PO	A	E	DP
Bonvechio	1.000	3	3	2	0	1
Carrasco	.791	42	30	57	23	7
Contreras	.900	4	2	7	1	1
Davidiuk	.929	4	4	9	1	0
Gonzalez	.972	9	10	25	1	4

Shortstop	PCT	G	PO	A	E	DP
Bush	1.000	1	0	2	0	0
Contreras	.973	15	29	43	2	10
Davidiuk	.968	16	23	37	2	4
Gonzalez	1.000	1	0	1	0	0
Rivera	.950	6	15	23	2	3

	PCT	G	PO	A	E	DP
Rodriguez	.917	21	27	39	6	8

Outfield	PCT	G	PO	A	E	DP
Alley	.917	5	10	1	1	0
Angulo	.962	11	24	1	1	0
Bourassa	1.000	4	8	1	0	0
Burke	.966	43	53	4	2	0
Campbell	1.000	7	18	0	0	0
Carter	.964	30	49	4	2	0
Carvajal	.947	17	17	1	1	0
Durango	.939	28	60	2	4	2
Hunter	.948	25	52	3	3	0
Stokes	—	1	0	0	0	0
Wetzel	.750	3	3	0	1	0

BY ANDY BAGGARLY

After a second consecutive losing season, the Giants were forced to look in the mirror and admit the obvious: They cannot continue their organizational strategy of crowding older, short-term veterans around Barry Bonds.

Bonds climbed to No.2 on the all-time home run list, passing Babe Ruth with his 715th career round-tripper in June. But he wasn't able to carry the Giants to a winning record, and after missing nearly all of 2005 he was a non-factor through most of the summer.

Bonds heated up after his 42nd birthday in July and finished with 26 home runs. His final blast was the 734th of his career, breaking Hank Aaron's National League record and putting him within 22 of a new major league record.

But even with the cherished mark so close, Giants managing partner Peter Magowan appeared ready to cut ties with Bonds after the club finished with a 76-85 record, unless he returns at a significantly reduced salary.

"We need to go in a new direction," Magowan said. "The strategy has been one of having a great player—maybe the greatest player in the game—at the centerpiece and filling in with veteran players. For a long time that worked well. It caught up with us in the last couple of years. And now we do need to get younger and healthier."

That includes the manager. Felipe Alou, 71, was ushered out after four seasons, and he wasn't disappointed to go. He faced a daily battle writing a lineup because most of his older regulars were day-to-day or lost for long stretches. Moises Alou missed time with various leg injuries, Bonds dictated his availability and Mike Matheny was lost at the end of May with a concussion that could end his career.

ORGANIZATION LEADERS

BATTING		*Minimum 250 at-bats
*AVG	Janeway, Rich, AZL Giants	.324
R	Three players tied at	90
H	Minicozzi, Mark, San Jose	160
TB	Velez, Eugenio, Augusta	256
2B	Bowker, John, Fresno/San Jose	32
3B	Velez, Eugenio, Augusta	20
HR	Three players tied at	16
RBI	Minicozzi, Mark, San Jose	93
BB	Copeland, Ben, Augusta	73
SO	Maroul, David, Augusta	123
SB	Richardson, Antoan, Augusta	66
*OBP	Burriss, Emmanuel, Salem-Keizer	.384
*SLG	Witter, Adam, Salem-Keizer	.585
XBH	Velez, Eugenio, Augusta	63

PITCHING		#Minimum 75 innings
W	Martinez, Joseph, Augusta	15
L	Floyd, Jesse, Connecticut	14
#ERA	Cowart, Adam, Salem-Keizer	1.08
G	Hedrick, Justin, San Jose	64
CG	Begg, Chris, Connecticut	3
SV	Anderson, Brian, San Jose	37
IP	Begg, Chris, Connecticut	175
BB	Garcia, James, San Jose/Fresno/Connecticut	72
SO	Misch, Pat, Connecticut/Fresno	136
	Pereira, Nick, San Jose/Fresno	136
#AVG	Cowart, Adam, Salem-Keizer	.178

PLAYERS OF THE YEAR

MAJOR LEAGUE: Jason Schmidt, rhp

Schmidt wore the workhorse tag again in San Francisco in 2006. The 33-year-old tossed 213 innings, going 11-9, 3.59 and leading the club with 180 strikeouts. Schmidt ranked among the National League leaders in strikeouts, ERA and complete games, and he held opponents to a .238 average.

MINOR LEAGUE: Engenio Velez, 2b

Velez came to the Giants in the 2005 minor league Rule 5 draft and was a key part of low Class A Augusta's postseason run, batting .315/.369/.557. It was his best offensive year by far, as he led the South Atlantic League with 20 triples and added 145 hits, 29 doubles and 64 stolen bases.

Closer Armando Benitez also failed to stay healthy or productive and somehow managed to become more of a divisive clubhouse presence than Bonds.

Still, the starting pitching carried the club for most of the season and the Giants even managed to hold first place as late as July 22. Then they lost 16 of 19 and their pitchers ran out of gas down the final two weeks to kill their chances of contending in a weakened league.

The Giants finished 76-85 and in third place—a half-game ahead of the Diamondbacks and Rockies in the NL West. It was their worst finish with Bonds in the lineup since 1996. Even though Bonds posted a .454 on-base percentage, he didn't have the same game-changing effect.

While the Giants did not rule out re-signing Bonds after the season, they made it clear that he can no longer take up a quarter of the club's $85 million payroll. "He's one of 11 pieces of the puzzle," Magowan said, referring to the club's large number of free agents. "He's not even the centerpiece."

The Giants began their organizational shift in June, when they selected righthander Tim Lincecum with the 10th-round pick and gave him a club-record $2.025 million signing bonus. They broke the record a month later when they gave a $2.1 million bonus to 16-year-old Dominican infielder Angel Villalona.

General manager Brian Sabean reversed a habit of giving away draft picks as compensation for signing older free agents, but the Giants are paying the price after years of punting first-round talent with a farm system that ranks far behind their NL West rivals. The system was further set back by a rash of injuries that stunted the progress of well-regarded prospects Eddy Martinez-Esteve, Marcus Sanders, Merkin Valdez, Kelyn Acosta and Waldis Joaquin.

But the Giants always seem to graduate talented arms to the big leagues, and Jonathan Sanchez had an encouraging debut that suggests he could be a long-term option in the rotation. And Matt Cain has the look of an ace. In his first full season, the 21-year-old went 13-12, 4.15 and held opponents to a .222 average.

San Francisco Giants   MLB

National League

BATTING	B-T	HT	WT	DOB	AVG	vLH	vRH	G	AB	R	H	2B	3B	HR	RBI	BB	HBP	SH	SF	SO	SB	CS	SLG	OBP
Alfonzo, Eliezer..............	R-R	6-0	225	2-7-79	.266	.246	.271	87	286	27	76	17	2	12	39	9	7	4	3	74	1	0	.465	.302
Alou, Moises	R-R	6-3	225	7-3-66	.301	.349	.286	98	345	52	104	25	1	22	74	28	1	0	4	31	2	1	.571	.352
Bonds, Barry	L-L	6-2	230	7-24-64	.270	.255	.276	130	367	74	99	23	0	26	77	115	10	0	1	51	3	0	.545	.454
De La Rosa, Tomas	R-R	5-10	180	1-28-78	.313	.250	.333	16	16	1	5	0	0	0	1	1	0	0	0	3	0	0	.313	.353
Durham, Ray	B-R	5-8	190	11-30-71	.293	.341	.277	137	498	79	146	30	7	26	93	51	2	2	2	61	7	2	.538	.360
Ellison, Jason	R-R	5-10	180	4-4-78	.222	.269	.200	84	81	14	18	5	1	2	4	5	1	3	1	14	2	2	.383	.273
Feliz, Pedro	R-R	6-1	210	4-27-75	.244	.212	.253	160	603	75	147	35	5	22	98	33	1	1	6	112	1	1	.428	.281
Finley, Steve	L-L	6-1	195	3-12-65	.246	.255	.244	139	426	66	105	21	12	6	40	46	2	3	4	55	7	0	.394	.320
Frandsen, Kevin	R-R	6-0	175	5-24-82	.215	.200	.217	41	93	12	20	4	0	2	7	3	6	0	0	14	0	1	.323	.284
Greene, Todd	R-R	5-10	210	5-8-71	.289	.250	.301	61	159	16	46	12	2	2	17	10	1	0	0	45	0	0	.428	.335
Hillenbrand, Shea...........	R-R	6-1	210	7-27-75	.248	.339	.219	60	234	33	58	12	0	9	29	7	3	0	3	40	0	1	.415	.275
Ishikawa, Travis	L-L	6-3	210	9-24-83	.292	.400	.263	12	24	1	7	3	1	0	4	1	0	0	0	6	0	0	.500	.320
Knoedler, Justin	R-R	6-2	210	7-17-80	.143	.000	.167	5	7	0	1	0	0	0	0	0	0	0	0	1	0	0	.143	.143
Lewis, Fred....................	L-R	6-2	190	12-9-80	.455	.500	.444	13	11	5	5	1	0	0	2	0	0	0	0	3	0	0	.545	.455
Linden, Todd	B-R	6-3	220	6-30-80	.273	.208	.302	61	77	15	21	4	2	2	5	9	1	2	0	20	1	0	.455	.356
Matheny, Mike	R-R	6-3	225	9-22-70	.231	.364	.181	47	160	10	37	8	0	3	18	9	2	3	3	30	0	1	.338	.274
Niekro, Lance	R-R	6-3	225	1-29-79	.246	.246	.246	66	199	27	49	9	2	5	31	11	0	0	0	32	0	0	.387	.286
Ortmeier, Dan	B-L	6-4	215	5-11-81	.250	.000	.300	9	12	0	3	1	0	0	2	0	0	0	0	4	0	0	.333	.250
Santos, Chad	L-L	5-11	220	4-28-81	.429	.667	.250	3	7	2	3	0	0	1	2	1	0	0	0	2	0	0	.857	.500
Sweeney, Mark	L-L	6-1	215	10-26-69	.251	.135	.270	114	259	32	65	15	2	5	37	28	3	0	1	50	0	1	.382	.330
Vizcaino, Jose	B-R	6-1	190	3-26-68	.210	.231	.200	64	119	16	25	3	0	1	5	16	0	1	0	10	0	2	.261	.304
2-team (16 St. Louis)					.232	—	—	80	142	19	33	6	0	2	8	17	0	2	0	14	0	2	.317	.314
Vizquel, Omar	B-R	5-9	175	4-24-67	.295	.340	.281	153	579	88	171	28	7	4	58	56	6	13	5	51	24	7	.389	.361
Winn, Randy	B-R	6-2	195	6-9-74	.262	.219	.278	149	573	82	150	34	5	11	56	48	7	3	4	63	10	8	.396	.324

PITCHING	B-T	HT	WT	DOB	W	L	ERA	G	GS	CG	SV	IP	H	R	ER	HR	BB	SO	AVG	vLH	vRH	K/9	BB/9
Accardo, Jeremy	R-R	6-2	190	12-8-81	1	3	4.91	38	0	0	3	40	38	23	22	2	11	40	.247	.196	.276	8.93	2.45
Benitez, Armando..........	R-R	6-4	260	11-3-72	4	2	3.52	41	0	0	17	38	39	15	15	6	21	31	.267	.270	.265	7.28	4.93
Cain, Matt....................	R-R	6-3	235	10-1-84	13	12	4.15	32	31	1	0	191	157	93	88	18	87	179	.222	.217	.227	8.45	4.11
Chulk, Vinnie	R-R	6-1	195	12-19-78	0	3	5.24	28	0	0	0	22	17	13	13	2	15	25	.210	.154	.236	10.07	6.04
Correia, Kevin	R-R	6-2	200	8-24-80	2	2	3.49	48	0	0	0	70	64	27	27	5	22	57	.242	.275	.218	7.36	2.84
Fassero, Jeff	L-L	6-1	215	1-5-63	1	1	7.80	10	1	0	0	15	23	13	13	4	8	7	.365	.333	.381	4.20	4.80
Hennessey, Brad	R-R	6-2	195	2-7-80	5	6	4.26	34	12	0	1	99	92	53	47	12	42	42	.251	.230	.265	3.81	3.81
Kline, Steve	R-L	6-1	210	8-22-72	4	3	3.66	72	0	0	1	52	53	24	21	5	26	33	.275	.261	.287	5.75	4.53
Lowry, Noah	R-L	6-2	200	10-10-80	7	10	4.74	27	27	1	0	159	166	89	84	21	56	84	.273	.312	.262	4.74	3.16
Misch, Pat	R-L	6-2	195	8-18-81	0	0	0.00	1	0	0	0	1	2	0	0	0	0	1	.400	.000	.667	9.00	0.00
Morris, Matt	R-R	6-5	220	8-9-74	10	15	4.98	33	33	2	0	208	218	123	115	22	63	117	.268	.277	.261	5.07	2.73
Munter, Scott	R-R	6-6	260	3-7-80	0	1	8.74	27	0	0	0	23	30	22	22	1	18	7	.366	.405	.333	2.78	7.15
Sadler, Billy	R-R	6-0	190	9-21-81	0	0	6.75	5	0	0	0	4	5	3	3	2	2	6	.294	.250	.333	13.50	4.50
Sanchez, Jonathan	L-L	6-2	165	11-19-82	3	1	4.95	27	4	0	0	40	39	26	22	3	23	33	.250	.256	.248	7.43	5.18
Schmidt, Jason	R-R	6-5	210	1-29-73	11	9	3.59	32	32	3	0	213	189	94	85	21	80	180	.238	.262	.215	7.59	3.38
Stanton, Mike...............	L-L	6-1	215	6-2-67	4	2	3.09	26	0	0	8	23	23	8	8	1	6	18	.267	.280	.262	6.94	2.31
2-team (56 Washington)					7	7	3.99	82	0	0	8	67	70	30	30	2	27	48	—	—	—	6.38	3.59
Taschner, Jack	L-L	6-3	210	4-21-78	0	1	8.38	24	0	0	0	19	31	23	18	4	7	15	.344	.275	.400	6.98	3.26
Walker, Tyler	R-R	6-3	260	5-15-76	0	1	15.19	6	0	0	0	5	9	9	9	1	5	3	.391	.400	.385	5.06	8.44
Wilson, Brian	R-R	6-1	205	3-16-82	2	3	5.40	31	0	0	1	30	32	19	18	1	21	23	.281	.348	.235	6.90	6.30
Worrell, Tim	R-R	6-4	240	7-5-67	3	2	7.52	23	0	0	6	20	28	18	17	9	7	12	.308	.256	.354	5.31	3.10
Wright, Jamey	R-R	6-6	235	12-24-74	6	10	5.19	34	21	0	0	156	167	95	90	16	64	79	.282	.261	.300	4.56	3.69

FIELDING

Catcher	PCT	G	PO	A	E	DP	PB
Alfonzo	.992	84	567	31	5	3	1
Greene	.995	42	196	11	1	1	1
Knoedler	1.000	11	0	0	0	1	
Matheny	.996	46	250	19	1	2	2

First Base	PCT	G	PO	A	E	DP
Greene	1.000	5	10	3	0	1
Hillenbrand	.998	58	423	35	1	29
Ishikawa	1.000	10	51	8	0	6
Niekro	.989	58	419	36	5	38
Santos	.947	3	17	1	1	1
Sweeney	.995	53	362	36	2	35
Vizcaino	.975	10	77	1	2	7

Second Base	PCT	G	PO	A	E	DP
De La Rosa	1.000	2	0	2	0	1
Durham	.982	133	272	341	11	82
Frandsen	.977	28	35	51	2	7
Vizcaino	1.000	16	30	41	0	7

Third Base	PCT	G	PO	A	E	DP
De La Rosa	—	2	0	0	0	0
Feliz	.955	159	116	332	21	31
Hillenbrand	.923	8	4	8	1	0
Vizcaino	1.000	2	0	1	0	0

Shortstop	PCT	G	PO	A	E	DP
De La Rosa	.933	8	7	7	1	0
Feliz	1.000	2	4	0	0	0

	PCT	G	PO	A	E	DP
Frandsen	.889	3	3	5	1	2
Vizcaino	.961	19	15	34	2	3
Vizquel	.993	152	205	390	4	87

Outfield	PCT	G	PO	A	E	DP
Alou	.978	92	173	1	4	0
Bonds	.985	116	188	6	3	0
Ellison	.960	64	46	2	2	0
Feliz	1.000	3	1	0	0	0
Finley	.997	130	287	5	1	1
Lewis	.889	6	8	0	1	0
Linden	1.000	47	40	1	0	0
Ortmeier	1.000	3	4	0	0	0
Sweeney	.960	21	24	0	1	0
Winn	.992	141	348	8	3	1

Fresno Grizzlies   Triple-A

Pacific Coast League

BATTING	B-T	HT	WT	DOB	AVG	vLH	vRH	G	AB	R	H	2B	3B	HR	RBI	BB	HBP	SH	SF	SO	SB	CS	SLG	OBP
Alfonzo, Eliezer..............	R-R	6-0	225	2-7-79	.189	.143	.200	24	74	5	14	0	1	2	6	4	6	2	1	18	0	0	.297	.282
Armitage, Jon	B-R	6-5	210	10-29-80	.429	—	.429	4	7	3	3	0	0	1	4	3	0	0	1	2	0	0	.857	.545
Bowker, John	L-L	6-2	190	7-8-83	.500	.000	.667	2	4	0	2	0	0	0	0	0	0	0	0	0	0	0	.500	.500
Bush, Evan	R-R	6-2	195	4-25-84	.400	1.000	.250	3	5	1	2	0	0	0	0	1	0	0	0	1	0	0	1.000	.400
Cervelli, Mike	R-R	5-11	200	8-17-76	.283	.316	.274	68	269	36	76	17	1	8	53	13	1	0	6	37	0	0	.442	.311
Cordido, Julio	R-R	6-1	220	7-30-80	.333	.500	.286	3	9	2	3	0	0	0	0	0	0	0	0	0	0	0	.333	.400
Creswell, Tayler	R-R	6-0	170	2-11-87	.000	—	.000	1	1	0	0	0	0	0	0	0	0	0	0	0	0	0	.000	.000
De La Rosa, Tomas	R-R	5-10	180	1-28-78	.293	.286	.295	79	300	43	88	21	2	8	43	23	5	5	2	45	8	5	.457	.352

General manager: Brian Sabean. **Farm director:** Jack Hiatt. **Scouting director:** Matt Nerland.

Class	Team	League	W	L	PCT	Finish*	Manager	Affiliate Since
Majors	San Francisco	National	76	85	.472	10th	Felipe Alou	—
Triple-A	Fresno Grizzlies	Pacific Coast	61	83	.424	14th (16)	Shane Turner	1998
Double-A	Connecticut Defenders	Eastern	64	77	.454	10th (12)	Dave Machemer	2003
High A	San Jose Giants	California	82	58	.586	1st (10)	Lenn Sakata	1988
Low A	Augusta GreenJackets	South Atlantic	92	47	.662	1st (16)	Roberto Kelly	2005
Short-season	Salem-Keizer Volcanoes	Northwest	55	21	.724	+1st (8)	Steve Decker	1997
Rookie	AZL Giants	Arizona	33	22	.600	4th (9)	Bert Hunter	2000
OVERALL 2006 MINOR LEAGUE RECORD			387	308	.557	1st (30)		

*Finish in overall standings (No. of teams in league). +League champion

	B-T	HT	WT	DOB	AVG	OBP	SLG	G	AB	R	H	2B	3B	HR	RBI	BB	HBP	SH	SF	SO	SB	CS	vLH	vRH
Ellison, Jason	R-R	5-10	180	4-4-78	.406	.408	.406	46	192	41	78	18	2	1	18	14	3	1	1	20	7	4	.536	.452
Flores, Jose	R-R	5-11	185	6-28-73	.238	.222	.242	21	80	11	19	5	0	1	9	7	1	0	0	9	0	0	.338	.307
Frandsen, Kevin	R-R	6-0	175	5-24-82	.304	.311	.301	71	293	46	89	25	3	3	30	12	14	7	2	30	7	4	.440	.358
Haad, Yamid	R-R	6-2	220	9-2-77	.183	.263	.167	39	115	13	21	7	0	3	11	3	1	0	1	21	0	0	.322	.208
Hansen, Jed	R-R	6-1	190	8-19-72	.247	.218	.258	111	365	47	90	17	2	10	44	32	7	1	3	72	10	3	.386	.317
Hornostaj, Aaron	L-R	6-1	178	5-19-83	.225	.250	.219	18	40	5	9	0	0	0	5	6	0	0	2	10	0	0	.225	.313
Horwitz, Brian	R-R	6-1	180	11-7-82	.125	.167	.100	5	16	1	2	1	0	0	1	2	0	0	0	2	0	0	.188	.222
Hutting, Tim	R-R	6-0	190	10-29-81	.227	.238	.222	24	75	9	17	2	0	1	7	8	2	2	0	11	0	0	.293	.318
Knoedler, Justin	R-R	6-2	210	7-17-80	.253	.255	.253	71	233	32	59	13	4	4	27	22	1	4	1	58	4	0	.395	.319
Labarbera, Anthony	R-R	5-10	190	3-17-80	.152	.143	.154	20	46	6	7	1	0	0	2	6	0	0	0	9	0	0	.174	.250
Lewis, Fred	L-R	6-0	190	12-9-80	.276	.225	.291	120	439	85	121	20	11	12	56	68	4	2	4	105	18	8	.453	.375
Linden, Todd	B-R	6-3	220	6-30-80	.278	.273	.280	52	187	31	52	11	3	5	23	29	4	0	1	44	5	0	.449	.385
McMains, Derin	B-R	6-0	180	11-3-79	.143	.000	.167	4	14	0	2	0	0	0	2	1	1	0	1	2	0	0	.143	.235
Melo, Juan	B-R	6-1	160	10-11-76	.284	.263	.292	82	275	36	78	10	1	5	39	18	2	3	5	46	2	2	.382	.327
2-team (33 Colorado Springs)					.263	—		115	384	43	101	12	2	8	50	24	2	3	5	70	2	2	.367	.306
Niekro, Lance	R-R	6-3	225	1-29-79	.319	.306	.324	36	144	27	46	7	0	14	34	7	0	0	1	23	0	0	.660	.349
Nunez, Abraham	B-R	6-3	210	2-5-77	.279	.284	.278	78	283	44	79	19	3	12	57	41	0	0	2	65	5	3	.495	.368
Ortmeier, Dan	B-L	6-4	215	5-11-81	.244	.290	.230	68	262	37	64	14	3	6	33	16	3	0	2	40	8	6	.389	.293
Rodriguez, Guillermo	R-R	5-11	195	5-15-78	.220	.219	.221	39	127	20	28	8	1	8	16	12	4	0	2	25	0	1	.488	.303
Santos, Chad	L-L	5-11	220	4-28-81	.261	.209	.279	91	353	40	92	18	1	14	70	24	1	0	3	86	0	0	.436	.307
Shabala, Adam	L-R	6-1	190	2-6-78	.277	.234	.289	94	289	45	80	20	2	5	41	48	0	1	3	67	7	3	.412	.376
Timpner, Clay	L-L	6-2	195	5-13-83	.286	.278	.288	62	238	33	68	8	3	3	19	10	0	3	0	31	5	7	.382	.315

PITCHING	B-T	HT	WT	DOB	W	L	ERA	G	GS	CG	SV	IP	H	R	ER	HR	BB	SO	AVG	vLH	vRH	K/9	BB/9
Accardo, Jeremy	R-R	6-2	190	12-8-81	0	0	1.80	3	0	0	0	5	1	1	1	0	1	8	.278	.571	.091	14.40	1.80
Anderson, Matt	R-R	6-4	200	8-17-76	1	2	9.17	26	0	0	0	34	48	36	35	8	29	33	.340	.328	.351	8.65	7.60
Bergman, Dusty	L-L	6-5	200	2-1-78	0	1	13.09	14	0	0	0	11	21	19	16	0	11	12	.412	.353	.441	9.82	9.00
Cooper, Brian	R-R	6-1	185	8-19-74	4	9	4.82	27	19	0	0	123	144	83	66	22	42	71	.293	.306	.284	5.18	3.06
Garcia, James	R-R	6-2	190	2-3-80	5	3	5.73	12	12	0	0	60	55	44	38	8	37	47	.248	.297	.207	7.09	5.58
Hennessey, Brad	R-R	6-2	195	2-7-80	0	1	2.53	2	2	0	0	11	11	9	3	1	1	7	.250	.250	.250	5.91	0.84
Hines, Carlos	R-R	6-2	190	9-26-80	2	5	5.04	44	0	0	2	55	65	36	31	7	26	43	.294	.355	.262	6.99	4.23
Kinney, Matt	R-R	6-5	230	12-16-76	8	7	4.80	28	24	1	0	154	158	90	82	23	53	127	.261	.292	.237	7.44	3.10
Liriano, Pedro	R-R	6-2	170	10-23-80	1	6	5.37	24	10	0	0	67	84	51	40	5	29	38	.302	.341	.271	5.10	3.90
Lowry, Noah	R-L	6-2	200	10-10-80	0	0	4.50	1	1	0	0	6	5	3	3	1	1	6	.208	.375	.125	9.00	1.50
Miller, Jeff	R-R	6-4	200	2-1-80	1	2	3.27	15	0	0	0	22	19	9	8	4	5	13	.232	.267	.212	5.32	2.05
Misch, Pat	R-L	6-2	195	8-18-81	4	2	4.02	10	10	1	0	65	74	32	29	7	11	57	.287	.284	.288	7.89	1.52
Palmer, Matt	R-R	6-2	224	3-21-79	6	4	4.05	15	15	0	0	91	91	45	41	10	30	64	.265	.292	.246	6.33	2.97
Pannone, Anthony	R-R	6-3	212	7-7-81	0	0	0.00	1	0	0	0	1	1	0	0	0	0	0	.250	.000	.500	0.00	0.00
Pereira, Nick	R-R	6-0	190	9-22-82	4	3	5.92	15	15	0	0	79	87	55	52	10	48	60	.281	.301	.264	6.84	5.47
Petersen, Jeff	R-R	6-4	225	10-16-81	2	5	8.58	18	4	0	0	36	52	38	34	3	17	15	.356	.360	.360	3.79	4.29
Sadler, Billy	R-R	6-0	190	9-21-81	2	0	1.80	7	0	0	1	10	5	2	2	1	2	12	.156	.300	.091	10.80	1.80
Sanchez, Jonathan	L-L	6-2	165	11-19-82	2	2	3.80	6	6	0	0	24	13	10	10	1	13	28	.163	.238	.136	10.65	4.94
Simon, Alfredo	R-R	6-4	230	5-8-81	0	6	6.75	10	10	0	0	52	76	41	39	8	19	35	.349	.394	.307	6.06	3.29
Taschner, Jack	L-L	6-3	210	4-21-78	6	7	3.65	45	0	0	14	49	49	21	20	5	17	68	.263	.232	.277	12.41	3.10
Tejera, Michael	L-L	5-9	190	10-18-76	8	5	3.80	35	13	0	0	111	113	52	47	12	42	81	.267	.173	.299	6.55	3.40
Threets, Erick	L-L	6-5	240	11-4-81	2	1	2.87	49	0	0	0	63	51	26	20	4	44	51	.223	.232	.219	7.32	6.32
Valdez, Merkin	R-R	6-3	220	11-10-81	0	4	5.80	46	0	0	5	50	52	42	32	6	39	48	.268	.293	.250	8.70	7.07
Villafuerte, Brandon	R-R	5-11	195	12-17-75	2	5	4.59	49	0	0	2	67	60	34	34	2	18	60	.247	.236	.256	8.10	2.43
Wilson, Brian	R-R	6-1	205	3-16-82	1	3	2.89	24	0	0	7	28	20	9	9	2	14	30	.202	.170	.231	9.64	4.50

FIELDING

Catcher	PCT	G	PO	A	E	DP	PB
Alfonzo	.993	23	145	6	1	1	2
Haad	.972	25	125	13	4	2	2
Hansen	.955	9	38	4	2	0	0
Knoedler	.990	66	443	38	5	4	6
Rodriguez	.990	35	274	24	3	1	8

First Base	PCT	G	PO	A	E	DP
Cervenak	1.000	10	84	4	0	8
Haad	.842	2	16	0	3	1
Hansen	.974	16	103	10	3	10
Niekro	.979	34	257	26	6	24
Santos	.985	87	762	49	12	71

Second Base	PCT	G	PO	A	E	DP
Bush	1.000	1	1	3	0	2
Cervenak	1.000	1	3	1	0	0
De La Rosa	1.000	8	16	18	0	4
Frandsen	.975	48	106	131	6	28

	PCT	G	PO	A	E	DP
Hansen	.962	52	84	145	9	25
Hornostaj	1.000	12	22	41	0	11
Labarbera	.980	10	23	25	1	10
McMains	1.000	4	8	13	0	3
Melo	.989	17	48	38	1	14

Third Base	PCT	G	PO	A	E	DP
Cervenak	.945	56	39	99	8	5
Cordido	1.000	3	4	4	0	0
Frandsen	.882	13	10	20	4	3
Hansen	.919	21	9	48	5	2
Knoedler	1.000	2	3	1	0	0
Labarbera	1.000	5	0	1	0	0
Melo	.984	29	18	42	1	2
Shabala	.915	28	10	44	5	2

Shortstop	PCT	G	PO	A	E	DP
De La Rosa	.955	72	109	190	14	52
Flores	.963	21	20	58	3	11

	PCT	G	PO	A	E	DP
Frandsen	.980	12	13	37	1	6
Hansen	1.000	3	7	9	0	4
Hutting	.972	23	41	64	3	19
Labarbera	1.000	2	1	4	0	1
Melo	.946	18	37	33	4	6

Outfield	PCT	G	PO	A	E	DP
Armitage	1.000	3	2	1	0	0
Bowker	1.000	1	1	0	0	0
Ellison	1.000	44	103	5	0	3
Hansen	1.000	10	19	1	0	1
Horwitz	1.000	3	4	0	0	0
Lewis	.976	106	203	5	5	1
Linden	.982	48	111	1	2	1
Nunez	.960	68	114	5	5	0
Ortmeier	.977	64	124	4	3	0
Shabala	1.000	39	77	3	0	1
Timpner	.983	57	111	2	2	0

Eastern League

BATTING	B-T	HT	WT	DOB	AVG	vLH	vRH	G	AB	R	H	2B	3B	HR	RBI	BB	HBP	SH	SF	SO	SB	CS	SLG	OBP
Alfonzo, Eliezer	R-R	6-0	225	2-7-79	.277	.269	.282	20	65	8	18	3	0	0	7	7	1	0	1	16	1	0	.323	.351
Armitage, Jon	B-R	6-5	210	10-29-80	.189	.091	.231	20	37	3	7	1	1	0	1	7	0	1	1	5	1	1	.270	.311
Busch, Andy	R-R	6-2	205	10-28-81	.103	.056	.116	36	87	3	9	2	0	0	4	6	1	2	1	41	0	1	.126	.168
Buscher, Brian	L-R	6-0	200	4-18-81	.259	.246	.264	130	467	43	121	23	3	7	49	39	6	7	5	75	5	4	.366	.321
Foster, Quincy	L-R	6-2	185	10-30-74	.277	.194	.304	45	148	23	41	3	2	1	8	13	0	2	1	24	7	1	.345	.333
Hornostaj, Aaron	L-R	6-1	178	5-19-83	.077	.000	.080	9	26	2	2	0	1	0	2	2	2	0	0	7	0	0	.154	.200
Horwitz, Brian	R-R	6-1	180	11-7-82	.286	.329	.266	78	269	23	77	9	1	2	29	31	4	0	3	35	3	3	.349	.365
Ishikawa, Travis	L-L	6-3	210	9-24-83	.232	.197	.243	86	298	33	69	13	4	10	42	35	3	1	3	88	0	0	.403	.316
Jennings, Todd	R-R	6-0	190	12-10-81	.239	.289	.215	41	138	9	33	4	0	1	17	4	0	0	1	23	1	0	.290	.259
Knoedler, Justin	R-R	6-2	210	7-17-80	.211	.125	.236	21	71	7	15	6	0	1	8	4	1	0	0	24	1	1	.338	.263
Labarbera, Anthony	R-R	5-10	190	3-17-80	.500	.333	.667	3	6	0	3	0	0	0	0	2	0	0	0	0	0	0	.500	.625
Martinez-Esteve, Eddy	R-R	6-2	215	7-14-83	.272	.304	.261	27	92	8	25	10	0	2	11	9	0	0	4	14	0	0	.446	.324
McMains, Derin	B-R	6-0	180	11-3-79	.223	.259	.207	106	358	45	80	13	2	3	20	48	9	3	2	37	18	6	.296	.329
Munhall, Brian	R-R	6-0	190	6-17-80	.250	.220	.263	46	140	10	35	5	1	2	13	9	0	2	2	30	2	0	.343	.291
Ortmeier, Dan	B-L	6-4	215	5-11-81	.251	.179	.288	47	167	17	42	9	1	2	11	17	3	0	2	38	7	4	.353	.328
Requena, Alex	B-R	5-11	185	8-13-80	.226	.194	.245	25	84	12	19	4	0	1	4	7	0	0	0	18	6	4	.310	.286
Schierholtz, Nate	L-R	6-2	215	2-15-84	.270	.263	.274	125	470	55	127	25	7	14	54	27	12	0	1	81	8	3	.443	.325
Sisk, Aaron	R-R	6-0	190	9-17-78	.198	.173	.210	79	237	28	47	9	0	10	28	23	2	1	1	62	7	1	.363	.274
Timpner, Clay	L-L	6-2	195	5-13-83	.222	.189	.235	66	261	26	58	11	2	3	13	13	1	5	2	31	11	6	.314	.260
Von Schell, Tyler	R-R	6-3	229	7-7-79	.228	.229	.227	116	369	34	84	23	1	9	35	24	1	2	1	101	0	1	.369	.276
Wald, Jake	R-R	6-2	188	2-8-81	.202	.215	.197	134	435	42	88	19	3	4	30	35	10	6	0	112	7	7	.287	.277
Walter, Randy	R-R	6-1	212	4-14-81	.207	.207	.207	92	251	24	52	13	3	5	22	15	3	1	1	65	11	5	.343	.259

PITCHING	B-T	HT	WT	DOB	W	L	ERA	G	GS	CG	SV	IP	H	R	ER	HR	BB	SO	AVG	vLH	vRH	K/9	BB/9
Bateman, Joe	R-R	6-2	170	5-6-80	4	6	3.75	53	0	0	10	72	65	37	30	3	23	77	.238	.292	.204	9.63	2.88
Begg, Chris	R-R	6-4	195	9-12-79	13	10	3.40	26	26	3	0	175	159	78	66	8	31	97	.239	.237	.241	5.00	1.60
Broshuis, Garrett	R-R	6-2	185	12-18-81	7	10	4.97	27	27	1	0	152	160	92	84	12	41	104	.273	.303	.248	6.16	2.43
Espineli, Eugene	L-L	6-4	195	9-8-82	8	7	4.11	35	13	1	2	107	117	52	49	6	29	65	.283	.353	.255	5.45	2.43
Floyd, Jesse	R-R	6-5	185	1-2-81	4	14	4.00	25	25	2	0	135	125	66	60	9	38	100	.244	.256	.229	6.67	2.53
Garcia, James	R-R	6-2	210	2-3-80	3	8	3.89	15	15	0	0	81	78	46	35	6	31	65	.248	.308	.187	7.22	3.44
Matos, Osiris	R-R	6-1	189	8-6-84	0	0	3.72	6	0	0	2	10	11	4	4	0	2	5	.282	.188	.348	4.66	1.86
Misch, Patrick	R-L	6-2	195	8-18-81	5	4	2.26	18	17	0	0	104	95	32	26	7	24	79	.247	.254	.244	6.86	2.08
Montero, Oscar	R-R	6-2	175	5-9-78	2	1	4.30	32	0	0	1	46	45	24	22	4	20	63	.251	.289	.223	12.33	3.91
Munter, Scott	R-R	6-6	260	3-7-80	1	4	4.73	28	0	0	1	40	45	24	21	1	15	22	.292	.314	.274	4.95	3.38
Musgrave, Mike	R-R	6-2	185	4-10-84	0	0	5.63	9	2	0	0	24	27	15	15	4	9	15	.278	.241	.294	5.63	3.38
Palmer, Matt	R-R	6-2	224	3-21-79	5	3	1.30	15	9	0	0	62	50	20	9	1	10	51	.216	.150	.274	7.36	1.44
Petersen, Jeff	R-R	6-4	225	10-16-81	1	1	4.94	17	0	0	0	27	27	15	15	2	15	15	.270	.273	.268	4.94	4.94
Ramirez, Froilan	R-R	6-3	195	5-31-84	0	1	36.00	1	1	0	0	1	1	4	4	0	3	0	.333	.000	1.000	0.00	27.00
Sadler, Billy	R-R	6-0	190	9-21-81	3	2	2.56	44	0	0	20	46	23	14	13	1	29	67	.146	.154	.141	13.20	5.72
Sanchez, Jonathan	L-L	6-2	165	11-19-82	2	1	1.15	13	3	0	2	31	14	7	4	0	9	46	.137	.097	.155	13.21	2.59
Spiehs, R.D.	R-R	6-3	224	10-18-79	4	1	3.76	41	0	0	2	65	77	30	27	2	21	27	.304	.302	.306	3.76	2.92
Waddell, Jason	R-L	6-2	206	6-11-81	1	3	3.70	38	3	0	1	49	64	27	20	4	15	49	.323	.373	.293	9.06	2.77

FIELDING

Catcher	PCT	G	PO	A	E	DP	PB
Alfonzo	1.000	14	120	6	0	0	0
Busch	.978	33	159	22	4	4	3
Jennings	1.000	39	258	25	0	3	1
Knoedler	.982	21	150	11	3	0	3
Munhall	.990	46	292	13	3	2	3

First Base	PCT	G	PO	A	E	DP
Alfonzo	1.000	2	23	1	0	2
Armitage	1.000	3	17	2	0	1
Horwitz	.989	10	85	7	1	8
Ishikawa	.993	80	714	49	5	55
Sisk	1.000	1	3	0	0	1
Spiehs	1.000	1	1	0	0	0
Von Schell	.991	49	423	30	4	41

Second Base	PCT	G	PO	A	E	DP
Bateman	1.000	1	1	1	0	0
Hornostaj	1.000	7	19	24	0	4
Jennings	1.000	1	1	0	0	0
Labarbera	.909	3	5	5	1	0
McMains	.984	106	186	303	8	58
Sisk	.971	34	48	84	4	20

Third Base	PCT	G	PO	A	E	DP
Buscher	.958	127	85	254	15	20
Hornostaj	1.000	1	0	2	0	0
Jennings	1.000	1	0	2	0	0
Sisk	.813	17	11	15	6	1
Walter	.—	1	0	0	0	0

Shortstop	PCT	G	PO	A	E	DP
Sisk	.968	9	12	18	1	4

Wald	.962	134	206	395	24	77

Outfield	PCT	G	PO	A	E	DP
Armitage	1.000	9	10	0	0	0
Foster	.946	35	50	3	3	0
Horwitz	.981	55	103	2	2	0
Martinez-Esteve	1.000	26	42	0	0	0
Montero	1.000	1	1	0	0	0
Ortmeier	.990	43	99	0	1	0
Requena	.935	22	40	3	3	0
Schierholtz	.965	113	184	8	7	1
Sisk	.857	13	6	0	1	0
Timpner	.968	66	148	2	5	1
Waddell	.—	1	0	0	0	0
Walter	.967	69	109	8	4	0

California League

BATTING	B-T	HT	WT	DOB	AVG	vLH	vRH	G	AB	R	H	2B	3B	HR	RBI	BB	HBP	SH	SF	SO	SB	CS	SLG	OBP
Abreu, Johany	B-R	6-0	165	4-3-84	.203	.151	.233	41	143	14	29	3	2	1	7	9	1	5	0	29	3	3	.273	.255
Armitage, Jon	B-R	6-5	210	10-29-80	.128	.071	.160	13	39	3	5	3	0	1	4	2	0	0	0	15	2	1	.282	.171
Bowker, John	L-L	6-2	190	7-8-83	.284	.276	.287	112	462	61	131	32	6	7	66	37	2	7	3	100	6	3	.424	.337
Busch, Andy	R-R	6-2	205	10-28-81	.267	.200	.300	4	15	3	4	0	0	1	3	0	0	1	0	6	0	0	.467	.267
Cordido, Julio	R-R	6-1	220	7-30-80	.281	.292	.276	122	467	74	131	20	4	12	78	30	9	0	9	88	13	7	.418	.329
Dobson, Pat	R-R	6-3	210	12-8-80	.259	.338	.218	112	394	62	102	19	1	4	49	40	8	7	3	91	20	8	.343	.337
Dyche, Joseph	R-R	6-1	185	10-27-82	.225	.233	.222	47	169	23	38	4	1	3	15	10	3	1	0	37	13	4	.302	.280
Frandsen, Kevin	R-R	6-0	175	5-24-82	.429	1.000	.000	2	7	1	3	0	0	0	1	0	0	0	0	0	0	0	.429	.556
Haad, Yamid	R-R	6-2	220	9-2-77	.256	.375	.226	13	39	6	10	2	0	1	5	9	0	0	0	9	0	1	.385	.396
Haines, Kyle	L-R	6-1	170	7-28-82	.105	.200	.071	9	19	5	2	1	0	0	2	4	1	2	0	3	1	0	.158	.292
Holm, Stephen	R-R	6-0	206	10-21-79	.258	.236	.271	69	229	44	59	13	0	15	30	24	5	5	0	59	0	0	.511	.341
Horwitz, Brian	R-R	6-1	180	11-7-82	.324	.333	.321	56	207	26	67	11	2	2	31	30	4	0	3	23	0	2	.425	.414
Hutting, Tim	R-R	6-0	190	10-29-81	.266	.315	.238	69	252	29	67	10	0	4	32	24	4	8	1	55	5	1	.353	.338
Jennings, Todd	R-R	6-0	190	12-10-81	.280	.322	.267	64	239	35	67	15	2	0	26	15	8	5	1	40	4	0	.360	.342
Klink, Simon	B-R	6-1	215	12-21-81	.233	.213	.241	98	326	44	76	17	2	9	34	44	8	1	0	107	4	1	.380	.339

	B-T	HT	WT	DOB	AVG	vLH	vRH	G	AB	R	H	2B	3B	HR	RBI	BB	HBP	SH	SF	SO	SB	CS	SLG	OBP
La Torre, Tyler	L-R	6-0	210	4-22-83	.280	.000	.304	8	25	3	7	1	0	0	5	5	0	0	0	6	1	0	.320	.400
Minicozzi, Mark	R-R	6-1	210	2-11-83	.282	.326	.263	128	497	70	140	23	2	4	77	44	8	2	7	87	2	4	.360	.345
Requena, Alex	B-R	5-11	155	8-13-80	.307	.306	.307	51	212	29	65	5	2	0	19	19	1	2	0	53	22	5	.349	.366
Rodriguez, Guillermo	R-R	5-11	195	5-15-78	.364	.250	.385	26	77	20	28	1	0	5	21	10	3	0	1	12	1	0	.662	.451
Sanders, Marcus	R-R	6-0	160	8-25-85	.213	.326	.182	54	211	39	45	9	1	0	17	25	3	4	3	43	24	5	.265	.302
Santos, Chad	L-L	5-11	220	4-28-81	.236	.182	.273	14	55	5	13	3	1	2	11	2	1	0	1	18	0	0	.436	.271
Sosa, Carlos	L-R	6-1	195	10-20-81	.307	.230	.337	93	355	54	109	25	2	10	54	38	4	0	0	107	3	1	.473	.380
Thompson, William	L-L	6-1	180	11-20-82	.277	.314	.262	33	119	15	33	9	0	0	10	14	0	2	0	23	0	1	.353	.353
Wagner, Michael	R-R	6-3	200	9-13-81	.284	.372	.237	76	271	51	77	15	4	8	42	15	6	5	3	81	3	2	.458	.332

PITCHING

	B-T	HT	WT	DOB	W	L	ERA	G	GS	CG	SV	IP	H	R	ER	HR	BB	SO	AVG	vLH	vRH	K/9	BB/9
Acosta, Kelyn	R-R	6-1	205	4-24-85	0	1	6.75	6	6	0	0	9	10	8	7	2	4	11	.270	.263	.278	10.61	3.86
Anderson, Brian	R-R	6-3	210	5-25-83	1	1	1.86	54	0	0	37	68	44	14	14	5	17	85	.183	.216	.158	11.31	2.26
Bauer, Ricky	R-R	6-2	170	3-1-83	0	1	9.95	2	1	0	0	6	7	7	7	0	2	3	.280	.273	.286	4.26	2.84
Cox, Ben	R-R	6-2	220	9-20-81	4	3	3.31	31	0	0	2	49	48	24	18	7	24	45	.257	.216	.283	8.27	4.41
Garcia, James	R-R	6-2	210	2-3-80	0	1	6.23	3	1	0	0	4	3	3	3	0	4	6	.214	.429	.000	12.46	8.31
Gardner, Adam	L-L	6-0	185	2-14-82	4	3	4.86	40	2	0	0	67	56	45	36	7	39	52	.221	.253	.207	7.02	5.27
Grogan, Spencer	L-L	6-4	215	10-10-82	3	1	5.64	13	0	0	1	22	26	18	14	4	5	16	.289	.280	.292	6.45	2.01
Hedrick, Justin	R-R	6-3	225	6-8-82	6	4	2.00	56	0	0	6	86	53	19	19	3	30	110	.182	.180	.183	11.56	3.15
Hinshaw, Alex	L-L	6-4	190	10-31-82	6	3	4.26	30	10	0	0	70	58	48	33	6	60	78	.227	.282	.207	10.08	7.75
King, Thomas	R-R	6-5	205	12-5-83	3	4	3.67	50	0	0	0	81	70	40	33	3	46	66	.230	.272	.209	7.33	5.11
Lincecum, Tim	L-R	5-11	160	6-15-84	2	0	1.95	6	6	0	0	28	13	7	6	3	12	48	.135	.135	.136	15.61	3.90
Lowry, Noah	R-L	6-2	200	10-10-80	0	0	0.00	1	1	0	0	5	5	0	0	0	1	9	.250	.000	.278	17.36	1.93
Martinez, Gregorio	R-R	6-1	160	7-2-82	8	8	4.49	26	26	0	0	138	150	86	69	18	35	111	.270	.287	.255	7.22	2.28
McGrath, Ryan	R-R	6-3	200	12-20-82	0	0	0.00	2	0	0	0	4	4	1	0	0	1	1	.235	.333	.214	2.25	0.00
McNiven, Brooks	R-R	6-5	180	6-19-81	8	7	3.98	36	11	0	0	109	144	69	48	9	19	78	.310	.330	.297	6.46	1.57
Moreno, Anthony	R-R	5-11	198	5-4-83	11	7	4.21	32	23	0	0	137	150	73	64	10	54	115	.286	.296	.277	7.57	3.56
Pannone, Anthony	R-R	6-3	212	7-7-81	3	0	6.11	12	0	0	0	18	23	12	12	2	3	17	.319	.375	.292	8.66	1.53
Paul, Ryan	L-L	6-4	205	8-10-84	0	0	0.00	1	0	0	0	2	1	0	0	0	0	2	.167	.000	.250	9.00	13.50
Pendley, Nathan	L-L	6-4	220	9-5-81	1	0	2.68	23	0	0	1	40	31	13	12	1	17	45	.218	.224	.214	10.04	3.79
Pereira, Nick	R-R	6-0	190	9-22-82	7	1	2.06	13	13	0	0	79	65	21	18	1	16	76	.222	.256	.180	8.69	1.83
Reina, Jesus	L-L	6-2	175	4-20-84	5	4	5.94	18	17	1	0	86	100	60	57	9	47	74	.294	.288	.296	7.71	4.90
Rodriguez, Guillermo	R-R	5-11	195	5-15-78	0	0	9.82	3	0	0	0	4	3	4	4	1	4	4	.231	.222	.250	9.82	9.82
Sack, Darren	R-R	6-4	190	7-19-82	7	3	1.94	23	10	0	0	83	60	21	18	3	34	71	.205	.125	.262	7.67	3.67
Salankey, Caleb	R-R	6-1	180	10-10-82	0	0	5.56	3	2	0	0	11	10	7	7	1	6	11	.250	.240	.267	8.74	4.76
Serrato, Juan	R-R	6-3	205	11-4-81	1	1	7.94	3	3	0	0	11	14	10	10	0	11	6	.341	.333	.346	4.76	8.74
Simon, Alfredo	R-R	6-4	230	5-8-81	2	4	6.44	18	7	0	0	36	43	28	26	7	14	35	.299	.274	.317	8.67	3.47
Whitaker, Craig	R-R	6-4	170	11-19-84	0	0	4.50	1	1	0	0	2	2	1	1	0	1	1	.250	.200	.333	4.50	4.50
Wilson, Brian	R-R	6-1	205	3-16-82	0	0	9.00	1	0	0	0	1	1	1	1	0	1	1	.200	.000	.333	9.00	9.00

FIELDING

Catcher	PCT	G	PO	A	E	DP	PB
Busch	1.000	4	30	0	0	0	0
Haad	.993	13	123	11	1	1	2
Holm	.998	52	403	24	1	4	6
Jennings	.991	63	512	55	5	8	19
La Torre	.983	8	53	4	1	0	0
Rodriguez	1.000	9	69	7	0	2	1

First Base	PCT	G	PO	A	E	DP
Cordido	.991	61	505	35	5	54
Dobson	.991	45	312	18	3	25
Horwitz	.947	5	34	2	2	4
Santos	.984	14	115	6	2	7
Sosa	.913	2	20	1	2	0
Thompson	.990	23	184	10	2	22

Second Base	PCT	G	PO	A	E	DP
Haines	1.000	1	1	1	0	0
Hutting	.969	14	28	34	2	9
Minicozzi	.980	127	229	363	12	80

Third Base	PCT	G	PO	A	E	DP
Abreu	—	1	0	0	0	0
Cordido	.907	43	21	77	10	9
Holm	.941	7	7	9	1	2
Hutting	.903	16	6	22	3	1
Klink	.887	81	41	156	25	16

Shortstop	PCT	G	PO	A	E	DP
Abreu	.943	28	40	76	7	15
Cordido	.938	15	21	39	4	5
Frandsen	1.000	2	7	5	0	3

	PCT	G	PO	A	E	DP
Haines	.880	6	8	14	3	4
Hutting	.946	42	61	114	10	23
Sanders	.921	51	89	131	19	32

Outfield	PCT	G	PO	A	E	DP
Abreu	1.000	9	16	1	0	0
Armitage	1.000	2	3	0	0	0
Bowker	.984	108	181	6	3	2
Dobson	.987	70	146	8	2	2
Dyche	.976	47	117	3	3	0
Horwitz	1.000	37	54	4	0	0
Requena	.983	49	115	3	2	1
Sosa	.975	66	111	4	3	0
Wagner	.984	42	58	4	1	1

Augusta GreenJackets — Low Class A

South Atlantic League

BATTING	B-T	HT	WT	DOB	AVG	vLH	vRH	G	AB	R	H	2B	3B	HR	RBI	BB	HBP	SH	SF	SO	SB	CS	SLG	OBP
Abreu, Johany	B-R	6-0	165	4-3-84	.344	.417	.300	9	32	5	11	1	0	0	2	0	1	0	0	3	1	0	.438	.344
Armitage, Jon	B-R	6-5	210	10-29-80	.253	.217	.266	26	87	16	22	2	2	3	16	13	1	0	0	15	0	0	.425	.356
Benavidez, Julian	R-R	6-2	218	4-14-82	.258	.143	.299	40	132	12	34	7	0	5	24	13	4	0	5	27	0	0	.424	.331
Bocock, Brian	R-R	5-11	185	3-9-85	.000	.000	—	2	1	1	0	0	0	0	0	0	1	0	0	1	0	0	.000	.000
Borg, Hector	B-R	5-10	160	5-26-85	.200	.292	.115	17	50	4	10	0	0	0	2	3	2	1	1	7	4	2	.200	.268
Busch, Andy	R-R	6-2	205	10-28-81	.125	.200	.000	6	8	0	1	0	0	0	2	2	0	0	0	6	0	0	.125	.222
Conte, Nick	R-R	5-10	175	1-25-82	.153	.091	.171	49	144	13	22	2	0	0	7	15	2	1	0	32	0	2	.167	.242
Contreras, Anthony	L-R	5-11	185	9-26-83	.296	.258	.313	121	467	60	138	18	2	2	54	24	3	2	4	61	13	5	.355	.331
Copeland, Benjamin	L-L	5-11	195	12-17-83	.281	.286	.278	135	527	90	148	29	12	5	71	73	3	2	5	90	30	21	.410	.368
Gunther, Barry	B-R	6-0	190	3-18-82	.260	.271	.253	84	281	34	73	8	1	3	39	25	6	2	2	53	1	1	.327	.331
Haines, Kyle	L-R	6-1	170	7-28-82	.258	.255	.260	59	178	18	46	5	0	1	15	33	4	3	2	27	0	3	.303	.381
Hornostaj, Aaron	L-R	6-1	178	5-9-83	.400	.000	.444	4	10	1	4	0	0	0	3	1	0	0	0	1	0	0	.400	.455
Maroul, David	R-R	6-2	210	2-15-83	.249	.240	.253	106	393	58	98	21	3	11	67	25	8	6	7	123	4	1	.402	.303
McCarthy, Greg	R-R	6-4	215	5-10-83	.211	.333	.178	16	57	3	12	3	0	0	13	0	0	0	0	13	0	0	.263	.274
Mooney, Michael	R-R	6-0	205	6-8-83	.287	.289	.288	134	494	82	142	28	7	11	74	44	12	0	7	115	38	10	.439	.355
Paulino, Adalberto	R-R	5-11	179	9-6-82	.304	.250	.318	21	56	15	17	2	0	0	4	7	4	2	0	9	1	1	.393	.371
Requena, Alex	B-R	5-11	155	8-13-80	.268	.244	.286	26	97	18	26	1	0	0	8	10	3	1	1	27	11	4	.278	.351
Richardson, Antoan	B-R	5-8	165	10-8-83	.292	.279	.299	124	418	78	122	17	4	2	28	54	9	7	5	73	66	9	.366	.381
Sandoval, Pablo	S-R	5-11	180	8-11-86	.265	.201	.293	117	438	43	116	20	1	1	49	22	8	1	4	74	3	4	.322	.309
Velez, Eugenio	B-R	6-1	163	5-16-82	.315	.236	.359	126	460	90	145	29	20	14	90	30	1	0	5	81	64	15	.557	.369
Yens, Jose	R-R	6-1	190	10-16-82	.226	.284	.190	83	283	32	64	13	2	1	28	13	9	0	3	56	7	3	.297	.279

PITCHING	B-T	HT	WT	DOB	W	L	ERA	G	GS	CG	SV	IP	H	R	ER	HR	BB	SO	AVG	vLH	vRH	K/9	BB/9
Bauer, Ricky	R-R	6-2	170	3-1-83	0	0	4.91	19	0	0	0	18	22	12	10	0	3	12	.310	.423	.244	5.89	1.47
Cabeza, Manuel	R-R	6-2	180	2-6-85	0	0	20.25	1	1	0	0	1	3	3	3	0	1	2	.429	.250	.667	13.50	6.75

Name	B-T	HT	WT	DOB	W	L	ERA	G	GS	CG	SV	IP	H	R	ER	HR	BB	SO	AVG	vLH	vRH	K/9	BB/9
Clark, Jeff	R-R	6-6	247	5-6-80	0	1	7.71	2	2	0	0	5	6	4	4	0	2	2	.286	.500	.000	3.86	3.86
Cody, Buck	R-L	6-2	195	6-22-82	2	0	4.19	23	0	0	0	39	27	22	18	3	35	31	.196	.219	.189	7.22	8.15
Foltin, Wayne	R-R	6-2	200	12-11-82	5	2	3.14	43	0	0	17	52	39	23	18	3	25	44	.202	.205	.200	7.66	4.35
Grace, Robert	R-R	6-1	165	2-2-83	0	0	0.00	1	0	0	0	4	0	0	0	0	1	7	.000	.000	.000	17.18	2.45
Griffin, Daniel	R-R	6-7	225	9-29-84	5	5	4.46	16	16	1	0	73	78	44	36	7	33	78	.266	.268	.265	9.66	4.09
Martinez, Joseph	L-R	6-3	185	2-26-83	15	5	3.01	27	27	1	0	168	156	66	56	9	26	135	.246	.255	.240	7.25	1.40
Martis, Shairon	R-R	6-1	175	3-30-87	6	4	3.64	15	15	0	0	77	76	39	31	3	21	66	.257	.231	.271	7.75	2.47
2-team (4 Savannah)					7	5	3.67	19	19	0	0	98	99	48	40	5	25	80	—	—		7.35	2.30
Matos, Osiris	R-R	6-1	189	8-6-84	7	3	1.76	44	0	0	13	61	42	13	12	3	12	81	.193	.148	.219	11.89	1.76
McKae, Dave	R-R	6-2	190	11-24-81	8	2	1.80	18	14	0	0	85	74	24	17	1	17	71	.225	.195	.245	7.52	1.80
Millikan, Bryan	R-R	6-5	202	8-13-83	4	1	3.64	35	0	0	2	54	65	28	22	4	14	39	.301	.311	.292	6.46	2.32
Minor, Matthew	R-R	6-0	180	9-20-82	0	1	6.75	12	0	0	0	16	19	15	12	1	16	12	.302	.370	.250	6.75	9.00
Nieto, Ben	L-L	5-11	225	4-4-84	1	2	12.27	4	3	0	0	15	27	21	20	4	5	16	.370	.333	.382	9.82	3.07
Pichardo, Kelvin	R-R	6-0	160	10-13-85	2	4	3.19	12	5	0	0	37	31	15	13	1	17	35	.226	.233	.221	8.59	4.17
Quinowski, David	L-L	5-10	170	4-23-86	4	2	1.43	44	0	0	4	75	36	14	12	1	24	76	.145	.143	.145	9.08	2.87
Ray, Ronnie	R-R	6-3	195	5-11-84	8	6	3.53	27	26	0	0	148	154	65	58	8	47	112	.275	.261	.285	6.83	2.86
Romo, Sergio	R-R	5-11	185	3-4-83	10	2	2.53	31	10	0	4	103	78	33	29	9	19	95	.208	.262	.175	8.27	1.65
Shaver, Ryan	R-R	6-5	175	12-17-84	11	6	3.64	25	20	1	0	131	148	62	53	4	38	80	.289	.297	.283	5.50	2.54
Wilding, Taylor	R-R	6-1	190	10-22-84	4	1	2.66	24	0	0	3	47	47	15	14	3	12	40	.263	.329	.206	7.61	2.28

FIELDING

Catcher	PCT	G	PO	A	E	DP	PB
Busch	1.000	5	32	4	0	0	1
Conte	.976	47	331	37	9	6	9
Gunther	.992	80	563	70	5	4	9
McCarthy	.986	16	113	24	2	3	2

First Base	PCT	G	PO	A	E	DP
Armitage	.982	7	49	5	1	6
Benavidez	.964	8	51	3	2	8
Maroul	1.000	5	19	1	0	2
Sandoval	.992	93	811	43	7	66
Yens	.990	33	272	14	3	16

Second Base	PCT	G	PO	A	E	DP
Abreu	1.000	4	8	17	0	4
Bocock	1.000	1	3	4	0	1
Borg	.980	13	14	36	1	6

	PCT	G	PO	A	E	DP
Contreras	1.000	14	20	42	0	7
Haines	.958	42	63	119	8	21
Hornostaj	.889	2	4	4	1	1
Maroul	1.000	1	1	4	0	1
Paulino	1.000	2	3	3	0	1
Velez	.976	68	111	176	7	35

Third Base	PCT	G	PO	A	E	DP
Abreu	.857	2	4	2	1	1
Borg	1.000	5	1	10	0	0
Contreras	.912	23	19	33	5	3
Hornostaj	1.000	1	1	1	0	0
Maroul	.948	89	63	157	12	20
Paulino	1.000	1	1	0	0	0
Sandoval	.844	21	20	34	10	3
Velez	1.000	1	0	6	0	1

Shortstop	PCT	G	PO	A	E	DP
Abreu	1.000	1	0	2	0	0
Contreras	.963	82	109	229	13	34
Haines	.975	14	26	51	2	7
Maroul	.907	12	10	29	4	5
Velez	.911	32	51	82	13	24

Outfield	PCT	G	PO	A	E	DP
Abreu	1.000	2	2	0	0	0
Armitage	.929	9	12	1	1	0
Copeland	.982	132	212	9	4	2
Haines	1.000	1	2	0	0	0
Mooney	.953	127	227	15	12	1
Paulino	1.000	8	10	1	0	0
Requena	1.000	17	32	1	0	0
Richardson	.990	118	278	8	3	3
Yens	.889	10	13	3	2	0

Salem-Keizer Volcanoes — Short-Season

Northwest League

BATTING	B-T	HT	WT	DOB	AVG	vLH	vRH	G	AB	R	H	2B	3B	HR	RBI	BB	HBP	SH	SF	SO	SB	CS	SLG	OBP
Bocock, Brian	R-R	5-11	185	3-9-85	.223	.250	.206	39	103	12	23	6	0	0	7	12	1	3	2	29	6	1	.282	.305
Boyer, Bradley	L-R	6-0	185	10-4-83	.246	.263	.244	61	183	27	45	9	6	5	28	17	2	1	3	29	6	2	.443	.312
Burriss, Emmanuel	B-R	6-0	170	1-17-85	.307	.333	.297	65	254	50	78	8	2	1	27	27	6	4	2	22	35	11	.366	.384
Bush, Evan	R-R	6-2	195	4-25-84	.188	.231	.158	32	64	4	12	2	0	0	3	8	0	1	0	16	1	0	.219	.278
Davis, Robert	R-R	6-0	195	12-31-83	.171	.211	.125	14	35	3	6	1	0	0	2	2	1	0	0	3	0	0	.200	.237
Felmy, Robert	L-L	5-10	168	4-29-84	.281	.279	.281	55	196	38	55	8	1	8	33	19	4	0	1	34	10	1	.454	.355
Graham, Tyler	R-R	6-0	180	1-25-84	.240	.171	.274	50	125	23	30	3	0	0	9	11	6	7	2	38	14	4	.264	.326
Gutierrez-Portalatin, Henry ..	R-R	5-11	195	5-7-83	.380	.407	.365	25	79	10	30	2	1	0	12	3	2	0	2	7	3	0	.430	.407
Haad, Yamid	R-R	6-2	220	9-2-77	.000	.000	.000	6	16	0	0	0	0	0	0	1	0	0	0	4	0	0	.000	.059
La Torre, Tyler	L-R	6-0	210	4-22-83	.111	.000	.118	6	18	4	2	0	0	0	0	1	0	1	0	5	0	0	.222	.158
McBryde, Michael	R-R	6-1	170	3-22-85	.276	.189	.302	71	225	38	62	9	5	3	34	22	2	5	1	59	16	4	.400	.344
Neal, Thomas	R-R	6-1	205	8-17-87	.250	.280	.238	50	176	26	44	6	2	4	20	7	3	0	1	44	1	3	.375	.289
Pill, Brett	R-R	6-4	200	9-9-84	.220	.200	.225	60	223	37	49	16	0	5	35	22	3	0	2	39	3	2	.359	.296
Rohlinger, Ryan	R-R	6-1	185	10-7-83	.252	.243	.256	65	234	34	59	13	1	3	28	27	5	2	5	27	0	2	.355	.336
Rojas, Nestor	R-R	6-0	200	11-18-83	.250	.500	.167	4	8	1	2	0	0	0	1	0	0	0	0	2	0	0	.250	.250
Salsgiver, Lance	R-R	6-0	175	11-21-83	.197	.063	.308	35	71	7	14	3	1	0	4	5	3	0	0	9	1	0	.268	.278
Schoop, Sharlon	R-R	6-0	160	4-15-87	.286	—	.286	4	7	1	2	0	0	0	1	2	1	0	0	0	0	0	.286	.500
Thompson, William	L-L	6-0	180	11-20-82	.386	.348	.404	19	70	16	27	4	0	3	17	15	0	0	0	8	0	0	.571	.494
Todd, Christopher	B-R	5-10	170	9-20-82	.289	.217	.311	44	97	14	28	1	0	0	14	20	1	4	1	8	2	2	.299	.412
Weston, Matthew	L-L	6-3	215	5-20-84	.280	.263	.284	63	200	27	56	14	0	4	27	13	2	0	2	34	2	0	.410	.327
Witter, Adam	L-R	6-1	175	2-17-83	.285	.300	.281	61	207	40	59	12	1	16	52	25	2	0	1	41	2	3	.585	.366

PITCHING	B-T	HT	WT	DOB	W	L	ERA	G	GS	CG	SV	IP	H	R	ER	HR	BB	SO	AVG	vLH	vRH	K/9	BB/9
Calicutt, Steven	L-L	6-2	190	2-7-84	4	1	1.75	18	4	0	2	46	39	10	9	0	11	26	.238	.150	.266	5.05	2.14
Cowart, Adam	R-R	6-2	190	8-18-83	10	1	1.08	15	15	0	0	83	51	13	10	2	8	55	.178	.192	.171	5.94	0.86
Cranston, Jared	B-L	6-2	195	4-18-85	2	0	4.15	13	0	0	0	17	13	9	8	3	18	34	.213	.438	.133	17.65	9.35
English, Jesse	L-L	6-2	215	9-13-84	3	0	6.35	17	0	0	0	28	21	21	20	6	18	40	.208	.231	.200	12.71	5.72
Hobson, Gib	R-R	6-3	195	1-13-85	3	3	2.94	11	9	0	0	52	42	22	17	3	14	38	.225	.246	.213	6.58	2.42
Lincecum, Tim	L-R	5-11	160	6-15-84	0	0	0.00	2	2	0	0	4	1	0	0	0	0	6	.071	.167	.000	22.50	0.00
Lussier, Paul	R-R	6-2	220	11-7-85	4	1	2.90	22	0	0	4	40	30	14	13	4	14	35	.205	.175	.217	7.81	3.12
Newton, David	R-R	5-11	200	3-4-86	0	0	0.00	2	0	0	0	3	2	0	0	0	0	5	.182	.500	.000	15.00	0.00
Odom, John	R-R	6-2	185	1-6-82	6	3	3.05	15	15	0	0	74	72	30	25	4	16	51	.250	.252	.249	6.23	1.95
Oseguera, Paul	L-L	6-0	180	1-6-84	2	1	3.72	16	0	0	2	29	25	13	12	0	9	39	.225	.300	.198	12.10	2.79
Paul, Ryan	L-L	6-4	205	8-10-84	1	1	6.08	12	0	0	0	13	15	9	9	2	8	20	.283	.176	.333	13.50	5.40
Paul, Adam	R-R	6-6	214	2-17-84	1	3	3.86	23	0	0	1	37	34	18	16	1	14	26	.250	.265	.245	6.27	3.38
Pichardo, Kelvin	R-R	6-0	160	10-13-85	2	0	4.60	6	0	0	1	16	17	10	8	2	6	24	.266	.227	.286	13.79	3.45
Pucetas, Kevin	R-R	6-4	225	11-27-84	7	1	2.17	15	15	0	0	71	57	22	17	2	19	60	.222	.289	.186	7.64	2.42
Rodriguez, Wilmin	L-L	6-2	175	5-13-85	0	0	2.45	3	0	0	1	4	3	1	1	1	0	3	.214	.000	.333	7.36	0.00
Snyder, Benjamin	L-L	6-1	175	7-20-85	4	1	3.66	15	12	0	0	66	60	30	27	6	17	60	.242	.185	.258	7.87	2.31
Stolp, Eric	R-R	6-3	182	8-18-84	0	1	2.93	14	0	0	0	31	27	14	10	0	11	20	.239	.303	.213	5.87	3.23
Tanner, Clayton	R-L	6-1	180	12-5-87	2	2	3.46	13	0	0	1	26	17	11	10	1	8	25	.183	.227	.169	8.65	2.77
Trinidad, Juan	R-R	6-3	200	11-6-85	2	1	1.52	24	0	0	16	24	18	4	4	2	9	14	.209	.238	.200	5.32	1.52
Whitaker, Craig	R-R	6-4	170	11-19-84	2	1	3.86	4	4	0	0	19	13	9	8	1	13	15	.200	.222	.191	7.23	6.27

FIELDING

Catcher	PCT	G	PO	A	E	DP	PB
Davis	1.000	12	61	6	0	0	0
Gutierrez-Portalatin	1.000	24	148	8	0	1	3
Haad	1.000	6	33	2	0	0	1
La Torre	1.000	6	39	7	0	0	1
Rojas	1.000	4	16	0	0	0	0
Witter	.985	41	295	25	5	4	9

First Base	PCT	G	PO	A	E	DP
Bush	1.000	4	15	0	0	0
Pill	.995	58	538	46	3	54
Thompson	1.000	15	139	9	0	11
Witter	.972	5	33	2	1	4

Second Base	PCT	G	PO	A	E	DP
Bocock	.961	21	35	63	4	17
Boyer	.986	56	84	123	3	28
Bush	1.000	2	3	2	0	1
Todd	.981	15	14	37	1	5

Third Base	PCT	G	PO	A	E	DP
Bush	.813	10	1	12	3	2
Rohlinger	.950	65	51	156	11	11
Todd	.905	12	4	15	2	2

Shortstop	PCT	G	PO	A	E	DP
Bocock	.987	18	27	50	1	17

	PCT	G	PO	A	E	DP
Burriss	.952	62	99	200	15	38
Schoop	1.000	3	4	4	0	1
Todd	.875	3	3	4	1	2

Outfield	PCT	G	PO	A	E	DP
Bush	1.000	1	1	0	0	0
Felmy	.964	54	76	5	3	1
Graham	.984	48	61	2	1	0
McBryde	.959	70	131	11	6	4
Neal	.972	30	34	1	1	1
Salsgiver	1.000	30	25	1	0	1
Weston	1.000	42	36	0	0	0

AZL Giants — Rookie

Arizona League

BATTING

	B-T	HT	WT	DOB	AVG	vLH	vRH	G	AB	R	H	2B	3B	HR	RBI	BB	HBP	SH	SF	SO	SB	CS	SLG	OBP
Balmer, Allen	L-R	5-11	205	10-17-83	.231	.200	.240	30	65	11	15	4	0	0	8	14	2	0	0	7	1	1	.292	.383
Benavidez, Julian	R-R	6-2	218	4-14-82	.340	.200	.357	15	47	7	16	3	0	4	18	10	0	0	3	8	0	0	.660	.433
Borg, Hector	B-R	5-10	160	5-26-85	.221	.091	.246	20	68	7	15	3	2	0	13	3	0	1	0	9	2	4	.324	.254
Cividanes, Emmanuel	L-L	6-1	175	10-31-84	.309	.333	.306	29	97	26	30	5	1	0	14	20	0	1	0	11	5	1	.381	.427
Creswell, Tayler	R-R	6-0	170	2-11-87	.224	.280	.214	47	165	35	37	7	2	0	19	21	10	1	3	43	16	2	.291	.342
Davis, Robert	R-R	6-0	195	12-31-83	.500	.333	.583	8	18	5	9	4	0	0	5	1	0	0	1	0	0	0	.722	.526
De La Rosa, Tomas	R-R	5-10	180	1-28-78	.407	.800	.318	7	27	4	11	1	0	0	2	1	1	0	1	2	2	0	.444	.433
Downs, Matthew	R-R	6-2	190	3-19-84	.310	.296	.312	46	168	34	52	16	4	0	29	17	3	3	5	9	6	1	.452	.373
Flores, Jose	B-R	5-11	175	8-17-87	.289	.192	.314	34	128	19	37	1	0	1	21	7	2	1	2	14	4	1	.320	.331
Janeway, Rich	L-R	6-2	190	7-22-81	.324	.375	.315	43	148	19	48	12	3	2	39	15	1	4	4	15	5	3	.486	.381
Jean, Juan	L-R	6-1	180	9-14-85	.310	.300	.311	29	84	14	26	3	2	0	10	8	2	0	0	5	5	0	.393	.383
Klimas, Matthew	R-R	5-11	185	7-3-87	.348	.333	.353	20	46	8	16	2	0	0	4	4	3	1	1	7	3	0	.391	.426
La Torre, Tyler	L-R	6-0	210	4-22-83	.143	.000	.150	7	21	1	3	0	0	0	0	0	0	0	0	6	0	0	.143	.143
Luster, Jeremiah	R-R	5-10	175	8-31-86	.244	.400	.225	23	45	6	11	2	0	0	7	8	0	1	0	7	2	0	.289	.358
McCarthy, Greg	R-R	6-4	215	5-10-83	.226	.333	.214	9	31	3	7	1	0	1	6	1	1	0	0	4	0	0	.355	.273
Nunez, Abraham	B-R	6-3	210	2-5-77	.375	.250	.417	6	16	6	6	1	1	1	4	4	1	0	0	2	1	0	.750	.524
Nunez, Ariel	R-R	6-3	190	8-3-85	.203	.231	.196	23	59	8	12	3	0	0	4	3	2	1	0	23	4	2	.254	.266
Perez, Hector	R-R	6-2	186	3-3-86	.138	.143	.136	18	29	2	4	0	0	0	2	2	1	1	0	9	1	0	.138	.219
Rojas, Nestor	R-R	6-0	200	11-18-83	.241	.286	.234	25	54	6	13	1	0	0	1	8	0	0	0	5	1	0	.259	.339
Roundy, Joe	R-R	6-3	200	8-30-83	.244	.400	.215	38	127	16	31	9	2	5	17	7	7	0	3	26	4	3	.465	.313
Sanders, Marcus	B-R	6-0	160	8-25-85	.121	.000	.138	10	33	7	4	1	0	0	3	7	0	0	0	11	4	0	.152	.275
Sarmiento, Elio	B-R	6-0	200	6-20-86	.284	.250	.290	31	81	13	23	2	1	2	10	5	6	1	0	14	0	1	.407	.370
Schoop, Sharlon	R-R	6-0	160	4-15-87	.310	.412	.294	38	126	29	39	7	1	1	21	26	4	2	2	15	8	3	.405	.437
Simmons, James	R-R	6-3	190	9-3-85	.278	.286	.276	42	126	26	35	9	1	1	9	16	1	1	1	33	2	2	.389	.361
Van Elderen, Sean	R-R	6-3	225	9-21-82	.212	.526	.121	29	85	12	18	4	1	0	10	8	3	1	2	29	4	1	.282	.296

PITCHING

	B-T	HT	WT	DOB	W	L	ERA	G	GS	CG	SV	IP	H	R	ER	HR	BB	SO	AVG	vLH	vRH	K/9	BB/9
Acosta, Kelyn	R-R	6-1	205	4-24-85	0	0	0.00	1	0	0	0	1	1	4	0	0	1	0	.250	1.000	.000	0.00	13.50
Brinson, Morgan	R-R	6-3	181	12-11-86	0	0	16.62	7	0	0	0	4	6	9	8	1	13	4	.353	.375	.333	8.31	27.00
Cabeza, Manuel	R-R	6-2	180	2-6-85	7	0	3.38	11	8	0	0	45	43	18	17	1	10	40	.247	.206	.274	7.94	1.99
Clark, Jeffrey	R-R	6-6	247	5-6-85	0	1	0.00	4	4	0	0	9	7	2	1	0	1	10	.219	.167	.231	10.00	1.00
De La Rosa, Carlos	L-L	6-2	190	7-15-84	1	3	5.13	16	0	0	0	26	30	18	15	1	12	25	.288	.192	.320	8.54	4.10
Foeman, Kevin	R-R	6-6	215	4-2-84	0	1	10.62	13	3	0	0	20	29	28	24	1	19	15	.358	.263	.387	6.64	8.41
Grace, Timothy	R-R	6-1	165	2-2-83	1	0	2.25	4	1	0	0	8	8	2	2	0	4	5	.267	.364	.211	5.63	4.50
Martinez, Roberto	L-L	6-1	175	5-5-86	3	2	4.05	14	4	0	1	40	39	21	18	1	22	49	.253	.357	.230	11.03	4.95
Martinez, Lenny	L-L	6-5	230	9-25-85	1	0	3.94	15	0	0	0	16	14	7	7	1	6	20	.241	.125	.286	11.25	3.38
McGovern, Ryan	L-L	6-1	185	6-23-84	0	0	4.26	10	0	0	0	13	11	6	6	1	5	14	.234	.375	.205	9.95	3.55
McGrath, Ryan	R-R	6-3	200	12-20-82	5	3	2.94	13	7	0	0	52	52	21	17	1	15	29	.274	.284	.268	5.02	2.60
Newton, David	R-R	5-11	200	3-4-86	3	1	1.14	23	0	0	13	24	19	7	3	0	12	31	.211	.226	.203	11.79	4.56
Ortiz-Jusino, Adam	R-R	6-3	190	10-24-84	2	2	2.76	19	0	0	1	29	29	14	9	0	15	21	.269	.277	.262	6.44	4.60
Pannone, Anthony	R-R	6-3	212	7-7-81	0	0	23.14	3	0	0	0	2	5	6	6	1	2	5	.417	.600	.286	19.29	7.71
Paulino, Julio	R-R	6-4	190	1-2-87	1	0	7.30	8	0	0	0	12	16	11	10	1	9	9	.314	.318	.310	6.57	6.57
Ramirez, Froilan	R-R	6-3	195	5-31-84	0	0	4.38	11	0	0	0	12	9	7	6	1	8	8	.200	.313	.138	8.76	5.84
Rodriguez, Wilmin	L-L	6-2	175	5-13-85	3	3	5.66	12	6	0	1	35	44	25	22	0	15	23	.312	.333	.306	5.91	3.85
Rusova, Ivan	R-R	6-1	180	11-5-86	0	0	7.36	11	0	0	0	11	7	9	9	1	15	11	.194	.250	.179	9.00	12.27
Sosa, Henry	R-R	6-2	185	7-28-85	2	1	3.90	9	6	0	0	32	20	15	14	3	4	31	.177	.222	.147	11.41	3.34
Valdez, Jose	R-R	6-7	190	8-1-88	1	3	7.38	12	8	0	0	39	48	36	32	3	25	40	.304	.280	.315	9.23	5.77
Yntema, Orlando	R-R	6-3	180	2-21-86	4	3	3.79	12	8	0	1	55	56	25	23	2	15	42	.269	.260	.274	6.91	2.47

FIELDING

Catcher	PCT	G	PO	A	E	DP	PB
Davis	1.000	8	32	1	0	1	1
Klimas	.991	20	98	11	1	1	3
La Torre	1.000	7	52	7	0	1	3
McCarthy	1.000	4	14	2	0	0	0
Rojas	1.000	17	83	15	0	1	1
Sarmiento	.990	27	173	18	2	1	8

First Base	PCT	G	PO	A	E	DP
Benavidez	1.000	1	10	0	0	0
Janeway	.978	31	216	9	5	32
Rojas	.981	7	49	4	1	6
Van Elderen	.981	25	193	12	4	18

Second Base	PCT	G	PO	A	E	DP
Borg	1.000	11	20	30	0	5

	PCT	G	PO	A	E	DP
Flores	1.000	21	32	38	0	11
Jean	.965	27	50	61	4	20
Sarmiento	1.000	1	2	1	0	0
Schoop	.976	9	15	26	1	8

Third Base	PCT	G	PO	A	E	DP
Balmer	.913	12	8	13	2	2
Borg	.833	3	0	5	1	1
Downs	.922	43	23	72	8	10
Flores	.833	2	1	4	1	0
Sarmiento	—	2	0	0	0	0

Shortstop	PCT	G	PO	A	E	DP
Borg	.875	5	8	13	3	2
De La Rosa	.947	7	11	25	2	2
Flores	.977	11	19	24	1	7

	PCT	G	PO	A	E	DP
Sanders	.935	9	10	33	3	6
Schoop	.951	31	49	107	8	21

Outfield	PCT	G	PO	A	E	DP
Cividanes	1.000	28	41	2	0	0
Creswell	.976	47	76	5	2	0
Janeway	1.000	1	2	0	0	0
Luster	.938	17	14	1	1	0
Nunez	1.000	5	8	0	0	0
Nunez	.853	19	27	2	5	0
Perez	.875	11	7	0	1	0
Roundy	.933	35	37	5	3	2
Simmons	.969	40	58	4	2	1

SEATTLE MARINERS

BY SCOTT HANSON

The Mariners were nine wins better in 2006, enough to save the jobs of general manager Bill Bavasi and manager Mike Hargrove, but not enough to avoid their third consecutive last-place finish in the American League West.

At least the trend is heading in the right direction. After winning 63 games in 2004 and 69 in 2005, the Mariners improved to 78-84. While the team will retain Bavasi and Hargrove, they have been put on notice for next season.

"Let me be clear, I am disappointed with what's happened this season," Mariners chief executive officer Howard Lincoln told the Seattle Times. "I am tired of seeing the team lose."

Lincoln also said that both the general manager and manager are aware that they are on the hot seat entering 2007.

A franchise-worst 0-for-11 road trip in August, part of 20 straight losses to AL West teams, sent the Mariners from playoff contention to hopelessly out of the race and led to the trade of team icon Jamie Moyer, whose 145 wins with Seattle is a franchise record.

With the playoffs no longer a possibility, the Mariners played a lot of young players in the final two months and finished strong. They were 20-15 after the 0-11 road trip, and Lincoln said the good finish played a role in keeping his GM and manager.

The Mariners enjoyed a career year from left fielder Raul Ibanez, who had 33 homers and 123 RBIs. First baseman Richie Sexson and third baseman Adrian Beltre rebounded from poor starts to finish with fairly good

PLAYERS OF THE YEAR

MAJOR LEAGUE: Ichiro Suzuki, of

An all-star and Gold Glove winner in all six of his big league seasons, Suzuki led the Mariners with a .322 average, .370 on-base percentage, 110 runs, 224 hits and nine triples. He also stole 45 bases in 47 tries. Suzuki also played 39 games in center field, in advance of a 2007 move over from right.

MINOR LEAGUE: Adam Jones, of

Triple-A wasn't the only new experience for Jones last season. He also shifted from shortstop to center field, and the 21-year-old managed to hit .287/.345/.484 with 16 home runs and 13 stolen bases for Tacoma. Jones made his major league debut in August but struggled to a .216 average.

STEVE MOORE

numbers. Sexson had 34 homers and 107 RBIs and Beltre had 25 home runs and 87 RBIs.

New catcher Kenji Johjima made a smooth transition from Japan to the major leagues, hitting .291/.332/.451 with 18 homers and 76 RBIs. Outfielder Ichiro Suzuki put together a typically strong season, hitting .322 and collecting 224 hits. Maybe more important, Ichiro seemed fine moving to center field from right field at the end of August, and it appears he will start 2007 in center.

The 2007 rotation figures to be much different than it was to begin 2006. The only two holdovers will likely be 20-year-old Felix Hernandez and Jarrod Washburn. Neither had the season the Mariners were looking for. Hernandez, one of baseball's top young players, was inconsistent while compiling a 12-14, 4.52 record. Washburn went 8-14, 4.67 after signing a four-year, $37.5 million contract.

Jake Woods (7-4, 4.20) and minor league callup Cha Seung Baek (4-1, 3.67 in six Seattle starts) will get consideration to join them, but the Mariners are also expected to try to obtain pitching help via free agency.

Several minor league callups made good impressions in the final couple of months. None was better than reliever Mark Lowe, who began the season at Class A Inland Empire and proved to be a great set-up man, not allowing a run in his first 17⅔ innings with Seattle.

The Mariners have high hopes heading into next season. "I expect to be in the postseason next year," Ibanez told the Times. "That's what everybody's goal is."

The Mariners will have several changes in the minor leagues next season. Dave Brundage was fired after leading Triple-A Tacoma to a 74-70 record, and Dave Myers was fired after leading short-season Everett to a 31-45 record.

Two affiliates also ended six-year relationships with the club. The Double-A affiliation will move from San Antonio of the Texas League to West Tenn of the Southern League, and the high Class A affiliation switches Cal League outposts, from Inland Empire to High Desert.

In its last season as a Mariners affiliate, Inland Empire won the California League championship.

ORGANIZATION LEADERS

BATTING	*Minimum 250 at-bats	
*AVG	Chen, Yung Chi, Inland Empire/AZL/San Antonio	.324
R	Johnson, Brent, Inland Empire	82
H	LaHair, Bryan, San Antonio/Tacoma	145
TB	Wilson, Michael, Inland Empire/San Antonio	241
2B	Hubbard, Thomas, Inland Empire/San Antonio	32
3B	Boucher, Sebastien, San Antonio	9
	Womack, Josh, Inland Empire	9
HR	Wilson, Michael, Inland Empire/San Antonio	23
RBI	Wilson, Michael, Inland Empire/San Antonio	95
BB	Boucher, Sebastien, San Antonio	73
SO	Wilson, Michael, Inland Empire/San Antonio	156
SB	Boucher, Sebastien, San Antonio	27
	Sabatella, Bryan, Wisconsin/Everett	27
*OBP	White, Joseph, Everett	.424
*SLG	Peguero, Carlos, AZL Mariners/Everett	.520
XBH	Wilson, Michael, Inland Empire/San Antonio	56

PITCHING	#Minimum 75 innings	
W	Thomas, Justin, Wisconsin/Inland Empire	14
L	Fagan, Paul, Wisconsin	14
#ERA	Salinas, Doug, AZL Mariners	2.84
G	Woerman, Joseph, Wisconsin/Inland Empire	61
CG	Fagan, Paul, Wisconsin	3
SV	Huber, Jon, San Antonio/Tacoma	23
IP	Thomas, Justin, Wisconsin/Inland Empire	166
BB	Bello, Cibney, Inland Empire	82
SO	Cruceta, Francisco, Tacoma	185
#AVG	Salinas, Doug, AZL Mariners	.219

Seattle Mariners / **MLB**

American League

BATTING	B-T	HT	WT	DOB	AVG	vLH	vRH	G	AB	R	H	2B	3B	HR	RBI	BB	HBP	SH	SF	SO	SB	CS	SLG	OBP
Beltre, Adrian	R-R	5-11	220	4-7-79	.268	.280	.262	156	620	88	166	39	4	25	89	47	10	1	3	118	11	5	.465	.328
Betancourt, Yuniesky	R-R	5-10	190	1-31-82	.289	.240	.301	157	558	68	161	28	6	8	47	17	1	7	1	54	11	8	.403	.310
Bloomquist, Willie	R-R	5-11	195	11-27-77	.247	.253	.238	102	251	36	62	6	2	1	15	24	4	2	2	40	16	3	.299	.320
Bohn, T.J.	R-R	6-5	210	1-17-80	.143	.100	.250	18	14	2	2	0	0	1	2	2	0	0	0	8	0	0	.357	.250
Borchard, Joe	B-R	6-4	230	11-25-78	.222	.000	.333	6	9	3	2	0	0	0	0	0	0	0	0	3	0	1	.222	.222
Broussard, Ben	L-L	6-2	220	9-24-76	.238	.313	.230	56	164	17	39	7	0	8	17	9	2	0	2	45	2	0	.427	.282
2-team (88 Cleveland)					.289	—		144	432	61	125	21	0	21	63	26	3	0	4	103	2	1	.484	.331
Choo, Shin-Soo	L-L	5-11	210	7-13-82	.091	—	.091	4	11	0	1	1	0	0	0	1	0	0	0	4	0	0	.182	.167
2-team (45 Cleveland)					.280	—		49	157	23	44	12	3	3	22	18	2	1	1	50	5	3	.452	.360
Dobbs, Greg	L-R	6-1	205	7-2-78	.370	.000	.385	23	27	4	10	3	1	0	3	0	1	0	0	4	0	1	.556	.393
Everett, Carl	B-R	6-0	220	6-3-71	.227	.186	.243	92	308	37	70	8	0	11	33	29	3	0	3	57	1	3	.360	.297
Ibanez, Raul	L-R	6-2	220	6-2-72	.289	.243	.307	159	626	103	181	33	5	33	123	65	1	0	7	115	2	4	.516	.353
Johjima, Kenji	R-R	6-0	200	6-8-76	.291	.263	.299	144	506	61	147	25	1	18	76	20	13	0	3	46	3	1	.451	.332
Jones, Adam	R-R	6-2	200	8-1-85	.216	.235	.211	32	74	6	16	4	0	1	8	2	0	0	0	22	3	1	.311	.237
Lawton, Matt	L-R	5-10	190	11-30-71	.259	1.000	.231	11	27	5	7	0	0	0	1	2	0	0	0	2	0	0	.259	.310
Lopez, Jose	R-R	6-0	200	11-24-83	.282	.331	.265	151	603	78	170	28	8	10	79	26	9	12	5	80	5	2	.405	.319
Morse, Mike	R-R	6-4	225	3-22-82	.372	.438	.182	21	43	5	16	5	0	0	11	3	0	0	2	7	1	0	.488	.396
Navarro, Oswaldo	R-R	6-0	155	10-2-84	.667	—	.667	4	3	0	2	0	0	0	0	0	0	1	0	1	0	0	.667	.667
Perez, Eduardo	R-R	6-4	240	9-11-69	.195	.200	.182	43	87	6	17	1	0	1	11	13	1	0	1	22	0	1	.241	.304
2-team (37 Cleveland)					.253	—		80	186	22	47	10	0	9	33	18	3	0	3	33	0	1	.452	.324
Petagine, Roberto	L-L	6-1	170	6-2-71	.185	.000	.200	31	27	3	5	2	0	1	2	4	1	0	0	10	0	0	.370	.313
Quiroz, Guillermo	R-R	6-1	200	11-29-81	.000	—	.000	1	2	0	0	0	0	0	0	0	0	0	0	2	0	0	.000	.000
Reed, Jeremy	L-L	6-0	200	6-15-81	.217	.000	.249	67	212	27	46	6	5	6	17	11	2	2	2	31	2	3	.377	.260
Rivera, Rene	R-R	5-10	210	7-31-83	.152	.087	.171	35	99	8	15	4	0	2	4	3	1	3	0	29	1	0	.253	.184
Sexson, Richie	R-R	6-8	235	12-29-74	.264	.204	.280	158	591	75	156	40	0	34	107	64	4	0	4	154	1	1	.504	.338
Snelling, Chris	L-L	5-10	205	12-3-81	.250	.091	.271	36	96	14	24	6	1	3	8	13	4	5	1	38	2	1	.427	.360
Suzuki, Ichiro	L-R	5-9	170	10-22-73	.322	.352	.311	161	695	110	224	20	9	9	49	49	5	1	2	71	45	2	.416	.370

PITCHING	B-T	HT	WT	DOB	W	L	ERA	G	GS	CG	SV	IP	H	R	ER	HR	BB	SO	AVG	vLH	vRH	K/9	BB/9
Baek, Cha Seung	R-R	6-4	220	5-29-80	4	1	3.67	6	6	0	0	34	26	15	14	6	13	23	.208	.211	.206	6.03	3.41
Campillo, Jorge	R-R	6-1	190	8-10-78	0	0	15.43	1	0	0	0	2	4	4	4	0	0	1	.364	.250	.429	3.86	0.00
Chick, Travis	R-R	6-3	215	6-10-84	0	0	12.60	3	0	0	0	5	7	7	7	0	10	2	.333	.500	.182	3.60	18.00
Cruceta, Francisco	R-R	6-2	215	7-4-81	0	0	10.80	4	1	0	0	7	10	8	8	2	6	2	.370	.200	.471	2.70	8.10
Feierabend, Ryan	L-L	6-3	190	8-22-85	0	1	3.71	4	2	0	0	17	15	7	7	3	7	11	.231	.231	.231	5.82	3.71
Fruto, Emiliano	R-R	6-3	235	6-6-84	2	2	5.50	23	0	0	1	36	34	24	22	4	24	34	.246	.267	.237	8.50	6.00
Green, Sean	R-R	6-6	230	4-20-79	0	0	4.50	24	0	0	0	32	34	16	16	2	13	15	.279	.190	.325	4.22	3.66
Guardado, Eddie	R-L	6-0	205	10-2-70	1	3	5.48	28	0	0	5	23	29	14	14	8	11	22	.309	.286	.322	8.61	4.30
Harris, Jeff	R-R	6-1	190	7-4-74	0	0	5.40	3	0	0	0	3	3	2	2	0	0	1	.250	.000	.375	2.70	0.00
Hernandez, Felix	R-R	6-3	230	4-8-86	12	14	4.52	31	31	2	0	191	195	105	96	23	60	176	.262	.281	.241	8.29	2.83
Huber, Jon	R-R	6-2	195	7-7-81	2	1	1.08	16	0	0	0	17	10	3	2	0	6	11	.172	.067	.209	5.94	3.24
Jimenez, Cesar	L-L	5-11	180	11-12-84	0	0	14.73	4	1	0	0	7	13	12	12	4	4	3	.382	.167	.429	3.68	4.91
Livingston, Bobby	L-L	6-3	195	9-3-82	0	0	18.00	3	0	0	0	5	9	10	10	2	6	3	.375	.364	.385	5.40	10.80
Lowe, Mark	R-R	6-3	190	6-7-83	1	0	1.93	15	0	0	0	19	12	4	4	1	9	20	.190	.167	.205	9.64	4.34
Mateo, Julio	R-R	6-0	220	8-2-77	9	4	4.19	48	0	0	0	54	62	27	25	6	22	31	.297	.394	.246	5.20	3.69
Meche, Gil	R-R	6-3	220	9-8-78	11	8	4.48	32	32	1	0	187	183	106	93	24	84	156	.256	.240	.271	7.52	4.05
Moyer, Jamie	L-L	6-0	180	11-18-62	6	12	4.39	25	25	2	0	160	179	85	78	25	44	82	.285	.258	.294	4.61	2.48
Nageotte, Clint	R-R	6-3	225	10-25-80	0	0	27.00	1	0	0	0	1	2	3	3	1	2	1	.400	.500	.333	9.00	18.00
O'Flaherty, Eric	L-L	6-2	195	2-5-85	0	0	4.09	15	0	0	0	11	18	9	5	2	6	6	.360	.238	.448	4.91	4.91
Pineiro, Joel	R-R	6-1	200	9-25-78	8	13	6.36	40	25	1	1	166	209	123	117	23	64	87	.311	.287	.332	4.73	3.48
Putz, J.J.	R-R	6-5	250	2-22-77	4	1	2.30	72	0	0	36	78	59	20	20	4	13	104	.207	.211	.204	11.95	1.49
Sherrill, George	L-L	6-0	225	4-19-77	2	4	4.28	72	0	0	1	40	30	19	19	0	27	42	.213	.143	.297	9.45	6.08
Soriano, Rafael	R-R	6-1	220	12-19-79	1	2	2.25	53	0	0	2	60	44	15	15	6	21	65	.204	.244	.179	9.75	3.15
Washburn, Jarrod	L-L	6-1	190	8-13-74	8	14	4.67	31	31	0	0	187	198	103	97	25	55	103	.268	.317	.257	4.96	2.65
Woods, Jake	L-L	6-1	190	9-3-81	7	4	4.20	37	8	0	0	105	115	51	49	12	53	66	.278	.291	.273	5.66	4.54

FIELDING

Catcher	PCT	G	PO	A	E	DP	PB
Johjima	.993	144	882	58	7	9	10
Quiroz	1.000	1	5	0	0	0	0
Rivera	.987	35	220	14	3	3	6

First Base	PCT	G	PO	A	E	DP
Bloomquist	1.000	4	6	0	0	0
Broussard	.976	10	74	8	2	12
Dobbs	1.000	3	10	0	0	3
Morse	1.000	2	11	0	0	2
Perez	1.000	5	10	2	0	2
Petagine	1.000	9	23	4	0	3
Sexson	.997	150	1235	110	4	115

Second Base	PCT	G	PO	A	E	DP
Beltre	—	1	0	0	0	0

	PCT	G	PO	A	E	DP
Bloomquist	.962	15	20	31	2	6
Lopez	.978	150	282	417	16	95

Third Base	PCT	G	PO	A	E	DP
Beltre	.968	155	136	323	15	32
Bloomquist	1.000	12	5	15	0	4
Dobbs	1.000	1	0	0	0	0
Morse	1.000	5	0	3	0	1

Shortstop	PCT	G	PO	A	E	DP
Betancourt	.971	157	251	430	20	95
Bloomquist	1.000	17	9	23	0	3
Morse	—	1	0	0	0	0
Navarro	.750	2	0	3	1	2

Outfield	PCT	G	PO	A	E	DP
Bloomquist	1.000	59	104	2	0	0

	PCT	G	PO	A	E	DP
Bohn Jr.	.875	18	7	0	1	0
Borchard	1.000	3	4	1	0	0
Choo	.944	4	16	1	1	0
Dobbs	1.000	3	1	0	0	0
Everett	1.000	2	3	0	0	0
Ibanez	.994	158	301	11	2	0
Jones	.960	26	67	5	3	1
Lawton	7	11	0	0	0	
Morse	1.000	9	9	1	0	0
Reed	.992	64	129	3	1	0
Snelling	.979	34	45	1	1	1
Suzuki	.992	159	364	9	3	3

2006 PERFORMANCE

General manager: Bill Bavasi. **Farm director:** Frank Mattox. **Scouting director:** Bob Fontaine.

Class	Team	League	W	L	PCT	Finish*	Manager	Affiliate Since
Majors	Seattle	American	78	84	.481	10th (14)	Mike Hargrove	—
Triple-A	Tacoma Rainiers	Pacific Coast	74	70	.514	7th (16)	Dave Brundage	1995
Double-A	San Antonio Missions	Texas	60	78	.435	7th (8)	Daren Brown	2001
High A	Inland Empire 66ers	California	72	68	.514	+5th (10)	Gary Thurman	2001
Low A	Wisconsin Timber Rattlers	Midwest	54	86	.386	13th (14)	Jim Horner	1993
Short-season	Everett AquaSox	Northwest	31	45	.408	6th (8)	Dave Myers	1995
Rookie	AZL Mariners	Arizona	25	30	.455	5th (9)	Dana Williams	2001
OVERALL 2006 MINOR LEAGUE RECORD			316	377	.456	27th (30)		

*Finish in overall standings (No. of teams in league). +League champion

Tacoma Rainiers — Triple-A

ORGANIZATION STATISTICS

Pacific Coast League

BATTING	B-T	HT	WT	DOB	AVG	vLH	vRH	G	AB	R	H	2B	3B	HR	RBI	BB	HBP	SH	SF	SO	SB	CS	SLG	OBP
Arroyo, Jack	R-R	6-1	175	9-7-80	.000	—	.000	4	2	2	0	0	0	0	0	0	0	0	0	1	0	0	.000	.000
Beltran, Juan	R-R	6-0	165	8-26-86	.167	.000	.250	3	12	1	2	1	0	0	2	0	0	0	0	3	0	0	.250	.167
Bohn, T.J.	R-R	6-5	210	1-17-80	.283	.292	.280	97	378	53	107	20	1	9	43	33	4	2	2	81	15	3	.413	.345
Brown, Hunter	R-R	6-2	210	10-24-79	.262	.303	.250	107	385	64	101	30	2	7	48	55	3	2	2	89	12	5	.405	.357
Cabrera, Asdrubal	B-R	6-0	170	11-13-85	.236	.277	.224	60	203	27	48	12	2	3	22	24	3	1	2	51	7	5	.360	.323
Castro, Ismael	R-R	5-9	193	8-14-83	.303	.325	.296	49	175	24	53	16	2	4	21	5	3	1	1	21	3	1	.486	.332
Choo, Shin-Soo	L-L	5-11	210	7-13-82	.323	.185	.361	94	375	71	121	21	3	13	48	45	2	1	4	73	26	4	.499	.394
Clement, Jeff	L-R	6-1	210	8-21-83	.257	.192	.275	67	245	23	63	10	0	4	32	16	8	1	2	53	0	2	.347	.321
Dobbs, Greg	L-R	6-1	205	7-2-78	.314	.295	.321	99	379	60	119	19	3	9	55	37	2	0	3	58	14	5	.451	.375
Fernandez, Jair	R-R	6-1	170	12-10-86	.000	—	.000	1	3	0	0	0	0	0	0	1	0	0	0	1	0	0	.000	.250
Garciaparra, Michael	R-R	6-1	175	4-2-83	.316	.406	.288	42	136	26	43	5	0	1	10	22	3	1	0	26	3	3	.375	.422
Gary, Alex	R-R	6-3	225	10-11-83	.143	.000	.188	7	21	1	3	1	0	0	1	0	0	0	1	13	1	0	.190	.182
Guzman, Juan	B-R	5-10	175	4-10-82	.000	—	.000	1	4	0	0	0	0	0	0	0	0	0	0	0	0	0	.000	.000
Johnson, Rob	R-R	6-1	200	7-22-83	.231	.288	.216	97	337	28	78	9	4	4	33	13	1	6	2	74	14	7	.318	.261
Jones, Adam	R-R	6-2	200	8-1-85	.287	.173	.318	96	380	69	109	19	4	16	62	28	6	1	1	78	13	4	.484	.345
LaHair, Bryan	L-R	6-5	215	11-5-82	.327	.255	.348	54	202	36	66	10	0	10	44	23	1	1	3	49	3	0	.525	.393
Liverpool, Marquise	R-R	5-11	191	4-16-86	.000	—	.000	1	1	0	0	0	0	0	0	0	0	0	0	0	0	0	.000	.000
Miller, Corky	R-R	6-1	245	3-18-76	.333	1.000	.200	2	6	1	2	0	0	0	0	1	0	0	0	1	0	0	.333	.429
Monzon, Erick	R-R	6-0	190	11-30-81	.200	.000	.250	2	5	2	1	0	0	0	0	1	0	1	0	3	0	0	.200	.333
Morban, Jose	B-R	6-1	170	10-2-79	.244	.067	.286	26	78	16	19	4	2	1	9	11	2	1	0	26	2	3	.385	.352
Morse, Mike	R-R	6-4	225	3-22-82	.248	.286	.233	57	206	23	51	15	1	5	34	14	3	1	4	46	0	1	.403	.300
Navarro, Oswaldo	R-R	6-0	155	10-2-84	.246	.103	.285	55	183	15	45	9	0	2	21	19	1	2	4	33	1	2	.328	.314
Nelson, Jon	R-R	6-5	235	1-16-80	.284	.323	.272	74	271	43	77	15	4	14	46	12	8	0	1	83	3	3	.524	.332
Petagine, Roberto	L-L	6-1	170	6-2-71	.167	—	.167	4	6	1	1	0	0	0	4	0	0	0	1	0	0	.167	.500
Quiroz, Guillermo	R-R	6-1	200	11-29-81	.304	.326	.295	38	138	15	42	8	0	3	28	11	2	0	2	29	0	0	.428	.359
Reynolds, Kevin	L-L	6-1	185	7-1-82	.333	.500	.250	2	6	2	2	0	0	0	0	1	0	1	0	1	0	0	.333	.333
Rivera, Rene	R-R	5-10	210	7-31-83	.667	1.000	.000	1	3	1	2	1	0	0	0	0	0	0	0	1	0	0	1.000	.667
Schweiger, Brian	R-R	6-0	195	8-21-82	.417	1.000	.364	6	12	3	5	2	0	0	4	1	0	0	2	2	0	0	.583	.400
Sears, Todd	L-R	6-6	205	10-23-75	.267	.167	.300	45	172	25	46	9	1	5	26	14	1	1	1	37	3	0	.419	.324
Snelling, Chris	L-L	5-10	205	12-3-81	.216	.258	.200	69	241	36	52	13	1	5	39	31	11	2	5	60	4	2	.340	.326
Youngbauer, Scott	B-R	6-1	175	1-14-79	.235	.203	.245	72	243	38	57	11	3	9	23	18	5	3	2	57	3	4	.416	.299
Zorn, Dean	B-R	6-1	190	9-12-86	.059	.000	.091	5	17	2	1	0	0	0	0	0	0	0	0	7	0	0	.059	.059

PITCHING	B-T	HT	WT	DOB	W	L	ERA	G	GS	CG	SV	IP	H	R	ER	HR	BB	SO	AVG	vLH	vRH	K/9	BB/9
Appier, Kevin	R-R	6-2	220	12-6-67	1	2	4.54	10	5	0	0	36	39	20	18	0	24	26	.273	.267	.277	6.56	6.06
Asher, David	R-L	6-1	195	2-18-83	0	0	5.79	3	0	0	0	5	5	3	3	0	3	7	.263	.333	.250	13.50	5.79
Atchison, Scott	R-R	6-2	195	3-29-76	4	0	2.34	30	0	0	1	50	49	13	13	2	15	39	.253	.267	.237	7.02	2.70
Baek, Cha Seung	R-R	6-2	200	5-29-80	12	4	3.00	24	24	0	0	147	133	57	49	17	37	103	.241	.227	.254	6.31	2.27
Bibens-Dirkx, Austin	R-R	6-2	190	4-29-85	0	0	0.00	1	0	0	0	2	2	0	0	0	1	5	.250	.250	.250	22.50	4.50
Blackley, Travis	L-L	6-3	200	11-4-82	1	1	4.09	2	2	0	0	11	10	5	5	2	5	5	.233	.400	.211	4.09	4.09
Collis, Everett	R-R	6-2	215	1-14-84	0	0	0.00	2	0	0	0	2	0	0	0	0	1	0	.000	.000	.000	4.50	0.00
Cortez, Renee	R-R	6-4	180	12-9-82	5	3	4.18	31	0	0	5	52	61	29	24	3	28	50	.298	.266	.324	8.71	4.88
Cruceta, Francisco	R-R	6-2	215	7-4-81	13	9	4.38	28	28	1	0	160	150	81	78	25	76	185	.247	.225	.266	10.38	4.27
Dorman, Rich	R-R	6-2	210	9-30-78	7	7	4.55	31	16	1	1	119	101	66	60	13	67	114	.234	.237	.232	8.65	5.08
Flannery, Mike	R-R	6-2	225	9-20-79	0	3	5.32	16	0	0	0	24	27	20	14	2	21	18	.281	.255	.306	6.85	7.99
Foppert, Jesse	R-R	6-6	220	7-10-80	0	1	6.97	5	2	0	0	10	10	10	8	0	14	11	.270	.263	.278	9.58	12.19
Fruto, Emiliano	R-R	6-3	235	6-6-84	1	3	3.18	28	0	0	10	45	33	23	16	1	21	55	.204	.187	.218	10.92	4.17
Green, Sean	R-R	6-6	230	4-20-79	4	1	2.25	15	0	0	5	24	18	6	6	0	11	12	.225	.262	.184	4.50	4.13
Harris, Jeff	R-R	6-1	190	7-4-74	0	3	5.52	15	4	0	0	31	43	22	19	6	7	13	.319	.333	.304	3.77	2.03
Hrynio, Michael	R-R	6-2	213	11-18-82	0	0	9.00	2	0	0	0	3	3	3	3	0	5	0	.182	.333	.125	0.00	15.00
Huber, Jon	R-R	6-2	195	7-7-81	3	1	2.61	29	0	0	12	41	46	14	12	3	10	38	.280	.313	.247	8.27	2.18
Huisman, Justin	R-R	6-2	200	4-16-79	1	0	7.67	14	1	0	0	27	35	23	23	6	15	21	.315	.396	.241	7.00	5.00
Jimenez, Cesar	L-L	5-11	180	11-12-84	5	10	4.36	24	19	1	0	107	107	54	52	8	55	66	.266	.257	.269	5.53	4.61
Livingston, Bobby	L-L	6-3	195	9-3-82	8	11	4.59	23	22	0	0	135	165	74	69	18	36	69	.308	.297	.314	4.59	2.39
Looper, Aaron	R-R	6-2	210	9-7-76	0	2	5.98	41	0	0	0	65	89	50	43	9	22	36	.330	.316	.343	5.01	3.06
Nageotte, Clint	R-R	6-3	225	10-25-80	7	7	5.74	19	19	0	0	89	102	63	57	6	53	51	.295	.304	.284	5.14	5.34
Nannini, Mike	R-R	5-11	190	8-9-80	0	0	10.00	9	0	0	0	9	14	14	10	0	9	7	.368	.500	.273	7.00	9.00
O'Flaherty, Eric	L-L	6-2	195	2-5-85	1	0	0.00	2	0	0	0	1	4	0	0	0	1	4	.214	.333	.125	9.82	2.45
Oldham, Jonathan	L-L	6-2	210	5-18-82	1	1	6.87	12	1	0	0	18	24	20	14	6	10	14	.329	.333	.326	6.87	4.91
Parker, Terrence	R-R	6-3	205	4-8-85	0	0	0.00	1	0	0	0	1	0	0	0	0	0	0	.000	.000	.000	0.00	0.00
Snyder, Jason	R-R	6-6	205	4-6-83	1	1	1.50	2	1	0	0	6	7	4	1	0	2	4	.292	.250	.333	6.00	3.00
Wright, Dan	R-R	6-5	240	12-14-77	0	0	6.55	4	0	0	0	11	10	8	8	0	7	8	.263	.222	.300	6.55	5.73
Zapata, Juan	R-R	6-3	180	8-6-84	0	0	6.00	5	0	0	0	9	10	8	6	2	3	5	.278	.300	.250	8.00	3.00

FIELDING

Catcher

Catcher	PCT	G	PO	A	E	DP	PB
Beltran	1.000	3	19	3	0	0	1
Clement	.993	37	273	11	2	4	0
Fernandez	1.000	1	10	1	0	0	0
Johnson	.988	74	466	48	6	2	11
Miller	1.000	1	8	1	0	0	0
Quiroz	1.000	30	194	14	0	2	4
Rivera	1.000	1	8	0	0	0	0
Schweiger	.950	4	19	0	1	0	2

First Base

First Base	PCT	G	PO	A	E	DP
Brown	1.000	12	88	5	0	12
Dobbs	.997	31	258	27	1	34
LaHair	.998	52	444	37	1	59
Morse	.992	16	124	8	1	10
Nelson	1.000	5	35	1	0	3
Petagine	1.000	3	20	1	0	1
Schweiger	1.000	1	0	1	0	0
Sears	.993	32	259	24	2	20

Second Base

Second Base	PCT	G	PO	A	E	DP
Brown	.983	13	22	36	1	6
Castro	.969	40	67	121	6	39
Garciaparra	.966	40	70	98	6	19
Guzman	1.000	1	2	3	0	1
Monzon	1.000	1	0	4	0	1
Morban	.949	12	21	35	3	6
Youngbauer	.984	39	65	121	3	28
Zorn	1.000	3	7	13	0	3

Third Base

Third Base	PCT	G	PO	A	E	DP
Brown	.918	68	24	132	14	15
Castro	.818	4	2	7	2	0
Dobbs	.989	44	20	70	1	4
Morban	—	1	0	0	0	0
Morse	1.000	15	11	29	0	4
Youngbauer	.886	16	9	30	5	2

Shortstop

Shortstop	PCT	G	PO	A	E	DP
Cabrera	.986	60	130	157	4	48
Monzon	1.000	1	1	5	0	0

Second Base (cont.)

	PCT	G	PO	A	E	DP
Morban	.889	6	6	10	2	0
Morse	.969	12	15	47	2	10
Navarro	.971	55	82	153	7	40
Youngbauer	.986	15	23	45	1	10
Zorn	1.000	1	0	1	0	0

Outfield

Outfield	PCT	G	PO	A	E	DP
Bohn	.991	96	217	11	2	2
Brown	1.000	5	10	0	0	0
Choo	.971	93	130	2	4	0
Dobbs	.974	20	36	1	1	0
Gary	1.000	4	7	0	0	0
Johnson	1.000	2	1	0	0	0
Jones	.966	95	220	10	8	3
LaHair	1.000	1	3	0	0	0
Morban	.643	7	9	0	5	0
Morse	1.000	11	11	0	0	0
Nelson	.960	66	117	3	5	0
Reynolds	1.000	2	5	0	0	0
Snelling	.977	43	80	6	2	1

San Antonio Missions — Double-A

Texas League

BATTING	B-T	HT	WT	DOB	AVG	vLH	vRH	G	AB	R	H	2B	3B	HR	RBI	BB	HBP	SH	SF	SO	SB	CS	SLG	OBP
Arroyo, Jack	R-R	6-1	175	9-7-80	.135	.143	.130	15	37	4	5	0	0	0	3	1	2	0	6	1	1	.135	.220
Balentien, Wladimir	R-R	6-2	190	7-2-84	.230	.227	.230	121	444	76	102	23	1	22	82	70	4	0	4	140	14	7	.435	.337
Boucher, Sebastien	L-R	6-0	190	10-19-81	.248	.266	.243	110	416	60	103	9	6	1	29	65	2	9	2	91	26	9	.305	.351
Bourgeois, Jason	R-R	5-9	185	1-4-82	.277	.318	.266	107	411	65	114	22	7	4	38	37	3	4	5	66	23	7	.394	.338
Castro, Ismael	R-R	5-9	193	8-14-83	.241	.167	.250	31	112	13	27	6	1	1	9	5	0	0	0	22	4	2	.339	.274
Chen, Yung Chi	R-R	5-11	170	7-13-83	.295	.346	.285	40	149	22	44	9	2	3	22	18	0	4	3	23	5	3	.443	.365
Clement, Jeff	L-R	6-1	210	8-21-83	.288	.333	.273	15	59	7	17	6	1	2	10	7	3	0	1	8	0	0	.525	.386
Garciaparra, Michael	R-R	6-1	175	4-2-83	.305	.238	.321	28	105	13	32	3	1	1	16	8	5	1	2	21	1	1	.381	.375
Gregorio, Tom	R-R	6-2	215	5-5-77	.250	.333	.200	3	8	0	2	0	0	0	0	0	1	0	0	0	0	0	.250	.250
Guzman, Jesus	R-R	6-1	165	6-14-84	.257	.286	.250	115	408	57	105	18	3	9	55	46	4	9	4	74	7	3	.382	.335
Hargrove, Andy	R-L	6-1	240	10-31-81	.125	.000	.143	4	8	0	1	0	0	0	0	0	1	0	0	4	0	0	.125	.222
Harris, Gary	L-R	5-10	185	9-9-79	.206	.226	.202	42	160	15	33	6	1	0	12	6	2	1	1	28	8	3	.256	.243
Henson, Julian	R-R	5-10	190	4-10-87	.000	—	.000	1	1	0	0	0	0	0	0	0	0	0	0	0	0	0	.000	.000
Hubbard, Thomas	R-R	6-2	215	4-16-82	.289	.317	.284	65	242	29	70	15	1	5	33	30	1	1	1	58	0	2	.421	.369
LaHair, Bryan	L-R	6-5	215	11-5-82	.293	.159	.326	60	222	22	65	12	0	6	30	24	4	1	1	52	0	0	.428	.371
Liverpool, Marquise	R-R	5-11	191	4-16-86	.250	—	.250	2	4	1	1	0	0	0	0	1	0	0	0	1	0	0	.250	.250
Monzon, Erick	R-R	6-0	190	11-30-81	.245	.333	.223	78	269	32	66	17	2	3	29	25	2	2	3	48	9	0	.357	.311
Navarro, Oswaldo	R-R	6-1	175	10-2-84	.267	.229	.275	79	266	27	71	13	1	1	24	39	5	3	0	57	7	6	.335	.371
Nelson, Jon	R-R	6-5	235	1-16-80	.245	.333	.218	45	163	23	40	10	1	5	18	6	5	0	0	54	3	1	.411	.293
Oliveros, Luis	R-R	6-1	205	6-18-83	.176	.286	.152	46	153	8	27	3	0	0	5	2	4	3	1	18	0	0	.196	.206
Quiroz, Guillermo	R-R	6-1	200	11-29-81	.188	.056	.239	16	64	5	12	3	0	3	9	3	1	0	0	15	0	0	.375	.235
Reynolds, Kevin	L-L	6-1	185	7-1-82	.217	.250	.206	15	46	6	10	3	0	0	2	2	0	1	0	4	1	2	.283	.250
Rogelstad, Matt	R-R	6-3	185	9-13-82	.185	.438	.102	23	65	11	12	1	1	1	11	4	0	2	1	9	0	1	.277	.229
Ruchti, Justin	R-R	6-2	200	12-11-80	.222	.185	.231	42	144	13	32	5	0	3	17	6	1	1	0	33	0	0	.319	.258
Schweiger, Brian	R-R	6-0	195	8-21-82	.218	.417	.182	27	78	6	17	1	0	0	4	10	1	0	1	20	0	0	.231	.311
Tuiasosopo, Matt	R-R	6-2	210	5-10-86	.185	.146	.194	62	216	16	40	4	0	1	10	20	2	2	1	64	2	1	.218	.259
Wilson, Michael	B-R	6-1	238	6-29-83	.245	.280	.236	67	249	32	61	12	1	12	43	28	6	0	0	85	1	1	.446	.336
Youngbauer, Scott	B-R	6-1	175	1-14-79	.280	.273	.281	31	118	12	33	6	2	2	17	13	1	3	2	25	2	1	.415	.351

PITCHING	B-T	HT	WT	DOB	W	L	ERA	G	GS	CG	SV	IP	H	R	ER	HR	BB	SO	AVG	vLH	vRH	K/9	BB/9
Bazardo, Yorman	R-R	6-2	220	7-11-84	6	5	3.64	25	25	0	0	138	144	65	56	10	45	80	.275	.265	.284	5.20	2.93
Blackley, Travis	L-L	6-3	200	11-4-82	8	11	4.06	25	25	0	0	144	139	77	65	18	45	100	.255	.260	.253	6.25	2.81
Campillo, Jorge	R-R	6-1	190	8-10-78	2	0	2.53	2	2	0	0	11	12	4	3	0	2	3	.293	.333	.235	2.53	1.69
Chick, Travis	R-R	6-3	215	6-10-84	4	2	3.19	11	11	0	0	68	57	25	24	3	37	44	.230	.231	.229	5.85	4.92
Embry, Byron	R-R	6-2	240	9-5-76	0	1	2.31	12	0	0	5	12	8	3	3	0	4	20	.186	.167	.211	15.43	3.09
Feierabend, Ryan	L-L	6-3	190	8-22-85	9	12	4.28	28	28	0	0	154	156	87	73	16	55	127	.267	.275	.263	7.44	3.22
Fillinger, Chad	R-R	6-4	210	10-26-82	7	1	3.44	32	0	0	0	68	63	30	26	6	23	55	.249	.283	.227	7.28	3.04
Flannery, Mike	R-R	6-2	225	9-20-79	0	4	5.11	20	0	0	1	37	40	30	21	1	19	26	.290	.354	.256	6.32	4.62
Huber, Jon	R-R	6-2	195	7-7-81	0	3	4.88	21	0	0	11	24	30	13	13	0	4	19	.316	.250	.356	7.13	1.50
James, Craig	R-R	6-1	175	3-10-83	4	3	2.61	43	0	0	1	62	54	24	18	3	33	56	.237	.269	.220	8.13	4.79
Jimenez, Cesar	L-L	5-11	180	11-12-84	0	2	2.76	3	3	0	0	16	10	5	5	0	5	10	.179	.333	.122	5.51	2.76
Jordan, Justin	R-R	6-5	210	8-31-81	0	0	10.38	1	0	0	0	4	10	5	5	2	0	1	.435	.500	.412	2.08	0.00
Kahn, Stephen	R-R	6-3	215	12-14-83	1	3	6.23	31	0	0	0	39	50	30	27	3	31	33	.316	.310	.320	7.62	7.15
Lowe, Mark	R-R	6-3	190	6-7-83	0	2	2.16	11	0	0	4	17	14	4	4	1	3	14	.233	.115	.324	7.56	1.62
Mackintosh, Jason	R-L	6-0	205	7-2-80	4	5	3.38	36	11	0	0	99	97	44	37	8	34	59	.258	.295	.240	5.38	3.10
Mateo, Nathanel	R-R	6-1	160	12-24-82	3	7	5.80	26	7	0	0	68	78	50	44	10	30	60	.291	.297	.287	7.90	3.95
Moorhead, Brandon	R-R	6-2	215	1-23-80	2	3	6.02	9	8	0	0	40	51	28	27	3	17	25	.309	.240	.367	5.58	3.79
O'Flaherty, Eric	L-L	6-2	195	2-5-85	2	2	1.14	25	0	0	7	39	45	10	5	0	15	36	.300	.271	.319	8.24	3.43
Pettyjohn, Adam	R-R	6-3	190	6-11-77	2	4	2.91	17	3	0	1	53	46	18	17	5	14	45	.245	.218	.264	7.69	2.39
Rohrbaugh, Robert	R-L	6-2	195	12-28-83	5	5	3.78	14	14	0	0	86	87	37	36	9	27	64	.268	.324	.238	6.72	2.84
Rowland-Smith, Ryan	L-L	6-3	200	1-26-83	1	3	2.83	23	1	0	4	41	38	18	13	2	18	48	.241	.188	.277	10.45	3.92

FIELDING

Catcher	PCT	G	PO	A	E	DP	PB
Clement	.977	12	82	4	2	0	1
Gregorio	1.000	2	13	3	0	0	1
Henson	1.000	1	0	1	0	0	0
Oliveros	.995	45	341	22	2	4	11
Quiroz	.966	16	108	7	4	3	2
Ruchti	.989	42	238	23	3	2	3
Schweiger	.985	27	176	21	3	4	5

First Base	PCT	G	PO	A	E	DP
Hargrove	.971	4	31	2	1	2
Hubbard	.991	62	500	41	5	49
LaHair	.993	57	490	41	4	43
Monzon	.993	14	121	13	1	17
Nelson	.971	5	31	2	1	3
Rogelstad	1.000	3	17	2	0	2

Second Base	PCT	G	PO	A	E	DP
Bourgeois	.991	21	46	60	1	15

	PCT	G	PO	A	E	DP
Castro	.974	25	42	72	3	19
Chen	1.000	35	58	88	0	21
Garciaparra	.983	24	48	68	2	13
Guzman	.966	25	43	70	4	16
Monzon	1.000	3	8	8	0	2
Rogelstad	1.000	6	8	12	0	3
Youngbauer	.950	4	7	12	1	6

Third Base	PCT	G	PO	A	E	DP
Castro	—	1	0	0	0	0
Chen	—	1	0	0	0	0
Guzman	.948	71	31	132	9	10
Monzon	1.000	5	4	9	0	0
Rogelstad	1.000	6	6	12	0	1
Tuiasosopo	.907	57	42	95	14	7

Shortstop	PCT	G	PO	A	E	DP
Bourgeois	.750	1	0	3	1	0
Chen	1.000	3	5	6	0	0

	PCT	G	PO	A	E	DP
Garciaparra	.889	3	5	3	1	2
Monzon	.937	40	61	102	11	30
Navarro	.968	79	138	249	13	47
Youngbauer	.922	16	19	52	6	11

Outfield	PCT	G	PO	A	E	DP
Arroyo	1.000	10	12	3	0	0
Balentien	.960	114	248	17	11	6
Boucher	.990	104	275	9	3	3
Bourgeois	.964	41	75	5	3	1
Gregorio	—	1	0	0	0	0
Harris	1.000	35	86	4	0	1
Liverpool	—	1	0	0	0	0
Monzon	.882	8	14	1	2	0
Nelson	.982	33	54	2	1	0
Oliveros	—	1	0	0	0	0
Reynolds	1.000	12	19	3	0	1
Wilson	.944	60	91	10	6	4

Inland Empire 66ers — High Class A

California League

BATTING	B-T	HT	WT	DOB	AVG	vLH	vRH	G	AB	R	H	2B	3B	HR	RBI	BB	HBP	SH	SF	SO	SB	CS	SLG	OBP
Arroyo, Jack	R-R	6-1	175	9-7-80	.253	.255	.252	50	182	24	46	9	2	1	19	15	4	1	1	46	9	0	.341	.322
Chen, Yung Chi	R-R	5-11	170	7-13-83	.342	.303	.360	67	278	49	95	17	3	5	48	22	2	2	5	40	21	7	.478	.388
Colton, Chris	R-R	6-1	198	9-21-82	.239	.175	.261	110	381	56	91	22	1	5	42	38	3	5	5	92	17	9	.341	.309
Craig, Casey	L-R	6-1	185	1-12-85	.294	.222	.310	64	245	28	72	7	3	9	41	22	5	2	4	50	3	8	.457	.359
Dominguez, Jeffrey	B-R	6-2	153	7-31-86	.245	.276	.239	46	163	17	40	5	1	0	17	11	0	3	2	32	1	2	.288	.290
Eastley, Reed	L-R	6-2	210	7-24-83	.275	.299	.267	96	349	47	96	17	0	8	67	42	12	3	6	55	1	2	.393	.367
Falcon, Omar	B-R	6-1	210	9-1-82	.264	.250	.269	58	174	31	46	13	0	7	28	37	1	2	0	64	0	1	.460	.396
Fernandez, Jair	R-R	6-1	170	12-10-86	.074	.222	.000	8	27	3	2	1	0	0	1	2	0	1	0	8	0	0	.111	.138
Hargrove, Andy	R-L	6-1	240	10-31-81	.222	.160	.239	42	117	18	26	5	0	5	16	16	2	1	2	42	1	0	.393	.321
Heid, Trevor	R-R	6-3	210	4-30-82	.200	.000	.273	9	30	3	6	2	0	1	4	0	1	0	0	9	0	1	.367	.226
Hubbard, Thomas	L-R	6-2	215	4-16-82	.265	.297	.250	61	226	40	60	17	0	6	34	27	4	0	1	40	1	1	.420	.353
Johnson, Brent	R-R	6-2	185	5-21-82	.284	.271	.289	129	500	82	142	23	2	1	48	65	11	7	3	55	16	11	.344	.377
Limonta, Johan	L-L	6-0	205	8-4-83	.462	.500	.455	8	26	3	12	0	1	1	5	1	1	0	0	3	0	0	.654	.500
Meneses, Alex	R-R	5-10	185	12-21-83	.270	.269	.270	32	115	11	31	4	0	0	7	12	2	0	2	23	1	2	.304	.373
Monzon, Erick	R-R	6-0	190	11-30-81	.262	.242	.268	34	130	15	34	5	3	2	18	14	0	0	1	25	3	1	.392	.331
Oliveros, Luis	R-R	6-1	205	6-18-83	.248	.179	.272	42	153	12	38	8	0	1	17	4	2	5	0	19	1	2	.320	.277
Prettyman, Ronald	L-R	6-2	190	8-4-81	.275	.284	.272	100	378	45	104	20	2	1	37	21	2	4	3	55	10	4	.347	.314
Reynolds, Kevin	L-L	6-1	185	7-1-82	.333	.333	.333	7	18	4	6	1	0	0	1	5	0	1	0	2	0	1	.389	.478
Rogelstad, Matt	L-R	6-3	185	9-13-82	.260	.278	.253	36	127	19	33	8	2	0	18	10	0	1	3	25	0	1	.354	.307
Santin, Daniel	L-L	6-3	205	11-7-84	.167	.000	.250	2	6	0	1	0	0	0	0	0	0	0	0	1	0	0	.167	.167
Schweiger, Brian	R-R	6-0	195	8-21-82	.333	.417	.306	17	48	9	16	2	0	2	10	10	1	2	2	13	0	2	.500	.443
Tucker, J.B.	R-R	6-0	200	2-20-82	.201	.286	.200	51	154	21	31	4	2	3	17	18	3	4	0	42	2	1	.312	.297
Tuiasosopo, Matt	R-R	6-2	210	5-10-86	.306	.382	.272	59	232	31	71	14	0	1	34	14	5	2	0	58	5	6	.379	.359
Valbuena, Luis	L-R	5-10	160	11-30-85	.252	.375	.230	43	163	18	41	10	1	2	10	14	1	3	0	26	1	3	.362	.315
Wilson, Michael	B-R	6-1	238	6-29-83	.315	.296	.326	52	200	38	63	15	3	9	38	22	3	0	5	59	4	6	.555	.389
Womack, Josh	L-L	6-0	194	1-5-84	.286	.283	.288	116	412	66	118	15	9	6	43	40	4	5	3	90	17	14	.410	.353

PITCHING	B-T	HT	WT	DOB	W	L	ERA	G	GS	CG	SV	IP	H	R	ER	HR	BB	SO	AVG	vLH	vRH	K/9	BB/9
Arroyo, Jack	R-R	6-1	175	9-7-80	0	1	31.50	1	0	0	0	2	3	7	7	1	5	0	.375	.333	.400	0.00	22.50
Baldwin, Andrew	R-R	6-5	215	10-20-82	2	1	0.82	3	3	0	0	22	12	2	2	1	2	13	.160	.154	.163	5.32	0.82
Bello, Cibney	L-R	6-5	209	9-10-82	6	10	3.94	29	27	0	0	153	145	86	67	19	78	137	.247	.268	.232	8.06	4.59
Beltran, Saydel	L-L	5-11	175	1-23-83	1	0	1.42	12	0	0	0	13	8	3	2	1	9	10	.174	.063	.233	7.11	6.39
Beus, Lance	L-L	6-1	180	3-11-83	0	0	3.38	1	1	0	0	3	4	1	1	0	2	4	.333	.250	.375	13.50	6.75
Blanco, Ivan	R-R	6-1	190	9-24-83	5	3	3.66	20	8	0	1	71	55	37	29	7	38	50	.218	.233	.208	6.31	4.79
Campillo, Jorge	R-R	6-1	190	8-10-78	1	1	4.00	2	2	0	0	9	8	4	4	2	6	2	.222	.125	.300	6.00	2.00
De La Cruz, Jose	R-R	6-6	206	9-23-83	2	4	2.97	50	0	0	21	61	50	26	20	4	19	52	.220	.209	.228	7.71	2.82
Done, Juan	R-R	6-2	220	10-2-81	2	1	6.83	20	0	0	0	28	39	24	21	3	18	23	.339	.260	.378	7.48	5.84
Fillinger, Chad	R-R	6-4	210	10-26-82	1	1	2.61	2	2	0	0	10	12	6	3	0	1	6	.300	.320	.267	5.23	0.87
Gibson, Rollie	L-L	6-2	220	12-30-83	0	0	0.00	3	0	0	0	1	0	0	0	0	3	2	.000	—	.000	13.50	20.25
Hrynio, Marcus	R-R	6-2	213	11-18-82	0	0	4.64	14	0	0	0	21	15	11	11	1	18	18	.203	.222	.191	7.59	7.59
Jensen, Aaron	R-R	6-2	180	6-11-84	3	9	7.18	21	21	0	0	89	113	80	71	13	46	62	.310	.331	.294	6.27	4.65
Jordan, Justin	R-R	6-5	210	8-31-81	5	7	5.19	27	14	0	0	87	105	74	50	8	30	46	.294	.280	.305	4.78	3.12
Kahn, Stephen	L-R	6-3	215	12-14-83	2	0	1.95	20	0	0	8	28	16	7	6	1	15	35	.167	.250	.096	11.39	4.88
Lockwood, Jon	R-R	6-2	210	12-12-81	6	3	3.87	36	0	0	0	74	65	37	32	5	39	65	.238	.202	.259	7.87	4.72
Lowe, Mark	R-R	6-3	190	6-7-83	1	0	1.84	13	2	0	2	29	14	10	6	0	11	46	.132	.189	.101	14.11	3.38
Morrow, Brandon	R-R	6-3	175	7-26-84	0	0	0.00	1	1	0	0	3	0	0	0	0	0	4	.000	.000	.000	12.00	0.00
Nottingham, Shawn	L-L	6-1	190	1-22-85	5	12	4.17	26	26	1	0	155	164	90	72	13	52	136	.266	.205	.279	7.88	3.01
O'Flaherty, Eric	L-L	6-2	195	2-5-85	0	1	3.45	16	0	0	1	29	31	11	11	1	6	33	.292	.154	.338	10.36	1.88
Oldham, Thomas	L-L	6-2	210	5-18-82	0	1	4.82	5	0	0	1	9	11	5	5	1	0	9	.395	.500	.378	8.68	0.00
Rivera, Mumba	R-R	6-5	205	12-10-80	5	4	4.19	40	0	0	0	77	68	46	36	9	38	68	.239	.243	.236	7.91	4.42
Rohrbaugh, Robert	R-L	6-2	195	12-28-83	7	1	1.46	10	9	1	0	55	43	11	9	2	8	47	.214	.200	.216	7.64	1.30
Rowland-Smith, Ryan	L-L	6-3	200	1-26-83	0	1	5.68	7	0	0	0	6	7	4	4	1	2	9	.308	.111	.412	12.79	2.84
Santiago, Julio	L-L	6-0	155	12-8-85	3	1	2.89	7	7	0	0	28	29	12	9	0	15	31	.264	.200	.282	9.96	4.82
Sullivan, John	R-R	6-3	220	2-22-82	0	0	0.00	1	0	0	0	1	0	0	0	0	1	0	.000	.000	.000	0.00	9.00
Thomas, Justin	L-L	6-3	220	1-18-84	9	4	4.10	17	17	1	0	105	108	58	48	10	45	111	.269	.239	.273	9.48	3.84
Trolia, Aaron	R-R	6-2	210	5-10-81	4	2	4.80	34	0	0	1	54	69	35	29	9	23	59	.319	.300	.331	9.77	3.81
Woerman, Joseph	R-R	6-3	200	12-12-82	2	0	2.67	24	0	0	0	30	29	10	9	2	15	31	.250	.244	.253	9.20	4.45

ORGANIZATION STATISTICS

FIELDING

Catcher	PCT	G	PO	A	E	DP	PB
Falcon	.994	48	335	21	2	5	8
Fernandez	.981	7	47	5	1	0	0
Oliveros	.989	42	331	41	4	5	8
Santin	1.000	1	12	0	0	0	0
Schweiger	.953	12	84	17	5	0	4
Tucker	.994	44	306	27	2	2	8

First Base	PCT	G	PO	A	E	DP
Colton	.—	1	0	0	0	0
Eastley	.986	60	456	45	7	48
Hargrove	.975	38	253	15	7	33
Hubbard	.980	34	272	15	6	31
Johnson	.889	2	8	0	1	0
Limonta	1.000	6	48	2	0	1
Prettyman	1.000	3	17	2	0	0
Rogelstad	1.000	10	67	4	0	2

Second Base	PCT	G	PO	A	E	DP
Arroyo	.946	27	64	58	7	22
Chen	.971	62	115	154	8	45
Meneses	.915	11	21	22	4	2
Monzon	.946	9	15	20	2	6
Rogelstad	.939	9	14	17	2	5
Valbuena	.984	28	44	80	2	11

Third Base	PCT	G	PO	A	E	DP
Chen	1.000	3	2	3	0	1
Eastley	.885	14	9	14	3	0
Johnson	.920	21	13	33	4	4
Meneses	.813	6	3	10	3	0
Monzon	.944	7	5	12	1	1
Prettyman	.966	69	56	144	7	26
Rogelstad	1.000	8	4	15	0	0
Tuiasosopo	.930	15	9	31	3	1
Valbuena	1.000	4	0	4	0	0

Shortstop	PCT	G	PO	A	E	DP
Dominguez	.888	45	64	118	23	22
Meneses	.957	9	11	34	2	7

Outfield	PCT	G	PO	A	E	DP
Monzon	.959	14	22	25	2	6
Prettyman	.956	18	28	59	4	13
Rogelstad	1.000	6	10	11	0	1
Tuiasosopo	.906	38	68	105	18	27
Valbuena	.978	10	16	28	1	8
Arroyo	.938	7	15	0	1	0
Colton	.979	96	186	5	4	0
Craig	.977	60	126	2	3	2
Heid	.941	8	15	1	1	1
Johnson	.988	102	249	6	3	1
Limonta	1.000	1	2	0	0	0
Reynolds	1.000	6	12	0	0	0
Rogelstad	1.000	1	3	0	0	0
Wilson	.960	46	88	7	4	3
Womack	.984	102	177	4	3	1

Wisconsin Timber Rattlers — Low Class A

Midwest League

BATTING	B-T	HT	WT	DOB	AVG	vLH	vRH	G	AB	R	H	2B	3B	HR	RBI	BB	HBP	SH	SF	SO	SB	CS	SLG	OBP
Avila, Gerardo	L-L	6-2	185	7-15-86	.159	.167	.158	23	88	5	14	2	0	0	8	1	1	0	2	22	1	0	.182	.174
Craig, Casey	L-R	6-1	185	1-12-85	.259	.163	.282	62	220	32	57	13	3	5	35	22	1	0	5	47	15	4	.414	.323
Dominguez, Jeffrey	B-R	6-2	153	7-31-86	.263	.278	.259	68	247	30	65	7	0	0	16	26	1	0	3	45	11	7	.291	.332
Flaig, Jeffrey	R-R	6-2	170	3-3-85	.220	.205	.224	91	336	37	74	24	1	1	27	13	10	2	2	73	1	2	.307	.269
Garth, Ronald	R-R	5-11	165	11-5-84	.275	.289	.271	109	404	48	111	22	2	10	48	26	15	2	3	81	11	8	.413	.339
Gary, Alex	R-R	6-3	225	10-11-83	.163	.162	.163	41	129	20	21	3	0	5	12	11	4	2	3	64	2	5	.302	.245
Guzman, Juan	B-R	5-10	175	4-10-82	.125	—	.125	3	8	2	1	0	0	0	0	0	0	0	0	1	1	0	.125	.125
Henson, Julian	R-R	5-10	190	4-10-87	.000	—	.000	3	5	0	0	0	0	0	0	0	0	0	0	2	0	0	.000	.000
Hernandez, Eddy	L-L	6-3	170	8-4-84	.243	.235	.245	115	403	46	98	21	3	6	48	26	5	0	2	135	1	7	.355	.296
Hernandez, Jairo	R-R	6-3	185	5-8-85	.195	.171	.204	42	133	10	26	5	2	1	9	5	2	0	1	39	4	5	.286	.234
Hudson, Robert	R-R	6-0	170	8-31-83	.270	.309	.260	112	400	54	108	18	4	4	34	26	2	3	1	62	13	9	.365	.317
Ledbetter, Curtis	R-R	6-3	220	12-26-81	.247	.258	.245	54	174	19	43	6	3	5	22	12	4	1	3	48	2	2	.402	.306
Liddi, Alex	R-R	6-4	176	8-14-88	.184	.375	.133	11	38	4	7	1	0	0	2	1	0	0	1	8	0	1	.211	.200
Limonta, Johan	L-L	6-0	205	8-4-83	.241	.077	.277	58	212	18	51	9	2	6	24	19	1	0	1	53	1	1	.387	.305
Lo, Kuo Hui	R-R	6-2	188	9-26-85	.243	.250	.241	29	107	21	26	3	1	1	7	9	3	0	1	31	16	3	.318	.317
Minaker, Chris	R-R	6-0	195	3-24-84	.315	.455	.293	40	162	17	51	10	0	4	17	13	0	1	2	21	4	2	.451	.362
Moore, Adam	R-R	6-3	215	5-8-84	.267	.240	.271	44	165	21	44	6	0	7	24	14	6	0	2	38	0	0	.430	.342
Posluszny, Stan	R-R	6-3	220	11-14-82	.143	.250	.132	13	42	4	6	2	0	1	0	5	3	0	1	6	1	0	.238	.196
Prosise, Nicholas	R-R	6-2	220	4-12-84	.226	.174	.241	31	106	10	24	2	0	2	11	7	3	1	0	26	0	1	.302	.293
Reynolds, Kevin	L-L	6-1	185	7-1-82	.206	.200	.207	14	34	6	7	1	0	0	0	2	3	2	0	7	2	3	.235	.308
Sabatella, Bryan	R-R	6-4	220	11-1-84	.199	.143	.213	52	176	20	35	7	0	3	17	11	4	2	2	31	5	1	.290	.259
Saunders, Michael	L-R	6-4	205	11-19-86	.240	.261	.232	104	359	48	86	10	8	4	39	48	2	2	5	103	22	7	.345	.329
Schweiger, Brian	R-R	6-0	195	8-21-82	.500	.000	.667	2	4	0	2	0	0	0	0	1	0	0	0	2	0	0	.500	.600
Scott, Travis	L-R	6-3	220	4-24-85	.242	.227	.245	38	132	13	32	8	2	0	20	5	3	2	4	37	0	1	.333	.278
Tucker, J.B.	R-R	6-0	200	2-20-82	.250	.281	.240	39	128	24	32	8	2	4	19	19	7	1	2	33	3	0	.438	.372
Valbuena, Luis	L-R	5-10	160	11-30-85	.286	.310	.278	89	325	45	93	16	6	3	38	44	1	1	2	44	21	7	.400	.371
Wu, Chao Kuan	L-R	6-3	192	5-25-84	.195	.167	.197	22	77	9	15	3	1	0	9	4	0	1	2	13	1	1	.260	.229

PITCHING	B-T	HT	WT	DOB	W	L	ERA	G	GS	CG	SV	IP	H	R	ER	HR	BB	SO	AVG	vLH	vRH	K/9	BB/9
Allen, Nicholas	R-R	6-1	210	6-15-83	7	4	3.86	34	12	0	0	100	114	52	43	11	26	62	.291	.250	.317	5.56	2.33
Asher, David	R-L	6-1	195	2-18-83	1	2	4.31	30	11	0	0	86	93	50	41	7	27	60	.276	.244	.287	6.30	2.84
Beus, Lance	L-L	6-1	180	3-11-83	0	6	4.46	31	1	0	0	40	46	25	20	5	25	34	.282	.260	.292	7.59	5.58
Bibens-Dirkx, Austin	R-R	6-2	190	4-29-85	2	2	1.95	25	0	0	4	32	24	7	7	0	7	38	.200	.143	.250	10.58	1.95
Colon, Juan	R-R	6-1	170	10-19-81	1	2	6.04	17	2	0	0	28	29	21	19	1	17	18	.271	.227	.302	5.72	5.40
Escalona, Jose	L-L	5-11	165	1-7-86	7	12	4.06	26	26	0	0	126	128	68	57	12	60	110	.262	.267	.261	7.84	4.27
Fagan, Paul	L-L	6-5	195	4-13-85	5	14	4.94	28	28	3	0	166	188	109	91	12	63	100	.296	.268	.304	5.43	3.42
Flores, Ruben	R-R	6-4	165	5-19-84	1	9	5.04	34	8	0	0	75	68	49	42	5	53	93	.240	.218	.256	11.16	6.36
Gibson, Rollie	L-L	6-2	220	12-30-83	0	1	5.64	22	0	0	0	30	32	20	19	2	25	28	.281	.378	.234	8.31	7.42
Gilmore, Jeffrey	R-R	6-2	190	9-29-83	2	0	6.67	19	0	0	0	27	35	22	20	3	12	18	.307	.231	.347	6.00	4.00
Guaramato, Edgar	R-R	6-1	170	8-5-84	3	3	5.74	54	0	0	6	63	51	46	40	5	47	64	.226	.198	.243	9.19	6.75
Hudson, Robert	R-R	6-0	170	8-31-83	0	0	0.00	2	0	0	0	2	1	0	0	0	0	2	.143	.333	.000	9.00	0.00
Kappel, Brian	R-R	6-0	215	1-7-83	4	0	1.61	24	0	0	8	28	15	7	5	1	8	29	.156	.133	.176	9.32	2.57
Koliscak, Cory	R-R	6-2	200	11-30-81	2	0	3.68	10	0	0	5	15	16	7	6	1	6	6	.262	.259	.265	3.68	3.68
Martinez, Roman	R-R	6-3	160	8-9-84	2	3	3.98	35	1	0	1	52	45	28	23	2	12	49	.224	.156	.266	8.48	2.08
Ockerman, Justin	L-R	6-10	263	1-8-83	0	0	11.74	7	1	0	0	8	12	10	10	0	12	12	.375	.571	.320	14.09	14.09
Snyder, Jason	R-R	6-6	205	4-6-83	2	4	5.46	11	11	0	0	58	73	49	35	3	24	43	.311	.278	.339	6.71	3.75
Sullivan, John	R-R	6-3	220	2-22-82	0	0	0.00	3	0	0	1	4	2	0	0	0	7	6	.154	.000	.222	14.54	0.00
Thomas, Justin	L-L	6-3	220	1-18-84	5	5	3.10	11	11	0	0	61	69	29	21	4	17	51	.286	.245	.297	7.52	2.51
Vega, Marwin	R-R	6-0	175	10-27-86	5	10	5.34	20	20	0	0	98	111	71	58	4	37	71	.287	.311	.263	6.54	3.41
Williams, Harold	L-R	6-4	190	9-24-84	3	4	3.17	31	8	0	0	77	51	37	27	6	72	90	.191	.200	.187	10.57	8.45
Woerman, Joseph	R-R	6-3	200	12-12-82	2	2	2.12	28	0	0	7	34	19	12	8	1	14	54	.162	.114	.183	14.29	3.71
Wu, Chao Kuan	L-R	6-3	192	5-25-84	0	0	9.00	1	0	0	0	1	2	1	1	0	1	0	.400	.000	.667	0.00	9.00

FIELDING

Catcher	PCT	G	PO	A	E	DP	PB
Ledbetter	1.000	10	73	4	0	0	3
Moore	.993	31	252	26	2	3	4
Prosise	.985	30	177	20	3	4	5
Schweiger	1.000	2	12	1	0	0	0
Scott	.975	27	215	22	6	5	2
Tucker	.990	34	250	40	3	2	12
Wu	1.000	11	90	8	0	0	4

First Base	PCT	G	PO	A	E	DP
Avila	.989	20	171	9	2	18
Flaig	.984	32	287	18	5	22
Ledbetter	.981	15	98	8	2	10
Limonta	.965	28	237	10	9	21
Prosise	1.000	1	2	0	0	0
Sabatella	.984	45	337	23	6	40

	PCT	G	PO	A	E	DP
Wu	.982	5	53	3	1	6
Second Base						
Dominguez	.971	7	15	18	1	3
Garth	.955	41	79	89	8	21
Guzman	1.000	2	7	4	0	1
Hudson	.982	10	27	29	1	12
Valbuena	.979	82	157	225	8	57
Third Base						
Flaig	.879	38	22	65	12	6
Garth	.844	61	28	107	25	7
Hudson	.914	38	32	64	9	9
Liddi	.862	11	9	16	4	2
Shortstop						
Dominguez	.925	55	69	116	15	23
Garth	.857	2	3	3	1	1

	PCT	G	PO	A	E	DP
Hudson	.961	53	73	172	10	30
Minaker	.978	36	62	118	4	23
Outfield						
Avila	1.000	2	1	0	0	0
Craig	.974	59	107	6	3	2
Flaig	1.000	17	21	0	0	0
Gary	.986	39	69	3	1	1
Hernandez	.969	101	182	5	6	1
Hernandez	.932	37	68	1	5	0
Limonta	1.000	21	25	4	0	0
Lo	.930	29	49	4	4	1
Posluszny	1.000	13	12	2	0	0
Reynolds	1.000	11	14	0	0	0
Sabatella	1.000	2	3	0	0	0
Saunders	.986	99	196	9	3	0

Everett AquaSox   Short-Season

Northwest League

BATTING	B-T	HT	WT	DOB	AVG	vLH	vRH	G	AB	R	H	2B	3B	HR	RBI	BB	HBP	SH	SF	SO	SB	CS	SLG	OBP
Bonilla, Leury	R-R	6-3	170	2-8-85	.230	.259	.218	59	196	20	45	12	0	7	27	13	1	3	4	53	5	2	.398	.276
Diaz, Ogui	R-R	6-2	170	12-1-85	.240	.224	.246	64	225	15	54	8	1	0	10	8	3	2	0	54	7	5	.284	.275
Dickey, Gavin	R-R	5-11	200	9-29-83	.216	.163	.233	55	176	28	38	6	3	5	21	13	10	2	1	40	16	2	.369	.305
Fernandez, Jair	R-R	6-1	170	12-10-86	.230	.275	.211	43	135	15	31	9	0	1	19	16	6	2	2	26	0	1	.319	.333
Graterol, Jose	R-R	6-1	175	8-27-84	.205	.323	.140	28	88	12	18	5	0	0	4	12	2	1	0	27	5	2	.261	.314
Halman, Gregory	R-R	6-4	192	8-26-87	.259	.286	.253	28	116	19	30	6	4	5	15	3	3	1	0	32	10	4	.509	.295
Henson, Julian	R-R	5-10	190	4-10-87	.300	.000	.500	4	10	3	3	0	0	0	0	4	1	0	0	3	0	0	.300	.533
Ledbetter, Curtis	R-R	6-3	220	12-26-81	.222	.250	.212	13	45	7	10	3	0	2	9	3	0	0	0	13	1	0	.422	.271
Lo, Kuo Hui	R-R	6-2	188	9-26-85	.276	.200	.292	16	58	11	16	3	1	2	10	5	1	0	1	12	8	2	.466	.338
Minaker, Chris	R-R	6-0	195	3-24-84	.289	.320	.276	19	83	11	24	6	1	1	9	2	1	0	0	7	2	1	.422	.314
Moore, Adam	R-R	6-3	215	5-8-84	.317	.455	.288	16	63	8	20	9	0	0	9	2	1	0	0	10	0	0	.460	.348
Peguero, Carlos	L-L	6-5	210	2-22-87	.204	.179	.215	25	93	7	19	4	1	2	9	2	0	0	0	34	0	2	.333	.221
Pimentel, Manelik	R-R	6-2	185	10-19-84	.251	.188	.277	59	223	23	56	11	1	10	42	18	0	2	51	0	2	.444	.305
Reynolds, Kevin	L-l	6-1	185	7-1-82	.242	.130	.291	36	149	16	36	9	0	0	13	9	1	1	2	25	4	4	.302	.286
Sabatella, Bryan	R-R	6-4	220	11-1-84	.261	.270	.257	63	207	34	54	10	2	2	25	20	5	1	4	39	22	4	.357	.335
Santin, Daniel	L-L	6-3	205	11-7-84	.256	.263	.254	19	78	11	20	4	2	1	0	2	1	0	1	15	0	0	.385	.289
Scott, Travis	L-R	6-3	220	4-24-85	.000	—	.000	1	3	1	0	0	0	0	0	0	0	0	0	2	0	0	.000	.000
Villezcas, Marcos	B-R	5-11	180	12-10-83	.214	.033	.264	34	140	15	30	4	1	3	16	10	2	0	0	23	0	1	.321	.276
Vogel, Matthew	R-R	5-8	170	8-1-83	.100	.200	.000	4	10	0	1	0	0	0	0	0	0	0	0	4	0	0	.100	.100
White, Joseph	L-R	6-3	210	1-14-86	.250	.208	.264	60	196	29	49	5	0	7	21	56	4	1	7	56	0	3	.383	.424
Wu, Chao Kuan	L-R	6-3	192	5-25-84	.236	.304	.212	29	89	10	21	5	0	0	5	10	0	1	1	19	0	0	.292	.310
Zorn, Dean	B-R	6-1	190	9-12-86	.235	.180	.258	46	170	18	40	8	2	0	12	13	0	3	0	36	3	3	.306	.290

PITCHING	B-T	HT	WT	DOB	W	L	ERA	G	GS	CG	SV	IP	H	R	ER	HR	BB	SO	AVG	vLH	vRH	K/9	BB/9
Ball, Bryan	R-R	6-2	210	7-10-84	0	1	9.00	3	1	0	0	4	6	5	4	0	4	5	.316	.200	.357	11.25	9.00
Beltran, Saydel	L-L	5-11	175	1-23-83	0	1	13.50	5	0	0	0	5	9	8	7	1	1	6	.391	.167	.471	11.57	1.93
Bibens-Dirkx, Austin	R-R	6-2	190	4-29-85	0	0	0.00	3	0	0	1	4	1	0	0	0	1	6	.083	.000	.167	13.50	2.25
Butler, Anthony	L-L	6-7	205	11-18-87	1	2	2.76	9	9	0	0	42	23	16	13	2	25	52	.160	.172	.157	11.06	5.31
Colon, Juan	R-R	6-1	170	10-19-81	2	0	8.00	4	0	0	0	9	10	9	8	2	4	10	.270	.267	.273	10.00	4.00
Dilone, Natividad	R-R	6-0	160	9-8-82	3	6	3.38	14	13	0	0	64	62	29	24	3	25	35	.252	.233	.266	4.92	3.52
Fenton, Will	R-R	6-2	205	4-7-83	1	0	9.00	4	0	0	0	5	7	6	5	1	2	3	.333	.800	.188	5.40	3.60
Fiorenza, Andrew	R-R	6-2	210	6-24-84	1	1	4.55	16	2	0	0	30	26	18	15	2	17	14	.236	.289	.208	4.25	5.16
Fister, Douglas	L-R	6-8	200	2-4-84	3	5	2.25	20	4	0	4	40	35	18	10	2	11	35	.229	.241	.222	7.88	2.48
Gibson, Rollie	L-L	6-2	220	12-30-83	0	1	3.45	15	0	0	0	29	15	13	11	5	11	33	.153	.200	.127	10.36	3.45
Kafka, Ari	R-R	6-6	230	6-12-83	1	0	4.35	19	0	0	0	31	22	19	15	4	13	32	.190	.186	.192	9.29	3.77
Kantakevich, Joseph	R-R	6-2	195	5-9-84	2	0	2.48	20	0	0	1	33	39	14	9	4	11	40	.295	.265	.313	11.02	3.03
Kappel, Brian	R-R	6-0	215	1-7-83	0	1	0.00	7	0	0	5	9	6	2	0	0	3	16	.182	.231	.150	15.43	2.89
Mickolio, Kameron	R-R	6-9	256	5-10-84	1	0	2.78	21	0	0	4	32	34	14	10	1	7	26	.264	.227	.282	7.24	1.95
Nesbitt, Gregory	L-L	6-3	195	3-6-83	1	1	5.47	9	4	0	0	25	32	20	15	3	3	24	.320	.450	.288	8.76	1.09
Orta, Ricky	R-R	6-2	195	11-6-84	4	5	5.20	13	11	0	0	54	54	34	31	6	14	45	.265	.302	.237	7.55	2.35
Richard, Steven	R-R	6-3	240	3-7-85	1	2	6.08	14	0	0	0	27	31	26	18	4	16	29	.284	.361	.247	9.79	5.40
Schilling, Michael	R-R	6-5	240	1-15-84	3	8	6.25	13	12	0	0	59	75	52	41	8	16	43	.301	.304	.299	6.56	2.44
Solomon, Aaron	R-R	6-2	205	8-8-83	0	0	3.86	15	0	0	0	19	14	12	8	0	18	20	.194	.208	.188	9.64	8.68
Souza, Justin	R-R	6-1	185	10-22-85	2	2	4.99	17	0	0	1	31	32	21	17	5	13	33	.267	.295	.250	9.68	3.82
Suriel, Jose	L-L	6-3	170	3-30-84	1	0	3.69	23	0	0	1	32	36	18	13	3	11	28	.298	.324	.287	7.96	3.13
Tillman, Chris	R-R	6-5	195	4-15-88	1	2	7.70	6	6	0	0	20	23	17	17	4	15	29	.325	.387	.283	13.27	6.86
Uhlmansiek, Steven	L-L	6-3	185	2-10-83	3	6	4.07	15	15	0	0	66	57	32	30	3	38	60	.229	.333	.204	8.14	5.16
Vogel, Matthew	R-R	5-8	170	8-1-83	0	0	9.00	1	0	0	0	1	1	1	1	1	0	0	.250	—	.250	0.00	0.00

FIELDING

Catcher	PCT	G	PO	A	E	DP	PB
Fernandez	.987	37	273	34	4	2	13
Henson	1.000	3	21	3	0	0	1
Ledbetter	1.000	6	39	2	0	0	2
Moore	.989	10	80	8	1	0	2
Santin	.978	5	39	5	1	0	1
Wu	.983	20	159	12	3	1	2

First Base	PCT	G	PO	A	E	DP
Pimentel	.984	31	231	18	4	22
Sabatella	1.000	6	28	2	0	2
White	.992	44	354	26	3	31
Wu	1.000	1	11	0	0	0

Second Base	PCT	G	PO	A	E	DP
Bonilla	1.000	1	0	2	0	0
Diaz	1.000	1	1	3	0	0
Minaker	.971	12	31	37	2	10
Villezcas	.970	18	18	47	2	2
Vogel	1.000	4	8	4	0	1
Zorn	.975	43	74	121	5	20

Third Base	PCT	G	PO	A	E	DP
Bonilla	.898	51	36	105	16	9
Pimentel	.893	17	17	33	6	2
Sabatella	1.000	1	0	1	0	0
Villezcas	.840	9	7	14	4	1
Zorn	.667	1	1	1	1	0

Shortstop	PCT	G	PO	A	E	DP
Diaz	.916	63	102	161	24	33
Minaker	.913	6	10	11	2	2
Villezcas	.912	8	10	21	3	4

Outfield	PCT	G	PO	A	E	DP
Bonilla	.875	6	7	0	1	0
Dickey	.980	52	95	2	2	0
Graterol	.976	27	35	5	1	2
Halman	.981	27	51	0	1	0
Lo	.958	16	22	1	1	0
Peguero	.936	23	43	1	3	0
Reynolds	.988	36	76	3	1	0
Sabatella	.958	51	88	3	4	1

Arizona League

BATTING

	B-T	HT	WT	DOB	AVG	vLH	vRH	G	AB	R	H	2B	3B	HR	RBI	BB	HBP	SH	SF	SO	SB	CS	SLG	OBP
Avila, Gerardo	L-L	6-2	185	7-15-86	.326	.385	.311	32	132	22	43	6	2	7	29	7	2	0	0	35	3	2	.561	.369
Beltran, Juan	R-R	6-0	165	6-26-86	.258	.348	.227	26	89	9	23	3	0	1	7	4	1	1	1	18	2	3	.326	.295
Benitez, Deybis	R-R	6-2	170	4-23-87	.268	.250	.273	48	190	27	51	3	4	0	13	23	3	2	1	46	7	7	.326	.355
Bohn, T.J.	R-R	6-5	210	1-17-80	.250	.000	.333	4	16	4	4	3	1	0	1	1	0	0	0	8	3	0	.563	.294
Chen, Yung Chi	R-R	5-11	170	7-13-83	.273	.333	.200	3	11	1	3	1	1	0	2	1	1	0	0	0	0	0	.545	.385
Dominguez, Jeffrey	B-R	6-2	153	7-31-86	.273	.167	.400	3	11	3	3	2	0	0	0	2	0	0	0	2	0	0	.455	.385
Dotel, Welington	R-R	6-1	180	10-2-85	.261	.154	.286	52	207	40	54	10	6	7	31	13	5	2	1	69	7	7	.469	.319
Garciaparra, Michael	R-R	6-1	175	4-2-83	.313	.500	.250	4	16	3	5	3	0	1	2	1	0	0	0	1	1	.688	.353
Gary, Alex	R-R	6-3	225	10-11-83	.243	.143	.267	13	37	8	9	2	1	2	8	14	5	0	0	11	4	0	.514	.500
Graterol, Jose	R-R	6-1	175	8-27-84	.250	.143	.286	8	28	5	7	0	0	0	3	4	0	0	0	9	4	1	.250	.343
Guzman, Juan	B-R	5-10	175	4-10-82	.238	.333	.222	14	42	8	10	3	2	0	7	11	0	0	1	5	2	0	.405	.389
Henson, Julian	R-R	5-10	190	4-10-87	.203	.083	.228	27	69	8	14	0	1	0	5	13	8	0	1	14	3	3	.232	.385
Hernandez, Jairo	R-R	6-3	185	5-8-85	.216	.111	.238	13	51	10	11	1	1	0	5	5	0	0	0	15	2	1	.275	.286
Jacobo, Erwin	R-R	6-2	195	6-15-85	.222	.125	.243	17	45	7	10	2	0	2	9	11	2	1	0	18	0	2	.400	.397
Keck, Paul	R-R	6-3	205	6-16-84	.100	.250	.000	4	10	1	1	1	0	0	2	0	2	0	0	3	0	0	.200	.250
Liddi, Alex	R-R	6-4	176	8-14-88	.313	.293	.319	47	182	31	57	13	6	3	25	12	1	0	2	48	9	2	.500	.355
Liverpool, Marquise	R-R	5-11	191	4-16-86	.264	.286	.259	38	144	27	38	2	2	1	14	15	7	3	0	26	18	9	.326	.361
Meneses, Alex	R-R	5-10	185	12-21-83	.387	.400	.462	9	31	10	12	1	0	0	3	6	0	1	0	5	2	3	.419	.486
Morban, Jose	B-R	6-1	170	10-2-79	.286	.200	.304	8	28	7	8	1	4	0	3	5	0	1	0	13	3	0	.607	.394
Peguero, Carlos	L-L	6-5	210	2-22-87	.313	.241	.333	34	134	27	42	10	7	7	30	13	2	0	1	49	3	2	.649	.380
Posluszny, Stan	L-R	6-3	220	11-14-82	.305	.105	.379	34	141	17	43	6	2	2	18	5	0	0	0	26	1	2	.418	.329
Prettyman, Ronald	L-R	6-2	190	8-4-81	.333	.500	.300	4	12	2	4	0	0	0	3	1	0	0	5	0	1	.333	.500
Ruiz, Donato	R-R	6-3	170	3-17-83	.233	.154	.250	20	73	11	17	3	1	0	15	3	4	0	2	21	7	0	.301	.293
Santin, Daniel	L-L	6-3	205	11-7-84	.276	.000	.320	8	29	4	8	1	0	1	7	0	1	0	0	2	0	0	.414	.300
Villezcas, Marcos	B-R	5-11	180	12-10-83	.283	.300	.278	12	46	14	13	1	0	1	10	8	0	0	1	6	1	1	.370	.382
Vogel, Matthew	R-R	5-8	170	8-1-83	.241	.150	.261	31	108	9	26	3	0	0	8	4	1	5	0	13	4	3	.269	.274

PITCHING

	B-T	HT	WT	DOB	W	L	ERA	G	GS	CG	SV	IP	H	R	ER	HR	BB	SO	AVG	vLH	vRH	K/9	BB/9
Adcock, Nathan	R-R	6-5	190	2-25-88	0	2	3.31	10	6	0	0	35	33	21	13	1	16	31	.243	.319	.202	7.90	4.08
Ball, Bryan	R-R	6-2	210	7-10-84	1	0	0.00	3	0	0	0	4	2	1	0	0	2	4	.143	.286	.000	9.00	4.50
Blanco, Ivan	R-R	6-1	190	9-24-83	0	0	0.00	2	2	0	0	4	1	0	0	0	2	5	.083	.000	.125	11.25	4.50
Brown, Will	L-R	6-3	215	10-9-87	0	3	5.70	16	0	0	4	24	29	19	15	0	15	28	.287	.350	.272	10.65	5.70
Butler, Anthony	L-L	6-7	205	11-18-87	2	0	2.57	5	3	0	0	14	5	4	4	0	9	25	.116	.200	.105	16.07	5.79
Campillo, Jorge	R-R	6-1	190	8-10-78	0	0	4.15	6	5	0	0	13	13	6	6	0	0	15	.277	.375	.226	10.38	0.00
Collis, Everett	R-R	6-2	215	1-14-84	2	1	3.55	15	0	0	4	25	27	14	10	1	11	19	.267	.229	.288	6.75	3.91
Cortez, Renee	R-R	6-4	180	12-9-82	1	0	0.00	1	0	0	0	2	0	0	0	0	1	2	.000	.000	.000	9.00	4.50
Eichelberger, Jared	R-R	6-7	210	8-4-83	1	3	4.28	16	0	0	0	27	19	16	13	3	22	34	.196	.214	.182	11.20	7.24
Fenton, Will	R-R	6-2	205	4-7-83	0	1	9.39	4	0	0	0	8	13	10	8	0	4	3	.406	.294	.533	3.52	4.70
Frye, Randall	R-R	6-4	221	9-11-83	0	0	0.00	1	0	0	0	1	1	0	0	0	0	0	.250	.000	.500	0.00	0.00
Gaetano, Diomny	R-R	6-3	185	11-14-84	0	0	20.25	4	0	0	0	3	7	6	6	0	2	0	.500	.667	.455	0.00	6.75
Harmon, Robert	R-R	6-7	239	9-28-83	1	2	8.25	15	0	0	0	24	15	27	22	0	25	21	.188	.130	.211	7.88	9.38
Harris, Jeff	R-R	6-1	190	7-4-74	0	0	0.00	4	2	0	0	6	6	0	0	0	0	6	.250	.182	.308	9.00	0.00
Huisman, Justin	R-R	6-1	200	4-16-79	0	0	1.80	3	2	0	0	5	5	1	1	0	2	9	.263	.667	.188	16.20	3.60
Javier, Carlos	R-R	6-3	170	5-28-87	3	4	7.57	11	5	0	0	36	41	34	30	2	28	27	.295	.283	.302	6.81	7.07
Koliscak, Cory	R-R	6-2	200	11-30-81	0	1	1.29	5	0	0	0	7	5	3	1	0	4	5	.192	.091	.267	6.43	5.14
Morrow, Brandon	R-R	6-3	175	7-26-84	0	2	2.77	7	4	0	0	13	10	4	4	0	9	13	.227	.158	.280	9.00	6.23
Nageotte, Clint	R-R	6-3	225	10-25-80	0	0	1.80	2	2	0	0	5	4	1	1	0	2	2	.222	.250	.214	3.60	3.60
Parker, Terrence	R-R	6-3	205	4-8-85	0	3	3.94	16	0	0	1	30	28	17	13	0	17	33	.248	.200	.274	10.01	5.16
Pettis, Marquis	R-R	6-2	180	9-9-82	1	2	3.86	16	0	0	0	28	21	17	12	2	9	15	.206	.179	.216	4.82	2.89
Salinas, Doug	R-R	6-4	195	12-5-88	4	0	2.84	12	5	0	2	51	39	19	16	1	15	49	.219	.203	.231	8.70	2.66
Santiago, Julio	L-L	6-4	155	12-8-85	0	0	9.00	2	1	0	0	3	7	3	3	0	1	1	.438	.333	.462	3.00	3.00
Snyder, Jason	R-R	6-6	205	4-6-83	1	0	0.00	2	0	0	0	5	2	3	0	0	3	2	.125	.000	.167	3.60	5.40
Sullivan, John	R-R	6-3	220	2-22-82	0	1	1.29	6	0	0	0	7	7	1	1	0	1	6	.269	.364	.200	7.71	1.29
Tillman, Chris	R-R	6-5	195	4-15-88	2	0	0.82	5	0	0	0	11	9	4	1	0	5	16	.214	.250	.200	13.09	4.09
Torres, Leonardo	R-R	6-2	165	7-8-86	1	0	4.98	9	5	0	0	22	16	15	12	0	20	16	.203	.290	.146	6.65	8.31
Van Gaalen, Aric	R-L	6-6	195	8-25-84	3	1	2.45	5	4	0	0	26	32	11	7	0	2	19	.314	.250	.326	6.66	0.70
Varvaro, Anthony	R-R	6-0	180	10-31-84	0	2	1.64	5	3	0	0	11	7	3	2	0	5	11	.184	.231	.160	12.27	4.09
Winter, Haley	R-R	5-9	185	6-16-84	2	2	6.91	17	0	0	0	27	43	27	21	0	6	26	.347	.333	.353	8.56	1.98
Zapata, Juan	R-R	6-3	180	8-6-84	0	0	3.60	3	2	0	0	5	5	3	2	1	3	5	.278	.333	.222	9.00	5.40

FIELDING

Catcher	PCT	G	PO	A	E	DP	PB
Beltran	.990	21	156	40	2	5	3
Henson	.982	24	136	25	3	2	9
Jacobo	.950	15	117	15	7	0	10
Keck	1.000	4	24	5	0	1	1
Santin	1.000	1	4	0	0	0	0

First Base	PCT	G	PO	A	E	DP
Avila	.984	32	285	16	5	15
Beltran	.889	1	6	2	1	0
Jacobo	1.000	1	6	0	0	1
Liddi	.971	11	95	6	3	12
Ruiz	.967	11	106	10	4	11

Second Base	PCT	G	PO	A	E	DP
Beltran	.909	4	2	8	1	0
Chen	1.000	3	9	4	0	2

	PCT	G	PO	A	E	DP
Garciaparra	.895	4	9	8	2	5
Guzman	.982	12	21	35	1	6
Meneses	.966	9	21	36	2	7
Morban	.737	3	5	9	5	0
Villezcas	1.000	3	8	6	0	2
Vogel	.952	20	40	40	4	6

Third Base	PCT	G	PO	A	E	DP
Benitez	.793	11	5	18	6	1
Liddi	.933	37	28	69	7	3
Morban	.833	2	1	4	1	0
Prettyman	.900	3	3	6	1	2
Vogel	1.000	3	1	4	0	0

Shortstop	PCT	G	PO	A	E	DP
Benitez	.913	36	49	109	15	14
Dominguez	.955	3	10	11	1	2

	PCT	G	PO	A	E	DP
Morban	.833	2	2	3	1	1
Villezcas	.964	9	18	36	2	7
Vogel	.914	5	10	22	3	7

Outfield	PCT	G	PO	A	E	DP
Bohn Jr.	1.000	4	10	0	0	0
Dotel	.988	48	75	7	1	3
Gary	.950	13	18	1	1	1
Graterol	.833	6	5	0	1	0
Hernandez	.917	9	11	0	1	0
Liverpool	.940	37	61	2	4	0
Peguero	.977	31	38	5	1	0
Posluszny	1.000	8	13	0	0	0
Ruiz	1.000	7	10	0	0	0
Vogel	1.000	4	2	1	0	0

TAMPA BAY DEVIL RAYS

BY MARC TOPKIN

In Tampa Bay's first year under new ownership and management, the Devil Rays seemed to make progress everywhere but on the major league field.

Attendance and interest in the team increased and the organization added talent by trading veterans for prospects—resulting in more victories in the minor leagues.

But the Devil Rays won six fewer games than the season before, lost more than 100 games for the first time since 2002 and finished with sole possession of the worst record in the majors at 61-101 for the first time in their nine-season history.

Injuries–which exposed a lack of depth–were a key part of the overall problem, especially early in the season. With injuries to third baseman Aubrey Huff, shortstop Julio Lugo, second baseman Jorge Cantu and center fielder Rocco Baldelli, the Devil Rays didn't get their projected starting lineup on the field until June 7, their 60th game. Two members of the rotation—Scott Kazmir and Casey Fossum—were later sidelined, and overall Tampa Bay had 17 players on the DL and lost 965 days to injury-third most in the majors.

As if the injuries didn't hurt enough, the Devil Rays traded away several key veterans who they weren't planning to retain, including Huff, Lugo, catcher Toby Hall, lefthander Mark Hendrickson, outfielder Joey Gathright and infielder-outfielder Russell Branyan. Only five players on the Opening Day roster stayed active until the end of the season.

Through trades Tampa Bay added four players who were in the majors in 2006—Jae Seo, Dioner Navarro, J.P. Howell and Ben Zobrist—and several prospects, including Mitch Talbot and Joel Guzman.

The product on the field was often young and inexpe-

rienced, forcing first-year manager Joe Maddon to use 145 different lineups. The Devil Rays lost an American League record 60 games in which they had held the lead and were 20-61 in road games—the third-worst record since baseball expanded to a 162-game schedule in 1961. The Devil Rays, 41-40 at home, are the first team to lose 100 games with a winning home record.

Team officials felt the road record was the result of inexperience and an inability to execute in pressure situations in unfriendly settings. Maddon—whose upbeat, constantly positive style was a significant change from three years of Lou Piniella's reign—acknowledged that the team's lack of fundamentals was "really kind of staggering."

"The word is execution,"' Maddon said. "Offensively, pitching, defensively, we just have to be more consistent within the fundamentals of the game.''

Though the team's struggles were disappointing, some individual success stories did shine through. Carl Crawford increased his home run total and batting average for a fifth consecutive season. He led the AL with 58 steals and 16 triples, and ranked sixth with a .348 average with runners in scoring position, sixth with 59 multi-hit games, 10th with 189 hits and tied for 8th with 10 outfield assists.

Baldelli hit .302/.339/.533 after missing all of 2005 due to injury, yet the most encouraging performance for the future might have been the play of right fielder Delmon Young. The 21-year-old was vilified early in the season after throwing his bat at an umpire at Triple-A Durham and finished the year praised for his stellar play and good behavior during a month-long trial in the majors. The Devil Rays were impressed enough to limit Young's at-bats so he could retain eligibility for the 2007 Rookie of the Year award.

Among other minor league accomplishments, Double-A Montgomery won the Southern League championship and high Class A Visalia lost in the California League final. Two prospects earned most valuable player honors: shortstop Reid Brignac in the California League and first baseman/DH Kevin Witt in the International League.

ORGANIZATION LEADERS

BATTING		*Minimum 250 at-bats
*AVG	Ashley, Nevin, Princeton	.333
R	Perez, Fernando, Visalia	137
H	Perez, Fernando, Visalia	182
TB	Brignac, Reid, Visalia/Montgomery	281
2B	Nowak, Chris, Visalia	45
3B	Johnson, Elliot, Montgomery	10
HR	Witt, Kevin, Durham	36
RBI	Nowak, Chris, Visalia	103
BB	Perez, Fernando, Visalia	88
SO	Perez, Fernando, Visalia	149
SB	Upton, D.J., Durham	46
*OBP	Ashley, Nevin, Princeton	.440
*SLG	Witt, Kevin, Durham	.577
XBH	Witt, Kevin, Durham	66

PITCHING		#Minimum 75 innings
W	Sonnanstine, Andrew, Montgomery	15
L	Peguero, Tony, Montgomery	13
#ERA	Hellickson, Jeremy, Hudson Valley	2.43
G	Rodriguez, Jose, Montgomery/Durham	61
CG	Sonnanstine, Andrew, Montgomery	4
SV	Dupas, Greg, Southwest Michigan	25
IP	Sonnanstine, Andrew, Montgomery	186
BB	Mann, Brandon, Visalia	66
SO	McGee, Jacob, Southwest Michigan	171
#AVG	Hellickson, Jeremy, Hudson Valley	.193

Tampa Bay Devil Rays — MLB

American League

BATTING	B-T	HT	WT	DOB	AVG	vLH	vRH	G	AB	R	H	2B	3B	HR	RBI	BB	HBP	SH	SF	SO	SB	CS	SLG	OBP
Baldelli, Rocco	R-R	6-4	200	9-25-81	.302	.297	.303	92	364	59	110	24	6	16	57	14	7	0	2	70	10	1	.533	.339
Branyan, Russell	L-R	6-3	195	12-19-75	.201	.185	.204	64	169	23	34	10	0	12	27	19	2	1	2	62	2	0	.473	.286
Burroughs, Sean	L-R	6-2	180	9-12-80	.190	.000	.211	8	21	3	4	1	0	0	1	4	0	0	0	7	1	0	.238	.320
Cantu, Jorge	R-R	6-1	185	1-30-82	.249	.233	.256	107	413	40	103	18	2	14	62	26	3	0	6	91	1	1	.404	.295
Crawford, Carl	L-L	6-2	220	8-5-81	.305	.288	.311	151	600	89	183	20	16	18	77	37	4	9	2	85	58	9	.482	.348
Gathright, Joey	L-R	5-10	170	4-27-81	.201	.209	.198	55	154	25	31	6	0	0	13	20	3	5	0	30	12	3	.240	.305
2-team (79 Kansas City)					.238	—	—	134	383	99	91	12	3	1	41	42	7	9	4	75	22	9	.292	.321
Gomes, Jonny	R-R	6-1	205	11-22-80	.216	.297	.187	117	385	53	83	21	1	20	59	61	6	0	9	116	1	5	.431	.325
Green, Nick	R-R	6-0	175	9-10-78	.077	.056	.095	17	39	4	3	0	0	0	6	0	0	0	11	0	3	.077	.200
2-team (46 New York)					.184	—	—	63	114	12	21	5	0	2	4	11	1	1	0	40	1	4	.281	.262
Hall, Toby	R-R	6-3	240	10-21-75	.231	.250	.224	64	221	15	51	13	0	8	23	8	2	0	3	17	0	2	.398	.261
Hollins, Damon	R-L	5-11	180	6-12-74	.228	.240	.221	121	333	37	76	20	0	15	33	19	0	2	1	64	3	3	.423	.269
Huff, Aubrey	L-R	6-4	230	12-20-76	.283	.232	.304	63	230	26	65	15	1	8	28	24	0	0	2	25	0	0	.461	.348
Lee, Travis	L-L	6-3	225	5-26-75	.224	.226	.224	114	343	35	77	11	2	11	31	42	2	0	1	73	5	2	.364	.312
Lugo, Julio	R-R	6-1	175	11-16-75	.308	.323	.304	73	289	53	89	17	1	12	27	27	3	3	0	47	18	4	.498	.353
Navarro, Dioner	B-R	5-9	215	2-9-84	.244	.268	.237	56	193	23	47	7	0	4	20	20	1	1	1	33	1	1	.342	.316
Norton, Greg	B-R	6-1	200	7-6-72	.296	.283	.299	98	294	47	87	15	0	17	45	35	3	1	2	69	1	5	.520	.374
Ordaz, Luis	R-R	5-11	170	8-12-75	.000	—	.000	1	2	0	0	0	0	0	0	0	0	0	0	0	0	0	.000	.000
Paul, Josh	R-R	6-1	220	5-19-75	.260	.333	.234	58	146	15	38	9	0	1	8	14	1	3	1	39	1	2	.342	.327
Perez, Tomas	B-R	5-11	195	12-29-73	.212	.178	.226	99	241	31	51	12	0	2	16	5	0	4	4	44	1	0	.286	.224
Riggans, Shawn	R-R	6-2	190	7-25-80	.172	.000	.263	10	29	3	5	1	0	0	1	4	0	0	0	7	0	0	.207	.273
Upton, B.J.	R-R	6-3	180	8-21-84	.246	.298	.227	50	175	20	43	5	0	1	10	13	1	0	0	40	11	3	.291	.302
Wigginton, Ty	R-R	6-0	225	10-11-77	.275	.316	.260	122	444	55	122	25	1	24	79	32	6	1	3	97	4	3	.498	.330
Witt, Kevin	L-R	6-4	220	1-5-76	.148	.167	.145	19	61	5	9	2	0	2	5	0	0	0	0	21	0	0	.279	.148
Young, Delmon	R-R	6-3	205	9-14-85	.317	.379	.299	30	126	16	40	9	1	3	10	1	3	0	1	24	2	2	.476	.336
Zobrist, Ben	B-R	6-3	200	5-26-81	.224	.212	.229	52	183	10	41	6	2	2	18	10	1	0	2	33	2	3	.311	.260

PITCHING	B-T	HT	WT	DOB	W	L	ERA	G	GS	CG	SV	IP	H	R	ER	HR	BB	SO	AVG	vLH	vRH	K/9	BB/9
Camp, Shawn	R-R	6-1	200	11-18-75	7	4	4.68	75	0	0	4	75	93	43	39	9	19	53	.313	.370	.284	6.36	2.28
Childers, Jason	R-R	6-0	160	1-13-75	0	1	4.70	5	0	0	0	8	12	6	4	1	4	5	.343	.357	.333	5.87	4.70
Colome, Jesus	R-R	6-2	205	12-23-77	0	0	27.00	1	0	0	0	1	1	1	1	0	1	0	.000	—	.000	0.00	27.00
Corcoran, Tim	R-R	6-2	205	4-15-78	5	9	4.38	21	16	0	0	90	92	48	44	10	48	59	.271	.281	.262	5.88	4.78
Dunn, Scott	R-R	6-3	200	5-23-78	1	0	11.74	7	0	0	0	8	17	10	10	2	4	4	.436	.438	.435	4.70	4.70
Fossum, Casey	L-L	6-1	160	1-6-78	6	6	5.33	25	25	0	0	130	136	89	77	18	63	88	.265	.271	.263	6.09	4.36
Hammel, Jason	R-R	6-6	200	9-2-82	0	6	7.77	9	9	0	0	44	61	38	38	7	21	32	.333	.372	.299	6.55	4.30
Harper, Travis	L-R	6-4	190	5-21-76	2	0	4.93	30	0	0	0	42	62	27	23	6	13	32	.348	.400	.322	6.86	2.79
Harville, Chad	R-R	5-9	185	9-16-76	0	2	5.93	32	0	0	1	41	44	27	27	5	22	30	.277	.284	.272	6.59	4.83
Hendrickson, Mark	L-L	6-9	230	6-23-74	4	8	3.81	13	13	1	0	90	81	42	38	10	34	51	.241	.313	.223	5.12	3.41
Howell, J.P.	L-L	6-0	175	4-25-83	1	3	5.10	8	8	0	0	42	52	25	24	4	14	33	.310	.400	.281	7.02	2.98
Jackson, Edwin	R-R	6-3	190	9-9-83	0	0	5.45	23	1	0	0	36	42	27	22	2	25	27	.292	.233	.333	6.69	6.19
Kazmir, Scott	L-L	6-0	190	1-24-84	10	8	3.24	24	24	1	0	145	132	59	52	15	52	163	.240	.227	.242	10.14	3.24
Lugo, Ruddy	R-R	6-0	190	5-22-80	2	4	3.81	64	0	0	0	85	75	39	36	4	37	48	.240	.213	.264	5.08	3.92
McClung, Seth	R-R	6-6	250	2-7-81	6	12	6.29	39	15	0	6	103	120	77	72	14	68	59	.294	.299	.289	5.16	5.94
Meadows, Brian	R-R	6-3	240	11-21-75	3	6	5.17	53	0	0	8	70	90	43	40	14	15	35	.313	.254	.361	4.52	1.94
Miceli, Dan	R-R	6-0	225	9-9-70	1	2	3.94	33	0	0	4	32	25	17	14	4	20	18	.217	.130	.295	5.06	5.63
Orvella, Chad	R-R	5-11	190	10-1-80	1	5	7.40	22	0	0	0	24	36	23	20	6	20	17	.346	.275	.391	6.29	7.40
Salas, Juan	R-R	6-2	210	11-7-78	0	0	5.40	8	0	0	0	10	13	7	6	1	3	8	.295	.200	.421	7.20	2.70
Seo, Jae	R-R	6-0	230	5-24-77	1	8	5.00	17	16	0	0	90	122	56	50	17	31	39	.331	.346	.316	3.90	3.10
Shields, Jamie	R-R	6-4	215	12-20-81	6	8	4.84	21	21	1	0	125	141	69	67	18	38	104	.288	.266	.309	7.51	2.74
Stokes, Brian	R-R	6-1	205	9-7-79	1	0	4.88	5	4	0	0	24	31	13	13	2	9	15	.320	.302	.341	5.63	3.38
Switzer, Jon	L-L	6-3	190	8-13-79	2	2	4.54	40	0	0	0	35	34	19	17	5	19	18	.294	.220	.321	4.81	5.08
Waechter, Doug	R-R	6-4	210	1-28-81	1	4	6.62	11	10	0	0	53	67	40	39	6	19	25	.310	.284	.331	4.25	3.23
Walker, Tyler	R-R	6-3	260	5-15-76	1	3	4.95	20	0	0	10	20	18	11	11	0	7	16	.240	.314	.175	7.20	3.15

FIELDING

Catcher	PCT	G	PO	A	E	DP	PB
Hall	.991	61	310	22	3	2	3
Navarro	.981	54	330	34	7	2	5
Paul	1.000	52	301	24	0	5	0
Riggans	1.000	8	56	4	0	1	0

First Base	PCT	G	PO	A	E	DP
Branyan	1.000	2	8	0	0	1
Lee	.998	112	856	58	2	97
Norton	.994	25	154	9	1	12
Perez	1.000	1	8	0	0	0
Wigginton	.997	45	302	28	1	26
Witt	.935	5	28	1	2	1

Second Base	PCT	G	PO	A	E	DP
Cantu	.973	103	209	252	13	65
Green	1.000	4	7	8	0	3

	PCT	G	PO	A	E	DP
Perez	.988	22	27	58	1	12
Wigginton	1.000	43	66	116	0	31

Third Base	PCT	G	PO	A	E	DP
Branyan	.700	5	1	6	3	0
Burroughs	.963	7	6	20	1	4
Hall	—	1	0	0	0	0
Huff	.980	60	38	109	3	15
Perez	.963	40	15	37	2	4
Upton	.906	50	38	88	13	6
Wigginton	.940	34	16	63	5	7

Shortstop	PCT	G	PO	A	E	DP
Green	1.000	10	10	21	0	6
Lugo	.957	73	113	201	14	42
Ordaz	1.000	1	1	1	0	0
Perez	.966	36	47	96	5	25

	PCT	G	PO	A	E	DP
Zobrist	.963	52	86	148	9	31

Outfield	PCT	G	PO	A	E	DP
Baldelli	.979	91	228	6	5	3
Branyan	.969	55	89	5	3	0
Crawford	.991	148	304	10	3	0
Gathright	.994	54	155	2	1	2
Gomes	1.000	8	19	0	0	0
Green	1.000	1	1	0	0	0
Hollins	.982	115	216	5	4	1
Norton	.956	31	42	1	2	0
Paul	—	1	0	0	0	0
Perez	1.000	5	11	0	0	0
Wigginton	.913	12	19	2	2	0
Young	.983	30	54	4	1	0

General manager: Andrew Friedman. **Farm director:** Mitch Lukevics. **Scouting director:** R.J. Harrison.

Class	Team	League	W	L	PCT	Finish*	Manager	Affiliate Since
Majors	Tampa Bay	American	61	101	.377	14th (14)	Joe Maddon	—
Triple-A	Durham Bulls	International	64	78	.451	11th (14)	John Tamargo	1998
Double-A	Montgomery Biscuits	Southern	77	62	.554	+3rd (10)	Charlie Montoyo	2004
High A	Visalia Oaks	California	75	65	.536	2nd (10)	Joe Szekely	2005
Low A	Southwest Michigan Devil Rays	Midwest	62	77	.446	12th (14)	Skeeter Barnes	2005
Short-season	Hudson Valley Renegades	New York-Penn	31	43	.419	12th (14)	Matt Quatraro	1996
Rookie	Princeton Devil Rays	Appalachian	28	36	.438	9th (10)	Jamie Nelson	1997
OVERALL 2006 MINOR LEAGUE RECORD			337	361	.483	22nd (30)		

*Finish in overall standings (No. of teams in league). +League champion

Durham Bulls — Triple-A

International League

BATTING	B-T	HT	WT	DOB	AVG	vLH	vRH	G	AB	R	H	2B	3B	HR	RBI	BB	HBP	SH	SF	SO	SB	CS	SLG	OBP
Baldelli, Rocco	R-R	6-4	200	9-25-81	.404	.412	.400	12	47	7	19	5	0	0	4	4	0	0	0	10	0	1	.511	.451
Bankston, Wes	R-R	6-4	200	11-23-83	.297	.415	.254	52	195	22	58	13	0	5	29	10	1	0	1	40	0	1	.441	.333
Burroughs, Sean	L-R	6-2	180	9-12-80	.214	.256	.196	37	131	8	28	2	0	1	11	9	1	1	1	29	1	3	.252	.268
Butler, Brent	R-R	6-0	180	2-11-78	.269	.212	.295	120	439	39	118	26	3	2	38	23	1	7	1	45	3	5	.355	.306
Cash, Kevin	R-R	6-0	190	12-6-77	.183	.132	.207	78	240	17	44	10	1	2	21	24	5	3	1	74	1	2	.258	.270
Cortez, Fernando	L-R	6-1	175	8-10-81	.222	.120	.255	60	203	21	45	6	2	0	7	11	1	2	0	37	8	3	.271	.265
Dukes, Elijah	R-R	6-2	225	6-26-84	.293	.293	.294	80	283	58	83	15	5	10	50	44	7	0	0	47	9	4	.488	.395
Gathright, Joey	L-R	5-10	170	4-27-81	.258	.200	.313	10	31	5	8	2	0	0	1	6	2	1	0	3	6	2	.323	.410
Green, Nick	R-R	6-0	175	9-10-78	.238	.188	.269	10	42	2	10	0	0	1	2	0	1	1	0	14	0	0	.310	.256
2-team (14 Columbus)					.222			24	90	5	20	4	0	1	6	7	2	2	1	27	1	0	.300	.290
Guzman, Joel	R-R	6-6	250	11-24-84	.193	.280	.159	25	88	7	17	5	0	4	9	4	0	0	0	23	0	1	.386	.228
Hall, James	L-R	6-3	210	5-19-84	.182	.500	.111	4	11	0	2	0	0	0	1	0	1	0	0	4	1	0	.182	.250
Johnson, Joshua	R-R	6-0	205	11-3-82	.111	.000	.125	7	9	0	1	0	0	0	0	1	0	0	0	3	0	0	.111	.200
Knox, Ryan	R-R	6-1	184	6-28-77	.184	.233	.164	34	103	7	19	7	0	1	4	5	0	0	0	35	1	1	.282	.222
Maniscalco, Matthew	R-R	5-10	180	2-18-81	.182	.357	.122	21	55	4	10	0	0	0	3	2	0	2	0	14	0	0	.182	.211
McDonald, Darnell	R-R	5-11	210	11-17-78	.292	.308	.285	136	538	80	157	33	1	14	57	47	4	4	3	115	30	12	.435	.351
Norton, Greg	B-R	6-1	200	7-6-72	.111	.000	.200	3	9	1	1	0	0	0	0	1	1	0	0	3	0	0	.111	.200
Nye, Rodney	R-R	6-4	215	12-2-76	.245	.261	.239	49	159	16	39	9	1	2	14	12	2	0	2	45	0	0	.352	.303
2-team (43 Pawtucket)					.242			92	298	29	72	18	1	4	31	30	3	0	5	70	1	0	.349	.312
Ordaz, Luis	R-R	5-11	170	8-12-75	.339	.389	.317	17	59	5	20	4	1	0	1	6	1	0	1	3	1	0	.492	.344
Raburn, John	B-R	6-0	164	2-16-79	.194	.222	.178	24	72	6	14	2	0	0	1	11	0	1	0	14	6	2	.222	.301
Riggans, Shawn	R-R	6-2	190	7-25-80	.293	.296	.291	115	417	43	122	26	2	11	54	27	5	2	2	88	2	2	.444	.341
Rivas, Luis	R-R	5-11	180	8-30-79	.218	.228	.213	69	229	21	50	8	1	2	24	10	1	2	2	34	2	1	.288	.252
Romano, Jason	R-R	6-0	185	6-24-79	.105	.063	.136	13	38	2	4	0	0	0	4	0	1	0	9	0	1	.105	.190
Rose, Mike	B-R	6-1	225	8-25-76	.104	.143	.077	20	67	4	7	1	0	2	5	5	0	0	1	21	0	0	.209	.164
Upton, B.J.	R-R	6-3	180	8-21-84	.269	.303	.254	106	398	72	107	18	4	8	41	65	4	0	3	89	46	17	.394	.374
Wigginton, Ty	R-R	6-0	225	10-11-77	.375		.375	2	8	3	3	0	0	0	1	2	0	0	0	2	0	0	1.000	.375
Witt, Kevin	L-R	6-4	220	1-5-76	.291	.261	.305	128	485	82	141	29	1	36	99	50	4	0	3	132	0	1	.577	.360
Young, Delmon	R-R	6-3	205	9-14-85	.316	.300	.322	86	342	50	108	22	4	8	59	15	3	0	10	65	22	4	.474	.341
Zobrist, Ben	B-R	6-3	200	5-26-81	.304	.500	.255	18	69	12	21	3	1	0	6	10	1	2	0	9	4	1	.377	.400

PITCHING	B-T	HT	WT	DOB	W	L	ERA	G	GS	CG	SV	IP	H	R	ER	HR	BB	SO	AVG	vLH	vRH	K/9	BB/9
Cash, Kevin	R-R	6-0	190	12-6-77	1	0	0.00	1	0	0	0	1	0	0	0	0	0	0	.000	.000	.000	0.00	0.00
Childers, Jason	R-R	6-0	160	1-13-75	2	3	4.99	39	0	0	2	52	58	34	29	8	22	39	.278	.221	.317	6.71	3.78
Corcoran, Tim	R-R	6-2	205	4-15-78	5	1	1.91	19	3	0	1	38	30	13	8	2	9	32	.219	.250	.198	7.65	2.15
Cromer, Jason	R-L	6-4	226	12-11-80	0	1	4.74	12	1	0	0	19	18	14	10	2	11	19	.247	.100	.302	9.00	5.21
Dunn, Scott	R-R	6-3	200	5-23-78	4	2	2.73	38	1	0	0	66	57	21	20	2	28	70	.228	.224	.230	9.55	3.82
Flinn, Chris	R-R	6-2	197	8-18-80	0	0	3.86	8	1	0	0	12	12	5	5	1	7	7	.273	.313	.250	5.40	5.40
Hammel, Jason	R-R	6-6	200	9-2-82	5	9	4.23	24	24	1	0	128	133	71	60	11	36	117	.270	.263	.275	8.25	2.54
Harville, Chad	R-R	5-9	185	9-16-76	0	0	3.00	11	0	0	1	15	15	5	5	0	8	9	.263	.292	.242	5.40	4.80
Hines, Carlos	R-R	6-3	190	9-26-80	1	1	1.80	8	0	0	0	10	13	5	2	0	2	7	.302	.125	.407	6.30	1.80
Howell, J.P.	L-L	6-0	175	4-25-83	5	3	2.62	10	10	0	0	55	53	18	16	2	15	49	.260	.209	.273	8.02	2.45
Jackson, Edwin	R-R	6-3	190	9-9-83	3	7	5.55	22	13	0	0	73	84	55	45	7	35	66	.288	.248	.311	8.14	4.32
Johnson, Joshua	R-R	6-0	205	11-3-82	0	1	4.50	2	0	0	1	2	4	1	1	0	0	2	.364	.333	.400	9.00	0.00
Lynn, Kevin	R-R	5-11	185	11-12-78	0	0	4.50	1	0	0	0	2	2	1	1	0	0	2	.250	.000	.333	9.00	0.00
Magrane, Jim	R-R	6-2	204	7-23-78	1	4	5.70	7	7	0	0	43	52	32	27	5	8	30	.292	.295	.289	6.33	1.69
McClung, Seth	R-R	6-6	250	2-7-81	1	0	2.20	14	0	0	5	16	16	5	4	1	2	26	.242	.300	.194	14.33	1.10
Miadich, J.B.	R-R	6-4	225	2-3-76	0	6	4.26	26	0	0	10	25	18	15	12	1	25	30	.186	.135	.217	10.66	8.88
Miller, Justin	R-R	6-2	200	8-27-77	2	0	3.86	5	0	0	1	7	5	4	3	2	2	11	.192	.071	.333	14.14	2.57
Nye, Rodney	R-R	6-4	215	12-2-76	0	0	0.00	1	0	0	0	1	0	0	0	0	1	0	.250	.500	.000	9.00	9.00
2-team (1 Pawtucket)					0	0	0.00	2	0	0	0	3	3	0	0	0	1	2	—	—	—	6.00	3.00
Orvella, Chad	R-R	5-11	190	10-1-80	4	0	1.86	27	0	0	1	39	31	11	8	2	9	55	.217	.290	.160	12.80	2.09
Prochaska, Mike	L-L	6-1	210	5-23-80	1	3	5.10	7	4	0	0	30	31	18	17	4	12	20	.267	.222	.281	6.00	3.60
Reyes, Al	R-R	6-1	210	4-10-70	0	0	3.00	2	0	0	0	3	3	1	1	0	3	3	.273	.143	.500	9.00	9.00
Ridgway, Jeff	R-L	6-3	189	8-17-80	1	4	3.03	34	0	0	0	39	35	15	13	3	13	38	.238	.204	.258	8.84	3.03
Rodriguez, Jose	R-R	6-0	170	1-15-82	4	2	2.43	49	2	0	1	74	69	23	20	4	27	62	.251	.275	.237	7.54	3.28
Salas, Juan	R-R	6-2	210	11-7-78	1	1	1.57	27	0	0	3	29	15	5	5	3	11	33	.149	.192	.102	10.36	3.45
Seddon, Chris	L-L	6-3	190	10-13-83	9	9	4.72	28	28	1	0	154	168	92	81	20	46	108	.277	.252	.286	6.30	2.68
Shields, Jamie	R-R	6-4	215	12-20-81	3	2	2.64	10	10	0	0	61	60	24	18	3	6	64	.252	.289	.248	9.39	0.88
Stokes, Brian	R-R	6-1	205	9-7-79	7	7	4.11	29	23	0	0	134	134	75	61	8	49	103	.260	.270	.253	6.94	3.30
Switzer, Jon	L-L	6-3	190	8-13-79	3	0	0.87	26	0	0	3	31	22	4	3	1	13	29	.191	.132	.221	8.42	3.77
Waechter, Doug	R-R	6-4	210	1-28-81	1	12	8.32	17	15	1	0	79	129	82	73	7	24	45	.366	.381	.352	5.13	2.73

ORGANIZATION STATISTICS

Catcher

Catcher	PCT	G	PO	A	E	DP	PB
Cash	.992	50	317	42	3	4	12
Johnson	1.000	6	24	2	0	0	0
Riggans	.984	88	694	34	12	3	7
Rose	.984	7	58	2	1	0	1

First Base

First Base	PCT	G	PO	A	E	DP
Bankston	.977	47	356	25	9	22
Cash	1.000	2	16	0	0	1
Cortez	1.000	3	6	3	0	0
Norton	1.000	2	13	1	0	2
Nye	.960	3	22	2	1	0
Rose	.667	1	2	0	1	0
Wigginton	1.000	1	7	0	1	0
Witt	.988	88	717	54	9	84

Second Base

Second Base	PCT	G	PO	A	E	DP
Butler	1.000	31	53	60	0	13
Cortez	.976	48	91	151	6	36
Green	.929	3	6	7	1	2
Maniscalco	1.000	3	7	7	0	2
Raburn	1.000	2	2	3	0	1
Rivas	.964	64	109	161	10	30

Third Base

Third Base	PCT	G	PO	A	E	DP
Burroughs	.922	35	27	67	8	7
Butler	.933	32	23	61	6	5
Cash	.846	5	1	10	2	1
Cortez	.909	10	7	23	3	2
Guzman	.870	12	7	13	3	1
Nye	.962	29	14	61	3	7
Raburn	.824	7	2	12	3	2
Upton	.900	18	10	35	5	1

Shortstop

Shortstop	PCT	G	PO	A	E	DP
Butler	1.000	14	14	41	0	8
Green	1.000	1	3	1	0	0
Maniscalco	.935	17	20	38	4	4
Ordaz	1.000	16	21	30	0	7
Raburn	1.000	1	0	3	0	0
Upton	.930	84	133	237	28	67
Zobrist	.968	18	27	34	2	4

Outfield

Outfield	PCT	G	PO	A	E	DP
Baldelli	.917	7	11	0	1	0
Butler	1.000	36	55	2	0	0
Cash	1.000	2	3	0	0	0
Dukes	.949	78	142	7	8	2
Gathright	1.000	10	26	1	0	0
Green	1.000	5	8	1	0	0
Guzman	.920	12	21	2	2	0
Hall	1.000	4	4	0	0	0
Knox	1.000	31	44	3	0	0
McDonald	.990	134	301	4	3	0
Nye	1.000	9	11	0	0	0
Raburn	1.000	12	20	2	0	2
Romano	1.000	13	21	1	0	1
Young	.988	86	157	5	2	0

Montgomery Biscuits — Double-A

Southern League

BATTING

BATTING	B-T	HT	WT	DOB	AVG	vLH	vRH	G	AB	R	H	2B	3B	HR	RBI	BB	HBP	SH	SF	SO	SB	CS	SLG	OBP
Albernaz, Craig	R-R	5-8	177	10-30-82	.000	.000	—	2	3	0	0	0	0	0	0	0	0	0	0	1	0	0	.000	.000
Bankston, Wes	R-R	6-4	200	11-23-83	.263	.220	.278	45	167	20	44	7	1	4	19	12	3	0	1	37	4	1	.389	.322
Breen, Patrick	L-L	6-3	215	6-23-82	.217	.182	.230	24	83	13	18	4	2	5	16	7	2	0	0	34	0	1	.494	.293
Brignac, Reid	L-R	6-3	170	1-16-86	.300	.342	.278	28	110	18	33	6	2	3	16	7	3	0	1	31	3	0	.473	.355
Cantu, Jorge	R-R	6-1	185	1-30-82	.194	.333	.160	8	31	4	6	0	0	2	8	1	0	0	1	9	0	0	.387	.212
Christianson, Ryan	R-R	6-2	210	4-21-81	.195	.193	.196	95	328	38	64	9	0	14	38	31	3	0	3	110	9	1	.351	.268
Coleman, Michael	R-R	5-11	215	8-16-75	.239	.245	.236	121	435	51	104	25	3	17	61	41	0	0	2	93	6	0	.428	.313
Cuevas, Aneudi	R-R	6-1	182	10-6-81	.225	.083	.293	41	111	10	25	6	0	1	8	7	2	0	1	45	1	0	.306	.281
Isenia, Chairon	R-R	5-11	210	1-23-79	.236	.202	.254	78	288	25	68	13	0	3	26	17	1	1	2	50	2	0	.313	.279
Johnson, Elliot	B-R	6-0	171	3-9-84	.281	.312	.265	122	494	69	139	21	10	15	50	39	2	4	3	122	20	18	.455	.335
Johnson, Joshua	R-R	6-0	205	11-3-82	.235	.125	.333	7	17	2	4	0	0	0	3	1	0	0	1	8	0	0	.235	.381
Knox, Ryan	R-R	6-1	184	6-28-77	.149	.176	.132	25	87	8	13	3	0	2	7	9	4	1	1	21	4	1	.253	.257
Leandro, Francisco	L-L	5-10	180	7-19-80	.220	.177	.237	74	218	20	48	12	0	1	14	26	2	4	0	38	3	1	.289	.309
Longoria, Evan	R-R	6-2	180	10-7-85	.267	.233	.290	26	105	14	28	5	0	6	19	1	0	0	3	20	2	1	.486	.266
Maniscalco, Matthew	R-R	5-10	180	2-18-81	.235	.178	.262	103	332	27	78	10	4	0	30	42	6	7	4	64	9	6	.289	.328
Martinez, Gabriel	L-R	6-2	180	5-17-83	.266	.222	.284	126	425	59	113	25	1	10	46	65	4	2	7	126	5	1	.400	.363
Owens, Jeremy	R-R	6-1	200	12-9-76	.237	.300	.204	125	414	60	98	15	4	14	41	32	5	7	0	142	24	6	.394	.299
Pridie, Jason	L-R	6-1	190	10-9-83	.230	.223	.234	132	460	39	106	11	4	5	34	31	3	4	5	93	16	5	.304	.281
Raburn, John	B-R	6-0	164	2-16-79	.295	.346	.259	93	322	47	95	15	5	0	32	47	2	10	1	47	20	8	.373	.387
Ruggiano, Justin	R-R	6-2	205	4-12-82	.333	.439	.269	31	108	25	36	14	3	4	27	19	2	1	0	29	4	4	.630	.442
2-team (89 Jacksonville)					.280	—	—	120	400	76	112	32	6	13	72	65	7	1	3	103	14	9	.488	.387
Schleicher, Mark	R-R	6-1	180	1-1-82	.000	.000	.000	12	20	0	0	0	0	0	0	1	0	0	0	14	0	0	.000	.048

PITCHING

PITCHING	B-T	HT	WT	DOB	W	L	ERA	G	GS	CG	SV	IP	H	R	ER	HR	BB	SO	AVG	vLH	vRH	K/9	BB/9
Allen, Brian	R-R	6-3	175	9-15-79	0	0	9.00	1	0	0	1	1	1	1	1	0	0	0	.500	—	.500	0.00	0.00
Carvajal, Marcos	R-R	6-4	175	8-19-84	2	2	3.86	39	0	0	0	72	66	34	31	7	39	69	.239	.238	.240	8.59	4.85
Cromer, Jason	R-L	6-4	226	12-11-80	4	5	2.58	20	16	0	0	87	84	40	25	3	34	59	.254	.274	.246	6.08	3.50
Ferreras, Yorkin	L-L	6-1	155	1-28-81	1	3	10.13	17	0	0	0	21	39	28	24	3	12	18	.402	.438	.385	7.59	5.06
Flanagan, Jeremy	R-R	6-3	215	4-14-81	6	1	3.65	32	0	0	1	57	51	24	23	2	21	39	.241	.217	.252	6.19	3.34
Flinn, Chris	R-R	6-2	197	8-18-80	1	6	5.49	16	12	0	0	62	81	45	38	2	24	43	.319	.311	.325	6.21	3.47
Henderson, Brian	L-L	5-11	195	5-19-82	2	2	2.16	41	0	0	5	50	47	13	12	2	11	28	.253	.209	.277	5.04	1.98
Kranawetter, Josh	R-R	5-11	184	5-21-80	2	0	5.46	28	0	0	3	31	30	19	19	5	13	20	.254	.250	.257	5.74	3.73
Machi, Jean	R-R	6-0	170	2-1-83	6	1	2.64	49	0	0	16	72	68	25	21	2	37	68	.255	.271	.246	8.54	4.65
Magrane, Jim	R-R	6-2	204	7-23-78	11	8	2.98	21	21	0	0	130	110	46	43	6	43	90	.234	.207	.251	6.25	2.98
Miceli, Dan	R-R	6-0	225	9-9-70	0	0	0.00	1	0	0	0	5	3	0	0	0	1	5	.176	.250	.154	9.00	1.80
Niemann, Jeff	R-R	6-9	260	2-28-83	5	5	2.68	14	14	0	0	77	56	24	23	6	29	84	.202	.188	.212	9.78	3.38
Peguero, Tony	R-R	6-3	170	2-17-81	10	12	2.97	31	21	0	1	152	132	66	50	10	39	93	.229	.243	.219	5.52	2.31
Prochaska, Mike	L-L	6-1	210	5-23-80	4	4	4.48	17	13	0	0	74	72	41	37	7	32	42	.256	.247	.260	5.09	3.87
Ridgway, Jeff	R-L	6-3	189	8-17-80	1	0	2.33	16	0	0	2	19	10	5	5	1	7	29	.152	.067	.176	13.50	3.26
Rodriguez, Jose	R-R	6-0	170	1-15-82	0	0	4.05	5	0	0	1	7	5	3	3	1	3	6	.200	.091	.286	8.10	4.05
Salas, Juan	R-R	6-2	210	11-7-78	3	0	0.00	23	0	0	14	35	13	4	0	0	14	52	.110	.081	.123	13.50	3.63
Sonnanstine, Andrew	L-R	6-3	185	3-18-83	15	8	2.67	28	28	4	0	186	151	63	55	15	34	153	.224	.227	.222	7.42	1.65
Talbot, Mitch	R-R	6-2	175	10-17-83	4	3	1.90	10	10	0	0	66	51	16	14	2	18	59	.214	.170	.240	8.01	2.44
Tiffany, Chuck	L-L	6-1	195	1-25-85	0	2	6.89	4	4	0	0	16	20	15	12	3	14	12	.313	.125	.339	6.89	8.04

FIELDING

Catcher	PCT	G	PO	A	E	DP	PB
Albernaz	1.000	2	7	0	0	0	0
Christianson	.992	87	613	48	5	7	3
Isenia	.992	51	341	28	3	3	11
Johnson	.933	4	14	0	1	0	0

First Base	PCT	G	PO	A	E	DP
Bankston	.974	4	34	3	1	3
Coleman	.996	33	257	10	1	31
Isenia	.983	7	54	5	1	6
Martinez	.987	101	849	47	12	81
Raburn	1.000	8	60	4	0	10

Second Base	PCT	G	PO	A	E	DP
Cantu	1.000	5	10	6	0	4
Cuevas	1.000	2	4	3	0	0
Johnson	.976	113	213	325	13	89
Raburn	.946	22	38	67	6	13

Third Base	PCT	G	PO	A	E	DP
Bankston	.782	30	14	47	17	3
Cuevas	.921	32	22	48	6	4
Longoria	.946	25	11	59	4	12
Martinez	.893	28	20	55	9	5
Raburn	.894	37	21	72	11	8
Schleicher	.833	3	1	4	1	1

Shortstop	PCT	G	PO	A	E	DP
Brignac	.956	28	36	73	5	11
Maniscalco	.960	103	152	275	18	69
Raburn	.957	10	18	26	2	7
Schleicher	1.000	2	1	6	0	1

Outfield	PCT	G	PO	A	E	DP
Breen	.947	18	36	0	2	0
Coleman	.952	32	38	2	2	0
Cuevas	.833	6	10	0	2	0
Knox	.981	25	50	2	1	0
Leandro	.979	67	88	5	2	1
Martinez	1.000	1	1	0	0	0
Owens	.989	124	246	19	3	9
Pridie	.987	132	286	8	4	4
Raburn	.882	10	14	1	2	0
Ruggiano	1.000	27	50	2	0	1
Schleicher	1.000	3	6	0	0	0

California League

BATTING

BATTING	B-T	HT	WT	DOB	AVG	vLH	vRH	G	AB	R	H	2B	3B	HR	RBI	BB	HBP	SH	SF	SO	SB	CS	SLG	OBP
Arhart, Josh	R-R	6-1	220	9-13-79	.301	.342	.285	107	429	64	129	27	2	15	78	22	8	0	7	93	3	2	.478	.341
Asanovich, Josh	R-R	6-2	185	1-31-83	.293	.177	.329	107	406	66	119	27	2	5	58	48	5	2	5	63	16	4	.406	.371
Breen, Patrick	L-L	6-3	215	6-23-82	.282	.229	.297	94	326	61	92	18	1	21	63	52	4	0	2	105	8	5	.537	.385
Brignac, Reid	L-R	6-3	170	1-16-86	.326	.302	.332	100	411	82	134	26	3	21	83	35	4	2	3	82	12	6	.557	.382
Cardona, David	R-R	6-2	175	11-7-82	.254	.289	.233	33	118	19	30	5	1	3	20	10	0	2	2	44	1	1	.390	.308
Cottrell, Patrick	R-R	5-11	160	3-16-82	.266	.342	.240	114	440	66	117	19	2	7	54	14	3	3	1	58	6	7	.366	.293
Cumberland, Shaun	L-R	6-2	185	8-1-84	.258	.219	.270	126	520	86	134	18	3	16	98	42	6	3	133	29	9	.396	.319
Dufner, Kris	B-R	6-2	185	2-15-80	.175	.250	.156	23	80	7	14	1	0	0	7	8	2	1	2	22	1	0	.188	.261
Huff, Aubrey	L-R	6-4	230	12-20-76	.250	.000	.400	2	8	2	2	1	0	0	1	1	0	0	0	2	0	0	.375	.333
Jaso, John	L-R	6-2	205	9-19-83	.309	.234	.325	95	366	58	113	22	0	10	55	31	3	0	6	48	1	2	.451	.362
Johnson, Joshua	R-R	6-0	205	11-3-82	.212	.267	.167	11	33	3	7	4	0	0	3	5	1	0	0	12	0	0	.333	.333
Leandro, Francisco	L-L	5-10	180	7-19-80	.119	.143	.114	13	42	2	5	1	0	0	1	2	0	1	0	5	2	0	.143	.159
Longoria, Evan	R-R	6-2	180	10-7-85	.327	.360	.318	28	110	22	36	8	0	8	28	13	2	1	2	19	1	1	.618	.402
Lopez, Christian	R-R	6-1	185	10-10-84	.400	—	.400	1	5	1	2	1	0	0	1	0	0	0	0	0	0	0	.600	.400
Nowak, Chris	R-R	6-5	225	2-21-83	.308	.292	.313	130	494	93	152	45	3	11	103	69	9	2	8	83	17	6	.478	.397
Pedroza, Sergio	L-R	6-1	180	2-23-84	.313	.304	.316	29	99	23	31	9	1	4	9	20	4	1	0	26	0	2	.545	.447
Perez, Fernando	R-R	6-1	195	4-23-83	.307	.319	.303	133	547	123	168	19	9	4	56	78	6	8	2	134	33	16	.397	.398
Reiman, Joey	R-R	6-1	200	12-20-80	.306	.368	.279	59	186	31	57	10	2	1	29	24	11	4	2	50	0	2	.398	.413
Schleicher, Mark	R-R	6-1	180	1-1-82	.269	.245	.278	50	175	27	47	8	0	7	25	5	0	0	3	48	1	2	.434	.284
Simmons, Coltyn	R-R	6-0	205	12-4-83	.275	.238	.316	13	40	5	11	0	0	1	11	7	3	0	0	8	0	0	.350	.420
St. Clair, Jason	R-R	5-10	173	9-27-82	.222	.100	.250	18	54	10	12	1	0	0	4	1	4	0	1	14	1	1	.241	.283
Vick, Hunter	B-R	5-9	165	4-12-82	.300	.227	.342	17	60	10	18	0	0	1	7	9	1	0	0	12	2	0	.350	.400

PITCHING

PITCHING	B-T	HT	WT	DOB	W	L	ERA	G	GS	CG	SV	IP	H	R	ER	HR	BB	SO	AVG	vLH	vRH	K/9	BB/9
Allen, Brian	R-R	6-3	175	9-15-79	5	5	5.17	38	0	0	2	78	105	54	45	10	13	39	.322	.336	.312	4.48	1.49
Barratt, Jonathan	R-L	5-9	165	3-19-85	9	6	2.93	21	20	1	0	111	93	43	36	8	37	100	.229	.229	.229	8.13	3.01
De Los Santos, Richard	R-R	6-1	175	6-1-84	5	3	3.44	41	0	0	13	68	72	26	26	1	19	49	.270	.261	.278	6.49	2.51
Debarr, Nick	R-R	6-4	205	8-24-83	4	3	2.74	40	0	0	9	69	61	25	21	3	17	61	.244	.243	.244	7.96	2.22
Dufner, Kris	B-R	6-2	185	2-15-80	0	0	0.00	2	0	0	0	1	1	0	0	0	0	1	.200	1.000	.000	6.75	0.00
Feldkamp, Derek	R-R	6-4	210	5-9-83	8	6	6.41	28	28	0	0	138	176	112	98	21	56	91	.316	.337	.299	5.95	3.66
Gonzalez, Jino	L-L	6-2	210	9-5-82	6	7	5.53	30	8	1	0	86	101	76	53	12	40	53	.294	.210	.319	5.53	4.17
Houser, James	L-L	6-4	185	12-15-84	12	4	4.41	28	27	0	0	151	140	80	74	20	46	137	.246	.254	.244	8.17	2.74
Johnson, Joshua	R-R	6-0	205	11-3-82	0	0	0.00	1	0	0	0	1	0	0	0	0	0	0	.000	.000	—	0.00	0.00
Lugo, Ruddy	R-R	6-0	190	5-22-80	0	0	6.75	4	0	0	1	4	6	4	3	0	2	5	.316	.400	.222	11.25	4.50
Mann, Brandon	L-L	6-2	165	5-16-84	4	9	5.64	29	24	0	0	137	145	99	86	19	66	120	.270	.317	.250	7.86	4.33
Mason, Chris	R-R	6-0	185	7-1-84	12	10	5.02	28	27	0	0	152	177	96	85	17	44	111	.289	.326	.253	6.56	2.60
Matthews, Jarod	R-R	6-2	212	11-10-82	0	7	5.85	23	6	0	0	52	51	42	34	11	29	53	.246	.260	.234	9.11	4.99
Meek, Evan	R-R	6-1	190	5-12-83	0	1	9.00	2	0	0	0	5	6	5	5	0	4	7	.250	.300	.300	12.60	7.20
2-team (26 Lake Elsinore)					6	7	5.14	28	25	0	0	124	142	85	71	5	66	120	—	—	—	8.69	4.78
Moran, Nick	R-R	6-5	205	1-3-80	2	1	5.51	21	0	0	0	49	56	35	30	1	20	48	.295	.262	.321	8.82	3.67
Perez, Antonio	B-L	5-9	165	6-12-81	1	1	6.11	39	0	0	1	56	74	41	38	6	22	31	.323	.261	.350	4.98	3.54
Wayne, Brett	R-R	6-0	183	4-28-80	7	2	3.54	45	0	0	7	81	63	36	32	5	34	83	.216	.211	.220	9.18	3.76

FIELDING

Catcher	PCT	G	PO	A	E	DP	PB
Arhart	.992	86	598	62	5	3	9
Jaso	.963	24	163	17	7	2	3
Johnson	1.000	3	22	2	0	0	0
Lopez	1.000	1	5	0	0	0	0
Reiman	.991	33	198	17	2	4	2
Simmons	1.000	5	25	5	0	0	0

First Base	PCT	G	PO	A	E	DP
Dufner	.983	6	54	4	1	5
Johnson	.909	1	8	2	1	2
Nowak	.984	125	1074	87	19	92
Reiman	.991	11	97	10	1	10

Second Base	PCT	G	PO	A	E	DP
Asanovich	.977	91	162	255	10	57

	PCT	G	PO	A	E	DP	PB
Cottrell	1.000	7	18	26	0	5	
Dufner	.956	12	19	24	2	4	
Schleicher	.963	6	14	12	1	4	
St. Clair	.906	11	12	17	3	3	
Vick	.918	14	23	33	5	9	

Third Base	PCT	G	PO	A	E	DP
Cottrell	.972	103	76	233	9	23
Dufner	.909	5	3	7	1	1
Huff	1.000	2	1	2	0	0
Longoria	.984	21	9	53	1	4
Nowak	.933	4	3	11	1	1
Schleicher	.857	4	2	4	1	1
Vick	.800	3	2	2	1	0

Shortstop	PCT	G	PO	A	E	DP
Asanovich	.947	14	23	48	4	12

	PCT	G	PO	A	E	DP
Brignac	.940	100	139	287	27	53
Schleicher	.932	29	33	63	7	9
St. Clair	.727	2	1	7	3	2

Outfield	PCT	G	PO	A	E	DP
Breen	.944	92	162	5	10	0
Cardona	1.000	33	52	1	0	0
Cottrell	1.000	2	2	0	0	0
Cumberland	.960	126	268	18	12	9
Leandro	.857	10	12	0	2	0
Pedroza	.956	28	42	1	2	0
Perez	.966	131	329	8	12	1
Schleicher	.000	1	0	0	1	0
St. Clair	1.000	5	4	0	0	0

Midwest League

BATTING

BATTING	B-T	HT	WT	DOB	AVG	vLH	vRH	G	AB	R	H	2B	3B	HR	RBI	BB	HBP	SH	SF	SO	SB	CS	SLG	OBP
Bethel, Ryan	B-R	6-0	170	3-26-82	.103	.208	.063	30	87	7	9	1	0	0	3	13	2	4	0	14	2	1	.115	.235
Brennan, Jackson	R-R	6-0	185	8-28-82	.261	.394	.238	226	36	59	16	0	5	34	38	12	0	2	56	9	5	.398	.392
Cardona, David	R-R	6-2	175	11-7-82	.324	.222	.360	11	34	5	11	1	0	1	2	5	0	0	11	0	1	.441	.425
Cunningham, Chris	R-R	6-0	200	8-24-82	.249	.300	.234	83	257	34	64	14	1	3	20	35	4	2	0	69	2	3	.346	.348
Devins, Matthew	R-R	6-0	200	5-23-83	.227	.200	.235	81	211	16	48	4	0	0	22	36	6	5	4	38	5	5	.246	.350
Durante, Eric	R-R	5-10	175	7-11-84	.208	.136	.230	35	96	9	20	3	2	1	9	12	4	1	0	15	2	4	.313	.321
Groce, Garrett	R-R	6-1	190	4-24-83	.263	.258	.265	126	448	62	118	22	1	5	45	44	6	3	4	118	30	14	.350	.335
Hall, James	L-R	6-3	210	5-19-84	.274	.242	.292	116	423	43	116	30	4	8	62	31	9	1	1	92	7	15	.421	.336
Hughes, Rhyne	L-L	6-2	175	9-9-83	.233	.176	.249	114	386	22	90	16	4	3	39	33	3	0	6	102	1	8	.319	.294
Jamieson, Alex	L-R	5-11	205	4-7-83	.261	.259	.262	70	218	23	57	13	1	3	21	32	1	4	0	49	3	1	.372	.359
Lopez, Christian	R-R	6-1	185	10-10-84	.217	.194	.223	99	345	23	75	10	2	2	23	18	3	7	4	71	6	3	.275	.259
Matulia, John	L-L	6-0	175	8-19-86	.196	.171	.201	55	194	24	38	4	0	0	12	16	4	6	0	39	7	7	.216	.271
Rousseve, Brandon	R-R	6-1	175	8-4-84	.091	.143	.075	32	88	8	8	0	1	0	0	7	1	5	0	28	2	3	.114	.167
Simmons, Coltyn	R-R	6-0	205	12-4-83	.227	.290	.213	54	172	13	39	4	2	1	15	16	7	5	2	22	0	2	.291	.315

	B-T	HT	WT	DOB	AVG	vLH	vRH	G	AB	R	H	2B	3B	HR	RBI	BB	HBP	SH	SF	SO	SB	CS	SLG	OBP
Spring, Matthew	R-R	6-2	215	11-7-84	.205	.289	.176	48	176	14	36	11	0	4	13	7	1	0	2	67	3	0	.335	.237
St. Clair, Jason	R-R	5-10	173	9-27-82	.248	.286	.242	40	145	20	36	6	2	0	9	5	2	6	1	20	5	3	.317	.281
Suarez, Cesar	R-R	5-11	170	8-17-83	.294	.364	.278	89	350	47	103	25	2	4	35	15	6	4	0	39	5	9	.411	.334
Vick, Hunter	B-R	5-9	165	4-12-82	.213	.265	.198	62	160	14	34	6	0	0	10	15	1	10	0	28	2	2	.250	.284
Walton, Neil	R-R	6-5	180	2-23-84	.190	.207	.186	128	415	48	79	15	1	2	29	29	7	17	4	122	19	8	.246	.253

PITCHING	B-T	HT	WT	DOB	W	L	ERA	G	GS	CG	SV	IP	H	R	ER	HR	BB	SO	AVG	vLH	vRH	K/9	BB/9
Bethel, Ryan	B-R	6-0	170	3-26-82	0	0	0.00	1	0	0	0	1	0	0	0	0	1	0	.000	.000	.000	0.00	9.00
Bigda, Drew	R-L	6-0	215	5-16-83	1	4	5.30	40	0	0	1	56	48	43	33	2	55	55	.231	.193	.245	8.84	8.84
Cayton, Jason	L-R	6-5	200	3-5-84	0	3	8.35	5	4	0	0	18	24	22	17	1	17	12	.324	.276	.356	5.89	8.35
Davis, Wade	R-R	6-5	220	9-7-85	7	12	3.02	27	27	1	0	146	124	61	49	5	64	165	.234	.284	.193	10.17	3.95
De La Cruz, Eddie	R-R	6-3	161	10-6-81	2	3	4.65	43	0	0	2	62	64	45	32	3	39	64	.272	.315	.245	9.29	5.66
Dupas, Greg	R-R	6-6	230	1-31-84	4	2	1.93	48	0	0	25	56	43	20	12	3	13	59	.202	.218	.190	9.48	2.09
Evers, William	R-R	6-2	195	8-31-82	1	1	4.08	32	3	0	0	46	37	28	21	2	38	37	.213	.203	.219	7.19	7.38
Kamrath, Jeffrey	R-R	6-3	210	4-6-82	1	8	4.28	30	11	0	2	88	71	48	42	7	42	89	.216	.297	.171	9.07	4.28
Kelly, Chris	R-R	6-3	200	7-14-82	5	6	4.66	46	0	0	0	64	75	43	33	5	28	45	.291	.292	.290	6.36	3.96
Lynn, Kevin	R-R	5-11	185	11-12-78	8	1	1.90	43	0	0	5	71	57	16	15	3	8	74	.218	.208	.225	9.38	1.01
McGee, Jacob	L-L	6-3	190	8-6-86	7	9	2.96	26	26	0	0	134	103	54	44	7	65	171	.211	.260	.194	11.49	4.37
Reinhard, Gregory	L-R	6-1	205	8-11-83	6	10	4.50	27	26	0	0	142	142	76	71	8	54	134	.258	.183	.306	8.49	3.42
Rondon, Celso	R-R	5-11	170	4-7-84	0	1	4.70	6	0	0	1	8	15	8	4	0	1	8	.395	.444	.350	9.39	1.17
Vick, Hunter	B-R	5-9	165	4-12-82	0	0	9.00	1	0	0	0	1	3	2	1	0	0	1	.429	.333	.500	0.00	0.00
Walker, Matthew	R-R	6-3	193	8-16-86	5	5	3.18	15	15	0	0	82	66	34	29	5	41	68	.223	.198	.242	7.46	4.50
Walker, Aaron	L-L	6-3	210	2-4-82	6	2	5.17	49	0	0	2	78	83	51	45	8	23	85	.269	.279	.265	9.77	2.64
Wlodarczyk, Michael	L-L	6-5	230	12-2-82	9	10	3.29	27	27	0	0	153	142	77	56	5	56	123	.246	.195	.261	7.24	3.29

FIELDING

Catcher	PCT	G	PO	A	E	DP	PB
Jamieson	.990	23	180	22	2	3	0
Lopez	.984	80	634	99	12	5	14
Simmons	.983	12	109	9	2	1	1
Spring	.983	29	259	26	5	4	5

Devins	.930	14	18	22	3	5	
Durante	1.000	34	62	62	0	15	
Rousseve	.966	24	33	53	3	12	
St. Clair	.939	33	56	68	8	13	
Suarez	1.000	2	3	3	0	0	
Vick	.960	46	55	112	7	23	

Durante	.500	2	0	1	1	0	
Rousseve	.891	10	15	26	5	5	
St. Clair	.800	1	1	3	1	1	
Vick	.931	9	11	16	2	4	
Walton	.947	126	193	308	28	62	

First Base	PCT	G	PO	A	E	DP
Bethel	.987	11	66	12	1	7
Devins	.991	18	107	7	1	9
Hughes	.980	109	783	61	17	64
Jamieson	.970	15	92	6	3	8
Simmons	1.000	1	1	0	0	0
Suarez	1.000	1	8	0	0	2

Third Base	PCT	G	PO	A	E	DP
Bethel	.788	17	8	18	7	2
Devins	.875	43	40	51	13	5
Rousseve	—	1	0	0	0	0
Suarez	.899	86	69	144	24	11
Vick	1.000	9	6	7	0	1

Outfield	PCT	G	PO	A	E	DP
Brennan	.976	65	117	5	3	1
Cardona	1.000	8	11	0	0	0
Cunningham	.972	71	98	5	3	0
Groce	.983	121	227	6	4	1
Hall	.963	101	178	5	7	2
Matulla	.965	55	82	0	3	0
Simmons	1.000	1	4	0	0	0
St. Clair	.900	5	8	1	1	0
Vick	—	1	0	0	0	0

Second Base	PCT	G	PO	A	E	DP
Bethel	.938	7	6	9	1	1

Shortstop	PCT	G	PO	A	E	DP
Bethel	1.000	2	3	3	0	2
Devins	1.000	1	0	2	0	0

Hudson Valley Renegades

Short-Season

New York-Penn League

BATTING	B-T	HT	WT	DOB	AVG	vLH	vRH	G	AB	R	H	2B	3B	HR	RBI	BB	HBP	SH	SF	SO	SB	CS	SLG	OBP
Callender, Joseph	R-R	5-11	165	11-25-83	.209	.220	.206	64	234	27	49	0	2	1	17	10	1	6	1	25	5	2	.239	.244
de la Rosa, Jairo	R-R	6-2	170	9-8-85	.227	.219	.231	68	220	21	50	17	1	3	17	14	1	7	0	71	9	4	.355	.277
Dhaenens, Seth	L-R	6-2	175	5-20-84	.000	.000	.000	2	6	0	0	0	0	0	0	0	1	0	1	0	0	0	.000	.000
Durante, Eric	R-R	5-10	175	7-11-84	.183	.222	.164	22	82	4	15	3	0	1	4	8	3	0	0	15	3	0	.256	.280
Fields, Matthew	R-R	6-4	255	7-8-85	.241	.284	.224	69	266	28	64	17	0	7	29	7	6	0	2	80	4	2	.383	.274
Gummo, Scott	R-R	6-1	230	9-22-82	.163	.100	.181	30	92	6	15	3	0	0	4	9	2	0	1	21	0	0	.196	.250
Hamilton, Josh	L-L	6-4	205	5-21-81	.260	.200	.275	15	50	7	13	3	1	0	5	5	0	0	0	11	0	1	.360	.327
Kennedy, David	B-R	6-2	178	7-10-83	.200	.125	.217	32	85	11	17	3	0	0	3	7	3	1	1	27	3	1	.235	.281
Lagreid, Thomas	R-R	6-1	185	10-24-83	.165	.174	.162	28	91	8	15	7	0	0	3	8	1	2	0	23	1	1	.242	.240
Longoria, Evan	R-R	6-2	180	10-7-85	.424	.750	.320	8	33	5	14	1	1	4	11	5	0	0	1	5	1	0	.879	.487
Loyola, Maiko	R-R	5-11	174	7-19-85	.241	.271	.229	64	216	24	52	10	1	3	24	35	0	6	1	39	11	5	.338	.345
Matulla, John	L-L	6-0	175	8-19-86	.252	.239	.257	62	254	30	64	9	0	4	14	17	6	5	1	54	5	12	.287	.313
Mayer, James	R-R	5-11	165	3-8-84	.290	.200	.333	9	31	5	9	2	0	0	1	2	2	0	0	3	0	1	.355	.371
Paxton, Ian	R-R	6-1	210	9-4-83	.203	.071	.236	23	69	7	14	4	0	1	3	3	1	1	1	20	0	0	.304	.222
Rousseve, Brandon	R-R	6-1	175	8-4-84	.204	.209	.202	50	142	16	29	4	0	0	15	12	1	6	0	51	8	0	.232	.271
Royster, Ryan	R-R	6-2	205	7-25-86	.247	.230	.253	63	231	20	57	15	1	8	29	9	5	1	3	65	5	2	.424	.286
Spring, Matthew	R-R	6-2	215	11-7-84	.204	.231	.191	50	167	13	34	8	0	4	15	13	1	2	2	66	0	2	.323	.262
Stewart, William	R-R	6-0	190	8-28-83	.254	.224	.264	54	197	23	50	16	0	6	27	16	4	0	3	58	1	3	.426	.318

PITCHING	B-T	HT	WT	DOB	W	L	ERA	G	GS	CG	SV	IP	H	R	ER	HR	BB	SO	AVG	vLH	vRH	K/9	BB/9
Baker, Brian	R-R	6-5	190	1-10-83	0	1	2.93	21	0	0	6	31	17	11	10	2	11	31	.153	.209	.118	9.10	3.23
Butler, Joshua	R-R	6-5	195	12-11-84	0	3	5.40	5	2	0	0	13	13	9	8	0	7	12	.265	.333	.182	8.10	4.73
Falk, Matthew	L-R	6-3	190	8-25-84	4	4	3.90	17	6	0	0	58	59	28	25	2	10	47	.268	.324	.240	7.34	1.56
Fines, Woods	R-R	6-4	180	8-14-85	7	3	2.47	14	14	0	0	87	78	30	24	1	17	63	.246	.200	.285	6.49	1.75
Frontz, Neal	R-R	6-3	190	4-6-84	0	2	3.12	21	0	0	5	40	34	14	14	1	10	27	.228	.221	.235	6.02	2.23
Gil, Roberto	R-R	6-1	160	10-24-85	2	2	5.79	20	0	0	0	28	33	21	18	1	13	31	.280	.273	.286	9.96	4.18
Hellickson, Jeremy	R-R	6-1	185	4-8-87	4	3	2.43	15	14	0	0	78	55	24	21	3	16	96	.193	.223	.171	11.12	1.85
Lagreid, Thomas	R-R	6-1	185	10-24-83	0	0	40.50	1	0	0	0	1	4	3	3	1	0	0	.667	1.000	.500	0.00	0.00
Larson, Matt	R-R	6-4	215	4-9-81	0	0	3.00	6	0	0	0	6	7	5	2	0	3	4	.292	.083	.500	6.00	4.50
Morse, Ryan	L-L	6-3	200	5-21-83	1	2	2.50	3	3	0	0	18	17	8	5	1	3	12	.254	.118	.300	6.00	1.50
Muro, Joseph	R-R	6-0	161	2-16-84	1	1	4.15	15	0	0	0	17	14	10	8	0	16	17	.222	.261	.200	8.83	8.31
Nagy, Brett	R-R	6-1	190	11-10-84	1	3	6.46	22	0	0	0	31	35	25	22	7	11	31	.297	.269	.318	9.10	3.23
Owen, Ryan	L-R	6-4	200	7-26-84	5	3	2.65	15	13	0	0	71	63	26	21	2	11	57	.237	.196	.247	7.19	1.39
Reid, Ryan	L-R	5-11	215	4-24-85	1	9	6.24	15	12	0	0	53	60	42	37	2	24	43	.282	.277	.286	7.26	4.05
Rodriguez, Claudio	R-R	6-5	244	6-29-83	1	1	2.14	12	0	0	2	21	17	6	5	0	8	21	.224	.303	.163	9.00	3.43
Rollins, Lewis	R-R	6-1	190	5-25-85	1	3	4.08	12	10	0	0	46	44	25	21	3	14	48	.249	.226	.269	9.32	2.72
Rondon, Celso	R-R	5-11	170	4-7-84	0	1	1.93	14	0	0	1	23	21	9	5	1	8	21	.233	.205	.261	8.10	3.09
Rulon, Ben	L-L	6-2	175	5-25-82	0	1	9.82	4	0	0	0	4	4	4	4	0	1	3	.267	.500	.182	7.36	9.82
Walker, Erik	L-R	6-4	225	10-15-83	3	1	0.48	20	0	0	7	38	18	3	2	0	6	53	.141	.174	.122	12.66	1.43

FIELDING

Catcher	PCT	G	PO	A	E	DP	PB
Lagreid	.954	22	164	24	9	4	2
Paxton	.968	14	112	10	4	0	1
Spring	.989	42	320	46	4	1	8

First Base	PCT	G	PO	A	E	DP
Fields	.990	69	632	49	7	59
Gummo	.951	5	37	2	2	5
Lagreid	1.000	3	15	2	0	0

Second Base	PCT	G	PO	A	E	DP
Callender	.970	26	36	62	3	8

Third Base	PCT	G	PO	A	E	DP
Dhaenens	.917	2	5	6	1	2
Durante	.969	21	36	59	3	19
Rousseve	.963	31	38	65	4	18

Third Base	PCT	G	PO	A	E	DP
Callender	.946	41	27	60	5	6
Gummo	.894	21	10	32	5	1
Longoria	.944	5	4	13	1	4
Mayer	.850	9	4	13	3	0
Rousseve	.909	11	4	16	2	4

Shortstop	PCT	G	PO	A	E	DP
Callender	1.000	1	0	3	0	0
de la Rosa	.943	68	94	186	17	39
Rousseve	.967	7	9	20	1	6

Outfield	PCT	G	PO	A	E	DP
Hamilton	.857	6	6	0	1	0
Kennedy	.943	23	33	0	2	0
Loyola	.981	58	95	9	2	3
Matulia	.993	62	147	4	1	2
Royster	.924	56	73	0	6	0
Stewart	.974	27	38	0	1	0

Princeton Devil Rays — Rookie

Appalachian League

BATTING	B-T	HT	WT	DOB	AVG	vLH	vRH	G	AB	R	H	2B	3B	HR	RBI	BB	HBP	SH	SF	SO	SB	CS	SLG	OBP
Albernaz, Craig	R-R	5-8	177	10-30-82	.186	.143	.200	31	86	11	16	3	0	0	3	7	2	2	0	18	2	0	.221	.263
Ashley, Nevin	R-R	6-2	210	8-14-84	.333	.321	.340	47	153	25	51	8	1	4	28	21	9	1	1	40	7	3	.477	.440
Colon, Kevin	R-R	5-11	165	7-6-84	.169	.094	.216	28	83	7	14	1	1	0	4	9	1	3	0	18	4	5	.205	.258
De Leon, Epifanio	R-R	6-5	205	1-5-86	.210	.224	.200	41	143	15	30	9	1	2	20	6	3	2	1	52	3	0	.329	.255
Dhaenens, Seth	L-R	6-2	175	5-20-84	.233	.209	.240	50	172	19	40	2	1	0	24	16	2	1	1	32	5	8	.256	.304
Gustafson, Chris	L-R	6-1	170	11-2-84	.278	.200	.308	35	90	18	25	6	2	1	17	28	0	0	0	26	6	4	.422	.449
Jennings, Desmond	R-R	6-2	180	10-30-86	.277	.274	.278	56	213	48	59	10	1	4	20	22	6	4	1	39	32	5	.390	.360
Johnson, Joshua	R-R	6-0	205	11-3-82	.467	.750	.364	4	15	2	7	0	1	0	4	2	0	0	0	2	0	0	.600	.529
Lopez, Andrew	R-R	6-1	185	1-18-87	.256	.338	.216	56	199	27	51	11	3	4	27	25	7	1	2	65	9	3	.402	.356
Matthews, Brad	R-R	6-0	175	6-8-83	.300	.353	.231	22	60	9	18	1	0	0	1	4	1	2	0	14	3	1	.317	.354
McCormick, Michael	R-R	6-2	200	9-6-86	.275	.246	.286	62	222	34	61	18	0	10	39	26	7	2	3	64	7	7	.491	.364
O'Malley, Shawn	R-R	5-10	155	12-28-87	.213	.156	.235	50	160	28	34	4	1	1	10	16	7	5	1	38	10	3	.269	.310
Pickerell, Steven	R-R	6-3	215	2-5-82	.291	.259	.321	19	55	5	16	3	0	0	7	2	1	2	1	10	1	1	.345	.322
Sonoqui, Eligio	L-L	6-2	195	1-20-88	.201	.100	.231	40	134	3	27	2	0	0	9	6	0	0	0	43	2	2	.216	.236
Sullivan, Shane	L-L	6-4	215	5-8-86	.207	.364	.150	31	82	14	17	3	0	0	3	17	0	0	0	14	10	6	.244	.343
Wrigley, Henry	R-R	6-3	180	8-9-86	.250	.239	.256	54	188	22	47	9	1	5	26	7	0	3	3	39	5	2	.388	.273

PITCHING	B-T	HT	WT	DOB	W	L	ERA	G	GS	CG	SV	IP	H	R	ER	HR	BB	SO	AVG	vLH	vRH	K/9	BB/9
Andujar, Chris	R-R	6-2	180	8-24-87	3	5	5.66	12	11	0	0	48	52	32	30	2	25	37	.284	.329	.255	6.99	4.72
Barnett, Travis	R-R	6-7	215	10-2-83	1	2	4.24	17	0	0	4	17	20	18	8	0	14	12	.299	.333	.283	6.35	7.41
Cobb, Alexander	R-R	6-1	180	10-7-87	0	0	5.19	6	1	0	0	9	9	7	5	3	3	8	.265	.364	.217	8.31	3.12
Cuevas, Aneudi	R-R	6-1	182	10-6-81	0	0	0.84	11	0	0	0	11	8	5	1	0	6	10	.205	.222	.200	8.44	5.06
Fessler, Christopher	R-R	6-3	200	11-21-84	0	1	5.59	13	0	0	0	19	25	16	12	1	7	17	.301	.346	.281	7.91	3.26
Fisher, Matthew	R-R	6-2	195	9-6-83	0	0	6.48	15	0	0	1	17	16	12	12	1	12	8	.254	.438	.191	4.32	6.48
Florentino, Bladimir	R-R	6-2	187	9-20-84	1	3	3.00	8	5	0	0	27	19	14	9	2	18	29	.202	.257	.169	9.67	6.00
Hayes, Tyree	R-R	6-5	175	8-8-88	3	1	2.48	9	7	1	0	40	34	14	11	3	9	26	.230	.255	.215	5.85	2.03
Larson, Matt	R-R	6-4	215	4-9-81	0	0	5.00	9	0	0	0	9	9	5	5	0	6	2	.281	.143	.320	2.00	6.00
Martin, Troy	L-L	6-3	215	3-28-82	1	1	3.97	10	0	0	0	23	21	10	10	0	11	21	.244	.333	.225	8.34	4.37
Morse, Ryan	L-L	6-3	200	5-21-83	5	3	2.88	10	10	0	0	56	44	20	18	2	18	44	.221	.304	.210	7.03	2.88
Noel, Wilton	R-R	6-5	180	1-1-83	2	5	4.81	13	12	1	0	58	58	38	31	5	20	54	.256	.316	.235	8.38	3.10
Pendarvis, Chad	L-L	6-7	210	6-22-83	4	4	3.47	12	11	1	0	60	61	28	23	6	23	42	.280	.195	.299	6.34	3.47
Ragan, Jason	B-R	6-5	175	12-12-82	4	2	2.55	14	1	0	0	35	35	17	10	2	4	32	.248	.267	.240	8.15	1.02
Rodriguez, Claudio	R-R	6-5	244	6-29-83	0	0	4.66	6	0	0	0	10	11	6	5	2	5	11	.275	.250	.281	10.24	4.66
Suchowiecki, Mark	R-L	6-1	195	2-22-83	3	4	3.31	13	4	0	0	33	31	18	12	4	10	28	.244	.300	.234	7.71	2.76
Trafton, Alex	R-R	6-5	225	11-27-82	1	1	1.44	18	0	0	7	25	19	6	4	0	11	20	.218	.240	.210	7.20	3.96
Welch, Scott	R-R	6-4	180	11-8-82	0	4	4.86	15	2	0	0	33	33	19	18	2	9	24	.270	.306	.256	6.48	2.43
Zimmerman, Ryan	R-R	6-0	185	9-19-84	0	0	6.35	11	0	0	0	11	11	8	8	1	5	10	.256	.316	.208	7.94	3.97

FIELDING

Catcher	PCT	G	PO	A	E	DP	PB
Albernaz	.969	31	177	41	7	1	3
Ashley	.989	26	165	21	2	1	7
Johnson	1.000	4	27	5	0	1	1
Pickerell	.974	8	67	8	2	0	2

First Base	PCT	G	PO	A	E	DP
Sonoqui	.982	29	204	17	4	26
Wrigley	.994	40	330	22	2	32

Second Base	PCT	G	PO	A	E	DP
Colon	.857	3	3	9	2	1
Dhaenens	.982	50	103	112	4	32
Matthews	.959	15	30	41	3	12

Third Base	PCT	G	PO	A	E	DP
Colon	1.000	3	2	4	0	1
McCormick	.851	61	37	135	30	10

Shortstop	PCT	G	PO	A	E	DP
Colon	.954	20	37	46	4	13
O'Malley	.963	46	71	140	8	30

Outfield	PCT	G	PO	A	E	DP
De Leon	.968	40	88	2	3	0
Gustafson	1.000	26	40	2	0	1
Jennings	.983	54	112	1	2	0
Lopez	.961	56	68	5	3	1
Sullivan	.857	23	23	1	4	

TEXAS RANGERS

BY EVAN GRANT

The Rangers began 2006 with hopes of ending the longest playoff drought in the American League West and manager Buck Showalter proclaiming his club ready to play in October.

But the season ended as so many have for the Rangers: more disappointment and more changes on the way.

The Rangers, who have not been to the playoffs since 1999, had plenty of strong individual performances in 2006, but came up short again as a team. Texas finished third in the AL West at 80-82, and it ultimately cost Showalter his job. In four years under Showalter, Texas never finished higher than third in the four-team division.

Former Athletics third base coach Ron Washington replaced Showalter and becomes the Rangers' first black manager and the 11th in major league history. Washington will be charged with figuring out how to make the team's individual success translate into victories.

Among last season's highlights:

■ Michael Young had 200 hits for a fourth consecutive year, and the shortstop was the MVP of the All-Star Game in Pittsburgh. He also hit .300 for a fourth straight season and set a club record with 52 doubles while playing every game.

■ Gary Matthews Jr. set club records in almost every offensive category for leadoff hitters and was among the top defensive center fielders. Matthews made himself into a coveted free agent by hitting .313/.371/.495 with 44 doubles and making a handful of amazing catches. His grab well above the center field wall on Mike Lamb's

ORGANIZATION LEADERS

BATTING
*Minimum 250 at-bats

*AVG	Barrios, Victor, AZL Rangers	.307
R	Harrison, Ben, Bakersfield/Frisco	89
H	Harrison, Ben, Bakersfield/Frisco	164
TB	Harrison, Ben, Bakersfield/Frisco	287
2B	Mahar, Kevin, Frisco	38
	Murphy, Steven, AZL Rangers/Bakersfield	38
3B	Hulett Jr., Tim, Bakersfield/Frisco	11
HR	Gold, Nate, Frisco	34
RBI	Gold, Nate, Frisco	107
	Harrison, Ben, Bakersfield/Frisco	107
BB	Hulett, Tug, Bakersfield/Frisco	92
SO	Gac, Ian, Bakersfield/Clinton	179
SB	Guzman, Freddy, Portland/Oklahoma	31
*OBP	Hulett, Tug, Bakersfield/Frisco	.411
*SLG	Gold, Nate, Frisco	.564
XBH	Gold, Nate, Frisco	67

PITCHING
#Minimum 75 innings

W	Diamond, Thomas, Frisco	12
	Kometani, Paul, Bakersfield/Frisco	12
L	Rasner, Jacob, Clinton	16
#ERA	Volquez, Edinson, Oklahoma	3.21
G	Ramirez, Erasmo, Oklahoma	54
CG	Dickey, R.A., Oklahoma	3
SV	Corey, Bryan, Frisco/Oklahoma/Pawtucket	15
IP	Mathis, Douglas, Bakersfield/Frisco	161
BB	Diamond, Thomas, Frisco	78
SO	Danks, John, Frisco/Oklahoma	154
#AVG	Volquez, Edinson, Oklahoma	.203

MAJOR LEAGUE: Mark Teixeira, 1b

Teixeira bounced back from a tough first half to lead the Rangers in six offensive categories. Though his home run total dipped to 33 after he hit 43 in 2005, he ranked third in the American League with 79 extra-base hits and batted .282/.371/.514 overall with 110 RBIs and 45 doubles.

MINOR LEAGUE: Nate Gold, 1b

Gold has moved slowly, spending a full year at each level since being drafted in the 10th round in 2002. He finally reached Double-A at the end of 2005 and began to separate himself in 2006, leading the Texas League with 34 home runs and finishing second in RBIs (103) and slugging percentage (.582).

drive July 1 might have been the best defensive play of 2006.

■ Mark Teixeira won his second consecutive Gold Glove at first base and hit .282/.371/.514 with 33 homers, 45 doubles and 110 RBIs in what many termed a down year for the fourth-year player. He bounced back from a down first half to set personal best in several categories, though his home run numbers were down.

■ Kevin Millwood proved that big-time free agents could come to Texas and succeed. In the first year of a five-year, $60 million deal, the righthander went 16-12, 4.52 with 157 strikeouts in 215 innings.

The list didn't end there. Mark DeRosa (.296/.357/.456) had a breakout year, righthander Akinori Otsuka (32 saves) established himself as a legitimate closer and righthander Vicente Padilla (15-10, 4.50) proved to be a steal in his first season with the club.

And still the Rangers faded in the second half. After Millwood and Padilla, no other Rangers pitcher won more than seven games. And while the pitching was better, the team ERA still ranked last among the four AL West teams.

On the minor league side, even individual accomplishments were lacking. While lefthander John Danks (9-9, 4.24 at Triple-A Oklahoma and Double-A Frisco) continued to move forward, and righthander Eric Hurley (8-7, 3.53 at high Class A Bakersfield and Frisco) took a big step toward turning the Rangers' prized trio of pitching prospects into a quartet, two other members took step backward.

Righthander Edinson Volquez (1-6, 7.29 with the Rangers) struggled with control and was a significant flop in the major leagues. Righthander Thomas Diamond (12-5, 4.24 with 78 walks at Frisco) also had control problems. All four prospects are expected to start 2007 in the minor leagues.

The Rangers finished the minor league season with the worst winning percentage (.423) of any major league organization and didn't have a single affiliate make the postseason. In fact, four of their affiliates finished with the worst records in their leagues.

Texas Rangers   MLB

American League

BATTING	B-T	HT	WT	DOB	AVG	vLH	vRH	G	AB	R	H	2B	3B	HR	RBI	BB	HBP	SH	SF	SO	SB	CS	SLG	OBP
Arias, Joaquin	R-R	6-1	165	9-21-84	.545	.333	.800	6	11	4	6	1	0	0	1	1	0	0	0	0	0	1	.636	.583
Barajas, Rod	R-R	6-2	230	9-5-75	.256	.156	.279	97	344	49	88	20	0	11	41	17	4	5	1	51	0	0	.410	.298
Blalock, Hank	L-R	6-1	200	11-21-80	.266	.216	.284	152	591	76	157	26	3	16	89	51	2	0	2	98	1	0	.401	.325
Botts, Jason	B-R	6-5	250	7-26-80	.220	.100	.250	20	50	8	11	4	0	1	6	8	0	0	2	18	0	0	.360	.317
Brown, Adrian	B-R	6-0	190	2-7-74	.194	.133	.238	25	36	6	7	1	0	0	2	2	0	1	1	9	1	0	.222	.231
Cruz, Nelson	R-R	6-3	225	7-1-80	.223	.217	.226	41	130	15	29	3	0	6	22	7	0	0	1	32	1	0	.385	.261
DeRosa, Mark	R-R	6-1	205	2-26-75	.296	.342	.278	136	520	78	154	40	2	13	74	44	6	0	2	102	4	4	.456	.357
Guzman, Freddy	B-R	5-10	165	1-20-81	.286	.500	.000	9	7	1	2	0	0	0	0	1	1	0	0	1	0	0	.286	.444
Hairston, Jerry	R-R	5-10	185	5-29-76	.205	.139	.250	63	88	17	18	3	1	0	6	9	1	2	0	20	2	2	.261	.283
Hyzdu, Adam	R-R	6-2	220	12-6-71	.250	.000	.500	2	4	0	1	0	0	0	0	0	0	0	0	2	0	0	.250	.250
Jimenez, D'Angelo	B-R	6-0	215	12-21-77	.211	.200	.214	20	57	7	12	3	0	1	8	10	0	1	0	6	0	0	.316	.328
2-team (8 Oakland)					.183	—	—	28	71	8	13	3	0	1	8	16	0	1	0	13	0	0	.268	.333
Kinsler, Ian	R-R	6-0	200	6-22-82	.286	.271	.292	120	423	65	121	27	1	14	55	40	3	1	7	64	11	4	.454	.347
Laird, Gerald	R-R	6-1	225	11-13-79	.296	.400	.241	78	243	46	72	20	1	7	22	12	2	1	2	54	3	1	.473	.332
Lee, Carlos	R-R	6-2	240	6-20-76	.322	.339	.316	59	236	42	76	19	1	9	35	20	0	4	26	7	0		.525	.369
Matthews, Gary	B-R	6-3	225	8-25-74	.313	.314	.313	147	620	102	194	44	6	19	79	58	4	0	8	99	10	7	.495	.371
Mench, Kevin	R-R	6-0	225	1-7-78	.284	.333	.269	87	320	36	91	18	1	12	50	23	4	0	2	42	1	0	.459	.338
Meyer, Drew	L-R	5-10	200	8-29-81	.214	.333	.182	5	14	1	3	0	0	0	0	0	0	1	0	8	0	0	.214	.214
Nevin, Phil	R-R	6-3	220	1-19-71	.216	.267	.198	46	176	26	38	8	0	9	31	21	2	0	0	39	0	0	.415	.307
2-team (16 Minnesota)					.211	—	—	62	218	28	46	9	0	10	35	31	2	1	1	54	0	0	.390	.313
Nix, Laynce	L-L	6-0	200	10-30-80	.094	.250	.071	9	32	1	3	1	0	0	4	0	1	0	1	17	0	0	.125	.118
Ojeda, Miguel	R-R	6-1	230	1-29-75	.308	.250	.333	5	13	0	4	2	0	0	4	0	0	0	0	3	0	0	.462	.308
Stairs, Matt	L-R	5-9	215	2-27-68	.210	.188	.215	26	81	6	17	4	0	3	11	6	1	0	0	22	0	0	.370	.273
3-team (14 Detroit, 77 Kansas City)					.247	—	—	117	348	42	86	21	0	13	51	40	3	0	2	86	0	0	.420	.328
Teixeira, Mark	B-R	6-3	220	4-11-80	.282	.302	.275	162	628	99	177	45	1	33	110	89	4	0	6	128	2	1	.514	.371
Wilkerson, Brad	L-L	6-0	205	6-1-77	.222	.190	.230	95	320	56	71	15	2	15	44	37	3	2	3	116	3	2	.422	.306
Young, Eric	R-R	5-9	185	5-11-67	.200	.400	.000	4	10	1	2	1	1	0	2	1	0	1	0	1	0	0	.500	.273
Young, Michael	R-R	6-1	200	10-19-76	.314	.295	.320	162	691	93	217	52	3	14	103	48	1	0	8	96	7	3	.459	.356

PITCHING	B-T	HT	WT	DOB	W	L	ERA	G	GS	CG	SV	IP	H	R	ER	HR	BB	SO	AVG	vLH	vRH	K/9	BB/9
Alfonseca, Antonio	R-R	6-5	250	4-16-72	0	0	5.63	19	0	0	0	16	23	10	10	3	7	5	.348	.452	.257	2.81	3.94
Bauer, Rick	R-R	6-6	225	1-10-77	3	1	3.55	58	1	0	2	71	73	31	28	4	25	35	.272	.231	.299	4.44	3.17
Benoit, Joaquin	R-R	6-3	220	7-26-77	1	1	4.86	56	0	0	0	80	68	49	43	5	38	85	.224	.191	.245	9.60	4.29
Castro, Fabio	L-L	5-7	175	1-20-85	0	0	4.32	4	0	0	0	8	6	5	4	0	7	5	.200	.250	.192	5.40	7.56
Cordero, Francisco	R-R	6-2	235	5-11-75	7	4	4.81	49	0	0	6	49	49	27	26	5	16	54	.265	.280	.252	9.99	2.96
Corey, Bryan	R-R	6-0	180	10-21-73	1	1	2.60	16	0	0	0	17	15	5	5	0	8	13	.231	.147	.323	6.75	4.15
2-team (16 Boston)					2	1	3.69	32	0	0	0	39	35	16	16	1	15	28	—	—	—	6.46	3.46
Dickey, R.A.	R-R	6-3	220	10-29-74	0	1	18.90	1	1	0	0	3	8	7	7	6	1	1	.471	.000	.500	2.70	2.70
Eaton, Adam	R-R	6-2	200	11-23-77	7	4	5.12	13	13	0	0	65	78	38	37	11	24	43	.299	.320	.279	5.95	3.32
Feldman, Scott	L-R	6-6	225	2-7-83	0	2	3.92	36	0	0	0	41	42	19	18	4	10	30	.266	.280	.259	6.53	2.18
Francisco, Frank	R-R	6-2	235	9-11-79	0	1	4.91	8	0	0	0	7	8	4	4	2	2	6	.267	.000	.444	7.36	2.45
Koronka, John	L-L	6-1	180	7-3-80	7	7	5.69	23	23	0	0	125	145	80	79	17	47	61	.294	.274	.300	4.39	3.38
Littleton, Wes	R-R	6-2	210	9-2-82	2	1	1.73	33	0	0	1	36	23	7	7	2	13	17	.189	.256	.157	4.21	3.22
Loe, Kameron	R-R	6-7	240	9-10-81	3	6	5.86	15	15	1	0	78	105	54	51	10	22	34	.317	.313	.321	3.91	2.53
Mahay, Ron	L-L	6-2	190	6-28-71	1	3	3.95	62	0	0	0	57	54	30	25	7	28	56	.250	.240	.258	8.84	4.42
Masset, Nick	R-R	6-4	190	5-17-82	0	0	4.15	8	0	0	0	9	9	4	4	0	2	4	.300	.250	.357	4.15	2.08
Millwood, Kevin	R-R	6-4	230	12-24-74	16	12	4.52	34	34	2	0	215	228	114	108	23	53	157	.272	.285	.258	6.57	2.22
Otsuka, Akinori	R-R	6-0	210	1-13-72	2	4	2.11	63	0	0	32	60	53	17	14	3	11	47	.241	.287	.190	7.09	1.66
Padilla, Vicente	R-R	6-2	220	9-27-77	15	10	4.50	33	33	0	0	200	206	108	100	21	70	156	.266	.305	.228	7.02	3.15
Rheinecker, John	L-L	6-2	235	5-29-79	4	6	5.86	21	13	0	0	71	104	46	46	6	19	28	.349	.197	.392	3.57	2.42
Rupe, Josh	R-R	6-2	210	8-18-82	0	1	3.41	16	0	0	0	29	33	11	11	2	9	14	.287	.225	.320	4.34	2.79
Shouse, Brian	L-L	5-11	190	9-26-68	0	0	4.15	6	0	0	0	4	6	2	2	1	1	3	.316	.400	.222	6.23	2.08
Tejeda, Robinson	R-R	6-3	230	3-24-82	5	5	4.28	14	14	0	0	74	83	40	35	10	32	40	.288	.331	.250	4.89	3.91
Volquez, Edinson	R-R	6-0	200	7-3-83	1	6	7.29	8	8	0	0	33	52	28	27	7	17	15	.359	.361	.357	4.05	4.59
Wasdin, John	R-R	6-2	190	8-5-72	2	2	5.10	9	0	0	0	30	33	19	17	6	13	16	.266	.328	.212	4.80	3.90
Wells, Kip	R-R	6-3	205	4-21-77	1	0	5.63	2	2	0	0	8	15	6	5	0	3	4	.405	.278	.526	4.50	3.38
Wilson, C.J.	L-L	6-1	215	11-18-80	2	4	4.06	44	0	0	1	44	39	23	20	7	18	43	.234	.155	.292	8.73	3.65

FIELDING

Catcher	PCT	G	PO	A	E	DP	PB
Barajas	.984	94	591	35	10	2	5
Laird	.986	71	392	30	6	5	5
Ojeda	1.000	5	21	2	0	0	1

First Base	PCT	G	PO	A	E	DP
Barajas	1.000	5	14	1	0	0
DeRosa	1.000	1	4	1	0	1
Nevin	1.000	1	8	0	0	2
Stairs	1.000	1	2	0	0	1
Teixeira	.997	159	1480	88	4	158

Second Base	PCT	G	PO	A	E	DP
DeRosa	.993	26	50	86	1	16
Hairston Jr.	.800	1	2	2	1	1
Jimenez	.944	16	35	32	4	12
Kinsler	.973	119	247	393	18	94
Meyer	1.000	3	8	6	0	1

Young	1.000	1	2	6	0	2

Third Base	PCT	G	PO	A	E	DP
Arias	1.000	1	1	4	0	0
Blalock	.963	122	72	237	12	20
DeRosa	.971	40	19	82	3	6
Hairston Jr.	1.000	1	1	1	0	0
Jimenez	1.000	2	0	1	0	0

Shortstop	PCT	G	PO	A	E	DP
Arias	1.000	5	6	9	0	2
DeRosa	1.000	7	9	19	0	5
Hairston Jr.	1.000	3	4	6	0	3
Meyer	.000	1	0	1	0	0
Young	.981	155	241	492	14	113

Outfield	PCT	G	PO	A	E	DP
Botts	1.000	1	1	0	0	0
Brown	.971	24	31	3	1	1
Cruz	1.000	39	69	4	0	1
DeRosa	.993	64	132	5	1	1
Guzman	1.000	4	5	0	0	0
Hairston Jr.	1.000	52	53	8	0	2
Hyzdu	1.000	1	3	0	0	0
Laird	—	1	0	0	0	0
Lee	.976	51	82	1	2	0
Matthews	.980	145	340	8	7	2
Mench	.992	72	128	3	1	1
Meyer	1.000	1	0	0	0	0
Nix	1.000	9	21	2	0	2
Stairs	1.000	1	1	0	0	0
Wilkerson	.993	82	143	7	1	3
Young	1.000	1	4	0	0	0

General manager: Jon Daniels. **Farm director:** John Lombardo. **Scouting director:** Ron Hopkins.

Class	Team	League	W	L	PCT	Finish*	Manager	Affiliate Since
Majors	Texas	American	80	82	.494	9th (14)	Buck Showalter	—
Triple-A	Oklahoma RedHawks	Pacific Coast	74	70	.503	8th (16)	Tim Ireland	1983
Double-A	Frisco RoughRiders	Texas	72	68	.514	5th (8)	Darryl Kennedy	2003
High A	Bakersfield Blaze	California	58	82	.414	10th (10)	Arnie Beyeler	2005
Low A	Clinton LumberKings	Midwest	45	94	.324	14th (14)	Carlos Subero	2003
Short-season	Spokane Indians	Northwest	26	50	.342	8th (8)	Mike Micucci	2003
Rookie	AZL Rangers	Arizona	19	37	.339	9th (9)	Bob Skube	2003
OVERALL 2006 MINOR LEAGUE RECORD			294	401	.423	30th (30)		

*Finish in overall standings (No. of teams in league). +League champion

Oklahoma RedHawks — Triple-A

Pacific Coast League

BATTING	B-T	HT	WT	DOB	AVG	vLH	vRH	G	AB	R	H	2B	3B	HR	RBI	BB	HBP	SH	SF	SO	SB	CS	SLG	OBP
Arias, Joaquin	R-R	6-1	165	9-21-84	.268	.275	.265	124	493	56	132	14	10	4	49	19	4	2	7	64	26	10	.361	.296
Baldiris, Aarom	R-R	6-2	195	1-5-83	.216	.261	.200	78	264	20	57	9	1	2	23	11	3	3	3	46	1	2	.280	.253
Berg, Dave	R-R	5-11	205	9-3-70	.185	.250	.158	8	27	2	5	0	0	0	0	2	0	1	0	5	0	0	.185	.241
Botts, Jason	B-R	6-5	250	7-26-80	.309	.385	.282	63	220	43	68	19	1	13	39	31	4	0	4	61	6	0	.582	.398
Brewer, Jace	R-R	6-0	190	6-9-79	.242	.250	.239	65	194	15	47	8	2	2	17	10	2	6	2	36	1	4	.335	.284
Brown, Adrian	B-R	6-0	190	2-7-74	.295	.295	.295	36	122	15	36	4	1	1	11	17	0	2	1	18	11	1	.369	.379
Burke, Jamie	R-R	6-0	225	9-24-71	.278	.310	.267	102	370	46	103	21	1	10	49	22	3	3	1	41	0	0	.422	.323
DeRosa, Mark	R-R	6-1	205	2-26-75	.500	.571	.400	3	12	2	6	1	0	0	0	0	0	0	0	1	0	0	.583	.500
Diaz, Victor	R-R	6 0	200	12-10-81	.385	.500	.200	3	13	1	5	0	0	0	2	1	0	0	1	6	0	0	.385	.400
Durazo, Erubiel	L-L	6-3	240	1-23-75	.299	.125	.365	22	77	9	23	5	0	2	12	9	0	0	0	12	0	0	.442	.372
Eldridge, Rashad	B-R	6-1	185	10-16-81	.220	.229	.216	36	123	10	27	3	0	2	14	12	1	1	2	33	3	3	.293	.290
Gregorio, Tom	R-R	6-2	215	5-5-77	.218	.206	.224	37	110	8	24	2	0	2	15	10	0	2	2	23	0	0	.291	.279
Guzman, Freddy	B-R	5-10	165	1-20-81	.282	.244	.300	69	252	45	71	9	2	1	14	36	2	2	1	36	31	9	.345	.375
2-team (30 Portland)					.279	—	—	99	376	60	105	16	4	3	28	50	2	3	1	55	42	12	.367	.366
Harrigan, Hunter	R-R	6-1	210	4-17-83	.000	.000	.000	1	4	0	0	0	0	0	0	0	0	0	0	4	0	0	.000	.000
Hart, Jason	R-R	6-4	235	9-5-77	.254	.304	.237	88	307	39	78	19	1	14	45	23	5	2	1	61	1	1	.459	.315
Hatcher, Justin	R-R	5-10	200	5-12-80	.143	.000	.167	7	14	2	2	0	0	1	1	0	0	0	0	6	0	0	.357	.143
Hyzdu, Adam	R-R	6-2	220	12-6-71	.271	.413	.217	128	439	64	119	25	4	19	80	74	1	0	10	102	7	4	.476	.370
Kinsler, Ian	R-R	6-0	200	6-22-82	.256	.412	.136	10	39	7	10	3	0	2	6	2	0	0	5	1	1	.487	.293
Matthews, Gary	B-R	6-3	225	8-25-74	.429	.333	.500	6	21	10	9	2	0	1	4	1	0	0	0	2	0	.524	.538
McDougall, Marshall	R-R	6-1	200	12-19-78	.214	.400	.111	4	14	1	3	1	0	0	1	0	0	0	0	1	0	0	.286	.214
Meyer, Drew	L-R	5-10	200	8-29-81	.228	.256	.219	95	364	37	83	14	4	2	28	27	0	8	4	91	9	11	.305	.278
Morrissey, Adam	R-R	5-11	170	6-8-81	.236	.462	.152	42	144	13	34	8	1	1	15	11	2	1	2	38	2	3	.326	.296
Nix, Laynce	L-L	6-0	200	10-30-80	.269	.231	.284	77	286	39	77	14	1	10	55	18	6	1	3	77	4	1	.430	.323
2-team (18 Nashville)					.297	—	—	95	354	55	105	19	2	17	68	22	7	1	3	95	4	1	.506	.347
Ojeda, Miguel	R-R	6-1	230	1-29-75	.340	.467	.281	14	47	8	16	2	0	4	6	0	0	0	8	0	0	.383	.415
2-team (17 Colorado Springs)					.313	—	—	31	99	19	31	6	1	2	8	18	0	1	1	18	1	0	.455	.415
Olson, Tim	R-R	6-2	200	8-1-78	.128	.000	.156	13	39	2	5	0	0	0	1	2	0	0	0	9	1	0	.128	.171
Simon, Randall	L-L	6-0	240	5-25-75	.317	.238	.357	19	63	3	20	5	0	1	7	7	1	0	1	7	0	0	.444	.389
Sinisi, Vince	L-L	6-0	195	11-7-81	.220	.333	.184	14	50	6	11	4	0	0	7	5	0	0	1	9	0	0	.300	.298
Smith, Will	L-R	6-0	200	10-23-81	.280	.394	.242	43	132	14	37	7	0	3	15	15	0	0	1	26	0	0	.402	.351
Trzesniak, Nick	R-R	6-0	210	11-19-80	.255	.279	.246	50	161	20	41	9	0	1	12	15	0	3	1	29	4	2	.329	.316
2-team (18 Albuquerque)					.262	—	—	68	210	28	55	10	1	4	26	22	0	3	2	38	4	2	.376	.329
Wathan, Derek	B-R	6-3	190	12-13-76	.125	.000	.167	3	8	0	1	0	0	0	1	0	0	0	1	1	0	.125	.125
2-team (68 Memphis)					.267	—	—	71	258	26	69	16	7	5	20	10	0	2	0	42	9	3	.442	.295
Webster, Anthony	L-R	6-0	197	4-10-83	.269	.257	.273	69	242	30	65	15	2	3	19	13	4	6	0	36	16	4	.384	.317
Yan, Ruddy	B-R	6-0	160	1-13-82	.220	.278	.188	20	50	9	11	1	1	0	1	6	3	1	0	5	4	0	.280	.328
Young, Eric	R-R	5-9	185	5-11-67	.222	.167	.238	9	27	3	6	2	3	0	1	4	2	0	0	4	0	2	.519	.364

PITCHING	B-T	HT	WT	DOB	W	L	ERA	G	GS	CG	SV	IP	H	R	ER	HR	BB	SO	AVG	vLH	vRH	K/9	BB/9
Alfonseca, Antonio	R-R	6-5	250	4-16-72	0	1	6.00	3	0	0	0	3	4	2	2	0	1	1	.400	.333	.429	3.00	3.00
Baker, Chris	R-R	6-1	195	8-24-77	0	0	0.00	1	0	0	0	2	1	0	0	0	1	1	.143	.000	.167	4.50	4.50
2-team (26 Round Rock)					9	4	2.62	27	6	0	1	86	78	33	25	5	29	41	—	—	—	4.29	3.03
Bukvich, Ryan	R-R	6-2	250	5-13-78	3	2	6.11	31	0	0	0	35	44	27	24	8	22	37	.297	.359	.250	9.42	5.60
Bumstead, Michael	R-R	6-4	210	7-8-77	0	0	0.00	1	0	0	0	2	1	0	0	0	0	0	.143	.500	.000	0.00	0.00
Carlson, Jesse	L-L	6-1	160	12-31-80	0	0	0.00	10	0	0	0	11	6	0	0	0	4	5	.167	.182	.160	4.09	3.27
Castro, Fabio	L-L	5-7	175	1-20-85	0	0	4.91	1	1	0	0	4	5	2	2	0	1	5	.313	.250	.333	12.27	2.45
Chavez, Jesse	R-R	6-1	160	8-21-83	0	0	4.50	1	0	0	0	2	3	1	1	0	0	3	.333	.667	.167	13.50	0.00
Corey, Bryan	R-R	6-0	180	01-21-73	0	0	0.60	12	0	0	0	8	15	8	1	1	0	2	16	.163	.167	.161	9.60	1.20
Danks, John	L-L	6-1	200	4-15-85	4	5	4.33	14	13	0	0	71	67	43	34	11	34	72	.248	.177	.277	9.17	4.33
Diaz, Jose	R-R	6-0	240	4-13-80	0	0	3.28	28	1	0	4	36	28	14	13	2	46	42	.215	.185	.246	11.61	5.55
2-team (13 Omaha)					2	3	4.00	41	1	0	4	54	42	27	24	5	37	62	—	—	—	10.33	6.17
Dickey, R.A.	R-R	6-3	220	10-29-74	9	8	4.92	22	19	3	1	132	134	80	72	17	46	61	.272	.279	.267	4.17	3.14
Durocher, Jayson	R-R	6-3	230	8-18-74	1	0	7.94	4	0	0	0	6	5	6	5	1	3	7	.360	.500	.267	11.12	4.76
Eaton, Adam	R-R	6-2	200	11-23-77	0	0	1.50	2	2	0	0	6	3	1	1	0	2	8	.136	.273	.000	12.00	3.00
Feldman, Scott	L-R	6-6	225	2-7-83	2	2	1.98	23	0	0	4	27	20	9	6	2	9	24	.206	.276	.176	7.90	2.96
Gregorio, Tom	R-R	6-2	215	5-5-77	0	0	0.00	1	0	0	0	2	0	0	0	0	0	1	.167	.000	.333	9.00	4.50
Hudgins, John	R-R	6-2	195	8-31-81	1	1	6.38	7	2	0	0	18	18	17	13	3	7	16	.250	.222	.267	7.85	3.44
2-team (2 Portland)					2	2	5.40	9	4	0	0	25	29	25	15	4	8	23	—	—	—	8.28	2.88
Jimenez, Kelvin	R-R	6-0	180	10-27-80	4	2	5.21	26	0	0	1	38	40	22	22	4	24	40	.265	.204	.299	9.47	5.68
Knott, Eric	L-L	5-10	191	9-23-74	0	0	3.44	3	0	0	0	18	21	7	7	2	3	8	.292	.273	.300	3.93	1.47
Koronka, John	L-L	6-1	180	7-3-80	0	1	4.12	3	3	0	0	20	19	9	9	2	7	17	.260	.250	.263	7.78	3.20

	B-T	HT	WT	DOB	W	L	ERA	G	GS	CG	SV	IP	H	R	ER	HR	BB	SO	AVG	vLH	vRH	K/9	BB/9
Lee, Derek	L-L	6-3	208	8-20-74	6	12	4.26	29	23	1	0	144	156	73	68	15	53	92	.283	.255	.293	5.76	3.32
Leicester, Jon	R-R	6-2	230	2-7-79	0	1	10.00	2	2	0	0	9	17	11	10	0	3	7	.415	.294	.500	7.00	3.00
Littleton, Wes	R-R	6-2	210	9-2-82	4	1	2.16	13	0	0	2	17	14	4	4	3	5	15	.233	.273	.211	8.10	2.70
Loe, Kameron	R-R	6-7	240	9-10-81	1	2	9.13	13	3	0	1	23	32	24	23	3	13	21	.327	.300	.345	8.34	5.16
Mahay, Ron	L-L	6-2	190	6-28-71	0	1	1.42	5	0	0	2	6	5	4	1	0	0	11	.227	.222	.231	15.63	0.00
Masset, Nick	R-R	6-4	190	5-17-82	4	5	4.81	24	7	1	3	67	79	48	36	4	28	65	.293	.319	.267	8.69	3.74
Morrissey, Adam	R-R	5-11	170	6-8-81	1	0	0.00	1	0	0	0	1	0	0	0	0	3	0	.000	.000	.000	0.00	27.00
Ramirez, Erasmo	L-L	6-0	190	4-29-76	6	3	3.59	54	0	0	9	68	69	27	27	5	7	47	.262	.239	.275	6.25	0.93
Rheinecker, John	L-L	6-2	230	5-29-79	4	5	2.52	15	15	2	0	93	93	33	26	5	24	68	.266	.291	.259	6.58	2.32
Rupe, Josh	R-R	6-2	210	8-18-82	1	1	3.38	12	0	0	2	13	13	6	5	0	6	4	.271	.280	.261	2.70	4.05
Shouse, Brian	L-L	5-11	190	9-26-68	0	1	5.40	5	0	0	0	5	7	5	3	1	4	3	.318	.333	.316	5.40	7.20
Silva, Jose	R-R	6-6	235	12-19-73	0	0	6.75	3	0	0	0	7	11	6	5	0	1	4	.355	.000	.423	5.40	1.35
Tejeda, Robinson	R-R	6-3	230	3-24-82	6	2	3.15	15	15	0	0	80	61	30	28	7	42	79	.210	.211	.210	8.89	4.73
Volquez, Edinson	R-R	6-0	200	7-3-83	6	6	3.21	21	21	0	0	121	86	51	43	9	72	130	.203	.167	.235	9.70	5.37
Walker, Kevin	L-L	6-3	215	9-20-76	6	5	4.63	46	5	0	2	68	77	37	35	5	32	59	.296	.176	.361	7.81	4.24
Ward, Jeremy	R-R	6-3	235	2-24-78	1	0	5.40	4	0	0	2	8	13	7	5	0	2	4	.371	.250	.474	4.32	2.16
Wasdin, John	R-R	6-2	190	8-5-72	3	3	2.00	13	9	1	0	63	52	23	14	2	17	62	.225	.295	.176	8.86	2.43
Wilson, C.J.	L-L	6-1	215	11-18-80	1	0	2.45	9	0	0	2	11	10	3	3	0	5	17	.233	.067	.321	13.91	4.09

FIELDING

Catcher	PCT	G	PO	A	E	DP	PB
Burke	.987	55	418	33	6	5	7
Gregorio	.992	35	234	29	2	0	11
Harrigan	1.000	1	2	1	0	0	0
Hatcher	1.000	1	7	0	0	0	0
Ojeda	.991	14	96	12	1	3	0
Trzesniak	.992	45	327	26	3	2	5

First Base	PCT	G	PO	A	E	DP
Berg	1.000	6	49	4	0	3
Botts	.976	18	146	14	4	18
Brewer	1.000	3	23	3	0	1
Burke	1.000	18	148	11	0	18
Durazo	1.000	1	7	0	0	0
Hart	.997	85	727	36	2	69
Simon	.977	4	37	5	1	5
Sinisi	.990	12	95	4	1	11
Trzesniak	.929	3	23	3	2	2

Second Base	PCT	G	PO	A	E	DP
Baldiris	.950	8	17	21	2	8
Brewer	1.000	25	44	57	0	16
DeRosa	1.000	2	1	2	0	1

	PCT	G	PO	A	E	DP
Kinsler	.963	10	21	31	2	9
Meyer	.984	70	124	185	5	44
Morrissey	.971	36	51	81	4	23
Yan	.833	3	3	7	2	1
Young	1.000	2	3	7	0	2

Third Base	PCT	G	PO	A	E	DP
Baldiris	.943	70	39	127	10	3
Berg	1.000	2	0	2	0	1
Brewer	.957	33	13	54	3	5
Burke	.937	24	5	54	4	2
DeRosa	1.000	1	1	4	0	0
McDougall	1.000	4	3	7	0	1
Meyer	.923	5	4	8	1	1
Morrissey	.947	4	4	14	1	3
Olson	.952	8	5	15	1	2
Wathan	1.000	1	1	0	0	0
Young	1.000	1	1	2	0	0

Shortstop	PCT	G	PO	A	E	DP
Arias	.957	124	176	356	24	81
Brewer	1.000	4	1	10	0	2
Meyer	.967	19	23	64	3	16

	PCT	G	PO	A	E	DP
Wathan	1.000	1	0	2	0	1

Outfield	PCT	G	PO	A	E	DP
Botts	.957	27	42	2	2	0
Brewer	1.000	2	1	0	0	0
Brown	.981	28	53	0	1	0
Diaz	.500	1	1	0	1	0
Eldridge	.929	31	48	4	4	0
Guzman	.993	67	137	3	1	0
Hart	—	2	0	0	0	0
Hatcher	1.000	2	2	0	0	0
Hyzdu	.996	120	218	18	1	5
Matthews	.714	2	5	0	2	0
Meyer	.857	4	6	0	1	0
Nix	.986	68	133	3	2	1
Olson	1.000	1	1	0	0	0
Sinisi	1.000	3	5	0	0	0
Smith	.968	22	27	3	1	0
Webster	.943	56	97	2	6	2
Yan	1.000	16	29	1	0	0
Young	1.000	4	7	0	0	0

Frisco RoughRiders — Double-A

Texas League

BATTING	B-T	HT	WT	DOB	AVG	vLH	vRH	G	AB	R	H	2B	3B	HR	RBI	BB	HBP	SH	SF	SO	SB	CS	SLG	OBP
Baldiris, Aarom	R-R	6-2	195	1-5-83	.307	.417	.289	25	88	14	27	8	0	2	11	4	5	0	0	8	2	3	.466	.371
Benjamin, Casey	R-R	6-2	190	8-1-80	.283	.197	.308	92	329	48	93	21	2	7	46	34	1	7	3	56	4	3	.422	.349
Blalock, Jake	R-R	6-4	205	8-6-83	.266	.281	.260	110	376	37	100	19	0	7	41	40	3	1	3	85	8	3	.372	.339
Botts, Jason	B-R	6-5	250	7-26-80	.125	.000	.167	5	16	3	2	0	0	0	2	3	0	0	1	3	0	0	.125	.250
Brewer, Jace	R-R	6-0	190	6-9-79	.263	.143	.333	5	19	0	5	1	0	0	1	3	1	0	1	4	1	1	.316	.375
Cruz, Enrique	R-R	6-1	205	11-21-81	.270	.220	.295	76	281	32	76	17	1	3	32	19	3	4	0	82	8	6	.370	.323
Fasano, Jim	L-R	6-5	230	7-20-83	.244	.264	.239	96	365	48	89	27	0	8	55	31	4	1	2	93	2	0	.384	.308
Fox, Adam	R-R	6-0	195	11-23-81	.269	.333	.235	9	26	3	7	2	2	1	5	1	0	0	0	5	0	0	.615	.296
Gold, Nate	R-R	6-3	221	6-12-80	.292	.276	.298	120	452	74	132	27	1	34	103	55	9	1	5	85	3	4	.582	.376
Grayson, Luke	R-R	5-10	199	7-28-82	.233	.229	.234	55	176	24	41	11	0	4	20	14	5	1	2	43	7	4	.364	.305
Harrison, Ben	R-R	6-4	203	9-18-81	.282	.288	.279	42	163	27	46	8	1	8	27	10	5	0	1	32	6	1	.491	.341
Hulett, Tug	L-R	5-10	185	2-28-83	.308	.288	.316	48	185	36	57	8	4	0	15	31	1	3	3	36	9	2	.395	.405
Mahar, Kevin	R-R	6-4	215	6-8-81	.267	.267	.267	127	505	82	135	38	2	20	82	33	8	7	5	110	13	7	.469	.319
Metcalf, Travis	R-R	6-3	215	8-17-82	.221	.238	.216	121	425	51	94	16	2	8	37	45	3	0	4	112	9	7	.325	.298
Morrissey, Adam	R-R	5-11	170	6-8-81	.313	.258	.336	54	208	42	65	13	1	5	29	25	1	0	1	47	2	2	.457	.387
Nickeas, Mike	R-R	6-0	205	2-13-83	.248	.290	.232	39	113	15	28	7	0	2	15	21	6	3	4	22	1	1	.363	.382
Richardson, Kevin	R-R	6-3	228	9-12-80	.271	.378	.231	93	303	54	82	12	3	17	47	33	9	2	1	95	4	1	.498	.358
Ringe, Craig	R-R	5-9	180	3-16-80	.205	.286	.186	23	73	7	15	4	1	0	5	6	1	2	0	16	2	0	.288	.275
Sinisi, Vince	L-L	6-0	195	11-7-81	.309	.462	.273	18	68	9	21	2	1	0	9	6	1	0	0	11	2	2	.368	.373
Smith, Dustin	R-R	6-2	205	5-8-81	.200	.438	.114	19	60	3	12	0	0	0	2	2	1	0	1	11	0	0	.200	.234
Tingler, Jayce	L-L	5-8	155	11-28-80	.227	.250	.221	25	97	10	22	0	0	0	6	8	3	4	0	9	4	2	.227	.306
Valichka, Brian	R-R	6-3	200	8-21-83	.400	.000	.444	3	10	2	4	0	0	0	1	0	0	0	0	1	0	0	.400	.400
Webster, Anthony	L-R	6-0	197	4-10-83	.310	.308	.311	59	216	37	67	10	4	5	19	18	1	3	1	25	3	5	.463	.364
Yan, Ruddy	R-R	6-0	160	1-13-82	.257	.161	.295	49	202	33	52	7	1	0	17	18	2	5	3	24	11	5	.302	.320

PITCHING	B-T	HT	WT	DOB	W	L	ERA	G	GS	CG	SV	IP	H	R	ER	HR	BB	SO	AVG	vLH	vRH	K/9	BB/9
Alfonseca, Antonio	R-R	6-5	250	4-16-72	0	0	0.00	1	0	0	0	1	0	0	0	0	0	0	.000	.000	.000	0.00	0.00
Benjamin, Casey	R-R	6-2	190	8-1-80	0	0	13.50	2	0	0	0	1	2	2	2	0	1	1	.333	.500	.250	6.75	6.75
Bumstead, Michael	R-R	6-4	210	7-8-77	1	2	1.81	33	0	0	5	55	39	13	11	0	20	56	.199	.214	.188	9.22	3.29
Carlson, Jesse	L-L	6-1	160	12-31-80	6	5	4.66	43	0	0	3	58	65	39	30	7	18	45	.274	.281	.268	6.98	2.79
Castro, Fabio	L-L	5-7	175	1-20-85	0	1	1.98	5	4	0	0	14	14	7	3	1	8	10	.259	.222	.278	6.59	5.27
Chavez, Jesse	R-R	6-1	160	8-21-83	2	5	4.42	38	0	0	4	59	54	33	29	5	28	70	.245	.300	.200	10.68	4.27
Corey, Bryan	R-R	6-0	180	10-21-73	1	0	2.08	13	0	0	7	17	16	7	4	0	6	19	.242	.276	.216	9.87	3.12
Danks, John	L-L	6-1	200	4-15-85	5	4	4.15	13	13	0	0	69	74	38	32	11	22	82	.273	.300	.262	10.64	2.86
Diamond, Thomas	R-R	6-3	245	4-6-83	12	5	4.24	27	27	1	0	129	104	65	61	14	78	145	.219	.218	.220	10.09	5.43
Diaz, Jose	R-R	6-0	240	4-13-80	2	0	1.29	8	4	0	0	28	16	5	4	0	20	29	.174	.149	.200	9.32	6.43
Eaton, Adam	R-R	6-2	200	11-23-77	0	0	1.42	2	2	0	0	6	3	1	1	0	1	5	.269	.500	.071	7.11	1.42
Francisco, Frank	R-R	6-2	235	9-11-79	0	0	1.84	13	0	0	0	15	10	3	3	1	4	22	.189	.235	.167	13.50	2.45

ORGANIZATION STATISTICS

Name	B-T	HT	WT	DOB	W	L	ERA	G	GS	CG	SV	IP	H	R	ER	HR	BB	SO	AVG	vLH	vRH	K/9	BB/9
Galarraga, Armando	R-R	6-4	180	1-15-82	1	6	5.49	9	9	0	0	41	56	34	25	5	13	38	.327	.360	.293	8.34	2.85
Haigwood, Daniel	R-L	6-2	200	11-19-83	1	2	3.63	12	12	1	0	62	66	29	25	4	44	57	.280	.290	.275	8.27	6.39
Hurley, Eric	R-R	6-4	195	9-17-85	3	1	1.95	6	6	0	0	37	21	9	8	4	11	31	.168	.235	.122	7.54	2.68
Ingram, Jesse	R-R	6-1	200	4-27-82	3	2	5.21	15	0	0	4	19	20	13	11	2	5	22	.274	.250	.293	10.42	2.37
Jensen, Ryan	R-R	6-0	255	9-17-75	2	4	5.94	11	8	0	0	50	62	37	33	6	13	37	.295	.359	.246	6.66	2.34
Kometani, Paul	R-R	6-4	200	12-24-82	8	5	4.69	17	16	1	0	88	95	50	46	4	33	77	.275	.251	.296	7.85	3.36
Littleton, Wes	R-R	6-2	210	9-2-82	3	0	0.66	17	0	0	3	27	13	3	2	1	7	25	.137	.184	.105	8.23	2.30
Loe, Kameron	R-R	6-7	240	9-10-81	0	1	5.14	2	2	0	0	7	8	5	4	1	4	4	.286	.357	.214	5.14	5.14
Masset, Nick	R-R	6-4	190	5-17-82	2	2	2.06	8	8	0	0	48	38	16	11	0	20	40	.213	.256	.177	7.50	3.75
Mathis, Douglas	R-R	6-3	220	6-7-83	0	0	3.60	2	2	0	0	10	14	5	4	0	5	10	.326	.333	.313	9.00	4.50
Mendoza, Luis	L-R	6-3	180	10-31-83	2	4	7.75	7	7	0	0	38	55	33	33	2	11	21	.333	.356	.315	4.93	2.58
Pote, Lou	R-R	6-3	200	8-21-71	3	2	5.04	17	1	0	0	30	33	17	17	3	15	24	.287	.365	.222	7.12	4.45
Poveda, Omar	R-R	6-4	200	9-28-87	0	1	1.80	1	1	0	0	5	4	2	1	0	5	1	.222	.125	.300	1.80	9.00
Rowe, Steven	R-R	6-4	210	7-17-80	5	5	5.53	45	3	0	0	83	95	59	51	14	33	67	.288	.289	.287	7.27	3.58
Rupe, Josh	R-R	6-2	210	8-18-82	0	0	10.50	6	0	0	0	6	7	7	7	2	4	3	.280	.353	.125	4.50	6.00
Shouse, Brian	L-L	5-11	190	9-26-68	0	0	0.00	2	0	0	0	2	2	0	0	0	1	1	.286	.000	.500	4.50	4.50
Thompson, Travis	R-R	6-5	225	7-3-77	1	0	2.31	6	0	0	0	12	15	3	3	1	1	4	.326	.174	.478	3.09	0.77
Touchet, Danny	R-R	6-2	202	1-12-82	3	4	5.07	34	0	0	2	66	78	38	37	6	18	45	.297	.307	.290	6.17	2.47
Walker, Andy	R-R	6-1	175	4-20-83	4	4	5.81	20	15	0	0	93	119	67	60	21	21	52	.306	.300	.312	5.03	2.03
Wallace, Shane	L-L	6-2	225	12-29-80	0	1	10.57	7	0	0	0	8	12	9	9	1	5	4	.353	.500	.321	4.70	5.87
Ward, Jeremy	R-R	6-3	235	2-24-78	2	2	4.35	30	0	0	2	50	51	26	24	5	16	46	.270	.177	.336	8.34	2.90
Wilson, C.J.	L-L	6-1	215	11-18-80	0	0	2.70	4	0	0	0	3	3	1	1	0	2	6	.231	.125	.400	16.20	5.40

FIELDING

Catcher	PCT	G	PO	A	E	DP	PB
Nickeas	.994	39	281	27	2	1	3
Richardson	.992	89	703	56	6	8	6
Smith	.965	18	123	14	5	1	4
Valichka	1.000	3	16	2	0	0	1

First Base	PCT	G	PO	A	E	DP
Benjamin	1.000	2	5	0	0	0
Fasano	.990	27	182	19	2	12
Gold	.990	104	826	90	9	73
Sinisi	.991	13	107	9	1	9

Second Base	PCT	G	PO	A	E	DP
Baldiris	.947	25	51	75	7	14
Benjamin	.976	21	45	78	3	12

	PCT	G	PO	A	E	DP
Fox	1.000	2	3	4	0	0
Hulett Jr.	.996	47	99	131	1	35
Morrissey	.962	44	73	104	7	15
Ringe	.950	3	5	14	1	0

Third Base	PCT	G	PO	A	E	DP
Benjamin	.938	5	7	8	1	0
Cruz	.952	15	10	30	2	5
Fox	1.000	4	3	3	0	1
Gold	—	1	0	0	0	0
Metcalf	.946	120	76	185	15	14

Shortstop	PCT	G	PO	A	E	DP
Benjamin	.960	58	92	146	10	30
Brewer	.955	5	11	10	1	2

	PCT	G	PO	A	E	DP
Cruz	.929	59	81	140	17	31
Fox	1.000	2	2	5	0	1
Ringe	.863	20	17	52	11	9

Outfield	PCT	G	PO	A	E	DP
Benjamin	1.000	3	10	0	0	0
Blalock	.994	100	164	4	1	1
Botts	1.000	2	7	0	0	0
Grayson	.939	47	92	1	6	0
Harrlson	1.000	34	46	3	0	0
Mahar	.976	117	230	15	6	3
Sinisi	1.000	1	2	0	0	0
Tingler	.981	25	51	0	1	0
Webster	.957	51	87	3	4	0
Yan	.992	48	125	3	1	2

Bakersfield Blaze — High Class A

California League

BATTING

Name	B-T	HT	WT	DOB	AVG	vLH	vRH	G	AB	R	H	2B	3B	HR	RBI	BB	HBP	SH	SF	SO	SB	CS	SLG	OBP
Benjamin, Casey	R-R	6-2	190	8-1-80	.256	.214	.280	12	39	3	10	3	0	0	3	1	0	0	1	9	1	0	.333	.268
Boggs, Brandon	B-R	6-0	190	1-9-83	.261	.316	.240	78	284	48	74	20	4	8	37	40	1	0	2	63	13	4	.444	.352
Crabtree, Benjamin	R-R	6-0	210	11-2-82	.083	.000	.100	4	12	1	1	0	0	0	0	2	1	1	0	5	0	0	.083	.267
Creswell, Reese	L-R	6-3	205	7-5-85	.143	—	.143	2	7	1	1	0	0	0	1	0	0	0	4	0	0		.143	.143
Dominguez, Carlos	R-R	6-1	177	6-8-86	.214	.222	.200	5	14	1	3	0	0	0	0	0	0	1	3	0	0		.214	.200
Duran, German	R-R	5-10	185	8-3-84	.284	.257	.294	114	457	81	130	31	2	13	72	35	1	2	8	89	15	9	.446	.331
Fasano, Jim	L-R	6-5	230	7-20-83	.305	.176	.357	14	59	6	18	3	0	2	7	4	1	0	0	9	0	0	.458	.359
Fox, Adam	R-R	6-0	195	11-23-81	.256	.274	.251	77	289	38	74	21	1	7	35	27	4	2	4	51	7	4	.408	.324
Frostad, Emerson	L-R	6-1	210	1-13-83	.320	.365	.307	79	291	46	93	30	1	12	51	36	0	1	5	68	3	7	.553	.389
Furtado, Micah	L-R	5-7	170	6-9-82	.249	.300	.228	103	382	59	95	19	3	8	42	44	5	7	2	81	11	10	.377	.333
Gac, Ian	R-R	6-3	245	8-10-85	.188	.277	.147	55	208	24	39	4	1	9	23	13	3	0	3	97	3	0	.346	.242
Gomez, Mauro	R-R	6-2	190	9-7-84	.258	.326	.240	59	213	25	55	14	2	4	25	6	1	0	2	71	1	0	.399	.279
Gonzalez, Juan	R-R	6-0	165	2-23-82	.237	.233	.238	59	211	31	50	13	1	1	17	22	2	3	3	58	9	2	.322	.311
Grayson, Luke	R-R	5-10	199	7-28-82	.225	.238	.221	51	178	24	40	13	1	6	22	10	6	4	0	60	2	3	.410	.289
Harrison, Ben	R-R	6-4	203	9-18-81	.293	.303	.289	87	331	52	97	19	1	18	74	49	10	0	3	85	9	3	.520	.395
Hatcher, Justin	R-R	5-10	180	5-12-80	.228	.257	.212	32	101	13	23	1	0	0	9	12	1	0	0	26	2	1	.238	.316
Hawke, Phillip	L-L	6-3	240	8-22-83	.220	.270	.200	36	132	10	29	3	1	2	15	19	0	2	0	40	1	0	.303	.318
Hooft, Joseph	R-R	5-10	175	8-30-82	.093	.056	.120	13	43	4	4	1	0	0	3	4	1	0	1	8	0	1	.116	.216
Hulett, Tug	R-L	5-10	185	2-28-83	.291	.273	.299	77	289	46	84	19	7	2	37	61	3	4	4	61	15	5	.426	.415
Martinez, Alberto	R-R	6-1	191	8-27-86	.267	.462	.188	12	45	5	12	3	0	0	3	1	0	1	0	9	0	3	.333	.283
Murphy, Steven	L-R	6-2	210	4-22-84	.283	.215	.310	116	470	73	133	36	5	19	68	31	7	3	2	102	10	8	.506	.335
Napoli, Joe	R-R	6-4	230	10-4-82	.313	.667	.231	5	16	1	5	1	0	0	0	2	0	0	0	5	0	0	.375	.421
Nickeas, Mike	R-R	6-0	205	2-13-83	.297	.278	.304	17	64	6	19	4	0	0	6	5	0	1	0	17	0	0	.359	.395
Peterson, David	R-R	5-10	170	8-22-83	.125	.000	.154	7	16	1	2	0	0	0	0	3	0	0	0	9	0	1	.125	.263
Thon, Freddie	L-L	6-2	215	4-9-84	.321	.289	.329	53	218	21	70	16	0	2	32	5	1	0	3	35	2	3	.422	.335
Tingler, Jayce	L-L	5-8	155	11-28-80	.330	.292	.349	56	224	40	74	4	3	0	17	36	4	6	0	16	5	7	.375	.432
Valichka, Brian	R-R	6-3	200	8-21-83	.179	.000	.250	9	28	3	5	1	0	0	2	0	1	0	1	6	1	0	.214	.200
Valiente, Roberto	R-R	6-0	185	3-4-83	.287	.360	.261	57	188	27	54	11	1	1	12	12	3	1	0	41	4	3	.372	.340
Washington, Johnny	R-R	5-11	165	5-6-84	.139	.200	.095	16	36	3	5	2	0	0	0	2	0	1	0	11	0	1	.194	.184

PITCHING

Name	B-T	HT	WT	DOB	W	L	ERA	G	GS	CG	SV	IP	H	R	ER	HR	BB	SO	AVG	vLH	vRH	K/9	BB/9
Bannister, John	R-R	6-4	198	1-20-84	5	8	5.87	18	18	0	0	97	109	69	63	9	53	109	.286	.321	.258	10.15	4.93
Bukvich, Ryan	R-R	6-2	250	5-13-78	2	0	2.70	6	0	0	0	10	6	4	3	0	5	4	.167	.200	.143	4.50	4.50
Coffman, Broc	L-L	6-2	215	3-28-85	5	9	7.24	19	18	0	0	83	110	85	67	11	40	67	.313	.346	.303	7.24	4.32
Farnum, Matt	R-R	6-2	195	6-1-81	0	1	3.42	30	0	0	5	50	51	21	19	3	19	54	.263	.282	.250	9.72	3.42
Fogle, Nathan	R-R	6-4	225	12-27-83	0	0	5.63	6	0	0	3	8	6	5	5	0	9	15	.194	.143	.235	16.88	10.13
Galarraga, Armando	R-R	6-4	180	1-15-82	0	1	6.23	2	2	0	0	9	6	9	6	2	7	7	.176	.091	.217	7.27	7.27
Herrera, Danny Ray	L-L	5-8	145	10-21-84	4	2	1.35	14	5	0	1	53	39	16	8	0	12	61	.201	.143	.217	10.29	2.03
Hurley, Eric	R-R	6-4	195	9-17-85	5	6	4.11	18	18	1	0	101	92	60	46	12	32	106	.239	.251	.229	9.48	2.86

Name	B-T	HT	WT	DOB	W	L	ERA	G	GS	CG	SV	IP	H	R	ER	HR	BB	SO	AVG	vLH	vRH	K/9	BB/9
Ingram, Jesse	R-R	6-1	200	4-27-82	6	0	2.43	27	0	0	9	59	34	20	16	3	22	95	.163	.170	.158	14.41	3.34
Izquierdo, Ivan	R-R	6-1	205	10-14-83	0	0	9.00	1	0	0	0	1	2	1	1	0	0	2	.400	.250	1.000	18.00	0.00
Kometani, Paul	R-R	6-4	200	12-24-82	4	2	3.30	10	10	0	0	60	69	27	22	3	13	56	.286	.313	.262	8.40	1.95
Lamacchia, Marc	R-R	6-1	190	3-27-82	1	3	6.32	12	2	0	0	31	42	31	22	5	18	27	.318	.273	.364	7.76	5.17
Lujan, John	R-R	6-1	200	5-10-84	1	4	5.74	38	0	0	4	69	75	51	44	8	43	58	.281	.304	.265	7.57	5.61
Mathis, Douglas	R-R	6-3	220	6-7-83	10	7	4.18	26	25	2	0	151	160	76	70	14	47	109	.275	.286	.267	6.51	2.81
Morla, Wandy	R-R	6-3	195	10-22-83	1	2	6.34	18	3	0	0	38	47	34	27	7	19	26	.301	.286	.314	6.10	4.46
Padgett, Mike	R-R	6-4	210	5-6-82	0	3	2.77	7	0	0	2	13	15	11	4	2	3	13	.278	.286	.269	9.00	2.08
Pote, Lou	R-R	6-3	200	8-21-71	2	1	3.75	9	0	0	1	24	24	10	10	1	8	25	.282	.323	.259	9.38	3.00
Rodriguez, William	L-L	6-0	189	5-8-84	2	2	6.61	13	0	0	0	16	18	13	12	3	10	12	.273	.348	.233	6.61	5.51
Schlact, Michael	R-R	6-7	205	12-9-85	4	13	5.99	26	26	0	0	138	179	112	92	15	61	81	.317	.349	.290	5.27	3.97
Touchet, Danny	R-R	6-2	202	1-12-82	1	2	3.07	9	0	0	1	15	12	5	5	1	5	11	.226	.222	.231	6.75	3.07
Vera, Edwin	R-R	5-11	170	2-26-83	0	10	5.21	35	11	0	1	93	106	67	54	6	67	93	.296	.273	.315	8.97	6.46
Walker, Andy	R-R	6-1	215	4-20-83	1	1	4.50	9	2	0	0	28	25	15	14	3	7	22	.245	.271	.222	7.07	2.25
Wallace, Shane	L-L	6-2	225	12-29-80	1	2	7.50	21	0	0	0	30	47	30	25	4	12	31	.359	.257	.396	9.30	3.60
Wilson, Jon	R-R	6-1	200	4-28-83	1	3	4.53	31	0	0	3	54	72	39	27	4	23	37	.329	.368	.303	6.20	3.86
Wirth, Shannon	R-R	6-0	215	5-27-84	2	0	6.30	5	0	0	0	10	14	11	7	4	1	5	.311	.286	.323	4.50	0.90

FIELDING

Catcher	PCT	G	PO	A	E	DP	PB
Crabtree	.971	4	28	5	1	1	2
Creswell	1.000	2	12	1	0	0	2
Dominguez	1.000	5	34	7	0	0	2
Frostad	.981	71	562	51	12	6	33
Hatcher	.988	29	222	25	3	1	8
Martinez	1.000	12	77	8	0	0	2
Nickeas	.993	16	125	13	1	1	2
Valichka	.987	9	67	7	1	1	2

First Base	PCT	G	PO	A	E	DP
Fasano	.982	5	48	7	1	4
Fox	1.000	1	1	1	0	0
Gac	.975	47	393	28	11	32
Gomez	.985	28	247	22	4	28
Gonzalez	1.000	2	3	1	0	0
Hawke	.975	26	218	17	6	31
Thon	.985	34	298	20	5	37

Second Base	PCT	G	PO	A	E	DP
Duran	.984	46	103	147	4	36
Furtado	.968	72	141	191	11	49
Hulett Jr.	.966	23	40	72	4	13
Washington	.929	10	8	18	2	5

Third Base	PCT	G	PO	A	E	DP
Benjamin	.947	10	4	14	1	0
Duran	1.000	1	1	3	0	2
Fox	.927	64	39	139	14	15
Furtado	.903	11	7	21	3	3
Gomez	.766	16	10	26	11	3
Hooft	.889	12	7	25	4	3
Hulett Jr.	.938	35	15	60	5	9

Shortstop	PCT	G	PO	A	E	DP
Benjamin	.900	2	6	3	1	2
Duran	.905	54	66	135	21	26
Fox	.859	12	18	37	9	11
Gonzalez	.935	57	74	158	16	37
Hooft	1.000	1	2	5	0	0
Hulett Jr.	.961	18	21	53	3	10
Peterson	.960	7	6	18	1	6

Outfield	PCT	G	PO	A	E	DP
Boggs	.959	77	135	6	6	0
Grayson	.949	49	85	8	5	3
Harrison	.978	75	127	4	3	1
Murphy	.972	111	199	12	6	2
Napoli	1.000	4	8	0	0	0
Tingler	.981	54	102	4	2	1
Valiente	.969	55	90	4	3	0

Clinton LumberKings — Low Class A

Midwest League

BATTING	B-T	HT	WT	DOB	AVG	vLH	vRH	G	AB	R	H	2B	3B	HR	RBI	BB	HBP	SH	SF	SO	SB	CS	SLG	OBP
Blunt, Terrance	B-R	6-1	185	8-14-82	.271	.269	.272	115	395	53	107	28	1	1	43	49	3	4	1	63	14	9	.354	.355
Crabtree, Benjamin	R-R	6-0	210	11-2-82	.245	.263	.233	62	196	10	48	6	0	2	24	9	4	3	1	53	3	2	.306	.290
Dominguez, Carlos	R-R	6-1	177	6-8-86	.255	.200	.270	15	47	6	12	2	0	1	5	1	1	1	1	12	0	1	.362	.280
Gac, Ian	R-R	6-3	245	8-10-85	.197	.132	.219	54	208	21	41	8	2	7	26	8	1	0	3	69	0	1	.356	.227
Gerrard, Grant	L-L	6-4	220	5-1-84	.298	.261	.309	28	104	16	31	5	0	2	16	11	1	0	0	23	2	1	.404	.371
Herren, K.C.	L-R	6-1	215	8-21-85	.221	.176	.239	87	303	24	67	10	3	2	21	36	1	4	0	81	3	6	.294	.306
Hooft, Joseph	R-R	5-10	175	8-30-82	.000	.000	.000	4	14	0	0	0	0	0	0	0	0	0	0	2	1	0	.000	.000
Kemp, Joseph	L-L	6-1	195	2-22-82	.248	.175	.268	77	262	31	65	14	6	4	35	20	6	2	0	66	7	7	.393	.316
Kemp, Chris	L-R	6-4	210	8-24-83	.226	.154	.239	24	84	10	19	4	0	2	13	6	2	0	2	19	1	0	.345	.287
Killian, Billy	L-R	6-1	190	6-12-86	.164	.077	.188	17	61	4	10	2	2	0	6	4	0	0	0	20	1	0	.262	.215
Martinez, Alberto	R-R	6-1	191	8-27-86	.094	.182	.048	22	64	3	6	1	0	0	2	2	0	2	0	20	0	1	.109	.121
Mayberry, John	R-R	6-6	230	12-21-83	.268	.290	.259	126	459	77	123	26	4	21	77	59	9	0	6	117	9	3	.479	.358
Mehl, Truan	L-R	6-2	200	3-20-83	.252	.189	.270	102	333	36	84	12	4	3	32	14	1	6	6	56	15	5	.339	.280
Peterson, David	R-R	5-10	170	8-22-83	.231	.269	.200	64	208	17	48	6	2	0	7	10	1	9	0	43	2	4	.279	.269
Smith, Matt	L-R	5-10	172	6-12-83	.267	.279	.263	124	457	57	122	14	3	3	27	58	3	8	3	89	20	13	.330	.351
Thon, Freddie	L-L	6-2	215	4-9-84	.280	.291	.275	69	261	29	73	11	0	7	33	10	2	0	3	39	2	2	.402	.308
Valichka, Brian	R-R	6-3	200	8-21-83	.231	.274	.204	65	221	22	51	12	0	6	31	17	5	3	1	46	4	2	.367	.299
Vallejo, Jose	R-R	6-0	172	9-11-86	.234	.220	.240	127	496	62	116	11	4	2	29	32	7	7	1	104	24	9	.284	.289
Whittleman, John	L-R	6-2	195	2-11-87	.227	.243	.222	130	466	56	106	21	3	9	43	60	0	0	4	97	7	6	.343	.313

PITCHING	B-T	HT	WT	DOB	W	L	ERA	G	GS	CG	SV	IP	H	R	ER	HR	BB	SO	AVG	vLH	vRH	K/9	BB/9
Altman, Kevin	R-R	6-2	170	12-24-84	3	8	4.85	34	6	0	2	85	94	49	46	6	23	78	.281	.290	.274	8.23	2.43
Byrd, Cain	R-R	6-3	210	1-6-85	0	0	8.10	2	0	0	0	3	2	3	3	1	3	3	.200	.500	.125	8.10	8.10
Coffman, Broc	L-L	6-2	215	3-28-85	3	1	0.47	4	1	0	0	19	12	3	1	0	4	15	.171	.150	.180	6.98	1.86
Cordero, Julian	L-L	6-0	165	9-28-84	2	5	2.91	27	5	0	0	68	65	31	22	3	26	49	.248	.206	.263	6.49	3.44
Crabtree, Benjamin	R-R	6-0	210	11-2-82	0	0	0.00	1	0	0	0	1	0	0	0	0	0	0	.000	.000	—	0.00	18.00
Diaz, J.B.	R-R	6-2	185	6-9-83	5	4	4.26	36	2	0	0	74	83	43	35	5	28	41	.280	.252	.297	4.99	3.41
Fogle, Nathan	R-R	6-4	225	12-27-83	0	0	0.00	8	0	0	0	14	6	1	0	0	7	20	.125	.200	.071	12.86	4.50
Garcia, Juan Carlos	B-R	6-2	177	10-10-82	1	3	6.28	24	0	0	2	43	51	41	30	5	23	37	.287	.314	.269	7.74	4.81
Giles, Josh	R-R	6-1	175	8-3-84	2	1	3.88	28	0	0	2	46	44	22	20	5	15	47	.256	.309	.221	9.13	2.91
Hollis, Jonathan	R-R	6-3	240	9-17-83	1	1	1.93	7	0	0	1	14	11	4	3	1	5	6	.212	.167	.235	3.86	3.21
Hooft, Joseph	R-R	5-10	175	8-30-82	0	0	0.00	1	0	0	0	1	0	0	0	0	0	0	.000	—	.000	0.00	0.00
Jimenez, Juan	R-R	6-2	180	5-18-86	4	11	5.25	22	19	0	0	117	123	73	68	13	43	73	.277	.271	.281	5.63	3.32
Kemp, Joseph	L-L	6-1	195	2-22-82	0	0	13.50	2	0	0	0	2	1	3	3	1	3	3	.143	.000	.167	13.50	13.50
Kirkman, Michael	L-L	6-3	185	9-18-86	0	3	6.98	6	6	0	0	19	23	17	15	0	24	22	.303	.350	.286	10.24	11.17
Marte, Jose	R-R	6-5	185	9-4-83	6	7	3.51	39	0	0	12	67	59	33	26	1	34	71	.242	.234	.247	9.59	4.59
McLaughlin, Joey	R-R	6-0	185	2-11-82	1	0	4.50	15	1	0	0	32	32	18	16	5	12	29	.256	.341	.214	8.16	3.38
2-team (16 Lansing)					4	1	3.84	31	1	0	0	58	57	28	25	6	24	46	—	—		7.06	3.68
Oakes, Gerry	L-R	6-5	191	4-29-82	1	2	8.08	30	0	1	0	42	39	44	38	5	46	31	.247	.283	.224	6.59	9.78
Phillips, Zachary	L-L	6-1	178	9-21-86	5	12	5.96	28	28	0	0	142	178	106	94	5	66	126	.315	.372	.301	7.99	4.18
Poveda, Omar	R-R	6-4	190	9-28-87	4	13	4.88	26	26	0	0	149	167	92	81	12	37	133	.286	.255	.306	8.02	2.23
Rasner, Jacob	R-R	6-4	195	12-4-86	6	16	5.41	27	27	1	0	145	154	102	87	14	52	117	.274	.282	.269	7.28	3.24
Rogers, Kyle	R-R	6-3	190	9-23-85	1	6	4.67	22	18	0	0	104	87	68	54	6	61	87	.228	.241	.219	7.53	5.28
Swanson, Glenn	L-L	6-1	175	5-15-83	0	1	2.12	8	0	0	1	17	14	7	4	1	4	25	.212	.167	.238	13.24	2.12

FIELDING

Catcher	PCT	G	PO	A	E	DP	PB
Crabtree	.979	45	288	42	7	3	9
Dominguez	.991	14	94	15	1	2	6
Killian	.993	17	142	6	1	0	0
Martinez	.972	22	149	22	5	6	6
Valichka	.993	49	353	49	3	2	6

First Base	PCT	G	PO	A	E	DP
Blunt	1.000	14	83	1	0	10
Gac	.978	48	374	28	9	36
Kemp	1.000	12	104	4	0	7
Thon	.983	63	473	39	9	48
Valichka	.940	9	59	4	4	5

Second Base	PCT	G	PO	A	E	DP
Blunt	1.000	3	8	3	0	2
Peterson	.988	21	35	47	1	11
Vallejo	.976	118	237	337	14	78

Third Base	PCT	G	PO	A	E	DP
Blunt	1.000	2	1	4	0	0
Hooft	1.000	1	1	0	0	0
Mehl	—	1	0	0	0	0
Peterson	.902	17	17	29	5	3
Whittleman	.891	121	74	203	34	18

Shortstop	PCT	G	PO	A	E	DP
Blunt	—	1	0	0	0	0

	PCT	G	PO	A	E	DP
Peterson	.920	18	28	41	6	12
Smith	.948	120	159	300	25	65
Vallejo	.833	2	2	3	1	1

Outfield	PCT	G	PO	A	E	DP
Blunt	.966	77	164	5	6	1
Gerrard	.945	26	51	1	3	0
Herren	.978	66	129	7	3	1
Hooft	1.000	1	2	0	0	0
Kemp	.957	59	109	2	5	0
Mayberry	.979	114	233	5	5	1
Mehl	.985	83	185	6	3	0

Spokane Indians — Short-Season

Northwest League

BATTING	B-T	HT	WT	DOB	AVG	vLH	vRH	G	AB	R	H	2B	3B	HR	RBI	BB	HBP	SH	SF	SO	SB	CS	SLG	OBP
Backman II, Wally	L-R	6-2	215	1-7-86	.202	.167	.213	62	208	26	42	4	1	5	24	31	2	0	4	69	7	6	.303	.306
Berkery, Thomas	R-R	6-1	180	9-29-82	.248	.245	.249	65	238	30	59	11	1	4	27	31	8	0	3	47	7	2	.353	.350
Cadena, Nickolas	R-R	6-1	185	11-17-82	.259	.286	.252	54	189	31	49	16	1	3	26	23	5	0	2	49	3	5	.402	.352
Davis, Chris	L-R	6-3	210	3-17-86	.277	.328	.260	69	253	38	70	18	1	15	42	23	3	0	1	65	2	3	.534	.343
Gentry, Craig	R-R	6-2	190	11-29-83	.281	.286	.279	56	221	27	62	15	4	0	13	9	15	0	1	37	20	6	.385	.350
Gerrard, Grant	L-L	6-4	220	5-1-84	.278	.280	.277	29	108	18	30	7	3	1	14	15	1	0	0	26	7	2	.426	.371
Harrigan, Hunter	R-R	6-1	210	4-17-83	.130	.077	.146	19	54	4	7	2	0	1	4	4	6	0	0	26	0	2	.222	.266
Heafner, Jay	R-R	5-10	175	1-1-84	.242	.277	.230	51	186	26	45	12	1	0	17	15	2	0	2	40	1	1	.317	.302
Herren, K.C.	L-R	6-1	215	8-21-85	.268	.172	.301	31	112	15	30	3	3	3	13	11	0	0	0	31	4	2	.429	.333
Hooft, Joseph	R-R	5-10	175	8-30-82	.188	.259	.165	34	112	11	21	3	0	1	13	9	2	3	19	1	5	.241	.254
Kemp, Chris	L-R	6-4	210	8-24-83	.218	.318	.198	36	133	10	29	5	0	3	15	9	2	0	1	31	1	0	.323	.276
Killian, Billy	L-R	6-1	190	6-12-86	.244	.207	.255	38	127	10	31	8	2	0	12	6	1	0	1	38	2	2	.339	.281
Marquardt, Steven	R-R	6-2	210	6-11-86	.257	.340	.230	59	218	28	56	15	3	3	25	22	3	0	2	42	5	3	.394	.331
Napoli, Joe	R-R	6-4	230	10-4-82	.224	.207	.232	26	85	7	19	0	2	1	9	11	3	0	0	26	1	0	.306	.333
Nelson, Brian	R-R	6-3	225	5-18-84	.219	.000	.250	9	32	5	7	0	0	0	4	4	1	0	0	6	1	0	.219	.324
Santana, Julio	B-R	6-1	175	12-26-85	.133	.000	.182	5	15	1	2	0	0	0	2	0	0	0	0	10	0	1	.133	.235
Tracy, Chad	R-R	6-3	200	7-4-85	.262	.158	.292	66	252	41	66	14	1	11	35	23	7	0	1	46	4	1	.456	.339
Washington, Johnny	R-R	5-11	165	5-6-84	.167	.250	.143	6	18	2	3	1	0	0	2	0	0	0	1	7	1	0	.222	.158

PITCHING	B-T	HT	WT	DOB	W	L	ERA	G	GS	CG	SV	IP	H	R	ER	HR	BB	SO	AVG	vLH	vRH	K/9	BB/9
Ballard, Michael	R-L	6-2	180	2-6-84	2	7	5.68	18	13	0	0	63	78	49	40	7	19	41	.304	.309	.302	5.83	2.70
Crow, Craig	R-R	6-2	200	11-25-83	1	3	6.66	13	4	0	0	26	35	25	19	0	12	25	.315	.395	.265	8.77	4.21
Donovan, Patrick	L-L	6-1	185	2-22-84	0	1	4.88	27	0	0	2	48	61	30	26	5	6	26	.308	.380	.284	4.88	1.13
Francisco, Frank	R-R	6-2	235	9-11-79	0	0	0.00	4	0	0	0	4	3	0	0	0	0	6	.200	.167	.222	13.50	0.00
Galarraga, Armando	R-R	6-4	180	1-15-82	0	1	4.50	1	1	0	0	4	4	2	2	1	0	3	.250	.000	.308	6.75	0.00
Garcia, Juan Carlos	B-R	6-2	177	10-10-82	0	5	8.21	9	7	0	0	34	48	36	31	4	15	16	.338	.296	.364	4.24	3.97
Garr, Brennan	R-R	6-2	190	2-22-84	2	0	4.85	17	0	0	0	26	30	20	14	1	14	29	.280	.350	.239	10.04	4.85
Haar, Jeremiah	L-R	6-2	190	12-29-84	1	1	2.60	8	3	0	0	28	24	17	8	3	8	22	.220	.245	.200	7.16	2.60
Harrigan, Hunter	R-R	6-1	210	4-17-83	0	0	0.00	1	0	0	0	0	0	0	0	0	0	0	.000	—	.000	0.00	0.00
Jaimes, Jose	R-R	6-2	180	6-26-84	2	1	2.25	4	4	0	0	16	9	4	4	0	9	18	.164	.133	.175	10.13	5.06
James, Brandon	R-R	6-3	207	9-5-86	0	0	6.75	1	1	0	0	4	6	3	3	1	3	1	.353	.400	.333	2.25	6.75
Jones, Derrick	R-R	6-1	190	6-11-84	1	0	2.66	14	0	0	1	24	18	9	7	2	13	13	.217	.205	.227	4.94	4.94
Kiker, Kasey	L-L	5-10	170	11-19-87	0	7	4.13	16	15	0	0	52	44	34	24	5	35	51	.232	.222	.234	8.77	6.02
Morla, Wandy	R-R	6-3	195	10-22-83	2	1	6.00	4	0	0	0	18	23	13	12	1	10	10	.319	.259	.356	5.00	5.00
Rogers, Kyle	R-R	6-3	190	9-23-85	2	2	2.86	6	4	0	0	22	15	7	7	2	5	18	.197	.250	.159	7.36	2.05
Schaecher, Adam	R-R	6-3	200	1-22-84	2	3	4.83	22	0	0	1	54	73	40	29	3	10	28	.323	.257	.355	4.67	1.67
Slusarz, John	R-R	6-3	170	7-19-84	3	4	5.55	24	0	0	1	47	61	40	29	4	19	37	.300	.290	.306	7.09	3.64
Swanson, Glenn	L-L	6-1	175	5-15-83	1	0	4.23	13	0	0	0	28	28	16	13	4	9	26	.257	.304	.244	8.46	2.93
Wagner, Michael	R-R	6-1	190	12-17-84	4	7	6.38	17	16	0	0	66	88	54	47	5	22	73	.319	.434	.254	9.90	2.98
Weilep, Austin	R-R	6-1	210	3-20-85	3	2	4.67	25	0	0	4	54	70	36	28	2	18	41	.310	.311	.309	6.83	3.00
Wirth, Shannon	R-R	6-0	215	5-27-84	0	3	8.66	10	0	0	0	18	26	23	17	0	12	7	.329	.429	.275	3.57	6.11
Zamzow, Brett	R-R	6-5	200	12-19-84	0	2	2.86	15	4	0	2	28	24	15	9	2	16	26	.231	.361	.162	8.26	5.08

FIELDING

Catcher	PCT	G	PO	A	E	DP	PB
Harrigan	.969	18	113	10	4	1	6
Killian	.977	26	162	8	4	2	10
Tracy	.986	38	260	19	4	2	4

First Base	PCT	G	PO	A	E	DP
Backman II	.983	14	106	12	2	8
Berkery	1.000	1	2	0	0	0
Cadena	1.000	1	3	0	0	0
Davis	.984	32	234	16	4	28
Harrigan	1.000	1	3	2	0	1
Kemp	.970	32	226	30	8	24
Nelson	1.000	2	13	1	0	0

Second Base	PCT	G	PO	A	E	DP
Berkery	.943	30	61	87	9	20
Cadena	.979	8	21	25	1	8
Heafner	.926	15	18	32	4	4
Hooft	.938	17	38	37	5	10
Santana	.938	5	8	7	1	1
Washington	.957	5	8	14	1	3

Third Base	PCT	G	PO	A	E	DP
Cadena	.815	21	15	29	10	3
Hooft	.963	9	7	19	1	1
Marquardt	.821	49	34	85	26	7

Shortstop	PCT	G	PO	A	E	DP
Berkery	.921	34	43	85	11	18

	PCT	G	PO	A	E	DP
Cadena	1.000	1	0	1	0	0
Heafner	.949	38	53	97	8	25
Hooft	.786	6	7	15	6	2

Outfield	PCT	G	PO	A	E	DP
Backman II	.961	49	96	2	4	2
Cadena	1.000	10	17	1	0	0
Davis	.924	36	58	3	5	0
Gentry	.993	55	147	5	1	2
Gerrard	.925	27	62	0	5	0
Herren	.983	30	59	0	1	0
Hooft	1.000	1	6	0	0	0
Marquardt	—	1	0	0	0	0
Napoli	.981	23	52	1	1	0
Nelson	.833	7	10	0	2	0

Arizona League

BATTING	B-T	HT	WT	DOB	AVG	vLH	vRH	G	AB	R	H	2B	3B	HR	RBI	BB	HBP	SH	SF	SO	SB	CS	SLG	OBP
Anderson, Ronnie	R-R	5-11	162	11-1-86	.210	.263	.204	40	119	20	25	3	1	0	8	20	1	2	4	37	10	3	.252	.319
Baldiris, Aarom	R-R	6-2	195	1-5-83	.571	.000	.667	2	7	1	4	1	0	0	1	2	1	0	0	2	0	0	.714	.700
Barrios, Victor	R-R	5-11	175	9-29-86	.307	.185	.324	50	176	28	54	10	2	2	23	11	6	1	2	32	14	3	.420	.364
Botts, Jason	B-R	6-5	250	7-26-80	.250	.167	.333	3	12	1	3	2	0	0	1	2	0	0	0	1	0	0	.417	.357
Bradbury, Josh	R-R	6-2	210	3-2-85	.191	.238	.180	35	110	11	21	3	1	1	15	10	2	1	0	31	2	0	.264	.270
Creswell, Reese	L-R	6-3	205	7-5-85	.192	.278	.167	25	73	5	14	3	2	0	7	10	0	1	1	31	0	0	.288	.286
Dominguez, Carlos	R-R	6-1	177	6-8-86	.281	.375	.268	18	64	7	18	2	0	1	9	2	1	0	2	5	1	2	.359	.304
Estrella, Julio	R-R	6-2	170	3-17-82	.188	.333	.178	24	48	12	9	2	0	0	4	8	3	2	0	20	3	4	.229	.339
Gomez, Mauro	R-R	6-2	190	9-7-84	.409	.750	.333	11	44	9	18	3	0	3	14	5	1	0	0	5	1	1	.682	.480
Gossage, Kevin	R-R	6-4	190	2-16-87	.222	.176	.236	29	72	8	16	6	0	0	4	13	0	0	0	24	1	1	.306	.341
Hooft, Joseph	R-R	5-10	175	8-30-82	.290	.167	.320	11	31	0	9	2	0	0	5	1	0	1	0	6	2	2	.355	.313
Jaimes, Matthew	R-R	6-0	190	1-9-88	.247	.167	.259	29	93	14	23	2	1	1	11	14	1	0	0	19	4	4	.323	.352
James, Andres	B-R	5-9	150	11-25-87	.231	.286	.218	38	147	14	34	2	0	0	14	5	0	5	0	38	3	6	.245	.257
Lemon, Marcus	L-R	5-11	173	6-2-88	.310	.273	.328	24	84	16	26	4	2	0	9	16	0	1	0	10	11	2	.405	.420
Martinez, Alberto	R-R	6-1	191	8-27-86	.000	.000	.000	5	5	1	0	0	0	0	0	1	0	2	0	2	0	0	.000	.167
Murphy, Steven	L-R	6-2	210	4-22-84	.333	—	.333	1	3	0	1	0	0	0	1	1	0	0	1	1	0	0	.333	.400
Napoli, Joe	R-R	6-4	230	10-4-82	.308	.333	.303	10	39	5	12	6	0	0	5	1	3	0	0	13	1	2	.462	.372
Nelson, Brian	R-R	6-3	220	5-18-84	.247	.222	.254	29	85	4	21	0	0	0	4	9	5	2	0	19	2	1	.247	.354
Osuna, Renny	R-R	6-0	172	4-24-85	.234	.333	.213	21	77	10	18	6	0	0	6	5	1	0	0	8	3	1	.312	.289
Pina, Manuel	R-R	5-11	165	6-5-87	.244	.100	.286	14	45	1	11	4	0	0	3	2	2	0	1	4	0	0	.333	.300
Podraza, Cody	R-R	5-8	185	11-6-87	.321	.455	.301	24	84	18	27	6	2	0	6	8	11	1	1	15	12	4	.440	.424
Rodriguez, Timothy	R-R	6-2	210	1-24-87	.196	.273	.188	31	97	11	19	1	1	2	10	6	4	2	0	24	1	3	.289	.271
Rodriguez, Jose	R-R	6-0	200	2-14-88	.266	.206	.282	49	184	22	49	6	3	0	20	14	1	0	1	44	3	4	.332	.320
Simon, Randall	L-L	6-0	240	5-25-75	.278	.333	.267	5	18	2	5	1	0	0	3	1	0	0	0	0	0	0	.333	.316
Teagarden, Taylor	R-R	6-1	200	12-21-83	.050	.000	.083	7	20	4	1	0	0	0	1	9	0	0	0	7	1	0	.050	.345
Trzesniak, Nick	R-R	6-0	210	11-19-80	.400	1.000	.333	7	20	4	8	5	0	0	2	4	0	0	1	1	0	0	.650	.500
Yan, Ruddy	B-R	6-0	160	1-13-82	.278	.333	.250	5	18	4	5	0	0	0	2	6	0	0	3	4	2	.278	.458
Yan, Johan	R-R	6-3	185	9-27-84	.218	.222	.220	39	119	20	26	5	1	2	12	11	5	1	0	50	0	1	.328	.311

PITCHING	B-T	HT	WT	DOB	W	L	ERA	G	GS	CG	SV	IP	H	R	ER	HR	BB	SO	AVG	vLH	vRH	K/9	BB/9
Bannister, John	R-R	6-4	198	1-20-84	0	0	4.50	1	0	0	0	2	1	1	1	0	0	6	.143	—	.143	27.00	0.00
Brigham, Jacob	R-R	6-3	190	2-10-88	2	6	3.70	14	11	0	0	58	54	37	24	5	19	58	.236	.270	.219	8.95	2.93
Bukvich, Ryan	R-R	6-2	250	5-13-78	0	0	0.00	1	0	0	0	2	1	0	0	0	0	1	.200	.000	.333	5.40	0.00
Castillo, Fabio	R-R	6-1	190	2-19-89	0	0	0.00	1	1	0	0	3	1	0	0	0	2	4	.100	.250	.000	12.00	6.00
Ford, Patrick	L-L	6-1	175	5-26-84	0	2	6.21	11	0	0	1	29	39	32	20	0	22	30	.317	.385	.299	9.31	6.83
Funk, Shane	R-R	6-6	235	5-9-87	0	9	9.00	15	10	0	0	39	55	48	39	5	35	36	.333	.293	.373	8.31	8.08
Galarraga, Armando	R-R	6-4	180	1-15-82	0	2	3.31	6	6	0	0	16	18	8	6	0	6	16	.290	.344	.233	8.82	3.31
Gudex, Timothy	L-L	6-0	165	9-23-82	2	0	0.00	7	0	0	1	14	5	1	0	0	4	18	.114	.000	.135	11.57	2.57
Haar, Jeremiah	L-R	6-2	190	12-29-84	3	0	7.23	10	0	0	0	19	30	17	15	2	8	14	.357	.455	.323	6.75	3.86
Herrera, Danny Ray	L-L	5-8	145	10-21-84	0	1	2.08	3	0	0	2	9	5	2	2	0	0	11	.172	.250	.160	11.42	0.00
Hoben, Daniel	L-L	5-11	185	6-29-87	1	0	4.44	11	4	0	2	26	23	13	13	0	9	28	.235	.261	.227	9.57	3.08
Hollis, Jonathan	R-R	6-3	240	9-17-83	1	0	8.38	9	0	0	0	19	25	18	18	0	8	21	.321	.366	.270	9.78	3.72
Izquierdo, Ivan	R-R	6-1	205	10-14-83	2	0	5.91	11	0	0	0	21	23	16	14	0	9	18	.267	.308	.234	7.53	3.80
James, Brandon	R-R	6-3	207	9-5-86	2	4	5.40	14	8	0	1	62	81	41	37	4	17	33	.321	.375	.284	4.82	2.48
Jensen, Ryan	R-R	6-0	255	9-17-75	0	0	4.50	1	1	0	0	2	2	1	1	0	1	0	.286	.667	.000	0.00	4.50
Kirkman, Michael	L-L	6-3	185	9-18-86	1	2	13.20	8	4	0	0	15	21	27	22	0	27	8	.333	.625	.291	4.80	16.20
Locke, Jared	L-L	6-6	225	8-14-84	3	4	4.56	14	7	0	0	47	50	29	24	2	22	40	.275	.231	.287	7.61	4.18
Nevarez, Matthew	R-R	6-5	220	2-26-87	0	0	9.00	1	0	0	0	1	2	1	1	1	0	2	.400	.500	.000	18.00	0.00
Rice, Forrest	L-L	6-0	180	11-29-85	0	1	5.60	14	0	0	0	35	50	24	22	2	12	19	.331	.363	.354	4.84	3.06
Rojas, Cesar	R-R	6-3	205	7-15-86	0	0	4.76	2	2	0	0	6	8	4	3	0	2	4	.320	.500	.286	6.35	3.18
Santana, Julio	B-R	6-1	175	12-26-85	1	2	3.45	10	0	0	1	16	7	7	6	1	13	16	.132	.000	.189	9.19	7.47
Tejeda, Robinson	R-R	6-3	230	3-24-82	0	0	6.75	2	2	0	0	4	4	3	3	0	0	6	.250	.250	.250	13.50	0.00
Ueno, Keisuke	R-R	6-4	205	3-6-86	1	3	4.95	13	0	0	2	36	37	24	20	3	22	29	.261	.319	.232	7.18	5.45
Wirth, Shannon	R-R	6-0	215	5-27-84	0	1	1.74	5	0	0	2	10	11	2	2	0	2	12	.262	.368	.174	10.45	1.74

FIELDING

Catcher	PCT	G	PO	A	E	DP	PB
Creswell	.955	22	144	27	8	1	9
Dominguez	.966	13	69	17	3	0	2
Gossage	.984	27	165	21	3	1	7
Martinez	.964	4	20	7	1	1	1
Trzesniak	.966	5	22	6	1	1	0

First Base	PCT	G	PO	A	E	DP
Bradbury	.949	6	53	3	3	3
Creswell	1.000	1	7	0	0	0
Gomez	.980	7	45	5	1	4
Jaimes	1.000	1	1	0	0	0
Nelson	.970	27	183	10	6	17
Rodriguez	.979	20	131	11	3	9
Simon	1.000	5	29	3	0	2

Second Base	PCT	G	PO	A	E	DP
Baldiris	1.000	2	1	7	0	0
Hooft	.949	11	20	17	2	7
Jaimes	1.000	3	8	4	0	2
James	.905	16	34	33	7	8
Osuna	.960	21	40	56	4	13
Yan	.946	9	13	22	2	2

Third Base	PCT	G	PO	A	E	DP
Bradbury	1.000	3	0	3	0	0
Gomez	1.000	4	3	8	0	0
Jaimes	.800	4	3	5	2	0
Rodriguez	.942	32	22	59	5	4
Yan	.857	19	14	22	6	2

Shortstop	PCT	G	PO	A	E	DP
Jaimes	1.000	2	7	3	0	0

James	.918	24	35	77	10	12
Lemon	.896	24	37	58	11	10
Yan	.794	12	23	27	13	7

Outfield	PCT	G	PO	A	E	DP
Anderson	.965	37	78	4	3	1
Barrios	.986	44	69	4	1	1
Botts	1.000	3	3	0	0	0
Bradbury	.953	24	41	0	2	0
Estrella	.912	20	31	0	3	0
Jaimes	.955	18	21	0	1	0
Murphy	1.000	1	4	0	0	0
Napoli	.933	10	14	0	1	0
Podraza	.982	24	52	3	1	2
Rodriguez	1.000	1	3	0	0	0
Yan	1.000	5	12	1	0	0

BY LARRY MILLSON

The Blue Jays had their best finish in the American League East since 1993—when they won their second World Series—but still missed the playoffs as they finished second to the Yankees and behind the Tigers for the wild card.

They won 87 games, the most since 1998 when they won 88, but postseason appearances since the World Series years continue to elude them. The season was considered a step forward, but to continue to progress the team will need to further improve its rotation.

The Jays had high hopes for 2006 after winning 80 games in 2005. They made a big splash during the off-season by signing free-agent pitchers B.J. Ryan and A.J. Burnett. They also traded for third baseman Troy Glaus (who hit 38 home runs with 104 RBIs) and first baseman Lyle Overbay (who hit .312) and signed catcher Bengie Molina (who hit .284 with 19 home runs) as a free agent.

Ryan performed as expected with 38 saves in 42 opportunities. But Burnett missed nearly half of the season because his surgically repaired elbow acted up, and he went 10-8, 3.96. Two other members of the rotation also had disappointing seasons. Lefthander Gustavo Chacin was limited to 17 starts because of an elbow injury. Josh Towers was not injured but pitched poorly and twice cleared waivers on an outright assignment to Triple A Syracuse.

Staff ace Roy Halladay was the first major league pitcher to reach 16 wins—reaching the mark on Aug. 20—but he did not win in six starts after that and missed his final two starts of the season with a forearm strain. He finished 16-5, 3.19.

PLAYERS OF THE YEAR

MAJOR LEAGUE: Roy Halladay, rhp

Seven of Halladay's 32 starts came against the Yankees and Red Sox, and 17 were at Rogers Centre, one of the most hitter-friendly environments in the American League. That he paced the Blue Jays with 220 innings, 16 wins and a 3.19 ERA—second in the AL— underlines how vital he is to the club's success.

MINOR LEAGUE: Adam Lind, of

Lind turned his power up a notch in 2006, hitting 26 home runs between Double-A, Triple-A and Toronto to more than double his previous high. He led the Eastern League with a .543 slugging percentage—a big reason why he was named MVP—and challenged for the triple crown before a July promotion.

Lefthander Ted Lilly won a career-high 15 against 13 losses, with an ERA of 4.31. He showed improvement after a tiff with manager John Gibbons, when he was removed from a start after letting an 8-0 lead slip away.

It was the second problem Gibbons had with a player during the 2006 season. Shea Hillenbrand was traded to the Giants in late July after the he expressed his unhappiness with then organization and Gibbons challenged him in the clubhouse.

Opening Day shortstop Russ Adams, the club's first-round pick in 2002, struggled at the plate (batting .219) and in the field, and he also was twice sent to Syracuse and will go into 2007 needing to earn a spot on the team. If he has a future with the organization it will be at second base.

Vernon Wells was solid in center field again, and after a winter of hard work and an appearance in the World Baseball Classic he had a good April, a month when he has struggled in recent years. He ended up batting .303/.357/.542 with 32 home runs and 106 RBIs.

Left fielder Reed Johnson showed he could be an everyday player, and Alexis Rios batted .302 in a breakout season in which he was chosen to play in the All-Star Game. He had to miss the game because a staph infection in his leg put him in hospital and on the disabled list. He took time to regain his groove after leaving the DL.

In September the Blue Jays got a glimpse of the future in left fielder Adam Lind, who batted .367 in 18 games. He was the player of the year in the Double-A Eastern League with New Hampshire, where he batted .310 before going to Triple-A Syracuse, where he batted .394. He was one of the organization's two players of the year. Outfielder Travis Snider, the team's first-round pick in June, won the award in the Rookie-level Appalachian League by hitting .325 for Pulaski.

Blue Jays prospects won't be performing in Pulsaki in future years, however, because the organization dropped its Appy League operation after the season. The organization intends to go with just five minor league affiliates in 2007.

ORGANIZATION LEADERS

BATTING	*Minimum 250 at-bats	
*AVG	Lind, Adam, New Hampshire/Syracuse	.330
R	Cannon, Chip, New Hampshire	94
H	Patterson, Ryan, Dunedin/New Hampshire	161
TB	Patterson, Ryan, Dunedin/New Hampshire	285
2B	Patterson, Ryan, Dunedin/New Hampshire	42
3B	Lydon, Wayne, Syracuse	12
HR	Cannon, Chip, New Hampshire	34
RBI	Patterson, Ryan, Dunedin/New Hampshire	93
BB	Majewski, Dustin, Dunedin/New Hampshire	100
SO	Cannon, Chip, New Hampshire	176
SB	Klosterman, Ryan, Dunedin/New Hampshire	27
*OBP	Emanuele, Chris, Pulaski/Auburn	.412
	Snider, Travis, Pulaski	.412
*SLG	Snider, Travis, Pulaski	.567
XBH	Patterson, Ryan, Dunedin/New Hampshire	70

PITCHING	#Minimum 75 innings	
W	MacDonald, Michael, New Hampshire	13
	Trias, Orlando, Dunedin	13
L	Isenberg, Kurt, New Hampshire/Dunedin	12
	Purcey, David, Syracuse/New Hampshire	12
#ERA	Ramirez, Ismael, New Hampshire/Syracuse	2.42
G	Thorpe, Tracy, New Hampshire	60
CG	Litsch, Jesse, New Hampshire/Dunedin	3
SV	Tavarez, Milton, Dunedin	21
IP	MacDonald, Michael, New Hampshire	171
BB	Purcey, David, Syracuse/New Hampshire	82
SO	Cheng, Chi-Hung, Lansing	154
#AVG	Carnline, William, Lansing/Dunedin	.220

Toronto Blue Jays — MLB

American League

BATTING	B-T	HT	WT	DOB	AVG	vLH	vRH	G	AB	R	H	2B	3B	HR	RBI	BB	HBP	SH	SF	SO	SB	CS	SLG	OBP
Adams, Russ	L-R	6-0	195	8-30-80	.219	.135	.234	90	251	31	55	14	1	3	28	22	1	3	3	41	1	2	.319	.282
Alfonzo, Edgardo	R-R	5-11	210	11-8-73	.162	.222	.143	12	37	4	6	1	0	0	4	5	1	0	0	10	0	0	.189	.279
2-team (18 Los Angeles)					.126	—	—	30	87	5	11	2	0	0	5	7	1	0	0	4	0	0	.149	.200
Barker, Kevin	L-L	6-1	235	7-26-75	.235	.000	.250	12	17	3	4	1	0	1	1	1	0	0	0	10	0	0	.471	.278
Catalanotto, Frank	L-R	6-0	195	4-27-74	.300	.237	.306	128	437	56	131	36	2	7	56	52	4	2	4	37	1	3	.439	.376
Figueroa, Luis	B-R	5-9	165	2-16-74	.111	.000	.143	8	9	1	1	1	0	0	0	0	0	0	0	2	0	0	.222	.111
Glaus, Troy	R-R	6-5	240	8-3-76	.252	.292	.238	153	540	105	136	27	0	38	104	86	3	0	5	134	3	2	.513	.355
Hattig, John	B-R	6-2	230	2-27-80	.333	.000	.381	13	24	2	8	1	0	0	3	5	0	0	0	8	0	0	.375	.448
Hill, Aaron	R-R	5-11	195	3-21-82	.291	.298	.288	155	546	70	159	28	3	6	50	42	9	4	5	66	5	2	.386	.349
Hillenbrand, Shea	R-R	6-1	210	7-27-75	.301	.337	.286	81	296	40	89	15	1	12	39	14	6	0	3	40	1	2	.480	.342
Hinske, Eric	L-R	6-2	235	8-5-77	.264	.135	.294	78	197	35	52	9	2	12	29	27	0	0	0	49	1	1	.513	.353
2-team (31 Boston)					.271	—	—	109	277	43	75	17	2	13	34	35	0	0	0	79	2	2	.487	.353
Johnson, Reed	R-R	5-10	180	12-8-76	.319	.323	.316	134	461	86	147	34	2	12	49	33	21	1	1	81	8	2	.479	.390
Lind, Adam	L-L	6-2	195	7-17-83	.367	.444	.353	18	60	8	22	8	0	2	8	5	0	0	1	12	0	0	.600	.415
McDonald, John	R-R	5-11	185	9-24-74	.223	.230	.220	104	260	35	58	7	3	3	23	16	2	6	2	41	7	2	.308	.271
Molina, Bengie	R-R	5-11	225	7-20-74	.284	.358	.246	117	433	44	123	20	1	19	57	19	4	0	2	47	1	1	.467	.319
Mottola, Chad	R-R	6-3	235	10-15-71	.250	.182	.400	10	16	3	4	2	0	0	0	0	0	0	0	3	0	0	.375	.250
Overbay, Lyle	L-L	6-2	235	1-28-77	.312	.284	.322	157	581	82	181	46	1	22	92	55	2	0	2	96	5	3	.508	.372
Phillips, Jason	R-R	6-1	210	9-27-76	.250	.290	.176	25	48	4	12	6	0	0	6	1	1	0	1	5	0	1	.375	.275
Rios, Alex	R-R	6-5	195	2-18-81	.302	.295	.305	128	450	68	136	33	6	17	82	35	3	0	10	89	15	6	.516	.349
Roberts, Ryan	R-R	5-11	190	9-19-80	.077	—	.077	9	13	1	1	0	0	1	1	1	0	0	0	4	0	0	.308	.143
Wells, Vernon	R-R	6-1	225	12-8-78	.303	.330	.292	154	611	91	185	40	5	32	106	54	3	0	9	90	17	4	.542	.357
Zaun, Gregg	B-R	5-10	190	4-14-71	.272	.373	.251	99	290	39	79	19	0	12	40	41	3	0	5	42	0	2	.462	.363

PITCHING	B-T	HT	WT	DOB	W	L	ERA	G	GS	CG	SV	IP	H	R	ER	HR	BB	SO	AVG	vLH	vRH	K/9	BB/9
Accardo, Jeremy	R-R	6-2	190	12-8-81	1	1	5.97	27	0	0	0	29	38	19	19	5	9	14	.325	.288	.354	4.40	2.83
Burnett, A.J.	R-R	6-4	230	1-3-77	10	8	3.98	21	21	2	0	136	138	67	60	14	39	118	.264	.261	.267	7.83	2.59
Chacin, Gustavo	L-L	5-11	195	12-4-80	9	4	5.05	17	17	0	0	87	90	51	49	19	38	47	.266	.268	.266	4.84	3.92
Chulk, Vinnie	R-R	6-1	195	12-19-78	1	0	5.25	20	0	0	0	24	29	16	14	4	5	18	.293	.243	.323	6.75	1.88
Downs, Scott	L-L	6-2	190	3-17-76	6	2	4.09	59	5	0	1	77	73	38	35	9	30	61	.249	.232	.258	7.13	3.51
Frasor, Jason	R-R	5-10	170	8-9-77	3	2	4.32	51	0	0	0	50	47	24	24	8	17	51	.244	.211	.262	9.18	3.06
Halladay, Roy	R-R	6-6	225	5-14-77	16	5	3.19	32	32	4	0	220	208	82	78	19	34	132	.251	.259	.244	5.40	1.39
Janssen, Casey	R-R	6-4	205	9-17-81	6	10	5.07	19	17	0	0	94	103	58	53	12	21	44	.275	.292	.261	4.21	2.01
League, Brandon	R-R	6-2	195	3-16-83	1	2	2.53	33	0	0	1	43	34	17	12	3	9	29	.214	.276	.178	6.12	1.90
Lilly, Ted	L-L	6-1	190	1-4-76	15	13	4.31	32	32	0	0	182	179	98	87	28	81	160	.254	.202	.265	7.93	4.01
Marcum, Shaun	R-R	6-0	190	12-14-81	3	4	5.06	21	14	0	0	78	87	44	44	14	38	65	.279	.303	.256	7.47	4.37
McGowan, Dustin	R-R	6-2	215	3-24-82	1	2	7.24	16	3	0	0	27	35	27	22	2	25	22	.304	.327	.283	7.24	8.23
Romero, Davis	L-L	5-10	170	3-30-83	1	0	3.86	7	0	0	0	16	19	7	7	1	6	10	.297	.318	.286	5.51	3.31
Rosario, Francisco	R-R	6-1	215	9-28-80	1	2	6.65	17	1	0	0	23	24	17	17	4	16	21	.264	.310	.242	8.22	6.26
Ryan, B.J.	L-L	6-6	260	12-28-75	2	2	1.37	65	0	0	38	72	42	12	11	3	20	86	.169	.120	.182	10.70	2.49
Schoeneweis, Scott	L-L	6-0	190	10-2-73	2	2	6.51	55	0	0	1	37	39	27	27	3	16	18	.273	.257	.290	4.34	3.86
Speier, Justin	R-R	6-4	205	11-6-73	2	0	2.98	58	0	0	0	51	47	18	17	5	21	55	.235	.183	.264	9.64	3.68
Tallet, Brian	L-L	6-6	215	9-21-77	3	0	3.81	44	1	0	0	54	45	24	23	5	31	37	.238	.220	.246	6.13	5.13
Taubenheim, Ty	R-R	6-6	250	11-17-82	1	5	4.89	12	7	0	0	35	40	22	19	5	18	26	.282	.262	.296	6.69	4.63
Towers, Josh	R-R	6-1	180	2-26-77	2	10	8.42	15	12	0	0	62	93	62	58	17	17	35	.343	.325	.357	5.08	2.47
Walker, Pete	R-R	6-2	195	4-8-69	1	1	5.40	23	0	0	1	30	37	24	18	5	13	27	.296	.318	.284	8.10	3.90

FIELDING

Catcher	PCT	G	PO	A	E	DP	PB
Molina	.997	99	614	48	2	6	11
Phillips	1.000	9	41	1	0	0	0
Zaun	.994	72	437	32	3	2	4

First Base	PCT	G	PO	A	E	DP
Barker	1.000	2	13	0	0	0
Hillenbrand	.987	19	136	12	2	14
Hinske	1.000	4	15	0	0	1
Overbay	.994	145	1357	93	9	124
Phillips	.958	6	23	0	1	1

Second Base	PCT	G	PO	A	E	DP
Adams	.987	50	59	98	2	18

	PCT	G	PO	A	E	DP
Alfonzo	1.000	12	14	31	0	4
Figueroa	.900	3	4	5	1	2
Hill	.987	112	174	345	7	93
McDonald	1.000	10	11	15	0	3
Roberts	1.000	8	8	11	0	3

Third Base	PCT	G	PO	A	E	DP
Glaus	.963	145	95	271	14	37
Hattig	1.000	10	4	14	0	1
Hillenbrand	.828	17	6	18	5	2
Hinske	1.000	10	3	14	0	1
McDonald	—	2	0	0	0	0

Shortstop	PCT	G	PO	A	E	DP
Adams	.928	36	41	88	10	18

	PCT	G	PO	A	E	DP
Figueroa	1.000	2	2	2	0	0
Glaus	1.000	8	5	18	0	2
Hill	.941	63	60	130	12	19
McDonald	.960	90	105	231	14	57

Outfield	PCT	G	PO	A	E	DP
Barker	.500	1	0	1	0	0
Catalanotto	.994	102	143	10	1	3
Hinske	1.000	30	41	2	0	1
Johnson	.996	133	213	12	1	2
Lind	1.000	2	4	0	0	0
Mottola	1.000	5	3	0	0	0
Rios	.996	125	224	8	1	2
Wells	.988	150	332	4	4	3

Syracuse SkyChiefs — Triple-A

International League

BATTING	B-T	HT	WT	DOB	AVG	vLH	vRH	G	AB	R	H	2B	3B	HR	RBI	BB	HBP	SH	SF	SO	SB	CS	SLG	OBP
Adams, Russ	L-R	6-0	195	8-30-80	.311	.321	.305	42	161	21	50	9	3	0	15	17	0	0	1	23	3	2	.404	.374
Barker, Kevin	L-L	6-1	235	7-26-75	.275	.270	.277	130	473	72	130	39	2	18	76	80	2	0	4	119	5	3	.480	.379
Cosby, Rob	R-R	6-1	215	4-2-81	.252	.291	.235	123	453	54	114	24	1	18	66	21	6	5	1	97	1	3	.428	.293
Figueroa, Luis	B-R	5-9	165	2-16-74	.276	.290	.270	93	377	39	104	22	3	6	38	24	2	8	6	35	11	9	.398	.318
Griffin, John-Ford	L-L	6-2	220	11-19-79	.225	.231	.221	60	227	30	51	14	0	6	22	19	2	0	1	59	2	0	.388	.289
Hattig, John	B-R	6-2	230	2-27-80	.276	.250	.287	103	373	48	103	30	1	4	36	35	2	3	0	108	0	1	.394	.341
Jova, Maikel	R-R	6-0	205	3-5-81	.233	.200	.240	9	30	1	7	0	0	0	0	5	0	0	0	5	0	0	.233	.233
Kratz, Erik	R-R	6-4	240	6-15-80	.250	.385	.185	12	40	12	10	2	0	1	7	5	0	0	2	4	0	0	.375	.319
Lind, Adam	L-L	6-2	195	7-17-83	.394	.265	.453	34	109	20	43	7	0	5	18	23	2	0	3	18	1	0	.596	.496
Lydon, Wayne	B-R	6-2	195	4-17-81	.263	.310	.245	132	513	80	135	16	12	9	46	53	3	10	1	120	26	10	.394	.335

General manager: J.P. Ricciardi. **Farm director:** Dick Scott. **Scouting director:** Jon Lalonde.

Class	Team	League	W	L	PCT	Finish*	Manager	Affiliate Since
Majors	Toronto	American	87	75	.537	7th (14)	John Gibbons	—
Triple-A	Syracuse SkyChiefs	International	64	79	.448	12th (14)	Michael Basso	1978
Double-A	New Hampshire Fisher Cats	Eastern	68	73	.482	7th (12)	Doug Davis	2003
High A	Dunedin Blue Jays	Florida State	68	69	.496	8th (12)	Omar Malave	1987
Low A	Lansing Lugnuts	Midwest	72	65	.526	7th (12)	Ken Joyce	2005
Short-season	Auburn Doubledays	New York-Penn	42	32	.568	3rd (14)	Dennis Holmberg	2001
Rookie	Pulaski Blue Jays	Appalachian	35	33	.515	3rd (10)	Dave Pano	2003
OVERALL 2006 MINOR LEAGUE RECORD			349	351	.499	16th (30)		

*Finish in overall standings (No. of teams in league). +League champion

	B-T	HT	WT	DOB				G	AB	R	H	2B	3B	HR	RBI	BB	HBP	SH	SF	SO	SB	CS	SLG	OBP
Mahoney, Mike	R-R	6-0	200	12-5-72	.200	.274	.172	70	225	17	45	8	0	1	17	12	3	1	4	53	0	2	.249	.246
Mottola, Chad	R-R	6-3	235	10-15-71	.265	.305	.248	110	431	48	114	27	2	16	65	30	2	0	1	103	8	0	.448	.315
Phillips, Jason	R-R	6-1	210	9-27-76	.273	.270	.274	70	249	31	68	11	0	7	40	22	4	5	1	43	1	1	.402	.341
Rios, Alex	R-R	6-5	195	2-18-81	.300	.333	.250	3	10	0	3	1	0	0	1	1	0	0	0	3	0	0	.400	.364
Roberts, Ryan	R-R	5-11	190	9-19-80	.273	.283	.270	98	362	44	99	28	1	10	49	30	2	6	3	86	5	3	.439	.330
Santos, Sergio	R-R	6-3	225	7-4-83	.214	.267	.194	128	481	48	103	24	1	5	38	24	2	2	0	96	1	3	.299	.254
Schneider, John	R-R	6-3	250	2-14-80	.200	.000	.333	3	10	0	2	1	0	0	2	0	0	0	0	2	0	0	.300	.333
Singleton, Justin	L-R	6-2	190	4-10-79	.205	.250	.195	58	200	25	41	8	1	6	18	21	1	2	0	81	2	0	.345	.284
Solano, Danny	R-R	6-0	200	12-3-75	.222	.227	.220	26	72	6	16	3	0	1	4	6	1	1	1	18	0	0	.306	.288
Sweppenhiser, Kelly	R-R	6-0	185	11-25-83	.000	.000	—	1	1	0	0	0	0	0	0	0	0	0	1	0	0	.000	.000
Thigpen, Curtis	R-R	5-10	185	4-19-83	.264	.438	.189	13	53	3	14	3	0	1	9	2	1	0	0	9	0	1	.377	.304

PITCHING	B-T	HT	WT	DOB	W	L	ERA	G	GS	CG	SV	IP	H	R	ER	HR	BB	SO	AVG	vLH	vRH	K/9	BB/9
Baldwin, James	R-R	6-3	265	7-15-71	0	0	3.38	2	0	0	0	3	4	3	1	1	0	1	.267	.500	.231	3.38	0.00
Banks, Josh	R-R	6-3	215	7-18-82	10	11	5.17	29	29	0	0	171	184	108	98	35	28	126	.267	.255	.277	6.64	1.48
Burnett, A.J.	R-R	6-4	230	1-3-77	1	0	0.00	1	1	0	0	5	0	0	0	0	1	7	.000	.000	.000	12.60	1.80
Burnside, Adrian	R-L	6-4	210	3-15-77	3	0	3.48	33	0	0	0	34	26	17	13	4	13	32	.208	.195	.214	8.55	3.48
Chacin, Gustavo	L-L	5-11	195	12-4-80	0	3	10.13	4	4	0	0	11	22	12	12	1	3	11	.400	.308	.429	9.28	2.53
Chulk, Vinnie	R-R	6-1	195	12-19-78	3	2	2.25	19	0	0	1	32	20	8	8	4	14	43	.175	.214	.153	12.09	3.94
De Jong, Jordan	R-R	6-2	200	4-12-79	2	0	4.12	22	0	0	0	39	38	19	18	3	13	33	.259	.270	.250	7.55	2.97
Figueroa, Luis	B-R	5-9	165	2-16-74	0	0	—	1	0	0	0	1	1	1	0	0	0	0	1.000	—	1.000	—	—
Frasor, Jason	R-R	5-10	170	8-9-77	3	1	3.98	18	0	0	1	20	21	10	9	1	13	33	.266	.194	.313	14.61	5.75
Gronkiewicz, Lee	R-R	5-10	200	8-21-78	2	3	3.27	41	0	0	17	44	47	18	16	4	8	33	.272	.222	.300	6.75	1.64
Houston, Ryan	R-R	6-4	230	9-22-79	2	4	3.68	46	0	0	2	66	68	37	27	2	38	68	.262	.288	.244	9.27	5.18
Howard, Ben	R-R	6-2	200	1-15-79	1	1	8.82	11	0	0	0	17	20	18	17	6	8	7	.323	.316	.333	4.41	3.86
2-team (34 Buffalo)					3	2	5.37	45	0	0	11	57	59	36	34	7	21	29	—	—	—	4.58	3.32
Janssen, Casey	R-R	6-4	205	9-17-81	1	5	4.85	9	9	0	0	43	47	23	23	3	8	32	.283	.277	.287	6.75	1.69
League, Brandon	R-R	6-2	195	3-16-83	3	2	2.14	31	1	0	8	55	57	19	13	0	15	43	.273	.272	.273	7.08	2.47
Marcum, Shaun	R-R	6-0	190	12-14-81	4	0	3.42	18	5	0	0	53	48	20	20	6	9	60	.241	.224	.250	10.25	1.54
McGowan, Dustin	R-R	6-2	215	3-24-82	4	5	4.39	23	13	0	1	84	77	45	41	7	39	86	.238	.254	.227	9.21	4.18
Ormond, Rodney	R-R	6-4	220	6-17-77	0	1	6.75	4	0	0	0	5	7	4	4	2	3	4	.304	.333	.286	6.75	5.06
Purcey, David	L-L	6-5	235	4-22-82	2	7	5.40	12	12	1	0	52	49	41	31	7	38	45	.249	.237	.252	7.84	6.62
Ramirez, Ismael	R-R	6-2	205	3-3-81	2	0	4.50	3	3	0	0,	18	16	9	9	3	3	8	.242	.278	.200	4.00	1.50
Romero, Davis	L-L	5-10	170	3-30-83	4	4	3.83	18	3	0	1	45	46	25	19	3	7	36	.264	.119	.311	7.25	1.41
Rosario, Francisco	R-R	6-1	215	9-28-80	0	3	2.79	14	8	0	1	42	29	14	13	2	13	50	.196	.132	.232	10.71	2.79
Savickas, Russ	R-R	6-4	190	7-30-83	0	1	7.36	1	1	0	0	4	4	3	3	1	0	3	.286	.286	.286	0.00	7.36
Scobie, Jason	R-R	6-1	195	9-1-79	2	7	4.63	12	8	1	1	56	60	31	29	10	16	36	.268	.231	.300	5.75	2.56
2-team (16 Norfolk)					3	18	6.53	28	23	1	1	133	177	101	97	19	47	83	—	—	—	5.59	3.16
Solano, Danny	R-R	5-9	200	12-3-75	0	0	27.00	1	0	0	0	1	3	1	1	0	1	0	.750	.500	1.000	0.00	27.00
Tallet, Brian	L-L	6-6	215	9-21-77	1	2	5.68	20	0	0	3	25	32	17	16	4	10	21	.317	.333	.312	7.46	3.55
Taubenheim, Ty	R-R	6-6	250	11-17-82	2	4	2.85	18	14	0	0	76	75	25	24	9	18	48	.261	.264	.259	5.71	2.14
Towers, Josh	R-R	6-1	195	2-26-77	5	5	4.00	15	15	0	0	101	121	53	45	12	11	76	.300	.286	.311	6.75	0.98
Vermilyea, James	R-R	6-4	200	2-10-82	6	7	3.85	25	17	0	1	115	129	57	49	9	28	64	.291	.313	.273	5.02	2.20
Weber, Ben	R-R	6-4	205	11-17-69	1	1	4.33	12	0	0	1	44	48	27	21	5	10	42	.276	.344	.239	8.66	2.06

FIELDING

Catcher	PCT	G	PO	A	E	DP	PB
Kratz	1.000	12	99	5	0	0	
Mahoney	.991	64	428	30	4	3	7
Phillips	.989	56	435	22	5	2	3
Schneider	1.000	3	17	1	0	0	1
Thigpen	.990	13	95	2	1	0	0

First Base	PCT	G	PO	A	E	DP
Barker	.989	103	843	79	10	91
Cosby	1.000	8	64	6	0	9
Hattig	.981	23	195	12	4	20
Mottola	1.000	1	3	0	0	0
Phillips	.991	12	110	2	1	13

Second Base	PCT	G	PO	A	E	DP
Adams	.951	39	59	114	9	17
Figueroa	.958	25	61	77	6	26
Roberts	.977	75	149	231	9	56
Solano	1.000	5	13	15	0	5

Third Base	PCT	G	PO	A	E	DP
Cosby	.977	45	30	95	3	8
Figueroa	.958	29	29	63	4	8
Hattig	.929	53	29	101	10	6
Roberts	.778	5	3	4	2	0
Solano	.917	16	9	24	3	2
Sweppenhiser	—	1	0	0	0	0

Shortstop	PCT	G	PO	A	E	DP
Figueroa	.974	17	22	52	2	12
Santos	.952	126	176	356	27	87

Outfield	PCT	G	PO	A	E	DP
Cosby	.976	54	76	5	2	0
Griffin	.952	55	95	4	5	0
Jova	1.000	7	10	0	0	0
Lind	.988	34	76	3	1	1
Lydon	.977	131	280	12	7	4
Mottola	.977	97	163	7	4	2
Rios	1.000	1	1	0	0	0
Singleton	.991	57	107	5	1	0
Solano	1.000	2	1	0	0	0

New Hampshire Fisher Cats — Double-A

Eastern League

BATTING	B-T	HT	WT	DOB	AVG	vLH	vRH	G	AB	R	H	2B	3B	HR	RBI	BB	HBP	SH	SF	SO	SB	CS	SLG	OBP
Alfonzo, Edgardo	R-R	5-11	210	11-8-73	.000	.000	.000	3	8	1	0	0	0	0	0	2	0	0	0	1	0	0	.000	.200
Arnold, Eric	R-R	6-1	195	7-9-80	.255	.289	.240	44	141	14	36	10	0	5	26	10	1	3	4	48	0	3	.433	.301
Cannon, Chip	L-R	6-5	225	11-30-81	.248	.265	.242	135	475	78	118	25	1	27	69	51	11	1	1	158	0	2	.476	.335

	B-T	HT	WT	DOB	AVG	vLH	vRH	G	AB	R	H	2B	3B	HR	RBI	BB	HBP	SH	SF	SO	SB	CS	SLG	OBP
Chiaravalloti, Vito	R-R	6-3	225	10-26-80	.190	.189	.190	42	137	17	26	3	0	6	18	14	2	1	2	45	0	0	.343	.271
Corrente, David	R-R	6-2	210	10-13-83	.333	—	.333	1	3	0	1	1	0	0	1	1	0	0	0	2	0	0	.667	.500
Cota, Carlo	R-R	5-9	185	9-18-80	.198	.158	.222	73	202	31	40	10	1	1	12	34	2	6	1	67	4	0	.272	.318
Davenport, Ron	L-R	6-2	210	10-16-81	.181	.158	.190	41	138	9	25	4	0	3	15	9	0	1	4	25	0	1	.275	.225
Hassey, Brad	R-R	5-10	180	11-28-79	.196	.228	.184	102	331	33	65	15	0	2	22	19	7	8	0	45	1	2	.260	.255
Jova, Maikel	R-R	6-0	205	3-5-81	.192	.098	.241	31	120	11	23	9	0	0	14	3	0	0	0	23	0	0	.267	.211
Klosterman, Ryan	R-R	5-11	185	5-28-82	.248	.111	.282	43	137	22	34	5	0	4	16	17	7	3	1	37	7	3	.372	.358
Kratz, Erik	R-R	6-4	240	6-15-80	.225	.265	.206	71	258	34	58	10	0	6	27	16	8	1	1	54	1	0	.333	.290
Kuzmic, Craig	B-R	6-0	180	5-2-77	.105	.000	.125	6	19	4	2	1	0	0	2	5	1	0	0	10	0	0	.158	.320
Lind, Adam	L-L	6-2	195	7-17-83	.310	.267	.328	91	348	43	108	24	0	19	71	25	2	0	3	87	2	1	.543	.357
Majewski, Dustin	L-L	5-11	205	8-16-81	.233	.238	.231	65	236	44	55	8	1	13	33	51	2	1	1	56	1	1	.441	.372
Mayorson, Manuel	R-R	5-10	185	3-10-83	.277	.232	.296	125	477	48	132	19	1	2	55	21	5	11	3	44	12	11	.333	.312
Miller, Tony	R-R	5-9	200	8-18-80	.241	.298	.214	43	145	25	35	7	0	0	8	37	1	4	0	55	6	4	.290	.399
Negron, Miguel	L-L	6-2	170	8-22-82	.215	.302	.172	33	130	12	28	5	0	2	12	9	0	0	0	25	2	5	.300	.266
Olson, Tim	R-R	6-2	200	8-1-78	.268	.244	.276	48	168	19	45	11	0	6	18	15	0	1	1	43	5	2	.440	.326
Patterson, Ryan	R-R	5-11	205	5-2-83	.257	.271	.252	49	187	19	48	14	1	6	20	13	2	2	1	50	2	0	.439	.310
Schneider, John	R-R	6-3	250	2-14-80	.222	.313	.172	15	45	4	10	5	0	1	4	6	1	0	1	20	0	1	.400	.321
Singleton, Justin	L-R	6-2	190	4-10-79	.194	.000	.214	9	31	4	6	3	0	0	4	4	0	1	0	8	0	0	.290	.286
Smith, David	R-R	6-2	190	1-12-81	.253	.320	.223	130	483	67	122	33	1	19	74	40	7	0	3	118	7	4	.443	.317
Solano, Danny	R-R	5-9	200	12-3-75	.161	.000	.185	21	62	5	10	4	0	0	4	7	1	0	0	18	1	0	.226	.257
Thigpen, Curtis	R-R	5-10	185	4-19-83	.259	.352	.220	87	309	49	80	25	5	5	36	52	4	5	3	61	5	1	.421	.390
Urgelles, Jeff	R-R	6-1	200	6-19-82	.500	—	.500	2	2	0	1	0	0	0	0	0	0	0	0	0	0	0	.500	.500

PITCHING	B-T	HT	WT	DOB	W	L	ERA	G	GS	CG	SV	IP	H	R	ER	HR	BB	SO	AVG	vLH	vRH	K/9	BB/9
Arnold, Jason	R-R	6-3	210	5-2-79	0	2	1.90	12	2	0	0	24	17	6	5	1	10	29	.207	.216	.200	11.03	3.80
Bullard, Jim	L-L	6-7	225	12-29-79	2	2	3.46	32	0	0	2	26	25	15	10	2	13	29	.250	.341	.186	10.04	4.50
Burnett, A.J.	R-R	6-4	230	1-3-77	1	0	1.50	1	1	0	0	6	2	2	1	1	3	9	.105	.000	.143	13.50	4.50
De Jong, Jordan	R-R	6-2	200	4-12-79	0	0	1.45	23	0	0	0	37	26	6	6	2	14	38	.188	.186	.191	9.16	3.38
Fahrner, Evan	R-R	6-2	200	3-4-78	0	0	6.35	3	0	0	0	6	7	5	4	0	4	5	.304	.400	.231	7.94	6.35
2-team (33 Reading)..					1	4	3.71	36	0	0	3	51	45	27	21	3	28	55	—	—	—	9.71	4.94
Falkenbach, Connor	R-R	6-0	185	2-22-82	0	0	6.75	7	0	0	0	9	14	8	7	0	5	5	.350	.357	.346	4.82	4.50
Hill, Danny	R-R	6-0	205	11-5-81	3	7	5.54	44	3	0	0	75	90	49	46	10	30	62	.299	.308	.291	7.47	3.62
Houston, Ryan	R-R	6-4	230	9-22-79	1	0	2.70	5	0	0	0	7	6	2	2	1	2	11	.231	.353	.000	14.85	2.70
Isenberg, Kurt	R-L	6-0	190	1-15-82	3	9	5.67	20	14	0	0	87	121	57	55	5	22	55	.330	.339	.326	5.67	2.27
James, Justin	R-R	6-3	215	9-13-81	2	0	2.38	24	0	0	0	42	42	11	11	2	10	38	.264	.297	.242	8.21	2.16
Kratz, Erik	R-R	6-4	240	6-15-80	0	0	27.00	1	0	0	0	1	4	3	3	0	1	1	.571	.000	.800	9.00	9.00
Litsch, Jesse	R-R	6-1	205	3-9-85	3	4	5.06	12	12	1	0	69	85	44	39	6	13	54	.309	.310	.308	7.01	1.69
MacDonald, Michael	R-R	6-1	195	10-29-81	13	9	3.94	28	28	2	0	171	180	85	75	9	37	103	.271	.341	.198	5.41	1.94
Ormond, Rodney	R-R	6-4	220	6-17-77	6	5	2.44	51	0	0	6	74	53	25	20	8	15	54	.205	.157	.243	6.60	1.83
Phillips, Paul	R-R	6-2	225	1-26-84	0	0	7.71	3	0	0	0	2	3	2	2	0	3	5	.222	.250	.200	19.29	11.57
Purcey, David	L-L	6-5	235	4-22-82	4	5	5.60	16	16	0	0	88	101	59	55	9	44	81	.287	.319	.275	8.25	4.48
Ramirez, Ismael	R-R	6-2	205	3-3-81	7	5	2.08	20	19	0	0	108	85	31	25	10	32	75	.218	.226	.212	6.23	2.66
Romero, Davis	L-L	5-10	170	3-30-83	6	5	2.93	12	12	1	0	74	57	27	24	3	19	70	.213	.188	.223	8.55	2.32
Romero, Ricardo	R-L	6-1	195	11-6-84	2	7	5.08	12	12	0	0	67	65	43	38	7	26	41	.256	.200	.279	5.48	3.48
Scobie, Jason	R-R	6-1	195	9-1-79	1	0	1.50	1	1	0	0	6	8	1	1	0	0	2	.320	.583	.077	3.00	0.00
Thorpe, Tracy	R-R	6-4	255	12-15-80	3	1	2.91	54	0	0	18	56	33	20	18	4	29	62	.169	.184	.160	10.02	4.69
Vermilyea, James	R-R	6-4	200	2-10-82	0	0	1.65	5	1	0	1	16	15	4	3	0	0	7	.242	.235	.250	3.86	0.00
Wolfe, Brian	R-R	6-3	225	11-29-80	1	3	5.74	24	2	0	0	42	54	30	27	5	15	34	.302	.329	.277	7.23	3.19
Yates, Kyle	R-R	5-11	190	1-8-83	6	9	3.75	28	18	1	1	127	118	60	53	10	38	102	.246	.219	.273	7.21	2.69

FIELDING

Catcher	PCT	G	PO	A	E	DP	PB
Corrente	1.000	1	9	1	0	0	0
Kratz	.993	58	410	36	3	5	8
Kuzmic	.933	2	14	0	1	0	0
Schneider	.986	9	66	5	1	0	0
Thigpen	.987	73	509	42	7	5	13
Urgelles	1.000	2	6	0	0	0	0

First Base	PCT	G	PO	A	E	DP
Cannon	.985	117	999	84	16	83
Chiaravalloti	1.000	21	184	15	0	13
Olson	1.000	8	37	2	0	6
Schneider	1.000	1	10	0	0	1
Solano	.800	1	4	0	1	0

Second Base	PCT	G	PO	A	E	DP
Alfonzo	1.000	3	5	8	0	3
Cota	.977	73	113	222	8	46
Hassey	.986	18	32	39	1	9
Klosterman	.987	17	29	48	1	7
Mayorson	.989	21	28	60	1	9
Olson	.963	17	32	47	3	13

Third Base	PCT	G	PO	A	E	DP
Arnold	.899	44	19	79	11	6
Hassey	.995	70	57	132	1	12
Kuzmic	1.000	3	4	7	0	1
Olson	.843	21	10	33	8	1
Schneider	.667	1	0	2	1	1
Solano	.974	14	9	29	1	1

Shortstop	PCT	G	PO	A	E	DP
Hassey	.985	16	30	37	1	11
Klosterman	.983	26	42	75	2	12
Mayorson	.972	102	129	288	12	51

Outfield	PCT	G	PO	A	E	DP
Davenport	.959	28	43	4	2	2
Hassey	1.000	5	2	0	0	0
Jova	1.000	26	52	3	0	1
Lind	.985	80	129	1	2	0
Majewski	.993	57	128	5	1	0
Miller	.979	40	89	4	2	0
Negron	1.000	32	64	1	0	1
Patterson	.945	43	66	3	4	0
Singleton	1.000	8	13	0	0	0
Smith	.971	111	192	10	6	4

Dunedin Blue Jays — High Class A

Florida State League

BATTING	B-T	HT	WT	DOB	AVG	vLH	vRH	G	AB	R	H	2B	3B	HR	RBI	BB	HBP	SH	SF	SO	SB	CS	SLG	OBP
Armstrong, Jason	R-R	6-0	185	11-13-81	.154	.353	.098	23	78	7	12	1	0	0	6	5	2	0	0	13	1	1	.167	.224
Arnold, Eric	R-R	6-1	195	7-9-80	.226	.192	.239	49	186	24	42	14	0	7	27	12	0	0	2	62	0	1	.414	.270
Bormaster, Brian	R-R	5-9	205	10-19-81	.000	.000	.000	2	5	0	0	0	0	0	0	0	0	0	0	2	0	0	.000	.000
Butler, Jacob	R-R	6-1	200	2-9-83	.145	.176	.132	17	55	7	8	2	1	1	12	5	0	0	2	17	0	0	.273	.210
Corrente, David	R-R	6-2	210	10-13-83	.319	.423	.289	35	116	13	37	7	0	7	31	7	1	1	3	19	0	0	.560	.354
Cota, Carlo	R-R	5-9	185	9-18-80	.242	.242	.242	41	157	22	38	7	0	2	27	22	3	1	1	43	4	4	.325	.344
Davenport, Ron	L-R	6-2	210	10-16-81	.321	.405	.303	56	237	42	76	24	0	11	40	12	3	0	2	34	2	0	.561	.358
Diaz, Robinzon	R-R	5-11	210	9-19-83	.306	.349	.295	104	418	59	128	21	1	3	44	20	3	4	2	37	8	1	.383	.341
Dirosa, Mike	R-R	5-11	190	1-17-80	.214	.000	.231	4	14	3	3	2	0	0	2	0	0			6	0	0	.357	.313
Dragicevich, Scott	R-R	6-3	205	6-28-80	.257	.277	.250	54	171	27	44	11	0	3	15	23	2	0	0	48	0	1	.374	.352
Gutierrez, Chris	R-R	5-10	170	3-12-84	.221	.304	.204	81	281	36	62	9	0	1	19	38	7	1	2	45	1	2	.263	.326
Hatch, Anthony	L-R	6-4	185	8-30-83	.500	.500	.500	3	8	3	4	2	0	0	3	0	0	0	0	0	0	0	.750	.600
Klosterman, Ryan	R-R	5-11	185	5-28-82	.287	.207	.304	85	321	55	92	27	3	12	64	24	8	0	1	78	19	0	.502	.350
Kreuzer, Josh	R-R	6-5	235	9-28-82	.257	.220	.270	52	187	30	48	19	0	7	31	21	7	0	1	46	1	0	.471	.352

	B-T	HT	WT	DOB	AVG	vLH	vRH	G	AB	R	H	2B	3B	HR	RBI	BB	HBP	SH	SF	SO	SB	CS	SLG	OBP
Lex, Joshua	R-R	6-0	230	10-7-81	.333	—	.333	1	3	0	1	0	0	0	0	0	0	1	0	0	0	0	.333	.500
Majewski, Dustin	L-L	5-11	205	8-16-81	.271	.289	.268	64	221	38	60	16	2	7	41	49	0	4	39	3	3		.457	.398
Mathews, Aaron	R-R	5-10	200	5-10-82	.282	.252	.291	111	461	68	130	23	5	9	38	35	1	1	3	58	9	7	.412	.332
Nielsen, Eric	R-R	6-0	225	11-14-81	.286	.323	.275	115	402	62	115	16	1	6	47	56	15	0	2	76	3	0	.376	.392
Patterson, Ryan	R-R	5-11	205	5-2-83	.288	.274	.292	84	354	65	102	25	0	19	69	20	1	4	1	61	2	4	.520	.327
Patton, Cory	L-L	5-8	215	6-18-82	.247	.292	.229	61	235	28	58	10	2	11	44	16	1	0	3	59	4	2	.447	.294
Peralta, Juan	B-R	6-0	185	6-24-83	.251	.330	.226	109	391	47	98	16	3	3	41	28	1	6	2	92	13	7	.330	.301
Schneider, John	R-R	6-3	250	2-14-80	.250	.111	.282	16	48	7	12	1	0	4	13	12	0	0	0	20	0	0	.521	.400
Singleton, Justin	L-R	6-2	190	4-10-79	.214	.000	.231	4	14	2	3	1	0	0	2	3	0	0	0	5	0	0	.286	.353
Snavely, Christian	L-R	6-2	205	5-7-82	.228	.225	.228	82	272	41	62	18	1	7	41	41	2	0	5	77	2	3	.379	.328
Zaun, Gregg	B-R	5-10	190	4-14-71	.000	.000	.000	1	4	0	0	0	0	0	0	0	0	0	0	1	0	0	.000	.000

PITCHING	B-T	HT	WT	DOB	W	L	ERA	G	GS	CG	SV	IP	H	R	ER	HR	BB	SO	AVG	vLH	vRH	K/9	BB/9
Berroa, Yesson	R-R	6-5	230	7-30-82	0	0	1.74	13	0	0	0	21	14	4	4	1	6	21	.194	.179	.205	9.15	2.61
Burnett, A.J.	R-R	6-4	230	1-3-77	0	0	3.38	2	2	0	0	8	9	3	3	0	2	6	.290	.273	.300	6.75	2.25
Carnline, William	R-R	6-3	205	1-3-84	4	3	3.47	10	10	0	0	57	58	26	22	6	16	31	.261	.247	.272	4.89	2.53
Chacin, Gustavo	L-L	5-11	195	12-4-80	0	0	9.64	1	1	0	0	5	6	5	5	0	4	6	.300	.200	.333	9.64	7.71
Core, Danny	R-R	6-1	205	7-17-81	5	4	4.41	40	7	0	0	80	73	47	39	8	35	87	.244	.267	.230	9.83	3.95
Duff, Matt	R-R	6-1	215	10-6-74	0	0	6.75	6	0	0	0	7	8	5	5	0	3	8	.308	.375	.278	10.80	4.05
Falkenbach, Connor	R-R	6-0	185	2-22-82	6	0	1.94	47	0	0	8	56	49	14	12	1	12	40	.239	.253	.231	6.47	1.94
Fowler, Eric	L-L	6-3	220	3-18-83	8	11	3.74	28	27	1	0	149	164	82	62	10	36	116	.274	.326	.258	7.01	2.17
Gornati, T.J.	R-R	6-1	210	3-16-81	2	3	3.94	40	0	0	0	64	66	35	28	6	25	41	.273	.257	.285	5.77	3.52
Harang, Daryl	L-L	6-2	225	11-19-82	4	4	3.16	45	0	0	1	63	61	26	22	2	17	50	.251	.260	.247	7.18	2.44
Isenberg, Kurt	R-L	6-0	190	1-15-82	2	3	3.30	11	8	0	0	46	49	21	17	3	14	36	.277	.219	.290	6.99	2.72
James, Justin	R-R	6-3	215	9-13-81	0	2	4.12	24	0	0	0	44	39	21	20	2	15	34	.235	.241	.231	7.01	3.09
Keng, Po-Hsuan	R-R	6-1	235	10-15-84	0	1	10.38	7	0	0	0	9	16	10	10	3	2	3	.410	.389	.429	2.08	3.12
King, Jeremy	R-R	6-2	210	11-12-81	1	1	7.71	6	1	0	0	14	17	12	12	2	6	6	.321	.227	.387	3.86	3.86
2-team (9 Tampa)					3	3	5.58	15	6	0	0	50	60	33	31	3	19	35	—	—	—	6.30	3.42
Litsch, Jesse	R-R	6-1	205	3-9-85	6	6	3.53	16	15	2	0	89	94	39	35	5	8	81	.267	.277	.257	8.16	0.81
Mumma, Bradley	L-L	6-4	250	4-1-81	1	3	5.80	26	0	0	0	36	43	24	23	4	14	33	.293	.275	.302	8.33	3.53
Phillips, Paul	R-R	6-2	225	1-26-84	1	3	6.97	15	0	0	0	21	27	17	16	1	7	21	.314	.375	.278	9.15	3.05
Ray, Robert	R-R	6-5	185	1-21-84	2	4	4.99	14	0	0	0	49	59	34	27	2	13	37	.306	.347	.265	6.84	2.40
Romero, Ricardo	R-L	6-1	200	11-6-84	2	1	2.47	10	10	1	0	58	48	17	16	5	14	61	.224	.278	.213	9.41	2.16
Savickas, Russ	R-R	6-4	190	7-30-83	6	4	4.11	13	13	0	0	66	73	40	30	7	28	34	.280	.295	.268	4.66	3.84
Sowers, Joshua	R-R	6-0	170	5-17-83	0	0	0.00	1	0	0	0	3	5	2	0	0	1	1	.455	.375	.667	3.00	3.00
Tate, Derek	R-L	5-11	190	12-19-81	0	0	5.87	5	0	0	0	8	11	5	5	0	5	7	.333	.250	.360	5.62	5.62
Tavarez, Milton	R-R	6-2	235	3-29-82	2	4	6.71	49	0	0	21	51	63	46	38	9	29	65	.296	.340	.259	11.47	5.12
Trias, Orlando	R-R	6-3	215	3-16-84	13	8	3.82	27	27	0	0	153	161	67	65	10	48	88	.272	.290	.254	5.17	2.82
Wolfe, Brian	R-R	6-3	225	11-29-80	1	4	6.00	5	5	0	0	24	33	20	16	3	3	17	.317	.283	.364	6.38	1.13
Yates, Kyle	R-R	5-11	190	1-8-83	2	0	0.64	4	2	0	0	14	8	1	1	0	0	13	.163	.000	.211	8.36	0.00

FIELDING

Catcher	PCT	G	PO	A	E	DP	PB
Bormaster	1.000	2	12	1	0	0	0
Corrente	.986	34	202	12	3	1	4
Diaz	.983	88	619	65	12	3	13
Dirosa	1.000	4	18	0	0	0	0
Lex	1.000	1	9	0	0	0	0
Schneider	1.000	12	94	12	0	2	4
Zaun	1.000	1	5	0	0	0	0

First Base	PCT	G	PO	A	E	DP
Davenport	.976	20	155	7	4	14
Dragicevich	.994	18	145	13	1	16
Kreuzer	.989	37	334	23	4	30
Schneider	1.000	2	16	1	0	1
Snavely	.987	64	563	40	8	38

Second Base	PCT	G	PO	A	E	DP
Cota	.964	41	98	115	8	25
Dragicevich	1.000	1	0	2	0	0
Gutierrez	1.000	23	39	65	0	13
Peralta	.991	72	120	219	3	32

Third Base	PCT	G	PO	A	E	DP
Armstrong	.873	23	9	53	9	4
Arnold	.884	32	21	78	13	8
Diaz	.818	9	4	14	4	2
Dragicevich	.943	31	20	63	5	7
Gutierrez	.913	45	27	78	10	5
Hatch	1.000	3	0	2	0	0

Shortstop	PCT	G	PO	A	E	DP
Dragicevich	1.000	4	4	9	0	2

	PCT	G	PO	A	E	DP
Gutierrez	.968	14	16	44	2	12
Klosterman	.960	85	122	259	16	45
Peralta	.976	34	63	103	4	17
Snavely	1.000	1	2	8	0	0

Outfield	PCT	G	PO	A	E	DP
Butler	.960	13	20	4	1	1
Davenport	.960	25	47	1	2	0
Majewski	1.000	62	158	5	0	2
Mathews	.976	96	197	9	5	2
Nielsen	.970	91	155	7	5	2
Patterson	.975	77	114	5	3	1
Patton	.963	47	76	3	3	0
Singleton	.667	3	3	1	2	0
Snavely	—	1	0	0	0	0

Lansing Lugnuts — Low Class A

Midwest League

BATTING	B-T	HT	WT	DOB	AVG	vLH	vRH	G	AB	R	H	2B	3B	HR	RBI	BB	HBP	SH	SF	SO	SB	CS	SLG	OBP
Armstrong, Jason	R-R	6-0	185	11-13-81	.270	.270	.270	49	200	20	54	5	0	1	16	14	4	0	4	30	5	5	.310	.324
Bell, Josh	R-R	6-0	220	7-3-84	.273	.321	.260	75	264	29	72	15	1	10	30	11	3	0	0	90	1	2	.451	.309
Bormaster, Brian	R-R	5-9	205	10-19-81	.189	.149	.199	74	233	20	44	12	0	5	22	38	3	0	2	66	1	4	.305	.308
Butler, Jacob	R-R	6-1	200	2-9-83	.251	.245	.258	98	375	45	94	21	2	11	78	43	5	1	5	110	4	4	.405	.332
Garibaldi, Anthony	R-R	6-1	200	12-19-80	.210	.259	.198	95	305	37	64	11	1	8	29	24	13	2	3	91	9	4	.331	.293
Gonzalez, Jesus	R-R	6-4	200	7-9-84	.239	.242	.239	95	309	43	74	14	1	3	28	15	7	4	5	77	11	2	.320	.286
Gutierrez, Chris	R-R	5-10	170	3-12-84	.320	.400	.291	18	75	11	24	7	3	0	9	8	0	2	0	14	3	3	.493	.376
Hatch, Anthony	L-R	6-4	185	8-30-83	.314	.320	.312	70	239	46	75	23	4	9	37	35	0	1	1	37	5	1	.548	.406
Hetherington, Luke	R-R	6-0	210	4-13-83	.297	.246	.309	91	293	52	87	18	2	5	31	38	6	0	4	79	21	10	.423	.384
Hicks, David	L-L	6-5	235	11-22-81	.237	.152	.256	108	375	34	89	24	1	3	42	30	0	0	3	42	9	4	.331	.292
Kalter, Zachary	L-R	6-2	200	9-19-84	.240	.000	.261	25	75	9	18	3	0	0	9	7	0	0	0	16	1	3	.280	.296
Metropoulos, Joey	R-R	6-2	265	10-7-83	.270	.312	.257	114	396	55	107	27	1	11	56	61	12	0	7	91	7	4	.427	.378
Patton, Cory	L-L	5-8	215	6-18-82	.290	.151	.330	62	241	37	70	19	2	9	46	40	5	0	4	50	3	2	.510	.337
Pettway, Brian	R-R	6-1	225	7-29-83	.246	.168	.266	125	452	58	111	31	6	16	54	39	13	0	5	145	1	5	.447	.320
Quintana, Al	R-R	6-0	220	11-9-82	.176	.091	.200	18	51	8	9	0	0	0	3	10	0	0	0	11	1	1	.176	.311
Rodriguez, Yuber	B-R	6-0	200	11-17-83	.223	.222	.223	103	310	38	69	8	3	2	28	35	3	4	4	91	24	8	.287	.304
Sena, Emmanuel	B-R	6-1	180	10-15-84	.143	.250	.100	6	14	3	2	1	0	0	0	0	0	0	0	5	1	0	.214	.143
Shoffit, Sean	L-R	6-2	195	6-9-85	.246	.221	.253	104	390	63	96	17	7	4	41	50	2	6	0	109	15	10	.356	.335
Urgelles, Jeff	R-R	6-0	220	6-19-82	.000	.000	.000	2	7	0	0	0	0	0	0	0	0	0	0	1	0	0	.000	.000

PITCHING	B-T	HT	WT	DOB	W	L	ERA	G	GS	CG	SV	IP	H	R	ER	HR	BB	SO	AVG	vLH	vRH	K/9	BB/9
Bell, Kristian	R-R	6-1	190	1-11-84	6	6	3.73	23	23	0	0	128	111	59	53	7	65	86	.238	.261	.219	6.05	4.57
Berroa, Yesson	R-R	6-5	230	7-30-82	3	2	1.49	22	0	0	3	36	26	6	6	1	13	43	.206	.220	.197	10.65	3.22
Carnline, William	R-R	6-3	205	1-3-84	5	4	2.70	15	10	0	1	67	44	26	20	7	12	66	.182	.171	.191	8.91	1.62

Name	B-T	HT	WT	DOB	W	L	ERA	G	GS	CG	SV	IP	H	R	ER	HR	BB	SO	AVG	vLH	vRH	K/9	BB/9
Cheng, Chi-Hung	L-L	6-1	200	6-20-85	11	5	2.70	28	28	0	0	143	129	57	43	5	68	154	.244	.201	.259	9.67	4.27
Delgadillo, Hector	R-R	6-0	200	1-2-83	3	1	4.23	7	5	0	0	28	25	16	13	3	13	19	.250	.275	.233	6.18	4.23
Dicken, Randy	R-R	6-1	195	8-19-82	0	1	4.91	4	0	0	0	7	5	4	4	0	4	9	.192	.000	.294	11.05	4.91
Hicks, David	L-L	6-5	235	11-22-81	0	0	0.00	1	0	0	0	1	0	0	0	0	0	1	.000	.000	.000	9.00	0.00
Keng, Po-Hsuan	R-R	6-1	235	10-15-84	1	4	2.33	32	0	0	3	70	61	26	18	4	18	60	.235	.176	.272	7.75	2.33
Martin, Adrian	R-R	6-1	175	9-2-84	8	3	4.37	27	9	0	1	95	111	56	46	13	19	62	.293	.327	.271	5.89	1.81
McKenzie, Casey	R-R	6-2	215	7-26-82	3	5	3.18	13	12	0	0	65	68	32	23	7	21	45	.276	.347	.228	6.23	2.91
McLaughlin, Joey	R-R	6-0	185	2-11-82	3	1	3.04	16	0	0	0	27	25	10	9	1	12	17	.255	.237	.267	5.74	4.05
2-team (15 Clinton)					4	1	3.84	31	1	0	0	58	57	28	25	6	24	46	—			7.06	3.68
Mumma, Bradley	L-L	6-4	250	4-1-81	0	0	4.00	5	0	0	1	9	12	5	4	0	7	11	.308	.333	.286	11.00	7.00
Phillips, Paul	R-R	6-2	225	1-26-84	5	3	2.01	31	0	0	14	40	36	12	9	2	13	37	.231	.203	.250	8.26	2.90
Rodriguez, Edward	R-R	6-4	185	10-6-84	1	5	4.20	25	0	0	4	41	48	23	19	2	19	27	.291	.347	.240	5.98	4.20
Rogers, Adam	R-R	6-4	185	10-2-84	1	0	0.00	2	0	0	0	4	3	1	0	0	0	2	.200	.000	.231	4.91	0.00
Roy, Scott	R-R	6-1	235	8-15-82	0	0	0.00	2	0	0	0	3	2	0	0	1	0	3	.167	.000	.222	6.00	3.00
Savickas, Russ	R-R	6-4	190	7-30-83	2	2	3.18	14	14	0	0	76	79	32	27	3	28	73	.275	.331	.229	8.61	3.30
Serro, Ted	R-R	6-4	205	10-2-84	0	2	4.94	14	0	0	0	27	27	20	15	1	9	23	.245	.367	.148	7.57	2.96
Sowers, Joshua	R-R	6-0	170	5-17-83	0	2	5.56	18	0	0	0	34	44	23	21	1	10	21	.317	.373	.275	5.56	2.65
Stidfole, Sean	R-R	6-3	195	3-12-84	7	7	4.83	31	10	0	3	88	85	51	47	5	35	89	.262	.241	.296	9.14	3.59
Tate, Derek	R-L	5-11	190	12-19-81	0	2	6.75	6	0	0	1	7	8	5	5	0	8	4	.286	.200	.333	5.40	10.80
Timm, Jordan	L-L	6-6	240	1-15-81	4	2	5.02	40	1	0	2	66	80	42	37	7	21	45	.299	.277	.310	6.11	2.85
Tressler, Aaron	R-R	6-1	185	3-28-82	8	4	1.90	23	15	0	0	109	95	30	23	3	16	96	.233	.213	.250	7.95	1.33
Wice, Joe	L-L	6-6	230	9-1-85	0	0	0.00	1	0	0	0	2	0	0	0	0	0	2	.000	.000	.000	9.00	0.00
Wideman, Aaron	R-L	5-11	190	6-8-85	1	4	5.00	11	10	0	0	45	53	30	25	2	18	39	.298	.257	.308	7.80	3.60

FIELDING

Catcher	PCT	G	PO	A	E	DP	PB
Bell	.982	66	487	50	10	5	13
Bormaster	.986	70	515	53	8	7	10
Quintana	.985	9	58	8	1	1	3
Urgelles	1.000	1	3	0	0	1	0

First Base	PCT	G	PO	A	E	DP
Hicks	.985	99	806	77	13	80
Metropoulos	.988	44	360	43	5	33

Second Base	PCT	G	PO	A	E	DP
Armstrong	.936	20	42	46	6	12
Garibaldi	1.000	1	2	5	0	1
Gutierrez	1.000	1	2	2	0	0
Hatch	.964	15	22	32	2	10

	PCT	G	PO	A	E	DP
Sena	.900	2	2	7	1	1
Shoffit	.947	102	213	266	27	67

Third Base	PCT	G	PO	A	E	DP
Armstrong	.885	26	26	43	9	3
Garibaldi	.959	73	57	154	9	18
Gutierrez	.967	11	7	22	1	1
Hatch	.929	28	19	46	5	3
Quintana	1.000	7	1	5	0	1
Sena	1.000	1	1	0	0	0
Urgelles	1.000	1	0	4	0	0

Shortstop	PCT	G	PO	A	E	DP
Armstrong	1.000	1	0	5	0	0
Garibaldi	.966	18	48	64	4	19

	PCT	G	PO	A	E	DP
Gonzalez	.943	94	142	290	26	49
Gutierrez	1.000	7	17	23	0	3
Hatch	.948	27	49	61	6	19

Outfield	PCT	G	PO	A	E	DP
Butler	.979	83	132	8	3	3
Hatch	—	1	0	0	0	0
Hetherington	.986	85	134	6	2	0
Kalter	.914	23	31	1	3	1
Patton	.971	46	65	3	2	1
Pettway	.960	99	135	8	6	2
Rodriguez	.955	99	184	5	9	0
Sena	—	1	0	0	0	0

Auburn Doubledays — Short-Season

New York-Penn League

BATTING	B-T	HT	WT	DOB	AVG	vLH	vRH	G	AB	R	H	2B	3B	HR	RBI	BB	HBP	SH	SF	SO	SB	CS	SLG	OBP
Baksh, Jonathan	R-R	6-1	205	3-1-85	.280	.343	.267	52	182	25	51	11	3	0	18	17	1	0	1	36	5	2	.374	.343
Barron, Raul	B-R	6-0	170	4-4-86	.267	.000	.308	4	15	0	4	0	0	0	1	0	0	0	0	4	0	0	.267	.267
Calderone, Adam	L-R	6-2	195	3-17-84	.248	.204	.259	70	246	34	61	12	6	2	25	17	2	8	4	52	7	2	.370	.297
Campbell, Scott	R-R	5-11	190	9-25-84	.292	.208	.314	68	240	39	70	14	0	1	18	33	11	6	3	31	2	10	.350	.397
Diaz, Jonathan	R-S	5-8	160	4-10-85	.200	.075	.240	73	220	34	44	7	0	1	26	30	12	10	2	55	5	5	.245	.326
Emanuele, Chris	R-R	6-0	180	2-17-84	.357	.000	.500	6	14	2	5	1	0	1	3	0	0	0	0	2	0	1	.643	.357
Fernandez, Luis	R-R	6-0	150	11-16-87	.125	.000	.167	4	8	1	1	0	0	0	1	0	0	0	0	2	0	0	.125	.125
Hall, Brian	R-R	6-0	190	2-1-82	.242	.235	.245	18	66	9	16	4	0	1	6	2	0	0	0	8	0	0	.348	.265
Hopkins, Luke	L-R	6-2	255	4-15-85	.239	.233	.241	71	251	35	60	16	2	6	42	40	1	0	6	72	0	0	.390	.337
Jerolaman, Brian	R-R	6-0	195	5-10-85	.241	.167	.261	45	141	27	34	10	1	0	21	26	1	1	0	38	0	0	.326	.363
Kalter, Zachary	L-R	6-2	200	9-19-84	.283	.250	.286	21	46	10	13	0	1	0	3	11	0	2	0	10	1	1	.326	.421
Lane, Matthew	L-R	6-2	225	5-23-84	.194	.064	.230	64	222	26	43	9	2	4	27	9	6	0	3	60	1	0	.306	.242
Liuzza, Matt	R-R	6-0	215	2-3-84	.268	.321	.246	55	194	25	52	14	1	6	37	16	3	0	0	56	0	0	.443	.333
Looze, Christopher	L-L	6-2	205	12-23-81	.222	—	.222	8	18	2	4	0	0	0	1	2	0	0	0	5	0	0	.222	.300
Quintana, Al	R-R	6-0	220	11-9-82	.300	.667	.143	6	10	1	3	0	0	0	1	1	0	0	0	3	0	0	.300	.364
Scobee, Shawn	R-R	6-1	210	10-11-84	.212	.143	.240	56	170	23	36	10	2	4	25	16	14	2	0	68	3	1	.365	.330
Sena, Emmanuel	B-R	6-1	180	10-15-84	.207	.375	.143	18	29	3	6	0	0	0	4	3	0	0	1	8	1	1	.207	.273
Stone, Wesley	R-R	5-10	195	4-16-87	.154	.000	.286	5	13	2	2	0	0	0	0	1	0	0	0	3	0	0	.154	.214
Sweppenhiser, Kelly	R-R	6-0	185	11-25-83	.213	.185	.226	44	80	8	17	2	0	0	5	9	7	2	1	16	0	1	.238	.340
Zeskind, Benjamin	B-R	6-0	180	1-19-83	.278	.420	.241	66	237	31	66	18	5	4	28	26	2	10	2	60	3	3	.447	.352

PITCHING	B-T	HT	WT	DOB	W	L	ERA	G	GS	CG	SV	IP	H	R	ER	HR	BB	SO	AVG	vLH	vRH	K/9	BB/9
Aguirre, Wilfreddy	L-L	6-1	210	11-8-86	3	4	2.19	13	11	1	0	53	43	15	13	2	16	27	.230	.231	.230	4.56	2.70
Alfaro, Gabriel	R-R	6-3	215	6-14-83	0	1	2.89	6	0	0	0	9	11	6	3	1	1	8	.282	.167	.333	7.71	0.96
Benson, Shane	R-R	6-4	210	12-15-86	3	1	3.47	9	7	0	1	36	35	15	14	1	6	28	.246	.226	.258	6.94	1.49
Bigley, Dennis	R-R	6-4	230	8-18-83	1	0	1.54	16	0	0	7	23	17	4	4	0	7	24	.198	.179	.207	9.26	2.70
Bull, Brian	L-L	6-1	185	12-29-83	1	3	4.38	18	8	0	0	51	53	32	25	2	16	25	.262	.209	.277	4.38	2.81
Byrnes, Scott	R-R	6-1	210	2-18-83	0	1	4.67	19	0	0	3	27	29	17	14	1	13	19	.261	.129	.313	6.33	4.33
Delgadillo, Hector	R-R	6-0	200	1-2-83	3	2	4.73	7	7	0	0	32	31	19	17	2	8	27	.254	.267	.247	7.52	2.23
Dials, Zachary	R-R	6-1	205	7-22-85	4	3	1.89	15	5	0	3	38	27	14	8	0	11	23	.190	.304	.135	5.43	2.61
Dicken, Randy	R-R	6-1	195	8-19-82	1	0	6.75	2	0	0	0	1	1	1	1	0	4	0	.200	.000	.333	0.00	27.00
Ginley, Kyle	R-R	6-2	225	9-1-86	1	0	0.00	2	1	0	0	10	5	0	0	0	5	6	.147	.143	.150	5.40	4.50
Harrison, Benjamin	L-L	6-1	190	4-14-84	0	1	1.13	21	0	0	0	32	25	12	4	0	8	27	.208	.194	.213	7.59	2.25
Lirette, Chase	R-R	6-3	210	6-9-85	4	1	2.23	10	6	0	1	40	32	11	10	1	7	37	.219	.182	.250	8.26	1.56
Lowe, Ronald	R-L	6-0	210	9-6-83	4	2	4.21	22	3	0	0	36	35	22	17	0	11	26	.252	.176	.276	6.44	2.72
Magee, Brandon	R-R	6-5	205	7-26-83	3	1	3.10	11	11	0	0	52	51	23	18	1	19	40	.254	.280	.238	6.88	3.27
McGuigan, Patrick	R-R	6-1	185	9-8-84	0	0	1.86	7	0	0	2	10	9	2	2	1	2	11	.250	.250	.250	10.24	1.86
McKenzie, Casey	R-R	6-2	215	7-26-82	1	0	1.64	7	0	0	0	11	9	2	2	0	0	9	.237	.200	.250	7.36	0.00
Nieves, Javier	R-R	5-10	190	2-5-84	1	1	3.08	16	0	0	0	26	29	11	9	1	10	28	.287	.303	.279	9.57	3.42
O'Brien, Daniel	L-L	5-10	195	9-12-84	0	3	11.91	5	3	0	0	11	16	16	15	1	7	8	.333	.375	.325	6.35	5.56

Name	B-T	HT	WT	DOB	W	L	ERA	G	GS	CG	SV	IP	H	R	ER	HR	BB	SO	AVG	vLH	vRH	K/9	BB/9
Overbey, Seth	L-R	6-2	165	4-30-84	4	2	2.42	23	0	0	4	45	37	16	12	3	12	29	.227	.263	.208	5.84	2.42
Reddout, Chris	L-L	6-6	215	12-15-82	3	2	3.50	10	10	0	0	46	50	26	18	1	11	21	.262	.367	.225	4.08	2.14
Rodriguez, Edward	R-R	6-4	185	10-6-84	0	0	0.00	3	0	0	2	6	3	0	0	0	1	6	.158	.125	.182	9.00	1.50
Serro, Ted	R-R	6-4	205	10-2-84	2	0	0.00	4	0	0	1	13	2	0	0	0	3	12	.050	.000	.067	8.10	2.03
Sowers, Joshua	R-R	6-0	170	5-17-83	1	0	0.00	1	0	0	0	2	1	0	0	0	1	0	.143	.250	.000		3.86
Starner, Nathan	L-L	6-2	190	5-29-84	0	0	3.86	3	0	0	0	2	0	1	1	0	1	2	.000	.000	.000	7.71	3.86
Tritz, John	R-R	5-10	220	2-19-84	2	4	5.81	20	0	0	0	26	31	23	17	1	11	19	.310	.360	.293	6.49	3.76

FIELDING

Catcher	PCT	G	PO	A	E	DP	PB
Jeroloman	.991	35	201	29	2	3	3
Lane	1.000	18	95	4	0	1	1
Liuzza	.995	30	172	13	1	1	4
Quintana	1.000	2	8	0	0	1	

First Base	PCT	G	PO	A	E	DP
Hall	1.000	1	2	0	0	0
Hopkins	.988	62	603	34	8	37
Lane	.980	14	90	9	2	11
Liuzza	1.000	2	19	2	0	1
Looze	.909	2	10	0	1	0

Second Base	PCT	G	PO	A	E	DP
Campbell	.964	61	121	203	12	37

Fernandez	1.000	4	7	6	0	2
Hall	.915	11	22	32	5	6
Sena	1.000	2	4	4	0	2
Stone	1.000	2	7	10	0	3

Third Base	PCT	G	PO	A	E	DP
Barron	.800	4	0	4	1	0
Campbell	1.000	8	4	14	0	1
Lane	.821	32	13	42	12	2
Quintana	1.000	2	0	3	0	0
Sena	.933	9	2	12	1	0
Stone	1.000	3	1	6	0	0
Sweppenhiser	.911	42	15	57	7	5

Shortstop	PCT	G	PO	A	E	DP
Diaz	.958	73	118	266	17	39
Fernandez	1.000	1	0	1	0	0
Sena	1.000	1	2	4	0	0

Outfield	PCT	G	PO	A	E	DP
Baksh	.967	42	83	6	3	3
Calderone	.978	65	132	3	3	0
Emanuele	1.000	6	9	0	0	0
Hall	1.000	2	2	0	0	0
Kalter	.944	18	16	1	1	0
Scobee	.944	48	65	2	4	0
Sena	1.000	1	2	0	0	0
Zeskind	.963	59	75	2	3	0

Pulaski Blue Jays — Rookie

Appalachian League

BATTING

Name	B-T	HT	WT	DOB	AVG	vLH	vRH	G	AB	R	H	2B	3B	HR	RBI	BB	HBP	SH	SF	SO	SB	CS	SLG	OBP
Aguilar, Heliezer	R-R	5-11	225	3-9-84	.194	.238	.175	42	139	21	27	6	1	1	15	9	4	0	2	30	1	1	.273	.260
Barron, Raul	B-R	6-0	170	4-4-86	.295	.262	.313	51	193	26	57	7	2	0	21	21	0	4	1	30	3	3	.352	.363
Chavez, Yohermyn	R-R	6-3	200	1-26-89	.276	.235	.296	36	105	19	29	9	0	0	18	9	8	2	2	23	1	2	.362	.371
Del Campo, Jonathan	B-R	6-2	185	5-18-88	.206	.118	.239	26	63	4	13	0	0	1	4	11	0	0	0	12	0	1	.254	.324
Ebarb, Roger	L-R	5-11	215	6-11-83	.229	.350	.197	35	96	15	22	3	1	2	12	20	0	0	1	17	0	0	.344	.359
Emanuele, Chris	R-R	6-0	180	2-17-84	.323	.367	.307	60	226	42	73	16	4	2	23	30	6	0	1	40	10	2	.456	.414
Fernandez, Luis	R-R	6-0	150	11-16-87	.263	.225	.274	50	175	24	46	5	0	0	16	20	2	3	3	17	3	4	.291	.340
Franko, Paul	R-R	6-1	200	6-7-84	.236	.255	.227	44	148	25	35	8	0	1	17	17	10	1	1	37	0	0	.311	.352
Frost, Baron	R-R	6-0	190	2-19-84	.320	.375	.294	38	125	21	40	11	4	4	31	16	2	0	4	24	0	0	.520	.395
Garbarino, Mikal	B-R	5-11	180	4-7-88	.000	.000	—	1	1	0	0	0	0	0	0	0	0	0	0	0	0	0	.000	.000
Jaspe, Jonathan	B-R	5-11	205	4-11-85	.290	.267	.301	60	238	37	69	22	2	7	48	18	2	0	1	40	0	2	.487	.344
Lex, Joshua	R-R	6-0	230	10-7-81	.238	.222	.245	47	151	30	36	11	0	2	25	26	8	2	0	46	1	0	.351	.378
Sanchez, Luis	B-R	6-0	150	5-27-87	.140	.059	.192	13	43	4	6	0	0	0	2	4	1	3	1	10	1	0	.140	.224
Santana, Victor	R-R	6-4	210	2-25-84	.254	.227	.265	39	142	24	36	5	2	5	24	15	0	1	0	52	1	1	.423	.325
Snider, Travis	L-L	5-11	245	2-2-88	.325	.313	.331	54	194	36	63	12	1	11	41	30	0	0	2	47	6	3	.567	.412
Soto, Leance	R-R	6-2	220	6-13-85	.190	.100	.221	34	116	11	22	3	0	1	15	8	2	0	1	36	1	0	.241	.252
Stone, Wesley	R-R	5-10	195	4-16-87	.216	.167	.239	48	171	31	37	7	0	0	16	36	0	1	3	43	2	2	.257	.348

PITCHING

Name	B-T	HT	WT	DOB	W	L	ERA	G	GS	CG	SV	IP	H	R	ER	HR	BB	SO	AVG	vLH	vRH	K/9	BB/9
Barbara, Michael	R-R	6-3	170	4-27-85	2	2	4.80	13	13	0	0	51	55	32	27	6	21	44	.271	.273	.270	7.82	3.73
Bigley, Dennis	R-R	6-4	230	8-18-83	2	0	2.16	6	0	0	1	8	7	4	2	1	0	7	.206	.250	.182	7.56	0.00
Dials, Zachary	R-R	6-1	205	7-22-85	0	0	0.00	3	0	0	1	3	1	0	0	0	1	2	.125	.000	.200	6.00	3.00
Estanga, Edgar	L-L	5-10	230	10-18-85	0	3	3.49	24	0	0	1	28	26	15	11	4	3	30	.241	.160	.265	9.53	0.95
Foster, Matt	L-L	6-3	220	9-4-81	0	0	2.19	13	0	0	0	12	9	3	3	0	4	12	.205	.400	.103	8.76	2.92
Gilmore, Jeffrey	R-R	6-2	190	9-29-84	2	1	3.63	17	0	0	0	22	19	11	9	2	8	25	.226	.200	.234	10.07	3.22
Ginley, Kyle	R-R	6-2	225	9-1-86	1	1	4.73	8	1	0	0	27	22	14	14	3	11	42	.222	.143	.235	14.18	3.71
Gonzalez, Reidier	R-R	5-11	215	11-1-85	3	5	4.26	13	13	0	0	61	75	41	29	2	16	50	.301	.278	.314	7.34	2.35
Mateo, Francisco	L-L	5-11	220	5-7-84	5	2	4.18	14	14	0	0	65	66	38	30	4	21	59	.261	.306	.253	8.21	2.92
McGuigan, Patrick	R-R	6-1	185	9-8-84	1	0	1.53	17	0	0	7	18	13	5	3	1	3	21	.194	.077	.222	10.70	1.53
McRobbie, Alex	R-R	6-2	185	1-16-83	4	3	4.27	14	14	0	0	65	76	33	31	5	19	56	.289	.303	.282	7.71	2.62
Melek, Nathan	R-R	5-11	170	2-24-84	1	1	2.60	21	0	0	0	35	24	19	10	2	12	22	.190	.200	.188	5.71	3.12
Reddout, Chris	L-L	6-6	215	12-15-82	1	0	0.00	2	0	0	0	5	2	0	0	0	0	6	.105	.000	.154	10.13	0.00
Rogers, Adam	R-R	6-4	235	10-2-84	4	2	3.74	21	0	0	0	34	28	15	14	4	2	22	.215	.091	.241	5.88	0.53
Serro, Ted	R-R	6-4	205	10-2-84	0	0	0.00	2	0	0	0	2	1	0	0	0	2	2	.125	.000	.167	7.71	7.71
Starner, Nathan	L-L	6-2	190	5-29-84	1	4	3.28	24	0	0	0	25	15	14	9	0	16	41	.163	.222	.149	14.96	5.84
Stidfole, Alan	L-L	6-2	190	3-12-84	1	2	3.60	14	0	0	1	20	19	10	8	2	9	10	.253	.300	.236	9.90	2.70
Tate, Derek	R-L	5-11	190	12-19-81	0	0	23.14	3	0	0	0	2	6	6	1	7	2		.000	.333	1.000	7.71	27.00
Taylor, Drew	L-L	6-5	225	8-2-82	1	3	3.95	23	1	0	1	27	21	14	12	2	11	37	.208	.214	.205	12.18	3.62
Walter, Kyle	R-L	6-3	195	7-16-84	0	3	4.37	11	11	0	0	23	19	12	11	1	20	10	.244	.000	.257	7.94	7.94
Wice, Joe	L-L	6-6	230	9-1-85	4	1	3.75	20	1	0	0	36	35	20	15	2	9	42	.254	.000	.304	10.50	2.25
Zinnicker, John	R-L	6-2	180	7-10-84	2	0	3.25	26	0	0	1	28	34	15	10	0	10	24	.298	.216	.338	7.81	3.25

FIELDING

Catcher	PCT	G	PO	A	E	DP	PB
Ebarb	1.000	21	152	19	0	2	2
Jaspe	.982	40	336	38	7	8	7
Lex	.980	13	87	12	2	0	1

First Base	PCT	G	PO	A	E	DP
Franko	.983	39	333	15	6	29
Jaspe	1.000	8	60	4	0	4
Lex	.970	27	185	12	6	14

Second Base	PCT	G	PO	A	E	DP
Barron	.944	8	10	24	2	7
Del Campo	.928	19	26	38	5	9

Fernandez	.882	4	8	7	2	3
Stone	.966	44	70	102	6	24

Third Base	PCT	G	PO	A	E	DP
Barron	.958	28	15	76	4	3
Del Campo	.615	4	4	4	5	0
Fernandez	.500	2	0	1	1	0
Jaspe	.875	4	1	6	1	0
Soto	.830	32	21	57	16	4
Stone	.588	4	1	9	7	1

Shortstop	PCT	G	PO	A	E	DP
Barron	.959	15	30	40	3	7

Del Campo	—	1	0	0	0	0
Fernandez	.913	44	72	106	17	31
Sanchez	.953	13	16	45	3	8

Outfield	PCT	G	PO	A	E	DP
Aguilar	.950	36	55	2	3	0
Chavez	.929	32	36	3	3	0
Emanuele	.981	58	103	1	2	0
Frost	.818	12	9	0	2	0
Santana	.964	37	50	4	2	2
Snider	.966	44	80	4	3	3

BY LACY LUSK

For one series, a change in ownership looked like all the Nationals franchise needed to turn into a winner.

A group led by developer Ted Lerner and his family was about to take over the club in late July when the team held what it called a grand re-opening at RFK Stadium. The players did their part with a sweep of the Cubs, but the revival was short-lived as the club finished 71-91 in its second season in Washington—10 games worse than in its debut.

"This is an exciting challenge," new team president Stan Kasten said. "Now that all the T's are crossed and all the I's are dotted, the real fun work begins to make this franchise a long-term success on and off the field."

The 2006 Nationals were not without notable achievements despite a third consecutive last-place finish in the National League East and the end of manager Frank Robinson's five-year tenure.

Alfonso Soriano, acquired from the Rangers in the offseason, was an all-star as a left fielder after initially refusing to take the field at that position in a spring training game. The former second baseman relented and went on to hit 46 home runs and steal 41 bases in becoming the fourth member of the 40-40 club. He was the first of that group to also have at least 40 doubles.

Ryan Zimmerman, the fourth pick in the 2005 draft, was handed the third-base job and exceeded expectations by hitting .287/.351/.471 with 20 homers, 47 doubles and 110 RBIs while providing stellar defense. First baseman Nick Johnson hit .290/.428/.520 in the first season when he did not go on the disabled list. In the next-to-last weekend, though, he broke his right leg in a collision

ORGANIZATION LEADERS

BATTING		*Minimum 250 at-bats
*AVG	Broadway, Larry, New Orleans	.288
R	Casto, Kory, Harrisburg	89
H	Casto, Kory, Harrisburg	142
TB	Casto, Kory, Harrisburg	243
2B	Powell, Brandon, Potomac	34
3B	Godwin, Tyrell, New Orleans	7
	Pahuta, Tim, Savannah	7
HR	Casto, Kory, Harrisburg	21
	Whitesell, Josh, Harrisburg	21
RBI	Casto, Kory, Harrisburg	89
BB	Casto, Kory, Harrisburg	90
SO	Whitesell, Josh, Harrisburg	139
SB	Dorta, Melvin, Harrisburg/New Orleans	36
*OBP	Casto, Kory, Harrisburg	.392
*SLG	Casto, Kory, Harrisburg	.479
XBH	Casto, Kory, Harrisburg	53

PITCHING		#Minimum 75 innings
W	Bouknight, Kip, Harrisburg/New Orleans	9
	Good, Andrew, New Orleans	9
L	Trahan, David, Savannah/Potomac	13
#ERA	Perez, Beltran, Harrisburg	3.11
G	Gryboski, Kevin, New Orleans	52
CG	Bouknight, Kip, Harrisburg/New Orleans	2
SV	Corcoran, Roy, Harrisburg/New Orleans	27
IP	Bouknight, Kip, Harrisburg/New Orleans	158
BB	Echols, Justin, New Orleans/Harrisburg	81
SO	Martinez, Anastacio, Harrisburg/New Orleans	126
#AVG	Martinez, Anastacio, Harrisburg/New Orleans	.249

PLAYERS OF THE YEAR

MAJOR LEAGUE: Alfonso Soriano, of

With 46 home runs and 41 stolen bases, Soriano joined Jose Canseco, Barry Bonds and Alex Rodriguez as the only members of the 40-40 club. He had a monster season despite playing for a new team and switching from second base to left field. His 89 extra-base hits led the National League.

MINOR LEAGUE: Kory Casto, 3b/of

With Ryan Zimmerman entrenched at third base, Casto moved back to the outfield, the position he played in college. It has mattered little to Casto, as he's hit wherever he's played. He led the Eastern League with 81 walks and finished second with 84 runs and third with 80 RBIs and a .379 on-base percentage.

RICH ABEL

with right fielder Austin Kearns. Johnson was expected to be ready by the start of spring training in 2007.

Kearns, shortstop Felipe Lopez and reliever Ryan Wagner joined the Nationals in an eight-player trade with the Reds on July 13. General manager Jim Bowden looked into other possible trades, especially involving Soriano, who instead remained in Washington and entered the offseason as a free agent.

Bowden was retained by the new owners and is working closely with Kasten, who was president of the Braves for 17 years and envisions an organization being built much like Atlanta's—primarily through a strong farm system. The new owners, who paid $450 million for the team, quickly showed a willingness to spend money in the international market, announcing a $1.4 million signing bonus for 16-year-old Dominican shortstop Esmailyn Gonzalez, and spending freely in the draft.

"This was a very different experience for a lot of us in the room because we haven't been a big market team before," Bowden said. "Philosophically, this was the first time we were allowed to take the best player on the board regardless—and we did that."

Former Diamondbacks scouting director Mike Rizzo took a job in the front office as assistant GM, with Dana Brown remaining as scouting director. Rizzo's knowledge of Arizona's farm system helped the Nationals with their biggest waiver deal in August, a trade that sent veteran righthander Livan Hernandez west for Double-A pitchers Garrett Mock and Matt Chico.

Kory Casto, blocked by Zimmerman at third base, returned to the outfield in midseason with Double-A Harrisburg and won the Eastern League rookie of the year award. The Nationals also selected him as their minor league player of the year and righthanded reliever Zech Zinicola, a 2006 sixth-round pick from Arizona State, who jumped from short-season ball to Double-A, as pitcher of the year.

After the season, the Nationals improved the locations of their Triple-A and low Class A clubs. They signed two-year deals with Columbus of the International League and Hagerstown of the South Atlantic League.

National League

BATTING	B-T	HT	WT	DOB	AVG	vLH	vRH	G	AB	R	H	2B	3B	HR	RBI	BB	HBP	SH	SF	SO	SB	CS	SLG	OBP
Anderson, Marlon	L-R	5-11	200	1-6-74	.274	.255	.280	109	215	31	59	13	2	5	23	18	1	3	2	41	2	4	.423	.331
2-team (25 Los Angeles)					.297	—	—	134	279	43	83	16	4	12	38	25	1	4	3	49	4	6	.513	.354
Byrd, Marlon	R-R	6-0	235	8-30-77	.223	.188	.242	78	197	28	44	8	1	5	18	22	6	1	2	47	3	3	.350	.317
Castro, Bernie	B-R	5-10	165	7-14-79	.227	.182	.258	42	110	18	25	1	3	0	10	9	0	1	0	18	7	2	.291	.286
Church, Ryan	L-L	6-1	220	10-14-78	.276	.265	.279	71	196	22	54	17	1	10	35	26	3	3	2	60	6	1	.526	.366
Clayton, Royce	R-R	6-0	200	1-2-70	.269	.365	.232	87	305	36	82	22	1	0	27	19	4	5	5	53	8	3	.348	.315
2-team (50 Cincinnati)					.258	—	—	137	454	49	117	30	1	2	40	30	5	7	6	85	14	6	.341	.307
Dorta, Melvin	R-R	5-11	160	1-15-82	.211	.333	.154	15	19	3	4	1	0	0	0	1	0	0	0	2	0	2	.263	.250
Escobar, Alex	R-R	6-1	190	9-6-78	.356	.400	.333	33	87	14	31	3	2	4	18	8	0	0	4	18	2	0	.575	.394
Fick, Robert	L-R	6-1	205	3-15-74	.266	.273	.262	60	128	14	34	4	0	2	9	10	1	2	0	24	1	1	.344	.324
Gonzalez, Wiki	R-R	5-11	205	5-17-74	.229	.222	.231	12	35	3	8	0	0	0	2	2	0	0	1	5	0	0	.229	.263
Guillen, Jose	R-R	5-11	195	5-17-76	.216	.200	.221	69	241	28	52	15	1	9	40	15	7	0	5	48	1	0	.398	.276
Harper, Brandon	R-R	6-4	200	4-29-76	.293	.258	.400	18	41	6	12	3	0	2	6	4	1	0	1	4	0	0	.512	.362
Harris, Brendan	R-R	6-1	200	8-26-80	.250	.250	.250	17	32	3	8	2	0	0	2	3	1	0	0	3	0	0	.313	.333
2-team (8 Cincinnati)					.238	—	—	25	42	5	10	2	0	1	3	4	1	0	0	7	0	0	.357	.319
Jackson, Damian	R-R	5-11	185	8-16-73	.198	.233	.178	67	116	16	23	6	1	4	10	12	4	3	0	39	1	3	.371	.295
Johnson, Nick	L-L	6-3	225	9-19-78	.290	.303	.285	147	500	100	145	46	0	23	77	110	13	2	3	99	10	3	.520	.428
Kearns, Austin	R-R	6-3	235	5-20-80	.250	.368	.206	63	212	33	53	12	1	8	36	41	5	1	2	50	2	3	.429	.381
2-team (87 Cincinnati)					.264	—	—	150	537	86	142	33	2	24	86	76	10	1	5	135	9	4	.467	.363
LeCroy, Matthew	R-R	6-2	230	12-13-75	.239	.229	.250	39	67	5	16	3	0	2	9	11	1	0	1	17	0	0	.373	.350
Logan, Nook	B-R	6-3	180	11-28-79	.300	.350	.286	27	90	13	27	3	1	1	8	6	0	1	2	20	2	1	.389	.337
Lombard, George	L-R	6-0	210	9-14-75	.143	.000	.250	20	21	2	3	0	0	1	1	5	0	0	0	10	2	0	.286	.308
Lopez, Felipe	B-R	6-1	185	5-12-80	.281	.289	.277	71	274	43	77	13	2	2	22	34	2	8	2	60	21	6	.365	.362
2-team (85 Cincinnati)					.274	—	—	156	617	98	169	27	3	11	52	81	2	11	3	126	44	12	.381	.358
Mateo, Henry	B-R	6-0	175	10-14-76	.154	.214	.083	22	26	5	4	2	0	1	3	2	0	1	0	3	0	0	.346	.214
Matos, Luis	R-R	6-0	215	10-30-78	.200	.182	.250	14	15	2	3	2	0	0	0	0	0	0	0	3	0	0	.333	.200
Schneider, Brian	L-R	6-1	195	11-26-76	.256	.271	.251	124	410	30	105	18	0	4	55	38	2	2	3	67	2	2	.329	.320
Soriano, Alfonso	R-R	6-1	180	1-7-76	.277	.293	.271	159	647	119	179	41	2	46	95	67	9	2	3	160	41	17	.560	.351
Vento, Mike	R-R	6-0	195	5-25-78	.278	.250	.300	9	18	3	5	1	0	1	4	0	0	0	0	5	0	0	.333	.409
Vidro, Jose	B-R	5-11	195	8-27-74	.289	.323	.276	126	463	52	134	26	1	7	47	41	3	0	4	48	1	0	.395	.348
Ward, Daryle	L-L	6-2	240	6-27-75	.308	.083	.337	78	104	15	32	9	0	6	19	14	2	0	3	21	0	1	.567	.390
2-team (20 Atlanta)					.308	—	—	98	130	17	40	10	0	7	26	15	2	0	3	27	0	1	.546	.380
Watson, Brandon	L-R	6-1	170	9-30-81	.179	.000	.208	9	28	0	5	0	0	0	0	0	0	0	0	3	0	2	.179	.207
Zimmerman, Ryan	R-R	6-3	210	9-28-84	.287	.280	.289	157	614	84	176	47	3	20	110	61	2	1	4	120	11	8	.471	.351

PITCHING	B-T	HT	WT	DOB	W	L	ERA	G	GS	CG	SV	IP	H	R	ER	HR	BB	SO	AVG	vLH	vRH	K/9	BB/9
Armas, Tony	R-R	6-3	225	4-29-78	9	12	5.03	30	30	0	0	154	167	96	86	19	64	97	.279	.274	.284	5.67	3.74
Astacio, Pedro	R-R	6-2	210	11-28-69	5	5	5.98	17	17	1	0	90	109	64	60	14	31	42	.301	.270	.330	4.18	3.09
Bergmann, Jason	R-R	6-4	190	9-25-81	0	2	6.68	29	6	0	0	65	81	49	48	12	27	54	.312	.257	.351	7.52	3.76
Booker, Chris	R-R	6-3	235	12-9-76	0	0	3.68	10	0	0	0	7	5	3	3	1	1	7	.192	.222	.176	8.59	1.23
Bowie, Micah	L-L	6-4	205	11-10-74	0	1	1.37	15	0	0	0	20	11	3	3	1	7	11	.164	.273	.111	5.03	3.20
Bray, Bill	L-L	6-3	215	6-5-83	1	1	3.91	19	0	0	0	23	24	11	10	2	9	16	.273	.286	.264	6.26	3.52
2-team (29 Cincinnati)					3	2	4.09	48	0	0	2	50	57	27	23	5	18	39	—	—	—	6.93	3.20
Campbell, Brett	R-R	6-0	170	10-17-81	0	0	10.38	4	0	0	0	4	4	5	5	1	2	4	.250	.333	.143	8.31	4.15
Corcoran, Roy	R-R	5-10	170	5-11-80	0	1	11.12	6	0	0	0	6	12	8	7	1	4	6	.414	.625	.154	9.53	6.35
Cordero, Chad	R-R	6-0	200	3-18-82	7	4	3.19	68	0	0	29	73	59	27	26	13	22	69	.215	.219	.212	8.47	2.70
Day, Zach	R-R	6-4	215	6-15-78	1	3	4.73	5	5	0	0	27	29	15	14	2	11	13	.276	.318	.246	4.39	3.71
Drese, Ryan	R-R	6-3	235	4-5-76	0	2	5.19	2	2	0	0	9	9	8	5	0	8	5	.290	.250	.304	5.19	8.31
Eischen, Joey	L-L	6-0	215	5-25-70	0	1	8.59	22	0	0	0	15	18	18	14	2	19	18	.295	.087	.421	11.05	11.66
Gryboski, Kevin	R-R	6-5	230	11-15-73	0	0	14.29	10	0	0	0	6	14	11	9	3	2	4	.452	.500	.400	6.35	3.18
Hernandez, Livan	R-R	6-2	245	2-20-75	9	8	5.34	24	24	0	0	147	176	94	87	22	52	89	.298	.310	.287	5.46	3.19
2-team (10 Arizona)					13	13	4.83	34	34	0	0	216	246	125	116	29	78	128	—	—	—	5.33	3.25
Hill, Shawn	R-R	6-2	185	4-28-81	1	3	4.66	6	6	0	0	37	43	20	19	2	12	16	.297	.324	.268	3.93	2.95
Hughes, Travis	R-R	6-5	235	5-25-78	0	0	6.35	8	0	0	0	11	13	8	8	2	6	4	.310	.182	.450	3.18	4.76
Majewski, Gary	R-R	6-1	215	2-26-80	3	2	3.58	46	0	0	0	55	49	24	22	4	25	34	.233	.256	.219	5.53	4.07
2-team (19 Cincinnati)					4	4	4.61	65	0	0	0	70	72	38	36	5	29	43	—	—	—	5.50	3.71
O'Connor, Michael	L-L	6-3	170	8-17-80	3	8	4.80	21	20	0	0	105	96	61	56	19	35	60	.244	.253	.242	5.06	3.86
Ortiz, Ramon	R-R	6-0	175	5-23-73	11	16	5.57	33	33	0	0	191	230	127	118	31	64	104	.297	.316	.278	4.91	3.02
Patterson, John	R-R	6-5	210	1-30-78	1	2	4.43	8	8	0	0	41	36	21	20	4	9	42	.237	.299	.188	9.30	1.99
Perez, Beltran	R-R	6-2	180	10-24-81	2	1	3.86	8	3	0	0	21	16	9	9	3	13	9	.222	.270	.171	3.86	5.57
Ramirez, Santiago	R-R	5-11	210	8-15-78	0	0	8.10	4	0	0	0	3	6	3	3	1	2	1	.375	.500	.300	2.70	5.40
Rauch, Jon	R-R	6-11	260	9-27-78	4	5	3.35	85	0	0	2	91	74	37	34	13	36	86	.231	.254	.216	8.47	3.55
Rivera, Saul	B-R	5-11	150	12-7-77	3	0	3.43	54	0	0	1	60	59	28	23	4	32	41	.250	.194	.290	6.12	4.77
Rodriguez, Felix	R-R	6-1	210	9-9-72	1	1	7.67	31	0	0	0	29	32	25	25	5	16	15	.281	.314	.254	4.60	4.91
Schroder, Chris	R-R	6-3	210	8-20-78	0	2	6.35	21	0	0	0	23	23	21	20	7	15	39	.223	.261	.193	12.39	4.76
Stanton, Mike	L-L	6-1	215	6-2-67	3	5	4.47	56	0	0	0	44	47	22	22	1	21	30	.278	.267	.284	6.09	4.26
2-team (26 San Francisco)					7	7	3.99	82	0	0	0	67	70	30	30	2	27	48	—	—	—	6.38	3.59
Traber, Billy	L-L	6-5	200	9-18-79	4	3	6.44	15	8	0	0	43	53	33	31	5	14	25	.301	.263	.312	5.19	2.91
Wagner, Ryan	R-R	6-4	225	7-15-82	3	3	4.70	26	0	0	0	31	36	21	16	3	15	20	.293	.197	.387	5.87	4.40

FIELDING

Catcher	PCT	G	PO	A	E	DP	PB
Fick	.991	26	102	8	1	2	4
Gonzalez	.972	12	62	8	2	0	2
Harper	.987	14	77	1	1	0	0
LeCroy	.968	13	60	1	2	0	0
Schneider	.993	123	691	56	5	8	5

First Base	PCT	G	PO	A	E	DP
Anderson	1.000	2	2	0	0	0
Fick	1.000	13	57	5	0	4
Johnson	.988	147	1165	93	15	91
LeCroy	.952	6	19	1	1	2
Schneider	1.000	1	1	0	0	0
Vidro	1.000	8	54	3	0	7

	PCT	G	PO	A	E	DP
Ward	.968	6	29	1	1	2
Second Base	**PCT**	**G**	**PO**	**A**	**E**	**DP**
Anderson	.961	32	51	71	5	13
Castro	.984	29	65	58	2	13
Harris	1.000	4	5	4	0	0
Jackson	1.000	11	9	18	0	3
Vidro	.990	107	224	250	5	53

General manager: Jim Bowden. **Farm director:** Andy Dunn. **Scouting director:** Dana Brown.

Class	Team	League	W	L	PCT	Finish*	Manager	Affiliate Since
Majors	Washington	National	71	91	.438	14th (16)	Frank Robinson	—
Triple-A	New Orleans Zephyrs	Pacific Coast	72	71	.503	9th (16)	Tim Foli	2005
Double-A	Harrisburg Senators	Eastern	67	75	.472	9th (12)	John Stearns	1991
High A	Potomac Nationals	Carolina	64	76	.457	6th (8)	Randy Knorr	2005
Low A	Savannah Sand Gnats	South Atlantic	56	83	.403	15th (16)	Bobby Williams	2003
Short-season	Vermont Expos	New York-Penn	23	52	.307	14th (14)	Jose Alguacil	1994
Rookie	GCL Nationals	Gulf Coast	23	31	.426	10th (13)	Bob Henley	1998

OVERALL 2006 MINOR LEAGUE RECORD 305 388 .440 28th (30)

*Finish in overall standings (No. of teams in league). +League champion

Third Base	PCT	G	PO	A	E	DP
Dorta	1.000	3	0	3	0	0
Harris	1.000	3	1	5	0	0
Jackson	.600	6	1	5	4	1
Mateo	1.000	2	0	1	0	0
Zimmerman	.965	157	152	260	15	30

Shortstop	PCT	G	PO	A	E	DP
Clayton	.970	86	110	240	11	39
Dorta	.909	3	1	9	1	0
Harris	.923	5	5	7	1	1

	PCT	G	PO	A	E	DP
Jackson	.833	16	8	12	4	0
Lopez	.947	71	89	162	14	34
Mateo	.875	3	4	3	1	1
Outfield	**PCT**	**G**	**PO**	**A**	**E**	**DP**
Anderson	.914	17	30	2	3	2
Byrd	.987	71	150	1	2	0
Castro	.—	2	0	0	0	0
Church	.986	62	144	2	2	1
Escobar	.984	23	62	1	1	0
Fick	1.000	6	4	0	0	0

	PCT	G	PO	A	E	DP
Guillen	.988	68	163	3	2	0
Jackson	.957	26	44	0	2	0
Kearns	.968	60	147	3	5	1
Logan	.983	26	59	0	1	0
Lombard	.933	8	13	1	1	0
Mateo	.—	1	0	0	0	0
Matos	1.000	4	4	1	0	0
Soriano	.969	158	326	22	11	9
Vento	1.000	8	13	0	0	0
Ward	1.000	12	18	0	0	0
Watson	1.000	8	17	0	0	0

New Orleans Zephyrs   Triple-A

Pacific Coast League

BATTING	B-T	HT	WT	DOB	AVG	vLH	vRH	G	AB	R	H	2B	3B	HR	RBI	BB	HBP	SH	SF	SO	SB	CS	SLG	OBP
Broadway, Larry	L-L	6-4	230	12-17-80	.288	.344	.266	123	444	60	128	25	2	15	78	45	2	3	5	116	5	1	.455	.353
Byrd, Marlon	R-R	6-0	235	8-30-77	.271	.275	.270	46	155	22	42	9	0	7	29	16	7	0	1	31	3	1	.465	.363
Castillo, Alberto	R-R	6-0	215	2-10-70	.268	.282	.262	88	254	33	68	17	0	0	30	35	1	6	2	42	1	2	.335	.356
Castro, Bernie	B-R	5-10	165	7-14-79	.284	.329	.265	69	268	36	76	5	3	2	25	18	0	6	0	34	22	2	.347	.329
Church, Ryan	L-L	6-1	205	10-14-78	.246	.204	.262	53	175	29	43	6	0	7	29	25	3	0	3	41	5	1	.400	.345
Cleveland, Russ	R-R	6-3	215	12-26-79	.196	.273	.171	21	46	6	9	1	0	0	1	1	0	0	0	12	1	0	.217	.213
DeMent, Dan	R-R	5-10	191	6-17-78	.177	.053	.217	22	79	7	14	1	0	2	10	6	0	1	0	22	0	2	.266	.235
Dorta, Melvin	R-R	5-11	160	1-15-82	.433	.250	.462	8	30	6	13	1	0	1	3	1	0	2	1	2	3	2	.567	.438
Fick, Robert	L-R	6-1	205	3-15-74	.143	.000	.167	2	7	0	1	0	0	0	0	1	0	0	0	2	1	0	.143	.250
Fitzpatrick, Reginald	L-L	5-11	180	2-28-83	.192	.000	.263	13	26	3	5	1	0	0	2	2	0	1	0	6	1	0	.231	.250
Godwin, Tyrell	L-R	6-0	200	7-10-79	.248	.250	.248	126	411	59	102	22	7	7	45	32	4	0	2	68	19	6	.387	.307
Gonzalez, Wiki	R-R	5-11	205	5-17-74	.298	.276	.309	26	84	9	25	4	0	4	16	9	4	0	2	9	1	0	.488	.384
Harper, Brandon	R-R	6-4	200	4-29-76	.292	.233	.311	43	120	18	35	10	0	2	11	15	6	1	1	21	3	1	.425	.394
Harris, Brendan	R-R	6-1	200	8-26-80	.283	.315	.273	59	219	37	62	14	0	5	32	26	9	1	2	56	3	2	.416	.379
Kelly, Kenny	R-R	6-2	190	1-26-79	.248	.216	.264	110	351	47	87	13	2	1	34	43	2	12	1	75	19	8	.305	.332
Labandeira, Josh	R-R	5-7	180	2-25-79	.276	.292	.270	120	395	49	109	17	2	3	44	37	10	11	3	52	11	13	.352	.351
Larson, Brandon	R-R	6-0	210	5-24-76	.268	.266	.269	117	380	58	102	17	1	20	76	38	2	0	2	101	4	3	.476	.336
LeCroy, Matthew	R-R	6-2	230	12-13-75	.267	.286	.250	5	15	0	4	1	0	0	2	0	0	0	0	4	0	0	.333	.267
Lombard, George	L-R	6-0	210	9-14-75	.302	.367	.279	62	189	35	57	10	1	10	24	23	5	3	0	49	18	2	.524	.392
Mateo, Henry	B-R	6-0	175	10-14-76	.254	.365	.214	113	433	55	110	21	6	2	35	38	4	12	3	78	33	11	.344	.318
Medrano, Anthony	R-R	5-10	170	12-8-74	.227	.214	.234	39	75	9	17	1	0	0	7	11	0	1	0	7	1	1	.240	.326
Raines, Tim	B-R	5-10	195	8-31-79	.227	.111	.271	26	66	8	15	4	0	1	5	3	0	1	0	13	5	0	.333	.261
San Pedro, Erick	R-R	6-0	205	10-5-83	.115	.000	.158	12	26	0	3	1	0	0	2	2	0	1	0	10	0	0	.154	.179
Sorensen, Logan	L-L	6-1	195	8-12-81	.400	.000	.500	3	5	1	2	0	0	0	1	0	0	0	2	1	0	0	.400	.500
Thissen, Greg	R-R	6-4	185	6-1-81	.220	.286	.194	23	50	3	11	2	0	0	5	1	0	0	6	1	1	0	.260	.235
Vento, Mike	R-R	6-0	195	5-25-78	.341	.368	.331	62	217	34	74	14	0	7	33	20	1	0	2	35	3	4	.502	.396
Watson, Brandon	L-R	6-1	170	9-30-81	.305	.400	.292	21	82	11	25	3	1	0	13	3	0	1	1	10	2	1	.366	.326

PITCHING	B-T	HT	WT	DOB	W	L	ERA	G	GS	CG	SV	IP	H	R	ER	HR	BB	SO	AVG	vLH	vRH	K/9	BB/9
Astacio, Pedro	R-R	6-2	210	11-28-69	1	1	6.43	3	3	0	0	14	17	10	10	1	3	4	.304	.321	.286	2.57	1.93
Beltran, Francis	R-R	6-2	230	11-29-79	0	0	4.50	4	0	0	0	6	6	4	3	0	5	4	.286	.429	.214	6.00	7.50
Bergmann, Jason	R-R	6-4	190	9-25-81	8	2	3.28	26	4	0	4	60	54	22	22	5	20	62	.244	.211	.262	9.25	2.98
Booker, Chris	R-R	6-3	235	12-9-76	2	2	3.94	15	0	0	0	16	14	7	7	0	13	29	.237	.250	.229	16.31	7.31
Bouknight, Kip	R-R	6-0	190	11-16-78	3	0	4.64	6	6	0	0	33	30	17	17	5	13	23	.242	.291	.203	6.27	3.55
Bowie, Micah	L-L	6-4	205	11-10-74	2	0	3.83	31	0	0	1	42	33	20	18	0	24	57	.213	.188	.224	12.12	5.10
Bray, Bill	L-L	6-3	215	6-5-83	4	1	3.98	21	0	0	5	32	26	14	14	5	9	45	.217	.286	.188	12.79	2.56
Campbell, Brett	R-R	6-0	170	10-17-81	0	1	3.92	15	0	0	0	21	14	9	9	1	11	19	.189	.111	.234	8.7	4.79
Corcoran, Roy	R-R	5-10	170	5-11-80	2	4	2.41	28	0	0	11	34	24	11	9	0	25	37	.202	.140	.246	9.89	6.68
Denney, Kyle	R-R	6-2	190	7-27-77	0	2	3.33	6	6	0	0	27	28	15	10	2	18	32	.267	.259	.269	10.67	6.00
Echols, Justin	R-R	6-3	200	10-6-80	1	0	5.40	1	1	0	0	5	4	3	3	1	4	3	.211	.000	.400	5.40	7.20
Figueroa, Nelson	R-R	6-1	180	5-18-74	3	5	4.38	16	11	0	0	76	76	41	37	12	21	44	.260	.254	.265	5.21	2.49
Foli, Daniel	R-R	6-2	180	3-30-81	0	0	0.00	1	0	0	1	3	2	0	0	0	4	0	.182	.167	.200	12.00	12.00
Gil, David	R-R	6-4	215	10-1-78	2	3	4.34	12	10	0	0	56	67	30	27	8	10	36	.294	.288	.299	5.79	1.61
Good, Andrew	R-R	6-1	210	9-19-79	9	9	4.81	28	26	0	0	148	176	90	79	22	35	93	.292	.263	.311	5.67	2.13
Gryboski, Kevin	R-R	6-5	230	11-15-73	4	6	3.71	52	0	0	7	61	67	31	25	3	26	43	.284	.291	.278	6.38	3.86
Hill, Shawn	R-R	6-2	185	4-28-81	0	0	3.60	1	1	0	0	5	6	2	2	0	2	2	.286	.250	.308	3.60	3.60
Hughes, Travis	R-R	6-5	235	5-25-78	2	6	2.32	51	0	0	4	74	50	30	19	3	41	87	.192	.196	.188	10.63	5.01
Martinez, Anastacio	R-R	6-2	185	11-3-78	5	11	4.48	24	24	0	0	129	121	71	64	13	58	115	.251	.303	.214	8.04	4.06
Norderum, Jason	L-L	6-3	220	11-21-81	0	0	2.08	4	0	0	0	9	9	2	2	1	5	8	.310	.200	.368	5.19	8.31
O'Connor, Michael	L-L	6-3	170	8-17-80	1	0	2.73	6	4	0	0	26	21	10	8	2	11	28	.221	.158	.237	9.57	3.76
Patterson, John	R-R	6-5	210	1-30-78	0	0	1.93	1	1	0	0	5	4	1	1	0	3	3	.222	.300	.125	5.79	3.86
Perrin, Devin	R-R	6-7	225	5-14-81	0	0	5.40	2	1	0	0	5	5	3	3	0	3	1	.286	.400	.222	7.20	8.10

ORGANIZATION STATISTICS

	B-T	HT	WT	DOB	W	L	ERA	G	GS	CG	SV	IP	H	R	ER	HR	BB	SO	AVG	vLH	vRH	K/9	BB/9
Ramirez, Santiago	R-R	5-11	210	8-15-78	2	1	0.99	19	0	0	7	27	16	3	3	1	4	28	.174	.139	.196	9.22	1.32
Rivera, Saul	B-R	5-11	150	12-7-77	1	1	1.59	12	2	0	1	28	25	7	5	1	12	25	.236	.250	.226	7.94	3.81
Rodriguez, Felix	R-R	6-1	210	9-9-72	0	0	7.84	8	0	0	0	10	14	10	9	1	10	7	.326	.333	.320	6.10	8.71
Rueckel, Danny	R-R	6-0	175	9-25-79	3	1	3.38	15	0	0	0	21	16	8	8	2	11	21	.203	.206	.200	8.86	4.64
Schroder, Chris	R-R	6-3	210	8-20-78	2	1	1.52	28	0	0	1	47	25	9	8	2	16	60	.152	.188	.125	11.41	3.04
Thompson, Chris	R-R	6-3	195	1-2-82	1	0	7.59	5	0	0	0	11	11	9	9	2	9	11	.289	.400	.217	9.28	7.59
Traber, Billy	L-L	6-5	200	9-18-79	7	7	4.05	21	21	1	0	124	143	62	56	8	26	102	.289	.162	.338	7.38	1.88
Wagner, Ryan	R-R	6-4	225	7-15-82	0	0	4.00	6	0	0	0	9	8	4	4	0	2	5	.250	.273	.238	5.00	2.00
Watkins, Steve	R-R	6-4	215	7-19-78	7	7	3.85	21	20	0	0	112	105	58	48	10	41	78	.246	.242	.250	6.25	3.28

FIELDING

Catcher	PCT	G	PO	A	E	DP	PB
Castillo	.991	79	584	50	6	5	10
Cleveland	1.000	11	50	8	0	0	2
Gonzalez	.991	23	196	13	2	2	4
Harper	.992	34	237	21	2	2	5
Harris	—	1	0	0	0	0	0
San Pedro	.971	12	61	5	2	0	1

First Base	PCT	G	PO	A	E	DP
Broadway	.993	120	988	75	8	82
Cleveland	1.000	2	3	2	0	1
DeMent	1.000	1	1	0	0	0
Fick	1.000	1	11	0	0	0
Harper	1.000	2	8	0	0	0
Harris	.909	1	9	1	1	2
Larson	.992	19	111	11	1	13
LeCroy	1.000	2	11	3	0	0
Mateo	1.000	5	19	1	0	1
Sorensen	1.000	3	13	2	0	1
Thissen	.875	2	6	1	1	1
Vento	.981	9	49	4	1	2

Second Base	PCT	G	PO	A	E	DP
Castro	.974	56	105	118	6	24
DeMent	.944	17	26	41	4	6
Harris	1.000	10	18	25	0	5
Labandeira	.800	1	3	1	1	0
Mateo	.966	59	103	149	9	33
Medrano	1.000	14	14	12	0	3
Raines	.982	20	21	33	1	6
Thissen	1.000	3	0	1	0	0

Third Base	PCT	G	PO	A	E	DP
Cleveland	.923	4	6	6	1	0
DeMent	1.000	9	2	7	0	0
Dorta	.923	6	3	9	1	1
Harris	.955	37	22	62	4	5
Labandeira	—	5	0	0	0	0
Larson	.934	69	33	108	10	5
Mateo	1.000	35	16	50	0	6
Medrano	1.000	11	2	9	0	1
Thissen	.938	8	3	12	1	1

Shortstop	PCT	G	PO	A	E	DP
DeMent	1.000	1	2	4	0	1
Dorta	1.000	4	4	18	0	5
Harris	.938	15	26	34	4	10
Labandeira	.956	115	142	318	21	63
Mateo	.943	11	13	20	2	3
Medrano	.972	12	15	20	1	4

Outfield	PCT	G	PO	A	E	DP
Broadway	1.000	1	1	0	0	0
Byrd	.986	35	70	2	1	1
Castro	.950	13	19	0	1	0
Church	.970	44	95	3	3	1
Fick	1.000	1	1	0	0	0
Fitzpatrick	1.000	10	14	1	0	0
Godwin	.960	114	161	6	7	1
Harper	1.000	2	2	0	0	0
Kelly	.985	99	191	4	3	1
Labandeira	1.000	2	3	0	0	0
Lombard	.989	51	90	2	1	1
Mateo	1.000	24	26	0	0	0
Raines	1.000	7	16	0	0	0
Schroder	1.000	1	3	0	0	0
Thissen	1.000	5	4	0	0	0
Vento	.989	50	86	3	1	0
Watson	1.000	20	30	1	0	0

Harrisburg Senators — Double-A

Eastern League

BATTING	B-T	HT	WT	DOB	AVG	vLH	vRH	G	AB	R	H	2B	3B	HR	RBI	BB	HBP	SH	SF	SO	SB	CS	SLG	OBP
Blanco, Tony	R-R	6-1	175	11-10-81	.290	.273	.300	9	31	2	9	0	2	8	2	1	0	0	11	0	0	.516	.353
Bynum, Seth	R-R	6-0	185	12-19-80	.232	.268	.212	72	203	19	47	10	0	0	11	30	2	1	0	46	4	2	.281	.336
Casto, Kory	L-R	6-1	195	12-8-81	.272	.189	.303	140	489	84	133	24	6	20	80	81	8	4	8	104	6	5	.468	.379
Chavez, Ender	L-L	5-11	155	3-9-81	.143	.125	.147	22	42	6	6	1	0	2	5	0	0	0	9	1	1	.214	.234
Church, Ryan	L-L	6-1	220	10-14-78	.211	.000	.235	5	19	3	4	0	0	2	3	3	0	0	5	1	0	.526	.318
Cleveland, Russ	R-R	6-3	215	12-26-79	.036	.000	.053	10	28	0	1	0	0	0	0	0	0	0	7	0	0	.036	.100
DeMent, Dan	R-R	5-10	191	6-17-78	.234	.260	.226	115	397	61	93	16	3	18	52	45	7	7	2	114	6	7	.426	.322
Desmond, Ian	R-R	6-2	185	9-20-85	.182	.138	.196	37	121	8	22	4	1	0	3	5	0	6	0	35	4	1	.231	.214
Diaz, Frank	R-R	6-2	180	10-6-83	.259	.304	.240	107	402	44	104	17	1	9	50	19	3	2	2	59	5	5	.373	.296
Dorta, Melvin	R-R	5-11	160	1-15-82	.257	.218	.272	108	404	54	104	15	3	5	30	30	1	5	3	34	33	10	.347	.307
Emmerick, Joshua	R-R	6-4	190	2-22-81	.175	.208	.158	53	143	7	25	4	0	1	8	12	0	1	0	44	0	0	.224	.259
Escobar, Alex	R-R	6-1	190	9-6-78	.311	.355	.297	35	122	21	38	11	0	5	26	20	8	0	0	23	2	2	.525	.440
Feliciano, Jesus	L-L	6-0	174	6-6-79	.230	.292	.221	64	178	15	41	3	0	1	13	10	1	3	1	15	3	5	.264	.274
Fick, Robert	L-R	6-1	205	3-15-74	.281	.118	.350	16	57	11	16	1	0	1	4	8	0	0	2	8	2	1	.351	.369
Guerrero, Cristian	R-R	6-7	175	7-12-80	.257	.429	.200	43	140	14	36	4	4	5	20	10	0	0	6	45	4	3	.450	.307
Lane, Richard	L-L	6-3	205	1-4-80	.202	.302	.178	116	228	18	46	11	2	2	27	12	1	3	2	50	1	1	.294	.243
Manriquez, Salomon	R-R	6-1	190	9-15-82	.257	.299	.242	100	339	39	87	18	0	10	45	32	1	2	3	86	0	0	.398	.320
Raines, Tim	B-R	6-0	195	8-31-79	.292	.323	.281	65	240	40	70	11	0	6	23	23	0	5	1	54	25	5	.413	.352
Redman, Prentice	R-R	6-3	195	8-23-79	.286	.316	.276	83	297	40	85	22	1	11	45	38	5	0	2	63	8	8	.478	.374
Rodriguez, Robert	R-R	5-10	180	12-17-80	.000	.000	—	1	1	0	0	0	0	0	0	0	0	0	0	0	0	0	.000	.000
Thissen, Greg	R-R	6-4	185	6-1-81	.195	.247	.203	39	82	9	16	3	0	2	6	18	0	4	1	15	1	1	.305	.337
Vidro, Jose	B-R	5-11	195	8-27-74	.250	—	.250	3	8	0	2	0	0	0	0	1	0	0	0	0	0	0	.250	.400
Webb, Trey	R-R	6-0	170	2-11-82	.200	.417	.107	10	40	3	8	0	0	0	1	0	0	0	0	11	0	0	.200	.200
Whitesell, Josh	L-L	6-3	215	4-14-82	.264	.267	.263	127	402	47	106	11	0	19	56	53	4	6	2	125	2	6	.433	.354
Yepez, Marcos	B-R	5-10	160	12-29-81	.275	.455	.217	27	91	13	25	1	2	1	3	7	0	3	1	28	5	2	.363	.323

PITCHING	B-T	HT	WT	DOB	W	L	ERA	G	GS	CG	SV	IP	H	R	ER	HR	BB	SO	AVG	vLH	vRH	K/9	BB/9
Alvarez, Oscar	L-L	6-0	165	9-17-80	8	8	5.25	30	23	1	0	134	148	83	78	16	38	89	.285	.250	.296	5.99	2.56
Armas, Tony	R-R	6-3	225	4-29-78	0	0	7.71	1	1	0	0	3	2	2	2	0	1	4	.300	.333	.286	11.43	3.86
Astacio, Pedro	R-R	6-2	210	11-28-69	0	0	2.25	1	1	0	0	4	1	1	1	0	2	0	.077	.143	.000	4.50	0.00
Balester, Collin	R-R	6-5	190	6-6-86	1	0	1.83	3	3	0	0	20	15	5	4	0	6	10	.231	.220	.250	4.58	2.75
Bouknight, Kip	R-R	6-0	190	11-16-78	6	8	4.55	21	21	2	0	125	127	67	63	10	39	92	.261	.271	.252	6.64	2.82
Campbell, Brett	R-R	6-0	170	10-17-81	0	3	3.14	13	0	0	0	8	14	16	6	5	0	11	20	.276	.308	.250	12.56	6.91
Chico, Matt	L-L	5-11	200	6-10-83	2	0	3.27	4	4	0	0	22	28	9	8	3	8	13	.318	.417	.281	5.32	3.27
Corcoran, Roy	R-R	5-10	170	5-11-80	0	2	0.35	21	0	0	16	26	12	6	1	1	10	40	.138	.135	.140	13.85	3.46
DeMent, Dan	R-R	5-10	191	6-17-78	0	0	8.31	5	0	0	0	4	6	5	4	2	1	0	.316	.222	.400	0.00	2.08
Drese, Ryan	R-R	6-3	235	4-5-76	0	2	3.86	3	3	0	0	9	11	7	4	1	6	4	.306	.364	.214	3.86	5.79
Echols, Justin	R-R	6-3	200	10-6-80	5	8	4.36	24	22	0	0	120	113	64	58	13	77	117	.252	.294	.209	8.80	5.79
Felfoldi, Jonathan	L-L	6-1	183	7-6-81	0	1	10.80	1	1	0	0	5	9	7	6	0	2	5	.375	.600	.316	9.00	3.60
Foli, Daniel	R-R	6-2	180	3-30-81	5	1	5.11	23	0	0	2	44	48	26	25	2	25	45	.267	.214	.313	9.20	5.11
Gil, David	R-R	6-4	210	10-1-78	1	1	3.00	8	0	0	0	15	9	6	5	0	6	14	.173	.087	.241	8.40	3.60
Hill, Shawn	R-R	6-2	185	4-28-81	3	3	2.68	10	10	0	0	50	46	20	15	2	5	32	.237	.299	.175	5.72	0.89
Kolb, Dan	R-R	6-1	190	6-5-80	4	2	3.66	40	0	0	8	79	60	37	32	6	33	82	.211	.229	.196	9.38	3.78
Martinez, Anastacio	R-R	6-1	175	11-3-78	2	0	3.65	2	2	0	0	12	10	5	5	1	3	11	.222	.227	.217	8.03	2.19
Martis, Shairon	R-R	6-1	175	3-30-87	0	1	12.60	1	1	0	0	5	8	7	7	4	3	1	.348	.316	.500	1.80	5.40
Maust, David	L-R	6-2	205	11-6-78	6	10	4.81	24	24	0	0	122	125	69	65	16	38	63	.267	.268	.266	4.66	2.81
Mock, Garrett	R-R	6-4	205	4-25-83	0	0	10.26	4	4	0	0	17	24	19	18	6	9	15	.387	.355	.409	4.86	2.70
Morales, Alexis	R-R	5-11	170	12-8-82	0	0	5.74	2	0	0	0	16	16	10	10	3	21	15	.267	.250	.278	8.62	12.06

ORGANIZATION STATISTICS

Morales, Ricardo	L-L	6-1	170	12-9-83	1	0	0.00	1	1	0	0	6	4	0	0	0	1	2	.190	.111	.250	3.00	1.50
Norderum, Jason	L-L	6-3	220	11-21-81	1	0	4.54	15	1	0	0	40	40	22	20	2	19	20	.263	.293	.245	4.54	4.31
Nyquist, Brett	L-L	6-7	205	5-7-81	0	0	9.00	2	0	0	0	6	9	9	6	0	4	0	.346	.667	.304	0.00	6.00
Ovalles, Juan	R-R	6-0	165	5-15-82	0	0	6.75	4	0	0	0	4	4	3	3	0	7	3	.286	.167	.375	6.75	15.75
Perez, Beltran	R-R	6-2	180	10-24-81	8	6	3.11	31	16	1	1	122	127	53	42	8	40	107	.267	.260	.273	7.92	2.96
Perrin, Devin	R-R	6-7	225	5-14-81	3	4	4.72	35	0	0	3	55	56	37	29	6	42	48	.265	.304	.235	7.81	6.83
Plexico, Gerald	L-L	6-4	210	2-24-80	4	3	3.99	34	0	0	3	65	65	30	29	5	24	47	.270	.272	.268	6.47	3.31
Rueckel, Danny	R-R	6-0	175	9-25-79	4	4	4.20	26	2	0	1	45	50	22	21	4	12	35	.287	.307	.273	7.00	2.40
Schroder, Chris	R-R	6-3	210	8-20-78	2	0	5.02	9	0	0	1	14	18	9	8	2	6	13	.300	.296	.303	8.16	3.77
Sylvester, Billy	R-R	6-5	210	10-1-76	0	2	13.50	2	2	0	0	8	10	13	12	2	15	7	.313	.235	.400	7.88	16.88
Thompson, Chris	R-R	6-3	195	1-2-82	0	1	15.63	4	0	0	0	6	8	12	11	0	10	6	.348	.500	.231	8.53	14.21
Zinicola, Zechry	R-R	6-1	220	3-2-85	1	1	2.70	10	0	0	5	10	11	6	3	0	11	8	.256	.261	.250	7.20	9.90

FIELDING

Catcher	PCT	G	PO	A	E	DP	PB
Cleveland	1.000	7	42	4	0	1	0
Emmerick	.987	46	279	14	4	1	5
Fick	1.000	7	50	0	0	0	2
Manriquez	.979	94	596	58	14	3	17
Rodriguez	1.000	1	1	0	0	0	0

First Base	PCT	G	PO	A	E	DP
Dorta	1.000	5	7	0	0	1
Emmerick	.875	4	7	0	1	2
Fick	.947	3	15	3	1	2
Lane	.978	84	416	34	10	44
Thissen	1.000	1	1	0	0	0
Whitesell	.981	93	663	59	14	74

Second Base	PCT	G	PO	A	E	DP
Bynum	1.000	1	1	0	0	0
DeMent	.973	110	219	251	13	70
Dorta	.946	19	25	28	3	9
Thissen	1.000	3	5	3	0	1
Vidro	1.000	3	6	4	0	1
Webb	.979	10	25	22	1	7
Yepez	1.000	11	13	17	0	5

Third Base	PCT	G	PO	A	E	DP
Casto	.933	103	43	166	15	21
Dorta	.967	32	15	44	2	1
Thissen	.934	33	23	48	5	7
Yepez	.778	5	0	7	2	1

Shortstop	PCT	G	PO	A	E	DP
Bynum	.951	68	98	174	14	45
Desmond	.924	37	53	81	11	20
Dorta	.976	43	43	78	3	21
Yepez	.981	13	23	30	1	6

Outfield	PCT	G	PO	A	E	DP
Casto	.991	55	107	4	1	1
Chavez	.962	14	25	0	1	0
Church	1.000	5	10	1	0	0
Diaz	.989	106	270	7	3	1
Dorta	1.000	31	40	1	0	0
Echols	1.000	1	1	0	0	0
Escobar	.972	34	66	4	2	0
Feliciano	.989	54	86	4	1	1
Fick	1.000	2	4	0	0	0
Guerrero	.960	39	70	2	3	0
Lane	.929	18	12	1	1	0
Raines	.992	58	116	3	1	1
Redman	.992	61	126	1	1	0

Potomac Nationals — High Class A

Carolina League

BATTING	B-T	HT	WT	DOB	AVG	vLH	vRH	G	AB	R	H	2B	3B	HR	RBI	BB	HBP	SH	SF	SO	SB	CS	SLG	OBP
Baez, Edgardo	R-R	6-2	190	7-12-85	.103	.000	.156	20	68	4	7	2	0	2	3	8	0	1	0	26	0	0	.221	.197
Bernadina, Rogearvin	L-L	6-0	175	6-12-84	.270	.232	.288	123	434	60	117	19	3	6	42	56	4	6	4	98	28	11	.369	.355
Blanco, Tony	R-R	6-1	175	11-10-81	.255	.270	.248	54	196	24	50	13	0	8	32	14	3	0	1	61	3	0	.444	.313
Brown, Dee	R-R	6-0	230	10-21-82	.303	.367	.250	32	109	16	33	4	1	4	24	6	5	0	1	27	2	1	.468	.364
Bynum, Seth	R-R	6-0	185	12-19-80	.244	.227	.253	34	119	16	29	7	1	1	6	10	1	1	0	39	6	3	.345	.308
Castro, Jonathan	B-R	6-1	160	11-29-83	.300	.333	.286	5	10	0	3	1	0	0	2	0	0	0	0	2	0	0	.400	.300
Chavez, Ender	L-L	5-11	155	3-9-81	.276	.253	.286	81	279	50	77	9	1	1	24	57	1	6	0	46	20	10	.326	.401
Cleveland, Russ	R-R	6-3	215	12-26-79	.222	.231	.214	10	27	4	6	1	0	1	1	1	0	1	0	7	0	0	.370	.250
Desmond, Ian	R-R	6-2	185	9-20-85	.244	.197	.269	92	365	50	89	20	2	9	45	29	9	2	3	79	14	8	.384	.313
Fitzpatrick, Reginald	L-L	5-11	180	2-28-83	.229	.176	.254	33	105	16	24	4	1	1	13	5	1	0	0	25	9	0	.314	.270
German, Agustin	R-R	6-0	180	12-13-85	.000	.000	.000	2	4	0	0	0	0	0	0	0	0	0	0	2	0	0	.000	.000
Guerrero, Cristian	R-R	6-7	175	7-12-80	.231	.205	.242	37	130	23	30	3	2	3	16	11	2	3	1	33	6	2	.354	.299
Guillen, Jose	R-R	5-11	195	5-17-76	.500	.750	.000	3	6	2	3	0	0	2	3	1	0	0	0	0	0	0	1.500	.571
Ivany, Devin	R-R	6-2	185	7-27-82	.262	.278	.255	115	446	62	117	19	3	6	55	25	7	3	1	64	12	3	.359	.311
Lowrance, Marvin	L-L	6-0	215	7-16-84	.257	.250	.261	112	377	47	97	20	3	5	48	43	6	1	2	75	2	0	.366	.341
Martinez, Michael	B-R	5-9	145	9-16-82	.217	.100	.308	7	23	1	5	2	0	0	2	1	1	0	0	1	1	0	.304	.280
Montz, Luke	R-R	6-2	205	7-7-83	.229	.250	.219	131	449	59	103	27	3	16	76	51	8	2	9	91	3	3	.410	.313
Mortimer, Steve	L-L	6-3	215	6-10-81	.224	.116	.260	60	174	27	39	9	0	6	23	15	11	1	0	62	3	2	.379	.325
Nunez, Alex	L-R	5-11	170	4-30-81	.265	.188	.333	13	34	0	9	0	0	0	1	3	1	1	0	7	2	1	.265	.342
Powell, Brandon	L-R	6-0	191	8-15-80	.280	.246	.294	126	460	64	129	34	4	14	71	37	7	5	3	124	30	9	.463	.341
Rodriguez, Robert	R-R	5-10	180	12-17-80	.105	.136	.063	20	38	1	4	0	0	0	4	2	0	0	1	7	0	0	.105	.146
Schneider, Brian	L-R	6-1	195	11-26-76	.222	.333	.167	2	9	1	2	1	0	0	1	0	0	0	0	2	0	0	.333	.222
Thissen, Greg	R-R	6-4	185	6-1-81	.200	.200	.200	6	20	4	4	0	0	0	3	1	0	0	1	3	0	0	.200	.227
Vidro, Jose	B-R	5-11	195	8-27-74	.333	—	.333	1	3	0	1	1	0	0	0	0	0	0	0	0	0	0	.667	.333
Vroman, Douglas	R-R	6-2	200	2-9-81	.150	.211	.095	18	40	4	6	2	0	0	0	7	0	1	0	6	1	0	.200	.277
Webb, Trey	R-R	6-0	170	2-11-82	.257	.259	.256	112	416	53	107	28	5	6	47	30	11	0	4	81	20	8	.392	.321
Yepez, Marcos	B-R	5-10	160	12-29-81	.268	.225	.288	87	287	35	77	14	2	4	37	25	4	1	3	94	20	12	.373	.332

PITCHING	B-T	HT	WT	DOB	W	L	ERA	G	GS	CG	SV	IP	H	R	ER	HR	BB	SO	AVG	vLH	vRH	K/9	BB/9
Astacio, Pedro	R-R	6-2	210	11-28-69	0	0	0.00	1	1	0	0	3	3	0	0	0	0	2	.250	.400	.143	6.00	0.00
Balester, Collin	R-R	6-5	190	6-6-86	4	5	5.20	23	22	0	0	118	126	71	68	12	53	87	.280	.264	.293	6.65	4.05
Bunn, Greg	R-R	6-1	210	2-3-83	1	1	7.22	15	1	0	1	29	39	25	23	5	19	21	.331	.283	.361	6.59	5.97
Campbell, Brett	R-R	6-0	170	10-17-81	3	1	2.38	19	0	0	8	23	22	7	6	3	2	27	.253	.270	.240	10.72	0.79
De Los Santos, Juan	R-L	6-0	184	1-15-83	1	0	7.36	4	0	0	0	4	2	3	3	0	5	4	.167	.200	.143	9.82	12.27
Everts, Clint	B-R	6-2	170	8-10-84	5	10	6.00	20	19	0	0	90	96	69	60	11	53	92	.264	.232	.287	9.20	5.30
Felfoldi, Jonathan	L-L	6-1	183	7-6-81	3	8	5.10	20	19	0	0	108	114	67	61	9	54	70	.273	.354	.249	5.85	4.51
Foli, Daniel	R-R	6-2	180	3-30-81	0	0	3.52	6	0	0	0	8	13	4	3	0	8	7	.382	.273	.435	8.22	9.39
Henderson, Jim	L-R	6-5	190	10-21-82	2	2	4.50	25	1	0	1	52	44	31	26	4	22	56	.222	.222	.222	9.69	3.81
Hinckley, Michael	R-L	6-3	170	10-5-82	6	8	5.52	28	28	0	0	148	178	102	91	18	63	79	.303	.237	.322	4.79	3.82
Kolb, Dan	R-R	6-1	190	6-5-80	0	0	0.00	4	0	0	2	11	7	0	0	0	1	10	.175	.143	.182	8.44	0.84
Martinez, Carlos	R-R	6-4	177	3-30-84	1	0	5.40	1	1	0	0	5	6	3	3	1	2	3	.300	.364	.222	5.40	3.60
Martis, Shairon	R-R	6-1	175	3-30-87	0	2	3.00	2	2	0	0	12	9	5	4	0	3	7	.209	.067	.286	5.25	2.25
Morales, Alexis	R-R	5-11	170	12-8-82	3	2	2.17	32	0	0	2	46	30	15	11	3	25	49	.189	.227	.161	9.66	4.93
Morales, Ricardo	L-L	6-1	170	12-9-83	6	10	4.70	25	23	1	0	132	150	84	69	13	42	69	.287	.291	.286	4.70	2.86
Norderum, Jason	L-L	6-3	220	11-21-81	3	5	4.01	13	9	0	0	58	54	33	26	3	31	40	.251	.273	.246	6.17	4.78
Nyquist, Brett	L-L	6-7	205	5-7-81	0	3	6.93	11	2	0	0	25	37	19	19	2	12	10	.356	.343	.362	3.65	4.38
Ovalles, Juan	R-R	6-0	165	5-15-82	6	8	3.30	38	1	0	7	63	50	25	23	3	32	80	.219	.245	.197	11.49	4.60
Patterson, John	R-R	6-5	210	1-30-78	0	1	5.19	2	2	0	0	9	12	7	5	1	2	11	.324	.375	.286	11.42	2.08
Pearson, Anthony	R-R	6-3	190	8-14-81	0	1	6.11	16	1	0	0	28	31	19	19	2	24	26	.290	.275	.299	8.36	7.71
Perrault, Josh	R-R	6-3	205	6-11-82	2	0	1.02	14	0	0	3	18	14	2	2	1	9	14	.219	.160	.256	7.13	4.58
Plexico, Gerald	L-L	6-4	210	2-24-80	3	0	1.93	9	0	0	0	14	11	3	3	3	4	15	.220	.167	.237	9.64	2.57
Reid, Brett	R-R	5-11	200	10-18-79	0	2	5.40	12	0	0	0	20	18	14	12	1	12	14	.250	.292	.229	6.30	5.40

Name	B-T	HT	WT	DOB	W	L	ERA	G	GS	CG	SV	IP	H	R	ER	HR	BB	SO	AVG	vLH	vRH	K/9	BB/9
Rodriguez, Felix	R-R	6-1	210	9-9-72	0	0	9.00	1	1	0	0	1	2	2	1	1	0	0	.400	.000	1.000	0.00	0.00
Stammen, Craig	R-R	6-3	200	3-9-84	0	2	5.76	7	6	0	0	30	34	20	19	5	7	16	.288	.246	.333	4.85	2.12
Strayhorn, Kole	R-R	6-0	196	10-1-82	1	1	5.74	15	0	0	0	27	32	20	17	2	12	26	.294	.286	.300	8.78	4.05
Thompson, Chris	R-R	6-3	195	1-2-82	4	2	3.00	29	0	0	1	42	29	18	14	0	28	31	.201	.155	.233	6.64	6.00
Trahan, David	R-R	6-3	185	2-27-81	1	0	10.00	4	1	0	0	9	15	11	10	1	9	3	.366	.591	.105	3.00	9.00
Wilson, Thomas	R-L	6-2	185	5-21-82	6	2	3.80	43	0	0	0	64	63	33	27	4	37	49	.259	.221	.277	6.89	5.20
Zinicola, Zechry	R-R	6-1	220	3-2-85	3	0	1.98	9	0	0	3	14	11	3	3	0	3	13	.229	.235	.226	8.56	1.98

FIELDING

Catcher	PCT	G	PO	A	E	DP	PB
Cleveland	.974	7	35	2	1	0	0
Ivany	.987	97	664	76	10	3	10
Montz	.985	29	167	26	3	2	4
Rodriguez	1.000	20	93	16	0	1	3

First Base	PCT	G	PO	A	E	DP
Ivany	1.000	3	17	2	0	0
Montz	.990	84	640	48	7	50
Mortimer	.995	56	411	30	2	47
Powell	.957	4	21	1	1	2
Thissen	1.000	1	5	2	0	1
Yepez	1.000	3	17	0	0	0

Second Base	PCT	G	PO	A	E	DP
Castro	.500	1	1	0	1	0

Second Base (cont.)	PCT	G	PO	A	E	DP
Martinez	1.000	7	11	18	0	4
Nunez	.975	8	15	24	1	7
Thissen	1.000	1	3	1	0	0
Webb	.970	109	219	271	15	61
Yepez	.956	19	31	34	3	7

Third Base	PCT	G	PO	A	E	DP
Bynum	.667	1	0	2	1	0
Nunez	1.000	3	0	3	0	1
Powell	.912	112	66	183	24	11
Thissen	—	1	0	0	0	0
Yepez	.882	30	15	45	8	6

Shortstop	PCT	G	PO	A	E	DP
Bynum	.950	33	46	88	7	16
Castro	1.000	3	5	4	0	1
Desmond	.932	91	138	219	26	55

	PCT	G	PO	A	E	DP
Yepez	.983	18	18	40	1	7

Outfield	PCT	G	PO	A	E	DP
Baez	.949	20	36	1	2	0
Bernadina	.983	123	289	5	5	1
Brown	.932	31	69	0	5	0
Chavez	.984	80	171	8	3	1
Cleveland	—	1	0	0	0	0
Fitzpatrick	1.000	30	57	1	0	0
Guerrero	1.000	36	62	2	0	0
Guillen	1.000	2	1	0	0	0
Lowrance	.973	88	137	8	4	0
Mortimer	.917	5	11	0	1	0
Thissen	1.000	1	2	0	0	0
Vroman	.971	17	32	1	1	1
Yepez	.969	12	27	4	1	1

Savannah Sand Gnats — Low Class A

South Atlantic League

BATTING	B-T	HT	WT	DOB	AVG	vLH	vRH	G	AB	R	H	2B	3B	HR	RBI	BB	HBP	SH	SF	SO	SB	CS	SLG	OBP
Baez, Edgardo	R-R	6-2	190	7-12-85	.279	.309	.265	94	355	46	99	22	2	6	44	30	3	2	5	80	3	2	.403	.336
Brown, Dee	R-R	6-0	230	10-21-82	.278	.308	.263	103	385	55	107	22	5	6	51	18	13	0	7	90	12	4	.408	.326
Carr, Adam	R-R	6-1	185	4-1-84	.250	.200	.308	7	28	1	7	1	0	1	2	0	0	0	0	11	0	0	.393	.250
Castro, Jonathan	B-R	6-1	160	11-29-83	.212	.235	.200	14	52	7	11	2	1	0	3	4	0	0	0	17	0	1	.288	.268
Castro, Ofilio	R-R	6-0	160	8-18-83	.253	.213	.273	123	459	61	116	16	6	5	57	60	4	3	6	65	11	2	.346	.342
Contreras, Jose	B-R	6-0	170	4-26-85	.201	.204	.199	96	279	32	56	5	2	0	15	56	0	7	1	69	11	5	.233	.333
Daniel, Michael	L-R	6-3	180	8-17-84	.193	.173	.202	52	181	20	35	5	1	4	16	26	2	2	0	52	8	4	.298	.301
Davis, Leonard	L-R	5-10	195	12-24-83	.225	.170	.249	83	289	32	65	12	4	8	38	21	5	2	5	87	4	5	.377	.284
De la Cruz, Jorge	R-R	6-3	210	10-2-85	.125	.000	.200	8	24	2	3	1	0	0	0	2	0	0	0	8	0	0	.167	.192
Fitzpatrick, Reginald	L-L	5-11	180	2-28-83	.287	.297	.283	47	150	20	43	4	2	5	23	15	1	1	2	42	8	4	.440	.351
French, Christopher	R-R	5-8	175	6-1-84	.750	1.000	.667	2	4	1	3	0	0	0	0	0	0	0	0	1	0	0	.750	.750
Guzman, Francisco	R-R	6-4	195	12-21-83	.146	.231	.107	13	41	4	6	0	0	1	4	5	1	0	0	13	2	0	.220	.255
Howell, John-Michael	R-R	6-3	200	12-30-82	.190	.242	.167	28	105	8	20	4	0	1	13	7	2	1	1	28	0	0	.257	.252
Martinez, Michael	B-R	5-9	145	9-16-82	.172	.231	.148	30	87	9	15	0	0	4	7	0	6	0	1	10	4	3	.172	.234
Maxwell, Justin	R-R	6-5	225	11-6-83	.172	.133	.186	17	58	8	10	2	2	1	7	8	2	0	0	23	1	0	.328	.294
Nunez, Alex	L-R	5-11	170	4-30-81	.265	.189	.286	72	249	30	66	12	3	2	19	25	2	6	1	38	10	6	.361	.336
Pahuta, Tim	L-R	6-4	225	5-3-83	.265	.241	.275	77	268	37	71	14	7	5	30	23	2	2	1	71	1	0	.425	.327
Peacock, Brian	R-R	6-1	185	8-26-84	.232	.225	.236	88	314	46	73	15	2	12	42	24	8	0	4	102	1	0	.408	.300
Plasencia, Francisco	L-L	6-1	192	6-19-84	.261	.204	.286	132	502	69	131	25	6	6	45	66	9	6	5	124	12	12	.371	.354
Poppert, John	R-R	6-0	185	4-14-82	.210	.155	.237	69	210	28	44	8	0	8	23	28	4	4	1	58	0	0	.362	.313
San Pedro, Erick	R-R	6-0	205	10-5-83	.164	.214	.128	22	67	4	11	1	0	1	7	7	1	0	0	21	0	0	.224	.253
Sandora, Robert	L-R	6-0	200	8-5-81	.263	.000	.319	19	57	6	15	0	0	1	7	5	1	1	0	9	0	0	.316	.333
Schade, Scott	R-R	6-1	220	2-22-82	.221	.210	.226	71	258	27	57	14	3	6	34	19	4	0	2	75	1	0	.368	.283
Sorensen, Logan	L-L	6-1	195	8-12-81	.276	.429	.227	24	87	4	24	6	0	2	9	6	0	0	1	8	1	2	.345	.340
2-team (72 Greenville)					.247	—		96	344	37	85	17	4	1	35	42	0	0	2	51	11	4	.328	.327
Torres, Carlos	R-R	6-4	190	4-3-84	.241	.375	.077	9	29	7	7	1	0	2	4	4	1	0	0	11	0	0	.483	.353

PITCHING	B-T	HT	WT	DOB	W	L	ERA	G	GS	CG	SV	IP	H	R	ER	HR	BB	SO	AVG	vLH	vRH	K/9	BB/9
Bunn, Greg	R-R	6-1	210	2-3-83	0	1	11.12	8	0	0	0	11	17	14	14	5	5	10	.354	.278	.400	7.94	3.97
Carr, Adam	R-R	6-1	185	4-1-84	0	0	2.25	6	0	0	0	8	4	2	2	0	4	8	.267	.182	.316	9.00	4.50
Cook, Steven	R-R	6-4	205	11-26-81	2	0	6.75	10	0	0	0	15	19	13	11	2	5	9	.311	.310	.313	5.52	3.07
De Los Santos, Juan	R-L	6-0	184	1-15-83	1	0	1.98	8	0	0	1	14	6	3	3	0	13	20	.133	.154	.125	13.17	8.56
Estrada, Marco	R-R	6-0	180	7-5-83	1	4	5.59	8	8	0	0	37	44	23	23	6	14	29	.301	.271	.316	7.05	3.41
Foli, Daniel	R-R	6-2	180	3-30-81	0	2	5.68	6	0	0	0	6	10	7	4	0	2	7	.345	.250	.412	9.95	2.84
Garza, Rudy	R-R	6-2	190	4-10-84	2	1	6.87	9	0	0	1	18	26	14	14	5	4	9	.342	.346	.340	4.42	1.96
Henderson, Jim	L-R	6-5	190	10-21-82	0	1	3.38	3	0	0	0	5	6	2	2	1	0	6	.300	.500	.214	10.13	0.00
Hlebovy, Gus	R-R	5-11	165	7-6-82	2	2	5.14	11	0	0	0	14	17	8	8	1	8	12	.315	.333	.308	7.71	5.14
Jackson, Aaron	B-R	6-9	175	3-28-86	0	1	4.50	1	1	0	0	4	2	2	2	0	2	3	.154	.200	.125	6.75	4.50
Lambert, Bryan	R-R	6-2	240	10-19-81	3	10	5.46	34	11	0	2	91	99	65	55	10	32	58	.281	.257	.297	5.76	3.18
Lannan, John	L-L	6-5	200	9-27-84	6	8	4.76	27	25	1	0	138	149	83	73	11	54	114	.275	.266	.281	7.43	3.52
Lehman, Jamie	R-R	6-2	185	3-14-85	4	2	2.62	21	0	0	4	45	48	21	13	1	8	26	.273	.256	.286	5.24	1.61
Levinski, Don	R-R	6-4	200	10-20-82	2	1	3.48	27	0	0	1	41	26	20	16	0	27	46	.187	.231	.161	10.02	5.88
Lira, Oscar	R-R	6-3	185	7-17-82	0	0	1.29	3	1	0	0	7	3	1	1	0	6	7	.125	.000	.188	9.00	7.71
Martinez, Carlos	R-R	6-4	177	3-30-84	6	7	4.87	27	23	0	0	118	131	75	64	7	42	64	.281	.286	.276	4.87	3.19
Martis, Shairon	R-R	6-1	175	3-30-87	1	1	3.80	4	4	0	0	21	23	9	9	2	4	14	.284	.333	.250	5.91	1.69
Mavroulis, Coby	L-L	6-3	180	2-7-83	0	0	4.17	28	0	0	4	37	37	17	17	2	18	25	.268	.258	.271	6.14	4.42
Meque, Jacobo	L-L	6-2	175	10-1-83	2	2	11.49	18	0	0	4	16	23	22	20	3	15	21	.354	.350	.356	12.06	8.62
Nyquist, Brett	L-L	6-2	205	5-7-81	6	3	3.69	22	5	0	0	64	60	24	19	5	13	46	.246	.149	.269	6.50	1.84
Peralta, Yader	R-R	6-1	170	2-22-86	0	0	13.50	2	0	0	0	2	3	3	3	1	2	2	.286	.333	.250	9.00	9.00
Perrault, Josh	R-R	6-3	205	6-11-82	0	0	3.74	33	0	0	4	46	41	21	19	3	9	42	.230	.289	.186	8.28	1.77
Poppert, John	R-R	6-0	185	4-14-82	0	0	0.00	1	0	0	0	1	0	0	0	0	0	0	.500	1.000	.000	0.00	0.00
Reid, Brett	R-R	5-11	200	10-18-79	0	2	6.39	11	0	0	2	13	16	9	9	2	5	10	.308	.278	.324	7.11	3.55
Shefka, Ricky	B-R	6-2	200	1-16-84	2	5	6.42	17	8	0	0	55	73	49	39	6	14	27	.324	.296	.346	4.45	2.30
Spradlin, Jack	R-L	6-2	170	9-23-84	2	3	6.22	20	3	0	0	46	62	36	32	5	14	39	.316	.282	.325	7.58	2.72
Stammen, Craig	R-R	6-3	200	3-9-84	6	9	3.58	21	21	0	0	113	110	55	45	10	29	93	.251	.262	.242	7.41	2.31
Thompson, Chris	R-R	6-3	195	1-2-82	0	0	0.00	5	0	0	0	7	5	0	0	0	3	7	.083	.111	.067	11.74	8.22

Trahan, David	R-R	6-3	185	2-27-81	1	13	4.99	28	19	1	0	115	144	79	64	7	43	90	.308	.300	.315	7.02	3.36
Yost, Gene	R-L	6-3	185	6-23-81	7	5	3.83	33	10	0	1	89	81	41	38	8	35	73	.244	.229	.248	7.35	3.53

FIELDING

Catcher	PCT	G	PO	A	E	DP	PB
Peacock	.988	46	301	27	4	2	4
Poppert	.995	63	392	45	2	2	5
San Pedro	.974	21	130	17	4	0	9
Sandora	.992	18	107	15	1	4	3

First Base	PCT	G	PO	A	E	DP
Howell	.993	26	266	24	2	23
Nunez	.929	2	13	0	1	1
Pahuta	.996	62	529	38	2	54
Poppert	.972	4	31	4	1	4
Sandora	1.000	1	2	0	0	0
Schade	.997	31	274	14	1	28
Sorensen	1.000	11	89	8	0	8
Torres	.988	9	75	5	1	12

Second Base	PCT	G	PO	A	E	DP
Castro	1.000	2	4	2	0	2
Castro	.968	53	92	147	8	38
Contreras	.948	21	42	50	5	19
Davis	1.000	9	16	20	0	5
Nunez	.973	59	109	181	8	42

Third Base	PCT	G	PO	A	E	DP
Castro	.946	40	18	70	5	7
Davis	.900	68	44	145	21	16
Nunez	1.000	2	0	4	0	0
Pahuta	.964	9	5	22	1	1
Schade	.965	27	22	61	3	2

Shortstop	PCT	G	PO	A	E	DP
Castro	.957	12	24	43	3	11
Castro	.972	33	44	96	4	18

	PCT	G	PO	A	E	DP
Contreras	.933	70	85	222	22	38
Martinez	.922	28	50	103	13	28
Nunez	.909	1	3	7	1	3

Outfield	PCT	G	PO	A	E	DP
Baez	.960	87	160	6	7	1
Brown	.973	90	136	9	4	1
Daniel	.989	49	81	6	1	1
Davis	1.000	1	1	0	0	0
De la Cruz	1.000	8	18	0	0	0
Fitzpatrick	.952	35	56	3	3	0
French	1.000	1	3	0	0	0
Guzman	1.000	8	14	1	0	1
Maxwell	1.000	10	21	0	0	0
Pahuta	1.000	1	1	0	0	0
Plasencia	.984	121	246	8	4	1
Sorensen	1.000	14	13	1	0	0

Vermont Lake Monsters — Short-Season

New York-Penn League

BATTING	B-T	HT	WT	DOB	AVG	vLH	vRH	G	AB	R	H	2B	3B	HR	RBI	BB	HBP	SH	SF	SO	SB	CS	SLG	OBP
Caputo, Richard	R-R	6-1	185	10-3-84	.180	.150	.191	48	150	14	27	5	1	2	8	10	2	3	0	26	0	0	.267	.241
Castro, Jonathan	R-R	6-1	160	11-29-83	.214	.145	.250	52	154	15	33	7	0	0	9	15	2	4	0	45	3	8	.260	.292
Conway, Brandon	L-R	6-3	190	11-9-83	.196	.222	.186	26	97	10	19	1	0	2	8	4	0	0	0	27	0	1	.268	.228
Daniel, Michael	L-R	6-3	180	8-17-84	.304	.250	.331	53	181	29	55	8	3	3	18	16	5	1	0	52	13	4	.431	.376
De la Cruz, Jorge	R-R	6-3	210	10-26-85	.083	.000	.125	4	12	0	1	1	0	0	1	0	0	0	1	4	0	0	.167	.077
Delaughter, Ryan	R-R	6-2	210	12-31-86	.227	.254	.213	59	203	18	46	7	1	2	22	17	3	2	2	75	0	3	.300	.293
German, Agustin	R-R	6-0	180	12-13-85	.147	.000	.200	12	34	4	5	1	0	1	2	1	1	1	0	11	0	0	.265	.194
Goldschmeding, Jeremy	R-R	6-2	190	12-28-83	.215	.288	.170	64	228	27	49	4	2	0	17	15	4	7	0	55	8	4	.250	.275
Guzman, Francisco	R-R	6-4	195	12-21-86	.261	.281	.258	65	230	23	60	11	1	5	35	15	4	4	4	48	4	1	.383	.316
Jacobsen, Robert	R-R	6-1	205	8-30-84	.244	.143	.296	13	41	5	10	2	0	0	2	2	0	0	0	18	1	0	.293	.279
Logan, Brett	R-R	6-2	215	12-31-82	.087	.200	.056	16	46	2	4	1	0	0	2	4	0	0	0	14	0	0	.109	.160
Martinez, Jonathan	B-R	6-0	170	9-23-84	.236	.270	.222	35	123	17	29	3	1	0	9	15	2	3	1	30	7	3	.276	.326
Martinez, Michael	B-R	5-9	145	9-16-82	.321	.255	.352	45	159	26	51	5	2	1	19	9	2	8	1	28	6	8	.396	.363
Maxwell, Justin	R-R	6-5	225	11-6-83	.269	.313	.243	74	271	36	73	11	3	4	33	27	6	0	2	61	20	5	.376	.346
McMillan, Brett	L-R	6-5	215	11-18-83	.227	.125	.268	62	220	17	50	12	1	0	20	17	2	1	2	35	3	3	.291	.288
Nichols, Patrick	R-R	6-2	210	9-12-84	.191	.275	.143	34	110	11	21	5	1	2	7	5	1	1	0	32	0	0	.309	.233
Ogando, Cristian	R-R	6-2	175	8-5-86	.171	.286	.143	11	35	1	6	0	1	0	2	3	0	0	0	11	0	1	.229	.237
Rooney, Sean	B-R	5-10	205	4-12-86	.237	.000	.321	12	38	3	9	3	0	0	4	4	0	0	1	12	0	0	.316	.302
San Pedro, Erick	R-R	6-0	205	10-5-83	.185	.000	.266	28	92	4	17	2	0	0	6	7	2	1	2	27	0	0	.207	.252

PITCHING	B-T	HT	WT	DOB	W	L	ERA	G	GS	CG	SV	IP	H	R	ER	HR	BB	SO	AVG	vLH	vRH	K/9	BB/9
Anderson, Cory	R-R	6-4	220	12-18-83	1	1	3.93	13	0	0	0	18	23	15	8	1	8	13	.303	.424	.209	6.38	3.93
Arnesen, Erik	R-R	6-3	260	3-19-84	1	3	4.56	12	8	0	0	49	61	28	25	2	11	32	.307	.324	.287	5.84	2.01
Baldwin, Zachary	R-L	6-5	225	5-21-83	1	5	3.81	14	8	0	0	54	58	25	23	3	15	40	.270	.264	.272	6.63	2.48
De Los Santos, Juan	R-L	6-0	184	1-15-83	0	3	5.68	25	0	0	3	25	20	21	16	2	32	25	.225	.150	.246	8.88	11.37
Engles, Terrence	R-R	6-4	170	11-12-82	2	8	5.43	14	12	0	0	60	70	43	36	3	15	41	.290	.274	.306	6.18	2.26
Enriquez, Andre	R-R	6-3	212	5-15-84	0	0	27.00	1	0	0	0	1	2	2	2	0	2	0	1.000	—	1.000	0.00	27.00
Garza, Rudy	R-R	6-2	190	4-10-84	2	2	5.96	14	0	0	1	23	29	23	15	1	7	17	.319	.368	.283	6.75	2.78
Gibson, Glenn	L-L	6-4	195	9-21-87	0	0	0.00	3	3	0	0	6	2	0	0	0	0	7	.100	.111	.091	10.50	0.00
Harrison, Ryan	R-R	6-2	190	7-12-86	0	0	12.71	7	0	0	0	6	6	9	8	0	5	3	.261	.364	.167	4.76	7.94
Jackson, Aaron	B-R	6-0	175	3-28-86	3	5	3.11	13	11	0	0	64	65	29	22	1	16	48	.265	.267	.264	6.79	2.26
Kimball, Cole	R-R	6-3	225	8-1-85	1	4	5.82	16	5	0	0	34	43	26	22	3	24	28	.307	.342	.266	7.41	6.35
Lugo, Chris	R-R	6-1	185	11-10-86	1	4	2.54	23	0	0	3	39	35	15	11	1	9	33	.248	.220	.265	7.62	2.08
Meque, Jacobo	L-L	6-4	175	10-1-83	2	3	5.13	17	0	0	2	26	21	17	15	0	20	34	.216	.188	.231	11.62	6.84
Novoa, Yunior	L-L	6-4	180	9-11-84	0	1	7.36	1	0	0	0	4	5	3	3	1	4	1	.357	.000	.400	2.45	9.82
Peralta, Yader	R-R	6-1	170	2-22-86	2	3	4.70	23	0	0	0	38	35	26	20	2	14	39	.236	.241	.233	9.16	3.29
Perks, Matthew	R-R	6-7	200	8-20-85	0	1	1.64	5	1	0	0	11	13	8	2	0	3	4	.283	.217	.348	3.27	2.45
Pfau, Daniel	R-L	6-0	190	6-12-84	2	0	2.56	19	0	0	0	32	26	9	9	0	8	26	.222	.256	.205	7.39	2.27
Shefka, Ricky	B-R	6-3	200	1-16-84	0	0	0.00	1	1	0	0	3	1	0	0	0	0	2	.100	.167	.000	6.00	0.00
Spradlin, Jack	R-L	6-2	170	9-23-84	2	3	1.69	10	10	0	0	48	40	19	9	3	10	31	.217	.188	.224	5.81	1.88
Taylor, Jeffrey	R-R	6-9	245	10-8-83	1	2	4.19	19	0	0	1	19	24	17	9	1	7	17	.286	.256	.268	7.91	3.26
Thompson, Daryl	R-R	6-1	170	11-2-85	0	1	6.75	4	4	0	0	7	5	5	5	0	6	8	.200	.250	.154	10.80	6.75
Van Allen, Cory	L-L	6-3	180	12-24-84	1	4	4.06	13	9	0	0	58	53	29	26	5	16	41	.248	.240	.248	6.40	2.50
White, Demetri	R-L	6-1	175	6-12-82	1	0	5.27	4	0	0	0	14	16	10	8	0	12	19	.291	.231	.310	12.51	7.90
Zinicola, Zechry	R-R	6-1	220	3-2-85	0	0	0.00	8	0	0	4	9	6	0	0	0	1	10	.182	.364	.091	10.00	1.00

FIELDING

Catcher	PCT	G	PO	A	E	DP	PB
German	1.000	1	8	0	0	0	1
Logan	.992	16	109	15	1	2	2
Nichols	.968	26	162	18	6	3	7
Rooney	.985	9	50	14	1	1	3
San Pedro	.990	25	168	23	2	2	9

First Base	PCT	G	PO	A	E	DP
Conway	.974	9	70	6	2	8
De la Cruz	1.000	1	8	0	0	1
Jacobsen	.971	4	30	4	1	1
Martinez	1.000	4	35	2	0	3
McMillan	.983	60	494	35	9	45

Second Base	PCT	G	PO	A	E	DP
Caputo	1.000	1	0	1	0	0
Castro	.955	24	50	55	5	17
Conway	1.000	7	11	17	0	2
Martinez	.962	21	42	60	4	13
Martinez	.955	26	57	70	6	22

Third Base	PCT	G	PO	A	E	DP
Caputo	.915	33	28	58	8	5
Castro	.946	20	10	43	3	6
Conway	.840	9	8	13	4	4
De la Cruz	.500	1	0	1	1	0
Goldschmeding	.850	4	4	13	3	0
Martinez	1.000	8	3	13	0	0

	PCT	G	PO	A	E	DP
Martinez	1.000	1	0	1	0	0

Shortstop	PCT	G	PO	A	E	DP
Castro	1.000	1	2	2	0	1
Goldschmeding	.940	54	67	137	13	28
Martinez	1.000	3	5	7	0	2
Martinez	.888	19	41	62	13	14

Outfield	PCT	G	PO	A	E	DP
Daniel	.978	49	88	1	2	0
Delaughter	.932	44	65	3	5	0
Guzman	.933	54	93	4	7	0
Jacobsen	1.000	6	6	0	0	0
Maxwell	.969	72	155	3	5	1
Ogando	1.000	5	5	0	0	0

Gulf Coast League

BATTING	B-T	HT	WT	DOB	AVG	vLH	vRH	G	AB	R	H	2B	3B	HR	RBI	BB	HBP	SH	SF	SO	SB	CS	SLG	OBP
Alvarez, Jean	R-R	6-2	185	2-15-87	.219	.256	.206	48	146	26	32	2	0	2	8	25	5	3	1	46	0	3	.274	.350
Carr, Adam	R-R	6-1	185	4-1-84	.343	.300	.360	15	35	5	12	4	0	2	10	5	0	0	0	5	0	0	.629	.425
Cruz, Frank	B-R	6-0	156	1-8-89	.104	.000	.128	23	48	7	5	1	1	0	3	11	0	2	1	20	0	0	.167	.267
De Castro, Angel	R-R	6-1	177	1-22-85	.239	.286	.219	18	46	7	11	1	0	0	2	7	0	1	0	11	0	0	.261	.340
De la Cruz, Jorge	R-R	6-3	210	10-2-85	.220	.163	.243	46	164	15	36	11	0	2	26	13	2	1	7	43	0	1	.323	.274
Englund, Stephen	R-R	6-3	190	6-6-88	.183	.222	.170	35	115	16	21	3	0	1	12	17	4	1	1	41	5	1	.235	.307
Escobar, Alex	R-R	6-1	190	9-6-78	.143	.000	.250	3	7	1	1	0	0	0	1	2	0	0	1	0	0	0	.143	.333
Figuereo, Johan	R-R	6-2	195	3-2-86	.200	.227	.190	48	165	17	33	8	0	1	12	15	1	3	1	39	1	1	.267	.269
French, Chris	R-R	5-8	175	6-1-84	.171	.217	.151	34	76	8	13	0	0	1	4	10	1	2	1	28	2	1	.211	.273
German, Agustin	R-R	6-0	180	12-13-85	.211	.182	.222	14	38	3	8	2	1	0	6	6	0	1	0	9	0	1	.316	.318
Hidalgo, Richard	R-R	6-2	180	7-24-87	.173	.161	.177	32	110	9	19	6	0	2	9	3	2	0	1	35	0	0	.282	.207
Jacobsen, Robert	R-R	6-1	205	8-30-84	.249	.235	.254	51	193	24	48	8	0	6	16	18	3	4	1	53	14	1	.290	.321
Logan, Brett	R-R	6-2	215	12-31-82	.364	.000	.421	14	22	3	8	1	0	0	2	5	0	1	0	2	0	0	.409	.481
Lombard, George	L-R	6-0	210	9-14-75	.176	.250	.154	6	17	1	3	1	0	0	1	6	1	0	0	3	1	0	.235	.417
Lopez, Yhonson	L-L	6-1	160	10-27-88	.167	.000	.200	6	6	2	1	0	0	0	0	1	0	0	0	4	0	0	.167	.286
Louisa, Lorvin	R-R	6-4	200	2-7-83	.400	.400	.400	6	15	2	6	1	0	0	3	2	0	1	0	5	0	1	.467	.471
Mancebo, Melvin	R-R	6-1	190	9-8-83	.800	—	.800	2	5	2	4	2	0	0	1	0	0	0	0	0	0	0	1.200	.800
Marrero, Christopher	R-R	6-3	210	7-2-88	.309	.100	.377	22	81	10	25	9	0	0	16	8	1	0	1	19	0	0	.420	.374
Martinez, Jonathan	B-R	6-0	170	9-23-84	.214	.192	.222	28	98	15	21	1	1	0	7	17	2	3	0	24	1	2	.245	.342
Mateo, Johan	R-R	6-0	180	5-28-86	.167	—	.167	2	6	1	1	0	0	0	0	0	0	0	0	0	0	0	.167	.167
Ogando, Cristian	R-R	6-2	175	8-5-86	.333	.250	.385	8	21	4	7	1	0	0	2	1	0	0	0	6	0	0	.381	.364
Rooney, Sean	B-R	5-10	205	4-12-86	.241	.340	.200	44	170	19	41	5	2	3	26	14	1	1	0	25	2	2	.347	.303
Solano, Jhonatan	R-R	—	—	8-12-85	.256	.229	.266	37	129	16	33	3	0	0	11	6	3	4	2	15	3	1	.279	.300
Vento, Mike	R-R	6-0	195	5-25-78	.250	.333	.235	6	20	3	5	0	0	1	4	4	0	0	1	0	0	0	.400	.375
Vizcaino, Francisco	—	—	—	11-28-84	.167	.091	.200	17	36	3	6	0	0	0	2	6	0	3	0	13	5	3	.167	.286
Watson, Brandon	L-R	6-1	170	9-30-81	.333	.000	.400	2	6	1	2	0	0	0	0	1	0	0	1	0	0	0	.333	.429

PITCHING	B-T	HT	WT	DOB	W	L	ERA	G	GS	CG	SV	IP	H	R	ER	HR	BB	SO	AVG	vLH	vRH	K/9	BB/9
Abreu, Edulin	R-R	6-3	160	8-8-84	3	2	1.91	10	5	0	0	33	34	12	7	1	8	26	.256	.304	.221	7.09	2.18
Almonte, Robert	R-R	6-1	195	5-10-86	0	1	2.13	7	0	0	0	13	7	3	3	1	8	10	.171	.167	.174	7.11	5.68
Alvarez, Manuel	R-R	5-11	175	12-18-85	2	3	2.79	14	0	0	0	19	14	7	6	1	8	15	.203	.133	.222	6.98	3.72
Anderson, Cory	R-R	6-4	220	12-18-83	0	1	0.00	3	0	0	0	3	1	2	0	0	1	2	.083	.000	.143	6.75	3.38
Armas, Tony	R-R	6-3	225	4-29-78	0	1	5.40	1	1	0	0	5	8	3	3	0	1	7	.348	.385	.300	12.60	1.80
Beltran, Francis	R-R	6-6	230	11-29-79	0	0	1.29	6	1	0	0	7	7	1	1	0	2	5	.269	.200	.313	6.43	2.57
Bravo, Wuillys	L-L	6-0	160	7-9-87	1	1	2.54	9	8	0	0	39	32	15	11	1	16	30	.229	.167	.241	6.92	3.69
Buchter, Ryan	L-L	6-1	185	2-13-87	1	1	7.24	11	1	0	0	14	18	11	11	1	13	12	.321	.364	.311	7.90	8.56
Carr, Adam	R-R	6-1	185	4-1-84	1	0	3.06	10	0	0	1	18	13	6	6	1	7	19	.200	.214	.189	9.68	3.57
Cuello, Yonatan	R-R	6-4	190	2-3-84	2	1	1.50	8	1	0	1	18	14	5	3	3	14	.209	.154	.244	7.00	1.50
Estrada, Marco	R-R	6-0	180	7-5-83	2	0	1.52	5	4	0	0	24	14	4	4	1	6	27	.165	.176	.157	10.27	2.28
Garza, Rudy	R-R	6-2	190	4-10-84	0	0	0.00	1	0	0	1	2	2	0	0	0	3	.250	.000	.286	11.57	0.00
Harrison, Ryan	R-R	6-2	190	7-12-86	0	0	5.79	3	0	0	0	5	5	3	3	0	2	3	.313	.286	.333	3.86	5.79
Hlebovy, Gus	R-R	5-11	165	7-6-82	1	0	1.59	9	0	0	2	11	11	2	2	0	1	8	.262	.125	.294	6.35	0.79
Jones, Desmond	R-R	6-2	195	3-16-86	1	1	6.23	8	0	0	0	9	9	8	6	1	11	15	.273	.308	.250	15.58	11.42
Lira, Oscar	R-R	6-3	185	7-17-82	4	5	3.88	12	6	0	0	46	48	26	20	0	17	30	.267	.338	.226	5.83	3.30
Matias, Randy	R-R	6-0	180	9-19-86	0	1	10.24	9	0	0	0	10	17	11	11	1	6	5	.405	.389	.417	4.66	5.59
Novoa, Yunior	L-L	6-4	180	9-11-84	1	1	1.74	7	6	0	0	31	25	8	6	0	9	35	.221	.190	.228	10.16	2.61
Perks, Matthew	R-R	6-7	200	8-20-85	2	2	1.71	6	4	0	0	26	27	11	5	0	8	19	.257	.235	.268	6.49	2.73
Pichardo, Eduardo	R-R	6-0	175	8-1-87	0	0	18.47	7	0	0	0	6	4	13	13	0	16	7	.182	.333	.125	9.95	22.74
Pinkston, Friedel	R-R	6-3	200	2-3-84	0	0	13.50	1	0	0	0	1	2	2	2	0	3	2	.333	—	.333	13.50	20.25
Rincon, Jonathan	R-R	6-1	200	2-15-85	1	3	6.17	7	4	0	0	23	37	16	16	2	4	13	.359	.383	.339	5.01	1.54
Sanchez, Jose	R-R	6-1	202	10-11-81	1	2	2.52	8	5	0	0	36	30	17	10	1	5	33	.221	.341	.163	8.33	1.26
Sosa, Gabriel	L-L	5-9	170	9-27-85	0	0	6.75	4	0	0	0	3	2	4	2	0	5	5	.200	.250	.167	16.88	16.88
Taylor, Rhys	R-R	6-3	154	10-9-85	0	0	1.42	3	1	0	0	6	8	2	1	0	2	3	.296	.100	.412	4.26	2.84
Watkins, Michael	R-R	6-1	187	11-20-87	0	0	—	1	0	0	0	0	0	1	1	0	1	0	—	—	—	—	—
Welsh, Joseph	L-L	6-4	180	9-29-84	0	2	1.08	11	1	0	1	25	16	6	3	0	10	20	.184	.286	.152	7.20	3.60
Wilkie, Josh	R-R	6-2	190	7-22-84	2	2	4.94	13	1	0	2	27	33	19	15	0	11	31	.289	.282	.293	10.21	3.62
Willems, Colton	R-R	6-3	175	7-30-88	0	1	3.38	5	5	0	0	16	23	8	6	1	3	8	.338	.267	.395	4.50	1.69

FIELDING

Catcher	PCT	G	PO	A	E	DP	PB
German	.987	10	61	14	1	0	3
Logan	1.000	9	47	7	0	1	1
Rooney	1.000	21	150	16	0	3	9
Solano	.989	21	157	21	2	5	4

First Base	PCT	G	PO	A	E	DP
De la Cruz	.952	4	18	2	1	3
Figuereo	1.000	1	7	0	0	0
Jacobsen	.977	51	445	22	11	32

Second Base	PCT	G	PO	A	E	DP
Alvarez	.952	5	9	11	1	3
Cruz	.917	21	25	41	6	4
De Castro	1.000	4	3	11	0	1
Figuereo	1.000	2	2	3	0	0

	PCT	G	PO	A	E	DP
French	.933	4	7	7	1	2
Martinez	.959	28	67	75	6	16

Third Base	PCT	G	PO	A	E	DP
Alvarez	1.000	1	0	1	0	0
De la Cruz	.852	12	6	17	4	1
Figuereo	.889	43	32	88	15	8
Mateo	.750	2	3	3	2	0

Shortstop	PCT	G	PO	A	E	DP
Alvarez	.939	45	65	120	12	17
Cruz	.667	1	0	4	2	0
De Castro	.857	13	12	30	7	9

Outfield	PCT	G	PO	A	E	DP
De la Cruz	.982	30	49	5	1	2
Englund	.972	35	66	3	2	0
Escobar	1.000	3	3	1	0	1
French	.943	22	33	0	2	0
Hidalgo	.931	32	51	3	4	1
Lombard	1.000	4	4	0	0	0
Lopez	1.000	5	4	0	0	0
Louisa	1.000	6	8	0	0	0
Mancebo	1.000	2	2	1	0	0
Marrero	.967	22	29	0	1	0
Martinez	1.000	1	1	0	0	0
Ogando	1.000	8	7	1	0	1
Vento	1.000	3	4	0	0	0
Vizcaino	.960	14	24	0	1	0
Watson	1.000	2	3	0	0	0

MINOR
LEAGUES

End of longtime Triple-A deals tops busy affiliation shuffle

BY WILL LINGO

As the game of affiliation changing wrapped up, the big stories came from the end of longtime relationships.

Minor league and major league teams can sign new player-development contracts with each other every two years. And while the movement after the 2006 season involved several teams at every level, some of those changes were more significant than others. One, the Dodgers leaving the Florida State League for the California League, was interesting not just because they've had an affiliate in Vero Beach since 1980, but because it looks like the first step in the Dodgers moving to a new spring training home in Arizona.

And in the International League, three of the most stable affiliations in the minor leagues ended, resulting in the most significant changes in Triple-A since the classification was realigned from three leagues to two and added two new franchises in 1998. The movement left the following changes in place for the 2007 season: the Phillies from Scranton/Wilkes-Barre to Ottawa, the Orioles from Ottawa to Norfolk, the Mets from Norfolk to New Orleans, the Nationals from New Orleans to Columbus, and the Yankees from Columbus to Scranton.

That left some clear winners and losers in the process.

The biggest loser was the Mets, who lost their low Class A affiliation in Hagerstown and ended up in Savannah, but much more significantly lost their Triple-A affiliation in Norfolk and ended up in New Orleans.

In Norfolk, the Tides closed the book on 37 years with the Mets when they announced a new affiliation with the Orioles. The Mets had been affiliated with the Norfolk franchise (which has also been known as Tidewater during its history) since it joined the International League in 1969, but Norfolk officials complained about a lack of communication and cooperation from the Mets this year. The Virginian-Pilot newspaper reported that neither general manager Omar Minaya nor assistant GM Tony Bernazard had visited Norfolk this season.

"They took us for granted," Tides general manager Dave Rosenfield told the newspaper.

Aside from the end of a such a long relationship, the move to New Orleans increases the Mets' Triple-A-to-big league commute by nearly 1,000 miles and puts them in the Pacific Coast League, which will further increase travel.

The Mets took the public-relations offensive, announc-

New lease on life for Scranton/Wilkes-Barre
The Yankees move to Lackawanna County Stadium after 27 years in Columbus

ing their new affiliation before the Tides and Orioles held their press conference in Norfolk, but it was clear the Mets wanted to stay with the Tides when they enlisted area native David Wright to make a last-ditch plea for them.

Without a doubt, the biggest winner in all the movement was Scranton, which had looked like a sad sack at the beginning of the season. The Phillies had already let the Red Barons know they were on the way out, making that the first of the long-term marriages to break up.

The Phillies had been in Scranton since the team joined the IL in 1989, but no one could blame them for looking for greener pastures. Philadelphia will be Ottawa's major league partner next season, but the Ottawa franchise will move to Allentown, Pa., in 2008, putting the Phillies even closer to home and in a brand-new ballpark.

Meanwhile, Lackawanna County Stadium was showing its age and the Red Barons franchise had become more of a political football than anything else. It looked like the Nationals or the Orioles were going to be the best options for new affiliates, but as the year wore on the expected renewal of the Yankees-Columbus affiliation never came.

Suddenly, the Red Barons were the Yankees' best option, and it all came together in September. Local fans were excited, and the Red Barons' phones immediately started ringing with ticket requests.

And yet that might not be the most significant change to happen to the franchise this offseason. Lost in all the hoopla was the announcement that Mandalay Baseball will take over operation of the franchise, which will mean higher ticket prices for local fans but also a more professional operation.

Mandalay, which already owns five minor league teams, is also taking over management of the New York-Penn League's Staten Island Yankees. The New York Yankees are buying that club and turning over the operation to Mandalay.

The Clippers, who had been the Yankees' Triple-A affiliate since 1979, signed a two-year agreement with the Nationals. The Phillies will move their Triple-A affiliation to Ottawa and play there for a year before the team is expected to move to Allentown, Pa., for the 2008 season.

Clippers general manager Ken Schnacke has already said the team will be interested in talking to the Indians

MINOR LEAGUES

and Reds in 2008, when their Triple-A affiliations could be available again. The Clippers will also have a new stadium by then—it will open either in 2008 or '09.

Jays Drop Out Of Appalachian League

Before the affiliation shuffle officially got under way, a major alteration took place in the Appalachian League.

The Blue Jays notified the league that they won't be back in Pulaski next year, and they likely will drop to five affiliates for 2007, rather than the conventional six. That left the Appy League to look for another major league organization to come in and take the Blue Jays' place.

"They have shown their intent to leave Pulaski, and we are exploring options to replace them," league president Lee Landers said. "One is good and two are bad."

The good one was simply finding another major league team to take the Blue Jays' place. But that didn't happen because other teams' affiliations were set. With the Blue Jays dropping an affiliate, there was no domino effect to push a team to Pulaski.

So the less palatable options had come into play: operating a co-op club in Pulaski, or playing with just nine teams. The co-op situation, in which a number of major league clubs would supply players for Pulaski, is more attractive to Landers than going back to nine teams.

"The worst-case scenario is playing with nine clubs," he said. "To me, that's unacceptable."

But that was looking like the most likely option as the winter wore on. While a nine-team league is inconvenient, supplying players for a 10th team might cost more money than teams want to spend.

"When you look at the dollars and cents, some farm directors will say no because they don't have it in their budget," Landers said.

Landers was working on trying to show the teams that any additional costs would only offset what would be increased travel costs if the league drops to nine teams. Additionally, a nine-team league would lead to day games with smaller gates, and would impair the league's chances of getting stadium upgrades at other cities in the future.

That would also mean an empty stadium in Pulaski, where the city has put more than $750,000 into ballpark improvements over the last decade.

Looking for a 10th team
Lee Landers

"I think there is a credibility issue here," he said. "We have made improvements throughout our league, so these cities deserve to have teams."

Interestingly, Pulaski returned to the Appy League a decade ago to help out MLB, which faced a shortage of affiliates after the expansion involving the Devil Rays and Diamondbacks. The Rangers were squeezed out in the affiliation shuffle following the 1996 season, so the league returned to Pulaski to give the Rangers another affiliate. The move also benefited the league because it operated with nine teams in 1996, after the franchise in Huntington, W.Va., folded. The Blue Jays replaced the Rangers in 2003.

The Appy League already went through one change after the season, with the Royals replacing the Indians in

Burlington. The Indians are dropping from seven affiliates to six, while the Royals want to move up to seven.

Rays Prospects Misbehave In Durham

After a season that featured three of the Durham Bulls' top prospects ending up in trouble, the Devil Rays fired the entire Bulls coaching staff.

Manager John Tamargo, hitting coach Richie Hebner, pitching coach Joe Coleman and trainer Tom Tinsdale were all let go after a season in which outfielder Delmon Young was suspended for 50 games for throwing a bat that struck an umpire; shortstop/third baseman B.J. Upton was arrested and charged with driving while impaired; and outfielder Elijah Dukes was disciplined multiple times, and was quoted in USA Today complaining of taking showers in sewer water in Durham.

On the field, the Bulls finished 64-78, the team's worst record in 10 years as a Triple-A franchise.

"I wasn't totally surprised," Tamargo told the Durham Herald-Sun. "I knew they were going to do something. I'm going to miss the Bulls organization and the fans in Durham. The situation (with the players) was not good. Durham is a great place to manage. I just wish I had another chance."

Tamargo was in his first year as Bulls manager after replacing Bill Evers, who joined the Devil Rays major league coaching staff. Hebner had worked with the Bulls for four years, while Coleman had been in Durham for seven seasons.

With new ownership and management in place, the Devil Rays adopted the slogan "Under Construction" before the 2006 season, and based on all the incidents the organization endured, it was clear the Rays are still a work in progress.

Most notably, Young drew national attention for tossing his bat at the home-plate umpire in an April game against Pawtucket, striking him in the chest. He was suspended for 50 games and only threw more light on the problems of his teammates.

Upton was arrested in Chapel Hill, N.C., in the early morning hours of June 16 and charged with driving while impaired. Dukes was suspended or disciplined several times during the season before finally being sent home in August. Tamargo himself was suspended 10 games for a run-in with an umpire in May.

"They don't understand the value of respect. Respect for their teammates, respect for the game and respect for themselves," another International League manager said. "There is no question all three of them are going to be big leaguers, but there is certainly cause for worry."

Young expressed remorse for his actions and was adamant about putting the incident behind him.

"It's a lot easier to deal with the media now. You guys already got the worst on me, so it makes it a lot easier to deal with you . . . I'm just out here making sure I make the right judgments," he said. "We're all role models for everybody, so you've got to do the best you can to keep a positive image. I messed up, so now I have to try to regain that image, keep my nose clean and play baseball and play hard."

Young spent time doing community service during his suspension, dividing his work between the Durham Bulls

ORGANIZATION STANDINGS

Cumulative farm club records for the 30 major league organizations, with winning percentages going back five years. Every organization has six affiliates, except for the Indians and Mets, who have seven.

	2006 W	L	PCT	2005	2004	2003	2002
1. San Francisco	387	308	.557	.555	.471	.454	.463
2. Houston	389	310	.557	.494	.533	.500	.535
3. N.Y. Yankees	378	308	.551	.541	.514	.501	.530
4. Detroit	365	315	.537	.555	.467	.481	.509
5. Cleveland	404	349	.537	.525	.540	.576	.577
6. Minnesota	365	319	.534	.535	.502	.503	.540
7. Oakland	367	326	.530	.545	.576	.532	.509
8. Philadelphia	359	323	.526	.429	.467	.462	.525
9. Arizona	373	338	.525	.496	.489	.513	.454
10. Chi. Cubs	362	329	.524	.492	.538	.474	.529
11. Cincinnati	358	332	.519	.454	.470	.480	.528
12. San Diego	354	336	.513	.472	.501	.476	.513
13. Boston	349	341	.506	.512	.503	.496	.454
14. L.A. Dodgers	345	340	.504	.490	.502	.485	.563
15. St. Louis	348	349	.499	.492	.520	.451	.509
16. Toronto	349	351	.499	.523	.572	.531	.480
17. Kansas City	343	349	.496	.500	.501	.527	.521
18. Milwaukee	336	343	.495	.473	.453	.469	.462
19. Pittsburgh	336	348	.491	.519	.511	.581	.571
20. L.A. Angels	339	353	.490	.489	.455	.510	.472
21. Colorado	346	365	.487	.501	.482	.508	.473
22. Tampa Bay	337	361	.483	.464	.472	.497	.445
23. Baltimore	338	364	.481	.498	.458	.486	.434
24. N.Y. Mets	360	394	.477	.509	.547	.503	.496
25. Atlanta	321	356	.474	.482	.514	.497	.512
26. Florida	316	363	.465	.501	.455	.502	.491
27. Seattle	316	377	.456	.517	.508	.527	.471
28. Washington	305	388	.440	.438	.424	.437	.477
29. Chi. White Sox	296	399	.426	.504	.504	.494	.466
30. Texas	294	401	.423	.491	.549	.547	.498

Youth Athletic League and the Miracle League of Gulf Beaches in Florida. He also made a donation (of an undisclosed amount) to the home plate umpire's Little League.

"It was a good opportunity to help out others," Young said. "I went out and helped kids and adults that don't really get a chance to play. They got more out of it than I ever thought they would, so that's the least I got out of it."

No One Wins In Umpire Strike

After two months on strike, minor league umpires finally approved a new labor agreement in May, agreeing to terms remarkably similar to the ones they rejected a few weeks earlier.

"We are happy to have reached a deal that will assure labor peace with our umpires through the 2011 season," Minor League Baseball vice president Pat O'Conner said. "We look forward to continuing another great season of baseball without the distraction of a strike."

The umpires didn't report for duty at the beginning of the 2006 season as they sought higher pay and better benefits from the Professional Baseball Umpire Corp., the organization that manages umpires for Minor League Baseball. The two sides negotiated throughout the winter, and negotiations stagnated in the spring until a federal mediator brought the two sides to the table at the end of April.

Negotiators reached a tentative deal then, but the membership of the Association of Minor League Umpires rejected the deal by about a two-to-one margin. Union leadership recommended that it be adopted, but union members decided the agreement did not show enough improvement over previous proposals.

The two sides returned to mediation and came up with another tentative deal, one with few significant changes from the earlier deal. The new agreement provides for salary increases of $100 a month and per diem (meal money) increase of about $3 a day. Per diem payments go up in each year of the agreement.

Minor league teams used local replacements to fill in for the striking umpires this season. While many players and managers complained about the quality of their work, games went on with few hiccups during the strike.

At its most comical, the strike sparked stories of replacement umpires who didn't understand some of the basic nuances of the professional game. In the Texas League, for example, players told the story of a catcher who reached back over his shoulder for a baseball after a ball was fouled off. The replacement ump shook his hand.

On the more serious side, however, the inferior umpiring could have affected the development of players had it gone on all season. The lowest moment probably came when manager Chris Cron pulled his Birmingham team off the field in a Southern League game that was marred by bad calls and fights, resulting in a forfeit.

Whatever bargaining position the umpires had disappeared after their mediation session at the end of April, however. Negotiations had reached an impasse when a federal mediator brokered a deal, but the union rank-and-file rejected the new contract.

That left union negotiators with nothing to do.

Gordon does it all in first pro season

Kansas City Royals fans have salivated over the thought of watching Alex Gordon, the No. 2 overall pick in 2005, play at Kauffman Stadium. They've dreamed of how he'll turn around the organization, become a mainstay at third base, lead the team to the playoffs. Just like Hall of Famer George Brett did.

PLAYER OF THE YEAR

Those are pretty high expectations that carry a hefty amount of pressure, but Gordon has certainly done nothing to prove those diehards wrong, earning Baseball America's Minor League Player of the Year award.

"He's very impressive," Royals farm director J.J. Picollo said. "He's got that rare combination of speed and power. He's very well-rounded . . . I don't know what you could ask anyone else to do in his first full season."

It wouldn't have surprised anyone if Gordon had stumbled a bit in 2006. While he was BA's College Player of the Year in 2005 at Nebraska, this is professional baseball and he opened the year in Double-A Wichita after making his debut on the opposite side of the infield in the Arizona Fall League last October.

It's quite a jump to make, it's a tiring process playing 140 regular season games when you're used to playing half that, and the pressure was intense. The media wanted him constantly, whether they were newspaper writers, TV or radio stations from Wichita, Kansas City, Lincoln, Neb., or ESPN2. Fans' expectations were fierce. Everyone wanted a piece. Yet all Gordon did was go out and impress. Again, and again and again.

"He's been solid in everything, basestealing, hitting for average, hitting for power," said Frank White, Double-A Wichita manager and former Royals second baseman. "Definitely all phases of his game have been solid.

"He's done an outstanding job, he works hard in

Everything the Royals were looking for Alex Gordon gives Kansas City fans hope

practice, he takes this game seriously and he comes to win every day. That's what stands out, that he's been able to maintain it all, and he's been strong in the clutch, too."

By the numbers, Gordon had a great year: He hit .325 with 111 runs, 158 hits, 39 doubles, 29 homers, 22 stolen bases, 72 walks and 100 RBIs. He also had a .588 slugging percentage and .427 on-base percentage.

Gordon, who was also the Texas League player of the year, ranked in the top five in the TL in 10 categories: average, runs, hits, doubles, homers, RBIs, walks, slugging percentage and on-base percentage.

"This kid can pretty much do everything," said Tulsa manager Stu

Cole. "He can hit for power, he can hit for average, he can steal a base. And he's played pretty good third base against us."

It would have been easy for the Royals to rush Gordon up to Kansas City and enjoy the hype that would have come with the move. Brett was so taken with Gordon that he added fuel to fans' fever by saying in April that he believed Gordon, based on his athletic ability and baseball skills, could have joined the Royals then.

"I didn't think I was as good as he was," Brett said. "At age 22, I wasn't. It took me a while to become a good player; it's going to take him awhile. But he's so much farther ahead defensively than I was at 22, the difference is day and night."

Moving slowly was a decision solidified by new general manager Dayton Moore. "When you're dealing with the future of young players, you don't want to make mistakes, so you err on the side of caution," he said.

As much talk as there has been about Gordon's offense, he's no slouch defensively. Oh, he made 16 errors and needs to work on his one weakness, his backhand. Overall, though, he's a highly skilled defender.

"He can do everything," White said. "He makes the routine play, he makes the difficult play, he makes the play when he dives left or right. He catches pop-ups over his head down the line, his throws are accurate, his footwork is good.

"I mean, he's done everything probably over and above the expectations coming out of spring training."

Which means Gordon has whet the appetite of Royals fans even more. It's hard to blame them for their high hopes; Gordon can do little wrong.

PREVIOUS **WINNERS**
1981—Mike Marshall, 1b, Albuquerque (Dodgers)
1982—Ron Kittle, of, Edmonton (White Sox)
1983—Dwight Gooden, rhp, Lynchburg (Mets)
1984—Mike Bielecki, rhp, Hawaii (Pirates)
1985—Jose Canseco, of, Huntsville/Tacoma (Athletics)
1986—Gregg Jefferies, ss, Columbia/Lynchburg/Jackson (Mets)
1987—Gregg Jefferies, ss, Jackson/Tidewater (Mets)
1988—Tom Gordon, rhp, Appleton/Memphis/Omaha (Royals)
1989—Sandy Alomar, c, Las Vegas (Padres)
1990—Frank Thomas, 1b, Birmingham (White Sox)
1991—Derek Bell, of, Syracuse (Blue Jays)
1992—Tim Salmon, of, Edmonton (Angels)
1993—Manny Ramirez, of, Canton/Charlotte (Indians)
1994—Derek Jeter, ss, Tampa/Albany/Columbus (Yankees)
1995—Andruw Jones, of, Macon (Braves)
1996—Andruw Jones, of, Durham/Greenville/Richmond (Braves)
1997—Paul Konerko, 1b, Albuquerque (Dodgers)
1998—Eric Chavez, 3b, Huntsville/Edmonton (Athletics)
1999—Rick Ankiel, lhp, Arkansas/Memphis (Cardinals)
2000—Jon Rauch, rhp, Winston-Salem/Birmingham (White Sox)
2001—Josh Beckett, rhp, Brevard County/Portland (Marlins)
2002—Rocco Baldelli, of, Bakersfield/Orlando/Durham (Devil Rays)
2003—Joe Mauer, c, Fort Myers/New Britain (Twins)
2004—Jeff Francis, lhp, Tulsa/Colorado Springs(Rockies)
2005—Delmon Young, of, Montgomery/Durham (Devil Rays)

MINOR LEAGUES

Ledford leads Sacramento to top

Some decisions are agonized over and others are no-brainers. Extending their Triple-A affiliation with the Pacific Coast League's Sacramento River Cats through 2010, as the Athletics did in September, falls in the latter category.

Not only is Sacramento less than 100 miles from Oakland, making it an ideal destination for major league reinforcements, but it's also arguably the minor leagues' most successful franchise—on the field and off. And those are just a couple of the reasons Baseball America is honoring River Cats president and general manager Alan Ledford as our Minor League Executive of the Year.

EXECUTIVE OF THE YEAR

Sacramento's Raley Field has been the most popular fan destination in the minor leagues since it opened in 2000. The River Cats have led all minor league teams in attendance in each of their seven seasons and have drawn a total of more than 5.5 million fans.

They've done it by bringing a major league-quality operation to the minor leagues and refusing to rest on their laurels. Ledford deflects the credit to his staff, the quality of the Sacramento market, and the natural appeal of minor league baseball, which provides an opportunity to be irreverent as well as giving fans a much closer relationship with the players on the field.

"We're very fortunate to be in a market that allows us the opportunity to take the best of both worlds," he said.

Ledford, a graduate of the University of California, began overseeing the day-to-day operations of the River Cats in September 2002, first as president and chief operating officer. He added GM to his job title in 2004. But he's really been with the River Cats since day one. Prior to officially joining the front office, Ledford was executive vice president of MGO Marketing Group, a sports and entertainment consulting group based in Lafayette, Calif.

Ledford's ties to the A's run deeper still. He spent 15 years prior to his time at MGO with Oakland, rising to the position of vice president of business operations.

"What it gave me, No. 1, was a passion for the sport," Ledford said. "I gained an appreciation for baseball beyond what you have as a fan, and saw the role baseball can play in the community. Baseball can really play an important role in people's lives."

Passion for baseball
Alan Ledford

The River Cats have been able to build on their success each year by continuing to innovate both at the ballpark and in the community. That's what the River Cats did as part of hosting the 2005 Triple-A all-star game. "We were looking for a project that would give the game a legacy and provide a benefit for the community, as well as a presence for the team on a grassroots level," he said.

So River Cats Independence Field was born. It's a field where children with disabilities can play baseball, and the River Cats not only gave money to help build the field, but also helped raise the profile for the community center that wanted to build it.

And it's one of the many reasons Ledford and the River Cats continue to thrive in Sacramento, and show no signs of giving up the minor league attendance crown anytime soon.

"That's something we take a tremendous amount of pride in," he said. "We have an incredible product in the minor leagues, and to continue to grow, teams must continue to innovate and take advantage of the grassroots appeal of the sport and the product."

PREVIOUS WINNERS

2002—Randy Mobley, International League
2003—Chuck Domino, Reading (Eastern)
2004—Chris Kemple, Wilmington Blue Rocks (Carolina)
2005—Jay Miller, Round Rock Express (Pacific Coast)

Management had already sweetened its offer a bit, and when the union leaders weren't able to deliver on their deal they were basically paralyzed.

"Minor League Baseball did everything right and our union did everything wrong," said one of the striking umpires, on condition of anonymity. "I guess we can chalk this up to a learning experience. I'm excited about going back to work because there's nothing like being between the white lines. It's when I get back to my hotel that I'll regret it. We're getting the same exact money and this didn't resolve anything. We all just caved to get back for the all-star games."

Another Record-Breaking Year At The Gate

The minor leagues continued their impressive attendance run, setting a record for the third straight season.

The 176 teams in 15 leagues drew 41,710,357 fans, an increase of 377,078 fans over 2005's record-setting total. Five of the top six attendance marks of all time have come in the past five years, as the minor leagues have shown steady growth.

The minors can thank the Mexican League's Monterrey Sultans for the new record this time. Monterrey drew 989,454 fans, an increase of 481,816 over last year. Monterrey averaged 17,990 fans per game, easily best in the minors.

If you take the Mexican League out of the equation, attendance for the U.S. leagues actually dropped 104,738 from last year's total. The Florida State League, Pioneer League and South Atlantic League showed the largest percentage gains from last year, while the Eastern, International and Midwest Leagues showed the largest percentage declines.

Daytona, Clearwater, St. Lucie and Fort Myers all set

attendance records in the Florida State League, thanks to improved promotional schedules and better weather.

"Those were the four teams that really pushed it. The one that really surprised me is Daytona," Florida State League president Chuck Murphy said. "Daytona is not an easy town (to sell in). To bring fans in, you have to really beat the bushes. How they did it, I don't know."

The Greenville Drive (South Atlantic), which opened a new stadium this season, showed the biggest increase in average attendance this season. The team had drawn 4,789 fans per game this year, compared with an average of 1,685 fans last year.

The second-largest increase belonged to the Winston-Salem Warthogs (Carolina), who were drawing 25 percent more fans a game. Unlike the Drive, the Warthogs can't point to a new stadium as a reason for the increase—in fact, the Warthogs have managed to increase their attendance in each of the past two seasons despite having a new ballpark open in nearby Greensboro in 2005.

The reason for the Warthogs increase? An increased reliance on reading programs and ballpark buyouts by companies in the community has turned Monday and Tuesday games into successful draws instead of black holes in the schedule.

"We had some dates in April and May that were competing with our July 4 attendance figures," Warthogs general manager Ryan Manuel said.

And of course, for the seventh straight season, Sacramento led the way in attendance among U.S. minor league teams. The RiverCats drew 728,227 fans, topping fellow Pacific Coast League member Memphis (692,426 fans) for the crown.

Triple-A Championship Comes Back Strong

The return of the Triple-A championship was a success on and off the field.

Pacific Coast League champion Tucson defeated International League champ Toledo 5-2 in the event dubbed the Bricktown Showdown, in a game broadcast nationally on ESPN.

But probably more importantly, the game—following in the footsteps of the Triple-A World Series, which was

Tucson dominates with prospects

Two weeks into the 2006 season, Tucson looked much better on paper than it did on the field.

Despite having such prospects as shortstop Stephen Drew, second baseman Alberto Callaspo, outfielders Carlos Quentin and Scott Hairston, first baseman Chris Carter, third baseman Brian Barden and righthander Dustin Nippert, the Sidewinders sputtered early, winning just four of their first 15 games.

But with the addition of outfielder Chris Young, as well as huge years by veterans like catcher Robby Hammock and pitchers Randy Choate, Mike Bacsik, Kevin Jarvis and Mike Koplove—not to mention the occasional prospect callup from Double-A Tennessee—Tucson finished the season with nothing more than a few bumps in the road en route to a 91-53 record, the best in Triple-A.

TEAM OF THE **YEAR**

That final record, along with the Sidewinders' first Pacific Coast League title in 13 years, earned Tucson Baseball America's 2006 Team of the Year. Just for good measure, Tucson also beat Toledo in a one-game showdown for the overall Triple-A championship.

Sidewinders manager Chip Hale was named the PCL's manager of the year after Tucson topped the 90-win plateau for the first time in the franchise's 39-year history. The Sidewinders became just the third team in Tucson franchise history to win the PCL championship following the Tucson Toros in 1991 and 1993.

"The year was truly remarkable," Diamondbacks farm director A.J. Hinch said. "When you consider the record, individual statistics, the way they always played the game hard and with an attitude really is a tribute to the job the player-development staff did with that club."

A lot of the success Tucson enjoyed this season also came down to good timing. The Diamondbacks have one of the top farm systems in the game today, and many of their upper-tier prospects saw time in southeastern Arizona in 2006.

While that started with Drew—Arizona's No. 1 prospect heading into the year—the catalyst turned out to be Callaspo, who finished among the minor league leaders in average (.337) and hits (165). The 23-year-old Venezuelan infielder carried a 27-56 strikeout-walk ratio, and wound up leading the minors by whiffing once in every 20.52 plate appearances.

Though the Sidewinders benefited from Callaspo's .404 on-base percentage, they also featured several bigtime power hitters. Six players topped double-digits in home runs, with Hairston leading the way with 26. Carter and Barden totaled 35 homers and 65 doubles between them.

The club also got a further offensive boost when catcher Miguel Montero was promoted from Double-A. Montero, who is solid defensively in his own right, contributed by hitting .321/.396/.515.

Offense may have been Tucson's defining team trait, but the Sidewinders pitching staff was the truly remarkable part of the 2006 season. Led by Nippert and righthander Micah Owings—as well as a deep corps of dependable relievers—Tucson's staff finished fourth in the league with a 3.88 ERA.

Both were horses, as Nippert tossed 140 innings and Owings added 87 frames after being called up from Tennessee. Combined, the two righthanders went 23-8, 4.42 while the bullpen of Choate, Bacsik, Koplove, Greg Aquino, Jeff Bajenaru, Mike Schultz, Casey Daigle, Tony Pena, Doug Slaten, Jose Valverde, Bill Murphy and newcomer Evan MacLane combined to carry a 3.55 ERA in 545 total innings.

PREVIOUS **WINNERS**

1993—Harrisburg/Eastern (Expos)
1994—Wilmington/Carolina (Royals)
1995—Norfolk/International (Mets)
1996—Edmonton/Pacific Coast (Athletics)
1997—West Michigan/Midwest (Tigers)
1998—Mobile/Southern (Padres)
1999—Trenton/Eastern (Red Sox)
2000—Round Rock/Texas (Astros)
2001—Lake Elsinore/California (Padres)
2002—Akron/Eastern (Indians)
2003—Sacramento/Pacific Coast (Athletics)
2004—Lancaster/California (Diamondbacks)
2005—Jacksonville/Southern (Dodgers)

MINOR LEAGUES

Selected by Baseball America

Matt Garza

Chris Iannetta

Hunter Pence

Chris Young

FIRST TEAM

Pos.	Player, Team (Organization)	AVG	OBP	SLG	AB	R	H	2B	3B	HR	RBI	BB	SO	SB
C	Chris Iannetta, Tulsa/Colo. Springs (Rockies)	.336	.433	.564	307	61	103	22	3	14	48	48	55	1
1B	Joey Votto, Chattanooga (Reds)	.319	.408	.547	508	85	162	46	2	22	77	78	109	24
2B	Howie Kendrick, Salt Lake (Angels)	.369	.408	.631	290	57	107	25	6	13	62	12	48	11
3B	Alex Gordon, Wichita (Royals)	.325	.427	.588	486	111	158	39	1	29	100	72	113	22
SS	Reid Brignac, Visalia/Montgomery (Devil Rays)	.321	.376	.539	521	100	167	32	5	24	99	42	113	15
OF	Jay Bruce, Dayton (Reds)	.291	.355	.516	444	69	129	42	5	16	81	44	106	19
OF	Adam Lind, New Hamp./Syracuse (Blue Jays)	.330	.394	.556	457	63	151	31	0	24	89	48	105	3
OF	Hunter Pence, Corpus Christi (Astros)	.283	.357	.533	523	97	148	31	8	28	95	60	109	17
DH	Kevin Kouzmanoff, Akron/Buffalo (Indians)	.379	.437	.656	346	68	131	28	1	22	75	33	46	4

Pos.	Pitcher, Team (Organization)	W	L	ERA	G	GS	SV	IP	H	HR	BB	SO	GO/AO	AVG
SP	Homer Bailey, Sarasota/Chattanooga (Reds)	10	6	2.47	26	26	0	139	99	7	50	156	1.12	.198
SP	Yovani Gallardo, Brev. Co./Huntsville (Brewers)	11	5	1.86	26	26	0	155	104	6	51	188	1.18	.192
SP	Matt Garza, Ft. Myers/N.B./Roch. (Twins)	14	4	1.99	23	23	0	136	87	6	32	154	0.89	.179
SP	Philip Hughes, Tampa/Trenton (Yankees)	12	6	2.16	26	26	0	146	92	5	34	168	1.42	.179
RP	Juan Salas, Montgomery/Durham (Devil Rays)	4	1	0.71	50	0	17	63	28	3	25	85	1.13	.128

SECOND TEAM

Pos.	Player, Team (Organization)	AVG	OBP	SLG	AB	R	H	2B	3B	HR	RBI	BB	SO	SB
C	Carlos Ruiz, Scranton/W-B (Phillies)	.307	.389	.505	368	56	113	25	0	16	69	42	56	4
1B	James Loney, Las Vegas (Dodgers)	.380	.426	.546	366	64	139	33	2	8	67	32	34	9
2B	Alberto Callaspo, Tucson (Diamondbacks)	.337	.404	.478	490	93	165	24	12	7	68	56	27	8
3B	Josh Fields, Charlotte (White Sox)	.305	.379	.515	462	85	141	32	4	19	70	54	136	28
SS	Brandon Wood, Arkansas (Angels)	.276	.355	.552	453	74	125	42	4	25	83	54	149	19
OF	Brian Barton, Kinston/Akron (Indians)	.323	.412	.511	446	88	144	21	3	19	83	52	109	41
OF	Terry Evans, P.B./Spring./Ark. (Cardinals/Angels)	.309	.377	.565	501	104	155	23	3	33	87	41	127	37
OF	Chris Young, Tucson (Diamondbacks)	.276	.363	.532	402	78	111	32	4	21	77	52	71	17
DH	Mark Reynolds, Lancaster/Tenn. (Diamondbacks)	.318	.401	.633	387	87	123	25	2	31	98	52	109	1

Pos.	Pitcher, Team (Organization)	W	L	ERA	G	GS	SV	IP	H	HR	BB	SO	GO/AO	AVG
SP	Nick Adenhart, Cedar Rap./Rancho Cuca. (Angels)	15	4	2.56	25	25	0	158	135	3	42	145	1.58	.229
SP	Chuck Lofgren, Kinston (Indians)	17	5	2.32	25	25	0	140	108	5	54	125	0.73	.217
SP	Adam Miller, Akron/Buffalo (Indians)	15	6	2.84	27	25	0	158	133	9	46	161	1.57	.227
SP	Kevin Slowey, Fort Myers/New Britain (Twins)	8	5	1.88	23	23	0	149	102	8	22	151	0.69	.188
RP	Brian Anderson, San Jose (Giants)	1	1	1.86	54	0	37	68	44	5	17	85	0.80	.183

canceled five years ago because of financial problems and dwindling attendance in Las Vegas—drew 12,572 fans, a near sellout to Oklahoma City's Bricktown Ballpark.

"This was a great idea that was very well executed," PCL president Branch Rickey proudly proclaimed.

The revised Triple-A championship format was a winner-take-all single game played in the Oklahoma RedHawks' stylish downtown stadium.

The Tucson pitchers, limiting Toledo to a single run and only a half dozen hits through the first eight innings, led the way. Micah Owings, who went undefeated in 10 PCL decisions while compiling a combined 16-2 minor league record for the season, burned through the power-packed Toledo lineup with ease to get the victory. He struck out six, three coming as the final outs of innings, while allowing a single run, ultimately leaving after five frames as his pitch count hit 100. Minor control problems, which led to four walks, accelerated the pitch count but Toledo could only manage four singles and a double off Owings.

The game's unlikely home run hero, Tucson catcher Juan Brito, outhomered the entire Toledo team. Brito who hit eight home runs during the regular season and none during the PCL playoffs, lined a shot into the left-field bleachers in the fifth inning to allow Tucson to retake the lead after Toledo got on the scoreboard.

"I wasn't trying to hit a home run because that's really

Since Alfonso Soriano homered twice in the inaugural 1999 contest, the All-Star Futures Game has served as more of a showcase for pitchers than hitters.

But a potent U.S. lineup wasn't to be denied at PNC Park this year. Led by several of the game's top offensive prospects, the United States established a new Futures Game record for runs while outslugging the World for an 8-5 victory at PNC Park. The United States now has won five times in eight games.

"That American team has some bats, now," World first-base coach and Triple-A Charlotte manager Razor Shines said. "That's some big power over there in that clubhouse. I've been telling people all year how Josh Fields has been carrying our team and he comes into a game like this as basically just one of the guys."

Outfielder Billy Butler became the second straight Royals prospect to win the MVP award, following Justin Huber. Butler went 2-for-3, including a two-run homer in the bottom of the second that erased a 1-0 lead the World had taken in the top half. The blast traveled 394 feet to center field off Jose Garcia (Marlins).

The United States never looked back, breaking the game open with five runs in the third. Davis Romero (Blue Jays) retired Pirates catcher Neil Walker on a groundout before running into the top of the U.S. lineup. Diamondbacks shortstop Stephen Drew singled and Angels second baseman Howie Kendrick walked before Royals third baseman Alex Gordon, Astros right fielder Hunter Pence and White Sox DH Josh Fields followed with consecutive RBI singles to make it 5-1.

Fields was erased on a cutoff play, but Rockies first baseman Joe Koshansky drilled a 396-foot homer to right field, chasing Romero. Butler and Tigers outfielder Cameron Maybin delivered consecutive singles off Carlos Carrasco (Phillies), who finally escaped by getting Walker on a popup.

The World pitching staff wasn't as loaded as it was in the previous two Futures Games, when the World did not allow an earned run. But the outburst was impressive nonetheless. In the first seven Futures Games, the United States managed to score five runs in a game just once, in 2001.

Though the U.S. staff had more power arms than the World, it too had trouble keeping runs off the board. Homer Bailey (Reds) threw bullets during his one-inning stint, but surrendered the second-inning run when Padres catcher George Kottaras doubled on a 97 mph fastball and Dodgers shortstop Chin Lung Hu followed with another on a 94 mph heater.

Kottaras also ignited a three-run rally in the fourth off Philip Hughes (Yankees), whose fastball sat at 93-95 mph. Diamondbacks outfielder Carlos Gonzalez singled with one out and scored on a double by Mariners DH Wladimir Balentien. Kottaras then planted a pitch 406 feet over the fence in left-center to cut the U.S. lead to 7-4. Gordon got a run back for the United States with an RBI double off Edgar Martinez (Red Sox) in the bottom half before the World made another charge in the fifth. Eric Hurley (Rangers) got two outs but also put two runners on base via a single and a walk, and Balentien greeted Sean Smith (Indians) with an RBI double to make it 8-5.

Bringing home the hardware
Royals prospect Billy Butler won Futures Game MVP honors

UNITED STATES ROSTER

Pitchers: Nick Adenhart (Angels), Homer Bailey (Reds), Gio Gonzalez (Phillies), Jason Hirsh (Astros), Philip Hughes (Yankees), Eric Hurley (Rangers), Matt Lindstrom (Mets), Nick Pereira (Giants), Josh Sharpless (Pirates), Sean Smith (Indians).
Catchers: Kurt Suzuki (Athletics), Neil Walker (Pirates).
Infielders: Ryan Braun (Brewers), Stephen Drew (Diamondbacks), Josh Fields (White Sox), Alex Gordon (Royals), Howie Kendrick (Angels), Joe Koshansky (Rockies), Eric Patterson (Cubs), Troy Tulowitzki (Rockies).
Outfielders: Travis Buck (Athletics), Billy Butler (Royals), Cameron Maybin (Tigers), Hunter Pence (Astros), Nolan Reimold (Orioles).

WORLD ROSTER

Pitchers: Carlos Carrasco (Phillies), Jaime Garcia (Cardinals), Yovani Gallardo (Brewers), Jose Garcia (Marlins), Radhames Liz (Orioles), Edgar Martinez (Red Sox), Davis Romero (Blue Jays), Jae Kuk Ryu (Cubs), Juan Salas (Devil Rays), Humberto Sanchez (Tigers).
Catchers: George Kottaras (Padres), Salomon Manriquez (Nationals).
Infielders: Joaquin Arias (Rangers), Wladimir Balentien (Mariners), Yung Chi Chen (Mariners), Luis Cruz (Padres), Yunel Escobar (Braves), Joel Guzman (Dodgers), Chin Lung Hu (Dodgers), Pablo Sandoval (Giants), Joey Votto (Reds).
Outfielders: Anderson Gomes (White Sox), Carlos Gonzalez (Diamondbacks), Trent Oeltjen (Twins), Jose Tabata (Yankees).

8TH ANNUAL ALL-STAR FUTURES GAME
PNC Park, Pittsburgh • July 9, 2006

United States 8, World 5

World	AB	R	H	BI	United States	AB	R	H	BI
Oeltjen, lf	2	0	0	0	Drew, ss	3	1	1	0
Gomes, lf	2	0	0	0	Tulowitzki, ss	0	0	0	0
Chen, 2b	2	0	0	0	Kendrick, 2b	2	2	0	0
Cruz, 2b	2	0	0	0	Patterson, 2b	1	0	0	0
Votto, 1b	2	0	1	0	Gordon, 3b	3	1	2	2
Sandoval, 1b	2	1	1	0	Braun, 3b	1	0	0	0
Guzman, 3b	2	0	0	0	Pence, rf	3	1	1	1
Escobar, 3b	1	0	0	0	Reimold, rf	1	0	0	0
Gonzalez, rf	4	1	1	0	Fields, dh	3	1	2	1
Balentien, dh	3	1	2	2	Koshansky, 1b	3	1	1	2
Kottaras, c	2	2	2	2	Butler, lf	3	1	2	2
Manriquez, c	0	0	0	0	Buck, lf	0	0	0	0
Hu, ss	3	0	1	1	Maybin, cf	3	0	2	0
Tabata, cf	3	0	1	0	Walker, c	2	0	0	0
					Suzuki, c	1	0	0	0
Totals	**30**	**5**	**9**	**5**	**Totals**	**29**	**8**	**11**	**8**

World				
World	001	021	0—4	
United States	000	000	0—0	

2B: Fields, Gordon, Kottaras, Hu, Balentien. **HR:** Butler, Koshansky, Kottaras. **LOB:** World 6, **U.S.** 6.
E: Hu.

WORLD	IP	H	R	ER	BB	SO	USA	IP	H	R	ER	BB	SO
Sanchez	1	0	0	0	0	2	Hirsh	1	1	0	0	0	1
Garcia, Jose L	1	2	2	2	0	0	Bailey W	1	2	1	1	0	1
Romero	⅓	5	5	5	1	0	Gonzalez	1	0	0	0	0	1
Carrasco	⅔	2	0	0	0	0	Hughes	1	4	3	3	0	2
Martinez	1	1	1	0	1	0	Hurley	⅔	1	0	0	1	0
Gallardo	1	1	0	0	1	0	Smith	0	1	0	0	1	0
Liz	⅔	0	0	0	0	1	Sharpless	1⅓	0	0	0	0	0
Salas	½	0	0	0	0	0	Lindstrom S	1	0	0	0	0	2

T: 2:24.

CLASSIFICATION ALL-STARS

Selected by Baseball America

Triple-A — International League, Pacific Coast League

Pos.	Player, Team (Organization)	AVG	OBP	SLG	AB	R	H	2B	3B	HR	RBI	BB	SO	SB
C	Carlos Ruiz, Scranton/W-B (Phillies)	.307	.389	.505	368	56	113	25	0	16	69	42	56	4
1B	James Loney, Las Vegas (Dodgers)	.380	.426	.546	366	64	139	33	2	8	67	32	34	9
2B	Howie Kendrick, Salt Lake (Angels)	.369	.408	.631	290	57	107	25	6	13	62	12	48	11
3B	Josh Fields, Charlotte (White Sox)	.305	.379	.515	462	85	141	32	4	19	70	54	136	28
SS	Stephen Drew, Tucson (Diamondbacks)	.284	.340	.462	342	55	97	16	3	13	51	33	50	3
OF	Chris Young, Tucson (Diamondbacks)	.276	.363	.532	402	78	111	32	4	21	77	52	71	17
OF	Carlos Quentin, Tucson (Diamondbacks)	.289	.424	.487	318	66	92	30	3	9	52	45	46	5
OF	Shin-Soo Choo, Tacoma (Mariners)	.323	.394	.499	375	71	121	21	3	13	48	45	73	26
DH	Kevin Witt, Durham (Devil Rays)	.291	.360	.577	485	82	141	29	1	36	99	50	132	0

Pos.	Pitcher, Team (Organization)	W	L	ERA	G	GS	SV	IP	H	HR	BB	SO	GO/AO	AVG
SP	Jason Hirsh, Round Rock (Astros)	13	2	2.10	23	23	0	137	94	5	51	118	0.78	.193
SP	Rich Hill, Iowa (Cubs)	7	1	1.80	15	15	0	100	62	3	21	135	1.05	.179
SP	Jeremy Sowers, Buffalo (Indians)	9	1	1.39	15	15	0	97	78	1	29	54	1.44	.224
SP	Jered Weaver, Salt Lake (Angels)	6	1	2.10	12	11	0	77	63	7	10	93	0.64	.223
RP	Pat Neshek, Rochester (Twins)	6	2	1.95	33	0	14	60	41	7	14	87	1.42	.189

Player of the Year: Howie Kendrick, 2b, Salt Lake (Angels). **Manager of the Year:** Chip Hale, Tucson (Diamondbacks). **Team of the Year:** Tucson (Diamondbacks)

PLAYER OF THE YEAR
Howie Kendrick, 2b
Salt Lake

Double-A — Eastern League, Southern League, Texas League

Pos.	Player, Team (Organization)	AVG	OBP	SLG	AB	R	H	2B	3B	HR	RBI	BB	SO	SB
C	Kurt Suzuki, Midland (Athletics)	.285	.392	.415	376	64	107	26	1	7	55	58	50	5
1B	Joey Votto, Chattanooga (Reds)	.319	.408	.547	508	85	162	46	2	22	77	78	109	24
2B	Elliot Johnson, Montgomery (Devil Rays)	.281	.335	.455	494	69	139	21	10	15	50	39	122	20
3B	Alex Gordon, Wichita (Royals)	.325	.427	.588	486	111	158	39	1	29	100	72	113	22
SS	Brandon Wood, Arkansas (Angels)	.276	.355	.552	453	74	125	42	4	25	83	54	149	19
OF	Hunter Pence, Corpus Christi (Astros)	.283	.357	.533	523	97	148	31	8	28	95	60	109	17
OF	Billy Butler, Wichita (Royals)	.331	.388	.499	477	82	158	33	1	15	96	41	67	1
OF	Terry Evans, Spring./Ark. (Cardinals/Angels)	.308	.380	.578	263	61	81	13	2	18	42	21	77	16
DH	Kevin Kouzmanoff, Akron (Indians)	.389	.449	.660	244	46	95	19	1	15	55	23	34	2

Pos.	Pitcher, Team (Organization)	W	L	ERA	G	GS	SV	IP	H	HR	BB	SO	GO/AO	AVG
SP	Adam Miller, Akron (Indians)	15	6	2.75	26	24	0	154	129	9	43	157	1.59	.226
SP	Philip Hughes, Trenton (Yankees)	10	3	2.25	21	21	0	116	73	5	32	138	1.49	.179
SP	Homer Bailey, Chattanooga (Reds)	7	1	1.59	13	13	0	68	50	1	28	77	1.33	.208
SP	Yovani Gallardo, Huntsville (Brewers)	5	2	1.63	13	13	0	77	50	2	28	85	0.77	.187
RP	Juan Salas, Montgomery (Devil Rays)	3	0	0.00	23	0	14	35	13	0	14	52	1.43	.110

Player of the Year: Alex Gordon, 3b, Wichita (Royals). **Manager of the Year:** Todd Claus, Portland (Red Sox). **Team of the Year:** Montgomery (Devil Rays).

PLAYER OF THE YEAR
Alex Gordon, 3b
Wichita

High Class A — California League, Carolina League, Florida State League

Pos.	Player, Team (Organization)	AVG	OBP	SLG	AB	R	H	2B	3B	HR	RBI	BB	SO	SB
C	Jake Fox, Daytona (Cubs)	.313	.383	.574	249	45	78	15	1	16	61	27	49	4
1B	Chris Nowak, Visalia (Devil Rays)	.308	.397	.478	494	93	152	45	3	11	103	69	83	17
2B	Emilio Bonifacio, Lancaster (Diamondbacks)	.321	.375	.449	546	117	175	35	7	7	50	44	104	61
3B	Chase Headley, Lake Elsinore (Padres)	.291	.389	.434	484	79	141	33	0	12	73	74	96	4
SS	Reid Brignac, Visalia (Devil Rays)	.326	.382	.557	411	82	134	26	3	21	83	35	82	12
OF	Carlos Gonzalez, Lancaster (Diamondbacks)	.300	.356	.563	403	82	121	35	4	21	94	30	104	15
OF	Brian Barton, Kinston (Indians)	.308	.410	.515	295	56	91	16	3	13	57	39	83	26
OF	Mark Reynolds, Lancaster (Diamondbacks)	.337	.422	.670	273	64	92	18	2	23	77	41	72	1
DH	Sean Rodriguez, Rancho Cuca. (Angels)	.301	.377	.545	455	78	137	29	5	24	77	47	124	15

Pos.	Pitcher, Team (Organization)	W	L	ERA	G	GS	SV	IP	H	HR	BB	SO	GO/AO	AVG
SP	Chuck Lofgren, Kinston (Indians)	17	5	2.32	25	25	0	140	108	5	54	125	0.73	.217
SP	Greg Smith, Lancaster (Diamondbacks)	9	0	1.63	13	13	0	88	57	3	31	71	1.42	.190
SP	Scott Lewis, Kinston (Indians)	3	3	1.48	27	26	0	116	84	3	28	123	0.89	.203
SP	Kevin Slowey, Fort Myers (Twins)	4	2	1.01	14	14	0	89	52	2	9	99	0.70	.164
RP	Brian Anderson, San Jose (Giants)	1	1	1.86	54	0	37	68	44	5	17	85	0.80	.183

Player of the Year: Chuck Lofgren, lhp, Kinston (Indians). **Manager of the Year:** Lenn Sakata, San Jose (Giants). **Team of the Year:** Kinston (Indians).

PLAYER OF THE YEAR
Chuck Lofgren, lhp
Kinston

not my game," Brito said. "But it just happened and the fact it put us back ahead was great. I was just happy to be able to do my part to help the team."

Tucson, using four singles and two Toledo errors, put the game away in the ninth, scoring three times to make it 5-1. Toledo attempted a bottom of the ninth rally but could only come up with a single run via David Espinosa's RBI double.

The resounding success of the event in its new form seems certain to make it a minor league cornerstone for years to come.

"I think we've got a winner, both for tonight and far into the future," International League president Randy

Mobley said.

With a packed stadium and an ESPN television audience watching, the one-game, winner-take-all Triple-A championship certainly appeared to be a total triumph. What wasn't as apparent to outside observers was just how much time and energy went into achieving the success.

"There have been a lot of people involved in coming up with the concept and even more directly involved in making it a reality," Mobley said. "I think all the different perspectives and input allowed us to create something very special that will only grow in size and significance in the future."

CLASSIFICATION ALL-STARS

Low Class A — Midwest League, South Atlantic League

Pos.	Player, Team (Organization)	AVG	OBP	SLG	AB	R	H	2B	3B	HR	RBI	BB	SO	SB
C	J.R. Towles, Lexington (Astros)	.317	.382	.525	284	39	90	19	2	12	55	21	46	13
1B	Erik Lis, Beloit (Twins)	.326	.402	.547	411	69	134	37	3	16	70	51	83	4
2B	Eugenio Velez, Augusta (Giants)	.315	.369	.557	460	90	145	29	20	14	90	34	81	64
3B	Jeff Baisley, Kane County (Athletics)	.298	.382	.519	466	86	139	35	1	22	110	62	86	6
SS	Brent Lillibridge, Hickory (Pirates)	.299	.414	.522	274	59	82	18	5	11	43	51	61	29
OF	Will Venable, Fort Wayne (Padres)	.314	.389	.477	472	86	148	34	5	11	91	55	81	18
OF	Jay Bruce, Dayton (Reds)	.291	.355	.516	444	69	129	42	5	16	81	44	106	19
OF	Cameron Maybin, West Mich. (Tigers)	.304	.387	.457	385	59	117	20	6	9	69	50	116	27
DH	Sergio Pedroza, Columbus (Dodgers)	.281	.437	.562	317	61	89	24	1	21	75	73	91	2

Pos.	Pitcher, Team (Organization)	W	L	ERA	G	GS	SV	IP	H	HR	BB	SO	GO/AO	AVG
SP	Matt Maloney, Lakewood (Phillies)	16	9	2.03	27	27	0	169	120	5	73	180	1.04	.194
SP	Carlos Carrasco, Lakewood (Phillies)	12	6	2.26	26	26	0	159	103	6	65	159	1.07	.182
SP	Will Inman, West Virginia (Brewers)	10	2	1.71	23	20	0	111	75	3	24	134	0.71	.190
SP	Nick Adenhart, Cedar Rapids (Angels)	10	2	1.95	16	16	0	106	84	2	26	99	1.33	.215
RP	Yohan Pino, Beloit (Twins)	14	2	1.91	42	7	3	94	69	4	20	99	0.79	.198

Player of the Year: Jay Bruce, of, Dayton (Reds). **Manager of the Year:** Matt Walbeck, West Michigan (Tigers). **Team of the Year:** Lakewood (Phillies).

PLAYER OF THE YEAR
Jay Bruce, of
Dayton

Short-Season — New York-Penn League, Northwest League

Pos.	Player, Team (Organization)	AVG	OBP	SLG	AB	R	H	2B	3B	HR	RBI	BB	SO	SB
C	Adam Witter, Salem-Keizer (Giants)	.285	.366	.585	207	40	59	12	1	16	52	25	41	2
1B	Chris Davis, Spokane (Rangers)	.277	.343	.534	253	38	70	18	1	15	42	23	65	2
2B	Wilmer Pino, Staten Island (Yankees)	.326	.363	.410	227	43	74	15	2	0	31	7	35	18
3B	Mitch Hilligoss, Staten Island (Yankees)	.292	.357	.352	267	40	78	8	1	2	36	24	47	12
SS	Scott Sizemore, Oneonta (Tigers)	.327	.394	.435	294	49	96	15	4	3	37	32	47	7
OF	Jordan Parraz, Tri-City (Astros)	.336	.421	.494	253	46	85	18	2	6	38	33	44	23
OF	Cyle Hankerd, Yakima (Diamondbacks)	.384	.424	.519	216	24	83	17	0	4	38	13	54	0
OF	Tyler Colvin, Boise (Cubs)	.268	.313	.483	265	50	71	12	6	11	53	17	55	12
DH	Chad Huffman, Eugene (Padres)	.343	.439	.576	198	41	68	17	1	9	40	25	34	2

Pos.	Pitcher, Team (Organization)	W	L	ERA	G	GS	SV	IP	H	HR	BB	SO	GO/AO	AVG
SP	Adam Cowart, Salem-Keizer (Giants)	10	1	1.08	15	15	0	83	51	2	8	55	2.58	.178
SP	Chris Salamida, Tri-City (Astros)	10	1	1.06	14	14	0	68	44	2	23	53	0.54	.189
SP	George Kontos, Staten Island (Yankees)	7	3	2.64	14	14	0	78	64	3	19	82	1.64	.227
SP	Jeremy Hellickson, Hud. Valley (Devil Rays)	3	3	2.43	15	14	0	78	55	3	16	96	1.48	.193
RP	Justin Masterson, Lowell (Red Sox)	3	1	0.85	14	0	0	32	20	0	2	33	2.81	.174

Player of the Year: Cyle Hankerd, of, Yakima (Diamondbacks). **Manager of the Year:** Steve Decker, Salem-Keizer (Giants). **Team of the Year:** Salem-Keizer (Giants).

PLAYER OF THE YEAR
Cyle Hankerd, of
Yakima

Rookie — Appalachian League, Arizona League, Gulf Coast League, Pioneer League

Pos.	Player, Team (Organization)	AVG	OBP	SLG	AB	R	H	2B	3B	HR	RBI	BB	SO	SB
C	Nevin Ashley, Princeton (Devil Rays)	.333	.440	.477	153	25	51	8	1	4	28	21	40	7
1B	Chris Carter, Great Falls (White Sox)	.299	.398	.570	251	37	75	21	1	15	59	34	70	4
2B	Justin Turner, Billings (Reds)	.338	.411	.511	231	53	78	16	3	6	41	23	38	12
3B	Billy Rowell, Bluefield (Orioles)	.329	.422	.507	152	38	50	15	3	2	26	25	47	3
SS	Chris Valaika, Billings (Reds)	.324	.387	.520	275	58	89	22	4	8	60	24	61	2
OF	Ryan Rogowski, Ogden (Dodgers)	.312	.429	.471	263	64	82	14	8	4	36	52	40	30
OF	Cedric Hunter, AZL Padres (Padres)	.371	.467	.484	213	46	79	13	4	1	44	40	22	17
OF	Travis Snider, Pulaski (Blue Jays)	.325	.412	.567	194	36	63	12	1	11	41	30	47	6
DH	Matt Sweeney, AZL/Orem (Angels)	.335	.426	.563	176	38	59	11	7	5	39	23	29	4

Pos.	Pitcher, Team (Organization)	W	L	ERA	G	GS	SV	IP	H	HR	BB	SO	GO/AO	AVG
SP	Vladimir Veras, AZL Angels (Angels)	8	2	1.35	12	12	0	60	46	0	13	58	1.26	.210
SP	Jamie Richmond, Danville (Braves)	7	1	1.21	14	12	0	67	51	0	4	52	2.11	.210
SP	Brent Fisher, AZL/Idaho Falls (Royals)	3	1	2.12	15	14	1	72	43	3	19	107	0.88	.169
SP	Tommy Hanson, Danville (Braves)	4	1	2.09	13	8	0	52	42	2	9	56	0.76	.218
RP	Danny Hernandez, Elizabethton (Twins)	1	1	3.81	28	0	18	28	20	2	9	40	1.25	.190

Player of the Year: Travis Snider, of, Pulaski (Blue Jays). **Manager of the Year:** Ray Smith, Elizabethton (Twins). **Team of the Year:** Danville (Braves).

PLAYER OF THE YEAR
Travis Snider, of
Pulaski

MINOR LEAGUES

MIKE JAMES

FSL Move Could Signal End Of Dodgertown

The Vero Beach Dodgers are no more, but the Los Angeles Dodgers are staying in town—at least for the time being.

The Los Angeles Dodgers announced they will move their high Class A affiliate to Inland Empire in the California League, while the Devil Rays will move into Dodgertown and add Vero Beach in the Florida State League.

Dodgers officials said the decision was not based on a desire for the club to leave Vero Beach, but people outside the organization interpret the move as the team's first step toward moving its spring training base to Arizona.

"The primary reason for moving the team is to have the prospects closer to our baseball operations folks, so it is a little easier to monitor their development," said Camille Johnston, Dodgers senior vice president of communications. "It also provides an opportunity for some of our major league players to have a quick rehab stint nearby."

The Dodgers will return to Vero Beach for spring training in 2007, and their Rookie-level Gulf Coast League team and minor league rehabilitation site will remain at Dodgertown. "At this point there is no change in that status," she said.

But the Dodgers have been linked to potential spring training sites in Glendale and Goodyear, two Phoenix

Claus brings winning approach to his teams

Winner on and off the field
Portland manager Todd Claus

Since his playing days, Todd Claus has always been a gamer.

A nondrafted free agent out of North Florida signed by Angels scout Tom Kotchman, Claus played for three years as a middle infielder and never made it above Double-A.

MANAGER OF THE YEAR
"I always wanted to play in the big leagues, but I knew at a young age that I would eventually be a coach because my talent was minimal," said Claus, 37.

Still, that didn't stop him from leaving it out on the field until Super Bowl Sunday in early 1994, when he got a call from the Angels asking him to take the hitting coach job at short-season Boise.

Claus served as hitting coach for two seasons at Boise (where Kotchman was the manager), and progressed up the ladder to being the Double-A hitting coach by 1998. From 1999-2001, he went back to coaching short-season ball to accommodate spring scouting duties in South Florida the organization had added.

Claus moved on to the managing ranks in 2002 at low Class A Cedar Rapids, and after two seasons with the Kernels, Claus was suddenly fired by the Angels and immediately hired by the Red Sox.

He stayed one season at high Class A Sarasota before moving to Double-A Portland—leading the Sea Dogs to the Eastern League playoff the past two years. Portland won it all in 2006 with a club that didn't have the elite talent of its opponent, Akron.

His scouting background, success as a manager and ability to deal with the adversity of leaving the Angels has prompted Baseball America to name Claus as its Minor League Manager of the Year.

"This is a team that went through a 10-game losing streak in August, and he and the staff deserve a lot of credit for turning that around," Red Sox farm director Mike Hazen said. "He's the guy that drives that team for 142 games every season. You know he expects the energy, the intensity and the effort every night.

"We can't replicate the environment in Boston, but Todd's done an outstanding job of developing our players and putting them in the postseason

where they can perform in pressure-type situations."

Claus has always been a fiery guy. That comes across in his demeanor on the field, his preparation by breaking down his own scouting reports and those from advance scouts for every game.

And he's always been a winner.

As an amateur, he played at Cardinal Gibbons (Fla.) High, which took home its first state championship in 10 years in 1987. He then played a year at Indian River (Fla.) Junior College before heading to North Florida.

Then there is the scouting background. Claus signed Angels catcher Mike Napoli in the 17th round and outfielder Tommy Murphy in the third round in 2000.

"It's tough enough to get one guy who makes it to the big leagues," Kotchman said. "But this guy had two guys debut up there on the same day.

"He's made the most of every opportunity and dealt well with everything that's been thrown his way. On top of that, he throws a great BP—he's an exceptional coach, an exceptional manager and an exceptional human being."

PREVIOUS WINNERS

1981—Ed Nottle, Tacoma (Athletics)	
1982—Eddie Haas, Richmond (Braves)	
1983—Bill Dancy, Reading (Phillies)	
1984—Sam Perlozzo, Jackson (Mets)	
1985—Jim Lefebvre, Phoenix (Giants)	
1986—Brad Fischer, Huntsville (Athletics)	
1987—Dave Trembley, Harrisburg (Pirates)	
1988—Joe Sparks, Indianapolis (Expos)	
1989—Buck Showalter, Albany (Yankees)	
1990—Kevin Kennedy, Albuquerque (Dodgers)	
1991—Butch Hobson, Pawtucket (Red Sox)	
1992—Grady Little, Greenville (Braves)	
1993—Terry Francona, Birmingham (White Sox)	
1994—Tim Ireland, El Paso (Brewers)	
1995—Marc Bombard, Indianapolis (Reds)	
1996—Carlos Tosca, Portland (Marlins)	
1997—Gary Jones, Edmonton (Athletics)	
1998—Terry Kennedy, Iowa (Cubs)	
1999—John Mizerock, Wichita (Royals)	
2000—Joel Skinner, Buffalo (Indians)	
2001—Jackie Moore, Round Rock (Astros)	
2002—John Russell, Edmonton (Twins)	
2003—Dave Brundage, San Antonio (Mariners)	
2004—Marty Brown, Buffalo (Indians)	
2005—Ken Oberkfell, Norfolk (Mets)	

suburbs trying to get state money to build two-team complexes. The Indians have already signed an agreement to move to Goodyear if that complex gets built, but the Dodgers are believed to prefer Glendale.

Vero Beach city manager Jim Gabbard said Craig Callan, Dodgers vice president of spring training and minor league facilities, told him about a week ago that the Vero Beach Dodgers were leaving and he informed council members then.

"Obviously, we love the Dodgers and would have liked to have kept the team here, but I think it's basically a

business decision," Gabbard said.

At the same time, Gabbard said he is excited about the Devil Rays minor league affiliate coming to town. "We are just glad to have baseball, and we think it will be a smooth transition," he said.

Indian River County administrator Joe Baird said the county's agreement with the Dodgers allows for the affiliation change, but he said the county tried to keep the Dodgers in Vero Beach.

"There is a lot of tradition with the Vero Beach Dodgers; that is the bad part," Baird said. "It is disappointing, but sometimes you have to accept what is going to happen and move on."

Baird also confirmed with Callan the Dodgers will remain in Vero Beach for spring training for now. He said he believes the Dodgers will eventually move elsewhere for spring training, however, and the county is already considering who might replace them.

"It appears more and more that they are leaving, and we are going to look at other teams," Baird said.

The Devil Rays happily return to the Florida State League after six seasons in the Cal League. The Vero Beach franchise will get a new name, but that has not been settled on yet.

Devil Rays senior vice president of baseball operations Gerry Hunsicker said the change in affiliation worked out well for both teams involved.

"From a timing standpoint, (for) both our affiliate in Visalia and the Dodgers in Vero Beach, those agreements

were up, and it was a matter of the Dodgers wanting to get to California, and we were trying to get closer to home," Hunsicker said.

Though the Dodgers had an Florida State League team in Vero Beach since 1980, the opportunity to return to California was appealing. The Dodgers used to operate two Class A franchises—one in the FSL and another in the Cal League (San Bernardino) from 1995-2000—but beginning in 2001 Major League Baseball required each organization to maintain one high and one low Class A affiliate.

The Devil Rays signed an agreement in September to move their spring training operations to a renovated complex in Port Charlotte, Fla., beginning in 2009. Such a move could coincide with the Dodgers' move to Arizona, with the Vero Beach franchise moving to Port Charlotte, a more natural fit if the team remains a Devil Rays affiliate.

MINOR LEAGUE ALL-STAR GAMES

For Kevin Witt, the 2006 Triple-A all-star game provided a bit of redemption.

Witt collected three of the 11 hits in the contest, including a two-run homer in the third, as the International League stars claimed a 6-0 victory over the best from the Pacific Coast League at Toledo's Fifth Third Field on July 12.

Despite hard rains that soaked Toledo most of the day, as well as a gullywasher shortly before the game began, the soggy conditions did not dampen the spirits of the 11,500 fans in attendance.

Nor did the rain affect the performance of Witt, who rebounded from a disappointing effort in the home run derby two days earlier to earn IL MVP honors. The Durham Bulls first baseman also had a first-inning single and opposite-field RBI double in the fifth to finish just a triple short of hitting for the cycle.

"I caught a lot of heat for not performing in the home run derby," Witt said. "Hopefully this will make my teammates back in Durham give me a little better welcome when I come back home."

The IL squad broke in front with three unearned runs in the third inning. Charlotte's Jorge Velandia led off with a single against Nashville's Ben Hendrickson, and Chris Denorfia hit a grounder to third that looked like a double play ball. But Justin Leone of Portland threw the ball wildly to second, allowing Velandia to move to third.

Hendrickson threw a wild pitch that scored Velandia, and two outs later Witt launched a long home run to right-center.

The International League staff combined to tie a Triple-A all-star game record by allowing PCL hitters just two hits. Two Charlotte pitchers, knuckleballer Charlie Haeger and lefty Heath Phillips, retired the first 12 PCL hitters in order.

The International League staff allowed only three other baserunners the rest of the night and erased two of them on double plays. The PCL never advanced a runner past second.

Iowa's Rich Hill, the starter for the PCL, was named that squad's MVP after throwing two scoreless innings and striking out a pair.

ALL-STAR ROUNDUP

EASTERN LEAGUE: Altoona outfielder Brett Roneberg's two-out single in the sixth inning provided the go-ahead runs as the South beat the North 5-3 in the Eastern League all-star game at Portland, Maine. Roneberg, the game's MVP, had three singles in five at-bats, with three RBIs. The North jumped to a 3-1 lead, but Roneberg's sixth-inning hit and three shutout innings from Kip Bouknight led the South to victory.

SOUTHERN LEAGUE: The North scored early and often to easily capture the Southern League all-star game 9-4 in Montgomery, Ala. The North scored at least one run in the second through seventh innings as eight players collected hits. The attack was led by West Tenn's Scott Moore, who was MVP after recording three hits, including two home runs.

TEXAS LEAGUE: The South rose again in the Texas League all-star game, defeating the North 1-0 in Little Rock, Ark. While top hitting prospects like Brandon Wood, Troy Tulowitzki, Alex Gordon, Billy Butler, and Hunter Pence were present, pitching was the centerpiece of the contest. Josh Anderson, one of nine Corpus Christi players on the South team, was named MVP after driving in the game's only run.

CALIFORNIA-CAROLINA LEAGUE: The Carolina Leaguers won their second straight all-star game against the California League, winning 6-3 at Salem, Va. The Cal League jumped off to an early 1-0 lead in the first, but Carolina came roaring back with a pair of runs in the bottom half—highlighted by Kinston outfielder Brian Barton's RBI triple. Frederick outfielder Nolan Reimold went 2-for-3 with an RBI and was named the CL star of the game. Reid Brignac, who went 2-for-4 at the plate, was the Cal League star of the game.

FLORIDA STATE LEAGUE: Pitching dominated the FSL all-star game until the West finally emerged for a 7-4 win in Lakeland, Fla. Lakeland outfielder Jeff Frazier wowed the hometown fans, hitting a two-run homer off St. Lucie righthander Jose Sanchez to win the game's MVP.

MIDWEST LEAGUE: Dayton's Jay Bruce helped the East defeat the West in the Midwest League all-star game, 7-1 in Davenport, Iowa. The 19-year-old was the youngest player in the game, but he did not perform like it as he went 3-for-5 with a home run, a double and two stolen bases. The Reds prospect was named the game's MVP.

SOUTH ATLANTIC LEAGUE: The North defeated the South 4-0 in the Sally League all-star game at Eastlake, Ohio, in a game that took just 2:15 to play. Marlins lefthander Aaron Thompson got the win as he combined with eight other pitchers on a three-hitter. West Virginia third baseman Mat Gamel earned MVP honors by going 2-for-4 with a double.

MINOR LEAGUES

MINOR LEAGUE
DEPARTMENT LEADERS
Full-season teams only

TEAM

WINS
Augusta (South Atlantic) 92
Tucson (Pacific Coast) 91
West Michigan (Midwest) 89
Akron (Eastern) 87
Jacksonville (Southern) 86

LONGEST WINNING STREAK
Jacksonville (Southern) 15
Salem (Carolina) 14
Binghamton (Eastern) 12
Brooklyn (New York-Penn) 12
Charlotte (International)................................12
Salem-Keizer (Northwest) 12

LOSSES
Clinton (Midwest) 94
Kannapolis (South Atlantic) 94
Omaha (Pacific Coast) 91
Arkansas (Texas) 87
Three teams tied at 86

LONGEST LOSING STREAK
Huntsville (Southern)...................................14
Kannapolis (South Atlantic) 12
Richmond (International) 12
San Antonio (Texas) 12
Three teams tied at 11

BATTING AVERAGE*
Lancaster (California)................................ .303
Tucson (Pacific Coast) 289
Visalia (California) 289
Albuquerque (Pacific Coast) 288
Las Vegas (Pacific Coast) 288

RUNS
Lancaster (California) 872
Visalia (California) 861
Tucson (Pacific Coast) 844
Salt Lake (Pacific Coast) 798
Sacramento (Pacific Coast) 794

HOME RUNS
Portland (Pacific Coast) 175
Lancaster (California) 171
Round Rock (Pacific Coast) 170
Tucson (Pacific Coast) 160
Arkansas (Texas) 158

STOLEN BASES
Asheville (South Atlantic)...........................266
Augusta (South Atlantic) 244
Cedar Rapids (Midwest) 201
Nashville (Pacific Coast) 196
Lynchburg (Carolina) 194

EARNED RUN AVERAGE*
West Tenn (Southern) 2.84
West Michigan (Midwest) 2.96
Jacksonville (Southern) 2.98
Lakewood (South Atlantic) 3.10
Beloit (Midwest) 3.18

STRIKEOUTS
Southwest Michigan (Midwest) 1189
San Jose (California) 1177
Lakewood (South Atlantic) 1176
Vero Beach (Florida State) 1171
Jacksonville (Southern) 1135

INDIVIDUAL BATTING

BATTING AVERAGE*
James Loney (Las Vegas) 380
Kevin Kouzmanoff (Akron/Buffalo)..............379
Matt Kemp (Las Vegas/Jacksonville) .... .346
J.R. House (Round Rock/Corpus Christi) .345
Corey Coles (St. Lucie) 341
Norris Hopper (Louisville/Chattanooga).....340
Alberto Callaspo (Tucson) 337

Luis Perez (Stockton) 334
Michel Abreu (St. Lucie/Binghamton) .... .332
Billy Butler (Wichita) 331

RUNS
Fernando Perez (Visalia) 123
Emilio Bonifacio (Lancaster) 117
Brian Burgamy (Reading/Clearwater)..........112
Alex Gordon (Wichita) 111
Brent Lillibridge (Hickory, Lynchburg)........106

HITS
Chris Rahl (Lancaster) 186
Emilio Bonifacio (Lancaster) 175
Josh Anderson (Corpus Christi)..................173
J.R. House (Round Rock/Corpus Christi) ..170
Fernando Perez (Visalia) 168

TOP HITTING STREAKS
Jorge Cortes (Corpus Christi) 27
Darnell McDonald (Durham) 27
Ben Francisco (Buffalo) 25
Nate Schierholtz (Connecticut) 25
Three players tied at 22

TOTAL BASES
Sean Rodriguez (R.C./Ark./Salt Lake) 291
Alex Gordon (Wichita) 286
Chris Rahl (Lancaster) 285
Brooks Conrad (Round Rock) 284
Terry Evans (P.B./Spring./Arkansas) 283

EXTRA-BASE HITS
Brooks Conrad (Round Rock) 79
Brandon Wood (Arkansas)...........................71
Jon Knott (Portland) 70
Joey Votto (Chattanooga) 70
Alex Gordon (Wichita) 69

DOUBLES
Seth Smith (Tulsa) 46
Joey Votto (Chattanooga) 46
Chris Nowak (Visalia)..................................45
Chris Rahl (Lancaster) 44
Jeremy Slayden (Lakewood) 44

TRIPLES
Eugenio Velez (Augusta) 20
Vic Buttler (Altoona/Indianapolis) 15
Brooks Conrad (Round Rock) 15
Michael Bourn (Reading/Scranton) 13
Michael Hollimon (West Michigan) 13

HOME RUNS
Kevin Witt (Durham) 36
Nate Gold (Frisco) 34
Terry Evans (P.B./Spring./Arkansas) 33
Jon Knott (Portland) 32
Joseph Koshansky (Tulsa) 31
Mark Reynolds (Lancaster/Tennessee) 31

RUNS BATTED IN
Jon Knott (Portland) 113
Jeffrey Baisley (Kane County) 110
Joseph Koshansky (Tulsa)..........................109
Jeff Baker (Colorado Springs) 108
Scott McClain (Sacramento) 107

MOST RBIs IN A GAME
Cory Patton (Dunedin) 10
Jordan Renz (Cedar Rapids) 10
Ryan Patterson (Dunedin) 9
Five players tied at 8

STOLEN BASES
Eric Young Jr. (Oklahoma)............................87
Darren Ford (West Virginia)..........................69
Justin Christian (Trenton) 68
Antoan Richardson (Augusta) 66
Eugenio Velez (Augusta) 64

CAUGHT STEALING
Eric Young Jr. (Oklahoma)............................31
Dexter Fowler (Asheville).............................23
Christopher Walker (West Tenn) 23

James Loney

Nyjer Morgan (Altoona, Lynchburg) 22
Bradley Coon (Cedar Rapids).......................21
Benjamin Copeland (Augusta) 21

HIT BY PITCH
Michael Collins (Rancho Cucamonga) 33
Carlos Quentin (Tucson) 31
Brandon Burgess (Lancaster) 28
Jason Mooneyham (Columbus/Vero Beach) 27
Chris Gimenez (Lake County)........................26

WALKS
Jack Cust (Portland) 143
Jeff Natale (Greenville, Wilmington) 103
Sergio Pedroza (Columbus/Vero/Visalia) 101
Dustin Majewski (Dunedin/New Hamp.) 100
Jeffrey Corsaletti (Wilmington) 97

STRIKEOUTS
Brandon Szymanski (Dayton) 191
Charlton Jimerson (Round Rock) 183
Corey Ragsdale (Binghamton) 182
Ian Gac (Bakersfield/Clinton) 179
Jordan Renz (Cedar Rapids) 178

SACRIFICE FLIES
J.R. House (Round Rock/Corpus Christi) 12
Brad Miller (Yakima) 12
Four players tied at 11

SACRIFICE HITS
Jose Coronado (St. Lucie) 31
Jose Castro (Hagerstown) 21
Joshua Johnson (Burlington) 19
Five players tied at 17

SLUGGING PERCENTAGE*
Kevin Kouzmanoff (Akron/Buffalo)............ .656
Mark Reynolds (Lancaster/Tennessee) .... .633
Scott Hairston (Tucson)...............................591
Alex Gordon (Wichita) 588
Terrmel Sledge (Portland) 583

ON-BASE PERCENTAGE*
Jack Cust (Portland) 467
Reggie Willits (Salt Lake) 448
Jeff Natale (Wilmington/Greenville) 446
Kevin Kouzmanoff (Akron/Buffalo)............ .437
Ole Sheldon (Salem/Lexington) 430

ON BASE PLUS SLUGGING (OPS)*
Kevin Kouzmanoff (Akron/Buffalo) 1.093
Mark Reynolds (Lancaster/Tennessee) 1.034
Jack Cust (Portland) 1.016
Alex Gordon (Wichita) 1.016
Scott Hairston (Tucson)...............................997

BATTING AVERAGE BY POSITION*

Catchers
J.R. House (Round Rock/Corpus Christi) .345
Branden Florence (Reading/Clearwater) .. .324
John Jaso (Visalia) .... .309
Carlos Ruiz (Scranton/WB) .... .307
Robinzon Diaz (Dunedin) .... .306

First Basemen
James Loney (Las Vegas) .... .380
Michel Abreu (St. Lucie/Binghamton) ...... .332
Erik Lis (Beloit) .... .326
Carlos Rivera (Rome) .... .325
Mike Eylward (Arkansas/Salt Lake) ...... .324

Second Basemen
Alberto Callaspo (Tucson) .... .337
Edgar V. Gonzalez (Jup./Carolina/Albuq.) .327
Corey Wimberly (Modesto) .... .325
Yung Chi Chen (Inland Empire/San Ant.).. .324
Scott Hairston (Tucson) .... .323

Third Basemen
Kevin Kouzmanoff (Akron/Buffalo) .... .379
Billy Butler (Wichita) .... .331
Alex Gordon (Wichita) .... .325
Mark Reynolds (Lancaster/Tennessee) .... .318
Andy LaRoche (Las Vegas/Jacksonville) .. .315

Shortstops
Ben Zobrist (Durham/Corpus Christi) ...... .323
Reid Brignac (Visalia/Montgomery) .... .321
Alexi Casilla (Fort Myers/New Britain) ...... .318
Eugenio Velez (Augusta) .... .315
Sean Rodriguez (R.C./Ark./Salt Lake) ...... .307

Outfielders
Matt Kemp (Las Vegas/Jacksonville) .... .346
Corey Coles (St. Lucie) .... .341
Norris Hopper (Louisville/Chattanooga) .. .340
Luis Perez (Stockton) .... .334
Adam Lind (New Hampshire/Syracuse) .... .330

INDIVIDUAL PITCHING

EARNED RUN AVERAGE*
Scott Lewis (Kinston) 1.48
Yovani Gallardo (Brevard Co./Huntsville) .. 1.86
Kevin Slowey (Fort Myers/New Britain) 1.88
Chase Wright (Tampa) 1.88
Matt Garza (Ft. Myers/New Brit./Roch.) 1.99
Matthew Maloney (Lakewood) 2.03
Jason Hirsh (Round Rock) 2.10
Brian Mazone (Reading/Scranton) 2.11
Michael Devaney (Binghamton/St. Lucie) .. 2.13
Philip Hughes (Tampa/Trenton) 2.16
Donald Veal (Peoria/Daytona) 2.16

WORST ERA*
Harold Eckert (Las Vegas) 7.49

Jacob McGee

Christopher Hunter (Arkansas) 7.45
Michael Madsen (Midland/Stockton) 7.34
Luis Cota (High Desert) 7.09
Kellen Raab (Lancaster) 6.84

WINS
Charles Lofgren (Kinston) 17
Jason Windsor (Sacramento/Midland) 17
Matthew Maloney (Lakewood) 16
Micah Owings (Tucson/Tennessee) 16
Zach Segovia (Reading/Clearwater) 16

LOSSES
Jason Scobie (New Hamp./Syr./Norfolk) 18
Jacob Rasner (Clinton) 16
Ryan Rote (Kannapolis/Great Falls) 15
Dennis Tankersley (Memphis) 15
Robert Brownlie (West Tenn/Iowa) 14
Nathan Bumstead (Erie) 14
Jorge De Paula (Columbus/Trenton) 14
Paul Fagan (Wisconsin) 14
Jesse Floyd (Connecticut) 14
Matt Ginter (Indianapolis/Pawtucket) 14
Dirk Hayhurst (Lake Elsinore/Port./Mobile) .. 14
Christopher Hunter (Arkansas) 14
Ray Liotta (Birmingham/Winston-Salem) 14
Omar Poveda (Clinton/Frisco) 14
Errol Simonitsch (New Britain) 14
Chris Waters (Mississippi) 14

GAMES
Neil Jamison (Lake Elsinore/Fort Wayne) 65
Jason Karnuth (Sacramento/Toledo) 62
Joshua Newman (Tulsa) 62
J.B. Miadich (Durham/Albuquerque) 61
Clay Rapada (West Tenn/Iowa) 61
Ehren Wassermann (Birmingham) 61

COMPLETE GAMES
Tim Redding (Charlotte) 5
Eight players tied at 4

SAVES
Brian Anderson (San Jose) 37
Mike Sillman (Palm Beach) 35
Neil Jamison (Lake Elsinore/Fort Wayne) 34
Jim Hoey (Bowie, Delmarva/Frederick) 33
Marcus McBeth (Stockton/Midland/Sac.) 32

SHUTOUTS
Andrew Sonnanstine (Montgomery) 4
Johnny Cueto (Dayton/Sarasota) 3
Michael Devaney (Binghamton/St. Lucie) 3
13 players tied at 2

INNINGS PITCHED
Tim Redding (Charlotte) 187.2
Andrew Sonnanstine (Montgomery) 185.2
Chad Durbin (Toledo) 185.0
Ross Ohlendorf (Tucson/Tennessee) 182.2
Robert Mosebach (R.C./Cedar Rapids) 182.1

WALKS
Stephen Randolph (Charlotte) 114
Corwin Malone (Birmingham) 94
Matt DeSalvo (Columbus/Trenton) 93
Samuel Deduno (Modesto) 92
Franklin Morales (Modesto) 89
Tyler Pelland (Chattanooga) 89

STRIKEOUTS
Yovani Gallardo (Brevard Co./Huntsville) 188
Francisco Cruceta (Tacoma) 185
Matthew Maloney (Lakewood) 180
Franklin Morales (Modesto) 179
Tyler Clippard (Trenton) 175

HITS ALLOWED
A.J. Shappi (Lancaster/Tennessee) 205
Kyle Middleton (Wichita/Omaha) 203
Jesse Smith (Salt Lake/Arkansas) 203
Jordan Pals (Springfield) 201
John Webb (Memphis) 201

STRIKEOUTS PER NINE INNINGS (Starters)*
Jacob McGee (Southwest Michigan) 11.49
Yovani Gallardo (Brevard Co./Huntsville) 10.92
Clay Buchholz (Wilmington/Greenville) 10.59
Brandon Erbe (Delmarva) 10.53
Scott Elbert (Vero Beach/Jacksonville) 10.52

Yovani Gallardo

STRIKEOUTS PER NINE INNINGS (Relievers)*
Paul Estrada (Corpus Christi) 13.60
Mike Sillman (Palm Beach) 13.50
Jesse Ingram (Bakersfield/Frisco) 13.44
Pat Neshek (Rochester) 13.05
Richard Aldridge (R.C./Cedar Rapids) 12.84

BATTING AVERAGE AGAINST (Starters)*
Donald Veal (Peoria/Daytona) .... .175
Philip Hughes (Trenton/Tampa) .... .179
Matt Garza (Ft. Myers/New Britain/Roch.) .179
Carlos Carrasco (Lakewood) .... .182
Kevin Slowey (Fort Myers/New Britain) ...... .188

BATTING AVERAGE AGAINST (Relievers)*
Troy Cate (Palm Beach/Springfield) .... .127
Juan Salas (Durham/Montgomery) .... .128
David Quinowski (Augusta) .... .145
Gabe DeHoyos (High Desert/Wichita) ...... .159

MOST STRIKEOUTS IN A GAME
Franklin Morales (Modesto) 16
Eric Hurley (Bakersfield) 15
Rich Dorman (Tacoma) 14
Cole Hamels (Scranton/Wilkes-Barre) 14
Rich Hill (Iowa) 14
Brent Leach (Columbus) 14
Adam Thomas (Vero Beach) 14
Jered Weaver (Salt Lake) 14

WILD PITCHES
Samuel Deduno (Modesto) 34
Adam Daniels (Quad Cities) 28
Jordan Pratt (Columbus) 26
Cibney Bello (Inland Empire) 24
Franklin Morales (Modesto) 24

BALKS
Franklin Morales (Modesto) 10
Jaime Garcia (Palm Beach/Quad Cities) 9
Matt Harrison (Mississippi/Myrtle Beach) 6
Four players tied at 5

HIT BATTERS
Samuel Deduno (Modesto) 22
Virgil Vasquez (Erie) 20
Sean Tracey (Charlotte) 19
Omar Diaz (VSL Cardinals) 18
Tyler Clippard (Trenton) 17
Edgar Guaramato (Wisconsin) 17
Adam Harben (New Britain) 17
Frank Herrmann (Lake County) 17
Todd Redmond (Hickory) 17

INDIVIDUAL FIELDING

MOST ERRORS
Pedro Ciriaco (South Bend) 45
Mike Bell (West Virginia) 41
Christopher Nelson (Asheville) 41
Eduardo Nunez (Charleston/Tampa) 40
Jeffrey Dominguez (Inland Empire/Wisc.) 39

MINOR LEAGUES

MINOR LEAGUE BEST TOOLS

Full season leagues only

	International/AAA	Pacific Coast/AAA	Eastern/AA	Southern/AA	Texas/AA	California/A	Carolina/A	Florida State/A	Midwest/A	South Atlantic/A
Best Batting Prospect	Josh Fields, Charlotte	Howie Kendrick, Salt Lake	Adam Lind, New Hampshire	Joey Votto, Chattanooga	Billy Butler, Wichita	Carlos Gonzalez, Lancaster	Trevor Crowe, Kinston	Ryan Braun, Brevard County	Jay Bruce, Dayton	Jose Tabata, Charleston
Best Power Prospect	Scott Thorman, Richmond	Nelson Cruz, Nashville	Adam Lind, New Hampshire	Matt Kemp, Jacksonville	Joe Koshansky, Tulsa	Ben Harrison, Bakersfield	Brandon Jones, Myrtle Beach	Terry Evans, Palm Beach	Jay Bruce, Dayton	Sergio Pedroza, Columbus
Best Strike-Zone Judgment	Chris Denorfia, Louisville	Alberto Callaspo, Tucson	Kory Casto, Harrisburg	Danny Richar, Tennessee	Ben Zobrist, Corpus Christi	Tug Hulett, Bakersfield	Trevor Crowe, Kinston	Cory Dunlap, Vero Beach	Joshua Johnson, Burlington	Gaby Sanchez, Greensboro
Best Baserunner	Jerry Owens, Charlotte	Charlton Jimerson, Round Rock	Justin Christian, Trenton	Eric Patterson, West Tenn	Josh Anderson, Corpus Christi	Emilio Bonifacio, Lancaster	Jacoby Ellsbury, Wilmington	Brett Gardner, Tampa	Cameron Maybin, West Michigan	Eric Young Jr., Asheville
Fastest Baserunner	Rajai Davis, Indianapolis	Freddy Guzman, Oklahoma	Michael Bourn, Reading	Chris Walker, West Tenn	Josh Anderson, Corpus Christi	Corey Wimberly, Modesto	Jacoby Ellsbury, Wilmington	Alexi Casilla, Fort Myers	Cameron Maybin, West Michigan	Eric Young Jr., Asheville
Best Pitching Prospect	Jeremy Sowers, Buffalo	Jered Weaver, Salt Lake	Philip Hughes, Trenton	Anibal Sanchez, Carolina	Ubaldo Jimenez, Tulsa	Greg Smith, Lancaster	Chuck Lofgren, Kinston	Homer Bailey, Sarasota	Nick Adenhart, Cedar Rapids	Will Inman, West Virginia
Best Fastball	Brandon League, Syracuse	Chad Billingsley, Las Vegas	Matt Lindstrom, Binghamton	Juan Mateo, West Tenn	Juan Morillo, Tulsa	Jose Arredondo, Rancho Cucamonga	Radhames Liz, Frederick	Homer Bailey, Sarasota	Jake McGee, Southwest Michigan	Brandon Erbe, Delmarva
Best Breaking Pitch	J.D. Durbin, Rochester	Rich Hill, Iowa	Philip Hughes, Trenton	Lance Broadway, Birmingham	Paul Estrada, Corpus Christi	Mark Lowe, Inland Empire	Jimmy Barthmaier, Salem	Matt Garza, Fort Myers	Matt Walker, Southwest Michigan	Clay Buchholz, Greenville
Best Control	Jeremy Sowers, Buffalo	Jason Hirsh, Round Rock	Matt Garza, New Britain	Andy Sonnanstine, Montgomery	Ryan Feierabend, San Antonio	Nick Pereira, San Jose	Scott Lewis, Kinston	Kevin Slowey, Fort Myers	Ramon Garcia, West Michigan	Tip Fairchild, Lexington
Best Reliever	Pat Neshek, Rochester	Jack Taschner, Fresno	Matt Lindstrom, Binghamton	Juan Salas, Montgomery	Manuel Corpas, Tulsa	Mark Lowe, Inland Empire	James Hoey, Frederick	Mike Sillman, Palm Beach	Ed Campusano, Peoria	James Hoey, Delmarva
Best Defensive Catcher	Shawn Riggans, Durham	Jeff Mathis, Salt Lake	Curtis Thigpen, New Hampshire	Miguel Perez, Chattanooga	Kurt Suzuki, Midland	Landon Powell, Stockton	Wyatt Toregas, Kinston	Tuffy Gosewisch, Clearwater	Christian Lopez, Southwest Michigan	J.R. Towles, Lexington
Best Defensive First Baseman	Casey Rogowski, Charlotte	James Loney, Las Vegas	Travis Ishikawa, Connecticut	Joey Votto, Chattanooga	Brant Colamarino, Midland	Chris Nowak, Visalia	Ian Bladergroen, Wilmington	Mike Carp, St. Lucie	Ryan Norwood, Peoria	Logan Sorensen, Greenville
Best Defensive Second Baseman	Anderson Hernandez, Norfolk	Alberto Callaspo, Tucson	Eider Torres, Akron	Tony Abreu, Jacksonville	Kevin Melillo, Midland	Gregorio Petit, Stockton	J.C. Holt, Myrtle Beach	Alexi Casilla, Fort Myers	Joshua Johnson, Burlington	Eric King, Lexington
Best Defensive Third Baseman	Andy Marte, Buffalo	Brendan Harris, New Orleans	Brian Buscher, Connecticut	Scott Moore, West Tenn	Alex Gordon, Wichita	Freddy Sandoval, Rancho Cucamonga	Van Pope, Myrtle Beach	Mike Costanzo, Clearwater	Jeff Baisley, Kane County	Marcos Vechionacci, Charleston
Best Defensive Shortstop	Danny Sandoval, Scranton/Wilkes-Barre	Stephen Drew, Tucson	Tony Giarratano, Erie	Chin Lung-Hu, Jacksonville	Oswaldo Navarro, San Antonio	Jonathan Herrera, Modesto	Edwin Maysonet, Salem	Alcides Escobar, Brevard County	Justin Sellers, Kane County	Tommy Manzella, Lexington
Best Infield Arm	Sergio Santos, Syracuse	Erick Aybar, Salt Lake	Kody Kirkland, Erie	Yunel Escobar, Mississippi	Troy Tulowitzki, Tulsa	Cliff Pennington, Stockton	Van Pope, Myrtle Beach	Mike Costanzo, Clearwater	Matt Bush, Fort Wayne	Marcos Vechionacci, Charleston
Best Defensive Outfielder	Chris Denorfia, Louisville	Adam Jones, Tacoma	Frank Diaz, Harrisburg	Chris Walker, West Tenn	Reid Gorecki, Springfield	Fernando Perez, Visalia	Jacoby Ellsbury, Wilmington	Brett Gardner, Tampa	Jose Duarte, Burlington	Jordan Schafer, Rome
Best Outfield Arm	Keith Reed, Ottawa	Shin Soo Choo, Tacoma	Brent Clevlen, Erie	Jerry Gil, Tennessee	Wladimir Balentien, San Antonio	Carlos Gonzalez, Lancaster	Mickey Hall, Wilmington	Brett Carroll, Jupiter	Leyson Septimo, South Bend	Mike Mooney, Augusta
Most Exciting Player	Lastings Milledge, Norfolk	Howie Kendrick, Salt Lake	Philip Hughes, Trenton	Matt Kemp, Jacksonville	Hunter Pence, Corpus Christi	Carlos Gonzalez, Lancaster	Trevor Crowe, Kinston	Alexi Casilla, Fort Myers	Cameron Maybin, West Michigan	Dexter Fowler, Asheville
Best Manager Prospect	Torey Lovullo, Buffalo	Craig Colbert, Portland	Tim Bogar, Akron	Gary Jones, Mobile	Daren Brown, San Antonio	Gary Thurman, Inland Empire	Chad Epperson, Wilmington	Pop Warner, Palm Beach	Matt Walbeck, West Michigan	Travis Barbary, Columbus

Selected at midseason 2006 by Baseball America in consultation with minor league managers

FREITAS AWARDS

Baseball America's annual Bob Freitas Awards are presented to franchises that show sustained excellence in the business of minor league baseball.

They were first presented in 1989, shortly after the death of Freitas, a longtime minor league operator, promoter and ambassador. Franchises must be in operation for at least five seasons before they're eligible to win.

■ By now, everyone is familiar with the phenomenon that is the Durham Bulls. But soon after the team's new ballpark opened in the mid-1990s came the opportunity to move up to Triple-A. And here's where the next chapter of Durham Bulls history began.

The Bulls joined the International League as a Devil Rays affiliate in 1998 and went from drawing around 350,000 fans a season in their first few years in the new ballpark as a Carolina League franchise, to draw about 500,000 fans a season as an International League franchise. (The Carolina League franchise moved to South Carolina and became the Myrtle Beach Pelicans.)

One thing hasn't changed, though, and that's the team's commitment to its community. "If anyone in the community asks us to do something for them, we bend over backwards to help them," Bulls vice president George Habel said. "We're serious about that; it's the way our company operates."

■ From the very first game at Blair County Ballpark, the Altoona Curve has been a success story. The club drew 6,171 fans that first night in 1999, despite frigid temperatures and intermittent rain, and finished the season drawing 323,932 fans.

The club was sold to an ownership group headed by Pittsburgh lawyer Chuck Greenberg in 2002, and the Pirates have been so impressed with Altoona's operation that they renewed their affiliation for another four years in September.

For Altoona, a city of roughly 50,000 with a history steeped in the railroad industry, the Curve provided an economic boon. GM Todd Parnell said the organization's philosophy stems directly from Greenberg, who is as visible and accessible as it gets among minor league owners.

"It all starts with fun, and that whole deal comes from Chuck," Parnell said. "I mean, it's capital punishment for any front-office employee who stays in their office during the game. For those three hours, we're on—it's game time and you should want to be seen and have an impact on fans."

■ When you go to a Daytona Cubs game, there isn't a whole lot that would feel out of place at any other well-run minor league park. As Daytona Cubs general manager Bill Papierniak explains, "It's not rocket science."

But the details are important, which is why the Daytona Cubs emphasize them. And as Papierniak sees it, they are a big reason the club has seen its attendance double in the past five years: while playing in 76-year-old Jackie Robinson Stadium and in the Florida State League, which is known as the place where the crowds disappear when the big league clubs pack up spring training.

■ From their first game in 2002, it was clear the Aberdeen IronBirds were a special operation. The maiden franchise of Ripken Baseball has been nothing but a success since its debut. The Orioles affiliate was able to sell out its 6,300-seat ballpark for every game from day one. In the process, the IronBirds built up a season-ticket waiting list to maintain the demand for the tickets. Since then, they have built up a waiting list of 1,800 seats.

Ripken Stadium is now the centerpiece of Ripken Center, a facility that also features a youth baseball complex dedicated to teaching baseball "The Ripken Way."

PREVIOUS WINNERS

Triple-A

Year	Team
1989	Columbus (International)
1990	Pawtucket (International)
1991	Buffalo (American Association)
1992	Iowa (American Association)
1993	Richmond (International)
1994	Norfolk (International)
1995	Albuquerque (Pacific Coast)
1996	Indianapolis (American Association)
1997	Rochester (International)
1998	Salt Lake (Pacific Coast)
1999	Louisville (International)
2000	Edmonton (Pacific Coast)
2001	Buffalo (International)
2002	Memphis (Pacific Coast)
2003	Pawtucket (International)
2004	Sacramento (Pacific Coast)
2005	Toledo (International)

Double-A

Year	Team
1989	El Paso (Texas)
1990	Arkansas (Texas)
1991	Reading (Eastern)
1992	Tulsa (Texas)
1993	Harrisburg (Eastern)
1994	San Antonio (Texas)
1995	Midland (Texas)
1996	Carolina (Southern)
1997	Bowie (Eastern)
1998	Trenton (Eastern)
1999	Portland (Eastern)
2000	Reading (Eastern)
2001	Mobile (Southern)
2002	Chattanooga (Southern)
2003	New Britain (Eastern)
2004	Round Rock (Texas)
2005	Tulsa (Texas)

Class A

Year	Team
1989	Durham (Carolina)
1990	San Jose (California)
1991	Asheville (South Atlantic)
1992	Springfield (Midwest)
1993	South Bend (Midwest)
1994	Kinston (Carolina)
1995	Kane County (Midwest)
1996	Wisconsin (Midwest)
1997	Rancho Cucamonga (California)
1998	West Michigan (Midwest)
1999	Wilmington (Carolina)
2000	Charleston, S.C. (South Atlantic)
2001	Delmarva (South Atlantic)
2002	Fort Myers (Florida State)
2003	Modesto (California)
2004	Dayton (Midwest)
2005	Lakewood (South Atlantic)

Short-Season

Year	Team
1989	Eugene (Northwest)
1990	Salt Lake City (Pioneer)
1991	Spokane (Northwest)
1992	Boise (Northwest)
1993	Billings (Pioneer)
1994	Everett (Northwest)
1995	Great Falls (Pioneer)
1996	Bluefield (Appalachian)
1997	Oneonta (New York-Penn)
1998	Hudson Valley (New York-Penn)
1999	Portland (Northwest)
2000	Lowell (New York-Penn)
2001	Salem-Keizer (Northwest)
2002	Ogden (Pioneer)
2003	Spokane (Northwest)
2004	Burlington (Appalachian)
2005	Brooklyn (New York-Penn)

INTERNATIONAL LEAGUE
TRIPLE-A

BY MATT EDDY

The Toledo Mud Hens featured no award winners, their hitters led the International League in strikeouts by more than 100 and they finished with the league's fifth-best record. Oh, and they didn't even qualify for the play-offs at the conclusion of the regular season.

Like the parent Detroit Tigers, the Mud Hens were in many ways the most surprising team in their league, and their IL championship equally so. Toledo won it all in 2005, too, becoming the first team to win consecutive Governor's Cups since the 2002-03 Durham Bulls. With the win, the Mud Hens earned the right to square off against Tucson, the Pacific Coast League champion, in the inaugural Bricktown Showdown in Oklahoma City. They lost that game, but that did little to obscure Toledo's remarkable season.

Indianapolis tied with Toledo atop the Western Division on the final day of the season, when the Indians won and the Mud Hens lost. Toledo then won a play-in game 4-0 to move on, in typical Toledo fashion: They bludgeoned their opponent with home runs. Because while the Mud Hens often struck out, they also hit a league-leading 152 home runs. Outfielder Ryan Ludwick and third baseman Mike Hessman, who finished second and third in the league with 28 and 24 round-trippers, each went deep in the play-in game. DH Josh Phelps had been the club's other big bopper, and sole postseason all-star, hitting .308/.370/.532 with 24 home runs and 90 RBIs.

The Mud Hens upended the favored Charlotte Knights in four games in the first round, then dispatched the Rochester Red Wings in five for the title. The Mud Hens erased a 2-1 series deficit to Rochester, a deficit they fell into by facing righthander Kevin Slowey and lefthander Glen Perkins, both among the Twins' top prospects and both recent callups from Double-A New Britain.

The Mud Hens responded in Games Four and Five, outscoring the Red Wings by a combined 16-1. When the dust settled, the top four playoff sluggers were all Mud Hens: Hessman, with five home runs; Phelps, with four; outfielder Dustan Mohr, four; and outfielder David Espinosa, three. The same four, plus second baseman Jack Hannahan, also were among the playoff leaders in RBIs, extra-base hits and slugging percentage.

Rochester had advanced to the finals by defeating Scranton/Wilkes-Barre, which at 84-58 sported the IL's best record, in the first round. Red Barons manager John Russell was named league manager of the year.

Toledo also played host to the Triple-A all-star game in July, when the IL triumphed 6-0 against a listless PCL squad that collected just two hits. Durham first baseman Kevin Witt was the game's MVP with three hits, including a double and a two-run home run. (Witt would also win league MVP honors at season's end for hitting .291/.360/.577 with a minor league-leading 36 home runs.) Ludwick lost to Buffalo third baseman Andy Marte in the home run derby the night before.

Charlotte had been the IL's strongest outfit for much of the season but lost two key contributors—right fielder Ryan Sweeney (.296/.350/.452) and knuckleballer Charlie Haeger (14-6, 3.07)—to big league promotions just before the playoffs began. Manager Razor Shines still had the league's most valuable pitcher, lefthander Heath Phillips (13-5, 2.96), and rookie of the year, third baseman Josh Fields (.305/.379/.515 with 19 home runs and 28 stolen bases).

TOP 20 PROSPECTS

1. Delmon Young, of, Durham (Devil Rays)
2. Lastings Milledge, of, Norfolk (Mets)
3. Jeremy Sowers, lhp, Buffalo (Indians)
4. Tom Gorzelanny, lhp, Indianapolis (Pirates)
5. Ryan Sweeney, of, Charlotte (White Sox)
6. Josh Fields, 3b, Charlotte (White Sox)
7. Hayden Penn, rhp, Ottawa (Orioles)
8. Andy Marte, 3b, Buffalo (Indians)
9. Humberto Sanchez, rhp, Toledo (Tigers)
10. Jamie Shields, rhp, Durham (Devil Rays)
11. Elijah Dukes, of, Durham (Devil Rays)
12. Scott Thorman, 1b/of, Richmond (Braves)
13. Brandon League, rhp, Syracuse (Blue Jays)
14. Jason Hammel, rhp, Durham (Devil Rays)
15. Dustin McGowan, rhp, Syracuse (Blue Jays)
16. Pat Neshek, rhp, Rochester (Twins)
17. Michael Bourn, of, Scranton/Wilkes-Barre (Phillies)
18. Dustin Pedroia, ss/2b, Pawtucket (Red Sox)
19. Charlie Haeger, rhp, Charlotte (White Sox)
20. Chris Denorfia, of, Louisville (Reds)

STANDINGS

Page	NORTH	W	L	PCT	GB	Manager	Attendance	Average	Last Penn.
197	Scranton/W-B Red Barons (Phillies)	84	58	.592	—	John Russell	376,284	5,534	None
166	Rochester Red Wings (Twins)	79	64	.552	5½	Stan Cliburn	463,836	6,626	1997
101	Buffalo Bisons (Indians)	73	68	.518	10½	Torey Lovullo	607,929	8,811	2004
62	Ottawa Lynx (Orioles)	74	69	.517	10½	Dave Trembley	122,574	1,915	1995
70	Pawtucket Red Sox (Red Sox)	69	75	.479	16	Ron Johnson	613,065	9,289	1984
257	Syracuse SkyChiefs (Blue Jays)	64	79	.448	20½	Michael Basso	347,699	5,349	1976
Page	SOUTH	W	L	PCT	GB	Manager	Attendance	Average	Last Penn.
85	Charlotte Knights (White Sox)	79	62	.560	—	Razor Shines	303,086	4,736	1999
243	Durham Bulls (Devil Rays)	64	78	.451	15½	John Tamargo	507,547	7,356	2003
174	Norfolk Tides (Mets)	57	84	.404	22	Ken Oberkfell	463,769	6,922	1985
55	Richmond Braves (Braves)	57	86	.399	23	Brian Snitker	321,696	4,731	1994
Page	WEST	W	L	PCT	GB	Manager	Attendance	Average	Last Penn.
205	Indianapolis Indians (Brewers)	76	66	.535	—	Trent Jewett	547,768	7,608	2000
115	Toledo Mud Hens (Tigers)	76	66	.535	—	Larry Parrish	569,380	8,134	2006
93	Louisville Bats (Reds)	75	68	.524	1½	Rick Sweet	652,692	9,193	2001
183	Columbus Clippers (Yankees)	69	73	.486	7	Dave Miley	518,875	7,520	1996

PLAYOFFS—Semifinals: Rochester defeated Scranton/Wilkes-Barre 3-1 and Toledo defeated Charlotte 3-1 in best-of-five series. **Finals:** Toledo defeated Rochester 3-2 in best-of-five series.

NOTE: Teams' individual batting and pitching statistics can be found on page indicated in lefthand column.

2006 INTERNATIONAL LEAGUE STATISTICS

CLUB BATTING

	AVG	G	AB	R	H	2B	3B	HR	BB	SO	SB	OBP	SLG
Louisville	.270	143	4749	578	1283	240	24	96	399	844	103	.331	.391
Charlotte	.267	141	4728	673	1264	280	22	119	431	968	155	.334	.411
Rochester	.264	143	4831	614	1273	254	37	84	399	903	71	.322	.384
Durham	.263	142	4767	592	1256	248	27	111	400	1007	143	.324	.397
Ottawa	.261	143	4678	589	1223	240	20	105	380	825	127	.323	.389
Scranton/WB	.260	142	4710	574	1225	268	42	83	377	912	106	.320	.388
Buffalo	.259	141	4733	646	1224	289	16	138	460	982	80	.331	.414
Toledo	.259	143	4807	652	1245	267	38	152	465	1194	118	.330	.425
Syracuse	.258	143	4850	599	1252	282	27	114	427	1083	66	.321	.398
Richmond	.255	143	4800	510	1223	214	18	68	421	903	90	.319	.349
Columbus	.254	142	4704	620	1197	244	25	129	505	941	78	.334	.399
Indianapolis	.252	142	4689	578	1180	247	30	88	473	992	180	.325	.373
Pawtucket	.252	144	4749	581	1195	235	30	107	546	935	111	.333	.381
Norfolk	.240	141	4519	497	1084	209	21	76	454	955	85	.314	.346

CLUB PITCHING

	ERA	G	CG	SHO	SV	IP	H	R	ER	HR	BB	SO	AVG
Scranton/WB	3.28	142	7	13	51	1250	1112	503	455	95	393	897	.240
Rochester	3.31	143	10	16	38	1264	1173	533	465	81	452	973	.244
Buffalo	3.44	141	4	12	29	1246	1169	555	476	79	426	943	.248
Indianapolis	3.55	142	2	14	48	1257	1170	541	496	105	393	974	.248
Louisville	3.58	143	2	12	40	1245	1248	567	495	119	436	916	.264
Ottawa	3.59	143	4	15	44	1233	1214	557	492	89	462	953	.259
Charlotte	3.66	141	10	9	38	1230	1108	571	500	123	549	1018	.244
Toledo	3.74	142	5	12	43	1260	1228	582	524	120	399	893	.258
Durham	3.99	142	3	8	34	1237	1268	649	548	99	421	1078	.264
Syracuse	4.09	143	2	7	38	1257	1300	664	571	144	370	1046	.265
Norfolk	4.17	141	2	14	31	1209	1284	619	560	102	390	908	.274
Columbus	4.24	142	5	5	35	1239	1293	655	583	107	430	981	.270
Pawtucket	4.29	144	3	14	37	1249	1263	653	596	111	498	914	.265
Richmond	4.32	143	2	11	30	1255	1294	654	602	96	518	950	.268

CLUB FIELDING

	PCT	PO	A	E	DP		PCT	PO	A	E	DP
Indianapolis	.982	3772	1439	95	135	Louisville	.978	3734	1537	119	151
Scranton/WB	.981	3750	1422	98	123	Norfolk	.978	3627	1494	115	145
Charlotte	.980	3691	1437	104	126	Rochester	.977	3790	1470	122	115
Ottawa	.980	3699	1511	107	141	Columbus	.976	3716	1448	129	126
Pawtucket	.980	3747	1363	106	126	Buffalo	.974	3739	1553	139	144
Richmond	.979	3766	1450	112	115	Syracuse	.974	3772	1467	138	138
Toledo	.979	3781	1579	117	146	Durham	.971	3711	1383	150	124

INDIVIDUAL BATTING LEADERS
(Minimum 446 Plate Appearances)

	AVG	G	AB	R	H	2B	3B	HR	RBI	BB	SO	SB
Phelps, Josh, Toledo	.308	126	464	60	143	26	3	24	90	38	124	6
Fields, Josh, Charlotte	.305	124	462	85	141	32	4	19	70	54	136	28
Pedroia, Dustin, Pawtucket	.305	111	423	55	129	30	3	5	50	48	27	1
Sweeney, Ryan, Charlotte	.296	118	449	64	133	25	3	13	70	35	73	7
Riggans, Shawn, Durham	.293	115	417	43	122	26	2	11	54	27	88	2
McDonald, Darnell, Durham	.292	136	538	80	157	33	1	14	57	47	115	30
Witt, Kevin, Durham	.291	128	485	82	141	29	1	36	99	52	132	0
Velandia, Jorge, Charlotte	.291	122	475	69	138	25	1	10	56	28	85	15
Calloway, Ron, Pawtucket	.288	114	406	49	117	27	3	4	49	40	77	9
Gutierrez, Jesse, Louisville	.282	119	397	46	112	27	2	10	61	49	74	0

INDIVIDUAL PITCHING LEADERS
(Minimum 115 Innings)

	W	L	ERA	G	GS	CG	SV	IP	H	R	ER	BB	SO
Mazone, Brian, Scranton/WB	13	3	2.03	20	20	0	0	128	108	40	29	36	85
Phillips, Heath, Charlotte	13	5	2.96	25	24	2	0	155	152	62	51	39	102
Michalak, Chris, Louisville	9	5	2.99	23	22	0	0	132	142	56	44	28	61
Haeger, Charlie, Charlotte	14	6	3.07	26	25	2	0	170	143	71	58	78	130
Durbin, Chad, Toledo	11	8	3.11	28	28	2	0	185	169	72	64	46	149
Guthrie, Jeremy, Buffalo	9	5	3.14	21	20	2	0	123	104	50	43	48	88
Brito, Eude, Scranton/WB	10	8	3.17	26	23	2	1	148	116	60	52	55	103
Bowles, Brian, Ottawa	10	10	3.23	30	26	1	0	156	156	66	56	53	78
Wilson, Kris, Columbus	9	6	3.40	21	21	2	0	132	120	54	50	24	103
Redding, Tim, Charlotte	12	10	3.40	29	28	5	0	188	168	77	71	56	148

ALL-STAR TEAM

C—Carlos Ruiz, Scranton/Wilkes-Barre. **1B**—Kevin Witt, Durham. **2B**—Joe Thurston, Scranton/Wilkes-Barre. **3B**—Josh Fields, Charlotte. **SS**—Jorge Velandia, Charlotte. **OF**—Jason Dubois, Buffalo; Norris Hopper, Louisville; Darnell McDonald, Durham. **DH**—Josh Phelps, Toledo. **Utility**—Dustin Pedroia, Pawtucket. **SP**—Heath Phillips, Charlotte. **RP**—Pat Neshek, Rochester.

Most Valuable Player: Kevin Witt, Durham. **Most Valuable Pitcher:** Heath Phillips, Charlotte. **Rookie of the Year:** Josh Fields, Charlotte. **Manager of the Year:** John Russell, Scranton/Wilkes-Barre.

DEPARTMENT LEADERS

BATTING

OBP	Young, Ernie, Charlotte	.405
SLG	Witt, Kevin, Durham	.577
R	Fields, Josh, Charlotte	85
H	McDonald, Darnell, Durham	157
TB	Witt, Kevin, Durham	280
XBH	Witt, Kevin, Durham	66
2B	Barker, Kevin, Syracuse	39
3B	Lydon, Wayne, Syracuse	12
HR	Witt, Kevin, Durham	36
RBI	Witt, Kevin, Durham	99
SAC	Hooper, Kevin, Toledo	15
SF	Two players tied at	10
BB	Barker, Kevin, Syracuse	80
IBB	Murphy, David, Pawtucket	8
	Witt, Kevin, Durham	8
HBP	Garko, Ryan, Buffalo	19
SO	Ludwick, Ryan, Toledo	167
SB	Upton, B.J., Durham	46
CS	Upton, B.J., Durham	17
GIDP	Gutierrez, Jesse, Louisville	23
AB/SO	Pedroia, Dustin, Pawtucket	15.67

PITCHING

G	Chiasson, Scott, Louisville	60
GS	Banks, Josh, Syracuse	29
	Munro, Pete, Rochester	29
CG	Redding, Tim, Charlotte	5
SHO	Durbin, Chad, Toledo	2
	Sowers, Jeremy, Buffalo	2
GF	Chiasson, Scott, Louisville	49
	Gardner, Lee, Toledo	49
SV	Gardner, Lee, Toledo	30
	Manon, Julio, Ottawa	30
W	Haeger, Charlie, Charlotte	14
L	Scobie, Jason, Syracuse	18
IP	Redding, Tim, Charlotte	187.2
H	Munro, Pete, Rochester	188
R	Banks, Josh, Syracuse	108
ER	Banks, Josh, Syracuse	98
HB	Tracey, Sean, Charlotte	19
BB	Randolph, Stephen, Charlotte	114
SO	Durbin, Chad, Toledo	149
SO/9 (SP)	Gorzelanny, Tom, Indianapolis	8.49
SO/9 (SP)	Bell, Heath, Norfolk	14.4
WP	Tracey, Sean, Charlotte	20
BK	Phillips, Heath, Charlotte	4

FIELDING

C	PCT	Maldonado, Carlos, Indianapolis	.996
	PO	Riggans, Shawn, Durham	694
	A	Whiteside, Eli, Ottawa	58
	E	Nieves, Wil, Columbus	13
	DP	Nieves, Wil, Columbus	10
		Sardinha, Dane, Louisville	10
	PB	Matos, Pascual, Charlotte	17
		Stewart, Chris, Charlotte	17
	CS%	Molina, Gustavo, Charlotte	53%
1B	PCT	Tracy, Andy, Ottawa	.997
	PO	Rogowski, Casey, Charlotte	1055
	A	Jones, Garrett, Rochester	124
	E	Rogowski, Casey, Charlotte	11
	DP	Rogowski, Casey, Charlotte	102
2B	PCT	Thurston, Joe, Scranton/WB	.979
	PO	Thurston, Joe, Scranton/WB	292
	A	Thurston, Joe, Scranton/WB	325
	E	Garcia, Danny, Columbus	16
	DP	Thurston, Joe, Scranton/WB	75
3B	PCT	Hessman, Mike, Toledo	.973
	PO	Hessman, Mike, Toledo	82
	A	Snyder, Earl, Louisville	224
	E	Marte, Andy, Buffalo	19
	DP	Marte, Andy, Buffalo	25
SS	PCT	Velandia, Jorge, Charlotte	.979
	PO	Santos, Sergio, Syracuse	176
	A	Santos, Sergio, Syracuse	356
	E	Upton, B.J., Durham	28
	DP	Santos, Sergio, Syracuse	87
OF	PCT	Davis, Rajai, Indianapolis	.991
	PO	McDonald, Darnell, Durham	301
	A	Ludwick, Ryan, Toledo	14
	E	Dukes, Elijah, Durham	8
		Roberson, Chris, Scranton/WB	8
	DP	Four players tied at	4

MINOR LEAGUES

BY WILL LINGO

Tucson will need to add a new shelf to its trophy case for all the hardware it brought home in 2006.

The Sidewinders brought home their first Pacific Coast League title since 1993, and then they went on to capture the overall Triple-A championship by winning the inaugural Bricktown Showdown over Toledo. The honors continued rolling in after the season, with Chip Hale winning PCL manager of the year honors, three players (Alberto Callaspo, Stephen Drew and Scott Hairston) earning spots on the PCL all-star team and the entire squad capturing Baseball America's Minor League Team of the Year award.

Tucson enjoyed a bumper crop of Diamondbacks prospects in 2006 and cruised to a 91-53 record, easily the best record in Triple-A and the best record in the minor leagues overall. The Sidewinders dispatched Salt Lake in the semifinals before meeting Round Rock for the PCL championship. The Express had the second-best record in the league and had been led by Jason Hirsh and Chris Sampson—who finished 1-2 in the league ERA race—during most of the season.

But Hirsh was gone by the time the playoffs rolled around, and Sampson had been reduced to a relief role, so the Sidewinders hit their way past Round Rock to win the title 6-3 in a three-game sweep.

The Express jumped out to a 3-1 lead in the clincher, but Kenny Perez and Callaspo led off the seventh with back-to-back singles,

advanced on a wild pitch, then scored when right fielder Jon Weber delivered a single up the middle. That was followed by back-to-back blasts by Brian Barden and Robby Hammock to give the Sidewinders a 6-3 lead, and that's the way the game ended.

Tucson used a similar formula to win the Triple-A title over the International League's Toledo MudHens 5-2 in front of 12,572 fans in Oklahoma City. Righthander Micah Owings, who went 10-0, 3.70 with the Sidewinders after a midseason promotion to Double-A, was the pitcher of the game after allowing one run in five innings and striking out six. Hairston was the MVP after going 2-for-4 with a double and an RBI.

The outstanding individual performance in the league came from Las Vegas first baseman James Loney, who batted .380 to take the overall minor league batting title. League MVP honors went to veteran Scott McClain, who hit 28 homers and drove in 107 runs for Sacramento, which again led the minors in attendance.

The league will see only one affiliation change in 2007, with the Mets taking over from the Nationals at New Orleans. The Zephyrs had a successful season in their return to New Orleans after Hurricane Katrina, becoming the first professional franchise to play a game back in the city when they took the field on Opening Day. Zephyr Field was used as a staging area for recovery efforts but was back and better than ever by the beginning of the season.

TOP 20 **PROSPECTS**

1. Stephen Drew, ss, Tucson (Diamondbacks)
2. Jered Weaver, rhp, Salt Lake (Angels)
3. Howie Kendrick, 2b, Salt Lake (Angels)
4. Chad Billingsley, rhp, Las Vegas (Dodgers)
5. Andy LaRoche, 3b, Las Vegas (Dodgers)
6. Matt Kemp, of, Las Vegas (Dodgers)
7. Chris Young, of, Tucson (Diamondbacks)
8. Adam Jones, of, Tacoma (Mariners)
9. Jason Hirsh, rhp, Round Rock (Astros)
10. Carlos Quentin, of, Tucson (Diamondbacks)
11. Felix Pie, of, Iowa (Cubs)
12. James Loney, 1b, Las Vegas (Dodgers)
13. Anthony Reyes, rhp, Memphis (Cardinals)
14. John Danks, lhp, Oklahoma (Rangers)
15. Erick Aybar, ss, Salt Lake (Angels)
16. Rich Hill, lhp, Iowa (Cubs)
17. Miguel Montero, c, Tucson (Diamondbacks)
18. Chris Iannetta, c, Colorado Springs (Rockies)
19. Edinson Volquez, rhp, Oklahoma (Rangers)
20. Joel Guzman, 3b/of, Las Vegas (Dodgers)

STANDINGS

AMERICAN CONFERENCE

Page	NORTH	W	L	PCT	GB	Manager	Attendance	Average	Last Penn.
160	Nashville Sounds (Brewers)	76	68	.528	—	Frank Kremblas	410,569	5,950	2005
78	Iowa Cubs (Cubs)	76	68	.528	—	Bobby Dickerson	546,554	8,038	None
212	Memphis Redbirds (Cardinals)	58	86	.403	18	Danny Sheaffer	692,426	9,752	2000
138	Omaha Royals (Royals)	53	91	.368	23	Mike Jirschele	319,777	4,634	None

Page	SOUTH	W	L	PCT	GB	Manager(s)	Attendance	Average	Last Penn.
130	Round Rock Express (Astros)	85	59	.590	—	Jackie Moore	677,706	9,413	2002
250	Oklahoma RedHawks (Rangers)	74	70	.514	11	Tim Ireland/Mike Boulanger	526,932	7,422	None
265	New Orleans Zephyrs (Nationals)	72	71	.503	12½	Tim Foli	361,493	5,164	2001
122	Albuquerque Isotopes (Marlins)	70	72	.493	14	Dean Treanor	581,308	8,304	None

PACIFIC CONFERENCE

Page	NORTH	W	L	PCT	GB	Manager	Attendance	Average	Last Penn.
144	Salt Lake Stingers (Angels)	81	63	.563	—	Brian Harper	451,938	6,550	1979
235	Tacoma Rainiers (Mariners)	74	70	.514	7	Dave Brundage	313,031	4,537	2001
220	Portland Beavers (Padres)	68	76	.472	13	Todd Claus	401,092	5,649	1994
109	Colorado Springs Sky Sox (Rockies)	66	77	.462	14½	Tom Runnells	265,500	3,848	1995

Page	SOUTH	W	L	PCT	GB	Manager	Attendance	Average	Last Penn.
48	Tucson Sidewinders (Diamondbacks)	91	53	.632	—	Chip Hale	271,698	4,055	2006
190	Sacramento River Cats (Athletics)	78	66	.542	13	Tony DeFrancesco	728,227	10,257	2004
152	Las Vegas 51s (Dodgers)	67	77	.465	24	Jerry Royster	365,659	5,079	1988
227	Fresno Grizzlies (Giants)	61	83	.424	30	Shane Turner	499,595	7,037	None

PLAYOFFS—Semifinals: Round Rock defeated Nashville 3-2 and Tucson defeated Salt Lake 3-1 in best-of-five series. Final: Tucson defeated Round Rock 3-0 in best-of-five series.

NOTE: Teams' individual batting and pitching statistics can be found on page indicated in lefthand column.

MINOR LEAGUES

2006 PACIFIC COAST LEAGUE STATISTICS

CLUB BATTING

	AVG	G	AB	R	H	2B	3B	HR	BB	SO	SB	OBP	SLG
Tucson	.289	144	5056	844	1461	296	36	160	540	840	72	.364	.457
Albuquerque	.288	142	4882	723	1405	283	41	118	471	1092	76	.357	.435
Las Vegas	.288	144	4978	735	1432	284	25	106	476	845	119	.352	.419
Salt Lake	.285	144	4897	798	1397	289	46	136	463	1011	142	.352	.446
Colorado Springs	.276	143	4880	696	1348	261	44	124	460	992	101	.342	.424
Tacoma	.273	144	4826	706	1316	260	33	124	440	1060	127	.339	.417
Round Rock	.271	144	4881	753	1323	274	42	170	476	1162	117	.339	.449
Sacramento	.270	144	4851	794	1311	261	19	157	612	1011	87	.357	.429
Fresno	.268	144	4937	712	1322	269	43	127	437	957	86	.332	.417
Nashville	.265	144	4786	656	1270	230	24	108	504	1050	196	.338	.391
New Orleans	.264	143	4812	643	1268	225	25	96	460	978	168	.334	.381
Portland	.263	144	4876	732	1282	252	25	175	653	1079	55	.353	.433
Iowa	.262	144	4812	609	1261	248	24	120	490	1004	81	.334	.398
Oklahoma	.261	144	4728	579	1232	226	35	96	415	901	131	.323	.384
Omaha	.261	144	4770	578	1245	225	34	108	420	789	65	.325	.390
Memphis	.243	144	4832	555	1175	222	25	122	471	1041	77	.315	.375

CLUB PITCHING

	ERA	G	CG	SHO	SV	IP	H	R	ER	HR	BB	SO	AVG
Nashville	3.62	144	8	12	35	1275	1188	594	513	114	471	1052	.248
Round Rock	3.78	144	4	12	46	1275	1226	613	536	115	485	924	.254
New Orleans	3.84	143	1	6	42	1276	1221	622	545	112	498	1114	.252
Tucson	3.88	144	6	6	36	1272	1301	627	548	90	420	975	.267
Oklahoma	3.89	144	8	12	42	1251	1227	633	541	111	506	1057	.259
Iowa	3.91	144	2	9	40	1278	1294	612	555	113	448	1066	.266
Memphis	4.29	144	5	6	26	1278	1348	684	609	142	434	941	.274
Tacoma	4.42	144	3	9	37	1243	1295	688	611	133	558	970	.271
Sacramento	4.56	144	2	10	38	1260	1349	709	639	117	472	986	.274
Albuquerque	4.58	142	4	8	31	1244	1354	730	633	128	492	975	.281
Omaha	4.58	144	2	4	28	1235	1360	734	628	137	424	843	.283
Salt Lake	4.65	144	7	10	33	1258	1357	739	650	150	427	930	.278
Las Vegas	4.69	144	3	9	38	1271	1330	776	663	139	621	1071	.272
Fresno	4.88	144	2	3	31	1274	1359	788	691	150	550	1015	.275
Portland	4.92	144	1	8	32	1272	1415	774	695	158	494	983	.283
Colorado Springs	5.15	143	2	5	36	1255	1424	790	718	138	488	910	.289

CLUB FIELDING

	PCT	PO	A	E	DP		PCT	PO	A	E	DP
Nashville	.982	3826	1550	100	128	Portland	.977	3817	1460	124	140
Round Rock	.980	3825	1519	108	147	Albuquerque	.977	3732	1565	127	157
Sacramento	.980	3781	1397	107	101	Las Vegas	.977	3813	1453	126	159
Iowa	.980	3834	1509	110	134	New Orleans	.977	3829	1446	122	119
Tacoma	.979	3730	1485	110	151	Memphis	.976	3835	1592	134	147
Tucson	.979	3815	1525	116	145	Fresno	.975	3822	1440	135	130
Colorado Springs	.979	3765	1662	119	170	Salt Lake	.974	3775	1528	144	173
Oklahoma	.977	3752	1504	125	140	Omaha	.972	3706	1576	150	166

INDIVIDUAL BATTING LEADERS
(Minimum 446 Plate Appearances)

	AVG	G	AB	R	H	2B	3B	HR	RBI	BB	SO	SB
Callaspo, Alberto, Tucson	.337	114	490	93	165	24	12	7	68	56	27	8
Rivera, Carlos, Colorado Springs	.325	120	421	54	137	25	1	9	70	18	51	3
McEwing, Joe, Round Rock	.315	112	422	64	133	21	1	10	46	23	65	16
Eylward, Mike, Salt Lake	.314	109	405	57	127	22	0	8	63	43	60	1
Rottino, Vinny, Nashville	.314	117	398	55	125	25	2	7	42	40	74	12
Allen, Chad, Omaha	.314	105	417	39	131	26	4	14	78	32	60	1
McAnulty, Paul, Portland	.310	125	478	76	148	34	5	19	79	62	79	1
Baker, Jeff, Colorado Springs	.305	128	482	71	147	30	4	20	108	46	110	7
Carter, Chris, Tucson	.301	136	509	87	153	30	3	19	97	78	69	10
Gwynn, Tony, Nashville	.300	112	447	73	134	21	5	4	42	42	84	30

INDIVIDUAL PITCHING LEADERS
(Minimum 115 Innings)

	W	L	ERA	G	GS	CG	SV	IP	H	R	ER	BB	SO
Hirsh, Jason, Round Rock	13	2	2.10	23	23	1	0	137	94	37	32	51	118
Sampson, Chris, Round Rock	12	3	2.51	27	18	2	4	126	110	48	35	14	68
Saunders, Joe, Salt Lake	10	4	2.67	21	20	1	0	135	117	44	40	38	97
Baek, Cha Seung, Tacoma	12	4	3.00	24	24	0	0	147	133	57	49	37	103
Volquez, Edinson, Oklahoma	6	6	3.21	21	21	0	0	121	86	51	43	72	130
Ryu, Jae Kuk, Iowa	8	8	3.23	24	23	1	0	139	123	54	50	51	114
Fernandez, Jared, Nashville	6	4	3.27	24	15	4	3	129	141	64	47	23	76
Hampson, Justin, Colorado Springs	8	4	3.33	31	13	0	0	122	121	57	45	39	95
Hendrickson, Ben, Nashville	9	8	3.36	23	23	1	0	139	121	60	52	46	97
Sarfate, Dennis, Nashville	10	7	3.67	34	21	0	0	125	125	63	51	78	117

ALL-STAR TEAM

C—Jeff Mathis, Salt Lake. **1B**—James Loney, Las Vegas. **2B**—Alberto Callaspo, Tucson. **3B**—Scott McClain, Sacramento. **SS**—Stephen Drew, Tucson. **OF**—Jeff Baker, Colorado Springs; Scott Hairston, Tucson; Reggie Willits, Salt Lake. **DH**—Jon Knott, Portland. **RHP**—Jason Hirsh, Round Rock. **LHP**—Rich Hill, Iowa. **RP**—Nate Field, Colorado.

Most Valuable Player: Scott McClain, Sacramento. **Pitcher of the Year:** Jason Hirsh, Round Rock. Rookie of the Year: Howie Kendrick, Salt Lake. **Manager of the Year:** Chip Hale, Tucson.

BATTING

OBP	Cust, Jack, Portland	.467
SLG	Hairston, Scott, Tucson	.591
R	Conrad, Brooks, Round Rock	.100
H	Callaspo, Alberto, Tucson	.165
TB	Conrad, Brooks, Round Rock	.284
XBH	Conrad, Brooks, Round Rock	.79
2B	Young, Delwyn, Las Vegas	.42
3B	Conrad, Brooks, Round Rock	.15
HR	Knott, Jon, Portland	.32
RBI	Knott, Jon, Portland	.113
SAC	Valdez, Wilson, Las Vegas	.14
SF	Hyzdu, Adam, Oklahoma	.10
BB	Cust, Jack, Portland	.143
IBB	Loney, James, Las Vegas	.7
HBP	Quentin, Carlos, Tucson	.31
SO	Jimerson, Charlton, Round Rock	.183
SB	Guzman, Freddy, Oklahoma	.42
CS	Aybar, Erick, Salt Lake	.18
GIDP	Knott, Jon, Portland	.22
	Wood, Jason, Albuquerque	.22
AB/SO	Callaspo, Alberto, Tucson	.18.15

PITCHING

G	Anderson, Jason, Portland	.60
GS	Houlton, D.J., Las Vegas	.29
CG	Fernandez, Jared, Nashville	.4
SHO	Four players tied at	.2
GF	Clontz, Brad, Albuquerque	.50
SV	Field, Nate, Colorado Springs	.25
W	Five players tied at	.13
L	Tankersley, Dennis, Memphis	.15
IP	Webb, John, Memphis	.176.2
H	Webb, John, Memphis	.201
R	Houlton, D.J., Las Vegas	.115
ER	Esposito, Mike, Colorado Springs	.104
HB	Fulchino, Jeff, Albuquerque	.15
BB	Sarfate, Dennis, Nashville	.78
SO	Cruceta, Francisco, Tacoma	.185
SO/9(SP)	Hill, Rich, Iowa	.12.15
SO/9(SP)	Wuertz, Michael, Iowa	.14.47
WP	Cruceta, Francisco, Tacoma	.18
BK	Wilhite, Matt, Salt Lake	.3

FIELDING

C	PCT	Quintero, Humberto, Round Rock	.993
	PO	Soto, Geovany, Iowa	.712
	A	Soto, Geovany, Iowa	.69
	E	Hoover, Paul, Albuquerque	.12
	DP	Mathis, Jeff, Salt Lake	.9
		Soto, Geovany, Iowa	.9
	PB	Three players tied at	.11
	CS%	Quiroz, Guillermo, Tacoma	.56%
1B	PCT	Broadway, Larry, New Orleans	.993
	PO	Carter, Chris, Tucson	.1042
	A	Rivera, Carlos, Colo. Springs	.83
	E	Carter, Chris, Tucson	.15
	DP	Carter, Chris, Tucson	.106
2B	PCT	Conrad, Brooks, Round Rock	.987
	PO	Nix, Jayson, Colorado Springs	.225
	A	Nix, Jayson, Colorado Springs	.369
	E	Spivey, Junior, Memphis	.13
	DP	Nix, Jayson, Colorado Springs	.88
3B	PCT	McClain, Scott, Sacramento	.977
	PO	McClain, Scott, Sacramento	.102
	A	McGehee, Casey, Iowa	.248
	E	Aviles, Mike, Omaha	.20
	DP	McGehee, Casey, Iowa	.31
SS	PCT	Ojeda, Augie, Iowa	.984
	PO	Valdez, Wilson, Las Vegas	.215
	A	Andino, Robert, Albuquerque	.361
	E	Arias, Joaquin, Oklahoma	.24
	DP	Valdez, Wilson, Las Vegas	.83
OF	PCT	Hyzdu, Adam, Oklahoma	.996
	PO	Pie, Felix, Iowa	.333
	A	Hyzdu, Adam, Oklahoma	.18
		Pie, Felix, Iowa	.18
	E	Young, Delwyn, Las Vegas	.9
	DP	Pie, Felix, Iowa	.8

MINOR LEAGUES

BY ALAN MATTHEWS

A year after a bevy of the Red Sox' top prospects lost to Akron in the Eastern League championship series, a Portland Sea Dogs team whose best prospect never played a game came away with the championship.

Portland manager Todd Claus, Baseball America's 2006 Minor League Manager of the Year, captained a blue-collar group of players to an unlikely three games to two series victory over Akron in the EL finals.

Brandon Moss

"I told the guys before the series they had no business being here," Claus told the Portland fans over the Hadlock Field public-address system after the Sea Dogs held off the Aeros in Game Five. "It is with heart and character that we're standing here right now."

Though Akron led the league in wins after compiling an 87-55 regular season record, Portland jumped on Akron's ace, righthander Adam Miller, for four runs in the first three innings in Game One and carried a 2-0 advantage back to Portland.

Akron won the next two games, forcing a decisive fifth game that Miller was expected to start before the Indians elected to shut him down for the season, opting to preserve an arm that had already logged more than 166 innings. In Game Five, Portland used a pair of four-run innings and eight strong innings from righthander Devern Hansack to sew up the series. Hansack won both of his starts, and was promoted to Boston after the series.

Portland outfielder Brandon Moss was named MVP of the post-season. In 10 playoff games, Moss was 13-for-36 with a double, five home runs, 10 RBIs, nine runs and four walks. He homered twice in Game Four against Akron, which was played on his 23rd birthday.

The Aeros, who were making their fourth postseason appearance in the past five seasons, including EL titles in 2003 and 2005, edged Altoona three games to two to take the Southern Division title. Portland's first-round series win over Trenton not only pitted a Yankees farm team against the rival Red Sox, but was also won in the 10th inning on a Moss walk-off home run in Game Four.

The blast ended Trenton's season, which saw the Thunder overcome a 1-13 start to win 80 games, keyed by the EL's most successful pitching twosome of Philip Hughes and Tyler Clippard.

Hughes was the league's top prospect and one of a handful of potential front-of-the-rotation starters to appear in the EL in 2006. He led the circuit in ERA (2.25), finished fourth in strikeouts (138) and helped the Thunder to the league's best team ERA (3.20). Clippard also ranked among the league's elite arms after winning 12 games and posting 175 strikeouts, a league-high.

New Britain righthander Matt Garza made just 10 starts in Double-A on his way to the big leagues, but made quite an impact nonetheless, racking up 68 strikeouts and 14 walks in 57 innings. Binghamton's Mike Pelfrey and Bowie lefty Adam Loewen also pitched briefly in the EL before climbing to the majors later in the summer.

The regular season ended on a sad note in Reading when baseball legend "Broadway" Charlie Wagner passed away. The 93-year-old former Red Sox great, a fixture at Reading games for decades, died while sitting in his car in the parking lot outside Reading's FirstEnergy Stadium after attending a game.

TOP 20 PROSPECTS

1. Philip Hughes, rhp, Trenton (Yankees)
2. Matt Garza, rhp, New Britain (Twins)
3. Mike Pelfrey, rhp, Binghamton (Mets)
4. Adam Miller, rhp, Akron (Indians)
5. Adam Loewen, lhp, Bowie (Orioles)
6. Adam Lind, of, New Hampshire (Blue Jays)
7. Jacoby Ellsbury, of, Portland (Red Sox)
8. Carlos Gomez, of, Binghamton (Mets)
9. Humberto Sanchez, rhp, Erie (Tigers)
10. Tyler Clippard, rhp, Trenton (Yankees)
11. Jonathan Sanchez, lhp, Connecticut (Giants)
12. Trevor Crowe, of, Akron (Indians)
13. Kevin Kouzmanoff, 3b, Akron (Indians)
14. Kory Casto, 3b/of, Harrisburg (Nationals)
15. Alexi Casilla, ss, New Britain (Twins)
16. Scott Mathieson, rhp, Reading (Phillies)
17. Jair Jurrjens, rhp, Erie (Tigers)
18. Gio Gonzalez, lhp, Reading (Phillies)
19. Radhames Liz, rhp, Bowie (Orioles)
20. Garrett Olson, lhp, Bowie (Orioles)

STANDINGS

Page	NORTH	W	L	PCT	GB	Manager	Attendance	Average	Last Penn.
184	Trenton Thunder (Yankees)	80	62	.563	—	Bill Masse	413,068	5,986	None
71	Portland Sea Dogs (Red Sox)	72	67	.518	6½	Todd Claus	400,534	6,358	2006
175	Binghamton Mets (Mets)	70	70	.500	9	Juan Samuel	215,336	3,214	1994
258	New Hampshire Fisher Cats (Blue Jays)	68	73	.482	11½	Doug Davis	300,049	4,616	2004
229	Connecticut Defenders (Giants)	64	77	.454	15½	Dave Machemer	170,807	2,755	2002
167	New Britain Rock Cats (Twins)	64	78	.451	16	Riccardo Ingram	328,406	5,052	2001

Page	SOUTH	W	L	PCT	GB	Manager	Attendance	Average	Last Penn.
102	Akron Aeros (Indians)	87	55	.613	—	Tim Bogar	412,995	6,354	2005
206	Altoona Curve (Pirates)	75	64	.540	10½	Tim Leiper	365,407	5,536	None
199	Reading Phillies (Phillies)	71	69	.507	15	P.J. Forbes	460,216	6,670	2001
63	Bowie Baysox (Orioles)	67	74	.475	19½	Don Werner	285,277	4,389	None
266	Harrisburg Senators (Nationals)	67	75	.472	20	John Stearns	253,937	3,790	1999
116	Erie SeaWolves (Tigers)	60	81	.426	26½	Duffy Dyer	206,875	3,088	None

PLAYOFFS—Semifinals: Portland defeated Trenton 3-1 and Akron defeated Altoona 3-2 in best-of-five series. **Finals:** Portland defeated Akron 3-2 in best-of-five series.

NOTE: Teams' individual batting and pitching statistics can be found on page indicated in lefthand column.

2006 EASTERN LEAGUE STATISTICS

CLUB BATTING

	AVG	G	AB	R	H	2B	3B	HR	BB	SO	SB	OBP	SLG
Akron	.271	142	4754	679	1288	253	27	114	459	985	176	.340	.407
Altoona	.262	139	4628	607	1212	213	50	92	439	942	103	.330	.389
Reading	.260	140	4680	613	1216	218	35	88	440	848	81	.328	.378
New Britain	.257	142	4598	581	1180	221	35	87	432	934	134	.327	.377
Trenton	.257	142	4790	659	1229	253	32	121	475	989	117	.330	.399
Portland	.256	139	4598	654	1175	289	20	90	456	888	86	.330	.386
Bowie	.255	141	4637	589	1181	219	24	100	411	1002	100	.323	.377
Binghamton	.247	140	4612	558	1138	224	23	102	427	1174	92	.320	.372
Harrisburg	.246	142	4614	563	1137	188	24	120	469	1036	113	.320	.376
New Hampshire	.241	141	4592	593	1108	251	11	127	461	1100	56	.317	.384
Erie	.236	141	4612	573	1087	216	25	128	438	1192	102	.308	.377
Connecticut	.232	141	4582	460	1064	208	32	77	385	973	96	.298	.342

CLUB PITCHING

	ERA	G	CG	SHO	SV	IP	H	R	ER	HR	BB	SO	AVG
Trenton	3.20	142	3	19	38	1253	1044	514	445	95	451	1107	.226
Altoona	3.56	139	2	11	49	1210	1104	561	479	98	421	970	.243
Binghamton	3.61	140	6	12	38	1227	1155	561	492	95	404	977	.249
Connecticut	3.70	141	7	10	41	1226	1183	587	504	70	365	947	.254
Akron	3.74	142	4	17	38	1250	1162	580	519	101	466	1080	.247
Bowie	3.81	141	3	14	32	1244	1156	587	518	109	488	1080	.251
Portland	3.83	139	2	16	28	1196	1127	592	509	126	460	978	.249
Reading	3.86	140	6	9	42	1237	1154	595	530	128	414	1023	.247
New Hampshire	3.91	141	5	14	28	1221	1210	598	530	95	385	972	.259
New Britain	3.92	142	9	13	29	1215	1214	639	530	93	448	982	.260
Erie	4.12	141	9	11	33	1215	1256	630	557	122	458	981	.269
Harrisburg	4.44	142	4	8	48	1231	1250	685	607	114	532	966	.264

CLUB FIELDING

	PCT	PO	A	E	DP		PCT	PO	A	E	DP
New Hampshire	.978	3664	1499	117	120	Reading	.975	3710	1367	130	119
Bowie	.977	3671	1456	121	138	Binghamton	.974	3682	1482	139	125
Trenton	.977	3758	1364	119	113	Harrisburg	.974	3693	1319	136	135
Erie	.976	3646	1501	129	155	Altoona	.973	3629	1457	139	116
Akron	.976	3749	1505	127	113	New Britain	.972	3646	1422	148	133
Connecticut	.976	3679	1463	126	119	Portland	.971	3587	1322	149	119

INDIVIDUAL BATTING LEADERS
(Minimum 440 Plate Appearances)

	AVG	G	AB	R	H	2B	3B	HR	RBI	BB	SO	SB
Abreu, Michel, Binghamton	.332	111	398	62	132	26	1	17	70	45	87	0
Roneberg, Brett, Altoona	.303	109	400	63	121	19	1	10	74	51	58	9
Oeltjen, Trent, New Britain	.299	113	401	61	120	16	10	3	44	36	58	23
Padilla, Jorge, Binghamton	.295	129	482	66	142	26	1	10	54	42	87	8
Keylor, Cory, Bowie	.294	124	446	58	131	20	2	10	68	48	92	6
Buttler, Vic, Altoona	.292	109	411	52	120	20	14	5	51	33	53	21
Ruiz, Randy, Trenton	.286	119	468	72	134	35	1	26	87	41	132	2
Span, Denard, New Britain	.285	134	536	80	153	16	6	2	45	40	78	24
Moss, Brandon, Portland	.285	133	508	76	145	36	3	12	83	56	108	8
Deeds, Doug, New Britain	.282	132	440	71	124	35	3	14	72	70	107	4

INDIVIDUAL PITCHING LEADERS
(Minimum 114 Innings)

	W	L	ERA	G	GS	CG	SV	IP	H	R	ER	BB	SO
Hughes, Philip, Trenton	10	3	2.25	21	21	0	0	116	73	30	29	32	138
Miller, Adam, Akron	15	6	2.75	26	24	1	0	154	129	56	47	43	157
Perez, Beltran, Harrisburg	8	6	3.11	31	16	1	1	122	127	53	42	40	107
Collazo, Willie, Binghamton	7	6	3.11	18	18	1	0	119	104	44	41	16	79
Jacobsen, Landon, Altoona	14	9	3.21	26	25	1	0	154	144	64	55	55	80
Hansack, Devern, Portland	8	7	3.26	31	18	0	1	132	122	55	48	36	124
Clippard, Tyler, Trenton	12	10	3.35	28	28	1	0	166	118	72	62	55	175
Begg, Chris, Connecticut	13	10	3.40	26	26	3	0	175	159	78	66	31	97
Finch, Brian, Bowie	6	12	3.65	27	26	1	0	146	146	83	59	69	83
Vasquez, Virgil, Erie	7	12	3.73	27	27	3	0	174	174	79	72	50	129

ALL-STAR TEAM

ALL-STAR TEAM: C—Curtis Thigpen, New Hampshire. **1B**—Michel Abreu, Binghamton. **2B**—Eider Torres, Akron. **3B**—Kevin Kouzmanoff, Akron. **SS**—Manuel Mayorson, New Hampshire. **OF**—Vic Buttler, Altoona; Kory Casto, Harrisburg; Adam Lind, New Hampshire. **DH**—Randy Ruiz, Trenton. **Utility**—Melvin Dorta, Harrisburg. **RHP**—Adam Miller, Akron. **LHP**—Shane Youman, Altoona. **RP**—Henry Owens, Binghamton.

Most Valuable Player: Adam Lind, New Hampshire. **Pitcher of the Year:** Adam Miller, Akron. **Rookie of the Year:** Kory Casto, Harrisburg. **Manager of the Year:** Tim Bogar, Akron.

BATTING

OBP	Abreu, Michel, Binghamton	.404
SLG	Ruiz, Randy, Trenton	.532
R	Snyder, Brad, Akron	.86
H	Span, Denard, New Britain	153
TB	Ruiz, Randy, Trenton	249
XBH	Ruiz, Randy, Trenton	62
2B	Moss, Brandon, Portland	36
3B	Buttler, Vic, Altoona	14
HR	Cannon, Chip, New Hampshire	27
RBI	Ruiz, Randy, Trenton	87
SAC	Molina, Felix, New Britain	16
SF	Two players tied at	9
BB	Airoso, Kurt, Erie	81
	Casto, Kory, Harrisburg	81
IBB	Abreu, Michel, Binghamton	9
HBP	Bacani, David, Portland	20
	Gomez, Carlos, Binghamton	20
SO	Ragsdale, Corey, Binghamton	182
SB	Christian, Justin, Trenton	68
CS	Blue, Vincent, Erie	14
GIDP	Mayorson, Manuel, New Hampshire	20
AB/SO	Dorta, Melvin, Harrisburg	11.88

PITCHING

G	Warden, Jim Ed, Akron	55
GS	Clippard, Tyler, Trenton	28
	MacDonald, Michael, New Hampshire	28
CG	Four players tied at	3
SHO	Devaney, Michael, Binghamton	2
	DuBose, Eric, Bowie	2
GF	Knight, Brandon, Altoona	41
SV	Knight, Brandon, Altoona	27
W	Miller, Adam, Akron	15
L	Three players tied at	14
IP	Begg, Chris, Connecticut	175
H	Simonitsch, Errol, New Britain	186
R	Bumstead, Nathan, Erie	102
ER	Bumstead, Nathan, Erie	86
HB	Vasquez, Virgil, Erie	14
BB	Gonzalez, Gio, Reading	81
SO	Clippard, Tyler, Trenton	175
SO/9 (SP)	Hughes, Philip, Trenton	10.71
SO/9 (SP)	Owens, Henry, Binghamton	16.65
WP	Echols, Justin, Harrisburg	20
BK	Smith, Chris, Portland	3

FIELDING

C	PCT	Santos, Omir, Trenton	.996
	PO	Santos, Omir, Trenton	.755
	A	Brown, Dustin, Portland	68
	E	Manriquez, Salomon, Harrisburg	14
	DP	Hubele, Ryan, Bowie	11
	PB	Manriquez, Salomon, Harrisburg	17
	CS%	Gradoville, Tim, Reading	53%
1B	PCT	Pond, Simon, Altoona	.995
	PO	Cannon, Chip, New Hampshire	999
	A	Pond, Simon, Altoona	87
	E	Cannon, Chip, New Hampshire	16
		Jimenez, Luis Antonio, Portland	16
	DP	Hunt, Kelly, Erie	107
2B	PCT	McMains, Derin, Connecticut	.984
	PO	Lopez, Gabe, Trenton	248
	A	Batista, Wilson, Binghamton	334
	E	Batista, Wilson, Binghamton	20
	DP	Molina, Felix, New Britain	71
3B	PCT	Buscher, Brian, Connecticut	.958
	PO	Buscher, Brian, Connecticut	85
	A	Buscher, Brian, Connecticut	254
	E	Kirkland, Kody, Erie	24
	DP	Casto, Kory, Harrisburg	21
SS	PCT	Mayorson, Manuel, New Hamp.	.972
	PO	Ragsdale, Corey, Binghamton	221
	A	Wald, Jake, Connecticut	395
	E	Borowiak, Zach, Portland	25
	DP	Ragsdale, Corey, Binghamton	81
OF	PCT	Christian, Justin, Trenton	.993
	PO	Span, Denard, New Britain	306
	A	Goleski, Ryan, Akron	12
	E	Snyder, Brad, Akron	8
	DP	Span, Denard, New Britain	5

MINOR LEAGUES

SOUTHERN LEAGUE
DOUBLE-A

BY CHRIS KLINE

The way the Chattanooga Lookouts performed over the course of the 2006 season, it was easy to pick them as the favorites to win the Southern League crown for the first time since 1988.

After finishing the 2005 season with the worst record in the Southern League and in the Reds organization, the Lookouts rebounded to win the first-half division title and finished with an 81-59 record, second in the league behind Jacksonville.

But even with the bat of league MVP Joey Votto, who led the league in most offensive categories, and the late addition of righthander Homer Bailey—one of the top pitching prospects in the minors—Chattanooga lost in the first round to Huntsville.

The Stars boasted a big power bat and righthander of their own, as third baseman Ryan Braun more than doubled his home run total from the high Class A Florida State League and Yovani Gallardo finished 5-2, 1.63 in 77 innings during the second half.

But even Huntsville couldn't touch the Montgomery rotation during the league finals, as the Biscuits toppled the Stars 3-1 to win their first title since the club's inception in 2004.

Led by starters Andrew Sonnanstine (15-8, 2.67), Jeff Niemann (5-5, 2.68) and Mitch Talbot (4-3, 1.90), as well as an offensive infusion from shortstop Reid Brignac and 2006 first-rounder Evan Longoria ran away with the title, losing just once in the postseason.

Talbot, who came over from the Astros to the Devil Rays in a dead-line deal involving Aubrey Huff, had arguably the best playoff performances in the minors, as he tossed back-to-back shutouts in his two starts. The first came in the clincher for the Southern Division title over Jacksonville, and the second in Game Three of the finals against Huntsville.

"I told my teammates before the game, 'Give me two runs and I'll guarantee you a win,' " Talbot said after the Jacksonville start. He didn't need to say it a second time, blanking the Stars and finishing the postseason with a 24-2 strikeout-walk ratio in 18 innings.

"What he was able to do . . . it's very rare," Montgomery manager Charlie Montoyo said. "He was our blood and guts out there. He fed life into every other part of our club with those outings. It was unreal to watch."

Longoria, the third overall pick out of Long Beach State, batted .345 and hit three homers in the playoffs. Outfielder/first baseman Michael Coleman hit four home runs while batting .364. And Jason Pridie was the club's biggest contributor in the postseason, hitting .423 with seven runs.

"We had a little bit of everything clicking," Montoyo said. "But the one thing we really had was leadership on this team. Pridie was one of those guys, Sonnanstine was one of those guys. When we needed someone to step up, they hit that next level."

Several affiliations in the SL changed after the 2006 season, as the Padres left Mobile in favor of the Texas League's San Antonio Missions. The Diamondbacks moved from Tennessee to take the Mobile vacancy, while the Cubs moved from West Tenn to Tennessee. The Mariners moved from the TL to the SL, signing a two-year deal with West Tenn.

STANDINGS: SPLIT SEASON

FIRST HALF					SECOND HALF				
NORTH	**W**	**L**	**PCT**	**GB**	**NORTH**	**W**	**L**	**PCT**	**GB**
Chattanooga	44	26	.629	—	Huntsville	43	26	.623	—
West Tenn	43	27	.614	1	Tennessee	38	31	.551	5
Carolina	32	38	.457	12	Chattanooga	37	33	.529	6½
Tennessee	32	38	.457	12	West Tenn	32	38	.457	11½
Huntsville	24	45	.348	19½	Carolina	29	41	.414	14½
SOUTH	**W**	**L**	**PCT**	**GB**	**SOUTH**	**W**	**L**	**PCT**	**GB**
Jacksonville	48	22	.686	—	Montgomery	41	29	.586	—
Montgomery	36	33	.522	11½	Jacksonville	38	32	.543	3
Mississippi	31	38	.449	16½	Mobile	35	34	.507	5½
Birmingham	31	39	.443	17	Birmingham	28	42	.400	13
Mobile	27	42	.391	20½	Mississippi	27	42	.391	13½

PLAYOFFS—Semifinals: Huntsville defeated Chattanooga 3-0 and Montgomery defeated Jacksonville 3-0 in best-of-five series. **Final:** Montgomery defeated Huntsville 3-1 in best-of-five series.

TOP 20 PROSPECTS

1. Homer Bailey, rhp, Chattanooga (Reds)
2. Yovani Gallardo, rhp, Huntsville (Brewers)
3. Scott Elbert, lhp, Jacksonville (Dodgers)
4. Matt Kemp, of, Jacksonville (Dodgers)
5. Andy LaRoche, 3b, Jacksonville (Dodgers)
6. Ryan Braun, 3b, Huntsville (Brewers)
7. Joey Votto, 1b, Chattanooga (Reds)
8. Jeff Niemann, rhp, Montgomery (Devil Rays)
9. Anibal Sanchez, rhp, Carolina (Marlins)
10. Jarrod Saltalamacchia, c, Mississippi (Braves)
11. Miguel Montero, c, Tennessee (Diamondbacks)
12. Sean Gallagher, rhp, West Tenn (Cubs)
13. Tyler Lumsden, lhp, Birmingham (White Sox)
14. George Kottaras, c, Mobile (Padres)
15. Alberto Gonzalez, ss, Tennessee (Diamondbacks)
16. Mitch Talbot, rhp, Montgomery (Devil Rays)
17. Eric Patterson, 2b, West Tenn (Cubs)
18. Juan Salas, rhp, Montgomery (Devil Rays)
19. Andy Sonnanstine, rhp, Montgomery (Devil Rays)
20. Lance Broadway, rhp, Birmingham (White Sox)

STANDINGS: OVERALL

Page		W	L	PCT	GB	Manager	Attendance	Average	Last Penn.
153	Jacksonville Suns (Dodgers)	86	54	.614	—	John Shoemaker	404,992	5,869	2005
94	Chattanooga Lookouts (Reds)	81	59	.579	5	Jayhawk Owens	231,421	3,354	1988
244	Montgomery Biscuits (Devil Rays)	77	62	.554	8½	Charlie Montoyo	313,795	4,615	2006
79	West Tenn Diamond Jaxx (Cubs)	75	65	.536	11	Pat Listach	95,486	1,404	2000
49	Tennessee Smokies (Diamondbacks)	70	69	.504	15½	Bill Plummer	255,906	3,763	2004
161	Huntsville Stars (Brewers)	67	71	.486	18	Don Money	158,775	2,481	2001
221	Mobile BayBears (Padres)	62	76	.449	23	Gary Jones	207,597	3,009	2004
124	Carolina Mudcats (Marlins)	61	79	.436	25	Luis Dorante	246,569	3,680	2003
87	Birmingham Barons (White Sox)	59	81	.421	27	Chris Cron	282,304	4,033	2002
56	Mississippi Braves (Braves)	58	80	.420	27	Jeff Blauser	248,955	3,716	1997

NOTE: Teams' individual batting and pitching statistics can be found on page indicated in lefthand column.

2006 SOUTHERN LEAGUE STATISTICS

CLUB BATTING

	AVG	G	AB	R	H	2B	3B	HR	BB	SO	SB	OBP	SLG
Chattanooga	.263	140	4676	597	1228	262	31	95	435	1083	109	.328	.393
Tennessee	.255	139	4595	604	1173	221	17	127	422	928	44	.324	.394
Jacksonville	.252	140	4703	646	1187	241	18	98	565	1008	78	.338	.374
West Tenn	.251	140	4634	521	1162	238	34	72	436	1031	162	.319	.363
Mississippi	.247	140	4616	492	1140	208	28	65	378	1009	73	.308	.346
Huntsville	.247	138	4527	578	1119	205	23	75	512	1008	115	.327	.352
Carolina	.246	140	4513	503	1109	246	19	78	454	1079	106	.322	.361
Montgomery	.246	139	4558	549	1120	201	39	106	438	1134	131	.317	.377
Birmingham	.245	140	4617	501	1132	208	28	82	434	961	105	.314	.356
Mobile	.240	138	4502	529	1080	236	20	88	523	1071	45	.323	.360

CLUB PITCHING

	ERA	G	CG	SHO	SV	IP	H	R	ER	HR	BB	SO	AVG
West Tenn	2.84	140	4	13	43	1249	1123	459	394	70	443	1086	.242
Jacksonville	2.98	140	5	16	49	1256	1038	486	416	95	469	1135	.227
Montgomery	3.21	139	4	19	44	1220	1090	512	435	81	425	969	.239
Huntsville	3.30	138	3	11	32	1204	1135	537	442	86	391	1017	.251
Chattanooga	3.37	140	1	12	47	1235	1133	553	463	78	528	1090	.246
Mobile	3.58	138	7	11	32	1201	1134	578	478	93	435	1032	.249
Tennessee	3.59	139	6	11	35	1215	1191	548	484	95	397	1013	.260
Carolina	3.74	140	5	14	33	1210	1169	593	503	94	502	1036	.255
Mississippi	3.87	138	2	10	36	1217	1177	604	524	108	472	1037	.256
Birmingham	4.10	140	2	9	37	1238	1260	650	564	86	535	897	.267

CLUB FIELDING

	PCT	PO	A	E	DP		PCT	PO	A	E	DP
West Tenn	.980	3746	1483	109	125	Birmingham	.974	3714	1547	140	137
Tennessee	.978	3645	1511	114	123	Montgomery	.972	3662	1418	148	144
Huntsville	.978	3613	1372	112	121	Mississippi	.972	3652	1309	145	123
Jacksonville	.978	3768	1461	116	137	Chattanooga	.972	3705	1476	147	118
Carolina	.975	3629	1390	131	101	Mobile	.969	3603	1491	162	105

INDIVIDUAL BATTING LEADERS
(Minimum 434 Plate Appearances)

	AVG	G	AB	R	H	2B	3B	HR	RBI	BB	SO	SB
Votto, Joey, Chattanooga	.319	136	508	85	162	46	2	22	77	78	109	24
D'Antona, James, Tennessee	.310	126	461	72	143	29	0	17	67	54	88	2
Walker, Christopher, West Tenn	.292	131	513	70	150	22	11	2	35	40	102	50
Richar, Danny, Tennessee	.292	130	480	79	140	25	5	8	42	52	77	15
Anderson, Drew, Huntsville	.291	108	402	60	117	24	4	6	43	39	80	17
Gonzalez, Alberto, Tennessee	.290	129	434	67	126	20	3	6	50	37	42	5
Abreu, Tony, Jacksonville	.287	118	457	66	131	24	3	6	55	33	69	8
Varner, Noochie, Chattanooga	.285	133	460	63	131	33	2	10	73	33	90	2
Johnson, Elliot, Montgomery	.281	122	494	69	139	21	10	15	50	39	122	20
Ruggiano, Justin, Jacksonville-Montgomery	.280	120	400	76	112	32	6	13	72	65	103	14

INDIVIDUAL PITCHING LEADERS
(Minimum 112 Innings)

	W	L	ERA	G	GS	CG	SV	IP	H	R	ER	BB	SO
Lundberg, Spike, Jacksonville	15	2	2.27	24	24	1	0	151	124	42	38	42	110
Jackson, Steven, Tennessee	8	11	2.65	24	24	1	0	150	131	52	44	45	125
Sonnanstine, Andrew, Montgomery	15	8	2.67	28	28	4	0	186	151	63	55	34	153
Lumsden, Tyler, Birmingham	9	4	2.69	20	20	0	0	124	114	47	37	40	72
Broadway, Lance, Birmingham	8	8	2.74	25	25	2	0	154	160	59	47	40	111
Nall, T.J., Jacksonville	10	7	2.82	29	19	2	2	141	116	51	44	30	155
Thurman, Corey, Huntsville	5	9	2.96	24	24	0	0	140	129	56	46	42	124
Peguero, Tony, Montgomery	10	12	2.97	31	21	0	1	152	132	66	50	39	93
Magrane, Jim, Montgomery	11	8	2.98	21	21	0	0	130	110	46	43	43	90
Shaver, Chris, West Tenn	7	10	2.99	26	26	1	0	150	146	62	50	56	120

ALL-STAR TEAM

C—Miguel Montero, Tennessee. **1B**—Joey Votto, Chattanooga. **2B**—Danny Richar, Tennessee. **3B**—Scott Moore, West Tenn. **SS**—Chin-Lung Hu, Jacksonville. **OF**—Jery Gil, Tennessee, Ricardo Nanita, Birmingham, Christopher Walker, West Tenn. **DH**—Craig Brazell, Jacksonville. **Utility**—Jamie D'Antona, Tennessee. **RHP**—Andy Sonnanstine, Montgomery. **LHP**—Tyler Lumsden, Birmingham. **RP**—David Shafer, Chattanooga.

Most Valuable Player: Joey Votto, Chattanooga. **Most Outstanding Pitcher:** Spike Lundberg, Jacksonville. **Manager of the Year:** John Shoemaker, Jacksonville.

BATTING

OBP	Votto, Joey, Chattanooga	.408
SLG	Votto, Joey, Chattanooga	.547
R	Votto, Joey, Chattanooga	.85
H	Votto, Joey, Chattanooga	.162
TB	Votto, Joey, Chattanooga	.278
XBH	Votto, Joey, Chattanooga	.70
2B	Votto, Joey, Chattanooga	.46
3B	Walker, Christopher, West Tenn	.11
HR	Gil, Jerry, Tennessee	.26
RBI	Brazell, Craig, Jacksonville	.91
SAC	Crabbe, Callix, Huntsville	.16
SF	Varner, Noochie, Chattanooga	.11
BB	Votto, Joey, Chattanooga	.78
IBB	Moore, Scott, West Tenn	.7
HBP	Murillo, Agustin, Tennessee	.12
SO	Owens, Jeremy, Montgomery	.142
SB	Walker, Christopher, West Tenn	.50
CS	Walker, Christopher, West Tenn	.23
GIDP	Escobar, Yunel, Mississippi	.20
AB/SO	Getz, Christopher, Birmingham	.10.81

PITCHING

G	Wassermann, Ehren, Birmingham	.61
GS	Four players tied at	.28
CG	Ohlendorf, Ross, Tennessee	.4
	Sonnanstine, Andrew, Montgomery	.4
SHO	Sonnanstine, Andrew, Montgomery	.4
GF	Wassermann, Ehren, Birmingham	.54
SV	Thayer, Dale, Mobile	.27
W	Lundberg, Spike, Jacksonville	.15
	Sonnanstine, Andrew, Montgomery	.15
L	Waters, Chris, Mississippi	.14
IP	Sonnanstine, Andrew, Montgomery	186
H	Ohlendorf, Ross, Tennessee	.180
R	Waters, Chris, Mississippi	.90
ER	Waters, Chris, Mississippi	.83
HB	Bostick II, Adam, Carolina	.10
	Broadway, Lance, Birmingham	.10
BB	Malone, Corwin, Birmingham	.94
SO	Nall, T.J., Jacksonville	.155
SO/9 (SP)	Nall, T.J., Jacksonville	.9.62
SO/9 (SP)	Alexander, Mark, Jacksonville	.13.79
WP	Ohlendorf, Ross, Tennessee	.15
BK	Harrison, Matt, Mississippi	.5

FIELDING

C	PCT	Montero, Miguel, Tennessee	.997
	PO	Perez, Miguel, Chattanooga	.864
	A	Molina, Gustavo, Birmingham	.78
	E	Perez, Miguel, Chattanooga	.14
	DP	Perez, Miguel, Chattanooga	.14
	PB	Ellis, A.J., Jacksonville	.14
		Fox, Jacob, West Tenn	.14
	CS%	Gutierrez, Gabriel, Jacksonville	.69%
1B	PCT	Bear, Ryan, Carolina	.992
	PO	Votto, Joey, Chattanooga	1068
	A	Votto, Joey, Chattanooga	.127
	E	Votto, Joey, Chattanooga	.14
	DP	Votto, Joey, Chattanooga	.99
2B	PCT	Richar, Danny, Tennessee	.986
	PO	Crabbe, Callix, Huntsville	.237
		Patterson, Eric, West Tenn	.237
	A	Crabbe, Callix, Huntsville	.352
	E	Abreu, Tony, Jacksonville	.16
	DP	Johnson, Elliot, Montgomery	.89
3B	PCT	Mitchell, Lee, Carolina	.972
	PO	Schnurstein, Micah, Birm.	.97
	A	Schnurstein, Micah, Birm.	.268
	E	Schnurstein, Micah, Birm.	.28
	DP	Schnurstein, Micah, Birm.	.20
SS	PCT	Hu, Chin Lung, Jacksonville	.981
	PO	Gonzalez, Alberto, Tennessee	.212
	A	Gonzalez, Alberto, Tennessee	.391
	E	Ciriaco, Juan, Mobile	.25
	DP	Gonzalez, Alberto, Tennessee	.82
OF	PCT	Acuna, Ron, Huntsville	1.000
	PO	Pridie, Jason, Montgomery	.286
	A	Three players tied at	.19
	E	Campusano, Jose, Carolina	.9
	DP	Owens, Jeremy, Montgomery	.9

MINOR LEAGUES

BY WILL LINGO

The Double-A Texas League had plenty of talent this season, most of it concentrated among four teams.

While Tulsa (six players among the league's top 20 prospects), Corpus Christi (four), Midland and Wichita (three each) had a host of interesting players on their rosters, the prospects were sparse at other league stops. The talent also showed on the field, as those four teams made the playoffs, with Corpus Christi beating Wichita in the championship series.

Tulsa had one of the most loaded teams in the minors in the first half, going 41-29. But key players such as righthander Ubaldo Jimenez and catcher Chris Iannetta were promoted by midseason, and the Drillers played .500 ball in the second half. They then bowed to Wichita in the first round of the playoffs.

Corpus Christi also lost a lot of talent to callups and trades as the season went on, but a complement of veterans such as Walter Young and midseason promotions like Troy Patton pushed the Hooks to the title.

Ben Zobrist was the team's offensive sparkplug and finished second in the TL batting race at .327, but he was part of the trade that brought Aubrey Huff to the Astros at midseason along with righthander Mitch Talbot, costing the Hooks one of their best hitters and best pitchers. Both players ended up making significant contributions in the Devil Rays organization in the second half of the season.

Corpus Christi also lost two key performers who were promoted to Triple-A in the second half. Matt Albers finished as the league's ERA leader and pitcher of the year with a record of 10-2, 2.17, and veteran J.R. House rejuvenated his career by batting .325 with 10 home runs.

But by the end of the year it was a different cast that led the Hooks to the title, and for juggling all the talent but still winning, Dave Clark was named the league's manager of the year. They won in a memorable final game, edging Wichita 8-7 in 14 innings to win Game Four and the title in the team's second season in Corpus Christi.

Shortstop Wade Robinson singled in outfielder Jorge Cortes in

the 14th for the win, but that was only the final act in an amazing game. The Wranglers took a 6-5 lead into the eighth, but Corpus Christi tied the game thanks to a pair of walks and a pair of hit batters.

Wichita seemed to be in position to send the series to a deciding Game Five in the ninth, as Minor League Player of the Year Alex Gordon came up with no outs and runners at second and third. But Gordon lined to first baseman Josh Bonifay, who stepped on first, then threw to second to complete a triple play.

Wichita's triple threat of first-round picks in Gordon, Billy Butler and Chris Lubanski not only helped the Wranglers to the second-best record in the league but also gave hope to Royals fans that a brighter future could be on the way. Gordon was also the league's player of the year.

The future is not so bright in Wichita, however, as the club announced it will be moving to a new ballpark in Springdale, Ark., after the 2007 season—the Wranglers' 20-year anniversary as a member of the Texas League.

For the most part, there was stability on the affiliation front after the 2006 season, with only San Antonio looking for a new partner after becoming disenchanted with the Mariners. The Missions were an attractive option as the westernmost Double-A affiliate on the market, and they ended up signing a two-year agreement with the Padres.

STANDINGS: SPLIT SEASON

FIRST HALF					SECOND HALF				
EAST	**W**	**L**	**PCT**	**GB**	**EAST**	**W**	**L**	**PCT**	**GB**
Tulsa	41	29	.586	—	Wichita	43	26	.623	—
Springfield	39	29	.574	1	Tulsa	34	35	.493	9
Wichita	34	36	.486	7	Arkansas	27	42	.391	16
Arkansas	24	45	.348	16½	Springfield	27	43	.386	16½
WEST	**W**	**L**	**PCT**	**GB**	**WEST**	**W**	**L**	**PCT**	**GB**
Corpus Christi	41	28	.594	—	Midland	42	27	.609	—
Midland	36	34	.514	5½	Frisco	37	33	.529	5½
Frisco	35	35	.500	6½	Corpus Christi	35	35	.500	7½
San Antonio	27	41	.397	13½	San Antonio	33	37	.471	9½

PLAYOFFS—Semifinals: Wichita defeated Tulsa 3-1 and Corpus Christi defeated Midland 3-0 in best-of-five series. **Final:** Corpus Christi defeated Midland 3-1 in best-of-five series.

TOP 20 PROSPECTS

1. Alex Gordon, 3b, Wichita (Royals)
2. Brandon Wood, ss, Arkansas (Angels)
3. Troy Tulowitzki, ss, Tulsa (Rockies)
4. Billy Butler, of, Wichita (Royals)
5. Travis Buck, of, Midland (Athletics)
6. Ubaldo Jimenez, rhp, Tulsa (Rockies)
7. John Danks, lhp, Frisco (Rangers)
8. Hunter Pence, of, Corpus Christi (Astros)
9. Juan Gutierrez, rhp, Corpus Christi (Astros)
10. Ian Stewart, 3b, Tulsa (Rockies)
11. Chris Iannetta, c, Tulsa (Rockies)
12. Mitch Talbot, rhp, Corpus Christi (Astros)
13. Joe Koshansky, 1b, Tulsa (Rockies)
14. Kurt Suzuki, c, Midland (Athletics)
15. Matt Albers, rhp, Corpus Christi (Astros)
16. Chris Lubanski, of, Wichita (Royals)
17. Juan Morillo, rhp, Tulsa (Rockies)
18. Marcus McBeth, rhp, Midland (Athletics)
19. Terry Evans, of, Springfield/Arkansas (Cardinals/Angels)
20. Wladimir Balentien, of, San Antonio (Mariners)

STANDINGS: OVERALL

Page		W	L	PCT	GB	Manager	Attendance	Average	Last Penn.
192	Midland RockHounds (Athletics)	78	61	.561	—	Von Hayes	266,700	3,922	2005
139	Wichita Wranglers (Royals)	77	62	.554	1	Frank White	177,758	2,653	1999
132	Corpus Christi Hooks (Astros)	76	63	.547	2	Dave Clark	506,398	7,234	2006
110	Tulsa Drillers (Rockies)	75	64	.540	3	Stu Cole	333,763	4,982	1998
251	Frisco RoughRiders (Rangers)	72	68	.514	6½	Darryl Kennedy	580,480	8,413	2004
214	Springfield Cardinals (Cardinals)	66	72	.478	11½	Chris Maloney	492,372	7,349	1994
236	San Antonio Missions (Mariners)	60	78	.435	17½	Daren Brown	277,035	3,958	2003
146	Arkansas Travelers (Angels)	51	87	.370	26½	Tyrone Boykin	207,507	3,294	2001

NOTE: Teams' individual batting and pitching statistics can be found on page indicated in lefthand column.

MINOR LEAGUES

2006 TEXAS LEAGUE STATISTICS

CLUB BATTING

	AVG	G	AB	R	H	2B	3B	HR	BB	SO	SB	OBP	SLG
Corpus Christi	.279	139	4738	645	1324	257	37	119	431	821	113	.343	.425
Wichita	.277	140	4796	785	1329	260	29	124	512	832	69	.350	.421
Midland	.275	139	4818	715	1323	288	34	116	614	950	72	.363	.421
Tulsa	.272	139	4721	726	1286	301	31	150	475	962	71	.346	.445
Arkansas	.268	139	4685	689	1255	293	25	158	421	1078	129	.339	.442
Frisco	.267	140	4756	671	1272	258	26	131	460	1015	101	.339	.415
Springfield	.262	138	4626	665	1213	249	21	128	515	975	92	.341	.408
San Antonio	.247	138	4617	576	1142	207	32	85	477	1029	114	.323	.361

CLUB PITCHING

	ERA	G	CG	SHO	SV	IP	H	R	ER	HR	BB	SO	AVG
San Antonio	3.85	138	0	7	34	1220	1229	607	522	100	461	925	.266
Corpus Christi	3.92	139	3	10	37	1227	1194	627	535	111	483	1069	.255
Midland	4.16	139	4	6	43	1255	1294	643	580	99	446	972	.271
Tulsa	4.25	139	8	8	36	1221	1186	678	577	140	473	959	.257
Frisco	4.30	140	3	6	30	1238	1268	676	591	121	493	1099	.264
Springfield	4.33	138	1	3	37	1212	1252	668	583	130	481	927	.268
Wichita	4.59	140	2	4	38	1240	1287	701	632	132	542	948	.270
Arkansas	5.65	139	3	5	26	1215	1434	872	763	178	526	763	.298

CLUB FIELDING

	PCT	PO	A	E	DP		PCT	PO	A	E	DP
Midland	.982	3765	1489	98	135	Springfield	.973	3635	1501	140	132
Wichita	.978	3719	1560	121	148	Frisco	.973	3714	1385	139	107
Tulsa	.976	3663	1480	127	156	Arkansas	.972	3645	1462	145	177
San Antonio	.974	3659	1483	137	134	Corpus Christi	.968	3682	1387	167	125

INDIVIDUAL BATTING LEADERS
(Minimum 434 Plate Appearances)

	AVG	G	AB	R	H	2B	3B	HR	RBI	BB	SO	SB
Butler, Billy, Wichita	.331	119	477	82	158	33	1	15	96	41	67	1
Gordon, Alex, Wichita	.325	130	486	111	158	39	1	29	101	72	113	22
Ash, Jonathan, Corpus Christi	.314	112	392	40	123	22	5	1	28	25	36	5
Richardson, Juan, Springfield	.311	121	444	71	138	31	1	17	78	46	114	0
Anderson, Josh, Corpus Christi	.308	130	561	83	173	26	4	3	50	27	73	43
Spanos, Vasili, Midland	.308	120	439	70	135	29	1	9	67	52	73	0
Maier, Mitch, Wichita	.306	138	543	95	166	35	7	14	92	41	96	13
Rodland, Eric, Arkansas	.300	118	397	64	119	22	2	8	51	58	54	2
Porter, Gregory, Arkansas	.298	118	440	73	131	28	0	20	71	26	103	4
Stavinoha, Nick, Springfield	.297	111	417	55	124	26	3	12	73	28	81	2

INDIVIDUAL PITCHING LEADERS
(Minimum 112 Innings)

	W	L	ERA	G	GS	CG	SV	IP	H	R	ER	BB	SO
Albers, Matt, Corpus Christi	10	2	2.17	19	19	0	0	116	96	40	28	47	95
Ziegler, Brad, Midland	9	6	3.37	23	22	1	0	142	151	60	53	37	88
Douglass, Chance, Corpus Christi	7	8	3.52	28	26	2	0	161	144	67	63	56	102
Bazardo, Yorman, San Antonio	6	5	3.64	25	25	0	0	138	144	65	56	45	80
Knox, Brad, Midland	12	5	3.67	27	25	1	0	162	154	74	66	62	100
Ulloa, Enmanuel, Tulsa	7	6	3.91	23	23	0	0	127	125	65	55	35	112
Blackley, Travis, San Antonio	8	11	4.06	25	25	0	0	144	139	77	65	45	100
Miller, Joshua, Corpus Christi	11	10	4.14	33	22	1	0	152	163	83	70	41	103
Kaiser, Marc, Tulsa	10	10	4.15	25	25	4	0	165	174	89	76	40	73
Diamond, Thomas, Frisco	12	5	4.24	27	27	1	0	129	104	65	61	78	145

ALL-STAR TEAM

C—Kurt Suzuki, Midland. **1B**—Joe Koshansky, Tulsa. **2B**—Jonny Ash, Corpus Christi. **3B**—Alex Gordon, Wichita. **SS**—Brandon Wood, Arkansas. **OF**—Josh Anderson, Corpus Christi; Billy Butler, Wichita; Hunter Pence, Corpus Christi. **DH**—Nate Gold, Frisco. **Utility**—Ben Zobrist, Corpus Christi.

Player of the Year: Alex Gordon, Wichita. **Pitcher of the Year:** Matt Albers, Corpus Christi. **Manager of the Year:** Dave Clark, Corpus Christi.

BATTING
OBP	Zobrist, Ben, Corpus Christi	.434
SLG	Gordon, Alex, Wichita	.588
R	Gordon, Alex, Wichita	111
H	Anderson, Josh, Corpus Christi	173
TB	Gordon, Alex, Wichita	286
XBH	Wood, Brandon, Arkansas	71
2B	Smith, Seth, Tulsa	46
3B	Lubanski, Chris, Wichita	11
HR	Gold, Nate, Frisco	34
RBI	Koshansky, Joseph, Tulsa	109
SAC	McCoy, Mike, Springfield	16
SF	Three players tied at	10
BB	Gordon, Alex, Wichita	72
	Lubanski, Chris, Wichita	72
IBB	Pence, Hunter, Corpus Christi	6
HBP	Spanos, Vasili, Midland	25
SO	Wood, Brandon, Arkansas	149
SB	Anderson, Josh, Corpus Christi	43
CS	Anderson, Josh, Corpus Christi	13
GIDP	Butler, Billy, Wichita	25
AB/SO	Ash, Jonathan, Corpus Christi	10.89

PITCHING
G	Newman, Joshua, Tulsa	62
GS	Aguilar, Ray, Midland	28
	Feierabend, Ryan, San Antonio	28
CG	Kaiser, Marc, Tulsa	4
SHO	Douglass, Chance, Corpus Christi	2
GF	Worrell, Mark, Springfield	51
SV	Worrell, Mark, Springfield	27
W	Five players tied at	12
L	Hunter, Christopher, Arkansas	14
IP	Kaiser, Marc, Tulsa	164.2
H	Pals, Jordan, Springfield	201
R	Register, Steven, Tulsa	114
ER	Hunter, Christopher, Arkansas	104
HB	Blackley, Travis, San Antonio	15
BB	Morillo, Juan, Tulsa	80
SO	Diamond, Thomas, Frisco	145
SO/9(SP)	Diamond, Thomas, Frisco	10.09
SO/9(SP)	Estrada, Paul, Corpus Christi	13.6
WP	Cedeno, Juan, Wichita	16
BK	Mansfield, Monte, Corpus Christi	4

FIELDING
C	PCT	Suzuki, Kurt, Midland	.997
	PO	Richardson, Kevin, Frisco	.703
	A	Wilson, Bobby, Arkansas	63
	E	Johnson, Gabe, Springfield	9
		Wilson, Bobby, Arkansas	9
	DP	Franco, Iker, Springfield	10
	PB	Colina, Alvin, Tulsa	11
		Oliveros, Luis, San Antonio	11
	CS%	Espino, Damaso, Wichita	49
1B	PCT	Richardson, Juan, Springfield	.993
	PO	Koshansky, Joseph, Tulsa	1108
	A	Koshansky, Joseph, Tulsa	96
	E	Koshansky, Joseph, Tulsa	11
	DP	Koshansky, Joseph, Tulsa	126
2B	PCT	Melillo, Kevin, Midland	.990
	PO	Melillo, Kevin, Midland	249
	A	Melillo, Kevin, Midland	363
	E	Hoffpauir, Jarrett, Springfield	23
	DP	Rodland, Eric, Arkansas	111
3B	PCT	Gordon, Alex, Wichita	.955
	PO	Brown, Matthew, Arkansas	96
	A	Stewart, Ian, Tulsa	252
	E	Brown, Matthew, Arkansas	27
	DP	Stewart, Ian, Tulsa	38
SS	PCT	Merrill Jr., Ronnie, Midland	.974
	PO	Wood, Brandon, Arkansas	219
	A	Sanchez, Angel, Wichita	423
	E	McCoy, Mike, Springfield	27
		Wood, Brandon, Arkansas	27
	DP	Sanchez, Angel, Wichita	99
		Wood, Brandon, Arkansas	99
OF	PCT	Blalock, Jake, Frisco	.994
	PO	Maier, Mitch, Wichita	333
	A	Balentien, Wladimir, San Antonio	17
	E	Balentien, Wladimir, San Antonio	11
	DP	Balentien, Wladimir, San Antonio	6

BY AARON FITT

The Inland Empire 66ers got hot at the right time.

The Mariners affiliate won the California League's first-half Southern Division title by just a half-game, then was ravaged by the promotions of standouts Yung-Chi Chen, Matt Tuiasosopo and Mark Lowe. The 66ers went just 34-37 in the second half and limped into the playoffs with an overall record that was 10 games worse than San Jose.

But the resilient 66ers saved their best baseball for the postseason, eliminating Lake Elsinore three games to one and advancing to a championship series showdown against juggernaut Visalia. The Oaks won the first two games of the series to force Inland Empire to the brink of elimination, but the 66ers won the final three games to capture the Cal League title.

Four 66ers pitchers combined to shut down the potent Visalia offense in the decisive fifth game, allowing just five hits and issuing three walks while striking out 10 in a 2-1 win. Outfielder Josh Womack got the 66ers on the board with an inside-the-park home run down the right-field line in the fifth inning. Then, in the eighth, first baseman Johan Limonta broke a 1-1 tie with an RBI double that proved to be the game-winner.

The outcome might have been different if Visalia still had infielders Reid Brignac and Evan Longoria on its roster. Brignac, a 20-year-old shortstop, won Cal League MVP honors despite spending the final month of the season at Double-A Montgomery. Longoria, the third overall pick in the 2006 draft, hit eight home runs in just 28 games for the Oaks before punching his ticket to Montgomery.

Longoria was part of a major talent infusion from the 2006 draft in the second half. No. 2 overall pick Greg Reynolds gave Modesto's staff a boost, and No. 11 pick Tim Lincecum became San Jose's best pitcher as soon as he joined the team. Of that threesome, only Reynolds played enough to qualify for the league's top prospects list, checking in at No. 8 behind a solid group of 20-year-olds. But pickings were slim outside the top 10.

A year after Brandon Wood, Howie Kendrick, Stephen Drew and Billy Butler headlined a Cal League bumper crop, the talent level dipped quite a bit in 2006. There remained a few very good prospects at the top of the league, namely 20-year-old sluggers Brignac and Gonzalez and 20-year-old pitchers Franklin Morales, Nick Adenhart and Eric Hurley, but there were plenty of question marks after that.

The league will see several significant affiliation changes in 2007, most notably with the Dodgers returning to Inland Empire and abandoning their Vero Beach affiliate in the Florida State League.

The Mariners will leave Indland Empire and switch their affiliation to High Desert, after the Royals left the Mavericks to return to Wilmington in the Carolina League. The Red Sox, who left Wilmington, will come to the league at Lancaster. The Diamondbacks will leave Lancaster and replace the Devil Rays in Visalia. Bringing things full circle, the Devil Rays go to the FSL to replace the Dodgers affiliation at Vero Beach.

MINOR LEAGUES

STANDINGS: SPLIT SEASON

FIRST HALF

NORTH	W	L	PCT	GB
San Jose	41	29	.586	—
Modesto	35	35	.500	6
Stockton	35	35	.500	6
Visalia	33	37	.471	8
Bakersfield	28	42	.400	13
SOUTH	**W**	**L**	**PCT**	**GB**
Inland Empire	39	31	.557	—
High Desert	39	31	.557	—
Lake Elsinore	36	34	.514	3
Lancaster	32	38	.457	7
Rancho Cuca.	32	38	.457	7

SECOND HALF

NORTH	W	L	PCT	GB
Visalia	42	28	.600	—
San Jose	41	29	.586	1
Stockton	34	36	.486	8
Modesto	31	39	.443	11
Bakersfield	30	40	.429	12
NORTH	**W**	**L**	**PCT**	**GB**
Lake Elsinore	38	32	.543	—
Lancaster	36	34	.514	2
High Desert	34	36	.486	4
Inland Empire	33	37	.471	5
Rancho Cuca.	31	39	.443	7

PLAYOFFS—Division series: Lake Elsinore defeated High Desert 2-1 and Visalia defeated Stockton 2-1 in best-of-three series. **Semifinals:** Inland Empire defeated Lake Elsinore 3-1 and Visalia defeated San Jose 3-2 in best-of-five series. **Finals:** Inland Empire defeated Visalia 3-2 in best-of-five series.

TOP 20 PROSPECTS

1. Reid Brignac, ss, Visalia (Devil Rays)
2. Carlos Gonzalez, of, Lancaster (Diamondbacks)
3. Franklin Morales, lhp, Modesto (Rockies)
4. Nick Adenhart, rhp, Rancho Cucamonga (Angels)
5. Eric Hurley, rhp, Bakersfield (Rangers)
6. Travis Buck, of, Stockton (Athletics)
7. Jose Arredondo, rhp, Rancho Cucamonga (Angels)
8. Greg Reynolds, rhp, Modesto (Rockies)
9. Greg Smith, lhp, Lancaster (Diamondbacks)
10. Jonathan Herrera, ss, Modesto (Rockies)
11. Emilio Bonifacio, 2b, Lancaster (Diamondbacks)
12. Sean Rodriguez, ss, Rancho Cucamonga (Angels)
13. Mark Reynolds, if, Lancaster (Diamondbacks)
14. Ben Harrison, of, Bakersfield (Rangers)
15. Landon Powell, c, Stockton (Athletics)
16. Yung Chi Chen, 2b, Inland Empire (Mariners)
17. Fernando Perez, of, Visalia (Devil Rays)
18. Samuel Deduno, rhp, Modesto (Rockies)
19. Cesar Ramos, lhp, Lake Elsinore (Rockies)
20. Chase Headley, 3b, Lake Elsinore (Padres)

STANDINGS: OVERALL

Page	Team	W	L	PCT	GB	Manager(s)	Attendance	Average	Last Penn.
229	San Jose Giants (Giants)	82	58	.586	—	Lenn Sakata	157,216	2,347	2005
245	Visalia Oaks (Devil Rays)	75	65	.536	7	Joe Szekely	61,958	898	1978
222	Lake Elsinore Storm (Padres)	74	66	.529	8	Rick Renteria	233,318	3,381	2001
140	High Desert Mavericks (Royals)	73	67	.521	9	Jeff Carter	122,574	1,751	1997
237	Inland Empire 66ers (Mariners)	72	68	.514	10	Gary Thurman	186,065	2,697	2006
192	Stockton Ports (Athletics)	69	71	.493	13	Todd Steverson	213,724	3,097	2002
50	Lancaster Jethawks (Diamondbacks)	68	72	.486	14	Brett Butler	117,123	1,722	None
110	Modesto Nuts (Rockies)	66	74	.471	16	Chad Kreuter/Glenallen Hill	144,637	2,191	2004
146	Rancho Cucamonga Quakes (Angels)	63	77	.450	19	Bobby Mitchell	260,474	3,721	1994
252	Bakersfield Blaze (Rangers)	58	82	.414	24	Carlos Subero	76,629	1,111	1989

NOTE: Teams' individual batting and pitching statistics can be found on page indicated in lefthand column.

2006 CALIFORNIA LEAGUE STATISTICS

CLUB BATTING

	AVG	G	AB	R	H	2B	3B	HR	BB	SO	SB	OBP	SLG
Lancaster	.303	140	4942	872	1499	291	41	171	434	1045	147	.368	.483
Visalia	.289	140	4949	861	1430	270	29	135	496	1061	134	.359	.437
High Desert	.277	140	4814	729	1334	259	32	109	470	957	104	.346	.412
Stockton	.276	140	4787	779	1320	266	26	127	535	983	81	.355	.422
Inland Empire	.273	140	4834	690	1321	244	35	76	487	974	114	.346	.385
San Jose	.271	140	4829	716	1308	246	35	87	450	1092	126	.341	.390
Rancho Cucamonga	.270	140	4828	713	1303	257	41	114	458	1089	129	.346	.411
Bakersfield	.268	140	4845	693	1299	294	34	114	486	1141	114	.339	.413
Modesto	.266	140	4701	704	1249	246	42	97	510	1066	152	.345	.398
Lake Elsinore	.259	140	4782	689	1240	257	33	87	608	1089	107	.350	.381

CLUB PITCHING

	ERA	G	CG	SHO	SV	IP	H	R	ER	HR	BB	SO	AVG
San Jose	3.85	140	1	9	47	1256	1194	640	537	102	509	1177	.250
Lake Elsinore	3.90	140	2	10	42	1240	1297	648	538	89	362	960	.271
Inland Empire	4.04	140	3	10	35	1255	1230	700	563	108	541	1113	.256
Rancho Cucamonga	4.54	140	4	10	25	1245	1329	731	628	99	554	920	.275
Modesto	4.61	140	1	8	34	1234	1304	743	632	72	530	1113	.272
Bakersfield	4.83	140	3	5	30	1242	1360	823	667	120	536	1132	.279
Visalia	4.83	140	2	5	33	1241	1327	774	666	134	449	989	.275
Stockton	4.90	140	2	3	37	1223	1400	754	665	121	443	1025	.290
High Desert	4.95	140	3	3	42	1226	1354	742	674	143	441	1133	.282
Lancaster	5.60	140	2	5	38	1222	1508	891	760	129	569	935	.303

CLUB FIELDING

	PCT	PO	A	E	DP		PCT	PO	A	E	DP
High Desert	.974	3679	1502	138	144	Inland Empire	.968	3766	1363	170	133
Modesto	.972	3701	1517	151	124	Lancaster	.968	3666	1434	170	144
Lake Elsinore	.970	3720	1533	165	137	Visalia	.967	3722	1461	178	123
Stockton	.970	3668	1415	158	131	Rancho Cuca.	.967	3736	1514	180	144
San Jose	.969	3768	1408	163	128	Bakersfield	.963	3725	1524	204	144

INDIVIDUAL BATTING LEADERS
(Minimum 434 Plate Appearances)

	AVG	G	AB	R	H	2B	3B	HR	RBI	BB	SO	SB
Rahl, Chris, Lancaster	.327	131	568	101	186	44	8	13	83	35	119	19
Brignac, Reid, Visalia	.326	100	411	82	134	26	3	21	83	35	82	12
Bonifacio, Emilio, Lancaster	.321	130	546	117	175	35	7	7	50	44	104	61
Herrera, Jonathan, Modesto	.310	127	487	87	151	20	8	7	77	58	67	34
Nowak, Chris, Visalia	.308	130	494	93	152	45	3	11	103	69	83	17
Perez, Fernando, Visalia	.307	133	547	123	168	19	9	4	56	78	134	33
Nicolas, Cesar, Lancaster	.302	120	434	78	131	34	0	14	80	60	81	1
Rodriguez, Sean, Rancho Cuca.	.301	116	455	78	137	29	5	24	77	47	124	15
Arhart, Josh, Visalia	.301	107	429	64	129	27	2	15	78	22	93	3
Gonzalez, Carlos, Lancaster	.300	104	403	82	121	35	4	21	94	30	104	15

INDIVIDUAL PITCHING LEADERS
(Minimum 112 Innings)

	W	L	ERA	G	GS	CG	SV	IP	H	R	ER	BB	SO
Morales, Franklin, Modesto	10	9	3.68	27	26	0	0	154	126	77	63	89	179
Ramos, Cesar, Lake Elsinore	7	8	3.70	26	24	0	0	141	161	72	58	44	70
Bello, Cibney, Inland Empire	6	10	3.94	29	27	0	0	153	145	86	67	78	137
Nottingham, Shawn, Inland Empire	5	12	4.17	26	26	1	0	155	164	90	72	52	136
Mathis, Douglas, Bakersfield	10	7	4.18	26	25	2	0	151	160	76	70	47	109
Moreno, Anthony, San Jose	11	7	4.21	32	23	0	0	137	150	73	64	54	115
Gragg III, John, High Desert	8	9	4.29	20	20	1	0	130	142	66	62	36	95
Houser Jr., James, Visalia	12	4	4.41	28	27	0	0	151	140	80	74	46	137
Cardenas, Humberto, Modesto	8	8	4.44	28	16	0	0	130	150	73	64	29	80
Martinez, Gregorio, San Jose	8	8	4.49	26	26	0	0	138	150	86	69	35	111

ALL-STAR TEAM

ALL-STAR TEAM: C—Landon Powell, Stockton. **1B**—Mike Stodolka, High Desert. **2B**—Emilio Bonifacio, Lancaster. **3B**—Chase Headley, Lake Elsinore. **SS**—Reid Brignac, Visalia. **OF**—Carlos Gonzalez, Lancaster; Matt Miller, Modesto; Chris Rahl, Lancaster. **DH**—Sean Rodriguez, Rancho Cucamonga. **Utility**—Mark Reynolds, Lancaster. **P**—Brian Anderson, San Jose; Jose Arredondo, Rancho Cucamonga; Gregorio Martinez, San Jose; Greg Smith, Lancaster.

Most Valuable Player: Reid Brignac, Visalia. **Pitcher of the Year:** Brian Anderson, San Jose. **Rookie of the Year:** Reid Brignac, Visalia. **Managers of the Year:** Joe Szekely, Visalia/Gary Thurman, Inland Empire.

DEPARTMENT LEADERS

BATTING
OBP	Brown, Tim, Lake Elsinore	.427
SLG	Gonzalez, Carlos, Lancaster	.563
R	Perez, Fernando, Visalia	123
H	Rahl, Chris, Lancaster	186
TB	Rahl, Chris, Lancaster	285
XBH	Rahl, Chris, Lancaster	65
2B	Nowak, Chris, Visalia	45
3B	Three players tied at	9
HR	Burgess, Brandon, Lancaster	26
RBI	Nowak, Chris, Visalia	103
SAC	Frey, Christopher, Modesto	17
SF	Two players tied at	10
BB	Brown, Tim, Lake Elsinore	79
IBB	Gonzalez, Carlos, Lancaster	7
HBP	Collins, Michael, Rancho Cucamonga	33
SO	Nelson, Justin, Modesto	156
SB	Bonifacio, Emilio, Lancaster	61
CS	Perez, Fernando, Visalia	16
	Wimberly, Corey, Modesto	16
GIDP	Leslie, Myron, Stockton	19
AB/SO	Falu, Irving, High Desert	11.54

PITCHING
G	Jamison, Neil, Lake Elsinore	61
GS	Three players tied at	28
CG	Mathis, Douglas, Bakersfield	2
	Smith, Gregory, Lancaster	2
SHO	Smith, Gregory, Lancaster	2
GF	Jamison, Neil, Lake Elsinore	54
SV	Anderson, Brian, San Jose	37
W	Houser Jr., James, Visalia	12
	Mason, Christopher, Visalia	12
L	Rodriguez, Francisco, Rancho Cucamonga	13
	Schlact, Michael, Bakersfield	13
IP	Rodriguez Jr., Fernando, Rancho Cucamonga	163.1
H	Mattheus, Ryan, Modesto	198
R	Cota, Luis, High Desert	113
ER	Cota, Luis, High Desert	104
HB	Deduno, Samuel, Modesto	22
BB	Deduno, Samuel, Modesto	92
SO	Morales, Franklin, Modesto	179
SO/9 (SP)	Arredondo, Jose, Rancho Cucamonga	11.5
SO/9 (SP)	Ingram, Jesse, Bakersfield	14.41
WP	Deduno, Samuel, Modesto	34
BK	Morales, Franklin, Modesto	10

FIELDING
C	PCT	Powell, Landon, Stockton	.994
	PO	Powell, Landon, Stockton	611
	A	Powell, Landon, Stockton	69
	E	Frostad, Emerson, Bakersfield	12
	DP	Donachie, Adam, High Desert	11
	PB	Frostad, Emerson, Bakersfield	33
	CS%	Schweiger, Brian, Inland Empire	60%
1B	PCT	Nicolas, Cesar, Lancaster	.991
	PO	Nowak, Chris, Visalia	1074
	A	Everidge, Tommy, Stockton	95
	E	Nowak, Chris, Visalia	19
	DP	Everidge, Tommy, Stockton	108
2B	PCT	Minicozzi, Mark, San Jose	0.98
	PO	Bonifacio, Emilio, Lancaster	277
	A	Kazmar, Sean, Lake Elsinore	375
	E	Kazmar, Sean, Lake Elsinore	22
	DP	Kazmar, Sean, Lake Elsinore	91
3B	PCT	Cottrell, Patrick, Visalia	.972
	PO	Lucas, Edward, High Desert	85
	A	Lucas, Edward, High Desert	268
	E	Klink, Simon, San Jose	25
	DP	Lucas, Edward, High Desert	27
SS	PCT	Falu, Irving, High Desert	.971
	PO	Herrera, Jonathan, Modesto	208
	A	Adams, Skip, Lake Elsinore	413
	E	Adams, Skip, Lake Elsinore	29
		Rodriguez, Sean, Rancho Cucamonga	29
	DP	Adams, Skip, Lake Elsinore	86
OF	PCT	Johnson, Brent, Inland Empire	.988
	PO	Perez, Fernando, Visalia	329
	A	Cumberland, Shaun, Visalia	18
	E	Cumberland, Shaun, Visalia	12
		Gonzalez, Carlos, Lancaster	12
		Perez, Fernando, Visalia	12
	DP	Cumberland, Shaun, Visalia	9

BY CHRIS KLINE

It seemed nothing could stop the Kinston Indians in 2006.

Kinston won its second title in three years in a rematch of the 2005 Mills Cup championship series, knocking off 2005 champion Frederick.

The K-Tribe has enjoyed a remarkable run during its 20-year affiliation with the Indians, advancing to the championship series 11 times. Kinston did not lose in the postseason, first sweeping Salem for the Southern Division title, then winning the first three games of the Mills Cup to sweep the Keys as well.

"This is a testament to all the hard work every single one of these players put in every day," Kinston manager Mike Sarbaugh said. "There was a little bit of everything that went into this season—strong individual performances, solid fundamentals and really just staying loose and having fun."

Kinston dominated the first half, going 47-23, but as usual the Indians called up impact players like Trevor Crowe, Brian Barton, Ryan Goleski and Wyatt Toregas. The team stumbled at times down the stretch—including losing three straight to Frederick in August.

But the Indians had two constants in the rotation in lefthanders Chuck Lofgren and Scott Lewis. Lofgren, a fourth-round pick in 2004, displayed power stuff from the left side, topping out at 94 mph with his fastball. The 20-year-old lefthander wound up winning 17 games, tying Triple-A Sacramento righthander Jason Windsor for the minor league lead. Lofgren would have had more wins, but the bullpen blew four saves when Lofgren started.

"Everybody wants to move up, but this is where I work," Lofgren said. "I just try to go out and give this club my best every fifth day. It was a great season, a great team to be a part of for the entire season."

On the flip side of Lofgren was Lewis, a soft-tossing lefty whose strong suit is pinpoint command. Lewis, the Indians' third-round pick in 2004, might not have had the record he would have liked because his pitch count was limited as he came back from arm problems, but he wound up winning the minor league ERA title with a 1.48 mark in 116 innings.

"The biggest thing for him is that he proved he was healthy and he bounced back well between starts," Kinston pitching coach Steve Lyons said. "But having the minor league wins leader and the minor league ERA leader on the same club? One of this club's strongest suits was its starting pitching, no question."

Strong pitching was certainly the Carolina League's biggest asset in 2006, as Salem also boasted prospects Troy Patton, Chad Reineke, Jimmy Barthmaier and Felipe Paulino on its staff. Throw in Myrtle Beach lefthander Matt Harrison, Potomac righthander Collin Balester and the Frederick duo of Radhames Liz and Garrett Olson, and it's easy to see how dominant the arms were.

"Looking back on my two years in this league, I'll automatically think of the lefties," Salem pitching coach Stan Boroski said. "When was the last time you had so many lefthanders so young, that have that kind of talent."

That's not to say the hitters were slouches, but the league lost speedy outfielders Jacoby Ellsbury (Wilmington) and Crowe by mid-season. Frederick outfielder Nolan Reimold had an up and down season and hit .255, and Lynchburg catcher Neil Walker missed the first month of the season with a wrist injury and never met expectations.

Wilmington switched affiliations after just two seasons with the Red Sox. The Blue Rocks returned to their roots, going back to a Kansas City affiliate—the club they were affiliated with since their inception in 1993 until 2004.

STANDINGS: SPLIT SEASON

FIRST HALF

NORTH	W	L	PCT	GB
Wilmington	35	35	.500	—
Lynchburg	34	36	.486	1
Potomac	33	37	.471	2
Frederick	26	43	.337	8½

SOUTH	W	L	PCT	GB
Kinston	47	23	.671	—
Winston-Salem	37	32	.536	9½
Myrtle Beach	35	35	.500	12
Salem	32	38	.457	15

SECOND HALF

NORTH	W	L	PCT	GB
Frederick	35	34	.507	—
Wilmington	32	36	.471	2½
Potomac	31	39	.443	4½
Lynchburg	29	39	.426	5½

SOUTH	W	L	PCT	GB
Salem	44	23	.657	—
Kinston	38	31	.551	7
Myrtle Beach	37	33	.529	8½
Winston-Salem	29	40	.420	16

PLAYOFFS—Semifinals: Frederick defeated Wilmington 2-1 and Kinston defeated Salem 2-0 in best-of-three series. **Final:** Kinston defeated Frederick 3-0 in best-of-five series.

TOP 20 PROSPECTS

1. Chuck Lofgren, lhp, Kinston (Indians)
2. Jacoby Ellsbury, of, Wilmington (Red Sox)
3. Troy Patton, lhp, Salem (Astros)
4. Trevor Crowe, of, Kinston (Indians)
5. Jimmy Barthmaier, rhp, Salem (Astros)
6. Nolan Reimold, of, Frederick (Orioles)
7. Matt Harrison, lhp, Myrtle Beach (Braves)
8. Neil Walker, c, Lynchburg (Pirates)
9. Radhames Liz, rhp, Frederick (Orioles)
10. Scott Lewis, lhp, Kinston (Indians)
11. Brandon Jones, of, Myrtle Beach (Braves)
12. Collin Balester, rhp, Potomac (Nationals)
13. Van Pope, 3b, Myrtle Beach (Braves)
14. Felipe Paulino, rhp, Salem (Astros)
15. Garrett Olson, lhp, Frederick (Orioles)
16. Brian Barton, of, Kinston (Indians)
17. Brett Lillibridge, ss, Lynchburg (Pirates)
18. Chad Reineke, rhp, Salem (Astros)
19. Brian Bixler, ss, Lynchburg (Pirates)
20. Jed Lowrie, ss, Wilmington (Red Sox)

STANDINGS: OVERALL

Page		W	L	PCT	GB	Manager	Attendance	Average	Last Penn.
103	Kinston Indians (Indians)	85	54	.612	—	Mike Sarbaugh	112,253	1,651	2006
132	Salem Avalanche (Astros)	76	61	.555	8	Jim Pankovits	237,724	3,602	2001
57	Myrtle Beach Pelicans (Braves)	72	68	.514	13½	Rocket Wheeler	200,152	3,079	2000
72	Wilmington Blue Rocks (Red Sox)	67	71	.486	17½	Chad Epperson	312,258	4,525	1999
88	Winston-Salem Warthogs (White Sox)	66	72	.478	18½	Rafael Santana	149,755	2,415	2003
267	Potomac Nationals (Nationals)	64	76	.457	21½	Randy Knorr	151,507	2,367	1989
207	Lynchburg Hillcats (Pirates)	63	75	.457	21½	Gary Green	157,744	2,354	2002
64	Frederick Keys (Orioles)	61	77	.442	23½	Bien Figueroa	280,034	4,376	2005

NOTE: Teams' individual batting and pitching statistics can be found on page indicated in lefthand column.

2006 CAROLINA LEAGUE STATISTICS

CLUB BATTING

	AVG	G	AB	R	H	2B	3B	HR	BB	SO	SB	OBP	SLG
Kinston	.272	139	4639	744	1263	248	41	102	597	914	154	.360	.409
Lynchburg	.266	138	4556	652	1211	253	27	72	469	881	194	.342	.381
Myrtle Beach	.257	140	4594	599	1182	223	18	82	484	884	152	.333	.367
Salem	.253	137	4484	582	1133	289	19	86	452	903	125	.327	.383
Potomac	.252	140	4628	623	1168	240	31	95	438	1062	182	.326	.379
Frederick	.252	138	4599	637	1159	248	16	112	519	952	94	.335	.386
Wilmington	.251	138	4621	614	1161	263	44	80	519	981	85	.334	.379
Winston-Salem	.251	138	4421	566	1108	243	28	100	409	857	120	.322	.386

CLUB PITCHING

	ERA	G	CG	SHO	SV	IP	H	R	ER	HR	BB	SO	AVG
Salem	3.38	137	2	12	41	1200	1075	518	450	66	484	978	.242
Kinston	3.44	139	2	10	37	1208	1098	544	462	77	446	1023	.244
Winston-Salem	3.48	138	2	9	35	1180	1128	577	456	67	463	887	.251
Wilmington	3.82	138	3	6	32	1217	1202	601	517	85	434	937	.258
Frederick	4.34	138	0	6	31	1210	1203	711	583	126	481	987	.258
Myrtle Beach	4.44	140	6	8	41	1210	1229	673	597	99	518	872	.267
Lynchburg	4.45	138	3	5	30	1200	1198	678	593	101	487	819	.263
Potomac	4.68	140	1	6	28	1207	1252	715	627	108	574	931	.269

CLUB FIELDING

	PCT	PO	A	E	DP		PCT	PO	A	E	DP
Kinston	.979	3625	1400	109	121	Wilmington	.974	3652	1393	136	110
Salem	.978	3600	1430	111	132	Potomac	.971	3620	1345	147	111
Lynchburg	.975	3599	1429	127	120	Frederick	.966	3630	1370	177	111
Myrtle Beach	.975	3630	1344	128	119	Winston-Salem	.966	3541	1598	180	143

INDIVIDUAL BATTING LEADERS
(Minimum 434 Plate Appearances)

	AVG	G	AB	R	H	2B	3B	HR	RBI	BB	SO	SB
Loadenthal, Carl, Myrtle Beach	.323	106	365	64	118	13	2	7	48	62	67	25
Torbert, Wallace, Salem	.305	119	455	69	139	31	1	5	52	24	71	24
Brown, Jordan, Kinston	.290	125	473	71	137	26	7	15	59	59	4	
Otness, John, Wilmington	.281	105	402	48	113	24	2	3	45	29	40	1
Young, Matt, Myrtle Beach	.281	118	424	65	119	30	2	2	52	71	55	21
Powell, Brandon, Potomac	.280	126	460	64	129	34	4	14	71	37	124	30
Pinckney, Brandon, Kinston	.277	100	382	57	106	26	2	5	55	35	54	5
Carlin, Michael, Lynchburg	.274	116	423	70	116	23	6	13	74	51	78	11
Mercedes, Victor, Winston-Salem	.273	137	521	68	142	34	8	10	52	36	69	20
Sellers, Neil, Salem	.271	127	451	53	122	40	2	2	61	48	60	10

INDIVIDUAL PITCHING LEADERS
(Minimum 112 Innings)

	W	L	ERA	G	GS	CG	SV	IP	H	R	ER	BB	SO
Lewis, Scott, Kinston	3	3	1.48	27	26	0	0	116	84	24	19	28	123
Lofgren, Charles, Kinston	17	5	2.32	25	25	1	0	140	108	51	36	54	125
Hottovy, Thomas, Wilmington	8	6	2.80	21	21	2	0	122	109	49	38	35	91
Egbert, Jack, Winston-Salem	9	8	2.94	25	25	0	0	141	131	57	46	46	120
Whisler, Wesley, Winston-Salem	10	7	2.97	20	20	1	0	118	112	52	39	44	57
Ness, Joe, Kinston	9	6	3.62	26	26	0	0	139	128	64	56	55	120
Barthmaier, James, Salem	11	8	3.62	27	27	0	0	147	137	64	59	67	134
Villa, Kelvin, Myrtle Beach	8	6	3.83	25	19	0	1	120	121	65	51	47	86
Dobies, Andrew, Wilmington	8	6	3.98	21	21	0	0	118	124	58	52	33	77
Ramirez, Luis, Frederick	8	9	4.23	23	23	0	0	126	107	68	59	42	122

ALL-STAR TEAM

ALL-STAR TEAM: C—Lou Santangelo, Salem. **1B**—Chris Kelly, Winston-Salem. **2B**—Paco Figueroa, Frederick. **3B**—Brandon Powell, Potomac. **SS**—Brian Bixler, Lynchburg. **OF**—Jordan Brown, Kinston; Carl Loadenthal, Myrtle Beach; Beau Torbert, Salem. **DH**—Jason Fransz, Frederick. **Utility IF**—Van Pope, Myrtle Beach. **Utility OF**—Brian Barton, Kinston. **SP**—Chuck Lofgren, Kinston. **RP**—Michael James, Wilmington.

Most Valuable Player: Jordan Brown, Kinston. **Pitcher of the Year:** Chuck Lofgren, Kinston. **Manager of the Year:** Jim Pankovits, Salem.

BATTING

OBP	Loadenthal, Carl, Myrtle Beach	.425
SLG	Santangelo, Louis, Salem	.473
R	Pope, Van, Myrtle Beach	.78
H	Mercedes, Victor, Winston-Salem	.142
TB	Brown, Jordan, Kinston	.222
	Mercedes, Victor, Winston-Salem	.222
XBH	Caraballo, Francisco, Salem	.58
2B	Caraballo, Francisco, Salem	.40
	Sellers, Neil, Salem	.40
3B	Mercedes, Victor, Winston-Salem	.8
HR	Fransz, Jason, Frederick	.24
RBI	Brown, Jordan, Kinston	.87
SAC	Three players tied at	.17
SF	Carlin, Michael, Lynchburg	.10
BB	Corsaletti, Jeffrey, Wilmington	.97
IBB	Jones, Brandon, Myrtle Beach	.6
	Sutton, Drew, Salem	.6
HBP	Smith, Sean, Winston-Salem	.18
SO	Whitney, Matthew, Kinston	.131
SB	Powell, Pedro, Lynchburg	.63
CS	Powell, Pedro, Lynchburg	.16
GIDP	Pinckney, Andrew, Wilmington	.18
AB/SO	Otness, John, Wilmington	.10.05

PITCHING

G	Marshall, Jay, Winston-Salem	.58
GS	Hinckley, Michael, Potomac	.28
CG	Four players tied at	.2
SHO	Four players tied at	.1
GF	James, Michael, Wilmington	.43
SV	James, Michael, Wilmington	.25
W	Lofgren, Charles, Kinston	.17
L	Three players tied at	.11
IP	Hart, Kevin, Frederick	.148
	Hinckley, Michael, Potomac	.148
H	Hinckley, Michael, Potomac	.178
R	Hinckley, Michael, Potomac	.102
ER	Hinckley, Michael, Potomac	.91
HB	Morales, Ricardo, Potomac	.12
	Richardson, Jason, Wilmington	.12
BB	Barthmaier, James, Salem	.67
SO	Barthmaier, James, Salem	.134
SO/9(SP)	Lewis, Scott, Kinston	.9.24
SO/9(SP)	Jackson, Kyle, Wilmington	.13.3
WP	Sturge, Justin, Wilmington	.16
BK	Hinckley, Michael, Potomac	.5

FIELDING

C	PCT	Otness, John, Wilmington	.993
	PO	Santangelo, Louis, Salem	.703
	A	Ivany, Devin, Potomac	.76
	E	Lucy, Donny, Winston-Salem	.14
	DP	Sammons, Clint, Myrtle Beach	.9
	PB	Sammons, Clint, Myrtle Beach	.21
	CS%	Rodriguez, Robert, Potomac	.50%
1B	PCT	Bladergroen, Ian, Wilmington	.993
	PO	Head, Stephen, Winston	.907
	A	Kelly, Christopher, Winston-Salem	.86
	E	Pearce, Steven, Lynchburg	.10
	DP	Head, Stephen, Winston	.86
2B	PCT	Sutton, Drew, Salem	.978
	PO	Webb, Trey, Potomac	.219
	A	Sutton, Drew, Salem	.361
	E	Figueroa, Paco, Frederick	.20
	DP	Sutton, Drew, Salem	.65
3B	PCT	Pope, Van, Myrtle Beach	.962
	PO	Pope, Van, Myrtle Beach	.113
	A	Rooi, Vince, Lynchburg	.215
	E	Powell, Brandon, Potomac	.24
		Whitney, Matthew, Kinston	.24
	DP	Rooi, Vince, Lynchburg	.20
SS	PCT	Maysonet, Edwin, Salem	.975
	PO	Mercedes, Victor, Winston-Salem	.190
	A	Mercedes, Victor, Winston-Salem	.445
	E	Mercedes, Victor, Winston-Salem	.35
	DP	Mercedes, Victor, Winston-Salem	.97
OF	PCT	Alcantara, Ervin, Salem	.993
	PO	Powell, Pedro, Lynchburg	.296
	A	Powell, Pedro, Lynchburg	.16
	E	Reimold, Nolan, Frederick	.7
	DP	Alcantara, Ervin, Salem	.4

MINOR LEAGUES

BY J.J. COOPER

In his first season as a manager in 2005, Gary Carter led the Rookie-level Gulf Coast League Mets to a division title as he was named manager of the year.

In his second year, he did one better. Carter's St. Lucie Mets swept Dunedin in three games to claim the Florida State League title.

Catcher Jesus Flores batted .471 in five playoff games including a 4-for-4 effort in the deciding Game Three as St. Lucie pounded Dunedin 6-2 in the clincher.

St. Lucie was a perfect 5-0 in the playoffs, after also sweeping Palm Beach in the best-of-three semifinals. Reliever Carlos Muniz saved all five victories.

In the regular season, as usual, pitching was the story of the league. The FSL has always been a nightmare for hitters. Spacious major league spring-training parks turn home runs into long outs, several of the stadiums have prevailing winds that blow in, and the heat and humidity sap hitters' bat speed as the long season rolls along.

But hitters this year had extra reason to feel they were being picked on. Because the league has some of the best April weather in the minors, teams stocked their FSL affiliates with a slew of the best pitching prospects in baseball.

Homer Bailey, Philip Hughes, Yovanni Gallardo, Matt Garza, Cole Hamels, Andrew Miller and Mike Pelfrey all made appearances in the league. Fort Myers in particular seemed to run out quality arm after quality arm, as Garza and Kevin Slowey and Jose Mijares were joined by Kyle Waldrop, Anthony Swarzak, Oswaldo Sosa and Kyle Aselton.

Slowey was the league's most effective pitcher. The Twins righthander went 4-2, 1.01 in 14 starts with an amazing 99-to-9 strikeout-to-walk ratio.

The midseason all-star game also came down to pitching. Over the first six innings 12 pitchers limited opposing batters to just one run each before the West finally emerged for a 7-4 win at Joker Marchant Stadium in Lakeland, Fla.

Led by Slowey and Bailey, 10 West pitchers combined to strike out 15 in all. Lakeland outfielder Jeff Frazier wowed the hometown fans, hitting a two-run homer in the bottom of the sixth off St. Lucie righthander Jose Sanchez. The Tigers' third-round pick in 2004 out of Rutgers was named the game's MVP.

Like most of the other top arms, Slowey was promoted to Double-A during the season, which opened the way for Yankees lefthander Chase Wright to win the ERA title with a 12-3, 1.88 season. Wright was named the league's pitcher of the year. His teammate Cody Ehlers was the league MVP as the Tampa first baseman hit .298-18-106.

After the season, the Dodgers announced they were leaving the Florida State League after 26 seasons at Vero Beach's Dodgertown. The Devil Rays signed an affiliation agreement with Vero Beach to replace the Dodgers in the FSL. "There is a lot of tradition with the Vero Beach Dodgers; that is the bad part," Indian River County administrator Joe Baird said. "It is disappointing, but sometimes you have to accept what is going to happen and move on."

STANDINGS: SPLIT SEASON

FIRST HALF					SECOND HALF			
EAST	W	L	PCT	GB	**EAST**	W	L	PCT	GB
St. Lucie	40	30	.571	—	Palm Beach	36	29	.554	—
Palm Beach	39	31	.557	1	Daytona	36	31	.537	1
Brevard Co.	35	31	.530	3	St. Lucie	37	32	.536	1
Daytona	35	35	.500	5	Brevard Co.	29	34	.460	6
Jupiter	31	38	.449	8	Vero Beach	25	38	.397	10
Vero Beach	26	42	.382	13	Jupiter	24	42	.364	12½
WEST	W	L	PCT	GB	**WEST**	W	L	PCT	GB
Dunedin	38	32	.543	—	Fort Myers	42	28	.600	—
Fort Myers	38	32	.543	—	Tampa	41	28	.594	½
Lakeland	37	32	.536	½	Clearwater	36	34	.514	6
Tampa	34	34	.500	3	Sarasota	36	34	.514	6
Clearwater	31	38	.449	6½	Lakeland	31	36	.463	9½
Sarasota	30	39	.435	7½	Dunedin	30	37	.448	10½

PLAYOFFS—Semifinals: St. Lucie defeated Palm Beach 2-0 and Dunedin defeated Fort Myers 2-1 in best-of-three series. **Finals:** St. Lucie defeated Dunedin 3-0 in best-of-five series.

TOP 20 PROSPECTS

1. Homer Bailey, rhp, Sarasota (Reds)
2. Yovanni Gallardo, rhp, Brevard County (Brewers)
3. Scott Elbert, lhp, Vero Beach (Dodgers)
4. Ryan Braun, 3b, Brevard County (Brewers)
5. Donald Veal, lhp, Daytona (Cubs)
6. Colby Rasmus, of, Palm Beach (Cardinals)
7. Mark Rogers, rhp, Brevard County (Brewers)
8. Mike Carp, 1b, St. Lucie (Mets)
9. Blake DeWitt, 2b/3b, Vero Beach (Dodgers)
10. Kevin Slowey, rhp, Fort Myers (Twins)
11. Sean Gallagher, rhp, Daytona (Cubs)
12. Terry Evans, of, Palm Beach (Cardinals)
13. Gaby Hernandez, rhp, Jupiter (Marlins)
14. Johnny Cueto, rhp, Sarasota (Reds)
15. Jaime Garcia, lhp, Palm Beach (Cardinals)
16. Jair Jurrjens, rhp, Lakeland (Tigers)
17. Jose Mijares, lhp, Fort Myers (Twins)
18. Alexi Casilla, ss/2b, Fort Myers (Twins)
19. Ryan Patterson, of, Dunedin (Blue Jays)
20. Greg Golson, of, Clearwater (Phillies)

STANDINGS: OVERALL

Page		W	L	PCT	GB	Manager(s)	Attendance	Average	Last Penn.
168	Fort Myers (Twins)	80	60	.571	—	Kevin Boles	116,397	1,791	1985
214	Palm Beach (Cardinals)	75	60	.556	2½	Ron Warner	105,122	1,593	2005
176	St. Lucie (Mets)	77	62	.554	2½	Gary Carter	100,518	1,523	2006
185	Tampa (Yankees)	75	62	.547	3½	Luis Sojo	105,647	1,601	2004
80	Daytona (Cubs)	71	66	.518	7½	Don Buford/Buddy Bailey	147,677	2,238	2004
117	Lakeland (Tigers)	68	68	.500	10	Mike Rojas	32,179	495	1992
259	Dunedin (Blue Jays)	68	69	.496	10½	Omar Malave	27,529	430	None
162	Brevard County (Brewers)	64	65	.496	10½	Ramon Aviles	88,726	1,504	2001
200	Clearwater (Phillies)	67	72	.482	12½	Greg Legg	159,067	2,339	1993
95	Sarasota (Reds)	66	73	.475	13½	Donnie Scott	34,620	533	1963
124	Jupiter (Marlins)	55	80	.407	22½	Tim Cossins	95,656	1,518	1991
154	Vero Beach (Dodgers)	51	80	.389	24½	Luis Salazar	64,985	1,000	1990

NOTE: Teams' individual batting and pitching statistics can be found on page indicated in lefthand column.

2006 FLORIDA STATE LEAGUE STATISTICS

CLUB BATTING

	AVG	G	AB	R	H	2B	3B	HR	BB	SO	SB	OBP	SLG
Dunedin	.266	137	4639	686	1235	272	19	120	453	938	72	.337	.411
Brevard County	.262	129	4293	555	1126	187	25	56	402	905	144	.333	.357
Daytona	.260	137	4551	634	1185	216	28	81	439	954	107	.332	.374
Clearwater	.260	139	4670	631	1213	230	27	89	496	949	106	.338	.378
Tampa	.260	137	4594	633	1195	205	36	95	440	889	169	.329	.382
St. Lucie	.258	139	4542	608	1174	243	24	102	390	1037	84	.328	.390
Vero Beach	.257	141	4387	577	1128	209	20	112	468	917	93	.332	.390
Fort Myers	.256	140	4648	630	1190	196	40	85	446	912	140	.326	.370
Palm Beach	.250	135	4528	619	1134	211	29	99	455	997	112	.325	.375
Sarasota	.248	139	4621	566	1147	234	39	88	358	979	161	.312	.373
Lakeland	.245	136	4521	562	1109	224	36	84	448	1125	176	.318	.367
Jupiter	.231	135	4436	501	1025	202	19	68	401	1123	124	.304	.331

CLUB PITCHING

	ERA	G	CG	SHO	SV	IP	H	R	ER	HR	BB	SO	AVG
Tampa	3.35	137	2	7	33	1216	1121	553	452	65	425	1051	.244
St. Lucie	3.39	139	5	11	46	1190	1133	546	448	94	400	871	.251
Fort Myers	3.55	140	4	15	43	1216	1111	583	479	79	480	1077	.243
Jupiter	3.58	135	2	8	33	1193	1164	611	475	74	417	951	.254
Palm Beach	3.65	135	3	12	41	1187	1163	573	482	75	378	960	.258
Brevard County	3.66	129	0	11	26	1123	1042	540	457	83	448	1093	.246
Lakeland	3.85	136	9	3	34	1200	1168	621	514	90	396	823	.255
Sarasota	3.97	139	3	10	34	1207	1186	637	533	111	458	954	.256
Dunedin	3.99	137	4	9	30	1192	1254	623	529	90	364	941	.270
Clearwater	4.01	139	5	7	33	1220	1180	639	544	112	401	959	.255
Daytona	4.03	137	1	7	42	1190	1188	635	533	95	502	964	.262
Vero Beach	4.44	131	0	2	25	1139	1151	671	562	111	527	1171	.262

CLUB FIELDING

	PCT	PO	A	E	DP		PCT	PO	A	E	DP
Brevard County	.973	3368	1257	130	101	Fort Myers	.972	3649	1417	146	118
Clearwater	.973	3660	1416	143	125	St. Lucie	.970	3571	1411	153	122
Tampa	.973	3647	1446	139	121	Sarasota	.969	3622	1330	161	128
Palm Beach	.972	3561	1524	145	128	Vero Beach	.967	3417	1180	158	101
Dunedin	.972	3576	1468	147	115	Lakeland	.967	3601	1519	175	146
Daytona	.972	3570	1472	144	134	Jupiter	.966	3578	1401	177	117

INDIVIDUAL BATTING LEADERS
(Minimum 434 Plate Appearances)

	AVG	G	AB	R	H	2B	3B	HR	RBI	BB	SO	SB
Coles, Corey, St. Lucie	.341	124	458	65	156	26	4	1	45	48	59	21
Florence, Branden, Clearwater	.327	130	496	46	162	30	2	7	86	31	62	6
Iribarren, Hernan, Brevard County	.319	108	398	50	127	12	4	2	50	39	57	19
Diaz, Robinzon, Dunedin	.306	104	418	59	128	21	1	3	44	20	37	8
Ehlers, Cody, Tampa	.298	134	497	68	148	38	1	18	106	64	88	5
Roberts, Brandon, Sara.-Fort Myers	.293	131	532	80	156	17	2	4	49	36	82	50
Peterson, Brock, Fort Myers	.291	121	447	65	130	21	4	21	75	40	93	6
Katin, Brendan, Brevard County	.289	116	450	64	130	34	3	13	75	34	112	4
Lucena, Juan, Palm Beach	.288	120	490	58	141	16	2	3	49	21	34	1
Carp, Mike, St. Lucie	.287	137	491	69	141	27	1	17	88	51	107	2

INDIVIDUAL PITCHING LEADERS
(Minimum 112 Innings)

	W	L	ERA	G	GS	CG	SV	IP	H	R	ER	BB	SO
Wright, Chase, Tampa	12	3	1.88	37	14	1	0	120	95	32	25	43	100
Aguilar, Salvador, St. Lucie	7	5	3.25	20	19	0	0	114	124	48	41	32	65
Swarzak, Anthony, Fort Myers	11	7	3.27	27	27	2	0	146	131	56	53	60	131
Trahern, Dallas, Lakeland	6	11	3.30	25	25	4	0	145	129	66	53	41	86
Boggs, Mitchell, Palm Beach	10	6	3.41	27	27	1	0	145	153	69	55	51	126
Lecure, Sam, Sarasota	7	12	3.43	27	27	0	0	142	130	63	54	46	115
Kendrick, Kyle, Clearwater	9	7	3.53	21	20	2	0	130	117	59	51	37	79
Hernandez, Gabriel, Jupiter	9	7	3.68	21	20	0	0	120	120	60	49	35	115
Fowler, Eric, Dunedin	8	11	3.74	28	27	1	0	149	164	82	62	36	116
Smith, Brett, Tampa	8	9	3.81	28	26	0	0	158	166	82	67	56	119

ALL-STAR TEAM

ALL-STAR TEAM: C—Robinzon Diaz, Dunedin; Jesus Flores, St. Lucie. **1B**—Cody Ehlers, Tampa. **2B**—Hernan Iribarren, Brevard County. **3B**—Blake DeWitt, Vero Beach. **SS**—Ryan Klosterman, Dunedin. **OF**—Corey Coles, St. Lucie; Ryan Harvey, Daytona; Brandon Roberts, Fort Myers. **Utility IF**—Alexi Casilla. **Utility OF**—Branden Florence, Clearwater. **DH**—Brendan Katin, Brevard County. **SP**—Mitchell Boggs, Palm Beach; Anthony Swarzak, Fort Myers; Orlando Trias, Dunedin; Chase Wright, Tampa. **RP**—Carlos Muniz, St. Lucie; Mike Sillman, Palm Beach.

Most Valuable Player: Cody Ehlers, Tampa. **Most Valuable Pitcher:** Chase Wright, Tampa. **Manager of the Year:** Gary Carter, St. Lucie.

DEPARTMENT LEADERS

BATTING

OBP	Dunlap, Cory, Vero Beach	.435
SLG	Patterson, Ryan, Dunedin	.520
R	Burgamy, Brian, Clearwater	110
H	Florence, Branden, Clearwater	162
TB	Ehlers, Cody, Tampa	242
XBH	Ehlers, Cody, Tampa	57
	Strait, Cody, Sarasota	57
2B	Ehlers, Cody, Tampa	38
3B	Pickrel, Jeremy, Fort Myers	10
HR	Three players tied at	21
RBI	Ehlers, Cody, Tampa	106
SAC	Coronado, Jose, St. Lucie	31
SF	Florence, Branden, Clearwater	10
BB	Burgamy, Brian, Clearwater	88
	Dunlap, Cory, Vero Beach	88
IBB	Ehlers, Cody, Tampa	9
HBP	Carp, Mike, St. Lucie	25
SO	Dlugach, Brent, Lakeland	144
SB	Roberts, Brandon, Fort Myers	50
	Strait, Cody, Sarasota	50
CS	Iribarren, Hernan, Brevard County	15
	Paul, Xavier, Vero Beach	15
GIDP	Frazier, Jeffrey, Lakeland	25
AB/SO	Lucena, Juan, Palm Beach	14.41

PITCHING

G	Sillman, Mike, Palm Beach	57
GS	Six players tied at	27
CG	Trahern, Dallas, Lakeland	4
SHO	14 players tied at	1
GF	Sillman, Mike, Palm Beach	54
SV	Sillman, Mike, Palm Beach	35
W	Trias, Orlando, Dunedin	13
L	Lecure, Sam, Sarasota	12
IP	Smith, Brett, Tampa	158
H	Ardoin, Kevin, Lakeland	176
R	Griffith, Derek, Clearwater	85
ER	Griffith, Derek, Clearwater	76
HB	Holliman, Mark, Daytona	14
	Trahern, Dallas, Lakeland	14
BB	Webber, Nicholas, Palm Beach	63
SO	Swarzak, Anthony, Fort Myers	131
SO/9 (SP)	Bastardo, Alberto, Vero Beach	10.05
SO/9 (SP)	Ramirez, Edwar, Tampa	13.79
WP	Berg, Justin, Daytona	19
BK	Garcia, Jaime, Palm Beach	5

FIELDING

C	PCT	Pilittere, Peter, Tampa	.998
	PO	Davis, Bradley, Jupiter	726
	A	Flores, Jesus, St. Lucie	85
	E	Diaz, Robinzon, Dunedin	12
	DP	Four players tied at	7
	PB	Purdom, John, Sarasota	21
	CS%	Gutierrez, Gabriel, Vero	59%
1B	PCT	Ehlers, Cody, Tampa	.994
	PO	Larish, Jeffrey, Lakeland	1245
	A	Larish, Jeffrey, Lakeland	92
	E	Carp, Mike, St. Lucie	14
	DP	Larish, Jeffrey, Lakeland	128
2B	PCT	Lucena, Juan, Palm Beach	.975
	PO	Lucena, Juan, Palm Beach	230
	A	Lucena, Juan, Palm Beach	312
	E	Mejia, Gilberto, Lakeland	22
	DP	Lucena, Juan, Palm Beach	76
3B	PCT	Spearman, Jemel, Daytona	.933
	PO	Costanzo, Michael, Clearwater	79
	A	Costanzo, Michael, Clearwater	242
	E	Costanzo, Michael, Clearwater	25
	DP	Costanzo, Michael, Clearwater	21
		Spearman, Jemel, Daytona	21
SS	PCT	Nicholson, David, Vero Beach	.953
	PO	Coronado, Jose, St. Lucie	233
	A	Dlugach, Brent, Lakeland	423
	E	Harman, Brad, Clearwater	36
	DP	Dlugach, Brent, Lakeland	92
OF	PCT	Miller, Jai, Jupiter	.996
	PO	Thomas, Clete, Lakeland	321
	A	Strait, Cody, Sarasota	23
	E	Danielson, Sean, Palm Beach	12
	DP	Strait, Cody, Sarasota	6
		Thomas, Clete, Lakeland	6

BY WILL LINGO

West Michigan had the best record in the Midwest League during the regular season, so it was fitting that the Whitecaps cruised to the title. After losing Game One of the finals to Kane County, West Michigan stormed back to win the next three games.

West Michigan finished off the Cougars with eight runs over the first four innings of Game Four and got six strong innings from Eric Averill who went 2-0, 0.00 in the playoffs. Shortstop Mike Hollimon slugged four homers in the postseason to power the offense.

The Whitecaps have become one of the league's flagship franchises on and off the field, annually ranking among the league attendance leaders and winning four Midwest League titles since 1996. And more than 4,000 fans turned out for the finale as everyone on the team contributed to the win.

The club's 2.96 team ERA was easily the best in the league, and Burke Badenhop led the rotation with a 14-3 record and 2.84 ERA. Orlando Perdomo was the workhorse in the bullpen, piling up 28 saves to lead the league, though he wasn't around for the stretch drive.

The team's best prospect also happened to be one of its best offensive performers, with dynamic outfielder Cameron Maybin batting .304 with 20 doubles and 27 steals even though he missed more than a month with a finger injury.

The league as a whole has offered some strong outfield crops in recent years, including groups featuring Adam Dunn and Austin Kearns in 2000 and Carlos Gonzalez and Travis Buck last season. But the MWL never had outfield talent to match what it had in 2006. Maybin, Dayton's Jay Bruce, South Bend's Justin Upton and Quad Cities' Colby Rasmus spent their first full seasons terrorizing MWL pitchers and wowing everyone else.

The outfielders aside, the league's pitching was much deeper in talent than its position players. Its best mound prospect was clear cut, with Cedar Rapids righthander Nick Adenhart a nearly unanimous pick. His teammate Stephen Marek is not as highly regarded as a prospect, but he was the league's ERA leader with a 10-2, 1.96 season. And it was Kane County's Jeff Baisley, who piled up 22 home runs and 110 RBIs, who won league MVP honors.

The league will see just one franchise and affiliation change for 2007—at the same place. The Southwest Michigan Devil Rays, a franchise known by a variety of names as it struggled in Battle Creek, Mich.—will move to Midland, Mich., and become the Great Lakes Loons. The Devil Rays also left as the team's affiliate, with the Dodgers stepping in.

STANDINGS: SPLIT SEASON

FIRST HALF

EAST	W	L	PCT	GB
West Michigan	41	26	.612	—
Fort Wayne	40	27	.597	1
Dayton	35	35	.500	7½
South Bend	33	33	.500	7½
SW Michigan	32	37	.464	10
Fort Wayne	31	36	.463	10

WEST	W	L	PCT	GB
Peoria	41	28	.594	—
Kane County	40	29	.580	1
Burlington	35	32	.522	5
Beloit	35	33	.515	5
Quad Cities	34	34	.500	6½
Cedar Rapids	31	39	.443	10½
Wisconsin	27	43	.386	14½
Clinton	23	46	.333	18

SECOND HALF

EAST	W	L	PCT	GB
West Michigan	48	22	.686	—
South Bend	41	29	.586	7
Fort Wayne	40	30	.571	8
Dayton	32	38	.457	16
Lansing	32	38	.457	16
SW Michigan	30	40	.429	18

WEST	W	L	PCT	GB
Quad Cities	42	27	.609	—
Beloit	39	31	.557	3½
Kane County	39	31	.557	3½
Cedar Rapids	34	35	.493	8
Peoria	34	36	.486	8½
Burlington	29	41	.414	13½
Wisconsin	27	43	.386	15½
Clinton	22	48	.314	20½

PLAYOFFS—Division series: Beloit defeated Peoria 2-1, West Michigan defeated Fort Wayne 2-1, Lansing defeated South Bend 2-0, Kane County defeated Quad Cities 2-1 in best-of-three series. **Semifinals:** West Michigan defeated Lansing 2-0, Kane County defeated Beloit 2-0 in best-of-three series. **Final:** West Michigan defeated Kane County 3-1 in best-of-five series.

TOP 20 PROSPECTS

1. Jay Bruce, of, Dayton (Reds)
2. Cameron Maybin, of, West Michigan (Tigers)
3. Justin Upton, of, South Bend (Diamondbacks)
4. Colby Rasmus, of, Quad Cities (Cardinals)
5. Nick Adenhart, rhp, Cedar Rapids (Angels)
6. Jacob McGee, lhp, Southwest Michigan (Devil Rays)
7. Jaime Garcia, lhp, Quad Cities (Cardinals)
8. Wade Davis, rhp, Southwest Michigan (Devil Rays)
9. Donald Veal, lhp, Peoria (Cubs)
10. Matt Walker, rhp, Southwest Michigan (Devil Rays)
11. Stephen Marek, rhp, Cedar Rapids (Angels)
12. Johnny Cueto, rhp, Dayton (Reds)
13. Bryan Anderson, c, Quad Cities (Cardinals)
14. Oswaldo Sosa, rhp, Beloit (Twins)
15. John Mayberry Jr., of, Clinton (Rangers)
16. Justin Sellers, ss, Kane County (Athletics)
17. Eduardo Morlan, rhp, Beloit (Twins)
18. Paul Kelly, ss, Beloit (Twins)
19. Pedro Ciriaco, ss, South Bend (Diamondbacks)
20. Jeff Baisley, 3b, Kane County (Athletics)

STANDINGS: OVERALL

Page	Team	W	L	PCT	GB	Manager	Attendance	Average	Last Penn.
118	West Michigan Whitecaps (Tigers)	89	48	.650	—	Matt Walbeck	356,155	5,238	2006
193	Kane County Cougars (Athletics)	79	60	.568	11	Aaron Nieckula	500,052	7,354	2001
215	Swing of the Quad Cities (Cardinals)	76	61	.555	13	Keith Mitchell	146,688	2,328	1990
51	South Bend Silver Hawks (Diamondbacks)	74	62	.544	14½	Mark Haley	164,168	2,565	2005
81	Peoria Chiefs (Cubs)	75	64	.540	15	Jody Davis	235,031	3,406	2002
169	Beloit Snappers (Twins)	74	64	.536	15½	Jeff Smith	84,547	1,281	1995
260	Lansing Lugnuts (Blue Jays)	72	65	.526	17	Ken Joyce	331,503	4,948	2003
223	Fort Wayne Wizards (Padres)	71	66	.518	18	Randy Ready	253,564	3,842	None
96	Dayton Dragons (Reds)	67	73	.479	23½	Billy Gardner	582,903	8,448	None
147	Cedar Rapids Kernels (Angels)	65	74	.468	25	Bobby Magallanes	176,021	2,589	1994
140	Burlington Bees (Royals)	64	73	.467	25	Jim Gabella	65,190	1019	1999
245	Southwest Michigan Devil Rays (Devil Rays)	62	77	.446	28	Skeeter Barnes	84,969	1,328	2000
238	Wisconsin Timber Rattlers (Mariners)	54	86	.386	38½	Jim Horner	209,033	3,216	1984
253	Clinton LumberKings (Royals)	45	94	,324	46	Andy Fox	108,301	1,570	1991

NOTE: Teams' individual batting and pitching statistics can be found on page indicated in lefthand column.

2006 MIDWEST LEAGUE STATISTICS

CLUB BATTING

	AVG	G	AB	R	H	2B	3B	HR	BB	SO	SB	OBP	SLG
Quad Cities	.272	137	4686	694	1274	253	30	90	430	841	146	.341	.396
Kane County	.267	139	4637	720	1239	244	27	80	531	925	106	.348	.383
Fort Wayne	.263	137	4663	672	1226	261	31	81	506	954	91	.342	.384
South Bend	.259	136	4615	627	1193	231	21	85	462	958	77	.334	.373
Beloit	.259	138	4716	602	1221	229	43	65	399	990	115	.326	.367
West Michigan	.254	137	4666	620	1186	222	48	81	508	1066	123	.331	.374
Dayton	.253	140	4721	609	1194	258	36	91	393	1061	90	.317	.381
Lansing	.252	137	4604	608	1159	256	33	98	476	1156	122	.329	.386
Peoria	.250	139	4579	564	1143	213	22	72	373	998	119	.315	.353
Cedar Rapids	.245	139	4625	592	1131	208	50	78	418	1113	201	.314	.362
Wisconsin	.245	140	4614	563	1129	207	41	71	368	1072	138	.308	.353
Clinton	.243	139	4639	534	1129	193	34	72	406	1032	114	.309	.346
Burlington	.242	137	4484	539	1084	166	28	52	488	955	158	.324	.326
Southwest Michigan	.235	139	4431	468	1040	201	23	42	407	1000	110	.309	.319

CLUB PITCHING

	ERA	G	CG	SHO	SV	IP	H	R	ER	HR	BB	SO	AVG
West Michigan	2.96	137	6	15	49	1236	1115	492	407	64	325	962	.241
Beloit	3.18	138	5	14	35	1250	1142	531	442	69	396	1128	.242
Lansing	3.44	137	0	15	33	1217	1177	566	465	74	430	1033	.255
Quad Cities	3.45	137	4	11	30	1207	1099	577	463	58	446	1034	.243
Burlington	3.47	137	1	8	34	1214	1127	551	468	90	400	940	.247
Cedar Rapids	3.57	139	8	9	32	1252	1217	572	496	84	359	942	.258
Peoria	3.67	139	2	9	44	1212	1153	567	494	84	455	931	.251
Dayton	3.70	140	3	12	44	1225	1133	591	503	90	401	1089	.244
Southwest Michigan	3.76	139	1	9	38	1207	1097	628	504	64	545	1189	.241
Fort Wayne	3.76	137	3	15	27	1198	1225	612	501	82	395	884	.266
Kane County	3.90	139	6	8	40	1208	1180	616	523	61	494	999	.259
South Bend	3.93	136	5	9	36	1207	1214	629	527	66	387	938	.260
Wisconsin	4.41	140	3	4	27	1211	1224	720	593	85	565	1039	.264
Clinton	4.81	139	1	6	22	1205	1245	760	644	89	518	1013	.268

CLUB FIELDING

	PCT	PO	A	E	DP		PCT	PO	A	E	DP
Burlington	.974	3641	1371	135	116	Dayton	.967	3674	1472	173	112
Cedar Rapids	.973	3755	1597	147	145	Clinton	.967	3615	1335	169	120
West Michigan	.973	3707	1438	142	118	Lansing	.966	3651	1535	181	131
Kane County	.972	3623	1472	149	138	Quad Cities	.965	3621	1459	182	125
Peoria	.971	3637	1377	151	92	Wisconsin	.965	3632	1449	184	132
Fort Wayne	.971	3595	1560	156	143	SW Michigan	.964	3620	1317	184	103
South Bend	.968	3622	1392	167	107	Beloit	.964	3749	1438	191	116

INDIVIDUAL BATTING LEADERS
(Minimum 434 Plate Appearances)

	AVG	G	AB	R	H	2B	3B	HR	RBI	BB	SO	SB
Lis, Erik, Beloit	.326	105	411	69	134	37	3	16	70	51	83	4
Venable, William, Fort Wayne	.314	124	472	86	148	34	5	11	91	55	81	18
Norwood, Ryan, Peoria	.307	134	505	62	155	28	0	15	69	27	106	5
Maybin, Cameron, West Michigan	.304	101	385	59	117	20	6	9	69	50	116	27
Valdez, Jesus, Peoria	.302	130	510	63	154	25	1	5	61	22	73	10
Baisley, Jeffrey, Kane County	.298	124	466	86	139	35	1	22	110	62	86	6
Statia, Hainley, Cedar Rapids	.297	111	417	68	124	31	1	1	38	52	54	23
Justice, Justin, West Michigan	.295	112	414	51	122	22	9	6	67	41	101	15
Bruce, Jay, Dayton	.291	117	444	69	129	42	5	16	81	44	106	19
Recker, Anthony, Kane County	.287	109	407	52	117	24	3	14	57	42	115	5

INDIVIDUAL PITCHING LEADERS
(Minimum 112 Innings)

	W	L	ERA	G	GS	CG	SV	IP	H	R	ER	BB	SO
Marek, Stephen, Cedar Rapids	10	2	1.96	19	19	1	0	119	95	27	26	24	100
Hearne, Trey, Quad Cities	12	3	2.25	31	17	0	0	128	102	42	32	34	106
Atkins, Mitch, Peoria	13	4	2.41	25	25	0	0	138	110	47	37	53	127
Rosa, Carlos, Burlington	8	6	2.53	24	24	1	0	139	121	50	39	54	102
Cheng, Chi-Hung, Lansing	11	5	2.70	28	28	0	0	143	129	57	43	68	154
Sosa, Oswaldo, Beloit	9	7	2.75	20	20	1	0	118	102	44	36	36	95
Fisher, Carlos, Dayton	12	5	2.76	27	27	0	0	150	133	53	46	38	122
Nicoll, Christopher, Burlington	4	9	2.82	23	23	0	0	134	105	49	42	40	140
Badenhop, Burke, West Michigan	14	3	2.84	27	27	3	0	171	170	59	54	31	124
McGee, Jacob, Southwest Michigan	7	9	2.96	26	26	0	0	134	103	54	44	65	171

ALL-STAR TEAM

C—Bryan Anderson, Quad Cities. **1B**—Erik Lis, Beloit. **2B**—Josh Johnson, Burlington. **SS**—Mike Hollimon, West Michigan. **3B**—Jeff Baisley, Kane County. **OF**—Jay Bruce, Dayton; Cameron Maybin, West Michigan; Will Venable, Fort Wayne. **DH**—Randy Roth, Quad Cities. **RHP**—Nick Adenhart, Cedar Rapids. **LHP**—Jake McGee, Southwest Michigan. **RP**—Ed Campusano, Peoria; Greg Dupas, Southwest Michigan; Orlando Perdomo, West Michigan.

Most Valuable Player: Jeff Baisley, Kane County. **Prospect of the Year:** Cameron Maybin, West Michigan. **Manager of the Year:** Matt Walbeck, West Michigan.

DEPARTMENT LEADERS

BATTING
OBP	Lis, Erik, Beloit .... .402
SLG	Lis, Erik, Beloit .... .547
R	Baisley, Jeffrey, Kane County 86
	Venable, William, Fort Wayne 86
H	Norwood, Ryan, Peoria 155
TB	Baisley, Jeffrey, Kane County 242
XBH	Bruce, Jay, Dayton 63
2B	Bruce, Jay, Dayton 42
3B	Hollimon, Michael, West Michigan......13
HR	Renz, Jordan, Cedar Rapids...............24
RBI	Baisley, Jeffrey, Kane County 110
SAC	Johnson, Joshua, Burlington..............19
SF	Baisley, Jeffrey, Kane County 10
BB	Johnson, Joshua, Burlington..............93
IBB	Hollimon, Michael, West Michigan......6
	Lis, Erik, Beloit...................................6
HBP	Ovalle, Edward, Beloit 20
SO	Szymanski, Brandon, Dayton 191
SB	Coon, Bradley, Cedar Rapids 55
CS	Coon, Bradley, Cedar Rapids 21
GIDP	Hendricks, Trey, South Bend 17
AB/SO	Cotto, Pedro, West Michigan 14.52

PITCHING
G	Guaramato, Edgar, Wisconsin...........54
GS	Five players tied at 28
CG	Four players tied at 3
SHO	Cueto, Johnny, Dayton.......................2
	Garcia, Ramon, West Michigan.........2
GF	Dupas, Greg, Southwest Michigan...42
SV	Perdomo, Orlando, West Michigan...28
W	Badenhop, Burke, West Michigan 14
	Pino, Yohan, Beloit 14
L	Rasner, Jacob, Clinton 17
IP	Averill, Erik, West Michigan 171
H	Shields, Trey, Kane County 190
R	Fagan, Paul, Wisconsin 109
ER	Phillips, Zachary, Clinton 94
HB	Guaramato, Edgar, Wisconsin...........17
BB	Santo, Joel, Peoria.............................74
SO	McGee, Jacob, Southwest Michigan..171
SO/9 (SP)	McGee, Jacob, Southwest Michigan..11.49
SO/9 (SP)	Woerman, Joseph, Wisconsin 14.29
WP	Daniels, Adam, Quad Cities...............28
BK	Yepez, Jesus, Peoria............................5

FIELDING
C	PCT Reed, Mark, Peoria 993
	PO Tatum, Craig, Dayton......................699
	A Lopez, Christian, SW Michigan 99
	E Lopez, Christian, SW Michigan.........12
	Recker, Anthony, Kane County 12
	DP Martinez, Brett, Cedar Rapids 9
	Tatum, Craig, Dayton..........................9
	PB Anderson, Bryan, Quad Cities 17
	CS% Muyco, Jake, Peoria 54%
1B	PCT Norwood, Ryan, Peoria............. .991
	PO Trumbo, Mark, Cedar Rapids.......1033
	A Kleen, Steve, Kane County 83
	E Lis, Erik, Beloit...................................19
	DP Kleen, Steve, Kane County 96
2B	PCT Johnson, Joshua, Burlington..... .982
	PO Vallejo, Jose, Clinton 237
	A Vallejo, Jose, Clinton 337
	E Shoffit, Sean, Lansing 27
	DP Rhymes, William, West Michigan .80
3B	PCT Baisley, Jeffrey, Kane County ... .963
	PO Lisson, Mario, Burlington...............111
	A Baisley, Jeffrey, Kane County 243
	E Whittleman, John, Clinton 34
	DP Morris, Dallas, Cedar Rapids 28
SS	PCT Statia, Hainley, Cedar Rapids... .972
	PO Sellers, Justin, Kane County 217
	A Hollimon, Michael, West Michigan...394
	E Ciriaco, Pedro, South Bend 45
	DP Sellers, Justin, Kane County 81
OF	PCT Gregg, Davy, Peoria .... .989
	PO Duarte, Jose, Burlington................300
	A Duarte, Jose, Burlington 22
	E Tintor, Eli, Beloit 10
	DP Duarte, Jose, Burlington....................7

BY MATT MEYERS

Since moving to Lakewood in 2001, the BlueClaws had been a powerhouse at the box office but a laughingstock on the field. With an overall record 312-379 in its first five seasons, Lakewood never finished higher than third in any half-season in the South Atlantic League.

It's amazing what a little pitching can do.

Led by righthander Carlos Carrasco and lefthanders Matt Maloney and Josh Outman, the BlueClaws had the lowest ERA in the league at 3.10 and went 47-23 in the second half of the season to storm into the playoffs for the first time since moving to the Jersey Shore.

The BlueClaws took down Lexington in the first round with a two-game sweep to set up a showdown with Augusta, which had swept Rome. The two teams had the best overall records in the league, and in fact, Augusta had been the more dominant team after going 92-47 on the season and 53-16 in the second half.

Augusta's offense proved no match for the Lakewood pitching in the final, however, as the GreenJackets could muster only two runs in their three losses. The BlueClaws won the best-of-five series 3-1.

The finale was a coronation of sorts for Maloney, who threw his best start of the season in his biggest start of the season. The Mississippi product threw a shutout and fanned 12 in a 5-0 victory. During the regular season, Maloney almost won the pitching triple crown, leading the league in wins (16) and strikeouts (180) but finishing second in ERA to West Virginia's Will Inman.

Maloney's performance stood out in a league loaded with pitching prospects. In fact, the trio at Lakewood might not have been the most talented pitching staff in the league. Greensboro opened the season with four first-rounders (Chris Volstad, Aaron Thompson, Sean West and Ryan Tucker) from the 2005 draft and later added Brett Sinkbeil, a first-rounder from the 2006 draft.

However, any discussion of prospects in the SAL in 2006 begins with a trio of players who were 17 for the most of the season. Outfielders Jose Tabata (Charleston) and Fernando Martinez (Hagerstown) and shortstop Elvis Andrus (Rome) were the talk of the league, with Tabata barely edging the other two in the league top 20 rankings.

The SAL added another new stadium in 2006, and this was one of the most ambitious ever. With the Red Sox affiliate now in Greenville, the Drive built their new park in the mold of Fenway Park. The new stadium helped give them the fifth-best attendance in the SAL.

STANDINGS: SPLIT SEASON

FIRST HALF					SECOND HALF				
NORTH	W	L	PCT	GB	**NORTH**	W	L	PCT	GB
Lexington	44	25	.638	—	Lakewood	47	23	.671	—
West Virginia	39	30	.565	5	West Virginia	35	32	.522	10½
Delmarva	37	31	.544	6½	Lake County	35	33	.515	11
Lakewood	37	32	.536	7	Hickory	34	34	.500	12
Greensboro	36	34	.514	8½	Greensboro	32	35	.478	13½
Hickory	33	36	.478	11	Lexington	31	38	.449	15½
Lake County	29	41	.414	15½	Hagerstown	30	40	.429	17
Hagerstown	28	42	.400	16½	Delmarva	27	42	.391	19½
SOUTH	W	L	PCT	GB	**SOUTH**	W	L	PCT	GB
Rome	42	28	.600	—	Augusta	53	16	.768	—
Augusta	39	31	.557	3	Asheville	39	28	.582	13
Charleston	38	32	.543	4	Charleston	40	30	.571	13½
Columbus	37	33	.529	5	Columbus	35	35	.500	18½
Asheville	35	35	.500	7	Greenville	32	38	.457	21½
Greenville	35	35	.500	7	Rome	29	40	.420	24
Savannah	28	42	.400	14	Savannah	28	41	.406	25
Kannapolis	20	50	.286	22	Kannapolis	22	44	.333	291

PLAYOFFS—Semifinals: Lakewood defeated Lexington 2-0 and Augusta defeated Rome 2-0 in best-of-three series. **Final:** Lakewood defeated Augusta 3-1 in best-of-five series.

TOP 20 PROSPECTS

1. Andrew McCutchen, of, Hickory (Pirates)
2. Jose Tabata, of, Charleston (Yankees)
3. Fernando Martinez, of, Hagerstown (Mets)
4. Elvis Andrus, ss, Rome (Braves)
5. Carlos Carrasco, rhp, Lakewood (Phillies)
6. Chris Volstad, rhp, Greensboro (Marlins)
7. Will Inman, rhp, West Virginia (Brewers)
8. Sean West, lhp, Greensboro (Marlins)
9. Brandon Erbe, rhp, Delmarva (Orioles)
10. Dexter Fowler, of, Asheville (Rockies)
11. Deolis Guerra, rhp, Hagerstown (Mets)
12. John Drennen, of, Lake County (Indians)
13. Clay Buchholz, rhp, Greenville (Red Sox)
14. Lorenzo Cain, of, West Virginia (Brewers)
15. Michael Bowden, rhp, Greenville (Red Sox)
16. Ryan Tucker, rhp, Greensboro (Marlins)
17. Eric Campbell, 3b, Rome (Braves)
18. Aaron Thompson, lhp, Greensboro (Marlins)
19. Matt Maloney, lhp, Lakewood (Phillies)
20. Josh Outman, lhp, Lakewood (Phillies)

STANDINGS: OVERALL

Page	Team	W	L	PCT	GB	Manager(s)	Attendance	Average	Last Penn.
230	Augusta GreenJackets (Giants)	92	47	.662	—	Roberto Kelly	155,910	2,475	1999
201	Lakewood BlueClaws (Phillies)	84	55	.604	8	Dave Huppert	448,310	6,691	2006
186	Charleston RiverDogs (Yankees)	78	62	.557	14½	Bill Mosiello/Pat Roessler	267,908	3,999	None
133	Lexington Legends (Astros)	75	63	.543	16½	Jack Lind	376,702	5,540	2001
162	West Virginia (Brewers)	74	62	.544	16½	Mike Guerrero	239,721	3,756	1990
111	Asheville Tourists (Rockies)	74	63	.540	17	Joe Mikulik	167,745	2,581	1984
155	Columbus Catfish (Dodgers)	72	68	.514	20½	Travis Barbary	66,516	1,039	None
58	Rome Braves (Braves)	71	68	.511	21	Randy Ingle	232,259	3,416	2003
126	Greensboro Grasshoppers (Marlins)	68	69	.496	23	Brandon Hyde	427,890	6,386	1982
208	Hickory Crawdads (Pirates)	67	70	.489	24	Jeff Branson	173,137	2,623	2004
73	Greenville Drive (Red Sox)	67	73	.479	25½	Luis Alicea	330,078	4,784	1998
65	Delmarva Shorebirds (Orioles)	64	73	.467	27	Gary Kendall	217,980	3,406	2000
104	Lake County Captains (Indians)	64	74	.464	27½	Lee May Jr.	346,519	5,172	None
177	Hagerstown Suns (Mets)	58	82	.414	34½	Frank Cacciatore	149,188	2,260	None
268	Savannah Sand Gnats (Nationals)	56	83	.403	36	Bobby Williams	84,642	1,302	1996
88	Kannapolis Intimidators (White Sox)	42	94	.309	48½	Omer Munoz	111,045	1,735	2005

NOTE: Teams' individual batting and pitching statistics can be found on page indicated in lefthand column.

2006 SOUTH ATLANTIC LEAGUE STATISTICS

CLUB BATTING

	AVG	G	AB	R	H	2B	3B	HR	BB	SO	SB	OBP	SLG
West Virginia	.277	136	4574	691	1265	256	34	79	500	882	184	.353	.399
Augusta	.271	139	4621	673	1252	206	55	60	413	896	244	.338	.378
Asheville	.271	137	4573	755	1239	285	25	98	455	1032	266	.347	.408
Columbus	.267	140	4697	711	1253	237	28	104	569	908	100	.355	.396
Hickory	.265	137	4648	702	1230	237	26	111	419	1018	115	.335	.398
Lakewood	.256	139	4678	637	1197	279	29	66	486	1059	131	.334	.370
Greenville	.255	140	4803	675	1226	255	39	104	504	1057	99	.335	.390
Rome	.254	139	4636	645	1176	228	34	101	409	1064	174	.321	.383
Charleston	.253	140	4612	633	1168	196	33	61	513	1005	188	.336	.350
Greensboro	.250	137	4556	606	1137	219	24	114	443	984	114	.324	.383
Lexington	.250	138	4579	618	1144	264	23	87	396	961	172	.319	.375
Lake County	.245	138	4579	568	1123	195	29	87	525	1077	102	.329	.358
Savannah	.241	139	4538	564	1095	192	46	81	469	1113	90	.319	.357
Kannapolis	.240	136	4505	546	1083	213	31	91	356	1062	117	.305	.362
Hagerstown	.238	140	4542	522	1083	218	16	83	415	987	98	.313	.348
Delmarva	.237	137	4423	582	1047	231	27	79	534	1068	101	.325	.355

CLUB PITCHING

	ERA	G	CG	SHO	SV	IP	H	R	ER	HR	BB	SO	AVG
Lakewood	3.10	139	5	19	44	1231	1010	509	424	51	490	1176	.223
Charleston	3.20	140	2	11	34	1221	1132	562	434	80	448	1026	.246
Augusta	3.26	139	3	17	43	1208	1128	518	437	64	367	1034	.247
Greenville	3.55	140	0	7	27	1233	1116	608	486	101	418	1063	.240
Lexington	3.58	138	3	9	40	1205	1140	586	480	108	472	1041	.249
Lake County	3.60	138	1	8	32	1222	1167	593	489	86	411	943	.252
Greensboro	3.74	137	2	11	32	1204	1160	601	501	105	439	1069	.255
Delmarva	3.76	137	2	4	36	1194	1159	623	499	76	471	1015	.255
Hagerstown	3.79	140	4	8	32	1207	1135	604	509	84	517	994	.250
West Virginia	3.87	136	2	10	31	1178	1124	615	507	87	483	1026	.251
Asheville	4.03	137	1	4	45	1193	1249	662	535	89	442	924	.270
Rome	4.21	139	4	8	29	1211	1209	665	567	76	534	1018	.261
Hickory	4.31	137	3	2	36	1198	1225	716	574	119	413	884	.263
Savannah	4.65	139	2	7	25	1198	1286	718	619	103	434	921	.275
Columbus	4.70	140	4	4	32	1212	1214	743	633	94	569	1102	.262
Kannapolis	4.75	136	1	4	24	1183	1264	805	624	83	498	937	.272

CLUB FIELDING

	PCT	PO	A	E	DP		PCT	PO	A	E	DP
Greensboro	.974	3613	1491	135	126	Delmarva	.968	3580	1375	166	111
Lake County	.973	3667	1485	143	130	Columbus	.967	3637	1445	172	161
Augusta	.973	3624	1416	141	116	Lexington	.966	3616	1454	178	129
Savannah	.972	3593	1566	151	144	Asheville	.966	3580	1624	182	121
Lakewood	.970	3693	1350	158	131	West Virginia	.964	3535	1328	184	134
Charleston	.969	3662	1515	164	135	Hagerstown	.963	3622	1498	194	147
Greenville	.969	3700	1556	169	131	Hickory	.961	3594	1570	210	108
Rome	.969	3633	1373	161	141	Kannapolis	.959	3548	1413	213	111

INDIVIDUAL BATTING LEADERS
(Minimum 434 Plate Appearances)

	AVG	G	AB	R	H	2B	3B	HR	RBI	BB	SO	SB
Spidale, Mike, Lakewood	.345	80	313	58	108	19	3	1	37	37	33	29
Velez, Eugenio, Augusta	.315	126	460	90	145	29	20	14	90	34	81	64
Slayden, Jeremy, Lakewood	.310	107	400	65	124	44	3	10	81	41	89	5
Cain, Lorenzo, West Virginia	.307	132	527	91	162	36	4	6	60	58	104	34
Garner, Cole, Asheville	.302	120	464	100	140	40	2	19	88	25	127	35
Delaney, Jason, Hickory	.300	128	456	64	137	27	3	9	75	56	79	5
Brantley, Michael, West Virginia	.300	108	360	47	108	10	2	0	42	61	51	24
Jones, Ben, Charleston	.298	110	383	63	114	18	4	21	88	59	85	0
Fowler, Dexter, Asheville	.296	99	405	92	120	31	6	8	46	43	79	43
Campbell, Eric, Rome	.296	116	449	83	133	27	3	22	77	23	68	18

INDIVIDUAL PITCHING LEADERS
(Minimum 112 Innings)

	W	L	ERA	G	GS	CG	SV	IP	H	R	ER	BB	SO
Maloney, Matthew, Lakewood	16	9	2.03	27	27	2	0	169	120	54	38	73	180
Carrasco, Carlos, Lakewood	12	6	2.26	26	26	2	0	159	103	50	40	65	159
Redmond, Todd, Hickory	13	6	2.75	27	27	0	0	160	137	64	49	33	148
Outman, Joshua, Lakewood	14	6	2.95	27	27	1	0	155	119	61	51	75	161
Martinez, Joseph, Augusta	15	5	3.01	27	27	1	0	168	156	66	56	26	135
Arias, Wilkins, Charleston	9	6	3.01	31	22	1	2	141	118	50	47	53	114
Volstad, Christopher, Greensboro	11	8	3.08	26	26	0	0	152	161	73	52	36	99
Deters, James, Lake County	12	9	3.11	28	28	1	0	168	178	77	58	29	106
Erbe, Brandon, Delmarva	5	9	3.22	28	27	0	0	115	88	47	41	47	133
Murdy, Garrett, Lexington	6	5	3.34	32	14	0	2	114	112	57	43	37	75

ALL-STAR TEAM

C—Angel Salome, West Virginia. **1B**—Ben Jones, Charleston. **2B**—Eugenio Velez, Augusta. **SS**—Tommy Manzella, Lexington. **3B**—Mat Gamel, West Virginia. **OF**—Lorenzo Cain, West Virginia; Cole Garner, Asheville; Andrew McCutchen, Hickory. **Utility IF**—Eric Campbell, Rome. **Utility OF**—Dexter Fowler, Asheville. **DH**—Brad Corley, Hickory. **RHP**—Will Inman, West Virginia. **LHP**—Matt Maloney; Lakewood.

Most Valuable Player: Eugenio Velez, Augusta. **Most Outstanding Pitcher:** Matt Maloney, Lakewood. **Manager of the Year:** Roberto Kelly, Augusta.

BATTING

OBP	Pedroza, Sergio, Columbus	.437
SLG	Pedroza, Sergio, Columbus	.562
R	Garner, Cole, Asheville	.100
H	Cain, Lorenzo, West Virginia	.162
TB	Velez, Eugenio, Augusta	.256
XBH	Velez, Eugenio, Augusta	.63
2B	Slayden, Jeremy, Lakewood	.44
3B	Velez, Eugenio, Augusta	.20
HR	Campbell, Eric, Rome	.22
RBI	Corley, Brad, Hickory	.100
SAC	Castro, Jose, Hagerstown	.21
SF	Harris, Clay, Lakewood	.11
BB	Finan, Ryan, Delmarva	.85
IBB	Gamel, Mat, West Virginia	.8
HBP	Gimenez, Chris, Lake County	.26
SO	Baez, Welinson, Lakewood	.158
SB	Young Jr., Eric, Asheville	.87
CS	Young Jr., Eric, Asheville	.31
GIDP	Bell, Mike, West Virginia	.20
	Castro, Ofilio, Savannah	.20
AB/SO	Ascencion, Quincy, Delmarva	.8.51

PITCHING

G	Chirino, Israel, Kannapolis	.57
GS	Deters, James, Lake County	.28
	Hernandez, David, Delmarva	.28
CG	Five players tied at	.2
SHO	14 players tied at	.1
GF	Davis, Matt, Lake County	.51
SV	Davis, Matt, Lake County	.26
W	Maloney, Matthew, Lakewood	.16
L	Four players tied at	.13
IP	Maloney, Matthew, Lakewood	.168.2
H	Deters, James, Lake County	.178
R	Brooks, Richard, Kannapolis	.104
ER	Alvarez, Mario, Columbus	.84
HB	Herrmann, Frank, Lake County	.17
	Redmond, Todd, Hickory	.17
BB	Jones, Beau, Rome	.83
SO	Maloney, Matthew, Lakewood	.180
SO/9 (SP)	Inman, William, West Virginia	.10.71
SO/9 (RP)	Doolittle, Michael, Greensboro	.12.26
WP	Pratt, Jordan, Columbus	.26
BK	Cline, Zachary, Lakewood	.4

FIELDING

C	PCT	Clark, Cody, Rome	.998
	PO	Marson, Lou, Lakewood	.868
	A	Hernandez, Francisco, Kannapolis	95
	E	Salome, Angel, West Virginia	.15
	DP	Butera, Andrew, Hagerstown	.14
	PB	Lerud, Steven, Hickory	.35
	CS%	McCarthy, Greg, Augusta	.52%
1B	PCT	Pacheco, Fernando, Lake Co.	.994
	PO	Evans, Nick, Hagerstown	.1124
	A	Evans, Nick, Hagerstown	.81
	E	Allen, Brandon, Kannapolis	.16
	DP	Evans, Nick, Hagerstown	.109
2B	PCT	Asprilla, Avelino, Lakewood	.980
		King, Eric, Lexington	.980
	PO	Young Jr., Eric, Asheville	.267
	A	Young Jr., Eric, Asheville	.369
	E	Pellot, Hector, Hagerstown	.28
	DP	Asprilla, Avelino, Lakewood	.74
3B	PCT	Finan, Ryan, Delmarva	.957
	PO	Granadillo, Tony, Greenville	.86
	A	Baez, Welinson, Lakewood	.248
	E	Ventura, Leivi, Hagerstown	.36
	DP	Ventura, Leivi, Hagerstown	.31
SS	PCT	Romero, Niuman, Lake County	.966
	PO	Andrus, Elvis, Rome	.208
		De Jesus, Ivan, Columbus	.208
	A	Castro, Jose, Hagerstown	.350
	E	Nelson, Christopher, Asheville	.41
	DP	De Jesus, Ivan, Columbus	.86
OF	PCT	Schafer, Jordan, Rome	.993
	PO	Ford, Darren, West Virginia	.289
	A	Cain, Lorenzo, West Virginia	.15
		Mooney, Michael, Augusta	.15
	E	Four players tied at	.12
	DP	Cain, Lorenzo, West Virginia	.6

MINOR LEAGUES

NEW YORK-PENN LEAGUE
SHORT-SEASON

BY JOHN MANUEL

The Yankees have rarely had trouble winning big league titles, even in the New York-Penn League. Staten Island took home its second straight title after defeating Tri-City (Astros) two out of three games.

Righthander George Kontos, a fifth-round pick out of Northwestern in 2006, got the win in the deciding game for Staten Island as he struck out 11 in six innings for his second win of the playoffs in a 2-0 victory. First baseman Kyle Larsen drove home both runs for the Yankees and finished the postseason with a .389 average along with two homers and seven RBIs.

Kyle Larsen

Among prospects, pitchers and catchers stood out the most in the league, where the position talent was on par with most years and the pitching seemed a bit stronger than normal, albeit with a paucity of quality lefthanders.

The best player in the league probably was Hudson Valley third baseman Evan Longoria, the No. 3 overall pick in the 2006 draft. He dazzled in his pro debut with 21 homers overall, including four in eight NY-P games before moving on.

"I only saw him for three games, but he just jumped out at me," said a scout who popped in for some rare NY-P coverage. "He really opened my eyes with his power. He just really handled a wood bat very well."

Some might argue Longoria

wasn't even the best third-base prospect, however. Aberdeen's Billy Rowell, the ninth overall pick in June, showed similar hitting ability from the left side as a 17-year-old. As with Longoria, Rowell's 11-game cameo was too short to qualify for BA's Top 20 Prospects list, but he left an impression nonetheless.

"He opened my eyes right away," Vermont manager Jose Alguacil said. "He hit the ball with real authority."

The league's most intriguing player, though, was Longoria's Renegades teammate, outfielder Josh Hamilton. The No. 1 overall pick in 1999, Hamilton had previously played low Class A ball with his Hudson Valley manager, Matt Quatraro. Hamilton hit a soft .260 before needing arthroscopic knee surgery, another obstacle on his long road to recovery from back and shoulder injuries and drug addiction.

"All the tools are still there," Quatraro said. "He's more mature, more patient at the plate now. He's better equipped now to deal with it all. It's just a shame he got hurt."

Tri-City had one of the league's better stories in 13th-round pick Chris Salamida, who went to school at nearby SUNY Oneonta and grew up about 15 minutes from the team's home ballpark. Salamida dominated the league, going 10-1, 1.06 to lead the NY-P in victories and ERA.

The league saw a three-way affiliation shuffle after the season, with the Pirates moving into nearby State College—which drew 138,000 fans in its first season in the league in 2006—followed by the Phillies taking the Pirates' place in Williamsport, and the Cardinals filling the vacancy in Batavia.

TOP 20 PROSPECTS

1. Jeremy Hellickson, rhp, Hudson Valley (Devil Rays)
2. Pedro Beato, rhp, Aberdeen (Orioles)
3. Matt McBride, c, Mahoning Valley (Indians)
4. Max Sapp, c, Tri-City (Astros)
5. Kris Johnson, lhp, Lowell (Red Sox)
6. Justin Masterson, rhp, Lowell (Red Sox)
7. Jordan Parraz, of, Tri-City (Astros)
8. Adam Ottavino, rhp, State College (Cardinals)
9. Scott Sizemore, ss/2b, Oneonta (Tigers)
10. Joe Smith, rhp, Brooklyn (Mets)
11. Tim Norton, rhp, Staten Island (Yankees)
12. Mark Hamilton, 1b, State College (Cardinals)
13. Justin Maxwell, of, Vermont (Nationals)
14. Jason Berken, rhp, Aberdeen (Orioles)
15. George Kontos, rhp, Staten Island (Yankees)
16. Chris Vinyard, 1b, Aberdeen (Orioles)
17. Mitch Hilligoss, ss/3b, Staten Island (Yankees)
18. Chris Salamida, lhp, Tri-City (Astros)
19. Wilmer Pino, 2b, Staten Island (Yankees)
20. Neil Wagner, rhp, Mahoning Valley (Indians)

STANDINGS

Page	McNAMARA	W	L	PCT	GB	Manager	Attendance	Average	Last Penn.
187	Staten Island Yankees	45	29	.608	—	Gaylen Pitts	115,395	3,394	2006
178	Brooklyn Cyclones (Mets)	41	33	.554	4½	George Greer	289,323	7,820	2001
66	Aberdeen IronBirds (Orioles)	41	34	.547	4½	Andy Etchebarren	235,905	6,376	1983
246	Hudson Valley Renegades (Devil Rays)	31	43	.419	14	Matt Quatraro	164,425	4,444	1999

Page	PINCKNEY	W	L	PCT	GB	Manager	Attendance	Average	Last Penn.
261	Auburn Doubledays (Blue Jays)	42	32	.568	—	Dennis Holmberg	63,267	1,861	1998
105	Mahoning Valley Scrappers (Indians)	40	36	.526	3	Rouglas Odor	129,719	3,603	2004
216	State College Spikes (Cardinals)	39	36	.520	3½	Mark Dejohn	138,619	3,851	1994
202	Batavia Muckdogs (Phillies)	35	38	.479	6½	Steve Roadcap	39,094	1,150	1963
127	Jamestown Jammers (Marlins)	33	39	.458	8	Bo Porter	45,128	1,410	1991
209	Williamsport Crosscutters (Pirates)	28	47	.373	14½	Tom Prince	69,510	1,931	2003

Page	STEDLER	W	L	PCT	GB	Manager	Attendance	Average	Last Penn.
134	Tri-City ValleyCats (Astros)	43	31	.581	—	Greg Langbehn	129,126	3,490	1997
119	Oneonta Tigers	40	34	.541	3	Tom Brookens	39,499	1,162	1998
74	Lowell Spinners (Red Sox)	39	36	.520	4½	Bruce Crabbe	192,387	5,344	None
269	Vermont Lake Monsters (Nationals)	23	52	.307	20½	Jose Alguacil	100,570	2,794	1996

PLAYOFFS—Semifinals: Tri-City defeated Auburn 2-0 and Staten Island defeated Brooklyn 2-0, in best-of-three series. **Finals:** Staten Island defeated Tri-City 2-1 in best-of-three series.

NOTE: Teams' individual batting and pitching statistics can be found on page indicated in lefthand column.

2006 NEW YORK-PENN LEAGUE STATISTICS

CLUB BATTING

	AVG	G	AB	R	H	2B	3B	HR	BB	SO	SB	OBP	SLG
Staten Island	.267	74	2494	365	667	119	15	29	228	508	70	.339	.362
Oneonta	.265	74	2586	348	684	117	30	25	281	560	40	.343	.362
Lowell	.258	75	2497	321	644	111	15	31	254	514	37	.337	.352
Tri-City	.248	74	2487	321	617	114	15	32	244	552	90	.323	.345
Auburn	.245	74	2402	337	588	128	23	29	259	589	28	.330	.353
Mahoning Valley	.245	76	2467	297	605	109	20	30	196	475	56	.309	.342
State College	.241	75	2427	299	586	113	19	33	215	502	77	.313	.344
Jamestown	.237	72	2362	302	560	102	22	21	220	515	63	.312	.326
Batavia	.234	73	2318	289	542	101	17	19	189	498	85	.300	.317
Vermont	.233	75	2424	262	565	89	17	22	186	611	65	.296	.311
Brooklyn	.231	74	2429	251	562	105	17	19	230	509	44	.307	.312
Aberdeen	.231	75	2531	309	585	124	20	29	202	627	58	.301	.330
Williamsport	.229	75	2461	243	564	97	23	17	177	549	57	.284	.308
Hudson Valley	.227	74	2466	255	561	122	7	38	178	635	56	.288	.329

CLUB PITCHING

	ERA	G	CG	SHO	SV	IP	H	R	ER	HR	BB	SO	AVG
Batavia	2.86	73	3	5	20	623	548	254	198	27	188	551	.235
Brooklyn	2.96	74	2	10	24	663	619	284	218	27	184	541	.245
Tri-City	3.03	74	0	9	21	666	560	276	224	39	244	565	.230
Aberdeen	3.08	75	0	2	28	683	577	285	234	32	275	626	.231
Auburn	3.12	74	1	5	24	643	582	288	223	19	191	462	.240
Oneonta	3.14	74	1	4	23	666	646	302	232	17	182	504	.257
Williamsport	3.24	75	1	4	18	652	565	279	235	29	228	575	.234
Staten Island	3.29	74	0	6	18	646	554	277	236	22	251	586	.233
Mahoning Valley	3.39	76	0	9	27	648	591	297	244	32	203	540	.240
Hudson Valley	3.43	74	0	6	20	664	593	303	253	27	192	617	.238
Lowell	3.50	75	0	2	27	665	622	317	259	25	217	549	.246
State College	3.71	75	2	3	22	648	619	321	267	23	226	515	.250
Jamestown	4.00	72	0	5	15	623	595	337	277	26	234	494	.251
Vermont	4.03	75	0	5	14	647	659	379	290	29	244	519	.263

CLUB FIELDING

	PCT	PO	A	E	DP		PCT	PO	A	E	DP
Tri-City	.979	1997	803	60	52	Mahoning Valley	.967	1943	746	92	47
Staten Island	.976	1938	772	67	47	Oneonta	.966	1998	877	100	78
Williamsport	.970	1955	850	88	72	State College	.966	1945	807	98	60
Aberdeen	.969	2049	841	91	72	Brooklyn	.964	1989	877	108	66
Batavia	.968	1870	722	85	42	Lowell	.964	1996	867	106	55
Hudson Valley	.968	1993	792	92	70	Jamestown	.961	1869	765	107	66
Auburn	.967	1929	873	95	57	Vermont	.960	1941	769	114	66

INDIVIDUAL BATTING LEADERS
(Minimum 236 Plate Appearances)

	AVG	G	AB	R	H	2B	3B	HR	RBI	BB	SO	SB
Parraz, Jordan, Tri-City	.336	70	253	46	85	18	2	6	38	33	44	23
Sizemore, Scott, Oneonta	.327	70	294	49	96	15	4	3	37	32	47	7
Pino, Wilmer, Staten Island	.326	61	227	43	74	15	2	0	31	7	35	18
Martin, Dustin, Brooklyn	.315	72	251	22	79	15	7	2	35	28	50	7
Taylor, Eric, Tri-City	.315	68	251	42	79	18	1	2	20	27	40	9
Southard, Nathan, State College	.306	66	242	43	74	21	4	5	44	27	42	16
Denham, Jason, Mahoning Valley	.302	53	215	22	65	9	2	0	14	18	34	6
Blackwood, Jacob, Jamestown	.300	69	267	30	80	16	1	2	32	11	33	5
Lytle, Andrew, Mahoning Valley	.292	65	236	36	69	10	0	1	22	20	34	10
Hilligoss, Mitchell, Staten Island	.292	67	267	40	78	8	1	2	36	24	47	12

INDIVIDUAL PITCHING LEADERS
(Minimum 61 Innings)

	W	L	ERA	G	GS	CG	SV	IP	H	R	ER	BB	SO
Salamida, Christopher, Tri-City	10	1	1.06	14	14	0	0	68	44	12	8	23	53
Brown, Eric, Brooklyn	7	1	1.16	10	10	1	0	70	53	16	9	4	55
Tomlin, Joshua, Mahoning Valley	8	2	2.09	15	15	0	0	77	56	24	18	15	69
Stoner, Tobi, Brooklyn	6	2	2.15	14	14	1	0	84	66	25	20	17	62
Bresnahan, Patrick, Williamsport	4	5	2.25	15	10	0	0	68	50	21	17	17	59
Qualben, David, Tri-City	5	5	2.25	14	14	0	0	72	54	26	18	20	43
Moore, Jeffrey, Aberdeen	6	2	2.29	15	13	0	0	79	65	26	20	5	60
Beazley, Travis, Lowell	3	2	2.39	14	13	0	0	68	68	26	18	19	59
Hellickson, Jeremy, Hudson Valley	4	3	2.43	15	14	0	0	78	55	24	21	16	96
Hallberg, Bryan, Tri-City	4	3	2.44	15	12	0	1	70	63	23	19	21	53

MINOR LEAGUES

NORTHWEST LEAGUE
SHORT-SEASON

BY AARON FITT

Salem-Keizer, a Giants affiliate loaded with experienced, accomplished college stars making their pro debuts, was the Northwest League's dominant team from wire to wire in 2007.

The Volcanoes, who went 55-21 in the regular season to win the Western Division by 12 games, capped off their impressive season by winning the NWL championship in four games against Boise.

Righthander Kevin Pucetas, a 17th-round pick in June out of Limestone (S.C.) College, struck out four and allowed five hits over six shutout innings in the Volcanoes' 6-4 win in the championship clincher. Emmanuel Burriss and Adam Witter had two hits apiece to lead the Salem-Keizer offense, and center fielder Michael McBryde preserved the

BILL MITCHELL

Emmanuel Burriss

win with a diving catch in the eighth inning, robbing Steven Clevenger of a likely two-run double that would have tied the game.

Burriss, the Giants' first-round pick in June out of Kent State, was the catalyst for the league's highest-scoring offense. The speedy shortstop led the NWL with 35 stolen bases—though he also led the league by getting caught 11 times—and ranked as the league's No. 4 prospect. Witter provided the muscle, tying for the league lead with 16 home runs and leading by himself with a .585 slugging percentage, while making the conversion to catcher.

On the mound, Salem-Keizer was just as strong, leading the league with a 2.95 team ERA. (To complete their dominance, the Volcanoes were also the league's best defensive team.)

Juan Trinidad led the league with 16 saves to anchor the Salem-Keizer bullpen, and the rotation was anchored by soft-tossing submariner Adam Cowart, a 35th-round pick out of Kansas State.

Cowart did not allow an earned run in his first four starts (spanning 21 innings), then reeled off an even longer stretch of five starts (28 innings) without yielding an earned run. On his way to winning pitcher of the year honors, Cowart won his first 10 professional decisions before losing in his final outing of the regular season. Still, his 10 wins led the league, as did his .178 opponent average.

Despite his success, Cowart ranked as just the No. 20 prospect in the league, as scouts question whether he's got enough stuff to get batters out at higher levels.

That was also because there was plenty of talent at the top of the NWL.

College players making their pro debuts traditionally dominate the league, and that doesn't figure to change. Even in 2006, when the league featured two impressive high school pitchers (Tony Butler and Kasey Kiker) making their pro debuts and a third who was a first-rounder in 2005 (Mark Pawelek), 14 of the 20 best prospects were college products.

One of those college players, five-tool Boise outfielder Tyler Colvin, grabbed the top prospect mantle from Tri-City righthander Shane Lindsay, an Australian dynamo who utterly dominated the NWL in 2005 and returned while rehabbing a shoulder injury. Lindsay ranked as the league's top pitching prospect again, posting a 2.79 ERA in 29 innings before he moved on to low Class A Asheville.

Yakima outfielder Cyle Hankerd was the NWL's other major story in 2006. A third-round pick out of Southern California in June, Hankerd terrorized Northwest League pitchers, winning the batting title by 41 points on his way to league MVP honors.

Hankerd batted .384 even though he was the only real threat in a Yakima lineup that batted .242 as a team.

The NWL remained one of the most stable league in the minors, with no affiliation changes or franchise movement either before or after the season. The league hasn't added a new franchise since Tri-City joined in 2001.

TOP 20 PROSPECTS

1. Tyler Colvin, of, Boise (Cubs)
2. Shane Lindsay, rhp, Tri-City (Rockies)
3. Matt Sulentic, of, Vancouver (Athletics)
4. Emmanuel Burriss, ss, Salem-Keizer (Giants)
5. Clye Hankerd, of, Yakima (Diamondbacks)
6. Tony Butler, lhp, Everett (Mariners)
7. Kasey Kiker, lhp, Spokane (Rangers)
8. Matt Antonelli, 3b, Eugene (Padres)
9. Mark Pawelek, lhp, Boise (Cubs)
10. Jermaine Mitchell, of, Vancouver (Athletics)
11. Josh Sullivan, rhp, Tri-City (Rockies)
12. Chris Davis, 1b/of, Spokane (Rangers)
13. Chad Tracy, c, Spokane (Rangers)
14. Chad Huffman, of, Eugene (Padres)
15. Daniel Mayora, ss, Tri-City (Rockies)
16. Brooks Brown, rhp, Yakima (Diamondbacks)
17. Andrew Bailey, rhp, Vancouver (Athletics)
18. Scott Deal, rhp, Vancouver (Athletics)
19. Kam Mickolio, rhp, Everett (Mariners)
20. Adam Cowart, rhp, Salem-Keizer (Giants)

STANDINGS

Page	EAST	W	L	PCT	GB	Manager	Attendance	Average	Last Penn.
82	Boise Hawks (Cubs)	44	32	.579	—	Steve McFarland	108,876	2,865	2004
134	Tri-City Dust Devils (Rockies)	38	38	.500	6	Freddie Ocasio	67,545	1,778	None
51	Yakima Bears (Diamondbacks)	28	48	.368	16	Jay Gainer	63,400	1,668	2000
254	Spokane Indians (Rangers)	26	50	.342	18	Mike Micucci	182,091	4,792	2005
Page	WEST	W	L	PCT	GB	Manager	Attendance	Average	Last Penn.
231	Salem-Keizer Volcanoes (Giants)	55	21	.724	—	Steve Decker	118,622	3,122	2001
224	Eugene Emeralds (Padres)	43	33	.566	12	Doug Dascenzo	122,734	3,230	1980
194	Vancouver Canadians (Athletics)	39	37	.513	16	Rick Magnante	123,878	3,260	None
239	Everett AquaSox (Mariners)	31	45	.408	24	Dave Myers	106,675	2,883	1985

PLAYOFFS: Salem-Keizer defeated Boise 3-1 in best-of-five series.

NOTE: Teams' individual batting and pitching statistics can be found on page indicated in lefthand column.

MINOR LEAGUES

2006 NORTHWEST LEAGUE STATISTICS

CLUB BATTING

	AVG	G	AB	R	H	2B	3B	HR	BB	SO	SB	OBP	SLG
Boise	.268	76	2583	397	691	127	26	46	223	480	89	.332	.390
Salem-Keizer	.264	76	2591	412	683	119	20	52	259	457	101	.338	.385
Eugene	.256	76	2621	391	671	156	8	51	299	576	43	.341	.380
Vancouver	.246	76	2565	342	631	137	17	33	253	536	67	.318	.351
Spokane	.245	76	2561	330	628	134	23	51	248	615	67	.324	.375
Yakima	.242	76	2591	318	626	113	10	40	254	645	50	.318	.339
Everett	.241	76	2553	313	615	127	17	49	221	581	83	.310	.362
Tri-City	.239	76	2553	301	611	125	19	33	239	661	73	.317	.342

CLUB PITCHING

	ERA	G	CG	SHO	SV	IP	H	R	ER	HR	BB	SO	AVG
Salem-Keizer	2.95	76	0	8	29	683	557	260	224	39	206	598	.223
Tri-City	3.04	76	3	8	17	681	566	290	230	30	243	667	.224
Eugene	3.54	76	0	5	24	687	655	339	270	38	252	561	.253
Vancouver	3.66	76	0	5	20	681	641	332	277	47	250	504	.248
Boise	3.80	76	0	6	18	673	634	337	284	44	242	526	.248
Yakima	3.89	76	3	1	11	674	683	369	291	41	269	554	.261
Everett	4.29	76	0	4	17	669	652	404	319	64	279	624	.253
Spokane	4.99	76	0	1	11	664	768	473	368	52	255	517	.287

CLUB FIELDING

	PCT	PO	A	E	DP		PCT	PO	A	E	DP
Salem-Keizer	.977	2050	879	69	79	Eugene	.963	2060	818	111	69
Boise	.967	2018	821	98	73	Everett	.961	2006	767	113	61
Tri-City	.966	2043	753	97	68	Yakima	.961	2022	848	116	68
Vancouver	.965	2044	778	103	68	Spokane	.950	1992	725	143	68

INDIVIDUAL BATTING LEADERS
(Minimum 236 Plate Appearances)

	AVG	G	AB	R	H	2B	3B	HR	RBI	BB	SO	SB
Hankerd, Cyle, Yakima	.384	54	216	24	83	17	0	4	38	13	54	0
Huffman, Chad, Eugene	.343	54	198	41	68	17	1	9	40	35	34	2
Cooper, Craig, Eugene	.320	60	231	45	74	18	1	6	46	32	44	5
Burriss, Emmanuel, Salem-Keizer	.307	65	254	50	78	8	2	1	27	27	22	35
Joseph, Alfred, Boise	.306	67	229	35	70	14	2	3	29	17	35	8
Mayora, Daniel, Tri-City	.304	74	276	40	84	19	2	5	30	23	70	8
Cobb, Larry, Vancouver	.292	63	253	42	74	14	2	1	14	27	49	9
Camp, Matt, Boise	.289	74	301	51	87	12	2	1	37	27	32	22
Clevenger, Steven, Boise	.286	63	220	35	63	8	1	2	21	26	28	5
Antonelli, Matt, Eugene	.286	55	189	38	54	12	1	0	22	46	31	9

INDIVIDUAL PITCHING LEADERS
(Minimum 61 Innings)

	W	L	ERA	G	GS	CG	SV	IP	H	R	ER	BB	SO
Cowart, Adam, Salem-Keizer	10	1	1.08	15	15	0	0	83	51	13	10	8	55
Pucetas, Kevin, Salem-Keizer	7	1	2.17	15	15	0	0	71	57	22	17	19	60
Dove, Shane, Yakima	5	6	2.26	16	14	1	0	88	78	38	22	18	72
Dunn, Brooks, Eugene	5	6	2.41	19	12	0	1	78	68	34	21	19	45
Pawelek, Mark, Boise	3	5	2.51	15	12	0	0	61	54	24	17	23	52
Sullivan, Joshua, Tri-City	3	4	2.71	13	13	0	0	70	49	30	21	21	74
Odom, John, Salem-Keizer	6	3	3.05	15	15	0	0	74	72	30	25	16	51
Breit, Aaron, Eugene	2	3	3.08	18	12	0	0	64	60	31	22	22	69
Valdez, Cesar, Yakima	7	5	3.15	16	16	2	0	97	97	43	34	20	81
Dilone, Natividad, Everett	3	5	3.38	14	13	0	0	64	62	29	24	25	35

ALL-STAR TEAM

C—Chad Tracy, Spokane. **1B**—Craig Cooper, Eugene. **2B**—Emmanuel Burriss, Salem-Keizer. **3B**—Alex Valdez, Vancouver. **SS**—Daniel Mayora, Tri-City. **OF**—Cyle Hankerd, Yakima; Chad Huffman, Eugene; Matt Sulentic, Vancouver. **DH**—Russ Canzler, Boise; Chris Davis, Spokane. **LHP**—Shane Dove, Yakima. **RHP**—Adam Cowart, Salem-Keizer. **LHRP**—Jeremy Papelbon, Boise. **RHRP**—Juan Trinidad, Salem-Keizer.

Most Valuable Player: Cyle Hankerd, Yakima. **Managers of the Year:** Doug Dascenzo, Eugene/Steve Decker, Salem-Keizer.

DEPARTMENT LEADERS

BATTING

OBP	Huffman, Chad, Eugene	.439
SLG	Witter, Adam, Salem-Keizer	.585
R	Epping, Michael, Eugene	.53
H	Camp, Matt, Boise	.87
TB	Canzler, Russell, Boise	.152
XBH	Canzler, Russell, Boise	.42
2B	Canzler, Russell, Boise	.22
3B	Boyer, Bradley, Salem-Keizer	.6
	Colvin, Tyler, Boise	.6
HR	Canzler, Russell, Boise	.16
	Witter, Adam, Salem-Keizer	.16
RBI	Canzler, Russell, Boise	.61
SAC	Affronti, Michael, Vancouver	.9
SF	Miller, Brad, Yakima	.12
BB	White, Joseph, Everett	.56
IBB	Mitchell, Jermaine, Vancouver	.3
HBP	Gentry, Craig, Spokane	.15
SO	Ferrante, Victor, Tri-City	.89
SB	Burriss, Emmanuel, Salem-Keizer	.35
CS	Burriss, Emmanuel, Salem-Keizer	.11
GIDP	Rohlinger, Ryan, Salem-Keizer	.13
AB/SO	Burriss, Emmanuel, Salem-Keizer	11.55

PITCHING

G	Katz, Ethan, Tri-City	.29
GS	Three players tied at	.16
CG	Kreidermacher, Andrew, Tri-City	.2
	Valdez, Cesar, Yakima	.2
GF	Rodriguez, R.J., Eugene	.24
SV	Trinidad, Juan, Salem-Keizer	.16
W	Cowart, Adam, Salem-Keizer	.10
L	Schilling, Michael, Everett	.8
	Souther, Scott, Yakima	.8
IP	Valdez, Cesar, Yakima	.97
H	Valdez, Cesar, Yakima	.97
R	Wagner, Michael, Spokane	.54
ER	Wagner, Michael, Spokane	.47
HB	Pawelek, Mark, Boise	.12
BB	Butler, Eric, Yakima	.46
SO	Valdez, Cesar, Yakima	.81
SO/9 (SP)	Wagner, Michael, Spokane	9.92
SO/9 (RP)	Cranston, Jared, Salem-Keizer	17.65
WP	Slusarz, John, Spokane	.14
BK	Quezada, Jackson, Eugene	.3
	Valdez, Rolando, Eugene	.3

FIELDING

C	PCT	Smith, Jacob, Vancouver	.994
	PO	McKenry, Michael, Tri-City	.426
	A	Smith, Jacob, Vancouver	.36
	E	Valverde, Kody, Eugene	.7
	DP	Canepa, Matthew, Boise	.6
	PB	Fernandez, Jair, Everett	.13
	CS%	Fernandez, Jair, Everett	48%
1B	PCT	Pill, Brett, Salem-Keizer	.995
	PO	Canzler, Russell, Boise	.621
	A	Pill, Brett, Salem-Keizer	.46
	E	Dowling, Greg, Vancouver	.13
	DP	Dowling, Greg, Vancouver	.56
2B	PCT	Boyer, Bradley, Salem-Keizer	.986
	PO	Clevenger, Steven, Boise	.133
	A	Clevenger, Steven, Boise	.180
	E	Batten, Joseph, Yakima	.13
	DP	Clevenger, Steven, Boise	.41
3B	PCT	Rohlinger, Ryan, Salem-Keizer	.950
	PO	Rohlinger, Ryan, Salem-Keizer	.51
	A	Rohlinger, Ryan, Salem-Keizer	156
	E	Marquardt, Steven, Spokane	.26
	DP	Lansford, Joshua, Boise	.14
		Valdez, Alexander, Vancouver	.14
SS	PCT	Matulia, Matt, Boise	.960
	PO	Diaz, Ogui, Everett	.102
	A	Sharpe, Blake, Yakima	.227
	E	Diaz, Ogui, Everett	.24
	DP	Three players tied at	.38
OF	PCT	Cobb, Larry, Vancouver	.993
		Gentry, Craig, Spokane	.993
	PO	Camp, Matt, Boise	.156
	A	McBryde, Michael, Salem-Keizer	.11
	E	Crafort, Willy, Eugene	.6
		McBryde, Michael, Salem-Keizer	.6
	DP	McBryde, Michael, Salem-Keizer	.4

BY MATT EDDY

Some things in baseball happen as if scripted. The Braves and Twins played for the league championship for the second consecutive season in 2006, with the Braves emerging as victors and winning the first league title in Danville history.

Both organizations have proven themselves behemoths of player development, and their Appalachian League affiliates are annually among the league's best teams. Danville took the season series between the two clubs, four games to two, and the club, which has been a Braves farm team since 1993, is managed by former major league infielder Paul Runge.

The Braves entered the finals as favorites, having scored the most runs in the league and allowed the second fewest, but were two-time losers in the league finals. Danville had lost in three-game sets to Greeneville and Elizabethton in 2004 and 2005.

Because of Tropical Storm Ernesto, the two teams had to decide the 2006 championship in a doubleheader after the Braves had won the opener. The Twins took the first game of the doubleheader to tie the series at 1-1. In the nightcap—with the league title on the line and the score tied 3-3 in the seventh—Braves third baseman Danny Brezeale connected for the go-ahead home run. Atlanta's 19th-round pick in 2004, Brezeale was 7-for-10 with three RBIs in the series.

Danville's offensive attack revolved around outfielders Larry Williams, who led the league in hits (90), at-bats (266) and total bases (117), and Willie Cabrera, who finished third with 72 hits, and shortstop Chase Fontaine, the Braves' second-round pick last year. The pitching staff was even better, fronted by righthanders Jamie Richmond—the league's pitcher of the year who led the league with a 1.21 ERA and finished second with seven wins—and Tommy Hanson, the top pitching prospect in the league. Righthander Kris Medlen posted a 0.41 ERA and was 10-for-10 in

saves.

The Twins' ties to Elizabethton date to 1974, and the club has not had a losing season since 1988. Manager Ray Smith is a six-time winner of the league's manager of the year award.

While Danville and Elizabethton again dominated the standings, it was a pair of lefthanded-hitting high school sluggers taken in the top half of the 2006 draft who made the strongest impression. Pulaski outfielder Travis Snider, taken 14th overall by the Blue Jays, and Bluefield third baseman Bill Rowell, who went ninth overall to the Orioles, were above-average hitters and both project to hit for more power as they mature. Snider won league player of the year honors by hitting .325/.412/.567. His 11 home runs ranked second in the league, and he might have finished first had he not missed the final week with wrist tendinitis.

The Orioles and White Sox each sent their top-drafted lefthander to the league: third-round picks Zach Britton and Justin Edwards spent their entire summers in the league. In all, clubs sent six players drafted in the top three rounds to the Appalachian League—the others were Bluefield second baseman Ryan Adams and Fontaine—and that group didn't include first-round picks Chris Parmelee (Twins) and Max Sapp (Astros), who jumped over the league entirely. Princeton featured three promising 18-year-old righthanders, including two sons of former major leaguers: Chris Andujar, son of Joaquin; Alex Cobb; and Tyree Hayes, an eighth-round pick and son of Charlie.

While the Appy League hopes to field 10 teams in 2007, two of them would feature new affiliations. The Royals will take over the Burlington franchise from the Indians, while the Blue Jays won't be back in Pulaski after four years there. The league was left looking for a replacement major league organization, but if one is not found, then the league would either drop to nine teams or operate Pulaski as a co-op.

TOP 20 PROSPECTS

1. Travis Snider, of, Pulaski (Blue Jays)
2. Bill Rowell, 3b, Bluefield (Orioles)
3. Kieron Pope, of, Bluefield (Orioles)
4. Tommy Hanson, rhp, Danville (Braves)
5. Jamie Richmond, rhp, Danville (Braves)
6. Daryl Jones, of, Johnson City (Cardinals)
7. Desmond Jennings, of, Princeton (Devil Rays)
8. Chase Fontaine, ss, Danville (Braves)
9. Jon Edwards, of, Johnson City (Cardinals)
10. Zach Britton, lhp, Bluefield (Orioles)
11. Emmanuel Garcia, ss/2b, Kingsport (Mets)
12. Blake King, rhp, Johnson City (Cardinals)
13. Tyler Herron, rhp, Johnson City (Cardinals)
14. Brian Kirwan, rhp, Elizabethton (Twins)
15. Alex Burnett, rhp, Elizabethton (Twins)
16. Justin Edwards, lhp, Bristol (White Sox)
17. Ronald Ramirez, ss/2b, Greeneville (Astros)
18. Yohermyn Chavez, of, Pulaski (Blue Jays)
19. Nevin Ashley, c, Princeton (Devil Rays)
20. Sergio Sevrino, lhp, Greeneville (Astros)

STANDINGS

Page	EAST	W	L	PCT	GB	Manager(s)	Attendance	Average	Last Penn.
59	Danville Braves	40	27	.597	—	Paul Runge	40,131	1,180	2006
262	Pulaski Blue Jays	35	33	.515	5½	Dave Pano	28,852	902	None
105	Burlington Indians	34	33	.507	6	Kevin Higgins	37,463	1,171	1993
67	Bluefield Orioles	31	37	.456	9½	Gary Allenson	25,902	893	2001
247	Princeton Devil Rays	28	36	.438	10½	Jamie Nelson	27,148	936	1994

Page	WEST	W	L	PCT	GB	Manager	Attendance	Average	Last Penn.
170	Elizabethton Twins	42	26	.618	—	Ray Smith	28,551	892	2005
135	Greeneville Astros	34	33	.507	7½	Ivan DeJesus	51,633	1,519	2004
179	Kingsport Mets	34	33	.507	7½	Donovan Mitchell	39,439	1,195	1995
217	Johnson City Cardinals	34	34	.500	8	Dan Radison	23,009	719	1976
90	Bristol White Sox	22	42	.344	18	Nick Leyva	20,012	667	2002

PLAYOFFS: Danville defeated Elizabethton 2-1 in best-of-three series.

NOTE: Teams' individual batting and pitching statistics can be found on page indicated in lefthand column.

2006 APPALACHIAN LEAGUE STATISTICS

CLUB BATTING

	AVG	G	AB	R	H	2B	3B	HR	BB	SO	SB	OBP	SLG
Danville	.285	67	2256	380	642	135	10	48	213	451	35	.354	.417
Kingsport	.264	67	2227	357	589	115	16	40	278	495	79	.353	.384
Pulaski	.263	68	2326	370	611	125	14	37	290	494	30	.352	.376
Elizabethton	.258	68	2313	361	596	119	18	47	205	501	32	.328	.386
Burlington	.253	67	2305	340	584	98	7	40	246	442	75	.332	.354
Bluefield	.251	68	2218	304	557	121	19	31	245	582	31	.331	.365
Princeton	.250	64	2055	287	513	90	13	31	214	514	106	.332	.351
Johnson City	.244	68	2295	314	560	112	17	48	200	525	57	.315	.370
Greeneville	.241	67	2269	279	546	101	18	34	214	550	65	.318	.346
Bristol	.238	64	2104	256	501	96	12	24	211	495	29	.319	.329

CLUB PITCHING

	ERA	G	CG	SHO	SV	IP	H	R	ER	HR	BB	SO	AVG
Greeneville	3.31	67	0	5	18	599	567	282	220	30	188	507	.248
Danville	3.67	67	0	4	18	579	558	286	236	31	217	548	.252
Kingsport	3.70	67	0	4	17	578	580	301	238	43	230	448	.260
Pulaski	3.83	68	0	1	17	597	569	321	254	42	202	588	.247
Princeton	3.87	64	3	5	12	540	516	293	232	36	216	435	.254
Bluefield	4.20	68	0	3	20	572	575	355	267	30	255	464	.256
Burlington	4.23	67	0	3	14	601	625	347	282	55	225	492	.267
Johnson City	4.35	68	1	3	16	598	565	364	289	34	295	522	.247
Elizabethton	4.46	68	1	7	23	589	575	320	292	44	205	566	.256
Bristol	4.98	64	0	4	8	549	569	379	304	35	283	479	.261

CLUB FIELDING

	PCT	PO	A	E	DP		PCT	PO	A	E	DP
Elizabethton	.970	1768	708	76	69	Burlington	.960	1802	806	108	80
Danville	.964	1737	683	90	55	Johnson City	.959	1794	726	109	66
Greeneville	.962	1797	709	98	62	Pulaski	.955	1792	718	119	63
Princeton	.962	1620	665	91	63	Bristol	.953	1647	688	115	53
Kingsport	.961	1735	759	100	60	Bluefield	.945	1715	776	146	70

INDIVIDUAL BATTING LEADERS
(Minimum 211 Plate Appearances)

	AVG	G	AB	R	H	2B	3B	HR	RBI	BB	SO	SB
Williams, Larry, Danville	.338	66	266	36	90	17	2	2	46	23	46	2
Snider, Travis, Pulaski	.325	54	194	36	63	12	1	11	41	30	47	6
Emanuele, Chris, Pulaski	.323	60	226	42	73	16	4	2	23	30	40	10
Ramirez, Ronald, Greeneville	.314	57	229	23	72	20	2	3	33	11	42	7
Valencia, Daniel, Elizabethton	.311	48	190	30	59	13	0	8	29	15	34	0
Gartrell, Maurice, Bristol	.308	61	214	41	66	16	1	4	33	43	48	4
Cabrera, Willie, Danville	.308	60	234	35	72	13	1	7	37	11	32	3
Brown, Steve, Greeneville	.306	54	193	36	59	3	2	1	12	9	35	12
Buckman, Brandon, Johnson City	.300	62	230	33	69	17	0	8	34	24	31	0
Garcia, Felipe, Burlington	.298	59	235	26	70	10	1	7	41	17	34	1

INDIVIDUAL PITCHING LEADERS
(Minimum 54 Innings)

	W	L	ERA	G	GS	CG	SV	IP	H	R	ER	BB	SO
Richmond, Jamie, Danville	7	1	1.21	14	12	0	0	67	51	11	9	4	52
Clark, Zach, Bluefield	5	4	2.11	13	13	0	0	64	56	26	15	19	58
Trinidad, Polin, Greeneville	4	4	2.39	13	13	0	0	75	59	24	20	10	66
Maria, Jose, Bluefield	4	6	2.55	14	14	0	0	71	67	33	20	17	53
Morse, Ryan, Princeton	5	3	2.88	10	10	0	0	56	44	20	18	18	44
Severino, Sergio, Greeneville	6	3	2.90	13	13	0	0	68	50	24	22	27	90
King, Blake, Johnson City	4	3	3.02	13	13	0	0	63	37	25	21	29	74
Mullens, Greg, Kingsport	7	2	3.06	12	12	0	0	62	73	32	21	17	38
Castillo, Jose, Elizabethton	4	3	3.17	13	12	0	0	71	64	28	25	23	56
Pendarvis, Chad, Princeton	4	3	3.47	12	11	1	0	60	61	28	23	23	42

ALL-STAR TEAM

C—Nevin Ashley, Princeton. **1B**—Brandon Buckman, Johnson City. **2B**—Ronald Ramirez, Greeneville. **3B**—Danny Valencia, Elizabethton. **SS**—Chase Fontaine, Danville. **OF**—Willie Cabrera, Danville; Kieron Pope, Bluefield; Larry Williams, Danville. **DH**—Felipe Garcia, Burlington. **Util**—Emmanuel Garcia, Kingsport. **LHP**—Polin Trinidad, Greeneville. **RHP**—Jamie Richmond, Danville. **RP**—Danny Hernandez, Elizabethton.

Player of the Year: Travis Snider, Pulaski. **Pitcher of the Year:** Jamie Richmond, Danville. **Manager of the Year:** Ray Smith, Elizabethton.

DEPARTMENT LEADERS

BATTING
OBP	Ashley, Nevin, Princeton	.440
SLG	Snider, Travis, Pulaski	.567
R	Jennings, Desmond, Princeton	48
H	Williams, Larry, Danville	90
TB	Williams, Larry, Danville	117
XBH	Jaspe, Jonathan, Pulaski	31
2B	Jaspe, Jonathan, Pulaski	22
3B	Four players tied at	5
HR	Shorey, Mark, Johnson City	13
RBI	Head, Jerad, Burlington	52
SAC	Two tied at	6
SF	Three tied at	5
BB	Gartrell, Maurice, Bristol	43
IBB	Snider, Travis, Pulaski	4
HBP	Inouye, Matthew, Bristol	11
SO	Cruz, Cirilo, Greeneville	78
SB	Jennings, Desmond, Princeton	32
CS	Caipen, Brandon, Greeneville	9
GIDP	Mortensen, Trevor, Burlington	12
AB/SO	Garcia, Isaias, Johnson City	14.77

PITCHING
G	Hernandez, Danny, Elizabethton	28
GS	Five players tied at	14
CG	Five players tied at	1
SHO	Three players tied at	1
GF	Hernandez, Danny, Elizabethton	25
SV	Hernandez, Danny, Elizabethton	18
W	Lugo, Jose, Elizabethton	8
L	Carter, Anthony, Bristol	8
	Ouellette, Ryan, Bluefield	8
IP	Trinidad, Polin, Greeneville	75.1
H	Carter, Anthony, Bristol	88
R	Carter, Anthony, Bristol	58
ER	Carter, Anthony, Bristol	54
HB	Storey, Mike, Burlington	12
BB	Stires, Justin, Bristol	35
SO	Severino, Sergio, Greeneville	90
SO/9 (SP)	Severino, Sergio, Greeneville	11.85
SO/9 (RP)	Wilson, Tyler, Danville	16.12
WP	Stires, Justin, Bristol	11
BK	Brujan, Rafael, Bristol	4

FIELDING
C	PCT	Henriquez, Ralph, Greeneville	.990
	PO	Britton, Phillip, Danville	373
	A	Britton, Phillip, Danville	43
	E	Britton, Phillip, Danville	8
	DP	Jaspe, Jonathan, Pulaski	8
	PB	Caldera, Ciro, Johnson City	13
		Tavarez, Aregenis, Burlington	13
	CS%	Christy, Jeffrey, Elizabethton	.58%
1B	PCT	Buckman, Brandon, Johnson City	.989
	PO	Cruz, Cirilo, Greeneville	516
	A	Buckman, Brandon, Johnson City	37
	E	Cruz, Cirilo, Greeneville	9
	DP	Buckman, Brandon, Johnson City	51
		Cruz, Cirilo, Greeneville	51
2B	PCT	Dhaenens, Seth, Princeton	.982
	PO	Dhaenens, Seth, Princeton	103
	A	Ramirez, Reinaldo, Greeneville	136
	E	Enuco, Matthew, Bristol	14
	DP	Kinning, Brett, Burlington	37
3B	PCT	Brezeale, Danny, Danville	.942
	PO	Caipen, Brandon, Greeneville	45
	A	Zuaznabar, Alejandro, Kingsport	146
	E	McCormick, Michael, Princeton	30
	DP	Zuaznabar, Alejandro, Kingsport	13
SS	PCT	O'Malley, Shawn, Princeton	.963
	PO	Infante, Jansy, Burlington	82
	A	Garcia, Emmanuel, Kingsport	167
	E	Pham, Thomas, Johnson City	34
	DP	Infante, Jansy, Burlington	34
OF	PCT	Mortensen, Trevor, Burl.	.987
	PO	Rosales, Orlando, Greeneville	122
	A	Rosales, Orlando, Greeneville	7
	E	Gartrell, Maurice, Bristol	6
		Rodriguez, Concepcion, Danville	6
	DP	Rosales, Orlando, Greeneville	4
		Shorey, Mark, Johnson City	4

PIONEER LEAGUE
ROOKIE

BY WILL LINGO

Missoula rode the pitching of Osbek Castillo and Hector Ambriz and the hitting of Shea McFeely to its first Pioneer League title in eight years.

The Diamondbacks sent a talented team to Missoula, including players with a track record of success. McFeely, who helped lead Oregon State to the College World Series championship in June, hit a three-run homer in the fifth inning of the clincher to seal the title for the Osprey. Castillo, a Cuban defector, and Ambriz, a fifth-round pick out of UCLA in June, combined on a four-hitter as

BILL MITCHELL
Sean O'Sullivan

Missoula beat Idaho Falls 4-2 in Game Two as Missoula rolled to the league title with a couple of two-game sweeps.

The Osprey's win was a team effort because the team had few of the league's individual honors. Only Daniel Stange, who led the league with 13 saves, was at the top of any of the PL's major statistical categories.

Billings had the league's most potent offense and finished with the best overall record, with Daniel Dorn leading the league in batting at .354 and Justin Turner and Logan Parker finishing in the top 10. Dorn also led the league with a .573 slugging percentage. The Mustangs batted .288 as a team and scored 464 runs, 26 more than the next closest team.

Billings also had the league's MVP in shortstop Chris Valaika, who hit .324 with 22 doubles and 60 RBIs and set a league record with a 32-game hitting streak. He also tied for the league lead in both hits (with 89) and total bases (with 143).

As impressive as Billings' offense was, Orem's pitching was just as dominant during the regular season. Orem also won its division in both halves, and like Billings fell in the first round of the playoffs.

Despite a rotation featuring no four-year college players, the Owlz pitching staff was easily the best in the league, leading in ERA by

0.25. Sean O'Sullivan, Kenneth Herndon and Trevor Bell finished first, second and eighth in the league in ERA, while Jeremy Haynes, who just missed qualifying, would have been ranked fourth.

But the league's pitcher of the year was Casper's Brandon Hynick, who went 4-3, 2.39 with 70 strikeouts against just eight walks in 64 innings.

As a general rule, though, the Pioneer League favors hitters, and they dominated the league prospect list, claiming seven of the 10 spots. But most people in the league said the high-end talent was down compared to seasons past.

"In other years, I've seen a greater number of blue-chip prospects come from the Pioneer League," Casper manager P.J. Carey said. "There still are some very good prospects, but I think it's down from other years."

As more teams are easing high school draft picks into pro ball, the Pioneer League is becoming less dependent on the current year's draft for prospects. The 2005 draft class put eight players among the top 20, while Ogden righthander Bryan Morris (the No. 1 prospect) and Herndon were highly regarded 2005 draft-and-follows who went early in the 2006 draft after failing to sign.

The league's best off-field news came after the season, when voters in Billings approved up to $12.5 million to help pay for a new stadium to replace outdated Cobb Field, which opened in 1948.

STANDINGS: SPLIT SEASON

FIRST HALF

NORTH	W	L	PCT	GB
Billings	23	15	.605	—
Great Falls	18	20	.474	5
Missoula	18	20	.474	5
Helena	15	23	.395	8

SOUTH	W	L	PCT	GB
Orem	23	15	.605	—
Idaho Falls	22	16	.579	1
Ogden	18	20	.474	5
Casper	15	23	.395	8

SECOND HALF

NORTH	W	L	PCT	GB
Billings	28	10	.737	—
Missoula	24	14	.632	4
Great Falls	19	19	.500	9
Helena	10	28	.263	18

SOUTH	W	L	PCT	GB
Orem	22	16	.579	—
Ogden	19	19	.500	3
Idaho Falls	18	20	.474	4
Casper	12	26	.316	10

PLAYOFFS—Semifinals: Missoula defeated Billings 2-0 and Idaho Falls defeated Orem 2-0 in best-of-three series. **Final:** Missoula defeated Idaho Falls 2-0 in best-of-three series.

TOP 20 PROSPECTS

1. Bryan Morris, rhp, Ogden (Dodgers)
2. Josh Bell, 3b, Ogden (Dodgers)
3. Hector Gomez, ss/3b, Casper (Rockies)
4. Sean O'Sullivan, rhp, Orem (Angels)
5. Gerardo Parra, of, Missoula (Diamondbacks)
6. Peter Bourjos, of, Orem (Angels)
7. Drew Stubbs, of, Billings (Reds)
8. Andrew Fie, 3b, Missoula (Diamondbacks)
9. Jeremy Haynes, rhp, Orem (Angels)
10. Ryan Mount, ss, Orem (Angels)
11. Cole Gillespie, of, Helena (Brewers)
12. Kenneth Herndon, rhp, Orem (Angels)
13. Chris Valaika, ss, Billings (Reds)
14. Chris Carter, 1b, Great Falls (White Sox)
15. Steven Johnson, rhp, Ogden (Dodgers)
16. Trevor Bell, rhp, Orem (Angels)
17. Pedro Strop, rhp, Casper (Rockies)
18. Stephen Chapman, of, Helena (Brewers)
19. Brandon Hynick, rhp, Casper (Rockies)
20. Hector Ambriz, rhp, Missoula

STANDINGS: OVERALL

Page	Team	W	L	PCT	GB	Manager	Attendance	Average	Last Penn.
97	Billings Mustangs (Reds)	51	25	.671	—	Rick Burleson	93,256	2,520	2001
148	Orem Owlz (Angels)	45	31	.592	6	Tom Kotchman	102,631	2,701	2005
52	Missoula Osprey (Diamondbacks)	42	34	.553	9	Hector De La Cruz	70,062	1,894	2006
141	Idaho Falls Chukars (Royals)	40	36	.526	11	Brian Rupp	73,802	1,942	2000
156	Ogden Raptors (Dodgers)	37	39	.487	14	Lance Parrish	134,961	3,552	None
163	Helena Brewers (Brewers)	34	42	.447	17	Eddie Sedar	36,270	954	1984
89	Great Falls White Sox (Diamondbacks)	28	48	.368	23	Bobby Tolan	93,619	2,464	2002
113	Casper Rockies (Rockies)	27	49	.355	24	Paul Carey	57,023	1,501	None

NOTE: Teams' individual batting and pitching statistics can be found on page indicated in lefthand column.

MINOR LEAGUES

314 • BASEBALL AMERICA 2007 ALMANAC

2006 PIONEER LEAGUE STATISTICS

CLUB BATTING

	AVG	G	AB	R	H	2B	3B	HR	BB	SO	SB	OBP	SLG
Billings	.288	76	2609	464	752	142	21	53	298	527	61	.369	.420
Idaho Falls	.273	76	2614	423	713	136	25	36	343	554	133	.362	.385
Ogden	.272	76	2596	438	706	126	23	65	303	574	82	.357	.413
Great Falls	.269	76	2595	369	697	149	17	58	225	593	76	.338	.406
Helena	.261	76	2610	409	680	121	17	55	327	530	84	.355	.383
Missoula	.258	76	2561	408	660	127	25	57	263	547	109	.339	.394
Orem	.257	76	2614	398	673	133	27	48	285	652	71	.342	.384
Casper	.236	76	2534	334	598	107	20	41	262	694	71	.315	.343

CLUB PITCHING

	ERA	G	CG	SHO	SV	IP	H	R	ER	HR	BB	SO	AVG
Orem	3.65	76	0	2	23	678	632	344	275	55	271	587	.245
Billings	3.90	76	0	4	27	672	625	359	291	56	291	556	.250
Missoula	3.98	76	0	6	27	670	640	364	296	45	319	618	.251
Ogden	4.40	76	0	2	13	673.2	724	411	329	43	288	667	.272
Helena	4.57	76	1	1	17	674	726	416	342	56	285	455	.277
Idaho Falls	4.62	76	0	4	18	668	703	385	343	48	215	569	.273
Great Falls	4.75	76	0	3	15	670	734	474	354	51	319	614	.276
Casper	5.75	76	1	4	8	662	695	490	423	59	318	605	.269

CLUB FIELDING

	PCT	PO	A	E	DP		PCT	PO	A	E	DP
Missoula	.969	2009	823	90	71	Orem	.964	2034	844	109	66
Idaho Falls	.967	2004	866	99	80	Casper	.962	1986	820	112	75
Billings	.967	2016	832	98	88	Ogden	.960	2021	760	116	62
Helena	.965	2022	912	105	72	Great Falls	.947	2011	874	163	85

INDIVIDUAL BATTING LEADERS
(Minimum 236 Plate Appearances)

	AVG	G	AB	R	H	2B	3B	HR	RBI	BB	SO	SB
Dorn, Daniel, Billings	.354	60	206	48	73	17	2	8	40	36	36	3
Mertins, Kurt, Idaho Falls	.342	61	225	46	77	11	3	1	26	18	39	26
Turner, Justin, Billings	.338	60	231	53	78	16	3	6	41	23	38	12
Pettit, Christopher, Orem	.336	68	226	41	76	25	3	7	54	31	48	5
Maddox, Marc, Idaho Falls	.336	62	232	46	78	22	4	3	40	33	31	7
Parker, Logan, Billings	.329	66	231	43	76	12	3	9	51	41	47	2
Parra, Gerardo, Missoula	.328	69	271	46	89	18	4	4	43	25	30	23
Valaika, Chris, Billings	.324	70	275	58	89	22	4	8	60	24	61	2
Errecart, Chris, Helena	.316	70	272	49	86	16	0	13	61	25	56	5
Rogowski, Ryan, Ogden	.312	70	263	64	82	14	8	4	36	52	40	30

INDIVIDUAL PITCHING LEADERS
(Minimum 61 Innings)

	W	L	ERA	G	GS	CG	SV	IP	H	R	ER	BB	SO
O'Sullivan, Sean, Orem	4	0	2.14	14	14	0	0	71	65	23	17	7	55
Herndon, Kenneth, Orem	5	2	2.21	14	14	0	0	69	65	25	17	10	36
Hynick, Brandon, Casper	4	3	2.39	12	12	0	0	64	55	23	17	8	70
Hardy, Rowdy, Idaho Falls	5	3	2.80	15	15	0	0	80	79	29	25	5	52
Castillo, Jesus, Ogden	2	5	2.88	14	14	0	0	72	65	29	23	25	55
Smith, Jordan, Billings	6	3	3.01	14	14	0	0	69	58	29	23	20	49
Norberto, Jordan, Missoula	3	3	3.09	16	16	0	0	76	59	30	26	40	64
Bell, Trevor, Orem	4	2	3.50	16	16	0	0	82	82	35	32	15	53
Teaford, Everett, Idaho Falls	5	1	3.71	15	12	0	0	63	54	29	26	20	51
Fournier, Daniel, Missoula	4	3	3.77	15	15	0	0	76	74	43	32	39	43

ALL-STAR TEAM

C—Andy Bouchie, Helena. **1B**—Chris Carter, Great Falls. **2B**—Justin Turner, Billings. **3B**—Josh Bell, Ogden. **SS**—Chris Valaika, Billings. **OF**—Chris Errecart, Helena; Gerrardo Parra, Missoula; Chris Pettit, Orem. **DH**—Hector Gomez, Casper. **P**—Osbek Castillo, Missoula; Rowdy Hardy, Idaho Falls; Brandon Hynick, Casper; Sean O'Sullivan, Orem; Jordan Smith, Billings.

Most Valuable Player: Chris Valaika, Billings. **Pitcher of the Year:** Brandon Hynick, Casper. **Managers of the Year:** Rick Burleson, Billings/Tom Kotchman, Orem.

DEPARTMENT LEADERS

BATTING

OBP	Gillespie, Cole, Helena	.464
SLG	Dorn, Daniel, Billings	.573
R	Rogowski, Ryan, Ogden	.64
H	Parra, Gerardo, Missoula	.89
	Valaika, Chris, Billings	.89
TB	Carter, Christopher, Great Falls	.143
	Valaika, Chris, Billings	.143
XBH	Carter, Christopher, Great Falls	.37
2B	Pettit, Christopher, Orem	.25
3B	Chapman, Stephen, Helena	.8
	Rogowski, Ryan, Ogden	.8
HR	Carter, Christopher, Great Falls	.15
RBI	Errecart, Chris, Helena	.61
SAC	Heisey, Chris, Billings	.9
SF	Two players tied at	.6
BB	Rogowski, Ryan, Ogden	.52
IBB	Two players tied at	.5
HBP	Errecart, Chris, Helena	.16
SO	Christensen, David, Casper	.93
SB	Gilbert, Archie, Great Falls	.35
CS	Three players tied at	.8
GIDP	De La Cruz, Fredy, Helena	.12
AB/SO	Parra, Gerardo, Missoula	.9.03

PITCHING

G	Walters, Nick, Great Falls	.28
GS	Bell, Trevor, Orem	.16
	Norberto, Jordan, Missoula	.16
CG	Jean, Chris, Helena	.1
	Rogers, Esmil, Casper	.1
GF	Stange, Daniel, Missoula	.24
SV	Stange, Daniel, Missoula	.13
W	Six players tied at	.6
L	Lopez, Ronny, Casper	.10
IP	Bell, Trevor, Orem	.82.1
H	Lopez, Ronny, Casper	.104
R	Lopez, Ronny, Casper	.81
ER	Lopez, Ronny, Casper	.69
HB	Rogers, Esmil, Casper	.13
BB	Neighborgall, Jason, Missoula	.46
SO	Johnson, Steven, Ogden	.86
SO/9 (SP)	Morris, Bryan, Ogden	.11.92
SO/9 (SP)	Roenicke, Joshua, Billings	.13.79
WP	Neighborgall, Jason, Missoula	.22
BK	Castillo, Osbek, Missoula	.4
	Silano, Yull, Casper	.4

FIELDING

C	PCT	Hester, John, Missoula	.997
		Medero-Stullz, Carlos, Ogden	.997
	PO	Knazek, Scott, Orem	.438
	A	Knazek, Scott, Orem	.41
	E	Agustin, Jhayson, Casper	.8
	DP	Three players tied at	.4
	PB	Agustin, Jhayson, Casper	.17
	CS%	Gonzalez, Rey, Billings	.50%
1B	PCT	Turner, Jase, Idaho Falls	.992
	PO	Carter, Christopher, Great Falls	558
	A	Taloa, Rick, Ogden	.45
	E	Carter, Christopher, Great Falls	.16
	DP	Carter, Christopher, Great Falls	.62
2B	PCT	Cabrera, Everth, Casper	.977
	PO	Green, Taylor, Helena	.125
	A	Green, Taylor, Helena	.179
	E	Soto, Jesus, Ogden	.12
	DP	Green, Taylor, Helena	.45
3B	PCT	De La Cruz, Fredy, Helena	.933
	PO	Herrera, Brenan, Idaho Falls	.45
	A	Fie, Andrew, Missoula	.166
	E	Grace, Michael, Great Falls	.27
	DP	Fie, Andrew, Missoula	.15
SS	PCT	Mount, Ryan, Orem	.961
	PO	Valaika, Chris, Billings	.99
	A	Oxendine, Matthew, Missoula	.197
	E	McConnell, Christopher, Idaho Falls	.18
	DP	Valaika, Chris, Billings	.51
OF	PCT	Marrero, Christian, Great Falls	.1.000
	PO	Bourjos, Peter, Orem	.138
	A	Cruz, Lee, Great Falls	.13
	E	Cruz, Lee, Great Falls	.10
	DP	Dorn, Daniel, Billings	.5

MINOR LEAGUES

ARIZONA LEAGUE
ROOKIE

BY JOHN MANUEL

The Padres had the talent. The Padres had the stats. And the Padres also showed on the field they had the Arizona League's best team.

The Padres defeated the Angels 5-2 in a one-game playoff to determine the Arizona League champion. They got seven strikeouts in 5⅓ innings from starter Pablo Menchaca and 3⅔ innings of scoreless relief from Matthew Huff and Matt Handley to seal the victory.

The Padres won the league's first-half title by one game, and the Angels edged the Royals for the second-half title, keeping the Royals at home for the one-game playoff even though they had the league's second-best record.

San Diego's Rookie-level affiliate had the league's best batting average (.290) and on-base percentage (.391) and led the league in runs (382). Manager Sixto Lezcano's lineup featured the league's top hitter in speedster Luis Durango (.378/.470/.448) as well as its MVP, fellow outfielder Cedric Hunter (.371/.467/.484). Each player had 17 stolen bases.

An All-American in high school during the spring, Hunter is considered the better prospect.

"I had Alex Rodriguez when he first signed, and Cedric is right up there with A-Rod in terms of his aptitude," Lezcano said, "He learns very, very quickly. He wasn't just all about BP. He learned to run the bases better, take leads, throw to the right bases. He was very coachable."

Durango and Hunter upstaged teammate and fellow outfielder Kyle Burke, a supplemental first-rounder who was one of three 2006 first-rounders to play in the AZL long enough to qualify for consideration in the league's Top 10 Prospects list.

Pitchers dominated the prospect list in 2005 with Mark Pawelek, Nick Adenhart and Craig Italiano rating 1-2-3. But 2006 saw a reversal, as position players took seven of the top nine spots. Angels catcher Hank Conger

DAVID STONER

Cedric Hunter

showed all-around skills before breaking the hamate bone in his right wrist 19 games into his pro debut. He missed the title game. Burke also cracked the top 10 and finished on a high note with two hits in the game.

Another first-rounder, Brewers righthander Jeremy Jeffress, ranked as the AZL's top pitcher. He drew attention for a fastball that reached triple digits on several teams' radar guns.

However, like other Brewers pitchers, he had trouble throwing strikes. The Brewers staff posted a 6.31 ERA and walked 330 (while striking out just 379) while throwing 112 wild pitches in 488 innings. Just seven full-season clubs (with twice the schedule) had more wild pitches as a staff. Brewers righthander Rolando Pascual led the league with 20.

Two players who repeated the AZL intrigued managers. Still teenagers, Royals lefthander Brent Fisher and Giants shortstop Sharlon Schoop both have rare skill sets and enough ability to project as big leaguers. They made the top 20 prospects list in 2005 as well, Schoop at No. 11 and Fisher at No. 18.

Schoop moved up to No. 7 in 2006 and was the league's only player to hit for the cycle, turning the trick July 2 against the Royals. Fisher led all short-season pitchers, averaging 12.9 strikeouts per nine innings. The Arizona native repeated the league so he could work closely with former Cy Young Award winner Mark Davis, the AZL Royals' pitching coach.

STANDINGS: SPLIT SEASON

FIRST HALF	W	L	PCT	GB	SECOND HALF	W	L	PCT	GB
Padres	18	10	.643	—	Angels	19	8	.704	—
Giants	17	11	.607	1	Royals	19	9	.679	½
Royals	17	11	.607	1	Padres	18	9	.667	1
Angels	15	13	.536	3	Giants	16	11	.593	3
Brewers	14	14	.500	4	Athletics	14	13	.519	5
Mariners	14	14	.500	4	Cubs	11	16	.407	8
Rangers	11	17	.393	7	Mariners	11	16	.407	8
Athletics	10	18	.357	8	Rangers	8	20	.286	11½
Cubs	10	18	.357	8	Brewers	7	21	.250	12½

PLAYOFFS: The Padres defeated the Angels in a one-game playoff to claim the league championship.

TOP 20 PROSPECTS

1.	Hank Conger, c, Angels
2.	Jeremy Jeffress, rhp, Brewers
3.	Cedric Hunter, of, Padres
4.	Marcus Lemon, ss, Rangers
5.	Brent Fisher, lhp, Royals
6.	Matt Sweeney, 3b/1b, Angels
7.	Sharlon Schoop, ss, Giants
8.	Kyler Burke, of, Padres
9.	Jason Taylor, 3b, Royals
10.	Vladimir Veras, rhp, Angels
11.	Brent Brewer, ss, Brewers
12.	Gerardo Avila, 1b, Mariners
13.	Luis Durango, of, Padres
14.	Jose Ceda, lhp, Cubs
15.	Manuel Cabeza, rhp, Giants
16.	Derrick Robinson, of, Royals
17.	Nick Van Stratten, of, Royals
18.	Carlos Peguero, of, Mariners
19.	Warner Madrigal, rhp, Angels
20.	Felix Carrasco, 3b, Padres

STANDINGS: OVERALL

Page	Team	Complex	W	L	PCT	GB	Manager	Last Penn.
225	Padres	Peoria	36	19	.655	—	Carlos Lezcano	2006
142	Royals	Surprise	36	20	.643	½	Lloyd Simmons	2003
149	Angels	Mesa	34	21	.618	2	Ever Magallanes	None
232	Giants	Scottsdale	33	22	.600	3	Bert Hunter	2005
240	Mariners	Peoria	25	30	.455	11	Dana Williams	2000
195	Athletics	Phoenix	24	31	.436	12	Juan Dilone	2001
83	Cubs	Mesa	21	34	.382	15	Carmelo Martinez	2002
164	Brewers	Phoenix	21	35	.375	15½	Charlie Greene	1990
255	Rangers	Surprise	19	37	.339	17½	Bob Skube	None

NOTE: Teams' individual batting and pitching statistics can be found on page indicated in lefthand column.

MINOR LEAGUES

2006 ARIZONA LEAGUE STATISTICS

CLUB BATTING

	AVG	G	AB	R	H	2B	3B	HR	BB	SO	SB	OBP	SLG
Padres	.290	55	1959	382	569	90	26	23	305	432	56	.391	.398
Mariners	.274	55	1882	315	516	81	41	35	184	465	86	.351	.417
Brewers	.273	56	1948	321	532	96	30	22	204	446	91	.352	.387
Giants	.273	55	1894	324	518	101	21	18	216	315	80	.358	.378
Angels	.271	55	1850	312	502	101	38	26	222	432	68	.360	.409
Royals	.268	56	1909	365	512	80	36	15	272	396	130	.373	.371
Rangers	.252	56	1894	252	477	85	16	12	197	450	82	.336	.333
Cubs	.240	55	1816	258	435	84	23	11	207	466	78	.331	.329
Athletics	.237	55	1844	252	437	91	19	14	219	482	66	.332	.330

CLUB PITCHING

	ERA	G	CG	SHO	SV	IP	H	R	ER	HR	BB	SO	AVG
Angels	3.39	55	0	7	14	486	449	234	183	19	177	455	.244
Royals	3.57	56	1	4	18	499	499	254	198	25	155	445	.258
Padres	4.14	55	1	1	7	464	509	285	227	21	183	428	.267
Mariners	4.19	55	0	1	12	481	452	290	224	11	241	452	.250
Cubs	4.56	55	0	1	9	478	509	309	242	16	200	374	.273
Giants	4.57	55	0	2	17	487	493	291	247	20	236	446	.266
Athletics	5.25	55	0	3	11	483	506	342	282	22	264	475	.268
Rangers	5.36	56	0	0	12	492	553	356	293	25	240	430	.282
Brewers	6.31	56	0	1	8	488	528	422	342	17	330	379	.272

CLUB FIELDING

	PCT	PO	A	E	DP		PCT	PO	A	E	DP
Giants	.965	1460	604	75	62	Angels	.948	1459	603	114	44
Royals	.960	1497	569	86	48	Athletics	.948	1449	542	109	42
Padres	.956	1481	573	95	45	Rangers	.945	1476	605	122	44
Cubs	.953	1434	659	104	47	Brewers	.944	1464	638	125	43
Mariners	.951	1442	635	106	47						

INDIVIDUAL BATTING LEADERS
(Minimum 174 Plate Appearances)

	AVG	G	AB	R	H	2B	3B	HR	RBI	BB	SO	SB
Hunter, Cedric, Padres	.371	52	213	46	79	13	4	1	44	40	22	17
Sweeney, Matthew, Angels	.341	44	170	38	58	11	7	5	39	23	27	4
Hunt, Jeremy, Padres	.323	45	164	32	53	8	3	5	32	28	37	0
Contreras, Rayner, Padres	.316	44	171	36	54	9	3	2	52	20	34	4
Liddi, Alex, Mariners	.313	47	182	31	57	13	6	3	25	12	48	9
Downs, Matthew, Giants	.310	46	168	34	52	16	4	0	29	17	9	6
Barrios, Victor, Rangers	.307	50	176	28	54	10	2	2	23	11	32	14
Alonso, John, Brewers	.301	47	176	27	53	17	2	6	35	10	31	0
Lewis, Christopher, Angels	.295	42	156	24	46	10	5	2	23	18	26	9
Van Stratten, Nick, Royals	.292	54	209	46	61	8	7	3	35	25	17	14

INDIVIDUAL PITCHING LEADERS
(Minimum 45 Innings)

	W	L	ERA	G	GS	CG	SV	IP	H	R	ER	BB	SO
Veras, Nicolas, Angels	8	2	1.35	12	12	0	0	60	46	15	9	13	58
Schoeninger, Timothy, Angels	6	2	1.79	14	13	0	0	75	64	22	15	4	64
Fisher, Brent, Royals	3	1	2.11	14	14	0	0	68	41	18	16	19	98
Parker, Taylor, Cubs	2	2	2.35	14	8	0	0	54	49	16	14	13	39
Salinas, Doug, Mariners	4	0	2.84	12	5	0	2	51	39	19	16	15	49
McGrath, Ryan, Giants	5	3	2.94	13	7	0	0	52	52	21	17	15	29
Raglione, Paul, Royals	3	0	3.11	10	7	0	2	46	53	27	16	10	48
Menchaca, Pablo, Padres	3	1	3.35	13	7	0	0	51	52	23	19	9	39
Cabeza, Manuel, Giants	7	0	3.38	11	8	0	0	45	43	18	17	10	40
Jimenez, Esmerlin, Angels	5	3	3.57	14	13	0	0	63	60	29	25	17	60

ALL-STAR TEAM

C—Blake Parker, Cubs. **1B**—Gerardo Avila, Mariners. **2B**—Raynor Contreras, Padres. **3B**—Matt Sweeney, Angels. **SS**—Sharlon Schoop, Giants. **OF**—Luis Durango, Padres; Cedric Hunter, Padres; Carlos Peguero, Mariners. **DH**—John Alonso, Brewers **LHP**—Brent Fisher, Royals. **RHP**—Vladimir Veras, Angels. **LHRP**—Taylor Parker, Cubs. **RHRP**—David Newton, Giants.

Most Valuable Player: Cedric Hunter, Padres. **Manager of the Year:** Ever Magallanes, Angels.

DEPARTMENT LEADERS

BATTING

OBP	Durango, Luis, Padres	.470
SLG	Sweeney, Matthew, Angels	.576
R	Hunter, Cedric, Padres	.46
	Van Stratten, Nick, Royals	.46
H	Hunter, Cedric, Padres	.79
TB	Hunter, Cedric, Padres	.103
XBH	Alonso, John, Brewers	.25
2B	Alonso, John, Brewers	.17
3B	Lucas, Scott, Royals	.9
HR	Three players tied at	.7
RBI	Contreras, Rayner, Padres	.52
SAC	Six players tied at	.5
SF	Three players tied at	.5
BB	Doscher, Nicholas, Royals	.41
IBB	Schoop, Sharlon, Giants	.2
HBP	Lucas, Scott, Royals	.15
SO	Dotel, Welington, Mariners	.69
SB	Goetz, Mike, Brewers	.31
CS	Robinson, Derrick, Royals	.14
GIDP	Rodriguez, Jose, Rangers	.7
AB/SO	Downs, Matthew, Giants	.18.67

PITCHING

G	Huff, Matthew, Padres	.23
	Newton, David, Giants	.23
GS	Fisher, Brent, Royals	.14
	Morales, Angelo, Royals	.14
CG	Morales, Angelo, Royals	.1
	Salazar, Yesid, Padres	.1
SHO	Morales, Angelo, Royals	.1
GF	Newton, David, Giants	.23
SV	Newton, David, Giants	.13
W	Veras, Nicolas, Angels	.8
L	Funk, Shane, Rangers	.9
IP	Morales, Angelo, Royals	.76
H	Morales, Angelo, Royals	.98
R	Pascual, Rolando, Brewers	.51
ER	Pascual, Rolando, Brewers	.46
HB	Harmon, Robert, Mariners	.13
BB	Rodriguez, Henry Alberto, Athletics	.50
SO	Fisher, Brent, Royals	.98
SO/9(SP)	Fisher, Brent, Royals	.12.91
SO/9(RP)	Corchado, Jose, Athletics	.15.98
WP	Pascual, Rolando, Brewers	.20
BK	Renshaw, Jacob, Cubs	.4
	Valdez, Jose, Giants	.4

FIELDING

C	PCT	Doscher, Nicholas, Royals	.986
	PO	Doscher, Nicholas, Royals	.329
	A	Beltran, Juan, Mariners	.40
	E	Rivera, Julio, Athletics	.10
	DP	Beltran, Juan, Mariners	.5
	DP	De Los Santos, Anel, Angels	.5
	PB	Whiteside, Brett, Brewers	.24
	CS%	Hackstedt, Adam, Cubs	.62%
1B	PCT	Hunt, Jeremy, Padres	.992
	PO	Lucas, Scott, Royals	.463
	A	Alonso, John, Brewers	.29
	E	Alonso, John, Brewers	.10
	DP	Lucas, Scott, Royals	.41
2B	PO	Perez, Alwin, Royals	.62
	A	Felix, Jovanny, Brewers	.99
	E	Felix, Jovanny, Brewers	.13
	DP	Perez, Alwin, Royals	.26
3B	PCT	Downs, Matthew, Giants	.922
	PO	Taylor, Jason, Royals	.32
	A	Taylor, Jason, Royals	.78
	E	Carrasco, Felix, Padres	.23
	DP	Downs, Matthew, Giants	.10
SS	PCT	Juan, Manuel, Royals	.923
	PO	Juan, Manuel, Royals	.70
	A	Brewer, Brent, Brewers	.116
	E	Brewer, Brent, Brewers	.24
	DP	Juan, Manuel, Royals	.23
OF	PCT	Van Stratten, Nick, Royals	.989
	PO	Goetz, Mike, Brewers	.117
	A	Dyson, Jarrod, Royals	.11
	E	Fuller, Clayton, Angels	.7
	DP	Ortiz, Norberto, Angels	.4

MINOR LEAGUES

BY ALAN MATTHEWS

It won't make up for their big league club fading down the stretch, but the Red Sox managed to beat the Dodgers in three games to win the Gulf Coast League title—and the Yankees didn't even make the playoffs.

The Red Sox got an automatic bid to the finals by finishing with the league's best record, and the Dodgers beat the Tigers 4-2 in a one-game playoff between the league's other two division winners to capture the other bid to the championship series.

The Dodgers took the first game of the series by scoring two runs in the top of the ninth, highlighted by Preston Mattingly's RBI double. Brian Matthews, who hit the winning homer in the 10th inning of the playoff against the Tigers, followed with a single, advancing Mattingly to third. The No. 31 pick in the 2006 draft scored an insurance run on a wild pitch by reliever Mauricio Mendez.

Joseph Guerra and Miguel Socolovich combined on a four-hitter as the Red Sox tied the series by beating the Dodgers 5-1 in the second game. Guerra allowed one run on four hits in six innings, retiring 10 of the final 11 batters he faced. Socolovich tossed three hitless frames to earn the save.

The clincher was anticlimactic, as the Sox trounced the Dodgers 11-2. Jorge Rodriguez took a no-hitter into the sixth inning and Pedro Vasquez hit a grand slam to lead the way. Rodriguez earned the win, allowing a run on one hit over six frames. His bid for a no-hitter was foiled in the sixth,

Preston Mattingly

when Trayvon Robinson led off with a double and scored on Francisco Lizarraga's groundout.

In the fourth, Michael Jones launched a solo homer to put the Red Sox ahead for good. The homer was the highlight of a stellar day for Jones, who went 5-for-5.

For the second year in a row, the GCL was loaded with prospects, many of whom reported to Florida after being drafted in the early rounds in June. Seven first-rounders, including No. 7 overall selection Clayton Kershaw, made their pro debuts in the GCL.

A Dodgers lefthander, Kershaw was the unequivocal No. 1 prospect, dominating the league right out of high school.

Three other first-round choices—Twins outfielder/first baseman Chris Parmelee, Nationals outfielder Chris Marrero and Red Sox outfielder Jason Place—ranked among the GCL's top five prospects.

The league's Latin American contingent was equally promising. Tigers outfielder Gorkys Hernandez, a 19-year-old from Venezuela, won the batting title. Hernandez' teammate, Audy Ciriaco, was one of several Latino shortstops who drew consideration for the list, along with Lizarraga, Carlos Rivero (Indians), Danny Garcia (Marlins) and Jose de los Santos (Pirates).

The Tigers also placed three players on the league all-star team, with Hernandez an easy choice in the outfield. Ciriaco couldn't beat out the Phillies' Adrian Cardenas for the shortstop spot, but first baseman Chris Carlson and reliever Alfredo Figaro also won spots on the team.

Yankees pitchers Grant Duff and Angel Reyes were 1-2 in the league ERA race at 1.14 and 1.35.

"I thought players got better and the level of play got better from the beginning to the end," Indians manager Chris Tremie said, "and to me that's a sign of a productive league."

TOP 20 PROSPECTS

1. Clayton Kershaw, lhp, Dodgers
2. Chris Parmelee, of/1b, Twins
3. Gorkys Hernandez, of, Tigers
4. Chris Marrero, of, Nationals
5. Jason Place, of, Red Sox
6. Dellin Betances, rhp, Yankees
7. Adrian Cardenas, ss, Phillies
8. Neftali Feliz, rhp, Braves
9. Jhonny Nunez, rhp, Dodgers
10. Tom Hickman, of, Marlins
11. Preston Mattingly, ss, Dodgers
12. Kyle Drabek, rhp, Phillies
13. Steven Evarts, lhp, Braves
14. Jesus Sanchez, c, Phillies
15. Chad Rodgers, lhp, Braves
16. Josue Calzado, of, Yankees
17. D'Arby Myers, of, Phillies
18. Zach McAllister, rhp, Yankees
19. Carlos Monasterios, rhp, Yankees
20. Joe Benson, of, Twins

· STANDINGS

Page	EAST	Complex Site	W	L	PCT	GB	Manager	Last Penn.
157	Dodgers	Vero Beach	32	22	.593	—	Juan Bustabad	1990
128	Marlins	Jupiter	29	24	.547	2½	Edwin Rodriguez	None
180	Mets	St. Lucie	23	30	.434	8½	Bobby Floyd	None
270	Nationals	Melbourne	23	31	.426	9	Bobby Henley	1991
Page	NORTH	Complex Site	W	L	PCT	GB	Manager	Last Penn.
120	Tigers	Lakeland	32	18	.640	—	Kevin Bradshaw	None
188	Yankees	Tampa	31	20	.608	1½	Matt Martin	2005
60	Braves	Kissimmee	23	27	.460	9	Luis Ortiz	2003
106	Indians	Winter Haven	21	29	.420	11	Chris Tremie	None
203	Phillies	Clearwater	18	31	.367	13½	Jim Morrison	2002
Page	SOUTH	Complex Site	W	L	PCT	GB	Manager	Last Penn.
74	Red Sox	Fort Myers	35	19	.648	—	Dave Tomlin	2006
210	Pirates	Bradenton	27	26	.509	7½	Pete Mackanin	None
171	Twins	Fort Myers	26	27	.491	8½	Nelson Prada	None
98	Reds	Sarasota	18	34	.346	16	Luis Aguayo	None

PLAYOFFS—Semifinals: Dodgers defeated Tigers 4-2 in one-game playoff. Final: Red Sox defeated Dodgers 2-1 in best-of-three series.

NOTE: Teams' individual batting and pitching statistics can be found on page indicated in lefthand column.

MINOR LEAGUES

2006 GULF COAST LEAGUE STATISTICS

CLUB BATTING

	AVG	G	AB	R	H	2B	3B	HR	BB	SO	SB	OBP	SLG
Pirates	.268	53	1756	233	471	83	13	22	152	337	65	.336	.368
Dodgers	.267	54	1801	272	480	87	16	20	185	388	57	.340	.366
Red Sox	.260	54	1751	244	456	85	19	33	165	378	48	.329	.387
Tigers	.258	50	1671	254	431	76	13	35	134	352	91	.319	.382
Reds	.255	53	1747	209	446	86	15	15	145	361	40	.321	.347
Indians	.254	50	1664	240	423	73	8	24	144	374	79	.320	.351
Yankees	.243	51	1645	241	400	82	9	20	210	323	59	.339	.340
Twins	.242	54	1743	257	422	72	21	24	180	397	61	.324	.349
Mets	.234	53	1782	227	417	66	16	13	207	430	41	.320	.311
Braves	.233	50	1686	213	392	72	7	20	173	400	60	.318	.319
Marlins	.231	53	1702	199	394	57	13	15	191	363	43	.315	.307
Phillies	.227	49	1584	180	359	68	9	14	138	389	93	.297	.307
Nationals	.226	54	1775	220	402	70	5	15	202	450	34	.312	.297

CLUB PITCHING

	ERA	G	CG	SHO	SV	IP	H	R	ER	HR	BB	SO	AVG
Marlins	2.86	53	0	0	18	460	391	196	146	12	151	419	.226
Yankees	2.92	51	0	4	15	444	361	176	144	27	123	442	.220
Red Sox	3.02	54	1	2	17	461	435	198	155	20	129	354	.252
Dodgers	3.03	54	1	6	16	469	382	198	158	15	193	428	.219
Tigers	3.03	50	1	6	14	430	363	176	145	16	174	372	.228
Pirates	3.29	53	0	3	14	457	420	214	167	22	150	372	.245
Nationals	3.35	54	0	3	9	476	461	226	177	14	188	406	.252
Braves	3.74	50	0	7	15	443	394	224	184	18	164	366	.238
Reds	4.04	53	0	1	9	457	434	254	205	20	196	377	.252
Twins	4.29	54	2	4	15	468	506	277	223	32	167	370	.276
Phillies	4.46	49	2	1	10	422	466	275	209	27	159	311	.278
Indians	4.58	50	0	3	13	431	421	278	219	25	179	347	.250
Mets	4.73	53	0	4	11	461	459	298	242	22	253	378	.261

CLUB FIELDING

	PCT	PO	A	E	DP		PCT	PO	A	E	DP
Yankees	.970	1333	522	58	38	Braves	.957	1328	515	82	49
Pirates	.967	1371	570	67	51	Nationals	.955	1428	577	94	45
Tigers	.967	1290	537	62	49	Reds	.955	1370	587	92	40
Red Sox	.966	1384	591	69	52	Phillies	.952	1265	556	91	46
Dodgers	.965	1407	515	69	35	Twins	.951	1404	567	102	44
Mets	.965	1381	574	71	41	Indians	.951	1292	529	94	38
Marlins	.963	1380	539	74	36						

INDIVIDUAL BATTING LEADERS
(Minimum 167 Plate Appearances)

	AVG	G	AB	R	H	2B	3B	HR	RBI	BB	SO	SB
Hernandez, Gorkys, Tigers	.327	50	205	41	67	9	2	5	23	10	27	20
Cardenas, Adrian, Phillies	.318	41	154	22	49	5	4	2	21	17	28	13
Romero, Deibinson, Twins	.313	50	176	37	55	10	2	4	38	13	37	6
Pena, Roman, Indians	.311	43	151	27	47	12	1	5	23	22	48	6
Carlson, Christopher, Tigers	.311	49	177	27	55	16	0	11	47	24	31	3
Arlet, Luis, Tigers	.300	44	160	33	48	4	3	6	20	9	54	20
Fernandez-Oliva, Carlos, Red Sox	.297	43	155	33	46	12	2	3	23	20	26	9
Perez, Smelin, Pirates	.295	47	190	27	56	8	3	1	13	12	23	13
Cabrera, Angel, Reds	.293	48	167	31	49	15	2	3	17	24	31	2
Mattingly, Preston, Dodgers	.290	47	186	22	54	12	3	1	29	9	39	12

INDIVIDUAL PITCHING LEADERS
(Minimum 43 Innings)

	W	L	ERA	G	GS	CG	SV	IP	H	R	ER	BB	SO
Duff, Grant, Yankees	5	1	1.14	11	8	0	0	47	26	12	6	17	59
Reyes, Angel, Yankees	3	2	1.35	11	5	0	3	47	25	10	7	14	45
Nunez, Jhonny, Dodgers	6	0	1.58	10	7	0	0	57	35	12	10	19	56
Aponte, Eleazar, Tigers	4	0	1.77	8	6	1	0	46	37	10	9	7	33
Fountain, Joel, Marlins	3	2	2.30	10	6	0	1	43	31	12	11	9	32
Rodriguez, Jorge, Red Sox	4	1	2.35	9	6	0	0	46	38	20	12	18	34
Rodriguez, Dionis, Pirates	3	3	2.36	11	9	0	0	46	43	18	12	12	41
Righter, Matthew, Tigers	4	1	2.47	10	10	0	0	47	44	19	13	17	27
Gomez, Jeanmar, Indians	4	3	2.48	11	9	0	0	54	50	24	15	12	34
Doubront, Felix, Red Sox	2	3	2.52	11	11	0	0	54	41	17	15	13	36

ALL-STAR TEAM

C—Wilson Ramos, Twins. **1B**—Chris Carlson, Tigers. **2B**—Elian Herrera, Dodgers. **3B**—Deibinson Romero, Twins. **SS**—Adrian Cardenas, Phillies. **OF**—Justin Byler, Pirates; Gorkys Hernandez, Tigers; D'Arby Myers, Phillies. **SP**—Jhonny Nunez, Dodgers. **RP**—Alfredo Figaro, Tigers.

Manager of the Year: Dave Tomlin, Red Sox.

BATTING
OBP	Pena, Roman, GCL Indians	.408
SLG	Carlson, Christopher, GCL Tigers	.588
R	Hernandez, Gorkys, GCL Tigers	41
H	Hernandez, Gorkys, GCL Tigers	67
TB	Carlson, Christopher, GCL Tigers	104
XBH	Carlson, Christopher, GCL Tigers	27
2B	Carlson, Christopher, GCL Tigers	16
3B	Montero, Juan, GCL Mets	6
	Reed, Justin, GCL Reds	6
HR	Carlson, Christopher, GCL Tigers	11
RBI	Carlson, Christopher, GCL Tigers	47
SAC	Lizarraga, Francisco, GCL Dodgers	11
SF	De la Cruz, Jorge, GCL Nationals	7
BB	Hickman, Thomas, GCL Marlins	30
	Hollingsworth, Donald, GCL Yankees	30
IBB	Calzado, Josue, GCL Yankees	3
HBP	Santiago, Eric, GCL Twins	14
SO	Arlet, Luis, GCL Tigers	54
SB	Montero, Lucas, GCL Indians	23
CS	Benson, Joe, GCL Twins	10
GIDP	Two players tied at	7
AB/SO	Ramos, Wilson, GCL Twins	11

PITCHING
G	Zabala, Felix, GCL Marlins	20
GS	Doubront, Felix, GCL Red Sox	11
	Rondon, Hector, GCL Indians	11
CG	Bromberg, David, GCL Twins	2
SHO	Aponte, Eleazar, GCL Tigers	1
	Bromberg, David, GCL Twins	1
GF	Tippett, Bradley, GCL Twins	18
SV	Tippett, Bradley, GCL Twins	10
W	Nunez, Jhonny, GCL Dodgers	6
L	Newman, Justin, GCL Reds	6
IP	Nunez, Jhonny, GCL Dodgers	57
H	Rondon, Hector, GCL Indians	62
R	Rondon, Hector, GCL Indians	34
ER	Rondon, Hector, GCL Indians	30
HB	Rondon, Hector, GCL Indians	8
BB	Roth, Robert, GCL Phillies	31
SO	Duff, Grant, GCL Yankees	59
SO/9 (SP)	Alcala, Omar, GCL Twins	6.47
SO/9 (RP)	Perdomo, Luis, GCL Indians	13.05
WP	Beattie, Eric, GCL Tigers	16
	Holdzkom, John, GCL Mets	16
BK	Alcala, Omar, GCL Twins	4

FIELDING
C	PCT	Bowen, Joseph, GCL Tigers	.989
	PO	Jansen, Kenley, GCL Dodgers	262
	A	Ramos, Wilson, GCL Twins	36
	E	Dominguez, Javier, GCL Mets	9
	DP	Solano, Jhonatan, GCL Nationals	5
	PB	Castillo, Alex, GCL Indians	9
		Rooney, Sean, GCL Nationals	9
	CS%	Garcia, Aaron, GCL Mets	53%
1B	PCT	Carlson, Christopher, GCL Tigers	.987
	PO	Jacobsen, Robert, GCL Nationals	.445
	A	Parliament, Adam, GCL Braves	24
	E	Jacobsen, Robert, GCL Nationals	11
	DP	Carlson, Christopher, GCL Tigers	36
2B	PCT	Voyles, Jeffery, GCL Mets	.980
	PO	Perez, Smelin, GCL Pirates	105
	A	Perez, Smelin, GCL Pirates	107
	E	Chiang, Chih-Hsien, GCL Red Sox	10
		Lawman, Matthew, GCL Twins	10
	DP	Perez, Smelin, GCL Pirates	29
3B	PCT	Giarraputo, Nicholas, GCL Mets	.931
	PO	Giarraputo, Nicholas, GCL Mets	47
	A	Figuereo, Johan, GCL Nationals	88
	E	Figuereo, Johan, GCL Nationals	15
	DP	Francisco, Juan, GCL Reds	10
		Giarraputo, Nicholas, GCL Mets	10
SS	PCT	Alvarez, Jean, GCL Nationals	.939
	PO	Cabrera, Angel, GCL Reds	81
	A	Cabrera, Angel, GCL Reds	160
	E	Cabrera, Angel, GCL Reds	20
	DP	Ciriaco, Audy, GCL Tigers	31
OF	PCT	Koko, Rubi, GCL Braves	1
	PO	Benson, Joe, GCL Twins	116
	A	Parmelee, Chris, GCL Twins	11
	E	Hernandez, Ramon, GCL Indians	7
	DP	Rosario, Jovanny, GCL Dodgers	4

MINOR LEAGUES

DOMINICAN SUMMER LEAGUE

CIBAO	W	L	PCT	GB
Royals	47	21	.691	—
Braves	35	33	.515	12
Marlins	28	42	.400	20
White Sox	28	42	.400	20

SAN PEDRO DE MACORIS	W	L	PCT	GB
Pirates	48	19	.716	—
Angels	47	20	.701	1
Astros	36	30	.545	11½
Rangers	21	44	.323	26
Orioles	13	52	.200	34

SANTO DOMINGO NORTH	W	L	PCT	GB
Mariners	42	24	.636	—
Phillies	40	26	.606	2
Athletics1	33	32	.508	8½
Cardinals	30	35	.462	11½
Athletics2	18	46	.281	23

SANTO DOMINGO WEST	W	L	PCT	GB
Tigers	48	18	.727	—
Mets	33	33	.500	15
Padres	32	33	.492	15½
Nationals1	30	35	.462	17½
Nationals2	21	45	.318	27

BOCA CHICA	W	L	PCT	GB
Yankees1	49	20	.71	—
Indians	44	27	.62	6
Blue Jays	44	29	.603	7
Twins	43	29	.597	7½
Yankees2	41	30	.577	9
Rockies	36	36	.5	14½
Giants	32	34	.485	15½
Reds	31	36	.463	17
Dodgers	30	42	.417	20½
Cubs	25	46	.352	25
Diamondbacks	24	46	.343	25½
Red Sox	23	47	.329	26½

PLAYOFFS—First round: Mariners defeated Royals 2-1 and Yankees1 defeated Indians 2-1 in best-of-three series. **Semifinals:** Mariners defeated Tigers 2-1 and Yankees1 defeated Pirates 2-0 in best-of-three series. **Finals:** Yankees1 defeated DSL Mariners 3-1 in a best-of-five series.

INDIVIDUAL BATTING LEADERS
(Minimum 178 At-Bats)

	AVG	AB	R	H	2B	3B	HR	RBI	SB
Diaz, Kelvin, Indians	.382	204	43	78	13	1	9	62	4
Sosa, Pablo, Marlins	.333	213	30	71	10	7	1	25	11
Leveret, Rene, Twins	.331	254	31	84	22	0	7	55	2
Cruz, Diego, Royals	.330	206	29	68	14	0	0	40	0
Dionicio, Andres, Yankees1	.330	233	37	77	15	0	8	42	1
Nunez, Luis, Mariners	.326	190	46	62	10	3	0	22	21
Lara, Elvis, Cubs	.325	255	41	83	11	6	2	46	10
Farias, Dany, Blue Jays	.325	265	52	86	17	1	5	42	14
Rojas, Francis, Cardinals	.321	215	23	69	13	1	6	36	2
Rincon, Ambiorix, Phillies	.320	256	48	82	22	1	5	31	12
Vargas, Hancer, White Sox	.318	233	46	74	6	3	1	12	10
Collado, Keyter, Dodgers	.314	191	29	60	12	0	2	23	3
Santana, Ramoncito, Twins	.313	176	35	55	10	2	8	30	2
Castro, Ivan, Cardinals	.313	195	24	61	9	1	3	34	3
Gil, Leonardo, Athletics1	.308	182	26	56	4	1	0	15	3
Parra, Camilo, Braves	.304	204	24	62	10	2	3	31	4
Bernardo, Luis, Orioles	.304	168	23	51	9	4	1	20	1
Bejarano, Enderson, Royals	.304	191	35	58	14	1	1	29	1
Luna, Migeul, White Sox	.303	178	32	54	19	0	1	22	6
Vargas, Alex, Pirates	.300	240	39	72	11	1	0	35	11
Puello, Alberto, Rangers	.298	188	22	56	7	2	1	25	4
Molina, Yeldrys, Royals	.296	247	58	73	18	2	1	33	15
Velasquez, Isaias, Indians	.292	267	60	78	8	3	0	20	25
Benzant, Hector, Athletics2	.291	172	21	50	7	1	1	8	6
Perez, Yensy, Blue Jays	.291	237	40	69	7	4	1	24	9
Hernandez, Deivi, Braves	.290	193	25	56	15	3	1	25	2
Rodriguez, Angel, Indians	.290	231	39	67	12	3	0	30	7
Gomez, Leuris, Rockies	.290	224	39	65	7	3	0	13	17
De Los Santos, Joel, Marlins	.290	245	45	71	8	2	1	15	27

Medrano, Ignacio, Mets	.289	194	33	56	10	0	0	25	9
Burgos, Ricardo, Red Sox	.288	184	28	53	14	3	4	39	3
Garzon, Edgar, Padres	.286	199	17	57	15	0	0	28	3
Rodriguez, Yunior, Athletics1	.284	190	25	54	11	2	1	17	3
Pena, Silvio, Pirates	.283	223	36	63	9	2	1	22	18
Ramirez, Alvaro, Yankees2	.282	181	25	51	4	4	0	15	12
Martinez, Eduard, Phillies	.282	227	39	64	7	1	0	16	6
Castillo, Alcibiades, Rangers	.281	167	28	47	11	3	2	21	18
Puga, Jaspher, Angels	.280	189	29	53	9	2	0	28	8
Paulino, Yancarlos, Angels	.280	164	39	46	9	3	0	18	18
Nicolas, Bartolo, Blue Jays	.280	264	42	74	9	3	3	39	14
Navarro, Yamaico, Red Sox	.279	201	29	56	13	5	3	37	5
Perez, Juan Carlos, Marlins	.279	208	29	58	7	0	0	21	1
Cuello, Prilys, Yankees2	.279	215	43	60	18	4	7	38	8
Florentino, Yoeli, Padres	.279	222	33	62	14	0	4	31	5
Reyes, Leonardo, Rockies	.278	227	26	63	11	1	1	22	9
Solarte, Yangervis, Twins	.278	194	32	54	9	2	2	29	2
Medina, Jose, Giants	.278	216	42	60	8	5	6	35	8
Silverio, Alfredo, Dodgers	.276	225	36	62	12	6	6	48	6
Serrano, Victor, Red Sox	.275	229	43	63	7	1	1	18	15
Rosario, Ebert, Astros	.275	200	26	55	6	2	1	21	5
Rosario, Alberto, Angels	.275	178	28	49	5	4	0	23	3
Peguero, Francisco, Giants	.275	182	24	50	10	3	4	16	3
Arias, Renny, Royals	.273	194	37	53	10	2	2	24	9
Brito, Jeanfred, Twins	.273	242	55	66	6	11	0	17	17
Andres, Graviel, Athletics2	.273	161	29	44	8	3	1	15	7
Santa, Luis, Phillies	.272	169	26	46	8	1	0	15	8
Reyes, Jesus, Cubs	.270	196	36	53	8	1	2	16	16
Herrera, Julian, Yankees2	.270	211	27	57	9	4	2	28	3
Quezada, Andres, Cubs	.268	198	31	53	9	5	2	27	5
Diaz, Wilmer, Giants	.267	172	23	46	10	2	1	18	5
Constanza, Jose, Tigers	.266	173	37	46	5	1	0	28	27
Jimenez, Antonio, Royals	.264	174	31	46	9	3	3	35	3
Mata, Argenis, Blue Jays	.264	174	36	46	11	1	0	23	6
Montesino, Isidro, Tigers	.263	179	32	47	6	0	2	23	17
Peguero, Fausto, Royals	.263	194	36	51	6	4	0	24	17
Mejia, Juan, Phillies	.263	232	34	61	15	1	2	40	12
Veloz, Greg, Mets	.262	221	50	58	16	1	4	28	28
Gomez, Roy, Yankees1	.262	221	28	58	11	0	1	34	8
Guzman, Joaquin, Tigers	.261	157	19	41	5	2	1	30	5
Chourio, Segundo, Twins	.261	234	25	61	15	2	4	37	0
Ramirez, Welinton, Blue Jays	.261	241	31	63	13	4	3	46	7
Perez, Miguel, Rockies	.258	248	33	64	13	3	0	22	20
Bermudez, Ronald, Red Sox	.257	179	30	46	9	5	0	12	7
Soto, Victor, Royals	.257	210	33	54	16	4	2	30	9
Guzman, Jose, Tigers	.256	219	31	56	9	1	4	25	3
Contreras, Ivan, Angels	.255	196	39	50	8	10	1	15	8
Lagares, Juan, Mets	.255	204	36	52	7	8	3	33	12
Sandoval, Orlando, Rockies	.254	232	30	59	15	2	5	34	9
Kirindongo, Randolph, Marlins	.254	205	28	52	11	2	1	27	6
Almonte, Abraham, Yankees1	.254	209	51	53	11	3	8	26	36
Rodriguez, Keyter, Athletics1	.254	181	25	46	10	2	1	24	3
Mathiw, Santos, Phillies	.254	209	35	53	13	3	3	30	8
Encarnacion, Jairo, Pirates	.254	213	36	54	11	0	5	23	8
Ramirez, Ramon, Diamondbacks	.253	233	23	59	11	6	0	23	7
Sanchez, Karexon, Indians	.253	233	47	59	9	2	6	35	22
Cruz, Jose, Tigers	.253	182	49	46	6	0	1	20	16
Sierra, Moises, Blue Jays	.253	245	35	62	16	1	4	26	17
Peguero, Luis, Mariners	.252	163	33	41	5	3	1	19	10
Solorzano, Luis, Nationals1	.252	214	25	54	6	1	0	17	17
Guzman, Amauri, Dodgers	.251	191	36	48	6	0	2	20	16
Sierra, Raddy, Angels	.250	152	20	38	8	2	1	23	7
Vasquez, Carlos, Blue Jays	.250	200	33	50	7	0	1	21	17
Rosario, Wilin, Rockies	.249	213	28	53	7	0	3	25	5
Urena, Ariel, Diamondbacks	.247	215	33	53	12	1	6	19	11
De Los Santos, Vladimir, Phillies	.247	247	39	61	9	3	1	29	15

INDIVIDUAL PITCHING LEADERS
(Minimum 53 Innings)

	W	L	ERA	G	SV	IP	H	BB	SO
Bautista, Juan, Nationals1	4	0	0.75	13	1	60	34	16	70
Pinales, Agustin, Astros	3	3	0.78	11	0	58	37	13	41
Jimenez, Arbert, Red Sox	2	1	0.99	14	1	54	40	10	50
Fernandez, Eddy, Mariners	8	2	1.06	12	0	68	46	10	73
Beltre, Omar, Rangers	2	3	1.23	13	1	66	42	7	80
Diaz, Jose, Pirates	8	2	1.23	16	1	88	67	13	71
Cedeno, Santo, Twins	10	0	1.23	15	0	95	52	17	62
Acosta, Richard, Pirates	7	1	1.27	11	0	71	59	9	80

Name	W	L	ERA	G	SV	IP	H	BB	SO
Frias, Santo, Indians	4	4	1.30	11	0	55	37	18	44
Chevalier, Juan, Angels	5	0	1.31	10	0	55	38	12	54
Abad, Fernando, Astros	5	2	1.32	15	1	61	50	7	64
Perez, Luis, Blue Jays	4	0	1.38	14	0	85	47	23	107
Marte, Luis, Tigers	8	0	1.38	11	0	65	41	15	90
Castro, Angel, Tigers	4	1	1.39	9	0	58	34	10	71
Florentino, Antonio, Phillies	7	2	1.44	15	0	81	47	26	65
Duran, Jose, Astros	6	1	1.47	13	0	61	31	21	67
Rondon, Danny, Twins	4	4	1.48	13	0	67	66	16	43
Chacin, Jhoulys, Rockies	4	1	1.49	12	0	73	60	18	67
Perez, Jose, Angels	6	1	1.52	12	0	71	37	17	59
Carreno, Joel, Blue Jays	8	3	1.53	15	0	82	48	28	86
Paulino, Eduardo, Royals	9	1	1.55	17	0	70	54	12	44
Rojas, Jonathan, Braves	7	0	1.57	12	0	63	40	19	47
Alvarez, Jose, Red Sox	2	1	1.61	15	0	62	46	19	64
Rosario, Frank, White Sox	4	1	1.62	13	0	72	57	8	67
Guanchez, Wilmer, Twins	4	1	1.69	14	0	75	53	23	58
Matos, Miguel, Phillies	6	1	1.71	13	0	53	40	8	54
Molina, Robin, Angels	7	2	1.76	14	0	82	61	19	43
Del Rosario, Enerio, Reds	5	1	1.78	13	0	71	51	15	59
Soto, Eleno, Rangers	4	3	1.79	11	0	55	46	15	44
Rodriguez, Mario, Giants	5	2	1.79	14	0	55	48	21	54
Soto, Jesus, Padres	3	2	1.84	15	0	64	59	9	93
Hidalgo, Charles, Pirates	5	2	1.86	20	6	58	43	22	51
Paniagua, Onarkys, White Sox	4	2	1.88	14	0	62	52	23	59
Paulino, Ricardo, Pirates	6	2	1.93	13	0	75	58	11	67
Figuereo, Freddy, Pirates	4	2	1.97	13	0	59	43	10	40
Villegas, Juan, Athletics1	3	7	2.01	16	2	72	60	21	55
Obispo, Wirfin, Reds	4	5	2.04	14	0	79	47	18	93
Viola, Pedro, Reds	5	5	2.04	15	0	62	50	20	77
Flande, Yohan, Phillies	6	1	2.08	13	0	65	55	12	60
Reyes, Henry, Twins	6	2	2.09	15	0	77	43	33	71
Beltre, Cristian, Diamondbacks	4	4	2.23	13	0	65	67	11	44
Urena, Jose, Indians	5	6	2.26	14	0	56	46	27	40
Cabrera, Alberto, Cubs	5	6	2.27	15	0	71	69	18	55
Cabrera, Francis, Angels	6	2	2.28	14	0	83	57	23	76
Martinez, Anillins, Indians	7	0	2.28	17	2	71	49	29	75
Ramirez, Wilfredo, Indians	8	1	2.31	14	0	82	73	13	70
Nunez, Eddy, Pirates	2	2	2.35	12	1	54	38	15	53
Noboa, Pedro, Dodgers	3	2	2.38	10	0	64	51	10	70
Alcantara, Ariel, Mariners	3	3	2.39	12	0	60	34	23	54
Montas, Wiston, Royals	3	2	2.41	15	2	60	44	15	48
Ramirez, Wiliam, Braves	6	2	2.47	13	0	69	59	15	48
Vasquez, Daniel, Diamondbacks	4	6	2.51	19	0	65	46	17	72
Dominguez, Kelvin, Dodgers	2	2	2.56	14	0	53	34	36	75
Campos, Jose, Rockies	6	5	2.58	14	0	84	77	14	62
Luna, Daury, Phillies	5	4	2.59	15	0	87	65	27	88
Guzman, Kelvin, Rockies	4	5	2.60	11	0	62	52	20	52
Patino, Geomar, Giants	5	2	2.62	23	3	65	49	24	53
Arrioja, Jorge, A's1/A's 2	2	6	2.65	16	0	54	44	18	59
Castillo, Noel, Yankees1	3	1	2.67	14	0	54	40	8	43
Mercedes, Bruno, Mariners	6	3	2.72	11	0	60	52	18	52
Ciriaco, Edwin, Astros	3	4	2.75	13	0	59	35	32	69
Corporan, Moises, Nationals1	3	4	2.75	12	0	56	39	20	44
Infante, Edilmar, Cubs	1	5	2.78	18	1	55	55	10	21
Bustamante, Juan, Blue Jays	6	5	2.80	16	1	71	58	29	84
Romero, Alvaro, Athletics1	3	5	2.83	13	0	60	56	19	37
Noel, Luis, Orioles	2	5	2.85	18	2	60	53	26	46
Mieses, Santo, Tigers	4	3	2.90	12	0	59	34	29	90
Vasquez, Alberto, Royals	3	3	2.94	14	1	52	62	5	26
Agudo, Juan, Twins	4	6	2.97	14	0	58	52	22	40

Name	AVG	AB	R	H	2B	3B	HR	RBI	SB
Morales, Jaime, Phillies	.316	228	38	72	17	0	1	27	19
Gonzalez, Orlando, Tigers/Marlins	.314	185	22	58	12	0	4	31	5
Hidalgo, Anderson, Twins/Jays	.310	242	28	75	13	0	3	43	17
Mendez, Carlos, Reds	.309	230	26	71	16	0	1	29	1
Gomez, Luis, Reds	.307	244	39	75	11	4	0	33	9
Tang, Jorge, Reds	.306	216	45	66	6	3	0	17	16
Morillo, Domingo, Twins/Jays	.305	223	43	68	9	1	1	29	14
Carrera, Ezequiel, Mets	.301	216	41	65	4	5	1	19	22
Murillo, Francisco, Phillies	.299	221	39	66	11	2	10	56	9
Munoz, Joe, Pirates	.295	196	42	58	11	1	0	23	23
Chourio, Anderson, Pirates	.295	227	53	67	8	1	0	25	38
Armas, Herman, Astros	.295	234	48	69	19	4	5	34	15
Bonfante, Ricardo, Astros	.291	268	48	78	11	2	0	41	33
Rojas, Jesus, Tigers/Marlins	.290	221	38	64	11	1	5	34	5
Agudelo, Jorge, Mariners	.290	186	32	54	6	0	0	14	6
Quiroz, Arlon, Phillies	.288	243	52	70	12	4	2	18	31
Gualdron, Jose, Reds	.288	278	38	80	16	6	6	44	11
Contreras, Efrain, Reds	.287	164	37	47	8	2	5	26	6
Bonevacia, Arthur, Orioles/W. Sox	.287	174	28	50	5	6	0	25	4
Medrano, Jhonny, Astros	.286	238	38	68	17	2	3	49	12
Tello, Renzo, Astros	.285	253	55	72	19	3	7	46	4
Guilarte, Danny, Mets	.281	199	29	56	6	5	1	19	21
Rodriguez, Yonderman, Phillies	.279	208	28	58	4	0	0	19	8
Espinoza, Humberto, Mariners	.276	156	29	43	2	3	0	14	1
Mavares, Dixon, Pirates	.273	183	39	50	8	3	0	15	11
Fuentes, Cesar, Mariners	.273	183	25	50	3	2	1	20	5
Sanchez, Juan, Twins/Blue Jays	.269	238	39	64	14	4	1	30	8
Colina, Edilio, Mariners	.268	179	39	48	5	2	1	24	4
Palacios, Luis, Tigers/Marlins	.266	229	43	61	12	1	2	11	17
Martina, Quincy, Cardinals	.266	188	22	50	6	2	1	15	7
Hernandez, Xavier, Reds	.266	188	24	50	8	0	4	24	0
Zavala, Gabriel, Mets	.263	213	36	56	15	4	8	42	6
Landoni, Emerson, Tigers/Marlins	.263	198	25	52	7	1	0	18	6
Figueroa, Oscar, Astros	.263	213	30	56	9	3	2	34	7
Blanco, Robert, Astros	.262	225	38	59	13	0	1	29	8
Blanco, Jourik, Orioles/White Sox	.262	172	28	45	13	0	4	28	1
Trinidad, Michaelangel, Pirates	.261	218	34	57	15	0	5	36	3
Extrano, Jetsy, Mariners	.261	157	24	41	8	2	0	23	6
Omana, Gustavo, Reds	.254	201	26	51	7	0	1	24	4
Conde, Edwin, Cardinals	.254	173	17	44	11	0	7	30	2
Martinez, Mario, Reds	.253	174	13	44	8	2	0	20	5
Pinto, Josmil, Twins/Blue Jays	.251	195	25	49	7	1	3	30	3
Britton, Dwight, Mariners	.251	227	39	57	10	2	4	28	13
Murakami, Fabio, Phillies	.249	173	28	43	6	0	1	19	4
Vargas, Marcos, Mets	.247	215	27	53	15	0	7	22	5
Garcia, Jose, Cardinals	.241	203	27	49	12	0	1	16	7
Bolivar, Dognnt, Cardinals	.239	230	26	55	7	2	8	29	8
Yepez, Mario, Mariners	.227	172	11	39	7	2	1	26	6
Requena, Jonathan, Twins/Jays	.225	187	19	42	4	0	0	20	4
Stephenson, Zuriel, Tigers/Marlins	.218	170	15	37	11	0	3	17	3

INDIVIDUAL PITCHING LEADERS
(Minimum 58 Innings)

Name	W	L	ERA	G	SV	IP	H	BB	SO
Ramirez, Juan, Mariners	5	1	1.66	14	0	65	43	35	56
Castro, Oscar, Reds	6	2	2.04	14	0	62	48	15	30
Olivares, Manuel, Mets	6	3	2.14	12	0	63	51	14	45
Melendez, Moises, Phillies	8	2	2.18	15	0	91	72	33	104
Olivero, Yovanny, Mariners	4	6	2.18	14	0	70	68	17	48
Ortiz, Wilson, Pirates	4	1	2.25	16	2	60	51	22	61
Mendoza, Wladimir, Cardinals	6	4	2.26	14	0	76	50	10	67
Escalona, Sergio, Phillies	3	4	2.29	14	1	71	63	25	71
Perez, Carlos, Orioles/White Sox	6	2	2.48	15	0	87	92	16	64
Orman, Conrad, Orioles/White Sox	6	2	2.57	12	0	70	61	21	85
Romero, Mauricio, Phillies	5	2	2.59	14	0	83	83	22	75
Venegas, Alfredo, Mariners	4	4	2.76	17	1	75	70	13	53
Teller, Carlos, Mariners	2	0	2.86	15	0	63	40	41	73
Pereira, Nelson, Pirates	3	5	2.95	17	0	58	53	20	39
Echarry, Johnattan, Astros	4	1	3.03	12	0	62	61	19	40
Carrillo, Matias, Mets	3	5	3.38	12	0	69	76	8	35
Martinez, Joucer, Orioles/White Sox	5	4	3.48	16	2	75	76	23	54
Ballestas, Freddy, Phillies	5	4	3.60	14	0	75	89	23	39
Figueroa, Rogers, Mets	6	4	3.71	13	0	68	67	16	48
Rivero, Raul, Orioles/White Sox	4	5	3.78	16	0	79	68	20	72
Prieto, Ramon, Astros	1	6	3.82	14	0	68	62	22	33
Rodriguez, Carlos, Twins/Blue Jays	2	3	4.21	17	2	58	59	13	38
Rada, Jose, Cardinals	2	6	4.48	16	1	66	87	13	44
Sanchez, Angelo, Twins/Blue Jays	3	7	4.55	15	0	65	69	34	39
Linares, Kristhiam, Tigers/Marlins	3	3	4.57	13	0	65	60	16	37
Marquez, Winston, Twins/Blue Jays	1	5	4.82	18	0	65	63	45	68
Munoz, Miguel, Twins/Blue Jays	3	6	4.91	16	0	66	64	43	42
Diaz, Omar, Cardinals	2	8	5.02	17	0	66	74	37	56
Ibarra, Edgar, Twins/Blue Jays	2	6	5.49	19	0	59	72	23	29
Marquez, Angel, Tigers/Marlins	3	5	5.71	13	0	65	84	13	55

VENEZUELAN SUMMER LEAGUE

CIBAO	W	L	PCT	GB
Phillies	41	25	.621	—
Pirates	41	25	.621	—
Orioles/White Sox	41	29	.586	2
Mariners	37	28	.569	3½
Mets	37	32	.536	5½
Reds	35	31	.530	6
Astros	37	34	.521	6½
Tigers/Marlins	25	46	.352	18½
Cardinals	24	46	.343	19
Twins/Blue Jays	23	45	.338	19

PLAYOFFS: Phillies defeated Pirates 2-0 in a best-of-three series.

INDIVIDUAL BATTING LEADERS
(Minimum 194 Plate Appearances)

Name	AVG	AB	R	H	2B	3B	HR	RBI	SB
Moreno, Wilfredo, Orioles/W. Sox	.389	198	43	77	13	0	5	40	4
Paisano, David, Orioles/White Sox	.338	195	36	66	13	7	0	17	8
Rocero, Ciro, Pirates	.321	237	50	76	10	2	3	44	34

ARIZONA FALL LEAGUE

The players and contributing organizations may change each season, but the Phoenix Desert Dogs continue to dominate the Arizona Fall League. Consisting of prospects from the Athletics, Blue Jays, Devil Rays, Reds and Tigers, the Phoenix team this time around captured its third straight championship by defeating the Grand Canyon Rafters, 6-2, in front of 1,181 fans at Scottsdale Stadium.

The way in which the Desert Dogs, representing the AFL's East Division, won the championship game was indicative of the way they played all season.

"We got the hits when we needed them," manager Tony DeFrancesco (A's) said. "We had the number one pitching in the league and the number one defense, and we came out and proved that's what it takes. In games like this, it's going to take a mistake or a big hit . . . They made the first mistake and we took advantage of it."

The Desert Dogs made the most of their four hits, getting on the board with three unearned runs on only one hit in the third inning. Fernando Perez (Devil Rays) had a two-run single off Rafters starter (and losing pitcher) A.J. Murray (Rangers), and a pair of errors helped the rally.

Grand Canyon got on the board in the top of the fifth, ending a 28-inning scoreless streak by Desert Dogs starter Virgil Vasquez (Tigers), the game's winning pitcher. Vasquez held the Rafters hitless through the first four innings before Jeff Fiorentino (Orioles) led off the fifth with a single, advanced to second on a ground out, and scored on a Cortez double.

Vasquez, who was slated to stay in the game for 75 pitches, was nearly pulled after Cortez' hit due to cramping in his leg and fingers, but toughed it out to complete the fifth inning.

"I had fun out here," said the righthander, who pitched at Double-A Erie during the regular season said. "We had a great team. I kept telling the guys before the game that I wish we could have this team during the season because we had so much fun together . . . If you have fun and stay loose, you're going to succeed as a team."

Pitching was supposed to be the theme of the Fall League for once, as top prospects such as righthanders Luke Hochever (Royals), Philip Humber (Mets) and Mike Pelfrey (Mets) were sent to Arizona expected to make up for time lost to injuries or holdouts. All three went home early, though, due to arm soreness that

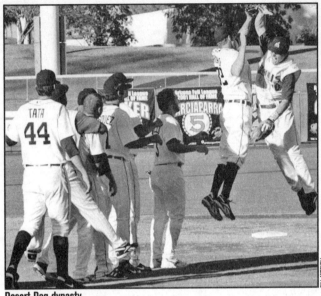

Desert Dog dynasty
Phoenix captured its third straight Arizona Fall League championship

their clubs hoped was minor.

Despite their departures, scouts considered the '06 AFL talent crop a solid one, though it fell short of the star-studded 2005 crew that included Ryan Zimmerman (Nationals), Howie Kendrick (Angels) and Stephen Drew (Diamondbacks). Rockies shortstop Troy Tulowitzki earned the nod from scouts as the No. 1 prospect in the league.

"In terms of sudden-impact players, last year's group was one for the ages," a scout from an American League club said. "But this is just as deep—I just don't think you have as many stars here. But in terms of talent that will make some kind of impact in the major leagues, it's all here."

Desert Dogs first baseman Chip Cannon (Blue Jays) was named the league MVP after leading the league in home runs (11), RBIs (29) and slugging percentage (.714).

Scottsdale infielder Kevin Frandsen (Giants) went hitless in his last two games, and Peoria Javelinas infielder Yunel Escobar (Braves) passed him in the season's final days to capture the league batting crown. Frandsen, however, was named the league's Dernell Stenson Sportsmanship award winner, in recognition of the AFL player who best exemplifies unselfishness, hard work and leadership.

The league also instituted its first all-star game, called the Rising Stars Showcase, with the East beating the West 3-1.

—BILL MITCHELL

TOP 20 PROSPECTS

1. Troy Tulowitzki, ss, Grand Canyon (Rockies)
2. Ryan Braun, 3b, Scottsdale (Brewers)
3. Fernando Martinez, of, Mesa (Mets)
4. Jacoby Ellsbury, of, Peoria Javelinas (Red Sox)
5. Trevor Crowe, of, Peoria Javelinas (Indians)
6. Elijah Dukes, of, Phoenix (Devil Rays)
7. Hunter Pence, of, Mesa (Astros)
8. Gio Gonzalez, lhp, Peoria Saguaros (Phillies)
9. Matt Albers, rhp, Mesa (Astros)
10. Kevin Slowey, rhp, Mesa (Twins)
11. Troy Patton, lhp, Mesa (Astros)
12. Jonathan Meloan, rhp, Mesa (Dodgers)
13. Joe Koshansky, 1b, Grand Canyon (Rockies)
14. Kory Casto, of, Peoria Saguaros (Nationals)
15. Neil Walker, c, Grand Canyon (Pirates)
16. Mark Reynolds, 2b, Scottsdale (Diamondbacks)
17. Nolan Reimold, of, Grand Canyon (Orioles)
18. Jeff Fiorentino, of, Grand Canyon (Orioles)
19. Brett Gardner, of, Peoria Saguaros (Yankees)
20. Eric Patterson, 2b, Mesa (Cubs)

EAST	W	L	PCT	GB
Phoenix Desert Dogs	20	11	.645	—
Mesa Solar Sox	15	16	.484	5
Scottsdale Scorpions	15	17	.469	5½

WEST	W	L	PCT	GB
Grand Canyon Rafters	16	16	.500	—
Peoria Saguaros	15	17	.469	1
Peoria Javelinas	14	18	.438	2

PLAYOFFS: Phoenix defeated Grand Canyon 6-2 in one-game championship.

INDIVIDUAL BATTING LEADERS
(Minimum 86 Plate Appearances)

	AVG	G	AB	R	H	HR	RBI
Escobar, Yunel, Javelinas	.407	22	86	16	35	2	22
Frandsen, Kevin, Scorpions	.388	23	85	18	33	4	19
Zobrist, Ben, Desert Dogs	.366	27	101	29	37	2	21
Cannon, Chip, Desert Dogs	.352	29	105	22	37	11	29
Maier, Mitch, Rafters	.350	23	100	19	35	0	6
Marti, Amaury, Saguaros	.345	21	84	16	29	4	14
Patterson, Eric, Solar Sox	.345	28	113	27	39	1	13
Crowe, Trevor, Javelinas	.329	21	79	18	26	0	14
Tulowitzki, Troy, Rafters	.329	22	79	8	26	1	10
Reynolds, Mark, Scorpions	.327	27	101	15	33	5	26

INDIVIDUAL PITCHING LEADERS
(Minimum 20 Innings)

	W	L	ERA	IP	H	BB	SO
Musser, Neal, Rafters	0	2	2.61	21	22	2	18
Tata, Jordan, Desert Dogs	1	2	2.63	24	24	7	12
Vasquez, Virgil, Desert Dogs	2	1	2.81	26	17	5	19
Simonitsch, Errol, Solar Sox	0	1	3.91	23	24	7	18
Rasner, Darrell, Saguaros	0	0	4.18	24	20	12	17
Palmer, Matt, Scorpions	0	1	4.29	21	18	15	20
Pelland, Tyler, Desert Dogs	0	1	4.95	20	25	11	15
Pauley, David, Javelinas	0	3	5.06	27	36	6	14
Muegge, Danny, Solar Sox	0	2	5.16	23	31	8	13
Malone, Corwin, Scorpions	0	4	5.16	23	32	10	7

GRAND CANYON RAFTERS

BATTING	AVG	AB	R	H	2B	3B	HR	RBI	BB	SO	SB
Bass, Bryan, ss/2b	.119	42	8	5	2	1	0	2	9	28	1
Cortez, Fernando, 2b	.333	78	10	26	2	0	0	8	6	8	5
Donachie, Adam, c	.360	25	7	9	3	0	1	4	7	10	1
Eldred, Brad, 1b	.231	65	7	15	5	0	1	8	7	13	3
Fiorentino, Jeff, of	.263	95	18	25	8	0	3	11	15	16	1
Koshansky, Joe, 1b	.227	97	10	22	3	0	5	21	10	30	0
Lubanski, Chris, of	.185	27	4	5	1	1	0	1	4	11	0
Maier, Mitch, of	.350	100	19	35	5	1	0	6	4	20	9
Metcalf, Travis, 3b	.258	93	8	24	6	0	3	23	4	16	0
Miller, Matthew, of	.322	59	13	19	3	0	4	14	4	10	1
Reimold, Nolan, of	.284	88	15	25	7	0	1	9	16	20	1
Richardson, Kevin, c	.278	36	3	10	5	0	0	9	6	12	0
Stansberry, Craig, 2b	.128	78	14	10	2	0	1	9	11	13	5
Tulowitzki, Troy, ss	.329	79	8	26	6	1	1	10	11	11	2
Walker, Neil, c	.290	69	8	20	5	1	0	8	2	12	0
Webster, Anthony, of	.286	56	9	16	0	0	1	4	5	10	5
Yount, Dustin, 1b	.192	26	3	5	0	0	0	4	3	4	1

PITCHING	W	L	ERA	G	GS	SV	IP	H	BB	SO
Chavez, Jesse	3	0	0.64	12	0	4	14	6	3	11
Christensen, Daniel	0	0	1.80	5	2	0	10	7	1	6
Davidson, David	2	2	5.17	9	3	0	16	16	6	14
DeHoyos, Gabe	0	0	3.07	14	0	0	15	15	10	10
Finch, Brian	2	2	5.50	11	2	0	18	25	5	8
Hochevar, Luke	0	0	8.64	3	3	0	8	13	2	8
Ingram, Jesse	0	0	12.41	13	0	0	12	19	7	6
Keefer, Ryan	0	1	5.54	12	0	0	13	14	5	10
Koronka, John	0	1	5.29	5	5	0	17	17	7	4
Lowery, Devon	0	1	8.44	5	0	0	5	5	2	4
McCurdy, Nick	0	1	4.08	15	0	2	18	22	3	14
Miller, Jim	1	1	7.20	15	0	0	15	17	6	8
Morris, Cory	0	2	3.07	5	5	0	15	15	7	18
Murray, A.J.	3	2	5.30	9	3	0	19	25	6	17
Musser, Neal	0	2	2.61	9	3	0	21	22	2	18
Newman, Joshua	0	0	0.79	12	0	0	11	9	6	15
Rogers, Brian	2	0	0.00	6	0	0	8	2	3	6
Shortslef, Josh	0	1	2.65	6	5	0	17	15	10	7
Songster, Judd	1	0	6.00	11	1	0	15	16	7	17
Speier, Ryan	0	0	4.50	8	0	0	8	5	2	11
Touchet, Danny	2	0	6.06	12	0	1	16	17	10	12

MESA SOLAR SOX

BATTING	AVG	AB	R	H	2B	3B	HR	RBI	BB	SO	SB
Abreu, Michel, 1b	.280	93	16	26	7	0	6	25	12	11	1
Conrad, Brooks, of/2b	.359	39	8	14	6	2	1	4	10	9	2
Deeds, Doug, of	.216	37	6	8	0	1	2	6	2	8	1
Ellis, A.J., c	.346	52	10	18	1	0	2	9	14	7	0
Fox, Jacob, c	.250	64	8	16	5	0	1	18	3	11	1
Hu, Chin Lung, ss	.193	57	7	11	2	0	0	2	4	5	3
Malek, Bobby, of	.227	88	9	20	6	1	1	12	9	17	0
Martinez, Fernando, of	.253	87	16	22	5	0	2	7	5	17	1
Moore, Scott, 3b/1b	.250	104	22	26	8	2	3	13	15	28	4
Moses, Matt, 3b	.297	74	9	22	4	0	1	13	6	13	1
Patterson, Eric, 2b	.345	113	27	39	6	2	1	13	12	16	15
Pence, Hunter, of	.339	62	10	21	3	1	3	11	4	15	6
Raglani, Anthony, of	.237	76	10	18	5	1	2	11	7	25	0
Rodriguez, Mike, of	.214	14	3	3	0	0	0	0	1	0	1
Santangelo, Louis, c	.182	22	1	4	0	0	0	1	7	0	0
Tolbert, Matt, ss/2b	.313	96	16	30	6	0	1	11	15	15	6
Winfree, David, 3b/1b	.176	68	8	12	3	1	3	17	10	20	1

PITCHING	W	L	ERA	G	GS	SV	IP	H	BB	SO
Akin, Brian	1	3	3.65	12	0	0	12	15	12	10
Albers, Matt	0	1	3.94	6	6	0	16	14	6	9
Cameron, Kevin	1	1	8.59	11	0	0	15	23	8	16
Harben, Adam	0	1	6.43	3	3	0	7	10	4	7
Holdzkom, Lincoln	2	0	7.08	13	0	0	20	20	13	21
Hoorelbeke, Casey	1	0	2.84	14	0	1	19	15	12	17
Humber, Philip	0	0	4.50	1	1	0	2	2	1	3
McGinley, Blake	1	1	2.70	6	1	0	10	6	4	12
McLemore, Mark	2	0	4.76	10	1	0	17	13	8	16
Meloan, Jonathan	2	0	1.96	14	0	1	18	12	8	21
Muegge, Danny	0	2	5.16	8	4	0	23	31	8	13
Mulvey, Kevin	0	0	6.00	5	5	0	15	17	8	7
Nall, Brandon	1	0	0.00	2	0	0	2	1	1	0
Patton, Troy	2	0	4.80	9	0	1	15	12	8	17
Pelfrey, Mike	0	0	0.00	2	1	0	4	1	2	2
Pignatiello, Carmen	0	0	0.87	10	0	0	10	4	4	15
Rapada, Clay	1	1	3.07	16	0	0	15	12	3	17
Reineke, Chad	1	1	6.39	12	0	0	13	16	6	15
Sawatski, Jay	0	1	11.77	14	0	0	13	28	6	10
Simonitsch, Errol	0	1	3.91	7	7	0	23	24	7	18
Slowey, Kevin	0	1	2.37	8	3	1	19	19	2	12

PEORIA SAGUAROS

BATTING	AVG	AB	R	H	2B	3B	HR	RBI	BB	SO	SB
Brown, Dee, of	.125	24	3	3	0	0	1	4	2	0	0
Bynum, Seth, 2b/ss	.257	74	8	19	4	0	0	5	11	19	1
Casto, Kory, of	.302	53	8	16	4	0	1	9	17	12	0
Ciriaco, Juan, 2b	.197	61	9	12	1	0	2	7	4	15	1
Duncan, Eric, 1b/3b	.257	113	16	29	3	1	2	18	9	16	0
Gardner, Brett, of	.250	108	26	27	4	2	1	10	27	22	6
Headley, Chase, 3b	.257	101	15	26	6	0	3	12	18	22	1
Jaramillo, Jason, c	.379	66	14	25	8	0	2	17	9	11	0
Cazana-Marti, Amaury, of	.345	84	16	29	7	0	4	14	3	23	0
Morton, Colt, c	.269	52	7	14	4	0	2	8	5	19	0
Pilittere, P.J., c	.394	33	4	13	2	0	1	8	3	5	0
Ryan, Brendan, ss	.310	126	19	39	6	1	2	20	7	19	3
Sinisi, Vince, of	.264	72	11	19	2	0	1	5	8	11	0
Stavinoha, Nick, of	.218	78	4	17	2	1	1	8	6	15	0
Whitesell, Josh, 1b	.262	84	15	22	9	0	2	17	9	21	0

PITCHING	W	L	ERA	G	GS	SV	IP	H	BB	SO
Beam, T.J.	2	1	0.60	11	0	2	15	11	6	17
Bisenius, Joseph	1	1	11.57	4	0	0	5	7	4	6
Dove, Dennis	1	0	1.93	6	0	0	9	4	4	7
Ellis, Jonathan	0	0	9.00	2	0	0	2	1	1	1
Felfoldi, Jonathan	2	0	7.47	7	0	0	16	25	3	13
Floyd, Gavin	0	1	5.59	6	6	0	19	17	10	14
Foli, Daniel	2	0	6.92	9	0	1	13	17	6	8
Gonzalez, Gio	0	0	2.81	6	5	0	16	13	10	20
Haberer, Jonathan	0	0	4.50	7	0	0	10	12	7	6
Happ, J.A.	1	0	5.02	5	4	0	14	17	5	10
Henn, Sean	3	1	7.43	9	0	0	13	16	11	12
Kendrick, Kyle	2	0	6.75	7	0	0	11	17	5	4
Kennard, Jeff	1	2	6.89	10	0	0	16	21	9	16
Key, Chris	0	0	6.75	6	0	0	11	13	3	5
Parisi, Mike	0	0	7.88	9	0	0	16	18	7	14
Perrault, Josh	0	0	5.40	6	0	0	10	12	3	3
Perrin, Devin	0	2	7.59	9	0	0	11	16	10	11
Pomeranz, Stuart	1	2	9.00	6	6	0	17	30	8	3
Rasner, Darrell	0	0	4.18	6	6	0	24	20	12	17
Rosales, Leonel	0	2	2.57	13	0	7	14	10	6	17
Segovia, Zach	1	1	0.93	6	0	0	10	4	3	7
Wells, Jared	0	2	5.28	6	5	0	15	20	10	14

MINOR LEAGUES

PEORIA JAVELINAS

BATTING

	AVG	AB	R	H	2B	3B	HR	RBI	BB	SO	SB
Brown, Dustin, c	.239	67	8	16	1	1	1	6	10	14	1
Burrus, Josh, of	.261	88	17	23	3	2	4	24	7	24	4
Carroll, Brett, of	.284	74	9	21	6	0	3	16	3	10	1
Cleveland, Brian, ss	.125	8	2	1	0	0	0	0	0	2	0
Crowe, Trevor, of	.329	79	18	26	2	2	0	14	18	10	3
Ellsbury, Jacoby, of	.276	105	18	29	4	3	0	3	8	16	7
Escobar, Yunel, ss/2b	.407	86	16	35	3	2	2	22	9	7	3
Garciaparra, Michael, ss/2b	.342	79	13	27	4	0	1	13	1	13	2
Herrera, Javi, c	.296	27	9	8	1	0	0	3	9	6	0
Holt, J.C., 2b	.388	67	14	26	3	1	1	8	6	16	3
Inglett, Joe, ss	.417	48	9	20	1	0	0	6	8	6	1
Kouzmanoff, Kevin, 1b/3b	.382	55	14	21	7	0	2	10	4	5	0
Saltalamacchia, Jarrod, c	.565	23	8	13	1	0	3	12	5	2	0
Sanchez, Gabriel, 1b	.279	111	19	31	7	0	2	20	19	15	0
Spann, Chad, 3b/1b	.268	82	11	22	5	1	1	12	9	21	1
Tuiasosopo, Matt, 3b	.167	78	9	13	1	1	0	4	6	22	0
Wilson, Michael, of	.243	74	10	18	2	1	3	19	13	27	1

PITCHING

	W	L	ERA	G	GS	SV	IP	H	BB	SO
Bostick, Adam	0	0	5.66	6	6	0	21	24	10	16
Collins, Kyle	1	1	7.84	11	0	1	10	15	6	8
Devine, Joey	0	0	4.50	7	0	2	8	6	7	9
DiNardo, Lenny	1	0	2.70	10	0	0	13	12	5	16
Dittler, Jake	0	1	11.25	2	2	0	4	6	3	4
Edell, Ryan	0	1	3.78	5	5	0	17	18	5	9
Hertzler, Barry	1	0	3.31	11	1	0	16	15	9	17
Jackson, Kyle	6	0	6.23	11	0	0	17	21	10	11
James, Craig	0	0	3.60	10	0	0	10	10	6	7
Kahn, Stephen	0	0	8.64	9	0	0	8	14	8	7
Lerew, Anthony	1	2	5.52	11	0	0	15	17	12	8
Livingston, Bobby	1	3	10.45	6	6	0	21	37	3	17
Nestor, Scott	0	1	17.10	10	0	0	10	19	8	8
Pauley, David	0	3	5.06	7	7	0	27	36	6	14
Rowland-Smith, Ryan	1	0	5.40	12	0	0	15	19	8	16
Santos, Reid	0	1	2.53	10	0	1	11	9	6	7
Sipp, Tony	0	0	4.35	10	0	1	10	4	9	16
Startup, Will	1	1	13.00	9	0	0	9	16	6	6
Tyler, Scott	1	0	7.59	10	0	1	11	11	8	9
White, Sean	0	3	6.35	5	5	0	17	18	11	12
Yourkin, Matt	1	0	3.97	9	0	0	11	15	6	10

PHOENIX DESERT DOGS

BATTING

	AVG	AB	R	H	2B	3B	HR	RBI	BB	SO	SB
Anderson, Drew, 2b	.269	67	7	18	2	2	0	3	5	17	4
Bankston, Wes, 1b	.083	12	1	1	0	0	0	2	1	3	0
Buck, Travis, of	.259	27	6	7	2	0	1	7	1	4	0
Cannon, Chip, 1b	.352	105	22	37	5	0	11	29	21	33	2
Clevlen, Brent, of	.250	92	13	23	1	0	2	20	18	35	2
Dukes, Elijah, 1b/of	.313	32	10	10	4	0	2	8	6	10	1
Hubele, Ryan, c	.182	22	1	4	2	0	0	2	2	4	0
Kirkland, Kody, 3b	.200	90	13	18	5	1	2	14	11	38	2
Klosterman, Ryan, util	.308	26	3	8	0	0	0	3	4	10	1
Melillo, Kevin, 2b/3b	.245	94	12	23	4	0	2	10	7	15	2
Moran, Javon, of	.224	58	4	13	2	0	0	10	2	11	2
Perez, Fernando, of	.241	108	23	26	2	0	0	6	21	28	12
Powell, Landon, c	.170	53	4	9	2	0	0	2	9	12	1
Rabelo, Mike, c	.143	7	1	1	0	0	0	3	2	1	0
Robnett, Richie, of	.429	14	1	6	2	2	1	5	3	5	0
Strait, Cody, of	.257	109	19	28	6	1	1	12	14	28	12
Thigpen, Curtis, c	.307	88	16	27	9	1	2	21	12	14	1
Zobrist, Ben, ss	.366	101	29	37	7	1	2	21	23	15	3

PITCHING

	W	L	ERA	G	GS	SV	IP	H	BB	SO
Burton, Jared	1	2	4.38	10	0	1	12	10	6	11
Coutlangus, Jon	1	0	2.70	12	0	0	10	11	5	12
De Jong, Jordan	3	0	4.50	13	0	0	16	11	5	12
Dumatrait, Phil	2	0	5.59	7	5	0	19	27	13	12
Flanagan, Jeremy	1	0	4.32	10	0	0	8	6	6	6
Hamman, Corey	1	0	2.77	15	0	0	13	12	5	11
Henderson, Brian	1	0	5.40	13	0	0	12	14	8	6
Larrison, Preston	0	0	6.17	13	0	0	12	16	6	9
McBeth, Marcus	1	0	4.50	11	0	2	10	7	3	11
McGowan, Dustin	1	3	5.59	5	5	0	19	18	9	18
Medlock, Calvin	0	1	4.30	10	1	0	15	14	1	13
Mitchell, Michael	1	1	2.61	12	0	0	10	10	3	10
Niemann, Jeff	0	0	2.70	2	2	0	7	7	2	8
Pelland, Tyler	0	1	4.95	7	4	0	20	25	11	15
Ridgway, Jeff	1	0	3.48	13	0	1	10	6	4	11
Robertson, Connor	1	0	7.59	12	0	1	11	13	6	13
Tata, Jordan	1	2	2.63	6	6	0	24	24	7	12
Thorpe, Tracy	0	0	4.38	12	0	2	12	10	5	18
Vasquez, Virgil	2	1	2.81	6	5	0	26	17	5	19
Yates, Kyle	2	0	1.13	6	4	0	24	19	6	25

SCOTTSDALE SCORPIONS

BATTING

	AVG	AB	R	H	2B	3B	HR	RBI	BB	SO	SB
Braun, Ryan, 3b	.326	92	19	30	9	1	6	25	11	23	4
Brown, Matthew, 3b	.295	78	15	23	4	0	1	6	4	16	1
Cook, David, of	.191	68	16	13	7	0	3	6	10	26	3
Coon, Bradley, of	.257	35	7	9	2	0	0	5	10	10	6
D'Antona, Jamie, c/1b	.224	76	6	17	6	0	2	9	3	9	0
Evans, Terry, of	.280	25	3	7	2	0	1	7	1	9	1
Frandsen, Kevin, ss/2b	.388	85	18	33	3	1	4	19	12	4	8
Gonzalez, Andy, ss	.170	53	6	9	3	0	0	7	6	6	6
Ishikawa, Travis, 1b	.186	59	5	11	3	1	0	7	4	17	1
Lewis, Fred, of	.273	55	9	15	2	3	2	7	7	10	2
Moss, Steve, of	.190	63	13	12	3	0	0	1	12	17	5
Myers, Michael, ss/of	.176	17	2	3	2	0	0	1	3	4	2
Owens, Jerry, of	.310	58	5	18	2	0	0	4	4	9	10
Reynolds, Mark, 1b/2b/of	.327	101	15	33	7	1	5	26	9	26	1
Richar, Danny, 2b	.247	81	16	20	5	1	2	8	5	17	5
Rottino, Vinny, c/of	.213	80	13	17	8	0	1	9	8	16	5
Wilson, Bobby, c	.286	56	5	16	5	0	2	8	7	9	0

PITCHING

	W	L	ERA	G	GS	SV	IP	H	BB	SO
Bray, Steve	1	1	4.38	13	0	0	12	14	3	7
Davidson, Daniel	0	1	7.00	6	6	0	18	29	6	15
Day, Dewon	0	0	7.71	12	0	0	12	10	10	15
Edwards, Bill	0	0	4.50	10	1	0	12	6	9	13
Elliott, Matt	1	2	10.64	13	0	1	11	19	8	16
Hedrick, Justin	1	1	4.63	14	0	0	12	13	3	8
Jackson, Steven	0	2	7.11	6	6	0	19	24	9	13
Kinsey, Chris	2	0	6.60	10	0	0	15	14	7	15
Malone, Corwin	0	4	5.16	7	7	0	23	32	10	7
Misch, Patrick	1	1	2.79	13	0	0	10	8	5	11
Narron, Sam	0	0	27.00	1	0	0	1	0	0	0
Palmer, Matt	1	1	4.29	7	7	0	21	18	15	20
Parra, Manuel	0	1	6.14	5	5	0	15	19	9	13
Russell, Adam	2	0	3.65	13	0	0	12	11	5	8
Sadler, Billy	2	0	1.29	12	0	3	14	9	4	22
Sarfate, Dennis	1	0	4.20	14	0	3	15	15	8	23
Schultz, Mike	1	1	5.25	12	0	0	12	13	8	13
Thompson, Richard	0	1	10.13	11	0	0	13	24	3	14
Whisler, Wesley	1	1	3.97	13	0	0	11	7	10	2
Wilhite, Matt	1	0	3.86	12	0	0	12	10	6	9
Zumwalt, Alec	0	0	7.62	13	0	0	13	16	15	3

HAWAII WINTER BASEBALL

Hawaii Winter Baseball returned to the baseball landscape for the first time since 1997, and by almost all accounts it was a success.

Though some complained about limited pregame access to the field for workouts, as well as difficulty finding enough at-bats to go around on crowded rosters, the league was praised as being a positive alternative to instructional league for promising prospects in Class A.

The talent level in HWB was better than expected, as the Yankees, Rockies and Braves sent several top prospects to the island state. Also, many U.S. position players gained the experience of hitting against older, polished pitchers from Japan. Japanese clubs sent 30 players in all to Hawaii, adding an interesting twist to the league.

For the 120 or so players, the coaching staffs and the four umpires lucky to draw a Hawaii assignment, it was a no-brainer to accept the offer to play in the developmental league.

"It didn't take me long to think about it," said West Oahu CaneFires manager Todd Claus. "Hawaii? You kidding me? I'd jump on that opportunity. When I found out I was selected, I was elated. I brought my family with me. Got a 6-year old son. He's enjoying the beaches, doing some skim-boarding and snorkeling. Of course, the wife loves it here. I'm very lucky, very honored to be here."

But forget the perks, such as 80-degree days in October and a five-minute walk to the beach from where most of the players found rentals in Waikiki. The players were legitimate prospects.

"(The league) might have better talent in terms of potential than the Arizona Fall League," said Bill Geivett, the Rockies' assistant general manager/vice president of baseball operations.

Waikiki BeachBoys manager Lenn Sakata agreed. "This is pretty good baseball," said Sakata, a Hawaii resident and the manager of the Giants' high Class A club in San Jose. "We have some good players here and they're extremely young. That's what's amazing."

During the league's first stint from 1993-97, 138 players found their way to the big leagues. Angels catcher Jorge Fabregas was the first alumnus to reach the bigs in 1994. More notable products include Ichiro Suzuki, Jason Giambi, Todd Helton, Mark Kotsay and Derrek Lee.

When the Hawaiian league folded after the 1997 season, Major League Baseball tried other markets for a fall developmental league, first in Maryland in 1998, then in California in 1999. Neither fared well, and the Arizona Fall League was the only game in town for prospects in the U.S. ever since.

The original HWB had teams on four islands in Oahu, Maui, Kauai and Hawaii (also known as the Big Island), with Kauai eventually giving way to a second team on Oahu. The Honolulu Sharks and West Oahu CaneFires are the only teams left from the previous stint. The Waikiki BeachBoys and North Shore Honu (Hawaiian word for turtle) were the new teams.

League owner Duane Kurisu said he would eventually like to expand by reviving teams on the other islands. Part of the agreement with Major League Baseball was to keep the league on one island for at least two seasons so that front-office personnel and scouts don't have to island-hop to monitor their players. The original league ceased because of financial reasons. Kurisu only agreed to revive the league if MLB was willing to pay the players' salaries.

As with anything new, there were kinks to work out. Hans L'Orange Park was a county playground with a baseball diamond. It had been refurbished during the league's first time around, but still needed some work for the 2006 season. At Murakami Stadium, the University of Hawaii was holding fall workouts, so the league couldn't take the field for pregame until 90 minutes before games. To get in their work, one team took batting practice in the covered batting cage, while the other does it the usual way on the field. In a workout before the season started on Oct. 1, Sakata held a practice at a public park near the Waialae Country Club.

The league also got shaken in October after an earthquake struck Hawaii. The quake, which registered 6.6 on the Richter Scale and was the largest to hit the islands since 1983, started at 7:07 a.m. local time, and both games on the Hawaii Winter Baseball schedule were postponed.

While each island in the chain was shaken by the quake, a 12-hour power outage was the worst the Honolulu area had to endure.

"It wasn't too much," Sakata said. "The power outage lasted about 12 hours, so there was obvious chaos about that—people not being prepared, that sort of thing. There was some damage and things were shaking, but it wasn't nearly as bad as it could have been. It's just one of those lessons that makes you remember there are a lot of things you can't control."

The league's season ended in late November.

TOP 15 PROSPECTS

1. Troy Tulowitzki, ss, Grand Canyon (Rockies)
1. Joba Chamberlain, rhp, West Oahu (Yankees)
2. John Mayberry Jr., of, West Oahu (Rangers)
3. Dexter Fowler, of, Waikiki (Rockies)
4. Jeff Marquez, rhp, West Oahu (Yankees)
5. Eric Young Jr., 2b, Waikiki (Rockies)
6. Rick Vanden Hurk, rhp, Waikiki (Marlins)
7. Mike Carp, 1b, North Shore (Mets)
8. Ian Kennedy, rhp, West Oahu (Yankees)
9. Blake DeWitt, 2b, North Shore (Dodgers)
10. Marco Estrada, rhp, Waikiki (Nationals)
11. Will Venable, of, West Oahu (Padres)
12. Lorenzo Cain, of, North Shore (Brewers)
13. Jeff Clement, c, Waikiki (Mariners)
14. Johnny Whittleman, 3b, West Oahu (Rangers)
15. Zach Hammes, rhp, North Shore (Dodgers)

INDEPENDENT
LEAGUES

After offseason of indy upheaval net result doesn't change much

BY J.J. COOPER

The winter before the 2006 season proved to be the busiest in more than a decade for the independent minor leagues. The Northern League, the original independent league, lost four teams that left to form a new league. The surprise move came just after the 2005 season ended, leaving independent league fans wondering who would be playing where in 2006.

While that was going on, the United League emerged, lining up stadium deals in three former Central League cities in addition to several cities from the defunct Texas-Louisiana League. That move came as the Central League disbanded, with most of the remaining teams joining the Northern League's refugees to form the new American Association.

Big draw in Fort Worth
Luke Hochevar's draft holdout proved beneficial on and off the field for indy ball

In a much less contentious move, the Atlantic League's Nashua Pride shifted to the Can-Am League for economic reasons, while the Golden League dropped three teams and added one for its second season.

But for all of the changes, once the season began and all of the offseason wrangling and shuffling had settled down, the actual on-field product didn't end up being much different from past years.

In 2005, there were 56 independent teams in six leagues. In 2006, there were 56 independent teams in seven leagues—it's just that the names of some of the leagues had changed. And the moves didn't dent independent baseball's growing popularity, as more than 7.55 million fans attended independent league games in 2006, a gain of 42,000 from 2005's record numbers.

For the past several seasons, a lack of work visas thinned out the talent pool for independent leagues, but the situation returned to normal this season. Tweaks to the visa rules allowed teams to acquire more foreign players, after two seasons when visas were nearly unattainable.

That helped in two different ways. Teams were able to sign Dominican, Venezuelan and Canadian players again, but more importantly, the loosening of the visa rules also meant affiliated clubs were more willing to release players at the end of spring training. In 2005, affiliated teams kept more veterans on rosters or in extended spring training, worried that injuries would leave them unable to fill roster holes later in the season.

"I think it was more normal this year than last year," Joliet manager Hal Lanier said. "More people were released (by affiliated teams) this year."

United League Gets Off To Solid Debut

The United League's inaugural season began on schedule, which immediately put it beyond a number of independent leagues that never made it to Opening Day. But the league was forced to scramble when a court fight kept the status of the Edinburg Coyotes up in the air until less than two weeks before Opening Day. While the league eventually got the legal issues cleared up when the bankrupt Edinburg Roadrunners (a former Central League franchise) dropped their case, the delay left the new team way behind in ticket and advertising sales.

The six-team league drew an average of 1,800 fans a game, led by Amarillo, which drew more than 2,500 a game.

"We didn't have an overall number, but we were thinking if we could get it up to the old standards of the last year of the Texas-Louisiana League, that would be our goal. We're more than succeeding at that," United League chief executive Byron Pierce said during the season.

Hochevar Brings Fort Worth Attention

When the Royals selected Luke Hochevar with the No. 1 pick in the 2006 draft, some regarded it as bad news that the industry was rewarding a draft holdout. But it was great news for independent leagues.

Hochevar, who was taken by the Dodgers in the supplemental first round last year, agreed to and then turned down a $2.98 million deal with the club last summer, opting to return to the draft. To prove that his stuff was just as good as it was last year, Hochevar signed with the American Association's Fort Worth Cats in the spring. Hochevar ended up signing with the Royals for $5.3 million after a relatively short negotiation.

"It seemed to play out perfectly for everybody. For Luke hopefully and for the Cats," Cats general manager Monty Clegg said.

Hochevar was not the first player to go the indy ball route when contract negotiations broke down. J.D. Drew (Northern League) and his brother Stephen (Atlantic) both used strong indy ball efforts to land large contracts, while the threat of playing helped Jason Varitek (Northern) and Jered Weaver (Atlantic) land deals.

But Hochevar's rise up the draft charts while pitching

INDEPENDENT LEAGUES

in the independent leagues may pave the way for further draft double-dippers. After all, Hochevar entered the season in a similar situation to Wade Townsend a year earlier. Townsend, the No. 8 pick in the 2004 draft out of Rice, did not pitch competitively again after negotiations between him and the Orioles broke down that fall, although he did throw on the side. He eventually was drafted by the Devil Rays with the eighth pick in the 2005 draft, but signed for below slot money.

"I think it will open up for players that aren't satisfied with their draft stats to look at indy ball. It's got to be a college player who can come to indy ball and learn from it," American Association commissioner Miles Wolff said.

For his part, Hochevar seemed to enjoy his experience in indy ball, which helped him get used to the pro game.

"Going to Fort Worth was a great experience," he said. "Those hitters, they're older, they're experienced and they're a lot smarter. I learned a great deal playing there due to the discipline of the hitters—they control the strike zone a lot better. The speed of the game overall, I believe has helped me a significant amount."

Hochevar fit in quickly with his teammates.

"Even in a month and a half he was here, I think three or four guys on the team are lifelong friends with him," Cats reliever Zane Carlson said. "He was just another weird dude that hangs out. But I've never played with a guy so focused. He's writing notes after he throws. Working out every day. It was a good example to see what it takes."

And Hochevar was popular for another reason. Usually, an indy league is lucky if a scout stops by every couple of weeks. Every time Hochevar pitched, almost every team in baseball had a scout behind the plate. While they were all there to see Hochevar, it still gave other Cats a chance to show what they can do.

Indy Teams Grab For Attention

While Hochevar was a point of pride for indy ball, there were many other attention grabbers—most of them not as legitimate as baseball stories.

Aside from the usual wacky promotions, skier Bode Miller, former Negro Leaguer Buck O'Neill and 83-year-old Jim Eriotes all made brief appearances in indy league games as publicity stunts.

But the publicity stunt of the year, for good or bad, was

Church swings for attention

Every week, as Ian Church continued to hit home run after home run, and double after double, Kalamazoo manager Fran Riordan prepared to see him leave.

He figured that any week some

PLAYER
OF THE **YEAR**

major league club would sign the Kings star center fielder. But the inquiry never came, as Church put together one of the best seasons in Frontier League history.

"For whatever reasons, Ian was able to put up these numbers consistently and no major league baseball team took notice. I think it was a pretty special season," Riordan said.

But while Church never got the call to affiliated ball, his season did stand out. He led all independent leagues with 31 home runs and a .668 slugging percentage while finishing second in the Frontier League with a .317 batting average. For his efforts, he earned our Independent Leagues Player of the Year award.

Church was named MVP of the Frontier League and was also MVP of the all-star game. His victory at the all-star game's home run derby answered questions about his power numbers, which were aided by playing at the relatively

Ian Church

small Homer Stryker Field. The park features an inviting left field fence just 306 feet from home plate.

"He hit some home runs at some pretty big ballparks. He hit a lot of home runs to dead center. I'd say one home run was a home run that wouldn't have been one anywhere else. The other 30 would have been out of anywhere. He wasn't hitting wall-scrapers," Riordan said.

Church hasn't always been a power hitter. He showed up at Stetson University as a developmental player who hoped to contribute. After sitting on the bench as a freshman, he became a top-of-the-order speedster as a sophomore, but didn't show any power until his senior season.

"The thing I loved about Ian is he was such a blue collar guy," Stetson coach Pete Dunn said. "He would run through a wall for you. He was a guy that got the most out of his ability. He wasn't gifted with a cannon; he had better than average speed but he wasn't a burner. He would get himself in trouble chasing pitches, but worked to become more selective."

A similar story happened once he came to independent ball after going undrafted. He spent much of the past two years on Northern League benches before getting his chance to star this season. Now he'll spend the winter playing in the Mexican Pacific League, hoping that a strong winter will further convince scouts that he's worthy of a chance.

the Schaumburg Flyers' decision to align with an online network that allowed fans to make all the key decisions for the team by Web vote. The idea, understandably, was not exactly a hit with the team, which won the first-half division title, then quickly fell to last place in the division once the fans were given the vote.

"It's not ideal from a manager's standpoint," Schaumburg manager Andy McCauley told the Fargo Forum. "I don't think any manager in the league would think that it is."

AMERICAN ASSOCIATION

When the new American Association formed out of the remnants of the Central League and four teams that split off from the Northern League, the assumption was that Central League teams would have a tough time keeping up with the ex-Northern Leaguers. After all, the Northern League teams had a longer history, and traditionally had spent more money on their clubs.

But when it was all over, the Fort Worth Cats, the 2005 Central League champs, were hoisting the first American Association trophy.

Fort Worth beat St. Paul 2-1 in a winner-take-all Game Five. After falling behind 1-0, Shawn Williams tied up the game for the Cats with a home run in the fifth, and indy league veteran Marc Mirizzi doubled in Terence Green with the winning run in the sixth.

Playoff heroics in St. Paul are nothing new for Mirizzi. In 2004, he hit a walk-off grand slam in the deciding Game Five as St. Paul beat Schaumburg for the Northern League title. Mirizzi, who was 9-for-23 (.391) in the series, was the finals MVP. He also hit .299/.361/.431 for the season.

Lincoln first baseman Pichi Balet was the league MVP after he led the league with a .378 average.

STANDINGS

NORTH	W	L	PCT	GB
*#Lincoln	65	31	.677	—
St. Paul	54	42	.563	11
St. Joe	49	46	.516	15½
Sioux City	43	53	.448	22
Sioux Falls	34	62	.354	31

SOUTH	W	L	PCT	GB
#Fort Worth	56	39	.589	—
*Shreveport	54	39	.581	1
Coastal Bend	49	47	.510	7½
Pensacola	39	57	.406	17½
El Paso	33	60	.355	22

* First-half winner # Second-half winner

PLAYOFFS: Semifinals—St. Paul defeated Lincoln 3-1; and Fort Worth defeated Shreveport 3-2. **Finals**—Fort Worth defeated St. Paul 3-2.

MANAGERS: Coastal Bend—John Harris; **El Paso**—Mike Marshall/Butch Henry; **Fort Worth**—Stan Hough; **Lincoln**—Tim Johnson; **Pensacola**—Kash Beauchamp; **St. Joseph**—Chris Carminucci; **St. Paul**—George Tsamis; **Shreveport**—Bob Flori; **Sioux City**—Ed Nottle; **Sioux Falls**—Mike Pinto.

ATTENDANCE: St. Paul 288,171; Lincoln 190,873; Fort Worth 177,894; El Paso 155,651; Sioux Falls 120,536; Sioux City 88,408; Coastal Bend 85,862; Pensacola 78,755; St. Joe 59,264; Shreveport 53,107.

ALL-STAR TEAM: C—Chris Grossman, Sioux City; **1B**—Pichi Balet, Lincoln; **2B**—Alex Llanos, Sioux City; **3B**—Trino Aguilar, Pensacola; **SS**—Carlos Mendoza, Pensacola; **OF**—Chad Hermanse, Sioux Falls; Will Quintana, St. Joe's; Brian Sprout, Pensacola. **DH**—Jorge Alvarez, El Paso. **LHP**—Lindsay Gulin, Lincoln; **RHP**—Cory Walters, Fort Worth; **RP**—Tony Pierce, Pensacola.

Player of the Year: Pichi Balet, Lincoln. **Rookie Player of the Year:** Jimmy Mojica, St. Joe's. **Rookie Pitcher of the Year:** Jason Howerton, Lincoln. **Manager of the Year:** Tim Johnson, Lincoln.

INDIVIDUAL BATTING LEADERS

Batter, Team	AVG	G	AB	R	H	HR	RBI
Balet, Pichi, Linc	.378	86	360	67	136	9	82
Olow, Adam, SP	.360	58	214	49	77	5	33
Sprout, Brian, SP	.350	91	337	64	118	10	59
Mendoza, Carlos, Pens	.346	68	260	40	90	3	34
Schmidt, J.P., EP	.345	87	313	61	108	2	48
Llanos, Alex, SC	.341	83	314	48	107	10	43
Warner, Bryan, Linc	.338	94	394	56	133	9	79
Tartaglia, Evan, Linc	.335	73	319	80	107	1	28
Corbeil, Al, Shreve	.332	78	304	43	101	2	52
Alvarez, Jorge, EP	.330	93	379	68	125	6	78

INDIVIDUAL PITCHING LEADERS

Pitcher, Team	W	L	ERA	IP	H	BB	SO
Gulin, Lindsay, Linc	13	2	2.10	120	90	20	104
Blitstein, Jeffrey, Linc	8	2	2.31	140	138	33	61
Nussbeck, Mark, SJ	8	3	2.97	97	77	19	105

	W	L	ERA	IP	H	BB	SO
Cogan, Tony, SF	7	5	3.02	92	100	30	43
Walters, Cory, FW	14	4	3.08	132	118	25	111
Snow, Bert, Shreve	9	3	3.13	109	99	45	86
Litchfield, B.J., CB	5	4	3.21	81	81	28	59
Hull, Kevin, FW	7	4	3.25	111	110	51	78
Flores, Pedro, CB	6	6	3.27	127	129	63	77
Neitz, Josh, Shreve	4	5	3.34	94	81	27	53

COASTAL BEND AVIATORS

BATTING	AVG	AB	R	H	2B	3B	HR	RBI	SB
Burwell, Wilson, 3b	.291	158	23	46	5	2	0	12	2
Carter, Charles, of	.222	9	1	2	0	0	0	1	0
Connor, Nick, of	.167	24	0	4	1	0	0	4	1
Creighton, Matt, 2b	.258	330	44	85	15	1	7	44	1
Davis, Brett, 3b	.182	11	2	2	1	0	0	3	0
Fryer, Brian, of	.313	371	52	116	16	3	4	41	33
Gallardo, Carlos, of	.283	60	12	17	5	1	1	9	0
Garanzuay, Hector, 2b	.176	51	5	9	0	0	0	6	0
Heaston, Bryan, 1b	.143	7	2	1	1	0	0	0	0
Joffrion, Jack, ss	.257	191	21	49	5	2	4	35	1
2-team (15 El Paso)	.261	241	28	63	11	3	4	39	2
Jones, Jacob, of	.095	21	6	2	0	1	0	2	0
Landin, Jaime, ss	.292	243	35	71	12	1	3	20	9
Lehr, Ryan, 3b	.208	53	6	11	4	0	0	6	0
Medina, Rodney, of	.279	229	36	64	11	4	0	18	13
Morales, Steve, c	.301	256	31	77	13	1	6	35	0
O'Sullivan, Pat, of	.465	101	16	47	7	0	5	25	2
Ontiveros, Jeff, c	.245	184	25	45	7	0	5	25	2
Ruiz, Ryan, of	.276	163	34	45	5	1	1	12	11
2-team (38 Sioux City)	.258	302	53	78	10	2	1	18	15
Russ, Ryan, of	.160	75	7	12	3	0	1	5	3
Smith, Bryon, 1b	.292	360	54	105	20	1	5	53	3
Tartaglia, Evan, of	.280	75	13	21	2	1	0	5	13
Van Dusen,Derrick, 2b	.100	10	1	0	1	0	0	0	0
Wilson, Andy, 3b	.270	204	23	55	6	1	5	35	5
York, Andrew, c	.162	99	8	16	3	0	0	5	0

PITCHING	W	L	ERA	G	SV	IP	H	BB	SO
Beseda, Adam	0	0	0.00	3	0	1	2	1	0
Clay, Trevor	0	1	5.31	12	0	20	22	7	15
Flores, Pedro	6	6	3.27	21	0	127	129	63	77
Goodmann, Joe	0	0	1.31	18	6	21	16	4	25
Heaston, Bryan	7	4	5.12	35	2	95	96	53	74
Henderson, Dan	0	0	27.00	1	0	1	4	0	0
Lira, James	2	0	2.00	16	11	18	13	7	18
Litchfield, B.J.	5	4	3.32	53	7	81	82	28	59
Lopez, Jose	4	6	4.48	15	0	76	77	30	81
McGough, Tim	2	4	3.43	12	0	66	60	30	49
McGowan, Mike	1	0	8.85	9	0	20	31	8	20
Morgan, Lavelle	3	1	5.82	11	0	22	31	13	16
Nesloney, Ryan	0	0	13.50	1	0	2	5	2	1
Pello, Brandon	1	3	5.17	20	1	54	76	27	44
Pickens, J.R.	9	6	2.45	40	1	59	59	27	50
Pluta, Tony	0	2	9.00	5	0	12	16	13	12
Stover, Ricky	5	6	5.60	18	0	100	103	47	70
Van Dusen, Derrick	3	4	4.55	9	0	55	51	31	38
Wiebe, Jonathan	1	0	6.52	7	0	10	11	10	5

EL PASO DIABLOS

BATTING	AVG	AB	R	H	2B	3B	HR	RBI	SB
Alvarez, Jorge, 1b	.330	379	68	125	33	1	6	78	9
Camacho, Juan, 1b	.444	54	11	24	4	1	4	19	0
Castillo, Braulio, of	.283	166	28	47	12	0	8	29	0
Conley, Evan, 3b	.231	78	10	18	3	0	0	7	0
Drew, Kory, of	.254	323	45	82	14	3	2	32	5
Eichel, Matt, c	.223	175	24	39	10	0	2	19	1
Flowers, Brett, 1b	.260	50	5	13	2	1	1	5	0
Fulton, Josh, 2b	.177	164	30	29	2	0	0	14	7
Harkins, Mike, 1b	.299	157	16	47	6	0	4	30	1
Haygood, Brandon, 2b	.283	120	18	34	3	0	1	18	4
2-team (9 Shreveport)	.279	147	19	41	3	0	1	18	4
Joffrion, Jack, ss	.280	50	7	14	6	1	0	4	1
Klimkiewicz, Josh, 3b	.667	3	0	2	1	0	0	2	0
Machado, Albenis, ss	.314	229	49	72	16	3	4	41	13
Mangum, Greg, 2b	.267	15	2	4	1	0	0	1	0
Rosenthal, Ben, c	.233	253	42	59	14	1	6	36	1
Schmidt, J.P., 3b	.345	313	61	108	15	4	2	48	26
Sepulveda, Carlos, of	.256	277	47	71	13	5	3	44	2
Smith, Dustin, 2b	.204	49	7	10	4	0	0	5	0
Wood, Logan, of	.280	250	44	70	14	3	4	29	4
Wragg, Curtis, 2b	.000	4	0	0	0	0	0	0	0

PITCHING	W	L	ERA	G	SV	IP	H	BB	SO
Abbott, Justin	1	8	5.97	18	1	60	94	18	35
Acierno, Marc	0	0	11.25	2	0	4	8	1	1
Brower, Kevin	1	2	8.55	34	1	40	60	27	23

INDEPENDENT LEAGUES

	W	L	ERA	G	SV	IP	H	BB	SO
Cameron, Dustin	4	3	3.86	33	1	58	57	23	48
Cherry, William	0	0	7.96	19	1	26	37	12	18
Craker, Justin	0	2	9.31	2	0	10	21	4	6
Darley, Ned	0	0	1.23	6	3	7	7	4	5
Ebers, Eric	1	2	10.97	5	0	11	20	8	8
2-team (6 Lincoln)	1	2	10.06	11	0	17	27	14	13
Figueroa, Juan	1	0	3.60	5	0	5	4	5	5
Garcia, Jose	1	3	9.21	7	0	28	40	18	11
Griffith, Dustin	0	1	13.50	2	0	1	3	0	2
Harkins, Mike	0	0	4.50	1	0	2	2	1	2
Martin, Larry	0	0	8.31	4	0	4	4	6	1
McWatters, David	3	11	7.98	23	0	103	170	28	46
Mendible, Frank	0	0	162.00	2	0	0	2	5	0
3-team (3 FtW, 2 Shreve.)	0	0	27.00	5	0	4	6	10	3
Parris, Matt	1	6	7.43	7	0	40	56	29	11
Ramirez, Joslin	1	5	5.76	30	7	66	73	25	47
Reeves, Mike	0	1	10.80	6	0	12	24	10	7
Rogers, Joe	0	0	5.49	12	0	20	32	3	12
Tate, Alex	0	0	27.00	3	0	1	5	1	1
Testa, Chris	0	0	9.53	7	0	6	7	8	4
Torres, Andy	9	5	4.38	18	0	115	153	27	59
Trevino, Chris	3	3	4.91	19	1	62	68	30	58
Wachman, Robert	5	3	2.73	14	1	59	60	32	39
Wiedmeyer, Jason	2	5	6.07	9	0	46	73	17	32

FORT WORTH CATS

BATTING	AVG	AB	R	H	2B	3B	HR	RBI	SB
Adolfo, Carlos, of	.291	275	52	80	19	0	9	50	5
Carter, Charles, of	.289	45	4	13	4	0	0	6	0
2-team (3 Coastal Bend)	.278	54	5	15	4	0	0	7	0
Foster, Jordan, 1b	.313	364	70	114	24	2	9	51	7
Goree, Trenton, c	.400	5	0	2	0	0	0	0	0
Green, Terence, 3b	.314	392	64	123	21	3	5	53	28
Harkrider, Kip, 2b	.317	331	51	105	14	2	1	31	5
Hatcher, Justin, c	.429	14	3	6	1	0	0	1	1
Karr, Palmer, of	.237	76	12	18	1	0	3	12	1
2-team (15 Pensacola)	.218	110	16	24	2	0	3	16	5
Keesee, David, 2b	.220	118	18	26	3	0	0	10	4
Lup, Ken, c	.228	189	17	43	4	0	0	8	1
Miller, Adam, of	.213	122	9	26	4	2	2	11	4
Mirizzi, Marc, ss	.299	355	38	106	20	0	9	60	6
Mota, Tony, of	.297	327	51	97	18	2	7	36	27
Rogers, Drew, of	.187	91	7	17	4	0	3	11	1
Sepulveda, Carlos, of	.231	26	7	6	1	1	0	2	1
2-team (77 El Paso)	.254	303	54	77	14	6	3	46	3
Smith, Dustin, c	.333	21	2	7	1	0	0	1	0
Spencer, Matthew, of	.245	204	24	50	13	1	4	26	3
Von Behren, Jason, 2b/c	.250	4	7	1	0	0	0	0	4
Wallis, Jacob, c	.240	50	6	12	1	0	0	4	3
Williams, Shawn, 1b	.317	164	26	52	8	0	1	23	2
Zacuto, Kris, c	.228	123	9	28	7	0	4	27	0

PITCHING	W	L	ERA	G	SV	IP	H	BB	SO
Carlson, Zane	3	4	6.28	31	0	29	31	23	33
Casey, James	0	0	6.84	19	1	26	33	11	21
Garcia, Justin	0	3	7.77	19	1	24	34	13	17
Grybash, Dan	6	7	3.98	24	0	93	83	65	64
Harrington, Matt	6	1	2.90	39	2	50	37	23	56
Hochevar, Luke	1	1	2.38	4	0	23	20	11	34
Hull, Kevin	7	4	3.25	19	0	111	110	51	78
Kirsten, Joel	7	4	3.90	22	1	113	109	30	63
Montani, Jeff	2	1	6.00	17	0	21	30	10	13
Newman, Brandon	0	0	2.59	21	0	24	24	14	11
Valentin, Dan	4	1	3.89	13	0	44	50	16	32
2-team (2 Sioux Falls)	4	2	6.22	15	0	51	67	19	37
Walters, Cory	14	4	3.08	19	0	132	118	25	111
Weems, Ryan	3	9	5.80	20	0	104	128	39	75
Wilkerson, Steven	3	0	3.06	43	19	50	42	19	44

LINCOLN SALTDOGS

BATTING	AVG	AB	R	H	2B	3B	HR	RBI	SB
Balet, Pichi, 1b	.378	360	67	136	21	3	9	82	5
Cooley, Brett, 1b	.307	290	47	89	16	0	16	69	0
Duchek, Matt, c	.159	69	6	11	2	0	0	2	0
Fox, Ben, of	.000	1	1	0	0	0	0	0	0
Gordon, Casey, ss	.240	96	23	23	1	1	3	15	1
Harris, Cory, of	.248	270	38	67	15	1	11	38	5
Lopez, Luis, dh	.216	51	7	11	1	0	1	4	0
Patton, Josh, 2b	.326	371	67	121	26	6	11	64	9
Pierre, Michael, ss	.000	12	2	0	0	0	0	1	2
Powell, Paul, of	.301	339	59	102	30	1	7	45	1
Priddy, Ryan, ss	.279	129	13	36	4	0	0	9	1
Sullivan, Kevin, c	.308	318	56	98	24	2	5	47	13
Tartaglia, Evan, of	.352	244	67	86	13	7	1	23	32
2-team (18 Coastal Bend)	.335	319	80	107	15	8	1	28	45

	AVG	AB	R	H	2B	3B	HR	RBI	SB
Torres, Jose, of	.262	141	30	37	6	1	4	23	3
Warner, Bryan, of	.338	394	56	133	21	1	9	79	8
Yaconetti, Jay, 3b	.288	330	52	95	24	1	10	56	1

PITCHING	W	L	ERA	G	SV	IP	H	BB	SO
Blitstein, Jeffrey	8	2	2.31	21	1	140	138	33	61
Cooley, Brett	0	0	0.00	2	0	3	1	2	3
Ebers, Eric	0	0	8.53	6	0	6	7	6	5
Fitch, Mike	0	1	0.00	1	0	0	0	4	0
Fox, Ben	10	3	4.34	20	0	114	129	49	69
Fuell, Jerrod	0	2	4.05	28	11	27	27	3	28
Gardner, Jarrett	2	2	2.38	16	1	34	38	7	35
Gulin, Lindsay	13	2	2.10	19	0	120	90	20	104
Howerton, Jason	4	0	2.61	16	0	21	23	5	12
2-team (13 Sioux City)	4	2	3.77	29	1	43	56	18	17
Lincoln, Roger	6	5	3.50	17	0	93	101	28	63
Marsden, Aaron	0	0	6.94	7	0	12	20	6	12
Nowicki, Nate	0	1	6.75	4	0	4	6	0	1
Rodaway, Brian	8	3	3.53	17	0	107	100	40	89
Russ, Christopher	2	1	5.57	33	0	42	51	23	24
Ruwe, Kyle	10	6	3.91	41	1	90	90	12	54
Tichota, Clay	0	1	13.50	3	0	2	0	2	2
Turino, Yoankis	0	0	3.60	4	0	5	4	3	5
Vandermeer, Scott	1	3	4.54	39	4	42	42	19	23

PENSACOLA PELICANS

BATTING	AVG	AB	R	H	2B	3B	HR	RBI	SB
Aguilar, Trino, 3b	.322	363	59	117	23	3	8	51	12
Avila, Rolo, of	.259	313	48	81	9	0	1	29	20
Bethea, Larry, 1b	.298	235	30	70	10	0	7	36	9
Branch, George, of	.266	256	36	68	16	0	11	46	3
Brown, Bo, 2b	.157	229	37	36	9	2	3	23	1
Dorn, Tim, 1b	.327	312	43	102	24	1	10	43	6
Karr, Palmer, of	.176	34	4	6	1	0	0	4	4
Koehler, Jim, c	.211	19	3	4	1	0	1	3	0
McMillan, Beau, 2b	.083	12	0	1	1	0	0	1	0
Mendoza, Carlos, ss	.346	260	40	90	20	0	3	34	21
Montague, Ed, of	.326	267	47	87	19	4	6	35	14
Pasieka, Jon, c	.286	21	4	6	0	0	0	4	1
Priddy, Ryan, ss	.111	9	0	1	0	0	0	0	0
Rocha, Juan, c	.282	337	45	95	13	1	13	50	5
Salvo, Andrew, 2b	.222	108	17	24	5	0	0	7	3
Stevens, Greg, c	.257	35	4	9	1	0	0	4	1
Wade, Drake, of	.235	162	30	38	6	2	3	25	14
Woodruff, Bud, c	.275	40	4	11	2	0	3	6	0
Yepez, Jose, c	.283	198	22	56	9	0	3	34	4

PITCHING	W	L	ERA	G	SV	IP	H	BB	SO
Allen, Blake	1	3	5.92	9	0	38	50	20	21
Androsko, Todd	3	6	5.20	19	0	90	95	51	74
Begnaud, Russell	6	2	2.70	8	0	50	45	17	39
Brown, Bo	0	0	2.35	2	0	8	2	5	1
Courage, Josh	1	1	4.43	18	0	22	18	14	12
Dobson, Richard	2	5	3.96	40	0	77	89	26	47
Dorn, Tim	0	0	0.00	3	0	3	4	4	5
Girardeau, Clark	2	8	5.77	12	0	69	77	29	48
Hyle, Michael	2	3	5.24	8	0	45	44	33	31
Lane, Andrew	0	0	14.81	8	0	10	25	8	3
Luke, Bryan	0	0	4.00	6	0	9	13	8	6
Maness, Nick	2	4	4.62	8	0	37	44	20	24
Martin, Chris	1	1	4.96	10	0	16	19	12	7
O'Neal, Charles	0	0	2.16	4	0	8	9	7	7
Perdue, Matt	0	1	9.50	16	0	18	28	10	13
Pierce, Tony	2	4	1.83	37	21	34	25	21	53
Scheafer, Carl	4	2	3.53	20	0	43	46	18	16
Smith, Sam	5	7	4.46	25	0	113	134	41	56
Sodowsky, Clint	5	1	2.85	11	0	60	49	19	60
Stephens, Trey	0	0	4.26	7	0	6	5	4	3
Vose, Jake	1	3	6.46	14	0	24	30	17	22
Walker, Benny	2	6	5.47	25	0	53	46	40	45

ST. JOSEPHS BLACKSNAKES

BATTING	AVG	AB	R	H	2B	3B	HR	RBI	SB
Buhagiar, Joshua, of	.250	20	1	5	0	0	0	1	0
Burke, Mark, 1b	.307	309	40	95	23	1	5	62	2
Dworken, Mikalea, c	.235	213	13	50	5	1	1	28	1
Harris, Cory, of	.279	111	14	31	9	0	4	22	3
2-team (64 Lincoln)	.257	381	52	98	24	1	15	60	8
Huguet, J.C., c	.000	5	0	0	0	0	0	0	0
Infante, Jefferson, c	.198	106	8	21	4	0	1	16	1
Johnson, Matt, c	.000	2	0	0	0	0	0	0	0
Jordan, Scooter, of	.289	350	67	101	10	3	0	24	33
Kitch, Denver, 2b	.243	305	39	74	12	6	1	21	5
Merriman, Terrell, of	.240	204	38	49	9	3	0	23	5
Mitsumori, Shingo, of	.000	0	1	0	0	0	0	0	0

BATTING	AVG	AB	R	H	2B	3B	HR	RBI	SB
Mojica, Jimmy, ss	.299	294	44	88	10	5	0	32	17
Mulhern, Bryan, c	.167	12	1	2	0	0	0	1	0
Nowlin, Cody, 1b	.254	268	35	68	14	4	4	33	2
Quintana, Wil, of	.271	354	63	96	24	3	21	71	3
Thomas, Ben, 3b	.279	355	66	99	28	1	5	51	9
Whitesides, Jake, 2b	.299	338	48	101	13	13	6	59	12

PITCHING	W	L	ERA	G	SV	IP	H	BB	SO
Balbuena, Caleb	0	0	2.57	18	0	21	13	6	17
Conrad, Jason	0	0	24.75	3	0	4	11	3	4
DeChristofaro, Vinnie	0	1	4.10	36	1	37	34	24	28
Edwards, Andrew	2	5	4.94	14	0	58	62	35	27
Graves, Donovan	8	7	4.21	21	0	133	153	28	66
Huguet, J.C.	7	3	3.54	40	4	89	73	35	79
Jarman, Josh	0	1	5.58	19	0	31	31	28	22
Johnson, Matt	6	3	5.73	43	0	60	73	25	27
Kupper, Dustin	1	1	4.37	5	0	23	22	19	8
Merle, Jesen	4	7	6.38	30	0	72	102	24	36
Mitsumori, Shingo	4	5	5.83	30	0	71	91	25	36
Mojica, Jimmy	0	0	0.00	1	0	1	0	0	0
Nussbeck, Mark	8	3	2.97	18	0	97	77	19	105
Thomas, Evan	4	7	6.19	13	0	77	94	34	50
Tricoglou, Jamie	5	3	2.52	43	19	64	52	34	67

ST. PAUL SAINTS

BATTING	AVG	AB	R	H	2B	3B	HR	RBI	SB
Balkan, Adam, ph	.000	0	1	0	0	0	0	0	0
Becker, Brian, 1b	.300	150	22	45	12	0	4	20	0
Brice, Thomas, of	.238	21	6	5	0	0	1	7	2
Buchanan, Brian, 1b	.292	185	31	54	7	0	11	48	2
Butler, Steve, ss	.254	134	21	34	3	0	0	11	0
Cox, Billy, c	.299	117	16	35	5	0	2	20	0
Fischer, Rob, of	.257	230	34	59	9	4	5	31	6
Forbes, Mike, of	.185	81	6	15	2	0	0	1	1
Frost, Jeremy, c	.269	323	49	87	14	1	9	44	16
Gretz, Nick, 1b	.304	247	35	75	14	1	4	44	0
Lytle, Chaz, of	.297	165	32	49	7	0	0	17	16
Olow, Adam, of	.360	214	49	77	14	1	5	33	7
Renick, Josh, 2b	.287	376	59	108	12	3	1	46	9
Rodriguez, Victor, 3b	.287	216	25	62	12	0	3	28	0
Scalabrini, Pat, 3b	.313	367	54	115	20	1	8	57	12
Sprout, Brian, of	.350	337	64	118	28	1	10	59	10
Torres, Jose, of	.232	112	14	26	6	0	2	14	3
2-team (42 Lincoln)	.249	253	44	63	12	1	6	37	6
White, Derrick, of	.364	33	10	12	4	0	3	9	0
Willis, Derek, of	.188	16	5	3	0	0	0	3	1

PITCHING	W	L	ERA	G	SV	IP	H	BB	SO
Boughner, Anthony	9	7	3.55	20	0	122	136	21	67
Butler, Steve	0	0	0.00	2	0	3	2	0	3
Eikum, Gabe	0	0	14.40	1	0	5	12	3	5
Hammons, Matt	3	1	3.73	41	22	41	40	16	35
Hernandez, Ivan	4	2	3.07	38	0	59	56	23	47
Lord, Justin	11	3	4.20	19	0	120	130	20	55
Lubrano, Paul	0	0	7.00	9	0	9	12	7	11
Meyer, Mike	10	8	5.11	21	0	130	159	24	55
Peck, Mike	0	1	7.36	5	0	7	10	4	7
Pike, Matthew	2	4	3.32	41	3	65	54	25	51
Rival, Kevin	2	2	6.15	22	1	34	36	18	25
Ruud, Charlie	8	6	3.75	21	0	132	143	28	96
Stanton, T.J.	5	7	5.90	16	0	82	103	36	49
Tisch, Tim	0	0	0.00	1	0	1	2	0	1
Whinnery, Brian	1	1	4.95	6	0	20	28	5	16
Willis, Derek	0	0	0.00	1	0	1	1	0	0

SHREVEPORT SPORTS

BATTING	AVG	AB	R	H	2B	3B	HR	RBI	SB
Brown, Neb, 2b	.294	303	66	89	21	2	3	40	28
Bryant, Tommy, c	.278	209	32	58	11	0	4	37	0
Corbeil, Al, 1b	.332	304	43	101	22	0	2	52	0
Corbeil, Nick, c	.133	15	2	2	0	0	1	3	0
Easley, Austin, of	.277	321	53	89	14	4	7	43	9
Falu, Melvin, 3b	.301	266	41	80	9	0	6	39	3
Fenwick, Ron, ss	.273	187	29	51	9	0	1	17	2
Gambill, Chad, dh	.262	381	61	100	23	0	10	74	1
Haygood, Brandon, 2b	.259	27	1	7	0	0	0	0	0
Humphries, Justin, 1b	.249	201	27	50	15	4	7	35	0
Neitz, Josh, of	.000	2	0	0	0	0	0	0	0
Polanco, Enohel, ss	.325	308	51	100	14	7	5	53	14
Reyes, Melvin, 2b	.056	18	1	1	0	0	0	0	0
Self, Todd, of	.320	222	43	71	16	3	7	46	6
Smith, Coby, of	.275	335	60	92	7	0	2	25	42
Torres, Jason, c	.269	67	2	18	2	0	0	5	0
Willis, Mike, 2b-OF	.000	4	0	0	0	0	0	0	0

PITCHING	W	L	ERA	G	SV	IP	H	BB	SO
Cunningham, Aaron	0	4	3.16	24	5	31	33	6	17
Cunningham, Derek	3	3	2.77	18	1	52	37	30	48
Freeman, Dan	0	2	7.11	15	2	13	18	8	10
Hendricks, Thomas	7	4	3.45	18	0	104	120	26	39
Kirkland, Aaron	2	3	3.81	40	0	52	49	22	51
Little, Jeff	2	0	3.43	15	1	21	19	3	20
Mendible, Frank	0	0	10.13	2	0	3	3	3	2
Mercedes, Gerson	3	1	2.38	32	8	42	29	15	35
Mozingo, Dan	0	2	10.80	6	0	17	26	11	3
Neitz, Josh	4	5	3.34	19	0	94	81	27	53
Nieto, Jose	0	1	13.50	2	0	1	2	4	0
Snow, Bert	9	3	3.13	18	0	109	99	45	86
Snyder, Ryan	6	6	3.77	14	0	74	89	14	36
Tyson, Leo	3	0	5.79	27	1	42	48	23	28
Westbrook, Nick	0	0	2.45	3	0	4	5	2	0
Wikstrom, Eric	11	3	3.95	19	0	114	122	39	55
Winters, Mal	4	2	2.75	11	0	36	30	4	27

SIOUX CITY EXPLORERS

BATTING	AVG	AB	R	H	2B	3B	HR	RBI	SB
Burress, J.J., ss	.274	277	34	76	7	2	0	26	11
Carlson, Jason, 2b	.239	46	4	11	4	0	1	3	0
Daubert, Jake, of	.294	177	28	52	11	1	3	24	1
Gripp, Ryan, 3b	.293	324	47	95	25	0	13	55	0
Grossman, Chris, c	.305	351	61	107	30	2	14	56	2
Guzman, Freddy, of	.333	3	1	1	0	0	0	0	0
Henry, Kevin, of	.215	274	40	59	12	3	14	49	0
Keppinger, Billy, of	.161	31	3	5	1	0	0	5	0
Llanos, Alex, 2b	.341	314	48	107	13	1	10	43	15
McCarthy, Joey, 2b	.200	5	0	1	0	0	0	0	0
Meier, Dan, 1b	.241	253	34	61	13	1	5	38	0
Mendoza, Robert, 2b	.198	172	17	34	6	0	5	21	0
Moreno, Jorge, of	.302	364	77	110	24	2	19	65	16
Pace, Zack, of	.233	189	33	44	6	0	0	14	9
Richardson, Mike, of	.270	244	34	66	10	2	9	33	3
Ruiz, Ryan, of	.237	139	19	33	5	1	0	6	4
Scholten, J.D., of	.333	3	1	1	0	0	0	0	0
Shay, Nick, 1b	.125	32	1	4	2	0	0	3	0
Thames, Julius, 2b	.295	95	14	28	3	0	0	6	3

PITCHING	W	L	ERA	G	SV	IP	H	BB	SO
Dillard, Johnny	0	0	4.05	4	0	7	7	6	3
Ferguson, Keith	0	1	9.82	10	0	11	13	9	8
Gaarder, Karsten	1	5	6.47	19	0	88	122	45	54
Holguin, Nathan	4	2	7.88	12	0	48	71	13	24
Howerton, Jason	2	2	4.84	13	1	22	33	13	5
Howerton, John	6	3	4.18	36	0	56	69	21	28
Keppinger, Billy	9	5	3.42	22	0	142	143	25	96
Kramer, Sean	2	3	4.46	36	15	36	32	22	40
Lipari, Thomas	6	8	4.77	19	0	117	149	44	60
Marcotte, Trevor	1	4	5.58	12	0	69	80	30	29
Marotz, Ty	1	0	0.00	6	0	12	2	5	16
Marsden, Aaron	3	7	7.01	14	0	69	102	28	39
2-team (7 Lincoln)	3	7	7.00	21	0	81	122	34	51
Mattison, Kieran	1	2	7.94	4	0	17	27	9	5
Nunes, Mike	3	5	4.26	37	1	51	57	20	32
Scholten, J.D.	5	4	5.54	24	0	75	89	33	33
Swiatkiewicz, Chris	1	2	11.33	5	0	27	43	8	10

SIOUX FALLS CANARIES

BATTING	AVG	AB	R	H	2B	3B	HR	RBI	SB
Anderson, Dennis, c	.322	230	33	74	10	1	7	37	6
Arroyo, Abner, 1b	.330	351	58	116	32	1	13	65	0
Bays, Leonard, 2b	.000	3	0	0	0	0	0	0	0
Clemente, Edgard, of	.237	97	16	23	7	0	1	12	0
Cogan, Tony, 1b	.500	4	1	2	1	0	0	0	0
Delucchi, Dustin, of	.284	95	12	27	4	0	0	12	2
Eriotes, Jim, dh	.000	1	0	0	0	0	0	0	0
Fermin, Angel, ss	.250	232	30	58	7	4	3	23	6
Hall, Chris, 3b	.239	355	42	85	19	2	4	40	7
Hermansen, Chad, of	.317	375	77	119	35	3	19	72	4
Hernandez, Alexis, c	.306	36	3	11	1	2	1	6	0
Hoffman, David, c	.226	159	15	36	6	0	0	14	3
Juarez, Sammy, ss	.122	49	0	6	1	0	0	2	0
Kaplan, Jonathan, of	.000	19	1	0	0	0	0	1	1
Kmiecik, Kyle, 2b	.141	64	5	9	0	0	1	4	0
Monegan, Anthony, of	.294	136	16	40	5	0	0	15	8
Montgomery, Matt, of	.333	3	1	1	0	0	0	0	0
Santana, Ralph, 2b	.276	373	56	103	11	1	1	28	40
Schmitz, John, c	.268	209	28	56	9	2	1	24	4
Schuda, Justin, 1b	.257	70	6	18	8	0	1	14	0
Smith, Bubba, 1b	.306	108	17	33	2	0	8	22	0
Smith, Jake, c	.268	41	5	11	0	0	1	1	1
Sugden, Jason, of	.213	127	13	27	8	3	2	19	4
Suzumegano, Kenta, 2b	.145	55	7	8	2	0	1	5	0
Weber, Chris, 2b	.274	84	17	23	0	2	1	8	1

INDEPENDENT LEAGUES

PITCHING	W	L	ERA	G	SV	IP	H	BB	SO
Barrett, Robert	2	2	7.24	10	0	32	45	13	28
Bauer, Peter	1	4	4.41	6	0	35	45	9	10
Bays, Leonard	2	4	4.50	41	3	58	71	18	46
Beard, Jabe	1	2	6.75	12	1	20	27	7	11
Carter, Eric	0	0	15.88	5	0	6	10	8	3
Cierlik, Jason	3	4	2.68	30	2	40	30	21	27
Cogan, Tony	7	5	3.02	16	0	92	100	30	43
Donlin, Sean	0	7	5.93	27	0	85	86	42	70
Garrison, Aaron	6	7	5.31	21	0	102	103	50	77
Greusel, Evan	0	2	11.57	4	0	19	34	9	12
Hoffman, David	0	0	18.00	1	0	1	3	1	0
Johnson, Doug	5	8	4.68	17	0	98	109	49	65
Juarez, Sammy	0	0	0.00	1	0	1	1	0	0
Koziara, Matt	3	5	6.14	10	0	59	79	19	16
Kupper, Dustin	0	1	17.18	2	0	4	5	5	2
2-team (5 St. Joe's)	1	2	6.15	7	0	26	27	24	10
Marcus, Clint	1	1	7.92	10	0	25	39	14	12
Montgomery, Matt	0	1	3.95	14	9	14	15	5	13
Ortiz, John	0	0	6.00	4	0	3	10	1	2
Perez, Alex	0	2	7.27	2	0	9	8	11	3
Petrusek, Matt	2	3	5.05	30	3	73	79	28	59
Rodriguez, Mike	0	1	8.10	2	0	7	7	5	4
Scarbery, Chad	1	1	4.88	4	0	24	24	12	20
Valentin, Dan	0	1	21.60	2	0	7	17	3	5
Wall, Jason	0	1	9.82	1	0	4	10	0	2
Weber, Chris	0	0	0.00	1	0	1	1	1	0
Wesley, John	0	0	1.42	13	6	13	7	3	15

ATLANTIC LEAGUE

In their second season, the Lancaster Barnstormers rolled through the Atlantic League playoffs on the way to their first title.

In the championship series, Lancaster swept Bridgeport in three games, thanks to an offense that scored 27 runs. Denny Harriger finished off the Bluefish in the deciding game, allowing two runs on nine hits. Harriger, 37, has bounced around the minor leagues for 20 years, but did earn a four-game stint with the Tigers in 1998. He spent three games with Monclova of the Mexican League in 2006, and when that didn't work out, he headed to Lancaster, where he went 17-4, 2.63.

Harriger told some of his teammates that this would be his swan song, but that doesn't mean that his teammates aren't going lobby him to come back.

"He says he's done," Barnstormers pitcher Scott Sobkowiak told the Lancaster New Era. "But me and Cam (Smith) are going to work on him this offseason. He's just too good. He's so much fun to watch. He's probably the best teammate I've ever had."

The Barnstormers won their title at home, in front of a crowd of 6,558. "They were screaming. They were focused on every pitch. We truly had a home field advantage," general manager Joe Pinto said.

Lincoln Mikkelsen, one of two players still playing from the original 1993 season of the Northern League, was named both the player and pitcher of the year after a 15-5, 1.85 season for Atlantic City.

STANDINGS

NORTH	W	L	PCT	GB
*Bridgeport	75	49	.605	
&Long Island	73	51	.589	2
Newark	42	83	.336	34
Road Warriors	42	83	.336	34

SOUTH	W	L	PCT	GB
*&Lancaster	75	51	.595	
Atlantic City	69	57	.548	6
Somerset	65	61	.516	10
Camden	61	65	.484	14

&First-half champion. *Second-half champion.

Playoffs—Semifinals: Lancaster defeated Atlantic City 2-0 and Bridgeport defeated Long Island 2-0 in best-of-three series. **Finals:** Lancaster defeated Bridgeport 3-0 in best-of-five series.

MANAGERS: Atlantic City—Jeff Ball; **Bridgeport**—Dave LaPoint; **Camden**—Wayne Krenchicki; **Lancaster**—Tom Herr; **Long Island**—Don McCormack; **Newark**—Chris Jones; **Road Warriors**—Jeff Scott; **Somerset**—Sparky Lyle.

ATTENDANCE: Long Island 419,150; Lancaster 370,176; Somerset 362,585; Camden 253,013; Bridgeport 193,096; Newark 178,132; Atlantic City 134,900.

ALL-STAR TEAM: C—John Pachot, Camden; **1B**—Mike Huggings, Road Warriors; **2B**—Steve Hine, Bridgeport; **3B**—Jeff Nettles, Somerset; **SS**—Raul Marval, Atlantic City; **OF**—Ryan Radmanovich, Somerset; Mel Stocker, Long Island; Reggie Taylor, Lancaster; Denny Abreu, Camden. **DH**—Bucky Jacobsen, Long Island. **Util**—Joe Jiannetti, Atlantic City. **Starting Pitcher**—Denny Harriger, Lancaster; Lincoln Mikkelsen, Atlantic City. **Relief Pitcher**—Chris Fussell, Camden.

Player of the Year: Lincoln Mikklesen, Atlantic City. **Manager of the Year:** Dave LaPoint, Bridgeport.

INDIVIDUAL BATTING LEADERS

Batter, Team	AVG	G	AB	R	H	HR	RBI
Abreu, Denny, Cam	.323	105	396	70	128	15	56
Jiannetti, Joe, AC	.319	119	439	67	140	21	79
Hine, Steve, Bridge	.315	115	391	70	123	10	64
Cruz, Deivi, Bridge	.307	90	368	57	113	9	63
Stocker, Mel, LI	.303	110	442	87	134	3	39
Ortiz, Nick, Somer	.303	110	412	51	125	8	55
Taylor, Reggie, Lanc	.302	115	430	87	130	23	77
Almonte, Erick, LI	.302	111	404	73	122	9	77
Radmanovich, Ryan, Somer	.302	98	334	70	101	27	66
Marval, Raul, AC	.298	124	490	88	146	17	73

INDIVIDUAL PITCHING LEADERS

Pitcher, Team	W	L	ERA	IP	H	BB	SO
Mikkelsen, Lincoln, AC	15	5	1.85	175	127	46	122
Harriger, Denny, Lanc	17	4	2.63	181	191	29	82
Hodges, Kevin, Bridge	12	7	3.01	137	147	43	70
Difelice, Mark, Camden	12	9	3.19	158	163	24	132
Powell, Greg, Camden	5	11	3.22	142	147	40	74
Persails, Mark, AC	7	5	3.43	139	127	60	116
Ahearne, Pat, LI	12	4	3.47	156	176	28	105
Crockett, Ben, Somer.	8	11	3.51	164	178	31	113
Costello, Ryan, Camden	7	9	3.62	159	154	56	95
McDonald, Jon, Camden.	8	7	3.64	134	157	35	50

ATLANTIC CITY SURF

BATTING	AVG	AB	R	H	2B	3B	HR	RBI	SB
Benjamin, Al, of	.123	57	6	7	1	0	2	4	0
Delgado, Dario, 1b	.274	168	28	46	13	0	8	35	1
2-team (66 Newark)	.260	396	55	103	30	0	15	68	2
Heath, Demetrius, 2b	.293	478	74	140	14	5	0	29	71
Housel, David, of	.208	96	11	20	1	1	1	8	8
Imwalle, Matt, 3b	.264	110	8	29	7	2	1	7	2
Jiannetti, Joe, 3b	.319	439	67	140	29	6	21	79	8
Johnson, Gary, of	.247	434	43	107	18	2	8	40	7
Leathers, Todd, 1b	.263	437	64	115	20	1	14	67	4
MacLeod, John, c	.184	87	11	16	4	0	0	8	0
Maddox, Dusty, of	.226	164	20	37	7	2	1	19	11
Marval, Raul, ss	.298	490	88	146	22	2	17	73	5
Nichols, Joe, of	.000	12	3	0	0	0	0	0	0
Polanco, Enohel. 3b/ss	.190	21	4	4	0	0	0	1	0
Rosario, Mel, c	.306	157	20	48	16	1	7	26	3
Timmons, Ozzie, of	.269	412	62	111	29	0	19	63	1
Torrealba, Steve, c	.200	95	9	19	3	1	3	10	0
Torres, Jason, c	.242	95	12	23	6	0	2	14	1
Williams, Clyde, of	.266	447	68	119	21	3	20	67	20

PITCHERS	W	L	ERA	G	SV	IP	H	BB	SO
Acosta, Domingo	6	4	3.61	26	2	42	45	11	36
Balbuena, Caleb	0	0	1.69	10	1	11	9	3	8
Bell, Gary	2	1	7.18	22	0	31	41	24	26
Blitstein, Jeffrey	2	1	3.79	3	0	19	16	7	11
Brunet, Mike	0	0	1.46	10	1	12	11	5	20
Corrado, Rob	6	5	5.48	32	0	67	69	47	56
DiAngelo, Jason	2	1	3.44	30	6	37	33	14	44
Dougherty, Kevin	1	4	2.60	6	0	28	30	14	14
Estrella, Leo	4	5	4.85	23	1	72	80	26	59
Grezlovski, Ben	4	6	3.42	54	12	68	58	33	58
Hesseltine, Charlie	3	2	5.06	12	0	21	27	8	14
High, Andy	7	7	3.94	25	0	144	138	60	89
MacLeod, John	0	0	0.00	1	0	1	0	0	0
Marcotte	1	0	16.20	2	0	2	6	0	3
Mikkelsen, Lincoln	15	5	1.85	25	0	175	127	46	122
Persails, Mark	7	5	3.43	21	0	139	127	60	116
Pierce, Tony	0	1	2.61	9	2	10	7	9	12
Schurman, Ryan	7	6	4.06	24	0	146	148	60	109
Steward, Jaime	1	3	5.83	12	0	46	57	23	22

	W	L	ERA	G	SV	IP	H	BB	SO
Swayze, Jeff	0	0	3.38	4	0	5	4	5	2
Tricoglou, Jamie	1	0	1.42	10	3	13	5	5	22
Ward, Jeremy	0	0	0.00	5	2	5	0	3	6
Weber, Ben	0	1	8.53	9	0	13	15	2	10

BRIDGEPORT BLUEFISH

BATTING	AVG	AB	R	H	2B	3B	HR	RBI	SB
Alfonzo, Edgardo, 2b	.286	14	1	4	2	0	0	4	0
Boehringer, Brian, 2b	.000	1	0	0	0	0	0	0	0
Brinkley, Darryl, of	.232	56	8	13	2	0	1	3	0
Burnham, Gary, 1b/of	.319	72	7	23	5	0	1	10	0
Cruz, Deivi, ss	.307	368	57	113	23	2	9	63	2
Darula, Bobby, of	.358	81	11	29	4	0	0	10	4
Echevarria, Angel, 1b	.275	171	20	47	7	0	4	24	0
Espada, Angel, of	.266	271	40	72	7	1	0	28	18
Fernandez, Alex, of	.222	72	9	16	5	0	0	8	1
Figueroa, Luis, 3b	.319	116	14	37	2	0	3	17	0
Hannahan, Buzz, ss	.263	99	18	26	4	0	1	13	4
Hine, Steve, 2b	.315	391	70	123	29	4	10	64	14
Hutchins, Norm, of	.230	291	46	67	13	2	8	43	9
Kuilan, Hector, c	.291	213	19	62	10	0	2	24	0
Layfield, Scotty,	.000	1	0	0	0	0	0	0	0
Mota, Tony, of	.172	29	5	5	1	0	0	2	3
Nathans, John, of	.230	126	12	29	4	0	0	8	1
2-team (13 Newark)	.215	163	17	35	5	0	1	11	1
Nelson, Bryant, 3b	.284	363	61	103	23	0	8	44	13
Otanez, Willis, 1b	.350	163	34	57	9	2	12	33	0
Pogue, Jamie, c	.253	190	37	48	11	0	6	19	0
Rios, Brian, ph	.000	1	1	0	0	0	0	0	0
Rodriguez, Carlos, of	.214	70	6	15	3	1	3	10	4
Rolls, Damian, 1b	.315	279	41	88	15	4	5	38	8
Rose, P.J., 1b	.299	194	29	58	12	0	7	33	0
Sanchez, Tino, 1b	.324	145	20	47	7	0	3	21	1
Simontacchi, Jason, 1b	.000	0	1	0	0	0	0	0	0
Wesson, Barry, of	.288	406	70	117	14	8	10	55	17

PITCHING	W	L	ERA	G	SV	IP	H	BB	SO
Anderson, Matt	1	1	4.11	15	2	15	12	8	17
Beech, Matt	7	6	4.34	19	0	114	114	51	86
Bierbrodt, Nick	1	0	3.21	12	0	14	17	11	18
2-team (6 Somerset)	1	1	4.91	18	0	18	24	19	21
Boehringer, Brian	2	1	2.05	5	0	31	25	12	24
Borbon, Pedro	0	0	2.25	2	0	4	2	3	5
Cunnane, Will	2	0	2.25	2	0	12	11	2	11
Fesh, Sean	3	3	3.57	51	0	45	45	17	42
Hackman, Luther	8	0	2.81	27	8	74	63	31	60
Hodges, Kevin	12	7	3.01	22	0	137	147	43	70
Hutchins, Norm	0	1	9.00	2	0	3	5	4	2
Journell, Jimmy	4	4	3.69	47	6	83	74	40	93
Krines, Dan	3	3	6.86	32	0	59	75	9	28
Layfield, Scotty	4	1	3.86	52	0	49	49	23	26
Mathews, T.J.	12	7	3.79	24	0	145	140	36	109
Montgomery, Matt	2	2	5.17	30	1	31	24	13	23
Norton, Phil	0	0	13.50	2	0	1	4	0	0
Osborne, Donovan	2	1	2.64	7	0	48	36	8	39
Porzio, Mike	8	6	3.93	26	1	126	130	68	90
Ramos, Eddy	2	5	3.72	36	15	46	47	24	37
Simontacchi, Jason	1	0	0.84	10	2	11	6	0	10
Villacis, Eduardo	0	1	5.40	4	0	7	9	1	4
Young, Colin	1	0	5.91	24	0	32	43	13	21

CAMDEN RIVERSHARKS

BATTING	AVG	AB	R	H	2B	3B	HR	RBI	SB
Abreu, Denny, of	.323	396	70	128	19	4	15	56	26
Aquilino, Anthony, 2b	.130	23	1	3	0	0	0	0	0
Barrett, Rich, of	.233	386	52	90	10	6	2	24	15
Biernbaum, L.J., of	.310	29	5	9	2	0	3	7	0
Connell, Lino, 2b	.269	375	44	101	24	1	6	50	15
Conti, Jason, of	.228	101	8	23	7	0	0	7	2
Davidson, Cleatus, 2b	.150	40	7	6	2	0	0	4	1
Demarco, Matt, 3b	.239	218	21	52	7	2	4	31	1
Floyd, Mike, of	.192	52	5	10	0	2	0	3	0
Freire, Alejandro, 1b	.289	187	26	54	9	0	10	41	1
Jones, Ryan, 1b	.224	388	50	87	21	1	9	41	2
Lopez, Luis, 3b	.226	62	7	14	2	0	2	10	0
Maness, Dwight, of	.274	416	63	114	24	6	12	57	21
McGarvey, Randy, c	.234	107	13	25	1	1	0	11	1
O'Sullivan, Patrick, of	.368	19	2	7	1	0	1	2	0
Pachot, John, c	.282	386	35	109	20	1	10	52	1
Rodriguez, Javy, ss	.197	188	20	37	3	0	13	16	
Skrehot, Shaun, ss	.286	231	40	66	10	1	6	24	10
Strauss, Brad, 3b	.257	307	37	79	16	1	3	31	4
Swann, Pedro, of	.293	208	34	61	15	3	7	31	5
Torres, Jason, c	.095	21	2	2	0	0	0	0	0

PITCHING	W	L	ERA	G	SV	IP	H	BB	SO
Axelson, Josh	1	3	4.50	33	0	54	62	38	34
Babula, Shaun	0	0	4.50	3	0	2	3	2	2
Barrett, Rich	0	0	0.00	1	0	1	0	2	1
Bechtel, Chuck	0	2	3.42	22	1	26	21	11	15
Conti, Jason	1	0	0.00	1	0	3	1	2	1
Costello, Ryan	7	9	3.62	26	0	159	154	56	95
Currier, Rik	2	0	3.79	3	0	19	13	8	19
Davis, Brendon	3	7	3.51	26	0	77	62	52	49
Demarco, Matt	0	0	54.00	1	0	0	2	0	1
Difelice, Mark	12	9	3.19	25	0	158	163	24	132
Donaldson, Bo	0	0	2.51	18	0	32	29	20	31
Fussell, Chris	8	4	3.78	56	23	67	60	27	81
Ion, Mark	4	2	3.42	34	0	55	33	40	52
McDonald, Jon	8	7	3.64	23	0	134	157	35	50
Myers, Damian	4	4	5.09	24	0	35	40	20	26
Phelps, Travis	0	1	0.00	2	0	8	6	5	8
Powell, Greg	5	11	3.22	22	0	142	147	40	74
Rizzo, Todd	0	0	5.06	2	0	5	4	4	2
Stocks, Nick	6	6	4.96	17	0	105	105	42	64

LANCASTER BARNSTORMERS

BATTING	AVG	AB	R	H	2B	3B	HR	RBI	SB
Ackerman, Eric, of	.000	1	0	0	0	0	0	0	0
Bowers, Jason, ss	.277	148	28	41	4	2	5	23	7
Burkhart, Lance, c	.222	315	52	70	20	0	16	57	3
Crozier, Brandon, of	.291	227	38	66	13	4	7	25	6
Derhak, Alex, c	.000	18	1	0	0	0	0	1	0
Dufner, Kris, 2b	.245	204	30	50	6	1	8	21	1
Foster, Quincy, of	.302	248	42	75	6	3	5	29	20
Gonzalez, Danny, ss	.319	254	44	81	5	2	8	27	6
Hake, Travis, 2b	.241	290	42	70	12	1	1	34	18
Hernandez, Alex, 1b	.261	69	7	18	3	0	2	12	2
Hileman, Jutt, of	.286	433	55	124	22	1	8	58	11
Maxwell, Keith, 1b	.270	137	21	37	10	0	4	20	1
2-team (18 Newark)	.235	196	28	46	12	0	5	24	1
Ortiz, Jose, 3b	.289	384	64	111	24	1	18	80	5
Santana, Manny, c	.250	252	33	63	16	1	10	40	1
Taylor, Reggie, of	.302	430	87	130	27	6	23	77	25
Todd, Jeremy, 1b	.322	258	59	83	20	2	16	63	4
Van Note, Note, 3b	.238	248	35	59	12	2	4	29	4
Van Rossum, Rossum, of	.242	277	53	67	12	1	12	37	13
Wilson, Kevin, ss	.333	9	1	3	0	0	0	1	0

PITCHING	W	L	ERA	G	SV	IP	H	BB	SO
Ackerman, Eric	6	5	4.60	37	0	78	101	28	36
Boker, John	2	0	3.10	5	0	29	27	9	15
Clem, Christopher	0	0	4.10	15	1	26	36	9	10
2-team (15 Road Warriors)	1	1	5.48	30	1	44	62	16	22
Dooley, Joe	1	1	7.77	6	0	24	19	14	16
Evert, Brett	0	0	6.00	1	0	6	4	1	5
Harriger, Denny	17	4	2.63	26	0	181	191	29	82
Hassett, Steve	0	0	13.50	6	0	7	15	5	4
Henkel, Rob	7	4	4.23	27	1	72	75	27	43
Henriquez, Oscar	1	0	2.70	3	0	3	2	4	2
Knox, Matt	2	3	3.09	41	9	55	44	16	52
Lira, James	0	1	1.86	7	1	10	6	4	10
Patterson, Scott	2	0	0.78	20	14	23	13	5	31
Peeples, Ross	0	0	3.55	23	1	25	28	10	12
Pennington, Todd	0	1	2.08	13	0	17	13	14	14
Smith, Cam	5	6	4.60	28	0	76	57	74	74
Sobkowiak, Scott	9	7	4.61	26	0	131	139	48	86
Stevens, Josh	2	0	2.63	2	0	14	11	5	5
Weatherby, Charlie	3	3	3.13	63	15	75	71	21	67
Whitaker, Brian	12	7	4.98	27	0	150	177	64	64
Zwirchitz, Andy	6	10	6.26	29	0	94	85	54	71

LONG ISLAND DUCKS

BATTING	AVG	AB	R	H	2B	3B	HR	RBI	SB
Almonte, Erick, 3b	.302	404	73	122	24	4	9	77	16
Ambrosini, Dominick, of	.317	249	41	79	16	3	8	48	6
Bass, Jayson, of	.366	41	11	15	4	0	2	13	1
Cafiero, Rob, 1b	.270	111	14	30	5	0	0	19	0
Connors, Greg, c	.264	258	30	68	15	0	6	39	0
Goelz, Bryan, of	.254	142	19	36	6	1	1	12	5
2-team (51 Road Warriors)	.240	304	34	73	10	3	4	26	8
Goelz, Jim, 2b-SS	.267	30	4	8	2	0	0	4	0
Gonzalez, Juan, of	.323	130	23	42	7	0	6	23	0
Haverbusch, Kevin, of	.252	326	43	82	28	3	9	55	3
Hernandez, Carlos, 2b	.280	443	62	124	23	2	4	57	32
Jacobsen, Bucky, 1b	.291	413	72	120	22	2	21	89	6
King, Brad, c	.259	232	34	60	16	0	7	36	3
Mahomes, Pat, of	.500	2	4	1	0	0	0	0	0
Navarrete, Ray, 3b	.284	162	29	46	12	2	2	21	7
Ortiz, Nick, 3b	.450	20	4	9	2	0	3	8	0

	AVG	AB	R	H	2B	3B	HR	RBI	SB
Pena, Elvis, 2b	.255	361	63	92	19	3	1	27	38
Rodriguez, Henry, 1b	.287	355	53	102	19	0	12	59	0
Schrager, Tony, ss	.297	192	35	57	11	0	5	33	1
Stocker, Mel, of	.303	442	87	134	19	8	3	39	56

PITCHING	W	L	ERA	G	SV	IP	H	BB	SO
Ahearne, Pat	12	4	3.47	23	0	156	175	28	105
Arroyo, Luis	1	0	2.70	3	0	10	6	3	3
Bailey, Cory	0	2	3.64	16	1	30	36	11	21
Batson, Byron	0	1	5.57	4	0	21	24	2	11
Blanton, Jason	0	0	9.00	2	0	2	2	1	4
Cafiero, Rob	0	0	3.38	10	0	16	16	6	10
Cain, Tim	5	4	6.61	25	0	67	97	17	45
Crudale, Mike	5	4	5.37	47	1	52	50	13	40
Erdos, Todd	5	3	4.97	25	8	25	29	9	16
Figueroa, Nelson	0	1	2.79	2	0	10	9	3	9
Fiore, Tony	7	2	2.71	9	0	63	54	13	39
Freed, Mark	0	0	9.26	13	1	12	13	25	6
Hartmann, Pete	10	6	4.19	40	0	118	126	29	100
Jensen, Ryan	2	2	4.21	5	0	26	33	9	23
Lorraine, Andrew	2	1	3.12	9	0	43	55	13	19
Mahomes, Pat	11	4	3.87	21	0	140	145	42	74
Mann, Jim	0	2	11.57	7	0	12	18	8	7
Manning, David	2	0	4.32	8	1	17	13	4	11
Mannix, Kevin	2	1	4.06	38	1	89	87	35	51
Modica, Greg	3	2	3.48	5	0	34	31	8	15
2-team (6 Road Warriors)	4	3	3.61	11	0	67	55	24	43
Moss, Damian	0	5	7.67	6	0	29	33	19	27
Pizarro, Mel	0	0	6.75	3	0	4	6	0	4
Pulsipher, Bill	4	4	4.15	12	0	74	78	23	53
Runion, Tony	0	0	2.70	10	1	10	8	3	6
Tolar, Kevin	2	1	1.60	36	17	39	42	12	44
Young, Colin	1	0	18.90	5	0	3	10	3	4
Ziegler, Mike	1	3	7.13	4	0	18	21	9	5
2-team (6 Road Warriors)	2	5	3.98	10	0	43	39	15	21

NEWARK BEARS

BATTING	AVG	AB	R	H	2B	3B	HR	RBI	SB
Benjamin, Al, of	.269	357	44	96	23	3	12	53	8
2-team (16 AC)	.249	414	50	103	24	3	14	57	8
Booth, Jeremy, c	.245	53	8	13	5	0	3	8	0
Brunson, Matt, 2b	.286	220	44	63	5	0	2	9	16
Delgado, Dario, 1b	.250	228	27	57	17	0	7	33	1
Devore, Doug, of	.229	96	9	22	4	0	4	11	1
Hernandez, Alexis, 1b	.307	306	41	94	10	0	11	47	0
Herrera, Jose, of	.305	259	45	79	11	1	13	50	0
Maxwell, Keith, 1b	.153	59	7	9	2	0	1	4	0
Mendez, Donaldo, ss	.272	184	32	50	15	2	5	23	18
Miller, Orlando, 3b	.163	49	4	8	2	0	0	1	2
Moore, Mike, of	.240	125	15	30	6	0	5	14	2
Nathans, John, c	.162	37	5	6	1	0	1	3	0
Nava, Lipso, 3b	.239	188	20	45	8	2	7	31	1
Pennyfeather, Will, of	.288	364	51	105	19	0	13	65	7
Rodriguez, Liu, 2b	.318	214	36	68	8	1	2	11	1
Rodriguez, Vic, 3b	.371	186	27	69	20	0	6	33	0
Sanchez, Marcos, c	.226	31	3	7	1	0	0	3	0
Sanders, Anthony, of	.284	211	36	60	12	5	3	25	5
Santora, Jack, ss	.174	293	38	51	5	0	0	17	17
Steppe, Nicholas, of	.239	113	13	27	4	0	0	12	0
Thomas, Jonathan, c	.244	127	16	31	4	0	1	13	3
Torres, Chris, c	.222	99	8	22	3	0	3	19	0
Valencia, Vic, c	.233	227	34	53	11	1	17	40	3
Velez, Kelvyn, 2b	.100	20	3	2	0	0	0	0	0

PITCHING	W	L	ERA	G	SV	IP	H	BB	SO
Acosta, Domingo	1	2	9.37	15	0	16	23	9	10
2-team (26 AC)	7	6	5.22	41	2	59	68	20	46
Babula, Shaun	0	2	4.26	21	0	25	28	10	24
Babula, Shaun	0	2	4.28	24	0	27	31	12	26
Cedeno, Blas	0	1	43.20	2	0	2	6	3	1
Censale, Silvio	3	1	8.07	32	0	32	44	31	24
Cole, Joey	3	2	4.82	50	20	52	53	30	64
Cosgrove, Michael	0	7	9.75	9	0	36	57	12	19
Daneker, Pat	5	10	5.51	21	0	116	138	32	59
Delgado, Ernie	0	4	12.30	12	0	26	48	27	11
Gannon, Joe	6	11	5.11	27	0	153	143	96	101
Glick, David	0	1	6.57	10	0	12	11	8	8
Granado, Jan	1	1	7.77	5	0	22	33	11	14
Hill, Jeremy	7	5	3.62	56	3	65	56	30	46
Maness, Nick	2	2	5.35	19	0	34	30	17	17
Martinez, Samuel	0	0	16.43	6	0	8	15	7	2
Matos, Josue	0	1	2.31	2	0	12	7	6	8
Mendoza, Hatuey	0	2	6.31	12	0	26	30	12	17
Mirabal, Carlos	4	6	5.51	18	0	87	92	31	47
Pacheco, Enemencio	3	2	7.77	31	0	44	68	28	21
Rijo, Fernando	0	2	4.11	15	0	35	30	21	33

	AVG	AB	R	H	2B	3B	HR	RBI	SB
Robertson, Jeriome	0	0	2.25	2	0	12	11	5	15
Sauer, Marc	0	0	13.50	2	0	2	6	1	2
Shepard, David	5	14	5.18	28	0	158	182	41	96
Steppe, Nicholas	0	0	0.00	1	0	0	0	0	0
Torres, Chris	0	0	2.84	4	0	6	7	1	4
Wade, Travis	2	7	5.08	64	1	73	76	20	53

ROAD WARRIORS

BATTING	AVG	AB	R	H	2B	3B	HR	RBI	SB
Aracena, Sandy, c	.239	348	33	83	18	2	9	56	1
Barrows, Derek, ss	.241	373	25	90	10	4	4	37	1
Bryan, Jason, of	.210	381	43	80	17	1	9	43	1
Carrion, Jackson, 2b	.215	107	12	23	0	1	0	4	2
Fulse, Sheldon, of	.235	417	73	98	14	2	10	39	50
Goelz, Bryan, of	.228	162	15	37	4	2	3	14	3
Gonzalez, Bernie, of	.256	418	54	107	26	2	8	43	5
Housel, David, 3b	.203	177	17	36	9	0	0	13	4
2-team (33 AC)	.205	273	28	56	10	1	1	21	12
Huggins, Mike, 1b	.284	443	74	126	23	0	20	69	4
Jarosinski, Brian, of	.156	45	4	7	2	1	0	0	0
Martinez, Felix, ss	.271	181	23	49	9	3	2	26	9
Mejia, Manuel, c	.289	367	49	106	15	1	7	42	2
Nichols, Joe, 3b	.172	29	4	5	0	1	0	3	0
2-team (7 AC)	.122	41	7	5	0	1	0	3	0
Olivares, Teuris, 2b	.282	415	62	117	25	2	15	52	14
Ortiz, Nick, ss	.288	306	37	88	16	0	4	34	8
Sanchez, Marcos, c	.152	66	4	10	3	0	1	5	0
2-team (10 Newark)	.175	97	7	17	4	0	1	8	0

PITCHING	W	L	ERA	G	SV	IP	H	BB	SO
Baez, Benito	3	1	1.27	27	0	28	19	16	28
Burrows, Angelo	3	2	4.09	23	0	44	41	19	45
Castillo, Alberto	4	3	5.31	16	1	59	74	28	32
Clem, Christopher	1	1	7.50	15	0	18	26	7	12
Corrado, Tom	1	1	10.64	3	0	11	18	10	7
Eickhorst, Chris	1	15	5.44	25	0	134	150	90	88
Garay, Bernardo	0	0	19.29	3	0	5	12	7	2
Garay, Kelvin	0	0	7.71	2	0	2	4	1	1
Goldwater, Kyle	8	10	5.37	26	0	166	173	61	86
Gonzalez, Bernie	0	0	0.00	2	0	1	0	0	1
Guerrero, Julio	2	1	3.54	55	4	61	47	20	46
Herrera, Cesar	2	5	4.31	32	1	48	34	43	35
Marcotte, Trevor	0	0	1.80	4	0	10	6	4	11
Martinez, Feli	1	0	11.57	5	0	9	14	9	8
Martinez, Miguel	1	4	7.66	36	1	47	42	54	28
Miller, Brian	1	4	11.29	10	0	18	33	16	10
Modica, Greg	1	1	3.74	6	0	34	24	16	28
Nina, Elvin	2	3	4.13	11	0	57	55	23	45
Pizarro, Melvin	4	9	3.98	50	10	52	61	23	35
Rodriguez, Feli	0	0	6.00	6	0	9	3	11	3
Scheuing, Matt	6	11	6.45	20	0	105	157	44	55
Soto, Darwin	0	2	4.50	12	2	12	12	3	15
Steinborn, Chris	1	8	6.11	16	0	71	89	37	35
Young, Colin	0	0	1.72	9	0	16	9	3	12
2-team (24 Bridgeport)	2	0	5.47	38	0	51	62	19	37
Ziegler, Mike	1	2	1.78	6	0	25	18	6	16

SOMERSET PATRIOTS

BATTING	AVG	AB	R	H	2B	3B	HR	RBI	SB
Anderson, Travis, c	.248	339	43	84	18	1	3	34	2
Ayala, Elliott, of	.233	43	9	10	2	1	0	1	2
Barnes, Larry, of	.272	478	68	130	27	5	17	83	7
Booth, Jeremy, c	.077	13	0	1	0	0	0	0	0
2-team (19 Newark)	.212	66	8	14	5	0	3	8	0
Boran, Patrick, of	.229	354	45	81	18	0	3	23	17
Buckley, Jim, c	.211	76	5	16	2	0	2	7	0
Burt, James, 1b	.203	301	33	61	16	1	4	32	5
Clemente, Edgard, of	.265	68	13	18	4	0	3	5	1
Gsell, Tony, of	.168	101	9	17	4	0	3	15	2
Lockwood, Mike, of	.336	134	20	45	7	0	6	15	8
Lucca, Joe, 1b	.314	35	4	11	0	0	3	8	0
Lunar, Fernando, c	.193	212	14	41	9	0	2	18	2
McDermond, Ryan, c	.000	1	0	0	0	0	0	0	0
Nettles, Jeff, 3b	.277	383	67	106	26	0	21	69	2
Nicholson, Kevin, ss	.244	405	54	99	26	2	3	44	0
3Ortiz, Nick, ss	.326	86	10	28	3	1	1	13	4
3-team (6 LI, 78 RW)	.303	412	51	125	21	1	8	55	12
Radmanovich, Ryan, of	.302	334	70	101	24	0	27	66	0
Rojas, Tommy, c	.239	46	10	11	2	0	5	9	0
Sandberg, Jared, 1b	.206	34	2	7	1	1	1	6	0
Sandel, George, 2b	.230	400	27	92	12	0	2	41	3
Stanley, Henri, of	.261	272	50	71	13	6	5	21	11

PITCHING	W	L	ERA	G	SV	IP	H	BB	SO
Almonte, Hector	5	1	2.33	33	15	39	24	18	56
Averette, Robert	5	1	3.40	10	0	53	51	21	32

	W	L	ERA	G	SV	IP	H	BB	SO
Bierbrodt, Nick	0	1	10.38	6	0	4	7	8	3
Boran, Patrick	0	0	0.00	1	0	1	2	0	0
Crockett, Ben	8	11	3.51	27	0	164	178	31	113
Davis, Kane	0	0	4.20	13	1	15	16	12	20
Elder, Dave	2	4	4.39	20	1	41	42	22	50
Gsell, Tony	0	0	0.00	1	0	1	1	0	0
Johnson, Mike	5	4	4.34	34	9	37	39	8	42
Larson, Adam	0	1	13.50	3	0	2	4	1	1
Marquez, Robert	2	1	2.84	12	1	13	8	2	13
Mcconnell, Sam	1	4	3.79	12	0	74	81	14	43
Moser, Todd	6	6	4.27	27	0	97	102	34	58
Mounce, Tony	0	1	7.71	6	0	5	5	6	4
Olson, Jason	5	4	3.99	36	1	56	51	25	60
Pratt, Andy	3	1	5.81	25	0	31	39	11	21
Ramsey, Keith	6	7	3.76	24	0	156	157	37	96
Shiell, Jason	3	2	2.92	9	0	52	54	18	32
Solveson, Saul	5	4	3.11	42	0	46	42	19	21
Sylvester, Billy	3	1	2.48	11	0	58	39	29	65
Urban, Jeff	3	1	3.23	28	1	64	57	18	51
Van Hekken, Andy	3	6	5.56	13	0	81	91	18	64
Wechsler, Justin	0	1	8.00	9	0	9	13	9	7

CAN-AM LEAGUE

The Quebec Capitales used the motivation of a tough loss in 2005 to help push them to a title in 2006.

The Capitales had the best record in the Can-Am League in 2005 but were swept in the championship series by the Worcester Tornadoes. They won it in 2006, as Ed Montague singled in T.J. Simizu in the ninth inning to give the Capitales a 5-4 win in the deciding Game Five. Brockton had won two straight do-or-die games to tie the series at 2-2.

"When we played North Shore (in the Can-Am semifinals) we felt when we got ahead we were going to win the game," Quebec manager Michel Laplante told the Brockton Enterprise. "You can't have that feeling against Brockton. They reflect (manager) Chris Miyake's personality. They don't panic when they get behind. I have not been in many sudden-death games, but to me, there couldn't have been a better game."

The leader of the 2006 Capitales was a familiar face. Third baseman Eddie Lantigua, the 2005 Independent League Player of the Year, was the Can-Am's MVP for the second consecutive season. Lantigua led the league in batting (.343), on-base percentage (.424) and slugging percentage (.547).

STANDINGS

	W	L	PCT	GB
*North Shore	58	32	.644	—
New Haven	53	38	.582	5½
Brockton	49	43	.533	11
Quebec	44	44	.500	14
Worcester	41	49	.456	17
Nashua	40	48	.455	17
Sussex	32	58	.356	26

*First and second-half champion

PLAYOFFS: Semifinals—Quebec defeated North Shore and Brockton defeated New Haven 3-1 in best-of-5 series. **Finals**—Quebec defeated Brockton 3-2 in best-of-5 series.

ATTENDANCE: Brockton 157,462; Quebec 138,376; Worcester 116,712; North Shore 102,639; Sussex 85,126; New Jersey 89,385; New Haven County 62,356; Nashua 57,975.

MANAGERS: Brockton—Chris Miyake; **Nashua**—Butch Hobson; **New Haven County**—Mike Church; **New Jersey**—Joe Calfapietra; **North Shore**—John Kennedy; **Quebec**—Michel Laplante; **Sussex**—Brian Drahman; **Worcester**—Rich Gedman.

All-STAR TEAM: C—Alex Trezza, North Shore; **1B**—Vic Davilla, North Shore; **2B**—Ricardo Cordova, North Shore; **3B**—Eddie Lantigua, Quebec; **SS**—Chris Rowan, North Shore; **OF**—Josh Beauregard, Worcester; Horace Lawrence, New Haven County; Jason Tuttle, New Jersey; **DH**—Guye Senjem, Brockton. **LHP**—Bryan Morse, North Shore; **RHP**—Gabe Ribas, Quebec; **RP**—Kevin Fitzgerald, North Shore.

Player of the Year: Vic Davilla, North Shore. **Rookie Player of the Year:** Jeremy Terni, New Haven County. **Rookie Pitcher of the Year:** Shaun McNamara, North Shore. **Manager:** John Kennedy, North Shore.

INDIVIDUAL BATTING LEADERS

BATTER, TEAM	AVG	G	AB	R	H	HR	RBI
Lantigua, Eddie, Quebec	.343	83	300	55	103	11	61
Brooks, Jeff, NS	.319	86	323	38	103	7	53
Lawrence, Horace, NH	.318	87	311	48	99	5	41
Lindsey, John, NJ	.311	69	238	37	74	10	41
Grimes, Scott, Suss	.310	72	210	40	65	3	17
Cordova, Ricardo, NS	.306	80	288	33	88	5	41
Colabello, Chris, Worc	.305	90	344	52	105	7	58
Tuttle, Jason, NJ	.303	87	346	46	105	0	26
Davilla, Vic, NS	.299	88	321	56	96	12	61
Terni, Jeremy, NH	.295	71	261	36	77	8	42

INDIVIDUAL PITCHING LEADERS

PITCHER, TEAM	W	L	ERA	IP	H	BB	SO
Guerrero, Junior, Worc	9	4	1.89	105	90	44	79
Morse, Bryan, NS	11	5	2.16	117	103	25	87
Weagle, Matt, Worc	3	2	2.51	90	82	18	37
Viera, Rolando, Brock	9	7	2.65	126	113	48	110
Kelly, John, Brock	10	3	2.65	122	116	49	95
Valles, Rolando, NH	9	5	2.81	118	103	23	74
Ribas, Gabe, Quebec	10	3	2.84	133	115	30	106
Pavlik, Isaac, NJ	6	2	2.86	72	65	17	65
Bennett, Joel, NJ	7	3	2.91	96	79	27	85
Guy, Brad, Brock	9	5	2.93	153	149	20	75

BROCKTON ROX

BATTING	AVG	AB	R	H	2B	3B	HR	RBI	SB
Brachold, Keith, of	.200	180	28	36	4	2	5	22	9
Brunson, Matt, 2b	.224	67	7	15	3	0	0	4	2
Daubert, Jake, 1b	.221	113	8	25	10	0	1	12	2
George, Kyle, 2b-3B	1.000	1	0	1	0	0	0	0	0
Gulick, Travis, of	.132	38	2	5	1	0	0	4	0
Hough, Joe, of	.265	166	28	44	5	0	5	21	16
Julien, Eugene, of	.286	318	42	91	15	4	1	27	16
Keesee, David, 2b	.208	24	5	5	1	0	0	0	1
Larue, Jeff, 3b	.320	25	2	8	3	0	0	3	1
Lebron, Francisco, 1b	.322	236	38	76	19	0	7	40	0
2-team (24 Quebec)	.286	315	43	90	21	0	9	50	0
Medina, Junior, of	.000	3	1	0	0	0	0	0	0
Milbury, Joe, 3b	.200	10	0	2	0	0	0	2	0
Radwan, Jason, c	.282	319	45	90	16	1	10	51	5
Rosenblat, Brad, of	.237	274	37	65	13	3	8	31	13
Scanzano, Mike, ss	.278	313	51	87	13	0	0	29	9
Schmitz, John, of	.217	23	1	5	2	0	0	2	1
Senjem, Guye, of	.289	322	48	93	10	1	14	55	1
Strong, Zach, 3b	.211	171	22	36	5	0	2	17	6
2-team (21 Worcester)	.221	249	29	55	5	2	3	27	7
Torres, Mike, 2b	.267	318	28	85	21	2	1	30	7
Trupiano, Brian, 3b	.167	6	0	1	0	0	0	1	0
Williams, Simon, of	.200	80	9	16	3	2	1	11	2
Wong, Andrew, 2b	.000	1	1	0	0	0	0	0	0
Zacuto, Kris, of	.129	62	6	8	3	0	0	4	0

PITCHING	W	L	ERA	G	SV	IP	H	BB	SO
Averette, Robert	1	3	3.96	6	0	39	49	9	25
Baker, Joey	2	5	4.41	18	0	51	62	21	22
Boker, John	7	3	4.98	18	0	87	82	36	60
Carter, Eric	1	1	4.76	8	0	11	7	11	7
Daws, Josh	0	0	18.00	1	0	1	1	3	2
George, Kyle	3	3	3.43	33	3	42	41	22	37
Gonzalez, Santos	0	1	5.30	13	0	19	29	16	14
Guy, Brad	9	5	2.93	21	0	153	149	20	75
Henry, Mike	0	1	6.91	3	0	14	20	9	10
Kelly, John	8	1	1.92	15	1	89	78	32	71
2-team (6 New Jersey)	10	3	2.65	21	1	122	116	49	95
Koch, Jon	4	2	4.05	39	14	47	40	30	50
Lipson, David	0	0	9.00	1	0	1	3	0	1
Lundgren, Wayne	2	6	3.80	24	0	69	68	16	44
Morel, Edwin	1	0	2.50	8	1	18	26	4	12
Rispoli, Tom	0	1	3.38	11	0	16	18	8	13
Strong, Zach	0	0	0.00	3	0	2	1	1	0
Torres, Mike	0	0	18.00	1	0	1	4	0	1
Trevino, Chris	0	1	9.95	1	0	6	9	0	1
Viera, Rolando	9	7	2.65	21	0	126	113	48	110
Wylie, Jason	2	3	4.15	12	2	17	20	8	8

NASHUA PRIDE

BATTING	AVG	AB	R	H	2B	3B	HR	RBI	SB
Ayala, Elliott, of	.269	167	17	45	11	0	0	18	9
Baker, Jamie, of	.333	3	1	1	0	0	0	1	1
Baker, Steve, of	.187	75	7	14	1	0	0	4	4
Bass, Jayson, of	.353	85	26	30	6	1	6	15	9
Becher, William, 1b	.227	282	35	64	13	1	9	47	3

BATTING	AVG	AB	R	H	2B	3B	HR	RBI	SB
Bergeron, Jabe, of	.094	32	3	3	0	0	1	3	0
Bethea, Larry, dh	.308	117	22	36	5	1	8	26	3
Branch, George, of	.125	24	1	3	1	0	1	0	0
Brown, Mark, c	.133	60	2	8	1	0	0	1	0
Carter, Lenny, of	.000	8	1	0	0	0	0	0	0
Cordova, Ricardo, 2b	.340	53	6	18	2	0	1	2	6
Creighton, Jack, 2b	.000	5	0	0	0	0	0	0	0
Creighton, Tom, 2b	.257	319	41	82	12	1	3	28	15
Davis, Brett, 3b	.091	11	0	1	0	0	0	1	0
DePriest, Derrick, 1b	.000	2	0	0	0	0	0	0	0
Dillard, Andy, 3b	.283	269	40	76	12	2	5	33	6
Dobson, Sean, of	.274	288	39	79	14	1	1	32	14
Duplissie, Bryan, of	.250	180	26	45	11	0	4	18	3
Hamilton, Mark, of	.371	97	12	36	4	0	2	11	1
Hernandez, Alexis, c	.343	35	2	12	3	0	1	9	0
Johnson, Jared, of	.226	62	11	14	3	0	0	2	5
Johnson, Kade, c	.133	15	1	2	1	0	0	0	1
Kartler, Bryce, of	.375	8	1	3	2	0	0	1	0
Lofton, James, ss	.253	281	43	71	14	0	5	33	8
Miller, Bode, of	.000	2	0	0	0	0	0	0	0
Murray, Glenn, of	.234	171	33	40	10	0	5	31	5
Page, Miles, c	.316	19	2	6	0	0	0	1	0
Rojas, Tommy, c	.320	197	31	63	13	1	5	27	2
Shea, Elliot, of	.191	47	5	9	1	0	0	4	5
Stevens, Josh, of	.000	1	0	0	0	0	0	0	0
Thigpen, Josh, of	.200	5	1	1	0	1	0	1	0

PITCHING	W	L	ERA	G	SV	IP	H	BB	SO
Baker, Jamie	3	1	1.82	34	2	35	21	22	31
Blanton, Jason	2	1	5.12	35	0	39	50	25	33
Brown, Mark	0	0	13.50	1	0	1	3	0	0
Carter, Lenny	0	3	6.35	30	1	45	55	24	22
Connolly, Jon	1	0	1.29	1	0	7	2	1	8
Creighton, Jack	0	1	19.29	2	0	2	4	5	2
Davis, Vince	4	5	4.28	23	1	67	54	33	36
DePriest, Derrick	1	2	4.50	24	14	28	27	6	37
Duplissie, Bryan	0	0	7.80	4	0	15	25	7	5
Fuda, Giorgio	0	0	15.00	9	0	6	8	12	3
Goetz, Geoff	0	0	9.00	3	0	2	1	4	0
Hamilton, Mark	9	6	4.33	18	0	114	121	34	73
Jobin, Kevin	0	0	6.75	2	0	3	2	4	4
Johnson, Jared	0	0	0.00	1	0	1	1	0	0
Kartler, Bryce	0	0	5.00	10	0	9	7	10	13
Lavergne, Jarrad	2	6	4.91	10	0	44	49	29	30
2-team (8 North Shore)	4	8	4.43	18	0	85	95	51	59
Leclair, Aric	0	0	5.11	13	0	12	14	6	7
Lipson, David	0	2	6.55	7	0	11	9	8	4
Pahucki, David	0	1	18.00	5	0	3	5	8	3
Paul, Jason	2	3	3.51	23	0	49	41	21	31
Reichert, Dan	8	5	3.86	20	0	121	100	47	93
Shepard, Kevin	0	0	10.80	2	0	2	3	6	2
Slack, Nic	0	4	5.40	11	2	12	19	4	12
Stevens, Josh	5	3	4.46	13	0	71	89	8	55
Thigpen, Josh	0	1	8.41	5	0	20	18	20	14
Valdes, Raul	2	1	5.09	4	0	23	30	11	17
Wade, Terrell	1	1	12.34	3	0	12	27	4	11

NEW HAVEN COUNTY CROSS CUTTERS

BATTING	AVG	AB	R	H	2B	3B	HR	RBI	SB
Bailey, D.J., 2b	.271	96	19	26	5	1	0	9	5
Benes, Richie, 2b	.000	5	0	0	0	0	0	0	0
Boston, D.J., 1b	.333	48	8	16	4	0	2	13	0
Cirella, Eric, of	.250	4	1	1	0	0	0	0	0
DeLeon, Sandy, c	.310	116	15	36	6	0	0	14	4
Delgado, Jose, 2b	.249	325	50	81	15	2	2	27	32
Encarnacion, Orlando, of	.220	245	36	54	12	0	7	35	3
Esposito, Vinny, 3b	.226	31	2	7	1	0	0	0	0
Gaskin, Christopher, 1b	.268	127	15	34	8	0	3	18	3
Gibson, Derrick, of	.280	275	43	77	19	0	14	48	8
Hackney, Matt, c	.227	128	11	29	2	2	1	12	4
Lawrence, Horace, of	.318	311	48	99	15	4	5	41	24
Maduro, Jorge, c	.263	38	2	10	1	1	0	1	0
Mayo, Jeff, c	.087	23	1	2	0	0	0	0	0
Nettles, Marcus, of	.288	222	29	64	6	2	0	12	45
Story-Harden, Thomari, 2b	.249	229	27	57	13	0	8	41	3
Terni, Chas, ss	.247	275	42	68	19	0	6	36	1
Terni, Jeremy, 3b	.295	261	36	77	18	0	8	42	4
Valles, Rolando, of	.000	1	0	0	0	0	0	0	0
Vroman, Douglas, of	.217	189	21	41	8	1	1	18	6

PITCHING	W	L	ERA	G	SV	IP	H	BB	SO
Bonesio, Ryan	3	2	2.96	27	0	52	45	22	33
Comolli, Mark	2	0	1.79	36	1	50	38	24	40
Gonzalez, Saul	0	0	9.00	1	0	3	4	1	2
Hall, Courtney	5	4	3.61	19	0	110	102	46	86
Keinath, Tim	7	6	4.09	18	0	103	121	42	38
Knoff, Justin	9	5	3.16	30	1	80	67	23	72
Lawrence, Horace	0	0	0.00	1	0	0	0	1	0
Stawarz, Jarrett	6	5	5.46	24	0	86	94	37	61
Valles, Rolando	9	5	2.81	18	0	118	103	23	74
Vroman, Douglas	0	0	9.00	1	0	1	2	1	1
Weimer, Andrew	3	4	2.76	47	20	46	39	18	27
Whitworth, Brad	4	4	3.83	15	0	80	68	37	60
Willey, Cory	5	3	2.55	41	1	42	43	20	44

NEW JERSEY JACKALS

BATTING	AVG	AB	R	H	2B	3B	HR	RBI	SB
Baker, Casey, of	.130	23	3	3	1	0	0	0	0
Belcher, Jason, c	.286	213	34	61	13	0	4	31	1
Bellis, John, c	.000	2	1	0	0	0	0	0	0
Cordova, Ricardo, 2b	.346	81	11	28	7	0	1	16	3
Fernandez, Alex, of	.303	152	23	46	10	1	4	19	0
Gomes, Joey, of	.262	107	4	28	9	1	2	15	0
Howdeshell, Andy, 3b	.188	16	2	3	1	0	0	2	0
2-team (18 North Shore)	.099	81	10	8	1	0	0	4	0
Kartler, Bryce, of	.321	28	5	9	0	2	1	3	0
2-team (12 Nashua)	.333	36	6	12	2	2	1	4	0
Kuklick, Clay, c	.306	170	14	52	9	0	2	25	0
Lindsey, John, of	.311	238	37	74	20	0	10	41	0
Mihalics, Joseph, 2b	.251	267	43	67	9	4	1	27	4
Milsom, Geoff, of	.000	9	0	0	0	0	0	0	0
Nesbit, Mike, of	.333	63	14	21	4	0	0	7	5
Peavey, Bill, 1b	.264	303	44	80	13	0	8	45	1
Prosise, Nicholas, c	.000	4	0	0	0	0	0	0	0
Reyes, Guillermo, ss	.283	314	42	89	17	1	6	47	16
Santiago, Jayson, of	.250	4	1	1	0	0	0	0	0
Schade, Ryan, of	.067	15	0	1	1	0	0	0	0
Smithlin, Zach, of	.223	283	40	63	4	1	0	21	28
Tuttle, Jason, of	.303	346	46	105	10	2	0	26	21
Veras, Wilton, 3b	.258	325	47	84	23	0	3	46	1

PITCHING	W	L	ERA	G	SV	IP	H	BB	SO
Bennett, Joel	7	3	2.91	14	0	96	79	27	85
Brey, Josh	0	3	6.57	7	0	25	29	10	18
Brown, Jared	1	5	5.17	15	0	31	32	18	26
Dixon, Ryan	0	0	11.05	7	0	7	11	8	7
Espinal, Willy	0	0	5.86	24	1	28	34	14	23
Gaal, Bryan	0	1	19.29	1	0	2	8	1	0
Goodmann, Joe	0	0	7.11	6	0	6	6	6	6
Kartler, Bryce	0	0	5.00	10	0	9	7	10	13
Kelly, John	2	2	4.59	0	0	33	38	17	24
Mondesir, James	0	4	3.78	17	0	33	27	21	28
Myers, Aaron	4	9	6.70	18	0	86	92	28	49
Nikolic, Adam	2	0	3.86	31	0	37	29	28	52
Orloski, Joe	6	9	4.08	24	0	124	125	36	41
Pavlik, Isaac	6	2	2.86	12	0	72	65	17	65
Schwartz, Josh	2	2	2.54	14	0	28	19	13	20
Stanton, T.J.	0	1	6.75	2	0	11	14	3	3
Thomas, Jared	1	1	0.00	5	2	6	4	5	3
Tisch, Tim	0	0	4.05	5	0	7	8	4	0
Valdes, Raul	7	3	2.81	17	0	83	82	22	62
Vicaro, Michael	1	0	4.43	8	0	22	18	16	29
Wylie, Jason	4	3	6.57	24	7	25	27	11	24
2-team (12 Brockton)	6	6	5.57	36	9	42	47	19	32

NORTH SHORE SPIRIT

BATTING	AVG	AB	R	H	2B	3B	HR	RBI	SB
Anderson, Charlie, 1b	.000	4	0	0	0	0	0	0	0
Batz, Daniel, of	.235	34	6	8	1	0	0	7	0
Bensko, Dusty, ph	.000	1	0	0	0	0	0	1	0
Bethel, Ryan, of	.257	175	29	45	11	0	1	20	4
Brooks, Jeff, 1b	.319	323	38	103	22	1	7	53	0
Brown, Morgan, ss	.206	63	7	13	2	1	0	4	2
Cordova, Ricardo, 2b	.258	62	3	16	2	0	1	7	1
4-team (14 Nash., 24 Worc., 24 N.J.)	.306	288	33	88	15	3	5	41	16
Davilla, Vic, 1b	.299	321	56	96	18	1	12	61	3
DeVries, Jonathan, c	.203	128	12	26	3	0	2	13	0
Fischer, Rob, of	.292	72	17	21	2	0	3	10	7
Galemba, Leon, c	.000	2	0	0	0	0	0	0	0
Gray, Antoin, 3b	.367	30	3	11	1	0	1	8	0
Howdeshell, Andy, ss	.077	65	8	5	0	0	0	2	0
Reininger, Jarrett, 3b	.134	67	8	9	0	0	4	13	0
Rowan, Chris, ss	.273	231	40	63	14	4	8	35	3
Sabino, Luis, of	.245	200	27	49	9	4	1	19	11
Trezza, Alex, c	.259	259	39	67	17	0	19	44	0
Weed, Brian, of	.264	299	53	79	16	1	6	34	24
Weir, Garrett, of	.242	236	36	57	9	3	0	14	4
Whealy, Blake, 3b	.000	9	0	0	0	0	0	0	0
Wishy, Andrew, of	.270	307	46	83	27	0	7	44	3
Wolff, John, 3b-SS	.200	5	0	1	0	0	0	0	0

PITCHING	W	L	ERA	G	SV	IP	H	BB	SO
Bicondoa, Ryan	6	0	1.57	8	0	57	36	12	63
Bishop, Matthew	6	1	1.74	8	0	47	34	10	30
Brooks, Jake	0	2	19.64	3	0	4	9	5	0
Drown, Erik	3	1	2.01	12	0	22	13	17	27
Dugan, Tim	0	1	3.14	15	0	29	35	6	26
Farley, Chris	6	3	3.42	12	0	71	58	22	46
Fitzgerald, Kevin	0	1	2.14	42	27	42	30	16	36
Lavergne, Jarrad	2	2	3.92	8	0	41	46	22	29
McNamara, Shawn	5	0	2.15	10	0	46	37	20	27
Morse, Bryan	11	5	2.16	18	0	117	103	25	87
Rival, Kevin	1	0	1.40	12	0	19	11	4	25
Robinson, Dennis	5	4	2.28	30	2	59	55	14	34
Siak, Joey	8	7	3.22	18	0	117	119	21	62
Smith, Sam	2	0	1.93	2	0	14	14	2	7
Trout, Jared	3	5	4.18	23	0	80	84	38	46

QUEBEC CAPITALES

BATTING	AVG	AB	R	H	2B	3B	HR	RBI	SB
Bergeron, Mathieu, 1b	.253	217	22	55	7	1	7	36	2
Emond, Benoit, of	.194	144	19	28	6	0	0	16	8
Galemba, Leon, c	.000	2	0	0	0	0	0	0	0
Garcia, Alex, of	.206	175	16	36	1	1	0	14	9
Gunning, Matt, dh	.200	5	1	1	0	0	0	0	0
Huguet, JC, of	.000	3	0	0	0	0	0	0	0
James, Willie, ss	.215	284	41	61	8	0	0	15	29
Jensen, Marcus, 1b	.167	24	2	4	1	0	1	1	1
Kurhan, Mick, 3b	.150	40	1	6	3	0	0	7	0
Lamarche, Maxime, c	1.000	1	0	1	0	0	0	0	0
Lantigua, Eddie, 1b	.343	300	55	103	26	1	11	61	2
Lebron, Francisco, 1b	.177	79	5	14	2	0	2	10	0
Legare, Simon, of	.216	185	18	40	12	0	1	16	9
Lehr, Ryan, 3b	.250	92	12	23	3	1	1	16	2
2-team (40 Sussex)	.281	231	31	65	13	1	3	39	2
Lepine, Olivier, c	.235	268	31	63	11	0	7	31	2
Montague, Ed, of	.500	32	9	16	6	1	2	13	1
Scalabrini, Dany, 2b	.259	309	41	80	15	0	0	21	7
Shimizu, T.J., 2b	.244	127	21	31	3	2	0	13	11
Smith, Nestor, of	.293	157	22	46	10	0	2	26	4
Tomlinson, Goefrey, of	.276	337	61	93	19	7	2	44	19
Trainor, Nick, of	.197	61	7	12	1	1	2	6	3
Woodruff, Bud, c	.326	46	4	15	3	0	0	2	0

PITCHING	W	L	ERA	G	SV	IP	H	BB	SO
Beavers, Kevin	4	4	5.92	10	0	49	60	17	32
Benson, Jason	0	0	16.50	3	0	6	17	5	1
Cyr, Eric	1	0	0.00	1	0	8	2	0	4
DeMontigny, Mathieu	1	1	6.48	2	0	8	13	1	3
Dumesnil, Brian	0	0	1.80	14	1	15	14	2	13
Dunn, Keith	6	11	4.25	18	0	112	118	27	67
Forbes, Terry	0	0	27.00	1	0	0	2	1	0
Gomez, Deibis	0	1	5.52	6	0	15	21	3	4
Hernandez, Juan	2	0	4.50	2	0	4	3	5	4
Huguet, J.C.	0	0	0.00	2	0	7	4	3	7
Kemlo, Chris	0	2	12.75	4	0	12	24	8	7
Kurhan, Mick	0	0	0.00	1	0	2	1	0	2
Lang, Blair	1	0	5.04	14	0	25	20	15	18
Laplante, Michel	0	0	6.75	1	0	4	5	1	4
Lipson, David	0	0	10.13	1	0	3	1	4	3
3-team (7 Nashua, 1 Brockton)	0	2	7.36	9	0	15	13	12	8
Major, Marc	3	5	3.71	18	0	53	42	30	52
Mendoza, Cristian	3	1	2.12	32	16	34	26	7	40
Ough, Wayne	1	2	4.70	3	0	15	19	7	16
Pello, Brandon	3	1	1.80	10	0	15	14	6	6
Perez, Jorge	0	1	1.93	2	0	14	13	3	13
Pilkington, Jason	4	2	2.93	23	0	55	56	24	47
Purcell, Brad	2	4	5.85	11	0	48	51	20	15
Ribas, Gabe	10	3	2.84	20	0	133	115	30	106
Ryan, Shawn	1	1	3.88	20	0	51	25	47	40
Stanton, T.J.	1	0	1.00	4	1	9	2	3	11
2-team (2 New Jersey)	1	1	4.12	6	1	20	16	6	14
Tucker, Julien	1	5	5.87	10	0	54	70	20	23

SUSSEX SKYHAWKS

BATTING	AVG	AB	R	H	2B	3B	HR	RBI	SB
Agramonte, Marcos, 2b	.287	310	35	89	12	2	1	31	21
Alcott, Jason, c	.218	110	6	24	3	0	0	9	0
Ayala, Abraham, c	.268	224	22	60	8	0	1	27	0
Booth, Jeremy, 1b	.222	63	1	14	2	0	0	7	0
Cabrera, Mayke, 3b	.264	106	9	28	4	0	0	6	1
Cooper, James, of	.272	345	63	94	21	5	3	32	22
Corporan, Elvis, 3b	.226	243	32	55	15	0	4	37	1
Daly, Rich, 1b	.217	295	31	64	15	1	7	49	0
Grimes, Scott, of	.310	210	40	65	10	2	3	17	2
Gutierrez, Jose, of	.375	8	3	3	1	0	0	1	1

BATTING	AVG	AB	R	H	2B	3B	HR	RBI	SB
Kinsolving, Darin, of	.201	139	9	28	3	0	0	10	0
Lehr, Ryan, 1b	.302	139	19	42	10	0	2	23	0
LeNoir, Bobby, ss	.265	344	47	91	12	2	3	39	13
Martinez, Candido, of	.143	28	2	4	0	0	0	1	0
Mears, Magic, 2b	.156	45	6	7	3	1	0	3	0
Ury, Josh, of	.269	357	45	96	14	4	2	37	6

PITCHING	W	L	ERA	G	SV	IP	H	BB	SO
Brooks, Jake	1	1	5.40	9	2	10	11	2	7
Campos, David	0	1	10.22	5	0	12	15	18	10
Correa, Jose	7	4	3.75	20	0	86	86	31	74
Ford, Brian	5	7	4.02	18	0	101	115	36	41
Gault, Joe	2	3	5.24	16	1	34	32	25	26
Greenhouse, Michael	1	6	5.70	12	0	54	66	24	35
Hawk, Derek	0	6	5.31	18	0	61	66	34	45
Howell, Michael	1	0	4.20	5	0	15	17	4	7
Jimenez, Elvis	0	1	2.25	16	0	24	26	11	22
Mincks, Lincoln	1	9	5.09	17	0	106	147	30	43
Musialowski, Jay	0	2	10.50	4	0	6	13	2	2
Olsen, Kevin	4	0	2.45	6	0	33	30	4	28
Perez, Julio	4	4	3.28	34	7	47	44	12	50
Price, Reid	0	1	1.69	7	0	16	13	6	10
Renery, Mike	0	1	16.20	3	0	3	5	5	4
Smith, Alex	1	1	5.52	14	0	29	36	19	15
Tierney, Christopher	1	2	3.06	6	0	18	12	9	15
Tisch, Tim	1	5	7.29	10	0	42	52	26	22
2-team (5 New Jersey)	1	5	6.84	15	0	49	60	30	22
Upwood, Jake	0	2	7.71	15	1	19	23	15	13
Ury, Josh	0	0	3.00	2	0	3	4	0	1
Zallie, Chris	3	2	2.48	8	0	40	34	17	27

WORCESTER TORNADOES

BATTING	AVG	AB	R	H	2B	3B	HR	RBI	SB
Beauregard, Josh, of	.274	351	63	96	15	8	6	42	22
Beauregard, Keith, of	.228	228	23	52	3	0	0	22	7
Bergeron, Jabe, of	.262	141	12	37	10	0	1	16	0
Colabello, Chris, 1b	.305	344	52	105	26	2	7	58	4
Cordova, Ricardo, ss	.283	92	13	26	4	3	2	16	6
Frawley, Tucker, 2b	.222	90	11	20	0	0	0	9	2
Lahair, Jeff, 2b	.255	274	33	70	12	1	2	34	7
Laurent, Phillip, of	.083	24	1	2	0	0	0	0	0
Lemieux, Jared, of	.250	16	3	4	0	0	0	0	1
Loiseau, Scott, 2b	.186	43	4	8	1	1	0	2	0
Mercado, Oni, c	.263	179	17	47	13	1	4	25	1
Montalbano, Greg, c	.000	1	0	0	0	0	0	0	0
Page, Miles, c	.170	47	5	8	3	0	0	4	0
Pena, Alex, of	.400	15	3	6	1	0	1	3	0
Perry, Patrick, c	.246	122	16	30	2	0	0	11	1
Reynoso, Danilo, c	.077	26	0	2	0	0	0	2	0
Rios, Brian, 3b	.246	114	9	28	5	1	1	15	1
Rodriguez, Marcos, of	.200	30	5	6	1	0	0	7	0
Shank, Chris, of	.333	3	0	1	0	0	0	1	0
Shea, Elliot, of	.356	59	8	21	5	0	2	9	2
Strong, Zach, 3b	.244	78	7	19	0	2	1	10	1
Taylor, Lucas, of	.213	239	44	51	6	1	0	18	32
Tewksbary, Bob, ss	.234	188	31	44	12	4	1	19	4
Wasserman, Austin, of	.261	203	34	53	11	3	0	20	4

PITCHING	W	L	ERA	G	SV	IP	H	BB	SO
Byard, David	1	6	4.93	33	6	38	47	19	27
Guerrero, Junior	9	4	1.89	18	0	105	90	44	79
Jimenez, Elvis	3	3	5.46	13	0	28	32	18	15
Mahan, Dallas	2	2	4.74	29	2	44	47	13	29
Mattox, D.J.	2	9	4.83	18	0	91	102	62	71
Meagher, Mike	1	7	4.47	24	0	44	58	24	35
Merchant, Jamie	3	1	2.22	28	5	53	41	17	51
Montalbano, Greg	5	3	1.80	13	0	55	43	14	46
Pena, Alex	6	4	3.08	20	1	111	100	49	75
Shank, Chris	2	3	3.91	27	1	48	54	21	48
Weagle, Matt	3	2	2.51	23	2	90	82	18	37
Willett, Reid	4	5	6.42	20	0	69	89	31	53

FRONTIER LEAGUE

The Evansville Otters couldn't say they were the most dominant team in the Frontier League, but the Otters did have a knack for winning at the right times.

Evansville finished the regular season with a 46-50 record, but sneaked into the playoffs as a wild card because only one of the four teams in the West finished with a winning record.

The Otters then dropped their first two games of their first-round playoff series against Rockford, won the next two, then found themselves trailing 3-2 with two outs in the ninth of the deciding game. But Frank Scott drew a walk, moved to second on a wild pitch and scored on an error. The Otters ended up winning 6-3 in the 13th.

After that, the championship series was anticlimactic. Evansville swept Chillicothe in three games for their first league title. DH Jeff Goldbach was named the series MVP.

Ian Church was named the league MVP after he led all independent leagues with 31 home runs.

STANDINGS

NORTH DIVISION	W	L	PCT	GB
*Bridgeport	75	49	.605	
&Long Island	73	51	.589	2
Newark	42	83	.336	34
Road Warriors	42	83	.336	34
SOUTH DIVISION	**W**	**L**	**PCT**	**GB**
*&Lancaster	75	51	.595	
Atlantic City	69	57	.548	6
Somerset	65	61	.516	10
Camden	61	65	.484	14

&First-half champion. *Second-half champion.

Playoffs—Semifinals: Lancaster defeated Atlantic City 2-0 and Bridgeport defeated Long Island 2-0 in best-of-three series. **Finals:** Lancaster defeated Bridgeport 3-0 in best-of-five series.

MANAGERS: Atlantic City—Jeff Ball; **Bridgeport**—Dave LaPoint; **Camden**—Wayne Krenchicki; **Lancaster**—Tom Herr; **Long Island**—Don McCormack; **Newark**—Chris Jones; **Road Warriors**—Jeff Scott; **Somerset**—Sparky Lyle.

ATTENDANCE: Long Island 419,150; Lancaster 370,176; Somerset 362,585; Camden 253,013; Bridgeport 193,096; Newark 178,132; Atlantic City 134,900.

ALL-STAR TEAM: C—John Pachot, Camden; **1B**—Mike Huggings, Road Warriors; **2B**—Steve Hine, Bridgeport; **3B**—Jeff Nettles, Somerset; **SS**—Raul Marval, Atlantic City; **OF**—Ryan Radmanovich, Somerset; Mel Stocker, Long Island; Reggie Taylor, Lancaster; Denny Abreu, Camden. **DH**—Bucky Jacobsen, Long Island. **Util**—Joe Jiannetti, Atlantic City. **SP**—Denny Harriger, Lancaster; Lincoln Mikkelsen, Atlantic City. **RP**—Chris Fussell, Camden.

Player of the Year: Lincoln Mikklesen, Atlantic City. **Manager of the Year:** Dave LaPoint, Bridgeport.

INDIVIDUAL BATTING LEADERS

Batter, Team	AVG	G	AB	R	H	HR	RBI
Abreu, Denny, Cam	.323	105	396	70	128	15	56
Jiannetti, Joe, AC	.319	119	439	67	140	21	79
Hine, Steve, Bridge	.315	115	391	70	123	10	64
Cruz, Deivi, Bridge	.307	90	368	57	113	9	63
Stocker, Mel, LI	.303	110	442	87	134	3	39
Ortiz, Nick, Somer	.303	110	412	51	125	8	55
Taylor, Reggie, Lanc	.302	115	430	87	130	23	77
Almonte, Erick, LI	.302	111	404	73	122	9	77
Radmanovich, Ryan, Somer	.302	98	334	70	101	27	66
Marval, Raul, AC	.298	124	490	88	146	17	73

INDIVIDUAL PITCHING LEADERS

Pitcher, Team	W	L	ERA	IP	H	BB	SO
Mikkelsen, Lincoln, AC	15	5	1.85	175	127	46	122
Harriger, Denny, Lanc	17	4	2.63	181	191	29	82
Hodges, Kevin, Bridge	12	7	3.01	137	147	43	70
Difelice, Mark, Camden	12	9	3.19	158	163	24	132
Powell, Greg, Camden	5	11	3.22	142	147	40	74
Persails, Mark, AC	7	5	3.43	139	127	60	116
Ahearne, Pat, LI	12	4	3.47	156	176	28	105
Crockett, Ben, Camden	8	11	3.51	164	178	31	113
Costello, Ryan, Camden	7	9	3.62	159	154	56	95
McDonald, Jon, Camden	8	7	3.64	134	157	35	50

CHILLICOTHE PAINTS

BATTING	AVG	AB	R	H	2B	3B	HR	RBI	SB
Barganier, Brandon, of	.241	203	23	49	6	4	2	16	4
Baywal, Tim, 1b-of	.224	49	3	11	6	0	0	5	0
Brotherton, Jeremy, 2b	.130	77	8	10	1	0	0	4	2
Cantu, Adrian, 3b	.259	259	32	67	16	0	6	37	3
Clifford, Travis, dh	.250	4	0	1	0	0	0	0	0
Colopy, Brian, 3b	.269	223	40	60	9	1	3	22	4
Cooksey, Matt, of	.282	181	44	51	6	0	1	13	28
Dixon, D.J., c	.158	38	3	6	0	0	1	2	0
Drabek, Justin, 2b	.200	60	4	12	0	0	0	2	1
Funaro, Jeff, c	.252	111	8	28	5	0	1	12	3
Garcia, Travis, ss	.289	350	48	101	26	1	11	66	7

	AVG	AB	R	H	2B	3B	HR	RBI	SB
Gonzalez, Eddie, c	.176	74	4	13	2	0	2	11	0
2-team (27 River City)	.199	166	12	33	3	0	3	19	1
Graves, T.J., 3b	.000	5	0	0	0	0	0	1	0
2-team (25 River City)	.259	147	24	38	9	0	3	18	2
Grullon, Leo, of	.284	67	9	19	4	0	1	9	1
Johnson, Taylor, of	.269	78	12	21	3	1	4	20	3
2-team (64 Gateway)	.299	321	50	96	28	1	7	56	13
Kane, Ryan, of	.272	92	15	25	0	2	0	4	10
Martin, Steve, of	.207	111	12	23	6	0	1	10	2
Mendoza, Jaziel, 1b	.200	145	20	29	4	1	3	21	2
Parrish, Jeff, c	.211	175	20	37	7	1	5	19	3
Paterson, Tommy, of	.143	21	2	3	1	0	0	0	0
Rafferty, Ryan, 1b	.143	7	0	1	0	0	0	0	0
Ramistella, John, of	.283	314	61	89	20	4	13	60	41
Richards, Jud, 1b	.217	69	3	15	3	0	0	3	0
Rutgers, Paul, 2b	.285	281	42	80	12	3	7	36	14
Sellers, Daniel, of	.158	19	4	3	0	0	0	3	3

PITCHING	W	L	ERA	G	SV	IP	H	BB	SO
Baywal, Tim	0	0	36.00	1	0	1	3	1	0
Beans, Shane	0	0	13.50	2	0	1	3	2	0
Cavanaugh, Nick	2	1	2.24	28	8	64	38	34	88
Coffey, Andrew	3	2	3.00	7	0	33	33	20	20
Cunningham, Perry	9	6	2.30	20	0	129	95	33	83
Drabek, Justin	1	1	1.32	5	0	14	13	6	8
Flanigan, Ryan	0	0	5.40	7	0	10	12	5	2
Harrison, Shea	0	0	5.40	1	0	3	6	1	3
Hartfelder, Kurt	10	5	1.67	18	0	118	103	27	67
Hines, Jacob	2	3	5.00	11	0	45	57	29	18
Jackson, Drew	2	1	1.93	6	1	19	10	7	22
2-team (32 Florence)	6	2	2.47	38	5	69	46	33	75
Johnson, Bryan	1	1	0.00	7	1	8	3	4	9
Juske, Ted	0	0	6.75	2	0	1	4	1	0
2-team (19 Gateway)	3	1	5.16	21	0	23	23	19	18
Lipson, David	0	0	10.80	2	0	2	2	4	1
Lovell, Ben	3	2	3.19	20	0	48	39	21	26
Martinez, John	5	0	2.09	9	0	39	34	10	17
2-team (4 Windy City)	5	4	3.59	13	0	63	60	19	25
Meigs, Tyler	0	1	5.84	9	0	12	8	8	11
Moenter, Curtis	2	1	4.05	5	0	20	13	12	14
2-team (32 Florence)	10	7	2.75	37	7	85	65	51	75
Morgan, Lavelle	3	3	3.05	8	0	41	30	19	36
Palmer, Lucas	4	3	3.04	24	1	92	73	41	73
Plouffe, Marshall	5	2	2.54	41	3	57	44	22	42
Puskar, Dallas	0	0	2.70	2	1	3	1	2	0
Putman, Rickey	0	0	6.23	4	0	4	9	3	3
Rafferty, Ryan	2	2	7.50	17	0	18	20	21	17
Ramistella, John	0	0	0.00	1	0	0	0	0	0
Teall, Eric	4	3	1.96	34	14	46	30	12	49

EVANSVILLE OTTERS

BATTING	AVG	AB	R	H	2B	3B	HR	RBI	SB
Balkan, Adam, of	.087	23	1	2	0	0	0	1	0
2-team (55 Windy City)	.246	183	14	45	4	0	0	20	2
Berry, Vince, of	.000	4	1	0	0	0	0	1	0
Blacken, Beau, of	.279	247	32	69	12	1	4	34	3
Bubalo, Ty, c	.200	50	6	10	1	0	2	9	2
Burgess, Tim, of	.243	37	2	9	3	0	0	2	0
Burnau, Ryan,	1.000	1	0	1	0	0	0	0	0
Clinton, Ricky, c	.203	118	10	24	4	1	0	11	1
Cook, Riley, of	.375	16	1	6	0	0	0	2	1
Desmond, Geoff, 1b	.167	6	1	1	0	0	0	0	0
2-team (36 River City)	.203	123	20	25	4	0	4	21	1
Edwards, Jeff, 3b	.300	327	51	98	26	4	12	54	3
Funaro, Jeff, c	.310	29	3	9	2	0	3	6	1
2-team (45 Chillicothe)	.264	140	11	37	7	0	4	18	4
Galloway, Mike, of	.233	86	11	20	1	0	1	8	0
2-team (44 Florence)	.277	253	38	70	9	0	4	37	3
Goldbach, Jeff, 1b	.306	353	56	108	21	1	17	69	11
Heffron, Aaron, of	.243	169	22	41	7	5	6	23	1
Hickey, Jon, 3b	.125	8	1	1	0	0	0	0	1
Jacobs, Elliot, of	.105	19	2	2	0	0	0	0	0
McKenna, Brian, ss	.258	337	40	87	12	0	2	26	3
Milsom, Geoff, 3b-OF	.038	26	1	1	1	0	0	0	0
Mueller, Dale, of	.245	335	34	82	7	0	1	24	27
Pennino, Tom, c	.190	147	10	28	3	0	2	8	0
Prady, Ricky, of	.154	26	1	4	0	0	0	2	0
Rembert, Grant, of	.258	124	16	32	3	0	1	16	2
Scott, Frank, 2b	.246	338	57	83	8	1	0	22	21
Shaffer, Eric,	.000	4	0	0	0	0	0	0	0
Smith, Kyle, 3b	.221	149	16	33	5	0	1	9	7
Spry, Michael, of	.236	148	19	35	7	1	4	33	1
Stewart, Josh, of	.200	50	7	10	2	0	1	2	0
Stone, Nathan,	1.000	1	0	1	1	0	0	0	0

INDEPENDENT LEAGUES

PITCHING	W	L	ERA	G	SV	IP	H	BB	SO
Abrams, Casey	0	2	6.75	4	0	21	25	10	15
Arnold, Nathan	2	0	1.37	4	0	26	20	4	14
Bille, Michael	2	5	2.01	41	20	45	35	19	47
Blackard, Cody	5	5	3.44	13	0	71	76	23	34
Bolton, Dustin	0	0	0.00	1	0	4	4	4	4
Brazell, Landon	3	5	4.44	15	0	81	73	53	58
Burnau, Ryan	5	4	1.37	31	0	46	21	15	50
Del Prete, Anthony	1	2	2.25	30	0	44	46	14	30
Foster, Ben	1	1	6.17	2	0	12	10	6	8
Gillis, Chad	1	1	6.11	7	0	18	19	7	9
Greenhouse, Michael	3	2	3.73	6	0	31	29	16	17
Haggerty, Jake	5	4	3.67	20	0	98	97	52	68
Johnson, Donnie	2	0	1.80	4	0	5	2	2	4
Langdon, Donny	3	3	2.74	30	1	49	38	17	65
Mueller, Dale	0	0	0.00	1	0	1	2	1	1
Pawelczyk, Kyle	1	2	2.84	11	0	19	18	5	25
Pillsbury, Chris	6	4	2.71	18	0	110	112	53	96
Restivo, Matt	5	5	3.16	15	0	88	93	36	58
Shaffer, Eric	0	1	4.46	12	0	36	36	16	43
Souther, Scott	0	0	3.60	1	0	5	4	3	3
Stone, Nathan	1	4	3.66	21	0	32	32	17	14

FLORENCE FREEDOM

BATTING	AVG	AB	R	H	2B	3B	HR	RBI	SB
Abbott, Chad, c	.308	13	1	4	0	0	0	1	0
Allen, Trevor, of	.200	35	6	7	1	0	0	3	0
Blacken, Beau, of	.229	70	9	16	4	0	1	11	1
2-team (74 Evansville)	.268	317	41	85	16	1	5	45	4
Brown, Chris, of	.284	169	22	48	10	0	2	25	3
Buscher, Gregory, 3b	.252	143	15	36	10	0	5	25	1
Chauncey, Clint, c	.197	279	28	55	8	1	5	25	3
Connor, Nick, of	.253	154	20	39	6	1	1	11	2
Cooksey, Matt, of	.304	69	11	21	2	1	0	8	10
2-team (64 Chillicothe)	.288	250	55	72	8	1	1	21	38
Draska, Chris, of	.400	10	1	4	2	0	0	0	0
Galloway, Mike, of	.299	167	27	50	8	0	3	29	3
Geswein, Kyle, 1b	.210	309	35	65	14	0	9	42	1
Hall, Trevor, 1b	.245	110	10	27	4	0	1	4	0
Hanson, Ryan, c	.216	37	6	8	2	0	0	5	0
Hiter, Nick, c	.125	8	1	1	0	0	0	2	0
Holland, Joe, 2b	.235	34	3	8	0	0	0	2	0
Hurst, Jason, of	.207	111	11	23	1	0	3	16	1
Kim, Eddie, 1b	.190	121	14	23	1	0	1	6	0
2-team (47 River City)	.264	295	44	78	13	0	6	32	1
McGheehan, Conor, 1b-C	.333	3	1	1	0	0	0	1	0
Novotny, Jerred, of	.115	26	3	3	1	0	1	1	0
Quigg, Wally, of	.232	314	29	73	12	1	1	30	2
Sanchez, Josh, ss	.204	280	23	57	10	0	0	21	2
Stone, Greg, 3b	.275	342	41	94	14	1	2	34	13
Vetter, Scott, 2b	.250	20	1	5	0	0	0	1	0
Watson, Reggie, of	.271	277	43	75	13	5	1	21	27

PITCHING	W	L	ERA	G	SV	IP	H	BB	SO
Adkins, Luke	0	2	7.46	5	0	25	36	10	14
Bowlin, Jason	5	9	3.28	19	0	129	107	46	71
Burris, Bob	0	0	23.14	3	0	2	5	3	2
Castle, Cody	2	1	2.34	26	2	42	37	20	31
Church, B.J.	4	5	3.30	15	0	76	62	37	54
Clayton, Patrick	0	0	6.43	6	0	7	3	14	9
DeMark, Mike	1	4	3.22	41	1	64	44	30	59
Easton, Aaron	0	1	11.37	4	0	6	12	9	6
Eger, Mark	0	0	0.00	1	0	0	0	1	0
Freedman, Coogie	0	1	13.50	3	0	2	5	0	1
Geswein, Kyle	0	0	0.00	1	0	1	0	0	1
Goins, Mitch	7	7	3.95	20	0	121	128	44	61
Jackson, Drew	4	1	2.66	32	4	51	36	26	53
Laycock, Keegan	0	0	27.00	1	0	1	4	0	1
Leatherwood, Chase	1	2	6.10	11	0	21	21	13	9
Lovell, Ben	1	3	6.11	5	0	18	33	7	10
2-team (20 Chillicothe)	4	5	3.97	25	0	66	72	28	36
Moenter, Curtis	8	6	2.35	32	7	65	52	39	61
Parfett, Rob	0	0	9.95	4	0	6	10	1	2
Payton, Grant	1	2	9.00	5	0	17	25	11	12
Roelle, Justin	0	3	8.10	6	0	17	20	9	6
Rosell, Rick	0	0	5.87	12	0	15	17	12	12
Thomas, Steve	0	0	3.86	2	0	2	3	3	3
Troop, Jon	1	1	3.50	25	1	44	39	26	35
Watts, Joey	2	4	4.68	9	0	33	31	18	14
Webb, Chris	1	6	3.99	11	0	65	59	36	29
3-team (7 Kalamazoo, 3 RC)	2	8	5.19	21	0	85	93	45	40

GATEWAY GRIZZLIES

BATTING	AVG	AB	R	H	2B	3B	HR	RBI	SB
Arnold, David, of	.254	138	28	35	5	1	3	21	12
2-team (5 River City)	.247	150	29	37	5	1	3	21	14
Arrowood, Jason, c	.260	204	18	53	9	0	2	20	1
Bransfield, Matt, 3b	.228	127	18	29	4	0	2	9	0
Breyman, Mike, 1b	.310	294	48	91	17	2	12	55	2
Colbert, Justin, 3b	.221	95	12	21	3	1	0	2	3
Colvin, Brooks, ss	.221	280	45	62	8	2	3	27	3
Derhak, Alex, c	.140	43	6	6	2	0	0	1	1
Garrett, Matt, of	.200	5	1	1	0	0	0	0	1
Gilbert, Gary, 3b	.220	59	3	13	4	0	0	5	0
Gilliam, Bobby, of	.286	98	14	28	2	0	0	10	4
Hopkins, Trave, c	.308	13	1	4	0	0	0	0	0
House, Kevin, of	.263	179	32	47	7	2	5	19	20
Isaacson, Greg, 2b	.274	361	47	99	27	2	4	49	7
Johnson, Taylor, of	.309	243	38	75	25	0	3	36	10
Lopez, Freddy, of	.238	277	28	66	8	0	8	35	2
Martin, Mike, c	.176	17	1	3	1	0	0	4	0
Rafferty, Ryan, 1b	.143	7	0	1	0	0	0	0	0
Roberts, Dustin, of	.275	218	29	60	11	2	11	41	3
Sellers, Daniel, of	.205	73	4	15	0	1	0	1	3
2-team (8 Chillicothe)	.196	92	8	18	0	1	0	4	6
Stevens, Greg, c	.292	72	12	21	5	1	2	8	1
Stewart, Alex, 3b	.158	57	5	9	0	0	0	2	1
Wirth, Robert, 3b	.296	270	43	80	12	0	12	44	2

PITCHING	W	L	ERA	G	SV	IP	H	BB	SO
Barriger, Marcus	0	0	2.92	9	0	12	15	9	9
Basta, E.J.	1	2	5.73	6	0	11	11	5	12
Blumberg, Rob	0	0	13.00	6	0	9	13	9	5
Brewer, Dale	0	0	18.00	4	0	4	9	7	1
Castorri, Christian	3	4	4.89	23	1	53	57	15	41
Dessau, Erik	6	7	3.97	18	0	113	116	35	74
Galle, Andy	1	1	5.19	5	0	9	9	6	5
Hagan, Ian	0	0	63.00	1	0	1	7	2	0
Himes, Andrew	2	2	3.18	7	0	40	40	7	20
Juske, Ted	3	1	5.06	19	0	21	19	18	18
Little, Chris	3	2	2.78	14	0	58	51	23	40
Mayfield, Brian	0	1	7.47	15	0	16	15	17	9
Mlotkowski, Mike	3	0	2.78	4	0	23	22	20	23
2-team (15 Windy City)	5	6	4.05	19	0	96	90	68	83
Nicholson, Scott	3	0	5.83	18	1	42	46	22	37
Pennington, Todd	1	2	4.15	26	17	30	25	17	32
Rafferty, Ryan	1	0	0.00	11	7	14	4	5	23
2-team (17 Chillicothe)	3	2	4.18	28	7	32	24	26	40
Rasmussen, Jordan	0	1	7.71	3	0	12	17	4	8
Rebyanski, Anthony	2	4	3.62	19	1	27	17	19	36
Roush, Nathan	6	5	3.49	19	1	119	99	38	73
2-team (19 Windy City)	1	3	3.34	25	0	35	30	33	43
Russo, Noah	0	1	6.00	6	0	12	11	14	14
Soja, Steve	8	7	3.55	20	0	129	134	41	54
Stapleton, Chilion	0	4	9.77	5	0	16	21	22	12
Stein, Todd	2	5	6.38	10	0	42	54	23	27

KALAMAZOO KINGS

BATTING	AVG	AB	R	H	2B	3B	HR	RBI	SB
Baker, Casey W., ss	.247	186	35	46	2	1	6	14	13
Baker, Casey C., of	.333	264	30	88	18	2	2	25	7
Blakeley, Damian, c	.000	7	1	0	0	0	0	1	0
Carroll, Justin, c	.282	316	51	89	19	1	13	44	0
Church, Ian, of	.317	379	77	120	38	1	31	78	5
Eastman, Trevor, c	.204	147	9	30	5	0	0	8	0
Gill, Ray, 1b	.244	295	37	72	10	0	19	64	1
Hughes, Michael, 1b	.219	96	12	21	2	2	2	13	0
Johnson, Jared, 3b	.217	115	10	25	6	0	0	10	3
Kmiecik, Lee, 2b	.252	210	15	53	7	0	3	24	5
Krohn, Jason, ss	.222	9	2	2	1	0	0	1	0
Leavitt, Adam, 2b	.236	267	33	63	7	3	4	20	10
Mezistrano, Lee, dh	.222	9	3	2	0	0	0	0	0
Pirman, Pete, of	.286	360	58	103	25	1	11	46	27
Ramos, Joseph, 3b	.283	318	50	90	14	5	8	37	29
Russell, Mike, c	.262	126	24	33	10	0	8	23	0
Ryan, Tim, of	.000	2	0	0	0	0	0	0	0
Shick, Cameron, of	.133	15	2	2	0	0	1	5	0
Thompson, Lance, of	.182	11	1	2	1	0	0	1	0
Wolff, John, ss	.207	111	13	23	1	1	1	6	0

PITCHING	W	L	ERA	G	SV	IP	H	BB	SO
Acierno, Marc	0	2	6.75	4	0	15	21	4	5
Baker, Casey	0	0	9.00	1	0	5	9	2	2
Blackwell, Brad	2	0	1.86	31	22	29	21	13	27
Caldwell, Daniel	3	2	5.94	34	1	77	85	39	50
Cervera, Michael	6	7	5.57	21	0	95	125	47	73
DeValk, Dane	7	5	3.92	20	0	124	127	29	92
Dow, Jeremy	2	3	2.55	7	0	25	20	21	18
Eddy, Cooper	2	5	3.74	50	0	65	70	23	64
Fogelson, Scott	6	4	3.53	25	0	92	86	39	84
Harris, Josh	0	2	8.86	5	0	21	27	11	15

	W	L	ERA	G	SV	IP	H	BB	SO
Hastings, Jon	0	0	13.50	5	0	3	5	6	3
Long, Jeffrey	4	8	3.75	38	0	58	50	22	39
Martin, Brandon	4	2	3.28	32	0	49	46	23	39
Martin, Josh	5	1	3.02	8	0	48	37	20	24
Mendola, Brandon	0	2	17.36	3	0	5	8	6	4
Merrell, Jon	3	2	3.99	8	0	47	44	29	24
Perez, Chris	2	2	5.92	9	0	38	34	23	38
Rose, Eli	0	1	8.38	8	0	10	11	11	7
Smith, Jared	0	0	8.59	4	0	7	9	4	3
Squires, Steven	0	0	9.00	3	0	9	14	2	3
Webb, Chris	1	1	9.00	7	0	10	11	6	5
Wernke, Casey	0	1	2.45	2	0	4	1	9	2

RIVER CITY RASCALS

BATTING	AVG	AB	R	H	2B	3B	HR	RBI	SB
Arnold, David, of	.167	12	1	2	0	0	0	0	2
Astrauskas, Wayne, c	.091	11	1	1	0	0	0	0	0
Bowling, Casey, of	.279	122	13	34	5	2	2	18	7
Boyd, Jason, of	.241	112	19	27	5	0	1	13	7
2-team (37 Washington)	.242	231	28	56	12	2	3	25	10
Brown, Chris, 1b	.249	173	21	43	4	0	6	26	1
2-team (46 Florence)	.266	342	43	91	14	0	8	51	4
Buscher, Gregory, 3b	.056	18	1	1	0	0	0	0	0
2-team (0 Florence)	.230	161	16	37	11	0	5	25	1
Castanon, Jose, 3b	.207	121	22	25	5	0	1	8	1
Chevalier, Eric, of	.256	297	44	76	19	4	9	49	13
Cockrell, Michael, ss	.266	290	38	77	11	1	4	34	17
Desmond, Geoff, 1b	.205	117	19	24	3	0	4	21	1
Episcopo, Ryan, of	.125	8	0	1	0	0	0	0	0
Gonzalez, Eddie, c	.217	92	8	20	1	0	1	8	1
Grullon, Leo, of	.238	80	15	19	5	0	2	9	1
Guessford, Eddie, of	.273	278	33	76	16	1	2	28	8
Hillman, Dusty, 2b	.189	53	5	10	1	0	0	3	2
Hopkins, Trave, of	.282	124	14	35	6	0	0	16	2
2-team (3 Gateway)	.285	137	15	39	6	0	0	16	2
Just, Mike, 2b	.317	205	26	65	12	3	1	18	2
Keating, Brian, 2b	.000	1	0	0	0	0	0	0	0
Keen, Kyle, of	.244	90	11	22	4	0	0	7	2
Kim, Eddie, 1b	.316	174	30	55	12	0	5	26	1
Madrid, Mike, 1b	.280	250	32	70	11	0	10	44	2
Marshall, Jon, c	.207	87	7	18	2	0	1	12	0
McConnell, Kirk, of	.283	53	13	15	3	0	1	5	2
McKinley, Justin, 3b	.273	183	31	50	11	1	2	24	14
Santor, John, 3b	.226	53	7	12	1	0	2	5	2
Slagle, Anthony, of	.240	129	22	31	8	0	2	13	1
Stevens, Jeff, c	.333	3	0	1	0	0	0	0	0
Yates, Adam, ss	.179	28	4	5	1	0	0	1	1

PITCHING	W	L	ERA	G	SV	IP	H	BB	SO
Alverson, Steve	1	1	5.09	14	0	23	22	13	20
Bolton, Dustin	1	2	9.00	8	0	11	17	5	9
2-team (1 Evansville)	1	2	6.75	9	0	15	21	9	13
Brook, Steven	6	6	4.11	21	0	136	127	34	100
Callahan, Shawn	0	0	4.07	18	0	24	32	7	13
Cassidy, Kevin	0	2	9.39	7	1	8	13	9	6
Cheek, Cameron	4	2	3.63	29	0	57	65	17	31
Evers, Patrick	3	7	2.91	42	19	53	48	11	37
Jefferson, Andrew	0	1	8.68	5	0	9	12	6	6
Johnson, Brian	4	3	3.90	23	0	62	71	22	27
Jones, Kyle	1	1	9.26	3	0	12	9	13	2
Keating, Brian	6	6	4.02	19	0	123	116	57	92
Kohorst, Pat	0	3	16.20	3	0	10	18	7	7
2-team (9 Washington)	5	7	6.75	12	0	52	63	22	23
Landavazo, Derrick	2	2	7.56	14	0	17	25	5	13
Lasinski, Greg	1	1	6.75	9	0	13	17	7	6
2-team (5 Washington)	2	1	4.32	14	0	25	26	16	14
Ledbetter, Aaron	4	6	2.73	14	0	106	98	22	72
McConnell, Caleb	2	1	4.01	6	0	25	23	14	10
Phillips, Shawn	3	0	0.86	7	0	31	24	5	22
2-team (1 Washington)	3	0	1.62	8	0	33	31	6	24
Renery, Mike	0	7	5.05	11	0	62	71	31	34
Tapper, Jon	1	2	7.45	8	0	10	12	9	5
Tyler, Adam	1	2	5.64	5	0	22	34	10	6
Webb, Chris	0	1	9.31	3	0	10	23	3	6

ROCKFORD RIVERHAWKS

BATTING	AVG	AB	R	H	2B	3B	HR	RBI	SB
Anthonsen, Joe, ss	.286	343	45	98	16	2	0	39	22
Besl, Joe, 3b	.200	25	0	5	0	0	0	1	0
Bidwell, Mike, 3b	.167	90	6	15	2	0	0	4	0
Bowen, Jake, 3b	.200	190	22	38	7	0	0	14	5
Brooks, Cody, 2b	.214	112	17	24	3	0	0	10	13
Cabrera, Mayke, 1b	.275	51	6	14	4	0	0	2	1
Cavers, Eric, c	.229	35	2	8	1	0	1	7	1
DiBlasi, Chris, 1b	.232	56	4	13	1	0	1	7	1

Dutton, Brad, 2b	.217	217	21	47	6	0	3	28	12
Flowers, Bo, of	.271	225	30	61	15	1	4	31	16
2-team (18 Windy City)	.265	291	40	77	17	2	4	37	22
Gerlits, Gooby, c	.228	228	18	52	7	0	9	36	2
Gipson, Ryan, 2b	.318	22	4	7	0	0	0	3	2
Holdren, Stephen, 1b	.242	62	13	15	3	0	2	8	4
Hunton, Bart, 1b	.226	84	5	19	6	0	0	8	2
Isoz, Pat, ph	.000	2	0	0	0	0	0	0	0
James, Jason, of	.341	123	21	42	7	2	0	16	6
Johnson, Nick, of	.307	349	40	107	26	3	3	47	17
Keesee, David, 3b	.361	61	8	22	3	0	0	3	3
Letler, Scott, 1b	.208	72	12	15	1	0	2	5	2
2-team (17 Windy City)	.216	134	17	29	5	0	3	10	2
Lewis, Chris, of	.129	31	3	4	1	0	0	3	1
Massey, Beau, 1b	.179	39	9	7	0	0	2	7	1
Quihuis-Bell, Richard, 1b	.247	97	9	24	7	0	1	7	0
Santana, Rico, of	.261	341	52	89	18	0	6	45	29
Sauls, Matt, of	.273	256	49	70	9	3	7	26	17
Vickers, Bryan, c	.234	47	8	11	0	0	2	5	0
VonTungeln, Cory, c	.188	32	3	6	0	0	0	0	1

PITCHING	W	L	ERA	G	SV	IP	H	BB	SO
Barbosa, Joe	3	3	3.07	0	0	41	50	9	25
Bauer, Garrett	6	5	2.82	19	0	121	94	55	85
Brnardic, Ryan	0	1	6.52	18	0	19	28	16	15
Darling, Bobby	0	2	6.00	11	0	15	13	11	4
Dowling, Dave	4	4	2.30	41	3	43	31	12	40
Endicott, Drew	0	2	4.66	2	0	10	14	4	4
James, Jason	1	2	3.00	6	0	9	6	8	6
Kroft, Adam	6	3	2.00	43	1	68	54	18	44
Lyons, Tom	0	0	4.40	13	0	14	12	14	9
Marksbury, Mike	2	0	2.87	29	12	31	23	11	34
Massey, Beau	2	1	3.62	32	5	37	32	21	30
Parker, Shaun	1	3	3.35	7	0	43	37	24	42
2-team (14 Traverse City)	4	7	4.74	21	1	104	105	58	81
Payton, Grant	0	0	5.29	11	0	17	21	11	11
Rodriguez, Augustine	3	0	4.55	16	1	32	40	5	17
Roper, Derek	6	7	2.79	19	0	126	115	25	101
Smith, John	2	1	3.14	13	0	14	16	4	15
Towery, Dane	5	8	4.28	19	0	109	133	31	57
Watson, Tanner	8	5	2.85	17	0	107	99	27	66

TRAVERSE CITY BEACH BUMS

BATTING	AVG	AB	R	H	2B	3B	HR	RBI	SB
Batkoski, Nick, 3b	.291	358	54	104	17	1	7	68	10
Blevins, Clay, c	.258	256	22	66	15	0	1	29	3
Draska, Chris, of	.167	18	4	3	1	0	0	0	0
2-team (3 Florence)	.250	28	5	7	3	0	0	0	0
Engers, John, of	.222	54	9	12	1	0	2	8	1
Garcia, Douglas, of	.276	315	35	87	15	1	5	54	10
Gergel, Kevin, c	.193	197	19	38	6	1	4	26	3
Gravley, Nathan, of	.284	222	28	63	13	2	0	20	7
Holmes, Justin, ss	.269	331	45	89	10	0	0	27	13
Meagher, Justin, of	.200	120	11	24	2	0	0	6	4
Mendoza, Jaziel, of	.169	65	10	11	2	0	1	5	0
2-team (52 Chillicothe)	.190	210	30	40	5	1	4	26	2
Reese, Mike, of	.269	327	66	88	10	4	7	41	33
Roach, Al, of	.233	257	38	60	14	2	3	39	2
Vericker, Brad, 1b	.294	228	37	67	13	0	9	44	3
White, Kevin, of	.240	96	12	23	5	0	1	7	0
Young, Stephen, 2b	.271	343	53	93	8	3	1	27	24

PITCHING	W	L	ERA	G	SV	IP	H	BB	SO
Ariail, Ryan	0	0	4.30	11	0	15	16	7	21
Barchus, Jon	1	0	15.43	4	0	5	9	4	1
Bucklew, Kory	1	0	3.62	17	1	27	35	5	10
Casoli, Tony	13	3	2.44	19	0	144	131	25	85
Davis, Hunter	5	3	2.65	42	9	54	41	22	51
Furrow, Jason	3	2	2.68	28	0	47	44	14	41
Gehring, Ryan	7	5	2.98	18	0	121	126	26	57
Joslyn, Kevin	0	0	10.50	5	1	6	7	3	6
Klovstad, Buddy	3	3	5.51	6	0	33	36	8	25
Lemieux, David	4	3	5.00	16	0	54	65	23	27
McClellan, Robbie	8	5	3.31	18	0	101	85	30	80
Mezzetta, Paul	0	1	4.38	26	1	51	57	13	32
Parker, Shaun	3	4	5.72	14	1	61	68	34	39
Shippey, Steven	8	5	3.77	20	3	91	85	23	61
Thomson, Jordan	1	5	5.35	34	10	39	34	11	34

WASHINGTON WILD THINGS

BATTING	AVG	AB	R	H	2B	3B	HR	RBI	SB
Arbinger, Mike, of	.273	348	60	95	22	8	8	53	5
Bok, Matt, c	.184	87	11	16	5	0	1	11	4
Boyd, Jason, of	.244	119	9	29	7	2	2	12	3
Bucholtz, Jason, 2b	.257	222	33	57	5	3	1	34	14
Butler, Kevin, c	.000	7	0	0	0	0	0	0	0

BATTING	AVG	AB	R	H	2B	3B	HR	RBI	SB
Carter, Chris, of	.314	309	61	97	9	6	8	48	7
Grandstrand, Brett, ss	.284	282	39	80	22	2	0	29	12
Hudak, Andy, 1b	.240	296	48	71	12	4	10	44	11
Ketron, Brandon, c	.330	203	33	67	11	4	5	32	2
Koenig, Lance, c	.279	337	62	94	11	6	5	47	17
Massari, Nick, 2b	.251	175	30	44	9	2	2	27	8
Peavey, Pat, 3b	.262	378	52	99	21	3	10	83	5
Sidick, Chris, of	.300	393	64	118	12	16	6	41	31
Taylor, Ryan, 2b	.267	30	4	8	1	0	0	0	0
Werman, Kyle, 2b	.254	130	16	33	2	1	0	14	1
Winkler, Shane, of	.125	32	2	4	0	1	0	2	0

PITCHING	W	L	ERA	G	SV	IP	H	BB	SO
Carter, Andy	0	0	3.38	2	0	8	7	1	7
Cochran, Tom	8	5	3.25	22	0	127	111	44	105
Gabel, Brent	2	2	6.33	9	0	27	29	20	16
Grijalva, Jon	0	1	3.86	7	0	12	9	7	7
Hahn, Cory	4	3	3.73	8	0	41	33	21	24
Hollenbeck, J.J.	3	0	2.70	12	0	27	29	7	13
Kohorst, Pat	5	4	4.50	9	0	42	45	15	16
Lasinski, Greg	1	0	1.54	5	0	12	9	9	8
Ledbetter, Aaron	4	1	2.12	7	0	51	43	6	25
2-team (14 River City)	8	7	2.53	21	0	157	141	28	97
Novosel, Walt	1	2	5.46	11	0	28	23	23	11
Ohalek, Corey	0	1	3.62	35	4	55	55	12	35
Phillips, Shawn	0	0	13.50	1	0	2	7	1	2
Popp, Jim	3	0	3.20	36	15	45	45	16	52
Sadler, Patrick	4	2	2.68	30	3	50	44	27	47
Schrader, Justin	0	0	12.71	3	0	6	12	1	2
Spragg, Stephen	6	7	2.09	43	4	82	63	33	37
Sprouse, Shannon	0	0	21.60	2	1	2	6	2	2
Squires, Matt	10	5	4.31	20	0	109	118	38	85
Stanley, Pat	8	4	2.72	22	0	136	101	53	111
Werman, Kyle	0	0	0.00	2	0	2	1	2	2

WINDY CITY THUNDERBOLTS

BATTING	AVG	AB	R	H	2B	3B	HR	RBI	SB
Albano, Anthony, of	.250	60	7	15	2	1	2	7	0
Balkan, Adam, of	.269	160	13	43	4	0	0	19	2
Bonilla, Clemente, 2b	.307	202	32	62	10	0	2	23	22
Buhagiar, Joshua, of	.194	98	16	19	3	0	2	8	2
Conley, Evan, 3b-ss	.000	4	0	0	0	0	0	1	0
Diggins, Ben, 1b	.209	67	10	14	1	0	1	8	1
Ewen, Nick, of	.255	110	13	28	3	1	0	9	3
Fiallo, Adriel, ss	.000	4	0	0	0	0	0	0	0
Flowers, Bo, of	.242	66	10	16	2	1	0	6	6
Forbes, Mike, of	.200	135	14	27	8	0	2	16	6
Gordon, Casey, ss	.125	8	0	1	0	0	0	2	0
Hall, Trevor, 1b	.286	56	7	16	2	0	1	4	0
2-team (28 Florence)	.259	166	17	43	6	0	2	8	0
Hill, Chad, ss	.176	34	2	6	1	0	0	0	1
Holdren, Stephen, of	.198	86	13	17	8	1	4	12	0
2-team (23 Rockford)	.216	148	26	32	11	1	6	20	4
House, Kevin, of	.229	83	14	19	4	2	1	10	7
2-team (44 Gateway)	.252	262	46	66	11	4	6	29	27
Ketter, Steve, c	.219	169	20	37	13	0	1	21	0
Klusaw, Nick, 1b	.235	119	10	28	4	1	3	17	1
Lefler, Scott, 1b	.226	62	5	14	4	0	1	5	0
Lisk, Charlie, 3b	.316	98	10	31	5	2	1	18	2
Lynch, Michael, c	.211	19	0	4	1	0	0	1	1
Mann, Jason, c	.187	187	13	35	4	0	2	17	0
McCarthy, John, 1b	.283	127	15	36	3	1	0	24	5
Navarro, Ramon, ss	.222	54	7	12	0	0	0	2	1
Price, Chris, of	.167	18	0	3	0	0	0	1	0
Santor, John, 3b	.231	281	35	65	21	1	5	43	0
2-team (14 River City)	.231	334	42	77	22	1	7	48	2
Schutt, Doug, of	.271	340	64	92	8	4	5	33	56
Seratelli, Anthony, 2b	.286	248	48	71	7	7	6	39	28
Shay, Nick, ss	.217	23	2	5	1	0	0	3	0
Solis, Eddie, 3b	.159	44	2	7	0	0	1	7	0
Vetter, Scott, ss	.253	198	33	50	8	1	0	16	13
Weber, Rick, of	.000	0	0	0	0	0	0	0	0

PITCHING	W	L	ERA	G	SV	IP	H	BB	SO
Baxter, Brian	1	1	5.40	4	0	18	26	4	9
Beuning, Brian	2	5	2.34	46	24	65	46	30	67
Causey, Mike	3	1	3.32	28	1	38	35	19	47
Coffey, Andrew	2	4	5.88	11	0	49	59	29	34
2-team (7 Chillicothe)	5	6	4.72	18	0	82	92	49	54
Estrada, Ignacio	2	2	4.66	17	1	19	18	15	10
Glynn, Josh	0	3	7.94	3	0	17	27	3	4
Hummel, John	1	3	7.48	5	0	22	34	15	11
Jones, Rustin	0	0	8.64	4	0	8	13	9	3
Kellbach, Brandon	4	4	5.69	37	0	55	58	32	40
Martinez, John	0	4	6.00	4	0	24	26	9	8
McMillan, Jason	1	1	3.02	24	0	42	30	22	36

PITCHING	W	L	ERA	G	SV	IP	H	BB	SO
Mlotkowski, Mike	2	6	4.44	15	0	73	68	48	60
Nicholson, Scott	1	0	4.97	5	0	13	11	9	11
2-team (18 Gateway)	1	3	5.63	23	1	54	57	31	48
Phillips, Billy	6	0	3.86	33	0	72	72	40	72
Pleeter, Gregg	0	0	0.00	1	0	1	3	0	0
Renault, Nick	2	6	4.39	12	0	70	71	32	62
Russo, Noah	1	2	1.96	19	0	23	19	19	29
Schutt, Doug	0	0	0.00	1	0	0	1	1	1
Simms, Scott	5	9	3.80	19	0	116	123	61	69
Trevino, Toro	3	7	3.86	15	0	96	85	31	68
Weber, Rick	1	0	4.32	34	1	25	28	22	26

GOLDEN LEAGUE

The Golden League's second season featured the return of Jose Canseco and the emergence of a dominant team.

Les Lancaster's Reno Silver Sox finished the season with the league's best record (47-33) and easily beat the Fullerton Flyers in the league's championship series. The Silver Sox also sold seven players to affiliated ball.

It was another accolade in an impressive managerial career for Lancaster, who has not had a losing season in seven years as a manager and won his second league title.

Reno rode the success of a lineup led by catcher Marcus Jensen (.340/.460/.597) and third baseman Edgar Varela (.348/.394/.607). Lancaster built an exceptional bullpen around Scott Schneider (2-4, 2.78, 19 saves), Mike McTamney (2-0, 1.47) and Nate Sevier (6-2, 2.25).

Canseco was signed early in the season by the San Diego Surf Dawgs, then traded to the Long Beach Armada. While his presence did bring some media attention, Canseco hit .169/.322/.380 in 71 at-bats. Less-accomplished former big leaguers like Jensen and Desi Wilson (.333/.392/.417) proved much more successful.

In its second season, the Golden League continued to struggle to draw fans. Yuma (2,142 fans a game) led the league in attendance but was the only team to draw more than 1,800 fans a game.

STANDINGS

	W	L	PCT	GB
*Reno	47	33	.588	—
Chico	46	34	.575	1
#Fullerton	43	37	.538	4
Long Beach	37	43	.463	10
San Diego	35	45	.438	12
Yuma	32	48	.400	15

* First-half winner. # Second-half winner

PLAYOFFS: Reno defeated Fullerton 3-1 in best-of-5 series.
ATTENDANCE: Yuma 79,244; Chico 64,701; Reno 62,903; Fullerton 59,071; Long Beach 57,141; San Diego 46,282.
MANAGER: Chico—Mark Parent; Fullerton—Garry Templeton; Long Beach—Darrell Evans; Reno—Les Lancaster; San Diego—Terry Kennedy; Yuma—Benny Castillo.
ALL-STAR TEAM: C—Marcus Jensen, Reno. 1B—Desi Wilson, Chico. 2B—Adam Mandel, San Diego. 3B—Henry Calderon, Yuma. SS—Bret LeVier, Fullerton. Util—Craig Kuzmic, Chico. OF—Seth Pietsch, San Diego; Jason Van Meetren, Chico; Jeff LaRue, Long Beach; Scott Goodman, San Diego. DH—Peanut Williams, Fullerton. SP—Chris Jakubaskaus, Fullerton; Andre Simpson, Long Beach; Ben Thurmond, Reno; Phil Springman, Chico; Brian Kroll, Chico; Nate Sevier, Reno. RP—Josh Rummonds, San Diego; Scott Schneider, Reno; E.J. Shanks, San Diego; Mike Peck, Long Beach; Wes Faust, Fullerton.

Player of the Year: Peanut Williams, Fullerton. Pitcher of the Year: Chris Jakubaskaus, Fullerton. Manager of the Year: Les Lancaster, Reno.

INDIVIDUAL BATTING LEADERS

BATTER, TEAM	AVG	G	AB	R	H	HR	RBI
Pietsch, Seth, SD	.353	51	201	30	71	5	27
Jensen, Marcus, Reno	.340	68	253	58	86	14	57
Wilson, Desi, Chico	.333	80	333	58	111	2	58
Mandel, Adam, SD	.324	75	321	59	104	3	35
Kuzmic, Craig, Chico	.319	72	270	60	86	12	53
Van Meetren, Jason, Chico	.311	77	283	46	88	4	51
Day, Johnny, SD	.309	56	207	24	64	0	22
Williams, Peanut, Full	.308	79	305	56	94	20	75
Templeton Jr., Garry, Full	.307	76	319	56	98	1	32

INDEPENDENT LEAGUES

INDIVIDUAL PITCHING LEADERS

PITCHER, TEAM	W	L	ERA	IP	H	BB	SO
Currier, Rik, LB	2	4	1.41	64	37	18	59
Singleton, Nick, Chico	7	6	2.77	107	94	38	75
Sugarman, Jeremy, Full	6	5	2.80	93	82	30	58
Springman, Phil, Chico	7	1	2.92	71	62	17	45
Jakubauskas, Chris, Full	8	1	3.09	96	89	21	76
Simpson, Andre, LB	7	6	3.28	123	102	44	140
Kroll, Brian, Chico	9	5	3.39	106	103	24	72
Claypool, Ryan, LB	4	5	3.39	98	96	56	61
Thurmond, Ben, Reno	8	4	3.43	100	101	21	83
Ramsey, Justin, LB	8	4	3.49	88	78	39	73

CHICO OUTLAWS

BATTING	AVG	AB	R	H	2B	3B	HR	RBI	SB
Booker, Steve, of	.276	127	22	35	4	0	2	15	4
Calderon, Henry, 3b	.273	22	6	6	0	1	1	1	0
2-team (72 Yuma)	.327	315	46	103	23	1	2	35	28
Draper, Tim, of	.000	1	0	0	0	0	0	0	0
Froloff, Alex, of	.265	136	20	36	4	1	2	17	6
Gandolfo, Rob, 2b	.287	331	60	95	16	3	0	25	18
Garcia, Lino, of	.240	192	31	46	11	2	4	32	10
Gossage, Todd, 3b	.262	187	35	49	9	3	2	31	4
Kovacs, Jesse, ss	.241	274	37	66	10	1	3	22	4
Kuzmic, Craig, c	.319	270	60	86	23	2	12	53	6
Mallory, Mike, of	.253	289	57	73	13	2	14	63	12
Matteucci, Jason, of	.252	147	21	37	7	0	2	17	3
Pierce, Whit, c	.221	68	11	15	2	0	0	9	0
Tavelli, Angelo, 2b-SS	.000	14	1	0	0	0	0	1	0
Van Meetren, Jason, of	.311	283	46	88	17	1	4	51	15
Wallace, Jim, c	.218	119	13	26	5	1	4	22	1
Wilson, Desi, 1b	.333	333	58	111	20	1	2	58	4

PITCHING	W	L	ERA	G	SV	IP	H	BB	SO
Ampi, A.J.	1	2	5.79	24	6	33	41	12	28
Anaya, Robert	0	2	5.53	19	0	41	47	25	26
Beavers, Kevin	0	0	12.00	4	0	3	7	3	0
Caughey, Trevor	1	0	2.12	8	0	17	16	0	17
Cosgrove, Mike	3	1	4.35	9	0	39	39	23	23
Gold, Adam	0	0	18.90	2	0	3	7	2	2
Gregg, Grant	6	5	4.40	17	0	110	133	23	60
Huguet, George	4	2	3.92	32	5	41	48	12	27
Kroll, Brian	9	5	3.39	17	0	106	103	24	72
McKinley, Jacob	0	4	4.40	23	1	45	35	15	39
Nagasaka, Hideki	5	3	4.15	9	0	56	51	23	46
2-team (32 Reno)	6	3	4.97	15	0	80	77	42	64
Perez, Alex	1	2	8.76	5	0	12	14	6	5
Searle, Chris	2	0	4.25	11	0	30	35	5	14
Singleton, Nick	7	6	2.77	17	0	107	94	38	75
Springman, Phil	7	1	2.92	16	1	71	62	17	45
Taylor, Aaron	0	1	13.50	4	0	3	4	3	3

FULLERTON FLYERS

BATTING	AVG	AB	R	H	2B	3B	HR	RBI	SB
Banach, John, 3b	.313	16	1	5	1	0	0	2	2
Bergstrom, Bub, of	.133	15	1	2	1	0	0	0	0
Bonilla, Clemente, 2b	.293	58	11	17	2	1	0	3	3
Chop, Chad, of	.291	151	20	44	3	0	6	19	3
DeLeon, Sandy, c	.167	24	2	4	0	0	0	2	0
Dennis, Bernard, c	.000	9	0	0	0	0	0	0	0
Dennis, Brian, c	.000	5	0	0	0	0	0	0	0
Elder, Rick, of	.200	75	12	15	3	2	3	12	1
Ferrara, Matt, ss	.211	175	25	37	3	1	3	15	11
Flowers, Brett	.133	15	0	2	0	0	0	0	0
Frazee, Joseph, of	.314	51	5	16	6	0	0	10	2
Gordon, Casey, 2b	.238	21	3	5	1	0	0	0	1
Hall, Trevor, of	.295	122	22	36	7	1	5	23	1
Hendricks, Joey, c	.317	41	4	13	1	0	0	4	1
LeVier, Brett, 3b	.274	325	54	89	13	2	2	39	6
Mayorga, Gabriel, 2b	.269	156	21	42	5	0	3	19	2
Morales, Buddy, c	.291	117	15	34	4	0	1	11	0
Pohle, Richard, of	.296	270	44	80	12	2	4	39	5
Sasa, Toshi, of	.271	118	15	32	6	1	0	15	5
Saunders, Nick, 3b	.238	42	6	10	1	0	0	4	0
Schmidt, Jesse, of	.328	137	23	45	7	2	1	30	12
Shorsher, Adam, c	.140	50	0	7	1	0	0	4	0
Templeton, Garry, of	.307	319	56	98	19	4	1	32	8
Wallis, Jacob, c	.191	68	11	13	4	0	2	10	0
Williams, Peanut, 1b	.308	305	56	94	9	2	20	75	4
Yamanaka, M, of	.250	4	0	1	0	0	0	0	0
Zamora, Hector, 3b	.342	111	18	38	4	0	4	10	2
2-team (14 Reno)	.331	157	24	52	9	0	5	16	2

PITCHING	W	L	ERA	G	SV	IP	H	BB	SO
Casanova, Nicholas	1	2	3.89	24	0	39	44	19	27
Dickert, Reed	1	0	1.40	11	0	19	10	10	20

	W	L	ERA	IP	H	BB	SO
Faust, Wes	7	3	3.98	30	11	61	69	25	59
Frydendall, Craig	4	6	4.09	17	0	95	106	19	50
Gelatka, Todd	4	5	5.21	16	0	74	86	36	56
Grijalva, Jon	3	2	4.75	20	2	30	29	14	29
Groeger, Jeff	7	4	3.82	21	0	78	68	32	76
Jakubauskas, Chris	8	1	3.09	15	1	96	89	21	76
Lincoln, Matthew	0	2	6.55	14	2	34	42	18	24
Mason, Robert	1	5	6.35	24	1	45	59	25	33
McTamney, Mike	0	0	7.32	10	1	20	24	10	19
Olson, Ryan	1	2	2.89	29	0	37	33	8	39
Sugarman, Jeremy	6	5	2.80	16	0	93	83	30	58

LONG BEACH ARMADA

BATTING	AVG	AB	R	H	2B	3B	HR	RBI	SB
Canseco, Jose, dh	.176	68	9	12	3	0	4	9	0
2-team (1 San Diego)	.169	71	9	12	3	0	4	9	0
Castro, Bobby, 2b	.183	142	10	26	6	0	0	5	1
Cicatelli, Cole, c	.290	107	13	31	4	1	0	15	2
Collette, Jason, c	.167	102	7	17	2	0	1	8	1
DiRosa, Mike, c	.162	37	1	6	1	0	1	2	0
Harrison, Adonis, 2b	.272	217	35	59	10	2	2	22	16
Hernandez, Jeremy, ss	.281	288	36	81	17	4	5	32	5
Klemm, Chris, of	.271	273	35	74	13	0	1	25	12
LaRue, Jeff, 1b	.296	294	49	87	26	1	13	58	12
Martinez, Jaime, 1b	.339	56	8	19	2	0	0	9	2
Peters, Samone, 1b	.235	166	23	39	10	1	6	29	0
Ramirez, David, c	.231	143	15	33	4	0	1	16	0
Shelley, Randall, 3b	.241	274	33	66	12	0	6	42	7
Stevenson, Ryan, of	.264	227	31	60	3	5	0	20	12
Wakeland, Chris, of	.314	35	4	11	3	0	1	6	0
Webb, Ryan, of	.274	321	44	88	12	2	3	29	16

PITCHING	W	L	ERA	G	SV	IP	H	BB	SO
Buchan, Paul	1	1	8.06	6	0	26	28	14	4
Canseco, Jose	0	1	4.15	1	0	4	2	5	1
Clark, Chad	1	0	9.00	7	0	7	4	18	6
Claypool, Ryan	4	5	3.39	16	0	98	96	56	61
Collette, Jason	0	1	9.00	1	0	1	2	0	0
Currier, Rik	2	4	1.41	11	0	64	37	18	59
Hoff, Brian	3	4	3.83	31	1	45	62	13	36
Leduc, Dennis	4	1	3.30	22	0	46	41	12	42
McDaniel, Denny	0	2	8.53	2	0	6	10	3	5
Newman, Alan	0	0	20.25	2	0	3	0	10	1
Peck, Mike	1	2	1.67	26	6	32	28	16	33
Pettyjohn, Adam	1	1	1.64	2	0	11	10	3	11
Pudewell, Nathaniel	2	4	6.09	17	0	65	80	26	36
Ramirez, David	0	0	0.00	1	0	1	0	1	0
Ramsey, Justin	8	4	3.49	21	0	88	78	39	73
Shelley, Randall	0	0	0.00	1	0	1	0	1	0
Simpson, Andre	7	6	3.28	18	0	123	102	44	140
Smith, Bud	2	4	2.70	10	0	53	50	14	38
Stevenson, Ryan	0	0	9.00	1	0	1	2	0	0
Testa, Chris	1	2	2.42	24	2	22	14	14	24
Zick, Jeremy	0	1	5.29	7	0	17	24	6	14

RENO SILVER SOX

BATTING	AVG	AB	R	H	2B	3B	HR	RBI	SB
Astrauskas, Wayne, c	.290	31	6	9	1	0	0	7	0
Booker, Steve, of	.213	80	10	17	3	0	0	8	3
2-team (32 Chico)	.251	207	32	52	7	0	2	23	7
Callan, Adam, ss	.000	10	0	0	0	0	0	2	0
Carmenates, Alberto, 2b	.000	10	0	0	0	0	0	0	0
Carter, Brandon, of	.207	29	5	6	0	0	0	2	1
Chikazawa, Masashi, c	.277	83	17	23	5	0	6	18	1
Dewey, Jason, c	.164	55	8	9	4	0	1	4	2
2-team (27 Yuma)	.236	157	22	37	7	1	5	16	4
Done, Mike, 2b	.272	224	37	61	14	2	2	35	4
Fisk, Nate, of	.310	29	5	9	2	1	0	5	0
Giannotti, Rich, of	.292	96	20	28	7	3	0	15	6
Grau, Philip, of	.264	235	47	62	15	1	7	37	8
Gredvig, Doug, 1b	.299	278	45	83	13	1	10	49	3
Hall, Victor, of	.365	74	23	27	1	3	3	15	15
Jensen, Marcus, c	.340	253	58	86	23	0	14	57	2
Koehler, James, c	.500	12	1	6	0	0	0	3	0
Lang, C.J., ss	.257	206	34	53	5	5	3	33	7
Lucca, Lou, 3b	.250	40	7	10	0	0	1	5	1
Madrid, Carlos, 2b	.301	226	43	68	15	0	1	35	16
Maher, Caleb, of	.233	90	14	21	6	0	1	13	0
Marini, Chris, ss	.353	17	5	6	0	1	1	2	0
Null, Brad, ph	.000	1	0	0	0	0	0	0	0
Rodriguez, Carlos, of	.288	52	11	15	2	1	3	9	2
Shanks, James, of	.279	179	34	50	12	1	6	29	11
Smith, Demond, of	.333	27	10	9	2	0	4	7	1
Sobel, Evan, ss	.243	144	16	35	5	1	0	14	2
Stacey, D.J., of	.222	36	6	8	0	1	1	5	1

	AVG	AB	R	H	2B	3B	HR	RBI	SB
Varela, Edgar, 3b	.348	178	31	62	19	0	9	43	0
Zamora, Hector, of	.304	46	6	14	5	0	1	6	0

PITCHING	W	L	ERA	G	SV	IP	H	BB	SO
Bonnell, Jared	4	2	5.52	16	1	59	71	20	30
Chavez, Carlos	6	5	6.01	13	0	70	95	25	47
Done, Mike	2	0	0.00	3	0	10	11	1	4
Harris, Nat	1	2	5.87	16	0	38	49	23	32
Johnson, James	4	3	4.70	12	0	69	87	23	50
Krout, William	1	1	9.53	6	0	6	11	1	3
Marini, Chris	6	4	4.81	18	1	82	93	26	70
Martinez, Jason	2	3	5.04	22	1	50	56	25	40
McKernan, Mike	0	0	6.19	9	0	16	18	8	12
McTamney, Mike	2	0	1.47	18	1	31	22	4	17
2-team (10 Fullerton)	2	0	3.75	28	2	50	46	14	36
Nagasaka, Hideki	1	0	6.94	6	0	23	26	19	18
Schneider, Scott	2	4	2.78	34	19	36	26	11	49
Sevier, Nate	6	2	2.25	32	2	56	43	29	48
Shackelford, Josh	0	0	8.31	4	0	4	7	5	2
Spiegel, Mike	0	1	8.20	4	0	19	24	16	9
Stull, Everett	2	2	4.15	8	0	35	35	17	21
Thurmond, Ben	8	4	3.43	16	0	100	101	21	83

SAN DIEGO SURF

BATTING	AVG	AB	R	H	2B	3B	HR	RBI	SB
Canseco, Jose, dh	.000	3	0	0	0	0	0	0	0
Ciarrachi, Kevin, c	.322	59	9	19	6	0	2	13	0
Connolly, Matt, of	.220	109	15	24	1	0	2	12	12
Day, Johnny, 2b	.309	207	24	64	11	1	0	22	5
Fox, Ryan, of	.215	65	12	14	3	0	3	7	2
Garcia, Tony, ss	.258	310	40	80	17	1	3	33	4
Goodman, Scott, of	.296	240	41	71	14	0	10	49	2
Guerra, Nick, c	.274	288	40	79	13	2	2	44	4
Henderson, Will, 1b	.264	87	15	23	3	0	5	9	0
Huskins, Joey, of	.325	117	18	38	5	2	2	19	1
Maloney, Matt, of	.324	170	33	55	9	1	7	38	7
Mandel, Adam, 2b	.324	321	59	104	11	3	3	35	10
McCann, Jeremy, 1b	.301	103	15	31	8	0	0	8	7
Montgomery, John, c	.000	2	0	0	0	0	0	0	0
Moore, Justin, ss	.118	17	0	2	0	0	0	0	0
Pietsch, Seth, of	.353	201	40	71	9	1	5	27	4
Pourciau, Brent, of	.000	2	0	0	0	0	0	0	0
Pyles, Derrick, of	.225	80	9	18	3	0	1	7	4
Quihuis-Bell, Richard, 1b	.216	74	6	16	1	0	1	6	0
2-team (16 Yuma)	.189	127	9	24	1	1	1	11	0
Reinking, Kevin, c	.216	51	6	11	1	1	0	4	0
Roldan, Victor, 3b	.291	175	20	51	4	1	3	23	1
Wheatland, Matt, 1b	.167	84	3	14	1	1	0	4	2
York, Andrew, 1b-c	.333	3	0	0	0	0	0	0	0

PITCHING	W	L	ERA	G	SV	IP	H	BB	SO
Carr, Will	0	2	10.67	8	0	14	23	9	5
Fox, Ryan	1	1	4.11	10	1	15	17	12	22
Gale, Chris	2	6	6.15	17	0	91	121	53	52
George, Chris	2	7	5.88	21	3	78	102	29	71
Guerra, Nick	0	0	0.00	1	0	1	1	2	1
Leishman, Mike	1	1	8.10	25	0	40	54	28	42
Mendoza, Marcos	2	4	8.65	9	0	34	46	27	36
Meyer, Jake	5	4	5.09	11	0	53	63	21	41
Ottman, Justin	3	5	5.77	14	0	69	91	20	32
Pourciau, Brent	4	6	7.01	26	1	68	81	42	41
Rummonds, Josh	1	1	2.08	26	13	26	22	14	35
Safken, Joe	3	0	5.74	24	0	58	68	23	35
Shanks, E.J.	6	1	1.78	30	3	51	41	15	38
Smyth, Steve	3	1	3.15	5	0	34	35	11	29
Turino, Yoankis	0	1	4.79	7	1	21	20	9	19

YUMA SCORPIONS

BATTING	AVG	AB	R	H	2B	3B	HR	RBI	SB
Calderon, Henry, 3b	.331	293	40	97	23	0	1	34	28
Dewey, Jason, c	.275	102	14	28	3	1	4	12	2
Guzman, Jacob, c	.284	243	39	69	18	0	11	53	1
Kovatch, Billy, of	.284	176	30	50	15	1	0	25	16
LeBron, Juan, of	.280	175	22	49	11	0	4	25	1
Lechepelle, , of	.000	3	0	0	0	0	0	0	0
Lopez, Javier, of	.280	311	49	87	20	3	9	45	17
Malone, Billy, of	.266	304	37	81	20	3	5	46	20
Munoz, Billy, 1b	.500	12	1	6	1	0	0	2	0
Norton, Kalen, of	.271	188	28	51	8	0	1	15	8
Pringle, Eric, 2b	.253	245	38	62	7	2	0	21	9
Quihuis-Bell, Richard, 1b	.151	53	3	8	0	1	0	5	0
Reinking, Kevin, c	.102	49	5	5	1	0	0	0	0
2-team (14 San Diego)	.160	100	11	16	2	1	0	4	0
Smith, Steve, c	.179	117	13	21	2	0	2	9	0
Tena, Hector, ss	.246	285	39	70	17	0	7	34	7
Wilson, Andy, of	.272	125	12	34	8	0	1	11	4

PITCHING	W	L	ERA	G	SV	IP	H	BB	SO
Amason, Ryan	5	4	6.07	12	0	67	91	27	30
Baca, Anthony	0	0	6.00	14	1	15	16	13	13
Bunyan, Brian	5	6	5.38	15	0	87	96	27	65
Dunham, Steve	4	7	4.60	15	0	90	103	33	44
Foor, Erik	0	1	4.79	13	0	21	27	12	14
Keeling, Justin	0	1	10.59	13	0	17	23	9	8
Langlois, Chris	4	9	4.80	18	0	105	110	21	84
Luque, Roger	0	3	3.78	13	0	17	18	9	8
Meacham, Rusty	0	1	19.29	1	0	2	7	0	1
Nolen, Walt	1	6	5.56	24	8	44	51	22	32
Perez, Jorge	6	4	3.69	15	0	98	98	35	62
Riley, Rob	1	0	8.84	17	0	19	35	13	13
Sander, Richard	1	1	5.06	14	0	21	21	20	14
Saucedo, Matthew	2	1	4.41	28	3	33	40	19	20
Terrebonne, Jared	1	5	2.93	37	1	40	34	29	41
Tucker, Cardoza	1	0	5.25	11	0	0	9	1	3

NORTHERN LEAGUE

Doug Simunic has never been the kind of manager who gives up on a guy in a slump. So when Mark Michael took the mound in the deciding game of the Northern League championship series, Simunic wasn't worried.

Michael had earned a spot in the all-star game with a 6-0, 2.37 start to the season. But in July, his season began to fall apart as he endured a stretch of miserable outings that saw his ERA rise to 4.72. Eventually, Simunic asked Michael to head to the bullpen so he could take a look at a couple of rookies.

Michael returned to the rotation in time to pitch the biggest game of the RedHawks season, a two-hitter as Fargo-Moorhead beat Gary 1-0 to win the title three games to one. Michael was named the championship series' outstanding player.

The title was the RedHawks third Northern League crown, and first since 2003. Fargo-Moorhead went 68-27 in 2005—the best record in independent baseball—but fell to Gary in the championship series three games to two, losing the final three games of the series.

The roster had changed significantly for 2006, but huge seasons by Joe Mathis, the league MVP, and Jesse Hoorelbeke helped Fargo-Moorhead finish 63-33, once again the best record in the league.

Mathis set a league record with 42 doubles as part of a .359/.442/.578 season. He also played a solid center field, serving as the team's sparkplug as the leadoff hitter. Hoorelbeke hit .332 while leading the league in home runs (21) and slugging percentage (.647) before signing with the Cubs in August.

STANDINGS

EAST	W	L	PCT	GB
#Gary	51	46	.526	—
*Schaumburg	46	50	.479	4½
Kansas City	45	51	.469	5½
Joliet	42	55	.433	9

WEST	W	L	PCT	GB
*#Fargo-Moorhead	63	33	.656	—
Winnipeg	52	44	.542	11
Edmonton	44	52	.458	19
Calgary	42	54	.438	21

* First-half winner # Second-half winner

PLAYOFFS: Semifinals—Fargo-Moorhead defeated Winnipeg 3-2; Gary defeated Schaumburg 3-2. **Finals**—Fargo-Moorhead defeated Gary 3-1.

MANAGERS: Calgary—Mike Busch; **Edmonton**—Terry Bevington; **Fargo-Moorhead**—Doug Simunic; **Gary**—Greg Tagert; **Joliet**—Steve Mallet; **Kansas City**—Al Gallagher; **Schaumburg**—Andy McCauley; **Winnipeg**—Rick Forney.

ATTENDANCE: Winnipeg 312,213; Kansas City 269,205; Schaumburg 200,591; Joliet 199,356; Fargo-Moorhead 171,877; Gary 163,133; Edmonton 65,930; Calgary 50,025.

ALL-STAR GAME: C—Craig Hurba, Kansas City; **1B**—Jesse Hoorelbeke, Fargo-Moorhead; **2B**—Manabu Kuramochi, Calgary; **3B**—Ruben Salazar, Fargo-Moorhead; **SS**—Stubby Clapp, Edmonton; **OF**—Greg Jacobs, Kansas

City; Fehlandt Lentini, Winnipeg; Joe Mathis, Fargo-Moorhead; **DH**—Jimmy Hurst, Winnipeg; **RHP**—Jonathan Krysa, Kansas City; **LHP**—Kris Regas, Gary; Luis Villareal, Joliet/Winnipeg.

Player of the Year: Joe Mathis, Fargo-Moorhead. **Pitcher of the Year:** Jonathan Krysa, Kansas City. **Manager of the Year:** Doug Simunic, Fargo-Moorhead.

INDIVIDUAL BATTING LEADERS

Batter, Team	AVG	G	AB	R	H	HR	RBI
Mathis, Joe, FM	.359	96	396	95	142	11	61
Jacobs, Greg, KC	.333	89	333	60	111	15	64
Hoorelbeke, Jesse, FM	.332	74	283	55	94	21	65
Weekly, Chris, Shaum	.328	88	338	59	111	10	61
Lentini, Fehlandt, Win	.325	96	418	93	136	6	49
Clapp, Stubby, Edmon	.323	79	303	61	98	1	34
Berrios, Harry, FM	.315	93	359	46	113	5	49
Hurst, Jimmy, Win	.307	94	335	74	103	18	78
McCallum, Geoff, Shaum	.305	54	220	41	67	1	24
Kuramochi, Manabu, Calg	.303	67	251	47	76	0	27

INDIVIDUAL PITCHING LEADERS

Pitcher, Team	W	L	ERA	IP	H	BB	SO
Villarreal, Luis, Win	6	5	2.71	90	88	33	63
Kerber, Travis, Gary	4	5	2.78	78	79	21	40
Williams, Blake, Shaum	6	5	2.92	96	91	29	69
George, Todd, FM	10	4	3.04	115	107	47	72
Henry, Mike, Edmon	5	3	3.20	79	68	26	43
Beshears, Josh, Win	5	5	3.25	119	106	50	85
Moore, Ben, Win	7	6	3.30	104	87	29	62
Goltz, Brandon, FM	9	2	3.47	106	93	54	56
Greusel, Evan, Calg	8	2	3.49	101	106	23	62
Schweitzer, Matt, Shaum	6	4	3.58	83	89	22	82

CALGARY VIPERS

BATTING	AVG	AB	R	H	2B	3B	HR	RBI	SB
Adriana, Sharnol, 1b	.341	91	17	31	3	0	3	13	8
Almario, Yosvany, of	.229	70	8	16	5	0	0	6	1
Ashman, Shaun, of	.180	61	8	11	1	0	1	4	1
Brinkley, Darryl, of	.368	125	24	46	11	0	2	15	12
Butts, Jeff, of	.240	167	26	40	7	2	0	17	8
Carter, Josh, of	.239	213	24	51	12	1	5	31	4
Castro, Nelson, ss	.257	342	51	88	23	3	6	43	13
Colson, Jason, 1b	.272	206	26	56	9	0	8	34	0
Duncan, Carlos, 3b	.272	302	55	82	15	2	12	59	33
Freeborn, Geoff, of	.000	3	0	0	0	0	0	0	0
Hosford, Clint, of	.000	4	0	0	0	0	0	0	0
Jamison, Ryan, ph	.000	1	0	0	0	0	0	0	0
Kuramochi, Manabu, 2b	.303	251	47	76	6	1	0	27	29
McEachran, Aaron, 3b	.270	359	49	97	21	2	9	57	1
Miller, Drew, of	.297	337	63	100	16	3	3	43	3
Mungle, Jonathan, of	.200	50	6	10	4	0	0	6	0
Rogers, Brandon, c	.277	310	37	86	16	2	0	27	0
Rosario, Sam, ss	.255	255	31	65	14	4	1	37	13
Shorsher, Adam, c	.248	141	15	35	8	0	1	16	0

PITCHING	W	L	ERA	G	SV	IP	H	BB	SO
Bobel, Jay	0	2	9.97	6	0	22	36	16	7
Brewer, Jeff	1	1	8.10	2	0	10	12	5	4
Brooks, Jake	0	2	10.80	5	1	7	9	5	3
Calvert, Klae	0	0	5.73	2	0	11	16	2	7
Crawford, Wesley	0	0	0.00	1	0	0	0	1	0
Danmiller, Beau	0	0	0.00	2	0	2	2	1	2
Daws, Josh	0	0	18.90	7	0	7	21	1	5
Douglas, James	0	1	27.00	3	0	2	3	5	2
Dowdy, Justin	2	2	4.45	19	0	28	28	8	20
Falconer, Kenny	0	0	9.00	1	0	1	2	1	1
Freeborn, Geoff	2	1	4.97	37	1	25	31	13	17
Glosser, Jason	2	0	9.95	7	0	6	13	3	5
Greusel, Evan	8	2	3.49	21	0	101	106	23	62
Hahn, Charlie	0	0	10.24	5	0	10	16	4	3
Hosford, Clint	5	5	4.62	29	0	74	77	30	52
Huizinga, Jon	2	4	3.29	40	12	55	44	27	58
James, Frank	1	2	6.09	11	0	34	44	14	11
Jamison, Ryan	2	2	3.67	11	1	49	50	12	18
Kobayashi, Ryokan	0	2	5.32	40	0	69	76	27	47
Lyons, Tom	1	8	6.54	12	0	52	66	37	17
Mattison, Kieran	0	0	4.96	14	2	16	19	12	11
Oldenburg, Quintin	2	4	7.98	15	0	44	74	18	22
Ortiz, Javier	2	3	4.36	7	0	43	45	12	12
Pluta, Anthony	0	1	20.25	4	0	5	7	10	3
Prata, Danny	3	0	10.91	4	0	16	26	13	9
Rogers, Brad	6	1	5.53	39	0	72	97	21	33
Sarver, Scott	3	5	3.12	10	0	49	42	22	29
Sobkow, Phil	1	1	5.87	8	0	8	9	5	6
2-team (5 Winnipeg)	1	2	5.34	13	0	29	35	19	16
White, Brett	2	1	5.02	3	0	14	15	5	4

EDMONTON CRACKER CATS

BATTING	AVG	AB	R	H	2B	3B	HR	RBI	SB
Becker, Chris, 2b	.242	347	37	84	12	1	4	40	7
Boudon, Chad, of	.284	88	14	25	7	0	0	10	2
Chappel, Dan, of	.220	100	12	22	4	0	0	8	0
Clapp, Stubby, ss	.323	303	61	98	19	5	1	34	32
Clark, Robert, c	.271	48	8	13	2	0	0	5	2
Eggleston, Aharon, of	.251	175	18	44	4	0	0	20	8
Emond, Benoit, of	.391	64	10	25	2	0	0	12	3
Freeman, Ashley, 3b	.270	393	64	106	17	0	5	51	13
Hanson, Ryan, c	.243	70	12	17	1	1	0	8	0
Hiter, Nick, c	.211	57	8	12	0	0	0	6	1
Lisk, Charlie, c	.214	84	11	18	4	3	2	8	1
McClain, Terrence, of	.282	362	50	102	22	5	7	59	4
Morrison, Greg, 1b	.231	346	52	80	12	3	8	53	7
Nichols, Kyle, 1b	.240	121	10	29	6	0	6	28	0
3-team (16 K.C., 38 Joliet)	.264	329	33	87	8	0	15	55	0
Patterson, Derek, dh	.240	229	35	55	10	1	2	38	7
Schifano, Tony, ss	.302	43	3	13	2	0	0	2	1
Shorsher, Adam, c	.264	87	11	23	2	0	2	3	0
2-team (37 Calgary)	.254	228	26	58	10	0	3	19	0
Ware, Jeremy, of	.283	314	50	89	23	2	7	40	9

PITCHING	W	L	ERA	G	SV	IP	H	BB	SO
Bissell, Brad	2	4	4.70	17	1	67	99	18	33
Cabrera, Nate	0	0	4.26	3	0	6	8	2	6
Cherry, Brad	0	0	7.06	12	0	22	25	8	14
DeVisser, John	0	1	5.40	5	0	8	12	3	3
Fauske, Josh	1	3	3.74	21	11	22	20	12	12
Gangi, Aaron	1	2	7.03	12	0	24	36	10	10
Gardner, Hayden	3	0	4.71	22	1	29	33	13	20
Harrison, James	1	1	7.08	14	0	20	23	11	13
2-team (11 Winnipeg)	1	1	7.96	25	0	32	41	15	20
Henry, Mike	5	3	3.20	12	0	79	68	26	43
Holmen, Ian	0	0	12.71	5	0	6	9	9	3
Judson, Scott	0	0	11.25	3	0	4	4	2	4
Kemlo, Chris	6	3	4.30	11	0	69	71	24	39
Kemp, Matt	0	0	9.28	3	0	11	16	7	4
Kusiewicz, Mike	3	1	3.72	4	0	29	31	4	16
Lawson, Brett	8	6	5.73	20	0	99	109	62	98
Little, Jeff	2	5	8.01	9	0	48	67	14	28
MacDonald, Jeff	0	0	27.00	1	0	2	2	0	0
Oldenburg, Quintin	2	0	3.63	20	0	40	48	20	18
2-team (15 Calgary)	4	4	5.92	35	0	84	122	38	40
Randall, Mark	0	0	0.00	6	0	7	7	0	2
Richmond, Scott	3	7	3.03	39	8	71	53	17	72
Rivard, Reggie	5	5	3.96	13	0	64	66	9	31
Tam, Brandon	0	0	18.00	2	0	3	7	1	1
White, Geoff	2	9	5.06	21	0	100	128	38	51

FARGO-MOORHEAD REDHAWKS

BATTING	AVG	AB	R	H	2B	3B	HR	RBI	SB
Austin, Richard, of	.296	362	75	107	24	2	13	69	22
Badger, Graig, 2b	.063	16	2	1	0	0	0	1	1
Berrios, Harry, 1b	.309	149	22	46	7	1	2	21	8
2-team (54 Winnipeg)	.315	359	46	113	13	2	5	49	8
DeNet, Billy, 2b	.357	14	1	5	0	0	0	0	0
Dormanen, Derek, 2b	.182	121	21	22	4	1	0	10	1
Goodman, Scott, of	.242	62	5	15	2	0	2	5	1
Hoorelbeke, Jesse, 1b	.332	283	55	94	24	1	21	65	1
Kofler, Eric, dh	.209	187	21	39	5	0	10	28	0
Krause, Brent, c	.282	404	68	114	30	6	6	64	22
Lopez, Robbie, c	.000	2	0	0	0	0	0	0	0
Mathis, Joe, of	.359	396	95	142	42	6	11	61	24
Mottram, Allen, c	.302	341	44	103	24	1	8	50	1
Peschel, Mike, of	.000	3	0	0	0	0	0	0	0
Ringe, Craig, 2b	.258	279	53	72	13	0	7	39	13
Salazar, Ruben, 3b	.295	370	52	109	21	0	2	75	2
Wayment, Kory, ss	.231	355	50	82	12	4	0	27	11

PITCHING	W	L	ERA	G	SV	IP	H	BB	SO
Adams, Brian	2	1	2.94	33	10	34	37	15	26
Culp, Brandon	6	5	4.44	24	6	77	78	37	46
Dormanen, Derek	0	0	4.50	2	0	4	2	1	1
George, Todd	10	4	3.04	19	0	115	107	47	72
Glosser, Jason	3	1	3.91	14	0	23	20	6	14
Goltz, Brandon	9	2	3.47	19	0	106	93	54	56
Gray, Josh	4	1	3.10	39	4	58	49	25	44
Harmsen, Brandon	3	3	3.89	30	1	39	34	11	35
Hewitt, Brian	1	3	3.18	46	1	65	52	33	50
Kemp, Matt	0	1	21.00	2	0	3	9	3	2
McLaughlin, Jeff	4	3	3.88	17	1	70	57	27	34
Michael, Mark	4	5	4.19	21	0	101	95	49	79
Peschel, Mike	9	4	4.03	27	0	87	88	48	65
Ryan, Shawn	2	1	3.00	5	0	21	9	19	19
Stevens, Josh	0	1	11.57	2	0	5	11	3	4

Treadway, Brion 4 0 1.76 6 0 41 35 18 20

GARY RAILCATS

BATTING	AVG	AB	R	H	2B	3B	HR	RBI	SB
Allensworth, Jermaine, of	.297	357	49	106	21	0	6	46	26
Booth, Steve, c	.256	133	24	34	11	0	2	17	0
Coles, Mike, of	.274	223	30	61	11	4	1	20	16
Curry, Chris, c	.285	256	35	73	14	0	6	32	3
Graham, Ryan, 2b	.214	28	3	6	0	0	0	2	1
Haake, Steve, 1b	.293	338	42	99	22	5	7	57	22
Haynes, Nathan, of	.263	114	24	30	4	1	5	17	8
Martin, Todd, of	.143	14	3	2	0	0	0	0	0
McNamee, Eric, 2b	.261	165	31	43	3	1	0	24	5
Patterson, Jarrod, 1b	.319	138	18	44	8	0	2	22	0
3-team (44 Schaum., 7 Joliet)	.275	335	42	92	23	2	5	61	0
Pecci, Jay, ss	.277	339	46	94	15	3	1	38	3
Rohleder, Andy, of	.269	320	39	86	9	1	6	46	12
Taylor, Alex, 2b	.238	227	37	54	5	2	2	25	17
Townsend, Tanner, 3b	.263	357	59	94	24	3	11	53	15
Vericker, Brad, 1b	.200	85	9	17	3	0	1	13	0
White, Kevin, of	.269	175	30	47	13	1	3	25	0

PITCHING	W	L	ERA	G	SV	IP	H	BB	SO
Brandt, Ryan	3	2	6.30	22	0	30	35	10	12
Burnau, Ryan	0	1	15.32	10	1	12	27	9	9
Carter, Andy	0	2	4.97	9	0	13	22	3	9
Edsall, Steve	3	2	4.27	40	0	59	47	23	29
Frendling, Neal	0	1	11.17	3	0	10	19	5	3
Garrett, Troy	0	0	9.00	1	0	1	2	0	0
Glen, Willie	11	5	3.75	25	0	149	123	60	122
Guthrie, Sazi	1	2	5.84	9	0	25	20	24	14
Habel, Josh	8	9	4.40	24	0	133	132	44	112
Kerber, Travis	4	5	2.78	41	9	78	79	21	40
Klovstad, Buddy	1	2	4.55	6	0	28	33	8	5
Mault, Jeff	2	2	4.91	8	0	18	24	5	5
Miller, Ryan	2	1	2.21	21	2	41	34	8	35
Mumma, Brad	0	0	20.25	1	0	1	3	0	2
Petty, Matt	0	0	10.80	3	0	5	10	1	3
Regas, Kris	5	2	2.36	56	4	61	51	14	52
Schauff, Ned	0	0	9.00	2	0	3	4	2	3
Schmidt, Jeremy	1	1	16.20	3	0	5	7	4	3
Shelley, Jason	12	8	3.75	25	0	154	142	51	145
Sikaras, Pete	0	1	2.53	21	9	21	21	9	17

JOLIET JACKHAMMERS

BATTING	AVG	AB	R	H	2B	3B	HR	RBI	SB
Amado, Jose, 3b	.325	123	23	40	7	0	3	18	2
Blackmon, Dennis, c	.257	171	24	44	10	0	1	12	0
Boyer, Billy, ss	.153	59	6	9	3	1	0	7	0
Brown, Chris, 3b	.333	78	15	26	5	1	0	11	4
Ciarrachi, Kevin, c	.214	14	1	3	0	0	0	0	0
Drobiak, Jayson, of	.247	235	28	58	13	1	9	33	9
Ehrnsberger, Chad, 2b	.294	252	44	74	17	0	12	48	2
Foust, J.D., of	.297	138	18	41	8	0	2	10	7
Gill, Blake, 2b	.298	262	39	78	15	1	4	39	0
Goss, Mike, of	.299	334	41	100	10	0	1	28	21
Harris, Gary, of	.235	34	1	8	0	0	0	3	0
Henderson, Will, 1b	.286	98	13	28	6	0	3	10	1
Hill, Chad, ss	.129	31	1	4	0	0	0	3	0
Jova, Maikel, of	.281	203	33	57	7	1	5	30	1
Lackaff, John, ss	.255	392	49	100	19	1	7	54	3
Landry, Michael, c	.158	19	4	3	1	1	0	5	0
Nichols, Kyle, of	.267	146	18	39	0	0	7	20	0
Nieves, Melvin, 1b	.146	48	11	7	1	0	3	3	1
Patterson, Jarrod, 3b	.154	26	3	4	2	0	0	2	0
Pietsch, Seth, of	.279	111	17	31	5	2	2	13	3
Romprey, Ed, ss	.313	16	4	5	0	0	0	1	0
Smith, Bubba, 1b	.292	209	21	61	11	1	4	25	1
Stevens, Greg, c	.243	115	11	28	3	0	1	9	2
Stratton, Rob, of	.236	148	23	35	9	0	8	31	0
Vickers, Bryan, of	.400	10	3	4	2	0	0	2	0
Wallis, Jake, c	.000	16	1	0	0	0	0	0	0

PITCHING	W	L	ERA	G	SV	IP	H	BB	SO
Blackmon, Dennis	0	0	9.00	1	0	1	3	0	0
Boss, Tommy	2	1	3.31	24	0	35	43	7	32
Cheppenko, Kevin	6	5	4.14	20	0	113	114	48	58
Ellison, Derrick	2	0	1.02	31	1	35	28	15	34
2-team (8 Schaumburg)	2	1	2.90	39	1	50	43	23	43
Fussell, Eric	1	1	3.42	19	0	50	49	18	26
Glosser, Jason	0	2	2.25	3	0	4	6	2	3
2-team (7 Calg., 14 F-M, 6 Winn.)	2	1	6.04	30	0	45	56	15	29
Hensen, Brian	0	0	27.00	3	0	1	3	1	0
Kleine, Victor	4	3	2.45	37	2	59	35	24	50
Luque, Roger	3	5	6.33	9	0	48	70	19	28
Manning, David	3	5	5.83	12	0	63	79	28	41
McCall, Derell	6	5	3.94	32	1	94	105	26	64
Moore, Ben	0	2	14.85	3	0	7	9	6	4
Morenko, Brad	4	8	5.40	21	0	78	101	17	46
Oropesa, Eddie	2	1	4.43	4	0	22	29	10	18
Ozias, Todd	0	3	7.52	4	0	20	26	6	17
Peller, Kevin	0	0	0.00	1	0	1	0	1	0
Romprey, Ed	0	0	9.00	3	0	5	5	4	1
Sauer, Marc	0	2	8.31	3	0	13	23	3	6
Smith, Matt	4	5	4.64	11	0	64	79	16	45
Stephens, Amad	1	4	1.99	39	21	45	36	10	44
Villarreal, Luis	4	5	2.76	14	0	78	76	30	54
Wernke, Casey	0	0	5.06	4	0	5	7	3	2

KANSAS CITY T-BONES

BATTING	AVG	AB	R	H	2B	3B	HR	RBI	SB
Acosta, Jesse, 2b	.205	73	13	15	1	1	2	6	0
Beever, James, c	.194	31	3	6	1	0	0	1	0
Dawson, Millard, of	.000	21	1	0	0	0	0	2	0
Delgado, Gabby, 2b	.214	14	3	3	1	0	0	1	0
Dreher, Doug, of	.285	333	44	95	21	0	1	29	2
Ebers, Eric, of	.000	1	0	0	0	0	0	0	0
Foust, J.D., of	.273	205	29	56	8	1	4	27	12
2-team (39 Joliet)	.283	343	47	97	16	1	6	37	19
Hurba, Craig, c	.269	346	51	93	20	4	18	47	6
Jacobs, Greg, of	.333	333	60	111	28	3	15	64	14
Jones, Brandon, 3b	.225	182	28	41	4	2	10	32	1
Knapp, Robbie, 3b	.250	76	13	19	0	0	1	10	0
Lawhorn, Darryl, of	.259	174	25	45	6	0	7	24	1
Magness, Pat, of	.269	145	29	39	6	0	6	21	0
Nichols, Kyle, of	.306	62	5	19	2	0	2	7	0
Norman, Zach, 3b	.207	116	14	24	2	1	2	10	1
Pearson, Eddie, 1b	.288	302	40	87	7	0	16	56	0
Peterson, Charles, 1b	.286	336	44	96	16	0	11	51	2
Sosebee, Chad, ss	.204	334	40	68	15	5	6	37	4
Spidale, Mike, of	.346	52	12	18	3	0	1	6	3
Vega, Eric, of	.071	42	10	3	0	0	0	1	3
Whealy, Blake, 2b	.232	56	9	13	4	0	0	6	3

PITCHING	W	L	ERA	G	SV	IP	H	BB	SO
Balbuena, Caleb	1	2	5.75	20	0	20	19	14	17
Beever, James	0	0	0.00	5	0	7	3	3	4
Bicknell, Greg	7	13	4.10	24	0	165	183	33	107
Blair, Tom	4	8	6.45	28	0	75	89	37	45
Bolton, Dustin	0	0	0.00	5	0	5	4	1	3
Ebers, Eric	0	1	6.48	13	0	25	41	13	17
Embry, Byron	4	2	1.27	29	14	35	19	19	51
Gilliland, Clint	0	0	7.94	3	0	6	12	0	4
Jones, Jaime	0	1	5.25	17	1	12	9	9	8
Krysa, Jonathan	13	5	3.74	23	0	161	164	51	129
Lewis, Lavon	0	0	4.05	11	0	20	17	10	14
McElwain, Logan	2	3	3.31	27	1	35	39	14	24
Morrison, James	4	4	3.75	42	6	62	65	10	37
Robles, Larry	5	6	3.71	16	0	90	94	46	64
Slack, Nick	0	0	13.50	2	0	2	4	0	2
Sosebee, Chad	0	0	0.00	1	0	0	1	0	1
Tauscher, Ryan	0	1	7.94	8	0	6	6	4	3
Viane, David	0	1	9.00	5	0	12	21	5	2
Waters, Christopher	0	0	0.00	1	0	1	0	1	0
Wichert, Justin	0	0	9.00	2	0	2	4	3	1
Woodman, Hank	5	4	4.66	14	0	87	97	40	84

SCHAUMBURG FLYERS

BATTING	AVG	AB	R	H	2B	3B	HR	RBI	SB
Almonte, Sandy, ss	.252	127	10	32	6	3	2	10	6
Bailie, Matt, of	.000	1	0	0	0	0	0	0	0
Blundell, Jordan, 3b	.154	13	1	2	0	0	0	1	1
Chappel, Dan, 2b	.182	11	2	2	1	0	0	1	1
2-team (29 Edmonton)	.216	111	14	24	5	0	0	9	1
Cole, Eric, of	.282	309	51	87	20	2	7	44	4
Dobosz, Dave, of	.000	0	1	0	0	0	0	0	0
Draska, Chris, of	.143	21	0	3	1	0	0	2	0
Gentry, Garett, of	.167	12	1	2	0	0	0	0	0
Gord, Nelson, of	.272	305	52	83	13	1	2	28	27
Hendrickson, Justin, of	.201	164	13	33	4	0	5	18	0
Hughes, Mike, of	.667	3	0	2	0	0	0	0	0
Jackson, Dan, of	.000	1	0	0	0	0	0	0	0
Lopez, Josue, 1b	.232	332	38	77	17	0	10	39	4
Marconi, Rob, 2b	.221	140	19	31	4	3	4	18	6
Marks, Tim, c	.256	215	25	55	7	1	0	8	0
McCallum, Geoff, ss	.305	220	41	67	9	1	1	24	15
Navarro, Ramon, 2b	.310	29	6	9	1	0	1	6	0
Patterson, Jarrod, 3b	.257	171	21	44	13	2	3	37	0
Sather, Todd, of	.250	8	0	2	0	0	0	0	0
Schweitzer, Matt, of	.333	3	0	1	0	0	0	0	0
Van Iderstine, Ben, of	.301	316	37	95	20	0	3	47	2

INDEPENDENT LEAGUES

	AVG	AB	R	H	2B	3B	HR	RBI	SB
Walker, Ryan, c	.228	219	21	50	5	0	2	25	0
Watson, Rob, 2b	.230	287	35	66	11	3	2	32	7
Weekly, Chris, 3b	.328	338	59	111	22	2	10	61	11

PITCHING	W	L	ERA	G	SV	IP	H	BB	SO
Andel, Chris	3	1	2.63	44	0	55	46	19	46
Bailie, Matt	2	5	4.11	9	0	50	58	16	46
Brunke, Jason	0	1	4.50	2	0	8	13	2	5
Cotton, Nate	1	1	0.67	25	17	27	12	9	32
DeHart, Rick	5	6	5.79	19	0	112	133	35	69
Dobosz, Dave	4	6	5.63	13	0	70	89	26	22
Durost, Kenny	3	1	2.03	7	0	40	30	17	43
Ellison, Derrick	0	1	7.53	8	0	14	15	8	9
Glick, David	1	1	1.89	3	0	19	17	10	7
2-team (5 Winnipeg)	2	4	4.50	8	0	38	45	23	18
Gord, Nelson	0	0	6.75	2	0	4	8	1	0
Hahn, Charlie	1	0	1.29	1	0	7	2	1	1
2-team (5 Calgary)	1	0	6.48	6	0	17	18	5	4
Holmen, Ian	0	2	9.00	5	0	17	21	19	12
Hummel, John	1	0	36.00	1	0	2	6	4	0
Jackson, Dan	5	4	3.78	47	6	48	59	17	43
Jefferson, Andrew	4	1	3.72	25	0	36	41	20	17
Jenkins, Raymond	7	8	4.66	21	0	112	120	59	69
Schweitzer, Matt	6	4	3.58	50	1	83	89	22	82
Swindle, Robert	2	2	3.41	5	0	32	32	8	22
Walker, Ryan	0	0	7.50	2	0	6	8	2	3
Watson, Rob	0	0	4.50	1	0	2	2	0	2
Williams, Blake	6	5	2.92	15	0	96	91	29	69

WINNIPEG GOLDEYES

BATTING	AVG	AB	R	H	2B	3B	HR	RBI	SB
Benick, Jon, 1b	.234	47	5	11	3	0	0	2	0
Berrios, Harry, of	.319	210	24	67	6	1	3	28	0
Gates, David, of	.245	188	33	46	10	0	5	29	4
Hamilton, Ryan, 2b	.234	175	16	41	5	0	0	15	1
Hurst, Jimmy, of	.307	335	74	103	19	1	18	78	11
Johnstone, Tyler, 2b OF	.000	2	0	0	0	0	0	0	0
Lentini, Fehlandt, of	.325	418	93	136	32	13	6	49	57
Mann, Matt, of	.279	358	44	100	23	0	9	59	11
Matos, Julius, 2b	.268	56	13	15	2	0	1	7	1
Maxwell, Keith, of	.293	99	14	29	4	0	4	17	0
Mendoza, Aaron, c	.318	217	31	69	17	1	3	32	4
Mercado, Oni, c	.194	31	2	6	1	0	0	1	0
Poulin, Ma, ss	.225	306	34	69	14	1	0	25	10
Quartararo, Daniel, 2b	.163	43	3	7	1	0	0	4	0
Ramon, Amos, 2b	.303	33	1	10	2	0	0	5	2
Sain, Greg, 1b	.205	156	19	32	9	0	6	27	2
Smith, Will, of	.265	196	28	52	11	0	4	22	3
Stang, Corey, of	.340	97	15	33	4	1	0	13	0
Walsh, Sean, 3b	.233	283	32	66	15	0	3	36	3

PITCHING	W	L	ERA	G	SV	IP	H	BB	SO
Beshears, Josh	10	5	3.25	19	0	119	106	50	85
Bott, Glenn	7	7	3.79	20	0	131	132	30	96
Brown, Joe	2	3	3.60	36	2	65	62	27	56
Chenard, Ken	3	3	4.30	6	0	29	24	8	37
Evans, Tony	5	3	4.58	14	0	73	68	27	64
Glick, David	1	3	7.11	5	0	19	28	13	11
Glosser, Jason	0	0	9.53	6	0	11	17	4	7
Harris, Reggie	0	0	27.00	1	0	1	3	1	1
Harrison, James	0	0	9.53	11	0	11	18	4	7
Kite, Josh	1	1	1.96	43	12	46	34	16	54
Litchfield, B.J.	1	0	9.00	1	0	1	2	0	1
Moore, Ben	7	4	2.51	19	0	97	78	23	58
2-team (3 Joliet)	7	6	3.30	22	0	104	87	29	62
Pence, Howard	7	4	2.34	38	1	50	41	27	37
Poulin, Ma	0	0	0.00	1	0	1	0	0	1
Ramon, Amos	0	0	0.00	1	0	2	1	0	1
Scarbery, Chad	2	2	5.14	12	0	61	71	26	37
Smith, Donnie	1	2	2.51	23	0	14	9	13	11
Sobkow, Phil	0	1	5.14	5	0	21	26	14	10
Soto, Darwin	1	2	5.48	23	9	23	36	7	15
Stirm, Brian	1	3	6.43	9	0	7	11	7	5
Velazquez, Juan	0	0	4.91	4	0	4	3	1	7
Villarreal, Luis	2	0	2.38	2	0	11	12	3	9
2-team (14 Joliet)	6	5	2.71	16	0	90	88	33	63
Wagner, Mike	1	1	2.55	37	1	49	39	11	42

UNITED LEAGUE

All season, Edinburg was the monster of the United League. The team started out 17-0 and had the best record in the league all season.

But when the playoffs came around, the third-seeded Alexandria Aces pulled off the upset, beating Edinburg in the league's first championship series.

"I knew all along we had a good chance of winning. We had two or three former big leaguers, three or four Triple-A guys and a number of Double-A guys, so they never panicked. Whether we won five in a row or lost five in a row, they kept an even keel," Alexandria manager Ricky Van Asselberg said.

Van Asselberg wasn't hired until just a couple of weeks before the season began. He was the team's third manager after one backed out and another resigned because of health reasons, so the team he fielded on Opening Day was the handiwork of others. He found himself with three rookies in his rotation when the season began.

So the Aces signed veteran catcher Ryan Smith to handle the pitching staff, then added Justin Dowdy as the closer. And when they found rookie pitcher Adam Frey, everything fell into place. The 22-year-old out of Division III Trinity College dominated older hitters with exceptional command of his 90 mph fastball.

Frey was on the mound in the championship series clincher. The game was closed out by Dowdy, another midseason addition. First baseman Josh Tranum was named the series MVP after hitting .714 (10-for-14), including a 5-for-5 night in the clincher.

STANDINGS

	W	L	PCT	GB
Edinburg	57	33	.633	—
San Angelo	46	44	.511	11
Alexandria	45	44	.506	11½
Laredo	44	46	.489	13
Amarillo	39	50	.438	17½
Rio Grande	38	52	.422	19

PLAYOFFS: Semifinals—Edinburg defeated Laredo 2-1 and Alexandria defeated San Angelo 2-1 in best-of-3 series. **Finals**—Alexandria defeated Edinburg 3-1 in best-of-5 series.

ATTENDANCE: Amarillo 106,797; Edinburg 93,474; Alexandria 79,071; San Angelo 74,687; Rio Grande 66,928; Laredo 54,591.

MANAGERS: Alexandria—Ricky VanAsselberg; **Amarillo**—Buddy Biancalana; **Edinburg**—Vince Moore; **Laredo**—Dan Shwam; **San Angelo**—Doc Edwards; **Rio Grande**—Eddie Dennis.

INDIVIDUAL BATTING LEADERS

BATTER, TEAM	AVG	G	AB	R	H	HR	RBI
Anderson, John, SA	.390	63	272	61	106	2	47
Figueroa, Carlos, Amar	.339	87	322	73	109	6	62
Bravo, Danny, Amar	.329	61	252	56	83	5	47
Sanguinetti, Tony, SA	.327	79	297	64	97	10	53
Anderson, Keto, Alex	.325	89	385	87	125	3	39
Schnedimiller, Gary, Amar	.323	78	260	66	84	9	56
Cairo, Sergio, RG	.322	59	227	28	73	2	33
Maldonado, Edwin, Lare	.315	89	356	70	112	13	73
Davis, John-Paul, Alex	.307	88	322	46	99	4	67
Beamon, Trey, Alex	.306	80	297	51	91	3	41

INDIVIDUAL PITCHING LEADERS

PITCHER, TEAM	W	L	ERA	IP	H	BB	SO
Steed, Eric, Edin	8	4	3.61	120	118	70	84
Harris, Ryan, Edin	10	6	3.86	131	124	48	108
Montoya, Eric, Edin	10	6	3.90	122	133	46	103
Hernandez, Santo, Alex	8	4	3.94	121	108	51	105
Doble, Clemente, RG	3	5	4.03	89	88	46	83
Flores, Neomar, Edin	9	5	4.12	116	125	43	89
Jones, Fontella, Alex	10	4	4.15	119	115	73	93
Batson, Byron, Lar	9	5	4.44	128	166	25	72
Roque, Darryl, Lar	10	9	4.47	137	151	33	79
Kesten, Michael, Amar	4	6	4.60	94	97	51	93

AMARILLO DILLAS

BATTING	AVG	AB	R	H	2B	3B	HR	RBI	SB
Bravo, Danny, 2b	.329	252	56	83	25	3	5	47	19
Cruz-Rivera, Kenneth, of	.000	5	1	0	0	0	0	0	0
Davis, Eric, of	.249	169	19	42	7	3	3	33	6
Davis, John-Paul, 1b	.307	322	46	99	14	0	4	67	12
Derhak, Alex, c	.125	24	1	3	1	0	0	2	0
Dickinson, Jake, of	.226	53	9	12	3	0	1	5	2

Batting	AVG	AB	R	H	2B	3B	HR	RBI	SB
Donahoo, Brett, of	.289	242	40	70	25	1	6	48	5
Figueroa, Carlos, 2b	.339	322	73	109	19	1	6	62	21
Griffin, Kevin, c	.191	68	4	13	1	1	0	7	0
Krog, John, of	.274	73	7	20	2	0	0	12	3
Lewis, Marcus, of	.278	234	57	65	5	4	0	24	31
2-team (18 Alexandria)	.276	268	61	74	6	4	0	27	31
Lindstrom, Josh, c	.210	62	11	13	2	0	1	8	5
McMullen, Ian, c	.400	5	1	2	0	0	0	0	0
Mendoza, Carlos, of	.338	74	9	25	8	0	0	14	1
2-team (14 Rio Grande)	.339	127	16	43	13	1	0	19	2
Miller, Gerald, of	.205	78	22	16	6	2	0	8	5
Morrison, Bryce, of	.263	167	26	44	12	3	4	25	7
2-team (35 San Angelo)	.289	298	52	86	23	6	7	47	9
Padilla, Eric, ss	.226	288	41	65	12	1	0	25	9
Ramos, Jordan, 2b	.256	133	25	34	8	1	0	14	2
2-team (19 San Angelo)	.241	195	39	47	12	1	0	19	4
Schneidmiller, Gary, 3b	.323	260	66	84	20	3	9	56	14
Smith, Ryan, ss	.200	75	9	15	1	1	1	10	1
Wenger, Justin, c	.260	104	10	27	6	1	0	11	1
Winkler, Shane, of	.077	13	4	1	1	0	0	0	2

Pitching	W	L	ERA	G	SV	IP	H	BB	SO
Agosto, Stevenson	4	6	6.44	14	0	80	103	39	54
Allen, Kyle	4	3	6.44	22	0	43	62	20	44
Allen, Taylor	9	4	4.71	18	0	107	107	67	81
Anderson, Danny	0	0	21.94	4	0	5	9	9	1
Anthony, Spencer	0	0	7.50	5	0	6	4	7	2
Beever, James	0	0	13.94	3	0	10	21	5	5
Davis, John-Paul	0	0	0.00	1	0	1	1	0	0
Griffin, Charles	7	5	5.50	22	0	87	104	34	65
Jensen, Jed	0	0	0.00	3	0	4	5	0	4
2-team (13 San Angelo)	1	3	4.71	16	2	29	36	5	19
Jessee, Clay	0	0	0.00	3	0	1	2	1	3
Kesten, Michael	4	6	4.60	19	1	94	97	51	93
Koshko, Darren	1	1	5.61	16	0	26	34	16	12
Lopez, Omar	0	4	10.20	4	0	15	18	10	10
Parker, Josh	5	8	4.64	23	2	111	124	46	102
Pearson, Craig	0	0	5.52	26	0	44	38	43	42
Perez, Ezequiel	1	0	3.00	4	0	6	7	7	1
Pineiro, Lazaro	0	1	10.29	7	0	7	9	6	4
2-team (7 Alexandria)	0	3	6.95	14	0	22	25	15	14
Pridgeon, Kip	0	0	3.60	5	0	5	3	5	6
Pusateri, Jonathan	1	1	5.59	2	0	10	11	6	3
Rodney, Lee	1	0	1.40	16	0	19	12	11	15
Rodriguez, Mike	1	3	5.21	6	0	38	36	26	34
Stern, Brian	0	0	21.60	2	0	2	5	1	0
Tillman, Derek	0	4	7.11	9	0	13	13	9	17
Waters, Christopher	1	4	3.22	28	13	36	37	11	42
Winings, Brian	0	0	9.00	1	0	1	1	2	0

ALEXANDRIA ACES

Batting	AVG	AB	R	H	2B	3B	HR	RBI	SB
Anderson, Keto, of	.325	385	87	125	11	5	3	39	50
Beamon, Trey, of	.306	297	51	91	11	2	3	41	3
Bonner, Adam, of	.276	261	44	72	24	1	2	25	4
Boyd, Jared, 3b	.141	71	9	10	1	0	0	1	0
Davidson, Cleatus, 2b	.268	306	64	82	14	1	3	37	29
Espinosa, Luis, c	.258	155	20	40	6	0	4	24	1
Griffin, Kevin, c	.242	66	9	16	1	1	0	13	0
Guance, Luis, ss	.297	316	61	94	20	3	11	67	26
Langaigne, Selwyn, of	.345	58	7	20	4	0	2	14	5
Lewis, Marcus, of	.265	34	4	9	1	0	0	3	0
Lynch, Mike, c	.214	14	1	3	0	0	0	2	0
McGuire, Cameron, c	.000	1	1	0	0	0	0	0	0
Mejias, Erick, of	.257	265	40	68	22	0	2	58	26
Paz, Rich, 3b	.305	305	56	93	21	1	5	64	3
Reinking, Kevin, c	.316	19	4	6	1	0	2	8	1
Smith, Ryan, c	.252	147	21	37	8	0	2	11	0
2-team (23 Amarillo)	.234	222	30	52	9	1	3	21	1
Tranum, Josh, 1b	.300	313	62	94	14	2	10	74	12
Van Asselberg, Ricky, c	.000	3	0	0	0	0	0	0	0

Pitching	W	L	ERA	G	SV	IP	H	BB	SO
Bengel, Buddy	5	8	6.08	19	0	90	107	37	50
Bonner, Adam	0	0	0.00	1	0	0	0	1	1
Borland, Curt	3	4	6.97	34	3	41	63	20	38
Boyd, Jared	0	0	9.00	5	0	7	11	4	2
Bridges, Donnie	0	2	16.00	10	0	18	18	11	11
Brownsten, Chris	0	0	8.59	2	0	7	9	2	4
Chivilli, Pedro	0	1	7.20	5	0	7	5	6	8
Cox, Adam	4	2	5.10	17	0	48	40	28	43
Desclouds, Danny	0	0	10.38	2	0	4	6	6	2
Dowdy, Justin	3	1	2.25	17	7	20	12	8	21
Duff, Matt	0	0	5.52	5	0	15	18	6	11
Frey, Adam	4	1	1.93	15	1	47	36	12	27
Garcia, Justin	1	1	3.29	18	1	27	23	13	28

Pitching	W	L	ERA	G	SV	IP	H	BB	SO
Hernandez, Santo	8	4	3.94	19	0	121	108	51	105
Jones, Fontella	10	4	4.15	22	0	119	115	73	93
Martin, Brian	1	5	6.75	7	0	31	34	15	25
Moody, Jason	1	4	4.86	31	0	33	37	20	27
Nourie, Jon	0	0	8.10	3	0	3	5	6	6
Paz, Rich	0	0	0.00	1	0	0	2	1	0
Pineiro, Lazaro	0	2	5.40	7	0	15	16	9	10
Rodriguez, Alejandro	0	2	9.28	3	0	11	15	5	7
Rodriguez, Luis	1	1	3.51	22	0	26	19	22	27
Shack, Jermaine	1	1	9.30	16	0	20	32	13	16
Smith, Mike	3	1	4.74	7	0	38	49	19	36
Smolar, Jordan	0	0	0.00	1	0	2	0	1	2
Snapp, Mike	0	0	0.00	4	0	5	5	4	5
Turney, Brad	0	0	10.80	8	0	8	16	8	5

EDINBURG COYOTES

Batting	AVG	AB	R	H	2B	3B	HR	RBI	SB
Acey, Jermy, ss	.240	154	27	37	8	1	3	31	9
Albertson, Eli, of	.260	281	51	73	12	0	4	32	4
Aranda, Nick, of	.288	59	13	17	5	1	1	10	10
Arias, Garvi, of	.250	112	14	28	4	0	1	14	4
Cancel, Robinson, c	.297	343	58	102	24	0	10	52	28
Cherry, Evan, of	.283	283	39	80	14	0	2	40	7
Gallardo, Carlos, 1b	.296	199	30	59	14	3	0	28	3
Gonzalez, Eric, of	.283	325	68	92	22	0	4	53	14
Grijalva, Lorenzo, 2b	.237	194	52	46	12	2	1	23	17
Lara, Eddie, 3b	.303	323	53	98	16	3	2	62	25
McSweeney, Skye, 1b	.172	29	4	5	2	0	0	2	0
2-team (6 Laredo)	.191	47	5	9	3	0	0	3	1
Medina, Rodney, of	.442	52	7	23	3	0	0	5	3
Olmeda, Jose, 3b	.299	361	61	108	17	1	17	72	5
Sandoval, Abigail, ss	.300	170	17	51	4	0	3	26	7
2-team (20 Rio Grande)	.282	248	27	70	5	0	4	37	9
Wilson, Eddie, c	.295	156	28	46	7	0	0	21	4

Pitching	W	L	ERA	G	SV	IP	H	BB	SO
Casares, Kelly	0	0	0.67	22	7	27	19	3	31
Castro, Julio	6	1	1.62	29	2	33	18	11	33
Clay, Adam	1	0	1.35	6	0	7	7	1	7
2-team (24 Rio Grande)	2	4	5.51	30	7	33	37	17	26
Daly, Brian	2	0	6.11	14	0	18	23	14	13
Flores, Neomar	9	5	4.12	18	0	116	125	43	89
Fox, John	2	3	6.54	9	0	43	49	19	39
Gonzalez, Eric	0	0	0.00	2	0	2	0	0	2
Guerra, Aaron	1	2	1.67	21	0	27	34	5	30
Harris, Ryan	10	6	3.86	19	0	131	124	48	108
Marshall, Jacoby	0	1	11.57	5	0	5	5	7	5
2-team (19 San Angelo)	4	1	8.86	24	0	44	68	37	38
Martin, Larry	1	1	5.63	16	1	16	12	18	17
Montoya, Eric	10	6	3.90	18	0	122	133	46	103
Nesloney, Ryan	1	0	6.35	15	0	17	29	12	11
Nieto, Jose	0	0	0.00	3	0	2	1	4	4
2-team (17 Laredo)	1	1	6.67	20	1	28	28	16	19
Noonan, Andy	2	3	7.78	30	0	57	79	45	47
Ramirez, Edward	1	1	1.07	25	16	25	14	10	46
Ruiz, Julio	4	0	1.93	5	0	28	21	16	13
Steed, Bric	8	4	3.61	18	0	120	118	70	84
Tijerina, Carlos	0	0	7.71	4	0	5	3	4	3

LAREDO BRONCOS

Batting	AVG	AB	R	H	2B	3B	HR	RBI	SB
Bennett, Anthony, of	.271	240	30	65	7	2	3	32	9
Cadena, Alex, c	.188	48	6	9	1	0	0	2	0
Cain, Wes, ss	.000	3	1	0	0	0	0	0	0
Correa, Dalphie, ss	.107	84	10	9	3	0	1	4	3
Cruz, Orlando, of	.287	282	43	81	13	0	10	45	13
Darrell, Ryan, of	.059	17	0	1	0	0	0	1	1
Eisenhower, Charlie, 2b	.000	6	0	0	0	0	0	0	0
Fowler, David, of	.260	127	24	33	7	4	1	16	16
Gibson, Kris, of	.148	27	3	4	0	0	1	4	1
Gram, Kevin, c	.130	23	1	3	0	0	0	0	0
Hough, Brad, of	.259	54	15	14	5	0	1	6	2
Judkins, Chris, 1b	.250	52	11	13	1	1	0	6	13
Karr, Palmer, of	.347	150	31	52	9	1	10	29	10
Khalil, Rashid, of	.074	27	0	2	1	0	0	3	0
Lebron, Hector, 1b	.167	6	0	1	0	0	0	0	0
Maldonado, Edwin, 2b	.315	356	70	112	29	2	13	73	12
Maldonado, Jose, c	.000	0	0	0	0	0	0	0	0
McGuire, Cameron, 1b	.258	159	18	41	12	0	2	18	0
2-team (1 Alexandria)	.256	160	19	41	12	0	2	18	0
McSweeney, Skye, 1b	.222	18	1	4	1	0	0	1	1
Memmert, Gabe, 1b	.253	186	23	47	9	1	3	21	0
Perez, Mark, of	.308	13	1	4	0	0	0	1	0
Ponce, Arnoldo, ss	.298	255	41	76	14	2	6	37	13
Salas, Jose, c	.290	341	51	99	24	2	6	57	5

PITCHING (BATTING cont.)	AVG	AB	R	H	2B	3B	HR	RBI	SB
Serrata, Mike, of	.263	243	63	64	11	2	1	13	16
Tinius, Ben, 3b	.290	317	39	92	17	1	8	52	4
Van Allen, Larry, of	.000	11	2	0	0	0	0	0	1
Zachary, Matt, 1b	.000	1	0	0	0	0	0	0	0

PITCHING	W	L	ERA	G	SV	IP	H	BB	SO
Anderson, Scott	1	2	8.53	11	0	25	40	21	9
Batson, Byron	9	5	4.44	20	0	128	166	25	72
Braun, Bart	0	0	7.36	6	0	7	8	6	5
Cain, Wes	0	1	27.00	4	0	1	1	5	1
Casey, James	0	2	18.78	4	0	8	17	10	6
Cress, Joey	0	1	5.87	9	0	31	44	12	18
Daly, Brian	4	6	6.34	14	0	77	106	30	44
2-team (14 Edinburg)	6	6	6.30	28	0	94	129	44	57
Dunn, James	4	0	1.35	11	0	20	16	4	23
Ferguson, Keith	0	0	14.09	3	0	8	23	3	5
Green, Brian	0	0	0.00	2	0	0	3	2	0
Hough, Brad	0	0	3.38	3	0	8	2	3	10
Johnson, Derrick	0	0	9.00	4	0	3	5	1	3
Kirsch, Brad	0	0	5.40	3	0	2	2	4	0
Laurel, Albert	0	1	7.45	9	0	10	9	8	5
Lewis, James	0	1	1.65	27	13	27	17	13	21
Matta, Felix	0	1	7.56	3	0	8	11	5	3
Nieto, Jose	1	1	7.27	17	1	26	27	12	15
Pusateri, Jonathan	2	2	5.31	23	0	39	44	21	25
Roque, Darryl	10	9	4.47	22	0	137	151	33	79
Serrata, Mike	0	0	4.50	1	0	2	2	0	1
Settle, Mike	0	0	23.14	2	0	2	6	2	0
Shaw, Elliott	5	7	5.74	19	0	105	107	71	74
Smiley, Wesley	1	1	4.34	7	0	19	14	15	24
Smith, John	1	2	7.71	8	1	7	10	5	5
Spaulding, Kevin	0	0	4.05	5	0	7	10	4	8
Stull, Everett	0	1	6.10	2	0	10	10	14	7
Valentin, Dan	1	1	3.44	8	1	18	15	6	16
Zachary, Matt	4	2	3.80	37	2	45	40	19	35

(PITCHING cont.)	W	L	ERA	G	SV	IP	H	BB	SO
2-team (9 Laredo)	5	7	6.30	22	0	90	116	39	51
Cumbie, Beau	0	0	8.04	13	0	16	17	14	15
Doble, Clemente	3	5	4.03	32	6	89	88	46	83
Estrada, Ignacio	2	1	7.94	5	0	11	13	10	9
Fernando, Pedro	1	0	3.18	2	0	6	5	1	4
Foor, Erik	1	1	7.07	6	0	14	15	15	6
Gore, Brian	0	0	14.54	4	0	4	5	7	6
Hanson, Adam	2	2	3.75	5	0	24	20	10	23
Henyan, Peter	0	3	3.66	9	0	47	40	26	42
Lantigua, Denys	1	0	5.19	5	0	9	10	1	4
Matta, Felix	0	2	4.64	14	0	21	20	17	12
2-team (3 Laredo)	0	3	5.46	17	0	30	31	22	15
Morillo, Roberto	0	0	0.00	1	0	1	0	2	0
Parfett, Rob	3	4	5.92	15	0	73	95	31	35
Rodriguez, Felix	0	0	6.35	6	0	6	6	11	1
Rogers, Joe	6	1	2.84	10	0	67	59	10	54
Templet, Jordy	1	2	8.18	4	0	22	23	17	20
Torres, Eduardo	0	0	37.80	2	0	2	4	4	0
Whiteside, Kevin	0	0	0.00	1	0	1	1	0	0
Williams, Julian	1	0	0.00	3	0	6	5	3	4

SAN ANGELO COLTS

BATTING	AVG	AB	R	H	2B	3B	HR	RBI	SB
Allain, Greg, 1b	.188	32	10	6	2	0	1	8	0
Anderson, John, 2b	.390	272	61	106	14	1	2	47	24
Baker, Brian, of	.245	343	57	84	19	5	17	68	2
Bass, Kevin, 1b	.305	298	57	91	21	0	8	49	0
Crosland, Jason, 3b	.300	363	65	109	28	0	21	78	1
Gaines, Ronny, of	.143	21	1	3	1	0	0	0	0
Griffin, Kevin, c	.143	7	1	1	0	0	0	3	0
Guiliano, Matt, ss	.226	208	30	47	7	1	0	22	2
Juarez, Sammy, 3b-SS	.228	79	11	18	1	1	1	8	0
Krause, Scott, 1b	.303	188	33	57	21	2	7	41	0
Lewis, Mark, ss	.111	9	2	1	0	0	0	0	0
Mandelbaum, Kyle, c	.333	3	0	1	1	0	0	2	0
Morrison, Bryce, of	.321	131	26	42	11	3	3	22	2
Palmer, Cody, of	.210	100	8	21	6	0	4	18	1
Pendergrass, Tyrone, of	.281	345	71	97	17	6	4	36	27
Ramos, Jordan, ss	.210	62	14	13	4	0	0	5	2
Rhomberg, Joe, 2b	.252	115	14	29	4	1	2	15	0
Rosario, Olmo, ss	.333	75	17	25	3	2	1	19	5
Sanguinetti, Tony, c	.327	297	64	97	15	5	10	53	0
Sherrill, J.J., of	.274	230	42	63	20	4	6	32	15
Watts, Corey, c	.222	9	2	2	1	0	0	0	0

PITCHING	W	L	ERA	G	SV	IP	H	BB	SO
Artz, Stephen	3	2	4.35	25	0	68	73	15	47
Beever, James	0	2	9.00	6	0	6	11	2	4
2-team (3 James Beever)	0	2	12.12	9	0	16	32	7	9
Ferreras, Yorkin	4	6	3.13	12	0	69	83	19	65
Glick, David	1	2	6.61	6	0	31	40	12	28
Goodman, Mark	2	3	5.40	26	3	77	111	14	36
Gore, Brian	2	1	9.64	4	0	5	3	4	2
Hanson, Adam	3	8	5.99	13	0	77	78	37	62
2-team (5 Rio Grande)	5	10	5.45	18	0	101	98	47	85
James, Frank	3	2	5.13	8	0	40	48	16	12
Jensen, Jed	1	3	5.47	13	2	25	31	5	15
Jernigan, Pat	0	0	7.71	4	0	7	11	2	4
Johnson, Carl	1	0	2.74	5	0	23	20	18	4
Jordan, Brantley	6	4	3.92	35	15	39	41	19	35
Keoppel, Trey	4	1	4.11	11	0	50	51	23	49
King, Ben	1	0	0.00	3	0	3	2	1	0
Lopez, Omar	2	1	5.40	6	0	18	18	13	11
2-team (4 Amarillo)	2	7	5.56	10	0	33	36	23	21
Marshall, Jacoby	4	0	8.54	19	0	39	63	30	33
Martin, Brian	0	0	9.00	2	0	3	5	1	1
2-team (1 Alexandria)	1	5	6.95	9	0	34	39	16	26
Monsma, Quinn	1	0	4.38	12	0	25	29	12	19
Moore, Eric	0	0	4.50	2	0	2	2	1	1
Mulle, Ryan	0	0	2.25	13	0	28	23	7	22
Palmer, Cody	0	0	36.00	1	0	1	6	0	0
Pridgeon, Kip	0	1	2.03	16	0	31	17	29	28
Pusateri, Jonathan	0	0	12.86	2	0	7	18	7	1
Richardson, Beau	0	0	5.40	2	0	2	2	1	1
Rodriguez, Alejandro	0	0	0.00	3	0	11	8	2	9
2-team (3 Alexandria)	0	2	4.64	6	0	21	23	7	16
Rodriguez, Mike	1	3	6.80	8	0	45	45	33	35
Rodriguez, Wil	0	0	12.79	3	0	6	10	9	7
Smith, John	1	2	1.54	17	2	23	19	13	25
Snapp, Mike	0	0	20.25	1	0	3	3	3	1
Walker, Edwin	2	0	5.14	6	0	28	32	17	26

RIO GRANDE VALLEY WHITEWINGS

BATTING	AVG	AB	R	H	2B	3B	HR	RBI	SB
Acey, Jermy, 3b	.310	168	30	52	10	3	4	27	10
2-team (41 Edinburg)	.276	322	57	89	18	4	7	58	19
Astrauskas, Wayne, 1b	.212	66	8	14	2	0	2	10	1
Barillas, Norlan, 1b	.200	15	2	3	1	0	1	3	0
Bergstrom, Bub, of	.269	26	5	7	0	1	0	2	1
Blanco, Luis, 1b	.235	153	19	36	6	0	6	21	0
Bozenhard, A.J., 3b	.200	5	0	1	0	0	0	0	1
Bramasco, Omar, ss	.286	283	65	81	28	1	6	35	13
Cairo, Sergio, of	.322	227	28	73	7	2	2	33	1
Castillo, Braulio, of	.331	163	32	54	13	4	6	31	0
Clary, Casey, c	.228	268	30	61	17	0	10	41	2
Doble, Clemente, of	.000	2	0	0	0	0	0	0	0
Downing, Juan, 3b	.156	32	2	5	1	0	0	2	0
Downing, Ramon, 2b	.174	23	3	4	1	0	0	4	0
Gray, Antoin, 2b	.298	319	80	95	22	1	21	80	10
4-team (41 Alex., 19 Amar., 2 SA)	.233	206	24	48	6	3	0	33	1
Griffin, Kevin, c	.277	65	10	18	4	1	0	10	1
Isoz, Pat, ss	.294	17	2	5	1	0	0	1	0
Jay, Scott, 1b	.228	57	3	13	3	0	1	9	0
Lantigua, Denys, of-C	.309	81	9	25	6	0	1	10	2
Lorenzo, Juan, of	.333	39	3	13	2	0	0	8	0
McLain, Sam, of	.286	231	41	66	19	2	3	26	7
Mejia, Jorge, 2b	.185	54	9	10	3	0	1	9	1
Mendoza, Carlos, of	.340	53	7	18	5	1	0	5	1
Morillo, Roberto, ss	.167	18	1	3	0	0	0	1	4
Nunez, Dimerson, of	.302	53	6	16	6	0	0	4	0
Peguero, Miguel, ss	.316	57	10	18	2	1	1	8	3
Pena, Waren, of	.263	99	13	26	4	0	0	8	0
Sandoval, Abigail, 3b	.244	78	10	19	1	0	1	11	2
Sena, Sonel, c	.188	16	1	3	0	0	0	1	0
Szabo, Jordan, of	.205	88	8	18	3	1	0	7	1
Whiteside, Kevin, of	.226	199	37	45	5	1	1	20	14
Williams, Julian, of	.254	63	13	16	4	0	0	8	0

PITCHING	W	L	ERA	G	SV	IP	H	BB	SO
Acosta, Nibaldo	1	2	3.11	19	0	46	46	26	44
Bennett, Ryan	1	1	4.32	11	0	25	26	19	24
Bonilla, Danny	2	8	7.16	19	0	99	110	67	114
Bowe, Brandon	3	4	9.24	15	2	25	27	22	20
Bozenhard, A.J.	3	6	6.22	15	0	68	90	26	28
Buitron, Andy	0	0	67.50	1	0	1	2	2	1
Cabaniel, Tomas	1	0	3.00	2	0	3	3	1	3
Clary, Casey	0	0	0.00	1	0	1	0	0	1
Clay, Adam	1	4	6.58	24	7	26	30	16	19
Cress, Joey	5	6	6.52	13	0	59	72	27	33

INTERNATIONAL
BASEBALL

Team USA's return to Olympics caps outstanding summer season

BY JOHN MANUEL

Shorn of its Cold War drama, the baseball rivalry between Cuba and the United States still burns bright, as high-quality players, tight games between the two in their rare meetings and 45 years of political tension stoke the fiery competition. The teams' meeting in the final game of the 2006 Americas Olympic Qualifier had little practical meaning, as both already had qualified for the 2008 Olympic field in Beijing, China.

But the game was about more than the rivalry between two teams, about more than just bragging rights. USA Baseball CEO Paul Seiler had explained the scope of the situation to the American team, full of minor league prospects such as Angels infielder Brandon Wood, Royals outfielder Billy Butler, catchers Jarrod Saltalamacchia (Braves) and Kurt Suzuki (Athletics), and Twins righthander Kevin Slowey, when it first gathered in Kissimmee, Fla.

"I had an American flag with me, and I just explained to the guys that we didn't qualify (for the 2004 Olympics) in 2003. That was tough to go through," Seiler said. "I sat there in Athens and watched the 2004 Games go on without the United States playing. I played soccer, and I watched this year's World Cup with the U.S. not getting out of the first round.

"I talked about what happened with the World Baseball Classic, about how great that was but how the U.S. went 3-3. I'm tired of watching the list of U.S. sports failures on TV. I told them we had an opportunity to go to Cuba and to not just qualify for the Olympics—though that was the primary goal—but to plant a stake in the ground, hang this American flag and say, 'We're back.' "

Consider it done. Slowey threw five steady innings, giving up only one run. Team USA usurped the usual Cuban game plan and sprinted out to a 5-1 lead, then stayed resilient when Cuba rallied to tie the game at 5. In the end, talent came to the forefront, as Wood clubbed a two-run homer in the eighth to break the tie. Saltalamacchia homered in the ninth, and American relievers Lee Gronkiewicz (Blue Jays) and Henry Owens (Mets) held on for an 8-5 victory.

Wood had struggled most of the tournament and had just five hits in 32 at-bats entering the eighth inning against Cuba when he faced ace reliever Pedro Luis Lazo. Suzuki had singled to lead off the frame, and U.S. manager Davey Johnson signaled for Wood to bunt the potential go-ahead runner over. Wood has three successful sacrifice hits the last two years in the minors to go with 172 extra-base hits, and true to form, he was more comfortable with the latter.

"Most of us learn all the signs just to stay interested in the game," said Slowey, who had given up one run in five innings in his start against Cuba only to see the Cubans battle back against relievers J. Brent Cox (Yankees) and Jeff Ridgway (Devil Rays). "We see Woody up and the first

September fist pump
Bobby Hill slides home with one of Team USA's runs in an 8-5 win over Cuba

pitch was up and in, and he missed it. The next one he couldn't get the bunt down. So now we're all saying, 'OK, 0-2, just hit one out now.' And the one he hit was just a towering shot, and when we saw their center fielder drop his head and watch it go out, we lost it.

"We were all running out there to home plate to meet him. You would never see that in a pro game. It was like we were all in college again. I was talking about it in the dugout with Nick Adenhart (Angels), we were like, 'Did we just do that?' "

The finale, which silenced an above-capacity crowd of 45,000 in Havana's Stadio Latinamericano, capped an impressive display by Team USA, just the second pro team since USA Baseball started using professionals in 1999 to win a significant international tournament. The first, of course, was the 2000 Olympic team.

That was the last time Team USA had beaten Cuba in any important international tournament, but in 2006, Cuba came up empty (though it had entered the Intercontinental Cup, played in November in Taiwan, an event that did not include the U.S. or any other North American or Caribbean nations). More shocking is three of the five major international events on the calendar—the Olympic qualifier, the FISU World University Championships (for college-aged players) and the World Junior Championships—all took place on Cuban soil, and Cuba won none of them. One veteran Cuban journalist said he could not remember a worse summer for Cuban baseball.

Few can remember one so successful for USA Baseball. Its teams also won the Pan American Youth (16-and-under) championship in Venezuela in August and the FISU championship, which marked the first time an American college team had won a tournament in Cuba.

The stellar summer was a welcome one for USA Baseball, which has endured choppy waters since the 2003 defeat Seiler told the team about. Manager Frank Robinson had a talented squad in '03 but it was eliminated in the quarterfinals of the Olympic qualifying event that year in Panama. Not only did USA Baseball not field

INTERNATIONAL BASEBALL

a team for the '04 Olympics, but it also lost the U.S. Olympic Committee funding that comes with being in the Games. Then baseball was removed from the Olympic program altogether, making Beijing the last scheduled Olympic baseball tournament.

But in 2006, USA Baseball began to rebound from those disappointments. It struck a partnership with Major League Baseball and will receive the bulk of its funding from MLB and the player's union. Construction on its new four-field complex in suburban Cary, N.C., neared completion, and then there was the success on the field.

The qualifier team lost only once, dropping a 12-9 decision to Venezuela in extra innings, when its bullpen faltered. Otherwise, the team had success behind a powerful offense that slugged 19 homers in nine games, including a walk-off game-winner by Suzuki against Brazil and five against Cuba in the finale—two by unlikely power source Michael Bourn (Phillies), who hit just five in 470 at-bats in the minor league season. Bourn was one of six Americans with two homers in the event, while Mark Reynolds (Diamondbacks) hit four to lead the team. Outfielder Skip Schumaker (Cardinals), called the team's MVP by both Slowey and Seiler, hit .405 and scored 15 runs as the team's sparkplug leadoff man, while second baseman Bobby Hill (Padres) led the event with a .522 average and .667 on-base percentage.

The pitching staff also delivered for the most part, as lefthander Heath Phillips (White Sox) and righty Zach Segovia (Phillies) won both of their starts and the staff overall delivered a 3-1 strikeout-walk ratio.

The event's top pitcher was Cuba's top performer, 21-year-old righthander Frank Montieth, fast emerging as the island nation's top young pitcher. He won both of his starts and pitched 13 scoreless innings in the tournament, walking two, giving up two hits and striking out 15.

Mexico—which didn't originally qualify for this tournament, gaining entry only when Aruba failed to field a team at the last minute and dropped out—and Canada kept their Olympic hopes alive by finishing third and fourth. They will play in a second-chance Olympic qualifier in 2007 in Taiwan. Venezuela (fifth place) and Panama (sixth) qualified for the 2007 World Cup, while seventh-place Nicaragua qualified for the 2007 Pan American Games in Brazil.

But only one team could be the winner, and this time, it was Team USA.

"It has been a good year," Seiler said. "If I had to pick three highlights of my tenure at USA Baseball, I'd definitely rank the bus-ride home after qualifying right up there with the '95 junior team at Fenway Park, which was just a special group and a special feeling, and Sydney 2000, because winning Olympic gold is the pinnacle of what we do.

"But that bus ride home was just filled with such positive energy, with some relief mixed in. Beating Cuba to win the thing was just icing on the cake, but it did make me think what a great year we've had."

Flexing In FISU

The college national team won its second straight FISU championship, following up the gold won in '04 in Taiwan by a team that featured an infield with current Nationals third baseman Ryan Zimmerman, Rockies

2006 AMERICAS OLYMPIC QUALIFIER

POOL PLAY STANDINGS

POOL A	W	L	POOL B	W	L
*Cuba	5	0	*United States	4	1
*Panama	4	1	*Mexico	4	1
*Nicaragua	3	2	*Canada	3	2
*Dominican Republic	2	3	*Venezuela	2	3
Colombia	1	4	Puerto Rico	1	4
Ecuador	0	5	Brazil	1	4

*Advanced to second round

SECOND-ROUND STANDINGS

	W	L
^$United States	6	1
^$Cuba	6	1
@$Mexico	5	2
@$Canada	4	3
$Venezuela	3	4
$Panama	2	5
Nicaragua	2	5
Dominican Republic	0	7

^Qualified for 2008 Olympics
@Qualified for 2007 second-stage Olympic qualifier
$Qualified for 2007 World Cup in Taiwan

INDIVIDUAL BATTING LEADERS
(Minimum 20 Plate Appearances)

	AVG	AB	R	H	2B	3B	HR	RBI	SB
Hill, Bobby, USA	.522	23	7	12	0	1	1	7	0
Agnoly, Earl, Pan	.471	34	11	16	2	0	1	6	0
Suzuki, Kurt, USA	.455	22	6	10	4	0	2	4	1
Quintero, Cesar, Pan	.452	31	5	14	2	1	1	5	2
Saunders, Michael, Can	.448	29	4	13	4	0	0	7	0
Duvergel, Girovis, Cuba	.429	28	9	12	1	1	1	5	0
Enriquez, Michel, Cuba	.429	35	10	15	1	1	1	8	0
Frostad, Emerson, Can	.421	19	8	8	0	0	2	3	1
DePaula, Luis, DR	.409	22	3	9	0	1	2	9	0
Schumaker, Skip USA	.405	37	15	15	2	1	1	8	0

INDIVIDUAL PITCHING LEADERS
(Minimum 10 Innings)

	W	L	ERA	SV	IP	H	BB	SO
Montieth, Frank, Cuba	2	0	0.00	0	13	2	2	15
Gonzalez, Norberto, Cuba	1	0	0.00	0	10	5	2	13
Ortega, Pablo, Mex	2	0	0.54	0	17	10	2	22
Palma, Adiel, Cuba	2	0	0.71	0	13	9	6	23
Begg, Chris, Can	2	0	1.35	0	13	11	2	12
Diaz, Rafael, Mex	3	0	1.38	0	13	11	2	10
Phillips, Heath, USA	2	0	1.38	0	13	8	1	8
Gray, Brett, Can	1	1	1.38	0	13	8	3	10
Pineda, Jairo, Nic	1	0	1.80	0	10	6	5	8
Cedeno, Bienvenido, Pan	1	0	1.80	0	10	5	5	9

TEAM USA STATISTICS

PLAYER	AVG	AB	R	H	2B	3B	HR	RBI	SB
Bobby Hill, 2b	.522	23	7	12	0	1	1	7	1
Kurt Suzuki, c	.455	22	6	10	4	0	2	4	0
Skip Schumaker, of	.405	37	15	15	2	1	1	8	0
Mike Kinkade, 3b	.333	30	8	10	3	0	0	11	0
Mark Reynolds, 2b/3b	.320	25	8	8	0	0	4	8	0
Billy Butler, of	.313	32	5	10	2	0	2	8	1
Jarrod Saltalamacchia, c	.250	32	5	8	2	0	1	4	0
Chad Allen, of	.250	24	3	6	0	0	2	10	0
Michael Bourn, of	.250	24	6	6	1	0	2	4	1
Bryan La Hair, 1b	.222	36	10	8	2	1	2	9	0
Brandon Wood, ss	.182	33	9	6	1	1	2	5	0
Matt Tupman, c	.000	2	0	0	0	0	0	0	0

PITCHERS	W	L	ERA	G	SV	IP	H	BB	SO
Nick Adenart, rhp	0	0	7.71	4	0	7	9	1	6
Mike Bacsik, lhp	0	1	9.00	2	1	5	7	1	5
J. Brent Cox, rhp	0	0	3.86	4	0	7	8	3	7
Jeff Farnsworth, rhp	1	0	3.00	4	0	3	4	1	4
Lee Gronkiewicz, rhp	1	0	5.40	5	0	5	6	1	7
Henry Owens, rhp	0	0	6.35	6	3	6	4	3	6
Heath Phillips, lhp	2	0	1.38	2	0	13	8	1	8
Jeff Ridgway, lhp	0	0	0.00	4	0	3	3	2	5
Zach Segovia, rhp	2	0	2.45	2	0	11	8	3	6
Kevin Slowey, rhp	0	0	4.50	2	0	10	10	2	7
Greg Smith, lhp	0	0	4.91	2	0	7	8	4	6
Nick Ungs, rhp	2	0	3.52	3	0	8	7	1	6

shortstop Troy Tulowitzki and Minor League Player of the Year Alex Gordon (Royals). The '06 club may not have had quite that level of talent, but it beat Taiwan 18-9 in

BATTING

Name	AVG	AB	R	H	2B	3B	HR	RBI
Michael Main	.500	10	4	5	1	0	0	1
Greg Peavey	.500	2	0	1	0	0	0	1
Daniel Elorriaga	.412	17	4	7	2	0	1	4
Justin Jackson	.310	29	5	9	1	0	0	5
Tommy Medica	.304	23	6	7	2	0	0	4
Christian Colon	.276	29	3	8	1	0	0	1
Matt Newman	.269	26	5	7	2	0	0	2
Matt Dominguez	.241	29	4	7	1	1	2	11
Mike Moustakas	.231	26	9	6	0	0	1	7
Victor Sanchez	.160	25	4	4	0	0	0	3
Freddie Freeman	.095	21	1	2	1	0	0	2
Hunter Morris	.000	7	1	0	0	0	0	0

PITCHING

Name	W	L	ERA	IP	H	BB	SO	AVG
Blake Beavan	2	1	0.00	15	10	3	14	.196
Tim Anderson	0	0	0.00	8	6	1	12	.188
Kevin Rhoderick	0	0	0.00	4	3	2	7	.231
Jarrod Parker	1	0	0.77	12	6	5	10	.154
Greg Peavey	1	1	1.29	7	3	1	12	.120
Neil Ramirez	2	0	2.89	9	5	8	10	.156
Matt Harvey	2	1	4.70	8	6	7	11	.214
Michael Main	0	0	7.71	2	1	2	3	.167

the FISU tournament finale to win the gold medal. Going 8-0 in the event, Team USA won its first-ever event in Cuba (though it did not play Cuba, eliminated in the semifinals) and went 28-2-1 overall on the summer, a .919 winning percentage, tops in program history.

Catcher J.P. Arencibia (Tennessee), playing his second summer with Team USA, emerged as one of the team's stars in Cuba, the nation of his parents' birth. He was the event's MVP after hitting .412 with four home runs and 23 RBIs in the event, and his nine home runs led Team USA for the summer. A pair of Vanderbilt stars led the Americans, as lefthander David Price was the team's top starter while third baseman Pedro Alvarez its top bat. Price went 5-1, 0.20 (a Team USA ERA record) with 61 strikeouts in 44 innings, while Alvarez led the team in batting (.379) and RBIs (43) while adding five homers.

"I definitely would have liked to play Cuba," said Team USA ace lefthander David Price, who was named Baseball America's Summer Player of the Year. "I didn't think they were very good—I would have liked to put a nice whuppin' on Cuba and have a nice crowd there, but I guess we beat Chinese Taipei for the ninth time (this summer). That's pretty good to beat a team nine times."

In the finale, Team USA set season highs for hits (22) and runs to overcome an early 3-0 deficit, scoring 13 unanswered runs to help lefthander Nick Schmidt (Arkansas) pick up his third victory of the summer. Schmidt pitched five innings and gave up just two hits and three unearned runs while striking out five and walking four.

"I remember during batting practice before that game," USA coach Tim Corbin said, "and the guys were just centering every ball, and I felt, 'We're going to win. We're going to score some runs today, I can feel it.' We fell behind 3-0 but came right back."

Team USA has won a silver medal

(2002) and two golds (2004, 2006) in the last three FISU World University Games.

Junior Team Settles For Silver

In the final international competition of the year—September's IBAF World Junior Championship in Sancti Spiritus, Cuba—Team USA went for one for the thumb, a fifth tournament championship. But even though Team USA once again successfully dispatched host Cuba's tournament entry, winning 4-0 in the tournament's quarterfinals, it couldn't close the deal. A two-strike, two-out grounder in the bottom of the ninth inning of the gold-medal game bounced over U.S. shortstop Justin Jackson (Asheville, N.C.) and into center field to bring home the winning run, ending the gold medal game 4-3 in favor of Korea.

"It was a two-hopper bringing the shortstop to the bag," said coach Jason Hisey (Pima, Ariz.) "He was going to catch it and touch second when it hit something and went over his head."

Team USA pitchers hit two batters and walked eight others while its offense stranded 14 runners, including two at second and third in the top of the ninth. It was a crushing close to a tumultuous tournament for Team USA.

America lost its first two games of the event during pool play, and barely qualified for the quarterfinals, as the No. 4 seed in one of two four-team brackets. Offense was the main culprit, as Team USA hit just .258 overall and endured a rain-shortened 3-0 shutout loss to Mexico.

Team USA rallied to win five games in a row, starting with a 2-1 victory against Canada that turned its tournament around. Its win against No. 1 overall seed Cuba followed a six-hour rain delay, much of which the team spent napping on a bus to avoid making the two-hour round-trip back to its hotel in Ciego de Avila.

"It was a tremendously emotional week," Hisey said. "Tremendous ups and incredibly scary downs. We just

PLAYER, Pos.	Yr.	SCHOOL	AVG	AB	R	H	2B	3B	HR	RBI	SB
Pedro Alvarez, 3b	Fr.	Vanderbilt	.382	110	26	42	11	2	5	40	9
Julio Borbon, of	So.	Tennessee	.345	116	35	40	1	4	4	20	14
Jemile Weeks, 2b	Fr.	Miami	.343	108	29	37	8	1	4	21	14
J.P. Arencibia, c	So.	Tennessee	.302	116	20	35	9	2	8	37	1
Roger Kieschnick, of	Fr.	Texas Tech	.290	62	8	18	4	1	1	14	2
Preston Clark, c	Fr.	Texas	.263	57	12	15	5	0	2	9	4
Darwin Barney, ss	So.	Oregon State	.258	93	17	24	6	0	1	8	6
Brandon Crawford, ss	Fr.	UCLA	.257	35	7	9	2	0	0	6	1
Sean Doolittle, 1b/lhp	So.	Virginia	.239	113	18	27	4	0	2	13	0
Tim Federowicz, c/rhp	Fr.	North Carolina	.226	31	5	7	2	0	0	7	0
Zack Cozart, ss	So.	Mississippi	.224	67	14	15	4	0	1	11	5
Todd Frazier, ss/of	So.	Rutgers	.224	76	14	17	1	1	3	9	4
Tommy Hunter, rhp	Fr.	Alabama	.000	1	0	0	0	0	0	0	0

PITCHERS	Yr.	SCHOOL	W	L	ERA	G	SV	IP	H	BB	SO
Tim Federowciz, rhp	Fr.	North Carolina	0	0	0.00	5	0	6	4	3	10
Andrew Brackman, rhp	So.	N. C. State	0	0	0.00	2	0	4	2	2	3
Sean Doolittle, lhp	So.	Virginia	0	0	0.00	1	0	2	0	0	4
Darwin Barney, rhp	So.	Oregon State	0	0	0.00	1	0	1	1	0	0
David Price, lhp	So.	Vanderbilt	5	1	0.20	8	0	44	21	7	61
Jake Arrieta, rhp	So.	Texas Christian	4	0	0.27	6	0	34	11	23	34
Cole St.Clair, lhp	So.	Rice	4	0	0.69	13	3	26	10	8	43
Daniel Moskos, lhp	Fr.	Clemson	0	0	0.96	17	6	19	6	4	31
Ross Detwiler, rhp	So.	Missouri State	2	0	1.00	5	0	18	8	7	20
Nick Hill, lhp	Jr.	Army	4	0	1.48	7	1	24	15	9	26
Nick Schmidt, lhp	So.	Arkansas	2	1	1.53	6	0	29	18	9	33
Wes Roemer, rhp	So.	Cal State Fullerton	2	0	2.01	4	0	22	15	6	18
Casey Weathers, rhp	Jr.	Vanderbilt	0	0	2.16	6	0	8	6	4	16
Bryan Augustein, rhp	So.	Florida	1	0	2.45	2	0	7	7	2	7
Tommy Hunter, rhp	Fr.	Alabama	3	0	3.80	14	0	21	19	4	23

Strong performance by junior national team, too
Matt Dominguez helped Team USA win silver in the World Juniors

Moustakas contributed a leaping catch in the third inning, preventing a home run, and Dominguez slammed a crucial three-run homer in the seventh inning to provide the game's key blow.

"I thought our boys stood toe-to-toe with them and punched back," Hisey said. "That, to me, was the determining factor in the game."

The next day, Team USA avenged its loss to Mexico with an 8-2 victory, as Dominguez slammed another three-run shot. But Korea beat Canada and 6-foot-7 ace Phillipe Aumont to reach the finale, and as was the case in 2000—when left-hander/outfielder Shin-Soo Choo, now of the Indians, led them to victory—the Koreans dashed American gold-medal hopes again.

"All four of their runs scored by walk, hit by pitch or errors," Hisey said. "We pitched so well for the whole tournament but just didn't command the strike zone all night (in the gold-medal game)."

It was the fourth world title for Korea. Canada won the bronze medal by defeating Mexico 6-2.

—ALAN MATTHEWS

Youth National Team Captures Gold

USA Baseball's youth national team completed its dominant run through the Pan Am Championships by pounding host Venezuela 13-3 in a game that lasted just seven innings because of the 10-run rule. Team USA trailed for just three innings in the entire tournament, during which it racked up a 9-0 record and won the gold medal.

Seven days removed from pitching the first no-hitter in the 10-year history of the youth national team against Venezuela, Ryan Weber (St. Petersburg, Fla.) threw a complete game to clinch Team USA's first Pan Am championship since 2000.

The closest game was an 8-5 victory against Cuba, which beat the U.S. in the 2005 finals of the World Youth Championship in Mexico. Eight runs tied for the fewest runs the U.S. scored in any game in the event. Team USA scored four runs in the first inning thanks to three Venezuela errors and never looked back.

"You're in a foreign country, and they focused on the white ball, and they accomplished everything that we set out to," U.S. coach Garye LaFevers said of his players. "The most enjoyable part of it was the domination of the tournament."

—AARON FITT

International Tidbits

■ The U.S. won the second Women's World Cup, played in Taiwan, by going 5-1 and beating Japan 13-11 in the final game. Righthander Trista Russo had two victories out of the bullpen to pace the Americans. Japan's Ayumi Ota hit the only home run in the event.

■ International Baseball Federation president Aldo Notari died July 25 in Italy. He was 74. Notari had presided over the IBAF in 1993, overseeing the evolution of international baseball from amateur to professional competitions. He also had lobbied hard, though unsuccessfully, to return baseball to the Olympics for the 2012 Games. USA Baseball had nominated Harvey Schiller, a former chairman of the U.S. Olympic Committee and commissioner of the Southeastern Conference, among other honors, to replace him.

came up one bad hop short."

The junior national team came in with great expectations, and great hopes. The senior class of 2007—which provided 17 of Team USA's 18 players in the 18-and-under tournament—is considered one of the most talented in years by pro scouts, and Team USA seemed to have its best chance in years to bring home a gold medal.

American junior teams had won five golds (this was the program's ninth silver medal), but the last gold came in 1999 in Taiwan. Since then, the U.S. has had plenty of talent come through its junior program, but no more gold medals. It seemed the talent on this team could end the drought, and it also seemed like USA Baseball's year.

But the U.S. avoided disaster in pool play by defeating Canada. The 2-1 victory kept the U.S. in the running for the medal round and got the team started on a hot streak that nearly earned it a gold medal.

Chatsworth (Calif.) High teammates Mike Moustakas and Matt Dominguez led the way with key plays, as Moustakas drove in five runs in an 18-1 rout of Italy, while Dominguez added a three-run double. Dominguez then kicked off an 11-1 rout of Spain with a two-run triple, backing the 12-strikeout effort by righthander Greg Peavey (Vancouver, Wash.).

That set up a quarterfinal matchup against the host Cubans, and the Cuban junior team—led by 17-year-old man-child Dayan Viciedo, who nearly made Cuba's World Baseball Classic roster in March—was undefeated leading into the game. But righthander Blake Beavan (Irving, Texas) pitched fearlessly, using his low arm angle to confound Cuba's hitters in a 4-0 shutout. He gave up just seven hits and struck out 11, and called the victory "one of the best experiences of my life."

Yucatan gets back to pinnacle

BY WILL LINGO

Jesus Castillo gave Yucatan its first Mexican League championship in 22 years, hitting a walk-off homer in the 14th inning of Game Five of the league championship series to push the Lions to a 2-1 win over Monterrey.

MEXICO The teams combined for 17 hits and five errors in the decisive game, but could manage just three runs, none after the second inning—until Castillo's blast.

Castillo led off the 14th by taking Miguel Rubio's 1-2 pitch over the right-field fence. The 23-year-old was 0-for-4 with a walk in the game, and had just one home run in 166 regular season at-bats.

Yucatan won the best-of-seven final series four games to one to claim its third title and first since 1984.

Jose Vargas got his fourth postseason win in the game, shutting down the Sultans over the final five innings. Yucatan starter Oscar Rivera allowed one run on six hits and three walks while fanning eight in seven innings. Over the final three games of the series, Yucatan's starting pitchers gave up one run in 19 innings of work.

The Lions took advantage of two miscues in the second to get on the board. Willie Romero reached on second baseman Miguel Flores' throwing error and advanced two bases on an errant pickoff attempt by Felix Heredia. Raul Sanchez followed with a sacrifice fly to tie the game. Francisco Mendez drove in what proved to be Monterrey's only run in the top of the inning when he singled home Luis Garcia.

The Sultans nearly regained the lead in the 11th when Garcia tried to score from second base on Carlos Rodriguez' infield hit. But second baseman Oswaldo Morejon threw him out.

STANDINGS

FIRST HALF

NORTH	W	L	PCT	GB
Monterrey	39	16	.709	—
Puebla	34	22	.607	5½
Saltillo	34	22	.607	5½
Tijuana	32	24	.571	7½
San Luis Potosi	27	29	.482	12½
Monclova	24	32	.429	15½
Laguna	22	34	.393	17½
Aguascalientes	13	42	.236	26

SOUTH	W	L	PCT	GB
Mexico	35	20	.636	—
Angelopolis	32	24	.571	3½
Oaxaca	31	25	.554	4½
Yucatan	29	26	.527	6
Campeche	24	32	.429	11½
Tabasco	24	32	.429	11½
Veracruz	23	32	.418	12
Cordoba	22	33	.400	13

SECOND HALF

NORTH	W	L	PCT	GB
Monterrey	40	14	.741	—
Puebla	30	22	.577	9
Saltillo	28	23	.549	10½
Laguna	28	25	.528	11½
Tijuana	26	28	.481	14
Monclova	24	28	.462	15
San Luis Potosi	22	32	.407	18
Aguascalientes	14	39	.264	25½

SOUTH	W	L	PCT	GB
Oaxaca	32	19	.627	—
Mexico	31	20	.608	1
Angelopolis	29	21	.580	2½
Yucatan	29	25	.537	4½
Veracruz	26	26	.500	6½
Campeche	23	29	.442	9½
Cordoba	21	31	.404	11½
Tabasco	15	36	.294	17

PLAYOFFS—First round: Saltillo defeated Puebla 4-3, Yucatan defeated Mexico 4-3, Monterrey defeated Tijuana 4-1, and Angelopolis defeated Oaxaca 4-2 in best-of-seven series. **Semifinals:** Monterrey defeated Saltillo 4-1 and Yucatan defeated Angelopolis 4-1 in best-of-seven series. **Finals:** Yucatan defeated Monterrey 4-1 in a best-of-seven series.

ATTENDANCE—Monterrey 1,003,161; Saltillo 581,309; Tijuana 475,508; Laguna 287,671; Monclova 224,642; Yucatan 210,658; Mexico 184,642; Veracruz 174,291; Oaxaca 127,144; Cordoba 125,806; Angelopolis 122,427; Aguascalientes 118,486; Tabasco 117,059; Puebla 114,317; San Luis Potosi 71,686; Campeche 52,470

INDIVIDUAL BATTING LEADERS
(Minimum 341 Plate Appearances)

	AVG	AB	R	H	2B	3B	HR	RBI	SB
Gil, Geronimo, Mexico	.387	310	58	120	32	0	12	71	1
Robles, Javier, Angelopolis	.381	323	71	123	22	2	23	81	4
Martinez, Abel, Aguascalientes	.372	325	50	121	16	3	2	57	7
Lopez, Raul, Monclova	.372	301	53	112	22	1	10	55	2
Cesar, Dionys, Monterrey	.370	440	87	163	31	1	10	72	42
Arredondo, Luis, Yucatan	.370	419	66	155	17	11	3	54	18
Amado, Jose, Cordoba	.364	398	74	145	27	1	20	81	11
Amador, Jose, Laguna	.363	432	83	157	27	1	9	61	8
Lopez, Mendy, Monterrey	.363	353	92	128	23	0	30	94	2
Valdes, Pedro, Oaxaca	.362	370	74	134	34	1	14	100	3
Valle, Jorge Luis, Saltillo	.361	385	71	139	31	2	12	60	0
Brinkley, Darryl, San Luis Potosi	.355	440	72	156	35	1	6	60	24
Adriana, Sharnol, San Luis Potosi	.354	407	79	144	24	3	22	91	31
Otanez, Willis, Veracruz	.354	381	70	135	23	0	19	76	0
O'Sullivan, Pat, San Luis Potosi	.353	344	61	125	21	2	16	60	14
Rodriguez, Serafin, Angelopolis	.353	306	52	108	20	0	6	50	12
Ahumada, Alejandro, S.L. Potosi	.351	413	68	145	20	2	6	49	14
Orantes, Ramon, Monterrey	.351	333	47	117	20	3	5	55	3
Martinez, Manny, Puebla	.348	385	89	134	32	0	15	84	26
Guzman, Edwards, Puebla	.346	407	75	141	20	0	14	78	3
Brena, Jaime, Oaxaca	.345	371	80	128	22	1	2	46	8
Espinoza, Efren, Oaxaca	.342	368	80	126	23	4	23	81	15
Guerrero, Sergio, Saltillo	.341	340	58	116	20	1	8	53	0
Terrazas, Ivan, Monclova	.338	342	80	129	30	5	13	53	8
Iturbe, Pedro, Puebla	.338	373	65	126	18	1	15	76	1
Bullett, Scott, Tabasco/Yucatan	.336	393	60	131	22	2	19	78	3
Vizcarra, Roberto, Campeche	.334	419	65	140	24	0	14	59	5
Castaneda, Rafael, Laguna	.334	371	48	124	26	1	6	69	2
Quintero, Christian, Oaxaca	.332	455	79	151	26	3	8	52	20
Presichi, Cristhian, Saltillo	.332	370	59	123	20	2	17	64	16
Romero, Willie, Yucatan	.331	390	61	129	19	3	7	61	24
Garanzuay, Hector, Monclova	.331	366	53	121	21	2	12	61	4
Saenz, Ricardo, Monclova	.331	357	68	118	26	0	21	85	1

Quintero, Edgar, Monterrey .... .330 367 65 121 26 0 22 94 5
Rios, Eduardo, Aguascalientes...... .329 425 90 140 34 2 33 112 7
Soto, Saul, Mexico .... .329 328 42 108 19 0 17 62 1
Contreras, Albino, Puebla .... .328 344 64 113 25 8 3 38 15
Munoz, Noe, Saltillo...................... .326 362 56 118 19 0 5 52 1
Gomez, Heber, Monterrey .... .326 347 64 113 23 0 5 59 9
Valencia, Carlos, Mexico .... .325 375 60 122 31 1 11 58 0
Meyers, Chad, Veracruz................ .325 338 71 110 24 1 4 37 32
Sievers, Carlos, Tabasco .... .325 302 36 98 18 0 11 53 3
Saucedo, Robert, Mexico .... .324 413 78 134 25 1 27 89 4
Meza, Gonzalo, Monclova .... .321 302 58 97 16 2 8 50 1
Gonzalez, Roman, Aguascalientes... .319 445 77 142 20 4 1 49 9
Martinez, Grimaldo, Aguas. .... .318 377 54 120 20 0 4 43 4
Mendez, Roberto, Monclova .... .317 303 71 96 8 3 13 59 8
Leon, Donny, Puebla .... .316 380 72 120 17 0 23 86 0
Villalobos, Carlos, San Luis Potosi .312 298 41 93 17 2 10 55 3
Langaigne, Selwyn, Cordoba .... .311 392 60 122 29 5 2 39 5
Perez, Robert, Campeche/Yucatan .311 338 43 105 16 0 14 52 3
Sandoval, Jose Luis, Mexico .... .311 299 51 93 19 1 12 53 1
Mata, Noe, Cordoba .... .308 364 45 112 22 2 8 55 4
Espinoza, Jose, Tijuana................ .307 313 61 96 23 2 6 40 1
Castellano, Pedro, Yucatan .... .306 392 62 120 28 1 15 87 0
Cervantes, Ivan, Oaxaca.............. .305 348 55 106 17 0 1 35 4
Latham, Chris, Oaxaca.................. .301 366 76 110 25 4 18 77 19
Gonzalez, Santiago, Veracruz....... .301 346 56 104 25 0 4 29 20
Buelna, Lorenzo, Puebla .... .300 433 71 130 26 6 6 58 8
Flores, Miguel, Monterrey .... .300 350 69 105 14 4 2 40 20
Martinez, Luis Carlos, Puebla ...... .300 313 43 94 16 2 6 34 7
Morejon, Oswaldo, Yucatan .... .299 401 55 120 24 1 5 51 6
Acuna, Jose, Cordoba .... .296 318 58 94 12 7 0 22 12
Burkhart, Morgan, Saltillo/Camp... .294 309 44 91 21 0 8 44 1
Cervantes, Refugio, Agua./Saltillo .292 408 54 119 14 1 17 73 0
Evans, Tom, Tabasco/Saltillo........ .292 359 79 105 21 3 25 68 8
Pellow, Kit, Saltillo........................ .291 306 68 89 17 1 21 66 1
French, Anton, Campeche .... .290 321 67 93 13 6 15 55 22
Diaz, Eddy, Laguna .... .289 398 56 115 20 0 10 71 0
Alvarez, Hector, San Luis Potosi .. .287 303 39 87 15 1 4 31 5
Castro, Domingo, Monclova .... .286 381 45 109 11 2 0 40 16
Salas, Heriberto, Tijuana .... .284 331 60 94 16 0 2 41 2
Sanchez, Roque, Campeche .... .283 332 45 94 19 0 5 39 3
Gastelum, Carlos Alberto, Angel... .282 394 75 111 18 5 1 40 11
Paez, Hector, Campeche/Tijuana .. .280 350 41 98 23 1 11 47 3
Santana, Mario, Tabasco .... .279 330 40 92 18 0 3 39 5
Valdez, Francisco, Cordoba .... .279 298 21 83 11 0 6 47 2
Borges, Luis, Yucatan .... .274 412 53 113 19 2 0 41 3
Diaz, Pedro, Monclova .... .273 377 60 103 21 0 13 56 2
Arias, George, Tijuana .... .272 302 61 82 14 2 19 71 1
Canizalez, Juan, Yucatan/Veracruz .271 317 40 86 16 3 3 43 4
Diaz, Remigio, Tabasco .... .269 335 32 90 18 1 2 27 2
Jimenez, Eduardo, Tijuana .... .263 304 37 80 10 0 15 65 0
Hernandez, Hector, Veracruz .... .260 366 49 95 17 1 4 35 11
Munoz, Jose, Saltillo...................... .260 354 55 92 15 1 6 34 5
Fentanes, Oscar, Cordoba .... .255 322 33 82 8 0 4 37 1
Vazquez, Gregorio, Tabasco.......... .245 298 35 73 7 0 1 25 10
Guizar, Hector, Cordoba .... .244 308 22 75 11 0 4 34 0

OTHER SELECT PLAYERS

	AVG	AB	R	H	2B	3B	HR	RBI	SB
White, Derrick, Tijuana................	.407	285	68	116	31	0	19	73	5
McDonald, Donzell, Yucatan	.326	242	54	79	17	8	5	31	29
Simon, Randall, Tijuana................	.348	233	46	81	13	0	18	69	1
Gil, Benji, Monterrey	.374	198	45	74	9	1	11	45	8
Leon, Jose, Campeche..................	.348	178	34	62	9	0	17	49	2
Smith, Demond, Laguna	.353	156	27	55	16	3	6	27	8
Torrealba, Steve, Aguascalientes ..	.250	124	20	31	6	0	5	13	0
Toca, Jorge, Tabasco....................	.355	124	19	44	9	0	5	21	1
Bass, Jayson, Monclova	.350	120	32	42	7	0	9	24	8
Nunnally, Jon, Campeche	.209	67	12	14	4	0	3	12	0
Swann, Pedro, Tabasco	.296	54	12	16	9	1	1	9	2
Minor, Damon, Campeche	.200	45	8	9	3	0	3	9	0
Valenzuela, Mario, Saltillo	.208	24	3	5	1	0	0	0	0

INDIVIDUAL PITCHING LEADERS
(Minimum 88 Innings)

	W	L	ERA	G	SV	IP	H	BB	SO
Izquierdo, Hansel, Cordoba 9		6	2.92	18	0	129	131	39	80
Garcia, Alfredo, Monterrey 10		2	2.94	20	0	89	104	20	29
Castellanos, Hugo, Tijuana...........6		0	3.17	22	1	111	105	39	111
Robles, Salvador, Mexico 11		4	3.21	23	0	112	119	36	84
Gonzalez, Vinicio, Tabasco...........8		7	3.24	30	2	122	124	45	78
Garcia, Adolfo, Cordoba 4		3	3.25	28	0	89	91	32	22
Elizalde, Carlos, Oaxaca 13		7	3.33	21	0	135	134	41	78
Rios, Alejandro, Saltillo 11		3	3.43	22	1	113	128	42	67
Knott, Eric, Puebla 9		7	3.48	20	0	122	149	21	69
Montano, Ignacio, Veracruz 9		3	3.54	22	0	127	127	48	83
Alvarez, Juan Jesus, Campeche 8		5	3.63	21	0	131	133	51	69
Gonzalez, Rudy, Mexico 7		3	3.64	21	0	106	121	34	89
Campos, Francisco, Camp./Mont...11		5	3.65	19	0	118	111	39	74
Mendoza, Mario, Saltillo...............9		7	3.70	23	0	141	149	45	82
Rivera, Oscar, Yucatan.................9		7	3.73	21	0	121	114	38	112
Silva, Walter, Monterrey...............11		7	3.93	21	0	126	130	50	89
Acosta, Jasiel, Monclova 9		5	3.99	20	0	122	141	43	64
Manrique, Alberto, Laguna 6		3	4.14	24	0	104	101	37	37
Martinez, Juan, Cordoba 5		4	4.21	16	0	88	98	29	32
Moreno, Leobardo, Veracruz 6		8	4.23	19	0	104	110	35	44
Kamar, Emil, Puebla...................11		5	4.24	22	0	140	161	49	59
Alvarez, Victor, Mexico 8		4	4.27	20	0	110	144	32	40
Rivera, Oscar, Tabasco 2		10	4.35	20	0	99	117	54	44
Quinones, Enrique, S.L. Potosi......5		9	4.47	23	0	103	130	23	28
Aceves, Alfredo, Monterrey 8		5	4.50	19	0	124	126	26	95
Quintanilla, Juan, Oaxaca 8		7	4.50	21	0	116	136	27	97
Beltran, Alonso, Tijuana 13		5	4.50	21	0	108	116	42	91
Villalobos, Fernando, Yucatan 8		7	4.51	23	0	108	114	64	58
Santiago, Jose, Tabasco 7		7	4.55	34	0	146	195	23	84
Pulido, Carlos, Monclova 9		8	4.60	22	0	139	176	20	78
Ruiz, Miguel, Campeche...............7		8	4.61	19	0	113	118	43	67
Arellano, Salvador, Yucatan 12		5	4.63	22	0	113	134	45	78
Montemayor, Humberto, Cam./Mon...7		6	4.69	19	1	96	118	27	65
Bourgeois, Steve, Saltillo............10		5	4.75	22	0	121	141	49	86
Cordova, Francisco, Mexico 9		7	4.89	21	0	103	116	30	49
Lopez, Emigdio, Veracruz.............8		5	4.90	19	0	97	112	27	33
Valdez, Armando, Puebla 6		5	4.98	23	0	99	114	40	45
Guzman, Jesus, Angelopolis 11		4	5.11	20	0	92	106	26	50
Coco, Pasqual, Monclova/Cord...10		10	5.15	26	4	117	135	54	86
Garcia, Ramon Antonio, Laguna...8		8	5.19	22	0	127	153	62	45
Renovato, Nestor, S.L. Potosi 4		10	5.22	24	0	117	141	28	57
Navarro, Hector, Veracruz 1		11	5.62	24	0	99	120	47	55
Medrano, Leo, San Luis Potosi 5		7	5.76	28	0	106	134	38	83
Moreno, Claudio, Tijuana 6		10	5.79	24	0	111	133	39	55
Flores, Jorge, Monclova 6		7	6.11	30	1	88	126	37	40
Leyva, Edgar, San Luis Potosi 7		10	6.23	20	0	108	143	31	58
Ramirez, Roberto, Mexico 10		6	6.26	20	0	119	172	26	68
Ortega, Pablo, Angelopolis...........5		6	6.27	21	0	93	121	39	50
Delgadillo, Juan, Tabasco 4		12	6.33	28	0	114	154	45	78
Rodriguez, Raul, Angel./Mon. 5		8	6.35	22	0	95	121	31	56
Elvira, Narciso, Campeche 5		10	6.38	17	0	91	102	43	56
Salgado, Eduardo, Aguas. 4		9	7.17	22	0	117	164	27	56
Perez, Guadalupe, Cordoba 6		6	7.61	20	0	89	121	40	29

OTHER SELECT PLAYERS

	W	L	ERA	G	SV	IP	H	BB	SO
Silva, Jose, Monterrey 1		1	0.82	24	2	22	15	8	15
Yabu, Keiichi, Tijuana..................0		0	3.00	11	5	12	14	2	9
Suzuki, Mac, Tijuana 4		5	3.48	27	11	67	51	39	50
De Los Santos, Valerio, Mont. 6		0	3.54	9	0	53	43	20	37
Beltran, Rigo, Saltillo 2		4	7.58	15	0	59	88	35	37
Dorame, Randey, Monclova 0		0	7.71	22	0	33	43	17	12
Roberts, Willis, Campeche 0		2	8.74	11	3	11	17	7	10
Harriger, Denny, Monclova 1		1	9.26	3	0	12	23	3	9

Another U.S. skipper makes mark

BY WAYNE GRACZYK

For the second consecutive season in Japanese professional baseball, an American manager has taken a Pacific League team to a national title. Following the accomplishment of Bobby Valentine, who led the Chiba Lotte Marines to victory in the 2005 Japan Series, Trey Hillman guided the Hokkaido Nippon Ham Fighters to an easy five-game win over the Central League Chunichi Dragons in 2006.

JAPAN

Hillman, in his fourth year managing the Fighters, took the Nippon Ham franchise to its second Japan championship and its first since 1962 when the club was based in Tokyo and known as the Toei Flyers.

Now in Sapporo on Japan's northernmost main island of Hokkaido, the Fighters won it all with a late regular season surge that allowed them to clinch first place and the number one seed in the three-team post-season P.L. playoffs, a sweep of the Fukuoka SoftBank Hawks in those playoffs and four straight wins over Chunichi after the losing Game one of the Japan Series to the Dragons on the road at Nagoya Dome.

Nippon Ham rode the arms of young pitchers Yu Darvish (a 20-year-old righthander with an Iranian father and a Japanese mother), who posted a regular season record of 12-5, and 23-year-old rookie lefty Tomoya Yagi. Yagi was 12-8.

Spearheading the team's offense was first baseman Michihiro Ogasawara who led the Pacific League with 32 home runs and 100 RBIs while hitting .313, Panamanian slugger Fernando Seguignol (.295, 26 homers) and the Fighters most popular player, former New York Mets and San Francisco Giants outfielder Tsuyoshi Shinjo, also contributed.

One-time Minnesota Twins righty Micheal Nakamura, now the Fighters closer, racked up 39 saves.

Chunichi won its second Central League pennant in three years under manager Hiromitsu Ochiai. The Dragons were led by ace righthander Kenshin Kawkami (17-7), batting champion Kosuke Fukudome (.351) and the league's home run king and RBI leader, former Montreal Expos and Baltimore Orioles farmhand and Korea Baseball Organization star Tyrone Woods, who slammed a Dragons franchise record 47 home runs and drove in 144 while batting .310.

A total of 55 North American and Australian players saw action in Japanese pro baseball in 2006, along with three managers from the U.S. Besides Hillman and Valentine, Marty Brown served as field boss of the Hiroshima Carp for whom he played from 1992-1994.

Among foreign players who stood out this season were first baseman Alex Cabrera of the Seibu Lions (.315, 31, 100) who tied Ogasawara for the Pacific League RBI lead, Hanshin Tigers first baseman Andy Sheets, and infielders Rick Short and Jose Fernandez of the Tohoku Rakuen Golden Eagles, all of whom hit better than .300.

Another first sacker, Adam Riggs of the Yakult Swallows, belted 39 homers to finish third in the Central division behind Woods and Korean slugger Lee Seung Yeop. Lee hit 41 for the Yomiuri Giants and was runner-up in the batting race behind Fukudome with a .323 average.

Non-Japanese pitching standouts included Giants starter Jeremy Powell (10-10), Orix Buffaloes righthander Tom Davey (10-8) and Yokohama BayStars closer Marc Kroon (27 saves). Former U.S. minor leaguer Rick Guttormson threw a no-hitter for the Yakult Swallows during an interleague game against Rakuten.

A trio of Japanese righthanded pitchers caught the eyes of scouts from major league teams who visited Japan throughout the year.

About-to-become free agent Hiroki Kuroda of the Hiroshima Carp led the Central League with a 1.85 ERA while posting a 13-6 record.

Seibu Lions fireballer Daisuke Matsuzaka went 17-5 with a 2.13 ERA and was expected to be posted for major league service following the season.

Though not often mentioned as an immediate candidate for MLB, Kazumi Saito of the Fukuoka SoftBank Hawks topped the Pacific loop with a mark of 18-5, 1.75 and 205 strikeouts in 201 innings pitched.

As the 2006 season was winding down, plans were being made for 2007, with the Central League deciding to join its Pacific cousin in establishing two stages of playoffs to decide its Japan Series representative. The C.L. will adopt the same format as its opposite number, with the top three teams in the regular season standings qualifying for postseason play.

It was also agreed to reduce the number of interleague games, begun in 2005, from 36 to 24, with each club playing four games, rather than six, against each team in the opposite league.

In an apparent continuing trend, another American manager has been hired. Former Houston Astros and Los Angeles Angels skipper Terry Collins has taken over as field boss of the Orix Buffaloes and will battle the language and cultural barriers overcome by Valentine, Hillman and Brown.

CENTRAL LEAGUE

STANDINGS

	W	L	T	PCT.	GB
Chunichi Dragons	87	54	5	.617	—
Hanshin Tigers	84	58	4	.592	3½
Yakult Swallows	70	73	3	.490	18
Yomiuri Giants	65	79	2	.451	23½
Hiroshima Carp	62	79	5	.440	25
Yokohama BayStars	58	84	4	.408	29½

INDIVIDUAL BATTING LEADERS
(Minimum 452 Plate Appearances)

	AVG.	AB	R	H	2B	3B	HR	RBI	SB
Fukudome, Kosuke, Dragons	.351	496	117	174	47	5	31	104	11
Lee, Seung Yeop, Giants	.323	524	101	169	30	0	41	108	5
Aoki, Norichika, Swallows	.321	599	112	192	26	3	13	62	41
Maeda, Tomonori, Carp	.314	472	66	148	22	1	23	75	2

	AVG	AB	R	H	2B	3B	HR	RBI	SB
Iwamura, Akinori, Swallows	.311	546	84	170	27	2	32	77	8
Sheets, Andy, Tigers	.310	580	87	180	31	1	19	75	0
Woods, Tyrone, Dragons	.310	523	85	162	29	0	47	144	1
Kanemoto, Tomoaki, Tigers	.303	545	85	165	24	4	26	98	2
Hamanaka, Osamu, Tigers	.302	486	71	147	26	1	20	75	2
Araki, Masahiro, Dragons	.300	464	69	139	19	1	2	31	30
Arai, Takahiro, Carp	.299	566	78	169	23	2	25	100	1
Riggs, Adam, Swallows	.294	591	111	174	39	0	39	94	11
Abe, Shinnosuke, Giants	.294	452	39	133	26	2	10	56	0
Toritani, Takashi, Tigers	.289	543	65	157	28	2	15	58	5
Soyogi, Eishin, Carp	.289	450	78	130	20	8	8	36	13
Nioka, Tomohiro, Giants	.289	551	67	159	26	0	25	79	0
Ishii, Takuro, BayStars	.288	604	91	174	30	0	6	32	12
Ibata, Hirozaku, Dragons	.283	573	97	162	19	2	8	48	17
Higashide, Akihiro, Carp	.282	504	57	142	10	1	0	23	11
Morino, Masahiko, Dragons	.280	428	58	120	19	0	10	52	0
Miyade, Ryuji, Swallows	.275	422	49	116	22	3	9	59	1
Yano, Akihiro, Tigers	.274	453	42	124	20	3	17	78	0
Ochoa, Alex, Dragons	.273	523	57	143	30	1	15	77	2
Shima, Shigenobu, Carp	.269	495	56	133	12	0	24	69	2
Akahoshi, Norihiro, Tigers	.269	566	84	152	13	3	0	20	35
Kinjo, Tatsuhiko, BayStars	.268	552	60	148	22	2	11	59	2
Ramirez, Alex, Swallows	.267	603	79	161	28	2	26	112	0
Murata, Shuichi, BayStars	.266	545	83	145	30	3	34	114	1
Tanishige, Motonobu, Dragons	.234	428	48	100	22	1	9	38	0

REMAINING U.S. AND LATIN PLAYERS
	AVG	AB	R	H	2B	3B	HR	RBI	SB
LaRocca, Greg, Swallows	.285	379	58	108	14	0	18	63	2
Spencer, Shane, Tigers	.222	108	12	24	5	0	6	17	1
Dillon, Joe, Giants	.195	87	9	17	3	1	2	7	0
Arias, George, Giants	.167	60	5	10	2	0	2	5	0

INDIVIDUAL PITCHING LEADERS
(Minimum 146 Innings)
	W	L	ERAG	SV	IP	H	BB	SO
Kuroda, Hiroki, Carp	13	6	1.85	26	1	189	169	21	144
Fukuhara, Shinobu, Tigers	12	5	2.09	24	0	155	143	42	119
Kawakami, Kenshin, Dragons	17	7	2.51	29	0	215	166	39	194
Utsumi, Tetsuya, Giants	12	13	2.78	31	0	194	163	52	179
Asakura, Kenta, Dragons	13	6	2.79	25	0	155	155	33	107
Guttormson, Rick, Swallows	9	10	2.85	25	0	174	145	38	127
Igawa, Kei, Tigers	14	9	2.97	29	0	209	180	49	194
Shimoyanagi, Tsuyoshi, Tigers	12	11	3.17	25	0	150	154	55	86
Uehara, Koji, Giants	8	9	3.21	24	0	168	157	21	151
Powell, Jeremy, Giants	10	10	3.31	28	0	187	196	31	131
Yamamoto, Masahiro, Dragons	11	7	3.32	27	1	171	147	36	124
Ishii, Kazuhisa, Swallows	11	7	3.44	28	0	178	177	59	170
Miura, Daisuke, BayStars	8	12	3.45	30	0	217	227	44	160
Sasaoka, Shinji, Carp	8	8	4.09	27	0	150	155	29	82
Ishikawa, Masanori, Swallows	10	10	4.53	29	0	151	191	17	81
Kadokura, Ken, BayStars	10	9	4.84	28	0	154	187	51	114
Otake, Kan, Carp	6	13	4.93	30	0	157	172	54	110

REMAINING U.S., AUSTRALIAN AND LATIN PLAYERS
	W	L	ERAG	SV	IP	H	BB	SO
Marte, Victor, Carp	0	1	1.59	12	0	11	5	6	5
Williams, Jeff, Tigers	3	2	1.90	47	3	47	37	15	49
Bale, John, Carp	1	2	2.93	30	6	43	45	11	46
Kroon, Marc, BayStars	2	5	3.0047		27	48	38	8	70
Gonzalez, Dicky, Swallows	9	7	3.15	17	0	114	118	25	95
Douglass, Sean, Carp	9	6	3.41	20	0	98	85	30	71
Cubillan, Darwin, Tigers	1	2	3.79	49	2	74	58	29	55
Sonnier, Shawn, BayStars	1	0	3.82	27	0	31	29	13	37
Guzman, Domingo, Dragons	2	2	3.93	4	0	18	19	2	13
Martinez, Luis, Dragons	6	9	4.25	23	0	112	126	41	75
Glover, Gary, Giants	5	7	4.97	20	0	96	125	23	63
Oxspring, Chris, Tigers	4	3	5.12	16	0	77	78	23	51
Romano, Mike, Carp	5	9	5.64	31	0	104	122	45	65
Feliciano, Juan, Carp	0	1	7.39	12	0	35	50	12	11
Beverlin, Jason, BayStars	0	4	11.13	8	0	32	58	5	29
Galva, Claudio, Dragons	0	0	11.25	3	0	4	5	1	5

PACIFIC LEAGUE

STANDINGS

PACIFIC LEAGUE
	W	L	T	Pct.	GB
Hokkaido Nippon Ham Fighters	82	54	0	.603	—
Seibu Lions	80	54	2	.597	1
Fukuoka SoftBank Hawks	75	56	5	.573	4½
Chiba Lotte Marines	65	70	1	.481	16½
Orix Buffaloes	52	81	3	.391	28½
Tohoku Rakuten Golden Eagles	47	85	4	.356	33

PLAYOFFS—SoftBank defeated Seibu 2-1 in best-of-three series; Nippon Ham defeated SoftBank 2-0 (with one-game pre-series advantage) in best-of-five series for league championship.

INDIVIDUAL BATTING LEADERS
(Minimum 421 Plate Appearances)
	AVG	AB	R	H	2B	3B	HR	RBI	SB
Matsunaga, Nobuhiko, Hawks	.324	447	79	145	32	1	19	76	2
Cabrera, Alex, Lions	.315	466	74	147	21	1	31	100	0
Short, Rick, Eagles	.314	401	33	126	27	0	4	34	5
Ogasawara, Michihiro, Fighters	.313	496	77	155	31	1	32	100	4
Fukuura, Kazuya, Marines	.312	436	43	136	20	1	4	52	0
Kawasaki, Munenori, Hawks	.312	449	69	140	21	7	3	27	24
Inaba, Atsunori, Fighters	.307	473	66	145	22	2	26	75	5
Nakajima, Hiroyuki, Lions	.306	412	76	126	22	1	16	63	14
Tsuchiya, Teppei, Eagles	.303	396	44	120	17	7	2	29	10
Muramatsu, Arihito, Buffaloes	.303	400	52	121	11	4	3	28	13
Fernandez, Jose, Eagles	.302	490	72	148	33	0	28	88	2
Tanaka, Kensuke, Fighters	.301	376	68	113	10	6	7	42	21
Takasu, Yosuke, Eagles	.300	403	41	121	16	2	1	38	10
Wada, Kazuhiro, Lions	.298	484	72	144	34	2	19	95	3
Seguignol, Fernando, Fighters	.295	485	60	143	37	0	26	77	0
Omura, Naoyuki, Hawks	.294	562	74	165	19	3	6	60	22
Akada, Shogo, Lions	.293	451	50	132	16	7	2	34	16
Kataoka, Yasuyuki, Lions	.292	404	57	118	21	4	4	44	28
Morimoto, Hichori, Fighters	.285	520	84	148	28	6	9	42	13
Nishioka, Tsuyoshi, Marines	.282	426	58	120	20	7	4	27	33
Zuleta, Julio, Hawks	.281	466	59	131	22	0	29	91	1
Agbayani, Benny, Eagles	.281	417	59	117	18	1	17	65	4
Shiozaki, Makoto, Buffaloes	.278	410	46	114	14	2	9	31	1
Tani, Yoshitomo, Buffaloes	.267	434	45	116	16	0	6	30	1
Imae, Toshiaki, Marines	.267	457	49	122	25	2	9	47	3
Satozaki, Tomoya, Marines	.264	382	50	101	23	1	17	56	2
Shinjo, Tsuyoshi, Fighters	.258	438	47	113	21	0	16	62	2
Kaneko, Makoto, Fighters	.254	393	44	100	26	3	6	40	7
Yamasaki, Takeshi, Eagles	.241	419	40	101	21	1	19	67	0

REMAINING U.S. AND LATIN PLAYERS
	AVG	AB	R	H	2B	3B	HR	RBI	SB
Watson, Matt, Marines	.274	186	14	51	12	0	5	20	0
Franco, Matt, Marines	.263	274	33	72	8	0	7	20	0
Cabrera, Jolbert, Hawks	.260	342	41	89	21	1	8	50	6
Liefer, Jeff, Lions	.252	143	24	36	9	1	13	32	0
Garcia, Karim, Buffaloes	.249	301	33	75	10	0	13	37	0
Macias, Jose, Fighters	.229	227	24	52	15	1	3	21	3
Brumbaugh, Cliff, Buffaloes	.223	121	13	27	3	0	5	12	1
Pascucci, Val, Marines	.222	203	26	45	9	1	13	32	0
Valent, Eric, Eagles	.189	74	8	14	2	0	1	5	1
Grabowski, Jason, Buffaloes	.146	89	10	13	4	0	4	7	0

INDIVIDUAL PITCHING LEADERS
(Minimum 136 Innings)
	W	L	ERA	G	SV	IP	H	BB	SO
Saito, Kazumi, Hawks	18	5	1.75	26	0	201	147	46	205
Matsuzaka, Daisuke, Lions	17	5	2.13	25	0	186	138	34	200
Yagi, Tomoya, Fighters	12	8	2.48	26	0	171	134	51	108
Davey, Tom, Buffaloes	10	8	2.62	24	0	165	159	53	77
Ono, Shingo, Marines	7	7	2.66	22	0	146	131	29	61
Kobayashi, Hiroyuki, Marines	10	7	2.78	20	0	143	129	27	120
Darvish, Yu, Fighters	12	5	2.89	25	0	150	128	64	115
Wada, Tsuyoshi, Hawks	14	6	2.98	24	0	163	137	42	136
Arakaki, Nagisa, Hawks	13	5	3.01	23	0	155	132	46	151
Kawagoe, Hidetaka, Buffaloes	9	9	3.14	24	0	163	169	29	74
Wakui, Hideaki, Lions	12	8	3.24	26	0	178	161	53	136
Shimizu, Naoyuki, Lions	10	8	3.42	25	0	171	178	36	137
Nishiguchi, Fumiya, Lions	9	9	3.55	26	0	177	175	65	154
Hirano, Yoshihisa, Buffaloes	7	11	3.81	26	0	172	182	39	105
Watanabe, Shunsuke, Marines	5	11	4.35	23	0	147	155	35	105
Ichiba, Yasuhiro, Eagles	7	14	4.37	30	0	194	205	71	151
Kubo, Yasutomo, Fighters	7	13	4.55	23	0	140	153	32	119
Yamamura, Hiroki, Eagles	7	10	5.35	30	0	136	157	46	57

REMAINING U.S., AUSTRALIAN AND LATIN PLAYERS
	W	L	ERA	G	SV	IP	H	BB	SO
Lee, Corey, Fighters	5	3	3.43	11	0	63	58	32	41
Thomas, Brad, Fighters	4	1	3.74	40	1	46	50	23	43
Gissell, Chris, Lions	6	4	3.96	18	0	109	112	30	85
Glynn, Ryan, Eagles	7	7	3.96	21	0	127	143	36	121
Graman, Alex, Lions	4	6	4.26	13	0	74	87	19	41
Beirne, Kevin, Marines	3	5	4.41	28	0	65	60	27	48
Diaz, Felix, Fighters	3	5	4.91	8	0	44	47	16	22
Obermueller, Wes, Buffaloes	1	6	5.31	14	0	42	46	29	27
Serafini, Dan, Buffaloes	0	4	5.97	7	0	22	34	11	11
Miller, Justin, Marines	0	1	10.80	12	0	12	18	10	11
Carrasco, D.J., Hawks	0	3	14.81	3	0	10	22	10	9

Lions take back-to-back titles

The Samsung Lions went back to back in 2006, defending their Korea Baseball Organization title by edging the Hanwha Eagles 3-2 in Game Six of the Korean Series in Seoul.

Following a 15-inning draw, the Lions scored three runs in the first and second innings and held on to wrap up the best-of-seven series four games to one.

KOREA

It was the Lions' fourth title (the others were 1985, 2002 and 2005), and they became the third club in Korean history to win back-to-back titles.

The series MVP award went to shortstop Park Jin-man, who hit a game-winning single in the 12th inning of Game Three and batted .280 in the series.

The league MVP for the season, however, was Ryu Hyun-jin of the Hanwha Eagles, who became the first player in Korea Baseball Organization history to win the MVP and rookie of the year awards in the same season.

Ryu, 19, edged Lotte Giants' Lee Dae-ho, who led the league in homers, RBIs, batting and slugging percentage. The 24-year-old Lee was the first player to win the league's triple crown since former Lion Lee Man-soo in 1984. Oh Seung-hwan of the Samsung Lions, who set the Asian record for the most saves with 47, finished third in the voting.

Ryu, who came into the league directly out of high school, matched Lee's feat by winning the pitching triple crown. He led the league with 18 wins, 204 strikeouts and a 2.23 ERA and became the first pitcher to accomplish the feat since 1991, when it was done by Sun Dong-yol, who now manages the Lions.

Ryu helped the Eagles to place third in the regular season and advance to the Korean Series for the first time since 1999. He started four times in the playoffs but did not record a win.

The Lions leaned on pitching, even though Bae Young-soo, who had two wins and one save with a 0.87 ERA in the Korean Series. A strong bullpen composed of closer Oh Seung-hwan, who saved 47, the most saves in Asia, and reliever Kwon Oh-joon also hellped the team.

The Korean Series created controversy in the nation because two of the six games in the finals were played in Seoul, even though the Lions are based in Taegu and the Eagles are based in Taejon. The KBO gets a cut of playoff ticket sales, so it schedules any finals games beyond the first four in Seoul's 30,000-seat Chamsil Stadium. The first four games of the series were played at the teams' home parks.

If a Seoul-based team advances to the Korean Series, the teams play a traditional schedule in their home parks. But the league says guaranteeing games in a bigger stadium in Seoul gives more fans a chance to see the games

Yet the biggest story in Korean baseball in 2006 did not happen in Korea at all, but in the World Baseball Classic. Korea was a darkhorse in the competition but ended up as one of the tournament's biggest stories,

reaching the semifinals without a loss before losing to Japan.

In the first round, Asian home run king Lee Seung Yeop—who plays professionally in Japan—belted a come-from-behind, two-run home run off Hirotoshi Ishii to give Korea a dramatic 3-2 win over a shocked Japan and first place (3-0 record) in Asian pool play at Tokyodome.

Five Korean pitchers scattered seven hits and held the powerful Japanese team to a run each in the first two innings, then kept Japan scoreless through the ninth. The visitors put a run on the board with a sacrifice fly in the fifth, and Lee turned the tables with his eighth-inning shot into the right-field bleachers.

Both Korea and Japan advanced to the second round, where they were in a pool with the United States and Mexico in Southern California. They again shocked the world by going 3-0 to win the pool, including a win over the United States, behind the slugging of Lee (who ended the tournament with five home runs in seven games) and an outstanding defense that did not commit any errors. Major leaguer Chan Ho Park was the team's leading pitcher, allowing no runs in 10 innings of work.

But the single-elimination semifinals became Korea's undoing against archrival Japan, as righthander Koji Uehara shut them out 6-0 over seven masterful, three-hit innings.

Korea finished with the best record in the Classic (6-1) and beat Japan twice in the first two rounds, but had to fly home with only the consolation of having proven its baseball worthiness not just in Asia, but globally.

"I didn't anticipate that we would be where we are today," Korean manager In Sik Kim said. "I did not expect that at all."

The success in the World Baseball Classic gave the Lions hope that they would dominate Asian baseball at the Konami Cup Asia Series in November, which pits the professional champions from Japan, Taiwan and Korea, as well as an all-star team from China, against each other.

But Korea was upset by Taiwan's champion La New Bears and failed to advance to the finals, which were won by Japan's Nippon Ham Fighters. The Lions were hamstrung by weak offense and by injuries, which kept players like Bae out of the series.

STANDINGS

	W	L	T	PCT	GB
Samsung Lions	73	50	3	.593	—
Hyundai Unicorns	70	55	1	.560	4
Hanwha Eagles	67	57	2	.540	6 ½
Kia Tigers	64	59	3	.520	9
Doosan Bears	63	60	3	.512	10
SK Wyverns	60	65	1	.480	14
Lotte Giants	50	73	3	.407	23
LG Twins	47	75	4	.385	25 ½

PLAYOFFS: First round—Hanwha defeated Kia 3-1 in best-of-five series. **Semifinals**—Hanwha defeated Hyundai 3-1 in best-of-five series. **Finals**—Samsung defeated Hanwha 4-1 in best-of-seven series.

Veteran sluggers highlight season

BY PETER BJARKMAN

The hottest on-field race in Cuba during the 45th Serie Nacional (National Series) was the head-to-head individual clash between long-time national team stars Michel Enríquez, the third baseman for Isla de la Juventud, and Las Tunas outfielder Osmani Urrutia.

CUBA After helping lead Cuba to a surprise second-place finish in March's inaugural World Baseball Classic, the two veteran sluggers staged a down-to-the-wire race for the batting title. When the dust settled, Enríquez claimed his first hitting crown with a .447 mark, the third-best single season performance in league history. Urrutia finished the year at .425 and logged a league-leading 135 base hits, but his string of five straight batting crowns ended despite hitting .400 or better for the fifth time in the last six seasons.

Sancti Spiritus second baseman Yulieski Gourriel, just 22, also made some headlines of his own in the shadows of Enríquez and Urrutia, pacing the circuit in homers (27), triples (11), RBIs (92) and runs scored (89).

For all the hitting heroics, 2006 was a year equally noted for managerial musical chairs on the Cuban national team scene. Long-time manager Higinio Vélez was riding high after Cuba's WBC performance, then quickly fell from grace due to much second guessing of his handling of pitchers during the WBC finals loss to Japan. Industriales skipper Rey Anglada inherited the national team by early summer and soon directed a gold-medal finish in the Central American Games in Colombia, though his team lost to Team USA in the finals of the Americas Olympic Qualifier in Havana. The 1970s-era national team second baseman was once banned from Cuban League play after his 1979 implication in a game-fixing scandal and subsequently served three decades of penance before re-emerging as the Industriales skipper in 2002. Anglada has now directed fan-favorite Havana Industriales to three league pennants in four seasons since his surprising return.

On the pennant race front, Industriales was back on top, finishing two games off the pace in Group B during the 90-game regular season, but charging through the playoffs on the strength of its corps of promising young pitchers and finally upending defending champion Santiago in the six-game finale. The title was the 10th overall for Industriales—the league high water mark—and third of the current decade.

The best series of the postseason was the semifinal shootout between Industriales and Group B rival Sancti Spíritus, featuring sluggers Gourriel and Frederich Cepeda, and managed by 1980s national team hero Lourdes Gourriel. Road teams won all seven games, and the talented young Industriales pitching featuring Frank Montieth, Deinys Suárez and Yadel Martí stemmed the Sancti Spíritus slugging onslaught on the road, with Montieth (pronounced Mon-tee-yeah) authoring a gritty performance in the 4-3 deciding game.

STANDINGS

WEST

GROUP A	W	L	PCT.	GB
Isla de la Juventud	54	35	.607	—
Pinar del Río	48	42	.533	6½
Matanzas	29	61	.322	25½
Metropolitanos	19	69	.216	34½

GROUP B	W	L	Pct.	GB
Sancti Spíritus	58	32	.644	—
Industriales	56	34	.622	2
Habana Province	51	38	.573	6½
Cienfuegos	35	54	.393	22½

EAST

GROUP C	W	L	Pct.	GB
Villa Clara	58	32	.644	—
Ciego de Ávila	53	37	.589	5
Las Tunas	47	43	.522	11
Camagüey	41	49	.456	17

GROUP D	W	L	Pct.	GB
Santiago de Cuba	56	34	.611	—
Granma	51	38	.556	4½
Guantánamo	34	56	.367	22
Holguín	27	63	.411	29

PLAYOFFS—Quarterfinals: Industriales defeated Isla de la Juventud 3-2; Sancti Spíritus defeated Habana Province 3-1; Santiago de Cuba defeated Ciego de Avila 3-1; Granma defeated Villa Clara 3-2. Semifinals: Santiago de Cuba defeated Granma 4-0; Industriales defeated Sancti Spíritus 4-3. Finals: Industriales defeated Santiago de Cuba 4-2.

INDIVIDUAL BATTING LEADERS
(Minimum 238 Plate Appearances)

	AVG	AB	R	H	2B	3B	HR	RBI
Michel Enríquez, Isla Juventud	.447	255	77	114	26	0	12	58
Osmani Urrutia, LasTunas	.425	318	52	135	22	0	13	71
Yoandry Garlobo, Matanzas	.407	236	52	96	12	1	12	49
Pedro Poll, Santiago de Cuba	.366	325	57	119	27	0	7	82
Leslie Anderson, Camagüey	.363	336	67	122	22	2	15	62
Yoandry Urgellés, Industriales	.362	301	58	109	19	1	5	66
José Julio Ruiz, Santiago de Cuba	.357	241	45	86	14	4	2	48
Alexis Laborde, Guantánamo	.353	331	48	117	16	1	11	74
Joan Carlos Pedroso, Las Tunas	.353	272	68	96	19	2	22	72
Vladimir García, Isla Juventud	.352	247	33	87	16	0	4	60
Yohenis Céspedes, Granma	.351	339	89	119	24	4	23	78
Loidel Chapellí, Camagüey	.351	285	51	100	20	1	8	53
Robelquiz Videaux, Guantánamo	.351	276	51	97	22	2	9	47
Ariel Borrero, Villa Clara	.346	286	53	99	13	1	11	61
Yorelvis Charles, Ciego de Avila	.344	358	66	123	14	1	16	72
Yaibel Tamayo, Ciego de Avila	.344	241	44	83	17	4	5	40
Amaury Suárez, Las Tunas	.340	356	63	121	18	3	9	56
Yordanis Samón, Granma	.340	329	64	112	16	3	12	80
Rolando Meriño, Santiago de Cuba	.340	297	68	101	26	2	7	57
Dayan Viciedo, Villa Clara	.337	323	54	109	16	4	14	58
José Abreu, Cienfuegos	.337	312	53	105	20	5	11	64
Marino Luis Marquez, Camagüey	.336	333	62	112	8	1	2	35
Yasser Pérez, Matanzas	.334	314	51	105	19	4	3	33
Adalberto Ibarra, Industriales	.333	318	43	106	19	5	1	41

INDIVIDUAL PITCHING LEADERS
(Minimum 88 Innings)

	W	L	ERA	G	IP	BB	SO
Noelvis Hernández, Sancti Spíritus	7	2	2.29	14	94	23	56
Yosvani Pérez, Cienfuegos	9	5	2.30	15	98	24	58
Maikel Folich, Ciego de Avila	11	0	2.43	16	118	54	59
Luis Borroto, Villa Clara	11	5	2.45	17	125	59	117
Yadel Martí, Industriales	9	5	2.69	17	117	23	85
Pedro Luis Lazo, Pinar del Río	12	8	2.78	21	156	26	110
Raidel Miranda, Pinar del Río	5	5	2.95	18	92	42	82
Vladimir Baños, Rinar del Río	8	5	3.13	17	106	23	63
Ormari Romero, Santiago de Cuba	8	6	3.33	16	114	22	51
Yosvani Aragón, Sancti Spíritus	9	6	3.38	18	123	29	89
Ismel Jimenes, Sancti Spíritus	7	3	3.43	30	94	32	58
Robelto Carrillo, Villa Clara	6	2	3.47	19	99	34	69
Alien Mora, Ciego de Avila	9	6	3.54	18	119	27	59
Jonder Martínez, Habana Province	10	3	3.55	18	122	27	84

INTERNATIONAL BASEBALL

Rimini rides hot streak to title

Rimini just barely made the Serie A/1 playoffs, but once they did, they rode a hot streak to the Italy Series title, knocking off pennant winner Bologna in the semifinals and Grosseto in the championship series for their 11th national title.

Former major leaguer Brian Looney was 2-0, 0.00 in the Italy Series. The 37-year old southpaw made two long relief appearances giving up five hits in eight innings. Fellow big league alumnus Jaime Navarro lost twice in the championship series, although he threw a complete game in each and allowed a total of three earned runs.

ITALY

The Italy Series was a good example of good pitching beating good hitting. Grosseto topped Serie A/1 with a .266 team batting average during the regular season. But the Rimini pitching staff, owners of the third-best ERA (2.81), held Grosseto to just four earned runs in the finals. Rimini hit a meager .187 in the Italy Series and had the worst team batting average (.229) in the league.

Newly promoted Godo had a fine Serie A/1 debut and finished only one game out of the playoffs. Godo received big contributions on the mound from former Bologna righty Cristian Mura (9-4, 2.54) and ex-minor leaguers like Cody Cillo (7-4, 2.59) and Felix Romero (4-4, 2.21). Left fielder Quinn Ciccarelli (.333, 2 homers, 16 RBIs), a product of Cal State Northridge, was second in Serie A/1 with 29 stolen bases. San Marino finished out of the playoffs but won the European Cup by defeating hosts Grosseto 3-0 in an all-Serie A/1 final.

STANDINGS

Team	W	L	PCT	GB
Bologna	30	18	.625	—
Nettuno	28	20	.583	2
Grosseto	28	20	.583	2
Rimini	25	23	.521	5
Godo	24	24	.500	6
Modena	23	25	.479	7
Parma	22	26	.458	8
San Marino	22	26	.458	8
Anzio	14	34	.292	16

PLAYOFFS: Semifinals—Grosseto defeated Nettuno 4-1 and Rimini defeated Bologna 4-2 in best-of-five series. **Finals**—Rimini defeated Grosseto 4-1 in best-of-five series.

INDIVIDUAL BATTING LEADERS

PLAYER, TEAM	AVG	AB	R	H	HR	RBI	SB
Gomez, Adolfo, Modena	.371	197	48	73	1	16	6
McNamara, James, Nettuno	.348	187	26	65	1	26	7
Ciccarelli, Quinn, Godo	.333	192	40	64	2	16	29
Dallospedale, Davide, Bologna	.330	188	22	62	0	27	9
Buccheri, James Rimini	.324	185	38	60	1	25	35
Chiarini, Mario, Rimini	.318	148	21	47	2	28	11
Gerali, Michele, Modena	.316	155	21	49	0	13	10
Gutierrez, Victor, Grosseto	.313	144	28	45	1	19	8
Lollio, Gino, Grosseto	.310	184	27	57	5	40	6
Munoz, Orlando, Modena	.306	160	23	49	1	21	8

INDIVIDUAL PITCHING LEADERS

PITCHER, TEAM	W	L	ERA	SV	G	IP	H	BB	SO
Looney, Brian, Rimini	2	2	0.75	4	16	48	23	10	53
Matos, Jesus, Bologna	7	4	1.47	0	16	110	88	15	136
Florian, Frailyn, Anzio	5	2	1.84	1	16	83	55	41	83
Roman, Herazo, Modena	9	5	1.87	0	16	106	85	30	96
Ventura, Cipriano, Nettuno	3	3	1.88	1	14	53	42	9	38
Arias Victor, Nettuno	9	2	1.94	0	16	102	80	30	93
Figueroa, Bautista, San Marino	6	6	2.06	0	14	96	87	21	87

Kinheim finally wins third title

Kinheim defeated the Hoofddorp Pioniers three games to two in the Holland Series to capture their first Dutch major league championship since 1994. It was just the third national title in the Haarlem club's 71-year history.

The visiting team won each of the first four games of the series. In coming back from a two-games-to-one deficit, Kinheim duplicated a feat that they had achieved twelve years earlier. No other DML club has come from behind in such a manner since the Holland Series became a best-of-five series in 1990.

Kinheim lefty Patrick Beljaards went the distance in Game Two. The 28-year old Haarlem native was 2-0, 0.55 in the Holland Series and 3-0, 0.74 overall in the postseason. The Pioniers defeated Neptunus in the other semifinal. As a result, Neptunus was finally dethroned after winning seven straight DML titles. Hoofddorp southpaw Richard Orman was 2-0, 1.15 in the semis. The 37-year-old Aruba native became the DML's all-time wins leader among lefthanders.

HOLLAND

Former Blue Jay minor leaguer Diegomar Markwell was ineffective in the playoffs for Neptunus, going 0-2, 4.97 after a stellar regular season (12-2, 1.58). Several Japanese players have enjoyed success in the league in recent years, and outfielder Yuji Nerei became the first Japanese position player to make a big splash in the league.

DUTCH MAJOR LEAGUE

STANDINGS

	W	L	T	PCT	GB
Kinheim	33	7	2	.810	—
Neptunus	29	11	1	.720	4
Hoofddorp Pioniers	25	17	0	.595	9
ADO	23	19	0	.548	11
HCAW	19	21	2	.476	14
Almere	14	26	1	.354	19
Sparta/Feyenoord	11	31	0	.262	23
Amsterdam Pirates	10	32	0	.238	24

INDIVIDUAL BATTING LEADERS

PLAYER, TEAM	AVG	G	AB	R	H	HR	RBI	SB
Raily Legito, Nept	.366	40	161	36	59	3	36	17
Benjamin Dille, Nept	.358	40	162	32	58	1	28	6
Johnny Balentina, Nept	.356	40	177	40	63	0	21	23
Glenn Romney, Hoofd	.352	37	142	21	50	1	20	2
Yuji Nerei, Nept	.351	40	151	34	53	3	31	2
Tjerk Smeets, Kinh	.349	41	152	25	53	1	36	4
Derick Francisca, Amster	.337	42	163	20	55	2	14	8
Eugene Kingsale, Almere	.333	32	108	25	36	1	12	8

INDIVIDUAL PITCHING LEADERS

PITCHER, TEAM	ERA	G	W	L	SV	IP	H	BB	SO
Akira Okamoto, ADO	1.11	13	6	1	0	105	62	28	100
Nick Stuifbergen, HCAW	1.36	13	5	1	0	73	55	13	53
Diegomar Markwell, Nept	1.58	17	12	2	1	108	89	34	82
Rob Cordemans, ADO	1.72	18	9	3	0	131	93	25	127
Patrick Beljaards, Kinh	1.76	17	12	2	0	123	102	18	62
David Bergman, Kinh	1.94	16	12	1	0	107	98	22	72
Erik Remmerswaal, ALM	2.02	11	3	1	0	58	48	23	28

Lions win as league tries to build

On a scorching July 1 afternoon in this port city about an hour's train ride southeast of Beijing, two baseball teams took part in what an American passerby might have assumed to be a high school game. An important game, perhaps, given the energy of the crowd, but judging by the dilapidated concrete stands alone, a high school game nonetheless.

CHINA In fact, the two teams that took the field were engaged in something more important than a mere high school drama: They were squaring off in the 2006 China Baseball League World Series.

After dropping two games at home the weekend before in the best of five series, it was the visiting Guangdong Leopards who needed to score first. But with two runs in the bottom of the second, the Tianjin Lions beat them to the punch. The Leopards answered with a three-run home run the following inning to take a one-run lead, and that's where the score remained for five innings.

With two on and two out in the bottom of the eighth, Tianjin used a double down the third base line to score two runs. After Guangdong's scoreless ninth, the Lions had won 4-3 and celebrated with fireworks—the China Baseball League crown was theirs.

Established in 2002 and expanded in 2005, the CBL includes four teams in addition to Tianjin and Guangdong: the Beijing Tigers and Shanghai Golden Eagles, members of the league since its inception, and the Sichuan Dragons and China Hopestars, who joined for the 2005 season. The teams play a regular season schedule of roughly 30 games—something that many point to as one of the league's weaknesses.

Nonetheless, the league has helped to raise the level of play in China. Under the stewardship of former big lea-guers Jim Lefebvre and Bruce Hurst—who will shepherd the nation's baseball team through the 2008 Olympics in Beijing—China finished third at the 23rd Asian Baseball Championship in Japan in 2005.

Only a year later, however, it was pummeled by Japan, Korea and Taiwan in the World Baseball Classic, failing to advance out of pool play. To be fair, Japan went on to win the event while Korea went to the semifinals, but clearly China can't count itself among the world's finest just yet. And given the number of obstacles China faces in bringing its baseball program up to par, it's difficult to predict just when that time might be.

As Shen Wei sees it, a number of problems stem from baseball's idiosyncrasies, which clash with China's culture of conformity. In her capacity as secretary general of the Chinese Baseball Association, the country's administrative body for baseball, she spends her days fighting to build baseball's popularity, but often finds it to be a hard sell due to its irregularities.

Wei said through a translator that one of the main problems in trying to spread the sport's popularity, for example, is the fact that a baseball field can vary in size and that it can take up more space than a soccer field or basketball court, the country's two most popular sports. That makes it more difficult to find room for baseball fields in already overcrowded country.

Similarly, when baseball officials try to convince television stations to broadcast CBL games, baseball's irregular game length is also a strike against it as officials cannot say exactly how long any particular game will be. Finally, there's a lack of play at the youth level. Because baseball, unlike basketball and soccer, isn't played at most primary and secondary schools, Chinese don't become familiar with the sport until much later in life, if ever.

Bears complete dominant season

Chen Chin-fong's two-run homer off the President Lions' Pan "Du Du" Wei-luen tied the game at 3-3 in the top of the sixth and sparked a six-run rally, as the La New Bears beat the Lions 7-3 to complete a four-game sweep of the 2006 Taiwan Series at Tainan.

It was the first Taiwan title for the Bears, completing a worst to first run for the team, which

TAIWAN also won both halves of the Taiwan regular season.

The Bears rallied back from deficits as large as three runs in three of the four wins against the Lions, treating fans around the nation to some of the best late-game finishes in postseason history.

American righthander Anthony Fiore pitched 4⅓ innings of shutout ball in relief to earn the win.

The championship featured a potent La New offense that stormed through the regular season with a 62-34-4 record, comfortably ahead of the second-place Lions (48-45-7). The Lions swept the Sinon Bulls in three games in the first round of the playoffs to advance to the finals.

The Lions were led by the pitching of Du Du and American lefty Jeriome Robertson, while the Bears lineup featured former major leaguer Chen, who posted a league-best 81 RBIs, 20 homers and 20 stolen bases.

The Bears then scored an even bigger victory for baseball in Taiwan in the annual Asian Series in Tokyo in November, when the champions of the professional leagues in Japan, Korea, China and Taiwan faced off.

The Bears advanced to the final after Taiwan's best showing in the two-year history of the tournament. Taiwan's champs scored a 3-2 defeat over the Samsung Lions to advance to the final against Japan's Nippon Ham Fighters.

"I guess a lot of people predicted we would finish third," Bears manager Hong I-Chung told the Taipei Times. "But from the beginning I said, 'I am not (going to Japan as) a tourist. I am going to fight. We practiced hard and we showed what we can do."

Taiwan's best did not advance out of pool play in March's World Baseball Classic. Taiwan defeated China but lost to Japan and Korea to finish the event with a 1-2 record.

INTERNATIONAL BASEBALL

Venezuela takes Caribbean crown

Dominican Republic pitching coach Mark Brewer couldn't have been more right in his prediction prior to the Caribbean Series finale.

"This game is going to come down to relief pitching or defense," Brewer said.

And so it was, with Venezuela coming from behind in the ninth inning to topple the Dominican Republic 5-4 to claim its first Caribbean Series title since 1989.

Alex Gonzalez (Red Sox) knotted the score in the ninth by driving in William Bergolla (Reds), who pinch-ran for Ramon Hernandez (Orioles). Then Henry Blanco (Cubs), who drove in the go-ahead run against Puerto Rico the night before, popped a fly ball to shallow left that hit shortstop Erick Aybar (Angels) on the head, then rolled toward the outfield, along with Dominican Republic's championship hopes.

First title for Venezuela since 1989
Alex Gonzalez scored the winning run against the Dominican

Gonzalez scored from first base to give Venezuela its first series crown in 17 years and Caracas' first since 1982. The seats at Estadio Jose Perez Colmenares couldn't contain the fans, who mobbed their Caracas Lions in a celebration as only can be seen in winter ball.

Despite the strange ending—Blanco was credited with a double—Venezuela deserved every bit of this Caribbean Series championship.

To appreciate Caracas' accomplishment, consider that manager Carlos Subero took over the helm on Dec. 9 after a devastating loss the night before that left Caracas 21-22 on the season and seemingly out of playoff contention.

Behind its new manager, Caracas won 14 of its final 19 games to qualify for the round robin, where it faced further obstacles.

The Lions finished 6-6 in the Venezuelan postseason, and had to win four straight in the round-robin tournament to squeeze into the final against the Aragua Tigers—who were vying for their third consecutive league crown. After losing the opener, the underdogs looked dominant, winning the next four.

Then came the Caribbean Series.

Venezuela rocked Mexico 17-1 in the opener, handled Puerto Rico 6-1, and came from behind to smash Dominican Republic 11-9 in Game Three.

In the next three games, Venezuela scooted by a pesky Mexico team 4-3 in extra innings and overcame a tough Puerto Rico club 5-1 before bringing down the house with its 5-4 come-from-behind thriller to clinch the Caribbean Series for this baseball-crazy nation.

Hernandez, who was named series MVP, summed up his teammates' sentiment—being driven to win it all for national pride.

"I've never won a Caribbean Series and I've played in six," Hernandez said. "Everyone wants to be champion once for his country."

Both teams went at it full throttle, beginning with the starting pitchers. Veteran Geremi Gonzalez (Mets) threw eight innings, giving up four runs on seven hits for Caracas. Juan Cruz (Athletics) didn't throw as long but gave his team a slight edge, allowing two runs on four hits in 5⅔ innings. The Lions' tying run came off righthander Jose Valverde (Diamondbacks).

The Dominicans scored in the first inning thanks to some small ball and an error by the home team. Anderson Hernandez (Mets) slapped a base hit past Gonzalez and moved

2005-06 WINTER ALL-STARS

Angels' shortstop Brandon Wood might have set an Arizona Fall League record with 14 homers, but Pirates utilityman Yurendell De Caster came within two home runs of the Venezuelan League mark. While it was close between the two players—not to mention the postseason heroics of Mets' infielder Anderson Hernandez and the numbers White Sox outfielder Jerry Owens put up—De Caster is our Winter Player of the Year based on his numbers, as well as the level of competition he played against in the Venezuelan League.

Pos.	Player, Team (League)	Organization	AVG	AB	H	HR	RBI	SB
C	Mike Napoli, Aguilas (D.R.)	Angels	.342	79	27	5	19	0
1B	Jesse Gutierrez, Navajoa (Mex.)	Reds	.293	184	54	15	40	0
2B	Esteban German, Azucareros (D.R.)	Royals	.331	181	60	0	19	30
3B	Eric Duncan, Grand Canyon (AFL)	Yankees	.362	94	34	8	27	0
SS	Brandon Wood, Surprise (AFL)	Angels	.307	114	35	14	32	0
OF	Yurendell De Caster, Oriente (Ven.)	Pirates	.325	209	68	17	47	11
OF	Luis A. Garcia, Hermosillo (Mex.)	None	.320	219	70	18	57	0
OF	Luke Scott, Magallanes (Ven.)	Astros	.345	119	41	12	30	0
DH	Luis Figueroa, Mayaguez (P.R.)	Red Sox	.417	163	68	1	22	5

Pos.	Player, Team (League)	Organization	W	L	ERA	IP	H	BB	SO
SP	William Collazo, Carolina (P.R.)	Angels	5	2	2.35	57	51	8	33
SP	Harold Eckert, Zulia (Ven.)	Dodgers	4	4	2.78	74	62	21	94
SP	Willie Eyre, Aragua (Ven.)	Twins	9	0	1.26	64	56	13	39
SP	Spike Lundberg, Gusave (Mex.)	Blue Jays	9	3	2.23	93	77	22	61
RP	Yhency Brazoban, Licey (D.R.)	Dodgers	3	2	1.64	22	21	6	21

to second on a bunt by Aybar. Miguel Tejada (Orioles) muscled a flare over to second where Marco Scutaro (Athletics) botched it, allowing Hernandez to score.

Jose Offerman, who spent the 2005 season with the Mets, hit a sacrifice fly in the fourth that brought in Ron Belliard (Indians) to make it 3-0.

Hernandez followed in the Venezuelan fourth by whacking a Cruz pitch over the left-field wall to put Venezuela on the board.

Although the ninth made the difference, the sixth proved to be a key inning.

With two outs and men at the corners, outfielder Franklin Gutierrez (Indians) greeted Valverde with a line drive to right field that got past a diving Timo Perez, who spent last season with the White Sox. Scutaro and Hernandez scored and Gutierrez ended up on third with a bases-clearing triple to tie the game at 3.

"It came down to the pitching in the sixth, which couldn't contain the Venezuelan offense," Dominican manager Rafael Landestoy said. "Perez was just being aggressive (with his dive)."

Sandy Martinez, who spent 2005 with the Pirates, gave the Dominicans the lead again with a solo shot off Gonzalez in the seventh that set up the dramatic ending to the series.

Perez' dive turned out to be a grave miscalculation, considering the circumstances. But the Dominicans were still up 4-3 going into the ninth where its relief pitching and defense failed. After Jorge Sosa (Devil Rays) allowed Venezuela two legitimate hits in the ninth, Aybar's mishap sealed the victory.

In all, Venezuela outscored its opponents 45-15, hit nine home runs in the series, compiled a team batting average of .327 and its pitching staff finished with a 2.62 ERA.

The Dominicans finished second in the tournament, with their only two losses coming against Venezuela. Puerto Rico finished third, while Mexico's Mazatlan Deer—last year's Caribbean Series champion—went 0-6 in series play and finished last.

Even though Mexico did not win a single game in the tournament, second baseman Edgar Gonzalez was named to the series all-star team. Rounding out the all-star honors were catcher Sandy Martinez (Dominican Republic), first baseman Ramon Hernandez (Venezuela), shortstop Alex Gonzalez (Venezuela), third baseman Luis Rodriguez (Venezuela), outfielders Napoleon Calzado, Alexis Gomez, Timo Perez (Dominican Republic) and designated hitter Alex Cabrera. The two pitchers named to the squad were righthander Geremi Gonzalez (Venezuela) and lefthander William Collazo (Puerto Rico).

De Caster Blasts Way To Top

Among all the big names playing winter ball this year, Pirates utilityman Yurendell De Caster was a name often overlooked. But after an impressive performance in the Venezuelan League, De Caster has at last made a lasting impression, and was named Baseball America's Winter Player of the Year to fortify his growing reputation.

De Caster, 26, has come a long way since signing with the Devil Rays in 1996 out of his native Curacao. The Pirates plucked him in a minor league phase of the Rule 5 draft in 2000. He climbed steadily through the system, spending two years at high Class A Lynchburg, another

season in Double-A Altoona before debuting at Triple-A Indianapolis last year.

Pirates farm director Brian Graham likens him to teammate Ronny Paulino, who has also followed a similar development path.

"Both he and Paulino are classic player development cases," Graham said. "They've come a long way with learning the culture, the language—and sometimes it takes some guys longer to really get a handle on where they are as a player. I think what you're seeing from both these players is they're finally comfortable with their plan and their approach and we're seeing them begin to put up some numbers as a result."

Putting up numbers wasn't a problem for De Caster in Venezuela this winter. Playing mostly the outfield for Oriente, De Caster batted .325 with 17 homers and 47 RBIs in 209 at-bats. He tied for the league lead in homers—falling two shy of the league record—tied for the lead in steals, and finished second in runs and RBIs.

Originally signed as a third baseman, De Caster has become one of the most versatile players in the Pirates organization. During the 2005 season at Indianapolis, De Caster played both corner infield positions, and even filled-in in right field late in the summer when the Indians were making their push to the International League playoffs.

"He was just about as valuable of a player as we had last year," Indianapolis manager Trent Jewett said. "He didn't put up gaudy numbers—in fact, just the fact that he's so versatile probably took a toll on the numbers. But he handled it well. I knew on any given day I could put him somewhere in the field, somewhere in the order, and he'd be fine.

"And if you watched him closely, those numbers he put up in winter ball were in there. It's his approach and how he operates."

CARIBBEAN SERIES

Maracay and Valencia, Venezuela, Feb. 2-7, 2006

	W	L	PCT
Venezuela	6	0	1.000
Dominican Republic	4	2	.667
Puerto Rico	2	4	.333
Mexico	0	6	.000

INDIVIDUAL BATTING LEADERS
(Minimum 16 Plate Appearances)

Player, Team	AVG	G	AB	R	H	HR	RBI
Ramon Hernandez, VZ	.542	6	24	6	13	3	8
Edgar Gonzalez, Mex	.524	6	21	4	11	3	3
Alexis Gomez, DR	.500	6	20	6	10	0	4
Alex Gonzalez, VZ	.409	6	22	5	9	1	7
Luis Cruz, Mex	.375	4	16	3	6	2	5
Ruben Gotay, PR	.368	5	19	4	7	1	3
Luis Figueroa, PR	.364	6	22	2	8	1	5
Franklin Gutierrez, VZ	.364	6	22	4	8	0	4
Alex Cabrera, VZ	.360	6	25	5	9	2	7
Anderson Hernandez, DR	.333	6	30	6	10	1	4

INDIVIDUAL PITCHING LEADERS
(Minimum 4 Innings)

Player, Team	W	L	ERA	IP	H	BB	SO
Geremi Gonzalez, VZ	1	0	1.20	15	10	3	12
Landon Jacobsen, VZ	0	0	1.29	7	3	1	3
Albert Vargas, VZ	0	0	1.69	5	2	0	1
Daniel Cabrera, DR	1	0	1.80	5	2	2	5
Orlando Trias, VZ	1	0	1.80	5	6	1	1
Federico Baez, DR	0	1	2.25	12	5	3	6
Danny Tamayo, DR	1	0	3.00	6	5	0	4
William Collazo, PR	0	1	3.38	11	10	4	6
Roman Colon, DR	0	1	3.60	5	4	2	3
Edgar Gonzalez, Mex	0	0	3.86	7	6	2	3

INTERNATIONAL BASEBALL

DOMINICAN LEAGUE

STANDINGS

REGULAR SEASON	W	L	PCT	GB
Licey	32	18	.640	—
Aguilas	27	23	.540	5
Escogido	26	23	.531	5½
Azucareros	25	24	.510	6½
Estrellas	22	28	.440	10
Gigantes	17	33	.340	15

PLAYOFFS	W	L	PCT	GB
Aguilas	12	5	.706	—
Licey	10	8	.556	2½
Escogido	7	10	.412	5
Azucareros	6	12	.333	6½

CHAMPIONSHIP SERIES: Licey defeated Aguilas 4-2 in best-of-seven series for league championship.

MEXICAN PACIFIC LEAGUE

STANDINGS

REGULAR SEASON	W	L	PCT	GB
*Navojoa	39	29	.574	—
Guasave	36	32	.529	3
#Mazatlan	35	32	.522	3½
Hermosillo	34	33	.507	4½
Mochis	34	34	.500	5
Obregon	33	35	.485	6
Culiacan	31	36	.463	7½
Mexicali	28	39	.418	10 ?

*First-half champion. #Second-half champion.

PLAYOFFS—Quarterfinals: Navojoa defeated Culiacan 4-1; Guasave defeated Mochis 4-2 and Hermosillo defeated Mazatlan 4-2 in best-of-seven series. **Semifinals:** Mazatlan defeated Navojoa 4-2 and Guasave defeated Hermosillo 4-3 in best-of-seven series. **Final:** Mazatlan defeated Gusave 4-1 in best-of-seven series.

INDIVIDUAL BATTING LEADERS
(Minimum 184 Plate Appearances)

	AVG	AB	R	H	2B	3B	HR	RBI	SB
Canizalez, Juan Carlos, Hermosillo	.337	255	41	86	10	1	12	50	0
Johnson, Rontrez, Mochis	.333	174	40	58	7	0	9	27	7
Clark, Howie, Mexicali	.333	171	26	57	6	3	9	30	1
Cruz, Luis A., Navojoa	.327	211	33	69	16	1	10	37	2
Clark, Douglas, Navojoa	.324	204	41	66	14	1	11	42	11
Hopper, Norris, Navojoa	.320	231	36	74	6	0	1	21	12
Garcia, Luis A., Hermosillo	.320	219	49	70	9	0	18	57	0
Holbert, Aaron, Navojoa	.314	172	31	54	9	1	6	32	8
Orantes, Ramon, Mochis	.312	231	36	72	7	1	9	46	0
Valenzuela, Mario, Guasave	.310	242	39	75	12	0	16	48	1
Munoz, Noe, Guasave	.310	239	32	74	10	0	6	34	0
Rivera, Ruben, Culiacan	.308	227	42	70	8	1	16	44	9
Roberson, Chris, Hermosillo	.307	192	32	59	14	0	4	19	9
Gonzalez, Adrian, Mazatlan	.306	258	31	79	15	2	10	43	0
Quintero, Christian, Mochis	.306	245	44	75	11	1	6	32	2
Bojorquez, Victor, Mochis	.302	242	30	73	9	0	9	40	0
Amezaga, Alfredo, Obregon	.294	265	36	78	12	4	5	33	17
Gutierrez, Jesse, Navojoa	.293	184	31	54	7	0	15	40	0
Gastelum, Carlos, Hermosillo	.292	264	38	77	7	1	0	13	6
Francisco, Ben, Culiacan	.291	247	34	72	11	1	13	31	11

INDIVIDUAL PITCHING LEADERS
(Minimum 54 Innings)

	W	L	ERA	G	SV	IP	H	BB	SO
Lundberg, Spike, Guasave	9	3	2.23	13	0	93	77	22	61
Ortega, Pablo, Mazatlan	4	5	2.49	13	0	94	96	21	47
Campos, Francisco, Mazatlan	4	6	2.60	14	0	93	75	41	78
Elizalde, Christian, Obregon	3	2	2.76	12	0	72	55	18	46
Izquierdo, Hansel, Navojoa	4	6	3.05	20	1	62	50	27	42
Difelice, Mark, Obregon	5	2	3.14	12	0	77	70	17	56
Silva, Walter, Mazatlan	7	3	3.33	13	0	84	69	26	61
Montemayor, Humberto, Navojoa	6	4	3.52	14	0	77	74	24	47
Rodriguez, Jesus, Obregon	4	4	3.81	15	0	76	67	33	50
Gonzalez, Vinicio, Navojoa	7	4	3.90	12	0	65	57	25	39
Rodriguez, Francisco, Mochis	7	5	3.92	15	0	67	60	33	37
Alvarez, Azael, Hermosillo	5	4	4.02	12	0	63	54	32	46
Castellanos, Jonathan, Hermosillo	5	4	4.05	15	0	80	84	22	50

PUERTO RICAN LEAGUE

STANDINGS

REGULAR SEASON	W	L	PCT	GB
Manati	24	17	.585	—
Carolina	23	18	.561	1
Ponce	21	22	.488	4
Caguas	20	21	.488	4
Mayaguez	19	23	.452	5½
Arecibo	17	23	.425	6½

PLAYOFFS—Semifinals: Ponce defeated Manati 4-0 and Carolina defeated Caguas 4-1 in best-of-seven series. **Final:** Carolina defeated Ponce 5-3 in best-of-nine series.

INDIVIDUAL BATTING LEADERS
(Minimum 108 Plate Appearances)

	AVG	AB	R	H	2B	3B	HR	RBI	SB
Figueroa, Luis A., Mayaguez	.417	163	28	68	14	2	1	22	5
Garcia, Omar, Arecibo	.361	108	13	39	7	0	5	14	0
Redman, Tike, Ponce	.356	177	24	63	9	1	2	17	7
Valentin, Javier, Manati	.336	134	19	45	6	0	7	30	0
Willits, Reggie, Manati	.333	93	20	31	4	2	1	6	8
Ruiz, Randy, Mayaguez	.320	128	16	41	12	0	5	29	0
Martinez, Gabriel, Caguas	.319	119	14	38	9	2	2	17	2
Cora, Alex, Caguas	.319	116	28	37	8	0	0	11	2
Pachot, John, Manati	.318	148	21	47	9	1	9	26	0
Torres, Andres, Mayaguez	.316	95	24	30	3	2	1	8	10
Figueroa, Luis D., Carolina	.312	141	20	44	8	0	3	24	0
Velazquez, Jose, Arecibo	.310	113	20	35	4	1	6	18	4
Guzman, Edwards, Arecibo	.301	136	16	41	10	1	1	15	0
Rodriguez, Victor, Carolina	.301	133	6	40	6	0	1	14	0
Munoz, Jose, Caguas	.299	154	26	46	5	0	2	17	2
Nieves, Wil, Mayaguez	.297	145	18	43	7	1	4	18	0
Crespo, Cesar, Carolina	.294	160	26	47	11	1	3	18	7
Leon, Donny, Caguas	.293	150	21	44	13	0	4	26	0
Maysonet, Edwin, Arecibo	.293	99	15	29	5	1	0	18	0
Padilla, Jorge, Arecibo	.291	127	20	37	7	0	5	17	2

INDIVIDUAL PITCHING LEADERS
(Minimum 32 Innings)

	W	L	ERA	G	SV	IP	H	BB	SO
Middleton, Kyle, Manati	1	0	1.91	8	0	38	35	16	20
Matos, Josue, Carolina	4	0	2.27	11	0	44	38	8	31
Collazo, William, Carolina	5	2	2.35	11	0	57	51	8	33
Soler, Alay, Ponce	3	2	2.37	8	0	38	24	11	25
Cyr, Eric, Arecibo	5	2	2.95	9	0	40	47	10	29
Pulsipher, Bill, Mayaguez	3	4	3.08	10	0	53	57	12	33
Agosto, Stevenson, Arecibo	0	2	3.09	17	0	32	20	18	19
Roman, Orlando, Caguas	5	2	3.14	9	0	49	45	20	28
MaGrane, Jim, Carolina	2	2	3.18	10	1	45	46	10	23
Alvarado, Carlo, Ponce	6	2	3.46	11	0	55	53	27	45
Maduro, Calvin, Manati	3	2	3.51	9	0	41	44	10	24
Baez, Federico, Manati	2	2	3.59	9	0	48	45	10	36
Valentin, Dan, Mayaguez	1	4	3.72	14	0	36	28	18	20
Floyd, Gavin, Arecibo	1	1	3.89	8	0	35	32	17	21

VENEZUELAN LEAGUE

STANDINGS

WESTERN DIVISION	W	L	PCT	GB
Aragua	38	24	.613	—
Lara	27	35	.435	11
Occidente	23	38	.377	14½
Zulia	23	39	.371	15

EASTERN DIVISION	W	L	PCT	GB
Magallanes	39	23	.629	—
Caracas	34	27	.557	4½
Oriente	32	30	.516	7
La Guaira	31	31	.500	8

PLAYOFFS	W	L	PCT	GB
Aragua	10	6	.625	—
Caracas	10	6	.625	—
Magallanes	9	7	.563	1
Lara	7	9	.467	3
Oriente	4	12	.250	6

CHAMPIONSHIP SERIES: Caracas defeated Aragua 4-1 in best-of-seven series for league championship.

COLLEGE
BASEBALL

Believe it's the Beavers
Oregon State rallied to become just the second team in the last 26 years to win the CWS after dropping its Omaha opener

Beavers cap amazing Omaha run with one final drama-packed win

BY WILL KIMMEY

Bill Rowe's father Douglas is an actor who has made appearances in "M*A*S*H*," "Star Trek" and "ER." So naturally, Oregon State's senior first baseman was asked what kind of script he'd write for the Beavers before the best-of-3 finals of the College World Series against North Carolina.

"I told him Jonah would come back on short days' rest and Gundy would come in with two on and two out," Rowe said. "I was standing there at first base watching it happen."

If Rowe hadn't been, he might not have believed the ending. Starter Jonah Nickerson worked into the seventh inning for the third time in eight days, and closer Kevin Gunderson came out of the bullpen with two on in the ninth—but there was only one out, not two.

The one thing Rowe left out was the excitement he'd feel rounding third base with the go-ahead run in the bottom of the eighth inning. He scored when North Carolina second baseman Bryan Steed fielded a routine grounder with two outs but threw wide of first base and the ball glanced off Tim Federowicz' glove into foul territory.

Rowe raced home to score from second base, and Oregon State held on for a 3-2 win to earn its first national title in baseball and the second in school history. (The other one was a 1961 cross country title.) Just as it had in bracket play, Oregon State lost the first game of the championship series to North Carolina, but didn't

Right out of a Hollywood script
Bill Rowe scored the winning run

lose again. That included an 11-7 win in the second game, in which the Beavers fell behind 5-0 before storming back with a seven-run fourth inning capped by a three-run homer by Rowe.

"The will of this team, we tried to compete hard and never give up," said center fielder Tyler Graham, who capped a CWS of outstanding defensive plays by catching the final out. "We can play with anyone in the country. We never doubted ourselves and from there we just took the national championship."

Oregon State's path to becoming the Northern-most national champion since Minnesota won it all in 1964 was nearly as unlikely as a team from that latitude winning a title in a sport dominated by teams from California, Florida, Texas and the rest of the sun belt. The Beavers set a record by winning six elimination games and became the first team to lose two games in Omaha and still leave as champions. They also tied Stanford's 2003 mark by playing eight times at Rosenblatt Stadium.

"I'm sick of Rosenblatt Stadium," righthander Dallas Buck told his celebrating teammates during the trophy presentation. "Let's get the hell out of here."

Many predicted that might happen much earlier for Oregon State, which lost its first CWS game 11-1 to Miami. Instead, Oregon State became the second team in the last 26 years to win the College World Series after losing its first game. Southern California turned the trick in 1998.

DENNIS HUBBARD

The little man who could
Kevin Gunderson came up big for OSU

The Beavers followed their opening-game loss by winning four elimination games in four days, toppling Georgia, Miami and top-ranked Rice twice. Nickerson started that run with a win against Georgia. He came back on two days' rest as Oregon State beat Rice a second time to advance to the championship series against a North Carolina team that was undefeated in the NCAA tournament and fully rested on the mound, where it owned the luxury of sending out two first-round draft picks in the finals.

Nickerson To The Rescue

Oregon State proved just as strong on the mound. After North Carolina earned a 4-3 win in the opener, it didn't look like Nickerson would even get the chance to make his CWS-record tying third start, in which he went 6⅔ innings and allowed two unearned runs. Nickerson, the CWS most outstanding player, finished with a 2-0, 0.84 record after throwing 323 pitches in eight days and allowing no earned runs over his the final 16⅔ innings.

Nickerson didn't earn the win in the finale, but he kept his team in position to do so. North Carolina got to him in the top of the fifth inning, a frame that saw two impressive Oregon State streaks end. Jay Cox reached on the first OSU error in 51⅓ innings in Omaha. He scored two batters later on an RBI double by Seth Williams that represented the first run scored against Nickerson in 14 CWS innings. That run, and the one that followed it to tie the score that inning, was unearned, the first such runs the Beavers had allowed in the NCAA tournament.

Nickerson's night brought back memories of Stanford's John Hudgins throwing 334 pitches over 10 days and three starts in the 2003 CWS. Unlike Hudgins, Nickerson produced his heroics for the winning team.

"I knew if I pitched my best, we would keep playing," said Nickerson, who paid $85 for a massage at the team hotel the day before the championship series began.

Nickerson's relief pitched with only slightly more rest than he did. Buck, who went 6⅓ innings in the first game of the championship series, started lobbying to enter the game in the sixth inning. He got his wish in the eighth, entering with two runners on and no outs. He struck out two batters to escape, with the final K coming as UNC's Josh Horton raced down the third-base line in an attempt to steal home. Buck earned his first winning decision in four career appearances in Omaha to improve to 13-3 in his junior season.

"Dallas Buck is a warrior," Oregon State pitching coach Dan Spencer said. "He bleeds winning. I felt so good for him to get in the game and go do the things he did . . . because he hadn't had much luck here."

Gunderson, who pitched a season-long 5⅓ innings to

COLLEGE WORLD SERIES

Rosenblatt Stadium, Omaha, June 16-26

BRACKET ONE	W	L	RF	RA
North Carolina	3	0	15	10
Cal State Fullerton	2	2	23	21
Clemson	1	2	14	13
Georgia Tech	0	2	9	15

Bracket One Final: North Carolina 6, Cal State Fullerton 5.

BRACKET TWO	W	L	RF	RA
Oregon State	4	1	21	15
Rice	2	2	9	13
Miami	1	2	14	12
Georgia	0	2	7	11

Bracket Two Final: Oregon State 5, Rice 0; Oregon State 2, Rice 0.

CHAMPIONSHIP SERIES
(Best of 3)

June 24: North Carolina 4, Oregon State 3
June 25: Oregon State 11, North Carolina 7
June 26: Oregon State 3, North Carolina 2

INDIVIDUAL BATTING LEADERS
(Minimum 10 At-Bats)

Player, Team	AVG	AB	R	H	2B	3B	HR	RBI	BB
David Cooper, Cal State Fullerton	.533	15	2	8	0	0	1	5	0
Danny Dorn, Cal State Fullerton	.471	17	6	8	2	0	0	2	5
John Curtis, Cal State Fullerton	.429	14	0	6	2	0	0	1	0
Bill Rowe, Oregon State	.407	27	7	11	2	1	1	8	3
Chad Flack, North Carolina	.379	29	6	11	1	2	0	1	0
Seth Williams, North Carolina	.375	24	2	9	2	0	0	2	2
Justin Turner, Cal State Fullerton	.364	22	2	8	1	0	0	1	0
Stan Widmann, Clemson	.364	11	0	4	1	0	0	0	1
Shea McFeely, Oregon State	.333	27	4	9	2	0	2	5	2
Mitch Canham, Oregon State	.333	27	1	9	2	0	0	4	3

INDIVIDUAL PITCHING LEADERS
(Minimum 6 Innings)

Pitcher, Team	W	L	ERA	G	SV	IP	H	BB	SO
Bryce Cox, Rice	1	0	0.00	3	1	9.2	5	0	9
Scott Maine, Miami	1	0	0.00	1	0	7	4	2	3
Jonathan Hovis, North Carolina	1	0	0.00	4	0	6	6	4	2
Jonah Nickerson, Oregon State	2	0	0.84	3	0	21.1	12	4	19
Daniel Turpen, Oregon State	1	0	0.96	3	0	9.1	7	3	4
Danny Gil, Miami	0	1	1.35	1	0	6.2	5	1	6
Stephen Faris, Clemson	0	1	2.25	1	0	8	7	1	5
Kevin Gunderson, Oregon State	1	0	2.45	5	3	11	7	1	6
Lee Hyde, Georgia Tech	0	0	2.57	1	0	7	3	5	6
Robert Woodard, North Carolina	1	0	3.00	2	0	12	9	5	8

ALL-TOURNAMENT TEAM

C—Tim Federowicz, North Carolina. **1B**—Bill Rowe, Oregon State. **2B**—Justin Turner, Cal State Fullerton. **SS**—Josh Horton, North Carolina. **3B**—Shea McFeely, Oregon State. **OF**—Jay Cox, North Carolina; Danny Dorn, Cal State Fullerton; Cole Gillespie, Oregon State. **DH**—David Cooper, Cal State Fullerton. **P**—Kevin Gunderson, Oregon State; Jonah Nickerson, Oregon State.
Most Outstanding Player—Jonah Nickerson, rhp, Oregon State.

earn the win in the second game of the championship series, came out of the bullpen to get the final two outs with two runners on base.

Coach Pat Casey—Baseball America's Coach of the Year—said it was fitting that Nickerson, Buck and Gunderson all contributed to the team's final win in a 50-16 season. Their belief in Casey and commitment to the school played a major role in its reaching Omaha in 2005 for the first time since 1952.

"I really don't know what to say," Casey said. "It's an unbelievable feeling. These young men worked their fannies off. I told them at the beginning of the year, if you give 100 percent and never allow your opponent to be tougher than you, we'll win a lot of games."

Filling The Seats

The 2005 College World Series set session attendance records nearly every day, but the 2006 event ended up out-drawing it to set an all-time record with 310,609 visitors to Rosenblatt Stadium.

Yes, the 2006 event included one more game than the previous year's event, but the 2005 total of 266,998 was surpassed during the first game of the championship series when 26,808 fans came to set a finals record thanks to an influx of Oregon State and North Carolina fans eager to watch the two first-time finalists.

All those fans were able to spend plenty of time at Rosenblatt, as two of the longest games in CWS history took place this year. North Carolina beat Cal State Fullerton 7-5 in 13 innings on the first day of the event in a game that lasted four hours, 53 minutes and came up 20 minutes shy of becoming the longest game in College World Series history.

Fullerton's 7-6 come-from-behind win to eliminate Clemson lasted four hours and five minutes, the third-longest nine-inning game in CWS history.

Close Games, Closely Watched

The 8.3 runs per game scored at the 2005 CWS were the fewest since the aluminum bat era began in 1974, and the 2006 event was on pace to challenge that mark before an 11-7 Oregon State victory against North Carolina in the second game of the championship series. A 3-2 final helped pull the average back down, and the 8.9 runs per game ranks as the second fewest over the last three decades.

The low scores also brought close games, with 11 of

COLLEGE WORLD SERIES CHAMPIONS: 1947-2006

Year	Champion	Coach	Record	Runner-Up	MVP
1947	California*	Clint Evans	31-10	Yale	None selected
1948	Southern California	Sam Barry	40-12	Yale	None selected
1949	Texas*	Bibb Falk	23-7	Wake Forest	Charles Teague, 2b, Wake Forest
1950	Texas	Bibb Falk	27-6	Washington State	Ray VanCleef, of, Rutgers
1951	Oklahoma*	Jack Baer	19-9	Tennessee	Sid Hatfield, 1b-p, Tennessee
1952	Holy Cross	Jack Barry	21-3	Missouri	Jim O'Neill, p, Holy Cross
1953	Michigan	Ray Fisher	21-9	Texas	J.L. Smith, p, Texas
1954	Missouri	Hi Simmons	22-4	Rollins	Tom Yewcic, c, Michigan State
1955	Wake Forest	Taylor Sanford	29-7	Western Michigan	Tom Borland, p, Oklahoma State
1956	Minnesota	Dick Siebert	33-9	Arizona	Jerry Thomas, p, Minnesota
1957	California*	George Wolfman	35-10	Penn State	Cal Emery, 1b-p, Penn State
1958	Southern California	Rod Dedeaux	35-7	Missouri	Bill Thom, p, Southern California
1959	Oklahoma State	Toby Greene	27-5	Arizona	Jim Dobson, 3b, Oklahoma State
1960	Minnesota	Dick Siebert	34-7	Southern California	John Erickson, 2b, Minnesota
1961	Southern California*	Rod Dedeaux	43-9	Oklahoma State	Littleton Fowler, p, Oklahoma State
1962	Michigan	Don Lund	31-13	Santa Clara	Bob Garibaldi, p, Santa Clara
1963	Southern California	Rod Dedeaux	37-16	Arizona	Bud Hollowell, c, Southern California
1964	Minnesota	Dick Siebert	31-12	Missouri	Joe Ferris, p, Maine
1965	Arizona State	Bobby Winkles	54-8	Ohio State	Sal Bando, 3b, Arizona State
1966	Ohio State	Marty Karow	27-6	Oklahoma State	Steve Arlin, p, Ohio State
1967	Arizona State	Bobby Winkles	53-12	Houston	Ron Davini, c, Arizona State
1968	Southern California*	Rod Dedeaux	45-14	Southern Illinois	Bill Seinsoth, 1b, Southern California
1969	Arizona State	Bobby Winkles	56-11	Tulsa	John Dolinsek, of, Arizona State
1970	Southern California	Rod Dedeaux	51-13	Florida State	Gene Ammann, p, Florida State
1971	Southern California	Rod Dedeaux	53-13	Southern Illinois	Jerry Tabb, 1b, Tulsa
1972	Southern California	Rod Dedeaux	50-13	Arizona State	Russ McQueen, p, Southern California
1973	Southern California*	Rod Dedeaux	51-11	Arizona State	Dave Winfield, of-p, Minnesota
1974	Southern California	Rod Dedeaux	50-20	Miami	George Milke, p, Southern California
1975	Texas	Cliff Gustafson	56-6	South Carolina	Mickey Reichenbach, 1b, Texas
1976	Arizona	Jerry Kindall	56-17	Eastern Michigan	Steve Powers, dh-p, Arizona
1977	Arizona State	Jim Brock	57-12	South Carolina	Bob Horner, 3b, Arizona State
1978	Southern California*	Rod Dedeaux	54-9	Arizona State	Rod Boxberger, p, Southern California
1979	Cal State Fullerton	Augie Garrido	60-14	Arkansas	Tony Hudson, p, Cal State Fullerton
1980	Arizona	Jerry Kindall	45-21	Hawaii	Terry Francona, of, Arizona
1981	Arizona State	Jim Brock	55-13	Oklahoma State	Stan Holmes, of, Arizona State
1982	Miami*	Ron Fraser	57-18	Wichita State	Dan Smith, p, Miami (Fla.)
1983	Texas*	Cliff Gustafson	66-14	Alabama	Calvin Schiraldi, p, Texas
1984	Cal State Fullerton	Augie Garrido	66-20	Texas	John Fishel, of, Cal State Fullerton
1985	Miami (Fla.)*	Ron Fraser	64-16	Texas	Greg Ellena, dh, Miami (Fla.)
1986	Arizona	Jerry Kindall	49-19	Florida State	Mike Senne, of, Arizona
1987	Stanford	Mark Marquess	53-17	Oklahoma State	Paul Carey, of, Stanford
1988	Stanford	Mark Marquess	46-23	Arizona State	Lee Plemel, p, Stanford
1989	Wichita State	Gene Stephenson	68-16	Texas	Greg Brummett, p, Wichita State
1990	Georgia	Steve Webber	52-19	Oklahoma State	Mike Rebhan, p, Georgia
1991	Louisiana State*	Skip Bertman	55-18	Wichita State	Gary Hymel, c, Louisiana State
1992	Pepperdine*	Andy Lopez	48-11	Cal State Fullerton	Phil Nevin, 3b, Cal State Fullerton
1993	Louisiana State	Skip Bertman	53-17	Wichita State	Todd Walker, 2b, Louisiana State
1994	Oklahoma*	Larry Cochell	50-17	Georgia Tech	Chip Glass, of, Oklahoma
1995	Cal State Fullerton*	Augie Garrido	57-9	Southern California	Mark Kotsay, of-p, Cal State Fullerton
1996	Louisiana State*	Skip Bertman	52-15	Miami	Pat Burrell, 3b, Miami
1997	Louisiana State*	Skip Bertman	57-13	Alabama	Brandon Larson, ss, Louisiana State
1998	Southern California	Mike Gillespie	49-17	Arizona State	Wes Rachels, 2b, Southern California
1999	Miami*	Jim Morris	50-13	Florida State	Marshall McDougall, 2b, Florida State
2000	Louisiana State*	Skip Bertman	52-17	Stanford	Trey Hodges, rhp, Louisiana State
2001	Miami*	Jim Morris	53-12	Stanford	Charlton Jimerson, of, Miami
2002	Texas*	Augie Garrido	57-15	South Carolina	Huston Street, rhp, Texas
2003	Rice	Wayne Graham	58-12	Stanford	John Hudgins, rhp, Stanford
2004	Cal State Fullerton	George Horton	47-22	Texas	Jason Windsor, rhp, Cal State Fullerton
2005	Texas*	Augie Garrido	56-16	Florida	David Maroul, 3b, Texas
2006	Oregon State	Pat Casey	50-16	North Carolina	Jonah Nickerson, rhp, Oregon State

*Undefeated

the 16 games decided by one or two runs, the most in CWS history. That type of drama helped the Monday night finale average 1,979,000 households for a 2.2 rating. It marked ESPN's most-viewed and third highest-rated college baseball game ever. The second game of the championship series, telecast Sunday on ESPN2, rated as that network's most-viewed and highest-rated college baseball game. Overall households and ratings increased 25 percent and 22 percent on ESPN and 18 percent and 14 percent on ESPN2.

Year Of The Pitcher–Just Not In Omaha

The College World Series didn't go that well for the three first-team All-America pitchers that advanced, as Andrew Miller, Wes Roemer and Eddie Degerman combined for an 0-2 record in six combined starts.

Saving his best for last
Daniel Bard nearly pitched UNC to a title

North Carolina won both times Miller started, but the College Player of the Year didn't earn a decision either time. He allowed eight runs on 13 hits in 12⅓ innings over two starts and gave up three homers after yielding only one all season.

Fullerton's Roemer allowed nine hits and five runs over 8⅔ innings in two starts against North Carolina. The Tar Heels hit four homers off Roemer, who had allowed three previous home runs on the season.

Rice's Degerman allowed four hits over two starts, but didn't win either of them. He got a no decision in 6-4 win against Georgia in which he took a no-hitter into the seventh inning (but walked a season-high eight) and lost to Oregon State 2-0 on a night when he yielded three hits.

Daniel Bard, Miller's teammate and fellow first-round pick, gave up five runs on 12 hits in his first CWS start, but rebounded with one of the best performances of his career in the 3-2 loss to Oregon State. He allowed six hits and a walk over 7⅔ innings, and while Oregon State scored three times against him, only one of the runs was earned. He became the hard-luck loser when Bill Rowe, whom he walked with two outs in the eighth, came around to score on Steed's throwing error.

Bard and Miller were two of the 11 college pitchers who were drafted in the first round in June—16 if you count supplemental first-rounders. That is a reflection of a remarkable year for elite pitchers in college baseball. No. 4 overall pick Brad Lincoln of Houston ranked in the nation's top 10 in wins and ERA, and No. 10 pick Tim Lincecum of Washington led the nation with 199 strikeouts. Lincecum finished his sterling collegiate career with 491 career strikeouts, the most in Pacific-10 conference history.

Other college arms who went in the first 10 picks of the draft include Stanford righthander Greg Reynolds (No. 2), California righthander Brandon Morrow (5) and Miller (6).

Mainieri Embraces Bertman's Shadow

Skip Bertman knows it takes a special person to serve as Louisiana State's baseball coach from his experience in that capacity and now as the school's athletics director. The job requires a coach who can win games while handling the constant pressure to win national championships, something he did five times from 1991-2000.

Bertman believes he found that man in Paul Mainieri, who left Notre Dame after 12 seasons to replace Smoke Laval as LSU's coach.

"Let's face it, the Skip Bertman shadow is huge," Mainieri said. "I realize what I am getting into. A lot of

RPI RANKINGS

The Ratings Percentage Index (RPI) is an important tool used by the NCAA in selecting at-large teams for the 64-team Division I regional field. This chart shows the official 2006 RPI rankings, with records against Division I opponents (ties are not included), as of the NCAA tournament selection day and at the end of the season. The ranking in the Baseball America Top 25 at the time is indicated in parentheses. Asterisks denote teams that did not get a regional bid. College World Series teams are in boldface.

Selection Day (May 29)		Final (June 29)	
RPI Ranking	Record	RPI Ranking	Record
1. Clemson (3)	47-14	1. Clemson (5)	53-16
2. Rice (1)	49-10	2. Rice (4)	56-13
3. Texas (4)	40-19	3. Cal State Fullerton (3)	50-15
4. Cal State Fullerton (2)	43-13	4. North Carolina (2)	54-14
5. Georgia Tech (10)	45-16	5. Georgia Tech (7)	50-18
6. Alabama (6)	41-19	6. Alabama (10)	44-21
7. Nebraska (9)	41-15	7. Oklahoma (9)	45-22
8. Georgia (8)	41-19	8. Miami (8)	42-24
9. Florida State	42-19	9. Georgia (6)	47-23
10. Oklahoma (17)	40-19	10. Florida State	44-21
11. North Carolina (11)	45-13	11. Texas (12)	41-21
12. Virginia (12)	46-13	12. Oregon State (1)	50-16
13. Miami	36-21	13. Nebraska (15)	41-17
14. North Carolina State	38-21	14. North Carolina State	40-23
15. Arkansas (21)	38-19	15. College of Charleston (14)	46-17
16. Mississippi (7)	40-20	16. Virginia (16)	47-15
17. Oklahoma State (20)	39-18	17. Winthrop	46-18
18. Pepperdine (18)	40-19	18. Mississippi (11)	44-22
19. Winthrop	44-16	19. Oklahoma State (23)	41-20
20. Houston (14)	39-20	20. Arkansas	39-21
21. College of Charleston (24)	43-35	21. Troy	47-16
22. Troy	45-14	22. Pepperdine (21)	42-21
23. UCLA	32-23	23. UCLA	33-25
24. Elon	44-16	24. Elon	45-18
25. *Wake Forest	33-22	25. Houston (24)	39-22
26. Tulane (23)	41-19	26. South Carolina (13)	41-25
27. Kentucky (13)	42-15	27. *Wake Forest	33-22
28. Arizona State (16)	36-19	28. Kentucky (20)	44-17
29. South Carolina	37-22	29. Tulane	43-21
30. Oregon State (5)	39-14	30. Fresno State (22)	45-18
31. Fresno State (19)	43-16	31. *Baylor	37-26
32. *Baylor	32-32	32. Arizona State	37-21
33. Kansas (22)	39-23	33. Kansas	40-25
34. Mississippi State	35-21	34. Vanderbilt	38-27
35. Vanderbilt	36-25	35. Mississippi State	37-23
36. Hawaii	42-15	36. Hawaii	44-17
37. *Louisiana State	35-24	37. Stanford (19)	33-27
38. South Alabama	38-19	38. *Louisiana State	35-24
39. Southern Mississippi	38-21	39. South Alabama	39-21
40. UC Irvine	36-22	40. Southern Mississippi	39-23
41. *Florida	28-28	41. Oral Roberts (17)	38-16
42. Notre Dame (15)	44-15	42. Missouri (18)	35-28
43. Jacksonville	42-17	43. UC Irvine	36-24
44. Stanford	30-25	44. *Florida	28-28
45. Wichita State	43-20	45. Notre Dame	44-17
46. UNC Wilmington	41-20	46. Wichita State (25)	45-22
47. *Long Beach State	29-27	47. San Francisco	39-23
48. Oral Roberts	35-14	48. Jacksonville	43-19
49. Missouri	31-25	49. UNC Wilmington	42-22
50. Michigan	42-19	50. *Long Beach State	29-27

COLLEGE BASEBALL

THE ROAD TO OMAHA

June 9-12. 16 teams, eight best-of-3 series.
Winners advance to College World Series.

REGIONALS

June 2-5. 64 teams, 16 double-elimination tournaments.
Winners advance to super-regionals. *Automatic qualifier.

CAL STATE FULLERTON

■ **Super Regional Site:** Fullerton, Calif. (Cal State Fullerton).
Participants: Missouri (35-26) at Cal State Fullerton (46-13).
(Cal State Fullerton wins 2-0, advances to College World Series).
■ **Regional Site:** Malibu, Calif. (Pepperdine).
Participants: *No. 1 Pepperdine (40-19), No. 2 UCLA (33-23), No.
3 UC Irvine (36-22), No. 4 Missouri (31-25).
Champion: Missouri (4-1). **Runner-Up:** Pepperdine (2-2).
Outstanding Player: Brock Bond, 2b, Missouri.
■ **Regional Site:** Fullerton, Calif. (Cal State Fullerton).
Participants: *No. 1 Cal State Fullerton (43-13), No. 2 Fresno St.
(43-16), No. 3 San Diego (32-23), No. 4 St. Louis (32-27).
Champion: Cal State Fullerton (3-0).
Runner-Up: Fresno St. (2-2).
Outstanding Player: Blake Davis, ss, Cal State Fullerton.

CLEMSON

■ **Super Regional Site:** Clemson, S.C. (Clemson).
Participants: Oral Roberts (41-14) at Clemson (50-14).
(Clemson wins 2-0, advances to College World Series).
■ **Regional Site:** Fayetteville, Ark. (Arkansas).
Participants: No. 1 Oklahoma St. (39-18), *No. 2 Arkansas (38-19),
No. 3 Oral Roberts (39-14), No. 4 Princeton (19-24-1).
Champion: Oral Roberts (3-0). **Runner-Up:** Oklahoma St. (2-2).
Outstanding Player: Chad Rothford, 1b, Oral Roberts.
■ **Regional Site:** Clemson, S.C. (Clemson).
Participants: *No. 1 Clemson (47-14), No. 2 Elon (44-16), No. 3
Mississippi St. (35-21), No. 4 UNC Asheville (28-33).
Champion: Clemson (3-0). **Runner-Up:** Mississippi St. (2-2).
Outstanding Player: Michael Johnson, 1b, Clemson.

GEORGIA

■ **Super Regional Site:** Athens, Ga. (Georgia).
Participants: South Carolina (40-23) at Georgia (45-20).
(Georgia wins 2-1, advances to College World Series).
■ **Regional Site:** Charlottesville, Va. (Virginia).
Participants: *No. 1 Virginia (46-13), No. 2 South Carolina (37-22),
No. 3 Evansville (40-20), No. 4 Lehigh (28-26).
Champion: South Carolina (3-2). **Runner-Up:** Evansville (2-2).
Outstanding Player: Phil Disher, dh, South Carolina.
■ **Regional Site:** Athens, Ga. (Georgia).
Participants: *No. 1 Georgia (41-19), No. 2 Florida State (42-19),
No. 3 Jacksonville (42-17), No. 4 Sacred Heart (26-28).
Champion: Georgia (3-1). **Runner-Up:** Florida State (3-1).
Outstanding Player: Joey Side, of, Georgia.

GEORGIA TECH

■ **Super Regional Site:** Atlanta (Georgia Tech).
Participants: Col. of Charleston (46-15) at Georgia Tech (48-16)
(Georgia Tech wins 2-0, advances to College World Series).
■ **Regional Site:** Lexington, Ky. (Kentucky).
Participants: *No. 1 Kentucky (42-15), No. 2 Col. of Charleston
(43-15), No. 3 Notre Dame 945-15), No. 4 Ball St. (37-20).
Champion: Col. of Charleston (3-0). **Runner-Up:** Kentucky (2-2).
Outstanding Player: Alex Garabedian, c, Col. of Charleston.

■ **Regional Site:** Atlanta (Georgia Tech).
Participants: *No. 1 Georgia Tech (45-16), No. 2 Vanderbilt (36-25), No. 3 Michigan (42-19), No. 4 Stetson (38-22).
Champion: Georgia Tech (3-0). **Runner-Up:** Vanderbilt (2-2).
Outstanding Player: Matt Wieters, c/p, Georgia Tech.

MIAMI (FLA.)

■ **Super Regional Site:** Oxford, Miss. (Mississippi).
Participants: Miami (Fla.) (39-21) at Mississippi (43-20)
(Miami wins 2-1, advances to College World Series).
■ **Regional Site:** Lincoln, Neb. (Nebraska).
Participants: *No. 1 Nebraska (42-15), No. 2 Miami (Fla.) (36-21),
No. 3 San Francisco (38-21), No. 4 Manhattan (32-21).
Champion: Miami (3-0). **Runner-Up:** Manhattan (2-2).
Outstanding Player: Jemile Weeks, 2b, Miami.
■ **Regional Site:** Oxford, Miss. (Mississippi).
Participants: *No. 1 Mississippi (40-20), No. 2 Tulane (41-19),
No. 3 South Alabama (38-19), No. 4 Bethune-Cookman (30-25).
Champion: Mississippi (3-0). **Runner-Up:** Tulane (2-2).
Outstanding Player: Justin Brashear, c, Mississippi.

NORTH CAROLINA

■ **Super Regional Site:** Tuscaloosa, Ala. (Alabama).
Participants: North Carolina (48-13) at Alabama (44-19)
(North Carolina wins 2-0, advances to College World Series).
■ **Regional Site:** Chapel Hill, N.C. (North Carolina).
Participants: *No. 1 North Carolina (45-13), No. 2 Winthrop (44-16), No. 3 UNC Wilmington (41-20), No. 4 Maine (35-20-1).
Champion: North Carolina (3-0). **Runner-Up:** Winthrop (2-2).
Outstanding Player: Jay Cox, of, North Carolina.
■ **Regional Site:** Tuscaloosa, Ala. (Alabama).
Participants: *No. 1 Alabama (41-19), No. 2 Troy (45-14), No. 3
Southern Mississippi (38-21), No. 4 Jacksonville (35-22).
Champion: Alabama (3-0). **Runner-Up:** Troy (2-2).
Outstanding Player: Kody Valverde, c, Alabama.

OREGON STATE

■ **Super Regional Site:** Corvallis, Ore. (Oregon State).
Participants: Stanford (33-25) at Oregon State (42-14)
(Oregon State wins 2-0).
■ **Regional Site:** Austin, Texas (Texas).
Participants: *No. 1 Texas (40-19), No. 2 NC State (38-21), No.
3 Stanford (30-25), No. 4 Texas-Arlington (29-34).
Champion: Stanford (3-0). **Runner-Up:** NC State (2-2).
Outstanding Player: Chris Minaker, ss, Stanford.
■ **Regional Site:** Corvallis, Ore. (Oregon State).
Participants: *No. 1 Oregon State (39-14), No. 2 Kansas (42-23),
No. 3 Hawaii (43-15), No. 4 Wright St. (32-25).
Champion: Oregon State (3-0). **Runner-Up:** Hawaii (2-2).
Outstanding Player: Chris Kunda, 2b, Oregon State.

RICE

■ **Super Regional Site:** Houston, Texas (Rice).
Participants: Oklahoma (44-20) at Rice (53-10)
(Rice wins 2-1, advances to College World Series).
■ **Regional Site:** Norman, Okla. (Oklahoma).
Participants: *No. 1 Oklahoma (40-19), No. 2 Houston (39-20),
No. 3 Wichita St. (44-20), No. 4 Texas Christian (38-21).
Champion: Oklahoma (4-1). **Runner-Up:** Wichita St. (2-2).
Outstanding Player: Ryan Rohlinger, 3b, Oklahoma.
■ **Regional Site:** Houston, Texas (Rice).
Participants: *No. 1 Rice (50-10), No. 2 Arizona St. (36-19),
No. 3 Baylor (35-24), No. 4 Prairie View (33-20).
Champion: Rice (3-0). **Runner-Up:** Baylor (2-2).
Outstanding Player: Eddie Degerman, rhp, Rice.

people might be afraid of that. I am going to stand here and tell you that I am not afraid of that."

Laval won more Southeastern Conference games than any other coach during his five-year tenure and advanced to the CWS twice, but he was pressured to resign on the heels of declining attendance and LSU's missing the NCAA tournament in 2006 for the first time since 1988 following a 35-24 season.

Mainieri, 48, guided Notre Dame to nine NCAA tournaments, 533 wins and the 2002 College World Series in his time in South Bend, Ind. His 2006 team went 45-17-1.

Mainieri was replaced at Notre Dame by former Evansville coach Dave Schrage, a former assistant to Mainieri at St. Thomas (Fla.) in the 1980s.

COACHING CAROUSEL

Division I coaching changes at the end of the 2006 season:

School	New Coach (Previous School/Job)	Former Coach (Reason)
Alabama A&M	Jay Martin (Alabama A&M football assist.)	Thomas Wesley (not renewed)
Alabama-Birmingham	Brian Shoop (Birmingham-Southern)	Larry Giangrosso (retired)
Boston College	Mikio Aoki (BC assistant)	Pete Hughes (to Virginia Tech)
Cleveland State	Kevin Kocks (NAIA Spalding)	Jay Murphy (not renewed)
Coppin State	Vacant	Guy Robertson (resigned)
Evansville	David Seifert (UE assistant)	Dave Schrage (Notre Dame)
Georgia State	Greg Frady (GSU assistant)	Mike Hurst (became GSU assistant AD)
Indiana State	Lindsay Meggs (Chico State)	Bob Warn (retired)
Grambling State	Barret Rey (Southern pitching coach)	James Randall (not renewed)
Jackson State	Omar Johnson (JSU assistant)	Mark Salter (not renewed)
Lipscomb	Jeff Forehand (NAIA Trevecca Nazarene)	Wynn Fletcher (resigned)
Louisiana State	Paul Mainieri (Notre Dame)	Smoke Laval (resigned)
Louisville	Dan McDonnell (Mississippi assistant)	Lelo Prado (to South Florida)
Marshall	Jeff Waggoner (N.C. State assistant)	Dave Piepenbrink (took job outside baseball)
Maryland-Eastern Shore	Will Gardner (Delaware State assistant)	Bobby Rodriguez (resigned)
Notre Dame	Dave Schrage (Evansville)	Paul Mainieri (to LSU)
Richmond	Mark McQueen (Virginia Commonwealth)	Ron Atkins (retiring after 2007 season)
Sam Houston State	Mark Johnson (former Texas A&M coach)	Chris Rupp (resigned)
South Florida	Lelo Prado (Louisville)	Eddie Cardieri (resigned)
Southern California	Chad Krueter (Rockies, high Class A)	Mike Gillespie (retired)
Valparaiso	Tracy Woodson	Paul Twenge (resigned)
Virginia Tech	Pete Hughes (Boston College)	Chuck Hartman (retired)
Wisconsin-Milwaukee	Scott Doffek (UW-M assistant)	Jerry Augustine (took job outside baseball)

Legendary Coaches Pass

College baseball's greatest leader and amateur baseball's greatest ambassador, former Southern California coach Rod Dedeaux, died in January of complications from a stroke he suffered the previous month. Dedeaux was 91.

Dedeaux was the Trojans coach for 45 seasons from 1942-86, winning 11 College World Series crowns and 28 conference titles. (Curiously, the NCAA only recognizes Dedeaux with 10 titles, crediting co-coach Sam Barry with USC's first title even though Dedeaux actually ran the team.) He posted an overall record of 1,332-571-11 for a .699 winning percentage, and retired with more wins than any other college baseball coach.

"Rod not only was college baseball's greatest coach, he was the sport's and USC's greatest ambassador," said Trojans coach Mike Gillespie, who played for Dedeaux and was a member of the 1961 championship team. Gillespie retired after the season and handed the reigns of the tradition-rich USC program over to his son-in-law Chad Kreuter.

In all Dedeaux coached 59 big leaguers. The list includes Hall of Fame pitcher Tom Seaver, as well as future Hall of Famers Randy Johnson and Mark McGwire, Dave Kingman and Bill "Spaceman" Lee.

Dedeaux wasn't the only college baseball coaching heavyweight to pass away in 2006. Former East Carolina coach Keith LeClair lost his battle with amyotrophic lateral sclerosis (ALS) in July at age 40.

LeClair had two significant careers in college baseball, first as an all-conference player at Western Carolina, then as a head coach at his alma mater and later East Carolina.

He was part of 13 NCAA tournament teams as a player and coach, and as a player, the former walk-on set single-season Western Carolina records for hits and total bases. As a coach, his Pirates teams included Diamondbacks infielder Chad Tracy and a slew of players who followed him into coaching, such as Eric Bakich (Vanderbilt), Cliff Godwin (LSU) and Joe Hastings (Boston College).

When LeClair's career was at its peak, in 2001, his East Carolina team went 47-13, losing to Tennessee in a super-regional played in Kinston, N.C., with East Carolina as the host.

LeClair officially gave up his post in June 2002, though assistant coaches Kevin McMullen (now at Virginia) and Tommy Eason (now at Pitt, N.C., Community College) piloted the team for much of the season. That last club went 43-20-1, bringing LeClair's career record to 441-231-3 in just 11 seasons.

Birmingham Southern Drops To D-III

Citing financial disappointments, the board of trustees at Birmingham-Southern College voted in June to drop its athletic program from NCAA Division I to Division III, affecting 193 athletes at the small liberal arts school. Player defections then caused the school to suspend its baseball program for 2007.

The decision came after the school's first internal review since 1999, when the school began a transition from the NAIA to Division I. No sport at Birmingham-Southern has been as successful as its baseball program, a team that won the Big South regular-season conference title in two of the three seasons in which it competed. Coach Brian Shoop led the program to an at-large bid to the NCAA tournament in 2004 after regular-season wins against Georgia, Mississippi State and Alabama.

Shoop left after the season to take over the head coaching job at Alabama-Birmingham.

APR Makes Its Mark

A pair of 2005 College World Series participants—Texas and Tennessee—were among 21 NCAA Division I baseball programs that lost scholarships based on the Academic Progress Report released by the NCAA in March.

Ten baseball programs—including Texas and Tennessee—lost the maximum of 1.17 scholarships, a figure based on 10 percent of the sport's limit of 11.7 scholarships. The NCAA said the one-year reduction in scholarships had to be taken in either 2006 or 2007.

The APR reflected data for the 2003-2004 and 2004-2005 academic years, and measured a school's retention of student-athletes and their progress toward graduation.

2006 COLLEGE ALL-AMERICA TEAM

Selected by Baseball America

Wade LeBlanc | Tim Lincecum | Brad Lincoln | Evan Longoria | Drew Stubbs

FIRST TEAM

POS	Player, School	YR	Hometown	AVG	AB	R	H	2B	3B	HR	RBI	BB	SO	SB
C	Matt Wieters, Georgia Tech	So.	Goose Creek, S.C.	.355	251	72	92	20	0	15	71	56	39	3
1B	Mark Hamilton, Tulane	Jr.	Bellaire, Texas	.336	235	61	79	12	0	29	69	51	42	2
2B	Jim Negyrch, Pittsburgh	Jr.	Buffalo, N.Y.	.396	182	41	72	14	0	11	60	40	42	6
3B	Pedro Alvarez, Vanderbilt	Fr.	New York, N.Y.	.329	240	70	79	15	1	22	64	57	64	7
SS	Brian Friday, Rice	So.	Houston, Texas	.353	269	66	95	22	3	9	57	30	51	17
OF	Kellen Kulbacki, James Madison	So.	Hershey, Pa.	.464	194	68	90	17	2	24	75	30	32	13
OF	Cole Gillespie, Oregon State	Jr.	West Linn, Ore.	.374	238	83	89	25	5	13	57	46	37	15
OF	Tyler Colvin, Clemson	Jr.	North Augusta, S.C.	.356	281	64	100	22	5	13	70	28	42	23
DH	Ryan Strieby, Kentucky	Jr.	Brier, Wash.	.343	233	60	80	22	1	20	77	46	39	2
UT	Brad Lincoln, Houston	Jr.	Clute, Texas	.295	224	35	66	12	0	14	53	24	41	5

POS	Player, School	YR	Hometown	W	L	ERA	G	GS	CG	SV	IP	H	BB	SO
SP	Andrew Miller, North Carolina	Jr.	Gainesville, Fla.	13	2	2.48	20	18	0	1	123	100	40	133
SP	Tim Lincecum, Washington	Jr.	Renton, Wash.	12	4	1.94	22	17	3	3	125	75	63	199
SP	Eddie Degerman, Rice	Sr.	Granada Hills, Calif.	13	2	2.00	20	19	0	0	131	78	56	172
SP	Wes Roemer, Cal State Fullerton	So.	Glendora, Calif.	13	3	2.38	21	20	3	1	155	126	7	145
RP	Cole St. Clair, Rice	So.	Santa Ana, Calif.	7	2	1.82	37	2	0	11	74	39	26	100
UT	Brad Lincoln, Houston	Jr.	Clute, Texas	12	2	1.69	17	17	3	0	128	91	32	152

SECOND TEAM

POS	Player, School	YR	Hometown	AVG	AB	R	H	2B	3B	HR	RBI	BB	SO	SB
C	Kody Valverde, Alabama	Sr.	Baton Rouge, La.	.347	219	58	76	17	2	12	59	42	36	1
1B	Craig Cooper, Notre Dame	Sr.	Plainview, N.Y.	.425	228	79	97	19	3	9	41	10	14	9
2B	Justin Turner, Cal State Fullerton	Sr.	Bellflower, Calif.	.355	287	63	102	19	4	4	43	16	31	20
3B	Evan Longoria, Long Beach State	Jr.	Downey, Calif.	.353	201	42	71	13	2	11	43	40	29	3
SS	Emmanuel Burris, Kent State	Jr.	Washington, D.C.	.360	239	70	86	10	3	4	28	23	22	42
OF	Jacob Dempsey, Winthrop	Sr.	Chesapeake, Va.	.403	248	71	100	28	2	17	78	49	36	8
OF	Jon Jay, Miami	Jr.	Miami, Fla.	.361	227	77	82	14	2	6	46	39	30	31
OF	Drew Stubbs, Texas	Jr.	Atlanta, Texas	.342	243	65	83	14	4	12	58	41	60	26
DH	Josh Horton, North Carolina	So.	Hillsborough, N.C.	.395	271	62	107	17	1	7	59	33	28	12
UT	Sean Doolittle, Virginia	So.	Tabernacle, J.J.	.324	216	49	70	15	1	4	57	54	28	2

POS	Player, School	YR	Hometown	W	L	ERA	G	GS	CG	SV	IP	H	BB	SO
SP	Jake Arrieta, Texas Christian	So.	Plano, Texas	14	4	2.35	19	17	1	1	111	96	37	111
SP	Jonah Nickerson, Oregon State	Jr.	Oregon City, Ore.	13	4	2.34	20	20	3	0	137	114	38	131
SP	Nick Schmidt, Arkansas	So.	St. Louis, Mo.	9	3	3.01	17	17	1	0	117	90	50	145
SP	Steven Wright, Hawaii	Jr.	Moreno Valley, Calif.	11	2	2.30	16	15	2	1	110	80	19	123
RP	Don Czyz, Kansas	Sr.	Overland Park, Kan.	6	0	1.56	37	0	0	19	63	49	15	60
UT	Sean Doolittle, Virginia	So.	Tabernacle, J.J.	11	2	2.38	18	15	0	1	91	64	21	108

THIRD TEAM

POS	Player, School	YR	Hometown	AVG	AB	R	H	2B	3B	HR	RBI	BB	SO	SB
C	Jordan Newton, Western Kentucky	Jr.	Hodgenville, Ky.	.324	176	50	57	14	5	14	58	45	43	6
1B	Andy D'Alessio, Clemson	Jr.	Naples, Fla.	.312	250	55	78	15	0	23	85	30	60	7
2B	Damon Sublett, Wichita State	So.	Wichita, Kan.	.394	165	45	65	9	1	10	45	31	34	12
3B	Josh Rodriguez, Rice	Jr.	Houston, Texas	.344	262	62	90	21	3	11	64	42	47	10
SS	Zach Cozart, Mississippi	So.	Collierville, Tenn.	.338	272	57	92	16	1	10	64	17	28	24
OF	Corey Brown, Oklahoma State	So.	Tampa, Fla.	.347	216	68	75	13	6	13	40	42	58	14
OF	John Raynor, UNC Wilmington	Sr.	Benson, N.C.	.370	262	63	97	17	2	12	69	22	41	42
OF	Joey Side, Georgia	Jr.	Loganville, Ga.	.352	315	57	111	20	9	13	54	23	46	7
DH	Chad Huffman, Texas Christian	Jr.	Missouri City, Texas	.388	209	58	81	16	2	18	71	38	31	6
UT	Mike Felix, Troy	Jr.	Panama City, Fla.	.381	168	36	64	14	1	5	31	18	34	3

POS	Player, School	YR	Hometown	W	L	ERA	G	GS	CG	SV	IP	H	BB	SO
SP	Lauren Gagnier, Cal State Fullerton	Jr.	Santa Cruz, Calif.	14	5	2.80	21	19	0	0	132	109	25	105
SP	Danny Ray Herrera, New Mexico	Jr.	Odessa, Texas	10	0	2.24	17	17	3	0	128	112	29	104
SP	Wade LeBlanc, Alabama	Jr.	Lake Charles, La.	11	1	2.92	18	18	3	0	129	100	43	128
SP	P.J. Walters, South Alabama	Jr.	Daphne, Ala.	11	3	3.20	19	19	5	0	152	159	33	166
RP	Josh Fields, Georgia	So.	Hull, Ga.	3	2	1.80	35	0	0	15	50	36	11	56
UT	Mike Felix, Troy	Jr.	Panama City, Fla.	9	4	3.45	28	8	1	4	102	85	49	134

Miller leads Tar Heels back to Omaha

Andrew Miller's 13-2, 2.11 season stands as a key reason for North Carolina's first College World Series berth since 1989. But the junior lefthander would rather be known as one of many Tar Heels piled atop one another after Chad Flack's game-ending home run to clinch a super-regional series win at Alabama.

PLAYER *OF THE* **YEAR** "I think he kind of feels uncomfortable talking about himself," North Carolina coach Mike Fox said of his junior lefthander. "You know how kids can be, they don't want people to think they think they're better than anybody. His parents said he's always been like that. Even in high school he didn't really want the attention. He's a big kid at heart and a great teammate."

But Miller, all 6 feet and 6 inches of him, can't hide from the attention now. His dominant junior season, in which he posted a 119-36 strikeout-walk ratio and allowed seven extra-base hits (and only one home run) in 111 innings, not only helped him meet a personal goal of reaching Omaha, but also earned him Baseball America's College Player of the Year award.

"I appreciate all the awards and the accolades, but the biggest memory for me is going to be we went to Omaha and what we accomplished there," Miller said. "I certainly wouldn't want to have a good year on a team that's not as good. I've never really been a part of a team like this."

Miller becomes the sixth pitcher to win the award in the last 25 years and the first lefthander to ever claim the award. The honor—and humility—came in the middle of perhaps the best week in Miller's life.

The Tigers drafted him sixth overall on a Tuesday, and three days later he struck out 11 Alabama batters over seven innings without allowing an earned run to put his team just one game from Omaha. He used his mid-90s four-seam fastball, 88-90 mph two-seamer and power slider to dominate the Crimson Tide, recording three strikeouts against leadoff man Emeel Salem.

"There's a reason he's the sixth pick in the draft. He's a great pitcher. And it's really hard to solve a guy like that," said Salem, who hit .356 and was the only consensus selection on the all-Southeastern Conference first team.

"He has three pitches and even movement on a 97 mile an hour fastball. We didn't capitalize when we had chances but he didn't make enough mistakes for us to get anything going."

Good luck blending in after a game like that. Even Alabama fans were asking for Miller's autograph the next day. After honoring those requests, Miller settled into the North Carolina bullpen. Mr. All-American (the only player on both BA's preseason and postseason first-teams) was down there holding a walkie-talkie, serving as the team's communicator by relaying the coaches' wishes from the

Humility in the face of acclaim
Andrew Miller just wants to be one of the guys

dugout as to which relievers should warm up.

That perch gave Miller a great viewpoint to watch Flack's heroics. "A great performance in the most exciting baseball game I've ever seen," Miller said of the sophomore first baseman giving UNC a 5-4 lead with a three-run homer in the eighth inning and then turning a 7-6 deficit into an 8-7 win with a two-out, two-run walk-off homer in the bottom of the ninth to clinch the super-regional.

"I just ran in from the bullpen as fast as I could," Miller said. "I basically was right with Chad rounding third base. It was a unique feeling I don't think I've ever had.

"That's been our goal all year to get to Omaha. A lot of people started to think that Carolina is a team that never really makes it—a pretty talented team that falls apart at the end of the year. We're finally going to Omaha and I can't wait."

Fox, who was coaching third base, said he'll never forget the look on Miller's face as he sprinted past, walkie-talkie still in hand, to join Flack and the rest of the team in a giant celebratory mass. It was all arms, legs, hats and cleats. Nearly impossible to discern any particular player. Just all Tar Heels.

Just the way Miller likes it.

PREVIOUS WINNERS

1981	Mike Sodders, 3b, Arizona State
1982	Jeff Ledbetter, of/lhp, Florida State
1983	Dave Magadan, 1b, Alabama
1984	Oddibe McDowell, of, Arizona State
1985	Pete Incaviglia, of, Oklahoma State
1986	Casey Close, of, Michigan
1987	Robin Ventura, 3b, Oklahoma State
1988	John Olerud, 1b/lhp, Washington State
1989	Ben McDonald, rhp, Louisiana State
1990	Mike Kelly, of, Arizona State
1991	David McCarty, 1b, Stanford
1992	Phil Nevin, 3b, Cal State Fullerton
1993	Brooks Kieschnick, dh/rhp, Texas
1994	Jason Varitek, c, Georgia Tech
1995	Todd Helton, 1b/lhp, Tennessee
1996	Kris Benson, rhp, Clemson
1997	J.D. Drew, of, Florida State
1998	Jeff Austin, rhp, Stanford
1999	Jason Jennings, rhp, Baylor
2000	Mark Teixeira, 3b, Georgia Tech
2001	Mark Prior, rhp, Southern California
2002	Khalil Greene, ss, Clemson
2003	Rickie Weeks, 2b, Southern
2004	Jered Weaver, rhp, Long Beach State
2005	Alex Gordon, 3b, Nebraska

Casey works magic at Oregon State

Just a few years ago, Pat Casey thought about leaving Oregon State.

Maybe he could find more success in pro ball, working as an instructor. He was sick of identifying talented players, selling them on a school in which he believed and then losing out on the players because another program offered a better history or better weather.

COACH
OF THE **YEAR**

Casey sure is glad he kept believing. His 12th Oregon State team beat North Carolina twice after losing the first game of the College World Series championship series to win the school a second national title to go along with a 1961 cross country championship. Oregon State (50-16), which won consecutive Pacific-10 Conference titles for the first time in school history in 2006, was the only team to reach the College World Series in 2005 and 2006. Not bad for a program whose only previous CWS trip had come in 1952. For those successes, Casey earns Baseball America's 2006 College Coach of the Year award.

"I sat with him in a restaurant in 2000 in Corvallis, he was down and out and thinking 'Can I do it here?' I quite frankly didn't think he could do it there with Oregon kids," Arizona State coach Pat Murphy said. "But he did. And he didn't do it with any funny business. He did it straight up, the right way."

Reaching the pinnacle
Pat Casey built the Beavers into a power

Casey might have done it the right way, but his 2006 team also did it the hard way in Omaha. It won a CWS-record six elimination games after dropping its first game in bracket play and again losing its opener in the championship series.

"If you're going to coach, you better be able to lead," Casey said. "After we lost that first game to North Carolina, I told them to walk off the bus proud. Then they bowed their necks and played like champions."

The Beavers believed, and they persevered. Just as Casey had a few years before in coming off a 19-35 season in 1999, the first year the Pac-10's Northern and Southern teams competed as a full league.

"In '99, I'm on a plane flying back from getting our tails whipped and I questioned it for a moment," Casey said. "But it's about leading

young men. If you don't believe you can do it, players can see it in your eyes. If you don't believe, they won't either."

Casey stuck it out. He measured the program's success incrementally. Winning a game against Stanford or Arizona State. Getting to 10 wins in conference play. Then it happened in 2005. A collection of 2003 recruits formed the axis of a strong pitching rotation: Dallas Buck, Jonah Nickerson and closer Kevin Gunderson. He remembers Gunderson saying he'd always wanted to play at Stanford.

"I said, 'OK, we play there, you'll just be wearing our uniform,' " Casey said, and it's worth noting Oregon State went 8-3 against Stanford over the last three years.

The first series win against the Cardinal came last season, when the Beavers went 46-12, 19-5 in the Pac-10 and showed up in Omaha as the story of the year.

"Last year everyone was happy for us and it was a fun story, and this year there are more critics saying we can't do it or players aren't as good as they were," Casey said. "It comes with success. When you have that bulls-eye on your back, it makes a difference every game. Teams are gunning for us, every game they're giving us their best."

But Oregon State's best proved the best of all.

Baylor's Thompson honored as assistant coach

The 2003 murder of Baylor basketball player Patrick Dennehy by teammate Carlton Dotson and the subsequent misconduct and resignation of basketball coach Dave Bliss made Mitch Thompson's job quite a bit more difficult. Baylor's baseball program had nothing to do with any of that, of course, yet the Bears suffered on the recruiting trail from the PR fallout.

But the stellar group of players that Thompson brought to Waco in 2002 helped pull Baylor through that rough period, leading the Bears to the College World Series in 2005. All of a sudden, the Bears found themselves out of basketball's dark shadow, and the difference was apparent on

Thompson

the recruiting trail.

"It was quite a time, because we'd make an offer to a kid and he'd accept it," Thompson said. "We didn't lose a single kid that we offered."

Now Baylor is harvesting the fruits of that 2005 CWS run and the ensuing recruiting boon. With four elite recruits and a number of other potential high-impact players, Baylor's 2006 haul ranks as the nation's best.

And for helping turn Baylor into a national powerhouse in his 14 seasons as recruiting coordinator in Waco, Thompson earned the 2006 American Baseball Coaches Association/Baseball America Assistant Coach of the Year award.

Alvarez tears apart SEC

When the Vanderbilt players were asked to vote for the players they'd like to see in the starting lineup in surveys at the end of fall ball, Pedro Alvarez didn't win the vote at third base. He didn't even come close.

"I think 70 percent of the votes went to another guy," Commodores coach Tim Corbin said. "There were mixed reviews on (Alvarez)—he didn't have a whole lot of success. In the fall he hit .170, so he was struggling a little bit.

"It didn't worry me too much, because I felt like he was going to

FRESHMAN OF THE YEAR

play his way into the position. I had seen enough of him before."

It turns out Corbin's instinct was right. Not only did Alvarez earn the starting third base job, but he also went on to slug 22 home runs—tops among all third basemen in the nation and more than a third of Vanderbilt's team total. He also led the Commodores in on-base percentage (.456), slugging percentage (.675), RBIs (64) and runs (70) in an All-America season that also earned him Baseball America's Freshman of the Year award.

It was quite a turnaround from the fall, when Alvarez admitted to being a little anxious.

"We have about 14, 15 pitchers—probably half are lefties—and they were all throwing real well," the left-handed-hitting Alvarez said. "We would face them in scrimmages, and I said to myself, 'Well, if the pitching is like this in every other school, it's going to be a long year.' But I got used to the pitching, what pitchers like to do, like to throw."

It didn't happen right away. At a season-opening tourna-

ment in Los Angeles, Alvarez went 1-for-9 with four strikeouts and a pair of errors in three games. His bat started to come around during the next 15 games, all of which were home games for the Commodores. He began recognizing pitches better, cutting down on his strikeouts and increasing his walks.

It took a little longer for him to settle in defensively, and he made two errors at Mississippi in Vandy's Southeastern Conference opener, bringing his season total to seven.

But soon Alvarez found his comfort zone, especially at the plate. He tore through the SEC, batting .360-7-27. His defense was steady too, as he made just four more errors in his next 29 conference games.

"I've told everyone I've spoken to about him, his defense is as good as his offense," Corbin said. "He's definitely married to the game, and he likes to work on the defensive part of the game too."

Alvarez' work ethic and humility have always made him stand out, even more than his immense talent. He impressed scouts with his respectful nature and lack of ego last year, even though he slipped to the Red Sox in the 14th round because of his strong commitment to Vanderbilt.

"The way he carries himself and handles himself, it's something to really admire about the kid, on top of the type of baseball player he's supposed to be," Red Sox scouting director Jason McLeod said.

Slow start, torrid finish
Pedro Alvarez found his comfort zone

FRESHMAN ALL-AMERICA TEAM

FIRST TEAM

Pos.	Player, School	AVG	OBP	SLG	AB	R	H	HR	RBI	SB
C	Tim Federowicz, North Carolina	.320	.383	.532	250	35	80	12	62	2
1B	Justin Smoak, South Carolina	.303	.407	.586	244	61	74	17	63	1
2B	Jemile Weeks, Miami	.354	.448	.564	243	66	86	6	40	12
3B	Pedro Alvarez, Vanderbilt	.329	.456	.675	240	70	79	22	64	7
SS	Gordon Beckham, Georgia	.280	.348	.490	286	61	80	12	54	5
OF	Aaron Luna, Rice	.322	.447	.638	199	48	64	16	50	4
OF	Warren McFadden, Tulane	.382	.457	.513	238	53	91	1	50	6
OF	Jared Prince, Washington St.	.401	.492	.618	207	50	83	9	58	10
DH	Alex Buchholz, Delaware	.378	.433	.721	222	62	84	18	64	8
UT	Luis Flores, Houston	.288	.392	.500	156	24	45	8	30	2

Pos.	Player, School	W	L	ERA	SV	IP	H	BB	SO	AVG
SP	Christian Friedrich, Eastern Ken.	10	2	1.98	0	82	64	24	118	.204
SP	Aaron Shafer, Wichita St.	11	3	2.63	0	99.1	87	22	77	.238
SP	Jacob Thompson, Virginia	10	4	2.60	0	100.1	82	29	77	.225
SP	Alex Wilson, Winthrop	13	3	3.78	0	138	127	50	143	.247
RP	Kyle Weiland, Notre Dame	2	4	2.37	16	49.1	39	20	48	.224
UT	Luis Flores, Houston	6	3	3.00	0	87	76	17	67	.239

SECOND TEAM

C—Preston Paramore, Arizona State (.318-3-35). **1B**—Allan Dykstra, Wake Forest (.324-15-56). **2B**—David Adams, Virginia (.318-5-49). **3B**—Kevin McAvoy, Maine (.369-10-64). **SS**—Brandon Crawford, UCLA (.318-6-30). **OF**—Mike Bianucci, Auburn (.359-8-31), Jericho Jones, Louisiana Tech (.357-16-56), Kyle Russell, Texas (.276-10-42). **DH**—Ike Davis, Arizona State (.329-9-65). **UT**—J.B. Shuck, Ohio State (.325-0-19).

SP—Chris Fetter, Michigan (5-2, 2.22), Scott Gorgen, UC Irvine (7-5, 2.54), Tommy Hunter, Alabama (10-3, 3.30), Brian Matusz, San Diego (4-3, 4.25). **RP**—Brett Hunter, Pepperdine (5-3, 2.83, 11 SV). **UT**—J.B. Shuck, Ohio State (8-5, 2.51).

NCAA DIVISION I LEADERS

TEAM BATTING

TEAM BATTING	G	AVG
Jackson State	39	.359
West Virginia	58	.339
North Carolina State	63	.333
Alcorn State	47	.333
Ohio State	58	.332
Troy	63	.332
Winthrop	64	.329
St. John's (N.Y.)	59	.327
Oral Roberts	57	.327
South Alabama	60	.326

RUNS SCORED	G	R
Georgia Tech	68	594
Troy	63	579
UNC Wilmington	64	560
North Carolina State	63	538
Rice	70	523
James Madison	59	516
New Mexico	59	507
Kentucky	61	500
Southern Mississippi	62	492
Oklahoma	67	492

DOUBLES	G	2B
Rice	70	162
Troy	63	157
UNC Wilmington	64	156
Georgia Tech	68	156
James Madison	59	149
North Carolina State	63	148
Kentucky	61	146
Mississippi	66	145
Delaware	54	143
Wisconsin-Milwaukee	57	143
Clemson	69	143

TRIPLES	G	3B
Arizona	55	34
Oklahoma State	61	32
Baylor	63	32
Oregon State	66	31
Alcorn State	47	29
Michigan State	56	29
Dallas Baptist	56	28
Arizona State	58	28
Va. Commonwealth	58	27
Georgia	70	27

HOME RUNS	G	HR
Delaware	54	111
James Madison	59	101
Kentucky	61	99
South Carolina	66	92
Georgia Tech	68	90
Dallas Baptist	56	86
Washington	61	86
Troy	63	86
Oklahoma State	61	84
North Carolina	69	83

STOLEN BASES	G	SB	AT
Prairie View	55	218	253
Mississippi Valley	56	191	224
New Orleans	56	160	204
Jackson State	39	143	156
McNeese State	55	142	183
Southern Utah	54	137	172
Wichita State	68	137	160
Indiana	56	135	176
UNC Wilmington	64	133	158
College of Charleston	63	128	164

TEAM PITCHING

WINNING PERCENTAGE	W	L	PCT
Rice	57	13	.814
North Carolina	54	15	.783
Cal State Fullerton	50	15	.769
Clemson	53	16	.768
Virginia	47	15	.768
Oregon State	50	16	.758
Troy	47	16	.746
Georgia Tech	50	18	.735
Le Moyne	38	14	.731
College of Charleston	46	17	.730

EARNED RUN AVERAGE	G	ERA
Cal State Fullerton	65	2.73
College of Charleston	63	3.02
Virginia	62	3.04
Rice	70	3.16
St. John's (N.Y.)	59	3.21
Clemson	69	3.26
Army	51	3.28
Monmouth	49	3.34
North Carolina	69	3.35
Le Moyne	52	3.36

TEAM FIELDING

FIELDING PERCENTAGE	G	PCT
Oklahoma	67	.983
San Jose State	59	.979
Tulane	64	.978
South Carolina	66	.978
UCLA	58	.977
Cal State Fulleton	65	.977
Gonzaga	53	.976
Oregon State	66	.975
Michigan	47	.975
Pepperdine	63	.975

Menace to opposing pitchers
Kellen Kulbacki was a force in 2006

INDIVIDUAL BATTING

BATTING AVERAGE
(Minimum 150 At-Bats)

	YR	AVG	G	AB	R	H	2B	3B	HR	RBI	BB	SO	SB
Mike Goetz, Wisc.-Milwaukee	Sr.	.493	57	225	67	111	23	6	3	33	9	20	0
Kellen Kulbacki, James Madison	So.	.464	53	194	68	90	17	2	24	75	30	32	13
Joaquin Rodriguez, Jackson State	Jr.	.457	39	140	50	64	15	2	3	54	22	8	19
Shundell Russaw, Jackson State	Sr.	.440	38	141	50	62	11	2	2	35	14	11	18
Ryah Khoury, Utah	Sr.	.438	56	224	73	98	18	4	13	54	39	28	16
Craig Cooper, Notre Dame	Sr.	.425	57	228	.79	97	19	3	9	41	38	14	9
Marcus Davis, Alcorn State	Jr.	.424	23	89	30	35	8	3	8	34	7	27	6
Nate Schill, James Madison	Jr.	.419	58	227	50	95	16	0	14	68	9	28	7
Matt McBride, Lehigh	Jr.	.417	56	211	56	88	19	0	12	61	21	15	22
Bradley Hubbert, Alcorn State	Jr.	.416	27	99	29	40	10	0	6	36	8	26	12
Ronnie Bourquin, Ohio State	Sr.	.416	58	219	54	91	15	2	8	66	32	24	3
Tom King, Troy	Jr.	.411	62	285	75	117	35	1	8	73	27	28	3
Mark Shorey, High Point	Sr.	.408	56	213	41	87	19	0	20	62	36	34	5
Chris Pieper, Bucknell	So.	.406	36	101	18	41	7	2	3	20	2	17	1
Erik Huber, Eastern Illinois	Jr.	.404	55	198	32	80	9	0	2	39	25	17	7
Jacob Dempsey, Winthrop	Sr.	.403	64	248	71	100	28	2	17	78	49	36	8
Casey Bowling, West Virginia	Sr.	.403	55	206	45	83	15	2	7	43	17	25	5
Luke Hopkins, New Mexico State	So.	.403	44	149	46	60	11	0	16	65	53	27	0
Ryan Rizzo, Quinnipiac	Jr.	.402	46	184	43	74	12	0	4	26	16	15	6
Mike Preist, Campbell	Sr.	.402	56	224	62	90	16	3	13	53	31	28	13
Jared Prince, Washington St	Fr	.400	56	207	50	83	16	1	9	58	30	25	10
David Doss, South Alabama	Fr.	.400	44	175	39	70	19	1	7	39	11	26	4
Mike Epping, New Orleans	Sr.	.400	55	205	56	82	12	1	8	58	25	25	42
Sergio Miranda, Va. Commonwealth	So.	.400	58	250	50	100	20	4	4	40	26	24	15
Daniel Murphy, Jacksonville	Jr.	.398	57	221	54	88	10	1	6	55	34	13	15
Chris Joachim, St. John's (N.Y.)	Jr.	.398	58	216	52	86	12	2	1	46	25	21	20
Jermaine Mitchell, UNC Greensboro	Jr.	.397	59	234	43	93	11	7	5	41	42	43	24
Ben Trotter, Illinois-Chicago	Jr.	.397	42	141	30	56	9	1	2	34	9	14	1
Parker Gargis, Samford	Jr.	.396	58	202	45	80	15	1	5	55	16	24	2
Jim Negrych, Pittsburgh	Jr.	.396	50	182	41	72	14	0	11	60	40	42	6
Brandon Menchaca, Delaware	So.	.395	54	220	61	87	20	9	16	64	23	37	28
Adam Amar, Memphis	Jr.	.395	55	210	40	83	17	3	10	66	31	26	2
Jeff Beachum, Middle Tennessee State	Sr.	.395	54	248	62	98	18	1	3	39	16	14	10
Daniel Nava, Santa Clara	Sr.	.395	54	200	47	79	10	4	3	37	31	29	15
Tim Ryan, Centenary (La.)	Sr.	.395	53	195	47	77	13	3	3	36	36	19	12
Josh Horton, North Carolina	So.	.395	68	271	62	107	17	1	7	59	33	28	12
Anthony McLin, Jackson State	Jr.	.395	33	114	26	45	9	0	2	32	12	11	18
Justin Johnson, Illinois-Chicago	Sr.	.395	50	185	52	73	18	3	11	57	22	19	3
Nick Massari, Monmouth	Jr.	.395	49	185	48	73	14	3	8	51	21	20	21
Charlie Yarbrough, Eastern Kentucky	Jr.	.391	55	207	49	81	18	0	18	69	32	42	0
Greg Sexton, William & Mary	Jr.	.391	52	197	47	77	19	1	6	59	20	23	12
Michael McKenry, Middle Tenn. State	Jr.	.390	55	210	42	82	13	4	13	68	38	24	2
Bryan Tews, Brown	Sr.	.390	38	146	35	57	10	1	4	25	11	24	1
Blake Lalli, Gardner-Webb	Sr.	.389	55	208	39	81	13	1	11	39	35	16	3
Dustin Martin, Sam Houston St.	Sr.	.389	54	208	45	81	16	2	6	40	29	32	13
Joe Roundy, Kansas State	Sr.	.389	52	198	46	77	16	2	8	51	15	20	10
Mike Affronti, Le Moyne	Sr.	.389	52	198	52	77	12	3	12	54	12	19	17
Scott Campbell, Gonzaga	Jr.	.389	53	211	48	82	9	0	4	24	39	17	6
Wilson Tucker, Belmont	Jr.	.388	55	227	40	88	20	5	10	53	14	27	1

RUNS	YR	G	R
Cole Gillespie, Oregon State	Jr.	63	83
Craig Cooper, Notre Dame	Sr.	57	79
Jordan Pacheco, New Mexico	So.	59	79
Shane Robinson, Florida State	Jr.	65	79
Tyler Jones, South Alabama	Jr.	60	78
Jon Jay, Miami (Fla.)	Jr.	66	77
Jeff Kindel, Georgia Tech	Sr.	68	77
Aaron Bates, North Carolina State	Jr.	63	76
Tom King, Troy	Jr.	63	75
Chris Coghlan, Mississippi	Jr.	66	75

HITS	YR	G	H
Tom King, Troy	Jr.	63	117
Chad Flack, North Carolina	So.	67	112
Mike Goetz, Wisconsin-Milwaukee	Sr.	57	111
Joey Side, Georgia	Sr.	70	111
Josh Horton, North Carolina	So.	68	107
Justin Turner, Cal State Fullerton	Jr.	65	102
Greg Buchanan, Rice	Sr.	70	102
Matt Camp, North Carolina State	Jr.	63	101
Emeel Salem, Alabama	Jr.	65	101
Tyler Colvin, Clemson	Jr.	69	100
Jacob Dempsey, Winthrop	Sr.	64	100
Sergio Miranda, Va. Common.	So.	58	100

Andy D'Alessio: 85 RBIs

TONY FARLOW

SLUGGING PERCENTAGE

(Minimum 150 At-Bats)	YR	G	PCT
Kellen Kulbacki, James Madison	So.	53	.943
Marcus Davis, Alcorn State	Jr.	43	.847
Shawn Scobee, Nevada	Sr.	53	.847
Luke Hopkins, New Mexico State	So.	44	.799
Brandon Menchaca, Delaware	So.	54	.786
Mark Shorey, High Point	Sr.	56	.779
Drew Holder, Dallas Baptist	Sr.	56	.755
Luke Cannon, Texas State	Sr.	54	.753
Jeremy Hunt, Villanova	Sr.	54	.743
Chad Huffman, Texas Christian	Jr.	55	.742

ON-BASE PERCENTAGE

(Minimum 150 At-Bats)	YR	G	PCT
Mike Goetz, Wisconsin-Milwaukee	Sr.	57	.579
Kellen Kulbacki, James Madison	So.	53	.568
Ryan Khoury, Utah	Sr.	56	.549
Luke Hopkins, New Mexico State	So.	44	.548
Shawn Scobee, Nevada	Sr.	53	.538
Craig Cooper, Notre Dame	Sr.	57	.522
Jim Negrych, Pittsburgh	Jr.	50	.515
Rich Russell, Marshall	Sr.	54	.513
Greg Dowling, Georgia Southern	Sr.	58	.511
Mark Shorey, High Point	Sr.	56	.504

DOUBLES	YR	G	2B
Tom King, Troy	Jr.	63	35
Jay Miller, Washington State	Sr.	59	28
Jacob Dempsey, Winthrop	Sr.	64	28
Phillip Laurent, Liberty	Sr.	60	27
Joe Fowler, UMBC	So.	52	26
Matt Maloney, Gardner-Webb	Sr.	55	26
Tyler Henley, Rice	So.	70	26
Todd Davison, Delaware	Sr.	54	25
Justin Jenkins, West Virginia	Sr.	58	25
Daniel Stovall, New Mexico	Jr.	59	25
Carson Kainer, Texas	Jr.	61	25
Cole Gillespie, Oregon State	Jr.	63	25
Danny Worth, Pepperdine	So.	63	24
Bill Moss, Memphis	Jr.	58	24

Warren McFadden, Tulane	Fr.	64	24
Josh Yates, Arkansas State	Jr.	50	23
Case Caseedy, Furman	Sr.	54	23
Galen Schumm, Dayton	Sr.	55	23
Mike Goetz, Wisconsin-Milwaukee	Sr.	57	23

TRIPLES	YR	G	3B
Marcus Davis, Alcorn State	Jr.	43	12
Tyler Jones, Alcorn State	Jr.	60	11
Chris Swauger, Citadel	So.	61	10
Seth Fortenberry, Baylor	Sr.	63	10
Justin Newman, Georgia State	Sr.	44	9
Bray Boyer, Arizona	Sr.	53	9
Brendon Menchaca, Delaware	So.	54	9
Zach Penprase, Mississippi Valley	Jr.	55	9
Joey Side, Georgia	Jr.	70	9

HOME RUNS	YR	G	HR
Kellen Kulbacki, James Madison	So.	53	24
Michael Cowgill, James Madison	Sr.	59	23
Quinn Stewart, LSU	Sr.	59	23
Josh Morris, Georgia	Jr.	67	23
Andy D'Alessio, Clemson	Jr.	69	23
Shawn Scobee, Nevada	Sr.	53	22
Pedro Alvarez, Vanderbilt	Fr.	64	22
Chris Carlson, New Mexico	Jr.	59	21
Ben Saylor, Brigham Young	Sr.	59	21
Brad Miller, Ball State	Sr.	60	21
Drew Holder, Dallas Baptist	Sr.	56	20
Mark Shorey, High Point	Sr.	56	20
Zach Clem, Washington	Sr.	57	20
Ryan Strieby, Kentucky	Jr.	61	20
Mark Hamilton, Tulane	Sr.	64	20

RUNS BATTED IN	YR	G	RBI
Andy D'Alessio, Clemson	Jr.	69	85
Chris Carlson, New Mexico	Jr.	59	79
Mark Wright, Mississippi	Jr.	63	79
Jacob Dempsey, Winthrop	Sr.	64	78
Ryan Strieby, Kentucky	Jr.	61	77
Brad Miller, Ball State	Sr.	60	76
Kellen Kulbacki, James Madison	So.	53	75
Drew Holder, Dallas Baptist	Sr.	56	75
Daniel Stovall, New Mexico	Jr.	59	75
David Freese, South Alabama	Jr.	60	73
Phillip Laurent, Liberty	Sr.	60	73
Tom King, Troy	Jr.	63	73
Ben Humphrey, Central Michigan	Jr.	56	72
James McOwen, Florida Int'l	So.	60	71
Keith Smith, UNLV	Jr.	56	71
Chad Huffman, TCU	Sr.	57	71
Cody Montgomery, Dallas Baptist	Sr.	54	70
Brendan Murphy, Marshall	Jr.	54	70
Logan Parker, Cincinnati	Sr.	58	69
Dennis Guinn, Florida State	Sr.	60	69
Charlie Yarbrough, Eastern Kentucky	Jr.	55	69

WALKS	YR	G	BB
Pedro Alvarez, Vanderbilt	Fr.	64	57
Matt Wieters, Georgia Tech	So.	68	56
Logan Parker, Cincinnati	Sr.	58	54
Sean Doolittle, Virginia	So.	62	54
Luke Hopkins, New Mexico State	So.	44	53
Greg Dowling, Ga. Southern	Sr.	58	53
Zach Dillon, Baylor	Sr.	63	53

Jake Arrieta: 14 wins

ANDREW WOOLLEY

Emmanuel Burris: 42 stolen bases

Cat Everett, Tulane	So.	64	53
Matt Rizzotti, Manhattan	So.	57	52
Bryan Cartie, McNeese State	So.	51	51
Allan Dykstra, Wake Forest	Fr.	55	51

TOUGHEST TO STRIKE OUT

(Minimum 125 At-Bats)	YR	AB	SO	RATIO
Mark Hallberg, Illinois-Chicago	So.	217	6	36.2
Christopher Acker, Dela. State	Sr.	204	7	29.1
Mike Kenefick, NYIT	Sr.	133	5	26.6
Kraig Binick, NYIT	Jr.	164	7	23.4
Brandon Paritz, Stetson	Sr.	250	11	22.7
Ryan Sterling, Georgia State	Sr.	214	10	21.4
Keoni Ruth, San Diego	Jr.	229	11	20.8
Vince Chiera, Akron	So.	187	9	20.8
Isa Garcia, Houston	Sr.	227	11	20.6
Matt Cusick, Southern Calif.	Sr.	225	11	20.5

STOLEN BASES	YR	G	SB	AT
Calvin Lester, Prairie View	Jr.	54	56	65
Zach Penprase, Mississippi Valley	Jr.	55	56	63
Mike Epping, New Orleans	Sr.	55	42	49
Emmanuel Burriss, Kent State	Jr.	56	42	44
John Raynor, UNC Wilmington	Sr.	63	42	44
Michael Richard, Prairie View	Sr.	55	41	53
Jimmy Miles, Old Dominion	Jr.	56	39	45
Eric Nieto, Manhattan	So.	57	39	43
K.K. Chalmers, Memphis	So.	60	39	43
Kenny Waddell, Wichita State	Sr.	65	38	46
Reggie Watson, Indiana	Sr.	56	36	42
Phillip Coker, Coll. of Charleston	Sr.	63	36	37
Emeel Salem, Alabama	Jr.	65	36	47

HIT BY PITCH	YR	G	HBP
Colt Sedbrook, Arizona	So.	55	26
Aaron Luna, Rice	Fr.	64	25
Logan Johnson, Louisville	Jr.	60	24
B.T. Good, VMI	Sr.	55	23
Alex Nettey, Notre Dame	Sr.	62	23
Jon Jay, Miami (Fla.)	Jr.	66	23
Brian Kimutis, Akron	Sr.	50	22
Rich Russell, Marshall	Sr.	54	22
Steve Hook, Rutgers	Sr.	58	22
Cody Merrell, Texas State	Sr.	59	22
Robbie Wilder, Hawaii	Sr.	59	22
Kirk Bacsu, Evansville	Jr.	62	22

WINS	YR	W	L
Jake Arrieta, TCU	So.	14	4
Lauren Gagnier, Cal State Fullerton	Jr.	14	5
Eddie Degerman, Rice	Sr.	13	2
Barry Enright, Pepperdine	So.	13	2
Andrew Miller, North Carolina	Jr.	13	2
Wes Remer, Cal State Fullerton	So.	13	2
Eddie Romero, Fresno State	Jr.	13	2
Dallas Buck, Oregon State	Jr.	13	3
Alex Wilson, Winthrop	Fr.	13	3
Jonah Nickerson, Oregon State	Jr.	13	4
Heath Rollins, Winthrop	Jr.	13	4

APPEARANCES	YR	G
John Dunn, Southern California	Fr.	40
Ryan Paul, Cal State Fullerton	Sr.	39
Jonathan Hovis, North Carolina	Sr.	38
Patrick Currin, UNC Greensboro	Sr.	38
Adam Worthington, Illinois-Chicago	Fr.	38

EARNED RUN AVERAGE
(Minimum 60 Innings)

	YR	W	L	ERA	G	GS	CG	SV	IP	H	R	ER	BB	SO
Jonathan Hovis, North Carolina	Sr.	8	2	1.17	38	0	0	2	69	47	13	9	23	58
Steve Holmes, Rhode Island	Jr.	10	2	1.30	14	13	5	1	104	72	23	15	20	93
Nick Chigges, College of Charleston	Jr.	11	2	1.40	17	16	2	0	116	86	28	18	48	100
Chris Cody, Manhattan	Sr.	12	2	1.42	14	13	9	0	108	76	24	17	23	105
Ben Hunter, Wake Forest	So.	1	2	1.47	33	0	0	14	55	38	16	9	17	70
Derrik Lutz, George Washington	Jr.	6	4	1.54	14	13	4	1	100	65	38	17	30	89
Justin Piggott, Mississippi State	So.	7	1	1.66	19	5	3	2	65	57	16	12	4	41
Brad Lincoln, Houston	Jr.	12	2	1.69	17	17	3	0	128	91	29	24	32	152
Mitch Harris, Navy	So.	10	3	1.74	13	13	6	0	83	57	22	16	20	113
Cole St.Clair, Rice	So.	7	2	1.82	37	2	0	11	74	39	19	15	26	100
Zachary Groh, Binghamton	So.	5	3	1.85	11	11	4	0	63	41	18	13	15	71
Jamie Degidio, Rhode Island	So.	7	2	1.86	15	7	1	2	63	50	17	13	11	62
Tim Lincecum, Washington	Jr.	12	4	1.94	22	17	3	3	125	75	39	27	63	199
Jeff Fischer, Eastern Michigan	So.	9	4	1.97	17	12	5	0	110	90	35	24	24	103
Christian Friedrich, Eastern Kentucky	Fr.	10	2	1.98	15	14	3	0	82	64	28	18	24	110
Eddie Degerman, Rice	Sr.	13	2	2.00	20	19	0	0	131	78	35	29	58	172
Wade Korpi, Notre Dame	So.	7	2	2.01	14	12	1	0	76	55	20	17	27	94
Tim Norton, Connecticut	Sr.	7	2	2.04	14	13	4	0	93	62	23	21	24	96
Brandon Morrow, California	Jr.	7	4	2.05	14	14	2	0	97	72	34	22	39	97
Sam Shorts, Miami (Ohio)	Sr.	5	2	2.05	20	6	0	2	65	53	18	15	13	40
Quinn Leath, Western Illinois	Jr.	8	2	2.06	18	13	1	1	79	64	29	18	33	54
Danny Farquhar, La-Lafayette	Fr.	6	1	2.17	20	6	0	4	62	56	16	15	20	55
Buddy Glass, La-Lafayette	So.	8	3	2.17	14	14	5	0	108	84	31	26	20	83
Chris Ashman, Oral Roberts	Sr.	10	1	2.17	19	11	3	1	99	82	35	24	27	75
Austin Creps, Texas A&M	Jr.	3	4	2.20	11	11	0	0	70	64	23	17	13	51
Danny Otoro, Duke	Jr.	5	4	2.20	15	9	2	0	74	76	34	18	6	45
Chris Fetter, Michigan	Fr.	5	2	2.22	16	10	1	1	73	66	25	18	14	48
Jonah Nickerson, Oregon State	Jr.	13	4	2.24	20	20	3	0	137	114	40	34	38	131
Danny Ray Herrera, New Mexico	Jr.	10	0	2.24	17	17	3	0	128	112	41	32	29	104
Max Scherzer, Missouri	Jr.	7	3	2.25	14	13	1	0	80	57	22	20	23	78
Justin Segal, UC Santa Barbara	Jr.	5	3	2.29	36	0	0	7	55	46	20	14	13	33
Steven Wright, Hawaii	Jr.	11	2	2.30	16	15	2	1	110	80	32	28	19	123
Jake Arrieta, TCU	So.	14	4	2.35	19	17	1	1	111	96	40	29	37	111
Paul Hammond, Michicagn	Sr.	8	4	2.36	15	13	6	1	84	79	30	22	24	68
Stephen Faris, Clemson	Jr.	9	3	2.36	18	18	1	0	103	77	36	27	20	86
Wes Remer, Cal State Fullerton	So.	13	2	2.38	21	20	3	1	155	126	43	41	7	145
Sean Doolittle, Virginia	So.	11	2	2.38	18	15	0	1	91	64	29	24	21	108
Cole DeVries, Minnesota	Jr.	7	3	2.42	14	14	3	0	93	76	31	25	32	72
Zach Peterson, Illinois-Chicago	Jr.	9	3	2.42	17	15	4	0	108	107	37	29	12	73
Danny Davis, McNeese State	Jr.	8	0	2.43	25	0	0	7	56	47	20	15	23	46
John Zinnicker, St. Bonaventure	Sr.	8	2	2.44	16	12	2	2	85	86	35	23	24	59
Brad Brach, Monmouth	So.	6	4	2.44	13	13	6	0	85	69	28	23	10	82
Harold Mozingo, VCU	Jr.	7	1	2.45	14	13	5	0	96	54	30	26	18	101
Josh Faiola, Dartmouth	Sr.	6	2	2.45	9	8	5	0	70	68	30	19	14	38
Brett Sinkbeil, Missouri State	Jr.	5	1	2.45	11	11	1	0	70	45	24	19	23	75
Derek McDaid, Charlotte	Sr.	9	4	2.45	16	15	5	0	103	97	39	28	24	69
Tim Bascom, UCF	Jr.	5	6	2.47	14	14	1	0	80	62	25	22	25	90
Andrew Miller, North Carolina	Jr.	13	2	2.48	20	18	0	1	123	100	50	34	40	133
Aaron Poreda, San Francisco	So.	8	5	2.49	18	17	2	0	112	116	46	31	28	75

David Price: 155 strikeouts

Brooks Brown, Georgia	Jr.	19	123
Adam Ottavino, Northeastern	Jr.	14	120
Joshua Froneberger, Ala. State	So.	19	119
Christian Friedrich, Eastern Ky.	Fr.	15	118
Scott Moore, Texas State	Sr.	16	118
Michael Hauff, N.C. A&T	Sr.	22	117
Mitch Harris, Navy	So.	13	113
Jeff Manship, Notre Dame	Jr.	15	111
Sean Doolittle, Virginia	So.	18	108

STRIKEOUTS	YR	IP	SO
Tim Lincecum, Washington	Jr.	125	199
Eddie Degerman, Rice	Sr.	131	172
P.J. Walters, South Alabama	Jr.	152	166
David Price, Vanderbilt	So.	110	155
Brad Lincoln, Houston	Jr.	128	152
Jason Godin, Old Dominion	Jr.	115	146
Nick Schmidt, Arkansas	So.	116	145
Heath Rollins, Winthrop	Jr.	123	143
Mike Felix, Troy	Jr.	102	134
Andrew Miller, North Carolina	Jr.	123	133
Josh Ehmke, Samford	Jr.	109	132
Brad Furnish, TCU	Jr.	100	125
Ryan Reid, James Madison	So.	94	124
Steven Wright, Hawaii	Jr.	110	123
Brooks Brown, Georgia	Jr.	111	123
Adam Ottavino, Northeastern	Jr.	94	120

STRIKEOUTS/9 INNINGS			
(Minimum 50 innings)	IP	SO	AVG
Tim Lincecum, Washington	125	199	14.3
Christian Friedrich, Ea. Kentucky	82	118	13
David Price, Vanderbilt	110	155	12.6
Mitch Harris, Navy	82	113	12.3
Cole St. Clair, Rice	74	100	12.1
Mike Felix, Troy	101	134	11.9
Eddie Degerman, Rice	130	172	11.8
Ryan Reid, James Madison	94	124	11.8
Adam Ottavino, Northeastern	93	120	11.5
Ben Hunter, Wake Forest	55	70	11.5

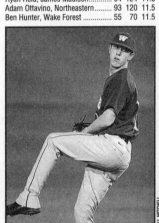

Tim Lincecum: 199 innings pitched

Jonathan Hovis: 1.17 ERA

Kevin Gunderson, Oregon State	Jr.	37
Cole St.Clair, Rice	So.	37
Robbi Elsemiller, Stetson	So.	37
Brad Rulon, Georgia Tech	So.	37
Jason Foster, Illinois-Chicago	Sr.	37
Don Czyz, Kansas	Jr.	37
Chris Perez, Miami (Fla.)	Jr.	37
David Cogswell, Georgia Southern	Sr.	37

SAVES	YR	G	SV
Kevin Gunderson, Oregon State	Jr.	37	20
Don Czyz, Kansas	Sr.	37	19
Kyle Weiland, Notre Dame	Fr.	30	16
Adrew Urena, Mercer	Sr.	30	15
Josh McLaughlin, Coll. of Charleston	Jr.	31	15
Andrew Carnignan, North Carolina	So.	32	15
Link Saunders, Citadel	Jr.	33	15
Joshua Fields, Georgia	So.	35	15
Ryan Davis, Kent State	Jr.	27	14
Ben Hunter, Wake Forest	So.	33	14
Daniel Latham, Tulane	Jr.	35	14
Robbie Elsemiller, Stetson	So.	37	14

INNINGS PITCHED	YR	G	IP
Tim Lincecum, Washington	Jr.	22	199
Eddie Degerman, Rice	Sr.	20	172
P.J. Walters, South Alabama	Jr.	19	166
David Price, Vanderbilt	So.	19	155
Brad Lincoln, Houston	Jr.	17	152
Jason Godin, Old Dominion	Jr.	15	146
Nick Schmidt, Arkansas	So.	17	145
Heath Rollins, Wintthrop	Jr.	22	143
Mike Felix, Troy	Jr.	28	134
Andrew Miller, North Carolina	Jr.	20	133
Josh Ehmke, Samford	Jr.	16	132
Brad Furnish, TCU	Jr.	20	125
Ryan Reid, James Madison	So.	14	124
Steven Wright, Hawaii	Jr.	16	123

COLLEGE
TOP 25

Boldface indicates selected in 2006 draft.

1. OREGON STATE

Coach: Pat Casey **Record:** 50-16

BATTING	YR	AVG	AB	R	H	2B	3B	HR	RBI	SB
Cole Gillespie, of/inf	Jr.	.374	238	83	89	25	5	13	57	15
Bill Rowe, 1b	Sr.	.341	229	49	78	22	4	6	56	1
Erik Ammon, c	So.	.333	15	2	5	1	0	0	4	0
Darwin Barney, ss	Jr.	.330	261	53	86	11	3	0	36	16
John Wallace, of	Fr.	.326	132	27	43	2	1	0	19	5
Tyler Graham, of	Jr.	.323	124	24	40	3	1	1	20	11
Mike Lissman, of	Sr.	.316	95	17	30	3	1	0	10	3
Mitch Canham, lf/c	So.	.299	224	41	67	13	5	7	54	10
Shea McFeely, 3b	Sr.	.296	260	50	77	7	6	4	51	5
Chris Kunda, 2b	Sr.	.273	194	41	53	16	2	2	41	2
Scott Santschi, of	Jr.	.271	181	27	49	13	3	2	29	4
Koa Kahalenhoe, of	Fr.	.263	57	5	15	0	0	0	8	1
Geoff Wagner, of	Sr.	.242	91	16	22	4	0	1	10	2
Ryan Gipson, 2b	Sr.	.207	92	15	19	4	0	0	14	3
Casey Priseman, c	So.	.200	25	2	5	1	0	0	3	0
Greg Laybourn, of	Fr.	.176	17	3	3	0	0	0	0	0
Lonnie Lechelt, if		.087	23	5	2	0	0	0	0	1

PITCHING	YR	W	L	ERA	G	SV	IP	H	BB	SO
Jonah Nickerson, rhp	Jr.	13	4	2.24	20	0	137	114	38	131
Kevin Gunderson, lhp	Jr.	3	2	2.36	37	20	53	38	17	45
Daniel Turpen, rhp	So.	3	0	2.90	13	0	31	30	6	14
Mike Stutes, rhp	So.	8	2	3.10	17	0	81	74	37	77
Dallas Buck, rhp	Jr.	13	3	3.44	21	0	128	101	60	97
Eddie Kunz, rhp	So.	5	1	3.61	29	0	42	39	21	30
Joe Paterson, lhp	So.	1	1	4.11	26	1	31	23	14	21
Greg Keim, rhp	Jr.	0	0	4.80	10	0	15	20	6	8
Mark Grbavac, rhp	Fr.	1	0	5.11	11	0	12	10	5	8
Anton Maxwell, lhp	Jr.	3	3	5.50	10	0	34	38	22	21
Jon Koller, rhp	Sr.	0	0	8.49	11	0	12	13	5	3
Brian Budrow, rhp		0	0	10.12	7	0	8	9	5	6

2. NORTH CAROLINA

Coach: Mike Fox **Record:** 54-15

BATTING	YR	AVG	AB	R	H	2B	3B	HR	RBI	SB
Josh Horton, ss	So.	.395	271	62	107	17	1	7	59	12
Chad Flack, 1b/3b	Jr.	.384	292	68	112	18	5	13	68	15
Jay Cox, of	Jr.	.375	232	56	87	15	0	15	65	7
Kyle Shelton, ss/2b	So.	.328	119	27	39	3	1	1	16	5
Tim Federowicz, c/1b	Fr.	.320	250	35	80	17	0	12	62	2
Mike Cavasinni, of/2b	Jr.	.317	199	43	63	3	0	0	18	16
Seth Williams, of	So.	.298	171	20	51	12	1	3	23	4
Reid Fronk, 3b	So.	.292	233	68	68	19	1	9	44	4
Matt Spencer, of/1b/lhp/of	So.	.278	176	39	49	9	1	6	29	15
Garrett Gore, if/of	Fr.	.227	75	10	17	3	0	0	10	0
Benji Johnson, c	So.	.273	209	36	57	9	2	14	44	4
Bryan Steed, 2b	Jr.	.265	147	30	39	9	0	2	23	4
Matt Iannetta, c/of	So.	.226	31	7	7	1	0	1	9	2
Joe Pietropaoli, 2b/3b	Jr.	.174	23	3	4	1	0	0	2	0

PITCHING	YR	W	L	ERA	G	SV	IP	H	BB	SO
Brian Farrell, lhp	Fr.	0	0	1.50	8	0	6	2	4	6
Jonathan Hovis, rhp	Sr.	8	2	1.17	38	2	69	47	23	59
Andrew Miller, lhp	Jr.	13	2	2.48	20	1	123	100	40	133
Luke Putkonen, rhp	Fr.	6	0	3.08	13	0	61	50	22	36
Andrew Carignan, rhp	So.	2	3	3.21	32	15	34	18	15	44
Robert Woodard, rhp	Jr.	7	1	3.43	18	0	108	107	24	55
Tyler Trice, rhp	So.	1	0	3.57	16	0	18	22	8	13
Daniel Bard, rhp	Jr.	9	4	3.64	19	0	101	92	37	94
Mike Facchinei, rhp	So.	0	1	4.63	9	0	12	12	8	16
Adam Warren, rhp	Fr.	1	0	4.81	15	0	24	29	13	15
Matt Danford, rhp	Jr.	7	2	5.27	33	0	55	54	26	51
Rob Wooten, rhp	So.	0	0	9.82	10	0	7	12	8	14
Matt Cox, lhp/1b	Fr.	0	0	11.12	9	0	6	6	4	7

3. CAL STATE FULLERTON

Coach: George Horton **Record:** 50-15

BATTING	YR	AVG	AB	R	H	2B	3B	HR	RBI	SB
Justin Turner, 2b	Sr.	.355	287	63	102	19	4	4	43	20

BATTING	YR	AVG	AB	R	H	2B	3B	HR	RBI	SB
Blake Davis, ss	Jr.	.351	259	64	91	13	5	5	39	15
Danny Dorn, of	Sr.	.351	174	37	61	13	1	4	43	7
Brett Pill, 1b	Jr.	.328	253	52	83	23	3	5	40	11
Brandon Tripp, of	Jr.	.321	221	44	71	11	6	9	42	10
David Cooper, 1b/lhp	Fr.	.305	151	16	46	9	0	2	37	0
Cory Vanderhook, c	So.	.304	69	12	21	5	0	1	17	1
Evan McArthur, 3b/dh	Jr.	.303	228	44	69	13	1	7	36	7
Bryan Harris, if	Jr.	.295	88	10	26	5	2	0	15	2
Joe Scott, if	Fr.	.286	14	5	4	0	0	0	3	2
Jared Clark, rhp/of	Fr.	.277	166	29	46	5	1	5	30	3
John Curtis, c	Jr.	.277	166	25	46	7	0	0	23	2
Matthew Fahey, of/c	Fr.	.238	21	2	5	0	0	1	4	0
Joe Turgeon, of	Sr.	.233	30	4	7	0	0	0	6	2
Clark Hardman, of/rhp	Jr.	.224	147	20	33	5	0	0	12	8

PITCHING	YR	W	L	ERA	G	SV	IP	H	BB	SO
Vinnie Pestano, rhp	Jr.	2	1	0.97	29	13	37	19	14	43
Ryan Paul, lhp	Jr.	3	1	1.01	39	2	36	20	13	43
Adam Jorgenson, rhp	So.	2	0	1.48	20	0	30	20	7	21
Wes Roemer, rhp	So.	13	2	2.38	21	1	155	126	7	145
Cory Arbiso, rhp	Fr.	0	0	2.65	10	2	17	23	6	8
Lauren Gagnier, rhp	Jr.	14	5	2.80	21	0	132	109	25	105
Dustin Miller, rhp	Sr.	12	1	3.13	18	0	98	85	26	52
Bryan Harris, rhp	Jr.	1	2	3.60	8	0	10	11	3	4
Justin Klipp, rhp	Jr.	2	1	4.00	20	0	27	29	9	25
John Estes, lhp	Sr.	1	1	4.07	24	0	24	23	7	18
Dave Pherrin, lhp	Jr.	0	0	4.61	6	0	14	12	5	11
Jared Clark, rhp	So.	0	1	15.00	4	0	6	15	5	3

4. RICE

Coach: Wayne Graham **Record:** 57-13

BATTING	YR	AVG	AB	R	H	2B	3B	HR	RBI	SB
Brian Friday, ss/3b	So.	.353	269	66	95	22	3	9	57	17
Greg Buchanan, 2b	Sr.	.346	295	64	102	9	3	5	42	13
Josh Rodriguez, ss/2b	Jr.	.344	262	62	90	21	3	11	64	10
Tyler Henley, of	So.	.336	274	74	92	26	7	8	54	6
Joe Savery, p/1b	So.	.335	254	61	85	20	1	9	66	7
Aaron Luna, if	Fr.	.322	199	48	64	13	1	16	50	4
Adam Zornes, c	Fr.	.302	96	19	29	4	0	5	23	1
Jordan Dodson, ut/p	Jr.	.297	229	35	68	16	2	6	41	8
Travis Reagan, c/if	Jr.	.294	85	12	25	5	1	0	12	0
Danny Lehmann, c	So.	.278	158	32	44	12	0	3	31	1
Bobby Bramhall, of	So.	.258	31	7	8	2	0	0	4	0
Kenny Ford, c	Fr.	.235	51	7	12	3	0	1	9	0
Derek Myers, 2b	Fr.	.222	18	10	4	0	0	0	2	3
Chad Lembeck, if	So.	.215	135	25	29	9	2	6	29	5
Trey Sperring, if	Fr.	.077	13	1	1	0	0	1	1	0

PITCHING	YR	W	L	ERA	G	SV	IP	H	BB	SO
Cole St. Clair, lhp	So.	7	2	1.82	37	11	74	39	26	100
Eddie Degerman, rhp	Sr.	13	2	2.00	20	0	131	78	58	172
Bobby Bramhall, lhp	So.	4	2	2.36	26	3	53	36	26	47
Joe Savery, lhp	So.	5	1	2.76	13	0	62	55	24	62
Will McDaniel, rhp	So.	5	1	3.34	19	0	59	53	23	40
Bryce Cox, rhp	Sr.	5	3	3.48	32	4	52	41	25	62
Craig Crow, rhp	Jr.	8	2	3.53	24	0	82	85	35	88
Bobby Bell, rhp	Jr.	8	0	4.17	18	3	73	77	21	61
Daniel Cooper, rhp	So.	0	0	4.32	6	0	8	6	3	5
Kyle Gunderson, rhp	Jr.	0	0	7.50	6	0	6	9	0	2
Bryan Price, rhp	Fr.	0	1	14.14	8	0	7	15	8	10
Kurt Pessa, rhp	So.	0	1	16.88	1	0	1	1	0	1

5. CLEMSON

Coach: Jack Leggett **Record:** 53-16

BATTING	YR	AVG	AB	R	H	2B	3B	HR	RBI	SB
Tyler Colvin, of/1b	Jr.	.356	281	64	100	22	5	13	70	23
Brad Chalk, of	So.	.353	238	67	84	9	4	0	20	18
Travis Storrer, of	Sr.	.321	165	29	53	10	1	9	45	2
Taylor Harbin, 2b/ss	So.	.319	254	54	81	20	2	9	47	13
Andy D'Alessio, 1b	Jr.	.312	250	55	78	15	0	23	85	7
Stan Widmann, ss	So.	.307	241	39	74	12	2	1	30	15
Herman Demmink, 3b	Sr.	.296	280	60	83	16	4	5	32	13
Marquez Smith, if	Jr.	.291	223	53	65	20	1	10	48	5

COLLEGE BASEBALL

BATTING	YR	AVG	AB	R	H	2B	3B	HR	RBI	SB
D.J. Mitchell, of	Fr.	.289	90	20	26	3	0	0	12	8
Adrian Casanova, c	Sr.	.249	205	25	51	10	1	5	34	1
Ben Hall, 2b/1b	Sr.	.226	62	8	14	2	0	2	9	1
Alex Burg, c/of	Fr.	.219	32	5	7	3	0	1	8	1
Doug Hogan, c	So.	.143	28	3	4	1	0	1	6	0
Tanner Leggett, ss/2b	Fr.	.133	15	3	2	0	0	1	1	0
Jameson Smith, if/of	Fr.	.125	16	0	2	0	0	0	0	0
John Ingram, if/of	Fr.	.100	10	0	1	0	0	0	0	0

PITCHING	YR	W	L	ERA	G	SV	IP	H	BB	SO
Stephen Faris, rhp	Jr.	9	3	2.36	18	0	103	77	20	86
Sean Clark, rhp	Jr.	2	0	2.50	11	0	36	28	10	30
Daniel Moskos, lhp	Fr.	5	5	2.52	33	10	54	44	21	54
Stephen Clyne, rhp	Jr.	1	1	2.59	16	0	24	17	5	26
P.J. Zoochi, rhp	So.	6	0	2.81	18	1	67	65	26	66
Josh Cribb, rhp	Sr.	9	0	3.09	16	0	87	70	26	83
Jason Berken, rhp	Jr.	9	3	3.22	18	0	81	83	34	75
Ryan Hinson, lhp	Fr.	4	0	3.82	19	1	31	24	18	31
Steve Richard, rhp	Jr.	0	1	4.30	21	4	23	29	9	14
David Kopp, rhp	So.	6	2	4.32	20	0	58	59	21	46
Alex Martin, lhp	Fr.	2	0	4.42	14	0	18	21	8	8
Drew Fiorenza, rhp	Sr.	0	0	6.60	12	1	15	18	5	15
Matt Vaughn, rhp	Fr.	0	1	10.12	13	0	13	22	7	15

6. GEORGIA
Coach: David Perno   Record: 47-23

BATTING	YR	AVG	AB	R	H	2B	3B	HR	RBI	SB
Jonathan Wyatt, of	Jr.	.360	267	57	96	7	2	4	40	10
Joey Side, of	Jr.	.352	315	57	111	20	9	13	54	7
Jason Jacobs, c	Jr.	.331	248	56	82	18	1	7	48	7
Matt Olson, of	So.	.326	86	15	28	5	1	1	19	1
Ryan Pelsel, 3b	so.	.310	274	45	85	16	1	2	45	3
Josh Morris, 1b	Jr.	.309	272	62	84	16	3	23	68	3
Matt Robbins, of	Jr.	.301	133	23	40	9	1	2	24	5
Bobby Felmy, of	Jr.	.292	264	49	77	11	2	9	52	10
Gordon Beckham, ss	Fr.	.280	286	61	80	18	3	12	54	5
Kyle Keen, rf/dh	Sr.	.279	136	30	38	4	3	4	26	5
Matthew Dunn, 2b	Jr.	.261	230	34	60	9	1	1	26	6
Joe Billick, c	So.	.077	13	0	1	1	0	0	1	0

PITCHING	YR	W	L	ERA	G	SV	IP	H	BB	SO
Joshua Fields, rhp	So.	3	2	1.80	35	15	50	36	11	56
Nick DeSilvio, lhp	Fr.	0	0	1.93	9	0	9	6	6	6
Rip Warren, lhp	Jr.	8	3	3.25	34	0	75	64	21	77
Brooks Brown, rhp	Jr.	8	4	4.07	19	0	111	101	44	123
Stephen Dodson, rhp	Jr.	1	0	4.66	19	1	48	62	6	28
Trevor Holder, rhp	Fr.	5	3	4.70	21	0	59	67	14	23
Jason Leaver, lhp	Fr.	3	2	4.95	18	0	44	51	14	35
Mickey Westphal, lhp	Sr.	7	3	5.24	17	0	93	121	19	44
Nathan Moreau, lhp	Fr.	8	1	5.50	20	0	69	80	20	40
Jason Fellows, lhp	Sr.	1	0	6.30	12	0	21	30	10	6
Adam McDaniel, rhp	Jr.	2	1	8.53	21	0	32	35	25	25
Ben Jeffers, rhp	Fr.	1	1	9.26	8	1	12	17	10	11
Iain Sebastian, rhp	Fr.	0	3	18.00	5	0	6	16	9	4

7. GEORGIA TECH
Coach: Danny Hall   Record: 50-18

BATTING	YR	AVG	AB	R	H	2B	3B	HR	RBI	SB
Danny Payne, of/lhp	Jr.	.356	180	56	64	14	1	11	44	20
Matt Wieters, c/rhp	So.	.355	259	72	92	20	0	15	71	3
Whit Robbins, 1b	Jr.	.352	247	71	87	19	1	13	67	2
Luke Murton, 1b	Fr.	.339	171	42	58	10	0	6	44	6
Jeff Kindel, of/lhp	Jr.	.337	273	77	92	18	1	14	55	0
Wally Crancer, of	Jr.	.321	159	32	51	11	0	6	30	2
Mike Trapani, 2b	Jr.	.311	222	45	69	12	0	5	43	2
Russell Harben, if	Fr.	.300	10	1	3	0	0	0	2	0
Steven Blackwood, of	Sr.	.271	255	55	69	17	0	7	52	5
Michael Fisher, ss	Sr.	.268	235	52	63	10	1	1	39	8
Ryan Tinkoff, if	Fr.	.261	23	7	6	1	0	0	2	0
Andy Hawranick, c	Sr.	.259	108	19	28	3	0	0	18	3
Chris House, of	Fr.	.250	20	4	5	0	0	0	5	0
Brad Feltes, if	So.	.118	17	6	2	0	0	1	4	0

PITCHING	YR	W	L	ERA	G	SV	IP	H	BB	SO
Brad Rulon, rhp	So.	5	0	2.20	37	2	49	36	27	51
Lee Hyde, lhp	Jr.	6	0	3.02	25	1	86	75	42	72
Matt Wieters, rhp	So.	1	3	3.41	21	7	32	35	8	35
John Goodman, rhp	So.	2	0	3.68	8	0	15	10	5	11
Danny Payne, lhp	So.	0	0	3.86	7	1	7	4	5	8
Tim Gustafson, rhp	So.	2	0	3.94	15	4	30	33	6	16
Tim Ladd, lhp	So.	5	3	4.27	22	0	46	62	15	32
Jared Hyatt, rhp	Jr.	3	0	4.66	23	2	46	49	24	51
Blake Wood, rhp	Jr.	11	4	4.79	19	0	115	138	41	95
Chris Hicks, rhp	Fr.	4	1	5.31	23	2	46	49	24	51

PITCHING (cont.)	YR	W	L	ERA	G	SV	IP	H	BB	SO
David Duncan, lhp	Fr.	7	2	5.50	19	0	72	88	25	51
Ryan Turner, lhp	Jr.	4	4	5.55	18	0	60	69	22	46
Michael Hutts, lhp	Fr.	0	1	9.00	4	1	8	10	1	9

8. MIAMI
Coach: Jim Morris   Record: 42-24

BATTING	YR	AVG	AB	R	H	2B	3B	HR	RBI	SB
Jon Jay, of	Jr.	.361	227	77	82	14	2	6	46	31
Jemile Weeks, 2b	Fr.	.352	256	69	90	18	8	6	40	13
Tommy Giles, of	Jr.	.339	233	46	79	20	2	9	45	11
Danny Valencia, 3b	Jr.	.324	244	47	79	10	0	9	61	8
Eddy Rodriguez, c	Jr.	.318	201	37	64	13	0	9	34	1
Yonder Alonso, 3b	Fr.	.295	244	48	72	18	0	10	69	4
Blake Tekotte, of	Fr.	.286	199	36	57	6	4	4	30	10
Dennis Raben, of	Fr.	.285	179	32	51	12	0	8	32	1
Walter Diaz, 2b/ss	So.	.284	102	12	29	7	0	0	12	6
Gus Menendez, 3b	Sr.	.284	74	13	21	4	0	1	12	1
Roger Tomas, ss	Jr.	.283	152	28	43	5	1	0	16	3
Richrd O' Brien Jr., c	Jr.	.252	111	18	28	3	0	5	22	1
Chris Petralli, 1b	Jr.	.182	11	1	2	0	0	0	2	0
Nick Freitas, of	Fr.	.077	13	1	1	0	0	0	0	0

PITCHING	YR	W	L	ERA	G	SV	IP	H	BB	SO
Chris Perez, rhp	Jr.	4	1	1.79	37	12	55	35	30	67
Danny Gil, rhp	Jr.	4	3	2.66	36	0	68	49	34	59
Jon McLean, rhp	Sr.	1	0	3.92	28	0	41	32	11	29
Manny Miguelez, lhp	So.	8	4	4.31	20	0	104	89	37	78
Carlos Gutierrez, rhp	So.	9	7	4.40	17	0	88	81	33	62
Andrew Lane, lhp	Sr.	1	1	4.56	34	1	26	29	18	25
Scott Maine, lhp	Sr.	12	3	4.57	18	0	106	97	39	76
Marcelo Albir, rhp	Sr.	0	1	5.48	15	0	21	25	17	10
Ricky Orta, rhp	Jr.	2	2	6.11	18	1	53	60	23	47
Jason Santana, rhp	Fr.	1	1	7.07	9	0	14	18	6	8
Raudel Alfonso, rhp	So.	0	1	7.11	6	0	6	5	9	5

9. OKLAHOMA
Coach: Sunny Golloway   Record: 45-22

BATTING	YR	AVG	AB	R	H	2B	3B	HR	RBI	SB
Ryan Rohlinger, 3b	Sr.	.387	256	69	99	16	2	13	67	8
Joseph Hughes, lhp	Jr.	.370	81	17	30	4	1	0	20	1
Russell Raley, 2b	Sr.	.360	178	40	54	6	1	2	28	7
Chuckie Caufield, of	Sr.	.351	271	68	95	17	3	9	50	19
Brandon Moss, c	Fr.	.343	67	16	23	0	1	3	17	0
Ryan Mottern, rhp	So.	.323	62	9	20	5	1	1	16	5
Kevin Smith, 3b/1b/dh	Jr.	.319	260	47	83	19	4	9	70	2
Aaron Reza, 2b	Sr.	.318	217	47	69	12	2	1	33	8
Freddy Rodriguez, ss	Sr.	.311	193	26	60	3	1	1	37	2
Jarod Freeman, dh/rhp	Sr.	.308	13	2	4	2	0	0	2	0
Kody Kaiser, of	So.	.305	245	53	75	16	5	7	42	14
Joe Dunigan, of	So.	.297	118	18	35	6	1	4	27	4
Jackson Williams, c	Jr.	.292	202	38	59	15	0	3	36	5
Aaron Ivey, of	Jr.	.279	104	25	29	4	0	1	10	9
Cory Williamson, of	Sr.	.158	19	4	3	0	0	0	2	1
Scott Rooker, of	Jr.	.136	22	9	3	1	0	0	1	0
John Shackelford, c	Sr.	.133	15	4	2	1	0	0	2	0

PITCHING	YR	W	L	ERA	G	SV	IP	H	BB	SO
Matt Lovelady, rhp	Jr.	0	0	3.38	7	0	5	5	5	4
Steven Guerra, rhp	Sr.	11	4	4.04	19	0	107	103	29	73
Daniel McCutchen, rhp	Sr.	10	8	4.06	21	1	149	142	42	147
Joseph Hughes, rhp	Jr.	0	0	4.86	12	0	17	23	7	16
John Brownell, rhp	Sr.	5	1	5.01	34	2	83	93	27	67
P.J. Sandoval, rhp	Sr.	6	5	5.47	18	0	81	101	17	50
Will Savage, rhp	Sr.	7	2	5.49	36	10	57	79	16	47
Nate Hammons, lhp	Fr.	2	0	6.06	18	0	16	19	7	11
Nich Conway, rhp	Fr.	0	0	7.20	9	0	5	6	1	5
Ryan Mottern, rhp	So.	4	2	7.88	13	0	38	45	22	36
Jimmy Rollins, lhp	Jr.	0	0	8.31	10	0	13	13	7	9
Brad Burns, rhp	So.	0	0	8.38	7	0	10	16	7	7

10. ALABAMA
Coach: Jim Wells   Record: 44-21

BATTING	YR	AVG	AB	R	H	2B	3B	HR	RBI	SB
Jeff Texada, ss/2b	Fr.	.571	7	4	4	1	0	0	1	0
Emeel Salem, of	Jr.	.356	284	67	101	14	7	2	32	36
Kody Valverde, c	Sr.	.347	219	58	76	17	2	12	59	1
Spencer Pennington, 1b/dh	Jr.	.303	175	20	53	4	0	4	26	2
Matt Downs, if/rhp	Sr.	.298	252	52	75	16	2	7	62	6
Ryan Rhoden, c/of	Jr.	.285	200	31	57	5	2	1	24	1
Greg Paiml, ss	Jr.	.284	215	45	61	8	5	3	35	6
Wes Henderson, 1b/dh	Jr.	.273	22	1	6	2	0	0	3	0
Alex Avila, 3b	Fr.	.271	203	41	55	14	1	5	42	2
Evan Bush, 2b	Jr.	.265	253	43	67	12	1	6	48	5
Brandon Belcher, of/lhp	Jr.	.259	212	36	55	6	1	3	24	7

Davud Ferazza, c	Sr.	.259	58	11	15	3	0	4	12	0
Matt Bentley, 1b	So.	.217	46	8	10	3	0	1	8	0
Kyle Moore, ss/2b	Fr.	.212	33	3	7	0	0	1	8	1
Kent Matthes, of/inf	Fr.	.200	55	7	11	1	0	1	8	0
Allen Ponder, if	Jr.	.200	5	1	1	0	0	0	2	0
Andrew Rodgers, of	So.	.176	17	1	3	0	0	0	0	0
PITCHING	YR	W	L	ERA	G	SV	IP	H	BB	SO
Jake McCarter, rhp	Jr.	6	1	2.32	20	1	62	52	40	78
Austin Graham, rhp	Fr.	2	1	2.87	4	0	16	15	5	8
Wade LeBlanc, lhp	Jr.	11	1	2.92	18	0	129	100	43	128
David Robertson, rhp	So.	4	4	3.02	29	10	54	32	29	65
Tommy Hunter, rhp	Fr.	10	3	3.30	20	1	117	115	22	80
Josh Copeland, rhp	So.	1	0	3.38	13	0	21	19	12	19
Miers Quigley, lhp	Fr.	1	2	3.75	7	0	24	24	8	21
Patrick Kelly, rhp	Jr.	0	0	4.34	10	0	19	16	10	14
Kenneth Brown, lhp	Sr	0	0	4.50	2	0	2	2	3	1
Bernard Robert, rhp	Jr.	8	6	4.72	17	0	101	115	40	78
Jordan Davis, rhp	Sr.	1	3	5.40	24	2	37	42	24	26

11. MISSISSIPPI

Coach: Mike Bianco **Record:** 44-22

BATTING	YR	AVG	AB	R	H	2B	3B	HR	RBI	SB
Chris Coghlan, 3b	Jr.	.350	263	75	92	22	3	5	50	24
Zack Cozart, ss	So.	.338	272	57	92	16	1	10	64	15
C.J. Ketchum, dh/1b/3b	Jr.	.337	261	30	88	13	0	2	36	2
Alex Presley, of	Jr.	.336	253	61	85	18	7	6	61	20
Justin Henry, dh/1b	So.	.332	268	65	89	12	3	1	30	18
Logan Power, of	Fr.	.328	119	28	39	9	0	2	23	5
Mark Wright, of	Jr.	.305	226	48	69	19	1	16	79	2
Jon-Jon Hancock, of/rhp	So.	.272	158	19	43	15	0	2	33	1
Evan Button, if	Jr.	.265	117	19	31	3	3	0	19	5
Justin Brashear, c	Jr.	.253	198	42	50	13	1	12	42	1
Brett Basham, c	Fr.	.250	32	3	8	1	0	0	1	0
Peyton Farr, if	So.	.250	16	8	4	0	0	1	5	0
Cody Overbeck, of	Fr.	.218	55	9	12	2	0	2	3	0
Alex Kliman, c/inf	So.	.167	24	2	4	1	0	0	3	0
JoJo Tann, if	Fr.	.167	12	13	2	0	0	0	2	2
PITCHING	YR	W	L	ERA	G	SV	IP	H	BB	SO
Jesse Simpson, rhp	Fr.	1	0	2.48	15	2	29	24	9	22
Garrett White, lhp	Jr.	3	1	3.39	29	11	58	50	19	69
Will Kline, rhp	So.	5	2	3.71	22	3	68	69	22	76
Brett Bukvich, lhp	Fr.	6	6	4.50	18	0	92	116	23	74
Nick Hetland, rhp	Jr.	1	1	4.85	4	0	13	12	10	9
Lance Lynn, rhp	Fr.	7	3	4.96	18	1	85	87	51	76
C. Satterwhite, rhp	Fr.	11	2	5.00	23	2	63	68	34	46
Stoney Stone, rhp	Sr.	2	0	5.25	22	1	36	42	12	27
Craig Rodriguez, lhp	Jr.	5	3	5.53	20	0	81	88	22	59
Tommy Baumgardner, lhp	Sr.	3	4	5.81	14	0	48	55	26	35

12. TEXAS

Coach: Augie Garrido **Record:** 41-21

BATTING	YR	AVG	AB	R	H	2B	3B	HR	RBI	SB
Hunter Harris, rhp	Fr.	.371	70	13	26	5	1	1	19	1
Carson Kainer, of	Jr.	.364	231	37	84	25	3	4	66	4
Drew Stubbs, of	Jr.	.342	243	65	83	14	4	12	58	26
Jordan Danks, of	Fr.	.319	116	31	37	7	5	2	21	7
Bradley Suttle, dh	Jr.	.301	226	31	68	15	1	4	36	2
Nick Peoples, if/of	Jr.	.289	228	56	66	6	4	3	27	19
Chance Wheeless, 1b	Jr.	.283	219	47	62	13	1	2	30	5
Preston Clark, c/3b	Jr.	.273	216	27	59	12	2	5	30	1
Brett Lewis, c/inf	Jr.	.247	97	13	24	3	0	0	11	2
Clay Van Hook, 2b/3b/c	Jr.	.244	45	9	11	2	0	0	4	3
Chais Fuller, ss/2b	Jr.	.244	172	27	42	6	1	0	10	2
Preston Pehrson, c	Jr.	.185	27	2	5	1	0	0	4	0
PITCHING	YR	W	L	ERA	G	SV	IP	H	BB	SO
Keith Shinaberry, lhp	Fr.	2	0	1.35	5	0	7	9	0	4
Joseph Krebs, lhp	Jr.	2	1	2.73	23	2	33	36	9	31
Austin Wood, lhp	Fr.	4	3	3.15	35	7	46	40	19	37
Randy Boone, rhp	Jr.	4	2	3.59	22	2	43	41	12	41
Kyle McCulloch, rhp	Jr.	8	5	3.61	19	1	110	113	32	82
Kenn Kasparek, rhp	So.	5	2	3.80	23	3	64	65	28	39
Joey Parigi, lhp	Fr.	1	2	3.86	22	1	35	36	15	25
Jordan Street, lhp	So.	0	0	3.86	7	0	7	10	0	2
Kyle Walker, lhp	Fr.	4	1	3.89	20	0	39	23	33	48
Adrian Alaniz, rhp	So.	7	4	4.18	20	3	97	89	44	70
Riley Boening, rhp	Fr.	4	1	5.26	19	0	63	64	41	58

13. SOUTH CAROLINA

Coach: Ray Tanner **Record:** 41-25

BATTING	YR	AVG	AB	R	H	2B	3B	HR	RBI	SB
Michael Campbell, of	Sr.	.364	209	52	76	13	3	4	49	5
Chris Brown, 2b/dh/3b	Sr.	.358	137	41	49	10	1	5	19	2

Neil Giesler, 1b/3b	Sr.	.352	250	48	88	9	0	4	39	1
Trent Kline, c	Sr.	.336	149	27	50	5	4	4	22	0
Andrew Crisp, if	Fr.	.328	174	31	57	11	0	7	22	3
Ian Paxton, c	Sr.	.319	94	15	30	7	0	5	17	0
Jon Willard, of	Jr.	.304	46	10	14	0	0	7	18	0
Justin Smoak, 1b	Fr.	.303	244	61	74	18	0	17	63	1
Bobbie Grinestaff, if/of	Jr.	.297	202	51	60	8	1	17	58	1
Cheyne Hurst, of	Jr.	.292	212	40	62	10	3	4	38	5
Drew Martin, 1b	Jr.	.276	76	9	21	7	0	3	28	0
Phil Disher, c	So.	.262	65	14	17	3	0	6	17	1
Reese Havens, if	Fr.	.259	239	40	62	12	1	4	40	0
James Darnell, if	Fr.	.239	113	20	27	4	0	3	18	2
Jonathan Ratledge, of	Fr.	.214	14	5	3	0	0	0	3	0
Mark Stanley, c	Jr.	.211	95	20	20	3	1	2	5	3
Harley Lail, if	Jr.	.100	10	1	1	0	1	0	0	0
PITCHING	YR	W	L	ERA	G	SV	IP	H	BB	SO
Arik Hempy, lhp	Jr.	2	1	2.65	7	0	34	22	11	47
Harris Honeycutt, rhp	So.	7	0	3.33	16	0	68	62	32	65
Andrew Cruse, rhp	So.	4	3	3.79	20	3	55	57	21	51
Mike Cisco, rhp	Fr.	7	5	3.96	18	0	89	78	23	76
Wynn Pelzer, rhp	So.	5	5	4.15	20	5	80	66	42	66
Conor Lalor, rhp	Jr.	0	1	4.32	19	0	28	26	16	24
Brandon Todd, rhp	Jr.	0	0	4.63	10	0	12	15	5	9
Shawn Valdes-Fauli, rhp	So.	1	0	4.76	12	3	11	9	4	7
Will Atwood, rhp	Fr.	4	2	5.47	14	0	49	58	10	29
Forrest Beverly, lhp	Jr.	6	3	5.60	17	0	63	72	24	55
Jeff Jeffords, rhp	Jr.	0	1	5.79	18	0	23	26	15	17
Dan Luczak, rhp	So.	2	0	5.79	9	0	14	9	9	14
Kyle Brown, rhp	Fr.	0	1	6.00	10	0	9	9	4	10
Andy Lambert, rhp	Sr.	2	2	6.75	14	0	25	35	11	25
Chase Tucker, lhp	Jr.	0	1	7.13	20	0	18	18	4	25
Alex Farotto, lhp	Fr.	1	0	8.25	12	0	12	17	8	13

14. COLLEGE OF CHARLESTON

Coach: John Pawlowski **Record:** 46-17

BATTING	YR	AVG	AB	R	H	2B	3B	HR	RBI	SB
Alex Garabedian, c	So.	.366	246	47	90	11	1	6	51	5
Larry Cobb, of	Jr.	.357	235	58	84	19	6	7	38	21
Jess Easterling, 3b	Sr.	.346	237	36	82	17	1	6	45	2
Joey Friddle, of	Jr.	.343	233	48	80	15	0	3	37	17
Phillip Coker, of	Sr.	.337	258	57	87	17	0	3	39	36
Chris Campbell, 2b	Jr.	.319	248	41	79	15	1	4	58	6
Jedd Cordisco, of	Fr.	.316	19	2	6	1	0	0	3	1
Oliver Marmol, ss	Jr.	.314	194	51	61	12	3	2	33	26
Graham Maiden, 1b	Jr.	.302	126	20	38	3	0	2	15	2
Matt Kirkpatrick, c	Jr.	.296	54	9	16	3	1	0	9	0
Clay McCord, of	Jr.	.286	126	17	36	3	1	1	11	12
Ben Lasater, if	Jr.	.282	177	31	50	11	0	3	22	0
Michael Harrington, of	So.	.260	50	8	13	1	0	1	11	0
Steve Trask, if	Fr.	.154	13	1	2	1	0	1	3	0
PITCHING	YR	W	L	ERA	G	SV	IP	H	BB	SO
Tim McCarty, rhp	Jr.	1	0	0.00	3	0	6	4	5	9
Josh McLaughlin, rhp	Jr.	1	4	1.27	31	15	57	36	23	71
Nick Chigges, rhp	Jr.	11	2	1.40	17	0	116	86	48	100
Wes Braden, rhp	Sr.	1	0	2.00	2	0	9	6	1	2
Danny Meszaros, rhp	So.	9	2	3.22	16	1	87	77	35	86
Jeff Beliveau, lhp	Fr.	6	4	3.40	16	0	77	77	39	61
Quinn Monsma, lhp	Sr.	7	2	3.41	30	4	58	51	27	42
Graham Godfrey, rhp	So.	8	2	3.57	16	0	98	91	42	101
Brendan Stines, rhp	Fr.	2	0	4.15	14	0	13	13	8	9
Mitch Besselievre, rhp	Fr.	0	0	4.38	10	0	12	15	4	9
Drew Shamrock, lhp	Sr.	0	0	6.61	12	0	16	23	12	15
Jake Goldberg, rhp	So.	0	1	7.77	11	0	22	31	9	22

15. NEBRASKA

Coach: **Record:** 42-17

BATTING	YR	AVG	AB	R	H	2B	3B	HR	RBI	SB
Ryan Wehrle, 2b	So.	.367	226	50	83	22	1	8	48	14
Luke Gorsett, of	Jr.	.348	207	44	72	14	1	15	48	8
Nick Jaros, of	Jr.	.342	190	41	65	13	1	4	33	10
Brandon Buckman, dh/1b	Sr.	.339	230	43	78	8	1	14	51	3
Nick Sullivan, of	Fr.	.318	66	8	21	3	0	2	12	3
Jeff Lanning, c	Fr.	.300	20	4	6	2	0	0	2	2
Andrew Brown, 1b	Jr.	.298	141	24	42	4	1	9	30	1
Jake Opitz, if	So.	.293	205	27	60	9	3	2	27	8
Andy Gerch, of	So.	.290	131	25	38	8	2	4	18	0
Jeff Christy, c	So.	.284	201	36	57	11	1	8	32	8
Jake Mort, lhp	So.	.265	136	20	36	6	0	0	24	9
Steve Edlefsen, if	So.	.260	73	9	19	3	1	1	7	3
Bryce Nimmo, of	So.	.259	205	39	53	7	2	3	21	16
PITCHING	YR	W	L	ERA	G	SV	IP	H	BB	SO
Erik Bird, rhp	Fr.	0	2	0.82	24	1	22	17	4	9

	YR	W	L	ERA	G	SV	IP	H	BB	SO
Zach Herr, lhp	Fr.	0	0	2.05	24	0	22	17	7	18
Brett Jensen, rhp	Sr.	5	0	2.56	27	13	46	27	10	41
Tony Watson, lhp	So.	10	2	2.78	17	0	100	88	24	69
Luke Wertz, rhp	So.	1	0	3.00	12	1	15	13	7	13
Matt Foust, rhp	So.	0	0	3.18	3	1	6	2	4	3
Charlie Shirek, rhp	Fr.	4	2	3.23	18	1	70	66	20	29
Tim Radmacher, rhp	Fr.	1	0	3.60	4	0	10	5	14	9
Jon Klausing, rhp	So.	4	2	3.65	9	0	25	24	9	16
Johnny Dorn, rhp	So.	9	4	3.89	14	0	83	89	26	49
Joba Chamberlain, rhp	Jr.	6	5	3.93	14	0	89	84	34	102
Mike Harmelink, rhp	Jr.	0	0	5.68	8	0	13	13	2	13
Jared Cranston, lhp	Jr.	2	0	6.46	21	0	15	24	15	15
Dan Jennings, lhp	Fr.	0	0	8.22	7	0	8	9	10	2

16. VIRGINIA

Coach: Brian O'Connor   Record: 47-15

BATTING	YR	AVG	AB	R	H	2B	3B	HR	RBI	SB
John Scaglione, if	Jr.	0.412	17	4	7	0	0	0	9	0
Brandon Marsh, of	Jr.	.380	208	51	79	13	3	2	30	14
Tom Hagan, 1b/of	Sr.	.357	210	41	75	12	3	0	41	19
Mattt Bernstine, c	Sr.	.353	17	5	6	1	0	0	3	0
Patrick Wingfield, if	Jr.	.342	76	16	26	6	0	0	10	5
Brandon Guyer, of	So.	.336	238	53	80	19	4	7	57	17
Jeremy Farrell, if	Fr.	.324	148	19	48	9	1	2	32	2
Sean Doolittle, 1b/lhp	Jr.	.324	216	49	70	15	1	4	57	2
David Adams, if	Fr.	.318	239	57	76	8	4	5	49	7
Tim Henry, of	Jr.	.318	195	39	62	11	2	1	39	12
Mike Mitchell, of	Jr.	.317	104	34	33	5	2	0	11	15
Greg Miclat, if	Fr.	.316	215	53	68	11	2	0	22	21
Ryan Hudson, of	Jr.	.275	40	11	11	4	0	2	12	1
Mike Campagna, if	Sr.	.256	39	9	10	0	0	0	9	0
Beau Seabury, c	Jr.	.213	164	23	35	8	0	2	34	0

PITCHING	YR	W	L	ERA	G	SV	IP	H	BB	SO
Josh Myers, rhp	Sr.	3	1	0.00	10	0	17	8	8	20
Sean Doolittle, lhp	So.	11	2	2.38	18	1	91	64	21	108
Jacob Thompson, rhp	Fr.	10	4	2.60	16	0	100	82	29	77
Pat McAnaney, rhp	So.	5	1	2.79	19	1	58	53	11	55
Casey Lambert, lhp	Jr.	3	2	2.79	28	10	39	41	11	44
Alex Smith, lhp	Jr.	0	1	2.79	11	0	10	10	2	12
Andrew Carraway, rhp	Fr.	2	0	2.91	19	0	34	33	6	33
Michael Schwimer, rhp	So.	3	1	3.12	36	0	61	45	14	56
Mike Ballard, lhp	Sr.	9	3	4.09	16	0	92	92	25	69
Shooter Hunt, rhp	Fr.	0	0	4.72	17	0	34	35	15	33
Robert Poutier, rhp	So.	1	0	6.55	4	0	11	10	13	7

17. ORAL ROBERTS

Coach: Rob Watson   Record: 41-16

BATTING	YR	AVG	AB	R	H	2B	3B	HR	RBI	SB
Andy Bouchie, c	Jr.	.376	229	52	86	16	1	12	54	0
Brendan Duffy, of	So.	.358	212	67	76	12	3	1	40	14
Chad Rothford, 1b	Sr.	.332	217	38	72	16	0	13	62	0
Jake Kahaulelio, 2b	Jr.	.323	229	53	74	20	2	4	40	1
Carter McQuigg, 3b/of	Jr.	.319	166	33	53	9	0	7	33	3
Travis DeBondt, of/lhp	Sr.	.315	165	37	52	14	3	3	33	4
Tim Torres, ss	Sr.	.314	226	56	71	15	1	10	39	12
Brian Agualiar, c	Jr.	.313	166	35	52	8	2	3	37	2
Kelly Minissale, of	So.	.311	206	40	64	6	2	3	38	3
Ben Baker, if	Fr.	.281	57	12	16	3	0	0	6	0
Pat Warfle, of	Jr.	.279	129	23	36	12	1	3	22	2

PITCHING	YR	W	L	ERA	G	SV	IP	H	BB	SO
Chance Chapman, rhp	Jr.	5	1	1.55	15	0	46	38	22	36
Chris Ashman, rhp	Sr.	10	1	2.17	19	1	99	82	27	75
Sean Jarrett, rhp	Sr.	7	2	2.63	24	7	62	51	10	71
Daniel Greenwalt, rhp	Jr.	6	2	3.41	15	0	71	71	27	39
Nick Jones, rhp	Sr.	7	4	3.89	15	0	90	89	32	90
Erik Crichton, rhp	Sr.	5	1	4.33	22	1	52	49	16	43
Taylor McIntyre, lhp	Jr.	1	4	7.42	14	0	47	51	32	39
Ronnie Ball, rhp	Jr.	0	0	10.29	6	0	7	7	12	10

18. MISSOURI

Coach: Tim Jamieson   Record: 35-28

BATTING	YR	AVG	AB	R	H	2B	3B	HR	RBI	SB
Brock Bond, if	So.		201	45	68	11	0	2	29	11
Evan Frey, of	So.	.337	190	36	64	4	3	0	22	9
Ryan Lollis, lhp/of	Fr.	.327	101	21	33	6	1	1	20	2
Zane Taylor, of	Sr.	.324	244	47	79	19	2	2	41	14
Derek Chambers, 1b	Sr.	.300	223	36	67	10	0	6	38	1
Jacob Priday, of/c	So.	.283	233	42	66	13	0	11	49	7
Gary Arndt, ss	Jr.	.280	218	33	61	9	1	5	43	6
Hunter Mense, of	Jr.	.258	213	31	55	14	4	2	37	17
John McKee, 3b	Jr.	.240	100	19	24	9	0	3	25	0
Trevor Helms, 2b	Sr.	.237	173	37	41	4	2	1	15	6

	YR	AVG	AB	R	H	2B	3B	HR	RBI	SB
J.C. Field, c	Sr.	.236	161	19	38	7	0	4	24	0
Kyle Mach, if	Fr.	.219	32	9	7	0	0	1	5	0
David Cales, if/rhp	Fr.	.167	30	8	5	1	0	1	8	0
Dan Pietroburgo, c	So.	.154	13	4	2	0	0	0	2	0
Bryson LeBlanc, of	Sr.	.136	22	7	3	0	0	0	1	0

PITCHING	YR	W	L	ERA	G	SV	IP	H	BB	SO
Travis Wendte, rhp	Sr.	2	2	1.86	32	2	48	46	13	40
Max Scherzer, rhp	Jr.	7	3	2.25	14	0	80	57	23	78
Nick Admire, rhp	Sr.	0	0	2.31	11	0	12	10	5	10
David Cales, rhp	Fr.	2	3	2.83	23	1	41	25	14	49
Rick Zagone, lhp	Fr.	6	3	3.28	18	0	69	72	23	48
Nathan Culp, lhp	Jr.	11	6	3.40	20	1	124	115	17	84
Taylor Parker, lhp	Sr.	4	4	3.50	34	5	54	46	23	42
Brant Combs, lhp	Fr.	0	0	3.72	21	0	19	18	8	20
Aaron Crow, rhp	Fr.	1	4	4.06	19	0	78	94	20	60
Brett Reynolds, rhp	Jr.	0	0	4.50	9	0	10	10	4	8
Stephan Holst, rhp	Jr.	1	2	6.75	4	0	15	16	4	16
John Thies, lhp	So.	1	1	8.16	10	0	14	21	6	18

19. STANFORD

Coach: Mark Marquess   Record: 33-27

BATTING	YR	AVG	AB	R	H	2B	3B	HR	RBI	SB
Grant Escue, if	Fr.	.422	45	8	19	1	0	0	8	0
Chris Minaker, ss	Sr.	.364	258	47	94	21	3	11	64	5
Michael Taylor, of	So.	.325	228	36	74	15	3	5	39	2
Ryan Seawell, of/1b	Jr.	.313	166	34	52	9	3	2	14	5
Randy Molina, 2b/inf	Jr.	.308	130	23	40	5	0	0	10	0
Chris Lewis, 2b	Sr.	.306	219	31	67	14	2	8	48	2
Jason Castro, c/1b	Fr.	.283	159	27	45	5	2	3	19	5
Joey August, of	Fr.	.273	110	26	30	2	0	1	6	2
Brendan Domaracki, of	So.	.267	45	3	12	2	0	1	7	0
John Hester, c	Sr.	.264	193	29	51	12	0	2	25	5
Jim Rapoport, of	Jr.	.251	203	31	51	8	2	3	32	3
Brian Juhl, c	So.	.217	46	8	10	2	0	1	3	0
Brent Milleville, c/1b	Fr.	.198	106	13	21	5	0	2	12	2
Cord Phelps, if	Fr.	.196	92	10	18	0	0	0	10	0
J.J. Jelmini, if	Fr.	.182	11	2	2	1	0	0	2	0
Austin Yount, if/rhp	Fr.	.139	36	3	5	3	1	1	7	0
Sean Ratliff, lhp/of	Fr.	.000	14	2	0	0	0	0	1	0

PITCHING	YR	W	L	ERA	G	SV	IP	H	BB	SO
Austin Yount, rhp	Fr.	4	0	2.84	16	1	25	18	9	15
Greg Reynolds, rhp	Jr.	7	6	3.31	18	0	128	118	32	108
Nolan Gallagher, rhp	So.	5	5	3.99	22	0	65	68	28	51
Jeremy Bleich, lhp	Fr.	4	4	4.05	24	7	60	63	16	37
David Stringer, rhp	So.	3	4	4.34	19	1	48	49	15	47
Matt Leva, rhp	Jr.	2	1	4.43	11	0	41	36	23	28
Erik Davis, rhp	So.	1	1	4.91	22	4	33	40	17	22
Matt Manship, rhp	Sr.	2	6	5.51	19	0	67	93	16	50
Max Fearnow, rhp	Fr.	2	0	5.91	16	0	21	29	9	19
Sean Ratlif, rhp	Fr.	2	0	6.75	19	0	28	39	13	30
Blake Holler, lhp	Jr.	1	0	8.86	11	0	21	39	8	18

20. KENTUCKY

Coach: John Cohen   Record: 44-17

BATTING	YR	AVG	AB	R	H	2B	3B	HR	RBI	SB
Ryan Strieby, if	Jr.	.343	233	60	80	22	1	20	77	2
Michael Bertram, 3b	Jr.	.340	197	39	67	16	0	5	37	6
Sean Coughlin, c	Jr.	.325	203	52	66	13	0	17	55	0
Antone DeJesus, of	So.	.323	223	67	72	16	3	5	36	11
Matt McKinney, if	So.	.300	80	18	24	4	0	2	14	2
Collin Cowgill, of	So.	.298	225	62	67	15	1	16	61	6
Billy Grace, of	So.	.297	155	31	46	12	1	6	28	1
John Shelby, if/of	Jr.	.291	213	56	62	18	0	18	56	12
Brian Hastings, c/inf	So.	.276	58	13	16	6	0	0	14	2
Ryan Wilkes, if/rhp	So.	.265	189	34	50	11	0	1	26	2
Shaun Lehmann, if/of	Sr.	.244	172	43	42	6	3	8	32	7
Steve Deaton, if	So.	.235	17	6	4	1	0	1	1	0
Justin Scutchfiel, c	Sr.	.217	60	10	13	4	0	0	11	0
Mike Brown, if	Jr.	.207	29	9	6	2	0	0	7	1

PITCHING	YR	W	L	ERA	G	SV	IP	H	BB	SO
Dewayne Oxford, rhp	Jr.	0	0	2.35	16	1	23	31	2	12
Greg Dombrowski, rhp	So.	10	2	2.83	15	0	102	113	11	54
Brock Baber, rhp	So.	4	0	3.10	23	4	29	36	6	11
Craig Snipp, lhp	Sr.	7	5	3.48	16	0	106	125	25	83
Tommy Warner, lhp	So.	3	3	3.51	9	0	33	35	6	20
Zach Dials, rhp	Jr.	1	1	3.97	21	1	34	33	8	25
Chris Rusin, lhp	Fr.	5	0	4.03	16	0	38	44	14	25
Matt Robinson, lhp	So.	6	1	4.65	22	0	50	54	21	53
Aaron Tennyson, lhp	Sr.	4	3	5.00	17	0	81	101	26	45
Andrew Albers, lhp	So.	3	3	5.40	21	7	30	39	14	28
Troy Ragle, lhp	Jr.	1	1	9.31	10	0	10	17	3	4
Adam Revelette, lhp	Sr.	0	0	11.12	12	0	6	13	4	3

21. PEPPERDINE

Coach: Steve Rodriguez   **Record:** 42-21

BATTING	YR	AVG	AB	R	H	2B	3B	HR	RBI	SB
Danny Kelly, if	Jr.	0.4	10	0	4	0	0	0	2	0
David Uribes, 2b/ss	Sr.	.374	227	53	85	12	1	1	25	22
Nick Kliebert, dh/2b	Sr.	.340	191	31	65	11	0	0	38	4
Adrian Ortiz, of	So.	.340	194	32	66	3	1	1	28	10
Chad Tracy, c	Jr.	.315	254	39	80	20	4	6	46	11
Danny Worth, if	Jr.	.310	252	47	78	24	0	3	38	1
Matt Aidem, if	So.	.292	65	8	19	2	0	1	11	0
Denny Duron, if	Fr.	.290	62	6	18	3	1	0	6	0
Luke Salas, of	Jr.	.288	212	28	61	7	4	1	32	13
Chase d'Arnaud, if	Fr.	.282	195	30	55	14	0	2	22	2
Donald Brown, of	So.	.276	192	36	53	11	2	2	36	4
Justin Tellam, c	Jr.	.233	146	22	34	7	0	8	26	0
Michael Beattie, of/dh	Jr.	.232	69	6	16	3	0	0	7	0
Brandon Daguio, of	Sr.	.208	53	13	11	5	0	0	4	1
Mike Craig, if	Jr.	.179	39	6	7	1	0	1	3	0
Tony Asaro, ut	Fr.	.100	10	2	1	1	0	0	2	0

PITCHING	YR	W	L	ERA	G	SV	IP	H	BB	SO
Paul Coleman, lhp	Sr.	8	5	2.59	17	0	115	89	37	97
Brian Ozols, rhp	So.	1	0	2.83	20	1	29	34	16	53
Brett Hunter, rhp	Fr.	5	3	2.83	29	11	60	52	16	53
Bob Della Grotta, rhp	Jr.	0	2	2.84	3	0	6	8	3	2
James Johnson, rhp	Sr.	6	2	3.24	19	1	89	90	14	54
Bryan Minkel, lhp/inf	Sr.	0	1	3.32	16	0	19	6	8	15
Jason Dominguez, of/rhp	Sr.	6	1	3.52	24	2	54	59	23	33
Barry Enright, rhp	So.	13	2	4.05	21	0	124	145	22	68
Adam Olbrychowski, rhp	So.	2	4	4.61	11	0	41	53	17	20
Bryce Stowell, rhp	Fr.	1	1	7.16	11	0	16	22	8	13

22. FRESNO STATE

Coach: Mike Batesole   **Record:** 45-18

BATTING	YR	AVG	AB	R	H	2B	3B	HR	RBI	SB
Justin Wilson, if/lhp	Fr.	.412	17	2	7	3	0	0	5	0
Beau Mills, if	So.	.355	200	42	71	21	1	14	58	3
Brian Lapin, of	So.	.349	172	34	60	10	1	3	42	5
Christian Vitters, if	Jr.	.340	212	51	72	13	0	11	58	10
Chase Moore, of	So.	.333	48	7	16	3	0	2	9	1
Kent Sakamoto, if	Sr.	.332	253	55	84	18	1	6	46	9
Ozzie Lewis, of	So.	.331	151	30	50	8	3	6	23	0
Steve Susdorf, of	So.	.329	225	63	74	15	1	14	49	4
Erik Wetzel, if	Fr.	.325	203	48	66	11	2	1	27	10
Loren Storey, of	Jr.	.306	186	38	57	5	1	2	18	21
Nick Moresi, of	Jr.	.301	176	36	53	4	0	4	27	4
Frank LoNigro, c	Jr.	.267	172	23	46	6	1	8	45	4
Ryan Overland, c	Jr.	.267	30	2	8	3	0	0	9	0
Todd Sandell, if	So.	.200	75	8	15	3	0	1	6	2
Adam O'Daniel, if	Fr.	.196	51	7	10	0	0	1	4	3
Gavin Hedstrom, if	Jr.	.182	11	4	2	0	0	0	1	1
Jared Halpert, of	Jr.	.176	17	7	3	2	0	0	1	1
Danny Grubb, c	Fr.	.156	32	3	5	1	0	0	0	0

PITCHING	YR	W	L	ERA	G	SV	IP	H	BB	SO
Brandon Miller, lhp	Jr.	0	2	2.79	18	2	19	22	1	10
Andy Underwood, rhp	Jr.	12	3	3.40	20	1	132	131	37	110
Jason Breckley, rhp	So.	3	0	3.50	25	3	36	33	13	40
Justin Wilson, lhp	Fr.	0	0	3.60	17	0	25	24	19	34
Eddie Romero, lhp	Jr.	13	2	3.72	21	0	126	136	46	89
Brandon Burke, rhp	So.	8	5	3.88	24	6	67	71	18	54
Doug Fister, rhp	Sr.	8	6	4.10	20	0	116	118	47	108
Holden Sprague, rhp	Fr.	0	0	5.88	16	0	26	33	4	23
Tanner Scheppers, rhp	Fr.	1	0	9.00	12	0	15	17	15	16

23. OKLAHOMA STATE

Coach: Frank Anderson   **Record:** 41-20

BATTING	YR	AVG	AB	R	H	2B	3B	HR	RBI	SB
Tyler Mach, 3b	Jr.	.364	250	47	91	18	0	16	66	2
Deik Scram, of	Jr.	.363	168	37	61	13	7	6	35	8
Corey Brown, of	So.	.347	216	68	75	13	6	13	40	14
Keanon Simon, of	Jr.	.336	220	55	74	10	6	6	25	15
Rebel Ridling, 1b	Jr.	.324	108	19	35	13	0	2	21	0
Shelby Ford, ss	Jr.	.319	213	50	68	12	3	12	60	7
Ty Wright, of	Jr.	.316	228	41	72	12	0	6	47	6
John Schindler, c	Jr.	.291	55	7	16	1	1	1	9	0
Adam Carr, 1b	Sr.	.290	200	37	58	13	4	12	42	1
Kendall Horner, if	Fr.	.286	21	3	6	1	0	1	0	0
Matt Clarkson, c	Jr.	.279	140	21	39	7	2	3	18	0
Jordy Mercer, ss	Fr.	.270	200	33	54	7	1	6	24	7
Ryan Flavell, c	Jr.	.267	15	2	4	2	0	0	5	0
Justin Colbert, 2b	Sr.	.243	70	16	17	1	2	1	12	2
Steve Ptak, of	So.	.234	47	7	11	3	0	0	2	0

PITCHING	YR	W	L	ERA	G	SV	IP	H	BB	SO
Jared Swart, rhp	Jr.	1	0	1.93	5	0	14	14	2	14
Jeff Breedlove, rhp	Fr.	2	1	3.32	24	0	43	46	18	27
Brett McDonald, rhp	Sr.	1	0	3.68	10	0	15	14	8	11
Brae Wright, lhp	Sr.	8	4	3.99	15	0	99	106	19	59
Oliver Odle, rhp	Jr.	5	4	4.15	20	3	82	99	10	39
DeWayne Carver, rhp	So.	0	0	4.22	7	0	11	11	3	6
Matt Gardner, rhp	So.	7	3	4.43	18	0	83	88	22	51
Charles Benoit, lhp	So.	5	4	4.56	13	0	51	50	25	45
Jordy Mercer, rhp	Fr.	5	0	4.74	12	5	19	14	8	17
Trent Lare, lhp	So.	0	0	5.21	15	0	19	19	3	16
Rick Rivas, rhp	Sr.	2	2	5.30	5	0	19	19	4	8
Dusty Barnard, rhp	Sr.	2	0	5.40	10	0	20	26	6	14
Josh Fritsche, lhp	Jr.	2	2	6.04	13	0	28	36	11	26
Kyle Hollander, rhp	Jr.	0	0	7.04	7	0	8	10	4	6
Joe Kent, lhp	Fr.	1	0	8.31	9	0	13	15	10	8
Brandon Gaviglio, rhp	Fr.	0	0	10.50	5	0	6	9	3	9

24. HOUSTON

Coach: Rayner Noble   **Record:** 39-22

BATTING	YR	AVG	AB	R	H	2B	3B	HR	RBI	SB
Isa Garcia, 2b	Sr.	.357	227	51	81	13	4	4	30	19
Bryan Tully, of	So.	.322	199	34	64	14	1	6	28	8
Jake Stewart, of	Jr.	.321	224	44	72	15	1	7	33	13
Josh Stirneman, if	Jr.	.315	168	24	53	7	3	7	25	6
Matt Weston, of	Jr.	.314	175	39	55	10	1	16	51	3
Brad Lincoln, rhp/inf	Jr.	.295	224	35	66	12	0	14	53	5
Dustin Kingsbury, if	Jr.	.290	245	37	71	16	2	5	31	14
Luis Flores, c/rhp/inf	Fr.	.288	156	24	45	9	0	8	30	2
Brett Logan, c	Sr.	.284	102	15	29	5	1	0	9	4
Travis Cougot, if	Fr.	.283	152	28	43	5	2	2	16	9
Bryan Pounds, if	So.	.231	65	7	15	0	0	0	5	0
Brian Temko, c/inf	Jr.	.189	37	4	7	4	0	1	4	0
Matt Farrington, lhp	Sr.	.182	22	9	4	0	1	0	0	2
Chris Joseph, of	So.	.171	41	3	7	1	0	0	3	0

PITCHING	YR	W	L	ERA	G	SV	IP	H	BB	SO
Brad Lincoln, rhp	Jr.	12	2	1.69	17	0	128	91	32	152
Luis Flores, rhp	Fr.	6	3	3.00	15	0	87	76	17	67
Ricky Hargrove, rhp	So.	8	6	3.31	22	1	101	97	27	82
Sean McLemore, rhp	So.	0	0	3.52	7	1	8	9	1	9
Clayton Boone, rhp	Jr.	3	1	3.72	25	4	29	29	17	31
Matt Farrington, lhp	Sr.	5	4	4.36	17	1	66	76	24	36
Brady Glos, rhp	So.	0	4	4.76	9	0	6	5	7	5
Shea Hancock, rhp	Jr.	2	3	4.85	22	2	43	41	22	44
Aaron Brown, rhp	Jr.	3	6	6.07	28	1	43	46	23	50
Barry Laird, rhp	Fr.	1	0	6.32	16	0	16	14	12	7
Stephen Whalen, rhp	So.	0	0	11.12	7	0	6	14	4	7

25. WICHITA STATE

Coach: Gene Stephenson   **Record:** 46-22

BATTING	YR	AVG	AB	R	H	2B	3B	HR	RBI	SB
Damon Sublett, if/rhp	So.	.394	165	45	65	9	1	10	45	12
Conor Gillaspie, 3b/of	Fr.	.352	261	41	92	18	3	7	67	5
Matt Brown, rhp/of	So.	.335	278	55	93	23	6	4	57	15
Blake Hurlbutt, of	Jr.	.330	91	19	30	1	0	0	8	5
Derek Schermerhorn, if	Jr.	.329	222	41	73	14	0	0	29	17
Josh Workman, ss/2b	Fr.	.317	262	70	83	9	4	4	39	35
Tyler Weber, c	Jr.	.305	105	19	32	4	0	1	21	1
Tyler Hill, lhp/1b/of	Jr.	.286	224	38	64	5	4	1	39	4
Kenny Waddell, of	Sr.	.282	255	48	72	4	1	0	21	38
Brandon Hall, c/3b	Jr.	.272	136	21	37	2	0	3	30	1
Noah Krol, if/rhp	Jr.	.247	166	28	41	6	1	2	20	3
Brian Spear, 3b	So.	.244	127	17	31	7	0	2	23	1
Danny Jackson, 1b/rhp	Jr.	.179	39	5	7	1	0	0	4	0
Tony Pechek, c	Fr.	.083	24	0	2	0	0	0	1	1

PITCHING	YR	W	L	ERA	G	SV	IP	H	BB	SO
Damon Sublett, rhp	So.	1	0	0	14	7	12	5	10	23
Anthony Capra, lhp	Fr.	2	2	1.76	30	2	51	45	14	39
Noah Booth, lhp	Jr.	1	1	2.5	28	7	54	45	15	44
Matt Smith, rhp	Fr.	1	0	2.55	14	0	25	21	14	18
Aaron Shafer, rhp	Fr.	11	3	2.63	16	0	99	87	22	77
Noah Krol, rhp	Jr.	0	1	2.95	18	4	21	24	5	20
Max Hutson, lhp	Jr.	3	0	3.76	13	0	26	23	14	12
Travis Banwart, rhp	Jr.	9	4	3.87	18	1	100	91	29	81
Khol Nanney, rhp	So.	2	1	3.97	25	1	34	35	10	24
Rob Musgrave, lhp	So.	6	3	4.11	16	0	77	77	22	54
Kris Johnson, lhp	So.	6	2	4.86	15	0	54	57	21	45
Kyle Touchatt, lhp	Jr.	4	1	6.75	20	1	31	39	12	20
Jared Simon, rhp	Jr.	0	1	8.71	10	0	10	16	3	6
Jereme Foster, rhp	Sr.	0	3	11.17	4	0	10	15	7	6

2006 CONFERENCE
STANDINGS & LEADERS

*Won conference tournament

Boldface: NCAA regional participant/conference department leader

AMERICA EAST CONFERENCE

	Conference		Overall	
	W	L	W	L
Vermont	16	8	19	34
Stony Brook	15	9	25	29
*Maine	13	9	35	22
Albany	12	10	20	32
Binghamton	12	11	27	23
Hartford	8	16	11	38
Maryland-Baltimore County	5	17	18	34

ALL-CONFERENCE TEAM: C—Tom Hill, Albany. 1B—Brendon Hitchcock, Binghamton. 2B—Chris Sipp, Stony Brook. 3B—Kevin McAvoy, Maine. SS—Justin Smucker, Binghamton. OF—Joe Hough, Maine; Joe Fowler, UMBC; Kyle Brault, Vermont. DH—Nate Olson, Albany. SP—Zach Groh, Binghamton; Joe Serafin, Vermont. RP—Gary Novakowski, Stony Brook.

Player of the Year: Kyle Brault, Vermont. **Pitcher of the Year:** Zach Groh, Binghamton. **Rookie of the Year:** Kevin McAvoy, Maine. **Coach of the Year:** Bill Currier, Vermont.

INDIVIDUAL BATTING LEADERS
(Minimum 125 At-Bats)

	AVG	AB	R	H	2B	3B	HR	RBI	SB
Smith, Curt, Maine	.386	223	56	86	17	6	5	55	19
Hill, Tom, Albany	.372	180	45	67	13	1	11	46	5
McAvoy, Kevin, Maine	.369	198	39	73	12	1	10	64	4
Barrett, Joel, Maine	.368	223	57	82	19	3	5	50	0
Hitchcock, Brendon, Binghamton	.363	182	38	66	13	1	7	46	5
Brault, Kyle, Vermont	.357	182	38	65	19	0	11	52	4
Smucker, Justin, Binghamton	.352	176	45	62	7	3	3	27	6
Wyland, Steve, Albany	.345	171	47	59	7	0	1	25	4
Fowler, Joe, UMBC	.345	200	43	69	26	2	8	36	7
Clark, Zach, UMBC	.341	170	28	58	11	1	6	33	1
Hough, Joe, Maine	.341	220	62	75	12	3	8	37	26
DiBiaso, Chris, Stony Brook	.341	179	25	61	9	1	7	40	2
McGraw, Matt, Maine	.333	201	55	67	12	2	5	39	17
Carey, Jason, Vermont	.333	189	45	63	14	1	6	33	10
Donovan, Sean, Albany	.329	143	22	47	5	3	1	28	3
Pasieka, Jon, Stony Brook	.327	156	24	51	15	1	1	27	3
Perez, Andres, Stony Brook	.327	199	38	65	11	2	7	29	5
Quintal, Ryan, Maine	.322	205	49	66	11	5	9	60	5
Bowen, Steve, UMBC	.320	181	26	58	13	1	8	38	6
Corvino, Leo, Albany	.312	154	30	48	8	3	1	20	5
Sipp, Chris, Stony Brook	.311	196	30	61	6	0	0	16	8
Pennino, Tom, Stony Brook	.310	171	22	53	11	0	3	30	2
Chapman, Jim, Vermont	.309	191	34	59	15	0	1	27	0
Fortuna, Isidro, Stony Brook	.306	183	35	56	9	3	5	28	3
Leonard, Robert, Stony Brook	.306	157	29	48	10	2	3	17	1
Simek, Matt, Binghamton	.305	177	32	54	16	0	4	31	7
Wertepny, Jeff, Binghamton	.298	151	23	45	3	0	3	23	2
Daniels, Brad, Albany	.297	148	27	44	7	3	2	23	10
Massie, Kyle, Vermont	.297	172	22	51	5	0	0	27	2
Menendez, Danny, Maine	.295	193	33	57	8	2	0	29	9
Sobocinski, Ben, Hartford	.291	175	24	51	9	1	2	19	8

INDIVIDUAL PITCHING LEADERS
(Minimum 50 Innings)

	W	L	ERA	G	SV	IP	H	BB	SO
Groh, Zach, Binghamton	5	3	1.85	11	0	63	41	15	71
Restivo, Matt, Stony Brook	3	7	2.62	14	0	82	68	28	64
Van Gorder, Mike, Binghamton	6	1	2.79	11	1	52	42	16	39
Suchowiecki, Mark, Albany	6	4	3.21	14	0	81	75	39	63
Szymanski, Weston, Hartford	6	4	3.38	18	0	61	65	9	27
Clark, Zach, UMBC	1	6	3.86	12	1	54	58	8	53
Browne, Chris, Hartford	3	6	4.23	20	0	55	54	24	13
Serafin, Joe, Vermont	5	3	4.23	14	0	89	88	33	84
Errigo, Mike, Stony Brook	3	4	4.52	13	0	64	76	15	50
Bakey, Kris, Stony Brook	4	4	4.57	13	0	65	74	18	43
Pavlis, Jon, UMBC	5	6	4.78	16	0	90	119	13	60
Bach, Eddie, UMBC	3	5	4.89	19	2	74	72	34	63
Bayer, Jeremiah, Vermont	2	8	4.98	22	0	56	64	28	44
Diamond, Scott, Binghamton	5	6	5.14	12	0	75	74	21	44
Koehler, Tom, Stony Brook	4	5	5.17	14	0	71	83	31	57

ATLANTIC COAST CONFERENCE

ATLANTIC	Conference		Overall	
	W	L	W	L
*Clemson	24	6	53	16
Florida State	16	13	44	21
NC State	16	13	40	23
Wake Forest	16	13	33	22
Boston College	9	21	28	25
Maryland	8	22	26	30
COASTAL				
North Carolina	22	8	54	15
Virginia	21	9	47	15
Georgia Tech	19	11	50	18
Miami	17	13	43	23
Duke	6	24	15	40
Virginia Tech	4	25	20	33

ALL-CONFERENCE TEAM: C—Eddy Rodriguez, Miami. 1B—Andy D'Alessio, Clemson. 2B—Ramon Corona, NC State. SS—Josh Horton, North Carolina. 3B—Matt Antonelli, Wake Forest. DH—Tom Hagan, Virginia. OF—Matt Camp, NC State; Jay Cox, North Carolina; Danny Payne, Georgia Tech; Shane Robinson, Florida State; Jon Jay, Miami. SP—Josh Cribb, Clemson; Sean Dolittle, Virginia; Bryan Henry, Florida State; Andrew Miller, North Carolina. RP—Ben Hunter, Wake Forest.

Player of the Year: Sean Doolittle, Virginia. **Pitcher of the Year:** Andrew Miller, North Carolina

Coach of the Year: Jack Legget, Clemson. **Freshman of the Year:** Allan Dykstra, Wake Forest

INDIVIDUAL BATTING LEADERS
(Minimum 125 At-Bats)

	AVG	AB	R	H	2B	3B	HR	RBI	SB
Horton, Josh, North Carolina	.395	271	62	107	17	1	7	59	12
Camp, Matt, NC State	.387	261	64	101	22	1	2	46	9
Flack, Chad, North Carolina	.384	292	68	112	18	5	13	68	15
Marsh, Brandon, Virginia	.380	208	51	79	13	3	2	30	14
Cox, Jay, North Carolina	.375	232	56	87	15	0	15	65	7
Jay, Jon , Miami	.361	227	77	82	14	2	6	46	31
Robinson, Shane, Florida State	.361	269	79	97	15	3	7	38	32
Hagan, Tom, Virginia	.357	210	41	75	12	3	0	41	19
Colvin, Tyler, Clemson	.356	281	64	100	22	5	13	70	23
Wieters, Matt, Georgia Tech	.355	259	72	92	20	0	15	71	3
Bates, Aaaron, NC State	.354	243	76	86	20	0	10	54	6
Mangum, Caleb, NC State	.354	181	31	64	8	1	4	34	1
Chalk, Brad, Clemson	.353	238	67	84	9	4	0	21	18
Corona, Ramon, NC State	.353	278	71	98	19	5	6	57	9
Robbins, Whit, Georgia Tech	.352	247	71	87	19	1	13	67	2
Weeks, Jemile, Miami	.352	256	69	90	18	8	6	40	13
Still, Jon, NC State	.350	214	58	75	15	0	8	58	3
Posey, Buster, Florida State	.346	246	58	85	14	2	4	48	9
Magini, Matt, NC State	.343	239	46	82	16	4	7	60	1
Ayers, Johnny, Boston College	.340	215	55	73	11	4	0	20	17
Murton, Luke, Georgia Tech	.339	171	42	58	10	0	6	45	6
Giles, Tommy, Miami	.339	233	46	79	20	2	9	45	11
Melvin, Dan, Maryland	.338	204	34	69	10	1	5	30	8
Rye, Jack, Florida State	.338	222	63	75	16	2	12	46	6
Kindel, Jeff, Georgia Tech	.337	273	77	92	18	1	14	55	0
Guyer, Brandon, Virginia	.336	238	53	80	19	4	7	57	17
Guinn, Dennis, Florida State	.335	236	49	79	17	3	12	69	4
Antonelli, Matt, Wake Forest	.333	219	64	73	18	2	11	38	15
Hodges, Wes, Georgia Tech	.329	219	49	72	20	0	11	67	0
Aragon, Brian, NC State	.325	237	49	77	15	1	9	54	6
Dykstra, Allan, Wake Forest	.324	185	45	60	17	1	15	56	2
Doolittle, Sean, Virginia	.324	216	49	70	15	1	4	57	2
Valencia, Danny, Miami	.324	244	47	79	10	0	9	61	8
McGill, Shawn, Boston College	.322	214	33	69	15	2	3	37	12
Ruiz, Jett, Boston College	.321	168	21	54	16	0	3	18	2
Federowicz, Tim, North Carolina	.320	250	35	80	17	0	12	62	2

INDIVIDUAL PITCHING LEADERS
(Minimum 50 Innings)

	W	L	ERA	G	SV	IP	H	BB	SO
Hovis, Jonathan, North Carolina	8	2	1.17	38	2	69	47	23	59
Hunter, Ben, Wake Foers	1	2	1.47	33	14	55	38	17	70
Otero, Danny, Duke	5	4	2.20	15	0	74	76	6	45

384 • BASEBALL AMERICA 2007 ALMANAC

COLLEGE BASEBALL

Name	W	L	ERA	G	SV	IP	H	BB	SO
Faris, Stephen, Clemson	9	3	2.36	18	0	103	77	20	86
Doolittle, Sean, Virginia	11	2	2.38	18	1	91	64	21	108
Miller, Andrew, North Carolina	13	2	2.48	20	1	123	100	40	133
Thompson, Jacob, Virginia	10	4	2.60	16	0	100	82	29	77
Gil, Danny, Miami	4	3	2.66	36	0	68	49	34	59
Henry, Bryan, Florida State	9	4	2.88	18	0	116	98	30	98
Chambliss, Tyler, Florida State	12	4	2.97	19	0	115	105	50	117
Hyde, Lee, Georgia Tech	6	0	3.02	25	1	86	75	42	72
Cribb, Josh, Clemson	9	0	3.09	16	0	87	70	26	83
Berken, Jason, Clemson	9	3	3.22	18	0	81	83	34	75
Ratliff, Ted, Boston College	4	1	3.29	14	1	55	41	25	47
Young, Kyle, Wake Forest	4	3	3.36	28	1	64	66	15	32
Woodard, Robert, North Carolina	7	1	3.43	18	0	108	107	24	55
Doyle, Terry , Boston College	5	5	3.44	13	0	89	80	28	72
Bard, Daniel, North Carolina	9	4	3.64	18	0	101	92	37	94
Ballard, Mike, Virginia	9	3	4.09	16	0	92	92	25	69
Miguelez, Manny, Miami	8	4	4.31	20	0	104	89	37	78
Gutierrez, Carlos, Miami	9	7	4.40	17	0	88	81	33	62
McConnell, Eryk, NC State	7	6	4.5	15	0	88	95	22	65
Maine, Scott, Miami	12	3	4.57	18	0	106	97	39	76
Niesen, Eric, Wake Forest	3	2	4.68	22	0	58	49	35	50
Hobson, Gib, NC State	10	2	4.74	21	0	99	108	30	66
Houston, Dan, Boston College	2	6	4.78	13	0	64	78	21	42

ATLANTIC SUN CONFERENCE

	Conference		Overall	
	W	L	W	L
Jacksonville	23	7	43	19
North Florida	20	10	34	21
Mercer	19	11	34	26
*Stetson	16	14	38	24
East Tennessee State	14	16	31	27
Florida Atlantic	14	16	30	28
Campbell	13	17	19	38
Gardner-Webb	12	18	24	31
Kennesaw State	12	18	24	32
Belmont	11	19	24	31
Lipscomb	11	19	22	32

ALL-CONFERENCE TEAM: C—Blake Lalli, Gardner-Webb. **1B**—Chris Johnson, Stetson. **2B**—Aaron Lautman, Belmont. **SS**—Matt Oxendine, North Florida. **3B**—Daniel Murphy, Jacksonville. **OF**—Pete Clifford, Jacksonville; Wilson Tucker, Belmont; Jordan Hafer, Florida Atlantic. **DH**—Mike Armstrong, Mercer. **LHP**—Matt Dobbins, Jacksonville. **RHP**—Brantley New, Mercer; Andrew Urena, Mercer; Brad Johnson, North Florida.

Player of the Year: Daniel Murphy, Jacksonville. **Pitcher of the Year:** Matt Dobbins, Jacksonville. **Freshman of the Year:** Derek Wiley, Belmont. **Coach of the Year:** Terry Alexander, Jacksonville.

INDIVIDUAL BATTING LEADERS
(Minimum 125 At-Bats)

Name	AVG	AB	R	H	2B	3B	HR	RBI	SB
Priest, Mike, Campbell	.402	224	62	90	16	3	13	53	13
Murphy, Daniel, Jacksonville	.398	221	54	88	10	1	6	55	15
Lalli, Blake, Gardner-Webb	.389	208	39	81	13	1	11	39	3
Tucker, Wilson, Belmont	.388	227	40	88	20	5	10	53	1
Johnson, Chris, Stetson	.376	245	47	92	16	1	11	66	4
Barrett, Shawn, Mercer	.371	210	40	78	16	0	3	32	2
Armstrong, Mike, Mercer	.368	171	30	63	11	0	9	30	1
Scott, Brandon, Campbell	.364	231	46	84	10	7	4	26	25
Hodach, Johnathan, North Florida	.364	176	35	64	16	0	4	35	2
McCann, Jeremy, Gardner-Webb	.360	197	40	71	16	2	9	51	10
Gronkowski, Gordie, Jacksonville	.358	246	59	88	19	1	10	51	2
Holt, Tim, Campbell	.357	238	55	85	15	2	3	29	8
Traylor, Matt, East Tenn.	.352	159	39	56	6	0	4	29	6
Byrne, Shane, East Tenn.	.345	249	51	86	15	4	8	49	15
Lee, C.J., East Tennessee State	.345	232	40	80	10	2	6	43	14
Lautman, Aaron, Belmont	.344	157	23	54	8	0	1	16	6
Hafer, Jordan, Florida Atlantic	.344	195	34	67	14	2	9	34	4
Maloney, Matt, Gardner-Webb	.342	228	44	78	26	4	9	43	4
Wiley, Derek, Belmont	.342	199	29	68	12	0	14	48	0
Mitchell, Ryan, Lipscomb	.341	176	47	60	10	0	7	30	6
Dallas, Matt, Kennesaw State	.335	227	43	76	18	0	4	27	9
Glanville, Jimmy, North Florida	.333	210	44	70	13	1	4	32	7
Thompson, Josh, Mercer	.332	223	47	74	16	0	15	53	2
McCallister, Mike, Jacksonville	.332	223	44	74	14	1	10	54	7
Miller, Zac, Lipscomb	.331	181	38	60	13	0	8	35	0
Lepage, Thomas, Jacksonville	.330	218	40	72	12	0	2	45	5
Stevens, Tyler, Florida Atlantic	.329	152	17	50	5	0	0	21	4
Renfroe, Eric, Mercer	.324	224	46	73	10	1	4	40	11
Bocock, Brian, Stetson	.324	250	47	81	16	2	0	30	19
Lopez, Matt, Jacksonville	.322	233	36	75	5	2	1	44	6
Douglas, Stephen, East Tenn.	.322	230	47	74	14	2	9	41	33
Oxendine, Matt, North Florida	.320	222	47	71	16	1	6	26	8

Name	AVG	AB	R	H	2B	3B	HR	RBI	SB
Morrow, Jay, Kennesaw State	.318	211	40	67	16	0	2	45	4
Clifford, Pete, Jacksonville	.317	262	61	83	21	3	5	38	21
Church, Blake, East Tenn.	.316	228	54	72	14	3	11	50	0
Jordan, Shane, Stetson	.315	260	53	82	14	1	0	25	19
Albano, Anthony, Florida Atlantic	.314	172	25	54	15	3	2	30	5
Petsch, Ben, Belmont	.313	227	44	71	21	2	4	37	11
Hamme, Ryan, Campbell	.312	186	19	58	8	3	2	31	4
Ramirez, Ovy, Florida Atlantic	.310	200	28	62	14	1	5	40	5
McCarty, Tyler, Mercer	.309	175	29	54	7	0	0	25	3

INDIVIDUAL PITCHING LEADERS
(Minimum 50 Innings)

Name	W	L	ERA	G	SV	IP	H	BB	SO
Urena, Andrew, Mercer	4	2	1.30	30	15	48	36	27	59
Camp, Jon, Belmont	0	1	1.54	8	1	11	8	6	9
Young, Justin, Jacksonville	2	1	1.66	22	3	38	28	14	26
Frawley, John, North Florida	1	0	1.96	14	0	23	23	3	17
Papelbon, Jeremy, North Florida	5	4	2.43	16	0	89	76	14	88
Elsemiller, Robbie, Stetson	7	3	2.56	37	14	70	63	17	54
Johnson, Brad, North Florida	9	1	2.65	15	0	88	81	23	79
Paplebon, Josh, North Florida	4	2	2.81	29	8	42	39	14	40
Parvey, Aaron, Jacksonville	6	1	3.32	30	1	62	56	27	27
Williams, Charles, Lipscomb	2	3	3.38	17	4	59	72	20	30
Dobbins, Matt, Jacksonville	12	2	3.45	22	1	120	111	50	74
New, Brantley, Mercer	9	3	3.60	16	0	100	100	40	95
Kluber, Corey, Stetson	6	5	3.61	17	0	92	78	31	76
Ingolglia, Christ, Stetson	6	2	3.76	22	0	103	119	25	72
Storey, Mickey, Florida Atlantic	7	9	3.84	17	0	120	127	30	125
Brown, Tim, Jacksonville	3	3	3.90	23	2	62	70	20	36
Moffitt, Josh, Belmont	5	4	3.90	15	0	90	99	30	64
Lee, Charles, Belmont	4	8	4.00	15	0	101	108	28	61
Schmal, Joel, Florida Atlantic	6	2	4.18	18	1	67	72	21	52
Meador, Ben, Belmont	5	3	4.36	20	0	74	82	7	39
Abercrombie, Hunter, Mercer	7	4	4.41	24	2	82	112	19	35
LeSage, Quinn, Campbell	5	4	4.47	17	0	87	104	20	48
Nery, Nathan, Stetson	7	5	4.53	26	0	87	94	35	70
Ackley, D.J., Jacksonville	7	4	4.68	23	0	110	113	25	89
Cooney, Brandon, Florida Atlantic	4	6	4.71	18	1	73	79	30	58
Schnelly, Matt, Lipscomb	4	7	4.88	17	1	96	107	30	91

ATLANTIC-10 CONFERENCE

	Conference		Overall	
	W	L	W	L
Rhode Island	19	6	34	16
St. Bonaventure	18	8	29	21
Dayton	18	9	33	24
Charlotte	18	9	35	20
*Saint Louis	18	9	35	20
George Washington	13	12	25	34
Fordham	13	14	24	32
La Salle	12	14	20	31
Duquesne	12	15	19	33
Richmond	12	15	22	23
Massachusetts	11	16	14	30
Saint Joseph's	9	18	17	39
Xavier	9	18	19	37
Temple	6	19	12	41

ALL-CONFERENCE TEAM: C—Bill Musselman, Saint Louis; Rich Prall, La Salle. **1B**—Brian Pellegrini, St. Bonaventure. **2B**—Galen Schumm, Dayton. **SS**—Mike Ambrose, Charlotte; Mike Massa, Dayton. **3B**—Dan Brady, Temple. **DH**—Greg Rodgers, Saint Louis. **OF**—Joe Rizzo, St. Bonaventure; Greg Smith, Fordham; Spencer Steedley, Charlotte. **SP**—Steve Holmes, Rhode Island; Derrik Lutz, George Washington. **RP**—Craig Rohren, Dayton.

Player of the Year: Brian Pellegrini, St. Bonaventure. **Pitcher of the Year:** Steve Holmes, Rhode Island. **Freshman of the Year:** Aaron Bray, Charlotte. **Coach of the Year:** Larry Sudbrook, St. Bonaventure.

INDIVIDUAL BATTING LEADERS
(Minimum 125 At-Bats)

Name	AVG	AB	R	H	2B	3B	HR	RBI	SB
Zeskind, Ben, Richmond	.379	235	57	89	17	5	10	40	19
Smith, Greg, Fordham	.376	181	46	68	17	1	13	48	4
Pellegrini, Brian, St. Bonaventure	.367	188	46	69	15	0	13	57	6
Ambrose, Mike, Charlotte	.366	227	48	83	16	6	2	31	17
Bray, Aaron, Charlotte	.365	222	59	81	8	4	0	29	17
Moley, Randy, St. Bonaventure	.360	189	46	68	11	0	2	21	13
Lane, Cory, Charlotte	.357	224	59	80	8	6	4	39	14
Zaneski, Zach, Rhode Island	.357	129	23	46	8	1	2	18	1
Mahoney, Joe, Richmond	.356	222	43	79	14	1	5	49	1
Musselman, Bill, Saint Louis	.344	189	27	65	11	0	2	27	3

COLLEGE BASEBALL

INDIVIDUAL PITCHING LEADERS
(Minimum 50 Innings)

	W	L	ERA	G	SV	IP	H	BB	SO
Holmes, Steve, Rhode Island	10	2	1.30	14	1	104	72	20	93
Lutz, Derrik, George Washington	6	4	1.54	14	1	100	65	30	89
Degidio, Jamie, Rhode Island	7	2	1.86	15	2	63	50	11	62
McDaid, Derek, Charlotte	9	4	2.45	16	0	103	97	24	69
Wilkie, Josh, George Washington	5	5	2.57	14	0	98	88	27	97
Vincent, Cody, St. Bonaventure	6	5	2.58	17	1	98	95	23	62
Bird, Ryan, Saint Louis	8	6	2.75	18	0	124	122	41	100
Waters, Dan, La Salle	4	5	2.79	16	0	87	78	18	90
Mills, Adam, Charlotte	8	5	3.00	17	0	114	100	19	111
Trubee, Luke, Dayton	9	6	3.95	17	0	107	115	22	82
Martinez, Javier, Fordham	6	6	4.17	14	0	86	61	64	84
Creevy, Mike, Xavier	3	9	4.26	16	1	101	120	29	74
Sever, Dave, Saint Louis	7	3	4.40	16	0	92	100	35	46
Hessler, Jason, St. Joseph's	4	7	4.77	15	0	89	100	26	82
Lucas, Michael, Xavier	2	8	4.79	17	1	92	103	35	71

BIG EAST CONFERENCE

	Conference		Overall	
	W	L	W	L
*Notre Dame	21	5	45	17
Connecticut	18	6	39	18
Louisville	17	10	31	29
St. John's	16	10	40	19
West Virginia	14	13	36	22
Rutgers	13	14	29	28
Cincinnati	13	14	32	26
South Florida	12	15	23	35
Pittsburgh	10	17	23	29
Georgetown	10	17	24	32
Villanova	8	18	27	27
Seton Hall	7	20	17	34

ALL-CONFERENCE TEAM: C—David Carpenter, West Virginia. 1B—Craig Cooper, Notre Dame. 2B—Jim Negrych, Pittsburgh. SS—Todd Frazier, Rutgers. 3B—Justin Jenkins, West Virginia. DH—Anthony Smith, St. John's. OF—Will Vogl, St. John's; Casey Bowling, West Virginia; Stan Posluszny, West Virginia. P—Tim Norton, Connecticut; Nick Tucci, Connecticut; Jeff Manship, Notre Dame; Jeff Samardzija, Notre Dame.

Player of the Year: Craig Cooper, Notre Dame. Pitcher of the Year: Jeff Manship, Notre Dame. Freshman of the Year: Addison Maruscak, South Florida. Coach of the Year: Jim Penders, Connecticut.

INDIVIDUAL BATTING LEADERS
(Minimum 125 At-Bats)

	AVG	AB	R	H	2B	3B	HR	RBI	SB
Cooper, Craig, Notre Dame	.425	228	79	97	19	3	9	41	9
Bowling, Casey, West Virginia	.403	206	45	83	15	2	7	43	4
Joachim, Chris, St. John's	.398	216	52	86	12	2	1	46	20
Negrych, Jim, Pittsburgh	.396	182	41	72	14	0	11	60	6
Hunt, Jeremy, Villanova	.385	187	52	72	14	4	15	56	2
Vogl, Will, St. John's	.382	233	64	89	18	6	14	62	10
Jenkins, Justin, West Virginia	.376	250	62	94	25	0	10	49	8
White, Adam, West Virginia	.368	201	48	74	6	3	1	27	19
Harrison, Josh, Cincinnati	.367	229	67	84	14	0	5	43	10
Frazier, Todd, Rutgers	.366	227	62	83	14	3	11	51	21
Smith, Anthony, St. John's	.366	186	40	68	6	1	8	46	3
Kuhn, Tyler, West Virginia	.365	252	59	92	20	3	3	50	8
Mayer, Jimmy, Pittsburgh	.357	213	52	76	16	1	2	29	15
Molloy, Kris, Villanova	.356	174	37	62	4	5	2	24	14
Farkes, Josh, Connecticut	.349	152	35	53	9	0	5	31	6
Dirr, Bryan, St. John's	.347	167	31	58	6	0	0	22	8
Parker, Logan, Cincinnati	.344	221	61	76	18	7	11	69	13
Donovan, Dennis, Connecticut	.341	214	45	73	17	1	5	42	3
Deluca, Sam, St. John's	.339	242	53	82	11	3	1	41	14
Maler, Bryan, Connecticut	.338	216	47	73	14	2	1	35	22
Querns, Tim, Rutgers	.337	190	23	64	5	1	0	36	2
Grose, Jeff, Rutgers	.336	235	52	79	15	2	2	30	10
Bransfield, Matt, Notre Dame	.333	204	34	68	19	1	6	45	4
Posluszny, Stan, West Virginia	.332	241	54	80	22	0	10	60	6
Cates, Chris, Louisville	.332	232	47	77	14	2	1	32	3
Day, Larry, Connecticut	.332	229	34	76	12	1	1	51	3
McDonald, Dan, Seton Hall	.330	179	29	59	16	3	1	34	5
Mirsky, Craig, Villanova	.328	195	41	64	5	4	0	32	9
Mahoney, Pat, Connecticut	.328	229	49	75	17	1	4	33	2
Helms, Doug, West Virginia	.325	255	38	83	13	1	3	44	4
Shunk, Derek, Villanova	.325	203	40	66	9	0	3	44	0
Arcadia, Ryan, Villanova	.324	216	55	70	7	1	0	31	19
Dressman, Danny, Notre Dame	.321	187	38	60	9	2	0	36	6
Lilley, Brett, Notre Dame	.320	203	39	65	6	0	2	32	5
Muscenti, Mark, Cincinnati	.320	175	48	56	13	1	1	30	3
Gaston, Sean, Notre Dame	.319	163	27	52	8	1	1	30	4

INDIVIDUAL PITCHING LEADERS
(Minimum 50 Innings)

	W	L	ERA	G	SV	IP	H	BB	SO
Korpi, Wade, Notre Dame	7	2	2.00	14	0	76	55	27	94
Norton, Tim, Connecticut	7	2	2.04	14	0	93	62	24	96
Muldowney, Billy, Pittsburgh	5	4	3.16	16	0	83	80	24	99
Manship, Jeff, Notre Dame	9	2	3.26	15	0	94	78	28	111
Mulvey, Kevin, Villanova	3	8	3.61	14	0	92	91	23	88
Sirois, Rich, Connecticut	6	3	3.64	13	0	84	93	24	45
Barnes, Scott, St. John's	3	2	3.66	15	0	64	51	35	74
Tucci, Nick, Connecticut	9	2	3.67	14	0	83	87	23	43
Yurish, Matt, West Virginia	6	3	3.84	13	0	73	63	42	71
Thornton, Tom, Notre Dame	7	3	3.94	15	0	82	93	7	58
Tosoni, Matt, St. John's	3	3	3.94	13	1	64	66	16	40
Delaney, Robb, St. John's	7	3	4.01	15	0	76	89	20	78
McDonald, Dan, Seton Hall	1	10	4.11	14	1	81	80	49	65
Young, Corey, Seton Hall	4	3	4.21	15	1	68	75	27	59
Samardzija, Jeff, Notre Dame	8	2	4.33	15	0	98	101	37	61
Higgins, Yuri, South Florida	3	3	4.38	27	0	72	61	55	66
Hudspeth, Casey, South Florida	7	7	4.38	16	0	99	100	41	105
Durst, Kenny, West Virginia	5	4	4.39	14	0	68	70	30	48
Merklinger, Dan, Seton Hall	4	7	4.57	14	0	81	77	53	83
Landis, Kyle, Pittsburgh	3	2	4.63	21	1	56	58	22	57
Halford, Brian, Louisville	5	4	4.69	26	2	86	84	24	74

BIG SOUTH CONFERENCE

	Conference		Overall	
	W	L	W	L
Birmingham-Southern	18	6	33	22
Winthrop	17	7	46	18
Coastal Carolina	15	9	30	27
High Point	14	10	27	32
Liberty	13	11	39	21
*UNC Asheville	10	14	28	35
Virginia Military Institute	9	15	30	25
Charleston Southern	8	16	18	38
Radford	4	20	7	41

ALL-CONFERENCE TEAM: C—Blake Burton, Birmingham-Southern. 1B—Heath Rollins, Winthrop. 2B—Chris Carrara, Winthrop. SS—Matt Repec, Winthrop. 3B—Kelly Sweppenhiser, Virginia Military Institute. DH—Chris Norwood, High Point. OF—Mark Shorey, High Point; Jacob Dempsey, Winthrop; Tommy Lentz, Winthrop. P—Alex Wilson, Winthrop; Heath Rollins, Winthrop; Brandon Hynick, Birmingham-Southern.

Player of the Year: Heath Rollins, Winthrop. Player of the Year: Mark Shorey, High Point. Freshman of the Year: Alex Wilson, Winthrop. Coach of the Year: Sal Bando Jr., High Point.

INDIVIDUAL BATTING LEADERS
(Minimum 125 At-Bats)

	AVG	AB	R	H	2B	3B	HR	RBI	SB
Shorey, Mark, High Point	.408	213	41	87	19	0	20	62	5
Dempsey, Jacob, Winthrop	.403	248	71	100	28	2	17	78	8
Tommy Lentz, Winthrop	.379	232	51	88	17	1	8	51	10
Just, Michael, Liberty	.379	248	64	94	16	3	4	53	8
Laurent, Phillip, Liberty	.377	239	44	90	27	0	10	73	5
Carrara, Chris, Winthrop	.364	269	73	98	13	5	7	34	33
Goforth, Mark, Birm.-Southern	.363	226	56	82	8	3	0	20	27
Fyle, Justin, Charleston Southern	.352	227	48	80	11	1	8	46	6
Arrington, Elliott, UNC Asheville	.352	256	41	90	23	1	7	47	1
Sweppenhiser, Kelly, VMI	.350	206	58	72	13	1	7	41	8
Grijalva, Aaaron, Liberty	.347	222	56	77	19	5	7	51	23
Hardy, Brint, Birm.-Southern	.346	162	29	56	6	0	1	31	18
Brundridge, Wes, Charl. Southern	.342	228	44	78	13	0	5	36	8
Repec, Matt, Winthrop	.341	255	55	87	21	1	8	67	3
Miller, Chad, Liberty	.339	239	68	81	15	5	5	47	24
Billak, Scott, Birm.-Southern	.336	211	48	71	16	5	9	45	14
Reed, Klint, VMI	.332	211	45	70	21	1	2	39	9
Vernon, Rob, UNC Asheville	.330	179	37	59	14	2	7	35	6
Rollins, Heath, Winthrop	.328	232	64	76	11	5	4	31	25
Fields, Jacoby, VMI	.327	202	43	66	12	1	2	36	5
Norwood, Chris, High Point	.325	243	55	79	10	3	6	33	16
Vrable, Adam, Coastal Carolina	.324	188	29	61	7	1	1	25	11
Carey, Phil, Winthrop	.324	176	32	57	8	3	7	45	5
Crumpler, Robert, VMI	.321	187	40	60	15	1	6	41	1
Cowan, Jeff, High Point	.319	235	54	75	16	2	2	27	9
Good, B.T., VMI	.318	195	37	62	12	1	1	36	21
Mattison, Kevin, UNC Asheville	.317	224	49	71	14	8	8	43	13
Sappelt, David, Coastal Carolina	.315	178	28	56	3	4	5	37	5
Barber, Matt, Birm.-Southern	.310	197	33	61	12	1	6	36	6
John, Phil, Liberty	.308	159	39	49	8	0	2	30	8
Schwartz, Randy, High Point	.306	222	24	68	12	0	5	23	5
Perkins, David, Char. Southern	.302	162	15	49	13	0	6	30	1
Hynick, Brandon, Birm.-Southern	.301	173	45	52	12	0	15	50	3

Gaillard, Patrick, Liberty	.299	244	55	73	14	3	4	32	16
Rice, Chad, VMI	.294	211	56	62	7	1	4	29	11
Toth, Nate, Radford	.293	174	35	51	12	1	4	31	0

INDIVIDUAL PITCHING LEADERS
(Minimum 50 Innings)

	W	L	ERA	G	SV	IP	H	BB	SO
Hynick, Brandon, Birm.-Southern	6	6	**2.59**	15	0	101	90	26	89
Gagg, Bobby, Coastal Carolina	4	1	2.95	17	0	76	32	27	49
Fleet, Austin, Coastal Carolina	4	2	3.39	14	0	66	71	21	53
Rollins, Heath, Winthrop	**13**	4	3.51	22	1	123	109	46	**143**
Barham, Trey, VMI	7	5	3.53	18	1	94	78	36	98
Page, Ryan, Liberty	9	2	3.59	17	0	73	76	20	39
Wilson, Alex, Winthrop	**13**	3	3.78	20	0	**138**	127	50	**143**
Portice, Eammon, High Point	7	5	3.86	18	0	110	109	32	112
Sowers, Ryan, Charleston Southern	5	6	4.12	16	2	94	105	47	46
Horne, David, Birmingham-Southern	10	3	4.26	16	0	95	51	40	63
DeLaGarza, Andy, Coastal Carolina	3	6	4.29	20	1	92	93	38	62
Smink, Travis, VMI	7	4	4.4	21	2	73.2	79	32	38
Solbach, Michael, Liberty	7	4	4.66	15	0	85	97	25	71
Salmon, Kevin, Coastal Carolina	4	4	4.68	21	0	57	53	35	49
Hollenbeck, J.J., VMI	3	5	4.71	15	1	63	66	23	40
DeRatt, Alan, UNC Asheville	8	5	4.77	20	0	115	154	26	71
Christie, Matt, High Point	3	2	4.84	16	0	80	87	31	52
Umberger, Dustin, Liberty	4	2	4.99	20	2	83	100	27	47
Thompson, Phillip, Liberty	6	7	5.15	24	0	93	114	21	77
O'Donnell, Bubba, High Point	2	1	5.51	**30**	5	67	81	36	50
Nigro, Chris, UNC Asheville	5	11	5.57	19	1	103	134	40	67

BIG 10 CONFERENCE

	Conference		Overall	
	W	L	W	L
*Michigan	23	9	43	19
Northwestern	21	11	26	33
Ohio State	19	12	37	21
Minnesota	17	14	34	26
Purdue	15	17	31	27
Illinois	15	17	29	29
Michigan State	13	19	26	30
Penn State	13	19	20	36
Iowa	12	20	23	33
Indiana	11	21	22	34

ALL-CONFERENCE TEAM: C—Jeff Kunkel, Michigan. 1B—Pat McMahon, Northwestern. 2B—Jason Zoeller, Ohio State. SS—Mitch Hilligoss, Purdue. 3B—Ronnie Bourquin, Ohio State. DH—Antonio Mule, Northwestern. OF—Matt Angle, Ohio State; Eric Rose, Michigan; Ryan Basham, Michigan State. SP—Chris Fetter, Michigan; Paul Hammond, Michigan; Dan Delucia, Ohio State. RP—Tim Gudex, Iowa.

Player of the Year: Ronnie Bourquin, Ohio State. **Pitcher of the Year:** Dan Brauer, Northwestern. **Freshman of the Year:** J.B. Shuck, Ohio State. **Coach of the Year:** Paul Stevens, Northwestern.

INDIVIDUAL BATTING LEADERS
(Minimum 125 At-Bats)

	AVG	AB	R	H	2B	3B	HR	RBI	SB
Bourquin, Ronnie, Ohio State	**.416**	219	54	**91**	15	2	8	**66**	3
Hilligoss, Mitch, Purdue	.386	228	62	88	16	5	6	41	18
Recknagel, Nate, Michigan	.372	218	40	81	19	0	8	41	4
Angle, Matt, Ohio State	.369	214	**63**	79	13	1	0	27	25
Fryer, Eric, Ohio State	.368	212	46	78	14	4	5	52	5
Basham, Ryan, Michigan State	.363	201	44	73	12	2	0	53	9
Thompson, Lance, Penn State	.362	213	30	77	16	2	4	45	2
Mule, Antonio, Northwestern	.357	213	34	76	8	4	**11**	47	2
Krider, Troy, Michigan State	.355	211	40	75	11	1	1	21	19
Haas, Keith, Indiana	.353	187	37	66	5	0	1	21	24
White, Ryne, Purdue	.352	196	33	69	12	3	6	45	1
Hunter, Andy, Minnesota	.344	192	41	66	10	1	5	41	1
Stephen, Jedidiah, Ohio State	.342	216	37	74	19	3	9	49	3
Snowden, Ryan, Illinois	.342	222	53	76	**20**	2	1	28	10
Cattrysse, Alan, Michigan State	.342	193	31	66	10	3	2	40	11
Watson, Reggie, Indiana	.341	205	46	70	6	4	2	20	**36**
Zoeller, Jason, Ohio State	.337	178	30	60	13	4	5	27	2
Wolfe, Eric, Purdue	.337	181	36	61	8	2	4	38	4
Kunkel, Jeff, Michigan	.335	230	38	77	15	0	8	28	4
McMahon, Pat, Northwestern	.333	219	31	73	14	1	5	41	3
Roof, Shawn, Illinois	.333	207	39	69	7	2	0	22	25
Gerstenberger, Steve, Mich. State	.331	166	36	55	5	**7**	4	30	9
Rose, Eric, Michigan	.329	213	43	70	7	1	2	44	32
Ingaldson, Spencer, Purdue	.327	171	28	56	7	0	2	22	2
Mahler, Leif, Michigan	.325	212	35	69	8	0	0	25	2
Hunter, John, Purdue	.322	199	26	64	10	1	4	33	1
Owens, Jake, Northwestern	.319	235	48	75	11	2	1	16	9
Hastings, Ryan, Illinois	.319	210	34	67	10	6	1	35	4
MacLean, Luke, Minnesota	.316	196	37	62	3	2	0	30	9

Day, Kyle, Michigan State	.315	200	52	63	11	5	3	33	10
Rhode, Mike, Illinois	.315	216	48	68	14	1	3	38	6
Gummo, Scott, Penn State	.314	175	28	55	13	0	5	28	1
Fields, Caleb, Northwestern	.308	208	32	64	4	0	5	27	4
Davis, Lars, Illinois	.307	205	25	63	7	2	5	38	3
Wine, Cory, Penn State	.306	186	20	57	14	2	0	22	2
Ernst, Brian, Penn State	.305	197	20	60	8	1	1	24	6

INDIVIDUAL PITCHING LEADERS
(Minimum 50 Innings)

	W	L	ERA	G	SV	IP	H	BB	SO
Fetter, Chris, Michigan	5	2	**2.22**	16	1	73	66	14	48
Hammond, Paul, Michigan	8	4	2.36	15	1	84	79	24	68
DeVries, Cole, Minnesota	7	3	2.42	14	0	93	76	32	72
Shuck, J.B., Ohio State	8	5	2.51	15	0	79	75	33	57
Fleenor, Doug, Indiana	4	3	2.57	17	0	56	**47**	15	30
Dauby, Trae, Purdue	4	7	2.76	24	1	51	62	22	53
Bull, Brian, Minnesota	7	4	3.01	14	0	87	82	23	50
Sattler, Dan, Purdue	5	7	3.14	13	0	77	83	30	60
DeLucia, Dan, Ohio State	**10**	2	3.25	15	0	**108**	103	25	69
Brauer, Dan, Northwestern	7	2	3.30	15	0	93	88	45	**90**
Luebke, Cory, Ohio State	7	6	3.38	13	0	85	87	25	65
Hale, Jake, Ohio State	4	5	3.38	14	0	64	57	29	39
Buente, Jay, Purdue	6	4	3.40	13	0	77	73	23	70
Maitland, Jeff, Iowa	6	4	3.55	13	0	76	81	21	48
Siberio, Julio, Northwestern	4	2	3.69	18	5	68	74	**9**	55
Brabender, Dustin, Minnesota	6	5	3.96	14	0	77	67	23	59
Stidfole, Alan, Penn State	3	5	4.06	14	0	93	107	27	70
Seward, Austin, Iowa	6	6	4.08	15	0	64	62	24	32
Crosier, Clint, Indiana	3	6	4.14	14	0	63	65	23	34
Heines, Ricky, Purdue	5	3	4.16	14	0	63	69	32	35
Wyner, Mark, Penn State	3	8	4.45	15	1	79	74	32	72
Lewis, Josh, Indiana	4	7	4.56	14	0	77	86	27	49
Brookes, Craig, Michigan State	2	4	4.56	14	0	73	99	19	54
O'Loughlin, Luke, Iowa	2	6	5.17	16	0	71	77	37	32
Kontos, George, Northwestern	3	**10**	5.29	16	0	95	107	53	84
Gerbe, Jeff, Michigan State	4	7	5.38	13	0	79	110	25	32

BIG 12 CONFERENCE

	Conference		Overall	
	W	L	W	L
Texas	19	7	41	21
Oklahoma State	18	9	41	20
Oklahoma	17	10	45	22
Nebraska	17	10	42	17
Baylor	13	14	37	26
*Kansas	13	14	43	25
Missouri	12	15	35	28
Texas Tech	9	16	31	26
Kansas State	8	17	31	20
Texas A&M	6	20	25	30

ALL-CONFERENCE TEAM: C—Zach Dillon, Baylor. 1B—Brandon Buckman, Nebraska; Chance Wheeless, Texas. 2B—Jared Schweitzer, Kansas. SS—Ryan Wehrele, Nebraska. 3B—Tyler Mach, Oklahoma State. DH—Jacob Priday, Missouri; Hunter Harris, Texas. OF—Luke Gorsett, Nebraska; Drew Stubbs, Texas; Roger Kieschnick, Texas Tech. UTIL—Jordy Mercer, Oklahoma State. SP—Tony Watson, Nebraska; Kyle McCulloch, Texas; Nathan Culp, Missouri. RP—Don Czyz, Kansas; Brett Jensen, Nebraska.

Players of the Year: Drew Stubbs, Texas; Tyler Mach, Oklahoma State. **Pitcher of the Year:** Kyle McCulloch, Texas. **Coach of the Year:** Augie Garrido, Texas. **Freshman of the Year:** Roger Kieschnick, Texas Tech. **Freshman Pitcher of the Year:** Miles Morgan, Texas Tech. **Newcomer of the Year:** Tyler Mach, Oklahoma State.

INDIVIDUAL BATTING LEADERS
(Minimum 125 At-Bats)

	AVG	AB	R	H	2B	3B	HR	RBI	SB
Roundy, Joe, Kansas State	.391	197	46	77	16	2	8	51	10
Rohlinger, Ryan, Oklahoma	.387	256	**69**	**99**	16	2	13	67	7
Smith, Matt, Texas Tech	.377	183	38	69	16	1	7	69	0
Schweitzer, Jared, Kansas	.369	241	53	89	14	1	11	41	1
Rice, Barrett, Kansas State	.368	190	36	70	18	2	3	34	6
Wehrle, Ryan, Nebraska	.367	226	50	83	22	1	8	48	14
Dillon, Zach, Baylor	.364	206	41	75	14	1	4	47	3
Mach, Tyler, Oklahoma State	.364	250	47	91	18	0	**16**	66	2
Kainer, Carson, Texas	.364	231	37	84	**25**	3	5	66	4
Scram, Deik, Oklahoma State	.363	168	37	61	13	7	6	35	8
Raley, Russell, Oklahoma	.360	178	40	64	6	1	2	28	7
Kieschnick, Roger, Texas Tech	.359	237	54	85	14	2	9	55	8
Capps, Brian, Texas Tech	.353	218	47	77	12	4	2	34	9
Caufield, Chuckie, Oklahoma	.351	271	68	95	17	3	9	50	19
Gorsett, Luke, Nebraska	.348	207	44	72	14	1	15	48	8
Brown, Corey, Oklahoma State	.347	216	68	75	13	6	13	40	14

	AVG	AB	R	H	2B	3B	HR	RBI	SB
Jaros, Nick, Nebraska	.342	190	41	65	13	1	4	33	10
Stubbs, Drew, Texas	.342	243	65	83	14	4	12	58	26
Buckman, Brandon, Nebraska	.339	230	43	78	8	1	14	51	3
Bond, Brock, Missouri	.338	201	45	68	10	0	2	29	11

INDIVIDUAL PITCHING LEADERS
(Minimum 50 Innings)

	W	L	ERA	G	SV	IP	H	BB	SO
Creps, Austin, Texas A&M	3	4	2.20	11	0	70	64	13	51
Scherzer, Max, Missouri	7	3	2.25	14	0	80	57	23	78
Watson, Tony, Nebraska	10	2	2.78	17	0	100	88	24	69
Meyer, Jason, Texas A&M	3	4	2.90	23	1	78	65	22	58
Hynes, Colt, Texas Tech	5	3	2.93	21	2	71	56	18	39
Cowart, Adam, Kansas State	6	7	3.22	14	0	89	98	11	72
Shirek, Charlie, Nebraska	4	2	3.23	18	1	70	66	20	29
Zagone, Rick, Missouri	6	3	3.28	18	0	69	72	23	48
Culp, Nathan, Missouri	11	6	3.40	20	1	124	115	17	84
Linebaugh, Randall, Baylor	6	1	3.42	20	0	71	71	30	65
Bayuk, Chase, Kansas State	7	2	3.52	15	0	72	79	24	53
McCulloch, Kyle, Texas	8	5	3.61	19	1	110	113	32	82
Quick, Kodiak, Kansas	11	4	3.62	19	0	112	131	40	68
Morgan, Miles, Texas Tech	6	7	3.63	17	0	107	113	31	103
LaMotta, Ryan, Baylor	7	6	3.73	16	0	99	98	39	60
Kasparek, Kenn, Texas	5	2	3.80	23	3	64	65	28	39
Dorn, Johnny, Nebraska	9	4	3.89	14	0	83	89	26	49
Chamberlain, Joba, Nebraska	6	5	3.93	14	0	89	84	34	102
Wright, Brae, Oklahoma State	8	4	3.99	15	0	99	106	19	59
Hutt, Brad, Kansas State	7	4	4.01	13	0	85	88	13	46

BIG WEST CONFERENCE

	Conference		Overall	
	W	L	W	L
*Cal State Fullerton	18	3	50	14
Long Beach State	12	9	29	27
UC Irvine	11	10	36	24
Cal Poly	10	11	29	27
Pacific	9	12	30	25
UC Riverside	9	12	29	25
UC Santa Barbara	9	12	26	28
Cal State Northridge	6	15	26	30

ALL-CONFERENCE TEAM: C—Matt Canepa, Cal Poly. **1B**—Brett Pill, Cal State Fullerton. **2B**—Justin Turner, Cal State Fullerton. **SS**—Blake Davis, Cal State Fullerton; Chris Valaika, UC Santa Barbara. **3B**—Evan Longoria, Long Beach State. **DH**—Matt Berezay, Pacific. **UTIL**—Jimmy Van Ostrand, Cal Poly. **OF**—Brett Bigler, UC Riverside; DJ Hollingsworth, UC Riverside; Brandon Tripp, Cal State Fullerton. **SP**—Andrew Carpenter, Long Beach State; Lauren Gagnier, Cal State Fullerton; Wes Roemer, Cal State Fullerton. **RP**—Vinnie Pestano, Cal State Fullerton.

Players of the Year: Justin Turner, Cal State Fullerton; Evan Longoria, Long Beach State. **Pitcher of the Year:** Wes Roemer, Cal State Fullerton. **Coach of the Year:** George Horton, Cal State Fullerton. **Freshman Player of the Year:** Danny Espinosa, Long Beach State. **Freshman Pitcher of the Year:** Scott Gorgen, UC Irvine.

INDIVIDUAL BATTING LEADERS
(Minimum 125 At-Bats)

	AVG	AB	R	H	2B	3B	HR	RBI	SB
Bigler, Brett, UC Riverside	.356	205	45	73	11	4	0	35	27
Turner, Justin, Cal State Fullerton	.355	287	63	102	19	4	4	43	20
Cipriano, Cody, UC Irvine	.354	192	31	68	18	1	4	36	16
Longoria, Evan, Long Beach State	.353	201	42	71	13	2	11	43	3
Lansford, Josh, Cal Poly	.353	235	33	83	12	3	7	39	5
Pedroza, Jaime, UC Riverside	.352	159	29	56	11	3	2	31	6
Davis, Blake, Cal State Fullerton	.351	259	64	91	13	5	5	39	15
Hollingsworth, D.J., UC Riverside	.351	185	39	65	15	1	5	39	24
Dorn, Danny, Cal State Fullerton	.351	174	37	61	13	1	4	43	7
Carrithers, Alden, UC Santa Barbara	.342	196	60	67	12	1	2	30	6
Valaika, Chris, UC Santa Barbara	.335	227	44	76	12	1	10	57	4
Glasgow, Ramon, Pacific	.333	162	25	54	8	0	0	16	7
Blauer, Robbie, UC Santa Barbara	.332	184	38	61	11	0	2	29	2
Dudrey, Gary, UC Irvine	.331	142	35	47	9	3	1	14	24
Pill, Brett, Cal State Fullerton	.328	253	52	83	23	3	5	40	11
Canepa, Matt, Cal Poly	.326	178	21	58	7	0	1	35	1
Emerick, Matt, UC Santa Barbara	.325	191	31	62	11	4	2	27	7
Berezay, Matt, Pacific	.322	242	42	65	18	1	11	39	6
Tripp, Brandon, Cal State Fullerton	.321	221	44	71	11	6	9	42	10
Lyons, Scott, Cal State Northridge	.321	156	22	50	3	0	1	30	4
Andrade Jr., Jorge, Cal State North.	.320	203	34	65	12	1	3	19	3
Steinmeyer, Brian, UC Riverside	.309	207	40	64	10	0	3	32	4
Perry, Robert, Long Beach State	.309	204	43	63	7	4	3	33	9
Cline, Matt, Long Beach State	.308	146	26	45	4	0	0	14	5
Ching, Adam, Pacific	.308	224	40	69	15	1	0	23	10
Cooper, David, Cal State Fullerton	.305	151	16	46	9	0	2	37	0

INDIVIDUAL PITCHING LEADERS
(Minimum 50 Innings)

	W	L	ERA	G	SV	IP	H	BB	SO
Segal, Justin, UC Santa Barbara	5	3	2.29	36	7	55	46	13	33
Roemer, Wes, Cal State Fullerton	13	2	2.38	21	1	155	126	7	145
Gorgen, Scott, UC Irvine	7	5	2.54	19	0	110	93	33	87
Centanni, Joey, Pacific	6	4	2.77	18	0	88	77	26	40
Gagnier, Lauren, Cal State Fullerton	14	5	2.80	21	0	132	109	25	105
Swanson, Glenn, UC Irvine	9	4	2.86	21	0	91	94	15	69
Carpenter, Anderw, Long Beach State	7	4	2.91	16	0	118	102	20	99
Simmons, James, UC Riverside	9	5	2.96	16	0	109	108	19	94
Braun, Jeff, UC Santa Barbara	2	2	3.11	9	0	55	56	17	31
Miller, Dustin, Cal State Fullerton	12	1	3.13	18	0	98	85	26	52
Cassel, Justin, UC Irvine	7	9	3.43	18	0	134	136	25	99
Huges, Jared, Long Beach State	8	4	3.67	16	0	108	97	33	77
Worley, Vance, Long Beach State	4	7	3.82	21	1	73	78	28	37
Baker, Craig, Cal State Northridge	6	9	3.97	18	0	102	105	33	102
Bills, Taylor, UC Riverside	5	5	4.11	15	1	81	78	25	42
Brettl, Jimmy, Cal State Northridge	4	2	4.38	30	3	76	88	25	53
Fien, Casey, Cal Poly	6	5	4.44	30	2	99	113	14	53
Fick, Chuckie, Cal State Northridge	6	7	4.48	15	0	90	80	36	72
Quirarte, Edwin, Cal State Northridge	4	7	4.50	18	0	78	81	23	46
Norris, Bud, Cal Poly	8	6	4.55	18	0	111	118	57	61
Massetti, Luke, Pacific	5	5	4.65	14	0	89	99	22	62
Tracy, Brian, UC Santa Barbara	3	7	4.89	17	0	77	88	34	29
Graham, Andy, UC Santa Barbara	6	7	5.11	16	0	99	115	42	55
Fleming, Bryan, UC Santa Barbara	2	7	5.34	17	0	67	74	21	40
Winter, Haley, UC Riverside	4	4	5.42	14	0	83	117	14	61
Daley, Casey, Cal Poly	7	8	5.48	19	0	110	124	61	110
Harris, Ty'Relle, Pacific	4	5	5.97	15	0	63	74	40	50

COLONIAL ATHLETIC ASSOCIATION

	Conference		Overall	
	W	L	W	L
James Madison	22	8	38	21
Old Dominion	21	9	39	17
Northeastern	19	10	27	23
Virginia Commonwealth	18	11	34	24
*UNC Wilmington	17	13	42	22
Georgia State	13	17	26	31
Delaware	12	18	30	24
George Mason	12	18	20	31
William & Mary	11	19	24	31
Hofstra	11	19	24	31
Towson	8	22	20	34

ALL-CONFERENCE TEAM: C—Chris Hatcher, UNC Wilmington. **1B**—Nate Schill, James Madison. **2B**—Michael Cowgill, James Madison. **SS**—Sergio Miranda, Virginia Commonwealth. **3B**—Matt Poulk, UNC Wilmington. **DH**—Tim St. Clair, Virginia Commonwealth. **UTIL**—Alex Buchholz, Delawre. **OF**—Brandon Menchaca, Delaware; Kellen Kulbacki, James Madison; John Raynor, UNC Wilmington. **SP**—Harold Mozingo, Virginia Commonwealth; Adam Ottavino, Northeastern. **RP**—Dana Arrowood, Old Dominon.

Player of the Year: Kellen Kulbacki, James Madison. **Defensive Player of the Year:** Sergio Miranda, Virginia Commonwealth. **Freshman of the Year:** Alex Buchholz, Delaware. **Coach of the Year:** Jerry Myers, Old Dominion.

INDIVIDUAL BATTING LEADERS
(Minimum 125 At-Bats)

	AVG	AB	R	H	2B	3B	HR	RBI	SB
Kulbacki, Kellen, James Madison	.464	194	68	90	17	2	24	75	13
Schill, Nate, James Madison	.419	227	50	95	16	0	14	68	7
Miranda, Sergio, VCU	.400	250	50	100	20	4	4	40	15
Menachaca, Brandon, Delaware	.395	220	61	87	20	0	9	16	64	28
Sexton, Greg, William & Mary	.391	197	47	77	19	0	6	56	12
Bolden, Jared, VCU	.385	221	46	85	13	7	7	45	12
Bucholz, Alex, Delaware	.378	222	62	84	16	3	18	64	8
Raynor, John, UNC Wilmington	.370	262	63	97	17	2	12	69	42
Hargrave, Daniel, UNC Wilmington	.360	139	43	50	13	0	12	43	5
Davidson, Todd, Delaware	.357	235	66	84	25	2	11	42	13
Tamsin, Mike, Northeastern	.353	173	28	61	15	0	3	34	1
Heffron, Adam, Towson	.350	197	34	69	9	4	6	38	5
Miles, Jimmy, Old Dominion	.348	267	53	93	19	4	4	32	39
Hatcher, Chris, UNC Wilmington	.348	264	60	92	18	1	7	55	17
McLean, Lee, UNC Wilmington	.346	159	51	55	14	0	8	43	8
Lunardi, Jeff , William & Mary	.343	210	48	72	14	0	3	38	10
Sheridan, Mike, William & Mary	.339	127	25	43	6	0	3	33	2
St. Clair, Tim, VCU	.335	209	27	70	17	2	8	46	4
Skellchock, Kyle, Towson	.330	215	37	71	18	0	2	33	6
Rocon-Salvas, J.M., Georgia State	.330	215	47	71	7	3	2	36	9
Tinnerella, A.J., Towson	.330	215	25	71	10	0	2	46	0

	AVG	AB	R	H	2B	3B	HR	RBI	SB
Appel, Jason, UNC Wilmington	.330	188	37	62	8	1	3	27	12
Zahm, Mike, Old Dominion	.328	235	54	77	15	5	6	43	9
Newman, Justin, Georgia State	.327	171	26	56	11	9	5	33	6
Lake, Joe, James Madison	.327	205	50	67	15	2	0	26	6
Sluder, Matt, James Madison	.326	190	46	62	18	1	4	40	2
Jacobsen, Robby, George Mason	.326	218	42	71	16	1	11	37	20
Stoneburner, Davis, Jas. Madison	.325	126	37	41	10	2	6	30	6
Poulk, Matt, UNC Wilmington	.324	225	58	73	15	2	14	45	13
Caputo, Ricky, Hofstra	.324	204	48	66	11	1	12	47	13
Maliniak, Greg, William & Mary	.322	177	29	57	10	3	4	34	5
Altieri, Rob, James Madison	.321	134	31	43	8	1	3	20	1
Wilson, Wesley, Georgia State	.321	159	29	51	15	2	4	36	4
Suttle, Eric, Georgia State	.319	235	46	75	8	2	4	38	5
Batts, Jonathan, UNC Wilmington	.319	229	65	73	18	1	12	56	10

INDIVIDUAL PITCHING LEADERS
(Minimum 50 Innings)

	W	L	ERA	G	SV	IP	H	BB	SO
Mozingo, Harold, VCU	7	1	**2.45**	14	0	96	54	18	101
Bowen, Evan , Delaware	2	1	2.95	5	0	58	**46**	35	42
Ottavino, Adam, Northeastern	4	5	2.98	14	0	94	71	33	120
Pellegrine, Dave, Northeastern	6	5	3.02	13	0	92	84	42	69
Vernon, Pete, William & Mary	4	1	3.06	32	0	53	48	16	38
Braxton, Brett, UNC Wilmington	6	1	3.22	13	0	59	47	21	52
Hudson, Dan, Old Dominion	7	3	3.28	14	0	93	43	26	79
Paul, Adam, UNC Wilmington	7	3	3.31	**36**	**9**	54	53	16	36
Reid, Ryan, James Madison	**10**	4	3.43	14	0	94	80	43	124
Gunter, Kevin, Old Dominion	6	5	3.46	15	0	104	99	30	101
Holt, Bradley, UNC Wilmington	3	3	3.48	14	0	54	54	28	42
Nesbitt, Greg, James Madison	6	3	3.54	13	0	81	84	22	80
Houck, Kurt, James Madison	2	2	3.55	14	0	51	40	29	38
Leonard, John, VCU	7	5	3.56	17	1	96	50	39	91
Miller, Travis, James Madison	6	2	3.67	9	0	56	**46**	19	60
Drabowiecki, Kris, Northeastern	6	2	3.76	12	0	81	85	22	68
Benton, Thomas, UNC Wilmington	9	5	3.80	20	0	**121**	116	35	101
Smith, Trevor, Northeastern	7	4	3.88	23	3	53	**46**	32	50
Rogers, Patrick, Hofstra	2	3	3.89	13	0	69	70	19	25
Godin, Jason, Old Dominion	8	3	4.06	15	0	115	116	38	**146**
Eppley, Cody, VCU	6	1	4.44	17	0	71	77	15	53
Kantakevich, Joe, William & Mary	4	3	4.61	25	5	70	71	28	61
Heppner, Matt, Delaware	4	3	4.81	17	1	77	80	25	56
Hicks, Romas, Georgia State	4	4	4.91	13	0	77	90	29	67
Bennett, Bobby, Georgia State	5	3	4.93	28	1	66	71	45	40
Shunick, Clayton, Georgia State	5	7	4.94	17	0	95	121	42	69

CONFERENCE USA

	Conference		Overall	
	W	L	W	L
*Rice	22	2	57	13
Houston	18	6	39	22
Tulane	15	9	43	21
Memphis	13	11	31	28
Southern Mississippi	13	11	39	22
East Carolina	10	14	33	26
Marshall	6	18	22	32
Alabama-Birmingham	6	18	19	38
Central Florida	5	19	23	33

ALL-CONFERENCE TEAM: C—Jake Smith, East Carolina. IF—Adam Amar, Memphis; Brian Friday, Rice; Isa Garcia, Houston; Mark Hamilton, Tulane; Marc Maddox, Southern Mississippi. DH—Brad Lincoln, Houston. OF—Toddric Johnson, Southern Mississippi; Warren McFadden, Tulane; Matt Weston, Houston. P—Tim Bascom, Central Florida Eddie Degerman, Rice; Brad Lincoln, Houston; Sean Morgan, Tulane. RP—Cole St. Clair, Rice.

Player of the Year: Mark Hamilton, Tulane. **Pitcher of the Year:** Brad Lincoln, Houston. **Freshman of the Year:** Warren McFadden, Tulane. **Coach of the Year:** Wayne Graham, Rice.

INDIVIDUAL BATTING LEADERS
(Minimum 125 At-Bats)

	AVG	AB	R	H	2B	3B	HR	RBI	SB
Amar, Adam, Memphis	.395	210	40	83	17	3	10	66	2
McFadden, Warren, Tulane	.382	238	53	91	24	2	1	50	6
Sutton, Trey, Southern Miss.	.375	240	50	90	14	2	4	32	4
Dozier, Brian, Southern Miss.	.368	209	39	77	8	4	3	39	11
Moss, Bill, Memphis	.365	233	49	85	24	0	6	45	2
Friday, Brian, Rice	.365	255	65	93	21	3	9	56	17
Johnson, Toddric, Southern Miss.	.363	259	65	94	10	3	11	52	9
Garcia, Isa, Houston	.357	227	51	81	13	4	4	30	19
Friday, Brian, Rice	.353	269	66	95	22	3	9	57	17
Russell, Rich, Marshall	.347	173	49	60	9	0	6	34	3
Buchanan, Greg, Rice	.346	295	64	**102**	9	3	5	42	13
Federick, Adam, Marshall	.345	203	54	70	16	0	9	38	10
Smith, Jake, East Carolina	.344	218	41	75	16	1	13	65	0
Rodriguez, Josh, Rice	.344	262	62	90	21	3	11	64	10
Donahue, John Wayne, Ala.-Birm.	.343	102	19	35	7	0	4	23	1
Southard, Nathan, Tulane	.342	240	55	82	16	5	7	48	27
Eldridge, Harrison, East Carolina	.336	217	44	73	13	0	2	26	12
Hamilton, Mark, Tulane	.336	235	61	79	12	0	**20**	69	2
Petersen, Will, Memphis	.336	253	64	85	22	0	10	47	12
Batts, Stephen, East Carolina	.336	131	26	44	6	1	1	15	6
Henley, Tyler, Rice	.336	274	**74**	92	**26**	**7**	5	54	6
Savery, Joe, Rice	.335	254	61	85	20	1	9	66	7
Guidry, Tim, Tulane	.333	153	28	51	12	0	3	39	4
Henderson, Brandon, East Carolina	.326	132	23	43	9	1	4	24	3
Norrid, Kyle, Memphis	.324	247	46	80	14	2	4	45	4
Auer, Tyson, Central Florida	.323	164	30	53	5	6	2	28	17
Luna, Aaron, Rice	.322	199	48	64	13	1	16	50	4
Tully, Bryan, Houston	.322	199	34	64	14	1	6	28	8
Stewart, Jake, Houston	.321	224	44	72	15	1	7	33	13
Bono, Ryan, Central Florida	.320	200	31	64	14	0	6	33	0
Lieberman, Joey, Memphis	.319	135	28	43	7	0	13	42	1
Stirneman, Josh, Houston	.315	168	24	53	7	3	7	24	6
Murphy, Brendan, Marshall	.315	203	40	64	19	1	15	**70**	2
Weston, Matt, Houston	.314	175	39	55	10	1	16	51	3
Ewing, Michael, Southern Miss.	.313	182	40	57	15	1	8	41	1
Maddox, Marc, Southern Miss.	.313	246	61	77	7	2	18	**70**	14
Chalmers, K.K., Memphis	.312	237	61	74	12	6	6	30	**39**

INDIVIDUAL PITCHING LEADERS
(Minimum 50 Innings)

	W	L	ERA	G	SV	IP	H	BB	SO
Lincoln, Brad, Houston	12	2	**1.69**	17	0	128	91	32	152
St. Clair, Cote, Rice	7	2	1.82	**37**	11	74	39	26	100
Degerman, Eddie, Rice	**13**	2	2.00	20	0	**131**	78	58	**172**
Best, Daniel, Southern Mississippi	6	2	2.20	31	13	53	45	11	50
Martin, Trey, Tulane	6	0	2.32	29	0	62	48	21	37
Bramhall, Bobby, Rice	4	2	2.36	26	3	53	36	26	47
Bascom, Tim, Central Florida	5	6	2.47	14	0	80	62	25	90
Savery, Joe, Rice	5	1	2.76	13	0	62	55	24	62
Flores, Luis, Houston	6	3	3.00	15	0	87	76	17	67
Taylor, Brody, East Carolina	8	2	3.12	14	0	92	81	21	68
Hargrove, Ricky, Houston	8	6	3.31	22	1	101	97	27	82
McDaniel, Will, Rice	7	1	3.34	19	0	59	53	23	40
Cox, Bryce, Rice	5	1	3.48	32	4	52	41	25	62
Morgan, Sean, Tulane	8	6	3.51	17	0	118	96	39	125
Crow, Craig, Rice	8	2	3.53	24	0	82	85	35	88
Belanger, Ryan, Southern Miss.	8	3	3.82	24	1	66	86	24	62
Hose, T.J., East Carolina	3	4	3.88	15	0	67	68	27	51
Mohl, Billy, Tulane	9	0	4.03	18	0	105	114	21	67
Crew, Jim, Alabama-Birmingham	6	4	4.07	17	0	77	64	60	49
Bell, Bobby, Rice	8	0	4.17	18	3	73	77	21	61
Russum, Cliff, Southern Miss.	8	6	4.23	16	0	94	90	40	54
Houck, Mitch, Central Florida	3	4	4.24	14	0	64	57	34	70
Farrington, Matt, Houston	5	4	4.36	17	1	66	76	24	36
Bowden, Barry, Southern Miss.	3	2	4.37	13	0	58	57	30	48
Sweat, Kyle, Central Florida	3	4	4.52	15	0	72	80	22	36
Sasser, Dustin, East Carolina	5	7	4.55	16	0	85	96	36	52

HORIZON LEAGUE

	Conference		Overall	
	W	L	W	L
Illinois-Chicago	22	7	35	20
Wisconsin-Milwaukee	18	12	32	25
*Wright State	17	13	32	27
Youngstown State	16	13	26	29
Butler	9	21	21	36
Cleveland State	6	22	10	42

ALL-CONFERENCE TEAM: C—Justin Johnson, Illinois-Chicago. 1B—Joe Nowicki, Wisconsin-Milwaukee. 2B—Mark Hallberg, Illinois-Chicago. SS—Joe Pauley, Butler. 3B—Dan Biedenharn, Wright State. DH—Erich Diedrich, Youngstown State. UT—Brandon Caipen, Youngstown State. OF—Bart Babineauz, Illinois-Chicago; Larry Gempp Jr., Illinois-Chicago; Mike Goetz, Wisconsin-Milwaukee. P—Zach Peterson, Illinois-Chicago; Joe Smith, Wright State.

Player of the Year: Mike Goetz, Wisconsin-Milwaukee. **Pitcher of the Year:** Joe Smith, Wright State. **Newcomer of the Year:** Chad Schroeder, Illinois-Chicago. **Coach of the Year:** Mike Dee, Illinois-Chicago.

INDIVIDUAL BATTING LEADERS
(Minimum 125 At-Bats)

	AVG	AB	R	H	2B	3B	HR	RBI	SB
Goetz, Mike, Wis.-Milwaukee	.493	225	**67**	**111**	23	**6**	3	33	**17**
Trotter, Ben, Illinois-Chicago	.397	141	30	56	9	1	2	33	1
Johnson, Justin, Illinois-Chicago	.395	185	52	73	18	3	11	57	3
Nowicki, Joe, Wis.-Milwaukee	.376	229	61	86	21	2	11	57	9
Hallberg, Mark, Illinois-Chicago	.373	217	56	81	19	1	3	41	6
Oeder, Ross, Wright State	.366	213	49	78	14	5	1	28	9

COLLEGE BASEBALL

	AVG	AB	R	H	2B	3B	HR	RBI	SB
Diedrich, Erich, Youngs. State	.357	210	41	75	14	2	9	58	0
Rosinski, Ted, Illinois-Chicago	.353	156	22	55	8	1	3	27	2
Chinn, Steve, Cleveland State	.350	203	24	71	10	2	3	28	6
Page, Josh, Youngstown State	.346	214	34	74	9	0	1	22	8
Babineaux, Bart, Illinois-Chicago	.340	197	52	67	10	3	18	65	10
Garcia, Aaron, Wright State	.333	207	29	69	18	0	5	40	2
Caipen, Brandon, Youngs. State	.332	229	47	76	18	1	5	45	6
Banks, Justin, Youngstown State	.332	202	30	69	13	2	4	29	4
Abusalem, Amin, Wright State	.327	223	30	73	13	1	7	41	5

INDIVIDUAL PITCHING LEADERS
(Minimum 50 Innings)

	W	L	ERA	G	SV	IP	H	BB	SO
Peterson, Zach, Illinois-Chicago	9	3	2.42	17	0	108	107	12	73
Barrett, Robert, Wright State	9	3	2.69	19	0	87	72	25	64
Foster, Jason, Illinois-Chicago	2	3	3.00	37	3	58	55	9	32
Shaffer, Eric, Youngstown State	4	5	3.35	17	0	80	97	17	44
Skinner, Joe, Illinois-Chicago	7	5	3.74	20	0	84	95	18	34
Schanz, Erich, Wright State	6	4	4.08	16	0	82	98	33	59
Engle, Lucas, Youngstown State	4	4	4.35	19	0	99	115	19	72
Deter, Brian, Butler	5	7	4.52	17	1	80	90	35	45
Sorenson, Aaron, Wisc.-Milwaukee	5	4	4.64	14	0	83	94	19	60
Cavaiani, Rick, Wisc.-Milwaukee	8	2	4.84	15	0	80	99	19	66
Bokowy, Bryan, Butler	3	5	4.93	15	0	88	114	27	57
Sokolowski, Matt, Butler	0	5	5.19	17	0	59	72	25	26
Snyder, Chris, Wright State	5	7	5.24	17	0	79	89	30	44
Rauwerdink, Mike, Wisc.-Milwaukee	4	4	5.37	15	0	69	71	31	50
Phillis, Don, Illinois-Chicago	7	4	6.28	16	0	62	70	20	29

IVY LEAGUE

	Conference		Overall	
GEHRIG	W	L	W	L
*Princeton	11	9	19	26
Pennsylvania	7	13	12	27
Columbia	6	14	13	32
Cornell	6	14	10	29
ROLFE				
Harvard	14	6	21	20
Dartmouth	13	7	20	19
Brown	12	8	16	24
Yale	11	9	26	19

ALL-CONFERENCE TEAM: C—Devin Thomas, Brown . **1B**—Josh Klimkiewicz, Harvard; Marc Sawyer, Yale. **2B**—Bryan Tews, Brown . SS—Morgan Brown, Harvard. **3B**—Steffan Wilson, Harvard. **DH**—Dan Neczypor, Columbia; Stephen Wendell, Princeton. **UT**—Jeff Dietz, Brown . **OF**—Will Bashelor, Dartmouth; Paul Christian, Brown; Matt Vance, Harvard. **P**—Josh Faiola, Dartmouth; Shawn Haviland, Harvard. **RP**—Matt Fealey, Yale.

Player of the Year: Marc Sawyer, Yale. **Pitcher of the Year:** Shawn Haviland, Harvard. **Freshmen of the Year:** Adam Cole, Harvard; Steve Daniels, Brown.

INDIVIDUAL BATTING LEADERS
(Minimum 125 At-Bats)

	AVG	AB	R	H	2B	3B	HR	RBI	SB
Tews, Bryan, Brown	.390	146	35	57	10	1	4	25	0
Bashelor, Will, Dartmouth	.382	144	42	55	11	5	2	32	18
Sawyer, Marc, Yale	.378	172	30	65	16	2	3	33	7
Wright, Damon, Dartmouth	.377	151	24	57	6	3	0	34	5
Dietz, Jeff, Brown	.364	121	20	44	7	0	4	33	0
Christian, Paul, Brown	.360	164	31	59	16	2	8	37	5
Boaen, Joey , Pennsylvania	.349	109	29	38	9	3	4	23	3
Corn, Josh, Pennsylvania	.346	133	30	46	10	1	3	26	5
Salsgiver, Lance, Harvard	.342	149	37	51	9	1	4	18	18
Wendkos, Zack, Princeton	.339	168	31	57	13	2	8	39	0
Weiss, Michael, Cornell	.333	111	10	37	6	2	0	20	1
Wilson, Steffan, Harvard	.331	160	32	53	17	1	6	43	10
Hughes, Danny, Brown	.331	136	20	45	8	0	5	29	3
Klimkiewicz, Josh, Harvard	.331	118	28	39	6	0	7	41	2
Prince, Aaron, Princeton	.327	165	30	54	9	3	1	19	9
Kaufman, Brian , Cornell	.326	138	45	45	8	6	9	38	11
Williams, Ron, Columbia	.326	132	18	43	8	2	0	21	2
Salini, Andrew, Columbia	.325	169	36	55	13	1	6	37	10
Thomas, Devin, Brown	.324	136	32	44	12	2	5	29	7
Vance, Matt, Harvard	.318	151	39	48	10	5	1	21	25
Myette, Tommy, Dartmouth	.308	143	32	44	10	0	3	30	9
Perkins, Henry, Columbia	.305	141	26	43	9	3	1	16	9
Nwaka, Alex , Pennsylvania	.304	148	26	45	11	1	3	26	12
Cox, Josh, Yale	.301	166	28	50	12	2	1	28	14
Gorynski, P.J., Yale	.301	173	32	52	9	0	1	21	5

INDIVIDUAL PITCHING LEADERS
(Minimum 50 Innings)

	W	L	ERA	G	SV	IP	H	BB	SO
Faiola, Josh, Dartmouth	6	2	2.45	9	0	70	68	14	38

	W	L	ERA	G	SV	IP	H	BB	SO
Staehely, Christian, Princeton	5	2	2.57	13	0	74	54	34	49
Young, Russell, Dartmouth	3	3	3.44	12	2	50	64	10	29
Stiller, Erik, Princeton	4	4	3.45	11	0	73	73	17	70
Walz, Eric, Princeton	2	2	3.72	13	1	68	62	29	46
Haviland, Shawn, Harvard	4	6	4.06	14	1	62	64	18	50
Cole, Adam, Harvard	2	4	4.32	13	0	50	45	31	40
Smith, Alec, Yale	4	4	4.33	10	0	54	54	14	46
Collis, Rocky, Cornell	3	3	4.56	9	0	53	60	18	41
Purdy, Bill, Columbia	2	7	4.94	14	0	71	81	18	37
Tews, Bryan, Brown	3	5	5.10	9	0	55	79	17	35
McNamara, Shaun, Brown	2	4	5.75	9	0	56	62	21	45
Baumann, John, Columbia	3	3	5.95	19	1	56	79	17	41

METRO ATLANTIC CONFERENCE

	Conference		Overall	
	W	L	W	L
LeMoyne	21	5	38	14
*Manhattan	17	9	34	23
Rider	17	10	25	31
Niagara	17	10	28	26
Marist	16	10	24	28
Fairfield	12	14	18	29
Siena	12	15	23	31
Canisius	9	18	18	36
Iona	8	18	12	42
Saint Peter's	3	23	10	41

ALL-CONFERENCE TEAM: C—Nick Derba, Manhattan. **1B**—Matt Rizzotti, Manhattan. **2B**—Andy Parrino, Le Moyne. **SS**—Mike Affronti, Le Moyne. **3B**—Patrick Feeney, Marist. **DH**—John Fitzpatrick, Manhattan. **UTIL**—Andrew MacNevin, Niagara. **OF**—Matt Mazurek, Canisius; Mike Alati, Niagara; Jeff Vincent, Niagara; Gabe Perez, Siena. **P**—Bobby Blevins, Le Moyne; Chris Cody, Manhattan.

Player of the Year: Mike Affronti, Le Moyne. **Pitcher of the Year:** Chris Cody, Manhattan. **Relief Pitcher of the Year:** Ryan Woods, Le Moyne. **Freshman of the Year:** Jamie Hayes, Rider. **Coaches of the Year:** Steve Owens , Le Moyne; Barry Davis, Rider

INDIVIDUAL BATTING LEADERS
(Minimum 125 At-Bats)

	AVG	AB	R	H	2B	3B	HR	RBI	SB
Affronti, Michael, Le Moyne	.389	198	52	77	142	3	12	54	17
Alati, Mike, Niagara	.374	198	37	74	16	1	7	51	7
Feeney, Pat, Marist	.372	191	37	71	13	1	3	32	4
Hayes, James, Rider	.372	191	41	71	14	0	3	38	18
Parrino, Andy, Le Moyne	.363	201	49	73	17	2	4	29	7
Vincent, Jeff, Niagara	.361	191	47	69	19	5	7	34	33
Mazurek, Matt, Canisius	.358	190	33	68	12	0	2	44	18
Willis, Jake, Siena	.356	188	35	67	16	0	8	48	1
Lepore, Justin, Marist	.349	169	34	59	7	1	9	42	0
MacNevin, Andrew, Niagara	.344	195	43	67	11	0	6	47	4
Rizzotti, Matt, Manhattan	.340	203	57	69	15	3	9	43	5
Poalise, Mike, Rider	.338	210	46	71	8	1	0	33	12
Conte, Nick, Iona	.335	161	22	54	10	0	6	31	7
Letizia, Tom, Rider	.330	206	43	68	11	1	0	15	11
LaSala, James, Iona	.330	197	26	65	16	0	1	26	3
Fitzpatrick, John, Manhattan	.325	200	45	65	14	2	18	66	2
Perez, Gabe, Siena	.324	188	51	61	6	3	11	38	23
Parsons, Daniel, Niagara	.324	204	51	66	9	1	1	17	12
Crimoli, Gene, Rider	.324	170	39	55	4	1	6	36	5
Crawford, Stephen, Le Moyne	.320	172	29	55	8	1	1	29	8
Maertz, Santo, St. Peter's	.319	135	19	43	7	0	1	25	4
Musolf, Travis, Marist	.316	193	40	61	10	3	1	36	9
Mahoney, Kevin, Canisius	.313	201	42	63	7	1	7	39	7
King, Ryan, Siena	.311	177	37	55	11	2	3	19	15
Connors, Keith, Le Moyne	.310	187	51	58	12	4	9	41	8
Rose, Jamie, Le Moyne	.310	168	36	52	13	2	0	21	14
Lombardi, Dom, Manhattan	.305	203	35	62	8	0	3	29	14
Alexander, Dennis, St. Peter's	.305	177	38	54	4	0	0	15	11
Derba, Nick, Manhattan	.304	204	42	62	8	2	3	34	6
McGuire, Mike, St. Peter's	.301	156	22	47	11	0	2	25	10
DeSimone, Albie, Fairfield	.299	134	26	40	6	1	0	20	14

INDIVIDUAL PITCHING LEADERS
(Minimum 50 Innings)

	W	L	ERA	G	SV	IP	H	BB	SO
Cody, Chris, Manhattan	12	2	1.42	14	0	108	76	23	105
Blevins, Bobby, Le Moyne	10	2	2.57	14	0	98	80	22	95
Sheridan, T.J., Le Moyne	8	1	2.76	13	0	78	51	37	88
Nevins, Matt, Manhattan	3	6	3.44	21	2	55	62	24	47
Sawatzky, Josh, Niagra	8	5	3.54	15	0	89	88	42	57
Darcy, Jesse, Manhattan	5	3	4.03	15	0	92	91	34	69
Kennedy, Jim, Rider	6	3	4.07	14	0	77	92	19	46
Rickards, Josh, Marist	3	1	4.11	17	0	57	61	23	28
Heath, George, Marist	6	4	4.28	13	0	69	75	7	49

	W	L	ERA	G	SV	IP	H	BB	SO
Smith, Jonathan, Marist	4	7	4.42	13	0	75	80	13	40
Santerre, Josh, Manhattan	4	4	4.44	13	0	53	51	20	33
Kamintzky, Ed, Fairfield	4	5	4.47	14	0	91	98	37	76
Falasca, Michael, Le Moyne	5	4	4.48	13	0	70	72	27	46
Radanovic, Mike, Niagra	5	4	4.63	15	0	93	90	35	89
Reid, Trevor, Siena	3	4	4.64	14	0	54	59	23	21
Moberg, Matt, Siena	4	4	4.79	12	0	68	43	34	37

MID-AMERICAN CONFERENCE

	Conference		Overall	
EAST	**W**	**L**	**W**	**L**
Kent State	19	7	38	19
Miami (Ohio)	17	10	33	25
Ohio	14	13	22	25
Bowling Green	11	16	26	27
Akron	8	18	15	36
Buffalo	6	21	15	37
WEST				
Central Michigan	17	9	35	23
*Ball State	16	9	38	22
Western Michigan	16	9	30	22
Eastern Michigan	14	12	27	27
Toledo	11	15	26	27
Northern Illinois	8	18	24	31

ALL-CONFERENCE TEAM: C—Todd Balduf, Kent State. 1B—Brad Miller, Ball State. 2B—Drew Saylor, Kent State. SS—Emmanuel Burriss, Kent State. 3B—Andrew Davis, Kent State. DH—Anthony Gressick, Ohio. UTIL—Ben Humphrey, Central Michigan. OF—Kurt Eichorn, Kent State; Bryan MItzel, Central Michigan; Brian Toner, Northern Illinois. SP—John Ely, Miami (Ohio); Jeff Fischer, Eastern Michigan; Ethan Hollingsworth, Western Michigan; Dan O'Brien, Western Michigan; Chad Wagler, Kent State. RP—Matt German, Northern Illinois.

Player of the Year: Emmanuel Burriss, Kent State. **Pitcher of the Year:** Jeff Fischer, Eastern Michigan. **Coach of the Year:** Scott Stricklin, Kent State. **Freshman of the Year:** Ethan Hollingsworth, Western Michigan.

INDIVIDUAL BATTING LEADERS
(Minimum 125 At-Bats)

	AVG	AB	R	H	2B	3B	HR	RBI	SB
Walker, Willie, Ohio	.377	154	38	58	10	4	4	39	6
Davis, Andrew, Kent State	.376	221	47	83	18	1	3	47	2
Saylor, Drew, Kent State	.374	246	67	**92**	**20**	3	14	68	2
Toner, Brian, Northern Illinois	.373	185	40	69	10	3	9	41	11
Gressick, Anthony, Ohio	.372	196	45	73	16	1	8	43	11
Watson, Jason, Toledo	.366	205	33	75	12	2	3	46	5
Burriss, Emmanuel, Kent State	.360	239	**70**	86	10	3	4	28	**42**
Bradshaw, Steve, Eastern Mich.	.356	194	25	69	17	0	3	40	5
Lawson, Eric, Bowling Green	.355	186	42	66	14	0	5	30	5
Witt, Bryant, Ohio	.349	166	36	58	8	2	2	27	1
Marquardt, Nathan, West. Michigan	.349	189	28	66	10	1	6	37	2
Rogers, Justin, Ball State	.347	213	42	74	13	2	5	44	3
Lankford, Noah, Central Michigan	.347	199	43	69	13	2	5	34	7
Wasserman, Tyler, Bowling Green	.345	165	27	57	10	0	0	24	4
Kingsley, James, Buffalo	.343	204	35	70	15	2	7	38	2
Eichorn, Kurt, Kent State	.341	211	64	72	9	3	14	61	11
Moratti, Troy, Central Michigan	.341	217	52	74	9	1	2	39	6
Davidson, Kurt, Akron	.338	207	37	70	11	0	12	47	2
Humphrey, Ben, Central Michigan	.338	222	45	75	15	**5**	13	72	3
Hammond, Dusty, Ohio	.335	182	26	61	7	2	0	18	6
Miller, Brad, Ball State	.335	245	67	82	19	1	**21**	**76**	1
Jones, J.T., Central Michigan	.330	233	57	77	10	1	0	44	15
Simon, Scott, Northern Illinois	.329	213	44	70	18	0	7	38	2
Gentile, Zach, Western Michigan	.329	207	41	68	6	1	5	39	8
Balduf, Todd, Kent State	.328	186	37	61	12	1	9	56	0
Orr, Geoff, Miami Ohio	.327	220	38	72	17	2	6	41	5
Wells, Kurt , Bowling Green	.326	181	32	59	7	0	1	29	6
Maunus, Kyle, Western Michigan	.326	178	21	58	10	1	4	26	0
Sullivan, Mike, Ball State	.326	**258**	61	84	14	0	3	40	15
Swint, Jake, Toledo	.323	201	35	65	7	2	2	28	9
Dygert, Kyle, Ball State	.316	215	38	68	7	3	7	34	1
Hoisington, Drew, Toledo	.316	209	45	66	1	3	3	20	10
Chiera, Vince, Akron	.316	187	24	59	5	1	1	29	2
Hillier, Brandon, Miami Ohio	.313	233	30	73	10	1	1	37	5
Lehrman, Derek, Eastern Michigan	.313	166	25	52	14	2	2	24	2

INDIVIDUAL PITCHING LEADERS
(Minimum 50 Innings)

	W	L	ERA	G	SV	IP	H	BB	SO
Fischer, Jeff, Eastern Michigan	**9**	4	**1.97**	17	0	110	90	24	102
Shorts, Sam, Miami Ohio	5	2	2.06	21	0	62	55	13	40
Silverman, Yale, Ohio	4	3	2.62	20	2	72	64	15	45
O'Brien, Dan, Western Michigan	6	3	2.68	14	0	87	82	23	93
Wagler, Chad, Kent State	**10**	3	2.68	15	0	104	93	20	69

	W	L	ERA	G	SV	IP	H	BB	SO
Brech, Alan, Bowling Green	4	1	2.69	13	0	80	76	27	52
Taylor, Graham, Miami Ohio	8	5	3.15	14	0	103	100	21	70
Hollingsworth, Ethan, West. Mich.	9	3	3.21	13	0	81	74	26	66
Collmenter, Josh, Central Michigan	8	5	3.41	15	0	95	91	38	94
Hangbers, Brian, Bowling Green	4	4	3.42	17	1	55	**54**	22	22
Rawlings, Kyle, Toledo	7	3	3.52	12	0	72	67	26	36
Ely, John, Miami Ohio	8	2	3.57	12	0	76	76	21	80
Pacella, John, Kent State	5	1	3.65	12	1	67	59	17	40
Liersemann, Ross, Akron	6	5	3.78	14	0	**112**	104	22	95
Biddle, George, Eastern Michigan	5	6	3.85	18	0	91	88	19	52
Weiser, Keith, Miami Ohio	3	6	4.23	15	0	94	98	24	79
Snyder, Ben, Ball State	8	5	4.45	19	0	109	101	40	**108**
Gressick, Anthony, Ohio	4	1	4.47	9	0	54	65	20	49
Curry, Levi, Toledo	4	5	4.50	13	0	70	85	20	27
Lauscher, Kurt, Central Michigan	5	3	4.60	14	0	78	81	27	53
Pritchard, Tyler, Ball State	7	3	4.93	22	0	80	95	27	51
Welsh, Joe, Toledo	4	7	4.96	13	0	78	91	44	39
Witt, Derek, Ohio	6	4	5.01	13	0	92	105	21	66
DeGeeter, Ryan, Ball State	3	5	5.02	15	0	75	83	27	44
McWilliams, Sean, Buffalo	4	6	5.11	22	1	88	112	39	66

MID-CONTINENT CONFERENCE

	Conference		Overall	
	W	**L**	**W**	**L**
*Oral Roberts	17	2	41	16
Western Ilinois	14	8	32	32
Oakland	13	11	20	38
Centenary	11	11	23	30
Southern Utah	11	13	26	28
Valparaiso	9	14	17	34
Chicago State	2	18	7	44

ALL-CONFERENCE TEAM: C—Andy Bouchie, Oral Roberts. 1B—Chad Rothford, Oral Roberts. 2B—Jake Kahaulelio, Oral Roberts. SS—Tim Torres, Oral Roberts. 3B—Jimmy Baker, Centenary. DH—Justin Darr, Centenary. UTIL—Kevin Carkeek, Oakland. OF—Brendan Duffy, Oral Roberts; Tim Ryan, Centenary; Justin Sotelo, Southern Utah. SP—Chris Ashman, Oral Roberts; Nick Jones, Oral Roberts; Quinn Leath, Western Illinois. RP—Scott Boleski, Oakland; Chance Chapman, Oral Roberts.

Players of the Year: Chris Ashman, Oral Roberts; Chad Rothford, Oral Roberts. **Pitcher of the Year:** Chris Ashman, Oral Roberts. **Newcomers of the Year:** Andy Bouchie, Oral Roberts; Chad Rothford, Oral Roberts. **Coach of the Year:** Rob Walton, Oral Roberts.

INDIVIDUAL BATTING LEADERS
(Minimum 125 At-Bats)

	AVG	AB	R	H	2B	3B	HR	RBI	SB
Ryan, Tim, Centenary	.395	195	44	77	13	3	3	36	12
Sotelo, Justin, Southern Utah	.378	195	40	74	**20**	**5**	4	43	21
Bouchie, Andy, Oral Roberts	.376	**229**	52	**86**	16	1	12	54	0
Check, Ryan, Western Illinois	.369	198	39	73	10	4	6	33	15
Manthei, Ryan, Valparaiso	.363	146	29	53	13	0	9	31	2
Duffy, Brendand, Oral Roberts	.358	212	**67**	76	12	3	1	40	14
Crepeau, Kyle, Oral Roberts	.350	177	23	63	5	0	0	19	14
Kutansky, Kevin, Valparaiso	.342	184	40	63	9	4	3	28	7
Darr, Justin, Centenary	.339	177	25	60	5	1	0	37	8
Grow, Justin, Chicago State	.339	189	28	64	10	1	0	23	2
Wilson, Justin, Oakland	.337	175	42	59	5	1	6	26	15
Rothford, Chad, Oral Roberts	.332	217	38	72	16	0	13	**62**	0
Knapp, Steve, Western Illinois	.327	205	44	67	9	3	3	42	30
Latino, Roc, Chicago State	.326	187	42	61	12	2	7	34	9
Oliverson, Jeff, Southern Utah	.325	154	29	50	12	1	3	30	10
Kahaulelio, Jake, Oral Roberts	.323	**229**	53	74	**20**	2	4	50	1
Burgess, Amos, Southern Utah	.320	203	33	65	15	3	4	34	20
McQuigg, Carter, Oral Roberts	.319	166	33	53	9	0	7	33	3
Maldonado, Alex, Centenary	.318	157	31	50	5	0	0	34	4
DeBondt, Travis, Oral Roberts	.315	165	37	52	14	3	3	33	4
Carkeek, Kevin, Oakland	.315	197	35	62	13	0	6	43	3
Baker, Jimmy, Centenary	.315	197	42	62	14	1	4	43	3
Torres, Tim, Oral Roberts	.314	226	56	71	15	1	10	39	12
Aguailar, Brian, Oral Roberts	.313	166	35	52	8	2	3	37	2
Williams, Torey, Centenary	.312	125	22	39	5	1	0	16	4
Minissale, Kelly, Oral Roberts	.311	206	40	64	6	2	3	38	3
Hahl, Charlie, Southern Utah	.309	175	41	54	7	4	2	22	**33**
Webb, Matt, Centenary	.308	185	45	57	13	2	4	29	17
Huff, Justin, Centenary	.307	179	29	55	11	2	0	21	9
Dimick, Trever, Southern Utah	.304	204	40	62	8	4	3	41	17
Wilson, Chester, Centenary	.304	135	25	41	15	1	1	22	1
Jenison, Drew, Oakland	.301	133	16	40	9	2	3	24	5
Newquist, Matt, Western Illinois	.299	214	37	64	19	2	4	42	1
Schmidgall, Ryan, Western Illinois	.297	185	38	55	8	3	2	18	8
Torres, John, Chicago State	.297	172	34	51	8	2	**14**	36	7
Marulli, Bryan, Oakland	.294	136	26	40	5	0	1	15	4

COLLEGE BASEBALL

INDIVIDUAL PITCHING LEADERS
(Minimum 50 Innings)

	W	L	ERA	G	SV	IP	H	BB	SO
Leath, Quinn, Western Illinois	8	2	**2.06**	18	1	79	64	33	54
Ashman, Chris, Oral Roberts	10	1	2.17	19	1	**99**	82	27	75
Jarrett, Sean, Oral Roberts	7	2	2.63	24	**7**	62	**52**	**10**	71
Greenwalt, Daniel, Oral Roberts	6	2	3.41	15	0	71	71	27	39
Kaage, Will, Centenary	4	4	3.53	13	0	59	81	18	24
Schmidgall, Ryan, Western Illinois	5	5	3.57	15	0	63	72	13	60
Johnson, Rob, Western Illinois	4	2	3.62	21	3	60	57	14	55
Jones, Nick, Oral Roberts	7	3	3.89	15	0	90	89	32	**90**
Crichton, Erik, Oral Roberts	5	1	4.33	22	1	52	49	16	43
Shore, John Paul, Western Illinois	7	5	4.84	19	0	74	74	28	40
Wilson, Matt, Southern Utah	5	4	4.98	14	1	69	105	20	50
Yergin, Harvey, Valaparaiso	2	8	5.02	13	0	75	93	35	45
Fulenchek, Brandon, Centenary	3	6	5.40	16	0	70	81	21	37
Noel, Brad, Oakland	4	5	5.40	19	0	50	50	37	30
Mahon, Bobby, Western Illinois	5	6	5.45	23	4	69	84	38	53
Calhoun, Kris, Centenary	4	5	5.45	**31**	1	66	74	21	47

MID-EASTERN ATHLETIC CONFERENCE

	Conference		Overall	
	W	L	W	L
*Bethune-Cookman	15	0	30	27
Norfolk State	11	7	23	28
Coppin State	7	8	13	41
Maryland -Eastern Shore	8	10	17	34
Delaware State	7	11	18	37
North Carolina A&T	6	12	22	36
Florida A&M	6	12	13	34

ALL-CONFERENCE TEAM: C—Jorge Mico, Bethune-Cookman. **IF**—Brandon Gravely, Delaware State; Ernie Banks, Norfolk State; Moriba George, Norfolk State; Charlie Gamble, North Carolina A&T. **DH**—John Boyd, Norfolk State. **OF**—Nabil Sagbini, Bethune-Cookman; Ryan Deakyne, Coppin State; Joseph McIntyre, North Carolina A&T. **P**—Richard Rodriguez, Bethune-Cookman; Francisco Rodriguez, Bethune-Cookman. **RP**—Francisco Gomez, Bethune-Cookman.

Player of the Year: Nabil Sagbini, Bethune-Cookman. **Freshman of the Year:** Jose Ortiz-Rivera, Bethune-Cookman. **Coach of the Year:** Mervyl Melendez, Bethune-Cookman.

INDIVIDUAL BATTING LEADERS
(Minimum 125 At-Bats)

	AVG	AB	R	H	2B	3B	HR	RBI	SB
Starkey, T.J. , Norfolk State	**.382**	157	42	60	12	1	0	19	12
McIntyre, Joe, N.C. A&T	.371	224	47	83	15	0	10	35	5
Banks, Ernie, Norfolk State	.370	173	31	64	11	5	2	30	1
Gamble, Charlie, N.C. A&T	.364	**231**	48	**84**	**21**	6	8	**54**	16
Sagbini, Nabil, Bethune-Cookman	.363	193	42	70	11	5	11	40	12
Hoban, Justin, Md.-Eastern Shore	.354	178	25	63	14	3	1	24	3
George, Moriba, Norfolk State	.344	186	42	64	9	3	3	38	18
Guastella, Peter, Florida A&M	.343	143	19	49	6	1	2	22	6
Savage, Rocco, Norfolk State	.341	126	25	43	8	1	3	22	0
McFadden, Corey, Florida A&M	.341	173	36	59	8	1	2	22	21
Boyd, John, Norfolk State	.338	130	20	44	8	0	7	33	1
Mico, Jorge, Bethune-Cookman	.335	197	34	66	21	0	7	46	8
Acker, C.J., Delaware State	.333	204	44	68	13	0	1	31	13
Deakyne, Ryan, Coppin State	.332	208	33	69	14	**7**	3	45	5
Oates, Patrick, N.C. A&T	.323	229	42	74	20	0	9	40	5
Decambra, Allen, Florida A&M	.323	161	29	52	6	2	3	24	4
Hostetter, Tyler, Delaware State	.321	215	34	69	14	1	1	36	8
Clethan, Kevin, Florida A&M	.319	160	23	51	8	2	1	25	6
Gravely, Brandon, Delaware State	.319	204	39	65	13	1	**12**	48	6
Greene, Corey, Coppin State	.316	187	23	59	7	3	6	33	6
Schirmer, Morgan, Md.-ES	.314	140	22	44	9	1	0	20	3
Irvine, Colin, Coppin State	.308	201	32	62	11	2	4	32	7
Gaines, Eric, Md.-Eastern Shore	.300	200	35	60	10	6	0	26	14
Traynum, Amiel, Coppin State	.296	206	38	61	10	3	0	17	23

INDIVIDUAL PITCHING LEADERS
(Minimum 50 Innings)

	W	L	ERA	G	SV	IP	H	BB	SO
Rodriguez, Francisco, Beth.-Cook.	**9**	1	**3.06**	17	0	82	75	14	60
Young, Mark, Norfolk State	4	5	3.21	14	0	70	63	41	51
Williams, De'Mece, Norfolk State	6	4	3.49	14	0	90	83	40	68
Rodriguez, Richard, Beth.-Cookman	.8	5	3.62	19	0	109	106	29	111
Blackwell, Dustin, Beth.-Cookman	7	7	3.67	16	0	88	99	14	43
Hauff, Michael, N.C. A&T	6	7	4.13	22	1	100	107	34	**117**
Register, Stephen, Florida A&M	2	2	4.15	22	1	52	71	28	54
Longchamps, Dustin, Md.-ES	7	6	4.4	15	0	86	81	54	60
Primus, John, N.C. A&T	6	6	4.51	17	0	**110**	131	19	90
Seal, Joey , Norfolk State	3	6	4.93	17	1	84	85	59	67
Caldeyro, Frankie, Norfolk State	2	5	5.43	18	0	53	59	41	38
Keyes, Billy, Delaware State	6	8	5.44	20	0	103	114	48	75

	W	L	ERA	G	SV	IP	H	BB	SO
Bitter, Nick, Delaware State	6	7	5.52	18	0	104	138	28	86
Smith, Chad, Florida A&M	3	7	5.54	15	2	76	90	29	40
Bellon, Matt, Coppin State	5	4	5.71	21	0	87	102	35	55
Auch, Bill, Coppin State	4	**11**	5.98	20	2	87	123	26	39

MISSOURI VALLEY CONFERENCE

	Conference		Overall	
	W	L	W	L
Evansville	16	8	43	22
Missouri State	15	8	33	22
*Wichita State	15	9	46	22
Creighton	13	11	31	21
Southern Illinois	12	12	33	25
Bradley	11	12	26	31
Northern Iowa	10	14	28	27
Illinois State	10	14	20	33
Indiana State	5	19	20	34

ALL-CONFERENCE TEAM: C—Nevin Ashley, Indiana State 1B—Kasey Whal, Evansville 2B—Damon Sublett, Wichita State SS—Brandon Douglas, Northern Iowa 3B—Conor Gillaspie, Wichita State DH—Pat Tumilty, Evansville. UTIL—Zach Daeges, Creighton. OF—Matt Brown, Wichita State; Grant Gerrard, Southern Illinois; Nolan Keane, Missouri State. SP—Marc Lewis, Creighton; Brandon Magee, Bradley; Aaron Shafer, Wichita State. RP—Chris Krawczyk, Missouri State; Scott Souther, Evansville.

Player of the Year: Damon Sublett, Wichita State. **Pitcher of the Year:** Aaron Shafer, Wichita State. **Newcomer of the Year:** Ben Norton, Evansville. **Freshman of the Year:** Aaron Shafer, Wichita State.

INDIVIDUAL BATTING LEADERS
(Minimum 125 At-Bats)

	AVG	AB	R	H	2B	3B	HR	RBI	SB
Sublett, Damon, Wichita State	**.394**	165	45	65	9	1	10	45	12
Ashley, Nevin, Indiana State	.382	199	41	76	10	**7**	10	42	3
Wahl, Kasey, Evansville	.371	245	45	91	20	2	7	55	1
Douglas, Brandon, Northern Iowa	.370	211	51	78	11	1	4	33	10
Elmendorf, Scott, Southern Illinois	.353	207	54	73	9	0	0	23	7
Gillaspie, Conor, Wichita State	.352	261	41	92	18	3	7	**67**	4
Douglas, Brett, Northern Iowa	.351	151	21	53	7	0	1	21	5
Daeges, Zach, Creighton	.350	180	59	63	13	1	**13**	49	8
Brewer, Dan, Bradley	.347	196	42	68	20	3	5	35	8
Gerrard, Grant, Southern Illinois	.344	224	54	77	15	2	5	55	15
Brown, Matt, Wichita State	.335	**278**	55	**93**	**23**	6	4	57	15
Bradley, Curt, Northern Iowa	.331	172	25	57	6	5	1	23	7
Keane, Nolan, Missouri State	.331	142	24	47	11	2	6	34	2
Lawson, Matt, Missouri State	.330	227	43	75	19	3	1	28	20
Schermerhorn, Derek, Wich. State	.329	222	41	73	14	0	0	29	17
Newburger, Jason, Bradley	.327	171	32	56	7	0	4	30	7
Anetsberger, Ryan, Illinois State	.327	205	25	67	12	3	1	25	4
Tumilty, Pat, Evansville	.325	212	55	69	16	2	**13**	49	6
Frieske, Mark, Northern Iowa	.319	216	39	69	8	0	1	20	8
Workman, Haywood, Wich. State	.317	262	**70**	83	9	4	4	39	35
Odenreider, Chase, Creighton	.315	203	38	64	10	0	6	38	4
Featherston, Brett, Northern Iowa	.315	178	34	56	19	0	6	48	2
Brewer, Tim, Indiana State	.313	211	41	66	3	6	5	21	28
Curry, Ryan, Bradley	.307	212	25	65	12	2	1	36	6
Watts, Kern, Evansville	.306	232	49	71	10	3	2	41	13
Koski, Kevin, Southern Illinois	.300	237	56	71	11	2	1	30	13

INDIVIDUAL PITCHING LEADERS
(Minimum 50 Innings)

	W	L	ERA	G	SV	IP	H	BB	SO
Sinkbeil, Brett, Missouri State	5	1	2.45	11	0	70	45	23	75
Schaecher, Adam, Creighton	5	3	2.54	15	0	85	68	18	36
Shafer, Aaron, Wichita State	**11**	3	2.63	16	0	99	87	22	77
Magee, Brandon, Bradley	8	4	2.66	14	0	105	109	28	**101**
Detwiler, Ross Missouri State	7	4	2.81	14	0	93	73	47	99
Lewis, Marc, Creighton	7	0	2.81	14	0	64	61	32	46
Krawczyk, Chris, Missouri State	6	5	2.84	22	**9**	70	61	16	66
Brinkman, Matt, Evansville	6	5	2.97	22	3	91	80	20	77
Venditte, Pat, Creighton	4	3	3.02	30	2	63	61	18	54
Jenkins, Aaron, Northern Iowa	4	1	3.09	17	0	58	**37**	50	70
Norton, Ben, Evansville	9	3	3.23	19	1	98	87	33	73
Rogers, Adam, Evansville	7	5	3.63	17	0	**117**	125	19	81
Jevne, Zach, Northern Iowa	7	5	3.64	14	0	89	95	24	77
Hayes, Ryan, Indiana State	3	5	3.66	15	1	84	82	27	51
Carroll, Scott, Missouri State	6	4	3.73	14	0	82	79	32	65
Banwart, Travis, Wichita State	9	4	3.87	18	1	100	91	29	81

MOUNTAIN WEST CONFERENCE

	Conference		Overall	
	W	L	W	L
*Texas Christian	17	5	39	23

Brigham Young	14	8	33	28
San Diego State	14	8	23	36
Nevada-Las Vegas	12	10	29	30
New Mexico	10	12	30	29
Utah	9	13	28	28
Air Force	1	21	10	38

ALL-CONFERENCE TEAM: C—Andew Walker, Texas Christian. **1B**—Chad Huffman, Texas Christian. **2B**—Jordan Pacheco, New Mexico. **SS**—Ryan Khoury, Utah. **3B**—Ian Hollick, New Mexico. **DH**—Chris Carlson, New Mexico. **OF**—Ben Saylor, Brigham Young; Austin Adams, Texas Christian; Keith Smith, Nevada-Las Vegas. **P**—Danny Ray Herrera, New Mexico; Bruce Billings, San Diego State; Jake Arrieta, Texas Christian. **RP**—Sam Demel, Texas Christian; Jabe Beard, Nevada-Las Vegas.

Player of the Year: Ryan Khoury, Utah. **Pitchers of the Year:** Danny Ray Herrera, New Mexico; Jake Arrieta , Texas Christian. **Coach of the Year:** Jim Schlossnagle, Texas Christian

INDIVIDUAL BATTING LEADERS
(Minimum 125 At-Bats)

	AVG	AB	R	H	2B	3B	HR	RBI	SB
Khoury, Ryan, Utah	.438	224	73	98	18	4	13	56	16
Huffman, Chad, Texas Christian	.388	209	58	81	16	2	18	71	6
Hollick, Ian, New Mexico	.376	221	49	83	16	3	11	65	5
Smyth, Paul, San Diego State	.370	227	48	84	19	6	11	63	6
Carlson, Chris, New Mexico	.366	235	63	86	16	1	21	79	0
Lang, C.J., Nevada-Las Vegas	.362	235	66	85	12	2	8	42	16
Smith, Keith, Nevada-Las Vegas	.359	223	60	80	18	4	14	71	2
Baldwin, Bret, Utah	.358	165	36	59	16	5	4	28	2
Brossman, Jay, Utah	.354	229	46	81	18	1	10	57	11
Pacheco, Jordan, New Mexico	.351	248	79	87	21	1	5	43	11
Saylor, Ben, Brigham Young	.350	237	58	83	17	2	21	66	8
Carpenter, Matt, Texas Christian	.349	241	40	84	11	1	1	36	5
Adams, Austin, Texas Christian	.347	193	39	67	12	0	4	27	1
Banks, Stetson, Brigham Young	.333	165	26	55	6	2	1	24	18
Kervin, Bryan, Texas Christian	.329	258	49	85	16	1	2	41	4
Berry, Quintin, San Diego State	.329	240	61	79	16	4	5	35	31
Barba, Ray, New Mexico	.329	219	56	72	10	3	9	43	3
Welsh, John, Utah	.326	221	44	72	17	2	8	41	6
Borba, Zach, Nevada-Las Vegas	.324	173	42	56	10	2	2	25	9
Stovall, Daniel, New Mexico	.323	266	51	86	25	2	10	75	0
Crosby, Blake, Brigham Young	.322	152	17	49	9	0	0	23	2
Walker, Braden, Texas Christian	.321	165	37	53	11	4	3	37	3
Kowalski, Ryan, Nevada-Las Vegas	.319	191	43	61	4	0	3	18	14
Mozeleski, Joe, Utah	.319	188	42	60	10	1	4	34	1
Nelson, Casey, Brigham Young	.318	179	30	57	13	0	4	27	1
Steglich, Corey, Texas Christian	.318	170	36	54	9	2	2	34	4

INDIVIDUAL PITCHING LEADERS
(Minimum 50 Innings)

	W	L	ERA	G	SV	IP	H	BB	SO
Herrera, Danny Ray, New Mexico	10	0	2.24	17	0	128	112	29	104
Arrieta, Jake, Texas Christian	14	4	2.35	19	1	111	96	37	111
Billings, Bruce, San Diego State	6	3	3.43	15	0	81	71	43	85
Muir, Jordan, Brigham Young	6	0	3.97	18	0	68	66	34	57
Demel, Sam, Texas Christian	6	5	4.08	23	6	93	93	37	100
Cooper, Josh, Utah	7	6	4.32	16	0	90	93	49	78
Furnish, Brad, Texas Christian	8	6	4.32	20	3	100	82	49	125
Craig, Jesse, Brigham Young	7	7	4.70	16	0	103	122	25	80
Masterson, Justin, San Diego State	6	7	4.81	17	1	116	124	26	108
Trinnaman, Lucas, Utah	3	4	5.08	15	0	78	73	30	60
Wells, Patrick, Brigham Young	7	6	5.21	15	0	78	85	38	50
King, Eric, Utah	4	8	5.25	16	0	72	97	39	39
Brown, Mitch, Air Force	3	10	5.65	16	0	72	94	30	51
Tabor, Ryan, Nevada-Las Vegas	3	4	5.70	16	0	73	94	24	40
Skogley, Kevin, Nevada-Las Vegas	3	5	6.52	20	0	77	85	36	60
Saddoris, Chris, Nevada-Las Vegas	6	8	7.1	20	0	77	110	36	47

NORTHEAST CONFERENCE

	Conference		Overall	
	W	L	W	L
Central Connecticut State	16	7	33	18
Quinnipiac	14	8	22	24
Wagner	15	9	18	34
Monmouth	14	9	27	22
*Sacred Heart	14	9	26	30
Mount St. Mary's	12	11	23	24
Long Island	10	13	13	33
Fairleigh Dickinson	6	18	10	43
St. Francis	3	20	6	39

ALL-CONFERENCE TEAM: C—Mike Hussa, Monmouth. **1B**—Josh Vittek, Mount St. Mary's. **2B**—Jason Maiella, Sacred Heart. **SS**—Nick Massari, Monmouth. **3B**—John Delaney, Quinnipiac. **DH**—Rick Niederhaus, Monmouth. **UTIL**—Matt Born, Fairleigh Dickinson. **OF**—Tim Binkoski,

Quinnipiac; Ryan Rizzo, Quinnipiac; Patrick Sullivan, Monmouth. **RHP**—Evan Scribner, Central Connecticut St. **LHP**—Dustin Pease, Mount St. Mary's.

Player of the Year: Nick Massari, Monmouth. **Pitcher of the Year:** Dustin Pease, Mount St. Mary's. **Freshman of the Year:** Rick Niederhaus, Monmouth. **Coach of the Year:** Charlie Hickey, Central Connecticut St.

INDIVIDUAL BATTING LEADERS
(Minimum 125 At-Bats)

	AVG	AB	R	H	2B	3B	HR	RBI	SB
Rizzo, Ryan, Quinnipiac	.402	184	43	74	12	0	4	26	6
Massari, Nick, Monmouth	.395	185	48	73	14	3	8	51	21
Niederhaus, Rick, Monmouth	.383	141	19	54	4	3	4	28	4
Salvatore, Sean, Central Conn. St.	.378	180	47	68	15	0	4	34	9
Roman, John, Central Conn. St.	.355	172	30	61	9	1	4	43	0
Delaney, John, Quinnipiac	.353	156	31	55	8	1	0	19	3
Brown, Seth, Central Conn. St.	.347	176	47	61	6	0	0	28	7
Hanson, Jeff, Sacred Heart	.345	165	25	57	17	1	5	40	3
Binkoski, Tim, Quinnipiac	.345	174	36	60	11	0	5	31	4
DiGeronimo, Joseph, Wagner	.344	195	27	67	12	1	2	19	21
Vittek, Josh, Mount St. Mary's	.340	162	31	55	20	0	7	39	0
McKee, Bobby, Sacred Heart	.339	174	36	59	14	5	2	29	4
Hussa, Mike, Monmouth	.331	181	34	60	6	0	4	31	6
Taha, Adam, Central Conn. St.	.331	157	49	52	9	0	1	31	4
Sullivan, Patrick, Monmouth	.328	192	37	63	11	6	1	38	9
Schillaci, Jay, Central Conn. St.	.319	185	34	59	12	0	3	44	8
Kaloyanides, David, Sacred Heart	.316	155	31	49	11	1	4	16	13
Memoli, Matt, Central Conn. St.	.315	184	37	58	9	5	2	43	8
Fay, Stephan, Mount St. Mary's	.314	156	25	49	16	0	2	31	0
Maiella, Jason, Sacred Heart	.312	192	31	60	16	2	3	34	6
Trusch, Matt, Mount St. Mary's	.310	145	19	45	3	0	0	15	5
Marchese, Phil, St. Francis	.309	162	33	50	14	0	2	17	13
Matos, Wilson, Quinnipiac	.308	172	29	53	12	1	4	35	3
Coppola, Ricky, Quinnipiac	.307	163	32	50	15	0	0	16	7
Durkin, Sean, Long Island	.302	179	32	54	8	1	0	20	8
Rowen, Robert, Long Island	.296	155	50	50	7	0	1	24	8

INDIVIDUAL PITCHING LEADERS
(Minimum 50 Innings)

	W	L	ERA	G	SV	IP	H	BB	SO
Brach, Brad, Monmouth	6	4	2.44	13	0	85	69	10	82
Gianni, Matt, Central Connecticut St.	9	4	2.75	14	0	85	64	28	60
Cummings, Joe, Monmouth	6	3	3.08	14	0	91	89	13	59
Scribner, Evan, Central Conn. St.	7	4	3.25	17	2	91	103	18	57
Monti, Jay, Sacred Heart	8	5	3.30	15	1	95	103	19	91
Pease, Dustin, Mount St. Mary's	10	4	3.42	21	0	92	85	11	73
Aldrich, Chris, Sacred Heart	7	3	3.44	14	0	89	85	23	59
Maynard, Mike, Long Island	5	1	3.60	14	0	70	72	25	55
Wakefield, Chris, Quinnipiac	5	3	4.01	9	0	52	52	23	40
Piechowski, Adam, Central Conn. St.	5	1	4.16	16	2	67	70	38	53
Coulson, Matt, Monmouth	5	4	4.21	12	0	58	61	20	22
Testa, Joe, Wagner	7	4	4.38	17	0	88	86	40	98
Mayer, Andy, Quinnipiac	6	4	4.48	13	0	72	82	22	38
Eng, Stephen, Fairfield Dickinson	2	7	4.65	11	0	60	79	8	35
Honeyman, Brian, St. Francis	1	5	4.96	16	0	53	72	19	37
O'Hara, John, Fairleigh Dickinson	3	7	5.13	14	1	74	72	38	75

OHIO VALLEY CONFERENCE

	Conference		Overall	
	W	L	W	L
Samford	21	6	34	25
*Jacksonville State	19	8	35	24
Eastern Illinois	17	10	31	24
Eastern Kentucky	16	10	29	26
Austin Peay State	14	13	32	27
Southeast Missouri	11	16	23	33
Tennessee Tech	11	16	18	36
Tennessee-Martin	9	18	20	35
Morehead State	8	18	17	36
Murray State	8	19	15	40

ALL-CONFERENCE TEAM: C—Levi Olson, Southeast Missouri. **1B**—Charlie Yarbrough, Eastern Kentucky. **2B**—Omar Padilla, Southeast Missouri. **SS**—Michael Marseco, Samford. **3B**—Parker Gargis, Samford. **DH**—Chris O'Dell, Eastern Kentucky. **UT**—Ryan Gilboy, Austin Peay. **OF**—Mark Chagnon, Eastern Illinois; Nick Cleckler, Jacksonville State; Brett Bolger, Eastern Kentucky. **SP**—Josh Ehmke, Samford; Christian Friedrich, Eastern Kentucky. **RP**—Joseph Edens, Samford.

Player of the Year: Charlie Yarbrough, Eastern Kentucky. **Pitcher of the Year:** Josh Ehmke, Samford. **Freshman of the Year:** Christian Friedrich, Eastern Kentucky. **Coach of the Year:** Casey Dunn, Samford.

COLLEGE BASEBALL

INDIVIDUAL BATTING LEADERS
(Minimum 125 At-Bats)

	AVG	AB	R	H	2B	3B	HR	RBI	SB
Huber, Erick, Eastern Illinois	.404	198	32	80	9	0	2	39	7
Gargis, Parker, Samford	.396	202	45	80	15	1	5	55	2
Yarbrough, Charlie, Eastern Ky.	.389	208	49	81	18	0	18	69	0
Chagnon, Mark, Eastern Illinois	.380	200	46	76	13	1	3	43	7
Cleckler, Nick, Jacksonville State	.373	220	63	82	9	6	2	33	22
Gilboy, Ryan, Austin Peay State	.366	194	34	71	10	3	5	54	8
Wells, Tony, Eastern Kentucky	.363	160	22	58	5	5	5	36	13
Kane, Ryan, Austin Peay State	.355	217	52	77	12	5	2	49	26
Bolger, Brett, Eastern Kentucky	.351	205	47	72	5	1	3	31	16
Youngblood, Cody, APS	.350	214	62	75	7	2	4	29	25
Olson, Levi, Southeast Missouri	.343	166	31	57	20	0	2	32	0
Padilla, Omar, SE Missouri	.340	203	42	69	18	0	4	25	9
Meyer, Blake, Eastern Illinois	.327	171	29	56	1	1	0	11	5
Whittemore, Clay, JSU	.327	217	39	71	16	3	3	40	10
Nommensen, Brett, Eastern Ill.	.325	194	46	63	9	3	1	27	11
Schroeder, Jacob, APS	.324	182	34	59	16	1	5	27	2
New, Jake, Tennessee Tech	.319	191	23	61	15	0	2	21	1
Pritchett, Dustin, SE Missouri	.319	141	22	45	14	2	2	22	6
Smith, Bert, Jacksonville State	.316	234	55	74	10	1	0	39	22
Bass, Garrett, Jacksonville State	.316	155	41	49	8	6	7	25	8
Turner, Richard, JSU	.315	165	31	52	11	0	1	22	2
Beck, Eric, Jacksonville State	.313	179	35	56	7	2	8	60	0
Rojas, Louis , Samford	.309	204	43	63	11	2	5	42	3
Renton, Lance, Tennessee-Martin	.307	189	26	58	10	1	2	28	2
Morgan, John, Samford	.306	209	50	64	11	2	3	16	9
Kinder, Ryan, Morehead State	.304	204	34	62	12	1	8	35	2

INDIVIDUAL PITCHING LEADERS
(Minimum 50 Innings)

	W	L	ERA	G	SV	IP	H	BB	SO
Friedrich, Christian, Eastern Ky.	10	2	1.98	15	0	82	64	24	118
Daniel, Brad, Austin Peay State	6	3	2.55	28	6	71	59	32	59
Hardy, Rowdy, Austin Peay State	9	3	2.58	18	0	101	111	18	68
Hand, Donovan, Jacksonville State	9	5	2.80	18	0	103	113	34	89
Ehmke, Josh, Samford	11	2	3.15	16	0	109	93	63	132
Kelley, Shawn, Austin Peay State	5	6	3.30	18	0	95	102	26	89
Hash, Eric, Eastern Kentucky	6	1	3.8	14	0	64	73	16	54
Knapp, David, Samford	7	4	3.94	17	0	75	75	20	74
Gierich, Drew, Eastern Illinois	1	2	4.11	16	0	77	84	35	45
Ledlow, Adam, Tennessee-Martin	2	10	4.12	16	0	90	106	39	46
Vaculik, Chris, Eastern Illinois	5	7	4.13	28	8	70	68	32	57
Clements, Jon, Jacksonville State	4	2	4.21	17	1	68	77	21	55
McAlister, Jamie, SE Missouri	4	12	4.36	23	3	109	135	23	80
Reynolds, Matt, Austin Peay State	4	4	4.42	17	0	59	73	20	45
Mabee, Henry, Morehead State	5	8	4.43	16	1	87	103	23	83
Gibson, Kalen, Murray State	4	8	4.59	16	0	98	113	37	66
Lassiter, Eric, Samford	5	5	4.75	18	1	91	104	23	54
Darwin, Matt, Jacksonville State	6	1	4.83	16	0	73	86	18	45
Perconte, Michal, Murray State	4	7	4.92	18	3	86	99	21	58
Lucci, Shane, Morehead State	6	9	5.01	15	0	97	120	27	72
Smith, Matt, Tennessee Tech	4	5	5.07	17	1	55	63	11	40

PACIFIC-10 CONFERENCE

	Conference		Overall	
	W	L	W	L
*Oregon State	16	7	50	16
Arizona State	14	10	37	21
UCLA	13	10	33	25
Arizona	12	12	27	28
Stanford	11	13	33	27
Southern California	11	13	25	33
Washington	11	13	36	25
Washington State	10	14	36	23
California	9	15	26	28

ALL-CONFERENCE TEAM: C—Ryan Babineau, UCLA; Preston Paramore, Arizona State. **1B**—Curt Rindal, Washington. **INF**—Darwin Barney, Oregon State; Matt Cusick, Southern California; Chris Minaker, Stanford; Eric Sogard, Arizona State. **DH**—Hector Ambriz, UCLA. **OF**—Zach Clem, Washington; Colin Curtis, Arizona State; Matt Hague, Washington; Cyle Hankerd, Southern California; Jay Miller, Washington State. **RHP/OF**—Jared Prince, Washington State. **LHP/OF**—Ike Davis, Arizona State. **SP**—Dallas Buck, Oregon State; Dave Huff, UCLA; Tim Lincecum, Washington; Brandon Morrow, California; Jonah Nickerson, Oregon State. **RP**—Kevin Gunderson, Oregon State.

Player of the Year: Cole Gillespie, Oregon State. **Pitcher of the Year:** Tim Lincecum, Washington. **Freshman of the Year:** Ike Davis, Arizona State. **Defensive Player of the Year:** Chris Kunda, Oregon State. **Coach of the Year:** Pat Casey, Oregon State.

INDIVIDUAL BATTING LEADERS
(Minimum 125 At-Bats)

	AVG	AB	R	H	2B	3B	HR	RBI	SB
Prince, Jared, Washington State	.401	207	50	83	16	1	9	58	10
Hankerd, Cyle, So. California	.383	230	58	88	15	1	10	55	2
Hague, Matt, Washington	.381	226	53	86	17	1	6	45	8
Gillespie, Cole, Oregon State	.374	238	83	89	25	5	13	57	15
Wallace, Brett, Arizona State	.371	151	31	56	11	0	7	32	3
Cusick, Matt, Southern California	.369	225	63	83	10	2	4	35	6
Minaker, Chris, Stanford	.364	258	47	94	21	3	11	68	5
Miller, Jay, Washington State	.361	244	49	88	28	0	0	37	17
Sogard, Eric, Arizona State	.353	184	47	65	13	5	9	50	2
Rindal, Curt, Washington	.350	234	43	82	21	1	10	48	3
Coulter, Travis, Washington State	.345	226	54	78	5	1	2	27	10
Craig, Allen, California	.344	221	39	76	15	0	11	32	6
Rowe, Bill, Oregon State	.341	229	49	78	22	4	6	56	1
Sedbrook, Colt, Arizona	.339	192	48	65	8	5	6	34	3
Perales, Daniel, So. California	.337	196	32	66	6	1	4	37	7
Curtis, Colin, Arizona State	.335	239	60	80	15	5	6	54	21
Murphy, Jim, Washington State	.333	210	34	70	13	1	8	46	2
Rhinehart, Bill, Arizona	.333	174	40	58	14	3	6	48	0
Donald, Jason, Arizona	.332	229	42	76	19	4	6	49	7
Barney, Darwin, Oregon State	.330	261	53	86	11	3	0	36	16
Davis, Ike, Arizona State	.329	240	39	79	20	2	9	65	2
Jensen, Chris, UCLA	.325	234	45	76	13	0	6	36	0
Taylor, Michael, Stanford	.325	228	36	74	15	3	5	39	2
Sharpe, Blake, Southern California	.323	232	49	75	9	3	0	32	5
Boyer, Brad, Arizona	.323	223	65	72	8	9	2	38	21
Sferra, J.J., Arizona State	.323	155	28	50	5	3	0	15	5
Crawford, Brandon, UCLA	.318	242	42	77	14	6	6	30	7
Paramoer, Preston, Arizona State	.318	173	35	55	10	0	3	35	3
Seawell, Ryan, Stanford	.313	166	34	52	9	3	2	14	5
Boesch, Brennan, California	.313	214	35	67	11	0	10	42	7
Fox, Willy, Arizona State	.312	173	49	54	9	5	2	32	11
Steele, T.J. , Arizona	.312	173	33	54	13	5	0	33	5
Frost, Baron, Southern California	.310	213	39	66	15	0	6	47	6
Vieira, Darin, Southern California	.310	197	23	61	12	1	0	31	1
Lewis, Chris, Stanford	.306	219	31	67	14	2	8	48	2
Clem, Zach, Washington	.304	217	52	66	12	1	20	53	4

INDIVIDUAL PITCHING LEADERS
(Minimum 50 Innings)

	W	L	ERA	G	SV	IP	H	BB	SO
Lincecum, Tim, Washington	12	4	1.94	22	3	125	75	63	199
Nickerson, Jonah, Oregon State	13	4	2.24	20	0	137	114	38	131
Gunderson, Kevin, Oregon State	3	2	2.36	37	20	53	38	17	45
Huff, Dave, UCLA	7	4	2.98	16	0	130	121	27	100
Stutes, Mike, Oregon State	8	2	3.10	17	0	81	74	37	77
Bordes, Brett, Arizona State	7	1	3.15	31	4	54	41	32	47
Ross, Tyson, California	4	6	3.19	15	0	85	74	41	85
Reynolds, Greg, Stanford	7	6	3.31	18	0	128	118	32	108
Buck, Dallas, Oregon State	13	3	3.44	21	0	128	101	60	97
Ambriz, Hector, UCLA	8	7	3.65	20	2	113	105	41	97
Cribby, Elliott, Washington	7	6	3.76	29	10	69	68	27	44
Kennedy, Ian, Southern California	5	7	3.90	16	0	102	100	36	102
Gallagher, Nolan, Stanford	5	5	3.99	22	0	65	68	28	51
Dunn, John, Southern California	3	2	4.00	40	0	63	58	32	33
Bleich, Jeremy, Stanford	4	4	4.05	24	7	60	63	16	37
Miller, Jayson, Washington State	2	1	4.11	19	1	50	51	7	31

PATRIOT LEAGUE

	Conference		Overall		
	W	L	W	L	Tie
*Lehigh	13	7	28	28	
Bucknell	13	7	24	24	
Lafayette	11	9	27	24	
Army	10	10	30	20	
Navy	8	12	32	21	1
Holy Cross	5	15	16	26	1

ALL-CONFERENCE TEAM: C—Matt McBride, Lehigh. **1B**—Cole White, Army. **2B**—Mike Sandonato, Lehigh. **SS**—Matt Capece, Bucknell; Ian Law, Lafayette. **3B**—Matt Geiger, Lehigh. **DH**—Chris Pieper, Bucknell; Kevin Leasure, Lafayette. **OF**—Milan Dinga, Army; Kyle Walter, Bucknell; Tom Hayes , Lafayette. **SP**—Nick Hill, Army; Matt Kamine, Lafayette; Mitch Harris, Navy. **RP**—Jason Buursma, Bucknell.

Player of the Year: Matt McBride, Lehigh. **Pitcher of the Year:** Mitch Harris, Navy. **Freshman of the Year:** Tyler Stampone, Holy Cross. **Coach of the Year:** Sean Leary, Lehigh.

INDIVIDUAL BATTING LEADERS
(Minimum 125 At-Bats)

	AVG	AB	R	H	2B	3B	HR	RBI	SB
McBride, Matt, Lehigh	.417	211	56	88	19	0	12	61	22
Dinga, Milan, Army	.385	174	44	67	10	5	7	35	4

COLLEGE BASEBALL

	AVG	AB	R	H	2B	3B	HR	RBI	SB
Frawley, Tucker, Holy Cross	.380	171	28	65	10	2	0	37	4
Law, Ian , Lafayette	.340	194	54	66	15	0	5	32	12
Ercolano, Joe, Lehigh	.339	186	60	63	14	2	5	22	14
Walter, Kyle, Bucknell	.335	173	33	58	18	3	3	37	10
Capece, Matt, Bucknell	.335	176	31	59	8	2	0	26	17
McGinn, Ryan, Navy	.333	186	29	62	16	4	2	40	7
Geiger, Matt, Lehigh	.323	158	31	51	6	4	1	26	8
Sandonato, Mike, Lehigh	.321	190	31	61	6	2	2	24	11
White, Cole, Army	.320	175	26	56	13	1	6	33	3
Grandizio, Chris, Bucknell	.320	150	26	48	13	1	0	12	3
Johnston, Jonathan, Navy	.317	202	51	64	10	3	1	27	35
Bet, Nick, Leg	.311	196	41	61	13	2	2	38	8
Munde, Jared, Navy	.311	206	37	64	15	3	5	41	17
Leasure, Kevin, Lafayette	.303	152	26	46	11	0	4	34	5
Hollins, Renaldo, Navy	.302	205	41	62	5	3	0	21	20
Hamilton, Thomas, Navy	.290	186	26	54	10	2	2	29	5
Simmons, Chris, Army	.283	180	27	51	8	2	4	34	5
Buursma, Jason, Bucknell	.268	164	26	44	8	4	4	23	2
O'Connor, Liam, Navy	.265	162	22	43	1	1	0	19	16

INDIVIDUAL PITCHING LEADERS
(Minimum 50 Innings)

	W	L	ERA	G	SV	IP	H	BB	SO
Harris, Mitch, Navy	10	3	1.74	13	0	83	57	20	113
White, Cole, Army	5	4	2.48	11	0	58	59	16	50
Rutherford, Patrick, Holy Cross	1	1	2.89	13	2	47	38	14	26
Davitt, Jed, Lafayette	3	2	2.95	16	0	58	60	22	30
Reese, Kevin , Lafayette	3	1	3.14	13	1	57	59	8	47
Moss, Jacob, Bucknell	4	3	3.33	10	0	54	59	28	32
Hill, Nick, Army	6	4	3.34	11	0	67	54	24	65
McCoy, Mark, Navy	5	2	3.42	14	1	76	79	20	63
Kamine, Matt, Lafayette	4	3	3.62	10	0	60	60	8	41
Curry, Matt, Bucknell	3	6	3.69	11	0	61	71	12	27
Matteo, Joe, Lehigh	8	3	3.80	15	0	85	104	22	56
Revelle, Matt, Lafayette	4	4	3.91	12	0	76	80	16	33
Hampe, Scott, Holy Cross	3	3	4.15	9	0	61	54	18	37
Mayhew, Ben, Army	4	5	4.45	12	0	61	70	13	55
Collina, Kyle, Lehigh	6	6	4.52	15	0	86	88	36	87
Gjeldum, Ted, Lafayette	5	4	5.04	11	0	55	70	15	31
Mittag, Nathan, Bucknell	5	5	5.09	12	0	64	78	15	31

SOUTHEASTERN CONFERENCE

	Conference		Overall	
EAST	**W**	**L**	**W**	**L**
Kentucky	20	10	44	17
Georgia	18	12	47	23
Vanderbilt	16	14	38	27
South Carolina	15	15	41	25
Tennessee	11	18	31	24
Florida	10	20	28	28
WEST				
Alabama	20	10	44	21
Arkansas	18	12	39	21
*Mississippi	17	13	44	22
Louisiana State	13	17	35	24
Mississippi State	12	17	37	23
Auburn	9	21	22	34

ALL-CONFERENCE TEAM: C—J.P. Arencibia, Tennessee. **1B**—Ryan Strieby, Kentucky. **2B**—Jeffrey Rea, Mississippi State. **SS**—Zack Cozart, Mississippi; Thomas Berkery , Mississippi State. **3B**—Pedro Alvarez, Vanderbilt. **DH**—Mike Biannucci, Auburn. **OF**—Emeel Salem, Alabama; Quinn Stewart, Louisiana State; Michael Campbell, South Carolina. **P**—Nick Schmidt, Arkansas; Wade LeBlanc, Alabama. **RP**—Joshua Fields, Georgia.

Player of the Year: Ryan Strieby, Kentucky. **Pitcher of the Year:** Nick Schmidt, Arkansas. **Freshman of the Year:** Pedro Alvarez, Vanderbilt. **Scholar-Athlete of the Year:** Emeel Salem, Alabama. **Coach of the Year:** John Cohen, Kentucky.

INDIVIDUAL BATTING LEADERS
(Minimum 125 At-Bats)

	AVG	AB	R	H	2B	3B	HR	RBI	SB
Berkery, Thomas, Mississippi State	.383	230	48	88	17	2	7	44	2
Rea, Jeffery, Mississippi State	.372	253	58	94	12	1	2	27	14
Borbon, Julio, Tennessee	.366	235	45	86	14	5	1	30	19
Campbell, Michael, South Carolina	.364	209	54	76	13	3	4	49	5
Wyatt, Johnathan, Georgia	.361	266	57	96	7	3	4	40	10
Bianucci, Mike, Auburn	.359	181	27	65	13	0	8	31	0
Salem, Emeel, Alabama	.356	284	67	101	14	7	2	32	36
Side, Joey, Georgia	.352	315	57	111	20	9	13	54	8
Giesler, Neil, South Carolina	.352	250	48	88	9	0	4	39	1
Arencibia, J.P., Tennessee	.352	216	44	76	17	0	11	52	0
Coghlan, Chris , Mississippi	.350	263	75	92	22	3	5	51	24
Valverde, Kody, Alabama	.347	219	58	76	17	2	12	59	1
Strieby, Ryan, Kentucky	.343	233	60	80	22	1	20	77	2

	AVG	AB	R	H	2B	3B	HR	RBI	SB
Bertram, Michael, Kentucky	.340	197	39	67	16	0	5	37	6
Flaherty, Ryan, Vanderbilt	.339	227	43	77	19	1	2	49	2
Cozart, Zack, Mississippi	.338	272	57	92	16	1	10	64	15
Ketchum, C.J., Misssissippi	.337	261	30	88	13	0	2	36	2
Easley, Edward, Mississippi State	.336	247	60	83	18	0	4	42	2
Presley, Alex, Mississippi	.336	253	61	85	18	7	6	61	20
Delmonico, Tony, Tennessee	.335	203	39	68	10	2	3	36	7
Henry, Justin, Mississippi	.332	268	65	89	12	3	1	30	18
Johnstone, Tyler, Auburn	.332	229	43	76	10	1	1	29	15
Jacobs, Jason, Georgia	.331	248	56	82	18	1	7	47	7
Alvarez, Pedro, Vanderbilt	.329	240	70	79	15	1	22	64	7
Macias, David, Vanderbilt	.328	238	49	78	6	2	1	23	9
Crisp, Andrew, South Carolina	.328	174	31	57	11	0	7	22	3
Robin, Shea, Vanderbilt	.327	217	39	71	16	2	5	36	0
Gentry, Craig, Arksansas	.326	178	37	58	15	3	3	23	16
Sean Coughlin, Kentucky	.325	203	52	66	13	0	17	55	0
DeJesus, Antone, Kentucky	.323	223	67	72	16	3	5	37	11
Davis, Ryan, Vanderbilt	.323	186	28	60	10	1	4	31	2
Feinberg, Alex, Vanderbilt	.322	199	38	64	10	1	1	23	2
Waguespack, Steven, LSU	.321	162	26	52	8	1	3	20	7
Bogany, Jarred, Louisiana State	.319	163	21	52	6	3	0	16	6
de la Osa, Dominic, Vanderbilt	.319	251	48	80	14	1	9	46	13
Hollensworth, Chris, Arkansas	.318	151	31	48	18	1	2	17	6
Dugger, Jake, Arkansas	.317	208	43	66	11	1	12	44	5
Liuzza, Matt, Louisiana State	.317	183	28	58	13	0	3	21	1
Rivera, Michael, Tennessee	.316	212	33	67	12	1	4	36	5
Butts, Jeff, Mississippi State	.316	209	39	66	14	3	7	45	10
Kemp, Chris, Tennessee	.314	204	35	64	9	0	11	41	0
Dixon, Russell, Auburn	.313	198	24	62	19	0	4	31	0
Peisel, Ryan, Georgia	.310	274	45	85	16	1	2	45	3
LaNinfa, Brian, Mississippi State	.309	165	30	51	11	0	11	50	0
Morris, Josh, Georgia	.309	272	62	84	16	3	23	68	3
Wright, Mark, Mississippi	.305	226	48	69	19	1	16	79	2
Dickey, Gavin, Florida	.304	181	36	55	7	2	11	41	8
Smoak, Justin, South Carolina	.303	244	61	74	18	0	17	63	1
Pennington, Spencer, Auburn	.303	175	20	53	4	0	4	26	2
Mayer, Jordan, Louisiana State	.301	176	35	53	8	0	6	30	2
Hernandez, Brian, Vanderbilt	.301	256	37	77	21	2	3	43	5
Edmundson, Kelly, Tennessee	.301	183	35	55	16	0	9	39	0

INDIVIDUAL PITCHING LEADERS
(Minimum 50 Innings)

	W	L	ERA	G	SV	IP	H	BB	SO
Pigott, Justin , Mississippi State	7	1	1.66	19	2	65	57	4	41
Seibert, Shaun, Arkansas	4	0	2.79	17	0	61	59	15	62
Dombrowski, Greg, Kentucky	10	2	2.83	15	0	102	113	11	54
LeBlanc, Wade, Alabama	11	1	2.92	18	0	129	100	43	128
Schmidt, Nick, Arkansas	9	3	3.01	17	0	117	90	50	145
Augenstein, Bryan, Florida	9	6	3.07	15	0	111	102	24	98
Edmondson, Josh, Florida	5	0	3.21	35	2	67	70	10	37
Warren, Rip, Georgia	8	3	3.25	34	3	75	64	21	77
Hunter, Tommy, Alabama	10	3	3.30	20	1	117	115	22	80
Cobb, Craig, Tennessee	9	3	3.31	26	1	111	117	21	64
Honeycutt, Harris, South Carolina	7	0	3.33	16	0	68	62	32	65
Snipp, Craig, Kentucky	7	5	3.48	16	0	106	125	25	83
Olvey, Derik, Louisiana State	6	2	3.50	12	0	69	63	14	55
Kline, Will, Mississippi	5	2	3.71	22	3	68	69	22	76
Heath, Deunte, Tennessee	4	3	3.86	15	0	56	52	22	39
Davis, Ty, Vanderbilt	5	5	3.91	24	1	71	66	28	71
Crowell, Cody, Vanderbilt	6	3	3.95	17	0	84	91	21	52
Buschmann, Matt, Vanderbilt	6	4	3.95	15	0	96	91	29	88
Cisco, Mike, South Carolina	7	5	3.96	18	0	89	78	23	76
Brown, Brooks, Georgia	8	4	4.07	19	0	111	101	44	123
Pelzer, Wynn, South Carolina	5	5	4.15	20	5	80	66	42	66
Price, David, Vanderbilt	9	5	4.32	19	0	110	96	43	155
Crawford, Evan, Auburn	5	8	4.35	15	0	79	87	40	55
Dunn, Brooks, Mississippi State	8	6	4.40	15	0	94	99	32	71
Adkins, James, Tennessee	8	6	4.50	16	0	106	96	42	112
Bukvich, Brett, Mississippi	8	6	4.50	18	0	92	116	23	74

SOUTHERN CONFERENCE

	Conference		Overall	
	W	**L**	**W**	**L**
Elon	21	6	45	18
*College of Charleston	20	7	46	17
Furman	16	11	32	23
Georgia Southern	16	11	31	27
The Citadel	15	12	34	27
Western Carolina	14	13	33	27
UNC Greensboro	13	14	26	33
Appalachian State	9	18	24	31
Davidson	6	21	18	33
Wofford	5	22	20	37

ALL-CONFERENCE TEAM: C—Tony Maccani, Furman. **1B**—Greg

Dowling, Georgia Southern. 2B—Ronnie Shore, Davidson. SS—A.J. Davidiuk, Furman. 3B—Jonathan Greene, Western Carolina. DH—Robert Rodebaugh, Elon. OF—Chris Swauger, The Citadel; Chris Price, Elon; Jermaine Mitchell, UNC Greensboro; Steven Strausbaugh, Western Carolina. P—Nick Chigges, College of Charleston; Everett Teaford, Georgia Southern. RP—Josh McLaughlin, College of Charleston.

Player of the Year: A.J. Davidiuk, Furman. **Pitcher of the Year:** Nick Chigges, College of Charleston. **Freshman of the Year:** Steven Hensely, Elon. **Coach of the Year:** Mike Kennedy, Elon.

INDIVIDUAL BATTING LEADERS
(Minimum 125 At-Bats)

	AVG	AB	R	H	2B	3B	HR	RBI	SB
Mitchell, Jermaine, UNC-G	.397	234	43	93	11	7	5	41	23
Dowling, Greg, Georgia Southern	.377	212	59	80	11	0	11	50	6
Shore, Ronnie, Davidson	.367	218	52	80	17	1	2	22	18
Cassedy, Case, Furman	.366	213	43	78	23	2	7	58	6
Garabedian, Alex, Charleston	.366	246	47	90	11	1	6	51	5
Davidiuk, A.J., Furman	.362	207	48	75	15	0	11	48	3
Cobb, Larry, Charleston	.357	235	58	84	19	6	7	38	21
McDaniel, Trey, Western Carolina	.356	233	55	83	14	1	13	55	1
Swauger, Chris, Citadel	.356	239	54	85	21	10	7	43	8
Shaft, Barrett, Western Carolina	.354	243	68	86	17	1	1	37	7
Maccani, Tony, Furman	.352	193	40	68	13	1	6	47	2
Miller, Matt, Georgia Southern	.351	171	39	60	12	0	4	21	1
Shehan, Chris, Georgia Southern	.350	203	39	71	10	1	2	32	6
Terry, Ben, Furman	.349	192	47	67	9	2	1	23	5
Easterling, Jess, Charleston	.346	237	36	82	17	1	6	45	2
Robinson, Joey, Appalachian State	.345	200	32	69	13	1	1	29	6
Friddle, Joey, Charleston	.343	233	48	80	15	0	3	37	17
Rodebaugh, Robert, Elon	.340	203	47	69	21	0	11	60	0
Strausbaugh, Steven, W. Carolina	.340	209	61	71	17	1	17	64	2
Price, Chris, Elon	.339	236	51	80	18	2	12	61	0
Greene, Jonathan, W. Carolina	.338	240	41	81	13	0	14	54	10
Coker, Philip, Charleston	.337	258	57	87	17	0	3	39	36
Daysh, Joe, Furman	.333	189	42	63	9	2	6	45	6
Crissey, Alden, Davidson	.332	202	31	67	16	0	7	44	0
Weaver, Adam, Elon	.329	219	53	72	13	0	3	47	6
Hollis, Chris, Georgia Southern	.324	173	47	56	9	3	0	18	17
Vasami, Chris, Elon	.322	233	43	75	12	4	14	57	0
Kirkley, Shane, Wofford	.322	202	44	65	14	0	12	40	10
Heafner, Jay, Davidson	.321	187	55	60	11	2	8	35	14
Borden, Wes, Appalachian State	.321	156	27	50	13	0	0	26	2
Zage, Gregory, Davidson	.320	178	33	57	15	2	12	49	0
Arnold, Matt, Citadel	.319	160	27	51	3	3	3	26	0
Campbell, Chris, Charleston	.319	248	41	79	15	1	4	58	6
Murphy, Blake, Western Carolina	.316	215	39	68	17	4	10	59	12
Rembert, Grant, Elon	.315	238	51	75	13	1	9	44	10
Marmol, Oliver, Charleston	.314	194	51	61	12	3	2	33	26

INDIVIDUAL PITCHING LEADERS
(Minimum 50 Innings)

	W	L	ERA	G	SV	IP	H	BB	SO
Chigges, Nick, Charleston	11	2	1.40	17	0	116	86	48	100
Chastain, Matt, Charleston	10	2	2.81	16	0	106	111	32	57
Currin, Patrick, UNC Greensboro	10	3	2.93	38	8	83	68	14	71
Smith, Justin, Citadel	8	2	3.14	36	3	86	83	32	94
Meszaros, Danny, Charleston	9	2	3.22	16	1	87	77	35	86
Hudson, Ryan, Furman	2	1	3.30	24	0	59	55	23	39
Beliveau, Jeff, Charleston	6	4	3.40	16	0	77	77	39	61
Godfrey, Graham, Charleston	8	2	3.57	16	0	98	90	42	101
Wrenn, Wes, Citadel	6	2	3.88	15	0	97	105	24	74
Klinker, Matt, Furman	6	4	3.90	16	0	88	106	25	65
Teaford, Everett, Georgia Southern	10	4	3.96	19	0	120	110	28	122
Sexton, Tyler, Western Carolina	8	6	4.04	16	0	91	115	13	79
Crim, Matt, Citadel	5	1	4.08	17	0	71	81	26	51
Sherrill, Garrett, Appalachian State	7	5	4.11	21	2	96	93	41	53
Smith, Mason, Furman	3	4	4.30	15	0	67	82	24	43
Owens, Ryan, Citadel	4	8	4.41	18	1	96	105	41	82
Hodinka, Ryan, Furman	9	2	4.53	21	0	87	101	27	46
Cole, Lance, Elon	8	3	4.57	20	0	91	89	23	53
Rook, Jason, Appalachian State	4	5	4.71	16	0	84	87	54	66
Redwine, Austin, Wofford	5	8	4.80	18	0	99	112	38	85
Thornburg, Brock, Western Carolina	3	3	4.84	17	2	71	76	22	54
Wilson, Rob, Davidson	4	8	4.99	18	0	97	136	21	90
Starnes, Nick, UNC Greensboro	4	5	5.18	18	0	80	89	44	73
Hensley, Steven, Elon	6	5	5.29	19	0	99	104	35	96
Reeder, Jonathan, Appalachian State	4	7	6.10	21	1	93	114	28	57
McCullen, Brian, Western Carolina	6	1	6.11	32	1	63	83	23	59

SOUTHLAND CONFERENCE

	Conference		Overall	
	W	L	W	L
McNeese State	22	8	35	20

Texas-San Antonio	20	10	37	22
Texas State	20	10	29	30
Lamar	19	11	35	23
*Texas-Arlington	16	12	29	36
Northwestern State	15	15	33	28
Southeastern Louisiana	14	16	23	32
Louisiana-Monroe	12	16	18	37
Sam Houston State	12	18	23	31
Stephen F. Austin	7	23	15	41
Nicholls State	6	24	13	40

ALL-CONFERENCE TEAM: C—Adam Moore, Texas-Arlington. **1B**—Lee Todesco, Texas-San Antonio. **2B**—Brandon Morgan, Northwestern State. **SS**—Ben Soignier, Louisiana-Monroe. **3B**—Bryan Cartie, McNeese State. **DH**—Will Henderson , Lamar. **OF**—Colin DeLome, Lamar; Dustin Martin, Sam Houston State; Charlie Kingrey, McNeese State. **P**—William Delage, Lamar; Danny Davis, McNeese State; Josh Ruffin, Texas-San Antonio.

Player of the Year: Collin DeLome, Lamar. **Hitter of the Year,** Colin DeLome, Lamar. **Pitcher of the Year:** Danny Davis, McNeese State. **Freshman of the Year:** Ben Soignier, Louisiana-Monroe. **Newcomer of the Year:** Adam Moore, Texas-Arlington. **Coach of the Year:** Chad Clement, McNeese State.

INDIVIDUAL BATTING LEADERS
(Minimum 125 At-Bats)

	AVG	AB	R	H	2B	3B	HR	RBI	SB
Martin, Dustin, Sam Houston	.389	208	45	81	16	2	6	40	13
DeLome, Collin, Lamar	.376	237	57	89	16	6	11	56	5
McKennon, Michael, Texas-SA	.371	240	50	89	12	5	11	54	8
Todesco, Lee, Texas-San Antonio	.368	209	33	77	13	1	7	51	2
Kanaby, Erick, Lamar	.356	225	54	80	9	3	0	23	17
Rockett, Michael, Texas-SA	.352	196	32	69	7	2	5	32	5
Morgan, Brandon, NW Louisiana	.352	196	48	69	16	5	9	48	11
Morrison, Josh, La.-Monroe	.352	179	30	63	15	0	6	30	2
Moore, Adam, Texas-Arlington	.350	254	54	89	22	1	10	50	3
Miguera, Jose, Nicholls State	.350	180	38	63	9	2	3	33	7
Hernandez, Dan, Lamar	.350	183	45	64	9	0	9	42	0
Palermo, Michael, NW Louisiana	.349	218	50	76	13	2	1	15	17
Soignier, Ben, Lamar	.348	204	44	71	40	1	5	30	19
Hill, Steven, Stephen F. Austin	.348	207	43	72	16	2	14	44	10
Cannon, Luke, Texas State	.347	190	45	66	11	6	18	65	8
Bowman, Brent, Lamar	.345	148	24	51	6	5	1	27	4
Jeans, David, Stephen F. Austin	.341	179	31	61	3	1	1	14	9
Cartie, Bryan, McNeese State	.339	177	53	60	17	1	2	33	22
Kingrey, Charlie, McNeese State	.338	198	39	67	14	1	9	51	13
Krailo, Karl, Sam Houston State	.333	210	33	70	20	0	7	60	1
Dugas, Tyler, McNeese State	.333	138	18	46	9	0	4	28	3
Henderson, Will, Lamar	.332	226	43	75	15	0	13	65	2
Winn, Robby, Texas-Arlington	.329	216	32	71	12	0	4	38	0
Reider, Daniel, Texas-Arlington	.318	264	42	84	13	0	4	34	2
Jones, Kyle, Texas State	.318	217	34	69	4	0	2	29	15
Wood, David, Texas State	.311	190	27	59	13	1	7	39	0

INDIVIDUAL PITCHING LEADERS
(Minimum 50 Innings)

	W	L	ERA	G	SV	IP	H	BB	SO
Davis, Danny, McNeese State	8	0	2.43	25	7	56	47	23	46
Fiske, Justin, Texas State	2	7	2.56	32	6	60	44	24	71
Blacksher, Derek, McNeese State	7	3	3.01	16	0	99	91	19	79
Delage, William, Lamar	9	4	3.12	17	0	110	103	34	102
Ruffin, Josh, Texas-San Antonio	8	3	3.17	21	0	116	104	47	73
Robinson, Fraser, NW Louisiana	5	5	3.27	15	0	107	103	24	61
Moore, Scott, Texas State	10	4	3.34	16	0	102	88	62	118
Harrington, Allen, Lamar	3	3	3.39	24	5	72	70	33	75
Lehmann, Erich, Stephen F. Austin	8	3	3.4	24	1	77	93	14	63
Prihoda, Luke, Sam Houston State	3	6	3.49	28	4	57	50	10	52
Hart, Matt, Texas State	4	2	3.52	19	1	77	77	23	51
Vasquez, Steven, Texas-San Antonio	4	1	3.66	13	0	76	84	17	76
Brannon, Blake, Texas-San Antonio	8	6	3.77	22	0	100	87	37	67
Minell, Jeremy, SE Louisiana	6	4	3.97	16	0	102	116	33	80
Steinocher, Brian, Stephen F. Austin	3	10	4.05	16	0	102	86	45	75
Adkisson, Zach, Sam Houston State	4	5	4.05	14	0	67	81	24	32
Gray, Timothy, Sam Houston State	7	4	4.33	10	0	100	106	30	59
Stephens, James, Lamar	6	4	4.50	19	0	86	100	30	52
Province, Chris, SE Louisiana	4	7	4.50	22	5	70	95	22	49
Soignier, Ben, Lamar	1	5	4.50	14	1	58	57	17	49
Brown, Drew, NW Lousiana	5	7	4.6	18	0	76	75	51	73

SOUTHWESTERN ATHLETIC CONFERENCE

	Conference		Overall	
EAST	W	L	W	L
Mississippi Valley State	20	4	24	32
Alcorn State	18	6	26	21
Alabama State	11	12	11	34
Alabama A&M	9	14	8	26

Jackson State	1	23	22	17

WEST

	W	L	W	L
*Prairie View A&M	17	7	33	22
Southern	17	8	26	20
Texas Southern	15	9	19	30
Arkansas-Pine Bluff	8	15	14	25
Grambling State	3	21	6	35

ALL-CONFERENCE TEAM: C—Bradley Roper-Hubbert, Alcorn State. IF—Joaquin Rodriguez, Jackson State; Zach Penprase, Mississippi ValleyState; Brandon Revis, Southern; Michael Richard, Prairie View A&M; Gregory White, Alcorn State. **DH**—J.D. Stewart, Texas Southern. **OF**—Shundell Russaw, Jackson State; Marcus Davis, Alcorn State; Calvin Lester, Prairie View A&M. **P**—Wrandal Taylor, Prairie View A&M; Isaac Daniels, Texas Southern; Joshua Froenberger, Alabama State.

Player of the Year: Joaquin Rodriguez, Jackson State. **Pitcher of the Year:** Wrandal Taylor, Prairie View A&M. **Newcomer of the Year:** Bradley Roper-Hubbert, Alcorn State. **Coach of the Year:** Calvin Anderson, Southern.

INDIVIDUAL BATTING LEADERS
(Minimum 125 At-Bats)

	AVG	AB	R	H	2B	3B	HR	RBI	SB
Rodriguez, Joaquin, Jackson State	.457	140	50	64	15	2	3	54	19
Russaw, Shundell, Jackson State	.440	141	50	62	11	2	2	35	18
Davis, Marcus, Alcorn State	.424	170	56	72	15	12	11	64	14
Roper-Hubbert, Bradley, Alcorn State	.416	166	48	69	15	2	10	60	22
McLin, Anthony, Jackson State	.395	114	26	45	9	0	2	32	18
Pearson, Selmon, Alabama State	.373	153	33	57	15	1	10	42	5
Rivera, Jose, Arkansas-Pine Bluff	.367	120	33	44	9	0	2	21	17
White, Wilford, Prairie View A&M	.357	171	49	61	7	2	2	33	33
Penprase, Zach, Miss. Valley State	.354	195	41	69	5	9	1	36	56
Russell, Malcom, Ark.-Pine Bluff	.348	112	18	39	6	1	2	19	6
Edwards, Eugene, Pr. View A&M	.348	187	51	65	13	2	5	46	15
Taylor, Shawn, Alcorn State	.346	185	50	64	12	8	4	61	11
Coats, Demarcus, Southern	.345	174	43	60	11	4	3	33	11
Coachman, Herman, Texas So.	.344	128	17	44	10	0	4	29	1
White, Gregory, Alcorn State	.343	166	55	57	14	3	0	23	23
Lester, Calvin, Prairie View A&M	.341	179	55	61	2	3	1	37	56
Richard, Michael, Pr. View A&M	.338	195	47	66	14	4	0	48	41
Betschart, Caleb, Alcorn State	.335	167	52	56	12	1	1	46	11
Wright, Aaron, Ark.-Pine Bluff	.333	120	25	40	4	2	4	17	4
Shinhoster, Anton, Jackson State	.329	143	35	47	9	4	0	39	15
Sellers, Adam, Texas Southern	.326	138	21	45	4	2	3	30	8
Gause, Gerard, Alcorn State	.324	145	32	47	9	1	5	26	14
Revis, Brandon, Southern	.323	155	37	50	8	0	4	24	15
Clark, Darren, Southern	.319	141	31	45	11	0	13	47	1
Stamps, Chris, Jackson State	.317	126	28	40	8	1	2	40	10
Shamsud-Din, Furquan, Ala. State	.316	136	29	43	5	1	4	26	2
Jones, Jeffery, Alcorn State	.314	121	21	38	9	0	0	23	1
Weeks, Derrick, Miss.Valley State	.307	163	29	50	10	0	2	27	8
Spillars, Scott, Alcorn State	.305	151	27	45	13	0	1	36	2
Barker, Reggi, Ark.-Pine Bluff	.304	135	23	41	8	2	0	11	10
Green, Donald, Texas Southern	.300	130	24	39	8	3	1	20	16

INDIVIDUAL PITCHING LEADERS
(Minimum 50 Innings)

	W	L	ERA	G	SV	IP	H	BB	SO
Daniels, Isaac, Texas Southern	7	6	2.89	22	2	100	81	26	104
Taylor, Wrandal , Pr. View A&M	10	2	3.99	22	2	99	84	21	90
Donaby, Christopher, Southern	3	2	4.47	13	0	48	42	37	24
Stapleton, Ashkelton, Jackson State	6	1	4.72	16	0	53	59	24	23
Terry, Aaron, Arkansas-Pine Bluff	5	5	4.78	13	0	53	56	23	39
Finch, Micah, Alcorn State	5	1	4.92	22	0	57	72	34	47
Klassen, Trevor, Alcorn State	5	2	4.96	16	0	53	55	17	35
Kirk, Josha, Southern	5	5	5.05	12	0	57	68	20	44
Chase, Matthew, Prairie View A&M	6	6	5.12	19	1	78	85	38	63
Moring, Justin, Arkansas-Pine Bluff	2	6	5.31	15	4	61	68	33	55
Terrell, Joshua, Prairie View A&M	5	4	5.34	20	2	56	62	22	55
Merritt, Roydrick, Southern	7	1	5.34	12	0	56	66	26	54
Jordan, Darryl, Alcorn State	5	6	5.54	17	0	88	96	49	58
Canales, Adrian, Prairie View A&M	6	7	5.93	18	0	85	104	36	53
Stapleton, Charles, Jackson State	5	3	6.14	15	0	56	59	58	58
Froneberger, Josh, Alabama State	6	8	6.31	19	0	108	118	70	119

SUN BELT CONFERENCE

	Conference		Overall	
	W	L	W	L
*Troy	20	4	47	16
Louisiana-Lafayette	19	5	39	20
South Alabama	16	7	39	21
Florida International	12	12	36	24
New Orleans	12	12	30	28
Middle Tennessee	10	13	30	25
Arkansas State	7	16	22	30
Western Kentucky	5	18	22	30
Arkansas-Little Rock	5	19	24	30

ALL-CONFERENCE TEAM: C—Michael McKenry, Middle Tennessee. **1B**—Jeff Cunningham, South Alabama. **2B**—Brett Kinning , Arkansas State. **SS**—Tom King, Troy. **3B**—David Freese, South Alabama. **DH**—Josh Yates, Arkansas State. **UTIL**—Josh Dew, Troy. **OF**—Michael Epping, New Orleans; Mike Felix, Troy; Tyler Jones, South Alabama. **SP**—Hunter Moody, Louisiana-Lafayette; P.J. Walters, South Alabama. **RP**—Chase Christianson, South Alabama.

Player of the Year: David Freese, South Alabama. **Pitchers of the Year:** P.J. Walters, South Alabama; Hunter Moody, Louisiana-Lafayette. **Freshman of the Year:** David Doss, South Alabama. **Newcomer of the Year:** Tom King, Troy. **Coach of the Year:** Bobby Pierce, Troy.

INDIVIDUAL BATTING LEADERS
(Minimum 125 At-Bats)

	AVG	AB	R	H	2B	3B	HR	RBI	SB
Freese, David, South Alabama	.414	239	73	99	21	1	12	73	6
King, Tom, Troy	.411	285	75	117	35	1	8	35	3
Epping, Michael, New Orleans	.400	205	56	82	12	1	8	58	42
Doss, David, South Alabama	.400	175	39	70	19	1	7	39	4
Beachum, Jeff, Middle Tennessee	.395	248	62	98	18	1	3	39	10
McKenry, Michael, Mid. Tennessee	.390	210	42	82	13	4	13	68	2
Felix, Mike, Troy	.381	168	36	64	14	1	5	31	3
Martin, Todd, Middle Tennessee	.377	199	44	75	13	1	15	60	2
Yates, Josh, Arkansas State	.376	194	38	73	23	2	13	62	6
Dunn, Chris, Florida International	.376	210	53	79	6	2	2	36	29

INDIVIDUAL PITCHING LEADERS
(Minimum 50 Innings)

	W	L	ERA	G	SV	IP	H	BB	SO
Farquhar, Danny, La.-Lafayette	6	1	2.17	20	4	62	56	20	55
Glass, Buddy, Louisiana-Lafayette	8	3	2.17	14	0	108	84	20	83
Moody, Hunter, La.-Lafayette	12	2	2.63	15	0	113	101	26	86
Cryer, Bryan, New Orleans	7	1	2.72	17	0	109	104	21	108
Fernandez, Jason, La.-Lafayette	9	2	2.86	16	0	91	77	37	101
Walters, P.J., South Alabama	11	3	3.2	19	0	152	159	33	166
Felix, Mike, Troy	9	4	3.45	28	4	102	85	49	134
Turner, Dustin, Ark.-Little Rock	4	5	3.83	20	3	56	53	28	39
Christianson, Chase, South Alabama	6	5	3.88	32	6	60	72	12	59
Scott, Matt, Middle Tennesee	7	4	3.88	16	0	93	101	16	58

WEST COAST CONFERENCE

	Conference		Overall	
	W	L	W	L
Pepperdine	15	6	42	21
*San Francisco	15	6	39	23
San Diego	13	8	33	25
Loyola Marymount	11	10	24	32
Gonzaga	9	12	29	24
Santa Clara	9	12	28	26
Saint Mary's College	9	12	26	25
Portland	3	18	15	37

ALL-CONFERENCE TEAM: C—Kris Watts, Santa Clara. **1B**—Nick Kliebert, Pepperdine. **2B**—Kenoi Ruth, San Diego; David Uribes, Pepperdine. **SS**—Steve Singleton, San Diego. **3B**—Chase d'Arnaud, Pepperdine. **UTIL**—Scott Cousins, San Francisco. **OF**—Stefan Gartrell, San Francisco; Erik Johnson, Loyola Marymount; Daniel Nava, Santa Clara. **P**—Barry Enright, Pepperdine; Patrick McGuigan, San Francisco; Aaron Poreda , San Francisco. **RP**—Brett Hunter , Pepperdine.

Player of the Year: Scott Cousins, San Francisco. **Pitcher of the Year:** Barry Enright, Pepperdine; Patrick McGuigan, San Francisco. **Freshman of the Year:** Josh Romanski, San Diego. **Coach of the Year:** Nino Giarratano, San Francisco.

INDIVIDUAL BATTING LEADERS
(Minimum 125 At-Bats)

	AVG	AB	R	H	2B	3B	HR	RBI	SB
Nava, Daniel, Santa Clara	.395	200	47	79	10	4	3	37	15
Campbell, Scott, Gonzaga	.389	211	48	82	9	0	4	24	6
Uribes, David, Pepperdine	.374	227	53	58	12	1	1	25	22
Singleton, Steve, San Diego	.363	245	40	89	17	2	5	41	.4
Ruth, Keoni, San Diego	.358	229	51	82	12	1	2	34	17
Frederick, Orben, St. Mary's	.357	210	34	75	12	0	0	39	6
Carter, Sam, St. Mary's College	.356	191	49	68	15	0	11	51	6
Johnson, Erik, Loyola Marymount	.351	202	35	71	16	0	4	45	6
Cousins, Scott, San Francisco	.343	236	53	81	12	2	7	46	21
Kliebert, Nick, Pepperdine	.340	191	31	65	11	0	0	38	4
Ortin, Adrian, Pepperdine	.340	194	32	66	3	1	1	28	10
Holcomb, Darin, Gonzaga	.338	228	48	77	14	0	7	57	0
Railey, Joey, San Francisco	.338	240	46	81	12	2	2	31	14
Watts, Kris, Santa Clara	.336	211	40	71	18	0	9	54	4
Long, Matt, Santa Clara	.336	211	30	71	9	3	0	23	7
Gartrell, Stefan, San Francisco	.335	233	49	78	15	2	6	62	8

	AVG	AB	R	H	2B	3B	HR	RBI	SB
Farris, Eric, Loyola Marymount	.332	220	36	73	9	1	1	28	18
Peters, Matthew, Portland	.332	187	31	62	12	1	9	46	1
Wiegand, Ryan, Gonzaga	.330	191	29	63	15	0	1	45	2
Gallagher, Delaney, St. Mary's	.326	184	38	60	11	1	3	36	2
Carlson, Bobby, Gonzaga	.323	201	37	65	13	0	8	39	3
Smith, Andrew, San Francisco	.322	143	28	46	0	1	1	14	12
Tracy, Chad, Pepperdine	.315	254	39	80	20	4	6	46	11
Wilson, Brian, Loyola Marymount	.315	162	21	51	7	0	1	22	1
Abruzzo, Jordan, San Diego	.314	239	36	75	18	0	8	58	5
Brennan, Jackson, Gonzaga	.314	204	54	64	19	4	11	39	6

INDIVIDUAL PITCHING LEADERS
(Minimum 50 Innings)

	W	L	ERA	G	SV	IP	H	BB	SO
Poreda, Aaron, San Francisco	8	5	2.49	18	0	112	116	28	75
Coleman, Paul, Pepperdine	8	5	2.59	17	0	115	89	37	97
Hunter, Brett, Pepperdine	5	3	2.83	29	11	60	52	16	53
Lewis, Dan, St. Mary's College	5	3	2.91	24	4	68	57	27	56
Butler, Josh, San Diego	8	5	3.15	19	1	109	112	34	99
Donovan, Patrick, Gonzaga	8	4	3.22	16	0	106	100	40	50
Meyers, Brad, Loyola Marymount	8	4	3.23	17	0	111	117	30	62
Johnson, James, Pepperdine	6	2	3.24	19	1	89	90	14	54
Harmon, Brandon, Gonzaga	2	2	3.25	26	3	55	57	11	35
McGuigam, Patrick, San Francisco	12	3	3.28	25	5	115	119	21	73
Madden, Corey, St. Mary's College	6	2	3.30	13	0	85	79	32	76
Dominques, Jason, Pepperdine	6	1	3.52	24	2	54	59	23	33
Wickswat, Matt, Santa Clara	9	2	3.54	14	0	84	82	22	66
Couch, Matt, San Diego	7	5	4.00	21	3	108	107	23	71
Cousins, Scott, San Francisco	4	3	4.02	14	0	87	92	21	61
Lombard, Jeff, Santa Clara	2	1	4.02	29	1	54	62	18	46
Enright, Barry, Pepperdine	13	2	4.05	21	0	124	145	22	68
Dirkx, Austin, Portland	1	5	4.19	26	7	69	64	27	61
Anderson, Brian, San Francisco	6	0	4.21	21	2	51	45	23	30
Matusz, Brian, San Diego	4	3	4.25	15	1	89	85	39	93
Macias, Daniel, Loyola Marymount	5	8	4.35	18	0	93	102	31	36

WESTERN ATHLETIC CONFERENCE

	Conference		Overall	
	W	L	W	L
*Fresno State	18	6	45	18
Hawaii	17	6	45	17
San Jose State	12	12	33	26
Nevada	11	12	26	28
Louisiana Tech	11	13	33	25
Sacramento State	8	16	20	37
New Mexico State	6	18	19	36

ALL-CONFERENCE TEAM: C—Buddy Morales, Sacramento State. **1B**—Luis Avila, Hawaii. **2B**—Erik Wetzel, Fresno State. **SS**—Christian Vitters, Fresno State. **3B**—Beau Mills, Fresno State. **DH**—Steve Susdorf, Fresno State. **UTIL**—Brandon Hudson, Louisiana Tech. **OF**—Shawn Scobee, Nevada; Jericho Jones, Louisiana Tech; Robbie Wilder, Hawaii; Loren Storey, Fresno State. **SP**—Steven Wright, Hawaii; Doug Fister, Fresno State; Andy Underwood, Fresno State. **RP**—Tyler Davis, Hawaii.

Player of the Year: Christian Vitters, Fresno State. **Pitcher of the Year:** Steven Wright, Hawaii. **Freshman of the Year:** Jericho Jones, Louisiana Tech. **Coach of the Year:** Mike Trapsasso, Hawaii.

INDIVIDUAL BATTING LEADERS
(Minimum 125 At-Bats)

	AVG	AB	R	H	2B	3B	HR	RBI	SB
Hopkins, Luke, New Mexico State	.403	149	46	60	11	0	16	65	0
Bowman, Matt, Nevada	.376	218	48	82	17	1	8	40	11
Scobee, Shawn, Nevada	.371	170	53	63	15	0	22	53	3
Frash, Justin, Hawaii	.359	217	49	78	13	2	3	56	2
Jones, Jericho, Louisiana Tech	.357	185	45	66	10	0	16	56	3
Mills, Beau, Fresno State	.355	200	42	71	20	1	14	58	3
Hamilton, Ryan, Louisiana Tech	.351	228	47	80	16	0	7	45	2
Lapin, Brian, Fresno State	.349	172	34	60	10	1	3	42	4
Inouye, Matt, Hawaii	.347	193	32	67	17	2	2	40	15
Hudson, Brandon, Louisiana Tech	.347	170	24	59	7	1	5	33	3
Morales, Buddy, Sacramento State	.344	189	38	65	14	0	4	23	0
Ramon, Amos, Louisiana Tech	.342	196	45	67	13	0	7	35	8
Vitters, Christian, Fresno State	.340	212	51	72	13	0	11	58	10
Harvey, Adam, New Mexico State	.333	207	33	69	17	0	12	54	2
Sakamoto, Kent, Fresno State	.332	253	55	84	18	1	6	46	9
Wilder, Robbie, Hawaii	.332	208	62	69	9	1	2	20	15
Flores, David, Sacramento State	.331	163	29	54	16	0	3	28	3
Susdorf, Steve, Fresno State	.329	225	63	74	15	1	14	49	4
Aquirre, Abe, New Mexico State	.329	216	42	71	19	1	4	29	1
Wetzel, Erik, Fresno State	.325	203	48	66	11	2	1	27	10
Rike, Brian, Louisiana Tech	.322	171	36	55	8	2	8	34	7
Lance, Brandon, New Mexico State	.319	210	32	67	11	0	6	42	0
Angel, Ryan, San Jose State	.318	233	43	74	20	1	5	36	16
Johnson, Gary, Sacramento State	.312	221	32	69	12	1	2	18	8

	AVG	AB	R	H	2B	3B	HR	RBI	SB
Cobb, Adam, Louisiana Tech	.312	218	49	68	12	2	2	22	3
McCarthy, Joey, Louisiana Tech	.311	151	30	47	7	2	2	21	3
Dupree, Derek, Hawaii	.311	180	29	56	6	2	1	27	5
Storey, Loren, Fresno State	.306	186	38	57	5	1	2	18	21
Moresi, Nick, Fresno State	.303	175	36	53	4	0	4	27	4
Strombach, Jim, Sacramento State	.302	162	21	49	13	3	1	22	13
Christensen, Eli, Hawaii	.301	173	29	52	9	1	2	34	3

INDIVIDUAL PITCHING LEADERS
(Minimum 50 Innings)

	W	L	ERA	G	SV	IP	H	BB	SO
Wright, Steven, Hawaii	11	2	2.30	16	1	110	80	19	123
Alsup, Andrew, Louisiana Tech	5	1	3.05	23	4	62	59	19	39
Joyce, Mick, Sacramento State	5	1	3.09	10	0	64	54	28	34
Dewing, Branden, San Jose State	7	6	3.15	19	1	114	114	31	72
Underwood, Andy, Fresno State	12	3	3.40	20	1	132	131	37	110
Romero, Eddie, Fresno State	13	2	3.72	21	0	126	136	46	89
Burke, Brandon, Fresno State	4	5	3.88	24	6	67	71	18	54
Harrington, Ian, Hawaii	9	3	3.99	17	0	104	114	12	54
Fister, Doug, Fresno State	8	6	4.02	20	0	116	118	47	108
Schoeninger, Tim, Nevada	5	6	4.14	18	0	104	117	21	83
Amberson, Josh, San Jose State	6	4	4.22	16	0	75	71	28	74
Burnett, Luke, Louisiana Tech	4	6	4.23	15	1	72	60	39	73
Costi, Justin, Hawaii	8	2	4.41	15	0	82	79	23	69
Lacy, Matt, Louisiana Tech	5	2	4.68	14	0	85	110	21	62
Rodriguez, Ryan, Nevada	7	7	4.87	17	0	92	129	28	67
Moneypenny, Loren, San Jose State	4	6	5.29	17	0	99	105	26	80

INDEPENDENTS

	Conference		Overall	
	W	L	W	L
Dallas Baptist	7	1	33	23
Texas-Pan American	6	2	24	29
UC Davis	2	1	18	34
Northern Colorado	7	4	21	30
New York Tech	4	3	31	22
Utah Valley State	5	4	19	37
South Dakota State	7	8	23	29
North Dakota State	6	7	12	41
Indiana-Purdue-Fort Wayne	1	3	21	28
Savannah State	0	0	30	19
Longwood	0	0	23	27
Texas A&M-Corpus Christi	0	9	20	31
Hawaii-Hilo	0	3	15	34

ALL-INDEPENDENT TEAM: C—John Keene, Savannah State. **IF**—Dan Bulow, Utah Valley State; Tyson Fisher, South Dakota State; Brennan Garr, Northern Colorado; Cody Montgomery, Dallas Baptist. **DH**—Zach Harris, Northern Colorado; Joe Esposito, New York Tech. **OF**—Nick Connor, Utah Valley State; Drew Holder, Dallas Baptist; Austin Krum, Dallas Baptist; Tyler LaTorre, UC Davis; Jared Sullivan, North Dakota State. **P**—Marcus Cortes, Savannah State; Brian McCullough, Longwood; Chris Perez, New York Tech; Michael Potter, UC Davis. **RP**—Tim Haines, Texas-Pan American.

Player of the Year: Drew Holder, Dallas Baptist. **Pitcher of the Year:** Chris Perez, New York Tech. **Newcomer of the Year:** Seth Tartler, Northern Colorado. **Coach of the Year:** Eric Newman, Dallas Baptist.

INDIVIDUAL BATTING LEADERS
(Minimum 125 At-Bats)

	AVG	AB	R	H	2B	3B	HR	RBI	SB
Connor, Nick, Utah Valley State	.434	159	31	69	16	1	1	31	7
Krum, Austin, Dallas Baptist	.368	242	67	89	16	1	9	30	19
Benson, Chris, Utah Valley State	.367	188	31	69	13	4	1	36	4
Holder, Drew, Dallas Baptist	.364	220	73	80	20	3	20	75	7
Fisher, Tyson, South Dakota State	.363	190	50	69	13	4	9	48	6
LaTorre, Tyler, UC Davis	.363	182	37	66	8	0	3	32	6
MacMillan, Mike, NY Tech	.361	208	39	75	10	2	2	44	9
Binick, Kraig, NY Tech	.354	164	42	58	9	2	2	24	25
Alamia, Louie, Texas-Pan American	.352	193	32	68	11	3	2	25	5
Sullivan, Jared, North Dakota State	.351	174	32	61	21	0	7	41	4

INDIVIDUAL PITCHING LEADERS
(Minimum 50 Innings)

	W	L	ERA	G	SV	IP	H	BB	SO
Potter, Michael, UC Davis	5	3	2.77	12	0	75	70	18	59
McCullough, Brian, Longwood	7	3	3.11	18	1	110	107	21	97
Chris Perez, NY Tech	10	2	3.21	14	0	81	64	39	90
Moore, Alan, Longwood	6	5	3.25	21	2	55	59	22	35
Farrell, John, Longwood	3	3	3.51	14	0	51	61	15	28
Esposito, Joe, NY Tech	5	4	3.51	14	0	82	56	48	71
Uebelhor, Cole, IUPU-Fort Wayne	3	4	3.93	16	0	66	79	18	32
Norman, Will, Texas A&M-CC	4	6	4.22	16	0	81	85	27	70
Cortes, Marcus, Savannah State	9	5	4.63	17	0	101	111	47	68
Allen, Roy, Northern Colorado	3	3	4.64	12	0	52	65	9	49

NCAA Division II

Tampa was down often in the 2006 NCAA Division II Championship Tournament, but it was never out. For the third time in four tournament games, the Spartans rallied in their last at-bat, beating Chico State 3-2 in the final game in Montgomery, Ala.

Top-seeded Tampa advanced its record to 54-6 en route to winning the school's fourth championship. The game ended a wild run for No. 5 Chico State, who had entered 2006 without a tournament win since losing in the 2002 championship.

Down 2-1 in the ninth inning, Tampa started a two-out rally against Chico State reliever Billy Spottiswood, hitting three straight singles to tie the game. After a single and a walk in the tenth inning, Tampa's Chris Rosenbaum, making his first appearance of the tournament, hit the go-ahead RBI single.

Not surprisingly, it was tournament MVP Lee Cruz that scored the game's final run, capping off a record-setting season for the outfielder. Chosen in the 10th round by the White Sox, Cruz had surpassed Tampa records for hits, RBIs, and home runs in a season. Tino Martinez had previously held the home run record.

In his first relief appearance of the season, Tampa righthander Sergio Perez allowed just a double before securing the Spartans' win. The second-round draft choice by the Astros was the starter in the semifinal game, notching the win against Franklin Pierce. He came in relief of Aaron Cook, who won his third game of the tournament.

Tampa had survived numerous scares during the week, including in the first round, when Cruz hit a two-out home run to win the game against Francis Marion, 4-3. Montevallo swore not to make the same mistake in the second round, intentionally walking Cruz, which opened the door for a game-winning RBI single by freshman Jose Jimenez.

Chico State faced similar drama in its tournament run, using its own RBI single to overcome Division II Pitcher of the Year Gabriel Medina of Emporia State 2-1 in the first round.

While Chico State did not have a player drafted in 2006, the Spartans had five, including Perez, Cruz, and Cook (35th round, Angels) as well as Orlando Rosales (19th round, Astros) and Nick Peterson (12th round, Yankees).

WORLD SERIES
Site: Montgomery, Ala.
Participants: Tampa (54-6), Francis Marion, S.C. (41-18), Montevallo, Ala. (43-18), West Chester, Penn. (39-20), Ashland, Ohio (48-17), Franklin Pierce, N.H. (46-13), Chico State, Calif. (46-21), Emporia State, Kan. (48-13).
Champion: Tampa
Runner-Up: Chico State
Outstanding Player: Lee Cruz, Tampa

FIRST ROUND
Tampa 4, Francis Marion 3
Montevallo 3, West Chester 2
Ashland 14, Franklin Pierce 4
Chico State 2, Emporia State 1

SECOND ROUND
West Chester 3, Francis Marion 2 (Francis Marion eliminated)
Tampa 5, Montevallo 4
Franklin Pierce 4, Emporia State 0 (Emporia State eliminated)
Chico State 8, Ashland 4

THIRD ROUND
Franklin Pierce 7, Ashland 2 (Ashland eliminated)
Montevallo 10, West Chester 3 (West Chester eliminated)

SEMIFINALS
Chico State 9, Montevallo 5 (Montevallo eliminated)
Tampa 13, Franklin Pierce 3 (Franklin Pierce eliminated)

CHAMPIONSHIP
Tampa 3, Chico State 2

NCAA Division III

Twenty years removed from its previous championship, Marietta College restored glory to its program with an undefeated run through the NCAA Division III tournament, capped off by a 7-2 victory over Wheaton College.

Junior righthander Mike Eisenberg, an eighth-round pick by the Indians, struck out 12 batters to lead the Pioneer charge. The win was yet another in Eisenberg's storied career, which included winning the national Pitcher of the Year honors for Division III.

Eisenberg went 2-0 in the tournament, allowing just two earned runs over 16 innings, beating the Wisconsin-Stevens Point to open the tournament. His 23 strikeouts were a tournament high, as the 6-7 hurler shared co-Most Outstanding Player honors with teammate Justin Steranka.

"Nobody's more important than anybody else in our program, but he's our No. 1 pitcher," Marietta coach Brian Brewer said. "He's performed like it all year and he performed like it today. He's just a super kid and a great competitor."

Steranka shared the Outstanding Player award thanks to two home runs in the final game, raising his tournament average to .500. The home runs provided enough offense for the Pioneers to win their first championship since 1986, and their fourth overall. The school joined Eastern Connecticut State as the only D-III programs with as many championships.

Wheaton College had an admirable run in the tournament, reaching the finals in the program's ninth year of existence. The team's first appearance in the championship game ended a dominant season for the Lyons, during which they lost just 10 games.

Chris McDonough took the loss for Wheaton, but still was one of two Lyons on the all-tournament team, thanks to an earlier win against North Carolina Wesleyan. Pitcher Louie Bernardini, whose win against Wisconsin-Stevens Point had secured a place in the finals, joined McDonough on the team.

WORLD SERIES
Site: Appleton, Wes.
Participants: Aurora, Ill. (34-12), Chapman, Calif. (31-11), Eastern Connecticut State (35-18), Marietta, Ohio (39-11), Montclair State, N.J. (33-17-2), North Carolina Wesleyan (31-17), Wisconsin-Stevens Point (34-16), Wheaton, Mass. (38-8).
Champion: Marietta
Runner-Up: Wheaton
Co-Outstanding Players: Mike Eisenberg and Justin Steranka, Marietta

FIRST ROUND
Chapman 6, E. Connecticut State 3
Wheaton 2, North Carolina Wesleyan 0
Montclair State 7, Aurora 2
Marietta 2, Wisconsin-Stevens Point 1

SECOND ROUND
E. Connecticut State 9, North Carolina Wesleyan 8 (N.C. Wesleyan eliminated)
Wisconsin-Stevens Point 12, Aurora 3 (Aurora eliminated)
Chapman 3, Wheaton 0
Marietta 7, Montclair State (4)

THIRD ROUND
Wheaton 5, Wisconsin-Stevens Point 4 (Wisconsin-Stevens Point eliminated)
Montclair State 5, E. Connecticut State 4 (E. Connecticut State eliminated)

FOURTH ROUND
Marietta 10, Chapman 4
Wheaton 13, Montclair State 4 (Montclair State eliminated)

SEMIFINAL
Wheaton 4, Chapman 3 (Chapman eliminated)

CHAMPIONSHIP
Marietta 7, Wheaton 2

COLLEGE BASEBALL

NAIA

There was no more fitting victor in the NAIA's 50th annual postseason tournament than Lewis-Clark (Idaho) State College, whose dramatic 5-4 win against Cumberland (Tenn.) was the school's record-setting 14th championship.

The Warriors survived a first-round loss to take the title, winning five consecutive games, including head coach Ed Cheff's 1500th. The win over Cumberland came in the 11th inning, when Lewis-Clark's Jose Castenon drew a bases-loaded walk to win. The inning was led off by a hit batsman, the ninth of the game.

Lewis-Clark State had been ranked atop the NAIA for the entire season, but was shocked in the opening round by Lubbock Christian. The team reached the championship with a win against the University of British Columbia, led by Chris Kissock's 169-pitch gem, only one day after the sophomore had closed out a victory against Embry-Riddle (Fla.).

WORLD SERIES

Site: Lewiston, Idaho
Participants: Concordia, Calif. (33-15-1), Seton Hill, Pa. (45-18), Cumberland, Tenn. (47-16), Auburn Montgomery, Ala. (47-18), Lubbock Christian, Tex. (47-15), Lewis-Clark State, Idaho (42-7), Bellevue, Neb. (40-17), Saint Xavier, Ill. (33-25), Embry-Riddle, Fla. (49-13), British Columbia (48-11).
Champion: Lewis-Clark State
Runner-Up: Cumberland
Outstanding Player: Allen Balmer, Lewis-Clark State

FIRST ROUND
Concordia 5, Seton Hill 4
Cumberland 7, Auburn Montgomery 1
Lubbock Christian 4, Lewis-Clark State 3
Bellevue 6, Saint Xavier 3

SECOND ROUND
Auburn Montgomery 14, Seton Hill 9 (Seton Hill eliminated)
Lewis-Clark State 9, Saint Xavier 3 (Saint Xavier eliminated)
Embry-Riddle 7, Concordia 4
British Columbia 13, Bellevue 11

THIRD ROUND
Auburn Montgomery 7, Bellevue 6 (Bellevue eliminated)
Lewis-Clark State 17, Concordia 2 (Concordia eliminated)
Cumberland 7, Embry-Riddle 2
British Columbia 23, Lubbock Christian 5

FOURTH ROUND
Lubbock Christian 7, Auburn Montgomery 6 (Auburn Montgomery eliminated)
Lewis-Clark State 11, Embry-Riddle 10 (Embry-Riddle eliminated)
Cumberland 10, British Columbia 6

FIFTH ROUND
Lewis-Clark State 4, British Columbia 1 (British Columbia eliminated)
Lubbock Christian 6, Cumberland 5

SEMIFINAL
Cumberland 12, Lubbock Christian 1 (Lubbock Christian eliminated)

CHAMPIONSHIP
Lewis-Clark State 5, Cumberland 4.

Junior College

With six players under the control of major league teams, many considered Yavapai (Ariz.) JC the heavy favorite in the NJCAA Division I World Series. However, with a 7-6 win in the final game, Walters State (Tenn.) CC won the title, shocking the Roughriders en route to its 61st win of the season.

The Senators broke open a 5-5 tie in the eighth inning behind a Justin Pickett home run and Nick Belcher's RBI sacrifice bunt. Yavapai answered with one in the eighth, but could not tie the game against Walters State's Zane Stone,

who picked up his second win of the tournament.

Yavapai had been shocked in the first round of the tournament by Wallace State (Ala.) CC, but rebounded with four emphatic wins, including a 9-0 win against Walters State. However, the team could not make it two in a row, as Yavapai could not find enough offense to pull out the victory.

Site: Grand Junction, Colo.
Participants: San Jacinto-North, Texas. (36-23-1), Temple, Texas. (44-16), Walters State, Tenn. (56-7), Connors State, Okla. (36-20), South Suburban, Ill. (50-11), Potomac State, W.V. (40-12), Broward, Fla. (37-14), Butler, Kan. (37-17), Yavapai, Ariz. (47-9), Wallace State, Ala. (35-17)
Champion: Walters State
Runner-Up: Parkland
Outstanding Player: Jack Tilghman, Walters State

DIVISION II

Louisiana State-Eunice won its first NJCAA Division II title with a 3-0 win against powerhouse Grand Rapids (Mich.) CC, who had captured the previous three championships. LSU-Eunice was led by pitcher Brett Durand, who threw a complete-game, two-hit shutout to earn the victory. Grand Rapids had not been shut out in its previous 33 tournament games, dating back to 1993.

Site: Millington, Tenn.
Participants: Elgin, Ill. (46-14), Mesa, Ariz. (46-16), Lousiana State-Eunice (47-10), St. Louis-Forest Park, Mo. (35-18), Grand Rapids, Mich. (37-19), Iowa Central (43-16), Brookdale, N.J. (40-8), Alleghany, Penn. (47-9).
Champion: LSU-Eunice
Runner-Up: Grand Rapids
Outstanding Player: Brett Durand, LSU-Eunice

DIVISION III WORLD SERIES

Tournament MVP Ronny Hawley's first-inning home run was all the offense that Eastfield JC needed in winning the NJCAA Division III championship, a 4-2 win against Gloucester CC in Glens Falls, N.Y.

Site: Glens Falls, N.Y.
Participants: Herkimer, N.Y. (34-7-2), Joliet, Ill. (44-21), Eastfield, Tex. (38-16), Montgomery, Mary. (36-21), Ridgewater, Minn. (30-8), Suffolk, N.Y. (30-8), Gloucester, N.J. (34-7), Northern Essex, Mass.
Champion: Eastfield
Runner-Up: Gloucester
Outstanding Player: Ronny Hawley, Eastfield College

CALIFORNIA COMMUNITY COLLEGE CHAMPIONSHIP

On the heels of the 30th anniversary of its last championship, Long Beach City again won the California Community College title in an 8-1 blowout against Sacramento City. The victory prevented a remarkable Sac City comeback story; the Panthers started the season 8-14 and entered the Regional Playoffs as the #11 seed.

In the end, the Vikings were just too tough, as the championship was the club's 41st win—a school record. After losing to Sacramento City in the first finals game, the bats came alive for Long Beach in the winner-take-all finale, led by tournament MVP Jovanny Bramasco. The shortstop started the scoring with a solo home run in the second inning, and ended the game with 4 RBIs, giving him 10 for the tournament. The Vikings offense paved the way to their title, scoring 31 runs in 4 tournament games.

Site: Fresno.
Participants: Sierra (35-16), Sacramento City (28-22), Long Beach City (41-9), Cypress (42-12)
Champion: Long Beach City
Runner-Up: Sacramento City
Outstanding Player: Jovanny Bramasco

SUMMER LEAGUES

COMPILED BY AARON FITT

A year ago, 6-foot-6 sophomore lefthander Andrew Miller posted an utterly dominant summer and captured Baseball America's Summer Player of the Year award, then went on to win BA's College Player of the Year award the following spring while leading his team to the College World Series.

David Price can certainly entertain thoughts of following in Miller's footsteps, and he's well on his way. Price, a 6-6 lefty from Vanderbilt, was nearly untouchable for Team USA this year, going 5-1, 0.20 with 61 strikeouts and seven walks in 44 innings to win BA's Summer Player of the Year award for 2006.

"He's very deserving," said Team USA coach Tim Corbin, who also coaches Price at Vanderbilt. "He was very consistent—our No. 1 pitcher at the beginning of the summer, and our No. 1 pitcher at the end. I think David was a leader, kind of a go-to guy. He had done this before, and he felt comfortable in this situation."

Price found himself on the national team last summer after going 2-4, 2.86 with 90 strikeouts in 69 innings for the Commodores as a freshman. He led Team USA starters with 39 strikeouts and a 1.26 ERA in 29 innings, further fueling expectations for his sophomore season.

And for a while, Price lived up to those expectations. After his masterful 17-strikeout performance against Arkansas on April 7, Price was sitting pretty at 5-2, 1.81 with a 97-17 K-BB ratio in 60 innings.

Then, all of a sudden, the meat of the Southeastern Conference schedule hit him hard. He allowed five earned runs against Georgia. Then Alabama roughed him up for eight earned. Kentucky put up four earned against him, and Tennessee posted another eight-spot. Price was reeling, so Vanderbilt moved him out of his Friday starter role. He rebounded with three solid starts down the stretch before giving up seven more earned runs in his final start of the year, an NCAA regionals loss to Georgia Tech. Price finished 9-5, 4.16 with 155 strikeouts and 43 walks in 110 innings.

"I just felt like every game I got into sped up on me so much, I couldn't slow it back down," Price said. "The game would just get real quick, you don't take time between pitches, you just don't think. You just keep going through the motions, even though they're the wrong motions, and you don't make any adjustments."

Price sat down with Vandy pitching coach Derek Johnson after the spring was over and broke down his season. Price said he realized his mechanics would get out of whack when the game sped up on him—his hips would flatten out, taking the sharpness off his slider and velocity off his fastball. But Johnson helped Price put his struggles in perspective and regroup.

"After everything was said and done, I'm glad it happened my sophomore year instead of my freshman year, and I'm glad it happened my sophomore year instead of my junior year," Price said. "Now I know what it feels like to have a game speed up like that."

The summer was a different story, as Price came out and dominated wire to wire. He was able to blow away most batters with his two plus offerings—a mid-90s fastball and a vicious slider—but after facing teams like

Nearly untouchable
David Price was Team USA's ace

Taiwan and Japan a half-dozen or more times, Price needed to show another look. He worked hard with Team USA pitching coach Jim Schlossnagle to refine his changeup, and by the end of the summer it was a go-to pitch for him.

More importantly, Price sustained his success all summer, avoiding the big-inning meltdowns that plagued him in the SEC season this spring.

"He's starting to slow himself down. He realizes that if he has a tough inning it's not the end of the world, he just has to refocus, slow everything down, focus on the things that make him a good pitcher," Corbin said. "This year, if he had a tough outing, he would try to correct right away, work too hard and do too much, and sometimes it would blow up on him. Rarely do things blow up on David. I think the experiences of the spring helped him in summer."

Y-D Wins Cape Title Again

The Yarmouth-Dennis Red Sox won the Cape Cod League championship for the second time in three years with a 5-1 victory against Wareham.

Terry Doyle (Boston College) picked up the win for Yarmouth-Dennis by allowing just one run while striking out nine in six innings. He was perfect through four innings and struck out six of the first 12 batters he faced.

Doyle's replacement, David Robertson (Alabama), was even better, striking out seven in three perfect innings of relief to pick up the save and lock up the title. That performance helped earn Robertson playoff MVP honors.

Y-D capitalized on sloppy defense by the Gatemen to score four unearned runs in the deciding third game of the championship series. The Red Sox, who posted the league's best regular-season record at 28-16, dropped the

COLLEGE BASEBALL

LARRY GOREN

opener before winning the next two. Y-D had also lost the first game of the best-of-three East Division playoff series against Brewster before battling back with consecutive wins to advance to the championships.

Foresters Take NBC Title

Coach Bill Pintard's Santa Barbara Foresters, the class of the California Collegiate summer league, claimed their first championship at the National Baseball Congress World Series in Wichita.

In his 13th season as coach, Pintard finally got to hoist the title trophy, particularly sweet after the Foresters, needing one win, lost twice in the championship. The Foresters beat the Derby (Kan.) Twins 8-7 (after nearly squandering an 8-2 lead) to finish the event undefeated and claim the tournament title.

"I've had so many former players call me over the last few days, telling me I deserved to get this one," Pintard told the Wichita Eagle. "I don't know if I deserved it or not, but I know it's nice to have for all of those guys who didn't get to dogpile here, too. It's for everyone."

McKinney Pitchers Whiff 19 In TCL Finals

Three McKinney Marshals pitchers combined to strike out 19 batters in a 6-0 win against Denton as McKinney captured its first Texas Collegiate League championship.

Allen Harrington (Lamar) captured championship series outstanding player honors by striking out 16, walking two and allowing one hit over 7⅔ shutout innings. Relievers Michael Gunter (Blinn Junior College) and Matt Smith (Wichita State) struck out three more to set a TCL record

TOM PRIDDY

Justin Smoak

for most strikeouts in a game.

McKinney avenged a loss to Denton in last year's championship series with a two-game sweep of the Outlaws this year. The Marshals won the first game of the series 11-1.

That offensive outburst was quite a shift from McKinney's performance in the Tris Speaker Division playoffs, when the Marshals beat Coppell 2-0 despite being no-hit by Randy Boone (Texas) and James Russell (Texas).

Honkers Win Fourth Title

The Rochester Honkers won their Northwoods League-record fourth title—but first since 1999—with a 5-3 win against Thunder Bay, sweeping the best-of-three championship series. The big blow was a three-run homer by catcher Bill Musselman (St. Louis) in the second inning, and a solo shot by outfielder Chris Jones (Cal State Fullerton) in the fourth gave Rochester all the runs it needed.

Rochester closer Jake Toohey (Illinois) rode a strong second half of the spring season all through the summer, breaking the NWL single-season saves record with 24. Toohey was named the Honkers' pitcher of the year, as Rochester broke the NWL single-season wins record with 50, eclipsing the previous mark of 46 held by the 1998 Waterloo Bucks.

COLLEGE
SUMMER LEAGUES

CAPE COD LEAGUE

EAST	W	L	T	PCT	PTS
Yarmouth-Dennis Red Sox	28	16	0	.636	56
Brewster Whitecaps	24	18	2	.545	50
Orleans Cardinals	22	21	1	.512	45
Chatham Athletics	21	22	1	.488	43
Harwich Mariners	20	24	0	.455	40

WEST	W	L	T	PCT	PTS
Cotuit Kettleers	27	16	1	.628	55
Wareham Gatemen	24	19	1	.558	49
Falmouth Commodores	22	21	1	.512	45
Hyannis Mets	16	24	3	.400	35
Bourne Braves	9	32	2	.220	20

PLAYOFFS—Semifinals: Wareham defeated Cotuit 2-0 and Yarmouth-Dennis defeated Brewster 2-1 in best-of-three series. **Finals:** Yarmouth-Dennis defeated Wareham 2-0 in best-of-three series.

TOP 30 PROSPECTS: 1. Justin Smoak, 1b, Cotuit (South Carolina). 2. Andrew Brackman, rhp, Orleans (North Carolina State). 3. Matt Wieters, c, Orleans (Georgia Tech). 4. Joshua Fields, rhp, Yarmouth-Dennis (Georgia). 5. Matt Mangini, 3b, Hyannis (North Carolina State/transferring to Oklahoma State). 6. Brett Cecil, lhp, Orleans (Maryland). 7. Eddie Kunz, rhp, Falmouth (Oregon State). 8. James Simmons, rhp, Cotuit (UC Riverside). 9. Shooter Hunt, rhp, Falmouth (Virginia/transferring to Tulane). 10. Charlie Furbush, lhp, Hyannis (St. Joseph's, Maine/transferring to Louisiana State). 11. Josh Donaldson, 3b/c, Harwich (Auburn). 12. Josh Horton, ss, Harwich (North Carolina). 13. Mitch Canham, c, Falmouth (Oregon State). 14. Tony Watson, lhp, Harwich (Nebraska). 15. Matt LaPorta, 1b, Brewster (Florida). 16. Reese Havens, ss, Cotuit (South Carolina). 17. Dan Merklinger, lhp, Harwich (Seton Hall). 18. Terry Doyle, rhp, Yarmouth-Dennis (Boston College). 19. Jeremy Bleich, lhp, Wareham (Stanford). 20. Nolan Gallagher, rhp, Yarmouth-Dennis (Stanford). 21. Conor Graham, rhp, Wareham (Miami,

Ohio). 22. Brad Suttle, 3b, Wareham (Texas). 23. Buster Posey, ss/rhp, Yarmouth-Dennis (Florida State). 24. Tyler Henley, of, Yarmouth-Dennis (Rice). 25. Warren McFadden, of, Falmouth (Tulane). 26. Brad Emaus, inf, Yarmouth-Dennis (Tulane). 27. Vance Worley, rhp, Chatham (Long Beach State). 28. Paul Koss, rhp, Chatham (Southern California). 29. Cory Gearrin, rhp, Cotuit (Young Harris, Ga., JC/transferring to Mercer). 30. Ryan Flaherty, ss, Hyannis (Vanderbilt).

INDIVIDUAL BATTING LEADERS
(Minimum 119 Plate Appearances)

	AVG	G	AB	R	H	HR	RBI
Mangini, Matt, Hyannis	.310	40	155	11	48	2	16
Wieters, Matt, Orleans	.307	35	127	19	39	8	21
Chalk, Brad, Falmouth	.305	36	151	18	46	0	12
Cusick, Matt, Brewster	.304	39	135	17	41	2	12
Donaldson, Josh, Harwich	.302	39	149	23	45	4	21
Canham, Mitch, Falmouth	.300	28	110	22	33	4	16
Farris, Eric, Cotuit	.298	42	151	17	45	1	18
Angle, Matt, Cotuit	.292	42	137	23	40	1	11
Posey, Buster, Yarmouth-Dennis	.289	44	159	23	46	2	16
Smoak, Justin, Cotuit	.286	39	154	25	44	11	27

INDIVIDUAL PITCHING LEADERS
(Minimum 35 Innings)

	W	L	ERA	IP	H	BB	SO
Seibert, Shaun, Brewster	6	0	0.39	46	26	28	36
Hargrove, Ricky, Chatham	2	1	1.03	44	22	16	35
Simmons, James, Cotuit	4	2	1.18	53	34	5	44
Merklinger, Dan, Harwich	4	1	1.21	45	31	21	47
Atwood, Will, Brewster	2	0	1.29	35	16	14	29
Cribby, Elliott, Chatham	3	2	1.61	45	36	8	25
Farmer, Tom, Bourne	1	3	1.75	46	25	25	36
Furbush, Charlie, Hyannis	3	2	1.83	54	41	13	50

Staehely, Christian, Cotuit 5 1 2.09 52 41 15 28
Bleich, Jeremy, Wareham 1 1 2.09 43 34 15 31

BOURNE

BATTING

	AVG	AB	R	H	2B	3B	HR	RBI	SB
Bartles, Brett	.247	150	9	37	7	1	1	18	6
Cash, David	.280	107	14	30	4	1	0	6	3
Davis, Drew	.107	75	9	8	1	0	0	1	0
DiFazio, Vincent	.083	12	1	1	0	0	0	0	0
Everett, Cat	.177	113	9	20	0	0	0	6	1
Florio, Joe	.050	20	1	1	0	0	0	0	0
Goff, Andy	.176	136	7	24	5	0	0	10	2
Hall, Matt	.153	131	4	20	4	0	1	5	3
Krum, Austin	.234	128	18	30	3	1	1	9	5
Lanto, Hank	.250	4	0	1	0	0	0	0	0
Laplante, Adam	.235	17	1	4	1	0	0	3	0
(2-team/Brewster)	.121	33	2	4	1	0	0	3	0
Leclerc, Brian	.200	85	13	17	3	0	0	5	10
Linnenkohl, Brett	.154	26	1	4	0	1	0	1	1
Mooreland, Mitch	.239	138	17	33	8	0	4	20	2
Murphy, Blake	.000	9	0	0	0	0	0	0	0
Spiers, Joe	.286	7	0	2	0	0	0	0	1
Stewart, Jake	.100	20	0	2	0	0	0	2	0
Vicaro, Andrew	.250	12	1	3	0	0	0	2	0
Weglarz, Matt	.132	38	3	5	1	0	2	3	0
Wehrle, Ryan	.185	27	1	5	2	0	0	3	0
Wright, Ty	.250	104	4	26	4	0	0	10	1

PITCHING

	W	L	ERA	G	SV	IP	H	BB	SO
Bell, Bobby	1	3	3.82	7	1	31	25	17	34
Breedlove, Jeff	1	1	2.95	13	0	18	18	4	12
Carignan, Andrew	0	3	2.45	12	3	18	16	10	19
Curran, Tom	0	0	8.31	3	0	4	6	1	3
Farmer, Tom	1	3	1.75	8	0	46	25	25	36
Gardner, Matt	2	5	3.06	9	0	50	47	14	32
Holder, Trevor	0	1	2.38	11	0	23	19	11	26
Hunter, Ben	0	1	7.15	11	0	11	12	4	10
Lee, Michael	1	1	6.52	5	0	10	6	7	5
Mooreland, Mitch	0	1	3.00	7	1	9	7	4	10
Perinar, Gary	0	0	9.00	3	0	6	11	4	5
Portice, Eammon	0	5	6.30	7	0	30	34	9	45
Recchia, Nick	0	0	0.00	1	0	3	2	0	0
Salberg, Chris	0	1	3.25	14	0	28	30	10	29
Storey, Mickey	2	3	3.64	11	0	47	44	15	48
Tucker, Luke	0	1	3.68	6	1	7	2	6	8
Walker, Kyle	1	3	6.16	9	0	38	41	29	35
Wright, Ty	0	0	0.00	1	0	2	2	0	1

BREWSTER

BATTING

	AVG	AB	R	H	2B	3B	HR	RBI	SB
Adams, David	.214	117	10	25	2	0	0	13	4
Babineau, Ryan	.197	71	8	14	3	0	1	9	0
Clark, Jared	.197	61	7	12	1	0	3	7	2
Cooper, David	.304	69	8	21	3	0	1	10	0
Corder, Jason	.171	41	4	7	1	0	1	6	0
Cowgill, Colin	.244	135	18	33	7	1	2	13	1
Cusick, Matt	.304	135	17	41	6	0	2	12	3
Fisher, Michael	.230	100	11	23	3	2	1	14	4
Hall, Tavo	.181	83	10	15	1	0	0	11	3
Kline, Trent	.175	63	8	11	0	1	0	3	0
Laplante, Adam	.000	16	1	0	0	0	0	0	0
LaPorta, Matthew	.250	108	17	27	5	0	6	19	0
Romine, Andrew	.244	119	19	29	5	0	0	12	9
Sedbrook, Colt	.182	121	17	22	3	0	1	10	9
Snyder, Justin	.247	158	20	39	7	1	2	14	4
Yagjian, Jake	.200	10	0	2	1	0	0	2	0

PITCHING

	W	L	ERA	G	SV	IP	H	BB	SO
Atwood, Will	2	0	1.29	16	1	35	16	14	29
Bravo, Jonny	1	0	1.35	2	0	7	8	5	7
Clark, Jared	0	0	0.00	1	0	1	1	0	0
Conway, Nick	0	0	1.50	2	0	6	4	5	1
Cooper, David	1	0	0.00	1	0	2	1	1	3
Crabtree, Adam	0	0	0.00	3	0	3	1	1	2
Crowell, Cody	2	2	3.14	8	0	49	39	19	46
Davis, Erick	0	0	5.79	2	0	5	2	2	4
DeVries, Cole	3	2	3.31	8	0	49	50	5	50
Enright, Barry	3	3	3.82	7	1	33	45	5	23
Hynes, Colt	0	2	7.01	15	3	35	60	12	21
Maine, Scott	3	1	1.80	4	0	25	21	13	19
McDaniel, Adam	1	1	2.00	14	8	18	5	12	17
Morgan, Miles	0	2	7.71	2	0	7	12	4	4
Pannell, J.J.	1	3	3.21	9	0	33	3	6	2
Rulon, Brad	1	3	2.84	14	2	25	19	12	19
Sedbrook, Colt	0	0	5.40	4	1	5	3	2	6

CHATHAM

BATTING

	AVG	AB	R	H	2B	3B	HR	RBI	SB
Brown, Corey	.192	130	13	25	8	1	2	16	13
Carrara, Chris	.264	125	26	33	4	0	0	6	17
Derba, Nick	.119	84	9	10	4	0	2	7	0
Dykstra, Allan	.232	142	22	33	4	0	7	29	0
Easley, Edward	.269	52	5	14	2	0	1	4	0
Espinosa, Danny	.252	163	21	41	7	2	1	15	8
Frazier, Todd	.136	22	3	3	0	0	0	3	2
Fronk, Reid	.284	109	15	31	3	1	0	10	1
Ortiz, Adrian	.224	143	15	32	1	1	1	8	10
Pickens, Doug	.215	130	14	28	7	1	0	13	3
Reza, Aaron	.358	53	4	19	2	0	0	4	3
Rizzotti, Matt	.214	140	18	30	6	1	4	27	0
Tri, Rich	.350	20	5	7	1	0	1	3	1
Williams, David	.100	30	3	3	0	0	0	3	0
Williams, Seth	.178	90	6	16	2	0	1	8	0

PITCHING

	W	L	ERA	G	SV	IP	H	BB	SO
Cribby, Elliott	3	2	1.61	7	0	45	36	8	25
Giannini, Matt	0	1	4.03	11	2	22	20	18	20
Hargrove, Ricky	2	1	1.03	8	0	44	22	16	35
Koss, Paul	0	0	0.00	11	4	14	6	7	17
Lutz, Derrik	0	0	1.23	6	2	7	2	1	9
Moreau, Nathan	1	3	2.53	5	0	32	27	10	22
Niesen, Eric	2	3	4.87	16	1	20	19	11	28
Segal, Justin	1	1	0.84	17	0	21	15	10	13
Sirois, Rich	2	2	3.86	8	0	54	55	13	37
Terletzky, Josh	0	2	2.84	2	0	6	6	2	1
(2-team)	0	0	4.15	6	0	8.2	11	3	6
Wiman, Chris	2	4	4.74	8	0	38	37	12	29
Woodard, Robert	3	3	2.32	6	0	43	29	7	39
Worley, Vance	3	2	3.03	14	2	36	26	11	36

COTUIT

BATTING

	AVG	AB	R	H	2B	3B	HR	RBI	SB
Angle, Matt	.292	137	23	40	5	0	1	11	13
Delmonico, Tony	.303	33	6	10	0	0	0	5	2
Dunbar, Jeff	.368	19	1	7	1	0	0	6	0
Farris, Eric	.298	151	17	45	8	0	1	18	17
Gaston, Sean	.266	139	20	37	5	0	2	17	1
Havens, Reese	.266	124	15	33	4	0	2	16	4
Hula, Josh	.182	22	2	4	0	0	0	3	0
Kulbacki, Kellen	.240	150	24	36	6	0	7	18	4
Lilley, Brett	.182	77	10	14	0	0	0	7	1
Rea, Jeffrey	.242	161	27	39	4	2	0	19	8
Russell, Kyle	.206	126	14	26	8	0	3	18	4
Smoak, Justin	.286	154	25	44	10	0	11	27	0
Thomas, Tony Jr	.224	107	19	24	1	1	1	10	6
Tucker, Wilson	.250	24	1	6	1	0	0	2	0

PITCHING

	W	L	ERA	G	SV	IP	H	BB	SO
Bramhall, Bobby	0	0	3.00	1	0	3	5	1	3
Brown, Jay	3	2	1.47	10	1	31	20	6	24
Cisco, Michael	4	0	2.90	9	0	40	36	8	27
Costello, Matt	0	0	0.00	3	0	4	3	1	2
Delmonico, Tony	0	0	0.00	1	0	1	0	0	0
Delucia, Dan	2	3	3.55	10	0	38	31	13	23
Duncan, Dave	3	2	3.06	7	0	32	27	11	27
Gearrin, Cory	2	1	1.67	18	8	27	15	14	41
Godfrey, Graham	1	1	3.54	6	0	20	24	9	16
Ladd, Tim	1	2	1.20	9	0	15	13	5	6
Lilley, Brett	0	0	4.50	2	0	2	3	1	1
Mathews, Shane	2	1	2.82	13	0	38	34	20	27
Perinar, Gary	0	0	0.00	1	0	1	2	0	1
Runzler, Dan	0	0	2.45	15	2	26	23	17	24
Sattler, Dan	0	1	7.20	1	0	5	9	1	5
Simmons, James	4	2	1.18	8	0	53	34	5	44
Staehely, Christian	5	1	2.09	9	0	52	41	15	28

FALMOUTH

BATTING

	AVG	AB	R	H	2B	3B	HR	RBI	SB
Anetsberger, Ryan	.224	134	11	30	4	0	2	15	1
Barto, Aja	.216	116	18	25	4	0	3	9	4
Canham, Mitch	.300	110	22	33	5	1	4	16	4
Chalk, Brad	.305	151	18	46	5	1	0	12	6
Coogan, Hank	.154	13	0	2	0	0	0	1	0
Diaz, Mike	.217	23	1	5	1	0	0	1	1
Farrell, Jeremy	.180	122	15	22	2	0	4	12	3
Graceffa, Chris	.000	2	0	0	0	0	0	1	0

Seibert, Shaun 6 0 0.39 8 0 46 26 28 36
Stallings, Jeff 0 0 9.00 3 0 5 6 5 6
Turner, Ryan 1 2 3.57 7 0 40 44 11 15

BATTING	AVG	AB	R	H	2B	3B	HR	RBI	SB
Harbin, Taylor	.275	131	14	36	6	1	3	14	5
LaDow, Kelly	.000	1	0	0	0	0	0	0	0
McFadden, Warren	.239	159	29	38	4	2	8	21	3
Nuzzo, Matt	.230	74	9	17	1	0	3	9	1
Ocheltree, Evan	.313	16	1	5	1	0	0	2	1
Sweet, Travis	.176	34	4	6	0	0	1	2	3
Walker, Andrew	.271	140	16	38	12	0	2	19	0
Wallace, Brett	.248	145	19	36	7	0	5	22	1
Widmann, Stan	.286	112	12	32	5	1	0	8	7

PITCHING	W	L	ERA	G	SV	IP	H	BB	SO
Bartleski, Phil	0	1	5.14	2	0	7	6	4	1
Bramhall, Bobby	0	2	3.26	4	0	19	12	10	17
Carroll, Scott	0	0	8.44	2	0	5	8	3	4
Chalk, Brad	0	0	0.00	1	0	1	0	2	1
Copp, Brandon	0	1	2.25	7	0	12	10	14	7
Curran, Tom	0	1	13.50	2	0	1	2	1	1
(2-team/Bourne)	0	1	9.53	5	0	6	8	2	4
Demel, Sam	1	2	1.73	25	12	26	14	12	38
Detwiler, Ross	1	0	1.74	2	0	10	6	3	14
Dobrowiecki, Kris	0	3	7.53	10	0	35	40	15	25
Gomes, Brandon	2	2	3.62	16	0	32	29	14	43
Graceffa, Chris	0	0	27.00	1	0	1	2	4	1
Hunt, Shooter	3	0	3.38	11	0	40	19	30	54
Kopp, David	2	3	2.31	9	1	35	34	9	22
Kunz, Eddie	0	1	1.71	15	0	21	14	11	22
Luebke, Cory	3	2	2.84	7	0	38	29	14	32
Morgan, Sean	3	1	6.11	9	0	18	16	17	16
Paterson, Joe	3	0	2.28	9	0	28	26	8	25
Riordan, Cory	3	1	2.70	9	0	43	36	12	34
Schneider, Craig	0	2	3.86	3	0	12	13	7	4
Sweet, Travis	1	0	1.04	5	0	9	6	7	8

HARWICH

BATTING	AVG	AB	R	H	2B	3B	HR	RBI	SB
Amar, Adam	.261	46	4	12	1	0	1	4	0
Arcadia, Ryan	.000	3	1	0	0	0	0	0	0
D'Alessio, Andrew	.344	61	4	21	3	0	1	10	0
DeJesus, Antone	.234	124	16	29	6	1	0	4	5
Donaldson, Josh	.302	149	23	45	11	0	4	21	4
Flack, Chad	.205	44	3	9	1	0	0	3	3
Fryer, Eric	.253	91	13	23	4	0	2	9	0
Giavotella, Johnny	.153	111	11	17	1	1	2	10	4
Guyer, Brandon	.210	124	11	26	5	1	1	9	6
Horton, Josh	.209	86	8	18	4	1	0	8	8
Menchaca, Brandon	.171	105	7	18	2	1	2	7	12
Miranda, Sergio	.225	160	17	36	6	0	1	14	6
Schaeffer, Warren	.224	49	7	11	1	0	0	3	1
Spencer, Matt	.197	76	11	15	0	1	0	5	6
Swauger, Chris	.195	41	4	8	2	1	0	0	3
Thomas, Devin	.263	118	12	31	6	0	0	11	3

PITCHING	W	L	ERA	G	SV	IP	H	BB	SO
Asjes, Arshwin	0	1	5.40	5	0	15	12	7	18
Brant, Robert	0	4	5.79	11	0	28	28	24	24
Brookens, Joel	2	1	3.62	18	0	27	24	17	27
Cremins, Matt	0	0	6.23	1	0	4	7	2	3
Danford, Matt	2	1	3.16	6	0	26	21	14	24
Dorn, Johnny	1	5	4.70	10	0	46	48	11	21
Ellis, Josh	1	3	1.60	21	2	34	15	21	41
Hessler, Jason	1	1	1.42	5	0	13	12	4	13
Hill, Nick	1	1	2.70	2	0	10	9	2	11
Leonard, John	0	2	4.12	5	0	20	14	7	19
McCloud, Jimmy	1	0	3.86	3	0	7	8	2	5
McDonald, Dan	2	0	1.04	10	3	17	9	5	18
Menchaca, Brandon	0	0	5.40	1	0	2	2	1	3
Merklinger, Dan	4	1	1.21	8	0	45	31	21	47
Oates, Brian	0	0	20.25	2	0	3	2	6	3
Spencer, Matt	0	0	0.00	3	0	3	1	7	4
Sublett, Damon	0	0	0.00	8	5	8	2	1	17
Watson, Tony	5	2	2.44	8	0	48	38	10	46
Zocchi, P.J.	0	2	2.87	7	1	38	36	18	33

HYANNIS

BATTING	AVG	AB	R	H	2B	3B	HR	RBI	SB
Arsenault, Max	.500	4	1	2	0	0	0	0	0
Corona, Ramon	.236	123	14	29	6	1	1	19	4
Darnell, James	.246	126	11	31	9	0	2	15	2
Flaherty, Ryan	.250	132	17	33	6	2	0	18	4
Juhl, Brian	.179	78	7	14	2	0	2	6	0
Leonard, Brandon	.250	4	0	1	0	0	0	1	0
Macias, David	.281	160	21	45	3	0	0	10	4
Mangini, Matt	.310	155	11	48	7	0	2	16	4
McGonigle, Mark	.240	104	15	25	2	0	1	7	0
McGuire, Jared	.269	145	26	39	7	0	2	15	4

BATTING	AVG	AB	R	H	2B	3B	HR	RBI	SB
O'Brien, Sean	.266	143	12	38	7	1	0	10	0
Townsend, Jon	.186	70	5	13	2	0	1	4	3
Williams, Jackson	.245	102	8	25	1	0	0	9	1

PITCHING	W	L	ERA	G	SV	IP	H	BB	SO
Brown, Aaron	0	4	3.42	10	0	47	38	25	37
Collmenter, Josh	1	1	2.42	5	0	26	21	8	26
Daly, Matt	1	0	5.03	12	0	39	42	31	33
Dinga, Milan	1	0	1.35	13	0	20	18	6	16
Furbush, Charlie	3	2	1.83	9	0	54	41	13	50
Hale, Alex	1	3	4.75	10	0	30	30	15	33
Jeffers, Ben	0	2	4.58	18	1	20	17	18	27
Latham, Daniel	2	1	1.50	16	8	18	16	3	16
Lee, Gary	3	3	3.30	17	0	44	46	11	27
Porlier, Steve	2	3	4.91	7	0	26	29	8	35
Reifer, Adam	2	1	3.22	16	0	22	25	8	14
Rucker, Peden	0	1	13.50	1	0	2	2	4	0
Wood, Austin	0	1	5.32	7	0	24	29	13	16

ORLEANS

BATTING	AVG	AB	R	H	2B	3B	HR	RBI	SB
Braun, Steve	.205	39	2	8	2	0	0	5	1
Buschini, Shane	.091	11	2	1	0	0	0	0	0
Davis, Andrew	.200	125	6	25	3	0	0	10	3
Day, Larry	.141	78	5	11	0	0	0	2	2
Dunigan, Joe	.208	130	12	27	3	0	2	13	11
Gillin, Jim	.167	6	1	1	0	0	0	1	0
Hallberg, Mark	.236	165	23	39	7	0	0	8	3
Kaiser, Kody	.243	140	17	34	6	1	3	17	17
Mahoney, Joe	.233	129	20	30	5	0	2	10	3
Pond, Ryan	.220	91	7	20	4	0	0	2	1
Satin, Josh	.255	149	19	38	14	0	0	20	2
Scogin, Kyle	.197	66	8	13	1	0	0	4	2
Sontag, Ryan	.221	136	13	30	4	0	0	11	9
Spiers, John	.000	5	0	0	0	0	0	0	0
Valencia, Danny	.269	26	4	7	0	1	3	9	0
Wieters, Matt	.307	127	19	39	5	0	8	21	0

PITCHING	W	L	ERA	G	SV	IP	H	BB	SO
Baber, Brock	1	0	5.70	17	2	30	32	16	18
Betourne, Cameron	0	0	2.70	5	0	3	1	9	0
Brackman, Andrew	1	0	1.06	6	0	17	7	9	11
Cecil, Brett	1	0	2.17	19	11	29	18	9	40
Coulon, David	0	3	3.38	3	0	16	15	10	11
Davis, Ty	3	2	2.28	8	0	43	32	22	38
Goodman, John	0	1	7.36	7	0	11	12	11	10
Gustafson, Tim	1	0	3.27	6	0	11	8	7	13
Hyde, Trey	3	3	7.03	8	0	32	48	10	17
Martin, Trey	1	0	5.59	6	0	10	15	3	8
Miguelez, Emmanuel	2	2	3.21	6	0	28	16	14	21
Pond, Ryan	2	2	2.11	7	0	43	32	12	23
Scogin, Kyle	0	0	13.50	1	0	1	1	0	0
Shunick, Clayton	4	5	2.21	10	0	57	44	12	36
Sontag, Ryan	0	0	9.00	1	0	1	2	1	1
Surkamp, Eric	3	2	2.37	13	0	38	23	23	38
Villanueva, Elih	0	1	3.95	13	0	27	25	9	33

WAREHAM

BATTING	AVG	AB	R	H	2B	3B	HR	RBI	SB
De la Osa, Dominic	.270	141	17	38	8	2	0	12	8
Anderson, Matt	.000	4	0	0	0	0	0	0	0
Collins, Joel	.247	93	7	23	4	0	1	8	3
Dodson, Jordan	.158	57	8	9	3	0	1	2	4
Fon, Diallo	.180	111	8	20	2	0	1	14	5
Glover, Brandon	.231	121	14	28	4	0	1	10	14
Gotcher, Ryan	.232	151	17	35	7	1	1	15	15
Henry, Seth	.185	108	18	20	4	0	1	10	8
Lara, Robert	.170	47	5	8	1	0	0	3	2
Murton, Luke	.234	128	13	30	7	1	1	11	1
Ogata, Jason	.316	76	16	24	7	0	0	9	7
Parker, Michael	.000	5	2	0	0	0	0	0	0
Sawyer, Marc	.200	10	0	2	1	0	0	3	0
Suttle, Bradley	.226	137	22	31	10	0	5	18	3
Weems, Beamer	.243	107	18	26	9	2	0	16	5
Wilson, Steffan	.241	137	8	33	9	0	0	18	3

PITCHING	W	L	ERA	G	SV	IP	H	BB	SO
Banwart, Travis	3	2	1.06	7	0	34	29	8	31
Barham, Trey	0	2	2.08	3	0	4	2	4	1
Beno, Martin	2	0	0.50	9	2	18	11	7	14
Bleich, Jeremy	1	1	2.09	10	0	43	34	15	31
Boening, Riley	4	3	2.53	10	0	57	47	17	46
Cassavechia, Nick	1	2	1.72	23	3	31	23	10	35
Ely, John	1	3	3.70	11	0	49	47	19	45
Graham, Connor	3	0	3.60	19	5	20	18	14	24
Hamilton, Blake	0	0	3.38	2	0	3	1	3	2

Haviland, Shawn	0	0	2.45	1	0	4	3	5	1
Hicks, Chris	2	1	1.47	7	0	18	13	7	13
Lalor, John	3	1	4.40	9	1	29	33	10	22
Matthews, Tim	3	1	3.56	19	1	48	51	12	46
Putkonen, Luke	1	5	3.29	7	0	38	36	14	28
Schwartz, Steven	0	0	13.50	1	0	1	3	0	0

YARMOUTH-DENNIS

BATTING	AVG	AB	R	H	2B	3B	HR	RBI	SB
Bianucci, Michael	.258	89	19	23	5	0	4	8	2
Carrithers, Alden	.268	112	20	30	4	0	0	9	8
Carroll, Jeff	.133	15	1	2	0	0	0	0	0
Clement, Scott	.211	19	1	4	0	0	1	3	1
Emaus, Brad	.247	150	19	37	7	1	6	28	5
Etheredge, Zach	.129	31	5	4	1	0	0	1	5
Godfrey, Brandon	.267	15	2	4	0	0	0	2	0
Henley, Tyler	.286	105	23	30	5	1	7	19	6
Hollandar, Michael	.200	35	3	7	0	0	0	5	1
Lehmann, Danny	.207	87	11	18	4	0	1	7	3
McArthur, Evan	.258	89	9	23	6	0	2	11	2
Pacheco, Jordan	.190	116	18	22	5	1	1	8	5
Petrie, Chris	.000	2	0	0	0	0	0	0	0
Posey, Buster	.289	159	23	46	8	0	2	16	4
Sommer, Luke	.258	97	12	25	4	0	2	13	1
Strausbaugh, Steven	.225	129	13	29	5	1	4	15	3
Taylor, Michael	.243	115	14	28	7	0	4	19	6
Wallach, Matt	.229	48	6	11	3	0	2	9	0
Wingfield, Patrick	.500	6	1	3	0	0	0	0	0

PITCHING	W	L	ERA	G	SV	IP	H	BB	SO
Bianucci, Michael	0	0	0.00	1	0	1	1	1	0
Boggan, Kevin	2	1	3.82	12	0	35	34	15	35
Boman, Nate	3	2	2.94	8	0	34	22	18	38
Corgan, Chance	1	0	0.00	2	0	14	6	3	19
Crawford, Evan	0	1	6.43	2	0	7	9	2	4
Doyle, Terry	5	1	2.89	8	0	47	23	23	52
Drag, Devin	1	0	4.91	7	0	11	14	6	8
Etheredge, Zach	0	0	18.00	1	0	1	4	0	0
Fields, Joshua	0	1	2.55	16	13	18	10	5	27
Gallagher, Nolan	3	3	4.08	9	0	40	32	15	40
Greinke, Luke	1	2	3.57	8	1	23	21	8	23
Henry, Bryan	4	0	2.41	7	0	37	34	17	22
Hume, Donnie	4	0	2.40	7	0	45	36	20	41
Meyer, Matt	0	0	9.00	2	1	1	2	0	2
Pacheco, Jordan	2	0	1.35	4	0	7	6	5	6
Perkins, Adam	0	1	7.20	1	0	5	7	1	8
Posey, Buster	0	1	3.12	4	0	9	7	7	7
Ratliff, Sean	1	1	4.50	11	0	18	16	7	20
Robertson, David	0	2	2.79	16	5	29	21	20	46
Sommer, Luke	0	0	0.00	3	0	4	3	0	2
Strausbaugh, Steven	0	0	0.00	1	0	1	0	1	0
Turpin, Daniel	1	0	3.86	3	0	5	6	0	6
Van Slyke, Eric	0	0	13.50	2	0	2	4	0	1

ALASKA LEAGUE

	W	L	PCT	GB
Kenai Peninsula Oilers	23	12	.657	—
Anchorage Bucs	20	14	.588	2 ½
Mat-Su Miners	19	15	.559	3 ½
Alaska Goldpanners	15	18	.455	7
Anchorage Glacier Pilots	15	19	.441	7 ½
Athletes In Action	10	24	.294	12 ½

TOP 10 PROSPECTS: 1. Beau Mills, 3b/1b, Alaska Goldpanners (Lewis-Clark, Idaho, State). 2. Duke Welker, rhp, Anchorage Glacier Pilots (Arkansas). 3. Mark Willinsky, rhp, Mat-Su (Santa Clara). 4. Casey Weathers, rhp, Anchorage Glacier Pilots (Vanderbilt). 5. Chris Wietlispach, rhp, Mat-Su (Yale). 6. Xavier Scruggs, 1b/3b, Athletes In Action (UNLV). 7. Daniel Turpen, rhp, Mat-Su (Oregon State). 8. Chase d'Arnaud, ss, Anchorage Glacier Pilots (Pepperdine). 9. Blake Stauffer, util, Athletes In Action (Texas A&M). 10. Ike Davis, of, Anchorage Bucs (Arizona State).

INDIVIDUAL BATTING LEADERS
(Minimum 100 Plate Appearances)

	AVG	AB	R	H	2B	3B	HR	RBI	SB
Petersen, Bryan, Bucs	.365	137	27	50	10	4	0	24	10
Waters, Lucas, Pilots	.350	143	29	50	7	1	1	14	33
Nelson, Chris, Oilers	.347	121	23	42	11	2	0	18	12
Ercolano, Joe, Miners	.344	154	29	53	6	2	0	10	10
Koski, Kevin, Bucs	.329	170	34	56	5	2	1	15	27
Persichina, Joe, Panners	.328	122	24	40	8	1	1	17	4
Chu, Yuan-Chin, Panners	.317	142	18	45	7	2	0	22	6
Fox, Chris, Panners	.316	114	19	36	3	0	0	13	3
Simpson, Rick, AIA	.307	137	25	42	8	2	1	18	19
Thompson, Mark, Panners	.296	135	34	40	4	2	0	17	16

INDIVIDUAL PITCHING LEADERS
(Minimum 30 Innings)

	W	L	ERA	G	SV	IP	BB	SO
Timmons, Sean, Panners	5	0	1.17	6	0	46	10	20
Cogdill, Wes, AIA	1	0	1.29	18	3	35	10	26
Kissock, Chris, Panners	4	2	1.41	8	1	51	11	37
Welker, Duke, Pilots	1	2	1.46	9	0	49	23	35
Gruener, David, Miners	3	2	1.54	8	0	47	10	41
Wietlispach, Chris, Miners	4	2	1.65	7	0	44	27	45
Hernandez, Kevin, Panners	5	1	1.78	9	0	51	17	37
Smith, Tim, Miners	4	0	2.20	5	0	41	14	23
Tatusko, Ryan, Oilers	4	1	2.30	10	1	43	8	42
Laughlin, Levi, Pilots	3	1	2.32	8	0	50	9	27

ATLANTIC COLLEGIATE LEAGUE

WOLFF	W	L	PCT	GB
Kutztown Rockies	33	6	.846	—
Lehigh Valley Catz	25	15	.625	8 ½
Quakertown Blazers	18	20	.474	14 ½
Jersey Pilots	18	22	.450	15 ½

KAISER	W	L	PCT	GB
Metro New York Cadets	21	14	.600	—
Stamford Robins	15	23	.395	7 ½
Long Island Stars	11	26	.297	11
New York Generals	11	26	.297	11

PLAYOFFS: Kutztown defeated Lehigh Valley in a one-game championship.

TOP 10 PROSPECTS: 1. Steve Gilman, rhp, Metro NY (Yale). 2. Josh Smith, rhp, Lehigh Valley (Arkansas). 3. Michael Whitney, rhp Lehigh Valley (Navarro, Ariz., Junior College). 4. Peter Kennelly, rhp, Stamford (Fordham). 5. Will Romanowicz, rhp, Kutztown (Elon). 6. Phil Rummel, rhp, Kutztown (Kutztown, Pa.). 7. Jimmy Principe, of, Lehigh Valley (Brookdale, N.J., CC). 8. Brendon Murphy, of-1b, Lehigh Valley (Marshall). 9. Perry Schatzow, ss, Jersey (Kean, N.J.). 10. Matt Gianini, lhp, Stamford (Central Connecticut State).

INDIVIDUAL BATTING LEADERS
(Minimum 100 Plate Appearances)

	AVG	AB	R	H	2B	3B	HR	RBI	SB
Iacono, Sal, Metro NY	.411	90	15	37	10	1	0	14	5
Maloney, Jess, New York	.369	122	22	45	11	0	2	21	3
Fester, Jonas, Kutztown	.366	131	25	48	15	3	1	25	8
Wyland, Ryan, Kutztown	.366	123	28	45	6	4	1	34	8
Smucker, Justin, Kutztown	.358	120	21	43	9	0	0	24	6
Krailo, Karl, Lehigh Valley	.350	123	29	43	17	1	4	28	0
Schatzow, Perry, Jersey	.346	107	18	37	6	0	0	6	3
Deboer, Jacob, Kutztown	.344	96	21	33	3	0	0	7	8
Varricchio, TJ, New York	.343	99	13	34	14	0	2	14	2
Gavlick, Dan, Kutztown	.342	114	17	39	9	1	0	22	3
Butler, Josh, Quakertown	.333	117	16	39	6	1	1	15	4
Lape, Nate, Long Island	.333	108	26	36	5	3	3	31	7
Principe, Jimmy, Lehigh Valley	.330	112	16	37	3	3	0	17	9
Kahn, John, Metro NY	.329	79	12	26	5	1	1	15	2
Murphy, Brendan, Lehigh Valley	.326	135	19	44	9	1	4	30	0

INDIVIDUAL PITCHING LEADERS
(Minimum 30 Innings)

	W	L	ERA	G	SV	IP	H	BB	SO
Rummel, Phil, Rockies	7	0	1.12	8	0	48	43	15	35
Romanowicz, Will, Rockies	4	0	1.29	8	1	42	22	13	47
Ginanini, Matt, Robins	6	2	1.40	11	0	58	36	16	52
Barry, Richard, Cadets	2	1	1.43	9	0	44	36	19	36
Burch, David, Generals	5	0	1.49	8	0	48	35	17	38
Augustine, Joseph, Pilots	6	0	1.61	7	0	45	36	17	44
Kennelly, Peter, Robins	3	3	1.79	8	0	40	27	22	40
John, Tim, Rockies	5	1	2.53	8	0	46	44	10	29
Catanese, Joe, Cadets	4	1	2.55	7	0	35	23	16	29
Van Es, Scott, Pilots	3	4	2.95	11	1	43	41	11	34

CAL RIPKEN SR LEAGUE

	W	L	PCT	GB
Bethesda Big Train	28	12	.700	—
Rockville Express	25	15	.625	3
Maryland Orioles	23	17	.575	5
College Park Bombers	20	20	.500	8
Silver Spring-Takoma Thunderbolts	14	26	.350	14
Maryland Redbirds	10	30	.250	18

TOP 10 PROSPECTS: 1. Neil Ramirez, rhp, Youse's Orioles (Kempsville High, Virginia Beach, Va.). 2. Mitch Harris, rhp, Youse's Orioles (Navy). 3. Evan Frederickson, lhp, Bethesda (Virginia Tech). 4. Hunter Harris, rhp, Youse's Orioles (Texas). 5. Vinny DiFazio, c, Youse's Orioles (Alabama). 6. Eddie Bach, lhp, Youse's Orioles (Maryland-Baltimore County). 7. Neal

Davis, lhp, Youse's Orioles (Virginia). 8. Preston Pehrson, c, Bethesda (Towson). 9. Ivor Hodgson, of, Rockville (Mount St. Mary's). 10. Jim Britton, rhp, College Park (St. Bonaventure).

INDIVIDUAL BATTING LEADERS
(Minimum 100 Plate Appearances)

	AVG	AB	R	H	2B	3B	HR	SB
Vincent DiFazio, Maryland	.400	70	20	28	4	3	2	3
Joe Van Meter, Maryland	.349	63	9	22	8	2	1	2
Matt Long, Bethesda	.342	120	26	41	8	3	1	7
Justin Bour, Maryland	.331	121	16	40	10	1	0	0
Luke Adkins, Bethesda	.328	128	22	42	8	2	1	1
Brian Conley, Maryland	.317	126	21	40	4	2	2	3
Josh Dietz, Bethesda	.313	83	18	26	5	0	4	0
Ivor Hodgson, Rockville	.313	96	16	30	4	0	0	14
Corey Greene, Silver Spring	.310	71	9	22	5	1	1	0
Mike Murphy, Rockville	.310	113	21	35	5	1	2	9
Michael Gilmartin, Rockville	.309	110	12	34	3	3	1	5
Rob Pietroforte, Rockville	.307	114	21	35	4	3	1	0
Charlie Lenhard, Silver Spring	.307	137	20	42	9	1	7	0
Matt Bodenchuk, College Park	.306	124	19	38	11	0	2	0
Thomas Dolan, College Park	.306	62	10	19	2	0	0	2

INDIVIDUAL PITCHING LEADERS
(Minimum 20 Innings)

	W	L	ERA	G	SV	IP	BB	SO
Chris Cullen, Bethesda	3	0	0.39	12	2	23	8	14
Brad Taylor, College Park	1	0	0.71	15	3	25	8	30
Aerik Taylor, Maryland	2	2	1.20	8	0	30	11	18
Hunter Harris, Maryland	3	1	1.59	8	0	40	14	42
Thomas Dolan, College Park	4	1	1.72	6	0	31	15	26
Brian Anderson, Bethesda	3	1	1.87	12	2	34	14	34
Jason Schnitzer, Rockville	4	0	1.93	8	0	28	11	20
Ryan Huston, Rockville	5	1	1.97	9	2	46	7	29
Austin Hinkle, Bethesda	4	1	2.06	15	2	35	7	30
Andrew Germuth, Silver Spring	2	0	2.06	14	1	35	8	18

CENTRAL ILLINOIS COLLEGIATE LEAGUE

	W	L	PCT	GB
Danville Dans	25	19	.568	—
DuPage Dragons	25	19	.568	—
Twin City Stars	24	20	.545	1
Quincy Gems	24	20	.545	1
Dubois County Bombers	23	21	.523	2
Springfield Rifles	17	26	.395	7 ½
Galesburg Pioneers	15	28	.349	9 ½

PLAYOFFS: Semifinals–Twin City defeated DuPage 2-1 and Danville defeated Quincy 2-0 best-of-3 series. **Final**–Twin City defeated Danville 2-0 in a best-of-3 series.

TOP 10 PROSPECTS: 1. Bryce Stowell, rhp, Danville (UC Irvine). 2. Kevin Dubler, c, Dupage (Illinois State). 3. Bobby Stevens, ss, Twin City (Northern Illinois). 4. Aaron Weatherford, rhp, Danville (Mississippi State). 5. Louis Coleman, rhp, Danville (Louisiana State). 6. Pat Venditte, rhp/lhp, Quincy (Creighton). 7. Dan Brewer, ss, Dupage (Bradley). 8. Adam Buschini, if, Dupage (Cal Poly). 9. Ricardo Pecina, lhp, Danville (San Diego). 10. D.J. Mauldin, rhp, Dupage (Cal Poly).

INDIVIDUAL BATTING LEADERS
(Minimum 100 Plate Appearances)

	AVG	AB	R	H	2B	3B	HR	RBI	SB
Simon, Scott, Quincy	.337	187	33	63	15	1	6	28	2
White, Ryne, DuPage	.329	158	29	52	11	0	4	28	6
Stevens, Bobby, Twin City	.326	175	39	57	9	1	3	26	9
Spears, Casey, Springfield	.323	127	21	41	2	0	0	11	29
Goldsmith, Bradley, Dubois	.321	137	22	44	10	1	0	15	23
Quinn, Dan, Quincy	.319	138	28	44	7	1	7	24	0
Dudley, Kyle, Springfield	.315	127	19	40	5	1	0	15	9
Brewer, Dan, DuPage	.314	175	31	55	10	2	2	27	26
Meade, Frankie, Galesburg	.313	99	17	31	9	0	4	13	2
Law, Eric, Quincy	.311	90	27	28	4	0	3	23	14
Irvin, Josh, Dubois	.309	149	19	46	16	1	1	16	2
Angel, Ricky, Twin City	.308	169	26	52	8	1	1	25	0
Railey, Joey, Twin City	.306	186	39	57	10	2	1	23	12
Stead, Zach, Springfield	.303	99	15	30	4	0	0	18	1
Diggs, Wyn, Danville	.300	120	17	36	9	0	0	18	1

INDIVIDUAL PITCHING LEADERS
(Minimum 30 Innings)

	W	L	ERA	APP	SV	IP	H	BB	SO
Stowell, Bryce, Danville	5	1	1.52	10	0	53	35	13	69
Fields, Davy, Galesburg	4	2	1.60	27	0	39	26	6	25
Venditte, Pat, Quincy	2	1	1.66	30	0	43	29	11	46
Reilley, Brett, Dubois	5	1	1.80	8	0	50	39	10	35
Mauldin, D.J., DuPage	3	3	1.93	11	2	61	44	23	56

Vaculik, Chris, Dubois	4	2	2.14	14	4	42	29	16	38
Guttosch, Alex, Twin City	2	3	2.26	15	0	52	46	20	33
Pecina, Ricardo, Danville	7	1	2.35	11	0	57	57	20	56
Beatty, Andrew, DuPage	7	1	2.38	13	0	57	57	18	33
Myers, Ryan, Quincy	6	1	3.08	8	0	50	40	27	48

COASTAL PLAIN LEAGUE

NORTH	W	L	PCT	GB
*Peninsula Pilots	34	20	.630	—
+Edenton Steamers	35	16	.686	2 ½
Wilson Tobs	29	24	.547	4 ½
Outer Banks Daredevils	19	36	.345	15 ½
Petersburg Generals	18	36	.333	16

SOUTH	W	L	PCT	GB
+*Fayetteville SwampDogs	39	12	.765	—
Florence RedWolves	32	18	.640	6 ½
Columbia Blowfish	22	30	.423	17 ½
New Bern River Rats	20	34	.370	20 ½
Wilmington Sharks	19	34	.358	21

WEST	W	L	PCT	GB
+*Martinsville Mustangs	35	16	.686	—
Thomasville Hi-Toms	33	22	.600	4
Asheboro Copperheads	23	29	.442	12 ½
Spartanburg Stingers	21	29	.420	13 ½
Gastonia Grizzlies	14	37	.275	21

+First-half champion. *Second-half champion.

PETIT CUP TOURNAMENT: Thomasville (4-1) defeated Peninsula (3-1) in championship game of eight-team tournament.

TOP 10 PROSPECTS: 1. Keon Graves, 3b, Spartanburg (Spartanburg, S.C., Methodist). 2. Jimmy Gallagher, of, Peninsula (Duke). 3. Luke Prihoda, rhp, Fayetteville (Sam Houston State). 4. Nate Parks, of, Outer Banks (Virginia Tech). 5. C.J. Ziegler, 1b, Asheboro (Arizona). 6. Zach Brown, 1b, Thomasville (The Citadel). 7. Scott Diamond, lhp, Martinsville (Binghamton). 8. Steve Condotta, ss, Martinsville (Florida Tech). 9. Jeff Fischer, rhp, Edenton (Eastern Michigan). 10. Mike Flye, rhp, Wilson (East Carolina).

INDIVIDUAL BATTING LEADERS
(Minimum 100 Plate Appearances)

	AVG	AB	R	H	RBI	2B	3B	HR	SB
Gallagher, Jimmy, Peninsula	.423	175	40	74	45	13	0	5	13
Condotta, Steve, Martinsville	.355	138	28	49	20	8	1	0	10
Ziegler, C.J., Asheville	.352	165	40	58	32	9	1	13	2
Ray, Jamie, Martinsville	.350	180	27	63	34	12	1	1	17
Kennamer, Derek, Edenton	.345	142	33	49	12	1	1	0	25
Ashcraft, Trent, Florence	.340	191	26	65	27	5	0	2	20
Folli, Mike, Outer Banks	.330	197	26	65	29	8	5	0	15
Boyd, Wilson, Thomasville	.324	182	37	59	31	7	0	4	7
Leake, Matt, Martinsville	.320	178	27	57	28	13	5	3	11
Banks, Ernie, Peninsula	.318	154	24	49	36	12	1	3	0

INDIVIDUAL PITCHING LEADERS
(Minimum 30 Innings)

	W	L	ERA	G	SV	IP	H	BB	SO
Diamond, Scott, Martinsville	5	0	0.50	10	0	54	34	13	55
Dougher, Jimmy, Peninsula	7	1	0.79	11	0	57	35	5	45
Owen, Dylan, Florence	6	0	0.81	9	0	67	45	17	78
Scribner, Evan, Edenton	6	1	1.17	11	0	46	31	8	50
Anderson, David, Columbia	6	2	1.24	9	0	65	44	18	64
Clark, Craig, Peninsula	7	1	1.54	12	0	76	43	22	68
Lovett, Aaron, Fayetteville	6	2	1.56	10	0	58	43	29	58
Martin, Aaron, Fayetteville	5	1	1.59	11	0	45	28	18	33
Nehls, Brock, Fayetteville	6	0	1.60	15	1	67	42	23	55
McCullough, Brian, Outer Banks	5	3	1.64	10	0	66	52	24	54

FLORIDA COLLEGIATE SUMMER LEAGUE

	W	L	PCT	GB
Altamonte Springs Snappers	26	8	.765	—
Winter Park Diamond Dawgs	23	13	.639	4
Orlando Shockers	19	16	.543	7 ½
Winter Pines Warthogs	14	17	.452	10 ½
Sanford River Rats	16	20	.444	11 ½
Orlando Hammers	5	29	.147	21 ½

PLAYOFFS: Winter Park defeated Altamonte Springs in the championship game of a six-team tournament.

TOP 10 PROSPECTS: 1. Jon Lucroy, c, Winter Park (Louisiana-Lafayette). 2. Ty Pryor, rhp, Winter Pines, (North Florida). 3. Alan Farina, rhp, Orlando, (Clemson). 4. William Jackel, rhp, Winter Park, (Tallahassee CC). 5. Gene Howard, util, Winter Park, (Rollins College). 6. Andrew Laughter, rhp, Winter Park (Louisiana-Lafayette). 7. Kent Matthes, of, Winter Pines, (Alabama). 8. Avery Barnes, 2b, Altamonte Springs (Florida).

9. Mark Gildea, of, Altamonte Springs, (Florida State). 10. Mike Marseco, ss, Sanford (Samford).

INDIVIDUAL BATTING LEADERS
(Minimum 80 Plate Appearances)

	AVG	AB	R	H	2B	3B	HR	RBI	SB
Anthony Ottrando, Alt. Springs	.390	105	24	41	10	2	1	25	10
Avery Barnes, Alt. Springs	.361	108	37	39	9	1	2	24	24
Robby Perez, Winter Park	.353	136	29	48	6	1	5	20	8
Chadd Hartman, Sanford	.329	79	15	26	5	2	0	10	8
James Rowe, Alt. Springs	.317	82	16	26	6	0	0	9	7
Josh Spivey, Alt. Springs	.314	86	19	27	6	2	2	15	4
Andrew Turner, Winter Park	.308	117	16	36	7	0	3	23	2
Dwayne Bailey, Winter Park	.302	96	27	29	6	1	0	10	1
Jonathan Lucroy, Winter Park	.300	110	14	33	5	1	6	30	1
Matt Floyd, Hammers	.300	110	11	33	4	1	0	14	7
Cody Wheeler, Winter Pines	.299	77	18	23	8	0	2	9	1
Michael Marseco, Sanford	.296	135	20	40	5	4	0	15	7
Will Breslin, Shockers	.292	106	20	41	6	1	0	16	2
Ryan Richardson, Sanford	.291	110	13	32	7	1	1	13	14
Gene Howard, Winter Park	.291	117	17	34	4	2	1	23	0

INDIVIDUAL PITCHING LEADERS
(Minimum 20 Innings)

	W	L	ERA	G	SV	IP	H	BB	SO
Chas Spottswood, Alt. Springs	4	0	1.02	9	2	35	29	14	28
Ryan Vaughn, Sanford	2	1	1.04	11	2	26	19	7	31
J.J. Crumbley, Altamonte Springs	3	1	1.17	20	6	31	29	4	34
Ryan Horton, Winter Park	6	1	1.36	8	0	40	25	13	28
Ray Garcia, Altamonte Springs	5	0	1.38	6	0	39	25	10	58
Brad Johnson, Alatamonte Springs	6	1	1.42	8	0	44	34	9	47
Chris Smith, Sanford	2	4	1.74	6	0	31	26	13	15
Alan Farina, Shockers	3	1	2.11	8	1	38	26	18	42
Sean Bryant, Sanford	3	2	2.18	9	0	41	47	12	34
Shane Buriff, Shockers	2	1	2.19	7	1	25	19	8	32

GREAT LAKES LEAGUE

EAST	W	L	T	PCT	GB
Columbus All-Americans	28	12	0	.700	—
Lima Locos	23	14	1	.618	3 ½
Cincinnati Steam	22	18	0	.550	6
Delaware Cows	21	19	0	.525	7
Southern Ohio Copperheads	21	19	0	.525	7
Grand Lake Mariners	20	19	1	.513	7
Lake Erie Monarchs	17	21	0	.447	10
Xenia Athletes In Action	12	26	2	.325	15
Granville Settlers	12	28	0	.300	16

PLAYOFFS: Grand Lake defeated Lima in an eight team, double-elimination tournament.

TOP 10 PROSPECTS: 1. J.B Shuck, lhp/of, Columbus (Ohio State). 2. Damon Brewer, lhp, Lima (Bethune-Cookman). 3. John Baird, rhp, Delaware (Cincinnati). 4. Chris Kupillas, rhp, Grand Lake (Central Michigan). 5. Kyle Maunus, 3b, Cincinnati (Western Michigan). 6. Josh Harrison, if, Southern Ohio (Cincinnati). 7. Mike Wilson, rhp, Great Lakes (Michigan). 8. Travis Jones, 2b, Lima (South Carolina). 9. Matt Stiffler, of, Southern Ohio (Ohio). 10. Mark Sorensen, rhp, Columbus (Michigan State).

INDIVIDUAL BATTING LEADERS
(Minimum 80 Plate Appearances)

	AVG	AB	R	H	2B	3B	HR	RBI	SB
Damon Wright, Columbus	.374	99	15	37	6	2	0	10	5
Jacob Robbins, Lima	.371	116	21	43	2	0	0	7	14
Matt Stiffler, Southern Ohio	.367	120	20	44	12	2	0	20	9
J.B. Shuck, Columbus	.364	99	19	36	3	0	1	9	11
Joshua Harrison, Cincinnati	.347	118	21	41	2	2	1	14	11
Chris Dunn, Columbus	.346	81	9	28	4	1	0	8	8
Evan Armitage, Lima	.345	55	7	19	1	1	0	12	5
Kyle Maunus, Lake Erie	.327	98	22	32	5	0	1	17	5
Daniel Webb, Delaware	.323	133	17	43	9	0	0	15	3
Dusty Hammond, Grand Lake	.320	100	14	32	5	0	0	13	7

INDIVIDUAL PITCHING LEADERS
(Minimum 30 Innings)

	W	L	ERA	G	IP	H	BB	SO	SV
Chris Kupillas, Grand Lake	3	1	1.47	8	43	29	14	52	0
Dan Barker, Lima	2	0	1.63	8	39	28	16	20	0
Mark Sorensen, Columbus	6	0	1.71	7	47	31	9	28	0
Brett Lester, Xenia	3	3	1.74	10	47	39	21	38	1
Matt Marksbury, Cincinnati	3	3	2.05	8	48	34	9	24	1
Jay Clites, Lake Erie	1	4	2.23	7	40	29	6	17	0
Ben Buchanan, Southern Ohio	3	2	2.23	7	44	42	10	43	0
Kyle Pfirrman, Cincinnati	4	3	2.50	8	54	48	18	37	0
Chris Rubio, Lima	3	2	3.03	8	39	39	4	22	0

JAYHAWK LEAGUE

	W	L	PCT	GB
Hays Larks	25	13	.658	—
Liberal BeeJays	24	16	.600	2
El Dorado Broncos	20	19	.513	5 ½
Derby Twins	19	19	.500	6
Southwest Slashers	15	25	.375	11
Nevada Griffons	14	25	.359	11 ½

TOP 10 PROSPECTS: 1. Sam Elam, lhp, Hays (Notre Dame). 2. Matt Brown, of, El Dorado (Wichita State). 3. Brian Rike, of, Liberal (Louisiana Tech). 4. Cliff Springston, lhp, Hays (Baylor). 5. Kyle Day, c, Hays (Michigan state). 6. Dusty Renfrow, rhp, Nevada (Southeast Missouri State). 7. Dylan Moseley, rhp, Liberal (Louisiana Tech). 8. Noah Krol, rhp, El Dorado (Wichita State). 9. Drew Bowman, lhp, Liberal (Nebraska). 10. Derek Schermerhorn, 3b, El Dorado (Wichita State).

INDIVIDUAL BATTING LEADERS
(Minimum 100 Plate Appearances)

	AVG	AB	R	H	2B	3B	HR	RBI	SB
Clark, Chris, Derby	.430	107	28	46	11	0	5	20	4
Stovall, Dan, Hays	.394	109	22	43	9	0	6	28	0
Brown, Matt, El Dorado	.385	96	29	37	8	0	9	36	11
Day, Kyle, Hays	.371	124	31	46	12	1	7	27	3
Rike, Brian, Liberal	.362	105	26	38	9	2	3	18	13
Fry, Matt, Liberal	.351	114	23	40	10	0	1	15	0
Julius, Jacob, Southwest	.342	79	16	27	6	2	1	18	3
Phillips, Josh, Derby	.339	124	24	42	0	1	2	20	12
Schimiho, Derek El Dorado	.330	100	27	33	6	3	2	19	13
Ellrich, Justin, Nevada	.319	72	7	23	5	0	6	18	0
Wagner, Matt, Nevada	.318	107	12	34	6	0	1	12	1
Williams, Bo, Derby	.314	105	20	33	12	0	6	27	4
Wilson, Blaine, Liberal	.312	93	15	29	8	0	3	13	2
Christison, Dallas, Hays	.308	133	34	41	7	0	5	16	17
Brezovsky, Ross, Hays	.308	78	18	24	2	0	2	12	1

INDIVIDUAL PITCHING LEADERS
(Minimum 30 Innings)

	W	L	ERA	G	SV	IP	H	BB	SO
Elam, Sam, Hays	5	0	0.95	10	2	29	8	7	42
Springston, Cliff, Hays	3	1	1.35	7	0	40	30	18	31
Speak, Matt, Joplin	3	1	1.73	12	2	26	19	10	24
Longacre, Chad, Derby	1	0	2.51	13	0	29	27	2	13
Maclas, Danny, El Dorado	2	0	2.77	5	1	26	28	5	16
Allen, Lucas, Nevada	0	4	2.88	6	0	34	38	10	18
Grijalva, Fito, Hays	4	1	2.98	9	0	42	46	10	16
Moseley, Dylan, Liberal	4	2	3.25	7	0	44	41	9	27
Renfrow, Dustin, Nevada	2	1	3.27	6	0	33	28	8	16
Bowman, Drew, Liberal	3	1	3.31	6	0	35	34	18	27

NEW ENGLAND COLLEGIATE LEAGUE

NORTH	W	L	PCT	GB
Vermont Mountaineers	27	15	.643	—
Sanford Mainers	26	16	.619	1
Keene Swamp Bats	22	20	.524	5
Holyoke Giants	17	25	.405	10
Lowell All-Americans	16	26	.381	11
Concord Quarry Dogs	14	27	.341	12 ½

SOUTH	W	L	PCT	GB
Newport Gulls	32	10	.762	—
North Adams Steeplecats	25	17	.595	7
Torrington Twisters	23	18	.560	8 ½
Manchester Silkworms	21	20	.512	10 ½
Danbury Westerners	14	27	.341	17 ½
Pittsfield Dukes	13	29	.310	19

PLAYOFFS—Quaterfinals: Vermont beat Holyoke 2-0, Sanford beat Keene 2-0, Newport beat Manchester 3-2 and Torrington beat North Adams 2-0 in best-of-three series. **Semifinals:** Vermont beat Sanford 2-1 and Torrington beat Newport 2-0 in best-of-three series. **Final:** Vermont beat Torrington in a best-of-three series.

TOP 10 PROSPECTS: 1. Chris Friedrich, lhp, Vermont (Eastern Kentucky). 2. Andres Perez, 3b/of, Torrington (Stony Brook). 3. Curt Smith, 3b, Vermont (Maine). 4. Chris Dominguez, 3b, Newport (Louisville). 5. Pat McAnaney, lhp, Newport (Virginia). 6. Jay Monti, rhp, Holyoke (Sacred Heart). 7. Jim Murphy, 1B, Newport (Washington State). 8. Mark Murray, rhp, Vermont (Evansville). 9. Brendan McKearney, rhp, Newport (Washington). 10. Willy Fox, util, Pittsfield (Wake Forest).

INDIVIDUAL BATTING LEADERS
(Minimum 100 Plate Appearances)

	AVG	AB	R	H	2B	3B	HR	RBI	SB
Jim Murphy, Newport	.358	148	22	53	14	0	9	40	0
Andres Perez, Torrington	.355	110	24	39	8	1	6	20	5

	AVG	AB	R	H	2B	3B	HR	RBI	SB
Cheyne Hurst, Keene	.354	130	21	46	6	1	1	16	22
Aaron Garza, Manchester	.348	161	18	56	15	2	2	28	5
Willy Fox, Pittsfield	.341	129	20	44	8	3	2	19	17
Gil Zayas, Manchester	.333	168	22	56	7	0	8	27	0
Mike Tamsin, Danbury	.323	127	15	41	9	0	4	17	0
Curt Smith, Vermont	.323	155	26	50	8	2	1	18	20
Justin Lepore, Torrington	.319	113	18	36	4	0	1	23	0
Troy Krider, Vermont	.317	126	22	40	6	1	0	8	10
Matt S Miller, Sanford	.313	147	21	46	5	0	1	20	6
Jerod Edmondson, Sanford	.310	126	23	39	4	2	0	16	12
Zach Zaneski, Vermont	.309	110	11	34	5	0	0	20	1
Matt Karl, Keene	.308	107	16	33	3	0	6	15	1
Greg Miclat, Keene	.305	118	20	36	2	0	0	8	12

INDIVIDUAL PITCHING LEADERS
(Minimum 30 Innings)

	W	L	ERA	G	SV	IP	H	BB	SO
John Hernandez, Lowell	3	1	1.41	13	3	45	29	21	42
Brandon Harmon, North Adams	3	2	1.47	8	0	49	46	5	36
Jay Monti, Holyoke	5	1	1.62	7	0	50	26	9	59
Tom Close, Sanford	2	1	1.71	16	2	42	30	10	37
Pat McAnaney, Newport	7	0	1.74	9	0	52	33	9	55
Andrew Albers, Torrington	5	1	1.81	8	0	45	34	10	45
Dan Houston, Newport	2	1	1.90	10	0	47	41	23	44
Paul Nardozzi, Newport	5	1	2.05	9	1	48	34	14	27
Jacob Cook, Manchester	4	1	2.14	14	1	46	29	27	49
Joe Esposito, Vermont	4	3	2.19	8	0	53	39	31	61

NORTHWOODS LEAGUE

NORTH	W	L	PCT	GB
+Duluth Huskies	43	25	.632	—
Alexandria Beetles	39	29	.574	4
St. Cloud River Bats	33	34	.493	10
Mankato MoonDogs	32	35	.478	11 ½
*Thunder Bay Border Cats	29	38	.433	14 ½
Brainerd Blue Thunder	27	41	.397	16 ½

SOUTH	W	L	PCT	GB
*+Rochester Honkers	50	17	.746	—
Madison Mallards	36	32	.529	14 ½
La Crosse Loggers	34	34	.500	16 ½
Eau Claire Express	29	38	.433	21
Waterloo Bucks	28	40	.412	22 ½
Wisconsin Woodchucks	25	42	.373	25

*First-half champion. +Second-half champion

PLAYOFFS—Semifinals: Thunder Bay defeated Duluth 2-1 and Rochester defeated Madison 2-0 in best-of-three series. **Final:** Rochester defeated Thunder Bay 2-0 in best-of-three series.

TOP 10 PROSPECTS: 1. Jordan Zimmerman, rhp, Eau Claire (Wisconsin-Stevens Point). 2. Charlie Shirek, rhp, Duluth (Nebraska). 3. Brett Hunter, rhp, Alexandria (Pepperdine). 4. Steven Hensley, rhp, Duluth (Elon). 5. Chad Dawson, rhp, St. Cloud (Indiana State). 6. Tim Smith, of, Mankato (Arizona State). 7. Tim Murphy, of/lhp, Duluth (UCLA). 8. Jeff Richard, rhp, Waterloo (Central Michigan). 9. Chris Jones, of, Rochester (Cal State Fullerton). 10. Byron Wiley, of, Duluth (Kansas State).

INDIVIDUAL BATTING LEADERS
(Minimum 184 Plate Appearances)

	AVG	AB	R	H	2B	3B	HR	RBI	SB
Worth, Danny	.344	189	32	65	13	2	1	26	29
Loberg, Mike	.325	206	22	67	17	1	1	31	5
Pattock, Tod	.318	214	21	68	2	0	1	15	5
Dirks, Andy	.308	240	56	74	13	4	2	18	34
Smith, Tim	.300	250	33	75	9	1	3	19	19
Cutler, Charlie	.299	234	33	70	11	0	1	27	5
Wiley, Byron	.299	164	27	49	10	1	3	25	14
Frew, Bryan	.294	194	30	57	7	0	0	15	6
Huber, Erik	.292	240	27	70	8	0	2	37	9
White, Jason	.289	194	49	56	8	2	3	21	21
Curry, Caleb	.286	220	36	63	7	0	0	19	15
Hart, Jesse	.286	220	21	63	8	0	1	16	6
Cartie, Bryan	.285	221	30	63	15	2	1	22	6
Marchant, Gabe	.284	225	39	64	8	5	4	18	30
Podmolik, Andy	.283	233	28	66	7	1	1	20	10

INDIVIDUAL PITCHING LEADERS
(Minimum 54 Innings)

	W	L	ERA	G	SV	IP	H	BB	SO
Zimmermann, Jordan	4	2	1.01	11	0	80	42	28	92
Nihsen, Mike	9	2	1.04	14	6	78	50	16	40
McConnell, Eryk	5	2	1.38	10	0	59	52	10	34
Brummett, Tyson	4	4	1.40	9	0	64	49	17	54
Hunter, Brett	4	2	1.53	10	1	59	38	16	47
Reynolds, Matthew	5	1	1.62	12	0	83	70	15	48

	W	L	ERA	G	SV	IP	H	BB	SO
Sullivan, Jake	6	3	1.64	12	0	66	51	19	41
Huber, Tim	5	2	1.67	12	0	76	57	29	56
Dominguez, Jason	2	3	1.77	13	1	76	60	25	61
Salas, Steve	4	5	1.80	13	1	80	65	24	68

TEXAS COLLEGIATE LEAGUE

ROGERS HORNSBY	W	L	PCT	GB
Denton Outlaws	28	20	.583	—
Graham Roughnecks	21	27	.438	7
Mineral Wells Steam	20	28	.417	8
Weatherford Wranglers	20	28	.417	8

TRIS SPEAKER	W	L	PCT	GB
Coppell Copperheads	31	17	.646	—
McKinney Marshals	30	18	.625	1
Euless LoneStars	26	22	.542	5
Duncanville Deputies	21	27	.438	10
Plano Blue Sox	19	29	.396	12

PLAYOFFS: First round: Denton defeated Graham 2-0 and McKinney defeated Coppell 2-0 in best-of-three series. **Final:** McKinney defeated Denton 2-0 in best-of-three series.

TOP 10 PROSPECTS: 1. Randy Boone, rhp, Coppell (Texas). 2. Aaron Luna, 2b/of, Euless (Rice). 3. Brian Friday, ss, Duncanville (Rice). 4. Seth Garrison, rhp, Duncanville (Texas Christian). 5. Jess Todd, rhp, Coppell (Arkansas). 6. Jeff Nutt, c, Coppell (Arkansas). 7. Kirkland Rivers, lhp/cf, Mineral Wells (Texas A&M). 8. Matt Willard, ss, Euless (Arkansas). 9. Justin Garcia, rhp, Graham (New Orleans). 10. Wade Mackey, rhp, Mineral Wells (Baylor).

INDIVIDUAL BATTING LEADERS
(Minimum 100 Plate Appearances)

	AVG	AB	R	H	2B	3B	HR	RBI	SB
Davis, Aljay, Denton	.355	169	47	60	8	2	2	27	23
Cavagnaro, Matt, McKin	.345	174	37	60	7	5	2	23	11
Willard, Matt, Euless	.336	128	21	43	5	1	0	11	12
Hernandez, Jose, Denton	.327	159	30	52	8	1	5	41	9
Freeman, Jarod, Graham	.318	154	24	49	15	0	3	30	2
Richard, Michael, McKin	.315	124	28	39	9	0	0	16	28
Hill, Tyler, Coppell	.315	143	17	45	12	1	0	18	1
Cline, Matt, Denton	.306	147	33	45	6	1	1	17	10
Maitland, Ben, Plano	.305	154	15	47	11	2	1	26	2
Nutt, Jeff, Coppell	.303	152	23	46	15	0	3	33	3
Grijalva, Aaron, McKin	.300	120	17	36	3	1	1	19	10
Sebek, Todd, Coppell	.298	124	13	37	4	1	1	23	12
Vern, Matt, Euless	.294	153	20	45	9	1	0	22	8
Baker, Ryan, Denton	.293	164	27	48	10	0	1	19	3
Moss, Brandon, Euless	.292	137	22	40	11	0	0	21	0

INDIVIDUAL PITCHING LEADERS
(Minimum 30 Innings)

	W	L	ERA	G	SV	IP	H	BB	SO
Pessa, Kurt, Denton	4	0	0.00	7	0	34	12	8	33
Boone, Randy, Coppell	6	0	1.09	8	0	58	31	11	65
Ary, Brice, Denton	2	0	1.21	19	0	37	22	19	15
Wortham, Jake, Plano	3	0	1.49	17	3	31	23	6	24
Furrow, Donald, Weath	5	2	1.52	16	0	83	55	26	74
Farish, Dillon, Euless	2	1	1.55	22	6	24	19	6	24
Grace, Jason, Weath	3	2	1.60	9	1	45	33	9	5
Brancheau, Paul, Graham	0	1	1.61	16	0	28	14	17	16
Schneider, Paul, Plano	1	2	1.65	5	0	28	20	5	15
Doll, Mark, Plano	5	3	1.71	9	0	64	48	20	50

VALLEY LEAGUE

NORTH	W	L	PCT	GB
New Market Rebels	32	10	.762	—
Haymarket Senators	22	20	.524	10
Luray Wranglers	21	21	.500	11
Winchester Royals	21	21	.500	11
Front Royal Cardinals	15	27	.357	17

SOUTH	W	L	PCT	GB
Waynesboro Generals	27	15	.643	—
Harrisonburg Turks	25	17	.595	2
Covington Lumberjacks	21	21	.500	6
Staunton Braves	15	27	.357	12
Woodstock River Bandits	11	31	.262	16

PLAYOFFS: Quarterfinals—New Market defeated Winchester 2-1, Luray defeated Haymarket 2-0, Staunton defeated Waynesboro 2-1 and Harrisonburg defeated Covington 2-1 in best-of-three series. **Semifinals:** Staunton defeated Harrisonburg 2-0 and Luray defeated New Market 2-0 in best-of-three series. **Final:** Luray defeated Staunton 3-2 in a best-of-five series.

TOP 10 PROSPECTS: 1. Yonder Alonso, 1b, Luray (Miami). 2. Blake

Tekotte, of, Woodstock (Miami). 3. Paul Burnside, rhp, Winchester (Auburn). 4. Tyler Kuhn, ss, Luray (West Virginia). 5. Brandon Dickson, rhp, New Market (Tusculum, Tenn., College). 6. Jamie McOwen, of, Luray (Florida International). 7. Josh Dew, rhp/3b, Harrisonburg (Troy). 8. Adam White, of, Waynesboro (West Virginia). 9. Jordan Karnofsky, 1b/of, Front Royal (California). 10. Clint Robinson, 1b, Harrisonburg (Troy).

INDIVIDUAL BATTING LEADERS
(Minimum 100 Plate Appearances)

	AVG	AB	R	H	2B	3B	HR	RBI	SB
Candlin, Drew, Haymarket........	.365	156	23	57	6	0	4	25	3
Kuhn, Tyler, Luray..................	.363	223	42	81	13	5	7	25	3
Spain, Bobby, Harrisonburg	.348	158	28	55	9	0	3	24	0
Tollison, Michael, Haymarket ..	.331	172	30	57	10	0	9	29	1
Wingfield, Patrick, Winchester	.331	157	22	52	8	0	4	20	20
Anninos, Chris, Waynesboro....	.310	155	23	48	8	0	1	22	3
LeBlanc, Evan, Harrisonburg....	.308	146	23	45	11	1	2	23	3
Wilkins, Chris, Staunton	.308	172	28	53	6	2	1	22	15
Rachal, Ryan, Harrisonburg	.307	153	22	47	10	1	1	28	4
Davidson, Kurt, Waynesboro....	.304	158	23	48	12	1	4	31	2
Karnofsky, Jordan, Front Royal	.302	149	26	45	12	0	5	24	2
Beck, Chris, New Market..........	.302	126	17	38	9	1	0	15	10
Geiger, Jon, New Market..........	.301	146	27	44	8	2	2	11	23
Dennis, David, Harrisonburg....	.299	177	18	53	10	0	3	27	0
Querns, Timothy, Haymarket....	.298	161	23	48	7	0	0	24	2

INDIVIDUAL PITCHING LEADERS
(Minimum 30 Innings)

	W	L	ERA	G	SV	IP	H	BB	SO
Dages, Jon, Waynesboro	4	0	1.60	9	0	45	29	12	38
Davis, Dusty, Luray	4	1	1.65	11	0	55	50	15	44
Burnside, Paul, Winchester	2	2	1.70	10	0	58	41	17	55
Perkins, Adam, Waynesboro	5	1	1.86	9	1	48	34	19	38
Judy, Josh, Haymarket..................	4	1	1.91	8	0	47	36	10	40
Brackman, Mark, New Market	5	2	2.09	10	0	60	55	8	35
Barham, Trey, Front Royal	3	1	2.36	7	0	42	32	13	50
Ducey, John, New Market............	5	3	2.73	11	0	63	58	12	42
Moffitt, Josh, Waynesboro	3	2	2.81	12	0	48	44	19	40
Wheeler, Tim, Harrisonburg	4	2	2.88	9	0	56	53	17	49

WEST COAST COLLEGIATE

	W	L	PCT	GB
Spokane RiverHawks	28	14	.667	—
Wenatchee AppleSox	27	15	.643	1
Aloha Knights	25	17	.595	3
Bend Elks	24	18	.571	4
Kitsap BlueJackets	24	18	.571	4
Moses Lake Pirates	16	26	.381	12
Kelowna Falcons	13	29	.310	15
Bellingham Bells	11	31	.262	17

PLAYOFFS—Wenatchee defeated Spokane 2-0 in best-of-three championship series.

TOP 10 PROSPECTS: 1. Jared Prince, of/rhp, Aloha (Washington State). 2. Darin Holcomb, 3b, Spokane (Gonzaga). 3. Joey Wong, 2b, Bend (Oregon State). 4. Marc Rzepczynski, lhp, Aloha (UC Riverside). 5. Eric Sogard, 3b, Bend (Arizona State). 6. D.J. Lidyard, rhp, Wenatchee (Oregon State). 7. Jorge Reyes, rhp, Moses Lake (Oregon State). 8. Danny Cox, ss, Bend (Washington). 9. James Wallace, rhp, Aloha (College of Southern Idaho). 10. Kyle Paul, c, Kelowna (Missouri State).

INDIVIDUAL BATTING LEADERS
(Minimum 80 Plate Appearances)

	AVG	AB	R	H	RBI	2B	3B	HR
Eric Sogard, Bend	.347	118	22	41	19	10	1	0
Darin Holcomb, Spokane	.324	139	23	45	34	12	1	6
Hawkins Gebbers, Wenatchee...........	.322	143	18	46	20	9	0	1
Brent Mertens, Spokane	.321	137	21	44	21	5	5	0
Grant Desme, Bend	.318	157	30	50	32	8	5	3
Joey Wong, Bend	.310	116	19	36	16	3	0	0
Brett Munster, Moses Lake	.310	142	16	44	23	8	0	0
Jared Prince, Aloha	.308	78	12	24	13	6	1	0
Doug Buser, Kitsap	.306	134	28	41	9	3	0	0
Greg Biagi, Spokane	.303	119	16	36	11	6	0	0
Jamie Nilsen, Kitsap	.302	139	20	42	13	5	3	1
Carl Uhl, Spokane	.301	146	24	44	16	1	1	1
Ryan Fobert, Moses Lake	.301	113	4	34	21	3	0	0
Danny Meier, Kitsap	.295	156	22	46	21	6	0	2
Tyler Dean, Bend..............................	.294	119	24	35	13	6	1	0

INDIVIDUAL PITCHING LEADERS
(Minimum 30 Innings)

	W	L	ERA	G	SV	IP	H	BB	SO
Cory Powell, Spokane....................	4	2	1.31	8	0	55	48	18	36
Jeremy Hefner, Spokane	5	2	1.54	8	1	53	27	21	40
Blaine Hardy, Wenatchee	4	3	1.60	11	2	51	40	19	36
Clayton Mortenson, Wenatchee ...	4	2	1.62	11	0	61	43	30	38
Ross Humes, Kitsap	5	0	1.76	13	0	72	47	11	64
Matt Fields, Wenatchee	5	2	1.92	8	0	52	36	14	56
Marc Rzepczynski, Aloha	5	0	2.06	7	0	48	40	24	50
Brett Armour, Bellingham	5	3	2.41	10	0	60	40	25	57
Ross Black, Bellingham	1	6	2.44	9	0	48	48	8	27
D.J. Lidyard, Wenatchee	4	4	2.47	9	0	66	46	21	86
Chad Hunter, Moses Lake............	1	4	2.57	9	0	49	41	16	33
Luke Farden, Spokane	5	1	2.58	8	0	59	54	16	40
Tommy Milone, Wenatchee	5	1	2.61	11	2	52	44	10	36
Kyle Howe, Kitsap.........................	4	3	2.81	9	0	58	47	16	37
Geoff Nichols, Aloha.....................	2	2	2.93	9	0	46	42	17	34

HIGH SCHOOL/ YOUTH
BASEBALL

The Woodlands answers questions and stakes claim to national title

ROUND ROCK, Texas—Clutch is not a word those familiar with The Woodlands High baseball program often use to describe the perennial Houston-area power. Since the Highlanders' Class 5-A Texas state championship club of 2000, the program has consistently failed in those proverbial "clutch" situations.

Despite a wealth of talent and resources that produced district champions, nationally ranked teams, draft picks and a bevy of college players, the Highlanders had failed to advance past the regional semifinals of the Texas playoffs in five years.

So when The Woodlands went down 3-0 after two innings against Midland High in the state semifinals, a feeling of 'here we go again' consumed the crowd at Dell Diamond.

Then something happened—something The Woodlands had long been missing.

Trailing 3-2 in the top of the fifth inning, The Woodlands first baseman Brett Parsons delivered a perfect relay throw to catcher Mickey Armstrong to cut down Midland's Alex Lopez at the plate.

The Highlanders answered with three runs in the bottom of the inning to erase the deficit, their reputation and any doubt about who the nation's No. 1 high school team of 2006 was.

Following their comeback against Midland, the Highlanders defeated Katy High 5-3 in the 5-A state title game to wrap up the school's second state championship and its first final No. 1 ranking in the Baseball America/National High School Baseball Coaches Association poll.

"This group's a little different this year," said coach Ron Eastman following the 38-1 season. "They've been able to maintain when they've been down to teams. This group just has that sense that they're not going to quit. It's a great, very unselfish group of guys."

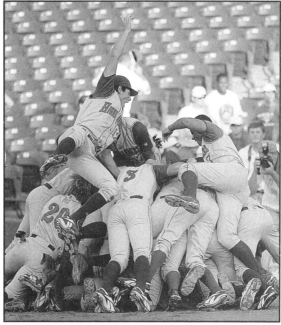

Coming through in the clutch
The Woodlands ran to Texas and national championships in 2006

Texas-sized Delivery

The Woodlands began the year ranked No. 7 and steadily climbed the rankings as the top teams from California, Florida and Arizona stumbled. By April 3, it had moved into the No. 1 spot and never relinquished the perch.

"They worked hard and came together as a team, really like no other I've ever seen," Eastman said. "It's very gratifying, and I'm just so happy for this group. They've worked so hard to get here. Our teams before this have had great kids and hard workers, but there's something special when a team comes together."

In Eastman's estimation, that happened sometime

around March 11, when the Highlanders downed defending 5-A champ Kingwood High 9-1 at the Minute Maid High School Classic at Minute Maid Park. The victory against Kingwood came a week after The Woodlands lost its only game of the season to Flower Mound, and was the fifth of 31 wins in a row it would tally to finish the championship season. The talented individuals meshed to form a unified team and that—universally voiced by players and coaches alike—was the linchpin.

"The younger guys in this group definitely got along with the older guys better," said senior righthander Steven Maxwell. "That's the main thing. We hung out together every single weekend, and we just got along better. When it came down to it, the team was what mattered the most."

Aptitude And Attitude

Fostering that atmosphere at The Woodlands isn't easy. From the time players reach high school in Houston they're well seasoned on the spirit of competition. Youth and prep travel teams endure arduous summer and fall schedules that make Texas' brand of high school baseball sharp, clean and generally well

PREVIOUS **WINNERS**

Previous No. 1 teams in the year-end Baseball America/National High School Baseball Coaches Association poll:

Year	Team
1992	Westminster Christian HS, Miami
1993	Greenway HS, Phoenix
1994	Sarasota (Fla.) HS
1995	Germantown (Tenn.) HS
1996	Westminster Christian HS, Miami
1997	Jesuit HS, Tampa
1998	Vestavia Hills (Ala.) HS
1999	Lassiter HS, Marietta, Ga.
2000	Gloucester Catholic HS, Gloucester City, N.J.
2001	Seminole (Fla.) HS
2002	Elkins HS, Missouri City, Texas
2003	Chatsworth (Calif.) HS
2004	Chatsworth (Calif.) HS
2005	Russell County (Ala.) HS

Cardenas emerges to take award

At first glance, Adrian Cardenas spent the fall and winter months leading up to his senior season in similar fashion to most high school players. He took hack after hack in the batting cage, exercised, lifted weights, fielded ground balls ad infinitum, fine-tuned his swing

PLAYER *OF THE* **YEAR**

and practiced practically every other physical aspect of the game imaginable.

It was how Cardenas prepared himself off the field that, in his estimation, made the difference.

He entered the season as a top-100 prospect, but not in consideration as a high-round draft choice. He wasn't even considered the best player on his high school team.

After the dust settled, he had set school, state and Dade County records, led his team to a state championship, been drafted in the supplemental first round, and been named Baseball America's High School Player of the Year.

"Oh my God, it's been unbelievable, and now with the draft it has all been amazing," he said. "This has truly been a Cinderella season."

Cardenas' unlikely tale can be traced to his evenings at his suburban Miami home prior to his senior season at Monsignor Pace High. With an intellect as remarkable as his athleticism, Cardenas, who graduated in the top 10 percent of his class, decided sharpening the mental side of his game was the step necessary to maximize his potential as a player.

"I love to analyze things," he said. "I basically wanted to carry the team on my back, and there was no time to be doubting or second-guessing yourself. I became so zeroed in on the game that day that I guess you have no option but to succeed."

And with that, Cardenas embarked on an otherworldly season. He homered seven times in his first eight games and was 28-for-34 without a strikeout a month into the season.

Positioned in the Spartans' three-hole in front of cleanup hitter Chris Marrero, Cardenas was getting pitches to hit, and punishing them with his strong, quick, lefthanded swing.

"It was like, 'Is this guy ever going to make an out,' " said Spartans coach Tom Duffin, who, like Cardenas, started at shortstop at Monsignor Pace back in 1985, the last time the school claimed the state championship.

The hits kept coming for Cardenas, who obliterated Duffin's school record for batting average, hitting .647

(75-for-116). He set a new Dade County home run mark with 18 and capped the season with a 5-for-5 performance in Monsignor Pace's championship game victory in Sarasota. He drove in 65 runs, scored another 52, hit 18 doubles, three triples and stole 14 bases.

Adrian Cardenas

At the season's outset, all the attention was on Marrero, whom Cardenas credits for inspiring him. Cardenas knew his friend was more talented and ranked higher as a pro prospect, and he was determined to show the nation that he not only could complement Marrero, but he was capable of outperforming him, as well.

"I love proving people wrong, and I knew the scouts were all there in the beginning to see Marrero," Cardenas said. "I wanted them to go there to see me just as much as Marrero."

Cardenas' declarations come with conviction, as Duffin and scouts alike will attest. He possesses a focus and outlook uncanny among players his age, instilled in part by his parents. A physical therapist and nurse, Cardenas' father and mother are the antithesis of the prototypical parents of a competitive, high-profile high school player. Cuban descendants, Juan and Aida Cardenas pointed their son in a completely different direction than the one that has become his livelihood.

Adrian began taking piano lessons as a three-year-old and performed in formal recitals up to the time he was a junior in high school. At a party to celebrate his selection in the draft, he entertained his friends and family by performing some of his favorite pieces by composers such as George Gershwin and Franz Liszt.

Cardenas points out that his parents' influence precipitated his mature, cerebral approach to the game, and he takes pride and satisfaction in knowing the path he has pursued—to play baseball professionally—was one he embraced with their encouragement, rather than their insistence.

"They don't know much about baseball, they just kind of follow it through me," Cardenas said with a laugh. "In some cases it might be the father or the mother pushing their son. With me, I haven't become the hitter that I am or the player I am because my father tells me to go take groundballs or hit. I became the player I am because I wanted to work at it and get to that level of being one of the best. That's very reassuring."

As the 37th overall pick (by the Phillies in the supplemental first round), he has the opportunity to follow his chosen path. His performance this spring, built on his hard work and solid foundation away from the game, makes it easy to believe in Cardenas' outlook.

"I know it's going to take a couple of years to develop, and I know I'm not going to hit no .647 when I get to the minors," he said. "But with time . . . I know I can rise to the occasion in the minor leagues and hopefully in the major leagues."

— ALAN MATTHEWS

PREVIOUS **WINNERS**

1992—Preston Wilson, of-rhp, Bamberg-Ehrhardt (S.C.) HS
1993—Trot Nixon, of-lhp, New Hanover HS, Wilmington, N.C.
1994—Doug Million, lhp, Sarasota (Fla.) HS
1995—Ben Davis, c, Malvern (Pa.) Prep
1996—Matt White, rhp, Waynesboro Area (Pa.) HS
1997—Darnell McDonald, of, Cherry Creek HS, Englewood, Colo.
1998—Drew Henson, 3b-rhp, Brighton (Mich.) HS
1999—Josh Hamilton, of-lhp, Athens Drive HS, Raleigh, N.C.
2000—Matt Harrington, rhp, Palmdale (Calif.) HS
2001—Joe Mauer, c, Cretin-Derham Hall, St. Paul, Minn.
2002—Scott Kazmir, lhp, Cypress Falls HS, Houston
2003—Jeff Allison, rhp, Veterans Memorial HS, Peabody, Mass.
2004—Homer Bailey, rhp, LaGrange (Texas) HS
2005—Justin Upton, ss, Great Bridge (Va.) HS

These were the top 50 high school teams in the nation at the end of the 2006 season. The staff of Baseball America and the National High School Baseball Coaches Association have compiled the national top 50 ranking since 1991.

Rank	School	Final Record	Accomplishment
1.	The Woodlands (Texas) HS	38-1	State 5-A champion
2.	Jackson HS, Mill Creek, Wash.	27-0	State 4-A champion
3.	Flanagan HS, Pembroke Pines, Fla.	29-3	State 6-A champion
4.	Chaparral HS, Scottsdale, Ariz.	31-3	State 5-A champion
5.	Monsignor Pace HS, Opa Locka, Fla.	28-4	State 4-A champion
6.	Lassiter HS, Marietta, Ga.	32-4	State 5-A champion
7.	Bellarmine Prep, San Jose, Calif.	34-4	CIF D-I sectional champion
8.	Brenham (Texas) HS	34-4	State 4-A regional finalist
9.	Chatsworth (Calif.) HS	31-3	CIF D-I sectional runner up
10.	Palm Beach Central HS, Wellington, Fla.	29-2	State 6-A regional finalist
11.	Riverside HS, Greer, S.C.	31-2	State 3-A champion
12.	Greenbrier HS, Augusta, Ga.	35-1	State 4-A champion
13.	Cypress (Calif.) HS	23-4	CIF D-II sectional second round
14.	Starr's Mill HS, Fayetteville, Ga.	38-2	State 5-A second round
15.	Bishop Kelley HS, Tulsa	38-2	State 5-A champion
16.	Massapequa (N.Y.) HS	31-0	State 2-A champion
17.	Owasso (Okla.) HS	35-2	State 6-A runner up
18.	Nova HS, Davie, Fla.	26-2	State 5-A regional quarterfinalist
19.	Lakewood (Calif.) HS	30-5	CIF sectional champion
20.	James Monroe HS, Bronx, N.Y.	50-2	State public school A champion
21.	Poly HS, Riverside, Calif.	25-5	CIF D-I sectional semifinalist
22.	Christian Brothers HS, Memphis	39-3	State D-II private school champion
23.	Captain Shreve HS, Shreveport, La.	37-3	State 3-A state champion
24.	Brophy Prep, Phoenix	30-5	State D-I 5-A champion
25.	Barbe HS, Lake Charles, La.	37-7	State 5-A champion
26.	Scotland HS, Laurinburg, N.C.	29-4	State 4-A champion
27.	Archbishop Rummel HS, Metairie, La.	33-5	State 5-A semifinalist
28.	Walsh Jesuit HS, Cuyahoga Falls, Ohio	30-2	State D-II champion
29.	Fallbrook (Calif.) HS	28-7	CIF D-I sectional runner up
30.	Arundel HS, Gambrills, Md.	22-3	State 4-A champion
31.	Osbourn HS, Manassas, Va.	24-2	State 3-A runner up
32.	La Cueva HS, Albuquerque	26-4	State 5-A champion
33.	Bishop Gorman HS, Las Vegas	35-7	State 4-A champion
34.	Bishop Moore HS, Orlando	29-2	State 4-A semifinalist
35.	El Camino Real HS, Woodland Hills, Calif.	26-6	CIF D-I semifinalist
36.	Barron Collier HS, Naples, Fla.	28-4	State 5-A semifinalist
37.	Jasper (Ind.) HS	34-1	State 3-A champion
38.	Free State HS, Lawrence, Kan.	22-3	State 6-A champion
39.	New Braunfels (Texas) HS	31-5	State 5-A champion
40.	Illinois Valley Central HS, Chillicothe, Ill.	30-1	State A champion
41.	North Forsyth HS, Winston-Salem, N.C.	30-2	State 4-A semifinalist
42.	Seton Hall Prep, West Orange, N.J.	23-4	State public school A champion
43.	Vianney HS, St. Louis	24-3	State Class 4 champion
44.	Old Tappan (N.J.) HS	29-2	State Group III semifinalist
45.	Pace HS, Milton, Fla.	29-3	State 5-A champion
46.	Sarasota (Fla.) HS	27-5	State 6-A runner up
47.	Torrey Pines HS, Encinitas, Calif.	28-6	CIF D-I sectional semifinalist
48.	Grosse Point N. HS, G.P. Woods, Mich.	37-1	State D-I champion
49.	Cherry Creek HS, Englewood, Colo.	20-2	District 5-A finalist
50.	Notre Dame Academy, Middleburg, Va.	28-5	State D-II champion

season in which he matched Drabek win for win, and finished 14-0, 1.27.

He and Drabek accounted for 28 of The Woodlands' 38 wins. Senior third baseman Paul Goldschmidt batted .315-8-44 and was lauded for his leadership, not on easy task on a team with such talent.

Six starters from the title game returned in 2007, including an outfield of Brett Eibner, David Alleman and Taylor Grote, significant players as juniors in 2006. The pieces are in place for Eastman again, and he hopes to clutch them together just as he did in 2006.

– JASON BECKER

Head Of State

The Woodlands was one of few favorites to finish what it started, as many of the nation's top high school teams found upsets awaiting them in their respective state playoffs. Perhaps no other state offered a more balanced, competitive field of teams that Louisiana and California in 2006.

Louisiana's playoff scene concluded with an unlikely scenario. Lake Charles' Barbe High came from behind in four of its five playoff games and knocked off the state's top-ranked team on its way to the Class 5-A title. The Bucs beat No. 27 Archbishop Rummel High (Metairie) 7-4 in the semifinals, thanks to a six-run fifth inning and nine stolen bases.

Another upset, this time of New Orleans' Jesuit High in front of more than 2,000 fans at Louisiana-Lafayette's Indian Field, by Sulphur (La.) High, landed Sulpher in the 5-A finals against Barbe.

Barbe pulled out a 2-1 win, marking the school's fourth state title and third in seven years. "It's amazing the obstacles this team had to face, and we're not the only ones," said Barbe coach Glenn Cecchini, who said the school's baseball field was destroyed during Hurricane Rita. "We had total devastation. It looked like a bomb had been dropped."

played. Even though Eastman is annually inheriting underclassmen who are above-average players, they often come from wealthy homes with egos that might match their baseball acumen.

This group had it all, however, playing with talent and chemistry and were led by righthander Kyle Drabek, the son of the 1990 National League Cy Young award winner Doug Drabek. Just 72 hours removed from being the Phillies' first-round draft pick, Kyle got the win against Midland in the semifinals and hit a three-run homer in the first inning against Katy.

Kyle is as well known for his thunderbolt arm as his combustible temperament, and he etched his name into Texas high school baseball lore by going 14-0, 1.00 as a senior with 155 strikeouts in 91 innings.

In the championship game, however, it was the Texas Christian-bound Maxwell who got the ball and he went the distance against Katy, scattering seven hits to cap a

Barbe played its first 28 games away from home while its field was rebuilt, and slipped out of the BA/NHSBCA poll when it lost five starters during the season's first month due to various injuries and illnesses. Yet its 37 victories were a state record. "It's been an unbelievable year," Cecchini said.

Texas signee Josh Prince hit .425 with a .500 on-base percentage, 19 walks, 13 strikeouts, 20 extra-base hits and 55 stolen bases for the Bucs, who posted a final ranking of No. 25. One of the top defensive infielders in the Class of 2006, Prince had a .956 fielding percentage, with nine errors in 261 innings at shortstop. His older brother Dooley played two seasons locally at McNeese State before transferring to Texas in 2004.

■ No. 23 Captain Shreve High (Shreveport, La.) won the Class 4-A championship and tied Barbe for a new state record for wins in a season with 37. Captain Shreve won its first state championship in baseball with the 7-0

2006 HIGH SCHOOL ALL-AMERICA TEAM

Cedric Hunter

Chris Parmelee

Clayton Kershaw

Kasey Kiker

Selected by Baseball America

FIRST TEAM

Pos., Player, School	Class	B-T	Ht.	Wt.	AVG	AB	R	H	2B	3B	HR	RBI	SB	Drafted
C Max Sapp, Bishop Moore HS, Orlando	Sr.	L-R	6-2	225	.591	71	14	42	11	0	10	48	0	Astros (1)
1B Lars Anderson, Jesuit HS, Carmichael, Calif.	Sr.	L-L	6-5	190	.429	84	44	36	2	1	15	45	6	Red Sox (18)
IF Adrian Cardenas, Mons. Pace HS, Opa Locka, Fla.	Sr.	L-R	6-0	190	.647	116	52	75	18	3	18	65	14	Phillies (1S)
IF Chris Marrero, Monsignor Pace HS, Opa Locka, Fla.	Sr.	R-R	6-3	215	.379	103	30	39	7	0	13	35	8	Nationals (1)
IF Bill Rowell, Bishop Eustace Prep, Pennsauken, N.J.	Sr.	L-R	6-4	198	.541	61	27	33	9	1	4	29	21	Orioles (1)
OF Cedric Hunter, Martin Luther King HS, Decatur, Ga.	Sr.	L-L	6-0	190	.580	69	49	40	9	2	12	28	20	Padres (3)
OF Chris Parmelee, Chino Hills (Calif.) HS	Sr.	L-L	6-1	195	.407	59	28	24	5	0	11	26	24	Twins (1)
OF Travis Snider, Jackson HS, Mill Creek, Wash.	Sr.	L-L	6-0	230	.500	84	50	42	9	2	11	45	8	Blue Jays (1)
UT Kyle Drabek, The Woodlands (Texas) High	Sr.	R-R	6-1	190	.427	131	32	56	11	2	12	41	1	Phillies (1)

Pos., Player, School	Class	B-T	Ht.	Wt.	W	L	ERA	G	SV	IP	H	BB	SO	Drafted
P Brett Anderson, Stillwater (Okla.) HS	Sr.	L-L	6-4	205	9	0	0.37	12	2	57	27	9	102	D-backs (2)
P Jeremy Jeffress, Halifax County HS, S. Boston, Va.	Sr.	R-R	6-0	174	9	1	0.44	10	0	64	22	24	121	Brewers (1)
P Clayton Kershaw, Highland Park HS, Dallas	Sr.	L-L	6-3	210	13	0	0.77	15	0	64	23	26	139	Dodgers (1)
P Kasey Kiker, Russell County HS, Seale, Ala.	Sr.	L-L	5-11	181	7	4	0.92	13	0	70	43	24	143	Rangers (1)
P Colton Willems, John Carroll Cath. HS, Ft. Pierce, Fla.	Sr.	R-R	6-4	185	7	1	0.68	9	0	51	16	6	99	Nationals (1)
UT Kyle Drabek, The Woodlands (Texas) High	Sr.	R-R	6-1	190	14	0	1.00	14	0	91	51	34	155	Phillies (1)

SECOND TEAM

Pos., Player, School	Class	B-T	Ht.	Wt.	AVG	AB	R	H	2B	3B	HR	RBI	SB	Drafted
C Hank Conger, Huntington Beach (Calif.) HS	Sr.	B-R	6-2	205	.449	78	25	35	7	1	11	27	1	Angels (1)
1B Cody Johnson, Mosley HS, Lynn Haven Fla.	Sr.	L-R	6-4	200	.522	67	44	35	6	0	15	43	10	Braves (1)
IF Lonnie Chisenhall, W. Carteret HS, Morehead Cty, N.C.	Sr.	L-R	6-1	175	.574	—	36	39	9	4	9	37	11	Pirates (11)
IF Tommy Pham, Durango HS, Las Vegas	Sr.	R-R	6-2	185	.581	110	53	64	17	7	10	56	28	Cardinals (16)
IF John Tolisano, Estero (Fla.) HS	Jr.	B-R	6-0	190	.623	—	33	48	10	2	7	45	—	Not eligible
OF Jason Place, Wren HS, Piedmont, S.C.	Sr.	R-R	6-3	200	.544	57	32	31	6	1	4	20	10	Red Sox (1)
OF Justin Reed, Hillcrest Christian HS, Jackson, Miss.	Sr.	L-R	5-11	185	.458	118	57	54	6	5	7	34	40	Reds (4)
OF Matt Sulentic, Hillcrest HS, Dallas	Sr.	L-R	5-10	175	.654	81	49	53	6	3	20	59	17	Athletics (3)
UT Kyler Burke, Ooltewah (Tenn.) HS	Sr.	L-L	6-2	198	.459	111	55	51	9	6	20	58	9	Padres (1S)

Pos., Player, School	Class	B-T	Ht.	Wt.	W	L	ERA	G	SV	IP	H	BB	SO	Drafted
P Kyle Blair, Los Gatos (Calif.) HS	Jr.	R-R	6-3	200	10	1	0.19	12	0	76	—	14	119	Not eligible
P Steve Evarts, Robinson HS, Tampa	Sr.	L-L	6-4	185	9	3	0.62	13	1	77	—	12	141	Braves (1S)
P Matt Latos, Coconut Creek (Fla.) HS	Sr.	R-R	6-5	208	7	3	0.64	12	2	66	23	14	110	Padres (11)
P Jeff Locke, Kennett HS, Center Conway, N.H.	Sr.	L-L	6-2	175	9	0	0.69	12	0	68	22	12	131	Braves (2)
P Cory Rasmus, Russell County HS, Seale, Ala.	Sr.	R-R	6-0	195	10	3	0.57	13	0	74	28	31	130	Braves (1S)
UT Kyler Burke, Ooltewah (Tenn.) HS	Sr.	L-L	6-2	198	9	1	1.36	10	0	61	27	29	101	Padres (1S)

THIRD TEAM

Pos., Player, School	Class	B-T	Ht.	Wt.	AVG	AB	R	H	2B	3B	HR	RBI	SB	Drafted
C Torre Langley, Alexander HS, Douglasville, Ga.	Sr.	R-R	5-9	175	.633	79	17	50	14	2	15	55	1	Marlins (3)
1B Aaron Miller, Channelview (Texas) HS	Sr.	L-L	6-3	205	.581	98	54	52	11	2	14	49	20	Rockies (11)
IF Marcus Lemon, Eustis (Fla.) HS	Sr.	L-R	5-11	170	.451	91	49	41	12	1	6	24	23	Rangers (4)
IF Russ Moldenhauer, Boerne (Texas) HS	Sr.	L-R	5-11	205	.510	100	36	51	10	0	8	27	8	Angels (3)
IF Nick Noonan, Francis Parker HS, San Diego	Jr.	L-R	6-1	170	.491	108	36	53	16	3	5	30	30	Not eligible
OF Joe Benson, Joliet Catholic HS, Joliet, Ill.	Sr.	R-R	6-2	200	.489	92	49	45	12	3	7	47	16	Twins (2)
OF Michael Burgess, Hillsborough HS, Tampa	Jr.	L-L	5-11	190	.511	88	—	45	11	0	12	48	24	Not eligible
OF Tom Hickman, Pepperell HS, Lindale, Ga.	Sr.	L-L	6-0	180	.520	111	44	38	8	3	12	53	10	Marlins (2)
UT Alex White, Conley HS, Greenville, N.C.	Sr.	R-R	6-4	185	.506	85	37	43	12	0	13	37	1	Dodgers (14)

Pos., Player, School	Class	B-T	Ht.	Wt.	W	L	ERA	G	SV	IP	H	BB	SO	Drafted
P Brandon Belt, Hudson HS, Lufkin, Texas	Sr.	L-L	6-5	188	10	0	0.24	11	0	58	8	17	117	Red Sox (11)
P Caleb Clay, Cullman (Ala.) HS	Sr.	R-R	6-2	185	10	1	1.29	21	5	87	39	21	112	Red Sox (1S)
P Alex Cobb, Vero Beach (Fla.) HS	Sr.	R-R	6-1	175	5	3	1.09	13	1	74	24	31	139	Devil Rays (4)
P Glenn Gibson, Center Moriches (N.Y.) HS	Sr.	L-L	6-4	200	8	1	0.23	11	0	61	7	11	145	Nationals (4)
P Jordan Walden, Mansfield (Texas) HS	Sr.	R-R	6-4	230	8	1	1.04	11	0	54	26	25	102	Angels (12)
UT Alex White, Conley HS, Greenville, N.C.	Sr.	R-R	6-4	185	10	0	0.46	10	3	76	34	11	136	Dodgers (14)

HIGH SCHOOL BASEBALL

victory over Marrero's Archbishop Shaw.

■ Louisiana's Class 3-A playoffs were more predictable, as Parkview Baptist High (Baton Rouge) rebounded from a slow start to win its fifth straight state title. Parkview Baptist junior lefthander/first baseman Forrest Moore posted a 12-0 record, while senior righthander/shortstop Kellen Bozeman went 8-0, and enrolled at Louisiana State. The Eagles finished 32-5 and have won 25 consecutive playoff games.

■ Eight of the nine California schools that were ranked in the May 22 BA/NHSBCA Top 50 poll lost in the playoffs, making for an unpredictable finish to California's prep baseball season.

The marquee matchup took place at Angels Stadium, where Lakewood (Calif.) High clinched the California Interscholastic Federation Division I Southern Section championship (California doesn't have a state championship, but rather 10 sections broken down into regions, which have as many as six divisions, with Division I being the largest schools) with a 2-1 victory against Agoura (Calif.) High.

Agoura junior righthander Robert Stock, BA's 2005 Youth Player of the Year, carried a 1-0 lead to the bottom of the seventh inning. But No. 19 Lakewood pieced together three consecutive hits—a leadoff bloop double to left field, a bunt single and a two-run ground ball hit down the right-field line—to come from behind.

"There's nothing you can really say to take the pain away from a loss like this," Agoura coach Scott Deck told the (Agoura Hills) Acorn.

Perhaps Lakewood's victory was foreshadowed. Earlier the same day, Damion Easley, the star of the 1987 Lakewood team that won the school's last sectional championship, hit three home runs for the Diamondbacks.

The team featured just two seniors in the starting lineup, with its nucleus comprised primarily of a group of juniors who won the Pony League World Series in 2003.

■ Kennedy High (Granada Hills, Calif.) was no-hit for five innings before rallying in the sixth to defeat ninthranked Chatsworth High 4-2 to take the Division I Los Angeles City Section title. Chatsworth senior righthander Josh Ravin surrendered a pair of singles, a walk and doubles to Kennedy sophomores Carlos Gonzalez and Chris Ornelas in the sixth.

■ California's highest-ranked team was No. 7 Bellarmine Prep (San Jose), which went 34-4 on its way to the Division I Central Coast section title.

Poll Positioning

■ The nation's second-ranked team, Jackson High of Mill Creek, Wash., completed its season undefeated. Jackson pasted Auburn High 7-1 to claim Washington's Class 4-A championship. Jackson junior lefthander Geoff Brown allowed one run in five-plus innings and drilled a two-run home run to cap Jackson's season with a 27-0 record. The title was the 12-year-old school's first in any sport.

■ Starr's Mill High (Fayetteville, Ga.) carried a perfect record and No. 3 national ranking into Georgia's Class 5-A playoffs, but was dramatically bounced in the second round by Tift County High. Starr's Mill won the three-game series opener and was one strike away from sweeping Tift County when Christian Glisson delivered a two-out, two-strike, two-run homer in the bottom of the seventh inning for a 4-3 victory.

From prep standout to Southern California
Robert Stock skipped his senior season of high school

The Devils trailed 4-3 in the top of the seventh inning of the decisive third game but again rallied, this time for three runs, more than enough for senior Austin Smith, who polished off a complete game and ended the Panthers' (28-2) season.

Starr's Mill, which finished the season ranked No. 14, was playing without four starters and senior righty Andrew Robinson. "I said to someone in an e-mail, 'We're riding on three flat tires right now,' " Starr's Mill coach Brent Moseley told the Atlanta Journal-Constitution.

Tift County (25-8) ran out of magic in the quarterfinals and was swept by Marietta's Kell High, 12-0 and 17-2. Kell advanced to the championship round, where it fell to fellow Marietta, Ga., power Lassiter High 10-9, 9-5. Lassiter finished ranked No. 6 nationally.

■ Florida's state tournament featured plenty of highlights, including a pair of much-anticipated pitching matchups in the Class 6-A semifinals. The day began with defending champion Flanagan (Pembroke Pines) and Hialeah High. Flanagan junior lefty D.J. Swatscheno tossed a two-hit shutout, out-dueling Hialeah senior lefty Nick Hernandez 1-0.

In the other 6-A semifinal, Sarasota High senior lefty Eric Erickson bested DeLand High junior righthander/outfielder Michael Main 7-0. Erickson, who enrolled at Miami, allowed three hits with 11 strikeouts, and Sarasota junior first baseman Evan Stobbs hit a two-run home run off Main, one of the best high school juniors in the country.

Main lasted 6⅓ innings, surrendering five hits and five runs with 13 punchouts. He was limited to 31 innings this season because of tendinitis in his rotator cuff, but racked up a 62-7 strikeout-walk ratio and batted .402 in 92 at-bats. Main's fastball was clocked as high as 97 mph against Oviedo High in the postseason.

No. 3 Flanagan beat No. 46 Sarasota High 7-1 for its second consecutive 6-A crown.

HIGH SCHOOL BASEBALL

■ In a wild Class 4-A title game, No. 5 Monsignor Pace (Opa Locka) outslugged Bishop Kenny (Jacksonville) 15-9. The Spartans (27-4) led 8-0 before the Crusaders (27-4) scored seven runs after two were out in the second inning to cut the lead to one. Monsignor Pace pulled away behind senior shortstop Adrian Cardenas, who went 5-for-5 with three doubles, a triple and five RBIs.

"It's incredible," Cardenas told the Miami Herald. "You can never understand how good it feels until you finally win it." Cardenas finished his senior season with a school-record .630 batting average, eclipsing the mark set by Monsignor Pace coach Tom Duffin. Cardenas clubbed 18 home runs, setting a new Dade County record, as well.

■ Pace High of Milton defeated Tampa's Hillsborough High 11-7 to claim the Class 5-A championship, finishing 29-4 and ranked No. 45.

■ Tulsa's Union High upset No. 17 Owasso High in Oklahoma's Class 6-A playoffs, squeaking out a 4-3 victory in extra innings to secure its second straight 6-A crown.

Oklahoma's 5-A title went to Tulsa's Bishop Kelley High, which defeated Albert High of Midwest City, 3-1. Bishop Kelley senior Jeff Scardino had a two-run single in the bottom of the sixth inning to provide the final margin. The Comets finished with a 38-2 mark and a No. 15 ranking.

■ Heading into New Jersey's postseason, it appeared the Garden State would boast a new school as its top team. But a month later, it was the state's perennial power, Seton Hall Prep, once again finishing as New Jersey's highest-ranked club and repeating as state champs.

The private, West Orange, N.J., school relied on a Division-I signee, senior Mike Ness (Duke), and two potential high-round draft picks in junior righthanders Rick Porcello and Evan Daneli, on its way to a 23-4 record and a No. 42 ranking. Porcello went 6-0 with an 0.30 ERA, including a pair of wins in the postseason. Seton Hall Prep won the Parochial A, Non-Public Class A championship, its fourth in the past six years. It marked the third time in the past four years Seton Hall Prep finished in the top 50 in the final poll, including a No. 9 finish in 2003.

Old Tappan (N.J) High was off to a 28-0 start before dropping two of its last three games, ending its season in the Group III semifinals. Old Tappan fell to Morristown High, which went on to the Group III title. The Colonials (26-7) came from behind in 20 of their 26 wins.

Stock Passes Up On Draft, Prep Glory

Across America in the fall of 2006, millions of teenagers were preparing for their final year of high school, brushing up on their calculus and narrowing their list of colleges to attend.

Robert Stock was a year ahead of them.

The 16-year-old catcher/righthander from Westlake Village, Calif., enrolled at Southern California, opting to skip his senior year at Agoura High. Instead, Stock attended his first college class—Writing 140—and will be eligible to play baseball for the Trojans when their 2007 season begins.

"I have a grasp on it," Stock said, "but I'm sure within the next week or so, it's really going to hit me that, 'Wow, I'm in college right now.'

"Missing my senior year in high school, not getting to take part in all these activities . . . I will definitely miss not going to the prom with my girlfriend; I've known her since the sixth grade. And I'll definitely miss playing baseball with my little brother (Richard). I haven't played with him since I was little, and I definitely will miss that."

Stock, who was named Baseball America's Youth Player of the Year in 2005 as a 15-year-old, met early academic admission requirements based on several criteria outlined in Rule 14.3.1.4 of the NCAA's early admission program. Stock ranked in the top 20 percent of his high school class and completed each of his core class requirements, except English. He also had the required GPA of at least 3.5 in each of his last four high school semesters. He then had to apply for a waiver from the NCAA that would grant him eligibility to play baseball at USC, which he received. His 1410 SAT score helped him overcome the final stumbling block of getting into Southern California through its Resident Honors Program, which allows about 30 elite students who have demonstrated exceptional maturity to enroll in the university a year early.

The Stocks were the ones who first broached the possibility of early enrollment with the USC coaching staff, and they were told the Trojans had no more scholarship money to give out. But the Stocks decided getting to school early was important enough that they would pay Robert's way his first year.

"If he (went) and played at Agoura this year, and then gets drafted in his normal class, I think baseball-wise, three more years would be one too many," said his father Gregg Stock. "He's ready to play Division I baseball this year. Being at that level for three years (beginning in the fall of 2007) would hold him back. It's much more tempting to sign (a professional contract after being drafted in) June 2007, versus going to college for three more years.

"The idea is to get our cake and eat it too."

Stock will be draft-eligible following his junior season at USC in 2009. If he had not signed out of high school in 2007 and waited until that fall to enroll, he would not be eligible to be drafted again until 2010. This decision negates any leverage he would have in 2007, but allows him to gain three years of college experience and enter the draft a year earlier than he would have, had Stock gone the conventional path. Gregg's assertion that his son is physically ready to compete against Pacific-10 Conference competition isn't debated by those in the scouting community, though the decision won't come without controversy.

"That has some validity," said a crosschecker with an National League club in response to Gregg Stock's sentiment. "He has played against the best competition and obviously he's an advanced player. But obviously when someone makes that kind of comment, it's going to make him a target in the college baseball world. I think he has enough ability that he would be able to back it up.

"Say he has a great year at Agoura and continues to develop as a catcher. There are clubs out there that might like him a lot and take him in the first 10 picks. We're talking anywhere from $2.1 to more than $3 million. I would hate to close that option. That's a pretty good start on life. But to each his own. That's the bottom line. I just hope it doesn't open a can of worms for

Talented '07 Class Emerges At Aflac Classic

SAN DIEGO—Reggie Jackson was a fitting choice as the honorary chairman for the fourth annual Aflac All-American Classic. Jackson spoke to 38 of the best rising high school seniors before the game at San Diego State, and they clearly listened closely.

Jackson, who slugged 563 home runs, also quipped about his 2,597 career strikeouts before the game. The cream of the high school Class of 2007 then went out showed a similar feast or famine approach in the West's 9-8 victory over the East at Tony Gywnn Stadium.

There were plenty of extra-base hits (11) and plenty of strikeouts (29), as 10 different pitchers hit 93 mph or better. The unpredictable, high-energy action was representative of the premium talent expected to be available in the 2007 draft.

"The pitching was a pleasant surprise here, especially from the East, and they had the better ones from the West and I think they showed us some impressive bats here today," said a crosschecker with a National League organization.

Facing one of the nation's most talented pitchers, the West scored four runs off Deland (Fla.) High's Michael Main in the first inning, keyed by back-to-back RBI doubles by Cypress (Calif.) High's Josh Vitters and Iowa City High's Jon Gilmore, and a run-scoring triple by Brett Kill (Aliso Niguel High, Aliso Viejo, Calif.). The West, which has won three Aflac games in a row, never relinquished the lead.

Main had plenty of velocity, touching 95 and pitching at 93, as well as control, finding the strike zone with 31 of his 45 first-inning pitches, but he lacked command, something the loaded West lineup wouldn't let him get away with.

"They sat on the fastball and they turned it around for some quality hits," Main said. "I mean, they really hit the ball with some intensity."

Potent Western Attack

Vitters blistered a double into left field off a 93 mph Main fastball to plate Christian Colon, and Gilmore followed with a sharp double of his own before Krill served a Main offering to the right-center field alley to make it 4-2.

Vitters, who tacked on two more doubles as part of his 3-for-4 afternoon, was one of a handful of West position players that looked right at home facing the hardest throwers in the high school class.

"The pitchers are probably supposed to dominate us because they're just a higher level than we're used

to facing, so it feels really good to come out here and hold my own," said Vitters, out of Cypress (Calif.) High. "I just make sure I get the front foot down early so I'm not late and just kind of look dead red."

The strategy worked, as the West piled up 13 hits, even touching up East righthander Rick Porcello, who ran his fastball up to 96, for a pair of runs in the sixth inning.

"People (might have been) trying to do too much, especially the pitchers," a scout said. "There was very little command today, but there are some good arms, just very fair pitchability until the end. And that happens when you try to grunt up and muscle up, play for the (radar) gun or play for the power."

Colon, who like Vitters hails from Orange County, went 2-for-3 with three stolen bases and three runs scored and was named MVP, an award he sheepishly accepted. "I really thought that (Vitters) was going to get it, and you know we both played really good," Colon said.

Looking Forward To Next June

After a down year for talent in the 2006 draft class, the 2007 crop of high school players could be the best of the decade. Most of the top players have made positive impressions all summer on the showcase and tournament circuit, and unlike in years past when most of the teens seemed exhausted by the time the summer's crowning event rolled around, swings were crisp and pitchers had plenty of heat.

Righthander Neil Ramirez (Kempsville, Va., High) breezed through the third inning off a low-90s fastball and pinpoint command, an inning trumped in the top of the fourth by Tim Alderson, a 6-foot-6 righthander from Horizon High in Scottsdale, Ariz. Alderson struck out two of the three batters he faced, dealing seven strikes in an eight-pitch inning.

Two of the class' most decorated prospects also rose to the occasion. Robert Stock (Agoura, Calif., High) ripped Porcello's 92 mph fastball over the center-field wall for a solo homer to lead off the seventh. An inning later, John Tolisano (Estero, Fla., High) took Tomball, Texas, High lefty Drake Britton deep.

"I thought it was a joke when they said they were going to have a home run derby," said West manager Dennis Pugh, a 33-year coaching veteran from San Diego. "But these kids can flat-out hit."

—ALAN MATTHEWS

other kids thinking that they can do this same thing."

Stock has been the talk of amateur baseball for more than three years. His fastball was clocked as high as 90 mph when he was 14, and he has developed a penchant for performing well on the biggest of stages. He started on the mound for the West in August's Aflac All-American game and homered to center field in the seventh inning. This spring as a junior at Agoura (Calif.) High, Stock came down with an inflamed rotator cuff in his right shoulder and decided it was best to concentrate

on hitting and catching this summer.

Since Stock carried a no-hitter into the sixth inning of the California Interscholastic Federation Southern Section Division I championship game in May, he toed a rubber less than a handful of times. The scouting consensus suggests his future is behind the plate, and the Stocks are convinced his best source of instruction is at USC. There Stock can learn from coach Chad Kreuter, who spent 16 seasons catching in the major leagues.

"My career goal is not to make money," Stock said,

"but to play in the major leagues, and going to college will make those chances higher."

Kreuter said the Trojans' primary goal is to get Stock ready to catch in the Pac-10, but Stock also will factor into USC's bullpen mix along with junior closer Paul Koss and incoming freshman Hector Rabago.

"How can you not want to use that resource? He's 93-95 off the mound," Kreuter said. "I know that one of the starting pitchers at Agoura got hurt last year, so he threw a lot, and he only threw once this summer because his arm was dead, so we will be careful with his arm.

"First and foremost for us is getting him ready behind the plate. I'm confident his bat will be fine, and we'll get him work off the mound, but we'll ease him into that. We have a situation now where we'll have three guys who can close games."

Stock's catch and throw skills are unrefined, but his arm strength serves him well as a catcher. His footwork and exchange can be cleaned up, which would improve his pop times from home to second. He's athletic and agile enough to block balls adequately presently. His instincts, work ethic and championship-caliber makeup should serve him well as he continues to develop.

"I think what's going to happen is he's going to catch every day, he's been a pitcher and this last year, he has put all of his time in catching, so you have to understand how little time he's had back there," the crosschecker said. "I think he's going to hit as much as (former USC All-America and current Mariners catcher) Jeff Clement with the power that Clement hit with, and be a better catcher than Clement."

—ALAN MATTHEWS

New Showcase For Black Preps

In an effort to improve the exposure of black baseball players from neighborhoods that lack well-structured youth and high school baseball programs, two black businessmen, along with black coaches and scouts, organized the inaugural Mentoring Viable Prospects showcase. The three-day event featured eight teams of rising high school juniors and seniors from Florida, New Orleans, the Southeast and St. Louis, and was held at Georgia Perimeter College's Clarkston campus outside of Atlanta.

The showcase's concept was spawned by Atlanta businessmen Milt Sanders and Melvin Treynum as well as Greg Goodwin, a high school coach and assistant principal.

"The point is to give those kids an opportunity to go to college, and if some of those kids go on to play professionally, all the better for the players," said Steve Williams, a Tigers crosschecker who was enlisted to aid in the event's organization and promotion. "A lot of these kids can't afford to (play) on some of these select teams, and we wanted to have the (historic black colleges and universities), junior colleges and four-year colleges come in and see them.

"It came out really, really well. It was very well organized and the kids had a great time."

Sanders' objective was not only to help black players receive scholarship offers, but to teach players and parents about the recruiting process, and provide coaches affordable ways to improve instruction.

In addition to the exposure the players received, Southern head coach Roger Cador, Rockies assistant

scouting director Danny Montgomery, Lake City (Fla.) Community College coach Tom Clark and an NCAA compliance representative spoke to coaches, players and parents at a symposium.

Class Of 2007 Shines At Area Codes

Long Beach State's Blair Field is notorious for being one of the best pitcher's parks on the West Coast, a fact that made the soaring home runs hit during the 20th annual Area Code Games a telling sign.

"Nobody hits them out here, and especially not high school players," said a veteran American League scout in attendance.

The consensus among scouts over the summer has been that the high school Class of 2007 is deep in high-ceiling talent, and the performances of many Southern California position players in the final major showcase of the summer reinforced that sentiment.

In 1996, Milton Bradley, Nick Johnson, Jimmy Rollins, Eric Chavez, Brad Cresse, Bobby Hill, Eric Munson and Freddy Sanchez were all drafted out of California high schools (Cresse, Hill, Munson and Sanchez chose to attend college before signing), and with each sharply hit line drive at this year's Area Code Games came whispers that this year's class could be comparable.

"I would concur with that," said a crosschecker with a National League organization. "When you see Vitters, Dominguez, Freeman, Noonan, Lambo, Stanton . . . Southern California is loaded with hitters this year, and there's a lot of people excited about next year's draft. Last year I don't think there were a lot of people excited about the draft."

Third basemen Matt Dominguez (Chatsworth High) and Josh Vitters (Cypress High) could be the cream of the crop.

Dominguez, who already holds a share of Chatsworth's career home run record and has homered the past two seasons in the California high school play-offs at Dodger Stadium, comes with a proven track record, bat speed and an aggressive approach. He's also above-average defensively. Vitters' feel for hitting is slightly better than Dominguez', and he also has outstanding bat speed and made consistent hard contact during the showcase.

El Modena High's Freddie Freeman and Newbury Park High's Andrew Lambo are both lefthanded-hitting first basemen with plus raw power. Lambo is smooth around the bag, while Freeman has well-above-average arm strength.

Nick Noonan (Parker High) entered his senior year as San Diego's top prep prospect. His tools are less impressive than many of his peers', but he centers balls with wood bats well and shows soft hands and good instincts at shortstop.

Sherman Oaks, Calif., product Mike Stanton offers intriguing upside. He had little trouble clearing the left-field wall in batting practice. The athletic, strong 6-foot-5, 205-pound Stanton generates above-average bat speed and has plus raw power.

Georgia Takes Little League World Series

Cody Walker's two-run home run was all the offense needed for Southeast pitcher Kyle Carter, who scattered three hits and fanned eleven as Columbus Northern Little League defeated Kawaguchi Little League of Japan,

AMATEUR/YOUTH CHAMPIONS 2006

TEAM USA

JUNIOR TEAM (18-and-Under)

Event	Site	Champion	Runner-up
Tournament of Champions	Joplin, Mo.	AABC	USA Stars
IBAF World Junior Championship	Sancti Spiritus, Cuba	Korea	United States

YOUTH TEAM (16-and-Under)

Event	Site	Champion	Runner-up
COPABE Pan-Am Championship	Barquisimeto, Venezuela	USA	Venezuela
USA Junior Olympics—East	Jupiter, Fla.	All-American Prospects	Tampa Bay Raiders
USA Junior Olympics—West	Peoria/Sunrise, Ariz.	NorCal Red	Anderson Bats

ALL-AMERICAN AMATEUR BASEBALL ASSOCIATION (AAABA) HEADQUARTERS: Zanesville, Ohio

Event	Site	Champion	Runner-up
World Series (21-and-Under)	Johnstown, Pa.	Maryland Orioles	Chicago Glen Ellyn Jam

AMATEUR ATHLETIC UNION (AAU) HEADQUARTERS: Lake Buena Vista, Fla.

Event	Site	Champion	Runner-up
10-and-Under (65-foot)	Charlotte	NC Cleveland Indians	Carolina Angels
11-and-Under (70-foot)	Orlando	Central Florida Express	East Cobb (Ga.) Astros
12-and-Under	Burnsville, Minn.	Baltimore Buzz	South Shore (Mass.) Seadogs
13-and-Under (80-foot)	Burlington, N.C.	East Cobb (Ga.) Astros	Team Tennessee
13-and-Under (90-foot)	Myrtle Beach, S.C.	Massachusetts Lightning Baseball	Central Florida Indians
14-and-Under (90-foot)	Sarasota, Fla.	California Starmaker Titans	Team Easton Florida
15-and-Under	Roanoke, Va.	NorCal	Team Charlotte (N.C.)
Junior Olympics/16 & U	New Orleans	East Cobb (Ga.) Astros	OTC (Ga.) Bearcats
17-and-Under	Louisville	Tri State (N.J.) Arsenal	Ohio All Pro Freight
18-and-Under	Orlando	Brandon (Fla.) Blaze	Brazos Valley (Texas) Renegades

AMERICAN AMATEUR BASEBALL CONGRESS (AABC) HEADQUARTERS: Farmington, N.M.

Event	Site	Champion	Runner-up
Pee Wee Reese (11 & U)	Brooklyn, N.Y.	Brooklyn (N.Y.) Metro	Germantown, Md.
Pee Wee Reese (12 & U)	Toa Baja, P.R.	Georgia Padres	Tulsa Lookouts
Sandy Koufax (13 & U)	Battle Creek, Mich.	Detroit Eagles	Burtonville (Ind.) Dawgs
Sandy Koufax (14 & U)	Douglasville, Ga.	Puerto Rico Potros	Seattle Stars
Mickey Mantle (15 & U)	Owasso, Okla.	Dallas Mustangs	Owasso (Okla.) Rams
Mickey Mantle (16 & U)	McKinney, Texas	Dallas-Bat	Trombly (Calif.) Cubs
Connie Mack (18 & U)	Farmington, N.M.	Arizona Firebirds	Trombly (Calif.) Braves
Stan Musial (open)	Huntsville, Texas	Long Island Storm	Tampa Elite

(continued on Page 420)

2-1, for the 60th Little League Baseball World Series championship in Williamsport, Pa.

With the win, Kyle became the only pitcher in Little League Baseball World Series history to win four games in one series.

Asia broke on top in the third inning with a run-scoring single by Go Matsumota, bringing in Seigo Yada from second base. As a pitcher, Go was nearly as effective as Kyle, giving up three hits while striking out nine.

But Josh Lester's single and Cody Walker's homer put Southeast ahead for good in the bottom half of the inning.

The title was the second for a Georgia team in as many tries. East Marietta National Little League of Marietta, Ga., won the championship game 3-1 against a team from the Dominican Republic.

It also is the first time since 1992-93 that U.S. teams have won back-to-back Little League World Series championships.

The game was to have been played on a Sunday, but rain forced postponement until the next day. Still, a crowd of 4,725 was on hand. The attendance for the entire 32-game series was more than 200,000.

Little League Baseball also made news after the series by becoming the first youth circuit to institute pitch limits, which will go into effect for 2007 play.

New Orleans Team Captures Legion Series

The American Legion team from the New Orleans suburb of Metairie had already survived Hurricane Katrina the year before, so losing the first game of the 2006 American Legion World Series was hardly an obstacle for them.

The Louisiana team scored three runs in the bottom of the eighth inning to beat Terre Haute, Ind., 6-4, in the championship game of the series in Cedar Rapids, Iowa, making it all the way back from that opening loss.

Matt Brown pitched a complete game to help Metairie claim the first World Series title in team history. Metairie lost to Terre Haute in the opening round of the tournament and had to come back through the loser's bracket by beating the Indiana team twice in the last two days of the Series.

"We lost the first game of this tournament, but it was never out of sight for us," said Brown, a sophomore at Calhoun Junior College in Decatur, Ala. "And we're going home with a nice trophy."

Metairie coach David Baudry said his team didn't get discouraged after losing to Terre Haute in the first round. Baudry, who coaches at Metairie's Archbishop Rummel High, where most of his players come from, said he has watched the movie "Field of Dreams" more than 100 times and got to visit the movie site in Dyersville during the series. He said that was almost as good as winning the title.

Metairie shortstop Mike Liberto was named the MVP of the tournament.

HIGH SCHOOL BASEBALL

AMERICAN LEGION BASEBALL — HEADQUARTERS: Indianapolis

Event	Site	Champion	Runner-up
World Series (19 & U)	Cedar Rapids, Iowa	Enid, Okla.	Twin Cities, Wash.

BABE RUTH BASEBALL — HEADQUARTERS: Trenton, N.J.

Event	Site	Champion	Runner-up
Cal Ripken (10 & U)	Lafayette, La.	Visalia, Calif.	New Canaan, Conn.
Cal Ripken (11-12)	Aberdeen, Md.	Hilo, Hawaii	Mexico
13-year-old	Hamilton Township, N.J.	Tri Valley, Calif.	
14-year-old	Wilson, N.C.	Citrus Valley, Calif.	
13-15-year-olds	Clifton Park, N.Y.	Torrance, Calif.	
16-year-old	Monticello, Ark.	Newark, Ohio	Mid-County, Texas
16-18-year-old	Newark, Ohio	San Gabriel Valley, Calif.	Licking County, Ohio

CONTINENTAL AMATEUR BASEBALL ASSOCIATION (CABA) — HEADQUARTERS: Westerville, Ohio

Event	Site	Champion	Runner-up
9-and-Under	Charles City, Iowa	Hawaii Warriors	Cincinnati Flames
10-and-Under	Lynwood, Ill.	Iowa Sun Devils	Naperville (Ill.) Wheatland Ducks
11-and-Under	Crystal Lake, Ill.	Toa Baja (P.R.) Apaches	Waco (Texas) Wolves
12-and-Under	Cincinnati	Union (Ohio) Post 79	Carolina (P.R.) Angeles
13-and-Under	Knoxville, Tenn.	Team Knoxville	Atlanta Bulls
14-and-Under (54-foot)	Dublin, Ohio	Brooklyn Bergen Beach	Columbus Cobras
15-and-Under	Crystal Lake, Ill.	East Cobb (Ga.) Astros	Hamlin Park (Ill.) All-Stars
16-and-Under	Marietta, Ga.	East Cobb (Ga.) Yankees	Columbus Sharks
High school age	Euclid, Ohio	Brooklyn Bergen Beach	Ohio Thunder/Orange
18-and-Under (wood)	Charleston, S.C.	South Carolina Diamond Devils/18	Midland (Ohio) Indians

LITTLE LEAGUE BASEBALL — HEADQUARTERS: Williamsport, Pa.

Event	Site	Champion	Runner-up
Little League (11-12)	Williamsport, Pa.	Columbus, Ga.	Kawaguchi City, Japan
Junior League (13-14)	Taylor, Mich.	El Campo, Texas	Sonora, Mexico
Senior League (15-16)	Bangor, Me.	Falcon, Venezuela	Pearl City, Hawaii
Big League (17-18)	Easley, S.C.	Thousand Oaks, Calif.	Puerto Rico

NATIONAL AMATEUR BASEBALL FEDERATION (NABF) — HEADQUARTERS: Bowie, Md.

Event	Site	Champion	Runner-up
Freshman (12 & U)	Hopkinsville, Ky.	Baltimore Buzz	Hit after Hit (Tenn.)
Sophomore (14 & U)	Joplin, Mo.	Bayside (N.Y.) Yankees	Xtreme (Ohio) Yankees
Junior (16 & U)	Northville, Mich.	Kinect Nationals, Ohio	Bayside (N.Y.) Yankees Nationals
High School (17 & U)	Greensboro, N.C.	Midville Dodgers	Frederick (Md.) Hustlers
Senior (18 & U)	Jackson, Miss.	Jackson (Miss.) 96ers	Bayside (N.Y.) Yankees
College (22 & U)	Toledo	Pittsburgh Pandas	Long Island (N.Y.) Astros
Major (open)	Louisville	Cleveland Mosquitoes	Detroit Jet Box

PERFECT GAME/WORLD WOOD BAT ASSOCIATION SUMMER CHAMPIONSHIPS — HEADQUARTERS: Cedar Rapids, Iowa

Event	Site	Champion	Runner-up
15-and-Under	Marietta, Ga.	Team Georgia	Lids Indiana Bulls
16-and-Under (East)	Marietta, Ga.	East Cobb (Ga.) Astros	Brentwood (Tenn.) A's
16-and-Under (West)	Fallbrook Calif.	NorCal Red Sox	NorCal Black Sox
17-and-Under	Marietta, Ga.	All-American Prospects	Impact (N.C.) Dirtbags
18-and-Under	Marietta, Ga.	Florida Bombers	Florida Magic

PONY BASEBALL — HEADQUARTERS: Washington, Pa.

Event	Site	Champion	Runner-up
Mustang (9-10)	Irving, Texas	Caguas, P.R.	Fountain Valley, Calif.
Bronco (11-12)	Monterey, Calif.	Tami Ami, Fla.	Taiwan
Pony (13)	Chino Hills, Calif.	San Juan, P.R.	Simi Valley, Calif.
Pony (13-14)	Washington, Pa.	Caguas, P.R.	Simi Valley, Calif.
Colt (15-16)	Lafayette, Ind.	Tampa	Greensboro, N.C.
Palomino (17-18)	Santa Clara, Calif.	Taiwan	Harlingen, Texas

REVIVING BASEBALL IN INNER CITIES (RBI) — HEADQUARTERS: New York

Event	Site	Champion	Runner-up
Junior (13-15)	Compton, Calif.	Detroit	Pawtucket, R.I.
Senior (16-18)	Compton, Calif.	Los Angeles	Philadelphia

U.S. SPECIALTY SPORTS ASSOCIATION (USSSA) — HEADQUARTERS: Petersburg, Va.

Event	Site	Champion	Runner-up
11-and-Under/Majors Elite	Orlando	Houston Banditos Black	West Covina (Calif.) Bombers
12-and-Under/Majors Elite	Orlando	Houston Banditos Black	OC (Calif.) Juice
13-and-Under/Majors Elite	Orlando	So Cal Redwings	Oklahoma Elite Black
14-and-Under/Majors Elite	Orlando	East Cobb (Ga.) Astros	Team (Texas) Kelley

HIGH SCHOOL BASEBALL

DRAFT

Hochevar's return to draft pool results in big splash with Royals

Luke Hochevar's holdout had a happy ending after the Royals selected the former Tennessee righthander with the first overall pick in the 2006 draft.

Hochevar played college ball at Tennessee and played in the spring of 2006 at Fort Worth in the independent American Association. He made four starts there, and was 1-1, 2.38 with 34 strikeouts and 11 walks in 23 innings.

He was pitching at Fort Worth because he couldn't come to an agreement with the Dodgers, who drafted him 40th overall in 2005. He became the highest-drafted player out of an independent league, surpassing J.D. Drew, who went fifth overall in 1998. Like Drew, Hochevar is represented by Scott Boras. And like Drew, he had acrimonious negotiations in his first try at the draft out of college.

Hochevar held out until Labor Day 2005, then switched agents, going from Boras to Matt Sosnick. Sosnick and the Dodgers quickly came to terms of a $2.98 million bonus, which would have been $50,000 more than that of the No. 4 overall pick, Nationals third baseman Ryan Zimmerman. He ended up reneging on that agreement, returning to Boras and never signing with the Dodgers

After being picked first overall, Hochevar said he was humbled to be picked so high and hadn't forgotten about his yearlong holdout.

"I learned a great deal of lessons (from my negotiations). I learned what people I can trust, (one of) which is Scott Boras," he said. "In the negotiations with the Dodgers, the scouting director (Logan White) felt I was not worthy to be paid with the top pitchers in the draft."

Royals scouting director Deric Ladnier said Hochevar

No waiting around this time
Luke Hochevar signed quickly with the Royals

PAUL GERHART

"needed to get out and play," then corrected himself: "I suppose he doesn't 'need' to, but I would say it would be career suicide" if he held out again.

That didn't happen, as Hochevar signed in early August, in time to pitch in the Royals farm system as well as the Arizona Fall League. Hochevar signed a major league contract (through 2009) that was similar to the deal signed by Mets righthander Mike Pelfrey, which was worth a guaranteed $5.3 million, with a bonus of $3.5 million.

Like Pelfrey, Hochevar was a first-team All-American, is represented by Boras and was a first-round pick in 2005. Pelfrey went ninth overall and already has pitched in the major leagues.

As with several other Boras holdouts, the maneuver worked for Hochevar. He flashed three plus pitches in indy ball and improved his draft standing. He not only went No. 1 overall, but he signed a contract that guarantees him more than 60 percent more money than he declined from the Dodgers. His contract also is believed to have escalator

YEAR-BY-YEAR BONUS PROGRESSION

Signing bonuses have grown exponentially since 1965, when the draft was instituted—to curtail the growth of signing bonuses. From a first-round average of less than $50,000 in the first several years of the draft, that average grew to more than $2 million by 2001. But Major League Baseball's efforts to curb bonuses in recent years—chiefly through setting recommended payments for each pick in the first 10 rounds—have slowed growth and even led to a decline in some years.

Following is a year-by-year breakdown of average first-round signing bonuses and the annual percentage change:

Year	Average	Change	Year	Average	Change	Year	Average	Change
1965	$42,516	—	1979	68,094	+0.2	1993	613,037	+27.2
1966	44,430	+4.5%	1980	74,025	+8.7	1994	790,357	+28.9
1967	42,898	-3.4	1981	78,573	+6.1	1995	918,019	+16.1
1968	43,850	+2.2	1982	82,615	+5.1	1996@	944,404	+2.9
1969	43,504	-0.8	1983	87,236	+5.6	1997	1,325,536	+40.4
1970	45,230	+3.9	1984	105,392	+20.8	1998	1,637,667	+23.1
1971	45,197	-0.1	1985	118,115	+12.1	1999	1,809,767	+10.5
1972	44,952	-0.5	1986	116,300	-1.6	2000	1,872,586	+3.5
1973	48,832	+8.6	1987	128,480	+10.5	2001	2,154,280	+15.0
1974	53,333	+9.2	1988	142,540	+10.9	2002	2,106,793	-2.2
1975	49,333	-7.5	1989	176,008	+23.5	2003	1,765,667	-16.2
1976	49,631	+0.6	1990	252,577	+43.5	2004	1,958,448	+10.9
1977	48,813	-1.6	1991	365,396	+44.7	2005	2,018,000	+3.0
1978	67,892	+39.1	1992	481,893	+31.9	2006*	1,896,552	-6.0

@ Does not include four loophole free agents.* Does not include one unsigned pick expected to sign.
NOTE: The signing bonus average for first-round picks from 1965-82 includes the value of college scholarship plans and incentive bonus plans, in addition to the cash bonus paid. From 1983-2005, the amount represents only the cash bonus paid.

clauses in it for being on the 25-man big league roster, which could swell the overall value of the deal to close to $7 million.

"We are excited to get Luke signed in a timely fashion, which is a tribute to Luke and the Glass family," Ladnier said. "We see Luke as a top-flight talent and a key part to our future success. We're pleased he'll be able to perform this season and begin working toward reaching the major leagues."

Hochevar is the fourth No. 1 overall pick in the last 20 years to sign a major league contract, joining Delmon Young (2003), Pat Burrell (1998) and Alex Rodriguez (1993).

"I understand there is a business side and I understand the business side well after going through last year," Hochevar said after signing. "I understand it requires patience. In my mind, I just had to stay locked in to what I had to do as a baseball player to get myself ready. When it all comes down to it, that's what I am."

Ladnier's peers refused to be critical of the Royals for taking a holdout with the No. 1 overall pick. They argued the Royals needed to make the best pick for them, and that the move would not be a trendsetter for future drafts (and future holdouts). They agreed with Ladnier's assessment that while North Carolina lefthander Andrew Miller was the consensus top talent available, he didn't do enough to set himself apart from the crowd—other than set the highest bonus demand.

Miller's representatives hoped rumors of his high demands (a major league contract worth as much as eight figures) would drive their client down the draft to the Yankees or Red Sox, but the Tigers stepped in at No. 6 and picked him, high demands or not.

"We were going to take the best player on our board, and that was Andrew Miller," Chadd said after the draft. "The reason he slid to us, you could argue, is signability. I was stunned."

Miller also signed in August and ended up pitching in the big leagues for the Tigers as they drove toward the playoffs in September, capping off an amazing year. The North Carolina lefthander was Baseball America's College Player of the Year, led the Tar Heels to the College World Series championship series and was the No. 6 overall pick in the draft.

Then he signed the largest guaranteed contract of any 2006 draft pick, just edging out Hochevar, who signed with the Royals a day before Miller's contract became official.

The Tigers signed Miller to a major league contract that included a $3.55 million bonus and a guaranteed September callup. According to a source familiar with the negotiations, the contract guarantees Miller more than $5.4 million, and with escalator clauses tied to his pres-

ence on the 25-man roster, Miller could earn nearly $7.3 million. His contract also allows him to opt out early for arbitration.

"(Getting to pitch in Detroit) is why I'm so happy to be a Tiger right now," Miller told reporters on a conference call. "The future certainly is bright in Detroit and I hope I can be part of that."

Miller, an unsigned third-round pick out of high school in 2003 by the Devil Rays, went 13-2, 2.48 for the Tar Heels in 2006, striking out 133 in 123 innings. North Carolina's all-time strikeouts leader (325) was 27-9, 2.85 in his three-year career.

Miller's contract was the second-largest of the 2006 draft, surpassed only by Cubs righthander (and Notre Dame wide receiver) Jeff Samardzija. That contract would pay Samardzija a record $7.25 million over five years if Samardzija commits fulltime to baseball. Both are clients of agents Darek Braunecker, Jim Lindell and Mark Rodgers, whose firm, Frontline Athlete Management, also negotiated the record $1.3 million deal of Cubs 11th-round pick Chris Huseby.

RECORD-BREAKING BONUSES

The Athletics paid Rick Monday, the first pick in the first draft, a signing bonus of $100,000. The figure stood as a draft record for 10 years but has since been broken many times over. This chart traces the progression of the bonus record from Monday to Jeff Samardzija, who potentially set a new record in 2006.

The figures represent cash bonuses, with no regard to benefits from college scholarship plans or incentives—or guaranteed money if a player signed a major league contract (such players are denoted with an asterisk). The list considers only players who signed with the clubs that drafted them and does not include the four loophole free agents from 1996. Among that group is former Devil Rays righthander Matt White, who established a bonus standard that still stands when he signed for $10.2 million.

Year	Player, Pos., Club (Round)	Bonus
1965	Rick Monday, of, Athletics (1)	$100,000
1975	Danny Goodwin, c, Angels (1)	$125,000
1978	Kirk Gibson, of, Tigers (1)	$150,000
	*Bob Horner, 3b, Braves (1)	$162,000
1979	Bill Bordley, lhp, Giants (1#)	$200,000
	Todd Demeter, 1b, Yankees (2)	$208,000
1988	Andy Benes, rhp, Padres (1)	$235,000
1989	Tyler Houston, c, Braves (1)	$241,500
	*Ben McDonald, rhp, Orioles (1)	$350,000
	*John Olerud, 1b, Blue Jays (3)	$575,000
1991	Mike Kelly, of, Braves (1)	$575,000
	Brien Taylor, lhp, Yankees (1)	$1,550,000
1994	Paul Wilson, rhp, Mets (1)	$1,550,000
	Josh Booty, 3b, Marlins (1)	$1,600,000
1996	Kris Benson, rhp, Pirates (1)	$2,000,000
1997	Rick Ankiel, lhp, Cardinals (2)	$2,500,000
	Matt Anderson, rhp, Tigers (1)	$2,505,000
1998	*J.D. Drew, of, Cardinals (1)	$3,000,000
	*Pat Burrell, 3b, Phillies (1)	$3,150,000
	Mark Mulder, lhp, Athletics (1)	$3,200,000
	Corey Patterson, of, Cubs (1)	$3,700,000
1999	Josh Hamilton, of, Devil Rays (1)	$3,960,000
2000	Joe Borchard, of, White Sox (1)	$5,300,000
2005	Justin Upton, ss, Diamondbacks (1)	$6,100,000
2006	†Jeff Samardzija, rhp, Cubs (5)	$7,250,000

*Major league contract. #January draft.

†Samardzija is guaranteed his full bonus amount only if he does not pursue an NFL career and remains with the Cubs through 2010.

FIRST-ROUND TRENDS

Year	College	High School	Hitters	Pitchers	Average Bonus	Change
2000	12	18	13	17	$1,872,586	+3.5%
2001	18	12	10	*20	*$2,154,280	+15.0%
2002	14	16	14	16	$2,106,793	-2.2%
2003	18	12	*20	10	$1,765,667	*-16.2%
2004	17	13	11	19	$1,958,448	+10.9%
2005	19	10	17	13	$2,018,000	+3.0%
2006	16	13	12	18	#$1,896,552	-6.0%

*Draft record.

#Does not include first-rounder Max Scherzer, still in negotiations.

Note: College includes junior college selections.

DRAFT '06 TOP 100 PICKS

Signing bonuses do not include scholarships, incentive bonus plans or salaries from a major league contract. Ages as of Oct. 1, 2006.

FIRST ROUND

Selection, Team: Player, Pos.	School	Age	Bonus	Comment
1. Royals: Luke Hochevar, rhp	Fort Worth (American Association)	23	$3,500,000	Gamble to turn down $2.98 million from Dodgers in '05 paid off with $5.25 million deal
2. Rockies: Greg Reynolds, rhp	Stanford	21	$3,250,000	Size/stuff/command combo thrills scouts, lack of strikeouts worries statheads
3. Devil Rays: Evan Longoria, 3b	Long Beach State	20	$3,000,000	Had best pro debut among '06 crop, hitting .315 with 18 HR while reaching Double-A
4. Pirates: Brad Lincoln, rhp	Houston	21	$2,750,000	Should move quickly after recovering from strained oblique that marred his debut
5. Mariners: Brandon Morrow, rhp	California	22	$2,450,000	High-90s fastball, mid-80s slider make him Mariners' closer of not-too-distant future
6. Tigers: Andrew Miller, lhp	North Carolina	21	$3,550,000	After stealing Carreron Maybin at No. 10 in '05, Tigers has top '06 prospect at No. 6
7. Dodgers: Clayton Kershaw, lhp	HS—Dallas	18	$2,300,000	First high school pick quickly established himself as one of minors' best southpaws
8. Reds: Drew Stubbs, of	Texas	21	$2,000,000	Gifted athlete didn't answer worries about bat by hitting .252 in Pioneer League
9. Orioles: Bill Rowell, 3b	HS—Pennsauken, N.J.	18	$2,100,000	As good as advertised: batted .328/.415/.503 and reached short-season ball
10. Giants: Tim Lincecum, rhp	Washington	22	$2,025,000	Followed spectacular spring with spectacular debut: 1.71 ERA, 58 K, 14 H in 32 IP
11. Diamondbacks: Max Scherzer, rhp	Missouri	22	Unsigned	Still expected to sign, his extended negotiations come as no surprise
12. Rangers: Kasey Kiker, lhp	HS—Seale, Ala.	18	$1,600,000	Just 5-foot-11 but unleashes 90-94 mph fastballs with little effort in delivery
13. Cubs: Tyler Colvin, of	Clemson	21	$1,475,000	Biggest surprise in first round rated as No. 1 prospect in Northwest League
14. Blue Jays: Travis Snider, of	HS—Everett, Wash.	18	$1,700,000	Won MVP award, edged Rowell for top-prospect honors in Appalachian League
15. Nationals: Chris Marrero, of	HS—Opa Locka, Fla.	18	$1,625,000	Best all-around prep position player moved to outfield, contracted viral meningitis
16. Brewers: Jeremy Jeffress, rhp	HS—South Boston, Va.	19	$1,550,000	Hit 99 mph with fastball, continued to draw Dwight Gooden comparisons in pro debut
17. Padres: Matt Antonelli, 3b	Wake Forest	21	$1,575,000	Athlete with gap power and on-base skills fits offensive profile better at second base
18. Phillies: Kyle Drabek, rhp/ss	HS—The Woodlands, Texas	18	$1,550,000	As talented as any draftee, but has makeup issues and had 7.71 ERA in Rookie ball
19. Marlins: Brett Sinkbeil, rhp	Missouri State	21	$1,525,000	One of five first-rounders in low Class A Greensboro rotation at season's end
20. Twins: Chris Parmelee, of/1b	HS—Chino Hills, Calif.	18	$1,500,000	Advanced high school hitter homered in first pro AB, kept going from there
21. Yankees: Ian Kennedy, rhp	Southern California	21	$2,250,000	Agreed to over-slot deal in June, but it curiously wasn't announced until mid-August
22. Nationals: Colton Willems, rhp	HS—Fort Pierce, Fla.	18	$1,425,000	His pure arm strength (fastballs up to 97 mph) ranked with best of high school crop
23. Astros: Max Sapp, c	HS—Orlando	18	$1,400,000	Held his own with bat, led New York-Penn League with 68 percent CS percentage
24. Braves: Cody Johnson, 1b	HS—Lynn Haven, Fla.	18	$1,375,000	Has big-time raw power and holes in swing; latter more obvious as he hit .184 in debut
25. Angels: Hank Conger, c	HS—Huntington Beach, Calif.	18	$1,350,000	Continued to hit and improve defensively before breaking hamate bone in right wrist
26. Dodgers: Bryan Morris, rhp	Motlow State (Tenn.) CC	19	$1,325,000	Agreed to $1.4 million bonus last year, but Devil Rays failed to close deal and lost him
27. Red Sox: Jason Place, of	HS—Piedmont, S.C.	18	$1,300,000	One of draft's better athletes answered some questions about his bat with solid debut
28. Red Sox: Daniel Bard, rhp	North Carolina	21	$1,550,000	Mariners considered him at No. 5, got mid-round bonus despite startling fall to No. 28
29. White Sox: Kyle McCulloch, rhp	Texas	21	$1,050,000	More steady than spectacular, should move quickly and already got to high Class A

SUPPLEMENTAL

Selection, Team: Player, Pos.	School	Age	Bonus	Comment
30. Cardinals: Adam Ottavino, rhp	Northeastern	20	$950,000	Focusing more on command than velo, didn't allow earned run in first four pro starts
31. Dodgers: Preston Mattingly, ss	HS—Evansville, Ind.	19	$1,000,000	Despite being Don's son and three-sport athlete, flew under radar for most of spring
32. Orioles: Pedro Beato, rhp	St. Petersburg (Fla.) JC	19	$1,000,000	Top draft-and-follow from 2005 turned down $800,000 offer from Mets
33. Giants: Emmanuel Burriss, ss	Kent State	21	$1,000,000	Speedster won stolen base crowns in Mid-American Conference (42), NWL (35)
34. Diamondbacks: Brooks Brown, rhp	Georgia	21	$900,000	Starter in college profiles better as late-inning reliever with sinker-curveball mix
35. Padres: Kyler Burke, of	HS—Ooltewah, Tenn.	18	$950,000	Tremendous athlete still has work to do at plate after hitting .209 in Rookie ball
36. Marlins: Chris Coghlan, 3b	Mississippi	21	$950,000	Won '05 Cape Cod batting title (.326) and hit .297 in pro debut—also slugged just .366
37. Phillies: Adrian Cardenas, ss	HS—Opa Locka, Fla.	18	$925,000	High School Player of Year outperformed prep teammate Marrero in pro ball, too
38. Braves: Cory Rasmus, rhp	HS—Seale, Ala.	18	$900,000	Starred with Kiker and brother Colby ('05 first-rounder) on '05 national prep champs
39. Indians: David Huff, lhp	UCLA	22	$900,000	Nearly doubled $500,000 he turned down as Phillies 19th-rounder a year ago
40. Red Sox: Kris Johnson, lhp	Wichita State	21	$850,000	Tommy John survivor had mid-first-round potential for 2007 if he returned to school
41. Yankees: Joba Chamberlain, rhp	Nebraska	21	$1,100,000	Had chance to go in top 10 picks before medical concerns heightened just before draft
42. Cardinals: Chris Perez, rhp	Miami	21	$800,000	First college closer selected posted 1.84 ERA, 12 saves in two months in low Class A
43. Braves: Steve Evarts, lhp	HS—Tampa	18	$800,000	Dastardly changeup is typical of crafty lefthander, while his low-90s fastball is not
44. Red Sox: Caleb Clay, rhp	HS—Cullman, Ala.	18	$775,000	Mostly an outfielder before this spring, when he started dealing heavy 90-94 mph heat
45. Royals: Jason Taylor, of	HS—Virginia Beach	18	$762,500	Athleticism has drawn comparisons to that of fellow Virginia prep product Justin Upton
46. Rockies: David Christensen, of	HS—Parkland, Fla.	18	$750,000	Swing-and-miss reputation persists after .198 average, 93 K in 58 pro games
47. Devil Rays: Josh Butler, rhp	San Diego	21	$725,000	Key will be throwing with less effort after late-spring fade carried over into summer

SECOND ROUND

Selection, Team: Player, Pos.	School	Age	Bonus	Comment
48. Pirates: Mike Felix, lhp	Troy	21	$725,000	Highest-drafted player ever out of Troy was two-way star who projects as reliever
49. Mariners: Chris Tillman, rhp	HS—Fountain Valley, Calif.	18	$680,000	Southern California's top prospect entering 2006 had uneven senior year, pro debut
50. Tigers: Ronnie Bourquin, 3b	Ohio State	21	$690,000	Batted .416/.492/.612 as Big 10 player of year, .266/.391/.349 in first taste of pro ball

DRAFT '06 TOP 100 PICKS

Signing bonuses do not include scholarships, incentive bonus plans or salaries from a major league contract. Ages as of Oct. 1, 2006

SECOND ROUND

Selection, Team: Player, Pos.	School	Age	Bonus	Comment
51. Braves: Jeff Locke, lhp	HS—Conway, N.H.	18	$675,000	Looks like best pitcher to come out of New Hampshire since Chris Carpenter
52. Reds: Sean Watson, rhp	Tennessee	21	$670,000	With Reds needing bullpen help, could get to majors quicker than most 2006 draftees
53. Padres: Chad Huffman, of	Texas Christian	21	$660,000	Former college quarterback has potent bat, led NWL with .439 on-base percentage
54. Cardinals: Brad Furnish, lhp	Texas Christian	21	$600,000	Horned Frogs teammates Huffman, Furnish went off board little sooner than expected
55. Diamondbacks: Brett Anderson, lhp	HS—Stillwater, Okla.	18	$950,000	Expected to go in first round, very refined lefty could prove to be a steal in second
56. Indians: Steven Wright, rhp	Hawaii	22	$630,000	Projected reliever sat out summer regaining strength after getting mono in spring
57. Indians: Josh Rodriguez, ss	Rice	21	$625,000	Played variety of infield positions in college, probably fits best at second base
58. Orioles: Ryan Adams, 2b	HS—New Orleans	19	$675,000	One of draft's better-hitting infielders honed hand-eye skills by playing ping pong
59. Nationals: Sean Black, rhp	HS—Medford, N.J.	18	Did Not Sign	Highest-drafted player not to sign wanted $1 million bonus; now at Seton Hall
60. Brewers: Brent Brewer, ss	HS—Tyrone, Ga.	18	$600,000	Florida State wide receiver recruit has more savvy than many prominent two-sporters
61. Padres: Wade LeBlanc, lhp	Alabama	22	$590,000	Finesse lefty lives off his changeup, posted 2.20 ERA in seven low Class A starts
62. Mets: Kevin Mulvey, rhp	Villanova	21	$585,000	Top Mets pick signed late but still found time to make three starts in Double-A
63. Marlins: Tom Hickman, of	HS—Lindale, Ga.	18	$575,000	Shoulder stiffness made it difficult for most teams to get good look at him this spring
64. Twins: Joe Benson, of	HS—Joliet, Ill.	18	$575,000	Could have played college football; brings that mentality and athleticism to diamond
65. Phillies: Drew Carpenter, rhp	Long Beach State	21	$570,000	Splitter stands out most in five-pitch arsenal; allowed just one run in five pro outings
66. Athletics: Trevor Cahill, rhp	HS—Vista, Calif.	18	$560,000	Athletics were last team to make a pick, used top choice to woo Cahill from Dartmouth
67. Astros: Sergio Perez, rhp	Tampa	21	$550,000	After saving clinching game of Division II World Series, handled low Class A with ease
68. Braves: Dustin Evans, rhp	Georgia Southern	22	$530,000	Recovered from stress fracture in elbow during spring to touch 95 mph with fastball
69. Indians: Wes Hodges, 3b	Georgia Tech	22	$1,000,000	Leg injury knocked him out of first round, but he got highest bonus in second round
70. Nationals: Stephen Englund, of	HS—Bellevue, Wash.	18	$515,000	Tools continue to outshine skills; batted .183 with 41 K in 35 games in Rookie ball
71. Red Sox: Justin Masterson, rhp	San Diego State	21	$510,000	Cape Cod's breakout player of 2005 could be Boston's long-term answer at closer
72. Braves: Chase Fontaine, ss	Daytona Beach (Fla.) CC	20	$500,000	Offensive-minded infielder turned down Rangers as 18th-round draft-and-follow
73. White Sox: Matt Long, rhp	Miami (Ohio)	22	$330,000	First senior drafted has recovered from Tommy John surgery in 2004 to touch 96 mph
74. Cardinals: Jon Jay, of	Miami	21	$480,000	Bat may be lone plus tool, but it could carry him; he hit .342/.416/.462 in low Class A

SUPPLEMENTAL
THIRD ROUND

Selection, Team: Player, Pos.	School	Age	Bonus	Comment
75. Indians: Matt McBride, c	Lehigh	21	$445,000	Best all-around college catcher in draft had sore shoulder but hit well in pro debut
76. Cardinals: Mark Hamilton, 1b	Tulane	22	$465,000	Bashed 31 homers between Tulane and pros this year, tied for NY-P lead with eight
77. Royals: Blake Wood, rhp	Georgia Tech	21	$460,000	Top winner on Tech's College World Series team isn't afraid to knock hitters off plate
78. Rockies: Keith Weiser, lhp	Miami (Ohio)	22	$455,000	Four-pitch lefty throws strikes, just needs to trust fastball and keep his pitches down
79. Devil Rays: Nick Fuller, rhp	HS—Marietta, Ga.	18	Did Not Sign	Compared to Brad Lidge, now at forefront of banner South Carolina recruiting class
80. Pirates: Shelby Ford, 2b	Oklahoma State	21	$450,000	Switch-hitter with some pop has played shortstop, could wind up as utilityman
81. Mariners: Tony Butler, lhp	HS—Oak Creek, Wis.	18	$445,000	Late bloomer pitched at 86-87 mph for most of spring before rocketing to 93-95
82. Tigers: Brennan Boesch, of	California	21	$445,000	Highly touted since high school, never has quite put it all together to satisfy scouts
83. Red Sox: Aaron Bates, 1b	North Carolina State	22	$440,000	Turned down Marlins as eighth-rounder, won Cape Cod League home run derby in '05
84. Reds: Chris Valaika, ss	UC Santa Barbara	21	$437,500	Won Pioneer League MVP award, set league mark with 32-game hit streak
85. Orioles: Zach Britton, lhp	HS—Weatherford, Texas	18	$435,000	Fastball jumped from 86-87 in 2005 to 92-93 this spring, with room for more growth
86. Diamondbacks: Dallas Buck, rhp	Oregon State	21	$250,000	First-rounder until elbow problems cropped up, still helped Beavers win national title
87. Diamondbacks: Cyle Hankerd, of	Southern California	21	$430,000	Won MVP award and batting title (.384) in NWL, then hit .369 in high Class A
88. Rangers: Chad Tracy, c	Pepperdine	21	$427,500	Son of Pirates manager Jim Tracy had first-round aspirations before late fade in spring
89. Giants: Clayton Tanner, lhp	HS—Concord, Calif.	18	$425,000	Likened to Noah Lowry, another California lefty who has worked out well for Giants
90. Marlins: Torre Langley, c	HS—Douglasville, Ga.	18	$422,500	Draft's best defensive catcher still has questions about bat after hitting .179 in debut
91. Nationals: Stephen King, ss	HS—Winter Park, Fla.	18	$750,000	It took highest bonus in third round to steer his quality bat away from Louisiana State
92. Brewers: Cole Gillespie, of	Oregon State	22	$417,500	Top hitter for College World Series champion Beavers batted .344 in debut
93. Padres: Cedric Hunter, of	HS—Decatur, Ga.	18	$415,000	Won Arizona League MVP award, reached base safely in first 49 games as pro
94. Mets: Joe Smith, rhp	Wright State	22	$410,000	Has better velo, slider than most sidearmers; could get look in big league camp
95. Marlins: Scott Cousins, of	San Francisco	21	$407,500	If he can't improve on .211/.253/.256 debut, he has shown low-90s fastball as lefty
96. Twins: Tyler Robertson, lhp	HS—Fair Oaks, Calif.	18	$405,000	Son of Rangers special assistant Jay confounds hitters with unorthodox delivery
97. Phillies: Jason Donald, ss	Arizona	21	$400,000	Turned down more money out of high school as 20th-round pick of Angels
98. Athletics: Matt Sulentic, of	HS—Dallas	18	$395,000	Precocious hitter batted .354 against older NWL competition, reached low Class A
99. Astros: Nick Moresi, of	Fresno State	21	$390,000	Broken hamate bone, inconsistent contact led to diminished college, pro numbers
100. Braves: Chad Rodgers, lhp	HS—Stow, Ohio	18	$385,000	Very polished for a high school lefty, had no problems making transition to pros

Draft Changes Ahead

The biggest draft news of the year may have come in the midst of the World Series, however, when several player-development changes were made as part of a new Collective Bargaining Agreement.

Overshadowed by more wide-ranging issues and the sheer euphoria of an agreement between Major League Baseball and the Players Association being reached with no rancor or threats of a work stoppage, the new labor agreement included significant changes to baseball's amateur draft and player-development pipeline.

Several draft alterations, ranging from a uniform Aug. 15 signing deadline to compensation for unsigned picks, will change how both teams and players experience the process, as well as how much and when money changes hands.

The most notable changes are those that deal with draft-pick compensation—both for teams that fail to sign a high pick as well as those who lose major league free agents in the offseason.

Teams that fail to sign a first-round pick no longer receive an extra pick after the first round as compensation, but instead a virtually identical pick the following year; for example, a team that fails to sign the No. 5 pick one year will receive the No. 6 pick the next, rather than one in the 30s or 40s. The same compensation also now exists for unsigned second-round picks, while a team that fails to sign a third-round pick will receive a sandwich pick between the third and fourth rounds.

The new system should decrease the growth of bonus payments to amateurs, as teams can walk away from negotiations with the reassurance of having a similar pick the next year. (Although that compensation pick, if unsigned, is not subject to compensation, which keeps clubs from using it over and over.) Clubs have for years wanted a system of prescribed, slotted bonuses for every high pick but learned early in the negotiations that the union would not accept it, so instead focused on stronger compensation rules.

"The concern with clubs was to get that club that was drafting as much leverage that they can have, so they

can select the best player they possibly can," said former Cubs president Andy MacPhail, a member of ownership's negotiation team. To the extent that bonus offers will probably either decrease or not grow as quickly because teams can walk away more comfortably, union executive director Donald Fehr said, "It will clearly have an effect. It will clearly not put (players) in the position that they would have been in had slotting been accepted. You have to find compromises."

One other change to the amateur draft is a uniform signing date of Aug. 15 for all players (other than college seniors), replacing the longtime and clumsy deadline of the moment a player attends his first four-year college class. In addition to creating some order for all involved—from teams to players to college coaches wanting an earlier idea of their incoming class—this also eliminates the junior-college, draft-and-follow rule in which players who attended two-year schools could sign with their drafting club until one week before the following draft.

Several ideas that have been discussed over the years, such as the trading of draft picks and an either supplemental or combined draft of all players worldwide, were not adopted. Also, the draft will continue to be held in June rather than be moved to July.

"The changes in the draft will help the teams in the bottom of the industry," MLB CEO Bob DuPuy said, "because they're getting better draft picks."

Some changes have been made to the draft-pick compensation afforded teams that lose major league free agents. Type C free agents have been eliminated, while teams that lose Type B free agents, which had previously received a pick from the signing club, will now get a sandwich pick between the first and second rounds. (This was pursued by the union to remove the disincentive for teams to sign those players.) Those changes go into effect immediately.

The number of players deemed Type A and B has been tweaked as well. Type A free agents, whose former team continues to receive a first- or second-round pick from the signing club as well as an extra pick between the first and second rounds, will be reduced from the 30 percent of players (as determined by a statistical formula) to 20; the Type B band is reduced from 31-50 percent to 21-40.

These changes will take effect after the 2007 season, allowing clubs which lose free agents this winter the same compensation they had always expected. Teams must still offer players salary arbitration to receive draft-pick compensation, though the deadline for that offer was moved up from Dec. 7 to Dec. 1.

The first-year player draft, also known as the Rule 4 draft, was not the only draft process altered by the new CBA. The major league portion of the Rule 5 draft will be affected by giving teams one extra year to protect players from it.

Rather than teams being allowed three years (for players signed at age 19 or older) or four years (for players 18 and younger) before leaving them off the 40-man roster subjects them to the Rule 5 draft, those periods have been lengthened to four and five. Ownership considered this a significant boost in their efforts to operate their minor league systems more effectively.

"That was one of the major things we had to give up, no question about it—to me it was the worst thing we had to give up," said Diamondbacks infielder Craig Counsell, a player representative to the union negotiating team. "Some players, especially immediately, are going to be hurt by that—this year. But in the end, you have to give up something to get something."

Draft Trends

Hochevar was the first of 18 pitchers selected in the first round, which fell two shy of the draft record of 20. That was something of a surprise, and the unexpected names that found their way into the first round were almost all hitters.

"All analysis of the draft is subjective, and some clubs

Nice surprise
Tyler Colvin provided good early returns for the Cubs

like certain types of players and judge them a certain way," Padres scouting director Grady Fuson said. "I do think there was a consensus as far as the top end of the draft was concerned, that there was pitching of every shape and size and type available. But we felt there was some offense to get, and I think other clubs felt the same way."

The surprise names started with the Cubs at No. 13, the Cubs' only pick until the fifth round. New scouting director Tim Wilken rolled the dice and selected Clemson outfielder Tyler Colvin, whose stock rose significantly in the weeks leading up to the draft as his production (.362, 13 homers, 23 stolen bases) started to match his tools and pro body.

More surprises appeared when three straight high school hitters went at spots 23-25: prep catchers Max Sapp (Astros, 23) and Hank Conger (Angels, 25) and outfielder Cody Johnson (Braves, 24).

"With such a dearth of position players in this draft, it was our aim to take the kids as quick as you could in the positional sense," said Astros scouting director Paul Ricciarini, who took Sapp 23rd overall. "It was easier for us to come back and get pitching later in the draft.

"The cynics are all saying how bad of a draft this is, but I totally disagree. I saw some nice bats in this draft. Now you have to look at it objectively and make sure you're not reaching for it too much. You have to ask yourself, 'Are we compromising talent to get an attractive positional need?' But that wasn't the case for us personally."

Fuson agreed with Ricciarini that while the strength of the draft might have been pitching depth, there were hitters to be had. Teams just had to be aggressive to get them, as San Diego was in picking Wake Forest infielder Matt Antonelli, a consensus first-round talent, 17th

BONUS RECORDS BY ROUND

Round	Player, Pos, Team	Year	Bonus
1st	Justin Upton, ss, Diamondbacks	2005	$6,100,000
Supp. 1st	Michael Garciaparra, ss, Mariners	2001	$2,000,000
2nd	Jason Young, rhp, Rockies	2000	$2,750,000
3rd	Matt Tuiasosopo, ss, Mariners	2004	$2,290,000
4th	Zach Miner, rhp, Braves	2000	$1,250,000
5th	#Jeff Samardzija, rhp, Cubs	2006	$7,250,000
6th	Quan Cosby, of, Angels	2001	$825,000
7th	Tyler Adamczyk, rhp, Cardinals	2001	$1,000,000
8th	Dellin Betances, rhp, Yankees	2006	$1,000,000
9th	Jason Middlebrook, rhp, Padres	1996	$750,000
10th	*Luis Cota, rhp, Royals	2003	$1,050,000
11th	Chris Huseby, rhp, Cubs	2006	$1,300,000
12th	Mike Rozier, lhp, Red Sox	2004	$1,575,000
13th	Jimmy Barthmaier, rhp, Astros	2003	$750,000
14th	Dexter Fowler, of, Rockies	2004	$925,000
Post-14th	*Sean Henn, lhp, Yankees	2000	$1,701,000

*Signed next year as draft-and-follow.

#Samardzija is guaranteed $7.25 million if he does not pursue an NFL career and remains with the Cubs through 2010.

BILL MITCHELL

FIRST OVERALL PICKS: THROUGH THE YEARS

Following is a year-by-year breakdown of the first overall pick in the June regular phase and his cash bonus, his highest level attained and his 2006 status. If a different player earned the largest bonus in that year, that player is noted along with the order he was picked and his bonus.

Year	No. 1 Pick	School	Hometown	Bonus	Highest Level	2006 Team	Largest Bonus (Pick Number)	Amount
1965	Rick Monday, of, Athletics	Arizona State U.	Santa Monica, Calif.	$100,000	Majors	Out of Baseball	same	
1966	Steve Chilcott, c, Mets	Antelope Valley HS	Lancaster, Calif.	75,000	Triple-A	Out of Baseball	Reggie Jackson, of, Athletics (2)	$80,000
1967	Ron Blomberg, 1b, Yankees	Druid Hills HS	Atlanta	65,000	Majors	Out of Baseball	#Mike Adamson, rhp, Orioles	75,000
1968	Tim Foli, ss, Mets	Notre Dame HS	Sherman Oaks, Calif.	74,000	Majors	Out of Baseball	Lloyd Allen, rhp, Angels (12)	75,000
1969	Jeff Burroughs, of, Senators	Wilson HS	Long Beach, Calif.	88,000	Majors	Out of Baseball	same	
1970	Mike Ivie, c, Padres	Walker HS	Decatur, Ga.	75,000	Majors	Out of Baseball	#Dave Kingman, 1b, Giants	80,000
1971	Danny Goodwin, c, White Sox	Central HS	Peoria, Ill.	DNS	Majors	Out of Baseball	Ed Kurpiel, 1b, Cardinals (8)	83,750
1972	Dave Roberts, 3b, Padres	U. of Oregon	Corvallis, Ore.	70,000	Majors	Out of Baseball	Jamie Quirk, ss, Royals (18)	78,000
1973	*David Clyde, lhp, Rangers	Westchester HS	Houston	65,000	Majors	Out of Baseball	^Alan Bannister, ss, Phillies	85,000
1974	*Bill Almon, ss, Padres	Brown U.	Warwick, R.I.	90,000	Majors	Out of Baseball	Willie Wilson, of, Royals (18)	90,000
1975	*Danny Goodwin, c, Angels	Southern U.	Peoria, Ill.	125,000	Majors	Out of Baseball	same	
1976	Floyd Bannister, lhp, Astros	Arizona State U.	Seattle	100,000	Majors	Out of Baseball	same	
1977	Harold Baines, of, White Sox	St. Michaels HS	St. Michaels, Md.	32,000	Majors	Out of Baseball	Paul Molitor, ss, Twins (3)	77,500
1978	*Bob Horner, 3b, Braves	Arizona State U.	Glendale, Ariz.	162,000	Majors	Out of Baseball	same	
1979	Al Chambers, 1b, Mariners	Harris HS	Harrisburg, Pa.	60,000	Majors	Out of Baseball	Todd Demeter, 1b, Yankees (51)	208,000
1980	Darryl Strawberry, of, Mets	Crenshaw HS	Los Angeles	152,500	Majors	Out of Baseball	same	
1981	Mike Moore, rhp, Mariners	Oral Roberts U.	Eakly, Okla.	100,000	Majors	Out of Baseball	Terry Blocker, of, Mets (4)	127,500
1982	Shawon Dunston, ss, Cubs	Jefferson HS	New York	135,000	Majors	Out of Baseball	Kenny Williams, of, Wh. Sox (78)	160,000
1983	Tim Belcher, rhp, Twins	Mt. Vernon Nazarene Coll.	Sparta, Ohio	DNS	Majors	Out of Baseball	Kurt Stillwell, ss, Reds (2)	135,000
1984	Shawn Abner, of, Mets	Mechanicsburg HS	Mechanicsburg, Pa.	150,500	Majors	Out of Baseball	same	
1985	B.J. Surhoff, c, Brewers	U. of North Carolina	Rye, N.Y.	150,000	Majors	Out of Baseball	Bobby Witt, rhp, Rangers (3)	179,000
1986	Jeff King, 3b, Pirates	U. of Arkansas	Colorado Springs	180,000	Majors	Out of Baseball	same	
1987	Ken Griffey Jr., of, Mariners	Moeller HS	Cincinnati	160,000	Majors	Reds	Mark Merchant, of, Pirates (2)	165,000
							Jack McDowell, rhp, Wh. Sox (5)	165,000
1988	Andy Benes, rhp, Padres	U. of Evansville	Evansville, Ind.	235,000	Majors	Out of Baseball	same	
1989	*Ben McDonald, rhp, Orioles	Louisiana State U.	Denham Springs, La.	350,000	Majors	Out of Baseball	*John Olerud, 1b, Blue Jays (79)	575,000
1990	Chipper Jones, ss, Braves	The Bolles School	Jacksonville	275,000	Majors	Braves	*Todd Van Poppel, rhp, A's (14)	500,000
							Tony Clark, 1b, Tigers (2)	500,000
1991	Brien Taylor, lhp, Yankees	East Carteret HS	Beaufort, N.C.	1,550,000	Double-A	Out of Baseball	same	
1992	Phil Nevin, 3b, Astros	Cal State Fullerton	Placentia, Calif.	700,000	Majors	Twins	Jeffrey Hammonds, of, Orioles (4)	975,000
1993	Alex Rodriguez, ss, Mariners	Westminster Christian HS	Miami	1,000,000	Majors	Yankees	Darren Dreifort, rhp, Dodgers (2)	1,300,000
1994	Paul Wilson, rhp, Mets	Florida State U.	Orlando, Fla.	1,550,000	Majors	Reds	Josh Booty, ss, Marlins (5)	1,600,000
1995	Darin Erstad, of, Angels	U. of Nebraska	Jamestown, N.D.	1,575,000	Majors	Angels	same	
1996	@Kris Benson, rhp, Pirates	Clemson U.	Kennesaw, Ga.	2,000,000	Majors	Orioles	Matt White, rhp, Giants (7)	10,200,000
1997	Matt Anderson, rhp, Tigers	Rice U.	Louisville	2,505,000	Majors	Giants (AAA)	same	
1998	*Pat Burrell, 3b, Phillies	U. of Miami	Boulder Creek, Calif.	3,150,000	Majors	Phillies	Corey Patterson, of, Cubs (3)	3,700,000
1999	Josh Hamilton, of, Devil Rays	Athens Drive HS	Raleigh, N.C.	3,960,000	Double-A	Out of Baseball	same	
2000	Adrian Gonzalez, 1b, Marlins	Eastside HS	Chula Vista, Calif.	3,000,000	Majors	Padres	Joe Borchard, of, White Sox (12)	5,300,000
2001	Joe Mauer, c, Twins	Cretin-Derham Hall	St. Paul, Minn.	5,150,000	Majors	Twins	same	
2002	Bryan Bullington, rhp, Pirates	Ball State U.	Fishers, Ind.	4,000,000	Majors	Pirates	B.J. Upton, ss, Devil Rays (2)	4,600,000
2003	*Delmon Young, of, Devil Rays	Camarillo HS	Camarillo, Calif.	3,700,000	Majors	Devil Rays	same	
2004	Matt Bush, ss, Padres	Mission Bay HS	El Cajon, Calif.	3,150,000	Class A	Padres (A)	Jered Weaver, rhp, Angels	4,000,000
							Stephen Drew, ss, D-backs	4,000,000
2005	Justin Upton, ss, D'backs	Great Bridge HS	Chesapeake, Va.	6,100,000	Class A	Diamondbacks (A)	same	

* Signed major league contract; cash bonus only reported. # Selected in June secondary phase. @ Includes four loophole free agents; White signed with Devil Rays.
^ Selected in January draft.

Rick Monday

LARRY GOREN

Chipper Jones

MORRIS FOSTOFF

Joe Mauer

overall. The Braves felt the same way about Johnson, whose stock had seemingly fallen during an inconsistent spring. Still, Clark said the Braves considered Johnson the premier power bat in the draft and decided they couldn't wait to take him.

There were some shocks on the pitcher side as well, starting when the Giants, usually hard to predict in the draft, took Tim Lincecum at the 10th overall pick. BA had ranked Lincecum as the draft's No. 2 prospect but also found several clubs leery of his size (listed at 6-foot-1, 160 pounds) and unconventional pinwheel delivery. As usual, the Giants went for a power arm that they liked more than other clubs.

"We like Tim's arm, stuff and athleticism," Giants vice president of player personnel Dick Tidrow said. "He's got a power arm with good breaking stuff. He's a fast mover who can pitch in either a starting or relief role."

Signability was a significant factor in the first round again. The Rockies, Devil Rays and Pirates all had pre-draft deals in place with their picks—in order, Stanford righthander Greg Reynolds ($3.25 million at No. 2 overall), Long Beach State infielder Evan Longoria ($3 million) and Houston righthander Brad Lincoln ($2.75 million). All three bonuses were below the figures players received in the same spots a year ago, when the 2-3-4 picks (Gordon, Mariners catcher Jeff Clement and Nationals third baseman Ryan Zimmerman) got $4 million, $3.4 million and $2.975 million.

The numbers would change when Diamondbacks first-rounder Max Scherzer signed (as expected), but overall the first-round bonuses saw their second-largest percentage drop in draft history.

Cubs Take Some Chances

The Colvin pick was just the beginning of a Cubs draft that was heavy on creativity and resourcefulness. Having lost his second-, third- and fourth-round picks because of major league free-agent signings, Wilken was left with a gaping hole at the top of his board in his first draft with the Cubs.

After taking Colvin, Wilken and the Cubs had to wait until the fifth round—136 picks later—before making their next choice. With fewer early picks, the Cubs had money in their signing budget to spread out to later picks.

So in the fifth round, the Cubs made Notre Dame righthander Jeff Samardzija their choice. Less than three weeks after the draft they signed the two-sport standout to a contract that will allow him to continue his standout football career with the Fighting Irish while pursuing professional baseball.

While Samardzija promptly drove to Boise, Idaho, where he made his pro pitching debut with the Cubs' short-season affiliate there, he has committed to return to South Bend for the start of football practice on Aug. 1.

Samardzija would receive $7.25 million if he makes baseball his primary sport. The Cubs have five years to pay him under baseball's rules for distributing signing bonuses to two-sport players, and the deal is backloaded, with Samardzija receiving less than $1 million in the first year of the deal, according to sources with knowledge of the contract.

The record for a signing bonus for a player that signed with the club that drafted him is $6.1 million, set in January 2006 by the Diamondbacks and 2005 No. 1

overall pick Justin Upton. The largest bonus in history given to a drafted player remains $10.2 million, which the Devil Rays gave loophole free agent Matt White in 1996.

One source indicated the size of the contract—clearly above the slot recommended by Major League Baseball—caused friction between the Cubs and MLB, with commissioner Bud Selig becoming personally involved in the negotiations.

Samardzija wasn't the only surprise the Cubs had planned for the draft's first day. With their 11th-round pick, they drafted a high school righthander who had thrown fewer than nine innings combined over his junior and senior seasons.

Chris Huseby, out of Martin County High in Stuart, Fla., was a household name in scouting circles in the spring of 2005. As a 6-foot-5 underclassman, he had the frame and had flashed the stuff to be a premium pick following his senior season. But Huseby came up lame early in his junior season, required Tommy John surgery and figured to be bound for Auburn after making a late-season return to the mound this spring. That changed when the Cubs offered him a $1.3 million bonus.

Cubs area scout Rolando Pino had tracked Huseby since 2004 and scouted him again this season when he finally returned to the mound. His familiarity with Huseby compelled him to get detailed information on Huseby's health in April. The reports were good, and Pino alerted Wilken that Huseby could be a perfect supplement to the club's thin draft.

Red Sox, Yankees Spend Big In Draft Too

The Yankees-Red Sox rivalry extends beyond their major league stadiums, and in 2006 it played out in the draft as both teams handed out huge bonuses to boost their draft classes.

The Yankees made waves on draft day with several picks, starting with Southern California righthander Ian Kennedy with the 21st overall pick. Kennedy wasn't a consensus first-round talent due to his smallish (6-foot-1, 195 pounds) frame, which offers little projection, and because his performance fell in his junior season. Then the Yankees took Nebraska righthander Joba Chamberlain—whose top-10 draft stock fell late due to injuries—in the supplemental first round, grabbed New York City prep righthander Dellin Betances in the eighth round, and snagged righty Mark Melancon in the ninth round—eight rounds later than the Arizona righthander might have gone if not for his elbow injury.

They ended up spending nearly $7 million to sign all their picks. Kennedy signed for a $2.25 million bonus—which the Yankees didn't announce for weeks after the deal was done—and Chamberlain signed for $1.1 million, while Betances agreed to a $1 million bonus, a record for an eighth-round pick. (It broke the mark the Yankees set with last year's eighth-rounder, Oklahoma prep outfielder Austin Jackson.) Melancon signed for $600,000.

With extra picks in the first and third rounds, as well

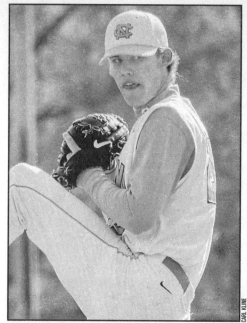

Big-money draft for Red Sox
Daniel Bard signed out of North Carolina for $1.55 million

as two supplemental first-rounders, the Red Sox ended up with a class that could be even better. Boston scouting director Jason McLeod said ownership gave his department the support to pursue talent in later rounds, with sluggers a priority.

"We were looking for guys with impact ability," McLeod said. "We have a system devoid of power hitters, and we looked in the later rounds to see who had power: Matt LaPorta, Lars Anderson, Ty Weeden. We spent a lot of time scouting these kids in the summer. We saw Lars and Ty for 20 games each with wood bats. That helped us evaluate them."

Boston paid well over slot money to sign three high school position players. Ryan Kalish, a ninth-round outfielder from New Jersey, signed for $600,000, while Ty Weeden, a 16th-round catcher from Oklahoma, signed for $420,000.

The biggest coup was 18th-rounder Lars Anderson, a first baseman from California. Considered a supplemental first-round pick until his reported bonus demands of $1 million scared teams off, Anderson signed for $825,000.

The Red Sox also took North Carolina righthander Daniel Bard with the 28th overall pick when his signing demands pushed him down the draft board, and they signed him at the end of the summer for $1.55 million, about $350,000 over the slot offer the Red Sox initially made. Bard was reported to be asking for more, perhaps a major league deal in the $4 million range, but he still received more than the Red Sox gave to their first first-round pick, prep outfielder Jason Place. Taken one spot ahead of Bard, Place signed for a $1.3 million bonus.

The signing of Bard left Diamondbacks pick Max Scherzer, the righthander out of Missouri, as the only unsigned first-round pick, but he was expected to sign rather than going back into the 2007 proceedings.

DRAFT ORDER 2007

A final weekend sweep of the Tigers not only kept Detroit from winning the American League Central, relegating it to the wild card, but it also helped the Royals avoid draft history. Kansas City lost 100 games, one fewer than the Devil Rays. So Tampa Bay picks No. 1 overall for the third time (1999, 2003) in its short history, while the Royals avoid being the first club to ever pick No. 1 overall in back-to-back years. The Royals picked second in 2005 and first in '06.

The order in the second half of the first round (picks 16-30) could change if those teams sign free agents that require compensation in the form of draft picks. For teams that had identical records in 2006, priority is given to the team that had the earlier first-round selection in 2005.

1. Devil Rays	(61-101)	16. Rangers	(80-82)
2. Royals	(62-100)	17. Astros	(82-80)
3. Cubs	(66-96)	18. Cardinals	(83-78)
4. Pirates	(67-95)	19. Phillies	(85-77)
5. Orioles	(70-92)	20. Red Sox	(86-76)
6. Nationals	(71-91)	21. Blue Jays	(87-75)
7. Brewers	(75-87)	22. Dodgers	(88-74)
8. Rockies	(76-86)	23. Padres	(88-74)
9. Diamondbacks	(76-86)	24. Angels	(89-73)
10. Giants	(76-85)	25. White Sox	(90-72)
11. Mariners	(78-84)	26. Athletics	(93-69)
12. Marlins	(78-84)	27. Tigers	(95-67)
13. Indians	(78-84)	28. Twins	(96-66)
14. Braves	(79-83)	29. Mets	(97-65)
15. Reds	(80-82)	30. Yankees	(97-65)

DRAFT 2006

CLUB-BY-CLUB SELECTIONS

Number represents order of selection • **Boldface** indicates player signed

ARIZONA DIAMONDBACKS (11)

1. Max Scherzer, rhp, Missouri
1s. **Brooks Brown, rhp, Georgia** (Supplemental choice—34th overall—for loss of Type A free agent Tim Worrell)
2. **Brett Anderson, lhp, Stillwater (Okla.) HS**
3. **Dallas Buck, rhp, Oregon State** (Choice from Giants as compensation for Worrell)
3. **Cyle Hankerd, of, Southern California**
4. **Bryant Thompson, rhp, Pensacola (Fla.) JC**
5. **Hector Ambriz, rhp, UCLA**
6. **Joey Side, of, Georgia**
7. **Daniel Stange, rhp, UC Riverside**
8. **Chase Christianson, rhp, South Alabama**
9. **Eddie Romero, lhp, Fresno State**
10. **Tony Barnette, rhp, Arizona State**
11. **Daniel Fournier, rhp, Franklin Pierce (N.H.) College**
12. **Andrew Fie, 3b, Trinity Christian Academy, Addison, Texas**
13. **John Hester, c, Stanford**
14. **Chad Beck, rhp, Louisiana-Lafayette**
15. **Matthew Oxedine, ss, North Florida**
16. **Blake Sharpe, 2b, Southern California**
17. **Brett Reynolds, rhp, Missouri**
18. **Brad Miller, 1b, Ball State**
19. **Tyler Jones, of, South Alabama**
20. Enrique Garcia, rhp, Potomac State (W.Va.) JC
21. **Sean Smith, 2b, UCLA**
22. **Danny Perales, of, Southern California**
23. **Derrick Walker, of, Wabash Valley (Ill.) JC**
24. **Andrew Beshenich, rhp, Norristown (Pa.) HS**
25. **Shane Byrne, of, East Tennessee State**
26. Frank Corolla, rhp, Magnolia (Texas) HS
27. **Connor Janes, of, Univ. of British Columbia**
28. **Shea McFeely, 3b, Oregon State**
29. Andrew Hayes, ss, McKenzie (Tenn.) HS
30. **Clay Zavada, lhp, Southern Illinois-Edwardsville**
31. Kiel Roling, c, Central Arizona JC
32. Osmany Masso, ss, Miami (No school)
33. **Osbek Castillo, rhp, Encino, Calif. (No school)**
34. **Tito Cruz, c, Long Beach State**
35. Casey Whitmer, rhp, Kilgore (Texas) HS
36. Jason Durst, rhp, Lake Sumter (Fla.) JC
37. Tyler Kmetko, 2b, Utah
38. Michael Guerrero, of, Meridian (Miss.) CC
39. Riley Etchebarren, of, Paradise Valley HS, Phoenix
40. Nick Cejka, c, Columbia Basin (Wash.) CC
41. Quinton Marsh, lhp, Wickenburg (Ariz.) HS
42. Sean Coughlin, c, Kentucky
43. Jason Stidham, ss, Melbourne (Fla.) HS
44. **Justin Brashear, c, Mississippi**
45. Clayton Conner, 3b, Okaloosa-Walton (Fla.) CC
46. Alvaro Garcia, rhp, Pima (Ariz.) CC
47. David Mixon, rhp, Louisiana-Monroe
48. Michael Solbach, rhp, Liberty
49. Dominic Piazza, c, Notre Dame
50. Kendall Volz, rhp, Smithson Valley HS, Spring Branch, Texas

ATLANTA BRAVES (24)

1. **Cody Johnson, 1b, Mosley HS, Lynn Haven, Fla.**
1s. **Cory Rasmus, rhp, Russell County HS, Seale, Ala.** (Supplemental choice—38th overall—for loss of Type A free agent Kyle Farnsworth)
1s. **Steve Evarts, lhp, Robinson HS, Tampa** (Supplemental choice—43rd overall—for loss of Type A free agent Rafael Furcal)
2. **Jeff Locke, lhp, Kennett HS Conway, N.H.** (Choice from Dodgers as compensation for Furcal)
2. **Dustin Evans, rhp, Georgia Southern**
2. **Chase Fontaine, ss, Daytona Beach (Fla.) CC** (Choice from Yankees as compensation for Farnsworth)
3. **Chad Rodgers, lhp, Walsh Jesuit HS, Stow, Ohio**
4. **Lee Hyde, lhp, Georgia Tech**
5. **Kevin Gunderson, lhp, Oregon State**
6. **Steven Figueroa, rhp, Edgewater HS, Orlando**
7. **Adam Coe, 3b, Russell County HS, Seale, Ala.**
8. **Casey Beck, rhp, San Jacinto (Texas) JC**
9. **Tim Gustafson, rhp, Georgia Tech**

10. **Kristopher Medlen, rhp, Santa Ana (Calif.) JC**
11. **Mike Mehlich, rhp, Bishop Moore HS, Orlando**
12. **Josh Morris, 1b, Georgia**
13. **Joseph Johnson, rhp, Louisburg (N.C.) JC**
14. Matt Small, rhp, Ipswich (Mass.) HS
15. **Stephen Shults, 3b, Walters State (Tenn.) CC**
16. **Jack Tilghman, rhp, Walters State (Tenn.) CC**
17. Clayton McMillian, lhp, Texarkana (Texas) JC
18. J.B. Paxson, c, Walters State (Tenn.) CC
19. **Deunte Heath, rhp, Tennessee**
20. Jonathan Cluff, ss, Bingham HS, South Jordan, Utah
21. Jordan Brown, rhp, Meridian (Miss.) CC
22. Cole Rohrbough, lhp, Western Nevada CC
23. Blake Guthrie, c, Louisburg (N.C.) JC
24. Zack Oliver, lhp, Paris (Texas) JC
25. Kyle Witten, rhp, Liberty HS, Bakersfield, Calif.
26. **Ryne Reynoso, rhp, Boston College**
27. Jake Rodriguez, rhp, Whittier (Calif.) HS
28. Adam Milligan, of, Hardin County HS, Savannah, Tenn.
29. Andrew Dunn, rhp, Logan (Ill.) JC
30. David Berres, of, South Suburban (Ill.) JC
31. Eric Barrett, lhp, Logan (Ill.) JC
32. Brendon Porch, rhp, East Union HS, Blue Springs, Miss.
33. Jordan Poirrier, ss, Riverside Academy, Coushatta, La.
34. Matt Morgal, rhp, Seminole State (Okla.) JC
35. Aroyo Fleming, rhp, Central HS, Baton Rouge, La.
36. Samson Williams, of, Laney HS, Wilmington, N.C.
37. Eric Broberg, 1b, Bishop Moore HS, Orlando
38. Josh Ashton, of, Rose HS, Greenville, N.C.
39. Daniel Davidson, rhp, Southern Union State (Ala.) CC
40. Tyreace House, of, Palmdale HS
41. Keegan Dennis, rhp, White County HS, Carmi, Ill.
42. Ralph West, lhp, Gar-Field HS, Woodbridge, Va.
43. L.V. Ware, of, Okaloosa-Walton (Fla.) CC
44. Kristopher Cichoski, rhp, CC of Southern Nevada
45. Mason Tobin, rhp, Western Nevada CC
46. Tyler Musselwhite, rhp, Chipola (Fla.) JC
47. John Kessick, rhp, Lake Michigan JC
48. Travis Tucker, rhp, McLennan (Texas) CC
49. Blake Holt, of, Temple (Texas) CC
50. Matt Jordan, lhp, Hinds (Miss.) CC

BALTIMORE ORIOLES (9)

1. **Bill Rowell, 3b, Bishop Eustace Prep, Pennsauken, N.J.**
1s. **Pedro Beato, rhp, St. Petersburg (Fla.) JC** (Supplemental choice—32nd overall—for loss of Type A free agent B.J. Ryan)
2. (Choice to Padres as compensation for Type A free agent Ramon Hernandez)
2. **Ryan Adams, ss, Jesuit HS, New Orleans** (Choice from Blue Jays as compensation for Ryan)
3. **Zach Britton, lhp, Weatherford (Texas) HS**
4. **Blake Davis, ss, Cal State Fullerton**
5. **Bobby Henson, ss, Tuttle (Okla.) HS**
6. **James Berken, rhp, Clemson**
7. **Josh Tamba, rhp, Cypress (Calif.) JC**
8. **Jedidiah Stephen, ss, Ohio State**
9. **Brett Bordes, lhp, Arizona State**
10. Emeel Salem, of, Alabama
11. **Anthony Martinez, 1b, Louisburg (N.C.) JC**
12. **Brandon Tripp, of, Cal State Fullerton**
13. **Ryan Ouellette, rhp, Indian River (Fla.) CC**
14. **Brent Allar, rhp, Texas Christian**
15. Dustin Black, c, Cleveland State (Tenn.) CC
16. **Justin Johnson, c, Illinois-Chicago**
17. Tony Watson, lhp, Nebraska
18. **Nathan Nery, lhp, Stetson**
19. **Todd Davison, ss, Delaware**
20. **Zach Dillon, c, Baylor**
21. **Luis Lopez, of, Dra Maria Cadilla de Martinez HS, Arecibo, P.R.**
22. Chris Salberg, lhp, Florida Atlantic
23. **Aubrey Miller, rhp, Arkansas Tech**
24. **Josh Faiola, rhp, Dartmouth**
25. Donald Anderson, rhp, Southwestern (Calif.) JC
26. Kipp Schutz, of, Harrison HS, Evansville, Ind.
27. **Zach Jevne, rhp, Northern Iowa**

28. **Michael Pierce, c, Fresno Pacific (Calif.)**
29. Brandon Kimbrel, rhp, Yoe HS, Cameron, Texas
30. Chris Cassidy, lhp, Riverside (Calif.) CC
31. Zach Gerler, ss, Howell Central HS, St. Charles, Mo.
32. Barrett Dail, rhp, Millbrook HS, Raleigh, N.C.
33. Drew Conklin, rhp, South Mountain (Ariz.) CC
34. Tyler Blandford, rhp, Daviess County HS, Owensboro, Ky.
35. Matt Drummond, lhp, Paso Robles (Calif.) HS
36. Patrick Egan, rhp, Quinnipiac (Conn.)
37. Michael Lane, of, Daviess County HS, Owensboro, Ky.
38. Adam Urnberg, rhp, Southern Idaho JC
39. Neal Davis, lhp, Catonsville HS, Baltimore
40. **David Cash, 2b, Florida**
41. Scott Migl, rhp, Saint Pius X HS, Houston
42. Jordan Durrance, lhp, Sierra HS, Manteca, Calif.
43. Jose Kianes, of, Martin County HS, Stuart, Fla.
44. Travis Lamar, rhp, Harrison HS, Evansville, Ind.
45. Isaiah Stanback, of, Washington
46. Vincent DiFazio, c, Indian River (Fla.) CC
47. Troy Burki, lhp, Gig Harbor (Wash.) HS
48. Jason Mills, rhp, George Mason
49. Dan Watson, rhp, Manatee (Fla.) HS
50. Orlando Rodriguez, c, Domenech HS, Isabela, P.R.

BOSTON RED SOX   (27)

1. **Jason Place, of, Wren HS, Piedmont, S.C.**
1. **Daniel Bard, rhp, North Carolina** (Choice from Yankees as compensation for Type A free agent Johnny Damon)
1s. **Kris Johnson, lhp, Wichita State** (Supplemental choice—40th overall—for loss of Damon)
1s. **Caleb Clay, rhp, Cullman (Ala.) HS** (Supplemental choice—44th overall—for loss of Type A free agent Bill Mueller)
2. **Justin Masterson, rhp, San Diego State**
3. **Aaron Bates, 1b, North Carolina State** (Choice from Dodgers as compensation for Mueller)
3. **Bryce Cox, rhp, Rice**
4. **Jon Still, c, North Carolina State**
5. **Dustin Richardson, lhp, Texas Tech**
6. **Zach Daeges, 3b, Creighton**
7. **Kristopher Negron, ss, Cosumnes River (Calif.) JC**
8. **Rafael Cabreja, of, Monroe HS, New York**
9. **Ryan Kalish, of, Red Bank (N.J.) Catholic HS**
10. Kyle Snyder, rhp, Wellington (Fla.) Community HS
11. Brandon Belt, lhp, Hudson HS, Lufkin, Texas
12. **Ryan Khoury, ss, Utah**
13. **Jordan Craft, rhp, Dallas Baptist**
14. Matt LaPorta, 1b, Florida
15. **Jorge Jimenez, 3b, Porterville (Calif.) JC**
16. **Tyler Weeden, c, Santa Fe HS, Edmond, Okla.**
17. **William Reddick, of, Middle Georgia JC**
18. **Lars Anderson, 1b, Jesuit HS, Carmichael, Calif.**
19. **Richie Lentz, rhp, Washington**
20. Kyle Gilligan, ss, Etobicoke Collegiate Institute, Toronto
21. **Brian Steinocher, rhp, Stephen F. Austin**
22. Michael Christl, rhp, Bradley
23. **Paul Smyth, of, San Diego State**
24. Robert Phares, rhp, Shelton State (Ala.) CC
25. Sam Gleason, rhp, Lamar (Colo.) CC
26. Chad Gross, 1b, Claremont (Calif.) HS
27. Charles New, rhp, Mercer (Ga.)
28. Carmine Giardina, lhp, Durant HS, Plant City, Fla.
29. Devin Foreman, 1b, Hales Franciscan HS, Chicago
30. **Ryne Lawson, rhp, West Alabama**
31. Logan Shafer, of, Cuesta (Calif.) JC
32. **Mike Chambers, 2b, Franklin Pierce (N.H.) College**
33. Jeff Rea, 2b, Mississippi State
34. Bryan Morgado, lhp, Florida Christian HS, Tallahassee, Fla.
35. Jeremy Rahman, of, Hazelwood Central HS, Florissant, Mo.
36. Darren Blocker, 3b, Connors State (Okla.) JC
37. Justin Markes, lhp, Owensboro (Ky.) Catholic HS
38. **Travis Beazley, rhp, Randolph-Macon (Va.) College**
39. Jordan Abruzzo, c, San Diego
40. Corey Davisson, c, West HS, Fresno, Calif.
41. Peter Tountas, ss, Jefferson (Mo.) CC
42. Doug Graybill, lhp, Sarasota (Fla.) HS
43. **Jeff Vincent, of, Niagara**
44. Andrew Leart, rhp, Sierra Vista HS, Las Vegas
45. Jake McCarter, rhp, Alabama
46. Junior Rodriguez, 3b, Coral Gables (Fla.) HS
47. Nick Hill, lhp, Army
48. **Josh Papelbon, rhp, North Florida**
49. P.J. Thomas, rhp, Wabash Valley (Ill.) CC
50. Darrell Fisherbaugh, rhp, Hawaii

CHICAGO CUBS   (13)

1. **Tyler Colvin, of, Clemson**
2. (Choice to Indians as compensation for Type A free agent Bob Howry)
3. (Choice to Giants as compensation for Type A free agent Scott Eyre)
4. (Choice to Twins as compensation for Type B free agent Jacque Jones)
5. **Jeff Samardzija, rhp, Notre Dame**
6. **Josh Lansford, 3b, Cal Poly**
7. **Steven Clevenger, ss, Chipola (Fla.) JC**
8. **Billy Muldowney, rhp, Pittsburgh**
9. **Cliff Anderson, of, Cottonwood HS, Salt Lake City**
10. **Jacob Renshaw, rhp, Ventura (Calif.) CC**
11. **Chris Huseby, rhp, Martin County HS, Stuart, Fla.**
12. **Kitt Kopach, rhp, Illinois State**
13. **Matthew Camp, of, North Carolina State**
14. **Drew Rundle, of, Bend (Ore.) HS**
15. **Matt Canepa, c, Cal Poly**
16. **Blake Parker, c, Arkansas**
17. Keoni Ruth, 2b, San Diego
18. Jose Hernandez, rhp, Edgewater HS, Orlando
19. **Jeremy Papelbon, lhp, North Florida**
20. **Kevin Kreier, rhp, Foothill HS, Henderson, Nev.**
21. **Taylor Parker, lhp, Missouri**
22. Jovan Rosa, 3b, Lake City (Fla.) CC
23. **Chuckie Platt, rhp, Lamar**
24. **Matt Matulia, ss, The Citadel**
25. Jamie Bagley, rhp, Hargrave HS, Huffman, Texas
26. **Michael Cooper, rhp, California**
27. Cedric Redmond, rhp, Joliet (Ill.) Township HS
28. Brett Summers, rhp, South Suburban (Ill.) CC
29. Jordan Latham, rhp, JC of Southern Idaho
30. **Donny Walters, rhp, Richland (Texas) JC**
31. Bryan Collins, rhp, Alvin (Texas) CC
32. **Cesar Valentin, ss, Catalina Morales de Flore HS, Moca, P.R.**
33. **Ron Clipp, rhp, Point Loma Nazarene (Calif.)**
34. **Nate Samson, ss, Ocala Forest HS, Ocala, Fla.**
35. Marquez Smith, 3b, Clemson
36. **Miguel Cuevas, rhp, Los Angeles Pierce JC**
37. David Francis, rhp, St. Joseph SS, Mississauga, Ontario
38. Ben Feltner, of, Temple (Texas) JC
39. Marcus Hatley, rhp, Mission Hills HS, San Marcos, Calif.
40. **Eli Diaz, rhp, Texarkana CC**
41. Jonathan Negron, rhp, Puerto Rican Baseball Academy, Guaynabo, P.R.
42. Ben Ornelas, of, Cypress (Calif.) JC
43. Anthony Morel, ss, Riverside (Calif.) CC
44. Daniel Berlind, rhp, Calabasas (Calif.) HS
45. **Elliot Shea, of, Franklin Pierce (N.H.) College**
46. Ryan Shook, lhp, Valley Christian Academy, Roseville, Calif.
47. **Andrew McCormick, rhp, Pikeville (Ky.) College**
48. Kenneth Goodline, rhp, North Monterey County HS, Castroville, Calif.
49. **Ryne Malone, 3b, Florida State**
50. Ryan Davis, lhp, East Lake HS, Sammamish, Wash.

CHICAGO WHITE SOX   (29)

1. **Kyle McCulloch, rhp, Texas**
2. **Matt Long, rhp, Miami (Ohio)**
3. **Justin Edwards, lhp, Olympia HS, Orlando**
4. **Tyler Reves, c, Texas Tech**
5. **John Shelby, 2b, Kentucky**
6. **Brian Omogrosso, rhp, Indiana State**
7. **Justin Cassel, rhp, UC Irvine**
8. **Kent Gerst, of, Fort Zumwalt West HS, O'Fallon, Mo.**
9. Chris Duffy, 3b, Cypress Creek HS, Orlando
10. **Lee Cruz, of, Tampa**
11. **Andrew Urena, rhp, Mercer**
12. Sergio Morales, of, Broward (Fla.) CC
13. **Tyson Corley, rhp, South Mountain (Ariz.) CC**
14. **Mike Grace, 1b, Florida Southern College**
15. Yasser Clor, rhp, Wilcox HS, Santa Clara, Calif
16. Jose Jimenez, 3b, Monsignor Edward Pace HS, Opa Locka, Fla.
17. **Kylee Hash, c, Basic HS, Henderson, Nev.**
18. Lucas Luetge, lhp, San Jacinto (Texas) JC
19. Jeff Dunbar, c, UC Riverside
20. Wade Kapteyn, rhp, Illiana Christian HS, Lansing, Ill.
21. **Matthew Inouye, c, Hawaii**
22. **Kanekoa Texeira, rhp, Saddleback (Calif.) CC**
23. Brandon Villalobos, lhp, Chaffey (Calif.) JC
24. **Michael Rocco, rhp, Cal State San Bernardino**
25. **Joseph Hunter, of, Mississippi State**
26. **David Wasylak, rhp, Lubbock Christian (Texas)**
27. Tyler Herriage, lhp, Marcus HS, Flower Mound, Texas
28. Jedon Matthews, 3b, Horizon HS, San Diego
29. **Garrett Johnson, lhp, Orme HS, Mayer, Ariz.**

30. Hector Santiago, lhp, Essex County Vocational Technical HS, Bloomfield, N.J.
31. Stefan Gartrell, of, San Francisco
32. Alex Curry, rhp, Canyon HS, Anaheim
33. Chris Ulrey, of, New Palestine (Ind.) HS
34. Tyler Wright, of, South Florida CC
35. Adam Heisler, of, Baker HS, Mobile, Ala.
36. Matthew Enuco, 2b, Rowan (N.J.)
37. Adam Severino, of, Broward (Fla.) CC
38. Jacob Petricka, rhp, Faribault (Minn.) HS
39. Clint Cisper, rhp, Northeastern State (Okla.)
40. Andy Mead, of, SUNY Cortland
41. Mike Bolsenbroek, rhp, Santa Ana (Calif.) CC
42. Jose Jackson, 2b, South Florida CC
43. Jordan Cheatham, of, Pike HS, Indianapolis
44. Andy Fernandez, rhp, Hialeah (Fla.) HS
45. Raul Duran, of, Saddleback HS, Santa Ana, Calif.
46. Michael Cerda, 3b, Beyer HS, Modesto, Calif.
47. Kyle Williams, 2b, Chaparral HS, Scottsdale, Ariz.
48. Rafael Reyes, c, Palmer Trinity HS, Miami
49. Rafael Vera, 2b, Manatee (Fla.) CC
50. Brendon O'Donnell, of, UT Permian Basin

CINCINNATI REDS (8)

1. **Drew Stubbs, of, Texas**
2. **Sean Watson, rhp, Tennessee**
3. **Chris Valaika, ss, UC Santa Barbara**
4. **Justin Reed, of, Hillcrest Christian HS, Jackson, Miss.**
5. **Josh Ravin, rhp, Chatsworth (Calif.) HS**
6. **Jordan Smith, rhp, Southern Nevada CC**
7. **Justin Turner, 2b, Cal State Fullerton**
8. **Travis Webb, rhp, Washington State**
9. **Jeremy Burchett, rhp, California**
10. **Josh Roenicke, rhp, UCLA**
11. **Brandon Rice, rhp, Spalding HS, Griffin, Ga.**
12. **Logan Parker, 1b, Cincinnati**
13. **Kevin Gunter, rhp, Old Dominion**
14. **Carson Kainer, of, Texas**
15. **Rafael Sanchez, 3b, Queensborough (N.Y.) CC**
16. **Jamie Arneson, lhp, Bakersfield (Calif.) CC**
17. **Chris Heisey, of, Messiah (Pa.) College**
18. Ryan Wehrle, ss, Nebraska
19. **Derrik Lutz, rhp, George Washington**
20. **Eddy Rodriguez, c, Miami**
21. **Christopher White, rhp, Texas A&M Kingsville**
22. **Adam Pointer, rhp, Alvin (Texas) CC**
23. Tony Brown, of, Crestview (Fla.) HS
24. **Anthony Esquer, c, Cal Poly Pomona**
25. **Michael McKennon, of, UT San Antonio**
26. **Anthony Gressick, rhp, Ohio**
27. **Keltavious Jones, of, Darton (Ga.) JC**
28. **Tyler Hauschild, c, Edmonds (Wash.) CC**
29. **Jason Louwsma, 3b, Florida Gulf Coast Univ.**
30. **Lee Tabor, lhp, Francis Marion (S.C.)**
31. **Eric Schaler, rhp, Dallas Baptist**
32. **Danny Dorn, of, Cal State Fullerton**
33. Justin Curry, rhp, Buford (Ga.) HS
34. Ben Ihde, 1b, Neenah (Wis.) HS
35. John Touchston, rhp, Kingwood (Texas) HS
36. Nicholas Wandless, rhp, South Carolina-Aiken
37. Jarrod Gaskey, of, Azle (Texas) HS
38. Trevor Coleman, c, Dripping Springs (Texas) HS
39. Todd Waller, 3b, Cape Coral (Fla.) HS
40. Tyler Dewitt, of, Ponderosa HS, Shingle Springs, Calif.
41. Jeremy Erben, rhp, New Braunfels (Texas) HS
42. John Housey, rhp, Nova HS, Davie, Fla.
43. Geraldo Leal, rhp, Mission (Texas) HS
44. Jason Chapman, of, Truckee (Calif.) HS
45. Mike Lachapelle, lhp, Sahuaro HS, Tuscon, Ariz.
46. Jordan Tiegs, rhp, Sauk Valley (Ill.) CC
47. Frueny Parra, c, Connors State (Okla.) JC
48. Jordan Shadle, ss, Green River (Wash.) CC
49. Cameron Bayne, of, St. Louis HS, Honolulu
50. Blake Benveniste, 3b, Chaminade Prep, West Hills, Calif.

CLEVELAND INDIANS (25)

1. (Choice to Angels as compensation for Type B free agent Paul Byrd)
1s. David Huff, lhp, UCLA (Supplemental choice—39th overall—for loss of Type A free agnet Bob Howry)
2. **Steven Wright, rhp, Hawaii** (Choice from Rangers as compensation for Type B free agent Kevin Millwood)
2. **Josh Rodriguez, 2b, Rice** (Choice from Cubs as compensation for Howry)
2. **Wes Hodges, 3b, Georgia Tech**

2s. Matt McBride, c, Lehigh (Supplemental choice for loss of Type C free agent Scott Elarton)
3. **Adam Davis, ss, Florida**
4. **Ryan Morris, lhp, South Mecklenburg HS, Charlotte, N.C.**
5. **Chris Archer, rhp, Clayton (N.C.) HS**
6. **Austin Creps, rhp, Texas A&M**
7. **Robert Alcombrack, c, Bear River HS, Grass Valley, Calif.**
8. **Mike Eisenberg, rhp, Marietta (Ohio) College**
9. **Jared Goedert, 3b, Kansas State**
10. **Paolo Espino, rhp, The Pendleton School, Bradenton, Fla.**
11. **Kelly Edmundson, c, Tennessee**
12. **Dan Frega, rhp, Illinois State**
13. Brant Rustich, rhp, UCLA
14. **William Delage, lhp, Lamar**
15. **Matt Meyer, lhp, Boston College**
16. **Stephen Douglas, of, East Tennessee State**
17. **Kyle Harper, rhp, Orange Coast (Calif.) CC**
18. **Daryl King, of, Benicia (Calif.) HS**
19. **Josh Tomlin, rhp, Texas Tech**
20. **Vinnie Pestano, rhp, Cal State Fullerton**
21. **John Gaub, lhp, Minnesota**
22. **Charles Hargis, ss, East Tennessee State**
23. **Derrick Loop, lhp, Cal State Los Angeles**
24. **Christopher Nash, 1b, Johnson County (Kan.) CC**
25. Alex Jordan, rhp, Cypress (Calif.) JC
26. Ty Pryor, rhp, Tennessee
27. Chris Roberts, of, West HS, Oshkosh, Wis.
28. **Dustin Realini, 3b, Santa Clara**
29. Thomas Benton, rhp, UNC Wilmington
30. Brett Carlin, lhp, Fullerton (Calif.) JC
31. Easton Gust, 2b, Cottonwood HS, Salt Lake City
32. David Uribes, 2b, Pepperdine
33. Jarett Jackson, of, Jefferson HS, Auburn, Wash.
34. Michael Bolsinger, rhp, McKinney North HS, McKinney, Texas
35. Alan Brech, lhp, Bowling Green State
36. Ryan Miller, lhp, Blinn (Texas) JC
37. Brett Kinning, 2b, Arkansas State
38. Nathan Bunton, rhp, Midland (Texas) Lutheran College
39. Jimmy Brettl, lhp, Cal State Northridge
40. Josh Yates, c, Arkansas State
41. Kyle Paul, c, Vernon (Texas) CC
42. Roderick Barcelo, of, Rivera HS, Vega Baja, P.R.
43. Mike Pontius, rhp, Holt HS, Wentzville, Mo.
44. Brad Reid, rhp, Decatur HS, Federal Way, Wash.
45. Zach Barger, of, Grossmont (Calif.) JC
46. Daniel Miltenberger, rhp, UCLA
47. Eric McKinney, of, Spiro (Okla.) HS
48. Travis Turek, rhp, Santa Barbara (Calif.) CC
49. Ryan Mottern, rhp, Oklahoma
50. Vinnie Catricala, 3b, Jesuit HS, Carmichael, Calif.

COLORADO ROCKIES (2)

1. **Greg Reynolds, rhp, Stanford**
2. **David Christensen, of, Douglas HS Parkland, Fla.**
3. **Keith Weiser, lhp, Miami (Ohio)**
4. **Craig Baker, rhp, Cal State Northridge**
5. **Helder Velazquez, ss, Puerto Rico Baseball Academy**
6. **Kevin Clark, of, Manatee (Fla.) JC**
7. **Michael McKenry, c, Middle Tennessee State**
8. **Brandon Hynick, rhp, Birmingham-Southern**
9. **Will Harris, rhp, Louisiana State**
10. **David Arnold, rhp, Lincoln Trail (Ill.) CC**
11. Aaron Miller, of, Channelview (Texas) HS
12. **Austin Rauch, c, El Capitan HS, Lakeside, Calif.**
13. **Spence Nagy, ss, Tallahassee (Fla.) CC**
14. **Jeff Kindel, of, Georgia Tech**
15. **Victor Ferrante, of, Solano (Calif.) JC**
16. **Anthony Jackson, of, Pacific**
17. **Michael Gibbs, rhp, Virginia Commonwealth**
18. Andrew Cashner, rhp, Angelina (Texas) JC
19. Zack Murry, ss, Chanute (Kan.) HS
20. **Sean Jarrett, rhp, Oral Roberts**
21. **Andrew Graham, rhp, UC Santa Barbara**
22. **Jay Cox, of, North Carolina**
23. Scott Maine, lhp, Miami
24. Shane Dyer, rhp, Eaton (Colo.) HS
25. Jeremy Jones, of, North Carolina A&T
26. **Devin Collis, lhp, Arkansas**
27. **Matt Repec, ss, Winthrop**
28. **Tommy Baumgardner, rhp, Mississippi**
29. **Shane Lowe, ss, New Bloomfield (Mo.) HS**
30. Scott Robinson, of, Henry County HS, McDonough, Ga.
31. Curtis Dupart, of, Woodinville (Wash.) HS
32. Miguel Valcarcel, rhp, Perkiomen School, Pennsburg, Pa.

33. Drew Shetrone, rhp, Cumberland (Tenn.) U.
34. Jamie Niley, lhp, Elk Grove (Calif.) Sr. HS
35. **Josh Banda, 1b, California Baptist**
36. Michael Diaz, c, Luis Munoz Marin HS, Barranquitas, P.R.
37. Zach Helton, 2b, Central HS, Knoxville, Tenn.
38. Jon Hesketh, lhp, Vernon (Texas) JC
39. Jason Fuqua, lhp, Sterling HS, Houston
40. David Luna, c, Piedmont Hills HS, San Jose, Calif.
41. Jay Taylor, rhp, West Seattle HS
42. Sean Halton, 1b, Fresno (Calif.) CC
43. Bryan Jaeger, of, Louisiana State-Eunice JC
44. Scott Bachman, lhp, Rocky Mountain HS, Fort Collins, Colo.
45. James Manning, rhp, Wallace State (Ala.) CC
46. Damion Carter, of, Southern Mississippi
47. Justin Miller, rhp, Bakersfield (Calif.) JC
48. Jesus Cebollero, rhp, Puerto Rico Baseball Academy, San Sebastian, P.R.
49. Paul Dickey, rhp, Lower Columbia (Wash.) CC
50. Jamie Johnson, of, West Ouachita HS, West Monroe, La.

DETROIT TIGERS (6)

1. **Andrew Miller, lhp, North Carolina**
2. **Ronald Borquin, 3b, Ohio State**
3. **Brennan Boesch, of, California**
4. **Ryan Strieby, 1b, Kentucky**
5. **Scott Sizemore, 2b, Virginia Commonwealth**
6. **Jordan Newton, c, Western Kentucky**
7. **Jonah Nickerson, rhp, Oregon State**
8. **Chris Cody, lhp, Manhattan**
9. **Zach Piccola, lhp, South Alabama**
10. **Lauren Gagnier, rhp, Cal State Fullerton**
11. **Hayden Parrott, 2b, Desert Mountain HS, Scottsdale, Ariz.**
12. **Joe Bowen, c, Vanguard HS, Ocala, Fla.**
13. **Angel Castro, rhp, Western Oklahoma State JC**
14. **Brett Jensen, rhp, Nebraska**
15. Franco Valdes, c, Monsignor Edward Pace HS, Opa Locka, Fla.
16. **Jeff Gerbe, rhp, Michigan State**
17. Ben Petralli, c, Sacramento CC
18. **Deik Scram, of, Oklahoma State**
19. **Duane Below, lhp, Lake Michigan JC**
20. **Casey Fien, rhp, Cal Poly**
21. **Thomas Thorton, lhp, Notre Dame**
22. **Chris Krawczyk, rhp, Missouri State**
23. **Aaron Furhman, lhp, Pleasant Valley HS, Brodheadsville, Pa.**
24. **Joe Tucker, of, Kent State**
25. Casey Weathers, rhp, Vanderbilt
26. Daniel Renfroe, of, Tattnall Square Academy, Macon, Ga.
27. Ryan Lindgren, rhp, Seminole (Okla.) JC
28. **Derek Witt, rhp, Ohio**
29. **Chris Carlson, 1b, New Mexico**
30. Phil Ortez, of, Scottsdale (Ariz.) CC
31. **Mike Sullivan, of, Ball State**
32. **Rudy Darrow, rhp, Nicholls State**
33. Kodiak Quick, rhp, Kansas
34. Brandon Johnson, rhp, Butler County (Kan.) CC
35. **Paul Hammond, lhp, Michigan**
36. Charles Nading, rhp, East HS, Anchorage, Alaska
37. Ryan LaMotta, rhp, Baylor
38. **Dana Arrowood, rhp, Old Dominion**
39. **Michael Bertram, 3b, Kentucky**
40. **Adrian Casanova, c, Clemson**
41. John Freeman, c, Carney (Okla.) HS
42. Kevin Chapman, lhp, Westminster Academy, Fort Lauderdale, Fla.
43. David Mattox, rhp, Connors State (Okla.) JC
44. Ryan Kilmer, rhp, Midwest City (Okla.) HS
45. Lance Durham, of, Bacon HS, Cincinnati
46. Kent Williamson, rhp, Cowley County (Kan.) CC
47. **Alec Shepherd, rhp, South Mountain (Ariz.) CC**
48. Matthew McDonald, rhp, Ulster County (N.Y.) CC
49. Kyle Peter, of, Cloud County (Kan.) CC
50. Alan Oaks, of, Divine Child HS, Dearborn, Mich.

FLORIDA MARLINS (19)

1. **Brett Sinkbeil, rhp, Missouri State**
1s. **Chris Coghlan, 3b, Mississippi** (Supplemental choice—36th overall—for loss of Type A free agent A.J. Burnett)
2. **Tom Hickman, of, Pepperell HS, Lindale, Ga.**
3. **Torre Langley, c, Alexander HS, Douglasville, Ga.** (Choice from Blue Jays as compensation for Burnett)
3. **Scott Cousins, of, San Francisco**
4. **Hector Correa, rhp, Lorenzo Coballes Gandia HS, Hatillo, P.R.**
5. **David Hatcher, c, UNC Wilmington**
6. **Justin Jacobs, ss, Chino (Calif.) HS**
7. **Don Czyz, rhp, Kansas**

8. **Dan Garcia, ss, Nogales HS, La Puente, Calif.**
9. **John Raynor, of, UNC Wilmington**
10. **Graham Taylor, lhp, Miami**
11. **Osvaldo Martinez, ss, Porterville (Calif.) JC**
12. **Brad Stone, rhp, Quincy (Ill.)**
13. **Andrew Saylor, 2b, Kent State**
14. **Jay Buente, rhp, Purdue**
15. **Guillermo Martinez, ss, South Alabama**
16. **Jacob Blackwood, 3b, Maplewoods (Mo.) CC**
17. **Hunter Mense, of, Missouri**
18. **Ross Liesermann, rhp, Akron**
19. **Jordan Davis, rhp, Alabama**
20. Steven Sultzbaugh, of, Westwood HS, Austin, Texas
21. **Corey Madden, rhp, St. Mary's**
22. **Kevan Kelley, lhp, Cal State San Bernardino**
23. Rylan Hanks, lhp, Cal State San Bernardino
24. Ernesto Rivera, of, Puerto Rico Baseball Academy, Canovanas, P.R.
25. **Joel Fountain, rhp, St. Mary's**
26. **Andy Jackson, lhp, Central Arkansas**
27. Jeremy Hall, rhp, East Tennessee State
28. Kedrick Martin, lhp, Meridian (Miss.) CC
29. Johnathan van Looy, lhp, John Swett HS, Crockett, Calif.
30. Quinn Harris, ss, Elizabethtown (Ky.) HS
31. William Mays, of, Sinclair (Ohio) CC
32. **Alejandro Sanabia, rhp, Castle Park HS, Chula Vista, Calif.**
33. Eric Basurto, rhp, Chabot (Calif.) CC
34. T.J. Kelly, rhp, Bakersfield (Calif.) JC
35. Christopher Evans, c, Serrano HS, Phelan, Calif.
36. David Williams, of, Rutgers
37. James Wallace, rhp, JC of Southern Idaho
38. Jeremy Tice, 3b, Tallahassee (Fla.) CC
39. **Brandon McDougall, of, UC Irvine**
40. **Tony Suarez, rhp, Southeastern Louisiana**
41. Kyle Barry, rhp, Madison Area (Wisc.) Tech CC
42. Ryan Kussmaul, rhp, Madison Area Tech (Wis.) CC
43. William Jackel, rhp, Tallahassee (Fla.) CC
44. T.J. Forrest, rhp, Haughton (La.) HS
45. Kyle Price, 2b, Eastern Oklahoma State JC
46. Mitch MacDonald, 3b, Monterey Peninsula (Calif.) JC
47. Brooks Martin, rhp, Streator (Ill.) HS
48. Lance Hanmer, ss, Greensburg (Ind.) HS
49. Michael Hubbard, of, Arkansas-Fort Smith JC
50. Andrew Raponi, 1b, Monte Vista HS, Danville, Calif.

HOUSTON ASTROS (23)

1. **Max Sapp, c, Bishop Moore HS, Orlando**
2. **Sergio Perez, rhp, Tampa**
3. **Nick Moresi, of, Fresno State**
4. **Chris Johnson, 3b, Stetson**
5. **Casey Hudspeth, rhp, South Florida**
6. **Bud Norris, rhp, Cal Poly**
7. **David Qualben, lhp, Pace (N.Y.)**
8. **Jimmy Van Ostrand, of, Cal Poly**
9. **Greg Buchanan, 2b, Rice**
10. Nathan Karns, rhp, Martin Senior HS, Arlington, Texas
11. **Tom Vessella, lhp, Whittier (Calif.) College**
12. **Bryan Hallberg, rhp, Pace (N.Y.)**
13. **Christopher Salamida, lhp, Oneonta State (N.Y.)**
14. **Justin Tellam, c, Pepperdine**
15. **Kevin Fox, lhp, Biola (Calif.)**
16. **Drew Holder, of, Dallas Baptist**
17. **Justin Stiver, rhp, Florida Gulf Coast Univ.**
18. **Colt Adams, rhp, Dixie State (Utah) JC**
19. **Orlando Rosales, of, Tampa**
20. Mark Sobolewski, ss, Sarasota (Fla.) HS
21. **Anthony Bello, lhp, Nova Southeastern (Fla.)**
22. **Chad Wagler, rhp, Kent State**
23. **Tim Torres, ss, Oral Roberts**
24. John Wiedenbauer, lhp, Seabreeze HS, Daytona Beach, Fla.
25. Jamaal Hollis, rhp, Whitney Young HS, Chicago
26. Lenell McGee, 3b, Mount Carmel (Ill.) HS
27. **Cirilo Cruz, 1b, Cumberland (Tenn.)**
28. **Brandon Caipen, 3b, Youngstown State**
29. Rafael Parks, of, Greenbrier HS, Evans, Ga.
30. **Eric Taylor, 3b, UCLA**
31. **Kyle Deyoung, rhp, Florida Southern College**
32. **Adam Hale, rhp, Texas A&M**
33. Codi Harshman, of, Sabino HS, Tucson
34. John Anderson, rhp, Captain Shreve HS, Shreveport, La.
35. Patrick Allen, of, Everett (Wash.) CC
36. Johnathan Moore, c, Lamar HS, Arlington Texas
37. Trent Henderson, ss, Newport (Wash.) HS
38. Casey Anderson, c, West Quacita HS, West Monroe, La.
39. Will Kline, rhp, Mississippi

40. Steve Detwiler, ss, San Rafael (Calif.) HS
41. Axel Gonzalez, of, Martinez HS, Guaynabo, P.R.
42. Kevin Sullivan, c, York HS, Elmhurst, Ill.
43. Greg Joseph, of, Mount San Jacinto (Calif.) CC
44. Adam Pilate, of, Sylacauga (Ala.) HS
45. Cody Madison, of, Vista Del Lago HS, Moreno Valley, Calif.
46. Joey Wong, ss, Sprague HS, Salem, Ore.
47. Mike Pericht, c, Providence Catholic HS, New Lenox, Ill.
48. Jerry Quinones, lhp, Compton (Calif.) CC
49. Andy Launier, 1b, Sierra (Calif.) JC
50. Paul Henley, of, Rice

KANSAS CITY ROYALS (1)

1. **Luke Hochevar, rhp, Fort Worth Cats (American Association)**
2. **Jason Taylor, of, Kellam HS Virginia Beach**
3. **Blake Wood, rhp, Georgia Tech**
4. **Derrick Robinson, of, Yonge HS, Gainesville, Fla.**
5. **Jason Godin, rhp, Old Dominion**
6. **Harold Mozingo, rhp, Virginia Commonwealth**
7. **Brett Bigler, of, UC Riverside**
8. **Josh Cribb, rhp, Clemson**
9. **Marc Maddox, 2b, Southern Mississippi**
10. **Nicholas Van Stratten, of, St. Louis CC-Meramec**
11. **Tyler Chambliss, rhp, Florida State**
12. **Everett Teaford, lhp, Georgia Southern**
13. **Kurt Mertins, 2b, JC of the Desert (Calif.)**
14. **Daniel Best, rhp, Southern Mississippi**
15. **Nick Francis, of, Pensacola (Fla.) JC**
16. **Tyrone Wilson, ss, Southern HS, Durham, N.C.**
17. **Matt Morizio, c, Northeastern**
18. Chase Larsson, of, Kitsilano SS, Vancouver, B.C.
19. Jeff Inman, rhp, Garces Memorial HS, Bakersfield, Calif.
20. Brad Boxberger, rhp, Foothill HS, Santa Ana, Calif.
21. **Burke Baldwin, lhp, Elgin (Ill.) CC**
22. **Romas Hicks, rhp, Georgia State**
23. **Aaron Hartsock, rhp, California Baptist**
24. Tyler Moyneur, c, Arizona Western JC
25. Rafael Valenzuela, ss, Nogales (Ariz.) HS
26. Darrell Lockett, of, Weatherford (Texas) HS
27. Colby Killian, rhp, Warren County HS, McMinnville, Tenn.
28. Michael Wheeler, of, Walters State (Tenn.) CC
29. Steve Rinaudo, ss, American River (Calif.) CC
30. Tyler Pearson, rhp, Northern Colorado
31. **Brandon Lance, c, New Mexico State**
32. Fernando Garcia, 2b, Immaculada HS, Arecibo, P.R.
33. Harold Smith, of, Palmetto (Fla.) HS
34. Jared Grace, 1b, Pensacola (Fla.) JC
35. Anthony Stovall, rhp, Kailua (Hawaii) HS
36. Manuel Garcia, rhp, Cochise (Ariz.) JC
37. Kaleb Harst, c, St. Thomas More HS, Lafayette, La.
38. Mike Dabbs, of, Cowley County (Kan.) CC
39. Steven Moore, rhp, Thomasville (Ga.) HS
40. Chris Snipes, lhp, Warner Robins (Ga.) HS
41. Jeremy Toole, rhp, Huntsville (Texas) HS
42. Todd McBride, of, The Dalles (Ore.)-Wahtonka Union HS
43. Brennan Thorpe, rhp, Saddleback (Calif.) CC
44. Bryan Paukovits, rhp, Southwestern (Calif.) CC
45. Eric Martinez, rhp, Southwestern (Calif.) JC
46. Chase Lehr, rhp, Centennial HS, Peoria, Ariz.
47. Ryan Cisterna, c, Chandler-Gilbert (Ariz.) CC
48. Colby Ho, 3b, Kaiser HS, Honolulu
49. Rocky Gale, c, North Salem HS, Salem, Ore.
50. **Jarrod Dyson, of, Southwest Mississippi JC**

LOS ANGELES ANGELS (26)

1. **Hank Conger, c, Huntington Beach (Calif.) HS** (Choice from Indians as compensation for Type B free agent Paul Byrd)
1. (Choice to Dodgers as compensation for Type A free agent Jeff Weaver)
2. (Choice to Nationals as compensation for Type B free agent Hector Carrasco)
3. Russ Moldenhauer, of, Boerne (Texas) HS
4. **Clay Fuller, of, Smithson Valley HS, Spring Branch, Texas**
5. **Kenneth Herndon, rhp, Gulf Coast (Fla.) CC**
6. **Robert Fish, lhp, Miller HS, San Bernardino, Calif.**
7. Jarrad Page, of, Cal State Los Angeles
8. **Matt Sweeney, 1b, Magruder HS, Rockville, Md.**
9. **Nate Boman, lhp, San Diego**
10. **Leonardo Calderon, lhp, Lake City (Fla.) CC**
11. **David Pellegrine, rhp, Northeastern**
12. Jordan Walden, rhp, Mansfield (Texas) HS
13. **Blake Holler, lhp, Stanford**
14. **Chris Armstrong, lhp, Owasso (Okla.) HS**
15. **Scott Knazek, c, Rider**

16. Scott Carroll, rhp, Missouri State
17. **Tadd Brewer, 2b, Lipscomb**
18. Charles Brewer, rhp, Chaparral HS, Scottsdale, Ariz.
19. **Chris Pettit, of, Loyola Marymount**
20. James Reichenbach, lhp, Central Bucks East HS, Doylestown, Penn.
21. John Vincent, of, New Mexico State
22. Michael Thomas, rhp, Marshall HS, Missouri City, Texas
23. **Tim Schoeninger, rhp, Nevada**
24. John Curtis, c, Cal State Fullerton
25. Jason Jarvis, rhp, Chaparral HS, Scottsdale, Ariz.
26. Ryan Kelley, lhp, Indian River (Fla.) CC
27. **Matt Reilly, rhp, Pace (N.Y.)**
28. **Barret Browning, lhp, Florida State**
29. Michael Davitt, rhp, Okaloosa-Walton (Fla.) CC
30. Kevin Skogley, lhp, Nevada Las Vegas
31. Dylan Lindsey, rhp, Broward (Fla.) CC
32. **Chris Lewis, 2b, Stanford**
33. **Wilberto Ortiz, ss, Dowling (N.Y.) College**
34. Bobby Wagner, of, Douglas (B.C.) JC
35. **Aaron Cook, rhp, Tampa**
36. **Alex Fonseca, ss, Florida Atlantic**
37. Ronnie Welty, of, Mesquite HS, Gilbert, Ariz.
38. **Eduardo Chile, rhp, Rollins (Fla.) College**
39. Rian Kiniry, of, Broward (Fla.) CC
40. Jake Locker, rhp, Ferndale (Wash.) HS
41. Brian Hobbs, of, Chipola (Fla.) JC
42. Jonathan Conaster, rhp, Tallahassee (Fla.) CC
43. **Doug Brandt, lhp, Cal State San Bernardino**
44. Dwain Green, rhp, Chipola (Fla.) JC
45. Matthew McCracken, lhp, Florida CC
46. Ryan Lipkin, c, Solano (Calif.) JC
47. Jonathan Plefka, rhp, Texas Tech
48. Abraham Gonzalez, rhp, Coachella Valley HS, Thermal, Calif.
49. **Gordon Gronkowski, 1b, Jacksonville**
50. Timothy Brewer, lhp, Kean HS, St. Thomas, Virgin Islands

LOS ANGELES DODGERS (7)

1. **Clayton Kershaw, lhp, Highland Park HS, Dallas**
1. **Bryan Morris, rhp, Motlow State (Tenn.) CC** (Choice from Angels as compensation for Type A free agent Jeff Weaver)
1S. **Preston Mattingly, ss, Evansville (Ind.) Central HS** (Supplemental choice—31st overall—for loss of Weaver)
2. (Choice to Braves as compensation for Type A free agent Rafael Furcal)
3. (Choice to Red Sox as compensation for Type A free agent Bill Mueller)
4. **Kyle Orr, 1b, Lambrick Park SS, Victoria, B.C.**
5. **Kyle Smit, rhp, Spanish Springs HS, Sparks, Nev.**
6. **Garrett White, lhp, Mississippi**
7. **Jamie Ortiz, 1b, San Alfonso de Ligorio HS, Guayama, P.R.**
8. **Tommy Giles, of, Miami**
9. **Bridger Hunt, 3b, Central Missouri State**
10. Andy D'Alessio, 1b, Clemson
11. **Justin Fuller, ss, Lewis-Clark (Idaho) State College**
12. **Paul Coleman, lhp, Pepperdine**
13. Nicholas Akins, ss, Los Angeles HS
14. Alex White, rhp, Conley HS, Greenville, N.C.
15. Gorman Erickson, c, Westview HS, San Diego
16. Justin Coats, ss, Texas HS, Texarkana, Texas
17. **Michael Rivera, 2b, Tennessee**
18. **Joe Jones, rhp, Portland**
19. Martin Beno, rhp, Mississippi Gulf Coast JC
20. Billy Bullock, rhp, Riverview (Fla.) HS
21. **Matthew Berezay, of, Pacific**
22. **Chris Jensen, of, UCLA**
23. **Eric Thompson, rhp, Roseburg (Ore.) HS**
24. **John Martin, c, Emporia State (Kan.)**
25. **Esteban Lopez, c, Hawaii**
26. Kody Kaiser, 2b, Oklahoma
27. A.J. Casario, c, Overbrook Senior HS, Pine Hill, N.J.
28. Taylor Lewis, rhp, Canyon del Oro HS, Oro Valley, Ariz.
29. Roberto Perez, c, Eugenio Maria de Hostos HS, Mayaguez, P.R.
30. Alex Burkard, lhp, Milton HS, Alpharetta, Ga.
31. Jonathan Wilson, 3b, St. Charles (Mo.) HS
32. Jordan Kopycinski, c, St. Thomas HS, Houston
33. Kurt Bradley, 2b, Northern Iowa
34. Luke Yoder, of, Liberty HS, Bakersfield, Calif.
35. Nick Buss, of, San Diego Mesa JC
36. Robert Taylor, c, Laredo (Texas) CC
37. Anthony Benner, 3b, Southwestern (Calif.) JC
38. Kameron Forte, c, Texas HS, Texarkana, Texas
39. Jake Debus, rhp, Moraine Valley (Ill.) CC
40. Chris Jones, ss, Redan HS, Stone Mountain, Ga.
41. Todd McCraw, c, Saint James HS, Myrtle Beach, S.C.
42. Joe Dispensa, of, St. Rita HS, Chicago

43. Jordan Chambless, rhp, Texas A&M
44. Aaron Barrett, rhp, Central HS, Evansville, Ind.
45. Greg Hendrix, lhp, North Atlanta HS
46. Ryan Aguayo, 2b, Servite HS, Anaheim
47. Brett Sowers, 3b, Cherry Creek HS, Englewood, Colo.
48. Tanner Biagini, 3b, Conley HS, Greenville, N.C.
49. Paul Goldschmidt, 1b, The Woodlands (Texas) HS
50. Kurt Benton, of, West Stanly HS, Oakboro, N.C.

MILWAUKEE BREWERS (16)

1. **Jeremy Jeffress, rhp, Halifax County HS, South Boston, Va.**
2. **Brent Brewer, ss, Sandy Creek HS, Tyrone, Ga.**
3. **Cole Gillespie, of, Oregon State**
4. **Evan Anundsen, rhp, Columbine HS, Littleton, Colo.**
5. **Chris Errecart, of, California**
6. **Brae Wright, lhp, Oklahoma State**
7. **Andrew Bouchie, c, Oral Roberts**
8. **Shane Hill, rhp, Florida Christian HS, Miami**
9. **Shawn Ferguson, rhp, Texas Christian**
10. **Michael McClendon, rhp, Seminole (Fla.) JC**
11. **Zach Clem, of, Washington**
12. Chad Robinson, rhp, Silverado HS, Las Vegas
13. **Chris Toneguzzi, rhp, Purdue**
14. **Hector Bernal, ss, El Paso (Texas) CC**
15. **Brett Whiteside, c, Mesquite HS, Gilbert, Ariz.**
16. **R.J. Seidel, rhp, Central HS, LaCrosse, Wisc.**
17. Aaron Tullo, rhp, St. Peterburg (Fla.) HS
18. Andrew Clark, 1b, New Palestine (Ind.) HS
19. Lee Haydel, of, Riverside Academy, Coushatta, La.
20. Mehdi Djebbar, lhp, Ahuntsic (Quebec) JC
21. **Jesse D'Amico, c, Mohawk HS, Bessemer, Pa.**
22. **Johnathan King, rhp, Northeastern Oklahoma A&M JC**
23. Scott Shuman, rhp, Tift County HS, Tifton, Ga.
24. **Travis Wendte, rhp, Missouri**
25. **Mike Goetz, of, Wisconsin-Milwaukee**
26. Marc Lewis, lhp, Creighton
27. Thomas Macy, rhp, Scottsdale (Ariz.) CC
28. Terrell Alliman, of, Bluevale (Ontario) Collegiate Institute
29. David Newmann, lhp, Texas A&M
30. **Jordan Swaydan, c, San Diego State**
31. Rob Bryson, rhp, William Penn HS, New Castle, Del.
32. Nick Tyson, rhp, Timber Creek Regional HS, Erial, N.J.
33. **Eric Newton, 2b, Santa Clara**
34. **Stuart Sutherland, rhp, Dallas Baptist**
35. Sanduan Dubose, 3b, Stillman (Ala.) College
36. Clay Jones, c, Bibb County HS, Centreville, Ala.
37. Weston Munson, ss, Fond du Lac (Wis.) HS
38. Todd Fitzgerald, lhp, San Jose (Calif.) CC
39. **Chuckie Caufield, of, Oklahoma**
40. Alex Koronis, rhp, Monsignor Edward Pace HS, Opa Locka, Fla.
41. John Poulk, 3b, UNC Wilmington
42. Matt Peck, rhp, Cowley County (Kan.) CC
43. **Dustin Lidyard, rhp, Lower Columbia (Wash.) JC**
44. Bryan Crosby, 3b, William Blount HS, Maryville, Tenn.
45. Matt Thompson, ss, Aztec (N.M.) HS
46. Aaron Johnson, c, Lethbridge (Alberta) CC
47. Matthew Coburn, rhp, San Jacinto (Texas) JC
48. Brandon Owens, rhp, Heritage HS, Conyers, Ga.
49. Nicholas Spears, ss, Poway (Calif.) HS
50. Ricky Alvernaz, 3b, Tamanawis SS, Vancouver, B.C.

MINNESOTA TWINS (20)

1. **Chris Parmelee, of/1b, Chino Hills (Calif.) HS**
2. **Joe Benson, of, Joliet (Ill.) Catholic HS**
3. **Tyler Robertson, lhp, Bella Vista HS, Fair Oaks, Calif.**
4. **Whit Robbins, 1b, Georgia Tech (Choice from Cubs as compensation for Type B free agent Jacque Jones)**
4. **Garrett Olson, 3b, Franklin Pierce (N.H.) College**
5. Devin Shepherd, of, Oxnard (Calif.) HS
6. **Jeff Christy, c, Nebraska**
7. **Jonathan Waltenbury, 1b, Henry Street HS, Whitby, Ontario**
8. **Brian Dinkleman, 2b, McKendree (Ill.) College**
9. **Sean Land, lhp, Kansas**
10. Jared Mitchell, of, Westgate HS, New Iberia, La.
11. **Steve Singleton, ss, San Diego**
12. **Kevin Harrington, of, Royal HS, Simi Valley, Calif.**
13. Aaron Senne, of, Mayo HS, Rochester, Minn.
14. **Jeff Manship, rhp, Notre Dame**
15. **Mark Dolenc, of, Minnesota State-Mankato**
16. Shayne Willson, of, Earl Marriott SS, Surrey, B.C.
17. Andy Oliver, lhp, Vermillion (Ohio) HS
18. Chris Anderson, lhp, Northern Essex (Mass.) CC
19. **Danny Valencia, 3b, Miami**
20. Gilbert Buenrostro, c, Cuesta (Calif.) JC

21. Eric Santiago, ss, Miami Dade CC South
22. Aaron Tennyson, lhp, Kentucky
23. **Thomas Wright, rhp, McGavock HS, Nashville**
24. **Nick Papasan, ss, Granbury (Texas) HS**
25. Dillon Baird, 3b, Prescott (Ariz.) HS
26. Kyle Mitchell, rhp, Mosley HS, Panama City, Fla.
27. Joseph Tribou, c, Northeast HS, St. Petersburg, Fla.
28. Dustin Williams, c, Woodlawn HS, Rison, Ark.
29. Braxton Chisholm, c, St. Cloud (Fla.) HS
30. Michael Mopas, lhp, Golden West (Calif.) JC
31. Kyle Thornton, rhp, Cowley County (Kan.) CC
32. Andres Diaz, c, Santaluces HS, Palm Beach, Fla.
33. Alberto Espinso, c, Brito HS, Miami
34. Marcel Champagnie, ss, Kaskaskia (Ill.) CC
35. Robby Donovan, rhp, Royal Palm Beach HS, West Palm Beach, Fla.
36. Julio Martinez, of, Flanagan HS, Pembroke Pines, Fla.
37. Aaron Baker, c, Denton (Texas) HS
38. Randy Boone, rhp, Texas
39. Anthony Slama, rhp, San Diego
40. **Michael Cowgill, 2b, James Madison**
41. Joan Ortiz, rhp, Juan Ponce de Leon HS, San Juan, P.R.
42. Robert Anderson, rhp, Rider HS, Wichita Falls, Texas
43. Francis Berry, rhp, First Colonial HS, Virginia Beach
44. Isaac Castillo, 2b, Waimea HS, Kauai, Hawaii
45. Brandon Trodick, rhp, CC of Southern Nevada
46. Richard Breton, of, Keystone Heights (Fla.) HS
47. Josh Chester, of, Cypress Bay HS, Weston, Fla.
48. Stephen Vento, rhp, Palm Beach (Fla.) CC
49. Calvin Culver, of, Quartz Hill HS, Lancaster, Calif.
50. Derek McCallum, ss, Hill-Murray HS, St. Paul, Minn.

NEW YORK METS (18)

1. (Choice to Phillies as compensation for Type A free agent Billy Wagner)
2. **Kevin Mulvey, rhp, Villanova**
3. **Joe Smith, rhp, Wright State**
4. **John Holdzkom, rhp, Salt Lake CC**
5. **Stephen Holmes, rhp, Rhode Island**
6. **Scott Schafer, rhp, Memorial HS, Pasadena, Texas**
7. **Daniel Stegall, of, Greenwood (Ark.) HS**
8. **Nathan Hedrick, rhp, Barton County (Kan.) CC**
9. Jeremy Barfield, of, Klein HS, Spring, Texas
10. Phillips Orta, rhp, Western Nebraska CC
11. Andy Moye, rhp, Alpharetta (Ga.) HS
12. **Nick Giarraputo, 3b, Simi Valley (Calif.) HS**
13. **Daniel Murphy, 3b, Jacksonville**
14. **Todd Privett, lhp, JC of Southern Idaho**
15. Justin Dalles, c, Park Vista Community HS, Boynton Beach, Fla.
16. **Tobi Stoner, rhp, Davis & Elkins (W.Va.) College**
17. **Stephen Puhl, c, St. Edward's (Texas)**
18. **Ritchie Price, ss, Kansas**
19. Justin Woodall, lhp, Lafayette HS, Oxford, Miss.
20. **Jason Jacobs, c, Georgia**
21. Joel Wells, 1b, Abilene Christian (Texas)
22. **Timothy Stronach, rhp, Worcester State (Mass.) College**
23. **Nick Waechter, rhp, Western Oregon State**
24. **Valentin Ramos, 1b, Sallisaw (Okla.) HS**
25. **Steven Cheney, rhp, Gulf Coast (Fla.) CC**
26. **Dustin Martin, of, Sam Houston State**
27. **Tim Haines, rhp, UT Pan American**
28. **William Bashelor, of, Dartmouth**
29. **Jake Eigsti, ss, Indiana State**
30. **Ricky Sparks, rhp, Dallas Baptist**
31. Jeremy Hambrice, of, Southern Arkansas
32. Bradley Roper-Hubbert, c, Alcorn State
33. Teddy Dziuba, c, Babson (Mass.) College
34. J.R. Voyles, 2b, Texas-San Antonio
35. James Newman, 2b, Erskine (S.C.) College
36. Edgar Ramirez, rhp, Louisiana State
37. Josh Stinson, rhp, Northwood HS, Shreveport, La.
38. J.J. Leaper, rhp, Sentinel (Oklahoma) HS
39. Donald Green, of, Texas Southern
40. Tyler Binkley, rhp, St. Mary's HS, Sault Ste. Marie, Ontario
41. Victor Black, rhp, Amarillo (Texas) HS
42. Terrell Stringer, rhp, Smith Station HS, Smiths, Ala.
43. Albert Cartwright, 2b, American Heritage Boca-Delray HS, Delray Beach, Fla.
44. Brad Schwarzenbach, rhp, Cerritos (Calif.) CC
45. Beau Pender, rhp, Gulf Coast (Fla.) CC
46. **Kyle Johnson, rhp, Chapman (Calif.) Univ.**
47. Shay Conder, c, CC of Southern Nevada
48. **Jonathan Koller, rhp, Oregon State**
49. Johnny Monell, c, Seminole (Fla.) CC
50. Ryan Wolfe, lhp, Winter Park (Fla.) HS

NEW YORK YANKEES (28)

1. **Ian Kennedy, rhp, Southern California** (Choice from Phillies as compensation for Type A free agent Tom Gordon)
1. (Choice to Red Sox as compensation for Type A free agent Johnny Damon)
1s. **Joba Chamberlain, rhp, Nebraska** (Supplemental choice—41st overall—for loss of Gordon)
2. (Choice to Braves as compensation for Type A free agent Kyle Farnsworth)
3. **Zach McAllister, rhp, Illinois Valley Central HS, Chillicothe, Ill.**
4. **Colin Curtis, of, Arizona State**
5. **George Kontos, rhp, Northwestern**
6. **Mitch Hilligoss, ss, Purdue**
7. **Tim Norton, rhp, Connecticut**
8. **Dellin Betances, rhp, Grand Street HS, New York**
9. **Mark Melancon, rhp, Arizona**
10. **Casey Erickson, rhp, Springfield (Ill.) JC**
11. **Seth Fortenberry, of, Baylor**
12. **Nick Peterson, rhp, Tampa**
13. **Daniel McCutchen, rhp, Oklahoma**
14. **Donald Hollingsworth, of, UC Riverside**
15. **Gabriel Medina, rhp, Emporia State (Kan.)**
16. **Paul David Patterson, rhp, Northern Kentucky**
17. **David Robertson, rhp, Alabama**
18. Paul Howell, lhp, American Christian Academy, Tuscaloosa, Ala.
19. **Chris Kunda, 2b, Oregon State**
20. **Kevin Russo, 2b, Baylor**
21. **Russel Raley, 2b, Oklahoma**
22. **Brian Aragon, of, North Carolina State**
23. **Brandon Thomson, lhp, Chandler-Gilbert (Ariz.) CC**
24. **Brian Baisley, c, South Florida**
25. Kevin Carby, ss, Texarkana (Texas) CC
26. Tim Dennehy, lhp, Chandler-Gilbert (Ariz.) CC
27. Michael Lee, rhp, Bellevue (Wash.) CC
28. Barrett Bruce, lhp, Flower Mound (Texas) HS
29. Orlando Torres, c, Puerto Rico Baseball Academy, Santa Isabell, P.R.
30. **Brock Ungricht, c, San Diego State**
31. Zak Presley, of, Carroll HS, Southlake, Texas
32. Thomas Palica, lhp, Golden West (Calif.) JC
33. **Luke Trubee, rhp, Dayton**
34. Tyler Ladendorf, ss, Maine West HS, Des Plaines, Ill.
35. Jimmy Van Ostrand, 3b, Hancock (Calif.) JC
36. Jared Rogers, rhp, Duncanville (Texas) HS
37. **Tim O'Brien, 3b, San Diego State**
38. **Nick Diyorio, of, Florida Southern College**
39. **Kevin Smith, 1b, Oklahoma**
40. Tanner Chitwood, lhp, Sulphur (Okla.) HS
41. Ohmed Danesh, of, Dr. Phillips HS, Orlando
42. Dan Duffy, ss, Mountain Ridge HS, Glendale, Ariz.
43. Eric Erickson, lhp, Sarasota (Fla.) HS
44. **James Lasala, c, Iona**
45. Nathan Albert, rhp, Bakersfield (Calif.) JC
46. Jeff Ludlow, rhp, Palm Harbor (Fla.) University HS
47. Charles Smith, c, Second Baptist HS, Houston
48. Jeffrey Loveys, rhp, Ball State
49. **Chase Odenreider, of, Creighton**
50. Sam Honeck, 1b, Grayson County (Texas) JC

OAKLAND ATHLETICS (22)

1. (Choice to Nationals as compensation for Type B free agent Esteban Loaiza)
2. **Trevor Cahill, rhp, Vista (Calif.) HS**
3. **Matt Sulentic, of, Hillcrest HS, Dallas**
4. **Chad Lee, rhp, Barton County (Kan.) CC**
5. **Jermaine Mitchell, of, UNC Greensboro**
6. **Andrew Bailey, rhp, Wagner (N.Y.) College**
7. Michael Leake, rhp, Fallbrook (Calif.) Union HS
8. **Angel Sierra, of, Puerto Rico Baseball Academy, Cayey, P.R.**
9. Danny Hamblin, 1b, Arkansas
10. **Christian Vitters, ss, Fresno State**
11. **Jason Fernandez, rhp, Louisiana-Lafayette**
12. **Shane Presutti, rhp, Franklin Pierce (N.H.) College**
13. **Ben Jukich, lhp, Dakota Wesleyan (S.D.)**
14. **Toddric Johnson, of, Southern Mississippi**
15. **Kyle Christensen, rhp, Millikan HS, Long Beach**
16. **Branden Dewing, lhp, San Jose State**
17. **Michael Affronti, ss, Le Moyne**
18. Michael Ambort, rhp, Lamar
19. **Greg Dowling, 1b, Georgia Southern**
20. **Josh McLaughlin, rhp, College of Charleston**
21. **Jacob Smith, c, East Carolina**
22. **Patrick Currin, rhp, UNC Greensboro**
23. **Scott Moore, rhp, Texas State**

24. **Earl Oakes, rhp, Pace (N.Y.)**
25. Aaron Odom, lhp, Texas Tech
26. **Derrick Gordon, lhp, Lamar**
27. **Larry Cobb, of, College of Charleston**
28. **Lorenzo Macias, of, Mount San Antonio (Calif.) CC**
29. **Matt Manship, rhp, Stanford**
30. **Josh Morgan, rhp, Missouri St. Louis**
31. Jonathan Pigott, of, Seabreeze HS, Daytona Beach, Fla.
32. Nicholas Hernandez, lhp, Hialeah (Fla.) Senior HS
33. Burke Lieppman, 1b, Prescott (Ariz.) HS
34. Steve Cochrane, c, Mission Viejo (Calif.) HS
35. Carlos Hernandez, lhp, West Valley (Calif.) JC
36. Jean Diaz, 3b, Perpetuo Socorro HS, San Juan P.R.
37. David Fry, of, Bishop Gorman HS, Las Vegas
38. Rylan Sandoval, if, Chabot (Calif.) JC
39. Dante Love, c, San Diego CC
40. Goldy Simmons, rhp, Monta Vista HS, Spring Valley, Calif.
41. Jeremy Weih, c, Wilton (Iowa) HS

PHILADELPHIA PHILLIES (21)

1. **Kyle Drabek, rhp/ss, The Woodlands (Texas) HS** (Choice from Mets as compensation for Type A free agent Billy Wagner)
1. (Choice to Yankees as compensation for Type A free agent Tom Gordon)
1s. **Adrian Cardenas, ss, Monsignor Pace HS, Opa Locka, Fla.** (Supplemental choice—37th overall—for loss of Wagner)
2. **Drew Carpenter, rhp, Long Beach State**
3. **Jason Donald, ss, Arizona**
4. **D'Arby Myers, of, Westchester HS, Los Angeles**
5. **Quintin Berry, of, San Diego State**
6. **Daniel Brauer, lhp, Northwestern**
7. **Charlie Yarborough, 1b, Eastern Kentucky**
8. **Terrance Warren, of, Bethel HS, Vallejo, Calif.**
9. **Andrew Cruse, rhp, South Carolina**
10. **Sam Walls, rhp, North Carolina State**
11. **Jarrod Freeman, rhp, Alta HS, Sandy, Utah**
12. **Darin McDonald, of, Cherry Creek HS, Englewood, Colo.**
13. **Zachary Penprase, ss, Mississippi Valley State**
14. **Ken Milner, of, Kansas**
15. Riley Cooper, of, Clearwater (Fla.) Central Catholic HS
16. **Cody Montgomery, 3b, Dallas Baptist**
17. **Jay Miller, of, Washington State**
18. Michael Dubee, rhp, Okaloosa-Walton (Fla.) CC
19. **Robert Roth, rhp, Lewiston (Idaho) HS**
20. **Dominic Brown, rhp, Redan HS, Stone Mountain, Ga.**
21. **Jacob Dempsey, of, Winthrop**
22. **Ben Pfinsgraff, rhp, Maryland**
23. **Shawn McGill, c, Boston College**
24. **Garet Hill, rhp, Biola (Calif.)**
25. Billy Mohl, rhp, Tulane
26. **Will Savage, rhp, Oklahoma**
27. **John Brownell, rhp, Oklahoma**
28. **Herman Demmink, 3b, Clemson**
29. **Mike Fuentes, c, Coastal Carolina**
30. **Brian Capps, of, Texas Tech**
31. Bruce Billings, rhp, San Diego State
32. **Alan Robbins, c, Winthrop**
33. **Mike Deveaux, ss, Georgia College & State U.**
34. Josh Thraikill, rhp, Roberson HS, Asheville, N.C.
35. Rashad Taylor, of, Skyline (Calif.) JC
36. Kyle Gibson, rhp, Greenfield (Ind.) Central HS
37. Shawn Epps, rhp, Northern Oklahoma JC
38. Bobby Haney, ss, Kings Park (N.Y.) HS
39. Gerard Mohrmann, rhp, Manitou Springs (Colo.) HS
40. Nathan Solow, lhp, La Cueva HS, Albuquerque, N.M.
41. Michael Antonini, lhp, Georgia College & State U.
42. Daniel Faulkner, rhp, Bishop Noll Institute, Hammond, Ind.
43. Yazy Arbelo, 1b, John Carroll HS, Fort Pierce, Fla.
44. Mike Petello, of, Saguaro HS, Scottsdale, Ariz.
45. Patrick Murray, 1b, Santa Ana (Calif.) JC
46. Trayvon Johnson, c, Community Harvest Charter School, Los Angeles
47. Tylien Manumaleuna, 3b, Dixie HS, St. George, Utah
48. Nick Morreale, c, Vernon Hills (Ill.) HS
49. Oliver Routhier-Pare, lhp, Ahuntsic (Quebec) JC
50. Matt Adams, 2b, Kings Academy, West Palm Beach, Fla.

PITTSBURGH PIRATES (4)

1. **Brad Lincoln, rhp, Houston**
2. **Mike Felix, lhp, Troy**
3. **Shelby Ford, 2b, Oklahoma State**
4. **Jared Hughes, rhp, Long Beach State**
5. **Patrick Bresnehan, rhp, Arizona State**
6. **Jim Negrych, 2b, Pittsburgh**
7. **Austin McClune, of, Santa Fe HS, Edmond, Okla.**

8. Alex Presley, of, Mississippi
9. Steve MacFarland, rhp, Lamar
10. Charles Benoit, lhp, Oklahoma State
11. Lonnie Chisenhall, 3b, West Carteret HS, Morehead City, N.C.
12. Kent Sakamoto, 1b, Fresno State
13. Brandon Holden, rhp, Douglas HS, Parkland, Fla.
14. Gregory Smith, 1b, Fordham
15. James Barksdale, of, North Alabama
16. Kris Watts, c, Santa Clara
17. Michael Crotta, rhp, Florida Atlantic
18. Francisco Ortiz, rhp, Puerto Rico Baseball Academy, Toa Alta, P.R.
19. Jason Moseby, of, Newport HS, Bellevue, Wash.
20. Matt Clarkson, c, Oklahoma State
21. Kody Paul, rhp, Glynn Academy, Brunswick, Ga.
22. Miles Durham, of, Northwestern State
23. Preston Claiborne, 3b, Newman Smith HS, Carrolton, Texas
24. Scott Massey, rhp, Southern Mississippi
25. Adam Simon, rhp, San Diego State
26. Ryan Kelly, rhp, Hilton Head (S.C.) HS
27. Cache Breedlove, 3b, Santa Fe HS, Edmond, Okla.
28. Rudy Owens, lhp, Mesa (Ariz.) HS
29. Brandon Williams, rhp, South Carolina-Upstate
30. Alphonso Owens, of, Dillon (S.C.) HS
31. Jared Keel, 3b, Troy
32. Jorge Charry, rhp, Lake City (Fla.) CC
33. Victor Alvarez, ss, Cumberland (Tenn.)
34. Pernell Halliman, rhp, West Hills (Calif.) JC
35. Josue Peley, ss, Seminole State (Okla.) JC
36. Chadwick Arnold, rhp, Southridge HS, Kennewick, Wash.
37. Damian Walcott, of, Brookdale (N.J.) CC
38. Brian McCullen, rhp, Western Carolina
39. Tom Hagan, of, Virginia
40. Phillip Brannon, rhp, Broome HS, Spartanburg, S.C.
41. Scott Kuhns, rhp, Parkland (Ill.) CC
42. Jon Harmston, lhp, Bullard HS, Fresno, Calif.
43. Devin Copley, rhp, Gulf Coast (Fla.) CC
44. Tanner Hines, ss, Hudson HS, Lufkin, Texas
45. Paul-Michael Klingsberg, 1b, Notre Dame HS, Sherman Oaks, Calif.
46. Ryan Groth, of, Indian River (Fla.) CC
47. Brandon Wilkerson, ss, Lamar HS, Arlington, Texas
48. Kenneth Wieda, rhp, Vernon (Texas) JC
49. Carson Middelton, rhp, Lindale (Texas) HS
50. Marquise Zachery, of, Lake City (Fla.) CC

ST. LOUIS CARDINALS (30)

1. Adam Ottavino, rhp, Northeastern
1s. Chris Perez, rhp, Miami (Supplemental choice—42nd overall—for loss of Type A free agent Matt Morris)
2. Brad Furnish, lhp, Texas Christian (Choice from Giants as compensation for Morris)
3. Jon Jay, of, Miami
2s. Mark Hamilton, 1b, Tulane (Supplemental choice for loss of Type C free agent Abraham Nunez)
3. Gary Daley, rhp, Cal Poly
4. Eddie Degerman, rhp, Rice
5. Shane Robinson, of, Florida State
6. Tyler Norrick, lhp, Southern Illinois
7. Luke Gorsett, of, Nebraska
8. Allen Craig, ss, California
9. Matt North, rhp, Deer Valley HS, Antioch, Calif.
10. Blair Erickson, rhp, UC Irvine
11. P.J. Walters, rhp, South Alabama
12. David Carpenter, c, West Virginia
13. Travis Mitchell, of, Parkway Central HS, Chesterfield, Mo.
14. Jon Edwards, of, Keller (Texas) HS
15. Lance Zawadzki, ss, San Diego State
16. Tommy Pham, ss, Durango HS, Las Vegas
17. Nathan Southard, of, Tulane
18. Amaury Cazana Marti, of, Miami (No school)
19. Brandon Buckman, 1b, Nebraska
20. Brandon Cooney, rhp, Florida Atlantic
21. Mark Diapoules, rhp, Martin County HS, Stuart, Fla.
22. Casey Mulligan, rhp, Valencia (Calif.) HS
23. LaCurtis Mayes, rhp, Poly HS, Riverside, Calif.
24. Roberto Gomez, lhp, UT Pan American
25. D'Marcus Ingram, of, North Little Rock (Ark.) HS
26. Garrett Bussiere, c, California
27. Christian Reyes, c, Porterville (Calif.) JC
28. Lucas Gregerson, rhp, Saint Xavier (Ill.) Univ.
29. Will Groff, 2b, SUNY Cortland
30. Jared Schweitzer, 3b, Kansas
31. Mark Shorey, of, High Point
32. Ross Smith, of, Dodge County HS, Eastman, Ga.
33. Brian Schroeder, lhp, UCLA

34. Isa Garcia, 2b, Houston
35. Jim Rapoport, of, Stanford
36. Adrian Alaniz, rhp, Texas
37. Logan Collier, rhp, Guilford (N.C.) College
38. Scott Thomas, c, Missouri Baptist
39. Matt Michael, lhp, Grand Canyon (Ariz.)
40. Tyler Mach, 3b, Oklahoma State
41. Mitch Canham, c, Oregon State
42. Kyle Mura, rhp, Loyola Marymount
43. Gabe Torres, ss, St. Peter's Prep, Jersey City, N.J.
44. Cameron Grant, of, Hermitage HS, Richmond, Va.
45. John Goodman, rhp, Georgia Tech
46. Robert Woodard, rhp, North Carolina
47. Nicholas Additon, lhp, Western HS, Davie, Fla.
48. Gary Thomas, lhp, Pine Bluff (Ark.) HS
49. Gary Taylor, of, Holmes (Miss.) JC
50. Charles Matthews, rhp, Athens (Ga.) Academy

SAN DIEGO PADRES (17)

1. Matt Antonelli, 3b, Wake Forest
1s. Kyler Burke, of, Ooltewah (Tenn.) HS (Supplemental choice—35th overall—for loss of Type A free agent Ramon Hernandez)
2. Chad Huffman, 2b, Texas Christian (Choice from Orioles as compensation for Hernandez)
2. Wade LeBlanc, lhp, Alabama
3. Cedric Hunter, of, King HS, Decatur, Ga.
4. Nate Culp, lhp, Missouri
5. Andy Underwood, rhp, Fresno State
6. Tim Bascom, rhp, Central Florida
7. Craig Cooper, 1b, Notre Dame
8. Tom King, ss, Troy
9. David Freese, 3b, South Alabama
10. Kody Valverde, c, Alabama
11. Matt Latos, rhp, Coconut Creek (Fla.) HS
12. Stephen Faris, rhp, Clemson
13. Michael Epping, of, New Orleans
14. Grant Green, ss, Canyon HS, Carlsbad, Calif.
15. Matt Buschmann, rhp, Vanderbilt
16. Ray Stokes, 2b, Cal State East Bay
17. Tyler Mead, rhp, Skyview (Wash.) HS
18. Garner Wetzel, of, Millsaps (Miss.) College
19. Brian Hernandez, c, Vanderbilt
20. Michael Campbell, of, South Carolina
21. Luke Cannon, of, Texas State
22. Justin Pickett, 1b, Walters State (Tenn.) CC
23. Brooks Dunn, lhp, Mississippi State
24. Nick Tucci, rhp, Connecticut
25. Nick Kliebert, 2b, Pepperdine
26. Jeremy McBryde, rhp, Rose State (Okla.) JC
27. Matt Huff, rhp, Regis (Colo.)
28. Jeremy Hunt, 1b, Villanova
29. A.J. Davidiuk, 3b, Furman
30. Joe Cates, rhp, Palomar (Calif.) JC
31. Jon Kirby, rhp, Lee (Tenn.)
32. Jordan Rogers, rhp, San Jacinto (Texas) JC
33. Sean Finefrock, rhp, Blanchard (Okla.) HS
34. Casey Haerther, 1b, Chaminade Prep HS, Chatsworth, Calif.
35. Joseph Cruz, rhp, South Hills HS, West Covina, Calif.
36. Daniel Johansen, rhp, Woodinville (Wash.) HS
37. Miguel Flores, rhp, St. John Bosco HS, Bellflower, Calif.
38. Ben Francis, rhp, Mosley HS, Lynn Haven, Fla.
39. Chance Deason, lhp, Piedmont (Okla.) HS
40. Josh Casas, lhp, South El Monte (Calif.) HS
41. Mike Freeman, ss, Edgewater HS, Orlando
42. Luke Stewart, 3b, Normal (Ill.) Community West HS
43. Jeff Ramirez, ss, El Camino HS, South San Francisco
44. Jeff Hart, ss, Puyallup (Wash.) HS
45. Bryce Lefebvre, 3b, Scottsdale (Ariz.) CC

SAN FRANCISCO GIANTS (10)

1. Tim Lincecum, rhp, Washington
1s. Emmanuel Burriss, ss, Kent State (Supplemental choice—33rd overall—for loss of Type A free agent Scott Eyre)
2. (Choice to Cardinals as compensation for Type A free agent Matt Morris)
3. (Choice to Diamondbacks as compensation for Type A free agent Tim Worrell)
3. Clayton Tanner, lhp, De la Salle HS, Concord, Calif. (Choice from Cubs as compensation for Eyre)
4. Ben Snyder, lhp, Ball State
5. Michael McBryde, of, Florida Atlantic
6. Ryan Rohlinger, ss, Oklahoma
7. Brett Pill, 1b, Cal State Fullerton
8. Matt Klimas, c, Texarkana (Texas) JC

9. Brian Bocock, ss, Stetson
10. Ryan Paul, lhp, Cal State Fullerton
11. Gib Hobson, rhp, North Carolina State
12. Matt Weston, of, Houston
13. Brad Boyer, 2b, Arizona
14. Eric Stolp, rhp, Pacific
15. Andrew Barbosa, lhp, Riverview HS, Sarasota, Fla.
16. Paul Oseguera, lhp, UCLA
17. Kevin Pucetas, rhp, Limestone (S.C.) College
18. Jeff Stallings, rhp, North Carolina State
19. Tyler Graham, of, Oregon State
20. Adam Paul, rhp, UNC Wilmington
21. Steven Calicutt, lhp, East Tennessee State
22. Bobby Felmy, of, Georgia
23. E.B. Crow, rhp, Sitka (Alaska) HS
24. Jeff Walters, rhp, Olympia HS, Orlando
25. Joseph Moos, ss, Williston (Fla.) HS
26. Shane Matthews, rhp, East Carolina
27. Sean Van Elderen, of, Mesa State (Colo.) College
28. Dusty Harvard, of, Natrona County HS, Casper, Wyo.
29. Nick Liles, 2b, Scotland HS, Laurinburg, N.C.
30. Daryl Maday, rhp, Arkansas
31. Matt McMurtry, lhp, Minnesota State-Mankato
32. Matthew Fairel, lhp, Winter Haven (Fla.) HS
33. Chris Siewart, c, Tennessee
34. Jared Cranston, lhp, Nebraska
35. Adam Cowart, rhp, Kansas State
36. Matt Downs, 3b, Alabama
37. Lance Salsgiver, of, Harvard
38. Ryan Butner, rhp, Hialeah (Fla.) Senior HS
39. Lee Darracott, ss, Vernon (Texas) JC
40. Jon Amaya, of, Diamond Bar (Calif.) HS
41. Bo Merrell, ss, Seward County (Kan.) CC
42. Brandon Grabham, rhp, Grayson County (Texas) JC
43. Kevin Boggan, rhp, Boston College
44. Kyle Lafrenz, c, Marshalltown (Iowa) CC
45. Matt Speake, rhp, New Mexico JC
46. Taylor Hammack, lhp, Angleton (Texas) HS
47. Ryan Bradley, lhp, Mattoon (Ill.) HS
48. Evan Bush, 2b, Alabama
49. Jonathan Batts, c, UNC Wilmington
50. Robert Davis, c, South Carolina-Aiken

SEATTLE MARINERS (5)

1. Brandon Morrow, rhp, California
2. Chris Tillman, rhp, Fountain Valley (Calif.) HS
3. Tony Butler, lhp, Oak Creek (Wis.) HS
4. Ricky Orta, rhp, Miami
5. Nathan Adcock, rhp, North Hardin HS, Elizabethtown, Ky.
6. Adam Moore, c, Texas-Arlington
7. Doug Fister, rhp, Fresno State
8. Steve Richard, rhp, Clemson
9. Justin Souza, rhp, Sacramento CC
10. Chris Minaker, ss, Stanford
11. Aaron Solomon, rhp, Cumberland (Tenn.)
12. Gavin Dickey, of, Florida
13. Joseph Kantakevich, rhp, College of William and Mary
14. Jared Baehl, 3b, North Posey HS, Poseyville, Ind.
15. Drew Fiorenza, rhp, Clemson
16. Austin Dirkx, rhp, Portland
17. Daniel Runzler, lhp, UC Riverside
18. Kam Mickolio, rhp, Utah Valley State
19. Cam Nobles, rhp, Jackson HS, Mill Creek, Wash.
20. Johan Limonta, 1b, Miami Dade CC South
21. Brent Gaphardt, lhp, Delaware
22. Fabian Williamson, lhp, Kennedy HS, Granada Hills, Calif.
23. Marcos Villezcas, ss, Brigham Young
24. Kyle Parker, rhp, Washington
25. Tyson Gilles, of, Mountain HS, Vancouver
26. Greg Moviel, lhp, Vanderbilt
27. Bryan Ball, rhp, Florida
28. Rocky Collis, rhp, Cornell
29. Greg Nesbitt, lhp, James Madison
30. Matt Vogel, ss, Lewis-Clark (Idaho) State
31. David McClain, rhp, San Jacinto (Texas) JC
32. Joe Agreste, 1b, Potomac State (W.Va.) JC
33. Robert Harmon, rhp, Arkansas-Little Rock
34. Stan Posluszny, of, West Virginia
35. Alex Meneses, ss, Barry (Fla.)
36. Kyle Haas, rhp, Douglas (B.C.) CC
37. Chris Walden, rhp, Bellefontaine (Ohio) HS
38. Mike Drake, of, Consumnes River (Calif.) JC
39. Philip Roy, rhp, Miami Dade CC South
40. Haley Winter, rhp, UC Riverside

41. Brandon Fromm, 1b, San Jose State
42. Shane Cox, rhp, Alvin (Texas) CC
43. Clint Straka, rhp, Northern Oklahoma-Enid JC
44. Bryan Earley, rhp, Elder HS, Cincinnati
45. Jeremy Camacho, ss, Eagle Rock HS, Los Angeles
46. Robbie Dominguez, rhp, Cerritos (Calif.) JC
47. Sean Ward, of, Evans (Ga.) HS
48. Jeremy Beeching, lhp, Volunteer State (Tenn.) CC
49. Ryne Tacker, rhp, Rice
50. Tyler Sanford, c, Saguaro HS, Scottsdale, Ariz.

TAMPA BAY DEVIL RAYS (3)

1. Evan Longoria, 3b/2b, Long Beach State
2. Josh Butler, rhp, San Diego
3. Nick Fuller, rhp, Kell HS, Marietta, Ga.
4. Alex Cobb, rhp, Vero Beach (Fla.) HS
5. Shawn O'Malley, ss, South Ridge HS, Kennewick, Wash.
6. Nevin Ashley, c, Indiana State
7. Ryan Reid, rhp, James Madison
8. Tyree Hayes, rhp, Tomball (Texas) HS
9. Eligio Sonoqui, 1b, Chavez HS, Laveen, Ariz.
10. Desmond Jennings, of, Itawamba (Miss.) CC
11. Heath Rollins, rhp, Winthrop
12. Teddy Hubbard, rhp, Hooks (Texas) HS
13. Mikie Minor, lhp, Forrest HS, Lewisburg, Tenn.
14. Travis Barnett, rhp, Salt Lake City
15. K.D. Kang, of, Parkview HS, Lilburn, Ga.
16. Ryan Owen, lhp, Cal State Dominguez Hills
17. Ryan Thornton, of, American River (Calif.) JC
18. Jay Brown, rhp, Young Harris (Ga.) JC
19. Robi Estrada, ss, El Segundo (Calif.) HS
20. Erik Walker, rhp, UNC Charlotte
21. Joey Callender, 2b, Texas Tech
22. Mark Thomas, c, Alpharetta (Ga.) HS
23. Matthew McCarney, of, Holy Trinity Catholic HS, Kanata, Ont.
24. Angel Chapa, rhp, Treasure Valley (Ore.) CC
25. Blaine Howell, rhp, Reynolds HS, Asheville, N.C.
26. Johnathon Parker, rhp, Lord Tweedsmuir HS, Surrey, B.C.
27. Luis Lopez, of, St. Francis HS, Carolina, P.R.
28. Andrew Hagins, of, Oak Park (Ill.) River Forest HS
29. Leon Johnson, of, Thatcher, Ariz. (No school)
30. Jimmy Mayer, ss, Pittsburgh
31. Justin Reynolds, of, Mount Hood (Ore.) CC
32. Emmanuel Morales, of, Puerto Rico Baseball Academy, Aguas Buenas, P.R.
33. Brooks Lindsay, 2b, Mount Hood (Ore.) CC
34. Stephen McCray, rhp, Parkview HS, Lilburn, Ga.
35. Michael Ross, 2b, Northwest Mississippi CC
36. Walter Marciel, lhp, Iolani HS, Honolulu
37. Kalvin Johnson, 1b, Iowa Western CC
38. Chris Dennis, 1b, St. Thomas of Villanova SS, Lasalle, Ontario
39. Matt Miraldi, of, Bear River HS, Grass Valley, Calif.
40. Brando Casalicchio, rhp, Cold Spring Harbor HS, Long Island, N.Y.
41. Michael Dufek, of, Desert Mountain HS, Scottsdale, Ariz.
42. Brandon Vernon, c, Overton HS, Nashville
43. Victor Ramos, of, Miami Senior HS
44. Neil Hardon, of, Saguaro HS, Scottsdale, Ariz.
45. Chris Wilson, rhp, Trinidad State (Colo.) JC
46. Candy Maldonado, of, Porterville (Calif.) JC
47. Brandon Brown, 3b, Tate HS, Cantonment, Fla.
48. Alex McRee, lhp, Chestatee HS, Gainesville, Ga.
49. Ryan Fraser, rhp, Walker Valley HS, Cleveland, Tenn.
50. Travis Tartamella, c, Los Osos HS, Rancho Cucamonga, Calif.

TEXAS RANGERS (12)

1. Kasey Kiker, lhp, Russell County HS, Seale, Ala.
2. (Choice to Indians as compensation for Type B free agent Kevin Millwood)
3. Chad Tracy, c, Pepperdine
4. Marcus Lemon, ss, Eustis (Fla.) HS
5. Chris Davis, 1b, Navarro (Colo.) JC
6. Jake Brigham, rhp, Central Florida Christian Academy, Ocoee, Fla.
7. Grant Gerrard, of, Southern Illinois
8. Josh Bradbury, of, Orange Coast (Calif.) CC
9. Brennan Garr, rhp, Northern Colorado
10. Craig Gentry, of, Arkansas
11. Craig Crow, rhp, Rice
12. Matt Jaimes, 3b, Chino (Calif.) HS
13. Kevin Angelle, lhp, Bridge City (Texas) HS
14. Mike Ballard, lhp, Virginia
15. Cody Himes, ss, JC of San Mateo (Calif.)
16. Cody Podraza, of, Tomball (Texas) HS
17. John Maschino, rhp, Seminole State (Okla.) CC
18. Mike Wagner, rhp, Washington State

19. Miguel Velazquez, of, Gabriel Mistral HS, San Juan, P.R.
20. Tyler Fleming, rhp, Cowley County (Kan.) CC
21. Brandt Walker, rhp, St. Stephen's Episcopal HS, Austin
22. Cory Luebke, lhp, Ohio State
23. **Jay Heafner, ss, Davidson**
24. Robert McClain, lhp, Walters State (Tenn.) CC
25. Derek Holland, lhp, Wallace State (Ala.) CC
26. Ken Gregory, 1b, Immaculata HS, Sommerville, N.J.
27. Jared Olson, 3b, Frederick (Md.) CC
28. William Hall, lhp, Lee's Summit (Mo.) HS
29. **Daniel Hoben, lhp, Chandler-Gilbert (Ariz.) CC**
30. **Nick Cadena, 3b, Florida International**
31. **Adam Schaecher, rhp, Creighton**
32. **Shannon Wirth, rhp, Lewis-Clark (Idaho) State College**
33. Eric Fry, of, San Jacinto (Texas) JC
34. **Austin Weilep, rhp, Lewis-Clark (Idaho) State College**
35. **Brian Nelson, of, Corban (Ore.) College**
36. **John Slusarz, rhp, Connecticut**
37. John Lambert, lhp, Chesterton (Ind.) HS
38. **Jon Hollis, rhp, Yale**
39. Gary Poynter, rhp, Weatherford (Texas) JC
40. Chris Dennis, rhp, Auburn
41. Brandon Gribbin, rhp, Golden West (Calif.) CC
42. Lance West, of, Captain Shreve HS, Shreveport, La.
43. Shawn Sanford, rhp, Cinnaminson (N.J.) HS
44. Dan Sattler, rhp, Purdue
45. **Danny Ray Herrera, lhp, New Mexico**
46. Clifton Thomas, of, El Cajon (Calif.) Valley HS
47. Joey Norwood, 3b, Modesto (Calif.) JC
48. Ryan Ostrosky, rhp, Lethbridge (Alberta) CC
49. Clint Stubbs, of, Atlanta (Texas) HS
50. **Patrick Donovan, lhp, Gonzaga**

TORONTO BLUE JAYS

1. **Travis Snider, of, Jackson HS, Everett, Wash.**
2. (Choice to Orioles as compensation for Type A free agent B.J. Ryan)
3. (Choice to Marlins as compensation for Type A free agent A.J. Burnett)
4. **Brandon Magee, rhp, Bradley**
5. **Luke Hopkins, 1b, New Mexico State**
6. **Brian Jeroloman, c, Florida**
7. **Jonathan Baksh, of, Florida Tech**
8. **Dan O'Brien, lhp, Western Michigan**
9. Cole Figueroa, ss, Lincoln HS, Tallahassee, Fla.
10. **Scott Campbell, 2b, Gonzaga**
11. **Matt Lane, c, Washington**
12. **Jonathan Diaz, ss, North Carolina State**
13. **Mikal Garbarino, of, San Dimas (Calif.) HS**
14. **Shawn Scobee, of, Nevada**
15. **Seth Overbey, rhp, Maryland**
16. **Chase Lirette, rhp, South Florida**
17. **Kyle Ginley, rhp, St. Petersburg (Fla.) JC**
18. **Kyle Walter, lhp, Bucknell**
19. **Matt Liuzza, c, Louisiana State**
20. **Jonathan Del Campo, ss, Cibola HS, Yuma, Ariz.**
21. **Ronald Lowe, lhp, Saint Leo (Fla.)**
22. Brad Mills, lhp, Arizona
23. **Adam Calderon, of, Florida Southern College**
24. Keith Demorgandie, rhp, Orange Coast (Calif.) JC
25. **Luis Fernandez, ss, Cervantes HS, San Juan, P.R.**
26. **Chris Emanuele, of, Northeastern**
27. **Pat McGuigan, rhp, San Francisco**
28. **Zach Dials, rhp, Kentucky**
29. Ryan Basham, of, Michigan State
30. **Raul Barron, ss, Pasadena (Calif.) CC**
31. **Adam Rogers, rhp, Evansville**
32. **John Tritz, rhp, UT San Antonio**
33. Greg Lopez, ss, Notre Dame
34. **Graham Godfrey, rhp, College of Charleston**
35. **John Zinnicker, lhp, St. Bonaventure**
36. Domonique Rodgers, of, Sacramento CC
37. **Ben Zeskind, of, Richmond**

38. Kevin Denis-Fortier, 1b, Crowder (Mo.) JC
39. Luke Tucker, rhp, Florida State
40. **Ted Serro, rhp, Franklin & Marshall (Pa.) College**
41. **Roger Ebarb, c, Lamar**
42. Justin Figueroa, 2b, Lincoln HS, Tallahassee, Fla.
43. **Nate Melek, rhp, New Mexico**
44. **Kelly Sweppenhiser, 3b, Virginia Military Institute**
45. Lee Verweel, lhp, Malvern Collegiate Institute, Toronto
46. Mace Thurman, lhp, McLennan (Texas) CC
47. Wilberto Morales, 1b, Arizona Western JC
48. Jonathan Fernandez, ss, American Heritage HS, Delray Beach, Fla.
49. **Kyle Cuthbertson, rhp, Midland (Texas) JC**
50. **Baron Frost, of, Southern California**

WASHINGTON NATIONALS (15)

1. **Chris Marrero, 3b, Monsignor Pace HS, Opa Locka, Fla.**
1. **Colton Willems, rhp, John Carroll Catholic HS, Fort Pierce, Fla.** (Choice from Athletics as compensation for Type B free agent Esteban Loaiza)
2. Sean Black, rhp, Lenape HS, Medford, N.J.
2. **Stephen Englund, of, Bellevue (Wash.) HS** (Choice from Angels as compensation for Type B free agent Hector Carrasco)
3. **Stephen King, ss, Winter Park (Fla.) HS**
4. **Glenn Gibson, lhp, Center Moriches (N.Y.) HS**
5. **Cory Van Allen, lhp, Baylor**
6. **Zech Zinicola, rhp, Arizona State**
7. Samuel Brown, rhp, Millbrook HS, Raleigh, N.C.
8. **Sean Rooney, c, Saddleback (Calif.) CC**
9. Joey Rosas, lhp, Yavapai (Ariz.) JC
10. Marcus Salmon, rhp, Sunset HS, Miami
11. **Desmond Jones, rhp, Middle Georgia JC**
12. **Cole Kimball, rhp, Centenary College**
13. **Hassan Pena, rhp, Palm Beach (Fla.) CC**
14. **Brett McMillan, 1b, UCLA**
15. Dustin Dickerson, 3b, Midway HS, Henrietta, Texas
16. **Patrick Nichols, c, Old Dominion**
17. **Erik Arnesen, rhp, Grove City (N.J.) College**
18. **Adam Carr, rhp, Oklahoma State**
19. Sam Dyson, rhp, Jesuit HS, Tampa
20. **Alberto Tavarez, rhp, Western Oklahoma State JC**
21. **Christopher French, of, New Mexico JC**
22. **Robert Jacobsen, 1b, George Mason**
23. Forrest Beverly, lhp, South Carolina
24. **Richard Caputo, 3b, Hofstra**
25. Jim Birmingham, lhp, Overbrook HS, Pine Hill, N.J.
26. **Brett Logan, c, Houston**
27. **Dan Pfau, lhp, George Washington**
28. Michael Robinns, lhp, Meridian (Miss.) CC
29. Khris Davis, of, Deer Valley HS, Glendale, Ariz.
30. Burt Reynolds, ss, Essex County Vocational Technical HS, Bloomfield, N.J.
31. **Zach Baldwin, lhp, West Virginia State**
32. **Joseph Welsh, lhp, Toledo**
33. Tyler Moore, 1b, Meridian (Miss.) CC
34. Taylor Kinzer, of, Homestead HS, Fort Wayne, Ind.
35. D'Vontrey Richardson, of, Lee County HS, Leesburg, Ga.
36. **Jeremy Goldschmeding, ss, Dallas Baptist**
37. Austin Hudson, rhp, Boone HS, Orlando
38. Zach Von Tersch, rhp, Cedar Falls (Iowa) HS
39. Andrew Doyle, rhp, Alleman HS, Rock Island, Ill.
40. Nick Pierce, rhp, DeMatha Catholic HS, Hyattsville, Md.
41. Brad Peacock, c, Palm Beach Central HS, Wellington, Fla.
42. Javier Martinez, rhp, Fordham
43. **Cory Anderson, rhp, U.S. Coast Guard Academy (Conn.)**
44. Chad Jenkins, lhp, Caravel Academy HS, Bear, Del.
45. Adam Kramer, rhp, New Mexico JC
46. Jayson Brugman, ss, South Mountain (Ariz.) CC
47. Josh Rodriguez, c, Red Mountain HS, Mesa, Ariz.
48. Kyle Page, of, Brevard County (Fla.) CC
49. Jarred Holloway, lhp, Russellville (Ark.) HS
50. J.J. Pannell, rhp, George Mason

APPENDIX

OBITUARIES

NOVEMBER 2005 - OCTOBER 2006

Bill Abernathie, a righthander who made one appearance in the major leagues, died Feb. 19 in Yucaipa, Calif. He was 77. Abernathie appeared with the Indians in 1952, allowing three runs in two innings. It was his only taste of the big leagues, as he spent the majority of his career in the high minors.

Oscar Acosta, who managed the Yankees affiliate in the Gulf Coast League, died April 19 near Santo Domingo, Dominican Republic. He was 48. Acosta, who also served as the club's player development coordinator in the Dominican, had been with the Yankees since 2004. Previously, he had worked as the pitching coach for the Cubs (2000-01) and Rangers (2002-03). As a player, the righthander pitched parts of three seasons in the Phillies farm system.

Earl Allen, a righthander who made three appearances with the Phillies in 1937, died Oct. 30 in Chesapeake, Va. He was 91. Allen went 0-1, 6.75 in 12 innings with Philadelphia.

Elden Auker, a righthander who won 130 major league games in 10 seasons, died Aug. 4 in Vero Beach, Fla. He was 95. Nicknamed Submarine for the underhand pitching style he developed because of a college football injury, Auker broke in with the Tigers in 1933 at age 22. The Tigers would win the American League pennant in 1934 and the World Series in 1935 with Auker making 43 starts in that span. In the former season, Auker compiled his personal best ERA (3.42, fifth-best in the AL); in the latter, he posted the league's top winning percentage by going 18-7 (.720). Auker also pitched for the Red Sox and Browns.

Dewayne "Beetle" Bailey, a former Louisiana State assistant coach, died Dec. 12 in Baton Rouge, La. He was 60. Bailey coached at LSU from 1988-95, helping lead the Tigers to national titles in 1991 and 1993. He later served as an athletics administrator until retiring in 2001. Before coming to LSU, Bailey was the head coach at Denham Springs (La.) High from 1980-87, where he coached righthander Ben McDonald, the first overall pick of the Orioles in the 1989 draft.

Dave Bartosch, outfielder for the St. Louis Cardinals in 1945 when he hit .255 in 24 games, died April 30 in Nashville. He was 89.

Bob Bellizzi, who established baseball at the College of Saint Rose, died May 7. He was 57. Bellizzi led the program from club level to NAIA to its present Division-II classification, where the Golden Knights had gone 418-259 over 14 seasons. The club made four NCAA Tournament appearances under Bellizzi: 1994, '95, '97 and 2000.

Vic Bernal, a righthander who pitched in 15 major league games for the Padres in 1977, died Sept. 2 in Los Angeles. He was 52. The fifth-round pick of the Padres in the 1975 draft out of Cal Poly, Bernal went 1-1, 5.31 in 20 innings.

Bud Black, a righthander who had three stints with the Tigers, died Oct. 2, 2005, in St. Louis. He was 73. Black made two appearances for the Tigers in 1952, going 0-1, 10.13 then missed the next two seasons because of military service. He was 2-3, 4.22 in 10 career games.

Johnny Callison, a productive outfielder for 16 major league seasons, died Oct. 12 in Philadelphia. He was 67. The White Sox signed Callison in 1957 and he needed just two and a half minor league seasons to make the majors, though Chicago traded him in 1959, just before he broke out. He would would play for the Phillies from 1960-69. He led the National League in doubles with 40 in 1966, and twice led in triples with 10 in 1962 and 16 in 1965. Callison's biggest year was 1964 when he hit .274/.316/.492 with career-high totals of 31 home runs and 104 RBIs. He received two first-place votes for NL MVP, but finished second to Cardinals third baseman Ken Boyer. Callison slugged 226 home runs and compiled a career line of .264/.331/.441 in 1,886 big league games. Callison would play for the Cubs and the Yankees before retiring after the 1973 season.

Frank Campos, an outfielder who spent parts of three seasons with the Senators, died Jan. 28 in Miami. He was 81. Campos played in 71 games with Washington altogether from 1951-1953, hitting .279/.298/.367.

Paul Campbell, a first baseman who spent three seasons each with the Red Sox and Tigers, died June 22 in Charlotte. He was 88. Campbell spent four of his major league seasons as a part-time player—and totaled just four games in his other two—hitting .255/.308/.358 in 380 career at-bats.

Dan Carnevale, a longtime minor league player, manager and executive as well as a major league scout, died Dec. 29 in Buffalo. He was 87. Carnevale spent 14 years in the minors as a shortstop and as player-manager led four teams in four different leagues to league titles. He took over as general manager for Buffalo (International) in 1956 before taking a job as a scout with the Athletics. He also scouted for the Orioles and Indians, and worked as a first-base coach for the A's in 1970. He retired from the game in 2001.

Bob Carpenter, a righthander who spent five seasons in the National League, died Oct. 19 in Evergreen Park, Ill. He was 87. Carpenter spent nearly five seasons with the Giants (and four games with the Cubs) from 1940-47, missing three seasons because of World War II. He went 25-20, 3.60 in 400 innings. His best season was 1942, when he went 11-10, 3.15.

Merv Connors, one of the most prolific home run hitters in minor league history, died Jan. 8 in Berkeley, Calif. He was 91. Connors led his league in home runs in six different seasons, tied for sixth most in minor league history, and his 400 minor league home runs rank fifth all time, according to The Minor League Register. Despite his hefty power numbers, Connors made it to the majors for just 52 games, hitting .279/.367/.485 with eight home runs for the White Sox in 1937 and 1938. Connors missed two seasons because of military service during World War II, but returned to action in 1946.

Sandy Consuegra, a righthander who spent nearly a decade in the majors, died Nov. 18 in Miami. He was 85. Consuegra, a Cuban native, didn't make it to the majors until he was 30, going 7-8, 4.39 for the Senators in 1950. He had his best season for the White Sox in

APPENDIX

1954. That season, Consuegra was an American League all-star, going 16-3, 2.69 to lead the league in winning percentage while finishing second in the ERA race. Consuegra also played for the Orioles and Giants.

Tony Currry, an outfielder who played for the Phillies and Indians in three major league seasons, died Oct. 16 in Nassau, Bahamas. He was 67. One of six Bahamas-born players to play in the majors, Curry excelled in the minor leagues before earning his first big league callup by the Phillies in 1960. Curry hit .246/.295/.374 in 297 at-bats and he never found regular work with the Phillies in 1960 or 1961 or with the Indians in 1966.

Jerry Dahlke, a righthander who pitched in five games for the White Sox, died Sept. 2 in Batesville, Miss. He was 77. His stint with White Sox covered just two innings in the 1956 season.

James Delsing, a longtime outfielder for several American League clubs, died May 4 in Chesterfield, Mo. He was 80. Delsing earned a 20-game audition with the White Sox in 1948, but didn't hit. A trade to the St. Louis Browns in 1950 gave him his first shot as an everyday outfielder, but he became most famous for replacing Gaedel after he had walked. Gaedel was the only midget to ever play in a major league game. Delsing spent five seasons as an everyday outfielder with the Browns and Tigers. He played for 10 seasons and hit .255/.339/.366 with 40 home runs in 822 games.

Con Dempsey, a righthander who pitched in three games for the Pirates, died Aug. 5 in Redwood City, Calif. He was 83. He made his major league debut in 1951 and pitched just seven innings before being returned to the minors.

Conrad Dettling, a White Sox scout who had been with the organization for 25 years, died June 4 in Reading, Pa. He was 75. He also worked as an associate scout for the Indians and Padres.

Dutch Fehring, who had one at-bat with the White Sox in 1934 and later served as Stanford's baseball coach, died April 14 in Palo Alto, Calif. He was 93. Fehring served as Stanford University baseball coach from 1954-1966, and was an assistant football coach there for 17 years, beginning in 1949.

Bill Fleming, a righthander who worked the war years in the majors, died June 4 in Reno, Nev. He was 92. The Red Sox called him up in 1940, and from 1942 to 1946 Fleming pitched for the Cubs. Fleming spent 1945—the year the Cubs last appeared in the World Series—in military service. He was 16-21, 3.79 in 442 big league innings.

Stan Gale, a shortstop who briefly played with the Senators, died Jan. 28 in Mobile, Ala. He was 86. Gale hit .111-0-1 in 18 at-bats with the Senators in 1942 in his only big league appearance.

Howdy Groskloss, the oldest living ex-major leaguer, died July 15 in Vero Beach, Fla. He was 100. Groskloss hit .280 in 161 at-bats for the Pirates in 1931 as a shortstop-second baseman. He would spend limited time with Pittsburgh in both 1930 and 1932. He also was a practicing physician.

Curt Gowdy, the longtime voice of the Red Sox and a member of the broadcaster's wing of the Baseball Hall of Fame, died Feb. 20 in West Palm Beach, Fla. He was 86. Gowdy was named the 1984 Ford Frick Award winner, capping a lengthy career filled with highlights. He

had gotten his start broadcasting six-man football in Cheyenne, Wyo., but before long he was broadcasting minor league baseball in Oklahoma City. He worked as Mel Allen's Yankees broadcasting partner for two years before becoming voice of the Red Sox in 1951, a post he held for 15 years. Gowdy would go on broadcast 13 World Series and 16 All-Star Games, as well as the Olympics, the Super Bowl and the NCAA Final Four.

Chet Hajduk, an outfielder-corner infielder who got one pinch-hit at-bat for the White Sox in 1941, died July 5 in Chicago. He was 87. From 1942-945 Hajduk served in the military.

Barry Halper, a long-time baseball memorabilia collector and limited partner in the Yankees, died Dec. 18 in Livingston, N.J. He was 66. Halper had one of the most distinguished collections in the world, eventually selling part of it to the Baseball Hall of Fame, while auctions of the rest of his collection garnered nearly $22 million in sales.

Al Heist, a part-time outfielder in three major league seasons, died Oct. 2 in Cookson, Okla. He was 78. Despite a successful minor league record, Heist saw action in just 177 big league games with the Cubs and Astros, hitting .255/.327/.368 from 1960 through 1962.

Elrod Hendricks, a player and coach who was one of most beloved members of the Orioles, died Dec. 21 in Glen Burnie, Md. He was 64. Hendricks spent the majority of his 12-year major league career as the Orioles catcher. Though the Milwaukee Braves signed Hendricks in 1959, it wasn't until the Orioles took him in the 1967 Rule 5 draft that he finally got a shot at the big leagues. By 1969, he was the O's regular catcher. He was traded away from the Orioles twice, but always found his way back to Baltimore. He finished his playing career as a player-coach in 1979. He remained as the team's bullpen coach through the 2005 season, making him the longest-tenured uniformed Oriole player or coach.

Billy Hitchcock, the first manager of the Atlanta Braves and a nine-year journeyman infielder in the American League, died April 9 in Opelika, Ala. He was 89. He played for the Tigers, Senators, Browns, Red Sox and Philadelphia Athletics in a career that spanned 1942-53. Hitchcock's career was interrupted by military service from 1943-45. He also managed the Orioles (1962-63) before his Braves stint (1966-67). His brother Jimmy also played in the majors.

Steve Howe

Steve Howe, a lefthander who pitched for the Dodgers, Twins, Rangers and Yankees in a 12-year major league career, died April 28 in Coachella, Callif. He was 48. Howe won National League Rookie of the Year honors in 1980 and recorded the final out in the Dodgers championship the following season. He was an All-Star in '82. But Howe gained notoriety for his drug addictions, which resulted in seven suspensions. In 1992 he was banned for life—the first player to incur the penalty for drugs. An arbitrator reinstated him after the season. Howe pitched from 1980-1996, appearing in 497 games with a 3.03 ERA.

Robert Johnson, author of the book that led to increased recognition for the Negro Leagues, died Feb. 11. He was 80. In 1970 Johnson finished "Only the Ball Was White," the first extensive history of the Negro Leagues. Just a year later, Satchel Paige became the first Negro League great to be inducted into the Hall of Fame.

Walt Kellner, a righthander who tossed seven innings for the Philadelphia Athletics over the 1952 and 1953 seasons, died June 19 in Tucson, Ariz. He was 77. After spending much of 1951 in the military, Kellner returned in 1952 to pitch for the A's. Kellner was a teammates of brother Alex, who won 101 games in a 12-year career, on the 1952 and 1953 A's.

Thornton Kipper, who pitched briefly for the Phillies from 1953-55, died March 29 in Scottsdale, Ariz. He was 77.

Joe Koppe, the primary shortstop for the Angels in their first two seasons and an eight-year major league veteran, died Sept. 27 in Ann Arbor, Mich. He was 75. Koppe also played for the Braves and Phillies, hitting just .236/.324/.324 for his major league career, which lasted from 1958 to 1965. He was noted more for his glovework and versatility, with more than 30 career games at second base, third base and shortstop.

Craig Kusick, a first baseman who spent seven seasons as a part-time player for the Twins and Blue Jays in the 1970s, died Sept. 27 in Minneapolis. He was 57. Kusick batted .235/.342/.392 in 497 major league games and amassed 46 home runs, 194 walks and 228 strikeouts. Kusick's best season was 1977, when he hit .254/.370/.433 with 12 home runs in 268 at-bats. Kusick spent 23 years as baseball coach at Rosemount (Minn.) High.

Swede Larsen, a second baseman for the Braves, died Oct. 8 in Tucson. He was 94. After playing semipro baseball, Larsen made the Boston Braves in 1936 without playing a minor league game. He went 0-for-1 in his brief, three-game career.

Keith LeClair, head coach at East Carolina University from 1997 to 2002 and a part of 13 regional teams as a player and coach, died July 17 in Greenville, N.C. He was 40. When LeClair's career was at its peak, in 2001, his East Carolina team went 47-13, losing to Tennessee in a super-regional played in Wilson, N.C., with East Carolina as the host. A walk-on at Western Carolina University, LeClair set the school single-season marks for hits and total bases and was signed by Smokey Burgess as a nondrafted free agent for the Braves in 1988. LeClair played just one pro season then joined the coaching staff at his alma mater, where he ascended to head coach.

Jim Lemon, a power-hitting outfielder who played 12 seasons in the majors for the Indians, Senators, Twins, Phillies and White Sox, died May 14 in Brandon, Miss. He was 78. Lemon finished 10th in American League MVP balloting in 1960 for the Senators, a season in which he was named an all-star and finished third in home runs (38), fourth in RBIs (100), sixth in slugging percentage (.508), fifth in total bases (268) and second in strikeouts (114). Lemon spent 1951-52 in military service and didn't get his first real chance in the majors until 1956 with the Senators. He hit .262/.332/.460 with 164 home runs.

Cory Lidle, a righthander who pitched for seven teams in nine big league seasons, going a career 82-72, 4.57, died Oct. 11 in New York. He was 34. Lidle toiled for six years (and three organizations) in the minor leagues before debuting with the 1997 Mets. He got his first regular major league gig in the Athletics' 2001 rotation. Teamed with pitching coach Rick Peterson, Lidle would have his best season, going 13-6, 3.59 in 188 innings for the AL wild-card winner. While extremely durable, Lidle never quite reached the heights of his Oakland years, and finished his career pitching for the Blue Jays, Reds, Phillies and Yankees.

Don Lindberg, a long-time scout for several major league teams and who played parts of four seasons in the minors, died May 31 in Anaheim. He was 91.

Paul Lindblad, a lefthander who spent more than a decade with the Athletics, died Jan. 1 in Arlington, Texas. He was 65. Lindblad's tenure with the A's stretched from their hapless days in Kansas City to their early-1970s rise in Oakland. He settled into the big leagues for good in 1966, going 5-10, 4.17 in 121 innings. Lindblad spent 14 seasons in the American League, working predominantly as a middle reliever. He led the league in appearances in 1972, going 5-8, 2.61 for the Rangers in 66 games. He finished his career with a 68-63, 3.29 record and 64 saves.

Royce Lint, a veteran minor league lefthander who appeared in 30 games for the Cardinals in 1954, died April 3 in Portland, Ore. He was 85. Lint went 2-3, 4.86 in 70 career innings.

Eddie Malone, a catcher who played briefly for the White Sox and who was a nine-year veteran of the Pacific Coast League, died June 1 in League Hills, Calif. He was 85. Malone saw his only major league time in 1949 and 1950, when he got into 86 games for the White Sox. But from 1943 until 1954—with the exception of 1945, which was spent in the military—Malone was a fixture of the PCL.

Carlos Martinez, a third baseman who played for a number of American League teams in the 1980s and 1990s, died Jan. 24 in Vargas, Venezuela. He was 41. A top prospect when he signed with the Yankees in 1983, Martinez was dealt to the White Sox in 1986. He saw spot time with the White Sox in 1988 and 1989 before winning a full-time job in 1989. He played three seasons with the Indians then spent part of the 1995 season with the Angels before retiring after a brief stint in the Mexican League in 1996. He hit .258/.293/.359 with 25 home runs in seven major league seasons.

Paul Minner, a lefthander who spent 10 seasons with the Brooklyn Dodgers and the Cubs, died March 28 in Lemoyne, Pa. He was 82. He appeared in Game Five of the 1949 World Series for the Dodgers, but was best known as a mainstay in the Cubs rotations of the 1950s. He had one winning season (14-9 in '52) for Chicago teams than never won more than they lost.

Herb Moford, a righthander who spent four seasons in the majors, died Dec. 3 in Cincinnati. He was 78. Moford went 1-1, 7.88 in 24 innings with the Cardinals in 1955, a rough enough debut that it took him a couple of years to work his way back to the big leagues. He went 5-13, 5.03 overall in 157 innings.

Seth Morehead, a lefthander who spent five seasons in the majors, died Jan. 17 in Shreveport, La. He was 71. Morehead worked as a reliever/spot starter for the

Phillies, Cubs and Braves from 1957-61. His best season was his debut in 1957, when he went 1-1, 3.66. He also went 2-9, 3.95 for the Cubs in 1960 in his most extensive major league work.

Bubba Morton, an outfielder who spent six seasons in the majors, died Jan. 14 in Seattle. He was 73. Morton made it to the majors with the Tigers in 1961 and was dealt to the Braves in 1963. Morton hit his way back to the big leagues after a 1964 demotion to the minors and spent most of 1967 and all of 1968-1969 with the Angels before wrapping up his career with one season playing in Japan. Morton would become the first African-American coach at Washington, where he coached the Huskies baseball team from 1972-76.

Ron Mrozinski, a lefthander who had brief stints with the Phillies, died Oct. 19 in Washington, N.J. He was 75. Mrozinski went 1-3, 5.76 in 82 innings with the Phillies. He made his debut in 1954, going 1-1, 4.50 after a mid-June callup. He spent the entire 1955 season with the Phillies, going 0-2, 6.62 as a reliever.

Mike Naymick, a righthander who spent four seasons with the Indians and Browns, died Oct. 12 in Stockton, Calif. He was 89. Naymick was 5-7, 3.93 in 112 innings in his major league career. Almost all of his work came with the Indians. Naymick struggled in 1944 with the Indians and was sent to the Browns, where after one appearance he was released and was out of baseball.

Joe Niekro, a longtime knuckleballer who won 221 major league games, died Oct. 27 in Tampa. He was 61. He was a rotation regular for the Cubs, Padres and Tigers from 1967-72. Once teamed with older brother Phil in Atlanta in 1973, though, Joe began to thrive after he re-learned the knuckleball their father had taught them. Unlike Phil, Joe had enough fastball, and a pretty good changeup, to not have to rely on the knuckleball exclusively. The Astros purchased Niekro from the Braves in 1975 and, armed with a perfected knuckleball, he became one of Houston's finest pitchers. He went 21-11, 3.00 and made the National League all-star team at age 34 in 1979, finishing runner-up to Cubs closer Bruce Sutter in NL Cy Young voting. Niekro followed up by going 20-12, 3.55 in 1980, becoming the first pitcher in Astros history to post back-to-back 20-win seasons. Niekro would pitch for the Yankees and Twins before retiring following the 1988 season, capping a 22-year big league career in which he went 221-204, 3.59 in 500 starts and 3,584 innings. Niekro combined with brother Phil to win 539 games, the most ever by a pair of brothers. Joe was the father of Giants first baseman Lance Niekro.

Milt Nielsen, an outfielder who got 15 at-bats for the Indians in a nine-year pro career, died Aug. 1, 2005, in Mankato, Minn. He was 80. Nielsen collected just one hit in those at-bats, which were divided between the 1949 and 1951 seasons.

Buck O'Neil, a celebrated and highly visible baseball personality whose impact as a player, manager, coach, scout and all-around ambassador for the game extended far beyond his playing days, died Oct. 6 in Kansas City, Mo. He was 94. O'Neil's playing and managing career spanned more than 25 years—playing in various leagues and for various independent and barnstorming teams—beginning in the late 1920s until his retirement as a player in 1955. He lost the 1943 through 1945 seasons to military service. He latched on with the Kansas City Monarchs of the Negro American League in 1938, where he spent the remainder of his career as a first baseman and manager. He won a batting title in 1946 with a .353 average and helped lead the Monarchs to four consecutive pennants from 1939-42. O'Neil became the first black major league coach when he joined the Cubs' staff in 1962. During his tenure as scout for the organization, which began in 1956, O'Neil scouted and signed two Hall of Famers: shortstop Ernie Banks and outfielder Lou Brock. Until the time of his death, O'Neil served on the Hall of Fame's Veterans' Committee and was chairman of the board for the Negro Leagues Museum in Kansas City.

Eddie Pellagrini, a rookie infielder for the pennant-winning 1946 Red Sox and later head coach at Boston College, died Oct. 11 in Weymouth, Mass. He was 88. Pellagrini amassed 563 games in the major leagues over an eight-year career, playing for the Browns, Phillies, Pirates and, most notably, his hometown Red Sox. He spent three years in the Navy during World War II then homered in his first major league at-bat in 1946. Pellagrini would finish at .226/.295/.316 overall. Pellagrini became BC's head coach in 1957. He took the Eagles to three College World Series appearances before his retirement in 1988.

Buddy Peterson, a shortstop who appeared in 13 major league games with the White Sox and Orioles and later starred in Japan, died Sept. 19 in Sacramento. He was 81. Peterson hit .237 in 38 big league at-bats, 21 of them with the White Sox in 1955 and the other 17 with the Orioles in 1957.

Bill Pierro, a righthander who played briefly for the Pirates and who twice led his minor league in strikeouts, died April 1 in Brooklyn. He was 79. Pierro appeared in just 12 games for the Pirates in 1950, walking 28 batters, compared with 13 strikeouts, which contributed to a 10.55 ERA. Pierro's career ended in '52 when he was diagnosed with encephalitis.

Vic Power, a smooth-fielding first baseman with the Athletics and Indians in the 1950s and 1960s, died Nov. 28 in Bayamon, Puerto Rico. He was 78. Power won seven straight Gold Gloves as the American League's best defensive first baseman of the early 1960s. Power could have been one of the first black players on the Yankees, but the team never called him up. In December 1953 he was traded to the Philadelphia Athletics, who gave him a chance to play in the majors. Power was a four-time all-star and led the American League in triples (10) in 1958. He played four seasons with the Indians, and finished his career with stints with the Twins, Angels and Phillies. He hit .284/.315/.411 with 126 home runs in a 12-year career.

Kirby Puckett, a Hall of Fame outfielder for the Twins, died March 6 in Phoenix. He was 45. Puckett spent his entire 12-year career with the Twins, winning World Series titles in 1987 and 1991. He hit .309 with five home runs and 15 RBIs in 24 postseason games. Puckett, who collected 2,304 hits

Kirby Puckett

and was a .318/.360/.477 lifetime hitter, appeared in 10 All-Star Games and won six Gold Gloves. He became the second-youngest player to die after being enshrined in Cooperstown. Only Lou Gehrig, 37 when he died in 1941, was younger. Always a fan favorite, the short and stocky Puckett was forced from the game in 1996 when glaucoma caused blindness in his right eye.

Billy Queen, a longtime minor league shortstop-outfielder who had a brief stint with the Milwaukee Braves in 1954, died April 23 in Gastonia, N.C. He was 77. His major league career consisted of three games with the Braves, in which he went 0-for-2 as a pinch hitter and made one appearance as a defensive replacement in the outfield.

Walter Rabb, the winningest baseball coach in University of North Carolina history, died April 4. He was 91. A North Carolina native, Rabb was a shortstop for North Carolina State in his playing days and he played two seasons in the Yankees farm system. Rabb joined the UNC physical education staff in 1942 and became Tar Heels head coach in 1957. He was 540-358 over his 31-year career and led UNC to four NCAA tournament appearances and two appearances in Omaha.

Billy Reed, who played 15 games for the Boston Braves in 1952, died Dec. 5 in Houston. He was 83. A second baseman, Reed played 10 seasons in the minors.

Bob Repass, a shortstop who spent two seasons in the big leagues, died Jan. 16 in Wethersfield, Conn. He was 88. Repass hit .230 for the Senators in 1942 in his only extensive big league action. He also had a brief appearance with the Cardinals in 1939, hitting .333 in three games.

Xavier Rescigno, a righthander who spent three seasons with the Pirates, died Dec. 24 in Sun City West, Ariz. He was 92. Rescigno spent nearly a decade in the minors before making it to the majors. He went 19-22, 4.13 in 335 innings for the Pirates from 1943-45.

Dino Restelli, an outfielder who slugged 13 home runs in two stints with the Pirates, died Aug. 8 in San Carlos, Calif. He was 81. Restelli made the most of 232 big league at-bats in 1949 by hitting .250/.358/.453 with 12 home runs and 40 RBIs. He would next play in the majors in 1951 when he hit .184 with a lone home run in 38 at-bats. For his career, Restelli hit .241/.341/.430.

Henry Rountree, a longtime minor league and College World Series umpire, died Aug. 17 in Blairsville, Ga. He was 75. Rountree umpired in the Carolina and Southern leagues from 1964-72, and was a substitute umpire in the National League from 1978-79 and in the American League in 1991.

Roland Seidler, son-in-law of former Dodgers owner Walter O'Malley and a member of the club's board of directors from 1975-98, died June 8. He was 77.

Sebastian Sisti, a utility player for the Boston Braves who played in the 1948 World Series, died April 24 in Amherst, N.Y. He was 85. In 13 major league seasons with the Braves, Sisti hit .244 and played every position but pitcher and catcher. He made the majors in 1939 at age 18.

Willie Smith, one of the few players to successfully work in the majors as a two-way player, died Jan. 16 in Anniston, Ala. He was 66. Smith was one of the last Negro Leaguers and moved to the affiliated minors in 1960. He went 1-0, 4.50 for the Tigers in 1963, but beginning in 1964 Smith was used much more as an outfielder. Smith spent seven seasons playing for the Angels, Indians, Cubs and Reds. Smith hit .248 with 46 home runs in nine major league seasons, while going 2-4, 3.10 in 61 innings as a pitcher.

Junior Thompson, a righthander who won 47 major league games for the Reds and New York Giants, died Aug. 24 in Scottsdale, Ariz. He was 89. Thompson won 13 games as a Reds rookie in 1939, and followed that up by going 16-9, 3.32 the next season. He pitched two more seasons for the Reds before moving on to the Giants, but not before serving in the military from 1943-45. For his career, he posted a 3.26 ERA in 687 innings.

Jake Wade, a lefthander who played eight seasons in the American League, died Feb. 1 in Wildwood, N.C. He was 93. Wade spent most of his major league career with the Tigers and White Sox, but also spent time with the Red Sox, Browns, Yankees and Senators. His best season was 1943, when he went 3-7, 3.00 for the White Sox. He missed the 1945 season because of World War II.

Chuck Wagner, who spent 71 years with the Red Sox as a righthander, scout and assistant farm director, died Aug. 30 in Reading, Pa. He was 93. Wagner was named Boston's assistant farm director in 1947 and stayed with the team as special assignment scout, minor league pitching instructor, major league pitching coach and, most recently, special minor league spring training consultant. Wagner had a rough major league rookie season in 1938, in which he posted an 8.27 ERA in 37 innings for the Red Sox. He would struggle in 1939 and 1940, too, with ERAs of 4.26 and 5.59. Wagner broke through with Boston in 1941 and 1942, when he went 12-8, 3.08 in 187 innings and 14-11, 3.29 in 205 innings. Wagner struggled to regain his form when he returned to the Red Sox in 1946, after serving three years in the military during World War II, and he retired following that season.

Leo Wells, who played shortstop for the 1942 and 1946 White Sox, died June 27 in St. Paul, Minn. He was 88. Wells' major league career was interrupted by military service from 1943 to 1945.

Cy Williams, who spent 42 years as a pro scout and signed or recommended 45 players who became big leaguers, including Andy Van Slyke, died May 8 in Buffalo. He was 92.Williams played five seasons in the minor leagues between 1936-43.

Brian Wilson, the Reds scout who signed Homer Bailey and Jay Bruce, the club's two most recent first round picks, died June 17. He was 33. Wilson attended Texas-San Antonio and was the 33rd-round pick of the Reds in the 1994 draft. He joined the organization's scouting staff following the 2006 season, his last as a player.

Junior Wooten, an outfielder-first baseman who played in parts of two seasons with the Senators, died Aug. 12 in Williamston, S.C. He was 82. Wooten appeared in six games with the Senators in 1947 and spent the entire 1948 season in the majors, hitting .256/.324/.322 in 258 at-bats. He also pitched two innings, giving up two runs, walking two and striking out one.

APPENDIX